New York Criminal Statutes and Rules

LexisNexis Colorbook

2015 GRAYBOOK
BENDER PAMPHLET EDITION

CRIMINAL PROCEDURE LAW

PENAL LAW

RELATED SECTIONS FROM:

Correction Law, Executive Law, Judiciary Law, Public Health Law, and Vehicle and Traffic Law

Uniform Rules for Courts Exercising Criminal Jurisdiction

Sentencing Guides by Hon. Barry Kamins

Court Directory

As amended by the 2014 Regular Legislative Session

(Current through Laws of 2014, Chapters 1 through 422)

QUESTIONS ABOUT THIS PUBLICATION?

For questions about the **Editorial Content** appearing in these volumes or reprint permission, please call:

Jeanine M. Schupbach, J.D., at .... 1-800-306-5230 (ext. 6733377)
Email: .... jeanine.schupbach@lexisnexis.com
Kathryn A. Calista, J.D. at .... 1-800-424-4200 (ext. 3465)
Email: .... kathryn.calista@lexisnexis.com
Outside the United States and Canada, please call .... (973) 820-2000

For assistance with replacement pages, shipments, billing or other customer service matters, please call:

Customer Services Department at .... (800) 833-9844
Outside the United States and Canada, please call .... (518) 487-3000
Fax Number .... (518) 487-3584
Customer Service Website .... http://www.lexisnexis.com/custserv/

For information on other Matthew Bender publications, please call:
Your account manager or .... (800) 223-1940
Outside the United States and Canada, please call .... (518) 487-3000

Library of Congress Card Number: 2001208776
ISBN: 978-0-7698-8977-1 (print)
ISBN: 978-1-6328-1124-0 (eBook)

Cite this publication as:

New York Criminal Statutes and Rules (2015 Graybook) (Matthew Bender)

Editorial Offices
630 Central Ave., New Providence, NJ 07974 (908) 464-6800
201 Mission St., San Francisco, CA 94105-1831 (415) 908-3200
www.lexisnexis.com

MATTHEW●BENDER

(2014–Pub.459)

TABLE OF CONTENTS

TABLE OF CONTENTS

TABLE OF LEGISLATIVE AMENDMENTS

A-1

TABLE OF 2014 AMENDMENTS

Current through Laws 2014, Chapters 1 through 422

CRIMINAL PROCEDURE LAW

Section	Effect	Chapter
2.10	eff. date amended	325
2.15(3), (7)	amended	262
30.10(3)(b)	amended	55
170.30(4)	added	402
170.80	amended	402
190.25(3)(h)	amended	347
200.50(4)	amended	55
216.00	eff. date amended	90
216.00(1), opening par.	amended	90
410.70(1), (5)	amended	17
410.91(5)	amended	90
420.35(2)	amended	385
700.05(8)(c)	amended	37
700.05(8)(f)	amended	55
700.05(8)(u)	added	55
720.15(4)	added	402
720.25	added	402
720.35(1)	amended	402

PENAL LAW

Section	Effect	Chapter
60.02(4)	added	402
65.00(4)	amended	17
80.00(1)	amended	55
80.10(1)	amended	55
110.05	amended	55
120.05	eff. date amended	197
120.05(3), (11)	amended	196
120.05(3-b), (11-b)	added	197
120.45	amended	184
130.53	amended	192

CORRECTION LAW

500	amended	131
500-a	eff. date amended	155
500-a(2-m)	added	346
500-b(4), (8)(3), (13)	amended	55
500-c(19)	added	346
500-o	eff. date amended	155

EXECUTIVE LAW

Section	Effect	Chapter
631(12)	amended	188

PUBLIC HEALTH LAW

Section	Effect	Chapter
3302(42), (43)	added	60
3309	amended	42
3309(3)-(5)	(3) added; former subds. (3) and (4) renumbered (4) and (5)	34
3318(2), opening par.	amended	60
3320(1)	amended	60
3321(1)(a)	amended	60
3322	amended	60
Art. 33, Tit. V-A	added	90
3360	added	90
3361	added	90
3362	added	90
3363	added	90
3364	added	90
3365	added	90
3366	added	90
3367	added	90
3368	added	90
3369	added	90
3369-a	added	90
3369-b	added	90
3369-c	added	90
3369-d	added	90
3369-e	added	90
3371(2)	amended	90

VEHICLE AND TRAFFIC LAW

PART I
CRIMINAL PROCEDURE LAW
AND PENAL LAW

CRIMINAL PROCEDURE LAW

LAWS 1970, CHAPTER 996, EFFECTIVE SEPTEMBER 1, 1971.

SYNOPSIS OF ARTICLES

PART ONE   General Provisions

Title A
Short Title, Applicability and Definitions

Title B
The Criminal Courts

Title C
General Principles Relating to Requirements For and Exemptions From Criminal Prosecution

Title D
Rules of Evidence, Standards of Proof and Related Matters

HISTORY: Add, L 1970, ch 996, § 1, eff Sept 1, 1971.

TITLE A   Short Title, Applicability and Definitions

ARTICLE 1
SHORT TITLE, APPLICABILITY AND DEFINITIONS

ARTICLE 2
PEACE OFFICERS

HISTORY: Add, L 1970, ch 996, § 1, eff Sept 1, 1971.

ARTICLE 1   SHORT TITLE, APPLICABILITY AND DEFINITIONS

HISTORY: Add, L 1970, ch 996, § 1, eff Sept 1, 1971.

§ 1.00. Short title

This chapter shall be known as the criminal procedure law, and may be cited as "CPL".

HISTORY: Add, L 1970, ch 996, § 1, eff Sept 1, 1971, with substance derived from Crim C § 1.

§ 1.10. Applicability of chapter to actions and matter occurring before and after effective date

1. The provisions of this chapter apply exclusively to:

(a) All criminal actions and proceedings commenced upon or after the effective date thereof and all appeals and other post-judgment proceedings relating or attaching thereto; and

(b) All matters of criminal procedure prescribed in this chapter which do not constitute a part of any particular action or case, occurring upon or after such effective date.

2. The provisions of this chapter apply to (a) all criminal actions and proceedings commenced prior to the effective date thereof but still pending on such date, and (b) all appeals and other post-judgment proceedings commenced upon or after such effective date which relate or attach to criminal actions and proceedings commenced or concluded prior to such effective date; provided that, if application of such provisions in any particular case would not be feasible or would work injustice, the provisions of the code of criminal procedure apply thereto.

3. The provisions of this chapter do not impair or render ineffectual any proceedings or procedural matters which occurred prior to the effective date thereof.

HISTORY: Add, L 1970, ch 996, § 1, eff Sept 1, 1971.

§ 1.20. Definitions of terms of general use in this chapter

Except where different meanings are expressly specified in subsequent provisions of this chapter, the term definitions contained in section 10.00 of the penal law are applicable to this chapter, and, in addition, the following terms have the following meanings:

1. "Accusatory instrument" means an indictment, an indictment ordered reduced pursuant to subdivision one-a of section 210.20 of this chapter, an information, a simplified information, a prosecutor's information, a superior court information, a misdemeanor complaint or a felony complaint. Every accusatory instrument, regardless of the person designated therein as accuser, constitutes an accusation on behalf of the state as plaintiff and must be entitled "the people of the state of New York" against a designated person, known as the defendant.

2. "Local criminal court accusatory instrument" means any accusatory instrument other than an indictment or a superior court information.

3. "Indictment" means a written accusation by a grand jury, more fully defined and described in article two hundred, filed with a superior court, which charges one or more defendants with the commission of one or more offenses, at least one of which is a crime, and which serves as a basis for prosecution thereof.

3-a. "Superior court information" means a written accusation by a district attorney more fully defined and described in articles one hundred ninety-five and two hundred, filed with a superior court pursuant to article one hundred ninety-five, which charges one or more defendants with the commission of one or more offenses, at least one of which is a crime, and which serves as a basis for prosecution thereof.

4. "Information" means a verified written accusation by a person, more fully defined and described in article one hundred, filed with a local criminal court, which charges one or more defendants with the commission of one or more offenses, none of which is a felony, and which may serve both to commence a criminal action and as a basis for prosecution thereof.

5.* "Simplified traffic information" means a written accusation, more fully defined and described in article one hundred, by a police officer or other public servant authorized by law to issue same, filed with a local criminal court, which, being in a brief or simplified form prescribed by the commissioner of motor vehicles, charges a person with one or more traffic infractions or misdemeanors relating to traffic, and which may serve both to commence a criminal action for such offense and as a basis for prosecution thereof.

5.* (a) "Simplified information" means a simplified traffic information, a simplified parks information, or a simplified environmental conservation information.

(b) "Simplified traffic information" means a written accusation by a police officer, or other public servant authorized by law to issue same, more fully defined and described in article one hundred, filed with a local criminal court, which, being in a brief or simplified form prescribed by the commissioner of motor vehicles, charges a person with one or more traffic infractions or misdemeanors relating to traffic, and which may serve both to commence a criminal action for such offense and as a basis for prosecution thereof.

(c) "Simplified parks information" means a written accusation by a police officer, or other public servant authorized by law to issue same, filed with a local criminal court, which, being in a brief or simplified form prescribed by the commissioner of parks and recreation, charges a person with one or more offenses, other than a felony, for which a uniform simplified parks information may be issued pursuant to the parks and recreation law and the navigation law, and which may serve both to commence a criminal action for such offense and as a basis for prosecution thereof.

(d) "Simplified environmental conservation information" means a written accusation by a police officer, or other public servant authorized by law to issue same, filed with a local criminal court, which being in a brief or simplified form prescribed by the commissioner of environmental conservation, charges a person with one or more offenses, other than a felony,

---

* There are two subdivisions 5.
* There are two subdivisions 5.

for which a uniform simplified environmental conservation simplified* information may be issued pursuant to the environmental conservation law, and which may serve both to commence a criminal action for such offense and as a basis for prosecution thereof.

6. "Prosecutor's information" means a written accusation by a district attorney, more fully defined and described in article one hundred, filed with a local criminal court, which charges one or more defendants with the commission of one or more offenses, none of which is a felony, and which serves as a basis for prosecution thereof.

7. "Misdemeanor complaint" means a verified written accusation by a person, more fully defined and described in article one hundred, filed with a local criminal court, which charges one or more defendants with the commission of one or more offenses, at least one of which is a misdemeanor and none of which is a felony, and which serves to commence a criminal action but which may not, except upon the defendant's consent, serve as a basis for prosecution of the offenses charged therein.

8. "Felony complaint" means a verified written accusation by a person, more fully defined and described in article one hundred, filed with a local criminal court, which charges one or more defendants with the commission of one or more felonies and which serves to commence a criminal action but not as a basis for prosecution thereof.

9. "Arraignment" means the occasion upon which a defendant against whom an accusatory instrument has been filed appears before the court in which the criminal action is pending for the purpose of having such court acquire and exercise control over his person with respect to such accusatory instrument and of setting the course of further proceedings in the action.

10. "Plea," in addition to its ordinary meaning as prescribed in sections 220.10 and 340.20, means, where appropriate, the occasion upon which a defendant enters such a plea to an accusatory instrument.

11. "Trial." A jury trial commences with the selection of the jury and includes all further proceedings through the rendition of a verdict. A non-jury trial commences with the first opening address, if there be any, and, if not, when the first witness is sworn, and includes all further proceedings through the rendition of a verdict.

12. "Verdict" means the announcement by a jury in the case of a jury trial, or by the court in the case of a non-jury trial, of its decision upon the defendant's guilt or innocence of the charges submitted to or considered by it.

13. "Conviction" means the entry of a plea of guilty to, or a verdict of guilty upon, an accusatory instrument other than a felony complaint, or to one or more counts of such instrument.

14. "Sentence" means the imposition and entry of sentence upon a conviction.

15. "Judgment." A judgment is comprised of a conviction and the sentence imposed thereon and is completed by imposition and entry of the sentence.

16. "Criminal action." A criminal action (a) commences with the filing of an accusatory instrument against a defendant in a criminal court, as specified in subdivision seventeen; (b) includes the filing of all further accusatory instruments directly derived from the initial one, and all proceedings, orders and motions conducted or made by a criminal court in the course of

---

* So in original.

disposing of any such accusatory instrument, or which, regardless of the court in which they occurred or were made, could properly be considered as a part of the record of the case by an appellate court upon an appeal from a judgment of conviction; and (c) terminates with the imposition of sentence or some other final disposition in a criminal court of the last accusatory instrument filed in the case.

17. "Commencement of criminal action." A criminal action is commenced by the filing of an accusatory instrument against a defendant in a criminal court, and, if more than one accusatory instrument is filed in the course of the action, it commences when the first of such instruments is filed.

18. "Criminal proceeding" means any proceeding which (a) constitutes a part of a criminal action or (b) occurs in a criminal court and is related to a prospective, pending or completed criminal action, either of this state or of any other jurisdiction, or involves a criminal investigation.

19. "Criminal court" means any court defined as such by section 10.10.

20. "Superior court" means any court defined as such by subdivision two of section 10.10.

21. "Local criminal court" means any court defined as such by subdivision three of section 10.10.

22. "Intermediate appellate court" means any court possessing appellate jurisdiction, other than the court of appeals.

23. "Judge" means any judicial officer who is a member of or constitutes a court, whether referred to in another provision of law as a justice or by any other title.

24. "Trial jurisdiction." A criminal court has "trial jurisdiction" of an offense when an indictment or an information charging such offense may properly be filed with such court, and when such court has authority to accept a plea to, try or otherwise finally dispose of such accusatory instrument.

25. "Preliminary jurisdiction." A criminal court has "preliminary jurisdiction" of an offense when, regardless of whether it has trial jurisdiction thereof, a criminal action for such offense may be commenced therein, and when such court may conduct proceedings with respect thereto which lead or may lead to prosecution and final disposition of the action in a court having trial jurisdiction thereof.

26. "Appearance ticket" means a written notice issued by a public servant, more fully defined in section 150.10, requiring a person to appear before a local criminal court in connection with an accusatory instrument to be filed against him therein.

27. "Summons" means a process of a local criminal court or superior court, more fully defined in section 130.10, requiring a defendant to appear before such court for the purpose of arraignment upon an accusatory instrument filed therewith by which a criminal action against him has been commenced.

28. "Warrant of arrest" means a process of a local criminal court, more fully defined in section 120.10, directing a police officer to arrest a defendant and to bring him before such court for the purpose of arraignment upon an accusatory instrument filed therewith by which a criminal action against him has been commenced.

29. "Superior court warrant of arrest" means a process of a superior court directing a police

officer to arrest a defendant and to bring him before such court for the purpose of arraignment upon an indictment filed therewith by which a criminal action against him has been commenced.

30. "Bench warrant" means a process of a criminal court in which a criminal action is pending, directing a police officer, or a uniformed court officer, pursuant to paragraph b of subdivision two of section 530.70 of this chapter, to take into custody a defendant in such action who has previously been arraigned upon the accusatory instrument by which the action was commenced, and to bring him before such court. The function of a bench warrant is to achieve the court appearance of a defendant in a pending criminal action for some purpose other than his initial arraignment in the action.

31. "Prosecutor" means a district attorney or any other public servant who represents the people in a criminal action.

32. "District attorney" means a district attorney, an assistant district attorney or a special district attorney, and, where appropriate, the attorney general, an assistant attorney general, a deputy attorney general, a special deputy attorney general, or the special prosecutor and inspector general for the protection of people with special needs or his or her assistants when acting pursuant to their duties in matters arising under article twenty of the executive law.

33. "Peace officer" means a person listed in section 2.10 of this chapter.

34. "Police officer." The following persons are police officers:

(a) A sworn member of the division of state police;

(b) Sheriffs, under-sheriffs and deputy sheriffs of counties outside of New York City;

(c) A sworn officer of an authorized county or county parkway police department;

(d) A sworn officer of an authorized police department or force of a city, town, village or police district;

(e) A sworn officer of an authorized police department of an authority or a sworn officer of the state regional park police in the office of parks and recreation;

(f) A sworn officer of the capital police force of the office of general services;

(g) An investigator employed in the office of a district attorney;

(h) An investigator employed by a commission created by an interstate compact who is, to a substantial extent, engaged in the enforcement of the criminal laws of this state;

(i) The chief and deputy fire marshals, the supervising fire marshals and the fire marshals of the bureau of fire investigation of the New York City fire department;

(j) A sworn officer of the division of law enforcement in the department of environmental conservation;

(k) A sworn officer of a police force of a public authority created by an interstate compact;

(l) Long Island railroad police.

(m) A special investigator employed in the statewide organized crime task force, while performing his assigned duties pursuant to section seventy-a of the executive law.

(n) A sworn officer of the Westchester county department of public safety services who, on or prior to June thirtieth, nineteen hundred seventy-nine was appointed as a sworn officer of the division of Westchester county parkway police or who was appointed on or after July first, nineteen hundred seventy-nine to the title of police officer, sergeant, lieutenant, captain or inspector or who, on or prior to January thirty-first, nineteen hundred eighty-three, was appointed as a Westchester county deputy sheriff.

(o) A sworn officer of the water-supply police employed by the city of New York, appointed to protect the sources, works, and transmission of water supplied to the city of New York, and to protect persons on or in the vicinity of such water sources, works, and transmission.

(p) Persons appointed as railroad policemen pursuant to section eighty-eight of the railroad law.

(q) An employee of the department of taxation and finance (i) assigned to enforcement of the taxes imposed under or pursuant to the authority of article twelve-A of the tax law and administered by the commissioner of taxation and finance, taxes imposed under or pursuant to the authority of article eighteen of the tax law and administered by the commissioner, taxes imposed under article twenty of the tax law, or sales or compensating use taxes relating to petroleum products or cigarettes imposed under article twenty-eight or pursuant to the authority of article twenty-nine of the tax law and administered by the commissioner or (ii) designated as a revenue crimes specialist and assigned to the enforcement of the taxes described in paragraph (c) of subdivision four of section 2.10 of this title, for the purpose of applying for and executing search warrants under article six hundred ninety of this chapter, for the purpose of acting as a claiming agent under article thirteen-A of the civil practice law and rules in connection with the enforcement of the taxes referred to above and for the purpose of executing warrants of arrest relating to the respective crimes specified in subdivision four of section 2.10 of this title.

(r) Any employee of the Suffolk county department of parks who is appointed as a Suffolk county park police officer.

(s) A university police officer appointed by the state university pursuant to paragraph 1 of subdivision two of section three hundred fifty-five of the education law.

(t) A sworn officer of the department of public safety of the Buffalo municipal housing authority who has achieved or been granted the status of sworn police officer and has been certified by the division of criminal justice services as successfully completing an approved basic course for police officers.

(u) Persons appointed as Indian police officers pursuant to section one hundred fourteen of the Indian law.

(v) Supervisor of forest ranger services; assistant supervisor of forest ranger services; forest ranger 3; forest ranger 2; forest ranger 1 employed by the state department of environmental conservation or sworn officer of the division of forest protection and fire management in the department of environmental conservation responsible for wild land search and rescue, wild land fire management in the state as prescribed in subdivision eighteen of section 9-0105 and title eleven of article nine of the environmental conservation law, exercising care, custody and control of state lands administered by the department of environmental conservation.

34-a. "Geographical area of employment." The "geographical area of employment" of certain police officers is as follows:

(a) [Until Sept 1, 2015] Except as provided in paragraph (d) of this subdivision, New York state constitutes the "geographical area of employment" of any police officer employed as such by an agency of the state or by an authority which functions throughout the state, or a police officer designated by the superintendent of state police pursuant to section two hundred twenty-three of the executive law;

(a) [Eff Sept 1, 2015] Except as provided in paragraph (d), New York state constitutes the "geographical area of employment" of any police officer employed as such by an agency of the state or by an authority which functions throughout the state;

(b) A county, city, town or village, as the case may be, constitutes the "geographical area of employment" of any police officer employed as such by an agency of such political subdivision or by an authority which functions only in such political subdivision; and

(c) Where an authority functions in more than one county, the "geographical area of employment" of a police officer employed thereby extends through all of such counties.

(d) The geographical area of employment of a police officer appointed by the state university is the campuses and other property of the state university, including any portion of a public highway which crosses or abuts such property.

35. "Commitment to the custody of the sheriff," when referring to an order of a court located in a county or city which has established a department of correction, means commitment to the commissioner of correction of such county or city.

36. "County" ordinarily means (a) any county outside of New York City or (b) New York City in its entirety. Unless the context requires a different construction, New York City, despite its five counties, is deemed a single county within the meaning of the provisions of this chapter in which that term appears.

37. "Lesser included offense." When it is impossible to commit a particular crime without concomitantly committing, by the same conduct, another offense of lesser grade or degree, the latter is, with respect to the former, a "lesser included offense." In any case in which it is legally possible to attempt to commit a crime, an attempt to commit such crime constitutes a lesser included offense with respect thereto.

38. "Oath" includes an affirmation and every other mode authorized by law of attesting to the truth of that which is stated.

39. "Petty offense" means a violation or a traffic infraction.

40. "Evidence in chief" means evidence, received at a trial or other criminal proceeding in which a defendant's guilt or innocence of an offense is in issue, which may be considered as a part of the quantum of substantive proof establishing or tending to establish the commission of such offense or an element thereof or the defendant's connection therewith.

41. "Armed felony" means any violent felony offense defined in section 70.02 of the penal law that includes as an element either:

(a) possession, being armed with or causing serious physical injury by means of a deadly weapon, if the weapon is a loaded weapon from which a shot, readily capable of producing death or other serious physical injury may be discharged; or

(b) display of what appears to be a pistol, revolver, rifle, shotgun, machine gun or other firearm.

42. "Juvenile offender" means (1) a person, thirteen years old who is criminally responsible for acts constituting murder in the second degree as defined in subdivisions one and two of section 125.25 of the penal law, or such conduct as a sexually motivated felony, where authorized pursuant to section 130.91 of the penal law; and (2) a person fourteen or fifteen years old who is criminally responsible for acts constituting the crimes defined in subdivisions one and two of section 125.25 (murder in the second degree) and in subdivision three of such section provided that the underlying crime for the murder charge is one for which such person is criminally responsible; section 135.25 (kidnapping in the first degree); 150.20 (arson in the first degree); subdivisions one and two of section 120.10 (assault in the first degree); 125.20 (manslaughter in the first degree); subdivisions one and two of section 130.35 (rape in the first degree); subdivisions one and two of section 130.50 (criminal sexual act in the first degree); 130.70 (aggravated sexual abuse in the first degree); 140.30 (burglary in the first degree); subdivision one of section 140.25 (burglary in the second degree); 150.15 (arson in the second degree); 160.15 (robbery in the first degree); subdivision two of section 160.10 (robbery in the second degree) of the penal law; or section 265.03 of the penal law, where such machine gun or such firearm is possessed on school grounds, as that phrase is defined in subdivision fourteen of section 220.00 of the penal law; or defined in the penal law as an attempt to commit murder in the second degree or kidnapping in the first degree, or such conduct as a sexually motivated felony, where authorized pursuant to section 130.91 of the penal law.

43. "Judicial hearing officer" means a person so designated pursuant to provisions of article twenty-two of the judiciary law.

HISTORY: Add, L 1970, ch 996, § 1, eff Sept 1, 1971, with substance derived from Crim C § 2-a; amd, L 1970, ch 997, §§ 5–9, eff Sept 1, 1971, L 1971, ch 544, §§ 1, 2, L 1971, ch 795, § 1, L 1971, ch 884, §§ 1–4, L 1972, ch 383, § 2, L 1972, ch 315, § 3, L 1972, ch 564, § 1, L 1972, ch 589, § 1, L 1972, ch 661, §§ 28, 29, eff Sept 1, 1972, L 1972, ch 662, § 5, eff Sept 1, 1972, L 1972, ch 729, § 2, eff Jan 1, 1973, L 1972, ch 858, § 1, eff June 2, 1972, L 1973, ch 461, § 1, L 1973, ch 780 § 1, L 1973, ch 781, § 1, L 1973, ch 782, § 1, L 1973, ch 948, §§ 1, 2, L 1974, ch 22, § 1, eff Feb 26, 1974, L 1974, ch 250, § 1, eff April 30, 1974, L 1974, ch 281, § 1, L 1974, ch 282, §§ 1, 2, L 1974, ch 467, §§ 1–3, eff June 22, 1974, L 1974, ch 707, §§ 3, 4, eff Sept 1, 1974, L 1974, ch 877, §§ 1, 2, eff Sept 1, 1974, L 1975, ch 509, § 1, L 1975, ch 667, § 13, L 1976, ch 265, § 2, eff Sept 1, 1976, L 1976, ch 590, § 1, L 1977, ch 487, § 1, L 1978, ch 205, § 1, L 1978, ch 481, §§ 8, 32, eff Sept 1, 1978, L 1978, ch 655, § 39, L 1978, ch 756, § 1, L 1979, ch 330, § 1, L 1979, ch 411, § 7, L 1979, ch 533, § 6, L 1980, ch 285, § 1, eff June 19, 1980, L 1980, ch 843, § 1, eff Sept 1, 1980, L 1981, ch 335, § 2, eff Sept 1, 1981, L 1982, ch 658, § 1, L 1983, ch 840, § 9, eff April 1, 1983, L 1983, ch 969, §§ 7, 8, eff Aug 8, 1983, L 1985, ch 65, § 3, L 1986, ch 318, § 1, L 1988, ch 521, § 2, L 1990, ch 209, § 9, eff Sept 1, 1990, L 1991, ch 166, § 340, eff June 12, 1991, L 1991, ch 542, § 1, eff July 23, 1991, L 1993, ch 446, § 1, eff Nov 1, 1993, L 1993, ch 508, § 11, L 1995, ch 2, §§ 68, 69, eff Sept 1, 1995, L 1998, ch 424, §§ 1, 2, eff Jan 1, 1999, L 1998, ch 435, § 1, eff Nov 1, 1998, L 1999, ch 428, § 2, eff Nov 1, 1999, expires and repealed Sept 1, 2015, L 2000, ch 599, § 1, eff Dec 20, 2000, L 2001, ch 504, § 5, eff Nov 21, 2001, L 2002, ch 318, §§ 1, 2, eff Aug 6, 2002, L 2003, ch 121, § 1, eff July 1, 2003, L 2003, ch 264, § 35, eff Nov 1, 2003, L 2005, ch 558, § 2, eff Aug 23, 2005 L 2006, ch 693, § 1, eff Sept 13, 2006, L 2007, ch 7, § 46, eff April 13, 2007, L 2011, ch 61, § 55 (Part K), eff Sept 1, 2011, L 2012, ch 501, § 4 (Part A), eff June 30, 2013.

ARTICLE 2 PEACE OFFICERS

§ 2.20.   **Powers of peace officers**

§ 2.30.   **Training requirements for peace officers**

   HISTORY: Add, L 1980, ch 843, § 2, eff Sept 1, 1980.

§ 2.10. Persons designated as peace officers

   Notwithstanding the provisions of any general, special or local law or charter to the contrary, only the following persons shall have the powers of, and shall be peace officers:

   1. Constables or police constables of a town or village, provided such designation is not inconsistent with local law.

   2. The sheriff, undersheriff and deputy sheriffs of New York city and sworn officers of the Westchester county department of public safety services appointed after January thirty-first, nineteen hundred eighty-three to the title of public safety officer and who perform the functions previously performed by a Westchester county deputy sheriff on or prior to such date.

   3. Investigators of the office of the state commission of investigation.

   4. Employees of the department of taxation and finance designated by the commissioner of taxation and finance as peace officers and assigned by the commissioner of taxation and finance

      (a) to the enforcement of any of the criminal or seizure and forfeiture provisions of the tax law relating to (i) taxes imposed under or pursuant to the authority of article twelve-A of the tax law and administered by the commissioner, (ii) taxes imposed under or pursuant to the authority of article eighteen of the tax law and administered by the commissioner, (iii) taxes imposed under article twenty of the tax law, or (iv) sales or compensating use taxes relating to petroleum products or cigarettes imposed under article twenty-eight or pursuant to the authority of article twenty-nine of the tax law and administered by the commissioner or

      (b) to the enforcement of any provision of the penal law relating to any of the taxes described in paragraph (a) of this subdivision and relating to crimes effected through the use of a statement or document filed with the department in connection with the administration of such taxes or

      (c) as revenue crimes specialist and assigned to the enforcement of any of the criminal provisions of the tax law relating to taxes administered by the commissioner of taxation and finance other than those taxes set forth in paragraph (a) of this subdivision or any provision of the penal law relating to such taxes, and those provisions of the penal law (i) relating to any of the foregoing taxes and (ii) relating to crimes effected through the use of a statement or document filed with the department in connection with the administration of such foregoing taxes or

      (d) to the enforcement of any provision of law which is subject to enforcement by criminal penalties and which relates to the performance by persons employed by the department of taxation and finance of the duties of their employment.

   Provided, however, that nothing in this subdivision shall be deemed to authorize any such employee designated as a peace officer after November first, nineteen hundred eighty-five to carry, possess, repair or dispose of a firearm unless the appropriate license therefor has been issued pursuant to section 400.00 of the penal law, and further provided that, prior to such designation by the commissioner each such employee shall have successfully completed the training requirements specified in section 2.30 of this article. Provided, further, that any license issued to such employee pursuant to such peace officer designation by the commissioner shall relate only to the firearm issued to such employee by the department of taxation and finance and such permit shall not cover any other firearms. The foregoing sentence shall not be deemed to prohibit such peace officer from applying for a separate permit relating to non-departmental firearms.

5. Employees of the New York city department of finance assigned to enforcement of the tax on cigarettes imposed by title D of chapter forty-six of the administrative code of the city of New York by the commissioner of finance.

6. Confidential investigators and inspectors, as designated by the commissioner, of the department of agriculture and markets, pursuant to rules of the department.

7. Officers or agents of a duly incorporated society for the prevention of cruelty to animals.

7-a. [Expires and repealed Aug 11, 2019] Officers or agents of a duly incorporated society for the prevention of cruelty to children in Rockland county; provided, however, that nothing in this subdivision shall be deemed to authorize such officer or agent to carry, possess, repair, or dispose of a firearm unless the appropriate license therefor has been issued pursuant to section 400.00 of the penal law; and provided further that such officer or agent shall exercise the powers of a peace officer only when he is acting pursuant to his special duties.

8. Inspectors and officers of the New York city department of health when acting pursuant to their special duties as set forth in section 564-11.0 of the administrative code of the city of New York; provided, however, that nothing in this subdivision shall be deemed to authorize such officer to carry, possess, repair or dispose of a firearm unless the appropriate license therefor has been issued pursuant to section 400.00 of the penal law.

9. Park rangers in Suffolk county, who shall be authorized to issue appearance tickets, simplified traffic informations, simplified parks informations and simplified environmental conservation informations.

10. Broome county park rangers who shall be authorized to issue appearance tickets, simplified traffic informations, simplified parks informations, and simplified environmental conservation informations; provided, however, that nothing in this subdivision shall be deemed to authorize such officer to carry, possess, repair or dispose of a firearm unless the appropriate license therefor has been issued pursuant to section 400.00 of the penal law.

11. Park rangers in Onondaga and Cayuga counties, who shall be authorized to issue appearance tickets, simplified traffic informations, simplified parks informations and simplified environmental conservation informations, within the respective counties of Onondaga and Cayuga.

12. Special policemen designated by the commissioner and the directors of in-patient facilities in the office of mental health pursuant to section 7.25 of the mental hygiene law, and special policemen designated by the commissioner and the directors of facilities under his jurisdiction in the office of mental retardation and developmental disabilities pursuant to section 13.25 of the mental hygiene law; provided, however, that nothing in this subdivision shall be deemed to authorize such officers to carry, possess, repair or dispose of a firearm unless the appropriate license therefor has been issued pursuant to section 400.00 of the penal law.

13. Persons designated as special policemen by the director of a hospital in the department of health pursuant to section four hundred fifty-five of the public health law; provided, however, that nothing in this subdivision shall be deemed to authorize such officer to carry, possess, repair or dispose of a firearm unless the appropriate license therefor has been issued pursuant to section 400.00 of the penal law.

14. [Repealed]

15. Uniformed enforcement forces of the New York state thruway authority, when acting pursuant to subdivision two of section three hundred sixty-one of the public authorities law; provided, however, that nothing in this subdivision shall be deemed to authorize such officer to carry, possess, repair or dispose of a firearm unless the appropriate license therefor has been issued pursuant to section 400.00 of the penal law.

16. Employees of the department of health designated pursuant to section thirty-three hundred eighty-five of the public health law; provided, however, that nothing in this subdivision shall be deemed to authorize such officer to carry, possess, repair or dispose of a firearm unless the appropriate license therefor has been issued pursuant to section 400.00 of the penal law.

17. Uniformed housing guards of the Buffalo municipal housing authority.

18. Bay constable of the city of Rye, the villages of Mamaroneck, South Nyack and bay constables of the towns of East Hampton, Hempstead, Oyster Bay, Riverhead, Southampton, Southold, Islip, Shelter Island, Brookhaven, Babylon, Smithtown, Huntington and North Hempstead; provided, however, that nothing in this subdivision shall be deemed to authorize the bay constables in the city of Rye, the village of South Nyack or the towns of Brookhaven, Babylon, Southold, East Hampton, Riverhead, Islip, other than a bay constable of the town of Islip who prior to April third, nineteen hundred ninety-eight served as harbormaster for such town and whose position was reclassified as bay constable for such town prior to such date, Smithtown, Huntington and Shelter Island to carry, possess, repair or dispose of a firearm unless the appropriate license therefor has been issued pursuant to section 400.00 of the penal law.

19. Harbor masters appointed by a county, city, town or village.

20. Bridge and tunnel officers, sergeants and lieutenants of the Triborough bridge and tunnel authority.

21. a. Uniformed court officers of the unified court system.

    b. Court clerks of the unified court system in the first and second departments.

    c. Marshall, deputy marshall, clerk or uniformed court officer of a district court.

    (d)* Marshalls or deputy marshalls of a city court, provided, however, that nothing in this subdivision shall be deemed to authorize such officer to carry, possess, repair or dispose of a firearm unless the appropriate license therefor has been issued pursuant to section 400.00 of the penal law.

    e. Uniformed court officers of the city of Mount Vernon.

    f. Uniformed court officers of the city of Jamestown.

22. Patrolmen appointed by the Lake George park commission; provided however that nothing in this subdivision shall be deemed to authorize such officer to carry, possess, repair or dispose of a firearm unless the appropriate license therefor has been issued pursuant to section 400.00 of the penal law.

23. Parole officers or warrant officers in the department of corrections and community supervision.

---

* So in original.

23-a. Parole revocation specialists in the department of corrections and community supervision; provided, however, that nothing in this subdivision shall be deemed to authorize such employee to carry, possess, repair or dispose of a firearm unless the appropriate license therefor has been issued pursuant to section 400.00 of the penal law.

24. Probation officers.

25. Officials, as designated by the commissioner of the department of corrections and community supervision pursuant to rules of the department, and correction officers of any state correctional facility or of any penal correctional institution.

26. Peace officers designated pursuant to the provisions of the New York state defense emergency act, as set forth in chapter seven hundred eighty-four of the laws of nineteen hundred fifty-one, as amended, when acting pursuant to their special duties during a period of attack or imminent attack by enemy forces, or during official drills called to combat natural or man-made disasters, or during official drills in preparation for an attack by enemy forces or in preparation for a natural or man-made disaster; provided, however, that nothing in this subdivision shall be deemed to authorize such officer to carry, possess, repair or dispose of a firearm unless the appropriate license therefor has been issued pursuant to section 400.00 of the penal law; and provided further, that such officer shall have the powers set forth in section 2.20 of this article only during a period of imminent or actual attack by enemy forces and during drills authorized under section twenty-nine-b of article two-B of the executive law, providing for the use of civil defense forces in disasters. Notwithstanding any other provision of law, such officers shall have the power to direct and control traffic during official drills in preparation for an attack by enemy forces or in preparation for combating natural or man-made disasters; however, this grant does not include any of the other powers set forth in section 2.20 of this article.

27. New York city special patrolmen appointed by the police commissioner pursuant to subdivision c or e of section 434a-7.0 or subdivision c or e of section 14-106 of the administrative code of the city of New York; provided, however, that nothing in this subdivision shall be deemed to authorize such officer to carry, possess, repair or dispose of a firearm unless the appropriate license therefor has been issued pursuant to section 400.00 of the penal law and the employer has authorized such officer to possess a firearm during any phase of the officers on-duty employment. Special patrolmen shall have the powers set forth in section 2.20 of this article only when they are acting pursuant to their special duties; provided, however, that the following categories of New York city special patrolmen shall have such powers whether or not they are acting pursuant to their special duties: school safety officers employed by the board of education of the city of New York; parking control specialists, taxi and limousine inspectors, urban park rangers and evidence and property control specialists employed by the city of New York; and further provided that, with respect to the aforementioned categories of New York city special patrolmen, where such a special patrolman has been appointed by the police commissioner and, upon the expiration of such appointment the police commissioner has neither renewed such appointment nor explicitly determined that such appointment shall not be renewed, such appointment shall remain in full force and effect indefinitely, until such time as the police commissioner expressly determines to either renew or terminate such appointment.

28. All officers and members of the uniformed force of the New York city fire department as set forth and subject to the limitations contained in section 487a-15.0 of the administrative code of the city of New York; provided, however, that nothing in this subdivision shall be deemed to authorize such officer to carry, possess, repair or dispose of a firearm unless the appropriate license therefor has been issued pursuant to section 400.00 of the penal law.

29. Special policemen for horse racing, appointed pursuant to the provisions of the pari-mutuel revenue law as set forth in chapter two hundred fifty-four of the laws of nineteen hundred forty, as amended; provided, however, that nothing in this subdivision shall be deemed to authorize such officer to carry, possess, repair or dispose of a firearm unless the appropriate license therefor has been issued pursuant to section 400.00 of the penal law.

30. Supervising fire inspectors, fire inspectors, the fire marshal and assistant fire marshals, all of whom are full-time employees of the county of Nassau fire marshal's office.

31. [Repealed]

32. Investigators of the department of motor vehicles, pursuant to section three hundred ninety-two-b of the vehicle and traffic law; provided, however, that nothing in this subdivision shall be deemed to authorize such officer to carry, possess, repair or dispose of a firearm unless the appropriate license therefor has been issued pursuant to section 400.00 of the penal law.

33. A city marshal of the city of New York who has received training in firearms handling from the federal bureau of investigation or in the New York city police academy, or in the absence of the available training programs from the federal bureau of investigation and the New York city police academy, from another law enforcement agency located in the state of New York, and who has received a firearms permit from the license division of the New York city police department.

34. Waterfront and airport investigators, pursuant to subdivision four of section ninety-nine hundred six of the unconsolidated laws; provided, however, that nothing in this subdivision shall be deemed to authorize such officer to carry, possess, repair or dispose of a firearm unless the appropriate license therefor has been issued pursuant to section 400.00 of the penal law.

35. Special investigators appointed by the state board of elections, pursuant to section 3-107 of the election law.

36. Investigators appointed by the state liquor authority, pursuant to section fifteen of the alcoholic beverage control law; provided, however, that nothing in this subdivision shall be deemed to authorize such officer to carry, possess, repair or dispose of a firearm unless the appropriate license therefor has been issued pursuant to section 400.00 of the penal law.

37. Special patrolmen of a political subdivision, appointed pursuant to section two hundred nine-v of the general municipal law; provided, however, that nothing in this subdivision shall be deemed to authorize such officer to carry, possess, repair or dispose of a firearm unless the appropriate license therefor has been issued pursuant to section 400.00 of the penal law.

38. A special investigator of the New York city department of investigation who has received training in firearms handling in the New York police academy and has received a firearms permit from the license division of the New York city police department.

39. Broome county special patrolman, appointed by the Broome county attorney; provided, however, that nothing in this subdivision shall be deemed to authorize such officer to carry, possess, repair or dispose of a firearm unless the appropriate license therefor has been issued pursuant to section 400.00 of the penal law.

40. Special officers employed by the city of New York or by the New York city health and hospitals corporation; provided, however, that nothing in this subdivision shall be deemed to authorize such officer to carry, possess, repair or dispose of a firearm unless the appropriate license therefor has been issued pursuant to section 400.00 of the penal law. The New York city

health and hospitals corporation shall employ peace officers appointed pursuant to this subdivision to perform the patrol, investigation, and maintenance of the peace duties of special officer, senior special officer and hospital security officer, provided however that nothing in this subdivision shall prohibit managerial, supervisory, or state licensed or certified professional employees of the corporation from performing such duties where they are incidental to their usual duties, or shall prohibit police officers employed by the city of New York from performing these duties.

41. Fire police squads organized pursuant to section two hundred nine-c of the general municipal law, at such times as the fire department, fire company or an emergency rescue and first aid squad of the fire department or fire company are on duty, or when, on orders of the chief of the fire department or fire company of which they are members, they are separately engaged in response to a call for assistance pursuant to the provisions of section two hundred nine of the general municipal law; provided, however, that nothing in this subdivision shall be deemed to authorize such officer to carry, possess, repair or dispose of a firearm unless the appropriate license therefor has been issued pursuant to section 400.00 of the penal law.

42. Special deputy sheriffs appointed by the sheriff of a county within which any part of the grounds of Cornell university or the grounds of any state institution constituting a part of the educational and research plants owned or under the supervision, administration or control of said university are located pursuant to section fifty-seven hundred nine of the education law; provided, however, that nothing in this subdivision shall be deemed to authorize such officer to carry, possess, repair or dispose of a firearm unless the appropriate license therefor has been issued pursuant to section 400.00 of the penal law.

43. Housing patrolmen of the Mount Vernon housing authority, acting pursuant to rules of the Mount Vernon housing authority; provided, however, that nothing in this subdivision shall be deemed to authorize such officer to carry, possess, repair or dispose of a firearm unless the appropriate license therefor has been issued pursuant to section 400.00 of the penal law.

44. The officers, employees and members of the New York city division of fire prevention, in the bureau of fire, as set forth and subject to the limitations contained in subdivision one of section 487a-1.0 of the administrative code of the city of New York; provided, however, that nothing in this subdivision shall be deemed to authorize such officer to carry, possess, repair or dispose of a firearm unless the appropriate license therefor has been issued pursuant to section 400.00 of the penal law.

45. Persons appointed and designated as peace officers by the Niagara frontier transportation authority, pursuant to subdivision thirteen of section twelve hundred ninety-nine-e of the public authorities law.

46. Persons appointed as peace officers by the Sea Gate Association pursuant to the provisions of chapter three hundred ninety-one of the laws of nineteen hundred forty, provided, however, that nothing in this subdivision shall be deemed to authorize such officer to carry, possess, repair or dispose of a firearm unless the appropriate license therefor has been issued pursuant to section 400.00 of the penal law.

47. Employees of the department of financial services when designated as peace officers by the superintendent of financial services and acting pursuant to their special duties as set forth in article four of the financial services law; provided, however, that nothing in this subdivision shall be deemed to authorize such officer to carry, possess, repair or dispose of a firearm unless the appropriate license therefor has been issued pursuant to section 400.00 of the penal law.

48. New York state air base security guards when they are designated as peace officers under military regulations promulgated by the chief of staff to the governor and when performing their duties as air base security guards pursuant to orders issued by appropriate military authority; provided, however, that nothing in this subdivision shall be deemed to authorize such guards to carry, possess, repair or dispose of a firearm unless the appropriate license therefor has been issued pursuant to section 400.00 of the penal law.

49. Members of the army national guard military police and air national guard security personnel belonging to the organized militia of the state of New York when they are designated as peace officers under military regulations promulgated by the adjutant general and when performing their duties as military policemen or air security personnel pursuant to orders issued by appropriate military authority; provided, however, that nothing in this subdivision shall be deemed to authorize such military police or air security personnel to carry, possess, repair or dispose of a firearm unless the appropriate license therefor has been issued pursuant to section 400.00 of the penal law.

50. Transportation supervisors in the city of White Plains appointed by the commissioner of public safety in the city of White Plains; provided, however, that nothing in this subdivision shall be deemed to authorize such officer to carry, possess, repair or dispose of a firearm unless the appropriate license therefor has been issued pursuant to section 400.00 of the penal law.

51. Officers and members of the fire investigation division of the fire department of the city of Rochester, the city of Binghamton and the city of Utica, when acting pursuant to their special duties in matters arising under the laws relating to fires, the extinguishment thereof and fire perils; provided, however, that nothing in this subdivision shall be deemed to authorize such officer to carry, possess, repair or dispose of a firearm unless the appropriate license therefor has been issued pursuant to section 400.00 of the penal law.

52. Security hospital treatment assistants, as so designated by the commissioner of the office of mental health while transporting persons convicted of a crime to court, to other facilities within the jurisdiction of the office of mental health, or to any state or local correctional facility; provided, however, that nothing in this subdivision shall be deemed to authorize such employee to carry, possess, repair or dispose of a firearm unless the appropriate license therefor has been issued pursuant to section 400.00 of penal law.

53. Authorized agents of the municipal directors of weights and measures in the counties of Suffolk, Nassau and Westchester when acting pursuant to their special duties as set forth in section one hundred eighty-one of the agriculture and markets law; provided, however, that nothing in this subdivision shall be deemed to authorize such officer to carry, possess, repair or dispose of a firearm unless the appropriate license therefor has been issued pursuant to section 400.00 of the penal law.

54. Special policemen appointed pursuant to section one hundred fifty-eight of the town law; provided, however, that nothing in this subdivision shall be deemed to authorize such officer to carry, possess, repair or dispose of a firearm unless the appropriate license therefor has been issued pursuant to section 400.00 of the penal law.

55. [Expired]

56. Dog control officers of the town of Brookhaven, who at the discretion of the town board may be designated as constables for the purpose of enforcing article twenty-six of the agriculture and markets law and for the purpose of issuing appearance tickets permitted under article seven of such law; provided, however, that nothing in this subdivision shall be deemed

to authorize such officer to carry, possess, repair or dispose of a firearm unless the appropriate license therefor has been issued pursuant to section 400.00 of the penal law.

57. Harbor Park rangers employed by the Snug Harbor cultural center in Richmond county and appointed as New York city special patrolmen by the police commissioner pursuant to subdivision c of section 14-106 of the administrative code of the city of New York. Notwithstanding any provision of law, rule or regulation, such officers shall be authorized to issue appearance tickets pursuant to section 150.20 of this chapter, and shall have such other powers as are specified in section 2.20 of this article only when acting pursuant to their special duties. Nothing in this subdivision shall be deemed to authorize such officers to carry, possess, repair or dispose of a firearm unless the appropriate license therefor has been issued pursuant to section 400.00 of the penal law and the employer has authorized such officer to possess a firearm during any phase of the officer's on-duty employment.

57-a.* Seasonal park rangers of the Westchester county department of public safety while employed as authorized by the commissioner of public safety/sheriff of the county of Westchester; provided, however, that nothing in this subdivision shall be deemed to authorize such officer to carry, possess, repair or dispose of a firearm unless the appropriate license therefor has been issued pursuant to section 400.00 of the penal law.

57-a.* Officers of the Westchester county public safety emergency force, when activated by the commissioner of public safety/sheriff of the county of Westchester; provided, however that nothing in this subdivision shall be deemed to authorize such officer to carry, possess, repair or dispose of a firearm unless the appropriate license therefor has been issued pursuant to section 400.00 of the penal law.

58. Uniformed members of the security force of the Troy housing authority provided, however, that nothing in this subdivision shall be deemed to authorize such officer to carry, possess, repair or dispose of a firearm unless the appropriate license therefor has been issued pursuant to section 400.00 of the penal law.

59. Officers and members of the sanitation police of the department of sanitation of the city of New York, duly appointed and designated as peace officers by such department; provided, however, that nothing in this subdivision shall be deemed to authorize such officer to carry, possess, repair or dispose of a firearm unless the appropriate license therefor has been issued pursuant to section 400.00 of the penal law. Provided, further, that nothing in this subdivision shall be deemed to apply to officers and members of the sanitation police regularly and exclusively assigned to enforcement of such city's residential recycling laws.

60. [Repealed]

61. Chief fire marshall, assistant chief fire marshall, fire marshall II and fire marshall I, all of whom are full-time employees of the Suffolk county department of fire, rescue and emergency services, when acting pursuant to their special duties in matters arising under the laws relating to fires, the extinguishment thereof and fire perils; provided, however, that nothing in this subdivision shall be deemed to authorize such officer to carry, possess, repair or dispose of a firearm unless the appropriate license therefor has been issued pursuant to section 400.00 of the penal law.

---

* There are two subdivisions 57-a.

* There are two subdivisions 57-a.

62.* Chief fire marshall, assistant chief fire marshall, fire marshall II and fire marshall I, all of whom are full-time employees of the town of Babylon, when acting pursuant to their special duties in matters arising under the laws relating to fires, the extinguishment thereof and fire perils; provided, however, that nothing in this subdivision shall be deemed to authorize such officer to carry, possess, repair or dispose of a firearm unless the appropriate license therefor has been issued pursuant to section 400.00 of the penal law.

62.* Employees of the division for youth assigned to transport and warrants units who are specifically designated by the director in accordance with section five hundred four-b of the executive law, provided, however, that nothing in this subdivision shall be deemed to authorize such employees to carry, possess, repair or dispose of a firearm unless the appropriate license therefor has been issued pursuant to section 400.00 of the penal law.

63.* Uniformed members of the fire marshal's office in the town of Southampton and the town of Riverhead, when acting pursuant to their special duties in matters arising under the laws relating to fires, the extinguishment thereof and fire perils; provided, however that nothing in this subdivision shall be deemed to authorize such officer to carry, possess, repair or dispose of a firearm unless the appropriate license therefor has been issued pursuant to section 400.00 of the penal law.

63.* Employees of the town court of the town of Greenburgh serving as a security officer; provided, however, that nothing in this subdivision will be deemed to authorize such officer to carry, possess, repair or dispose of a firearm unless the appropriate license therefor has been issued pursuant to section 400.00 of the penal law or to authorize such officer to carry or possess a firearm except while on duty.

64. Cell block attendants employed by the city of Buffalo police department; provided, however, that nothing in this subdivision shall be deemed to authorize such officer to carry, possess, repair or dispose of a firearm unless the appropriate license therefor has been issued pursuant to section 400.00 of the penal law.

65. Chief fire marshall, assistant chief fire marshall, fire marshall II and fire marshall I, all of whom are full-time employees of the town of Brookhaven, when acting pursuant to their special duties in matters arising under the laws relating to fires, the extinguishment thereof and fire perils; provided, however, that nothing in this subdivision shall be deemed to authorize such officer to carry, possess, repair or dispose of a firearm unless the appropriate license thereof has been issued pursuant to section 400.00 of the penal law.

66. Employees of the village court of the village of Spring Valley serving as security officers at such village court; provided, however, that nothing in this subdivision shall be deemed to authorize such officer to carry, possess, repair or dispose of a firearm unless the appropriate license therefor has been issued pursuant to section 400.00 of the penal law.

67. Employees of the town court of the town of Putnam Valley serving as a security officer; provided, however, that nothing in this subdivision will be deemed to authorize such officer to carry, possess, repair or dispose of a firearm unless the appropriate license therefor has been

---

* There are two subdivisions 62.

* There are two subdivisions 62.

* There are two subdivisions 63.

* There are two subdivisions 63.

issued pursuant to section 400.00 of the penal law or to authorize such officer to carry or possess a firearm except while on duty.

68.* Employees of the town court of the town of Southampton serving as uniformed court officers at such town court; provided, however, that nothing in this subdivision shall be deemed to authorize such officer to carry, possess, repair or dispose of a firearm unless the appropriate license therefor has been issued pursuant to section 400.00 of the penal law.

68.* The state inspector general and investigators designated by the state inspector general; provided, however, that nothing in this subdivision shall be deemed to authorize the state inspector general or such investigators to carry, possess, repair or dispose of a firearm unless the appropriate license therefor has been issued pursuant to section 400.00 of the penal law.

68.* Dog control officers of the town of Arcadia, who at the discretion of the town board may be designated as constables for the purpose of enforcing article twenty-six of the agriculture and markets law and for the purpose of issuing appearance tickets permitted under article seven of such law; provided, however, that nothing in this subdivision shall be deemed to authorize such officer to carry, possess, repair or dispose of a firearm unless the appropriate license therefor has been issued pursuant to section 400.00 of the penal law.

68.* Employees appointed by the sheriff of Livingston county, when acting pursuant to their special duties serving as uniformed marine patrol officers; provided, however, that nothing in this subdivision shall be deemed to authorize such officer to carry, possess, repair or dispose of a firearm unless the appropriate license has been issued pursuant to section 400.00 of the penal law or to authorize such officer to carry or possess a firearm except while on duty.

68.* Persons employed by the Chautauqua county sheriff's office serving as court security officers; provided, however, that nothing in this subdivision shall be deemed to authorize such officer to carry, possess, repair or dispose of a firearm unless the appropriate license therefor has been issued pursuant to section 400.00 of the penal law.

69. Employees of the village court of the village of Amityville serving as uniformed court officers at such village court; provided, however, that nothing in this subdivision shall be deemed to authorize such officer to carry, possess, repair or dispose of a firearm unless the appropriate license therefor has been issued pursuant to section 400.00 of the penal law.

70. Employees appointed by the sheriff of Yates county, pursuant to their special duties serving as uniformed marine patrol officers; provided, however, that nothing in this subdivision shall be deemed to authorize such officer to carry, possess, repair or dispose of a firearm unless the appropriate license has been issued pursuant to section 400.00 of the penal law or to authorize such officer to carry or possess a firearm except while on duty.

71. Town of Smithtown fire marshalls when acting pursuant to their special duties in matters arising under the laws relating to fires, the extinguishment thereof and fire perils; provided, however, that nothing in this subdivision shall be deemed to authorize such officers to carry,

---

* There are five subdivisions 68.
* There are five subdivisions 68.
* There are five subdivisions 68.
* There are five subdivisions 68.
* There are five subdivisions 68.

possess, repair or dispose of a firearm unless the appropriate license therefor has been issued pursuant to section 400.00 of the penal law.

72. Persons employed by Canisius college as members of the security force of such college; provided, however, that nothing in this subdivision shall be deemed to authorize such officer to carry, possess, repair or dispose of a firearm unless the appropriate license therefor has been issued pursuant to section 400.00 of the penal law.

73. Employees of the town court of the town of Newburgh serving as uniformed court officers at such town court; provided, however, that nothing in this subdivision shall be deemed to authorize such officer to carry, possess, repair or dispose of a firearm unless the appropriate license therefor has been issued pursuant to section 400.00 of the penal law.

74.* a. Special deputy sheriffs appointed by the sheriff of Tompkins county pursuant to paragraphs b and c of this subdivision; provided, however, that nothing in this subdivision shall be deemed to authorize such officer to carry, possess, repair or dispose of a firearm unless the appropriate license therefor has been issued pursuant to section 400.00 of the penal law.

b. For the protection of the grounds, buildings and property of Ithaca college the prevention of crime and the enforcement of law and order, and for the enforcement of such rules and regulations as the board of trustees of Ithaca college shall from time to time make, the sheriff of Tompkins county may appoint and remove following consultation with Ithaca college such number of special deputy sheriffs as is determined by the sheriff to be necessary for the maintenance of public order at Ithaca college, such appointments to be made from persons nominated by the president of Ithaca college. Such special deputy sheriffs shall comply with requirements as established by the sheriff and shall act only within Tompkins county. Such special deputy sheriffs so appointed shall be employees of the college and subject to its supervision and control as outlined in the terms and conditions to be mutually agreed upon between the sheriff and Ithaca college. Such special deputy sheriffs shall have the powers of peace officers and shall act solely within the said grounds or premises owned or administered by Ithaca college, except in those rare and special situations when requested by the sheriff to provide assistance on any public highway which crosses or adjoins such property. Ithaca college will provide legal defense and indemnification, and hold harmless the county of Tompkins, its officers and employees and the Tompkins county sheriff, its officers and employees, from all claims arising out of conduct by or injury to, such personnel while carrying out their law enforcement functions except in those situations when they are acting under the direct supervision and control of the county or sheriff's department.

c. Every special deputy sheriff so appointed shall, before entering upon the duties of his or her office, take and subscribe the oath of office prescribed by article thirteen of the constitution of the state of New York which oath shall be filed in the office of the county clerk of Tompkins county. Every special deputy sheriff appointed under this subdivision when on regular duty shall wear conspicuously a metallic shield with a designating number and the words "Special Deputy Sheriff Ithaca College" thereon.

74.* Parks and recreation forest rangers employed by the office of parks, recreation and historic preservation; provided, however, that nothing in this subdivision shall be deemed to

---

* There are four subdivisions 74.

* There are four subdivisions 74.

authorize such individuals to carry, possess, repair or dispose of a firearm unless the appropriate license therefor has been issued pursuant to section 400.00 of the penal law.

74.* Employees of the village court of the village of Quogue, town of Southampton serving as uniformed court officers at such village court; provided, however, that nothing in this subdivision shall be deemed to authorize such officer to carry, possess, repair or dispose of a firearm unless the appropriate license therefor has been issued pursuant to section 400.00 of the penal law.

74.* Employees of the town court of the town of East Hampton serving as uniformed court officers at such town court; provided, however, that nothing in this subdivision shall be deemed to authorize such officer to carry, possess, repair or dispose of a firearm unless the appropriate license therefor has been issued pursuant to section 400.00 of the penal law.

75.* Dog control officers of the town of Clarence, who at the discretion of the town board may be designated as constables for the purpose of enforcing article twenty-six of the agriculture and markets law and for the purpose of issuing appearance tickets permitted under article seven of the agriculture and markets law; provided, however, that nothing in this subdivision shall be deemed to authorize such officers to carry, possess, repair or dispose of a firearm unless the appropriate license therefor has been issued pursuant to section 400.00 of the penal law.

75.* Airport security guards, senior airport security guards, airport security supervisors, retired police officers, and supervisors of same, who are designated by resolution of the town board of the town of Islip to provide security at Long Island MacArthur Airport when acting pursuant to their duties as such, and such authority being specifically limited to the grounds of the said airport. However, nothing in this subdivision shall be deemed to authorize such officer to carry, possess, repair or dispose of a firearm unless the appropriate license therefor has been issued pursuant to section 400.00 of the penal law.

75.* Officers and members of the fire investigation unit of the fire department of the city of Buffalo when acting pursuant to their special duties in matters arising under the laws relating to fires, the extinguishment thereof and fire perils; provided, however, that nothing in this subdivision shall be deemed to authorize such officer to carry, possess, repair or dispose of a firearm unless the appropriate license therefor has been issued pursuant to section 400.00 of the penal law.

76.* Employees of the village court of the village of Southampton, town of Southampton serving as uniformed court officers at such village court; provided, however, that nothing in this subdivision shall be deemed to authorize such officer to carry, possess, repair or dispose of a firearm unless the appropriate license therefor has been issued pursuant to section 400.00 of the penal law.

---

* There are four subdivisions 74.
* There are four subdivisions 74.
* There are three subdivisions 75.
* There are three subdivisions 75.
* There are three subdivisions 75.
* There are two subdivisions 76.

76.* Animal control officers employed by the city of Peekskill; provided, however, that nothing in this subdivision shall be deemed to authorize such individuals to carry, possess, repair or dispose of a firearm unless the appropriate license therefor has been issued pursuant to section 400.00 of the penal law.

77.* (a) Syracuse University peace officers appointed by the chief law enforcement officer of the city of Syracuse pursuant to paragraphs (b), (c) and (d) of this subdivision, who shall be authorized to issue appearance tickets and simplified traffic informations; provided, however, that nothing in this subdivision shall be deemed to authorize any such officer to carry, possess, repair or dispose of a firearm unless the appropriate license therefor has been issued pursuant to section 400.00 of the penal law.

(b) For the protection of the grounds, buildings and property of Syracuse University, the prevention of crime and the enforcement of law and order, and for the enforcement of such rules and regulations as Syracuse University shall from time to time establish, the chief law enforcement officer of the city of Syracuse may appoint and remove, following consultations with Syracuse University; such number of Syracuse University peace officers as is determined by the chief law enforcement officer of the city of Syracuse to be necessary for the maintenance of public order at such university, such appointments to be made from persons nominated by the chancellor of Syracuse University. Such peace officers shall comply with such requirements as shall be established by the chief law enforcement officer of the city of Syracuse. Such Syracuse University peace officers so appointed shall be employees of such university, and subject to its supervision and control and the terms and conditions to be mutually agreed upon between the chief law enforcement officer of the city of Syracuse and Syracuse University. Nothing in this paragraph shall limit the authority of Syracuse University to remove such peace officers. Such Syracuse University peace officers shall have the powers of peace officers within the geographical area of employment of the grounds or premises owned, controlled or administrated by Syracuse University within the county of Onondaga, except in those situations when requested by the chief law enforcement officer of the city of Syracuse or his or her designee, including by means of written protocols agreed to by the chief law enforcement officer of the city of Syracuse and Syracuse University, to provide assistance on any public highway which crosses or adjoins such grounds or premises. Syracuse University shall provide legal defense and indemnification, and hold harmless the city of Syracuse, and its officers and employees from all claims arising out of conduct by or injury to, such peace officers while carrying out their law enforcement functions, except in those situations when they are acting under the direct supervision and control of the chief law enforcement officer of the city of Syracuse, or his or her designee.

(c) Every Syracuse University peace officer so appointed shall, before entering upon the duties of his or her office, take and subscribe the oath of office prescribed by article thirteen of the state constitution, which oath shall be filed in the office of the county clerk of the county of Onondaga. Every such peace officer appointed pursuant to this subdivision when on regular duty shall conspicuously wear a metallic shield with a designating number and the words "Syracuse University Peace Officer" engraved thereon.

(d) To become eligible for appointment as a Syracuse University peace officer a candidate shall, in addition to the training requirements as set forth in section 2.30 of this article,

---

* There are two subdivisions 76.

* There are two subdivisions 77.

complete the course of instruction in public and private law enforcement established pursuant to paragraph (c) of subdivision five of section sixty-four hundred fifty of the education law.

77.* Chief fire marshal, assistant chief fire marshal, and fire marshals, all of whom are full-time employees of the town of East Hampton, when acting pursuant to their special duties in matters arising under the laws relating to fires, the extinguishment thereof and fire perils; provided, however, that nothing in this subdivision shall be deemed to authorize such officer to carry, possess, repair or dispose of a firearm unless the appropriate license therefor has been issued pursuant to section 400.00 of the penal law.

78. A security officer employed by a community college who is specifically designated as a peace officer by the board of trustees of a community college pursuant to subdivision five-a of section sixty-three hundred six of the education law, or by a community college regional board of trustees pursuant to subdivision four-a of section sixty-three hundred ten of the education law; provided, however, that nothing in this subdivision shall be deemed to authorize such officer to carry, possess, repair or dispose of a firearm unless the appropriate license therefor has been issued pursuant to section 400.00 of the penal law.

79.* Court security officers employed by the Wayne county sheriff's office; provided however, that nothing in this subdivision shall be deemed to authorize such officer to carry, possess, repair or dispose of a firearm unless the appropriate license therefor has been issued pursuant to section 400.00 of the penal law.

79.* Supervisors and members of the arson investigation bureau and fire inspection bureau of the office of fire prevention and control when acting pursuant to their special duties in matters arising under the laws relating to fires, their prevention, extinguishment, investigation thereof, and fire perils; provided, however, that nothing in this subdivision shall be deemed to authorize such employees to carry, possess, repair, or dispose of a firearm unless the appropriate license therefor has been issued pursuant to section 400.00 of the penal law.

79.* Peace officers appointed by the city university of New York pursuant to subdivision sixteen of section sixty-two hundred six of the education law, who shall have the powers set forth in section 2.20 of this article whether or not they are acting pursuant to their special duties; provided, however, that nothing in this subdivision shall be deemed to authorize such officer to carry, possess, repair or dispose of a firearm unless the appropriate license therefor has been issued pursuant to section 400.00 of the penal law.

79.* Animal control officers of the city of Elmira, who at the discretion of the city council of the city of Elmira may be designated as constables for the purpose of enforcing article twenty-six of the agriculture and markets law, and for the purpose of issuing appearance tickets permitted under article seven of such law; provided, however, that nothing in this subdivision shall be deemed to authorize such officer to carry, possess, repair or dispose of a firearm unless the appropriate license therefor has been issued pursuant to section 400.00 of the penal law.

---

* There are two subdivisions 77.
* There are four subdivisions 79.
*' There are four subdivisions 79.
* There are four subdivisions 79.
* There are four subdivisions 79.

80. Employees of the Onondaga county sheriff's department serving as uniformed court security officers at Onondaga county court facilities; provided, however, that nothing in this subdivision shall be deemed to authorize such officers to carry, possess, repair or dispose of a firearm unless the appropriate license therefor has been issued pursuant to section 400.00 of the penal law.

81.* Members of the security force employed by Erie County Medical Center; provided however, that nothing in this subdivision shall be deemed to authorize such officer to carry, possess, repair or dispose of a firearm unless the appropriate license therefor has been issued pursuant to section 400.00 of the penal law.

81.* Employees of the town of Riverhead serving as court officers at town of Riverhead court facilities; provided, however, that nothing in this subdivision shall be deemed to authorize such officers to carry, possess, repair or dispose of a firearm unless the appropriate license therefor has been issued pursuant to section 400.00 of the penal law.

81.* Employees of the town court of the town of Southold serving as uniformed court officers at such town court; provided, however, that nothing in this subdivision shall be deemed to authorize such officer to carry, possess, repair or dispose of a firearm unless the appropriate license therefor has been issued pursuant to section 400.00 of the penal law.

81.* Commissioners of and court officers in the department of public safety for the town of Rye when acting pursuant to their special duties in matters arising under the laws relating to maintaining the safety and security of citizens, judges and court personnel in the town court, and effecting the safe and secure transport of persons under the custody of said department; provided, however, that nothing in this subdivision shall be deemed to authorize such employees to carry, possess, repair, or dispose of a firearm unless the appropriate license therefor has been issued pursuant to section 400.00 of the penal law.

81.* Employees of the town of Yorktown serving as court attendants at town of Yorktown court facilities; provided, however, that nothing in this subdivision shall be deemed to authorize such employees to carry, possess, repair or dispose of a firearm unless the appropriate license therefor has been issued pursuant to section 400.00 of the penal law.

81.* Employees of the Lewis county sheriff's department serving as uniformed court security officers at Lewis county court facilities; provided, however, that nothing in this subdivision shall be deemed to authorize such officers to carry, possess, repair or dispose of a firearm unless the appropriate license therefor has been issued pursuant to section 400.00 of the penal law.

82. Employees of the New York city business integrity commission designated as peace officers by the chairperson of such commission; provided, however, that nothing in this subdivision shall be deemed to authorize such officer to carry, possess, repair or dispose of a firearm unless the appropriate license therefor has been issued pursuant to section 400.00 of the penal law.

---

* There are six subdivisions 81.
* There are six subdivisions 81.
* There are six subdivisions 81.
* There are six subdivisions 81.
* There are six subdivisions 81.
* There are six subdivisions 81.

83.* Members of the security force employed by Kaleida Health within and directly adjacent to the hospital buildings on the medical campus located between East North Street, Goodell Street, Main Street and Michigan Avenue. These officers shall only have the powers listed in paragraph (c) of subdivision one of section 2.20 of this article, as well as the power to detain an individual for a reasonable period of time while awaiting the arrival of law enforcement, provided that the officer has actual knowledge, or probable cause to believe, that such individual has committed an offense; provided however, that nothing in this subdivision shall be deemed to authorize such officer to carry, possess, repair or dispose of a firearm unless the appropriate license therefor has been issued pursuant to section 400.00 of the penal law.

83.* (a) Security services officers employed by the University of Rochester who are designated as peace officers by the board of trustees of the University of Rochester pursuant to paragraphs (b), (c), (d) and (e) of this subdivision; provided, however, that nothing in this subdivision shall be deemed to authorize any such officer to carry, possess, repair or dispose of a firearm unless the appropriate license therefor has been issued pursuant to section 400.00 of the penal law.

(b) For the protection of the grounds, buildings and property of the University of Rochester, the prevention of crime and the enforcement of law and order, the board of trustees of the University of Rochester may appoint and remove such number of security services officers designated as peace officers as is determined by the board of trustees to be necessary for the maintenance of public order consistent with this subdivision. Such peace officers shall comply with such requirements as shall be mutually agreed upon between the chief law enforcement officers of the applicable local law enforcement jurisdictions and the University of Rochester. Such University of Rochester peace officers so appointed shall be employees of the University of Rochester and subject to its supervision and control. Such University of Rochester peace officers shall have the powers of peace officers within the geographic area of employment of the grounds or premises owned, controlled or administered by the University of Rochester within the county of Monroe except as provided in paragraph (c) of this subdivision; provided, however, such peace officers shall have the powers of peace officers beyond such geographic area upon the request of the chief law enforcement officer of the local law enforcement jurisdiction or his or her designee, for the purpose of transporting an individual who has been arrested in accordance with section 140.27 of this chapter and when no local law enforcement officer is available for transporting such individual in a timely manner.

(c) University of Rochester peace officers who are assigned to work at Strong Memorial Hospital shall only have the powers in section 9.41 of the mental hygiene law and the powers listed in paragraphs (a), (c) and (h) of subdivision one of section 2.20 of this article. Provided that in order to exercise the power set forth in paragraph (a) of subdivision one of section 2.20 of this article, the officer has actual knowledge, or probable cause to believe, that such individual has committed an offense.

(d) The University of Rochester shall provide legal defense and indemnification to applicable municipality and its officers and employees, and hold them harmless, against all claims arising out of conduct by or injury to such peace officers while carrying out their special duties, except in those situations when they are acting as agents of the chief law

---

* There are two subdivisions 83.

* There are two subdivisions 83.

enforcement officer of the applicable local law enforcement jurisdiction or his or her designee.

(e) To become eligible for designation as a University of Rochester peace officer, a candidate shall, in addition to the training requirements as set forth in section 2.30 of this article, complete the course of instruction in public and private law enforcement established pursuant to subdivision three of section sixty-four hundred thirty-five of the education law.

HISTORY: Add, L 1980, ch 843, § 2, eff Sept 1, 1980; amd, L 1981, ch 175, §§ 6, 8, 9, eff July 2, 1981 and applicable to offenses committed on or after such date; amd, L 1981, ch 175, § 7, L 1981, ch 462, § 1, L 1981, ch 470, § 1, L 1981, ch 523, § 1, L 1981, ch 720, § 5, eff Nov 1, 1981, L 1982, ch 658, § 2, retroactive to and deemed to have been in full force and effect on and after July 1, 1979, L 1983, ch 969, §§ 3–6, 9, eff Aug 8, 1983, L 1984, ch 740, § 1, L 1985, ch 65, § 4, eff April 17, 1985, L 1985, ch 266, § 1, L 1986, ch 318, § 2, eff July 17, 1986, L 1986, ch 364, § 1, L 1987, ch 617, § 11, eff Jan 1, 1988, L 1987, ch 734, §§ 1, 2, L 1987, ch 734, § 2, eff Nov 1, 1987 eff Nov 1, 1987, L 1988, ch 141, § 70, eff June 20, 1988, L 1988, ch 438, § 1, eff July 29, 1988, L 1988, ch 274, § 1, L 1988, ch 695, § 3, eff Jan 1, 1989, L 1989, ch 188, § 1, eff June 24, 1989, L 1989, ch 189, § 1, L 1989, ch 285, § 1, L 1989, ch 426, § 1, L 1990, ch 931, § 1, eff Oct 15, 1990, L 1991, ch 166, § 341, eff June 12, 1991, expired Nov 1, 1993, L 1992, ch 93, § 1, eff May 17, 1992, L 1992, ch 257, § 1, eff June 30, 1992, L 1992, ch 294, § 1, eff June 30, 1992, L 1992, ch 321, § 4, eff July 17, 1992, L 1992, ch 487, § 1, eff July 17, 1992, L 1992, ch 858, § 1, eff Dec 23, 1992, L 1993, ch 157, § 1, eff July 28, 1993, L 1993, ch 204, § 1, eff July 6, 1993, L 1993, ch 508, § 12, L 1993, ch 687, § 9, eff Dec 2, 1993, L 1994, ch 466, § 1, eff July 20, 1994, expired and repealed Jan 31, 1995, L 1994, ch 519, § 1, eff July 26, 1994, L 1994, ch 620, § 1, eff July 26, 1994, L 1994, ch 665, § 1, eff Aug 2, 1994, L 1994, ch 668, § 1, L 1995, ch 2, §§ 70 and 71, eff Sept 1, 1995, L 1995, ch 206, § 1, eff Sept 24, 1995, L 1995, ch 457, § 1, eff Aug 2, 1995, L 1995, ch 462, § 1, eff Aug 2, 1995, L 1995, ch 521, § 1, eff Aug 2, 1995, L 1995, ch 658, § 1, eff Aug 8, 1995, L 1996, ch 314, § 1, eff July 17, 1996, L 1996, ch 379, § 1, eff July 30, 1996, L 1997, ch 378, § 1, eff Aug 5, 1997, L 1997, ch 555, § 1, eff Sept 10, 1997, L 1997, ch 562, § 1, eff Sept 10, 1997, L 1998, ch 224, § 1, eff July 7, 1998, L 1998, ch 424, § 3, eff Jan 1, 1999, L 1995, ch 206, § 1, eff Sept 24, 1995, L 1999, ch 212, § 2, eff July 6, 1999, L 1999, ch 584, § 1, eff Nov 1, 1999, L 2000, ch 168, § 1, eff July 18, 2000, L 2000, ch 227, § 1, eff Aug 16, 2000, L 2000, ch 393, § 1, Aug 30, 2000, L 2000, ch 385, § 1, eff Aug 30, 2000, L 2000, ch 404, § 1, eff Aug 30, 2000, L 2001, ch 120, § 1, eff Aug 6, 2001, L 2001, ch 481, § 1, eff Nov 21, 2001, L 2001, ch 548, § 1, eff Dec 12, 2001, L 2002, ch 260, § 1, eff July 30, 2002, L 2002, ch 261, § 1, eff July 30, 2002, L 2002, ch 318, §§ 3, 4, eff Aug 6, 2002, L 2002, ch 320, § 1, Aug 6, 2002, L 2002, ch 321, § 1, Aug 6, 2002, L 2002, ch 623, § 1, eff Oct 2, 2002, L 2002, ch 623, § 1, eff Oct 2, 2002, L 2003, ch 626, § 1, eff Sept 30, 2003, L 2003, ch 638, § 1, eff Oct 7, L 2003, ch 654, § 1, eff Oct 7, 2003, 2003, L 2003, ch 665, § 1, eff Oct 15, 2003, L 2003, ch 671, § 1, eff Oct 15, 2003, L 2003, ch 689, § 3, eff Oct 21, 2003, L 2004, ch 17, § 1, eff March 23, 2004, L 2004, ch 24, § 3, eff April 6, 2004, L 2004, ch 235, § 1, eff July 27, 2004, L 2004, ch 241, § 1, eff July 27, 2004, L 2004, ch 367, § 1, Aug 17, 2004, L 2004, ch 664, §§ 2, 3, eff Oct 26, 2004, L 2004, ch 752, § 1, eff Jan 28, 2005, L 2005, ch 557, § 1, eff Aug 23, 2005, L 2006, ch 438, § 1, eff July 26, 2006, expired and repealed Dec 31, 2006, L 2006, ch 467, § 1, eff Feb 12, 2007, L 2006, ch 482, § 1, eff Aug 16, 2006, L 2006, ch 501, § 1, eff Aug 16, 2006, L 2006, ch 581, § 1, eff Aug 16, 2006, L 2006, ch 584, § 1, eff Aug 16, 2006, L 2006, ch 653, § 1, eff Sept 13, 2006, L 2006, ch 693, § 2, eff Sept 13, 2006, L 2008, ch 564, § 1, eff Sept 4, 2008, L 2009, ch 329, § 7, eff Aug 8, 2009, L 2009, ch 329, § 8, eff Aug 11, 2009, expires and repealed Aug 11, 2019, L 2010, ch 56, § 50 (Part B), eff July 1, 2010, L 2011, ch 61, § 56 (Part K), eff Sept 1, 2011, L 2011, ch 62, §§ 78, 78-a (Part A), eff Oct 3, 2011, L 2011, ch 62, § 70 (Part C, Subpart B), eff March 31, 2011, L 2012, ch 502, § 1, eff June 15, 2013, L 2012, ch 504, § 1, eff Dec 17, 2012.

§ 2.15. Federal law enforcement officers; powers

The following federal law enforcement officers shall have the powers set forth in paragraphs (a) (with the exception of the powers provided by paragraph (b) of subdivision one and paragraph (b) of subdivision three of section 140.25 of this chapter), (b), (c) and (h) of subdivision one of section 2.20 of this article:

1. Federal Bureau of Investigation special agents.

2. United States Secret Service special agents.

3. Immigration and Customs Enforcement special agents, deportation officers, and detention and deportation officers.

4. United States Marshals and Marshals Service deputies.

5. Drug Enforcement Administration special agents.

6. Federal Protective Officers, including law enforcement security officers, criminal investigators and police officers of the Federal Protective Service.

7. United States Customs and Border Protection Officers and United States Customs and Border Protection Border Patrol agents.

8. United States Postal Service police officers and inspectors.

9. United States park police; provided, however that, notwithstanding any provision of this section to the contrary, such park police shall also have the powers set forth in paragraph (b) of subdivision one of section 140.25 of this chapter and the powers set forth in paragraphs (d), (e) and (g) of subdivision one of section 2.20 of this article.

10. United States probation officers.

11. United States General Services Administration special agents.

12. United States Department of Agriculture special agents.

13. Bureau of Alcohol, Tobacco and Firearms special agents.

14. Internal Revenue Service special agents and inspectors.

15. Officers of the United States bureau of prisons.

16. United States Fish and Wildlife special agents.

17. United States Naval Investigative Service special agents.

18. United States Department of State special agents.

19. Special agents of the defense criminal investigative service of the United States department of defense.

20. United States Department of Commerce, Office of Export Enforcement, special agents.

21. United States Department of Veterans Administration police officers employed at the Veterans Administration Medical Center in Batavia.

22. Federal Reserve law enforcement officers.

23. Federal air marshal program special agents.

24.* United States department of transportation federal police officers and police supervisors assigned to the United States Merchant Marine Academy in Kings Point, New York; provided, however that, notwithstanding any provision of this section to the contrary, such police shall also have the powers set forth in paragraph (b) of subdivision one of section 140.25 of this chapter and the powers set forth in paragraphs (d), (e) and (g) of subdivision one of section 2.20

---

* There are two subdivisions 24.

of this article when acting pursuant to their special duties within the geographical area of their employment or within one hundred yards of such geographical area.

24.* United States Coast Guard Investigative Service special agents.

25. United States Department of Commerce, special agents and enforcement officers of the National Oceanic and Atmospheric Administration's Fisheries Office for Law Enforcement.

26. Department of the Army special agents, detectives and police officers.

27. United States Department of Interior, park rangers with law enforcement authority.

28. United States Environmental Protection Agency special agents with law enforcement authority.

HISTORY: Add, L 1982, ch 474, § 1; amd, L 1983, ch 68, § 1, eff May 3, 1983, L 1985, ch 205, § 1, L 1985, ch 392, § 1, eff July 19, 1985, L 1986, ch 420, § 1, L 1987, ch 644, § 1, eff Nov 1, 1987 L 1995, ch 177, § 1, eff July 19, 1995, L 1995, ch 522, § 1, eff Aug 2, 1995, L 1997, ch 549, § 1, eff Sept 10, 1997, L 2002, ch 92, § 1, eff June 24, 2002, L 2003, ch 299, § 1, eff Aug 5, 2003, L 2004, ch 110, § 1, eff June 15, 2004; amd, L 2004, ch 178, § 2, eff June 15, 2004, L 2004, ch 720, § 1, eff Nov 24, 2004, L 2005, ch 43, § 1, eff May 24, 2005, L 2005, ch 735, § 1, eff Oct 11, 2005, L 2006, ch 486, § 1, eff Aug 16, 2006, L 2007, ch 550, § 1, eff Aug 15, 2007, L 2011, ch 407, § 1, eff Aug 17, 2011, L 2013, ch 366, § 1, eff Sept 27, 2013, L 2014, ch 262, § 1, eff Aug 11, 2014.

§ 2.16. Watershed protection and enforcement officers; powers, duties, jurisdiction for arrests

1. Watershed protection and enforcement officers appointed by the city of Peekskill shall have the powers set forth in paragraphs (a), (b), (c), (f), (g), and (h) of subdivision one of section 2.20 of this article; provided, however, that nothing in this section shall be deemed to authorize such officer to carry, possess, repair, or dispose of a firearm unless the appropriate license therefor has been issued pursuant to section 400.00 of the penal law. Watershed protection and enforcement officers shall complete the training requirements set forth in section 2.30 of this article.

2. The city of Peekskill may appoint the following persons as watershed protection and enforcement officers:

(a) the water superintendent;

(b) the deputy assistant to the water superintendent; and

(c) the watershed inspector or inspectors.

3. The duties of the watershed protection and enforcement officers shall be to enforce those provisions of the environmental conservation law and the penal law which relate to the contamination of water in those areas of the Hollow Brook watershed located within the city of Peekskill, including its reservoirs, shoreline, and tributaries, and those areas of the Hollow Brook watershed and Wiccopee reservoir located outside of the city of Peekskill in the counties of Putnam and Westchester, including its reservoirs, shoreline, and tributaries.

4. Notwithstanding paragraph (b) of subdivision thirty-four-a of section 1.20 of this title and paragraph (b) of subdivision five of section 140.25 of this chapter, watershed protection and enforcement officers are authorized to make arrests and issue appearance tickets in those areas of the Hollow Brook watershed and Wiccopee reservoir located outside of the city of Peekskill in the counties of Putnam and Westchester, including along its reservoirs, shoreline, and tributaries.

---

* There are two subdivisions 24.

HISTORY: Add, L 2004, ch 347, § 1, eff Aug 10, 2004.

§ 2.20. Powers of peace officers

1. The persons designated in section 2.10 of this article shall have the following powers:

(a) The power to make warrantless arrests pursuant to section 140.25 of this chapter.

(b) The power to use physical force and deadly physical force in making an arrest or preventing an escape pursuant to section 35.30 of the penal law.

(c) The power to carry out warrantless searches whenever such searches are constitutionally permissible and acting pursuant to their special duties.

(d) The power to issue appearance tickets pursuant to subdivision three of section 150.20 of this chapter, when acting pursuant to their special duties. New York city special patrolmen shall have the power to issue an appearance ticket only when it is pursuant to rules and regulations of the police commissioner of the city of New York.

(e) The power to issue uniform appearance tickets pursuant to article twenty-seven of the parks, recreation and historic preservation law and to issue simplified traffic informations pursuant to section 100.25 of this chapter and section two hundred seven of the vehicle and traffic law whenever acting pursuant to their special duties.

(f) The power to issue a uniform navigation summons and/or complaint pursuant to section nineteen of the navigation law whenever acting pursuant to their special duties.

(g) The power to issue uniform appearance tickets pursuant to article seventy-one of the environmental conservation law, whenever acting pursuant to their special duties.

(h) The power to possess and take custody of firearms not owned by the peace officer, for the purpose of disposing, guarding, or any other lawful purpose, consistent with his duties as a peace officer.

(i) Any other power which a particular peace officer is otherwise authorized to exercise by any general, special or local law or charter whenever acting pursuant to his special duties, provided such power is not inconsistent with the provisions of the penal law or this chapter.

(j) Uniformed court officers shall have the power to issue traffic summonses and complaints for parking, standing, or stopping violations pursuant to the vehicle and traffic law whenever acting pursuant to their special duties.

2. For the purposes of this section a peace officer acts pursuant to his special duties when he performs the duties of his office, pursuant to the specialized nature of his particular employment, whereby he is required or authorized to enforce any general, special or local law or charter, rule, regulation, judgment or order.

3. A peace officer, whether or not acting pursuant to his special duties, who lawfully exercises any of the powers conferred upon him pursuant to this section, shall be deemed to be acting within the scope of his public employment for purposes of defense and indemnification rights and benefits that he may be otherwise entitled to under the provisions of section fifty-k of the general municipal law, section seventeen or eighteen of the public officers law, or any other applicable section of law.

HISTORY: Add, L 1980, ch 843, § 2, eff Sept 1, 1980. Sub 1, formerly opening par, so numbered, L 1985, ch 722, § 1, eff Aug 1, 1985. Former sub 1, redesignated sub 1, par (a), L 1985, ch 722, § 1, eff Aug 1, 1985. Sub 1, par (a), formerly sub 1, redesignated sub 1, par (a), L 1985, ch 722, § 1, eff Aug 1, 1985. Sub 1, par (b), formerly sub 2, redesignated sub 1, par (b), L 1985, ch 722, § 1, eff Aug 1, 1985. Sub 1, par (c), formerly sub 3, redesignated sub 1, par (c), L 1985, ch 722, § 1, eff Aug 1, 1985. Sub 1, par (d), formerly sub 4, redesignated sub 1, par (d), L 1985, ch 722, § 1, eff Aug 1, 1985. Sub 1, par (e), formerly sub 5, redesignated sub 1, par (e) and amd, L 1985, ch 722, § 1, eff Aug 1, 1985. Sub 1, par (f), formerly sub 6, redesignated sub 1, par (f), L 1985, ch 722, § 1, eff Aug 1, 1985. Sub 1, par (g), formerly sub 7, redesignated sub 1, par (g), L 1985, ch 722, § 1, eff Aug 1, 1985. Sub 1, par (h), formerly sub 8, redesignated sub 1, par (h), L 1985, ch 722, § 1, eff Aug 1, 1985. Sub 1, par (i), formerly sub 9, redesignated sub 1, par (i), L 1985, ch 722, § 1, eff Aug 1, 1985. Sub 1, par (j), add, L 2005, ch 685, § 1, eff Oct 4, 2005. Sub 2, formerly last undesignated par, so numbered, L 1985, ch 722, § 1, eff Aug 1, 1985. Former sub 2, designated sub 1, par (b), L 1985, ch 722, § 1, eff Aug 1, 1985. Sub 3, add, L 1985, ch 722, § 1, eff Aug 1, 1985. Former sub 3, redesignated sub 1, par (c), L 1985, ch 722, § 1, eff Aug 1, 1985. Subs 4–9, redesignated sub 1, pars (d)–(i), L 1985, ch 722, § 1, eff Aug 1, 1985.

§ 2.30. Training requirements for peace officers

1. Every peace officer in the state of New York must successfully complete a training program, a portion of which shall be prescribed by the municipal police training council and a portion of which shall be prescribed by his or her employer. The portion prescribed by the municipal police training council shall be comprised of subjects, and the hours each is to be taught, that shall be required of all types or classes of peace officers. The hours of instruction required by the municipal police training council shall not exceed one hundred eighty, unless a greater amount is either required by law or regulation, or is requested by the employer.

The segment prescribed by the employer for its employees shall be comprised of subjects, and the hours each is to be taught, relating to the special nature of the duties of the peace officers employed by it provided, however, that when the subjects prescribed by the employer are identical to the subjects in the training program required by the municipal police training council, the employer shall not be required to provide duplicate training for those subjects.

2. Each state or local agency, unit of local government, state or local commission, or public authority, or public or private organization which employs peace officers shall provide the training mandated by this section, the cost of which will be borne by the employer. Each peace officer satisfactorily completing the course prescribed by the municipal police training council shall be awarded a certificate by the division of criminal justice services attesting to that effect, and no person appointed as a peace officer shall exercise the powers of a peace officer, unless he or she has received such certification within twelve months of appointment.

3. No employer shall allow any peace officer it employs to carry or use a weapon during any phase of the officer's official duties, which constitutes on-duty employment, unless the officer has satisfactorily completed a course of training approved by the municipal police training council in the use of deadly physical force and firearms and other weapons, and annually receives instruction in deadly physical force and the use of firearms and other weapons as approved by the municipal police training council.

4. Upon the failure or refusal to comply with the requirements of this section, the commissioner of the division of criminal justice services shall apply to the supreme court for an order directed to the person responsible requiring compliance. Upon such application, the court may issue such order as may be just, and a failure to comply with the order of the court shall be a contempt of court and punishable as such.

5. Every employer of peace officers shall report to the division of criminal justice services, in such form and at such time as the division may by regulation require, the names of all peace officers who have satisfactorily completed any of the training requirements prescribed by this section.

6. A certificate attesting to satisfactory completion of the training requirements imposed under this section awarded to any peace officer by the executive director of the municipal police training council pursuant to this section shall remain valid:

(a) during the holder's continuous service as a peace officer; and

(b) for two years after the date of the commencement of an interruption in such service where the holder had, immediately prior to such interruption, served as a peace officer for less than two consecutive years; or

(c) for four years after the date of the commencement of an interruption in such service where the holder had, immediately prior to such interruption, served as a peace officer for two consecutive years or longer.

As used in this subdivision, the term "interruption" shall mean a period of separation from employment as a peace officer by reason of such officer's leave of absence, resignation or removal, other than removal for cause.

HISTORY: Add, L 1980, ch 843, § 2, eff Sept 1, 1980. Amd, L 2010, ch 491, § 3, eff Jan 1, 2011. Sub 1, amd, L 1989, ch 766, § 1, eff Sept 9, 1989. Sub 1, second undesignated par, amd, L 1989, ch 766, § 1, eff Sept 9, 1989. Sub 1, third undesignated par, amd, L 1991, ch 219, § 1, L 1991, ch 474, § 1, eff Nov 1, 1991. Sub 5, add, L 1987, ch 543, § 1, eff Nov 1, 1987. Sub 6, add, L 1988, ch 735, § 2, eff Jan 1, 1989.

TITLE B   The Criminal Courts

ARTICLE 10
THE CRIMINAL COURTS

HISTORY: Add, L 1970, ch 996, § 1, eff Sept 1, 1971.

ARTICLE 10   THE CRIMINAL COURTS

HISTORY: Add, L 1970, ch 996, § 1, eff Sept 1, 1971.

§ 10.10. The criminal courts; enumerated and definitions

1. The "criminal courts" of this state are comprised of the superior courts and the local criminal courts.

2. "Superior court" means:

(a) The supreme court; or

(b) A county court.

3. "Local criminal court" means:

(a) A district court; or

(b) The New York City criminal court; or

(c) A city court; or

(d) A town court; or

(e) A village court; or

(f) A supreme court justice sitting as a local criminal court; or

(g) A county judge sitting as a local criminal court.

4. "City court" means any court for a city, other than New York City, having trial jurisdiction of offenses of less than felony grade only committed within such city, whether such court is entitled a city court, a municipal court, a police court, a recorder's court or is known by any other name or title.

5. "Town court." A "town court" is comprised of all the town justices of a town.

6. "Village court." A "village court" is comprised of the justice of a village, or all the justices thereof if there be more than one, or, at a time when he or they are absent, an acting justice of a village who is authorized to perform the functions of a village justice during his absence.

7. Notwithstanding any other provision of this section, a court specified herein which possesses civil as well as criminal jurisdiction does not act as a criminal court when acting solely in the exercise of its civil jurisdiction, and an order or determination made by such a court in its civil capacity is not an order or determination of a criminal court even though it may terminate or otherwise control or affect a criminal action or proceeding.

HISTORY: Add, L 1970, ch 996, § 1, eff Sept 1, 1971.

§ 10.20. Superior courts; jurisdiction

1. Superior courts have trial jurisdiction of all offenses. They have:

    (a) Exclusive trial jurisdiction of felonies; and

    (b) Trial jurisdiction of misdemeanors concurrent with that of the local criminal courts; and

    (c) Trial jurisdiction of petty offenses, but only when such an offense is charged in an indictment which also charges a crime.

2. Superior courts have preliminary jurisdiction of all offenses, but they exercise such jurisdiction only by reason of and through the agency of their grand juries.

3. Superior court judges may, in their discretion, sit as local criminal courts for the following purposes:

    (a) conducting arraignments, as provided in subdivision two of section 170.15 and subdivision two of section 180.20 of this chapter;

    (b) issuing warrants of arrests, as provided in subdivision one of section 120.70 of this chapter; and

    (c) issuing search warrants, as provided in article six hundred ninety of this chapter.

    HISTORY: Add, L 1970, ch 996, § 1, eff Sept 1, 1971. Sub 3, add, L 1992, ch 815, § 1; amd, L 1992, ch 816, § 1, eff Nov 1, 1992. Sub 3, opening par, amd, L 1992, ch 816, § 1, eff Nov 1, 1992. Sub 3, par (a), amd, L 1992, ch 816, § 1, eff Nov 1, 1992.

§ 10.30. Local criminal courts; jurisdiction

1. Local criminal courts have trial jurisdiction of all offenses other than felonies. They have:

    (a) Exclusive trial jurisdiction of petty offenses except for the superior court jurisdiction thereof prescribed in paragraph (c) of subdivision one of section 10.20; and

    (b) Trial jurisdiction of misdemeanors concurrent with that of the superior courts but subject to divestiture thereof by the latter in any particular case.

2. Local criminal courts have preliminary jurisdiction of all offenses subject to divestiture thereof in any particular case by the superior courts and their grand juries.

3. Notwithstanding the provisions of subdivision one, a superior court judge sitting as a local criminal court does not have trial jurisdiction of any offense, but has preliminary jurisdiction only, as provided in subdivision two.

    HISTORY: Add, L 1970, ch 996, § 1, eff Sept 1, 1971.

§ 10.40. Chief administrator to prescribe forms

The chief administrator of the courts shall have the power to adopt, amend and rescind forms for the efficient and just administration of this chapter. A failure by any party to submit papers in compliance with forms authorized by this section shall not be grounds for that reason alone for denial or granting of any motion.

    HISTORY: Add, L 1984, ch 47, § 1, eff April 10, 1984.

TITLE C　General Principles Relating to Requirements For and Exemptions From Criminal Prosecution

ARTICLE 20
GEOGRAPHICAL JURISDICTION OF OFFENSES

ARTICLE 30
TIMELINESS OF PROSECUTIONS AND SPEEDY TRIAL

ARTICLE 40
EXEMPTION FROM PROSECUTION BY REASON OF PREVIOUS PROSECUTION

ARTICLE 50
COMPULSION OF EVIDENCE BY OFFER OF IMMUNITY

HISTORY: Add, L 1970, ch 996, § 1, eff Sept 1, 1971.

ARTICLE 20　GEOGRAPHICAL JURISDICTION OF OFFENSES

HISTORY: Add, L 1970, ch 996, § 1, eff Sept 1, 1971.

§ 20.10. Geographical jurisdiction of offenses; definitions of terms

The following definitions are applicable to this article:

1. "This state" means New York State as its boundaries are prescribed in the state law, and the space over it.

2. "County" means any of the sixty-two counties of this state as its boundaries are prescribed by law, and the space over it.

3. "Result of an offense." When a specific consequence, such as the death of the victim in a homicide case, is an element of an offense, the occurrence of such consequence constitutes the "result" of such offense. An offense of which a result is an element is a "result offense."

4. "Particular effect of an offense." When conduct constituting an offense produces consequences which, though not necessarily amounting to a result or element of such offense, have a materially harmful impact upon the governmental processes or community welfare of a particular jurisdiction, or result in the defrauding of persons in such jurisdiction, such conduct and offense have a "particular effect" upon such jurisdiction.

HISTORY: Add, L 1970, ch 996, § 1, eff Sept 1, 1971.

§ 20.20. Geographical jurisdiction of offenses; jurisdiction of state

Except as otherwise provided in this section and section 20.30, a person may be convicted in the criminal courts of this state of an offense defined by the laws of this state, committed either by his own conduct or by the conduct of another for which he is legally accountable pursuant to section 20.00 of the penal law, when:

1. Conduct occurred within this state sufficient to establish:

(a) An element of such offense; or

(b) An attempt to commit such offense; or

(c) A conspiracy or criminal solicitation to commit such offense, or otherwise to establish the complicity of at least one of the persons liable therefor; provided that the jurisdiction accorded by this paragraph extends only to conviction of those persons whose conspiratorial or other conduct of complicity occurred within this state; or

2. Even though none of the conduct constituting such offense may have occurred within this state:

(a) The offense committed was a result offense and the result occurred within this state. If the offense was one of homicide, it is presumed that the result, namely the death of the victim, occurred within this state if the victim's body or a part thereof was found herein; or

(b) The statute defining the offense is designed to prevent the occurrence of a particular effect in this state and the conduct constituting the offense committed was performed with intent that it would have such effect herein; or

(c) The offense committed was an attempt to commit a crime within this state; or

(d) The offense committed was conspiracy to commit a crime within this state and an overt act in furtherance of such conspiracy occurred within this state; or

3. The offense committed was one of omission to perform within this state a duty imposed by the laws of this state. In such case, it is immaterial whether such person was within or outside this state at the time of the omission.

HISTORY: Add, L 1970, ch 996, § 1, eff Sept 1, 1971.

§ 20.30. Geographical jurisdiction of offenses; effect of laws of other jurisdictions upon this state's jurisdiction

1. Notwithstanding the provisions of section 20.20, the courts of this state do not have jurisdiction to convict a person of an alleged offense partly committed within this state but consummated in another jurisdiction, or an offense of criminal solicitation, conspiracy or attempt in this state to commit a crime in another jurisdiction, or an offense of criminal facilitation in this state of a felony committed in another jurisdiction, unless the conduct constituting the consummated offense or, as the case may be, the conduct constituting the crime solicited, conspiratorially contemplated or facilitated, constitutes an offense under the laws of such other jurisdiction as well as under the laws of this state.

2. The courts of this state are not deprived of the jurisdiction accorded them by section 20.20 to convict a person of an offense defined by the laws of this state, partly committed in another jurisdiction but consummated in this state, or an offense of attempt or conspiracy in another jurisdiction to commit in this state a crime defined by the laws of this state, by the circumstance that the conduct constituting the consummated offense or, as the case may be, the crime attempted or conspiratorially contemplated, does not constitute an offense under the laws of such other jurisdiction.

HISTORY: Add, L 1970, ch 996, § 1, eff Sept 1, 1971.

§ 20.40. Geographical jurisdiction of offenses; jurisdiction of counties

A person may be convicted in an appropriate criminal court of a particular county, of an offense of which the criminal courts of this state have jurisdiction pursuant to section 20.20, committed either by his or her own conduct or by the conduct of another for which he or she is legally accountable pursuant to section 20.00 of the penal law, when:

1. Conduct occurred within such county sufficient to establish:

(a) An element of such offense; or

(b) An attempt or a conspiracy to commit such offense; or

2. Even though none of the conduct constituting such offense may have occurred within such county:

(a) The offense committed was a result offense and the result occurred in such county; or

(b) The offense committed was one of homicide and the victim's body or a part thereof was found in such county; or

(c) Such conduct had, or was likely to have, a particular effect upon such county or a political subdivision or part thereof, and was performed with intent that it would, or with knowledge that it was likely to, have such particular effect therein; or

(d) The offense committed was attempt, conspiracy or criminal solicitation to commit a crime in such county; or

(e) The offense committed was criminal facilitation of a felony committed in such county; or

3. The offense committed was one of omission to perform a duty imposed by law, which duty either was required to be or could properly have been performed in such county. In such case, it is immaterial whether such person was within or outside such county at the time of the omission; or

4. Jurisdiction of such offense is accorded to the courts of such county pursuant to any of the following rules:

(a) An offense of abandonment of a child or non-support of a child may be prosecuted in (i) any county in which such child resided during the period of abandonment or non-support, or (ii) any county in which such person resided during such period, or (iii) any county in which such person was present during such period, provided that he was arrested for such offense in such county or the criminal action therefor was commenced while he was present therein.

(b) An offense of bigamy may be prosecuted either in the county in which such offense was committed or in (i) any county in which bigamous cohabitation subsequently occurred, or (ii) any county in which such person was present after the commission of the offense, provided that he was arrested for such offense in such county or the criminal action therefor was commenced while he was present therein.

(c) An offense committed within five hundred yards of the boundary of a particular county, and in an adjoining county of this state, may be prosecuted in either such county.

(d) An offense committed anywhere on the Hudson river southward of the northern boundary of New York City, or anywhere on New York bay between Staten Island and Long Island, may be prosecuted in any of the five counties of New York City.

(e) An offense committed upon any bridge or in any tunnel having terminals in different counties may be prosecuted in any terminal county.

CPL

(f) An offense committed on board a railroad train, aircraft or omnibus operating as a common carrier may be prosecuted in any county through or over which such common carrier passed during the particular trip, or in any county in which such trip terminated or was scheduled to terminate.

(g) An offense committed in a private vehicle during a trip thereof extending through more than one county may be prosecuted in any county through which such vehicle passed in the course of such trip.

(h) An offense committed on board a vessel navigating or lying in any river, canal or lake flowing through or situated within this state, may be prosecuted in any county bordering upon such body of water, or in which it is located, or through which it passes; and if such offense was committed upon a vessel operating as a common carrier, it may be prosecuted in any county bordering upon any body of water upon which such vessel navigated or passed during the particular trip.

(i) An offense committed in the Atlantic Ocean within two nautical miles from the shore at high water mark may be prosecuted in an appropriate court of the county the shore line of which is closest to the point where the offense was committed. A crime committed more than two nautical miles from the shore but within the boundary of this state may be prosecuted in the supreme court of the county the shore line of which is closest to the point where the crime was committed.

(j) An offense of forgery may be prosecuted in any county in which the defendant, or another for whose conduct the defendant is legally accountable pursuant to section 20.00 of the penal law, possessed the instrument.

(k) An offense of offering of a false instrument for filing, or of larceny by means of a false pretense therein, may be prosecuted (i) in any county in which such instrument was executed, in whole or in part, or (ii) in any county in which any of the goods or services for which payment or reimbursement is sought by means of such instrument were purported to have been provided.

(l) An offense of identity theft or unlawful possession of personal identifying information and all criminal acts committed as part of the same criminal transaction as defined in subdivision two of section 40.10 of this chapter may be prosecuted (i) in any county in which part of the offense took place regardless of whether the defendant was actually present in such county, or (ii) in the county in which the person who suffers financial loss resided at the time of the commission of the offense, or (iii) in the county where the person whose personal identifying information was used in the commission of the offense resided at the time of the commission of the offense. The law enforcement agency of any such county shall take a police report of the matter and provide the complainant with a copy of such report at no charge.

(m) An offense under the tax law or the penal law of filing a false or fraudulent return, report, document, declaration, statement, or filing, or of tax evasion, fraud, or larceny resulting from the filing of a false or fraudulent return, report, document, declaration, or filing in connection with the payment of taxes to the state or a political subdivision of the state, may be prosecuted in any county in which an underlying transaction reflected, reported or required to be reflected or reported, in whole or part, on such return, report, document, declaration, statement, or filing occurred.

HISTORY: Add, L 1970, ch 996, § 1, eff Sept 1, 1971, with substance derived from Crim C

§§ 11-a, 134-a-137; amd, L 1985, ch 575, § 1, eff Nov 1, 1985, L 2002, ch 619, § 5, eff Nov 1, 2002; amd, L 2007, ch 346, § 2, eff July 18, 2007, L 2009, ch 57, § 1 (Part V-1, Subpart I), eff April 7, 2009, L 2011, ch 97, § 3 (Part C, Subpart C), eff June 24, 2011.

§ 20.50. Geographical jurisdiction of offenses; jurisdiction of cities, towns and villages

1. The principles prescribed in section 20.40, governing geographical jurisdiction over offenses as between counties of this state, are, where appropriate, applicable to the determination of geographical jurisdiction over offenses as between cities, towns and villages within a particular county unless a different determination is required by the provisions of some other express provision of statute.

2. Where an offense prosecutable in a local criminal court is committed in a city other than New York City, or in a town or village, but within one hundred yards of any other such political subdivision, it may be prosecuted in either such political subdivision.

HISTORY: Add, L 1970, ch 996, § 1, eff Sept 1, 1971.

§ 20.60. Geographical jurisdiction of offenses; communications and transportation of property between jurisdictions

For purposes of this article:

1. An oral or written statement made by a person in one jurisdiction to a person in another jurisdiction by means of telecommunication, mail or any other method of communication is deemed to be made in each such jurisdiction.

2. A person who causes property to be transported from one jurisdiction to another by means of mail, common carrier or any other method is deemed to have personally transported it in each jurisdiction, and if delivery is made in the second jurisdiction he is deemed to have personally made such delivery therein.

3. A person who causes by any means the use of a computer or computer service in one jurisdiction from another jurisdiction is deemed to have personally used the computer or computer service in each jurisdiction.

HISTORY: Add, L 1970, ch 996, § 1, eff Sept 1, 1971. Sub 3, add, L 1986, ch 514, § 7, eff Nov 1, 1986.

ARTICLE 30   TIMELINESS OF PROSECUTIONS AND SPEEDY TRIAL
§ 30.10.   Timeliness of prosecutions; periods of limitation
§ 30.20.   Speedy trial; in general
§ 30.30.   Speedy trial; time limitations
HISTORY: Add, L 1970, ch 996, § 1, eff Sept 1, 1971.

§ 30.10. Timeliness of prosecutions; periods of limitation

1. A criminal action must be commenced within the period of limitation prescribed in the ensuing subdivisions of this section.

2. Except as otherwise provided in subdivision three:

(a) A prosecution for a class A felony, or rape in the first degree as defined in section 130.35 of the penal law, or a crime defined or formerly defined in section 130.50 of the penal law, or aggravated sexual abuse in the first degree as defined in section 130.70 of the penal law, or course of sexual conduct against a child in the first degree as defined in section 130.75 of the penal law may be commenced at any time;

(b) A prosecution for any other felony must be commenced within five years after the commission thereof;

(c) A prosecution for a misdemeanor must be commenced within two years after the commission thereof;

(d) A prosecution for a petty offense must be commenced within one year after the commission thereof.

3. Notwithstanding the provisions of subdivision two, the periods of limitation for the commencement of criminal actions are extended as follows in the indicated circumstances:

(a) A prosecution for larceny committed by a person in violation of a fiduciary duty may be commenced within one year after the facts constituting such offense are discovered or, in the exercise of reasonable diligence, should have been discovered by the aggrieved party or by a person under a legal duty to represent him who is not himself implicated in the commission of the offense.

(b) A prosecution for any offense involving misconduct in public office by a public servant including, without limitation, an offense defined in article four hundred ninety-six of the penal law, may be commenced against a public servant, or any other person acting in concert with such public servant at any time during such public servant's service in such office or within five years after the termination of such service; provided however, that in no event shall the period of limitation be extended by more than five years beyond the period otherwise applicable under subdivision two of this section.

(c) A prosecution for any crime set forth in title twenty-seven or article seventy-one of the environmental conservation law may be commenced within four years after the facts constituting such crime are discovered or, in the exercise of reasonable diligence, should have been discovered by a public servant who has the responsibility to enforce the provisions of said title and article.

(d) A prosecution for any misdemeanor set forth in the tax law or chapter forty-six of the administrative code of the city of New York must be commenced within three years after the commission thereof.

(e) A prosecution for course of sexual conduct against a child in the second degree as defined in section 130.80 of the penal law may be commenced within five years of the commission of the most recent act of sexual conduct.

(f) As amended by L 2006, ch 3, § 2 and ch 320, § 10

For purposes of a prosecution involving a sexual offense as defined in article one hundred thirty of the penal law, other than a sexual offense delineated in paragraph (a) of subdivision two of this section, committed against a child less than eighteen years of age, incest in the first, second or third degree as defined in sections 255.27, 255.26 and 255.25 of the penal law committed against a child less than eighteen years of age, or use of a child in a sexual performance as defined in section 263.05 of the penal law, the period of limitation shall not begin to run until the child has reached the age of eighteen or the offense is reported to a law enforcement agency or statewide central register of child abuse and maltreatment, whichever occurs earlier.

(g) A prosecution for any felony defined in article four hundred ninety of the penal law must be commenced within eight years after the commission thereof provided, however, that in a prosecution for a felony defined in article four hundred ninety of the penal law, if the commission of such felony offense resulted in, or created a foreseeable risk of, death or serious physical injury to another person, the prosecution may be commenced at any time; provided, however, that nothing in this paragraph shall be deemed to shorten or otherwise lessen the period, defined in any other applicable law, in which a prosecution for a felony designated in this paragraph may be commenced.

4. In calculating the time limitation applicable to commencement of a criminal action, the following periods shall not be included:

(a) Any period following the commission of the offense during which (i) the defendant was continuously outside this state or (ii) the whereabouts of the defendant were continuously unknown and continuously unascertainable by the exercise of reasonable diligence. However, in no event shall the period of limitation be extended by more than five years beyond the period otherwise applicable under subdivision two.

(b) When a prosecution for an offense is lawfully commenced within the prescribed period of limitation therefor, and when an accusatory instrument upon which such prosecution is based is subsequently dismissed by an authorized court under directions or circumstances permitting the lodging of another charge for the same offense or an offense based on the same conduct, the period extending from the commencement of the thus defeated prosecution to the dismissal of the accusatory instrument does not constitute a part of the period of limitation applicable to commencement of prosecution by a new charge.

> **HISTORY:** Add, L 1970, ch 996, § 1, eff Sept 1, 1971; amd, L 1981, ch 719, § 2; amd, L 1985, ch 65, § 5, and applicable to all offenses committed on or after April 17, 1985, L 1985, ch 765, § 33, eff Aug 1, 1985 and applicable to all offenses committed on or after Aug 1, 1985, L 1986, ch 671, § 25, eff Nov 1, 1986, L 1996, ch 122, § 1, eff Aug 1, 1996, L 2004, ch 1, § 2 (Part A), eff July 23, 2004, L 2006, ch 3, §§ 1, 2, eff June 23, 2006, L 2006, ch 320, § 10, eff Nov 1, 2006, L 2008, ch 467, § 1, eff Aug 5, 2008, L 2014, ch 55, § 2 (Part H, Subpart A), eff April 30, 2014.

§ 30.20. Speedy trial; in general

1. After a criminal action is commenced, the defendant is entitled to a speedy trial.

2. Insofar as is practicable, the trial of a criminal action must be given preference over civil cases; and the trial of a criminal action where the defendant has been committed to the custody of the sheriff during the pendency of the criminal action must be given preference over other criminal actions.

> **HISTORY:** Add, L 1970, ch 996, § 1, eff Sept 1, 1971, with substance derived from Crim C § 8(1). Section heading, amd, L 1972, ch 184, § 1, eff April 28, 1972, with substance transferred from former § 30.30. Sub 1, formerly entire section, so designated, L 1972, ch 184, § 1, eff April 28, 1972. Sub 2, add, L 1972, ch 184, § 1, eff April 28, 1972.

§ 30.30. Speedy trial; time limitations

1. Except as otherwise provided in subdivision three, a motion made pursuant to paragraph (e) of subdivision one of section 170.30 or paragraph (g) of subdivision one of section 210.20 must be granted where the people are not ready for trial within:

(a) six months of the commencement of a criminal action wherein a defendant is accused of one or more offenses, at least one of which is a felony;

(b) ninety days of the commencement of a criminal action wherein a defendant is accused of one or more offenses, at least one of which is a misdemeanor punishable by a sentence of imprisonment of more than three months and none of which is a felony;

(c) sixty days of the commencement of a criminal action wherein the defendant is accused of one or more offenses, at least one of which is a misdemeanor punishable by a sentence of imprisonment of not more than three months and none of which is a crime punishable by a sentence of imprisonment of more than three months;

(d) thirty days of the commencement of a criminal action wherein the defendant is accused of one or more offenses, at least one of which is a violation and none of which is a crime.

2. Except as provided in subdivision three, where a defendant has been committed to the custody of the sheriff in a criminal action he must be released on bail or on his own recognizance, upon such conditions as may be just and reasonable, if the people are not ready for trial in that criminal action within:

(a) ninety days from the commencement of his commitment to the custody of the sheriff in a criminal action wherein the defendant is accused of one or more offenses, at least one of which is a felony;

(b) thirty days from the commencement of his commitment to the custody of the sheriff in a criminal action wherein the defendant is accused of one or more offenses, at least one of which is a misdemeanor punishable by a sentence of imprisonment of more than three months and none of which is a felony;

(c) fifteen days from the commencement of his commitment to the custody of the sheriff in a criminal action wherein the defendant is accused of one or more offenses, at least one of which is a misdemeanor punishable by a sentence of imprisonment of not more than three months and none of which is a crime punishable by a sentence of imprisonment of more than three months;

(d) five days from the commencement of his commitment to the custody of the sheriff in a criminal action wherein the defendant is accused of one or more offenses, at least one of which is a violation and none of which is a crime.

3. (a) Subdivisions one and two do not apply to a criminal action wherein the defendant is accused of an offense defined in sections 125.10, 125.15, 125.20, 125.25, 125.26 and 125.27 of the penal law.

(b) A motion made pursuant to subdivisions one or two upon expiration of the specified period may be denied where the people are not ready for trial if the people were ready for trial prior to the expiration of the specified period and their present unreadiness is due to some exceptional fact or circumstance, including, but not limited to, the sudden unavailability of evidence material to the people's case, when the district attorney has exercised due diligence to obtain such evidence and there are reasonable grounds to believe that such evidence will become available in a reasonable period.

(c) A motion made pursuant to subdivision two shall not:

(i) apply to any defendant who is serving a term of imprisonment for another offense;

(ii) require the release from custody of any defendant who is also being held in custody pending trial of another criminal charge as to which the applicable period has not yet elapsed;

(iii) prevent the redetention of or otherwise apply to any defendant who, after being released from custody pursuant to this section or otherwise, is charged with another crime or violates the conditions on which he has been released, by failing to appear at a judicial proceeding at which his presence is required or otherwise.

4. In computing the time within which the people must be ready for trial pursuant to subdivisions one and two, the following periods must be excluded:

(a) a reasonable period of delay resulting from other proceedings concerning the defendant, including but not limited to: proceedings for the determination of competency and the period during which defendant is incompetent to stand trial; demand to produce; request for a bill of particulars; pre-trial motions; appeals; trial of other charges; and the period during which such matters are under consideration by the court; or

(b) the period of delay resulting from a continuance granted by the court at the request of, or with the consent of, the defendant or his counsel. The court must grant such a continuance only if it is satisfied that postponement is in the interest of justice, taking into account the public interest in the prompt dispositions of criminal charges. A defendant without counsel must not be deemed to have consented to a continuance unless he has been advised by the court of his rights under these rules and the effect of his consent; or

(c) (i) the period of delay resulting from the absence or unavailability of the defendant. A defendant must be considered absent whenever his location is unknown and he is attempting to avoid apprehension or prosecution, or his location cannot be determined by due diligence. A defendant must be considered unavailable whenever his location is known but his presence for trial cannot be obtained by due diligence; or

(ii) where the defendant has either escaped from custody or has failed to appear when required after having previously been released on bail or on his own recognizance, and provided the defendant is not in custody on another matter, the period extending from the day the court issues a bench warrant pursuant to section 530.70 because of the defendant's failure to appear in court when required, to the day the defendant subsequently appears in the court pursuant to a bench warrant or voluntarily or otherwise; or

(d) a reasonable period of delay when the defendant is joined for trial with a co-defendant as to whom the time for trial pursuant to this section has not run and good cause is not shown for granting a severance; or

(e) the period of delay resulting from detention of the defendant in another jurisdiction provided the district attorney is aware of such detention and has been diligent and has made reasonable efforts to obtain the presence of the defendant for trial; or

(f) the period during which the defendant is without counsel through no fault of the court; except when the defendant is proceeding as his own attorney with the permission of the court; or

(g) other periods of delay occasioned by exceptional circumstances, including but not limited to, the period of delay resulting from a continuance granted at the request of a district attorney if (i) the continuance is granted because of the unavailability of evidence material to the people's case, when the district attorney has exercised due diligence to obtain such evidence and there are reasonable grounds to believe that such evidence will become available in a reasonable period; or (ii) the continuance is granted to allow the district attorney additional time to prepare the people's case and additional time is justified by the exceptional circumstances of the case.

(h) the period during which an action has been adjourned in contemplation of dismissal pursuant to sections 170.55, 170.56 and 215.10 of this chapter.

(i) The period prior to the defendant's actual appearance for arraignment in a situation in which the defendant has been directed to appear by the district attorney pursuant to subdivision three of section 120.20 or subdivision three of section 210.10.

(j) the period during which a family offense is before a family court until such time as an accusatory instrument or indictment is filed against the defendant alleging a crime constituting a family offense, as such term is defined in section 530.11 of this chapter.

5. For purposes of this section,

(a) where the defendant is to be tried following the withdrawal of the plea of guilty or is to be retried following a mistrial, an order for a new trial or an appeal or collateral attack, the criminal action and the commitment to the custody of the sheriff, if any, must be deemed to have commenced on the date the withdrawal of the plea of guilty or the date the order occasioning a retrial becomes final;

(b) where a defendant has been served with an appearance ticket, the criminal action must be deemed to have commenced on the date the defendant first appears in a local criminal court in response to the ticket;

(c) where a criminal action is commenced by the filing of a felony complaint, and thereafter, in the course of the same criminal action either the felony complaint is replaced with or converted to an information, prosecutor's information or misdemeanor complaint pursuant to article 180 or a prosecutor's information is filed pursuant to section 190.70, the period applicable for the purposes of subdivision one must be the period applicable to the charges in the new accusatory instrument, calculated from the date of the filing of such new accusatory instrument; provided, however, that when the aggregate of such period and the period of time, excluding the periods provided in subdivision four, already elapsed from the date of the filing of the felony complaint to the date of the filing of the new accusatory instrument exceeds six months, the period applicable to the charges in the felony complaint must remain applicable and continue as if the new accusatory instrument had not been filed;

(d) where a criminal action is commenced by the filing of a felony complaint, and thereafter, in the course of the same criminal action either the felony complaint is replaced with or converted to an information, prosecutor's information or misdemeanor complaint pursuant to article 180 or a prosecutor's information is filed pursuant to section 190.70, the period applicable for the purposes of subdivision two must be the period applicable to the charges in the new accusatory instrument, calculated from the date of the filing of such new accusatory instrument; provided, however, that when the aggregate of such period and the period of time, excluding the periods provided in subdivision four, already elapsed from the date of the filing of the felony complaint to the date of the filing of the new accusatory instrument exceeds ninety days, the period applicable to the charges in the felony complaint must remain applicable and continue as if the new accusatory instrument had not been filed.

(e) where a count of an indictment is reduced to charge only a misdemeanor or petty offense and a reduced indictment or a prosecutor's information is filed pursuant to subdivisions one-a and six of section 210.20, the period applicable for the purposes of subdivision one of this section must be the period applicable to the charges in the new accusatory instrument, calculated from the date of the filing of such new accusatory instrument; provided, however, that when the aggregate of such period and the period of time, excluding the periods provided in subdivision four of this section, already elapsed from the date of the filing of the indictment to the date of the filing of the new accusatory instrument exceeds six months, the period applicable to the charges in the indictment must remain applicable and continue as if the new accusatory instrument had not been filed;

(f) where a count of an indictment is reduced to charge only a misdemeanor or petty offense and a reduced indictment or a prosecutor's information is filed pursuant to subdivisions one-a and six of section 210.20, the period applicable for the purposes of subdivision two of this section must be the period applicable to the charges in the new accusatory instrument, calculated from the date of the filing of such new accusatory instrument; provided, however, that when the aggregate of such period and the period of time, excluding the periods provided in subdivision four of this section, already elapsed from the date of the filing of the indictment to the date of the filing of the new accusatory instrument exceeds ninety days, the period applicable to the charges in the indictment must remain applicable and continue as if the new accusatory instrument had not been filed.

6. The procedural rules prescribed in subdivisions one through seven of section 210.45 with respect to a motion to dismiss an indictment are also applicable to a motion made pursuant to subdivision two.

> **HISTORY:** Add, L 1972, ch 184, § 2, eff April 28, 1972. Former § 30.30, add, L 1971, ch 884, § 20; repealed, L 1972, ch 184, § 2, with substance transferred to § 30.20. Sub 3, par (a), amd, L 1974, ch 367, § 7, eff Sept 1, 1974. Sub 3, par (a), amd, L 2006, ch 93, § 3, eff June 7, 2006. Sub 4, par (a), amd, L 1979, ch 412, § 3, L 1982, ch 558, § 1, eff Oct 20, 1982. Sub 4, par (c), amd, L 1984, ch 670, § 1, eff Aug 1, 1984. Sub 4, par (c), subpar (i), formerly sub 4, entire par (c), so designated sub 4, par (c), subpar (i) and amd, L 1996, ch 631, § 1, eff Oct 4, 1996. Sub 4, par (c), subpar (ii), add, L 1996, ch 631, § 1, eff Oct 4, 1996. Sub 4, par (h), add, L 1986, ch 837, § 2, eff Nov 1, 1986. Sub 4, par (i), add, L 1993, ch 446, § 2, eff Nov 1, 1993. Sub 4, par (j), add, L 1994, ch 222, § 29, eff Jan 1, 1995. Sub 5, par (b), amd, L 1982, ch 109, § 1, eff May 18, 1982. Sub 5, par (e), add, L 1990, ch 209, § 10, eff Sept 1, 1990. Sub 5, par (f), add, L 1990, ch 209, § 10, eff Sept 1, 1990.

ARTICLE 40   EXEMPTION FROM PROSECUTION BY REASON OF PREVIOUS PROSECUTION

> **HISTORY:** Add, L 1970, ch 996, § 1, eff Sept 1, 1971.

§ 40.10. Previous prosecution; definitions of terms

The following definitions are applicable to this article:

1. "Offense." An "offense" is committed whenever any conduct is performed which violates a statutory provision defining an offense; and when the same conduct or criminal transaction violates two or more such statutory provisions each such violation constitutes a separate and distinct offense. The same conduct or criminal transaction also establishes separate and distinct offenses when, though violating only one statutory provision, it results in death, injury, loss or other consequences to two or more victims, and such result is an element of the offense as defined. In such case, as many offenses are committed as there are victims.

2. "Criminal transaction" means conduct which establishes at least one offense, and which is comprised of two or more or a group of acts either (a) so closely related and connected in point of time and circumstance of commission as to constitute a single criminal incident, or (b) so

closely related in criminal purpose or objective as to constitute elements or integral parts of a single criminal venture.

HISTORY: Add, L 1970, ch 996, § 1, eff Sept 1, 1971.

§ 40.20. Previous prosecution; when a bar to second prosecution

1. A person may not be twice prosecuted for the same offense.

2. A person may not be separately prosecuted for two offenses based upon the same act or criminal transaction unless:

(a) The offenses as defined have substantially different elements and the acts establishing one offense are in the main clearly distinguishable from those establishing the other; or

(b) Each of the offenses as defined contains an element which is not an element of the other, and the statutory provisions defining such offenses are designed to prevent very different kinds of harm or evil; or

(c) One of such offenses consists of criminal possession of contraband matter and the other offense is one involving the use of such contraband matter, other than a sale thereof; or

(d) One of the offenses is assault or some other offense resulting in physical injury to a person, and the other offense is one of homicide based upon the death of such person from the same physical injury, and such death occurs after a prosecution for the assault or other non-homicide offense; or

(e) Each offense involves death, injury, loss or other consequence to a different victim; or

(f) One of the offenses consists of a violation of a statutory provision of another jurisdiction, which offense has been prosecuted in such other jurisdiction and has there been terminated by a court order expressly founded upon insufficiency of evidence to establish some element of such offense which is not an element of the other offense, defined by the laws of this state; or

(g) The present prosecution is for a consummated result offense, as defined in subdivision three of section 20.10, which occurred in this state and the offense was the result of a conspiracy, facilitation or solicitation prosecuted in another state.

(h) One of such offenses is enterprise corruption in violation of section 460.20 of the penal law, racketeering in violation of federal law or any comparable offense pursuant to the law of another state and a separate or subsequent prosecution is not barred by section 40.50 of this article.

(i) One of the offenses consists of a violation of 18 U.S.C. 371, where the object of the conspiracy is to attempt in any manner to evade or defeat any federal income tax or the payment thereof, or a violation of 26 U.S.C. 7201, 26 U.S.C. 7202, 26 U.S.C. 7203, 26 U.S.C. 7204, 26 U.S.C. 7205, 26 U.S.C. 7206 or 26 U.S.C. 7212(A), where the purpose is to evade or defeat any federal income tax or the payment thereof, and the other offense is committed for the purpose of evading or defeating any New York state or New York city income taxes and is defined in article one hundred fifty-five of the penal law, article one hundred seventy of the penal law, article one hundred seventy-five of the penal law, article thirty-seven of the tax law or chapter forty of title eleven of the administrative code of the city of New York.

HISTORY: Add, L 1970, ch 996, § 1, eff Sept 1, 1971; amd, L 1984, ch 624, § 1, eff Nov 1, 1984, L 1986, ch 516, § 4, eff Nov 1, 1986, L 2011, ch 186, § 1, eff Oct 18, 2011.

§ 40.30. Previous prosecution; what constitutes

1. Except as otherwise provided in this section, a person "is prosecuted" for an offense, within the meaning of section 40.20, when he is charged therewith by an accusatory instrument filed in a court of this state or of any jurisdiction within the United States, and when the action either:

(a) Terminates in a conviction upon a plea of guilty; or

(b) Proceeds to the trial stage and a jury has been impaneled and sworn or, in the case of a trial by the court without a jury, a witness is sworn.

2. Despite the occurrence of proceedings specified in subdivision one, a person is not deemed to have been prosecuted for an offense, within the meaning of section 40.20, when:

(a) Such prosecution occurred in a court which lacked jurisdiction over the defendant or the offense; or

(b) Such prosecution was for a lesser offense than could have been charged under the facts of the case, and the prosecution was procured by the defendant, without the knowledge of the appropriate prosecutor, for the purpose of avoiding prosecution for a greater offense.

3. Despite the occurrence of proceedings specified in subdivision one, if such proceedings are subsequently nullified by a court order which restores the action to its pre-pleading status or which directs a new trial of the same accusatory instrument, the nullified proceedings do not bar further prosecution of such offense under the same accusatory instrument.

4. Despite the occurrence of proceedings specified in subdivision one, if such proceedings are subsequently nullified by a court order which dismisses the accusatory instrument but authorizes the people to obtain a new accusatory instrument charging the same offense or an offense based upon the same conduct, the nullified proceedings do not bar further prosecution of such offense under any new accusatory instrument obtained pursuant to such court order or authorization.

> **HISTORY:** Add, L 1970, ch 996, § 1, eff Sept 1, 1971. Sub 1, amd, L 1974, ch 80, § 1, eff March 19, 1974.

§ 40.40. Separate prosecution of jointly prosecutable offenses; when barred

1. Where two or more offenses are joinable in a single accusatory instrument against a person by reason of being based upon the same criminal transaction, pursuant to paragraph (a) of subdivision two of section 200.20, such person may not, under circumstances prescribed in this section, be separately prosecuted for such offenses even though such separate prosecutions are not otherwise barred by any other section of this article.

2. When (a) one of two or more joinable offenses of the kind specified in subdivision one is charged in an accusatory instrument, and (b) another is not charged therein, or in any other accusatory instrument filed in the same court, despite possession by the people of evidence legally sufficient to support a conviction of the defendant for such uncharged offense, and (c) either a trial of the existing accusatory instrument is commenced or the action thereon is disposed of by a plea of guilty, any subsequent prosecution for the uncharged offense is thereby barred.

3. When (a) two or more of such offenses are charged in separate accusatory instruments filed in the same court, and (b) an application by the defendant for consolidation thereof for trial purposes, pursuant to subdivision five of section 200.20 or section 100.45, is improperly denied, the commencement of a trial of one such accusatory instrument bars any subsequent prosecution upon any of the other accusatory instruments with respect to any such offense.

> **HISTORY:** Add, L 1970, ch 996, § 1, eff Sept 1, 1971.

§ 40.50. Previous prosecution; enterprise corruption

1. The following definitions are applicable to this section:

(a) A criminal act or offense is "specifically included" when a count of an accusatory instrument charging a person with enterprise corruption alleges a pattern of criminal activity and the act or offense is alleged to be a criminal act within such pattern.

(b) A criminal act is "a part of" a pattern of criminal activity alleged in a count of enterprise corruption when it is committed prior to commencement of the criminal action in which enterprise corruption is charged and was committed in furtherance of the same common scheme or plan or with intent to participate in or further the affairs of the same criminal enterprise to which the crimes specifically included in the pattern are connected.

(c) A person "is prosecuted" for an offense when he is prosecuted for it within the meaning of section 40.30 of this article or when an indictment or a count of an indictment charging that offense is dismissed pursuant to section 210.20 of this chapter without authorization to submit the charge to the same or another grand jury, or the indictment or the count of the indictment charging that offense is dismissed following the granting of a motion to suppress pursuant to article 710 of this chapter, unless an appeal from the order granting the motion to dismiss or suppress is pending.

(d) An offense was "not prosecutable" in an accusatory instrument in which a person was charged with enterprise corruption when there was no geographical jurisdiction of that offense in the county where the accusatory instrument was filed, or when the offense was prosecutable in the county and was not barred from prosecution by section 40.20 or 40.40 of this article or by any other provision of law but the prosecutor filing the accusatory instrument was not empowered by law to prosecute the offense.

2. A person who has been previously prosecuted for an offense may not be subsequently prosecuted for enterprise corruption based upon a pattern of criminal activity in which that prior offense, or another offense based upon the same act or criminal transaction, is specifically included unless:

(a) he was convicted of that prior offense; and

(b) the subsequent pattern of criminal activity in which he participated includes at least one criminal act for which he was not previously prosecuted, which was a felony, and which occurred after that prior conviction.

3. A person who has been previously prosecuted for enterprise corruption may not be subsequently prosecuted for an offense specifically included in the pattern of criminal activity upon which it was based, or another offense based upon the same act or criminal transaction, unless the offense is a class A felony and was not prosecutable in the accusatory instrument in which the person was charged with enterprise corruption.

4. A person may not be separately prosecuted for enterprise corruption and for an offense specifically included in the pattern of criminal activity upon which it is based or another offense based upon the same act or transaction, unless the offense is a class A felony and is not prosecutable in the accusatory instrument in which the person is charged with enterprise corruption.

5. A person who has been previously prosecuted for enterprise corruption may not be subsequently prosecuted for an offense which, while not specifically included in the pattern of criminal activity on which the prior charge of enterprise corruption was based, was nonetheless a part of that pattern, unless the offense was a class A or B felony and either the offense was not.

prosecutable in the accusatory instrument in which the person was charged with enterprise corruption or the people show, by clear and convincing evidence, that the prosecutor did not possess evidence legally sufficient to support a conviction of that offense at the time of the earlier prosecution and evidence of that offense was not presented as part of the case in chief in the earlier prosecution.

6. A person who has been previously prosecuted for enterprise corruption may not be subsequently prosecuted for enterprise corruption based upon a pattern of criminal activity that specifically includes a criminal act that was also specifically included in the pattern upon which the prior charge of enterprise corruption was based.

7. A person may not be separately prosecuted for enterprise corruption in two accusatory instruments based upon a pattern of criminal activity, alleged in either instrument, that specifically includes a criminal act that is also specifically included in the pattern upon which the other charge of enterprise corruption is based.

8. When a person is charged in an accusatory instrument with both one or more counts of enterprise corruption and with another offense or offenses specifically included in or otherwise a part of the pattern or patterns of criminal activity upon which the charge or charges of enterprise corruption is or are based, and the court orders that any of the counts be tried separately pursuant to subdivision one of section 200.40 of this chapter, this section shall not apply and subsequent prosecution of the remaining counts or offenses shall not be barred.

9. A person who has been previously prosecuted for racketeering pursuant to federal law, or any comparable offense pursuant to the law of another state may not be subsequently prosecuted for enterprise corruption based upon a pattern of criminal activity that specifically includes a criminal act that was also specifically included in the pattern of racketeering activity upon which the prior charge of racketeering was based provided, however, that this section shall not be construed to prohibit the subsequent prosecution of any other offense specifically included in or otherwise a part of a pattern of racketeering activity alleged in any such prior prosecution for racketeering or other comparable offense.

HISTORY: Add, L 1986, ch 516, § 5, eff Nov 1, 1986.

ARTICLE 50   COMPULSION OF EVIDENCE BY OFFER OF IMMUNITY

HISTORY: Add, L 1970, ch 996, § 1, eff Sept 1, 1971.

§ 50.10. Compulsion of evidence by offer of immunity; definitions of terms

The following definitions are applicable to this article:

1. "Immunity." A person who has been a witness in a legal proceeding, and who cannot, except as otherwise provided in this subdivision, be convicted of any offense or subjected to any penalty or forfeiture for or on account of any transaction, matter or thing concerning which he gave evidence therein, possesses "immunity" from any such conviction, penalty or forfeiture. A person who possesses such immunity may nevertheless be convicted of perjury as a result of having given false testimony in such legal proceeding, and may be convicted of or adjudged in contempt as a result of having contumaciously refused to give evidence therein.

2. "Legal proceeding" means a proceeding in or before any court or grand jury, or before any

body, agency or person authorized by law to conduct the same and to administer the oath or to cause it to be administered.

3. "Give evidence" means to testify or produce physical evidence.

HISTORY: Add, L 1970, ch 996, § 1, eff Sept 1, 1971.

§ 50.20. Compulsion of evidence by offer of immunity

1. Any witness in a legal proceeding, other than a grand jury proceeding, may refuse to give evidence requested of him on the ground that it may tend to incriminate him and he may not, except as provided in subdivision two, be compelled to give such evidence.

2. Such a witness may be compelled to give evidence in such a proceeding notwithstanding an assertion of his privilege against self-incrimination if:

(a) The proceeding is one in which, by express provision of statute, a person conducting or connected therewith is declared a competent authority to confer immunity upon witnesses therein; and

(b) Such competent authority (i) orders such witness to give the requested evidence notwithstanding his assertion of his privilege against self-incrimination, and (ii) advises him that upon so doing he will receive immunity.

3. A witness who is ordered to give evidence pursuant to subdivision two and who complies with such order receives immunity. Such witness is not deprived of such immunity because such competent authority did not comply with statutory provisions requiring notice to a specified public servant of intention to confer immunity.

4. A witness who, without asserting his privilege against self-incrimination, gives evidence in a legal proceeding other than a grand jury proceeding does not receive immunity.

5. The rules governing the circumstances in which witnesses may be compelled to give evidence and in which they receive immunity therefor in a grand jury proceeding are prescribed in section 190.40.

HISTORY: Add, L 1970, ch 996, § 1, eff Sept 1, 1971, with substance derived from Crim C §§ 10, 619-c.

§ 50.30. Authority to confer immunity in criminal proceedings; court a competent authority

In any criminal proceeding, other than a grand jury proceeding, the court is a competent authority to confer immunity in accordance with the provisions of section 50.20, but only when expressly requested by the district attorney to do so.

HISTORY: Add, L 1970, ch 996, § 1, eff Sept 1, 1971.

TITLE D   Rules of Evidence, Standards of Proof and Related Matters

ARTICLE 60
RULES OF EVIDENCE AND RELATED MATTERS

ARTICLE 65
[EXPIRES AND IS REPEALED SEPT 1, 2015] USE OF CLOSED-CIRCUIT
TELEVISION FOR CERTAIN CHILD WITNESSES

ARTICLE 70
STANDARDS OF PROOF

HISTORY: Add, L 1970, ch 996, § 1, eff Sept 1, 1971.

ARTICLE 60   RULES OF EVIDENCE AND RELATED MATTERS

HISTORY: Add, L 1970, ch 996, § 1, eff Sept 1, 1971.

§ 60.10. Rules of evidence; in general

Unless otherwise provided by statute or by judicially established rules of evidence applicable to criminal cases, the rules of evidence applicable to civil cases are, where appropriate, also applicable to criminal proceedings.

HISTORY: Add, L 1970, ch 996, § 1, eff Sept 1, 1971.

§ 60.15. Rules of evidence; what witnesses may be called

1. Unless otherwise expressly provided, in any criminal proceeding involving a defendant in which evidence is or may be received, both the people and the defendant may as a matter of right call and examine witnesses, and each party may cross-examine every witness called by the other party.

2. A defendant may testify in his own behalf, but his failure to do so is not a factor from which any inference unfavorable to him may be drawn.

> **HISTORY:** Add, L 1970, ch 996, § 1, eff Sept 1, 1971.

§ 60.20. Rules of evidence; testimonial capacity; evidence given by children

1. Any person may be a witness in a criminal proceeding unless the court finds that, by reason of infancy or mental disease or defect, he does not possess sufficient intelligence or capacity to justify the reception of his evidence.

2. Every witness more than nine years old may testify only under oath unless the court is satisfied that such witness cannot, as a result of mental disease or defect, understand the nature of an oath. A witness less than nine years old may not testify under oath unless the court is satisfied that he or she understands the nature of an oath. If under either of the above provisions, a witness is deemed to be ineligible to testify under oath, the witness may nevertheless be permitted to give unsworn evidence if the court is satisfied that the witness possesses sufficient intelligence and capacity to justify the reception thereof. A witness understands the nature of an oath if he or she appreciates the difference between truth and falsehood, the necessity for telling the truth, and the fact that a witness who testifies falsely may be punished.

3. A defendant may not be convicted of an offense solely upon unsworn evidence given pursuant to subdivision two.

> **HISTORY:** Add, L 1970, ch 996, § 1, eff Sept 1, 1971, with substance derived from Crim C § 392. Sub 2, amd, L 1975, ch 133, § 1, eff June 3, 1975. Sub 2, amd, L 2000, ch 1, § 11, eff Feb 1, 2001, L 2003, ch 264, § 36, eff Nov 1, 2003. Sub 3, amd, L 1975, ch 133, § 1, eff June 3, 1975.

§ 60.22. Rules of evidence; corroboration of accomplice testimony

1. A defendant may not be convicted of any offense upon the testimony of an accomplice unsupported by corroborative evidence tending to connect the defendant with the commission of such offense.

2. An "accomplice" means a witness in a criminal action who, according to evidence adduced in such action, may reasonably be considered to have participated in:

(a) The offense charged; or

(b) An offense based upon the same or some of the same facts or conduct which constitute the offense charged.

3. A witness who is an accomplice as defined in subdivision two is no less such because a prosecution or conviction of himself would be barred or precluded by some defense or exemption, such as infancy, immunity or previous prosecution, amounting to a collateral impediment to such a prosecution or conviction, not affecting the conclusion that such witness engaged in the conduct constituting the offense with the mental state required for the commission thereof.

> **HISTORY:** Add, L 1970, ch 996, § 1, eff Sept 1, 1971.

§ 60.25. Rules of evidence; identification by means of previous recognition, in absence of present identification

1. In any criminal proceeding in which the defendant's commission of an offense is in issue, testimony as provided in subdivision two may be given by a witness when:

(a) Such witness testifies that:

(i) He observed the person claimed by the people to be the defendant either at the time and place of the commission of the offense or upon some other occasion relevant to the case; and

(ii) On a subsequent occasion he observed, under circumstances consistent with such rights as an accused person may derive under the constitution of this state or of the United States, a person whom he recognized as the same person whom he had observed on the first or incriminating occasion; and

(iii) He is unable at the proceeding to state, on the basis of present recollection, whether or not the defendant is the person in question; and

(b) It is established that the defendant is in fact the person whom the witness observed and recognized on the second occasion. Such fact may be established by testimony of another person or persons to whom the witness promptly declared his recognition on such occasion.

2. Under circumstances prescribed in subdivision one, such witness may testify at the criminal proceeding that the person whom he observed and recognized on the second occasion is the same person whom he observed on the first or incriminating occasion. Such testimony, together with the evidence that the defendant is in fact the person whom the witness observed and recognized on the second occasion, constitutes evidence in chief.

HISTORY: Add, L 1970, ch 996, § 1, eff Sept 1, 1971. Sub 1, par (a), subpar (ii), amd, L 1977, ch 479, § 1, eff Sept 1, 1977.

§ 60.30. Rules of evidence; identification by means of previous recognition, in addition to present identification

In any criminal proceeding in which the defendant's commission of an offense is in issue, a witness who testifies that (a) he observed the person claimed by the people to be the defendant either at the time and place of the commission of the offense or upon some other occasion relevant to the case, and (b) on the basis of present recollection, the defendant is the person in question and (c) on a subsequent occasion he observed the defendant, under circumstances consistent with such rights as an accused person may derive under the constitution of this state or of the United States, and then also recognized him as the same person whom he had observed on the first or incriminating occasion, may, in addition to making an identification of the defendant at the criminal proceeding on the basis of present recollection as the person whom he observed on the first or incriminating occasion, also describe his previous recognition of the defendant and testify that the person whom he observed on such second occasion is the same person whom he had observed on the first or incriminating occasion. Such testimony constitutes evidence in chief.

HISTORY: Add, L 1970, ch 996, § 1; amd, L 1977, ch 479, § 2, eff Sept 1, 1977.

§ 60.35. Rules of evidence; impeachment of own witness by proof of prior contradictory statement

1. When, upon examination by the party who called him, a witness in a criminal proceeding gives testimony upon a material issue of the case which tends to disprove the position of such party, such party may introduce evidence that such witness has previously made either a written statement signed by him or an oral statement under oath contradictory to such testimony.

2. Evidence concerning a prior contradictory statement introduced pursuant to subdivision one may be received only for the purpose of impeaching the credibility of the witness with respect to

his testimony upon the subject, and does not constitute evidence in chief. Upon receiving such evidence at a jury trial, the court must so instruct the jury.

3. When a witness has made a prior signed or sworn statement contradictory to his testimony in a criminal proceeding upon a material issue of the case, but his testimony does not tend to disprove the position of the party who called him and elicited such testimony, evidence that the witness made such prior statement is not admissible, and such party may not use such prior statement for the purpose of refreshing the recollection of the witness in a manner that discloses its contents to the trier of the facts.

> **HISTORY:** Add, L 1970, ch 996, § 1, eff Sept 1, 1971, with substance derived from Crim C § 8-a.

§ 60.40. Rules of evidence; proof of previous conviction; when allowed

1. If in the course of a criminal proceeding, any witness, including a defendant, is properly asked whether he was previously convicted of a specified offense and answers in the negative or in an equivocal manner, the party adverse to the one who called him may independently prove such conviction. If in response to proper inquiry whether he has ever been convicted of any offense the witness answers in the negative or in an equivocal manner, the adverse party may independently prove any previous conviction of the witness.

2. If a defendant in a criminal proceeding, through the testimony of a witness called by him, offers evidence of his good character, the people may independently prove any previous conviction of the defendant for an offense the commission of which would tend to negate any character trait or quality attributed to the defendant in such witness' testimony.

3. Subject to the limitations prescribed in section 200.60, the people may prove that a defendant has been previously convicted of an offense when the fact of such previous conviction constitutes an element of the offense charged, or proof thereof is otherwise essential to the establishment of a legally sufficient case.

> **HISTORY:** Add, L 1970, ch 996, § 1, eff Sept 1, 1971.

§ 60.42. Rules of evidence; admissibility of evidence of victim's sexual conduct in sex offense cases

Evidence of a victim's sexual conduct shall not be admissible in a prosecution for an offense or an attempt to commit an offense defined in article one hundred thirty of the penal law unless such evidence:

    1. proves or tends to prove specific instances of the victim's prior sexual conduct with the accused; or

    2. proves or tends to prove that the victim has been convicted of an offense under section 230.00 of the penal law within three years prior to the sex offense which is the subject of the prosecution; or

    3. rebuts evidence introduced by the people of the victim's failure to engage in sexual intercourse, oral sexual conduct, anal sexual conduct or sexual contact during a given period of time; or

    4. rebuts evidence introduced by the people which proves or tends to prove that the accused is the cause of pregnancy or disease of the victim, or the source of semen found in the victim; or

    5. is determined by the court after an offer of proof by the accused outside the hearing of the

jury, or such hearing as the court may require, and a statement by the court of its findings of fact essential to its determination, to be relevant and admissible in the interests of justice.

HISTORY: Add, L 1975, ch 230, § 1, eff Sept 1, 1975. Sub 3, amd, L 2003, ch 264, § 37, eff Nov 1, 2003.

§ 60.43. Rules of evidence; admissibility of evidence of victim's sexual conduct in non-sex offense cases

Evidence of the victim's sexual conduct, including the past sexual conduct of a deceased victim, may not be admitted in a prosecution for any offense, attempt to commit an offense or conspiracy to commit an offense defined in the penal law unless such evidence is determined by the court to be relevant and admissible in the interests of justice, after an offer of proof by the proponent of such evidence outside the hearing of the jury, or such hearing as the court may require, and a statement by the court of its findings of fact essential to its determination.

HISTORY: Add, L 1990, ch 832, § 1, eff Nov 1, 1990.

§ 60.44. Use of anatomically correct dolls

Any person who is less than sixteen years old may in the discretion of the court and where helpful and appropriate, use an anatomically correct doll in testifying in a criminal proceeding based upon conduct prohibited by article one hundred thirty, article two hundred sixty or section 255.25, 255.26 or 255.27 of the penal law.

HISTORY: Add, L 1986, ch 358, § 1, eff Nov 1, 1986. Amd, L 2006, ch 320, § 11, eff Nov 1, 2006.

§ 60.45. Rules of evidence; admissibility of statements of defendants

1. Evidence of a written or oral confession, admission, or other statement made by a defendant with respect to his participation or lack of participation in the offense charged, may not be received in evidence against him in a criminal proceeding if such statement was involuntarily made.

2. A confession, admission or other statement is "involuntarily made" by a defendant when it is obtained from him:

(a) By any person by the use or threatened use of physical force upon the defendant or another person, or by means of any other improper conduct or undue pressure which impaired the defendant's physical or mental condition to the extent of undermining his ability to make a choice whether or not to make a statement; or

(b) By a public servant engaged in law enforcement activity or by a person then acting under his direction or in cooperation with him:

(i) by means of any promise or statement of fact, which promise or statement creates a substantial risk that the defendant might falsely incriminate himself; or

(ii) in violation of such rights as the defendant may derive from the constitution of this state or of the United States.

HISTORY: Add, L 1970, ch 996, § 1, eff Sept 1, 1971, with substance derived from Crim C § 395.

§ 60.46. Rules of evidence, family offense proceedings in family court

Evidence of a written or oral admission or any testimony given by either party, or evidence derived therefrom, in a proceeding under article eight of the family court act without the benefit of counsel in such proceeding may not be received into evidence in a criminal proceeding except for the purposes of impeachment unless such party waives the right to counsel on the record.

Nothing herein shall be deemed to prohibit any testimony or exhibits received into evidence in a criminal proceeding, or any orders, decisions or judgments arising from such proceeding from being received into evidence in any proceeding under article eight of the family court act.

> **HISTORY:** Add, L 1994, ch 222, § 30, eff Jan 1, 1995.

§ 60.48. Rules of evidence; admissibility of evidence of victim's manner of dress in sex offense cases

Evidence of the manner in which the victim was dressed at the time of the commission of an offense may not be admitted in a prosecution for any offense, or an attempt to commit an offense, defined in article one hundred thirty of the penal law, unless such evidence is determined by the court to be relevant and admissible in the interests of justice, after an offer of proof by the proponent of such evidence outside the hearing of the jury, or such hearing as the court may require, and a statement by the court of its findings of fact essential to its determination.

> **HISTORY:** Add, L 1994, ch 482, § 1, eff Nov 1, 1994.

§ 60.50. Rules of evidence; statements of defendants; corroboration

A person may not be convicted of any offense solely upon evidence of a confession or admission made by him without additional proof that the offense charged has been committed.

> **HISTORY:** Add, L 1970, ch 996, § 1, eff Sept 1, 1971, with substance derived from Crim C §§ 394, 395.

§ 60.55. Rules of evidence; psychiatric testimony in certain cases

1. When, in connection with the affirmative defense of lack of criminal responsibility by reason of mental disease or defect, a psychiatrist or licensed psychologist testifies at a trial concerning the defendant's mental condition at the time of the conduct charged to constitute a crime, he must be permitted to make a statement as to the nature of any examination of the defendant, the diagnosis of the mental condition of the defendant and his opinion as to the extent, if any, to which the capacity of the defendant to know or appreciate the nature and consequence of such conduct, or its wrongfulness, was impaired as a result of mental disease or defect at that time.

The psychiatrist or licensed psychologist must be permitted to make any explanation reasonably serving to clarify his diagnosis and opinion, and may be cross-examined as to any matter bearing on his competency or credibility or the validity of his diagnosis or opinion.

2. Any statement made by the defendant to a psychiatrist or licensed psychologist during his examination of the defendant shall be inadmissible in evidence on any issue other than that of the affirmative defense of lack of criminal responsibility, by reason of mental disease or defect. The statement shall, however, be admissible upon the issue of the affirmative defense of lack of criminal responsibility by reason of mental disease or defect, whether or not it would otherwise be deemed a privileged communication. Upon receiving the statement in evidence, the court must instruct the jury that the statement is to be considered only on the issue of such affirmative defense and may not be considered by it in its determination of whether the defendant committed the act constituting the crime charged.

> **HISTORY:** Add, L 1970, ch 996, § 1, eff Sept 1, 1971, with substance derived from Crim C § 398-b. Sub 1, formerly entire section, so numbered and amd, L 1980, ch 548, § 2, L 1984, ch 668, § 4, eff Nov 1, 1984 and not applicable to any criminal action or proceeding relating to an offense committed prior to Nov 1, 1984. Sub 2, add, L 1980, ch 548, § 2; amd, L 1984, ch 668, § 4, eff Nov 1, 1984 and not applicable to any criminal action or proceeding relating to an offense committed prior to Nov 1, 1984.

§ 60.60. Rules of evidence; certificates concerning judgments of conviction and fingerprints

1. A certificate issued by a criminal court, or the clerk thereof, certifying that a judgment of conviction against a designated defendant has been entered in such court, constitutes presumptive evidence of the facts stated in such certificate.

2. A report of a public servant charged with the custody of official fingerprint records which contains a certification that the fingerprints of a designated person who has previously been convicted of an offense are identical with those of a defendant in a criminal action, constitutes presumptive evidence of the fact that such defendant has previously been convicted of such offense.

> **HISTORY:** Add, L 1970, ch 996, § 1, eff Sept 1, 1971, with substance derived from Crim C §§ 482-a, 482-b.

§ 60.70. Rules of evidence; dangerous drugs destroyed pursuant to court order

The destruction of dangerous drugs pursuant to the provisions of article seven hundred fifteen hereof shall not preclude the admission on trial or in a proceeding in connection therewith of testimony or evidence where such testimony or evidence would otherwise have been admissible if such drugs had not been destroyed.

> **HISTORY:** Add, L 1973, ch 750, eff Sept 1, 1973.

§ 60.75. Rules of evidence; chemical test evidence

In any prosecution where two or more offenses against the same defendant are properly joined in one indictment or charged in two accusatory instruments properly consolidated for trial purposes and where one such offense charges a violation of any subdivision of section eleven hundred ninety-two of the vehicle and traffic law, chemical test evidence properly admissible as evidence of intoxication under subdivision one of section eleven hundred ninety-five of such law shall also, if relevant, be received in evidence with regard to the remaining charges in the indictments.

> **HISTORY:** Add, L 1984, ch 954, § 1, eff Sept 5, 1984.

§ 60.76. Rules of evidence; rape crisis counselor evidence in certain cases

Where disclosure of a communication which would have been privileged pursuant to section forty-five hundred ten of the civil practice law and rules is sought on the grounds that the privilege has been waived or that disclosure is required pursuant to the constitution of this state or the United States, the party seeking disclosure must file a written motion supported by an affidavit containing specific factual allegations providing grounds that disclosure is required. Upon the filing of such motion and affidavit, the court shall conduct an in camera review of the communication outside the presence of the jury and of counsel for all parties in order to determine whether disclosure of any portion of the communication is required.

> **HISTORY:** Add, L 1993, ch 432, § 2, eff Jan 22, 1994.

ARTICLE 65   [EXPIRES AND IS REPEALED SEPT 1, 2015] USE OF CLOSED-CIRCUIT TELEVISION FOR CERTAIN CHILD WITNESSES

> **HISTORY:** Add, L 1985, ch 505, § 1, eff July 24, 1985, expires and is repealed Sept 1, 2015.

§ 65.00. [Expires and is repealed Sept 1, 2015] Definitions

As used in this article:

1. "Child witness" means a person fourteen years old or less who is or will be called to testify in a criminal proceeding, other than a grand jury proceeding, concerning an offense defined in article one hundred thirty of the penal law or section 255.25, 255.26 or 255.27 of such law which is the subject of such criminal proceeding.

2. "Vulnerable child witness" means a child witness whom a court has declared to be vulnerable.

3. "Testimonial room" means any room, separate and apart from the courtroom, which is furnished comfortably and less formally than a courtroom and from which the testimony of a vulnerable child witness can be transmitted to the courtroom by means of live, two-way closed-circuit television.

4. "Live, two-way closed-circuit television" means a simultaneous transmission, by closed-circuit television, or other electronic means, between the courtroom and the testimonial room in accordance with the provisions of section 65.30.

5. "Operator" means the individual authorized by the court to operate the closed-circuit television equipment used in accordance with the provisions of this article.

6. A person occupies "a position of authority with respect to a child" when he or she is a parent, guardian or other person responsible for the custody or care of the child at the relevant time or is any other person who maintains an ongoing personal relationship with such parent, guardian or other person responsible for custody or care, which relationship involves his or her living, or his or her frequent and repeated presence, in the same household or premises as the child.

HISTORY: Add, L 1985, ch 505, § 1, eff July 24, 1985, expires and is repealed Sept 1, 2015.
Sub 1, amd, L 2004, ch 362, § 2, eff Nov 1, 2004, L 2006, ch 320, § 12, eff Nov 1, 2006.

§ 65.10. [Expires and is repealed Sept 1, 2015] Closed-circuit television; general rule; declaration of vulnerability

1. A child witness shall be declared vulnerable when the court, in accordance with the provisions of section 65.20, determines by clear and convincing evidence that it is likely that such child witness will suffer serious mental or emotional harm if required to testify at a criminal proceeding without the use of live, two-way closed-circuit television and that the use of such live, two-way closed-circuit television will diminish the likelihood or extent of, such harm.

2. When the court declares a child witness to be vulnerable, it shall, except as provided in subdivision four of section 65.30, authorize the taking of the testimony of the vulnerable child witness from the testimonial room by means of live, two-way closed-circuit television. Under no circumstances shall the provisions of this article be construed to authorize a closed-circuit television system by which events in the courtroom are not transmitted to the testimonial room during the testimony of the vulnerable child witness.

3. Nothing herein shall be contrued [construed]* to preclude the court from exercising its power to close the courtroom or from exercising any authority it otherwise may have to protect the well-being of a witness and the rights of the defendant.

_____

* The bracketed word has been inserted by the Publisher.

HISTORY: Add, L 1985, ch 505, § 1, eff July 24, 1985, expires and is repealed Sept 1, 2015. Sub 1, amd, L 2007, ch 548, § 1, eff Aug 15, 2007.

§ 65.20. [Expires and is repealed Sept 1, 2015] Closed-circuit television; procedure for application and grounds for determination

1. Prior to the commencement of a criminal proceeding; other than a grand jury proceeding, either party may apply to the court for an order declaring that a child witness is vulnerable.

2. A child witness should be declared vulnerable when the court, in accordance with the provisions of this section, determines by clear and convincing evidence that the child witness would suffer serious mental or emotional harm that would substantially impair the child witness' ability to communicate with the finder of fact without the use of live, two-way closed-circuit television.

3. A motion pursuant to subdivision one of this section must be made in writing at least eight days before the commencement of trial or other criminal proceeding upon reasonable notice to the other party and with an opportunity to be heard.

4. The motion papers must state the basis for the motion and must contain sworn allegations of fact which, if true, would support a determination by the court that the child witness is vulnerable. Such allegations may be based upon the personal knowledge of the deponent or upon information and belief, provided that, in the latter event, the sources of such information and the grounds for such belief are stated.

5. The answering papers may admit or deny any of the alleged facts and may, in addition, contain sworn allegations of fact relevant to the motion, including the rights of the defendant, the need to protect the child witness and the integrity of the truth-finding function of the trier of fact.

6. Unless all material facts alleged in support of the motion made pursuant to subdivision one of this section are conceded, the court shall, in addition to examining the papers and hearing oral argument, conduct an appropriate hearing for the purpose of making findings of fact essential to the determination of the motion. Except as provided in subdivision six of this section, it may subpoena or call and examine witnesses, who must either testify under oath or be permitted to give unsworn testimony pursuant to subdivision two of section 60.20 and must authorize the attorneys for the parties to do the same.

7. Notwithstanding any other provision of law, the child witness who is alleged to be vulnerable may not be compelled to testify at such hearing or to submit to any psychological or psychiatric examination. The failure of the child witness to testify at such hearing shall not be a ground for denying a motion made pursuant to subdivision one of this section. Prior statements made by the child witness relating to any allegations of conduct constituting an offense defined in article one hundred thirty of the penal law or incest as defined in section 255.25, 255.26 or 255.27 of such law or to any allegation of words or conduct constituting an attempt to prevent, impede or deter the child witness from cooperating in the investigation or prosecution of the offense shall be admissible at such hearing, provided, however, that a declaration that a child witness is vulnerable may not be based solely upon such prior statements.

8. (a) Notwithstanding any of the provisions of article forty-five of the civil practice law and rules, any physician, psychologist, nurse or social worker who has treated a child witness may testify at a hearing conducted pursuant to subdivision five of this section concerning the treatment of such child witness as such treatment relates to the issue presented at the hearing, provided that any otherwise applicable statutory privileges concerning communications between the child witness and such physician, psychologist, nurse or social worker in

connection with such treatment shall not be deemed waived by such testimony alone, except to the limited extent of permitting the court alone to examine in camera reports, records or documents, if any, prepared by such physician, psychologist, nurse or social worker. If upon such examination the court determines that such reports, records or documents, or any one or portion thereof, contain information material and relevant to the issue of whether the child witness is a vulnerable child witness, the court shall disclose such information to both the attorney for the defendant and the district attorney.

(b) At any time after a motion has been made pursuant to subdivision one of this section, upon the demand of the other party the moving party must furnish the demanding party with a copy of any and all of such records, reports or other documents in the possession of such other party and must, in addition, supply the court with a copy of all such reports, records or other documents which are the subject of the demand. At any time after a demand has been made pursuant to this paragraph, the moving party may demand that property of the same kind or character in possession of the party that originally made such demand be furnished to the moving party and, if so furnished, be supplied, in addition, to the court.

9. (a) Prior to the commencement of the hearing conducted pursuant to subdivision five of this section, the district attorney shall, subject to a protective order, comply with the provisions of subdivision one of section 240.45 of this chapter as they concern any witness whom the district attorney intends to call at the hearing and the child witness.

(b) Before a defendant calls a witness at such hearing, he or she must, subject to a protective order, comply with the provisions of subdivision two of section 240.45 of this chapter as they concern all the witnesses the defendant intends to call at such hearing.

10. The court may consider, in determining whether there are factors which would cause the child witness to suffer serious mental or emotional harm, a finding that any one or more of the following circumstances have been established by clear and convincing evidence:

(a) The manner of the commission of the offense of which the defendant is accused was particularly heinous or was characterized by aggravating circumstances.

(b) The child witness is particularly young or otherwise particularly subject to psychological harm on account of a physical or mental condition which existed before the alleged commission of the offense.

(c) At the time of the alleged offense, the defendant occupied a position of authority with respect to the child witness.

(d) The offense or offenses charged were part of an ongoing course of conduct committed by the defendant against the child witness over an extended period of time.

(e) A deadly weapon or dangerous instrument was allegedly used during the commission of the crime.

(f) The defendant has inflicted serious physical injury upon the child witness.

(g) A threat, express or implied, of physical violence to the child witness or a third person if the child witness were to report the incident to any person or communicate information to or cooperate with a court, grand jury, prosecutor, police officer or peace officer concerning the incident has been made by or on behalf of the defendant.

(h) A threat, express or implied, of the incarceration of a parent or guardian of the child witness, the removal of the child witness from the family or the dissolution of the family of the child witness if the child witness were to report the incident to any person or communicate information to or cooperate with a court, grand jury, prosecutor, police officer or peace officer concerning the incident has been made by or on behalf of the defendant.

(i) A witness other than the child witness has received a threat of physical violence directed at such witness or to a third person by or on behalf of the defendant.

(j) The defendant, at the time of the inquiry, (i) is living in the same household with the child witness, (ii) has ready access to the child witness or (iii) is providing substantial financial support for the child witness.

(k) The child witness has previously been the victim of an offense defined in article one hundred thirty of the penal law or incest as defined in section 255.25, 255.26 or 255.27 of such law.

(l) According to expert testimony, the child witness would be particularly suceptible [susceptible]* to psychological harm if required to testify in open court or in the physical presence of the defendant.

11. Irrespective of whether a motion was made pursuant to subdivision one of this section, the court, at the request of either party or on its own motion, may decide that a child witness may be vulnerable based on its own observations that a child witness who has been called to testify at a criminal proceeding is suffering severe mental or emotional harm and therefore is physically or mentally unable to testify or to continue to testify in open court or in the physical presence of the defendant and that the use of live, two-way closed-circuit television is necessary to enable the child witness to testify. If the court so decides, it must conduct the same hearing that subdivision five of this section requires when a motion is made pursuant to subdivision one of this section, and it must make findings of fact pursuant to subdivisions nine and eleven of this section, before determining that the child witness is vulnerable.

12. In deciding whether a child witness is vulnerable, the court shall make findings of fact which reflect the causal relationship between the existence of any one or more of the factors set forth in subdivision nine of this section or other relevant factors which the court finds are established and the determination that the child witness is vulnerable. If the court is satisfied that the child witness is vulnerable and that, under the facts and circumstances of the particular case, the defendant's constitutional rights to an impartial jury or of confrontation will not be impaired, it may enter an order granting the application for the use of live, two-way closed-circuit television.

13. When the court has determined that a child witness is a vulnerable child witness, it shall make a specific finding as to whether placing the defendant and the child witness in the same room during the testimony of the child witness will contribute to the likelihood that the child witness will suffer severe mental or emotional harm. If the court finds that placing the defendant and the child witness in the same room during the testimony of the child witness will contribute to the likelihood that the child witness will suffer severe mental or emotional harm, the order entered pursuant to subdivision eleven of this section shall direct that the defendant remain in the courtroom during the testimony of the vulnerable child witness.

HISTORY: Add, L 1985, ch 505, § 1, eff July 24, 1985, expires and is repealed Sept 1, 2015. Sub 2, add, L 2007, ch 548, § 2, eff Aug 15, 2007. Former sub 2, redesignated sub 3, L 2007, ch 548, § 2, eff Aug 15, 2007. Sub 3, formerly sub 2, so designated sub 3, L 2007, ch 548, § 2, eff Aug 15, 2007. Former sub 3, redesignated sub 4, L 2007, ch 548, § 2, eff Aug 15, 2007. Sub 4, formerly

---

* The bracketed word has been inserted by the Publisher.

sub 3, so designated sub 4, L 2007, ch 548, § 2, eff Aug 15, 2007. Former sub 4, redesignated sub 5, L 2007, ch 548, § 2, eff Aug 15, 2007. Sub 5, formerly sub 4, so designated sub 5, L 2007, ch 548, § 2, eff Aug 15, 2007. Former sub 5, redesignated sub 6, L 2007, ch 548, § 2, eff Aug 15, 2007. Sub 6, formerly sub 5, so designated sub 6, L 2007, ch 548, § 2, eff Aug 15, 2007. Former sub 6, redesignated sub 7, L 2007, ch 548, § 2, eff Aug 15, 2007. Sub 7, formerly sub 6, amd, L 2006, ch 320, § 13, eff Nov 1, 2006; so designated sub 7, L 2007, ch 548, § 2, eff Aug 15, 2007. Former sub 7, redesignated sub 8, L 2007, ch 548, § 2, eff Aug 15, 2007. Sub 8, formerly sub 7, so designated sub 8, L 2007, ch 548, § 2, eff Aug 15, 2007. Former sub 8, redesignated sub 9, L 2007, ch 548, § 2, eff Aug 15, 2007. Sub 9, formerly sub 8, so designated sub 9, L 2007, ch 548, § 2, eff Aug 15, 2007. Former sub 9, redesignated sub 10, L 2007, ch 548, § 2, eff Aug 15, 2007. Sub 10, formerly sub 9, amd, L 2006, ch 320, § 14, eff Nov 1, 2006; so designated sub 10, L 2007, ch 548, § 2, eff Aug 15, 2007. Former sub 10, redesignated sub 11, L 2007, ch 548, § 2, eff Aug 15, 2007. Sub 10, opening par, amd, L 2007, ch 548, § 3, eff Aug 15, 2007. Sub 11, formerly sub 10, amd, L 1991, ch 455, § 1, eff July 19, 1991. Sub 11, formerly sub 10, so designated sub 11, L 2007, ch 548, § 2, eff Aug 15, 2007. Former sub 11, redesignated sub 12, L 2007, ch 548, § 2, eff Aug 15, 2007. Sub 12, formerly sub 11, amd, L 1991, ch 455, § 1, eff July 19, 1991. Sub 12, formerly sub 11, so designated sub 12, L 2007, ch 548, § 2, eff Aug 15, 2007. Former sub 12, redesignated sub 13, L 2007, ch 548, § 2, eff Aug 15, 2007. Sub 13, formerly sub 12, so designated sub 13, L 2007, ch 548, § 2, eff Aug 15, 2007.

§ 65.30. [Expires and is repealed Sept 1, 2015] Closed-circuit television; special testimonial procedures

1. When the court has entered an order pursuant to section 65.20, the testimony of the vulnerable child witness shall be taken in the testimonial room and the image and voice of the vulnerable child witness, as well as the image of all other persons other than the operator present in the testimonial room, shall be transmitted live by means of closed-circuit television to the courtroom. The courtroom shall be equipped with monitors sufficient to permit the judge, jury, defendant and attorneys to observe the demeanor of the vulnerable child witness during his or her testimony. Unless the courtroom has been closed pursuant to court order, the public shall also be permitted to hear the testimony and view the image of the vulnerable child witness.

2. In all instances, the image of the jury shall be simultaneously transmitted to the vulnerable child witness in the testimonial room. If the court order issued pursuant to section 65.20 specifies that the vulnerable child witness shall testify outside the physical presence of the defendant, the image of the defendant and the image and voice of the person examining the vulnerable child witness shall also be simultaneously transmitted to the vulnerable child witness in the testimonial room.

3. The operator shall place herself or himself and the closed-circuit television equipment in a position that permits the entire testimony of the vulnerable child witness to be transmitted to the courtroom but limits the ability of the vulnerable child witness to see or hear the operator or the equipment.

4. Notwithstanding any provision of this article, if the court in a particular case involving a vulnerable child witness determines that there is no live, two-way closed-circuit television equipment available in the court or another court in the county or which can be transported to the court from another county or that such equipment, if available, is technologically inadequate to protect the constitutional rights of the defendant, it shall not permit the use of the closed-circuit television procedures authorized by this article.

5. If the order of the court entered pursuant to section 65.20 requires that the defendant remain in the courtroom, the attorney for the defendant and the district attorney shall also remain in the courtroom unless the court is satisfied that their presence in the testimonial room will not impede full and private communication between the defendant and his or her attorney and will not

encourage the jury to draw an inference adverse to the interest of the defendant.

6. Upon request of the defendant, the court shall instruct the jury that they are to draw no inference from the use of live, two-way closed-circuit television in the examination of the vulnerable child witness.

7. The vulnerable child witness shall testify under oath except as specified in subdivision two of section 60.20. The examination and cross-examination of the vulnerable child witness shall, in all other respects, be conducted in the same manner as if the vulnerable child witness had testified in the courtroom.

8. When the testimony of the vulnerable child witness is transmitted from the testimonial room into the courtroom, the court stenographer shall record the textimony [testimony]* in the same manner as if the vulnerable child witness had testified in the courtroom.

HISTORY: Add, L 1985, ch 505, § 1, eff July 24, 1985, expires and is repealed Sept 1, 2015.

ARTICLE 70   STANDARDS OF PROOF

§ 70.10.	Standards of proof; definitions of terms
§ 70.20.	Standards of proof for conviction

HISTORY: Add, L 1970, ch 996, § 1, eff Sept 1, 1971.

§ 70.10. Standards of proof; definitions of terms

The following definitions are applicable to this chapter:

1. "Legally sufficient evidence" means competent evidence which, if accepted as true, would establish every element of an offense charged and the defendant's commission thereof; except that such evidence is not legally sufficient when corroboration required by law is absent.

2. "Reasonable cause to believe that a person has committed an offense" exists when evidence or information which appears reliable discloses facts or circumstances which are collectively of such weight and persuasiveness as to convince a person of ordinary intelligence, judgment and experience that it is reasonably likely that such offense was committed and that such person committed it. Except as otherwise provided in this chapter, such apparently reliable evidence may include or consist of hearsay.

HISTORY: Add, L 1970, ch 996, § 1, eff Sept 1, 1971.

§ 70.20. Standards of proof for conviction

No conviction of an offense by verdict is valid unless based upon trial evidence which is legally sufficient and which establishes beyond a reasonable doubt every element of such offense and the defendant's commission thereof.

HISTORY: Add, L 1970, ch 996, § 1, eff Sept 1, 1971, with substance derived from Crim C § 389.

---

* The bracketed word has been inserted by the Publisher.

PART TWO   The Principal Proceedings

Title H
Preliminary Proceedings in Local Criminal Court

Title I
Preliminary Proceedings in Superior Court

Title J
Prosecution of Indictments in Superior Courts—Plea to Sentence

Title K
Prosecution of Informations in Local Criminal Courts—Plea to Sentence

Title L
Sentence

Title M Proceedings After Judgment

HISTORY: Add, L 1970, ch 996, § 1, eff Sept 1, 1971.

TITLE H   Preliminary Proceedings in Local Criminal Court

ARTICLE 100
COMMENCEMENT OF ACTION IN LOCAL CRIMINAL COURT—LOCAL CRIMINAL COURT ACCUSATORY INSTRUMENTS

ARTICLE 110
REQUIRING DEFENDANT'S APPEARANCE IN LOCAL CRIMINAL COURT FOR ARRAIGNMENT

ARTICLE 120
WARRANT OF ARREST

ARTICLE 130
THE SUMMONS

ARTICLE 140
ARREST WITHOUT A WARRANT

ARTICLE 150
THE APPEARANCE TICKET

ARTICLE 160
FINGERPRINTING AND PHOTOGRAPHING OF DEFENDANT AFTER ARREST—CRIMINAL IDENTIFICATION RECORDS AND STATISTICS

ARTICLE 170
PROCEEDINGS UPON INFORMATION, SIMPLIFIED TRAFFIC INFORMATION, PROSECUTOR'S INFORMATION AND MISDEMEANOR COMPLAINT FROM ARRAIGNMENT TO PLEA

ARTICLE 180
PROCEEDINGS UPON FELONY COMPLAINT FROM ARRAIGNMENT THEREON THROUGH DISPOSITION THEREOF

ARTICLE 182
[EXPIRES AND REPEALED SEPT 1, 2015] ALTERNATE METHOD OF COURT APPEARANCE

ARTICLE 185
[EXPIRED]

HISTORY: Add, L 1970, ch 996, § 1, eff Sept 1, 1971.

ARTICLE 100   COMMENCEMENT OF ACTION IN LOCAL CRIMINAL COURT—LOCAL CRIMINAL COURT ACCUSATORY INSTRUMENTS

HISTORY: Add, L 1970, ch 996, § 1, eff Sept 1, 1971.

§ 100.05. Commencement of action; in general

A criminal action is commenced by the filing of an accusatory instrument with a criminal court, and if more than one such instrument is filed in the course of the same criminal action, such action commences when the first of such instruments is filed. The only way in which a criminal action can be commenced in a superior court is by the filing therewith by a grand jury of an indictment against a defendant who has never been held by a local criminal court for the action of such grand jury with respect to any charge contained in such indictment. Otherwise, a criminal action can be commenced only in a local criminal court, by the filing therewith of a local criminal court accusatory instrument, namely:

1. An information; or

2. A simplified information; or

3. A prosecutor's information; or

4. A misdemeanor complaint; or

5. A felony complaint.

HISTORY: Add, L 1970, ch 996, § 1, eff Sept 1, 1971. Sub 2, amd, L 1972, ch 661, § 30, eff Sept 1, 1972.

§ 100.07. Commencement of action; effect of family court proceeding

A criminal court shall have concurrent jurisdiction over cognizable family offenses, as defined in subdivision one of section 530.11 of this chapter and in subdivision one of section eight hundred twelve of the family court act, notwithstanding the fact that a family court has or may be exercising jurisdiction over a petition under article eight of the family court act containing substantially the same allegations as are set forth in the accusatory instrument or indictment.

HISTORY: Add, L 1994, ch 222, § 31, eff Jan 1, 1995. Former § 100.07, add, L 1977, ch 449, § 10; amd, L 1978, ch 628, § 9, L 1978, ch 629, § 4, L 1990, ch 577, § 3; deleted, L 1994, ch 222, § 31, eff Jan 1, 1995.

§ 100.10. Local criminal court accusatory instruments; definitions thereof

1. An "information" is a verified written accusation by a person, filed with a local criminal court, charging one or more other persons with the commission of one or more offenses, none of which is a felony. It may serve as a basis both for the commencement of a criminal action and for the prosecution thereof in a local criminal court.

2. (a) A "simplified traffic information" is a written accusation by a police officer, or other public servant authorized by law to issue same, filed with a local criminal court, which charges a person with the commission of one or more traffic infractions and/or misdemeanors relating to traffic, and which, being in a brief or simplified form prescribed by the commissioner of motor vehicles, designates the offense or offenses charged but contains no factual allegations of an evidentiary nature supporting such charge or charges. It serves as a basis for commencement of a criminal action for such traffic offenses, alternative to the charging thereof by a regular information, and, under circumstances prescribed in section 100.25, it may serve, either in whole or in part, as a basis for prosecution of such charges.

(b) A "simplified parks information" is a written accusation by a police officer or other public servant authorized by law to issue same, filed with a local criminal court, which charges a person with the commission of one or more offenses, other than a felony, for which a uniform simplified parks information may be issued pursuant to the parks and recreation law and navigation law, and which being in a brief or simplified form prescribed by the commissioner of parks and recreation, designates the offense or offenses charged but contains no factual allegations of an evidentiary nature supporting such charge or charges. It serves as a basis for commencement of a criminal action for such offenses, alternative to the charging thereof by a regular information, and, under circumstances parescribed [prescribed]* in section 100.25, it may serve, either in whole or in part, as a basis for prosecution of such charges.

(c) A "simplified environmental conservation information" is a written accusation by a police officer or other public servant authorized by law to issue same, filed with a local criminal court, which charges a person with the commission of one or more offenses, other than a felony, for which a uniform simplified environmental conservation information may be issued pursuant to the environmental conservation law, and which being in a brief or simplified form prescribed by the commissioner of environmental conservation, designates the offense or offenses charged but contains no factual allegations of an evidentiary nature supporting such charge or charges. It serves as a basis for commencement of a criminal action for such offenses, alternative to the charging thereof by a regular information, and, under circumstances prescribed in section 100.25, it may serve, either in whole or in part, as a basis for prosecution of such charges.

3. A "prosecutor's information" is a written accusation by a district attorney, filed with a local criminal court, either (a) at the direction of a grand jury pursuant to section 190.70, or (b) at the direction of a local criminal court pursuant to section 180.50 or 180.70, or (c) at the district attorney's own instance pursuant to subdivision two of section 100.50, or (d) at the direction of a superior court pursuant to subdivision one-a of section 210.20, charging one or more persons with the commission of one or more offenses, none of which is a felony. It serves as a basis for the prosecution of a criminal action, but it commences a criminal action only where it results from a grand jury direction issued in a case not previously commenced in a local criminal court.

4. A "misdemeanor complaint" is a verified written accusation by a person, filed with a local criminal court, charging one or more other persons with the commission of one or more offenses, at least one of which is a misdemeanor and none of which is a felony. It serves as a basis for the commencement of a criminal action, but it may serve as a basis for prosecution thereof only where a defendant has waived prosecution by information pursuant to subdivision three of section 170.65.

5. A "felony complaint" is a verified written accusation by a person, filed with a local criminal court, charging one or more other persons with the commission of one or more felonies. It serves as a basis for the commencement of a criminal action, but not as a basis for prosecution thereof.

　　HISTORY: Add, L 1970, ch 996, § 1, eff Sept 1, 1971. Sub 2, amd, L 1972, ch 315, § 4, L 1972, ch 383, § 3, L 1972, ch 729, § 3, eff Jan 1, 1973. Sub 2, par (a), formerly entire subdivision, so lettered and amd, L 1972, ch 661, § 31, eff Sept 1, 1972. Sub 2, par (b), add, L 1972, ch 661, § 31, eff Sept 1, 1972. Sub 2, par (c), add, L 1974, ch 707, § 5, eff Sept 1, 1974. Sub 3, amd, L 1990, ch 209, § 11, eff Sept 1, 1990.

§ 100.15. Information, misdemeanor complaint and felony complaint; form and content

1. An information, a misdemeanor complaint and a felony complaint must each specify the name

_____

* The bracketed word has been inserted by the Publisher.

of the court with which it is filed and the title of the action, and must be subscribed and verified by a person known as the "complainant." The complainant may be any person having knowledge, whether personal or upon information and belief, of the commission of the offense or offenses charged. Each instrument must contain an accusatory part and a factual part. The complainant's verification of the instrument is deemed to apply only to the factual part thereof and not to the accusatory part.

2. The accusatory part of each such instrument must designate the offense or offenses charged. As in the case of an indictment, and subject to the rules of joinder applicable to indictments, two or more offenses may be charged in separate counts. Also as in the case of an indictment, such instrument may charge two or more defendants provided that all such defendants are jointly charged with every offense alleged therein.

3. The factual part of such instrument must contain a statement of the complainant alleging facts of an evidentiary character supporting or tending to support the charges. Where more than one offense is charged, the factual part should consist of a single factual account applicable to all the counts of the accusatory part. The factual allegations may be based either upon personal knowledge of the complainant or upon information and belief. Nothing contained in this section, however, limits or affects the requirement, prescribed in subdivision one of section 100.40, that in order for an information or a count thereof to be sufficient on its face, every element of the offense charged and the defendant's commission thereof must be supported by non-hearsay allegations of such information and/or any supporting depositions.

4. Where a felony complaint charges a violent felony offense defined in section 70.02 of the penal law and such offense is an armed felony as defined in subdivision forty-one of section 1.20,

   (a) the accusatory part of the instrument must designate the offense as an armed felony, and
   (b) the factual part of the instrument must allege facts of an evidentiary character supporting or tending to support such designation.

   HISTORY: Add, L 1970, ch 996, § 1, eff Sept 1, 1971. Sub 4, add, L 1978, ch 481, § 9, eff Sept 1, 1978.

§ 100.20. Supporting deposition; definition, form and content

A supporting deposition is a written instrument accompanying or filed in connection with an information, a simplified information, a misdemeanor complaint or a felony complaint, subscribed and verified by a person other than the complainant of such accusatory instrument, and containing factual allegations of an evidentiary character, based either upon personal knowledge or upon information and belief, which supplement those of the accusatory instrument and support or tend to support the charge or charges contained therein.

   HISTORY: Add, L 1970, ch 996, § 1; amd, L 1972, ch 661, § 32, eff Sept 1, 1972.

§ 100.25. Simplified information; form and content; defendant's right to supporting deposition; notice requirement

1. A simplified information must be substantially in the form prescribed by the commissioner of motor vehicles, the commissioner of parks and recreation, or the commissioner of environmental conservation, as the case may be.

2. A defendant charged by a simplified information is, upon a timely request, entitled as a matter of right to have filed with the court and served upon him, or if he is represented by an attorney, upon his attorney, a supporting deposition of the complainant police officer or public servant, containing allegations of fact, based either upon personal knowledge or upon information and belief, providing reasonable cause to believe that the defendant committed the offense or offenses

charged. To be timely, such a request must, except as otherwise provided herein and in subdivision three of this section, be made before entry of a plea of guilty to the charge specified and before commencement of a trial thereon, but not later than thirty days after the date the defendant is directed to appear in court as such date appears upon the simplified information and upon the appearance ticket issued pursuant thereto. If the defendant's request is mailed to the court, the request must be mailed within such thirty day period. Upon such a request, the court must order the complainant police officer or public servant to serve a copy of such supporting deposition upon the defendant or his attorney, within thirty days of the date such request is received by the court, or at least five days before trial, whichever is earlier, and to file such supporting deposition with the court together with proof of service thereof. Notwithstanding any provision to the contrary, where a defendant is issued an appearance ticket in conjunction with the offense charged in the simplified information and the appearance ticket fails to conform with the requirements of subdivision two of section 150.10, a request is timely when made not later than thirty days after (a) entry of the defendant's plea of not guilty when he or she has been arraigned in person, or (b) written notice to the defendant of his or her right to receive a supporting deposition when a plea of not guilty has been submitted by mail.

3. When at least one of the offenses charged in a simplified information is a misdemeanor, the court may, upon motion of the defendant, for good cause shown and consistent with the interest of justice, permit the defendant to request a supporting deposition beyond the thirty day request period set forth in subdivision two of this section provided, however, that no motion may be brought under this subdivision after ninety days has elapsed from the date the defendant is directed to appear in court as such date appears upon the simplified information and upon the appearance ticket issued pursuant thereto.

4. Notwithstanding any provision of law to the contrary, where a person is charged by a simplified information and is served with an appearance ticket as defined in section 150.10, such appearance ticket shall contain the following language: "NOTICE: YOU ARE ENTITLED TO RECEIVE A SUPPORTING DEPOSITION FURTHER EXPLAINING THE CHARGES PROVIDED YOU REQUEST SUCH SUPPORTING DEPOSITION WITHIN THIRTY DAYS FROM THE DATE YOU ARE DIRECTED TO APPEAR IN COURT AS SET FORTH ON THIS APPEARANCE TICKET. DO YOU REQUEST A SUPPORTING DEPOSITION? [   ]YES [   ]NO"

> **HISTORY:** Add, L 1970, ch 996, § 1; amd, L 1972, ch 661, § 33, eff Sept 1, 1972. Section heading, amd, L 1972, ch 661, § 33, L 1996, ch 67, § 1, eff Oct 20, 1996. Sub 1, amd, L 1974, ch 707, § 6, eff Sept 1, 1974. Sub 2, amd, L 1973, ch 614, § 1, L 1985, ch 225, § 1, L 1986, ch 431, § 1, L 1996, ch 67, § 2, eff Oct 20, 1996. Sub 3, add, L 1996, ch 67, § 3, eff Oct 20, 1996. Sub 4, add, L 1996, ch 67, § 3, eff Oct 20, 1996.

§ 100.30. Information, misdemeanor complaint, felony complaint, supporting deposition and proof of service of supporting deposition; verification

1. An information, a misdemeanor complaint, a felony complaint, a supporting deposition, and proof of service of a supporting deposition may be verified in any of the following manners:

(a) Such instrument may be sworn to before the court with which it is filed.

(b) Such instrument may be sworn to before a desk officer in charge at a police station or police headquarters or any of his superior officers.

(c) Where such instrument is filed by any public servant following the issuance and service of an appearance ticket, and where by express provision of law another designated public servant is authorized to administer the oath with respect to such instrument, it may be sworn to before such public servant.

(d) Such instrument may bear a form notice that false statements made therein are punishable as a class A misdemeanor pursuant to section 210.45 of the penal law, and such form notice together with the subscription of the deponent constitute a verification of the instrument.

(e) Such instrument may be sworn to before a notary public.

2. An instrument specified in subdivision one may be verified in any manner prescribed therein unless in a particular case the court expressly directs verification in a particular manner prescribed in said subdivision one.

> **HISTORY:** Add, L 1970, ch 996, § 1, eff Sept 1, 1971. Section heading, amd, L 1986, ch 71, § 1, eff Sept 1, 1986. Sub 1, opening par, amd, L 1986, ch 71, § 1, eff Sept 1, 1986. Sub 1, par (e), add, L 1984, ch 201, § 1, eff June 12, 1984.

§ 100.35. Prosecutor's information; form and content

A prosecutor's information must contain the name of the local criminal court with which it is filed and the title of the action, and must be subscribed by the district attorney by whom it is filed. Otherwise it should be in the form prescribed for an indictment, pursuant to section 200.50, and must, in one or more counts, allege the offense or offenses charged and a plain and concise statement of the conduct constituting each such offense. The rules prescribed in sections 200.20 and 200.40 governing joinder of different offenses and defendants in a single indictment are also applicable to a prosecutor's information.

> **HISTORY:** Add, L 1970, ch 996, § 1, eff Sept 1, 1971.

§ 100.40. Local criminal court accusatory instruments; sufficiency on face

1. An information, or a count thereof, is sufficient on its face when:

(a) It substantially conforms to the requirements prescribed in section 100.15; and

(b) The allegations of the factual part of the information, together with those of any supporting depositions which may accompany it, provide reasonable cause to believe that the defendant committed the offense charged in the accusatory part of the information; and

(c) Non-hearsay allegations of the factual part of the information and/or of any supporting depositions establish, if true, every element of the offense charged and the defendant's commission thereof.

2. A simplified information is sufficient on its face when, as provided by subdivision one of section 100.25, it substantially conforms to the requirement therefor prescribed by or pursuant to law; provided that when the filing of a supporting deposition is ordered by the court pursuant to subdivision two of said section 100.25, a failure of the complainant police officer or public servant to comply with such order within the time provided by subdivision two of said section 100.25 renders the simplified information insufficient on its face.

3. A prosecutor's information, or a count thereof, is sufficient on its face when it substantially conforms to the requirements prescribed in section 100.35.

4. A misdemeanor complaint or a felony complaint, or a count thereof, is sufficient on its face when:

(a) It substantially conforms to the requirements prescribed in section 100.15; and

(b) The allegations of the factual part of such accusatory instrument and/or any supporting depositions which may accompany it, provide reasonable cause to believe that the defendant committed the offense charged in the accusatory part of such instrument.

HISTORY: Add, L 1970, ch 996, § 1, eff Sept 1, 1971. Sub 2, amd, L 1972, ch 661, § 34, L 1985, ch 225, § 2, eff Nov 1, 1985.

§ 100.45. Information, prosecutor's information, misdemeanor complaint; severance, consolidation, amendment, bill of particulars

1. Where appropriate, the provisions of sections 200.20 and 200.40, governing severance of counts of an indictment and severance of defendants for trial purposes, and governing consolidation of indictments for trial purposes, apply to informations, to prosecutor's informations and to misdemeanor complaints.

2. The provisions of section 200.70 governing amendment of indictments apply to prosecutor's informations.

3. At any time before the entry of a plea of guilty to or the commencement of a trial of an information, the court may, upon application of the people and with notice to the defendant and opportunity to be heard, order the amendment of the accusatory part of such information by addition of a count charging an offense supported by the allegations of the factual part of such information and/or any supporting depositions which may accompany it. In such case, the defendant must be accorded any reasonable adjournment necessitated by the amendment.

4. The provisions of section 200.95, governing bills of particulars with respect to indictments, apply to informations, to misdemeanor complaints and to prosecutor's informations.

HISTORY: Add, L 1970, ch 996, § 1, eff Sept 1, 1971. Sub 4, amd, L 1982, ch 558, § 2, eff Oct 20, 1982.

§ 100.50. Superseding informations and prosecutor's informations

1. If at any time before entry of a plea of guilty to or commencement of a trial of an information or a prosecutor's information, another information or, as the case may be, another prosecutor's information is filed with the same local criminal court charging the defendant with an offense charged in the first instrument, the first such instrument is, with respect to such offense, superseded by the second and, upon the defendant's arraignment upon the latter, the count of the first instrument charging such offense must be dismissed by the court. The first instrument is not, however, superseded with respect to any count contained therein which charges an offense not charged in the second instrument.

2. At any time before entry of a plea of guilty to or commencement of a trial of an information, the district attorney may file with the local criminal court a prosecutor's information charging any offenses supported, pursuant to the standards prescribed in subdivision one of section 100.40, by the allegations of the factual part of the original information and/or any supporting depositions which may accompany it. In such case, the original information is superseded by the prosecutor's information and, upon the defendant's arraignment upon the latter, is deemed dismissed.

3. A misdemeanor complaint must or may be replaced and superseded by an information pursuant to the provisions of section 170.65.

HISTORY: Add, L 1970, ch 996, § 1, eff Sept 1, 1971. Sub 1, amd, L 1972, ch 610, § 1, eff May 24, 1972.

§ 100.55. Local criminal court accusatory instruments; in what courts filed

1. Any local criminal court accusatory instrument may be filed with a district court of a particular county when an offense charged therein was allegedly committed in such county or that

part thereof over which such court has jurisdiction.

2. Any local criminal court accusatory instrument may be filed with the New York City criminal court when an offense charged therein was allegedly committed in New York City.

3. Any local criminal court accusatory instrument may be filed with a city court of a particular city when an offense charged therein was allegedly committed in such city.

4. An information, a simplified information, a prosecutor's information or a misdemeanor complaint may be filed with a town court of a particular town when an offense charged therein was allegedly committed anywhere in such town other than in a village thereof having a village court.

5. An information, a simplified information, a prosecutor's information or a misdemeanor complaint may be filed with a village court of a particular village when an offense charged therein was allegedly committed in such village.

6. A felony complaint may be filed with any town court or village court of a particular county when a felony charged therein was allegedly committed in some town of such county. Such court need not be that of the town or village in which such felony was allegedly committed.

7. An information, a simplified information, a misdemeanor complaint or a felony complaint may be filed with a judge of a superior court sitting as a local criminal court when an offense charged therein was allegedly committed in a county in which such judge is then present and in which he either resides or is currently holding, or has been assigned to hold, a term of a superior court.

8. Where it is otherwise expressly provided by law that a particular kind of accusatory instrument may under given circumstances be filed with a local criminal court other than one authorized by this section, nothing contained in this section precludes the filing of such accusatory instrument accordingly.

9. In any case where each of two or more local criminal courts is authorized as a proper court with which to file an accusatory instrument, such an instrument may, in the absence of an express provision of law to the contrary, be filed with any one of such courts but not with more than one.

10. For purposes of this section, an offense is "committed in" a particular county, city, town, village or other specified political subdivision or area, not only when it is in fact committed therein but also when it is, for other reasons specified in sections 20.40 and 20.50, prosecutable in the criminal courts having geographical jurisdiction over such political subdivision or area.

HISTORY: Add, L 1970, ch 996, § 1, eff Sept 1, 1971. Sub 4, amd, L 1972, ch 661, § 35, eff Sept 1, 1972. Sub 5, amd, L 1972, ch 661, § 35, eff Sept 1, 1972. Sub 7, amd, L 1972, ch 661, § 35, eff Sept 1, 1972.

ARTICLE 110 REQUIRING DEFENDANT'S APPEARANCE IN LOCAL CRIMINAL COURT FOR ARRAIGNMENT

HISTORY: Add, L 1970, ch 996, § 1, eff Sept 1, 1971.

§ 110.10. Methods of requiring defendant's appearance in local criminal court for arraignment; in general

1. After a criminal action has been commenced in a local criminal court by the filing of an

accusatory instrument therewith, a defendant who has not been arraigned in the action and has not come under the control of the court may under certain circumstances be compelled or required to appear for arraignment upon such accusatory instrument by:

(a) The issuance and execution of a warrant of arrest, as provided in article one hundred twenty; or

(b) The issuance and service upon him of a summons, as provided in article one hundred thirty; or

(c) Procedures provided in articles five hundred sixty, five hundred seventy, five hundred eighty, five hundred ninety and six hundred for securing attendance of defendants in criminal actions who are not at liberty within the state.

2. Although no criminal action against a person has been commenced in any court, he may under certain circumstances be compelled or required to appear in a local criminal court for arraignment upon an accusatory instrument to be filed therewith at or before the time of his appearance by:

(a) An arrest made without a warrant, as provided in article one hundred forty; or

(b) The issuance and service upon him of an appearance ticket, as provided in article one hundred fifty.

HISTORY: Add, L 1970, ch 996, § 1, eff Sept 1, 1971.

§ 110.20. Local criminal court accusatory instruments; notice thereof to district attorney

When a criminal action in which a crime is charged is commenced in a local criminal court, other than the criminal court of the city of New York, a copy of the accusatory instrument shall be promptly transmitted to the appropriate district attorney upon or prior to the arraignment of the defendant on the accusatory instrument. If a police officer or a peace officer is the complainant or the filer of a simplified information, or has arrested the defendant or brought him before the local criminal court on behalf of an arresting person pursuant to subdivision one of section 140.20, such officer or his agency shall transmit the copy of the accusatory instrument to the appropriate district attorney. In all other cases, the clerk of the court in which the defendant is arraigned shall so transmit it.

HISTORY: Add, L 1977, ch 353, § 1; amd, L 1980, ch 843, § 7, eff Sept 1, 1980.

ARTICLE 120   WARRANT OF ARREST

HISTORY: Add, L 1970, ch 996, § 1, eff Sept 1, 1971.

§ 120.10. Warrant of arrest; definition, function, form and content

1. A warrant of arrest is a process issued by a local criminal court directing a police officer to arrest a defendant designated in an accusatory instrument filed with such court and to bring him before such court in connection with such instrument. The sole function of a warrant of arrest is to achieve a defendant's court appearance in a criminal action for the purpose of arraignment upon the accusatory instrument by which such action was commenced.

2. A warrant of arrest must be subscribed by the issuing judge and must state or contain (a) the name of the issuing court, and (b) the date of issuance of the warrant, and (c) the name or title of an offense charged in the underlying accusatory instrument, and (d) the name of the defendant to be arrested or, if such be unknown, any name or description by which he can be identified with reasonable certainty, and (e) the police officer or officers to whom the warrant is addressed, and (f) a direction that such officer arrest the defendant and bring him before the issuing court.

3. A warrant of arrest may be addressed to a classification of police officers, or to two or more classifications thereof, as well as to a designated individual police officer or officers. Multiple copies of such a warrant may be issued.

> **HISTORY:** Add, L 1970, ch 996, § 1, with substance derived from Crim C §§ 151, 152; amd, L 1980, ch 843, § 8, eff Sept 1, 1980. Amd, L 1998, ch 424, § 4, eff Jan 1, 1999. Sub 1, amd, L 1998, ch 424, § 4, eff Jan 1, 1999. Sub 2, amd, L 1998, ch 424, § 4, eff Jan 1, 1999. Sub 3, amd, L 1998, ch 424, § 4, eff Jan 1, 1999.

§ 120.20. Warrant of arrest; when issuable

1. When a criminal action has been commenced in a local criminal court by the filing therewith of an accusatory instrument, other than a simplified traffic information, against a defendant who has not been arraigned upon such accusatory instrument and has not come under the control of the court with respect thereto:

    (a) such court may, if such accusatory instrument is sufficient on its face, issue a warrant for such defendant's arrest; or

    (b) if such accusatory instrument is not sufficient on its face as prescribed in section 100.40, and if the court is satisfied that on the basis of the available facts or evidence it would be impossible to draw and file an accusatory instrument that is sufficient on its face, the court must dismiss the accusatory instrument.

2. Even though such accusatory instrument is sufficient on its face, the court may refuse to issue a warrant of arrest based thereon until it has further satisfied itself, by inquiry or examination of witnesses, that there is reasonable cause to believe that the defendant committed an offense charged. Upon such inquiry or examination, the court may examine, under oath or otherwise, any available person whom it believes may possess knowledge concerning the subject matter of the charge.

3. Notwithstanding the provisions of subdivision one, if a summons may be issued in lieu of a warrant of arrest pursuant to section 130.20, and if the court is satisfied that the defendant will respond thereto, it may not issue a warrant of arrest. Upon the request of the district attorney, in lieu of a warrant of arrest or summons, the court may instead authorize the district attorney to direct the defendant to appear for arraignment on a designated date if it is satisfied that the defendant will so appear.

> **HISTORY:** Add, L 1970, ch 996, § 1, eff Sept 1, 1971. Sub 1, opening par, formerly part of entire sub 1, so designated sub 1, opening par and amd, L 2000, ch 506, § 1, eff Nov 1, 2000. Sub 1, par (a), formerly part of entire sub 1, so designated sub 1, par (a) and amd, L 2000, ch 506, § 1, eff Nov 1, 2000. Sub 1, par (b), add, L 2000, ch 506, § 1, eff Nov 1, 2000. Sub 3, amd, L 1993, ch 446, § 3, eff Nov 1, 1993.

§ 120.30. Warrant of arrest; by what courts issuable and in what courts returnable

1. A warrant of arrest may be issued only by the local criminal court with which the underlying accusatory instrument has been filed, and it may be made returnable in such issuing court only.

2. The particular local criminal court or courts with which any particular local criminal court accusatory instrument may be filed for the purpose of obtaining a warrant of arrest are determined, generally, by the provisions of section 100.55. If, however, a particular accusatory instrument may pursuant to said section 100.55 be filed with a particular town court and such town court is not available at the time such instrument is sought to be filed and a warrant obtained, such accusatory instrument may be filed with the town court of any adjoining town of the same county. If such instrument may be filed pursuant to said section 100.55 with a particular village court and such village court is not available at the time, it may be filed with the town court of the town embracing such village, or if such town court is not available either, with the town court of any adjoining town of the same county.

HISTORY: Add, L 1970, ch 996, § 1, eff Sept 1, 1971.

§ 120.40. Warrant of arrest; attaching accusatory instrument to warrant of town court, village court or city court

A town court, village court or city court which issues a warrant of arrest may attach thereto a duplicate copy of the underlying accusatory instrument. If one or more duplicate copies of the warrant are issued, such court may attach as many copies of such accusatory instrument to copies of such warrant as it chooses. In any case where, pursuant to subdivision five of section 120.90, a defendant arrested upon such a warrant of arrest is brought before a local criminal court other than the town court, village court or city court in which the warrant is returnable, a copy of the accusatory instrument constitutes a valid basis for arraignment, as provided in subdivision one of section 170.15.

HISTORY: Add, L 1970, ch 996, § 1; amd, L 1973, ch 61, § 1, L 1988, ch 324, § 1, eff Nov 1, 1988. Section heading, amd, L 1988, ch 324, § 1, eff Nov 1, 1988.

§ 120.50. Warrant of arrest; to what police officers addressed

A warrant of arrest may be addressed to any police officer or classification of police officers whose geographical area of employment embraces either the place where the offense charged was allegedly committed or the locality of the court by which the warrant is issued.

HISTORY: Add, L 1970, ch 996, § 1; amd, L 1980, ch 843, § 9, eff Sept 1, 1980. Section heading, amd, L 1980, ch 843, § 9, eff Sept 1, 1980. Section heading, amd, L 1998, ch 424, § 5, eff Jan 1, 1999. Amd, L 1998, ch 424, § 5, eff Jan 1, 1999.

§ 120.55. Warrant of arrest; defendant under parole or probation supervision

If the defendant named within a warrant of arrest issued by a local criminal court pursuant to the provisions of this article, or by a superior court issued pursuant to subdivision three of section 210.10 of this chapter, is under the supervision of the state department of corrections and community supervision or a local or state probation department, then a warrant for his or her arrest may be executed by a parole officer or probation officer, when authorized by his or her probation director, within his or her geographical area of employment. The execution of the warrant by a parole officer or probation officer shall be upon the same conditions and conducted in the same manner as provided for execution of a warrant by a police officer.

HISTORY: Add, L 1979, ch 492, § 1; amd, L 1981, ch 456, § 1, eff July 7, 1981, L 2011, ch 62, § 71 (Part C, Subpart B), eff March 31, 2011.

§ 120.60. Warrant of arrest; what police officers may execute

1. A warrant of arrest may be executed by (a) any police officer to whom it is addressed, or (b) any other police officer delegated to execute it under circumstances prescribed in subdivisions two and three.

2. A police officer to whom a warrant of arrest is addressed may delegate another officer to whom it is not addressed to execute such warrant as his agent when:

(a) He has reasonable cause to believe that the defendant is in a particular county other than the one in which the warrant is returnable; and

(b) The warrant is, pursuant to section 120.70, executable in such other county without endorsement by a local criminal court thereof; and

(c) The geographical area of employment of the delegated police officer embraces the locality where the arrest is to be made.

3. Under circumstances specified in subdivision two, the police officer to whom the warrant is addressed may inform the delegated officer, by telecommunication, mail or any other means, of the issuance of the warrant, of the offense charged in the underlying accusatory instrument and of all other pertinent details, and may request him to act as his agent in arresting the defendant pursuant to such warrant. Upon such request, the delegated police officer is to the same extent as the delegating officer, authorized to make such arrest pursuant to the warrant within the geographical area of such delegated officer's employment. Upon so arresting the defendant, he must proceed as provided in subdivisions two and four of section 120.90.

HISTORY: Add, L 1970, ch 996, § 1; amd, L 1980, ch 843, § 10, eff Sept 1, 1980. Section heading, amd, L 1980, ch 843, § 10, eff Sept 1, 1980. Section heading, amd, L 1998, ch 424, § 6, eff Jan 1, 1999. Amd, L 1998, ch 424, § 6, eff Jan 1, 1999. Sub 1, amd, L 1998, ch 424, § 6, eff Jan 1, 1999. Sub 2, opening par, amd, L 1998, ch 424, § 6, eff Jan 1, 1999. Sub 2, par (c), amd, L 1998, ch 424, § 6, eff Jan 1, 1999. Sub 3, amd, L 1998, ch 424, § 6, eff Jan 1, 1999.

§ 120.70. Warrant of arrest; where executable

1. A warrant of arrest issued by a district court, by the New York City criminal court or by a superior court judge sitting as a local criminal court may be executed anywhere in the state.

2. A warrant of arrest issued by a city court, a town court or a village court may be executed:

(a) In the county of issuance or in any adjoining county; or

(b) Anywhere else in the state upon the written endorsement thereon of a local criminal court of the county in which the arrest is to be made. When so endorsed, the warrant is deemed the process of the endorsing court as well as that of the issuing court.

HISTORY: Add, L 1970, ch 996, § 1, eff Sept 1, 1971, with substance derived from Crim C §§ 155, 156.

§ 120.80. Warrant of arrest; when and how executed

1. A warrant of arrest may be executed on any day of the week and at any hour of the day or night.

2. Unless encountering physical resistance, flight or other factors rendering normal procedure impractical, the arresting police officer must inform the defendant that a warrant for his arrest for the offense designated therein has been issued. Upon request of the defendant, the officer must show him the warrant if he has it in his possession. The officer need not have the warrant in his possession, and, if he has not, he must show it to the defendant upon request as soon after the arrest as possible.

3. In order to effect the arrest, the police officer may use such physical force as is justifiable pursuant to section 35.30 of the penal law.

4. In order to effect the arrest, the police officer may, under circumstances and in the manner prescribed in this subdivision, enter any premises in which he reasonably believes the defendant to be present; provided, however, that where the premises in which the officer reasonably believes the defendant to be present is the dwelling of a third party who is not the subject of the arrest warrant, the officer shall proceed in the manner specified in article 690 of this chapter. Before such entry, he must give, or make reasonable effort to give, notice of his authority and purpose to an occupant thereof, unless there is reasonable cause to believe that the giving of such notice will:

(a) Result in the defendant escaping or attempting to escape; or

(b) Endanger the life or safety of the officer or another person; or

(c) Result in the destruction, damaging or secretion of material evidence.

5. If the officer is authorized to enter premises without giving notice of his authority and purpose, or if after giving such notice he is not admitted, he may enter such premises, and by a breaking if necessary.

HISTORY: Add, L 1970, ch 996, § 1, eff Sept 1, 1971, with substance derived from Crim C §§ 170–176. Sub 2, amd, L 1980, ch 843, § 11, eff Sept 1, 1980. Sub 3, amd, L 1980, ch 843, § 11, eff Sept 1, 1980. Sub 4, amd, L 1980, ch 843, § 11, L 1991, ch 504, § 1, eff Nov 1, 1991. Sub 4, opening par, amd, L 1991, ch 504, § 1, eff Nov 1, 1991. Sub 5, reenacted without change, L 1980, ch 843, § 11, eff Sept 1, 1980. Sub 2, amd, L 1998, ch 424, § 7, eff Jan 1, 1999. Sub 3, amd, L 1998, ch 424, § 7, eff Jan 1, 1999. Sub 4, opening par, amd, L 1998, ch 424, § 7, eff Jan 1, 1999.

§ 120.90. Warrant of arrest; procedure after arrest

1. Upon arresting a defendant for any offense pursuant to a warrant of arrest in the county in which the warrant is returnable or in any adjoining county, or upon so arresting him for a felony in any other county, a police officer, if he be one to whom the warrant is addressed, must without unnecessary delay bring the defendant before the local criminal court in which such warrant is returnable.

2. Upon arresting a defendant for any offense pursuant to a warrant of arrest in a county adjoining the county in which the warrant is returnable, or upon so arresting him for a felony in any other county, a police officer, if he be one delegated to execute the warrant pursuant to section 120.60, must without unnecessary delay deliver the defendant or cause him to be delivered to the custody of the officer by whom he was so delegated, and the latter must then proceed as provided in subdivision one.

3. Upon arresting a defendant for an offense other than a felony pursuant to a warrant of arrest in a county other than the one in which the warrant is returnable or one adjoining it, a police officer, if he be one to whom the warrant is addressed, must inform the defendant that he has a right to appear before a local criminal court of the county of arrest for the purpose of being released on his own recognizance or having bail fixed. If the defendant does not desire to avail himself of such right, the officer must request him to endorse such fact upon the warrant, and upon such endorsement the officer must without unnecessary delay bring him before the court in which the warrant is returnable. If the defendant does desire to avail himself of such right, or if he refuses to make the aforementioned endorsement, the officer must without unnecessary delay bring him before a local criminal court of the county of arrest. Such court must release the defendant on his own recognizance or fix bail for his appearance on a specified date in the court in which the warrant is returnable. If the defendant is in default of bail, the officer must without unnecessary

delay bring him before the court in which the warrant is returnable.

4. Upon arresting a defendant for an offense other than a felony pursuant to a warrant of arrest in a county other than the one in which the warrant is returnable or one adjoining it, a police officer, if he be one delegated to execute the warrant pursuant to section 120.60, may hold the defendant in custody in the county of arrest for a period not exceeding two hours for the purpose of delivering him to the custody of the officer by whom he was delegated to execute such warrant. If the delegating officer receives custody of the defendant during such period, he must proceed as provided in subdivision three. Otherwise, the delegated officer must inform the defendant that he has a right to appear before a local criminal court for the purpose of being released on his own recognizance or having bail fixed. If the defendant does not desire to avail himself of such right, the officer must request him to make, sign and deliver to him a written statement of such fact, and if the defendant does so, the officer must retain custody of him but must without unnecessary delay deliver him or cause him to be delivered to the custody of the delegating police officer. If the defendant does desire to avail himself of such right, or if he refuses to make and deliver the aforementioned statement, the delegated or arresting officer must without unnecessary delay bring him before a local criminal court of the county of arrest and must submit to such court a written statement reciting the material facts concerning the issuance of the warrant, the offense involved, and all other essential matters relating thereto. Upon the submission of such statement, such court must release the defendant on his own recognizance or fix bail for his appearance on a specified date in the court in which the warrant is returnable. If the defendant is in default of bail, the officer must retain custody of him but must without unnecessary delay deliver him or cause him to be delivered to the custody of the delegating officer. Upon receiving such custody, the latter must without unnecessary delay bring the defendant before the court in which the warrant is returnable.

5. Whenever a police officer is required pursuant to this section to bring an arrested defendant before a town court in which a warrant of arrest is returnable, and if such town court is not available at the time, such officer must, if a copy of the underlying accusatory instrument has been attached to the warrant pursuant to section 120.40, instead bring such defendant before any village court embraced, in whole or in part, by such town, or any local criminal court of an adjoining town or city of the same county or any village court embraced, in whole or in part, by such adjoining town. When the court in which the warrant is returnable is a village court which is not available at the time, the officer must in such circumstances bring the defendant before the town court of the town embracing such village or any other village court within such town or, if such town court or village court is not available either, before the local criminal court of any town or city of the same county which adjoins such embracing town or, before the local criminal court of any village embraced in whole or in part by such adjoining town. When the court in which the warrant is returnable is a city court which is not available at the time, the officer must in such circumstances bring the defendant before the local criminal court of any adjoining town or village embraced in whole or in part by such adjoining town of the same county.

6. Before bringing a defendant arrested pursuant to a warrant before the local criminal court in which such warrant is returnable, a police officer must without unnecessary delay perform all fingerprinting and other preliminary police duties required in the particular case. In any case in which the defendant is not brought by a police officer before such court but, following his arrest in another county for an offense specified in subdivision one of section 160.10, is released by a local criminal court of such other county on his own recognizance or on bail for his appearance on a specified date before the local criminal court before which the warrant is returnable, the latter court must, upon arraignment of the defendant before it, direct that he be fingerprinted by the appropriate officer or agency, and that he appear at an appropriate designated time and place for such purpose.

CPL

7. Upon arresting a juvenile offender, the police officer shall immediately notify the parent or other person legally responsible for his care or the person with whom he is domiciled, that the juvenile offender has been arrested, and the location of the facility where he is being detained.

8. Upon arresting a defendant, other than a juvenile offender, for any offense pursuant to a warrant of arrest, a police officer shall, upon the defendant's request, permit the defendant to communicate by telephone provided by the law enforcement facility where the defendant is held to a phone number located anywhere in the United States or Puerto Rico, for the purposes of obtaining counsel and informing a relative or friend that he or she has been arrested, unless granting the call will compromise an ongoing investigation or the prosecution of the defendant.

> **HISTORY:** Add, L 1970, ch 996, § 1; amd, L 1971, ch 762 § 1, 1979, ch 411, § 1, L 1980, ch 843, § 12, L 1984, ch 695, § 1, L 1986, ch 5, § 1, L 1987, ch 382, § 1, L 1988, ch 324, § 2, eff Nov 1, 1988, L 1988, ch 324, § 2, 1998, ch 424, § 8, eff Jan 1, 1999, L 2010, ch 94, § 1, eff July 24, 2010, L 2010, ch 96, § 1, eff July 24, 2010.

ARTICLE 130   THE SUMMONS

§ 130.10.   **Summons; definition, function, form and content**
§ 130.20.   **Summons; by what courts issuable and in what courts returnable**
§ 130.30.   **Summons; when issuable**
§ 130.40.   **Summons; service**
§ 130.50.   **Summons; defendant's failure to appear**
§ 130.60.   **Summons; fingerprinting of defendant**

> **HISTORY:** Add, L 1970, ch 996, § 1, eff Sept 1, 1971.

§ 130.10. Summons; definition, function, form and content

1. A summons is a process issued by a local criminal court directing a defendant designated in an information, a prosecutor's information, a felony complaint or a misdemeanor complaint filed with such court, or by a superior court directing a defendant designated in an indictment filed with such court, to appear before it at a designated future time in connection with such accusatory instrument. The sole function of a summons is to achieve a defendant's court appearance in a criminal action for the purpose of arraignment upon the accusatory instrument by which such action was commenced.

2. A summons must be subscribed by the issuing judge and must state or contain (a) the name of the issuing court, and (b) the name of the defendant to whom it is addressed, and (c) the name or title of an offense charged in the underlying accusatory instrument, and (d) the date of issuance of the summons, and (e) the date and time when it is returnable, and (f) a direction that the defendant appear before the issuing court at such time.

> **HISTORY:** Add, L 1970, ch 996, § 1, eff Sept 1, 1971. Sub 1, amd, L 1993, ch 446, § 4, eff Nov 1, 1993.

§ 130.20. Summons; by what courts issuable and in what courts returnable

A summons may be issued only by the local criminal court or superior court with which the accusatory instrument underlying it has been filed, and it may be made returnable in such issuing court only.

> **HISTORY:** Add, L 1970, ch 996, § 1; amd, L 1993, ch 446, § 5, eff Nov 1, 1993.

§ 130.30. Summons; when issuable

A local criminal court may issue a summons in any case in which, pursuant to section 120.20, it is authorized to issue a warrant of arrest based upon an information, a prosecutor's information, a felony complaint or a misdemeanor complaint. If such information, prosecutor's information, felony complaint or misdemeanor complaint is not sufficient on its face as prescribed in section 100.40, and if the court is satisfied that on the basis of the available facts or evidence it would be impossible to draw and file an authorized accusatory instrument that is sufficient on its face, the court must dismiss the accusatory instrument. A superior court may issue a summons in any case in which, pursuant to section 210.10, it is authorized to issue a warrant of arrest based upon an indictment.

> **HISTORY:** Add, L 1970, ch 996, § 1; amd, L 1993, ch 446, § 6, eff Nov 1, 1993. Amd, L 2000, ch 506, § 2, eff Nov 1, 2000.

§ 130.40. Summons; service

1. A summons may be served by a police officer, or by a complainant at least eighteen years old or by any other person at least eighteen years old designated by the court.

2. A summons may be served anywhere in the county of issuance or anywhere in an adjoining county.

> **HISTORY:** Add, L 1970, ch 996, § 1, eff Sept 1, 1971.

§ 130.50. Summons; defendant's failure to appear

If after the service of a summons the defendant does not appear in the designated local criminal court or superior court at the time such summons is returnable, the court may issue a warrant of arrest.

> **HISTORY:** Add, L 1970, ch 996, § 1; amd, L 1993, ch 446, § 7, eff Nov 1, 1993.

§ 130.60. Summons; fingerprinting of defendant

1. Upon the arraignment of a defendant whose court attendance has been secured by the issuance and service of a summons, based upon an indictment, a prosecutor's information or upon an information, felony complaint or misdemeanor complaint filed by a complainant who is a police officer, the court must, if an offense charged in the accusatory instrument is one specified in subdivision one of section 160.10, direct that the defendant be fingerprinted by the appropriate police officer or agency, and that he or she appear at an appropriate designated time and place for such purpose.

2. Upon the arraignment of a defendant whose court attendance has been secured by the issuance and service of a summons based upon an information or misdemeanor complaint filed by a complainant who is not a police officer, and who has not previously been fingerprinted, the court may, if it finds reasonable cause to believe that the defendant has committed an offense specified in subdivision one of section 160.10, direct that the defendant be fingerprinted by the appropriate police officer or agency and that he appear at an appropriate designated time and place for such purpose. A defendant whose court appearance has been secured by the issuance and service of a criminal summons based upon a misdemeanor complaint or information filed by a complainant who is not a police officer, must be directed by the court, upon conviction of the defendant, to be fingerprinted by the appropriate police officer or agency and the court must also direct that the defendant appear at an appropriate designated time and place for such purpose, if the defendant is convicted of any offense specified in subdivision one of section 160.10.

> **HISTORY:** Add, L 1970, ch 996, § 1; amd, L 1971, ch 762 § 2, eff Sept 1, 1971. Section heading, amd, L 1971, ch 762 § 2, eff Sept 1, 1971. Sub 1, formerly entire section, so numbered, L 1986, ch 396, § 1; amd, L 1991, ch 95, § 1, L 1993, ch 446, § 8, eff Nov 1, 1993. Sub 2, add, L 1986, ch 396, § 1; amd, L 1991, ch 95, § 1, eff Nov 1, 1991.

ARTICLE 140   ARREST WITHOUT A WARRANT

§ 140.05.   **Arrest without a warrant; in general**

HISTORY: Add, L 1970, ch 996, § 1, eff Sept 1, 1971.

§ 140.05. Arrest without a warrant; in general

A person who has committed or is believed to have committed an offense and who is at liberty within the state may, under circumstances prescribed in this article, be arrested for such offense although no warrant of arrest therefor has been issued and although no criminal action therefor has yet been commenced in any criminal court.

HISTORY: Add, L 1970, ch 996, § 1, eff Sept 1, 1971.

§ 140.10. Arrest without a warrant; by police officer; when and where authorized

1. Subject to the provisions of subdivision two, a police officer may arrest a person for:

(a) Any offense when he or she has reasonable cause to believe that such person has committed such offense in his or her presence; and

(b) A crime when he or she has reasonable cause to believe that such person has committed such crime, whether in his or her presence or otherwise.

2. A police officer may arrest a person for a petty offense, pursuant to subdivision one, only when:

(a) Such offense was committed or believed by him or her to have been committed within the geographical area of such police officer's employment or within one hundred yards of such geographical area; and

(b) Such arrest is made in the county in which such offense was committed or believed to have been committed or in an adjoining county; except that the police officer may follow such person in continuous close pursuit, commencing either in the county in which the offense was or is believed to have been committed or in an adjoining county, in and through any county of the state, and may arrest him or her in any county in which he or she apprehends him or her.

3. A police officer may arrest a person for a crime, pursuant to subdivision one, whether or not such crime was committed within the geographical area of such police officer's employment, and

he or she may make such arrest within the state, regardless of the situs of the commission of the crime. In addition, he or she may, if necessary, pursue such person outside the state and may arrest him or her in any state the laws of which contain provisions equivalent to those of section 140.55.

4. [*Expires and repealed Sept. 1, 2015*] Notwithstanding any other provisions of this section, a police officer shall arrest a person, and shall not attempt to reconcile the parties or mediate, where such officer has reasonable cause to believe that:

(a) a felony, other than subdivision three, four, nine or ten of section 155.30 of the penal law, has been committed by such person against a member of the same family or household, as member of the same family or household is defined in subdivision one of section 530.11 of this chapter; or

(b) a duly served order of protection or special order of conditions issued pursuant to subparagraph (i) or (ii) of paragraph (o) of subdivision one of section 330.20 of this chapter is in effect, or an order of which the respondent or defendant has actual knowledge because he or she was present in court when such order was issued, where the order appears to have been issued by a court of competent jurisdiction of this or another state, territorial or tribal jurisdiction; and

(i) Such order directs that the respondent or defendant stay away from persons on whose behalf the order of protection or special order of conditions has been issued and the respondent or defendant committed an act or acts in violation of such "stay away" provision of such order; or

(ii) The respondent or defendant commits a family offense as defined in subdivision one of section eight hundred twelve of the family court act or subdivision one of section 530.11 of this chapter in violation of such order of protection or special order of conditions.

The provisions of this subdivision shall apply only to orders of protection issued pursuant to sections two hundred forty and two hundred fifty-two of the domestic relations law, articles four, five, six and eight of the family court act and section 530.12 of this chapter, special orders of conditions issued pursuant to subparagraph (i) or (ii) of paragraph (o) of subdivision one of section 330.20 of this chapter insofar as they involve a victim or victims of domestic violence as defined by subdivision one of section four hundred fifty-nine-a of the social services law or a designated witness or witnesses to such domestic violence, and to orders of protection issued by courts of competent jurisdiction in another state, territorial or tribal jurisdiction. In determining whether reasonable cause exists to make an arrest for a violation of an order issued by a court of another state, territorial or tribal jurisdiction, the officer shall consider, among other factors, whether the order, if available, appears to be valid on its face or whether a record of the order exists on the statewide registry of orders of protection and warrants established pursuant to section two hundred twenty-one-a of the executive law or the protection order file maintained by the national crime information center; provided, however, that entry of the order of protection or special order of conditions into the statewide registry or the national protection order file shall not be required for enforcement of the order. When a special order of conditions is in effect and a defendant or respondent has been taken into custody pursuant to this paragraph, nothing contained in this paragraph shall restrict or impair a police officer from acting pursuant to section 9.41 of the mental hygiene law; or

(c) a misdemeanor constituting a family offense, as described in subdivision one of section 530.11 of this chapter and section eight hundred twelve of the family court act, has been committed by such person against such family or household member, unless the victim requests otherwise. The officer shall neither inquire as to whether the victim seeks an arrest of such person nor threaten the arrest of any person for the purpose of discouraging requests for police intervention. Notwithstanding the foregoing, when an officer has reasonable cause to believe that more than one family or household member has committed such a misdemeanor, the officer is not required to arrest each such person. In such circumstances, the officer shall attempt to identify and arrest the primary physical aggressor after considering: (i) the comparative extent of any injuries inflicted by and between the parties; (ii) whether any such person is threatening or has threatened future harm against another party or another family or household member; (iii) whether any such person has a prior history of domestic violence that the officer can reasonably ascertain; and (iv) whether any such person acted defensively to protect himself or herself from injury. The officer shall evaluate each complaint separately to determine who is the primary physical aggressor and shall not base the decision to arrest or not to arrest on the willingness of a person to testify or otherwise participate in a judicial proceeding.

Nothing contained in this subdivision shall be deemed to (a) require the arrest of any person when the officer reasonably believes the person's conduct is justifiable under article thirty-five of title C of the penal law; or (b) restrict or impair the authority of any municipality, political subdivision, or the division of state police from promulgating rules, regulations and policies requiring the arrest of persons in additional circumstances where domestic violence has allegedly occurred.

No cause of action for damages shall arise in favor of any person by reason of any arrest made by a police officer pursuant to this subdivision, except as provided in sections seventeen and eighteen of the public officers law and sections fifty-k, fifty-l, fifty-m and fifty-n of the general municipal law, as appropriate.

The protected party in whose favor the order of protection or temporary order of protection is issued may not be held to violate an order issued in his or her favor nor may such protected party be arrested for violating such order.

5. Upon investigating a report of a crime or offense between members of the same family or household as such terms are defined in section 530.11 of this chapter and section eight hundred twelve of the family court act, a law enforcement officer shall prepare and file a written report of the incident, on a form promulgated pursuant to section eight hundred thirty-seven of the executive law, including statements made by the victim and by any witnesses, and make any additional reports required by local law enforcement policy or regulations. Such report shall be prepared and filed, whether or not an arrest is made as a result of the officers' investigation, and shall be retained by the law enforcement agency for a period of not less than four years. Where the reported incident involved an offense committed against a person who is sixty-five years of age or older a copy of the report required by this subdivision shall be sent to the New York state committee for the coordination of police services to elderly persons established pursuant to section eight hundred forty-four-b of the executive law. Where the reported incident involved an offense committed by an individual known by the law enforcement officer to be under probation or parole supervision, he or she shall transmit a copy of the report as soon as practicable to the supervising probation department or the department of corrections and community supervision.

HISTORY: Add, L 1970, ch 996, § 1, eff Sept 1, 1971; amd, L 1970, ch 997, § 1, eff Sept 1, 1971, L 1994, ch 222, § 32, eff Jan 1, 1996, expires and repealed Sept 1, 2015, L 1994, ch 224, § 5-a, eff Oct 1, 1995, L 1994, ch 224, § 6, eff Jan 1, 1995, L 1995, ch 349, § 4, eff Jan 1, 1996, repealed Jan 1, 2005, L 1996, ch 511, § 1, eff Nov 6, 1996, L 1997, ch 4, §§ 1, 2, eff Jan 12, 1998, L 1997, ch 626, § 1, eff Sept 17, 1997, L 1998, ch 597, § 10, eff Dec 22, 1998, L 2003, ch 300, § 1, eff Nov 1, 2003, L 2004, ch 107, § 5, eff June 8, 2004, L 2004, ch 642, § 4 (repealed, L 2005, ch 87, § 3, eff June 7, 2005, deemed eff Oct 26, 2004), eff Oct 26, 2004, L 2009, ch 476, § 6, eff Dec 15, 2009, L 2011, ch 62, § 72 (Part C, Subpart B), eff March 31, 2011, L 2013, ch 480, § 12, eff Nov 13, 2013.

§ 140.15. Arrest without a warrant; when and how made by police officer

1. A police officer may arrest a person for an offense, pursuant to section 140.10, at any hour of any day or night.

2. The arresting police officer must inform such person of his authority and purpose and of the reason for such arrest unless he encounters physical resistance, flight or other factors rendering such procedure impractical.

3. In order to effect such an arrest, such police officer may use such physical force as is justifiable pursuant to section 35.30 of the penal law.

4. In order to effect such an arrest, a police officer may enter premises in which he reasonably believes such person to be present, under the same circumstances and in the same manner as would be authorized, by the provisions of subdivisions four and five of section 120.80, if he were attempting to make such arrest pursuant to a warrant of arrest.

> **HISTORY:** Add, L 1970, ch 996, § 1, eff Sept 1, 1971.

§ 140.20. Arrest without a warrant; procedure after arrest by police officer

1. Upon arresting a person without a warrant, a police officer, after performing without unnecessary delay all recording, fingerprinting and other preliminary police duties required in the particular case, must except as otherwise provided in this section, without unnecessary delay bring the arrested person or cause him to be brought before a local criminal court and file therewith an appropriate accusatory instrument charging him with the offense or offenses in question. The arrested person must be brought to the particular local criminal court, or to one of them if there be more than one, designated in section 100.55 as an appropriate court for commencement of the particular action; except that:

(a) If the arrest is for an offense other than a class A, B, C or D felony or a violation of section 130.25, 130.40, 205.10, 205.17, 205.19 or 215.56 of the penal law committed in a town, but not in a village thereof having a village court, and the town court of such town is not available at the time, the arrested person may be brought before the local criminal court of any village within such town or, any adjoining town, village embraced in whole or in part by such adjoining town, or city of the same county; and

(b) If the arrest is for an offense other than a class A, B, C or D felony or a violation of section 130.25, 130.40, 205.10, 205.17, 205.19 or 215.56 of the penal law committed in a village having a village court and such court is not available at the time, the arrested person may be brought before the town court of the town embracing such village or any other village court within such town, or, if such town or village court is not available either, before the local criminal court of any adjoining town, village embraced in whole or in part by such adjoining town, or city of the same county; and

(c) If the arrest is for an offense committed in a city, and the city court thereof is not available at the time, the arrested person may be brought before the local criminal court of any adjoining town or village, or village court embraced by an adjoining town, within the same county as such city; and

(d) If the arrest is for a traffic infraction or for a misdemeanor relating to traffic, the police officer may, instead of bringing the arrested person before the local criminal court of the political subdivision or locality in which the offense was allegedly committed, bring him before the local criminal court of the same county nearest available by highway travel to the point of arrest.

2. If the arrest is for an offense other than a class A, B, C or D felony or a violation of section 130.25, 130.40, 205.10, 205.17, 205.19 or 215.56 of the penal law, the arrested person need not be brought before a local criminal court as provided in subdivision one, and the procedure may instead be as follows:

    (a) A police officer may issue and serve an appearance ticket upon the arrested person and release him from custody, as prescribed in subdivision two of section 150.20; or

    (b) The desk officer in charge at a police station, county jail or police headquarters, or any of his superior officers, may, in such place fix pre-arraignment bail and, upon deposit thereof, issue and serve an appearance ticket upon the arrested person and release him from custody, as prescribed in section 150.30.

3. If (a) the arrest is for an offense other than a class A, B, C or D felony or a violation of section 130.25, 130.40, 205.10, 205.17, 205.19 or 215.56 of the penal law, and (b) owing to unavailability of a local criminal court the arresting police officer is unable to bring the arrested person before such a court with reasonable promptness, either an appearance ticket must be served unconditionally upon the arrested person or pre-arraignment bail must be fixed, as prescribed in subdivision two. If pre-arraignment bail is fixed but not posted, such arrested person may be temporarily held in custody but must be brought before a local criminal court without unnecessary delay. Nothing contained in this subdivision requires a police officer to serve an appearance ticket upon an arrested person or release him from custody at a time when such person appears to be under the influence of alcohol, narcotics or other drug to the degree that he may endanger himself or other persons.

4. If after arresting a person, for any offense, a police officer upon further investigation or inquiry determines or is satisfied that there is not reasonable cause to believe that the arrested person committed such offense or any other offense based upon the conduct in question, he need not follow any of the procedures prescribed in subdivisions one, two and three, but must immediately release such person from custody.

5. Before service of an appearance ticket upon an arrested person pursuant to subdivision two or three, the issuing police officer must, if the offense designated in such appearance ticket is one of those specified in subdivision one of section 160.10, cause such person to be fingerprinted in the same manner as would be required were no appearance ticket to be issued or served.

6. Upon arresting a juvenile offender without a warrant, the police officer shall immediately notify the parent or other person legally responsible for his care or the person with whom he is domiciled, that the juvenile offender has been arrested, and the location of the facility where he is being detained

7. Upon arresting a person, other than a juvenile offender, for any offense without a warrant, a police officer shall, upon the arrested person's request, permit him or her to communicate by telephone provided by the law enforcement facility where the defendant is held to a phone number located in the United States or Puerto Rico, for the purposes of obtaining counsel and informing a relative or friend that he or she has been arrested, unless granting the call will compromise an ongoing investigation or the prosecution of the defendant.

    HISTORY: Add, L 1970, ch 996, § 1; amd, L 1971, ch 762 §§ 3, 4, L 1979, ch 411, § 2, L 1984, ch 695, § 2, L 1986, ch 5, § 2, L 1987, ch 382, § 2, L 1987, ch 549,§§ 2, 3, L 1987, ch 550, §§ 4, 5, L 1988, ch 324, § 3, L 2010, ch 94, § 2, eff July 24, 2010, L 2010, ch 96, § 2, eff July 24, 2010.

§ 140.25.   Arrest without a warrant; by peace officer

1. A peace officer, acting pursuant to his special duties, may arrest a person for:

(a) Any offense when be has reasonable cause to believe that such person has committed such offense in his presence; and

(b) A crime when he has reasonable cause to believe that such person has committed such crime, whether in his presence or otherwise.

2. A peace officer acts "pursuant to his special duties" in making an arrest only when the arrest is for:

(a) An offense defined by a statute which such peace officer, by reason of the specialized nature of his particular employment or by express provision of law, is required or authorized to enforce; or

(b) An offense committed or reasonably believed by him to have been committed in such manner or place as to render arrest of the offender by such peace officer under the particular circumstances an integral part of his specialized duties.

3. A peace officer, whether or not he is acting pursuant to his special duties, may arrest a person for an offense committed or believed by him to have been committed within the geographical area of such peace officer's employment, as follows:

(a) He may arrest such person for any offense when such person has in fact committed such offense in his presence; and

(b) He may arrest such person for a felony when he has reasonable cause to believe that such person has committed such felony, whether in his presence or otherwise.

4. A peace officer, when outside the geographical area of his employment, may, anywhere in the state, arrest a person for a felony when he has reasonable cause to believe that such person has there committed such felony in his presence, provided that such arrest is made during or immediately after the allegedly criminal conduct or during the alleged perpetrator's immediate flight therefrom.

5. For the purposes of this section, the "geographical area of employment" of a peace officer is as follows:

(a) The "geographical area of employment" of any peace officer employed as such by any agency of the state consists of the entire state;

(b) The "geographical area of employment" of any peace officer employed as such by an agency of a county, city, town or village consists of (i) such county, city, town or village, as the case may be, and (ii) any other place where he is, at a particular time, acting in the course of his particular duties or employment;

(c) The "geographical area of employment" of any peace officer employed as such by any private organization consists of any place in the state where he is, at a particular time, acting in the course of his particular duties or employment.

HISTORY: Add, L 1970, ch 996, § 1; amd, L 1970, ch 997, § 2, L 1980, ch 843, § 13, eff Sept 1, 1980. Section heading, amd, L 1980, ch 843, § 13, eff Sept 1, 1980. Sub 3, add, L 1970, ch 997, § 2, eff Sept 1, 1971. Former sub 3, repealed, L 1970, ch 997, § 2, eff Sept 1, 1971. Sub 4, add, L 1970, ch 997, § 2, eff Sept 1, 1971. Former sub 4, repealed, L 1970, ch 997, § 2, eff Sept 1, 1971. Sub 5, add, L 1970, ch 997, § 2, eff Sept 1, 1971. Former sub 5, repealed, L 1970, ch 997, § 2, eff Sept 1, 1971. Sub 5, par (c), add, L 1980, ch 843, § 13, eff Sept 1, 1980.

§ 140.27. Arrest without a warrant; when and how made; procedure after arrest by peace officer

1. The rules governing the manner in which a peace officer may make an arrest, pursuant to section 140.25, are the same as those governing arrests by police officers, as prescribed in section 140.15.

2. Upon arresting a person without a warrant, a peace officer, except as otherwise provided in subdivision three, must without unnecessary delay bring him or cause him to be brought before a local criminal court, as provided in section 100.55 and subdivision one of section 140.20, and must without unnecessary delay file or cause to be filed therewith an appropriate accusatory instrument. If the offense which is the subject of the arrest is one of those specified in subdivision one of section 160.10, the arrested person must be fingerprinted and photographed as therein provided. In order to execute the required post-arrest functions, such arresting peace officer may perform such functions himself or he may enlist the aid of a police officer for the performance thereof in the manner provided in subdivision one of section 140.20.

3. If (a) the arrest is for an offense other than a class A, B, C or D felony or a violation of section 130.25, 130.40, 205.10, 205.17, 205.19 or 215.56 of the penal law and (b) owing to unavailability of a local criminal court such peace officer is unable to bring or cause the arrested person to be brought before such a court with reasonable promptness, the arrested person must be brought to an appropriate police station, county jail or police headquarters where he must be dealt with in the manner prescribed in subdivision three of section 140.20, as if he had been arrested by a police officer.

4. If the arrest is for an offense other than a class A, B, C or D felony or a violation of section 130.25, 130.40, 205.10, 205.17, 205.19 or 215.56 of the penal law, the arrested person need not be brought before a local criminal court as provided in subdivision two, and the procedure may instead be as follows:

(a) The arresting peace officer, where he is specially authorized by law to issue and serve an appearance ticket, may issue and serve an appearance ticket upon the arrested person and release him from custody; or

(b) The arresting peace officer, where he is not specially authorized by law to issue and serve an appearance ticket, may enlist the aid of a police officer and request that such officer issue and serve an appearance ticket upon the arrested person, and upon such issuance and service the latter must be released from custody.

5. Upon arresting a juvenile offender without a warrant, the peace officer shall immediately notify the parent or other person legally responsible for his care or the person with whom he is domiciled, that the juvenile offender has been arrested, and the location of the facility where he is being detained.

HISTORY: Add, L 1970, ch 997, § 3, eff Sept 1, 1971. Section heading, amd, L 1980, ch 843, § 14, eff Sept 1, 1980. Sub 1, amd, L 1980, ch 843, § 15, eff Sept 1, 1980. Sub 2, amd, L 1980, ch 843, § 15, eff Sept 1, 1980. Sub 3, amd, L 1987, ch 549, § 4, L 1987, ch 550, § 6, eff Nov 1, 1987. Sub 4, add, L 1975, ch 78, § 1; amd, L 1987, ch 549, § 5, L 1987, ch 550, § 7, eff Nov 1, 1987. Sub 4, opening par, amd, L 1987, ch 549, § 5, L 1987, ch 550, § 7, eff Nov 1, 1987. Sub 5, add, L 1979, ch 411, § 3, eff Aug 4, 1979.

§ 140.30. Arrest without a warrant; by any person; when and where authorized

1. Subject to the provisions of subdivision two, any person may arrest another person (a) for a felony when the latter has in fact committed such felony, and (b) for any offense when the latter

has in fact committed such offense in his presence.

2. Such an arrest, if for a felony, may be made anywhere in the state. If the arrest is for an offense other than a felony, it may be made only in the county in which such offense was committed.

HISTORY: Add, L 1970, ch 996, § 1, eff Sept 1, 1971, with substance derived from Crim C §§ 168, 183.

§ 140.35. Arrest without a warrant; by person acting other than as a police officer or a peace officer; when and how made

1. A person may arrest another person for an offense pursuant to section 140.30 at any hour of any day or night.

2. Such person must inform the person whom he is arresting of the reason for such arrest unless he encounters physical resistance, flight or other factors rendering such procedure impractical.

3. In order to effect such an arrest, such person may use such physical force as is justifiable pursuant to subdivision four of section 35.30 of the penal law.

HISTORY: Add, L 1970, ch 996, § 1, eff Sept 1, 1971. Section heading, amd, L 1980, ch 843, § 16, eff Sept 1, 1980.

§ 140.40. Arrest without a warrant; by person acting other than as a police officer or a peace officer; procedure after arrest

1. A person making an arrest pursuant to section 140.30 must without unnecessary delay deliver or attempt to deliver the person arrested to the custody of an appropriate police officer, as defined in subdivision five.* For such purpose, he may solicit the aid of any police officer and the latter, if he is not himself an appropriate police officer, must assist in delivering the arrested person to an appropriate officer. If the arrest is for a felony, the appropriate police officer must, upon receiving custody of the arrested person, perform all recording, fingerprinting and other preliminary police duties required in the particular case. In any case, the appropriate police officer, upon receiving custody of the arrested person, except as otherwise provided in subdivisions two and three, must bring him, on behalf of the arresting person, before an appropriate local criminal court, as defined in subdivision five,* and the arresting person must without unnecessary delay file an appropriate accusatory instrument with such court.

2. If (a) the arrest is for an offense other than a class A, B, C or D felony or a violation of section 130.25, 130.40, 205.10, 205.17, 205.19 or 215.56 of the penal law and (b) owing to unavailability of a local criminal court the appropriate police officer having custody of the arrested person is unable to bring him before such a court with reasonable promptness, the arrested person must be dealt with in the manner prescribed in subdivision three of section 140.20, as if he had been arrested by a police officer.

3. If the arrest is for an offense other than a class A, B, C or D felony or a violation of section 130.25, 130.40, 205.10, 205.17, 205.19 or 215.56 of the penal law, the arrested person need not be brought before a local criminal court, as provided in subdivision one, and the procedure may instead be as follows:

(a) An appropriate police officer may issue and serve an appearance ticket upon the arrested person and release him from custody, as prescribed in subdivision two of section 150.20; or

---

* Renumbered subd. 6 by L. 1979, Ch. 411, § 4.

* Renumbered subd. 6 by L. 1979, Ch. 411, § 4.

(b) The desk officer in charge at the appropriate police officer's station, county jail or police headquarters, or any of his superior officers, may, in such place, fix pre-arraignment bail and, upon deposit thereof, issue and serve an appearance ticket upon the arrested person and release him from custody, as prescribed in section 150.30.

4. Notwithstanding any other provision of this section, a police officer is not required to take an arrested person into custody or to take any other action prescribed in this section on behalf of the arresting person if he has reasonable cause to believe that the arrested person did not commit the alleged offense or that the arrest was otherwise unauthorized.

5. If a police officer takes an arrested juvenile offender into custody, the police officer shall immediately notify the parent or other person legally responsible for his care or the person with whom he is domiciled, that the juvenile offender has been arrested, and the location of the facility where he is being detained.

6. As used in this section:

(a) An "appropriate police officer" means one who would himself be authorized to make the arrest in question as a police officer pursuant to section 140.10;

(b) An "appropriate local criminal court" means one with which an accusatory instrument charging the offense in question may properly be filed pursuant to the provisions of section 100.55.

HISTORY: Add, L 1970, ch 996, § 1, eff Sept 1, 1971. Section heading, amd, L 1980, ch 843, § 17, eff Sept 1, 1980. Sub 1, amd, L 1971, ch 762, § 5, L 1975, ch 78, § 2, eff Sept 1, 1975. Sub 2, reenacted without change, L 1975, ch 78, § 2; amd, L 1987, ch 549, § 6, L 1987, ch 550, § 8, eff Nov 1, 1987. Sub 3, add, L 1975, ch 78, § 2; amd, L 1987, ch 549, § 7, L 1987, ch 550, § 9, eff Nov 1, 1987. Former sub 3, renumbered sub 4, L 1975, ch 78, § 2, eff Sept 1, 1975. Sub 3, opening par, amd, L 1987, ch 549, § 7, L 1987, ch 550, § 9, eff Nov 1, 1987. Sub 4, formerly sub 3, renumbered sub 4, L 1975, ch 78, § 2, eff Sept 1, 1975. Former sub 4, renumbered sub 5, L 1975, ch 78, § 2, eff Sept 1, 1975. Sub 5, add, L 1979, ch 411, § 4, eff Aug 4, 1979. Former sub 5, formerly sub 4, amd, L 1970, ch 997, § 4; renumbered sub 5, L 1975, ch 78, § 2; renumbered sub 6, L 1979, ch 411, § 4, eff Aug 4, 1979. Sub 6, formerly sub 4, amd, L 1970, ch 997, § 4; renumbered sub 5, L 1975, ch 78, § 2; renumbered sub 6, L 1979, ch 411, § 4, eff Aug 4, 1979.

§ 140.45. Arrest without a warrant; dismissal of insufficient local criminal court accusatory instrument

If a local criminal court accusatory instrument filed with a local criminal court pursuant to section 140.20, 140.25 or 140.40 is not sufficient on its face, as prescribed in section 100.40, and if the court is satisfied that on the basis of the available facts or evidence it would be impossible to draw and file an accusatory instrument which is sufficient on its face, it must dismiss such accusatory instrument and discharge the defendant.

HISTORY: Add, L 1970, ch 996, § 1; amd, L 1987, ch 549, § 8, L 1987, ch 550, § 10, eff Nov 1, 1987. Section heading, amd, L 1987, ch 550, § 10, eff Nov 1, 1987.

§ 140.50. Temporary questioning of persons in public places; search for weapons

1. In addition to the authority provided by this article for making an arrest without a warrant, a police officer may stop a person in a public place located within the geographical area of such officer's employment when he reasonably suspects that such person is committing, has committed or is about to commit either (a) a felony or (b) a misdemeanor defined in the penal law, and may demand of him his name, address and an explanation of his conduct.

2. Any person who is a peace officer and who provides security services for any court of the unified court system may stop a person in or about the courthouse to which he is assigned when

he reasonably suspects that such person is committing, has committed or is about to commit either (a) a felony or (b) a misdemeanor defined in the penal law, and may demand of him his name, address and an explanation of his conduct.

3. When upon stopping a person under circumstances prescribed in subdivisions one and two a police officer or court officer, as the case may be, reasonably suspects that he is in danger of physical injury, he may search such person for a deadly weapon or any instrument, article or substance readily capable of causing serious physical injury and of a sort not ordinarily carried in public places by law-abiding persons. If he finds such a weapon or instrument, or any other property possession of which he reasonably believes may constitute the commission of a crime, he may take it and keep it until the completion of the questioning, at which time he shall either return it, if lawfully possessed, or arrest such person.

4. In cities with a population of one million or more, information that establishes the personal identity of an individual who has been stopped, questioned and/or frisked by a police officer or peace officer, such as the name, address or social security number of such person, shall not be recorded in a computerized or electronic database if that individual is released without further legal action; provided, however, that this subdivision shall not prohibit police officers or peace officers from including in a computerized or electronic database generic characteristics of an individual, such as race and gender, who has been stopped, questioned and/or frisked by a police officer or peace officer.

> HISTORY: Add, L 1970, ch 996, § 1, eff Sept 1, 1971, with substance derived from Crim C § 180-a; amd, L 1972, ch 911, § 1; amd, L 1972, ch 911, § 1, eff Sept 1, 1972, L 1973, ch 159, § 1, L 1973, ch 159, § 1, L 1973, ch 714, § 1, eff Sept 1, 1973, L 1985, ch 237, § 1, eff Nov 1, 1985, L 2010, ch 176, § 1, eff July 16, 2010.

§ 140.55. Arrest without a warrant; by peace officers of other states for offense committed outside state; uniform close pursuit act

1. As used in this section, the word "state" shall include the District of Columbia.

2. Any peace officer of another state of the United States, who enters this state in close pursuit and continues within this state in such close pursuit of a person in order to arrest him, shall have the same authority to arrest and hold in custody such person on the ground that he has committed a crime in another state which is a crime under the laws of the state of New York, as police officers of this state have to arrest and hold in custody a person on the ground that he has committed a crime in this state.

3. If an arrest is made in this state by an officer of another state in accordance with the provisions of subdivision two, he shall without unnecessary delay take the person arrested before a local criminal court which shall conduct a hearing for the sole purpose of determining if the arrest was in accordance with the provisions of subdivision two, and not of determining the guilt or innocence of the arrested person. If such court determines that the arrest was in accordance with such subdivision, it shall commit the person arrested to the custody of the officer making the arrest, who shall without unnecessary delay take him to the state from which he fled. If such court determines that the arrest was unlawful, it shall discharge the person arrested.

4. This section shall not be construed so as to make unlawful any arrest in this state which would otherwise be lawful.

5. Upon the taking effect of this section it shall be the duty of the secretary of state to certify a copy of this section to the executive department of each of the states of the United States.

6. This section shall apply only to peace officers of a state which by its laws has made similar

provision for the arrest and custody of persons closely pursued within the territory thereof.

7. If any part of this section is for any reason declared void, it is declared to be the intent of this section that such invalidity shall not affect the validity of the remaining portions of this section.

8. This section may be cited as the uniform act on close pursuit.

> **HISTORY:** Add, L 1970, ch 996, § 1, eff Sept 1, 1971, with substance derived from Crim C § 860.

ARTICLE 150   THE APPEARANCE TICKET

> **HISTORY:** Add, L 1970, ch 996, § 1, eff Sept 1, 1971.

§ 150.10. Appearance ticket; definition, form and content

1. An appearance ticket is a written notice issued and subscribed by a police officer or other public servant authorized by state law or local law enacted pursuant to the provisions of the municipal home rule law to issue the same, directing a designated person to appear in a designated local criminal court at a designated future time in connection with his alleged commission of a designated offense. A notice conforming to such definition constitutes an appearance ticket regardless of whether it is referred to in some other provision of law as a summons or by any other name or title.

2. When an appearance ticket as defined in subdivision one of this section is issued to a person in conjunction with an offense charged in a simplified information, said appearance ticket shall contain the language, set forth in subdivision four of section 100.25, notifying the defendant of his right to receive a supporting deposition.

> **HISTORY:** Add, L 1970, ch 996, § 1; amd, L 1978, ch 495, § 1, eff July 20, 1978. Sub 1, formerly entire section, so designated, L 1996, ch 67, § 4, eff Oct 27, 1996. Sub 2, add, L 1996, ch 67, § 4, eff Oct 27, 1996.

§ 150.20. Appearance ticket; when and by whom issuable

1. Whenever a police officer is authorized pursuant to section 140.10 to arrest a person without a warrant for an offense other than a class A, B, C or D felony or a violation of section 130.25, 130.40, 205.10, 205.17, 205.19 or 215.56 of the penal law, he may, subject to the provisions of subdivisions three and four of section 150.40, instead issue to and serve upon such person an appearance ticket.

2. (a) Whenever a police officer has arrested a person without a warrant for an offense other than a class A, B, C or D felony or a violation of section 130.25, 130.40, 205.10, 205.17, 205.19 or 215.56 of the penal law pursuant to section 140.10, or (b) whenever a peace officer, who is not authorized by law to issue an appearance ticket, has arrested a person for an offense other than a class A, B, C or D felony or a violation of section 130.25, 130.40, 205.10, 205.17, 205.19

or 215.56 of the penal law pursuant to section 140.25, and has requested a police officer to issue and serve upon such arrested person an appearance ticket pursuant to subdivision four of section 140.27, or (c) whenever a person has been arrested for an offense other than a class A, B, C or D felony or a violation of section 130.25, 130.40, 205.10, 205.17, 205.19 or 215.56 of the penal law and has been delivered to the custody of an appropriate police officer pursuant to section 140.40, such police officer may, instead of bringing such person before a local criminal court and promptly filing or causing the arresting peace officer or arresting person to file a local criminal court accusatory instrument therewith, issue to and serve upon such person an appearance ticket. The issuance and service of an appearance ticket under such circumstances may be conditioned upon a deposit of pre-arraignment bail, as provided in section 150.30.

3. A public servant other than a police officer, who is specially authorized by state law or local law enacted pursuant to the provisions of the municipal home rule law to issue and serve appearance tickets with respect to designated offenses other than class A, B, C or D felonies or violations of section 130.25, 130.40, 205.10, 205.17, 205.19 or 215.56 of the penal law, may in such cases issue and serve upon a person an appearance ticket when he has reasonable cause to believe that such person has committed a crime, or has committed a petty offense in his presence.

HISTORY: Add, L 1970, ch 996, § 1, eff Sept 1, 1971. Sub 1, amd, L 1987, ch 549, § 9, L 1987, ch 550, § 11, eff Nov 1, 1987. Sub 2, amd, L 1972, ch 661, § 36, L 1975, ch 78, § 3, L 1987, ch 549, § 10, L 1987, ch 550, § 12, eff Nov 1, 1987. Sub 3, amd, L 1978, ch 495, § 2, L 1987, ch 549, § 11, L 1987, ch 550, § 13, eff Nov 1, 1987.

§ 150.30. Appearance ticket; issuance and service thereof after arrest upon posting of pre-arraignment bail

1. Issuance and service of an appearance ticket by a police officer following an arrest without a warrant, as prescribed in subdivision two of section 150.20, may be made conditional upon the posting of a sum of money, known as pre-arraignment bail. In such case, the bail becomes forfeit upon failure of such person to comply with the directions of the appearance ticket. The person posting such bail must complete and sign a form which states (a) the name, residential address and occupation of each person posting cash bail; and (b) the title of the criminal action or proceeding involved; and (c) the offense or offenses which are the subjects of the action or proceeding involved, and the status of such action or proceeding; and (d) the name of the principal and the nature of his involvement in or connection with such action or proceeding; and (e) the date of the principal's next appearance in court; and (f) an acknowledgement that the cash bail will be forfeited if the principal does not comply with the directions of the appearance ticket; and (g) the amount of money posted as cash bail. Such pre-arraignment bail may be posted as provided in subdivision two or three.

2. A desk officer in charge at a police station, county jail, or police headquarters, or any of his superior officers, may in such place, fix pre-arraignment bail, in an amount prescribed in this subdivision, and upon the posting thereof must issue and serve an appearance ticket upon the arrested person, give a receipt for the bail, and release such person from custody. Such pre-arraignment bail may be fixed in the following amounts:

(a) If the arrest was for a class E felony, any amount not exceeding seven hundred fifty dollars.

(b) If the arrest was for a class A misdemeanor, any amount not exceeding five hundred dollars.

(c) If the arrest was for a class B misdemeanor or an unclassified misdemeanor, any amount not exceeding two hundred fifty dollars.

(d) If the arrest was for a petty offense, any amount not exceeding one hundred dollars.

3. A police officer, who has arrested a person without a warrant pursuant to subdivision two of section 150.20 of this chapter for a traffic infraction, may, where he reasonably believes that such arrested person is not licensed to operate a motor vehicle by this state or any state covered by a reciprocal compact guaranteeing appearance as is provided in section five hundred seventeen of the vehicle and traffic law, fix pre-arraignment bail in the amount of fifty dollars; provided, however, such bail shall be posted by means of a credit card or similar device. Upon the posting thereof, said officer must issue and serve an appearance ticket upon the arrested person, give a receipt for the bail, and release such person from custody.

4. The chief administrator of the courts shall establish a system for the posting of pre-arraignment bail by means of credit card or similar device, as is provided by section two hundred twelve of the judiciary law. The head of each police department or police force and of any state department, agency, board, commission or public authority having police officers who fix pre-arraignment bail as provided herein may elect to use the system established by the chief administrator or may establish such other system for the posting of pre-arraignment bail by means of credit card or similar device as he or she may deem appropriate.

> **HISTORY:** Add, L 1970, ch 996, § 1, eff Sept 1, 1971. Sub 1, amd, L 1986, ch 708, § 1, L 1987, ch 111, § 1, eff Nov 1, 1987. Sub 2, amd, L 1986, ch 708, § 1, eff Nov 1, 1986. Sub 2, par (a), add, L 1987, ch 549, § 12, eff Nov 1, 1987. Former sub 2, par (a), relettered sub 2, par (b), L 1987, ch 549, § 12, eff Nov 1, 1987. Sub 2, par (b), formerly sub 2, par (a), relettered sub 2, par (b), L 1987, ch 549, § 12, eff Nov 1, 1987. Former sub 2, par (b), relettered sub 2, par (c), L 1987, ch 549, § 12, eff Nov 1, 1987. Sub 2, par (c), formerly sub 2, par (b), relettered sub 2, par (c), L 1987, ch 549, § 12, eff Nov 1, 1987. Former sub 2, par (c), relettered sub 2, par (d), L 1987, ch 549, § 12, eff Nov 1, 1987. Sub 2, par (d), formerly sub 2, par (c), relettered sub 2, par (d), L 1987, ch 549, § 12, eff Nov 1, 1987. Sub 3, add, L 1986, ch 708, § 1, eff Nov 1, 1986. Sub 4, add, L 1986, ch 708, § 1; amd, L 1987, ch 805, § 1, eff Aug 7, 1987.

§ 150.40. Appearance ticket; where returnable; how and where served

1. An appearance ticket must be made returnable in a local criminal court designated in section 100.55 as one with which an information for the offense in question may be filed.

2. An appearance ticket, other than one issued for a traffic infraction relating to parking, must be served personally, except that an appearance ticket issued for the violation of a local zoning ordinance or local zoning law, or of a building or sanitation code may be served in any manner authorized for service under section three hundred eight of the civil practice law and rules.

3. An appearance ticket may be served anywhere in the county in which the designated offense was allegedly committed or in any adjoining county, and may be served elsewhere as prescribed in subdivision four.

4. A police officer may, for the purpose of serving an appearance ticket upon a person, follow him in continuous close pursuit, commencing either in the county in which the alleged offense was committed or in an adjoining county, in and through any county of the state, and may serve such appearance ticket upon him in any county in which he overtakes him.

> **HISTORY:** Add, L 1970, ch 996, § 1, eff Sept 1, 1971. Sub 2, amd, L 2004, ch 415, § 1, eff Aug 24, 2004, L 2005, ch 642, § 1, eff Aug 30, 2005.

§ 150.50. Appearance ticket; filing a local criminal court accusatory instrument; dismissal of insufficient instrument

1. A police officer or other public servant who has issued and served an appearance ticket must, at or before the time such appearance ticket is returnable, file or cause to be filed with the local

criminal court in which it is returnable a local criminal court accusatory instrument charging the person named in such appearance ticket with the offense specified therein. Nothing herein contained shall authorize the use of a simplified information when not authorized by law.

2. If such accusatory instrument is not sufficient on its face, as prescribed in section 100.40, and if the court is satisfied that on the basis of the available facts or evidence it would be impossible to draw and file an accusatory instrument which is sufficient on its face, it must dismiss such accusatory instrument.

HISTORY: Add, L 1970, ch 996, § 1; amd, L 1987, ch 549, § 13, eff Nov 1, 1987. Section heading, amd, L 1987, ch 549, § 13, eff Nov 1, 1987. Sub 1, amd, L 1972, ch 661, § 37, L 1987, ch 549, § 13, eff Nov 1, 1987.

§ 150.60. Appearance ticket; defendant's failure to appear

If after the service of an appearance ticket and the filing of a local criminal court accusatory instrument charging the offense designated therein, the defendant does not appear in the designated local criminal court at the time such appearance ticket is returnable, the court may issue a summons or a warrant of arrest based upon the local criminal court accusatory instrument filed.

HISTORY: Add, L 1970, ch 996, § 1; amd, L 1987, ch 549, § 14, eff Nov 1, 1987.

§ 150.70. Appearance ticket; fingerprinting of defendant

Upon the arraignment of a defendant who has not been arrested and whose court attendance has been secured by the issuance and service of an appearance ticket pursuant to subdivision one of section 150.20, the court must, if an offense charged in the accusatory instrument is one specified in subdivision one of section 160.10, direct that the defendant be fingerprinted by the appropriate police officer or agency, and that he appear at an appropriate designated time and place for such purpose.

HISTORY: Add, L 1970, ch 996, § 1; amd, L 1971, ch 762 § 6, eff Sept 1, 1971. Section heading, amd, L 1971, ch 762 § 6, eff Sept 1, 1971.

§ 150.75. Appearance ticket; certain cases

1. The provisions of this section shall apply in any case wherein the defendant is alleged to have committed an offense defined in section 221.05 of the penal law, and no other offense is alleged, notwithstanding any provision of this chapter or any other law to the contrary.

2. Whenever the defendant is arrested without a warrant, an appearance ticket shall promptly be issued and served upon him, as provided in this article. The issuance and service of the appearance ticket may be made conditional upon the posting of pre-arraignment bail as provided in section 150.30 of this chapter but only if the appropriate police officer (a) is unable to ascertain the defendant's identity or residence address; or (b) reasonably suspects that the identification or residence address given by the defendant is not accurate; or (c) reasonably suspects that the defendant does not reside within the state. No warrant of arrest shall be issued unless the defendant has failed to appear in court as required by the terms of the appearance ticket or by the court.

HISTORY: Add, L 1977, ch 360, § 8, eff July 29, 1977, and applicable to acts committed on or after such date.

ARTICLE 160   FINGERPRINTING AND PHOTOGRAPHING OF DEFENDANT AFTER ARREST—CRIMINAL IDENTIFICATION RECORDS AND STATISTICS

HISTORY: Add, L 1970, ch 996, § 1, eff Sept 1, 1971.

§ 160.10. Fingerprinting; duties of police with respect thereto

1. Following an arrest, or following the arraignment upon a local criminal court accusatory instrument of a defendant whose court attendance has been secured by a summons or an appearance ticket under circumstances described in sections 130.60 and 150.70, the arresting or other appropriate police officer or agency must take or cause to be taken fingerprints of the arrested person or defendant if an offense which is the subject of the arrest or which is charged in the accusatory instrument filed is:

(a) A felony; or

(b) A misdemeanor defined in the penal law; or

(c) A misdemeanor defined outside the penal law which would constitute a felony if such person had a previous judgment of conviction for a crime; or

(d) Loitering for the purpose of engaging in a prostitution offense as defined in subdivision two of section 240.37 of the penal law.

(e) [Redesignated]

2. In addition, a police officer who makes an arrest for any offense, either with or without a warrant, may take or cause to be taken the fingerprints of the arrested person if such police officer:

(a) Is unable to ascertain such person's identity; or

(b) Reasonably suspects that the identification given by such person is not accurate; or

(c) Reasonably suspects that such person is being sought by law enforcement officials for the commission of some other offense.

3. Whenever fingerprints are required to be taken pursuant to subdivision one or permitted to be taken pursuant to subdivision two, the photograph and palmprints of the arrested person or the defendant, as the case may be, may also be taken.

4. The taking of fingerprints as prescribed in this section and the submission of available information concerning the arrested person or the defendant and the facts and circumstances of the crime charged must be in accordance with the standards established by the commissioner of the division of criminal justice services.

HISTORY: Add, L 1970, ch 996, § 1; amd, L 1971, ch 762, § 7, eff Sept 1, 1971, L 1972, ch 399, § 17, eff Sept 1, 1972 L 1976, ch 344, § 3, eff July 11, 1976, L 2010, ch 232, § 5, eff July 30, 2010.

§ 160.20. Fingerprinting; forwarding of fingerprints

Upon the taking of fingerprints of an arrested person or defendant as prescribed in section

160.10, the appropriate police officer or agency must without unnecessary delay forward two copies of such fingerprints to the division of criminal justice services.

> **HISTORY:** Add, L 1970, ch 996, § 1; amd, L 1971, ch 762 § 8, L 1972, ch 399, § 18, L 1973, ch 108, § 1, eff March 27, 1973. Section heading, amd, L 1971, ch 762 § 8, L 1973, ch 108, § 1, eff March 27, 1973.

§ 160.30. Fingerprinting; duties of division of criminal justice services

1. Upon receiving fingerprints from a police officer or agency pursuant to section 160.20 of this chapter, the division of criminal justice services must, except as provided in subdivision two of this section, classify them and search its records for information concerning a previous record of the defendant, including any adjudication as a juvenile delinquent pursuant to article three of the family court act, or as a youthful offender pursuant to article seven hundred twenty of this chapter, and promptly transmit to such forwarding police officer or agency a report containing all information on file with respect to such defendant's previous record, if any, or stating that the defendant has no previous record according to its files. Such a report, if certified, constitutes presumptive evidence of the facts so certified.

2. If the fingerprints so received are not sufficiently legible to permit accurate and complete classification, they must be returned to the forwarding police officer or agency with an explanation of the defects and a request that the defendant's fingerprints be retaken if possible.

> **HISTORY:** Add, L 1970, ch 996, § 1; amd, L 1971, ch 762, § 9, eff Sept 1, 1971. Section heading, amd, L 1971, ch 762, § 9, L 1972, ch 399, § 19, eff Sept 1, 1972. Sub 1, amd, L 1972, ch 399, § 19, L 1977, ch 447, § 5, L 1982, ch 920, § 73, eff July 1, 1983.

§ 160.40. Fingerprinting; transmission of report received by police

1. Upon receipt of a report of the division of criminal justice services as provided in section 160.30, the recipient police officer or agency must promptly transmit such report or a copy thereof to the district attorney of the county and two copies thereof to the court in which the action is pending.

2. Upon receipt of such report the court shall furnish a copy thereof to counsel for the defendant or, if the defendant is not represented by counsel, to the defendant.

> **HISTORY:** Add, L 1970, ch 996, § 1; amd, L 1971, ch 762, § 10, L 1972, ch 399, § 20, L 1975, ch 531, § 1, eff Aug 28, 1975. Section heading, amd, L 1971, ch 762, § 10, L 1975, ch 531, § 1, eff Aug 28, 1975. Sub 1, formerly entire section, so numbered and amd, L 1975, ch 531, § 1, eff Aug 28, 1975. Sub 2, add, L 1975, ch 531, § 1, eff Aug 28, 1975.

§ 160.45. Polygraph tests; prohibition against

1. No district attorney, police officer or employee of any law enforcement agency shall request or require any victim of a sexual assault crime to submit to any polygraph test or psychological stress evaluator examination.

2. As used in this section, "victim of a sexual assault crime" means any person alleged to have sustained an offense under article one hundred thirty or section 255.25, 255.26 or 255.27 of the penal law.

> **HISTORY:** Add, L 1987, ch 589, § 1; amd, L 1990, ch 78, § 1, eff Dec 1, 1990. Sub 1, amd, L 1996, ch 17, § 1, eff Feb 27, 1996. Sub 2, amd, L 1990, ch 78, § 1, eff Dec 1, 1990. Sub 2, amd, L 2006, ch 320, § 15, eff Nov 1, 2006.

§ 160.50. Order upon termination of criminal action in favor of the accused

1. Upon the termination of a criminal action or proceeding against a person in favor of such person, as defined in subdivision three of this section, unless the district attorney upon motion with

not less than five days notice to such person or his or her attorney demonstrates to the satisfaction of the court that the interests of justice require otherwise, or the court on its own motion with not less than five days notice to such person or his or her attorney determines that the interests of justice require otherwise and states the reasons for such determination on the record, the record of such action or proceeding shall be sealed and the clerk of the court wherein such criminal action or proceeding was terminated shall immediately notify the commissioner of the division of criminal justice services and the heads of all appropriate police departments and other law enforcement agencies that the action has been terminated in favor of the accused, and unless the court has directed otherwise, that the record of such action or proceeding shall be sealed. Upon receipt of notification of such termination and sealing:

(a) every photograph of such person and photographic plate or proof, and all palmprints and fingerprints taken or made of such person pursuant to the provisions of this article in regard to the action or proceeding terminated, except a dismissal pursuant to section 170.56 or 210.46 of this chapter, and all duplicates and copies thereof, except a digital fingerprint image where authorized pursuant to paragraph (e) of this subdivision, shall forthwith be, at the discretion of the recipient agency, either destroyed or returned to such person, or to the attorney who represented such person at the time of the termination of the action or proceeding, at the address given by such person or attorney during the action or proceeding, by the division of criminal justice services and by any police department or law enforcement agency having any such photograph, photographic plate or proof, palmprint or fingerprints in its possession or under its control;

(b) any police department or law enforcement agency, including the division of criminal justice services, which transmitted or otherwise forwarded to any agency of the United States or of any other state or of any other jurisdiction outside the state of New York copies of any such photographs, photographic plates or proofs, palmprints and fingerprints, including those relating to actions or proceedings which were dismissed pursuant to section 170.56 or 210.46 of this chapter, shall forthwith formally request in writing that all such copies be destroyed or returned to the police department or law enforcement agency which transmitted or forwarded them, and, if returned, such department or agency shall, at its discretion, either destroy or return them as provided herein, except that those relating to dismissals pursuant to section 170.56 or 210.46 of this chapter shall not be destroyed or returned by such department or agency;

(c) all official records and papers, including judgments and orders of a court but not including published court decisions or opinions or records and briefs on appeal, relating to the arrest or prosecution, including all duplicates and copies thereof, on file with the division of criminal justice services, any court, police agency, or prosecutor's office shall be sealed and not made available to any person or public or private agency;

(d) such records shall be made available to the person accused or to such person's designated agent, and shall be made available to (i) a prosecutor in any proceeding in which the accused has moved for an order pursuant to section 170.56 or 210.46 of this chapter, or (ii) a law enforcement agency upon ex parte motion in any superior court, if such agency demonstrates to the satisfaction of the court that justice requires that such records be made available to it, or (iii) any state or local officer or agency with responsibility for the issuance of licenses to possess guns, when the accused has made application for such a license, or (iv) the New York state department of corrections and community supervision when the accused is on parole supervision as a result of conditional release or a parole release granted by the New York state board of parole, and the arrest which is the subject of the inquiry is one which occurred while the accused was under such supervision or (v) any prospective employer of a police officer or peace officer as those terms are defined in subdivisions thirty-three and thirty-four of section 1.20 of this chapter, in relation to an application for employment as a police officer or peace officer; provided, however, that every person who is an applicant for the position of police officer or peace officer shall be furnished with a copy of all records obtained under this paragraph and afforded an opportunity to make an explanation thereto, or (vi) the probation department responsible for supervision of the accused when the arrest which is the subject of the inquiry is one which occurred while the accused was under such supervision; and

(e) where fingerprints subject to the provisions of this section have been received by the division of criminal justice services and have been filed by the division as digital images, such images may be retained, provided that a fingerprint card of the individual is on file with the division which was not sealed pursuant to this section or section 160.55 of this article.

2. A report of the termination of the action or proceeding in favor of the accused shall be sufficient notice of sealing to the commissioner of the division of criminal justice services unless the report also indicates that the court directed that the record not be sealed in the interests of justice. Where the court has determined pursuant to subdivision one of this section that sealing is not in the interest of justice, the clerk of the court shall include notification of that determination in any report to such division of the disposition of the action or proceeding.

3. For the purposes of subdivision one of this section, a criminal action or proceeding against a person shall be considered terminated in favor of such person where:

(a) an order dismissing the entire accusatory instrument against such person pursuant to article four hundred seventy was entered; or

(b) an order to dismiss the entire accusatory instrument against such person pursuant to section 170.30, 170.50, 170.55, 170.56, 180.70, 210.20, 210.46 or 210.47 of this chapter was entered or deemed entered, or an order terminating the prosecution against such person was entered pursuant to section 180.85 of this chapter, and the people have not appealed from such order or the determination of an appeal or appeals by the people from such order has been against the people; or

(c) a verdict of complete acquittal was made pursuant to section 330.10 of this chapter; or

(d) a trial order of dismissal of the entire accusatory instrument against such person pursuant to section 290.10 or 360.40 of this chapter was entered and the people have not appealed from such order or the determination of an appeal or appeals by the people from such order has been against the people; or

(e) an order setting aside a verdict pursuant to section 330.30 or 370.10 of this chapter was entered and the people have not appealed from such order or the determination of an appeal or appeals by the people from such order has been against the people and no new trial has been ordered; or

(f) an order vacating a judgment pursuant to section 440.10 of this chapter was entered and the people have not appealed from such order or the determination of an appeal or appeals by the people from such order has been against the people, and no new trial has been ordered; or

(g) an order of discharge pursuant to article seventy of the civil practice law and rules was entered on a ground which invalidates the conviction and the people have not appealed from such order or the determination of an appeal or appeals by the people from such order has been against the people; or

(h) where all charges against such person are dismissed pursuant to section 190.75 of this chapter. In such event, the clerk of the court which empaneled the grand jury shall serve a certification of such disposition upon the division of criminal justice services and upon the appropriate police department or law enforcement agency which upon receipt thereof, shall comply with the provisions of paragraphs (a), (b), (c) and (d) of subdivision one of this section in the same manner as is required thereunder with respect to an order of a court entered pursuant to said subdivision one; or

(i) prior to the filing of an accusatory instrument in a local criminal court against such person, the prosecutor elects not to prosecute such person. In such event, the prosecutor shall serve a certification of such disposition upon the division of criminal justice services and upon the appropriate police department or law enforcement agency which, upon receipt thereof, shall comply with the provisions of paragraphs (a), (b), (c) and (d) of subdivision one of this section in the same manner as is required thereunder with respect to an order of a court entered pursuant to said subdivision one.

(j) following the arrest of such person, the arresting police agency, prior to the filing of an accusatory instrument in a local criminal court but subsequent to the forwarding of a copy of the fingerprints of such person to the division of criminal justice services, elects not to proceed further. In such event, the head of the arresting police agency shall serve a certification of such disposition upon the division of criminal justice services which, upon receipt thereof, shall comply with the provisions of paragraphs (a), (b), (c) and (d) of subdivision one of this section in the same manner as is required thereunder with respect to an order of a court entered pursuant to said subdivision one.

(k) (i) The accusatory instrument alleged a violation of article two hundred twenty or section 240.36 of the penal law, prior to the taking effect of article two hundred twenty-one of the penal law, or a violation of article two hundred twenty-one of the penal law; (ii) the sole controlled substance involved is marijuana; (iii) the conviction was only for a violation or violations; and (iv) at least three years have passed since the offense occurred.

(l) An order dismissing an action pursuant to section 215.40 of this chapter was entered.

4. A person in whose favor a criminal action or proceeding was terminated, as defined in paragraph (a) through (h) of subdivision two of this section, prior to the effective date of this section, may upon motion apply to the court in which such termination occurred, upon not less than twenty days notice to the district attorney, for an order granting to such person the relief set forth in subdivision one of this section, and such order shall be granted unless the district attorney demonstrates to the satisfaction of the court that the interests of justice require otherwise. A person in whose favor a criminal action or proceeding was terminated, as defined in paragraph (i) or (j) of subdivision two of this section, prior to the effective date of this section, may apply to the appropriate prosecutor or police agency for a certification as described in said paragraph (i) or (j) granting to such person the relief set forth therein, and such certification shall be granted by such prosecutor or police agency.

HISTORY: Add, L 1976, ch 877, § 1, with substance derived from Civ R § 79-e; amd, L 1977, ch 835, § 1, L 1977, ch 905, § 1, eff Aug 11, 1977, L 1980, ch 192, § 2, L 1981, ch 122, § 1, L 1985, ch 208, § 1, applicable to all persons seeking appointment to position of police or peace officer on or after Nov 1, 1985; amd, L 1986, ch 294, § 1, L 1986, ch 837, § 3, L 1991, ch 142, §§ 1–3, L 1994, ch 169, § 80, eff June 9, 1994, deemed eff April 1, 1994, L 2001, ch 487, § 1, eff Nov 1, 2002, L 2004, ch 518, § 1, eff Nov 1, 2004, L 2011, ch 62, § 73 (Part C, Subpart B), eff March 31, 2011.

§ 160.55. Order upon termination of criminal action by conviction for noncriminal offense; entry of waiver; administrative findings

1. Upon the termination of a criminal action or proceeding against a person by the conviction of such person of a traffic infraction or a violation, other than a violation of loitering as described in paragraph (d) or (e) of subdivision one of section 160.10 of this chapter or the violation of operating a motor vehicle while ability impaired as described in subdivision one of section eleven hundred ninety-two of the vehicle and traffic law, unless the district attorney upon motion with not less than five days notice to such person or his or her attorney demonstrates to the satisfaction of the court that the interests of justice require otherwise, or the court on its own motion with not less than five days notice to such person or his or her attorney determines that the interests of justice require otherwise and states the reasons for such determination on the record, the clerk of the court wherein such criminal action or proceeding was terminated shall immediately notify the commissioner of the division of criminal justice services and the heads of all appropriate police departments and other law enforcement agencies that the action has been terminated by such conviction. Upon receipt of notification of such termination:

(a) every photograph of such person and photographic plate or proof, and all palmprints and fingerprints taken or made of such person pursuant to the provisions of this article in regard to the action or proceeding terminated, and all duplicates and copies thereof, except a digital fingerprint image where authorized pursuant to paragraph (e) of this subdivision, except for the palmprints and fingerprints concerning a disposition of harassment in the second degree as defined in section 240.26 of the penal law, committed against a member of the same family or household as the defendant, as defined in subdivision one of section 530.11 of this chapter, and determined pursuant to subdivision eight-a of section 170.10 of this title, shall forthwith be, at the discretion of the recipient agency, either destroyed or returned to such person, or to the attorney who represented such person at the time of the termination of the action or proceeding, at the address given by such person or attorney during the action or proceeding, by the division of criminal justice services and by any police department or law enforcement agency having any such photograph, photographic plate or proof, palmprints or fingerprints in its possession or under its control;

(b) any police department or law enforcement agency, including the division of criminal justice services, which transmitted or otherwise forwarded to any agency of the United States or of any other state or of any other jurisdiction outside the state of New York copies of any such photographs, photographic plates or proofs, palmprints and fingerprints, shall forthwith formally request in writing that all such copies be destroyed or returned to the police department or law enforcement agency which transmitted or forwarded them, and upon such return such department or agency shall, at its discretion, either destroy or return them as provided herein;

(c) all official records and papers relating to the arrest or prosecution, including all duplicates and copies thereof, on file with the division of criminal justice services, police agency, or prosecutor's office shall be sealed and not made available to any person or public or private agency;

(d) the records referred to in paragraph (c) of this subdivision shall be made available to the person accused or to such person's designated agent, and shall be made available to (i) a prosecutor in any proceeding in which the accused has moved for an order pursuant to section 170.56 or 210.46 of this chapter, or (ii) a law enforcement agency upon ex parte motion in any superior court, if such agency demonstrates to the satisfaction of the court that justice requires that such records be made available to it, or (iii) any state or local officer or agency with responsibility for the issuance of licenses to possess guns, when the accused has made application for such a license, or (iv) the New York state department of corrections and community supervision when the accused is under parole supervision as a result of conditional release or parole release granted by the New York state board of parole and the arrest which is the subject of the inquiry is one which occurred while the accused was under such supervision, or (v) the probation department responsible for supervision of the accused when the arrest which is the subject of the inquiry is one which occurred while the accused was under such supervision, or (vi) a police agency, probation department, sheriff's office, district attorney's office, department of correction of any municipality and parole department, for law enforcement purposes, upon arrest in instances in which the individual stands convicted of harassment in the second degree, as defined in section 240.26 of the penal law, committed against a member of the same family or household as the defendant, as defined in subdivision one of section 530.11 of this chapter, and determined pursuant to subdivision eight-a of section 170.10 of this title; and

(e) where fingerprints subject to the provisions of this section have been received by the division of criminal justice services and have been filed by the division as digital images, such images may be retained, provided that a fingerprint card of the individual is on file with the division which was not sealed pursuant to this section or section 160.50 of this article.

2. A report of the termination of the action or proceeding by conviction of a traffic violation or a violation other than a violation of loitering as described in paragraph (d) or (e) of subdivision one of section 160.10 of this title or the violation of operating a motor vehicle while ability impaired as described in subdivision one of section eleven hundred ninety-two of the vehicle and traffic law, shall be sufficient notice of sealing to the commissioner of the division of criminal justice services unless the report also indicates that the court directed that the record not be sealed in the interests of justice. Where the court has determined pursuant to subdivision one of this section that sealing is not in the interests of justice, the clerk of the court shall include notification of that determination in any report to such division of the disposition of the action or proceeding. When the defendant has been found guilty of a violation of harassment in the second degree and it was determined pursuant to subdivision eight-a of section 170.10 of this title that such violation was committed against a member of the same family or household as the defendant, the clerk of the court shall include notification of that determination in any report to such division of the disposition of the action or proceeding for purposes of paragraph (a) and subparagraph (vi) of paragraph (d) of subdivision one of this section.

3. A person against whom a criminal action or proceeding was terminated by such person's conviction of a traffic infraction or violation other than a violation of loitering as described in paragraph (d) or (e) of subdivision one of section 160.10 of this chapter or the violation of operating a motor vehicle while ability impaired as described in subdivision one of section eleven hundred ninety-two of the vehicle and traffic law, prior to the effective date of this section, may upon motion apply to the court in which such termination occurred, upon not less than twenty days notice to the district attorney, for an order granting to such person the relief set forth in subdivision one of this section, and such order shall be granted unless the district attorney demonstrates to the satisfaction of the court that the interests of justice require otherwise.

4. This section shall not apply to an action terminated in a manner described in paragraph (k) of subdivision two of section 160.50 of this chapter.

5. (a) When a criminal action or proceeding is terminated against a person by the entry of a waiver of a hearing pursuant to paragraph (c) of subdivision ten of section eleven hundred ninety-two of the vehicle and traffic law or section forty-nine-b of the navigation law, the record of the criminal action shall be sealed in accordance with this subdivision. Upon the entry of

such waiver, the court or the clerk of the court shall immediately notify the commissioner of the division of criminal justice services and the heads of all appropriate police departments and other law enforcement agencies that a waiver has been entered and that the record of the action shall be sealed when the person reaches the age of twenty-one or three years from the date of commission of the offense, whichever is the greater period of time. At the expiration of such period, the commissioner of the division of criminal justice services and the heads of all appropriate police departments and other law enforcement agencies shall take the actions required by paragraphs (a), (b) and (c) of subdivision one of section 160.50 of this article.

(b) Where a person under the age of twenty-one is referred by the police to the department of motor vehicles for action pursuant to section eleven hundred ninety-two-a or eleven hundred ninety-four-a of the vehicle and traffic law, or section forty-nine-b of the navigation law and a finding in favor of the motorist or operator is rendered, the commissioner of the department of motor vehicles shall, as soon as practicable, but not later than three years from the date of commission of the offense or when such person reaches the age of twenty-one, whichever is the greater period of time, notify the commissioner of the division of criminal justice services and the heads of all appropriate police departments and other law enforcement agencies that such finding in favor of the motorist or operator was rendered. Upon receipt of such notification, the commissioner of the division of criminal justice services and the heads of such police departments and other law enforcement agencies shall take the actions required by paragraphs (a), (b) and (c) of subdivision one of section 160.50 of this article.

(c) Where a person under the age of twenty-one is referred by the police to the department of motor vehicles for action pursuant to section eleven hundred ninety-two-a or eleven hundred ninety-four-a of the vehicle and traffic law, or section forty-nine-b of the navigation law, and no notification is received by the commissioner of the division of criminal justice services and the heads of all appropriate police departments and other law enforcement agencies pursuant to paragraph (b) of this subdivision, such commissioner of the division of criminal justice services and such heads of police departments and other law enforcement agencies shall, after three years from the date of commission of the offense or when the person reaches the age of twenty-one, whichever is the greater period of time, take the actions required by paragraphs (a), (b) and (c) of subdivision one of section 160.50 of this article.

    HISTORY: Add, L 1980, ch 192, § 1, eff Sept 1, 1980; amd, L 1981, ch 249, §§ 1, 2, L 1982, ch 174, § 1, L 1986, ch 294, § 2, L 1991, ch 142, §§ 4, 5, L 1992, ch 249, § 1, eff June 30, 1992, L 1994, ch 169, § 81, eff June 9, 1994, deemed eff April 1, 1994, L 1996, ch 196, §§ 22, 23, eff Nov 1, 1996, L 1998, ch 391, § 6, eff April 1, 1999, L 2009, ch 476, §§ 7, 8, 10, eff Jan 14, 2010, L 2011, ch 62, § 74 (Part C, Subpart B), eff March 31, 2011.

§ 160.58. Conditional sealing of certain controlled substance, marihuana or specified offense convictions

1. A defendant convicted of any offense defined in article two hundred twenty or two hundred twenty-one of the penal law or a specified offense defined in subdivision five of section 410.91 of this chapter who has successfully completed a judicial diversion program under article two hundred sixteen of this chapter, or one of the programs heretofore known as drug treatment alternative to prison or another judicially sanctioned drug treatment program of similar duration, requirements and level of supervision, and has completed the sentence imposed for the offense or offenses, is eligible to have such offense or offenses sealed pursuant to this section.

2. The court that sentenced the defendant to a judicially sanctioned drug treatment program may on its own motion, or on the defendant's motion, order that all official records and papers relating to the arrest, prosecution and conviction which resulted in the defendant's participation in the

judicially sanctioned drug treatment program be conditionally sealed. In such case, the court may also conditionally seal the arrest, prosecution and conviction records for no more than three of the defendant's prior eligible misdemeanors, which for purposes of this subdivision shall be limited to misdemeanor offenses defined in article two hundred twenty or two hundred twenty-one of the penal law. The court may only seal the records of the defendant's arrests, prosecutions and convictions when:

(a) the sentencing court has requested and received from the division of criminal justice services or the Federal Bureau of Investigation a fingerprint based criminal history record of the defendant, including any sealed or suppressed information. The division of criminal justice services shall also include a criminal history report, if any, from the Federal Bureau of Investigation regarding any criminal history information that occurred in other jurisdictions. The division is hereby authorized to receive such information from the Federal Bureau of Investigation for this purpose. The parties shall be permitted to examine these records;

(b) the defendant or court has identified the misdemeanor conviction or convictions for which relief may be granted;

(c) the court has received documentation that the sentences imposed on the eligible misdemeanor convictions have been completed, or if no such documentation is reasonably available, a sworn affidavit that the sentences imposed on the prior misdemeanors have been completed; and

(d) the court has notified the district attorney of each jurisdiction in which the defendant has been convicted of an offense with respect to which sealing is sought, and the court or courts of record for such offenses, that the court is considering sealing the records of the defendant's eligible misdemeanor convictions. Both the district attorney and the court shall be given a reasonable opportunity, which shall not be less than thirty days, in which to comment and submit materials to aid the court in making such a determination.

3. At the request of the defendant or the district attorney of a county in which the defendant committed a crime that is the subject of the sealing application, the court may conduct a hearing to consider and review any relevant evidence offered by either party that would aid the court in its decision whether to seal the records of the defendant's arrests, prosecutions and convictions. In making such a determination, the court shall consider any relevant factors, including but not limited to: (i) the circumstances and seriousness of the offense or offenses that resulted in the conviction or convictions; (ii) the character of the defendant, including his or her completion of the judicially sanctioned treatment program as described in subdivision one of this section; (iii) the defendant's criminal history; and (iv) the impact of sealing the defendant's records upon his or her rehabilitation and his or her successful and productive reentry and reintegration into society, and on public safety.

4. When a court orders sealing pursuant to this section, all official records and papers relating to the arrests, prosecutions, and convictions, including all duplicates and copies thereof, on file with the division of criminal justice services or any court shall be sealed and not made available to any person or public or private agency; provided, however, the division shall retain any fingerprints, palmprints and photographs, or digital images of the same.

5. When the court orders sealing pursuant to this section, the clerk of such court shall immediately notify the commissioner of the division of criminal justice services, and any court that sentenced the defendant for an offense which has been conditionally sealed, regarding the records that shall be sealed pursuant to this section.

6. Records sealed pursuant to this subdivision shall be made available to:

(a) the defendant or the defendant's designated agent;

(b) qualified agencies, as defined in subdivision nine of section eight hundred thirty-five of the executive law, and federal and state law enforcement agencies, when acting within the scope of their law enforcement duties; or

(c) any state or local officer or agency with responsibility for the issuance of licenses to possess guns, when the person has made application for such a license; or

(d) any prospective employer of a police officer or peace officer as those terms are defined in subdivisions thirty-three and thirty-four of section 1.20 of this chapter, in relation to an application for employment as a police officer or peace officer; provided, however, that every person who is an applicant for the position of police officer or peace officer shall be furnished with a copy of all records obtained under this paragraph and afforded an opportunity to make an explanation thereto.

7. The court shall not seal the defendant's record pursuant to this section while any charged offense is pending.

8. If, subsequent to the sealing of records pursuant to this subdivision, the person who is the subject of such records is arrested for or formally charged with any misdemeanor or felony offense, such records shall be unsealed immediately and remain unsealed; provided, however, that if such new misdemeanor or felony arrest results in a termination in favor of the accused as defined in subdivision three of section 160.50 of this article or by conviction for a non criminal offense as described in section 160.55 of this article, such unsealed records shall be conditionally sealed pursuant to this section.

HISTORY: Add, L 2009, ch 56, § 3 (Part AAA), eff June 6, 2009.

§ 160.60. Effect of termination of criminal actions in favor of the accused

Upon the termination of a criminal action or proceeding against a person in favor of such person, as defined in subdivision two of section 160.50 of this chapter, the arrest and prosecution shall be deemed a nullity and the accused shall be restored, in contemplation of law, to the status he occupied before the arrest and prosecution. The arrest or prosecution shall not operate as a disqualification of any person so accused to pursue or engage in any lawful activity, occupation, profession, or calling. Except where specifically required or permitted by statute or upon specific authorization of a superior court, no such person shall be required to divulge information pertaining to the arrest or prosecution.

HISTORY: Add, L 1976, ch 877, § 2, eff Sept 1, 1976.

ARTICLE 170   PROCEEDINGS UPON INFORMATION, SIMPLIFIED TRAFFIC INFORMATION, PROSECUTOR'S INFORMATION AND MISDEMEANOR COMPLAINT FROM ARRAIGNMENT TO PLEA

HISTORY: Add, L 1970, ch 996, § 1, eff Sept 1, 1971.

§ 170.10. Arraignment upon information, simplified traffic information, prosecutor's information or misdemeanor complaint; defendant's presence, defendant's rights, court's instructions and bail matters

1. Following the filing with a local criminal court of an information, a simplified information, a prosecutor's information or a misdemeanor complaint, the defendant must be arraigned thereon. The defendant must appear personally at such arraignment except under the following circumstances:

(a) In any case where a simplified information is filed and a procedure is provided by law which is applicable to all offenses charged in such simplified information and, if followed, would dispense with an arraignment or personal appearance of the defendant, nothing contained in this section affects the validity of such procedure or requires such personal appearance;

(b) In any case in which the defendant's appearance is required by a summons or an appearance ticket, the court in its discretion may, for good cause shown, permit the defendant to appear by counsel instead of in person.

2. Upon any arraignment at which the defendant is personally present, the court must immediately inform him, or cause him to be informed in its presence, of the charge or charges against him and must furnish him with a copy of the accusatory instrument.

3. The defendant has the right to the aid of counsel at the arraignment and at every subsequent stage of the action. If he appears upon such arraignment without counsel, he has the following rights:

(a) To an adjournment for the purpose of obtaining counsel; and

(b) To communicate, free of charge, by letter or by telephone provided by the law enforcement facility where the defendant is held to a phone number located in the United States, or Puerto Rico, for the purposes of obtaining counsel and informing a relative or friend that he or she has been charged with an offense; and

(c) To have counsel assigned by the court if he is financially unable to obtain the same; except that this paragraph does not apply where the accusatory instrument charges a traffic infraction or infractions only.

4. Except as provided in subdivision five, the court must inform the defendant:

(a) Of his rights as prescribed in subdivision three; and the court must not only accord him opportunity to exercise such rights but must itself take such affirmative action as is necessary to effectuate them; and

(b) Where a traffic infraction or a misdemeanor relating to traffic is charged, that a judgment of conviction for such offense would in addition to subjecting the defendant to the sentence provided therefor render his license to drive a motor vehicle and his certificate of registration subject to suspension and revocation as prescribed by law and that a plea of guilty to such offense constitutes a conviction thereof to the same extent as a verdict of guilty after trial; and

(c) Where the accusatory instrument is a simplified traffic information, that the defendant has a right to have a supporting deposition filed, as provided in section 100.25; and

(d) Where the accusatory instrument is a misdemeanor complaint, that the defendant may not be prosecuted thereon or required to enter a plea thereto unless he consents to the same, and that in the absence of such consent such misdemeanor complaint will for prosecution purposes have to be replaced and superseded by an information; and

(e) Where an information, a simplified information, a prosecutor's information, a misdemeanor complaint, a felony complaint or an indictment charges harassment in the second degree, as defined in section 240.26 of the penal law, if there is a judgment of conviction for such offense and such offense is determined to have been committed against a member of the same family or household as the defendant, as defined in subdivision one of section 530.11 of this chapter, the record of such conviction shall be accessible for law enforcement purposes and not sealed, as specified in paragraph (a) and subparagraph (vi) of paragraph (d) of subdivision one of section 160.55 of this title; and

5. In any case in which a defendant has appeared for arraignment in response to a summons or an appearance ticket, a printed statement upon such process of any court instruction required by the provisions of subdivision four, other than those specified in paragraphs (d) and (e) thereof, constitutes compliance with such provisions with respect to the instruction so printed.

6. If a defendant charged with a traffic infraction or infractions only desires to proceed without the aid of counsel, the court must permit him to do so. In all other cases, the court must permit the defendant to proceed without the aid of counsel if it is satisfied that he made such decision with knowledge of the significance thereof, but if it is not so satisfied it may not proceed until the defendant is provided with counsel, either of his own choosing or by assignment. Regardless of the kind or nature of the charges, a defendant who proceeds at the arraignment without counsel does not waive his right to counsel, and the court must inform him that he continues to have such right as well as all the rights specified in subdivision three which are necessary to effectuate it, and that he may exercise such rights at any stage of the action.

7. Upon the arraignment, the court, unless it intends to make a final disposition of the action immediately thereafter, must, as provided in subdivision one of section 530.20, issue a securing order either releasing the defendant on his own recognizance or fixing bail for his future

appearance in the action; except that where a defendant appears by counsel pursuant to paragraph (b) of subdivision one of this section, the court must release the defendant on his own recognizance.

8. Notwithstanding any other provision of law to the contrary, a local criminal court may not, at arraignment or within thirty days of arraignment on a simplified traffic information charging a violation of subdivision two, two-a, three, four or four-a of section eleven hundred ninety-two of the vehicle and traffic law and upon which a notation has been made pursuant to subdivision twelve of section eleven hundred ninety-two of the vehicle and traffic law, accept a plea of guilty to a violation of any subdivision of section eleven hundred ninety-two of the vehicle and traffic law, nor to any other traffic infraction arising out of the same incident, nor to any other traffic infraction, violation or misdemeanor where the court is aware that such offense was charged pursuant to an accident involving death or serious physical injury, except upon written consent of the district attorney.

8-a. (a) Where an information, a simplified information, a prosecutor's information, a misdemeanor complaint, a felony complaint or an indictment charges harassment in the second degree as defined in section 240.26 of the penal law, the people may serve upon the defendant and file with the court a notice alleging that such offense was committed against a member of the same family or household as the defendant, as defined in subdivision one of section 530.11 of this chapter. Such notice must be served within fifteen days after arraignment on an information, a simplified information, a prosecutor's information, a misdemeanor complaint, a felony complaint or an indictment for such charge and before trial. Such notice must include the name of the person alleged to be a member of the same family or household as the defendant and specify the specific family or household relationship as defined in subdivision one of section 530.11 of this chapter.

(b) If a defendant, charged with harassment in the second degree as defined in section 240.26 of the penal law stipulates, or admits in the course of a plea disposition, that the person against whom the charged offense is alleged to have been committed is a member of the same family or household as the defendant, as defined in subdivision one of section 530.11 of this chapter, such allegation shall be deemed established for purposes of paragraph (a) and subparagraph (vi) of paragraph (d) of subdivision one of section 160.55 of this title. If the defendant denies such allegation, the people may, by proof beyond a reasonable doubt, prove as part of their case that the alleged victim of such offense was a member of the same family or household as the defendant. In such circumstances, the trier of fact shall make its determination with respect to such allegation orally on the record or in writing.

9. Nothing contained in this section applies to the arraignment of corporate defendants, which is governed generally by the provisions of article six hundred.

   HISTORY: Add, L 1970, ch 996, § 1; amd, L 1972, ch 661, § 38, amd, L 1972, ch 243, § 1, L
   1972, ch 697, § 1, L 1992, ch 449, § 2, L 2006, ch 732, § 15, eff Nov 1, 2006, L 2009, ch 476, §§ 9,
   11, eff Oct 16, 2009, L 2010, ch 94, § 3, eff July 24, 2010.

§ 170.15. Removal of action from one local criminal court to another

Under circumstances prescribed in this section, a criminal action based upon an information, a simplified information, a prosecutor's information or a misdemeanor complaint may be removed from one local criminal court to another:

1. When a defendant arrested by a police officer for an offense other than a felony, allegedly committed in a city or town, has, owing to special circumstances and pursuant to law, not been brought before the particular local criminal court which by reason of the situs of such offense

has trial jurisdiction thereof, but, instead, before a local criminal court which does not have trial jurisdiction thereof, and therein stands charged with such offense by information, simplified information or misdemeanor complaint, such local criminal court must arraign him upon such accusatory instrument. If the defendant desires to enter a plea of guilty thereto immediately following such arraignment, such local criminal court must permit him to do so and must thereafter conduct the action to judgment. Otherwise, it must remit the action, together with all pertinent papers and documents, to the local criminal court which has trial jurisdiction of the action, and the latter court must then conduct such action to judgment or other final disposition.

2. When a defendant arrested by a police officer for an offense other than a felony has been brought before a superior court judge sitting as a local criminal court for arraignment upon an information, simplified information or misdemeanor complaint charging such offense, such judge must, as a local criminal court, arraign the defendant upon such accusatory instrument. Such judge must then remit the action, together with all pertinent papers and documents, to a local criminal court having trial jurisdiction thereof. The latter court must then conduct such action to judgment or other final disposition.

3. At any time within the period provided by section 255.20, where a defendant is arraigned upon an information, a simplified information, a prosecutor's information or a misdemeanor complaint pending in a city court, town court or a village court having trial jurisdiction thereof, a judge of the county court of the county in which such city court, town court or village court is located may, upon motion of the defendant or the people, order that the action be transferred for disposition from the court in which the matter is pending to another designated local criminal court of the county, upon the ground that disposition thereof within a reasonable time in the court from which removal is sought is unlikely owing to:

    (a) Death, disability or other incapacity or disqualification of all of the judges of such court; or

    (b) Inability of such court to form a jury in a case, in which the defendant is entitled to and has requested a jury trial.

4. Notwithstanding any provision of this section to the contrary, in any county outside a city having a population of one million or more, upon or after arraignment of a defendant on an information, a simplified information, a prosecutor's information or a misdemeanor complaint pending in a local criminal court, such court may, upon motion of the defendant and with the consent of the district attorney, order that the action be removed from the court in which the matter is pending to another local criminal court in the same county which has been designated a drug court by the chief administrator of the courts, and such drug court may then conduct such action to judgement or other final disposition; provided, however, that an order of removal issued under this subdivision shall not take effect until five days after the date the order is issued unless, prior to such effective date, the drug court notifies the court that issued the order that:

    (a) it will not accept the action, in which event the order shall not take effect, or

    (b) it will accept the action on a date prior to such effective date, in which event the order shall take effect upon such prior date.

Upon providing notification pursuant to paragraph (a) or (b) of this subdivision, the drug court shall promptly give notice to the defendant, his or her counsel and the district attorney.

HISTORY: Add, L 1970, ch 996, § 1, with substance derived from Crim C §§ 60, 702-a(2); amd, L 1972, ch 661, § 39, eff Sept 1, 1972. Sub 1, amd, L 1984, ch 695, § 3, eff Aug 1, 1984. Sub 3, amd, L 1974, ch 763, § 6, L 1974, ch 837, § 1, eff June 7, 1974. Sub 4, amd, L 2000, ch 67, § 1, eff Nov 1, 2000. Sub 4, opening par, formerly entire sub 4, add, L 1998, ch 77, § 1, eff June 2, 1998;

so designated sub 4, opening par and amd, L 1999, ch 565, § 1, eff Nov 1, 1999; amd, L 2000, ch 67, § 1, eff Nov 1, 2000. Sub 4, par (a), add, L 1999, ch 565, § 1, eff Nov 1, 1999. Sub 4, par (b), add, L 1999, ch 565, § 1, eff Nov 1, 1999. Sub 4, closing par, add, L 1999, ch 565, § 1, eff Nov 1, 1999.

§ 170.20. Divestiture of jurisdiction by indictment; removal of case to superior court at district attorney's instance

1. If at any time before entry of a plea of guilty to or commencement of a trial of a local criminal court accusatory instrument containing a charge of misdemeanor, an indictment charging the defendant with such misdemeanor is filed in a superior court, the local criminal court is thereby divested of jurisdiction of such misdemeanor charge and all proceedings therein with respect thereto are terminated.

2. At any time before entry of a plea of guilty to or commencement of a trial of an accusatory instrument specified in subdivision one, the district attorney may apply for an adjournment of the proceedings in the local criminal court upon the ground that he intends to present the misdemeanor charge in question to a grand jury with a view to prosecuting it by indictment in a superior court. In such case, the local criminal court must adjourn the proceedings to a date which affords the district attorney reasonable opportunity to pursue such action, and may subsequently grant such further adjournments for that purpose as are reasonable under the circumstances. Following the granting of such adjournment or adjournments, the proceedings must be as follows:

    (a) If such charge is presented to a grand jury within the designated period and either an indictment or a dismissal of such charge results, the local criminal court is thereby divested of jurisdiction of such charge, and all proceedings in the local criminal court with respect thereto are terminated.

    (b) If the misdemeanor charge is not presented to a grand jury within the designated period, the proceedings in the local criminal court must continue.

    HISTORY: Add, L 1970, ch 996, § 1, eff Sept 1, 1971, with substance derived from Crim C § 59.

§ 170.25. Divestiture of jurisdiction by indictment; removal of case to superior court at defendant's instance

1. At any time before entry of a plea of guilty to or commencement of a trial of a local criminal court accusatory instrument containing a charge of misdemeanor, a superior court having jurisdiction to prosecute such misdemeanor charge by indictment may, upon motion of the defendant made upon notice to the district attorney, showing good cause to believe that the interests of justice so require, order that such charge be prosecuted by indictment and that the district attorney present it to the grand jury for such purpose.

2. Such order stays the proceedings in the local criminal court pending submission of the charge to the grand jury. Upon the subsequent filing of an indictment in the superior court, the proceedings in the local criminal court terminate and the defendant must be required to appear for arraignment upon the indictment in the manner prescribed in subdivisions one and two of section 210.10. Upon the subsequent filing of a grand jury dismissal of the charge, the proceedings in the local criminal court terminate and the superior court must, if the defendant is not at liberty on his own recognizance, discharge him from custody or exonerate his bail, as the case may be.

3. At any time before entry of a plea of guilty to or commencement of a trial of or within thirty days of arraignment on an accusatory instrument specified in subdivision one, whichever occurs first, the defendant may apply to the local criminal court for an adjournment of the proceedings

therein upon the ground that he intends to make a motion in a superior court, pursuant to subdivision one, for an order that the misdemeanor charge be prosecuted by indictment. In such case, the local criminal court must adjourn the proceedings to a date which affords the defendant reasonable opportunity to pursue such action, and may subsequently grant such further adjournments for that purpose as are reasonable under the circumstances. Following the granting of such adjournment or adjournments, the proceedings must be as follows:

(a) If a motion in a superior court is not made by the defendant within the designated period, the proceedings in the local criminal court must continue.

(b) If a motion in a superior court is made by the defendant within the designated period, such motion stays the proceedings in the local criminal court until the entry of an order determining such motion.

(c) If the superior court enters an order granting the motion, such order stays the proceedings in the local criminal court as provided in subdivision two; and upon a subsequent indictment or dismissal of such charge by the grand jury, the proceedings in the local criminal court terminate as provided in subdivision two.

(d) If the superior court enters an order denying the motion, the proceedings in the local criminal court must continue.

4. Upon application of a defendant who on the basis of an order issued by a superior court pursuant to subdivision one is awaiting grand jury action, and who, at the time of such order or subsequent thereto, has been committed to the custody of the sheriff pending grand jury action, and who has been confined in such custody for a period of more than forty-five days without the occurrence of any grand jury action or disposition, the superior court which issued such order must release him on his own recognizance unless:

(a) The lack of a grand jury disposition during such period of confinement was due to the defendant's request, action or condition, or occurred with his consent; or

(b) The people have shown good cause why such order of release should not be issued. Such good cause must consist of some compelling fact or circumstance which precluded grand jury action within the prescribed period or rendered the same against the interest of justice.

HISTORY: Add, L 1970, ch 996, § 1, eff Sept 1, 1971, with substance derived from Crim C §§ 57, 58, 59. Sub 3, amd, L 1973, ch 592, § 1, eff Sept 1, 1973. Sub 4, add, L 1974, ch 509, § 1, eff Sept 1, 1974.

§ 170.30. Motion to dismiss information, simplified information, prosecutor's information or misdemeanor complaint

1. After arraignment upon an information, a simplified information, a prosecutor's information or a misdemeanor complaint, the local criminal court may, upon motion of the defendant, dismiss such instrument or any count thereof upon the ground that:

(a) It is defective, within the meaning of section 170.35; or

(b) The defendant has received immunity from prosecution for the offense charged, pursuant to sections 50.20 or 190.40; or

(c) The prosecution is barred by reason of a previous prosecution, pursuant to section 40.20; or

(d) The prosecution is untimely, pursuant to section 30.10; or

(e) The defendant has been denied the right to a speedy trial; or

(f) There exists some other jurisdictional or legal impediment to conviction of the defendant for the offense charged; or

(g) Dismissal is required in furtherance of justice, within the meaning of section 170.40.

2. A motion pursuant to this section, except a motion pursuant to paragraph (e) of subdivision one, should be made within the period provided by section 255.20. A motion made pursuant to paragraph (e) of subdivision one should be made prior to the commencement of trial or entry of a plea of guilty.

3. Upon the motion, a defendant who is in a position adequately to raise more than one ground in support thereof should raise every such ground upon which he intends to challenge the accusatory instrument. A subsequent motion based upon such a ground not so raised may be summarily denied, although the court, in the interest of justice and for good cause shown, may in its discretion entertain and dispose of such a motion on the merits notwithstanding.

4. After arraignment upon an information, a simplified information, a prosecutor's information or misdemeanor complaint on a charge of prostitution pursuant to section 230.00 of the penal law or loitering for the purposes of prostitution pursuant to subdivision two of section 240.37 of the penal law, provided that the person does not stand charged with loitering for the purpose of patronizing a prostitute, where such offense allegedly occurred when the person was sixteen or seventeen years of age, the local criminal court may dismiss such charge in its discretion in the interest of justice on the ground that a defendant participated in services provided to him or her.

HISTORY: Add, L 1970, ch 996, § 1, eff Sept 1, 1971. Section heading, amd, L 1972, ch 661, § 40, eff Sept 1, 1972. Sub 1, opening par, amd, L 1972, ch 661, § 40, eff Sept 1, 1972. Sub 2, amd, L 1972, ch 184, § 4, L 1974, ch 763, § 3, eff Sept 1, 1974. Sub 4, add, L 2014, ch 402, § 1, eff Oct 16, 2014.

§ 170.35. Motion to dismiss information, simplified information, prosecutor's information or misdemeanor complaint; as defective

1. An information, a simplified information, a prosecutor's information or a misdemeanor complaint, or a count thereof, is defective within the meaning of paragraph (a) of subdivision one of section 170.30 when:

(a) It is not sufficient on its face pursuant to the requirements of section 100.40; provided that such an instrument or count may not be dismissed as defective, but must instead be amended, where the defect or irregularity is of a kind that may be cured by amendment and where the people move to so amend; or

(b) The allegations demonstrate that the court does not have jurisdiction of the offense charged; or

(c) The statute defining the offense charged is unconstitutional or otherwise invalid.

2. An information is also defective when it is filed in replacement of a misdemeanor complaint pursuant to section 170.65 but without satisfying the requirements stated therein.

3. A prosecutor's information is also defective when:

(a) It is filed at the direction of a grand jury, pursuant to section 190.70, and the offense or offenses charged are not among those authorized by such grand jury direction; or

(b) It is filed by the district attorney at his own instance, pursuant to subdivision two of section 100.50, and the factual allegations of the original information underlying it and any supporting depositions are not legally sufficient to support the charge in the prosecutor's information.

HISTORY: Add, L 1970, ch 996, § 1, eff Sept 1, 1971. Section heading, amd, L 1972, ch 661, § 41, eff Sept 1, 1972. Sub 1, opening par, amd, L 1972, ch 661, § 41, eff Sept 1, 1972.

§ 170.40. Motion to dismiss information, simplified traffic information, prosecutor's information or misdemeanor complaint; in furtherance of justice

1. An information, a simplified traffic information, a prosecutor's information or a misdemeanor complaint, or any count thereof, may be dismissed in the interest of justice, as provided in paragraph (g) of subdivision one of section 170.30 when, even though there may be no basis for dismissal as a matter of law upon any ground specified in paragraphs (a) through (f) of said subdivision one of section 170.30, such dismissal is required as a matter of judicial discretion by the existence of some compelling factor, consideration or circumstance clearly demonstrating that conviction or prosecution of the defendant upon such accusatory instrument or count would constitute or result in injustice. In determining whether such compelling factor, consideration, or circumstance exists, the court must, to the extent applicable, examine and consider, individually and collectively, the following:

    (a) the seriousness and circumstances of the offense;

    (b) the extent of harm caused by the offense;

    (c) the evidence of guilt, whether admissible or inadmissible at trial;

    (d) the history, character and condition of the defendant;

    (e) any exceptionally serious misconduct of law enforcement personnel in the investigation, arrest and prosecution of the defendant;

    (f) the purpose and effect of imposing upon the defendant a sentence authorized for the offense;

    (g) the impact of a dismissal on the safety or welfare of the community;

    (h) the impact of a dismissal upon the confidence of the public in the criminal justice system;

    (i) where the court deems it appropriate, the attitude of the complainant or victim with respect to the motion;

    (j) any other relevant fact indicating that a judgment of conviction would serve no useful purpose.

2. An order dismissing an accusatory instrument specified in subdivision one in the interest of justice may be issued upon motion of the people or of the court itself as well as upon that of the defendant. Upon issuing such an order, the court must set forth its reasons therefor upon the record.

HISTORY: Add, L 1970, ch 996, § 1, eff Sept 1, 1971. Sub 1, amd, L 1979, ch 216, § 1, eff Jan 1, 1980.

§ 170.45. Motion to dismiss information, simplified traffic information, prosecutor's information or misdemeanor complaint; procedure

The procedural rules prescribed in section 210.45 with respect to the making, consideration and disposition of a motion to dismiss an indictment are also applicable to a motion to dismiss an information, a simplified traffic information, a prosecutor's information or a misdemeanor complaint.

HISTORY: Add, L 1970, ch 996, § 1, eff Sept 1, 1971.

§ 170.50. Motion in superior court to dismiss prosecutor's information

1. At any time after arraignment in a local criminal court upon a prosecutor's information filed at the direction of a grand jury and before entry of a plea of guilty thereto or commencement of a trial thereof, the local criminal court wherein the prosecutor's information is filed may, upon motion of the defendant, dismiss such prosecutor's information or a count thereof upon the ground that:

(a) The evidence before the grand jury was not legally sufficient to support the charge; or

(b) The grand jury proceeding resulting in the filing of such prosecutor's information was defective.

2. The criteria and procedures for consideration and disposition of such motion are the same as those prescribed in sections 210.30 and 210.35, governing consideration and disposition of a motion to dismiss an indictment on the ground of insufficiency of grand jury evidence or of a defective grand jury proceeding; and, where appropriate, the general procedural rules prescribed in section 210.45 for consideration and disposition of a motion to dismiss an indictment are also applicable.

3. Upon dismissing a prosecutor's information or a count thereof pursuant to this section, the court may, upon application of the people, in its discretion authorize the people to resubmit the charge or charges to the same or another grand jury. In the absence of such authorization, such charge or charges may not be resubmitted to a grand jury. The rules prescribed in subdivisions eight and nine of section 210.45 concerning the discharge of a defendant from custody or exoneration of bail in the absence of an authorization to resubmit an indictment to a grand jury, and concerning the issuance of a securing order and the effective period thereof where such an authorization is issued, apply equally where a prosecutor's information is dismissed pursuant to this section.

HISTORY: Add, L 1970, ch 996, § 1, eff Sept 1, 1971. Sub 1, amd, L 1973, ch 530, § 1, L 1981, ch 247, § 1, eff Jan 1, 1982. Sub 2, amd, L 1971, ch 788, § 2, eff Sept 1, 1971.

§ 170.55. Adjournment in contemplation of dismissal

1. Upon or after arraignment in a local criminal court upon an information, a simplified information, a prosecutor's information or a misdemeanor complaint, and before entry of a plea of guilty thereto or commencement of a trial thereof, the court may, upon motion of the people or the defendant and with the consent of the other party, or upon the court's own motion with the consent of both the people and the defendant, order that the action be "adjourned in contemplation of dismissal," as prescribed in subdivision two.

2. An adjournment in contemplation of dismissal is an adjournment of the action without date ordered with a view to ultimate dismissal of the accusatory instrument in furtherance of justice. Upon issuing such an order, the court must release the defendant on his own recognizance. Upon application of the people, made at any time not more than six months, or in the case of a family offense as defined in subdivision one of section 530.11 of this chapter, one year, after the issuance of such order, the court may restore the case to the calendar upon a determination that dismissal of the accusatory instrument would not be in furtherance of justice, and the action must thereupon proceed. If the case is not so restored within such six months or one year period, the accusatory instrument is, at the expiration of such period, deemed to have been dismissed by the court in furtherance of justice.

3. In conjunction with an adjournment in contemplation of dismissal the court may issue a temporary order of protection pursuant to section 530.12 or 530.13 of this chapter, requiring the defendant to observe certain specified conditions of conduct.

4. Where the local criminal court information, simplified information, prosecutor's information, or misdemeanor complaint charges a crime or violation between spouses or between parent and child, or between members of the same family or household, as the term "members of the same family or household" is defined in subdivision one of section 530.11 of this chapter, the court may as a condition of an adjournment in contemplation of dismissal order, require that the defendant participate in an educational program addressing the issues of spousal abuse and family violence.

5. The court may grant an adjournment in contemplation of dismissal on condition that the defendant participate in dispute resolution and comply with any award or settlement resulting therefrom.

6. The court may as a condition of an adjournment in contemplation of dismissal order, require the defendant to perform services for a public or not-for-profit corporation, association, institution or agency. Such condition may only be imposed where the defendant has consented to the amount and conditions of such service. The court may not impose such conditions in excess of the length of the adjournment.

6-a. The court may, as a condition of an authorized adjournment in contemplation of dismissal, where the defendant has been charged with an offense and the elements of such offense meet the criteria of an "eligible offense" and such person qualified as an "eligible person" as such terms are defined in section four hundred fifty-eight-l of the social services law, require the defendant to participate in an education reform program in accordance with section four hundred fifty-eight-l of the social services law.

7. The court may, as a condition of an adjournment in contemplation of dismissal order, where a defendant is under twenty-one years of age and is charged with (a) a misdemeanor or misdemeanors other than section eleven hundred ninety-two of the vehicle and traffic law, in which the record indicates the consumption of alcohol by the defendant may have been a contributing factor, or (b) a violation of paragraph (a) of subdivision one of section sixty-five-b of the alcoholic beverage control law, require the defendant to attend an alcohol awareness program established pursuant to subdivision (a) of section 19.07 of the mental hygiene law.

8. The granting of an adjournment in contemplation of dismissal shall not be deemed to be a conviction or an admission of guilt. No person shall suffer any disability or forfeiture as a result of such an order. Upon the dismissal of the accusatory instrument pursuant to this section, the arrest and prosecution shall be deemed a nullity and the defendant shall be restored, in contemplation of law, to the status he occupied before his arrest and prosecution.

9. Notwithstanding any other provision of this section, a court may not issue an order adjourning an action in contemplation of dismissal if the offense is for a violation of the vehicle and traffic law related to the operation of a motor vehicle (except one related to parking, stopping or standing), or a violation of a local law, rule or ordinance related to the operation of a motor vehicle (except one related to parking, stopping or standing), if such offense was committed by the holder of a commercial driver's license or was committed in a commercial motor vehicle, as defined in subdivision four of section five hundred one-a of the vehicle and traffic law.

HISTORY: Add, L 1970, ch 996, § 1, eff Sept 1, 1971; amd, L 1972, ch 661, § 42, eff Sept 1, 1972, L 1980, ch 24, § 1, L 1980, ch 530, § 13, L 1981, ch 847, § 2, L 1982, ch 134, § 1, L 1985, ch 672, § 5, eff Sept 30, 1985, L 1988, ch 39, § 1, eff April 1, 1989, L 1990, ch 683, § 3, eff Jan 18, 1991, L 1994, ch 222, § 33, eff Jan 1, 1995, L 1998, ch 383, § 8, eff April 1, 1999, L 2011, ch

58, § 8 (Part CC), eff May 30, 2011, L 2012, ch 55, § 7 (Part V), eff May 20, 2012.

§ 170.56. Adjournment in contemplation of dismissal in cases involving marihuana

1. Upon or after arraignment in a local criminal court upon an information, a prosecutor's information or a misdemeanor complaint, where the sole remaining count or counts charge a violation or violations of section 221.05, 221.10, 221.15, 221.35 or 221.40 of the penal law and before the entry of a plea of guilty thereto or commencement of a trial thereof, the court, upon motion of a defendant, may order that all proceedings be suspended and the action adjourned in contemplation of dismissal, or upon a finding that adjournment would not be necessary or appropriate and the setting forth in the record of the reasons for such findings, may dismiss in furtherance of justice the accusatory instrument; provided, however, that the court may not order such adjournment in contemplation of dismissal or dismiss the accusatory instrument if: (a) the defendant has previously been granted such adjournment in contemplation of dismissal, or (b) the defendant has previously been granted a dismissal under this section, or (c) the defendant has previously been convicted of any offense involving controlled substances, or (d) the defendant has previously been convicted of a crime and the district attorney does not consent or (e) the defendant has previously been adjudicated a youthful offender on the basis of any act or acts involving controlled substances and the district attorney does not consent.

2. Upon ordering the action adjourned in contemplation of dismissal, the court must set and specify such conditions for the adjournment as may be appropriate, and such conditions may include placing the defendant under the supervision of any public or private agency. At any time prior to dismissal the court may modify the conditions or extend or reduce the term of the adjournment, except that the total period of adjournment shall not exceed twelve months. Upon violation of any condition fixed by the court, the court may revoke its order and restore the case to the calendar and the prosecution thereupon must proceed. If the case is not so restored to the calendar during the period fixed by the court, the accusatory instrument is, at the expiration of such period, deemed to have been dismissed in the furtherance of justice.

3. Upon or after dismissal of such charges against a defendant not previously convicted of a crime, the court shall order that all official records and papers, relating to the defendant's arrest and prosecution, whether on file with the court, a police agency, or the New York state division of criminal justice services, be sealed and, except as otherwise provided in paragraph (d) of subdivision one of section 160.50 of this chapter, not made available to any person or public or private agency; except, such records shall be made available under order of a court for the purpose of determining whether, in subsequent proceedings, such person qualifies under this section for a dismissal or adjournment in contemplation of dismissal of the accusatory instrument.

4. Upon the granting of an order pursuant to subdivision three, the arrest and prosecution shall be deemed a nullity and the defendant shall be restored, in contemplation of law, to the status he occupied before his arrest and prosecution.

HISTORY: Add, L 1971, ch 1042, § 1, eff Sept 1, 1971. Sub 1, amd, L 1973, ch 276, § 22, L 1977, ch 360, § 9, eff July 29, 1977 and applicable to acts committed on or after such date. Sub 3, amd, L 1977, ch 905, § 2, eff Aug 11, 1977.

§ 170.60. Requirement of plea to information, simplified information or prosecutor's information

Unless an information, a simplified information or a prosecutor's information is dismissed or the criminal action thereon terminated or abated pursuant to a provision of this article or some other provision of law, the defendant must be required to enter a plea thereto.

HISTORY: Add, L 1970, ch 996, § 1; amd, L 1972, ch 661, § 43, eff Sept 1, 1972. Section heading, amd, L 1972, ch 661, § 43, eff Sept 1, 1972.

§ 170.65. Replacement of misdemeanor complaint by information and waiver thereof

1. A defendant against whom a misdemeanor complaint is pending is not required to enter a plea thereto. For purposes of prosecution, such instrument must, except as provided in subdivision three, be replaced by an information, and the defendant must be arraigned thereon. If the misdemeanor complaint is supplemented by a supporting deposition and such instruments taken together satisfy the requirements for a valid information, such misdemeanor complaint is deemed to have been converted to and to constitute a replacing information.

2. An information which replaces a misdemeanor complaint need not charge the same offense or offenses, but at least one count thereof must charge the commission by the defendant of an offense based upon conduct which was the subject of the misdemeanor complaint. In addition, the information may, subject to the rules of joinder, charge any other offense which the factual allegations thereof or of any supporting depositions accompanying it are legally sufficient to support, even though such offense is not based upon conduct which was the subject of the misdemeanor complaint.

3. A defendant who has been arraigned upon a misdemeanor complaint may waive prosecution by information and consent to be prosecuted upon the misdemeanor complaint. In such case, the defendant must be required, either upon the date of the waiver or subsequent thereto, to enter a plea to the misdemeanor complaint.

HISTORY: Add, L 1970, ch 996, § 1, eff Sept 1, 1971.

§ 170.70. Release of defendant upon failure to replace misdemeanor complaint by information

Upon application of a defendant against whom a misdemeanor complaint is pending in a local criminal court, and who, either at the time of his arraignment thereon or subsequent thereto, has been committed to the custody of the sheriff pending disposition of the action, and who has been confined in such custody for a period of more than five days, not including Sunday, without any information having been filed in replacement of such misdemeanor complaint, the criminal court must release the defendant on his own recognizance unless:

1. The defendant has waived prosecution by information and consented to be prosecuted upon the misdemeanor complaint, pursuant to subdivision three of section 170.65; or

2. The court is satisfied that there is good cause why such order of release should not be issued. Such good cause must consist of some compelling fact or circumstance which precluded replacement of the misdemeanor complaint by an information or a prosecutor's information within the prescribed period.

HISTORY: Add, L 1970, ch 996, § 1, eff Sept 1, 1971.

§ 170.75. [Repealed]

HISTORY: Add, L 1970, ch 996, § 1; repealed, L 1978, ch 481, § 10, eff Sept 1, 1978.

§ 170.80. Proceedings regarding certain prostitution charges; certain persons aged sixteen or seventeen

1. Notwithstanding any other provision of law, at any time at or after arraignment on a charge of prostitution pursuant to section 230.00 of the penal law or loitering for the purposes of prostitution pursuant to subdivision two of section 240.37 of the penal law, provided that the person does not stand charged with loitering for the purpose of patronizing a prostitute, where such

offense allegedly occurred when the person was sixteen or seventeen years of age except where, after consultation with counsel, a knowing and voluntary plea of guilty has been entered to such charge, any judge or justice hearing any stage of such case may, upon consent of the defendant after consultation with counsel:

(a) conditionally convert such charge in accordance with subdivision three of this section and retain it as a person in need of supervision proceeding for all purposes, and shall make such proceeding fully subject to the provisions and grant any relief available under article seven of the family court act; and/or

(b) order the provision of any of the specialized services enumerated in title eight-A of article six of the social services law, as may be reasonably available.

2. In the event of a conviction by plea or verdict to such charge or charges of prostitution or loitering for the purposes of prostitution as described in subdivision one of this section, the court must find that the person is a youthful offender for the purpose of such charge and proceed in accordance with article seven hundred twenty of this chapter, provided, however, that the available sentence shall be the sentence that may be imposed for a violation as defined in subdivision three of section 10.00 of the penal law. In such case, the records of the investigation and proceedings relating to such charge shall be sealed in accordance with section 720.35 of this chapter.

3. (a) When a charge of prostitution or loitering for the purposes of prostitution has been conditionally converted to a person in need of supervision proceeding pursuant to subdivision one of this section, the defendant shall be deemed a "sexually exploited child" as defined in subdivision one of section four hundred forty-seven-a of the social services law and therefore shall not be considered an adult for purposes related to the charges in the person in need of supervision proceeding. Sections seven hundred eighty-one, seven hundred eighty-two, seven hundred eighty-two-a, seven hundred eighty-three and seven hundred eighty-four of the family court act shall apply to any proceeding conditionally converted under this section.

(b) The court after hearing from the parties shall state the condition or conditions of such conversion, which may include the individual's participation in specialized services provided pursuant to title eight-A of article six of the social services law and other appropriate services available to persons in need of supervision in accordance with article seven of the family court act.

(c) (i) The court may, upon written application by the people at any time during the pendency of the person in need of supervision proceeding or during any disposition thereof, but in no event later than the individual's eighteenth birthday, restore the accusatory instrument if the court is satisfied by competent proof that the individual, without just cause, is not in substantial compliance with the condition or conditions of the conversion.

(ii) Notice of such an application to restore an accusatory instrument shall be served on the person and his or her counsel by the court. The notice shall include a statement setting forth a reasonable description of why the person is not in substantial compliance with the condition or conditions of the conversion and a date upon which such person shall appear before the court. The court shall afford the person the right to counsel and the right to be heard. Upon such appearance, the court must advise the person of the contents of the notice and the consequences of a finding of failure to substantially comply with the conditions of conversion. At the time of such appearance the court must ask the person whether he or she wishes to make any statement with respect to such alleged failure to substantially comply. In determining whether such person has failed to substantially comply with the terms of the conversion, the court shall conduct a hearing at which time such person may cross-examine witnesses and present evidence on his or her own behalf. Any findings the court shall make, shall be made on the court record. If the court finds that such person did not substantially comply, it may restore the accusatory instrument pursuant to subparagraph (i) of this paragraph, modify the terms of conversion in accordance with this section or otherwise continue such terms as in its discretion it deems just and proper.

(iii) If such accusatory instrument is restored pursuant to subparagraph (i) of this paragraph, the proceeding shall continue in accordance with subdivision two of this section. If the individual does not comply with services or does not return to court, the individual shall be returned in accordance with the provisions of article seven of the family court act.

4. At the conclusion of a person in need of supervision proceeding pursuant to this section, all records of the investigation and proceedings relating to such proceedings, including records created before the charge was conditionally converted, shall be sealed in accordance with section 720.35 of this chapter.

HISTORY: Add, L 2013, ch 555, § 1, eff Jan 10, 2014; amd, L 2014, ch 402, § 2, eff Oct 16, 2014.

ARTICLE 180   PROCEEDINGS UPON FELONY COMPLAINT FROM ARRAIGNMENT THEREON THROUGH DISPOSITION THEREOF

HISTORY: Add, L 1970, ch 996, § 1, eff Sept 1, 1971.

§ 180.10. Proceedings upon felony complaint; arraignment; defendant's rights, court's instructions and bail matters

1. Upon the defendant's arraignment before a local criminal court upon a felony complaint, the court must immediately inform him, or cause him to be informed in its presence, of the charge or charges against him and that the primary purpose of the proceedings upon such felony complaint is to determine whether the defendant is to be held for the action of a grand jury with respect to the charges contained therein. The court must furnish the defendant with a copy of the felony complaint.

2. The defendant has a right to a prompt hearing upon the issue of whether there is sufficient evidence to warrant the court in holding him for the action of a grand jury, but he may waive such right.

3. The defendant has a right to the aid of counsel at the arraignment and at every subsequent stage of the action, and, if he appears upon such arraignment without counsel, has the following rights:

(a) To an adjournment for the purpose of obtaining counsel; and

(b) To communicate, free of charge, by letter or by telephone provided by the law enforcement facility where the defendant is held to a phone number located in the United States or Puerto Rico, for the purpose of obtaining counsel and informing a relative or friend that he or she has been charged with an offense; and

(c) To have counsel assigned by the court in any case where he is financially unable to obtain the same.

4. The court must inform the defendant of all rights specified in subdivisions two and three. The court must accord the defendant opportunity to exercise such rights and must itself take such affirmative action as is necessary to effectuate them.

5. If the defendant desires to proceed without the aid of counsel, the court must permit him to do so if it is satisfied that he made such decision with knowledge of the significance thereof, but if it is not so satisfied it may not proceed until the defendant is provided with counsel, either of his own choosing or by assignment. A defendant who proceeds at the arraignment without counsel does not waive his right to counsel, and the court must inform him that he continues to have such right as well as all the rights specified in subdivision three which are necessary to effectuate it, and that he may exercise such rights at any stage of the action.

6. Upon the arraignment, the court, unless it intends immediately thereafter to dismiss the felony complaint and terminate the action, must issue a securing order which, as provided in subdivision two of section 530.20, either releases the defendant on his own recognizance or fixes bail or commits him to the custody of the sheriff for his future appearance in such action.

HISTORY: Add, L 1970, ch 996, § 1; amd, L 2010, ch 94, § 4, eff July 24, 2010.

§ 180.20. Proceedings upon felony complaint; removal of action from one local criminal court to another

Under circumstances prescribed in this section, a criminal action based upon a pending felony complaint may be removed from one local criminal court to another:

1. When a defendant arrested by a police officer for a felony allegedly committed in a town has not been brought before the town court of the town, or as the case may be before the village court of the village, in which the felony charged was allegedly committed, but, instead, to another local criminal court of the county and there stands charged with such offense by felony complaint, such latter court must arraign him upon such felony complaint. Such court must then either:

(a) Dispose of the felony complaint pursuant to this article. If such disposition results in a reduction of the felony charge and the filing of an information or prosecutor's information charging a misdemeanor or a petty offense pursuant to section 180.50 or subdivision two or three of section 180.70, such court must conduct the action to judgment or other final disposition; or

(b) Remit the action upon the felony complaint, together with all pertinent papers and documents, to the town court of the town, or as the case may be to the village court of the village, in which the felony charged was allegedly committed. In such case, the latter court must dispose of the felony complaint pursuant to this article.

1-a. When a defendant arrested by a police officer for a felony allegedly committed in a city has not been brought before the city court of such city but, instead, to the local criminal court of an adjoining town or village of the same county and there stands charged with such offense by felony complaint, such latter court must arraign him upon such felony complaint. Such court must then either:

(a) Dispose of the felony complaint pursuant to this article. If such disposition results in a reduction of the felony charge and the filing of an information or prosecutor's information charging a misdemeanor or a petty offense pursuant to section 180.50 or subdivision two or three of section 180.70 of this article, such court must conduct the action to judgment or other final disposition; or

(b) Remit the action upon the felony complaint, together with all pertinent papers and documents, to the city court of the city in which the felony charged was allegedly committed. In such case, the latter court must dispose of the felony complaint pursuant to this article.

2. When a defendant arrested by a police officer for a felony has been brought before a superior court judge sitting as a local criminal court for arraignment upon a felony complaint charging such felony, such judge must, as a local criminal court, arraign the defendant upon such felony complaint. Such court must then either:

(a) Dispose of the felony complaint pursuant to this article. If however, such disposition results in a reduction of the charge and the filing of an information or prosecutor's information charging a misdemeanor or a petty offense, such judge, after arraigning the defendant upon such accusatory instrument, must remit the action, together with all pertinent papers and documents, to a local criminal court having trial jurisdiction of the offense charged, and the latter court must then conduct the action to judgment or other final disposition; or

(b) Remit the action upon the felony complaint, together with all pertinent papers and documents, to a local criminal court having geographical jurisdiction over the area in which the felony charged was allegedly committed. In such case, such latter court must dispose of the felony complaint pursuant to this article.

3. Notwithstanding any provision of this section to the contrary, in any county outside a city having a population of one million or more, upon or after arraignment of a defendant on a felony complaint pending in a local criminal court having preliminary jurisdiction thereof, such court may, upon motion of the defendant and with the consent of the district attorney, order that the action be removed from the court in which the matter is pending to another local criminal court in the same county which has been designated a drug court by the chief administrator of the courts, and such drug court may then dispose of such felony complaint pursuant to this article; provided, however, that an order of removal issued under this subdivision shall not take effect until five days after the date the order is issued unless, prior to such effective date, the drug court notifies the court that issued the order that:

(a) it will not accept the action, in which event the order shall not take effect, or

(b) it will accept the action on a date prior to such effective date, in which event the order shall take effect upon such prior date.

Upon providing notification pursuant to paragraph (a) or (b) of this subdivision, the drug court shall promptly give notice to the defendant, his or her counsel and the district attorney.

HISTORY: Add, L 1970, ch 996, § 1, eff Sept 1, 1971. Sub 1, amd, L 1986, ch 5, § 3, eff June 12, 1986. Sub 1-a, add, L 1984, ch 695, § 4, eff Aug 1, 1984. Sub 3, amd, L 2000, ch 67, § 2, eff Nov 1, 2000. Sub 3, opening par, formerly entire sub 3, add, L 1998, ch 77, § 2, eff June 2, 1998; so designated sub 3, opening par and amd, L 1999, ch 565, § 2, eff Nov 1, 1999; amd, L 2000, ch 67, § 2, eff Nov 1, 2000. Sub 3, par (a), add, L 1999, ch 565, § 2, eff Nov 1, 1999. Sub 3, par (b), add, L 1999, ch 565, § 2, eff Nov 1, 1999. Sub 3, closing par, add, L 1999, ch 565, § 2, eff Nov 1, 1999.

§ 180.30. Proceedings upon felony complaint; waiver of hearing; action to be taken

If the defendant waives a hearing upon the felony complaint, the court must either:

1. Order that the defendant be held for the action of a grand jury of the appropriate superior court with respect to the charge or charges contained in the felony complaint. In such case, the court must promptly transmit to such superior court the order, the felony complaint, the supporting depositions and all other pertinent documents. Until such papers are received by the superior court, the action is deemed to be still pending in the local criminal court; or

2. Make inquiry, pursuant to section 180.50, for the purpose of determining whether the felony complaint should be dismissed and an information, a prosecutor's information or a misdemeanor complaint filed with the court in lieu thereof.

HISTORY: Add, L 1970, ch 996, § 1, eff Sept 1, 1971, with substance derived from Crim C § 190.

§ 180.40. Proceedings upon felony complaint; application in superior court following hearing or waiver of hearing

Where the local criminal court has held a defendant for the action of a grand jury, the district attorney may, at any time before such matter is submitted to the grand jury, apply, ex parte, to the appropriate superior court for an order directing that the felony complaint and other papers transmitted to such court pursuant to subdivision one of section 180.30 be returned to the local criminal court for reconsideration of the action to be taken. The superior court may issue such an order if it is satisfied that the felony complaint is defective or that such action is required in the interest of justice.

HISTORY: Add, L 1970, ch 996, § 1, with substance derived from Crim C § 190-a; amd, L 1974, ch 83, § 1, eff March 19, 1974. Section heading, amd, L 1974, ch 83, § 1, eff March 19, 1974.

§ 180.50. Proceedings upon felony complaint; reduction of charge

1. Whether or not the defendant waives a hearing upon the felony complaint, the local criminal court may, upon consent of the district attorney, make inquiry for the purpose of determining whether (a) the available facts and evidence relating to the conduct underlying the felony complaint provide a basis for charging the defendant with an offense other than a felony, and (b) if so, whether the charge should, in the manner prescribed in subdivision three, be reduced from one for a felony to one for a non-felony offense. Upon such inquiry, the court may question any person who it believes may possess information relevant to the matter, including the defendant if he wishes to be questioned.

2. If after such inquiry the court is satisfied that there is reasonable cause to believe that the defendant committed an offense other than a felony, it may order the indicated reduction as follows:

(a) If there is not reasonable cause to believe that the defendant committed a felony in addition to the non-felony offense in question, the court may as a matter of right order a reduction of the charge to one for the non-felony offense;

(b) If there is reasonable cause to believe that the defendant committed a felony in addition to the non-felony offense, the court may order a reduction of the charge to one for the non-felony offense only if (i) it is satisfied that such reduction is in the interest of justice, and (ii) the district attorney consents thereto; provided, however, that the court may not order such reduction where there is reasonable cause to believe that the defendant committed a class A felony, other than those defined in article two hundred twenty of the penal law, or any armed felony as defined in subdivision forty-one of section 1.20.

3. A charge is "reduced" from a felony to a non-felony offense, within the meaning of this section, by replacing the felony complaint with, or converting it to, another local criminal court accusatory instrument, as follows:

(a) If the factual allegations of the felony complaint and/or any supporting depositions are legally sufficient to support the charge that the defendant committed the non-felony offense in question, the court may:

(i) Direct the district attorney to file with the court a prosecutor's information charging the defendant with such non-felony offense; or

(ii) Request the complainant of the felony complaint to file with the court an information charging the defendant with such non-felony offense. If such an information is filed, any supporting deposition supporting or accompanying the felony complaint is deemed also to support or accompanying [accompany]* the replacing information; or

(iii) Convert the felony complaint, or a copy thereof, into an information by notations upon or attached thereto which make the necessary and appropriate changes in the title of the instrument and in the names of the offense or offenses charged. In case of such conversion, any supporting deposition supporting or accompanying the felony complaint is deemed also to support or accompany the information to which it has been converted;

(b) If the non-felony offense in question is a misdemeanor, and if the factual allegations of the felony complaint together with those of any supporting depositions, though providing reasonable cause to believe that the defendant committed such misdemeanor are not legally sufficient to support such misdemeanor charge, the court may cause such felony complaint to be replaced by or converted to a misdemeanor complaint charging the misdemeanor in question, in the manner prescribed in subparagraphs two and three of paragraph (a) of this subdivision.

(c) An information, a prosecutor's information or a misdemeanor complaint filed pursuant to this section may, pursuant to the ordinary rules of joinder, charge two or more offenses, and it may jointly charge with each offense any two or more defendants originally so charged in the felony complaint;

(d) Upon the filing of an information, a prosecutor's information or a misdemeanor complaint pursuant to this section, the court must dismiss the felony complaint from which such accusatory instrument is derived. It must then arraign the defendant upon the new accusatory instrument and inform him of his rights in connection therewith in the manner provided in section 170.10.

4. Upon making any finding other than that specified in subdivision two, the court must conduct a hearing upon the felony complaint, unless the defendant has waived the same. In the case of such waiver the court must order that the defendant be held for the action of a grand jury.

---

* The bracketed word has been inserted by the Publisher.

HISTORY: Add, L 1970, ch 996, § 1, eff Sept 1, 1971. Sub 2, par (b), amd, L 1978, ch 481, § 11, eff Sept 1, 1978.

§ 180.60. Proceedings upon felony complaint; the hearing; conduct thereof

A hearing upon a felony complaint must be conducted as follows:

1. The district attorney must conduct such hearing on behalf of the people.

2. The defendant may as a matter of right be present at such hearing.

3. The court must read to the defendant the felony complaint and any supporting depositions unless the defendant waives such reading.

4. Each witness, whether called by the people or by the defendant, must, unless he would be authorized to give unsworn evidence at a trial, testify under oath. Each witness, including any defendant testifying in his own behalf, may be cross-examined.

5. The people must call and examine witnesses and offer evidence in support of the charge.

6. The defendant may, as a matter of right, testify in his own behalf.

7. Upon request of the defendant, the court may, as a matter of discretion, permit him to call and examine other witnesses or to produce other evidence in his behalf.

8. Upon such a hearing, only non-hearsay evidence is admissible to demonstrate reasonable cause to believe that the defendant committed a felony; except that reports of experts and technicians in professional and scientific fields and sworn statements of the kinds specified in subdivisions two and three of section 190.30 are admissible to the same extent as in a grand jury proceeding, unless the court determines, upon application of the defendant, that such hearsay evidence is, under the particular circumstances of the case, not sufficiently reliable, in which case the court shall require that the witness testify in person and be subject to cross-examination.

9. The court may, upon application of the defendant, exclude the public from the hearing and direct that no disclosure be made of the proceedings.

10. Such hearing should be completed at one session. In the interest of justice, however, it may be adjourned by the court but, in the absence of a showing of good cause therefor, no such adjournment may be for more than one day.

HISTORY: Add, L 1970, ch 996, § 1; amd, L 1975, ch 307, § 1, eff June 24, 1975. Sub 8, amd, L 1975, ch 307, § 1, eff June 24, 1975.

§ 180.70. Proceedings upon felony complaint; disposition of felony complaint after hearing

At the conclusion of a hearing, the court must dispose of the felony complaint as follows:

1. If there is reasonable cause to believe that the defendant committed a felony, the court must, except as provided in subdivision three, order that the defendant be held for the action of a grand jury of the appropriate superior court, and it must promptly transmit to such superior court the order, the felony complaint, the supporting depositions and all other pertinent documents. Until such papers are received by the superior court, the action is deemed to be still pending in the local criminal court.

2. If there is not reasonable cause to believe that the defendant committed a felony but there is reasonable cause to believe that he committed an offense other than a felony, the court may, by means of procedures prescribed in subdivision three of section 180.50, reduce the charge to one for such non-felony offense.

3. If there is reasonable cause to believe that the defendant committed a felony in addition to a non-felony offense, the court may, instead of ordering the defendant held for the action of a grand jury as provided in subdivision one, reduce the charge to one for such non-felony offense as provided in subdivision two, if (a) it is satisfied that such reduction is in the interest of justice, and (b) the district attorney consents thereto; provided, however, that the court may not order such reduction where there is reasonable cause to believe the defendant committed a class A felony, other than those defined in article two hundred twenty of the penal law, or any armed felony as defined in subdivision forty-one of section 1.20.

4. If there is not reasonable cause to believe that the defendant committed any offense, the court must dismiss the felony complaint and discharge the defendant from custody if he is in custody, or, if he is at liberty on bail, it must exonerate the bail.

HISTORY: Add, L 1970, ch 996, § 1, eff Sept 1, 1971. Sub 3, amd, L 1978, ch 481, § 13, eff Sept 1, 1978.

§ 180.75. Proceedings upon felony complaint; juvenile offender

1. When a juvenile offender is arraigned before a local criminal court, the provisions of this section shall apply in lieu of the provisions of sections 180.30, 180.50 and 180.70 of this article.

2. If the defendant waives a hearing upon the felony complaint, the court must order that the defendant be held for the action of the grand jury of the appropriate superior court with respect to the charge or charges contained in the felony complaint. In such case the court must promptly transmit to such superior court the order, the felony complaint, the supporting depositions and all other pertinent documents. Until such papers are received by the superior court, the action is deemed to be still pending in the local criminal court.

3. If there be a hearing, then at the conclusion of the hearing, the court must dispose of the felony complaint as follows:

(a) If there is reasonable cause to believe that the defendant committed a crime for which a person under the age of sixteen is criminally responsible, the court must order that the defendant be held for the action of a grand jury of the appropriate superior court, and it must promptly transmit to such superior court the order, the felony complaint, the supporting depositions and all other pertinent documents. Until such papers are received by the superior court, the action is deemed to be still pending in the local criminal court; or

(b) If there is not reasonable cause to believe that the defendant committed a crime for which a person under the age of sixteen is criminally responsible but there is reasonable cause to believe that the defendant is a "juvenile delinquent" as defined in subdivision one of section 301.2 of the family court act, the court must specify the act or acts it found reasonable cause to believe the defendant did and direct that the action be removed to the family court in accordance with the provisions of article seven hundred twenty-five of this chapter; or

(c) If there is not reasonable cause to believe that the defendant committed any criminal act, the court must dismiss the felony complaint and discharge the defendant from custody if he is in custody, or if he is at liberty on bail, it must exonerate the bail.

4. Notwithstanding the provisions of subdivisions two and three of this section, a local criminal court shall, at the request of the district attorney, order removal of an action against a juvenile offender to the family court pursuant to the provisions of article seven hundred twenty-five of this chapter if, upon consideration of the criteria specified in subdivision two of section 210.43 of this chapter, it is determined that to do so would be in the interests of justice. Where, however, the

felony complaint charges the juvenile offender with murder in the second degree as defined in section 125.25 of the penal law, rape in the first degree as defined in subdivision one of section 130.35 of the penal law, criminal sexual act in the first degree as defined in subdivision one of section 130.50 of the penal law, or an armed felony as defined in paragraph (a) of subdivision forty-one of section 1.20 of this chapter, a determination that such action be removed to the family court shall, in addition, be based upon a finding of one or more of the following factors: (i) mitigating circumstances that bear directly upon the manner in which the crime was committed; or (ii) where the defendant was not the sole participant in the crime, the defendant's participation was relatively minor although not so minor as to constitute a defense to the prosecution; or (iii) possible deficiencies in proof of the crime.

5. Notwithstanding the provisions of subdivision two, three, or four, if a currently undetermined felony complaint against a juvenile offender is pending in a local criminal court, and the defendant has not waived a hearing pursuant to subdivision two and a hearing pursuant to subdivision three has not commenced, the defendant may move in the superior court which would exercise the trial jurisdiction of the offense or offenses charged were an indictment therefor to result, to remove the action to family court. The procedural rules of subdivisions one and two of section 210.45 of this chapter are applicable to a motion pursuant to this subdivision. Upon such motion, the superior court shall be authorized to sit as a local criminal court to exercise the preliminary jurisdiction specified in subdivisions two and three of this section, and shall proceed and determine the motion as provided in section 210.43 of this chapter; provided, however, that the exception provisions of paragraph (b) of subdivision one of such section 210.43 shall not apply when there is not reasonable cause to believe that the juvenile offender committed one or more of the crimes enumerated therein, and in such event the provisions of paragraph (a) thereof shall apply.

6. (a) If the court orders removal of the action to family court, it shall state on the record the factor or factors upon which its determination is based, and the court shall give its reasons for removal in detail and not in conclusory terms.

(b) the district attorney shall state upon the record the reasons for his consent to removal of the action to the family court where such consent is required. The reasons shall be stated in detail and not in conclusory terms.

(c) For the purpose of making a determination pursuant to subdivision four or five, the court may make such inquiry as it deems necessary. Any evidence which is not legally privileged may be introduced. If the defendant testifies, his testimony may not be introduced against him in any future proceeding, except to impeach his testimony at such future proceeding as inconsistent prior testimony.

(d) Where a motion for removal by the defendant pursuant to subdivision five has been denied, no further motion pursuant to this section or section 210.43 of this chapter may be made by the juvenile offender with respect to the same offense or offenses.

(e) Except as provided by paragraph (f), this section shall not be construed to limit the powers of the grand jury.

(f) Where a motion by the defendant pursuant to subdivision five has been granted, there shall be no further proceedings against the juvenile offender in any local or superior criminal court for the offense or offenses which were the subject of the removal order.

HISTORY: Add, L 1978, ch 481, § 33, eff Sept 1, 1978. Sub 3, par (b), amd, L 1982, ch 920, § 74, eff July 1, 1983. Sub 4, add, L 1979, ch 411, § 5, eff Aug 4, 1979. Former sub 4, repealed, L 1979, ch 411, § 5, eff Aug 4, 1979. Sub 4, amd, L 2003, ch 264, § 38, eff Nov 1, 2003. Sub 5, add, L 1979, ch 411, § 5, eff Aug 4, 1979. Former sub 5, repealed, L 1979, ch 411, § 5, eff Aug 4,

1979. Sub 6, add, L 1979, ch 411, § 5, eff Aug 4, 1979.

§ 180.80. Proceedings upon felony complaint; release of defendant from custody upon failure of timely disposition

Upon application of a defendant against whom a felony complaint has been filed with a local criminal court, and who, since the time of his arrest or subsequent thereto, has been held in custody pending disposition of such felony complaint, and who has been confined in such custody for a period of more than one hundred twenty hours or, in the event that a Saturday, Sunday or legal holiday occurs during such custody, one hundred forty-four hours, without either a disposition of the felony complaint or commencement of a hearing thereon, the local criminal court must release him on his own recognizance unless:

1. The failure to dispose of the felony complaint or to commence a hearing thereon during such period of confinement was due to the defendant's request, action or condition, or occurred with his consent; or

2. Prior to the application:

(a) The district attorney files with the court a written certification that an indictment has been voted; or

(b) An indictment or a direction to file a prosecutor's information charging an offense based upon conduct alleged in the felony complaint was filed by a grand jury; or

3. The court is satisfied that the people have shown good cause why such order of release should not be issued. Such good cause must consist of some compelling fact or circumstance which precluded disposition of the felony complaint within the prescribed period or rendered such action against the interest of justice.

HISTORY: Add, L 1970, ch 996, § 1; amd, L 1982, ch 556, § 1, eff Aug 21, 1982. Sub 2, amd, L 1982, ch 557, § 1, eff Aug 21, 1982.

§ 180.85. Termination of prosecution

1. After arraignment of a defendant upon a felony complaint, other than a felony complaint charging an offense defined in section 125.10, 125.15, 125.20, 125.25, 125.26 or 125.27 of the penal law, either party or the local criminal court or superior court before which the action is pending, on its own motion, may move in accordance with the provisions of this section for an order terminating prosecution of the charges contained in such felony complaint on consent of the parties.

2. A motion to terminate a prosecution pursuant to this section may only be made where the count or counts of the felony complaint have not been presented to a grand jury or otherwise disposed of in accordance with this chapter. Such motion shall be filed in writing with the local criminal court or superior court in which the felony complaint is pending not earlier than twelve months following the date of arraignment on such felony complaint. Upon the filing of such motion, the court shall fix a return date and provide the parties with at least thirty days' written notice of the motion and return date.

3. Where, upon motion to terminate a prosecution pursuant to this section, both parties consent to such termination, the court, on the return date of such motion, shall enter an order terminating such prosecution. For purposes of this subdivision, a party that is given written notice of a motion to terminate a prosecution shall be deemed to consent to such termination unless, prior to the return date of such motion, such party files a notice of opposition thereto with the court. Except as otherwise provided in subdivision four, where such a notice of opposition is filed, the court, on the

return date of the motion, shall enter an order denying the motion to terminate the prosecution.

4. Notwithstanding any other provision of this section, where the people file a notice of opposition pursuant to subdivision three, the court, on the return date of the motion, may defer disposition of such motion for a period of forty-five days. In such event, if the count or counts of such felony complaint are presented to a grand jury or otherwise disposed of within such period, the court, upon the expiration thereof, shall enter an order denying the motion to terminate the prosecution. If such count or counts are not presented to a grand jury or otherwise disposed of within such period, the court, upon the expiration thereof, shall enter an order terminating the prosecution unless, within the forty-five day period, the people, on at least five days' written notice to the defendant, show good cause for their failure to present or otherwise dispose of such count or counts. If such good cause is shown, the court, upon expiration of the forty-five day period, shall enter an order denying the motion to terminate the prosecution.

5. Notwithstanding any other provision of law, the defendant's appearance in court on the return date of the motion or on any other date shall not be required as a prerequisite to entry of an order under this section.

6. The period from the filing of a motion pursuant to this section until entry of an order disposing of such motion shall not, by reason of such motion, be considered a period of delay for purposes of subdivision four of section 30.30, nor shall such period, by reason of such motion, be excluded in computing the time within which the people must be ready for trial pursuant to such section 30.30.

7. Where a prosecution is terminated pursuant to this section, nothing contained herein shall preclude the people from subsequently filing an indictment charging the same count or counts provided such filing is in accordance with the provisions of this section, article thirty and any other relevant provisions of this chapter. Where the people indicate their intention to seek an indictment following the entry of an order terminating a prosecution pursuant to this section, the court shall, notwithstanding any provision of section 160.50 to the contrary, stay sealing under that section for a reasonable period not to exceed thirty days to permit the people an opportunity to pursue such indictment.

8. Where an order denying a party's motion to terminate a prosecution is entered pursuant to this section, such party may not file a subsequent motion to terminate the prosecution pursuant to this section for at least six months from the date on which such order is entered.

9. Notwithstanding any other provision of this section, where a motion to terminate a prosecution is filed with a local criminal court pursuant to subdivision two, and, prior to the determination thereof, such court is divested of jurisdiction by the filing of an indictment charging the offense or offenses contained in the felony complaint, such motion shall be deemed to have been denied as of the date of such divestiture.

10. The chief administrator of the courts, in consultation with the director of the division of criminal justice services and representatives of appropriate prosecutorial and criminal defense organizations in the state, shall adopt forms for the motion to terminate a prosecution authorized by subdivision one and for the notice of opposition specified in subdivision three.

HISTORY: Add, L 2004, ch 518, § 2, eff Nov 1, 2004. Sub 1, amd, L 2006, ch 93, § 4, eff June 7, 2006.

ARTICLE 182 [EXPIRES AND REPEALED SEPT 1, 2015] ALTERNATE METHOD OF COURT APPEARANCE

§ 182.10. [Expires and repealed Sept 1, 2015] Definition of terms

HISTORY: Add, L 1993, ch 689, § 1, eff Aug 4, 1993, deemed eff July 1, 1992, expires and repealed Sept 1, 2015. Former Art 182 (§§ 182.10–182.40), add, L 1990, ch 894, § 1; repealed, L 1993, ch 689, § 1, eff Aug 4, 1993.

§ 182.10. [Expires and repealed Sept 1, 2015] Definition of terms

As used in this article:

1. "Independent audio-visual system" means an electronic system for the transmission and receiving of audio and visual signals, encompassing encoded signals, frequency domain multiplexing or other suitable means to preclude the unauthorized reception and decoding of the signals by commercially available television receivers, channel converters, or other available receiving devices.

2. "Electronic appearance" means an appearance in which various participants, including the defendant, are not present in the court, but in which, by means of an independent audio-visual system, (a) all of the participants are simultaneously able to see and hear reproductions of the voices and images of the judge, counsel, defendant, police officer, and any other appropriate participant, and (b) counsel is present with the defendant, or if the defendant waives the presence of counsel on the record, the defendant and his or her counsel are able to see and hear each other and engage in private conversation.

HISTORY: Add, L 1993, ch 689, § 1, eff Aug 4, 1993, deemed eff July 1, 1992, expires and repealed Sept 1, 2015. Former § 182.10, add, L 1990, ch 894, § 1; repealed, L 1993, ch 689, § 1, eff Aug 4, 1993.

§ 182.20. [Expires and repealed Sept 1, 2015] Electronic appearance; general rule

1. Notwithstanding any other provision of law and except as provided in section 182.30 of this article, the court, in its discretion, may dispense with the personal appearance of the defendant, except an appearance at a hearing or trial, and conduct an electronic appearance in connection with a criminal action pending in Albany, Bronx, Broome, Erie, Kings, New York, Niagara, Oneida, Onondaga, Ontario, Orange, Putnam, Queens, Richmond, St. Lawrence, Tompkins, Chautauqua, Cattaraugus, Clinton, Essex, Montgomery, Rensselaer, Warren, Westchester, Suffolk,Herkimer or Franklin county, provided that the chief administrator of the courts has authorized the use of electronic appearance and the defendant, after consultation with counsel, consents on the record. Such consent shall be required at the commencement of each electronic appearance to such electronic appearance.

2. If, for any reason, the court determines on its own motion or on the motion of any party that the conduct of an electronic appearance may impair the legal rights of the defendant, it shall not permit the electronic appearance to proceed. If, for any other articulated reason, either party requests at any time during the electronic appearance that such appearance be terminated, the court shall grant such request and adjourn the proceeding to a date certain. Upon the adjourned date the proceeding shall be recommenced from the point at which the request for termination of the electronic appearance had been granted.

3. The electronic appearance shall be conducted in accordance with rules issued by the chief administrator of the courts.

4. When the defendant makes an electronic appearance, the court stenographer shall record any statements in the same manner as if the defendant had made a personal appearance. No electronic recording of any electronic appearance may be made, viewed or inspected except as may be authorized by the rules issued by the chief administrator of the courts.

HISTORY: Add, L 1993, ch 689, § 1, eff Aug 4, 1993, deemed eff July 1, 1992, expires and repealed Sept 1, 2015. Sub 1, amd, L 1994, ch 522, § 1, L 1995, ch 124, § 2, eff July 5, 1995, L 2009, ch 332, § 1, eff Aug 11, 2009. Former § 182.20, add, L 1990, ch 894, § 1; amd, L 1991, ch 432, § 1, L 1991 ch 440, § 1; repealed, L 1993, ch 689, § 1, eff Aug 4, 1993. Sub 1, amd, L 1998, ch 177, § 1, eff July 7, 1998, L 1998, ch 430, § 1, eff July 22, 1998, L 1998, ch 605, § 2, eff Sept 30, 1998, L 1999, ch 426, § 1, eff Aug 31, 1999, L 1999, ch 430, § 1, eff Aug 31, 1999, L 2000, ch 514, § 1, eff Oct 4, 2000, L 2001, ch 315, § 2, eff Sept 19, 2001, L 2002, ch 57, § 1, eff May 7, 2002, L 2002, ch 62, § 1, eff May 7, 2002, L 2004, ch 167, § 1, eff July 20, 2004, L 2006, ch 470, § 1, eff Aug 16, 2006, L 2006, ch 532, § 1, eff Aug 16, 2006, L 2007, ch 29, § 1, eff May 14, 2007, L 2008, ch 317, § 1, eff July 21, 2008.

§ 182.30. [Expires and repealed Sept 1, 2015] Electronic appearance; conditions and limitations

The following conditions and limitations apply to all electronic appearances:

1. The defendant may not enter a plea of guilty to, or be sentenced upon a conviction of, a felony.

2. The defendant may not enter a plea of not responsible by reason of mental disease or defect.

3. The defendant may not be committed to the state department of mental hygiene pursuant to article seven hundred thirty of this chapter.

4. The defendant may not enter a plea of guilty to a misdemeanor conditioned upon a promise of incarceration unless such incarceration will be imposed only in the event that the defendant fails to comply with a term or condition imposed under the original sentence.

5. A defendant who has been convicted of a misdemeanor may not be sentenced to a period of incarceration which exceeds the time the defendant has already served when sentence is imposed.

HISTORY: Add, L 1993, ch 689, § 1, eff Aug 4, 1993, deemed eff July 1, 1992, expires and repealed Sept 1, 2015. Former § 182.30, add, L 1990, ch 894, § 1; repealed, L 1993, ch 689, § 1, eff Aug 4, 1993.

§ 182.40. [Expires and repealed Sept 1, 2015] Approval by the chief administrator of the courts

1. The appropriate administrative judge shall submit to the chief administrator of the courts a written proposal for the use of electronic appearance in his or her jurisdiction. If the chief administrator of the courts approves the proposal, installation of an independent audio-visual system may begin.

2. Upon completion of the installation of an independent audio-visual system, the commission on cable television shall inspect, test, and examine the independent audio-visual system and certify to the chief administrator of the courts whether the system complies with the definition of an independent audio-visual system and is technically suitable for the conducting of electronic appearances as intended.

3. The chief administrator of the courts shall issue rules governing the use of electronic appearances.

HISTORY: Add, L 1993, ch 689, § 1, eff Aug 4, 1993, deemed eff July 1, 1992, expires and repealed Sept 1, 2015. Former § 182.40, add, L 1990, ch 894, § 1; repealed, L 1993, ch 689, § 1, eff Aug 4, 1993.

ARTICLE 185   [EXPIRED]

HISTORY: Add, L 1978, ch 416, § 1; expired, Sept 1, 1983.

TITLE I   Preliminary Proceedings in Superior Court

ARTICLE 190
THE GRAND JURY AND ITS PROCEEDINGS

ARTICLE 195
WAIVER OF INDICTMENT

ARTICLE 200
INDICTMENT AND RELATED INSTRUMENTS

ARTICLE 210
PROCEEDINGS IN SUPERIOR COURT FROM FILING OF INDICTMENT TO PLEA

ARTICLE 215
ADJOURNMENT IN CONTEMPLATION OF DISMISSAL FOR PURPOSES OF
REFERRING SELECTED FELONIES TO DISPUTE RESOLUTION

ARTICLE 216
JUDICIAL DIVERSION PROGRAM FOR CERTAIN FELONY OFFENDERS

HISTORY: Add, L 1970, ch 996, § 1, eff Sept 1, 1971.

ARTICLE 190   THE GRAND JURY AND ITS PROCEEDINGS

HISTORY: Add, L 1970, ch 996, § 1, eff Sept 1, 1971.

§ 190.05. Grand jury; definition and general functions

A grand jury is a body consisting of not less than sixteen nor more than twenty-three persons, impaneled by a superior court and constituting a part of such court, the functions of which are to hear and examine evidence concerning offenses and concerning misconduct, nonfeasance and neglect in public office, whether criminal or otherwise, and to take action with respect to such evidence as provided in section 190.60.

> **HISTORY:** Add, L 1970, ch 996, § 1, eff Sept 1, 1971, with substance derived from Crim C §§ 223, 224.

§ 190.10. Grand jury; for what courts drawn

The appellate division of each judicial department shall adopt rules governing the number and the terms for which grand juries shall be drawn and impaneled by the superior courts within its department; provided, however, that a grand jury may be drawn and impaneled for any extraordinary term of the supreme court upon the order of a justice assigned to hold such term.

> **HISTORY:** Add, L 1970, ch 996, § 1, eff Sept 1, 1971.

§ 190.15. Grand Jury; duration of term and discharge

1. A term of a superior court for which a grand jury has been impaneled remains in existence at least until and including the opening date of the next term of such court for which a grand jury has been designated. Upon such date, or within five days preceding it, the court may, upon declaration of both the grand jury and the district attorney that such grand jury has not yet completed or will be unable to complete certain business before it, extend the term of court and the existence of such grand jury to a specified future date, and may subsequently order further extensions for such purpose.

2. At any time when a grand jury is in recess and no other appropriate grand jury is in existence in the county, the court may, upon application of the district attorney or of a defendant held by a local criminal court for the action of a grand jury, order such grand jury reconvened for the purpose of dealing with a matter requiring grand jury action.

> **HISTORY:** Add, L 1970, ch 996, § 1, eff Sept 1, 1971, with substance derived from Crim C § 244.

§ 190.20. Grand jury; formation, organization and other matters preliminary to assumption of duties

1. The mode of selecting grand jurors and of drawing and impaneling grand juries is governed by the judiciary law.

2. Neither the grand jury panel nor any individual grand juror may be challenged, but the court may:

(a) At any time before a grand jury is sworn, discharge the panel and summon another panel if it finds that the original panel does not substantially conform to the requirements of the judiciary law; or

(b) At any time after a grand juror is drawn, refuse to swear him, or discharge him after he has been sworn, upon a finding that he is disqualified from service pursuant to the judiciary law, or incapable of performing his duties because of bias or prejudice, or guilty of misconduct in the performance of his duties such as to impair the proper functioning of the grand jury.

3. After a grand jury has been impaneled, the court must appoint one of the grand jurors as foreman and another to act as foreman during any absence or disability of the foreman. At some time before commencement of their duties, the grand jurors must appoint one of their number as secretary to keep records material to the conduct of the grand jury's business.

4. The grand jurors must be sworn by the court. The oath may be in any form or language which requires the grand jurors to perform their duties faithfully.

5. After a grand jury has been sworn, the court must deliver or cause to be delivered to each grand juror a printed copy of all the provisions of this article, and the court may, in addition, give the grand jurors any oral and written instructions relating to the proper performance of their duties as it deems necessary or appropriate.

6. If two or more grand juries are impaneled at the same court term, the court may thereafter, for good cause, transfer grand jurors from one panel to another, and any grand juror so transferred is deemed to have been sworn as a member of the panel to which he has been transferred.

    HISTORY: Add, L 1970, ch 996, § 1, eff Sept 1, 1971. Sub 5, amd, L 2000, ch 497, § 1, eff Nov 1, 2000.

§ 190.25. Grand jury; proceedings and operation in general

1. Proceedings of a grand jury are not valid unless at least sixteen of its members are present. The finding of an indictment, a direction to file a prosecutor's information, a decision to submit a grand jury report and every other affirmative official action or decision requires the concurrence of at least twelve members thereof.

2. The foreman or any other grand juror may administer an oath to any witness appearing before the grand jury.

3. Except as provided in subdivision three-a of this section, during the deliberations and voting of a grand jury, only the grand jurors may be present in the grand jury room. During its other proceedings, the following persons, in addition to witnesses, may, as the occasion requires, also be present:

    (a) The district attorney;

    (b) A clerk or other public servant authorized to assist the grand jury in the administrative conduct of its proceedings;

    (c) A stenographer authorized to record the proceedings of the grand jury;

    (d) An interpreter. Upon request of the grand jury, the prosecutor must provide an interpreter to interpret the testimony of any witness who does not speak the English language well enough to be readily understood. Such interpreter must, if he has not previously taken the constitutional oath of office, first take an oath before the grand jury that he will faithfully interpret the testimony of the witness and that he will keep secret all matters before such grand jury within his knowledge;

    (e) A public servant holding a witness in custody. When a person held in official custody is a witness before a grand jury, a public servant assigned to guard him during his grand jury appearance may accompany him in the grand jury room. Such public servant must, if he has not previously taken the constitutional oath of office, first take an oath before the grand jury that he will keep secret all matters before it within his knowledge.

    (f) An attorney representing a witness pursuant to section 190.52 of this chapter while that witness is present.

    (g) An operator, as that term is defined in section 190.32 of this chapter, while the videotaped examination of either a special witness or a child witness is being played.

    (h) A social worker, rape crisis counselor, psychologist or other professional providing emotional support to a child witness twelve years old or younger, or a social worker or informal caregiver, as provided in subdivision two of section two hundred six of the elder law, for a vulnerable elderly person as provided in subdivision three of section 260.31 of the penal law, who is called to give evidence in a grand jury proceeding concerning a crime defined in article one hundred twenty-one, article one hundred thirty, article two hundred sixty, section 120.10, 125.10, 125.15, 125.20, 125.25, 125.26, 125.27, 255.25, 255.26 or 255.27 of the penal law provided that the district attorney consents. Such support person shall not provide the witness with an answer to any question or otherwise participate in such proceeding and shall first take an oath before the grand jury that he or she will keep secret all matters before such grand jury within his or her knowledge.

3-a. Upon the request of a deaf or hearing-impaired grand juror, the prosecutor shall provide a sign language interpreter for such juror. Such interpreter shall be present during all proceedings of the grand jury which the deaf or hearing-impaired grand juror attends, including deliberation and voting. The interpreter shall, if he or she has not previously taken the constitutional oath of office, first take an oath before the grand jury that he or she will faithfully interpret the testimony of the witnesses and the statements of the prosecutor, judge and grand jurors; keep secret all matters before such grand jury within his or her knowledge; and not seek to influence the deliberations and voting of such grand jury.

4. (a) Grand jury proceedings are secret, and no grand juror, or other person specified in subdivision three of this section or section 215.70 of the penal law, may, except in the lawful discharge of his duties or upon written order of the court, disclose the nature or substance of any grand jury testimony, evidence, or any decision, result or other matter attending a grand jury proceeding. For the purpose of assisting the grand jury in conducting its investigation, evidence obtained by a grand jury may be independently examined by the district attorney, members of his staff, police officers specifically assigned to the investigation, and such other persons as the court may specifically authorize. Such evidence may not be disclosed to other persons without a court order. Nothing contained herein shall prohibit a witness from disclosing his own testimony.

(b) When a district attorney obtains evidence during a grand jury proceeding which provides reasonable cause to suspect that a child has been abused or maltreated, as those terms are defined by section ten hundred twelve of the family court act, he must apply to the court supervising the grand jury for an order permitting disclosure of such evidence to the state central register of child abuse and maltreatment. A district attorney need not apply to the court for such order if he has previously made or caused a report to be made to the state central register of child abuse and maltreatment pursuant to section four hundred thirteen of the social services law and the evidence obtained during the grand jury proceeding, or substantially similar information, was included in such report. The district attorney's application to the court shall be made ex parte and in camera. The court must grant the application and permit the district attorney to disclose the evidence to the state central register of child abuse and maltreatment unless the court finds that such disclosure would jeopardize the life or safety of any person or interfere with a continuing grand jury proceeding.

5. The grand jury is the exclusive judge of the facts with respect to any matter before it.

6. The legal advisors of the grand jury are the court and the district attorney, and the grand jury may not seek or receive legal advice from any other source. Where necessary or appropriate, the court or the district attorney, or both, must instruct the grand jury concerning the law with respect to its duties or any matter before it, and such instructions must be recorded in the minutes.

CPL

HISTORY: Add, L 1970, ch 996, § 1, eff Sept 1, 1971; amd, L 1977, ch 451, § 3, L 1978, ch 415, § 1, L 1978, ch 447, § 1, eff Sept 1, 1978, L 1984, ch 804, § 4, eff Nov 1, 1984, L 1985, ch 650, § 1, L 1985, ch 677, § 28, eff Jan 1, 1986, L 1986, ch 63, § 1, L 1987, ch 613, § 1, eff Aug 3, 1987, L 1994, ch 198, §§ 1, 2, eff Nov 1, 1994, L 2006, ch 93, § 5, eff June 7, 2006, L 2006, ch 320, § 16, eff Nov 1, 2006, L 2010, ch 405, § 3, eff Nov 11, 2010, L 2014, ch 347, § 1, eff Sept 4, 2014.

§ 190.30. Grand jury; rules of evidence

1. Except as otherwise provided in this section, the provisions of article sixty, governing rules of evidence and related matters with respect to criminal proceedings in general, are, where appropriate, applicable to grand jury proceedings.

2. A report or a copy of a report made by a public servant or by a person employed by a public servant or agency who is a physicist, chemist, coroner or medical examiner, firearms identification expert, examiner of questioned documents, fingerprint technician, or an expert or technician in some comparable scientific or professional field, concerning the results of an examination, comparison or test performed by him in connection with a case which is the subject of a grand jury proceeding, may, when certified by such person as a report made by him or as a true copy thereof, be received in such grand jury proceeding as evidence of the facts stated therein.

2-a. When the electronic transmission of a certified report, or certified copy thereof, of the kind described in subdivision two or three-a of this section or a sworn statement or copy thereof, of the kind described in subdivision three of this section results in a written document, such written document may be received in such grand jury proceeding provided that: (a) a transmittal memorandum completed by the person sending the report contains a certification that the report has not been altered and a description of the report specifying the number of pages; and (b) the person who receives the electronically transmitted document certifies that such document and transmittal memorandum were so received; and (c) a certified report or a certified copy or sworn statement or sworn copy thereof is filed with the court within twenty days following arraignment upon the indictment; and (d) where such written document is a sworn statement or sworn copy thereof of the kind described in subdivision three of this section, such sworn statement or sworn copy thereof is also provided to the defendant or his counsel within twenty days following arraignment upon the indictment.

3. A written or oral statement, under oath, by a person attesting to one or more of the following matters may be received in such grand jury proceeding as evidence of the facts stated therein:

(a) that person's ownership or lawful custody of, or license to occupy, premises, as defined in section 140.00 of the penal law, and of the defendant's lack of license or privilege to enter or remain thereupon;

(b) that person's ownership of, or possessory right in, property, the nature and monetary amount of any damage thereto and the defendant's lack of right to damage or tamper with the property;

(c) that person's ownership or lawful custody of, or license to possess property, as defined in section 155.00 of the penal law, including an automobile or other vehicle, its value and the defendant's lack of superior or equal right to possession thereof;

(d) that person's ownership of a vehicle and the absence of his consent to the defendant's taking, operating, exercising control over or using it;

(e) that person's qualifications as a dealer or other expert in appraising or evaluating a particular type of property, his expert opinion as to the value of a certain item or items of property of that type, and the basis for his opinion;

(f) that person's identity as an ostensible maker, drafter, drawer, endorser or other signator of a written instrument and its falsity within the meaning of section 170.00 of the penal law;

(g) that person's ownership of, or possessory right in, a credit card account number or debit card account number, and the defendant's lack of superior or equal right to use or possession thereof.

Provided, however, that no such statement shall be admitted when an adversarial examination of such person has been previously ordered pursuant to subdivision 8 of section 180.60, unless a transcript of such examination is admitted.

3-a. A sex offender registration form, sex offender registration continuation/supplemental form, sex offender registry address verification form, sex offender change of address form or a copy of such form maintained by the division of criminal justice services concerning an individual who is the subject of a grand jury proceeding, may, when certified by a person designated by the commissioner of the division of criminal justice services as the person to certify such records, as a true copy thereof, be received in such grand jury proceeding as evidence of the facts stated therein.

4. An examination of a child witness or a special witness by the district attorney videotaped pursuant to section 190.32 of this chapter may be received in evidence in such grand jury proceeding as the testimony of such witness.

5. Nothing in subdivisions two, three or four of this section shall be construed to limit the power of the grand jury to cause any person to be called as a witness pursuant to subdivision three of section 190.50.

6. Wherever it is provided in article sixty that the court in a criminal proceeding must rule upon the competency of a witness to testify or upon the admissibility of evidence, such ruling may in an equivalent situation in a grand jury proceeding, be made by the district attorney.

7. Wherever it is provided in article sixty that a court presiding at a jury trial must instruct the jury with respect to the significance, legal effect or evaluation of evidence, the district attorney, in an equivalent situation in a grand jury proceeding, may so instruct the grand jury.

8. (a) A business record may be received in such grand jury proceedings as evidence of the following facts and similar facts stated therein:

(i) a person's use of, subscription to and charges and payments for communication equipment and services including but not limited to equipment or services provided by telephone companies and internet service providers, but not including recorded conversations or images communicated thereby; and

(ii) financial transactions, and a person's ownership or possessory interest in any account, at a bank, insurance company, brokerage, exchange or banking organization as defined in section two of the banking law.

(b) Any business record offered for consideration by a grand jury pursuant to paragraph (a) of this subdivision must be accompanied by a written statement, under oath, that (i) contains a list or description of the records it accompanies, (ii) attests in substance that the person making the statement is a duly authorized custodian of the records or other employee or agent of the business who is familiar with such records, and (iii) attests in substance that such records were made in the regular course of business and that it was the regular course of such business to make such records at the time of the recorded act, transaction, occurrence or event, or within a reasonable time thereafter. Such written statement may also include a statement identifying the name and job description of the person making the statement, specifying the matters set forth in subparagraph (ii) of this paragraph and attesting that the business has made a diligent search and does not possess a particular record or records addressing a matter set forth in paragraph (a) of this subdivision, and such statement may be received at grand jury proceedings as evidence of the fact that the business does not possess such record or records. When records of a business are accompanied by more than one sworn written statement of its employees or agents, such statements may be considered together in determining the admissibility of the records under this subdivision. For the purpose of this subdivision, the term "business records" does not include any records prepared by law enforcement agencies or prepared by any entity in anticipation of litigation.

(c) Any business record offered to a grand jury pursuant to paragraph (a) of this subdivision that includes material beyond that described in such paragraph (a) shall be redacted to exclude such additional material, or received subject to a limiting instruction that the grand jury shall not consider such additional material in support of any criminal charge.

(d) No such records shall be admitted when an adversarial examination of such a records custodian or other employee of such business who was familiar with such records has been previously ordered pursuant to subdivision eight of section 180.60 of this chapter, unless a transcript of such examination is admitted.

(e) Nothing in this subdivision shall affect the admissibility of business records in the grand jury on any basis other than that set forth in this subdivision.

HISTORY: Add, L 1970, ch 996, § 1; amd, L 1971, ch 797, § 1, eff Sept 1, 1971. Sub 1, reenacted without change, L 1975, ch 307, § 2, eff June 24, 1975. Sub 2, reenacted without change, L 1975, ch 307, § 2, eff June 24, 1975. Sub 2-a, add, L 1987, ch 751, § 1, eff Nov 1, 1987. Sub 3, add, L 1975, ch 307, § 2; amd, L 1985, ch 188, § 1, eff June 11, 1985. Former sub 3, renumbered sub 5, L 1975, ch 307, § 2, eff June 24, 1975. Sub 3, par (e), add, L 1976, ch 586, § 1, eff July 21, 1976. Former sub 3, par (e), relettered sub 3, par (f), L 1976, ch 586, § 1, eff July 21, 1976. Sub 3, par (f), formerly sub 3, par (e), so relettered, L 1976, ch 586, § 1, eff July 21, 1976. Sub 4, add, L 1984, ch 804, § 1, eff Nov 1, 1984. Former sub 4, add, L 1975, ch 307, § 2; renumbered sub 5 and amd, L 1984, ch 804, § 1, eff Nov 1, 1984. Prior sub 4, renumbered sub 6, L 1975, ch 307, § 2, eff June 24, 1975. Sub 5, formerly sub 4, add, L 1975, ch 307, § 2; renumbered sub 5 and amd, L 1984, ch 804, § 1, eff Nov 1, 1984. Former sub 5, formerly sub 3, so renumbered, L 1975, ch 307, § 2; renumbered sub 6, L 1984, ch 804, § 2, eff Nov 1, 1984. Sub 6, formerly sub 3, renumbered sub 5, L 1975, ch 307, § 2, renumbered sub 6, L 1984, ch 804, § 2, eff Nov 1, 1984. Former sub 6, formerly sub 4, so renumbered, L 1975, ch 307, § 2; renumbered sub 7, L 1984, ch 804, § 2, eff Nov 1, 1984. Sub 7, formerly sub 4, renumbered sub 6, L 1975, ch 307, § 2, renumbered sub 7, L 1984, ch 804, § 2, eff Nov 1, 1984. Sub 2-a, amd, L 1998, ch 360, § 1, eff Nov 1, 1998, L 1999, ch 453, § 21, eff Jan 1, 2000. Sub 3, par (f), amd, L 2005, ch 690, § 1, eff Oct 4, 2005. Sub 3, par (g), add, L 2005, ch 690, § 1, eff Oct 4, 2005. Sub 3-a, add, L 1999, ch 453, § 22, eff Jan 1, 2000. Sub 8, add, L 2008, ch 279, § 14, Aug 6, 2008.

§ 190.32. Videotaped examination; definitions, application, order and procedure

(1) Definitions. As used in this section:

(a) "Child witness" means a person twelve years old or less whom the people intend to call as witness in a grand jury proceeding to give evidence concerning any crime defined in article one hundred thirty or two hundred sixty or section 255.25, 255.26 or 255.27 of the penal law of which the person was a victim.

(b) "Special witness" means a person whom the people intend to call as a witness in a grand jury proceeding and who is either:

(i) Unable to attend and testify in person in the grand jury proceeding because the person is either physically ill or incapacitated; or

(ii) More than twelve years old and who is likely to suffer very severe emotional or mental stress if required to testify in person concerning any crime defined in article one hundred thirty or two hundred sixty or section 255.25, 255.26 or 255.27 of the penal law to which the person was a witness or of which the person was a victim.

(c) "Operator" means a person employed by the district attorney who operates the video camera to record the examination of a child witness or a special witness.

2. In lieu of requiring a witness who is a child witness to appear in person and give evidence in a grand jury proceeding, the district attorney may cause the examination of such witness to be videotaped in accordance with the provisions of subdivision five of this section.

3. Whenever the district attorney has reason to believe that a witness is a special witness, he may make an ex parte application to the court for an order authorizing the videotaping of an examination of such special witness and the subsequent introduction in evidence in a grand jury proceeding of that videotape in lieu of the live testimony of such special witness. The application must be in writing, must state the grounds of the application and must contain sworn allegations of fact, whether of the district attorney or another person or persons, supporting such grounds. Such allegations may be based upon personal knowledge of the deponent or upon information and belief, provided, that in the latter event, the sources of such information and the grounds for such belief are stated.

4. If the court is satisfied that a witness is a special witness, it shall issue an order authorizing the videotaping of such special witness in accordance with the provisions of subdivision five of this section. The court order and the application and all supporting papers shall not be disclosed to any person except upon further court order.

5. The videotaping of an examination either of a child witness or a special witness shall proceed as follows:

(a) An examination of a child witness or a special witness which is to be videotaped pursuant to this section may be conducted anywhere and at any time provided that the operator begins the videotape by recording a statement by the district attorney of the date, time and place of the examination. In addition, the district attorney shall identify himself, the operator and all other persons present.

(b) An accurate clock with a sweep second hand shall be placed next to or behind the witness in such position as to enable the operator to videotape the clock and the witness together during the entire examination. In the alternative, a date and time generator shall be used to superimpose the day, hour, minute and second over the video portion of the recording during the entire examination.

(c) A social worker, rape crisis counselor, psychologist or other professional providing emotional support to a child witness or to a special witness, as defined in subparagraph (ii) of paragraph (b) of subdivision one of this section, or any of those persons enumerated in paragraphs (a), (b), (c), (d), (e), (f) and (g) of subdivision three of section 190.25 may be present during the videotaping except that a doctor, nurse or other medical assistant also may be present if required by the attendant circumstances. Each person present, except the witness, must, if he has not previously taken a constitutional oath of office or an oath that he will keep secret all matters before a grand jury, must take an oath on the record that he will keep secret the videotaped examination.

(d) The district attorney shall state for the record the name of the witness, and the caption and the grand jury number, if any, of the case. If the witness to be examined is a child witness, the date of the witness' birth must be recorded. If the witness to be examined is a special witness, the date of the order authorizing the videotaped examination and the name of the justice who issued the order shall be recorded.

(e) If the witness will give sworn testimony, the administration of the oath must be recorded. If the witness will give unsworn testimony, a statement that the testimony is not under oath must be recorded.

(f) If the examination requires the use of more than one tape, the operator shall record a statement of the district attorney at the end of each tape declaring that such tape has ended and referring to the succeeding tape. At the beginning of such succeeding tape, the operator shall record a statement of the district attorney identifying himself, the witness being examined and the number of tapes which have been used to record the examination of such witness. At the conclusion of the examination the operator shall record a statement of the district attorney certifying that the recording has been completed, the number of tapes on which the recording has been made and that such tapes constitute a complete and accurate record of the examination of the witness.

(g) A videotape of an examination conducted pursuant to this section shall not be edited unless upon further order of the court.

6. When the videotape is introduced in evidence and played in the grand jury, the grand jury stenographer shall record the examination in the same manner as if the witness had testified in person.

7. Custody of the videotape shall be maintained in the same manner as custody of the grand jury minutes.

HISTORY: Add, L 1984, ch 804, § 3, eff Nov 1, 1984. Sub 1, amd, L 2006, ch 320, § 17, eff Nov 1, 2006. Sub 1, par (a), amd, L 2006, ch 320, § 17, eff Nov 1, 2006. Sub 1, par (b), subpar (ii), amd, L 2006, ch 320, § 17, eff Nov 1, 2006. Sub 5, par (c), amd, L 1995, ch 91, § 1, eff June 28, 1995.

§ 190.35. Grand jury; definitions of terms

The term definitions contained in section 50.10 are applicable to sections 190.40, 190.45 and 190.50.

HISTORY: Add, L 1970, ch 996, § 1, eff Sept 1, 1971, with substance derived from Crim C § 619-c.

§ 190.40. Grand jury; witnesses, compulsion of evidence and immunity

1. Every witness in a grand jury proceeding must give any evidence legally requested of him regardless of any protest or belief on his part that it may tend to incriminate him.

2. A witness who gives evidence in a grand jury proceeding receives immunity unless:

(a) He has effectively waived such immunity pursuant to section 190.45; or

(b) Such evidence is not responsive to any inquiry and is gratuitously given or volunteered by the witness with knowledge that it is not responsive.

(c) The evidence given by the witness consists only of books, papers, records or other physical evidence of an enterprise, as defined in subdivision one of section 175.00 of the penal law, the production of which is required by a subpoena duces tecum, and the witness does not possess a privilege against self-incrimination with respect to the production of such evidence. Any further evidence given by the witness entitles the witness to immunity except as provided in subparagraph [paragraphs]* (a) and (b) of this subdivision.

     HISTORY: Add, L 1970, ch 996, § 1, eff Sept 1, 1971, with substance derived from Crim C § 619-c. Sub 2, par (c), add, L 1975, ch 454, § 1, eff July 24, 1975.

§ 190.45. Grand jury; waiver of immunity

1. A waiver of immunity is a written instrument subscribed by a person who is or is about to become a witness in a grand jury proceeding, stipulating that he waives his privilege against self-incrimination and any possible or prospective immunity to which he would otherwise become entitled, pursuant to section 190.40, as a result of giving evidence in such proceeding.

2. A waiver of immunity is not effective unless and until it is sworn to before the grand jury conducting the proceeding in which the subscriber has been called as a witness.

3. A person who is called by the people as a witness in a grand jury proceeding and requested by the district attorney to subscribe and swear to a waiver of immunity before giving evidence has a right to confer with counsel before deciding whether he will comply with such request, and, if he desires to avail himself of such right, he must be accorded a reasonable time in which to obtain and confer with counsel for such purpose. The district attorney must inform the witness of all such rights before obtaining his execution of such a waiver of immunity. Any waiver obtained, subscribed or sworn to in violation of the provisions of this subdivision is invalid and ineffective.

4. If a grand jury witness subscribes and swears to a waiver of immunity upon a written agreement with the district attorney that the interrogation will be limited to certain specified subjects, matters or areas of conduct, and if after the commencement of his testimony he is interrogated and testifies concerning another subject, matter or area of conduct not included in such written agreement, he receives immunity with respect to any further testimony which he may give concerning such other subject, matter or area of conduct and the waiver of immunity is to that extent ineffective.

     HISTORY: Add, L 1970, ch 996, § 1, eff Sept 1, 1971. Sub 4, amd, L 1974, ch 761, § 1, eff Sept 1, 1974.

§ 190.50. Grand jury; who may call witnesses; defendant as witness

1. Except as provided in this section, no person has a right to call a witness or appear as a witness in a grand jury proceeding.

2. The people may call as a witness in a grand jury proceeding any person believed by the district attorney to possess relevant information or knowledge.

3. The grand jury may cause to be called as a witness any person believed by it to possess relevant information or knowledge. If the grand jury desires to hear any such witness who was not called by the people, it may direct the district attorney to issue and serve a subpoena upon such witness, and the district attorney must comply with such direction. At any time after such a direction, however, or at any time after the service of a subpoena pursuant to such a direction and before the return date thereof, the people may apply to the court which impaneled the grand jury

---

     * The bracketed word has been inserted by the Publisher.

for an order vacating or modifying such direction or subpoena on the ground that such is in the public interest. Upon such application, the court may in its discretion vacate the direction or subpoena, attach reasonable conditions thereto, or make other appropriate qualification thereof.

4. Notwithstanding the provisions of subdivision three, the district attorney may demand that any witness thus called at the instance of the grand jury sign a waiver of immunity pursuant to section 190.45 before being sworn, and upon such demand no oath may be administered to such witness unless and until he complies therewith.

5. Although not called as a witness by the people or at the instance of the grand jury, a person has a right to be a witness in a grand jury proceeding under circumstances prescribed in this subdivision:

(a) When a criminal charge against a person is being or is about to be or has been submitted to a grand jury, such person has a right to appear before such grand jury as a witness in his own behalf if, prior to the filing of any indictment or any direction to file a prosecutor's information in the matter, he serves upon the district attorney of the county a written notice making such request and stating an address to which communications may be sent. The district attorney is not obliged to inform such a person that such a grand jury proceeding against him is pending, in progress or about to occur unless such person is a defendant who has been arraigned in a local criminal court upon a currently undisposed of felony complaint charging an offense which is a subject of the prospective or pending grand jury proceeding. In such case, the district attorney must notify the defendant or his attorney of the prospective or pending grand jury proceeding and accord the defendant a reasonable time to exercise his right to appear as a witness therein;

(b) Upon service upon the district attorney of a notice requesting appearance before a grand jury pursuant to paragraph (a), the district attorney must notify the foreman of the grand jury of such request, and must subsequently serve upon the applicant, at the address specified by him, a notice that he will be heard by the grand jury at a given time and place. Upon appearing at such time and place, and upon signing and submitting to the grand jury a waiver of immunity pursuant to section 190.45, such person must be permitted to testify before the grand jury and to give any relevant and competent evidence concerning the case under consideration. Upon giving such evidence, he is subject to examination by the people.

(c) Any indictment or direction to file a prosecutor's information obtained or filed in violation of the provisions of paragraph (a) or (b) is invalid and, upon a motion made pursuant to section 170.50 or section 210.20, must be dismissed; provided that a motion based upon such ground must be made not more than five days after the defendant has been arraigned upon the indictment or, as the case may be, upon the prosecutor's information resulting from the grand jury's direction to file the same. If the contention is not so asserted in timely fashion, it is waived and the indictment or prosecutor's information may not thereafter be challenged on such ground.

6. A defendant or person against whom a criminal charge is being or is about to be brought in a grand jury proceeding may request the grand jury, either orally or in writing, to cause a person designated by him to be called as a witness in such proceeding. The grand jury may as a matter of discretion grant such request and cause such witness to be called pursuant to subdivision three.

7. Where a subpoena is made pursuant to this section, all papers and proceedings relating to the subpoena and any motion to quash, fix conditions, modify or compel compliance shall be kept secret and not disclosed to the public by any public officer or public employee or any other individual described in section 215.70 of the penal law. This subdivision shall not apply where the

person subpoenaed and the prosecutor waive the provisions of this subdivision.

This subdivision shall not prevent the publication of decisions and orders made in connection with such proceedings or motions, provided the caption and content of the decision are written or altered by the court to reasonably preclude identification of the person subpoenaed.

HISTORY: Add, L 1970, ch 996, § 1, eff Sept 1, 1971. Sub 7, add, L 1978, ch 289, § 1, eff Sept 1, 1978.

§ 190.52. Grand jury; attorney for witness

1. Any person who appears as a witness and has signed a waiver of immunity in a grand jury proceeding, has a right to an attorney as provided in this section. Such a witness may appear with a retained attorney, or if he is financially unable to obtain counsel, an attorney who shall be assigned by the superior court which impaneled the grand jury. Such assigned attorney shall be assigned pursuant to the same plan and in the same manner as counsel are provided to persons charged with crime pursuant to section seven hundred twenty-two of the county law.

2. The attorney for such witness may be present with the witness in the grand jury room. The attorney may advise the witness, but may not otherwise take any part in the proceeding.

3. The superior court which impaneled the grand jury shall have the same power to remove an attorney from the grand jury room as such court has with respect to an attorney in a courtroom.

HISTORY: Add, L 1978, ch 447, § 2, eff Sept 1, 1978.

§ 190.55. Grand jury; matters to be heard and examined; duties and authority of district attorney

1. A grand jury may hear and examine evidence concerning the alleged commission of any offense prosecutable in the courts of the county, and concerning any misconduct, nonfeasance or neglect in public office by a public servant, whether criminal or otherwise.

2. District attorneys are required or authorized to submit evidence to grand juries under the following circumstances:

(a) A district attorney must submit to a grand jury evidence concerning a felony allegedly committed by a defendant who, on the basis of a felony complaint filed with a local criminal court of the county, has been held for the action of a grand jury of such county, except where indictment has been waived by the defendant pursuant to article one hundred ninety-five.

(b) A district attorney must submit to a grand jury evidence concerning a misdemeanor allegedly committed by a defendant who has been charged therewith by a local criminal court accusatory instrument, in any case where a superior court of the county has, pursuant to subdivision one of section 170.25, ordered that such misdemeanor charge be prosecuted by indictment in a superior court.

(c) A district attorney may submit to a grand jury any available evidence concerning an offense prosecutable in the courts of the county, or concerning misconduct, nonfeasance or neglect in public office by a public servant, whether criminal or otherwise.

HISTORY: Add, L 1970, ch 996, § 1, eff Sept 1, 1971. Sub 2, par (a), amd, L 1974, ch 467, § 4, eff June 22, 1974.

§ 190.60. Grand jury; action to be taken

After hearing and examining evidence as prescribed in section 190.55, a grand jury may:

1. Indict a person for an offense, as provided in section 190.65;

2. Direct the district attorney to file a prosecutor's information with a local criminal court, as provided in section 190.70;

3. Direct the district attorney to file a request for removal to the family court, as provided in section 190.71 of this article.

4. Dismiss the charge before it, as provided in section 190.75;

5. Submit a grand jury report, as provided in section 190.85.

HISTORY: Add, L 1970, ch 996, § 1, eff Sept 1, 1971. Sub 3, add, L 1978, ch 481, § 34, eff Sept 1, 1978. Former sub 3, renumbered sub 4, L 1978, ch 481, § 34, eff Sept 1, 1978. Sub 4, formerly sub 3, renumbered sub 4, L 1978, ch 481, § 34, eff Sept 1, 1978. Former sub 4, renumbered sub 5, L 1978, ch 481, § 34, eff Sept 1, 1978. Sub 5, formerly sub 4, renumbered sub 5, L 1978, ch 481, § 34, eff Sept 1, 1978.

§ 190.65. Grand jury; when indictment is authorized

1. Subject to the rules prescribing the kinds of offenses which may be charged in an indictment, a grand jury may indict a person for an offense when (a) the evidence before it is legally sufficient to establish that such person committed such offense provided, however, such evidence is not legally sufficient when corroboration that would be required, as a matter of law, to sustain a conviction for such offense is absent, and (b) competent and admissible evidence before it provides reasonable cause to believe that such person committed such offense.

2. The offense or offenses for which a grand jury may indict a person in any particular case are not limited to that or those which may have been designated, at the commencement of the grand jury proceeding, to be the subject of the inquiry; and even in a case submitted to it upon a court order, pursuant to the provisions of section 170.25, directing that a misdemeanor charge pending in a local criminal court be prosecuted by indictment, the grand jury may indict the defendant for a felony if the evidence so warrants.

3. Upon voting to indict a person, a grand jury must, through its foreman or acting foreman, file an indictment with the court by which it was impaneled.

HISTORY: Add, L 1970, ch 996, § 1, eff Sept 1, 1971. Sub 1, amd, L 1983, ch 28, § 1, eff April 5, 1983.

§ 190.70. Grand jury; direction to file prosecutor's information and related matters

1. Except in a case submitted to it pursuant to the provisions of section 170.25, a grand jury may direct the district attorney to file in a local criminal court a prosecutor's information charging a person with an offense other than a felony when (a) the evidence before it is legally sufficient to establish that such person committed such offense, and (b) competent and admissible evidence before it provides reasonable cause to believe that such person committed such offense. In such case, the grand jury must, through its foreman or acting foreman, file such direction with the court by which it was impaneled.

2. Such direction must be signed by the foreman or acting foreman. It must contain a plain and concise statement of the conduct constituting the offense to be charged, equivalent in content and precision to the factual statement required to be contained in an indictment pursuant to subdivision seven of section 200.50. Subject to the rules prescribed in sections 200.20 and 200.40 governing joinder in a single indictment of multiple offenses and multiple defendants, such grand jury direction may, where appropriate, specify multiple offenses of less than felony grade and multiple defendants, and may direct that the prospective prosecutor's information charge a single defendant with multiple offenses, or multiple defendants jointly with either a single offense or multiple offenses.

3. Upon the filing of such grand jury direction, the court must, unless such direction is insufficient on its face, issue an order approving such direction and ordering the district attorney to file such a prosecutor's information in a designated local criminal court having trial jurisdiction of the offense or offenses in question.

HISTORY: Add, L 1970, ch 996, § 1, eff Sept 1, 1971, with substance derived from Crim C § 61.

§ 190.71. Grand jury; direction to file request for removal to family court

(a) Except as provided in subdivision six of section 200.20 of this chapter, a grand jury may not indict (i) a person thirteen years of age for any conduct or crime other than conduct constituting a crime defined in subdivisions one and two of section 125.25 (murder in the second degree) or such conduct as a sexually motivated felony, where authorized pursuant to section 130.91 of the penal law; (ii) a person fourteen or fifteen years of age for any conduct or crime other than conduct constituting a crime defined in subdivisions one and two of section 125.25 (murder in the second degree) and in subdivision three of such section provided that the underlying crime for the murder charge is one for which such person is criminally responsible; 135.25 (kidnapping in the first degree); 150.20 (arson in the first degree); subdivisions one and two of section 120.10 (assault in the first degree); 125.20 (manslaughter in the first degree); subdivisions one and two of section 130.35 (rape in the first degree); subdivisions one and two of section 130.50 (criminal sexual act in the first degree); 130.70 (aggravated sexual abuse in the first degree); 140.30 (burglary in the first degree); subdivision one of section 140.25 (burglary in the second degree); 150.15 (arson in the second degree); 160.15 (robbery in the first degree); subdivision two of section 160.10 (robbery in the second degree) of the penal law; subdivision four of section 265.02 of the penal law, where such firearm is possessed on school grounds, as that phrase is defined in subdivision fourteen of section 220.00 of the penal law; or section 265.03 of the penal law, where such machine gun or such firearm is possessed on school grounds, as that phrase is defined in subdivision fourteen of section 220.00 of the penal law; or defined in the penal law as an attempt to commit murder in the second degree or kidnapping in the first degree, or such conduct as a sexually motivated felony, where authorized pursuant to section 130.91 of the penal law.

(b) A grand jury may vote to file a request to remove a charge to the family court if it finds that a person thirteen, fourteen or fifteen years of age did an act which, if done by a person over the age of sixteen, would constitute a crime provided (1) such act is one for which it may not indict; (2) it does not indict such person for a crime; and (3) the evidence before it is legally sufficient to establish that such person did such act and competent and admissible evidence before it provides reasonable cause to believe that such person did such act.

(c) Upon voting to remove a charge to the family court pursuant to subdivision (b) of this section, the grand jury must, through its foreman or acting foreman, file a request to transfer such charge to the family court. Such request shall be filed with the court by which it was impaneled. It must (1) allege that a person named therein did any act which, if done by a person over the age of sixteen, would constitute a crime; (2) specify the act and the time and place of its commission; and (3) be signed by the foreman or the acting foreman.

(d) Upon the filing of such grand jury request, the court must, unless such request is improper or insufficient on its face, issue an order approving such request and direct that the charge be removed to the family court in accordance with the provisions of article seven hundred twenty-five of this chapter.

HISTORY: Add, L 1978, ch 481, § 35, eff Sept 1, 1978. Sub (a), amd, L 1979, ch 411, § 8, L 1980, ch 136, § 1, L 1981, ch 335, § 3, eff Sept 1, 1981. Sub (a), amd, L 1998, ch 435, § 2, eff Nov 1, 1998, L 2003, ch 264, § 39, eff Nov 1, 2003, L 2007, ch 7, § 13, eff April 13, 2007.

§ 190.75. Grand jury; dismissal of charge

1. If upon a charge that a designated person committed a crime, either (a) the evidence before the grand jury is not legally sufficient to establish that such person committed such crime or any other offense, or (b) the grand jury is not satisfied that there is reasonable cause to believe that such person committed such crime or any other offense, it must dismiss the charge. In such case, the grand jury must, through its foreman or acting foreman, file its finding of dismissal with the court by which it was impaneled.

2. If the defendant was previously held for the action of the grand jury by a local criminal court, the superior court to which such dismissal is presented must order the defendant released from custody if he is in the custody of the sheriff, or, if he is at liberty on bail, it must exonerate the bail.

3. When a charge has been so dismissed, it may not again be submitted to a grand jury unless the court in its discretion authorizes or directs the people to resubmit such charge to the same or another grand jury. If in such case the charge is again dismissed, it may not again be submitted to a grand jury.

4. Whenever all charges against a designated person have been so dismissed, the district attorney must within ninety days of the filing of the finding of such dismissal, notify that person of the dismissal by regular mail to his last known address unless resubmission has been permitted pursuant to subdivision three of this section or an order of postponement of such service is obtained upon a showing of good cause and exigent circumstances.

> **HISTORY:** Add, L 1970, ch 996, § 1, eff Sept 1, 1971. Sub 4, add, L 1977, ch 907, § 1, eff Sept 1, 1977.

§ 190.80. Grand jury; release of defendant upon failure of timely grand jury action

Upon application of a defendant who on the basis of a felony complaint has been held by a local criminal court for the action of a grand jury, and who, at the time of such order or subsequent thereto, has been committed to the custody of the sheriff pending such grand jury action, and who has been confined in such custody for a period of more than forty-five days, or, in the case of a juvenile offender, thirty days, without the occurrence of any grand jury action or disposition pursuant to subdivision one, two or three of section 190.60, the superior court by which such grand jury was or is to be impaneled must release him on his own recognizance unless:

(a) The lack of a grand jury disposition during such period of confinement was due to the defendant's request, action or condition, or occurred with his consent; or

(b) The people have shown good cause why such order of release should not be issued. Such good cause must consist of some compelling fact or circumstance which precluded grand jury action within the prescribed period or rendered the same against the interest of justice.

> **HISTORY:** Add, L 1970, ch 996, § 1, eff Sept 1, 1971. Opening par, amd, L 1979, ch 411, § 9, eff Aug 4, 1979.

§ 190.85. Grand jury; grand jury reports

1. The grand jury may submit to the court by which it was impaneled, a report:

(a) Concerning misconduct, non-feasance or neglect in public office by a public servant as the basis for a recommendation of removal or disciplinary action; or

(b) Stating that after investigation of a public servant it finds no misconduct, non-feasance or neglect in office by him provided that such public servant has requested the submission of such report; or

(c) Proposing recommendations for legislative, executive or administrative action in the public interest based upon stated findings.

2. The court to which such report is submitted shall examine it and the minutes of the grand jury and, except as otherwise provided in subdivision four, shall make an order accepting and filing such report as a public record only if the court is satisfied that it complies with the provisions of subdivision one and that:

(a) The report is based upon facts revealed in the course of an investigation authorized by section 190.55 and is supported by the preponderance of the credible and legally admissible evidence; and

(b) When the report is submitted pursuant to paragraph (a) of subdivision one, that each person named therein was afforded an opportunity to testify before the grand jury prior to the filing of such report, and when the report is submitted pursuant to paragraph (b) or (c) of subdivision one, it is not critical of an identified or identifiable person.

3. The order accepting a report pursuant to paragraph (a) of subdivision one, and the report itself, must be sealed by the court and may not be filed as a public record, or be subject to subpoena or otherwise be made public until at least thirty-one days after a copy of the order and the report are served upon each public servant named therein, or if an appeal is taken pursuant to section 190.90, until the affirmance of the order accepting the report, or until reversal of the order sealing the report, or until dismissal of the appeal of the named public servant by the appellate division, whichever occurs later. Such public servant may file with the clerk of the court an answer to such report, not later than twenty days after service of the order and report upon him. Such an answer shall plainly and concisely state the facts and law constituting the defense of the public servant to the charges in said report, and, except for those parts of the answer which the court may determine to be scandalously or prejudicially and unnecessarily inserted therein, shall become an appendix to the report. Upon the expiration of the time set forth in this subdivision, the district attorney shall deliver a true copy of such report, and the appendix if any, for appropriate action, to each public servant or body having removal or disciplinary authority over each public servant named therein.

4. Upon the submission of a report pursuant to subdivision one, if the court finds that the filing of such report as a public record, may prejudice fair consideration of a pending criminal matter, it must order such report sealed and such report may not be subject to subpoena or public inspection during the pendency of such criminal matter, except upon order of the court.

5. Whenever the court to which a report is submitted pursuant to paragraph (a) of subdivision one is not satisfied that the report complies with the provisions of subdivision two, it may direct that additional testimony be taken before the same grand jury, or it must make an order sealing such report, and the report may not be filed as a public record, or be subject to subpoena or otherwise be made public.

HISTORY: Add, L 1970, ch 996, § 1, eff Sept 1, 1971, with substance derived from Crim C § 253-a.

§ 190.90. Grand jury; appeal from order concerning grand jury reports

1. When a court makes an order accepting a report of a grand jury pursuant to paragraph (a) of subdivision one of section 190.85, any public servant named therein may appeal the order; and when a court makes an order sealing a report of a grand jury pursuant to subdivision five of section 190.85, the district attorney or other attorney designated by the grand jury may appeal the order.

2. When a court makes an order sealing a report of a grand jury pursuant to subdivision five of

section 190.85, the district attorney or other attorney designated by the grand jury may, within ten days after service of a copy of the order and report upon each public servant named in the report, appeal the order to the appellate division of the department in which the order was made, by filing in duplicate a notice of appeal from the order with the clerk of the court in which the order was made and by serving a copy of such notice of appeal upon each such public servant. Notwithstanding any contrary provision of section 190.85, a true copy of the report of the grand jury shall be served, together with such notice of appeal, upon each such public servant.

3. The mode of and time for perfecting an appeal pursuant to this section, and the mode of and procedure for the argument thereof, are determined by the rules of the appellate division of the department in which the appeal is brought. Such rules shall prescribe the matters referred to in subdivision one of section 460.70 and in section 460.80, except that such appeal is a preferred cause and the appellate division of each department shall promulgate rules to effectuate such preference.

4. The record and all other presentations on appeal shall remain sealed, except that upon reversal of the order sealing the report or dismissal of the appeal of the named public servant by the appellate division, the report of the grand jury, with the appendix, if any, shall be filed as a public record as provided in subdivision three of section 190.85.

5. The procedure provided for in this section shall be the exclusive manner of reviewing an order made pursuant to section 190.85 and the appellate division of the supreme court shall be the sole court having jurisdiction of such an appeal. The order of the appellate division finally determining such appeal shall not be subject to review in any other court or proceeding.

6. The grand jury in an appeal pursuant to this section shall be represented by the district attorney unless the report relates to him or his office, in which event the grand jury may designate another attorney.

> **HISTORY:** Add, L 1970, ch 996, § 1, eff Sept 1, 1971, with substance derived from Crim C § 517-a. Sub 4, amd, L 1985, ch 517, § 1, eff Nov 1, 1985.

ARTICLE 195   WAIVER OF INDICTMENT

> **HISTORY:** Add, L 1974, ch 467, § 5, eff June 22, 1974.

§ 195.10. Waiver of indictment; in general

1. A defendant may waive indictment and consent to be prosecuted by superior court information when:

   (a) a local criminal court has held the defendant for the action of a grand jury; and

   (b) the defendant is not charged with a class A felony punishable by death or life imprisonment; and

   (c) the district attorney consents to the waiver.

2. A defendant may waive indictment pursuant to subdivision one in either:

   (a) the local criminal court in which the order was issued holding the defendant for action of a grand jury, at the time such order is issued; or

(b) the appropriate superior court, at any time prior to the filing of an indictment by the grand jury.

HISTORY: Add, L 1974, ch 467, § 5, eff June 22, 1974. Sub 1, amd, L 2008, ch 401, § 1, eff Nov 1, 2008. Sub 1, par (b), amd, L 2008, ch 401, § 1, eff Nov 1, 2008.

§ 195.20. Waiver of indictment; written instrument

A waiver of indictment shall be evidenced by a written instrument, which shall contain the name of the court in which it is executed, the title of the action, and the name, date and approximate time and place of each offense to be charged in the superior court information to be filed by the district attorney pursuant to section 195.40. The offenses named may include any offense for which the defendant was held for action of a grand jury and any offense or offenses properly joinable therewith pursuant to sections 200.20 and 200.40. The written waiver shall also contain a statement by the defendant that he is aware that:

(a) under the constitution of the state of New York he has the right to be prosecuted by indictment filed by a grand jury;

(b) he waives such right and consents to be prosecuted by superior court information to be filed by the district attorney;

(c) the superior court information to be filed by the district attorney will charge the offenses named in the written waiver; and

(d) the superior court information to be filed by the district attorney will have the same force and effect as an indictment filed by a grand jury.

The written waiver shall be signed by the defendant in open court in the presence of his attorney. The consent of the district attorney shall be endorsed thereon.

HISTORY: Add, L 1974, ch 467, § 5, eff June 22, 1974.

§ 195.30. Waiver of indictment; approval of waiver by the court

The court shall determine whether the waiver of indictment complies with the provisions of sections 195.10 and 195.20. If satisfied that the waiver complies with such provisions, the court shall approve the waiver and execute a written order to that effect. When the waiver is approved by a local criminal court, the local criminal court shall promptly transmit to the appropriate superior court the written waiver and order approving the waiver, along with all other documents pertinent to the action. Until such papers are received by the superior court, the action is deemed to be pending in the local criminal court.

HISTORY: Add, L 1974, ch 467, § 5, eff June 22, 1974.

§ 195.40. Waiver of indictment; filing of superior court information

When indictment is waived in a superior court the district attorney shall file a superior court information in such court at the time the waiver is executed. When indictment is waived in a local criminal court the district attorney shall file a superior court information in the appropriate superior court within ten days of the execution of the court order approving the waiver. Upon application of a defendant whose waiver of indictment has been approved by the court, and who, at the time of such approval or subsequent thereto, has been committed to the custody of the sheriff pending disposition of the action, and who has been confined in such custody for a period of more than ten days from the date of approval without the filing by the district attorney of a superior court information, the superior court must release him on his own recognizance unless:

(a) The failure of the district attorney to file a superior court information during such period of confinement was due to defendant's request, action or condition or occurred with his consent; or

(b) The people have shown good cause why such order of release should not be issued. Such good cause must consist of some compelling fact or circumstance which precluded the filing of the superior court information within the prescribed period.

HISTORY: Add, L 1974, ch 467, § 5, eff June 22, 1974.

ARTICLE 200   INDICTMENT AND RELATED INSTRUMENTS

HISTORY: Add, L 1970, ch 996, § 1, eff Sept 1, 1971.

§ 200.10. Indictment; definition

An indictment is a written accusation by a grand jury, filed with a superior court, charging a person, or two or more persons jointly, with the commission of a crime, or with the commission of two or more offenses at least one of which is a crime. Except as used in Article 190, the term indictment shall include a superior court information.

HISTORY: Add, L 1970, ch 996, § 1, with substance derived from Crim C § 247; amd, L 1974, ch 467, § 6, eff June 22, 1974.

§ 200.15. Superior court information; definition

A superior court information is a written accusation by a district attorney filed in a superior court pursuant to article one hundred ninety-five, charging a person, or two or more persons jointly, with the commission of a crime, or with the commission of two or more offenses, at least one of which is a crime. A superior court information may include any offense for which the defendant was held for action of a grand jury and any offense or offenses properly joinable therewith pursuant to sections 200.20 and 200.40, but shall not include an offense not named in the written waiver of indictment executed pursuant to section 195.20. A superior court information has the same force and effect as an indictment and all procedures and provisions of law applicable to indictments are also applicable to superior court informations, except where otherwise expressly provided.

HISTORY: Add, L 1974, ch 467, § 7, eff June 22, 1974.

§ 200.20. Indictment; what offenses may be charged; joinder of offenses and consolidation of indictments

1. An indictment must charge at least one crime and may, in addition, charge in separate counts one or more other offenses, including petty offenses, provided that all such offenses are joinable pursuant to the principles prescribed in subdivision two.

2. Two offenses are "joinable" when:

(a) They are based upon the same act or upon the same criminal transaction, as that term is defined in subdivision two of section 40.10; or

(b) Even though based upon different criminal transactions, such offenses, or the criminal transactions underlying them, are of such nature that either proof of the first offense would be material and admissible as evidence in chief upon a trial of the second, or proof of the second would be material and admissible as evidence in chief upon a trial of the first; or

(c) Even though based upon different criminal transactions, and even though not joinable pursuant to paragraph (b), such offenses are defined by the same or similar statutory provisions and consequently are the same or similar in law; or

(d) Though not directly joinable with each other pursuant to paragraph (a), (b) or (c), each is so joinable with a third offense contained in the indictment. In such case, each of the three offenses may properly be joined not only with each of the other two but also with any further offense joinable with either of the other two, and the chain of joinder may be further extended accordingly.

3. In any case where two or more offenses or groups of offenses charged in an indictment are based upon different criminal transactions, and where their joinability rests solely upon the fact that such offenses, or as the case may be at least one offense of each group, are the same or similar in law, as prescribed in paragraph (c) of subdivision two, the court, in the interest of justice and for good cause shown, may, upon application of either a defendant or the people, in its discretion, order that any such offenses be tried separately from the other or others thereof. Good cause shall include but not be limited to situations where there is:

(a) Substantially more proof on one or more such joinable offenses than on others and there is a substantial likelihood that the jury would be unable to consider separately the proof as it relates to each offense.

(b) A convincing showing that a defendant has both important testimony to give concerning one count and a genuine need to refrain from testifying on the other, which satisfies the court that the risk of prejudice is substantial.

(i) Good cause, under this paragraph (b), may be established in writing or upon oral representation of counsel on the record. Any written or oral representation may be based upon information and belief, provided the sources of such information and the grounds of such belief are set forth.

(ii) Upon the request of counsel, any written or recorded showing concerning the defendant's genuine need to refrain from testifying shall be ex parte and in camera. The in camera showing shall be sealed but a court for good cause may order unsealing. Any statements made by counsel in the course of an application under this paragraph (b) may not be offered against the defendant in any criminal action for impeachment purposes or otherwise.

4. When two or more indictments against the same defendant or defendants charge different offenses of a kind that are joinable in a single indictment pursuant to subdivision two, the court may, upon application of either the people or a defendant, order that such indictments be consolidated and treated as a single indictment for trial purposes. If such indictments, in addition to charging offenses which are so joinable charge other offenses which are not so joinable, they may nevertheless be consolidated for the limited purpose of jointly trying the joinable offenses. In such case, such indictments remain in existence with respect to any nonjoinable offenses and may be prosecuted accordingly. Nothing herein precludes the consolidation of an indictment with a superior court information.

5. A court's determination of an application for consolidation pursuant to subdivision four is discretionary; except that where an application by the defendant seeks consolidation with respect to offenses which are, pursuant to paragraph (a) of subdivision two, of a kind that are joinable in a single indictment by reason of being based upon the same act or criminal transaction, the court must order such consolidation unless good cause to the contrary be shown.

6. Where an indictment charges at least one offense against a defendant who was under the age of sixteen at the time of the commission of the crime and who did not lack criminal responsibility for such crime by reason of infancy, the indictment may, in addition, charge in separate counts one or more other offenses for which such person would not have been criminally responsible by reason of infancy, if:

(a) the offense for which the defendant is criminally responsible and the one or more other offenses for which he would not have been criminally responsible by reason of infancy are based upon the same act or upon the same criminal transaction, as that term is defined in subdivision two of section 40.10 of this chapter; or

(b) the offenses are of such nature that either proof of the first offense would be material and admissible as evidence in chief upon a trial of the second, or proof of the second would be material and admissible as evidence in chief upon a trial of the first.

HISTORY: Add, L 1970, ch 996, § 1, eff Sept 1, 1971. Sub 3, amd, L 1984, ch 672, § 1, eff Nov 1, 1984. Sub 3, par (a), add, L 1984, ch 672, § 1, eff Nov 1, 1984. Sub 3, par (b), add, L 1984, ch 672, § 1, eff Nov 1, 1984. Sub 4, amd, L 1974, ch 467, § 8, eff June 22, 1974. Sub 6, add, L 1980, ch 136, § 2, eff May 20, 1980.

§ 200.30. Indictment; duplicitous counts prohibited

1. Each count of an indictment may charge one offense only.

2. For purpose of this section, a statutory provision which defines the offense named in the title thereof by providing, in different subdivisions or paragraphs, different ways in which such named offense may be committed, defines a separate offense in each such subdivision or paragraph, and a count of an indictment charging such named offense which, without specifying or clearly indicating the particular subdivision or paragraph of the statutory provision, alleges facts which would support a conviction under more than one such subdivision or paragraph, charges more than one offense.

HISTORY: Add, L 1970, ch 996, § 1, eff Sept 1, 1971.

§ 200.40. Indictment; joinder of defendants and consolidation of indictments against different defendants

1. Two or more defendants may be jointly charged in a single indictment provided that:

(a) all such defendants are jointly charged with every offense alleged therein; or

(b) all the offenses charged are based upon a common scheme or plan; or

(c) all the offenses charged are based upon the same criminal transaction as that term is defined in subdivision two of section 40.10; or

(d) if the indictment includes a count charging enterprise corruption:

(i) all the defendants are jointly charged with every count of enterprise corruption alleged therein; and

(ii) every offense, other than a count alleging enterprise corruption, is a criminal act specifically included in the pattern of criminal activity on which the charge or charges of enterprise corruption is or are based; and

(iii) each such defendant could have been jointly charged with at least one of the other defendants, absent an enterprise corruption count, under the provisions of paragraph (a), (b) or (c) of this subdivision, in an accusatory instrument charging at least one such specifically included criminal act. For purposes of this subparagraph, joinder shall not be precluded on the ground that a specifically included criminal act which is necessary to permit joinder is not currently prosecutable, when standing alone, by reason of previous prosecution or lack of geographical jurisdiction.

Even in such case, the court, upon motion of a defendant or the people made within the period provided by section 255.20, may for good cause shown order in its discretion that any defendant be tried separately from the other or from one or more or all of the others. Good cause shall include, but not be limited to, a finding that a defendant or the people will be unduly prejudiced by a joint trial or, in the case of a prosecution involving a charge of enterprise corruption, a finding that proof of one or more criminal acts alleged to have been committed by one defendant but not one or more of the others creates a likelihood that the jury may not be able to consider separately the proof as it relates to each defendant, or in such a case, given the scope of the pattern of criminal activity charged against all the defendants, a particular defendant's comparatively minor role in it creates a likelihood of prejudice to him. Upon such a finding of prejudice, the court may order counts to be tried separately, grant a severance of defendants or provide whatever other relief justice requires.

2. When two or more defendants are charged in separate indictments with an offense or offenses but could have been so charged in a single indictment under subdivision one above, the court may, upon application of the people, order that such indictments be consolidated and the charges be heard in a single trial. If such indictments also charge offenses not properly the subject of a single indictment under subdivision one above, those offenses shall not be consolidated, but shall remain in existence and may be separately prosecuted. Nothing herein precludes the consolidation of an indictment with a superior court information.

HISTORY: Add, L 1970, ch 996, § 1, eff Sept 1, 1971, with substance derived from Crim C § 391. Sub 1, amd, L 1974, ch 763, § 9, L 1984, ch 672, § 2, L 1986, ch 516, § 6, eff Nov 1, 1986. Sub 1, par (b), add, L 1984, ch 672, § 2, eff Nov 1, 1984. Sub 1, par (c), add, L 1984, ch 672, § 2, eff Nov 1, 1984. Sub 1, par (d), add, L 1986, ch 516, § 6, eff Nov 1, 1986. Sub 2, amd, L 1974, ch 467, § 9, L 1984, ch 672, § 3, eff Nov 1, 1984.

§ 200.50. Indictment; form and content

An indictment must contain:

1. The name of the superior court in which it is filed; and

2. The title of the action and, where the defendant is a juvenile offender, a statement in the

title that the defendant is charged as a juvenile offender; and

3. A separate accusation or count addressed to each offense charged, if there be more than one; and

4. A statement in each count that the grand jury, or, where the accusatory instrument is a superior court information, the district attorney, accuses the defendant or defendants of a designated offense, provided that in any prosecution under article four hundred eighty-five of the penal law, the designated offense shall be the specified offense, as defined in subdivision three of section 485.05 of the penal law, followed by the phrase "as a hate crime", and provided further that in any prosecution under section 490.25 of the penal law, the designated offense shall be the specified offense, as defined in subdivision three of section 490.05 of the penal law, followed by the phrase "as a crime of terrorism"; and provided further that in any prosecution under section 130.91 of the penal law, the designated offense shall be the specified offense, as defined in subdivision two of section 130.91 of the penal law, followed by the phrase "as a sexually motivated felony"; and provided further that in any prosecution under section 496.06 of the penal law, the designated offense shall be the specified offense, as defined in subdivision two of such section, followed by the phrase "as a public corruption crime"; and

5. A statement in each count that the offense charged therein was committed in a designated county; and

6. A statement in each count that the offense charged therein was committed on, or on or about, a designated date, or during a designated period of time; and

7. A plain and concise factual statement in each count which, without allegations of an evidentiary nature,

    (a) asserts facts supporting every element of the offense charged and the defendant's or defendants' commission thereof with sufficient precision to clearly apprise the defendant or defendants of the conduct which is the subject of the accusation; and

    (b) in the case of any armed felony, as defined in subdivision forty-one of section 1.20, states that such offense is an armed felony and specifies the particular implement the defendant or defendants possessed, were armed with, used or displayed or, in the case of an implement displayed, specifies what the implement appeared to be; and

    (c) in the case of any hate crime, as defined in section 485.05 of the penal law, specifies, as applicable, that the defendant or defendants intentionally selected the person against whom the offense was committed or intended to be committed; or intentionally committed the act or acts constituting the offense, in whole or in substantial part because of a belief or perception regarding the race, color, national origin, ancestry, gender, religion, religious practice, age, disability or sexual orientation of a person; and

    (d) in the case of a crime of terrorism, as defined in section 490.25 of the penal law, specifies, as applicable, that the defendant or defendants acted with intent to intimidate or coerce a civilian population, influence the policy of a unit of government by intimidation or coercion, or affect the conduct of a unit of government by murder, assassination or kidnapping; and

    (e) in the case of a sexually motivated felony, as defined in section 130.91 of the penal law, asserts facts supporting the allegation that the offense was sexually motivated; and

8. The signature of the foreman or acting foreman of the grand jury, except where the

indictment has been ordered reduced pursuant to subdivision one-a of section 210.20 of this chapter or the accusatory instrument is a superior court information; and

9. The signature of the district attorney.

HISTORY: Add, L 1970, ch 996, § 1; amd, L 1974, ch 467, § 10, eff June 22, 1974, L 1978, ch 481, §§ 12, 36, eff Sept 1, 1978, L 1990, ch 209, § 12, eff Sept 1, 1990, L 2000, ch 107, § 7, eff Oct 8, 2000, L 2001, ch 300, § 5, eff Sept 17, 2001, L 2007, ch 7, § 31, eff April 13, 2007, L 2014, ch 55, § 15 (Part H, Subpart A), eff April 30, 2014.

§ 200.60. Indictment; allegations of previous convictions prohibited

1. When the fact that the defendant has been previously convicted of an offense raises an offense of lower grade to one of higher grade and thereby becomes an element of the latter, an indictment for such higher offense may not allege such previous conviction. If a reference to previous conviction is contained in the statutory name or title of such an offense, such name or title may not be used in the indictment, but an improvised name or title must be used which, by means of the phrase "as a felony" or in some other manner, labels and distinguishes the offense without reference to a previous conviction. This subdivision does not apply to an indictment or a count thereof that charges escape in the second degree pursuant to subdivision two of section 205.10 of the penal law, or escape in the first degree pursuant to section 205.15 thereof.

2. An indictment for such an offense must be accompanied by a special information, filed by the district attorney with the court, charging that the defendant was previously convicted of a specified offense. Except as provided in subdivision three, the people may not refer to such special information during the trial nor adduce any evidence concerning the previous conviction alleged therein.

3. After commencement of the trial and before the close of the people's case, the court, in the absence of the jury, must arraign the defendant upon such special information, and must advise him that he may admit the previous conviction alleged, deny it or remain mute. Depending upon the defendant's response, the trial of the indictment must then proceed as follows:

(a) If the defendant admits the previous conviction, that element of the offense charged in the indictment is deemed established, no evidence in support thereof may be adduced by the people, and the court must submit the case to the jury without reference thereto and as if the fact of such previous conviction were not an element of the offense. The court may not submit to the jury any lesser included offense which is distinguished from the offense charged solely by the fact that a previous conviction is not an element thereof.

(b) If the defendant denies the previous conviction or remains mute, the people may prove that element of the offense charged before the jury as a part of their case. In any prosecution under subparagraph (ix) of paragraph (a) of subdivision one of section 125.27 of the penal law, if the defendant denies the previous murder conviction or remains mute, the people may prove that element of the offense only after the jury has first found the defendant guilty of intentionally causing the death of a person as charged in the indictment, in which case the court shall then permit the people and the defendant to offer evidence and argument consistent with the relevant provisions of section 260.30 of this chapter with respect to the previous murder conviction.

4. Nothing contained in this section precludes the people from proving a prior conviction before a grand jury or relieves them from the obligation or necessity of so doing in order to submit a legally sufficient case.

HISTORY: Add, L 1970, ch 996, § 1, eff Sept 1, 1971, with substance derived from Crim C

§ 275-b. Sub 3, par (b), amd, L 1995, ch 1, § 8, eff Sept 1, 1995.

§ 200.61. Indictment; special information for operators of for-hire vehicles

1. The provisions of this section shall govern the procedures for determining whether a defendant is eligible to receive the sentence set forth in subdivision one of section 60.07 of the penal law upon conviction of a specified offense as defined in subdivision two of such section 60.07.

2. To receive the sentence set forth in subdivision one of section 60.07 of the penal law, an indictment for such specified offense must be accompanied by a special information, filed by the district attorney with the court, alleging that the victim of such offense was operating a for-hire vehicle in the course of providing for-hire vehicle services at the time of the commission of such offense.

3. Prior to the commencement of the trial, the court, in the absence of the jury, must arraign the defendant upon such special information, and must advise him that he may admit that the alleged victim of such offense was operating a for-hire vehicle in the course of providing for-hire vehicle services at the time of the alleged commission of such offense, deny such allegation or remain mute. Depending upon the defendant's response, the trial of the indictment must proceed as follows:

(a) If the defendant admits that the alleged victim of such specified offense charged was operating a for-hire vehicle in the course of providing for-hire vehicle services at the time of the commission of such alleged offense, such allegation, and only such allegation, shall be deemed established for purposes of eligibility, if the defendant is convicted of the underlying specified offense, for a sentence pursuant to subdivision one of section 60.07 of the penal law.

(b) If the defendant denies such allegation or remains mute, the people may, by proof beyond a reasonable doubt, prove as part of their case before the jury or, where the defendant has waived a jury trial, the court, that the alleged victim of such offense was operating a for-hire vehicle in the course of providing for-hire vehicle services at the time of the commission of the offense.

4. Where a jury, pursuant to paragraph (b) of subdivision three of this section, is charged with determining whether the alleged victim of such specified offense was operating a for-hire vehicle in the course of providing for-hire vehicle services, such jury shall consider and render its verdict on such matter only if it convicts the defendant of such specified offense or specified offenses charged.

5. For purposes of this section, the terms "for-hire vehicle", "for-hire vehicle services" and "specified offense" shall have the meanings set forth in section 60.07 of the penal law.

HISTORY: Add, L 2000, ch 148, § 5, eff Nov 1, 2000.

§ 200.62. Indictment; special information for child sexual assault offender

1. Whenever a person is charged with the commission or attempted commission of an offense defined in article one hundred thirty of the penal law which constitutes a felony and it appears that the victim of such offense was less than fifteen years old, an indictment for such offense may be accompanied by a special information, filed by the district attorney with the court, alleging that the victim was less than fifteen years old at the time of the commission of the offense; provided, however, that such an information need not be filed when the age of the victim is an element of the offense.

2. Prior to trial, or after the commencement of the trial but before the close of the people's case, the court, in the absence of the jury, must arraign the defendant upon such information and advise him or her that he or she may admit such allegation, deny it or remain mute. Depending upon the defendant's response, the trial of the indictment must proceed as follows:

(a) If the defendant admits that the alleged victim was less than fifteen years old at the time of the commission or attempted commission of the offense, that allegation shall be deemed established for all subsequent purposes, including sentencing pursuant to section 70.07 of the penal law.

(b) If the defendant denies such allegation or remains mute, the people may, by proof beyond a reasonable doubt, prove before the jury or, where the defendant has waived a jury trial, the court, that the alleged victim was less than fifteen years old at the time of the commission or attempted commission of the offense.

(c) Nothing in this subdivision shall prevent the people, in a trial before the court or a jury, from making reference to and introducing evidence of the victim's age.

3. Where a jury, pursuant to paragraph (b) of subdivision two of this section, makes the determination of whether the alleged victim of the offense was less than fifteen years old, such jury shall consider and render its verdict on such issue only after rendering its verdict with regard to the offense.

4. A determination pursuant to this section that the victim was less than fifteen years old at the time of the commission of the offense shall be binding in any future proceeding in which the issue may arise unless the underlying conviction or determination is vacated or reversed.

HISTORY: Add, L 2000, ch 1, § 47, eff Feb 1, 2001. Sub 2, opening par, amd, L 2003, ch 264, § 40, eff Nov 1, 2003. Sub 2, par (c), add, L 2003, ch 264, § 40, eff Nov 1, 2003.

§ 200.63. Indictment; special information for aggravated family offense

1. Whenever a person is charged with the commission or attempted commission of an aggravated family offense as defined in section 240.75 of the penal law, an indictment or information for such offense shall be accompanied by a special information, filed by the district attorney with the court, alleging that the defendant was previously convicted of a specified offense as defined in subdivision two of section 240.75 of the penal law, that at the time of the previous offense the defendant and the person against whom the offense was committed were members of the same family or household as defined in subdivision one of section 530.11 of this chapter, and that such previous conviction took place within the time period specified in subdivision one of section 240.75 of the penal law. Except as provided herein, the people may not refer to such special information during trial nor adduce any evidence concerning the allegations therein.

2. Prior to the commencement of the trial, the court, in the absence of the jury, must arraign the defendant upon such information and advise him or her that he or she may admit each such allegation, deny any such allegation or remain mute with respect to any such allegation. Depending upon the defendant's response, the trial of the indictment or information must then proceed as follows:

(a) (i) If the previous conviction is for an aggravated family offense as defined in section 240.75 of the penal law, and the defendant admits the previous conviction or that it took place within the time period specified in subdivision one of section 240.75 of the penal law, such admitted allegation or allegations shall be deemed established for the purposes of the present prosecution, including sentencing pursuant to section 70.00 of the penal law. The court must submit the case to the jury as if such admitted allegation or allegations were not elements of the offense.

(ii) If the defendant denies the previous conviction or remains mute with respect to it, the people may prove, beyond a reasonable doubt, that element of the offense before the jury as a part of their case.

(iii) If the defendant denies that the previous conviction took place within the time period specified in subdivision one of section 240.75 of the penal law, or remains mute with respect to that matter, the people may prove, beyond a reasonable doubt, before the jury as part of their case, that the previous conviction took place within the time period specified.

(b) (i) If the previous conviction is for a specified offense as defined in subdivision two of section 240.75 of the penal law, other than an aggravated family offense, and the defendant admits such previous conviction, that it took place within the time period specified in subdivision one of section 240.75 of the penal law, or that the defendant and the person against whom the offense was committed were members of the same family or household as defined in subdivision one of section 530.11 of this chapter, such admitted allegation or allegations shall be deemed established for the purposes of the present prosecution, including sentencing pursuant to section 70.00 of the penal law. The court must submit the case to the jury as if the admitted allegation or allegations were not elements of the offense.

(ii) If the defendant denies the previous conviction or remains mute with respect to it, the people may prove, beyond a reasonable doubt, that element of the offense before the jury as a part of their case.

(iii) If the defendant denies that the previous conviction took place within the time period specified in subdivision one of section 240.75 of the penal law, or remains mute with respect to that matter, the people may prove, beyond a reasonable doubt, before the jury as part of their case, that the previous conviction took place within the time period specified.

(iv) If the defendant denies that the defendant and the person against whom the previous offense was committed were members of the same family or household as defined in subdivision one of section 530.11 of this chapter, or remains mute with respect to that matter, the people may prove, beyond a reasonable doubt, that element of the offense before the jury as a part of their case.

HISTORY: Add, L 2012, ch 491, § 3 (Part D), eff Jan 23, 2013.

§ 200.65. Indictment; special information for enterprise corruption and criminal possession or use of a biological weapon or chemical weapon

When filing an indictment which charges enterprise corruption in violation of article four hundred sixty of the penal law, criminal possession of a chemical weapon or biological weapon in violation of section 490.37, 490.40, or 490.45 of the penal law, or criminal use of a chemical weapon or biological weapon in violation of section 490.47, 490.50, or 490.55 of the penal law, the district attorney must submit a statement to the court attesting that he or she has reviewed the substance of the evidence presented to the grand jury and concurs in the judgment that the charge is consistent with legislative findings in article four hundred sixty or four hundred ninety of the penal law, as applicable. For purposes of this section only, "district attorney" means the district attorney of the county, the attorney general, or the deputy attorney general in charge of the organized crime task force, or where such person is actually absent or disabled, the person authorized to act in his or her stead.

HISTORY: Add, L 1986, ch 516, § 7, eff Nov 1, 1986. Amd, L 2004, ch 1, § 10 (Part A), eff July

23, 2004. Section heading, amd, L 2004, ch 1, § 10 (Part A), eff July 23, 2004.

§ 200.70. Indictment; amendment of

1. At any time before or during trial, the court may, upon application of the people and with notice to the defendant and opportunity to be heard, order the amendment of an indictment with respect to defects, errors or variances from the proof relating to matters of form, time, place, names of persons and the like, when such an amendment does not change the theory or theories of the prosecution as reflected in the evidence before the grand jury which filed such indictment, or otherwise tend to prejudice the defendant on the merits. Where the accusatory instrument is a superior court information, such an amendment may be made when it does not tend to prejudice the defendant on the merits. Upon permitting such an amendment, the court must, upon application of the defendant, order any adjournment of the proceedings which may, by reason of such amendment, be necessary to accord the defendant adequate opportunity to prepare his defense.

2. An indictment may not be amended in any respect which changes the theory or theories of the prosecution as reflected in the evidence before the grand jury which filed it; nor may an indictment or superior court information be amended for the purpose of curing:

(a) A failure thereof to charge or state an offense; or

(b) Legal insufficiency of the factual allegations; or

(c) A misjoinder of offenses; or

(d) A misjoinder of defendants.

HISTORY: Add, L 1970, ch 996, § 1; amd, L 1974, ch 467, § 11, eff June 22, 1974.

§ 200.80. Indictment; superseding indictments

If at any time before entry of a plea of guilty to an indictment or commencement of a trial thereof another indictment is filed in the same court charging the defendant with an offense charged in the first indictment, the first indictment is, with respect to such offense, superseded by the second and, upon the defendant's arraignment upon the second indictment, the count of the first indictment charging such offense must be dismissed by the court. The first indictment is not, however, superseded with respect to any count contained therein which charges an offense not charged in the second indictment. Nothing herein precludes the filing of a superseding indictment when the first accusatory instrument is a superior court information.

HISTORY: Add, L 1970, ch 996, § 1, with substance derived from Crim C § 292-a; amd, L 1974, ch 467, § 12, eff June 22, 1974.

§ 200.90. [Repealed]

HISTORY: Add, L 1970, ch 996, § 1; amd, L 1974, ch 763, § 5, L 1979, ch 413, §§ 1, 2; repealed, L 1982, ch 558, § 3, eff Oct 20, 1982.

§ 200.95. Indictment; bill of particulars

1. Definitions.

(a) "Bill of particulars" is a written statement by the prosecutor specifying, as required by this section, items of factual information which are not recited in the indictment and which pertain to the offense charged and including the substance of each defendant's conduct encompassed by the charge which the people intend to prove at trial on their direct case, and whether the people intend to prove that the defendant acted as principal or accomplice or both, and items of factual information which are not recited in a special forfeiture information or prosecutor's forfeiture information containing one or more forfeiture counts and which pertain to the substance of each defendant's conduct giving rise to the forfeiture claim, the approximate value of property for which forfeiture is sought, the nature and extent of the defendant's interest in such property, and the extent of the defendant's gain, if any, from the offense charged. However, the prosecutor shall not be required to include in the bill of particulars matters of evidence relating to how the people intend to prove the elements of the offense charged or how the people intend to prove any item of factual information included in the bill of particulars.

(b) "Request for a bill of particulars" is a written request served by defendant upon the people, without leave of the court, requesting a bill of particulars, specifying the items of factual information desired, and alleging that defendant cannot adequately prepare or conduct his defense without the information requested.

2. Bill of particulars upon request. Upon a timely request for a bill of particulars by a defendant against whom an indictment is pending, the prosecutor shall within fifteen days of the service of the request or as soon thereafter as is practicable, serve upon the defendant or his attorney, and file with the court, the bill of particulars, except to the extent the prosecutor shall have refused to comply with the request pursuant to subdivision four of this section.

3. Timeliness of a request. A request for a bill of particulars shall be timely if made within thirty days after arraignment and before the commencement of trial. If the defendant is not represented by counsel, and has requested an adjournment to obtain counsel or to have counsel assigned, the thirty day period shall commence, for the purposes of a request for a bill of particulars by the defendant, on the date counsel initially appears on his behalf. However, the court may direct compliance with a request for a bill of particulars that, for good cause shown, could not have been made within the time specified.

4. Request refused. The prosecutor may refuse to comply with the request for a bill of particulars or any portion of the request for a bill of particulars to the extent he reasonably believes that the item of factual information requested is not authorized to be included in a bill of particulars, or that such information is not necessary to enable the defendant adequately to prepare or conduct his defense, or that a protective order would be warranted or that the demand is untimely. Such refusal shall be made in a writing, which shall set forth the grounds of such belief as fully as possible, consistent with the reason for the refusal. Within fifteen days of the request or as soon thereafter as practicable, the refusal shall be served upon the defendant and a copy shall be filed with the court.

5. Court ordered bill of particulars. Where a prosecutor has timely served a written refusal pursuant to subdivision four of this section and upon motion, made in writing, of a defendant, who has made a request for a bill of particulars and whose request has not been complied with in whole or in part, the court must, to the extent a protective order is not warranted, order the prosecutor to comply with the request if it is satisfied that the items of factual information requested are authorized to be included in a bill of particulars, and that such information is necessary to enable the defendant adequately to prepare or conduct his defense and, if the request was untimely, a finding of good cause for the delay. Where the prosecutor has not timely served a written refusal pursuant to subdivision four of this section the court must, unless it is satisfied that the people have shown good cause why such an order should not be issued, issue an order requiring the prosecutor to comply or providing for any other order authorized by subdivision one of section 240.70.

6. Motion procedure. A motion for a bill of particulars shall be made as prescribed in section 255.20. Upon an order granting a motion pursuant to this section, the prosecutor must file with the court a bill of particulars, reciting every item of information designated in the order, and serve a copy thereof upon the defendant. Pending such filing and service, the proceedings are stayed.

7. Protective order.

(a) The court in which the criminal action is pending may, upon motion of the prosecutor, or of any affected person, or upon determination of a motion of defendant for a court ordered bill of particulars, or upon its own initiative, issue a protective order denying, limiting, conditioning, delaying or regulating the bill of particulars for good cause, including constitutional limitations, danger to the integrity of physical evidence or a substantial risk of physical harm, intimidation, economic reprisal, bribery or unjustified annoyance or embarrassment to any person or an adverse effect upon the legitimate needs of law enforcement, including the protection of the confidentiality of informants, or any other factor or set of factors which outweighs the need for the bill of particulars.

(b) An order limiting, conditioning, delaying or regulating the bill of particulars may, among other things, require that any material copied or derived therefrom be maintained in the exclusive possession of the attorney for the defendant and be used for the exclusive purpose of preparing for the defense of the criminal action.

8. Amendment. At any time before commencement of trial, the prosecutor may, without leave of the court, serve upon defendant and file with the court an amended bill of particulars. At any time during trial, upon application of the prosecutor and with notice to the defendant and an opportunity for him to be heard, the court must, upon finding that no undue prejudice will accrue to defendant and that the prosecutor has acted in good faith, permit the prosecutor to amend the bill of particulars. Upon any amendment of the bill of particulars, the court must, upon application of defendant, order an adjournment of the proceedings or any other action it deems appropriate which may, by reason of the amendment, be necessary to accord the defendant an adequate opportunity to defend.

HISTORY: Add, L 1982, ch 558, § 3, eff Oct 20, 1982. Sub 1, par (a), amd, L 1990, ch 655, § 16, eff Nov 1, 1990.

ARTICLE 210   PROCEEDINGS IN SUPERIOR COURT FROM FILING OF INDICTMENT TO PLEA

HISTORY: Add, L 1970, ch 996, § 1, eff Sept 1, 1971.

§ 210.05. Indictment and superior court information exclusive methods of prosecution

The only methods of prosecuting an offense in a superior court are by an indictment filed therewith by a grand jury or by a superior court information filed therewith by a district attorney.

HISTORY: Add, L 1970, ch 996, § 1, with substance derived from Crim C § 222; amd, L 1974, ch 467, § 13, eff June 22, 1974. Section heading, amd, L 1974, ch 467, § 13, eff June 22, 1974.

§ 210.10. Requirement of and methods of securing defendant's appearance for arraignment upon indictment

After an indictment has been filed with a superior court, the defendant must be arraigned thereon. He must appear personally at such arraignment, and his appearance may be secured as follows:

1. If the defendant was previously held by a local criminal court for the action of the grand jury, and if he is confined in the custody of the sheriff pursuant to a previous court order issued in the same criminal action, the superior court must direct the sheriff to produce the defendant for arraignment on a specified date and the sheriff must comply with such direction. The court must give at least two days notice of the time and place of the arraignment to an attorney, if any, who has previously filed a notice of appearance in behalf of the defendant with such superior court, or if no such notice of appearance has been filed, to an attorney, if any, who filed a notice of appearance in behalf of the defendant with the local criminal court.

2. If a felony complaint against the defendant was pending in a local criminal court or if the defendant was previously held by a local criminal court for the action of the grand jury, and if the defendant is at liberty on his or her own recognizance or on bail pursuant to a previous court order issued in the same criminal action, the superior court must, upon at least two days notice to the defendant and his or her surety, to any person other than the defendant who posted cash bail and to any attorney who would be entitled to notice under circumstances prescribed in subdivision one, direct the defendant to appear before the superior court for arraignment on a specified date. If the defendant fails to appear on such date, the court may issue a bench warrant and, in addition, may forfeit the bail, if any. Upon taking the defendant into custody pursuant to such bench warrant, the executing police officer must without unnecessary delay bring the defendant before such superior court for arraignment. If such superior court is not available, the executing police officer may bring the defendant to the local correctional facility of the county in which such superior court sits, to be detained there until not later than the commencement of the next session of such court occurring on the next business day.

3. If the defendant has not previously been held by a local criminal court for the action of the grand jury and the filing of the indictment constituted the commencement of the criminal action, the superior court must order the indictment to be filed as a sealed instrument until the defendant is produced or appears for arraignment, and must issue a superior court warrant of arrest. Upon the request of the district attorney, in lieu of a superior court warrant of arrest, the court may issue a summons if it is satisfied that the defendant will respond thereto. Upon the request of the district attorney, in lieu of a warrant of arrest or summons, the court may instead authorize the district attorney to direct the defendant to appear for arraignment on a designated date if it is satisfied that the defendant will so appear. A superior court warrant of arrest is executable anywhere in the state. Such warrant may be addressed to any police officer whose geographical area of employment embraces either the place where the offense charged was allegedly committed or the locality of the court by which the warrant is issued. It must be executed in the same manner as an ordinary warrant of arrest, as provided in section 120.80,

and following the arrest the executing police officer must without unnecessary delay perform all recording, fingerprinting, photographing and other preliminary police duties required in the particular case, and bring the defendant before the superior court. If such superior court is not available, the executing police officer may bring the defendant to the local correctional facility of the county in which such superior court sits, to be detained there until not later than the commencement of the next session of such court occurring on the next business day.

4. A superior court warrant of arrest may be executed by (a) any police officer to whom it is addressed or (b) any other police officer delegated to execute it under circumstances prescribed in subdivisions five and six.

5. The issuing court may authorize the delegation of such warrant. Where the issuing court has so authorized, a police officer to whom a superior court warrant of arrest is addressed may delegate another police officer to whom it is not addressed to execute such warrant as his agent when:

(a) He has reasonable cause to believe that the defendant is in a particular county other than the one in which the warrant is returnable; and

(b) The geographical area of employment of the delegated police officer embraces the locality where the arrest is to be made.

6. Under circumstances specified in subdivision five, the police officer to whom the warrant is addressed may inform the delegated officer, by telecommunication, mail or any other means, of the issuance of the warrant, of the offense charged in the underlying accusatory instrument and of all other pertinent details, and may request such officer to act as his or her agent in arresting the defendant pursuant to such warrant. Upon such request, the delegated police officer is to the same extent as the delegating officer, authorized to make such arrest pursuant to the warrant within the geographical area of such delegated officer's employment. Upon so arresting the defendant, he or she must without unnecessary delay deliver the defendant or cause the defendant to be delivered to the custody of the police officer by whom he or she was so delegated, and the latter must then without unnecessary delay bring the defendant before a court in which such warrant is returnable. If such court is not available, the delegating officer may bring the defendant to the local correctional facility of the county in which such court sits, to be detained there until not later than the commencement of the next session of such court occurring on the next business day.

HISTORY: Add, L 1970, ch 996, § 1; amd, L 1974, ch 467, § 14, eff June 22, 1974. Sub 2, amd, L 1976, ch 696, § 1, L 1984, ch 384, § 1, L 1990, ch 681, § 1, eff Nov 1, 1990. Sub 3, amd, L 1990, ch 681, § 1, L 1993, ch 446, § 9, eff Nov 1, 1993. Sub 4, add, L 1988, ch 565, § 1, eff Nov 1, 1988. Sub 5, add, L 1988, ch 565, § 1, eff Nov 1, 1988. Sub 6, add, L 1988, ch 565, § 1; amd, L 1990, ch 681, § 1, eff Nov 1, 1990.

§ 210.15. Arraignment upon indictment; defendant's rights, court's instructions and bail matters

1. Upon the defendant's arraignment before a superior court upon an indictment, the court must immediately inform him, or cause him to be informed in its presence, of the charge or charges against him, and the district attorney must cause him to be furnished with a copy of the indictment.

2. The defendant has a right to the aid of counsel at the arraignment and at every subsequent stage of the action, and, if he appears upon such arraignment without counsel, has the following rights:

(a) To an adjournment for the purpose of obtaining counsel; and

(b) To communicate, free of charge, by letter or by telephone provided by the law enforcement facility where the defendant is held to a phone number located in the United States or Puerto Rico, for the purposes of obtaining counsel and informing a relative or friend that he or she has been charged with an offense; and

(c) To have counsel assigned by the court in any case where he is financially unable to obtain the same.

3. The court must inform the defendant of all rights specified in subdivision two. The court must accord the defendant opportunity to exercise such rights and must itself take such affirmative action as is necessary to effectuate them.

4. [Repealed]

5. If the defendant desires to proceed without the aid of counsel, the court must permit him to do so if it is satisfied that he made such decision with knowledge of the significance thereof, but if it is not so satisfied it may not proceed until the defendant is provided with counsel, either of his own choosing or by assignment. A defendant who proceeds at the arraignment without counsel does not waive his right to counsel, and the court must inform him that he continues to have such right as well as all the rights specified in subdivision two which are necessary to effectuate it, and that he may exercise such rights at any stage of the action.

6. Upon the arraignment, the court, unless it intends to make a final disposition of the action immediately thereafter, must, as provided in section 530.40, issue a securing order, releasing the defendant on his own recognizance or fixing bail or committing him to the custody of the sheriff for his future appearance in such action.

> **HISTORY:** Add, L 1970, ch 996, § 1; amd, L 1972, ch 697, § 2, L 1973, ch 472, § 1, L 2010, ch 94, § 5, eff July 24, 2010.

§ 210.16. Requirement of HIV related testing in certain cases

1. (a) In a case where an indictment or a superior court information has been filed with a superior court which charges the defendant with a felony offense enumerated in any section of article one hundred thirty of the penal law where an act of "sexual intercourse", "oral sexual conduct" or "anal sexual conduct," as those terms are defined in section 130.00 of the penal law, is required as an essential element for the commission thereof, the court shall, upon a request of the victim within six months of the date of the crimes charged, order that the defendant submit to human immunodeficiency virus (HIV) related testing. Testing of a defendant shall be ordered when the result would provide medical benefit to the victim or a psychological benefit to the victim. Medical benefit shall be found when the following elements are satisfied: (i) a decision is pending about beginning, continuing, or discontinuing a medical intervention for the victim; and (ii) the result of an HIV test of the accused could affect that decision, and could provide relevant information beyond that which would be provided by an HIV test of the victim. If testing the defendant would provide medical benefit to the victim or a psychological benefit to the victim, then the testing is to be conducted by a state, county, or local public health officer designated by the order. Test results, which shall not be disclosed to the court, shall be communicated to the defendant and the victim named in the order in accordance with the provisions of section twenty-seven hundred eighty-five-a of the public health law.

(b) For the purposes of this section, the terms "victim" and "applicant" mean the person with whom the defendant is charged to have engaged in an act of "sexual intercourse", "oral sexual conduct" or "anal sexual conduct", as those terms are defined in section 130.00 of the penal law, where such conduct with such victim was the basis for charging the defendant with an offense specified in paragraph (a) of this subdivision.

2. Any request made by the victim pursuant to this section must be in writing, filed with the court within six months of the date of the crimes charged, and provided by the court to the defendant or his or her counsel. The request must be filed with the court prior to or within forty-eight hours after the indictment or superior court information has been filed with the superior court; provided however that, for good cause shown, the court may permit such request to be filed at a later stage of the action within six months of the date of the crimes charged.

3. At any stage in the action within six months of the date of the crimes charged, prior to the final disposition of the indictment or superior court information and while the defendant is charged with an offense specified in paragraph (a) of subdivision one of this section, the victim may request that the defendant submit to a follow-up HIV related test. Such request must be in writing, filed with the court and provided by the court to the defendant or his or her counsel. Upon a finding that the follow-up HIV related test is medically appropriate the court must order that the defendant submit to such test. The court shall not make such finding of medical appropriateness unless the follow-up HIV related test is to be administered a sufficient time after the charged offense to be consistent with guidelines that may be issued by the commissioner of health. There shall be no more than one follow-up HIV related test absent a showing of extraordinary circumstances.

4. Any requests, related papers and orders made or filed pursuant to this section, together with any papers or proceedings related thereto, shall be sealed by the court and not made available for any purpose, except as may be necessary for the conduct of judicial proceedings directly related to the provisions of this section. All proceedings on such requests shall be held in camera.

5. The application for an order to compel a defendant to undergo an HIV related test may be made by the victim but, if the victim is an infant or incompetent person, the application may also be made by a representative as defined in section twelve hundred one of the civil practice law and rules. The application must state that: (a) the applicant was the victim of the offense enumerated in paragraph (a) of subdivision one of this section of which the defendant is charged; and (b) the applicant has been offered pre-HIV test counseling and post-HIV test counseling by a public health officer in accordance with article twenty-seven-F of the public health law and has been advised, in accordance with any guidelines that may be issued by the commissioner of health, of (i) the limitations on the information to be obtained through an HIV test on the proposed subject; (ii) current scientific assessments of the risk of transmission of HIV from the exposure he or she may have experienced; and (iii) the need for the applicant to undergo HIV related testing to definitively determine his or her HIV status.

6. The court shall conduct a hearing only if necessary to determine if the applicant is the victim of the offense of which the defendant is charged or to determine whether a follow-up test is medically appropriate. The court ordered test must be performed within forty-eight hours of the date on which the court ordered the test, provided, however, that whenever the defendant is not tested within the period prescribed by the court, the court must again order that the defendant undergo an HIV related test. The defendant shall be advised of information as to HIV testing and medical treatment in accordance with any guidelines that may be issued by the commissioner of health.

7. (a) Test results shall be disclosed subject to the following limitations, which shall be specified in any order issued pursuant to this section:

(i) disclosure of confidential HIV related information shall be limited to that information which is necessary to fulfill the purpose for which the order is granted; and

(ii) disclosure of confidential HIV related information shall be made to the defendant upon his or her request, and disclosure to a person other than the defendant shall be limited to the person making the application; redisclosure shall be permitted only to the victim, the victim's immediate family, guardian, physicians, attorneys, medical or mental health providers and to his or her past and future contacts to whom there was or is a reasonable risk of HIV transmission and shall not be permitted to any other person or the court.

(b) Unless inconsistent with this section, the court's order shall direct compliance with and conform to the provisions of article twenty-seven-F of the public health law. Such order shall include measures to protect against disclosure to others of the identity and HIV status of the applicant and of the person tested and may include such other measures as the court deems necessary to protect confidential information.

8. Any failure to comply with the provisions of this section or section twenty-seven hundred eighty-five-a of the public health law shall not impair or affect the validity of any proceeding upon the indictment or superior court information.

9. No information obtained as a result of a consent, hearing or court order for testing issued pursuant to this section nor any information derived therefrom may be used as evidence in any criminal or civil proceeding against the defendant which relates to events that were the basis for charging the defendant with an offense enumerated in paragraph (a) of subdivision one of this section, provided however that nothing in this section shall prevent prosecution of a witness testifying in any court hearing held pursuant to this section for perjury pursuant to article two hundred ten of the penal law.

HISTORY: Add, L 2007, ch 571, § 1, eff Nov 1, 2007.

§ 210.20. Motion to dismiss or reduce indictment

1. After arraignment upon an indictment, the superior court may, upon motion of the defendant, dismiss such indictment or any count thereof upon the ground that:

(a) Such indictment or count is defective, within the meaning of section 210.25; or

(b) The evidence before the grand jury was not legally sufficient to establish the offense charged or any lesser included offense; or

(c) The grand jury proceeding was defective, within the meaning of section 210.35; or

(d) The defendant has immunity with respect to the offense charged, pursuant to section 50.20 or 190.40; or

(e) The prosecution is barred by reason of a previous prosecution, pursuant to section 40.20; or

(f) The prosecution is untimely, pursuant to section 30.10; or

(g) The defendant has been denied the right to a speedy trial; or

(h) There exists some other jurisdictional or legal impediment to conviction of the defendant for the offense charged; or

(i) Dismissal is required in the interest of justice, pursuant to section 210.40.

1-a. After arraignment upon an indictment, if the superior court, upon motion of the defendant pursuant to this subdivision or paragraph b of subdivision one of this section challenging the legal sufficiency of the evidence before the grand jury, finds that the evidence before the grand jury was not legally sufficient to establish the commission by the defendant of the offense charged in any count contained within the indictment, but was legally sufficient to establish the commission of a lesser included offense, it shall order the count or counts of the indictment with respect to which the finding is made reduced to allege the most serious lesser included offense with respect to which the evidence before the grand jury was sufficient, except that where the most serious lesser included offense thus found is a petty offense, and the court does not find evidence of the commission of any crime in any other count of the indictment, it shall order the indictment dismissed and a prosecutor's information charging the petty offense filed in the appropriate local criminal court. The motion to dismiss or reduce any count of an indictment based on legal insufficiency to establish the offense charged shall be made in accordance with the procedure set forth in subdivisions one through seven of section 210.45, provided however, the court shall state on the record the basis for its determination. Upon entering an order pursuant to this subdivision, the court shall consider the appropriateness of any securing order issued pursuant to article 510 of this chapter.

2. A motion pursuant to this section, except a motion pursuant to paragraph (g) of subdivision one, should be made within the period provided in section 255.20. A motion made pursuant to paragraph (g) of subdivision one must be made prior to the commencement of trial or entry of a plea of guilty.

3. Upon the motion, a defendant who is in a position adequately to raise more than one ground in support thereof should raise every such ground upon which he intends to challenge the indictment. A subsequent motion based upon any such ground not so raised may be summarily denied, although the court, in the interest of justice and for good cause shown, may in its discretion entertain and dispose of such a motion on the merits notwithstanding.

4. Upon dismissing an indictment or a count thereof upon any of the grounds specified in paragraphs (a), (b), (c) and (i) of subdivision one, or, upon dismissing a superior court information or a count thereof upon any of the grounds specified in paragraphs (a) or (i) of subdivision one, the court may, upon application of the people, in its discretion authorize the people to submit the charge or charges to the same or another grand jury. When the dismissal is based upon some other ground, such authorization may not be granted. In the absence of authorization to submit or resubmit, the order of dismissal constitutes a bar to any further prosecution of such charge or charges, by indictment or otherwise, in any criminal court within the county.

5. If the court dismisses one or more counts of an indictment, against a defendant who was under the age of sixteen at the time of the commission of the crime and who did not lack criminal responsibility for such crime by reason of infancy, and one or more other counts of the indictment having been joined in the indictment solely with the dismissed count pursuant to subdivision six of section 200.20 is not dismissed, the court must direct that such count be removed to the family court in accordance with article seven hundred twenty-five of this chapter.

6. The effectiveness of an order reducing a count or counts of an indictment or dismissing an indictment and directing the filing of a prosecutor's information or dismissing a count or counts of an indictment charging murder in the first degree shall be stayed for thirty days following the entry of such order unless such stay is otherwise waived by the people. On or before the conclusion of such thirty-day period, the people shall exercise one of the following options:

(a) Accept the court's order by filing a reduced indictment, by dismissing the indictment and filing a prosecutor's information, or by filing an indictment containing any count or counts remaining after dismissal of the count or counts charging murder in the first degree, as appropriate;

(b) Resubmit the subject count or counts to the same or a different grand jury within thirty days of the entry of the order or such additional time as the court may permit upon a showing of good cause; provided, however, that if in such case an order is again entered with respect to such count or counts pursuant to subdivision one-a of this section, such count or counts may not again be submitted to a grand jury. Where the people exercise this option, the effectiveness of the order further shall be stayed pending a determination by the grand jury and the filing of a new indictment, if voted, charging the resubmitted count or counts;

(c) Appeal the order pursuant to subdivision one or one-a of section 450.20. Where the people exercise this option, the effectiveness of the order further shall be stayed in accordance with the provisions of subdivision two of section 460.40.

If the people fail to exercise one of the foregoing options, the court's order shall take effect and the people shall comply with paragraph (a) of this subdivision.

HISTORY: Add, L 1970, ch 996, § 1, eff Sept 1, 1971. Section heading, amd, L 1990, ch 209, § 13, eff Sept 1, 1990. Sub 1-a, add, L 1990, ch 209, § 14, eff Sept 1, 1990. Sub 2, amd, L 1972, ch 184, § 3, L 1974, ch 763, § 2, eff Sept 1, 1974. Sub 4, amd, L 1974, ch 467, § 15, eff June 22, 1974. Sub 5, add, L 1980, ch 136, § 3, eff May 20, 1980. Sub 6, add, L 1990, ch 209, § 14; amd, L 1995, ch 1, § 9, eff Sept 1, 1995. Sub 6, opening par, amd, L 1995, ch 1, § 9, eff Sept 1, 1995. Sub 6, par (a), amd, L 1995, ch 1, § 9, eff Sept 1, 1995. Sub 6, par (c), amd, L 1995, ch 1, § 9, eff Sept 1, 1995. Sub 6, closing par, add, L 1999, ch 563, § 1, eff Nov 1, 1999.

§ 210.25. Motion to dismiss indictment; as defective

An indictment or a count thereof is defective within the meaning of paragraph (a) of subdivision one of section 210.20 when:

1. It does not substantially conform to the requirements stated in article two hundred; provided that an indictment may not be dismissed as defective, but must instead be amended, where the defect or irregularity is of a kind that may be cured by amendment, pursuant to section 200.70, and where the people move to so amend; or

2. The allegations demonstrate that the court does not have jurisdiction of the offense charged; or

3. The statute defining the offense charged is unconstitutional or otherwise invalid.

HISTORY: Add, L 1970, ch 996, § 1, eff Sept 1, 1971.

§ 210.30. Motion to dismiss or reduce indictment on ground of insufficiency of grand jury evidence; motion to inspect grand jury minutes

1. A motion to dismiss an indictment or a count thereof pursuant to paragraph (b) of subdivision one of section 210.20 or a motion to reduce a count or counts of an indictment pursuant to subdivision one-a of section 210.20 must be preceded or accompanied by a motion to inspect the grand jury minutes, as prescribed in subdivision two of this section.

2. A motion to inspect grand jury minutes is a motion by a defendant requesting an examination by the court and the defendant of the stenographic minutes of a grand jury proceeding resulting in an indictment for the purpose of determining whether the evidence before the grand jury was legally sufficient to support the charges or a charge contained in such indictment.

3. Unless good cause exists to deny the motion to inspect the grand jury minutes, the court must grant the motion. It must then proceed to examine the minutes and to determine the motion to

dismiss or reduce the indictment. If the court, after examining the minutes, finds that release of the minutes, or certain portions thereof, to the parties is necessary to assist the court in making its determination on the motion, it may release the minutes or such portions thereof to the parties. Provided, however, such release shall be limited to that grand jury testimony which is relevant to a determination of whether the evidence before the grand jury was legally sufficient to support a charge or charges contained in such indictment. Prior to such release the district attorney shall be given an opportunity to present argument to the court that the release of the minutes, or any portion thereof, would not be in the public interest. For purposes of this section, the minutes shallinclude any materials submitted to the grand jury pursuant to subdivision eight of section 190.30 of this chapter.

4. If the court determines that there is not reasonable cause to believe that the evidence before the grand jury may have been legally insufficient, it may in its discretion either (a) deny both the motion to inspect and the motion to dismiss or reduce, or (b) grant the motion to inspect notwithstanding and proceed to examine the minutes and to determine the motion to dismiss or reduce.

5. In any case, the court must place on the record its ruling upon the motion to inspect.

6. The validity of an order denying any motion made pursuant to this section is not reviewable upon an appeal from an ensuing judgment of conviction based upon legally sufficient trial evidence.

7. Notwithstanding any other provision of law, where the indictment is filed against a juvenile offender, the court shall dismiss the indictment or count thereof where the evidence before the grand jury was not legally sufficient to establish the offense charged or any lesser included offense for which the defendant is criminally responsible. Upon such dismissal, unless the court shall authorize the people to resubmit the charge to a subsequent grand jury, and upon a finding that there was sufficient evidence to believe defendant is a juvenile delinquent as defined in subdivision (a) of section seven hundred twelve of the family court act and upon specifying the act or acts it found sufficient evidence to believe defendant committed, the court may direct that such matter be removed to family court in accordance with the provisions of article seven hundred twenty-five of this chapter.

HISTORY: Add, L 1970, ch 996, § 1, eff Sept 1, 1971. Section heading, amd, L 1990, ch 209, § 15, eff Sept 1, 1990. Sub 1, amd, L 1990, ch 209, § 15, eff Sept 1, 1990. Sub 2, amd, L 1980, ch 841, § 1, L 1980, ch 842, § 1, eff July 1, 1980. Sub 3, amd, L 1980, ch 841, § 2, L 1980, ch 842, § 1, L 1990, ch 209, § 15, eff Sept 1, 1990. Sub 3, amd, L 2008, ch 279, § 14-a, eff Jan 3, 2009. Sub 4, amd, L 1990, ch 209, § 15, eff Sept 1, 1990. Sub 7, add, L 1980, ch 136, § 4, eff May 20, 1980.

§ 210.35. Motion to dismiss indictment; defective grand jury proceeding

A grand jury proceeding is defective within the meaning of paragraph (c) of subdivision one of section 210.20 when:

1. The grand jury was illegally constituted; or

2. The proceeding is conducted before fewer than sixteen grand jurors; or

3. Fewer than twelve grand jurors concur in the finding of the indictment; or

4. The defendant is not accorded an opportunity to appear and testify before the grand jury in accordance with the provisions of section 190.50; or

5. The proceeding otherwise fails to conform to the requirements of article one hundred

ninety to such degree that the integrity thereof is impaired and prejudice to the defendant may result.

HISTORY: Add, L 1970, ch 996, § 1, eff Sept 1, 1971.

§ 210.40. Motion to dismiss indictment; in furtherance of justice

1. An indictment or any count thereof may be dismissed in furtherance of justice, as provided in paragraph (i) of subdivision one of section 210.20, when, even though there may be no basis for dismissal as a matter of law upon any ground specified in paragraphs (a) through (h) of said subdivision one of section 210.20, such dismissal is required as a matter of judicial discretion by the existence of some compelling factor, consideration or circumstance clearly demonstrating that conviction or prosecution of the defendant upon such indictment or count would constitute or result in injustice. In determining whether such compelling factor, consideration, or circumstance exists, the court must, to the extent applicable, examine and consider, individually and collectively, the following:

(a) the seriousness and circumstances of the offense;

(b) the extent of harm caused by the offense;

(c) the evidence of guilt, whether admissible or inadmissible at trial;

(d) the history, character and condition of the defendant;

(e) any exceptionally serious misconduct of law enforcement personnel in the investigation, arrest and prosecution of the defendant;

(f) the purpose and effect of imposing upon the defendant a sentence authorized for the offense;

(g) the impact of a dismissal upon the confidence of the public in the criminal justice system;

(h) the impact of a dismissal on the safety or welfare of the community;

(i) where the court deems it appropriate, the attitude of the complainant or victim with respect to the motion;

(j) any other relevant fact indicating that a judgment of conviction would serve no useful purpose.

2. In addition to the grounds specified in subdivision one of this section, a count alleging enterprise corruption in violation of article four hundred sixty of the penal law may be dismissed in the interest of justice where prosecution of that count is inconsistent with the stated legislative findings in said article. Upon a motion pursuant to this section, the court must inspect the evidence before the grand jury and such other evidence or information as it may deem proper.

3. An order dismissing an indictment in the interest of justice may be issued upon motion of the people or of the court itself as well as upon that of the defendant. Upon issuing such an order, the court must set forth its reasons therefor upon the record.

HISTORY: Add, L 1970, ch 996, § 1, eff Sept 1, 1971. Sub 1, amd, L 1979, ch 216, § 2, eff Jan 1, 1980. Sub 1, pars (a)–(j), add, L 1979, ch 216, § 2, eff Jan 1, 1980. Sub 2, add, L 1986, ch 516, § 8, eff Nov 1, 1986. Former sub 2, renumbered sub 3, L 1986, ch 516, § 8, eff Nov 1, 1986. Sub 3, formerly sub 2, renumbered sub 3, L 1986, ch 516, § 8, eff Nov 1, 1986.

§ 210.43. Motion to remove juvenile offender to family court

1. After a motion by a juvenile offender, pursuant to subdivision five of section 180.75 of this

chapter, or after arraignment of a juvenile offender upon an indictment, the superior court may, on motion of any party or on its own motion:

(a) except as otherwise provided by paragraph (b), order removal of the action to the family court pursuant to the provisions of article seven hundred twenty-five of this chapter, if, after consideration of the factors set forth in subdivision two of this section, the court determines that to do so would be in the interests of justice; or

(b) with the consent of the district attorney, order removal of an action involving an indictment charging a juvenile offender with murder in the second degree as defined in section 125.25 of the penal law; rape in the first degree, as defined in subdivision one of section 130.35 of the penal law; criminal sexual act in the first degree, as defined in subdivision one of section 130.50 of the penal law; or an armed felony as defined in paragraph (a) of subdivision forty-one of section 1.20, to the family court pursuant to the provisions of article seven hundred twenty-five of this chapter if the court finds one or more of the following factors: (i) mitigating circumstances that bear directly upon the manner in which the crime was committed; (ii) where the defendant was not the sole participant in the crime, the defendant's participation was relatively minor although not so minor as to constitute a defense to the prosecution; or (iii) possible deficiencies in the proof of the crime, and, after consideration of the factors set forth in subdivision two of this section, the court determined that removal of the action to the family court would be in the interests of justice.

2. In making its determination pursuant to subdivision one of this section the court shall, to the extent applicable, examine individually and collectively, the following:

(a) the seriousness and circumstances of the offense;

(b) the extent of harm caused by the offense;

(c) the evidence of guilt, whether admissible or inadmissible at trial;

(d) the history, character and condition of the defendant;

(e) the purpose and effect of imposing upon the defendant a sentence authorized for the offense;

(f) the impact of a removal of the case to the family court on the safety or welfare of the community;

(g) the impact of a removal of the case to the family court upon the confidence of the public in the criminal justice system;

(h) where the court deems it appropriate, the attitude of the complainant or victim with respect to the motion; and

(i) any other relevant fact indicating that a judgment of conviction in the criminal court would serve no useful purpose.

3. The procedure for bringing on a motion pursuant to subdivision one of this section, shall accord with the procedure prescribed in subdivisions one and two of section 210.45 of this article. After all papers of both parties have been filed and after all documentary evidence, if any, has been submitted, the court must consider the same for the purpose of determining whether the motion is determinable on the motion papers submitted and, if not, may make such inquiry as it deems necessary for the purpose of making a determination.

4. For the purpose of making a determination pursuant to this section, any evidence which is not

legally privileged may be introduced. If the defendant testifies, his testimony may not be introduced against him in any future proceeding, except to impeach his testimony at such future proceeding as inconsistent prior testimony.

5. a. If the court orders removal of the action to family court, it shall state on the record the factor or factors upon which its determination is based, and, the court shall give its reasons for removal in detail and not in conclusory terms.

b. The district attorney shall state upon the record the reasons for his consent to removal of the action to the family court. The reasons shall be stated in detail and not in conclusory terms.

HISTORY: Add, L 1979, ch 411, § 6, eff Aug 4, 1979. Sub 1, par (b), amd, L 2003, ch 264, § 41, eff Nov 1, 2003.

§ 210.45. Motion to dismiss indictment; procedure

1. A motion to dismiss an indictment pursuant to section 210.20 must be made in writing and upon reasonable notice to the people. If the motion is based upon the existence or occurrence of facts, the motion papers must contain sworn allegations thereof, whether by the defendant or by another person or persons. Such sworn allegations may be based upon personal knowledge of the affiant or upon information and belief, provided that in the latter event the affiant must state the sources of such information and the grounds of such belief. The defendant may further submit documentary evidence supporting or tending to support the allegations of the moving papers.

2. The people may file with the court, and in such case must serve a copy thereof upon the defendant or his counsel, an answer denying or admitting any or all of the allegations of the moving papers, and may further submit documentary evidence refuting or tending to refute such allegations.

3. After all papers of both parties have been filed, and after all documentary evidence, if any, has been submitted, the court must consider the same for the purpose of determining whether the motion is determinable without a hearing to resolve questions of fact.

4. The court must grant the motion without conducting a hearing if:

(a) The moving papers allege a ground constituting legal basis for the motion pursuant to subdivision one of section 210.20; and

(b) Such ground, if based upon the existence or occurrence of facts, is supported by sworn allegations of all facts essential to support the motion; and

(c) The sworn allegations of fact essential to support the motion are either conceded by the people to be true or are conclusively substantiated by unquestionable documentary proof.

5. The court may deny the motion without conducting a hearing if:

(a) The moving papers do not allege any ground constituting legal basis for the motion pursuant to subdivision one of section 210.20; or

(b) The motion is based upon the existence or occurrence of facts, and the moving papers do not contain sworn allegations supporting all the essential facts; or

(c) An allegation of fact essential to support the motion is conclusively refuted by unquestionable documentary proof.

6. If the court does not determine the motion pursuant to subdivision four or five, it must conduct a hearing and make findings of fact essential to the determination thereof. The defendant has a

right to be present in person at such hearing but may waive such right.

7. Upon such a hearing, the defendant has the burden of proving by a preponderance of the evidence every fact essential to support the motion.

8. When the court dismisses the entire indictment without authorizing resubmission of the charge or charges to a grand jury, it must order that the defendant be discharged from custody if he is in the custody of the sheriff, or if he is at liberty on bail it must exonerate the bail.

9. When the court dismisses the entire indictment but authorizes resubmission of the charge or charges to a grand jury, such authorization is, for purposes of this subdivision, deemed to constitute an order holding the defendant for the action of a grand jury with respect to such charge or charges. Such order must be accompanied by a securing order either releasing the defendant on his own recognizance or fixing bail or committing him to the custody of the sheriff pending resubmission of the case to the grand jury and the grand jury's disposition thereof. Such securing order remains in effect until the first to occur of any of the following:

(a) A statement to the court by the people that they do not intend to resubmit the case to a grand jury;

(b) Arraignment of the defendant upon an indictment or prosecutor's information filed as a result of resubmission of the case to a grand jury. Upon such arraignment, the arraigning court must issue a new securing order;

(c) The filing with the court of a grand jury dismissal of the case following resubmission thereof;

(d) The expiration of a period of forty-five days from the date of issuance of the order; provided that such period may, for good cause shown, be extended by the court to a designated subsequent date if such be necessary to accord the people reasonable opportunity to resubmit the case to a grand jury.

Upon the termination of the effectiveness of the securing order pursuant to paragraph (a), (c) or (d), the court must immediately order that the defendant be discharged from custody if he is in the custody of the sheriff, or if he is at liberty on bail it must exonerate the bail. Although expiration of the period of time specified in paragraph (d) without any resubmission or grand jury disposition of the case terminates the effectiveness of the securing order, it does not terminate the effectiveness of the order authorizing resubmission.

HISTORY: Add, L 1970, ch 996, § 1, eff Sept 1, 1971.

§ 210.46. Adjournment in contemplation of dismissal in marihuana cases in a superior court

Upon or after arraignment in a superior court upon an indictment where the sole remaining count or counts charge a violation or violations of section 221.05, 221.10, 221.15, 221.35 or 221.40 of the penal law and before the entry of a plea of guilty thereto or commencement of a trial thereof, the court, upon motion of a defendant, may order that all proceedings be suspended and the action adjourned in contemplation of dismissal or may dismiss the indictment in furtherance of justice, in accordance with the provisions of section 170.56 of this chapter.

HISTORY: Add, L 1973, ch 901, § 1; amd, L 1977, ch 360, § 10, eff July 29, 1977, and applicable to acts committed on or after such date.

§ 210.47. Adjournment in contemplation of dismissal in misdemeanor cases in superior court

Upon or after the arraignment in a superior court upon an indictment where the sole remaining count or counts charge a misdemeanor offense, and before the entry of a plea of guilty thereto or commencement of a trial thereof, the court, upon motion of the people or the defendant and with the consent of the other party, or upon the court's own motion with the consent of both the people and the defendant, may order that all proceedings be suspended and the action adjourned in contemplation of dismissal, in accordance with the provisions of section 170.55 of this chapter.

HISTORY: Add, L 2001, ch 487, § 2, eff Nov 1, 2002.

§ 210.50. Requirement of plea

Unless an indictment is dismissed or the criminal action thereon terminated or abated pursuant to the provisions of this article or some other provision of law, the defendant must be required to enter a plea thereto.

HISTORY: Add, L 1970, ch 996, § 1, eff Sept 1, 1971.

ARTICLE 215   ADJOURNMENT IN CONTEMPLATION OF DISMISSAL FOR PURPOSES OF REFERRING SELECTED FELONIES TO DISPUTE RESOLUTION

HISTORY: Add, L 1986, ch 837, § 1, eff Nov 1, 1986.

§ 215.10. Referral of selected felonies to dispute resolution

Upon or after arraignment in a local criminal court upon a felony complaint, or upon or after arraignment in a superior court upon an indictment or superior court information, and before final disposition thereof, the court, with the consent of the people and of the defendant, and with reasonable notice to the victim and an opportunity for the victim to be heard, may order that the action be adjourned in contemplation of dismissal, for the purpose of referring the action to a community dispute center established pursuant to article twenty-one-A of the judiciary law. Provided, however, that the court may not order any action adjourned in contemplation of dismissal if the defendant is charged therein with: (i) a class A felony, or (ii) a violent felony offense as defined in section 70.02 of the penal law, or (iii) any drug offense as defined in article two hundred twenty of the penal law, or (iv) a felony upon the conviction of which defendant must be sentenced as a second felony offender, a second violent felony offender, or a persistent violent felony offender pursuant to sections 70.06, 70.04 and 70.08 of the penal law, or a felony upon the conviction of which defendant may be sentenced as a persistent felony offender pursuant to section 70.10 of such law.

HISTORY: Add, L 1986, ch 837, § 1, eff Nov 1, 1986.

§ 215.20. Victim; definition

For purposes of section 215.10 of this article, "victim" means any person alleged to have sustained physical or financial injury to person or property as a direct result of the crime or crimes charged in a felony complaint, superior court information, or indictment.

HISTORY: Add, L 1986, ch 837, § 1, eff Nov 1, 1986.

§ 215.30. Adjournment in contemplation of dismissal; restoration to calendar; dismissal of action

Upon issuing an order adjourning an action in contemplation of dismissal pursuant to section 215.10 of this article, the court must release the defendant on his own recognizance and refer the action to a dispute resolution center established pursuant to article twenty-one-A of the judiciary law. No later than forty-five days after an action has been referred to a dispute resolution center, such center must advise the district attorney as to whether the charges against defendant have been resolved. Thereafter, if defendant has agreed to pay a fine, restitution or reparation, the district attorney must be advised every thirty days as to the status of such fine, restitution or reparation. Upon application of the people, made at any time not more than six months after the issuance of an order adjourning an action in contemplation of dismissal, the court may restore the action to the calendar upon a determination that dismissal of the accusatory instrument would not be in furtherance of justice, and the action must thereupon proceed. Notwithstanding the foregoing, where defendant has agreed to pay a fine, restitution, or reparation, but has not paid such fine, restitution or reparation, upon application of the people, made at any time not more than one year after the issuance of an order adjourning an action in contemplation of dismissal, the court may restore the action to the calendar upon a determination that defendant has failed to pay such fine, restitution, or reparation, and the action must thereupon proceed.

HISTORY: Add, L 1986, ch 837, § 1, eff Nov 1, 1986.

§ 215.40. Dismissal of action; effect thereof; records

If an action has not been restored to the calendar within six months, or where the defendant has agreed to pay a fine, restitution or reparation but has not paid such fine, restitution or reparation, within one year, of the issuance of an order adjourning the action in contemplation of dismissal, the accusatory instrument shall be deemed to have been dismissed by the court in furtherance of justice at the expiration of such six month or one year period, as the case may be. Upon dismissal of an action, the arrest and prosecution shall be deemed a nullity, and defendant shall be restored to the status he or she occupied before his or her arrest and prosecution. All papers and records relating to an action that has been dismissed pursuant to this section shall be subject to the sealing provisions of section 160.50 of this chapter.

HISTORY: Add, L 1986, ch 837, § 1, eff Nov 1, 1986.

ARTICLE 216   JUDICIAL DIVERSION PROGRAM FOR CERTAIN FELONY OFFENDERS

§ 216.00.   **Definitions**
§ 216.05.   **Judicial diversion program; court procedures**

HISTORY: Add, L 2009, ch 56, § 4 (Part AAA), eff Oct 7, 2009.

§ 216.00. Definitions

The following definitions are applicable to this article:

1. [Until July 5, 2021] "Eligible defendant" means any person who stands charged in an indictment or a superior court information with a class B, C, D or E felony offense defined in article one hundred seventy-nine, two hundred twenty or two hundred twenty-one of the penal law or any other specified offense as defined in subdivision four of section 410.91 of this chapter, provided, however, a defendant is not an "eligible defendant" if he or she:

1. [Eff July 5, 2021] "Eligible defendant" means any person who stands charged in an indictment or a superior court information with a class B, C, D or E felony offense defined in article two hundred twenty or two hundred twenty-one of the penal law or any other specified offense as defined in subdivision four of section 410.91 of this chapter, provided, however, a defendant is not an "eligible defendant" if he or she:

(a) within the preceding ten years, excluding any time during which the offender was incarcerated for any reason between the time of commission of the previous felony and the time of commission of the present felony, has previously been convicted of: (i) a violent felony offense as defined in section 70.02 of the penal law or (ii) any other offense for which a merit time allowance is not available pursuant to subparagraph (ii) of paragraph (d) of subdivision one of section eight hundred three of the correction law, or (iii) a class A felony offense defined in article two hundred twenty of the penal law; or

(b) has previously been adjudicated a second violent felony offender pursuant to section 70.04 of the penal law or a persistent violent felony offender pursuant to section 70.08 of the penal law.

A defendant who also stands charged with a violent felony offense as defined in section 70.02 of the penal law or an offense for which merit time allowance is not available pursuant to subparagraph (ii) of paragraph (d) of subdivision one of section eight hundred three of the correction law for which the court must, upon the defendant's conviction thereof, sentence the defendant to incarceration in state prison is not an eligible defendant while such charges are pending. A defendant who is excluded from the judicial diversion program pursuant to this paragraph or paragraph (a) or (b) of this subdivision may become an eligible defendant upon the prosecutor's consent.

2. "Alcohol and substance abuse evaluation" means a written assessment and report by a court-approved entity or licensed health care professional experienced in the treatment of alcohol and substance abuse, or by an addiction and substance abuse counselor credentialed by the office of alcoholism and substance abuse services pursuant to section 19.07 of the mental hygiene law, which shall include:

(a) an evaluation as to whether the defendant has a history of alcohol or substance abuse or alcohol or substance dependence, as such terms are defined in the diagnostic and statistical manual of mental disorders, fourth edition, and a co-occurring mental disorder or mental illness and the relationship between such abuse or dependence and mental disorder or mental illness, if any;

(b) a recommendation as to whether the defendant's alcohol or substance abuse or dependence, if any, could be effectively addressed by judicial diversion in accordance with this article;

(c) a recommendation as to the treatment modality, level of care and length of any proposed treatment to effectively address the defendant's alcohol or substance abuse or dependence and any co-occurring mental disorder or illness; and

(d) any other information, factor, circumstance, or recommendation deemed relevant by the assessing entity or specifically requested by the court.

HISTORY: Add, L 2009, ch 56, § 4 (Part AAA), eff Oct 7, 2009; amd, L 2014, ch 90, § 10, eff July 3, 2014, expires and repealed July 5, 2021.

§ 216.05. Judicial diversion program; court procedures

1. At any time after the arraignment of an eligible defendant, but prior to the entry of a plea of guilty or the commencement of trial, the court at the request of the eligible defendant, may order an alcohol and substance abuse evaluation. An eligible defendant may decline to participate in such an evaluation at any time. The defendant shall provide a written authorization, in compliance with the requirements of any applicable state or federal laws, rules or regulations authorizing disclosure of the results of the assessment to the defendant's attorney, the prosecutor, the local probation department, the court, authorized court personnel and other individuals specified in such authorization for the sole purpose of determining whether the defendant should be offered judicial

diversion for treatment for substance abuse or dependence, alcohol abuse or dependence and any co-occurring mental disorder or mental illness.

2. Upon receipt of the completed alcohol and substance abuse evaluation report, the court shall provide a copy of the report to the eligible defendant and the prosecutor.

3. (a) Upon receipt of the evaluation report either party may request a hearing on the issue of whether the eligible defendant should be offered alcohol or substance abuse treatment pursuant to this article. At such a proceeding, which shall be held as soon as practicable so as to facilitate early intervention in the event that the defendant is found to need alcohol or substance abuse treatment, the court may consider oral and written arguments, may take testimony from witnesses offered by either party, and may consider any relevant evidence including, but not limited to, evidence that:

(i) the defendant had within the preceding ten years (excluding any time during which the offender was incarcerated for any reason between the time of the acts that led to the youthful offender adjudication and the time of commission of the present offense) been adjudicated a youthful offender for: (A) a violent felony offense as defined in section 70.02 of the penal law; or (B) any offense for which a merit time allowance is not available pursuant to subparagraph (ii) of paragraph (d) of subdivision one of section eight hundred three of the correction law; and

(ii) in the case of a felony offense defined in subdivision four of section 410.91 of this chapter, any statement of or submitted by the victim, as defined in paragraph (a) of subdivision two of section 380.50 of this chapter.

(b) Upon completion of such a proceeding, the court shall consider and make findings of fact with respect to whether:

(i) the defendant is an eligible defendant as defined in subdivision one of section 216.00 of this article;

(ii) the defendant has a history of alcohol or substance abuse or dependence;

(iii) such alcohol or substance abuse or dependence is a contributing factor to the defendant's criminal behavior;

(iv) the defendant's participation in judicial diversion could effectively address such abuse or dependence; and

(v) institutional confinement of the defendant is or may not be necessary for the protection of the public.

4. When an authorized court determines, pursuant to paragraph (b) of subdivision three of this section, that an eligible defendant should be offered alcohol or substance abuse treatment, or when the parties and the court agree to an eligible defendant's participation in alcohol or substance abuse treatment, an eligible defendant may be allowed to participate in the judicial diversion program offered by this article. Prior to the court's issuing an order granting judicial diversion, the eligible defendant shall be required to enter a plea of guilty to the charge or charges; provided, however, that no such guilty plea shall be required when:

(a) the people and the court consent to the entry of such an order without a plea of guilty; or

(b) based on a finding of exceptional circumstances, the court determines that a plea of guilty shall not be required. For purposes of this subdivision, exceptional circumstances exist when, regardless of the ultimate disposition of the case, the entry of a plea of guilty is likely to result in severe collateral consequences.

5. The defendant shall agree on the record or in writing to abide by the release conditions set by the court, which, shall include: participation in a specified period of alcohol or substance abuse treatment at a specified program or programs identified by the court, which may include periods of detoxification, residential or outpatient treatment, or both, as determined after taking into account the views of the health care professional who conducted the alcohol and substance abuse evaluation and any health care professionals responsible for providing such treatment or monitoring the defendant's progress in such treatment; and may include: (i) periodic court appearances, which may include periodic urinalysis; (ii) a requirement that the defendant refrain from engaging in criminal behaviors.

6. Upon an eligible defendant's agreement to abide by the conditions set by the court, the court shall issue a securing order providing for bail or release on the defendant's own recognizance and conditioning any release upon the agreed upon conditions. The period of alcohol or substance abuse treatment shall begin as specified by the court and as soon as practicable after the defendant's release, taking into account the availability of treatment, so as to facilitate early intervention with respect to the defendant's abuse or condition and the effectiveness of the treatment program. In the event that a treatment program is not immediately available or becomes unavailable during the course of the defendant's participation in the judicial diversion program, the court may release the defendant pursuant to the securing order.

7. When participating in judicial diversion treatment pursuant to this article, any resident of this state who is covered under a private health insurance policy or contract issued for delivery in this state pursuant to article thirty-two, forty-three or forty-seven of the insurance law or article forty-four of the public health law, or who is covered by a self-funded plan which provides coverage for the diagnosis and treatment of chemical abuse and chemical dependence however defined in such policy; shall first seek reimbursement for such treatment in accordance with the provisions of such policy or contract.

8. During the period of a defendant's participation in the judicial diversion program, the court shall retain jurisdiction of the defendant, provided, however, that the court may allow such defendant to reside in another jurisdiction while participating in a judicial diversion program under conditions set by the court and agreed to by the defendant pursuant to subdivisions five and six of this section. The court may require the defendant to appear in court at any time to enable the court to monitor the defendant's progress in alcohol or substance abuse treatment. The court shall provide notice, reasonable under the circumstances, to the people, the treatment provider, the defendant and the defendant's counsel whenever it orders or otherwise requires the appearance of the defendant in court. Failure to appear as required without reasonable cause therefor shall constitute a violation of the conditions of the court's agreement with the defendant.

9. (a) If at any time during the defendant's participation in the judicial diversion program, the court has reasonable grounds to believe that the defendant has violated a release condition or has failed to appear before the court as requested, the court shall direct the defendant to appear or issue a bench warrant to a police officer or an appropriate peace officer directing him or her to take the defendant into custody and bring the defendant before the court without unnecessary delay. The provisions of subdivision one of section 530.60 of this chapter relating to revocation of recognizance or bail shall apply to such proceedings under this subdivision.

(b) In determining whether a defendant violated a condition of his or her release under the judicial diversion program, the court may conduct a summary hearing consistent with due process and sufficient to satisfy the court that the defendant has, in fact, violated the condition.

(c) If the court determines that the defendant has violated a condition of his or her release under the judicial diversion program, the court may modify the conditions thereof, reconsider the order of recognizance or bail pursuant to subdivision two of section 510.30 of this chapter, or terminate the defendant's participation in the judicial diversion program; and when applicable proceed with the defendant's sentencing in accordance with the agreement. Notwithstanding any provision of law to the contrary, the court may impose any sentence authorized for the crime of conviction in accordance with the plea agreement, or any lesser sentence authorized to be imposed on a felony drug offender pursuant to paragraph (b) or (c) of subdivision two of section 70.70 of the penal law taking into account the length of time the defendant spent in residential treatment and how best to continue treatment while the defendant is serving that sentence. In determining what action to take for a violation of a release condition, the court shall consider all relevant circumstances, including the views of the prosecutor, the defense and the alcohol or substance abuse treatment provider, and the extent to which persons who ultimately successfully complete a drug treatment regimen sometimes relapse by not abstaining from alcohol or substance abuse or by failing to comply fully with all requirements imposed by a treatment program. The court shall also consider using a system of graduated and appropriate responses or sanctions designed to address such inappropriate behaviors, protect public safety and facilitate, where possible, successful completion of the alcohol or substance abuse treatment program.

(d) Nothing in this subdivision shall be construed as preventing a court from terminating a defendant's participation in the judicial diversion program for violating a release condition when such a termination is necessary to preserve public safety. Nor shall anything in this subdivision be construed as precluding the prosecution of a defendant for the commission of a different offense while participating in the judicial diversion program.

(e) A defendant may at any time advise the court that he or she wishes to terminate participation in the judicial diversion program, at which time the court shall proceed with the case and, where applicable, shall impose sentence in accordance with the plea agreement. Notwithstanding any provision of law to the contrary, the court may impose any sentence authorized for the crime of conviction in accordance with the plea agreement, or any lesser sentence authorized to be imposed on a felony drug offender pursuant to paragraph (b) or (c) of subdivision two of section 70.70 of the penal law taking into account the length of time the defendant spent in residential treatment and how best to continue treatment while the defendant is serving that sentence.

10. Upon the court's determination that the defendant has successfully completed the required period of alcohol or substance abuse treatment and has otherwise satisfied the conditions required for successful completion of the judicial diversion program, the court shall comply with the terms and conditions it set for final disposition when it accepted the defendant's agreement to participate in the judicial diversion program. Such disposition may include, but is not limited to: (a) requiring the defendant to undergo a period of interim probation supervision and, upon the defendant's successful completion of the interim probation supervision term, notwithstanding the provision of any other law, permitting the defendant to withdraw his or her guilty plea and dismissing the indictment; or (b) requiring the defendant to undergo a period of interim probation supervision and, upon successful completion of the interim probation supervision term, notwithstanding the provision of any other law, permitting the defendant to withdraw his or her guilty plea, enter a guilty plea to a misdemeanor offense and sentencing the defendant as promised in the plea

agreement, which may include a period of probation supervision pursuant to section 65.00 of the penal law; or (c) allowing the defendant to withdraw his or her guilty plea and dismissing the indictment.

11. Nothing in this article shall be construed as restricting or prohibiting courts or district attorneys from using other lawful procedures or models for placing appropriate persons into alcohol or substance abuse treatment.

HISTORY: Add, L 2009, ch 56, § 4 (Part AAA), eff Oct 7, 2009; amd, L 2012, ch 347, § 2, eff Aug 1, 2012.

TITLE J　Prosecution of Indictments in Superior Courts—Plea to Sentence

ARTICLE 220
THE PLEA

ARTICLE 230
REMOVAL OF ACTION

ARTICLE 240
DISCOVERY

ARTICLE 250
PRE-TRIAL NOTICES OF DEFENSES

ARTICLE 255
PRE-TRIAL MOTIONS

ARTICLE 260
JURY TRIAL—GENERALLY

ARTICLE 270
JURY TRIAL-FORMATION AND CONDUCT OF JURY

ARTICLE 280
JURY TRIAL—MOTION FOR A MISTRIAL

ARTICLE 290
JURY TRIAL—TRIAL ORDER OF DISMISSAL

ARTICLE 300
JURY TRIAL—COURT'S CHARGE AND INSTRUCTIONS TO JURY

ARTICLE 310
JURY TRIAL—DELIBERATION AND VERDICT OF JURY

ARTICLE 320
WAIVER OF JURY TRIAL AND CONDUCT OF NON-JURY TRIAL

ARTICLE 330
PROCEEDINGS FROM VERDICT TO SENTENCE

HISTORY: Add, L 1970, ch 996, § 1, eff Sept 1, 1971.

ARTICLE 220　THE PLEA

HISTORY: Add, L 1970, ch 996, § 1, eff Sept 1, 1971.

§ 220.10. Plea; kinds of pleas

The only kinds of pleas which may be entered to an indictment are those specified in this section:

1. The defendant may as a matter of right enter a plea of "not guilty" to the indictment.

2. Except as provided in subdivision five, the defendant may as a matter of right enter a plea of "guilty" to the entire indictment.

3. Except as provided in subdivision five, where the indictment charges but one crime, the defendant may, with both the permission of the court and the consent of the people, enter a plea of guilty of a lesser included offense.

4. Except as provided in subdivision five, where the indictment charges two or more offenses in separate counts, the defendant may, with both the permission of the court and the consent of the people, enter a plea of:

(a) Guilty of one or more but not all of the offenses charged; or

(b) Guilty of a lesser included offense with respect to any or all of the offenses charged; or

(c) Guilty of any combination of offenses charged and lesser offenses included within other offenses charged.

5.   (a) (i) Where the indictment charges one of the class A felonies defined in article two hundred twenty of the penal law or the attempt to commit any such class A felony, then any plea of guilty entered pursuant to subdivision three or four of this section must be or must include at least a plea of guilty of a class B felony.

(ii) [Repealed]

(iii) Where the indictment charges one of the class B felonies defined in article two hundred twenty of the penal law then any plea of guilty entered pursuant to subdivision three or four must be or must include at least a plea of guilty of a class D felony.

(b) Where the indictment charges any class B felony, other than a class B felony defined in article two hundred twenty of the penal law or a class B violent felony offense as defined in subdivision one of section 70.02 of the penal law, then any plea of guilty entered pursuant to subdivision three or four must be or must include at least a plea of guilty of a felony.

(c) Where the indictment charges a felony, other than a class A felony or class B felony defined in article two hundred twenty of the penal law or class B or class C violent felony offense as defined in subdivision one of section 70.02 of the penal law, and it appears that the defendant has previously been subjected to a predicate felony conviction as defined in penal law section 70.06 then any plea of guilty entered pursuant to subdivision three or four must be or must include at least a plea of guilty of a felony.

(d) Where the indictment charges a class A felony, other than those defined in article two hundred twenty of the penal law, or charges a class B or class C violent felony offense as defined in subdivision one of section 70.02 of the penal law, then a plea of guilty entered pursuant to subdivision three or four must be as follows:

(i) Where the indictment charges a class A felony offense or a class B violent felony offense which is also an armed felony offense then a plea of guilty must include at least a plea of guilty to a class C violent felony offense;

(ii) Except as provided in subparagraph (i) of this paragraph, where the indictment charges a class B violent felony offense or a class C violent felony offense, then a plea of guilty must include at least a plea of guilty to a class D violent felony offense;

(iii) Where the indictment charges the class D violent felony offense of criminal possession of a weapon in the third degree as defined in subdivision four of section 265.02 of the penal law, and the defendant has not been previously convicted of a class A misdemeanor defined in the penal law in the five years preceding the commission of the offense, then a plea of guilty must be either to the class E violent felony offense of attempted criminal possession of a weapon in the third degree or to the class A misdemeanor of criminal possession of a weapon in the fourth degree as defined in subdivision one of section 265.01 of the penal law;

(iv) Where the indictment charges the class D violent felony offenses of criminal possession of a weapon in the third degree as defined in subdivision four of section 265.02 of the penal law and the provisions of subparagraph (iii) of this paragraph do not apply, or subdivision five, seven or eight of section 265.02 of the penal law, then a plea of guilty must include at least a plea of guilty to a class E violent felony offense.

(e) A defendant may not enter a plea of guilty to the crime of murder in the first degree as defined in section 125.27 of the penal law; provided, however, that a defendant may enter such a plea with both the permission of the court and the consent of the people when the agreed upon sentence is either life imprisonment without parole or a term of imprisonment for the class A-I felony of murder in the first degree other than a sentence of life imprisonment without parole.

(f) The provisions of this subdivision shall apply irrespective of whether the defendant is thereby precluded from entering a plea of guilty of any lesser included offense.

(g) Where the defendant is a juvenile offender, the provisions of paragraphs (a), (b), (c) and (d) of this subdivision shall not apply and any plea entered pursuant to subdivision three or four of this section, must be as follows:

(i) If the indictment charges a person fourteen or fifteen years old with the crime of murder in the second degree any plea of guilty entered pursuant to subdivision three or four must be a plea of guilty of a crime for which the defendant is criminally responsible;

(ii) If the indictment does not charge a crime specified in subparagraph (i) of this paragraph, then any plea of guilty entered pursuant to subdivision three or four of this section must be a plea of guilty of a crime for which the defendant is criminally responsible unless a plea of guilty is accepted pursuant to subparagraph (iii) of this paragraph;

(iii) Where the indictment does not charge a crime specified in subparagraph (i) of this paragraph, the district attorney may recommend removal of the action to the family court. Upon making such recommendation the district attorney shall submit a subscribed memorandum setting forth: (1) a recommendation that the interests of justice would best be served by removal of the action to the family court; and (2) if the indictment charges a thirteen year old with the crime of murder in the second degree, or a fourteen or fifteen year old with the crimes of rape in the first degree as defined in subdivision one of section 130.35 of the penal law, or criminal sexual act in the first degree as defined in subdivision one of section 130.50 of the penal law, or an armed felony as defined in paragraph (a) of subdivision forty-one of section 1.20 of this chapter specific factors, one or more of which reasonably supports the recommendation, showing, (i) mitigating circumstances that bear directly upon the manner in which the crime was committed, or (ii) where the defendant was not the sole participant in the crime, that the defendant's participation was relatively minor although not so minor as to constitute a defense to the prosecution, or (iii) possible deficiencies in proof of the crime, or (iv) where the juvenile offender has no previous adjudications of having committed a designated felony act, as defined in subdivision eight of section 301.2 of the family court act, regardless of the age of the offender at the time of commission of the act, that the criminal act was not part of a pattern of criminal behavior and, in view of the history of the offender, is not likely to be repeated.

If the court is of the opinion based on specific factors set forth in the district attorney's memorandum that the interests of justice would best be served by removal of the action to the family court, a plea of guilty of a crime or act for which the defendant is not criminally responsible may be entered pursuant to subdivision three or four of this section, except that a thirteen year old charged with the crime of murder in the second degree may only plead to a designated felony act, as defined in subdivision eight of section 301.2 of the family court act.

Upon accepting any such plea, the court must specify upon the record the portion or portions of the district attorney's statement the court is relying upon as the basis of its opinion and that it believes the interests of justice would best be served by removal of the proceeding to the family court. Such plea shall then be deemed to be a juvenile delinquency fact determination and the court upon entry thereof must direct that the action be removed to the family court in accordance with the provisions of article seven hundred twenty-five of this chapter.

(h) Where the indictment charges the class E felony offense of aggravated harassment of an employee by an inmate as defined in section 240.32 of the penal law, then a plea of guilty must include at least a plea of guilty to a class E felony.

6. The defendant may, with both the permission of the court and the consent of the people, enter a plea of not responsible by reason of mental disease or defect to the indictment in the manner prescribed in section 220.15 of this chapter.

HISTORY: Add, L 1970, ch 996, § 1, eff Sept 1, 1971. Sub 1, reenacted without change, L 1976, ch 480, § 1, eff July 1, 1976. Sub 2, amd, L 1974, ch 367, § 8, L 1976, ch 480, § 1, eff July 1, 1976. Sub 3, formerly sub 4, amd, L 1973, ch 276, § 23, L 1973, ch 277, § 12; so renumbered and amd, L 1976, ch 480, § 1, eff July 1, 1976. Former sub 3, repealed, L 1974, ch 367, § 9, eff Sept 1, 1974. Sub 4, formerly sub 5, amd, L 1973, ch 276, § 23, L 1973, ch 277, § 12; so renumbered and amd, L 1976, ch 480, § 1, eff July 1, 1976. Former sub 4, renumbered sub 3, L 1976, ch 480, § 1, eff July 1, 1976. Sub 5, formerly sub 6, add, L 1973, ch 276, § 23; so renumbered and amd, L 1976, ch 480, § 1, eff July 1, 1976. Former sub 5, renumbered sub 4, L 1976, ch 480, § 1, eff July 1, 1976. Sub 5, par (a), add, L 1979, ch 410, § 22, eff Sept 1, 1979. Former sub 5, par (a), formerly sub 6, par (a), add, L 1973, ch 276, § 23, reenacted without change, L 1973, ch 1051, § 16; deleted, L 1979, ch 410, § 22, eff Sept 1, 1979. Sub 5, par (b), formerly sub 5, par (c), add, L 1976, ch 480, § 1; amd, L 1976, ch 481, § 14; so relettered and amd, L 1979, ch 410, § 22, eff Sept 1, 1979. Former sub 5, par (b), add, L 1976, ch 480, § 1; deleted, L 1979, ch 410, § 22, eff Sept 1, 1979. Sub 5, par (c), formerly sub 5, par (d), so relettered and amd, L 1979, ch 410, § 22, eff Sept 1, 1979. Former sub 5, par (c), add, L 1976, ch 480, § 1; amd, L 1978, ch 481, § 14; relettered sub 5, par (b), L 1979, ch 410, § 22, eff Sept 1, 1979. Sub 5, par (d), add, L 1980, ch 233, § 18, eff Aug 12, 1980. Former sub 5, par (d), formerly sub 5, par (e), so relettered, L 1979, ch 410, § 22; repealed, L 1980, ch 233, § 18, eff Aug 12, 1980. Prior sub 5, par (d), formerly sub 6, par (b), so renumbered and amd, L 1976, ch 480, § 1; amd, L 1978, ch 481, § 14; relettered sub 5, par (c), L 1979, ch 410, eff Sept 1, 1979. Sub 5, par (d), subpar (iv), amd, L 1980, ch 234, § 3, L 1991, ch 496, § 6, eff Nov 1, 1991. Sub 5, par (e), formerly sub 5, par (f), so relettered, L 1979, ch 410, § 22; amd, L 1995, ch 1, § 10, eff Sept 1, 1995. Former sub 5, par (e), add, L 1978, ch 481, § 15; relettered sub 5, par (d), L 1979, ch 410,

§ 22, eff Sept 1, 1979. Prior sub 5, par (e), relettered sub 5, par (f), L 1978, ch 481, § 15, eff Sept 1, 1978. Sub 5, par (f), formerly sub 5, par (g), so relettered, L 1979, ch 410, § 22, eff Sept 1, 1979. Former sub 5, par (f), formerly sub 5, par (e), formerly sub 6, par (c), add, L 1974, ch 367, § 10; relettered sub 5, par (e), L 1976, ch 480, § 1; relettered sub 5, par (f), L 1978, ch 481, § 15; relettered sub 5, par (e), L 1979, ch 410, eff Sept 1, 1979. Sub 5, par (g), formerly sub 5, par (h), so relettered and amd, L 1979, ch 410, § 22, eff Sept 1, 1979. Former sub 5, par (g), formerly sub 5, par (f), formerly sub 6, par (d), relettered sub 5, par (f), L 1976, ch 480, § 1, relettered sub 5, par (g), L 1978, ch 481, § 15; relettered sub 5, par (f), L 1979, ch 410, § 22, eff Sept 1, 1979. Sub 5, par (g), subpar (iii), amd, L 1979, ch 411, § 10, L 1982, ch 920, § 75, eff July 1, 1983. [Editor's Note: L 1979, ch 411, § 10, purported to amend Sub 5, par (h), subpar (iii); however, L 1979, ch 410, § 22, had previously relettered par (h) as par (g).] Sub 5, par (g), second undesignated subpar, amd, L 1982, ch 920, § 75, eff July 1, 1983. Sub 5, par (g), closing subpar, amd, L 1979, ch 411, § 10, eff Aug 4, 1979. [Editor's Note: L 1979, ch 411, § 10, purported to amend sub 5, par (h), closing subpar; however, L 1979, ch 410, § 22, had previously relettered par (h) as par (g).] Sub 5, par (h), add, L 1996, ch 92, § 3, eff June 5, 1996. Former sub 5, par (h), add, L 1978, ch 481, § 37; relettered sub 5, par (g), L 1979, ch 410, § 22, eff Sept 1, 1979. Sub 6, add, L 1980, ch 548, § 3, eff Sept 1, 1980. Former sub 6, add, L 1973, ch 276, § 23, and L 1973, ch 277, § 12; amd, L 1973, ch 1051, § 16, L 1974, ch 367, § 10; renumbered sub 5, L 1976, ch 480, § 1, eff July 1, 1976. Former sub 6, par (b), add as sub 6, par (a), L 1973, ch 277, § 12; so relettered, L 1973, ch 1051, § 16, eff Sept 1, 1973. Former sub 6, par (c), add, L 1974, ch 367, § 10, eff Sept 1, 1974. Prior sub 6, par (c), add as sub 6, par (b), by L 1973, ch 276, § 23, and by L 1973, ch 277, § 12; relettered sub 6, par (c), L 1973, ch 1051, § 16, relettered sub 6, par (d), L 1974, ch 367, § 10, eff Sept 1, 1974. Former sub 6, par (d), formerly sub 6, par (c), so relettered, L 1974, ch 367, § 10, eff Sept 1, 1974. Sub 5, par (a), subpar (i), amd, L 2004, ch 738, § 16, eff Dec 27, 2004. Sub 5, par (a), subpar (ii), repealed, L 2004, ch 738, § 16, eff Dec 27, 2004. Sub 5, par (d), subpar (iv), amd, L 1999, ch 33, § 5, eff Nov 1, 1999, L 2000, ch 189, § 1, eff Nov 1, 2000. Sub 5, par (g), subpar (iii), amd, L 2003, ch 264, § 42, eff Nov 1, 2003.

§ 220.15. Plea; plea of not responsible by reason of mental disease or defect

1. The defendant may, with both the permission of the court and the consent of the people, enter a plea of not responsible by reason of mental disease or defect to the entire indictment. The district attorney must state to the court either orally on the record or in a writing filed with the court that the people consent to the entry of such plea and that the people are satisfied that the affirmative defense of lack of criminal responsibility by reason of mental disease or defect would be proven by the defendant at a trial by a preponderance of the evidence. The district attorney must further state to the court in detail the evidence available to the people with respect to the offense or offenses charged in the indictment, including all psychiatric evidence available or known to the people. If necessary, the court may conduct a hearing before accepting such plea. The district attorney must further state to the court the reasons for recommending such plea. The reasons shall be stated in detail and not in conclusory terms.

2. Counsel for the defendant must state that in his opinion defendant has the capacity to understand the proceedings and to assist in his own defense and that the defendant understands the consequences of a plea of not responsible by reason of mental disease or defect. Counsel for the defendant must further state whether in his opinion defendant has any viable defense to the offense or offenses charged in the indictment other than the affirmative defense of lack of criminal responsibility by reason of mental disease or defect. Counsel for the defendant must further state in detail the psychiatric evidence available to the defendant with respect to such latter affirmative defense.

3. Before accepting a plea of not responsible by reason of mental disease or defect, the court must address the defendant in open court and determine that he understands each of the following:

(a) The nature of the charge to which the plea is offered, and the consequences of such plea;

(b) That he has the right to plead not guilty or to persist in that plea if it has already been entered;

(c) That he has the right to be tried by a jury, the right to the assistance of counsel, the right to confront and cross-examine witnesses against him, and the right not to be compelled to incriminate himself;

(d) That if he pleads not responsible by reason of mental disease or defect there will be no trial with respect to the charges contained in the indictment, so that by offering such plea he waives the right to such trial;

(e) That if he pleads not responsible by reason of mental disease or defect the court will ask him questions about the offense or offenses charged in the indictment and that he will thereby waive his right not to be compelled to incriminate himself; and

(f) That the acceptance of a plea of not responsible by reason of mental disease or defect is the equivalent of a verdict of not responsible by reason of mental disease or defect after trial.

4. The court shall not accept a plea of not responsible by reason of mental disease or defect without first determining that there is a factual basis for such plea. The court must address the defendant personally in open court and determine that the plea is voluntary, knowingly made, and not the result of force, threats, or promises. The court must inquire whether the defendant's willingness to plead results from prior discussions between the district attorney and counsel for the defendant. The court must be satisfied that the defendant understands the proceedings against him, has sufficient capacity to assist in his own defense and understands the consequences of a plea of not responsible by reason of mental disease or defect. The court may make such inquiry as it deems necessary or appropriate for the purpose of making the determinations required by this section.

5. Before accepting a plea of not responsible by reason of mental disease or defect, the court must find and state each of the following on the record in detail and not in conclusory terms:

(a) That it is satisfied that each element of the offense or offenses charged in the indictment would be established beyond a reasonable doubt at a trial;

(b) That the affirmative defense of lack of criminal responsibility by reason of mental disease or defect would be proven by the defendant at a trial by a preponderance of the evidence;

(c) That the defendant has the capacity to understand the proceedings against him and to assist in his own defense;

(d) That such plea by the defendant is knowingly and voluntarily made and that there is a factual basis for the plea;

(e) That the acceptance of such plea is required in the interest of the public in the effective administration of justice.

6. When a plea of not responsible by reason of mental disease or defect is accepted by the court and recorded upon the minutes, the provisions of section 330.20 of this chapter shall govern all subsequent proceedings against the defendant.

HISTORY: Add, L 1980, ch 548, § 4, eff Sept 1, 1980. Sub 1, amd, L 1984, ch 668, § 5, eff Nov 1, 1984. Sub 2, amd, L 1984, ch 668, § 5, eff Nov 1, 1984. Sub 5, amd, L 1984, ch 668, § 5, eff Nov 1, 1984.

§ 220.20. Plea; meaning of lesser included offense for plea purposes

1. A "lesser included offense," within the meaning of subdivisions four and five of section

220.10 relating to the entry of a plea of guilty to an offense of lesser grade than one charged in a count of an indictment, means not only a "lesser included offense" as that term is defined in subdivision thirty-seven of section 1.20, but also one which is deemed to be such pursuant to the following rules:

(a) Where the only culpable mental state required for the crime charged is that the proscribed conduct be performed intentionally, any lesser offense consisting of reckless or criminally negligent, instead of intentional, performance of the same conduct is deemed to constitute a lesser included offense;

(b) Where the only culpable mental state required for the crime charged is that the proscribed conduct be performed recklessly, any lesser offense consisting of criminally negligent, instead of reckless, performance of the same conduct is deemed to constitute a lesser included offense;

(c) Where according to the allegations of a count a defendant's participation in the crime charged consisted in whole or in part of solicitation of another person to engage in the proscribed conduct, the offense of criminal solicitation, in any appropriate degree, is, with respect to such defendant, deemed to constitute a lesser included offense;

(d) Where according to the allegations of a count a defendant's participation in the crime charged consisted in whole or in part of conspiratorial agreement or conduct with another person to engage in the proscribed conduct, the crime of conspiracy, in any appropriate degree, is, with respect to such defendant, deemed to constitute a lesser included offense;

(e) Where according to the allegations of a count charging a felony a defendant's participation in such felony consisted in whole or in part of providing another person with means or opportunity for engaging in the proscribed conduct, the crime of criminal facilitation, in any appropriate degree, is, with respect to such defendant, deemed to constitute a lesser included offense;

(f) Where the crime charged is assault or attempted assault, in any degree, allegedly committed by intentionally causing or attempting to cause physical injury to a person by the immediate use of physical force against him, or where the crime charged is menacing, as defined in section 120.15 of the penal law, the offense of harassment, as defined in subdivision one of section 240.25 of the penal law, is deemed to constitute a lesser included offense;

(g) Where the crime charged is murder in the second degree as defined in subdivision three of section 125.25 of the penal law, allegedly committed in the course of the commission or attempted commission of a designated one of the underlying felonies enumerated in said subdivision, or during immediate flight therefrom, such designated underlying felony or attempted felony is deemed to constitute a lesser included offense. If such designated underlying felony is alleged to be robbery, burglary, kidnapping, or arson, without specification of the degree thereof, or an attempt to commit the same, a plea of guilty may be entered to the lowest degree thereof only, or as the case may be to attempted commission of such felony in its lowest degree, unless the allegations of the count clearly indicate the existence of all the elements of a higher degree;

(h) Where the crime charged is criminal sale of a controlled substance, any offense of criminal sale or possession of a controlled substance, in any degree, is deemed to constitute a lesser included offense.

(i) Where the crime charged is criminal possession of a controlled substance, any offense of criminal possession of a controlled substance, in any degree, is deemed to constitute a lesser included offense.

(j) Where the offense charged is unlawful disposal of hazardous wastes in violation of section 27-0914 of the environmental conservation law, any offense of unlawful disposal or possession of hazardous wastes as set forth in sections 71-2707, 71-2709, 71-2711 and 71-2713 of such law, in any degree, is deemed to constitute a lesser included offense;

(k) Where the offense charged is unlawful possession of hazardous wastes in violation of section 27-0914 of the environmental conservation law, any offense of unlawful possession of hazardous wastes as set forth in sections 71-2707 and 71-2709 of such law, in any degree, is deemed to constitute a lesser included offense.

2. An offense is deemed to be a lesser included offense with respect to a crime charged in an indictment, pursuant to the provisions of subdivision one, only for purposes of conviction upon a plea of guilty and not for purposes of conviction by verdict. For the latter purpose, an offense constitutes a lesser included one only when it conforms to the definition of that term contained in subdivision thirty-seven of section 1.20.

> **HISTORY:** Add, L 1970, ch 996, § 1, eff Sept 1, 1971. Sub 1, par (g), amd, L 1974, ch 367, § 11, eff Sept 1, 1974. Sub 1, par (h), add, L 1979, ch 410, § 23, eff Sept 1, 1979. Former sub 1, par (h), amd, L 1973, ch 276, § 24, L 1973, ch 1051, § 17; repealed, L 1979, ch 410, § 23, eff Sept 1, 1979. Sub 1, par (i), add, L 1979, ch 410, § 23, eff Sept 1, 1979. Former sub 1, par (i), add, L 1976, ch 480, § 2; repealed, L 1979, ch 410, § 23, eff Sept 1, 1979. Sub 1, pars (j) and (k), add, L 1981, ch 719, § 3, eff Sept 1, 1981.

§ 220.30. Plea; plea of guilty to part of indictment; plea covering other indictments

1. A plea of guilty not embracing the entire indictment, entered pursuant to the provisions of subdivision four or five of section 220.10, is a "plea of guilty to part of the indictment."

2. The entry and acceptance of a plea of guilty to part of the indictment constitutes a disposition of the entire indictment.

3. (a) (i) Except as provided in paragraph (b), or in paragraph (c) dealing with juvenile offenders, a plea of guilty, whether to the entire indictment or to part of the indictment, may, with both the permission of the court and the consent of the people, be entered and accepted upon the condition that it constitutes a complete disposition of one or more other indictments against the defendant then pending.

(ii) If the other indictment or indictments are pending in a different court or courts, they shall not be disposed of under this subdivision unless the other courts and the appropriate prosecutors also transmit their written permission and consent as provided in subdivision four of section 220.50 of this article; in such a case the court in which the plea is entered shall so notify the other courts which, upon such notice, shall dismiss the appropriate indictments pending therein.

(b) (i) A plea of guilty, whether to the entire indictment or to part of the indictment for any crime other than a class A felony, may not be accepted on the condition that it constitutes a complete disposition of one or more other indictments against the defendant wherein is charged a class A-I felony as defined in article two hundred twenty of the penal law or the attempt to commit any such class A-I felony, except that an eligible youth, as defined in subdivision two of section 720.10, may plea to a class B felony, upon consent of the district attorney, for purposes of adjudication as a youthful offender.

(ii) Where it appears that the defendant has previously been subjected to a predicate felony conviction as defined in paragraph (b) of subdivision (1) of section 70.06 of the penal law, a plea of guilty, whether to the entire indictment or to part of the indictment, of any offense other than a felony may not be accepted on the condition that it constitutes a complete disposition of one or more other indictments against the defendant wherein is charged a felony, other than a class A felony or a class B or class C violent felony offense as defined in subdivision one of section 70.02 of the penal law.

(iii) A plea of guilty, whether to the entire indictment or part of the indictment for any crime other than a class A felony or a class B or class C violent felony offense as defined in subdivision one of section 70.02 of the penal law, may not be accepted on the condition that it constitutes a complete disposition of one or more other indictments against the defendant wherein is charged a class A felony, other than those defined in article two hundred twenty of the penal law, or a class B violent felony offense which is also an armed felony offense.

(iv) Except as provided in subparagraph (iii) of this paragraph, a plea of guilty, whether to the entire indictment or part of the indictment, for any crime other than a class A felony or a class B, C, or D violent felony offense as defined in subdivision one of section 70.02 of the penal law, may not be accepted on the condition that it constitutes a complete disposition of one or more other indictments against the defendant wherein is charged a class B or class C violent felony offense as defined in subdivision one of section 70.02 of the penal law,

(v) A plea of guilty, whether to the entire indictment or part of the indictment, for any crime other than a violent felony offense as defined in section 70.02 of the penal law, may not be accepted on the condition that it constitutes a complete disposition of one or more other indictments against the defendant wherein is charged the class D violent felony offenses of criminal possession of a weapon in the third degree as defined in subdivision four, five, seven or eight of section 265.02 of the penal law; provided, however, a plea of guilty, whether to the entire indictment or part of the indictment, for the class A misdemeanor of criminal possession of a weapon in the fourth degree as defined in subdivision one of section 265.01 of the penal law may be accepted on the condition that it constitutes a complete disposition of one or more other indictments against the defendant wherein is charged the class D violent felony offense of criminal possession of a weapon in the third degree as defined in subdivision four of section 265.02 of the penal law when the defendant has not been previously convicted of a class A misdemeanor defined in the penal law in the five years preceding the commission of the offense.

(vi) A plea of guilty, whether to the entire indictment or to part of the indictment for any crime other than a felony, may not be accepted on the condition that it constitutes a complete disposition of one or more other indictments against the defendant wherein is charged a class B felony other than a class B violent felony offense as defined in subdivision one of section 70.02 of the penal law.

(vii) A defendant may not enter a plea of guilty to the crime of murder in the first degree as defined in section 125.27 of the penal law; provided, however, that a defendant may enter such a plea with both the permission of the court and the consent of the people when the agreed upon sentence is either life imprisonment without parole or a term of imprisonment for the class A-I felony of murder in the first degree other than a sentence of life imprisonment without parole.

(viii) A plea of guilty, whether to the entire indictment or to part of the indictment for any crime other than a class A or class B felony may not be accepted on condition that it constitutes a complete disposition of one or more other indictments against the defendant wherein is charged a class A-II felony defined in article two hundred twenty of the penal law or the attempt to commit any such felony.

(ix) A plea of guilty, whether to the entire indictment or to part of the indictment for any crime other than a class B, a class C, or a class D felony, may not be accepted on condition that it constitutes a complete disposition of one or more other indictments against the defendant wherein is charged a class B felony defined in article two hundred twenty of the penal law.

(c) Where the defendant is a juvenile offender, a plea of guilty, whether to the entire indictment or to part of the indictment, of any offense other than one for which the defendant is criminally responsible may not be accepted on the condition that it constitutes a complete disposition of one or more other indictments against the defendant.

HISTORY: Add, L 1970, ch 996, § 1, eff Sept 1, 1971. Sub 1, amd, L 1973, ch 276, § 25, L 1973, ch 277, § 13, L 1980, ch 548, § 5, eff Sept 1, 1980. Sub 2, re-enacted without change, L 1973, ch 276, § 25, L 1973, ch 277, § 13, eff Sept 1, 1973. Sub 3, par (a), formerly entire subdivision, so designated and amd, L 1973, ch 276, § 25, L 1973, ch 277, § 13, L 1976, ch 187, § 1, eff Sept 1, 1976. Sub 3, par (a), subpar (i), formerly part of sub 3, par (a), so designated and amd, L 1978, ch 481, § 38, eff Sept 1, 1978. Sub 3, par (a), subpar (ii), formerly part of sub 3, par (a), so designated and amd, L 1978, ch 481, § 38, eff Sept 1, 1978. Sub 3, par (b), subpar (i), add as sub 3, par (b), L 1973, ch 276, § 25; so designated, L 1973, ch 1051, § 18; amd, L 1976, ch 480, § 3, L 1979, ch 410, § 25, eff Sept 1, 1979. Sub 3, par (b), subpar (ii), add as sub 3, par (b), L 1973, ch 277, § 13; so designated, L 1973, ch 1051, § 18; amd, L 1978, ch 481, § 16, eff Sept 1, 1978. Sub 3, par (b), subpar (iii), add, L 1980, ch 233, § 19, eff Aug 12, 1980. Former sub 3, par (b), subpar (iii), add, L 1978, ch 481, § 17; repealed, L 1980, ch 233, § 19, eff Aug 12, 1980. Prior sub 3, par (b), subpar (iii), add, L 1974, ch 367, § 12; renumbered sub 3, par (b), subpar (v), L 1978, ch 481, § 17, eff Sept 1, 1978. Sub 3, par (b), subpar (iv), add, L 1980, ch 233, § 20, eff Aug 12, 1980. Former sub 3, par (b), subpar (iv), add, L 1976, ch 480, § 4; amd, L 1978, ch 481, § 16; renumbered sub 3, par (b), subpar (vi), L 1980, ch 233, § 20, eff Aug 12, 1980. Sub 3, par (b), subpar (v), add, L 1980, ch 233, § 20; amd, L 1980, ch 234, § 4, eff Aug 12, 1980. Former sub 3, par (b), subpar (v), formerly sub 3, par (b), subpar (iii), add, L 1974, ch 367, § 12; so renumbered, L 1978, ch 481, § 17; renumbered sub 3, par (b), subpar (vii), L 1980, ch 233, § 20, eff Aug 12, 1980. Sub 3, par (b), subpar (vi), formerly sub 3, par (b), subpar (iv), add, L 1976, ch 480, § 4; amd, L 1978, ch 481, § 16; so renumbered, L 1980, ch 233, § 20, eff Aug 12, 1980. Former sub 3, par (b), subpar (vi), formerly sub 3, par (b), subpar (v), add, L 1976, ch 480, § 4; so renumbered, L 1978, ch 481, § 17; renumbered sub 3, par (b), subpar (vii), L 1980, ch 233, § 20, eff Aug 12, 1980. Another sub 3, par (b), subpar (vi), repealed, L 1979, ch 410, § 24, eff Sept 1, 1979. Sub 3, par (b), subpar (vii), formerly sub 3, par (b), subpar (v), so renumbered, L 1980, ch 233, § 20; amd, L 1995, ch 1, § 11, eff Sept 1, 1995. Former sub 3, par (b), subpar (vii), renumbered sub 3, par (b), subpar (ix), L 1980, ch 233, § 20, eff Aug 12, 1980. Sub 3, par (b), subpar (viii), formerly sub 3, par (b), subpar (vi), add, L 1979, ch 410, § 26; so renumbered, L 1980, ch 233, § 20, eff Aug 12, 1980. Sub 3, par (b), subpar (ix), formerly sub 3, par (b), subpar (vii), add, L 1979, ch 410, § 26; so renumbered, L 1980, ch 233, § 20, eff Aug 12, 1980. Sub 3, par (c), add, L 1978, ch 481, § 39, eff Sept 1, 1978. Sub 3, par (b), subpar (v), amd, L 1999, ch 33, § 6, eff Nov 1, 1999, L 2000, ch 189, § 2, eff Nov 1, 2000.

§ 220.35. Hearing on predicate felony conviction

In any case where the defendant offers to enter a plea of guilty of a misdemeanor to constitute a disposition of the entire indictment or to constitute a complete disposition of one or more other indictments, or both, and the permission of the court and the consent of the people must be withheld solely upon the ground that it appears the defendant has previously been subjected to a predicate felony conviction as defined in paragraph (b) of subdivision one of section 70.06 of the penal law the court, if the defendant does not admit such predicate felony conviction, may conduct the hearing required by section 400.21 for the purpose of determining whether the plea may be entered or must be rejected. The finding upon any such hearing shall also be binding upon the defendant for the purpose of sentence.

HISTORY: Add, L 1973, ch 277, § 16, eff Sept 1, 1973.

§ 220.40. Plea; plea of not guilty; meaning

A plea of not guilty constitutes a denial of every allegation of the indictment.

HISTORY: Add, L 1970, ch 996, § 1, eff Sept 1, 1971, with substance derived from Crim C § 338.

§ 220.50. Plea; entry of plea

1. A plea to an indictment, other than one against a corporation, must be entered orally by the defendant in person; except that a plea to an indictment which does not charge a felony may, with the permission of the court, be entered by counsel upon submission by him of written authorization of the defendant.

2. A plea to an indictment against a corporation must be entered by counsel.

3. If a defendant who is required to enter a plea to an indictment refuses to do so or remains mute, the court must enter a plea of not guilty to the indictment in his behalf.

4. Where the permission of the court and the consent of the people are a prerequisite to the entry of a plea of guilty, the court and the prosecutor must either orally on the record or in a writing filed with the indictment state their reason for granting permission or consenting, as the case may be, to entry of the plea of guilty.

5. When a sentence is agreed upon by the prosecutor and a defendant as a predicate to entry of a plea of guilty, the court or the prosecutor must orally on the record, or in writing filed with the court, state the sentence agreed upon as a condition of such plea.

6. Where the defendant consents to a plea of guilty to the indictment, or part of the indictment, or consents to be prosecuted by superior court information as set forth in section 195.20 of this chapter, and if the defendant and prosecutor agree that as a condition of the plea or the superior court information certain property shall be forfeited by the defendant, the description and present estimated monetary value of the property shall be stated in court by the prosecutor at the time of plea. Within thirty days of the acceptance of the plea or superior court information by the court, the prosecutor shall send to the commissioner of the division of criminal justice services a document containing the name of the defendant, the description and present estimated monetary value of the property, and the date the plea or superior court information was accepted. Any property forfeited by the defendant as a condition to a plea of guilty to an indictment, or a part thereof, or to a superior court information, shall be disposed of in accordance with the provisions of section thirteen hundred forty-nine of the civil practice law and rules.

7. [Repealed Sept 1, 2015] Prior to accepting a defendant's plea of guilty to a count or counts of an indictment or a superior court information charging a felony offense, the court must advise the defendant on the record, that if the defendant is not a citizen of the United States, the defendant's plea of guilty and the court's acceptance thereof may result in the defendant's deportation, exclusion from admission to the United States or denial of naturalization pursuant to the laws of the United States. Where the plea of guilty is to a count or counts of an indictment charging a felony offense other than a violent felony offense as defined in section 70.02 of the penal law or an A-I felony offense other than an A-I felony as defined in article two hundred twenty of the penal law, the court must also, prior to accepting such plea, advise the defendant that, if the defendant is not a citizen of the United States and is or becomes the subject of a final order of

deportation issued by the United States Immigration and Naturalization Service, the defendant may be paroled to the custody of the Immigration and Naturalization Service for deportation purposes at any time subsequent to the commencement of any indeterminate or determinate prison sentence imposed as a result of the defendant's plea. The failure to advise the defendant pursuant to this subdivision shall not be deemed to affect the voluntariness of a plea of guilty or the validity of a conviction, nor shall it afford a defendant any rights in a subsequent proceeding relating to such defendant's deportation, exclusion or denial of naturalization.

> **HISTORY:** Add, L 1970, ch 996, § 1, eff Sept 1, 1971. Sub 4, add, L 1973, ch 276, § 26, L 1973, ch 277, § 14, eff Sept 1, 1973. Sub 5, add, L 1984, ch 671, § 1, eff Aug 31, 1984, but not applicable to appeals arising from any plea of guilty entered prior to such date. Sub 6, add, L 1990, ch 655, § 15, eff Nov 1, 1990. Sub 7, add, L 1995, ch 3, § 30, eff June 15, 1995, repealed Sept 1, 2015; amd, L 2004, ch 738, § 17, eff Dec 27, 2004.

§ 220.51. Notice before entry of plea or trial involving a public official

Prior to trial, and before accepting a defendant's plea to a count or counts of an indictment or a superior court information charging a felony offense, the court must individually advise the defendant, on the record, that if at the time of the alleged felony crime the defendant was a public official, as defined in subdivision six of section one hundred fifty-six of the retirement and social security law, the defendant's plea of guilty and the court's acceptance thereof or conviction after trial may result in proceedings for the reduction or revocation of such defendant's pension pursuant to article three-B of the retirement and social security law.

> **HISTORY:** Add, L 2011, ch 399, § 2, eff Nov 13, 2011.

§ 220.60. Plea; change of plea

1. A defendant who has entered a plea of not guilty to an indictment may as a matter of right withdraw such plea at any time before rendition of a verdict and enter a plea of guilty to the entire indictment pursuant to subdivision two, but subject to the limitation in subdivision five of section 220.10.

2. A defendant who has entered a plea of not guilty to an indictment may, with both the permission of the court and the consent of the people, withdraw such plea at any time before the rendition of a verdict and enter: (a) a plea of guilty to part of the indictment pursuant to subdivision three or four but subject to the limitation in subdivision five of section 220.10, or (b) a plea of not responsible by reason of mental disease or defect to the indictment pursuant to section 220.15 of this chapter.

3. At any time before the imposition of sentence, the court in its discretion may permit a defendant who has entered a plea of guilty to the entire indictment or to part of the indictment, or a plea of not responsible by reason of mental disease or defect, to withdraw such plea, and in such event the entire indictment, as it existed at the time of such plea, is restored.

4. When a special information has been filed pursuant to section 200.61 or 200.62 of this chapter, a defendant may enter a plea of guilty to the count or counts of the indictment to which the special information applies without admitting the allegations of the special information. Whenever a defendant enters a plea of guilty to the count or counts of the indictment to which the special information applies without admitting the allegations of the special information, the court must, unless the people consent otherwise, conduct a hearing in accordance with paragraph (b) of subdivision two of section 200.62 or paragraph (b) of subdivision three of section 200.61 of this chapter, whichever is applicable.

> **HISTORY:** Add, L 1970, ch 996, § 1; amd, L 1974, ch 367, § 13, L 1980, ch 548, § 6, eff Sept 1, 1980. Sub 2, formerly sub 3, amd, L 1973, ch 276, § 27, L 1973, ch 277, § 15, L 1973, ch 278,

§ 11; renumbered sub 2, L 1974, ch 367, § 13; amd, L 1995, ch 1, § 12, eff Sept 1, 1995. Former sub 2, deleted, L 1974, ch 367, § 13, eff Sept 1, 1974. Sub 3, formerly sub 4, renumbered sub 3, L 1974, ch 367, § 13, eff Sept 1, 1974. Former sub 3, amd, L 1973, ch 276, § 27, L 1973, ch 277, § 15, L 1973, ch 278, § 11; renumbered sub 2, L 1974, ch 367, § 13, eff Sept 1, 1974. Sub 4, add, L 2000, ch 1, § 55, eff Feb 1, 2001. Former sub 4, renumbered sub 3, L 1974, ch 367, § 13, eff Sept 1, 1974.

ARTICLE 230   REMOVAL OF ACTION

HISTORY: Add, L 1970, ch 996, § 1, eff Sept 1, 1971.

§ 230.10. Removal of action; from supreme court to county court and from county court to supreme court; at instance of court

Upon order of an appropriate court or judge, made at its or his own instance pursuant to rules established by the appellate division of the appropriate department, (a) an indictment filed with the supreme court at a term held in a particular county outside of New York City may, prior to entry of a plea of guilty thereto or commencement of a trial thereof, be removed to the county court of such county, and (b) an indictment filed in a county court may similarly be removed to the supreme court at a term held or to be held in the same county. Each of the appellate divisions of the second, third and fourth departments may establish rules authorizing such removals with respect to the superior courts within its department, and prescribing the courts or judges who may order such removals and other procedural matters involved therein.

HISTORY: Add, L 1970, ch 996, § 1, eff Sept 1, 1971.

§ 230.20. Removal of action; removal from county court to supreme court and change of venue; upon motion of party

1. At any time within the period provided by section 255.20, the appellate division of the department embracing the county, upon motion of either the defendant or the people, may, for good cause shown, order that the indictment and action be removed from the county court to the supreme court at a term held or to be held in the same county.

2. At any time within the period provided by section 255.20, the appellate division of the department embracing the county in which the superior court is located may, upon motion of either the defendant or the people demonstrating reasonable cause to believe that a fair and impartial trial cannot be had in such county, order either:

    (a) that the indictment and action be removed from such superior court to a designated superior court of or located in another county; or

    (b) that the commissioner of jurors of such county, in consultation with the appropriate administrative judge of the judicial district in which the county is located, expand the pool of jurors to encompass prospective jurors from the jury lists of counties that are within the judicial district in which, and that are geographically contiguous with the county in which, such superior court is located.

In making such determination the appellate division shall consider, among other factors, the hardship on potential jurors and the potential depletion of a county's qualified juror list that may result from an order expanding the jury pool. An order of removal under paragraph (a) herein must, if the defendant is in custody at the time, include a provision for transfer of custody by the sheriff or other appropriate public servant of the county of confinement to the sheriff or other appropriate public servant of the county to which the action has been removed. If the order is issued upon motion of the people, the appellate division may impose such conditions as it deems equitable and appropriate to insure that the removal does not subject the defendant to an unreasonable burden in making his defense. Any additional cost to the people incurred in complying with the order must be borne by the county from which the action originated.

3. Any motion made pursuant to this section must be based upon papers stating the grounds therefor, and must be made within the period provided by section 255.20 and upon five days notice thereof together with service of the moving papers upon, as the case may be, (a) the district attorney or (b) either the defendant or his counsel. In any case, the motion must be made returnable either during the appellate division term during which such moving papers are served or during the next term thereof.

4. If the appellate division grants the motion and orders a removal of the action, a certified copy of such order must be filed with the clerk of the superior court in which the indictment is pending. Such clerk must thereupon transmit such instrument, together with the pertinent papers and proceedings of the action, including all undertakings for appearances of the defendant and of the witnesses, or a certified copy or copies of the same, to the term of the superior court to which the action has been removed. Such latter court must then proceed to conduct the action to judgment or other final disposition.

> **HISTORY:** Add, L 1970, ch 996, § 1; amd, L 1974, ch 763, § 7, eff Sept 1, 1974. Sub 2, opening par, amd, L 1985, ch 257, § 1, eff Nov 1, 1985. Sub 2, par (a), formerly part of sub 2, opening par, so designated and amd, L 1985, ch 257, § 1, eff Nov 1, 1985. Sub 2, par (b), add, L 1985, ch 257, § 1, eff Nov 1, 1985. Sub 2, closing par, amd, L 1985, ch 257, § 1, eff Nov 1, 1985.

§ 230.30. Removal of action; stay of trial pending motion therefor

1. At any time when a timely motion for removal of an action from the county court to the supreme court or for a change of venue may be made pursuant to section 230.20, a justice holding a term of the supreme court in the district in which the indictment is pending, or a justice of the appellate division of the department in which the indictment is pending, upon application of either the defendant or the people, may, in his discretion and for good cause shown, order that the trial of such indictment be stayed for a designated period, not to exceed thirty days from the issuance of such order, to allow the applicant party to make a motion in the appropriate court for removal of the action from a county court to the supreme court or for a change of venue.

2. Such an order may be issued only upon an application made in writing and after reasonable notice and opportunity to be heard has been accorded the other party.

3. Upon issuing the order, the supreme court justice or appellate division justice must cause the order to be filed with the clerk of the court in which the indictment is pending. Thereafter, no further proceedings may be had in such court until a motion for removal or change of venue, as the case may be, if made within the designated period, has been determined, or until such designated period has expired without any such motion having been made.

4. When such an application for a stay has been made to and denied by a justice of the supreme court or a justice of the appellate division, a second such application may not be made to any other such justice.

> **HISTORY:** Add, L 1970, ch 996, § 1, eff Sept 1, 1971.

§ 230.40. Removal of action; determinations and rulings before and after removal; by which courts made

Upon any removal of an indictment and action from one superior court to another pursuant to the provisions of this article, determinations and rulings with respect to the action made before such removal are not thereby rendered invalid. All subsequent determinations and rulings must be made by the court to which the action is removed; and such latter court is deemed to have control of the grand jury minutes underlying the indictment for the purpose of determining post-removal motions addressed to the legal sufficiency of the grand jury evidence or the validity of the grand jury proceeding.

HISTORY: Add, L 1970, ch 996, § 1, eff Sept 1, 1971.

ARTICLE 240 DISCOVERY

HISTORY: Add, L 1979, ch 412, § 2, eff Jan 1, 1980. Former Art 240 (consisting of §§ 240.10–240.40), add, L 1970, ch 996, § 1; repealed, L 1979, ch 412, § 1, eff Jan 1, 1980.

§ 240.10. Discovery; definition of terms

The following definitions are applicable to this article:

1. "Demand to produce" means a written notice served by and on a party to a criminal action, without leave of the court, demanding to inspect property pursuant to this article and giving reasonable notice of the time at which the demanding party wishes to inspect the property designated.

2. "Attorneys' work product" means property to the extent that it contains the opinions, theories or conclusions of the prosecutor, defense counsel or members of their legal staffs.

3. "Property" means any existing tangible personal or real property, including, but not limited to, books, records, reports, memoranda, papers, photographs, tapes or other electronic recordings, articles of clothing, fingerprints, blood samples, fingernail scrapings or handwriting specimens, but excluding attorneys' work product.

4. "At the trial" means as part of the people's or the defendant's direct case.

HISTORY: Add, L 1979, ch 412, § 2, eff Jan 1, 1980. Former § 240.10, add, L 1970, ch 996, § 1; repealed, L 1979, ch 412, § 1, eff Jan 1, 1980.

§ 240.20. Discovery; upon demand of defendant

1. Except to the extent protected by court order, upon a demand to produce by a defendant against whom an indictment, superior court information, prosecutor's information, information, or simplified information charging a misdemeanor is pending, the prosecutor shall disclose to the defendant and make available for inspection, photographing, copying or testing, the following property:

(a) Any written, recorded or oral statement of the defendant, and of a co-defendant to be tried jointly, made, other than in the course of the criminal transaction, to a public servant engaged in law enforcement activity or to a person then acting under his direction or in cooperation with him;

(b) Any transcript of testimony relating to the criminal action or proceeding pending against the defendant, given by the defendant, or by a co-defendant to be tried jointly, before any grand jury;

(c) Any written report or document, or portion thereof, concerning a physical or mental examination, or scientific test or experiment, relating to the criminal action or proceeding which was made by, or at the request or direction of a public servant engaged in law enforcement activity, or which was made by a person whom the prosecutor intends to call as a witness at trial, or which the people intend to introduce at trial;

(d) Any photograph or drawing relating to the criminal action or proceeding which was made or completed by a public servant engaged in law enforcement activity, or which was made by a person whom the prosecutor intends to call as a witness at trial, or which the people intend to introduce at trial;

(e) Any photograph, photocopy or other reproduction made by or at the direction of a police officer, peace officer or prosecutor of any property prior to its release pursuant to the provisions of section 450.10 of the penal law, irrespective of whether the people intend to introduce at trial the property or the photograph, photocopy or other reproduction.

(f) Any other property obtained from the defendant, or a co-defendant to be tried jointly;

(g) Any tapes or other electronic recordings which the prosecutor intends to introduce at trial, irrespective of whether such recording was made during the course of the criminal transaction;

(h) Anything required to be disclosed, prior to trial, to the defendant by the prosecutor, pursuant to the constitution of this state or of the United States.

(i) The approximate date, time and place of the offense charged and of defendant's arrest.

(j) In any prosecution under penal law section 156.05 or 156.10, the time, place and manner of notice given pursuant to subdivision six of section 156.00 of such law.

(k) in any prosecution commenced in a manner set forth in this subdivision alleging a violation of the vehicle and traffic law, in addition to any material required to be disclosed pursuant to this article, any other provision of law, or the constitution of this state or of the United States, any written report or document, or portion thereof, concerning a physical examination, a scientific test or experiment, including the most recent record of inspection, or calibration or repair of machines or instruments utilized to perform such scientific tests or experiments and the certification certificate, if any, held by the operator of the machine or instrument, which tests or examinations were made by or at the request or direction of a public servant engaged in law enforcement activity or which was made by a person whom the prosecutor intends to call as a witness at trial, or which the people intend to introduce at trial.

2. The prosecutor shall make a diligent, good faith effort to ascertain the existence of demanded property and to cause such property to be made available for discovery where it exists but is not within the prosecutor's possession, custody or control; provided, that the prosecutor shall not be required to obtain by subpoena duces tecum demanded material which the defendant may thereby obtain.

HISTORY: Add, L 1979, ch 412, § 2, eff Jan 1, 1980. Former § 240.20, add, L 1970, ch 996, § 1; repealed, L 1979, ch 412, § 1, eff Jan 1, 1980. Sub 1, opening par, amd, L 1983, ch 317, § 1, eff July 21, 1983. Sub 1, par (c), amd, L 1982, ch 558, § 4, eff Oct 20, 1982. Sub 1, par (d), amd, L 1982, ch 558, § 4, eff Oct 20, 1982. Sub 1, par (e), add, L 1984, ch 795, § 3, eff Nov 1, 1984. Former sub 1, par (e), relettered sub 1, par (f), L 1984, ch 795, § 3, eff Nov 1, 1984. Sub 1, par (f), formerly sub 1, par (e), so relettered, L 1984, ch 795, § 3, eff Nov 1, 1984. Former sub 1, par (f), amd, L 1982, ch 558, § 4; relettered sub 1, par (g), L 1984, ch 795, § 3, eff Nov 1, 1984. Sub 1, par (g), formerly sub 1, par (f), amd, L 1982, ch 558, § 4; so relettered, L 1984, ch 795, § 3, eff Nov 1, 1984. Former sub 1, par (g), relettered sub 1, par (h), L 1984, ch 795, § 3, eff Nov 1, 1984. Sub 1, par (h), formerly sub 1, par (g), so relettered, L 1984, ch 795, § 3, eff Nov 1, 1984. Former sub 1, par (h), add, L 1982, ch 558, § 5; relettered sub 1, par (i), L 1984, ch 795, § 3, eff Nov 1, 1984. Sub 1, par (i), formerly sub 1, par (h), add, L 1982, ch 558, § 5; so relettered, L 1984, ch 795, § 3, eff Nov 1, 1984. Sub 1, par (j), add, L 1986, ch 514, § 8, eff Nov 1, 1986. Sub 1, par (k), add, L 1989, ch 536, § 1, eff Nov 1, 1989.

§ 240.30. Discovery; upon demand of prosecutor

1. Except to the extent protected by court order, upon a demand to produce by the prosecutor, a defendant against whom an indictment, superior court information, prosecutor's information, information, or simplified information charging a misdemeanor is pending shall disclose and make available for inspection, photographing, copying or testing, subject to constitutional limitations:

(a) any written report or document, or portion thereof, concerning a physical or mental examination, or scientific test, experiment, or comparisons, made by or at the request or direction of, the defendant, if the defendant intends to introduce such report or document at trial, or if the defendant has filed a notice of intent to proffer psychiatric evidence and such report or document relates thereto, or if such report or document was made by a person, other than defendant, whom defendant intends to call as a witness at trial; and

(b) any photograph, drawing, tape or other electronic recording which the defendant intends to introduce at trial.

2. The defense shall make a diligent good faith effort to make such property available for discovery where it exists but the property is not within its possession, custody or control, provided, that the defendant shall not be required to obtain by subpoena duces tecum demanded material that the prosecutor may thereby obtain.

HISTORY: Add, L 1979, ch 412, § 2, eff Jan 1, 1980. Former § 240.30, add, L 1970, ch 996, § 1; amd, L 1974, ch 763, § 4; repealed, L 1979, ch 412, § 1, eff Jan 1, 1980. Sub 1, amd, L 1980, ch 220, § 1, L 1982, ch 558, § 6, eff Oct 20, 1982. Sub 1, opening par, amd, L 1983, ch 317, § 2, eff July 21, 1983. Sub 1, par (a), formerly part of subdivision, so lettered and amd, L 1982, ch 558, § 6, eff Oct 20, 1982. Sub 1, par (b), add, L 1982, ch 558, § 6, eff Oct 20, 1982.

§ 240.35. Discovery; refusal of demand

Notwithstanding the provisions of sections 240.20 and 240.30, the prosecutor or the defendant, as the case may be, may refuse to disclose any information which he reasonably believes is not discoverable by a demand to produce, pursuant to section 240.20 or section 240.30 as the case may be, or for which he reasonably believes a protective order would be warranted. Such refusal shall be made in a writing, which shall set forth the grounds of such belief as fully as possible, consistent with the objective of the refusal. The writing shall be served upon the demanding party and a copy shall be filed with the court.

HISTORY: Add, L 1979, ch 412, § 2, eff Jan 1, 1980.

§ 240.40. Discovery; upon court order

1. Upon motion of a defendant against whom an indictment, superior court information, prosecutor's information, information, or simplified information charging a misdemeanor is pending, the court in which such accusatory instrument is pending:

(a) must order discovery as to any material not disclosed upon a demand pursuant to section 240.20, if it finds that the prosecutor's refusal to disclose such material is not justified; (b) must, unless it is satisfied that the people have shown good cause why such an order should not be issued, order discovery or any other order authorized by subdivision one of section 240.70 as to any material not disclosed upon demand pursuant to section 240.20 where the prosecutor has failed to serve a timely written refusal pursuant to section 240.35; (c) may order discovery with respect to any other property, which the people intend to introduce at the trial, upon a showing by the defendant that discovery with respect to such property is material to the preparation of his or her defense, and that the request is reasonable; and (d) where property in the people's possession, custody, or control that consists of a deoxyribonucleic acid ("DNA") profile obtained from probative biological material gathered in connection with the investigation or prosecution of the defendant and the defendant establishes that such profile complies with federal bureau of investigation or state requirements, whichever are applicable and as such requirements are applied to law enforcement agencies seeking a keyboard search or similar comparison, and that the data meets state DNA index system or national DNA index system criteria as such criteria are applied to law enforcement agencies seeking such a keyboard search or similar comparison, the court may order an entity that has access to the combined DNA index system or its successor system to compare such DNA profile against DNA databanks by keyboard searches, or a similar method that does not involve uploading, upon notice to both parties and the entity required to perform the search, upon a showing by the defendant that such a comparison is material to the presentation of his or her defense and that the request is reasonable. For purposes of this paragraph, a "keyboard search" shall mean a search of a DNA profile against the databank in which the profile that is searched is not uploaded to or maintained in the databank. Upon granting the motion pursuant to paragraph (c) of this subdivision, the court shall, upon motion of the people showing such to be material to the preparation of their case and that the request is reasonable, condition its order of discovery by further directing discovery by the people of property, of the same kind or character as that authorized to be inspected by the defendant, which he or she intends to introduce at the trial.

2. Upon motion of the prosecutor, and subject to constitutional limitation, the court in which an indictment, superior court information, prosecutor's information, information, or simplified information charging a misdemeanor is pending:

(a) must order discovery as to any property not disclosed upon a demand pursuant to section 240.30, if it finds that the defendant's refusal to disclose such material is not justified; and

(b) may order the defendant to provide non-testimonial evidence. Such order may, among other things, require the defendant to:

(i) Appear in a line-up;

(ii) Speak for identification by witness or potential witness;

(iii) Be fingerprinted;

(iv) Pose for photographs not involving reenactment of an event;

(v) Permit the taking of samples of blood, hair or other materials from his body in a manner not involving an unreasonable intrusion thereof or a risk of serious physical injury thereto;

(vi) Provide specimens of his handwriting;

(vii) Submit to a reasonable physical or medical inspection of his body.

This subdivision shall not be construed to limit, expand, or otherwise affect the issuance of a similar court order, as may be authorized by law, before the filing of an accusatory instrument consistent with such rights as the defendant may derive from the constitution of this state or of the United States. This section shall not be construed to limit or otherwise affect the administration of a chemical test where otherwise authorized pursuant to section one thousand one hundred ninety-four-a of the vehicle and traffic law.˙

3. An order pursuant to this section may be denied, limited or conditioned as provided in section 240.50.

> **HISTORY:** Add, L 1979, ch 412, § 2, eff Jan 1, 1980; amd, L 1982, ch 558, § 10, eff Oct 20, 1982, L 1983, ch 317, § 3, eff July 21, 1983, L 1983, ch 481, § 4, eff Oct 13, 1983, L 2012, ch 19, § 3, eff Aug 1, 2012.

§ 240.43. Discovery; disclosure of prior uncharged criminal, vicious or immoral acts

Upon a request by a defendant, the prosecutor shall notify the defendant of all specific instances of a defendant's prior uncharged criminal, vicious or immoral conduct of which the prosecutor has knowledge and which the prosecutor intends to use at trial for purposes of impeaching the credibility of the defendant. Such notification by the prosecutor shall be made immediately prior to the commencement of jury selection, except that the court may, in its discretion, order such notification and make its determination as to the admissibility for impeachment purposes of such conduct within a period of three days, excluding Saturdays, Sundays and holidays, prior to the commencement of jury selection.

> **HISTORY:** Add, L 1987, ch 222, § 1, eff Nov 1, 1987.

§ 240.44. Discovery; upon pre-trial hearing

Subject to a protective order, at a pre-trial hearing held in a criminal court at which a witness is called to testify, each party, at the conclusion of the direct examination of each of its witnesses, shall, upon request of the other party, make available to that party to the extent not previously disclosed:

1. Any written or recorded statement, including any testimony before a grand jury, made by such witness other than the defendant which relates to the subject matter of the witness's testimony.

2. A record of a judgment of conviction of such witness other than the defendant if the record of conviction is known by the prosecutor or defendant, as the case may be, to exist.

3. The existence of any pending criminal action against such witness other than the defendant if the pending criminal action is known by the prosecutor or defendant, as the case may be, to exist.

˙ Vehicle and traffic law § 1194-a was repealed by L 1988, ch 47, § 18, eff Nov 1, 1988. See now vehicle and traffic law article 31.

HISTORY: Add, L 1982, ch 558, § 7, eff Oct 20, 1982.

§ 240.45. Discovery; upon trial, of prior statements and criminal history of witnesses

1. After the jury has been sworn and before the prosecutor's opening address, or in the case of a single judge trial after commencement and before submission of evidence, the prosecutor shall, subject to a protective order, make available to the defendant:

(a) Any written or recorded statement, including any testimony before a grand jury and an examination videotaped pursuant to section 190.32 of this chapter, made by a person whom the prosecutor intends to call as a witness at trial, and which relates to the subject matter of the witness's testimony;

(b) A record of judgment of conviction of a witness the people intend to call at trial if the record of conviction is known by the prosecutor to exist;

(c) The existence of any pending criminal action against a witness the people intend to call at trial, if the pending criminal action is known by the prosecutor to exist.

The provisions of paragraphs (b) and (c) of this subdivision shall not be construed to require the prosecutor to fingerprint a witness or otherwise cause the division of criminal justice services or other law enforcement agency or court to issue a report concerning a witness.

2. After presentation of the people's direct case and before the presentation of the defendant's direct case, the defendant shall, subject to a protective order, make available to the prosecutor:

(a) any written or recorded statement made by a person other than the defendant whom the defendant intends to call as a witness at the trial, and which relates to the subject matter of the witness's testimony;

(b) a record of judgment of conviction of a witness, other than the defendant, the defendant intends to call at trial if the record of conviction is known by the defendant to exist;

(c) the existence of any pending criminal action against a witness, other than the defendant, the defendant intends to call at trial, if the pending criminal action is known by the defendant to exist.

HISTORY: Add, L 1979, ch 412, § 2; amd, L 1982, ch 558, § 8, eff Oct 20, 1982. Sub 1, par (a), amd, L 1984, ch 804, § 5, eff Nov 1, 1984. Sub 2, amd, L 1982, ch 558, § 8, eff Oct 20, 1982. Sub 2, par (a), formerly part of subdivision, so lettered and amd, L 1982, ch 558, § 8, eff Oct 20, 1982. Sub 2, par (b), add, L 1982, ch 558, § 8, eff Oct 20, 1982. Sub 2, par (c), add, L 1982, ch 558, § 8, eff Oct 20, 1982. Sub 3, deleted, L 1982, ch 558, § 8, eff Oct 20, 1982.

§ 240.50. Discovery; protective orders

1. The court in which the criminal action is pending may, upon motion of either party, or of any affected person, or upon determination of a motion of either party for an order of discovery, or upon its own initiative, issue a protective order denying, limiting, conditioning, delaying or regulating discovery pursuant to this article for good cause, including constitutional limitations, danger to the integrity of physical evidence or a substantial risk of physical harm, intimidation, economic reprisal, bribery or unjustified annoyance or embarrassment to any person or an adverse effect upon the legitimate needs of law enforcement, including the protection of the confidentiality of informants, or any other factor or set of factors which outweighs the usefulness of the discovery.

2. An order limiting, conditioning, delaying or regulating discovery may, among other things, require that any material copied or derived therefrom be maintained in the exclusive possession of

the attorney for the discovering party and be used for the exclusive purpose of preparing for the defense or prosecution of the criminal action.

3. A motion for a protective order shall suspend discovery of the particular matter in dispute.

4. Notwithstanding any other provision of this article, the personal residence address of a police officer or correction officer shall not be required to be disclosed except pursuant to an order issued by a court following a finding of good cause.

> **HISTORY:** Add, L 1979, ch 412, § 2, eff Jan 1, 1980. Sub 4, add, L 1981, ch 195, § 1; amd, L 1985, ch 348, § 1, eff Nov 1, 1985.

§ 240.60. Discovery; continuing duty to disclose

If, after complying with the provisions of this article or an order pursuant thereto, a party finds, either before or during trial, additional material subject to discovery or covered by such order, he shall promptly comply with the demand or order, refuse to comply with the demand where refusal is authorized, or apply for a protective order.

> **HISTORY:** Add, L 1979, ch 412, § 2, eff Jan 1, 1980.

§ 240.70. Discovery; sanctions; fees

1. If, during the course of discovery proceedings, the court finds that a party has failed to comply with any of the provisions of this article, the court may order such party to permit discovery of the property not previously disclosed, grant a continuance, issue a protective order, prohibit the introduction of certain evidence or the calling of certain witnesses or take any other appropriate action.

2. The failure of the prosecution to call as a witness a person specified in subdivision one of section 240.20 of this article or of any party to introduce disclosed material at the trial shall not, by itself, constitute grounds for any sanction or for adverse comment thereupon by any party in summation to the jury or at any other point.

3. A fee for copies of records required to be disclosed may be charged. Such fee shall not exceed twenty-five cents per photocopy not in excess of nine inches by fourteen inches, or the actual cost of reproducing any other record, except when a different fee is otherwise prescribed by law.

> **HISTORY:** Add, L 1979, ch 412, § 2, eff Jan 1, 1980.

§ 240.75. Discovery; certain violations

The failure of the prosecutor or any agent of the prosecutor to disclose statements that are required to be disclosed under subdivision one of section 240.44 or paragraph (a) of subdivision one of section 240.45 of this article shall not constitute grounds for any court to order a new pre-trial hearing or set aside a conviction, or reverse, modify or vacate a judgment of conviction in the absence of a showing by the defendant that there is a reasonable possibility that the non-disclosure materially contributed to the result of the trial or other proceeding; provided, however, that nothing in this section shall affect or limit any right the defendant may have to a re-opened pre-trial hearing when such statements were disclosed before the close of evidence at trial.

> **HISTORY:** Add, L 2000, ch 1, § 48, eff Feb 1, 2001.

§ 240.80. Discovery; when demand, refusal and compliance made

1. A demand to produce shall be made within thirty days after arraignment and before the commencement of trial. If the defendant is not represented by counsel, and has requested an adjournment to obtain counsel or to have counsel assigned, the thirty-day period shall commence,

for purposes of a demand by the defendant, on the date counsel initially appears on his behalf. However, the court may direct compliance with a demand to produce that, for good cause shown, could not have been made within the time specified.

2. A refusal to comply with a demand to produce shall be made within fifteen days of the service of the demand to produce, but for good cause may be made thereafter.

3. Absent a refusal to comply with a demand to produce, compliance with such demand shall be made within fifteen days of the service of the demand or as soon thereafter as practicable.

HISTORY: Add, L 1979, ch 412, § 2, eff Jan 1, 1980. Sub 2, amd, L 1982, ch 558, § 11, eff Oct 20, 1982. Sub 3, amd, L 1982, ch 558, § 11, eff Oct 20, 1982.

§ 240.90. Discovery; motion procedure

1. A motion by a prosecutor for discovery shall be made within forty-five days after arraignment, but for good cause shown may be made at any time before commencement of trial.

2. A motion by a defendant for discovery shall be made as prescribed in section 255.20 of this chapter.

3. Where the interests of justice so require, the court may permit a party to a motion for an order of discovery or a protective order, or other affected person, to submit papers or to testify ex parte or in camera. Any such papers and transcript of such testimony shall be sealed, but shall constitute a part of the record on appeal.

HISTORY: Add, L 1979, ch 412, § 2, eff Jan 1, 1980.

ARTICLE 250 PRE-TRIAL NOTICES OF DEFENSES

HISTORY: Add, L 1970, ch 996, § 1, eff Sept 1, 1971.

§ 250.10. Notice of intent to proffer psychiatric evidence; examination of defendant upon application of prosecutor

1. As used in this section, the term "psychiatric evidence" means:

(a) Evidence of mental disease or defect to be offered by the defendant in connection with the affirmative defense of lack of criminal responsibility by reason of mental disease or defect.

(b) Evidence of mental disease or defect to be offered by the defendant in connection with the affirmative defense of extreme emotional disturbance as defined in paragraph (a) of subdivision one of section 125.25 of the penal law and paragraph (a) of subdivision two of section 125.27 of the penal law.

(c) Evidence of mental disease or defect to be offered by the defendant in connection with any other defense not specified in the preceding paragraphs.

2. Psychiatric evidence is not admissible upon a trial unless the defendant serves upon the people and files with the court a written notice of his intention to present psychiatric evidence. Such notice must be served and filed before trial and not more than thirty days after entry of the plea of not guilty to the indictment. In the interest of justice and for good cause shown, however,

the court may permit such service and filing to be made at any later time prior to the close of the evidence.

3. When a defendant, pursuant to subdivision two of this section, serves notice of intent to present psychiatric evidence, the district attorney may apply to the court, upon notice to the defendant, for an order directing that the defendant submit to an examination by a psychiatrist or licensed psychologist as defined in article one hundred fifty-three of the education law designated by the district attorney. If the application is granted, the psychiatrist or psychologist designated to conduct the examination must notify the district attorney and counsel for the defendant of the time and place of the examination. Defendant has a right to have his counsel present at such examination. The district attorney may also be present. The role of each counsel at such examination is that of an observer, and neither counsel shall be permitted to take an active role at the examination.

4. After the conclusion of the examination, the psychiatrist or psychologist must promptly prepare a written report of his findings and evaluation. A copy of such report must be made available to the district attorney and to the counsel for the defendant. No transcript or recording of the examination is required, but if one is made, it shall be made available to both parties prior to the trial.

5. If the court finds that the defendant has willfully refused to cooperate fully in the examination ordered pursuant to subdivision three of this section it may preclude introduction of testimony by a psychiatrist or psychologist concerning mental disease or defect of the defendant at trial. Where, however, the defendant has other proof of his affirmative defense, and the court has found that the defendant did not submit to or cooperate fully in the examination ordered by the court, this other evidence, if otherwise competent, shall be admissible. In such case, the court must instruct the jury that the defendant did not submit to or cooperate fully in the pre-trial psychiatric examination ordered by the court pursuant to subdivison three of this section and that such failure may be considered in determining the merits of the affirmative defense.

> **HISTORY:** Add, L 1970, ch 996, § 1, eff Sept 1, 1971, with substance derived from Crim C § 336. Section heading, amd, L 1980, ch 548, § 7, eff Sept 1, 1980. Sub 1, formerly part of section, so numbered and amd, L 1980, ch 548, § 7, L 1982, ch 558, § 9, eff Oct 20, 1982. Sub 1, par (a), formerly part of subdivision, so lettered and amd, L 1982, ch 558, § 9, L 1984, ch 668, § 6, eff Nov 1, 1984. Sub 1, par (b), add, L 1982, ch 558, § 9, eff Oct 20, 1982. Sub 1, par (c), add, L 1982, ch 558, § 9, eff Oct 20, 1982. Sub 2, formerly part of section, so numbered and amd, L 1980, ch 548, § 7, eff Sept 1, 1980. Sub 3, add, L 1980, ch 548, § 7, eff Sept 1, 1980. Sub 4, add, L 1980, ch 548, § 7, eff Sept 1, 1980. Sub 5, add, L 1980, ch 548, § 7; amd, L 1984, ch 668, § 7, eff Nov 1, 1984.

§ 250.20. Notice of alibi

1. At any time, not more than twenty days after arraignment, the people may serve upon the defendant or his counsel, and file a copy thereof with the court, a demand that if the defendant intends to offer a trial defense that at the time of the commission of the crime charged he was at some place or places other than the scene of the crime, and to call witnesses in support of such defense, he must, within eight days of service of such demand, serve upon the people, and file a copy thereof with the court, a "notice of alibi," reciting (a) the place or places where the defendant claims to have been at the time in question, and (b) the names, the residential addresses, the places of employment and the addresses thereof of every such alibi witness upon whom he intends to rely. For good cause shown, the court may extend the period for service of the notice.

2. Within a reasonable time after receipt of the defendant's witness list but not later than ten days before trial, the people must serve upon the defendant or his counsel, and file a copy thereof with

the court, a list of the witnesses the people propose to offer in rebuttal to discredit the defendant's alibi at the trial together with the residential addresses, the places of employment and the addresses thereof of any such rebuttal witnesses. A witness who will testify that the defendant was at the scene of the crime is not such an alibi rebuttal witness. For good cause shown, the court may extend the period for service of the list of witnesses by the people.

3. If at the trial the defendant calls such an alibi witness without having served the demanded notice of alibi, or if having served such a notice he calls a witness not specified therein, the court may exclude any testimony of such witness relating to the alibi defense. The court may in its discretion receive such testimony, but before doing so, it must, upon application of the people, grant an adjournment not in excess of three days.

4. Similarly, if the people fail to serve and file a list of any rebuttal witnesses, the provisions of subdivision three, above, shall reciprocally apply.

5. Both the defendant and the people shall be under a continuing duty to promptly disclose the names and addresses of additional witnesses which come to the attention of either party subsequent to filing their witness lists as provided in this section.

> **HISTORY:** Add, L 1970, ch 996, § 1, with substance derived from Crim C § 295-l; amd, L 1974, ch 420, § 1, eff May 23, 1974. Sub 2, add, L 1974, ch 420, § 1, eff May 23, 1974. Former sub 2, renumbered sub 3, L 1974, ch 420, § 1, eff May 23, 1974. Sub 3, formerly sub 2, renumbered sub 3, L 1974, ch 420, § 1, eff May 23, 1974. Sub 4, add, L 1974, ch 420, § 1, eff May 23, 1974. Sub 5, add, L 1974, ch 420, § 1, eff May 23, 1974.

§ 250.30. Notice of defenses in offenses involving computers

1. In any prosecution in which the defendant seeks to invoke any of the defenses specified in section 156.50 of the penal law, the defendant must within forty-five days after arraignment and not less than twenty days before the commencement of the trial serve upon the people and file with the court a written notice of his intention to present such defense. For good cause shown, the court may extend the period for service of the notice.

2. The notice served must specify the subdivision or subdivisions upon which the defendant relies and must also state the reasonable grounds that led the defendant to believe that he had the authorization required by the statute or the right required by the statute to engage in such conduct.

3. If at the trial the defendant seeks to invoke any of the defenses specified in section 156.50 of the penal law without having served the notice as required, or seeks to invoke a subdivision or a ground not specified in the notice, the court may exclude any testimony or evidence in regard to the defense, or any subdivision or ground, not noticed. The court may in its discretion, for good cause shown, receive such testimony or evidence, but before doing so, it may, upon application of the people, grant an adjournment.

> **HISTORY:** Add, L 1986, ch 514, § 9, eff Nov 1, 1986.

§ 250.40. Notice of intent to seek death penalty

1. A sentence of death may not be imposed upon a defendant convicted of murder in the first degree unless, pursuant to subdivision two of this section, the people file with the court and serve upon the defendant a notice of intent to seek the death penalty.

2. In any prosecution in which the people seek a sentence of death, the people shall, within one hundred twenty days of the defendant's arraignment upon an indictment charging the defendant with murder in the first degree, serve upon the defendant and file with the court in which the indictment is pending a written notice of intention to seek the death penalty. For good cause shown

CPL

the court may extend the period for service and filing of the notice.

3. Notwithstanding any other provisions of law, where the people file a notice of intent to seek the death penalty pursuant to this section the defendant shall be entitled to an additional sixty days for the purpose of filing new motions or supplementing pending motions.

4. A notice of intent to seek the death penalty may be withdrawn at any time by a written notice of withdrawal filed with the court and served upon the defendant. Once withdrawn the notice of intent to seek the death penalty may not be refiled.

HISTORY: Add, L 1995, ch 1, § 13, eff Sept 1, 1995.

ARTICLE 255   PRE-TRIAL MOTIONS

§ 255.10.   **Definitions**
§ 255.20.   **Pre-trial motions; procedure**

    HISTORY: Add, L 1974, ch 763, § 1, eff Sept 1, 1974.

§ 255.10. Definitions

1.* "Pre-trial motion" as used in this article means any motion by a defendant which seeks an order of the court:

(a) dismissing or reducing an indictment pursuant to article 210 or removing an action to the family court pursuant to section 210.43; or

(b) dismissing an information, prosecutor's information, simplified information or misdemeanor complaint pursuant to article 170; or

(c) granting discovery pursuant to article 240; or

(d) granting a bill of particulars pursuant to sections [section]** 100.45 or 200.90***; or

(e) removing the action pursuant to sections [section]**** 170.15, 230.20 or 230.30; or

(f) suppressing the use at trial of any evidence pursuant to article 710; or

(g) granting separate trials pursuant to article 100 or 200.

    HISTORY: Add, L 1974, ch 763, § 1, eff Sept 1, 1974. Sub 1, par (a), amd, L 1979, ch 411, § 19, L 1990, ch 209, § 16, eff Sept 1, 1990.

§ 255.20. Pre-trial motions; procedure

1. Except as otherwise expressly provided by law, whether the defendant is represented by counsel or elects to proceed pro se, all pre-trial motions shall be served or filed within forty-five days after arraignment and before commencement of trial, or within such additional time as the court may fix upon application of the defendant made prior to entry of judgment. In an action in which an eavesdropping warrant and application have been furnished pursuant to section 700.70 or a notice of intention to introduce evidence has been served pursuant to section 710.30, such period shall be extended until forty-five days after the last date of such service. If the defendant is not represented by counsel and has requested an adjournment to obtain counsel or to have

---

*   So in original. There is no subdivision 2.

**   The bracketed word has been inserted by the Publisher.

***   § 200.90 was repealed by L 1982, ch 558, § 3, eff Oct 20, 1982. See CPL § 200.95.

****   The bracketed word has been inserted by the Publisher.

counsel assigned, such forty-five day period shall commence on the date counsel initially appears on defendant's behalf.

2. All pre-trial motions, with supporting affidavits, affirmations, exhibits and memoranda of law, whenever practicable, shall be included within the same set of motion papers, and shall be made returnable on the same date, unless the defendant shows that it would be prejudicial to the defense were a single judge to consider all the pre-trial motions. Where one motion seeks to provide the basis for making another motion, it shall be deemed impracticable to include both motions in the same set of motion papers pursuant to this subdivision.

3. Notwithstanding the provisions of subdivisions one and two hereof, the court must entertain and decide on its merits, at anytime [any time]* before the end of the trial, any appropriate pre-trial motion based upon grounds of which the defendant could not, with due diligence, have been previously aware, or which, for other good cause, could not reasonably have been raised within the period specified in subdivision one of this section or included within the single set of motion papers as required by subdivision two. Any other pre-trial motion made after the forty-five day period may be summarily denied, but the court, in the interest of justice, and for good cause shown, may, in its discretion, at any time before sentence, entertain and dispose of the motion on the merits.

4. Any pre-trial motion, whether made before or after expiration of the period specified in subdivision one of this section, may be referred by the court to a judicial hearing officer who shall entertain it in the same manner as a court. In the discharge of this responsibility, the judicial hearing officer shall have the same powers as a judge of the court making the assignment, except that the judicial hearing officer shall not determine the motion but shall file a report with the court setting forth findings of fact and conclusions of law. The rules of evidence shall be applicable at any hearing conducted hereunder by a judicial hearing officer. A transcript of any testimony taken, together with the exhibits or copies thereof, shall be filed with the report. The court shall determine the motion on the motion papers, affidavits and other documents submitted by the parties thereto, the record of the hearing before the judicial hearing officer, and the judicial hearing officer's report.

HISTORY: Add, L 1974, ch 763, § 1, eff Sept 1, 1974. Sub 1, amd, L 1976, ch 194, § 1, L 1982, ch 369, § 1, eff June 21, 1982. Sub 4, add, L 1983, ch 840, § 10, eff April 1, 1983.

ARTICLE 260   JURY TRIAL—GENERALLY

§ 260.10.	Jury trial; requirement thereof
§ 260.20.	Jury trial; defendant's presence at trial
§ 260.30.	Jury trial; in what order to proceed

HISTORY: Add, L 1970, ch 996, § 1, eff Sept 1, 1971.

§ 260.10. Jury trial; requirement thereof

Except as otherwise provided in section 320.10, every trial of an indictment must be a jury trial.

HISTORY: Add, L 1970, ch 996, § 1, eff Sept 1, 1971.

§ 260.20. Jury trial; defendant's presence at trial

A defendant must be personally present during the trial of an indictment; provided, however, that a defendant who conducts himself in so disorderly and disruptive a manner that his trial cannot be carried on with him in the courtroom may be removed from the courtroom if, after he has been warned by the court that he will be removed if he continues such conduct, he continues to engage in such conduct.

---

* The bracketed word has been inserted by the Publisher.

HISTORY: Add, L 1970, ch 996, § 1; amd, L 1971, ch 789, § 1, eff Sept 1, 1971.

§ 260.30. Jury trial; in what order to proceed

The order of a jury trial, in general, is as follows:

1. The jury must be selected and sworn.

2. The court must deliver preliminary instructions to the jury.

3. The people must deliver an opening address to the jury.

4. The defendant may deliver an opening address to the jury.

5. The people must offer evidence in support of the indictment.

6. The defendant may offer evidence in his defense.

7. The people may offer evidence in rebuttal of the defense evidence, and the defendant may then offer evidence in rebuttal of the people's rebuttal evidence. The court may in its discretion permit the parties to offer further rebuttal or surrebuttal evidence in this pattern. In the interest of justice, the court may permit either party to offer evidence upon rebuttal which is not technically of a rebuttal nature but more properly a part of the offering party's original case.

8. At the conclusion of the evidence, the defendant may deliver a summation to the jury.

9. The people may then deliver a summation to the jury.

10. The court must then deliver a charge to the jury.

11. The jury must then retire to deliberate and, if possible, render a verdict.

HISTORY: Add, L 1970, ch 996, § 1, eff Sept 1, 1971.

ARTICLE 270   JURY TRIAL-FORMATION AND CONDUCT OF JURY

HISTORY: Add, L 1970, ch 996, § 1, eff Sept 1, 1971.

§ 270.05. Trial jury; formation in general

1. A trial jury consists of twelve jurors, but "alternate jurors" may be selected and sworn pursuant to section 270.30.

2. The panel from which the jury is drawn is formed and selected as prescribed in the judiciary law. The first twelve members of the panel returned for the term who appear as their names are drawn and called, and who are not excluded as prescribed by this article, must be sworn and

thereupon constitute the trial jury.

HISTORY: Add, L 1970, ch 996, § 1, eff Sept 1, 1971.

§ 270.10. Trial jury; challenge to the panel

1. A challenge to the panel is an objection made to the entire panel of prospective trial jurors returned for the term and may be taken to such panel or to any additional panel that may be ordered by the court. Such a challenge may be made only by the defendant and only on the ground that there has been such a departure from the requirements of the judiciary law in the drawing or return of the panel as to result in substantial prejudice to the defendant.

2. A challenge to the panel must be made before the selection of the jury commences, and, if it is not, such challenge is deemed to have been waived. Such challenge must be made in writing setting forth the facts constituting the ground of challenge. If such facts are denied by the people, witnesses may be called and examined by either party. All issues of fact and law arising on the challenge must be tried and determined by the court. If a challenge to the panel is allowed, the court must discharge that panel and order another panel of prospective trial jurors returned for the term.

HISTORY: Add, L 1970, ch 996, § 1, eff Sept 1, 1971.

§ 270.15. Trial jury; examination of prospective jurors; challenges generally

1. (a) If no challenge to the panel is made as prescribed by section 270.10, or if such challenge is made and disallowed, the court shall direct that the names of not less than twelve members of the panel be drawn and called as prescribed by the judiciary law. Such persons shall take their places in the jury box and shall be immediately sworn to answer truthfully questions asked them relative to their qualifications to serve as jurors in the action. In its discretion, the court may require prospective jurors to complete a questionnaire concerning their ability to serve as fair and impartial jurors, including but not limited to place of birth, current address, education, occupation, prior jury service, knowledge of, relationship to, or contact with the court, any party, witness or attorney in the action and any other fact relevant to his or her service on the jury. An official form for such questionnaire shall be developed by the chief administrator of the courts in consultation with the administrative board of the courts. A copy of questionnaires completed by the members of the panel shall be given to the court and each attorney prior to examination of prospective jurors.

(b) The court shall initiate the examination of prospective jurors by identifying the parties and their respective counsel and briefly outlining the nature of case to all the prospective jurors. The court shall then put to the members of the panel who have been sworn pursuant to this subdivision and to any prospective jurors subsequently sworn, questions affecting their qualifications to serve as jurors in the action.

(c) The court shall permit both parties, commencing with the people, to examine the prospective jurors, individually or collectively, regarding their qualifications to serve as jurors. Each party shall be afforded a fair opportunity to question the prospective jurors as to any unexplored matter affecting their qualifications, but the court shall not permit questioning that is repetitious or irrelevant, or questions as to a juror's knowledge of rules of law. If necessary to prevent improper questioning as to any matter, the court shall personally examine the prospective jurors as to that matter. The scope of such examination shall be within the discretion of the court. After the parties have concluded their examinations of the prospective jurors, the court may ask such further questions as it deems proper regarding the qualifications of such prospective jurors.

1-a. The court may for good cause shown, upon motion of either party or any affected person or upon its own initiative, issue a protective order for a stated period regulating disclosure of the business or residential address of any prospective or sworn juror to any person or persons, other than to counsel for either party. Such good cause shall exist where the court determines that there is a likelihood of bribery, jury tampering or of physical injury or harassment of the juror.

2. Upon the completion of such examination by both parties, each, commencing with the people, may challenge a prospective juror for cause, as prescribed by section 270.20. If such challenge is allowed, the prospective juror must be excluded from service. After both parties have had an opportunity to challenge for cause, the court must permit them to peremptorily challenge any remaining prospective juror, as prescribed by section 270.25, and such juror must be excluded from service. The people must exercise their peremptory challenges first and may not, after the defendant has exercised his peremptory challenges, make such a challenge to any remaining prospective juror who is then in the jury box. If either party so requests, challenges for cause must be made and determined, and peremptory challenges must be made, within the courtroom but outside of the hearing of the prospective jurors in such manner as not to disclose which party made the challenge. The prospective jurors who are not excluded from service must retain their place in the jury box and must be immediately sworn as trial jurors. They must be sworn to try the action in a just and impartial manner, to the best of their judgment, and to render a verdict according to the law and the evidence.

3. The court may thereupon direct that the persons excluded be replaced in the jury box by an equal number from the panel or, in its discretion, direct that all sworn jurors be removed from the jury box and that the jury box be occupied by such additional number of persons from the panel as the court shall direct. In the court's discretion, sworn jurors who are removed from the jury box as provided herein may be seated elsewhere in the courtroom separate and apart from the unsworn members of the panel or may be removed to the jury room or be allowed to leave the courthouse. The process of jury selection as prescribed herein shall continue until twelve persons are selected and sworn as trial jurors. The juror whose name was first drawn and called must be designated by the court as the foreperson, and no special oath need be administered to him or her. If before twelve jurors are sworn, a juror already sworn becomes unable to serve by reason of illness or other incapacity, the court must discharge him or her and the selection of the trial jury must be completed in the manner prescribed in this section.

4. A challenge for cause of a prospective juror which is not made before he is sworn as a trial juror shall be deemed to have been waived, except that such a challenge based upon a ground not known to the challenging party at that time may be made at any time before a witness is sworn at the trial. If such challenge is allowed by the court, the juror shall be discharged and the selection of the trial jury shall be completed in the manner prescribed in this section, except that if alternate jurors have been sworn, the alternate juror whose name was first drawn and called shall take the place of the juror so discharged.

HISTORY: Add, L 1970, ch 996, § 1; amd, L 1981, ch 301, § 1, eff Jan 1, 1982. Sub 1, amd, L 1981, ch 301, § 1, L 1985, ch 173, § 1, L 1985, ch 467, § 1, eff Nov 1, 1985. Sub 1, par (a), formerly part of entire sub, so lettered and amd, L 1985, ch 173, § 1, L 1985, ch 467, § 1, eff Nov 1, 1985. Sub 1, par (b), add, L 1985, ch 173, § 1, eff Nov 1, 1985. Sub 1, par (c), formerly part of entire sub, so lettered and amd, L 1985, ch 173, § 1, eff Nov 1, 1985. Sub 1-a, add, L 1983, ch 684, § 1, eff Sept 1, 1983. Sub 2, amd, L 1981, ch 302, § 1, eff Sept 1, 1981. Sub 3, amd, L 1981, ch 301, § 1, L 1985, ch 516, § 1, eff Nov 1, 1985. Sub 3, amd, L 1997, ch 634, § 1, eff Sept 24, 1997.

§ 270.16. Capital cases; individual questioning for racial bias

1. In any case in which the crime charged may be punishable by death, the court shall, upon

motion of either party, permit the parties, commencing with the people, to examine the prospective jurors individually and outside the presence of the other prospective jurors regarding their qualifications to serve as jurors. Each party shall be afforded a fair opportunity to question a prospective juror as to any unexplored matter affecting his or her qualifications, including without limitation the possibility of racial bias on the part of the prospective juror, but the court shall not permit questioning that is repetitious or irrelevant, or questions as to a prospective juror's knowledge of rules of law. If necessary to prevent improper questioning as to any matter, the court shall personally examine the prospective jurors as to that matter. The scope of such examination shall be within the discretion of the court. After the parties have concluded their examinations of a prospective juror, the court may ask such further questions as it deems proper regarding the qualifications of the prospective juror.

2. The proceedings provided for in this section shall be conducted on the record; provided, however, that upon motion of either party, and for good cause shown, the court may direct that all or a portion of the record of such proceedings be sealed.

HISTORY: Add, L 1995, ch 1, § 14, eff Sept 1, 1995.

§ 270.20. Trial jury; challenge for cause of an individual juror

1. A challenge for cause is an objection to a prospective juror and may be made only on the ground that:

(a) He does not have the qualifications required by the judiciary law; or

(b) He has a state of mind that is likely to preclude him from rendering an impartial verdict based upon the evidence adduced at the trial; or

(c) He is related within the sixth degree by consanguinity or affinity to the defendant, or to the person allegedly injured by the crime charged, or to a prospective witness at the trial, or to counsel for the people or for the defendant; or that he is or was a party adverse to any such person in a civil action; or that he has complained against or been accused by any such person in a criminal action; or that he bears some other relationship to any such person of such nature that it is likely to preclude him from rendering an impartial verdict; or

(d) He was a witness at the preliminary examination or before the grand jury or is to be a witness at the trial; or

(e) He served on the grand jury which found the indictment in issue or served on a trial jury in a prior civil or criminal action involving the same incident charged in such indictment; or

(f) The crime charged may be punishable by death and the prospective juror entertains such conscientious opinions either against or in favor of such punishment as to preclude such juror from rendering an impartial verdict or from properly exercising the discretion conferred upon such juror by law in the determination of a sentence pursuant to section 400.27.

2. All issues of fact or law arising on the challenge must be tried and determined by the court. If the challenge is allowed, the court must exclude the person challenged from service. An erroneous ruling by the court allowing a challenge for cause by the people does not constitute reversible error unless the people have exhausted their peremptory challenges at the time or exhaust them before the selection of the jury is complete. An erroneous ruling by the court denying a challenge for cause by the defendant does not constitute reversible error unless the defendant has exhausted his peremptory challenges at the time or, if he has not, he peremptorily challenges such prospective juror and his peremptory challenges are exhausted before the selection of the jury is complete.

HISTORY: Add, L 1970, ch 996, § 1, eff Sept 1, 1971. Sub 1, par (e), amd, L 1989, ch 68, § 1, eff Nov 1, 1989. Sub 1, par (f), amd, L 1974, ch 367, § 14, L 1995, ch 1, § 15, eff Sept 1, 1995.

§ 270.25. Trial jury; peremptory challenge of an individual juror

1. A peremptory challenge is an objection to a prospective juror for which no reason need be assigned. Upon any peremptory challenge, the court must exclude the person challenged from service.

2. Each party must be allowed the following number of peremptory challenges:

(a) Twenty for the regular jurors if the highest crime charged is a class A felony, and two for each alternate juror to be selected.

(b) Fifteen for the regular jurors if the highest crime charged is a class B or class C felony, and two for each alternate juror to be selected.

(c) Ten for the regular jurors in all other cases, and two for each alternate juror to be selected.

3. When two or more defendants are tried jointly, the number of peremptory challenges prescribed in subdivision two is not multiplied by the number of defendants, but such defendants are to be treated as a single party. In any such case, a peremptory challenge by one or more defendants must be allowed if a majority of the defendants join in such challenge. Otherwise, it must be disallowed.

HISTORY: Add, L 1970, ch 996, § 1, eff Sept 1, 1971.

§ 270.30. Trial jury; alternate jurors

1. Immediately after the last trial juror is sworn, the court may in its discretion direct the selection of one or more, but not more than six additional jurors to be known as "alternate jurors", except that, in a prosecution under section 125.27 of the penal law, the court may, in its discretion, direct the selection of as many alternate jurors as the court determines to be appropriate. Alternate jurors must be drawn in the same manner, must have the same qualifications, must be subject to the same examination and challenges for cause and must take the same oath as the regular jurors. After the jury has retired to deliberate, the court must either (1) with the consent of the defendant and the people, discharge the alternate jurors or (2) direct the alternate jurors not to discuss the case and must further direct that they be kept separate and apart from the regular jurors.

2. In any prosecution in which the people seek a sentence of death, the court shall not discharge the alternate jurors when the jury retires to deliberate upon its verdict and the alternate jurors, in the discretion of the court, may be continuously kept together under the supervision of an appropriate public servant or servants until such time as the jury returns its verdict. If the jury returns a verdict of guilty to a charge for which the death penalty may be imposed, the alternate jurors shall not be discharged and shall remain available for service during any separate sentencing proceeding which may be conducted pursuant to section 400.27.

HISTORY: Add, L 1970, ch 996, § 1, with substance derived from Crim C § 358-a; amd, L 1979, ch 267, § 1, L 1992, ch 100, § 1, eff Nov 1, 1992. Sub 1, formerly entire section, so designated sub 1 and amd, L 1995, ch 1, § 16, eff Sept 1, 1995. Sub 2, add, L 1995, ch 1, § 16, eff Sept 1, 1995.

§ 270.35. Trial jury; discharge of juror; replacement by alternate juror

1. If at any time after the trial jury has been sworn and before the rendition of its verdict, a juror is unable to continue serving by reason of illness or other incapacity, or for any other reason is unavailable for continued service, or the court finds, from facts unknown at the time of the

selection of the jury, that a juror is grossly unqualified to serve in the case or has engaged in misconduct of a substantial nature, but not warranting the declaration of a mistrial, the court must discharge such juror. If an alternate juror or jurors are available for service, the court must order that the discharged juror be replaced by the alternate juror whose name was first drawn and called, provided, however, that if the trial jury has begun its deliberations, the defendant must consent to such replacement. Such consent must be in writing and must be signed by the defendant in person in open court in the presence of the court. If the discharged juror was the foreperson, the court shall designate as the new foreperson the juror whose name was second drawn and called. If no alternate juror is available, the court must declare a mistrial pursuant to subdivision three of section 280.10.

2. (a) In determining pursuant to this section whether a juror is unable to continue serving by reason of illness or other incapacity, or is for any other reason unavailable for continued service, the court shall make a reasonably thorough inquiry concerning such illness, incapacity or unavailability, and shall attempt to ascertain when such juror will be appearing in court. If such juror fails to appear, or if the court determines that there is no reasonable likelihood such juror will be appearing, in court within two hours of the time set by the court for the trial to resume, the court may presume such juror is unavailable for continued service and may discharge such juror. Nothing contained in this paragraph shall affect the court's discretion, under this or any other provision of law, to discharge a juror who repeatedly fails to appear in court in a timely fashion.

(b) The court shall afford the parties an opportunity to be heard before discharging a juror. If the court discharges a juror pursuant to this subdivision, it shall place on the record the facts and reasons for its determination that such juror is ill, incapacitated or unavailable for continued service.

(c) Nothing contained in this subdivision shall affect the requirements of subdivision one of this section pertaining to the discharge of a juror where the trial jury has begun its deliberations.

HISTORY: Add, L 1970, ch 996, § 1; amd, L 1975, ch 77, § 1, eff Sept 1, 1975. Sub 1, formerly entire section, so designated sub 1, L 1996, ch 630, § 1, eff Oct 4, 1996; amd, L 1999, ch 594, § 1, eff Nov 1, 1999. Former sub 1, redesignated as entire section, L 1975, ch 77, § 1, eff Sept 1, 1975. Sub 2, add, L 1996, ch 630, § 1, eff Oct 4, 1996. Former sub 2, deleted, L 1975, ch 77, § 1, eff Sept 1, 1975.

§ 270.40. Trial jury; preliminary instructions by court

After the jury has been sworn and before the people's opening address, the court must instruct the jury generally concerning its basic functions, duties and conduct. Such instructions must include, among other matters, admonitions that the jurors may not converse among themselves or with anyone else upon any subject connected with the trial; that they may not read or listen to any accounts or discussions of the case reported by newspapers or other news media; that they may not visit or view the premises or place where the offense or offenses charged were allegedly committed or any other premises or place involved in the case; that prior to discharge, they may not request, accept, agree to accept, or discuss with any person receiving or accepting, any payment or benefit in consideration for supplying any information concerning the trial; and that they must promptly report to the court any incident within their knowledge involving an attempt by any person improperly to influence any member of the jury.

HISTORY: Add, L 1970, ch 996, § 1; amd, L 1990, ch 305, § 1, eff Nov 11, 1990.

§ 270.45. Trial jury; when separation permitted

During the period extending from the time the jurors are sworn to the time they retire to deliberate upon their verdict, the court may in its discretion either permit them to separate during recesses and adjournments or direct that they be continuously kept together during such periods under the supervision of an appropriate public servant or servants. In the latter case, such public servant or servants may not speak to or communicate with any juror concerning any subject connected with the trial nor permit any other person to do so, and must return the jury to the court room at the next designated trial session.

> **HISTORY:** Add, L 1970, ch 996, § 1, eff Sept 1, 1971, with substance derived from Crim C § 414.

§ 270.50. Trial jury; viewing of premises

1. When the court is of the opinion that a viewing or observation by the jury of the premises or place where an offense on trial was allegedly committed, or of any other premises or place involved in the case, will be helpful to the jury in determining any material factual issue, it may in its discretion, at any time before the commencement of the summations, order that the jury be conducted to such premises or place for such purpose in accordance with the provisions of this section.

2. In such case, the jury must be kept together throughout under the supervision of an appropriate public servant or servants appointed by the court, and the court itself must be present throughout. The prosecutor, the defendant and counsel for the defendant may as a matter of right be present throughout, but such right may be waived.

3. The purpose of such an inspection is solely to permit visual observation by the jury of the premises or place in question, and neither the court, the parties, counsel nor the jurors may engage in discussion or argumentation concerning the significance or implications of anything under observation or concerning any issue in the case.

> **HISTORY:** Add, L 1970, ch 996, § 1, eff Sept 1, 1971, with substance derived from Crim C §§ 411, 412.

§ 270.55. Sentencing jury in capital cases

During the period extending from when a jury returns a verdict of guilty upon a count of an indictment charging murder in the first degree as defined by section 125.27 of the penal law until a jury retires to deliberate on the sentence pursuant to section 400.27, the court may in its discretion either permit the jurors to separate during recesses and adjournments or direct that they be continuously kept together during such periods under the supervision of an appropriate public servant or servants. In the latter case, such public servant or servants may not speak to or communicate with any juror concerning any subject connected with the sentencing proceeding nor permit any other person to do so, and must return the jury to the court room at the next designated session. Unless otherwise provided for in section 400.27, the provisions of sections 270.35, 270.40 and 270.50 shall govern the sentencing proceeding provided for in section 400.27.

> **HISTORY:** Add, L 1995, ch 1, § 17, eff Sept 1, 1995.

ARTICLE 280   JURY TRIAL—MOTION FOR A MISTRIAL

§ 280.10.   Motion for mistrial
§ 280.20.   Motion for mistrial; status of indictment upon new trial

> **HISTORY:** Add, L 1970, ch 996, § 1, eff Sept 1, 1971.

§ 280.10. Motion for mistrial

At any time during the trial, the court must declare a mistrial and order a new trial of the indictment under the following circumstances:

1. Upon motion of the defendant, when there occurs during the trial an error or legal defect in the proceedings, or conduct inside or outside the courtroom, which is prejudicial to the

defendant and deprives him of a fair trial. When such an error, defect or conduct occurs during a joint trial of two or more defendants and a mistrial motion is made by one or more but not by all, the court must declare a mistrial only as to the defendant or defendants making or joining in the motion, and the trial of the other defendant or defendants must proceed;

2. Upon motion of the people, when there occurs during the trial, either inside or outside the courtroom, gross misconduct by the defendant or some person acting on his behalf, or by a juror, resulting in substantial and irreparable prejudice to the people's case. When such misconduct occurs during a joint trial of two or more defendants, and when the court is satisfied that it did not result in substantial prejudice to the people's case as against a particular defendant and that such defendant was in no way responsible for the misconduct, it may not declare a mistrial with respect to such defendant but must proceed with the trial as to him;

3. Upon motion of either party or upon the court's own motion, when it is physically impossible to proceed with the trial in conformity with law.

HISTORY: Add, L 1970, ch 996, § 1, eff Sept 1, 1971.

§ 280.20. Motion for mistrial; status of indictment upon new trial

Upon a new trial resulting from an order declaring a mistrial, the indictment is deemed to contain all the counts which it contained at the time the previous trial was commenced, regardless of whether any count was thereafter dismissed by the court prior to the mistrial order.

HISTORY: Add, L 1970, ch 996, § 1, eff Sept 1, 1971.

ARTICLE 290   JURY TRIAL—TRIAL ORDER OF DISMISSAL
§ 290.10.   Trial order of dismissal
HISTORY: Add, L 1970, ch 996, § 1, eff Sept 1, 1971.

§ 290.10. Trial order of dismissal

1. At the conclusion of the people's case or at the conclusion of all the evidence, the court may, except as provided in subdivision two, upon motion of the defendant, (a) issue a "trial order of dismissal," dismissing any count of an indictment upon the ground that the trial evidence is not legally-sufficient to establish the offense charged therein or any lesser included offense, or (b) reserve decision on the motion until after the verdict has been rendered and accepted by the court. Where the court has reserved decision and the jury thereafter renders a verdict of guilty, the court shall proceed to determine the motion upon such evidence as it would have been authorized to consider upon the motion had the court not reserved decision. If the court determines that such motion should have been granted upon the ground specified in paragraph (a) herein, it shall enter an order both setting aside the verdict and dismissing any count of the indictment upon such ground. If the jury is discharged before rendition of a verdict the court shall proceed to determine the motion as set forth in this paragraph.

2. Despite the lack of legally sufficient trial evidence in support of a count of an indictment as described in subdivision one, issuance of a trial order of dismissal is not authorized and constitutes error when the trial evidence would have been legally sufficient had the court not erroneously excluded admissible evidence offered by the people.

3. When the court excludes trial evidence offered by the people under such circumstances that the substance or content thereof does not appear in the record, the people may, in anticipation of a possible subsequent trial order of dismissal emanating from the allegedly improper exclusion and erroneously issued in violation of subdivision two, and in anticipation of a possible appeal therefrom pursuant to subdivision two of section 450.20, place upon the record, out of the presence

of the jury, an "offer of proof" summarizing the substance or content of such excluded evidence. Upon the subsequent issuance of a trial order of dismissal and an appeal therefrom, such offer of proof constitutes a part of the record on appeal and has the effect and significance prescribed in subdivision two of section 450.40. In the absence of such an order and an appeal therefrom, such offer of proof is not deemed a part of the record and does not constitute such for purposes of an ensuing appeal by the defendant from a judgment of conviction.

4. Upon issuing a trial order of dismissal which dismisses the entire indictment, the court must immediately discharge the defendant from custody if he is in custody of the sheriff, or, if he is at liberty on bail, it must exonerate the bail.

> **HISTORY:** Add, L 1970, ch 996, § 1, eff Sept 1, 1971. Sub 1, amd, L 1983, ch 170, § 1, eff May 31, 1983.

ARTICLE 300 JURY TRIAL—COURT'S CHARGE AND INSTRUCTIONS TO JURY

> **HISTORY:** Add, L 1970, ch 996, § 1, eff Sept 1, 1971.

§ 300.10. Court's charge; in general

1. At the conclusion of the summations, the court must deliver a charge to the jury.

2. In its charge, the court must state the fundamental legal principles applicable to criminal cases in general. Such principles include, but are not limited to, the presumption of the defendant's innocence, the requirement that guilt be proved beyond a reasonable doubt and that the jury may not, in determining the issue of guilt or innocence, consider or speculate concerning matters relating to sentence or punishment. Upon request of a defendant who did not testify in his own behalf, but not otherwise, the court must state that the fact that he did not testify is not a factor from which any inference unfavorable to the defendant may be drawn. The court must also state the material legal principles applicable to the particular case, and, so far as practicable, explain the application of the law to the facts, but it need not marshal or refer to the evidence to any greater extent than is necessary for such explanation.

3. Where a defendant has raised the affirmative defense of lack of criminal responsibility by reason of mental disease or defect, as defined in section 40.15 of the penal law, the court must, without elaboration, instruct the jury as follows: "A jury during its deliberations must never consider or speculate concerning matters relating to the consequences of its verdict. However, because of the lack of common knowledge regarding the consequences of a verdict of not responsible by reason of mental disease or defect, I charge you that if this verdict is rendered by you there will be hearings as to the defendant's present mental condition and, where appropriate, involuntary commitment proceedings."

4. The court must specifically designate and submit, in accordance with the provisions of sections 300.30 and 300.40, those counts and offenses contained and charged in the indictment which the jury are to consider. Such determination must be made, and the parties informed thereof, prior to the summations. In its charge, the court must define each offense so submitted and, except as otherwise expressly provided, it must instruct the jury to render a verdict separately and

specifically upon each count submitted to it, and with respect to each defendant if there be more than one, and must require that the verdict upon each such count be one of the following:

(a) "Guilty" of the offense submitted, if there be but one; or

(b) Where appropriate, "guilty" of a specified one of two or more offenses submitted under the same count in the alternative pursuant to section 300.40; or

(c) "Not guilty"; or

(d) Where appropriate, "not responsible by reason of mental disease or defect."

5. Both before and after the court's charge, the parties may submit requests to charge, either orally or in writing, and the court must rule promptly upon each request. A failure to rule upon a request is deemed a denial thereof.

6. In a prosecution involving a charge of enterprise corruption, as defined in article four hundred sixty of the penal law, the court must specifically designate and separately submit for jury consideration those criminal acts which are contained and charged in the indictment and which are supported by legally sufficient trial evidence. Every criminal act which is not so supported shall be dismissed and stricken from the indictment. If legally sufficient trial evidence exists to support a lesser included offense which is also a criminal act within the meaning of subdivision one of section 460.10 of the penal law, such lesser offense shall be substituted. Such determination must be made and the parties informed thereof, prior to the summations. In its charge, the court must define each criminal act so submitted and, as when it may or must do so pursuant to sections 300.40 and 300.50 of this article, any lesser included offense that is also a criminal act within the meaning of subdivision one of section 460.10 of the penal law. It must instruct the jury to render a verdict separately and specifically upon each criminal act (and where necessary, any submitted lesser included offense) submitted to it with respect to each defendant. It must further explain to the jury that they may not consider a charge of enterprise corruption against any defendant until they have separately and unanimously agreed that the defendant has committed each of at least three criminal acts alleged as part of the pattern of criminal activity, including any submitted lesser included offenses.

> **HISTORY:** Add, L 1970, ch 996, § 1, eff Sept 1, 1971. Sub 3, add, L 1980, ch 548, § 8; amd, L 1984, ch 668, § 8, eff Nov 1, 1984. Former sub 3, renumbered sub 4, L 1980, ch 548, § 8, eff Sept 1, 1980. Sub 4, formerly sub 3, renumbered sub 4, L 1980, ch 548, § 8, eff Sept 1, 1980. Former sub 4, renumbered sub 5, L 1980, ch 548, § 8, eff Sept 1, 1980. Sub 4, par (d), amd, L 1980, ch 548, § 9, eff Sept 1, 1980. Sub 5, formerly sub 4, renumbered sub 5, L 1980, ch 548, § 8, eff Sept 1, 1980. Sub 6, add, L 1986, ch 516, § 9, eff Nov 1, 1986.

§ 300.30. Court's charge; submission of indictment to jury; definitions of terms

The following definitions are applicable to this article:

1. "Submission of a count" of an indictment means submission of the offense charged therein, or of a lesser included offense, or submission in the alternative of both the offense charged and a lesser included offense or offenses. When the court "submits a count," it must, at the least, submit the offense charged therein if such is supported by legally sufficient trial evidence, or if it is not, the greatest lesser included offense which is supported by legally sufficient trial evidence.

2. "Consecutive counts" means two or more counts of an indictment upon which consecutive sentences may be imposed in case of conviction thereon.

3. "Concurrent counts" means two or more counts of an indictment upon which concurrent

sentences only may be imposed in case of conviction thereon.

4. "Inclusory concurrent counts." Concurrent counts are "inclusory" when the offense charged in one is greater than any of those charged in the others and when the latter are all lesser offenses included within the greater. All other kinds of concurrent counts are "non-inclusory."

5. "Inconsistent counts." Two counts are "inconsistent" when guilt of the offense charged in one necessarily negates guilt of the offense charged in the other.

HISTORY: Add, L 1970, ch 996, § 1, eff Sept 1, 1971.

§ 300.40. Court's charge; submission of indictment to jury; counts to be submitted

The court may submit to the jury only those counts of an indictment remaining therein at the time of its charge which are supported by legally sufficient trial evidence, and every count not so supported should be dismissed by a trial order of dismissal. The court's determination as to which of the sufficient counts are to be submitted must be in accordance with the following rules:

1. If the indictment contains but one count, the court must submit such count.

2. If a multiple count indictment contains consecutive counts only, the court must submit every count thereof.

3. If a multiple count indictment contains concurrent counts of murder in the first degree, the court must submit every such count. In any other case, if a multiple count indictment contains concurrent counts only, the court must submit at least one such count, and may submit more than one as follows:

(a) With respect to non-inclusory concurrent counts, the court may in its discretion submit one or more or all thereof;

(b) With respect to inclusory concurrent counts, the court must submit the greatest or inclusive count and may or must, under circumstances prescribed in section 300.50, also submit, but in the alternative only, one or more of the lesser included counts. A verdict of guilty upon the greatest count submitted is deemed a dismissal of every lesser count submitted, but not an acquittal thereon. A verdict of guilty upon a lesser count is deemed an acquittal upon every greater count submitted.

4. If a multiple count indictment contains two or more groups of counts, with the counts within each group being concurrent as to each other but consecutive as to those of the other group or groups, the court must submit at least one count of each group, in the manner prescribed in subdivision three. If an indictment contains one or more of such groups of concurrent counts, and also one or more other counts each of which is consecutive as to every other count of the indictment, the court must submit each individual consecutive count and at least one count of each group of concurrent counts.

5. If an indictment contains two inconsistent counts, the court must submit at least one thereof. If a verdict of guilty upon either would be supported by legally sufficient trial evidence, the court may submit both counts in the alternative and authorize the jury to convict upon one or the other depending upon its findings of fact. In such case, the court must direct the jury that if it renders a verdict of guilty upon one such count it must render a verdict of not guilty upon the other. If the court is satisfied that a conviction upon one such count, though supported by legally sufficient trial evidence, would be against the weight of the evidence while a conviction upon the other would not, it may in its discretion submit the latter count only.

6. Notwithstanding any other provision of this section, the court is not required to submit any

particular count to the jury when:

(a) The people consent that it not be submitted; except that nothing contained in this paragraph limits the right accorded a defendant by section 300.50 to the submission, in certain situations, of counts charging lesser included offenses; or

(b) The number of counts or the complexity of the indictment requires selectivity of counts by the court in order to avoid placing an unduly heavy burden upon the jury in its consideration of the case. In such case, the court may submit to the jury a portion of the counts which are representative of the people's case.

7. Every count not submitted to the jury is deemed to have been dismissed by the court. Where the court, over objection of the people, refuses to submit a count which is consecutive as to every count actually submitted, such count is deemed to have been dismissed by a trial order of dismissal even though no such order was expressly made by the court.

HISTORY: Add, L 1970, ch 996, § 1, eff Sept 1, 1971. Sub 3, opening par, amd, L 1995, ch 1, § 18, eff Sept 1, 1995.

§ 300.50. Court's charge; submission of lesser included offenses

1. In submitting a count of an indictment to the jury, the court in its discretion may, in addition to submitting the greatest offense which it is required to submit, submit in the alternative any lesser included offense if there is a reasonable view of the evidence which would support a finding that the defendant committed such lesser offense but did not commit the greater. If there is no reasonable view of the evidence which would support such a finding, the court may not submit such lesser offense. Any error respecting such submission, however, is waived by the defendant unless he objects thereto before the jury retires to deliberate.

2. If the court is authorized by subdivision one to submit a lesser included offense and is requested by either party to do so, it must do so. In the absence of such a request, the court's failure to submit such offense does not constitute error.

3. The principles prescribed in subdivisions one and two apply equally where the lesser included offense is specifically charged in another count of the indictment.

4. Whenever the court submits two or more offenses in the alternative pursuant to this section, it must instruct the jury that it may render a verdict of guilty with respect to any one of such offenses, depending upon its findings of fact, but that it may not render a verdict of guilty with respect to more than one. A verdict of guilty of any such offense is not deemed an acquittal of any lesser offense submitted, but is deemed an acquittal of every greater offense submitted.

5. Where the indictment charges a crime committed by the defendant while he was under the age of sixteen but a lesser included offense would be one for which the defendant is not criminally responsible by reason of infancy, such lessor included offense may nevertheless be submitted to the jury in the same manner as an offense for which the defendant would be criminally responsible notwithstanding the fact that a verdict of guilty would not result in a criminal conviction.

6. For purposes of this section, the offenses of rape in the third degree as defined in subdivision three of section 130.25 of the penal law and criminal sexual act in the third degree as defined in subdivision three of section 130.40 of the penal law, are not lesser included offenses of rape in the first degree, criminal sexual act in the first degree or any other offense. Notwithstanding the foregoing, either such offense may be submitted as a lesser included offense of the applicable first degree offense when (i) there is a reasonable view of the evidence which would support a finding

that the defendant committed such lesser offense but did not commit the greater offense, and (ii) both parties consent to its submission.

HISTORY: Add, L 1970, ch 996, § 1, eff Sept 1, 1971, with substance derived from Crim C §§ 444, 445. Sub 5, add, L 1978, ch 481, § 40, eff Sept 1, 1978. Sub 6, add, L 2000, ch 1, § 46, eff Feb 1, 2001; amd, L 2003, ch 264, § 43, eff Nov 1, 2003.

ARTICLE 310   JURY TRIAL—DELIBERATION AND VERDICT OF JURY

HISTORY: Add, L 1970, ch 996, § 1, eff Sept 1, 1971.

§ 310.10. Jury deliberation; requirement of; where conducted

1. Following the court's charge, except as otherwise provided by subdivision two of this section, the jury must retire to deliberate upon its verdict in a place outside the courtroom. It must be provided with suitable accommodations therefor and must, except as otherwise provided in subdivision two of this section, be continuously kept together under the supervision of a court officer or court officers. In the event such court officer or court officers are not available, the jury shall be under the supervision of an appropriate public servant or public servants. Except when so authorized by the court or when performing administerial duties with respect to the jurors, such court officers or public servants, as the case may be, may not speak to or communicate with them or permit any other person to do so.

2. At any time after the jury has been charged or commenced its deliberations, and after notice to the parties and affording such parties an opportunity to be heard on the record outside of the presence of the jury, the court may declare the deliberations to be in recess and may thereupon direct the jury to suspend its deliberations and to separate for a reasonable period of time to be specified by the court, not to exceed twenty-four hours, except that in the case of a Saturday, Sunday or holiday, such separation may extend beyond such twenty-four hour period. Before each recess, the court must admonish the jury as provided in section 270.40 of this chapter and direct it not to resume its deliberations until all twelve jurors have reassembled in the designated place at the termination of the declared recess.

3. [Repealed]

HISTORY: Add, L 1970, ch 996, § 1, with substance derived from Crim C §§ 421, 423, 424; amd, L 1974, ch 214, § 1, L 1995, ch 83, § 209, eff July 5, 1995. Sub 1, formerly entire section, so designated and amd, L 1995, ch 83, § 209, eff July 5, 1995. Sub 2, add, L 1995, ch 83, § 209, eff July 5, 1995; L 2001, ch 47, § 2, eff May 30, 2001. Sub 3, add, L 1995, ch 83, § 209, eff July 5, 1995; repealed, L 2001, ch 47, § 3, eff May 30, 2001.

§ 310.20. Jury deliberation; use of exhibits and other material

Upon retiring to deliberate, the jurors may take with them:

1. Any exhibits received in evidence at the trial which the court, after according the parties an opportunity to be heard upon the matter, in its discretion permits them to take;

2. A written list prepared by the court containing the offenses submitted to the jury by the court in its charge and the possible verdicts thereon. Whenever the court submits two or more counts charging offenses set forth in the same article of the law, the court may set forth the dates, names of complainants or specific statutory language, without defining the terms, by which the counts may be distinguished; provided, however, that the court shall instruct the jury in its charge that the sole purpose of the notations is to distinguish between the counts; and

3. A written list prepared by the court containing the names of every witness whose testimony has been presented during the trial, if the jury requests such a list and the court, in its discretion, determines that such a list will assist the jury.

> **HISTORY:** Add, L 1970, ch 996, § 1, eff Sept 1, 1971. Amd, L 1999, ch 66, § 1, eff June 8, 1999. Sub 1, amd, L 1999, ch 66, § 1, eff June 8, 1999. Sub 2, amd, L 1996, ch 630, § 2, eff Oct 4, 1996, L 1999, ch 66, § 1, eff June 8, 1999, L 2002, ch 588, § 1, eff Sept 24, 2002. Sub 3, add, L 1999, ch 66, § 1, eff June 8, 1999.

§ 310.30. Jury deliberation; request for information

At any time during its deliberation, the jury may request the court for further instruction or information with respect to the law, with respect to the content or substance of any trial evidence, or with respect to any other matter pertinent to the jury's consideration of the case. Upon such a request, the court must direct that the jury be returned to the courtroom and, after notice to both the people and counsel for the defendant, and in the presence of the defendant, must give such requested information or instruction as the court deems proper. With the consent of the parties and upon the request of the jury for further instruction with respect to a statute, the court may also give to the jury copies of the text of any statute which, in its discretion, the court deems proper.

> **HISTORY:** Add, L 1970, ch 996, § 1, with substance derived from Crim C § 427; amd, L 1980, ch 208, § 1, eff June 9, 1980.

§ 310.40. Verdict; rendition thereof

1. The verdict must be rendered and announced by the foreperson of the jury in the courtroom in the presence of the court, a prosecutor, the defendant's counsel and the defendant; provided, however, that where the foreperson refuses or is unable to render and announce the verdict, the court may designate another member of the jury to do so.

2. Before rendering and announcing the verdict, the foreperson of the jury, or such other member of the jury as may be designated by the court pursuant to subdivision one, must be asked whether the jury has agreed upon a verdict and must answer in the affirmative.

> **HISTORY:** Add, L 1970, ch 996, § 1; amd, L 1976, ch 181, § 1, eff Sept 1, 1976. Sub 1, amd, L 2001, ch 488, § 1, eff Nov 21, 2001. Sub 2, amd, L 2001, ch 488, § 1, eff Nov 21, 2001.

§ 310.50. Verdict; form; reconsideration of defective verdict

1. The form of the verdict must be in accordance with the court's instructions, as prescribed in article three hundred.

2. If the jury renders a verdict which in form is not in accordance with the court's instructions or which is otherwise legally defective, the court must explain the defect or error and must direct the jury to reconsider such verdict, to resume its deliberation for such purpose, and to render a proper verdict. If the jury persists in rendering a defective or improper verdict, the court may in its discretion either order that the verdict in its entirety as to any defendant be recorded as an acquittal, or discharge the jury and authorize the people to retry the indictment or a specified count or counts thereof as to such defendant; provided that if it is clear that the jury intended to find a defendant not guilty upon any particular count, the court must order that the verdict be recorded

as an acquittal of such defendant upon such count.

3. If the court accepts a verdict which is defective or incomplete by reason of the jury's failure to render a verdict upon every count upon which it was instructed to do so, such verdict is deemed to constitute an acquittal upon every such count improperly ignored in the verdict.

4. In a prosecution involving a charge of enterprise corruption in violation of article four hundred sixty of the penal law, the jury must separately and specifically render a special verdict with regard to each criminal act and any lesser included offense submitted for its consideration as a part of a pattern of criminal activity in addition to its verdict on the charge of enterprise corruption. In the absence of a unanimous special verdict of guilty with regard to each of at least three criminal acts and/or lesser included offenses submitted for its consideration and legally sufficient to constitute a person's participation in a pattern of criminal activity within the meaning of subdivision four of section 460.10 of the penal law, the court must order that the verdict on the count charging enterprise corruption be recorded as an acquittal.

> **HISTORY:** Add, L 1970, ch 996, § 1, eff Sept 1, 1971. Sub 4, add, L 1986, ch 516, § 10, eff Nov 1, 1986.

§ 310.60. Discharge of jury before rendition of verdict and effect thereof

1. A deliberating jury may be discharged by the court without having rendered a verdict only when:

(a) The jury has deliberated for an extensive period of time without agreeing upon a verdict with respect to any of the charges submitted and the court is satisfied that any such agreement is unlikely within a reasonable time; or

(b) The court, the defendant and the people all consent to such discharge; or

(c) A mistrial is declared pursuant to section 280.10.

2. When the jury is so discharged, the defendant or defendants may be retried upon the indictment. Upon such retrial, the indictment is deemed to contain all counts which it contained, except those which were dismissed or were deemed to have resulted in an acquittal pursuant to subdivision one of section 290.10.

> **HISTORY:** Add, L 1970, ch 996, § 1, eff Sept 1, 1971. Sub 2, amd, L 1983, ch 170, § 2, eff May 31, 1983.

§ 310.70. Rendition of partial verdict and effect thereof

1. If a deliberating jury declares that it has reached a verdict with respect to one or more but not all of the offenses submitted to it, or with respect to one or more but not all of the defendants, the court must proceed as follows:

(a) If the possibility of ultimate agreement with respect to the other submitted offenses or defendants is so small and the circumstances are such that if they were the only matters under consideration the court would be authorized to discharge the jury pursuant to paragraph (a) of subdivision one of section 310.60, the court must terminate the deliberation and order the jury to render a partial verdict with respect to those offenses and defendants upon which or with respect to whom it has reached a verdict;

(b) If the court is satisfied that there is a reasonable possibility of ultimate agreement upon any of the unresolved offenses with respect to any defendant, it may either:

(i) Order the jury to render its verdict with respect to those offenses and defendants upon which or with respect to whom it has reached agreement and resume its deliberation upon the remainder; or

(ii) Refuse to accept a partial verdict at the time and order the jury to resume its deliberation upon the entire case.

2. Following the rendition of a partial verdict pursuant to subdivision one, a defendant may be retried for any submitted offense upon which the jury was unable to agree unless:

(a) A verdict of conviction thereon would have been inconsistent with a verdict, of either conviction or acquittal, actually rendered with respect to some other offense, or

(b) The submitted offense which was the subject of the disagreement, and some other submitted offense of higher or equal grade which was the subject of a verdict of conviction, were so related that consecutive sentences thereon could not have been imposed upon a defendant convicted of both such offenses.

3. As used in this section, a "submitted offense" means any offense submitted by the court to the jury, whether it be one which was expressly charged in a count of the indictment or a lesser included offense thereof submitted pursuant to section 300.50.

> **HISTORY:** Add, L 1970, ch 996, § 1, eff Sept 1, 1971. Sub 1, amd, L 1974, ch 762, § 1, eff Sept 1, 1974. Sub 2, amd, L 1974, ch 762, § 1, eff Sept 1, 1974. Sub 2, par (a), add, L 1974, ch 762, § 1, eff Sept 1, 1974. Sub 2, par (b), add, L 1974, ch 762, § 1, eff Sept 1, 1974. Sub 3, add, L 1974, ch 762, § 1, eff Sept 1, 1974.

§ 310.80. Recording and checking of verdict and polling of jury

After a verdict has been rendered, it must be recorded on the minutes and read to the jury, and the jurors must be collectively asked whether such is their verdict. Even though no juror makes any declaration in the negative, the jury must, if either party makes such an application, be polled and each juror separately asked whether the verdict announced by the foreman is in all respects his verdict. If upon either the collective or the separate inquiry any juror answers in the negative, the court must refuse to accept the verdict and must direct the jury to resume its deliberation. If no disagreement is expressed, the jury must be discharged from the case, except as otherwise provided in section 400.27.

> **HISTORY:** Add, L 1970, ch 996, § 1, with substance derived from Crim C §§ 450, 451; amd, L 1995, ch 1, § 19, eff Sept 1, 1995.

§ 310.85. Verdict of guilty where defendant not criminally responsible

1. Where a verdict of guilty is rendered with respect to a crime, but the defendant is not criminally responsible for such crime by reason of infancy, the court shall proceed as provided in this section.

2. If a verdict of guilty also is rendered with respect to a crime for which the defendant is criminally responsible, or if the defendant is awaiting sentence upon another criminal conviction or is under a sentence of imprisonment on another criminal conviction, the verdict rendered with respect to a crime for which he is not criminally responsible must be set aside and shall be deemed a nullity.

3. In any case where the verdict is not set aside pursuant to subdivision two of this section, the court must order that the verdict be deemed vacated and replaced by a juvenile delinquency fact determination. Upon so ordering, the court must direct that the action be removed to the family court in accordance with the provisions of article seven hundred twenty-five of this chapter.

> **HISTORY:** Add, L 1978, ch 481, § 41, eff Sept 1, 1978.

CPL

ARTICLE 320   WAIVER OF JURY TRIAL AND CONDUCT OF NON-JURY TRIAL

§ 320.10.   **Non-jury trial; when authorized**

§ 320.20.   **Non-jury trial; nature and conduct thereof**

HISTORY: Add, L 1970, ch 996, § 1, eff Sept 1, 1971.

§ 320.10. Non-jury trial; when authorized

1. Except where the indictment charges the crime of murder in the first degree, the defendant, subject to the provisions of subdivision two, may at any time before trial waive a jury trial and consent to a trial without a jury in the superior court in which the indictment is pending.

2. Such waiver must be in writing and must be signed by the defendant in person in open court in the presence of the court, and with the approval of the court. The court must approve the execution and submission of such waiver unless it determines that it is tendered as a stratagem to procure an otherwise impermissible procedural advantage or that the defendant is not fully aware of the consequences of the choice he is making. If the court disapproves the waiver, it must state upon the record its reasons for such disapproval.

HISTORY: Add, L 1970, ch 996, § 1, eff Sept 1, 1971. Sub 1, amd, L 1974, ch 367, § 15, eff Sept 1, 1974. Sub 3, repealed, L 1974, ch 367, § 16, eff Sept 1, 1974.

§ 320.20. Non-jury trial; nature and conduct thereof

1. A non-jury trial of an indictment must be conducted by one judge of the superior court in which the indictment is pending.

2. The court, in addition to determining all questions of law, is the execlusive [exclusive]* trier of all issues of fact and must render a verdict.

3. The order of the trial must be as follows:

(a) The court must permit the parties to deliver opening addresses in the order provided for a trial by jury pursuant to section 260.30.

(b) The order in which evidence must or may be offered by the respective parties is the same as that applicable to a jury trial of an indictment as prescribed in subdivisions five, six and seven of section 260.30.

(c) The court must permit the parties to deliver summations in the order provided for a trial by jury pursuant to section 260.30.

(d) The court must then consider the case and render a verdict.

4. The provisions governing motion practice and general procedure with respect to a jury trial are, wherever appropriate, applicable to a non-jury trial.

5. Before considering a multiple count indictment for the purpose of rendering a verdict thereon, and before the summations if there be any, the court must designate and state upon the record the counts upon which it will render a verdict and the particular defendant or defendants, if there be more than one, with respect to whom it will render a verdict upon any particular count. In determining what counts, offenses and defendants must be considered by it and covered by its verdict, and the form of the verdict in general, the court must be governed, so far as appropriate

---

* The bracketed word has been inserted by the Publisher.

and practicable, by the provisions of article three hundred governing the court's submission of counts and offenses to a jury upon a jury trial.

HISTORY: Add, L 1970, ch 996, § 1, eff Sept 1, 1971. Sub 3, par (a), amd, L 1981, ch 333, § 1, eff Sept 1, 1981. Sub 3, par (c), amd, L 1976, ch 320, § 1, eff Sept 1, 1976.

ARTICLE 330 PROCEEDINGS FROM VERDICT TO SENTENCE

HISTORY: Add, L 1970, ch 996, § 1, eff Sept 1, 1971.

§ 330.10. Disposition of defendant after verdict of acquittal

1. Upon a verdict of complete acquittal, the court must immediately discharge the defendant if he is in the custody of the sheriff, or, if he is at liberty on bail, it must exonerate the bail.

2. Upon a verdict of not responsible by reason of mental disease or defect, the provisions of section 330.20 of this chapter shall govern all subsequent proceedings against the defendant.

HISTORY: Add, L 1970, ch 996, § 1, eff Sept 1, 1971. Sub 2, amd, L 1980, ch 548, § 10, eff Sept 1, 1980.

§ 330.20. Procedure following verdict or plea of not responsible by reason of mental disease or defect

1. Definition of terms. As used in this section, the following terms shall have the following meanings:

(a) "Commissioner" means the state commissioner of mental health or the state commissioner of mental retardation and developmental disability.

(b) "Secure facility" means a facility within the state office of mental health or the state office of mental retardation and developmental disabilities which is staffed with personnel adequately trained in security methods and is so equipped as to minimize the risk or danger of escapes, and which has been so specifically designated by the commissioner.

(c) "Dangerous mental disorder" means: (i) that a defendant currently suffers from a "mental illness" as that term is defined in subdivision twenty of section 1.03 of the mental hygiene law, and (ii) that because of such condition he currently constitutes a physical danger to himself or others.

(d) "Mentally ill" means that a defendant currently suffers from a mental illness for which care and treatment as a patient, in the in-patient services of a psychiatric center under the jurisdiction of the state office of mental health, is essential to such defendant's welfare and that his judgment is so impaired that he is unable to understand the need for such care and treatment; and, where a defendant is mentally retarded, the term "mentally ill" shall also mean, for purposes of this section, that the defendant is in need of care and treatment as a resident in the in-patient services of a developmental center or other residential facility for the mentally retarded and developmentally disabled under the jurisdiction of the state office of mental retardation and developmental disabilities.

CPL

(e) "Examination order" means an order directed to the commissioner requiring that a defendant submit to a psychiatric examination to determine whether the defendant has a dangerous mental disorder, or if he does not have dangerous mental disorder, whether he is mentally ill.

(f) "Commitment order" or "recommitment order" means an order committing a defendant to the custody of the commissioner for confinement in a secure facility for care and treatment for six months from the date of the order.

(g) "First retention order" means an order which is effective at the expiration of the period prescribed in a commitment order for [or]* a recommitment order, authorizing continued custody of a defendant by the commissioner for a period not to exceed one year.

(h) "Second retention order" means an order which is effective at the expiration of the period prescribed in a first retention order, authorizing continued custody of a defendant by the commissioner for a period not to exceed two years.

(i) "Subsequent retention order" means an order which is effective at the expiration of the period prescribed in a second retention order or a prior subsequent retention order authorizing continued custody of a defendant by the commissioner for a period not to exceed two years.

(j) "Retention order" means a first retention order, a second retention order or a subsequent retention order.

(k) "Furlough order" means an order directing the commissioner to allow a defendant in confinement pursuant to a commitment order, recommitment order or retention order to temporarily leave the facility for a period not exceeding fourteen days, either with or without the constant supervision of one or more employees of the facility.

(l) "Transfer order" means an order directing the commissioner to transfer a defendant from a secure facility to a non-secure facility under the jurisdiction of the commissioner or to any non-secure facility designated by the commissioner.

(m) "Release order" means an order directing the commissioner to terminate a defendant's in-patient status without terminating the commissioner's responsibility for the defendant.

(n) "Discharge order" means an order terminating an order of conditions or unconditionally discharging a defendant from supervision under the provisions of this section.

(o) "Order of conditions" means an order directing a defendant to comply with this prescribed treatment plan, or any other condition which the court determines to be reasonably necessary or appropriate, and, in addition, where a defendant is in custody of the commissioner, not to leave the facility without authorization. In addition to such conditions, when determined to be reasonably necessary or appropriate, an order of conditions may be accompanied by a special order of conditions set forth in a separate document requiring that the defendant: (i) stay away from the home, school, business or place of employment of the victim or victims, or of any witness designated by the court, of such offense; or (ii) refrain from harassing, intimidating, threatening or otherwise interfering with the victim or victims of the offense and such members of the family or household of such victim or victims as shall be specifically named by the court in such special order. An order of conditions or special order of conditions shall be valid for five

---

* The bracketed word has been inserted by the Publisher.

years from the date of its issuance, except that, for good cause shown, the court may extend the period for an additional five years.

(p) "District attorney" means the office which prosecuted the criminal action resulting in the verdict or plea of not responsible by reason of mental disease or defect.

(q) "Qualified psychiatrist" means a physician who (i) is a diplomate of the American board of psychiatry and neurology or is eligible to be certified by that board; or (ii) is certified by the American osteopathic board of neurology and psychiatry or is eligible to be certified by that board.

(r) "Licensed psychologist" means a person who is registered as a psychologist under article one hundred fifty-three of the education law.

(s) "Psychiatric examiner" means a qualified psychiatrist or a licensed psychologist who has been designated by the commissioner to examine a defendant pursuant to this section, and such designee need not be an employee of the department of mental hygiene.

2. Examination order; psychiatric examiners. Upon entry of a verdict of not responsible by reason of mental disease or defect, or upon the acceptance of a plea of not responsible by reason of mental disease or defect, the court must immediately issue an examination order. Upon receipt of such order, the commissioner must designate two qualified psychiatric examiners to conduct the examination to examine the defendant. In conducting their examination, the psychiatric examiners may employ any method which is accepted by the medical profession for the examination of persons alleged to be suffering from a dangerous mental disorder or to be mentally ill or retarded. The court may authorize a psychiatrist or psychologist retained by a defendant to be present at such examination. The clerk of the court must promptly forward a copy of the examination order to the mental hygiene legal service and such service may thereafter participate in all subsequent proceedings under this section.

In all subsequent proceedings under this section, prior to the issuance of a special order of conditions, the court shall consider whether any order of protection had been issued prior to a verdict of not responsible by reason of mental disease or defect in the case, or prior to the acceptance of a plea of not responsible by reason of mental disease or defect in the case.

2-a. Firearm, rifle or shotgun surrender order. Upon entry of a verdict of not responsible by reason of mental disease or defect, or upon the acceptance of a plea of not responsible by reason of mental disease or defect, or upon a finding that the defendant is an incapacitated person pursuant to article seven hundred thirty of this chapter, the court shall revoke the defendant's firearm license, if any, inquire of the defendant as to the existence and location of any firearm, rifle or shotgun owned or possessed by such defendant and direct the surrender of such firearm, rifle or shotgun pursuant to subparagraph (f) of paragraph one of subdivision a of section 265.20 and subdivision six of section 400.05 of the penal law.

3. Examination order; place of examination. Upon issuing an examination order, the court must, except as otherwise provided in this subdivision, direct that the defendant be committed to a secure facility designated by the commissioner as the place for such psychiatric examination. The sheriff must hold the defendant in custody pending such designation by the commissioner, and when notified of the designation, the sheriff must promptly deliver the defendant to such secure facility. When the defendant is not in custody at the time of such verdict or plea, because he was previously released on bail or on his own recognizance, the court, in its discretion, may direct that such examination be conducted on an out-patient basis, and at such time and place as the commissioner shall designate. If, however, the commissioner informs the court that confinement of the defendant

is necessary for an effective examination, the court must direct that the defendant be confined in a facility designated by the commissioner until the examination is completed.

4. Examination order, duration. Confinement in a secure facility pursuant to an examination order shall be for a period not exceeding thirty days, except that, upon application of the commissioner, the court may authorize confinement for an additional period not exceeding thirty days when a longer period is necessary to complete the examination. If the initial hearing required by subdivision six of this section has not commenced prior to the termination of such examination period, the commissioner shall retain custody of the defendant in such secure facility until custody is transferred to the sheriff in the manner prescribed in subdivision six of this section. During the period of such confinement, the physician in charge of the facility may administer or cause to be administered to the defendant such emergency psychiatric, medical or other therapeutic treatment as in his judgment should be administered. If the court has directed that the examination be conducted on an out-patient basis, the examination shall be completed within thirty days after the defendant has first reported to the place designated by the commissioner, except that, upon application of the commissioner, the court may extend such period for a reasonable time if a longer period is necessary to complete the examination.

5. Examination order; reports. After he has completed his examination of the defendant, each psychiatric examiner must promptly prepare a report of his findings and evaluation concerning the defendant's mental condition, and submit such report to the commissioner. If the psychiatric examiners differ in their opinion as to whether the defendant is mentally ill or is suffering from a dangerous mental disorder, the commissioner must designate another psychiatric examiner to examine the defendant. Upon receipt of the examination reports, the commissioner must submit them to the court that issued the examination order. If the court is not satisfied with the findings of these psychiatric examiners, the court may designate one or more additional psychiatric examiners pursuant to subdivision fifteen of this section. The court must furnish a copy of the reports to the district attorney, counsel for the defendant and the mental hygiene legal service.

6. Initial hearing; commitment order. After the examination reports are submitted, the court must, within ten days of the receipt of such reports, conduct an initial hearing to determine the defendant's present mental condition. If the defendant is in the custody of the commissioner pursuant to an examination order, the court must direct the sheriff to obtain custody of the defendant from the commissioner and to confine the defendant pending further order of the court, except that the court may direct the sheriff to confine the defendant in an institution located near the place where the court sits if that institution has been designated by the commissioner as suitable for the temporary and secure detention of mentally disabled persons. At such initial hearing, the district attorney must establish to the satisfaction of the court that the defendant has a dangerous mental disorder or is mentally ill. If the court finds that the defendant has a dangerous mental disorder, it must issue a commitment order. If the court finds that the defendant does not have a dangerous mental disorder but is mentally ill, the provisions of subdivision seven of this section shall apply.

7. Initial hearing civil commitment and order of conditions. If, at the conclusion of the initial hearing conducted pursuant to subdivision six of this section, the court finds that the defendant is mentally ill but does not have a dangerous mental disorder, the provisions of articles nine or fifteen of the mental hygiene law shall apply at that stage of the proceedings and at all subsequent proceedings. Having found that the defendant is mentally ill, the court must issue an order of conditions and an order committing the defendant to the custody of the commissioner. The latter order shall be deemed an order made pursuant to the mental hygiene law and not pursuant to this section, and further retention, conditional release or discharge of such defendant shall be in

accordance with the provisions of the mental hygiene law. If, at the conclusion of the initial hearing, the court finds that the defendant does not have a dangerous mental disorder and is not mentally ill, the court must discharge the defendant either unconditionally or subject to an order of conditions.

7-a. Whenever the court issues a special order of conditions pursuant to this section, the commissioner shall make reasonable efforts to notify the victim or victims or the designated witness or witnesses that a special order of conditions containing such provisions has been issued, unless such victim or witness has requested that such notice should not be provided.

8. First retention order. When a defendant is in the custody of the commissioner pursuant to a commitment order, the commissioner must, at least thirty days prior to the expiration of the period prescribed in the order, apply to the court that issued the order, or to a superior court in the county where the secure facility is located, for a first retention order or a release order. The commissioner must give written notice of the application to the district attorney, the defendant, counsel for the defendant, and the mental hygiene legal service. Upon receipt of such application, the court may, on its own motion, conduct a hearing to determine whether the defendant has a dangerous mental disorder, and it must conduct such hearing if a demand therefor is made by the district attorney, the defendant, counsel for the defendant, or the mental hygiene legal service within ten days from the date that notice of the application was given to them. If such a hearing is held on an application for retention, the commissioner must establish to the satisfaction of the court that the defendant has a dangerous mental disorder or is mentally ill. The district attorney shall be entitled to appear and present evidence at such hearing. If such a hearing is held on an application for release, the district attorney must establish to the satisfaction of the court that the defendant has a dangerous mental disorder or is mentally ill. If the court finds that the defendant has a dangerous mental disorder it must issue a first retention order. If the court finds that the defendant is mentally ill but does not have a dangerous mental disorder, it must issue a first retention order and, pursuant to subdivision eleven of this section, a transfer order and an order of conditions. If the court finds that the defendant does not have a dangerous mental disorder and is not mentally ill, it must issue a release order and an order of conditions pursuant to subdivision twelve of this section.

9. Second and subsequent retention orders. When a defendant is in the custody of the commissioner pursuant to a first retention order, the commissioner must, at least thirty days prior to the expiration of the period prescribed in the order, apply to the court that issued the order, or to a superior court in the county where the facility is located, for a second retention order or a release order. The commissioner must give written notice of the application to the district attorney, the defendant, counsel for the defendant, and the mental hygiene legal service. Upon receipt of such application, the court may, on its own motion, conduct a hearing to determine whether the defendant has a dangerous mental disorder, and it must conduct such hearing if a demand therefor is made by the district attorney, the defendant, counsel for the defendant, or the mental hygiene legal service within ten days from the date that notice of the application was given to them. If such a hearing is held on an application for retention, the commissioner must establish to the satisfaction of the court that the defendant has a dangerous mental disorder or is mentally ill. The district attorney shall be entitled to appear and present evidence at such hearing. If such a hearing is held on an application for release, the district attorney must establish to the satisfaction of the court that the defendant has a dangerous mental disorder or is mentally ill. If the court finds that the defendant has a dangerous mental disorder it must issue a second retention order. If the court finds that the defendant is mentally ill but does not have a dangerous mental disorder, it must issue a second retention order and, pursuant to subdivision eleven of this section, a transfer order and an order of conditions. If the court finds that the defendant does not have a dangerous mental disorder and is not mentally ill, it must issue a release order and an order of conditions pursuant to

subdivision twelve of this section. When a defendant is in the custody of the commissioner prior to the expiration of the period prescribed in a second retention order, the procedures set forth in this subdivision for the issuance of a second retention order shall govern the application for and the issuance of any subsequent retention order.

10. Furlough order. The commissioner may apply for a furlough order, pursuant to this subdivision, when a defendant is in his custody pursuant to a commitment order, recommitment order, or retention order and the commissioner is of the view that, consistent with the public safety and welfare of the community and the defendant, the clinical condition of the defendant warrants a granting of the privileges authorized by a furlough order. The application for a furlough order may be made to the court that issued the commitment order, or to a superior court in the county where the secure facility is located. The commissioner must give ten days written notice to the district attorney, the defendant, counsel for the defendant, and the mental hygiene legal service. Upon receipt of such application, the court may, on its own motion, conduct a hearing to determine whether the application should be granted, and must conduct such hearing if a demand therefor is made by the district attorney. If the court finds that the issuance of a furlough order is consistent with the public safety and welfare of the community and the defendant, and that the clinical condition of the defendant warrants a granting of the privileges authorized by a furlough order, the court must grant the application and issue a furlough order containing any terms and conditions that the court deems necessary or appropriate. If the defendant fails to return to the secure facility at the time specified in the furlough order, then, for purposes of subdivision nineteen of this section, he shall be deemed to have escaped.

11. Transfer order and order of conditions. The commissioner may apply for a transfer order, pursuant to this subdivision, when a defendant is in his custody pursuant to a retention order or a recommitment order, and the commissioner is of the view that the defendant does not have a dangerous mental disorder or that, consistent with the public safety and welfare of the community and the defendant, the clinical condition of the defendant warrants his transfer from a secure facility to a non-secure facility under the jurisdiction of the commissioner or to any non-secure facility designated by the commissioner. The application for a transfer order may be made to the court that issued the order under which the defendant is then in custody, or to a superior court in the county where the secure facility is located. The commissioner must give ten days written notice to the district attorney, the defendant, counsel for the defendant, and the mental hygiene legal service. Upon receipt of such application, the court may, on its own motion, conduct a hearing to determine whether the application should be granted, and must conduct such hearing if the demand therefor is made by the district attorney. At such hearing, the district attorney must establish to the satisfaction of the court that the defendant has a dangerous mental disorder or that the issuance of a transfer order is inconsistent with the public safety and welfare of the community. The court must grant the application and issue a transfer order if the court finds that the defendant does not have a dangerous mental disorder, or if the court finds that the issuance of a transfer order is consistent with the public safety and welfare of the community and the defendant and that the clinical condition of the defendant, warrants his transfer from a secure facility to a non-secure facility. A court must also issue a transfer order when, in connection with an application for a first retention order pursuant to subdivision eight of this section or a second or subsequent retention order pursuant to subdivision nine of this section, it finds that a defendant is mentally ill but does not have a dangerous mental disorder. Whenever a court issues a transfer order it must also issue an order of conditions.

12. Release order and order of conditions. The commissioner may apply for a release order, pursuant to this subdivision, when a defendant is in his custody pursuant to a retention order or recommitment order, and the commissioner is of the view that the defendant no longer has a

dangerous mental disorder and is no longer mentally ill. The application for a release order may be made to the court that issued the order under which the defendant is then in custody, or to a superior court in the county where the facility is located. The application must contain a description of the defendant's current mental condition, the past course of treatment, a history of the defendant's conduct subsequent to his commitment, a written service plan for continued treatment which shall include the information specified in subdivision (g) of section 29.15 of the mental hygiene law, and a detailed statement of the extent to which supervision of the defendant after release is proposed. The commissioner must give ten days written notice to the district attorney, the defendant, counsel for the defendant, and the mental hygiene legal service. Upon receipt of such application, the court must promptly conduct a hearing to determine the defendant's present mental condition. At such hearing, the district attorney must establish to the satisfaction of the court that the defendant has a dangerous mental disorder or is mentally ill. If the court finds that the defendant has a dangerous mental disorder, it must deny the application for a release order. If the court finds that the defendant does not have a dangerous mental disorder but is mentally ill, it must issue a transfer order pursuant to subdivision eleven of this section if the defendant is then confined in a secure facility. If the court finds that the defendant does not have a dangerous mental disorder and is not mentally ill, it must grant the application and issue a release order. A court must also issue a release order when, in connection with an application for a first retention order pursuant to subdivision eight of this section or a second or subsequent retention order pursuant to subdivision nine of this section, it finds that the defendant does not have a dangerous mental disorder and is not mentally ill. Whenever a court issues a release order it must also issue an order of conditions. If the court has previously issued a transfer order and an order of conditions, it must issue a new order of conditions upon issuing a release order. The order of conditions issued in conjunction with a release order shall incorporate a written service plan prepared by a psychiatrist familiar with the defendant's case history and approved by the court, and shall contain any conditions that the court determines to be reasonably necessary or appropriate. It shall be the responsibility of the commissioner to determine that such defendant is receiving the services specified in the written service plan and is complying with any conditions specified in such plan and the order of conditions.

13. Discharge order. The commissioner may apply for a discharge order, pursuant to this subdivision, when a defendant has been continuously on an out-patient status for three years or more pursuant to a release order, and the commissioner is of the view that the defendant no longer has a dangerous mental disorder and is no longer mentally ill and that the issuance of a discharge order is consistent with the public safety and welfare of the community and the defendant. The application for a discharge order may be made to the court that issued the release order, or to a superior court in the county where the defendant is then residing. The commissioner must give ten days written notice to the district attorney, the defendant, counsel for the defendant, and the mental hygiene legal service. Upon receipt of such application, the court may, on its own motion, conduct a hearing to determine whether the application should be granted, and must conduct such hearing if a demand therefor is made by the district attorney. The court must grant the application and issue a discharge order if the court finds that the defendant has been continuously on an out-patient status for three years or more, that he does not have a dangerous mental disorder and is not mentally ill, and that the issuance of the discharge order is consistent with the public safety and welfare of the community and the defendant.

14. Recommitment order. At any time during the period covered by an order of conditions an application may be made by the commissioner or the district attorney to the court that issued such order, or to a superior court in the county where the defendant is then residing, for a recommitment order when the applicant is of the view that the defendant has a dangerous mental disorder. The

applicant must give written notice of the application to the defendant, counsel for the defendant, and the mental hygiene legal service, and if the applicant is the commissioner he must give such notice to the district attorney or if the applicant is the district attorney he must give such notice to the commissioner. Upon receipt of such application the court must order the defendant to appear before it for a hearing to determine if the defendant has a dangerous mental disorder. Such order may be in the form of a written notice, specifying the time and place of appearance, served personally upon the defendant, or mailed to his last known address, as the court may direct. If the defendant fails to appear in court as directed, the court may issue a warrant to an appropriate peace officer directing him to take the defendant into custody and bring him before the court. In such circumstance, the court may direct that the defendant be confined in an appropriate institution located near the place where the court sits. The court must conduct a hearing to determine whether the defendant has a dangerous mental disorder. At such hearing, the applicant, whether he be the commissioner or the district attorney must establish to the satisfaction of the court that the defendant has a dangerous mental disorder. If the applicant is the commissioner, the district attorney shall be entitled to appear and present evidence at such hearing; if the applicant is the district attorney, the commissioner shall be entitled to appear and present evidence at such hearing. If the court finds that the defendant has a dangerous mental disorder, it must issue a recommitment order. When a defendant is in the custody of the commissioner pursuant to a recommitment order, the procedures set forth in subdivisions eight and nine of this section for the issuance of retention orders shall govern the application for and the issuance of a first retention order, a second retention order, and subsequent retention orders.

15. Designation of psychiatric examiners. If, at any hearing conducted under this section to determine the defendant's present mental condition, the court is not satisfied with the findings of the psychiatric examiners, the court may direct the commissioner to designate one or more additional psychiatric examiners to conduct an examination of the defendant and submit a report of their findings. In addition, the court may on its own motion, or upon request of a party, may designate one or more psychiatric examiners to examine the defendant and submit a report of their findings. The district attorney may apply to the court for an order directing that the defendant submit to an examination by a psychiatric examiner designated by the district attorney, and such psychiatric examiner may testify at the hearing.

16. Rehearing and review. Any defendant who is in the custody of the commissioner pursuant to a commitment order, a retention order, or a recommitment order, if dissatisfied with such order, may, within thirty days after the making of such order, obtain a rehearing and review of the proceedings and of such order in accordance with the provisions of section 9.35 or 15.35 of the mental hygiene law.

17. Rights of defendants. Subject to the limitations and provisions of this section, a defendant committed to the custody of the commissioner pursuant to this section shall have the rights granted to patients under the mental hygiene law.

18. Notwithstanding any other provision of law, no person confined by reason of a commitment order, recommitment order or retention order to a secure facility may be discharged or released unless the commissioner shall deliver written notice, at least four days excluding Saturdays, Sundays and holidays, in advance of such discharge or release to all of the following:

   (a) the district attorney.

   (b) the police department having jurisdiction of the area to which the defendant is to be discharged or released.

(c) any other person the court may designate.

The notices required by this subdivision shall be given by the facility staff physician who was treating the defendant or, if unavailable, by the defendant's treatment team leader, but if neither is immediately available, notice must be given by some other member of the clinical staff of the facility. Such notice must be given by any means reasonably calculated to give prompt actual notice.

19. Escape from custody; notice requirements. If a defendant is in the custody of the commissioner pursuant to an order issued under this section, and such defendant escapes from custody, immediate notice of such escape shall be given by the department facility staff to: (a) the district attorney, (b) the superintendent of state police, (c) the sheriff of the county where the escape occurred, (d) the police department having jurisdiction of the area where the escape occurred, (e) any person the facility staff believes to be in danger, and (f) any law enforcement agency and any person the facility staff believes would be able to apprise such endangered person that the defendant has escaped from the facility. Such notice shall be given as soon as the facility staff know that the defendant has escaped from the facility and shall include such information as will adequately identify the defendant and the person or persons believed to be in danger and the nature of the danger. The notices required by this subdivision shall be given by the facility staff physician who was treating the defendant or, if unavailable, by the defendant's treatment team leader, but if neither is immediately available, notice must be given by some other member of the clinical staff of the facility. Such notice must be given by any means reasonably calculated to give prompt actual notice. The defendant may be apprehended, restrained, transported to, and returned to the facility from which he escaped by any peace officer, and it shall be the duty of the officer to assist any representative of the commissioner to take the defendant into custody upon the request of such representative.

20. Required affidavit. No application may be made by the commissioner under this section without an accompanying affidavit from at least one psychiatric examiner supportive of relief requested in the application, which affidavit shall be served on all parties entitled to receive the notice of application. Such affidavit shall set forth the defendant's clinical diagnosis, a detailed analysis of his or her mental condition which caused the psychiatric examiner to formulate an opinion, and the opinion of the psychiatric examiner with respect to the defendant. Any application submitted without the required affidavit shall be dismissed by the court.

21. Appeals.

(a) A party to proceedings conducted in accordance with the provisions of this section may take an appeal to an intermediate appellate court by permission of the intermediate appellate court as follows:

(i) the commissioner may appeal from any release order, retention order, transfer order, discharge order, order of conditions, or recommitment order, for which he has not applied;

(ii) a defendant, or the mental hygiene legal service on his or her behalf, may appeal from any commitment order, retention order, recommitment order, or, if the defendant has obtained a rehearing and review of any such order pursuant to subdivision sixteen of this section, from an order, not otherwise appealable as of right, issued in accordance with the provisions of section 9.35 or 15.35 of the mental hygiene law authorizing continued retention under the original order, provided, however, that a defendant who takes an appeal from a commitment order, retention order, or recommitment order may not subsequently obtain a rehearing and review of such order pursuant to subdivision sixteen of this section;

(iii) the district attorney may appeal from any release order, transfer order, discharge order, order of conditions, furlough order, or order denying an application for a recommitment order which he opposed.

(b) An aggrieved party may appeal from a final order of the intermediate appellate court to the court of appeals by permission of the intermediate appellate court granted before application to the court of appeals, or by permission of the court of appeals upon refusal by the intermediate appellate court or upon direct application.

(c) An appeal taken under this subdivision shall be deemed civil in nature, and shall be governed by the laws and rules applicable to civil appeals; provided, however, that a stay of the order appealed from must be obtained in accordance with the provisions of paragraph (d) hereof.

(d) The court from or to which an appeal is taken may stay all proceedings to enforce the order appealed from pending an appeal or determination on a motion for permission to appeal, or may grant a limited stay, except that only the court to which an appeal is taken may vacate, limit, or modify a stay previously granted. If the order appealed from is affirmed or modified, the stay shall continue for five days after service upon the appellant of the order of affirmance or modification with notice of its entry in the court to which the appeal was taken. If a motion is made for permission to appeal from such an order, before the expiration of the five days, the stay, or any other stay granted pending determination of the motion for permission to appeal, shall:

(i) if the motion is granted, continue until five days after the appeal is determined; or

(ii) if the motion is denied, continue until five days after the movant is served with the order of denial with notice of its entry.

22. Any special order of conditions issued pursuant tosubparagraph (i) or (ii) of paragraph (o) of subdivision one of this section shall bear in a conspicuous manner the term "special order of conditions" and a copy shall be filed by the clerk of the court with the sheriff's office in the county in which anyone intended to be protected by such special order resides, or, if anyone intended to be protected by such special order resides within a city, with the police department of such city. The absence of language specifying that the order is a "special order of conditions" shall not affect the validity of such order. A copy of such special order of conditions may from time to time be filed by the clerk of the court with any other police department or sheriff's office having jurisdiction of the residence, work place, or school of anyone intended to be protected by such special order. A copy of such special order may also be filed by anyone intended to be protected by such provisions at the appropriate police department or sheriff's office having jurisdiction. Any subsequent amendment or revocation of such special order may be filed in the same manner as provided in this subdivision. Such special order of conditions shall plainly state the date that the order expires.

HISTORY: Add, L 1980, ch 548, § 11, eff Sept 1, 1980; amd, L 1982, ch 526, §§ 1,–4, L 1983, ch 976, § 1, eff Aug 8, 1983, L 1985, ch 789, § 47, eff April 1, 1986, L 1989, ch 693, § 1, eff July 22, 1989, L 1993, ch 330, § 8, eff April 1, 1994, L 2003, ch 525, §§ 1–4, eff Sept 17, 2003, L 2004, ch 107, §§ 1–4, eff June 8, 2004, L 2013, ch 1, § 1, eff March 16, 2013.

§ 330.25. Removal after verdict

1. Where a defendant is a juvenile offender who does not stand convicted of murder in the second degree, upon motion and with the consent of the district attorney, the action may be removed to the family court in the interests of justice pursuant to article seven hundred twenty-five of this chapter notwithstanding the verdict.

2. If the district attorney consents to the motion for removal pursuant to this section, he shall file a subscribed memorandum with the court setting forth (1) a recommendation that the interests of justice would best be served by removal of the action to the family court; and (2) if the conviction is of an offense set forth in paragraph (b) of subdivision one of section 210.43 of this chapter, specific factors, one or more of which reasonably support the recommendation, showing, (i) mitigating circumstances that bear directly upon the manner in which the crime was committed, or (ii) where the defendant was not the sole participant in the crime, that the defendant's participation was relatively minor although not so minor as to constitute a defense to prosecution, or (iii) where the juvenile offender has no previous adjudications of having committed a designated felony act, as defined in subdivision eight of section 301.2 of the family court act, regardless of the age of the offender at the time of commission of the act, that the criminal act was not part of a pattern of criminal behavior and, in view of the history of the offender, is not likely to be repeated.

3. If the court is of the opinion, based upon the specific factors set forth in the district attorney's memorandum, that the interests of justice would best be served by removal of the action to the family court, the verdict shall be set aside and a plea of guilty of a crime or act for which the defendant is not criminally responsible may be entered pursuant to subdivision three or four of section 220.10 of this chapter. Upon accepting any such plea, the court must specify upon the record the portion or portions of the district attorney's statement the court is relying upon as the basis of its opinion and that it believes the interests of justice would best be served by removal of the proceeding to the family court. Such plea shall then be deemed to be a juvenile delinquency fact determination and the court upon entry thereof must direct that the action be removed to the family court in accordance with the provisions of article seven hundred twenty-five of this chapter.

HISTORY: Add, L 1978, ch 481, § 42, eff Sept 1, 1978. Sub 2, amd, L 1979, ch 411, § 11, L 1982, ch 920, § 76, eff July 1, 1983.

§ 330.30. Motion to set aside verdict; grounds for

At any time after rendition of a verdict of guilty and before sentence, the court may, upon motion of the defendant, set aside or modify the verdict or any part thereof upon the following grounds:

1. Any ground appearing in the record which, if raised upon an appeal from a prospective judgment of conviction, would require a reversal or modification of the judgment as a matter of law by an appellate court.

2. That during the trial there occurred, out of the presence of the court, improper conduct by a juror, or improper conduct by another person in relation to a juror, which may have affected a substantial right of the defendant and which was not known to the defendant prior to the rendition of the verdict; or

3. That new evidence has been discovered since the trial which could not have been produced by the defendant at the trial even with due diligence on his part and which is of such character as to create a probability that had such evidence been received at the trial the verdict would have been more favorable to the defendant.

HISTORY: Add, L 1970, ch 996, § 1, eff Sept 1, 1971.

§ 330.40. Motion to set aside verdict; procedure

1. A motion to set aside a verdict based upon a ground specified in subdivision one of section 330.30 need not be in writing, but the people must be given reasonable notice thereof and an opportunity to appear in opposition thereto.

2. A motion to set aside a verdict based upon a ground specified in subdivisions two and three

of section 330.30 must be made and determined as follows:

(a) The motion must be in writing and upon reasonable notice to the people. The moving papers must contain sworn allegations, whether by the defendant or by another person or persons, of the occurrence or existence of all facts essential to support the motion. Such sworn allegations may be based upon personal knowledge of the affiant or upon information and belief, provided that in the latter event the affiant must state the sources of such information and the grounds of such belief;

(b) The people may file with the court, and in such case must serve a copy thereof upon the defendant or his counsel, an answer denying or admitting any or all of the allegations of the moving papers;

(c) After all papers of both parties have been filed, the court must consider the same and, if the motion is determinable pursuant to paragraphs (d) or (e), must or may, as therein provided, determine the motion without holding a hearing to resolve questions of fact;

(d) The court must grant the motion if:

(i) The moving papers allege a ground constituting legal basis for the motion; and

(ii) Such papers contain sworn allegations of all facts essential to support such ground; and

(iii) All the essential facts are conceded by the people to be true.

(e) The court may deny the motion if:

(i) The moving papers do not allege any ground constituting legal basis for the motion; or

(ii) The moving papers do not contain sworn allegations of all facts essential to support the motion.

(f) If the court does not determine the motion pursuant to paragraphs (d) or (e), it must conduct a hearing and make findings of fact essential to the determination thereof;

(g) Upon such a hearing, the defendant has the burden of proving by a preponderance of the evidence every fact essential to support the motion.

　　HISTORY: Add, L 1970, ch 996, § 1, eff Sept 1, 1971.

§ 330.50. Motion to set aside verdict; order granting motion

1. Upon setting aside or modifying a verdict or a part thereof upon a ground specified in subdivision one of section 330.30, the court must take the same action as the appropriate appellate court would be required to take upon reversing or modifying a judgment upon the particular ground in issue.

2. Upon setting aside a verdict upon a ground specified in subdivision two of section 330.30, the court must order a new trial.

3. Upon setting aside a verdict upon a ground specified in subdivision three of section 330.30, the court must, except as otherwise provided in this subdivision, order a new trial. If a verdict is set aside upon the ground that had the newly discovered evidence in question been received at the trial the verdict probably would have been more favorable to the defendant in that the conviction probably would have been for a lesser offense than the one contained in the verdict, the court may

either (a) set aside such verdict or (b) with the consent of the people modify such verdict by reducing it to one of conviction of such lesser offense.

4. Upon a new trial resulting from an order setting aside a verdict, the indictment is deemed to contain all the counts and to charge all the offenses which it contained and charged at the time the previous trial was commenced, regardless of whether any count was dismissed by the court in the course of such trial, except those upon or of which the defendant was acquitted or is deemed to have been acquitted.

HISTORY: Add, L 1970, ch 996, § 1, eff Sept 1, 1971.

TITLE K   Prosecution of Informations in Local Criminal Courts—Plea to Sentence

ARTICLE 340
PRE-TRIAL PROCEEDINGS

ARTICLE 350
NON-JURY TRIALS

ARTICLE 360
JURY TRIAL

ARTICLE 370
PROCEEDINGS FROM VERDICT TO SENTENCE

HISTORY: Add, L 1970, ch 996, § 1, eff Sept 1, 1971.

ARTICLE 340   PRE-TRIAL PROCEEDINGS

HISTORY: Add, L 1970, ch 996, § 1, eff Sept 1, 1971.

§ 340.10. Definition of terms

The following definitions are applicable to this title:

1. "Information," in addition to its meaning as defined in subdivision one of section 100.10, includes (a) a simplified information and (b) a prosecutor's information and (c) a misdemeanor complaint upon which the defendant, by a waiver executed pursuant to subdivision three of section 170.65, has consented to be prosecuted.

2. "Single judge trial" means a trial in a local criminal court conducted by one judge sitting without a jury.

3. "Jury trial" means a trial in a local criminal court conducted by one judge sitting with a jury.

HISTORY: Add, L 1970, ch 996, § 1; amd, L 1971, ch 815, § 1, eff Sept 1, 1971. Sub 1, amd, L 1972, ch 661, § 44, eff Sept 1, 1972. Sub 3, formerly sub 4, renumbered sub 3 and amd, L 1971, ch 815, § 1, eff Sept 1, 1971. Former sub 3, deleted, L 1971, ch 815, § 1, eff Sept 1, 1971.

§ 340.20. The plea

1. Except as provided in subdivisions two and three, the provisions of article two hundred twenty, governing the kinds of pleas to indictments which may be entered and related matters, are, to the extent that they can be so applied, applicable to pleas to informations, and changes of pleas thereto, in local criminal courts.

2. A plea to an information, other than one against a corporation, must be entered in the following manner:

(a) Subject to the provisions of paragraph (b), a plea to an information must be entered orally by the defendant in person unless the court permits entry thereof by counsel upon the filing by him of a written and subscribed statement by the defendant declaring that he waives his right to plead to the information in person and authorizing his attorney to enter a plea on his behalf as set forth in the authorization.

(b) If the only offense or offenses charged are traffic infractions, the procedure provided in sections eighteen hundred five, eighteen hundred six and eighteen hundred seven of the vehicle and traffic law, relating to pleas in such cases, is, when appropriate, applicable and controlling.

3. A plea to an information against a corporation must be entered by counsel.

4. When a sentence is agreed upon by the prosecutor and a defendant as a predicate to entry of a plea of guilty, the court or the prosecutor must orally on the record, or in writing filed with the court, state the sentence agreed upon as a condition of such plea.

HISTORY: Add, L 1970, ch 996, § 1, eff Sept 1, 1971, with substance derived from Crim C §§ 335(1), 699(2), 700. Sub 2, par (a), amd, L 1974, ch 430, § 1, eff May 23, 1974. Sub 2, par (b), amd, L 1973, ch 61, § 2, eff Sept 1, 1973. Sub 4, add, L 1984, ch 671, § 2, eff Aug 31, 1984, and not applicable to appeals arising from any plea of guilty entered prior to such date.

§ 340.30. Pre-trial discovery and notices of defenses

The provisions of article two hundred forty, concerning pre-trial discovery by a defendant under indictment in a superior court, and article two hundred fifty, concerning pre-trial notice to the people by a defendant under indictment in a superior court who intends to advance a trial defense of mental disease or defect or of alibi, apply to a prosecution of an information in a local criminal court.

HISTORY: Add, L 1970, ch 996, § 1, eff Sept 1, 1971, with substance derived from Crim C § 336.

§ 340.40. Modes of trial

1. Except as otherwise provided in this section, a trial of an information in a local criminal court must be a single judge trial.

2. In any local criminal court a defendant who has entered a plea of not guilty to an information which charges a misdemeanor must be accorded a jury trial, conducted pursuant to article three hundred sixty, except that in the New York city criminal court, the trial of an information which charges a misdemeanor for which the authorized term of imprisonment is not more than six months must be a single judge trial. The defendant may at any time before trial waive a jury trial in the manner prescribed in subdivision two of section 320.10, and consent to a single judge trial.

3. A defendant entitled to a jury trial pursuant to subdivision two, shall be so entitled even though the information also charges an offense for which he is otherwise not entitled to a jury trial. In such case, the defendant is not entitled both to a jury trial and a separate single judge trial and the court may not order separate trials.

4. [Renumbered]

5, 6. [Deleted]

7. Notwithstanding any other provision of law, in any local criminal court the trial of a person who is an eligible youth within the meaning of the youthful offender procedure set forth in article seven hundred twenty and who has not prior to commencement of the trial been convicted of a crime or adjudicated a youthful offender must be a single judge trial.

HISTORY: Add, L 1970, ch 996, § 1; amd, L 1971, ch 815, § 2, eff Sept 1, 1971. Sub 2, amd, L 1984, ch 673, § 2,. Sub 3, formerly sub 4, renumbered sub 3 and amd, L 1971, ch 815, § 2, eff Sept 1, 1971. Former sub 3, deleted, L 1971, ch 815, § 2, eff Sept 1, 1971. Former sub 4, renumbered sub 3 and amd, L 1971, ch 815, § 2, eff Sept 1, 1971. Former subs 5 and 6, deleted, L 1971, ch 815, § 2, eff Sept 1, 1971. Sub 7, add, L 1971, ch 981, § 2, eff Sept 1, 1971.

§ 340.50. Defendant's presence at trial

1. Except as provided in subdivision two or three, a defendant must be personally present during the trial.

2. On motion of a defendant represented by counsel, the court may, in the absence of an objection by the people, issue an order dispensing with the requirement that the defendant be personally present at trial. Such an order may be made only upon the filing of a written and subscribed statement by the defendant declaring that he waives his right to be personally present at the trial and authorizing his attorney to conduct his defense.

3. A defendant who conducts himself in so disorderly and disruptive a manner that his trial cannot be carried on with him in the courtroom may be removed from the courtroom if, after he has been warned by the court that he will be removed if he continues such conduct, he continues to engage in such conduct.

> **HISTORY:** Add, L 1970, ch 996, § 1; amd, L 1971, ch 789, § 2, eff Sept 1, 1971. Sub 3, add, L 1971, ch 789, § 2, eff Sept 1, 1971.

ARTICLE 350   NON-JURY TRIALS

§ 350.10.   **Conduct of single judge trial**
§ 350.20.   **Trial by judicial hearing officer**

> **HISTORY:** Add, L 1970, ch 996, § 1, eff Sept 1, 1971.

§ 350.10. Conduct of single judge trial

1. A single judge trial of an information in a local criminal court must be conducted pursuant to this section.

2. The court, in addition to determining all questions of law, is the exclusive trier of all issues of fact and must render a verdict.

3. The order of the trial must be as follows:

(a) The court may in its discretion permit the parties to deliver opening addresses. If the court grants such permission to one party, it must grant it to the other also. If both parties deliver opening addresses, the people's address must be delivered first.

(b) The order in which evidence must or may be offered by the respective parties is the same as that applicable to a jury trial of an indictment as prescribed in subdivisions five, six and seven of section 260.30.

(c) The court may in its discretion permit the parties to deliver summations. If the court grants such permission to one party, it must grant permission to the other also. If both parties deliver summations, the defendant's summation must be delivered first.

(d) The court must then consider the case and render a verdict.

4. The provisions governing motion practice and general procedure with respect to a jury trial of an indictment are, wherever appropriate, applicable to a non-jury trial of an information.

5. If the information contains more than one count, the court must render a verdict upon each count not previously dismissed or must otherwise state upon the record its disposition of each such count. A verdict which does not so dispose of each count constitutes a verdict of not guilty with respect to each undisposed of count.

6. In rendering a verdict of guilty upon a count charging a misdemeanor, the court may find the defendant guilty of such misdemeanor if it is established by legally sufficient trial evidence, or guilty of any lesser included offense which is established by legally sufficient trial evidence.

HISTORY: Add, L 1970, ch 996, § 1, eff Sept 1, 1971.

§ 350.20. Trial by judicial hearing officer

1. Notwithstanding any provision of section 350.10 of this article, in any case where a single judge trial of an information in a local criminal court is authorized or required, the court may, upon agreement of the parties, assign a judicial hearing officer to conduct the trial. Where such assignment is made, the judicial hearing officer shall entertain the case in the same manner as a court and shall:

    (a) determine all questions of law;

    (b) act as the exclusive trier of all issues of fact; and

    (c) render a verdict.

2. In the discharge of this responsibility, the judicial hearing officer shall have the same powers as a judge of the court in which the proceeding is pending. The rules of evidence shall be applicable at a trial conducted by a judicial hearing officer.

3. Any action taken by a judicial hearing officer in the conduct of a trial shall be deemed the action of the court in which the proceeding is pending.

4. This section shall not apply where the single judge trial is of an information at least one count of which charges a class A misdemeanor.

5. [Effective until Suffolk county enacts a local law establishing a traffic and parking violations agency] Notwithstanding the provisions of subdivision one of this section, the administrative judge of Nassau county may, without the consent of the parties, assign matters involving traffic and parking infractions except those described in paragraphs (a), (b), (c)[,]* (d), (e) and (f) of subdivision two of section three hundred seventy-one of the general municipal law to a judicial hearing officer for all proceedings before the district court of Nassau county in accordance with the provisions of section sixteen hundred ninety of the vehicle and traffic law.

5. [Effective upon the enactment of a local law by Suffolk county establishing a traffic and parking violations agency] Notwithstanding the provisions of subdivision one of this section, for all proceedings before the district court of Nassau county the administrative judge of Nassau county may, and for all proceedings before the district court of Suffolk county, the administrative judge of Suffolk county may, without the consent of the parties, assign matters involving traffic and parking infractions except those described in paragraphs (a), (b), (c), (d), (e) and (f) of subdivision two of section three hundred seventy-one of the general municipal law to a judicial hearing officer in accordance with the provisions of section sixteen hundred ninety of the vehicle and traffic law.

    HISTORY: Add, L 1983, ch 840, § 11; amd, L 1990, ch 496, § 10, eff July 18, 1990, L 2012, ch 388, § 7, eff upon the enactment of a local law by Suffolk county establishing a traffic and parking violations agency.

    Editor's Note: Laws 2012, ch 388, § 13, eff April 1, 2013, provides as follows:

    "§ 13. This act shall take effect April 1, 2013; provided, however, the amendments to . . . subdivision 5 of section 350.20 of the criminal procedure law, as made by sections two, three, four, five, six and seven of this act, respectively, shall take effect only in the event that the county of Suffolk shall have by local law established a traffic and parking violations agency; provided that the legislature of the county of Suffolk shall notify the legislative bill drafting commission upon the occurrence of the enactment of the legislation provided for in

---

  * The bracketed punctuation has been inserted by the Publisher.

sections two, three, four, five, six and seven of this act in order that the commission may maintain an accurate and timely effective data base of the official text of the laws of the state of New York in furtherance of effectuating the provisions of section 44 of the legislative law and section 70-b of the public officers law; . . . ."

ARTICLE 360   JURY TRIAL

HISTORY: Add, L 1970, ch 996, § 1, eff Sept 1, 1971.

§ 360.05. Jury trial; order of trial

The provisions of section 260.30, governing the order of proceedings of a jury trial of an indictment in a superior court, are applicable to a jury trial of an information in a local criminal court.

HISTORY: Add, L 1970, ch 996, § 1, eff Sept 1, 1971.

§ 360.10. Trial jury; formation in general

1. A trial jury consists of six jurors, but "alternate jurors" may be selected and sworn pursuant to section 360.35.

2. The panel from which the jury is drawn is formed and selected as prescribed in the uniform district court act, uniform city court act, and uniform justice court act. In the New York city criminal court the panel from which the jury is drawn is formed and selected in the same manner as is prescribed for the formation and selection of a panel in the supreme court in counties within cities having a population of one million or more.

HISTORY: Add, L 1970, ch 996, § 1, eff Sept 1, 1971, with substance derived from Crim C §§ 703, 710. Sub 2, amd, L 1971, ch 815, § 4, eff Sept 1, 1971.

§ 360.15. Trial jury; challenge to the panel

1. A challenge to the panel is an objection made to the entire panel of prospective trial jurors returned for the trial of the action and may be taken to such panel or to any additional panel that may be ordered by the court. Such a challenge may be made only by the defendant and only on the ground that there has been such a departure from the requirements of the appropriate law in the drawing or return of the panel as to result in substantial prejudice to the defendant.

2. A challenge to the panel must be made before the selection of the jury commences, and, if it is not, such challenge is deemed to have been waived. Such challenge must be made in writing setting forth the facts constituting the ground of challenge. If such facts are denied by the people, witnesses may be called and examined by either party. All issues of fact and questions of law

arising on the challenge must be tried and determined by the court. If a challenge to the panel is allowed, the court must discharge that panel and order the return of another panel of prospective trial jurors.

HISTORY: Add, L 1970, ch 996, § 1, eff Sept 1, 1971.

§ 360.20. Trial jury; examination of prospective jurors; challenges generally

If no challenge to the panel is made as prescribed by section 360.15, or if such challenge is made and disallowed, the court must direct that the names of not less than six members of the panel be drawn and called. Such persons must take their places in the jury box and must be immediately sworn to answer truthfully questions asked them relative to their qualifications to serve as jurors in the action. The procedural rules prescribed in section 270.15 with respect to the examination of the prospective jurors and to challenges are also applicable to the selection of a trial jury in a local criminal court.

HISTORY: Add, L 1970, ch 996, § 1, eff Sept 1, 1971; amd, L 2013, ch 287, § 1, eff July 31, 2013.

§ 360.25. Trial jury; challenge for cause of an individual juror

1. A challenge for cause is an objection to a prospective member of the jury and may be made only on the ground that:

(a) He does not have the qualifications required by the judiciary law; or

(b) He has a state of mind that is likely to preclude him from rendering an impartial verdict based upon the evidence adduced at the trial; or

(c) He is related within the sixth degree by consanguinity or affinity to the defendant, or to the person allegedly injured by the crime charged, or to a prospective witness at the trial, or to counsel for the people or for the defendant; or that he is or was a party adverse to any such person in a civil action; or that he has complained against or been accused by any such person in a criminal action; or that he bears some other relationship to any such person of such nature that it is likely to preclude him from rendering an impartial verdict; or

(d) He is to be a witness at the trial; or where a prosecutor's information was filed at the direction of a grand jury, he was a witness before the grand jury or at the preliminary hearing; or

(e) He or she served on a trial jury in a prior civil or criminal action involving the same incident charged; or where a prosecutor's information was filed at the direction of a grand jury, he or she served on the grand jury which directed such filing.

2. All issues of fact or questions of law arising on the challenge must be tried and determined by the court. The provisions of subdivision two of section 270.20 with respect to challenges are also applicable to the selection of a trial jury in a local criminal court.

HISTORY: Add, L 1970, ch 996, § 1, eff Sept 1, 1971. Sub 1, par (e), amd, L 2006, ch 695, § 1, eff Nov 1, 2006.

§ 360.30. Trial jury; peremptory challenge of an individaul [individual]* juror

1. A peremptory challenge is an objection to a prospective juror for which no reason need be assigned. Upon any peremptory challenge, the court must exclude the person challenged from service.

---

* The bracketed word has been inserted by the Publisher.

2. Each party must be allowed three peremptory challenges. When two or more defendants are tried jointly, such challenges are not multiplied by the number of defendants, but such defendants are to be treated as a single party. In any such case, a peremptory challenge by one or more defendants must be allowed if a majority of the defendants join in such challenge. Otherwise, it must be disallowed.

HISTORY: Add, L 1970, ch 996, § 1, eff Sept 1, 1971.

§ 360.35. Trial jury; alternate juror

1. Immediately after the last trial juror is sworn, the court may in its discretion direct the selection of either one or two additional jurors to be known as "alternate jurors." The alternate jurors must be drawn in the same manner, must have the same qualifications, must be subject to the same examination and challenges for cause and must take the same oath as the regular jurors. Whether or not a party has used its peremptory challenge in the selection of the trial jury, one peremptory challenge is authorized in the selection of the alternate jurors.

2. The provisions of section 270.35 with respect to alternate jurors are also applicable to a trial jury in a local criminal court.

HISTORY: Add, L 1970, ch 996, § 1, eff Sept 1, 1971.

§ 360.40. Trial jury; conduct of jury trial in general

A jury trial of an information must be conducted generally in the same manner as a jury trial of an indictment, and the rules governing preliminary instructions by the court, supervision of the jury, motion practice and other procedural matters involved in the conduct of a jury trial of an indictment are, where appropriate, applicable to the conduct of a jury trial of an information.

HISTORY: Add, L 1970, ch 996, § 1, eff Sept 1, 1971.

§ 360.45. Court's charge and instructions; in general

The general principles, prescribed in section 300.10, governing the court's charge to the jury and requests to charge upon a trial of an indictment, are applicable to a jury trial of an information in a local criminal court.

HISTORY: Add, L 1970, ch 996, § 1, eff Sept 1, 1971.

§ 360.50. Court's submission of information to jury; counts and offenses to be submitted

1. The term definitions contained in section 300.30 are applicable to this section, except that the word "information" is to be substituted for the word "indictment" wherever the latter appears in said section 300.30.

2. The court may submit to the jury only those counts of an information remaining therein at the time of its charge which are supported by legally sufficient trial evidence, and every count not so supported should be dismissed by a trial order of dismissal. If the trial evidence is not legally sufficient to establish a misdemeanor charged in a particular count which the court would otherwise be required to submit pursuant to this section, but is legally sufficient to establish a lesser included offense, the court may submit such lesser included offense and, upon the people's request, must do so. In submitting a count charging a misdemeanor established by legally sufficient trial evidence, the court in its discretion may, in addition to submitting such misdemeanor, submit in the alternative any lesser included offense if there is a reasonable view of the evidence which would support a finding that the defendant committed such lesser offense but did not commit the misdemeanor charged.

3. If the information contains but one count, the court must submit such count.

4. If a multiple count information contains consecutive counts only, the court must submit every count thereof.

5. In any case where the information may be more complex by reason of concurrent counts or inconsistent counts or other factors indicated in subdivisions three, four and five of section 300.40, relating to multiple count indictments, the court, in its submission of such information to the jury, should, so far as practicable, be guided by the provisions of the said subdivisions of said section 300.40.

6. Notwithstanding any other provision of this section, the court is not required to submit to the jury any particular count of a multiple count information if the people consent that it not be submitted.

7. Every count not submitted to the jury is deemed to have been dismissed by the court. Where the court, over objection of the people, refuses to submit a count which is consecutive as to every count actually submitted, such count is deemed to have been dismissed by a trial order of dismissal even though no such order was expressly made by the court.

HISTORY: Add, L 1970, ch 996, § 1, eff Sept 1, 1971.

§ 360.55. Deliberation and verdict of jury

The provisions of article three hundred ten, governing the deliberation and verdict of a jury upon a jury trial of an indictment in a superior court, are applicable to a jury trial of an information in a local criminal court.

HISTORY: Add, L 1970, ch 996, § 1, eff Sept 1, 1971.

ARTICLE 370   PROCEEDINGS FROM VERDICT TO SENTENCE

§ 370.10.   **Proceedings from verdict to sentence**
§ 370.15.   **Procedure for determining whether certain misdemeanor crimes are crimes of domestic violence for purposes of federal law**

HISTORY: Add, L 1970, ch 996, § 1, eff Sept 1, 1971.

§ 370.10. Proceedings from verdict to sentence

The provisions of article three hundred thirty, governing the proceedings from verdict to sentence in an action prosecuted by indictment in a superior court, are applicable to a prosecution by information in a local criminal court; provided, however, where a judicial hearing officer has conducted the trial pursuant to section 350.20 of this chapter, all references to a court therein shall be deemed references to such judicial hearing officer.

HISTORY: Add, L 1970, ch 996, § 1; amd, L 1983, ch 840, § 12, eff April 1, 1983.

§ 370.15. Procedure for determining whether certain misdemeanor crimes are crimes of domestic violence for purposes of federal law

1. When a defendant has been charged with assault or attempted assault in the third degree as defined in sections 120.00 and 110.00 of the penal law, menacing or attempted menacing in the second degree as defined in sections 120.14 and 110.00 of the penal law, criminal obstruction of breathing or blood circulation or attempted criminal obstruction of breathing or blood circulation as defined in sections 121.11 and 110.00 of the penal law, or forcible touching or attempted forcible touching as defined in sections 130.52 and 110.00 of the penal law, the people may, at arraignment or no later than forty-five days after arraignment, for the purpose of notification to the division of criminal justice services pursuant to section 380.97 of this part, serve on the defendant and file with the court a notice alleging that the defendant is related or situated to the victim of the crime in the manner specified in 18 U.S.C. 921(a)(33)(A)(ii).

1. Such notice shall include the name of the person alleged to be the victim of such crime and shall specify the nature of the alleged relationship as set forth in 18 U.S.C. 921(a)(33)(A)(ii). Upon conviction of such offense, the court shall advise the defendant that he or she is entitled to a hearing on the allegation contained in the notice and, if necessary, an adjournment of the sentencing proceeding in order to prepare for such hearing, and that if such allegation is sustained, that determination and conviction will be reported to the division of criminal justice services.

3. After having been advised by the court as provided in subdivision two of this section, the defendant may stipulate or admit, orally on the record or in writing, that he or she is related or situated to the victim of such crime in the manner described in subdivision one of this section. In such case, such relationship shall be deemed established for purposes of section 380.97 of this part. If the defendant denies that he or she is related or situated to the victim of the crime as alleged in the notice served by the people, or stands mute with respect to such allegation, then the people shall bear the burden to prove beyond a reasonable doubt that the defendant is related or situated to the victim in the manner alleged in the notice. The court may consider reliable hearsay evidence submitted by either party provided that it is relevant to the determination of the allegation. Facts previously proven at trial or elicited at the time of entry of a plea of guilty shall be deemed established beyond a reasonable doubt and shall not be relitigated. At the conclusion of the hearing, or upon such a stipulation or admission, as applicable, the court shall make a specific written determination with respect to such allegation.

HISTORY: Add, L 2011, ch 258, § 1, eff Nov 29, 2011

TITLE L   Sentence

ARTICLE 380
SENTENCING IN GENERAL

ARTICLE 390
PRE-SENTENCE REPORTS

ARTICLE 400
PRE-SENTENCE PROCEEDINGS

ARTICLE 410
[UNTIL SEPT 1, 2015] SENTENCES OF PROBATION, CONDITIONAL DISCHARGE AND PAROLE SUPERVISION
[EFF SEPT 1, 2015] SENTENCES OF PROBATION AND CONDITIONAL DISCHARGE

ARTICLE 420 FINES, RESTITUTION AND REPARATION

ARTICLE 430 SENTENCES OF IMPRISONMENT

HISTORY: Add, L 1970, ch 996, § 1, eff Sept 1, 1971.

ARTICLE 380   SENTENCING IN GENERAL

HISTORY: Add, L 1970, ch 996, § 1, eff Sept 1, 1971.

§ 380.10. Applicability

1. In general. The procedure prescribed by this title applies to sentencing for every offense, whether defined within or outside of the penal law; provided, however, where a judicial hearing officer has conducted the trial pursuant to section 350.20 of this chapter, all references to a court herein shall be deemed references to such judicial hearing officer.

2. Exception. Whenever a different or inconsistent procedure is provided by any other law in

---

* There are two sections 380.95.

relation to sentencing for a non-criminal offense defined therein, such different or inconsistent procedure applies thereto.

> **HISTORY:** Add, L 1970, ch 996, § 1, eff Sept 1, 1971. Sub 1, amd, L 1983, ch 840, § 13, eff April 1, 1983.

§ 380.20. Sentence required

The court must pronounce sentence in every case where a conviction is entered. If an accusatory instrument contains multiple counts and a conviction is entered on more than one count the court must pronounce sentence on each count.

> **HISTORY:** Add, L 1970, ch 996, § 1, eff Sept 1, 1971.

§ 380.30. Time for pronouncing sentence

1. In general. Sentence must be pronounced without unreasonable delay.

2. Court to fix time. Upon entering a conviction the court must:

(a) Fix a date for pronouncing sentence; or

(b) Fix a date for one of the pre-sentence proceedings specified in article four hundred; or

(c) Pronounce sentence on the date the conviction is entered in accordance with the provisions of subdivision three.

3. Sentence on date of conviction. The court may sentence the defendant at the time the conviction is entered if:

(a) A pre-sentence report or a fingerprint report is not required; or

(b) Where any such report is required, the report has been received.

Provided, however, that the court may not pronounce sentence at such time without inquiring as to whether an adjournment is desired by the defendant. Where an adjournment is requested, the defendant must state the purpose thereof and the court may, in its discretion, allow a reasonable time.

4. Time for pre-sentence proceedings. The court may conduct one or more of the pre-sentence proceedings specified in article four hundred at any time before sentence is pronounced. Notice of any such proceeding issued after the date for pronouncing sentence has been fixed automatically adjourns the date for pronouncing sentence. In such case the court must fix a date for pronouncing sentence at the conclusion of such proceeding.

> **HISTORY:** Add, L 1970, ch 996, § 1, eff Sept 1, 1971. Sub 2, amd, L 1992, ch 55, § 282, eff April 10, 1992, expired March 31, 1994. Sub 2, par (c), add, L 1992, ch 55, § 282, eff April 10, 1992, expired March 31, 1994. Former sub 2, par (c), redesignated sub 2, par (d), L 1992, ch 55, § 282, eff April 10, 1992. Sub 2, par (d), formerly sub 2, par (c), so designated, L 1992, ch 55, § 282, eff April 10, 1992, expired March 31, 1994. Sub 3, add, L 1992, ch 55, § 283, eff April 10, 1992, expired March 31, 1994. Former sub 3, renumbered sub 4, L 1992, ch 55, § 283, eff April 10, 1992. Sub 4, formerly sub 3, renumbered sub 4, L 1992, ch 55, § 283, eff April 10, 1992, expired March 31, 1994. Former sub 4, renumbered sub 5, L 1992, ch 55, § 283, eff April 10, 1992. Sub 5, formerly sub 4, renumbered sub 5, L 1992, ch 55, § 283, eff April 10, 1992, expired March 31, 1994.

§ 380.40. Defendant's presence at sentencing

1. In general. The defendant must be personally present at the time sentence is pronounced.

2. Exception. Where sentence is to be pronounced for a misdemeanor or for a petty offense, the court may, on motion of the defendant, dispense with the requirement that the defendant be

personally present. Any such motion must be accompanied by a waiver, signed and acknowledged by the defendant, reciting the maximum sentence that may be imposed for the offense and stating that the defendant waives the right to be personally present at the time sentence is pronounced.

3. Corporations. Sentence may be pronounced against a corporation in the absence of counsel if counsel fails to appear on the date of sentence after reasonable notice thereof.

HISTORY: Add, L 1970, ch 996, § 1, eff Sept 1, 1971, with substance derived from Crim C § 473.

§ 380.50. Statements at time of sentence

1. At the time of pronouncing sentence, the court must accord the prosecutor an opportunity to make a statement with respect to any matter relevant to the question of sentence. The court must then accord counsel for the defendant an opportunity to speak on behalf of the defendant. The defendant also has the right to make a statement personally in his or her own behalf, and before pronouncing sentence the court must ask the defendant whether he or she wishes to make such a statement.

2. (a) For purposes of this section "victim" shall mean:

(1) the victim as indicated in the accusatory instrument; or

(2) if such victim is unable or unwilling to express himself or herself before the court or a person so mentally or physically disabled as to make it impracticable to appear in court in person or the victim is deceased, a member of the family of such victim, or the legal guardian or representative of the legal guardian of the victim where such guardian or representative has personal knowledge of and a relationship with the victim, unless the court finds that it would be inappropriate for such person to make a statement on behalf of the victim.

(b) If the defendant is being sentenced for a felony the court, if requested at least ten days prior to the sentencing date, shall accord the victim the right to make a statement with regard to any matter relevant to the question of sentence. The court shall notify the defendant no less than seven days prior to sentencing of the victim's intent to make a statement at sentencing. If the defendant does not receive timely notice pursuant to this subdivision, the defendant may request a reasonable adjournment.

(c) Any statement by the victim must precede any statement by counsel to the defendant or the defendant made pursuant to subdivision one of this section. The defendant shall have the right to rebut any statement made by the victim.

(d) Where the people and the defendant have agreed to a disposition which includes a sentence acceptable to the court, and the court intends to impose such sentence, any rebuttal by the defendant shall be limited to an oral presentation made at the time of sentencing.

(e) Where (1) the defendant has been found guilty after trial or there is no agreement between the people and the defendant as to a proposed sentence or the court, after the statement by the victim, chooses not to impose the proposed sentence agreed to by the parties; (2) the statement by the victim includes allegations about the crime that were not fully explored during the proceedings or that materially vary from or contradict the evidence at trial; and (3) the court determines that the allegations are relevant to the issue of sentencing, then the court shall afford the defendant the following rights:

(A) a reasonable adjournment of the sentencing to allow the defendant to present information to rebut the allegations by the victim; and

(B) allow the defendant to present written questions to the court that the defendant desires the court to put to the victim. The court may, in its discretion, decline to put any or all of the questions to the victim. Where the court declines to put any or all of the questions to the victim it shall state its reasons therefor on the record.

(f) If the victim does not appear to make a statement at the time of sentencing, the right to make a statement is waived. The failure of the victim to make a statement shall not be cause for delaying the proceedings against the defendant nor shall it affect the validity of a conviction, judgment or order.

3. The court may, either before or after receiving such statements, summarize the factors it considers relevant for the purpose of sentence and afford an opportunity to the defendant or his or her counsel to comment thereon.

4. Regardless of whether the victim requests to make a statement with regard to the defendant's sentence, where the defendant is committed to the custody of the department of corrections and community supervision upon a sentence of imprisonment for conviction of a violent felony offense as defined in section 70.02 of the penal law or a felony defined in article one hundred twenty-five of such law, or a sex offense as defined in subdivision (p) of section 10.03 of the mental hygiene law, within sixty days of the imposition of sentence the prosecutor shall provide the victim with a form, prepared and distributed by the commissioner of the department of corrections and community supervision, on which the victim may indicate a demand to be informed of the escape, absconding, discharge, parole, conditional release, release to post-release supervision, transfer to the custody of the office of mental health pursuant to article ten of the mental hygiene law, or release from confinement under article ten of the mental hygiene law of the person so imprisoned. If the victim submits a completed form to the prosecutor, it shall be the duty of the prosecutor to mail promptly such form to the department of corrections and community supervision.

5. Following the receipt of such form from the prosecutor, it shall be the duty of the department of corrections and community supervision or, where the person is committed to the custody of the office of mental health, at the time such person is discharged, paroled, conditionally released, released to post-release supervision, or released from confinement under article ten of the mental hygiene law, to notify the victim of such occurrence by certified mail directed to the address provided by the victim. In the event such person escapes or absconds from a facility under the jurisdiction of the department of corrections and community supervision, it shall be the duty of such department to notify immediately the victim of such occurrence at the most current address or telephone number provided by the victim in the most reasonable and expedient possible manner. In the event such escapee or absconder is subsequently taken into custody by the department of corrections and community supervision, it shall be the duty of such department to notify the victim of such occurrence by certified mail directed to the address provided by the victim within forty-eight hours of regaining such custody. In the case of a person who escapes or absconds from confinement under article ten of the mental hygiene law, the office of mental health shall notify the victim or victims in accordance with the procedures set forth in subdivision (g) of section 10.10 of the mental hygiene law. In no case shall the state be held liable for failure to provide any notice required by this subdivision.

6. Regardless of whether the victim requests to make a statement with regard to the defendant's sentence, where the defendant is sentenced for a violent felony offense as defined in section 70.02 of the penal law or a felony defined in article one hundred twenty-five of such law or any of the following provisions of such law sections 130.25, 130.30, 130.40, 130.45, 255.25, 255.26, 255.27, article two hundred sixty-three, 135.10, 135.25, 230.05, 230.06, subdivision two of section 230.30 or 230.32, the prosecutor shall, within sixty days of the imposition of sentence, provide the victim

with a form on which the victim may indicate a demand to be informed of any petition to change the name of such defendant. Such forms shall be maintained by such prosecutor. Upon receipt of a notice of a petition to change the name of any such defendant, pursuant to subdivision two of section sixty-two of the civil rights law, the prosecutor shall promptly notify the victim at the most current address or telephone number provided by such victim in the most reasonable and expedient possible manner of the time and place such petition will be presented to the court.

> **HISTORY:** Add, L 1970, ch 996, § 1, eff Sept 1, 1971; amd, L 1992, ch 307, § 1, eff Aug 16, 1992, L 1993, ch 499, § 1, eff Aug 25, 1993, L 1996, ch 173, § 1, eff July 18, 1996, L 1996, ch 198, § 1, eff July 25, 1996, L 1998, ch 1, § 41, eff Aug 6, 1998, L 2000, ch 549, § 5, eff Jan 24, 2001, L 2006, ch 320, § 18, eff Nov 1, 2006, L 2007, ch 7, § 12, eff April 13, 2007, L 2011, ch 62, § 75 (Part C, Subpart B), eff March 31, 2011.

§ 380.60. Authority for the execution of sentence

Except where a sentence of death is pronounced, a sentence and commitment or certificate of conviction showing the sentence pronounced by the court, or a certified copy thereof, constitutes the authority for execution of the sentence and serves as the order of commitment, and no other warrant, order of commitment or authority is necessary to justify or to require execution of the sentence.

> **HISTORY:** Add, L 1970, ch 996, § 1, eff Sept 1, 1971; amd, L 2011, ch 177, § 1, eff Sept 1, 2011.

§ 380.65. Sentence and commitment and order of protection to accompany defendant sentenced to imprisonment

A sentence and commitment or certificate of conviction, specifying the section, and to the extent applicable, the subdivision, paragraph and subparagraph of the penal law or other statute under which the defendant was convicted, or a certified copy thereof, and a copy of any order of protection or temporary order of protection issued against the defendant at the time of sentencing, must be delivered to the person in charge of the correctional facility or office of children and family services facility to which the defendant is committed at the time the defendant is delivered thereto. A sentence and commitment or certificate of conviction is not defective by reason of a failure to comply with the provisions of this section.

> **HISTORY:** Add, L 2011, ch 177, § 2, eff Sept 1, 2011.

§ 380.70. Minutes of sentence

[Until Sept 1, 2015] In any case where a person receives an indeterminate or determinate sentence of imprisonment, a certified copy of the stenographic minutes of the sentencing proceeding must be delivered by the court to the person in charge of the institution to which the defendant has been delivered within thirty days from the date such sentence was imposed.

[Eff Sept 1, 2015] In any case where a person receives an indeterminate sentence of imprisonment or a reformatory or alternative local reformatory sentence of imprisonment, a certified copy of the stenographic minutes of the sentencing proceeding must be delivered by the court to the person in charge of the institution to which the defendant has been delivered within thirty days from the date such sentence was imposed.

> **HISTORY:** First setout of section, add, L 1970, ch 996, § 1; amd, L 1995, ch 3, § 31, eff Oct 1, 1995, repealed Sept 1, 2015, L 2008, ch 56, § (Part D)3, eff April 23, 2008, L 2008, ch 141, § 1, eff June 30, 2008, L 2011, ch 177, § 3, eff Sept 1, 2011. Second setout of section, add, L 1970, ch 996, § 1; amd, L 2008, ch 56, § 4 (Part D), eff Sept 1, 2015, L 2008, ch 141, § 1-a, eff Sept 1, 2015, L 2011, ch 177, § 4, eff Sept 1, 2011.

§ 380.80. Reporting sentence to social services

Whenever a person receives a sentence of imprisonment, the court that has sentenced such person shall deliver the certificate of conviction and provide notification of the sentence imposed to the commissioner of social services who, in turn, shall deliver the certificate of conviction and provide notification of the sentence imposed to the appropriate local commissioner of social services.

> **HISTORY:** Add, L 1996, ch 700, § 2, eff Jan 7, 1997.

§ 380.85. Reporting sentences to office of professional medical conduct; licensed physician, physician assistant, or specialist assistant

Whenever a person who is a licensed physician, physician assistant, or specialist assistant or a physician who is practicing under a limited permit or as a medical resident is sentenced for a crime, the court that has sentenced such person shall deliver a copy of the certificate of conviction and provide notification of the conviction and sentence to the office of professional medical conduct.

> **HISTORY:** Add, L 2008, ch 477, § 26, eff Nov 3, 2008.

§ 380.90. Reporting sentences to schools

1. "Designated educational official" shall mean (a) an employee or representative of a school district who is designated by the school district or (b) an employee or representative of a charter school or private elementary or secondary school who is designated by such school to receive records pursuant to this section and to coordinate the student's participation in programs which may exist in the school district or community, including: non-violent conflict resolution programs, peer mediation programs and youth courts, extended day programs and other school violence prevention and intervention programs.

2. Whenever a person under the age of nineteen who is enrolled as a student in a public or private elementary or secondary school is sentenced for a crime, the court that has sentenced such person shall provide notification of the conviction and sentence to the designated educational official of the school in which such person is enrolled as a student. Such notification shall be used by the designated educational official only for purposes related to the execution of the student's educational plan, where applicable, successful school adjustment and reentry into the community. Such notification shall be kept separate and apart from such student's school records and shall be accessible only by the designated educational official. Such notification shall not be part of such student's permanent school record and shall not be appended to or included in any documentation regarding such student and shall be destroyed at such time as such student is no longer enrolled in the school district. At no time shall such notification be used for any purpose other than those specified in this subdivision.

> **HISTORY:** Add, L 2000, ch 181, § 14, eff Nov 1, 2000. Sub 1, amd, L 2001, ch 380, § 7, eff Oct 23, 2001, deemed eff on and after Nov 1, 2000.

§ 380.95. Reporting convictions of certain school employees[*]

Upon conviction of a teacher, as defined in subparagraph three of paragraph b of subdivision seven-a of section three hundred five of the education law, of a sex offense or sex offenses defined in subparagraph two of paragraph b of subdivision seven-a of section three hundred five of the education law, the district attorney or other prosecuting authority who obtained such conviction shall provide notice of such conviction to the commissioner of education identifying the sex offense or sex offenses of which the teacher has been convicted, the name and address of such offender and other identifying information prescribed by the commissioner of education, including the offender's date of birth and social security number, to the extent consistent with federal and

---

[*] There are two sections 380.95.

state laws governing personal privacy and confidentiality of information. Such district attorney or other prosecuting authority shall include in such notice the name and business address of the offender's counsel of record in the criminal proceeding.

   HISTORY: Add, L 2008, ch 296, § 3, eff July 21, 2008.

§ 380.95. Reporting convictions of certain school employees*

   Upon conviction of a school administrator or supervisor, as defined in subparagraph three of paragraph b of subdivision seven-b of section three hundred five of the education law, of an offense defined in subparagraph two of paragraph b of subdivision seven-b of section three hundred five of the education law, the district attorney or other prosecuting authority who obtained such conviction shall provide notice of such conviction to the commissioner of education identifying the offense of which the school administrator or supervisor has been convicted, the name and address of such offender and other identifying information prescribed by the commissioner of education, including the offender's date of birth and social security number, to the extent consistent with federal and state laws governing personal privacy and confidentiality of information. Such district attorney or other prosecuting authority shall include in such notice the name and business address of the offender's counsel of record in the criminal proceeding.

   HISTORY: Add, L 2008, ch 325, § 3, eff July 21, 2008.

§ 380.96. Obligation of sentencing court pursuant to article four hundred of the penal law

   Upon judgment of conviction of any offense which would require the seizure of firearms, shotguns or rifles from an individual so convicted, and the revocation of any license or registration issued pursuant to article four hundred of the penal law, the judge pronouncing sentence shall demand surrender of any such license or registration and all firearms, shotguns and rifles. The failure to so demand surrender shall not effect the validity of any revocation pursuant to article four hundred of the penal law.

   HISTORY: Add, L 2013, ch 1, § 2, eff March 16, 2013.

§ 380.97. Notification to division of criminal justice services of determinations in certain misdemeanor cases

   Upon judgment of conviction of assault or attempted assault in the third degree, as defined in sections 120.00 and 110.00 of the penal law, menacing or attempted menacing in the second degree, as defined in section 120.14 and 110.00 of the penal law, criminal obstruction of breathing or blood circulation or attempted criminal obstruction of breathing or blood circulation, as defined in sections 121.11 and 110.00 of the penal law, forcible touching or attempted forcible touching, as defined in sections 130.52 and 110.00 of the penal law, when the defendant has been determined, pursuant to section 370.15 of this part, to be related or situated to the victim of the offense in the manner specified in 18 U.S.C. 921(a)(33)(A)(ii), the clerk of the court shall include notification and a copy of the written determination in a report of such conviction to the division of criminal justice services to enable the division to report such determination to the federal bureau of investigation and assist the bureau in identifying persons prohibited from purchasing and possessing a firearm pursuant to the provisions of 18 U.S.C. 922.

   HISTORY: Add, L 2011, ch 258, § 2, eff Nov 29, 2011

ARTICLE 390   PRE-SENTENCE REPORTS

---

* There are two sections 380.95.

HISTORY: Add, L 1970, ch 996, § 1, eff Sept 1, 1971.

§ 390.10. Requirement of fingerprint report

In any case where the defendant is convicted of an offense specified in subdivision one of section 160.10, the court may not pronounce sentence until it has received a fingerprint report from the division of criminal justice services or a police department report with respect to the defendant's prior arrest record. For such purpose, the court may use the original fingerprint report obtained after the arrest or arraignment of the defendant, or it may direct that a new report be prepared and transmitted to it.

HISTORY: Add, L 1970, ch 996, § 1; amd, L 1971, ch 762, § 11, L 1972, ch 399, § 21, eff Sept 1, 1972.

§ 390.15. Requirement of HIV related testing in certain cases

1. (a) In any case where the defendant is convicted of a felony offense enumerated in any section of article one hundred thirty of the penal law, or any subdivision of section 130.20 of such law, where an act of "sexual intercourse", "oral sexual conduct" or "anal sexual conduct," as those terms are defined in section 130.00 of the penal law, is required as an essential element for the commission thereof, the court must, upon a request of the victim, order that the defendant submit to human immunodeficiency (HIV) related testing. The testing is to be conducted by a state, county, or local public health officer designated by the order. Test results, which shall not be disclosed to the court, shall be communicated to the defendant and the victim named in the order in accordance with the provisions of section twenty-seven hundred eighty-five-a of the public health law, but such results and disclosure need not be completed prior to the imposition of sentence.

(b) For the purposes of this section, the terms "defendant", "conviction" and "sentence" mean and include, respectively, an "eligible youth," a "youthful offender finding" and a "youthful offender sentence" as those terms are defined in section 720.10 of this chapter. The term "victim" means the person with whom the defendant engaged in an act of "sexual intercourse", "oral sexual conduct" or "anal sexual conduct", as those terms are defined in section 130.00 of the penal law, where such conduct with such victim was the basis for the defendant's conviction of an offense specified in paragraph (a) of this subdivision.

2. Any request made by the victim pursuant to this section must be in writing, filed with the court and provided by the court to the defendant or his or her counsel. The request must be filed with the court prior to or within ten days after entry of the defendant's conviction; provided that, for good cause shown, the court may permit such request to be filed at any time before sentence is imposed.

3. Any requests, related papers and orders made or filed pursuant to this section, together with any papers or proceedings related thereto, shall be sealed by the court and not made available for any purpose, except as may be necessary for the conduct of judicial proceedings directly related to the provisions of this section. All proceedings on such requests shall be held in camera.

4. The application for an order to compel a convicted person to undergo an HIV related test may be made by the victim but, if the victim is an infant or incompetent person, the application may

also be made by a representative as defined in section twelve hundred one of the civil practice law and rules. The application must state that (a) the applicant was the victim of the offense enumerated in paragraph (a) of subdivision one of this section of which the defendant stands convicted; and (b) the applicant has been offered counseling by a public health officer and been advised of (i) the limitations on the information to be obtained through an HIV test on the proposed subject; (ii) current scientific assessments of the risk of transmission of HIV from the exposure he or she may have experienced, and (iii) the need for the applicant to undergo HIV related testing to definitively determine his or her HIV status.

5. The court shall conduct a hearing only if necessary to determine if the applicant is the victim of the offense of which the defendant was convicted. The court ordered test must be performed within fifteen days of the date on which the court ordered the test, provided, however, that whenever the defendant is not tested within the period prescribed by the court, the court must again order that the defendant undergo an HIV related test.

6. (a) Test results shall be disclosed subject to the following limitations, which shall be specified in any order issued pursuant to this section:

(i) disclosure of confidential HIV related information shall be limited to that information which is necessary to fulfill the purpose for which the order is granted;

(ii) disclosure of confidential HIV related information shall be limited to the person making the application; redisclosure shall be permitted only to the victim, the victim's immediate family, guardian, physicians, attorneys, medical or mental health providers and to his or her past and future contacts to whom there was or is a reasonable risk of HIV transmission and shall not be permitted to any other person or the court.

(b) Unless inconsistent with this section, the court's order shall direct compliance with and conform to the provisions of article twenty-seven-F of the public health law. Such order shall include measures to protect against disclosure to others of the identity and HIV status of the applicant and of the person tested and may include such other measures as the court deems necessary to protect confidential information.

7. Any failure to comply with the provisions of this section or section twenty-seven hundred eighty-five-a of the public health law shall not impair or affect the validity of any sentence imposed by the court.

8. No information obtained as a result of a consent, hearing or court order for testing issued pursuant to this section nor any information derived therefrom may be used as evidence in any criminal or civil proceeding against the defendant which relates to events that were the basis for the defendant's conviction, provided however that nothing herein shall prevent prosecution of a witness testifying in any court hearing held pursuant to this section for perjury pursuant to article two hundred ten of the penal law.

HISTORY: Add, L 1995, ch 76, § 1, eff Aug 1, 1995. Sub 1, par (a), amd, L 2003, ch 264, § 44, eff Nov 1, 2003. Sub 1, par (b), amd, L 2003, ch 264, § 44, eff Nov 1, 2003.

§ 390.20. Requirement of pre-sentence report

1. Requirement for felonies. In any case where a person is convicted of a felony, the court must order a pre-sentence investigation of the defendant and it may not pronounce sentence until it has received a written report of such investigation.

2. Requirement for misdemeanors. Where a person is convicted of a misdemeanor a pre-sentence report is not required, but the court may not pronounce any of the following sentences

unless it has ordered a pre-sentence investigation of the defendant and has received a written report thereof:

    (a) A sentence of probation except where the provisions of subparagraph (ii) of paragraph (a) of subdivision four of this section apply;

    (b) A sentence of imprisonment for a term in excess of one hundred eighty days;

    (c) Consecutive sentences of imprisonment with terms aggregating more than ninety days.

3. Permissible in any case. For purposes of sentence, the court may, in its discretion, order a pre-sentence investigation and report in any case, irrespective of whether such investigation and report is required by subdivision one or two.

4. Waiver.

    (a) Notwithstanding the provisions of subdivision one or two of this section, a pre-sentence investigation of the defendant and a written report thereon may be waived by the mutual consent of the parties and with consent of the judge, stated on the record or in writing, whenever:

    (i) A sentence of imprisonment has been agreed upon by the parties and will be satisfied by the time served, or

    (ii) A sentence of probation has been agreed upon by the parties and will be imposed, or

    (iii) A report has been prepared in the preceding twelve months, or

    (iv) A sentence of probation is revoked.

[Until Sept 1, 2015] Provided, however, a pre-sentence investigation of the defendant and a written report thereon shall not be waived if an indeterminate or determinate sentence of imprisonment is to be imposed.

[Eff Sept 1, 2015] Provided, however, a pre-sentence investigation of the defendant and a written report thereon shall not be waived if an indeterminate sentence of imprisonment is to be imposed.

    (b) Whenever a pre-sentence investigation and report has been waived pursuant to subparagraph (i), (ii) or (iii) of paragraph (a) of this subdivision and the court determines that such information would be relevant to the court disposition, a victim impact statement shall be provided in accordance with this section.

5. Negotiated sentence of imprisonment. In any city having a population of one million or more and notwithstanding the provisions of subdivision one or two of this section, a pre-sentence investigation and written report thereon shall not be required where a negotiated sentence of imprisonment for a term of three hundred sixty-five days or less has been mutually agreed upon by the parties with consent of the judge, as a result of a conviction or revocation of a sentence of probation.

    HISTORY: Add, L 1970, ch 996, § 1; amd, L 1974, ch 652, § 9, L 1991, ch 413, §§ 78, 79, L 1995, ch 3, § 32, repealed eff Sept 1, 2015; amd, L 2010, ch 179,§ 1, eff July 15, 2010, L 2013, ch 556, § 6, eff April 10, 2014.

§ 390.30. Scope of pre-sentence investigation and report

1. The investigation. The pre-sentence investigation consists of the gathering of information with respect to the circumstances attending the commission of the offense, the defendant's history

of delinquency or criminality, and the defendant's social history, employment history, family situation, economic status, education, and personal habits. Such investigation may also include any other matter which the agency conducting the investigation deems relevant to the question of sentence, and must include any matter the court directs to be included.

2. Physical and mental examinations. Whenever information is available with respect to the defendant's physical and mental condition, the pre-sentence investigation must include the gathering of such information. In the case of a felony or a class A misdemeanor, or in any case where a person under the age of twenty-one is convicted of a crime, the court may order that the defendant undergo a thorough physical or mental examination in a designated facility and may further order that the defendant remain in such facility for such purpose for a period not exceeding thirty days.

3. The report and victim impact statement.

(a) The report of the pre-sentence investigation must contain an analysis of as much of the information gathered in the investigation as the agency that conducted the investigation deems relevant to the question of sentence. The report must also include any other imformation [information]* that the court directs to be included and the material required by paragraph (b) of this subdivision which shall be considered part of the report.

(b) The report shall also contain a victim impact statement, unless it appears that such information would be of no relevance to the recommendation or court disposition, which shall include an analysis of the victim's version of the offense, the extent of injury or economic loss and the actual out-of-pocket loss to the victim and the views of the victim relating to disposition including the amount of restitution and reparation sought by the victim after the victim has been informed of the right to seek restitution and reparation, subject to the availability of such information. In the case of a homicide or where the victim is unable to assist in the preparation of the victim impact statement, the information may be acquired from the victim's family. The victim impact statement shall be made available to the victim by the prosecutor pursuant to subdivision two of section 390.50 of this article. Nothing contained in this section shall be interpreted to require that a victim supply information for the preparation of this report.

4. In lieu of the procedure set forth in subdivisions one, two and three of this section, where the conviction is of a misdemeanor the scope of the pre-sentence investigation may be abbreviated and a short form report may be made. The use of abbreviated investigations and short form reports, the matters to be covered therein and the form of the reports shall be in accordance with the general rules regulating methods and procedures in the administration of probation as adopted from time to time by the commissioner of the division of criminal justice services pursuant to the provisions of article twelve of the executive law. No such rule, however, shall be construed so as to relieve the agency conducting the investigation of the duty of investigating and reporting upon:

(a) the extent of the injury or economic loss and the actual out-of-pocket loss to the victim including the amount of restitution and reparation sought by the victim, after the victim has been informed of the right to seek restitution and reparation, or

(b) any matter relevant to the question of sentence that the court directs to be included in particular cases.

5. [As amended, L 2010, ch 56, § 50 (Part A)] Information to be forwarded to the office of

---

* The bracketed word has been inserted by the Publisher.

CPL

probation and correctional alternatives. Investigating agencies under this article shall be responsible for the collection, and transmission to the office of probation and correctional alternatives, of data on the number of victim impact statements prepared, pursuant to regulations of the office. Such information shall be transmitted to the office of victim services and included in the office's annual report pursuant to subdivision twenty of section six hundred twenty-three of the executive law.

5. [As amended, L 2010, ch 56, § 29 (Part A-1)] Information to be forwarded to the state division of probation and correctional alternatives. Investigating agencies under this article shall be responsible for the collection, and transmission to the state division of probation and correctional alternatives, of data on the number of victim impact statements prepared. Such information shall be transmitted annually to the office of victim services and included in the office's annual report pursuant to subdivision twenty of section six hundred twenty-three of the executive law.

6. [As amended L 2009, ch 56, § 1 (Part O) and § 5 (Part AAA)] Interim probation supervision.

(a) In any case where the court determines that a defendant is eligible for a sentence of probation, the court, after consultation with the prosecutor and upon the consent of the defendant, may adjourn the sentencing to a specified date and order that the defendant be placed on interim probation supervision. In no event may the sentencing be adjourned for a period exceeding one year from the date the conviction is entered, except that upon good cause shown, the court may, upon the defendant's consent, extend the period for an additional one year where the defendant has agreed to and is still participating in a substance abuse treatment program in connection with a court designated a drug court by the chief administrator of the courts. When ordering that the defendant be placed on interim probation supervision, the court shall impose all of the conditions relating to supervision specified in subdivision three of section 65.10 of the penal law and the court may impose any or all of the conditions relating to conduct and rehabilitation specified in subdivisions two, four, five and five-a of section 65.10 of such law. The defendant must receive a written copy of any such conditions at the time he or she is placed on interim probation supervision. The defendant's record of compliance with such conditions, as well as any other relevant information, shall be included in the presentence report, or updated presentence report, prepared pursuant to this section, and the court must consider such record and information when pronouncing sentence. If a defendant satisfactorily completes a term of interim probation supervision, he or she shall receive credit for the time served under the period of interim probation supervision toward any probation sentence that is subsequently imposed in that case.

(b) In its discretion, the supervising probation department may utilize the provisions of sections 410.20, 410.30, 410.40, 410.50, 410.60 and 410.92 of this title, where applicable.

HISTORY: Add, L 1970, ch 996, § 1, eff Sept 1, 1971; amd, L 1971, ch 450, § 1, L 1982, ch 612, § 2, L 1985, ch 14, §§ 2, 3, eff Nov 1, 1985, L 1985, ch 134, § 26, eff April 1, 1985L 1991, ch 530, § 1, L 1992, ch 618, §§ 3, 4, eff Nov 1, 1992, L 1998, ch 159, § 1, eff Oct 5, 1998, L 1999, ch 216, § 1, eff Oct 4, 1999, L 2009, ch 56, § 1 (Part O), eff June 6, 2009, L 2009, ch 56, § 5 (Part AAA), eff April 7, 2009, L 2010, ch 56, § 50 (Part A), eff June 22, 2010, L 2010, ch 56, § 29 (Part A-1), eff June 22, 2010.

§ 390.40. Defendant's or prosecutor's pre-sentence memorandum

1. Either the defendant or prosecutor may, at any time prior to the pronouncement of sentence, file with the court a written memorandum setting forth any information he may deem pertinent to the question of sentence. Such memorandum may include information with respect to any of the matters described in section 390.30. The defendant may annex written statements by others in support of facts alleged in the memorandum.

2. The memorandum of the prosecutor shall be served on the defendant's attorney at least ten days prior to the date fixed for sentence.

3. The act of seeking health care for someone who is experiencing a drug or alcohol overdose or other life threatening medical emergency shall be considered by the court when presented as a mitigating factor in any criminal prosecution for a controlled substance, marihuana, drug paraphernalia, or alcohol related offense.

> **HISTORY:** Add, L 1970, ch 996, § 1, eff Sept 1, 1971; amd, L 1984, ch 263, § 1, eff Nov 1, 1984, L 2011, ch 154, § 3, eff Sept 18, 2011.

§ 390.50. Confidentiality of pre-sentence reports and memoranda

1. In general. Any pre-sentence report or memorandum submitted to the court pursuant to this article and any medical, psychiatric or social agency report or other information gathered for the court by a probation department, or submitted directly to the court, in connection with the question of sentence is confidential and may not be made available to any person or public or private agency except where specifically required or permitted by statute or upon specific authorization of the court. For purposes of this section, any report, memorandum or other information forwarded to a probation department within this state from a probation agency outside this state is governed by the same rules of confidentiality. Any person, public or private agency receiving such material must retain it under the same conditions of confidentiality as apply to the probation department that made it available.

2. Pre-sentence report; disclosure, victim access to impact statements; general principles.

(a) Not less than one court day prior to sentencing, unless such time requirement is waived by the parties, the pre-sentence report or memorandum shall be made available by the court for examination and for copying by the defendant's attorney, the defendant himself, if he has no attorney, and the prosecutor. In its discretion, the court may except from disclosure a part or parts of the report or memoranda which are not relevant to a proper sentence, or a diagnostic opinion which might seriously disrupt a program of rehabilitation, or sources of information which have been obtained on a promise of confidentiality, or any other portion thereof, disclosure of which would not be in the interest of justice. In all cases where a part or parts of the report or memoranda are not disclosed, the court shall state for the record that a part or parts of the report or memoranda have been excepted and the reasons for its action. The action of the court excepting information from disclosure shall be subject to appellate review. The pre-sentence report shall be made available by the court for examination and copying in connection with any appeal in the case, including an appeal under this subdivision. Upon written request, the court shall make a copy of the presentence report, other than a part or parts of the report redacted by the court pursuant to this paragraph, available to the defendant for use before the parole board for release consideration or an appeal of a parole board determination. In his or her written request to the court the defendant shall affirm that he or she anticipates an appearance before the parole board or intends to file an administrative appeal of a parole board determination. The court shall respond to the defendant's written request within twenty days from receipt of the defendant's written request.

(b) The victim impact statement prepared pursuant to subdivision three of section 390.30 of this article shall be made available by the prosecutor prior to sentencing to the victim or victim's family in accordance with his responsibilities under subdivision one of section 60.27 of the penal law and sections six hundred forty-one and six hundred forty-two of the executive law. The district attorney shall also give at least twenty-one days notice to the victim or victim's family of the date of sentencing and of the rights of the victim pursuant to subdivision two of section 380.50 of this chapter, including the victim or victim's family's obligation to inform the court of its intention, at least ten days prior to the sentencing date, to make a statement at sentencing. If the victim has not received timely notice pursuant to this paragraph, the court may proceed with sentencing if it determines that the victim and the defendant have received reasonable notice or may adjourn sentencing for no more than seven days in order to afford such reasonable notice. Failure to give notice shall not affect the validity of any sentence imposed.

3. Public agencies within this state. A probation department must make available a copy of its pre-sentence report and any medical, psychiatric or social agency report submitted to it in connection with its pre-sentence investigation or its supervision of a defendant, to any court, or to the probation department of any court, within this state that subsequently has jurisdiction over such defendant for the purpose of pronouncing or reviewing sentence and to any state agency to which the defendant is subsequently committed or certified or under whose care and custody or jurisdiction the defendant subsequently is placed upon the official request of such court or agency therefor. In any such case, the court or agency receiving such material must retain it under the same conditions of confidentiality as apply to the probation department that made it available, except that an agency with jurisdiction as that term is defined in subdivision (a) of section 10.03 of the mental hygiene law shall make such material available to the commissioner of mental health, attorney general, case review panel, or psychiatric examiners described in article ten of the mental hygiene law when such persons or entities request such material in the exercise of their statutory functions, powers, and duties under article ten of the mental hygiene law.

4. Public agencies outside this state. Upon official request of any probation, parole or public institutional agency outside this state, a probation department may make any information in its files available to such agency. Any such release of information shall be conditioned upon the agreement of the receiving agency to retain it under the same conditions of confidentiality as apply to the probation department that made it available.

5. Division of criminal justice services. Nothing contained in this section may be construed to prevent the voluntary submission by a probation department of data in its files to the division of criminal justice services.

6. Professional licensing agencies. Probation departments shall provide a copy of presentence reports prepared in the case of individuals who are known to be licensed pursuant to title eight of the education law to the state department of health if the licensee is a physician, a specialist's assistant or a physician's assistant, and to the state education department with respect to all other such licensees. Such reports shall be accumulated and forwarded every three months, shall be in writing, may be submitted in a hard copy or electronically, and shall contain the following information:

(a) the name of the licensee and the profession in which licensure is held,

(b) the date of the conviction and the nature thereof,

(c) the index or other identifying file number.

In any such case, the state department receiving such material must retain it under the same conditions of confidentiality as apply to the probation department that made it available.

HISTORY: Add, L 1970, ch 996, § 1, eff Sept 1, 1971; amd, L 1975, ch 310, § 1, L 1980, ch 866, § 9, eff Jan 1, 1981, L 1981, ch 581, § 1, L 1982, ch 157, § 1, eff June 1, 1982, L 1984, ch 132, § 1, L 1985, ch 14, § 4, eff Nov 1, 1985, L 1986, ch 224, § 1, L 1986, ch 369, §§ 1, 2, eff Nov 1, 1986, L 1992, ch 307, § 2, eff Aug 16, 1992, L 2007, ch 7, § 11, eff April 13, 2007, L 2010, ch 56, § 3 (Part D), eff Sept 20, 2010, L 2010, ch 56, § 5 (Part OO), eff July 22, 2010.

§ 390.60. Copy of reports to accompany defendant sentenced to imprisonment

1. Cases where copy of report is required. Whenever a person is sentenced to a term of imprisonment, a copy of any pre-sentence report prepared, a copy of any pre-sentence memorandum filed by the defendant and a copy of any medical, psychiatric or social agency report submitted to the court or to the probation department in connection with the question of sentence must be delivered to the person in charge of the correctional or division for youth facility to which the defendant is committed at the time the defendant is delivered thereto. When a person is committed to any hospital operated by the office of mental health or referred to any program established pursuant to section four hundred one of the correction law, from a correctional facility or division for youth facility, the person in charge of the correctional facility or division for youth facility shall ensure that a copy of any pre-sentence report concerning such person, a copy of any pre-sentence memorandum filed by such person, and a copy of any medical, psychiatric or social agency report submitted to the court or to the probation department in connection with the question of sentence is provided to such hospital or program.

2. Effect of failure to deliver required report. A commitment is not void by reason of failure to comply with the provisions of subdivision one, but the person in charge of the correctional facility to which the defendant has been delivered in execution of the sentence is authorized to refuse to accept custody of such person until the required report is delivered.

HISTORY: Add, L 1970, ch 996, § 1; amd, L 1984, ch 560, § 1, eff Nov 1, 1984. Sub 1, amd, L 1984, ch 560, § 1, L 1986, ch 62, § 1, L 1995, ch 181, § 1, eff July 19, 1995.

ARTICLE 400   PRE-SENTENCE PROCEEDINGS

HISTORY: Add, L 1970, ch 996, § 1, eff Sept 1, 1971.

§ 400.10. Pre-sentence conference

1. Authorization and purpose. Before pronouncing sentence, the court, in its discretion, may hold one or more pre-sentence conferences in open court or in chambers in order to (a) resolve any discrepancies between the pre-sentence report, or other information the court has received, and the defendant's or prosecutor's pre-sentence memorandum submitted pursuant to section 390.40, or

(b) assist the court in its consideration of any matter relevant to the sentence to be pronounced.

2. Attendance. Such conference may be held with the prosecutor and defense counsel in the absence of the defendant, or the court may direct that the defendant attend. The court may also direct that any person who has furnished or who can furnish information to the court concerning sentence attend. Reasonable notice of the conference must be given to the prosecutor and the defense counsel, who must be afforded an opportunity to participate therein.

3. Procedure at conference. The court may advise the persons present at the conference of the factual contents of any report or memorandum it has received and afford any of the participants an opportunity to controvert or to comment upon any fact. The court may also conduct a summary hearing at the conference on any matter relevant to sentence and may take testimony under oath. In the discretion of the court, all or any part of the proceedings at the conference may be recorded by a court stenographer and the transcript made part of the pre-sentence report.

4. Pre-sentence conditions. After conviction and prior to sentencing the court may adjourn sentencing to a subsequent date and order the defendant to comply with any of the conditions contained in paragraphs (a) through (f) and paragraph (1) of subdivision two of section 65.10 of the penal law. In imposing sentence, the court shall take into consideration the defendant's record of compliance with pre-sentence conditions ordered by the court.

> **HISTORY:** Add, L 1970, ch 996, § 1, eff Sept 1, 1971. Sub 1, amd, L 1984, ch 263, § 2, eff Nov 1, 1984. Sub 2, amd, L 1984, ch 263, § 2, eff Nov 1, 1984. Sub 4, add, L 1994, ch 509, § 1, eff July 26, 1994.

§ 400.14. [Expired]

> **HISTORY:** Add, L 1984, ch 673, § 3, eff Nov 1, 1984, expired July 1, 1990.

§ 400.15. Procedure for determining whether defendant is a second violent felony offender

1. Applicability. The provisions of this section govern the procedure that must be followed in any case where it appears that a defendant who stands convicted of a violent felony offense as defined in subdivision one of section 70.02 of the penal law has previously been subjected to a predicate violent felony conviction as defined in paragraph (b) of subdivision one of section 70.04 of the penal law and may be a second violent felony offender.

2. Statement to be filed. When information available to the court or to the people prior to sentencing for a violent felony offense indicates that the defendant may have previously been subjected to a predicate violent felony conviction, a statement must be filed by the prosecutor before sentence is imposed setting forth the date and place of each alleged predicate violent felony conviction. Where the provisions of subparagraph (v) of paragraph (c) of subdivision one of section 70.04 of the penal law apply, such statement also shall set forth the date of commencement and the date of termination as well as the place of imprisonment for each period of incarceration to be used for tolling of the ten year limitation set forth in subparagraph (iv) of paragraph (b) of such subdivision.

3. Preliminary examination. The defendant must be given a copy of such statement and the court must ask him whether he wishes to controvert any allegation made therein. If the defendant wishes to controvert any allegation in the statement, he must specify the particular allegation or allegations he wishes to controvert. Uncontroverted allegations in the statement shall be deemed to have been admitted by the defendant.

4. Cases where further hearing is not required. Where the uncontroverted allegations in the statement are sufficient to support a finding that the defendant has been subjected to a predicate violent felony conviction the court must enter such finding and when imposing sentence must

sentence the defendant in accordance with the provisions of section 70.04 of the penal law.

5. Cases where further hearing is required. Where the defendant controverts an allegation in the statement and the uncontroverted allegations in such statement are not sufficient to support a finding that the defendant has been subjected to a predicate violent felony conviction the court must proceed to hold a hearing.

6. Time for hearing. In any case where a copy of the statement was not received by the defendant at least two days prior to the preliminary examination, the court must upon request of the defendant grant an adjournment of at least two days before proceeding with the hearing.

7. Manner of conducting hearing.

(a) A hearing pursuant to this section must be before the court without jury. The burden of proof is upon the people and a finding that the defendant has been subjected to a predicate violent felony conviction must be based upon proof beyond a reasonable doubt by evidence admissible under the rules applicable to a trial of the issue of guilt.

(b) A previous conviction in this or any other jurisdiction which was obtained in violation of the rights of the defendant under the applicable provisions of the constitution of the United States must not be counted in determining whether the defendant has been subjected to a predicate violent felony conviction. The defendant may, at any time during the course of the hearing hereunder controvert an allegation with respect to such conviction in the statement on the grounds that the conviction was unconstitutionally obtained. Failure to challenge the previous conviction in the manner provided herein constitutes a waiver on the part of the defendant of any allegation of unconstitutionality unless good cause be shown for such failure to make timely challenge.

(c) At the conclusion of the hearing the court must make a finding as to whether or not the defendant has been subjected to a predicate violent felony conviction.

8. Subsequent use of predicate violent felony conviction finding. Where a finding has been entered pursuant to this section, such finding shall be binding upon that defendant in any future proceeding in which the issue may arise.

HISTORY: Add, L 1978, ch 481, § 18, eff Sept 1, 1978.

§ 400.16. Procedure for determining whether defendant is a persistent violent felony offender

1. Applicability. The provisions of this section govern the procedure that must be followed in any case where it appears that a defendant who stands convicted of a violent felony offense as defined in subdivision one of section 70.02 of the penal law has previously been subjected to two or more predicate violent felony convictions as defined in paragraph (b) of subdivision one of section 70.04, and may be a persistent violent felony offender as defined in section 70.08 of the penal law.

2. Statement; preliminary examination; hearing; subsequent use of predicate violent felony conviction finding. The requirements set forth in subdivisions two, three, four, five, six, seven and eight of section 400.15 with respect to the statement to be filed, preliminary examination, hearing and subsequent use of a predicate violent felony conviction finding in the case of a second violent felony offender, shall also apply to a determination of whether a defendant has been subjected to two or more violent predicate felony convictions and is a persistent violent felony offender.

HISTORY: Add, L 1978, ch 481, § 19, eff Sept 1, 1978.

§ 400.19. Procedure for determining whether defendant is a second child sexual assault felony offender

1. Applicability. The provisions of this section govern the procedure that must be followed in any case where it appears that a defendant who stands convicted of a felony offense for a sexual assault upon a child as defined in section 70.07 of the penal law has previously been convicted of a predicate felony for a sexual assault upon a child.

2. Statement to be filed. When information available to the people prior to the trial of a felony offense for a sexual assault against a child indicates that the defendant may have previously been subjected to a predicate felony conviction for a sexual assault against a child, a statement may be filed by the prosecutor at any time before trial commences setting forth the date and place of each alleged predicate felony conviction for a sexual assault against a child and a statement whether the defendant was eighteen years of age or older at the time of the commission of the predicate felony. Where the provisions of subparagraph (v) of paragraph (b) of subdivision one of section 70.06 of the penal law apply, such statement also shall set forth the date of commencement and the date of termination as well as the place of imprisonment for each period of incarceration to be used for tolling of the ten year limitation set forth in subparagraph (iv) of paragraph (b) of such subdivision.

3. Preliminary examination. The defendant must be given a copy of such statement and the court must ask him whether he wishes to controvert any allegation made therein. If the defendant wishes to controvert any allegation in the statement, he must specify the particular allegation or allegations he wishes to controvert. Uncontroverted allegations in the statement shall be deemed to have been admitted by the defendant.

4. Cases where further hearing is not required. Where the uncontroverted allegations in the statement are sufficient to support a finding that the defendant has been subjected to a predicate felony conviction for a sexual assault upon a child and that the defendant was 18 years of age or older at the time of the commission of the predicate felony, the court must enter such finding and when imposing sentence must sentence the defendant in accordance with the provisions of section 70.07 of the penal law.

5. Cases where further hearing is required. Where the defendant controverts an allegation in the statement, the court must proceed to hold a hearing.

6. Manner of conducting hearing.

(a) A hearing pursuant to this section must be before the court without jury. The burden of proof is upon the people and a finding that the defendant has been subjected to a predicate felony conviction for a sexual assault against a child as defined in subdivision two of section 70.07 of the penal law and that the defendant was 18 years of age or older at the time of the commission of the predicate felony must be based upon proof beyond a reasonable doubt by evidence admissible under the rules applicable to a trial of the issue of guilt.

(b) Regardless of whether the age of the victim is an element of the alleged predicate felony offense, where the defendant controverts an allegation that the victim of an alleged sexual assault upon a child was less than fifteen years old, the people may prove that the child was less than fifteen years old by any evidence admissible under the rules applicable to a trial of the issue of guilt. For purposes of determining whether a child was less than fifteen years old, the people shall not be required to prove that the defendant knew the child was less than fifteen years old at the time of the alleged sexual assault.

(c) A previous conviction in this or any other jurisdiction which was obtained in violation of the rights of the defendant under the applicable provisions of the constitution of the United States must not be counted in determining whether the defendant has been subjected to a predicate felony conviction for a sexual assault upon a child. The defendant may, at any time during the course of the hearing hereunder, controvert an allegation with respect to such conviction in the statement on the grounds that the conviction was unconstitutionally obtained. Failure to challenge the previous conviction in the manner provided herein constitutes a waiver on the part of the defendant of any allegation of unconstitutionality unless good cause be shown for such failure to make timely challenge.

(d) At the conclusion of the hearing the court must make a finding as to whether or not the defendant has been subjected to a predicate felony conviction for a sexual assault against a child as defined in subdivision two of section 70.07 of the penal law and whether the defendant was 18 years of age or older at the time of the commission of the predicate felony.

7. Subsequent use of predicate felony conviction finding. Where a finding has been entered pursuant to this section, such finding shall be binding in any future proceeding in which the issue may arise.

HISTORY: Add, L 2000, ch 1, § 51, eff Feb 1, 2001. Sub 2, amd, L 2003, ch 264, § 45, eff Nov 1, 2003. Sub 4, amd, L 2003, ch 264, § 45, eff Nov 1, 2003. Sub 6, amd, L 2003, ch 264, § 45, eff Nov 1, 2003. Sub 6, par (a), amd, L 2003, ch 264, § 45, eff Nov 1, 2003. Sub 6, par (d), amd, L 2003, ch 264, § 45, eff Nov 1, 2003.

§ 400.20. Procedure for determining whether defendant should be sentenced as a persistent felony offender

1. Applicability. The provisions of this section govern the procedure that must be followed in order to impose the persistent felony offender sentence authorized by subdivision two of section 70.10 of the penal law. Such sentence may not be imposed unless, based upon evidence in the record of a hearing held pursuant to this section, the court (a) has found that the defendant is a persistent felony offender as defined in subdivision one of section 70.10 of the penal law, and (b) is of the opinion that the history and character of the defendant and the nature and circumstances of his criminal conduct are such that extended incarceration and lifetime supervision of the defendant are warranted to best serve the public interest.

2. Authorization for hearing. When information available to the court prior to sentencing indicates that the defendant is a persistent felony offender, and when, in the opinion of the court, the available information shows that a persistent felony offender sentence may be warranted, the court may order a hearing to determine (a) whether the defendant is in fact a persistent felony offender, and (b) if so, whether a persistent felony offender sentence should be imposed.

3. Order directing a hearing. An order directing a hearing to determine whether the defendant should be sentenced as a persistent felony offender must be filed with the clerk of the court and must specify a date for the hearing not less than twenty days from the date the order is filed. The court must annex to and file with the order a statement setting forth the following:

(a) The dates and places of the previous convictions which render the defendant a persistent felony offender as defined in subdivision one of section 70.10 of the penal law; and

(b) The factors in the defendant's background and prior criminal conduct which the court deems relevant for the purpose of sentencing the defendant as a persistent felony offender.

4. Notice of hearing. Upon receipt of the order and statement of the court, the clerk of the court must send a notice of hearing to the defendant, his counsel and the district attorney. Such notice must specify the time and place of the hearing and the fact that the purpose of the hearing is to

determine whether or not the defendant should be sentenced as a persistent felony offender. Each notice required to be sent hereunder must be accompanied by a copy of the statement of the court.

5. Burden and standard of proof; evidence. Upon any hearing held pursuant to this section the burden of proof is upon the people. A finding that the defendant is a persistent felony offender, as defined in subdivision one of section 70.10 of the penal law, must be based upon proof beyond a reasonable doubt by evidence admissible under the rules applicable to the trial of the issue of guilt. Matters pertaining to the defendant's history and character and the nature and circumstances of his criminal conduct may be established by any relevant evidence, not legally privileged, regardless of admissibility under the exclusionary rules of evidence, and the standard of proof with respect to such matters shall be a preponderance of the evidence.

6. Constitutionality of prior convictions. A previous conviction in this or any other jurisdiction which was obtained in violation of the rights of the defendant under the applicable provisions of the Constitution of the United States may not be counted in determining whether the defendant is a persistent felony offender. The defendant may, at any time during the course of the hearing hereunder controvert an allegation with respect to such conviction in the statement of the court on the grounds that the conviction was unconstitutionally obtained. Failure to challenge the previous conviction in the manner provided herein constitutes a waiver on the part of the defendant of any allegation of unconstitutionality unless good cause be shown for such failure to make timely challenge.

7. Preliminary examination. When the defendant appears for the hearing the court must ask him whether he wishes to controvert any allegation made in the statement prepared by the court, and whether he wishes to present evidence on the issue of whether he is a persistent felony offender or on the question of his background and criminal conduct. If the defendant wishes to controvert any allegation in the statement of the court, he must specify the particular allegation or allegations he wishes to controvert. If he wishes to present evidence in his own behalf, he must specify the nature of such evidence. Uncontroverted allegations in the statement of the court are deemed evidence in the record.

8. Cases where further hearing is not required. Where the uncontroverted allegations in the statement of the court are sufficient to support a finding that the defendant is a persistent felony offender and the court is satisfied that (a) the uncontroverted allegations with respect to the defendant's background and the nature of his prior criminal conduct warrant sentencing the defendant as a persistent felony offender, and (b) the defendant either has no relevant evidence to present or the facts which could be established through the evidence offered by the defendant would not affect the court's decision, the court may enter a finding that the defendant is a persistent felony offender and sentence him in accordance with the provisions of subdivision two of section 70.10 of the penal law.

9. Cases where further hearing is required. Where the defendant controverts an allegation in the statement of the court and the uncontroverted allegations in such statement are not sufficient to support a finding that the defendant is a persistent felony offender as defined in subdivision one of section 70.10 of the penal law, or where the uncontroverted allegations with respect to the defendant's history and the nature of his prior criminal conduct do not warrant sentencing him as a persistent felony offender, or where the defendant has offered to present evidence to establish facts that would affect the court's decision on the question of whether a persistent felony offender sentence is warranted, the court may fix a date for a further hearing. Such hearing shall be before the court without a jury and either party may introduce evidence with respect to the controverted allegations or any other matter relevant to the issue of whether or not the defendant should be sentenced as a persistent felony offender. At the conclusion of the hearing the court must make a

finding as to whether or not the defendant is a persistent felony offender and, upon a finding that he is such, must then make such findings of fact as it deems relevant to the question of whether a persistent felony offender sentence is warranted. If the court both finds that the defendant is a persistent felony offender and is of the opinion that a persistent felony offender sentence is warranted, it may sentence the defendant in accordance with the provisions of subdivision two of section 70.10 of the penal law.

10. Termination of hearing. At any time during the pendency of a hearing pursuant to this section, the court may, in its discretion, terminate the hearing without making any finding. In such case, unless the court recommences the proceedings and makes the necessary findings, the defendant may not be sentenced as a persistent felony offender.

HISTORY: Add, L 1970, ch 996, § 1, eff Sept 1, 1971, with substance derived from Crim C § 470-a.

§ 400.21. Procedure for determining whether defendant is a second felony offender or a second felony drug offender

1. Applicability. The provisions of this section govern the procedure that must be followed in any case where it appears that a defendant who stands convicted of a felony has previously been convicted of a predicate felony and may be a second felony offender as defined in section 70.06 of the penal law or a second felony drug offender as defined in either paragraph (b) of subdivision one of section 70.70 of the penal law, or paragraph (b) of subdivision one of section 70.71 of the penal law.

2. Statement to be filed. When information available to the court or to the people prior to sentencing for a felony indicates that the defendant may have previously been subjected to a predicate felony conviction, a statement must be filed by the prosecutor before sentence is imposed setting forth the date and place of each alleged predicate felony conviction and whether the predicate felony conviction was a violent felony as that term is defined in subdivision one of section 70.02 of the penal law, or in any other jurisdiction of an offense which includes all of the essential elements of any such felony for which a sentence to a term of imprisonment in excess of one year or death was authorized and is authorized in this state regardless of whether such sentence was imposed. Where the provisions of subparagraph (v) of paragraph (b) of subdivision one of section 70.06 of the penal law apply, such statement also shall set forth the date of commencement and the date of termination as well as the state or local incarcerating agency for each period of incarceration to be used for tolling of the ten year limitation set forth in subparagraph (iv) of paragraph (b) of such subdivision.

3. Preliminary examination. The defendant must be given a copy of such statement and the court must ask him or her whether he or she wishes to controvert any allegation made therein. If the defendant wishes to controvert any allegation in the statement, he must specify the particular allegation or allegations he wishes to controvert. Uncontroverted allegations in the statement shall be deemed to have been admitted by the defendant.

4. Cases where further hearing is not required. Where the uncontroverted allegations in the statement are sufficient to support a finding that the defendant has been subjected to a predicate felony conviction the court must enter such finding, including a finding that the predicate felony conviction was of a violent felony as that term is defined in subdivision one of section 70.02 of the penal law, or in any other jurisdiction of an offense which includes all of the essential elements of any such felony for which a sentence to a term of imprisonment in excess of one year or death was authorized and is authorized in this state regardless of whether such sentence was imposed, and when imposing sentence must sentence the defendant in accordance with the applicable

provisions of section 70.06, 70.70 or 70.71 of the penal law.

5. Cases where further hearing is required. Where the defendant controverts an allegation in the statement and the uncontroverted allegations in such statement are not sufficient to support a finding that the defendant has been subjected to such a predicate felony conviction the court must proceed to hold a hearing.

6. Time for hearing. In any case where a copy of the statement was not received by the defendant at least two days prior to the preliminary examination, the court must upon request of the defendant grant an adjournment of at least two days before proceeding with the hearing.

7. Manner of conducting hearing.

(a) A hearing pursuant to this section must be before the court without jury. The burden of proof is upon the people and a finding that the defendant has been subjected to such a predicate felony conviction must be based upon proof beyond a reasonable doubt by evidence admissible under the rules applicable to a trial of the issue of guilt.

(b) A previous conviction in this or any other jurisdiction which was obtained in violation of the rights of the defendant under the applicable provisions of the constitution of the United States must not be counted in determining whether the defendant has been subjected to such a predicate felony conviction. The defendant may, at any time during the course of the hearing hereunder controvert an allegation with respect to such conviction in the statement on the grounds that the conviction was unconstitutionally obtained. Failure to challenge the previous conviction in the manner provided herein constitutes a waiver on the part of the defendant of any allegation of unconstitutionality unless good cause be shown for such failure to make timely challenge.

(c) At the conclusion of the hearing the court must make a finding as to whether or not the defendant has been subjected to a predicate felony conviction, including a finding as to whether or not the predicate felony conviction was of a violent felony as that term is defined in subdivision one of section 70.02 of the penal law, or in any other jurisdiction of an offense which includes all of the essential elements of any such felony for which a sentence to a term of imprisonment in excess of one year or death was authorized and is authorized in this state regardless of whether such sentence was imposed.

8. Subsequent use of predicate felony conviction finding. Where a finding has been entered pursuant to this section, such finding shall be binding upon that defendant in any future proceeding in which the issue may arise.

> **HISTORY:** Add, L 1973, ch 277, § 17, eff Sept 1, 1973. Amd, L 2004, ch 738, § 18, eff Jan 13, 2005. Section heading, amd, L 2004, ch 738, § 18, eff Jan 13, 2005. Sub 1, amd, L 2004, ch 738, § 18, eff Jan 13, 2005. Sub 2, amd, L 2004, ch 738, § 18, eff Jan 13, 2005. Sub 3, amd, L 2004, ch 738, § 18, eff Jan 13, 2005. Sub 4, amd, L 1973, ch 1051, § 19, eff Sept 1, 1973. Sub 4, amd, L 2004, ch 738, § 18, eff Jan 13, 2005. Sub 5, amd, L 2004, ch 738, § 18, eff Jan 13, 2005. Sub 7, par (a), amd, L 2004, ch 738, § 18, eff Jan 13, 2005. Sub 7, par (b), amd, L 2004, ch 738, § 18, eff Jan 13, 2005. Sub 7, par (c), amd, L 2004, ch 738, § 18, eff Jan 13, 2005.

§ 400.22. Evidence of imprisonment

The certificate of the commissioner of correction or of the warden or other chief officer of any prison, or of the superintendent or other chief officer of any penitentiary under the seal of his office containing name of person, a statement of the court in which conviction was had, the date and term of sentence, length of time imprisoned, and date of discharge from prison or penitentiary, shall be prima facie evidence of the imprisonment and discharge of any person under the conviction stated and set forth in such certificate for the purposes of any proceeding under section 400.20.

HISTORY: Add, L 1970, ch 996, § 1, with substance derived from Crim C § 470-b; amd, L 1984, ch 673, § 4, eff Nov 1, 1984, expired on July 1, 1990.

§ 400.27. Procedure for determining sentence upon conviction for the offense of murder in the first degree

1. Upon the conviction of a defendant for the offense of murder in the first degree as defined by section 125.27 of the penal law, the court shall promptly conduct a separate sentencing proceeding to determine whether the defendant shall be sentenced to death or to life imprisonment without parole pursuant to subdivision five of section 70.00 of the penal law. Nothing in this section shall be deemed to preclude the people at any time from determining that the death penalty shall not be sought in a particular case, in which case the separate sentencing proceeding shall not be conducted and the court may sentence such defendant to life imprisonment without parole or to a sentence of imprisonment for the class A-I felony of murder in the first degree other than a sentence of life imprisonment without parole.

2. The separate sentencing proceeding provided for by this section shall be conducted before the court sitting with the jury that found the defendant guilty. The court may discharge the jury and impanel another jury only in extraordinary circumstances and upon a showing of good cause, which may include, but is not limited to, a finding of prejudice to either party. If a new jury is impaneled, it shall be formed in accordance with the procedures in article two hundred seventy of this chapter. Before proceeding with the jury that found the defendant guilty, the court shall determine whether any juror has a state of mind that is likely to preclude the juror from rendering an impartial decision based upon the evidence adduced during the proceeding. In making such determination the court shall personally examine each juror individually outside the presence of the other jurors. The scope of the examination shall be within the discretion of the court and may include questions supplied by the parties as the court deems proper. The proceedings provided for in this subdivision shall be conducted on the record; provided, however, that upon motion of either party, and for good cause shown, the court may direct that all or a portion of the record of such proceedings be sealed. In the event the court determines that a juror has such a state of mind, the court shall discharge the juror and replace the juror with the alternate juror whose name was first drawn and called. If no alternate juror is available, the court must discharge the jury and impanel another jury in accordance with article two hundred seventy of this chapter.

3. For the purposes of a proceeding under this section each subparagraph of paragraph (a) of subdivision one of section 125.27 of the penal law shall be deemed to define an aggravating factor. Except as provided in subdivision seven of this section, at a sentencing proceeding pursuant to this section the only aggravating factors that the jury may consider are those proven beyond a reasonable doubt at trial, and no other aggravating factors may be considered. Whether a sentencing proceeding is conducted before the jury that found the defendant guilty or before another jury, the aggravating factor or factors proved at trial shall be deemed established beyond a reasonable doubt at the separate sentencing proceeding and shall not be relitigated. Where the jury is to determine sentences for concurrent counts of murder in the first degree, the aggravating factor included in each count shall be deemed to be an aggravating factor for the purpose of the jury's consideration in determining the sentence to be imposed on each such count.

4. The court on its own motion or on motion of either party, in the interest of justice or to avoid prejudice to either party, may delay the commencement of the separate sentencing proceeding.

5. Notwithstanding the provisions of article three hundred ninety of this chapter, where a defendant is found guilty of murder in the first degree, no presentence investigation shall be conducted; provided, however, that where the court is to impose a sentence of imprisonment, a

presentence investigation shall be conducted and a presentence report shall be prepared in accordance with the provisions of such article.

6. At the sentencing proceeding the people shall not relitigate the existence of aggravating factors proved at the trial or otherwise present evidence, except, subject to the rules governing admission of evidence in the trial of a criminal action, in rebuttal of the defendant's evidence. However, when the sentencing proceeding is conducted before a newly impaneled jury, the people may present evidence to the extent reasonably necessary to inform the jury of the nature and circumstances of the count or counts of murder in the first degree for which the defendant was convicted in sufficient detail to permit the jury to determine the weight to be accorded the aggravating factor or factors established at trial. Whenever the people present such evidence, the court must instruct the jury in its charge that any facts elicited by the people that are not essential to the verdict of guilty on such count or counts shall not be deemed established beyond a reasonable doubt. Subject to the rules governing the admission of evidence in the trial of a criminal action, the defendant may present any evidence relevant to any mitigating factor set forth in subdivision nine of this section; provided, however, the defendant shall not be precluded from the admission of reliable hearsay evidence. The burden of establishing any of the mitigating factors set forth in subdivision nine of this section shall be on the defendant, and must be proven by a preponderance of the evidence. The people shall not offer evidence or argument relating to any mitigating factor except in rebuttal of evidence offered by the defendant.

7. (a) The people may present evidence at the sentencing proceeding to prove that in the ten year period prior to the commission of the crime of murder in the first degree for which the defendant was convicted, the defendant has previously been convicted of two or more offenses committed on different occasions; provided, that each such offense shall be either (i) a class A felony offense other than one defined in article two hundred twenty of the penal law, a class B violent felony offense specified in paragraph (a) of subdivision one of section 70.02 of the penal law, or a felony offense under the penal law a necessary element of which involves either the use or attempted use or threatened use of a deadly weapon or the intentional infliction of or the attempted intentional infliction of serious physical injury or death, or (ii) an offense under the laws of another state or of the United States punishable by a term of imprisonment of more than one year a necessary element of which involves either the use or attempted use or threatened use of a deadly weapon or the intentional infliction of or the attempted intentional infliction of serious physical injury or death. For the purpose of this paragraph, the term "deadly weapon" shall have the meaning set forth in subdivision twelve of section 10.00 of the penal law. In calculating the ten year period under this paragraph, any period of time during which the defendant was incarcerated for any reason between the time of commission of any of the prior felony offenses and the time of commission of the crime of murder in the first degree shall be excluded and such ten year period shall be extended by a period or periods equal to the time served under such incarceration. The defendant's conviction of two or more such offenses shall, if proven at the sentencing proceeding, constitute an aggravating factor.

(b) In order to be deemed established, an aggravating factor set forth in this subdivision must be proven by the people beyond a reasonable doubt and the jury must unanimously find such factor to have been so proven. The defendant may present evidence relating to an aggravating factor defined in this subdivision and either party may offer evidence in rebuttal. Any evidence presented by either party relating to such factor shall be subject to the rules governing admission of evidence in the trial of a criminal action.

(c) Whenever the people intend to offer evidence of an aggravating factor set forth in this subdivision, the people must within a reasonable time prior to trial file with the court and serve upon the defendant a notice of intention to offer such evidence. Whenever the people intend to offer evidence of the aggravating factor set forth in paragraph (a) of this subdivision, the people shall file with the notice of intention to offer such evidence a statement setting forth the date and place of each of the alleged offenses in paragraph (a) of this subdivision. The provisions of section 400.15 of this chapter, except for subdivisions one and two thereof, shall be followed.

8. Consistent with the provisions of this section, the people and the defendant shall be given fair opportunity to rebut any evidence received at the separate sentencing proceeding.

9. Mitigating factors shall include the following:

(a) The defendant has no significant history of prior criminal convictions involving the use of violence against another person;

(b) The defendant was mentally retarded at the time of the crime, or the defendant's mental capacity was impaired or his ability to conform his conduct to the requirements of law was impaired but not so impaired in either case as to constitute a defense to prosecution;

(c) The defendant was under duress or under the domination of another person, although not such duress or domination as to constitute a defense to prosecution;

(d) The defendant was criminally liable for the present offense of murder committed by another, but his participation in the offense was relatively minor although not so minor as to constitute a defense to prosecution;

(e) The murder was committed while the defendant was mentally or emotionally disturbed or under the influence of alcohol or any drug, although not to such an extent as to constitute a defense to prosecution; or

(f) Any other circumstance concerning the crime, the defendant's state of mind or condition at the time of the crime, or the defendant's character, background or record that would be relevant to mitigation or punishment for the crime.

10. At the conclusion of all the evidence, the people and the defendant may present argument in summation for or against the sentence sought by the people. The people may deliver the first summation and the defendant may then deliver the last summation. Thereafter, the court shall deliver a charge to the jury on any matters appropriate in the circumstances. In its charge, the court must instruct the jury that with respect to each count of murder in the first degree the jury should consider whether or not a sentence of death should be imposed and whether or not a sentence of life imprisonment without parole should be imposed, and that the jury must be unanimous with respect to either sentence. The court must also instruct the jury that in the event the jury fails to reach unanimous agreement with respect to the sentence, the court will sentence the defendant to a term of imprisonment with a minimum term of between twenty and twenty-five years and a maximum term of life. Following the court's charge, the jury shall retire to consider the sentence to be imposed. Unless inconsistent with the provisions of this section, the provisions of sections 310.10, 310.20 and 310.30 shall govern the deliberations of the jury.

11. (a) The jury may not direct imposition of a sentence of death unless it unanimously finds beyond a reasonable doubt that the aggravating factor or factors substantially outweigh the mitigating factor or factors established, if any, and unanimously determines that the penalty of death should be imposed. Any member or members of the jury who find a mitigating factor to have been proven by the defendant by a preponderance of the evidence may consider such factor established regardless of the number of jurors who concur that the factor has been established.

(b) If the jury directs imposition of either a sentence of death or life imprisonment without parole, it shall specify on the record those mitigating and aggravating factors considered and those mitigating factors established by the defendant, if any.

(c) With respect to a count or concurrent counts of murder in the first degree, the court may direct the jury to cease deliberation with respect to the sentence or sentences to be imposed if the jury has deliberated for an extensive period of time without reaching unanimous agreement on the sentence or sentences to be imposed and the court is satisfied that any such agreement is unlikely within a reasonable time. The provisions of this paragraph shall apply with respect to consecutive counts of murder in the first degree. In the event the jury is unable to reach unanimous agreement, the court must sentence the defendant in accordance with subdivisions one through three of section 70.00 of the penal law with respect to any count or counts of murder in the first degree upon which the jury failed to reach unanimous agreement as to the sentence to be imposed.

(d) If the jury unanimously determines that a sentence of death should be imposed, the court must thereupon impose a sentence of death. Thereafter, however, the court may, upon written motion of the defendant, set aside the sentence of death upon any of the grounds set forth in section 330.30. The procedures set forth in sections 330.40 and 330.50, as applied to separate sentencing proceedings under this section, shall govern the motion and the court upon granting the motion shall, except as may otherwise be required by subdivision one of section 330.50, direct a new sentencing proceeding pursuant to this section. Upon granting the motion upon any of the grounds set forth in section 330.30 and setting aside the sentence, the court must afford the people a reasonable period of time, which shall not be less than ten days, to determine whether to take an appeal from the order setting aside the sentence of death. The taking of an appeal by the people stays the effectiveness of that portion of the court's order that directs a new sentencing proceeding.

(e) If the jury unanimously determines that a sentence of life imprisonment without parole should be imposed the court must thereupon impose a sentence of life imprisonment without parole.

(f) Where a sentence has been unanimously determined by the jury it must be recorded on the minutes and read to the jury, and the jurors must be collectively asked whether such is their sentence. Even though no juror makes any declaration in the negative, the jury must, if either party makes such an application, be polled and each juror separately asked whether the sentence announced by the foreman is in all respects his or her sentence. If, upon either the collective or the separate inquiry, any juror answers in the negative, the court must refuse to accept the sentence and must direct the jury to resume its deliberation. If no disagreement is expressed, the jury must be discharged from the case.

12. (a) Upon the conviction of a defendant for the offense of murder in the first degree as defined in section 125.27 of the penal law, the court shall, upon oral or written motion of the defendant based upon a showing that there is reasonable cause to believe that the defendant is mentally retarded, promptly conduct a hearing without a jury to determine whether the defendant is mentally retarded. Upon the consent of both parties, such a hearing, or a portion thereof, may be conducted by the court contemporaneously with the separate sentencing proceeding in the presence of the sentencing jury, which in no event shall be the trier of fact with respect to the hearing. At such hearing the defendant has the burden of proof by a preponderance of the evidence that he or she is mentally retarded. The court shall defer rendering any finding pursuant to this subdivision as to whether the defendant is mentally retarded until a sentence is imposed pursuant to this section.

(b) In the event the defendant is sentenced pursuant to this section to life imprisonment without parole or to a term of imprisonment for the class A-I felony of murder in the first degree other than a sentence of life imprisonment without parole, the court shall not render a finding with respect to whether the defendant is mentally retarded.

(c) In the event the defendant is sentenced pursuant to this section to death, the court shall thereupon render a finding with respect to whether the defendant is mentally retarded. If the court finds the defendant is mentally retarded, the court shall set aside the sentence of death and sentence the defendant either to life imprisonment without parole or to a term of imprisonment for the class A-I felony of murder in the first degree other than a sentence of life imprisonment without parole. If the court finds the defendant is not mentally retarded, then such sentence of death shall not be set aside pursuant to this subdivision.

(d) In the event that a defendant is convicted of murder in the first degree pursuant to subparagraph (iii) of paragraph (a) of subdivision one of section 125.27 of the penal law, and the killing occurred while the defendant was confined or under custody in a state correctional facility or local correctional institution, and a sentence of death is imposed, such sentence may not be set aside pursuant to this subdivision upon the ground that the defendant is mentally retarded. Nothing in this paragraph or paragraph (a) of this subdivision shall preclude a defendant from presenting mitigating evidence of mental retardation at the separate sentencing proceeding.

(e) The foregoing provisions of this subdivision notwithstanding, at a reasonable time prior to the commencement of trial the defendant may, upon a written motion alleging reasonable cause to believe the defendant is mentally retarded, apply for an order directing that a mental retardation hearing be conducted prior to trial. If, upon review of the defendant's motion and any response thereto, the court finds reasonable cause to believe the defendant is mentally retarded, it shall promptly conduct a hearing without a jury to determine whether the defendant is mentally retarded. In the event the court finds after the hearing that the defendant is not mentally retarded, the court must, prior to commencement of trial, enter an order so stating, but nothing in this paragraph shall preclude a defendant from presenting mitigating evidence of mental retardation at a separate sentencing proceeding. In the event the court finds after the hearing that the defendant, based upon a preponderance of the evidence, is mentally retarded, the court must, prior to commencement of trial, enter an order so stating. Unless the order is reversed on an appeal by the people or unless the provisions of paragraph (d) of this subdivision apply, a separate sentencing proceeding under this section shall not be conducted if the defendant is thereafter convicted of murder in the first degree. In the event a separate sentencing proceeding is not conducted, the court, upon conviction of a defendant for the crime of murder in the first degree, shall sentence the defendant to life imprisonment without parole or to a sentence of imprisonment for the class A-I felony of murder in the first degree other than a sentence of life imprisonment without parole. Whenever a mental retardation hearing is held and a finding is rendered pursuant to this paragraph, the court may not conduct a hearing pursuant to paragraph (a) of this subdivision. For purposes of this subdivision and paragraph (b) of subdivision nine of this section, "mental retardation" means significantly subaverage general intellectual functioning existing concurrently with deficits in adaptive behavior which were manifested before the age of eighteen.

(f) In the event the court enters an order pursuant to paragraph (e) of this subdivision finding that the defendant is mentally retarded, the people may appeal as of right from the order pursuant to subdivision ten of section 450.20 of this chapter. Upon entering such an order the court must afford the people a reasonable period of time, which shall not be less than ten days, to determine whether to take an appeal from the order finding that the defendant is mentally retarded. The taking of an appeal by the people stays the effectiveness of the court's order and any order fixing a date for trial. Within six months of the effective date of this subdivision, the court of appeals shall adopt rules to ensure that appeals pursuant to this paragraph are expeditiously perfected, reviewed and determined so that pretrial delays are minimized. Prior to adoption of the rules, the court of appeals shall issue proposed rules and receive written comments thereon from interested parties.

13. (a) As used in this subdivision, the term "psychiatric evidence" means evidence of mental disease, defect or condition in connection with either a mitigating factor defined in this section or a mental retardation hearing pursuant to this section to be offered by a psychiatrist, psychologist or other person who has received training, or education, or has experience relating to the identification, diagnosis, treatment or evaluation of mental disease, mental defect or mental condition.

(b) When either party intends to offer psychiatric evidence, the party must, within a reasonable time prior to trial, serve upon the other party and file with the court a written notice of intention to present psychiatric evidence. The notice shall include a brief but detailed statement specifying the witness, nature and type of psychiatric evidence sought to be introduced. If either party fails to serve and file written notice, no psychiatric evidence is admissible unless the party failing to file thereafter serves and files such notice and the court affords the other party an adjournment for a reasonable period. If a party fails to give timely notice, the court in its discretion may impose upon offending counsel a reasonable monetary sanction for an intentional failure but may not in any event preclude the psychiatric evidence. In the event a monetary sanction is imposed, the offending counsel shall be personally liable therefor, and shall not receive reimbursement of any kind from any source in order to pay the cost of such monetary sanction. Nothing contained herein shall preclude the court from entering an order directing a party to provide timely notice.

(c) When a defendant serves notice pursuant to this subdivision, the district attorney may make application, upon notice to the defendant, for an order directing that the defendant submit to an examination by a psychiatrist, licensed psychologist, or licensed clinical social worker designated by the district attorney, for the purpose of rebutting evidence offered by the defendant with respect to a mental disease, defect, or condition in connection with either a mitigating factor defined in this section, including whether the defendant was acting under duress, was mentally or emotionally disturbed or mentally retarded, or was under the influence of alcohol or any drug. If the application is granted, the district attorney shall schedule a time and place for the examination, which shall be recorded. Counsel for the people and the defendant shall have the right to be present at the examination. A transcript of the examination shall be made available to the defendant and the district attorney promptly after its conclusion. The district attorney shall promptly serve on the defendant a written copy of the findings and evaluation of the examiner. If the court finds that the defendant has wilfully refused to cooperate fully in an examination pursuant to this paragraph, it shall, upon request of the district attorney, instruct the jury that the defendant did not submit to or cooperate fully in such psychiatric examination. When a defendant is subjected to an examination pursuant to an order issued in accordance with this subdivision, any statement made by the defendant for the purpose of the examination shall be inadmissible in evidence against him in any criminal action or proceeding on any issue other than that of whether a mitigating factor has been established or whether the defendant is mentally retarded, but such statement is admissible upon such an issue whether or not it would otherwise be deemed a privileged communication.

14. (a) At a reasonable time prior to the sentencing proceeding or a mental retardation hearing:

(i) the prosecutor shall, unless previously disclosed and subject to a protective order, make available to the defendant the statements and information specified in subdivision one of section 240.45 and make available for inspection, photographing, copying or testing the property specified in subdivision one of section 240.20; and

(ii) the defendant shall, unless previously disclosed and subject to a protective order, make available to the prosecution the statements and information specified in subdivision two of section 240.45 and make available for inspection, photographing, copying or testing, subject to constitutional limitations, the reports, documents and other property specified in subdivision one of section 240.30.

(b) Where a party refuses to make disclosure pursuant to this section, the provisions of section 240.35, subdivision one of section 240.40 and section 240.50 shall apply.

(c) If, after complying with the provisions of this section or an order pursuant thereto, a party finds either before or during a sentencing proceeding or mental retardation hearing, additional material subject to discovery or covered by court order, the party shall promptly make disclosure or apply for a protective order.

(d) If the court finds that a party has failed to comply with any of the provisions of this section, the court may enter any of the orders specified in subdivision one of section 240.70.

15. The court of appeals shall formulate and adopt rules for the development of forms for use by the jury in recording its findings and determinations of sentence.

HISTORY: Add, L 1995, ch 1, § 20, eff Sept 1, 1995. Sub 7, par (a), formerly sub 7, par (b), so designated sub 7, par (a), L 2001, ch 300, § 7, eff Sept 17, 2001. Former sub 7, par (a), repealed, L 2001, ch 300, § 7, eff Sept 17, 2001. Sub 7, par (b), formerly sub 7, par (c), so designated sub 7, par (b), L 2001, ch 300, § 7, eff Sept 17, 2001. Sub 7, par (c), formerly sub 7, par (d), amd, L 2001, ch 300, § 6, eff Sept 17, 2001; so designated sub 7, par (c), L 2001, ch 300, § 7, eff Sept 17, 2001. Sub 7, par (d), redesignated sub 7, par (c), L 2001, ch 300, § 7, eff Sept 17, 2001. Sub 13, par (c), amd, L 2004, ch 230, § 2, eff July 27, 2004.

§ 400.30. Procedure for determining the amount of a fine based upon the defendant's gain from the offense

1. Order directing a hearing. In any case where the court is of the opinion that the sentence should consist of or include a fine and that, pursuant to article eighty of the penal law, the amount of the fine should be based upon the defendant's gain from the commission of the offense, the court may order a hearing to determine the amount of such gain. The order must be filed with the clerk of the court and must specify a date for the hearing not less than ten days after the filing of the order.

2. Notice of hearing. Upon receipt of the order, the clerk of the court must send a notice of the hearing to the defendant, his counsel and the district attorney. Such notice must specify the time and place of the hearing and the fact that the purpose thereof is to determine the amount of the defendant's gain from the commission of the offense so that an appropriate fine can be imposed.

3. Hearing. When the defendant appears for the hearing the court must ask him whether he wishes to make any statement with respect to the amount of his gain from the commission of the offense. If the defendant does make a statement, the court may accept such statement and base its finding thereon. Where the defendant does not make a statement, or where the court does not accept the defendant's statement, it may proceed with the hearing.

4. Burden and standard of proof; evidence. At any hearing held pursuant to this section the burden of proof rests upon the people. A finding as to the amount of the defendant's gain from the commission of the offense must be based upon a preponderance of the evidence. Any relevant evidence, not legally privileged, may be received regardless of its admissibility under the exclusionary rules of evidence.

5. Termination of hearing. At any time during the pendency of a hearing pursuant to this section the court may, in its discretion, terminate the hearing without making any finding.

> **HISTORY:** Add, L 1970, ch 996, § 1, eff Sept 1, 1971, with substance derived from Crim C § 470-c.

§ 400.40. Procedure for determining prior convictions for the purpose of sentence in certain cases

1. Applicability. Where a conviction is entered for an unclassified misdemeanor or for a traffic infraction and the authorized sentence depends upon whether the defendant has a previous judgment of conviction for an offense, or where a conviction is entered for a violation defined outside the penal law and the amount of the fine authorized by the law defining such violation depends upon whether the defendant has a previous judgment of conviction for an offense, such issue is determined as provided in this section.

2. Statement to be filed. If it appears that the defendant has a previous judgment of conviction and if the court is required, or in its discretion desires, to impose a sentence that would not be authorized in the absence of such previous judgment, a statement must be filed after conviction and before sentence setting forth the date and place of the previous judgment or judgments and the court must conduct a hearing to determine whether the defendant is the same person mentioned in the record of such judgment or judgments. In any case where an increased sentence is mandatory, the statement may be filed by the court or by the prosecutor. In any case where an increased sentence is discretionary, the statement may be filed only by the court.

3. Preliminary examination. The defendant must be given a copy of such statement and the court must ask him whether he admits or denies such prior judgment or judgments. If the defendant denies the same or remains mute, the court may proceed with the hearing and, where the increased sentence is mandatory, it must impose such.

4. Time for hearing. In any case where a copy of the statement was not received by the defendant at least two days prior to the preliminary examination, the court must upon request of the defendant grant an adjournment of at least two days before proceeding with the hearing.

5. Manner of conducting hearing. A hearing pursuant to this section must be before the court without a jury. The burden of proof is upon the people and a finding that the defendant has been convicted of any offense alleged in the statement must be based upon proof beyond a reasonable doubt by evidence admissible under the rules applicable to trial of the issue of guilt.

> **HISTORY:** Add, L 1970, ch 996, § 1, eff Sept 1, 1971, with substance derived from Crim C § 717(2).

ARTICLE 410 [UNTIL SEPT 1, 2015] SENTENCES OF PROBATION, CONDITIONAL DISCHARGE AND PAROLE SUPERVISION [EFF SEPT 1, 2015] SENTENCES OF PROBATION AND CONDITIONAL DISCHARGE

> **HISTORY:** Add, L 1970, ch 996, § 1; amd, L 1995, ch 3, § 33, eff Oct 1, 1995, repealed Sept 1, 2015.

§ 410.10. Specification of conditions of the sentence

1. When the court pronounces a sentence of probation or of conditional discharge it must specify as part of the sentence the conditions to be complied with. Where the sentence is one of probation, the defendant must be given a written copy of the conditions at the time sentence is imposed. In any case where the defendant is given a written copy of the conditions, a copy thereof must be filed with and become part of the record of the case, and it is not necessary to specify the conditions orally.

2. Commission of an additional offense, other than a traffic infraction, after imposition of a sentence of probation or of conditional discharge, and prior to expiration or termination of the period of the sentence, constitutes a ground for revocation of such sentence irrespective of whether such fact is specified as a condition of the sentence.

3. When the court pronounces a sentence of probation or conditional discharge for a specified crime defined in paragraph (e) of subdivision one of section six hundred thirty-two-a of the executive law, in addition to specifying the conditions of the sentence, the court shall provide written notice to such defendant concerning any requirement to report to the office of victim services funds of a convicted person as defined in section six hundred thirty-two-a of the executive law, the procedures for such reporting and any potential penalty for a failure to comply.

> **HISTORY:** Add, L 1970, ch 996, § 1, eff Sept 1, 1971, with substance derived from Crim C § 932; amd, L 2001, ch 62, § 12, eff June 25, 2001, L 2010, ch 56, § 51 (Part A), eff June 22, 2010, L 2010, ch 56, § 44 (Part A-1), eff June 22, 2010.

§ 410.11. [Repealed]

> **HISTORY:** Add, L 1973, ch 676, § 31; amd, L 1975, ch 667, § 14; repealed, L 1980, ch 471, § 28, eff July 23, 1980.

§ 410.20. Modification or enlargement of conditions

1. The court may modify or enlarge the conditions of a sentence of probation or of conditional discharge at any time prior to the expiration or termination of the period of the sentence. Such action may not, however, be taken unless the defendant is personally present, except that the defendant need not be present if the modification consists solely of the elimination or relaxation of one or more conditions. Whenever the defendant has not been present, the court shall notify the defendant in writing within twenty days of such modification specifying the nature of the elimination or relaxation of such condition or conditions and the effective date thereof. In any such case the modification or enlargement may be specified in the same manner as the conditions originally imposed and becomes part of the sentence.

2. The procedure set forth in this section applies to the imposition of an additional period of

conditional discharge as authorized by subdivision three of section 65.05 of the penal law.

HISTORY: Add, L 1970, ch 996, § 1, eff Sept 1, 1971, with substance derived from Crim C § 933. Sub 1, amd, L 1973, ch 127, § 1, L 1976, ch 640, § 1, eff Sept 1, 1976.

§ 410.30. Declaration of delinquency

If at any time during the period of a sentence of probation or of conditional discharge the court has reasonable cause to believe that the defendant has violated a condition of the sentence, it may declare the defendant delinquent and file a written declaration of delinquency. When the court receives a request for a declaration of delinquency by a probation officer, it shall make a decision on such request within seventy-two hours of its receipt of the request. Upon filing a written declaration of delinquency, the court must promptly take reasonable and appropriate action to cause the defendant to appear before it for the purpose of enabling the court to make a final determination with respect to the alleged delinquency in accordance with section 410.70 of this article.

HISTORY: Add, L 1970, ch 996, § 1, eff Sept 1, 1971, with substance derived from Crim C § 934-a. Amd, L 2008, ch 652, § 3, eff Nov 1, 2009.

§ 410.40. Notice to appear, warrant

1. Notice to appear. The court may at any time order that a person who is under a sentence of probation or of conditional discharge appear before it. Such order may be in the form of a written notice, specifying the time and place of appearance, mailed to or served personally upon the defendant as the court may direct. In the absence of a warrant issued pursuant to subdivision two of this section, where a probation officer has submitted a violation petition and report, the court shall promptly consider such petition and, where the court issues a notice to appear, the court shall direct that the defendant appear within ten business days of the court's order. When the order is in the form of such a notice, failure to appear as ordered without reasonable cause therefor constitutes a violation of the conditions of the sentence irrespective of whether such requirement is specified as a condition thereof.

2. Warrant. Where the probation officer has requested that a probation warrant be issued, the court shall, within seventy-two hours of its receipt of the request, issue or deny the warrant or take any other lawful action including issuance of a notice to appear pursuant to subdivision one of this section. If at any time during the period of a sentence of probation or of conditional discharge the court has reasonable grounds to believe that the defendant has violated a condition of the sentence, the court may issue a warrant to a police officer or to an appropriate peace officer directing him or her to take the defendant into custody and bring the defendant before the court without unnecessary delay; provided, however, if the court in which the warrant is returnable is a superior court, and such court is not available, and the warrant is addressed to a police officer or appropriate probation officer certified as a peace officer, such executing officer may bring the defendant to the local correctional facility of the county in which such court sits, to be detained there until not later than the commencement of the next session of such court occurring on the next business day; or if the court in which the warrant is returnable is a local criminal court, and such court is not available, and the warrant is addressed to a police officer or appropriate probation officer certified as a peace officer, such executing officer must without unnecessary delay bring the defendant before an alternate local criminal court, as provided in subdivision five of section 120.90 of this chapter. A court which issues such a warrant may attach thereto a summary of the basis for the warrant. In any case where a defendant arrested upon the warrant is brought before a local criminal court other than the court in which the warrant is returnable, such local criminal court shall consider such summary before issuing a securing order with respect to the defendant.

HISTORY: Add, L 1970, ch 996, § 1, eff Sept 1, 1971. Amd, L 2008, ch 652, § 4, eff Nov 1,

2009. Sub 1, amd, L 2008, ch 652, § 4, eff Nov 1, 2009. Sub 2, amd, L 1980, ch 843, § 18, L 1993, ch 161, § 1, L 1996, ch 115, § 1, eff June 4, 1996. Sub 2, amd, L 2008, ch 652, § 4, eff Nov 1, 2009.

§ 410.50. Custody and supervision of probationers

1. Custody. A person who is under a sentence of probation is in the legal custody of the court that imposed it pending expiration or termination of the period of the sentence.

2. Supervision. The probation department serving the court that imposed a sentence of probation has the duty of supervising the defendant during the period of such legal custody.

3. Search order. If at any time during the period of probation the court has reasonable cause to believe that the defendant has violated a condition of the sentence, it may issue a search order. Such order must be directed to a probation officer and may authorize such officer to search the person of the defendant and/or any premises in which he resides or any real or personal property which he owns or which is in his possession.

4. Taking custody without warrant. When a probation officer has reasonable cause to believe that a person under his supervision pursuant to a sentence of probation has violated a condition of the sentence, such officer may, without a warrant, take the probationer into custody and search his person.

5. Assistance by police officer. In executing a search order, or in taking a person into custody, pursuant to this section, a probation officer may be assisted by a police officer.

HISTORY: Add, L 1970, ch 996, § 1, eff Sept 1, 1971.

§ 410.60. Appearance before court

A person who has been taken into custody pursuant to section 410.40 or section 410.50 of this article for violation of a condition of a sentence of probation or a sentence of conditional discharge must forthwith be brought before the court that imposed the sentence. Where a violation of probation petition and report has been filed and the person has not been taken into custody nor has a warrant been issued, an initial court appearance shall occur within ten business days of the court's issuance of a notice to appear. If the court has reasonable cause to believe that such person has violated a condition of the sentence, it may commit him to the custody of the sheriff or fix bail or release such person on his own recognizance for future appearance at a hearing to be held in accordance with section 410.70 of this article. If the court does not have reasonable cause to believe that such person has violated a condition of the sentence, it must direct that he be released.

HISTORY: Add, L 1970, ch 996, § 1, eff Sept 1, 1971. Amd, L 2008, ch 652, § 5, eff Nov 1, 2009.

§ 410.70. Hearing on violation

1. In general. The court may not revoke a sentence of probation or a sentence of conditional discharge, or extend a period of probation, unless (a) the court has found that the defendant has violated a condition of the sentence and (b) the defendant has had an opportunity to be heard pursuant to this section. The defendant is entitled to a hearing in accordance with this section promptly after the court has filed a declaration of delinquency or has committed him or has fixed bail pursuant to this article.

2. Statement; preliminary examination. The court must file or cause to be filed with the clerk of the court a statement setting forth the condition or conditions of the sentence violated and a reasonable description of the time, place and manner in which the violation occurred. The defendant must appear before the court within ten business days of the court's issuance of the

notice to appear and the court must advise him of the contents of the statement and furnish him with a copy thereof. At the time of such appearance the court must ask the defendant whether he wishes to make any statement with respect to the violation. If the defendant makes a statement, the court may accept it and base its decision thereon. If the court does not accept it, or if the defendant does not make a statement, the court must proceed with the hearing. Provided, however, that upon request, the court must grant a reasonable adjournment to the defendant to enable him to prepare for the hearing.

3. Manner of conducting hearing. The hearing must be a summary one by the court without a jury and the court may receive any relevant evidence not legally privileged. The defendant may cross-examine witnesses and may present evidence on his own behalf. A finding that the defendant has violated a condition of his sentence must be based upon a preponderance of the evidence.

4. Counsel. The defendant is entitled to counsel at all stages of any proceeding under this section and the court must advise him of such right at the outset of the proceeding.

5. Revocation; modification; continuation. At the conclusion of the hearing the court may revoke, continue or modify the sentence of probation or conditional discharge. Where the court revokes the sentence, it must impose sentence as specified in subdivisions three and four of section 60.01 of the penal law. Where the court continues or modifies the sentence, it must vacate the declaration of delinquency and direct that the defendant be released. If the alleged violation is sustained and the court continues or modifies the sentence, it may extend the sentence up to the period of interruption specified in subdivision two of section 65.15 of the penal law, but any time spent in custody in any correctional institution pursuant to section 410.60 of this article shall be credited against the term of the sentence. Provided further, where the alleged violation is sustained and the court continues or modifies the sentence, the court may also extend the remaining period of probation up to the maximum term authorized by section 65.00 of the penal law. Provided, however, a defendant shall receive credit for the time during which he or she was supervised under the original probation sentence prior to any declaration of delinquency and for any time spent in custody pursuant to this article for an alleged violation of probation.

HISTORY: Add, L 1970, ch 996, § 1, eff Sept 1, 1971; amd, L 1977, ch 355, § 1, L 1985, ch 112, § 1, eff June 20, 1985, L 2008, ch 652, § 6, eff Nov 1, 2009, L 2013, ch 556, § 5, eff Feb 9, 2014, L 2014, ch 17, §§ 2, 3, eff Feb 9, 2014.

§ 410.80. Transfer of supervision of probationers

1. Authority to transfer supervision. Where a probationer at the time of sentencing or an interim probationer at the time of the imposition of the period of interim probation supervision resides in another jurisdiction within the state, the sentencing court shall transfer supervision to the appropriate probation department in such other jurisdiction. Where, after a probation sentence or interim probation supervision is pronounced, a probationer or interim probationer desires to reside in another jurisdiction within the state that is not served by the sentencing court, such court, in its discretion, may approve a change in residency and, upon approval, shall transfer supervision to the appropriate probation department serving the county of the probationer's proposed new residence. Any transfer under this subdivision must be in accordance with rules adopted by the commissioner of the division of criminal justice services.

2. Transfer of powers.

(a) Upon completion of transfer of probation as authorized pursuant to subdivision one, the probation department in the receiving jurisdiction shall assume all powers and duties of the probation department in the jurisdiction of the sentencing court. Upon completion of transfer, the appropriate court within the jurisdiction of the receiving probation department shall assume all powers and duties of the sentencing court and shall have sole jurisdiction in the case including jurisdiction over matters specified in article twenty-three of the correction law. Further, the sentencing court shall immediately forward its entire case record to the receiving court.

(i) In transfers involving a defendant sentenced to probation upon conviction of a felony, the receiving court served by the probation department to which supervision is transferred shall be the superior court within the jurisdiction of the probation department.

(ii) In transfers involving a defendant sentenced to probation upon conviction of a misdemeanor, the receiving court served by the probation department to which supervision is transferred shall be the appropriate criminal court within the jurisdiction of the probation department. The sending probation department shall consult with the probation department to which supervision will be transferred to determine the appropriate criminal court to receive the case.

(b) Where a transfer is authorized for a defendant on interim probation supervision pursuant to subdivision one of this section, the sentencing court shall retain jurisdiction during the period of interim probation. The probation department in the receiving jurisdiction shall assume all powers and duties of the original probation department in the jurisdiction of the sentencing court.

3. Interstate compact. Nothing contained in this section affects or limits the provisions of section two hundred fifty-nine-mm of the executive law relating to out-of-state probation supervision.

4. Federal transfer of custody and supervision. Notwithstanding the provisions of any other law, the court served by the probation department may consent to the transfer of custody and supervision of a probationer to the United States Department of Justice pursuant to the Witness Security Act of nineteen hundred eighty-four.

HISTORY: Add, L 1970, ch 996, § 1, eff Sept 1, 1971; amd, L 1972, ch 545, § 1, L 1978, ch 501, § 1, L 1980, ch 201, § 1, L 1981, ch 755, § 1, L 1985, ch 134, § 27, eff April 1, 1985, L 1986, ch 24, § 1, eff May 3, 1986, L 1988, ch 430, § 1, eff Nov 1, 1988, L 1993, ch 137, § 1, L 2007, ch 191, § 1, eff Sept 1, 2007, L 2010, ch 56, § 51 (Part A), eff June 22, 2010, L 2012, ch 347, § 1, eff Aug 1, 2012.

§ 410.90. Termination of sentence

1. The court may at any time terminate either a period of probation, other than a period of lifetime probation, for conviction to a crime or a period of conditional discharge for an offense.

2. The court may terminate a period of probation for a person who is subject to lifetime probation and who has been on unrevoked probation for at least five consecutive years.

3. (a) The court shall grant a request for termination of a sentence of probation under this section when, having regard to the conduct and condition of the probationer, the court is of the opinion that:

(i) the probationer is no longer in need of such guidance, training or other assistance which would otherwise be administered through probation supervision;

(ii) the probationer has diligently complied with the terms and conditions of the sentence of probation; and

(iii) the termination of the sentence of probation is not adverse to the protection of the public.

No such termination shall be granted unless the court is satisfied that the probationer, who is otherwise financially able to comply with an order of restitution or reparation, has made a good faith effort to comply therewith.

(b) The court shall grant a request for termination of a sentence of conditional discharge under this section when, having regard to the conduct and condition of the defendant, the court is of the opinion that:

(i) the defendant has diligently complied with the terms and conditions of the sentence of conditional discharge; and

(ii) termination of the sentence of conditional discharge is not adverse to protection of the public.

HISTORY: Add, L 1970, ch 996, § 1; amd, L 1973, ch 278, § 4, L 1980, ch 238, § 1, eff June 16, 1980. Sub 1, formerly entire section, so numbered and amd, L 1979, ch 410, § 27, eff Sept 1, 1979. Sub 2, add, L 1979, ch 410, § 27, eff Sept 1, 1979. Sub 3, add, L 1982, ch 782, § 3, eff Sept 1, 1982. Sub 3, par (a), amd, L 1992, ch 618, § 5, eff Nov 1, 1992. Sub 3, par (a), closing par, add, L 1992, ch 618, § 5, eff Nov 1, 1992.

§ 410.91. [Repealed Sept 1, 2015] Sentence of parole supervision

1. A sentence of parole supervision is an indeterminate sentence of imprisonment, or a determinate sentence of imprisonment imposed pursuant to paragraphs (b) and (d) of subdivision three of section 70.70 of the penal law, which may be imposed upon an eligible defendant, as defined in subdivision two of this section. If an indeterminate sentence, such sentence shall have a minimum term and a maximum term within the ranges specified by subdivisions three and four of section 70.06 of the penal law. If a determinate sentence, such sentence shall have a term within the ranges specified by subparagraphs (iii) and (iv) of paragraph (b) of subdivision three of section 70.70 of the penal law. Provided, however, if the court directs that the sentence be executed as a sentence of parole supervision, it shall remand the defendant for immediate delivery to a reception center operated by the state department of corrections and community supervision, in accordance with section 430.20 of this chapter and section six hundred one of the correction law, for a period not to exceed ten days. An individual who receives such a sentence shall be placed under the immediate supervision of the department of corrections and community supervision and must comply with the conditions of parole, which shall include an initial placement in a drug treatment campus for a period of ninety days at which time the defendant shall be released therefrom.

2. A defendant is an "eligible defendant" for purposes of a sentence of parole supervision when such defendant is a felony offender convicted of a specified offense or offenses as defined in subdivision five of this section, who stands convicted of no other felony offense, who has not previously been convicted of either a violent felony offense as defined in section 70.02 of the penal law, a class A felony offense or a class B felony offense other than a class B felony offense defined in article two hundred twenty of the penal law, and is not subject to an undischarged term of imprisonment.

3. When an indeterminate or determinate sentence of imprisonment is imposed upon an eligible defendant for a specified offense, as defined in subdivision five of this section, the court may direct that such sentence be executed as a sentence of parole supervision if the court finds (i) that the defendant has a history of controlled substance dependence that is a significant contributing factor to such defendant's criminal conduct; (ii) that such defendant's controlled substance dependence could be appropriately addressed by a sentence of parole supervision; and (iii) that imposition of such a sentence would not have an adverse effect on public safety or public confidence in the integrity of the criminal justice system.

4. [Repealed]

5. [Until July 5, 2021] For the purposes of this section, a "specified offense" is an offense defined by any of the following provisions of the penal law: burglary in the third degree as defined in section 140.20, criminal mischief in the third degree as defined in section 145.05, criminal mischief in the second degree as defined in section 145.10, grand larceny in the fourth degree as defined in subdivision one, two, three, four, five, six, eight, nine or ten of section 155.30, grand larceny in the third degree as defined in section 155.35 (except where the property consists of one or more firearms, rifles or shotguns), unauthorized use of a vehicle in the second degree as defined in section 165.06, criminal possession of stolen property in the fourth degree as defined in subdivision one, two, three, five or six of section 165.45, criminal possession of stolen property in the third degree as defined in section 165.50 (except where the property consists of one or more firearms, rifles or shotguns), forgery in the second degree as defined in section 170.10, criminal possession of a forged instrument in the second degree as defined in section 170.25, unlawfully using slugs in the first degree as defined in section 170.60, criminal diversion of medical marihuana in the first degree as defined in section 179.10 or an attempt to commit any of the aforementioned offenses if such attempt constitutes a felony offense; or a class B felony offense defined in article two hundred twenty where a sentence is imposed pursuant to paragraph (a) of subdivision two of section 70.70 of the penal law; or any class C, class D or class E controlled substance or marihuana felony offense as defined in article two hundred twenty or two hundred twenty-one.

5. [Eff July 5, 2021] For the purposes of this section, a "specified offense" is an offense defined by any of the following provisions of the penal law: burglary in the third degree as defined in section 140.20, criminal mischief in the third degree as defined in section 145.05, criminal mischief in the second degree as defined in section 145.10, grand larceny in the fourth degree as defined in subdivision one, two, three, four, five, six, eight, nine or ten of section 155.30, grand larceny in the third degree as defined in section 155.35 (except where the property consists of one or more firearms, rifles or shotguns), unauthorized use of a vehicle in the second degree as defined in section 165.06, criminal possession of stolen property in the fourth degree as defined in subdivision one, two, three, five or six of section 165.45, criminal possession of stolen property in the third degree as defined in section 165.50 (except where the property consists of one or more firearms, rifles or shotguns), forgery in the second degree as defined in section 170.10, criminal possession of a forged instrument in the second degree as defined in section 170.25, unlawfully using slugs in the first degree as defined in section 170.60, or an attempt to commit any of the aforementioned offenses if such attempt constitutes a felony offense; or a class B felony offense defined in article two hundred twenty where a sentence is imposed pursuant to paragraph (a) of subdivision two of section 70.70 of the penal law; or any class C, class D or class E controlled substance or marihuana felony offense as defined in article two hundred twenty or two hundred twenty-one.

6. Upon delivery of the defendant to the reception center, he or she shall be given a copy of the conditions of parole by a representative of the department of corrections and community supervision and shall acknowledge receipt of a copy of the conditions in writing. The conditions shall be established in accordance with article twelve-B of the executive law and the rules and regulations of the board of parole. Thereafter and while the parolee is participating in the intensive drug treatment program provided at the drug treatment campus, the department of corrections and community supervision shall assess the parolee's special needs and shall develop an intensive program of parole supervision that will address the parolee's substance abuse history and which shall include periodic urinalysis testing. Unless inappropriate, such program shall include the provision of treatment services by a community-based substance abuse service provider which has

a contract with the department of corrections and community supervision.

7. Upon completion of the drug treatment program at the drug treatment campus, a parolee will be furnished with money, clothing and transportation in a manner consistent with section one hundred twenty-five of the correction law to permit the parolee's travel from the drug treatment campus to the county in which the parolee's supervision will continue.

8. If the parole officer having charge of a person sentenced to parole supervision pursuant to this section has reasonable cause to believe that such person has violated the conditions of his or her parole, the procedures of subdivision three of section two hundred fifty-nine-i of the executive law shall apply to the issuance of a warrant and the conduct of further proceedings; provided, however, that a parole violation warrant issued for a violation committed while the parolee is being supervised at a drug treatment campus shall constitute authority for the immediate placement of the parolee into a correctional facility operated by the department of corrections and community supervision, which to the extent practicable shall be reasonably proximate to the place at which the violation occurred, to hold in temporary detention pending completion of the procedures required by subdivision three of section two hundred fifty-nine-i of the executive law.

HISTORY: Add, L 1995, ch 3, § 34, eff Oct 1, 1995, repealed Sept 1, 2015; amd, L 2009, ch 56, §§ 6–8 (Part AAA), eff April 7, 2009, L 2010, ch 121, §§ 1, 2, eff June 15, 2010, L 2011, ch 62, § 76 (Part C, Subpart B), eff March 31, 2011, L 2014, ch 90, § 11, eff July 3, 2014, expires and repealed July 5, 2021.

§ 410.92. [Repealed]

HISTORY: Add, L 2007, ch 377, § 2, eff July 18, 2007, expires and repealed March 31, 2010. Sub 2, amd, L 2008, ch 16, § 1, eff Feb 19, 2008.

ARTICLE 420   FINES, RESTITUTION AND REPARATION

HISTORY: Add, L 1970, ch 996, § 1; amd, L 1980, ch 290, § 2, eff Sept 1, 1980.

§ 420.05. Payment of fines, mandatory surcharges and fees by credit card.

When the court imposes a fine, mandatory surcharge or fee upon an individual who stands convicted of any offense, such individual may pay such fine, mandatory surcharge or fee by credit card or similar device. In such event, notwithstanding any other provision of law, he or she also may be required to pay a reasonable administrative fee. The amount of such administrative fee and the time and manner of its payment shall be in accordance with the system established by the chief administrator of the courts pursuant to paragraph (j) of subdivision two of section two hundred twelve of the judiciary law.

HISTORY: Add, L 1987, ch 805, § 2, eff Aug 7, 1987. Amd, L 2003, ch 537, § 1, eff Sept 17, 2003, L 2005, ch 457, § 3, eff Aug 9, 2005, L 2010, ch 528, § 5, eff Sept 17, 2010, deemed eff on and after Sept 1, 2009, amended L 2005, ch 457, § 7, so as to delete Aug 9, 2010, expiration date applicable to amendment of this section. Section heading, amd, L 2003, ch 537, § 1, eff Sept 17, 2003, L 2005, ch 457, § 3, eff Aug 9, 2005, L 2010, ch 528, § 5, eff Sept 17, 2010, deemed eff on and after Sept 1, 2009, amended L 2005, ch 457, § 7, so as to delete Aug 9, 2010, expiration date applicable to amendment of this section.

§ 420.10. Collection of fines, restitution or reparation

1. Alternative methods of payment. When the court imposes a fine upon an individual, it shall designate the official other than the district attorney to whom payment is to be remitted. When the court imposes restitution or reparation and requires that the defendant pay a designated surcharge thereon pursuant to the provisions of subdivision eight of section 60.27 of the penal law, it shall designate the official or organization other than the district attorney, selected pursuant to subdivision eight of this section, to whom payment is to be remitted.

(a) The court may direct:

(i) That the defendant pay the entire amount at the time sentence is pronounced;

(ii) That the defendant pay the entire amount at some later date; or

(iii) That the defendant pay a specified portion at designated periodic intervals.

(b) When the court imposes both (i) a fine and (ii) restitution or reparation and such designated surcharge upon an individual and imposes a schedule of payments, the court shall also direct that payment of restitution or reparation and such designated surcharge take priority over the payment of the fine.

(c) Where the defendant is sentenced to a period of probation as well as a fine, restitution or reparation and such designated surcharge, the court may direct that payment of the fine, restitution or reparation and such designated surcharge be a condition of the sentence.

(d) When a court requires that restitution or reparation and such designated surcharge be made it must direct that notice be given to a person or persons to whom it is to be paid of the conditions under which it is to be remitted; the name and address of the public official or organization to whom it is to be remitted for payment and the amount thereof; and the availability of civil proceedings for collection under subdivision six of this section. An official or organization designated to receive payment under this subdivision must report to the court any failure to comply with the order and shall cooperate with the district attorney pursuant to his responsibilities under subdivision six of this section.

(e) Where cash bail has been posted by the defendant as the principal and is not forfeited or assigned, the court at its discretion may order that bail be applied toward payment of any order of restitution or reparation or fine. If the court so orders, the bail proceeds shall be applied to payment first of the restitution or reparation and then of the fine.

2. Death of victim. In the event that the individual to whom restitution or reparation is to be made dies prior to completion of said restitution or reparation, the remaining payments shall be made to the estate of the deceased.

3. Imprisonment for failure to pay. Where the court imposes a fine, restitution or reparation, the sentence may provide that if the defendant fails to pay the fine, restitution or reparation in accordance with the direction of the court, the defendant must be imprisoned until the fine, restitution or reparation is satisfied. Such provision may be added at the time sentence is pronounced or at any later date while the fine, restitution or reparation or any part thereof remains unpaid; provided, however, that if the provision is added at a time subsequent to the pronouncement of sentence the defendant must be personally present when it is added. In any case where the defendant fails to pay a fine, restitution or reparation as directed the court may issue a warrant directing a peace officer, acting pursuant to his special duties, or a police officer, to take him into custody and bring him before the court; provided, however, if the court in which the warrant is

returnable is a city, town or village court, and such court is not available, and the warrant is addressed to a police officer, such executing police officer must without unnecessary delay bring the defendant before an alternate local criminal court, as provided in subdivision five of section 120.90 of this chapter; or if the court in which the warrant is returnable is a superior court, and such court is not available, and the warrant is addressed to a police officer, such executing police officer may bring the defendant to the local correctional facility of the county in which such court sits, to be detained there until not later than the commencement of the next session of such court occurring on the next business day. Such warrant may also be delegated in the same manner as a warrant pursuant to section 530.70 of this chapter. Where a sentence provides that the defendant be imprisoned for failure to pay a fine, the court shall advise the defendant that if he is unable to pay such fine, he has a right, at any time, to apply to the court to be resentenced as provided in subdivision five of this section.

4. Period of imprisonment. When the court directs that the defendant be imprisoned until the fine, restitution or reparation be satisfied, it must specify a maximum period of imprisonment subject to the following limits:

(a) Where the fine, restitution or reparation is imposed for a felony, the period may not exceed one year;

(b) Where the fine, restitution or reparation is imposed for a misdemeanor, the period may not exceed one-third of the maximum authorized term of imprisonment;

(c) Where the fine, restitution or reparation is imposed for a petty offense, the period may not exceed fifteen days; and

(d) Where a sentence of imprisonment as well as a fine, restitution or reparation is imposed, the aggregate of the period and the term of the sentence may not exceed the maximum authorized term of imprisonment.

(e) Jail time and good behavior time shall be credited against the full period of imprisonment, if served, as provided in section 70.30 of the penal law for definite sentences.

5. Application for resentence. In any case where the defendant is unable to pay a fine, restitution or reparation imposed by the court, he may at any time apply to the court for resentence. In such case, if the court is satisfied that the defendant is unable to pay the fine, restitution or reparation it must:

(a) Adjust the terms of payment; or

(b) Lower the amount of the fine, restitution or reparation; or

(c) Where the sentence consists of probation or imprisonment and a fine, restitution or reparation, revoke the portion of the sentence imposing the fine, restitution or reparation; or

(d) Revoke the entire sentence imposed and resentence the defendant. Upon such resentence the court may impose any sentence it originally could have imposed, except that the amount of any fine, restitution or reparation imposed may not be in excess of the amount the defendant is able to pay.

In any case where the defendant applies for resentencing with respect to any condition of the sentence relating to restitution or reparation the court must order that notice of such application and a reasonable opportunity to be heard be given to the person or persons given notice pursuant to subdivision one of this section. If the court grants the defendant's application by changing the original order for restitution or reparation in any manner, the court must place the reasons therefor on the record.

For the purposes of this subdivision, the court shall not determine that the defendant is unable to pay the fine, restitution or reparation ordered solely because of such defendant's incarceration but shall consider all the defendant's sources of income including, but not limited to, moneys in the possession of an inmate at the time of his admission into such facility, funds earned by him in a work release program as defined in subdivision four of section one hundred fifty of the correction law, funds earned by him as provided for in section one hundred eighty-seven of the correction law and any other funds received by him or on his behalf and deposited with the superintendent or the municipal official of the facility where the person is confined.

6. Civil proceeding for collection.

(a) A fine, restitution or reparation imposed or directed by the court shall be imposed or directed by a written order of the court containing the amount thereof required to be paid by the defendant. The court's order also shall direct the district attorney to file a certified copy of such order with the county clerk of the county in which the court is situate except where the court which issues such order is the supreme court in which case the order itself shall be filed by the clerk of the court acting in his or her capacity as the county clerk of the county in which the court is situate. Such order shall be entered by the county clerk in the same manner as a judgment in a civil action in accordance with subdivision (a) of rule five thousand sixteen of the civil practice law and rules. Even if the defendant was imprisoned for failure to pay such fine, restitution or reparation, or has served the period of imprisonment imposed, such order after entry thereof pursuant to this subdivision may be collected in the same manner as a judgment in a civil action by the victim, as defined in paragraph (b) of subdivision four of section 60.27 of the penal law, to whom restitution or reparation was ordered to be paid, the estate of such person or the district attorney. The entered order shall be deemed to constitute a judgment-roll as defined in section five thousand seventeen of the civil practice law and rules and immediately after entry of the order, the county clerk shall docket the entered order as a money judgment pursuant to section five thousand eighteen of such law and rules. Wherever appropriate, the district attorney shall file a transcript of the docket of the judgment with the clerk of any other county of the state. Such a restitution or reparation order, when docketed shall be a first lien upon all real property in which the defendant thereafter acquires an interest, having preference over all other liens, security interests, and encumbrances whatsoever, except:

(i) a lien or interest running to the benefit of the government of the United States or the state of New York, or any political subdivision or public benefit corporation thereof; or

(ii) a purchase money interest in any property.

(b) The district attorney may, in his or her discretion, and must, upon order of the court, institute proceedings to collect such fine, restitution or reparation.

7. Undisbursed restitution payments. Where a court requires that restitution or reparation be made by a defendant, the official or organization to whom payments are to be remitted pursuant to subdivision one of this section may place such payments in an interest-bearing account. The interest accrued and any undisbursed payments shall be designated for the payment of restitution orders that have remained unsatisfied for the longest period of time. For the purposes of this subdivision, the term "undisbursed restitution payments" shall mean those payments which have been remitted by a defendant but not disbursed to the intended beneficiary and such payment has gone unclaimed for a period of one year and the location of the intended beneficiary cannot be ascertained by such official or organization after using reasonable efforts.

8. Designation of restitution agency.

(a) The chief elected official in each county, and in the city of New York the mayor, shall designate an official or organization other than the district attorney to be responsible for the collection and administration of restitution and reparation payments under provisions of the penal law and this chapter. This official or organization shall be eligible for the designated surcharge provided for by subdivision eight of section 60.27 of the penal law.

(b) The restitution agency, as designated by paragraph (a) of this subdivision, shall be responsible for the collection of data on a monthly basis regarding the numbers of restitution and reparation orders issued, the numbers of satisfied restitution and reparation orders and information concerning the types of crimes for which such orders were required. A probation department designated as the restitution agency shall then forward such information to the office of probation and correctional alternatives within the first ten days following the end of each month. In all other cases the restitution agency shall report to the division of criminal justice services directly. The division of criminal justice services shall compile and review all such information and make recommendations to promote the use of restitution and encourage its enforcement.

> **HISTORY:** Add, L 1970, ch 996, § 1, with substance derived from Crim C § 470-d; amd, L 1977, ch 694, § 1, L 1980, ch 290, § 3, L 1980, ch 584, § 1, L 1980, ch 843, § 19, L 1983, ch 515, §§ 1, 2, L 1984, ch 335, § 3, eff July 3, 1984, L 1984, ch 965, § 3, L 1985, ch 134, § 2, L 1985, ch 233, §§ 1–5, L 1985, ch 506, § 1, eff Nov 1, 1985, L 1984, ch 965, § 2, L 1985, ch 233, § 4, L 1985, ch 506, § 1, eff Nov 1, 1985, L 1992, ch 618, § 6, eff Nov 1, 1992, L 1992, ch 378, § 1, eff Nov 1, 1992, L 1992, ch 618, §§ 7, 8, eff Nov 1, 1992, L 2010, ch 56, § 52 (Part A), eff June 22, 2010.

§ 420.20. Collection of fines, restitution or reparation imposed upon corporations

Where a corporation is sentenced to pay a fine, restitution or reparation, the fine, restitution or reparation must be paid at the time sentence is imposed. If the fine, restitution or reparation is not so paid, it may be collected in the same manner as a judgment in a civil action, and if execution issued upon such judgment be returned unsatisfied an action may be brought in the name of the people of the state of New York to procure a judgment sequestering the property of the corporation, as provided by the business corporation law. It is the duty of the attorney general in all criminal proceedings prosecuted by him, and, in all other proceedings, the county attorney for counties outside the city of New York, and, in the city of New York the corporation counsel of the city of New York, to institute proceedings to collect such fine, restitution or reparation.

> **HISTORY:** Add, L 1970, ch 996, § 1, with substance derived from Crim C § 682; amd, L 1973, ch 488, § 1, L 1980, ch 290, § 4, eff Sept 1, 1980. Section heading, amd, L 1980, ch 290, § 4, eff Sept 1, 1980.

§ 420.30. Remission of fines, restitution or reparation

1. Applicability. The procedure specified in this section governs remission of fines, restitution or reparation in all cases not covered by subdivision four of section 420.10.

2. Procedure.

(a) Any superior court which has imposed a fine, restitution or reparation for any offense may, in its discretion, on five days notice to the district attorney of the county in which such fine, restitution or reparation was imposed and to each person otherwise required to be given notice of restitution or reparation pursuant to subdivision one of section 420.10, remit such fine, restitution or reparation or any portion thereof. In case of a fine, restitution or reparation imposed by a local criminal court for any offense, a superior court holding a term in the county in which the fine, restitution or reparation was imposed may, upon like notice, remit such fine, restitution or reparation or any portion thereof.

(b) The court shall give each person given notice a reasonable opportunity to be heard on the question of remitting an order of restitution or reparation. If the court remits such restitution or reparation, or any part thereof, the reasons therefor shall be placed upon the record.

3. Restrictions. In no event shall a mandatory surcharge, sex offender registration fee, DNA databank fee or crime victim assistance fee be remitted provided, however, that a court may waive the crime victim assistance fee if such defendant is an eligible youth as defined in subdivision two of section 720.10 of this chapter, and the imposition of such fee would work an unreasonable hardship on the defendant, his or her immediate family, or any other person who is dependent on such defendant for financial support.

HISTORY: Add, L 1970, ch 996, § 1, with substance derived from Crim C § 470-c; amd, L 1980, ch 290, § 5, L 1995, ch 3, § 65, eff July 1, 1995. Section heading, amd, L 1980, ch 290, § 5, eff Sept 1, 1980. Sub 2, par (a), formerly sub 2, so designated, L 1992, ch 618, § 9, eff Nov 1, 1992. Sub 2, par (b), add, L 1992, ch 618, § 9; amd, L 1995, ch 3, § 65, eff July 1, 1995. Sub 3, add, L 1992, ch 794, § 2; amd, L 1993, ch 260, § 42, L 1995, ch 3, § 65, eff July 1, 1995. Sub 3, amd, L 2003, ch 62, § 6 (Part F), eff May 15, 2003, L 2004, ch 56, § 5 (Part F), eff Feb 16, 2005. Sub 4, add, L 1992, ch 794, § 2; deleted, L 1995, ch 3, § 65, eff July 1, 1995.

§ 420.35. Mandatory surcharge and crime victim assistance fee; applicability to sentences mandating payment of fines

1. The provisions of section 420.10 of this article governing the collection of fines and the provisions of section 420.40 of this article governing deferral of mandatory surcharges, sex offender registration fees, DNA databank fees and financial hardship hearings and the provisions of section 430.20 of this chapter governing the commitment of a defendant for failure to pay a fine shall be applicable to a mandatory surcharge, sex offender registration fee, DNA databank fee and a crime victim assistance fee imposed pursuant to subdivision one of section 60.35 of the penal law, subdivision twenty-a of section three hundred eighty-five of the vehicle and traffic law, subdivision nineteen-a of section four hundred one of the vehicle and traffic law, or a mandatory surcharge imposed pursuant to section eighteen hundred nine of the vehicle and traffic law or section 27.12 of the parks, recreation and historic preservation law. When the court directs that the defendant be imprisoned until the mandatory surcharge, sex offender registration fee or DNA databank fee is satisfied, it must specify a maximum period of imprisonment not to exceed fifteen days; provided, however, a court may not direct that a defendant be imprisoned until the mandatory surcharge, sex offender registration fee, or DNA databank fee is satisfied or otherwise for failure to pay the mandatory surcharge, sex offender registration fee or DNA databank fee unless the court makes a contemporaneous finding on the record, after according defendant notice and an opportunity to be heard, that the payment of the mandatory surcharge, sex offender registration fee or DNA databank fee upon defendant will not work an unreasonable hardship upon him or her or his or her immediate family.

2. Under no circumstances shall the mandatory surcharge, sex offender registration fee, DNA databank fee or the crime victim assistance fee be waived provided, however, that a court may waive the crime victim assistance fee if such defendant is an eligible youth as defined in subdivision two of section 720.10 of this chapter, and the imposition of such fee would work an unreasonable hardship on the defendant, his or her immediate family, or any other person who is dependent on such defendant for financial support. A court shall waive any mandatory surcharge and crime victim assistance fee when the court finds that a defendant is a victim of sex trafficking under section 230.34 of the penal law or a victim of trafficking in persons under the trafficking victims protection act (United States Code, Title 22, Chapter 78).

3. It shall be the duty of a court of record or administrative tribunal to report to the division of criminal justice services on the disposition and collection of mandatory surcharges, sex offender registration fees or DNA databank fees and crime victim assistance fees. Such report shall include, for all cases, whether the surcharge, sex offender registration fee, DNA databank fee or crime victim assistance fee levied pursuant to subdivision one of section 60.35 of the penal law or section eighteen hundred nine of the vehicle and traffic law has been imposed pursuant to law, collected, or is to be collected by probation or corrections or other officials. The form, manner and frequency of such reports shall be determined by the commissioner of the division of criminal justice services after consultation with the chief administrator of the courts and the commissioner of the department of motor vehicles.

HISTORY: Add, L 1982, ch 55, § 82; amd, L 1983, ch 15, § 3, L 1990, ch 696, § 9, eff Aug 19, 1990. Section heading, amd, L 1983, ch 15, § 3, L 1990, ch 190, § 320, L 1995, ch 3, § 66, eff July 1, 1995. Sub 1, formerly first undesignated par, so designated and amd, L 1990, ch 190, § 320, L 1990, ch 696, § 9; amd, L 1992, ch 55, § 355, L 1995, ch 3, § 66, eff July 1, 1995. Sub 2, formerly sub 4, so designated and amd, L 1995, ch 3, § 68, eff July 1, 1995. Former sub 2, formerly second undesignated par, add, L 1983, ch 15, § 3; so designated and amd, L 1990, ch 190, § 320, L 1990, ch 696, § 9; amd, L 1992, ch 55, § 355; repealed, L 1995, ch 3, § 67, eff July 1, 1995. Sub 3, formerly sub 6, so designated and amd, L 1995, ch 3, § 69, eff July 1, 1995. Former sub 3, add, L 1992, ch 794, § 3; amd, L 1993, ch 260, § 43; repealed, L 1995, ch 3, § 67, eff July 1, 1995. Prior sub 3, redesignated sub 4, L 1992, ch 794, § 3, eff Aug 7, 1992. Sub 4, add, L 1993, ch 260, § 43; redesignated sub 2, L 1995, ch 3, § 68, eff July 1, 1995. Former sub 4, formerly sub 3, add, L 1990, ch 190, § 320; amd, L 1991, ch 166, § 379, L 1992, ch 55, § 355; redesignated sub 4, L 1992, ch 794, § 3; redesignated sub 5, L 1993, ch 260, § 43, eff July 13, 1993, deemed eff July 1, 1993. Prior sub 4, redesignated sub 5, L 1992, ch 794, § 3, eff Aug 7, 1992. Sub 5, formerly sub 4, so designated, L 1993, ch 260, § 43; repealed, L 1995, ch 3, § 67, eff July 1, 1995. Former sub 5, formerly sub 4, add, L 1991, ch 166, § 379; so designated, L 1992, ch 794, § 3; redesignated sub 6, L 1993, ch 260, § 43, eff July 13, 1993, deemed eff July 1, 1993. Sub 6, formerly sub 5, so designated, L 1993, ch 260, § 43; redesignated sub 3, L 1995, ch 3, § 69, eff July 1, 1995. Sub 1, amd, L 2003, ch 62, § 7 (Part F), eff May 15, 2003. Sub 2, amd, L 2003, ch 62, § 7 (Part F), eff May 15, 2003, L 2004, ch 56, § 6 (Part F), eff Feb 16, 2005, L 2014, ch 385, § 1, eff Sept 23, 2014. Sub 3, amd, L 2003, ch 62, § 7 (Part F), eff May 15, 2003.

§ 420.40. Deferral of a mandatory surcharge; financial hardship hearings

1. Applicability. The procedure specified in this section governs the deferral of the obligation to pay all or part of a mandatory surcharge, sex offender registration fee or DNA databank fee imposed pursuant to subdivision one of section 60.35 of the penal law and financial hardship hearings relating to mandatory surcharges.

2. On an appearance date set forth in a summons issued pursuant to subdivision three of section 60.35 of the penal law, section eighteen hundred nine of the vehicle and traffic law or section 27.12 of the parks, recreation and historic preservation law, a person upon whom a mandatory surcharge, sex offender registration fee or DNA databank fee was levied shall have an opportunity to present on the record credible and verifiable information establishing that the mandatory surcharge, sex offender registration fee or DNA databank fee should be deferred, in whole or in part, because, due to the indigence of such person the payment of said surcharge, sex offender registration fee or DNA databank fee would work an unreasonable hardship on the person or his or her immediate family.

3. In assessing such information the superior court shall be mindful of the mandatory nature of the surcharge, sex offender registration fee and DNA databank fee, and the important criminal justice and victim services sustained by such fees.

4. Where a court determines that it will defer part or all of a mandatory surcharge, sex offender registration fee or DNA databank fee imposed pursuant to subdivision one of section 60.35 of the

penal law, a statement of such finding and of the facts upon which it is based shall be made part of the record.

5. A court which defers a person's obligation to pay a mandatory surcharge, sex offender registration fee or DNA databank fee imposed pursuant to subdivision one of section 60.35 of the penal law shall do so in a written order. Such order shall not excuse the person from the obligation to pay the surcharge, sex offender registration fee or DNA databank fee. Rather, the court's order shall direct the filing of a certified copy of the order with the county clerk of the county in which the court is situate except where the court which issues such order is the supreme court in which case the order itself shall be filed by the clerk of the court acting in his or her capacity as the county clerk of the county in which the court is situate. Such order shall be entered by the county clerk in the same manner as a judgment in a civil action in accordance with subdivision (a) of rule five thousand sixteen of the civil practice law and rules. The order shall direct that any unpaid balance of the mandatory surcharge, sex offender registration fee or DNA databank fee may be collected in the same manner as a civil judgment. The entered order shall be deemed to constitute a judgment-roll as defined in section five thousand seventeen of the civil practice law and rules and immediately after entry of the order, the county clerk shall docket the entered order as a money judgment pursuant to section five thousand eighteen of such law and rules.

HISTORY: Add, L 1995, ch 3, § 70, eff July 1, 1995. Sub 1, amd, L 2003, ch 62, § 8 (Part F), eff May 15, 2003. Sub 2, amd, L 2003, ch 62, § 8 (Part F), eff May 15, 2003. Sub 3, amd, L 2003, ch 62, § 8 (Part F), eff May 15, 2003. Sub 4, amd, L 2003, ch 62, § 8 (Part F), eff May 15, 2003. Sub 5, amd, L 2003, ch 62, § 8 (Part F), eff May 15, 2003.

ARTICLE 430   SENTENCES OF IMPRISONMENT

§ 430.10.   **Sentence of imprisonment not to be changed after commencement**
§ 430.20.   **Commitment of defendant**
§ 430.30.   **Duty to deliver defendant**

HISTORY: Add, L 1970, ch 996, § 1, eff Sept 1, 1971.

§ 430.10. Sentence of imprisonment not to be changed after commencement

Except as otherwise specifically authorized by law, when the court has imposed a sentence of imprisonment and such sentence is in accordance with law, such sentence may not be changed, suspended or interrupted once the term or period of the sentence has commenced.

HISTORY: Add, L 1970, ch 996, § 1, eff Sept 1, 1971.

§ 430.20. Commitment of defendant

1. In general. When a sentence of imprisonment is pronounced, or when th [the]* sentence consists of a fine and the court has directed that the defendant be imprisoned until it is satisfied, the defendant must forthwith be committed to the custody of the appropriate public servant and detained until the sentence is complied with.

2. [Until Sept 1, 2015] Indeterminate and determinate sentences. In the case of an indeterminate or determinate sentence of imprisonment, commitment must be to the custody of the state department of corrections and community supervision as provided in subdivision one of section 70.20 of the penal law. The order of commitment must direct that the defendant be delivered to an institution designated by the commissioner of corrections and community supervision in accordance with the provisions of the correction law.

2. [Eff Sept 1, 2015] Indeterminate sentences. In the case of an indeterminate sentence of

---

* The bracketed word has been inserted by the Publisher.

imprisonment, commitment must be to the custody of the state department of corrections and community supervision as provided in subdivision one of section 70.20 of the penal law. The order of commitment must direct that the defendant be delivered to an institution designated by the commissioner of corrections and community supervision in accordance with the provisions of the correction law.

3. Definite and intermittent sentences. In the case of a definite or intermittent sentence of imprisonment, commitment must be as follows:

(a) In counties contained within New York City or in any county that has a county department of correction, commitment must be to the custody of the department of correction of such city or county;

(b) In any other case, commitment must be to the county jail, workhouse or penitentiary, or to a penitentiary outside the county and the order of commitment must specify the institution to which the defendant is to be delivered.

4. [Until Sept 1, 2015] Certain resentences. When a sentence of imprisonment that has been imposed on a defendant is vacated and a new sentence is imposed on such defendant for the same offense, or for an offense based upon the same act, if the term of the new definite or determinate sentence or the maximum term of the new indeterminate sentence so imposed is less than or equal to that of the vacated sentence:

(a) where the time served by the defendant on the vacated sentence is equal to or greater than the term or maximum term of the new sentence, the new sentence shall be deemed to be served in its entirety and the defendant shall not be committed to a correctional facility pursuant to said sentence; and

(b) where the defendant was under the supervision of a local conditional release commission or the department of corrections and community supervision at the time the sentence was vacated, then the commitment shall direct that said conditional release or parole be recommenced, and the defendant shall not be committed to a correctional facility pursuant to said sentence, except as a result of revocation of parole or of conditional release; and

(c) where the defendant was not under the supervision of the department of corrections and community supervision at the time the indeterminate or determinate sentence was vacated, but would immediately be eligible for conditional release from the new indeterminate or determinate sentence, the court shall ascertain from the department of corrections and community supervision whether the defendant has earned a sufficient amount of good time under the vacated sentence so as to require the conditional release of the defendant under the new sentence; in the event the defendant has earned a sufficient amount of good time, the court shall stay execution of sentence until the defendant surrenders at a correctional facility pursuant to the direction of the department of corrections and community supervision, which shall occur no later than sixty days after imposition of sentence; upon said stay of execution, the court clerk shall immediately mail to the commissioner of corrections and community supervision a certified copy of the commitment reflecting said stay of execution and the name, mailing address and telephone number of the defendant's legal representative; in the event the defendant fails to surrender as directed by the department of corrections and community supervision, the department shall notify the court which shall thereafter remand the defendant to custody pursuant to section 430.30 of this article; and

(d) upon the resentence of a defendant as described in this subdivision, the court clerk shall immediately mail a certified copy of the commitment to the commissioner of corrections and community supervision if the vacated sentence or the new sentence is an indeterminate or determinate sentence and no mailing is required by paragraph (c) of this subdivision; additionally, the court clerk shall immediately mail a certified copy of the new commitment to the head of the appropriate local correctional facility if the vacated sentence or the new sentence is a definite sentence.

4. [Eff Sept 1, 2015] Certain resentences. When a sentence of imprisonment that has been imposed on a defendant is vacated and a new sentence is imposed on such defendant for the same offense, or for an offense based upon the same act, if the term of the new definite sentence or the maximum term of the new indeterminate sentence so imposed is less than or equal to that of the vacated sentence:

(a) where the time served by the defendant on the vacated sentence is equal to or greater than the term or maximum term of the new sentence, the new sentence shall be deemed to be served in its entirety and the defendant shall not be committed to a correctional facility pursuant to said sentence; and

(b) where the defendant was under the supervision of a local conditional release commission or the department of corrections and community supervision at the time the sentence was vacated, then the commitment shall direct that said conditional release or parole be recommenced, and the defendant shall not be committed to a correctional facility pursuant to said sentence, except as a result of revocation of parole or of conditional release; and

(c) where the defendant was not under the supervision of the department of corrections and community supervision at the time the indeterminate sentence was vacated, but would immediately be eligible for conditional release from the new indeterminate sentence, the court shall ascertain from the department of corrections and community supervision whether the defendant has earned a sufficient amount of good time under the vacated sentence so as to require the conditional release of the defendant under the new sentence; in the event the defendant has earned a sufficient amount of good time, the court shall stay execution of sentence until the defendant surrenders at a correctional facility pursuant to the direction of the department of corrections and community supervision, which shall occur no later than sixty days after imposition of sentence; upon said stay of execution, the court clerk shall immediately mail to the commissioner of corrections and community supervision a certified copy of the commitment reflecting said stay of execution and the name, mailing address and telephone number of the defendant's legal representative; in the event the defendant fails to surrender as directed by the department of corrections and community supervision, the department shall notify the court which shall thereafter remand the defendant to custody pursuant to section 430.30 of this article; and

(d) upon the resentence of a defendant as described in this subdivision, the court clerk shall immediately mail a certified copy of the commitment to the commissioner of corrections and community supervision if the vacated sentence or the new sentence is an indeterminate sentence and no mailing is required by paragraph (c) of this subdivision; additionally, the court clerk shall immediately mail a certified copy of the new commitment to the head of the appropriate local correctional facility if the vacated sentence or the new sentence is a definite sentence.

5. Commitment for failure to pay fine. Where the sentence consists of a fine and the court has directed that the defendant be imprisoned until it is satisfied, commitment must be as follows:

(a) If the sentence also includes a term of imprisonment, commitment must be to the same institution as is designated for service of the term of imprisonment, and the period of commitment commences (i) when the term of imprisonment is satisfied, or (ii) with the approval of the state board of parole, when the defendant becomes eligible for parole, or (iii) when the defendant becomes eligible for conditional release, whichever occurs first; provided, however, that the court may direct that the period of imprisonment for the fine run concurrently with the term of imprisonment; and

(b) In any other case, commitment must be to the agency or institution that would be designated in the case of a definite sentence.

HISTORY: Add, L 1970, ch 996, § 1, eff Sept 1, 1971; amd, L 1971, ch 788, § 1, eff Sept 1, 1971, L 1994, ch 370, § 1, L 1995, ch 3, § 35, eff Oct 1, 1995, repealed Sept 1, 2015, L 2011, ch 62, § 77 (Part C, Subpart B), eff March 31, 2011, L 2011, ch 62, § 78 (Part C, Subpart B), eff Sept 1, 2015.

§ 430.30. Duty to deliver defendant

In counties contained within New York City and in counties that have a commissioner of correction who is responsible for detention of defendants in criminal actions, it is the duty of the commissioner of correction of such city or county to deliver the defendant forthwith to the proper institution in accordance with the commitment. In all other counties it is the duty of the sheriff to deliver the defendant forthwith to the proper institution in accordance with the commitment.

HISTORY: Add, L 1970, ch 996, § 1, eff Sept 1, 1971.

TITLE M   Proceedings After Judgment
ARTICLE 440
POST-JUDGMENT MOTIONS

ARTICLE 450
APPEALS—IN WHAT CASES AUTHORIZED AND TO WHAT COURTS TAKEN

ARTICLE 460
APPEALS—TAKING AND PERFECTION THEREOF AND STAYS DURING PENDENCY THEREOF

ARTICLE 470
APPEALS—DETERMINATION THEREOF

HISTORY: Add, L 1970, ch 996, § 1, eff Sept 1, 1971.

ARTICLE 440   POST-JUDGMENT MOTIONS

HISTORY: Add, L 1970, ch 996, § 1, eff Sept 1, 1971.

§ 440.10. Motion to vacate judgment

1. At any time after the entry of a judgment, the court in which it was entered may, upon motion of the defendant, vacate such judgment upon the ground that:

(a) The court did not have jurisdiction of the action or of the person of the defendant; or

(b) The judgment was procured by duress, misrepresentation or fraud on the part of the court or a prosecutor or a person acting for or in behalf of a court or a prosecutor; or

(c) Material evidence adduced at a trial resulting in the judgment was false and was, prior to the entry of the judgment, known by the prosecutor or by the court to be false; or

(d) Material evidence adduced by the people at a trial resulting in the judgment was procured in violation of the defendant's rights under the constitution of this state or of the United States; or

(e) During the proceedings resulting in the judgment, the defendant, by reason of mental disease or defect, was incapable of understanding or participating in such proceedings; or

(f) Improper and prejudicial conduct not appearing in the record occurred during a trial resulting in the judgment which conduct, if it had appeared in the record, would have required a reversal of the judgment upon an appeal therefrom; or

(g) New evidence has been discovered since the entry of a judgment based upon a verdict of guilty after trial, which could not have been produced by the defendant at the trial even with due diligence on his part and which is of such character as to create a probability that had such evidence been received at the trial the verdict would have been more favorable to the defendant; provided that a motion based upon such ground must be made with due diligence after the discovery of such alleged new evidence; or

(g-1) Forensic DNA testing of evidence performed since the entry of a judgment, (1) in the case of a defendant convicted after a guilty plea, the court has determined that the defendant has demonstrated a substantial probability that the defendant was actually innocent of the offense of which he or she was convicted, or (2) in the case of a defendant convicted after a trial, the court has determined that there exists a reasonable probability that the verdict would have been more favorable to the defendant.

(h) The judgment was obtained in violation of a right of the defendant under the constitution of this state or of the United States; or

(i) The judgment is a conviction where the arresting charge was under section 240.37 (loitering for the purpose of engaging in a prostitution offense, provided that the defendant was not alleged to be loitering for the purpose of patronizing a prostitute or promoting prostitution) or 230.00 (prostitution) of the penal law, and the defendant's participation in the offense was a result of having been a victim of sex trafficking under section 230.34 of the penal law or trafficking in persons under the Trafficking Victims Protection Act (United States Code, title 22, chapter 78); provided that

(i) a motion under this paragraph shall be made with due diligence, after the defendant has ceased to be a victim of such trafficking or has sought services for victims of such trafficking, subject to reasonable concerns for the safety of the defendant, family members of the defendant, or other victims of such trafficking that may be jeopardized by the bringing of such motion, or for other reasons consistent with the purpose of this paragraph; and

(ii) official documentation of the defendant's status as a victim of sex trafficking or trafficking in persons at the time of the offense from a federal, state or local government agency shall create a presumption that the defendant's participation in the offense was a result of having been a victim of sex trafficking or trafficking in persons, but shall not be required for granting a motion under this paragraph.

2. Notwithstanding the provisions of subdivision one, the court must deny a motion to vacate a judgment when:

(a) The ground or issue raised upon the motion was previously determined on the merits upon an appeal from the judgment, unless since the time of such appellate determination there has been a retroactively effective change in the law controlling such issue; or

(b) The judgment is, at the time of the motion, appealable or pending on appeal, and sufficient facts appear on the record with respect to the ground or issue raised upon the motion to permit adequate review thereof upon such an appeal. This paragraph shall not apply to a motion under paragraph (i) of subdivision one of this section; or

(c) Although sufficient facts appear on the record of the proceedings underlying the judgment to have permitted, upon appeal from such judgment, adequate review of the ground or issue raised upon the motion, no such appellate review or determination occurred owing to the defendant's unjustifiable failure to take or perfect an appeal during the prescribed period or to his unjustifiable failure to raise such ground or issue upon an appeal actually perfected by him; or

(d) The ground or issue raised relates solely to the validity of the sentence and not to the validity of the conviction.

3. Notwithstanding the provisions of subdivision one, the court may deny a motion to vacate a judgment when:

(a) Although facts in support of the ground or issue raised upon the motion could with due diligence by the defendant have readily been made to appear on the record in a manner providing adequate basis for review of such ground or issue upon an appeal from the judgment, the defendant unjustifiably failed to adduce such matter prior to sentence and the ground or issue in question was not subsequently determined upon appeal. This paragraph does not apply to a motion based upon deprivation of the right to counsel at the trial or upon failure of the trial court to advise the defendant of such right, or to a motion under paragraph (i) of subdivision one of this section; or

(b) The ground or issue raised upon the motion was previously determined on the merits upon a prior motion or proceeding in a court of this state, other than an appeal from the judgment, or upon a motion or proceeding in a federal court; unless since the time of such determination there has been a retroactively effective change in the law controlling such issue; or

(c) Upon a previous motion made pursuant to this section, the defendant was in a position adequately to raise the ground or issue underlying the present motion but did not do so.

Although the court may deny the motion under any of the circumstances specified in this subdivision, in the interest of justice and for good cause shown it may in its discretion grant the motion if it is otherwise meritorious and vacate the judgment.

4. If the court grants the motion, it must, except as provided in subdivision five or six of this section, vacate the judgment, and must dismiss the accusatory instrument, or order a new trial, or take such other action as is appropriate in the circumstances.

5. Upon granting the motion upon the ground, as prescribed in paragraph (g) of subdivision one, that newly discovered evidence creates a probability that had such evidence been received at the trial the verdict would have been more favorable to the defendant in that the conviction would have been for a lesser offense than the one contained in the verdict, the court may either:

(a) Vacate the judgment and order a new trial; or

(b) With the consent of the people, modify the judgment by reducing it to one of conviction for such lesser offense. In such case, the court must re-sentence the defendant accordingly.

6. If the court grants a motion under paragraph (i) of subdivision one of this section, it must vacate the judgment and dismiss the accusatory instrument, and may take such additional action as is appropriate in the circumstances.

7. Upon a new trial resulting from an order vacating a judgment pursuant to this section, the indictment is deemed to contain all the counts and to charge all the offenses which it contained and charged at the time the previous trial was commenced, regardless of whether any count was dismissed by the court in the course of such trial, except (a) those upon or of which the defendant was acquitted or deemed to have been acquitted, and (b) those dismissed by the order vacating the judgment, and (c) those previously dismissed by an appellate court upon an appeal from the

judgment, or by any court upon a previous post-judgment motion.

8. Upon an order which vacates a judgment based upon a plea of guilty to an accusatory instrument or a part thereof, but which does not dismiss the entire accusatory instrument, the criminal action is, in the absence of an express direction to the contrary, restored to its prepleading status and the accusatory instrument is deemed to contain all the counts and to charge all the offenses which it contained and charged at the time of the entry of the plea, except those subsequently dismissed under circumstances specified in paragraphs (b) and (c) of subdivision six. Where the plea of guilty was entered and accepted, pursuant to subdivision three of section 220.30, upon the condition that it constituted a complete disposition not only of the accusatory instrument underlying the judgment vacated but also of one or more other accusatory instruments against the defendant then pending in the same court, the order of vacation completely restores such other accusatory instruments; and such is the case even though such order dismisses the main accusatory instrument underlying the judgment.

     HISTORY: Add, L 1970, ch 996, § 1; amd, L 2010, ch 332, §§ 1–5, L 2012, ch 19, § 4, eff Aug 1, 2012.

§ 440.20. Motion to set aside sentence; by defendant

1. At any time after the entry of a judgment, the court in which the judgment was entered may, upon motion of the defendant, set aside the sentence upon the ground that it was unauthorized, illegally imposed or otherwise invalid as a matter of law. Where the judgment includes a sentence of death, the court may also set aside the sentence upon any of the grounds set forth in paragraph (b), (c), (f), (g) or (h) of subdivision one of section 440.10 as applied to a separate sentencing proceeding under section 400.27, provided, however, that to the extent the ground or grounds asserted include one or more of the aforesaid paragraphs of subdivision one of section 440.10, the court must also apply subdivisions two and three of section 440.10, other than paragraph (d) of subdivision two of such section, in determining the motion. In the event the court enters an order granting a motion to set aside a sentence of death under this section, the court must either direct a new sentencing proceeding in accordance with section 400.27 or, to the extent that the defendant cannot be resentenced to death consistent with the laws of this state or the constitution of this state or of the United States, resentence the defendant to life imprisonment without parole or to a sentence of imprisonment for the class A-I felony of murder in the first degree other than a sentence of life imprisonment without parole. Upon granting the motion upon any of the grounds set forth in the aforesaid paragraphs of subdivision one of section 440.10 and setting aside the sentence, the court must afford the people a reasonable period of time, which shall not be less than ten days, to determine whether to take an appeal from the order setting aside the sentence of death. The taking of an appeal by the people stays the effectiveness of that portion of the court's order that directs a new sentencing proceeding.

2. Notwithstanding the provisions of subdivision one, the court must deny such a motion when the ground or issue raised thereupon was previously determined on the merits upon an appeal from the judgment or sentence, unless since the time of such appellate determination there has been a retroactively effective change in the law controlling such issue.

3. Notwithstanding the provisions of subdivision one, the court may deny such a motion when the ground or issue raised thereupon was previously determined on the merits upon a prior motion or proceeding in a court of this state, other than an appeal from the judgment, or upon a prior motion or proceeding in a federal court, unless since the time of such determination there has been a retroactively effective change in the law controlling such issue. Despite such determination, however, the court in the interest of justice and for good cause shown, may in its discretion grant the motion if it is otherwise meritorious.

4. An order setting aside a sentence pursuant to this section does not affect the validity or status of the underlying conviction, and after entering such an order the court must resentence the defendant in accordance with the law.

HISTORY: Add, L 1970, ch 996, § 1; amd, L 1995, ch 1, § 21, eff Sept 1, 1995.

§ 440.30. Motion to vacate judgment and to set aside sentence; procedure

1. (a) A motion to vacate a judgment pursuant to section 440.10 of this article and a motion to set aside a sentence pursuant to section 440.20 of this article must be made in writing and upon reasonable notice to the people. Upon the motion, a defendant who is in a position adequately to raise more than one ground should raise every such ground upon which he or she intends to challenge the judgment or sentence. If the motion is based upon the existence or occurrence of facts, the motion papers must contain sworn allegations thereof, whether by the defendant or by another person or persons. Such sworn allegations may be based upon personal knowledge of the affiant or upon information and belief, provided that in the latter event the affiant must state the sources of such information and the grounds of such belief. The defendant may further submit documentary evidence or information supporting or tending to support the allegations of the moving papers. The people may file with the court, and in such case must serve a copy thereof upon the defendant or his or her counsel, if any, an answer denying or admitting any or all of the allegations of the motion papers, and may further submit documentary evidence or information refuting or tending to refute such allegations. After all papers of both parties have been filed, and after all documentary evidence or information, if any, has been submitted, the court must consider the same for the purpose of ascertaining whether the motion is determinable without a hearing to resolve questions of fact.

(b) In conjunction with the filing or consideration of a motion to vacate a judgment pursuant to section 440.10 of this article by a defendant convicted after a trial, in cases where the court has ordered an evidentiary hearing upon such motion, the court may order that the people produce or make available for inspection property, as defined in subdivision three of section 240.10 of this part, in its possession, custody, or control that was secured in connection with the investigation or prosecution of the defendant upon credible allegations by the defendant and a finding by the court that such property, if obtained, would be probative to the determination of defendant's actual innocence, and that the request is reasonable. The court shall deny or limit such a request upon a finding that such a request, if granted, would threaten the integrity or chain of custody of property or the integrity of the processes or functions of a laboratory conducting DNA testing, pose a risk of harm, intimidation, embarrassment, reprisal, or other substantially negative consequences to any person, undermine the proper functions of law enforcement including the confidentiality of informants, or on the basis of any other factor identified by the court in the interests of justice or public safety. The court shall further ensure that any property produced pursuant to this paragraph is subject to a protective order, where appropriate. The court shall deny any request made pursuant to this paragraph where:

    (i) (1) the defendant's motion pursuant to section 440.10 of this article does not seek to demonstrate his or her actual innocence of the offense or offenses of which he or she was convicted that are the subject of the motion, or (2) the defendant has not presented credible allegations and the court has not found that such property, if obtained, would be probative to the determination of the defendant's actual innocence and that the request is reasonable;

    (ii) the defendant has made his or her motion after five years from the date of the judgment of conviction; provided, however, that this limitation period shall be tolled for five years if the defendant is in custody in connection with the conviction that is the subject of his or her motion, and provided further that, notwithstanding such limitation periods, the court may consider the motion if the defendant has shown: (A) that he or she has been pursuing his or her rights diligently and that some extraordinary circumstance prevented the timely filing of the motion; (B) that the facts upon which the motion is predicated were unknown to the defendant or his or her attorney and could not have been ascertained by the exercise of due diligence prior to the expiration of the statute of limitations; or (C) considering all circumstances of the case including but not limited to evidence of the defendant's guilt, the impact of granting or denying such motion upon public confidence in the criminal justice system, or upon the safety or welfare of the community, and the defendant's diligence in seeking to obtain the requested property or related relief, the interests of justice would be served by considering the motion;

(iii) the defendant is challenging a judgment convicting him or her of an offense that is not a felony defined in section 10.00 of the penal law; or

(iv) upon a finding by the court that the property requested in this motion would be available through other means through reasonable efforts by the defendant to obtain such property.

1-a. (a) (1) Where the defendant's motion requests the performance of a forensic DNA test on specified evidence, and upon the court's determination that any evidence containing deoxyribonucleic acid ("DNA") was secured in connection with the trial resulting in the judgment, the court shall grant the application for forensic DNA testing of such evidence upon its determination that if a DNA test had been conducted on such evidence, and if the results had been admitted in the trial resulting in the judgment, there exists a reasonable probability that the verdict would have been more favorable to the defendant.

(2) Where the defendant's motion for forensic DNA testing of specified evidence is made following a plea of guilty and entry of judgment thereon convicting him or her of: (A) a homicide offense defined in article one hundred twenty-five of the penal law, any felony sex offense defined in article one hundred thirty of the penal law, a violent felony offense as defined in paragraph (a) of subdivision one of section 70.02 of the penal law, or (B) any other felony offense to which he or she pled guilty after being charged in an indictment or information in superior court with one or more of the offenses listed in clause (A) of this subparagraph, then the court shall grant such a motion upon its determination that evidence containing DNA was secured in connection with the investigation or prosecution of the defendant, and if a DNA test had been conducted on such evidence and the results had been known to the parties prior to the entry of the defendant's plea and judgment thereon, there exists a substantial probability that the evidence would have established the defendant's actual innocence of the offense or offenses that are the subject of the defendant's motion; provided, however, that:

(i) the court shall consider whether the defendant had the opportunity to request such testing prior to entering a guilty plea, and, where it finds that the defendant had such opportunity and unjustifiably failed to do so, the court may deny such motion; and

(ii) a court shall deny the defendant's motion for forensic DNA testing where the defendant has made his or her motion more than five years after entry of the judgment of conviction; except that the limitation period may be tolled if the defendant has shown: (A) that he or she has been pursuing his or her rights diligently and that some extraordinary circumstance prevented the timely filing of the motion for forensic DNA testing; (B) that the facts upon which the motion is predicated were unknown to the defendant or his or her attorney and could not have been ascertained by the exercise of due diligence prior to the expiration of this statute of limitations; or (C) considering all circumstances of the case including but not limited to evidence of the defendant's guilt, the impact of granting or denying such motion upon public confidence in the criminal justice system, or upon the safety or welfare of the community, and the defendant's diligence in seeking to obtain the requested property or related relief, the interests of justice would be served by tolling such limitation period.

(b) In conjunction with the filing of a motion under this subdivision, the court may direct the people to provide the defendant with information in the possession of the people concerning the current physical location of the specified evidence and if the specified evidence no longer exists or the physical location of the specified evidence is unknown, a representation to that effect and information and documentary evidence in the possession of the people concerning the last known physical location of such specified evidence. If there is a finding by the court that the specified evidence no longer exists or the physical location of such specified evidence is unknown, such information in and of itself shall not be a factor from which any inference unfavorable to the people may be drawn by the court in deciding a motion under this section. The court, on motion of the defendant, may also issue a subpoena duces tecum directing a public or private hospital, laboratory or other entity to produce such specified evidence in its possession and/or information and documentary evidence in its possession concerning the location and status of such specified evidence.

(c) In response to a motion under this paragraph, upon notice to the parties and to the entity required to perform the search the court may order an entity that has access to the combined DNA index system ("CODIS") or its successor system to compare a DNA profile obtained from probative biological material gathered in connection with the investigation or prosecution of the defendant against DNA databanks by keyboard searches, or a similar method that does not involve uploading, upon a court's determination that (1) such profile complies with federal bureau of investigation or state requirements, whichever are applicable and as such requirements are applied to law enforcement agencies seeking such a comparison, and that the data meet state DNA index system and/or national DNA index system criteria as such criteria are applied to law enforcement agencies seeking such a comparison and (2) if such comparison had been conducted, and if the results had been admitted in the trial resulting in the judgment, a reasonable probability exists that the verdict would have been more favorable to the defendant, or in a case involving a plea of guilty, if the results had been available to the defendant prior to the plea, a reasonable probability exists that the conviction would not have resulted. For purposes of this subdivision, a "keyboard search" shall mean a search of a DNA profile against the databank in which the profile that is searched is not uploaded to or maintained in the databank.

2. If it appears by conceded or uncontradicted allegations of the moving papers or of the answer, or by unquestionable documentary proof, that there are circumstances which require denial thereof pursuant to subdivision two of section 440.10 or subdivision two of section 440.20, the court must summarily deny the motion. If it appears that there are circumstances authorizing, though not requiring, denial thereof pursuant to subdivision three of section 440.10 or subdivision three of section 440.20, the court may in its discretion either (a) summarily deny the motion, or (b) proceed to consider the merits thereof.

3. Upon considering the merits of the motion, the court must grant it without conducting a hearing and vacate the judgment or set aside the sentence, as the case may be, if:

(a) The moving papers allege a ground constituting legal basis for the motion; and

(b) Such ground, if based upon the existence or occurrence of facts, is supported by sworn allegations thereof; and

(c) The sworn allegations of fact essential to support the motion are either conceded by the people to be true or are conclusively substantiated by unquestionable documentary proof.

4. Upon considering the merits of the motion, the court may deny it without conducting a hearing if:

(a) The moving papers do not allege any ground constituting legal basis for the motion; or

(b) The motion is based upon the existence or occurrence of facts and the moving papers do not contain sworn allegations substantiating or tending to substantiate all the essential facts, as required by subdivision one; or

(c) An allegation of fact essential to support the motion is conclusively refuted by unquestionable documentary proof; or

(d) An allegation of fact essential to support the motion (i) is contradicted by a court record or other official document, or is made solely by the defendant and is unsupported by any other affidavit or evidence, and (ii) under these and all the other circumstances attending the case, there is no reasonable possibility that such allegation is true.

5. If the court does not determine the motion pursuant to subdivisions two, three or four, it must conduct a hearing and make findings of fact essential to the determination thereof. The defendant has a right to be present at such hearing but may waive such right in writing. If he does not so waive it and if he is confined in a prison or other institution of this state, the court must cause him to be produced at such hearing.

6. At such a hearing, the defendant has the burden of proving by a preponderance of the evidence every fact essential to support the motion.

7. Regardless of whether a hearing was conducted, the court, upon determining the motion, must set forth on the record its findings of fact, its conclusions of law and the reasons for its determination.

    HISTORY: Add, L 1970, ch 996, § 1; amd, L 1994, ch 737, § 2, L 2004, ch 138, § 2, L 2012, ch 19, §§ 1, 2, eff Aug 1, 2012.

§ 440.40. Motion to set aside sentence; by people

1. At any time not more than one year after the entry of a judgment, the court in which it was entered may, upon motion of the people, set aside the sentence upon the ground that it was invalid as a matter of law.

2. Notwithstanding the provisions of subdivision one, the court must summarily deny the motion when the ground or issue raised thereupon was previously determined on the merits upon an appeal from the judgment or sentence, unless since the time of such appellate determination there has been a retroactively effective change in the law controlling such issue.

3. Notwithstanding the provisions of subdivision one, the court may summarily deny such a motion when the ground or issue raised thereupon was previously determined on the merits upon a prior motion or proceeding in a court of this state, other than an appeal from the judgment or sentence, unless since the time of such determination there has been a retroactively effective change in the law controlling such issue. Despite such circumstance, however, the court, in the

interests of justice and for good cause shown, may in its discretion grant the motion if it is otherwise meritorious.

4. The motion must be made upon reasonable notice to the defendant and to the attorney if any who appeared for him in the last proceeding which occurred in connection with the judgment or sentence, and the defendant must be given adequate opportunity to appear in opposition to the motion. The defendant has a right to be present at such proceeding but may waive such right in writing. If he does not so waive it and if he is confined in a prison or other institution of this state, the court must cause him to be produced at the proceeding upon the motion.

5. An order setting aside a sentence pursuant to this section does not affect the validity or status of the underlying conviction, and after entering such an order the court must resentence the defendant in accordance with the law.

6. Upon a resentence imposed pursuant to subdivision five, the terms of which are more severe than those of the original sentence, the defendant's time for taking an appeal from the judgment is automatically extended in the manner prescribed in subdivision four of section 450.30.

HISTORY: Add, L 1970, ch 996, § 1, eff Sept 1, 1971.

§ 440.46. Motion for resentence; certain controlled substance offenders

1. Any person in the custody of the department of corrections and community supervision convicted of a class B felony offense defined in article two hundred twenty of the penal law which was committed prior to January thirteenth, two thousand five, who is serving an indeterminate sentence with a maximum term of more than three years, may, except as provided in subdivision five of this section, upon notice to the appropriate district attorney, apply to be resentenced to a determinate sentence in accordance with sections 60.04 and 70.70 of the penal law in the court which imposed the sentence.

2. As part of any such application, the defendant may also move to be resentenced to a determinate sentence in accordance with section 70.70 of the penal law for any one or more class C, D, or E felony offenses defined in article two hundred twenty or two hundred twenty-one of the penal law, the sentence or sentences for which were imposed by the sentencing court at the same time or were included in the same order of commitment as such class B felony.

3. The provisions of section twenty-three of chapter seven hundred thirty-eight of the laws of two thousand four shall govern the proceedings on and determination of a motion brought pursuant to this section; provided, however that the court's consideration of the institutional record of confinement of such person shall include but not be limited to such person's participation in or willingness to participate in treatment or other programming while incarcerated and such person's disciplinary history. The fact that a person may have been unable to participate in treatment or other programming while incarcerated despite such person's willingness to do so shall not be considered a negative factor in determining a motion pursuant to this section.

4. Subdivision one of section seven hundred seventeen and subdivision four of section seven hundred twenty-two of the county law, and the related provisions of article eighteen-A of such law, shall apply to the preparation of and proceedings on motions pursuant to this section, including any appeals.

5. The provisions of this section shall not apply to any person who is serving a sentence on a conviction for or has a predicate felony conviction for an exclusion offense. For purposes of this subdivision, an "exclusion offense" is:

(a) a crime for which the person was previously convicted within the preceding ten years, excluding any time during which the offender was incarcerated for any reason between the time of commission of the previous felony and the time of commission of the present felony, which was: (i) a violent felony offense as defined in section 70.02 of the penal law; or (ii) any other offense for which a merit time allowance is not available pursuant to subparagraph (ii) of paragraph (d) of subdivision one of section eight hundred three of the correction law; or

(b) a second violent felony offense pursuant to section 70.04 of the penal law or a persistent violent felony offense pursuant to section 70.08 of the penal law for which the person has previously been adjudicated.

> **HISTORY:** Add, L 2009, ch 56, § 9 (Part AAA); amd, L 2011, ch 62, § 79 (Part C, Subpart B), eff March 31, 2011.

§ 440.50. Notice to crime victims of case disposition

1. Upon the request of a victim of a crime, or in any event in all cases in which the final disposition includes a conviction of a violent felony offense as defined in section 70.02 of the penal law or a felony defined in article one hundred twenty-five of such law, the district attorney shall, within sixty days of the final disposition of the case, inform the victim by letter of such final disposition. If such final disposition results in the commitment of the defendant to the custody of the department of corrections and community supervision for an indeterminate sentence, the notice provided to the crime victim shall also inform the victim of his or her right to submit a written, audiotaped, or videotaped victim impact statement to the department of corrections and community supervision or to meet personally with a member of the state board of parole at a time and place separate from the personal interview between a member or members of the board and the inmate and make such a statement, subject to procedures and limitations contained in rules of the board, both pursuant to subdivision two of section two hundred fifty-nine-i of the executive law. The right of the victim under this subdivision to submit a written victim impact statement or to meet personally with a member of the state board of parole applies to each personal interview between a member or members of the board and the inmate.

2. As used in this section, "victim" means any person alleged or found, upon the record, to have sustained physical or financial injury to person or property as a direct result of the crime charged or a person alleged or found to have sustained, upon the record, an offense under article one hundred thirty of the penal law, or in the case of a homicide or minor child, the victim's family.

3. As used in this section, "final disposition" means an ultimate termination of the case at the trial level including, but not limited to, dismissal, acquittal, or imposition of sentence by the court, or a decision by the district attorney, for whatever reason, to not file the case.

> **HISTORY:** Add, L 1978, ch 496, § 1; amd, L 1985, ch 14, § 5, L 1985, ch 78, § 2, L 1994, ch 559, § 1, L 1998, ch 367, § 1, L 1998, ch 611, § 1, L 2005, ch 186, § 3, L 2011, ch 62, § 80 (Part C, Subpart B), eff March 31, 2011.

§ 440.55. Notice to education department where a licensed professional has been convicted of a felony

The district attorney shall give written notification to the department of education upon the conviction of a felony of any person holding a license pursuant to title eight of the education law. In addition, the district attorney shall give written notification to the department upon the vacatur or reversal of any felony conviction of any such person.

> **HISTORY:** Add, L 1996, ch 134, § 1, eff Aug 10, 1996.

§ 440.60. Notification of invalid sentences of probation

Whenever it shall appear to the satisfaction of the appropriate director of the probation department that a person sentenced pursuant to article sixty of the penal law has received a sentence which is invalid as a matter of law, it shall become his duty to notify the district attorney of the county in which such person was convicted. Upon such notification, the district attorney shall immediately investigate the matter and if such sentence of probation is in fact invalid as a matter of law, the district attorney shall immediately move to set aside such sentence pursuant to section 440.40 of this chapter.

HISTORY: Add, L 1984, ch 214, § 1, eff Nov 1, 1984.

§ 440.65. Notice to child protective agency of conviction for certain crimes against a child

Upon conviction of any person for a crime under article one hundred twenty, article one hundred twenty-five, article one hundred thirty, article two hundred sixty or article two hundred sixty-three of the penal law committed against a child under the age of eighteen by a person legally responsible for such child, as defined in subdivision three of section four hundred twelve of the social services law, the district attorney serving the jurisdiction in which such conviction is entered shall notify the local child protective services agency of such conviction including the name of the defendant, the name of the child, the court case number and the name of the prosecutor who appeared for the people.

HISTORY: Add, L 2006, ch 647, § 1, eff Oct 13, 2006.

§ 440.70. Notice to the secretary of state when false financing statement filed

Upon conviction of any person for a crime where the defendant intentionally filed or caused to be filed a financing statement pursuant to article nine of the uniform commercial code on form UCC1 that falsely claims that a person is indebted or obligated to such defendant, the court wherein such conviction is entered, or the clerk thereof, shall issue and cause to be filed a certificate with the New York secretary of state: (a) certifying that a judgment of conviction has been entered in such court against the defendant who was listed as the secured party in such form; and (b) specifying the date and location of the filing, any filing or indexing number assigned to such filing, the debtor named in such statement, and a description of the collateral encumbered by the instrument.

HISTORY: Add, L 2012, ch 113, § 1, eff July 18, 2012.

ARTICLE 450   APPEALS—IN WHAT CASES AUTHORIZED AND TO WHAT COURTS TAKEN

§ 450.90. Appeal to court of appeals from order of intermediate appellate court; in what cases authorized

HISTORY: Add, L 1970, ch 996, § 1, eff Sept 1, 1971.

§ 450.10. Appeal by defendant to intermediate appellate court; in what cases authorized as of right

An appeal to an intermediate appellate court may be taken as of right by the defendant from the following judgment, sentence and order of a criminal court:

1. A judgment other than one including a sentence of death, unless the appeal is based solely upon the ground that a sentence was harsh or excessive when such sentence was predicated upon entry of a plea of guilty and the sentence imposed did not exceed that which was agreed to by the defendant as a condition of the plea and set forth on the record or filed with the court as required by subdivision five of section 220.50 or subdivision four of section 340.20;

2. A sentence other than one of death, as prescribed in subdivision one of section 450.30, unless the appeal is based solely upon the ground that a sentence was harsh or excessive when such sentence was predicated upon entry of a plea of guilty and the sentence imposed did not exceed that which was agreed to by the defendant as a condition of the plea and set forth in the record or filed with the court as required by subdivision five of section 220.50 or subdivision four of section 340.20;

3. A sentence including an order of criminal forfeiture entered pursuant to section 460.30 of the penal law with respect to such forfeiture order.

4. An order, entered pursuant to section 440.40, setting aside a sentence other than one of death, upon motion of the People.

5. An order denying a motion, made pursuant to subdivision one-a of section 440.30, for forensic DNA testing of evidence.

HISTORY: Add, L 1970, ch 996, § 1, with substance derived from Crim C §§ 517, 750; amd, L 1971, ch 671, § 1, eff Sept 1, 1971. Section heading, amd, L 1971, ch 671, § 1, eff Sept 1, 1971. Sub 1, amd, L 1984, ch 671, § 3, eff Aug 31, 1984. Sub 2, amd, L 1971, ch 788, § 3, L 1984, ch 671, § 4, eff Aug 31, 1984. Sub 3, add, L 1986, ch 516, § 11, eff Nov 1, 1986. Former sub 3, formerly sub 5, renumbered sub 3, L 1971, ch 671, § 1, renumbered sub 4, L 1986, ch 516, § 11, eff Nov 1, 1986. Prior sub 3, deleted, L 1971, ch 671, § 1, eff Sept 1, 1971. Sub 4, formerly sub 5, renumbered sub 3, L 1971, ch 671, § 1, renumbered sub 4, L 1986, ch 516, § 11, eff Nov 1, 1986. Former sub 4, deleted, L 1971, ch 671, § 1, eff Sept 1, 1971. Sub 5, add, L 1999, ch 560, § 7, eff Dec 1, 1999. Former sub 5, renumbered sub 3, L 1971, ch 671, eff Sept 1, 1971.

§ 450.15. Appeal by defendant to intermediate appellate court; in what cases authorized by permission

If an appeal by defendant is not authorized as of right pursuant to section 450.10, the defendant may appeal from the following orders of a criminal court, provided that a certificate granting leave to appeal is issued pursuant to section 460.15:

1. An order denying a motion, made pursuant to section 440.10, to vacate a judgment other than one including a sentence of death;

2. An order denying a motion by the defendant made pursuant to section 440.20, to set aside a sentence other than one of death;

3. A sentence which is not otherwise appealable as of right pursuant to subdivision one or two of section 450.10.

HISTORY: Add, L 1971, ch 671, § 2; amd, L 1984, ch 671, § 5, eff Aug 31, 1984. Sub 3, add, L 1984, ch 671, § 5, eff Aug 31, 1984.

§ 450.20. Appeal by people to intermediate appellate court; in what cases authorized

An appeal to an intermediate appellate court may be taken as of right by the people from the following sentence and orders of a criminal court:

1. An order dismissing an accusatory instrument or a count thereof, entered pursuant to section 170.30, 170.50 or 210.20, or an order terminating a prosecution pursuant to subdivision four of section 180.85;

1-a. An order reducing a count or counts of an indictment or dismissing an indictment and directing the filing of a prosecutor's information, entered pursuant to subdivision one-a of section 210.20;

2. An order setting aside a verdict and dismissing an accusatory instrument or a count thereof, entered pursuant to paragraph (b) of subdivision one of section 290.10 or 360.40;

3. An order setting aside a verdict, entered pursuant to section 330.30 or 370.10;

4. A sentence other than one of death, as prescribed in subdivisions two and three of section 450.30;

5. An order, entered pursuant to section 440.10, vacating a judgment other than one including a sentence of death;

6. An order, entered pursuant to section 440.20, setting aside a sentence other than one of death;

7. An order denying a motion by the people, made pursuant to section 440.40, to set aside a sentence other than one of death;

8. An order suppressing evidence, entered before trial pursuant to section 710.20; provided that the people file a statement in the appellate court pursuant to section 450.50.

9. An order entered pursuant to section 460.30 of the penal law setting aside or modifying a verdict of forfeiture.

10. An order, entered pursuant to paragraph (e) of subdivision twelve of section 400.27, finding that the defendant is mentally retarded.

11. An order granting a motion, made pursuant to subdivision one-a of section 440.30, for forensic DNA testing of evidence.

HISTORY: Add, L 1970, ch 996, § 1, eff Sept 1, 1971, with substance derived from Crim C §§ 518, 750. Sub 1, amd, L 2004, ch 518, § 3, eff Nov 1, 2004. Sub 1-a, add, L 1990, ch 209, § 17, eff Sept 1, 1990. Sub 2, amd, L 1983, ch 170, § 3, eff May 31, 1983. Sub 9, add, L 1986, ch 516, § 12, eff Nov 1, 1986. Sub 10, add, L 1995, ch 1, § 22, eff Sept 1, 1995. Sub 11, add, L 1999, ch 560, § 8, eff Dec 1, 1999.

§ 450.30. Appeal from sentence

1. An appeal by the defendant from a sentence, as authorized by subdivision two of section 450.10, may be based upon the ground that such sentence either was (a) invalid as a matter of law, or (b) harsh or excessive. A sentence is invalid as a matter of law not only when the terms thereof are unauthorized but also when it is based upon an erroneous determination that the defendant had a previous valid conviction for an offense or, in the case of a resentence following a revocation of a sentence of probation or conditional discharge, upon an improper revocation of such original

sentence. An appeal by the defendant from a sentence, as authorized by subdivision three of section 450.15, may be based upon the ground that such sentence was harsh or excessive.

2. An appeal by the people from a sentence, as authorized by subdivision four of section 450.20, may be based only upon the ground that such sentence was invalid as a matter of law.

3. An appeal from a sentence, within the meaning of this section and sections 450.10 and 450.20, means an appeal from either the sentence originally imposed or from a resentence following an order vacating the original sentence. For purposes of appeal, the judgment consists of the conviction and the original sentence only, and when a resentence occurs more than thirty days after the original sentence, a defendant who has not previously filed a notice of appeal from the judgment may not appeal from the judgment, but only from the resentence.

4. When as a result of a successful appeal by the people from a sentence, the defendant receives a resentence the terms of which are more severe than those of the original or reversed sentence, the defendant, if he has not taken an appeal from the judgment, may, even though the period for doing so as prescribed in section 460.10 has expired, take such an appeal by filing and serving a notice of appeal, or an affidavit of errors as the case may be, within thirty days after imposition of the resentence. Upon such an appeal, only the conviction is reviewable; and any appellate challenge to the resentence must be made upon a separate appeal therefrom.

    HISTORY: Add, L 1970, ch 996, § 1, eff Sept 1, 1971. Sub 1, amd, L 1984, ch 671, § 6, eff Aug 31, 1984.

§ 450.40. Appeal by people from trial order of dismissal

1. An appeal by the people from a trial order of dismissal, as authorized by subdivision two of section 450.20, may, as indicated by section 290.10, be based either (a) upon the ground that the evidence adduced at the trial was legally sufficient to support the count or counts of the accusatory instrument dismissed by the order, or (b) upon the ground that, though not legally sufficient, such evidence would have been legally sufficient had the court not erroneously excluded admissible evidence offered by the people.

2. If the appeal is based upon the ground specified in paragraph (b) of subdivision one, and if the appellate court determines that the evidence unsuccessfully offered by the people was improperly excluded, and if at the trial the people made on offer of proof with respect thereto pursuant to subdivision three of section 290.10, the appellate court, in making its determination whether the people's evidence would have been legally sufficient had it not been for the improper exclusion, must treat the excluded evidentiary matter as it is summarized in the offer of proof as evidence constituting a part of the people's case.

    HISTORY: Add, L 1970, ch 996, § 1, eff Sept 1, 1971.

§ 450.50. Appeal by people from order suppressing evidence; filing of statement in appellate court

1. In taking an appeal, pursuant to subdivision eight of section 450.20, to an intermediate appellate court from an order of a criminal court suppressing evidence, the people must file, in addition to a notice of appeal or, as the case may be, an affidavit of errors, a statement asserting that the deprivation of the use of the evidence ordered suppressed has rendered the sum of the proof available to the people with respect to a criminal charge which has been filed in the court either (a) insufficient as a matter of law, or (b) so weak in its entirety that any reasonable possibility of prosecuting such charge to a conviction has been effectively destroyed.

2. The taking of an appeal by the people, pursuant to subdivision eight of section 450.20, from

an order suppressing evidence constitutes a bar to the prosecution of the accusatory instrument involving the evidence ordered suppressed, unless and until such suppression order is reversed upon appeal and vacated.

HISTORY: Add, L 1970, ch 996, § 1, eff Sept 1, 1971, with substance derived from Crim C §§ 518-a, 750.

§ 450.55. Appeal by people from order reducing a count of an indictment or directing the filing of a prosecutor's information

In taking an appeal to an intermediate appellate court pursuant to subdivision one-a of section 450.20, the people shall file a notice of appeal. Upon request of either party, the hearing and determination of such appeal shall be conducted in an expeditious manner. The chief administrator of the courts, with the advice and consent of the administrative board of the courts, shall adopt rules for the expeditious briefing, hearing and determination of such appeals.

HISTORY: Add, L 1990, ch 209, § 18, eff Sept 1, 1990.

§ 450.60. Appeal to intermediate appellate court; to what court taken

The particular intermediate appellate courts to which appeals authorized by sections 450.10 and 450.20 must be taken are as follows:

1. An appeal from a judgment, sentence or order of the supreme court must be taken to the appellate division of the department in which such judgment, sentence or order was entered.

2. An appeal from a judgment, sentence or order of a county court must be taken to the appellate division of the department in which such judgment, sentence or order was entered.

3. An appeal from a judgment, sentence or order of a local criminal court located outside of New York City must, except as otherwise provided in this subdivision, be taken to the county court of the county in which such judgment, sentence or order was entered.

If the appellate division of the second, third or fourth department has established an appellate term of the supreme court for its department, it may direct that appeals from such judgments, sentences and orders of such local criminal courts, or of particular classifications of such local criminal courts, be taken to such appellate term of the supreme court instead of to the county court; and in such case such an appeal must be so taken.

4. An appeal from a judgment, sentence or order of the New York City criminal court must be taken, if such judgment, sentence or order was entered at a term of such court held in New York or Bronx county, to the appellate division of the first department, and, if entered at a term of such court held in Kings, Queens or Richmond county, to the appellate division of the second department; except that if the appellate division of either such department has established an appellate term of the supreme court for its department, it may direct that all such appeals be taken thereto; and in such case such an appeal must be so taken.

HISTORY: Add, L 1970, ch 996, § 1, eff Sept 1, 1971. Sub 2, amd, L 1979, ch 74, § 1, eff Jan 1, 1980.

§ 450.70. Appeal by defendant directly to court of appeals; in what cases authorized

An appeal directly to the court of appeals may be taken as of right by the defendant from the following judgment and orders of a superior court:

1. A judgment including a sentence of death;

2. An order denying a motion, made pursuant to section 440.10, to vacate a judgment including a sentence of death;

3. An order denying a motion, made pursuant to section 440.20, to set aside a sentence of death;

4. An order denying a motion, made pursuant to paragraph (d) of subdivision eleven of section 400.27, to set aside a sentence of death.

HISTORY: Add, L 1970, ch 996, § 1, eff Sept 1, 1971, with substance derived from Crim C § 517. Sub 3, amd, L 1995, ch 1, § 23, eff Sept 1, 1995. Sub 4, add, L 1995, ch 1, § 23, eff Sept 1, 1995.

§ 450.80. Appeal by people directly to court of appeals; in what cases authorized

An appeal directly to the court of appeals may be taken as of right by the people from the following orders of a superior court:

1. An order, entered pursuant to section 440.10, vacating a judgment including a sentence of death;

2. An order, entered pursuant to section 440.20, setting aside a sentence of death;

3. An order, entered pursuant to paragraph (d) of subdivision eleven of section 400.27, setting aside a sentence of death;

4. An order, entered pursuant to subdivision twelve of section 400.27, setting aside a sentence of death.

HISTORY: Add, L 1970, ch 996, § 1, with substance derived from Crim C § 518; amd, L 1995, ch 1, § 24, eff Sept 1, 1995. Sub 2, amd, L 1995, ch 1, § 24, eff Sept 1, 1995. Sub 3, add, L 1995, ch 1, § 24, eff Sept 1, 1995. Sub 4, add, L 1995, ch 1, § 24, eff Sept 1, 1995.

§ 450.90. Appeal to court of appeals from order of intermediate appellate court; in what cases authorized

1. Provided that a certificate granting leave to appeal is issued pursuant to section 460.20, an appeal may, except as provided in subdivision two, be taken to the court of appeals by either the defendant or the people from any adverse or partially adverse order of an intermediate appellate court entered upon an appeal taken to such intermediate appellate court pursuant to section 450.10, 450.15, or 450.20, or from an order granting or denying a motion to set aside an order of an intermediate appellate court on the ground of ineffective assistance or wrongful deprivation of appellate counsel, or by either the defendant or the people from any adverse or partially adverse order of an intermediate appellate court entered upon an appeal taken to such intermediate appellate court from an order entered pursuant to section 440.46 of this chapter. An order of an intermediate appellate court is adverse to the party who was the appellant in such court when it affirms the judgment, sentence or order appealed from, and is adverse to the party who was the respondent in such court when it reverses the judgment, sentence or order appealed from. An appellate court order which modifies a judgment or order appealed from is partially adverse to each party.

2. An appeal to the court of appeals from an order of an intermediate appellate court reversing or modifying a judgment, sentence or order of a criminal court may be taken only if:

(a) The court of appeals determines that the intermediate appellate court's determination of reversal or modification was on the law alone or upon the law and such facts which, but for the determination of law, would not have led to reversal or modification; or

(b) The appeal is based upon a contention that corrective action, as that term is defined in section 470.10, taken or directed by the intermediate appellate court was illegal.

HISTORY: Add, L 1970, ch 996, § 1, eff Sept 1, 1971, with substance derived from Crim C §§ 519, 750. Sub 1, amd, L 1971, ch 671, § 3, eff Sept 1, 1971, L 2002, ch 498, § 1, eff Nov 1, 2002, L 2009, ch 56, § 10 (Part AAA), eff Oct 7, 2009. Sub 2, par (a), amd, L 1979, ch 651, § 1, eff Jan 1, 1980.

ARTICLE 460   APPEALS—TAKING AND PERFECTION THEREOF AND STAYS DURING PENDENCY THEREOF

HISTORY: Add, L 1970, ch 996, § 1, eff Sept 1, 1971.

§ 460.10. Appeal; how taken

1. Except as provided in subdivisions two and three, an appeal taken as of right to an intermediate appellate court or directly to the court of appeals from a judgment, sentence or order of a criminal court is taken as follows:

(a) A party seeking to appeal from a judgment or a sentence or an order and sentence included within such judgment, or from a resentence, or from an order of a criminal court not included in a judgment, must, within thirty days after imposition of the sentence or, as the case may be, within thirty days after service upon such party of a copy of an order not included in a judgment, file with the clerk of the criminal court in which such sentence was imposed or in which such order was entered a written notice of appeal, in duplicate, stating that such party appeals therefrom to a designated appellate court.

(b) If the defendant is the appellant, he must, within such thirty day period, serve a copy of such notice of appeal upon the district attorney of the county embracing the criminal court in which the judgment or order being appealed was entered. If the appeal is directly to the court of appeals, the district attorney, following such service upon him, must immediately give written notice thereof to the public servant having custody of the defendant.

(c) If the people are the appellant, they must, within such thirty day period, serve a copy of such notice of appeal upon the defendant or upon the attorney who last appeared for him in the court in which the order being appealed was entered.

(d) Upon filing and service of the notice of appeal as prescribed in paragraphs (a), (b) and (c), the appeal is deemed to have been taken.

(e) Following the filing with him of the notice of appeal in duplicate, the clerk of the court in which the judgment, sentence or order being appealed was entered or imposed, must endorse upon such instruments the filing date and must transmit the duplicate notice of appeal to the clerk of the court to which the appeal is being taken.

2. An appeal taken as of right to a county court or to an appellate term of the supreme court from a judgment, sentence or order of a local criminal court in a case in which the underlying

proceedings were recorded by a court stenographer is taken in the manner provided in subdivision one; except that where no clerk is employed by such local criminal court the appellant must file the notice of appeal with the judge of such court, and must further file a copy thereof with the clerk of the appellate court to which the appeal is being taken.

3. An appeal taken as of right to a county court or to an appellate term of the supreme court from a judgment, sentence or order of a local criminal court in a case in which the underlying proceedings were not recorded by a court stenographer is taken as follows:

(a) Within thirty days after entry or imposition in such local criminal court of the judgment, sentence or order being appealed, the appellant must file with such court either (i) an affidavit of errors, setting forth alleged errors or defects in the proceedings which are the subjects of the appeal, or (ii) a notice of appeal. Where a notice of appeal is filed, the appellant must serve a copy thereof upon the respondent in the manner provided in paragraphs (b) and (c) of subdivision one, and, within thirty days after the filing thereof, must file with such court an affidavit of errors.

(b) Not more than three days after the filing of the affidavit of errors, the appellant must serve a copy thereof upon the respondent or the respondent's counsel or authorized representative. If the defendant is the appellant, such service must be upon the district attorney of the county in which the local criminal court is located. If the people are the appellant, such service must be upon the defendant or upon the attorney who appeared for him in the proceedings in the local criminal court.

(c) Upon filing and service of the affidavit of errors as prescribed in paragraphs (a) and (b), the appeal is deemed to have been taken.

(d) Within ten days after the appellant's filing of the affidavit of errors with the local criminal court, such court must file with the clerk of the appellate court to which the appeal has been taken both the affidavit of errors and the court's return, and must deliver a copy of such return to each party or a representative thereof as indicated in paragraph (b). The court's return must set forth or summarize evidence, facts or occurrences in or adduced at the proceedings resulting in the judgment, sentence or order, which constitute the factual foundation for the contentions alleged in the affidavit of errors.

(e) If the local criminal court does not file such return within the prescribed period, or if it files a defective return, the appellate court, upon application of the appellant, must order such local criminal court to file a return or an amended return, as the case may be, within a designated time which such appellate court deems reasonable.

4. An appeal by a defendant to an intermediate appellate court by permission, pursuant to section 450.15, is taken as follows:

(a) Within thirty days after service upon the defendant of a copy of the order sought to be appealed, the defendant must make application, pursuant to section 460.15, for a certificate granting leave to appeal to the intermediate appellate court.

(b) If such application is granted and such certificate is issued, the defendant, within fifteen days after issuance thereof, must file with the criminal court in which the order sought to be appealed was rendered the certificate granting leave to appeal together with a written notice of appeal, or if the appeal is from a local criminal court in a case in which the underlying proceedings were not recorded by a court stenographer, either (i) an affidavit of errors, or (ii) a notice of appeal. In all other respects the appeal shall be taken as provided in subdivisions one, two and three.

5. An appeal to the court of appeals from an order of an intermediate appellate court is taken as follows:

(a) Within thirty days after service upon the appellant of a copy of the order sought to be appealed, the appellant must make application, pursuant to section 460.20, for a certificate granting leave to appeal to the court of appeals. The appellate division of each judicial department shall adopt rules governing the procedures for service of a copy of such order.

(b) If such application is granted, the issuance of the certificate granting leave to appeal shall constitute the taking of the appeal.

6. Where a notice of appeal, an affidavit of errors, an application for leave to appeal to an intermediate appellate court, or an application for leave to appeal to the court of appeals is premature or contains an inaccurate description of the judgment, sentence or order being or sought to be appealed, the appellate court, in its discretion, may, in the interest of justice, treat such instrument as valid. Where an appellant files a notice of appeal within the prescribed period but, through mistake, inadvertence or excusable neglect, omits to serve a copy thereof upon the respondent within the prescribed period, the appellate court to which the appeal is sought to be taken may, in its discretion and for good cause shown, permit such service to be made within a designated period of time, and upon such service the appeal is deemed to be taken.

HISTORY: Add, L 1970, ch 996, § 1; amd, L 1971, ch 671, § 4, eff Sept 1, 1971. Sub 1, par (a), amd, L 1992, ch 85, § 1, eff Aug 15, 1992. Sub 4, add, L 1971, ch 671, § 4, eff Sept 1, 1971. Former sub 4, renumbered sub 5, L 1971, ch 671, § 4, eff Sept 1, 1971. Sub 5, formerly sub 4, renumbered sub 5, L 1971, ch 671, § 4, eff Sept 1, 1971. Former sub 5, renumbered sub 6 and amd, L 1971, ch 671, § 4, eff Sept 1, 1971. Sub 5, par (a), amd, L 1994, ch 137, § 1, eff Aug 29, 1994. Sub 5, par (b), add, L 1977, ch 699, § 2, eff Sept 1, 1977. Former sub 5, par (b), repealed, L 1977, ch 699, § 1, eff Sept 1, 1977. Sub 5, pars (c)–(e), repealed, L 1977, ch 699, § 1, eff Sept 1, 1977. Sub 6, formerly sub 5, renumbered sub 6 and amd, L 1971, ch 671, § 4, eff Sept 1, 1971.

§ 460.15. Certificate granting leave to appeal to intermediate appellate court

1. A certificate granting leave to appeal to an intermediate appellate court is an order of one judge or justice of the intermediate appellate court to which the appeal is sought to be taken granting such permission and certifying that the case involves questions of law or fact which ought to be reviewed by the intermediate appellate court.

2. An application for such a certificate must be made in a manner determined by the rules of the appellate division of the department in which such intermediate appellate court is located. Not more than one application may be made for such a certificate.

HISTORY: Add, L 1971, ch 671, § 5, eff Sept 1, 1971.

§ 460.20. Certificate granting leave to appeal to court of appeals

1. A certificate granting leave to appeal to the court of appeals from an order of an intermediate appellate court is an order of a judge granting such permission and certifying that the case involves a question of law which ought to be reviewed by the court of appeals.

2. Such certificate may be issued by the following judges in the indicated situations:

(a) Where the appeal sought is from an order of the appellate division, the certificate may be issued by (i) a judge of the court of appeals or (ii) a justice of the appellate division of the department which entered the order sought to be appealed.

CPL

(b) Where the appeal sought is from an order of an intermediate appellate court other than the appellate division, the certificate may be issued only by a judge of the court of appeals.

3. An application for such a certificate must be made in the following manner:

(a) An application to a justice of the appellate division must be made upon reasonable notice to the respondent;

(b) An application seeking such a certificate from a judge of the court of appeals must be made to the chief judge of such court by submission thereof, either in writing or first orally and then in writing, to the clerk of the court of appeals. The chief judge must then designate a judge of such court to determine the application. The clerk must then notify the respondent of the application and must inform both parties of such designation.

4. A justice of the appellate division to whom such an application has been made, or a judge of the court of appeals designated to determine such an application, may in his discretion determine it upon such papers as he may request the parties to submit, or upon oral argument, or upon both.

5. Every judge or justice acting pursuant to this section shall file with the clerk of the court of appeals, immediately upon issuance, a copy of every certificate granting or denying leave to appeal.

> **HISTORY:** Add, L 1970, ch 996, § 1, eff Sept 1, 1971. Sub 5, add, L 1977, ch 699, § 3, eff Sept 1, 1977.

§ 460.30. Extension of time for taking appeal

1. Upon motion to an intermediate appellate court of a defendant who desires to take an appeal to such court from a judgment, sentence or order of a criminal court but has failed to file a notice of appeal, an application for leave to appeal, or, as the case may be, an affidavit of errors, with such criminal court within the prescribed period, or upon motion to the court of appeals of a defendant who desires to take an appeal to such court from an order of a superior court or of an intermediate appellate court, but has failed to make an application for a certificate granting leave to appeal to the court of appeals, or has failed to file a notice of appeal with the intermediate appellate court, within the prescribed period, such intermediate appellate court or the court of appeals, as the case may be, may order that the time for the taking of such appeal or applying for leave to appeal be extended to a date not more than thirty days subsequent to the determination of such motion, upon the ground that the failure to so file or make application in timely fashion resulted from (a) improper conduct of a public servant or improper conduct, death or disability of the defendant's attorney, or (b) inability of the defendant and his attorney to have communicated, in person or by mail, concerning whether an appeal should be taken, prior to the expiration of the time within which to take an appeal due to defendant's incarceration in an institution and through no lack of due diligence or fault of the attorney or defendant. Such motion must be made with due diligence after the time for the taking of such appeal has expired, and in any case not more than one year thereafter.

2. The motion must be in writing and upon reasonable notice to the people and with opportunity to be heard. The motion papers must contain sworn allegations of facts claimed to establish the improper conduct, inability to communicate, or other facts essential to support the motion, and the people may file papers in opposition thereto. After all papers have been filed, the court must consider the same for the purpose of ascertaining whether the motion is determinable without a hearing to resolve issues of fact.

3. If the motion papers allege facts constituting a legal basis for the motion, and if the essential

allegations are either conclusively substantiated by unquestionable documentary proof or are conceded by the people to be true, the court must grant the motion.

4. If the motion papers do not allege facts constituting a legal basis for the motion, or if an essential allegation is conclusively refuted by unquestionable documentary proof, the court may deny the motion.

5. If the court does not determine the motion pursuant to subdivision three or four, it must order the criminal court which entered or imposed the judgment, sentence or order sought to be appealed to conduct a hearing and to make and report findings of fact essential to the determination of such motion. Upon receipt of such report, the intermediate appellate court or the court of appeals, as the case may be, must determine the motion.

6. An order of an intermediate appellate court granting or denying a motion made pursuant to this section is appealable to the court of appeals if (a) such order states that the determination was made upon the law alone, and (b) a judge of the court of appeals, pursuant to procedure provided in section 460.20, of this chapter, issues a certificate granting leave to the appellant to appeal to the court of appeals.

HISTORY: Add, L 1970, ch 996, § 1; amd, L 1977, ch 699, § 4, eff Sept 1, 1977. Sub 1, amd, L 1971, ch 671, § 6, eff Sept 1, 1971.

§ 460.40. Effect of taking of appeal upon judgment or order of courts below; when stayed

1. The taking of an appeal by the defendant directly to the court of appeals, pursuant to subdivision one of section 450.70, from a superior court judgment including a sentence of death stays the execution of such sentence. Except as provided in subdivision two of this section, in no other case does the taking of an appeal, by either party, in and of itself stay the execution of any judgment, sentence or order of either a criminal court or an intermediate appellate court.

2. The taking of an appeal by the people to an intermediate appellate court pursuant to subdivision one-a of section 450.20, from an order reducing a count or counts of an indictment or dismissing an indictment and directing the filing of a prosecutor's information, stays the effect of such order. In addition, the taking of an appeal by the people to an intermediate appellate court pursuant to subdivision one of section 450.20, from an order dismissing a count or counts of an indictment charging murder in the first degree, stays the effect of such order.

3. Within six months of the effective date of this subdivision, the court of appeals shall adopt rules to ensure that a defendant is granted a stay of the execution of any death warrant issued pursuant to article twenty-two-B of the correction law to allow the defendant an opportunity to prepare and timely file an initial motion pursuant to section 440.10 or 440.20 seeking to set aside a sentence of death or vacate a judgment including a sentence of death and to allow the motion and any appeal from the denial thereof to be timely determined. The rules shall provide that in the event a defendant seeks to file any subsequent motion with respect to the judgment or sentence following a final determination of the defendant's initial motion pursuant to section 440.10 or 440.20, a motion for a stay of the execution of the death warrant may only be granted for good cause shown. The people and the defendant shall have a right to appeal to the court of appeals from orders granting or denying such stay motions and any rules adopted pursuant to this subdivision shall provide that the court of appeals may affirm such orders, reverse them or modify them upon such terms as the court deems appropriate and shall provide for the expeditious perfection and determination of such appeals. Prior to adoption of the rules, the court of appeals shall issue proposed rules and receive written comments thereon from interested parties.

HISTORY: Add, L 1970, ch 996, § 1, with substance derived from Crim C § 526; amd, L 1990, ch 209, § 19, eff Sept 1, 1990. Sub 1, formerly entire section, so designated and amd, L 1990, ch

209, § 19, eff Sept 1, 1990. Sub 2, add, L 1990, ch 209, § 19; amd, L 1995, ch 1, § 25, eff Sept 1, 1995. Sub 3, add, L 1995, ch 1, § 26, eff Sept 1, 1995.

§ 460.50. Stay of judgment pending appeal to intermediate appellate court

1. Upon application of a defendant who has taken an appeal to an intermediate appellate court from a judgment or from a sentence of a criminal court, a judge designated in subdivision two may issue an order both (a) staying or suspending the execution of the judgment pending the determination of the appeal, and (b) either releasing the defendant on his own recognizance or fixing bail pursuant to the provisions of article five hundred thirty. That phase of the order staying or suspending execution of the judgment does not become effective unless and until the defendant is released, either on his own recognizance or upon the posting of bail.

2. An order as prescribed in subdivision one may be issued by the following judges in the indicated situations:

(a) If the appeal is to the appellate division from a judgment or a sentence of either the supreme court or the New York City criminal court, such order may be issued by (i) a justice of the appellate division of the department in which the judgment was entered, or (ii) a justice of the supreme court of the judicial district embracing the county in which the judgment was entered;

(b) If the appeal is to the appellate division from a judgment or a sentence of a county court, such order may be issued by (i) a justice of such appellate division, or (ii) a justice of the supreme court of the judicial district embracing the county in which the judgment was entered, or (iii) a judge of such county court;

(c) If the appeal is to an appellate term of the supreme court from a judgment or sentence of the New York City criminal court, such order may be issued by a justice of the supreme court of the judicial district embracing the county in which the judgment was entered;

(d) With respect to appeals to county courts from judgments or sentences of local criminal courts, and with respect to appeals to appellate terms of the supreme court from judgments or sentences of any criminal courts located outside of New York City, the judges who may issue such orders in any particular situation are determined by rules of the appellate division of the department embracing the appellate court to which the appeal has been taken.

3. An application for an order specified in this section must be made upon reasonable notice to the people, and the people must be accorded adequate opportunity to appear in opposition thereto. Not more than one application may be made pursuant to this section.

4. Notwithstanding the provisions of subdivision one, if within one hundred twenty days after the issuance of such an order the appeal has not been brought to argument in or submitted to the intermediate appellate court, the operation of such order terminates and the defendant must surrender himself to the criminal court in which the judgment was entered in order that execution of the judgment be commenced or resumed; except that this subdivision does not apply where the intermediate appellate court has (a) extended the time for argument or submission of the appeal to a date beyond the specified period of one hundred twenty days, and (b) upon application of the defendant, expressly ordered that the operation of the order continue until the date of the determination of the appeal or some other designated future date or occurrence.

5. Where the defendant is at liberty during the pendency of an appeal as a result of an order issued pursuant to this section, the intermediate appellate court, upon affirmance of the judgment, must by appropriate certificate remit the case to the criminal court in which such judgment was

entered. The criminal court must, upon at least two days notice to the defendant, his surety and his attorney, promptly direct the defendant to surrender himself to the criminal court in order that execution of the judgment be commenced or resumed, and if necessary the criminal court may issue a bench warrant to secure his appearance.

6. Upon application of a defendant who has been granted a certificate granting leave to appeal pursuant to section 460.15 of this chapter, and in accordance with the procedures set forth in subdivisions three, four and five of this section, the intermediate appellate court may issue an order both (a) staying or suspending the execution of the judgment pending the determination of the appeal, and (b) either releasing the defendant on his own recognizance or fixing bail pursuant to the provisions of article five hundred thirty. That phase of the order staying or suspending execution of the judgment does not become effective unless and until the defendant is released, either on his own recognizance or upon the posting of bail.

   HISTORY: Add, L 1970, ch 996, § 1, eff Sept 1, 1971. Sub 1, amd, L 1971, ch 884, § 21, eff Sept 1, 1971. Sub 6, add, L 1981, ch 168, § 1, eff June 2, 1981.

§ 460.60. Stay of judgment pending appeal to court of appeals from intermediate appellate court

1. (a) A judge who, pursuant to section 460.20 of this chapter, has received an application for a certificate granting a defendant leave to appeal to the court of appeals from an order of an intermediate appellate court affirming or modifying a judgment including a sentence of imprisonment, a sentence of imprisonment, or an order appealed pursuant to section 450.15 of this chapter, of a criminal court, may, upon application of such defendant-appellant issue an order both (i) staying or suspending the execution of the judgment pending the determination of the application for leave to appeal, and, if that application is granted, staying or suspending the execution of the judgment pending the determination of the appeal, and (ii) either releasing the defendant on his own recognizance or continuing bail as previously determined or fixing bail pursuant to the provisions of article five hundred thirty. Such an order is effective immediately and that phase of the order staying or suspending execution of the judgment does not become effective unless and until the defendant is released, either on his own recognizance or upon the posting of bail.

   (b) If the application for leave to appeal is denied, the stay or suspension pending the application automatically terminates upon the signing of the certificate denying leave. Upon such termination, the certificate denying leave must be sent to the criminal court in which the original judgment was entered, and the latter must proceed in the manner provided in subdivision five of section 460.50 of this chapter.

2. An application pursuant to subdivision one must be made upon reasonable notice to the people, and the people must be accorded adequate opportunity to appear in opposition thereto. Such an application may be made immediately after the entry of the order sought to be appealed or at any subsequent time during the pendency of the appeal. Not more than one application may be made pursuant to this section.

3. Notwithstanding the provisions of subdivision one, if within one hundred twenty days after the issuance of a certificate granting leave to appeal, the appeal or prospective appeal has not been brought to argument in or submitted to the court of appeals, the operation of an order issued pursuant to subdivision one of this section terminates and the defendant must surrender himself to the criminal court in which the original judgment was entered in order that execution of such judgment be commenced or resumed; except that this subdivision does not apply where the court of appeals has (a) extended the time for argument or submission of the appeal to a date beyond the

specified period of one hundred twenty days and (b) upon application of the defendant expressly ordered that the operation of such order continue until the date of the determination of the appeal or some other designated future date or occurrence.

4. Where the defendant is at liberty during the pendency of an appeal as a result of an order issued pursuant to this section, the court of appeals upon affirmance of the judgment or order, must, by appropriate certificate, remit the case to the criminal court in which the judgment was entered, and the latter must proceed in the manner provided in subdivision five of section 460.50 of this chapter.

HISTORY: Add, L 1970, ch 996, § 1, eff Sept 1, 1971. Sub 1, amd, L 1981, ch 168, § 1, eff June 2, 1981. Sub 1, par (a), formerly entire subdivision, so designated and amd, L 1977, ch 699, § 4, eff Sept 1, 1977. Sub 1, par (b), add, L 1977, ch 699, § 4, eff Sept 1, 1977. Sub 2, amd, L 1977, ch 699, § 4, eff Sept 1, 1977. Sub 3, amd, L 1977, ch 699, § 4, eff Sept 1, 1977. Sub 4, amd, L 1977, ch 699, § 4, L 1981, ch 168, § 2, eff June 2, 1981.

§ 460.70. Appeal; how perfected

1. Except as provided in subdivision two, the mode of and time for perfecting an appeal which has been taken to an intermediate appellate court from a judgment, sentence or order of a criminal court are determined by rules of the appellate division of the department in which such appellate court is located. Among the matters to be determined by such court rules are the times when the appeal must be noticed for and brought to argument, the content and form of the records and briefs to be served and filed, and the time when such records and briefs must be served and filed.

When an appeal is taken by a defendant pursuant to section 450.10, a transcript shall be prepared and settled and shall be filed with the criminal court by the court reporter. The expense for such transcript and any reproduced copies of such transcript shall be paid by the defendant. Where the defendant is granted permission to proceed as a poor person by the appellate court, the court reporter shall promptly make and file with the criminal court a transcript of the stenographic minutes of such proceedings as the appellate court shall direct. The expense of transcripts and any reproduced copies of transcripts prepared for poor persons under this section shall be a state charge payable out of funds appropriated to the office of court administration for that purpose. The appellate court shall where such is necessary for perfection of the appeal, order that the criminal court furnish a reproduced copy of such transcript to the defendant or his counsel.

2. An appeal which has been taken to a county court or to an appellate term of the supreme court from a judgment, sentence or order of a local criminal court pursuant to subdivision three of section 460.10 is perfected as follows:

(a) After the local criminal court has, pursuant to paragraph (d) of subdivision three of section 460.10, filed its return with the clerk of the appellate court and delivered a copy thereof to the appellant, the appellant must file with such clerk, and serve a copy thereof upon the respondent, a notice of argument, noticing the appeal for argument at the term of such appellate court immediately following the term being held at the time of the appellant's receipt of the return. Upon motion of the appellant, however, such appellate court may for good cause shown enlarge the time to a subsequent term, in which case the appellant must notice the appeal for argument at such subsequent term;

(b) The appellant must further comply with all court rules applicable to the mode of perfecting such appeals;

(c) If the appellant does not file a notice of argument as provided in paragraph (a) or does not comply with all applicable court rules as provided in paragraph (b), the appellate court may, either upon motion of the respondent or upon its own motion, dismiss the appeal.

3. The mode of and time for perfecting any appeal which has been taken to the court of appeals are determined by the rules of the court of appeals. Among the matters to be determined by such court rules are the times when the appeal must be noticed for and brought to argument, the content, form and number of the records and briefs and copies thereof to be served and filed, and the times when such records and briefs must be served and filed.

When an appeal is taken by a defendant pursuant to section 450.70, the defendant shall cause to be prepared and printed or otherwise duplicated pursuant to rules of the court of appeals the record on appeal and the required number of copies thereof. If the defendant is granted permission to appeal as a poor person, the expense thereof shall be a state charge payable out of funds appropriated to the office of court administration for that purpose.

> **HISTORY:** Add, L 1970, ch 996, § 1, eff Sept 1, 1971. Sub 1, amd, L 1977, ch 695, § 1, applicable to all proceedings in which a notice of appeal is filed on or after that day, L 1995, ch 83, §§ 207, 208, eff June 20, 1995. Sub 3, amd, L 1977, ch 695, § 2, eff Sept, 1977, applicable to all proceedings in which a notice of appeal is filed on or after that day.

§ 460.80. Appeal; argument and submission thereof

The mode of and procedure for arguing or otherwise litigating appeals in criminal cases are determined by rules of the individual appellate courts. Among the matters to be determined by such court rules are the circumstances in which oral argument is required and those in which the case may be submitted by either or both parties without oral argument; the consequences or effect of failure to present oral argument when such is required; the amount of time for oral argument allowed to each party; and the number of counsel entitled to be heard.

> **HISTORY:** Add, L 1970, ch 996, § 1, eff Sept 1, 1971.

ARTICLE 470   APPEALS—DETERMINATION THEREOF

> **HISTORY:** Add, L 1970, ch 996, § 1, eff Sept 1, 1971.

§ 470.05. Determination of appeals; general criteria

1. An appellate court must determine an appeal without regard to technical errors or defects which do not affect the substantial rights of the parties.

2. For purposes of appeal, a question of law with respect to a ruling or instruction of a criminal court during a trial or proceeding is presented when a protest thereto was registered, by the party claiming error, at the time of such ruling or instruction or at any subsequent time when the court had an opportunity of effectively changing the same. Such protest need not be in the form of an "exception" but is sufficient if the party made his position with respect to the ruling or instruction known to the court, or if in reponse [response]* to a protest by a party, the court expressly decided the question raised on appeal. In addition, a party who without success has either expressly or impliedly sought or requested a particular ruling or instruction, is deemed to have thereby protested the court's ultimate disposition of the matter or failure to rule or instruct accordingly sufficiently to raise a question of law with respect to such disposition or failure regardless of whether any actual protest thereto was registered.

HISTORY: Add, L 1970, ch 996, § 1, eff Sept 1, 1971. Sub 2, amd, L 1986, ch 798, § 1, eff Aug 2, 1986 and applicable to all matters, actions or proceedings pending or commencing on and after Aug 2, 1986.

§ 470.10. Determination of appeals; definitions of terms

The following definitions are applicable to this article:

1. "Reversal" by an appellate court of a judgment, sentence or order of another court means the vacating of such judgment, sentence or order.

2. "Modification" by an appellate court of a judgment or order of another court means the vacating of a part thereof and affirmance of the remainder.

3. "Corrective action" means affirmative action taken or directed by an appellate court upon reversing or modifying a judgment, sentence or order of another court, which disposes of or continues the case in a manner consonant with the determinations and principles underlying the reversal or modification.

HISTORY: Add, L 1970, ch 996, § 1, eff Sept 1, 1971.

§ 470.15. Determination of appeals by intermediate appellate courts; scope of review

1. Upon an appeal to an intermediate appellate court from a judgment, sentence or order of a criminal court, such intermediate appellate court may consider and determine any question of law or issue of fact involving error or defect in the criminal court proceedings which may have adversely affected the appellant.

2. Upon such an appeal, the intermediate appellate court must either affirm or reverse or modify the criminal court judgment, sentence or order. The ways in which it may modify a judgment include, but are not limited to, the following:

(a) Upon a determination that the trial evidence adduced in support of a verdict is not legally sufficient to establish the defendant's guilt of an offense of which he was convicted but is legally sufficient to establish his guilt of a lesser included offense, the court may modify the judgment by changing it to one of conviction for the lesser offense:

(b) Upon a determination that the trial evidence is not legally sufficient to establish the defendant's guilt of all the offenses of which he was convicted but is legally sufficient to establish his guilt of one or more of such offenses, the court may modify the judgment by reversing it with respect to the unsupported counts and otherwise affirming it;

---

* The bracketed word has been inserted by the Publisher.

(c) Upon a determination that a sentence imposed upon a valid conviction is illegal or unduly harsh or severe, the court may modify the judgment by reversing it with respect to the sentence and by otherwise affirming it.

3. A reversal or a modification of a judgment, sentence or order must be based upon a determination made:

(a) Upon the law; or

(b) Upon the facts; or

(c) As a matter of discretion in the interest of justice; or

(d) Upon any two or all three of the bases specified in paragraphs (a), (b) and (c).

4. The kinds of determinations of reversal or modification deemed to be upon the law include, but are not limited to, the following:

(a) That a ruling or instruction of the court, duly protested by the defendant, as prescribed in subdivision two of section 470.05, at a trial resulting in a judgment, deprived the defendant of a fair trial;

(b) That evidence adduced at a trial resulting in a judgment was not legally sufficient to establish the defendant's guilt of an offense of which he was convicted;

(c) That a sentence was unauthorized, illegally imposed or otherwise invalid as a matter of law.

5. The kinds of determinations of reversal or modification deemed to be on the facts include, but are not limited to, a determination that a verdict of conviction resulting in a judgment was, in whole or in part, against the weight of the evidence.

6. The kinds of determinations of reversal or modification deemed to be made as a matter of discretion in the interest of justice include, but are not limited to, the following:

(a) That an error or defect occurring at a trial resulting in a judgment, which error or defect was not duly protested at trial as prescribed in subdivision two of section 470.05 so as to present a question of law, deprived the defendant of a fair trial;

(b) That a sentence, though legal, was unduly harsh or severe.

HISTORY: Add, L 1970, ch 996, § 1, eff Sept 1, 1971.

§ 470.20. Determination of appeals by intermediate appellate courts; corrective action upon reversal or modification

Upon reversing or modifying a judgment, sentence or order of a criminal court, an intermediate appellate court must take or direct such corrective action as is necessary and appropriate both to rectify any injustice to the appellant resulting from the error or defect which is the subject of the reversal or modification and to protect the rights of the respondent. The particular corrective action to be taken or directed is governed in part by the following rules:

1. Upon a reversal of a judgment after trial for error or defect which resulted in prejudice to the defendant or deprived him of a fair trial, the court must, whether such reversal be on the law or as a matter of discretion in the interest of justice, order a new trial of the accusatory instrument and remit the case to the criminal court for such action.

2. Upon a reversal of a judgment after trial for legal insufficiency of trial evidence, the court

must dismiss the accusatory instrument.

3. Upon a modification of a judgment after trial for legal insufficiency of trial evidence with respect to one or more but not all of the offenses of which the defendant was convicted, the court must dismiss the count or counts of the accusatory instrument determined to be legally unsupported and must otherwise affirm the judgment. In such case, it must either reduce the total sentence to that imposed by the criminal court upon the counts with respect to which the judgment is affirmed or remit the case to the criminal court for re-sentence upon such counts; provided that nothing contained in this paragraph precludes further sentence reduction in the exercise of the appellate court's discretion pursuant to subdivision six.

4. Upon a modification of a judgment after trial which reduces a conviction of a crime to one for a lesser included offense, the court must remit the case to the criminal court with a direction that the latter sentence the defendant accordingly.

5. Upon a reversal or modification of a judgment after trial upon the ground that the verdict, either in its entirety or with respect to a particular count or counts, is against the weight of the trial evidence, the court must dismiss the accusatory instrument or any reversed count.

6. Upon modifying a judgment or reversing a sentence as a matter of discretion in the interest of justice upon the ground that the sentence is unduly harsh or severe, the court must itself impose some legally authorized lesser sentence.

HISTORY: Add, L 1970, ch 996, § 1, eff Sept 1, 1971.

§ 470.25. Determination of appeals by intermediate appellate courts; form and content of order

1. An order of an intermediate appellate court which affirms a judgment, sentence or order of a criminal court need only state such affirmance.

2. An order of an intermediate appellate court which reverses or modifies a judgment, sentence or order of a criminal court must contain the following:

(a) A statement of whether the determination was upon the law or upon the facts or as a matter of discretion in the interest of justice, or upon any specified two or all three of such bases; and

(b) If the decision is rendered without opinion, a brief statement of the specific grounds of the reversal or modification; and

(c) A statement of the corrective action taken or directed by the court; and

(d) If the determination is exclusively upon the law, a statement of whether or not the facts upon which the criminal court's judgment, sentence or order is based have been considered and determined to have been established. In the absence of such a statement, it is presumed that the intermediate appellate court did not consider or make any determination with respect to such facts.

HISTORY: Add, L 1970, ch 996, § 1, eff Sept 1, 1971.

§ 470.30. Determination by court of appeals of appeals taken directly thereto from judgments and orders of criminal courts

1. Wherever appropriate, the rules set forth in sections 470.15 and 470.20, governing the consideration and determination by intermediate appellate courts of appeals thereto from judgments and orders of criminal courts, and prescribing their scope of review and the corrective

action to be taken by them upon reversal or modification, apply equally to the consideration and determination by the court of appeals of appeals taken directly thereto, pursuant to sections 450.70 and 450.80, from judgments and orders of superior criminal courts.

2. Whenever a sentence of death is imposed, the judgment and sentence shall be reviewed on the record by the court of appeals. Review by the court of appeals pursuant to subdivision one of section 450.70 may not be waived.

3. With regard to the sentence, the court shall, in addition to exercising the powers and scope of review granted under subdivision one of this section, determine:

(a) whether the sentence of death was imposed under the influence of passion, prejudice, or any other arbitrary or legally impermissible factor including whether the imposition of the verdict or sentence was based upon the race of the defendant or a victim of the crime for which the defendant was convicted;

(b) whether the sentence of death is excessive or disproportionate to the penalty imposed in similar cases considering both the crime and the defendant. In conducting such review the court, upon request of the defendant, in addition to any other determination, shall review whether the sentence of death is excessive or disproportionate to the penalty imposed in similar cases by virtue of the race of the defendant or a victim of the crime for which the defendant was convicted; and

(c) whether the decision to impose the sentence of death was against the weight of the evidence.

4. The court shall include in its decision: (a) the aggravating and mitigating factors established in the record on appeal; and (b) those similar cases it took into consideration.

5. In addition to exercising any other corrective action pursuant to subdivision one of this section, the court, with regard to review of a sentence of death, shall be authorized to:

(a) affirm the sentence of death; or

(b) set the sentence aside and remand the case for resentencing pursuant to the procedures set forth in section 400.27 for a determination as to whether the defendant shall be sentenced to death, life imprisonment without parole or to a term of imprisonment for the class A-I felony of murder in the first degree other than a sentence of life imprisonment without parole; or

(c) set the sentence aside and remand the case for resentencing by the court for a determination as to whether the defendant shall be sentenced to life imprisonment without parole or to a term of imprisonment for the class A-I felony of murder in the first degree other than a sentence of life imprisonment without parole.

HISTORY: Add, L 1970, ch 996, § 1, eff Sept 1, 1971. Sub 1, amd, L 1995, ch 1, § 27, eff Sept 1, 1995. Sub 2, add, L 1995, ch 1, § 27, eff Sept 1, 1995. Former sub 2, deleted, L 1995, ch 1, § 27, eff Sept 1, 1995. Sub 3, add, L 1995, ch 1, § 27, eff Sept 1, 1995. Sub 4, add, L 1995, ch 1, § 27, eff Sept 1, 1995. Sub 5, add, L 1995, ch 1, § 27, eff Sept 1, 1995.

§ 470.35. Determination by court of appeals of appeals from orders of intermediate appellate courts; scope of review

1. Upon an appeal to the court of appeals from an order of an intermediate appellate court affirming a judgment, sentence or order of a criminal court, the court of appeals may consider and determine not only questions of law which were raised or considered upon the appeal to the intermediate appellate court, but also any question of law involving alleged error or defect in the

criminal court proceedings resulting in the original criminal court judgment, sentence or order, regardless of whether such question was raised, considered or determined upon the appeal to the intermediate appellate court.

2. Upon an appeal to the court of appeals from an order of an intermediate appellate court reversing or modifying a judgment, sentence or order of a criminal court, the court of appeals may consider and determine:

(a) Any question of law which was determined by the intermediate appellate court and which, as so determined, constituted a basis for such court's order of reversal or modification; and

(b) Any other question of law involving alleged or possible error or defect in the criminal court proceedings resulting in the original judgment, sentence or order which may have adversely affected the party who was appellant in the intermediate appellate court and who is respondent in the court of appeals. The court of appeals is not precluded from considering and determining such a question by the circumstance that it was not considered or determined by the intermediate appellate court, or that it did not constitute a basis for such court's reversal or modification, or that the party who may have been adversely affected thereby is the respondent rather than the appellant in the court of appeals; and the court of appeals, even though rejecting the intermediate appellate court's reasons for its order of reversal or modification, may affirm or modify such order upon the basis of such other questions; and

(c) Any question concerning the legality of the corrective action taken by the intermediate appellate court.

3. Upon such an appeal, the court must affirm, reverse or modify the intermediate appellate court order.

HISTORY: Add, L 1970, ch 996, § 1, eff Sept 1, 1971.

§ 470.40. Determination by court of appeals of appeals from intermediate appellate courts; corrective action upon reversal or modification

1. Upon reversing or modifying an order of an intermediate appellate court affirming a criminal court judgment, sentence or order, the court of appeals must take or direct such corrective action as the intermediate appellate court would, pursuant to section 470.20, have been required or authorized to take or direct had it reversed or modified the criminal court judgment, sentence or order upon the same ground or grounds.

2. Upon reversing an order of an intermediate appellate court reversing or modifying a criminal court judgment, sentence or order upon the ground that questions of law were erroneously determined by the intermediate appellate court in favor of the party appellant therein, the court of appeals must take or direct corrective action as follows:

(a) If the facts underlying the original criminal court judgment, sentence or order were considered and determined to have been established by the intermediate appellate court, the court of appeals must reinstate and affirm the original criminal court judgment, sentence or order and remit the case to such criminal court for whatever further proceedings may be necessary to complete the action or proceedings therein; provided, however, that where such facts were applied to an erroneous determination of law, the court of appeals may remit the case to the intermediate appellate court for a further determination of the facts;

(b) If the facts underlying the original criminal court judgment, sentence or order were not, or are presumed not to have been, considered and determined by the intermediate appellate court, the court of appeals must remit the case to such intermediate appellate court for determination of the facts.

3. Upon modifying an intermediate appellate court order reversing or modifying a criminal court judgment or order, upon the ground that corrective action taken or directed by the intermediate appellate court was illegal, the court of appeals must either (a) itself take or direct the appropriate corrective action or (b) remit the case to the intermediate appellate court for appropriate corrective action by the latter.

HISTORY: Add, L 1970, ch 996, § 1, eff Sept 1, 1971, with substance derived from Crim C §§ 543-b, 546. Sub 2, par (a), amd, L 1979, ch 651, § 2, eff Jan 1, 1980.

§ 470.45. Remission of case by appellate court to criminal court upon reversal or modification of judgment; action by criminal court

Upon reversing or modifying a judgment and directing corrective action, an appellate court must remit the case to the criminal court in which the judgment was entered. Such criminal court must execute the direction of the appellate court and must, depending upon the nature of such direction, either discharge the defendant from custody, exonerate his bail or issue a securing order.

HISTORY: Add, L 1970, ch 996, § 1, eff Sept 1, 1971.

§ 470.50. Reargument of appeal; motion and criteria for

1. After its determination of an appeal taken pursuant to article four hundred fifty, an appellate court, in the interest of justice and for good cause shown, may in its discretion, upon motion of a party adversely affected by its determination, or upon its own motion, order a reargument or reconsideration of the appeal. Upon such an order the court may either direct further oral argument by the parties or confine its reconsideration to re-examination of the issues as previously argued or submitted upon the appeal proper. Upon ordering a reargument or reconsideration of an appeal, the court must again determine the appeal pursuant to the provisions of this article.

2. The court of appeals may promulgate rules limiting the time within which a motion for reargument of appeals determined by such court may be made, and the appellate division of each department may similarly promulgate such rules with respect to appeals determined by such appellate division and appeals determined by the other intermediate appellate courts located within such department. In the absence of any such rule of limitation, a motion for reargument may be made at any time.

HISTORY: Add, L 1970, ch 996, § 1, eff Sept 1, 1971.

§ 470.55. Status of accusatory instrument upon order of new trial or restoration of action to pre-pleading status

1. Upon a new trial of an accusatory instrument resulting from an appellate court order reversing a judgment and ordering such new trial, such accusatory instrument is deemed to contain all the counts and to charge all the offenses which it contained and charged at the time the previous trial was commenced, regardless of whether any count was dismissed by the court in the course of such trial, except (a) those upon or of which the defendant was acquitted or deemed to have been acquitted, and (b) those dismissed upon appeal or upon some other post-judgment order.

2. Upon an appellate court order which reverses a judgment based upon a plea of guilty to an accusatory instrument or a part thereof, but which does not dismiss the entire accusatory instrument, the criminal action is, in the absence of express appellate court direction to the contrary, restored to its pre-pleading status and the accusatory instrument is deemed to contain all the counts and to charge all the offenses which it contained and charged at the time of the entry of the plea, except those dismissed upon appeal or upon some other post-judgment order. Where

the plea of guilty was entered and accepted, pursuant to subdivision three of section 220.30, upon the condition that it constituted a complete disposition and dismissal not only of the accusatory instrument underlying the judgment reversed but also of one or more other accusatory instruments against the defendant then pending in the same court, the appellate court order of reversal completely restores such other accusatory instruments; and such is the case even where the order of reversal dismisses the entire accusatory instrument underlying the judgment reversed.

HISTORY: Add, L 1970, ch 996, § 1, eff Sept 1, 1971.

§ 470.60. Dismissal of appeal

1. At any time after an appeal has been taken and before determination thereof, the appellate court in which such appeal is pending may, upon motion of the respondent or upon its own motion, dismiss such appeal upon the ground of mootness, lack of jurisdiction to determine it, failure of timely prosecution or perfection thereof, or other substantial defect, irregularity or failure of action by the appellant with respect to the prosecution or perfection of such appeal.

2. Such motion must be made upon reasonable notice to the appellant and with opportunity to be heard. If the people are the appellant, such notice must be served upon the appropriate district attorney either personally or by ordinary mail. If the appellant is a defendant, such notice must be served upon him by ordinary mail at his last known place of residence or, if he is imprisoned, at the institution in which he is confined, and similar notice must be served upon the attorney, if any, who last appeared for him. Upon determination of the motion, a copy of the order entered thereon must similarly be served.

3. Provided that a certificate granting leave to appeal is issued pursuant to this subdivision, an appeal may be taken, in the manner prescribed in subdivision four of section 460.10, to the court of appeals from an order of an intermediate appellate court dismissing an appeal thereto. Such appeal may be based either upon the ground that the dismissal was invalid as a matter of law or upon the ground that it constituted an abuse of discretion. A certificate granting leave to appeal from such an order of dismissal may be issued only by a judge of the court of appeals upon an application made in the manner prescribed in paragraph (b) of subdivision three of section 460.20. Upon such an appeal, the court of appeals must either affirm or reverse the intermediate appellate court order.

HISTORY: Add, L 1970, ch 996, § 1, eff Sept 1, 1971.

PART THREE   Special Proceedings and Miscellaneous Procedures

Title P

Procedures for Securing Attendance at Criminal Actions and Proceedings of Defendants and Witnesses Under Control of Court—Recognizance, Bail and Commitment

Title Q

Procedures for Securing Attendance at Criminal Actions and Proceedings of Defendants not Securable by Conventional Means—and Related Matters

Title R

Procedures for Securing Attendance of Witnesses in Criminal Actions

Title S

Procedures for Securing Testimony for Future Use, and For Using Testimony Given in a Prior Proceeding

Title T

Procedures for Securing Evidence by Means of Court Order and for Suppressing Evidence Unlawfully or Improperly Obtained

Title U

Special Proceedings Which Replace, Suspend or Abate Criminal Actions

HISTORY: Add, L 1970, ch 996, § 1, eff Sept 1, 1971.

TITLE P   Procedures for Securing Attendance at Criminal Actions and Proceedings of Defendants and Witnesses Under Control of Court—Recognizance, Bail and Commitment

ARTICLE 500
RECOGNIZANCE, BAIL AND COMMITMENT—DEFINITION OF TERMS

ARTICLE 510
RECOGNIZANCE, BAIL AND COMMITMENT—DETERMINATION OF APPLICATION FOR RECOGNIZANCE OR BAIL, ISSUANCE OF SECURING ORDERS, AND RELATED MATTERS

ARTICLE 520
BAIL AND BAIL BONDS

ARTICLE 530
ORDERS OF RECOGNIZANCE OR BAIL WITH RESPECT TO DEFENDANTS IN CRIMINAL ACTIONS AND PROCEEDINGS—WHEN AND BY WHAT COURTS AUTHORIZED

ARTICLE 540
FORFEITURE OF BAIL AND REMISSION THEREOF

HISTORY: Add, L 1970, ch 996, § 1, eff Sept 1, 1971.

ARTICLE 500   RECOGNIZANCE, BAIL AND COMMITMENT—DEFINITION OF TERMS

§ 500.10.   **Recognizance, bail and commitment; definition of terms**

HISTORY: Add, L 1970, ch 996, § 1, eff Sept 1, 1971.

§ 500.10. Recognizance, bail and commitment; definition of terms

As used in this title, and in this chapter generally, the following terms have the following meanings:

1. "Principal" means a defendant in a criminal action or proceeding, or a person adjudged a material witness therein, or any other person so involved therein that he may by law be compelled to appear before a court for the purpose of having such court exercise control over his person to secure his future attendance at the action or proceeding when required, and who in fact either is before the court for such purpose or has been before it and been subjected to such control.

2. "Release on own recognizance." A court releases a principal on his own recognizance when, having acquired control over his person, it permits him to be at liberty during the pendency of the criminal action or proceeding involved upon condition that he will appear thereat whenever his attendance may be required and will at all times render himself amenable to the orders and processes of the court.

3. "Fix bail." A court fixes bail when, having acquired control over the person of a principal, it designates a sum of money and stipulates that, if bail in such amount is posted on behalf of the principal and approved, it will permit him to be at liberty during the pendency of the criminal action or proceeding involved.

4. "Commit to the custody of the sheriff." A court commits a principal to the custody of the sheriff when, having acquired control over his person, it orders that he be confined in the custody of the sheriff during the pendency of the criminal action or proceeding involved.

5. "Securing order" means an order of a court committing a principal to the custody of the

sheriff, or fixing bail, or releasing him on his own recognizance.

6. "Order of recognizance or bail" means a securing order releasing a principal on his own recognizance or fixing bail.

7. "Application for recognizance or bail" means an application by a principal that the court, instead of committing him to or retaining him in the custody of the sheriff, either release him on his own recognizance or fix bail.

8. "Post bail" means to deposit bail in the amount and form fixed by the court, with the court or with some other authorized public servant or agency.

9. "Bail" means cash bail or a bail bond.

10. "Cash bail" means a sum of money, in the amount designated in an order fixing bail, posted by a principal or by another person on his behalf with a court or other authorized public servant or agency, upon the condition that such money will become forfeit to the people of the state of New York if the principal does not comply with the directions of a court requiring his attendance at the criminal action or proceeding involved or does not otherwise render himself amenable to the orders and processes of the court.

11. "Obligor" means a person who executes a bail bond on behalf of a principal and thereby assumes the undertaking described therein. The principal himself may be an obligor.

12. "Surety" means an obligor who is not a principal.

13. "Bail bond" means a written undertaking, executed by one or more obligors, that the principal designated in such instrument will, while at liberty as a result of an order fixing bail and of the posting of the bail bond in satisfaction thereof, appear in a designated criminal action or proceeding when his attendance is required and otherwise render himself amenable to the orders and processes of the court, and that in the event that he fails to do so the obligor or obligors will pay to the people of the state of New York a specified sum of money, in the amount designated in the order fixing bail.

14. "Appearance bond" means a bail bond in which the only obligor is the principal.

15. "Surety bond" means a bail bond in which the obligor or obligors consist of one or more sureties or of one or more sureties and the principal.

16. "Insurance company bail bond" means a surety bond, executed in the form prescribed by the superintendent of insurance, in which the surety-obligor is a corporation licensed by the superintendent of insurance to engage in the business of executing bail bonds.

17. "Secured bail bond" means a bail bond secured by either:

(a) Personal property which is not exempt from execution and which, over and above all liabilities and encumbrances, has a value equal to or greater than the total amount of the undertaking; or

(b) Real property having a value of at least twice the total amount of the undertaking. For purposes of this paragraph, value of real property is determined by either:

(i) dividing the last assessed value of such property by the last given equalization rate or in a special assessing unit, as defined in article eighteen of the real property tax law, the appropriate class ratio established pursuant to section twelve hundred two of such law of the assessing municipality wherein the property is situated and by deducting from the resulting figure the total amount of any liens or other encumbrances upon such property; or

(ii) the value of the property as indicated in a certified appraisal report submitted by a state certified general real estate appraiser duly licensed by the department of state as provided in section one hundred sixty-j of the executive law, and by deducting from the appraised value the total amount of any liens or other encumbrances upon such property. A lien report issued by a title insurance company licensed under article sixty-four of the insurance law, that guarantees the correctness of a lien search conducted by it, shall be presumptive proof of liens upon the property.

18. "Partially secured bail bond" means a bail bond secured only by a deposit of a sum of money not exceeding ten percent of the total amount of the undertaking.

19. "Unsecured bail bond" means a bail bond, other than an insurance company bail bond, not secured by any deposit of or lien upon property.

20. "Court" includes, where appropriate, a judge authorized to act as described in a particular statute, though not as a court.

HISTORY: Add, L 1970, ch 996, § 1, eff Sept 1, 1971; amd, L 1992, ch 316, § 26, eff Nov 1, 1992, L 2011, ch 305, § 1, eff Aug 3, 2011.

ARTICLE 510   RECOGNIZANCE, BAIL AND COMMITMENT—DETERMINATION OF APPLICATION FOR RECOGNIZANCE OR BAIL, ISSUANCE OF SECURING ORDERS, AND RELATED MATTERS

HISTORY: Add, L 1970, ch 996, § 1, eff Sept 1, 1971.

§ 510.10. Securing order; when required

When a principal, whose future court attendance at a criminal action or proceeding is or may be required, initially comes under the control of a court, such court must, by a securing order, either release him on his own recognizance, fix bail or commit him to the custody of the sheriff. When a securing order is revoked or otherwise terminated in the course of an uncompleted action or proceeding but the principal's future court attendance still is or may be required and he is still under the control of a court, a new securing order must be issued. When the court revokes or otherwise terminates a securing order which committed the principal to the custody of the sheriff, the court shall give written notification to the sheriff of such revocation or termination of the securing order.

HISTORY: Add, L 1970, ch 996, § 1; amd, L 1984, ch 459, § 1, eff Nov 1, 1984.

§ 510.15. Commitment of principal under sixteen

1. When a principal who is under the age of sixteen is committed to the custody of the sheriff the court must direct that the principal be taken to and lodged in a place certified by the state division for youth as a juvenile detention facility for the reception of children. Where such a

direction is made the sheriff shall deliver the principal in accordance therewith and such person shall although lodged and cared for in a juvenile detention facility continue to be deemed to be in the custody of the sheriff. No principal under the age of sixteen to whom the provisions of this section may apply shall be detained in any prison, jail, lockup, or other place used for adults convicted of a crime or under arrest and charged with the commission of a crime without the approval of the state division for youth in the case of each principal and the statement of its reasons therefor. The sheriff shall not be liable for any acts done to or by such principal resulting from negligence in the detention of and care for such principal, when the principal is not in the actual custody of the sheriff.

2. Except upon consent of the defendant or for good cause shown, in any case in which a new securing order is issued for a principal previously committed to the custody of the sheriff pursuant to this section, such order shall further direct the sheriff to deliver the principal from a juvenile detention facility to the person or place specified in the order.

> **HISTORY:** Add, L 1978, ch 481, § 43; amd, L 1979, ch 411, § 12, eff Aug 4, 1979. Sub 1, formerly entire section, so designated, L 1980, ch 359, § 1, eff June 23, 1980. Sub 2, add, L 1980, ch 359, § 1, eff June 23, 1980.

§ 510.20. Application for recognizance or bail; making and determination thereof in general

1. Upon any occasion when a court is required to issue a securing order with respect to a principal, or at any time when a principal is confined in the custody of the sheriff as a result of a previously issued securing order, he may make an application for recognizance or bail.

2. Upon such application, the principal must be accorded an opportunity to be heard and to contend that an order of recognizance or bail must or should issue, that the court should release him on his own recognizance rather than fix bail, and that if bail is fixed it should be in a suggested amount and form.

> **HISTORY:** Add, L 1970, ch 996, § 1, eff Sept 1, 1971.

§ 510.30. Application for recognizance or bail; rules of law and criteria controlling determinations

1. Determinations of applications for recognizance or bail are not in all cases discretionary but are subject to rules, prescribed in article five hundred thirty and other provisions of law relating to specific kinds of criminal actions and proceedings, providing (a) that in some circumstances such an application must as a matter of law be granted, (b) that in others it must as a matter of law be denied and the principal committed to or retained in the custody of the sheriff, and (c) that in others the granting or denial thereof is a matter of judicial discretion.

2. To the extent that the issuance of an order of recognizance or bail and the terms thereof are matters of discretion rather than of law, an application is determined on the basis of the following factors and criteria:

(a) With respect to any principal, the court must consider the kind and degree of control or restriction that is necessary to secure his court attendance when required. In determining that matter, the court must, on the basis of available information, consider and take into account:

(i) The principal's character, reputation, habits and mental condition;

(ii) His employment and financial resources; and

(iii) His family ties and the length of his residence if any in the community; and

(iv) His criminal record if any; and

(v) His record of previous adjudication as a juvenile delinquent, as retained pursuant to section 354.2 of the family court act, or, of pending cases where fingerprints are retained pursuant to section 306.1 of such act, or a youthful offender, if any; and

(vi) His previous record if any in responding to court appearances when required or with respect to flight to avoid criminal prosecution; and

(vii) Where the principal is charged with a crime or crimes against a member or members of the same family or household as that term is defined in subdivision one of section 530.11 of this title, the following factors:

(A) any violation by the principal of an order of protection issued by any court for the protection of a member or members of the same family or household as that term is defined in subdivision one of section 530.11 of this title, whether or not such order of protection is currently in effect; and

(B) the principal's history of use or possession of a firearm; and

(viii) If he is a defendant, the weight of the evidence against him in the pending criminal action and any other factor indicating probability or improbability of conviction; or, in the case of an application for bail or recognizance pending appeal, the merit or lack of merit of the appeal; and

(ix) If he is a defendant, the sentence which may be or has been imposed upon conviction.

(b) Where the principal is a defendant-appellant in a pending appeal from a judgment of conviction, the court must also consider the likelihood of ultimate reversal of the judgment. A determination that the appeal is palpably without merit alone justifies, but does not require, a denial of the application, regardless of any determination made with respect to the factors specified in paragraph (a).

3. When bail or recognizance is ordered, the court shall inform the principal, if he is a defendant charged with the commission of a felony, that the release is conditional and that the court may revoke the order of release and commit the principal to the custody of the sheriff in accordance with the provisions of subdivision two of section 530.60 of this chapter if he commits a subsequent felony while at liberty upon such order.

HISTORY: Add, L 1970, ch 996, § 1; amd, L 1979, ch 411, § 13, L 1982, ch 920, § 77, eff July 1, 1983; amd, L 1977, ch 447, § 6, eff Sept 1, 1977, L 1981, ch 788, § 1, eff July 27, 1981, L 2012, ch 491, § 1 (Part D), eff Dec 24, 2012.

§ 510.40. Application for recognizance or bail; determination thereof, form of securing order and execution thereof

1. An application for recognizance or bail must be determined by a securing order which either:

(a) Grants the application and releases the principal on his own recognizance; or

(b) Grants the application and fixes bail; or

(c) Denies the application and commits the principal to, or retains him in, the custody of the sheriff.

2. Upon ordering that a principal be released on his own recognizance, the court must direct him to appear in the criminal action or proceeding involved whenever his attendance may be required and to render himself at all times amenable to the orders and processes of the court. If such principal is in the custody of the sheriff or at liberty upon bail at the time of the order, the court

must direct that he be discharged from such custody or, as the case may be, that his bail be exonerated.

3. Upon the issuance of an order fixing bail, and upon the posting thereof, the court must examine the bail to determine whether it complies with the order. If it does, the court must, in the absence of some factor or circumstance which in law requires or authorizes disapproval thereof, approve the bail and must issue a certificate of release, authorizing the principal to be at liberty, and, if he is in the custody of the sheriff at the time, directing the sheriff to discharge him therefrom. If the bail fixed is not posted, or is not approved after being posted, the court must order that the principal be committed to the custody of the sheriff.

HISTORY: Add, L 1970, ch 996, § 1, eff Sept 1, 1971.

§ 510.50. Enforcement of securing order

When the attendance of a principal confined in the custody of the sheriff is required at the criminal action or proceeding at a particular time and place, the court may compel such attendance by directing the sheriff to produce him at such time and place. If the principal is at liberty on his own recognizance or on bail, his attendance may be achieved or compelled by various methods, including notification and the issuance of a bench warrant, prescribed by law in provisions governing such matters with respect to the particular kind of action or proceeding involved.

HISTORY: Add, L 1970, ch 996, § 1, eff Sept 1, 1971.

ARTICLE 520   BAIL AND BAIL BONDS

HISTORY: Add, L 1970, ch 996, § 1, eff Sept 1, 1971.

§ 520.10. Bail and bail bonds; fixing of bail and authorized forms thereof

1. The only authorized forms of bail are the following:

(a) Cash bail.

(b) An insurance company bail bond.

(c) A secured surety bond.

(d) A secured appearance bond.

(e) A partially secured surety bond.

(f) A partially secured appearance bond.

(g) An unsecured surety bond.

(h) An unsecured appearance bond.

(i) Credit card or similar device; provided, however, that notwithstanding any other provision of law, any person posting bail by credit card or similar device also may be required to pay a reasonable administrative fee. The amount of such administrative fee and the time and manner of its payment shall be in accordance with the system established pursuant to subdivision four of section 150.30 of this chapter or paragraph (j) of subdivision two of section two hundred twelve of the judiciary law, as appropriate.

2. The methods of fixing bail are as follows:

(a) A court may designate the amount of the bail without designating the form or forms in which it may be posted. In such case, the bail may be posted in either of the forms specified in paragraphs (g) and (h) of subdivision one;

(b) The court may direct that the bail be posted in any one of two or more of the forms specified in subdivision one, designated in the alternative, and may designate different amounts varying with the forms;[.]*

HISTORY: Add, L 1970, ch 996, § 1, eff Sept 1, 1971. Sub 1, par (i), add, L 1986, ch 708, § 2; amd, L 1987, ch 805, § 3, eff Aug 7, 1987. Sub 1, par (i), amd, L 2005, ch 457, § 4, eff Jan 1, 2006, L 2010, ch 528, § 5, eff Sept 17, 2010, deemed eff on and after Sept 1, 2009, amended L 2005, ch 457, § 7, so as to delete Aug 9, 2010, expiration date applicable to amendment of Sub 1(i). Sub 2, par (a), amd, L 1972, ch 784, § 1, eff Sept 1, 1972. Sub 2, par (b), amd, L 1972, ch 784, § 1, eff Sept 1, 1972.

§ 520.15. Bail and bail bonds; posting of cash bail

1. Where a court has fixed bail pursuant to subdivision two of section 520.10, at any time after the principal has been committed to the custody of the sheriff pending the posting thereof, cash bail in the amount designated in the order fixing bail may be posted even though such bail was not specified in such order. Cash bail may be deposited with (a) the county treasurer of the county in which the criminal action or proceeding is pending or, in the city of New York with the commissioner of finance, or (b) the court which issued such order, or (c) the sheriff in whose custody the principal has been committed. Upon proof of the deposit of the designated amount the principal must be forthwith released from custody.

2. The person posting cash bail must complete and sign a form which states (a) the name, residential address and occupation of each person posting cash bail; and (b) the title of the criminal action or proceeding involved; and (c) the offense or offenses which are the subjects of the action or proceeding involved, and the status of such action or proceeding; and (d) the name of the principal and the nature of his involvement in or connection with such action or proceeding; and (e) that the person or persons posting cash bail undertake that the principal will appear in such action or proceeding whenever required and will at all times render himself amendable to the orders and processes of the court; and (f) the date of the principal's next appearance in court; and (g) an acknowledgment that the cash bail will be forfeited if the principal does not comply with any requirement or order of process to appear in court; and (h) the amount of money posted as cash bail.

3. Money posted as cash bail is and shall remain the property of the person posting it unless forfeited to the court.

HISTORY: Add, L 1970, ch 996, § 1; amd, L 1978, ch 655, § 40, eff July 25, 1978. Sub 1, formerly entire section, so designated, L 1984, ch 384, § 2, eff Sept 1, 1984. Sub 2, add, L 1984, ch 384, § 2, eff Sept 1, 1984. Sub 3, add, L 1984, ch 384, § 2, eff Sept 1, 1984.

§ 520.20. Bail and bail bonds; posting of bail bond and justifying affidavits; form and contents thereof

1. (a) Except as provided in paragraph (b) when a bail bond is to be posted in satisfaction of

---

* The bracketed punctuation has been inserted by the Publisher.

bail, the obligor or obligors must submit to the court a bail bond in the amount fixed, executed in the form prescribed in subdivision two, accompanied by a justifying affidavit of each obligor, executed in the form prescribed in subdivision four.

(b) When a bail bond is to be posted in satisfaction of bail fixed for a defendant charged by information or simplified information or prosecutor's information with one or more traffic infractions and no other offense, the defendant may submit to the court, with the consent of the court, an insurance company bail bond covering the amount fixed, executed in a form prescribed by the superintendent of insurance.

2. Except as provided in paragraph (b) of subdivision one, a bail bond must be subscribed and sworn to by each obligor and must state:

(a) The name, residential address and occupation of each obligor; and

(b) The title of the criminal action or proceeding involved; and

(c) The offense or offenses which are the subjects of the action or proceeding involved, and the status of such action or proceeding; and

(d) The name of the principal and the nature of his involvement in or connection with such action or proceeding; and

(e) That the obligor, or the obligors jointly and severally, undertake that the principal will appear in such action or proceeding whenever required and will at all times render himself amenable to the orders and processes of the court; and

(f) That in the event that the principal does not comply with any such requirement, order or process, such obligor or obligors will pay to the people of the state of New York a designated sum of money fixed by the court.

3. A bail bond posted in the course of a criminal action is effective and binding upon the obligor or obligors until the imposition of sentence or other termination of the action, regardless of whether the action is dismissed in the local criminal court after an indictment on the same charge or charges by a superior court, and regardless of whether such action is partially conducted or prosecuted in a court or courts other than the one in which the action was pending when such bond was posted, unless prior to such termination such order of bail is vacated or revoked or the principal is surrendered, or unless the terms of such bond expressly limit its effectiveness to a lesser period; provided, however, the effectiveness of such bond may only be limited to a lesser period if the obligor or obligors submit notice of the limitation to the court and the district attorney not less than fourteen days before effectiveness ends.

4. A justifying affidavit must be subscribed and sworn to by the obligor-affiant and must state his name, residential address and occupation. Depending upon the kind of bail bond which it justifies, such affidavit must contain further statements as follows:

(a) An affidavit justifying an insurance company bail bond must state:

(i) The amount of the premium paid to the obligor; and

(ii) All security and all promises of indemnity received by the surety-obligor in connection with its execution of the bond, and the name, occupation and residential and business addresses of every person who has given any such indemnifying security or promise.

An action by the surety-obligor against an indemnitor, seeking retention of security deposited by the latter with the former or enforcement of any indemnity agreement of a kind described in this sub-paragraph, will not lie except with respect to agreements and security specified in the justifying affidavit.

(b) An affidavit justifying a secured bail bond must state every item of personal property deposited and of real property pledged as security, the value of each such item, and the nature and amount of every lien or encumbrance thereon.

(c) An affidavit justifying a partially secured bail bond or an unsecured bail bond must state the place and nature of the obligor-affiant's business or employment, the length of time he has been engaged therein, his income during the past year, and his average income over the past five years.

HISTORY: Add, L 1970, ch 996, § 1, eff Sept 1, 1971. Sub 1, par (a), formerly entire subdivision, so lettered and amd, L 1973, ch 927, § 1, eff Sept 1, 1973. Sub 1, par (b), add, L 1973, ch 927, § 1, eff Sept 1, 1973. Sub 2, amd, L 1973, ch 927, § 1, eff Sept 1, 1973. Sub 3, amd, L 1973, ch 927, § 1, L 1974, ch 425, § 1, L 1981, ch 268, § 1, eff Aug 19, 1981. Sub 4, par (c), amd, L 1981, ch 145, § 1, eff June 25, 1981.

§ 520.30. Bail and bail bonds; examination as to sufficiency

1. Following the posting of a bail bond and the justifying affidavit or affidavits or the posting of cash bail, the court may conduct an inquiry for the purpose of determining the reliability of the obligors or person posting cash bail, the value and sufficiency of any security offered, and whether any feature of the undertaking contravenes public policy; provided that before undertaking an inquiry, of a person posting cash bail the court, after application of the district attorney, must have had reasonable cause to believe that the person posting cash bail is not in rightful possession of money posted as cash bail or that such money constitutes the fruits of criminal or unlawful conduct. The court may inquire into any matter stated or required to be stated in the justifying affidavits, and may also inquire into other matters appropriate to the determination, which include but are not limited to the following:

(a) The background, character and reputation of any obligor, and, in the case of an insurance company bail bond, the qualifications of the surety-obligor and its executing agent; and

(b) The source of any money or property deposited by any obligor as security, and whether any such money or property constitutes the fruits of criminal or unlawful conduct; and

(c) The source of any money or property delivered or agreed to be delivered to any obligor as indemnification on the bond, and whether any such money or property constitutes the fruits of criminal or unlawful conduct; and

(d) The background, character and reputation of any person who has indemnified or agreed to indemnify an obligor upon the bond; and whether any such indemnitor, not being licensed by the superintendent of insurance in accordance with the insurance law, has within a period of one month prior to such indemnity transaction given indemnification or security for like purpose in more than two cases not arising out of the same transaction; and

(e) The source of any money posted as cash bail, and whether any such money constitutes the fruits of criminal or unlawful conduct; and

(f) The background, character and reputation of the person posting cash bail.

2. Upon such inquiry, the court may examine, under oath or otherwise, the obligors and any other persons who may possess material information. The district attorney has a right to attend such inquiry, to call witnesses and to examine any witness in the proceeding. The court may, upon

application of the district attorney, adjourn the proceeding for a reasonable period to allow him to investigate the matter.

3. At the conclusion of the inquiry, the court must issue an order either approving or disapproving the bail.

HISTORY: Add, L 1970, ch 996, § 1; amd, L 1984, ch 384, § 3, eff Sept 1, 1984. Sub 1, par (e), add, L 1984, ch 384, § 3, eff Sept 1, 1984. Sub 1, par (f), add, L 1984, ch 384, § 3, eff Sept 1, 1984.

§ 520.40. Transfer of cash bail from local criminal court to superior court

When a local criminal court acquires control over the person of an accused and such court designates the amount of bail that the accused may post and such bail is posted in cash and subsequently the accused is arraigned in superior court where bail is fixed by such court, the accused may request that the cash bail posted in the local criminal court be transferred to the superior court. Notice of such request must be given to the person who posted cash bail. Upon such a request the superior court shall make an order directing the local criminal court to transfer the cash bail that it holds to the superior court for use in the superior court. If there is an overage, the superior court shall order it be paid over to the person who posted the cash bail in the local criminal court. If there is a deficiency, the accused shall post additional bail as directed by the superior court.

HISTORY: Add, L 1974, ch 219, § 1; amd, L 1984, ch 384, § 4, eff Sept 1, 1984.

[ARTICLE] 530*   ORDERS OF RECOGNIZANCE OR BAIL WITH RESPECT TO DEFENDANTS IN CRIMINAL ACTIONS AND PROCEEDINGS—WHEN AND BY WHAT COURTS AUTHORIZED

HISTORY: Add, L 1970, ch 996, § 1, eff Sept 1, 1971.

§ 530.10. Order of recognizance or bail; in general

Under circumstances prescribed in this article, a court, upon application of a defendant charged

---

* The bracketed word has been inserted by the Publisher.

with or convicted of an offense, is required or authorized to order bail or recognizance for the release or prospective release of such defendant during the pendency of either:

1. A criminal action based upon such charge; or

2. An appeal taken by the defendant from a judgment of conviction or a sentence or from an order of an intermediate appellate court affirming or modifying a judgment of conviction or a sentence.

HISTORY: Add, L 1970, ch 996, § 1, eff Sept 1, 1971.

§ 530.11. Procedures for family offense matters

1. The family court and the criminal courts shall have concurrent jurisdiction over any proceeding concerning acts which would constitute disorderly conduct, harassment in the first degree, harassment in the second degree, aggravated harassment in the second degree, sexual misconduct, forcible touching, sexual abuse in the third degree, sexual abuse in the second degree as set forth in subdivision one of section 130.60 of the penal law, stalking in the first degree, stalking in the second degree, stalking in the third degree, stalking in the fourth degree, criminal mischief, menacing in the second degree, menacing in the third degree, reckless endangerment, strangulation in the first degree, strangulation in the second degree, criminal obstruction of breathing or blood circulation, assault in the second degree, assault in the third degree, an attempted assault, identity theft in the first degree, identity theft in the second degree, identity theft in the third degree, grand larceny in the fourth degree, grand larceny in the third degree or coercion in the second degree as set forth in subdivisions one, two and three of section 135.60 of the penal law between spouses or former spouses, or between parent and child or between members of the same family or household except that if the respondent would not be criminally responsible by reason of age pursuant to section 30.00 of the penal law, then the family court shall have exclusive jurisdiction over such proceeding. Notwithstanding a complainant's election to proceed in family court, the criminal court shall not be divested of jurisdiction to hear a family offense proceeding pursuant to this section. For purposes of this section, "disorderly conduct" includes disorderly conduct not in a public place. For purposes of this section, "members of the same family or household" with respect to a proceeding in the criminal courts shall mean the following:

(a) persons related by consanguinity or affinity;

(b) persons legally married to one another;

(c) persons formerly married to one another regardless of whether they still reside in the same household;

(d) persons who have a child in common, regardless of whether such persons have been married or have lived together at any time; and

(e) persons who are not related by consanguinity or affinity and who are or have been in an intimate relationship regardless of whether such persons have lived together at any time. Factors the court may consider in determining whether a relationship is an "intimate relationship" include but are not limited to: the nature or type of relationship, regardless of whether the relationship is sexual in nature; the frequency of interaction between the persons; and the duration of the relationship. Neither a casual acquaintance nor ordinary fraternization between two individuals in business or social contexts shall be deemed to constitute an "intimate relationship".

2. Information to petitioner or complainant. The chief administrator of the courts shall designate the appropriate probation officers, warrant officers, sheriffs, police officers, district attorneys or any

other law enforcement officials, to inform any petitioner or complainant bringing a proceeding under this section before such proceeding is commenced, of the procedures available for the institution of family offense proceedings, including but not limited to the following:

(a) That there is concurrent jurisdiction with respect to family offenses in both family court and the criminal courts;

(b) That a family court proceeding is a civil proceeding and is for the purpose of attempting to stop the violence, end family disruption and obtain protection. That referrals for counseling, or counseling services, are available through probation for this purpose;

(c) That a proceeding in the criminal courts is for the purpose of prosecution of the offender and can result in a criminal conviction of the offender;

(d) That a proceeding or action subject to the provisions of this section is initiated at the time of the filing of an accusatory instrument or family court petition, not at the time of arrest, or request for arrest, if any;

(e) [Repealed]

(f) That an arrest may precede the commencement of a family court or a criminal court proceeding, but an arrest is not a requirement for commencing either proceeding.

(g) [Repealed]

(h) At such time as the complainant first appears before the court on a complaint or information, the court shall advise the complainant that the complainant may: continue with the proceeding in criminal court; or have the allegations contained therein heard in a family court proceeding; or proceed concurrently in both criminal and family court. Notwithstanding a complainant's election to proceed in family court, the criminal court shall not be divested of jurisdiction to hear a family offense proceeding pursuant to this section;

(i) Nothing herein shall be deemed to limit or restrict complainant's rights to proceed directly and without court referral in either a criminal or family court, or both, as provided for in section one hundred fifteen of the family court act and section 100.07 of this chapter;

(j) [Repealed]

2-a. Upon the filing of an accusatory instrument charging a crime or violation described in subdivision one of this section between members of the same family or household, as such terms are defined in this section, or as soon as the complainant first appears before the court, whichever is sooner, the court shall advise the complainant of the right to proceed in both the criminal and family courts, pursuant to section 100.07 of this chapter.

3. Official responsibility. No official or other person designated pursuant to subdivision two of this section shall discourage or prevent any person who wishes to file a petition or sign a complaint from having access to any court for that purpose.

4. When a person is arrested for an alleged family offense or an alleged violation of an order of protection or temporary order of protection or arrested pursuant to a warrant issued by the supreme or family court, and the supreme or family court, as applicable, is not in session, such person shall be brought before a local criminal court in the county of arrest or in the county in which such warrant is returnable pursuant to article one hundred twenty of this chapter. Such local criminal court may issue any order authorized under subdivision eleven of section 530.12 of this article, section one hundred fifty-four-d or one hundred fifty-five of the family court act or

subdivision three-b of section two hundred forty or subdivision two-a of section two hundred fifty-two of the domestic relations law, in addition to discharging other arraignment responsibilities as set forth in this chapter. In making such order, the local criminal court shall consider the bail recommendation, if any, made by the supreme or family court as indicated on the warrant or certificate of warrant. Unless the petitioner or complainant requests otherwise, the court, in addition to scheduling further criminal proceedings, if any, regarding such alleged family offense or violation allegation, shall make such matter returnable in the supreme or family court, as applicable, on the next day such court is in session.

5. Filing and enforcement of out-of-state orders of protection. A valid order of protection or temporary order of protection issued by a court of competent jurisdiction in another state, territorial or tribal jurisdiction shall be accorded full faith and credit and enforced as if it were issued by a court within the state for as long as the order remains in effect in the issuing jurisdiction in accordance with sections two thousand two hundred sixty-five and two thousand two hundred sixty-six of title eighteen of the United States Code.

(a) An order issued by a court of competent jurisdiction in another state, territorial or tribal jurisdiction shall be deemed valid if:

(i) the issuing court had personal jurisdiction over the parties and over the subject matter under the law of the issuing jurisdiction;

(ii) the person against whom the order was issued had reasonable notice and an opportunity to be heard prior to issuance of the order; provided, however, that if the order was a temporary order of protection issued in the absence of such person, that notice had been given and that an opportunity to be heard had been provided within a reasonable period of time after the issuance of the order; and

(iii) in the case of orders of protection or temporary orders of protection issued against both a petitioner, plaintiff or complainant and respondent or defendant, the order or portion thereof sought to be enforced was supported by: (A) a pleading requesting such order, including, but not limited to, a petition, cross-petition or counterclaim; and (B) a judicial finding that the requesting party is entitled to the issuance of the order which may result from a judicial finding of fact, judicial acceptance of an admission by the party against whom the order was issued or judicial finding that the party against whom the order was issued had given knowing, intelligent and voluntary consent to its issuance.

(b) Notwithstanding the provisions of article fifty-four of the civil practice law and rules, an order of protection or temporary order of protection issued by a court of competent jurisdiction in another state, territorial or tribal jurisdiction, accompanied by a sworn affidavit that upon information and belief such order is in effect as written and has not been vacated or modified, may be filed without fee with the clerk of the court, who shall transmit information regarding such order to the statewide registry of orders of protection and warrants established pursuant to section two hundred twenty-one-a of the executive law; provided, however, that such filing and registry entry shall not be required for enforcement of the order.

6. Notice. Every police officer, peace officer or district attorney investigating a family offense under this article shall advise the victim of the availability of a shelter or other services in the community, and shall immediately give the victim written notice of the legal rights and remedies available to a victim of a family offense under the relevant provisions of the criminal procedure law, the family court act and the domestic relations law. Such notice shall be prepared in Spanish

and English and if necessary, shall be delivered orally, and shall include but not be limited to the following statement:

"If you are the victim of domestic violence, you may request that the officer assist in providing for your safety and that of your children, including providing information on how to obtain a temporary order of protection. You may also request that the officer assist you in obtaining your essential personal effects and locating and taking you, or assist in making arrangements to take you, and your children to a safe place within such officer's jurisdiction, including but not limited to a domestic violence program, a family member's or a friend's residence, or a similar place of safety. When the officer's jurisdiction is more than a single county, you may ask the officer to take you or make arrangements to take you and your children to a place of safety in the county where the incident occurred. If you or your children are in need of medical treatment, you have the right to request that the officer assist you in obtaining such medical treatment. You may request a copy of any incident reports at no cost from the law enforcement agency. You have the right to seek legal counsel of your own choosing and if you proceed in family court and if it is determined that you cannot afford an attorney, one must be appointed to represent you without cost to you.

You may ask the district attorney or a law enforcement officer to file a criminal complaint. You also have the right to file a petition in the family court when a family offense has been committed against you. You have the right to have your petition and request for an order of protection filed on the same day you appear in court, and such request must be heard that same day or the next day court is in session. Either court may issue an order of protection from conduct constituting a family offense which could include, among other provisions, an order for the respondent or defendant to stay away from you and your children. The family court may also order the payment of temporary child support and award temporary custody of your children. If the family court is not in session, you may seek immediate assistance from the criminal court in obtaining an order of protection.

The forms you need to obtain an order of protection are available from the family court and the local criminal court (the addresses and telephone numbers shall be listed). The resources available in this community for information relating to domestic violence, treatment of injuries, and places of safety and shelters can be accessed by calling the following 800 numbers (the statewide English and Spanish language 800 numbers shall be listed and space shall be provided for local domestic violence hotline telephone numbers).

Filing a criminal complaint or a family court petition containing allegations that are knowingly false is a crime."

The division of criminal justice services in consultation with the state office for the prevention of domestic violence shall prepare the form of such written notice consistent with provisions of this section and distribute copies thereof to the appropriate law enforcement officials pursuant to subdivision nine of section eight hundred forty-one of the executive law.

Additionally, copies of such notice shall be provided to the chief administrator of the courts to be distributed to victims of family offenses through the criminal court at such time as such persons first come before the court and to the state department of health for distribution to all hospitals defined under article twenty-eight of the public health law. No cause of action for damages shall arise in favor of any person by reason of any failure to comply with the provisions of this subdivision except upon a showing of gross negligence or willful misconduct.

7. Rules of court regarding concurrent jurisdiction. The chief administrator of the courts, pursuant to paragraph (e) of subdivision two of section two hundred twelve of the judiciary law, shall promulgate rules to facilitate record sharing and other communication between the criminal

and family courts, subject to applicable provisions of this chapter and the family court act pertaining to the confidentiality, expungement and sealing of records, when such courts exercise concurrent jurisdiction over family offense proceedings.

HISTORY: Add, L 1980, ch 530, § 15; amd, L 1981, ch 416, § 20, L 1983, ch 925, § 2, eff Aug 8, 1983, L 1984, ch 948, § 13, eff Nov 1, 1984 and applicable to any action and proceeding commenced on or after Nov 1, 1984, L 1986, ch 847, § 2, L 1990, ch 667, § 1, L 1992, ch 345, § 6, L 1994, ch 222, §§ 34–39, eff Jan 1, 1995, L 1994, ch 224, § 7, eff Jan 1, 1995, L 1995, ch 349, § 5, eff July 28, 1995, L 1995, ch 440, § 2, eff Nov 1, 1995, L 1997, ch 186, §§ 7–9, eff July 8, 1997, L 1998, ch 597, § 11, eff Dec 22, 1998, L 1999, ch 125, §§ 1, 2, eff June 29, 1999, L 1999, ch 635, § 3, eff Dec 1, 1999, L 2007, ch 541, § 2, eff Nov 13, 2007, L 2008, ch 326, § 11, eff July 21, 2008, L 2009, ch 476, § 3, eff Dec 15, 2009, L 2010, ch 405, § 11, eff Nov 11, 2010, L 2013, ch 526, § 10, eff Dec 18, 2013.

§ 530.12. Protection for victims of family offenses

1. When a criminal action is pending involving a complaint charging any crime or violation between spouses, former spouses, parent and child, or between members of the same family or household, as members of the same family or household are defined in subdivision one of section 530.11 of this article, the court, in addition to any other powers conferred upon it by this chapter may issue a temporary order of protection in conjunction with any securing order committing the defendant to the custody of the sheriff or as a condition of any order of recognizance or bail or an adjournment in contemplation of dismissal.

(a) In addition to any other conditions, such an order may require the defendant:

(1) to stay away from the home, school, business or place of employment of the family or household member or of any designated witness, provided that the court shall make a determination, and shall state such determination in a written decision or on the record, whether to impose a condition pursuant to this paragraph, provided further, however, that failure to make such a determination shall not affect the validity of such temporary order of protection. In making such determination, the court shall consider, but shall not be limited to consideration of, whether the temporary order of protection is likely to achieve its purpose in the absence of such a condition, conduct subject to prior orders of protection, prior incidents of abuse, past or present injury, threats, drug or alcohol abuse, and access to weapons;

(2) to permit a parent, or a person entitled to visitation by a court order or a separation agreement, to visit the child at stated periods;

(3) to refrain from committing a family offense, as defined in subdivision one of section 530.11 of this article, or any criminal offense against the child or against the family or household member or against any person to whom custody of the child is awarded, or from harassing, intimidating or threatening such persons;

(4) to refrain from acts of commission or omission that create an unreasonable risk to the health, safety and welfare of a child, family or household member's life or health;

(5) to permit a designated party to enter the residence during a specified period of time in order to remove personal belongings not in issue in this proceeding or in any other proceeding or action under this chapter, the family court act or the domestic relations law;

(6) (A) to refrain from intentionally injuring or killing, without justification, any companion animal the defendant knows to be owned, possessed, leased, kept or held by the victim or a minor child residing in the household.

(B) "Companion animal", as used in this section, shall have the same meaning as in subdivision five of section three hundred fifty of the agriculture and markets law;

(7) (A) to promptly return specified identification documents to the protected party, in whose favor the order of protection or temporary order of protection is issued; provided, however, that such order may: (i) include any appropriate provision designed to ensure that any such document is available for use as evidence in this proceeding, and available if necessary for legitimate use by the party against whom such order is issued; and (ii) specify the manner in which such return shall be accomplished.

(B) For purposes of this subparagraph, "identification document" shall mean any of the following: (i) exclusively in the name of the protected party: birth certificate, passport, social security card, health insurance or other benefits card, a card or document used to access bank, credit or other financial accounts or records, tax returns, any driver's license, and immigration documents including but not limited to a United States permanent resident card and employment authorization document; and (ii) upon motion and after notice and an opportunity to be heard, any of the following, including those that may reflect joint use or ownership, that the court determines are necessary and are appropriately transferred to the protected party: any card or document used to access bank, credit or other financial accounts or records, tax returns, and any other identifying cards and documents.

(b) The court may issue an order, pursuant to section two hundred twenty-seven-c of the real property law, authorizing the party for whose benefit any order of protection has been issued to terminate a lease or rental agreement pursuant to section two hundred twenty-seven-c of the real property law.

(c) to refrain from committing a family offense, as defined in subdivision one of section 530.11 of this article, or any criminal offense against the child or against the family or household member or against any person to whom custody of the child is awarded, or from harassing, intimidating or threatening such persons;

(d) to refrain from acts of commission or omission that create an unreasonable risk to the health, safety and welfare of a child, family or household member's life or health;

(e) to permit a designated party to enter the residence during a specified period of time in order to remove personal belongings not in issue in this proceeding or in any other proceeding or action under this chapter, the family court act or the domestic relations law;

(f) 1. to refrain from intentionally injuring or killing, without justification, any companion animal the defendant knows to be owned, possessed, leased, kept or held by the victim or a minor child residing in the household.

2. "Companion animal", as used in this section, shall have the same meaning as in subdivision five of section three hundred fifty of the agriculture and markets law.

(g) The court may issue an order, pursuant to section two hundred twenty-seven-c of the real property law, authorizing the party for whose benefit any order of protection has been issued to terminate a lease or rental agreement pursuant to section two hundred twenty-seven-c of the real property law.

2. Notwithstanding any other provision of law, a temporary order of protection issued or continued by a family court pursuant to section eight hundred thirteen of the family court act shall continue in effect, absent action by the appropriate criminal court pursuant to subdivision three of

this section, until the defendant is arraigned upon an accusatory instrument filed pursuant to section eight hundred thirteen of the family court act in such criminal court.

3. The court may issue a temporary order of protection ex parte upon the filing of an accusatory instrument and for good cause shown. When a family court order of protection is modified, the criminal court shall forward a copy of such modified order to the family court issuing the original order of protection; provided, however, that where a copy of the modified order is transmitted to the family court by facsimile or other electronic means, the original copy of such modified order and accompanying affidavit shall be forwarded immediately thereafter.

3-a. Emergency powers when family court not in session; issuance of temporary orders of protection. Upon the request of the petitioner, a local criminal court may on an ex parte basis issue a temporary order of protection pending a hearing in family court, provided that a sworn affidavit, verified in accordance with subdivision one of section 100.30 of this chapter, is submitted: (i) alleging that the family court is not in session; (ii) alleging that a family offense, as defined in subdivision one of section eight hundred twelve of the family court act and subdivision one of section 530.11 of this article, has been committed; (iii) alleging that a family offense petition has been filed or will be filed in family court on the next day the court is in session; and (iv) showing good cause. Upon appearance in a local criminal court, the petitioner shall be advised that he or she may continue with the proceeding either in family court or upon the filing of a local criminal court accusatory instrument in criminal court or both. Upon issuance of a temporary order of protection where petitioner requests that it be returnable in family court, the local criminal court shall transfer the matter forthwith to the family court and shall make the matter returnable in family court on the next day the family court is in session, or as soon thereafter as practicable, but in no event more than four calendar days after issuance of the order. The local criminal court, upon issuing a temporary order of protection returnable in family court pursuant to this subdivision, shall immediately forward, in a manner designed to insure arrival before the return date set in the order, a copy of the temporary order of protection and sworn affidavit to the family court and shall provide a copy of such temporary order of protection to the petitioner; provided, however, that where a copy of the temporary order of protection and affidavit are transmitted to the family court by facsimile or other electronic means, the original order and affidavit shall be forwarded to the family court immediately thereafter. Any temporary order of protection issued pursuant to this subdivision shall be issued to the respondent, and copies shall be filed as required in subdivisions six and eight of this section for orders of protection issued pursuant to this section. Any temporary order of protection issued pursuant to this subdivision shall plainly state the date that such order expires which, in the case of an order returnable in family court, shall be not more than four calendar days after its issuance, unless sooner vacated or modified by the family court. A petitioner requesting a temporary order of protection returnable in family court pursuant to this subdivision in a case in which a family court petition has not been filed shall be informed that such temporary order of protection shall expire as provided for herein, unless the petitioner files a petition pursuant to subdivision one of section eight hundred twenty-one of the family court act on or before the return date in family court and the family court issues a temporary order of protection or order of protection as authorized under article eight of the family court act. Nothing in this subdivision shall limit or restrict the petitioner's right to proceed directly and without court referral in either a criminal or family court, or both, as provided for in section one hundred fifteen of the family court act and section 100.07 of this chapter.

3-b. Emergency powers when family court not in session; modifications of orders of protection or temporary orders of protection. Upon the request of the petitioner, a local criminal court may on an ex parte basis modify a temporary order of protection or order of protection which has been issued under article four, five, six or eight of the family court act pending a hearing in family court, provided that a sworn affidavit verified in accordance with subdivision one of section 100.30 of this chapter is submitted: (i) alleging that the family court is not in session and (ii) showing good cause, including a showing that the existing order is insufficient for the purposes of protection of the petitioner, the petitioner's child or children or other members of the petitioner's family or household. The local criminal court shall make the matter regarding the modification of the order returnable in family court on the next day the family court is in session, or as soon thereafter as practicable, but in no event more than four calendar days after issuance of the modified order. The court shall immediately forward a copy of the modified order, if any, and sworn affidavit to the family court and shall provide a copy of such modified order, if any, and affidavit to the petitioner; provided, however, that where copies of such modified order and affidavit are transmitted to the family court by facsimile or other electronic means, the original copies of such modified order and affidavit shall be forwarded to the family court immediately thereafter. Any modified temporary order of protection or order of protection issued pursuant to this subdivision shall be issued to the respondent and copies shall be filed as required in subdivisions six and eight of this section for orders of protection issued pursuant to this section.

4. The court may issue or extend a temporary order of protection ex parte or on notice simultaneously with the issuance of a warrant for the arrest of defendant. Such temporary order of protection may continue in effect until the day the defendant subsequently appears in court pursuant to such warrant or voluntarily or otherwise.

5. [Until Sept 1, 2015] Upon sentencing on a conviction for any crime or violation between spouses, between a parent and child, or between members of the same family or household as defined in subdivision one of section 530.11 of this article, the court may in addition to any other disposition, including a conditional discharge or youthful offender adjudication, enter an order of protection. Where a temporary order of protection was issued, the court shall state on the record the reasons for issuing or not issuing an order of protection. The duration of such an order shall be fixed by the court and: (A) in the case of a felony conviction, shall not exceed the greater of: (i) eight years from the date of such sentencing, or (ii) eight years from the date of the expiration of the maximum term of an indeterminate or the term of a determinate sentence of imprisonment actually imposed; or (B) in the case of a conviction for a class A misdemeanor, shall not exceed the greater of: (i) five years from the date of such sentencing, or (ii) five years from the date of the expiration of the maximum term of a definite or intermittent term actually imposed; or (C) in the case of a conviction for any other offense, shall not exceed the greater of: (i) two years from the date of sentencing, or (ii) two years from the date of the expiration of the maximum term of a definite or intermittent term actually imposed. For purposes of determining the duration of an order of protection entered pursuant to this subdivision, a conviction shall be deemed to include a conviction that has been replaced by a youthful offender adjudication. In addition to any other conditions, such an order may require the defendant:

5. [Eff Sept 1, 2015] Upon sentencing on a conviction for any crime or violation between spouses, between a parent and child, or between members of the same family or household as defined in subdivision one of section 530.11 of this article, the court may in addition to any other disposition, including a conditional discharge or youthful offender adjudication, enter an order of protection. Where a temporary order of protection was issued, the court shall state on the record the reasons for issuing or not issuing an order of protection. The duration of such an order shall be fixed by the court and, in the case of a felony conviction, shall not exceed the greater of: (i) five years from the date of such sentencing, or (ii) three years from the date of the expiration of the maximum term of an indeterminate sentence of imprisonment actually imposed; or in the case of a conviction for a class A misdemeanor, shall not exceed three years from the date of such sentencing; or in the case of a conviction for any other offense, shall not exceed one year from the

date of sentencing. For purposes of determining the duration of an order of protection entered pursuant to this subdivision, a conviction shall be deemed to include a conviction that has been replaced by a youthful offender adjudication. In addition to any other conditions, such an order may require the defendant:

(a) to stay away from the home, school, business or place of employment of the family or household member, the other spouse or the child, or of any witness designated by the court, provided that the court shall make a determination, and shall state such determination in a written decision or on the record, whether to impose a condition pursuant to this paragraph, provided further, however, that failure to make such a determination shall not affect the validity of such order of protection. In making such determination, the court shall consider, but shall not be limited to consideration of, whether the order of protection is likely to achieve its purpose in the absence of such a condition, conduct subject to prior orders of protection, prior incidents of abuse, extent of past or present injury, threats, drug or alcohol abuse, and access to weapons;

(b) to permit a parent, or a person entitled to visitation by a court order or a separation agreement, to visit the child at stated periods;

(c) to refrain from committing a family offense, as defined in subdivision one of section 530.11 of this article, or any criminal offense against the child or against the family or household member or against any person to whom custody of the child is awarded, or from harassing, intimidating or threatening such persons; or

(d) to refrain from acts of commission or omission that create an unreasonable risk to the health, safety and welfare of a child, family or household member's life or health;

(e) to permit a designated party to enter the residence during a specified period of time in order to remove personal belongings not in issue in this proceeding or in any other proceeding or action under this chapter, the family court act or the domestic relations law.

6. An order of protection or a temporary order of protection issued pursuant to subdivision one, two, three, four or five of this section shall bear in a conspicuous manner the term "order of protection" or "temporary order of protection" as the case may be and a copy shall be filed by the clerk of the court with the sheriff's office in the county in which the complainant resides, or, if the complainant resides within a city, with the police department of such city. The order of protection or temporary order of protection shall also contain the following notice: "This order of protection will remain in effect even if the protected party has, or consents to have, contact or communication with the party against whom the order is issued. This order of protection can only be modified or terminated by the court. The protected party cannot be held to violate this order nor be arrested for violating this order.". The absence of such language shall not affect the validity of such order. A copy of such order of protection or temporary order of protection may from time to time be filed by the clerk of the court with any other police department or sheriff's office having jurisdiction of the residence, work place, and school of anyone intended to be protected by such order. A copy of the order may also be filed by the complainant at the appropriate police department or sheriff's office having jurisdiction. Any subsequent amendment or revocation of such order shall be filed in the same manner as herein provided.

Such order of protection shall plainly state the date that such order expires.

6-a. The court shall inquire as to the existence of any other orders of protection between the defendant and the person or persons for whom the order of protection is sought.

7. A family offense subject to the provisions of this section which occurs subsequent to the issuance of an order of protection under this chapter shall be deemed a new offense for which the

complainant may seek to file a new accusatory instrument and may file a family court petition under article eight of the family court act as provided for in section 100.07 of this chapter.

8. In any proceeding in which an order of protection or temporary order of protection or a warrant has been issued under this section, the clerk of the court shall issue to the complainant and defendant and defense counsel and to any other person affected by the order a copy of the order of protection or temporary order of protection and ensure that a copy of the order of protection or temporary order of protection be transmitted to the local correctional facility where the individual is or will be detained, the state or local correctional facility where the individual is or will be imprisoned, and the supervising probation department or department of corrections and community supervision where the individual is under probation or parole supervision. The presentation of a copy of such order or a warrant to any peace officer acting pursuant to his or her special duties or police officer shall constitute authority for him or her to arrest a person who has violated the terms of such order and bring such person before the court and, otherwise, so far as lies within his or her power, to aid in securing the protection such order was intended to afford. The protected party in whose favor the order of protection or temporary order of protection is issued may not be held to violate an order issued in his or her favor nor may such protected party be arrested for violating such order.

9. If no warrant, order or temporary order of protection has been issued by the court, and an act alleged to be a family offense as defined in section 530.11 of this chapter is the basis of the arrest, the magistrate shall permit the complainant to file a petition, information or accusatory instrument and for reasonable cause shown, shall thereupon hold such respondent or defendant, admit to, fix or accept bail, or parole him or her for hearing before the family court or appropriate criminal court as the complainant shall choose in accordance with the provisions of section 530.11 of this chapter.

10. Punishment for contempt based on a violation of an order of protection or temporary order of protection shall not affect the original criminal action, nor reduce or diminish a sentence upon conviction for the original crime or violation alleged therein or for a lesser included offense thereof.

11. If a defendant is brought before the court for failure to obey any lawful order issued under this section, or an order of protection issued by a court of competent jurisdiction in another state, territorial or tribal jurisdiction, and if, after hearing, the court is satisfied by competent proof that the defendant has willfully failed to obey any such order, the court may:

(a) revoke an order of recognizance or revoke an order of bail or order forfeiture of such bail and commit the defendant to custody; or

(b) restore the case to the calendar when there has been an adjournment in contemplation of dismissal and commit the defendant to custody; or

(c) revoke a conditional discharge in accordance with section 410.70 of this chapter and impose probation supervision or impose a sentence of imprisonment in accordance with the penal law based on the original conviction; or

(d) revoke probation in accordance with section 410.70 of this chapter and impose a sentence of imprisonment in accordance with the penal law based on the original conviction. In addition, if the act which constitutes the violation of the order of protection or temporary order of protection is a crime or a violation the defendant may be charged with and tried for that crime or violation.

(e) [Repealed]

12. The chief administrator of the courts shall promulgate appropriate uniform temporary orders of protection and orders of protection forms to be used throughout the state. Such forms shall be promulgated and developed in a manner to ensure the compatability [compatibility]* of such forms with the statewide computerized registry established pursuant to section two hundred twenty-one-a of the executive law.

13. Notwithstanding the foregoing provisions, an order of protection, or temporary order of protection when applicable, may be entered against a former spouse and persons who have a child in common, regardless of whether such persons have been married or have lived together at any time, or against a member of the same family or household as defined in subdivision one of section 530.11 of this article.

14. The people shall make reasonable efforts to notify the complainant alleging a crime constituting a family offense when the people have decided to decline prosecution of such crime, to dismiss the criminal charges against the defendant or to enter into a plea agreement. The people shall advise the complainant of the right to file a petition in the family court pursuant to section 100.07 of this chapter and section one hundred fifteen of the family court act.

In any case where allegations of criminal conduct are transferred from the family court to the criminal court pursuant to paragraph (ii) of subdivision (b) of section eight hundred forty-six of the family court act, the people shall advise the family court making the transfer of any decision to file an accusatory instrument against the family court respondent and shall notify such court of the disposition of such instrument and the sentence, if any, imposed upon such respondent.

Release of a defendant from custody shall not be delayed because of the requirements of this subdivision.

15. Any motion to vacate or modify an order of protection or temporary order of protection shall be on notice to the non-moving party, except as provided in subdivision three-b of this section.

HISTORY: Add as § 530.11, L 1977, ch 449, § 11; amd, L 1978, ch 628, §§ 10, 11, L 1978, ch 629, § 5; renumbered § 530.12 and amd, L 1980, ch 530, § 14, eff June 24, 1980; amd, L 1981, ch 143, § 1, eff June 25, 1981, L 1981, ch 416, §§ 21, 22, eff Aug 6, 1981, L 1982, ch 516, § 4, eff July 13, 1982, L 1984, ch 388, § 1, L 1984, ch 948, § 14, eff Nov 1, 1984 and applicable to any action and proceeding commenced on or after Nov 1, 1984; amd, L 1985, ch 672, § 3, L 1986, ch 620, § 1, eff Nov 1, 1986, L 1986, ch 794, § 1, L 1988, ch 702, § 1, eff Sept 2, 1988, L 1989, ch 164, § 2, eff Oct 15, 1989, L 1990, ch 454, § 1, L 1993, ch 498, § 4, eff Nov 1, 1993, L 1994, ch 222, §§ 40–45, L 1994, ch 224, §§ 8, 14, eff Jan 1, 1995, L 1995, ch 3, § 36, eff Oct 1, 1995, repealed Sept 1, 2015, L 1995, ch 483, §§ 15, 16, eff Nov 1, 1995, L 1996, ch 511, § 2, eff Nov 6, 1996, L 1996, ch 644, §§ 1, 2, eff Nov 1, 1996, L 1997, ch 186, §§ 10–12, eff July 8, 1997, L 1997, ch 589, § 1, eff Sept 17, 1997, L 1998, ch 597, § 12, eff Dec 22, 1998, L 1998, ch 610, § 1, eff Oct 6, 1998, L 2001, ch 384, § 1, eff Nov 1, 2001, deemed repealed Sept 1, 2015, L 2001, ch 384, § 2, eff Sept 1, 2013, L 2006, ch 215, § 1, eff Aug 25, 2006, L 2006, ch 253, § 8, eff July 26, 2006, L 2007, ch 73, § 2, eff Oct 1, 2007, L 2007, ch 137, § 1, eff July 3, 2007, L 2008, ch 56, § 5 (Part D), eff April 23, 2008, L 2008, ch 326, § 12, eff July 21, 2008, L 2009, ch 476, § 12, eff Dec 15, 2009, L 2011, ch 9, § 1, eff May 13, 2011, repealed Sept 1, 2015, L 2011, ch 9, § 2, eff Sept 1, 2013, L 2011, ch 62, § 81 (Part C, Subpart B), eff March 31, 2011, L 2013, ch 480, § 13, eff Nov 13, 2013, L 2013, ch 526, § 11, eff Dec 18, 2013.

§ 530.13. Protection of victims of crimes, other than family offenses

1. When any criminal action is pending, and the court has not issued a temporary order of protection pursuant to section 530.12 of this article, the court, in addition to the other powers conferred upon it by this chapter, may for good cause shown issue a temporary order of protection

---

* The bracketed word has been inserted by the Publisher.

in conjunction with any securing order committing the defendant to the custody of the sheriff or as a condition of a pre-trial release, or as a condition of release on bail or an adjournment in contemplation of dismissal. In addition to any other conditions, such an order may require that the defendant:

(a) stay away from the home, school, business or place of employment of the victims of, or designated witnesses to, the alleged offense;

(b) refrain from harassing, intimidating, threatening or otherwise interfering with the victims of the alleged offense and such members of the family or household of such victims or designated witnesses as shall be specifically named by the court in such order;

(c) 1. to refrain from intentionally injuring or killing, without justification, any companion animal the defendant knows to be owned, possessed, leased, kept or held by such victim or victims or a minor child residing in such victim's or victims' household.

2. "Companion animal", as used in this section, shall have the same meaning as in subdivision five of section three hundred fifty of the agriculture and markets law.

In addition to the foregoing provisions, the court may issue an order, pursuant to section two hundred twenty-seven-c of the real property law, authorizing the party for whose benefit any order of protection has been issued to terminate a lease or rental agreement pursuant to section two hundred twenty-seven-c of the real property law.

2. The court may issue a temporary order of protection under this section ex parte upon the filing of an accusatory instrument and for good cause shown.

3. The court may issue or extend a temporary order of protection under this section ex parte simultaneously with the issuance of a warrant for the arrest of the defendant. Such temporary order of protection may continue in effect until the day the defendant subsequently appears in court pursuant to such warrant or voluntarily or otherwise.

4. [Until Sept 1, 2015] Upon sentencing on a conviction for any offense, where the court has not issued an order of protection pursuant to section 530.12 of this article, the court may, in addition to any other disposition, including a conditional discharge or youthful offender adjudication, enter an order of protection. Where a temporary order of protection was issued, the court shall state on the record the reasons for issuing or not issuing an order of protection. The duration of such an order shall be fixed by the court and; (A) in the case of a felony conviction, shall not exceed the greater of: (i) eight years from the date of such sentencing, or (ii) eight years from the date of the expiration of the maximum term of an indeterminate or the term of a determinate sentence of imprisonment actually imposed; or (B) in the case of a conviction for a class A misdemeanor, shall not exceed the greater of: (i) five years from the date of such sentencing, or (ii) five years from the date of the expiration of the maximum term of a definite or intermittent term actually imposed; or (C) in the case of a conviction for any other offense, shall not exceed the greater of: (i) two years from the date of sentencing, or (ii) two years from the date of the expiration of the maximum term of a definite or intermittent term actually imposed. For purposes of determining the duration of an order of protection entered pursuant to this subdivision, a conviction shall be deemed to include a conviction that has been replaced by a youthful offender adjudication. In addition to any other conditions such an order may require that the defendant:

4. [Eff Sept 1, 2015] Upon sentencing on a conviction for any offense, where the court has not issued an order of protection pursuant to section 530.12 of this article, the court may, in addition to any other disposition, including a conditional discharge or youthful offender adjudication, enter an order of protection. Where a temporary order of protection was issued, the court shall state on

the record the reasons for issuing or not issuing an order of protection. The duration of such an order shall be fixed by the court and, in the case of a felony conviction, shall not exceed the greater of: (i) five years from the date of such sentencing, or (ii) three years from the date of the expiration of the maximum term of an indeterminate sentence of imprisonment actually imposed; or in the case of a conviction for a class A misdemeanor, shall not exceed three years from the date of such sentencing; or in the case of a conviction for any other offense, shall not exceed one year from the date of sentencing. For purposes of determining the duration of an order of protection entered pursuant to this subdivision, a conviction shall be deemed to include a conviction that has been replaced by a youthful offender adjudication. In addition to any other conditions such an order may require that the defendant:

(a) stay away from the home, school, business or place of employment of the victim or victims, or of any witness designated by the court, of such offense;

(b) refrain from harassing, intimidating, threatening or otherwise interfering with the victim or victims of the offense and such members of the family or household of such victim or victims as shall be specifically named by the court in such order;

(c) 1. to refrain from intentionally injuring or killing, without justification, any companion animal the defendant knows to be owned, possessed, leased, kept or held by such victim or victims or a minor child residing in such victim's or victims' household.

2. "Companion animal", as used in this section, shall have the same meaning as in subdivision five of section three hundred fifty of the agriculture and markets law.

5. The court shall inquire as to the existence of any other orders of protection between the defendant and the person or persons for whom the order of protection is sought. An order of protection issued under this section shall plainly state the date that such order expires. Orders of protection issued to protect victims of domestic violence, as defined in section four hundred fifty-nine-a of the social services law, shall be on uniform statewide forms that shall be promulgated by the chief administrator of the courts in a manner to ensure the compatibility of such forms with the statewide registry of orders of protection and warrants established pursuant to section two hundred twenty-one-a of the executive law. A copy of an order of protection or a temporary order of protection issued pursuant to subdivision one, two, three, or four of this section shall be filed by the clerk of the court with the sheriff's office in the county in which such victim or victims reside, or, if the victim or victims reside within a city, with the police department of such city. A copy of such order of protection or temporary order of protection may from time to time be filed by the clerk of the court with any other police department or sheriff's office having jurisdiction of the residence, work place, and school of anyone intended to be protected by such order. A copy of the order may also be filed by the victim or victims at the appropriate police department or sheriff's office having jurisdiction. Any subsequent amendment or revocation of such order shall be filed in the same manner as herein provided.

6. In any proceeding in which an order of protection or temporary order of protection or a warrant has been issued under this section, the clerk of the court shall issue to the victim and the defendant and defense counsel and to any other person affected by the order, a copy of the order of protection or temporary order of protection and ensure that a copy of the order of protection or temporary order of protection be transmitted to the local correctional facility where the individual is or will be detained, the state or local correctional facility where the individual is or will be imprisoned, and the supervising probation department or department of corrections and community supervision where the individual is under probation or parole supervision. The presentation of a copy of such order or a warrant to any police officer or peace officer acting pursuant to his or

her special duties shall constitute authority for him or her to arrest a person who has violated the terms of such order and bring such person before the court and, otherwise, so far as lies within his or her power, to aid in securing the protection such order was intended to afford.

7. Punishment for contempt based upon a violation of an order or [of]* protection or temporary order of protection issued under this section shall not affect a pending criminal action, nor reduce or diminish a sentence upon conviction for any other crimes or offenses.

8. If a defendant is brought before the court for failure to obey any lawful order issued under this section and if, after hearing, the court is satisfied by competent proof that the defendant has willfully failed to obey any such order, the court may:

(a) revoke an order of recognizance or bail and commit the defendant to custody; or

(b) restore the case to the calendar when there has been an adjournment in contemplation of dismissal and commit the defendant to custody or impose or increase bail pending a trial of the original crime or violation; or

(c) revoke a conditional discharge in accordance with section 410.70 of this chapter and impose probation supervision or impose a sentence of imprisonment in accordance with the penal law based on the original conviction; or

(d) revoke probation in accordance with section 410.70 of this chapter and impose a sentence of imprisonment in accordance with the penal law based on the original conviction. In addition, if the act which constitutes the violation of the order of protection or temporary order of protection is a crime or a violation the defendant may be charged with and tried for that crime or violation.

9. The chief administrator of the courts shall promulgate appropriate uniform temporary order of protection and order of protection forms to be used throughout the state.

HISTORY: Add, L 1981, ch 575, § 1, eff Sept 1, 1981; amd, L 1984, ch 388, § 2, eff Sept 1, 1984, L 1985, ch 672, § 4, L 1986, ch 620, § 2, eff Nov 1, 1986, L 1986, ch 794, § 2, eff Nov 1, 1986, L 1990, ch 454, § 2, L 1995, ch 3, § 37, eff Oct 1, 1995, repealed Sept 1, 2015, L 1997, ch 589, § 2, eff Sept 17, 1997, L 1998, ch 610, § 2, eff Oct 6, 1998, L 2001, ch 384, § 3, eff Nov 1, 2001, deemed repealed Sept 1, 2015, L 2001, ch 384, § 4, eff Sept 1, 2015, L 2002, ch 462, § 1, eff Nov 18, 2002, L 2006, ch 215, § 2, eff Aug 25, 2006, L 2006, ch 253, § 9, eff July 26, 2006, L 2007, ch 137, § 1, eff July 3, 2007, add, L 2007, ch 616, § 2, eff Oct 1, 2007, L 2008, ch 56, § 6 (Part D), eff April 23, 2008, L 2009, ch 476, § 13, eff Dec 15, 2009, L 2011, ch 9, § 3, eff May 13, 2011, repealed Sept 1, 2015, L 2011, ch 9, § 4, eff Sept 1, 2015, L 2011, ch 62, § 82 (Part C, Subpart B), eff March 31, 2011.

§ 530.14. Suspension and revocation of a license to carry, possess, repair or dispose of a firearm or firearms pursuant to section 400.00 of the penal law and ineligibility for such a license; order to surrender firearms

1. Suspension of firearms license and ineligibility for such a license upon issuance of temporary order of protection. Whenever a temporary order of protection is issued pursuant to subdivision one of section 530.12 or subdivision one of section 530.13 of this article:

(a) the court shall suspend any such existing license possessed by the defendant, order the defendant ineligible for such a license and order the immediate surrender of any or all firearms owned or possessed where the court receives information that gives the court good cause to believe that (i) the defendant has a prior conviction of any violent felony offense as defined in

---

* The bracketed word has been inserted by the Publisher.

section 70.02 of the penal law; (ii) the defendant has previously been found to have willfully failed to obey a prior order of protection and such willful failure involved (A) the infliction of physical injury, as defined in subdivision nine of section 10.00 of the penal law, (B) the use or threatened use of a deadly weapon or dangerous instrument as those terms are defined in subdivisions twelve and thirteen of section 10.00 of the penal law, or (C) behavior constituting any violent felony offense as defined in section 70.02 of the penal law; or (iii) the defendant has a prior conviction for stalking in the first degree as defined in section 120.60 of the penal law, stalking in the second degree as defined in section 120.55 of the penal law, stalking in the third degree as defined in section 120.50 of the penal law or stalking in the fourth degree as defined in section 120.45 of such law; and

(b) the court shall where the court finds a substantial risk that the defendant may use or threaten to use a firearm unlawfully against the person or persons for whose protection the temporary order of protection is issued, suspend any such existing license possessed by the defendant, order the defendant ineligible for such a license and order the immediate surrender pursuant to subparagraph (f) of paragraph one of subdivision a of section 265.20 and subdivision six of section 400.05 of the penal law, of any or all firearms owned or possessed.

2. Revocation or suspension of firearms license and ineligibility for such a license upon issuance of an order of protection. Whenever an order of protection is issued pursuant to subdivision five of section 530.12 or subdivision four of section 530.13 of this article:

(a) the court shall revoke any such existing license possessed by the defendant, order the defendant ineligible for such a license and order the immediate surrender of any or all firearms owned or possessed where such action is required by section 400.00 of the penal law; and

(b) the court shall where the court finds a substantial risk that the defendant may use or threaten to use a firearm unlawfully against the person or persons for whose protection the order of protection is issued, (i) revoke any such existing license possessed by the defendant, order the defendant ineligible for such a license and order the immediate surrender of any or all firearms owned or possessed or (ii) suspend or continue to suspend any such existing license possessed by the defendant, order the defendant ineligible for such a license and order the immediate surrender pursuant to subparagraph (f) of paragraph one of subdivision a of section 265.20 and subdivision six of section 400.05 of the penal law, of any or all firearms owned or possessed.

3. Revocation or suspension of firearms license and ineligibility for such a license upon a finding of a willful failure to obey an order of protection. Whenever a defendant has been found pursuant to subdivision eleven of section 530.12 or subdivision eight of section 530.13 of this article to have willfully failed to obey an order of protection issued by a court of competent jurisdiction in this state or another state, territorial or tribal jurisdiction, in addition to any other remedies available pursuant to subdivision eleven of section 530.12 or subdivision eight of section 530.13 of this article:

(a) the court shall revoke any such existing license possessed by the defendant, order the defendant ineligible for such a license and order the immediate surrender of any or all firearms owned or possessed where the willful failure to obey such order involved (i) the infliction of physical injury, as defined in subdivision nine of section 10.00 of the penal law, (ii) the use or threatened use of a deadly weapon or dangerous instrument as those terms are defined in subdivisions twelve and thirteen of section 10.00 of the penal law, (iii) behavior constituting any violent felony offense as defined in section 70.02 of the penal law; or (iv) behavior constituting stalking in the first degree as defined in section 120.60 of the penal law, stalking in the second degree as defined in section 120.55 of the penal law, stalking in the third degree as defined in section 120.50 of the penal law or stalking in the fourth degree as defined in section 120.45 of such law; and

(b) the court shall where the court finds a substantial risk that the defendant may use or threaten to use a firearm unlawfully against the person or persons for whose protection the order of protection was issued, (i) revoke any such existing license possessed by the defendant, order the defendant ineligible for such a license and order the immediate surrender pursuant to subparagraph (f) of paragraph one of subdivision a of section 265.20 and subdivision six of section 400.05 of the penal law, of any or all firearms owned or possessed or (ii) suspend any such existing license possessed by the defendant, order the defendant ineligible for such a license and order the immediate surrender pursuant to subparagraph (f) of paragraph one of subdivision a of section 265.20 and subdivision six of section 400.05 of the penal law, of any or all firearms owned or possessed.

4. Suspension. Any suspension order issued pursuant to this section shall remain in effect for the duration of the temporary order of protection or order of protection, unless modified or vacated by the court.

5. Surrender.

(a) Where an order to surrender one or more firearms has been issued, the temporary order of protection or order of protection shall specify the place where such firearms shall be surrendered, shall specify a date and time by which the surrender shall be completed and, to the extent possible, shall describe such firearms to be surrendered, and shall direct the authority receiving such surrendered firearms to immediately notify the court of such surrender.

(b) The prompt surrender of one or more firearms pursuant to a court order issued pursuant to this section shall be considered a voluntary surrender for purposes of subparagraph (f) of paragraph one of subdivision a of section 265.20 of the penal law. The disposition of any such firearms shall be in accordance with the provisions of subdivision six of section 400.05 of the penal law.

(c) The provisions of this section shall not be deemed to limit, restrict or otherwise impair the authority of the court to order and direct the surrender of any or all pistols, revolvers, rifles, shotguns or other firearms owned or possessed by a defendant pursuant to sections 530.12 or 530.13 of this article.

6. Notice.

(a) Where an order of revocation, suspension or ineligibility has been issued pursuant to this section, any temporary order of protection or order of protection issued shall state that such firearm license has been suspended or revoked or that the defendant is ineligible for such license, as the case may be.

(b) The court revoking or suspending the license, ordering the defendant ineligible for such a license, or ordering the surrender of any firearm shall immediately notify the duly constituted police authorities of the locality concerning such action and, in the case of orders of protection and temporary orders of protection issued pursuant to section 530.12 of this article, shall immediately notify the statewide registry of orders of protection.

(c) The court revoking or suspending the license or ordering the defendant ineligible for such a license shall give written notice thereof without unnecessary delay to the division of state police at its office in the city of Albany.

(d) Where an order of revocation, suspension, ineligibility or surrender is modified or vacated, the court shall immediately notify the statewide registry of orders of protection and the duly constituted police authorities of the locality concerning such action and shall give written notice thereof without unnecessary delay to the division of state police at its office in the city of Albany.

7. Hearing. The defendant shall have the right to a hearing before the court regarding any revocation, suspension, ineligibility or surrender order issued pursuant to this section, provided that nothing in this subdivision shall preclude the court from issuing any such order prior to a hearing. Where the court has issued such an order prior to a hearing, it shall commence such hearing within fourteen days of the date such order was issued.

8. Nothing in this section shall delay or otherwise interfere with the issuance of a temporary order of protection or the timely arraignment of a defendant in custody.

HISTORY: Add, L 1996, ch 644, § 3, eff Nov 1, 1996; amd, L 1998, ch 597, § 13, eff Dec 22, 1998, L 1999, ch 635, § 4, eff Dec 1, 1999; L 2000, ch 434, § 1, eff Oct 20, 2000, L 2007, ch 198, § 1, eff Aug 2, 2007, L 2013, ch 1, §§ 13–15, eff March 16, 2013.

§ 530.20. Order of recognizance or bail; by local criminal court when action is pending therein

When a criminal action is pending in a local criminal court, such court, upon application of a defendant, must or may order recognizance or bail as follows:

1. When the defendant is charged, by information, simplified information, prosecutor's information or misdemeanor complaint, with an offense or offenses of less than felony grade only, the court must order recognizance or bail.

2. When the defendant is charged, by felony complaint, with a felony, the court may, in its discretion, order recognizance or bail except as otherwise provided in this subdivision:

(a) A city court, a town court or a village court may not order recognizance or bail when (i) the defendant is charged with a class A felony, or (ii) it appears that the defendant has two previous felony convictions;

(b) No local criminal court may order recognizance or bail with respect to a defendant charged with a felony unless and until:

(i) The district attorney has been heard in the matter or, after knowledge or notice of the application and reasonable opportunity to be heard, has failed to appear at the proceeding or has otherwise waived his right to do so; and

(ii) The court has been furnished with a report of the division of criminal justice services concerning the defendant's criminal record if any or with a police department report with respect to the defendant's prior arrest record. If neither report is available, the court, with the consent of the district attorney, may dispense with this requirement; provided, however, that in an emergency, including but not limited to a substantial impairment in the ability of such division or police department to timely furnish such report, such consent shall not be required if, for reasons stated on the record, the court deems it unnecessary. When the court has been furnished with any such report or record, it shall furnish a copy thereof to counsel for the defendant or, if the defendant is not represented by counsel, to the defendant.

HISTORY: Add, L 1970, ch 996, § 1; amd, L 1975, ch 531, § 2, eff Aug 28, 1975. Sub 1, amd, L 1972, ch 661, § 45, eff Sept 1, 1972. Sub 2, par (b), subpar (ii), amd, L 1971, ch 762 § 12, L 1972, ch 399, § 23, L 1979, ch 218, § 1, eff Jan 1, 1980.

§ 530.30. Order of recognizance or bail; by superior court judge when action is pending in local criminal court

1. When a criminal action is pending in a local criminal court, other than one consisting of a superior court judge sitting as such, a judge of a superior court holding a term thereof in the county, upon application of a defendant, may order recognizance or bail when such local criminal court:

(a) Lacks authority to issue such an order, pursuant to paragraph (a) of subdivision two of section 530.20; or

(b) Has denied an application for recognizance or bail; or

(c) Has fixed bail which is excessive. In such case, such superior court judge may vacate the order of such local criminal court and release the defendant on his own recognizance or fix bail in a lesser amount or in a less burdensome form.

2. Notwithstanding the provisions of subdivision one, when the defendant is charged with a felony in a local criminal court, a superior court judge may not order recognizance or bail unless and until the district attorney has had an opportunity to be heard in the matter and such judge has been furnished with a report as described in subparagraph (ii) of paragraph (b) of subdivision two of section 530.20.

3. Not more than one application may be made pursuant to this section.

HISTORY: Add, L 1970, ch 996, § 1, eff Sept 1, 1971. Sub 2, amd, L 1971, ch 762 § 13, eff Sept 1, 1971.

§ 530.40. Order of recognizance or bail; by superior court when action is pending therein

When a criminal action is pending in a superior court, such court, upon application of a defendant, must or may order recognizance or bail as follows:

1. When the defendant is charged with an offense or offenses of less than felony grade only, the court must order recognizance or bail.

2. When the defendant is charged with a felony, the court may, in its discretion, order recognizance or bail. In any such case in which an indictment (a) has resulted from an order of a local criminal court holding the defendant for the action of the grand jury, or (b) was filed at a time when a felony complaint charging the same conduct was pending in a local criminal court, and in which such local criminal court or a superior court judge has issued an order of recognizance or bail which is still effective, the superior court's order may be in the form of a direction continuing the effectiveness of the previous order.

3. Notwithstanding the provisions of subdivision two, a superior court may not order recognizance or bail, or permit a defendant to remain at liberty pursuant to an existing order, after he has been convicted of either: (a) a class A felony or (b) any class B or class C felony defined in article one hundred thirty of the penal law committed or attempted to be committed by a person eighteen years of age or older against a person less than eighteen years of age. In either case the court must commit or remand the defendant to the custody of the sheriff.

4. Notwithstanding the provisions of subdivision two, a superior court may not order recognizance or bail when the defendant is charged with a felony unless and until the district attorney has had an opportunity to be heard in the matter and such court has been furnished with a report as described in subparagraph (ii) of paragraph (b) of subdivision two of section 530.20.

HISTORY: Add, L 1970, ch 996, § 1, eff Sept 1, 1971. Sub 3, amd, L 2000, ch 1, § 12, eff Feb

1, 2001, L 2003, ch 264, § 46, eff Nov 1, 2003. Sub 4, amd, L 1971, ch 762, § 14, eff Sept 1, 1971.

§ 530.45. Order of recognizance or bail; after conviction and before sentence

1. When the defendant is at liberty in the course of a criminal action as a result of a prior order of recognizance or bail and the court revokes such order and then either fixes no bail or fixes bail in a greater amount or in a more burdensome form than was previously fixed and remands or commits defendant to the custody of the sheriff, a judge designated in subdivision two, upon application of the defendant following conviction of an offense other than a class A felony or a class B or class C felony offense defined in article one hundred thirty of the penal law committed or attempted to be committed by a person eighteen years of age or older against a person less than eighteen years of age, and before sentencing, may issue a securing order and either release defendant on his own recognizance, or fix bail, or fix bail in a lesser amount or in a less burdensome form than fixed by the court in which the conviction was entered.

2. An order as prescribed in subdivision one may be issued by the following judges in the indicated situations:

(a) If the criminal action was pending in supreme court or county court, such order may be issued by a justice of the appellate division of the department in which the conviction was entered.

(b) If the criminal action was pending in a local criminal court, such order may be issued by a judge of a superior court holding a term thereof in the county in which the conviction was entered.

3. An application for an order specified in this section must be made upon reasonable notice to the people, and the people must be accorded adequate opportunity to appear in opposition thereto. Not more than one application may be made pursuant to this section. Defendant must allege in his application that he intends to take an appeal to an intermediate appellate court immediately after sentence is pronounced.

4. Notwithstanding the provisions of subdivision one, if within thirty days after sentence the defendant has not taken an appeal to an intermediate appellate court from the judgment or sentence, the operation of such order terminates and the defendant must surrender himself to the criminal court in which the judgment was entered in order that execution of the judgment be commenced.

5. Notwithstanding the provisions of subdivision one, if within one hundred twenty days after the filing of the notice of appeal such appeal has not been brought to argument in or submitted to the intermediate appellate court, the operation of such order terminates and the defendant must surrender himself to the criminal court in which the judgment was entered in order that execution of the judgment be commenced or resumed; except that this subdivision does not apply where the intermediate appellate court has (a) extended the time for argument or submission of the appeal to a date beyond the specified period of one hundred twenty days, and (b) upon application of the defendant, expressly ordered that the operation of the order continue until the date of the determination of the appeal or some other designated future date or occurrence.

6. Where the defendant is at liberty during the pendency of an appeal as a result of an order issued pursuant to this section, the intermediate appellate court, upon affirmance of the judgment, must by appropriate certificate remit the case to the criminal court in which such judgment was entered. The criminal court must, upon at least two days notice to the defendant, his surety and his attorney, promptly direct the defendant to surrender himself to the criminal court in order that

execution of the judgment be commenced or resumed, and if necessary the criminal court may issue a bench warrant to secure his appearance.

HISTORY: Add, L 1974, ch 435, § 1, eff Sept 1, 1974. Sub 1, amd, L 2000, ch 1, § 13, eff Feb 1, 2001, L 2003, ch 264, § 47, eff Nov 1, 2003.

§ 530.50. Order of recognizance or bail; during pendency of appeal

A judge who is otherwise authorized pursuant to section 460.50 or section 460.60 to issue an order of recognizance or bail pending the determination of an appeal, may do so unless the defendant received a class A felony sentence or a sentence for any class B or class C felony offense defined in article one hundred thirty of the penal law committed or attempted to be committed by a person eighteen years of age or older against a person less than eighteen years of age.

HISTORY: Add, L 1970, ch 996, § 1, eff Sept 1, 1971. Amd, L 2000, ch 1, § 14, eff Feb 1, 2001, L 2003, ch 264, § 48, eff Nov 1, 2003.

§ 530.60. Order of recognizance or bail; revocation thereof

1. Whenever in the course of a criminal action or proceeding a defendant is at liberty as a result of an order of recognizance or bail issued pursuant to this chapter, and the court considers it necessary to review such order, it may, and by a bench warrant if necessary, require the defendant to appear before the court. Upon such appearance, the court, for good cause shown, may revoke the order of recognizance or bail. If the defendant is entitled to recognizance or bail as a matter of right, the court must issue another such order. If he or she is not, the court may either issue such an order or commit the defendant to the custody of the sheriff. Where the defendant is committed to the custody of the sheriff and is held on a felony complaint, a new period as provided in section 180.80 of this chapter shall commence to run from the time of the defendant's commitment under this subdivision.

2. (a) Whenever in the course of a criminal action or proceeding a defendant charged with the commission of a felony is at liberty as a result of an order of recognizance or bail issued pursuant to this article it shall be grounds for revoking such order that the court finds reasonable cause to believe the defendant committed one or more specified class A or violent felony offenses or intimidated a victim or witness in violation of sections 215.15, 215.16 or 215.17 of the penal law while at liberty. Before revoking an order of recognizance or bail pursuant to this subdivision, the court must hold a hearing and shall receive any relevant, admissible evidence not legally privileged. The defendant may cross-examine witnesses and may present relevant, admissible evidence on his own behalf. Such hearing may be consolidated with, and conducted at the same time as, a felony hearing conducted pursuant to article one hundred eighty of this chapter. A transcript of testimony taken before the grand jury upon presentation of the subsequent offense shall be admissible as evidence during the hearing. The district attorney may move to introduce grand jury testimony of a witness in lieu of that witness' appearance at the hearing.

(b) Revocation of an order of recognizance or bail and commitment pursuant to this subdivision shall be for the following periods, either:

(i) For a period not to exceed ninety days exclusive of any periods of adjournment requested by the defendant; or

(ii) Until the charges contained within the accusatory instrument have been reduced or dismissed such that no count remains which charges the defendant with commission of a felony; or

(iii) Until reduction or dismissal of the charges contained within the accusatory instrument charging the subsequent offense such that no count remains which charges the defendant with commission of a class A or violent felony offense.

Upon expiration of any of the three periods specified within this paragraph, whichever is shortest, the court may grant or deny release upon an order of bail or recognizance in accordance with the provisions of this article. Upon conviction to an offense the provisions of article five hundred thirty of this chapter shall apply.

(c) Notwithstanding the provisions of paragraph (a) of this subdivision a defendant, against whom a felony complaint has been filed which charges the defendant with commission of a class A or violent felony offense committed while he was at liberty as specified therein, may be committed to the custody of the sheriff pending a revocation hearing for a period not to exceed seventy-two hours. An additional period not to exceed seventy-two hours may be granted by the court upon application of the district attorney upon a showing of good cause or where the failure to commence the hearing was due to the defendant's request or occurred with his consent. Such good cause must consist of some compelling fact or circumstance which precluded conducting the hearing within the initial prescribed period.

HISTORY: Add, L 1970, ch 996, § 1, eff Sept 1, 1971. Sub 1, formerly entire section, so designated, L 1981, ch 788, § 2, eff July 27, 1981. Sub 2, add, L 1981, ch 788, § 2, eff July 27, 1981. Sub 2, par (a), amd, L 1986, ch 794, § 3, eff Nov 1, 1986, L 2011, ch 565, § 1, eff Oct 23, 2011.

§ 530.70. Order of recognizance or bail; bench warrant

1. A bench warrant issued by a superior court, by a district court, by the New York City criminal court or by a superior court judge sitting as a local criminal court may be executed anywhere in the state. A bench warrant issued by a city court, a town court or a village court may be executed in the county of issuance or any adjoining county; and it may be executed anywhere else in the state upon the written endorsement thereon of a local criminal court of the county in which the defendant is to be taken into custody. When so endorsed, the warrant is deemed the process of the endorsing court as well as that of the issuing court.

2. A bench warrant may be addressed to: (a) any police officer whose geographical area of employment embraces either the place where the offense charged was allegedly committed or the locality of the court by which the warrant is issued; or (b) any uniformed court officer for a court in the city of New York, the county of Nassau, the county of Suffolk or the county of Westchester or for any other court that is part of the unified court system of the state for execution in the building wherein such court officer is employed or in the immediate vicinity thereof. A bench warrant must be executed in the same manner as a warrant of arrest, as provided in section 120.80, and following the arrest, such executing police officer or court officer must without unnecessary delay bring the defendant before the court in which it is returnable; provided, however, if the court in which the bench warrant is returnable is a city, town or village court, and such court is not available, and the bench warrant is addressed to a police officer, such executing police officer must without unnecessary delay bring the defendant before an alternate local criminal court, as provided in subdivision five of section 120.90; or if the court in which the bench warrant is returnable is a superior court, and such court is not available, and the bench warrant is addressed to a police officer, such executing police officer may bring the defendant to the local correctional facility of the county in which such court sits, to be detained there until not later than the commencement of the next session of such court occurring on the next business day.

2-a. A court which issues a bench warrant may attach thereto a summary of the basis for the warrant. In any case where, pursuant to subdivision two of this section, a defendant arrested upon a bench warrant is brought before a local criminal court other than the court in which the warrant is returnable, such local criminal court shall consider such summary before issuing a securing order with respect to the defendant.

3. A bench warrant may be executed by (a) any officer to whom it is addressed, or (b) any other police officer delegated to execute it under circumstances prescribed in subdivisions four and five.

4. The issuing court may authorize the delegation of such warrant. Where the issuing court has so authorized, a police officer to whom a bench warrant is addressed may delegate another police officer to whom it is not addressed to execute such warrant as his or her agent when:

(a) He or she has reasonable cause to believe that the defendant is in a particular county other than the one in which the warrant is returnable; and

(b) The geographical area of employment of the delegated police officer embraces the locality where the arrest is to be made.

5. Under circumstances specified in subdivision four, the police officer to whom the bench warrant is addressed may inform the delegated officer, by telecommunication, mail or any other means, of the issuance of the warrant, of the offense charged in the underlying accusatory instrument and of all other pertinent details, and may request him or her to act as his or her agent in arresting the defendant pursuant to such bench warrant. Upon such request, the delegated police officer is to the same extent as the delegating officer, authorized to make such arrest pursuant to the bench warrant within the geographical area of such delegated officer's employment. Upon so arresting the defendant, he or she must without unnecessary delay deliver the defendant or cause him or her to be delivered to the custody of the police officer by whom he or she was so delegated, and the latter must then without unnecessary delay bring the defendant before the court in which such bench warrant is returnable.

6. A bench warrant may be executed by an officer of the state department of corrections and community supervision or a probation officer when the person named within the warrant is under the supervision of the department of corrections and community supervision or a department of probation and the probation officer is authorized by his or her probation director, as the case may be. The warrant must be executed upon the same conditions and in the same manner as is otherwise provided for execution by a police officer.

HISTORY: Add, L 1970, ch 996, § 1, eff Sept 1, 1971; amd, L 1976, ch 265, § 1, L 1979, ch 492, § 2, L 1981, ch 456, § 2, L 1981, ch 463, § 1, L 1988, ch 565, § 2, eff Nov 1, 1988, L 1988, ch 565, § 2, eff Nov 1, 1988, L 1990, ch 681, §§ 2, 3, eff Nov 1, 1990, L 1991, ch 352, § 1, eff Nov 1, 1991, L 2010, ch 10, § 1, eff May 22, 2010, L 2011, ch 62, § 83 (Part C, Subpart B), eff March 31, 2011.

§ 530.80. Order of recognizance or bail; surrender of defendant

1. At any time before the forfeiture of a bail bond, an obligor may surrender the defendant in his exoneration, or the defendant may surrender himself, to the court in which his case is pending or to the sheriff to whose custody he was committed at the time of giving bail, in the following manner:

(a) A certified copy of the bail bond must be delivered to the sheriff, who must detain the defendant in his custody thereon, as upon a commitment. The sheriff must acknowledge the surrender by a certificate in writing and must forthwith notify the court in which the case is pending that such surrender has been made.

(b) Upon the bail bond and the certificate of the sheriff, or upon the surrender to the court in which the case is pending, such court must, upon five days notice to the district attorney, order that the bail be exonerated. On filing such order, the bail is exonerated accordingly.

2. For the purpose of surrendering the defendant, an obligor or the person who posted cash bail for the defendant may take him into custody at any place within the state, or he may, by a written authority indorsed on a certified copy of the bail bond, empower any person over twenty years of age to do so.

3. At any time before the forfeiture of cash bail, the defendant may surrender himself or the person who posted bail for the defendant may surrender the defendant in the manner prescribed in subdivision one. In such case, the court must order a return of the money to the person who posted it, upon producing the certificate of the sheriff showing the surrender, and upon a notice of five days to the district attorney.

HISTORY: Add, L 1970, ch 996, § 1, eff Sept 1, 1971. Sub 2, amd, L 1984, ch 384, § 5, eff Sept 1, 1984. Sub 3, amd, L 1984, ch 384, § 5, eff Sept 1, 1984.

ARTICLE 540　FORFEITURE OF BAIL AND REMISSION THEREOF

§ 540.10.　　　　　　　Forfeiture of bail; generally
§ 540.20.　　　　　　　Forfeiture of bail; certain local criminal courts
§ 540.30.　　　　　　　Remission of forfeiture

HISTORY: Add, L 1970, ch 996, § 1, eff Sept 1, 1971.

§ 540.10. Forfeiture of bail; generally

1. If, without sufficient excuse, a principal does not appear when required or does not render himself amenable to the orders and processes of the criminal court wherein bail has been posted, the court must enter such facts upon its minutes and the bail bond or the cash bail, as the case may be, is thereupon forfeited.

2. If the principal appears at any time before the final adjournment of the court, and satisfactorily excuses his neglect, the court may direct the forfeiture to be discharged upon such terms as are just. If the forfeiture is not so discharged and the forfeited bail consisted of a bail bond, the district attorney, within one hundred twenty days after the adjournment of the court at which such bond was directed to be forfeited, must proceed against the obligor or obligors who executed such bond, in the manner prescribed in subdivision three. If the forfeited bail consisted of cash bail, the county treasurer with whom it is deposited shall give written notice of the forfeiture to the person who posted cash bail for the defendant may at any time after the final adjournment of the court or forty-five days after notice of forfeiture required herein has been given, whichever comes later, apply the money deposited to the use of the county.

3. A bail bond or cash bail, upon being forfeited, together with a certified copy of the order of the court forfeiting the same, must be filed by the district attorney in the office of the clerk of the county wherein such order was issued. Such clerk must docket the same in the book kept by him for docketing of judgments and enter therein a judgment against the obligor or obligors who executed such bail bond for the amount of the penalty of said bond or against the person who posted the cash bail for the amount of the cash bail, and the bond and the certified copy of the order of the court forfeiting the bond or the cash bail constitutes the judgment roll. Such judgment constitutes a lien on the real estate of the obligor or obligors who executed such bail bond from the time of the entry of the judgment. An execution may be issued to collect the amount of said bail bond in the same form and with the same effect as upon a judgment recovered in an action in said county upon a debt in favor of the people of the state of New York against such obligor or obligors.

HISTORY: Add, L 1970, ch 996, § 1, eff Sept 1, 1971. Sub 2, amd, L 1984, ch 384, § 6, eff Sept

1, 1984. Sub 2, amd, L 1998, ch 427, § 1, eff Oct 20, 1998. Sub 3, amd, L 1984, ch 384, § 6, eff Sept 1, 1984.

§ 540.20. Forfeiture of bail; certain local criminal courts

Nowithstanding the provisions of section 540.10, when bail has been posted in a city court, town court or village court in connection with a local criminal court accusatory instrument, other than a felony complaint, and thereafter such bail is forfeited, the following rules are applicable:

1. If such bail consists of a bail bond, the financial officer of such city, town or village must promptly commence an action for the recovery of the sum of money specified in such bond, and upon collection thereof shall pay the same over to the treasurer or financial officer of the city, the supervisor of the town or the treasurer of the village. Any amount recovered in such action, unless otherwise provided by law, shall be the property of the city, town or village in which the offense charged is alleged to have been committed.

2. If such bail consists of cash bail, the local criminal court must:

(a) If it is a city court, pay the forfeited bail to the treasurer or other financial officer of the city. Such forfeited bail, unless otherwise provided by law, is the property of such city.

(b) If it is a town court or a village court, pay the forfeited bail to the state comptroller on or before the tenth day of the month next succeeding such forfeiture. Such forfeited bail, unless otherwise provided by law, is the property of the town or village in which the offense charged is alleged to have been committed; provided, however, that when (i) a single amount of bail is posted for more than a single offense charged, and (ii) the town or village justice court does not attribute a specific amount of bail to each offense, and (iii) forfeited bail for at least two of the offenses would be the property of different governmental entities, the entire amount of forfeited bail shall be the property of the town or village in which the offenses charged are alleged to have been committed, except that, when forfeited bail for at least one of the offenses would be the property of the state, the entire amount of forfeited bail shall be the property of the state.

HISTORY: Add, L 1970, ch 996, § 1, eff Sept 1, 1971. Sub 2, amd, L 1991, ch 460, § 1, eff Nov 1, 1991. Sub 2, par (b), amd, L 1991, ch 460, § 1, eff Nov 1, 1991.

§ 540.30. Remission of forfeiture

1. After the forfeiture of a bail bond or cash bail, as provided in section 540.10, an application for remission of such forfeiture may be made to a court as follows:

(a) If the forfeiture has been ordered by a superior court, the application must be made in such court;

(b) If the forfeiture has been ordered by a local criminal court, the application must be made to a superior court in the county, except that if the local criminal court which ordered the forfeiture was a district court, the application may alternatively be made to that district court.

2. The application must be made within one year after the forfeiture of the bail is declared upon at least five days notice to the district attorney and service of copies of the affidavits and papers upon which the application is founded. The court may grant the application and remit the forfeiture or any part thereof, upon such terms as are just. The application may be granted only upon payment of the costs and expenses incurred in the proceedings for the enforcement of the forfeiture.

HISTORY: Add, L 1970, ch 996, § 1, eff Sept 1, 1971. Sub 1, par (b), amd, L 1980, ch 248, § 1, eff July 16, 1980.

TITLE Q　Procedures for Securing Attendance at Criminal Actions and Proceedings of Defendants not Securable by Conventional Means—and Related Matters

ARTICLE 550
SECURING ATTENDANCE OF DEFENDANTS—IN GENERAL

ARTICLE 560
SECURING ATTENDANCE OF DEFENDANTS CONFINED IN INSTITUTIONS WITHIN THE STATE

ARTICLE 570
SECURING ATTENDANCE OF DEFENDANTS WHO ARE OUTSIDE THE STATE BUT WITHIN THE UNITED STATES—RENDITION TO OTHER JURISDICTIONS OF DEFENDANTS WITHIN THE STATE—UNIFORM CRIMINAL EXTRADITION ACT

ARTICLE 580
SECURING ATTENDANCE OF DEFENDANTS CONFINED AS PRISONERS IN INSTITUTIONS OF OTHER JURISDICTIONS OF THE UNITED STATES–RENDITION TO OTHER JURISDICTIONS OF PERSONS CONFINED AS PRISONERS IN THIS STATE–AGREEMENT ON DETAINERS

ARTICLE 590
SECURING ATTENDANCE OF DEFENDANTS WHO ARE OUTSIDE THE UNITED STATES

ARTICLE 600
SECURING ATTENDANCE OF CORPORATE DEFENDANTS AND RELATED MATTERS

HISTORY: Add, L 1970, ch 996, § 1, eff Sept 1, 1971.

ARTICLE 550　SECURING ATTENDANCE OF DEFENDANTS—IN GENERAL

§ 550.10.　　　　　　**Securing attendance of defendants; in general**

HISTORY: Add, L 1970, ch 996, § 1, eff Sept 1, 1971.

§ 550.10. Securing attendance of defendants; in general

Depending upon the status of a criminal action pending against a defendant, the geographical location of the defendant at the time and other factors, his attendance thereat for purposes of arraignment or prosecution may be secured by the following methods:

1. If the defendant has never been arraigned in the action, and if he is at liberty within the state, his attendance may, under given circumstances, be secured by a warrant of arrest, as prescribed in article one hundred twenty, a superior court warrant of arrest, as prescribed in subdivision three of section 210.10, or a summons, as prescribed in article one hundred thirty.

2. If the defendant has been arraigned in the action and, by virtue of a securing order, is either in the custody of the sheriff or at liberty within the state on his own recognizance or on bail, his attendance may be secured as follows:

(a) If the defendant is confined in the custody of the sheriff, the court may direct the sheriff to produce him;

(b) If the defendant is at liberty within the state as a result of an order releasing him on his own recognizance or on bail, the court may secure his attendance by notification or by the issuance of a bench warrant.

3. If the defendant's attendance cannot be secured by methods described in subdivisions one and two, either because he is outside the state or because he is confined in an institution within the state as a result of an order issued in some other action, proceeding or matter, his attendance may, under indicated circumstances, be secured by procedures prescribed in the ensuing articles of this title.

HISTORY: Add, L 1970, ch 996, § 1, eff Sept 1, 1971.

ARTICLE 560   SECURING ATTENDANCE OF DEFENDANTS CONFINED IN INSTITUTIONS WITHIN THE STATE

§ 560.10.   **Securing attendance of defendants confined in institutions within the state**

HISTORY: Add, L 1970, ch 996, § 1, eff Sept 1, 1971.

§ 560.10. Securing attendance of defendants confined in institutions within the state

1. When a criminal action is pending against a defendant who is confined in an institution within the state pursuant to a court order issued in a different action, proceeding or matter, the following courts and judges may, under the indicated circumstances, order that the defendant be produced in the court in which the criminal action is pending for purposes of arraignment or prosecution therein:

(a) If the action is pending in a superior court or with a superior court judge sitting as a local criminal court, or in a district court or the New York City criminal court, such court may, upon application of the district attorney, order the production therein of a defendant confined in any institution within the state.

(b) If the action is pending in a city court or a town court or a village court, such court may, upon application of the district attorney, order production therein of a defendant confined in a county jail of such county. Production therein of a defendant confined in any other institution within the state may, upon application of the district attorney, be ordered by a judge of a superior court holding a term thereof in the county in which the action is pending.

2. An application by a district attorney, pursuant to subdivision one, for production of a defendant confined in an institution located in another county in connection with a criminal action or proceeding pending in such other county, must be made upon reasonable notice to the district attorney of such other county and to the attorney representing such defendant in or in connection with the action or proceeding pending therein, and the court or judge must accord them reasonable opportunity to be heard in the matter. If such court or judge determines that production of the defendant would result in an unreasonable interference with the conduct of the action in such other county, it must deny the application. If an order of production is issued, a justice of the appellate division, of either the department embracing the county of issuance thereof or of the department embracing the county of the defendant's confinement, upon application of the district attorney of the county of confinement or of the attorney representing the defendant in or in connection with the action pending therein, may for good cause shown vacate such order of production.

HISTORY: Add, L 1970, ch 996, § 1, eff Sept 1, 1971, with substance derived from Crim C §§ 10-b, 298-a, 298-b.

ARTICLE 570   SECURING ATTENDANCE OF DEFENDANTS WHO ARE OUTSIDE THE STATE BUT WITHIN THE UNITED STATES—RENDITION TO OTHER JURISDICTIONS OF DEFENDANTS WITHIN THE STATE—UNIFORM CRIMINAL EXTRADITION ACT

§ 570.02.   **Short title**

§ 570.04.   **Definitions**

HISTORY: Add, L 1970, ch 996, § 1, eff Sept 1, 1971, with substance derived from Crim C §§ 827-859.

§ 570.02. Short title

This article may be cited and referred to as the uniform criminal extradition act.

HISTORY: Add, L 1970, ch 996, § 1, eff Sept 1, 1971, with substance derived from Crim C § 827.

§ 570.04. Definitions

As used in this article, the following terms have the following meanings:

1. "Governor" includes any person performing the functions of governor by authority of the law of this state.

2. "Executive authority" includes the governor, and any person performing the functions of governor in a state other than this state.

3. "State," when referring to a state other than this state, includes any other state or territory, organized or unorganized, of the United States of America.

> **HISTORY:** Add, L 1970, ch 996, § 1, eff Sept 1, 1971, with substance derived from Crim C § 828.

§ 570.06. Fugitives from justice; duty of governor

Subject to the provisions of this article, the provisions of the constitution of the United States controlling, and any and all acts of congress enacted in pursuance thereof, it is the duty of the governor of this state to have arrested and delivered up to the executive authority of any other state of the United States any person charged in that state with treason, felony, or other crime, who has fled from justice and is found in this state.

> **HISTORY:** Add, L 1970, ch 996, § 1, eff Sept 1, 1971, with substance derived from Crim C § 829.

§ 570.08. Demand; form

No demand for the extradition of a person charged with crime in another state shall be recognized by the governor unless in writing alleging that the accused was present in the demanding state at the time of the commission of the alleged crime, and that thereafter he fled from the state, except in cases arising under section 570.14 or 570.16, and accompanied by a copy of an indictment found or by information supported by an affidavit in the state having jurisdiction of the crime, or by a copy of an affidavit made before a magistrate there, together with a copy of any warrant which was issued thereon, or by a copy of a judgment of conviction or of a sentence imposed in execution thereof, together with a statement by the executive authority of the demanding state that the person claimed has escaped from confinement or has broken the terms of his bail, probation or parole. The indictment, information or affidavit made before the magistrate must substantially charge the person demanded with having committed a crime under the law of that state; and the copy of the indictment, information, affidavit, judgment of conviction or sentence must be authenticated by the executive authority making the demand.

> **HISTORY:** Add, L 1970, ch 996, § 1, eff Sept 1, 1971, with substance derived from Crim C § 830.

§ 570.10. Investigation by governor

When a demand shall be made upon the governor of this state by the executive authority of another state for the surrender of a person so charged with crime, the governor may call upon the attorney general or any district attorney in this state to investigate or assist in investigating the demand, and to report to him the situation and circumstances of the person so demanded, and whether he ought to be surrendered.

> **HISTORY:** Add, L 1970, ch 996, § 1, eff Sept 1, 1971, with substance derived from Crim C § 831.

§ 570.12. Extradition of persons imprisoned or awaiting trial in another state

When it is desired to have returned to this state a person charged in this state with a crime and such person is imprisoned or is held under criminal proceedings then pending against him in another state, the governor of this state may agree with the executive authority of such other state for the extradition of such person before the conclusion of his term of sentence in such other state, upon condition that such person be returned to such other state at the expense of this state as soon as the prosecution in this state is terminated.

HISTORY: Add, L 1970, ch 996, § 1, eff Sept 1, 1971, with substance derived from Crim C § 832.

§ 570.14. Extradition of persons who left the demanding state under compulsion

The governor of this state may also surrender, on demand of the executive authority of any other state, any person in this state who is charged in the manner provided in section 570.08 with having violated the laws of the state whose executive authority is making the demand, even though such person left the demanding state involuntarily.

HISTORY: Add, L 1970, ch 996, § 1, eff Sept 1, 1971, with substance derived from Crim C § 833.

§ 570.16. Extradition of persons not present in demanding state at time of commission of crime

The governor of this state may also surrender, on demand of the executive authority of any other state, any person in this state charged in such other state in the manner provided in section 570.08 with committing an act in this state or in a third state, intentionally resulting in a crime in the state whose executive authority is making the demand, when the acts for which extradition is sought would be punishable by the laws of this state, if the consequences claimed to have resulted therefrom in the demanding state had taken effect in this state; and the provisions of this article not otherwise inconsistent, shall apply to such cases, even though the accused was not in that state at the time of the commission of the crime, and has not fled therefrom; provided, however, that the governor of this state may, in his discretion, make any such surrender conditional upon agreement by the executive authority of the demanding state, that the person so surrendered will be held to answer no criminal charges of any nature except those set forth in the requisition upon which such person is so surrendered, at least until such person has been given reasonable opportunity to return to this state after his acquittal, if he shall be acquitted, or if he shall be convicted, after he shall be released from confinement. Nothing in this section shall apply to the crime of libel.

HISTORY: Add, L 1970, ch 996, § 1, eff Sept 1, 1971, with substance derived from Crim C § 834.

§ 570.18. Issuance of warrant of arrest by governor; recitals therein

If the governor decides that the demand should be complied with, he shall sign a warrant of arrest, which shall be sealed with the state seal, and be directed to any police officer or other person whom he may think fit to entrust with the execution thereof. The warrant must substantially recite the facts necessary to the validity of its issuance.

HISTORY: Add, L 1970, ch 996, § 1, eff Sept 1, 1971, with substance derived from Crim C § 835.

§ 570.20. Execution of warrant; manner and place thereof

Such warrant shall authorize the police officer or other person to whom directed to arrest the accused at any time and any place where he may be found within the state and to command the aid of all police officers or other persons in the execution of the warrant, and to deliver the accused, subject to the provisions of this article to the duly authorized agent of the demanding state.

HISTORY: Add, L 1970, ch 996, § 1, eff Sept 1, 1971, with substance derived from Crim C § 836.

§ 570.22. Authority of arresting officer

Every such police officer or other person empowered to make the arrest, shall have the same authority, in arresting the accused to command assistance therein, as police officers have by law in the execution of any criminal process directed to them, with like penalties against those who refuse their assistance.

HISTORY: Add, L 1970, ch 996, § 1, eff Sept 1, 1971, with substance derived from Crim C § 837.

§ 570.24. Rights of accused person; application for writ of habeas corpus

No person arrested upon such warrant shall be delivered over to the agent whom the executive authority demanding him shall have appointed to receive him unless he shall first be taken forthwith before a justice or judge of a court of record in this state, who shall inform him of the demand made for his surrender and of the crime with which he is charged, and that he has the right to demand and procure legal counsel; and if the prisoner or his counsel shall state that he or they desire to test the legality of his arrest, the justice or judge of such court of record shall fix a reasonable time to be allowed within which to apply for a writ of habeas corpus. When such writ is applied for, notice thereof, and of the time and place of hearing thereon, shall be given to the district attorney of the county in which the arrest is made and in which the accused is in custody, and to the said agent of the demanding state.

HISTORY: Add, L 1970, ch 996, § 1, eff Sept 1, 1971, with substance derived from Crim C § 838.

§ 570.26. Noncompliance with preceding section; penalties for violation

Any officer who shall deliver to the agent for extradition of the demanding state a person in his custody under the governor's warrant, in disobedience of the preceding section, shall be guilty of a felony.

HISTORY: Add, L 1970, ch 996, § 1, eff Sept 1, 1971, with substance derived from Crim C § 839.

§ 570.28. Confinement of the accused in jail when necessary

The officer or persons executing the governor's warrant of arrest, or the agent of the demanding state to whom the prisoner may have been delivered may, when necessary, confine the prisoner in the jail of any county or city through which he may pass; and the keeper of such jail must receive and safely keep the prisoner until the officer or person having charge of him is ready to proceed on his route, such officer or person, however, being chargeable with the expense of keeping.

HISTORY: Add, L 1970, ch 996, § 1, eff Sept 1, 1971, with substance derived from Crim C § 840.

§ 570.30. Confinement of extradited persons passing through this state

The officer or agent of a demanding state to whom a prisoner may have been delivered following extradition proceedings in another state, or to whom a prisoner may have been delivered after waiving extradition in such other state, and who is passing through this state with such a prisoner for the purpose of immediately returning such prisoner to the demanding state may, when necessary, confine the prisoner in the jail of any county or city through which he may pass; and the keeper of such jail must receive and safely keep the prisoner until the officer or agent having charge of him is ready to proceed on his route, such officer or agent, however, being chargeable with the expense of keeping, provided, however, that such officer or agent shall produce and show to the keeper of such jail satisfactory written evidence of the fact that he is actually transporting such prisoner to the demanding state after a requisition by the executive authority of such demanding state or waiver thereof. Such person shall not be entitled to demand a new requisition while in this state.

HISTORY: Add, L 1970, ch 996, § 1, eff Sept 1, 1971, with substance derived from Crim C § 841.

§ 570.32. Arrest of accused before making of requisition

Whenever any person within this state shall be charged on the oath of any credible person before any local criminal court of this state with the commission of any crime in any other state and, except in cases arising under section 570.14 or 570.16, with having fled from justice, or, with having been convicted of a crime in that state and having escaped from confinement, or having broken the terms of his bail, probation or parole, or, whenever complaint shall have been made before any local criminal court in this state setting forth on the affidavit of any credible person in another state that a crime has been committed in such other state and that the accused has been charged in such other state with the commission of the crime, and, except in cases arising under section 570.14 or 570.16, has fled from justice, or with having been convicted of a crime in that state and having escaped from confinement or having broken the terms of his bail, probation or parole and is believed to be in this state, the local criminal court shall issue a warrant directed to any police officer directing him to apprehend the person named therein, wherever he may be found in this state, and to bring him before the same or any other local criminal court which may be available in or convenient of access to the place where the arrest may be made, to answer the charge or complaint and affidavit, and a certified copy of the sworn charge or complaint and affidavit upon which the warrant is issued shall be attached to such warrant.

> **HISTORY:** Add, L 1970, ch 996, § 1, eff Sept 1, 1971, with substance derived from Crim C § 842.

§ 570.34. Arrest of accused without warrant therefor

The arrest of a person in this state may be lawfully made also by any police officer or a private person, without a warrant, upon reasonable information that the accused stands charged in the courts of another state with a crime punishable by death or imprisonment for a term exceeding one year; but when so arrested the accused must be taken before a local criminal court with all practicable speed and complaint must be made against him under oath setting forth the ground for the arrest as in the preceding section; and, thereafter, his answers shall be heard as if he had been arrested on a warrant.

> **HISTORY:** Add, L 1970, ch 996, § 1, eff Sept 1, 1971, with substance derived from Crim C § 843.

§ 570.36. Commitment to await requisition; bail

If from the examination before the local criminal court it appears that the person held is the person charged with having committed the crime alleged, and, except in cases arising under section 570.14 or 570.16, that he has fled from justice, the local criminal court must, by a warrant reciting the accusation, commit him to the county jail for such a time not exceeding thirty days and specified in the warrant, as will enable the arrest of the accused to be made under a warrant of the governor on a requisition of the executive authority of the state having jurisdiction of the offense, unless the accused gives bail as provided in the next section, or until he shall be legally discharged.

> **HISTORY:** Add, L 1970, ch 996, § 1, eff Sept 1, 1971 with substance derived from Crim C § 844.

§ 570.38. Bail; in what cases; conditions of bond

Unless the offense with which the prisoner is charged is shown to be an offense punishable by death or life imprisonment under the laws of the state in which it was committed, a justice of the supreme court or county judge in this state may admit the person arrested to bail by bond or undertaking, with sufficient sureties, and in such sum as he deems proper, conditioned for his appearance before him at a time specified in such bond or undertaking but not later than thirty days after the examination referred to in section 570.36 and for his surrender, to be arrested upon the warrant of the governor of this state.

> **HISTORY:** Add, L 1970, ch 996, § 1, eff Sept 1, 1971, with substance derived from Crim C § 845.

§ 570.40. Extension of time of commitment; adjournment

If the accused is not arrested under warrant of the governor by the expiration of the time specified in the warrant, bond or undertaking, a local criminal court may discharge him or may recommit him for a further period of sixty days, or for further periods not to exceed in the aggregate sixty days, or a supreme court justice or county judge may again take bail for his appearance and surrender, as provided in section 570.38 but within a period not to exceed sixty days after the date of such new bond or undertaking.

> **HISTORY:** Add, L 1970, ch 996, § 1, eff Sept 1, 1971, with substance derived from Crim C § 846.

§ 570.42. Bail; when forfeited

If the prisoner is admitted to bail, and fails to appear and surrender himself according to the conditions of his bond or undertaking, the justice of the supreme court or county judge, by proper order, shall declare the bond forfeited and order his immediate arrest without warrant if he be within this state. Recovery may be had on such bond or undertaking in the name of the state as in the case of other bonds or undertakings given by the accused in criminal proceedings within this state.

> **HISTORY:** Add, L 1970, ch 996, § 1, eff Sept 1, 1971, with substance derived from Crim C § 847.

§ 570.44. Persons under criminal prosecution in this state at time of requisition

If a criminal prosecution has been instituted against such person under the laws of this state and is still pending, the governor, in his discretion, may either surrender him on demand of the executive authority of another state or hold him until he has been tried and discharged or convicted and punished in this state.

> **HISTORY:** Add, L 1970, ch 996, § 1, eff Sept 1, 1971, with substance derived from Crim C § 848.

§ 570.46. Guilt or innocence of accused; when inquired into

The guilt or innocence of the accused as to the crime with which he is charged may not be inquired into by the governor, or in any proceeding after the demand for extradition accompanied by a charge of crime in legal form as above provided shall have been presented to the governor, except as it may be involved in identifying the person held as the person charged with the crime.

> **HISTORY:** Add, L 1970, ch 996, § 1, eff Sept 1, 1971, with substance derived from Crim C § 849.

§ 570.48. Alias warrant of arrest

The governor may recall his warrant of arrest or may issue another warrant whenever he deems proper.

> **HISTORY:** Add, L 1970, ch 996, § 1, eff Sept 1, 1971, with substance derived from Crim C § 850.

§ 570.50. Written waiver of extradition proceedings

Any person arrested in this state charged with having committed any crime in another state or alleged to have escaped from confinement, or broken the terms of his bail, probation or parole, may waive the issuance and service of the warrant provided for in sections 570.18 and 570.20 and all other procedure incidental to extradition proceedings by executing or subscribing in the presence of a judge of any court of record within this state a writing which states that he consents to return to the demanding state, provided, however, that before such waiver shall be executed or subscribed by such person it shall be the duty of such judge to inform such person of his rights to the issuance and service of a warrant of extradition and to obtain a writ of habeas corpus as provided for in section 570.24.

If and when such consent has been duly executed it shall forthwith be forwarded to the office of the secretary of state of this state and filed therein. The judge shall direct the officer having such person in custody to deliver forthwith such person to the duly accredited agent or agents of the demanding state, and shall deliver or cause to be delivered to such agent or agents a copy of such consent. Provided, however, that nothing in this section shall be deemed to limit the rights of the accused person to return voluntarily and without formality to the demanding state, nor shall this waiver procedure be deemed to be an exclusive procedure or to limit the powers, rights or duties of the officers of the demanding state or of this state.

> **HISTORY:** Add, L 1970, ch 996, § 1, eff Sept 1, 1971, with substance derived from Crim C § 851.

§ 570.52. Fugitives from this state; duty of governor

Whenever the governor of this state shall demand a person charged with crime or with escaping from confinement or breaking the terms of his bail, probation or parole in this state from the executive authority of any other state, or from the chief justice or an associate justice of the supreme court of the District of Columbia authorized to receive such demand under the laws of the United States, he shall issue a warrant under the seal of this state to some agent commanding him to receive the person so charged, if delivered to him, and convey him to the proper officer of the county in this state in which the offense was committed.

> **HISTORY:** Add, L 1970, ch 996, § 1, eff Sept 1, 1971, with substance derived from Crim C § 852.

§ 570.54. Application for issuance of requisition; by whom made; contents

1. When the return to this state of a person charged with crime in this state is required, the district attorney of the county in which the offense was committed, or, if the offense is one which is cognizable by him or her, the attorney general shall present to the governor his or her written application for a requisition for the return of the person charged, in which application shall be stated the name of the person so charged, the crime charged against him or her, the approximate time, place and circumstances of its commission, the state in which he or she is believed to be, including the location of the accused therein at the time the application is made and certifying that, in the opinion of the said district attorney or attorney general the ends of justice require the arrest and return of the accused to this state for trial and that the proceeding is not instituted to enforce a private claim.

2. When there is required the return to this state of a person who has been convicted of a crime in this state and has escaped from confinement or broken the terms of his or her bail, probation or parole, the district attorney of the county in which the offense was committed, the warden of the institution or sheriff of the county, from which escape was made, or the commissioner of the state department of corrections and community supervision or his or her designee shall present to the governor a written application for a requisition for the return of such person, in which application shall be stated the name of the person, the crime of which he or she was convicted, the circumstances of his or her escape from confinement or of the breach of the terms of his or her bail, probation or parole, the state in which he or she is believed to be, including the location of the person therein at the time the application is made.

3. The application shall be verified by affidavit, shall be executed in duplicate and shall be accompanied by two certified copies of the accusatory instrument stating the offense with which the accused is charged, or of the judgment of conviction or of the sentence. The district attorney,

attorney general, warden, sheriff or the commissioner of the state department of corrections and community supervision or his or her designee may also attach such further affidavits and other documents in duplicate as he or she shall deem proper to be submitted with such application. One copy of the application, with the action of the governor indicated by endorsement thereon, and one of the certified copies of the accusatory instrument, or of the judgment of conviction or the sentence shall be filed in the office of the secretary of state to remain of record in that office. The other copies of all papers shall be forwarded with the governor's requisition.

HISTORY: Add, L 1970, ch 996, § 1, eff Sept 1, 1971, with substance derived from Crim C § 853; amd, L 1980, ch 2, § 1, eff Feb 8, 1980, L 2011, ch 62, § 84 (Part C, Subpart B), eff March 31, 2011.

§ 570.56. Expense of extradition

The expenses of extradition must be borne by the county from which the application for a requisition comes or, where the application is made by the attorney general, by the county in which the offense was committed. In the case of extradition of a person who has been convicted of a crime in this state and has escaped from a state prison or reformatory, the expense of extradition shall be borne by the department of corrections and community supervision. Where a person has broken the terms of his or her parole from a state prison or reformatory, the expense of extradition shall be borne by the state department of corrections and community supervision. Where a person has broken the terms of his or her bail or probation, the expense of extradition shall be borne by the county. Where a person has been convicted but not yet confined to a prison, or has been sentenced for a felony to a county jail or penitentiary and escapes, the expenses of extradition shall be charged to the county from whose custody the escape is effected. Nothing in this section shall preclude a county or the department of corrections and community supervision, as the case may be, from collecting the expenses involved in extradition from the person who was extradited.

HISTORY: Add, L 1970, ch 996, § 1, with substance derived from Crim C § 854; amd, L 1995, ch 193, § 1, eff Nov 1, 1995, L 2011, ch 62, § 85 (Part C, Subpart B), eff March 31, 2011.

§ 570.58. Immunity from service of process in certain civil actions

A person brought into this state on or after waiver of extradition based on a criminal charge shall not be subject to service of personal process in civil actions arising out of the same facts as the criminal proceeding to answer which he is being or has been returned until he has been convicted in the criminal proceeding, or if acquitted, until he has had reasonable opportunity to return to the state from which he was extradicted [extradited].*

HISTORY: Add, L 1970, ch 996, § 1, eff Sept 1, 1971, with substance derived from Crim C § 855.

§ 570.60. No immunity from other criminal prosecution while in this state

After a person has been brought back to this state by extradition proceedings, he may be tried in this state for other offenses which he may be charged with having committed here as well as that specified in the requisition for his extradition.

HISTORY: Add, L 1970, ch 996, § 1, eff Sept 1, 1971, with substance derived from Crim C § 856.

§ 570.62. Non-waiver by this state

Nothing in this article contained shall be deemed to constitute a waiver by this state of its right, power or privilege to try such demanded person for offenses committed within this state, or of its right, power or privilege to regain custody of such person by extradition proceedings or otherwise

---

* The bracketed word has been inserted by the Publisher.

for the purpose of trial, sentence or punishment for any offense committed within this state, nor shall any proceedings had under this article which result in, or fail to result in, extradition be deemed a waiver by this state of any of its rights, privileges or jurisdiction in any way whatsoever.

HISTORY: Add, L 1970, ch 996, § 1, eff Sept 1, 1971, with substance derived from Crim C § 857.

§ 570.64. Interpretation

The provisions of this article shall be so interpreted and construed as to effectuate its general purposes to make uniform the law of those states which enact it.

HISTORY: Add, L 1970, ch 996, § 1, eff Sept 1, 1971, with substance derived from Crim C § 858.

§ 570.66. Constitutionality

If any part of this article is for any reason declared void, such invalidity shall not affect the validity of the remaining portions thereof.

HISTORY: Add, L 1970, ch 996, § 1, eff Sept 1, 1971, with substance derived from Crim C § 859.

ARTICLE 580 SECURING ATTENDANCE OF DEFENDANTS CONFINED AS PRISONERS IN INSTITUTIONS OF OTHER JURISDICTIONS OF THE UNITED STATES–RENDITION TO OTHER JURISDICTIONS OF PERSONS CONFINED AS PRISONERS IN THIS STATE–AGREEMENT ON DETAINERS

HISTORY: Add, L 1970, ch 996, § 1, eff Sept 1, 1971.

§ 580.10. Securing attendance of defendants confined as prisoners in institutions of other jurisdictions of the United States; methods

The attendance in a criminal action pending in a court of this state of a defendant confined as a prisoner in an institution of another jurisdiction of the United States may, under prescribed circumstances, be secured pursuant to:

1. Section 570.12 of article five hundred seventy, known as the uniform criminal extradition act; or

2. Section 580.20, known as the agreement on detainers; or

3. Section 580.30.

HISTORY: Add, L 1970, ch 996, § 1, eff Sept 1, 1971.

§ 580.20. Agreement on detainers

The agreement on detainers is hereby enacted into law and entered into by this state with all other jurisdictions legally joining therein in the form substantially as follows:

TEXT OF THE AGREEMENT ON DETAINERS

The contracting states solemnly agree that:

Article I

The party states find that charges outstanding against a prisoner, detainers based on untried indictments, informations or complaints, and difficulties in securing speedy trial of persons already incarcerated in other jurisdictions, produce uncertainties which obstruct programs of prisoner treatment and rehabilitation. Accordingly, it is the policy of the party states and the purpose of this agreement to encourage the expeditious and orderly disposition of such charges and determination of the proper status of any and all detainers based on untried indictments, informations or complaints. The party states also find that proceedings with reference to such charges and detainers, when emanating from another jurisdiction, cannot properly be had in the absence of cooperative procedures. It is the further purpose of this agreement to provide such cooperative procedures.

Article II

As used in this agreement:

(a) "State" shall mean a state of the United States; the United States of America; a territory or possession of the United States; the District of Columbia; the Commonwealth of Puerto Rico.

(b) "Sending state" shall mean a state in which a prisoner is incarcerated at the time that he initiates a request for final disposition pursuant to Article III hereof or at the time that a request for custody or availability is initiated pursuant to Article IV hereof.

(c) "Receiving state" shall mean the state in which trial is to be had on an indictment, information or complaint pursuant to Article III or Article IV hereof.

Article III

(a) Whenever a person has entered upon a term of imprisonment in a penal or correctional institution of a party state, and whenever during the continuance of the term of imprisonment there is pending in any other party state any untried indictment, information or complaint on the basis of which a detainer has been lodged against the prisoner, he shall be brought to trial within one hundred eighty days after he shall have caused to be delivered to the prosecuting officer and the appropriate court of the prosecuting officer's jurisdiction written notice of the place of his imprisonment and his request for a final disposition to be made of the indictment, information or complaint; provided that for good cause shown in open court, the prisoner or his counsel being present, the court having jurisdiction of the matter may grant any necessary or reasonable continuance. The request of the prisoner shall be accompanied by a certificate of the appropriate official having custody of the prisoner, stating the term of commitment under which the prisoner is being held, the time already served, the time remaining to be served on the sentence, the amount of good time earned, the time of parole eligibility of the prisoner, and any decisions of the state parole agency relating to the prisoner.

(b) The written notice and request for final disposition referred to in paragraph (a) hereof shall be given or sent by the prisoner to the warden, commissioner of correction or other official having custody of him, who shall promptly forward it together with the certificate to the appropriate prosecuting official and court by registered or certified mail, return receipt requested.

(c) The warden, commissioner of correction or other official having custody of the prisoner shall promptly inform him of the source and contents of any detainer lodged against him and shall also inform him of his right to make a request for final disposition of the indictment, information or complaint on which the detainer is based.

(d) Any request for final disposition made by a prisoner pursuant to paragraph (a) hereof shall operate as a request for final disposition of all untried indictments, informations or complaints on the basis of which detainers have been lodged against the prisoner from the state to whose prosecuting official the request for final disposition is specifically directed. The warden, commissioner of correction or other official having custody of the prisoner shall forthwith notify all appropriate prosecuting officers and courts in the several jurisdictions within the state to which the prisoner's request for final disposition is being sent of the proceeding being initiated by the prisoner. Any notification sent pursuant to this paragraph shall be accompanied by copies of the prisoner's written notice, request, and the certificate. If trial is not had on any indictment, information or complaint contemplated hereby prior to the return of the prisoner to the original place of imprisonment, such indictment, information or complaint shall not be of any further force or effect, and the court shall enter an order dismissing the same with prejudice.

(e) Any request for final disposition made by a prisoner pursuant to paragraph (a) hereof shall also be deemed to be a waiver of extradition with respect to any charge or proceeding contemplated thereby or included therein by reason of paragraph (d) hereof, and a waiver of extradition to the receiving state to serve any sentence there imposed upon him, after completion of his term of imprisonment in the sending state. The request for final disposition shall also constitute a consent by the prisoner to the production of his body in any court where his presence may be required in order to effectuate the purposes of this agreement and a further consent voluntarily to be returned to the original place of imprisonment in accordance with the provisions of this agreement. Nothing in this paragraph shall prevent the imposition of a concurrent sentence if otherwise permitted by law.

(f) Escape from custody by the prisoner subsequent to his execution of the request for final disposition referred to in paragraph (a) hereof shall void the request.

Article IV

(a) The appropriate officer of the jurisdiction in which an untried indictment, information or complaint is pending shall be entitled to have a prisoner against whom he has lodged a detainer and who is serving a term of imprisonment in any party state made available in accordance with Article V(a) hereof upon presentation of a written request for temporary custody or availability to the appropriate authorities of the state in which the prisoner is incarcerated; provided that the court having jurisdiction of such indictment, information or complaint shall have duly approved, recorded and transmitted the request; and provided further that there shall be a period of thirty days after receipt by the appropriate authorities before the request be honored, within which period the governor of the sending state may disapprove the request for temporary custody or availability, either upon his own motion or upon motion of the prisoner.

(b) Upon receipt of the officer's written request as provided in paragraph (a) hereof, the appropriate authorities having the prisoner in custody shall furnish the officer with a certificate stating the term of commitment under which the prisoner is being held, the time already served, the time remaining to be served on the sentence, the amount of good time earned, the time of parole eligibility of the prisoner, and any decisions of the state parole agency relating to the prisoner. Said authorities simultaneously shall furnish all other officers and appropriate courts in the receiving state who have lodged detainers against the prisoner with similar certificates and with notices informing them of the request for custody or availability and of the reasons therefor.

(c) In respect of any proceeding made possible by this Article, trial shall be commenced within one hundred twenty days of the arrival of the prisoner in the receiving state, but for good cause shown in open court, the prisoner or his counsel being present, the court having jurisdiction of the matter may grant any necessary or reasonable continuance.

(d) Nothing contained in this Article shall be construed to deprive any prisoner of any right which he may have to contest the legality of his delivery as provided in paragraph (a) hereof but such delivery may not be opposed or denied on the ground that the executive authority of the sending state has not affirmatively consented to or ordered such delivery.

(e) If trial is not had on any indictment, information or complaint contemplated hereby prior to the prisoner's being returned to the original place of imprisonment pursuant to Article V(e) hereof, such indictment, information or complaint shall not be of any further force or effect, and the court shall enter an order dismissing the same with prejudice.

Article V

(a) In response to a request made under Article III or Article IV hereof, the appropriate authority in a sending state shall offer to deliver temporary custody of such prisoner to the appropriate authority in the state where such indictment, information or complaint is pending against such person in order that speedy and efficient prosecution may be had. If the request for final disposition is made by the prisoner, the offer of temporary custody shall accompany the written notice provided for in Article III of this agreement. In the case of a federal prisoner, the appropriate authority in receiving state shall be entitled to temporary custody as provided by this agreement or to the prisoner's presence in federal custody at the place for trial, whichever custodial arrangement may be approved by the custodian.

(b) The officer or other representative of a state accepting an offer of temporary custody shall present the following upon demand:

(1) Proper identification and evidence of his authority to act for the state into whose temporary custody the prisoner is to be given.

(2) A duly certified copy of the indictment, information or complaint on the basis of which the detainer has been lodged and on the basis of which the request for temporary custody of the prisoner has been made.

(c) If the appropriate authority shall refuse or fail to accept temporary custody of said person, or in the event that an action on the indictment, information or complaint on the basis of which the detainer has been lodged is not brought to trial within the period provided in Article III or Article IV hereof, the appropriate court of the jurisdiction where the indictment, information or complaint has been pending shall enter an order dismissing the same with prejudice, and any detainer based thereon shall cease to be of any force or effect.

(d) The temporary custody referred to in this agreement shall be only for the purpose of permitting prosecution on the charge or charges contained in one or more untried indictments, informations or complaints which form the basis of the detainer or detainers or for prosecution on any other charge or charges arising out of the same transaction. Except for his attendance at court and while being transported to or from any place at which his presence may be required, the prisoner shall be held in a suitable jail or other facility regularly used for persons awaiting prosecution.

(e) At the earliest practicable time consonant with the purposes of this agreement, the prisoner shall be returned to the sending state.

(f) During the continuance of temporary custody or while the prisoner is otherwise being made available for trial as required by this agreement, time being served on the sentence shall continue to run but good time shall be earned by the prisoner only if, and to the extent that, the law and practice of the jurisdiction which imposed the sentence may allow.

(g) For all purposes other than that for which temporary custody as provided in this agreement is exercised, the prisoner shall be deemed to remain in the custody of and subject to the jurisdiction of the sending state and any escape from temporary custody may be dealt with in the same manner as an escape from the original place of imprisonment or in any other manner permitted by law.

(h) From the time that a party state receives custody of a prisoner pursuant to this agreement until such prisoner is returned to the territory and custody of the sending state, the state in which the one or more untried indictments, informations or complaints are pending or in which trial is being had shall be responsible for the prisoner and shall also pay all costs of transporting, caring for, keeping and returning the prisoner. The provisions of this paragraph shall govern unless the states concerned shall have entered into a supplementary agreement providing for a different allocation of costs and responsibilities as between or among themselves. Nothing herein contained shall be construed to alter or affect any internal relationship among the departments, agencies and officers of and in the government of a party state, or between a party state and its subdivisions, as to the payment of costs, or responsibilities therefor.

Article VI

(a) In determining the duration and expiration dates of the time periods provided in Articles III and IV of this agreement, the running of said time periods shall be tolled whenever and for as long as the prisoner is unable to stand trial, as determined by the court having jurisdiction of the matter.

(b) No provision of this agreement, and no remedy made available by this agreement, shall apply to any person who is adjudged to be mentally ill.

Article VII

Each state party to this agreement shall designate an officer who, acting jointly with like officers of other party states, shall promulgate rules and regulations to carry out more effectively the terms and provisions of this agreement, and who shall provide, within and without the state, information necessary to the effective operation of this agreement.

Article VIII

This agreement shall enter into full force and effect as to a party state when such state has enacted the same into law. A state party to this agreement may withdraw herefrom by enacting a statute repealing the same. However, the withdrawal of any state shall not affect the status of any proceedings already initiated by inmates or by state officers at the time such withdrawal takes effect, nor shall it affect their rights in respect thereof.

Article IX

1. This agreement shall be liberally construed so as to effectuate its purposes. The provisions of this agreement shall be severable and if any phrase, clause, sentence or provision of this agreement is declared to be contrary to the constitution of any party state or of the United States or the applicability thereof to any government, agency, person or circumstance is held invalid, the validity of the remainder of this agreement and the applicability thereof to any government, agency, person or circumstance shall not be affected thereby. If this agreement shall be held contrary to the constitution of any state party hereto, the agreement shall remain in full force and effect as to the remaining states and in full force and effect as to the state affected as to all severable matters.

2. The phrase "appropriate court" as used in the agreement on detainers shall, with reference to the courts of this state, mean any court with criminal jurisdiction.

3. All courts, departments, agencies, officers and employees of this state and its political subdivisions are hereby directed to enforce the agreement on detainers and to cooperate with one another and with other party states in enforcing the agreement and effectuating its purposes.

4. Escape from custody while in another state pursuant to the agreement on detainers shall constitute an offense against the laws of this state to the same extent and degree as an escape from the institution in which the prisoner was confined immediately prior to having been sent to another

state pursuant to the provisions of the agreement on detainers and shall be punishable in the same manner as an escape from said institution.

5. It shall be lawful and mandatory upon the warden or other official in charge of a penal or correctional institution in this state to give over the person of any inmate thereof whenever so required by the operation of the agreement on detainers.

6. The governor is hereby authorized and empowered to designate an administrator who shall perform the duties and functions and exercise the powers conferred upon such person by Article VII of the agreement on detainers.

7. In order to implement Article IV(a) of the agreement on detainers, and in furtherance of its purposes, the appropriate authorities having custody of the prisoner shall, promptly upon receipt of the officer's written request, notify the prisoner and the governor in writing that a request for temporary custody has been made and such notification shall describe the source and contents of said request. The authorities having custody of the prisoner shall also advise him in writing of his rights to counsel, to make representations to the governor within thirty days, and to contest the legality of his delivery.

> **HISTORY:** Add, L 1970, ch 996, § 1, eff Sept 1, 1971, with substance derived from Crim C § 669-b.

§ 580.30. Securing attendance of defendants confined in federal prisons

1. A defendant against whom a criminal action is pending in a court of record of this state, and who is confined in a federal prison or custody either within or outside the state, may, with the consent of the attorney general of the United States, be produced in such court for the purpose of criminal prosecution, pursuant to the provisions of:

(a) Section four thousand eighty-five of title eighteen of the United States Code; or

(b) Subdivision two of this section.

2. When such a defendant is in federal custody as specified in subdivision one, a superior court, at a term held in the county in which the criminal action against him is pending, may, upon application of the district attorney of such county, issue a certificate, known as a writ of habeas corpus ad prosequendum, addressed to the attorney general of the United States, certifying that such defendant has been charged by the particular accusatory instrument filed against him in the specified court with the offense or offenses alleged therein, and that attendance of the defendant in such court for the purpose of criminal prosecution thereon is necessary in the interest of justice, and requesting the attorney general of the United States to cause such defendant to be produced in such court, under custody of a federal public servant, upon a designated date and for a period of time necessary to complete the prosecution. Upon issuing such a certificate, the court may deliver it, or cause or authorize it to be delivered, together with a certified copy of the accusatory instrument upon which it is based, to the attorney general of the United States or to his representative authorized to entertain the request.

> **HISTORY:** Add, L 1970, ch 996, § 1, eff Sept 1, 1971.

ARTICLE 590 SECURING ATTENDANCE OF DEFENDANTS WHO ARE OUTSIDE THE UNITED STATES

§ 590.10.   Securing attendance of defendants who are outside the United States

> **HISTORY:** Add, L 1970, ch 996, § 1, eff Sept 1, 1971.

§ 590.10. Securing attendance of defendants who are outside the United States

1. When a criminal action for an offense committed in this state is pending in a criminal court of this state against a defendant who is in a foreign country with which the United States has an extradition treaty, and when the accusatory instrument charges an offense which is declared in such treaty to be an extraditable one, the district attorney of the county in which such offense was allegedly committed may make an application to the Governor, requesting him to make an application to the President of the United States to institute extradition proceedings for the return of the defendant to this country and state for the purpose of prosecution of such action. The district attorney's application must comply with rules, regulations and guidelines established by the Governor for such applications and must be accompanied by all the accusatory instruments, affidavits and other documents required by such rules, regulations and guidelines.

2. Upon receipt of the district attorney's application, the Governor, if satisfied that the defendant is in the foreign country in question, that the offense charged is an extraditable one pursuant to the treaty in question, and that there are no factors or impediments which in law preclude such an extradition, may in his discretion make an application, addressed to the secretary of state of the United States, requesting that the President of the United States institute extradition proceedings for the return of the defendant from such foreign country. The Governor's application must comply with rules, regulations and guidelines established by the secretary of state for such applications and must be accompanied by all the accusatory instruments, affidavits and other documents required by such rules, regulations and guidelines.

3. If the Governor's application is granted and the extradition is achieved or attempted, all expenses incurred therein must be borne by the county from which the application emanated.

4. The provisions of this section apply equally to extradition or attempted extradition of a person who is a fugitive following the entry of a judgment of conviction against him in a criminal court of this state.

HISTORY: Add, L 1970, ch 996, § 1, eff Sept 1, 1971.

ARTICLE 600 SECURING ATTENDANCE OF CORPORATE DEFENDANTS AND RELATED MATTERS

§ 600.10.   Corporate defendants; securing attendance
§ 600.20.   Corporate defendants; prosecution thereof

HISTORY: Add, L 1970, ch 996, § 1, eff Sept 1, 1971.

§ 600.10. Corporate defendants; securing attendance

1. The court attendance of a corporation for purposes of commencing or prosecuting a criminal action against it may be accomplished by the issuance and service of a summons or an appearance ticket if such action has been or is about to be commenced in a local criminal court, and by a corporate summons if such action has been commenced in a superior court. Such process must be served upon the corporation by delivery thereof to an officer, director, managing or general agent, or cashier or assistant cashier of such corporation or to any other agent of such corporation authorized by appointment or by law to receive service of process.

2. A "corporate summons" is a process issued by a superior court directing a corporate defendant designated in an indictment to appear before it at a designated future time in connection with such indictment. A corporate summons must be generally in the form of a summons as prescribed in subdivision two of section 130.10. A corporate summons may be served by a public servant designated by the issuing court, and may be served anywhere in the state.

HISTORY: Add, L 1970, ch 996, § 1, eff Sept 1, 1971.

§ 600.20. Corporate defendants; prosecution thereof

At all stages of a criminal action, from the commencement thereof through sentence, a corporate defendant must appear by counsel. Upon failure of appearance at the time such defendant is required to enter a plea to the accusatory instrument, the court may enter a plea of guilty and impose sentence.

HISTORY: Add, L 1970, ch 996, § 1, eff Sept 1, 1971.

TITLE R   Procedures for Securing Attendance of Witnesses in Criminal Actions

ARTICLE 610
SECURING ATTENDANCE OF WITNESSES BY SUBPOENA

ARTICLE 620
SECURING ATTENDANCE OF WITNESSES BY MATERIAL WITNESS ORDER

ARTICLE 630
SECURING ATTENDANCE AS WITNESSES OF PERSONS CONFINED IN
INSTITUTIONS WITHIN THE STATE

ARTICLE 640
SECURING ATTENDANCE AS WITNESSES OF PERSONS AT LIBERTY OUTSIDE
THE STATE—RENDITION TO OTHER JURISDICTIONS OF WITNESSES AT
LIBERTY WITHIN THE STATE—UNIFORM ACT TO SECURE ATTENDANCE OF
WITNESSES FROM WITHOUT THE STATE IN CRIMINAL CASES

ARTICLE 650
SECURING ATTENDANCE AS WITNESSES OF PRISONERS CONFINED IN
INSTITUTIONS OF OTHER JURISDICTIONS OF THE UNITED
STATES—RENDITION TO OTHER JURISDICTIONS OF PRISONERS CONFINED IN
INSTITUTIONS WITHIN THE STATE

HISTORY: Add, L 1970, ch 996, § 1, eff Sept 1, 1971.

HISTORY: Add, L 1970, ch 996, § 1, eff Sept 1, 1971.

§ 610.10. Securing attendance of witnesses by subpoena; in general

1. Under circumstances prescribed in this article, a person at liberty within the state may be required to attend a criminal court action or proceeding as a witness by the issuance and service upon him of a subpoena.

2. A "subpoena" is a process of a court directing the person to whom it is addressed to attend and appear as a witness in a designated action or proceeding in such court, on a designated date and any recessed or adjourned date of the action or proceeding. If the witness is given reasonable notice of such recess or adjournment, no further process is required to compel his attendance on the adjourned date.

3. As used in this article, "subpoena" includes a "subpoena duces tecum." A subpoena duces tecum is a subpoena requiring the witness to bring with him and produce specified physical evidence.

HISTORY: Add, L 1970, ch 996, § 1, eff Sept 1, 1971.

§ 610.20. Securing attendance of witnesses by subpoena; when and by whom subpoena may be issued

1. Any criminal court may issue a subpoena for the attendance of a witness in any criminal action or proceeding in such court.

2. A district attorney, or other prosecutor where appropriate, as an officer of a criminal court in which he is conducting the prosecution of a criminal action or proceeding, may issue a subpoena of such court, subscribed by himself, for the attendance in such court or a grand jury thereof of any witness whom the people are entitled to call in such action or proceeding.

3. An attorney for a defendant in a criminal action or proceeding, as an officer of a criminal court, may issue a subpoena of such court, subscribed by himself, for the attendance in such court of any witness whom the defendant is entitled to call in such action or proceeding. An attorney for a defendant may not issue a subpoena duces tecum of the court directed to any department, bureau or agency of the state or of a political subdivision thereof, or to any officer or representative thereof. Such a subpoena duces tecum may be issued in behalf of a defendant upon order of a court pursuant to the rules applicable to civil cases as provided in section twenty-three hundred seven of the civil practice law and rules.

HISTORY: Add, L 1970, ch 996, § 1, eff Sept 1, 1971.

§ 610.25. Securing attendance of witness by subpoena; possession of physical evidence

1. Where a subpoena duces tecum is issued on reasonable notice to the person subpoenaed, the court or grand jury shall have the right to possession of the subpoenaed evidence. Such evidence may be retained by the court, grand jury or district attorney on behalf of the grand jury.

2. The possession shall be for a period of time, and on terms and conditions, as may reasonably be required for the action or proceeding. The reasonableness of such possession, time, terms, and conditions shall be determined with consideration for, among other things, (a) the good cause shown by the party issuing the subpoena or in whose behalf the subpoena is issued, (b) the rights and legitimate needs of the person subpoenaed and (c) the feasibility and appropriateness of making copies of the evidence. The cost of reproduction and transportation incident thereto shall be borne by the person or party issuing the subpoena unless the court determines otherwise in the interest of justice. Nothing in this article shall be deemed to prohibit the designation of a return date for a subpoena duces tecum prior to trial. Where physical evidence specified to be produced will be sought to be retained in custody, notice of such fact shall be given the subpoenaed party. In any case where the court receives or retains evidence prior to trial, it may, as may otherwise be authorized by law, grant the issuing party a reasonable opportunity to inspect such evidence.

HISTORY: Add, L 1977, ch 451, § 2, eff July 19, 1977. Sub 2, amd, L 1979, ch 413, § 3, eff Sept 1, 1979.

§ 610.30. Securing attendance of witnesses by subpoena; where subpoena may be served

1. A subpoena of any criminal court, issued pursuant to section 610.20, may be served anywhere in the county of issuance or anywhere in an adjoining county.

2. A subpoena of a superior court or of a superior court judge sitting as a local criminal court, issued pursuant to section 610.20, may be served anywhere in the state.

3. A subpoena of a district court or of the New York City criminal court, issued pursuant to section 610.20, may be served anywhere in the state; provided that, if such subpoena is issued by a prosecutor or by an attorney for a defendant, it may be served in a county other than the county of issuance or an adjoining county only if such court, upon application of such prosecutor or

attorney, endorses upon such subpoena an order for the attendance of the witness.

4. A subpoena of a city court or a town court or a village court, issued pursuant to section 610.20, may be served in a county other than the one of issuance or an adjoining county if a judge of a superior court, upon application of the issuing court or the district attorney or an attorney for the defendant, endorses upon such subpoena an order for the attendance of the witness.

> **HISTORY:** Add, L 1970, ch 996, § 1, eff Sept 1, 1971.

§ 610.40. Securing attendance of witnesses by subpoena; how and by whom subpoena may be served

A subpoena may be served by any person more than eighteen years old. Service must be made in the manner provided by the civil practice law and rules for the service of subpoenas in civil cases.

> **HISTORY:** Add, L 1970, ch 996, § 1, eff Sept 1, 1971.

§ 610.50. Securing attendance of witness by subpoena; fees

1. A witness subpoenaed by the people in a criminal action is entitled to the same fees and mileage as a witness in a civil action, payable by the treasurer of the county upon the certificate of the court or the clerk thereof, stating the number of days the witness actually attended and the number of miles traveled by him in order to attend. In any such action, the court may, by order, direct the county treasurer to pay to such witness a further reasonable sum for expenses, to be specified in the order, and the county treasurer, upon the production of the order or a certified copy thereof, must pay the witness the sum specified therein out of the county treasury. Such certificates shall only be issued by the court or the clerk thereof, upon the production of the affidavit of the witness, stating that he attended as such either on subpoena or request of the district attorney, the number of miles necessarily traveled and the duration of attendance. An officer in any state department who attends as a witness under this section in his official capacity, or in consequence of any official action taken by him, and who receives a fixed sum in lieu of expenses, or who is entitled to receive the actual expenses incurred by him in the discharge of his official duties, is not entitled to the compensation herein provided.

2. A witness subpoenaed by the defendant in a criminal action is not entitled as of right to witness and mileage fees, but the court may in its discretion, by order, direct the county treasurer to pay to such a witness a reasonable sum for expenses, to be specified in the order. Upon the production of the order or a certified copy thereof, the county treasurer must pay the witness the sum specified therein, out of the county treasury.

> **HISTORY:** Add, L 1970, ch 996, § 1, eff Sept 1, 1971, with substance derived from Crim C §§ 394, 616, 617.

ARTICLE 620   SECURING ATTENDANCE OF WITNESSES BY MATERIAL WITNESS ORDER

§ 620.70.   **Material witness order; compelling attendance of witness who fails to appear**

§ 620.80.   **Material witness order; witness fee**

HISTORY: Add, L 1970, ch 996, § 1, eff Sept 1, 1971.

§ 620.10. Material witness order; defined

A material witness order is a court order (a) adjudging a person a material witness in a pending criminal action and (b) fixing bail to secure his future attendance thereat.

HISTORY: Add, L 1970, ch 996, § 1, eff Sept 1, 1971.

§ 620.20. Material witness order; when authorized; by what courts issuable; duration thereof

1. A material witness order may be issued upon the ground that there is reasonable cause to believe that a person whom the people or the defendant desire to call as a witness in a pending criminal action:

(a) Possesses information material to the determination of such action; and

(b) Will not be amenable or responsive to a subpoena at a time when his attendance will be sought.

2. A material witness order may be issued only when:

(a) An indictment has been filed in a superior court and is currently pending therein; or

(b) A grand jury proceeding has been commenced and is currently pending; or

(c) A felony complaint has been filed with a local criminal court and is currently pending therein.

3. The following courts may issue material witness orders under the indicated circumstances:

(a) When an indictment has been filed, or a grand jury proceeding has been commenced, or a defendant has been held by a local criminal court for the action of a grand jury, a material witness order may be issued only by the superior court in which such indictment is pending or by which such grand jury has been or is to be impaneled;

(b) When a felony complaint is currently pending in a district court or in the New York City criminal court or before a superior court judge sitting as a local criminal court, a material witness order may be issued either by such court or by the superior court which would have jurisdiction of the case upon a holding of the defendant for the action of the grand jury;

(c) When a felony complaint is currently pending in a city court or a town court or a village court, a material witness order may be issued only by the superior court which would have jurisdiction of the case upon a holding of the defendant for the action of the grand jury.

4. Unless vacated pursuant to section 620.60, a material witness order remains in effect during the following periods of time under the indicated circumstances:

(a) An order issued by a superior court under the circumstances prescribed in paragraph (a) of subdivision three remains in effect during the pendency of the criminal action in such superior court;

(b) An order issued by a district court or the New York City criminal court or a superior court judge sitting as a local criminal court, under circumstances prescribed in paragraph (b) of subdivision three, remains in effect (i) until the disposition of the felony complaint pending in such court, and (ii) if the defendant is held for the action of a grand jury, during the pendency of the grand jury proceeding, and (iii) if an indictment results, for a period of ten days following the filing of such indictment, and (iv) if within such ten day period such order is indorsed by the superior court in which the indictment is pending, during the pendency of the action in such superior court. Upon such indorsement, the order is deemed to be that of the superior court.

(c) An order issued by a superior court under circumstances prescribed in paragraph (c) of subdivision three remains in effect (i) until the disposition of the felony complaint pending in the city, town or village court, and (ii) if the defendant is held for the action of the grand jury, during the pendency of the action in the superior court.

HISTORY: Add, L 1970, ch 996, § 1, eff Sept 1, 1971.

§ 620.30. Material witness order; commencement of proceeding by application; procurement of appearance of prospective witness

1. A proceeding to adjudge a person a material witness must be commenced by application to the appropriate court, made in writing and subscribed and sworn to by the applicant, demonstrating reasonable cause to believe the existence of facts, as specified in subdivision one of section 620.20, warranting the adjudication of such person as a material witness.

2. If the court is satisfied that the application is well founded, the prospective witness may be compelled to appear in response thereto as follows:

(a) The court may issue an order directing him to appear therein at a designated time in order that a determination may be made whether he should be adjudged a material witness, and, upon personal service of such order or a copy thereof within the state, he must so appear.

(b) If in addition to the allegations specified in subdivision one, the application contains further allegations demonstrating to the satisfaction of the court reasonable cause to believe that (i) the witness would be unlikely to respond to such an order, or (ii) after previously having been served with such an order, he did not respond thereto, the court may issue a warrant addressed to a police officer, directing such officer to take such prospective witness into custody within the state and to bring him before the court forthwith in order that a proceeding may be conducted to determine whether he is to be adjudged a material witness.

HISTORY: Add, L 1970, ch 996, § 1, eff Sept 1, 1971.

§ 620.40. Material witness order; arraignment

1. When the prospective witness appears before the court, the court must inform him of the nature and purpose of the proceeding, and that he is entitled to a prompt hearing upon the issue of whether he should be adjudged a material witness. The prospective witness possesses all the rights, and is entitled to all the court instructions, with respect to right to counsel, opportunity to obtain counsel and assignment of counsel in case of financial inability to retain such, which, pursuant to subdivisions three through five of section 180.10, accrue to a defendant arraigned upon a felony complaint in a local criminal court.

2. If the proceeding is adjourned at the prospective witness' instance, for the purpose of obtaining counsel or otherwise, the court must order him to appear upon the adjourned date. The court may further fix bail to secure his appearance upon such date or until the proceeding is completed and, upon default thereof, may commit him to the custody of the sheriff for such period.

HISTORY: Add, L 1970, ch 996, § 1, eff Sept 1, 1971.

§ 620.50. Material witness order; hearing, determination and execution of order

1. The hearing upon the application must be conducted as follows:

(a) The applicant has the burden of proving by a preponderance of the evidence all facts essential to support a material witness order, and any testimony so adduced must be given under oath;

(b) The prospective witness may testify under oath or may make an unsworn statement;

(c) The prospective witness may call witnesses in his behalf, and the court must cause process to be issued for any such witness whom he reasonably wishes to call, and any testimony so adduced must be given under oath;

(d) Upon the hearing, evidence tending to demonstrate that the prospective witness does or does not possess information material to the criminal action in issue, or that he will or will not be amenable or respond to a subpoena at the time his attendance will be sought, is admissible even though it consists of hearsay.

2. If the court is satisfied after such hearing that there is reasonable cause to believe that the prospective witness (a) possesses information material to the pending action or proceeding, and (b) will not be amenable or respond to a subpoena at a time when his attendance will be sought, it may issue a material witness order, adjudging him a material witness and fixing bail to secure his future attendance.

3. A material witness order must be executed as follows:

(a) If the bail is posted and approved by the court, the witness must, as provided in subdivision three of section 510.40, be released and be permitted to remain at liberty; provided that, where the bail is posted by a person other than the witness himself, he may not be so released except upon his signed written consent thereto;

(b) If the bail is not posted, or if though posted it is not approved by the court, the witness must, as provided in subdivision three of section 510.40, be committed to the custody of the sheriff.

HISTORY: Add, L 1970, ch 996, § 1, eff Sept 1, 1971.

§ 620.60. Material witness order; vacation, modification and amendment thereof

1. At any time after a material witness order has been issued the court must, upon application of such witness, with notice to the party upon whose application the order was issued, and with opportunity to be heard, make inquiry whether by reason of new or changed facts or circumstances the material witness order is no longer necessary or warranted, or, if it is, whether the original bail currently appears excessive. Upon making any such determination, the court must vacate the order. If its determination is that the order is no longer necessary or warranted, it must, as the situation requires, either discharge the witness from custody or exonerate the bail. If its determination is that the bail is excessive, it must issue a new order fixing bail in a lesser amount or on less burdensome terms.

2. At any time when a witness is at liberty upon bail pursuant to a material witness order, the court may, upon application of the party upon whose application the order was issued, with notice to the witness if possible and to his attorney if any and opportunity to be heard, make inquiry whether, by reason of new or changed facts or circumstances, the original bail is no longer sufficient to secure the future attendance of the witness at the pending action. Upon making such a determination, the court must vacate the order and issue a new order fixing bail in a greater amount or on terms more likely to secure the future attendance of the witness.

HISTORY: Add, L 1970, ch 996, § 1, eff Sept 1, 1971.

§ 620.70. Material witness order; compelling attendance of witness who fails to appear

If a witness at liberty on bail pursuant to a material witness order cannot be found or notified at the time his appearance as a witness is required, or if after notification he fails to appear in such action or proceeding as required, the court may issue a warrant, addressed to a police officer, directing such officer to take such witness into custody anywhere within the state and to bring him to the court forthwith.

HISTORY: Add, L 1970, ch 996, § 1, eff Sept 1, 1971.

§ 620.80. Material witness order; witness fee

A witness held in the custody of the sheriff as a result of a material witness order must be paid the sum of three dollars per day for each day of confinement in such custody. Such compensation is a county charge and is payable upon release of such material witness from custody or, in the discretion of the court, at any designated times or intervals during the confinement as the court may deem appropriate.

HISTORY: Add, L 1970, ch 996, § 1, eff Sept 1, 1971.

ARTICLE 630   SECURING ATTENDANCE AS WITNESSES OF PERSONS CONFINED IN INSTITUTIONS WITHIN THE STATE

HISTORY: Add, L 1970, ch 996, § 1, eff Sept 1, 1971.

§ 630.10. Securing attendance of witnesses confined in institutions within the state; in general

Under circumstances prescribed in this article, a person confined in an institution within this state pursuant to a court order may, upon application of a party to a criminal action or proceeding, demonstrating reasonable cause to believe that such person possesses information material thereto, be produced by court order and compelled to attend such action or proceeding as a witness.

HISTORY: Add, L 1970, ch 996, § 1, eff Sept 1, 1971, with substance derived from Crim C § 10-c.

§ 630.20. Securing attendance of witnesses confined in institutions within the state; when and by what courts order may be issued

The following courts and judges may, under the indicated circumstances, order production as witnesses of persons confined by court order in institutions within the state.

1. If the criminal action or proceeding is one pending in a superior court or with a superior court judge sitting as a local criminal court, such court may, except as provided in subdivision four, order the production as a witness therein of a person confined in any institution in the state.

2. If the criminal action or proceeding is one pending in a district court or the New York City criminal court, such court may order the production as a witness therein of a person confined in any institution within the state other than a state prison. Production therein of a prospective witness confined in a state prison may, except as provided in subdivision four, be ordered, upon application of the party desiring to call him, by a judge of a superior court holding a term thereof in the county in which the action or proceeding is pending.

3. If the criminal action or proceeding is one pending in a city court or a town court or a

village court, such court may order the production as a witness therein of a person confined in a county jail of such county. Production therein of a prospective witness confined in any other institution within the state may, except as provided in subdivision four, be ordered, upon application of the party desiring to call him, by a judge of a superior court holding a term thereof in the county in which the action or proceeding is pending.

4. Regardless of the court in which the criminal action or proceeding is pending, production as a witness therein of a prisoner who has been sentenced to death may be ordered, upon application of the party desiring to call him, only by a justice of the appellate division of the department in which the action or proceeding is pending. The application for such order, if made by the defendant, must be upon notice to the district attorney of the county.in which the action or proceeding is pending, and an application made by either party must be based upon a showing that the prisoner's attendance is clearly necessary in the interests of justice. Upon issuing such an order, the appellate division justice may fix and include therein any terms or conditions which he deems appropriate for execution thereof.

HISTORY: Add, L 1970, ch 996, § 1, eff Sept 1, 1971, with substance derived from Crim C § 10-c.

ARTICLE 640 SECURING ATTENDANCE AS WITNESSES OF PERSONS AT LIBERTY OUTSIDE THE STATE—RENDITION TO OTHER JURISDICTIONS OF WITNESSES AT LIBERTY WITHIN THE STATE—UNIFORM ACT TO SECURE ATTENDANCE OF WITNESSES FROM WITHOUT THE STATE IN CRIMINAL CASES

§ 640.10.　　　　　　　**Securing attendance of witnesses from within and without the state in criminal proceedings**

HISTORY: Add, L 1970, ch 996, § 1, eff Sept 1, 1971.

§ 640.10. Securing attendance of witnesses from within and without the state in criminal proceedings

1. As used in this section the following words shall have the following meanings unless the context requires otherwise.[:]*

"Witness" shall include a person whose testimony is desired in any proceeding or investigation by a grand jury or in a criminal action, prosecution or proceeding.

"State" shall include any territory of the United States and the District of Columbia.

"Subpoena" shall include a summons in any state where a summons is used in lieu of a subpoena.

2. Subpoenaing witness in this state to testify in another state. If a judge of a court of record in any state which by its laws has made provision for commanding persons within that state to attend and testify in this state certifies under the seal of such court that there is a criminal prosecution pending in such court, or that a grand jury investigation has commenced or is about to commence, that a person being within this state is a material witness in such prosecution, or grand jury investigation, and that his presence will be required for a specified number of days, upon presentation of such certificate to a justice of the supreme court or a county judge in the county in which such person is, such justice or judge shall fix a time and place for a hearing, and shall make an order directing the witness to appear at a time and place certain for the hearing.

If at such hearing the justice or judge determines that the witness is material and necessary, that

---

* The bracketed punctuation was inserted by the Publisher.

it will not cause undue hardship to the witness to be compelled to attend and testify in the prosecution or a grand jury investigation in the other state, and that the laws of the state in which the prosecution is pending, or grand jury investigation has commenced or is about to commence, will give to him protection from arrest and the service of civil and criminal process, he shall issue a subpoena, with a copy of the certificate attached, directing the witness to attend and testify in the court where the prosecution is pending, or where a grand jury investigation has commenced or is about to commence at a time and place specified in the subpoena. In any such hearing the certificate shall be prima facie evidence of all the facts stated therein.

If said certificate recommends that the witness be taken into immediate custody and delivered to an officer of the requesting state to assure his attendance in the requesting state such justice or judge may, in lieu of notification of the hearing, direct that such witness be forthwith brought before him for said hearing; and the justice or judge at the hearing being satisfied of the desirability of such custody and delivery, for which determination the certificate shall be prima facie proof of such desirability may, in lieu of issuing subpoena, order that said witness be forthwith taken into custody and delivered to an officer of the requesting state.

If the witness, who is subpoenaed as above provided, after being paid or tendered by some properly authorized person the sum of ten cents a mile for each mile and five dollars for each day that he is required to travel and attend as a witness fails without good cause to attend and testify as directed in the subpoena, he shall be punished in the manner provided for the punishment of any witness who disobeys a subpoena issued from a court of record in this state.

3. Witness from another state subpoenaed to testify in this state. If a person in any state, which by its laws has made provision for commanding persons within its borders to attend and testify in criminal prosecutions, or grand jury investigations commenced or about to commence, in this state, is a material witness in a prosecution pending in a court of record in this state, or in a grand jury investigation which has commenced or is about to commence, a judge of such court may issue a certificate under the seal of the court stating these facts and specifying the number of days the witness will be required. This certificate shall be presented to a judge of a court of record in the county in which the witness is found.

If said certificate recommends that the witness be taken into immediate custody and delivered to an officer of this state to assure his attendance in this state, such judge may direct that such witness be forthwith brought before him; and the judge being satisfied of the desirability of such custody and delivery, for which determination said certificate shall be prima facie proof, may order that said witness be forthwith taken into custody and delivered to an officer of this state, which order shall be sufficient authority to such officer to take such witness into custody and hold him unless and until he may be released by bail, recognizance, or order of the judge issuing the certificate.

If the witness is summoned to attend and testify in this state he shall be tendered the sum of ten cents a mile for each mile and five dollars for each day that he is required to travel and attend as a witness. Such fees shall be a proper charge upon the county in which such criminal prosecution or grand jury investigation is pending. A witness who has appeared in accordance with the provisions of the subpoena shall not be required to remain within this state a longer period of time than the period mentioned in the certificate, unless otherwise ordered by the court. If such witness fails without good cause to attend and testify as directed in this subpoena, he shall be punished in the manner provided for the punishment of any witness who disobeys a subpoena issued from a court of record in this state.

4. Exemption from arrest and service of process. If a person comes into this state in obedience to a subpoena directing him to attend and testify in this state he shall not while in this state pursuant

to such subpoena or order be subject to arrest or the service of process, civil or criminal, in connection with matters which arose before his entrance into this state under the subpoena.

If a person passes through this state while going to another state in obedience to a subpoena or order to attend and testify in that state or while returning therefrom, he shall not while so passing through this state be subject to arrest or the service of process, civil or criminal, in connection with matters which arose before his entrance into this state under the subpoena or order.

5. Uniformity of interpretation. This section shall be so interpreted and construed as to effectuate its general purpose to make uniform the law of the states which enact it.

6. Short title. This section may be cited as "Uniform act to secure the attendance of witnesses from without the state in criminal cases."

7. Constitutionality. If any part of this section is for any reason declared void, such invalidity shall not affect the validity of the remaining portions thereof.

HISTORY: Add, L 1970, ch 996, § 1, eff Sept 1, 1971, with substance derived from Crim C § 618-a.

ARTICLE 650   SECURING ATTENDANCE AS WITNESSES OF PRISONERS CONFINED IN INSTITUTIONS OF OTHER JURISDICTIONS OF THE UNITED STATES—RENDITION TO OTHER JURISDICTIONS OF PRISONERS CONFINED IN INSTITUTIONS WITHIN THE STATE

§ 650.10.   **Securing attendance of prisoner in this state as witness in proceeding without the state**

§ 650.20.   **Securing attendance of prisoner outside the state as witness in criminal action in the state**

§ 650.30.   **Securing attendance of prisoner in federal institution as witness in criminal action in the state**

HISTORY: Add, L 1970, ch 996, § 1, eff Sept 1, 1971.

§ 650.10. Securing attendance of prisoner in this state as witness in proceeding without the state

If a judge of a court of record in any other state, which by its laws has made provision for commanding a prisoner within that state to attend and testify in this state, certifies under the seal of that court that there is a criminal prosecution pending in such court or that a grand jury investigation has commenced, and that a person confined in a New York state correctional institution or prison within the department of corrections and community supervision, other than a person confined as criminally mentally ill, or as a defective delinquent, or confined in the death house awaiting execution, is a material witness in such prosecution or investigation and that his or her presence is required for a specified number of days, upon presentment of such certificate to a judge of a superior court in the county where the person is confined, upon notice to the attorney general, such judge, shall fix a time and place for a hearing and shall make an order directed to the person having custody of the prisoner requiring that such prisoner be produced at the hearing.

If at such hearing the judge determines that the prisoner is a material and necessary witness in the requesting state, the judge shall issue an order directing that the prisoner attend in the court where the prosecution or investigation is pending, upon such terms and conditions as the judge prescribes, including among other things, provision for the return of the prisoner at the conclusion of his or her testimony, proper safeguards on his or her custody, and proper financial reimbursement or other payment by the demanding jurisdiction for all expenses incurred in the production and return of the prisoner.

The attorney general is authorized as agent for the state of New York, when in his or her judgment it is necessary, to enter into such agreements with the appropriate authorities of the demanding jurisdiction as he or she determines necessary to ensure proper compliance with the order of the court.

HISTORY: Add, L 1970, ch 996, § 1, with substance derived from Crim C § 618-c; amd, L 1978, ch 550, § 12, eff July 24, 1978, L 2011, ch 62, § 86 (Part C, Subpart B), eff March 31, 2011.

§ 650.20. Securing attendance of prisoner outside the state as witness in criminal action in the state

1. When (a) a criminal action is pending in a court of record of this state, or a grand jury proceeding has been commenced, and (b) there is reasonable cause to believe that a person confined in a correctional institution or prison of another state, other than a person awaiting execution of a sentence of death or one confined as mentally ill or as a defective delinquent, possesses information material to such criminal action or proceeding, and (c) the attendance of such person as a witness in such action or proceeding is desired by a party thereto, and (d) the state in which such person is confined possesses a statute equivalent to section 650.10, the court in which such action or proceeding is pending may issue a certificate under the seal of such court, certifying all such facts and that the attendance of such person as a witness in such court is required for a specified number of days.

2. Such certificate may be issued upon application, of either the people or a defendant, demonstrating all the facts specified in subdivision one.

3. Upon issuing such a certificate, the court may deliver it, or cause or authorize it to be delivered, to a judge or a court of such other state who or which, pursuant to the laws thereof, is authorized to initiate or undertake legal action for the delivery of such prisoners to this state as witnesses.

HISTORY: Add, L 1970, ch 996, § 1, eff Sept 1, 1971.

§ 650.30. Securing attendance of prisoner in federal institution as witness in criminal action in the state

1. When (a) a criminal action is pending in a court of record of this state by reason of the filing therewith of an accusatory instrument, or a grand jury proceeding has been commenced, and (b) there is reasonable cause to believe that a person confined in a federal prison or other federal custody, either within or outside this state, possesses information material to such criminal action or proceeding, and (c) the attendance of such person as a witness in such action or proceeding is desired by a party thereto, a superior court, at a term held in the county in which such action or proceeding is pending, may issue a certificate, known as a writ of habeas corpus ad testificandum, addressed to the attorney general of the United States, certifying all such facts and requesting the attorney general of the United States to cause the attendance of such person as a witness in such court for a specified number of days under custody of a federal public servant.

2. Such a certificate may be issued upon application of either the people or a defendant, demonstrating all the facts specified in subdivision one.

3. Upon issuing such certificate, the court may deliver it, or cause or authorize it to be delivered, to the attorney general of the United States or to his representative authorized to entertain the request.

HISTORY: Add, L 1970, ch 996, § 1, eff Sept 1, 1971.

TITLE S   Procedures for Securing Testimony for Future Use, and For Using Testimony Given in a Prior Proceeding

ARTICLE 660
SECURING TESTIMONY FOR USE IN A SUBSEQUENT PROCEEDING—EXAMINATION OF WITNESSES CONDITIONALLY

ARTICLE 670
USE IN A CRIMINAL PROCEEDING OF TESTIMONY GIVEN IN A PREVIOUS PROCEEDING

ARTICLE 680
SECURING TESTIMONY OUTSIDE THE STATE FOR USE IN PROCEEDING WITHIN THE STATE—EXAMINATION OF WITNESSES ON COMMISSION

HISTORY: Add, L 1970, ch 996, § 1, eff Sept 1, 1971.

ARTICLE 660   SECURING TESTIMONY FOR USE IN A SUBSEQUENT PROCEEDING—EXAMINATION OF WITNESSES CONDITIONALLY

HISTORY: Add, L 1970, ch 996, § 1, eff Sept 1, 1971.

§ 660.10. Examination of witnesses conditionally; in general

After a defendant has been arraigned upon an accusatory instrument, and under circumstances prescribed in this article, a criminal court may, upon application of either the people or a defendant, order that a witness or prospective witness in the action be examined conditionally under oath in order that such testimony may be received into evidence at subsequent proceedings in or related to the action.

HISTORY: Add, L 1970, ch 996, § 1; amd, L 1980, ch 291, § 1, eff June 19, 1980.

§ 660.20. Examination of witnesses conditionally; grounds for order

An order directing examination of a witness conditionally must be based upon the ground that there is reasonable cause to believe that such witness:

1. Possesses information material to the criminal action or proceeding in issue; and

2. Will not be amenable or responsive to legal process or available as a witness at a time when his testimony will be sought, either because he is:

(a) About to leave the state and not return for a substantial period of time; or

(b) Physically ill or incapacited[incapacitated].*

HISTORY: Add, L 1970, ch 996, § 1, eff Sept 1, 1971.

§ 660.30. Examination of witnesses conditionally; when and to what courts application may be made

---

* The bracketed word has been inserted by the Publisher.

1. An application to examine a witness conditionally may be made at any time after the defendant has been arraigned upon an accusatory instrument and before termination of the action, or of a proceeding therein or related thereto, in which the witness's testimony is sought.

2. Such application must be made to and determined by the following courts under the indicated circumstances:

(a) If the action is pending in a local criminal court as a result of an accusatory instrument filed therewith, the application must be made to and determined by such local criminal court;

(b) If the defendant has been held by a local criminal court for the action of a grand jury on the basis of a felony complaint, or if an indictment has been filed against him, the application must be made to and determined by the superior court by which the grand jury was or is to be impaneled or in which the indictment is pending. If the superior court by which the grand jury is to be impaneled is the supreme court, the motion may, in the alternative, be made in the county court of the county in which the action is pending.

HISTORY: Add, L 1970, ch 996, § 1, eff Sept 1, 1971. Sub 2, amd, L 1973, ch 221, § 1, eff Sept 1, 1973.

§ 660.40. Examination of witnesses conditionally; application and notice

1. An application to examine a witness conditionally must be made in writing, must be subscribed and sworn to, and must contain:

(a) The title of the action, the offense or offenses charged, the nature and status of the action, and the name and residential address of the witness sought to be examined; and

(b) A statement that there is reasonable cause to believe that grounds for such an examination, as specified in section 660.20, exist, together with allegations of fact supporting such statement. Such allegations of fact may be those of the applicant, or those of another person in an accompanying deposition, or of both. They may be based either upon personal knowledge of the deponent or upon information and belief, provided that in the latter event the sources of such information and the grounds of such belief are stated.

2. The application may also contain a request that the examination, in addition to its being recorded in the same manner as would be required were the witness testifying at trial, also be recorded by videotape or other photographic method approved by and subject to standards and administrative policies promulgated pursuant to section twenty-eight of article six of the constitution.

3. A copy of the application, with reasonable notice and opportunity to be heard, must be served upon the other party to the action. If the defendant is the applicant, such service must be upon the district attorney. If the people are the applicant, such service must be upon the defendant and upon his attorney if any. The respondent party may file and serve a sworn written answer to the application.

HISTORY: Add, L 1970, ch 996, § 1; amd, L 1980, ch 291, § 2, eff June 19, 1980. Sub 2, add, L 1980, ch 291, § 2, eff June 19, 1980. Former sub 2, renumbered sub 3, L 1980, ch 291, § 2, eff June 19, 1980. Sub 3, formerly sub 2, renumbered sub 3, L 1980, ch 291, § 2, eff June 19, 1980.

§ 660.50. Examination of witnesses conditionally; determination of application

1. Before ruling upon the application, the court may, in addition to examining the papers and hearing oral argument, make any inquiry it deems appropriate for the purpose of making findings of fact essential to the determination. For such purpose, it may examine witnesses, under oath or

otherwise, subpoena or call witnesses and authorize the attorneys for the parties to do so.

2. If the court is satisfied that grounds for the application exist, it must order an examination of the witness conditionally at a designated time and place. Such examination must be conducted by the same court; except that, if it is to be held in another county, it may be conducted by a designated superior court of such other county.

3. The court must order that the examination be recorded in the same manner as would be required were the witness testifying at trial, and the court may, in addition, order that the examination also be recorded by videotape or other photographic method approved by and subject to standards and administrative policies promulgated pursuant to section twenty-eight of article six of the constitution.

4. Upon ordering the examination, the court must direct the party securing the order of examination to serve a copy of the order upon the respondent party and, if a defendant be such, upon his attorney also, and must either issue a subpoena for the witness' attendance thereat or authorize the applicant party's attorney do so.

HISTORY: Add, L 1970, ch 996, § 1; amd, L 1980, ch 291, § 3, eff June 19, 1980. Sub 3, add, L 1980, ch 291, § 3, eff June 19, 1980. Former sub 3, amd, L 1975, ch 181, § 1; renumbered sub 4, L 1980, ch 291, § 3, eff June 19, 1980. Sub 4, formerly sub 3, amd, L 1975, ch 181, § 1; renumbered sub 4, L 1980, ch 291, § 3, eff June 19, 1980.

§ 660.60. Examination of witnesses conditionally; the examination proceeding

1. The examination proceeding must be conducted in the same manner as would be required were the witness testifying at a trial, and must be recorded in such fashion as the court has directed pursuant to subdivision three of section 660.50 of this chapter. The witness must testify under oath. The applicant party must first examine the witness and the respondent party may then cross-examine him, with each party entitled to register objections and to receive rulings of the court thereon.

2. Upon conclusion of the examination, a transcript and any videotape or photographic recording thereof must be certified and filed with the court which ordered the examination.

HISTORY: Add, L 1970, ch 996, § 1; amd, L 1980, ch 291, § 4, eff June 19, 1980.

ARTICLE 670   USE IN A CRIMINAL PROCEEDING OF TESTIMONY GIVEN IN A PREVIOUS PROCEEDING

§ 670.10.   Use in a criminal proceeding of testimony given in a previous proceeding; when authorized

§ 670.20.   Use in a criminal proceeding of testimony given in a previous proceeding; procedure

HISTORY: Add, L 1970, ch 996, § 1, eff Sept 1, 1971.

§ 670.10. Use in a criminal proceeding of testimony given in a previous proceeding; when authorized

1. Under circumstances prescribed in this article, testimony given by a witness at (a) a trial of an accusatory instrument, or (b) a hearing upon a felony complaint conducted pursuant to section 180.60, or (c) an examination of such witness conditionally, conducted pursuant to article six hundred sixty, may, where otherwise admissible, be received into evidence at a subsequent proceeding in or relating to the action involved when at the time of such subsequent proceeding the witness is unable to attend the same by reason of death, illness or incapacity, or cannot with due diligence be found, or is outside the state or in federal custody and cannot with due diligence be brought before the court. Upon being received into evidence, such testimony may be read and

any videotape or photographic recording thereof played. Where any recording is received into evidence, the stenographic transcript of that examination shall also be received.

2. The subsequent proceedings at which such testimony may be received in evidence consist of:

(a) Any proceeding constituting a part of a criminal action based upon the charge or charges which were pending against the defendant at the time of the witness's testimony and to which such testimony related; and

(b) Any post-judgment proceeding in which a judgment of conviction upon a charge specified in paragraph (a) is challenged.

HISTORY: Add, L 1970, ch 996, § 1, eff Sept 1, 1971. Sub 1, amd, L 1971, ch 884 § 5, L 1980, ch 291, § 5, eff June 19, 1980.

§ 670.20. Use in a criminal proceeding of testimony given in a previous proceeding; procedure

1. In any criminal action or proceeding other than a grand jury proceeding, a party thereto who desires to offer in evidence testimony of a witness given in a previous action or proceeding as provided in section 670.10, must so move, either in writing or orally in open court, and must submit to the court, and serve a copy thereof upon the adverse party, an authenticated transcript of the testimony and any videotape or photographic recording thereof sought to be introduced. Such moving party must further state facts showing that personal attendance of the witness in question is precluded by some factor specified in subdivision one of section 670.10. In determining the motion, the court, with opportunity for both parties to be heard, must make inquiry and conduct a hearing to determine whether personal attendance of the witness is so precluded. If the court determines that such is the case and grants the motion, the moving party may introduce the transcript in evidence and read into evidence the testimony contained therein. In such case, the adverse party may register any objection or protest thereto that he would be entitled to register were the witness testifying in person, and the court must rule thereon.

2. Without obtaining any court order or authorization, a district attorney may introduce in evidence in a grand jury proceeding testimony of a witness given in a previous action or proceeding specified in subdivision one of section 670.10, provided that a foundation for such evidence is laid by other evidence demonstrating that personal attendance of such witness is precluded by some factor specified in subdivision one of section 670.10.

HISTORY: Add, L 1970, ch 996, § 1, eff Sept 1, 1971. Sub 1, amd, L 1980, ch 291, § 6, eff June 19, 1980.

ARTICLE 680   SECURING TESTIMONY OUTSIDE THE STATE FOR USE IN PROCEEDING WITHIN THE STATE—EXAMINATION OF WITNESSES ON COMMISSION

§ 680.80.   **Examination of witnesses on commission; use at trial of transcript of examination**

HISTORY: Add, L 1970, ch 996, § 1, eff Sept 1, 1971.

§ 680.10. Examination of witnesses on commission; in general

1. Under circumstances prescribed in this article, testimony material to a trial or pending trial of an accusatory instrument which charges a crime, may be taken by "examination on a commission" outside the state and received in evidence at such trial.

2. A "commission" is a process issued by a superior court designating one or more persons as commissioners and authorizing them to conduct a recorded examination of a witness or witnesses under oath, primarily on the basis of interrogatories annexed to the commission, and to remit to the issuing court the transcript of such examination.

HISTORY: Add, L 1970, ch 996, § 1, eff Sept 1, 1971.

§ 680.20. Examination of witnesses on commission; when commission issuable; form and content of application

1. Upon a pre-trial application of a defendant who has pleaded not guilty to an indictment or other accusatory instrument which charges a crime, the superior court in which such indictment is pending, or a superior court in the county in which such other accusatory instrument is pending, may issue a commission for examination of a designated person as a witness in the action, at a designated place outside this state, if it is satisfied that (a) such person possesses information material to the action which in the interest of justice should be disclosed at the trial, and (b) resides outside the state.

2. The application and moving papers must be in writing and must be subscribed and sworn to by the defendant or his attorney. A copy thereof must be served on the district attorney, with reasonable notice and opportunity to be heard. The moving papers must allege:

(a) The offense or offenses charged; and

(b) The status of the action; and

(c) The name of the prospective witness; and

(d) A statement that such prospective witness resides outside the state, and his address in the jurisdiction in which the examination sought is to occur; and

(e) A statement that he possesses information material to the action which in the interest of justice should be disclosed at the trial, together with a brief summary of the facts supporting such statement.

3. An application for issuance of a commission may request examination pursuant thereto of more than one person residing in the particular jurisdiction. In such case, it must contain allegations specified in subdivision two with respect to each such person, and the court must make separate rulings as to each.

HISTORY: Add, L 1970, ch 996, § 1, eff Sept 1, 1971.

§ 680.30. Examination of witnesses on commission; application by people for examination of witnesses

1. Upon granting the defendant's application for issuance of a commission, the court may, upon application of the people, determine that the commission shall also authorize examination of a person or persons designated by the people, who reside in the jurisdiction in which the examination

proceeding is to occur, if it is satisfied that such person or persons possess material information, reside outside the state and otherwise meet the standards for examination of witnesses on a commission as prescribed in subdivision one of section 680.20.

2. Such application and the moving papers must be in writing, must be subscribed and sworn to by the district attorney, and copies thereof must be served upon the defendant and his attorney, with reasonable notice and opportunity to be heard. The moving papers must contain all of the allegations required upon a defendant's application, as specified in subdivision two of section 680.20.

    HISTORY: Add, L 1970, ch 996, § 1, eff Sept 1, 1971.

§ 680.40. Examination of witnesses on commission; when commission issuable upon application of people

When a commission has been issued upon application of a defendant pursuant to section 680.20, the court may, upon application of the people, issue another commission for examination, either in the same or another jurisdiction, of a person designated by the people, under the same conditions as prescribed in said section 680.20. In such case, the court may, upon application of the defendant, determine, in the manner provided in section 680.30, that such commission shall also authorize examination of a person or persons designated by the defendant.

    HISTORY: Add, L 1970, ch 996, § 1, eff Sept 1, 1971.

§ 680.50. Examination of witnesses on commission; interrogatories

1. Following an order for the issuance of a commission and the court's designation of the witnesses to be examined thereon, each party must prepare interrogatories or questions to be asked of each witness who is to be examined upon his or its request, and must submit the same to the court and serve a copy thereof upon the other party. Following such submission and service, such other party may in the same manner submit and serve cross-interrogatories or questions, to be asked of the witness following his examination upon the direct inquiry.

2. After all such interrogatories and cross-interrogatories have been submitted and served, the court may examine them and, with opportunity for counsel to be heard, exclude and strike any question which it considers irrelevant, incompetent or otherwise improper or violative of the rules of evidence which prevail at a criminal trial.

    HISTORY: Add, L 1970, ch 996, § 1, eff Sept 1, 1971.

§ 680.60. Examination of witnesses on commission; form and content of the commission

1. The commission must be subscribed by the court and must contain:

    (a) The name and address of each witness to be examined; and

    (b) The name, or a descriptive title, of a commissioner or commissioners who, pursuant to subdivision two, are authorized to conduct the examination; and

    (c) A statement authorizing such commissioner or commissioners to administer the oath to witnesses; and

    (d) A direction that, upon completion of such examination, such commissioner or commissioners cause it to be transcribed and remit to the court the transcript, the commission, the interrogatories and all other pertinent instruments and documents.

2. The following persons may be designated commissioners:

    (a) If the examination is to occur within the United States or any territory thereof, any attorney authorized to practice law in the specified jurisdiction or any person authorized to administer oaths therein;

(b) If the examination is to occur in a foreign country, any diplomatic or consular agent or representative of the United States employed in such capacity in such country, or any commissioned officer of the armed forces.

3. The court must cause the commission to be delivered to a commissioner designated therein, together with a copy of this article.

HISTORY: Add, L 1970, ch 996, § 1, eff Sept 1, 1971.

§ 680.70. Examination of witnesses on commission; the examination

The examination on the commission must be conducted as follows:

1. Each witness must testify under oath, and the examination must be recorded and transcribed.

2. Each witness must first be asked all the questions contained in the interrogatories submitted by the party requesting his examination. He must then be asked all the questions contained in the cross-interrogatories, if any, submitted by the other party.

3. The defendant has a right to be represented by counsel at the examination, and the district attorney also has a right to be present, but both such rights may be waived. Upon the conclusion of the questioning of a witness upon the written interrogatories, he may be further examined by the attorney or representative of the party who requested his examination, and may then be cross-examined by the attorney or representative of the adverse party. Each such attorney or representative may register objections to the authority or qualifications of the commissioner, to the manner in which the examination is conducted, and to the admissibility of evidence, and all such objections must be recorded and transcribed.

4. Documentary or other physical evidence may be produced and submitted by a witness. Such evidence must be subscribed or otherwise identified by the witness, and certified by a commissioner and annexed to the transcript of the examination as a part of the record.

5. After the examination is transcribed, the commissioner or commissioners must subscribe and certify the transcript as an accurate record of the proceedings, and must then remit such transcript and all other pertinent instruments, documents and evidence to the court which issued the commission, in accordance with the directions thereof.

HISTORY: Add, L 1970, ch 996, § 1, eff Sept 1, 1971.

§ 680.80. Examination of witnesses on commission; use at trial of transcript of examination

1. When the transcript and record of the examination on commission are received by the superior court which issued the commission, they must be filed therewith if such court be the trial court, and, if not, transmitted to the trial court. A copy of the transcript must be delivered by the trial court to each party.

2. Upon the trial of the action, either party may, subject to the provisions of subdivision three, introduce and read into evidence the transcript or that portion thereof containing the testimony of a witness examined on the commission.

3. At any time prior to the introduction of such evidence, the trial court may examine the transcript and, upon according both parties opportunity to be heard and to register objections, may exclude and strike therefrom irrelevant, incompetent or otherwise inadmissible testimony. While

the transcript or any portion thereof is being read into evidence at the trial by a party, the other party may register any objection or protest thereto that he would be entitled to register were the witness testifying in person, regardless of whether such protest has previously been raised and passed upon by the court, and the court must rule thereon.

HISTORY: Add, L 1970, ch 996, § 1, eff Sept 1, 1971.

TITLE T   Procedures for Securing Evidence by Means of Court Order and for Suppressing Evidence Unlawfully or Improperly Obtained

ARTICLE 690
SEARCH WARRANTS

ARTICLE 700
EAVESDROPPING AND VIDEO SURVEILLANCE WARRANTS

ARTICLE 705
PEN REGISTERS AND TRAP AND TRACE DEVICES

ARTICLE 710
MOTION TO SUPPRESS EVIDENCE

ARTICLE 715
DESTRUCTION OF DANGEROUS DRUGS

HISTORY: Add, L 1970, ch 996, § 1, eff Sept 1, 1971.

ARTICLE 690   SEARCH WARRANTS

HISTORY: Add, L 1970, ch 996, § 1, eff Sept 1, 1971.

§ 690.05. Search warrants; in general; definition

1. Under circumstances prescribed in this article, a local criminal court may, upon application of a police officer, a district attorney or other public servant acting in the course of his official duties, issue a search warrant.

2. A search warrant is a court order and process directing a police officer to conduct:

(a) a search of designated premises, or of a designated vehicle, or of a designated person, for the purpose of seizing designated property or kinds of property, and to deliver any property so obtained to the court which issued the warrant; or

(b) a search of a designated premises for the purpose of searching for and arresting a person who is the subject of:

(i) a warrant of arrest issued pursuant to this chapter, a superior court warrant of arrest issued pursuant to this chapter, or a bench warrant for a felony issued pursuant to this chapter, where the designated premises is the dwelling of a third party who is not the subject of the arrest warrant; or

(ii) a warrant of arrest issued by any other state or federal court for an offense which would constitute a felony under the laws of this state, where the designated premises is the dwelling of a third party who is not the subject of the arrest warrant.

HISTORY: Add, L 1970, ch 996, § 1, eff Sept 1, 1971. Sub 2, amd, L 1980, ch 843, § 20, eff Sept 1, 1980. Sub 2, opening par, formerly part of sub 2, so designated and amd, L 1991, ch 504, § 2, eff Nov 1, 1991. Sub 2, opening par, amd, L 1998, ch 424, § 9, eff Jan 1, 1999. Sub 2, par (a), formerly part of sub 2, so designated and amd, L 1991, ch 504, § 2, eff Nov 1, 1991. Sub 2, par (b), add, L 1991, ch 504, § 2, eff Nov 1, 1991.

§ 690.10. Search warrants; property subject to seizure thereunder

Personal property is subject to seizure pursuant to a search warrant if there is reasonable cause to believe that it:

1. Is stolen; or

2. Is unlawfully possessed; or

3. Has been used, or is possessed for the purpose of being used, to commit or conceal the commission of an offense against the laws of this state or another state, provided however, that if such offense was against the laws of another state, the court shall only issue a warrant if the conduct comprising such offense would, if occurring in this state, constitute a felony against the laws of this state; or

4. Constitutes evidence or tends to demonstrate that an offense was committed in this state or another state, or that a particular person participated in the commission of an offense in this state or another state, provided however, that if such offense was against the laws of another state, the court shall only issue a warrant if the conduct comprising such offense would, if occurring in this state, constitute a felony against the laws of this state.

HISTORY: Add, L 1970, ch 996, § 1, eff Sept 1, 1971, with substance derived from Crim C § 792. Sub 3, amd, L 1994, ch 612, § 1, eff July 26, 1994. Sub 4, amd, L 1994, ch 612, § 1, eff July 26, 1994.

§ 690.15. Search warrants; what and who are subject to search thereunder

1. A search warrant must direct a search of one or more of the following:

(a) A designated or described place or premises;

(b) A designated or described vehicle, as that term is defined in section 10.00 of the penal law;

(c) A designated or described person.

2. A search warrant which directs a search of a designated or described place, premises or vehicle, may also direct a search of any person present thereat or therein.

HISTORY: Add, L 1970, ch 996, § 1, eff Sept 1, 1971.

§ 690.20. Search warrants; where executable

1. A search warrant issued by a district court, the New York City criminal court or a superior court judge sitting as a local criminal court may be executed pursuant to its terms anywhere in the state.

2. A search warrant issued by a city court, a town court or a village court may be executed pursuant to its terms only in the county of issuance or an adjoining county.

HISTORY: Add, L 1970, ch 996, § 1, eff Sept 1, 1971.

§ 690.25. Search warrants; to whom addressable and by whom executable

1. A search warrant must be addressed to a police officer whose geographical area of employment embraces or is embraced or partially embraced by the county of issuance. The warrant need not be addressed to a specific police officer but may be addressed to any police officer of a designated classification, or to any police officer of any classification employed or having general jurisdiction to act as a police officer in the county.

2. A police officer to whom a search warrant is addressed, as provided in subdivision one, may execute it pursuant to its terms anywhere in the county of issuance or an adjoining county, and he may execute it pursuant to its terms in any other county of the state in which it is executable if (a) his geographical area of employment embraces the entire county of issuance or (b) he is a member of the police department or force of a city located in such county of issuance.

3. [Repealed]

> **HISTORY:** Add, L 1970, ch 996, § 1, eff Sept 1, 1971. Sub 3, add, L 1980, ch 843, § 21, eff Sept 1, 1980. Sub 3, repealed, L 1998, ch 424, § 10, eff Jan 1, 1999.

§ 690.30. Search warrants; when executable

1. A search warrant must be executed not more than ten days after the date of issuance and it must thereafter be returned to the court without unnecessary delay.

2. A search warrant may be executed on any day of the week. It may be executed only between the hours of 6:00 A.M. and 9:00 P.M., unless the warrant expressly authorizes execution thereof at any time of the day or night, as provided in subdivision five of section 690.45.

> **HISTORY:** Add, L 1970, ch 996, § 1, eff Sept 1, 1971.

§ 690.35. Search warrants; the application

1. An application for a search warrant may be in writing or oral. If in writing, it must be made, subscribed and sworn to by a public servant specified in subdivision one of section 690.05. If oral, it must be made by such a public servant and sworn to and recorded in the manner provided in section 690.36.

2. The application shall be made to:

(a) A local criminal court, as defined in section 10.10 of this chapter, having preliminary jurisdiction over the underlying offense, or geographical jurisdiction over the location to be searched when the search is to be made for personal property of a kind or character described in section 690.10 of this article except that:

(i) if a town court has such jurisdiction but is not available to issue the search warrant, the warrant may be issued by the local criminal court of any village within such town or, any adjoining town, village embraced in whole or in part by such adjoining town, or city of the same county;

(ii) if a village court has such jurisdiction but is not available to issue the search warrant, the warrant may be issued by the town court of the town embracing such village or any other village court within such town, or, if such town or village court is not available either, before the local criminal court of any adjoining town, village embraced in whole or in part by such adjoining town, or city of the same county; and

(iii) if a city court has such jurisdiction but is not available to issue the search warrant, the warrant may be issued by the local criminal court of any adjoining town or village, or village court embraced by an adjoining town, within the same county as such city.

(b) A local criminal court, as defined in section 10.10 of this chapter, with geographical jurisdiction over the location where the premises to be searched is located, or which issued the underlying arrest warrant, when the search warrant is sought pursuant to paragraph (b) of subdivision two of section 690.05 of this article, for the purpose of arresting a wanted person.

Any search warrant issued pursuant to this section shall be subject to the territorial limitations provided by section 690.20 of this article.

3. The application must contain:

(a) The name of the court and the name and title of the applicant; and

(b) A statement that there is reasonable cause to believe that property of a kind or character described in section 690.10 may be found in or upon a designated or described place, vehicle or person or, in the case of an application for a search warrant as defined in paragraph (b) of subdivision two of section 690.05, a statement that there is reasonable cause to believe that the person who is the subject of the warrant of arrest may be found in the designated premises; and

(c) Allegations of fact supporting such statement. Such allegations of fact may be based upon personal knowledge of the applicant or upon information and belief, provided that in the latter event the sources of such information and the grounds of such belief are stated. The applicant may also submit depositions of other persons containing allegations of fact supporting or tending to support those contained in the application; and

(d) A request that the court issue a search warrant directing a search for and seizure of the property or person in question; and

(e) In the case of an application for a search warrant as defined in paragraph (b) of subdivision two of section 690.05, a copy of the warrant of arrest and the underlying accusatory instrument.

4. The application may also contain:

(a) A request that the search warrant be made executable at any time of the day or night, upon the ground that there is reasonable cause to believe that (i) it cannot be executed between the hours of 6:00 A.M. and 9:00 P.M., or (ii) the property sought will be removed or destroyed if not seized forthwith, or (iii) in the case of an application for a search warrant as defined in paragraph (b) of subdivision two of section 690.05, the person sought is likely to flee or commit another crime, or may endanger the safety of the executing police officers or another person if not seized forthwith or between the hours of 9:00 P.M. and 6:00 A.M.; and

(b) A request that the search warrant authorize the executing police officer to enter premises to be searched without giving notice of his authority and purpose, upon the ground that there is reasonable cause to believe that (i) the property sought may be easily and quickly destroyed or disposed of, or (ii) the giving of such notice may endanger the life or safety of the executing officer or another person, or (iii) in the case of an application for a search warrant as defined in paragraph (b) of subdivision two of section 690.05 for the purpose of searching for and arresting a person who is the subject of a warrant for a felony, the person sought is likely to commit another felony, or may endanger the life or safety of the executing officer or another person.

Any request made pursuant to this subdivision must be accompanied and supported by allegations of fact of a kind prescribed in paragraph (c) of subdivision two.

HISTORY: Add, L 1970, ch 996, § 1, eff Sept 1, 1971. Sub 1, amd, L 1982, ch 679, § 1, eff Sept 20, 1982. Sub 2, add, L 1992, ch 815, § 2; amd, L 1992, ch 816, § 2, eff Nov 1, 1992. Former sub 2, redesignated sub 3, L 1992, ch 815, § 2, eff Nov 1, 1992. Sub 2, par (a), formerly first undesignated par, opening par, so designated par (a), L 1992, ch 816, § 2, eff Nov 1, 1992. Sub 2, par (a), subpar (i), formerly par (a), so designated, L 1992, ch 816, § 2, eff Nov 1, 1992. Sub 2, par (a), subpar (ii), formerly par (b), so designated, L 1992, ch 816, § 2, eff Nov 1, 1992. Sub 2, par (a), subpar (iii), formerly par (c), so designated, L 1992, ch 816, § 2, eff Nov 1, 1992. Sub 2, par (b), add, L 1992, ch 816, § 2, eff Nov 1, 1992. Former sub 2, par (b), redesignated sub 2, par (a), subpar (ii), L 1992, ch 816, § 2, eff Nov 1, 1992. Sub 2, par (c), redesignated sub 2, par (a), subpar (iii), L 1992, ch 816, § 2, eff Nov 1, 1992. Sub 3, formerly sub 2, so designated, L 1992, ch 815, § 2, eff Nov 1, 1992. Former sub 3, amd, L 1980, ch 843, § 22; redesignated sub 4, L 1992, ch 815, § 2, eff Nov 1, 1992. Sub 3, par (b), formerly sub 2, par (b), amd, L 1991, ch 504, § 3, eff Nov 1, 1991. Sub 3, par (d), formerly sub 2, par (d), amd, L 1991, ch 504, § 4, eff Nov 1, 1991. Sub 3, par (e), formerly sub 2, par (e), add, L 1991, ch 504, § 4, eff Nov 1, 1991. Sub 4, formerly sub 3, so designated, L 1992, ch 815, § 2, eff Nov 1, 1992. Sub 4, par (a), formerly sub 3, par (a), amd, L 1991, ch 504, § 5, eff Nov 1, 1991. Sub 4, par (b), formerly sub 3, par (b), amd, L 1991, ch 504, § 5, eff Nov 1, 1991. Sub 4, par (b), amd, L 1998, ch 424, § 11, eff Jan 1, 1999.

§ 690.36. Search warrants; special provisions governing oral applications therefor

1. An oral application for a search warrant may be communicated to a judge by telephone, radio or other means of electronic communication.

2. Where an oral application for a search warrant is made, the applicant therefor must identify himself and the purpose of his communication. After being sworn as provided in subdivision three of this section, the applicant must also make the statement required by paragraph (b) of subdivision two of section 690.35 and provide the same allegations of fact required by paragraph (c) of such subdivision; provided, however, persons, properly identified, other than the applicant may also provide some or all of such allegations of fact directly to the court. Where appropriate, the applicant may also make a request specified in subdivision three of section 690.35.

3. Upon being advised that an oral application for a search warrant is being made, a judge shall place under oath the applicant and any other person providing information in support of the application. Such oath or oaths and all of the remaining communication must be recorded, either by means of a voice recording device or verbatim stenographic or verbatim longhand notes. If a voice recording device is used or a stenographic record made, the judge must have the record transcribed, certify to the accuracy of the transcription and file the original record and transcription with the court within twenty-four hours of the issuance of a warrant. If longhand notes are taken, the judge shall subscribe a copy and file it with the court within twenty-four hours of the issuance of a warrant.

HISTORY: Add, L 1982, ch 679, § 2, eff Sept 20, 1982.

§ 690.40. Search warrants; determination of application

1. In determining an application for a search warrant the court may examine, under oath, any person whom it believes may possess pertinent information. Any such examination must be either recorded or summarized on the record by the court.

2. If the court is satisfied that there is reasonable cause to believe that property of a kind or character referred to in section 690.10, and described in the application, may be found in or upon the place, premises, vehicle or person designated or described in the application, or, in the case of an application for a search warrant as defined in paragraph (b) of subdivision two of section 690.05, that there is reasonable cause to believe that the person who is the subject of a warrant of arrest, a superior court warrant of arrest, or a bench warrant for a felony may be found at the premises designated in the application, it may grant the application and issue a search warrant

directing a search of the said place, premises, vehicle or person and a seizure of the described property or the described person. If the court is further satisfied that grounds, described in subdivision four of section 690.35, exist for authorizing the search to be made at any hour of the day or night, or without giving notice of the police officer's authority and purpose, it may make the search warrant executable accordingly.

3. When a judge determines to issue a search warrant based upon an oral application, the applicant therefor shall prepare the warrant in accordance with section 690.45 and shall read it, verbatim, to the judge.

> **HISTORY:** Add, L 1970, ch 996, § 1, eff Sept 1, 1971. Sub 2, amd, L 1980, ch 843, § 23, L 1991, ch 504, § 6, eff Nov 1, 1991. Sub 3, add, L 1982, ch 679, § 3, eff Sept 20, 1982. Sub 2, amd, L 1998, ch 424, § 12, eff Jan 1, 1999.

§ 690.45. Search warrants; form and content

A search warrant must contain:

1. The name of the issuing court and, except where the search warrant has been obtained on an oral application, the subscription of the issuing judge; and

2. Where the search warrant has been obtained on an oral application, it shall so indicate and shall state the name of the issuing judge and the time and date on which such judge directed its issuance.

3. The name, department or classification of the police officer to whom it is addressed; and

4. A description of the property which is the subject of the search, or, in the case of a search warrant as defined in paragraph (b) of subdivision two of section 690.05, a description of the person to be searched for; and

5. A designation or description of the place, premises or person to be searched, by means of address, ownership, name or any other means essential to identification with certainty; and

6. A direction that the warrant be executed between the hours of 6:00 A.M. and 9:00 P.M., or, where the court has specially so determined, an authorization for execution thereof at any time of the day or night; and

7. An authorization, where the court has specially so determined, that the executing police officer enter the premises to be searched without giving notice of his authority and purpose; and

8. A direction that the warrant and any property seized pursuant thereto be returned and delivered to the court without unnecessary delay; and

9. In the case of a search warrant as defined in paragraph (b) of subdivision two of section 690.05, a copy of the warrant of arrest and the underlying accusatory instrument.

> **HISTORY:** Add, L 1970, ch 996, § 1, eff Sept 1, 1971, with substance derived from Crim C §§ 797, 799, 801. Sub 1, amd, L 1982, ch 679, § 4, eff Sept 20, 1982. Sub 2, add, L 1982, ch 679, § 5, eff Sept 20, 1982. Former sub 2, amd, L 1980, ch 843, § 24; renumbered sub 3, L 1982, ch 679, § 5, eff Sept 20, 1982. Sub 3, formerly sub 2, amd, L 1980, ch 843, § 24; renumbered sub 3, L 1982, ch 679, § 5, eff Sept 20, 1982. Former sub 3, renumbered sub 4, L 1982, ch 679, § 5, eff Sept 20, 1982. Sub 4, formerly sub 3, renumbered sub 4, L 1982, ch 679, § 5; amd, L 1991, ch 504, § 7, eff Nov 1, 1991. Former sub 4, renumbered sub 5, L 1982, ch 679, § 5, eff Sept 20, 1982. Sub 5, formerly sub 4, renumbered sub 5, L 1982, ch 679, § 5, eff Sept 20, 1982. Former sub 5, renumbered sub 6, L 1982, ch 679, § 5, eff Sept 20, 1982. Sub 6, formerly sub 5, renumbered sub 6, L 1982, ch 679, § 5, eff Sept 20, 1982. Former sub 6, amd, L 1980, ch 843, § 24; renumbered sub 7, L 1982, ch 679, § 5, eff Sept 20, 1982. Sub 7, formerly sub 6, amd, L 1980, ch 843, § 24; renumbered sub 7, L 1982, ch 679, § 5, eff Sept 20, 1982. Former sub 7, renumbered sub 8, L 1982, ch 679, § 5,

eff Sept 20, 1982. Sub 8, formerly sub 7, renumbered sub 8, L 1982, ch 679, § 5; amd, L 1991, ch 504, § 8, eff Nov 1, 1991. Sub 9, add, L 1991, ch 504, § 8, eff Nov 1, 1991. Sub 3, amd, L 1998, ch 424, § 13, eff Jan 1, 1999. Sub 7, amd, L 1998, ch 424, § 13, eff Jan 1, 1999.

§ 690.50. Search warrants; execution thereof

1. In executing a search warrant directing a search of premises or a vehicle, a police officer must, except as provided in subdivision two, give, or make reasonable effort to give, notice of his authority and purpose to an occupant thereof before entry and show him the warrant or a copy thereof upon request. If he is not thereafter admitted, he may forcibly enter such premises or vehicle and may use against any person resisting his entry or search thereof as much physical force, other than deadly physical force, as is necessary to execute the warrant; and he may use deadly physical force if he reasonably believes such to be necessary to defend himself or a third person from what he reasonably believes to be the use or imminent use of deadly physical force.

2. In executing a search warrant directing a search of premises or a vehicle, a police officer need not give notice to anyone of his authority and purpose, as prescribed in subdivision one, but may promptly enter the same if:

    (a) Such premises or vehicle are at the time unoccupied or reasonably believed by the officer to be unoccupied; or

    (b) The search warrant expressly authorizes entry without notice.

3. In executing a search warrant directing or authorizing a search of a person, a police officer must give, or make reasonable effort to give, such person notice of his authority and purpose and show him the warrant or a copy thereof upon request. If such person, or another, thereafter resists or refuses to permit the search, the officer may use as much physical force, other than deadly physical force, as is necessary to execute the warrant; and he may use deadly physical force if he reasonably believes such to be necessary to defend himself or a third person from what he reasonably believes to be the use or imminent use of deadly physical force.

4. Upon seizing property pursuant to a search warrant, a police officer must write and subscribe a receipt itemizing the property taken and containing the name of the court by which the warrant was issued. If property is taken from a person, such receipt must be given to such person. If property is taken from premises or a vehicle, such receipt must be given to the owner, tenant or other person in possession thereof if he is present; or if he is not, the officer must leave such a receipt in the premises or vehicle from which the property was taken.

5. Upon seizing property pursuant to a search warrant, a police officer must without unnecessary delay return to the court the warrant and the property, and must file therewith a written inventory of such property, subscribed and sworn to by such officer.

6. Upon arresting a person during a search for him or her pursuant to a search warrant as defined in paragraph (b) of subdivision two of section 690.05, a police officer shall comply with the terms of the warrant of arrest, superior court warrant of arrest, or bench warrant for a felony, and shall proceed in the manner directed by this chapter. Upon arresting such person, the police officer shall also, without unnecessary delay, file a written statement with the court which issued the search warrant, subscribed and sworn to by such officer, setting forth that the person has been arrested and duly brought before the appropriate court, return to the court the warrant and the property seized in the course of its execution, and file therewith a written inventory of any such property, subscribed and sworn to by such officer.

    HISTORY: Add, L 1970, ch 996, § 1, eff Sept 1, 1971, with substance derived from Crim C §§ 799, 803, 805. Sub 1, amd, L 1980, ch 843, § 25, eff Sept 1, 1980. Sub 2, opening par, amd, L

1980, ch 843, § 26, eff Sept 1, 1980. Sub 3, amd, L 1980, ch 843, § 27, eff Sept 1, 1980. Sub 4, amd, L 1980, ch 843, § 27, eff Sept 1, 1980. Sub 5, amd, L 1980, ch 843, § 27, eff Sept 1, 1980. Sub 6, add, L 1991, ch 504, § 9, eff Nov 1, 1991. Amd, L 1998, ch 424, § 14, eff Jan 1, 1999. Sub 1, amd, L 1998, ch 424, § 14, eff Jan 1, 1999. Sub 2, opening par, amd, L 1998, ch 424, § 14, eff Jan 1, 1999. Sub 3, amd, L 1998, ch 424, § 14, eff Jan 1, 1999. Sub 4, amd, L 1998, ch 424, § 14, eff Jan 1, 1999. Sub 5, amd, L 1998, ch 424, § 14, eff Jan 1, 1999. Sub 6, amd, L 1998, ch 424, § 14, eff Jan 1, 1999.

§ 690.55. Search warrants; dispositions of seized property

1. Upon receiving property seized pursuant to a search warrant, the court must either:

(a) Retain it in the custody of the court pending further disposition thereof pursuant to subdivision two or some other provision of law; or

(b) Direct that it be held in the custody of the person who applied for the warrant, or of the police officer who executed it, or of the governmental or official agency or department by which either such public servant is employed, upon condition that upon order of such court such property be returned thereto or delivered to another court.

2. A local criminal court which retains custody of such property must, upon request of another criminal court in which a criminal action involving or relating to such property is pending, cause it to be delivered thereto.

HISTORY: Add, L 1970, ch 996, § 1, eff Sept 1, 1971. Sub 1, par (b), amd, L 1980, ch 843, § 28, eff Sept 1, 1980. Sub 1, par (b), amd, L 1998, ch 424, § 15, eff Jan 1, 1999.

ARTICLE 700   EAVESDROPPING AND VIDEO SURVEILLANCE WARRANTS

HISTORY: Add, L 1970, ch 996, § 1, eff Sept 1, 1971. Article heading, amd, L 1988, ch 744, § 5, eff Dec 22, 1988.

§ 700.05. Eavesdropping and video surveillance warrants; definitions of terms

As used in this article, the following terms have the following meanings:

1. "Eavesdropping" means "wiretapping", "mechanical overhearing of conversation," or the "intercepting or accessing of an electronic communication", as those terms are defined in section 250.00 of the penal law, but does not include the use of a pen register or trap and trace device when authorized pursuant to article 705 of this chapter.

2. "Eavesdropping warrant" means an order of a justice authorizing or approving eavesdropping.

3. "Intercepted communication" means (a) a telephonic or telegraphic communication which was intentionally overheard or recorded by a person other than the sender or receiver thereof, without the consent of the sender or receiver, by means of any instrument, device or equipment, or (b) a conversation or discussion which was intentionally overheard or recorded, without the consent of at least one party thereto, by a person not present thereat, by means of any instrument, device or equipment; or (c) an electronic communication which was intentionally intercepted or accessed, as that term is defined in section 250.00 of the penal law. The term "contents," when used with respect to a communication, includes any information concerning the identity of the parties to such communications, and the existence, substance, purport, or meaning of that communication. The term "communication" includes conversation and discussion.

3-a. "Telephonic communication", "electronic communication", and "intentionally intercepted or accessed" have the meanings given to those terms by subdivisions three, five, and six respectively, of section 250.00 of the penal law.

4. "Justice," except as otherwise provided herein, means any justice of an appellate division of the judicial department in which the eavesdropping warrant is to be executed, or any justice of the supreme court of the judicial district in which the eavesdropping warrant is to be executed, or any county court judge of the county in which the eavesdropping warrant is to be executed. When the eavesdropping warrant is to authorize the interception of oral communications occurring in a vehicle or wire communications occurring over a telephone located in a vehicle, "justice" means any justice of the supreme court of the judicial department or any county court judge of the county in which the eavesdropping device is to be installed or connected or of any judicial department or county in which communications are expected to be intercepted. When such a justice issues such an eavesdropping warrant, such warrant may be executed and such oral or wire communications may be intercepted anywhere in the state.

5. "Applicant" means a district attorney or the attorney general or if authorized by the attorney general, the deputy attorney general in charge of the organized crime task force. If a district attorney or the attorney general is actually absent or disabled, the term "applicant" includes that person designated to act for him and perform his official function in and during his actual absence or disability.

6. "Law enforcement officer" means any public servant who is empowered by law to conduct an investigation of or to make an arrest for a designated offense, and any attorney authorized by law to prosecute or participate in the prosecution of a designated offense.

7. "Exigent circumstances" means conditions requiring the preservation of secrecy, and whereby there is a reasonable likelihood that a continuing investigation would be thwarted by alerting any of the persons subject to surveillance to the fact that such surveillance had occurred.

8. "Designated offense" means any one or more of the following crimes:

(a) A conspiracy to commit any offense enumerated in the following paragraphs of this subdivision, or an attempt to commit any felony enumerated in the following paragraphs of this subdivision which attempt would itself constitute a felony;

(b) Any of the following felonies: assault in the second degree as defined in section 120.05 of the penal law, assault in the first degree as defined in section 120.10 of the penal law, reckless endangerment in the first degree as defined in section 120.25 of the penal law, promoting a suicide attempt as defined in section 120.30 of the penal law, strangulation in the second degree as defined in section 121.12 of the penal law, strangulation in the first degree as defined in section 121.13 of the penal law, criminally negligent homicide as defined in section 125.10 of the penal law, manslaughter in the second degree as defined in section 125.15 of the penal law, manslaughter in the first degree as defined in section 125.20 of the penal law, murder in the second degree as defined in section 125.25 of the penal law, murder in the first degree as defined in section 125.27 of the penal law, abortion in the second degree as defined in section 125.40 of the penal law, abortion in the first degree as defined in section 125.45 of the penal law, rape in the third degree as defined in section 130.25 of the penal law, rape in the second degree as defined in section 130.30 of the penal law, rape in the first degree as defined in section 130.35 of the penal law, criminal sexual act in the third degree as defined in section 130.40 of the penal law, criminal sexual act in the second degree as defined in section 130.45 of the penal law, criminal sexual act in the first degree as defined in section 130.50 of the penal law, sexual abuse in the first degree as defined in section 130.65 of the penal law, unlawful imprisonment in the first degree as defined in section 135.10 of the penal law, kidnapping in the second degree as defined in section 135.20 of the penal law, kidnapping in the first degree as defined in section 135.25 of the penal law, labor trafficking as defined in section 135.35 of the penal law, custodial interference in the first degree as defined in section 135.50 of the penal law, coercion in the first degree as defined in section 135.65 of the penal law, criminal trespass in the first degree as defined in section 140.17 of the penal law, burglary in the third degree as defined in section 140.20 of the penal law, burglary in the second degree as defined in section 140.25 of the penal law, burglary in the first degree as defined in section 140.30 of the penal law, criminal mischief in the third degree as defined in section 145.05 of the penal law, criminal mischief in the second degree as defined in section 145.10 of the penal law, criminal mischief in the first degree as defined in section 145.12 of the penal law, criminal tampering in the first degree as defined in section 145.20 of the penal law, arson in the fourth degree as defined in section 150.05 of the penal law, arson in the third degree as defined in section 150.10 of the penal law, arson in the second degree as defined in section 150.15 of the penal law, arson in the first degree as defined in section 150.20 of the penal law, grand larceny in the fourth degree as defined in section 155.30 of the penal law, grand larceny in the third degree as defined in section 155.35 of the penal law, grand larceny in the second degree as defined in section 155.40 of the penal law, grand larceny in the first degree as defined in section 155.42 of the penal law, health care fraud in the fourth degree as defined in section 177.10 of the penal law, health care fraud in the third degree as defined in section 177.15 of the penal law, health care fraud in the second degree as defined in section 177.20 of the penal law, health care fraud in the first degree as defined in section 177.25 of the penal law, robbery in the third degree as defined in section 160.05 of the penal law, robbery in the second degree as defined in section 160.10 of the penal law, robbery in the first degree as defined in section 160.15 of the penal law, unlawful use of secret scientific material as defined in section 165.07 of the penal law, criminal possession of stolen property in the fourth degree as defined in section 165.45 of the penal law, criminal possession of stolen property in the third degree as defined in section 165.50 of the penal law, criminal possession of stolen property in the second degree as defined by section 165.52 of the penal law, criminal possession of stolen property in the first degree as defined by section 165.54 of the penal law, trademark counterfeiting in the second degree as defined in section 165.72 of the penal law, trademark counterfeiting in the first degree as defined in section 165.73 of the penal law, forgery in the second degree as defined in section 170.10 of the penal law, forgery in the first degree as defined in section 170.15 of the penal law, criminal possession of a forged instrument in the second degree as defined in section 170.25 of the penal law, criminal possession of a forged instrument in the first degree as defined in section 170.30 of the penal law, criminal possession of forgery devices as defined in section 170.40 of the penal law, falsifying business records in the first degree as defined in section 175.10 of the penal law, tampering with public records in the first degree as defined in section 175.25 of the penal law, offering a false instrument for filing in the first degree as defined in section 175.35 of the penal law, issuing a false certificate as defined in section 175.40 of the penal law, criminal diversion of prescription medications and prescriptions in the second degree as defined in section 178.20 of the penal law, criminal diversion of prescription medications and prescriptions in the first degree as defined in section 178.25 of the penal law, residential mortgage fraud in the fourth degree as defined in section 187.10 of the penal law, residential mortgage fraud in the third degree as defined in section 187.15 of the penal law, residential mortgage fraud in the second degree as defined in section 187.20 of the penal law, residential mortgage fraud in the first degree as defined in section 187.25 of the penal law, escape in the second degree as defined in section 205.10 of the penal law, escape in the first degree as defined in section 205.15 of the penal law, absconding from temporary release in the first degree as defined in section 205.17 of the penal law, promoting prison contraband in the first degree as defined in section 205.25 of the penal law, hindering prosecution in the second degree as defined in section 205.60 of the penal law, hindering prosecution in the first degree as defined in section 205.65 of the penal law, sex trafficking as defined in section 230.34 of the penal law, criminal possession of a weapon in the third degree as defined in subdivisions two, three and five of section 265.02 of the penal law, criminal possession of a weapon in the second degree as defined in section 265.03 of the penal law, criminal possession of a weapon in the first degree as defined in section 265.04 of the penal law, manufacture, transport, disposition and defacement of weapons and dangerous instruments and appliances defined as felonies in subdivisions one, two, and three of section 265.10 of the penal law, sections 265.11, 265.12 and 265.13 of the penal law, or prohibited use of weapons as defined in subdivision two of section 265.35 of the penal law, relating to firearms and other dangerous weapons, or failure to disclose the origin of a recording in the first degree as defined in section 275.40 of the penal law;

(c) Criminal possession of a controlled substance in the seventh degree as defined in section 220.03 of the penal law, criminal possession of a controlled substance in the fifth degree as defined in section 220.06 of the penal law, criminal possession of a controlled substance in the fourth degree as defined in section 220.09 of the penal law, criminal possession of a controlled substance in the third degree as defined in section 220.16 of the penal law, criminal possession of a controlled substance in the second degree as defined in section 220.18 of the penal law, criminal possession of a controlled substance in the first degree as defined in section 220.21 of the penal law, criminal sale of a controlled substance in the fifth degree as defined in section 220.31 of the penal law, criminal sale of a controlled substance in the fourth degree as defined in section 220.34 of the penal law, criminal sale of a controlled substance in the third degree as defined in section 220.39 of the penal law, criminal sale of a controlled substance in the second degree as defined in section 220.41 of the penal law, criminal sale of a controlled substance in the first degree as defined in section

220.43 of the penal law, criminally possessing a hypodermic instrument as defined in section 220.45 of the penal law, criminal sale of a prescription for a controlled substance or a controlled substance by a practitioner or pharmacist as defined in section 220.65 of the penal law, criminal possession of methamphetamine manufacturing material in the second degree as defined in section 220.70 of the penal law, criminal possession of methamphetamine manufacturing material in the first degree as defined in section 220.71 of the penal law, criminal possession of precursors of methamphetamine as defined in section 220.72 of the penal law, unlawful manufacture of methamphetamine in the third degree as defined in section 220.73 of the penal law, unlawful manufacture of methamphetamine in the second degree as defined in section 220.74 of the penal law, unlawful manufacture of methamphetamine in the first degree as defined in section 220.75 of the penal law, unlawful disposal of methamphetamine laboratory material as defined in section 220.76 of the penal law, operating as a major trafficker as defined in section 220.77 of the penal law, criminal possession of marihuana in the first degree as defined in section 221.30 of the penal law, criminal sale of marihuana in the first degree as defined in section 221.55 of the penal law, promoting gambling in the second degree as defined in section 225.05 of the penal law, promoting gambling in the first degree as defined in section 225.10 of the penal law, possession of gambling records in the second degree as defined in section 225.15 of the penal law, possession of gambling records in the first degree as defined in section 225.20 of the penal law, and possession of a gambling device as defined in section 225.30 of the penal law;

(d) Commercial bribing, commercial bribe receiving, bribing a labor official, bribe receiving by a labor official, sports bribing and sports bribe receiving, as defined in article one hundred eighty of the penal law;

(e) Criminal usury, as defined in article one hundred ninety of the penal law;

(f) Bribery in the third degree, bribery in the second degree, bribery in the first degree, bribe receiving in the third degree, bribe receiving in the second degree, bribe receiving in the first degree, bribe giving for public office, bribe receiving for public office and corrupt use of position or authority, as defined in article two hundred of the penal law;

(g) Bribing a witness, bribe receiving by a witness, bribing a juror and bribe receiving by a juror, as defined in article two hundred fifteen of the penal law;

(h) Promoting prostitution in the first degree, as defined in section 230.32 of the penal law, promoting prostitution in the second degree, as defined by subdivision one of section 230.30 of the penal law;

(i) Riot in the first degree and criminal anarchy, as defined in article two hundred forty of the penal law;

(j) Eavesdropping, as defined in article two hundred fifty of the penal law;

(k) Any of the acts designated as felonies in subdivisions two and four of section four hundred eighty-one of the tax law, which section relates to penalties under the tax on cigarettes imposed by article twenty of such law, and any of the acts designated as felonies in subdivision c of section 11-1317 of the administrative code of the city of New York, which section relates to penalties under the cigarette tax imposed by chapter thirteen of title eleven of such code.

(l) Scheme to defraud in the first degree as defined in article one hundred ninety of the penal law.

(m) Any of the acts designated as felonies in section three hundred fifty-two-c of the general business law.

(n) Any of the acts designated as felonies in title twenty-seven of article seventy-one of the environmental conservation law.

(o) Money laundering in the first degree, as defined in section 470.20 of the penal law, money laundering in the second degree as defined in section 470.15 of the penal law, money laundering in the third degree as defined in section 470.10 of such law, and money laundering in the fourth degree as defined in section 470.05 of such law, where the property involved represents or is represented to be the proceeds of specified criminal conduct which itself constitutes a designated offense within the meaning of this subdivision.

(p) Stalking in the second degree as defined in section 120.55 of the penal law, and stalking in the first degree as defined in section 120.60 of the penal law.

(q) Soliciting or providing support for an act of terrorism in the second degree as defined in section 490.10 of the penal law, soliciting or providing support for an act of terrorism in the first degree as defined in section 490.15 of the penal law, making a terroristic threat as defined in section 490.20 of the penal law, crime of terrorism as defined in section 490.25 of the penal law, hindering prosecution of terrorism in the second degree as defined in section 490.30 of the penal law, hindering prosecution of terrorism in the first degree as defined in section 490.35 of the penal law, criminal possession of a chemical weapon or biological weapon in the third degree as defined in section 490.37 of the penal law, criminal possession of a chemical weapon or biological weapon in the second degree as defined in section 490.40 of the penal law, criminal possession of a chemical weapon or biological weapon in the first degree as defined in section 490.45 of the penal law, criminal use of a chemical weapon or biological weapon in the third degree as defined in section 490.47 of the penal law, criminal use of a chemical weapon or biological weapon in the second degree as defined in section 490.50 of the penal law, and criminal use of a chemical weapon or biological weapon in the first degree as defined in section 490.55 of the penal law.

(r) Falsely reporting an incident in the second degree as defined in section 240.55 of the penal law, falsely reporting an incident in the first degree as defined in section 240.60 of the penal law, placing a false bomb in the second degree as defined in section 240.61 of the penal law, placing a false bomb in the first degree as defined in section 240.62 of the penal law, and placing a false bomb in a sports stadium or arena, mass transportation facility or enclosed shopping mall as defined in section 240.63 of the penal law.

(s) Identity theft in the second degree, as defined in section 190.79 of the penal law, identity theft in the first degree, as defined in section 190.80 of the penal law, unlawful possession of personal identification information in the second degree, as defined in section 190.82 of the penal law, and unlawful possession of personal identification information in the first degree, as defined in section 190.83 of the penal law.

(t) Menacing a police officer or peace officer as defined in section 120.18 of the penal law; aggravated criminally negligent homicide as defined in section 125.11 of the penal law; aggravated manslaughter in the second degree as defined in section 125.21 of the penal law; aggravated manslaughter in the first degree as defined in section 125.22 of the penal law; aggravated murder as defined in section 125.26 of the penal law.

CPL

(u) Any felony defined in article four hundred ninety-six of the penal law.

9. "Video surveillance" means the intentional visual observation by law enforcement of a person by means of a television camera or other electronic device that is part of a television transmitting apparatus, whether or not such observation is recorded on film or video tape, without the consent of that person or another person thereat and under circumstances in which such observation in the absence of a video surveillance warrant infringes upon such person's reasonable expectation of privacy under the constitution of this state or of the United States.

10. "Video surveillance warrant" means an order of a justice authorizing or approving video surveillance.

HISTORY: Add, L 1970, ch 996, § 1, eff Sept 1, 1971; amd, L 1972, ch 586, § 1, eff May 24, 1972, L 1973, ch 276, § 28, L 1978, ch 22, §§ 1, 2, eff Sept 1, 1978, L 1979, ch 410, § 28, L 1981, ch 565, § 1, eff Sept 1, 1981, L 1983, ch 105, § 1, eff May 17, 1983, L 1983, ch 646, § 1, L 1984, ch 919, § 1, eff Nov 1, 1984, L 1986, ch 671, § 26, eff Nov 1, 1986, L 1988, ch 744, §§ 6–10, eff Dec 22, 1988, L 1985, ch 611, § 1, L 1990, ch 154, § 1, eff May 17, 1990, L 1991, ch 496, § 7, L 1992, ch 490, § 2, L 1995, ch 1, § 28, eff Sept 1, 1995, L 1998, ch 2, § 40, eff Nov 1, 1998, L 1999, ch 635, § 5, eff Dec 1, 1999, L 2000, ch 489, § 2, eff Nov 1, 2000, L 2001, ch 300, § 8, eff Sept 17, 2001, L 2001, ch 301, § 9, eff Sept 17, 2001, L 2001, ch 302, § 4, eff Sept 17, 2001, L 2002, ch 619, § 6, eff Nov 1, 2002, L 2003, ch 246, § 49, eff Nov 1, 2003, L 2004, ch 1, § 3 (Part A), eff July 23, 2004, L 2005, ch 394, § 6, eff Oct 1, 2005, L 2005, ch 765, § 14, eff Dec 21, 2005, L 2006, ch 442, § 11, eff Nov 1, 2006, L 2007, ch 74, § 8, eff Nov 1, 2007, L 2007, ch 568, § 2, eff Nov 1, 2007, L 2007, ch 570, § 1, eff Nov 1, 2007, L 2008, ch 472, § 20, eff Nov 1, 2008, L 2009, ch 56, § 11 (Part AAA), eff Nov 1, 2009, L 2010, ch 405, § 4, eff Nov 11, 2010, L 2014, ch 37, § 1, eff June 23, 2014, L 2014, ch 55, §§ 9, 10 (Part H, Subpart A), eff April 30, 2014.

§ 700.10. Eavesdropping and video surveillance warrants; in general

1. Under circumstances prescribed in this article, a justice may issue an eavesdropping warrant or a video surveillance warrant upon ex parte application of an applicant who is authorized by law to investigate, prosecute or participate in the prosecution of the particular designated offense which is the subject of the application.

2. No eavesdropping or video surveillance warrant may authorize or approve the interception of any communication or the conducting of any video surveillance for any period longer than is necessary to achieve the objective of the authorization, or in any event longer than thirty days. Such thirty day period shall begin on the date designated in the warrant as the effective date, which date may be no later than ten days after the warrant is issued.

HISTORY: Add, L 1970, ch 996, § 1; amd, L 1988, ch 744, § 11, eff Dec 22, 1988. Section heading, amd, L 1988, ch 744, § 11, eff Dec 22, 1988. Sub 1, amd, L 1972, ch 586, § 2, L 1988, ch 744, § 11, eff Dec 22, 1988. Sub 2, amd, L 1988, ch 744, § 11, eff Dec 22, 1988.

§ 700.15. Eavesdropping and video surveillance warrants; when issuable

An eavesdropping or video surveillance warrant may issue only:

1. Upon an appropriate application made in conformity with this article; and

2. Upon probable cause to believe that a particularly described person is committing, has committed, or is about to commit a particular designated offense; and

3. Upon probable cause to believe that particular communications concerning such offense will be obtained through eavesdropping, or upon probable cause to believe that particular observations concerning such offense will be obtained through video surveillance; and

4. Upon a showing that normal investigative procedures have been tried and have failed, or reasonably appear to be unlikely to succeed if tried, or to be too dangerous to employ; and

5. Upon probable cause to believe that the facilities from which, or the place where, the communications are to be intercepted or the video surveillance is to be conducted, are being used, or are about to be used, in connection with the commission of such offense, or are leased to, listed in the name of, or commonly used by such person.

HISTORY: Add, L 1970, ch 996, § 1; amd, L 1988, ch 744, § 12, eff Dec 22, 1988. Section heading, amd, L 1988, ch 744, § 12, eff Dec 22, 1988. Opening par, amd, L 1988, ch 744, § 12, eff Dec 22, 1988. Sub 3, amd, L 1988, ch 744, § 12, eff Dec 22, 1988. Sub 5, amd, L 1988, ch 744, § 12, eff Dec 22, 1988.

§ 700.20. Eavesdropping and video surveillance warrants; application

1. An ex parte application for an eavesdropping or video surveillance warrant must be made to a justice in writing, except as provided in section 700.21 of this article, and must be subscribed and sworn to by an applicant.

2. The application must contain:

(a) The identity of the applicant and a statement of the applicant's authority to make such application; and

(b) A full and complete statement of the facts and circumstances relied upon by the applicant, to justify his belief that an eavesdropping or video surveillance warrant should be issued, including (i) a statement of facts establishing probable cause to believe that a particular designated offense has been, is being, or is about to be committed, (ii) a particular description of the nature and location of the facilities from which or the place where the communication is to be intercepted or the video surveillance is to be conducted, (iii) a particular description of the type of the communications sought to be intercepted or of the observations sought to be made, and (iv) the identity of the person, if known, committing such designated offense and whose communications are to be intercepted or who is to be the subject of the video surveillance; and

(c) A statement that such communications or observations are not otherwise legally privileged; and

(d) A full and complete statement of facts establishing that normal investigative procedures have been tried and have failed or reasonably appear to be unlikely to succeed if tried or to be too dangerous to employ, to obtain the evidence sought; and

(e) A statement of the period of time for which the eavesdropping or video surveillance is required to be maintained. If the nature of the investigation is such that the authorization for eavesdropping or video surveillance should not automatically terminate when the described type of communication has been first obtained or when the described type of observation has been first made, a particular description of facts establishing probable cause to believe that additional communications or observations of the same type will occur thereafter; and

(f) A full and complete statement of the facts concerning all previous applications, known to the applicant, for an eavesdropping or video surveillance warrant involving any of the same persons, facilities or places specified in the application, and the action taken by the justice on each such application.

3. Allegations of fact in the application may be based either upon the personal knowledge of the applicant or upon information and belief. If the applicant personally knows the facts alleged, it must be so stated. If the facts stated in the application are derived in whole or part from the statements of persons other than the applicant, the sources of such facts must be either disclosed

or described, and the application must contain facts establishing the existence and reliability of the informants or the reliability of the information supplied by them. The application must also state, so far as possible, the basis of the informant's knowledge or belief. Affidavits of persons other than the applicant may be submitted in conjunction with the application if they tend to support any fact or conclusion alleged therein. Such accompanying affidavits may be based either on personal knowledge of the affiant, or information and belief with the source thereof and the reason therefor specified.

> **HISTORY:** Add, L 1970, ch 996, § 1; amd, L 1988, ch 744, § 13, eff Dec 22, 1988. Section heading, amd, L 1988, ch 744, § 13, eff Dec 22, 1988. Sub 1, amd, L 1984, ch 897, § 1, L 1988, ch 744, § 13, eff Dec 22, 1988. Sub 2, amd, L 1988, ch 744, § 13, eff Dec 22, 1988. Sub 2, par (b), amd, L 1988, ch 744, § 13, eff Dec 22, 1988. Sub 2, par (c), amd, L 1988, ch 744, § 13, eff Dec 22, 1988. Sub 2, par (e), amd, L 1988, ch 744, § 13, eff Dec 22, 1988. Sub 2, par (f), amd, L 1988, ch 744, § 13, eff Dec 22, 1988.

§ 700.21. Temporary authorization for eavesdropping or video surveillance in emergency situations

1. In an emergency situation where imminent danger of death or serious physical injury exists and, under the circumstances, it is impractical for the applicant to prepare a written application without risk of such death or injury occurring, an application for an eavesdropping or video surveillance warrant need not be in writing but may be communicated to a justice by telephone, radio or other means of electronic communication.

2. Where an oral application for an eavesdropping or video surveillance warrant is made, the applicant therefor must identify himself and the purpose of his communication or observation, after being sworn as provided in subdivision three of this section. The application must meet the requirements of section 700.20 of this article and provide the same allegations of fact required by that section.

3. Upon being advised that an oral application for an eavesdropping or video surveillance warrant is being made, a justice shall place under oath the applicant and any other person providing information in support of the application. Such oath or oaths and all of the remaining communication must be recorded, either by means of a voice recording device or verbatim stenographic or verbatim longhand notes. If a voice recording device is used or a stenographic record made, the justice must have the record transcribed, certify to the accuracy of the transcription and file the original record and transcription with the court within twenty-four hours of the issuance of a warrant. If longhand notes are taken, the justice shall subscribe a copy and file it with the court within twenty-four hours of the issuance of a warrant.

4. Upon oral application, the court may, where it finds that an emergency situation exists and that the requirements of section 700.15 of this article have been satisfied, issue a temporary eavesdropping or video surveillance warrant authorizing eavesdropping or video surveillance for a period not to exceed twenty-four hours. Such eavesdropping or video surveillance warrant shall be executed in the manner prescribed by this article. The twenty-four hour period may not be extended nor may a temporary warrant be renewed except by written application in conformity with the requirements of this article.

> **HISTORY:** Add, L 1984, ch 897, § 2; amd, L 1988, ch 744, § 14, eff Dec 22, 1988. Section heading, amd, L 1988, ch 744, § 14, eff Dec 22, 1988. Sub 1, amd, L 1988, ch 744, § 14, eff Dec 22, 1988. Sub 2, amd, L 1988, ch 744, § 14, eff Dec 22, 1988. Sub 3, amd, L 1988, ch 744, § 14, eff Dec 22, 1988. Sub 4, amd, L 1988, ch 744, § 14, eff Dec 22, 1988.

§ 700.25. Eavesdropping warrants; determination of application

1. If the application conforms to section 700.20, the justice may require the applicant to furnish

additional testimony or documentary evidence in support of the application. He may examine, under oath, any person for the purpose of determining whether grounds exist for the issuance of the warrant pursuant to section 700.15. Any such examination must be either recorded or summarized in writing.

2. If the justice determines on the basis of the facts submitted by the applicant that grounds exist for the issuance of an eavesdropping warrant pursuant to section 700.15, the justice may grant the application and issue an eavesdropping warrant, in accordance with section 700.30.

3. If the application does not conform to section 700.20, or if the justice is not satisfied that grounds exist for the issuance of an eavesdropping warrant, the application must be denied.

HISTORY: Add, L 1970, ch 996, § 1, eff Sept 1, 1971.

§ 700.30.   Eavesdropping and video surveillance warrants; form and content

An eavesdropping or video surveillance warrant must contain:

1. The name of the applicant, date of issuance, and the subscription and title of the issuing justice; and

2. The identity of the person, if known, whose communications are to be intercepted or who is to be the subject of video surveillance; and

3. The nature and location of the communications facilities as to which, or the place where, authority to intercept or conduct video surveillance is granted; and

4. A particular description of the type of communications sought to be intercepted or of the type of observations to be made, and a statement of the particular designated offense to which it relates; and

5. The identity of the law enforcement agency authorized to intercept the communications or conduct the video surveillance; and

6. The period of time during which such interception or observation is authorized, including a statement as to whether or not the interception or video surveillance shall automatically terminate when the described communication has been first obtained or the described observation has been first made; and

7. A provision that the authorization to intercept or conduct video surveillance shall be executed as soon as practicable, shall be conducted in such a way as to minimize the interception of communications or the making of observations not otherwise subject to eavesdropping or video surveillance under this article, and must terminate upon attainment of the authorized objective, or in any event in thirty days; and

8. An express authorization to make secret entry upon a private place or premises to install an eavesdropping or video surveillance device, if such entry is necessary to execute the warrant; and

9. An order authorizing eavesdropping or video surveillance may direct that providers of wire or electronic communication services furnish the applicant information, facilities, or technical assistance necessary to accomplish the interception unobtrusively and with a minimum of interference with the services that the service provider accords the party whose communications are to be intercepted. The order shall not direct the service providers to perform the intercept or use the premises of the service provider for such activity.

HISTORY: Add, L 1970, ch 996, § 1; amd, L 1988, ch 744, § 15, eff Dec 22, 1988. Section heading, amd, L 1988, ch 744, § 15, eff Dec 22, 1988. Opening par, amd, L 1988, ch 744, § 15, eff Dec 22, 1988. Sub 2, amd, L 1988, ch 744, § 15, eff Dec 22, 1988. Sub 3, amd, L 1988, ch 744, § 15, eff Dec 22, 1988. Sub 4, amd, L 1988, ch 744, § 15, eff Dec 22, 1988. Sub 5, amd, L 1988, ch 744, § 15, eff Dec 22, 1988. Sub 6, amd, L 1988, ch 744, § 15, eff Dec 22, 1988. Sub 7, amd, L 1988, ch 744, § 15, eff Dec 22, 1988. Sub 8, amd, L 1988, ch 744, § 15, eff Dec 22, 1988. Sub 9, add, L 1988, ch 744, § 15, eff Dec 22, 1988.

§ 700.35. Eavesdropping and video surveillance warrants; manner and time of execution

1. An eavesdropping or video surveillance warrant must be executed according to its terms by a law enforcement officer who is a member of the law enforcement agency authorized in the warrant to intercept the communications or conduct the video surveillance.

2. Upon termination of the authorization in the warrant, eavesdropping or video surveillance must cease and as soon as practicable thereafter any device installed for such purpose either must be removed or must be permanently inactivated as soon as practicable by any means approved by the issuing justice. Entry upon a private place or premise for the removal or permanent inactivation of such device is deemed to be authorized by the warrant.

3. The contents of any communication intercepted or of any observation made by any means authorized by this article must, if possible, be recorded on tape or wire or other comparable device. The recording of the contents of any such communication or observation must be done in such way as will protect the recording from editing or other alterations.

4. In the event an intercepted communication is in a code or foreign language, and the services of an expert in that foreign language or code cannot reasonably be obtained during the interception period, where the warrant so authorizes and in a manner specified therein, the minimization required by subdivision seven of section 700.30 of this article may be accomplished as soon as practicable after such interception.

5. A good faith reliance by a provider of a wire or electronic communication service upon the validity of a court order issued pursuant to this article is a complete defense against any civil cause of action or criminal action based solely on a failure to comply with this article.

HISTORY: Add, L 1970, ch 996, § 1; amd, L 1988, ch 744, § 16, eff Dec 22, 1988. Section heading, amd, L 1988, ch 744, § 16, eff Dec 22, 1988. Sub 1, amd, L 1988, ch 744, § 16, eff Dec 22, 1988. Sub 2, amd, L 1988, ch 744, § 16, eff Dec 22, 1988. Sub 3, amd, L 1988, ch 744, § 16, eff Dec 22, 1988. Sub 4, add, L 1988, ch 744, § 16, eff Dec 22, 1988. Sub 5, add, L 1988, ch 744, § 16, eff Dec 22, 1988.

§ 700.40. Eavesdropping and video surveillance warrants; order of extension

At any time prior to the expiration of an eavesdropping or video surveillance warrant, the applicant may apply to the issuing justice, or, if he is unavailable, to another justice, for an order of extension. The period of extension shall be no longer than the justice deems necessary to achieve the purposes for which it was granted and in no event longer than thirty days. The application for an order of extension must conform in all respects to the provisions of section 700.20 and, in addition, must contain a statement setting forth the results thus far obtained from the interception, or a reasonable explanation of the failure to obtain such results. The provisions of sections 700.15 and 700.25 are applicable in the determination of such application. The order of extension must conform in all respects to the provisions of section 700.30. In the execution of such order of extension the provisions of section 700.35 are applicable.

HISTORY: Add, L 1970, ch 996, § 1; amd, L 1988, ch 744, § 17, eff Dec 22, 1988. Section heading, amd, L 1988, ch 744, § 17, eff Dec 22, 1988.

§ 700.50. Eavesdropping and video surveillance warrants; progress reports and notice

1. An eavesdropping or video surveillance warrant may require reports to be made to the issuing justice showing what progress has been made toward achievement of the authorized objective and the need for continued eavesdropping or video surveillance. Such reports shall be made at such intervals as the justice may require.

2. Immediately upon the expiration of the period of an eavesdropping or video surveillance warrant, the recordings of communications or observations made pursuant to subdivision three of section 700.35 must be made available to the issuing justice and sealed under his directions.

3. Within a reasonable time, but in no case later than ninety days after termination of an eavesdropping or video surveillance warrant, or expiration of an extension order, except as otherwise provided in subdivision four, written notice of the fact and date of the issuance of the eavesdropping or video surveillance warrant, and of the period of authorized eavesdropping or video surveillance, and of the fact that during such period communications were or were not intercepted or observation were or were not made, must be served upon the person named in the warrant and such other parties to the intercepted communications or subjects of the video surveillance as the justice may determine in his discretion is in the interest of justice. Service reasonably calculated to give affected parties the notice required by this subdivision shall be effected within the time limits provided for herein and in a manner prescribed by the justice. The justice, upon the filing of a motion by any person served with such notice, may in his discretion make available to such person or his counsel for inspection such portions of the intercepted communications or video surveillance, applications and warrants as the justice determines to be in the interest of justice.

4. On a showing of exigent circumstances to the issuing justice, the service of the notice required by subdivision three may be postponed by order of the justice for a reasonable period of time. Renewals of an order of postponement may be obtained on a new showing of exigent circumstances.

HISTORY: Add, L 1970, ch 996, § 1; amd, L 1988, ch 744, § 18, eff Dec 22, 1988. Section heading, amd, L 1988, ch 744, § 18, eff Dec 22, 1988. Sub 1, amd, L 1988, ch 744, § 18, eff Dec 22, 1988. Sub 2, amd, L 1988, ch 744, § 18, eff Dec 22, 1988. Sub 3, amd, L 1986, ch 388, § 1; L 1988, ch 744, § 18, eff Dec 22, 1988.

§ 700.55. Eavesdropping and video surveillance warrants; custody of warrants, applications and recordings

1. Applications made and warrants issued under this article shall be sealed by the justice. Any eavesdropping or video surveillance warrant, together with a copy of papers upon which the application is based, shall be delivered to and retained by the applicant as authority for the eavesdropping or video surveillance authorized therein. A copy of such eavesdropping or video surveillance warrant, together with all the original papers upon which the application was based, must be retained by the justice issuing the same, and, in the event of the denial of an application for such an eavesdropping or video surveillance warrant, a copy of the papers upon which the application was based must be retained by the justice denying the same. Such applications and warrants may be disclosed only upon a showing of good cause before a court and may not be destroyed except on order of the issuing or denying justice, and in any event must be kept for ten years.

2. Custody of the recordings made pursuant to subdivision three of section 700.35 may be wherever the justice orders. They may not be destroyed except upon an order of the justice who issued the warrant and in any event must be kept for ten years. Duplicate recordings may be made

for use or disclosure pursuant to the provisions of subdivisions one and two of section 700.65 for investigations.

> **HISTORY:** Add, L 1970, ch 996, § 1, eff Sept 1, 1971. Section heading, amd, L 1988, ch 744, § 19, eff Dec 22, 1988. Sub 1, amd, L 1988, ch 744, § 19, eff Dec 22, 1988.

§ 700.60. Eavesdropping warrants; reports to the administrative office of the United States courts

1. Within thirty days after the termination of an eavesdropping warrant or the expiration of an extension order, the issuing or denying justice must submit such report to the administrative office of the United States courts as is required by federal law.

2. In January of each year, the attorney general and each district attorney must submit such report to the administrative office of the United States courts as is required by federal law.

> **HISTORY:** Add, L 1970, ch 996, § 1; amd, L 1974, ch 615, § 10, eff May 30, 1974. Section heading, amd, L 1985, ch 421, § 1, eff July 19, 1985. Sub 1, amd, L 1985, ch 421, § 1, eff July 19, 1985. Sub 2, amd, L 1985, ch 421, § 1, eff July 19, 1985.

§ 700.65. Eavesdropping and video surveillance warrants; disclosure and use of information; order of amendment

1. Any law enforcement officer who, by any means authorized by this article, has obtained knowledge of the contents of any intercepted communication or video surveillance, or evidence derived therefrom, may disclose such contents to another law enforcement officer to the extent that such disclosure is appropriate to the proper performance of the official duties of the officer making or receiving the disclosure.

2. Any law enforcement officer who, by any means authorized by this article, has obtained knowledge of the contents of any intercepted communication or video surveillance, or evidence derived therefrom, may use such contents to the extent such use is appropriate to the proper performance of his official duties.

3. Any person who has received, by any means authorized by this article, any information concerning a communication or video surveillance, or evidence derived therefrom, intercepted or conducted in accordance with the provisions of this article, may disclose the contents of that communication or video surveillance, or such derivative evidence, while giving testimony under oath in any criminal proceeding in any court, in any grand jury proceeding or in any action commenced pursuant to article thirteen-A or thirteen-B of the civil practice law and rules; provided, however, that the presence of the seal provided for by subdivision two of section 700.50, or a satisfactory explanation of the absence thereof, shall be a prerequisite for the use or disclosure of the contents of any communication or video surveillance, or evidence derived therefrom; and provided further, however, that where a criminal court of competent jurisdiction has ordered exclusion or suppression of the contents of an intercepted communication or video surveillance, or evidence derived therefrom, such determination shall be binding in an action commenced pursuant to article thirteen-A or thirteen-B of the civil practice law and rules.

4. When a law enforcement officer, while engaged in intercepting communications or conducting video surveillance in the manner authorized by this article, intercepts a communication or makes an observation which was not otherwise sought and which constitutes evidence of any crime that has been, is being or is about to be committed, the contents of such communications or observation, and evidence derived therefrom, may be disclosed or used as provided in subdivisions one and two. Such contents and any evidence derived therefrom may be used under subdivision three when a justice amends the eavesdropping or video surveillance warrant to include such

contents. The application for such amendment must be made by the applicant as soon as practicable by giving notice to the court of the interception of the communication or the making of the observation and of the contents of such interception or observation; provided that during the period in which the eavesdropping or video surveillance is continuing, such notice must be given within ten days after probable cause exists to believe that a crime not named in the warrant has been, is being, or is about to be committed, or at the time an application for an order of extension is made pursuant to section 700.40 of this article, if such probable cause then exists, whichever is earlier. If the justice finds that such contents were otherwise intercepted in accordance with the provisions of this article, he may grant the application.

> **HISTORY:** Add, L 1970, ch 996, § 1; amd, L 1988, ch 744, § 20, eff Dec 22, 1988. Section heading, amd, L 1988, ch 744, § 20, eff Dec 22, 1988. Sub 1, amd, L 1988, ch 744, § 20, eff Dec 22, 1988. Sub 2, amd, L 1988, ch 744, § 20, eff Dec 22, 1988. Sub 3, amd, L 1986, ch 237, § 1, L 1988, ch 744, § 20, eff Dec 22, 1988. Sub 4, amd, L 1988, ch 744, § 20, eff Dec 22, 1988.

§ 700.70. Eavesdropping warrants; notice before use of evidence

The contents of any intercepted communication, or evidence derived therefrom, may not be received in evidence or otherwise disclosed upon a trial of a defendant unless the people, within fifteen days after arraignment and before the commencement of the trial, furnish the defendant with a copy of the eavesdropping warrant, and accompanying application, under which interception was authorized or approved. This fifteen day period may be extended by the trial court upon good cause shown if it finds that the defendant will not be prejudiced by the delay in receiving such papers.

> **HISTORY:** Add, L 1970, ch 996, § 1; amd, L 1976, ch 194, § 2, eff Sept 1, 1976.

ARTICLE 705   PEN REGISTERS AND TRAP AND TRACE DEVICES

> **HISTORY:** Add, L 1988, ch 744, § 21, eff Dec 22, 1988.

§ 705.00. Definitions

As used in this article, the following terms have the following meanings:

1. "Pen register" means a device which records or decodes electronic or other impulses which identify the numbers dialed or otherwise transmitted on the telephone line to which such device is attached, but such term does not include any device used by a provider or customer of a wire or electronic communication service for billing, or recording as an incident to billing, for communications services provided by such provider or any device used by a provider or customer of a wire communication service for cost accounting or other like purposes in the ordinary course of its business.

2. "Trap and trace device" means a device which captures the incoming electronic or other impulses which identify the originating number of an instrument or device from which a wire or electronic communication was transmitted.

3. "Applicant" means a district attorney, an assistant district attorney, and when empowered by law to conduct an investigation of or to prosecute or participate in the prosecution of a designated crime, the attorney general, an assistant attorney general, the deputy attorney general in charge of the statewide organized crime task force, or an assistant deputy attorney general of such task force.

4. "Law enforcement agency" means any agency which is empowered by law to conduct an investigation or to make an arrest for a felony, and any agency which is authorized by law to prosecute or participate in the prosecution of a felony.

5. "Designated crime" means any crime included within the definition of a "designated offense" in subdivision eight of section 700.05 of this chapter, any criminal act as defined in subdivision one of section 460.10 of the penal law, bail jumping in the first and second degree as defined in sections 215.57 and 215.56 of such law, or aggravated harassment as defined in subdivisions one and two of section 240.30 of such law.

6. "Justice" means justice as defined in subdivision four of section 700.05 of this chapter.

HISTORY: Add, L 1988, ch 744, § 21, eff Dec 22, 1988.

§ 705.05. Pen register and trap and trace authorizations; in general

Under circumstances prescribed in this article, a justice may issue an order authorizing the use of a pen register or a trap and trace device upon ex parte application of an applicant who is authorized by law to investigate, prosecute or participate in the prosecution of the designated crimes which are the subject of the application.

HISTORY: Add, L 1988, ch 744, § 21, eff Dec 22, 1988.

§ 705.10. Orders authorizing the use of a pen register or a trap and trace device; when issuable

An order authorizing the use of a pen register or a trap and trace device may issue only:

1. Upon an appropriate application made in conformity with this article; and

2. Upon a determination that an application sets forth specific, articulable facts, warranting the applicant's reasonable suspicion that a designated crime has been, is being, or is about to be committed and demonstrating that the information likely to be obtained by use of a pen register or trap and trace device is or will be relevant to an ongoing criminal investigation of such designated crime.

HISTORY: Add, L 1988, ch 744, § 21, eff Dec 22, 1988.

§ 705.15. Application for an order authorizing the use of a pen register or a trap and trace device

1. An ex parte application for an order or an extension of an order authorizing the use of a pen register or a trap and trace device must be made to a justice in writing, and must be subscribed and sworn to by the applicant.

2. The application must contain:

(a) The identity of the applicant and the identity of the law enforcement agency conducting the investigation; and

(b) A statement of facts and circumstances sufficient to justify the applicant's belief that an order authorizing the use of a pen register or a trap and trace device should be issued, including (i) a statement of the specific facts on the basis of which the applicant reasonably suspects that the designated crime has been, is being, or is about to be committed and demonstrating that the information likely to be obtained by use of a pen register or a trap and trace device is or will be relevant to an ongoing criminal investigation of such designated offense, (ii) the identity, if known, of the person to whom is leased or in whose name is listed the telephone line to which the pen register or trap and trace device is to be attached, (iii) the identity, if known, of the person who is the subject of the criminal investigation, (iv) the number and, if known, the physical location of the telephone line to which the pen register or trap and trace device is to be attached and, in the case of a trap and trace device, the geographic limits of the trap and trace order, and (v) a statement of the designated crime or crimes to which the information likely to be obtained by the use of the pen register or trap and trace device relates; and

(c) A statement of the period of time for which the authorization for the use of a pen register or a trap and trace device is required; and

(d) A statement of the facts concerning all previous applications, known to the applicant, for an order authorizing the use of a pen register or a trap and trace device involving any of the same persons or facilities specified in the application, and the action taken by the justice on each such application.

3. Allegations of fact in the application may be based either upon the personal knowledge of the applicant or upon information and belief. If the applicant personally knows the facts alleged, it must be so stated. If the facts stated in the application are derived in whole or in part from the statements of persons other than the applicant, the sources of such facts must be either disclosed or described.

HISTORY: Add, L 1988, ch 744, § 21, eff Dec 22, 1988.

§ 705.20. Orders authorizing the use of a pen register or a trap and trace device; determination of application

1. If the justice determines on the basis of the facts submitted by the applicant that grounds exist for the issue of an order authorizing the use of a pen register or a trap and trace device pursuant to section 705.10 of this article, the justice shall grant the application and issue an order authorizing the use of a pen register or a trap and trace device, in accordance with subdivision three of this section.

2. If the application does not conform to section 705.15 of this article, or if the justice is not satisfied that grounds exist for the issuance of an order authorizing the use of a pen register or a trap and trace device, the application must be denied.

3. An order issued under this section must contain:

(a) the name of the applicant, date of issuance, and the subscription and title of the issuing justice; and

(b) the identity, if known, of the person to whom is leased or in whose name is listed the telephone line to which the pen register or trap and trace device is to be attached; and

(c) the identity, if known, of the person who is the subject of the criminal investigation; and

(d) the number and, if known, the physical location of the telephone line to which the pen register or trap and trace device is to be attached and, in the case of a trap and trace device, the geographic limits of the trap and trace order; and

(e) a statement of the designated crime or crimes to which the information likely to be obtained by the pen register or trap and trace device relates.

4. An order issued under this section shall direct, upon the request of the applicant, the furnishing of information, facilities, and technical assistance necessary to accomplish the installation of the pen register or trap and trace device under section 705.25 of this article.

HISTORY: Add, L 1988, ch 744, § 21, eff Dec 22, 1988.

§ 705.25. Pen register or trap and trace device orders; time period and extensions

1. An order issued under this section shall authorize the installation and use of a pen register or a trap and trace device for a period not to exceed sixty days.

2. Extensions of such an order may be granted, but only upon an application for an order under section 705.05 of this article and upon the judicial finding required by subdivision one of section 705.10 of this article. The period of extension shall be for a period not to exceed sixty days.

HISTORY: Add, L 1988, ch 744, § 21, eff Dec 22, 1988.

§ 705.30. Nondisclosure of existence of pen register or a trap and trace device

An order authorizing or approving the installation and use of a pen register or a trap and trace device shall direct that:

1. the order be sealed until otherwise ordered by the court; and

2. the person owning or leasing the line to which the pen register or a trap and trace device is attached, or who has been ordered by the court to provide assistance to the applicant, not disclose the existence of the pen register or trap and trace device or the existence of the investigation to the listed subscriber, or to any other person, unless or until otherwise ordered by the court.

HISTORY: Add, L 1988, ch 744, § 21, eff Dec 22, 1988.

§ 705.35. Assistance in installation and use of a pen register or a trap and trace device

1. Upon the request of an applicant authorized to use a pen register under this article, a provider of a wire or electronic communication service, landlord, custodian, or other person shall furnish such applicant, or his agent, forthwith all information, facilities and technical assistance necessary to accomplish the installation of the pen register unobtrusively and with a minimum of interference with the services that the person so ordered by the court accords the party with respect to whom the installation and use is to take place, if such assistance is directed by a court order as provided in section 705.10 of this article.

2. Upon the request of an applicant authorized to receive the results of a trap and trace device under this article, a provider of a wire or electronic communication service, landlord, custodian, or other person shall install such device forthwith on the appropriate line and shall furnish such applicant forthwith all information, facilities and technical assistance including installation and operation of the device unobtrusively and with a minimum of interference with the services that the person so ordered by the court accords the party with respect to whom the installation and use is to take place, if such installation and assistance is directed by the court order as provided in section 705.10 of this article. Unless otherwise ordered by the court, the results of the trap and trace device shall be furnished to the applicant, or his agent, at reasonable intervals during regular business hours for the duration of the order.

CPL

3. A provider of a wire or electronic communication service, landlord, custodian, or other person who furnishes facilities or technical assistance pursuant to this section shall be reasonably compensated for such reasonable expenses incurred in providing such facilities and assistance.

4. No cause of action shall lie in any court against any provider of a wire or electronic communication service, its officers, employees, agents or other specified persons for providing information, facilities or assistance in accordance with the terms of a court order under this article. A good faith reliance by a provider of a wire or electronic communication service upon the validity of a court order issued pursuant to this article is a complete defense against any civil cause of action or criminal action based entirely on a failure to comply with this article.

    HISTORY: Add, L 1988, ch 744, § 21, eff Dec 22, 1988.

ARTICLE 710   MOTION TO SUPPRESS EVIDENCE

    HISTORY: Add, L 1970, ch 996, § 1, eff Sept 1, 1971.

§ 710.10. Motion to suppress evidence; definitions of terms

As used in this article, the following terms have the following meanings:

1. "Defendant" means a person who has been charged by an accusatory instrument with the commission of an offense.

2. "Evidence," when referring to matter in the possession of or available to a prosecutor, means any tangible property or potential testimony which may be offered in evidence in a criminal action.

3. "Potential testimony" means information or factual knowledge of a person who is or may be available as a witness.

4. "Eavesdropping" means "wiretapping", "mechanical overhearing of a conversation," or "intercepting or accessing of an electronic communication", as those terms are defined in section 250.00 of the penal law.

5. "Aggrieved." An "aggrieved person" includes, but is in no wise limited to, an "aggrieved person" as defined in subdivision two of section forty-five hundred six of the civil practice law and rules.

6. "Video surveillance" has the meaning given to that term by section 700.05 of this chapter.

7. "Pen register" and "trap and trace device" have the meanings given to those terms by subdivisions one and two respectively of section 705.00 of this chapter.

    HISTORY: Add, L 1970, ch 996, § 1, eff Sept 1, 1971. Sub 4, amd, L 1988, ch 744, § 22, eff Dec 22, 1988. Sub 6, add, L 1988, ch 744, § 23, eff Dec 22, 1988. Sub 7, add, L 1988, ch 744, § 23, eff Dec 22, 1988.

§ 710.20. Motion to suppress evidence; in general; grounds for

Upon motion of a defendant who (a) is aggrieved by unlawful or improper acquisition of evidence and has reasonable cause to believe that such may be offered against him in a criminal action, or (b) claims that improper identification testimony may be offered against him in a criminal action, a court may, under circumstances prescribed in this article, order that such evidence be suppressed or excluded upon the ground that it:

1. Consists of tangible property obtained by means of an unlawful search and seizure under circumstances precluding admissibility thereof in a criminal action against such defendant; or

2. Consists of a record or potential testimony reciting or describing declarations, conversations, or other communications overheard, intercepted, accessed, or recorded by means of eavesdropping, or observations made by means of video surveillance, obtained under circumstances precluding admissibility thereof in a criminal action against such defendant; or

3. Consists of a record or potential testimony reciting or describing a statement of such defendant involuntarily made, within the meaning of section 60.45; or

4. Was obtained as a result of other evidence obtained in a manner described in subdivisions one, two and three; or

5. Consists of a chemical test of the defendant's blood administered in violation of the provisions of subdivision three of section eleven hundred ninety-four of the vehicle and traffic law, subdivision eight of section forty-nine-a of the navigation law, subdivision seven of section 25.24 of the parks, recreation and historic preservation law, or any other applicable law; or

6. Consists of potential testimony regarding an observation of the defendant either at the time or place of the commission of the offense or upon some other occasion relevant to the case, which potential testimony would not be admissible upon the prospective trial of such charge owing to an improperly made previous identification of the defendant by the prospective witness.

7. Consists of information obtained by means of a pen register or trap and trace device installed or used in violation of the provisions of article seven hundred five of this chapter.

HISTORY: Add, L 1970, ch 996, § 1; amd, L 1976, ch 8, § 1, eff Feb 25, 1976. Sub 2, amd, L 1988, ch 744, § 24, eff Dec 22, 1988. Sub 3, amd, L 1982, ch 214, § 1, eff Sept 1, 1982. Sub 5, add, L 1983, ch 481, § 5; amd, L 1988, ch 47, § 3, L 1992, ch 805, § 49, eff Nov 1, 1992. Former sub 5, renumbered sub 6, L 1983, ch 481, § 5, eff Oct 13, 1983. Sub 6, formerly sub 5, renumbered sub 6, L 1983, ch 481, § 5, eff Oct 13, 1983. Sub 7, add, L 1988, ch 744, § 25, eff Dec 22, 1988. Sub 5, amd, L 1998, ch 629, § 4, eff Nov 1, 1999.

§ 710.30. Motion to suppress evidence; notice to defendant of intention to offer evidence

1. Whenever the people intend to offer at a trial (a) evidence of a statement made by a defendant to a public servant, which statement if involuntarily made would render the evidence thereof suppressible upon motion pursuant to subdivision three of section 710.20, or (b) testimony regarding an observation of the defendant either at the time or place of the commission of the offense or upon some other occasion relevant to the case, to be given by a witness who has previously identified him as such, they must serve upon the defendant a notice of such intention, specifying the evidence intended to be offered.

2. Such notice must be served within fifteen days after arraignment and before trial, and upon such service the defendant must be accorded reasonable opportunity to move before trial, pursuant to subdivision one of section 710.40, to suppress the specified evidence. For good cause shown, however, the court may permit the people to serve such notice, thereafter and in such case it must accord the defendant reasonable opportunity thereafter to make a suppression motion.

3. In the absence of service of notice upon a defendant as prescribed in this section, no evidence of a kind specified in subdivision one may be received against him upon trial unless he has, despite the lack of such notice, moved to suppress such evidence and such motion has been denied and the evidence thereby rendered admissible as prescribed in subdivision two of section 710.70.

HISTORY: Add, L 1970, ch 996, § 1, eff Sept 1, 1971. Section heading, amd, L 1976, ch 8, § 2, L 1976, ch 194, § 3, eff Sept 1, 1976. Sub 1, amd, L 1976, ch 8, § 2, eff Feb 25, 1976. Sub 2, reenacted without change, L 1976, ch 8, § 2; amd, L 1976, ch 194, § 3, eff Sept 1, 1976. Sub 3, reenacted without change, L 1976, ch 8, § 2; amd, L 1976, ch 194, § 3, eff Sept 1, 1976.

§ 710.40. Motion to suppress evidence; when made and determined

1. A motion to suppress evidence must be made after the commencement of the criminal action in which such evidence is allegedly about to be offered, and, except as otherwise provided in section 710.30 and in subdivision two of this section, it must be made within the period provided in subdivision one of section 255.20.

2. The motion may be made for the first time when, owing to unawareness of facts constituting the basis thereof or to other factors, the defendant did not have reasonable opportunity to make the motion previously, or when the evidence which he seeks to suppress is of a kind specified in section 710.30 and he was not served by the people, as provided in said section 710.30, with a pre-trial notice of intention to offer such evidence at the trial.

3. When the motion is made before trial, the trial may not be commenced until determination of the motion.

4. If after a pre-trial determination and denial of the motion the court is satisfied, upon a showing by the defendant, that additional pertinent facts have been discovered by the defendant which he could not have discovered with reasonable diligence before the determination of the motion, it may permit him to renew the motion before trial or, if such was not possible owing to the time of the discovery of the alleged new facts, during trial.

HISTORY: Add, L 1970, ch 996, § 1, eff Sept 1, 1971. Sub 1, amd, L 1974, ch 763, § 8, eff Sept 1, 1974. Sub 2, amd, L 1976, ch 194, § 4, eff Sept 1, 1976. Sub 3, amd, L 1977, ch 273, § 1, eff June 14, 1977.

§ 710.50. Motion to suppress evidence; in what courts made

1. The particular courts in which motions to suppress evidence must be made are as follows:

(a) If an indictment is pending in a superior court, or if the defendant has been held by a local criminal court for the action of a grand jury, the motion must be made in the superior court in which such indictment is pending or which impaneled or will impanel such grand jury. If the superior court which will impanel such grand jury is the supreme court, the motion may, in the alternative, be made in the county court of the county in which the action is pending;

(b) If a currently undetermined felony complaint is pending in a local criminal court, the motion must be made in the superior court which would have trial jurisdiction of the offense or offenses charged were an indictment therefor to result;

(c) If an information, a simplified information, a prosecutor's information or a misdemeanor complaint is pending in a local criminal court, the motion must be made in such court.

2. If after a motion has been made in and determined by a superior court a local criminal court acquires trial jurisdiction of the action by reason of an information, a prosecutor's information or a misdemeanor complaint filed therewith, such superior court's determination is binding upon such local criminal court. If, however, the motion has been made in but not yet determined by the

superior court at the time of the filing of such information, prosecutor's information or misdemeanor complaint, the superior court may not determine the motion but must refer it to the local criminal court of trial jurisdiction.

> **HISTORY:** Add, L 1970, ch 996, § 1, eff Sept 1, 1971. Sub 1, par (a), amd, L 1973, ch 221, § 2, eff Sept 1, 1973. Sub 1, par (c), amd, L 1972, ch 661, § 46, eff Sept 1, 1972.

§ 710.60. Motion to suppress evidence; procedure

1. A motion to suppress evidence made before trial must be in writing and upon reasonable notice to the people and with opportunity to be heard. The motion papers must state the ground or grounds of the motion and must contain sworn allegations of fact, whether of the defendant or of another person or persons, supporting such grounds. Such allegations may be based upon personal knowledge of the deponent or upon information and belief, provided that in the latter event the sources of such information and the grounds of such belief are stated. The people may file with the court, and in such case must serve a copy thereof upon the defendant or his counsel, an answer denying or admitting any or all of the allegations of the moving papers.

2. The court must summarily grant the motion if:

(a) The motion papers comply with the requirements of subdivision one and the people concede the truth of allegations of fact therein which support the motion; or

(b) The people stipulate that the evidence sought to be suppressed will not be offered in evidence in any criminal action or proceeding against the defendant.

3. The court may summarily deny the motion if:

(a) The motion papers do not allege a ground constituting legal basis for the motion; or

(b) The sworn allegations of fact do not as a matter of law support the ground alleged; except that this paragraph does not apply where the motion is based upon the ground specified in subdivision three or six of section 710.20.

4. If the court does not determine the motion pursuant to subdivisions [subdivision]* two or three, it must conduct a hearing and make findings of fact essential to the determination thereof. All persons giving factual information at such hearing must testify under oath, except that unsworn evidence pursuant to subdivision two of section 60.20 of this chapter may also be received. Upon such hearing, hearsay evidence is admissible to establish any material fact.

5. A motion to suppress evidence made during trial may be in writing and may be litigated and determined on the basis of motion papers as provided in subdivisions one through four, or it may, instead, be made orally in open court. In the latter event, the court must, where necessary, also conduct a hearing as provided in subdivision four, out of the presence of the jury if any, and make findings of fact essential to the determination of the motion.

6. Regardless of whether a hearing was conducted, the court, upon determining the motion, must set forth on the record its findings of fact, its conclusions of law and the reasons for its determination.

> **HISTORY:** Add, L 1970, ch 996, § 1, eff Sept 1, 1971. Sub 3, amd, L 1986, ch 776, § 1, eff Nov 1, 1986. Sub 4, amd, L 1975, ch 39, § 1, eff June 21, 1975.

---

* The bracketed word has been inserted by the Publisher.

§ 710.70. Motion to suppress evidence; orders of suppression; effects of orders and of failure to make motion

1. Upon granting a motion to suppress evidence, the court must order that the evidence in question be excluded in the criminal action pending against the defendant. When the order is based upon the ground specified in subdivision one of section 710.20 and excludes tangible property unlawfully taken from the defendant's possession, and when such property is not otherwise subject to lawful retention, the court may, upon request of the defendant, further order that such property be restored to him.

2. An order finally denying a motion to suppress evidence may be reviewed upon an appeal from an ensuing judgment of conviction notwithstanding the fact that such judgment is entered upon a plea of guilty.

3. A motion to suppress evidence made pursuant to this article is the exclusive method of challenging the admissibility of evidence upon the grounds specified in section 710.20, and a defendant who does not make such a motion before or in the course of a criminal action waives his right to judicial determination of any such contention.

Nothing contained in this article, however, precludes a defendant from attempting to establish at a trial that evidence introduced by the people of a pre-trial statement made by him should be disregarded by the jury or other trier of the facts on the ground that such statement was involuntarily made within the meaning of section 60.45. Even though the issue of the admissibility of such evidence was not submitted to the court, or was determined adversely to the defendant upon motion, the defendant may adduce trial evidence and otherwise contend that the statement was involuntarily made. In the case of a jury trial, the court must submit such issue to the jury under instructions to disregard such evidence upon a finding that the statement was involuntarily made.

HISTORY: Add, L 1970, ch 996, § 4, eff Sept 1, 1971.

ARTICLE 715   DESTRUCTION OF DANGEROUS DRUGS

HISTORY: Add, L 1973, ch 750, § 1, eff Sept 1, 1973.

§ 715.05. Dangerous drugs; definition

"Dangerous drugs" means any substance listed in schedule I, II, III, IV or V of section thirty-three hundred six of the public health law.

HISTORY: Add, L 1984, ch 851, § 1, eff Aug 5, 1984.

§ 715.10. Pretrial motion to destroy dangerous drugs

1. Subject to the limitations in paragraph (b) of subdivision two hereof a district attorney may move in a superior court for an order of destruction of the dangerous drugs in felony cases involving the possession or sale of such drugs.

2. A motion for an order of destruction of dangerous drugs shall be in writing, have attached thereto a copy of the report of analysis and shall be made in the following manner:

(a) Ex parte; where no defendants have been arrested in connection with the seizure of such drugs and a showing is made upon affidavit that the likelihood of any future arrest in connection therewith is nonexistent; or

(b) Upon notice, when a defendant has been arraigned in a superior court upon an indictment charging him with a felony involving the possession or sale of a dangerous drug and the dangerous drugs sought to be destroyed are material to the prosecution of said indictment.

3. When such motion is ex parte, the court may order the destruction of all or part of the subject drugs.

4. When such motion is upon notice, further proceedings shall be had as provided in section 715.20 hereof.

HISTORY: Add, L 1973, ch 750, § 1, eff Sept 1, 1973.

§ 715.20. Proceedings on motion upon notice

1. When such motion is on notice, a hearing thereon shall be held by the court before which it is returnable not later than thirty days after the return date and the defendant shall be present at such hearing.

2. A hearing held pursuant to this section shall be conducted and recorded in the same manner as would be required were the witnesses testifying at trial. The district attorney shall establish by competent evidence the nature and quantity of the dangerous drugs which are the subject of the motion. Each party shall have the right to call and cross examine witnesses and to register objections and to receive rulings of the court thereon.

3. If the court finds upon the conclusion of the hearing that neither the prosecution nor the defendant will be prejudiced thereby it may grant the motion and may make such order as it may deem appropriate for the destruction of part or all of such drugs.

4. A defendant may waive such hearing and consent to the granting of the motion and entry of an order of destruction either by sworn affidavit or by personal appearance in court and declaration on the record of such waiver and consent.

HISTORY: Add, L 1973, ch 750, § 1, eff Sept 1, 1973.

§ 715.30. Orders of the court

1. In any proceeding brought pursuant to this article, the court may grant or deny any motion made hereunder or the relief requested therein in whole or in part and issue any order thereon as it may deem proper and as the interests of justice may require in order to effectuate the provisions of this article.

2. An order of destruction of a dangerous drug issued by the court pursuant to this article shall state the time within which the provisions of such order are to be complied with. It shall direct the person having custody of the drug to make provision for the destruction thereof in the presence of at least two witnesses, at least one of whom shall be a police officer.

HISTORY: Add, L 1973, ch 750, § 1, eff Sept 1, 1973.

§ 715.40. Affidavit of destruction

An affidavit attesting to the date, time, place and manner of destruction of a dangerous drug pursuant to an order therefor and identifying the same by reference to the report of analysis or by other identifying number or system and the order of the court issued thereon, shall be filed with the court by the person who destroyed the drugs and by each of the witnesses required to be present by subdivision two of section 715.30 of this article.

HISTORY: Add, L 1973, ch 750, § 1, eff Sept 1, 1973.

§ 715.50. Analysis of dangerous drugs

1. On and after September first, nineteen hundred seventy-three, in every felony case involving the possession or sale of a dangerous drug, the head of the agency charged with custody of such drugs, or his designee, shall within forty-five days after receipt thereof perform or cause to be performed an analysis of such drugs, such analysis to include qualitative identification; weight and quantity where appropriate.

2. Within ten days after the report of such analysis is received by such agency, the head thereof or his designee shall forward a copy thereof to the appropriate district attorney and inform him of the location where the subject drugs are being held.

3. The failure to have an analysis made or to forward a copy thereof within the time specified in subdivisions one and two of this section shall not be deemed or construed to bar the making or granting of a motion pursuant to this article or to the prosecution of a case involving such drugs.

HISTORY: Add, L 1973, ch 750, § 1, eff Sept 1, 1973.

TITLE U   Special Proceedings Which Replace, Suspend or Abate Criminal Actions

ARTICLE 720
YOUTHFUL OFFENDER PROCEDURE

ARTICLE 725
REMOVAL OF PROCEEDING AGAINST JUVENILE OFFENDER TO FAMILY COURT

ARTICLE 730
MENTAL DISEASE OR DEFECT EXCLUDING FITNESS TO PROCEED

HISTORY: Add, L 1970, ch 996, § 1, eff Sept 1, 1971.

ARTICLE 720   YOUTHFUL OFFENDER PROCEDURE

     HISTORY: Add, L 1971, ch 981, § 1, eff Sept 1, 1971. Former Art 720 (consisting of §§ 720.05–720.70), add, L 1970, ch 996, § 1; repealed, L 1971, ch 981, § 1, eff Sept 1, 1971.

§ 720.05. [Repealed]

     HISTORY: Add, L 1970, ch 996, § 1; repealed, L 1971, ch 981, § 1, eff Sept 1, 1971, with substance transferred to § 720.10.

§ 720.10. Youthful offender procedure; definitions of terms

As used in this article, the following terms have the following meanings:

1. "Youth" means a person charged with a crime alleged to have been committed when he was at least sixteen years old and less than nineteen years old or a person charged with being a juvenile offender as defined in subdivision forty-two of section 1.20 of this chapter.

2. "Eligible youth" means a youth who is eligible to be found a youthful offender. Every youth is so eligible unless:

     (a) the conviction to be replaced by a youthful offender finding is for (i) a class A-I or class A-II felony, or (ii) an armed felony as defined in subdivision forty-one of section 1.20, except as provided in subdivision three, or (iii) rape in the first degree, criminal sexual act in the first degree, or aggravated sexual abuse, except as provided in subdivision three, or

     (b) such youth has previously been convicted and sentenced for a felony, or

     (c) such youth has previously been adjudicated a youthful offender following conviction of a felony or has been adjudicated on or after September first, nineteen hundred seventy-eight a juvenile delinquent who committed a designated felony act as defined in the family court act.

3. Notwithstanding the provisions of subdivision two, a youth who has been convicted of an

armed felony offense or of rape in the first degree, criminal sexual act in the first degree, or aggravated sexual abuse is an eligible youth if the court determines that one or more of the following factors exist: (i) mitigating circumstances that bear directly upon the manner in which the crime was committed; or (ii) where the defendant was not the sole participant in the crime, the defendant's participation was relatively minor although not so minor as to constitute a defense to the prosecution. Where the court determines that the eligible youth is a youthful offender, the court shall make a statement on the record of the reasons for its determination, a transcript of which shall be forwarded to the state division of criminal justice services, to be kept in accordance with the provisions of subdivision three of section eight hundred thirty-seven-a of the executive law.

4. "Youthful offender finding" means a finding, substituted for the conviction of an eligible youth, pursuant to a determination that the eligible youth is a youthful offender.

5. "Youthful offender sentence" means the sentence imposed upon a youthful offender finding.

6. "Youthful offender adjudication". A youthful offender adjudication is comprised of a youthful offender finding and the youthful offender sentence imposed thereon and is completed by imposition and entry of the youthful offender sentence.

HISTORY: Add, L 1971, ch 981, § 1, eff Sept 1, 1971, with substance transferred from § 720.05. Former § 720.10, add, L 1970, ch 996, § 1; repealed, L 1971, ch 981, § 1, eff Sept 1, 1971. Sub 1, amd, L 1979, ch 411, § 14, eff Aug 4, 1979. Sub 2, amd, L 1975, ch 832, § 1, L 1978, ch 481, § 58, L 1986, ch 416, § 1, eff Nov 1, 1986 and applicable to offenses committed on and after Nov 1, 1986. Sub 2, par (a), amd, L 2006, ch 316, § 1, eff July 26, 2006. Sub 2, par (c), add, L 1978, ch 481, § 58, eff Sept 1, 1978. Sub 3, add, L 1978, ch 481, § 59; amd, L 1986, ch 416, § 1, eff Nov 1, 1986 and applicable to offenses committed on and after Nov 1, 1986. Sub 3, amd, L 2003, ch 264, § 50, eff Nov 1, 2003. Former sub 3, renumbered sub 4, L 1978, ch 481, § 59, eff Sept 1, 1978. Sub 4, formerly sub 3, renumbered sub 4, L 1978, ch 481, § 59, eff Sept 1, 1978. Former sub 4, renumbered sub 5, L 1978, ch 481, § 59, eff Sept 1, 1978. Sub 5, formerly sub 4, renumbered sub 5, L 1978, ch 481, § 59, eff Sept 1, 1978. Former sub 5, renumbered sub 6, L 1978, ch 481, § 59, eff Sept 1, 1978. Sub 6, formerly sub 5, renumbered sub 6, L 1978, ch 481, § 59, eff Sept 1, 1978.

§ 720.15. Youthful offender procedure; sealing of accusatory instrument; privacy of proceedings; preliminary instructions to jury*

1. When an accusatory instrument against an apparently eligible youth is filed with a court, it shall be filed as a sealed instrument, though only with respect to the public.

2. When a youth is initially arraigned upon an accusatory instrument, such arraignment and all proceedings in the action thereafter may, in the discretion of the court and with the defendant's consent, be conducted in private.

3. The provisions of subdivisions one and two of this section requiring or authorizing the accusatory instrument filed against a youth to be sealed, and the arraignment and all proceedings in the action to be conducted in private shall not apply in connection with a pending charge of committing any felony offense as defined in the penal law. The provisions of subdivision one requiring the accusatory instrument filed against a youth to be sealed shall not apply where such youth has previously been adjudicated a youthful offender or convicted of a crime.

4. Notwithstanding any provision in this article, a person charged with prostitution as defined

---

* Editor's Note: L 1972, ch 937, § 1, eff Sept 1, 1972, repealed the provisions relating to preliminary instructions to the jury without a conforming amendment to the section catchline.

in section 230.00 of the penal law or loitering for the purposes of prostitution as defined in subdivision two of section 240.37 of the penal law, provided that the person does not stand charged with loitering for the purpose of patronizing a prostitute, and such person is aged sixteen or seventeen when such offense occurred, regardless of whether such person (i) had prior to commencement of trial or entry of a plea of guilty been convicted of a crime or found a youthful offender, or (ii) subsequent to such conviction for prostitution or loitering for prostitution is convicted of a crime or found a youthful offender, the provisions of subdivisions one and two of this section requiring or authorizing the accusatory instrument filed against a youth to be sealed, and the arraignment and all proceedings in the action to be conducted in private shall apply.

HISTORY: Add, L 1971, ch 981, § 1, eff Sept 1, 1971, with substance transferred from former §§ 720.15, 720.65. Former § 720.15, add, L 1970, ch 996, § 1; repealed, L 1971, ch 981, § 1, eff Sept 1, 1971. Sub 1, amd, L 1975, ch 832, § 2, eff Aug 9, 1975. Sub 1, amd, L 2008, ch 587, § 1, eff Jan 1, 2009. Sub 3, add, L 1978, ch 481, § 60; amd, L 1979, ch 411, § 15, L 1985, ch 774, § 1, eff Nov 1, 1985. Former sub 3, repealed, L 1972, ch 937, § 1, eff Sept 1, 1972. Sub 4, add, L 2014, ch 402, § 3, eff Oct 16, 2014.

§ 720.20. Youthful offender determination; when and how made; procedure thereupon

1. Upon conviction of an eligible youth, the court must order a pre-sentence investigation of the defendant. After receipt of a written report of the investigation and at the time of pronouncing sentence the court must determine whether or not the eligible youth is a youthful offender. Such determination shall be in accordance with the following criteria:

(a) If in the opinion of the court the interest of justice would be served by relieving the eligible youth from the onus of a criminal record and by not imposing an indeterminate term of imprisonment of more than four years, the court may, in its discretion, find the eligible youth is a youthful offender; and

(b) Where the conviction is had in a local criminal court and the eligible youth had not prior to commencement of trial or entry of a plea of guilty been convicted of a crime or found a youthful offender, the court must find he is a youthful offender.

2. Where an eligible youth is convicted of two or more crimes set forth in separate counts of an accusatory instrument or set forth in two or more accusatory instruments consolidated for trial purposes, the court must not find him a youthful offender with respect to any such conviction pursuant to subdivision one of this section unless it finds him a youthful offender with respect to all such convictions.

3. Upon determining that an eligible youth is a youthful offender, the court must direct that the conviction be deemed vacated and replaced by a youthful offender finding; and the court must sentence the defendant pursuant to section 60.02 of the penal law.

4. Upon determining that an eligible youth is not a youthful offender, the court must order the accusatory instrument unsealed and continue the action to judgment pursuant to the ordinary rules governing criminal prosecutions.

HISTORY: Add, L 1971, ch 981, § 1, eff Sept 1, 1971. Former § 720.20, add, L 1970, ch 996, § 1; repealed, L 1971, ch 981, § 1, eff Sept 1, 1971. Sub 1, amd, L 1974, ch 652, § 8, eff July 31, 1974 (Laws 1974, ch 653, § 8, changed effective date from May 30, 1974 to July 31, 1974.). Sub 3, amd, L 1974, ch 652, § 8, L 1980, ch 471, § 27, eff July 23, 1980.

§ 720.25. Youthful offender adjudication; certain exemptions.

Notwithstanding any inconsistent provisions of law:

1. where the court is required to find that a person is a youthful offender pursuant to section

170.80 of this chapter, the fact that such person has previously been convicted of a crime or adjudicated a youthful offender shall not prevent such person from being adjudicated a youthful offender as required by such section; and

2. a youthful offender adjudication pursuant to section 170.80 of this chapter shall not be considered in determining whether a person is an eligible youth, or in determining whether to find a person a youthful offender, in any subsequent youthful offender adjudication.

HISTORY: Add, L 2014, ch 402, § 4, eff Oct 16, 2014. Former § 720.25, add, L 1971, ch 981, § 1; repealed, L 1974, ch 652, § 3, eff July 31, 1974. Former § 720.25, add, L 1970, ch 996, § 1; repealed, L 1971, ch 981, § 1, eff Sept 1, 1971.

§ 720.30. Youthful offender adjudication; post-judgment motions and appeal

The provisions of this chapter, governing the making and determination of post-judgment motions and the taking and determination of appeals in criminal cases, apply to post-judgment motions and appeals with respect to youthful offender adjudications wherever such provisions can reasonably be so applied.

HISTORY: Add, L 1971, ch 981, § 1, eff Sept 1, 1971, with substance transferred from § 720.60. Former § 720.30, add, L 1970, ch 996, § 1; repealed, L 1971, ch 981, § 1, eff Sept 1, 1971.

§ 720.35. Youthful offender adjudication; effect thereof; records

1. A youthful offender adjudication is not a judgment of conviction for a crime or any other offense, and does not operate as a disqualification of any person so adjudged to hold public office or public employment or to receive any license granted by public authority but shall be deemed a conviction only for the purposes of transfer of supervision and custody pursuant to section two hundred fifty-nine-m of the executive law. A defendant for whom a youthful offender adjudication was substituted, who was originally charged with prostitution as defined in section 230.00 of the penal law or loitering for the purposes of prostitution as defined in subdivision two of section 240.37 of the penal law provided that the person does not stand charged with loitering for the purpose of patronizing a prostitute, for an offense allegedly committed when he or she was sixteen or seventeen years of age, shall be deemed a "sexually exploited child" as defined in subdivision one of section four hundred forty-seven-a of the social services law and therefore shall not be considered an adult for purposes related to the charges in the youthful offender proceeding or a proceeding under section 170.80 of this chapter.

2. Except where specifically required or permitted by statute or upon specific authorization of the court, all official records and papers, whether on file with the court, a police agency or the division of criminal justice services, relating to a case involving a youth who has been adjudicated a youthful offender, are confidential and may not be made available to any person or public or private agency, other than the designated educational official of the public or private elementary or secondary school in which the youth is enrolled as a student provided that such local educational official shall only have made available a notice of such adjudication and shall not have access to any other official records and papers, such youth or such youth's designated agent (but only where the official records and papers sought are on file with a court and request therefor is made to that court or to a clerk thereof), an institution to which such youth has been committed, the department of corrections and community supervision and a probation department of this state that requires such official records and papers for the purpose of carrying out duties specifically authorized by law; provided, however, that information regarding an order of protection or temporary order of protection issued pursuant to section 530.12 of this chapter or a warrant issued in connection therewith may be maintained on the statewide automated order of protection and warrant registry established pursuant to section two hundred twenty-one-a of the executive law during the period that such order of protection or temporary order of protection is in full force and effect or during

which such warrant may be executed. Such confidential information may be made available pursuant to law only for purposes of adjudicating or enforcing such order of protection or temporary order of protection and, where provided to a designated educational official, as defined in section 380.90 of this chapter, for purposes related to the execution of the student's educational plan, where applicable, successful school adjustment and reentry into the community. Such notification shall be kept separate and apart from such student's school records and shall be accessible only by the designated educational official. Such notification shall not be part of such student's permanent school record and shall not be appended to or included in any documentation regarding such student and shall be destroyed at such time as such student is no longer enrolled in the school district. At no time shall such notification be used for any purpose other than those specified in this subdivision.

3. If a youth who has been adjudicated a youthful offender is enrolled as a student in a public or private elementary or secondary school the court that has adjudicated the youth as a youthful offender shall provide notification of such adjudication to the designated educational official of the school in which such youth is enrolled as a student. Such notification shall be used by the designated educational official only for purposes related to the execution of the student's educational plan, where applicable, successful school adjustment and reentry into the community. Such notification shall be kept separate and apart from such student's school records and shall be accessible only by the designated educational official. Such notification shall not be part of such student's permanent school record and shall not be appended to or included in any documentation regarding such student and shall be destroyed at such time as such student is no longer enrolled in the school district. At no time shall such notification be used for any purpose other than those specified in this subdivision.

4. Notwithstanding subdivision two of this section, whenever a person is adjudicated a youthful offender and the conviction that was vacated and replaced by the youthful offender finding was for a sex offense as that term is defined in article ten of the mental hygiene law, all records pertaining to the youthful offender adjudication shall be included in those records and reports that may be obtained by the commissioner of mental health or the commissioner of developmental disabilities, as appropriate; the case review panel; and the attorney general pursuant to section 10.05 of the mental hygiene law.

HISTORY: Add, L 1971, ch 981, § 1, eff Sept 1, 1971, with substance transferred from § 720.70; amd, L 1972, ch 399, § 24, L 1980, ch 189, § 1, L 1992, ch 452, § 1, eff July 17, 1992, L 1996, ch 217, § 1, eff June 25, 1996, L 2000, ch 181, §§ 15, 16, eff Nov 1, 2000, L 2001, ch 412, § 1, eff Nov 1, 2001, L 2007, ch 7, § 14, eff April 13, 2007, L 2011, ch 62, § 87 (Part C, Subpart B), eff March 31, 2011. Sub 1, amd, L 2014, ch 402, § 5, eff Oct 16, 2014.

§§ 720.40–720.70. [Repealed]

HISTORY: Add, L 1970, ch 996, § 1; repealed, L 1971, ch 981, § 1, eff Sept 1, 1971, with substance transferred to §§ 720.25, 720.30, 720.15(2), 720.35, respectively.

ARTICLE 725   REMOVAL OF PROCEEDING AGAINST JUVENILE OFFENDER TO FAMILY COURT

HISTORY: Add, L 1978, ch 481, § 44, eff Sept 1, 1978.

§ 725.00. Applicability

The provisions of this article apply in any case where a court directs that an action or charge is to be removed to the family court under section 180.75, 190.71, 210.43, 220.10, 310.85 or 330.25 of this chapter.

HISTORY: Add, L 1978, ch 481, § 44; amd, L 1979, ch 411, § 17, eff Aug 4, 1979.

§ 725.05. Order of removal

When a court directs that an action or charge is to be removed to the family court the court must issue an order of removal in accordance with this section. Such order must be as follows:

1. It must provide that the action or charge is to be removed to the family court of the county in which such action or charge was pending, and it must specify the section pursuant to which the removal is authorized.

2. Where the direction is authorized pursuant to paragraph (b) of subdivision three of section 180.75 of this chapter, it must specify the act or acts it found reasonable cause to believe the defendant did.

3. Where the direction is authorized pursuant to subdivision four of section 180.75 of this chapter, it must specify the act or acts it found reasonable cause to allege.

4. Where the direction is authorized pursuant to section 190.71 of this chapter, the court shall annex to the order as part thereof a certified copy of the grand jury request.

4-a. Where the direction is authorized pursuant to subdivision seven of section 210.30 of this chapter, it must specify the act or acts for which there was sufficient evidence to believe that defendant did.

5. Where the direction is authorized pursuant to section 220.10, 310.85 or 330.25 of this chapter, it must specify the act or acts for which a plea or verdict of guilty was rendered or accepted and entered.

6. Where a securing order has not been made, the order of removal must provide that the police officer or peace officer who made the arrest or some other proper officer forthwith and with all reasonable speed take the juvenile to the designated family court or, where that cannot be done, it must provide for release or detention in the same manner as provided for a family court proceeding pursuant to section 320.5 of the family court act.

7. Whether or not a securing order has been made, the order of removal must specify a date certain within ten days from the date of the order of removal for the defendant's appearance in the family court and where the defendant is in detention or in the custody of the sheriff that date must be not later than the next day the family court is in session.

8. The order of removal must direct that all of the pleadings and proceedings in the action, or a certified copy of same be transferred to the designated family court and be delivered to and filed with the clerk of that court. For the purposes of this subdivision the term "pleadings and proceedings" includes the minutes of any hearing inquiry or trial held in the action, the minutes of any grand jury proceeding and the minutes of any plea accepted and entered.

9. The order of removal must be signed by a judge or justice of the court that directed the removal.

HISTORY: Add, L 1978, ch 481, § 44, eff Sept 1, 1978. Sub 4-a, add, L 1980, ch 136, § 5, eff May 20, 1980. Sub 6, amd, L 1980, ch 843, § 29, L 1982, ch 920, § 78, eff July 1, 1983. Sub 7, amd, L 1990, ch 223, § 4, eff June 13, 1990.

§ 725.10. Removal of action

1. When an order of removal is filed with the family court a proceeding pursuant to article three of the family court act must be originated. The family court thereupon must assume jurisdiction and proceed to render such judgment as the circumstances require, in the manner and to the extent provided by law.

2. Upon the filing of an order of removal in a criminal court the criminal action upon which the order is based shall be terminated, and there shall be no further criminal proceedings in any criminal court as defined in section 10.10 of this chapter with respect to the offense or offenses charged in the accusatory instrument which was the subject of removal. All further proceedings including motions and appeals shall be in accordance with laws appertaining to the family court and for this purpose all findings, determinations, verdicts and orders other than the order of removal, shall be deemed to have been made by the family court.

> **HISTORY:** Add, L 1978, ch 481, § 44, eff Sept 1, 1978. Sub 1, amd, L 1982, ch 920, § 79, eff July 1, 1983. Sub 2, amd, L 1979, ch 411, § 16, eff Aug 4, 1979.

§ 725.15. Sealing of records

Except where specifically required or permitted by statute or upon specific authorization of the court that directed removal of an action to the family court all official records and papers of the action up to and including the order of removal, whether on file with the court, a police agency or the division of criminal justice services, are confidential and must not be made available to any person or public or private agency, provided however that availability of copies of any such records and papers on file with the family court shall be governed by provisions that apply to family court records, and further provided that all official records and papers of the action shall be included in those records and reports that may be obtained upon request by the commissioner of mental health or commissioner of mental retardation and developmental disabilities, as appropriate; the case review panel; and the attorney general pursuant to section 10.05 of the mental hygiene law.

> **HISTORY:** Add, L 1978, ch 481, § 44, eff Sept 1, 1978. Amd, L 2007, ch 7, § 15, eff April 13, 2007.

§ 725.20. Record of certain actions removed

1. The provisions of this section shall apply in any case where an order of removal to the family court is entered pursuant to a direction authorized by subdivision four of section 180.75, or section 210.43, or subparagraph (iii) of paragraph (h) of subdivision five of section 220.10 of this chapter, or section 330.25 of this chapter.

2. When such an action is removed the court that directed the removal must cause the following additional records to be filed with the clerk of the county court or in the city of New York with the clerk of the supreme court of the county wherein the action was pending and with the division of criminal justice services:

(a) A certified copy of the order of removal;

(b) Where the direction is one authorized by subdivision four of section 180.75 of this chapter, a copy of the statement of the district attorney made pursuant to paragraph (b) of subdivision six of section 180.75 of this chapter;

(c) Where the direction is authorized by section 180.75, a copy of the portion of the minutes containing the statement by the court pursuant to paragraph (a) of subdivision six of such section 180.75;

(d) Where the direction is one authorized by subparagraph (iii) of paragraph (h) of subdivision five of section 220.10 or section 330.25 of this chapter, a copy of the minutes of the plea of guilty, including the minutes of the memorandum submitted by the district attorney and the court;

(e) Where the direction is one authorized by subdivision one of section 210.43 of this chapter, a copy of that portion of the minutes containing the statement by the court pursuant to paragraph (a) of subdivision five of section 210.43;

(f) Where the direction is one authorized by paragraph (b) of subdivision one of section 210.43 of this chapter, a copy of that portion of the minutes containing the statement of the district attorney made pursuant to paragraph (b) of subdivision five of section 210.43; and

(g) In addition to the records specified in this subdivision, such further statement or submission of additional information pertaining to the proceeding in criminal court in accordance with standards established by the commissioner of the division of criminal justice services, subject to the provisions of subdivision three of this section.

3. It shall be the duty of said clerk to maintain a separate file for copies of orders and minutes filed pursuant to this section. Upon receipt of such orders and minutes the clerk must promptly delete such portions as would identify the defendant, but the clerk shall nevertheless maintain a separate confidential system to enable correlation of the documents so filed with identification of the defendant. After making such deletions the orders and minutes shall be placed within the file and must be available for public inspection. Information permitting correlation of any such record with the identity of any defendant shall not be divulged to any person except upon order of a justice of the supreme court based upon a finding that the public interest or the interests of justice warrant disclosure in a particular cause for a particular case or for a particular purpose or use.

> **HISTORY:** Add, L 1978, ch 481, § 44, eff Sept 1, 1978. Sub 1, amd, L 1979, ch 411, § 18, eff Aug 4, 1979. Sub 2, amd, L 1979, ch 411, § 18, eff Aug 4, 1979. Sub 2, par (c), add, L 1979, ch 411, § 18, eff Aug 4, 1979. Former sub 2, par (c), relettered sub 2, par (d), L 1979, ch 411, § 18, eff Aug 4, 1979. Sub 2, par (d), formerly sub 2, par (c), so relettered, L 1979, ch 411, § 18, eff Aug 4, 1979. Sub 2, par (e), add, L 1979, ch 411, § 18, eff Aug 4, 1979. Sub 2, par (f), add, L 1979, ch 411, § 18, eff Aug 4, 1979. Sub 2, par (g), add, L 1979, ch 411, § 18, eff Aug 4, 1979.

ARTICLE 730   MENTAL DISEASE OR DEFECT EXCLUDING FITNESS TO PROCEED

> **HISTORY:** Add, L 1970, ch 996, § 1, eff Sept 1, 1971.

§ 730.10. Fitness to proceed; definitions

As used in this article, the following terms have the following meanings:

1. "Incapacitated person" means a defendant who as a result of mental disease or defect lacks capacity to understand the proceedings against him or to assist in his own defense.

2. "Order of examination" means an order issued to an appropriate director by a criminal court wherein a criminal action is pending against a defendant, or by a family court pursuant

to section 322.1 of the family court act wherein a juvenile delinquency proceeding is pending against a juvenile, directing that such person be examined for the purpose of determining if he is an incapacitated person.

3. "Commissioner" means the state commissioner of mental health or the state commissioner of mental retardation and developmental disabilities.

4. "Director" means (a) the director of a state hospital operated by the office of mental health or the director of a developmental center operated by the office of mental retardation and developmental disabilities, or (b) the director of a hospital operated by any local government of the state that has been certified by the commissioner as having adequate facilities to examine a defendant to determine if he is an incapacitated person, or (c) the director of community mental health services.

5. "Qualified psychiatrist" means a physician who:

(a) is a diplomate of the American board of psychiatry and neurology or is eligible to be certified by that board; or,

(b) is certified by the American osteopathic board of neurology and psychiatry or is eligible to be certified by that board.

6. "Certified psychologist" means a person who is registered as a certified psychologist under article one hundred fifty-three of the education law.

7. "Psychiatric examiner" means a qualified psychiatrist or a certified psychologist who has been designated by a director to examine a defendant pursuant to an order of examination.

8. "Examination report" means a report made by a psychiatric examiner wherein he sets forth his opinion as to whether the defendant is or is not an incapacitated person, the nature and extent of his examination and, if he finds that the defendant is an incapacitated person, his diagnosis and prognosis and a detailed statement of the reasons for his opinion by making particular reference to those aspects of the proceedings wherein the defendant lacks capacity to understand or to assist in his own defense. The state administrator and the commissioner must jointly adopt the form of the examination report; and the state administrator shall prescribe the number of copies thereof that must be submitted to the court by the director.

9. "Appropriate institution" means: (a) a hospital operated by the office of mental health or a developmental center operated by the office for people with developmental disabilities; or (b) a hospital licensed by the department of health which operates a psychiatric unit licensed by the office of mental health, as determined by the commissioner provided, however, that any such hospital that is not operated by the state shall qualify as an "appropriate institution" only pursuant to the terms of an agreement between the commissioner and the hospital. Nothing in this article shall be construed as requiring a hospital to consent to providing care and treatment to an incapacitated person at such hospital.

HISTORY: Add, L 1970, ch 996, § 1, eff Sept 1, 1971; amd, L 1973, ch 195, § 11, L 1974, ch 629, §§ 5, 6, L 1976, ch 435, § 4, eff June 23, 1976, L 1987, ch 440, § 1, eff April 1, 1988, L 1994, ch 566, § 1, eff July 26, 1994, L 2012, ch 56, § 1 (Part Q), eff March 30, 2012.

§ 730.20. Fitness to proceed; generally

1. The appropriate director to whom a criminal court issues an order of examination must be determined in accordance with rules jointly adopted by the judicial conference and the commissioner. Upon receipt of an examination order, the director must designate two qualified psychiatric examiners, of whom he may be one, to examine the defendant to determine if he is an

incapacitated person. In conducting their examination, the psychiatric examiners may employ any method which is accepted by the medical profession for the examination of persons alleged to be mentally ill or mentally defective. The court may authorize a psychiatrist or psychologist retained by the defendant to be present at such examination.

2. When the defendant is not in custody at the time a court issues an order of examination, because he was theretofore released on bail or on his own recognizance, the court may direct that the examination be conducted on an out-patient basis, and at such time and place as the director shall designate. If, however, the director informs the court that hospital confinement of the defendant is necessary for an effective examination, the court may direct that the defendant be confined in a hospital designated by the director until the examination is completed.

3. When the defendant is in custody at the time a court issues an order of examination, the examination must be conducted at the place where the defendant is being held in custody. If, however, the director determines that hospital confinement of the defendant is necessary for an effective examination, the sheriff must deliver the defendant to a hospital designated by the director and hold him in custody therein, under sufficient guard, until the examination is completed.

4. Hospital confinement under subdivisions two and three shall be for a period not exceeding thirty days, except that, upon application of the director, the court may authorize confinement for an additional period not exceeding thirty days if it is satisfied that a longer period is necessary to complete the examination. During the period of hospital confinement, the physician in charge of the hospital may administer or cause to be administered to the defendant such emergency psychiatric, medical or other therapeutic treatment as in his judgment should be administered.

5. Each psychiatric examiner, after he has completed his examination of the defendant, must promptly prepare an examination report and submit it to the director. If the psychiatric examiners are not unanimous in their opinion as to whether the defendant is or is not an incapacitated person, the director must designate another qualified psychiatric examiner to examine the defendant to determine if he is an incapacitated person. Upon receipt of the examination reports, the director must submit them to the court that issued the order of examination. The court must furnish a copy of the reports to counsel for the defendant and to the district attorney.

6. When a defendant is subjected to examination pursuant to an order issued by a criminal court in accordance with this article, any statement made by him for the purpose of the examination or treatment shall be inadmissible in evidence against him in any criminal action on any issue other than that of his mental condition, but such statement is admissible upon that issue whether or not it would otherwise be deemed a privileged communication.

7. A psychiatric examiner is entitled to his reasonable traveling expenses, a fee of fifty dollars for each examination of a defendant and a fee of fifty dollars for each appearance at a court hearing or trial but not exceeding two hundred dollars in fees for examination and testimony in any one case; except that if such psychiatric examiner be an employee of the state of New York he shall be entitled only to reasonable traveling expenses, unless such psychiatric examiner makes the examination or appears at a court hearing or trial outside his hours of state employment in a county in which the director of community mental health services certifies to the fiscal officer thereof that there is a shortage of qualified psychiatrists available to conduct examinations under the criminal procedure law in such county, in which event he shall be entitled to the foregoing fees and reasonable traveling expenses. Such fees and traveling expenses and the costs of sending a defendant to another place of detention or to a hospital for examination, of his maintenance therein

and of returning him shall, when approved by the court, be a charge of the county in which the defendant is being tried.

> **HISTORY:** Add, L 1970, ch 996, § 1, eff Sept 1, 1971. Sub 1, amd, L 1989, ch 693, § 2, eff July 22, 1989. Sub 5, amd, L 1989, ch 693, § 2, eff July 22, 1989. Sub 7, amd, L 1971, ch 884 § 6, L 1972, ch 692, § 1, eff July 1, 1972.

§ 730.30. Fitness to proceed; order of examination

1. At any time after a defendant is arraigned upon an accusatory instrument other than a felony complaint and before the imposition of sentence, or at any time after a defendant is arraigned upon a felony complaint and before he is held for the action of the grand jury, the court wherein the criminal action is pending must issue an order of examination when it is of the opinion that the defendant may be an incapacitated person.

2. When the examination reports submitted to the court show that each psychiatric examiner is of the opinion that the defendant is not an incapacitated person, the court may, on its own motion, conduct a hearing to determine the issue of capacity, and it must conduct a hearing upon motion therefor by the defendant or by the district attorney. If no motion for a hearing is made, the criminal action against the defendant must proceed. If, following a hearing, the court is satisfied that the defendant is not an incapacitated person, the criminal action against him must proceed; if the court is not so satisfied, it must issue a further order of examination directing that the defendant be examined by different psychiatric examiners designated by the director.

3. When the examination reports submitted to the court show that each psychiatric examiner is of the opinion that the defendant is an incapacitated person, the court may, on its own motion, conduct a hearing to determine the issue of capacity and it must conduct such hearing upon motion therefor by the defendant or by the district attorney.

4. When the examination reports submitted to the court show that the psychiatric examiners are not unanimous in their opinion as to whether the defendant is or is not an incapacitated person, or when the examination reports submitted to the superior court show that the psychiatric examiners are not unanimous in their opinion as to whether the defendant is or is not a dangerous incapacitated person, the court must conduct a hearing to determine the issue of capacity or dangerousness.

> **HISTORY:** Add, L 1970, ch 996, § 1, eff Sept 1, 1971. Sub 3, amd, L 1974, ch 629, § 7, eff May 30, 1974.

§ 730.40. Fitness to proceed; local criminal court accusatory instrument

1. When a local criminal court, following a hearing conducted pursuant to subdivision three or four of section 730.30 of this article, is satisfied that the defendant is not an incapacitated person, the criminal action against him or her must proceed. If it is satisfied that the defendant is an incapacitated person, or if no motion for such a hearing is made, such court must issue a final or temporary order of observation committing him or her to the custody of the commissioner for care and treatment in an appropriate institution for a period not to exceed ninety days from the date of the order, provided, however, that the commissioner may designate an appropriate hospital for placement of a defendant for whom a final order of observation has been issued, where such hospital is licensed by the office of mental health and has agreed to accept, upon referral by the commissioner, defendants subject to final orders of observation issued under this subdivision. When a local criminal court accusatory instrument other than a felony complaint has been filed against the defendant, such court must issue a final order of observation. When a felony complaint has been filed against the defendant, such court must issue a temporary order of observation committing him or her to the custody of the commissioner for care and treatment in an appropriate

institution or, upon the consent of the district attorney, committing him or her to the custody of the commissioner for care and treatment on an out-patient basis, for a period not to exceed ninety days from the date of such order, except that, with the consent of the district attorney, it may issue a final order of observation. Upon the issuance of a final order of observation, the district attorney shall immediately transmit to the commissioner, in a manner intended to protect the confidentiality of the information, a list of names and contact information of persons who may reasonably be expected to be the victim of any assault or any violent felony offense, as defined in the penal law, or any offense listed in section 530.11 of this chapter which would be carried out by the committed person; provided that the person who reasonably may be expected to be a victim does not need to be a member of the same family or household as the committed person.

2. When a local criminal court has issued a final order of observation, it must dismiss the accusatory instrument filed in such court against the defendant and such dismissal constitutes a bar to any further prosecution of the charge or charges contained in such accusatory instrument. When the defendant is in the custody of the commissioner pursuant to a final order of observation, the commissioner or his or her designee, which may include the director of an appropriate institution, immediately upon the discharge of the defendant, must certify to such court that he or she has complied with the notice provisions set forth in paragraph (a) of subdivision six of section 730.60 of this article. When the defendant is in the custody of the commissioner at the expiration of the period prescribed in a temporary order of observation, the proceedings in the local criminal court that issued such order shall terminate for all purposes and the commissioner must promptly certify to such court and to the appropriate district attorney that the defendant was in his or her custody on such expiration date. Upon receipt of such certification, the court must dismiss the felony complaint filed against the defendant.

3. When a local criminal court has issued an order of examination or a temporary order of observation, and when the charge or charges contained in the accusatory instrument are subsequently presented to a grand jury, such grand jury need not hear the defendant pursuant to section 190.50 unless, upon application by defendant to the superior court that impaneled such grand jury, the superior court determines that the defendant is not an incapacitated person.

4. When an indictment is filed against a defendant after a local criminal court has issued an order of examination and before it has issued a final or temporary order of observation, the defendant must be promptly arraigned upon the indictment, and the proceedings in the local criminal court shall thereupon terminate for all purposes. The district attorney must notify the local criminal court of such arraignment, and such court must thereupon dismiss the accusatory instrument filed in such court against the defendant. If the director has submitted the examination reports to the local criminal court, such court must forward them to the superior court in which the indictment was filed. If the director has not submitted such reports to the local criminal court, he must submit them to the superior court in which the indictment was filed.

5. When an indictment is timely filed against the defendant after the issuance of a temporary order of observation or after the expiration of the period prescribed in such order, the superior court in which such indictment is filed must direct the sheriff to take custody of the defendant at the institution in which he is confined and bring him before the court for arraignment upon the indictment. After the defendant is arraigned upon the indictment, such temporary order of observation or any order issued pursuant to the mental hygiene law after the expiration of the period prescribed in the temporary order of observation shall be deemed nullified. Notwithstanding any other provision of law, an indictment filed in a superior court against a defendant for a crime charged in the felony complaint is not timely for the purpose of this subdivision if it is filed more than six months after the expiration of the period prescribed in a temporary order of observation

issued by a local criminal court wherein such felony complaint was pending. An untimely indictment must be dismissed by the superior court unless such court is satisfied that there was good cause for the delay in filing such indictment.

HISTORY: Add, L 1970, ch 996, § 1, eff Sept 1, 1971; amd, L 2008, ch 231, § 1, eff Aug 6, 2008, L 2012, ch 56, § 2 (Part Q), eff March 30, 2012, L 2012, ch 476, § 1, eff Oct 3, 2012, L 2013, ch 7, §§ 1, 2, eff March 15, 2013.

§ 730.50. Fitness to proceed; indictment

1. When a superior court, following a hearing conducted pursuant to subdivision three or four of section 730.30 of this article, is satisfied that the defendant is not an incapacitated person, the criminal action against him or her must proceed. If it is satisfied that the defendant is an incapacitated person, or if no motion for such a hearing is made, it must adjudicate him or her an incapacitated person, and must issue a final order of observation or an order of commitment. When the indictment does not charge a felony or when the defendant has been convicted of an offense other than a felony, such court (a) must issue a final order of observation committing the defendant to the custody of the commissioner for care and treatment in an appropriate institution for a period not to exceed ninety days from the date of such order, provided, however, that the commissioner may designate an appropriate hospital for placement of a defendant for whom a final order of observation has been issued, where such hospital is licensed by the office of mental health and has agreed to accept, upon referral by the commissioner, defendants subject to final orders of observation issued under this subdivision, and (b) must dismiss the indictment filed in such court against the defendant, and such dismissal constitutes a bar to any further prosecution of the charge or charges contained in such indictment. Upon the issuance of a final order of observation, the district attorney shall immediately transmit to the commissioner, in a manner intended to protect the confidentiality of the information, a list of names and contact information of persons who may reasonably be expected to be the victim of any assault or any violent felony offense, as defined in the penal law, or any offense listed in section 530.11 of this chapter which would be carried out by the committed person; provided that the person who reasonably may be expected to be a victim does not need to be a member of the same family or household as the committed person. When the indictment charges a felony or when the defendant has been convicted of a felony, it must issue an order of commitment committing the defendant to the custody of the commissioner for care and treatment in an appropriate institution or, upon the consent of the district attorney, committing him or her to the custody of the commissioner for care and treatment on an out-patient basis, for a period not to exceed one year from the date of such order. Upon the issuance of an order of commitment, the court must exonerate the defendant's bail if he or she was previously at liberty on bail; provided, however, that exoneration of bail is not required when a defendant is committed to the custody of the commissioner for care and treatment on an out-patient basis. When the defendant is in the custody of the commissioner pursuant to a final order of observation, the commissioner or his or her designee, which may include the director of an appropriate institution, immediately upon the discharge of the defendant, must certify to such court that he or she has complied with the notice provisions set forth in paragraph (a) of subdivision six of section 730.60 of this article.

2. When a defendant is in the custody of the commissioner immediately prior to the expiration of the period prescribed in a temporary order of commitment and the superintendent of the institution wherein the defendant is confined is of the opinion that the defendant continues to be an incapacitated person, such superintendent must apply to the court that issued such order for an order of retention. Such application must be made within sixty days prior to the expiration of such period on forms that have been jointly adopted by the judicial conference and the commissioner. The superintendent must give written notice of the application to the defendant and to the mental

hygiene legal service. Upon receipt of such application, the court may, on its own motion, conduct a hearing to determine the issue of capacity, and it must conduct such hearing if a demand therefor is made by the defendant or the mental hygiene legal service within ten days from the date that notice of the application was given them. If, at the conclusion of a hearing conducted pursuant to this subdivision, the court is satisfied that the defendant is no longer an incapacitated person, the criminal action against him must proceed. If it is satisfied that the defendant continues to be an incapacitated person, or if no demand for a hearing is made, the court must adjudicate him an incapacitated person and must issue an order of retention which shall authorize continued custody of the defendant by the commissioner for a period not to exceed one year.

3. When a defendant is in the custody of the commissioner immediately prior to the expiration of the period prescribed in the first order of retention, the procedure set forth in subdivision two shall govern the application for and the issuance of any subsequent order of retention, except that any subsequent orders of retention must be for periods not to exceed two years each; provided, however, that the aggregate of the periods prescribed in the temporary order of commitment, the first order of retention and all subsequent orders of retention must not exceed two-thirds of the authorized maximum term of imprisonment for the highest class felony charged in the indictment or for the highest class felony of which he was convicted.

4. When a defendant is in the custody of the commissioner at the expiration of the authorized period prescribed in the last order of retention, the criminal action pending against him in the superior court that issued such order shall terminate for all purposes, and the commissioner must promptly certify to such court and to the appropriate district attorney that the defendant was in his custody on such expiration date. Upon receipt of such certification, the court must dismiss the indictment, and such dismissal constitutes a bar to any further prosecution of the charge or charges contained in such indictment.

5. When, on the effective date of this subdivision, any defendant remains in the custody of the commissioner pursuant to an order issued under former code of criminal procedure section six hundred sixty-two-b, the superintendent or director of the institution where such defendant is confined shall, if he believes that the defendant continues to be an incapacitated person, apply forthwith to a court of record in the county where the institution is located for an order of retention. The procedures for obtaining any order pursuant to this subdivision shall be in accordance with the provisions of subdivisions two, three and four of this section, except that the period of retention pursuant to the first order obtained under this subdivision shall be for not more than one year and any subsequent orders of retention must be for periods not to exceed two years each; provided, however, that the aggregate of the time spent in the custody of the commissioner pursuant to any order issued in accordance with the provisions of former code of criminal procedure section six hundred sixty-two-b and the periods prescribed by the first order obtained under this subdivision and all subsequent orders of retention must not exceed two-thirds of the authorized maximum term of imprisonment for the highest class felony charged in the indictment or the highest class felony of which he was convicted.

HISTORY: Add, L 1970, ch 996, § 1, eff Sept 1, 1971; amd, L 1972, ch 810, § 1, L 1974, ch 629, § 8, eff May 30, 1974, L 1985, ch 789, § 48, eff April 1, 1986, L 2008, ch 231, § 2, eff Aug 6, 2008, L 2012, ch 56, § 3 (Part Q), eff March 30, 2012, L 2013, ch 7, § 4, eff March 15, 2013.

§ 730.60. Fitness to proceed; procedure following custody by commissioner

1. When a local criminal court issues a final or temporary order of observation or an order of commitment, it must forward such order and a copy of the examination reports and the accusatory instrument to the commissioner, and, if available, a copy of the pre-sentence report. Upon receipt thereof, the commissioner must designate an appropriate institution operated by the department of

mental hygiene in which the defendant is to be placed, provided, however, that the commissioner may designate an appropriate hospital for placement of a defendant for whom a final order of observation has been issued, where such hospital is licensed by the office of mental health and has agreed to accept, upon referral by the commissioner, defendants subject to final orders of observation issued under this subdivision. The sheriff must hold the defendant in custody pending such designation by the commissioner, and when notified of the designation, the sheriff must deliver the defendant to the superintendent of such institution. The superintendent must promptly inform the appropriate director of the mental hygiene legal service of the defendant's admission to such institution. If a defendant escapes from the custody of the commissioner, the escape shall interrupt the period prescribed in any order of observation, commitment or retention, and such interruption shall continue until the defendant is returned to the custody of the commissioner.

2. Except as otherwise provided in subdivisions IV and V, when a defendant is in the custody of the commissioner pursuant to a temporary order of observation or an order of commitment or an order of retention, the criminal action pending against the defendant in the court that issued such order is suspended until the superintendent of the institution in which the defendant is confined determines that he is no longer an incapacitated person. In that event, the court that issued such order and the appropriate district attorney must be notified, in writing, by the superintendent of his determination. The court must thereupon proceed in accordance with the provisions of subdivision two of section 730.30 of this chapter; provided, however, if the court is satisfied that the defendant remains an incapacitated person, and upon consent of all parties, the court may order the return of the defendant to the institution in which he had been confined for such period of time as was authorized by the prior order of commitment or order of retention. Upon such return, the defendant shall have all rights and privileges accorded by the provisions of this article.

3. When a defendant is in the custody of the commissioner pursuant to an order issued in accordance with this article, the commissioner may transfer him to any appropriate institution operated by the department of mental hygiene, provided, however, that the commissioner may designate an appropriate hospital for placement of a defendant for whom a final order of observation has been issued, where such hospital is licensed by the office of mental health and has agreed to accept, upon referral by the commissioner, defendants subject to final orders of observation issued under this section. The commissioner may discharge a defendant in his custody under a final order of observation at any time prior to the expiration date of such order, or otherwise treat or transfer such defendant in the same manner as if he were a patient not in confinement under a criminal court order.

4. When a defendant is in the custody of the commissioner pursuant to an order of commitment or an order of retention, he may make any motion authorized by this chapter which is susceptible of fair determination without his personal participation. If the court denies any such motion it must be without prejudice to a renewal thereof after the criminal action against the defendant has been ordered to proceed. If the court enters an order dismissing the indictment and does not direct that the charge or charges be resubmitted to a grand jury, the court must direct that such order of dismissal be served upon the commissioner.

5. When a defendant is in the custody of the commissioner pursuant to an order of commitment or an order of retention, the superior court that issued such order may, upon motion of the defendant, and with the consent of the district attorney, dismiss the indictment when the court is satisfied that (a) the defendant is a resident or citizen of another state or country and that he will be removed thereto upon dismissal of the indictment, or (b) the defendant has been continuously confined in the custody of the commissioner for a period of more than two years. Before granting a motion under this subdivision, the court must be further satisfied that dismissal of the indictment

is consistent with the ends of justice and that custody of the defendant by the commissioner pursuant to an order of commitment or an order of retention is not necessary for the protection of the public and that care and treatment can be effectively administered to the defendant without the necessity of such order. If the court enters an order of dismissal under this subdivision, it must set forth in the record the reasons for such action, and must direct that such order of dismissal be served upon the commissioner. The dismissal of an indictment pursuant to this subdivision constitutes a bar to any further prosecution of the charge or charges contained in such indictment.

6. (a) Notwithstanding any other provision of law, no person committed to the custody of the commissioner pursuant to this article, or continuously thereafter retained in such custody, shall be discharged, released on condition or placed in any less secure facility or on any less restrictive status, including, but not limited to vacations, furloughs and temporary passes, unless the commissioner or his or her designee, which may include the director of an appropriate institution, shall deliver written notice, at least four days, excluding Saturdays, Sundays and holidays, in advance of the change of such committed person's facility or status, or in the case of a person committed pursuant to a final order of observation written notice upon discharge of such committed person, to all of the following:

(1) The district attorney of the county from which such person was committed;

(2) The superintendent of state police;

(3) The sheriff of the county where the facility is located;

(4) The police department having jurisdiction of the area where the facility is located;

(5) Any person who may reasonably be expected to be the victim of any assault or any violent felony offense, as defined in the penal law, or any offense listed in section 530.11 of this part which would be carried out by the committed person; provided that the person who reasonably may be expected to be a victim does not need to be a member of the same family or household as the committed person; and

(6) Any other person the court may designate.

Said notice may be given by any means reasonably calculated to give prompt actual notice.

(b) The notice required by this subdivision shall also be given immediately upon the departure of such committed person from the actual custody of the commissioner or an appropriate institution, without proper authorization. Nothing in this subdivision shall be construed to impair any other right or duty regarding any notice or hearing contained in any other provision of law.

(c) Whenever a district attorney has received the notice described in this subdivision, and the defendant is in the custody of the commissioner pursuant to a final order of observation or an order of commitment, he may apply within three days of receipt of such notice to a superior court, for an order directing a hearing to be held to determine whether such committed person is a danger to himself or others. Such hearing shall be held within ten days following the issuance of such order. Such order may provide that there shall be no further change in the committed person's facility or status until the hearing. Upon a finding that the committed person is a danger to himself or others, the court shall issue an order to the commissioner authorizing retention of the committed person in the status existing at the time notice was given hereunder, for a specified period, not to exceed six months. The district attorney and the committed person's attorney shall be entitled to the committed person's clinical records in the commissioner's custody, upon the issuance of an order directing a hearing to be held.

(d) Nothing in this subdivision shall be construed to impair any other right or duty regarding any notice or hearing contained in any other provision of law.

HISTORY: Add, L 1970, ch 996, § 1, eff Sept 1, 1971; amd, L 1973, ch 195 § 12, L 1974, ch 629, §§ 9, 10, eff May 30, 1974, L 1980, ch 549, §§ 2, 3, L 1981, ch 791, § 1, L 1984, ch 57, § 1, eff Nov 1, 1984 L 1985, ch 789, § 49, eff April 1, 1986, L 1987, ch 440, § 2, eff April 1, 1988, L 2008, ch 231, § 3, eff Aug 6, 2008, L 2012, ch 476, § 2, eff Oct 3, 2012, L 2013, ch 7, § 3, eff March 15, 2013.

§ 730.70. Fitness to proceed; procedure following termination of custody by commissioner

When a defendant is in the custody of the commissioner on the expiration date of a final or temporary order of observation or an order of commitment, or on the expiration date of the last order of retention, or on the date an order dismissing an indictment is served upon the commissioner, the superintendent of the institution in which the defendant is confined may retain him for care and treatment for a period of thirty days from such date. If the superintendent determines that the defendant is so mentally ill or mentally defective as to require continued care and treatment in an institution, he may, before the expiration of such thirty day period, apply for an order of certification in the manner prescribed in section 31.33 of the mental hygiene law.[*]

HISTORY: Add, L 1970, ch 996, § 1; amd, L 1973, ch 195 § 13, L 1974, ch 629, § 11, eff May 30, 1974. Sub 2, deleted, L 1974, ch 629, § 11, eff May 30, 1974.

---

[*] L 1977, ch 978, § 10, eff April 1, 1978, renumbered § 31.33 of the Mental Hygiene Law as § 9.33.

PENAL LAW

LAWS 1965, CHAPTER 1030, EFFECTIVE SEPTEMBER 1, 1967.

SYNOPSIS OF ARTICLES

PL

PART ONE   General Provisions

Title A
General Purposes, Rules of Construction, and Definitions

Title B
Principles of Criminal Liability

Title C
Defenses

HISTORY: Add, L 1965, ch 1030, eff Sept 1, 1967.

TITLE A   General Purposes, Rules of Construction, and Definitions

ARTICLE 1
GENERAL PURPOSES

ARTICLE 5
GENERAL RULES OF CONSTRUCTION AND APPLICATION

ARTICLE 10
DEFINITIONS

HISTORY: Add, L 1965, ch 1030, eff Sept 1, 1967.

ARTICLE 1   GENERAL PURPOSES

§ 1.00.   **Short title**
§ 1.05.   **General purposes**

HISTORY: Add, L 1965, ch 1030, eff Sept 1, 1967.

§ 1.00. Short title

This chapter shall be known as the "Penal Law."

HISTORY: Add, L 1965, ch 1030, eff Sept 1, 1967, with substance derived from former Penal Law § 1.

§ 1.05. General purposes

The general purposes of the provisions of this chapter are:

1. To proscribe conduct which unjustifiably and inexcusably causes or threatens substantial harm to individual or public interests;

2. To give fair warning of the nature of the conduct proscribed and of the sentences authorized upon conviction;

3. To define the act or omission and the accompanying mental state which constitute each offense;

4. To differentiate on reasonable grounds between serious and minor offenses and to prescribe proportionate penalties therefor;

5. To provide for an appropriate public response to particular offenses, including consideration of the consequences of the offense for the victim, including the victim's family, and the community; and

6. To insure the public safety by preventing the commission of offenses through the deterrent influence of the sentences authorized, the rehabilitation of those convicted, the promotion of their successfuland productive reentry and reintegration into society, and their confinement when required in the interests of public protection.

HISTORY: Add, L 1965, ch 1030, with substance derived from § 20; amd, L 1982, ch 612, § 1, eff Nov 1, 1982. Sub 4, amd, L 1982, ch 612, § 1, eff Nov 1, 1982. Sub 5, add, L 1982, ch 612, § 1, eff Nov 1, 1982. Former sub 5, renumbered sub 6, L 1982, ch 612, § 1, eff Nov 1, 1982. Sub 6, formerly sub 5, renumbered sub 6, L 1982, ch 612, § 1, eff Nov 1, 1982. Sub 6, amd, L 2006, ch 98, § 1, eff June 7, 2006.

ARTICLE 5   GENERAL RULES OF CONSTRUCTION AND APPLICATION

§ 5.00.   **Penal law not strictly construed**
§ 5.05.   **Application of chapter to offenses committed before and after enactment**
§ 5.10.   **Other limitations on applicability of this chapter**

HISTORY: Add, L 1965, ch 1030, eff Sept 1, 1967.

§ 5.00. Penal law not strictly construed

The general rule that a penal statute is to be strictly construed does not apply to this chapter, but the provisions herein must be construed according to the fair import of their terms to promote justice and effect the objects of the law.

HISTORY: Add, L 1965, ch 1030, eff Sept 1, 1967, with substance derived from § 21.

§ 5.05. Application of chapter to offenses committed before and after enactment

1. The provisions of this chapter shall govern the construction of and punishment for any offense defined in this chapter and committed after the effective date hereof, as well as the construction and application of any defense to a prosecution for such an offense.

2. Unless otherwise expressly provided, or unless the context otherwise requires, the provisions of this chapter shall govern the construction of and punishment for any offense defined outside of this chapter and committed after the effective date thereof, as well as the construction and application of any defense to a prosecution for such an offense.

3. The provisions of this chapter do not apply to or govern the construction of and punishment for any offense committed prior to the effective date of this chapter, or the construction and application of any defense to a prosecution for such an offense. Such an offense must be construed and punished according to the provisions of law existing at the time of the commission thereof in the same manner as if this chapter had not been enacted.

HISTORY: Add, L 1965, ch 1030, eff Sept 1, 1967, with substance derived in part from §§ 22 and 38.

§ 5.10. Other limitations on applicability of this chapter

1. Except as otherwise provided, the procedure governing the accusation, prosecution, conviction and punishment of offenders and offenses is not regulated by this chapter but by the criminal procedure law.

2. This chapter does not affect any power conferred by law upon any court-martial or other military authority or officer to prosecute and punish conduct and offenders violating military codes or laws.

3. This chapter does not bar, suspend, or otherwise affect any right or liability to damages, penalty, forfeiture or other remedy authorized by law to be recovered or enforced in a civil action, regardless of whether the conduct involved in such civil action constitutes an offense defined in this chapter.

4. Sections 120.45, 120.50, 120.55, 120.60 and 240.25, subdivisions two and three of section 240.26, and sections 240.70 and 240.71 of this chapter (a) do not apply to conduct which is otherwise lawful under the provisions of the National Labor Relations Act as amended, the National Railway Labor Act as amended, or the Federal Employment Labor Management Act as amended, and (b) do not bar any conduct, including, but not limited to, peaceful picketing or other peaceful demonstration, protected from legal prohibition by the federal and state constitutions.

HISTORY: Add, L 1965, ch 1030, eff Sept 1, 1967, with substance derived from §§ 23, 24, 37, 39, 41. Sub 1, amd, L 1971, ch 1097, § 72, eff Sept 1, 1971. Sub 4, add, L 1999, ch 635, § 12, eff Dec 1, 1999; amd, L 2000, ch 434, § 6, eff Oct 20, 2000.

ARTICLE 10   DEFINITIONS

§ 10.00.   **Definitions of terms of general use in this chapter**

HISTORY: Add, L 1965, ch 1030, eff Sept 1, 1967.

§ 10.00. Definitions of terms of general use in this chapter

Except where different meanings are expressly specified in subsequent provisions of this chapter, the following terms have the following meanings:

1. "Offense" means conduct for which a sentence to a term of imprisonment or to a fine is provided by any law of this state or by any law, local law or ordinance of a political subdivision of this state, or by any order, rule or regulation of any governmental instrumentality authorized by law to adopt the same.

2. "Traffic infraction" means any offense defined as "traffic infraction" by section one hundred fifty-five of the vehicle and traffic law.

3. "Violation" means an offense, other than a "traffic infraction," for which a sentence to a term of imprisonment in excess of fifteen days cannot be imposed.

4. "Misdemeanor" means an offense, other than a "traffic infraction," for which a sentence to a term of imprisonment in excess of fifteen days may be imposed, but for which a sentence to a term of imprisonment in excess of one year cannot be imposed.

5. "Felony" means an offense for which a sentence to a term of imprisonment in excess of one year may be imposed.

6. "Crime" means a misdemeanor or a felony.

7. "Person" means a human being, and where appropriate, a public or private corporation, an unincorporated association, a partnership, a government or a governmental instrumentality.

8. "Possess" means to have physical possession or otherwise to exercise dominion or control over tangible property.

9. "Physical injury" means impairment of physical condition or substantial pain.

10. "Serious physical injury" means physical injury which creates a substantial risk of death, or which causes death or serious and protracted disfigurement, protracted impairment of health or protracted loss or impairment of the function of any bodily organ.

11. "Deadly physical force" means physical force which, under the circumstances in which it is used, is readily capable of causing death or other serious physical injury.

12. "Deadly weapon" means any loaded weapon from which a shot, readily capable of producing death or other serious physical injury, may be discharged, or a switchblade knife, gravity knife, pilum ballistic knife, metal knuckle knife, dagger, billy, blackjack, plastic knuckles, or metal knuckles.

13. "Dangerous instrument" means any instrument, article or substance, including a "vehicle" as that term is defined in this section, which, under the circumstances in which it is used, attempted to be used or threatened to be used, is readily capable of causing death or other serious physical injury.

14. "Vehicle" means a "motor vehicle", "trailer" or "semi-trailer," as defined in the vehicle and traffic law, any snowmobile as defined in the parks and recreation law, any aircraft, or any vessel equipped for propulsion by mechanical means or by sail.

15. "Public servant" means (a) any public officer or employee of the state or of any political

subdivision thereof or of any governmental instrumentality within the state, or (b) any person exercising the functions of any such public officer or employee. The term public servant includes a person who has been elected or designated to become a public servant.

16. "Juror" means any person who is a member of any jury, including a grand jury, impaneled by any court in this state or by any public servant authorized by law to impanel a jury. The term juror also includes a person who has been drawn or summoned to attend as a prospective juror.

17. "Benefit" means any gain or advantage to the beneficiary and includes any gain or advantage to a third person pursuant to the desire or consent of the beneficiary.

18. "Juvenile offender" means (1) a person thirteen years old who is criminally responsible for acts constituting murder in the second degree as defined in subdivisions one and two of section 125.25 of this chapter or such conduct as a sexually motivated felony, where authorized pursuant to section 130.91 of the penal law; and (2) a person fourteen or fifteen years old who is criminally responsible for acts constituting the crimes defined in subdivisions one and two of section 125.25 (murder in the second degree) and in subdivision three of such section provided that the underlying crime for the murder charge is one for which such person is criminally responsible; section 135.25 (kidnapping in the first degree); 150.20 (arson in the first degree); subdivisions one and two of section 120.10 (assault in the first degree); 125.20 (manslaughter in the first degree); subdivisions one and two of section 130.35 (rape in the first degree); subdivisions one and two of section 130.50 (criminal sexual act in the first degree); 130.70 (aggravated sexual abuse in the first degree); 140.30 (burglary in the first degree); subdivision one of section 140.25 (burglary in the second degree); 150.15 (arson in the second degree); 160.15 (robbery in the first degree); subdivision two of section 160.10 (robbery in the second degree) of this chapter; or section 265.03 of this chapter, where such machine gun or such firearm is possessed on school grounds, as that phrase is defined in subdivision fourteen of section 220.00 of this chapter; or defined in this chapter as an attempt to commit murder in the second degree or kidnapping in the first degree, or such conduct as a sexually motivated felony, where authorized pursuant to section 130.91 of the penal law.

19. For the purposes of section 260.30 and 120.01 of this chapter the term "child day care provider" shall be defined as provided for in section three hundred ninety of the social services law.

20. For purposes of sections 120.13, 120.18, 125.11, 125.21 and 125.22 of this chapter, the term "peace officer" means a peace officer as defined in subdivision one, two, three, four, six, twelve, thirteen, fifteen, sixteen, seventeen, eighteen, nineteen, twenty, twenty-one, twenty-three, twenty-three-a, twenty-four, twenty-five, twenty-six, twenty-eight, twenty-nine, thirty, thirty-one, thirty-two, thirty-four, thirty-five, thirty-six, forty-three, forty-five, forty-seven, forty-eight, forty-nine, fifty-one, fifty-two, fifty-eight, sixty-one, as added by chapter two hundred fifty-seven of the laws of nineteen hundred ninety-two, sixty-one, as added by chapter three hundred twenty-one of the laws of nineteen hundred ninety-two, sixty-two, as added by chapter two hundred four of the laws of nineteen hundred ninety-three, sixty-two, as added by chapter six hundred eighty-seven of the laws of nineteen hundred ninety-three, sixty-three, as amended by chapter six hundred thirty-eight of the laws of two thousand three, sixty-four, sixty-five, sixty-eight, as added by chapter one hundred sixty-eight of the laws of two thousand, sixty-eight, as added by chapter three hundred eighty-one of the laws of two thousand, seventy, seventy-one, seventy-four, as added by chapter five hundred forty-eight of the laws of two thousand one, seventy-five, as added by chapter three hundred twenty-one of the laws of two thousand two, seventy-five, as added by chapter six hundred twenty-three of the laws of two thousand two, seventy-seven, as added by chapter three hundred sixty-seven of the laws of two

thousand four, seventy-eight or seventy-nine, as added by chapter two hundred forty-one of the laws of two thousand four, of section 2.10 of the criminal procedure law, as well as any federal law enforcement officer defined in section 2.15 of the criminal procedure law.

21. "Drug trafficking felony" means any of the following offenses defined in article two hundred twenty of this chapter: violation of use of a child to commit a controlled substance offense as defined in section 220.28; criminal sale of a controlled substance in the fourth degree as defined in section 220.34; criminal sale of a controlled substance in the third degree as defined in section 220.39; criminal sale of a controlled substance in the second degree as defined in section 220.41; criminal sale of a controlled substance in the first degree as defined in section 220.43; criminal sale of a controlled substance in or near school grounds as defined in section 220.44; unlawful manufacture of methamphetamine in the second degree as defined in section 220.74; unlawful manufacture of methamphetamine in the first degree as defined in section 220.75; or operating as a major trafficker as defined in section 220.77.

HISTORY: Add, L 1965, ch 1030; amd, L 1967, ch 791, § 1, eff Sept 1, 1967, L 1968, ch 73, § 9 L 1975, ch 686, § 1, L 1980, ch 295, § 1, eff June 19, 1980, L 1986, ch 328, § 1, L 1995, ch 219, § 1, eff Nov 1, 1995, L 1998, ch 435, § 3, eff Nov 1, 1998, L 1998, ch 600, § 4, eff Nov 1, 1998, L 2003, ch 264, § 1, eff Nov 1, 2003, L 2005, ch 765, § 11, eff Dec 21, 2005, L 2007, ch 7, § 47, eff April 13, 2007, L 2008, ch 257, § 1, eff Nov 1, 2008, L 2013, ch 1, § 26, eff March 16, 2013.

PL

TITLE B   Principles of Criminal Liability
ARTICLE 15
CULPABILITY

ARTICLE 20
PARTIES TO OFFENSES AND LIABILITY THROUGH ACCESSORIAL CONDUCT

HISTORY: Add, L 1965, ch 1030, eff Sept 1, 1967.

ARTICLE 15   CULPABILITY

HISTORY: Add, L 1965, ch 1030, eff Sept 1, 1967.

§ 15.00. Culpability; definitions of terms

The following definitions are applicable to this chapter:

1. "Act" means a bodily movement.

2. "Voluntary act" means a bodily movement performed consciously as a result of effort or determination, and includes the possession of property if the actor was aware of his physical possession or control thereof for a sufficient period to have been able to terminate it.

3. "Omission" means a failure to perform an act as to which a duty of performance is imposed by law.

4. "Conduct" means an act or omission and its accompanying mental state.

5. "To act" means either to perform an act or to omit to perform an act.

6. "Culpable mental state" means "intentionally" or "knowingly" or "recklessly" or with "criminal negligence," as these terms are defined in section 15.05.

HISTORY: Add, L 1965, ch 1030, eff Sept 1, 1967.

§ 15.05. Culpability; definitions of culpable mental states

The following definitions are applicable to this chapter:

1. "Intentionally." A person acts intentionally with respect to a result or to conduct described by a statute defining an offense when his conscious objective is to cause such result or to engage in such conduct.

2. "Knowingly." A person acts knowingly with respect to conduct or to a circumstance described by a statute defining an offense when he is aware that his conduct is of such nature or that such circumstance exists.

3. "Recklessly." A person acts recklessly with respect to a result or to a circumstance described by a statute defining an offense when he is aware of and consciously disregards a substantial and unjustifiable risk that such result will occur or that such circumstance exists. The risk must be of such nature and degree that disregard thereof constitutes a gross deviation from the standard of conduct that a reasonable person would observe in the situation. A person who

creates such a risk but is unaware thereof solely by reason of voluntary intoxication also acts recklessly with respect thereto.

4. "Criminal negligence." A person acts with criminal negligence with respect to a result or to a circumstance described by a statute defining an offense when he fails to perceive a substantial and unjustifiable risk that such result will occur or that such circumstance exists. The risk must be of such nature and degree that the failure to perceive it constitutes a gross deviation from the standard of care that a reasonable person would observe in the situation.

HISTORY: Add, L 1965, ch 1030, eff Sept 1, 1967.

§ 15.10. Requirements for criminal liability in general and for offenses of strict liability and mental culpability

The minimal requirement for criminal liability is the performance by a person of conduct which includes a voluntary act or the omission to perform an act which he is physically capable of performing. If such conduct is all that is required for commission of a particular offense, or if an offense or some material element thereof does not require a culpable mental state on the part of the actor, such offense is one of "strict liability." If a culpable mental state on the part of the actor is required with respect to every material element of an offense, such offense is one of "mental culpability."

HISTORY: Add, L 1965, ch 1030, eff Sept 1, 1967.

§ 15.15. Construction of statutes with respect to culpability requirements

1. When the commission of an offense defined in this chapter, or some element of an offense, requires a particular culpable mental state, such mental state is ordinarily designated in the statute defining the offense by use of the terms "intentionally," "knowingly," "recklessly" or "criminal negligence," or by use of terms, such as "with intent to defraud" and "knowing it to be false," describing a specific kind of intent or knowledge. When one and only one of such terms appears in a statute defining an offense, it is presumed to apply to every element of the offense unless an intent to limit its application clearly appears.

2. Although no culpable mental state is expressly designated in a statute defining an offense, a culpable mental state may nevertheless be required for the commission of such offense, or with respect to some or all of the material elements thereof, if the proscribed conduct necessarily involves such culpable mental state. A statute defining a crime, unless clearly indicating a legislative intent to impose strict liability, should be construed as defining a crime of mental culpability. This subdivision applies to offenses defined both in and outside this chapter.

HISTORY: Add, L 1965, ch 1030, eff Sept 1, 1967.

§ 15.20. Effect of ignorance or mistake upon liability

1. A person is not relieved of criminal liability for conduct because he engages in such conduct under a mistaken belief of fact, unless:

(a) Such factual mistake negatives the culpable mental state required for the commission of an offense; or

(b) The statute defining the offense or a statute related thereto expressly provides that such factual mistake constitutes a defense or exemption; or

(c) Such factual mistake is of a kind that supports a defense of justification as defined in article thirty-five of this chapter.

2. A person is not relieved of criminal liability for conduct because he engages in such conduct

under a mistaken belief that it does not, as a matter of law, constitute an offense, unless such mistaken belief is founded upon an official statement of the law contained in (a) a statute or other enactment, or (b) an administrative order or grant of permission, or (c) a judicial decision of a state or federal court, or (d) an interpretation of the statute or law relating to the offense, officially made or issued by a public servant, agency or body legally charged or empowered with the responsibility or privilege of administering, enforcing or interpreting such statute or law.

3. Notwithstanding the use of the term "knowingly" in any provision of this chapter defining an offense in which the age of a child is an element thereof, knowledge by the defendant of the age of such child is not an element of any such offense and it is not, unless expressly so provided, a defense to a prosecution therefor that the defendant did not know the age of the child or believed such age to be the same as or greater than that specified in the statute.

4. Notwithstanding the use of the term "knowingly" in any provision of this chapter defining an offense in which the aggregate weight of a controlled substance or marihuana is an element, knowledge by the defendant of the aggregate weight of such controlled substance or marihuana is not an element of any such offense and it is not, unless expressly so provided, a defense to a prosecution therefor that the defendant did not know the aggregate weight of the controlled substance or marihuana.

HISTORY: Add, L 1965, ch 1030, eff Sept 1, 1967. Sub 3, amd, L 1967, ch 791, § 2, eff Sept 1, 1967. Sub 4, add, L 1995, ch 75, § 19, eff June 10, 1995.

§ 15.25. Effect of intoxication upon liability

Intoxication is not, as such, a defense to a criminal charge; but in any prosecution for an offense, evidence of intoxication of the defendant may be offered by the defendant whenever it is relevant to negative an element of the crime charged.

HISTORY: Add, L 1965, ch 1030, eff Sept 1, 1967, with substance derived from § 1220.

ARTICLE 20   PARTIES TO OFFENSES AND LIABILITY THROUGH ACCESSORIAL CONDUCT

§ 20.00.	**Criminal liability for conduct of another**
§ 20.05.	**Criminal liability for conduct of another; no defense**
§ 20.10.	**Criminal liability for conduct of another; exemption**
§ 20.15.	**Convictions for different degrees of offense**
§ 20.20.	**Criminal liability of corporations**
§ 20.25.	**Criminal liability of an individual for corporate conduct**

HISTORY: Add, L 1965, ch 1030, eff Sept 1, 1967.

§ 20.00. Criminal liability for conduct of another

When one person engages in conduct which constitutes an offense, another person is criminally liable for such conduct when, acting with the mental culpability required for the commission thereof, he solicits, requests, commands, importunes, or intentionally aids such person to engage in such conduct.

HISTORY: Add, L 1965, ch 1030, eff Sept 1, 1967.

§ 20.05. Criminal liability for conduct of another; no defense

In any prosecution for an offense in which the criminal liability of the defendant is based upon the conduct of another person pursuant to section 20.00, it is no defense that:

1. Such other person is not guilty of the offense in question owing to criminal irresponsibility or other legal incapacity or exemption, or to unawareness of the criminal nature of the conduct

in question or of the defendant's criminal purpose or to other factors precluding the mental state required for the commission of the offense in question; or

2. Such other person has not been prosecuted for or convicted of any offense based upon the conduct in question, or has previously been acquitted thereof, or has legal immunity from prosecution therefor; or

3. The offense in question, as defined, can be committed only by a particular class or classes of persons, and the defendant, not belonging to such class or classes, is for that reason legally incapable of committing the offense in an individual capacity.

HISTORY: Add, L 1965, ch 1030, eff Sept 1, 1967.

§ 20.10. Criminal liability for conduct of another; exemption

Notwithstanding the provisions of sections 20.00 and 20.05, a person is not criminally liable for conduct of another person constituting an offense when his own conduct, though causing or aiding the commission of such offense, is of a kind that is necessarily incidental thereto. If such conduct constitutes a related but separate offense upon the part of the actor, he is liable for that offense only and not for the conduct or offense committed by the other person.

HISTORY: Add, L 1965, ch 1030, eff Sept 1, 1967.

§ 20.15. Convictions for different degrees of offense

Except as otherwise expressly provided in this chapter, when, pursuant to section 20.00, two or more persons are criminally liable for an offense which is divided into degrees, each person is guilty of such degree as is compatible with his own culpable mental state and with his own accountability for an aggravating fact or circumstance.

HISTORY: Add, L 1965, ch 1030, eff Sept 1, 1967.

§ 20.20. Criminal liability of corporations

1. As used in this section:

(a) "Agent" means any director, officer or employee of a corporation, or any other person who is authorized to act in behalf of the corporation.

(b) "High managerial agent" means an officer of a corporation or any other agent in a position of comparable authority with respect to the formulation of corporate policy or the supervision in a managerial capacity of subordinate employees.

2. A corporation is guilty of an offense when:

(a) The conduct constituting the offense consists of an omission to discharge a specific duty of affirmative performance imposed on corporations by law; or

(b) The conduct constituting the offense is engaged in, authorized, solicited, requested, commanded, or recklessly tolerated by the board of directors or by a high managerial agent acting within the scope of his employment and in behalf of the corporation; or

(c) The conduct constituting the offense is engaged in by an agent of the corporation while acting within the scope of his employment and in behalf of the corporation, and the offense is (i) a misdemeanor or a violation, (ii) one defined by a statute which clearly indicates a legislative intent to impose such criminal liability on a corporation, or (iii) any offense set forth in title twenty-seven of article seventy-one of the environmental conservation law.

HISTORY: Add, L 1965, ch 1030, eff Sept 1, 1967. Sub 2, par (c), amd, L 1981, ch 719, § 1, L 1986, ch 671, § 24, eff Nov 1, 1986; provided that all rules and regulations necessary for the implementation of this act are to be made on or before Nov 1, 1986.

§ 20.25. Criminal liability of an individual for corporate conduct

A person is criminally liable for conduct constituting an offense which he performs or causes to be performed in the name of or in behalf of a corporation to the same extent as if such conduct were performed in his own name or behalf.

HISTORY: Add, L 1965, ch 1030, eff Sept 1, 1967.

TITLE C   Defenses

ARTICLE 25
DEFENSES IN GENERAL

ARTICLE 30
DEFENSE OF INFANCY

ARTICLE 35
DEFENSE OF JUSTIFICATION

ARTICLE 40
OTHER DEFENSES INVOLVING LACK OF CULPABILITY

HISTORY: Add, L 1965, ch 1030, eff Sept 1, 1967.

ARTICLE 25   DEFENSES IN GENERAL

§ 25.00.   **Defenses; burden of proof**

HISTORY: Add, L 1965, ch 1030, eff Sept 1, 1967.

§ 25.00. Defenses; burden of proof

1. When a "defense," other than an "affirmative defense," defined by statute is raised at a trial, the people have the burden of disproving such defense beyond a reasonable doubt.

2. When a defense declared by statute to be an "affirmative defense" is raised at a trial, the defendant has the burden of establishing such defense by a preponderance of the evidence.

HISTORY: Add, L 1965, ch 1030, eff Sept 1, 1967.

ARTICLE 30   DEFENSE OF INFANCY

§ 30.00.   **Infancy**

§ 30.05.   **[Repealed]**

HISTORY: Add, L 1965, ch 1030, eff Sept 1, 1967. Article heading, amd, L 1984, ch 668, § 2, eff Nov 1, 1984, but not applicable to any criminal action or proceeding relating to an offense committed prior to Nov 1, 1984.

§ 30.00. Infancy

1. Except as provided in subdivision two of this section, a person less than sixteen years old is not criminally responsible for conduct.

2. A person thirteen, fourteen or fifteen years of age is criminally responsible for acts constituting murder in the second degree as defined in subdivisions one and two of section 125.25 and in subdivision three of such section provided that the underlying crime for the murder charge is one for which such person is criminally responsible or for such conduct as a sexually motivated felony, where authorized pursuant to section 130.91 of the penal law; and a person fourteen or fifteen years of age is criminally responsible for acts constituting the crimes defined in section 135.25 (kidnapping in the first degree); 150.20 (arson in the first degree); subdivisions one and two of section 120.10 (assault in the first degree); 125.20 (manslaughter in the first degree); subdivisions one and two of section 130.35 (rape in the first degree); subdivisions one and two of section 130.50 (criminal sexual act in the first degree); 130.70 (aggravated sexual abuse in the first degree); 140.30 (burglary in the first degree); subdivision one of section 140.25 (burglary in the second degree); 150.15 (arson in the second degree); 160.15 (robbery in the first degree); subdivision two of section 160.10 (robbery in the second degree) of this chapter; or section 265.03 of this chapter, where such machine gun or such firearm is possessed on school grounds, as that phrase is defined in subdivision fourteen of section 220.00 of this chapter; or defined in this chapter

as an attempt to commit murder in the second degree or kidnapping in the first degree, or for such conduct as a sexually motivated felony, where authorized pursuant to section 130.91 of the penal law.

3. In any prosecution for an offense, lack of criminal responsibility by reason of infancy, as defined in this section, is a defense.

HISTORY: Add, L 1965, ch 1030, with substance derived from § 2186; amd, L 1978, ch 481, § 28, eff Sept 1, 1978. Sub 2, add, L 1978, ch 481, § 28; amd, L 1979, ch 411, § 21, L 1981, ch 335, § 5, eff Sept 1, 1981. Former sub 2, renumbered sub 3, L 1978, ch 481, § 28, eff Sept 1, 1978. Sub 3, formerly sub 2, renumbered sub 3, L 1978, ch 481, § 28, eff Sept 1, 1978. Sub 2, amd, L 1998, ch 435, § 4, eff Nov 1, 1998, L 2003, ch 264, § 2, eff Nov 1, 2003, L 2007, ch 7, § 48, eff April 13, 2007.

§ 30.05. [Repealed]

HISTORY: Add, L 1965, ch 1030; repealed, L 1984, ch 668, § 1, eff Nov 1, 1984, but not applicable to any criminal action or proceeding relating to an offense committed prior to Nov 1, 1984.

ARTICLE 35   DEFENSE OF JUSTIFICATION

HISTORY: Add, L 1965, ch 1030, eff Sept 1, 1967. Article heading, amd, L 1968, ch 73, eff March 21, 1968.

§ 35.00. Justification; a defense

In any prosecution for an offense, justification, as defined in sections 35.05 through 35.30, is a defense.

HISTORY: Add, L 1965, ch 1030, eff Sept 1, 1967.

§ 35.05. Justification; generally

Unless otherwise limited by the ensuing provisions of this article defining justifiable use of physical force, conduct which would otherwise constitute an offense is justifiable and not criminal when:

1. Such conduct is required or authorized by law or by a judicial decree, or is performed by a public servant in the reasonable exercise of his official powers, duties or functions; or

2. Such conduct is necessary as an emergency measure to avoid an imminent public or private injury which is about to occur by reason of a situation occasioned or developed through no fault of the actor, and which is of such gravity that, according to ordinary standards of

intelligence and morality, the desirability and urgency of avoiding such injury clearly outweigh the desirability of avoiding the injury sought to be prevented by the statute defining the offense in issue. The necessity and justifiability of such conduct may not rest upon considerations pertaining only to the morality and advisability of the statute, either in its general application or with respect to its application to a particular class of cases arising thereunder. Whenever evidence relating to the defense of justification under this subdivision is offered by the defendant, the court shall rule as a matter of law whether the claimed facts and circumstances would, if established, constitute a defense.

HISTORY: Add, L 1965, ch 1030, eff Sept 1, 1967. Opening par, amd, L 1968, ch 73, § 2, eff March 21, 1968. Sub 1, amd, L 1968, ch 73, § 2, eff March 21, 1968.

§ 35.10. Justification; use of physical force generally

The use of physical force upon another person which would otherwise constitute an offense is justifiable and not criminal under any of the following circumstances:

1. A parent, guardian or other person entrusted with the care and supervision of a person under the age of twenty-one or an incompetent person, and a teacher or other person entrusted with the care and supervision of a person under the age of twenty-one for a special purpose, may use physical force, but not deadly physical force, upon such person when and to the extent that he reasonably believes it necessary to maintain discipline or to promote the welfare of such person.

2. A warden or other authorized official of a jail, prison or correctional institution may, in order to maintain order and discipline, use such physical force as is authorized by the correction law.

3. A person responsible for the maintenance of order in a common carrier of passengers, or a person acting under his direction, may use physical force when and to the extent that he reasonably believes it necessary to maintain order, but he may use deadly physical force only when he reasonably believes it necessary to prevent death or serious physical injury.

4. A person acting under a reasonable belief that another person is about to commit suicide or to inflict serious physical injury upon himself may use physical force upon such person to the extent that he reasonably believes it necessary to thwart such result.

5. A duly licensed physician, or a person acting under a physician's direction, may use physical force for the purpose of administering a recognized form of treatment which he or she reasonably believes to be adapted to promoting the physical or mental health of the patient if (a) the treatment is administered with the consent of the patient or, if the patient is under the age of eighteen years or an incompetent person, with the consent of the parent, guardian or other person entrusted with the patient's care and supervision, or (b) the treatment is administered in an emergency when the physician reasonably believes that no one competent to consent can be consulted and that a reasonable person, wishing to safeguard the welfare of the patient, would consent.

6. A person may, pursuant to the ensuing provisions of this article, use physical force upon another person in self-defense or defense of a third person, or in defense of premises, or in order to prevent larceny of or criminal mischief to property, or in order to effect an arrest or prevent an escape from custody. Whenever a person is authorized by any such provision to use deadly physical force in any given circumstance, nothing contained in any other such provision may be deemed to negate or qualify such authorization.

HISTORY: Add, L 1965, ch 1030, eff Sept 1, 1967. Sub 1, amd, L 1974, ch 930, § 1, eff Sept

1, 1974. Sub 5, amd, L 1974, ch 930, § 2, eff Sept 1, 1974. Sub 6, add, L 1968, ch 73, § 3, eff March 21, 1968. Former sub 6, repealed, L 1968, ch 73, § 3, eff March 21, 1968. Sub 5, amd, L 2004, ch 511, § 1, eff Sept 28, 2004. Sub 6, amd, L 2004, ch 511, § 1, eff Sept 28, 2004.

§ 35.15. Justification; use of physical force in defense of a person

1. A person may, subject to the provisions of subdivision two, use physical force upon another person when and to the extent he or she reasonably believes such to be necessary to defend himself, herself or a third person from what he or she reasonably believes to be the use or imminent use of unlawful physical force by such other person, unless:

(a) The latter's conduct was provoked by the actor with intent to cause physical injury to another person; or

(b) The actor was the initial aggressor; except that in such case the use of physical force is nevertheless justifiable if the actor has withdrawn from the encounter and effectively communicated such withdrawal to such other person but the latter persists in continuing the incident by the use or threatened imminent use of unlawful physical force; or

(c) The physical force involved is the product of a combat by agreement not specifically authorized by law.

2. A person may not use deadly physical force upon another person under circumstances specified in subdivision one unless:

(a) The actor reasonably believes that such other person is using or about to use deadly physical force. Even in such case, however, the actor may not use deadly physical force if he or she knows that with complete personal safety, to oneself and others he or she may avoid the necessity of so doing by retreating; except that the actor is under no duty to retreat if he or she is:

(i) in his or her dwelling and not the initial aggressor; or

(ii) a police officer or peace officer or a person assisting a police officer or a peace officer at the latter's direction, acting pursuant to section 35.30; or

(b) He or she reasonably believes that such other person is committing or attempting to commit a kidnapping, forcible rape, forcible criminal sexual act or robbery; or

(c) He or she reasonably believes that such other person is committing or attempting to commit a burglary, and the circumstances are such that the use of deadly physical force is authorized by subdivision three of section 35.20.

HISTORY: Add, L 1968, ch 73, § 4, eff March 21, 1968. Former § 36.15, add, L 1965, ch 1030, with substance derived from §§ 42, 246(3), 1055; amd, L 1965, ch 1039, § 1; repealed, L 1968, ch 73, § 4, eff March 21, 1968. Sub 1, amd, L 2004, ch 511, § 2, eff Sept 28, 2004. Sub 1, opening par, amd, L 2004, ch 511, § 2, eff Sept 28, 2004. Sub 1, par (a), amd, L 2004, ch 511, § 2, eff Sept 28, 2004. Sub 1, par (b), amd, L 2004, ch 511, § 2, eff Sept 28, 2004. Sub 2, amd, L 2004, ch 511, § 2, eff Sept 28, 2004. Sub 2, par (a), amd, L 2004, ch 511, § 2, eff Sept 28, 2004. Sub 2, par (a), subpar (i), amd, L 2004, ch 511, § 2, eff Sept 28, 2004. Sub 2, par (a), subpar (ii), amd, L 1980, ch 843, § 30, eff Sept 1, 1980. Sub 2, par (b), amd, L 2003, ch 264, § 3, eff Nov 1, 2003, L 2004, ch 511, § 2, eff Sept 28, 2004. Sub 2, par (c), amd, L 2004, ch 511, § 2, eff Sept 28, 2004.

§ 35.20. Justification; use of physical force in defense of premises and in defense of a person in the course of burglary

1. Any person may use physical force upon another person when he or she reasonably believes such to be necessary to prevent or terminate what he or she reasonably believes to be the

commission or attempted commission by such other person of a crime involving damage to premises. Such person may use any degree of physical force, other than deadly physical force, which he or she reasonably believes to be necessary for such purpose, and may use deadly physical force if he or she reasonably believes such to be necessary to prevent or terminate the commission or attempted commission of arson.

2. A person in possession or control of any premises, or a person licensed or privileged to be thereon or therein, may use physical force upon another person when he or she reasonably believes such to be necessary to prevent or terminate what he or she reasonably believes to be the commission or attempted commission by such other person of a criminal trespass upon such premises. Such person may use any degree of physical force, other than deadly physical force, which he or she reasonably believes to be necessary for such purpose, and may use deadly physical force in order to prevent or terminate the commission or attempted commission of arson, as prescribed in subdivision one, or in the course of a burglary or attempted burglary, as prescribed in subdivision three.

3. A person in possession or control of, or licensed or privileged to be in, a dwelling or an occupied building, who reasonably believes that another person is committing or attempting to commit a burglary of such dwelling or building, may use deadly physical force upon such other person when he or she reasonably believes such to be necessary to prevent or terminate the commission or attempted commission of such burglary.

4. As used in this section, the following terms have the following meanings:

(a) The terms "premises," "building" and "dwelling" have the meanings prescribed in section 140.00;

(b) Persons "licensed or privileged" to be in buildings or upon other premises include, but are not limited to:

(i) police officers or peace officers acting in the performance of their duties; and

(ii) security personnel or employees of nuclear powered electric generating facilities located within the state who are employed as part of any security plan approved by the federal operating license agencies acting in the performance of their duties at such generating facilities. For purposes of this subparagraph, the term "nuclear powered electric generating facility" shall mean a facility that generates electricity using nuclear power for sale, directly or indirectly, to the public, including the land upon which the facility is located and the safety and security zones as defined under federal regulations.

HISTORY: Add, L 1968, ch 73, § 5, eff March 21, 1968. Former § 35.20, add, L 1965, ch 1030, with substance derived from § 246(3); repealed, L 1968, ch 73, § 5, eff March 21, 1968. Sub 1, amd, L 2004, ch 511, § 3, eff Sept 28, 2004. Sub 2, amd, L 2004, ch 511, § 3, eff Sept 28, 2004. Sub 3, amd, L 2004, ch 511, § 3, eff Sept 28, 2004. Sub 4, par (b), amd, L 1980, ch 843, § 31, eff Sept 1, 1980. Sub 4, par (b), opening par, formerly part of entire sub 4, par (b), so designated sub 4, par (b) and amd, L 2004, ch 393, § 1, eff Aug 17, 2004. Sub 4, par (b), subpar (i), formerly part of entire sub 4, par (b), so designated sub 4, par (b), subpar (i) and amd, L 2004, ch 393, § 1, eff Aug 17, 2004. Sub 4, par (b), subpar (ii), add, L 2004, ch 393, § 1, eff Aug 17, 2004.

§ 35.25. Justification; use of physical force to prevent or terminate larceny or criminal mischief

A person may use physical force, other than deadly physical force, upon another person when and to the extent that he or she reasonably believes such to be necessary to prevent or terminate what he or she reasonably believes to be the commission or attempted commission by such other person of larceny or of criminal mischief with respect to property other than premises.

HISTORY: Add, L 1965, ch 1030, with substance derived from § 246(3); amd, L 1968, ch 73, § 6, eff March 21, 1968. Amd, L 2004, ch 511, § 4, eff Sept 28, 2004. Section heading, amd, L 1968, ch 73, § 6, eff March 21, 1968.

§ 35.27. Justification; use of physical force in resisting arrest prohibited

A person may not use physical force to resist an arrest, whether authorized or unauthorized, which is being effected or attempted by a police officer or peace officer when it would reasonably appear that the latter is a police officer or peace officer.

HISTORY: Add, L 1968, ch 73, § 7; amd, L 1980, ch 843, § 32, eff Sept 1, 1980.

§ 35.30. Justification; use of physical force in making an arrest or in preventing an escape

1. A police officer or a peace officer, in the course of effecting or attempting to effect an arrest, or of preventing or attempting to prevent the escape from custody, of a person whom he or she reasonably believes to have committed an offense, may use physical force when and to the extent he or she reasonably believes such to be necessary to effect the arrest, or to prevent the escape from custody, or in self-defense or to defend a third person from what he or she reasonably believes to be the use or imminent use of physical force; except that deadly physical force may be used for such purposes only when he or she reasonably believes that:

(a) The offense committed by such person was:

(i) a felony or an attempt to commit a felony involving the use or attempted use or threatened imminent use of physical force against a person; or

(ii) kidnapping, arson, escape in the first degree, burglary in the first degree or any attempt to commit such a crime; or

(b) The offense committed or attempted by such person was a felony and that, in the course of resisting arrest therefor or attempting to escape from custody, such person is armed with a firearm or deadly weapon; or

(c) Regardless of the particular offense which is the subject of the arrest or attempted escape, the use of deadly physical force is necessary to defend the police officer or peace officer or another person from what the officer reasonably believes to be the use or imminent use of deadly physical force.

2. The fact that a police officer or a peace officer is justified in using deadly physical force under circumstances prescribed in paragraphs (a) and (b) of subdivision one does not constitute justification for reckless conduct by such police officer or peace officer amounting to an offense against or with respect to innocent persons whom he or she is not seeking to arrest or retain in custody.

3. A person who has been directed by a police officer or a peace officer to assist such police officer or peace officer to effect an arrest or to prevent an escape from custody may use physical force, other than deadly physical force, when and to the extent that he or she reasonably believes such to be necessary to carry out such police officer's or peace officer's direction, unless he or she knows that the arrest or prospective arrest is not or was not authorized and may use deadly physical force under such circumstances when:

(a) He or she reasonably believes such to be necessary for self-defense or to defend a third person from what he or she reasonably believes to be the use or imminent use of deadly physical force; or

(b) He or she is directed or authorized by such police officer or peace officer to use deadly physical force unless heor she knows that the police officer or peace officer is not authorized to use deadly physical force under the circumstances.

4. A private person acting on his or her own account may use physical force, other than deadly physical force, upon another person when and to the extent that he or she reasonably believes such to be necessary to effect an arrest or to prevent the escape from custody of a person whom he or she reasonably believes to have committed an offense and who in fact has committed such offense; and may use deadly physical force for such purpose when he or she reasonably believes such to be necessary to:

(a) Defend himself, herself or a third person from what he or she reasonably believes to be the use or imminent use of deadly physical force; or

(b) Effect the arrest of a person who has committed murder, manslaughter in the first degree, robbery, forcible rape or forcible criminal sexual act and who is in immediate flight therefrom.

5. A guard, police officer or peace officer who is charged with the duty of guarding prisoners in a detention facility, as that term is defined in section 205.00, or while in transit to or from a detention facility, may use physical force when and to the extent that he or she reasonably believes such to be necessary to prevent the escape of a prisoner from a detention facility or from custody while in transit thereto or therefrom.

> **HISTORY:** Add, L 1968, ch 73, § 8; amd, L 1972, ch 598, § 1, L 1973, ch 676, § 27, L 1975, ch 667, § 32, eff Aug 6, 1975, deemed eff on and after April 1, 1975. Former § 35.30, add, L 1965, ch 1030, with substance derived in part from §§ 246(1), and 1055; repealed, L 1968, ch 73, § 8, eff March 21, 1968. Sub 1, opening par, amd, L 1980, ch 843, § 33, eff Sept 1, 1980. Sub 1, opening par, amd, L 2004, ch 511, § 5, eff Sept 28, 2004. Sub 1, par (c), amd, L 1980, ch 843, § 34, eff Sept 1, 1980. Sub 2, amd, L 1980, ch 843, § 35, eff Sept 1, 1980. Sub 2, amd, L 2004, ch 511, § 5, eff Sept 28, 2004. Sub 3, opening par, amd, L 1980, ch 843, § 35, eff Sept 1, 1980. Sub 3, opening par, amd, L 2004, ch 511, § 5, eff Sept 28, 2004. Sub 3, par (a), amd, L 2004, ch 511, § 5, eff Sept 28, 2004. Sub 3, par (b), amd, L 1980, ch 843, § 36, eff Sept 1, 1980. Sub 3, par (b), amd, L 2004, ch 511, § 5, eff Sept 28, 2004. Sub 4, opening par, amd, L 2004, ch 511, § 5, eff Sept 28, 2004. Sub 4, par (a), amd, L 2004, ch 511, § 5, eff Sept 28, 2004. Sub 4, par (b), amd, L 2003, ch 264, § 4, eff Nov 1, 2003. Sub 5, amd, L 1972, ch 598, § 1, L 1973, ch 676, § 27, L 1975, ch 667, § 32, L 1980, ch 471, § 16, L 1980, ch 843, § 37, eff Sept 1, 1980. Sub 5, amd, L 2004, ch 511, § 5, eff Sept 28, 2004.

§ 35.35. [Renumbered]

> **HISTORY:** Add, L 1965, ch 1030; renumbered § 40.00, L 1968, ch 73, eff March 21, 1968.

§ 35.40. [Renumbered]

> **HISTORY:** Add, L 1965, ch 1030; renumbered § 40.05, L 1968, ch 73, eff March 21, 1968.

§ 35.45. [Renumbered]

> **HISTORY:** Add, L 1965, ch 1030; renumbered § 40.10, L 1968, ch 73, eff March 21, 1968.

ARTICLE 40   OTHER DEFENSES INVOLVING LACK OF CULPABILITY

§ 40.00.	**Duress**
§ 40.05.	**Entrapment**
§ 40.10.	**Renunciation**
§ 40.15.	**Mental disease or defect**

> **HISTORY:** Add, L 1968, ch 73, § 10, eff March 21, 1968.

§ 40.00. Duress

1. In any prosecution for an offense, it is an affirmative defense that the defendant engaged in

the proscribed conduct because he was coerced to do so by the use or threatened imminent use of unlawful physical force upon him or a third person, which force or threatened force a person of reasonable firmness in his situation would have been unable to resist.

2. The defense of duress as defined in subdivision one of this section is not available when a person intentionally or recklessly places himself in a situation in which it is probable that he will be subjected to duress.

HISTORY: Added as § 35.35, L 1965, ch 1030, with substance derived from § 859; renumbered § 40.00, L 1968, ch 73, § 11, eff March 21, 1968.

§ 40.05. Entrapment

In any prosecution for an offense, it is an affirmative defense that the defendant engaged in the proscribed conduct because he was induced or encouraged to do so by a public servant, or by a person acting in cooperation with a public servant, seeking to obtain evidence against him for purpose of criminal prosecution, and when the methods used to obtain such evidence were such as to create a substantial risk that the offense would be committed by a person not otherwise disposed to commit it. Inducement or encouragement to commit an offense means active inducement or encouragement. Conduct merely affording a person an opportunity to commit an offense does not constitute entrapment.

HISTORY: Added as § 35.40, L 1965, ch 1030; renumbered § 40.05, L 1968, ch 73, § 11, eff March 21, 1968.

§ 40.10. Renunciation

1. In any prosecution for an offense, other than an attempt to commit a crime, in which the defendant's guilt depends upon his criminal liability for the conduct of another person pursuant to section 20.00, it is an affirmative defense that, under circumstances manifesting a voluntary and complete renunciation of his criminal purpose, the defendant withdrew from participation in such offense prior to the commission thereof and made a substantial effort to prevent the commission thereof.

2. In any prosecution for criminal facilitation pursuant to article one hundred fifteen, it is an affirmative defense that, prior to the commission of the felony which he facilitated, the defendant made a substantial effort to prevent the commission of such felony.

3. In any prosecution pursuant to section 110.00 for an attempt to commit a crime, it is an affirmative defense that, under circumstances manifesting a voluntary and complete renunciation of his criminal purpose, the defendant avoided the commission of the crime attempted by abandoning his criminal effort and, if mere abandonment was insufficient to accomplish such avoidance, by taking further and affirmative steps which prevented the commission thereof.

4. In any prosecution for criminal solicitation pursuant to article one hundred or for conspiracy pursuant to article one hundred five in which the crime solicited or the crime contemplated by the conspiracy was not in fact committed, it is an affirmative defense that, under circumstances manifesting a voluntary and complete renunciation of his criminal purpose, the defendant prevented the commission of such crime.

5. A renunciation is not "voluntary and complete" within the meaning of this section if it is motivated in whole or in part by (a) a belief that circumstances exist which increase the probability of detection or apprehension of the defendant or another participant in the criminal enterprise, or which render more difficult the accomplishment of the criminal purpose, or (b) a decision to postpone the criminal conduct until another time or to transfer the criminal effort to another victim or another but similar objective.

HISTORY: Added as § 35.45, L 1965, ch 1030; renumbered § 40.10, L 1968, ch 73, § 11, eff March 21, 1968.

§ 40.15. Mental disease or defect

In any prosecution for an offense, it is an affirmative defense that when the defendant engaged in the proscribed conduct, he lacked criminal responsibility by reason of mental disease or defect. Such lack of criminal responsibility means that at the time of such conduct, as a result of mental disease or defect, he lacked substantial capacity to know or appreciate either:

1. The nature and consequences of such conduct; or

2. That such conduct was wrong.

HISTORY: Add, L 1984, ch 668, § 3, eff Nov 1, 1984, but not applicable to any criminal action or proceeding relating to an offense committed prior to Nov 1, 1984.

PL

PART TWO   Sentences

Title E
Sentences

HISTORY: Add, L 1965, ch 1030, eff Sept 1, 1967.

TITLE E Sentences

ARTICLE 55
CLASSIFICATION AND DESIGNATION OF OFFENSES

ARTICLE 60
AUTHORIZED DISPOSITION OF OFFENDERS

ARTICLE 65
SENTENCES OF PROBATION, CONDITIONAL DISCHARGE AND UNCONDITIONAL DISCHARGE

ARTICLE 70
SENTENCES OF IMPRISONMENT

ARTICLE 75
[REPEALED]

ARTICLE 80
FINES

ARTICLE 85
SENTENCE OF INTERMITTENT IMPRISONMENT

HISTORY: Add, L 1965, ch 1030, eff Sept 1, 1967.

ARTICLE 55 CLASSIFICATION AND DESIGNATION OF OFFENSES

HISTORY: Add, L 1965, ch 1030, eff Sept 1, 1967.

§ 55.00. Applicability of article

The provisions of this article govern the classification and designation of every offense, whether defined within or outside of this chapter.

> **HISTORY:** Add, L 1967, ch 791, § 3, eff Sept 1, 1967. Former § 55.00, add, L 1965, ch 1030; repealed, L 1967, ch 791, § 3, eff Sept 1, 1967.

§ 55.05. Classifications of felonies and misdemeanors

1. Felonies. Felonies are classified, for the purpose of sentence, into five categories as follows:

   (a) Class A felonies;

   (b) Class B felonies;

   (c) Class C felonies;

   (d) Class D felonies; and

   (e) Class E felonies.

Class A felonies are subclassified, for the purpose of sentence, into two categories as follows: subclass I and subclass II, to be known as class A-I and class A-II felonies, respectively.

2. Misdemeanors. Misdemeanors are classified, for the purpose of sentence, into three categories as follows:

   (a) Class A misdemeanors;

   (b) Class B misdemeanors; and

(c) Unclassified misdemeanors.

HISTORY: Add, L 1965, ch 1030; amd, L 1973, ch 276, § 1, eff Sept 1, 1973. Sub 1, undesignated par, add, L 1973, ch 276, § 1; amd, L 1979, ch 410, § 1, eff Sept 1, 1979.

§ 55.10. Designation of offenses

1. Felonies.

(a) The particular classification or subclassification of each felony defined in this chapter is expressly designated in the section or article defining it.

(b) Any offense defined outside this chapter which is declared by law to be a felony without specification of the classification thereof, or for which a law outside this chapter provides a sentence to a term of imprisonment in excess of one year, shall be deemed a class E felony.

2. Misdemeanors.

(a) Each misdemeanor defined in this chapter is either a class A misdemeanor or a class B misdemeanor, as expressly designated in the section or article defining it.

(b) Any offense defined outside this chapter which is declared by law to be a misdemeanor without specification of the classification thereof or of the sentence therefor shall be deemed a class A misdemeanor.

(c) Except as provided in paragraph (b) of subdivision three, where an offense is defined outside this chapter and a sentence to a term of imprisonment in excess of fifteen days but not in excess of one year is provided in the law or ordinance defining it, such offense shall be deemed an unclassified misdemeanor.

3. Violations. Every violation defined in this chapter is expressly designated as such. Any offense defined outside this chapter which is not expressly designated a violation shall be deemed a violation if:

(a) Notwithstanding any other designation specified in the law or ordinance defining it, a sentence to a term of imprisonment which is not in excess of fifteen days is provided therein, or the only sentence provided therein is a fine; or

(b) A sentence to a term of imprisonment in excess of fifteen days is provided for such offense in a law or ordinance enacted prior to the effective date of this chapter but the offense was not a crime prior to that date.

4. Traffic infraction. Notwithstanding any other provision of this section, an offense which is defined as a "traffic infraction" shall not be deemed a violation or a misdemeanor by virtue of the sentence prescribed therefor.

HISTORY: Add, L 1965, ch 1030, eff Sept 1, 1967, with substance derived from §§ 1935, 1937. Sub 1, amd, L 1973, ch 276, § 2, eff Sept 1, 1973. Sub 2, amd, L 1967, ch 791, § 4, eff Sept 1, 1967. Sub 2, par (c), formerly sub 2, par (e), relettered sub 2, par (c), L 1978, ch 104, § 1, eff May 2, 1978. Sub 2, par (d), deleted, L 1967, ch 791, § 4, eff Sept 1, 1967. Sub 4, add, L 1967, ch 791, § 5, eff Sept 1, 1967.

ARTICLE 60   AUTHORIZED DISPOSITION OF OFFENDERS

HISTORY: Add, L 1967, ch 791, § 6, eff Sept 1, 1967. Former Art 60, add, L 1965, ch 1030; repealed, L 1967, ch 791, § 6, eff Sept 1, 1967.

§ 60.00. Applicability of provisions

1. The sentences prescribed by this article shall apply in the case of every offense, whether defined within or outside of this chapter.

2. The sole provision of this article that shall apply in the case of an offense committed by a juvenile offender is section 60.10 of this article and no other provisions of this article shall be deemed or construed to apply in any such case.

HISTORY: Add, L 1967, ch 791, § 6, eff Sept 1, 1967, with substance derived from § 60.00 in part. Former § 60.00, add, L 1965, ch 1030; repealed, L 1967, ch 791, § 6, eff Sept 1, 1967. Section heading, amd, L 1978, ch 481, § 29, eff Sept 1, 1978. Sub 1, formerly entire section, so designated, L 1978, ch 481, § 29, eff Sept 1, 1978. Sub 2, add, L 1978, ch 481, § 29, eff Sept 1, 1978.

§ 60.01. Authorized dispositions; generally

1. Applicability. Except as otherwise specified in this article, when the court imposes sentence upon a person convicted of an offense, the court must impose a sentence prescribed by this section.

2. Revocable dispositions.

(a) The court may impose a revocable sentence as herein specified:

(i) the court, where authorized by article sixty-five, may sentence a person to a period of probation or to a period of conditional discharge as provided in that article; or

(ii) the court, where authorized by article eighty-five, may sentence a person to a term of intermittent imprisonment as provided in that article.

(b) A revocable sentence shall be deemed a tentative one to the extent that it may be altered or revoked in accordance with the provisions of the article under which it was imposed, but for all other purposes shall be deemed to be a final judgment of conviction.

(c) In any case where the court imposes a sentence of probation, conditional discharge, or a sentence of intermittent imprisonment, it may also impose a fine authorized by article eighty.

(d) In any case where the court imposes a sentence of imprisonment not in excess of sixty days, for a misdemeanor or not in excess of six months for a felony or in the case of a sentence of intermittent imprisonment not in excess of four months, it may also impose a sentence of probation or conditional discharge provided that the term of probation or conditional discharge together with the term of imprisonment shall not exceed the term of probation or conditional discharge authorized by article sixty-five of this chapter. The sentence of imprisonment shall be a condition of and run concurrently with the sentence of probation or conditional discharge.

3. Other dispositions. When a person is not sentenced as specified in subdivision two, or when a sentence specified in subdivision two is revoked, the sentence of the court must be as follows:

(a) A term of imprisonment; or

(b) A fine authorized by article eighty, provided, however, that when the conviction is of a class B felony or of any felony defined in article two hundred twenty, the sentence shall not consist solely of a fine; or

(c) Both imprisonment and a fine; or

(d) Where authorized by section 65.20, unconditional discharge as provided in that section; or

(e) Following revocation of a sentence of conditional discharge imposed pursuant to section 65.05 of this chapter or paragraph (d) of subdivision two of this section, probation as provided in section 65.00 of this chapter or to the sentence of imprisonment and probation as provided for in paragraph (d) of subdivision two of this section.

4. In any case where a person has been sentenced to a period of probation imposed pursuant to section 65.00 of this chapter, if the part of the sentence that provides for probation is revoked, the court must sentence such person to imprisonment or to the sentence of imprisonment and probation as provided for in paragraph (d) of subdivision two of this section.

HISTORY: Added as § 60.10, L 1967, ch 791, § 6; amd, L 1970, ch 477, § 2; renumbered § 60.01 and amd, L 1973, ch 276, § 3, L 1973, ch 277, § 1, eff Sept 1, 1973. Sub 1, add, L 1973, ch 276, § 3, L 1973, ch 277, § 1, eff Sept 1, 1973. Former sub 1, renumbered sub 2 and amd, L 1973, ch 276, § 3, L 1973, ch 277, § 1, eff Sept 1, 1973. Sub 2, formerly sub 1, amd, L 1972, ch 157, § 1; renumbered sub 2 and amd, L 1973, ch 276, § 3, L 1973, ch 277, § 1, eff Sept 1, 1973. Sub 2, par (d), add, L 1974, ch 835, § 1; amd, L 1978, ch 274, § 1, L 1980, ch 86, § 1, L 1982, ch 65, § 1, eff Sept 1, 1982. Sub 3, formerly sub 2, first par, renumbered sub 3 and amd, L 1973, ch 276, § 3, L 1973, ch 277, § 1, eff Sept 1, 1973. Sub 3, par (a), amd, L 1984, ch 548, § 1, eff Nov 1, 1984. Sub 3, par (b), formerly sub 3, par (c), relettered sub 3, par (b), L 1974, ch 652, § 2, eff July 31, 1974 (Laws 1974, ch 653, § 8, changed the effective date from May 30, 1974 to July 31, 1974.). Former sub 3, par (b), repealed, L 1974, ch 652, § 2, eff July 31, 1974. Sub 3, par (c), formerly sub 3, par (d), relettered sub 3, par (c), L 1974, ch 652, § 2, eff July 31, 1974. Former sub 3, par (c), relettered sub 3, par (b), L 1974, ch 652, § 2, eff July 31, 1974. Sub 3, par (d), formerly sub 3, par (e), relettered sub 3, par (d), L 1974, ch 652, § 2; amd, L 1984, ch 548, § 1, eff Nov 1, 1984. Former sub 3, par (d), relettered sub 3, par (c), L 1974, ch 652, § 2, eff July 31, 1974. Sub 3, par (e), add, L 1984, ch 548, § 1, eff Nov 1, 1984. Sub 4, formerly sub 3, closing par, renumbered sub 4 and amd, L 1973, ch 276, § 3, L 1973, ch 277, § 1, L 1984, ch 548, § 2, eff Nov 1, 1984.

§ 60.02. Authorized disposition; youthful offender

When a person is to be sentenced upon a youthful offender finding, the court must impose a sentence as follows:

(1) If the sentence is to be imposed upon a youthful offender finding which has been substituted for a conviction of an offense other than a felony, the court must impose a sentence authorized for the offense for which the youthful offender finding was substituted, except that if the youthful offender finding was entered pursuant to paragraph (b) of subdivision one of section 720.20 of the criminal procedure law, the court must not impose a definite or intermittent sentence of imprisonment with a term of more than six months; or

(2) If the sentence is to be imposed upon a youthful offender finding which has been substituted for a conviction for any felony, the court must impose a sentence authorized to be imposed upon a person convicted of a class E felony provided, however, that the court must not impose a sentence of conditional discharge or unconditional discharge if the youthful offender finding was substituted for a conviction of a felony defined in article two hundred twenty of this chapter.

(3) The provisions of section 60.35 of this article shall apply to a sentence imposed upon a youthful offender finding and the amount of the mandatory surcharge and crime victim assistance fee which shall be levied at sentencing shall be equal to the amount specified in such section for the offense of conviction for which the youthful offender finding was substituted; provided, however that the court shall not impose the sex offender registration fee, DNA databank fee or supplemental sex offender victim fee, as defined in subparagraphs (iv) and (v) of paragraph (a) and paragraph (b) of subdivision one of section 60.35 of this article, for an offense in which the conviction was substituted with a youthful offender finding.

(4) Notwithstanding any other provision of law in this section, if the sentence is to be imposed upon a youthful offender finding which has been substituted for a conviction of prostitution or loitering for the purposes of prostitution provided that the person does not stand charged with loitering for the purpose of patronizing a prostitute, and such offense occurred when the person was sixteen or seventeen years of age, the court must impose a sentence authorized to be imposed upon a person convicted of a violation as defined in subdivision three of section 10.00 of the penal law and where the court imposes a revocable sentence authorized for a violation may order any of the specialized services enumerated in title eight-A of article six of the social services law or other appropriate services made available to persons in need

of super vision in accordance with article seven of the family court act.

HISTORY: Add, L 1979, ch 411, § 22; amd, L 1980, ch 471, § 17, eff July 23, 1980. Former § 60.02, add, L 1974, ch 652, § 4; amd, L 1974, ch 653, § 6; repealed, L 1979, ch 411, § 22, eff Aug 4, 1979. Sub (3), add, L 2004, ch 56, § 1 (Part F), eff Feb 16, 2005; amd, L 2008, ch 56, § 1 (Part Y), eff April 23, 2008, deemed eff Feb 16, 2005. Sub (4), add, L 2014, ch 402, § 6, eff Oct 16, 2014.

§ 60.03. [Repealed]

HISTORY: Add, L 1973, ch 676, § 28; amd, L 1974, ch 170, § 2, L 1974, ch 652, § 2, L 1975, ch 667, §§ 33, 34, L 1978, ch 269, § 1; repealed, L 1980, ch 471, § 18, eff July 23, 1980. Former § 60.03, formerly § 60.15, add, L 1967, ch 791, § 6; amd, L 1973, ch 195, § 26; renumbered § 60.03 and amd, L 1973, ch 276, § 4, L 1973, ch 277, § 2; repealed, L 1973, ch 676, § 28, eff Sept 1, 1973.

§ 60.04. Authorized disposition; controlled substances and marihuana felony offenses

1. Applicability. Notwithstanding the provisions of any law, this section shall govern the dispositions authorized when a person is to be sentenced upon a conviction of a felony offense defined in article two hundred twenty or two hundred twenty-one of this chapter or when a person is to be sentenced upon a conviction of such a felony as a multiple felony offender as defined in subdivision five of this section.

2. Class A felony. Every person convicted of a class A felony must be sentenced to imprisonment in accordance with section 70.71 of this title, unless such person is convicted of a class A-II felony and is sentenced to probation for life in accordance with section 65.00 of this title.

3. Class B felonies. Every person convicted of a class B felony must be sentenced to imprisonment in accordance with the applicable provisions of section 70.70 of this chapter, a definite sentence of imprisonment with a term of one year or less or probation in accordance with section 65.00 of this chapter provided, however, a person convicted of criminal sale of a controlled substance to a child as defined in section 220.48 of this chapter must be sentenced to a determinate sentence of imprisonment in accordance with the applicable provisions of section 70.70 of this chapter or to a sentence of probation in accordance with the opening paragraph of paragraph (b) of subdivision one of section 65.00 of this chapter.

4. Alternative sentence. Where a sentence of imprisonment or a sentence of probation as an alternative to imprisonment is not required to be imposed pursuant to subdivision two, three or five of this section, the court may impose any other sentence authorized by section 60.01 of this article, provided that when the court imposes a sentence of imprisonment, such sentence must be in accordance with section 70.70 of this title. Where the court imposes a sentence of imprisonment in accordance with this section, the court may also impose a fine authorized by article eighty of this title and in such case the sentence shall be both imprisonment and a fine.

5. Multiple felony offender. Where the court imposes a sentence pursuant to subdivision three of section 70.70 of this chapter upon a second felony drug offender, as defined in paragraph (b) of subdivision one of section 70.70 of this chapter, it must sentence such offender to imprisonment in accordance with the applicable provisions of section 70.70 of this chapter, a definite sentence of imprisonment with a term of one year or less, or probation in accordance with section 65.00 of this chapter, provided, however, that where the court imposes a sentence upon a class B second felony drug offender, it must sentence such offender to a determinate sentence of imprisonment in accordance with the applicable provisions of section 70.70 of this chapter or to a sentence of probation in accordance with the opening paragraph of paragraph (b) of subdivision one of section 65.00 of this chapter. When the court imposes sentence on a second felony drug offender pursuant to subdivision four of section 70.70 of this chapter, it must impose a determinate sentence of

imprisonment in accordance with such subdivision.

6. Substance abuse treatment. When the court imposes a sentence of imprisonment which requires a commitment to the state department of corrections and community supervision upon a person who stands convicted of a controlled substance or marihuana offense, the court may, upon motion of the defendant in its discretion, issue an order directing that the department of corrections and community supervision enroll the defendant in the comprehensive alcohol and substance abuse treatment program in an alcohol and substance abuse correctional annex as defined in subdivision eighteen of section two of the correction law, provided that the defendant will satisfy the statutory eligibility criteria for participation in such program. Notwithstanding the foregoing provisions of this subdivision, any defendant to be enrolled in such program pursuant to this subdivision shall be governed by the same rules and regulations promulgated by the department of corrections and community supervision, including without limitation those rules and regulations establishing requirements for completion and those rules and regulations governing discipline and removal from the program. No such period of court ordered corrections based drug abuse treatment pursuant to this subdivision shall be required to extend beyond the defendant's conditional release date.

7. a. Shock incarceration participation. When the court imposes a sentence of imprisonment which requires a commitment to the department of corrections and community supervision upon a person who stands convicted of a controlled substance or marihuana offense, upon motion of the defendant, the court may issue an order directing that the department of corrections and community supervision enroll the defendant in the shock incarceration program as defined in article twenty-six-A of the correction law, provided that the defendant is an eligible inmate, as described in subdivision one of section eight hundred sixty-five of the correction law. Notwithstanding the foregoing provisions of this subdivision, any defendant to be enrolled in such program pursuant to this subdivision shall be governed by the same rules and regulations promulgated by the department of corrections and community supervision, including without limitation those rules and regulations establishing requirements for completion and such rules and regulations governing discipline and removal from the program.

b. (i) In the event that an inmate designated by court order for enrollment in the shock incarceration program requires a degree of medical care or mental health care that cannot be provided at a shock incarceration facility, the department, in writing, shall notify the inmate, provide a proposal describing a proposed alternative-to-shock-incarceration program, and notify him or her that he or she may object in writing to placement in such alternative-to-shock-incarceration program. If the inmate objects in writing to placement in such alternative-to-shock-incarceration program, the department of corrections and community supervision shall notify the sentencing court, provide such proposal to the court, and arrange for the inmate's prompt appearance before the court. The court shall provide the proposal and notice of a court appearance to the people, the inmate and the appropriate defense attorney. After considering the proposal and any submissions by the parties, and after a reasonable opportunity for the people, the inmate and counsel to be heard, the court may modify its sentencing order accordingly, notwithstanding the provisions of section 430.10 of the criminal procedure law.

(ii) An inmate who successfully completes an alternative-to-shock-incarceration program within the department of corrections and community supervision shall be treated in the same manner as a person who has successfully completed the shock incarceration program, as set forth in subdivision four of section eight hundred sixty-seven of the correction law.

HISTORY: Add, L 2004, ch 738, § 20, eff Jan 13, 2005; amd, L 2009, ch 56, § 17 (Part AAA), eff April 7, 2009, L 2011, ch 62, § 120 (Part C, Subpart B), eff March 31, 2011.

§ 60.05. Authorized dispositions; other class A, B, certain C and D felonies and multiple felony offenders

1. Applicability. Except as provided in section 60.04 of this article governing the authorized dispositions applicable to felony offenses defined in article two hundred twenty or two hundred twenty-one of this chapter or in section 60.13 of this article governing the authorized dispositions applicable to felony sex offenses defined in paragraph (a) of subdivision one of section 70.80 of this title, this section shall govern the dispositions authorized when a person is to be sentenced upon a conviction of a class A felony, a class B felony or a class C, class D or class E felony specified herein, or when a person is to be sentenced upon a conviction of a felony as a multiple felony offender.

2. Class A felony. Except as provided in subdivisions three and four of section 70.06 of this chapter, every person convicted of a class A felony must be sentenced to imprisonment in accordance with section 70.00 of this title, unless such person is convicted of murder in the first degree and is sentenced in accordance with section 60.06 of this article.

3. Class B felony. Except as provided in subdivision six of this section, every person convicted of a class B violent felony offense as defined in subdivision one of section 70.02 of this title, must be sentenced to imprisonment in accordance with such section 70.02; and, except as provided in subdivision six of this section, every person convicted of any other class B felony must be sentenced to imprisonment in accordance with section 70.00of this title.

4. Certain class C felonies. Except as provided in subdivision six, every person convicted of a class C violent felony offense as defined in subdivision one of section 70.02 of this title, must be sentenced to imprisonment in accordance with section 70.02 of this title; and, except as provided in subdivision six of this section, every person convicted of the class C felonies of: attempt to commit any of the class B felonies of bribery in the first degree as defined in section 200.04, bribe receiving in the first degree as defined in section 200.12, conspiracy in the second degree as defined in section 105.15 and criminal mischief in the first degree as defined in section 145.12; criminal usury in the first degree as defined in section 190.42, rewarding official misconduct in the first degree as defined in section 200.22, receiving reward for official misconduct in the first degree as defined in section 200.27, attempt to promote prostitution in the first degree as defined in section 230.32, promoting prostitution in the second degree as defined in section 230.30, arson in the third degree as defined in section 150.10 of this chapter, must be sentenced to imprisonment in accordance with section 70.00 of this title.

5. Certain class D felonies. Except as provided in subdivision six of this section, every person convicted of the class D felonies of assault in the second degree as defined in section 120.05, strangulation in the second degree as defined in section 121.12 or attempt to commit a class C felony as defined in section 230.30 of this chapter, must be sentenced in accordance with section 70.00 or 85.00 of this title.

6. Multiple felony offender. When the court imposes sentence upon a second violent felony offender, as defined in section 70.04, or a second felony offender, as defined in section 70.06, the court must impose a sentence of imprisonment in accordance with section 70.04 or 70.06, as the case may be, unless it imposes a sentence of imprisonment in accordance with section 70.08 or 70.10.

7. Fines. Where the court imposes a sentence of imprisonment in accordance with this section,

the court also may impose a fine authorized by article eighty and in such case the sentence shall be both imprisonment and a fine.

HISTORY: Add, L 1973, ch 277, § 4, eff Sept 1, 1973; amd, L 1973, ch 278, § 1, L 1973, ch 1051, § 1, L 1974, ch 367, § 1, L 1974, ch 1041, § 9, L 1976, ch 424, § 3, L 1977, ch 22, § 1, L 1978, ch 481, § 1, L 1978 ch 627, § 6, L 1979, ch 410, § 2, L 1980, ch 233, § 1, eff Aug 12, 1980, L 1981, ch 711, § 9, eff July 1, 1982, provided that all steps necessary to prepare for the implementation of this act may be taken prior to the effective date, L 1995, ch 1, § 1, eff Sept 1, 1995, L 2004, ch 738, § 24, eff Jan 13, 2005, L 2007, ch 7, § 35, eff April 13, 2007, L 2010, ch 405, § 12, eff Nov 11, 2010.

§ 60.06. Authorized disposition; murder in the first degree offenders; aggravated murder offenders; certain murder in the second degree offenders; certain terrorism offenders; criminal possession of a chemical weapon or biological weapon offenders; criminal use of a chemical weapon or biological weapon offenders

When a defendant is convicted of murder in the first degree as defined in section 125.27 of this chapter, the court shall, in accordance with the provisions of section 400.27 of the criminal procedure law, sentence the defendant to death, to life imprisonment without parole in accordance with subdivision five of section 70.00 of this title, or to a term of imprisonment for a class A-I felony other than a sentence of life imprisonment without parole, in accordance with subdivisions one through three of section 70.00 of this title. When a person is convicted of murder in the second degree as defined in subdivision five of section 125.25 of this chapter or of the crime of aggravated murder as defined in subdivision one of section 125.26 of this chapter, the court shall sentence the defendant to life imprisonment without parole in accordance with subdivision five of section 70.00 of this title. When a defendant is convicted of the crime of terrorism as defined in section 490.25 of this chapter, and the specified offense the defendant committed is a class A-I felony offense, or when a defendant is convicted of the crime of criminal possession of a chemical weapon or biological weapon in the first degree as defined in section 490.45 of this chapter, or when a defendant is convicted of the crime of criminal use of a chemical weapon or biological weapon in the first degree as defined in section 490.55 of this chapter, the court shall sentence the defendant to life imprisonment without parole in accordance with subdivision five of section 70.00 of this title; provided, however, that nothing in this section shall preclude or prevent a sentence of death when the defendant is also convicted of murder in the first degree as defined in section 125.27 of this chapter. When a defendant is convicted of aggravated murder as defined in subdivision two of section 125.26 of this chapter, the court shall sentence the defendant to life imprisonment without parole or to a term of imprisonment for a class A-I felony other than a sentence of life imprisonment without parole, in accordance with subdivisions one through three of section 70.00 of this title.

HISTORY: Add, L 1974, ch 367, § 2; amd, L 1995, ch 1, § 2, eff Sept 1, 1995. Amd, L 2004, ch 1, § 4 (Part A), eff July 23, 2004, L 2004, ch 459, § 2, eff Nov 1, 2004, L 2005, ch 765, § 12, eff Dec 21, 2005, L 2009, ch 482, § 3, eff Oct 9, 2009. Section heading, amd, L 2004, ch 1, § 4 (Part A), eff July 23, 2004, L 2004, ch 459, § 2, eff Nov 1, 2004, L 2005, ch 765, § 12, eff Dec 21, 2005, L 2006, ch 93, § 1, eff June 7, 2006.

§ 60.07. Authorized disposition; criminal attack on operators of for-hire vehicles

1. Notwithstanding any other provision of law to the contrary, when a court has found, pursuant to the provisions of section 200.61 of the criminal procedure law, both that a person has been convicted of a specified offense as defined in subdivision two of this section and the victim of such offense was operating a for-hire vehicle in the course of providing for-hire vehicle services at the time of the commission of such offense, the sentence of imprisonment imposed upon conviction for such offense shall be the sentence authorized by the applicable provisions of article seventy of this chapter, provided, however, that the minimum term of an indeterminate sentence or minimum

determinate sentence shall be not less than three years nor more than five years greater than the minimum term or sentence otherwise required to be imposed pursuant to such provisions. The provisions of this subdivision shall not apply where the court, having regard to the nature and circumstances of the crime and the history and character of the defendant, finds on the record that such additional term or sentence would be unduly harsh and that not imposing such additional term or sentence would be consistent with the public safety and would not deprecate the seriousness of the crime.

2. For purposes of this section:

(a) the term "specified offense" shall mean an attempt to commit murder in the second degree as defined in section 125.25 of this chapter, gang assault in the first degree as defined in section 120.07 of this chapter, gang assault in the second degree as defined in section 120.06 of this chapter, assault in the first degree as defined in section 120.10 of this chapter, manslaughter in the first degree as defined in section 125.20 of this chapter, manslaughter in the second degree as defined in section 125.15 of this chapter, robbery in the first degree as defined in section 160.15 of this chapter, robbery in the second degree as defined in section 160.10 of this chapter, or the attempted commission of any of the following offenses: gang assault in the first degree as defined in section 120.07, assault in the first degree as defined in section 120.10, manslaughter in the first degree as defined in section 125.20 or robbery in the first degree as defined in section 160.15;

(b) the term "for-hire vehicle" shall mean a vehicle designed to carry not more than five passengers for compensation and such vehicle is a taxicab, as defined in section one hundred forty-eight-a of the vehicle and traffic law, a livery, as such term is defined in section one hundred twenty-one-e of the vehicle and traffic law, or a "black car", as such term is defined in paragraph (g) of this subdivision;

(c) the term "livery car base" shall mean a central facility, wherever located, that dispatches a livery operator to both pick-up and discharge passengers in the state;

(d) "for-hire vehicle services" shall mean:

(i) with respect to a taxicab, the transport of passengers pursuant to a license or permit issued by a local authority by a person duly authorized to operate such taxicab;

(ii) with respect to a livery, the transport of passengers by a livery operator while affiliated with a livery car base; or

(iii) with respect to a "black car", the transport of passengers by a "black car operator" pursuant to dispatches from or by a central dispatch facility regardless of where the pick-up and discharge occurs, and, with respect to dispatches from or by a central dispatch facility located outside the state, all dispatches involving a pick-up in the state, regardless of where the discharge occurs.

(e) "livery operator" shall mean the registered owner of a livery, as such term is defined in section one hundred twenty-one-e of the vehicle and traffic law, or a driver designated by such registered owner to operate the registered owner's livery as the registered owner's authorized designee, where such registered owner or driver provides services while affiliated with a livery car base;

(f) "black car operator" shall mean the registered owner of a "black car" or a driver designated by such registered owner to operate the registered owner's black car as the registered owner's authorized designee; and

(g) "black car" shall mean a for-hire vehicle dispatched from a central facility, which has certified to the satisfaction of the department of state pursuant to article six-F of the executive law that more than ninety percent of the central facility's for-hire business is on a payment basis other than direct cash payment by a passenger.

HISTORY: Add, L 2000, ch 148, § 6, eff Nov 1, 2000.

§ 60.08. Authorized dispositions; resentencing of certain controlled substance offenders

Any person convicted of an offense and sentenced to prison for an indeterminate sentence, the minimum of which was at least one year and the maximum of which was life imprisonment, which sentence was imposed pursuant to chapter two hundred seventy-six, two hundred seventy-seven, two hundred seventy-eight, or ten hundred fifty-one of the laws of nineteen hundred seventy-three, and for which such sentence was imposed upon conviction of the crime of criminal possession of a controlled substance in the first degree, criminal possession of a controlled substance in the second degree, criminal possession of a controlled substance in the third degree, criminal sale of a controlled substance in the first degree, criminal sale of a controlled substance in the second degree, or criminal sale of a controlled substance in the third degree, and the sole controlled substance involved was methadone, may apply, upon notice to the appropriate district attorney, for resentencing in the court which originally imposed sentence.

Such resentencing shall, unless substantial justice dictates otherwise, be pursuant to the current provisions of the penal law, and shall include credit for any jail time incurred upon the subject conviction as well as credit for any period of incarceration incurred pursuant to the sentence originally imposed.

In cases where the proof before the court is not available or is not sufficiently reliable to determine the amount of methadone present in any preparation, compound, mixture or substance containing methadone, there shall exist a rebuttable presumption that each ounce of the preparation, compound, mixture or substance contained sixty milligrams of methadone.

HISTORY: Add, L 1975, ch 783, § 1, eff Aug 9, 1975.

§ 60.09. Authorized dispositions; resentencing of certain persons convicted of specified controlled substance offenses

a. Any person convicted of an offense as defined in section 115.05, 220.16, 220.18, 220.39 or 220.41 of this chapter or of an attempt thereof, for an act committed on or after September first, nineteen hundred seventy-three but prior to the date on which the provisions of this section become effective, may, upon notice to the appropriate district attorney, apply for resentencing in the court which originally imposed sentence. Such resentencing shall be in accordance with the provisions of subdivision (b) of this section and shall include credit for any jail time incurred upon the subject conviction as well as credit for any period of incarceration incurred pursuant to the sentence originally imposed.

b. A court, upon an application specified in subdivision (a) of this section may resentence a person as follows:

(i) if the conviction was for a class A-III offense the court may impose a new maximum term which shall be no less than three times the amount of the minimum term imposed in the original sentence and no more than twenty-five years;

(ii) if the conviction was for a class A-II offense the court may impose a new minimum term which shall be no less than three years imprisonment and no more than eight and one-third years;

(iii) upon resentence of a person as specified in paragraph (i) of this subdivision the court shall resentence the person to the same minimum term previously imposed;

(iv) upon resentence of a person as specified in paragraph (ii) of this subdivision the court shall impose a maximum term of life imprisonment;

(v) if the conviction was for an offense as specified in section 115.05 of this chapter and the offense which was the object of the criminal facilitation was a class A-III felony then the court shall set aside the conviction and substitute it with a conviction for violation of section 115.01 or 115.00 of this chapter, whichever is appropriate under the facts of the case, and impose a sentence in accordance with those provisions.

c. Upon resentence as provided in this section the court may not impose a sentence greater than the sentence previously imposed.

    HISTORY: Add, L 1979, ch 410, § 3, eff Sept 1, 1979.

§ 60.10. Authorized disposition; juvenile offender

1. When a juvenile offender is convicted of a crime, the court shall sentence the defendant to imprisonment in accordance with section 70.05 or sentence him upon a youthful offender finding in accordance with section 60.02 of this chapter.

2. Subdivision one of this section shall apply when sentencing a juvenile offender notwithstanding the provisions of any other law that deals with the authorized sentence for persons who are not juvenile offenders. Provided, however, that the limitation prescribed by this section shall not be deemed or construed to bar use of a conviction of a juvenile offender, other than a juvenile offender who has been adjudicated a youthful offender pursuant to section 720.20 of the criminal procedure law, as a previous or predicate felony offender under section 70.04, 70.06, 70.08 or 70.10, when sentencing a person who commits a felony after he has reached the age of sixteen.

    HISTORY: Add, L 1978, ch 481, § 30; amd, L 1979, ch 411, § 23, eff Aug 4, 1979. Former § 60.10, add, L 1967, ch 791, § 6, with substance derived from § 60.00; renumbered § 60.01, L 1973, ch 276, § 3, L 1973, ch 277, eff Sept 1, 1973.

§ 60.11. Authorized dispositions; criminal possession of a weapon in the fourth degree

When a person is to be sentenced upon a conviction of the crime of criminal possession of a weapon in the fourth degree as defined in subdivision one of section 265.01 as a result of a plea of guilty entered in satisfaction of an indictment or count thereof charging the defendant with the class D violent felony offense of criminal possession of a weapon in the third degree as defined in subdivision four of section 265.02, the court must sentence the defendant in accordance with the provisions of section 70.15.

    HISTORY: Add, L 1980, ch 233, § 5, eff Aug 12, 1980.

§ 60.11-a. Authorized dispositions; certain criminal possession of a weapon in the third degree offenders

When a person is to be sentenced upon conviction of the crime of criminal possession of a weapon in the third degree as defined in subdivision ten of section 265.02 of this chapter, the court must sentence such defendant to a determinate sentence as provided in subparagraph (ii) of paragraph (c) of subdivision three of section 70.02 of this chapter, unless a greater minimum sentence is otherwise required by another provision of this chapter.

    HISTORY: Add, L 2013, ch 1, § 26-a, eff March 16, 2013.

§ 60.12. Authorized disposition; alternative indeterminate sentence of imprisonment; domestic violence cases

1. Notwithstanding any other provision of law, where a court is imposing sentence pursuant to section 70.02 upon a conviction for an offense enumerated in subdivision one of such section, other than an offense defined in article one hundred thirty of this chapter, and is authorized or required pursuant to such section to impose a determinate sentence of imprisonment for such offense, the court, upon a determination following a hearing that (a) the defendant was the victim of physical, sexual or psychological abuse by the victim or intended victim of such offense, (b) such abuse was a factor in causing the defendant to commit such offense and (c) the victim or intended victim of such offense was a member of the same family or household as the defendant as such term is defined in subdivision one of section 530.11 of the criminal procedure law, may, in lieu of imposing such determinate sentence of imprisonment, impose an indeterminate sentence of imprisonment in accordance with subdivisions two and three of this section.

2. The maximum term of an indeterminate sentence imposed pursuant to subdivision one of this section must be fixed by the court as follows:

(a) For a class B felony, the term must be at least six years and must not exceed twenty-five years;

(b) For a class C felony, the term must be at least four and one-half years and must not exceed fifteen years;

(c) For a class D felony, the term must be at least three years and must not exceed seven years; and

(d) For a class E felony, the term must be at least three years and must not exceed four years.

3. The minimum period of imprisonment under an indeterminate sentence imposed pursuant to subdivision one of this section must be fixed by the court at one-half of the maximum term imposed and must be specified in the sentence.

HISTORY: Add, L 1998, ch 1, § 1, eff Aug 6, 1998.

§ 60.13. Authorized dispositions; felony sex offenses

When a person is to be sentenced upon a conviction for any felony defined in article one hundred thirty of this chapter, including a sexually motivated felony, or patronizing a prostitute in the first degree as defined in section 230.06 of this chapter, incest in the second degree as defined in section 255.26 of this chapter, or incest in the first degree as defined in section 255.27 of this chapter, or a felony attempt or conspiracy to commit any of these crimes, the court must sentence the defendant in accordance with the provisions of section 70.80 of this title.

HISTORY: Add, L 2007, ch 7, § 34, eff April 13, 2007.

§ 60.15. [Repealed]

HISTORY: Add, L 1967, ch 791, § 6; amd, L 1973, ch 195, § 26; renumbered § 60.03, L 1973, ch 276, § 4, L 1973, ch 277, § 2, L 1973, ch 1051, § 20; repealed, L 1973, ch 676, § 28, eff Sept 1, 1973.

§ 60.20. Authorized dispositions; traffic infraction

1. When a person is convicted of a traffic infraction, the sentence of the court shall be as follows:

(a) A period of conditional discharge, as provided in article sixty-five; or

(b) Unconditional discharge as provided in section 65.20; or

(c) A fine or a sentence to a term of imprisonment, or both, as prescribed in and authorized by the provision that defines the infraction; or

(d) A sentence of intermittent imprisonment, as provided in article eighty-five.

2. Where a sentence of conditional discharge is imposed for a traffic infraction, all incidents of the sentence shall be the same as would be applicable if the sentence were for a violation.

HISTORY: Add, L 1967, ch 790, § 6, eff Sept 1, 1967. Sub 1, amd, L 1970, ch 477, § 3, eff May 8, 1970. Sub 1, par (d), add, L 1970, ch 477, § 3, eff May 8, 1970.

§ 60.21. Authorized dispositions; driving while intoxicated or aggravated driving while intoxicated

Notwithstanding paragraph (d) of subdivision two of section 60.01 of this article, when a person is to be sentenced upon a conviction for a violation of subdivision two, two-a or three of section eleven hundred ninety-two of the vehicle and traffic law, the court may sentence such person to a period of imprisonment authorized by article seventy of this title and shall sentence such person to a period of probation or conditional discharge in accordance with the provisions of section 65.00 of this title and shall order the installation and maintenance of a functioning ignition interlock device. Such period of probation or conditional discharge shall run consecutively to any period of imprisonment and shall commence immediately upon such person's release from imprisonment.

HISTORY: Add, L 2009, ch 496, § 13, eff Dec 18, 2009.

§ 60.25. Authorized dispositions; corporation

When a corporation is convicted of an offense, the sentence of the court shall be as follows:

(a) A fine authorized by section 80.10; or

(b) Where authorized by section 65.05, a period of conditional discharge as provided in that section; or

(c) Where authorized by section 65.20, unconditional discharge as provided in that section.

In any case where a corporation has been sentenced to a period of conditional discharge and such sentence is revoked, the court shall sentence the corporation to pay a fine.

HISTORY: Add, L 1967, ch 791, § 6, eff Sept 1, 1967, with substance derived from § 60.00 in part.

§ 60.27. Restitution and reparation

1. In addition to any of the dispositions authorized by this article, the court shall consider restitution or reparation to the victim of the crime and may require restitution or reparation as part of the sentence imposed upon a person convicted of an offense, and after providing the district attorney with an opportunity to be heard in accordance with the provisions of this subdivision, require the defendant to make restitution of the fruits of his or her offense or reparation for the actual out-of-pocket loss caused thereby and, in the case of a violation of section 190.78, 190.79, 190.80, 190.82 or 190.83 of this chapter, any costs or losses incurred due to any adverse action taken against the victim. The district attorney shall where appropriate, advise the court at or before the time of sentencing that the victim seeks restitution or reparation, the extent of injury or economic loss or damage of the victim, and the amount of restitution or reparation sought by the victim in accordance with his or her responsibilities under subdivision two of section 390.50 of the criminal procedure law and article twenty-three of the executive law. The court shall hear and consider the information presented by the district attorney in this regard. In that event, or when the victim impact statement reports that the victim seeks restitution or reparation, the court shall require, unless the interests of justice dictate otherwise, in addition to any of the dispositions authorized by this article that the defendant make restitution of the fruits of the offense and reparation for the actual out-of-pocket loss and, in the case of a violation of section 190.78, 190.79,

190.80, 190.82 or 190.83 of this chapter, any costs or losses incurred due to any adverse action, caused thereby to the victim. In the event that restitution or reparation are not ordered, the court shall clearly state its reasons on the record. Adverse action as used in this subdivision shall mean and include actual loss incurred by the victim, including an amount equal to the value of the time reasonably spent by the victim attempting to remediate the harm incurred by the victim from the offense, and the consequential financial losses from such action.

2. Whenever the court requires restitution or reparation to be made, the court must make a finding as to the dollar amount of the fruits of the offense and the actual out-of-pocket loss to the victim caused by the offense. In making this finding, the court must consider any victim impact statement provided to the court. If the record does not contain sufficient evidence to support such finding or upon request by the defendant, the court must conduct a hearing upon the issue in accordance with the procedure set forth in section 400.30 of the criminal procedure law.

3. The provisions of sections 420.10, 420.20 and 420.30 of the criminal procedure law shall apply in the collection and remission of restitution and reparation.

4. For purposes of the imposition, determination and collection of restitution or reparation, the following definitions shall apply:

(a) the term "offense" shall include the offense for which a defendant was convicted, as well as any other offense that is part of the same criminal transaction or that is contained in any other accusatory instrument disposed of by any plea of guilty by the defendant to an offense.

(b) the term "victim" shall include the victim of the offense, the representative of a crime victim as defined in subdivision six of section six hundred twenty-one of the executive law, an individual whose identity was assumed or whose personal identifying information was used in violation of section 190.78, 190.79 or 190.80 of this chapter, or any person who has suffered a financial loss as a direct result of the acts of a defendant in violation of section 190.78, 190.79, 190.80, 190.82 or 190.83 of this chapter, a good samaritan as defined in section six hundred twenty-one of the executive law and the office of victim services or other governmental agency that has received an application for or has provided financial assistance or compensation to the victim. A victim shall also mean any owner or lawful producer of a master recording, or a trade association that represents such owner or lawful producer, that has suffered injury as a result of an offense as defined in article two hundred seventy-five of this chapter.

5. (a) Except upon consent of the defendant or as provided in paragraph (b) of this subdivision, or as a condition of probation or conditional discharge as provided in paragraph (g) of subdivision two of section 65.10 of this chapter, the amount of restitution or reparation required by the court shall not exceed fifteen thousand dollars in the case of a conviction for a felony, or ten thousand dollars in the case of a conviction for any offense other than a felony. Notwithstanding the provisions of this subdivision, if an officer of a school district is convicted of violating any section of article one hundred fifty-five of this chapter where the victim of such crime is such officer's school district, the court may require an amount of restitution up to the full amount of the fruits of the offense or reparation up to the full amount of the actual out-of-pocket loss suffered by the victim, provided further that in such case the provisions of paragraph (b) of this subdivision shall not apply.

(b) The court in its discretion may impose restitution or reparation in excess of the amounts specified in paragraph (a) of this subdivision, provided however that the amount in excess must be limited to the return of the victim's property, including money, or the equivalent value thereof; and reimbursement for medical expenses actually incurred by the victim prior to sentencing as a result of the offense committed by the defendant.

6. Any payment made as restitution or reparation pursuant to this section shall not limit, preclude or impair any liability for damages in any civil action or proceeding for an amount in excess of such payment.

7. In the event that the court requires restitution or reparation to be made to a person and that person dies prior to the completion of said restitution or reparation, the remaining payments shall be made to the estate of the deceased.

8. The court shall in all cases where restitution or reparation is imposed direct as part of the disposition that the defendant pay a designated surcharge of five percent of the entire amount of a restitution or reparation payment to the official or organization designated pursuant to subdivision eight of section 420.10 of the criminal procedure law. The designated surcharge shall not exceed five percent of the amount actually collected. Upon the filing of an affidavit of the official or organization designated pursuant to subdivision eight of section 420.10 of the criminal procedure law demonstrating that the actual cost of the collection and administration of restitution or reparation in a particular case exceeds five percent of the entire amount of the payment or the amount actually collected, as the case may be, the court shall direct that the defendant pay an additional surcharge of not more than five percent of the entire amount of a restitution or reparation payment to such official or organization, or the actual cost of collection or administration, whichever is less unless, upon application of the defendant, the court determines that imposition of such additional surcharge would cause undue hardship to the defendant, or any other person who is financially supported by the defendant, or would otherwise not be in the interest of justice. Such additional surcharge, when added to the initial five percent surcharge, shall not exceed ten percent of the amount actually collected.

9. If the offense of which a person is convicted is a class A, class B, class C, or class D felony involving the sale of a controlled substance, as defined in article two hundred twenty of this chapter, and no other victim who is a person is seeking restitution in the case, the term "victim" as used in this section, in addition to its ordinary meaning, shall mean any law enforcement agency of the state of New York or of any subdivision thereof which has expended funds in the purchase of any controlled substance from such person or his agent as part of the investigation leading to such conviction. Any restitution which may be required to be made to a law enforcement agency pursuant to this section shall be limited to the amount of funds expended in the actual purchase of such controlled substance by such law enforcement agency, less the amount of any funds which have been or will be recovered from any other source, and shall not include a designated surcharge pursuant to subdivision eight of this section. Any law enforcement agency seeking restitution pursuant to this section shall file with the court and the district attorney an affidavit stating that funds expended in the actual purchase of a controlled substance for which restitution is being sought have not been and will not be recovered from any other source or in any other civil or criminal proceeding. Any law enforcement agency receiving restitution pursuant to this section shall promptly transmit to the commissioner of the division of criminal justice services a report stating the dollar amount of the restitution received.

10. If the offense of which a person is convicted is defined in section 150.10, 150.15 or 150.20 of this chapter, and no other victim who is a person is seeking restitution in the case, the term "victim" as used in this section, in addition to its ordinary meaning, shall mean any municipality or volunteer fire company which has expended funds or will expend funds for the purpose of restoration, rehabilitation or clean-up of the site of the arson. Any restitution which may be required to be made to a municipality or volunteer fire company pursuant to this section shall be limited to the amount of funds reasonably expended or to be expended for the purpose of

restoration, rehabilitation or clean- up of the site of the arson, less the amount of any funds which have been or will be recovered from any other source, and shall not include a designated surcharge pursuant to subdivision eight of this section. Any municipality or volunteer fire company seeking restitution pursuant to this section shall file with the court, district attorney and defense counsel an affidavit stating that the funds reasonably expended or to be expended for which restitution is being sought have not been and will not be recovered from any other source or in any other civil or criminal proceeding. For the purposes of this subdivision, "volunteer fire company" means a fire company as defined in paragraph a of subdivision two of section one hundred of the general municipal law.

11. Notwithstanding any other provision of this section to the contrary, when a person is convicted of harming an animal trained to aid a person with a disability in the second degree as defined in section 195.11 of this chapter, or harming an animal trained to aid a person with a disability in the first degree as defined in section 195.12 of this chapter, the court, in addition to any other sentence, shall order the payment of restitution to the person with a disability who was aided by such animal.

12. If the offense of which a person is convicted is defined in section 155.25, 155.30, 155.35, 155.40 or 155.42 of this chapter, and the property taken is timber, the court may upon conviction, in addition to any other sentence, direct the defendant to pay the rightful owner of such timber an amount equal to treble the stumpage value of the timber stolen as defined in section 71-0703 of the environmental conservation law and for any permanent and substantial damage caused to the land or the improvements thereon as a result of such violation. Such reparations shall be of such kind, nature and extent as will reasonably restore the lands affected by the violation to their condition immediately before the violation and may be made by physical restoration of such lands and/or by the assessment of monetary payment to make such restoration.

13. If the offense of which a person is convicted is defined in section 240.50, subdivision one or two of section 240.55, section 240.60, section 240.61, section 240.62 or section 240.63 of this chapter, and no other victim who is a person is seeking restitution in the case, the term "victim" as used in this subdivision, in addition to the ordinary meaning, shall mean any school, municipality, fire district, fire company, fire corporation, ambulance association, ambulance corporation, or other legal or public entity engaged in providing emergency services which has expended funds for the purpose of responding to a false report of an incident or false bomb as defined in section 240.50, subdivision one or two of section 240.55, section 240.60, section 240.61,section 240.62, or section 240.63 of this chapter. Any restitution which may be required to be made to a victim pursuant to this subdivision shall be limited to the amount of funds reasonably expended for the purpose of responding to such false report of incident or false bomb, less the amount of any funds which have been or will be recovered from any other source and shall not include a designated surcharge pursuant to subdivision eight of this section. Any victim seeking restitution pursuant to this subdivision shall file with the court, district attorney and defense counsel an affidavit stating that the funds reasonably expended for which restitution is being sought have not been and will not be recovered from any other source or in any other civil or criminal proceeding, except as provided for by section 3-112 of the general obligations law.

14. Where a transfer of probation has occurred pursuant to section 410.80 of the criminal procedure law and the probationer is subject to a restitution condition, the department of probation in the county in which the order of restitution was imposed shall notify the appropriate district attorney. Upon notification by the department of probation, such district attorney shall file a certified copy of the judgment with the clerk of the county in the receiving jurisdiction for purposes of establishing a first lien and to permit institution of civil proceedings pursuant to the provisions

of subdivision six of section 420.10 of the criminal procedure law.

> **HISTORY:** Add, L 1980, ch 290, § 1, eff Sept 1, 1980; amd, L 1983, ch 397, § 2, L 1983, ch 468, § 1, L 1984, ch 335, § 1, eff July 3, 1984, L 1984, ch 965, § 4, L 1985, ch 14, § 6, L 1985, ch 187, § 1, L 1985, ch 233, § 7, L 1985, ch 506, § 2, eff Nov 1, 1985, L 1986, ch 615, § 1, L 1991, ch 363, § 1, eff Nov 1, 1991, L 1991, ch 545, § 1, eff Nov 1, 1991, L 1992, ch 618, §§ 12, 13, 16, eff Nov 1, 1992, L 1996, ch 310, § 1, eff Nov 1, 1996, L 1999, ch 160, § 1, eff Nov 1, 1999, L 1999, ch 207, § 2, eff July 6, 1999, L 2002, ch 619, §§ 1, 2, eff Nov 1, 2002, L 2003, ch 602, § 14, eff March 1, 2004, L 2005, ch 499, § 2, eff Aug 16, 2005, L 2007, ch 519, § 1, eff Aug 15, 2007, L 2008, ch 279, § 7, eff Jan 3, 2009, L 2010, ch 56, § 41 (Part A-1), eff June 22, 2010, L 2010, ch 56, § 7 (Part D), eff Sept 20, 2010, L 2011, ch 313, § 2, eff Nov 1, 2011; L 2013, ch 356, § 1, eff Sept 27, 2013.

§ 60.28. Authorized disposition; making graffiti and possession of graffiti instruments

When a person is convicted of an offense defined in section 145.60 or 145.65 of this chapter, or of an attempt to commit such offense, and the sentence imposed by the court for such conviction includes a sentence of probation or conditional discharge, the court shall, where appropriate, include as a condition of such sentence the defendant's successful participation in a graffiti removal program pursuant to paragraph (h) of subdivision two of section 65.10 of this chapter.

> **HISTORY:** Add, L 1995, ch 536, § 1, eff Nov 1, 1995.

§ 60.29. Authorized disposition; cemetery desecration

When a person is convicted of an offense defined in section 145.22 or 145.23 of this chapter or of an attempt to commit such an offense, and the sentence imposed by the court for such conviction includes a sentence of probation or conditional discharge, such sentence shall, where appropriate, be in accordance with paragraph (h) of subdivision two of section 65.10 of this article as such section relates to cemetery crime.

> **HISTORY:** Add, L 1997, ch 165, § 4, eff Nov 1, 1997.

§ 60.30. Civil penalties

This article does not deprive the court of any authority conferred by law to decree a forfeiture of property, suspend or cancel a license, remove a person from office, or impose any other civil penalty and any appropriate order exercising such authority may be included as part of the judgment of conviction.

> **HISTORY:** Add, L 1967, ch 791, § 6, eff Sept 1, 1967, with substance derived from § 60.00, sub 6.

§ 60.35. Mandatory surcharge, sex offender registration fee, DNA databank fee, supplemental sex offender victim fee and crime victim assistance fee required in certain cases

1. (a) Except as provided in section eighteen hundred nine of the vehicle and traffic law and section 27.12 of the parks, recreation and historic preservation law, whenever proceedings in an administrative tribunal or a court of this state result in a conviction for a felony, a misdemeanor, or a violation, as these terms are defined in section 10.00 of this chapter, there shall be levied at sentencing a mandatory surcharge, sex offender registration fee, DNA databank fee and a crime victim assistance fee in addition to any sentence required or permitted by law, in accordance with the following schedule:

(i) a person convicted of a felony shall pay a mandatory surcharge of three hundred dollars and a crime victim assistance fee of twenty-five dollars;

(ii) a person convicted of a misdemeanor shall pay a mandatory surcharge of one hundred seventy-five dollars and a crime victim assistance fee of twenty-five dollars;

(iii) a person convicted of a violation shall pay a mandatory surcharge of ninety-five dollars and a crime victim assistance fee of twenty-five dollars;

(iv) a person convicted of a sex offense as defined by subdivision two of section one hundred sixty-eight-a of the correction law or a sexually violent offense as defined by subdivision three of section one hundred sixty-eight-a of the correction law shall, in addition to a mandatory surcharge and crime victim assistance fee, pay a sex offender registration fee of fifty dollars.

(v) a person convicted of a designated offense as defined by subdivision seven of section nine hundred ninety-five of the executive law shall, in addition to a mandatory surcharge and crime victim assistance fee, pay a DNA databank fee of fifty dollars.

(b) When the felony or misdemeanor conviction in subparagraphs (i), (ii) or (iv) of paragraph (a) of this subdivision results from an offense contained in article one hundred thirty of this chapter, incest in the third, second or first degree as defined insections 255.25, 255.26 and 255.27 of this chapter or an offense contained in article two hundred sixty-three of this chapter, the person convicted shall pay a supplemental sex offender victim fee of one thousand dollars in addition to the mandatory surcharge and any other fee.

2. Where a person is convicted of two or more crimes or violations committed through a single act or omission, or through an act or omission which in itself constituted one of the crimes or violations and also was a material element of the other, the court shall impose a mandatory surcharge and a crime victim assistance fee, and where appropriate a supplemental sex offender victim fee, in accordance with the provisions of this section for the crime or violation which carries the highest classification, and no other sentence to pay a mandatory surcharge, crime victim assistance fee or supplemental sex offender victim fee required by this section shall be imposed. Where a person is convicted of two or more sex offenses or sexually violent offenses, as defined by subdivisions two and three of section one hundred sixty-eight-a of the correction law, committed through a single act or omission, or through an act or omission which in itself constituted one of the offenses and also was a material element of the other, the court shall impose only one sex offender registration fee. Where a person is convicted of two or more designated offenses, as defined by subdivision seven of section nine hundred ninety-five of the executive law, committed through a single act or omission, or through an act or omission which in itself constituted one of the offenses and also was a material element of the other, the court shall impose only one DNA databank fee.

3. The mandatory surcharge, sex offender registration fee, DNA databank fee, crime victim assistance fee, and supplemental sex offender victim fee provided for in subdivision one of this section shall be paid to the clerk of the court or administrative tribunal that rendered the conviction. Within the first ten days of the month following collection of the mandatory surcharge, crime victim assistance fee, and supplemental sex offender victim fee, the collecting authority shall determine the amount of mandatory surcharge, crime victim assistance fee, and supplemental sex offender victim fee collected and, if it is an administrative tribunal, or a town or village justice court, it shall then pay such money to the state comptroller who shall deposit such money in the state treasury pursuant to section one hundred twenty-one of the state finance law to the credit of the criminal justice improvement account established by section ninety-seven-bb of the state finance law. Within the first ten days of the month following collection of the sex offender registration fee and DNA databank fee, the collecting authority shall determine the amount of the sex offender registration fee and DNA databank fee collected and, if it is an administrative tribunal, or a town or village justice court, it shall then pay such money to the state comptroller who shall deposit such money in the state treasury pursuant to section one hundred twenty-one of the state finance law to the credit of the general fund. If such collecting authority is any other court of the

unified court system, it shall, within such period, pay such money attributable to the mandatory surcharge or crime victim assistance fee to the state commissioner of taxation and finance to the credit of the criminal justice improvement account established by section ninety-seven-bb of the state finance law. If such collecting authority is any other court of the unified court system, it shall, within such period, pay such money attributable to the sex offender registration fee and the DNA databank fee to the state commissioner of taxation and finance to the credit of the general fund.

4. Any person who has paid a mandatory surcharge, sex offender registration fee, DNA databank fee, a crime victim assistance fee or a supplemental sex offender victim fee under the authority of this section based upon a conviction that is subsequently reversed or who paid a mandatory surcharge, sex offender registration fee, DNA databank fee, a crime victim assistance fee or supplemental sex offender victim fee under the authority of this section which is ultimately determined not to be required by this section shall be entitled to a refund of such mandatory surcharge, sex offender registration fee, DNA databank fee, crime victim assistance fee or supplemental sex offender victim fee upon application, in the case of a town or village court, to the state comptroller. The state comptroller shall require such proof as is necessary in order to determine whether a refund is required by law. In all other cases, such application shall be made to the department, agency or court that collected such surcharge or fee. Such department, agency or court shall initiate the refund process and the state comptroller shall pay the refund pursuant to subdivision fifteen of section eight of the state finance law.

5. [Until Sept 1, 2015]

(a) When a person who is convicted of a crime or violation and sentenced to a term of imprisonment has failed to pay the mandatory surcharge, sex offender registration fee, DNA databank fee, crime victim assistance fee or supplemental sex offender victim fee required by this section, the clerk of the court that rendered the conviction shall notify the superintendent or the municipal official of the facility where the person is confined. The superintendent or the municipal official shall cause any amount owing to be collected from such person during his or her term of imprisonment from moneys to the credit of an inmates' fund or such moneys as may be earned by a person in a work release program pursuant to section eight hundred sixty of the correction law. Such moneys attributable to the mandatory surcharge or crime victim assistance fee shall be paid over to the state comptroller to the credit of the criminal justice improvement account established by section ninety-seven-bb of the state finance law and such moneys attributable to the sex offender registration fee or DNA databank fee shall be paid over to the state comptroller to the credit of the general fund, except that any such moneys collected which are surcharges, sex offender registration fees, DNA databank fees, crime victim assistance fees or supplemental sex offender victim fees levied in relation to convictions obtained in a town or village justice court shall be paid within thirty days after the receipt thereof by the superintendent or municipal official of the facility to the justice of the court in which the conviction was obtained. For the purposes of collecting such mandatory surcharge, sex offender registration fee, DNA databank fee, crime victim assistance fee, and supplemental sex offender victim fee, the state shall be legally entitled to the money to the credit of an inmates' fund or money which is earned by an inmate in a work release program. For purposes of this subdivision, the term "inmates' fund" shall mean moneys in the possession of an inmate at the time of his or her admission into such facility, funds earned by him or her as provided for in section one hundred eighty-seven of the correction law and any other funds received by him or her or on his or her behalf and deposited with such superintendent or municipal official.

(b) The incarceration fee provided for in subdivision two of section one hundred eighty-nine of the correction law shall not be assessed or collected if any order of restitution or reparation, fine, mandatory surcharge, sex offender registration fee, DNA databank fee, crime victim assistance fee or supplemental sex offender victim fee remains unpaid. In such circumstances, any monies which may lawfully be withheld from the compensation paid to a prisoner for work performed while housed in a general confinement facility in satisfaction of such an obligation shall first be applied toward satisfaction of such obligation.

5. [Eff Sept 1, 2015] When a person who is convicted of a crime or violation and sentenced to a term of imprisonment has failed to pay the mandatory surcharge, sex offender registration fee, DNA databank fee, crime victim assistance fee or supplemental sex offender victim fee required by this section, the clerk of the court that rendered the conviction shall notify the superintendent or the municipal official of the facility where the person is confined. The superintendent or the municipal official shall cause any amount owing to be collected from such person during his or her term of imprisonment from moneys to the credit of an inmates' fund or such moneys as may be earned by a person in a work release program pursuant to section eight hundred sixty of the correction law. Such moneys attributable to the mandatory surcharge or crime victim assistance fee shall be paid over to the state comptroller to the credit of the criminal justice improvement account established by section ninety-seven-bb of the state finance law and such moneys attributable to the sex offender registration fee or DNA databank fee shall be paid over to the state comptroller to the credit of the general fund, except that any such moneys collected which are surcharges, sex offender registration fees, DNA databank fees, crime victim assistance fees or supplemental sex offender victim fees levied in relation to convictions obtained in a town or village justice court shall be paid within thirty days after the receipt thereof by the superintendent or municipal official of the facility to the justice of the court in which the conviction was obtained. For the purposes of collecting such mandatory surcharge, sex offender registration fee, DNA databank fee, crime victim assistance fee and supplemental sex offender victim fee, the state shall be legally entitled to the money to the credit of an inmates' fund or money which is earned by an inmate in a work release program. For purposes of this subdivision, the term "inmates' fund" shall mean moneys in the possession of an inmate at the time of his or her admission into such facility, funds earned by himor her as provided for in section one hundred eighty-seven of the correction law and any other funds received by him or her or on his or her behalf and deposited with such superintendent or municipal official.

6. Notwithstanding any other provision of this section, where a person has made restitution or reparation pursuant to section 60.27 of this article, such person shall not be required to pay a mandatory surcharge or a crime victim assistance fee.

7. Notwithstanding the provisions of subdivision one of section 60.00 of this article, the provisions of subdivision one of this section shall not apply to a violation under any law other than this chapter.

8. Subdivision one of section 130.10 of the criminal procedure law notwithstanding, at the time that the mandatory surcharge, sex offender registration fee or DNA databank fee, crime victim assistance fee or supplemental sex offender victim fee is imposed a town or village court may, and all other courts shall, issue and cause to be served upon the person required to pay the mandatory surcharge, sex offender registration fee or DNA databank fee, crime victim assistance fee or supplemental sex offender victim fee, a summons directing that such person appear before the court regarding the payment of the mandatory surcharge, sex offender registration fee or DNA databank fee, crime victim assistance fee or supplemental sex offender victim fee, if after sixty days from the date it was imposed it remains unpaid. The designated date of appearance on the summons shall be set for the first day court is in session falling after the sixtieth day from the imposition of the mandatory surcharge, sex offender registration fee or DNA databank fee, crime

victim assistance fee or supplemental sex offender victim fee. The summons shall contain the information required by subdivision two of section 130.10 of the criminal procedure law except that in substitution for the requirement of paragraph (c) of such subdivision the summons shall state that the person served must appear at a date, time and specific location specified in the summons if after sixty days from the date of issuance the mandatory surcharge, sex offender registration fee or DNA databank fee, crime victim assistance fee or supplemental sex offender victim fee remains unpaid. The court shall not issue a summons under this subdivision to a person who is being sentenced to a term of confinement in excess of sixty days in jail or in the department of corrections and community supervision. The mandatory surcharges, sex offender registration fee and DNA databank fees, crime victim assistance fees and supplemental sex offender victim fees for those persons shall be governed by the provisions of section 60.30 of this article.

9. Notwithstanding the provisions of subdivision one of this section, in the event a proceeding is in a town or village court, such court shall add an additional five dollars to the surcharges imposed by such subdivision one.

10. The provisions of this section shall apply to sentences imposed upon a youthful offender finding; provided, however that the court shall not impose the sex offender registration fee, DNA databank fee or supplemental sex offender victim fee, as defined in subparagraphs (iv) and (v) of paragraph (a) and paragraph (b) of subdivision one of this section, for an offense in which the conviction was substituted with a youthful offender finding.

> **HISTORY:** Add, L 1982, ch 55, § 81; amd, L 1983, ch 15, § 2, L 1983, ch 16, § 1, eff March 28, 1983, L 1985, ch 59, § 1, L 1989, ch 62, § 84, eff April 19, 1989, L 1990, ch 190, § 319, L 1991, ch 166, § 370, L 1992, ch 55, § 354, eff April 10, 1992, deemed eff April 1, 1992, L 1995, ch 3, § 56, eff June 10, 1995, expires Sept 1, 2015, L 1995, ch 3, § 71, eff July 1, 1995, L 1997, ch 452, § 2, eff Jan 1, 1998, L 1999, ch 385, § 2, eff July 27, 1999, L 1999, ch 385, § 3, eff Sept 1, 2009, L 2000, ch 57, § 1 (Part L), eff May 15, 2000, deemed eff on and after April 1, 2000, L 2003, ch 62, § 1 (Part F), eff May 15, 2003, L 2003, ch 62, §§ 1, 11 (Part M), eff Nov 11, 2003, L 2004, ch 56, § 1 (Part E), eff Aug 20, 2004, deemed eff on and after April 1, 2004, L 2004, ch 56, § 2 (Part E), eff Sept 1, 2005, L 2006, ch 320, § 2, eff Nov 1, 2006, L 2008, ch 56, § 1 (Part DD), eff July 1, 2008, L 2008, ch 56, § 2, eff April 23, 2008, deemed eff on and after Feb 16, 2005, L 2011, ch 62, § 121 (Part C, Subpart B), eff March 31, 2011, L 2013, ch 525, § 1, eff Dec 18, 2013.

§ 60.36. Authorized dispositions; driving while intoxicated offenses

Where a court is imposing a sentence for a violation of subdivision two, two-a, or three of section eleven hundred ninety-two of the vehicle and traffic law pursuant to sections 65.00 or 65.05 of this title and, as a condition of such sentence, orders the installation and maintenance of an ignition interlock device, the court may impose any other penalty authorized pursuant to section eleven hundred ninety-three of the vehicle and traffic law.

> **HISTORY:** Add, L 2009, ch 496, § 12, eff Dec 18, 2009.

§ 60.37. Authorized disposition; certain offenses

When a person has been charged with an offense and the elements of such offense meet the criteria of an "eligible offense" and such person qualifies as an "eligible person" as such terms are defined in section four hundred fifty-eight-l of the social services law, the court may, as a condition of adjournment in contemplation of dismissal in accordance with section 170.55 of the criminal procedure law, or a condition of probation or a conditional discharge, direct that the defendant participate in an education reform program pursuant to subdivision two of section four hundred fifty-eight-l of the social services law.

> **HISTORY:** Add, L 2011, ch 535, § 6, eff May 20, 2012; amd, L 2012, ch 55, § 6 (Part V), eff May 20, 2012.

ARTICLE 65   SENTENCES OF PROBATION, CONDITIONAL DISCHARGE AND UNCONDITIONAL DISCHARGE

HISTORY: Add, L 1965, ch 1030, eff Sept 1, 1967.

§ 65.00. Sentence of probation

1. Criteria.

   (a) Except as otherwise required by section 60.04 or 60.05 of this title, and except as provided by paragraph (b) hereof, the court may sentence a person to a period of probation upon conviction of any crime if the court, having regard to the nature and circumstances of the crime and to the history, character and condition of the defendant, is of the opinion that:

   (i) Institutional confinement for the term authorized by law of the defendant is or may not be necessary for the protection of the public;

   (ii) the defendant is in need of guidance, training or other assistance which, in his case, can be effectively administered through probation supervision; and

   (iii) such disposition is not inconsistent with the ends of justice.

   (b) The court, with the concurrence of either the administrative judge of the court or of the judicial district within which the court is situated or such administrative judge as the presiding justice of the appropriate appellate division shall designate, may sentence a person to a period of probation upon conviction of a class A-II felony defined in article two hundred twenty, the class B felony defined in section 220.48 of this chapter or any other class B felony defined in article two hundred twenty of this chapter where the person is a second felony drug offender as defined in paragraph (b) of subdivision one of section 70.70 of this chapter, if the prosecutor either orally on the record or in a writing filed with the indictment recommends that the court sentence such person to a period of probation upon the ground that such person has or is providing material assistance in the investigation, apprehension or prosecution of any person for a felony defined in article two hundred twenty or the attempt or the conspiracy to commit any such felony, and if the court, having regard to the nature and circumstances of the crime and to the history, character and condition of the defendant is of the opinion that:

   (i) Institutional confinement of the defendant is not necessary for the protection of the public;

   (ii) The defendant is in need of guidance, training or other assistance which, in his case, can be effectively administered through probation supervision;

   (iii) The defendant has or is providing material assistance in the investigation, apprehension or prosecution of a person for a felony defined in article two hundred twenty or the attempt or conspiracy to commit any such felony; and

   (iv) Such disposition is not inconsistent with the ends of justice.

   [Until Sept 1, 2015] Provided, however, that the court shall not, except to the extent authorized by paragraph (d) of subdivision two of section 60.01 of this chapter, impose a sentence of probation in any case where it sentences a defendant for more than one crime and imposes a sentence of imprisonment for any one of the crimes, or where the defendant is subject to an undischarged indeterminate or determinate sentence of imprisonment which was imposed at a previous time by a court of this state and has more than one year to run.

[Eff Sept 1, 2015] Provided, however, that the court shall not, except to the extent authorized by paragraph (d) of subdivision two of section 60.01 of this chapter, impose a sentence of probation in any case where it sentences a defendant for more than one crime and imposes a sentence of imprisonment for any one of the crimes, or where the defendant is subject to an undischarged indeterminate or reformatory sentence of imprisonment which was imposed at a previous time by a court of this state and has more than one year to run.

2. Sentence. When a person is sentenced to a period of probation the court shall, except to the extent authorized by paragraph (d) of subdivision two of section 60.01 of this chapter, impose the period authorized by subdivision three of this section and shall specify, in accordance with section 65.10, the conditions to be complied with. The court may modify or enlarge the conditions or, if the defendant commits an additional offense or violates a condition, revoke the sentence at any time prior to the expiration or termination of the period of probation.

3. Periods of probation. Unless terminated sooner in accordance with the criminal procedure law, the period of probation shall be as follows:

(a) (i) For a felony, other than a class A-II felony defined in article two hundred twenty of this chapter or the class B felony defined in section 220.48 of this chapter, or any other class B felony defined in article two hundred twenty of this chapter committed by a second felony drug offender, or a sexual assault, the period of probation shall be a term of three, four or five years;

(ii) For a class A-II felony drug offender as defined in paragraph (a) of subdivision one of section 70.71 of this chapter as described in paragraph (b) of subdivision one of this section, or a class B felony committed by a second felony drug offender described in paragraph (b) of subdivision one of this section, the period of probation shall be life and for a class B felony defined in section 220.48 of this chapter, the period of probation shall be twenty-five years;

(iii) For a felony sexual assault, the period of probation shall be ten years.

(b) (i) For a class A misdemeanor, other than a sexual assault, the period of probation shall be a term of two or three years;

(ii) For a class A misdemeanor sexual assault, the period of probation shall be six years.

(c) For a class B misdemeanor, the period of probation shall be one year, except the period of probation shall be no less than one year and no more than three years for the class B misdemeanor of public lewdness as defined in section 245.00 of this chapter;

(d) For an unclassified misdemeanor, the period of probation shall be a term of two or three years if the authorized sentence of imprisonment is in excess of three months, otherwise the period of probation shall be one year.

For the purposes of this section, the term "sexual assault" means an offense defined in article one hundred thirty or two hundred sixty-three, or in section 255.25, 255.26 or 255.27 of this chapter, or an attempt to commit any of the foregoing offenses.

4. If during the periods of probation referenced in subparagraph (i) of paragraph (a), subparagraph (i) of paragraph (b) and paragraph (d) of subdivision three of this section an alleged

violation is sustained following a hearing pursuant to section 410.70 of the criminal procedure law and the court continues or modifies the sentence, the court may extend the remaining period of probation up to the maximum term authorized by this section. Provided, however, a defendant shall receive credit for the time during which he or she was supervised under the original probation sentence prior to any declaration of delinquency and for any time spent in custody pursuant to this article for an alleged violation of probation.

5. In any case where a court pursuant to its authority under subdivision four of section 60.01 of this chapter revokes probation and sentences such person to imprisonment and probation, as provided in paragraph (d) of subdivision two of section 60.01 of this chapter, the period of probation shall be the remaining period of the original probation sentence or one year whichever is greater.

HISTORY: Add, L 1965, ch 1030, eff Sept 1, 1967, with substance derived from former Penal Law § 2188, and Criminal Code §§ 483, 933; amd, L 1971, ch 1097, § 73, L 1973, ch 276, § 7, L 1973, ch 277, § 5, L 1973, ch 278, eff Sept 1, 1973, L 1973, ch 676, § 29, eff Sept 1, 1973, L 1973, ch 1051, § 2, L 1974, ch 835, § 2, eff Sept 1, 1974, L 1979, ch 410, §§ 4, 5, eff Sept 1, 1979, L 1980, ch 471, §§ 19, 20, eff July 23, 1980, L 1985, ch 79, § 1, eff Nov 1, 1985, L 1995, ch 3, § 1-a, eff Oct 1, 1995, repealed eff Sept 1, 2015, L 2000, ch 1, § 10, eff Feb 1, 2001, L 2003, ch 264, § 5, eff Nov 1, 2003, L 2004, ch 568, § 1, eff Nov 1, 2004, L 2004, ch 738, § 25, eff Jan 13, 2005, L 2004, ch 738, § 26, eff Dec 27, 2004, L 2006, ch 320, § 3, eff Nov 1, 2006, L 2009, ch 56, §§ 19, 20 (Part AAA), eff April 7, 2009, L 2013, ch 556, §§ 1–4, eff Feb 9, 2014, L 2014, ch 17, § 1, eff Feb 9, 2014.

§ 65.05. Sentence of conditional discharge

1. Criteria.

(a) Except as otherwise required by section 60.05, the court may impose a sentence of conditional discharge for an offense if the court, having regard to the nature and circumstances of the offense and to the history, character and condition of the defendant, is of the opinion that neither the public interest nor the ends of justice would be served by a sentence of imprisonment and that probation supervision is not appropriate.

(b) When a sentence of conditional discharge is imposed for a felony, the court shall set forth in the record the reasons for its action.

2. Sentence. Except to the extent authorized by paragraph (d) of subdivision two of section 60.01 of this chapter, when the court imposes a sentence of conditional discharge the defendant shall be released with respect to the conviction for which the sentence is imposed without imprisonment or probation supervision but subject, during the period of conditional discharge, to such conditions as the court may determine. The court shall impose the period of conditional discharge authorized by subdivision three of this section and shall specify, in accordance with section 65.10, the conditions to be complied with. If a defendant is sentenced pursuant to paragraph (e) of subdivision two of section 65.10 of this chapter, the court shall require the administrator of the program to provide written notice to the court of any violation of program participation by the defendant. The court may modify or enlarge the conditions or, if the defendant commits an additional offense or violates a condition, revoke the sentence at any time prior to the expiration or termination of the period of conditional discharge.

3. Periods of conditional discharge. Unless terminated sooner in accordance with the criminal procedure law, the period of conditional discharge shall be as follows:

(a) Three years in the case of a felony; and

(b) One year in the case of a misdemeanor or a violation.

Where the court has required, as a condition of the sentence, that the defendant make restitution of the fruits of his or her offense or make reparation for the loss caused thereby and such condition has not been satisfied, the court, at any time prior to the expiration or termination of the period of conditional discharge, may impose an additional period. The length of the additional period shall be fixed by the court at the time it is imposed and shall not be more than two years. All of the incidents of the original sentence, including the authority of the court to modify or enlarge the conditions, shall continue to apply during such additional period.

> **HISTORY:** Add, L 1965, ch 1030, eff Sept 1, 1967, with substance derived from § 2188. Sub 1, add, L 1973, ch 277, § 6, eff Sept 1, 1973. Former sub 1, amd, L 1972, ch 157, § 2, L 1973, ch 276, § 8, L 1973, ch 1051, § 20; repealed, L 1973, ch 277, § 6, eff Sept 1, 1973. Sub 1, par (a), amd, L 1980, ch 471, § 21, L 1981, ch 742, § 1, eff Sept 1, 1981. Sub 2, amd, L 1972, ch 157, § 2, L 1974, ch 835, § 3, L 1981, ch 742, § 2, eff Sept 1, 1981. Sub 3, amd, L 1971, ch 1097, § 74, L 1992, ch 618, § 14, eff Nov 1, 1992. Sub 3, closing par, amd, L 1992, ch 618, § 14, eff Nov 1, 1992.

§ 65.10. Conditions of probation and of conditional discharge

1. In general. The conditions of probation and of conditional discharge shall be such as the court, in its discretion, deems reasonably necessary to insure that the defendant will lead a law-abiding life or to assist him to do so.

2. Conditions relating to conduct and rehabilitation. When imposing a sentence of probation or of conditional discharge, the court shall, as a condition of the sentence, consider restitution or reparation and may, as a condition of the sentence, require that the defendant:

(a) Avoid injurious or vicious habits;

(b) Refrain from frequenting unlawful or disreputable places or consorting with disreputable persons;

(c) Work faithfully at a suitable employment or faithfully pursue a course of study or of vocational training that will equip him for suitable employment;

(d) Undergo available medical or psychiatric treatment and remain in a specified institution, when required for that purpose;

(e) Participate in an alcohol or substance abuse program or an intervention program approved by the court after consultation with the local probation department having jurisdiction, or such other public or private agency as the court determines to be appropriate;

(e-1) Participate in a motor vehicle accident prevention course. The court may require such condition where a person has been convicted of a traffic infraction for a violation of article twenty-six of the vehicle and traffic law where the commission of such violation caused the serious physical injury or death of another person. For purposes of this paragraph, the term "motor vehicle accident prevention course" shall mean a motor vehicle accident prevention course approved by the department of motor vehicles pursuant to article twelve-B of the vehicle and traffic law;

(f) Support his dependents and meet other family responsibilities;

(g) Make restitution of the fruits of his or her offense or make reparation, in an amount he can afford to pay, for the actual out-of-pocket loss caused thereby. When restitution or reparation is a condition of the sentence, the court shall fix the amount thereof, the manner of performance, specifically state the date when restitution is to be paid in full prior to the expiration of the sentence of probation and may establish provisions for the early termination of a sentence of probation or conditional discharge pursuant to the provisions of subdivision three of section 410.90 of the criminal procedure law after the restitution and reparation part of a sentence of probation or conditional discharge has been satisfied. The court shall provide that in the event the person to whom restitution or reparation is to be made dies prior to the completion of said restitution or reparation, the remaining payments shall be made to the estate of the deceased.

(g-1) Reimburse a consumer credit reporting agency for the amount of the fee or fees that could have been charged by such agency to a domestic violence victim, as defined in section three hundred eighty-t of the general business law, had such victim not been eligible to receive security freeze services without charge pursuant to subdivision (n) of such section;

(h) Perform services for a public or not-for-profit corporation, association, institution or agency, including but not limited to services for the division of substance abuse services, services in an appropriate community program for removal of graffiti from public or private property, including any property damaged in the underlying offense, or services for the maintenance and repair of real or personal property maintained as a cemetery plot, grave, burial place or other place of interment of human remains. Provided however, that the performance of any such services shall not result in the displacement of employed workers or in the impairment of existing contracts for services, nor shall the performance of any such services be required or permitted in any establishment involved in any labor strike or lockout. The court may establish provisions for the early termination of a sentence of probation or conditional discharge pursuant to the provisions of subdivision three of section 410.90 of the criminal procedure law after such services have been completed. Such sentence may only be imposed upon conviction of a misdemeanor, violation, or class D or class E felony, or a youthful offender finding replacing any such conviction, where the defendant has consented to the amount and conditions of such service;

(i) If a person under the age of twenty-one years,

(i) resides with his parents or in a suitable foster home or hostel as referred to in section two hundred forty-four of the executive law,

(ii) attends school,

(iii) spends such part of the period of the sentence as the court may direct, but not exceeding two years, in a facility made available by the division for youth pursuant to article nineteen-G of the executive law, provided that admission to such facility may be made only with the prior consent of the division for youth,

(iv) attend a non-residential program for such hours and pursuant to a schedule prescribed by the court as suitable for a program of rehabilitation of youth,

(v) contribute to his own support in any home, foster home or hostel;

(j) Post a bond or other security for the performance of any or all conditions imposed;

(k) Observe certain specified conditions of conduct as set forth in an order of protection issued pursuant to section 530.12 or 530.13 of the criminal procedure law.

(k-1) Install and maintain a functioning ignition interlock device, as that term is defined in section one hundred nineteen-a of the vehicle and traffic law, in any vehicle owned or operated by the defendant if the court in its discretion determines that such a condition is necessary to ensure the public safety. The court may require such condition only where a person has been convicted of a violation of subdivision two, two-a or three of section eleven hundred ninety-two of the vehicle and traffic law, or any crime defined by the vehicle and traffic law or this chapter of which an alcohol-related violation of any provision of section eleven hundred ninety-two of the vehicle and traffic law is an essential element. The offender shall be required to install and operate the ignition interlock device only in accordance with section eleven hundred ninety-eight of the vehicle and traffic law.

(l) Satisfy any other conditions reasonably related to his rehabilitation.

3. Conditions relating to supervision. When imposing a sentence of probation the court, in addition to any conditions imposed pursuant to subdivision two of this section, shall require as conditions of the sentence, that the defendant:

(a) Report to a probation officer as directed by the court or the probation officer and permit the probation officer to visit him at his place of abode or elsewhere;

(b) Remain within the jurisdiction of the court unless granted permission to leave by the court or the probation officer. Where a defendant is granted permission to move or travel outside the jurisdiction of the court, the defendant shall sign a written waiver of extradition agreeing to waive extradition proceedings where such proceedings are the result of the issuance of a warrant by the court pursuant to subdivision two of section 410.40 of the criminal procedure law based on an alleged violation of probation. Where any county or the city of New York incurs costs associated with the return of any probationer based on the issuance of a warrant by the court pursuant to subdivision two of section 410.40 of the criminal procedure law, the jurisdiction may collect the reasonable and necessary expenses involved in connection with his or her transport, from the probationer; provided that where the sentence of probation is not revoked pursuant to section 410.70 of the criminal procedure law no such expenses may be collected.

(c) Answer all reasonable inquiries by the probation officer and notify the probation officer prior to any change in address or employment.

4. Electronic monitoring. When imposing a sentence of probation the court may, in addition to any conditions imposed pursuant to subdivisions two and three of this section, require the defendant to submit to the use of an electronic monitoring device and/or to follow a schedule that governs the defendant's daily movement. Such condition may be imposed only where the court, in its discretion, determines that requiring the defendant to comply with such condition will advance public safety, probationer control or probationer surveillance. Electronic monitoring shall be used in accordance with uniform procedures developed by the office of probation and correctional alternatives.

4-a. Mandatory conditions for sex offenders.

(a) When imposing a sentence of probation or conditional discharge upon a person convicted of an offense defined in article one hundred thirty, two hundred thirty-five or two hundred sixty-three of this chapter, or section 255.25, 255.26 or 255.27 of this chapter, and the victim of such offense was under the age of eighteen at the time of such offense or such person has been designated a level three sex offender pursuant to subdivision six of section 168-l of the correction law, the court shall require, as a mandatory condition of such sentence, that such sentenced offender shall refrain from knowingly entering into or upon any school grounds, as that term is defined in subdivision fourteen of section 220.00 of this chapter, or any other facility or institution primarily used for the care or treatment of persons under the age of eighteen while one or more of such persons under the age of eighteen are present, provided however, that when such sentenced offender is a registered student or participant or an employee of such facility or institution or entity contracting therewith or has a family member enrolled in such facility or institution, such sentenced offender may, with the written authorization of his or her probation officer or the court and the superintendent or chief administrator of such facility, institution or grounds, enter such facility, institution or upon such grounds for the limited purposes authorized by the probation officer or the court and superintendent or chief officer. Nothing in this subdivision shall be construed as restricting any lawful condition of supervision that may be imposed on such sentenced offender.

(b) When imposing a sentence of probation or conditional discharge upon a person convicted of an offense for which registration as a sex offender is required pursuant to subdivision two or three of section one hundred sixty-eight-a of the correction law, and the victim of such offense was under the age of eighteen at the time of such offense or such person has been designated a level three sex offender pursuant to subdivision six of section one hundred sixty-eight-l of the correction law or the internet was used to facilitate the commission of the crime, the court shall require, as mandatory conditions of such sentence, that such sentenced offender be prohibited from using the internet to access pornographic material, access a commercial social networking website, communicate with other individuals or groups for the purpose of promoting sexual relations with persons under the age of eighteen, and communicate with a person under the age of eighteen when such offender is over the age of eighteen, provided that the court may permit an offender to use the internet to communicate with a person under the age of eighteen when such offender is the parent of a minor child and is not otherwise prohibited from communicating with such child. Nothing in this subdivision shall be construed as restricting any other lawful condition of supervision that may be imposed on such sentenced offender. As used in this subdivision, a "commercial social networking website" shall mean any business, organization or other entity operating a website that permits persons under eighteen years of age to be registered users for the purpose of establishing personal relationships with other users, where such persons under eighteen years of age may: (i) create web pages or profiles that provide information about themselves where such web pages or profiles are available to the public or to other users; (ii) engage in direct or real time communication with other users, such as a chat room or instant messenger; and (iii) communicate with persons over eighteen years of age; provided, however, that, for purposes of this subdivision, a commercial social networking website shall not include a website that permits users to engage in such other activities as are not enumerated herein.

5. Other conditions. When imposing a sentence of probation the court may, in addition to any conditions imposed pursuant to subdivisions two, three and four of this section, require that the defendant comply with any other reasonable condition as the court shall determine to be necessary or appropriate to ameliorate the conduct which gave rise to the offense or to prevent the incarceration of the defendant.

5-a. Other conditions for sex offenders. When imposing a sentence of probation upon a person convicted of an offense for which registration as a sex offender is required pursuant to subdivision two or three of section one hundred sixty-eight-a of the correction law, in addition to any conditions required under subdivisions two, three, four, four-a and five of this section, the court may require that the defendant comply with a reasonable limitation on his or her use of the internet that the court determines to be necessary or appropriate to ameliorate the conduct which gave rise to the offense or to protect public safety, provided that the court shall not prohibit such sentenced offender from using the internet in connection with education, lawful employment or search for lawful employment.

HISTORY: Add, L 1965, ch 1030, eff Sept 1, 1967, with substance derived in part from §§ 2188, 2188-b; amd, L 1973, ch 676, § 30, L 1974, ch 930, § 3, L 1975, ch 667, § 35, L 1978, ch 500, § 1,

L 1980, ch 270, § 1, eff June 17, 1980, L 1980, ch 284, § 1, L 1980, ch 471, § 22, eff July 23, 1980, L 1980, ch 530, § 16, L 1981, ch 583, § 1, L 1981, ch 742, § 3, eff Sept 1, 1981, L 1982, ch 782, §§ 1, 2, L 1984, ch 335, § 2, L 1984, ch 417, § 1, eff Nov 1, 1984, L 1985, ch 672, §§ 1, 2, eff Sept 30, 1985, L 1986, ch 552, § 1, L 1989, ch 443, § 1, L 1992, ch 465, § 51, eff Jan 13, 1993, L 1992, ch 618, § 15, eff Nov 1, 1992, L 1995, ch 536, § 2, L 1996, ch 186, § 1, eff Nov 1, 1996, L 1996, ch 653, § 1, eff Sept 18, 1996, L 1997, ch 181, § 1, eff July 8, 1997, L 2000, ch 1, § 7, eff Feb 1, 2001, L 2001, ch 508, § 1, eff Jan 20, 2002, L 2005, ch 544, § 1, eff Sept 1, 2006, L 2006, ch 320, § 4, eff Nov 1, 2006, L 2006, ch 571, § 6, eff Nov 1, 2006, L 2007, ch 669, § 1, eff Oct 27, 2007, L 2008, ch 67, §§ 7, 8, eff April 28, 2008, L 2008, ch 406, § 2, eff Aug 5, 2008, L 2010, ch 56, § 46 (Part A), eff June 22, 2010, L 2010, ch 56, § 8 (Part D), eff Sept 20, 2010.

§ 65.15. Calculation of periods of probation and of conditional discharge

1. A period of probation or a period or additional period of conditional discharge commences on the day it is imposed. Multiple periods, whether imposed at the same or at different times, shall run concurrently.

2. When a person has violated the conditions of his probation or conditional discharge and is declared delinquent by the court, the declaration of delinquency shall interrupt the period of the sentence as of the date of the delinquency and such interruption shall continue until a final determination as to the delinquency has been made by the court pursuant to a hearing held in accordance with the provisions of the criminal procedure law.

3. [Until Sept 1, 2015] In any case where a person who is under a sentence of probation or of conditional discharge is also under an indeterminate or determinate sentence of imprisonment, imposed for some other offense by a court of this state the service of the sentence of imprisonment shall satisfy the sentence of probation or of conditional discharge unless the sentence of probation or of conditional discharge is revoked prior to the next to occur of parole or conditional release under, or satisfaction of, the sentence of imprisonment. Provided, however, that the service of an indeterminate or determinate sentence of imprisonment shall not satisfy a sentence of probation if the sentence of probation was imposed at a time when the sentence of imprisonment had one year or less to run.

3. [Eff Sept 1, 2015] In any case where a person who is under a sentence of probation or of conditional discharge is also under an indeterminate sentence of imprisonment, or a reformatory sentence of imprisonment authorized by section 75.00, imposed for some other offense by a court of this state the service of the sentence of imprisonment shall satisfy the sentence of probation or of conditional discharge unless the sentence of probation or of conditional discharge is revoked prior to the next to occur of parole or conditional release under, or satisfaction of, the sentence of imprisonment. Provided, however, that the service of an indeterminate or a reformatory sentence of imprisonment shall not satisfy a sentence of probation if the sentence of probation was imposed at a time when the sentence of imprisonment had one year or less to run.

   HISTORY: Add, L 1965, ch 1030, eff Sept 1, 1967. Sub 2, amd, L 1971, ch 1097, § 75, eff Sept 1, 1971. Sub 3, amd, L 1995, ch 3, § 1-b, eff Oct 1, 1995, repealed eff Sept 1, 2015.

§ 65.20. Sentence of unconditional discharge

1. Criteria. The court may impose a sentence of unconditional discharge in any case where it is authorized to impose a sentence of conditional discharge under section 65.05 if the court is of the opinion that no proper purpose would be served by imposing any condition upon the defendant's release.

When a sentence of unconditional discharge is imposed for a felony, the court shall set forth in the record the reasons for its action.

2. Sentence. When the court imposes a sentence of unconditional discharge, the defendant shall

be released with respect to the conviction for which the sentence is imposed without imprisonment, fine or probation supervision. A sentence of unconditional discharge is for all purposes a final judgment of conviction.

HISTORY: Add, L 1965, ch 1030, eff Sept 1, 1967.

ARTICLE 70   SENTENCES OF IMPRISONMENT

HISTORY: Add, L 1965, ch 1030, eff Sept 1, 1967.

§ 70.00. Sentence of imprisonment for felony

1. [Until Sept 1, 2015, as amended L 2004, ch 738, § 28 and L 2007, ch 7, § 36] Indeterminate sentence. Except as provided in subdivisions four, five and six of this section or section 70.80 of this article, a sentence of imprisonment for a felony, other than a felony defined in article two hundred twenty or two hundred twenty-one of this chapter, shall be an indeterminate sentence. When such a sentence is imposed, the court shall impose a maximum term in accordance with the provisions of subdivision two of this section and the minimum period of imprisonment shall be as provided in subdivision three of this section.

1. [Eff Sept 1, 2015, as amended L 2004, ch 738, § 29 and L 2007, ch 7, § 37] Indeterminate sentence. Except as provided in subdivisions four and five of this section or section 70.80 of this article, a sentence of imprisonment for a felony, other than a felony defined in article two hundred twenty or two hundred twenty-one of this chapter, shall be an indeterminate sentence. When such a sentence is imposed, the court shall impose a maximum term in accordance with the provisions of subdivision two of this section and the minimum period of imprisonment shall be as provided in subdivision three of this section.

2. Maximum term of sentence. The maximum term of an indeterminate sentence shall be at least

three years and the term shall be fixed as follows:

(a) For a class A felony, the term shall be life imprisonment;

(b) For a class B felony, the term shall be fixed by the court, and shall not exceed twenty-five years;

(c) For a class C felony, the term shall be fixed by the court, and shall not exceed fifteen years;

(d) For a class D felony, the term shall be fixed by the court, and shall not exceed seven years; and

(e) For a class E felony, the term shall be fixed by the court, and shall not exceed four years.

3. Minimum period of imprisonment. The minimum period of imprisonment under an indeterminate sentence shall be at least one year and shall be fixed as follows:

(a) In the case of a class A felony, the minimum period shall be fixed by the court and specified in the sentence.

(i) For a class A-I felony, such minimum period shall not be less than fifteen years nor more than twenty-five years; provided, however, that (A) where a sentence, other than a sentence of death or life imprisonment without parole, is imposed upon a defendant convicted of murder in the first degree as defined in section 125.27 of this chapter such minimum period shall be not less than twenty years nor more than twenty-five years, and, (B) where a sentence is imposed upon a defendant convicted of murder in the second degree as defined in subdivision five of section 125.25 of this chapter or convicted of aggravated murder as defined in section 125.26 of this chapter, the sentence shall be life imprisonment without parole, and, (C) where a sentence is imposed upon a defendant convicted of attempted murder in the first degree as defined in article one hundred ten of this chapter and subparagraph (i), (ii) or (iii) of paragraph (a) of subdivision one and paragraph (b) of subdivision one of section 125.27 of this chapter or attempted aggravated murder as defined in article one hundred ten of this chapter and section 125.26 of this chapter such minimum period shall be not less than twenty years nor more than forty years.

(ii) For a class A-II felony, such minimum period shall not be less than three years nor more than eight years four months, except that for the class A-II felony of predatory sexual assault as defined in section 130.95 of this chapter or the class A-II felony of predatory sexual assault against a child as defined in section 130.96 of this chapter, such minimum period shall be not less than ten years nor more than twenty-five years.

(b) For any other felony, the minimum period shall be fixed by the court and specified in the sentence and shall be not less than one year nor more than one-third of the maximum term imposed.

4. Alternative definite sentence for class D and E felonies. When a person, other than a second or persistent felony offender, is sentenced for a class D or class E felony, and the court, having regard to the nature and circumstances of the crime and to the history and character of the defendant, is of the opinion that a sentence of imprisonment is necessary but that it would be unduly harsh to impose an indeterminate or determinate sentence, the court may impose a definite sentence of imprisonment and fix a term of one year or less.

5. Life imprisonment without parole. Notwithstanding any other provision of law, a defendant sentenced to life imprisonment without parole shall not be or become eligible for parole or

conditional release. For purposes of commitment and custody, other than parole and conditional release, such sentence shall be deemed to be an indeterminate sentence. A defendant may be sentenced to life imprisonment without parole upon conviction for the crime of murder in the first degree as defined in section 125.27 of this chapter and in accordance with the procedures provided by law for imposing a sentence for such crime. A defendant must be sentenced to life imprisonment without parole upon conviction for the crime of terrorism as defined in section 490.25 of this chapter, where the specified offense the defendant committed is a class A-I felony; the crime of criminal possession of a chemical weapon or biological weapon in the first degree as defined in section 490.45 of this chapter; or the crime of criminal use of a chemical weapon or biological weapon in the first degree as defined in section 490.55 of this chapter; provided, however, that nothing in this subdivision shall preclude or prevent a sentence of death when the defendant is also convicted of the crime of murder in the first degree as defined in section 125.27 of this chapter. A defendant must be sentenced to life imprisonment without parole upon conviction for the crime of murder in the second degree as defined in subdivision five of section 125.25 of this chapter or for the crime of aggravated murder as defined in subdivision one of section 125.26 of this chapter. A defendant may be sentenced to life imprisonment without parole upon conviction for the crime of aggravated murder as defined in subdivision two of section 125.26 of this chapter.

6. [Repealed eff Sept 1, 2015] Determinate sentence. Except as provided in subdivision four of this section and subdivisions two and four of section 70.02, when a person is sentenced as a violent felony offender pursuant to section 70.02 or as a second violent felony offender pursuant to section 70.04 or as a second felony offender on a conviction for a violent felony offense pursuant to section 70.06, the court must impose a determinate sentence of imprisonment in accordance with the provisions of such sections and such sentence shall include, as a part thereof, a period of post-release supervision in accordance with section 70.45.

HISTORY: Add, L 1965, ch 1030, eff Sept 1, 1967. Section heading, amd, L 1973, ch 277, § 7, eff Sept 1, 1973. Sub 1, amd, L 1973, ch 277, § 7, with substance derived from § 2189, L 1995, ch 1, § 3, L 1995, ch 3, § 1-c, eff Oct 1, 1995, repealed eff Sept 1, 2015. Sub 1 [first setout], amd, L 2004, ch 738, § 28, eff Dec 14, 2004, expires and repealed, eff Sept 1, 2015, L 2007, ch 7, § 36, eff April 13, 2007. Sub 1 [second setout], amd, L 2004, ch 738, § 29, effective as stated in 2004 note below, L 2007, ch 7, § 37, effective as stated in 2007 note below. Sub 2, amd, L 1973, ch 276, § 9, eff Sept 1, 1973. Sub 2, amd, L 2004, ch 738, § 28, eff Dec 14, 2004. Sub 2, par (b), amd, L 1986, ch 280, § 1, eff Nov 1, 1986. Sub 2, par (b), amd, L 2004, ch 738, § 28, eff Dec 14, 2004. Sub 3, amd, L 1973, ch 276, § 9, eff Sept 1, 1973. Sub 3, amd, L 2004, ch 738, § 28, eff Dec 14, 2004. Sub 3, par (a), subpar (i), amd, L 1995, ch 1, § 4, eff Sept 1, 1995. Sub 3, par (a), amd, L 2006, ch 107, § 3, eff June 23, 2006. Sub 3, par (a), subpar (i), amd, L 2004, ch 459, § 3, eff Nov 1, 2004, L 2005, ch 765, § 2, eff Dec 21, 2005. Sub 3, par a, subpar (ii), amd, L 1979, ch 410, § 6, eff Sept 1, 1979. Sub 3, par (a), subpar (ii), amd, L 2006, ch 107, § 3, eff June 23, 2006. Sub 3, par a, subpar (iii), repealed, L 1979, ch 410, § 6, eff Sept 1, 1979. Sub 3, par (b), amd, L 1978, ch 481, § 2, L 1980, ch 873, § 1, L 1986, ch 280, § 2, L 1995, ch 3, § 2, eff Oct 1, 1995, repealed eff Sept 1, 2009. Sub 3, par (b), amd, L 1998, ch 1, § 2, eff Aug 6, 1998, L 2004, ch 738, § 28, eff Dec 14, 2004, L 2006, ch 746, § 3, eff Dec 15, 2006. Sub 3, par (c), repealed, L 1980, ch 873, § 2, eff Sept 1, 1980. Sub 4, formerly § 70.05, add, L 1965, ch 1030, with substance derived from §§ 2186, 2187; renumbered sub 4 and amd, L 1973, ch 277, § 8; amd, L 1976, ch 480, § 5, L 1983, ch 238, § 1, eff June 6, 1983. Sub 4, amd, L 1998, ch 1, § 3, eff Aug 6, 1998, L 2004, ch 738, § 28, eff Dec 14, 2004. Sub 5, add, L 1995, ch 1, § 5, eff Sept 1, 1995. Sub 5, amd, L 2004, ch 1, § 5 (Part A), eff July 23, 2004, L 2004, ch 459, § 3, eff Nov 1, 2004, L 2005, ch 765, § 3, eff Dec 21, 2005, L 2009, ch 482, § 2, eff Oct 9, 2009. Sub 6, add, L 1995, ch 3, § 3, eff Oct 1, 1995, repealed eff Sept 1, 2015; amd, L 1998, ch 1, § 4, eff Aug 6, 1998.

Editor's Notes:

Laws 2004, ch 738, § 41 (d-1) and (g), eff Dec 14, 2004, provides as follows:

§ 41. This act shall take effect immediately, provided that:

(d-1) the provisions of sections, twelve, fourteen, fifteen, eighteen, twenty, twenty-four, twenty-five, twenty-nine, thirty-three, thirty-five and thirty-six of this act shall take effect on the thirtieth day after it shall have become a law, and such provisions, with the exception of subdivision 6 of section 60.04 of the penal law as added by section twenty of this act, shall apply to crimes committed on or after the effective date thereof;

(g) the amendments to subdivision 1 of section 70.00 of the penal law made by section twenty-eight of this act shall be subject to the expiration and reversion of such subdivision pursuant to subdivision d of section 74 of chapter 3 of the laws of 1995, as amended, when upon such date the provisions of section twenty-nine of this act shall take effect;

Laws 2007, ch 7, §§ 1 and 52 (a), (b), eff April 13, 2007, provide as follows:

Section 1. Short title. This act shall be known and may be cited as the "sex offender management and treatment act."

§ 52. This act shall take effect on the thirtieth day after it shall have become a law; provided, however, that:

(a) the provisions of sections thirteen, twenty-nine, thirty, thirty-one, thirty-two, thirty-three, thirty-four, thirty-five, thirty-six, thirty-seven, thirty-eight, thirty-nine, thirty-nine-a, forty, forty-one, forty-two, forty-three, forty-four, forty-five, forty-six, forty-seven, forty-eight, forty-nine and fifty of this act shall only apply to crimes committed after the effective date of this act;

(b) the amendments to subdivision 1 of section 70.00 of the penal law made by section thirty-six of this act shall be subject to the expiration and reversion of such subdivision pursuant to subdivision d of section 74 of chapter 3 of the laws of 1995, as amended, when upon such date the provisions of section thirty-seven of this act shall take effect; . . . .

§ 70.02. Sentence of imprisonment for a violent felony offense

1. Definition of a violent felony offense. A violent felony offense is a class B violent felony offense, a class C violent felony offense, a class D violent felony offense, or a class E violent felony offense, defined as follows:

(a) Class B violent felony offenses: an attempt to commit the class A-I felonies of murder in the second degree as defined in section 125.25, kidnapping in the first degree as defined in section 135.25, and arson in the first degree as defined in section 150.20; manslaughter in the first degree as defined in section 125.20, aggravated manslaughter in the first degree as defined in section 125.22, rape in the first degree as defined in section 130.35, criminal sexual act in the first degree as defined in section 130.50, aggravated sexual abuse in the first degree as defined in section 130.70, course of sexual conduct against a child in the first degree as defined in section 130.75; assault in the first degree as defined in section 120.10, kidnapping in the second degree as defined in section 135.20, burglary in the first degree as defined in section 140.30, arson in the second degree as defined in section 150.15, robbery in the first degree as defined in section 160.15, incest in the first degree as defined in section 255.27, criminal possession of a weapon in the first degree as defined in section 265.04, criminal use of a firearm in the first degree as defined in section 265.09, criminal sale of a firearm in the first degree as defined in section 265.13, aggravated assault upon a police officer or a peace officer as defined in section 120.11, gang assault in the first degree as defined in section 120.07, intimidating a victim or witness in the first degree as defined in section 215.17, hindering prosecution of terrorism in the first degree as defined in section 490.35, criminal possession of a chemical weapon or biological weapon in the second degree as defined in section 490.40, and criminal use of a chemical weapon or biological weapon in the third degree as defined in section 490.47.

(b) Class C violent felony offenses: an attempt to commit any of the class B felonies set forth in paragraph (a) of this subdivision; aggravated criminally negligent homicide as defined in section 125.11, aggravated manslaughter in the second degree as defined in section 125.21, aggravated sexual abuse in the second degree as defined in section 130.67, assault on a peace officer, police officer, fireman or emergency medical services professional as defined in section

120.08, assault on a judge as defined in section 120.09, gang assault in the second degree as defined in section 120.06, strangulation in the first degree as defined in section 121.13, burglary in the second degree as defined in section 140.25, robbery in the second degree as defined in section 160.10, criminal possession of a weapon in the second degree as defined in section 265.03, criminal use of a firearm in the second degree as defined in section 265.08, criminal sale of a firearm in the second degree as defined in section 265.12, criminal sale of a firearm with the aid of a minor as defined in section 265.14, aggravated criminal possession of a weapon as defined in section 265.19, soliciting or providing support for an act of terrorism in the first degree as defined in section 490.15, hindering prosecution of terrorism in the second degree as defined in section 490.30, and criminal possession of a chemical weapon or biological weapon in the third degree as defined in section 490.37.

(c) Class D violent felony offenses: an attempt to commit any of the class C felonies set forth in paragraph (b); reckless assault of a child as defined in section 120.02, assault in the second degree as defined in section 120.05, menacing a police officer or peace officer as defined in section 120.18, stalking in the first degree, as defined in subdivision one of section 120.60, strangulation in the second degree as defined in section 121.12, rape in the second degree as defined in section 130.30, criminal sexual act in the second degree as defined in section 130.45, sexual abuse in the first degree as defined in section 130.65, course of sexual conduct against a child in the second degree as defined in section 130.80, aggravated sexual abuse in the third degree as defined in section 130.66, facilitating a sex offense with a controlled substance as defined in section 130.90, criminal possession of a weapon in the third degree as defined in subdivision five, six, seven, eight, nine or ten of section 265.02, criminal sale of a firearm in the third degree as defined in section 265.11, intimidating a victim or witness in the second degree as defined in section 215.16, soliciting or providing support for an act of terrorism in the second degree as defined in section 490.10, and making a terroristic threat as defined in section 490.20, falsely reporting an incident in the first degree as defined in section 240.60, placing a false bomb or hazardous substance in the first degree as defined in section 240.62, placing a false bomb or hazardous substance in a sports stadium or arena, mass transportation facility or enclosed shopping mall as defined in section 240.63, and aggravated unpermitted use of indoor pyrotechnics in the first degree as defined in section 405.18.

(d) Class E violent felony offenses: an attempt to commit any of the felonies of criminal possession of a weapon in the third degree as defined in subdivision five, six, seven or eight of section 265.02 as a lesser included offense of that section as defined in section 220.20 of the criminal procedure law, persistent sexual abuse as defined in section 130.53, aggravated sexual abuse in the fourth degree as defined in section 130.65-a, falsely reporting an incident in the second degree as defined in section 240.55 and placing a false bomb or hazardous substance in the second degree as defined in section 240.61.

2. Authorized sentence.

(a) [Until Sept 1, 2015] Except as provided in subdivision six of section 60.05, the sentence imposed upon a person who stands convicted of a class B or class C violent felony offense must be a determinate sentence of imprisonment which shall be in whole or half years. The term of such sentence must be in accordance with the provisions of subdivision three of this section.

(a) [Eff Sept 1, 2015] The sentence imposed upon a person who stands convicted of a class B or class C violent felony offense must be an indeterminate sentence of imprisonment. Except as provided in subdivision five of section 60.05, the maximum term of such sentence must be in accordance with the provisions of subdivision three of this section and the minimum period of imprisonment under such sentence must be in accordance with subdivision four of this section.

(b) Except as provided in paragraph (b-1) of this subdivision, subdivision six of section 60.05 and subdivision four of this section, the sentence imposed upon a person who stands convicted of a class D violent felony offense, other than the offense of criminal possession of a weapon in the third degree as defined in subdivision five, seven or eight of section 265.02 or criminal sale of a firearm in the third degree as defined in section 265.11, must be in accordance with the applicable provisions of this chapter relating to sentencing for class D felonies provided, however, that where a sentence of imprisonment is imposed which requires a commitment to the state department of corrections and community supervision, such sentence shall be a determinate sentence in accordance with paragraph (c) of subdivision three of this section.

(b-1) Except as provided in subdivision six of section 60.05, the sentence imposed upon a person who stands convicted of the class D violent felony offense of menacing a police officer or peace officer as defined in section 120.18 of this chapter must be a determinate sentence of imprisonment.

(c) Except as provided in subdivision six of section 60.05, the sentence imposed upon a person who stands convicted of the class D violent felony offenses of criminal possession of a weapon in the third degree as defined in subdivision five, seven, eight or nine of section 265.02, criminal sale of a firearm in the third degree as defined in section 265.11 or the class E violent felonies of attempted criminal possession of a weapon in the third degree as defined in subdivision five, seven, eight or nine of section 265.02 must be a sentence to a determinate period of imprisonment, or, in the alternative, a definite sentence of imprisonment for a period of no less than one year, except that:

    (i) the court may impose any other sentence authorized by law upon a person who has not been previously convicted in the five years immediately preceding the commission of the offense for a class A misdemeanor defined in this chapter, if the court having regard to the nature and circumstances of the crime and to the history and character of the defendant, finds on the record that such sentence would be unduly harsh and that the alternative sentence would be consistent with public safety and does not deprecate the seriousness of the crime; and

    (ii) the court may apply the provisions of paragraphs (b) and (c) of subdivision four of this section when imposing a sentence upon a person who has previously been convicted of a class A misdemeanor defined in this chapter in the five years immediately preceding the commission of the offense.

3. Term of sentence. The term of a determinate sentence for a violent felony offense must be fixed by the court as follows:

(a) For a class B felony, the term must be at least five years and must not exceed twenty-five years, provided, however, that the term must be: (i) at least ten years and must not exceed thirty years where the sentence is for the crime of aggravated assault upon a police officer or peace officer as defined in section 120.11 of this chapter; and (ii) at least ten years and must not exceed thirty years where the sentence is for the crime of aggravated manslaughter in the first degree as defined in section 125.22 of this chapter;

(b) For a class C felony, the term must be at least three and one-half years and must not exceed fifteen years, provided, however, that the term must be: (i) at least seven years and must not exceed twenty years where the sentence is for the crime of aggravated manslaughter in the second degree as defined in section 125.21 of this chapter; (ii) at least seven years and must not exceed twenty years where the sentence is for the crime of attempted aggravated assault upon a police officer or peace officer as defined in section 120.11 of this chapter; (iii) at least three and one-half years and must not exceed twenty years where the sentence is for the crime of aggravated criminally negligent homicide as defined in section 125.11 of this chapter; and (iv) at least five years and must not exceed fifteen years where the sentence is imposed for the crime of aggravated criminal possession of a weapon as defined in section 265.19 of this chapter;

(c) For a class D felony, the term must be at least two years and must not exceed seven years, provided, however, that the term must be: (i) at least two years and must not exceed eight years where the sentence is for the crime of menacing a police officer or peace officer as defined in section 120.18 of this chapter; and (ii) at least three and one-half years and must not exceed seven years where the sentence is imposed for the crime of criminal possession of a weapon in the third degree as defined in subdivision ten of section 265.02 of this chapter;

(d) For a class E felony, the term must be at least one and one-half years and must not exceed four years.

4. (a) Except as provided in paragraph (b) of this subdivision, where a plea of guilty to a class D violent felony offense is entered pursuant to section 220.10 or 220.30 of the criminal procedure law in satisfaction of an indictment charging the defendant with an armed felony, as defined in subdivision forty-one of section 1.20 of the criminal procedure law, the court must impose a determinate sentence of imprisonment.

(b) In any case in which the provisions of paragraph (a) of this subdivision or the provisions of subparagraph (ii) of paragraph (c) of subdivision two of this section apply, the court may impose a sentence other than a determinate sentence of imprisonment, or a definite sentence of imprisonment for a period of no less than one year, if it finds that the alternate sentence is consistent with public safety and does not deprecate the seriousness of the crime and that one or more of the following factors exist:

(i) mitigating circumstances that bear directly upon the manner in which the crime was committed; or

(ii) where the defendant was not the sole participant in the crime, the defendant's participation was relatively minor although not so minor as to constitute a defense to the prosecution; or

(iii) possible deficiencies in proof of the defendant's commission of an armed felony.

(c) The defendant and the district attorney shall have an opportunity to present relevant information to assist the court in making a determination pursuant to paragraph (b) of this subdivision, and the court may, in its discretion, conduct a hearing with respect to any issue bearing upon such determination. If the court determines that a determinate sentence of imprisonment should not be imposed pursuant to the provisions of such paragraph (b), it shall make a statement on the record of the facts and circumstances upon which such determination is based. A transcript of the court's statement, which shall set forth the recommendation of the district attorney, shall be forwarded to the state division of criminal justice services along with a copy of the accusatory instrument.

HISTORY: Add, L 1978, ch 481, § 3, eff Sept 1, 1978; amd, L 1980, ch 233, § 2, eff Aug 12, 1980, L 1980, ch 234, §§ 1, 2, L 1980, ch 583, § 1, L 1981, ch 175, § 1, L 1986, ch 124, § 1, L 1988, ch 450, § 3, L 1991, ch 496, § 4, L 1991, ch 521, § 1, L 1993, ch 291, §§ 1, 2, eff Nov 1, 1993, L 1995, ch 3, § 4, eff Oct 1, 1995, repealed eff Sept 1, 2015, L 1996, ch 122, § 2, L 1996, ch 181, § 1, eff Nov 1, 1996, L 1996, ch 632, § 1, L 1996, ch 646, § 1, L 1996, ch 647, § 1, eff Nov 1, 1996, L 1998, ch 1, §§ 5–9, eff Aug 6, 1998, L 1998, ch 378, § 2, eff Nov 1, 1998, L 1999, ch 33, §§ 1–4, eff Nov 1, 1999, L 1999, ch 635, § 10, eff Dec 1, 1999, L 2000, ch 189, §§ 6, 7, eff Nov 1, 2000, L 2001, ch 300, § 2, eff Sept 17, 2001, L 2001, ch 301, § 8, eff Sept 17, 2001, L 2003, ch 264, § 6, eff Nov 1, 2003, L 2003, ch 584, § 3, eff Nov 1, 2003, L 2004, ch 1, § 6 (Part A), eff July 23, 2004, L 2005, ch 764, §§ 1, 4, eff Dec, 21, 2005, L 2005, ch 765, §§ 4–6, eff Dec 21, 2005, L 2006, ch 110, § 2, eff Nov 1, 2006, L 2006, ch 320, § 5, eff Nov 1, 2006, L 2007, ch 7, § 32, eff April 13, 2007, L 2010, ch 405, § 1, eff Nov 11, 2010, L 2011, ch 62, § 122 (Part C, Subpart B), eff March 31, 2011, L 2011, ch 148, § 2, eff Nov 17, 2011, L 2013, ch 1, §§ 27–30, eff March 16, 2013.

§ 70.04. Sentence of imprisonment for second violent felony offender

1. Definiton of second violent felony offender.

(a) A second violent felony offender is a person who stands convicted of a violent felony offense as defined in subdivision one of section 70.02 after having previously been subjected to a predicate violent felony conviction as defined in paragraph (b) of this subdivision.

(b) For the purpose of determining whether a prior conviction is a predicate violent felony conviction the following criteria shall apply:

(i) The conviction must have been in this state of a class A felony (other than one defined in article two hundred twenty) or of a violent felony offense as defined in subdivision one of section 70.02, or of an offense defined by the penal law in effect prior to September first, nineteen hundred sixty-seven, which includes all of the essential elements of any such felony, or in any other jurisdiction of an offense which includes all of the essential elements of any such felony for which a sentence to a term of imprisonment in excess of one year or a sentence of death was authorized and is authorized in this state irrespective of whether such sentence was imposed;

(ii) Sentence upon such prior conviction must have been imposed before commission of the present felony;

(iii) Suspended sentence, suspended execution of sentence, a sentence of probation, a sentence of conditional discharge or of unconditional discharge, and a sentence of certification to the care and custody of the division of substance abuse services, shall be deemed to be a sentence;

(iv) Except as provided in subparagraph (v) of this paragraph, sentence must have been imposed not more than ten years before commission of the felony of which the defendant presently stands convicted;

(v) In calculating the ten year period under subparagraph (iv), any period of time during which the person was incarcerated for any reason between the time of commission of the previous felony and the time of commission of the present felony shall be excluded and such ten year period shall be extended by a period or periods equal to the time served under such incarceration;

(vi) An offense for which the defendant has been pardoned on the ground of innocence shall not be deemed a predicate violent felony conviction.

2. [Until Sept 1, 2015] Authorized sentence. When the court has found, pursuant to the provisions of the criminal procedure law, that a person is a second violent felony offender the court must impose a determinate sentence of imprisonment which shall be in whole or half years. Except where sentence is imposed in accordance with the provisions of section 70.10, the term of such sentence must be in accordance with the provisions of subdivision three of this section.

2. [Eff Sept 1, 2015] Authorized sentence. When the court has found, pursuant to the provisions of the criminal procedure law, that a person is a second violent felony offender the court must impose an indeterminate sentence of imprisonment. Except where sentence is imposed in accordance with the provisions of section 70.10, the maximum term of such sentence must be in accordance with the provisions of subdivision three of this section and the minimum period of imprisonment under such section must be in accordance with subdivision four of this section.

3. [Until Sept 1, 2015] Term of sentence. The term of a determinate sentence for a second violent felony offender must be fixed by the court as follows:

(a) For a class B felony, the term must be at least ten years and must not exceed twenty-five years;

(b) For a class C felony, the term must be at least seven years and must not exceed fifteen years; and

(c) For a class D felony, the term must be at least five years and must not exceed seven years.

(d) For a class E felony, the term must be at least three years and must not exceed four years.

3. [Eff Sept 1, 2015] Maximum term of sentence. The maximum term of an indeterminate sentence for a second violent felony offender must be fixed by the court as follows:

(a) For a class B felony, the term must be at least twelve years and must not exceed twenty-five years;

(b) For a class C felony, the term must be at least eight years and must not exceed fifteen years; and

(c) For a class D felony, the term must be at least five years and must not exceed seven years.

(d) For a class E felony, the term must be at least four years.

4. [Eff Sept 1, 2015] Minimum period of imprisonment. The minimum period of imprisonment under an indeterminate sentence for a second violent felony offender must be fixed by the court at one-half of the maximum term imposed and must be specified in the sentence.

HISTORY: Add, L 1978, ch 481, § 4, eff Sept 1, 1978. Sub 1, par (b), subpar (iii), amd, L 1980, ch 471, § 23, eff July 23, 1980. Sub 2, amd, L 1995, ch 3, § 5, eff Oct 1, 1995, repealed eff Sept 1, 2015. Sub 3, amd, L 1995, ch 3, § 5, eff Oct 1, 1995, repealed eff Sept 1, 2015. Sub 3, opening par, amd, L 1995, ch 3, § 5, eff Oct 1, 1995, repealed eff Sept 1, 2015. Sub 3, par (a), amd, L 1995, ch 3, § 5, eff Oct 1, 1995, repealed eff Sept 1, 2015. Sub 3, par (b), amd, L 1995, ch 3, § 5, eff Oct 1, 1995, repealed eff Sept 1, 2015. Sub 3, par (d), add, L 1980, ch 233, § 3; amd, L 1995, ch 3, § 5, eff Oct 1, 1995, repealed eff Sept 1, 2009. Sub 4, deleted, L 1995, ch 3, § 5, eff Oct 1, 1995.

§ 70.05. Sentence of imprisonment for juvenile offender

1. Indeterminate sentence. A sentence of imprisonment for a felony committed by a juvenile offender shall be an indeterminate sentence. When such a sentence is imposed, the court shall impose a maximum term in accordance with the provisions of subdivision two of this section and the minimum period of imprisonment shall be as provided in subdivision three of this section. The court shall further provide that where a juvenile offender is under placement pursuant to article three of the family court act, any sentence imposed pursuant to this section which is to be served consecutively with such placement shall be served in a facility designated pursuant to subdivision four of section 70.20 of this article prior to service of the placement in any previously designated facility.

2. Maximum term of sentence. The maximum term of an indeterminate sentence for a juvenile

offender shall be at least three years and the term shall be fixed as follows:

(a) For the class A felony of murder in the second degree, the term shall be life imprisonment;

(b) For the class A felony of arson in the first degree, or for the class A felony of kidnapping in the first degree the term shall be fixed by the court, and shall be at least twelve years but shall not exceed fifteen years;

(c) For a class B felony, the term shall be fixed by the court, and shall not exceed ten years;

(d) For a class C felony, the term shall be fixed by the court, and shall not exceed seven years; and

(e) For a class D felony, the term shall be fixed by the court and shall not exceed four years.

3. Minimum period of imprisonment. The minimum period of imprisonment under an indeterminate sentence for a juvenile offender shall be specified in the sentence as follows:

(a) For the class A felony of murder in the second degree, the minimum period of imprisonment shall be fixed by the court and shall be not less than five years but shall not exceed nine years provided, however, that where the sentence is for an offense specified in subdivision one or two of section 125.25 of this chapter and the defendant was fourteen or fifteen years old at the time of such offense, the minimum period of imprisonment shall be not less than seven and one-half years but shall not exceed fifteen years;

(b) For the class A felony of arson in the first degree, or for the class A felony of kidnapping in the first degree, the minimum period of imprisonment shall be fixed by the court and shall be not less than four years but shall not exceed six years; and

(c) For a class B, C or D felony, the minimum period of imprisonment shall be fixed by the court at one-third of the maximum term imposed.

HISTORY: Add, L 1978, ch 481, § 31, eff Sept 1, 1978. Former § 70.05, add, L 1965, ch 1030, with substance derived from §§ 2186, 2187; renumbered § 70.00, sub 4, L 1973, ch 277, § 8, eff Sept 1, 1973. Sub 1, amd, L 1984, ch 615, § 1, eff Nov 1, 1984. Sub 4, repealed, L 1981, ch 303, § 1, eff July 22, 1981, with substance transferred to § 70.20, sub 4. Sub 2, par (e), add, L 1998, ch 435, § 5, eff Nov 1, 1998. Sub 3, par (a), amd, L 2003, ch 174, § 1, eff Nov 1, 2003. Sub 3, par (c), amd, L 1998, ch 435, § 6, eff Nov 1, 1998.

§ 70.06. Sentence of imprisonment for second felony offender

1. Definition of second felony offender.

(a) A second felony offender is a person, other than a second violent felony offender as defined in section 70.04, who stands convicted of a felony defined in this chapter, other than a class A-I felony, after having previously been subjected to one or more predicate felony convictions as defined in paragraph (b) of this subdivision.

(b) For the purpose of determining whether a prior conviction is a predicate felony conviction the following criteria shall apply:

(i) The conviction must have been in this state of a felony, or in any other jurisdiction of an offense for which a sentence to a term of imprisonment in excess of one year or a sentence of death was authorized and is authorized in this state irrespective of whether such sentence was imposed;

(ii) Sentence upon such prior conviction must have been imposed before commission of the present felony;

(iii) Suspended sentence, suspended execution of sentence, a sentence of probation, a sentence of conditional discharge or of unconditional discharge, and a sentence of certification to the care and custody of the division of substance abuse services, shall be deemed to be a sentence;

(iv) Except as provided in subparagraph (v) of this paragraph, sentence must have been imposed not more than ten years before commission of the felony of which the defendant presently stands convicted;

(v) In calculating the ten year period under subparagraph (iv), any period of time during which the person was incarcerated for any reason between the time of commission of the previous felony and the time of commission of the present felony shall be excluded and such ten year period shall be extended by a period or periods equal to the time served under such incarceration;

(vi) An offense for which the defendant has been pardoned on the ground of innocence shall not be deemed a predicate felony conviction.

2. [Until Sept 1, 2015, as amended L 2007, ch 7, § 38] Authorized sentence. Except as provided in subdivision five or six of this section, or as provided in subdivision five of section 70.80 of this article, when the court has found, pursuant to the provisions of the criminal procedure law, that a person is a second felony offender the court must impose an indeterminate sentence of imprisonment. The maximum term of such sentence must be in accordance with the provisions of subdivision three of this section and the minimum period of imprisonment under such sentence must be in accordance with subdivision four of this section.

2. [Eff Sept 1, 2015, as amended L 2007, ch 7, § 39] Authorized sentence. Except as provided in subdivision five of this section, or as provided in subdivision five of section 70.80 of this article, when the court has found, pursuant to the provisions of the criminal procedure law, that a person is a second felony offender the court must impose an indeterminate sentence of imprisonment. The maximum term of such sentence must be in accordance with the provisions of subdivision three of this section and the minimum period of imprisonment under such sentence must be in accordance with subdivision four of this section.

3. [Until Sept 1, 2015, as amended L 2007, ch 7, § 38] Maximum term of sentence. Except as provided in subdivision five or six of this section, or as provided in subdivision five of section 70.80 of this article, the maximum term of an indeterminate sentence for a second felony offender must be fixed by the court as follows:

(a) For a class A-II felony, the term must be life imprisonment;

(b) For a class B felony, the term must be at least nine years and must not exceed twenty-five years;

(c) For a class C felony, the term must be at least six years and must not exceed fifteen years;

(d) For a class D felony, the term must be at least four years and must not exceed seven years; and

(e) For a class E felony, the term must be at least three years and must not exceed four years; provided, however, that where the sentence is for the class E felony offense specified in section 240.32 of this chapter, the maximum term must be at least three years and must not exceed five years.

3. [Eff Sept 1, 2015, as amended L 2007, ch 7, § 39] Maximum term of sentence. Except as

provided in subdivision five of this section, or as provided in subdivision five of section 70.80 of this article, the maximum term of an indeterminate sentence for a second felony offender must be fixed by the court as follows:

(a) For a class A-II felony, the term must be life imprisonment;

(b) For a class B felony, the term must be at least nine years and must not exceed twenty-five years;

(c) For a class C felony, the term must be at least six years and must not exceed fifteen years;

(d) For a class D felony, the term must be at least four years and must not exceed seven years; and

(e) For a class E felony, the term must be at least three years and must not exceed four years.

4. Minimum period of imprisonment

(a) The minimum period of imprisonment for a second felony offender convicted of a class A-II felony must be fixed by the court at no less than six years and not to exceed twelve and one-half years and must be specified in the sentence, except that for the class A-II felony of predatory sexual assault as defined in section 130.95 of this chapter or the class A-II felony of predatory sexual assault against a child as defined in section 130.96 of this chapter, such minimum period shall be not less than ten years nor more than twenty-five years.

(b) Except as provided in paragraph (a), the minimum period of imprisonment under an indeterminate sentence for a second felony offender must be fixed by the court at one-half of the maximum term imposed and must be specified in the sentence.

5. [Repealed]

6. [Repealed Sept 1, 2015] Determinate sentence. When the court has found, pursuant to the provisions of the criminal procedure law, that a person is a second felony offender and the sentence to be imposed on such person is for a violent felony offense, as defined in subdivision one of section 70.02, the court must impose a determinate sentence of imprisonment the term of which must be fixed by the court as follows:

(a) For a class B violent felony offense, the term must be at least eight years and must not exceed twenty-five years;

(b) For a class C violent felony offense, the term must be at least five years and must not exceed fifteen years;

(c) For a class D violent felony offense, the term must be at least three years and must not exceed seven years; and

(d) For a class E violent felony offense, the term must be at least two years and must not exceed four years.

7. [Repealed Sept 1, 2015] Notwithstanding any other provision of law, in the case of a person sentenced for a specified offense or offenses as defined in subdivision five of section 410.91 of the criminal procedure law, who stands convicted of no other felony offense, who has not previously been convicted of either a violent felony offense as defined in section 70.02 of this article, a class A felony offense or a class B felony offense, and is not under the jurisdiction of or awaiting delivery to the department of corrections and community supervision, the court may direct that such sentence be executed as a parole supervision sentence as defined in and pursuant to the

procedures prescribed in section 410.91 of the criminal procedure law.

HISTORY: Add, L 1973, ch 277, § 9, eff Sept 1, 1973; amd, L 1973, ch 278, § 8, L 1973, ch 1051, § 3, L 1975, ch 667, § 36, L 1975, ch 784, § 1, eff Aug 9, 1975, L 1978, ch 481, § 5, L 1979, ch 410, §§ 7–9, eff Sept 1, 1979, L 1980, ch 471, § 24, eff July 23, 1980, L 1996, ch 92, § 1, eff June 5, 1996, repealed Sept 30, 2005, L 1995, ch 3, §§ 6, 7, eff Oct 1, 1995, repealed Sept 1, 2015, L 2004, ch 738, § 31, eff Dec 27, 2004, L 2004, ch 738, § 32, eff Dec 14, 2004, L 2006, ch 107, § 4, eff June 23, 2006, L 2007, ch 7, § 38, eff April 13, 2007, L 2007, ch 7, § 39, eff Sept 11, 2015, L 2011, ch 62, § 123 (Part C, Subpart B), eff March 31, 2011.

Editor's Note:

Laws 2007, ch 7, §§ 1 and 52 (a), (c), eff April 13, 2007, provide as follows:

Section 1. Short title. This act shall be known and may be cited as the "sex offender management and treatment act."

§ 52. This act shall take effect on the thirtieth day after it shall have become a law; provided, however, that:

(a) the provisions of sections thirteen, twenty-nine, thirty, thirty-one, thirty-two, thirty-three, thirty-four, thirty-five, thirty-six, thirty-seven, thirty-eight, thirty-nine, thirty-nine-a, forty, forty-one, forty-two, forty-three, forty-four, forty-five, forty-six, forty-seven, forty-eight, forty-nine and fifty of this act shall only apply to crimes committed after the effective date of this act;

(c) the amendments to subdivisions 2 and 3 of section 70.06 of the penal law made by section thirty-eight of this act shall be subject to the expiration and reversion of such subdivisions pursuant to subdivision d of section 74 of chapter 3 of the laws of 1995, as amended, when upon such date the provisions of section thirty-nine of this act shall take effect; . . . .

§ 70.07. Sentence of imprisonment for second child sexual assault felony offender

1. A person who stands convicted of a felony offense for a sexual assault against a child, having been subjected to a predicate felony conviction for a sexual assault against a child, must be sentenced in accordance with the provisions of subdivision four or five of this section.

2. A "sexual assault against a child" means a felony offense, other than persistent sexual abuse as defined in section 130.53 of this chapter, (a) the essential elements of which include the commission or attempted commission of sexual conduct, as defined in subdivision ten of section 130.00 of this chapter, (b) committed or attempted to be committed against a child less than fifteen years old.

3. For purposes of determining whether a person has been subjected to a predicate felony conviction under this section, the criteria set forth in paragraph (b) of subdivision one of section 70.06 shall apply provided however that for purposes of this subdivision, the terms "ten year" or "ten years", as provided in subparagraphs (iv) and (v) of paragraph (b) of subdivision one of such section 70.06, shall be "fifteen year" or "fifteen years". The provisions of section 400.19 of the criminal procedure law shall govern the procedures that must be followed to determine whether a person who stands convicted of a sexual assault against a child has been previously subjected to a predicate felony conviction for such a sexual assault and whether such offender was eighteen years of age or older at the time of the commission of the predicate felony.

4. Where the court has found pursuant to subdivision three of this section that a person who stands convicted of a felony offense defined in article one hundred thirty of this chapter for the commission or attempted commission of a sexual assault against a child has been subjected to a predicate felony conviction for a sexual assault against a child, the court shall sentence the defendant as follows:

(a) where the defendant stands convicted of such sexual assault against a child and such conviction is for a class A-II or class B felony offense, and the predicate conviction for such sexual assault against a child is for a class A-II, class B or class C felony offense, the court shall impose an indeterminate sentence of imprisonment, the maximum term of which shall be life and the minimum period of which shall be at least fifteen years and no more than twenty-five years;

(b) where the defendant stands convicted of such sexual assault against a child and the conviction is for a class C felony offense, and the predicate conviction for such sexual assault against a child is for a class A-II, class B or class C felony offense, the court shall impose a determinate sentence of imprisonment, the term of which must be at least twelve years and must not exceed thirty years; provided however, that if the court determines that a longer sentence is warranted, the court shall set forth on the record the reasons for such determination and, in lieu of imposing such sentence of imprisonment, may impose an indeterminate sentence of imprisonment, the maximum term of which shall be life and the minimum period of which shall be at least fifteen years and no more than twenty-five years;

(c) where the defendant stands convicted of such sexual assault against a child and the conviction is for a class B felony offense, and the predicate conviction for such sexual assault against a child is for a class D or class E felony offense, the court shall impose a determinate sentence of imprisonment, the term of which must be at least twelve years and must not exceed thirty years;

(d) where the defendant stands convicted of such sexual assault against a child and the conviction is for a class C felony offense, and the predicate conviction for such sexual assault against a child is for a class D or class E felony offense, the court shall impose a determinate sentence of imprisonment, the term of which must be at least ten years and must not exceed twenty-five years;

(e) where the defendant stands convicted of such sexual assault against a child and the conviction is for a class D felony offense, and the predicate conviction for such sexual assault against a child is for a felony offense, the court shall impose a determinate sentence of imprisonment, the term of which must be at least five years and must not exceed fifteen years; and

(f) where the defendant stands convicted of such sexual assault against a child and the conviction is for a class E felony offense, and the predicate conviction for such sexual assault against a child is for a felony offense, the court shall impose a determinate sentence of imprisonment, the term of which must be at least four years and must not exceed twelve years.

5. Notwithstanding subdivision four of this section, where the court has found pursuant to subdivision three of this section that a person: (a) stands convicted of a felony offense defined in article one hundred thirty of this chapter for the commission or attempted commission of a sexual assault against a child; and (b) has been subjected to a predicate felony conviction for sexual assault against a child as defined in subdivision two of this section; and (c) who was under the age of eighteen years at the time of the commission of such predicate felony offense, then the court may, in lieu of the sentence authorized by subdivision four of this section, sentence the defendant to a term of imprisonment in accordance with the sentence authorized for the instant felony offense pursuant to subdivision three of section 70.04 of this article. The court shall set forth on the record the reasons for such determination.

HISTORY: Add, L 2000, ch 1, § 50, eff Feb 1, 2001. Sub 1, amd, L 2003, ch 264, § 7, eff Nov 1, 2003. Sub 2, amd, L 2003, ch 264, § 7, eff Nov 1, 2003. Sub 3, amd, L 2003, ch 264, § 7, eff Nov 1, 2003. Sub 4, par (a), amd, L 2006, ch 107, § 5, eff June 23, 2006. Sub 4, par (b), amd, L 2003, ch 264, § 8, eff Nov 1, 2003, L 2006, ch 107, § 5, eff June 23, 2006. Sub 5, add, L 2003, ch 264, § 9, eff Nov 1, 2003.

§ 70.08. Sentence of imprisonment for persistent violent felony offender; criteria

1. Definition of persistent violent felony offender.

(a) A persistent violent felony offender is a person who stands convicted of a violent felony offense as defined in subdivision one of section 70.02 or the offense of predatory sexual assault as defined in section 130.95 of this chapter or the offense of predatory sexual assault against a child as defined in section 130.96 of this chapter, after having previously been subjected to two or more predicate violent felony convictions as defined in paragraph (b) of subdivision one of section 70.04 of this article.

(b) For the purpose of determining whether a person has two or more predicate violent felony convictions, the criteria set forth in paragraph (b) of subdivision one of section 70.04 shall apply.

2. Authorized sentence. When the court has found, pursuant to the provisions of the criminal procedure law, that a person is a persistent violent felony offender the court must impose an indeterminate sentence of imprisonment, the maximum term of which shall be life imprisonment. The minimum period of imprisonment under such sentence must be in accordance with subdivision three of this section.

3. [Until Sept 1, 2015, as amended by L 2006, ch 107, § 7] Minimum period of imprisonment. The minimum period of imprisonment under an indeterminate life sentence for a persistent violent felony offender must be fixed by the court as follows:

(a) For the class A-II felony of predatory sexual assault as defined in section 130.95 of this chapter or the class A-II felony of predatory sexual assault against a child as defined in section 130.96 of this chapter, the minimum period must be twenty-five years;

(a-1) For a class B felony, the minimum period must be at least twenty years and must not exceed twenty-five years;

(b) For a class C felony, the minimum period must be at least sixteen years and must not exceed twenty-five years;

(c) For a class D felony, the minimum period must be at least twelve years and must not exceed twenty-five years.

3. [Eff Sept 1, 2015, as amended by L 2006, ch 107, § 8] Minimum period of imprisonment. The minimum period of imprisonment under an indeterminate life sentence for a persistent violent felony offender must be fixed by the court as follows:

(a) For the class A-II felony of predatory sexual assault as defined in section 130.95 of this chapter or the class A-II felony of predatory sexual assault against a child as defined in section 130.96 of this chapter, the minimum period must be twenty-five years;

(a-1) For a class B felony, the minimum period must be at least ten years and must not exceed twenty-five years;

(b) For a class C felony, the minimum period must be at least eight years and must not exceed twenty-five years;

(c) For a class D felony, the minimum period must be at least six years and must not exceed twenty-five years.

HISTORY: Add, L 1978, ch 481, § 6, eff Sept 1, 1978. Sub 1, par (a), amd, L 2006, ch 107, § 6, eff June 23, 2006. Sub 3 [first setout], amd, L 1995, ch 3, § 8, eff Oct 1, 1995, repealed eff Sept 1,

2015, L 2006, ch 107, § 7, eff June 23, 2006. Sub 3, par (a) [first setout], add, L 2006, ch 107, § 7, eff June 23, 2006. Former sub 3, par (a) [first setout], redesignated sub (a-1) [first setout], L 2006, ch 107, § 7, eff June 23, 2006. Sub 3, par (a-1)[first setout], formerly sub 3, par (a) [first setout], amd, L 1995, ch 3, § 8, eff Oct 1, 1995, repealed eff Sept 1, 2015; so designated sub 3, par (a-1) [first setout], L 2006, ch 107, § 7, eff June 23, 2006. Sub 3, par (b) [first setout], amd, L 1995, ch 3, § 8, eff Oct 1, 1995, repealed eff Sept 1, 2015. Sub 3, par (c) [first setout], amd, L 1995, ch 3, § 8, eff Oct 1, 1995, repealed eff Sept 1, 2015. Sub 3 [second setout], amd, L 2006, ch 107, § 8, eff Sept 1, 2015. Sub 3, par (a) [second setout], add, L 2006, ch 107, § 8, eff Sept 1, 2015. Former sub 3, par (a) [second setout], redesignated sub (a-1) [second setout], L 2006, ch 107, § 8, eff Sept 1, 2015. Sub 3, par (a-1)[second setout], formerly sub 3, par (a) [second setout], amd, L 1995, ch 3, § 8, eff Oct 1, 1995, repealed eff Sept 1, 2015; so designated sub 3, par (a-1) [second setout], L 2006, ch 107, § 8, eff Sept 1, 2015. Sub 3, par (b) [second setout], amd, L 1995, ch 3, § 8, eff Oct 1, 1995, repealed eff Sept 1, 2015. Sub 3, par (c) [second setout], amd, L 1995, ch 3, § 8, eff Oct 1, 1995, repealed eff Sept 1, 2015.

§ 70.10. Sentence of imprisonment for persistent felony offender

1. Definition of persistent felony offender.

(a) A persistent felony offender is a person, other than a persistent violent felony offender as defined in section 70.08, who stands convicted of a felony after having previously been convicted of two or more felonies, as provided in paragraphs (b) and (c) of this subdivision.

(b) A previous felony conviction within the meaning of paragraph (a) of this subdivision is a conviction of a felony in this state, or of a crime in any other jurisdiction, provided:

(i) that a sentence to a term of imprisonment in excess of one year, or a sentence to death, was imposed therefor; and

(ii) that the defendant was imprisoned under sentence for such conviction prior to the commission of the present felony; and

(iii) that the defendant was not pardoned on the ground of innocence; and

(iv) that such conviction was for a felony offense other than persistent sexual abuse, as defined in section 130.53 of this chapter.

(c) For the purpose of determining whether a person has two or more previous felony convictions, two or more convictions of crimes that were committed prior to the time the defendant was imprisoned under sentence for any of such convictions shall be deemed to be only one conviction.

2. Authorized sentence. When the court has found, pursuant to the provisions of the criminal procedure law, that a person is a persistent felony offender, and when it is of the opinion that the history and character of the defendant and the nature and circumstances of his criminal conduct indicate that extended incarceration and life-time supervision will best serve the public interest, the court, in lieu of imposing the sentence of imprisonment authorized by section 70.00, 70.02, 70.04, 70.06 or subdivision five of section 70.80 for the crime of which such person presently stands convicted, may impose the sentence of imprisonment authorized by that section for a class A-I felony. In such event the reasons for the court's opinion shall be set forth in the record.

HISTORY: Add, L 1965, ch 1030, eff Sept 1, 1967, with substance derived from §§ 1941, 1942. Sub 1, par (a), amd, L 1978, ch 481, § 7, eff Sept 1, 1978. Sub 1, par (b), subpar (iii), amd, L 2003, ch 264, § 69, eff Nov 1, 2003. Sub 1, par (b), subpar (iv), add, L 2003, ch 264, § 70, eff Nov 1, 2003. Sub 2, amd, L 1971, ch 1097, § 76, L 1973, ch 277, § 10, L 1973, ch 1051, § 4, L 1978, ch 481, § 7, eff Sept 1, 1978. Sub 2, amd, L 2007, ch 7, § 39-a, eff April 13, 2007.

§ 70.15. Sentences of imprisonment for misdemeanors and violation

1. Class A misdemeanor. A sentence of imprisonment for a class A misdemeanor shall be a definite sentence. When such a sentence is imposed the term shall be fixed by the court, and shall not exceed one year; provided, however, that a sentence of imprisonment imposed upon a conviction of criminal possession of a weapon in the fourth degree as defined in subdivision one of section 265.01 must be for a period of no less than one year when the conviction was the result of a plea of guilty entered in satisfaction of an indictment or any count thereof charging the defendant with the class D violent felony offense of criminal possession of a weapon in the third degree as defined in subdivision four of section 265.02, except that the court may impose any other sentence authorized by law upon a person who has not been previously convicted in the five years immediately preceding the commission of the offense for a felony or a class A misdemeanor defined in this chapter, if the court having regard to the nature and circumstances of the crime and to the history and character of the defendant, finds on the record that such sentence would be unduly harsh and that the alternative sentence would be consistent with public safety and does not deprecate the seriousness of the crime.

2. Class B misdemeanor. A sentence of imprisonment for a class B misdemeanor shall be a definite sentence. When such a sentence is imposed the term shall be fixed by the court, and shall not exceed three months.

3. Unclassified misdemeanor. A sentence of imprisonment for an unclassified misdemeanor shall be a definite sentence. When such a sentence is imposed the term shall be fixed by the court, and shall be in accordance with the sentence specified in the law or ordinance that defines the crime.

4. Violation. A sentence of imprisonment for a violation shall be a definite sentence. When such a sentence is imposed the term shall be fixed by the court, and shall not exceed fifteen days.

In the case of a violation defined outside this chapter, if the sentence is expressly specified in the law or ordinance that defines the offense and consists solely of a fine, no term of imprisonment shall be imposed.

HISTORY: Add, L 1965, ch 1030, eff Sept 1, 1967. Sub 1, amd, L 1980, ch 233, § 4, L 1981, ch 175, § 2, L 1984, ch 673, § 1, eff Nov 1, 1984, L 1993, ch 291, § 3, eff Nov 1, 1993.

§ 70.20. Place of imprisonment

1. [Until Sept 1, 2015]

(a) Indeterminate or determinate sentence. Except as provided in subdivision four of this section, when an indeterminate or determinate sentence of imprisonment is imposed, the court shall commit the defendant to the custody of the state department of corrections and community supervision for the term of his or her sentence and until released in accordance with the law; provided, however, that a defendant sentenced pursuant to subdivision seven of section 70.06 shall be committed to the custody of the state department of corrections and community supervision for immediate delivery to a reception center operated by the department.

(b) The court in committing a defendant who is not yet eighteen years of age to the department of corrections and community supervision shall inquire as to whether the parents or legal guardian of the defendant, if present, will grant to the minor the capacity to consent to routine medical, dental and mental health services and treatment.

(c) Notwithstanding paragraph (b) of this subdivision, where the court commits a defendant who is not yet eighteen years of age to the custody of the department of corrections and community supervision in accordance with this section and no medical consent has been obtained prior to said commitment, the commitment order shall be deemed to grant the capacity to consent to routine medical, dental and mental health services and treatment to the person so committed.

(d) Nothing in this subdivision shall preclude a parent or legal guardian of an inmate who is not yet eighteen years of age from making a motion on notice to the department of corrections and community supervision pursuant to article twenty-two of the civil practice law and rules and section one hundred forty of the correction law, objecting to routine medical, dental or mental health services and treatment being provided to such inmate under the provisions of paragraph (b) of this subdivision.

(e) Nothing in this section shall require that consent be obtained from the parent or legal guardian, where no consent is necessary or where the defendant is authorized by law to consent on his or her own behalf to any medical, dental, and mental health service or treatment.

1. [Eff Sept 1, 2015]

(a) Indeterminate sentence. Except as provided in subdivision four of this section, when an indeterminate sentence of imprisonment is imposed, the court shall commit the defendant to the custody of the state department of corrections and community supervision for the term of his or her sentence and until released in accordance with the law.

(b) The court in committing a defendant who is not yet eighteen years of age to the department of corrections and community supervision shall inquire as to whether the parents or legal guardian of the defendant, if present, will grant to the minor the capacity to consent to routine medical, dental and mental health services and treatment.

(c) Notwithstanding paragraph (b) of this subdivision, where the court commits a defendant who is not yet eighteen years of age to the custody of the department of corrections and community supervision in accordance with this section and no medical consent has been obtained prior to said commitment, the commitment order shall be deemed to grant the capacity to consent to routine medical, dental and mental health services and treatment to the person so committed.

(d) Nothing in this subdivision shall preclude a parent or legal guardian of an inmate who is not yet eighteen years of age from making a motion on notice to the department of corrections and community supervision pursuant to article twenty-two of the civil practice law and rules and section one hundred forty of the correction law, objecting to routine medical, dental or mental health services and treatment being provided to such inmate under the provisions of paragraph (b) of this subdivision.

(e) Nothing in this section shall require that consent be obtained from the parent or legal guardian, where no consent is necessary or where the defendant is authorized by law to consent on his or her own behalf to any medical, dental, and mental health service or treatment.

2.

(a) Definite sentence. Except as provided in subdivision four of this section, when a definite sentence of imprisonment is imposed, the court shall commit the defendant to the county or regional correctional institution for the term of his sentence and until released in accordance with the law.

(b) The court in committing a defendant who is not yet eighteen years of age to the local correctional facility shall inquire as to whether the parents or legal guardian of the defendant, if present, will grant to the minor the capacity to consent to routine medical, dental and mental health services and treatment.

(c) The court in committing a defendant who is not yet eighteen years of age to the local correctional facility shall inquire as to whether the parents or legal guardian of the defendant, if present, will grant to the minor the capacity to consent to routine medical, dental and mental health services and treatment.

2-a. Sentence of life imprisonment without parole. When a sentence of life imprisonment without parole is imposed, the court shall commit the defendant to the custody of the state department of corrections and community supervision for the remainder of the life of the defendant.

3. [Until Sept 1, 2015] Undischarged imprisonment in other jurisdiction. When a defendant who is subject to an undischarged term of imprisonment, imposed at a previous time by a court of another jurisdiction, is sentenced to an additional term or terms of imprisonment by a court of this state to run concurrently with such undischarged term, as provided in subdivision four of section 70.25, the return of the defendant to the custody of the appropriate official of the other jurisdiction shall be deemed a commitment for such portion of the term or terms of the sentence imposed by the court of this state as shall not exceed the said undischarged term. The defendant shall be committed to the custody of the state department of corrections and community supervision if the additional term or terms are indeterminate or determinate or to the appropriate county or regional correctional institution if the said term or terms are definite for such portion of the term or terms of the sentence imposed as shall exceed such undischarged term or until released in accordance with law. If such additional term or terms imposed shall run consecutively to the said undischarged term, the defendant shall be committed as provided in subdivisions one and two of this section.

3. [Eff Sept 1, 2015] Undischarged imprisonment in other jurisdiction. When a defendant who is subject to an undischarged term of imprisonment, imposed at a previous time by a court of another jurisdiction, is sentenced to an additional term or terms of imprisonment by a court of this state to run concurrently with such undischarged term, as provided in subdivision four of section 70.25, the return of the defendant to the custody of the appropriate official of the other jurisdiction shall be deemed a commitment for such portion of the term or terms of the sentence imposed by the court of this state as shall not exceed the said undischarged term. The defendant shall be committed to the custody of the state department of corrections and community supervision if the additional term or terms are indeterminate or to the appropriate county or regional correctional institution if the said term or terms are definite for such portion of the term or terms of the sentence imposed as shall exceed such undischarged term or until released in accordance with law. If such additional term or terms imposed shall run consecutively to the said undischarged term, the defendant shall be committed as provided in subdivisions one and two of this section.

4. (a) Notwithstanding any other provision of law to the contrary, a juvenile offender, or a juvenile offender who is adjudicated a youthful offender and given an indeterminate or a definite sentence, shall be committed to the custody of the commissioner of the office of children and family services who shall arrange for the confinement of such offender in secure facilities of the office. The release or transfer of such offenders from the office of children and family services shall be governed by section five hundred eight of the executive law.

(b) The court in committing a juvenile offender and youthful offender to the custody of the office of children and family services shall inquire as to whether the parents or legal guardian of the youth, if present, will consent for the office of children and family services to provide routine medical, dental and mental health services and treatment.

(c) Notwithstanding paragraph (b) of this subdivision, where the court commits an offender to the custody of the office of children and family services in accordance with this section and no medical consent has been obtained prior to said commitment, the commitment order shall be deemed to grant consent for the office of children and family services to provide for routine medical, dental and mental health services and treatment to the offender so committed.

(d) Nothing in this subdivision shall preclude a parent or legal guardian of an offender who is not yet eighteen years of age from making a motion on notice to the office of children and family services pursuant to article twenty-two of the civil practice law and rules objecting to routine medical, dental or mental health services and treatment being provided to such offender under the provisions of paragraph (b) of this subdivision.

(e) Nothing in this section shall require that consent be obtained from the parent or legal guardian, where no consent is necessary or where the offender is authorized by law to consent on his or her own behalf to any medical, dental and mental health service or treatment.

5. Subject to regulations of the department of health, routine medical, dental and mental health services and treatment is defined for the purposes of this section to mean any routine diagnosis or treatment, including without limitation the administration of medications or nutrition, the extraction of bodily fluids for analysis, and dental care performed with a local anesthetic. Routine mental health treatment shall not include psychiatric administration of medication unless it is part of an ongoing mental health plan or unless it is otherwise authorized by law.

HISTORY: Add, L 1965, ch 1030; amd, L 1975, ch 782, § 1; amd, L 1978, ch 268, § 1, L 1981, ch 303, § 2, eff July 22, 1981, L 1992, ch 465, § 52,L 1992, ch 465, § 52, L 1992, ch 479, § 3, eff July 17, 1992, deemed eff July 15, 1991, L 1995, ch 1, § 6, eff Sept 1, 1995, L 1995, ch 3, § 9, eff Oct 1, 1995, repealed eff Sept 1, 2015, L 1995, ch 516, §§ 2, 3, eff Aug 2, 1995, L 2011, ch 62, § 124 (Part C, Subpart B), eff March 31, 2011, L 2011, ch 62, § 125 (Part C, Subpart B), eff Sept 1, 2015, L 2013, ch 437, § 1, eff Oct 23, 2013.

§ 70.25. Concurrent and consecutive terms of imprisonment

1. Except as provided in subdivisions two, two-a and five of this section, when multiple sentences of imprisonment are imposed on a person at the same time, or when a person who is subject to any undischarged term of imprisonment imposed at a previous time by a court of this state is sentenced to an additional term of imprisonment, the sentence or sentences imposed by the court shall run either concurrently or consecutively with respect to each other and the undischarged term or terms in such manner as the court directs at the time of sentence. If the court does not specify the manner in which a sentence imposed by it is to run, the sentence shall run as follows:

(a) [Until Sept 1, 2015] An indeterminate or determinate sentence shall run concurrently with all other terms; and

(a) [Eff Sept 1, 2015] An indeterminate sentence shall run concurrently with all other terms; and

(b) A definite sentence shall run concurrently with any sentence imposed at the same time and shall be consecutive to any other term.

2. When more than one sentence of imprisonment is imposed on a person for two or more offenses committed through a single act or omission, or through an act or omission which in itself constituted one of the offenses and also was a material element of the other, the sentences, except if one or more of such sentences is for a violation of section 270.20 of this chapter, must run concurrently.

2-a. [*Until Sept. 1, 2015, as amended L 2004, ch 738, § 33, L 2007, ch 7, § 40 and L 2009, ch 495, § 1*] When an indeterminate or determinate sentence of imprisonment is imposed pursuant to section 70.04, 70.06, 70.07, 70.08, 70.10, subdivision three or four of section 70.70, subdivision three or four of section 70.71 or subdivision five of section 70.80 of this article, or is imposed for a class A-I felony pursuant to section 70.00 of this article, and such person is subject to an undischarged indeterminate or determinate sentence of imprisonment imposed prior to the date on which the present crime was committed, the court must impose a sentence to run consecutively with respect to such undischarged sentence.

2-a. [*Effective Sept. 1, 2015, as amended L 2004, ch 738, § 34, L 2007, ch 7, § 41 and L 2009, ch 495, § 2*] When an indeterminate or determinate sentence of imprisonment is imposed pursuant to section 70.04, 70.06, 70.07, 70.08, 70.10, subdivision three or four of section 70.70, subdivision three or four of section 70.71 or subdivision five of section 70.80 of this article, or is imposed for a class A-I felony pursuant to section 70.00 of this article, and such person is subject to an undischarged indeterminate sentence of imprisonment imposed prior to the date on which the present crime was committed, the court must impose a sentence to run consecutively with respect to such undischarged sentence.

2-b. [Until Sept 1, 2015] When a person is convicted of a violent felony offense committed after arraignment and while released on recognizance or bail, but committed prior to the imposition of sentence on a pending felony charge, and if an indeterminate or determinate sentence of imprisonment is imposed in each case, such sentences shall run consecutively. Provided, however, that the court may, in the interest of justice, order a sentence to run concurrently in a situation where consecutive sentences are required by this subdivision if it finds either mitigating circumstances that bear directly upon the manner in which the crime was committed or, where the defendant was not the sole participant in the crime, the defendant's participation was relatively minor although not so minor as to constitute a defense to the prosecution. The defendant and the district attorney shall have an opportunity to present relevant information to assist the court in making this determination and the court may, in its discretion, conduct a hearing with respect to any issue bearing upon such determination. If the court determines that consecutive sentences should not be ordered, it shall make a statement on the record of the facts and circumstances upon which such determination is based.

2-b. [Eff Sept 1, 2015] When a person is convicted of a violent felony offense committed after arraignment and while released on recognizance or bail, but committed prior to the imposition of sentence on a pending felony charge, and if an indeterminate sentence of imprisonment is imposed in each case, such sentences shall run consecutively. Provided, however, that the court may, in the interest of justice, order a sentence to run concurrently in a situation where consecutive sentences are required by this subdivision if it finds either mitigating circumstances that bear directly upon the manner in which the crime was committed or, where the defendant was not the sole participant in the crime, the defendant's participation was relatively minor although not so minor as to constitute a defense to the prosecution. The defendant and the district attorney shall have an opportunity to present relevant information to assist the court in making this determination and the court may, in its discretion, conduct a hearing with respect to any issue bearing upon such determination. If the court determines that consecutive sentences should not be ordered, it shall make a statement on the record of the facts and circumstances upon which such determination is based.

2-c. When a person is convicted of bail jumping in the second degree as defined in section 215.56 or bail jumping in the first degree as defined in section 215.57 committed after arraignment and while released on recognizance or bail in connection with a pending indictment or information charging one or more felonies, at least one of which he is subsequently convicted, and if an indeterminate sentence of imprisonment is imposed in each case, such sentences shall run consecutively. Provided, however, that the court may, in the interest of justice, order a sentence to run concurrently in a situation where consecutive sentences are required by this subdivision if it finds mitigating circumstances that bear directly upon the manner in which the crime was committed. The defendant and the district attorney shall have an opportunity to present relevant information to assist the court in making this determination and the court may, in its discretion, conduct a hearing with respect to any issue bearing upon such determination. If the court determines that consecutive sentences should not be ordered, it shall make a statement on the record of the facts and circumstances upon which such determination is based.

2-d. When a person is convicted of escape in the second degree as defined in section 205.10 or escape in the first degree as defined in section 205.15 committed after issuance of a securing order, as defined in subdivision five of section 500.10 of the criminal procedure law, in connection with a pending indictment or information charging one or more felonies, at least one of which he is subsequently convicted, and if an indeterminate sentence of imprisonment is imposed in each case, such sentences shall run consecutively. Provided, however, that the court may, in the interest of justice, order a sentence to run concurrently in a situation where consecutive sentences are required by this subdivision if it finds mitigating circumstances that bear directly upon the manner in which the crime was committed. The defendant and the district attorney shall have an opportunity to present relevant information to assist the court in making this determination and the court may, in its discretion, conduct a hearing with respect to any issue bearing upon such determination. If the court determines that consecutive sentences should not be ordered, it shall make a statement on the record of the facts and circumstances upon which such determination is based.

2-e. Whenever a person is convicted of course of sexual conduct against a child in the first degree as defined in section 130.75 or course of sexual conduct against a child in the second degree as defined in section 130.80 and any other crime under article one hundred thirty committed against the same child and within the period charged under section 130.75 or 130.80, the sentences must run concurrently.

2-f. Whenever a person is convicted of facilitating a sex offense with a controlled substance as defined in section 130.90 of this chapter, the sentence imposed by the court for such offense may be ordered to run consecutively to any sentence imposed upon conviction of an offense defined in article one hundred thirty of this chapter arising from the same criminal transaction.

2-g. Whenever a person is convicted of unlawful manufacture of methamphetamine in the third degree as defined in section 220.73 of this chapter, unlawful manufacture of methamphetamine in the second degree as defined in section 220.74 of this chapter, or unlawful manufacture of methamphetamine in the first degree as defined in section 220.75 of this chapter, or any attempt to commit any of such offenses, and such person is also convicted, with respect to such unlawful methamphetamine laboratory, of unlawful disposal of methamphetamine laboratory material as defined in section 220.76 of this chapter, the sentences must run concurrently.

3. Where consecutive definite sentences of imprisonment are not prohibited by subdivision two of this section and are imposed on a person for offenses which were committed as parts of a single incident or transaction, the aggregate of the terms of such sentences shall not exceed one year.

4. When a person, who is subject to any undischarged term of imprisonment imposed at a previous time by a court of another jurisdiction, is sentenced to an additional term or terms of imprisonment by a court of this state, the sentence or sentences imposed by the court of this state, subject to the provisions of subdivisions one, two and three of this section, shall run either concurrently or consecutively with respect to such undischarged term in such manner as the court directs at the time of sentence. If the court of this state does not specify the manner in which a sentence imposed by it is to run, the sentence or sentences shall run consecutively.

5. (a) [Until Sept 1, 2015] Except as provided in paragraph (c) of this subdivision, when a person is convicted of assault in the second degree, as defined in subdivision seven of section 120.05 of this chapter, any definite, indeterminate or determinate term of imprisonment which may be imposed as a sentence upon such conviction shall run consecutively to any undischarged term of imprisonment to which the defendant was subject and for which he was confined at the time of the assault.

(a) [Eff Sept 1, 2015] Except as provided in paragraph (c) of this subdivision, when a person is convicted of assault in the second degree, as defined in subdivision seven of section 120.05 of this chapter, any definite or indeterminate term of imprisonment which may be imposed as a sentence upon such conviction shall run consecutively to any undischarged term of imprisonment to which the defendant was subject and for which he was confined at the time of the assault.

(b) [Until Sept 1, 2015] Except as provided in paragraph (c) of this subdivision, when a person is convicted of assault in the second degree, as defined in subdivision seven of section 120.05 of this chapter, any definite, indeterminate or determinate term of imprisonment which may be imposed as a sentence upon such conviction shall run consecutively to any term of imprisonment which was previously imposed or which may be prospectively imposed where the person was confined within a detention facility at the time of the assault upon a charge which culminated in such sentence of imprisonment.

(b) [Eff Sept 1, 2015] Except as provided in paragraph (c) of this subdivision, when a person is convicted of assault in the second degree, as defined in subdivision seven of section 120.05 of this chapter, any definite or indeterminate term of imprisonment which may be imposed as a sentence upon such conviction shall run consecutively to any term of imprisonment which was previously imposed or which may be prospectively imposed where the person was confined within a detention facility at the time of the assault upon a charge which culminated in such sentence of imprisonment.

(c) Notwithstanding the provisions of paragraphs (a) and (b) of this subdivision, a term of imprisonment imposed upon a conviction to assault in the second degree as defined in subdivision seven of section 120.05 of this chapter may run concurrently to any other term of imprisonment, in the interest of justice, provided the court sets forth in the record its reasons for imposing a concurrent sentence. Nothing in this section shall require the imposition of a sentence of imprisonment where it is not otherwise required by law.

HISTORY: Add, L 1965, ch 1030, eff Sept 1, 1967. Sub 1, amd, L 1978, ch 481, § 22, L 1981, ch 372, § 1, eff Sept 1, 1981. Sub 1, par (a), amd, L 1995, ch 3, § 10, eff Oct 1, 1995, repealed eff Sept 1, 2015. Sub 2, amd, L 1984, ch 56, § 2, eff Nov 1, 1984. Sub 2-a, add, L 1978, ch 481, § 23; amd, L 1995, ch 3, § 11, eff Oct 1, 1995, repealed eff Sept 1, 2015. Sub 2-a [first setout], amd, L 2004, ch 738, § 33, eff Jan 13, 2005, expires and repealed Sept 1, 2015, L 2007, ch 7, § 40, eff April 13, 2007, L 2009, ch 495, § 1, eff Nov 16, 2009. Sub 2-a [second setout], amd, L 2004, ch 738, § 34, L 2007, ch 7, § 41, L 2009, ch 495, § 2, eff Sept 1, 2015. Sub 2-b, add L 1982, ch 559, § 1; amd, L 1995, ch 3, § 11, eff Oct 1, 1995, repealed eff Sept 1, 2015. Sub 2-c, add, L 1986, ch 795, § 1, eff Nov 1, 1986 and applicable to offenses committed on or after Nov 1, 1986. Sub 2-d, add, L 1986, ch 795, § 1, eff Nov 1, 1986 and applicable to offenses committed on or after Nov 1, 1986. Sub 2-e, add, L 1996, ch 122, § 3, eff Aug 1, 1996. Sub 2-f, add, L 2000, ch 1, § 52, eff Feb 1, 2001. Sub 2-g, add, L 2005, ch 394, § 5, eff Oct 1, 2005. Sub 4, add, L 1975, ch 782, § 2, eff Sept 1, 1975. Sub 5, add, L 1981, ch 372, § 2, eff Sept 1, 1981. Sub 5, par (a), amd, L 1995, ch 3, § 12, eff Oct 1, 1995, repealed eff Sept 1, 2015. Sub 5, par (b), amd, L 1995, ch 3, § 12, eff Oct 1, 1995, repealed eff Sept 1, 2015.

Editor's Notes:

Laws 2004, ch 738, § 41 (d-1) and (i), eff Jan 13, 2004, provides as follows:

§ 41. This act shall take effect immediately, provided that:

(d-1) the provisions of sections, twelve, fourteen, fifteen, eighteen, twenty, twenty-four, twenty-five, twenty-nine, thirty-three, thirty-five and thirty-six of this act shall take effect on the thirtieth day after it shall have become a law, and such provisions, with the exception of subdivision 6 of section 60.04 of the penal law as added by section twenty of this act, shall apply to crimes committed on or after the effective date thereof;

(i) the amendments to subdivision 2-a of section 70.25 of the penal law made by section thirty-three of this act shall be subject to the expiration and reversion of such subdivision pursuant to subdivision d of section 74 of chapter 3 of the laws of 1995, as amended, when upon such date the provisions of section thirty-four of this act shall take effect;

Laws 2007, ch 7, §§ 1 and 52 (a), (d), eff April 13, 2007, provide as follows:

Section 1. Short title. This act shall be known and may be cited as the "sex offender management and treatment act."

§ 52. This act shall take effect on the thirtieth day after it shall have become a law; provided, however, that:

(a) the provisions of sections thirteen, twenty-nine, thirty, thirty-one, thirty-two, thirty-three, thirty-four, thirty-five, thirty-six, thirty-seven, thirty-eight, thirty-nine, thirty-nine-a, forty, forty-one, forty-two, forty-three, forty-four, forty-five, forty-six, forty-seven, forty-eight, forty-nine and fifty of this act shall only apply to crimes committed after the effective date of this act;

d) the amendments to subdivision 2-a of section 70.25 of the penal law made by section forty of this act shall be subject to the expiration and reversion of such subdivision pursuant to subdivision d of section 74 of chapter 3 of the laws of 1995, as amended, when upon such date the provisions of section forty-one of this act shall take effect; . . . .

§ 70.30. Calculation of terms of imprisonment

1. [Until Sept 1, 2015] An indeterminate or determinate sentence of imprisonment commences when the prisoner is received in an institution under the jurisdiction of the state department of corrections and community supervision. Where a person is under more than one indeterminate or determinate sentence, the sentences shall be calculated as follows:

(a) If the sentences run concurrently, the time served under imprisonment on any of the sentences shall be credited against the minimum periods of all the concurrent indeterminate sentences and against the terms of all the concurrent determinate sentences. The maximum term or terms of the indeterminate sentences and the term or terms of the determinate sentences shall merge in and be satisfied by discharge of the term which has the longest unexpired time to run;

(b) If the defendant is serving two or more indeterminate sentences which run consecutively, the minimum periods of imprisonment are added to arrive at an aggregate minimum period of imprisonment equal to the sum of all the minimum periods, and the maximum terms are added to arrive at an aggregate maximum term equal to the sum of all the maximum terms, provided, however, that both the aggregate maximum term and the aggregate minimum period of imprisonment shall be subject to the limitations set forth in paragraphs (e) and (f) of this subdivision, where applicable;

(c) If the defendant is serving two or more determinate sentences of imprisonment which run consecutively, the terms of the determinate sentences are added to arrive at an aggregate maximum term of imprisonment, provided, however, that the aggregate maximum term of imprisonment shall be subject to the limitations set forth in paragraphs (e) and (f) of this subdivision, where applicable.

(d) If the defendant is serving one or more indeterminate sentences of imprisonment and one or more determinate sentence of imprisonment which run consecutively, the minimum term or terms of the indeterminate sentence or sentences and the term or terms of the determinate sentence or sentences are added to arrive at an aggregate maximum term of imprisonment, provided, however, (i) that in no event shall the aggregate maximum so calculated be less than the term or maximum term of imprisonment of the sentence which has the longest unexpired time to run; and (ii) that the aggregate maximum term of imprisonment shall be subject to the limitations set forth in paragraphs (e) and (f) of this subdivision, where applicable.

(e) (i) Except as provided in subparagraph (ii), (iii), (iv), (v), (vi) or (vii) of this paragraph, the aggregate maximum term of consecutive sentences, all of which are indeterminate sentences or all of which are determinate sentences, imposed for two or more crimes, other than two or more crimes that include a class A felony, committed prior to the time the person was imprisoned under any of such sentences shall, if it exceeds twenty years, be deemed to be twenty years, unless one of the sentences was imposed for a class B felony, in which case the aggregate maximum term shall, if it exceeds thirty years, be deemed to be thirty years. Where the aggregate maximum term of two or more indeterminate consecutive sentences is reduced by calculation made pursuant to this paragraph, the aggregate minimum period of imprisonment, if it exceeds one-half of the aggregate maximum term as so reduced, shall be deemed to be one-half of the aggregate maximum term as so reduced;

(ii) Where the aggregate maximum term of two or more consecutive sentences, one or more of which is a determinate sentence and one or more of which is an indeterminate sentence, imposed for two or more crimes, other than two or more crimes that include a class A felony, committed prior to the time the person was imprisoned under any of such sentences, exceeds twenty years, and none of the sentences was imposed for a class B felony, the following rules shall apply:

(A) if the aggregate maximum term of the determinate sentence or sentences exceeds twenty years, the defendant shall be deemed to be serving to [serving a]* a determinate sentence of twenty years.

(B) if the aggregate maximum term of the determinate sentence or sentences is less than twenty years, the defendant shall be deemed to be serving an indeterminate sentence the maximum term of which shall be deemed to be twenty years. In such instances, the minimum sentence shall be deemed to be ten years or six-sevenths of the term or aggregate maximum term of the determinate sentence or sentences, whichever is greater.

(iii) Where the aggregate maximum term of two or more consecutive sentences, one or more of which is a determinate sentence and one or more of which is an indeterminate sentence, imposed for two or more crimes, other than two or more crimes that include a class A felony, commmitted [committed]** prior to the time the person was imprisoned under any of such sentences, exceeds thirty years, and one of the sentences was imposed for a class B felony, the following rules shall apply:

(A) if the aggregate maximum term of the determinate sentence or sentences exceeds thirty years, the defendant shall be deemed to be serving a determinate sentence of thirty years;

(B) if the aggregate maximum term of the determinate sentence or sentences is less than thirty years, the defendant shall be deemed to be serving an indeterminate sentence

---

*   The bracketed words have been inserted by the Publisher.
** The bracketed word has been inserted by the Publisher.

the maximum term of which shall be deemed to be thirty years. In such instances, the minimum sentence shall be deemed to be fifteen years or six-sevenths of the term or aggregate maximum term of the determinate sentence or sentences, whichever is greater.

(iv) Notwithstanding subparagraph (i) of this paragraph, the aggregate maximum term of consecutive sentences, all of which are indeterminate sentences or all of which are determinate sentences, imposed for the conviction of two violent felony offenses committed prior to the time the person was imprisoned under any of such sentences and one of which is a class B violent felony offense, shall, if it exceeds forty years, be deemed to be forty years;

(v) Notwithstanding subparagraphs (ii) and (iii) of this paragraph, where the aggregate maximum term of two or more consecutive sentences, one or more of which is a determinate sentence and one or more of which is an indeterminate sentence, and where such sentences are imposed for the conviction of two violent felony offenses committed prior to the time the person was imprisoned under any such sentences and where one of which is a class B violent felony offense, the following rules shall apply:

(A) if the aggregate maximum term of the determinate sentence or sentences exceeds forty years, the defendant shall be deemed to be serving a determinate sentence of forty years;

(B) if the aggregate maximum term of the determinate sentence or sentences is less than forty years, the defendant shall be deemed to be serving an indeterminate sentence the maximum term of which shall be deemed to be forty years. In such instances, the minimum sentence shall be deemed to be twenty years or six-sevenths of the term or aggregate maximum term of the determinate sentence or sentences, whichever is greater.

(vi) Notwithstanding subparagraphs (i) and (iv) of this paragraph, the aggregate maximum term of consecutive sentences, all of which are indeterminate or all of which are determinate sentences, imposed for the conviction of three or more violent felony offenses committed prior to the time the person was imprisoned under any of such sentences and one of which is a class B violent felony offense, shall, if it exceeds fifty years, be deemed to be fifty years;

(vii) Notwithstanding subparagraphs (ii), (iii) and (v) of this paragraph, where the aggregate maximum term of two or more consecutive sentences, one or more of which is a determinate sentence and one or more of which is an indeterminate sentence, and where such sentences are imposed for the conviction of three or more violent felony offenses committed prior to the time the person was imprisoned under any such sentences and one of which is a class B violent felony offense, the following rules shall apply:

(A) if the aggregate maximum term of the determinate sentence or sentences exceeds fifty years, the defendant shall be deemed to be serving a determinate sentence of fifty years.

(B) if the aggregate maximum term of the determinate sentence or sentences is less than fifty years, the defendant shall be deemed to be serving an indeterminate sentence the maximum term of which shall be deemed to be fifty years. In such instances, the minimum sentence shall be deemed to be twenty-five years or six-sevenths of the term or aggregate maximum term of the determinate sentence or sentences, whichever is greater.

(viii) Notwithstanding any provision of this subdivision to the contrary where a person is serving two or more consecutive sentences, one or more of which is an indeterminate sentence and one or more of which is a determinate sentence, and if he would be eligible for a reduction provision pursuant to this subdivision if the maximum term or aggregate maximum term of the indeterminate sentence or sentences were added to the term or aggregate maximum term of the determinate sentence or sentences, the person shall be deemed to be eligible for the applicable reduction provision and the rules set forth in this subdivision shall apply.

(f) The aggregate maximum term of consecutive sentences imposed upon a juvenile offender for two or more crimes, not including a class A felony, committed before he has reached the age of sixteen, shall, if it exceeds ten years, be deemed to be ten years. If consecutive indeterminate sentences imposed upon a juvenile offender include a sentence for the class A felony of arson in the first degree or for the class A felony of kidnapping in the first degree, then the aggregate maximum term of such sentences shall, if it exceeds fifteen years, be deemed to be fifteen years. Where the aggregate maximum term of two or more consecutive sentences is reduced by a calculation made pursuant to this paragraph, the aggregate minimum period of imprisonment, if it exceeds one-half of the aggregate maximum term as so reduced, shall be deemed to be one-half of the aggregate maximum term as so reduced.

1. [Eff Sept 1, 2015] An indeterminate sentence of imprisonment commences when the prisoner is received in an institution under the jurisdiction of the state department of corrections and community supervision. Where a person is under more than one indeterminate sentence, the sentences shall be calculated as follows:

(a) If the sentences run concurrently, the time served under imprisonment on any of the sentences shall be credited against the minimum periods of all the concurrent sentences, and the maximum terms merge in and are satisfied by discharge of the term which has the longest unexpired time to run;

(b) If the sentences run consecutively, the minimum periods of imprisonment are added to arrive at an aggregate minimum period of imprisonment equal to the sum of all the minimum periods, and the maximum terms are added to arrive at an aggregate maximum term equal to the sum of all the maximum terms, provided, however, that both the aggregate maximum term and the aggregate minimum period of imprisonment shall be subject to the limitations set forth in paragraphs (c) and (d) of this subdivision, where applicable;

(c) (i) Except as provided in subparagraph (ii) or (iii) of this paragraph, the aggregate maximum term of consecutive sentences imposed for two or more crimes, other than two or more crimes that include a class A felony, committed prior to the time the person was imprisoned under any of such sentences shall, if it exceeds twenty years, be deemed to be twenty years, unless one of the sentences was imposed for a class B felony, in which case the aggregate maximum term shall, if it exceeds thirty years, be deemed to be thirty years. Where the aggregate maximum term of two or more consecutive sentences is reduced by calculation made pursuant to this paragraph, the aggregate minimum period of imprisonment, if it exceeds one-half of the aggregate maximum term as so reduced, shall be deemed to be one-half of the aggregate maximum term as so reduced;

(ii) Notwithstanding subparagraph (i) of this paragraph, the aggregate maximum term of consecutive sentences imposed for the conviction of two violent felony offenses committed prior to the time the person was imprisoned under any of such sentences and one of which is a class B violent felony offense, shall, if it exceeds forty years, be deemed to be forty years;

(iii) Notwithstanding subparagraphs (i) and (ii) of this paragraph, the aggregate maximum term of consecutive sentences imposed for the conviction of three or more violent felony offenses committed prior to the time the person was imprisoned under any of such sentences and one of which is a class B violent felony offense, shall, if it exceeds fifty years, be deemed to be fifty years;

(d) The aggregate maximum term of consecutive sentences imposed upon a juvenile offender for two or more crimes, not including a class A felony, committed before he has reached the age of sixteen, shall, if it exceeds ten years, be deemed to be ten years. If consecutive indeterminate sentences imposed upon a juvenile offender include a sentence for the class A felony of arson in the first degree or for the class A felony of kidnapping in the first degree, then the aggregate maximum term of such sentences shall, if it exceeds fifteen years, be deemed to be fifteen years. Where the aggregate maximum term of two or more consecutive sentences is reduced by a calculation made pursuant to this paragraph, the aggregate minimum period of imprisonment, if it exceeds one-half of the aggregate maximum term as so reduced, shall be deemed to be one-half of the aggregate maximum term as so reduced.

2. Definite sentences. A definite sentence of imprisonment commences when the prisoner is received in the institution named in the commitment. Where a person is under more than one definite sentence, the sentences shall be calculated as follows:

(a) If the sentences run concurrently and are to be served in a single institution, the terms merge in and are satisfied by discharge of the term which has the longest unexpired time to run;

(b) If the sentences run consecutively and are to be served in a single institution, the terms are added to arrive at an aggregate term and are satisfied by discharge of such aggregate term, or by service of two years imprisonment plus any term imposed for an offense committed while the person is under the sentences, whichever is less;

(c) If the sentences run concurrently and are to be served in more than one institution, the term of each such sentence shall be credited with the portion of any concurrent term served after that sentence was imposed;

(d) If the sentences run consecutively and are to be served in more than one institution, the aggregate of the time served in all of the institutions shall not exceed two years plus any term imposed for an offense committed while the person is under the sentences.

2-a. Undischarged imprisonment in other jurisdiction. Where a person who is subject to an undischarged term of imprisonment imposed at a previous time by a court of another jurisdiction is sentenced to an additional term or terms of imprisonment by a court of this state, to run concurrently with such undischarged term, such additional term or terms shall be deemed to commence when the said person is returned to the custody of the appropriate official of such other jurisdiction where the undischarged term of imprisonment is being served. If the additional term or terms imposed shall run consecutively to the said undischarged term, such additional term or terms shall commence when the prisoner is received in the appropriate institution as provided in subdivisions one and two of this section. The term or terms of such imprisonment shall be calculated and such other pertinent provisions of this section applied in the same manner as where a person is under more than one sentence in this state as provided in this section.

3. [Until Sept 1, 2015] The term of a definite sentence, a determinate sentence, or the maximum term of an indeterminate sentence imposed on a person shall be credited with and diminished by the amount of time the person spent in custody prior to the commencement of such sentence as a result of the charge that culminated in the sentence. In the case of an indeterminate sentence, if the

minimum period of imprisonment has been fixed by the court or by the board of parole, the credit shall also be applied against the minimum period. The credit herein provided shall be calculated from the date custody under the charge commenced to the date the sentence commences and shall not include any time that is credited against the term or maximum term of any previously imposed sentence or period of post-release supervision to which the person is subject. Where the charge or charges culminate in more than one sentence, the credit shall be applied as follows:

(a) If the sentences run concurrently, the credit shall be applied against each such sentence;

(b) If the sentences run consecutively, the credit shall be applied against the aggregate term or aggregate maximum term of the sentences and against the aggregate minimum period of imprisonment.

In any case where a person has been in custody due to a charge that culminated in a dismissal or an acquittal, the amount of time that would have been credited against a sentence for such charge, had one been imposed, shall be credited against any sentence that is based on a charge for which a warrant or commitment was lodged during the pendency of such custody.

3. [Eff Sept 1, 2015] Jail time. The term of a definite sentence or the maximum term of an indeterminate sentence imposed on a person shall be credited with and diminished by the amount of time the person spent in custody prior to the commencement of such sentence as a result of the charge that culminated in the sentence. In the case of an indeterminate sentence, if the minimum period of imprisonment has been fixed by the court or by the board of parole, the credit shall also be applied against the minimum period. The credit herein provided shall be calculated from the date custody under the charge commenced to the date the sentence commences and shall not include any time that is credited against the term or maximum term of any previously imposed sentence to which the person is subject. Where the charge or charges culminate in more than one sentence, the credit shall be applied as follows:

(a) If the sentences run concurrently, the credit shall be applied against each such sentence;

(b) If the sentences run consecutively, the credit shall be applied against the aggregate term or aggregate maximum term of the sentences and against the aggregate minimum period of imprisonment.

In any case where a person has been in custody due to a charge that culminated in a dismissal or an acquittal, the amount of time that would have been credited against a sentence for such charge, had one been imposed, shall be credited against any sentence that is based on a charge for which a warrant or commitment was lodged during the pendency of such custody.

4. [Until Sept 1, 2015] Good behavior time. Time allowances earned for good behavior, pursuant to the provisions of the correction law, shall be computed and applied as follows:

(a) In the case of a person serving an indeterminate or determinate sentence, the total of such allowances shall be calculated as provided in section eight hundred three of the correction law and the allowances shall be applied as provided in paragraph (b) of subdivision one of section 70.40;

(b) In the case of a person serving a definite sentence, the total of such allowances shall not exceed one-third of his term or aggregate term and the allowances shall be applied as a credit against such term.

4. [Eff Sept 1, 2015] Good behavior time. Time allowances earned for good behavior, pursuant to the provisions of the correction law, shall be computed and applied as follows:

(a) In the case of a person serving an indeterminate sentence, the total of such allowances shall not exceed one-third of his maximum or aggregate maximum term and the allowances shall be applied as provided in subdivision one (b) of section 70.40;

(b) In the case of a person serving a definite sentence, the total of such allowances shall not exceed one-third of his term or aggregate term and the allowances shall be applied as a credit against such term.

5. Time served under vacated sentence. When a sentence of imprisonment that has been imposed on a person is vacated and a new sentence is imposed on such person for the same offense, or for an offense based upon the same act, the new sentence shall be calculated as if it had commenced at the time the vacated sentence commenced, and all time credited against the vacated sentence shall be credited against the new sentence. In any case where a vacated sentence also includes a period of post-release supervision, all time credited against the period of post-release supervision shall be credited against the period of post-release supervision included with the new sentence. In the event a period of post-release supervision is not included with the new sentence, such period shall be credited against the new sentence.

6. Escape. When a person who is serving a sentence of imprisonment escapes from custody, the escape shall interrupt the sentence and such interruption shall continue until the return of the person to the institution in which the sentence was being served or, if the sentence was being served in an institution under the jurisdiction of the state department of corrections and community supervision, to an institution under the jurisdiction of that department. Any time spent by such person in custody from the date of escape to the date the sentence resumes shall be credited against the term or maximum term of the interrupted sentence, provided:

(a) That such custody was due to an arrest or surrender based upon the escape; or

(b) That such custody arose from an arrest on another charge which culminated in a dismissal or an acquittal; or

(c) That such custody arose from an arrest on another charge which culminated in a conviction, but in such case, if a sentence of imprisonment was imposed, the credit allowed shall be limited to the portion of the time spent in custody that exceeds the period, term or maximum term of imprisonment imposed for such conviction.

7. [Expires Sept 1, 2015] Absconding from temporary release or furlough program. When a person who is serving a sentence of imprisonment is permitted to leave an institution to participate in a program of work release or furlough program as such term is defined in section six hundred thirty-one of the correction law, or in the case of an institution under the jurisdiction of the state department of corrections and community supervision or a facility under the jurisdiction of the state office of children and family services to participate in a program of temporary release, fails to return to the institution or facility at or before the time prescribed for his or her return, such failure shall interrupt the sentence and such interruption shall continue until the return of the person to the institution in which the sentence was being served or, if the sentence was being served in an institution under the jurisdiction of the state department of corrections and community supervision or a facility under the jurisdiction of the state office of children and family services to an institution under the jurisdiction of that department or a facility under the jurisdiction of that office. Any time spent by such person in an institution from the date of his or her failure to return to the date his or her sentence resumes shall be credited against the term or maximum term of the interrupted sentence, provided:

(a) That such incarceration was due to an arrest or surrender based upon the failure to return; or

(b) That such incarceration arose from an arrest on another charge which culminated in a dismissal or an acquittal; or

(c) That such custody arose from an arrest on another charge which culminated in a conviction, but in such case, if a sentence of imprisonment was imposed, the credit allowed shall be limited to the portion of the time spent in custody that exceeds the period, term or maximum term of imprisonment imposed for such conviction.

> **HISTORY:** Add, L 1965, ch 1030, eff Sept 1, 1967; amd, L 1972, ch 339, § 9, expires Sept 1, 2011, L 1974, ch 465, eff May 23, 1974, L 1975, ch 782, § 3, eff Aug 9, 1975, L 1976, ch 21, § 1, L 1976, ch 145, § 2, eff July 1, 1976, L 1978, ch 481, §§ 24, 25, L 1979, ch 648, § 1, L 1980, ch 176, § 1, L 1983, ch 199, § 1, L 1983, ch 460, § 1, L 1984, ch 983, § 10, L 1988, ch 392, § 1, eff July 29, 1988, L 1995, ch 3, §§ 13–16, eff Oct 1, 1995, expires Sept 1, 2015, L 1998, ch 1, §§ 10, 11, eff Aug 6, 1998, L 2011, ch 62, § 126 (Part C, Subpart B), eff March 31, 2011, L 2011, ch 62, § 127 (Part C, Subpart B), eff Sept 1, 2013.

§ 70.35. Merger of certain definite and indeterminate or determinate sentences

[Until Sept 1, 2015, this section reads as follows:]

The service of an indeterminate or determinate sentence of imprisonment shall satisfy any definite sentence of imprisonment imposed on a person for an offense committed prior to the time the indeterminate or determinate sentence was imposed, except as provided in paragraph (b) of subdivision five of section 70.25 of this article. A person who is serving a definite sentence at the time an indeterminate or determinate sentence is imposed shall be delivered to the custody of the state department of corrections and community supervision to commence service of the indeterminate or determinate sentence immediately unless the person is serving a definite sentence pursuant to paragraph (b) of subdivision five of section 70.25 of this article. In any case where the indeterminate or determinate sentence is revoked or vacated, the person shall receive credit against the definite sentence for each day spent in the custody of the state department of corrections and community supervision.

[Eff Sept 1, 2015, this section will be recaptioned as "Merger of certain definite and indeterminate sentences" and it will read as follows:]

The service of an indeterminate sentence of imprisonment shall satisfy any definite sentence of imprisonment imposed on a person for an offense committed prior to the time the indeterminate sentence was imposed, except as provided in paragraph (b) of subdivision five of section 70.25 of this article. A person who is serving a definite sentence at the time an indeterminate sentence is imposed shall be delivered to the custody of the state department of corrections and community supervision to commence service of the indeterminate sentence immediately unless the person is serving a definite sentence pursuant to paragraph (b) of subdivision five of section 70.25 of this article. In any case where the indeterminate sentence is revoked or vacated, the person shall receive credit against the definite sentence for each day spent in the custody of the state department of corrections and community supervision.

> **HISTORY:** Add, L 1965, ch 1030; amd, L 1981, ch 372, § 3, L 1989, ch 527, § 1, L 1995, ch 3, § 17, eff Oct 1, 1995, repealed eff Sept 1, 2015, L 2011, ch 62, § 127-a (Part C, Subpart B), eff March 31, 2011, L 2011, ch 62, § 127-b (Part C, Subpart B), eff Sept 1, 2011.

§ 70.40. Release on parole; conditional release; presumptive release

1. Indeterminate sentence.

(a) [Until Sept 1, 2015] Release on parole shall be in the discretion of the state board of parole, and such person shall continue service of his or her sentence or sentences while on parole, in accordance with and subject to the provisions of the executive law and the correction law.

(i) A person who is serving one or more than one indeterminate sentence of imprisonment may be paroled from the institution in which he or she is confined at any time after the expiration of the minimum or the aggregate minimum period of the sentence or sentences or, where applicable, the minimum or aggregate minimum period reduced by the merit time allowance granted pursuant to paragraph (d) of subdivision one of section eight hundred three of the correction law.

(ii) A person who is serving one or more than one determinate sentence of imprisonment shall be ineligible for discretionary release on parole.

(iii) A person who is serving one or more than one indeterminate sentence of imprisonment and one or more than one determinate sentence of imprisonment, which run concurrently may be paroled at any time after the expiration of the minimum period of imprisonment of the indeterminate sentence or sentences, or upon the expiration of six-sevenths of the term of imprisonment of the determinate sentence or sentences, whichever is later.

(iv) A person who is serving one or more than one indeterminate sentence of imprisonment and one or more than one determinate sentence of imprisonment which run consecutively may be paroled at any time after the expiration of the sum of the minimum or aggregate minimum period of the indeterminate sentence or sentences and six-sevenths of the term or aggregate term of imprisonment of the determinate sentence or sentences.

(v) Notwithstanding any other subparagraph of this paragraph, a person may be paroled from the institution in which he or she is confined at any time on medical parole pursuant to section two hundred fifty-nine-r or section two hundred fifty-nine-s of the executive law or for deportation pursuant to paragraph (d) of subdivision two of section two hundred fifty-nine-i of the executive law or after the successful completion of a shock incarceration program pursuant to article twenty-six-A of the correction law.

(a) [Eff Sept 1, 2015]

(i) A person who is serving one or more than one indeterminate sentence of imprisonment may be paroled from the institution in which he or she is confined at any time after the expiration of the minimum or the aggregate minimum period of imprisonment of the sentence or sentences or after the successful completion of a shock incarceration program, as defined in article twenty-six-A of the correction law, whichever is sooner. Release on parole shall be in the discretion of the state board of parole, and such person shall continue service of his or her sentence or sentences while on parole, in accordance with and subject to the provisions of the executive law and the correction law.

(ii) A person who is serving one or more than one indeterminate sentence of imprisonment may be paroled from the institution in which he or she is confined at any time after the expiration of the minimum or the aggregate minimum period of the sentence or sentences.

(b) [Until Sept 1, 2015] A person who is serving one or more than one indeterminate or determinate sentence of imprisonment shall, if he or she so requests, be conditionally released from the institution in which he or she is confined when the total good behavior time allowed to him or her, pursuant to the provisions of the correction law, is equal to the unserved portion of his or her term, maximum term or aggregate maximum term; provided, however, that (i) in no event shall a person serving one or more indeterminate sentence of imprisonment and one or more determinate sentence of imprisonment which run concurrently be conditionally released until serving at least six-sevenths of the determinate term of imprisonment which has the longest unexpired time to run and (ii) in no event shall a person be conditionally released prior to the date on which such person is first eligible for discretionary parole release. The conditions of release, including those governing post-release supervision, shall be such as may be imposed by the state board of parole in accordance with the provisions of the executive law.

Every person so released shall be under the supervision of the state department of corrections and community supervision for a period equal to the unserved portion of the term, maximum term, aggregate maximum term, or period of post-release supervision.

(b) [Eff Sept 1, 2015] A person who is serving one or more than one indeterminate sentence of imprisonment shall, if he or she so requests, be conditionally released from the institution in which he or she is confined when the total good behavior time allowed to him or her, pursuant to the provisions of the correction law, is equal to the unserved portion of his or her maximum or aggregate maximum term. The conditions of release, including those governing post-release supervision, shall be such as may be imposed by the state board of parole in accordance with the provisions of the executive law.

Every person so released shall be under the supervision of the department of corrections and community supervision for a period equal to the unserved portion of the maximum, aggregate maximum term, or period of post-release supervision.

(c) [Repealedl Sept 1, 2015] A person who is serving one or more than one indeterminate sentence of imprisonment shall, if he or she so requests, be released from the institution in which he or she is confined if granted presumptive release pursuant to section eight hundred six of the correction law. The conditions of release shall be such as may be imposed by the state board of parole in accordance with the provisions of the executive law. Every person so released shall be under the supervision of the department of corrections and community supervision for a period equal to the unserved portion of his or her maximum or aggregate maximum term unless discharged in accordance with law.

2. Definite sentence. A person who is serving one or more than one definite sentence of imprisonment with a term or aggregate term in excess of ninety days, and is eligible for release according to the criteria set forth in paragraphs (a), (b) and (c) of subdivision one of section two hundred seventy-three of the correction law, may, if he or she so requests, be conditionally released from the institution in which he or she is confined at any time after service of sixty days of that term, exclusive of credits allowed under subdivisions four and six of section 70.30. In computing service of sixty days, the credit allowed for jail time under subdivision three of section 70.30 shall be calculated as time served. Conditional release from such institution shall be in the discretion of the parole board, or a local conditional release commission established pursuant to article twelve of the correction law, provided, however that where such release is by a local conditional release commission, the person must be serving a definite sentence with a term in excess of one hundred twenty days and may only be released after service of ninety days of such term. In computing service of ninety days, the credit allowed for jail time under subdivision three of section 70.30 of this article shall be calculated as time served. A conditional release granted under this subdivision shall be upon such conditions as may be imposed by the parole board, in accordance with the provisions of the executive law, or a local conditional release commission in accordance with the provisions of the correction law.

Conditional release shall interrupt service of the sentence or sentences and the remaining portion of the term or aggregate term shall be held in abeyance. Every person so released shall be under the supervision of the department of corrections and community supervision or a local probation department and in the custody of the local conditional release commission in accordance with article twelve of the correction law, for a period of one year. The local probation department shall cause complete records to be kept of every person released to its supervision pursuant to this subdivision. The department of corrections and community supervision may supply to a local probation department and the local conditional release commission custody information and records maintained on persons under the supervision of such local probation department to aid in the performance of its supervision responsibilities. Compliance with the conditions of release during the period of supervision shall satisfy the portion of the term or aggregate term that has been held in abeyance.

3. Delinquency.

(a) When a person is alleged to have violated the terms of presumptive release or parole and the state board of parole has declared such person to be delinquent, the declaration of delinquency shall interrupt the person's sentence as of the date of the delinquency and such interruption shall continue until the return of the person to an institution under the jurisdiction of the state department of corrections and community supervision.

(b) When a person is alleged to have violated the terms of his or her conditional release or post-release supervision and has been declared delinquent by the parole board or the local conditional release commission having supervision over such person, the declaration of delinquency shall interrupt the period of supervision or post-release supervision as of the date of the delinquency. For a conditional release, such interruption shall continue until the return of the person to the institution from which he or she was released or, if he or she was released from an institution under the jurisdiction of the state department of corrections and community supervision, to an institution under the jurisdiction of that department. Upon such return, the person shall resume service of his or her sentence. For a person released to post-release supervision, the provisions of section 70.45 shall apply.

(c) Any time spent by a person in custody from the time of delinquency to the time service of the sentence resumes shall be credited against the term or maximum term of the interrupted sentence, provided:

(i) that such custody was due to an arrest or surrender based upon the delinquency; or

(ii) that such custody arose from an arrest on another charge which culminated in a dismissal or an acquittal; or

(iii) that such custody arose from an arrest on another charge which culminated in a conviction, but in such case, if a sentence of imprisonment was imposed, the credit allowed shall be limited to the portion of the time spent in custody that exceeds the period, term or maximum term of imprisonment imposed for such such conviction.

HISTORY: Add, L 1965, ch 1030, eff Sept 1, 1967, with substance derived in part from § 2193(3); amd, L 1967, ch 324, § 3, L 1971, ch 425, § 1, L 1972, ch 295, § 1, L 1973, ch 468, eff June 5, 1973, L 1973, ch 478, § 1, eff June 5, 1973, L 1975, ch 148, § 1, L 1978, ch 481, § 26, L 1979, ch 467, §§ 1, 2, L 1987, ch 261, § 16, L 1989, ch 79, §§ 5, 6, eff May 1, 1989 and repealed eff Sept 1, 2005L 1992, ch 55, § 286, eff April 10, 1992, L 1995, ch 3, §§ 18, 19, eff Oct 1, 1995, repealed eff Sept 1, 2015, L 1997, ch 435, § 45, eff Aug 20, 1997, expires and repealed Sept 1, 2015, L 1998, ch 1, §§ 12, 13, eff Aug 6, 1998, L 2003, ch 62, §§ 12–14 (Part E), eff May 15, 2003, deemed eff on and after April 1, 2003, L 2009, ch 56, § 7 (Part J), eff April 7, 2009, L 2009, ch 56, §§ 4, 5 (Part SS), eff April 7, 2009, L 2011, ch 62, §§ 127-c, 127-d-1, 127-f (Part C, Subpart B), eff March 31, 2011, L 2011, ch 62, §§ 127-d, 127-e (Part C, Subpart B), eff Sept 1, 2015, L 2011, ch 62, §§ 127-g, 127-h (Part C, Subpart B), eff March 31, 2011.

§ 70.45. Determinate sentence; post-release supervision

1. In general. When a court imposes a determinate sentence it shall in each case state not only the term of imprisonment, but also an additional period of post-release supervision as determined pursuant to this article. Such period shall commence as provided in subdivision five of this section and a violation of any condition of supervision occurring at any time during such period of post-release supervision shall subject the defendant to a further period of imprisonment up to the balance of the remaining period of post-release supervision, not to exceed five years; provided, however, that a defendant serving a term of post-release supervision for a conviction of a felony sex offense, as defined in section 70.80 of this article, may be subject to a further period of imprisonment up to the balance of the remaining period of post-release supervision. Such maximum limits shall not preclude a longer period of further imprisonment for a violation where the defendant is subject to indeterminate and determinate sentences.

1-a. When, following a final hearing, a time assessment has been imposed upon a person convicted of a felony sex offense who owes three years or more on a period of post-release supervision, imposed pursuant to subdivision two-a of this section, such defendant, after serving three years of the time assessment, shall be reviewed by the board of parole and may be re-released to post-release supervision only upon a determination by the board of parole made in accordance with subdivision two of section two hundred fifty-nine-i of the executive law. If re-release is not granted, the board shall specify a date not more than twenty-four months from such determination for reconsideration, and the procedures to be followed upon reconsideration shall be the same. If a time assessment of less than three years is imposed upon such a defendant, the defendant shall be released upon the expiration of such time assessment, unless he or she is subject to further imprisonment or confinement under any provision of law.

2. Period of post-release supervision for other than felony sex offenses. The period of post-release supervision for a determinate sentence, other than a determinate sentence imposed for a felony sex offense as defined in paragraph (a) of subdivision one of section 70.80 of this article, shall be five years except that:

(a) such period shall be one year whenever a determinate sentence of imprisonment is imposed pursuant to subdivision two of section 70.70 of this article upon a conviction of a class D or class E felony offense;

(b) such period shall be not less than one year nor more than two years whenever a determinate sentence of imprisonment is imposed pursuant to subdivision two of section 70.70 of this article upon a conviction of a class B or class C felony offense;

(c) such period shall be not less than one year nor more than two years whenever a determinate sentence of imprisonment is imposed pursuant to subdivision three or four of section 70.70 of this article upon conviction of a class D or class E felony offense;

(d) such period shall be not less than one and one-half years nor more than three years whenever a determinate sentence of imprisonment is imposed pursuant to subdivision three or four of section 70.70 of this article upon conviction of a class B felony or class C felony offense;

(e) such period shall be not less than one and one-half years nor more than three years whenever a determinate sentence of imprisonment is imposed pursuant to subdivision three of section 70.02 of this article upon a conviction of a class D or class E violent felony offense;

(f) such period shall be not less than two and one-half years nor more than five years

PL

whenever a determinate sentence of imprisonment is imposed pursuant to subdivision three of section 70.02 of this article upon a conviction of a class B or class C violent felony offense.

2-a. Periods of post-release supervision for felony sex offenses. The period of post-release supervision for a determinate sentence imposed for a felony sex offense as defined in paragraph (a) of subdivision one of section 70.80 of this article shall be as follows:

(a) not less than three years nor more than ten years whenever a determinate sentence of imprisonment is imposed pursuant to subdivision four of section 70.80 of this article upon a conviction of a class D or class E felony sex offense;

(b) not less than five years nor more than fifteen years whenever a determinate sentence of imprisonment is imposed pursuant to subdivision four of section 70.80 of this article upon a conviction of a class C felony sex offense;

(c) not less than five years nor more than twenty years whenever a determinate sentence of imprisonment is imposed pursuant to subdivision four of section 70.80 of this article upon a conviction of a class B felony sex offense;

(d) not less than three years nor more than ten years whenever a determinate sentence is imposed pursuant to subdivision three of section 70.02 of this article upon a conviction of a class D or class E violent felony sex offense as defined in paragraph (b) of subdivision one of section 70.80 of this article;

(e) not less than five years nor more than fifteen years whenever a determinate sentence is imposed pursuant to subdivision three of section 70.02 of this article upon a conviction of a class C violent felony sex offense as defined in section 70.80 of this article;

(f) not less than five years nor more than twenty years whenever a determinate sentence is imposed pursuant to subdivision three of section 70.02 of this article upon a conviction of a class B violent felony sex offense as defined in section 70.80 of this article;

(g) not less than five years nor more than fifteen years whenever a determinate sentence of imprisonment is imposed pursuant to either section 70.04, section 70.06, or subdivision five of section 70.80 of this article upon a conviction of a class D or class E violent or non-violent felony sex offense as defined in section 70.80 of this article;

(h) not less than seven years nor more than twenty years whenever a determinate sentence of imprisonment is imposed pursuant to either section 70.04, section 70.06, or subdivision five of section 70.80 of this article upon a conviction of a class C violent or non-violent felony sex offense as defined in section 70.80 of this article;

(i) such period shall be not less than ten years nor more than twenty-five years whenever a determinate sentence of imprisonment is imposed pursuant to either section 70.04, section 70.06, or subdivision five of section 70.80 of this article upon a conviction of a class B violent or non-violent felony sex offense as defined in section 70.80 of this article; and

(j) such period shall be not less than ten years nor more than twenty years whenever any determinate sentence of imprisonment is imposed pursuant to subdivision four of section 70.07 of this article.

3. Conditions of post-release supervision. The board of parole shall establish and impose conditions of post-release supervision in the same manner and to the same extent as it may establish and impose conditions in accordance with the executive law upon persons who are granted parole or conditional release; provided that, notwithstanding any other provision of law,

the board of parole may impose as a condition of post-release supervision that for a period not exceeding six months immediately following release from the underlying term of imprisonment the person be transferred to and participate in the programs of a residential treatment facility as that term is defined in subdivision six of section two of the correction law. Upon release from the underlying term of imprisonment, the person shall be furnished with a written statement setting forth the conditions of post-release supervision in sufficient detail to provide for the person's conduct and supervision.

4. Revocation of post-release supervision. An alleged violation of any condition of post-release supervision shall be initiated, heard and determined in accordance with the provisions of subdivisions three and four of section two hundred fifty-nine-i of the executive law.

5. Calculation of service of period of post-release supervision. A period or periods of post-release supervision shall be calculated and served as follows:

(a) A period of post-release supervision shall commence upon the person's release from imprisonment to supervision by the department of corrections and community supervision and shall interrupt the running of the determinate sentence or sentences of imprisonment and the indeterminate sentence or sentences of imprisonment, if any. The remaining portion of any maximum or aggregate maximum term shall then be held in abeyance until the successful completion of the period of post-release supervision or the person's return to the custody of the department of corrections and community supervision, whichever occurs first.

(b) Upon the completion of the period of post-release supervision, the running of such sentence or sentences of imprisonment shall resume and only then shall the remaining portion of any maximum or aggregate maximum term previously held in abeyance be credited with and diminished by such period of post-release supervision. The person shall then be under the jurisdiction of the department of corrections and community supervision for the remaining portion of such maximum or aggregate maximum term.

(c) When a person is subject to two or more periods of post-release supervision, such periods shall merge with and be satisfied by discharge of the period of post-release supervision having the longest unexpired time to run; provided, however, any time served upon one period of post-release supervision shall not be credited to any other period of post-release supervision except as provided in subdivision five of section 70.30 of this article.

(d) When a person is alleged to have violated a condition of post-release supervision and the department of corrections and community supervision has declared such person to be delinquent: (i) the declaration of delinquency shall interrupt the period of post-release supervision; (ii) such interruption shall continue until the person is restored to post-release supervision; (iii) if the person is restored to post-release supervision without being returned to the department of corrections and community supervision, any time spent in custody from the date of delinquency until restoration to post-release supervision shall first be credited to the maximum or aggregate maximum term of the sentence or sentences of imprisonment, but only to the extent authorized by subdivision three of section 70.40 of this article. Any time spent in custody solely pursuant to such delinquency after completion of the maximum or aggregate maximum term of the sentence or sentences of imprisonment shall be credited to the period of post-release supervision, if any; and (iv) if the person is ordered returned to the department of corrections and community supervision, the person shall be required to serve the time assessment before being re-released to post-release supervision. In the event the balance of the remaining period of post-release supervision is six months or less, such time assessment may be up to six months unless a longer period is authorized pursuant to subdivision one of this section. The time assessment shall commence upon the issuance of a determination after a final hearing that the person has violated one or more conditions of supervision. While serving such assessment, the person shall not receive any good behavior allowance pursuant to section eight hundred three of the correction law. Any time spent in custody from the date of delinquency until return to the department of corrections and community supervision shall first be credited to the maximum or aggregate maximum term of the sentence or sentences of imprisonment, but only to the extent authorized by subdivision three of section 70.40 of this article. The maximum or aggregate maximum term of the sentence or sentences of imprisonment shall run while the person is serving such time assessment in the custody of the department of corrections and community supervision. Any time spent in custody solely pursuant to such delinquency after completion of the maximum or aggregate maximum term of the sentence or sentences of imprisonment shall be credited to the period of post-release supervision, if any.

(e) Notwithstanding paragraph (d) of this subdivision, in the event a person is sentenced to one or more additional indeterminate or determinate term or terms of imprisonment prior to the completion of the period of post-release supervision, such period of post-release supervision shall be held in abeyance and the person shall be committed to the custody of the department of corrections and community supervision in accordance with the requirements of the prior and additional terms of imprisonment.

(f) When a person serving a period of post-release supervision is returned to the department of corrections and community supervision pursuant to an additional consecutive sentence of imprisonment and without a declaration of delinquency, such period of post-release supervision shall be held in abeyance while the person is in the custody of the department of corrections and community supervision. Such period of post-release supervision shall resume running upon the person's re-release.

HISTORY: Add, L 1998, ch 1, § 15, eff Aug 6, 1998; amd, L 2004, ch 738, § 35, eff Jan 13, 2005, L 2007, ch 7, § 33, eff April 13, 2007, L 2007, ch 56, §§ 4, 5 (Part E), eff April 9, 2007, deemed eff on and after April 1, 2007, L 2008, ch 141, § 3, eff June 30, 2008, L 2011, ch 62, § 127-j (Part C, Subpart B), eff March 31, 2011.

§ 70.70. Sentence of imprisonment for felony drug offender other than a class A felony

1. For the purposes of this section, the following terms shall mean:

(a) "Felony drug offender" means a defendant who stands convicted of any felony, defined in article two hundred twenty or two hundred twenty-one of this chapter other than a class A felony.

(b) "Second felony drug offender" means a second felony offender as that term is defined in subdivision one of section 70.06 of this article, who stands convicted of any felony, defined in article two hundred twenty or two hundred twenty-one of this chapter other than a class A felony.

(c) "Violent felony" shall have the same meaning as that term is defined in subdivision one of section 70.02 of this article.

2. Except as provided in subdivision three or four of this section, a sentence of imprisonment for a felony drug offender shall be a determinate sentence as provided in paragraph (a) of this subdivision.

(a) Term of determinate sentence. Except as provided in paragraph (b) or (c) of this subdivision, the court shall impose a determinate term of imprisonment upon a felony drug offender which shall be imposed by the court in whole or half years, which shall include as a part thereof a period of post-release supervision in accordance with section 70.45 of this article. The terms of imprisonment authorized for such determinate sentences are as follows:

(i) for a class B felony, the term shall be at least one year and shall not exceed nine years, except that for the class B felony of criminal sale of a controlled substance in or near school grounds as defined in subdivision two of section 220.44 of this chapter or on a school bus as defined in subdivision seventeen of section 220.00 of this chapter or criminal sale of a controlled substance to a child as defined in section 220.48 of this chapter, the term shall be at least two years and shall not exceed nine years;

(ii) for a class C felony, the term shall be at least one year and shall not exceed five and one-half years;

(iii) for a class D felony, the term shall be at least one year and shall not exceed two and one-half years; and

(iv) for a class E felony, the term shall be at least one year and shall not exceed one and one-half years.

(b) Probation. Notwithstanding any other provision of law, the court may sentence a defendant convicted of a class B, class C, class D or class E felony offense defined in article two hundred twenty or two hundred twenty-one of this chapter to probation in accordance with the provisions of sections 60.04 and 65.00 of this chapter.

(c) Alternative definite sentence for class B, class C, class D, and class E felonies. If the court, having regard to the nature and circumstances of the crime and to the history and character of the defendant, is of the opinion that a sentence of imprisonment is necessary but that it would be unduly harsh to impose a determinate sentence upon a person convicted of a class C, class D or class E felony offense defined in article two hundred twenty or two hundred twenty-one of this chapter, or a class B felony defined in article two hundred twenty of this chapter, other than the class B felony defined in section 220.48 of this chapter, as added by a chapter of the laws of two thousand nine the court may impose a definite sentence of imprisonment and fix a term of one year or less.

(d) The court may direct that a determinate sentence imposed on a defendant convicted of a class B felony, other than the class B felony defined in section 220.48 of this chapter, pursuant to this subdivision be executed as a sentence of parole supervision in accordance with section 410.91 of the criminal procedure law.

3. Sentence of imprisonment for second felony drug offender.

(a) Applicability. This subdivision shall apply to a second felony drug offender whose prior felony conviction was not a violent felony.

(b) Authorized sentence. Except as provided in paragraphs (c), (d) and (e) of this subdivision, when the court has found pursuant to the provisions of section 400.21 of the criminal procedure law that a defendant is a second felony drug offender who stands convicted of a class B, class C, class D or class E felony offense defined in article two hundred twenty or two hundred twenty-one of this chapter the court shall impose a determinate sentence of imprisonment. Such determinate sentence shall include as a part thereof a period of post-release supervision in accordance with section 70.45 of this article. The terms of such determinate sentence shall be imposed by the court in whole or half years as follows:

(i) for a class B felony, the term shall be at least two years and shall not exceed twelve years;

(ii) for a class C felony, the term shall be at least one and one-half years and shall not exceed eight years;

(iii) for a class D felony, the term shall be at least one and one-half years and shall not exceed four years; and

(iv) for a class E felony, the term shall be at least one and one-half years and shall not exceed two years.

(c) Probation. Notwithstanding any other provision of law, the court may sentence a second felony drug offender convicted of a class B felony to lifetime probation in accordance with the provisions of section 65.00 of this chapter and may sentence a second felony drug offender convicted of a class C, class D or class E felony to probation in accordance with the provisions of section 65.00 of this chapter.

(d) Sentence of parole supervision. In the case of a person sentenced for a specified offense or offenses as defined in subdivision five of section 410.91 of the criminal procedure law, who stands convicted of no other felony offense, who has not previously been convicted of either a violent felony offense as defined in section 70.02 of this article, a class A felony offense or a class B felony offense, and is not under the jurisdiction of or awaiting delivery to the department of corrections and community supervision, the court may direct that a determinate sentence imposed pursuant to this subdivision shall be executed as a parole supervision sentence as defined in and pursuant to the procedures prescribed in section 410.91 of the criminal procedure law.

(e) Alternate definite sentence for class C, class D and class E felonies. If the court, having regard to the nature and circumstances of the crime and to the history and character of the defendant, is of the opinion that a sentence of imprisonment is necessary but that it would be unduly harsh to impose a determinate sentence upon a person convicted of a class C, class D or class E felony offense defined in article two hundred twenty or two hundred twenty-one of this chapter, the court may impose a definite sentence of imprisonment and fix a term of one year or less.

4. Sentence of imprisonment for second felony drug offender previously convicted of a violent felony.

(a) Applicability. This subdivision shall apply to a second felony drug offender whose prior felony conviction was a violent felony.

(b) Authorized sentence. When the court has found pursuant to the provisions of section 400.21 of the criminal procedure law that a defendant is a second felony drug offender whose prior felony conviction was a violent felony, who stands convicted of a class B, class C, class D or class E felony offense defined in article two hundred twenty or two hundred twenty-one of this chapter, the court shall impose a determinate sentence of imprisonment. Such determinate sentence shall include as a part thereof a period of post-release supervision in accordance with section 70.45 of this article. The terms of such determinate sentence shall be imposed by the court in whole or half years as follows:

(i) for a class B felony, the term shall be at least six years and shall not exceed fifteen years;

(ii) for a class C felony, the term shall be at least three and one-half years and shall not exceed nine years;

(iii) for a class D felony, the term shall be at least two and one-half years and shall not exceed four and one-half years; and

(iv) for a class E felony, the term shall be at least two years and shall not exceed two and one-half years.

HISTORY: Add, L 2004, ch 738, § 36, eff Jan 13, 2005; amd, L 2006, ch 436, § 1, eff Sept 1, 2006, L 2009, ch 56, §§ 21–25 (Part AAA), eff April 7, 2009, L 2011, ch 62, § 127-k (Part C, Subpart B), eff March 31, 2011.

§ 70.71. Sentence of imprisonment for a class A felony drug offender

1. For the purposes of this section, the following terms shall mean:

(a) "Felony drug offender" means a defendant who stands convicted of any class A felony as defined in article two hundred twenty of this chapter.

(b) "Second felony drug offender" means a second felony offender as that term is defined in subdivision one of section 70.06 of this article, who stands convicted of and is to be sentenced for any class A felony as defined in article two hundred twenty of this chapter.

(c) "Violent felony offense" shall have the same meaning as that term is defined in subdivision one of section 70.02 of this article.

2. Sentence of imprisonment for a first felony drug offender.

(a) Applicability. Except as provided in subdivision three, four or five of this section, this subdivision shall apply to a person convicted of a class A felony as defined in article two hundred twenty of this chapter.

(b) Authorized sentence. The court shall impose a determinate term of imprisonment which shall be imposed by the court in whole or half years and which shall include as a part thereof a period of post-release supervision in accordance with section 70.45 of this article. The terms authorized for such determinate sentences are as follows:

(i) for a class A-I felony, the term shall be at least eight years and shall not exceed twenty years;

(ii) for a class A-II felony, the term shall be at least three years and shall not exceed ten years.

(c) Lifetime probation. Notwithstanding any other provision of law, the court may sentence a defendant convicted of a class A-II felony defined in article two hundred twenty of this chapter to lifetime probation in accordance with the provisions of section 65.00 of this chapter.

3. Sentence of imprisonment for a second felony drug offender.

(a) Applicability. This subdivision shall apply to a second felony drug offender whose prior felony conviction or convictions did not include one or more violent felony offenses.

(b) Authorized sentence. When the court has found pursuant to the provisions of section 400.21 of the criminal procedure law that a defendant is a second felony drug offender who stands convicted of a class A felony as defined in article two hundred twenty or two hundred twenty-one of this chapter, the court shall impose a determinate sentence of imprisonment. Such determinate sentence shall include as a part thereof a period of post-release supervision in accordance with section 70.45 of this article. Such determinate sentence shall be imposed by the court in whole or half years as follows:

(i) for a class A-I felony, the term shall be at least twelve years and shall not exceed twenty-four years;

(ii) for a class A-II felony, the term shall be at least six years and shall not exceed fourteen years.

(c) Lifetime probation. Notwithstanding any other provision of law, the court may sentence a defendant convicted of a class A-II felony defined in article two hundred twenty of this chapter to lifetime probation in accordance with the provisions of section 65.00 of this chapter.

4. Sentence of imprisonment for a second felony drug offender previously convicted of a violent felony offense.

(a) Applicability. This subdivision shall apply to a second felony drug offender whose prior felony conviction was a violent felony.

(b) Authorized sentence. When the court has found pursuant to the provisions of section 400.21 of the criminal procedure law that a defendant is a second felony drug offender whose prior felony conviction was a violent felony, who stands convicted of a class A felony as defined in article two hundred twenty or two hundred twenty-one of this chapter, the court shall impose a determinate sentence of imprisonment. Such determinate sentence shall include as a part thereof a period of post-release supervision in accordance with section 70.45 of this article. Such determinate sentence shall be imposed by the court in whole or half years as follows:

(i) for a class A-I felony, the term shall be at least fifteen years and shall not exceed thirty years;

(ii) for a class A-II felony, the term shall be at least eight years and shall not exceed seventeen years.

5. Sentence of imprisonment for operating as a major trafficker.

(a) Applicability. This subdivision shall apply to a person convicted of the class A-I felony of operating as a major trafficker as defined in section 220.77 of this chapter.

(b) Authorized sentence. Except as provided in paragraph (c) of this subdivision, the court shall impose an indeterminate term of imprisonment for an A-I felony, in accordance with the provisions of section 70.00 of this article.

(c) Alternative determinate sentence. If a defendant stands convicted of violating section 220.77 of this chapter, and if the court, having regard to the nature and circumstances of the crime and the history and character of the defendant, is of the opinion that a sentence of imprisonment is necessary but that it would be unduly harsh to impose the indeterminate sentence for a class A-I felony specified under section 70.00 of this article, the court may instead impose the determinate sentence of imprisonment authorized by clause (i) of subparagraph (b) of subdivision two of this section for a class A-I drug felony; in such case, the reasons for the court's opinion shall be set forth on the record.

HISTORY: Add, L 2004, ch 738, § 36, eff Jan 13, 2005. Sub 2, par (a), amd, L 2009, ch 56, § 26 (Part AAA), eff Nov 1, 2009. Sub 5, add, L 2009, ch 56, § 26 (Part AAA), eff Nov 1, 2009.

§ 70.80. Sentences of imprisonment for conviction of a felony sex offense

1. Definitions.

(a) For the purposes of this section, a "felony sex offense" means a conviction of any felony defined in article one hundred thirty of this chapter, including a sexually motivated felony, or patronizing a prostitute in the first degree as defined in section 230.06 of this chapter, incest in the second degree as defined in section 255.26 of this chapter, or incest in the first degree as defined in section 255.27 of this chapter, or a felony attempt or conspiracy to commit any of the above.

(b) A felony sex offense shall be deemed a "violent felony sex offense" if it is for an offense defined as a violent felony offense in section 70.02 of this article, or for a sexually motivated felony as defined in section 130.91 of this chapter where the specified offense is a violent felony offense as defined in section 70.02 of this article.

(c) For the purposes of this section, a "predicate felony sex offender" means a person who stands convicted of any felony sex offense as defined in paragraph (a) of this subdivision, other than a class A-I felony, after having previously been subjected to one or more predicate felony convictions as defined in subdivision one of section 70.06 or subdivision one of section 70.04 of this article.

(d) For purposes of this section, a "violent felony offense" is any felony defined in subdivision one of section 70.02 of this article, and a "non-violent felony offense" is any felony not defined therein.

2. In imposing a sentence within the authorized statutory range for any felony sex offense, the court may consider all relevant factors set forth in section 1.05 of this chapter, and in particular, may consider the defendant's criminal history, if any, including any history of sex offenses; any mental illness or mental abnormality from which the defendant may suffer; the defendant's ability or inability to control his sexual behavior; and, if the defendant has difficulty controlling such behavior, the extent to which that difficulty may pose a threat to society.

3. Except as provided by subdivision four, five, six, seven or eight of this section, or when a defendant is being sentenced for a conviction of the class A-II felonies of predatory sexual assault and predatory sexual assault against a child as defined in sections 130.95 and 130.96 of this chapter, or for any class A-I sexually motivated felony for which a life sentence or a life without parole sentence must be imposed, a sentence imposed upon a defendant convicted of a felony sex offense shall be a determinate sentence. The determinate sentence shall be imposed by the court in whole or half years, and shall include as a part thereof a period of post-release supervision in accordance with subdivision two-a of section 70.45 of this article. Persons eligible for sentencing under section 70.07 of this article governing second child sexual assault felonies shall be sentenced under such section and paragraph (j) of subdivision two-a of section 70.45 of this article.

4. (a) Sentences of imprisonment for felony sex offenses. Except as provided in subdivision five, six, seven, or eight of this section, the term of the determinate sentence must be fixed by the court as follows:

(i) for a class B felony, the term must be at least five years and must not exceed twenty-five years;

(ii) for a class C felony, the term must be at least three and one-half years and must not exceed fifteen years;

(iii) for a class D felony, the term must be at least two years and must not exceed seven years; and

(iv) for a class E felony, the term must be at least one and one-half years and must not exceed four years.

(b) Probation. The court may sentence a defendant convicted of a class D or class E felony sex offense to probation in accordance with the provisions of section 65.00 of this title.

(c) Alternative definite sentences for class D and class E felony sex offenses. If the court, having regard to the nature and circumstances of the crime and to the history and character of the defendant, is of the opinion that a sentence of imprisonment is necessary but that it would be unduly harsh to impose a determinate sentence upon a person convicted of a class D or class E felony sex offense, the court may impose a definite sentence of imprisonment and fix a term of one year or less.

5. Sentence of imprisonment for a predicate felony sex offender.

(a) Applicability. This subdivision shall apply to a predicate felony sex offender who stands convicted of a non-violent felony sex offense and who was previously convicted of one or more felonies.

(b) Non-violent predicate felony offense. When the court has found, pursuant to the provisions of the criminal procedure law, that a person is a predicate felony sex offender, and the person's predicate conviction was for a non-violent felony offense, the court must impose a determinate sentence of imprisonment, the term of which must be fixed by the court as follows:

(i) for a class B felony, the term must be at least eight years and must not exceed twenty-five years;

(ii) for a class C felony, the term must be at least five years and must not exceed fifteen years;

(iii) for a class D felony, the term must be at least three years and must not exceed seven years; and

(iv) for a class E felony, the term must be at least two years and must not exceed four years.

(c) Violent predicate felony offense. When the court has found, pursuant to the provisions of the criminal procedure law, that a person is a predicate felony sex offender, and the person's predicate conviction was for a violent felony offense, the court must impose a determinate sentence of imprisonment, the term of which must be fixed by the court as follows:

(i) for a class B felony, the term must be at least nine years and must not exceed twenty-five years;

(ii) for a class C felony, the term must be at least six years and must not exceed fifteen years;

(iii) for a class D felony, the term must be at least four years and must not exceed seven years; and

(iv) for a class E felony, the term must be at least two and one-half years and must not exceed four years.

(d) A defendant who stands convicted of a non-violent felony sex offense, other than a class A-I or class A-II felony, who is adjudicated a persistent felony offender under section 70.10 of this article, shall be sentenced pursuant to the provisions of section 70.10 or pursuant to this subdivision.

6. Sentence of imprisonment for a violent felony sex offense. Except as provided in subdivisions seven and eight of this section, a defendant who stands convicted of a violent felony sex offense must be sentenced pursuant to the provisions of section 70.02, section 70.04, subdivision six of section 70.06, section 70.08, or section 70.10 of this article, as applicable.

7. Sentence for a class A felony sex offense. When a person stands convicted of a sexually motivated felony pursuant to section 130.91 of this chapter and the specified offense is a class A felony, the court must sentence the defendant in accordance with the provisions of:

(a) section 60.06 of this chapter and section 70.00 of this article, as applicable, if such offense is a class A-I felony; and

(b) section 70.00, 70.06 or 70.08 of this article, as applicable, if such offense is a class A-II felony.

8. Whenever a juvenile offender stands convicted of a felony sex offense, he or she must be sentenced pursuant to the provisions of sections 60.10 and 70.05 of this chapter.

9. Every determinate sentence for a felony sex offense, as defined in paragraph (a) of subdivision one of this section, imposed pursuant to any section of this article, shall include as a part thereof a period of post-release supervision in accordance with subdivision two-a of section 70.45 of this article.

HISTORY: Add, L 2007, ch 7, § 30, eff April 13, 2007.

§ 70.85. Transitional exception to determinate sentencing laws

This section shall apply only to cases in which a determinate sentence was imposed between September first, nineteen hundred ninety-eight, and the effective date of this section, and was required by law to include a term of post-release supervision, but the court did not explicitly state such a term when pronouncing sentence. When such a case is again before the court pursuant to section six hundred one-d of the correction law or otherwise, for consideration of whether to resentence, the court may, notwithstanding any other provision of law but only on consent of the district attorney, re-impose the originally imposed determinate sentence of imprisonment without any term of post-release supervision, which then shall be deemed a lawful sentence.

HISTORY: Add, L 2008, ch 141, § 2, eff June 30, 2008.

ARTICLE 75   [REPEALED]

HISTORY: Add, L 1965, ch 1030; repealed, L 1974, ch 652, § 7, L 1974, ch 653, § 7, eff July 31, 1974. (Laws 1974, ch 653, § 8, changed effective date from May 30, 1974 to July 31, 1974.).

ARTICLE 80   FINES

HISTORY: Add, L 1965, ch 1030, eff Sept 1, 1967.

§ 80.00. Fine for felony

1. A sentence to pay a fine for a felony shall be a sentence to pay an amount, fixed by the court, not exceeding the higher of

a. five thousand dollars; or

b. double the amount of the defendant's gain from the commission of the crime or, if the defendant is convicted of a crime defined in article four hundred ninety-six of this chapter, any higher amount not exceeding three times the amount of the defendant's gain from the commission of such offense; or

c. if the conviction is for any felony defined in article two hundred twenty or two hundred twenty-one of this chapter, according to the following schedule:

(i) for A-I felonies, one hundred thousand dollars;

(ii) for A-II felonies, fifty thousand dollars;

(iii) for B felonies, thirty thousand dollars;

(iv) for C felonies, fifteen thousand dollars.

When imposing a fine pursuant to the provisions of this paragraph, the court shall consider the profit gained by defendant's conduct, whether the amount of the fine is disproportionate to the conduct in which defendant engaged, its impact on any victims, and defendant's economic circumstances, including the defendant's ability to pay, the effect of the fine upon his or her immediate family or any other persons to whom the defendant owes an obligation of support.

2. As used in this section the term "gain" means the amount of money or the value of property derived from the commission of the crime, less the amount of money or the value of property returned to the victim of the crime or seized by or surrendered to lawful authority prior to the time sentence is imposed.

3. When the court imposes a fine for a felony pursuant to paragraph b of subdivision one of this section, the court shall make a finding as to the amount of the defendant's gain from the crime. If the record does not contain sufficient evidence to support such a finding or to permit adequate consideration of the matters specified in paragraph c of subdivision one of this section, the court may conduct a hearing upon such issues.

4. Exception. The provisions of this section shall not apply to a corporation.

5. All moneys in excess of five thousand dollars received or collected in payment of a fine imposed pursuant to paragraph c of subdivision one of this section are the property of the state and the state comptroller shall deposit all such fines to the rehabilitative alcohol and substance treatment fund established pursuant to section ninety-seven-cc of the state finance law.

6. Notwithstanding any inconsistent provision of subdivision one of this section a sentence to pay a fine for a felony set forth in the vehicle and traffic law shall be a sentence to pay an amount fixed by the court in accordance with the provisions of the law that defines the crime.

7. When the court imposes a fine pursuant to section 145.22 or 145.23 of this chapter, the court shall direct that no less than ten percent of such fine be credited to the state cemetery vandalism restoration and administration fund created pursuant to section ninety-seven-r of the state finance law.

HISTORY: Add, L 1965, ch 1030; amd, L 1977, ch 352, § 1, eff Sept 1, 1977, L 1989, ch 338, § 17, eff Nov 1, 1989, L 1990, ch 892, § 2, eff July 30, 1990, L 1997, ch 165, § 3, eff Nov 1, 1997, L 2014, ch 55, § 27 (Part H, Subpart A), eff April 30, 2014.

§ 80.05. Fines for misdemeanors and violation

1. Class A misdemeanor. A sentence to pay a fine for a class A misdemeanor shall be a sentence

to pay an amount, fixed by the court, not exceeding one thousand dollars, provided, however, that a sentence imposed for a violation of section 215.80 of this chapter may include a fine in an amount equivalent to double the value of the property unlawfully disposed of in the commission of the crime.

2. Class B misdemeanor. A sentence to pay a fine for a class B misdemeanor shall be a sentence to pay an amount, fixed by the court, not exceeding five hundred dollars.

3. Unclassified misdemeanor. A sentence to pay a fine for an unclassified misdemeanor shall be a sentence to pay an amount, fixed by the court, in accordance with the provisions of the law or ordinance that defines the crime.

4. Violation. A sentence to pay a fine for a violation shall be a sentence to pay an amount, fixed by the court, not exceeding two hundred fifty dollars.

In the case of a violation defined outside this chapter, if the amount of the fine is expressly specified in the law or ordinance that defines the offense, the amount of the fine shall be fixed in accordance with that law or ordinance.

5. Alternative sentence. If a person has gained money or property through the commission of any misdemeanor or violation then upon conviction thereof, the court, in lieu of imposing the fine authorized for the offense under one of the above subdivisions, may sentence the defendant to pay an amount, fixed by the court, not exceeding double the amount of the defendant's gain from the commission of the offense; provided, however, that the amount fixed by the court pursuant to this subdivision upon a conviction under section 11-1904 of the environmental conservation law shall not exceed five thousand dollars. In such event the provisions of subdivisions two and three of section 80.00 shall be applicable to the sentence.

6. Exception. The provisions of this section shall not apply to a corporation.

HISTORY: Add, L 1965, ch 1030, eff Sept 1, 1967. Sub 1, amd, L 1984, ch 669, § 2, eff Aug 1, 1984 and applicable to crimes committed on and after Aug 1, 1984. Sub 5, amd, L 1977, ch 352, § 2, eff Sept 1, 1977. Sub 5, amd, L 1999, ch 208, § 1, eff Nov 1, 1999.

§ 80.10. Fines for corporations

1. In general. A sentence to pay a fine, when imposed on a corporation for an offense defined in this chapter or for an offense defined outside this chapter for which no special corporate fine is specified, shall be a sentence to pay an amount, fixed by the court, not exceeding:

(a) Ten thousand dollars, when the conviction is of a felony;

(b) Five thousand dollars, when the conviction is of a class A misdemeanor or of an unclassified misdemeanor for which a term of imprisonment in excess of three months is authorized;

(c) Two thousand dollars, when the conviction is of a class B misdemeanor or of an unclassified misdemeanor for which the authorized term of imprisonment is not in excess of three months;

(d) Five hundred dollars, when the conviction is of a violation;

(e) Any higher amount not exceeding double the amount of the corporation's gain from the commission of the offense or, if the corporation is convicted of a crime defined in article four hundred ninety-six of this chapter, any higher amount not exceeding three times the amount of the corporation's gain from the commission of such offense.

2. Exception. In the case of an offense defined outside this chapter, if a special fine for a corporation is expressly specified in the law or ordinance that defines the offense, the fine fixed by the court shall be as follows:

(a) An amount within the limits specified in the law or ordinance that defines the offense; or

(b) Any higher amount not exceeding double the amount of the corporation's gain from the commission of the offense.

3. Determination of amount or value. When the court imposes the fine authorized by paragraph (e) of subdivision one or paragraph (b) of subdivision two for any offense the provisions of subdivision three of section 80.00 shall be applicable to the sentence.

HISTORY: Add, L 1965, ch 1030, eff Sept 1, 1967, with substance derived in part from § 1932; amd, L 2014, ch 55, § 28 (Part H, Subpart A), eff April 30, 2014.

§ 80.15. Multiple offenses

Where a person is convicted of two or more offenses committed through a single act or omission, or through an act or omission which in itself constituted one of the offenses and also was a material element of the other, and the court imposes a sentence of imprisonment or a fine or both for one of the offenses, a fine shall not be imposed for the other. The provisions of this section shall not apply to any offense or offenses set forth in the vehicle and traffic law.

HISTORY: Add, L 1965, ch 1030, with substance derived from § 1938; amd, L 1990, ch 892, § 3, eff July 30, 1990.

ARTICLE 85   SENTENCE OF INTERMITTENT IMPRISONMENT

HISTORY: Add, L 1970, ch 477, § 1, eff May 8, 1970.

§ 85.00. Sentence of intermittent imprisonment

1. Definition. A sentence of intermittent imprisonment is a revocable sentence of imprisonment to be served on days or during certain periods of days, or both, specified by the court as part of the sentence. A person who receives a sentence of intermittent imprisonment shall be incarcerated in the institution to which he is committed at such times as are specified by the court in the sentence.

2. Authorization for use of sentence. The court may impose a sentence of intermittent imprisonment in any case where:

(a) the court is imposing sentence, upon a person other than a second or persistent felony offender, for a class D or class E felony or for any offense that is not a felony; and

(b) the court is not imposing any other sentence of imprisonment upon the defendant at the same time; and

(c) the defendant is not under any other sentence of imprisonment with a term in excess of fifteen days imposed by any other court; and

3. Duration of sentence. A sentence of intermittent imprisonment may be for any term that could

be imposed as a definite sentence of imprisonment for the offense for which such sentence is imposed. The term of the sentence shall commence on the day it is imposed and shall be calculated upon the basis of the duration of its term, rather than upon the basis of the days spent in confinement, so that no person shall be subject to any such sentence for a period that is longer than a period that commences on the date the sentence is imposed and ends on the date the term of the longest definite sentence for the offense would have expired, after deducting the credit that would have been applicable to a definite sentence for jail time but without regard to any credit authorized to be allowed against the term of a definite sentence for good behavior. The provisions of section five hundred-1 of the correction law shall not be applicable to a sentence of intermittent imprisonment.

4. Imposition of sentence.

(a) When the court imposes a sentence of intermittent imprisonment the court shall specify in the sentence:

(i) that the court is imposing a sentence of intermittent imprisonment;

(ii) the term of such sentence;

(iii) the days or parts of days on which the sentence is to be served, but except as provided in paragraph (iv) hereof such specification need not include the dates on which such days fall; and

(iv) the first and last dates on which the defendant is to be incarcerated under the sentence.

(b) The court, in its discretion, may specify any day or days or parts thereof on which the defendant shall be confined and may specify a period to commence at the commencement of the sentence and not to exceed fifteen days during which the defendant is to be continuously confined.

HISTORY: Add, L 1970, ch 477, § 1, eff May 8, 1970. Sub 2, par (a), amd, L 1973, ch 277, § 11, eff Sept 1, 1973. Sub 2, par (d), repealed, L 1973, ch 523, § 1, eff Sept 1, 1973. Sub 3, amd, L 1987, ch 304, § 2, eff Sept 18, 1987.

§ 85.05. Modification and revocation of sentences of intermittent imprisonment

1. Authorization. A sentence of intermittent imprisonment may be modified by the court in its discretion upon application of the defendant; and the court on its own motion may modify or revoke any such sentence if:

(a) the court is satisfied during the term of the sentence that the defendant has committed another offense during such term;

(b) the defendant has failed to report to the institution to which he has been committed, or to the institution designated by the head of the agency to which he has been committed, on a day or dates specified in the commitment and is unable or unwilling to furnish a reasonable and acceptable explanation for such failure; or

(c) the defendant has violated a rule or regulation of the institution or agency to which he has been committed and the head of such institution or agency or someone delegated by him has reported such violation in writing to the court.

2. Interruption of sentence. In any case where the defendant fails to report to the institution or to an institution of the agency to which he has been committed, the term of the sentence shall be interrupted and such interruption shall continue until the defendant either reports to such institution

or appears before the court that imposed the sentence, whichever occurs first. If the defendant reports to the institution before he appears before the court, he shall be brought before the court.

3. Action by court. The court shall not modify or revoke a sentence of intermittent imprisonment unless the defendant has been afforded an opportunity to be heard. Any modification of a sentence of intermittent imprisonment:

(a) may provide (i) for different or additional or fewer days or parts of days on which the defendant is to be confined, or (ii) where the defendant has failed to report as specified in the sentence, an extension of the term of the sentence for the period during which it was interrupted, or (iii) for both; and

(b) shall be by written order of the court and shall be delivered and filed in the same manner as the original sentence, as specified in subdivision two of section 85.10 of this article.

4. Jail time. Where a sentence of intermittent imprisonment is revoked and a sentence of imprisonment is imposed in its place for the same offense, time spent in confinement under the sentence of intermittent imprisonment shall be calculated as jail time under subdivision three of section 70.30 of this chapter and shall be added to any jail time accrued against such sentence prior to imposition thereof.

HISTORY: Add, L 1970, ch 477, § 1, eff May 8, 1970.

§ 85.10. Commitment; notifications; warrants

1. Commitment. Commitment under a sentence of intermittent imprisonment and execution of the judgment shall be in accordance with the procedure applicable to a definite sentence of imprisonment, except that: (a) detention of the defendant under the judgment shall be executed during the times specified in the sentence; and (b) the court may provide that the defendant is to report to a specified institution on a specified date at a specified time to commence service of the sentence and in such case the defendant need not be taken into or retained in custody when sentence is imposed.

2. Notifications. A written copy of the sentence imposed by the court signed by the judge who imposed the sentence shall be delivered to the defendant and shall be annexed to the commitment and to each copy of the commitment required to be delivered or filed. When the defendant is not taken into or retained in custody at the time sentence is imposed, the commitment and copy of the sentence shall forthwith be delivered to the person whose duty it is to execute the judgment. If at any time the defendant fails to report for confinement as provided in the sentence the officer in charge of the institution or department to which such commitment is made or someone designated by such officer shall forthwith notify the court in writing of such failure to report.

3. Warrants. Upon receipt of any such notification the court may issue a warrant to an appropriate police officer or peace officer directing him to take the defendant into custody and bring him before the court. The court may then commit such person to custody or fix bail or release him on his own recognizance for future appearance before the court.

HISTORY: Add, L 1970, ch 477, § 1, eff May 8, 1970. Sub 3, amd, L 1980, ch 843, § 38, eff Sept 1, 1980.

§ 85.15. Subsequent sentences

1. [Until Sept 1, 2015] Indeterminate and determinate sentences. The service of an indeterminate or a determinate sentence of imprisonment shall satisfy any sentence of intermittent imprisonment imposed on a person for an offense committed prior to the time the indeterminate or determinate sentence was imposed. A person who is serving a sentence of intermittent imprisonment at the time

an indeterminate or a determinate sentence of imprisonment is imposed shall be delivered to the custody of the state department of corrections and community supervision to commence service of the indeterminate or determinate sentence immediately.

1. [Eff Sept 1, 2015] Indeterminate and reformatory sentences. The service of an indeterminate or a reformatory sentence of imprisonment shall satisfy any sentence of intermittent imprisonment imposed on a person for an offense committed prior to the time the indeterminate or reformatory sentence was imposed. A person who is serving a sentence of intermittent imprisonment at the time an indeterminate or a reformatory sentence of imprisonment is imposed shall be delivered to the custody of the state department of corrections and community supervision to commence service of the indeterminate or reformatory sentence immediately.

2. Definite sentences. If a definite sentence of imprisonment is imposed on a person who is under a previously imposed sentence of intermittent imprisonment, such person shall commence service of the definite sentence immediately. Where such definite sentence is for a term in excess of thirty days, the service of such sentence shall satisfy the sentence of intermittent imprisonment unless the sentence of intermittent imprisonment is revoked, or a warrant is issued pursuant to subdivision three of section 85.10 of this article and prior to satisfaction of, or conditional release under, such definite sentence of imprisonment.

HISTORY: Add, L 1970, ch 477, § 1, eff May 8, 1970; amd, L 1995, ch 3, § 20, eff Oct 1, 1995, repealed eff Sept 1, 2015, L 2011, ch 62, § 127-l (Part C, Subpart B), eff March 31, 2011, L 2011, ch 62, § 127-m (Part C, Subpart B), eff Sept 1, 2015.

§ 85.20. [Repealed]

HISTORY: Add, L 1970, ch 477, § 1; repealed, L 1973, ch 523, § 2, eff Sept 1, 1973.

PART THREE   Specific Offenses

Title G
Anticipatory Offenses

Title H
Offenses Against the Person Involving Physical Injury, Sexual Conduct, Restraint and Intimidation

Title I
Offenses Involving Damage to and Intrusion Upon Property

Title J
Offenses Involving Theft

Title K
Offenses Involving Fraud

Title L
Offenses Against Public Administration

Title M
Offenses Against Public Health and Morals

Title N
Offenses Against Public Order, Public Sensibilities and the Right to Privacy

Title O
Offenses Against Marriage, The Family, and The Welfare Of Children and Incompetents

Title P
Offenses Against Public Safety

HISTORY: Add, L 1965, ch 1030, eff Sept 1, 1967.

TITLE G   Anticipatory Offenses
ARTICLE 100
CRIMINAL SOLICITATION
ARTICLE 105
CONSPIRACY
ARTICLE 110
ATTEMPT
ARTICLE 115
CRIMINAL FACILITATION

HISTORY: Add, L 1965, ch 1030, eff Sept 1, 1967.

ARTICLE 100   CRIMINAL SOLICITATION

HISTORY: Add, L 1965, ch 1030, eff Sept 1, 1967.

§ 100.00. Criminal solicitation in the fifth degree

A person is guilty of criminal solicitation in the fifth degree when, with intent that another person engage in conduct constituting a crime, he solicits, requests, commands, importunes or otherwise attempts to cause such other person to engage in such conduct.

Criminal solicitation in the fifth degree is a violation.

HISTORY: Add, L 1965, ch 1030; amd, L 1978, ch 422, § 1, eff Sept 1, 1978. Section heading, amd, L 1978, ch 422, § 1, eff Sept 1, 1978.

§ 100.05. Criminal solicitation in the fourth degree

A person is guilty of criminal solicitation in the fourth degree when:

1. with intent that another person engage in conduct constituting a felony, he solicits, requests, commands, importunes or otherwise attempts to cause such other person to engage in such conduct; or

2. being over eighteen years of age, with intent that another person under sixteen years of age engage in conduct that would constitute a crime, he solicits, requests, commands, importunes or otherwise attempts to cause such other person to engage in such conduct.

Criminal solicitation in the fourth degree is a class A misdemeanor.

HISTORY: Add, L 1965, ch 1030; amd, L 1978, ch 422, § 2, eff Sept 1, 1978. Section heading, amd, L 1978, ch 422, § 2, eff Sept 1, 1978. Sub 1, formerly part of first par, so designated and amd, L 1978, ch 422, § 2, eff Sept 1, 1978. Sub 2, add, L 1978, ch 422, § 2, eff Sept 1, 1978.

§ 100.08. Criminal solicitation in the third degree

A person is guilty of criminal solicitation in the third degree when, being over eighteen years of age, with intent that another person under sixteen years of age engage in conduct that would constitute a felony, he solicits, requests, commands, importunes or otherwise attempts to cause such other person to engage in such conduct.

Criminal solicitation in the third degree is a class E felony.

HISTORY: Add, L 1978, ch 422, § 3, eff Sept 1, 1978.

§ 100.10. Criminal solicitation in the second degree

A person is guilty of criminal solicitation in the second degree when, with intent that another person engage in conduct constituting a class A felony, he solicits, requests, commands, importunes or otherwise attempts to cause such other person to engage in such conduct.

Criminal solicitation in the second degree is a class D felony.

HISTORY: Add, L 1965, ch 1030; amd, L 1972, ch 292, § 1, L 1978, ch 422, § 4, eff Sept 1, 1978. Section heading, amd, L 1978, ch 422, § 4, eff Sept 1, 1978.

§ 100.13. Criminal solicitation in the first degree

A person is guilty of criminal solicitation in the first degree when, being over eighteen years of age, with intent that another person under sixteen years of age engage in conduct that would constitute a class A felony, he solicits, requests, commands, importunes or otherwise attempts to cause such other person to engage in such conduct.

Criminal solicitation in the first degree is a class C felony.

HISTORY: Add, L 1978, ch 422, § 5, eff Sept 1, 1978.

§ 100.15. Criminal solicitation; no defense

It is no defense to a prosecution for criminal solicitation that the person solicited could not be guilty of the crime solicited owing to criminal irresponsibility or other legal incapacity or exemption, or to unawareness of the criminal nature of the conduct solicited or of the defendant's criminal purpose or to other factors precluding the mental state required for the commission of the crime in question.

HISTORY: Add, L 1965, ch 1030, eff Sept 1, 1967.

§ 100.20. Criminal solicitation; exemption

A person is not guilty of criminal solicitation when his solicitation constitutes conduct of a kind that is necessarily incidental to the commission of the crime solicited. When under such circumstances the solicitation constitutes an offense other than criminal solicitation which is related to but separate from the crime solicited, the actor is guilty of such related and separate offense only and not of criminal solicitation.

HISTORY: Add, L 1965, ch 1030, eff Sept 1, 1967.

ARTICLE 105   CONSPIRACY

HISTORY: Add, L 1965, ch 1030, eff Sept 1, 1967.

§ 105.00. Conspiracy in the sixth degree

A person is guilty of conspiracy in the sixth degree when, with intent that conduct constituting a crime be performed, he agrees with one or more persons to engage in or cause the performance of such conduct.

Conspiracy in the sixth degree is a class B misdemeanor.

> **HISTORY:** Add, L 1973, ch 1051, § 5; amd, L 1978, ch 422, § 6, eff Sept 1, 1978. Former § 105.00, add, L 1965, ch 1030, with substance derived from L 1909, § 580(1); amd, L 1973, ch 276, § 17, L 1973, ch 278, § 6; repealed, L 1973, ch 1051, § 5, eff Sept 1, 1973. Section heading, amd, L 1978, ch 422, § 6, eff Sept 1, 1978.

§ 105.05. Conspiracy in the fifth degree

A person is guilty of conspiracy in the fifth degree when, with intent that conduct constituting:

1. a felony be performed, he agrees with one or more persons to engage in or cause the performance of such conduct; or

2. a crime be performed, he, being over eighteen years of age, agrees with one or more persons under sixteen years of age to engage in or cause the performance of such conduct.

Conspiracy in the fifth degree is a class A misdemeanor.

> **HISTORY:** Add, L 1973, ch 1051, § 5; amd, L 1978, ch 422, § 6, eff Sept 1, 1978. Former § 105.05, add, L 1965, ch 1030, with substance derived from L 1909, §§ 580(1), 580-a; repealed, L 1973, ch 1051, § 5, eff Sept 1, 1973. (This section was also amended by L 1973, ch 276, § 17, which amendment was repealed by L 1973, ch 278, § 6, both eff Sept 1, 1973.). Section heading, amd, L 1978, ch 422, § 6, eff Sept 1, 1978. Sub 1, formerly part of first par, so designated and amd, L 1978, ch 422, § 6, eff Sept 1, 1978. Sub 2, add, L 1978, ch 422, § 6, eff Sept 1, 1978.

§ 105.10. Conspiracy in the fourth degree

A person is guilty of conspiracy in the fourth degree when, with intent that conduct constituting:

1. a class B or class C felony be performed, he or she agrees with one or more persons to engage in or cause the performance of such conduct; or

2. a felony be performed, he or she, being over eighteen years of age, agrees with one or more persons under sixteen years of age to engage in or cause the performance of such conduct; or

3. the felony of money laundering in the third degree as defined in section 470.10 of this chapter, be performed, he or she agrees with one or more persons to engage in or cause the performance of such conduct.

Conspiracy in the fourth degree is a class E felony.

> **HISTORY:** Add, L 1973, ch 1051, § 5; amd, L 1978, ch 422, § 6, eff Sept 1, 1978. Former § 105.10, add, L 1965, ch 1030, with substance derived from L 1909, §§ 580(1), 580-a; repealed, L 1973, ch 1051, § 5, eff Sept 1, 1973. (This section was also amended by L 1973, ch 276, § 17, which amendment was repealed by L 1973, ch 278, § 6, both eff Sept 1, 1973.). Amd, L 2000, ch 489, § 1, eff Nov 1, 2000. Section heading, amd, L 1978, ch 422, § 6, eff Sept 1, 1978. Sub 1, formerly part of first par, so designated and amd, L 1978, ch 422, § 6, eff Sept 1, 1978. Sub 1, amd, L 2000, ch 489, § 1, eff Nov 1, 2000. Sub 2, add, L 1978, ch 422, § 6, eff Sept 1, 1978. Sub 2, amd, L 2000, ch 489, § 1, eff Nov 1, 2000. Sub 3, add, L 2000, ch 489, § 1, eff Nov 1, 2000.

§ 105.13. Conspiracy in the third degree

A person is guilty of conspiracy in the third degree when, with intent that conduct constituting a class B or a class C felony be performed, he, being over eighteen years of age, agrees with one or more persons under sixteen years of age to engage in or cause the performance of such conduct.

Conspiracy in the third degree is a class D felony.

> **HISTORY:** Add, L 1978, ch 422, § 7, eff Sept 1, 1978.

§ 105.15. Conspiracy in the second degree

A person is guilty of conspiracy in the second degree when, with intent that conduct constituting a class A felony be performed, he agrees with one or more persons to engage in or cause the performance of such conduct.

Conspiracy in the second degree is a class B felony.

> **HISTORY:** Add, L 1973, ch 1051, § 5; amd, L 1978, ch 422, § 8, eff Sept 1, 1978. Former § 105.15, add, L 1965, ch 1030, with substance derived from L 1909, §§ 580(1), 580-a; amd, L 1972, ch 292, § 2, L 1973, ch 276, § 17, L 1973, ch 278, §§ 6, 7; repealed, L 1973, ch 1051, § 5, eff Sept 1, 1973. Section heading, amd, L 1978, ch 422, § 8, eff Sept 1, 1978.

§ 105.17. Conspiracy in the first degree

A person is guilty of conspiracy in the first degree when, with intent that conduct constituting a class A felony be performed, he, being over eighteen years of age, agrees with one or more persons under sixteen years of age to engage in or cause the performance of such conduct.

Conspiracy in the first degree is a class A-I felony.

> **HISTORY:** Add, L 1978, ch 422, § 9, eff Sept 1, 1978. Former § 105.17, add, L 1973, ch 276, § 17; repealed, L 1973, ch 278, § 6, eff Sept 1, 1973.

§ 105.20. Conspiracy; pleading and proof; necessity of overt act

A person shall not be convicted of conspiracy unless an overt act is alleged and proved to have been committed by one of the conspirators in furtherance of the conspiracy.

> **HISTORY:** Add, L 1965, ch 1030, eff Sept 1, 1967, with substance derived from § 583.

§ 105.25. Conspiracy; jurisdiction and venue

1. A person may be prosecuted for conspiracy in the county in which he entered into such conspiracy or in any county in which an overt act in furtherance thereof was committed.

2. An agreement made within this state to engage in or cause the performance of conduct in another jurisdiction is punishable herein as a conspiracy only when such conduct would constitute a crime both under the laws of this state if performed herein and under the laws of the other jurisdiction if performed therein.

3. An agreement made in another jurisdiction to engage in or cause the performance of conduct within this state, which would constitute a crime herein, is punishable herein only when an overt act in furtherance of such conspiracy is committed within this state. Under such circumstances, it is no defense to a prosecution for conspiracy that the conduct which is the objective of the conspiracy would not constitute a crime under the laws of the other jurisdiction if performed therein.

> **HISTORY:** Add, L 1965, ch 1030, eff Sept 1, 1967.

§ 105.30. Conspiracy; no defense

It is no defense to a prosecution for conspiracy that, owing to criminal irresponsibility or other legal incapacity or exemption, or to unawareness of the criminal nature of the agreement or the object conduct or of the defendant's criminal purpose or to other factors precluding the mental state required for the commission of conspiracy or the object crime, one or more of the defendant's co-conspirators could not be guilty of conspiracy or the object crime.

> **HISTORY:** Add, L 1965, ch 1030, eff Sept 1, 1967.

§ 105.35. Conspiracy; enterprise corruption: applicability

For purposes of this article, conspiracy to commit the crime of enterprise corruption in violation of section 460.20 of this chapter shall not constitute an offense.

> **HISTORY:** Add, L 1986, ch 516, § 3, eff Nov 1, 1986.

ARTICLE 110   ATTEMPT

§ 110.00.   **Attempt to commit a crime**
§ 110.05.   **Attempt to commit a crime; punishment**
§ 110.10.   **Attempt to commit a crime; no defense**

> **HISTORY:** Add, L 1965, ch 1030, eff Sept 1, 1967.

§ 110.00. Attempt to commit a crime

A person is guilty of an attempt to commit a crime when, with intent to commit a crime, he engages in conduct which tends to effect the commission of such crime.

> **HISTORY:** Add, L 1965, ch 1030, eff Sept 1, 1967, with substance derived from § 2 in part.

§ 110.05. Attempt to commit a crime; punishment

An attempt to commit a crime is a:

1. Class A-I felony when the crime attempted is the A-I felony of murder in the first degree, aggravated murder as defined in subdivision one of section 125.26 of this chapter, criminal possession of a controlled substance in the first degree, criminal sale of a controlled substance in the first degree, criminal possession of a chemical or biological weapon in the first degree or criminal use of a chemical or biological weapon in the first degree;

2. Class A-II felony when the crime attempted is a class A-II felony;

3. Class B felony when the crime attempted is a class A-I felony except as provided in subdivision one hereof;

4. Class C felony when the crime attempted is a class B felony;

5. Class D felony when the crime attempted is a class C felony;

6. Class E felony when the crime attempted is a class D felony;

7. Class A misdemeanor when the crime attempted is a class E felony;

8. Class B misdemeanor when the crime attempted is a misdemeanor;

9. Class D felony when the crime attempted is bribery in the third degree as defined in section 200.00 of this chapter, a class C felony when the crime attempted is bribery in the second degree as defined in section 200.03 of this chapter and a class B felony when the crime attempted is bribery in the first degree as defined in subdivision two of section 200.04 of this chapter.

> **HISTORY:** Add, L 1965, ch 1030, with substance derived from § 261; amd, L 1970, ch 112, § 1, eff Sept 1, 1970, L 1972, ch 292, § 3, L 1973, ch 276, § 12, eff Sept 1, 1973, L 1974, ch 367, § 3, eff Sept 1, 1974, L 1979, ch 410, § 10, eff Sept 1, 1979, L 2004, ch 1, § 11 (Part A), eff July 23, 2004, L 2006, ch 93, § 2, eff June 7, 2006, L 2014, ch 55, § 8 (Part H, Subpart A), eff March 30, 2014.

§ 110.10. Attempt to commit a crime; no defense

If the conduct in which a person engages otherwise constitutes an attempt to commit a crime pursuant to section 110.00, it is no defense to a prosecution for such attempt that the crime charged to have been attempted was, under the attendant circumstances, factually or legally impossible of commission, if such crime could have been committed had the attendant circumstances been as such person believed them to be.

HISTORY: Add, L 1965, ch 1030, eff Sept 1, 1967.

ARTICLE 115 CRIMINAL FACILITATION

HISTORY: Add, L 1965, ch 1030, eff Sept 1, 1967.

§ 115.00. Criminal facilitation in the fourth degree

A person is guilty of criminal facilitation in the fourth degree when, believing it probable that he is rendering aid:

1. to a person who intends to commit a crime, he engages in conduct which provides such person with means or opportunity for the commission thereof and which in fact aids such person to commit a felony; or

2. to a person under sixteen years of age who intends to engage in conduct which would constitute a crime, he, being over eighteen years of age, engages in conduct which provides such person with means or opportunity for the commission thereof and which in fact aids such person to commit a crime.

Criminal facilitation in the fourth degree is a class A misdemeanor.

HISTORY: Add, L 1965, ch 1030; amd, L 1978, ch 422, § 10, eff Sept 1, 1978. Section heading, amd, L 1978, ch 422, § 10, eff Sept 1, 1978. Sub 1, formerly part of first par, so designated and amd, L 1978, ch 422, § 10, eff Sept 1, 1978. Sub 2, add, L 1978, ch 422, § 10, eff Sept 1, 1978.

§ 115.01. Criminal facilitation in the third degree

A person guilty of criminal facilitation in the third degree, when believing it probable that he is rendering aid to a person under sixteen years of age who intends to engage in conduct that would constitute a felony, he, being over eighteen years of age, engages in conduct which provides such person with means or opportunity for the commission thereof and which in fact aids such person to commit a felony.

Criminal facilitation in the third degree is a class E felony.

HISTORY: Add, L 1978, ch 422, § 11, eff Sept 1, 1978.

§ 115.05. Criminal facilitation in the second degree

A person is guilty of criminal facilitation in the second degree when, believing it probable that he is rendering aid to a person who intends to commit a class A felony, he engages in conduct which provides such person with means or opportunity for the commission thereof and which in fact aids such person to commit such class A felony.

Criminal facilitation in the second degree is a class C felony.

HISTORY: Add, L 1965, ch 1030; amd, L 1972, ch 292, § 4, L 1978, ch 422, § 12, eff Sept 1, 1978. Section heading, amd, L 1978, ch 422, § 12, eff Sept 1, 1978.

§ 115.08. Criminal facilitation in the first degree

A person is guilty of criminal facilitation in the first degree when, believing it probable that he is rendering aid to a person under sixteen years of age who intends to engage in conduct that would constitute a class A felony, he, being over eighteen years of age, engages in conduct which provides such person with means or opportunity for the commission thereof and which in fact aids such person to commit such a class A felony.

Criminal facilitation in the first degree is a class B felony.

HISTORY: Add, L 1978, ch 422, § 13, eff Sept 1, 1978.

§ 115.10. Criminal facilitation; no defense

It is no defense to a prosecution for criminal facilitation that:

1. The person facilitated was not guilty of the underlying felony owing to criminal irresponsibility or other legal incapacity or exemption, or to unawareness of the criminal nature of the conduct in question or to other factors precluding the mental state required for the commission of such felony; or

2. The person facilitated has not been prosecuted for or convicted of the underlying felony, or has previously been acquitted thereof; or

3. The defendant himself is not guilty of the felony which he facilitated because he did not act with the intent or other culpable mental state required for the commission thereof.

HISTORY: Add, L 1965, ch 1030, eff Sept 1, 1967.

§ 115.15. Criminal facilitation; corroboration

A person shall not be convicted of criminal facilitation upon the testimony of a person who has committed the felony charged to have been facilitated unless such testimony be corroborated by such other evidence as tends to connect the defendant with such facilitation.

HISTORY: Add, L 1965, ch 1030, eff Sept 1, 1967.

§ 115.20. Criminal facilitation; definitions and construction

For purposes of this article, such conduct shall include, but not be limited to, making available, selling, exchanging, giving or disposing of a community gun, which in fact, aids a person to commit a crime. "Community gun" shall mean a firearm that is actually shared, made available, sold, exchanged, given or disposed of among or between two or more persons, at least one of whom is not authorized pursuant to law to possess such firearm. "Dispose of" shall have the same meaning as that term is defined in section 265.00 of this chapter. "Share" and "make available" shall, in the case of a firearm, be construed to include knowingly placing such firearm at a location accessible and known to one or more other persons.

HISTORY: Add, L 2013, ch 1, § 31, eff March 16, 2013.

TITLE H   Offenses Against the Person Involving Physical Injury, Sexual Conduct, Restraint and Intimidation

ARTICLE 120
ASSAULT AND RELATED OFFENSES

ARTICLE 121
STRANGULATION AND RELATED OFFENSES

ARTICLE 125
HOMICIDE, ABORTION AND RELATED OFFENSES

ARTICLE 130
SEX OFFENSES

ARTICLE 135
KIDNAPPING, COERCION AND RELATED OFFENSES

HISTORY: Add, L 1965, ch 1030, § 1, eff Sept 1, 1967.

ARTICLE 120   ASSAULT AND RELATED OFFENSES

§ 120.70.   Luring a child

HISTORY: Add, L 1965, ch 1030, eff Sept 1, 1967.

§ 120.00. Assault in the third degree

A person is guilty of assault in the third degree when:

1. With intent to cause physical injury to another person, he causes such injury to such person or to a third person; or

2. He recklessly causes physical injury to another person; or

3. With criminal negligence, he causes physical injury to another person by means of a deadly weapon or a dangerous instrument.

Assault in the third degree is a class A misdemeanor.

HISTORY: Add, L 1965, ch 1030, eff Sept 1, 1967, with substance derived in part from §§ 244, 245.

§ 120.01. Reckless assault of a child by a child day care provider

A person is guilty of reckless assault of a child when, being a child day care provider or an employee thereof, he or she recklessly causes serious physical injury to a child under the care of such provider or employee who is less than eleven years of age.

Reckless assault of a child by a child day care provider is a class E felony.

HISTORY: Add, L 1998, ch 600, § 3, eff Nov 1, 1998.

§ 120.02. Reckless assault of a child

1. A person is guilty of reckless assault of a child when, being eighteen years of age or more, such person recklessly causes serious physical injury to the brain of a child less than five years old by shaking the child, or by slamming or throwing the child so as to impact the child's head on a hard surface or object.

2. For purposes of subdivision one of this section, the following shall constitute "serious physical injury":

a. "serious physical injury" as defined in subdivision ten of section 10.00 of this chapter; or

b. extreme rotational cranial acceleration and deceleration and one or more of the following: (i) subdural hemorrhaging; (ii) intracranial hemorrhaging; or (iii) retinal hemorrhaging.

Reckless assault of a child is a class D felony.

HISTORY: Add, L 2006, ch 110, § 3, eff Nov 1, 2006.

§ 120.03. Vehicular assault in the second degree

A person is guilty of vehicular assault in the second degree when he or she causes serious physical injury to another person, and either:

(1) operates a motor vehicle in violation of subdivision two, three, four or four-a of section eleven hundred ninety-two of the vehicle and traffic law or operates a vessel or public vessel in violation of paragraph (b), (c), (d) or (e) of subdivision two of section forty-nine-a of the navigation law, and as a result of such intoxication or impairment by the use of a drug, or by the combined influence of drugs or of alcohol and any drug or drugs, operates such motor vehicle, vessel or public vessel in a manner that causes such serious physical injury to such other person, or

(2) operates a motor vehicle with a gross vehicle weight rating of more than eighteen thousand pounds which contains flammable gas, radioactive materials or explosives in violation of subdivision one of section eleven hundred ninety-two of the vehicle and traffic law, and such flammable gas, radioactive materials or explosives is the cause of such serious physical injury, and as a result of such impairment by the use ofalcohol, operates such motor vehicle in a manner that causes such serious physical injury to such other person, or

(3) operates a snowmobile in violation of paragraph (b), (c) or (d) of subdivision one of section 25.24 of the parks, recreation and historic preservation law or operates an all terrain vehicle as defined in paragraph (a) of subdivision one of section twenty-two hundred eighty-one of the vehicle and traffic law and in violation of subdivision two, three, four, or four-a of section eleven hundred ninety-two of the vehicle and traffic law, and as a result of such intoxication or impairment by the use of a drug, or by the combined influence of drugs or of alcohol and any drug or drugs, operates such snowmobile or all terrain vehicle in a manner that causes such serious physical injury to such other person.

If it is established that the person operating such motor vehicle, vessel, public vessel, snowmobile or all terrain vehicle caused such serious physical injury while unlawfully intoxicated or impaired by the use of alcohol or a drug, then there shall be a rebuttable presumption that, as a result of such intoxication or impairment by the use of alcohol or a drug, or by the combined influence of drugs or of alcohol and any drug or drugs, such person operated the motor vehicle, vessel, public vessel, snowmobile or all terrain vehicle in a manner that caused such serious physical injury, as required by this section.

Vehicular assault in the second degree is a class E felony.

HISTORY: Add, L 1983, ch 298, § 1; amd, L 1985, ch 507, § 1, L 1989, ch 393, § 1, L 1990, ch 173, § 81, L 1990, ch 452, § 2, L 1992, ch 427, § 3, L 1992, ch 805, § 47, eff Nov 1, 1992. Section heading, amd, L 1985, ch 507, § 1, eff Nov 1, 1985. Sub (1), amd, L 1990, ch 173, § 81, eff Aug 19, 1990. Sub (2), amd, L 1989, ch 393, § 1, L 1990, ch 173, § 81, L 1990, ch 452, § 2, L 1992, ch 805, § 47, eff Nov 1, 1992. Sub (3), formerly part of sub (2), so designated and amd, L 1990, ch 173, § 81, L 1990, ch 452, § 2; amd, L 1992, ch 427, § 3, eff Nov 1, 1992. Amd, L 2005, ch 39, § 2, eff June 8, 2005, L 2006, ch 732, § 21, eff Nov 1, 2006. Opening par amd, L 2005, ch 39, § 2, eff June 8, 2005. Sub (1), formerly sub (2), so designated sub (2) and amd, L 2005, ch 39, § 2, eff June 8, 2005, L 2006, ch 732, § 21, eff Nov 1, 2006. Former sub (1), deleted, L 2005, ch 39, § 2, eff June 8, 2005. Sub (2), formerly part of sub (3), amd, L 1998, ch 629, § 2, eff Nov 1, 1999; so designated sub (2) and amd, L 2005, ch 39, § 2, eff June 8, 2005, L 2006, ch 732, § 21, eff Nov 1, 2006. Former sub (2), redesignated sub (1), L 2005, ch 39, § 2, eff June 8, 2005. Sub (3), formerly part of entire sub (3), amd, L 1998, ch 629, § 2, eff Nov 1, 1999; so designated sub (3) and amd, L 2005, ch 39, § 2, eff June 8, 2005, L 2006, ch 732, § 21, eff Nov 1, 2006. Former sub (3), redesignated as part of subs 2 and 3, L 2005, ch 39, § 2, eff June 8, 2005. Second undesignated par, add, L 2005, ch 39, § 2, eff June 8, 2005; amd, L 2006, ch 732, § 21, eff Nov 1, 2006.

§ 120.04. Vehicular assault in the first degree

A person is guilty of vehicular assault in the first degree when he or she commits the crime of vehicular assault in the second degree as defined in section 120.03 of this article, and either:

(1) commits such crime while operating a motor vehicle while such person has.18 of one per centum or more by weight of alcohol in such person's blood as shown by chemical analysis of such person's blood, breath, urine or saliva made pursuant to the provisions of section eleven hundred ninety-four of the vehicle and traffic law;

(2) commits such crime while knowing or having reason to know that: (a) his or her license or his or her privilege of operating a motor vehicle in another state or his or her privilege of obtaining a license to operate a motor vehicle in another state is suspended or revoked and such suspension or revocation is based upon a conviction in such other state for an offense which

would, if committed in this state, constitute a violation of any of the provisions of section eleven hundred ninety-two of the vehicle and traffic law; or (b) his or her license or his or her privilege of operating a motor vehicle in the state or his or her privilege of obtaining a license issued by the commissioner of motor vehicles is suspended or revoked and such suspension or revocation is based upon either a refusal to submit to a chemical test pursuant to section eleven hundred ninety-four of the vehicle and traffic law or following a conviction for a violation of any of the provisions of section eleven hundred ninety-two of the vehicle and traffic law;

(3) has previously been convicted of violating any of the provisions of section eleven hundred ninety-two of the vehicle and traffic law within the preceding ten years, provided that, for the purposes of this subdivision, a conviction in any other state or jurisdiction for an offense which, if committed in this state, would constitute a violation of section eleven hundred ninety-two of the vehicle and traffic law, shall be treated as a violation of such law

(4) causes serious physical injury to more than one other person;

(5) has previously been convicted of violating any provision of this article or article one hundred twenty-five of this title involving the operation of a motor vehicle, or was convicted in any other state or jurisdiction of an offense involving the operation of a motor vehicle which, if committed in this state, would constitute a violation of this article or article one hundred twenty-five of this title; or

(6) commits such crime while operating a motor vehicle while a child who is fifteen years of age or less is a passenger in such motor vehicle and causes serious physical injury to such child.

If it is established that the person operating such motor vehicle caused such serious physical injury or injuries while unlawfully intoxicated or impaired by the use of alcohol or a drug, or by the combined influence of drugs or of alcohol and any drug or drugs, then there shall be a rebuttable presumption that, as a result of such intoxication or impairment by the use of alcohol or a drug, or by the combined influence of drugs or of alcohol and any drug or drugs, such person operated the motor vehicle in a manner that caused such serious physical injury or injuries, as required by this section and section 120.03 of this article.

Vehicular assault in the first degree is a class D felony.

HISTORY: Add, L 1985, ch 507, § 2, eff Nov 1, 1985. Amd, L 2005, ch 39, § 3, eff June 8, 2005, L 2006, ch 245, § 2, eff Nov 1, 2006, L 2006, ch 732, § 21, eff Nov 1, 2006, L 2006, ch 746, § 4, eff Dec 15, 2006, L 2009, ch 496, § 7, eff Dec 18, 2009. Opening par, amd, L 2005, ch 39, § 3, eff June 8, 2005, L 2006, ch 732, § 21, eff Nov 1, 2006, L 2006, ch 746, § 4, eff Dec 15, 2006. Sub (1), add, L 2006, ch 732, § 21, eff Nov 1, 2006; amd, L 2006, ch 746, § 4, eff Dec 15, 2006. Former sub (1) redesignated part of opening par, L 2006, ch 732, § 21, eff Nov 1, 2006. Sub (2), amd, L 1996, ch 528, § 1, eff Nov 1, 1996. Sub (2), amd, L 2005, ch 39, § 3, eff June 8, 2005, L 2006, ch 245, § 2, eff Nov 1, 2006, L 2006, ch 732, § 21, eff Nov 1, 2006, L 2006, ch 746, § 4, eff Dec 15, 2006. Sub (3), formerly sub (3) [first setout], add, L 2006, ch 245, § 2, eff Nov 1, 2006; amd, L 2006, ch 746, § 4, eff Dec 15, 2006, L 2009, ch 496, § 7, eff Dec 18, 2009. Sub (4), formerly sub (3) [second setout], add, L 2006, ch 732, § 21, eff Nov 1, 2006; so designated sub (4) and amd, L 2006, ch 746, § 4, eff Dec 15, 2006, L 2009, ch 496, § 7, eff Dec 18, 2009. Former sub (4), redesignated sub (5), L 2006, ch 746, § 4, eff Dec 15, 2006. Sub (5), formerly sub (4), add, L 2006, ch 732, § 21, eff Nov 1, 2006; so designated sub (5) and amd, L 2006, ch 746, § 4, eff Dec 15, 2006, L 2009, ch 496, § 7, eff Dec 18, 2009. Former sub (5), add, L 2006, ch 732, § 21, eff Nov 1, 2006; deleted, L 2006, ch 746, § 4, eff Dec 15, 2006. Sub (6), add, L 2009, ch 496, § 7, eff Dec 18, 2009. Second undesignated par, add, L 2005, ch 39, § 3, eff June 8, 2005; amd, L 2006, ch 732, § 21, eff Nov 1, 2006.

§ 120.04-a. Aggravated vehicular assault

A person is guilty of aggravated vehicular assault when he or she engages in reckless driving as defined by section twelve hundred twelve of the vehicle and traffic law, and commits the crime of vehicular assault in the second degree as defined in section 120.03 of this article, and either:

(1) commits such crimes while operating a motor vehicle while such person has.18 of one per centum or more by weight of alcohol in such person's blood as shown by chemical analysis of such person's blood, breath, urine or saliva made pursuant to the provisions of section eleven hundred ninety-four of the vehicle and traffic law;

(2) commits such crimes while knowing or having reason to know that: (a) his or her license or his or her privilege of operating a motor vehicle in another state or his or her privilege of obtaining a license to operate a motor vehicle in another state is suspended or revoked and such suspension or revocation is based upon a conviction in such other state for an offense which would, if committed in this state, constitute a violation of any of the provisions of section eleven hundred ninety-two of the vehicle and traffic law; or (b) his or her license or his or her privilege of operating a motor vehicle in this state or his or her privilege of obtaining a license issued by the commissioner of motor vehicles is suspended or revoked and such suspension or revocation is based upon either a refusal to submit to a chemical test pursuant to section eleven hundred ninety-four of the vehicle and traffic law or following a conviction for a violation of any of the provisions of section eleven hundred ninety-two of the vehicle and traffic law;

(3) has previously been convicted of violating any of the provisions of section eleven hundred ninety-two of the vehicle and traffic law within the preceding ten years, provided that, for the purposes of this subdivision, a conviction in any other state or jurisdiction for an offense which, if committed in this state, would constitute a violation of section eleven hundred ninety-two of the vehicle and traffic law, shall be treated as a violation of such law;

(4) causes serious physical injury to more than one other person;

(5) has previously been convicted of violating any provision of this article or article one hundred twenty-five of this title involving the operation of a motor vehicle, or was convicted in any other state or jurisdiction of an offense involving the operation of a motor vehicle which, if committed in this state, would constitute a violation of this article or article one hundred twenty-five of this title; or

(6) commits such crime while operating a motor vehicle while a child who is fifteen years of age or less is a passenger in such motor vehicle and causes serious physical injury to such child.

If it is established that the person operating such motor vehicle caused such serious physical injury or injuries while unlawfully intoxicated or impaired by the use of alcohol or a drug, or by the combined influence of drugs or of alcohol and any drug or drugs, then there shall be a rebuttable presumption that, as a result of such intoxication or impairment by the use of alcohol or a drug, or by the combined influence of drugs or of alcohol and any drug or drugs, such person operated the motor vehicle in a manner that caused such serious physical injury or injuries, as required by this section and section 120.03 of this article.

Aggravated vehicular assault is a class C felony.

HISTORY: Add, L 2007, ch 345, § 1, eff Nov 1, 2007, amd, L 2009, ch 496, § 8, eff Dec 18, 2009. Sub (4), amd, L 2009, ch 496, § 8, eff Dec 18, 2009. Sub (5), amd, L 2009, ch 496, § 8, eff Dec 18, 2009. Sub (6), add, L 2009, ch 496, § 8, eff Dec 18, 2009.

§ 120.05. Assault in the second degree

A person is guilty of assault in the second degree when:

1. With intent to cause serious physical injury to another person, he causes such injury to such person or to a third person; or

2. With intent to cause physical injury to another person, he causes such injury to such person or to a third person by means of a deadly weapon or a dangerous instrument; or

3. With intent to prevent a peace officer, a police officer, prosecutor as defined in subdivision thirty-one of section 1.20 of the criminal procedure law, registered nurse, licensed practical nurse, sanitation enforcement agent, New York city sanitation worker, a firefighter, including a firefighter acting as a paramedic or emergency medical technician administering first aid in the course of performance of duty as such firefighter, an emergency medical service paramedic or emergency medical service technician, or medical or related personnel in a hospital emergency department, a city marshal, a school crossing guard appointed pursuant to section two hundred eight-a of the general municipal law, a traffic enforcement officer or traffic enforcement agent, from performing a lawful duty, by means including releasing or failing to control an animal under circumstances evincing the actor's intent that the animal obstruct the lawful activity of such peace officer, police officer, prosecutor as defined in subdivision thirty-one of section 1.20 of the criminal procedure law, registered nurse, licensed practical nurse, sanitation enforcement agent, New York city sanitation worker, firefighter, paramedic, technician, city marshal, school crossing guard appointed pursuant to section two hundred eight-a of the general municipal law, traffic enforcement officer or traffic enforcement agent, he or she causes physical injury to such peace officer, police officer, prosecutor as defined in subdivision thirty-one of section 1.20 of the criminal procedure law, registered nurse, licensed practical nurse, sanitation enforcement agent, New York city sanitation worker, firefighter, paramedic, technician or medical or related personnel in a hospital emergency department, city marshal, school crossing guard, traffic enforcement officer or traffic enforcement agent; or

3-a. With intent to prevent an employee of a local social services district directly involved in investigation of or response to alleged abuse or neglect of a child, a vulnerable elderly person or an incompetent or physically disabled person, from performing such investigation or response, the actor, not being such child, vulnerable elderly person or incompetent or physically disabled person, or with intent to prevent an employee of a local social services district directly involved in providing public assistance and care from performing his or her job, causes physical injury to such employee including by means of releasing or failing to control an animal under circumstances evincing the actor's intent that the animal obstruct the lawful activities of such employee; or

3-b. With intent to prevent an employee of the New York city housing authority from performing his or her lawful duties while located on housing project grounds, real property, or a building owned, managed, or operated by such authority he or she causes physical injury to such employee; or

4. He recklessly causes serious physical injury to another person by means of a deadly weapon or a dangerous instrument; or

4-a. He recklessly causes physical injury to another person who is a child under the age of eighteen by intentional discharge of a firearm, rifle or shotgun; or

5. For a purpose other than lawful medical or therapeutic treatment, he intentionally causes stupor, unconsciousness or other physical impairment or injury to another person by administering to him, without his consent, a drug, substance or preparation capable of producing the same; or

6. In the course of and in furtherance of the commission or attempted commission of a felony, other than a felony defined in article one hundred thirty which requires corroboration for conviction, or of immediate flight therefrom, he, or another participant if there be any, causes physical injury to a person other than one of the participants; or

7. Having been charged with or convicted of a crime and while confined in a correctional facility, as defined in subdivision three of section forty of the correction law, pursuant to such charge or conviction, with intent to cause physical injury to another person, he causes such injury to such person or to a third person; or

8. Being eighteen years old or more and with intent to cause physical injury to a person less than eleven years old, the defendant recklessly causes serious physical injury to such person; or

9. Being eighteen years old or more and with intent to cause physical injury to a person less than seven years old, the defendant causes such injury to such person; or

10. Acting at a place the person knows, or reasonably should know, is on school grounds and with intent to cause physical injury, he or she:

(a) causes such injury to an employee of a school or public school district; or

(b) not being a student of such school or public school district, causes physical injury to another, and such other person is a student of such school who is attending or present for educational purposes. For purposes of this subdivision the term "school grounds" shall have the meaning set forth in subdivision fourteen of section 220.00 of this chapter.

11. With intent to cause physical injury to a train operator, ticket inspector, conductor, signalperson, bus operator or station agent employed by any transit agency, authority or company, public or private, whose operation is authorized by New York state or any of its political subdivisions, a city marshal, a school crossing guard appointed pursuant to section two hundred eight-a of the general municipal law, a traffic enforcement officer, traffic enforcement agent, prosecutor as defined in subdivision thirty-one of section 1.20 of the criminal procedure law, sanitation enforcement agent, New York city sanitation worker, registered nurse or licensed practical nurse he or she causes physical injury to such train operator, ticket inspector, conductor, signalperson, bus operator or station agent, city marshal, school crossing guard appointed pursuant to section two hundred eight-a of the general municipal law, traffic enforcement officer, traffic enforcement agent, prosecutor as defined in subdivision thirty-one of section 1.20 of the criminal procedure law, registered nurse, licensed practical nurse, sanitation enforcement agent or New York city sanitation worker, while such employee is performing an assigned duty on, or directly related to, the operation of a train or bus, or such city marshal, school crossing guard, traffic enforcement officer, traffic enforcement agent, prosecutor as defined in subdivision thirty-one of section 1.20 of the criminal procedure law, registered nurse, licensed practical nurse, sanitation enforcement agent or New York city sanitation worker, is performing an assigned duty.

11-a. With intent to cause physical injury to an employee of a local social services district directly involved in investigation of or response to alleged abuse or neglect of a child, vulnerable elderly person or an incompetent or physically disabled person, the actor, not being such child, vulnerable elderly person or incompetent or physically disabled person, or with intent to prevent an employee of a local social services district directly involved in providing public assistance and care from performing his or her job, causes physical injury to such employee; or

11-b. With intent to cause physical injury to an employee of the New York city housing authority performing his or her lawful duties while located on housing project grounds, real property, or a building owned, managed, or operated by such authority he or she causes physical injury to such employee; or

12. With intent to cause physical injury to a person who is sixty-five years of age or older, he or she causes such injury to such person, and the actor is more than ten years younger than such person.

Assault in the second degree is a class D felony.

HISTORY: Add, L 1965, ch 1030, with substance derived from §§ 2, 242, 243; amd, L 1967, ch 791, § 7, L 1968, ch 37, § 1, L 1972, ch 598, § 2, L 1974, ch 239, § 1, L 1974, ch 660, § 1, L 1975, ch 134, § 1, L 1975, ch 667, § 37, eff Aug 6, 1975, retroactive to and deemed to have been in full force and effect on and after April 1, 1975, L 1980, ch 471, § 25, L 1980, ch 843, § 39, L 1981, ch 372, §§ 4, 5, eff Sept 1, 1981, L 1984, ch 284, § 1, L 1985, ch 262, § 1, eff Sept 1, 1985, L 1990, ch 477, § 2, eff Nov 1, 1990, L 1996, ch 122, § 4, eff Aug 1, 1996, 1998, ch 269, § 1, eff Nov 1, 1998, L 1998, ch 287, § 1, eff Nov 1, 1998, L 2000, ch 181, § 13, eff Nov 1, 2000,L 2002, ch 598, § 1, eff Nov 1, 2002, L 2003, ch 607, § 1, eff Nov 1, 2003, L 2006, ch 100, § 1, eff Nov 1, 2006 L 2008, ch 45, § 1, eff July 22, 2008, L 2008, ch 68, § 1, eff June 29, 2008, L 2010, ch 318, §§ 1, 2, eff Nov 1, 2010, L 2010, ch 345, § 1, eff Sept 12, 2010, L 2012, ch 377, § 1, eff Sept 16, 2012, L 2012, ch 434, § 1, eff Nov 1, 2012, L 2013, ch 1, § 32, eff March 16, 2013, L 2013, ch 259, §§ 1, 2, eff Jan 27, 2014, L 2014, ch 196, § 1, eff Nov 1, 2014, L 2014, ch 197, § 1, eff Sept 3, 2014.

§ 120.06. Gang assault in the second degree

A person is guilty of gang assault in the second degree when, with intent to cause physical injury to another person and when aided by two or more other persons actually present, he causes serious physical injury to such person or to a third person.

Gang assault in the second degree is a class C felony.

HISTORY: Add, L 1996, ch 647, § 2, eff Nov 1, 1996.

§ 120.07. Gang assault in the first degree

A person is guilty of gang assault in the first degree when, with intent to cause serious physical injury to another person and when aided by two or more other persons actually present, he causes serious physical injury to such person or to a third person.

Gang assault in the first degree is a class B felony.

HISTORY: Add, L 1996, ch 647, § 2, eff Nov 1, 1996.

§ 120.08. Assault on a peace officer, police officer, fireman or emergency medical services professional

A person is guilty of assault on a peace officer, police officer, fireman or emergency medical services professional when, with intent to prevent a peace officer, police officer, a fireman, including a fireman acting as a paramedic or emergency medical technician administering first aid in the course of performance of duty as such fireman, or an emergency medical service paramedic or emergency medical service technician, from performing a lawful duty, he causes serious physical injury to such peace officer, police officer, fireman, paramedic or technician.

Assault on a peace officer, police officer, fireman or emergency medical services professional is a class C felony.

HISTORY: Add, L 1996, ch 632, § 2, eff Nov 1, 1996.

§ 120.09. Assault on a judge

A person is guilty of assault on a judge when, with intent to cause serious physical injury and prevent a judge from performing official judicial duties, he or she causes serious physical injury to such judge. For the purposes of this section, the term judge shall mean a judge of a court of record or a justice court.

Assault on a judge is a class C felony.

HISTORY: Add, L 2011, ch 148, § 1, eff Nov 17, 2011.

§ 120.10. Assault in the first degree

A person is guilty of assault in the first degree when:

1. With intent to cause serious physical injury to another person, he causes such injury to such person or to a third person by means of a deadly weapon or a dangerous instrument; or

2. With intent to disfigure another person seriously and permanently, or to destroy, amputate or disable permanently a member or organ of his body, he causes such injury to such person or to a third person; or

3. Under circumstances evincing a depraved indifference to human life, he recklessly engages in conduct which creates a grave risk of death to another person, and thereby causes serious physical injury to another person; or

4. In the course of and in furtherance of the commission or attempted commission of a felony or of immediate flight therefrom, he, or another participant if there be any, causes serious physical injury to a person other than one of the participants.

Assault in the first degree is a class B felony.

HISTORY: Add, L 1965, ch 1030, eff Sept 1, 1967, with substance derived from §§ 2, 240, 241, 1400. Sub 4, amd, L 1967, ch 791, § 8, eff Sept 1, 1967. Closing par, amd, L 1996, ch 646, § 2, eff Nov 1, 1996.

§ 120.11. Aggravated assault upon a police officer or a peace officer

A person is guilty of aggravated assault upon a police officer or a peace officer when, with intent to cause serious physical injury to a person whom he knows or reasonably should know to be a police officer or a peace officer engaged in the course of performing his official duties, he causes such injury by means of a deadly weapon or dangerous instrument.

Aggravated assault upon a police officer or a peace officer is a class B felony.

HISTORY: Add, L 1980, ch 233, § 6; amd, L 1981, ch 175, § 3, and shall be applicable to offenses committed on or after such date, L 1993, ch 283, § 1, eff Nov 1, 1993. Section heading, amd, L 1981, ch 175, § 3, eff July 2, 1981 and shall be applicable to offenses committed on or after such date.

§ 120.12. Aggravated assault upon a person less than eleven years old

A person is guilty of aggravated assault upon a person less than eleven years old when being eighteen years old or more the defendant commits the crime of assault in the third degree as defined in section 120.00 of this article upon a person less than eleven years old and has been previously convicted of such crime upon a person less than eleven years old within the preceding ten years.

Aggravated assault upon a person less than eleven years old is a class E felony.

HISTORY: Add, L 1990, ch 477, § 1, eff Nov 1, 1990, L 2013, ch 172, § 2, eff July 29, 2013.

§ 120.13. Menacing in the first degree

A person is guilty of menacing in the first degree when he or she commits the crime of menacing in the second degree and has been previously convicted of the crime of menacing in the second degree or the crime of menacing a police officer or peace officer within the preceding ten years.

Menacing in the first degree is a class E felony.

HISTORY: Add, L 1992, ch 345, § 1, eff Nov 1, 1992. Amd, L 2005, ch 765, § 8, eff Dec 21, 2005. First undesignated par, amd, L 2005, ch 765, § 8, eff Dec 21, 2005.

§ 120.14. Menacing in the second degree

A person is guilty of menacing in the second degree when:

1. He or she intentionally places or attempts to place another person in reasonable fear of physical injury, serious physical injury or death by displaying a deadly weapon, dangerous instrument or what appears to be a pistol, revolver, rifle, shotgun, machine gun or other firearm; or

2. He or she repeatedly follows a person or engages in a course of conduct or repeatedly commits acts over a period of time intentionally placing or attempting to place another person in reasonable fear of physical injury, serious physical injury or death; or

3. He or she commits the crime of menacing in the third degree in violation of that part of a duly served order of protection, or such order which the defendant has actual knowledge of because he or she was present in court when such order was issued, pursuant to article eight of the family court act, section 530.12 of the criminal procedure law, or an order of protection issued by a court of competent jurisdiction in another state, territorial or tribal jurisdiction, which directed the respondent or defendant to stay away from the person or persons on whose behalf the order was issued.

Menacing in the second degree is a class A misdemeanor.

HISTORY: Add, L 1992, ch 345, § 1; amd, L 1994, ch 222, § 46, eff Jan 1, 1995. Sub 2, amd, L 1994, ch 222, § 46, eff Jan 1, 1995. Sub 3, add, L 1994, ch 222, § 46, eff Jan 1, 1995. Sub 3, amd, L 1998, ch 597, § 14, eff Dec 22, 1998.

§ 120.15. Menacing in the third degree

A person is guilty of menacing in the third degree when, by physical menace, he or she intentionally places or attempts to place another person in fear of death, imminent serious physical injury or physical injury.

Menacing in the third degree is a class B misdemeanor.

HISTORY: Add, L 1965, ch 1030, eff Sept 1, 1967. Section heading, amd, L 1992, ch 345, § 2, eff Nov 1, 1992. First undesignated par, amd, L 1992, ch 345, § 2, eff Nov 1, 1992. Second undesignated par, amd, L 1992, ch 345, § 2, eff Nov 1, 1992.

§ 120.16. Hazing in the first degree

A person is guilty of hazing in the first degree when, in the course of another person's initiation into or affiliation with any organization, he intentionally or recklessly engages in conduct which creates a substantial risk of physical injury to such other person or a third person and thereby causes such injury.

Hazing in the first degree is a class A misdemeanor.

HISTORY: Add, L 1983, ch 716, § 1; amd, L 1988, ch 86, § 1, eff Nov 1, 1988. Section heading, amd, L 1988, ch 86, § 1, eff Nov 1, 1988.

§ 120.17. Hazing in the second degree

A person is guilty of hazing in the second degree when, in the course of another person's initiation or affiliation with any organization, he intentionally or recklessly engages in conduct which creates a substantial risk of physical injury to such other person or a third person.

Hazing in the second degree is a violation.

HISTORY: Add, L 1988, ch 86, § 1, eff Nov 1, 1988.

§ 120.18. Menacing a police officer or peace officer

A person is guilty of menacing a police officer or peace officer when he or she intentionally places or attempts to place a police officer or peace officer in reasonable fear of physical injury, serious physical injury or death by displaying a deadly weapon, knife, pistol, revolver, rifle, shotgun, machine gun or other firearm, whether operable or not, where such officer was in the course of performing his or her official duties and the defendant knew or reasonably should have known that such victim was a police officer or peace officer.

Menacing a police officer or peace officer is a class D felony.

HISTORY: Add, L 2005, ch 765, § 7, eff Dec 21, 2005.

§ 120.20. Reckless endangerment in the second degree

A person is guilty of reckless endangerment in the second degree when he recklessly engages in conduct which creates a substantial risk of serious physical injury to another person.

Reckless endangerment in the second degree is a class A misdemeanor.

HISTORY: Add, L 1965, ch 1030, eff Sept 1, 1967.

§ 120.25. Reckless endangerment in the first degree

A person is guilty of reckless endangerment in the first degree when, under circumstances evincing a depraved indifference to human life, he recklessly engages in conduct which creates a grave risk of death to another person.

Reckless endangerment in the first degree is a class D felony.

HISTORY: Add, L 1965, ch 1030, eff Sept 1, 1967.

§ 120.30. Promoting a suicide attempt

A person is guilty of promoting a suicide attempt when he intentionally causes or aids another person to attempt suicide.

Promoting a suicide attempt is a class E felony.

HISTORY: Add, L 1965, ch 1030, eff Sept 1, 1967, with substance derived from L 1909, § 2305.

§ 120.35. Promoting a suicide attempt; when punishable as attempt to commit murder

A person who engages in conduct constituting both the offense of promoting a suicide attempt and the offense of attempt to commit murder may not be convicted of attempt to commit murder unless he causes or aids the suicide attempt by the use of duress or deception.

HISTORY: Add, L 1965, ch 1030, eff Sept 1, 1967.

§ 120.40. Definitions

For purposes of sections 120.45, 120.50, 120.55 and 120.60 of this article:

1. "Kidnapping" shall mean a kidnapping crime defined in article one hundred thirty-five of this chapter.

2. "Unlawful imprisonment" shall mean an unlawful imprisonment felony crime defined in article one hundred thirty-five of this chapter.

3. "Sex offense" shall mean a felony defined in article one hundred thirty of this chapter, sexual misconduct, as defined in section 130.20 of this chapter, sexual abuse in the third degree

as defined in section 130.55 of this chapter or sexual abuse in the second degree as defined in section 130.60 of this chapter.

4. "Immediate family" means the spouse, former spouse, parent, child, sibling, or any other person who regularly resides or has regularly resided in the household of a person.

5. "Specified predicate crime" means:

a. a violent felony offense;

b. a crime defined in section 130.20, 130.25, 130.30, 130.40, 130.45, 130.55, 130.60, 130.70, 255.25, 255.26 or 255.27;

c. assault in the third degree, as defined in section 120.00; menacing in the first degree, as defined in section 120.13; menacing in the second degree, as defined in section 120.14; coercion in the first degree, as defined in section 135.65; coercion in the second degree, as defined in section 135.60; aggravated harassment in the second degree, as defined in section 240.30; harassment in the first degree, as defined in section 240.25; menacing in the third degree, as defined in section 120.15; criminal mischief in the third degree, as defined in section 145.05; criminal mischief in the second degree, as defined in section 145.10; criminal mischief in the first degree, as defined in section 145.12; criminal tampering in the first degree, as defined in section 145.20; arson in the fourth degree, as defined in section 150.05; arson in the third degree, as defined in section 150.10; criminal contempt in the first degree, as defined in section 215.51; endangering the welfare of a child, as defined in section 260.10; or

d. stalking in the fourth degree, as defined in section 120.45; stalking in the third degree, as defined in section 120.50; stalking in the second degree, as defined in section 120.55; or

e. an offense in any other jurisdiction which includes all of the essential elements of any such crime for which a sentence to a term of imprisonment in excess of one year or a sentence of death was authorized and is authorized in this state irrespective of whether such sentence was imposed.

HISTORY: Add, L 1999, ch 635, § 13, eff Dec 1, 1999. Sub 5, par b, amd, L 2006, ch 320, § 6, eff Nov 1, 2006.

§ 120.45 Stalking in the fourth degree

A person is guilty of stalking in the fourth degree when he or she intentionally, and for no legitimate purpose, engages in a course of conduct directed at a specific person, and knows or reasonably should know that such conduct:

1. is likely to cause reasonable fear of material harm to the physical health, safety or property of such person, a member of such person's immediate family or a third party with whom such person is acquainted; or

2. causes material harm to the mental or emotional health of such person, where such conduct consists of following, telephoning or initiating communication or contact with such person, a member of such person's immediate family or a third party with whom such person is acquainted, and the actor was previously clearly informed to cease that conduct; or

3. is likely to cause such person to reasonably fear that his or her employment, business or career is threatened, where such conduct consists of appearing, telephoning or initiating communication or contact at such person's place of employment or business, and the actor was previously clearly informed to cease that conduct.

For the purposes of subdivision two of this section, "following" shall include the unauthorized tracking of such person's movements or location through the use of a global positioning system or other device.

Stalking in the fourth degree is a class B misdemeanor.

HISTORY: Add, L 1999, ch 635, § 13, eff Dec 1, 1999; amd, L 2014, ch 184, § 1, eff Oct 21, 2014.

§ 120.50. Stalking in the third degree

A person is guilty of stalking in the third degree when he or she:

1. Commits the crime of stalking in the fourth degree in violation of section 120.45 of this article against three or more persons, in three or more separate transactions, for which the actor has not been previously convicted; or

2. Commits the crime of stalking in the fourth degree in violation of section 120.45 of this article against any person, and has previously been convicted, within the preceding ten years of a specified predicate crime, as defined in subdivision five of section 120.40 of this article, and the victim of such specified predicate crime is the victim, or an immediate family member of the victim, of the present offense; or

3. With intent to harass, annoy or alarm a specific person, intentionally engages in a course of conduct directed at such person which is likely to cause such person to reasonably fear physical injury or serious physical injury, the commission of a sex offense against, or the kidnapping, unlawful imprisonment or death of such person or a member of such person's immediate family; or

4. Commits the crime of stalking in the fourth degree and has previously been convicted within the preceding ten years of stalking in the fourth degree.

Stalking in the third degree is a class A misdemeanor.

HISTORY: Add, L 1999, ch 635, § 13, eff Dec 1, 1999.

§ 120.55. Stalking in the second degree

A person is guilty of stalking in the second degree when he or she:

1. Commits the crime of stalking in the third degree as defined in subdivision three of section 120.50 of this article and in the course of and in furtherance of the commission of such offense: (i) displays, or possesses and threatens the use of, a firearm, pistol, revolver, rifle, shotgun, machine gun, electronic dart gun, electronic stun gun, cane sword, billy, blackjack, bludgeon, plastic knuckles, metal knuckles, chuka stick, sand bag, sandclub, slingshot, slungshot, shirken, "Kung Fu Star", dagger, dangerous knife, dirk, razor, stiletto, imitation pistol, dangerous instrument, deadly instrument or deadly weapon; or (ii) displays what appears to be a pistol, revolver, rifle, shotgun, machine gun or other firearm; or

2. Commits the crime of stalking in the third degree in violation of subdivision three of section 120.50 of this article against any person, and has previously been convicted, within the preceding five years, of a specified predicate crime as defined in subdivision five of section 120.40 of this article, and the victim of such specified predicate crime is the victim, or an immediate family member of the victim, of the present offense; or

3. Commits the crime of stalking in the fourth degree and has previously been convicted of stalking in the third degree as defined in subdivision four of section 120.50 of this article against any person; or

4. Being twenty-one years of age or older, repeatedly follows a person under the age of fourteen or engages in a course of conduct or repeatedly commits acts over a period of time intentionally placing or attempting to place such person who is under the age of fourteen in reasonable fear of physical injury, serious physical injury or death; or

5. Commits the crime of stalking in the third degree, as defined in subdivision three of section 120.50 of this article, against ten or more persons, in ten or more separate transactions, for which the actor has not been previously convicted.

Stalking in the second degree is a class E felony.

HISTORY: Add, L 1999, ch 635, § 13, eff Dec 1, 1999. Sub 1, amd, L 2000, ch 434, § 4, eff Oct 20, 2000, L 2008, ch 257, § 2, eff Nov 1, 2008. Sub 4, amd, L 2003, ch 598, § 1, eff Nov 1, 2003. Sub 5, add, L 2003, ch 598, § 1, eff Nov 1, 2003.

§ 120.60. Stalking in the first degree

A person is guilty of stalking in the first degree when he or she commits the crime of stalking in the third degree as defined in subdivision three of section 120.50 or stalking in the second degree as defined in section 120.55 of this article and, in the course and furtherance thereof, he or she:

1. intentionally or recklessly causes physical injury to the victim of such crime; or

2. commits a class A misdemeanor defined in article one hundred thirty of this chapter, or a class E felony defined in section 130.25, 130.40 or 130.85 of this chapter, or a class D felony defined in section 130.30 or 130.45 of this chapter.

Stalking in the first degree is a class D felony.

HISTORY: Add, L 1999, ch 635, § 13, eff Dec 1, 1999; amd, L 2000, ch 434, § 5, eff Oct 20, 2000. Opening par, amd, L 2000, ch 434, § 5, eff Oct 20, 2000. Sub 1, amd, L 2000, ch 434, § 5, eff Oct 20, 2000. Sub 2, amd, L 2000, ch 434, § 5, eff Oct 20, 2000.

§ 120.70. Luring a child

1. A person is guilty of luring a child when he or she lures a child into a motor vehicle, aircraft, watercraft, isolated area, building, or part thereof, for the purpose of committing against such child any of the following offenses: an offense as defined in section 70.02 of this chapter; an offense as defined in section 125.25 or 125.27 of this chapter; a felony offense that is a violation of article one hundred thirty of this chapter; an offense as defined in section 135.25 of this chapter; an offense as defined in sections 230.30, 230.33 or 230.34 of this chapter; an offense as defined in sections 255.25, 255.26, or 255.27 of this chapter; or an offense as defined in sections 263.05, 263.10, or 263.15 of this chapter. For purposes of this subdivision "child" means a person less than seventeen years of age. Nothing in this section shall be deemed to preclude, if the evidence warrants, a conviction for the commission or attempted commission of any crime, including but not limited to a crime defined in article one hundred thirty-five of this chapter.

2. Luring a child is a class E felony, provided, however, that if the underlying offense the actor intended to commit against such child constituted a class A or a class B felony, then the offense of luring a child in violation of this section shall be deemed respectively, a class C felony or class D felony.

HISTORY: Add, L 2008, ch 405, § 1, eff Oct 4, 2008.

ARTICLE 121   STRANGULATION AND RELATED OFFENSES

§ 121.14.　　　　　Medical or dental purpose

HISTORY: Add, L 2010, ch 405, § 2, eff Nov 11, 2010.

§ 121.11. Criminal obstruction of breathing or blood circulation

A person is guilty of criminal obstruction of breathing or blood circulation when, with intent to impede the normal breathing or circulation of the blood of another person, he or she:

　　a. applies pressure on the throat or neck of such person; or

　　b. blocks the nose or mouth of such person.

Criminal obstruction of breathing or blood circulation is a class A misdemeanor.

HISTORY: Add, L 2010, ch 405, § 2, eff Nov 11, 2010.

§ 121.12. Strangulation in the second degree

A person is guilty of strangulation in the second degree when he or she commits the crime of criminal obstruction of breathing or blood circulation, as defined in section 121.11 of this article, and thereby causes stupor, loss of consciousness for any period of time, or any other physical injury or impairment.

Strangulation in the second degree is a class D felony.

HISTORY: Add, L 2010, ch 405, § 2, eff Nov 11, 2010.

§ 121.13. Strangulation in the first degree

A person is guilty of strangulation in the first degree when he or she commits the crime of criminal obstruction of breathing or blood circulation, as defined in section 121.11 of this article, and thereby causes serious physical injury to such other person.

Strangulation in the first degree is a class C felony.

HISTORY: Add, L 2010, ch 405, § 2, eff Nov 11, 2010.

§ 121.14. Medical or dental purpose

For purposes of sections 121.11, 121.12 and 121.13 of this article, it shall be an affirmative defense that the defendant performed such conduct for a valid medical or dental purpose.

HISTORY: Add, L 2010, ch 405, § 2, eff Nov 11, 2010.

ARTICLE 125　HOMICIDE, ABORTION AND RELATED OFFENSES

HISTORY: Add, L 1965, ch 1030, eff Sept 1, 1967.

§ 125.00. Homicide defined

Homicide means conduct which causes the death of a person or an unborn child with which a female has been pregnant for more than twenty-four weeks under circumstances constituting murder, manslaughter in the first degree, manslaughter in the second degree, criminally negligent homicide, abortion in the first degree or self-abortion in the first degree.

HISTORY: Add, L 1965, ch 1030, eff Sept 1, 1967, with substance derived from §§ 1042, 1043.

§ 125.05. Homicide, abortion and related offenses; definitions of terms

The following definitions are applicable to this article:

1. "Person," when referring to the victim of a homicide, means a human being who has been born and is alive.

2. "Abortional act" means an act committed upon or with respect to a female, whether by another person or by the female herself, whether she is pregnant or not, whether directly upon her body or by the administering, taking or prescription of drugs or in any other manner, with intent to cause a miscarriage of such female.

3. "Justifiable abortional act." An abortional act is justifiable when committed upon a female with her consent by a duly licensed physician acting (a) under a reasonable belief that such is necessary to preserve her life, or, (b) within twenty-four weeks from the commencement of her pregnancy. A pregnant female's commission of an abortional act upon herself is justifiable when she acts upon the advice of a duly licensed physician (1) that such act is necessary to preserve her life, or, (2) within twenty-four weeks from the commencement of her pregnancy. The submission by a female to an abortional act is justifiable when she believes that it is being committed by a duly licensed physician, acting under a reasonable belief that such act is necessary to preserve her life, or, within twenty-four weeks from the commencement of her pregnancy.

HISTORY: Add, L 1965, ch 1030, eff Sept 1, 1967. Sub 3, amd, L 1970, ch 127, § 1, eff July 1, 1970.

§ 125.10. Criminally negligent homicide

A person is guilty of criminally negligent homicide when, with criminal negligence, he causes the death of another person.

Criminally negligent homicide is a class E felony.

HISTORY: Add, L 1965, ch 1030, eff Sept 1, 1967, with substance derived from §§ 1052, 1053-a to 1053-f.

§ 125.11. Aggravated criminally negligent homicide

A person is guilty of aggravated criminally negligent homicide when, with criminal negligence, he or she causes the death of a police officer or peace officer where such officer was in the course of performing his or her official duties and the defendant knew or reasonably should have known that such victim was a police officer or peace officer.

Aggravated criminally negligent homicide is a class C felony.

HISTORY: Add, L 2005, ch 765, § 9, eff Dec 21, 2005.

§ 125.12. Vehicular manslaughter in the second degree

A person is guilty of vehicular manslaughter in the second degree when he or she causes the death of another person, and either:

(1) operates a motor vehicle in violation of subdivision two, three, four or four-a of section eleven hundred ninety-two of the vehicle and traffic law or operates a vessel or public vessel in violation of paragraph (b), (c), (d) or (e) of subdivision two of section forty-nine-a of the navigation law, and as a result of such intoxication or impairment by the use of a drug, or by the combined influence of drugs or of alcohol and any drug or drugs, operates such motor vehicle, vessel or public vessel in a manner that causes the death of such other person, or

(2) operates a motor vehicle with a gross vehicle weight rating of more than eighteen thousand pounds which contains flammable gas, radioactive materials or explosives in violation of subdivision one of section eleven hundred ninety-two of the vehicle and traffic law, and such flammable gas, radioactive materials or explosives is the cause of such death, and as a result of such impairment by the use of alcohol, operates such motor vehicle in a manner that causes the death of such other person, or

(3) operates a snowmobile in violation of paragraph (b), (c) or (d) of subdivision one of section 25.24 of the parks, recreation and historic preservation law or operates an all terrain vehicle as defined in paragraph (a) of subdivision one of section twenty-two hundred eighty-one of the vehicle and traffic law in violation of subdivision two, three, four, or four-a of section eleven hundred ninety-two of the vehicle and traffic law, and as a result of such intoxication or impairment by the use of a drug, or by the combined influence of drugs or of alcohol and any drug or drugs, operates such snowmobile or all terrain vehicle in a manner that causes the death of such other person.

If it is established that the person operating such motor vehicle, vessel, public vessel, snowmobile or all terrain vehicle caused such death while unlawfully intoxicated or impaired by the use of alcohol or a drug, then there shall be a rebuttable presumption that, as a result of such intoxication or impairment by the use of alcohol or a drug, or by the combined influence of drugs or of alcohol and any drug or drugs, such person operated the motor vehicle, vessel, public vessel, snowmobile or all terrain vehicle in a manner that caused such death, as required by this section.

Vehicular manslaughter in the second degree is a class D felony.

HISTORY: Add, L 1983, ch 298, § 2; amd, L 1985, ch 507, § 3, L 1989, ch 393, § 2, L 1990, ch 173, § 82, L 1990, ch 452, § 3, L 1992, ch 427, § 3, L 1992, ch 805, § 47, eff Nov 1, 1992. Section heading, amd, L 1985, ch 507, § 3, eff Nov 1, 1985. Sub (1), amd, L 1990, ch 173, § 82, eff Aug 19, 1990. Sub (2), amd, L 1989, ch 393, § 2, L 1990, ch 173, § 82, L 1990, ch 452, § 3, L 1992, ch 805, § 47, eff Nov 1, 1992. Sub (3), formerly part of sub (2), so designated and amd, L 1990, ch 173, § 82, L 1990, ch 452, § 3, L 1992, ch 427, § 3, eff Nov 1, 1992. Amd, L 2005, ch 39, § 4, eff June 8, 2005, L 2006, ch 732, § 22, eff Nov 1, 2006. Opening par, amd, L 2005, ch 39, § 4, eff June 8, 2005. Sub (1), formerly sub (2), so designated sub (1) and amd, L 2005, ch 39, § 4, eff June 8, 2005, L 2006, ch 732, § 22, eff Nov 1, 2006. Former sub (1), deleted, L 2005, ch 39, § 4, eff June 8, 2005. Sub (2), formerly part of sub (3), amd, L 1998, ch 629, § 3, eff Nov 1, 1999; so designated sub (2) and amd, L 2005, ch 39, § 4, eff June 8, 2005, L 2006, ch 732, § 22, eff Nov 1, 2006. Former sub (2), redesignated sub (1), L 2005, ch 39, § 4, eff June 8, 2005. Sub (3), formerly part of entire sub (3), amd, L 1998, ch 629, § 3, eff Nov 1, 1999; so designated sub (3) and amd, L 2005, ch 39,§ 4, eff June 8,2005, L 2006, ch 732, § 22, eff Nov 1, 2006. Former sub (3), redesignated as part of subs 2 and 3, L 2005, ch 39, § 4, eff June 8, 2005. Second undesignated par, add, L 2005, ch 39, § 4, eff June 8, 2005; amd, L 2006, ch 732, § 22, eff Nov 1, 2006.

§ 125.13. Vehicular manslaughter in the first degree

A person is guilty of vehicular manslaughter in the first degree when he or she commits the crime of vehicular manslaughter in the second degree as defined in section 125.12 of this article, and either:

(1) commits such crime while operating a motor vehicle while such person has.18 of one per centum or more by weight of alcohol in such person's blood as shown by chemical analysis of such person's blood, breath, urine or saliva made pursuant to the provisions of section eleven hundred ninety-four of the vehicle and traffic law;

(2) commits such crime while knowing or having reason to know that: (a) his or her license or his or her privilege of operating a motor vehicle in another state or his or her privilege of obtaining a license to operate a motor vehicle in another state is suspended or revoked and such suspension or revocation is based upon a conviction in such other state for an offense which would, if committed in this state, constitute a violation of any of the provisions of section eleven hundred ninety-two of the vehicle and traffic law; or (b) his or her license or his or her privilege of operating a motor vehicle in the state or his or her privilege of obtaining a license issued by the commissioner of motor vehicles is suspended or revoked and such suspension or revocation is based upon either a refusal to submit to a chemical test pursuant to section eleven hundred ninety-four of the vehicle and traffic law or following a conviction for a violation of any of the provisions of section eleven hundred ninety-two of the vehicle and traffic law;

(3) has previously been convicted of violating any of the provisions of section eleven hundred ninety-two of the vehicle and traffic law within the preceding ten years, provided that, for the purposes of this subdivision, a conviction in any other state or jurisdiction for an offense which, if committed in this state, would constitute a violation of section eleven hundred ninety-two of the vehicle and traffic law, shall be treated as a violation of such law;

(4) causes the death of more than one other person;

(5) has previously been convicted of violating any provision of this article or article one hundred twenty of this title involving the operation of a motor vehicle, or was convicted in any other state or jurisdiction of an offense involving the operation of a motor vehicle which, if committed in this state, would constitute a violation of this article or article one hundred twenty of this title; or

(6) commits such crime while operating a motor vehicle while a child who is fifteen years of age or less is a passenger in such motor vehicle and causes the death of such child.

If it is established that the person operating such motor vehicle caused such death or deaths while unlawfully intoxicated or impaired by the use of alcohol or a drug, or by the combined influence of drugs or of alcohol and any drug or drugs, then there shall be a rebuttable presumption that, as a result of such intoxication or impairment by the use of alcohol or a drug, or by the combined influence of drugs or of alcohol and any drug or drugs, such person operated the motor vehicle in a manner that caused such death or deaths, as required by this section and section 125.12 of this article.

Vehicular manslaughter in the first degree is a class C felony.

HISTORY: Add, L 1985, ch 507, § 4, eff Nov 1, 1985. Amd, L 2005, ch 39, § 5, eff June 8, 2005, L 2006, ch 245, § 3, eff Nov 1, 2006, L 2006, ch 732, § 22, eff Nov 1, 2006, L 2006, ch 746, § 5, eff Dec 15, 2006, L 2009, ch 496, § 9, eff Dec 18, 2009. Opening par, amd, L 2005, ch 39, § 5, eff June 8, 2005, L 2006, ch 732, § 22, eff Nov 1, 2006, L 2006, ch 746, § 5, eff Dec 15, 2006. Sub

(1), add, L 2006, ch 732, § 22, eff Nov 1, 2006; amd, L 2006, ch 746, § 5, eff Dec 15, 2006. Former sub (1), redesignated part of opening par, L 2006, ch 732, § 22, eff Nov 1, 2006. Sub (2), amd, L 1993, ch 678, § 1, L 1996, ch 528, § 2, eff Nov 1, 1996. Sub (2), amd, L 2005, ch 39, § 5, eff June 8, 2005, L 2006, ch 245, § 3, eff Nov 1, 2006, L 2006, ch 732, § 22, eff Nov 1, 2006, L 2006, ch 746, § 5, eff Dec 15, 2006. Sub (3), formerly sub (3) [first setout], add, L 2006, ch 245, § 3, eff Nov 1, 2006; amd, L 2006, ch 746, § 5, eff Dec 15, 2006, L 2009, ch 496, § 9, eff Dec 18, 2009. Sub (4), formerly sub (3) [second setout], add, L 2006, ch 732, § 22, eff Nov 1, 2006; so designated sub (4) and amd, L 2006, ch 746, § 5, eff Dec 15, 2006, L 2009, ch 496, § 9, eff Dec 18, 2009. Sub (5), formerly sub (4), add, L 2006, ch 732, § 22, eff Nov 1, 2006; so designated sub (5) and amd, L 2006, ch 746, § 5, eff Dec 15, 2006, L 2009, ch 496, § 9, eff Dec 18, 2009. Sub (6), add, L 2009, ch 496, § 9, eff Dec 18, 2009. Former sub (5), add, L 2006, ch 732, § 22, eff Nov 1, 2006; deleted, L 2006, ch 746, § 5, eff Dec 15, 2006. Second undesignated par, add, L 2005, ch 39, § 5, eff June 8, 2005; amd, L 2006, ch 732, § 22, eff Nov 1, 2006.

§ 125.14. Aggravated vehicular homicide

A person is guilty of aggravated vehicular homicide when he or she engages in reckless driving as defined by section twelve hundred twelve of the vehicle and traffic law, and commits the crime of vehicular manslaughter in the second degree as defined in section 125.12 of this article, and either:

(1) commits such crimes while operating a motor vehicle while such person has .18 of one per centum or more by weight of alcohol in such person's blood as shown by chemical analysis of such person's blood, breath, urine or saliva made pursuant to the provisions of section eleven hundred ninety-four of the vehicle and traffic law;

(2) commits such crimes while knowing or having reason to know that: (a) his or her license or his or her privilege of operating a motor vehicle in another state or his or her privilege of obtaining a license to operate a motor vehicle in another state is suspended or revoked and such suspension or revocation is based upon a conviction in such other state for an offense which would, if committed in this state, constitute a violation of any of the provisions of section eleven hundred ninety-two of the vehicle and traffic law; or (b) his or her license or his or her privilege of operating a motor vehicle in this state or his or her privilege of obtaining a license issued by the commissioner of motor vehicles is suspended or revoked and such suspension or revocation is based upon either a refusal to submit to a chemical test pursuant to section eleven hundred ninety-four of the vehicle and traffic law or following a conviction for a violation of any of the provisions of section eleven hundred ninety-two of the vehicle and traffic law;

(3) has previously been convicted of violating any of the provisions of section eleven hundred ninety-two of the vehicle and traffic law within the preceding ten years, provided that, for the purposes of this subdivision, a conviction in any other state or jurisdiction for an offense which, if committed in this state, would constitute a violation of section eleven hundred ninety-two of the vehicle and traffic law, shall be treated as a violation of such law;

(4) causes the death of more than one other person;

(5) causes the death of one person and the serious physical injury of at least one other person;

(6) has previously been convicted of violating any provision of this article or article one hundred twenty of this title involving the operation of a motor vehicle, or was convicted in any other state or jurisdiction of an offense involving the operation of a motor vehicle which, if committed in this state, would constitute a violation of this article or article one hundred twenty of this title; or

(7) commits such crime while operating a motor vehicle while a child who is fifteen years of age or less is a passenger in such motor vehicle and causes the death of such child.

If it is established that the person operating such motor vehicle caused such death or deaths while unlawfully intoxicated or impaired by the use of alcohol or a drug, or by the combined influence of drugs or of alcohol and any drug or drugs, then there shall be a rebuttable presumption that, as a result of such intoxication or impairment by the use of alcohol or a drug, or by the combined influence of drugs or of alcohol and any drug or drugs, such person operated the motor vehicle in a manner that caused such death or deaths, as required by this section and section 125.12 of this article.

Aggravated vehicular homicide is a class B felony.

HISTORY: Add, L 2007, ch 345, § 2, eff Nov 1, 2007; amd, L 2009, ch 496, § 10, eff Dec 18, 2009. Sub (5), amd, L 2009, ch 496, § 10, eff Dec 18, 2009. Sub (6), amd, L 2009, ch 496, § 10, eff Dec 18, 2009. Sub (7), add, L 2009, ch 496, § 10, eff Dec 18, 2009.

§ 125.15. Manslaughter in the second degree

A person is guilty of manslaughter in the second degree when:

1. He recklessly causes the death of another person; or

2. He commits upon a female an abortional act which causes her death, unless such abortional act is justifiable pursuant to subdivision three of section 125.05; or

3. He intentionally causes or aids another person to commit suicide.

Manslaughter in the second degree is a class C felony.

HISTORY: Add, L 1965, ch 1030, eff Sept 1, 1967, with substance derived from §§ 1050, 1053-a to 1053-f, 1391, 2304.

§ 125.20. Manslaughter in the first degree

A person is guilty of manslaughter in the first degree when:

1. With intent to cause serious physical injury to another person, he causes the death of such person or of a third person; or

2. With intent to cause the death of another person, he causes the death of such person or of a third person under circumstances which do not constitute murder because he acts under the influence of extreme emotional disturbance, as defined in paragraph (a) of subdivision one of section 125.25. The fact that homicide was committed under the influence of extreme emotional disturbance constitutes a mitigating circumstance reducing murder to manslaughter in the first degree and need not be proved in any prosecution initiated under this subdivision; or

3. He commits upon a female pregnant for more than twenty-four weeks an abortional act which causes her death, unless such abortional act is justifiable pursuant to subdivision three of section 125.05; or

4. Being eighteen years old or more and with intent to cause physical injury to a person less than eleven years old, the defendant recklessly engages in conduct which creates a grave risk of serious physical injury to such person and thereby causes the death of such person.

Manslaughter in the first degree is a class B felony.

HISTORY: Add, L 1965, ch 1030, eff Sept 1, 1967, with substance derived in part from § 1050. Sub 3, amd, L 1990, ch 477, § 3, eff Nov 1, 1990. Sub 4, add, L 1990, ch 477, § 3, eff Nov 1, 1990.

§ 125.21. Aggravated manslaughter in the second degree

A person is guilty of aggravated manslaughter in the second degree when he or she recklessly causes the death of a police officer or peace officer where such officer was in the course of performing his or her official duties and the defendant knew or reasonably should have known that such victim was a police officer or peace officer.

Aggravated manslaughter in the second degree is a class C felony.

HISTORY: Add, L 2005, ch 765, § 10, eff Dec 21, 2005.

§ 125.22. Aggravated manslaughter in the first degree

A person is guilty of aggravated manslaughter in the first degree when:

1. with intent to cause serious physical injury to a police officer or peace officer, where such officer was in the course of performing his or her official duties and the defendant knew or reasonably should have known that such victim was a police officer or a peace officer, he or she causes the death of such officer or another police officer or peace officer; or

2. with intent to cause the death of a police officer or peace officer, where such officer was in the course of performing his or her official duties and the defendant knew or reasonably should have known that such victim was a police officer or peace officer, he or she causes the death of such officer or another police officer or peace officer under circumstances which do not constitute murder because he or she acts under the influence of extreme emotional disturbance, as defined in paragraph (a) of subdivision one of section 125.25. The fact that homicide was committed under the influence of extreme emotional disturbance constitutes a mitigating circumstance reducing murder to aggravated manslaughter in the first degree or manslaughter in the first degree and need not be proved in any prosecution initiated under this subdivision.

Aggravated manslaughter in the first degree is a class B felony.

HISTORY: Add, L 2005, ch 765, § 10, eff Dec 21, 2005.

§ 125.25. Murder in the second degree

A person is guilty of murder in the second degree when:

1. With intent to cause the death of another person, he causes the death of such person or of a third person; except that in any prosecution under this subdivision, it is an affirmative defense that:

    (a) The defendant acted under the influence of extreme emotional disturbance for which there was a reasonable explanation or excuse, the reasonableness of which is to be determined from the viewpoint of a person in the defendant's situation under the circumstances as the defendant believed them to be. Nothing contained in this paragraph shall constitute a defense to a prosecution for, or preclude a conviction of, manslaughter in the first degree or any other crime; or

    (b) The defendant's conduct consisted of causing or aiding, without the use of duress or deception, another person to commit suicide. Nothing contained in this paragraph shall constitute a defense to a prosecution for, or preclude a conviction of, manslaughter in the second degree or any other crime; or

2. Under circumstances evincing a depraved indifference to human life, he recklessly engages in conduct which creates a grave risk of death to another person, and thereby causes the death of another person; or

3. Acting either alone or with one or more other persons, he commits or attempts to commit robbery, burglary, kidnapping, arson, rape in the first degree, criminal sexual act in the first degree, sexual abuse in the first degree, aggravated sexual abuse, escape in the first degree, or escape in the second degree, and, in the course of and in furtherance of such crime or of

immediate flight therefrom, he, or another participant, if there be any, causes the death of a person other than one of the participants; except that in any prosecution under this subdivision, in which the defendant was not the only participant in the underlying crime, it is an affirmative defense that the defendant:

(a) Did not commit the homicidal act or in any way solicit, request, command, importune, cause or aid the commission thereof; and

(b) Was not armed with a deadly weapon, or any instrument, article or substance readily capable of causing death or serious physical injury and of a sort not ordinarily carried in public places by law-abiding persons; and

(c) Had no reasonable ground to believe that any other participant was armed with such a weapon, instrument, article or substance; and

(d) Had no reasonable ground to believe that any other participant intended to engage in conduct likely to result in death or serious physical injury; or

4. Under circumstances evincing a depraved indifference to human life, and being eighteen years old or more the defendant recklessly engages in conduct which creates a grave risk of serious physical injury or death to another person less than eleven years old and thereby causes the death of such person; or

5. Being eighteen years old or more, while in the course of committing rape in the first, second or third degree, criminal sexual act in the first, second or third degree, sexual abuse in the first degree, aggravated sexual abuse in the first, second, third or fourth degree, or incest in the first, second or third degree, against a person less than fourteen years old, he or she intentionally causes the death of such person.

Murder in the second degree is a class A-I felony.

HISTORY: Add, L 1965, ch 1030; amd, L 1967, ch 791, § 9, eff Sept 1, 1967, with substance derived from §§ 1044, 1046. Section heading, amd, L 1974, ch 367, § 4, eff Sept 1, 1974. Opening par, amd, L 1974, ch 367, § 4, eff Sept 1, 1974. Sub 3, amd, L 1990, ch 477, § 4, eff Nov 1, 1990. Sub 3, opening par, amd, L 1984, ch 210, § 1, eff Nov 1, 1984, and applicable to all fact situations arising after the effective date of this act. Sub 3, opening par, amd, L 2003, ch 264, § 10, eff Nov 1, 2003. Sub 4, add, L 1990, ch 477, § 4, eff Nov 1, 1990. Sub 4, amd, L 2004, ch 459, § 4, eff Nov 1, 2004. Sub 5, add, L 2004, ch 459, § 4, eff Nov 1, 2004; amd, L 2006, ch 320, § 7, eff Nov 1, 2006. Concluding par, amd, L 1973, ch 276, § 13, L 1974, ch 367, § 4, eff Sept 1, 1974.

§ 125.26. Aggravated murder

A person is guilty of aggravated murder when:

1. With intent to cause the death of another person, he or she causes the death of such person, or of a third person who was a person described in subparagraph (i), (ii), (ii-a) or (iii) of paragraph (a) of this subdivision engaged at the time of the killing in the course of performing his or her official duties; and

(a) Either:

(i) the intended victim was a police officer as defined in subdivision thirty-four of section 1.20 of the criminal procedure law who was at the time of the killing engaged in the course of performing his or her official duties, and the defendant knew or reasonably should have known that the victim was a police officer; or

(ii) the intended victim was a peace officer as defined in paragraph a of subdivision twenty-one, subdivision twenty-three, twenty-four or sixty-two (employees of the division for youth) of section 2.10 of the criminal procedure law who was at the time of the killing engaged in the course of performing his or her official duties, and the defendant knew or reasonably should have known that the victim was such a uniformed court officer, parole officer, probation officer, or employee of the division for youth; or

(ii-a) the intended victim was a firefighter, emergency medical technician, ambulance driver, paramedic, physician or registered nurse involved in a first response team, or any other individual who, in the course of official duties, performs emergency response activities and was engaged in such activities at the time of killing and the defendant knew or reasonably should have known that the intended victim was such firefighter, emergency medical technician, ambulance driver, paramedic, physician or registered nurse; or

(iii) the intended victim was an employee of a state correctional institution or was an employee of a local correctional facility as defined in subdivision two of section forty of the correction law, who was at the time of the killing engaged in the course of performing his or her official duties, and the defendant knew or reasonably should have known that the victim was an employee of a state correctional institution or a local correctional facility; and

(b) The defendant was more than eighteen years old at the time of the commission of the crime; or

2. (a) With intent to cause the death of a person less than fourteen years old, he or she causes the death of such person, and the defendant acted in an especially cruel and wanton manner pursuant to a course of conduct intended to inflict and inflicting torture upon the victim prior to the victim's death. As used in this subdivision, "torture" means the intentional and depraved infliction of extreme physical pain that is separate and apart from the pain which otherwise would have been associated with such cause of death; and

(b) The defendant was more than eighteen years old at the time of the commission of the crime.

3. In any prosecution under subdivision one or two of this section, it is an affirmative defense that:

(a) The defendant acted under the influence of extreme emotional disturbance for which there was a reasonable explanation or excuse, the reasonableness of which is to be determined from the viewpoint of a person in the defendant's situation under the circumstances as the defendant believed them to be. Nothing contained in this paragraph shall constitute a defense to a prosecution for, or preclude a conviction of, aggravated manslaughter in the first degree, manslaughter in the first degree or any other crime except murder in the second degree; or

(b) The defendant's conduct consisted of causing or aiding, without the use of duress or deception, another person to commit suicide. Nothing contained in this paragraph shall constitute a defense to a prosecution for, or preclude a conviction of, aggravated manslaughter in the second degree, manslaughter in the second degree or any other crime except murder in the second degree.

Aggravated murder is a class A-I felony.

HISTORY: Add, L 2005, ch 765, § 13, eff Dec 21, 2005; amd, L 2009, ch 482, § 1, eff Oct 9, 2009, L 2013, ch 1, §§ 34, 35, eff March 16, 2013.

§ 125.27. Murder in the first degree

A person is guilty of murder in the first degree when:

1. With intent to cause the death of another person, he causes the death of such person or of a third person; and

(a) Either:

(i) the intended victim was a police officer as defined in subdivision 34 of section 1.20 of the criminal procedure law who was at the time of the killing engaged in the course of performing his official duties, and the defendant knew or reasonably should have known that the intended victim was a police officer; or

(ii) the intended victim was a peace officer as defined in paragraph a of subdivision twenty-one, subdivision twenty-three, twenty-four or sixty-two (employees of the division for youth) of section 2.10 of the criminal procedure law who was at the time of the killing engaged in the course of performing his official duties, and the defendant knew or reasonably should have known that the intended victim was such a uniformed court officer, parole officer, probation officer, or employee of the division for youth; or

(ii-a) the intended victim was a firefighter, emergency medical technician, ambulance driver, paramedic, physician or registered nurse involved in a first response team, or any other individual who, in the course of official duties, performs emergency response activities and was engaged in such activities at the time of killing and the defendant knew or reasonably should have known that the intended victim was such firefighter, emergency medical technician, ambulance driver, paramedic, physician or registered nurse; or

(iii) the intended victim was an employee of a state correctional institution or was an employee of a local correctional facility as defined in subdivision two of section forty of the correction law, who was at the time of the killing engaged in the course of performing his official duties, and the defendant knew or reasonably should have known that the intended victim was an employee of a state correctional institution or a local correctional facility; or

(iv) at the time of the commission of the killing, the defendant was confined in a state correctional institution or was otherwise in custody upon a sentence for the term of his natural life, or upon a sentence commuted to one of natural life, or upon a sentence for an indeterminate term the minimum of which was at least fifteen years and the maximum of which was natural life, or at the time of the commission of the killing, the defendant had escaped from such confinement or custody while serving such a sentence and had not yet been returned to such confinement or custody; or

(v) the intended victim was a witness to a crime committed on a prior occasion and the death was caused for the purpose of preventing the intended victim's testimony in any criminal action or proceeding whether or not such action or proceeding had been commenced, or the intended victim had previously testified in a criminal action or proceeding and the killing was committed for the purpose of exacting retribution for such prior testimony, or the intended victim was an immediate family member of a witness to a crime committed on a prior occasion and the killing was committed for the purpose of preventing or influencing the testimony of such witness, or the intended victim was an immediate family member of a witness who had previously testified in a criminal action or proceeding and the killing was committed for the purpose of exacting retribution upon such witness for such prior testimony. As used in this subparagraph "immediate family member" means a husband, wife, father, mother, daughter, son, brother, sister, stepparent, grandparent, stepchild or grandchild; or

(vi) the defendant committed the killing or procured commission of the killing pursuant to an agreement with a person other than the intended victim to commit the same for the receipt, or in expectation of the receipt, of anything of pecuniary value from a party to the agreement or from a person other than the intended victim acting at the direction of a party to such agreement; or

(vii) the victim was killed while the defendant was in the course of committing or attempting to commit and in furtherance of robbery, burglary in the first degree or second degree, kidnapping in the first degree, arson in the first degree or second degree, rape in the first degree, criminal sexual act in the first degree, sexual abuse in the first degree, aggravated sexual abuse in the first degree or escape in the first degree, or in the course of and furtherance of immediate flight after committing or attempting to commit any such crime or in the course of and furtherance of immediate flight after attempting to commit the crime of murder in the second degree; provided however, the victim is not a participant in one of the aforementioned crimes and, provided further that, unless the defendant's criminal liability under this subparagraph is based upon the defendant having commanded another person to cause the death of the victim or intended victim pursuant to section 20.00 of this chapter, this subparagraph shall not apply where the defendant's criminal liability is based upon the conduct of another pursuant to section 20.00 of this chapter; or

(viii) as part of the same criminal transaction, the defendant, with intent to cause serious physical injury to or the death of an additional person or persons, causes the death of an additional person or persons; provided, however, the victim is not a participant in the criminal transaction; or

(ix) prior to committing the killing, the defendant had been convicted of murder as defined in this section or section 125.25 of this article, or had been convicted in another jurisdiction of an offense which, if committed in this state, would constitute a violation of either of such sections; or

(x) the defendant acted in an especially cruel and wanton manner pursuant to a course of conduct intended to inflict and inflicting torture upon the victim prior to the victim's death. As used in this subparagraph, "torture" means the intentional and depraved infliction of extreme physical pain; "depraved" means the defendant relished the infliction of extreme physical pain upon the victim evidencing debasement or perversion or that the defendant evidenced a sense of pleasure in the infliction of extreme physical pain; or

(xi) the defendant intentionally caused the death of two or more additional persons within the state in separate criminal transactions within a period of twenty-four months when committed in a similar fashion or pursuant to a common scheme or plan; or

(xii) the intended victim was a judge as defined in subdivision twenty-three of section 1.20 of the criminal procedure law and the defendant killed such victim because such victim was, at the time of the killing, a judge; or

(xiii) the victim was killed in furtherance of an act of terrorism, as defined in paragraph (b) of subdivision one of section 490.05 of this chapter; and

(b) The defendant was more than eighteen years old at the time of the commission of the crime.

2. In any prosecution under subdivision one, it is an affirmative defense that:

(a) The defendant acted under the influence of extreme emotional disturbance for which there was a reasonable explanation or excuse, the reasonableness of which is to be determined from the viewpoint of a person in the defendant's situation under the circumstances as the defendant believed them to be. Nothing contained in this paragraph shall constitute a defense to a prosecution for, or preclude a conviction of, manslaughter in the first degree or any other crime except murder in the second degree; or

(b) The defendant's conduct consisted of causing or aiding, without the use of duress or deception, another person to commit suicide. Nothing contained in this paragraph shall constitute a defense to a prosecution for, or preclude a conviction of, manslaughter in the second degree or any other crime except murder in the second degree.

Murder in the first degree is a class A-I felony.

HISTORY: Add, L 1974, ch 367, § 5, eff Sept 1, 1974; amd, L 1995, ch 1, § 7, eff Sept 1, 1995, L 2001, ch 300, § 3, eff Sept 17, 2001, L 2003, ch 264, § 11, eff Nov 1, 2003, L 2013, ch 1, § 36, eff March 16, 2013.

§ 125.30. [Repealed]

HISTORY: Add, L 1967, ch 791, § 10, with substance derived from § 1045; amd, L 1968, ch 949, § 1, L 1971, ch 1205, § 1, L 1973, ch 276, § 16, L 1973, ch 278, § 10; repealed, L 1974, ch 367, § 6, eff Sept 1, 1974.

§ 125.35. [Repealed]

HISTORY: Add, L 1965, ch 1030, with substance derived from § 1045-a; amd, L 1967, ch 791, § 11; repealed, L 1974, ch 367, § 6, eff Sept 1, 1974.

§ 125.40. Abortion in the second degree

A person is guilty of abortion in the second degree when he commits an abortional act upon a female, unless such abortional act is justifiable pursuant to subdivision three of section 125.05.

Abortion in the second degree is a class E felony.

HISTORY: Add, L 1965, ch 1030, eff Sept 1, 1967, with substance derived from § 80.

§ 125.45. Abortion in the first degree

A person is guilty of abortion in the first degree when he commits upon a female pregnant for more than twenty-four weeks an abortional act which causes the miscarriage of such female, unless such abortional act is justifiable pursuant to subdivision three of section 125.05.

Abortion in the first degree is a class D felony.

HISTORY: Add, L 1965, ch 1030, eff Sept 1, 1967, with substance derived from §§ 80, 1050, 1051.

§ 125.50. Self-abortion in the second degree

A female is guilty of self-abortion in the second degree when, being pregnant, she commits or submits to an abortional act upon herself, unless such abortional act is justifiable pursuant to subdivision three of section 125.05.

Self-abortion in the second degree is a class B misdemeanor.

HISTORY: Add, L 1965, ch 1030, eff Sept 1, 1967, with substance derived from § 81.

§ 125.55. Self-abortion in the first degree

A female is guilty of self-abortion in the first degree when, being pregnant for more than twenty-four weeks, she commits or submits to an abortional act upon herself which causes her miscarriage, unless such abortional act is justifiable pursuant to subdivision three of section 125.05.

Self-abortion in the first degree is a class A misdemeanor.

HISTORY: Add, L 1965, ch 1030, eff Sept 1, 1967, with substance derived from §§ 81, 1052.

§ 125.60. Issuing abortional articles

A person is guilty of issuing abortional articles when he manufactures, sells or delivers any instrument, article, medicine, drug or substance with intent that the same be used in unlawfully procuring the miscarriage of a female.

Issuing abortional articles is a class B misdemeanor.

HISTORY: Add, L 1965, ch 1030, eff Sept 1, 1967, with substance derived from §§ 82, 1142.

ARTICLE 130   SEX OFFENSES

HISTORY: Add, L 1965, ch 1030, § 1, eff Sept 1, 1967.

§ 130.00. Sex offenses; definitions of terms

The following definitions are applicable to this article:

1. "Sexual intercourse" has its ordinary meaning and occurs upon any penetration, however slight.

2. (a) "Oral sexual conduct" means conduct between persons consisting of contact between the mouth and the penis, the mouth and the anus, or the mouth and the vulva or vagina.

   (b) "Anal sexual conduct" means conduct between persons consisting of contact between the penis and anus.

3. "Sexual contact" means any touching of the sexual or other intimate parts of a person for the purpose of gratifying sexual desire of either party. It includes the touching of the actor by the victim, as well as the touching of the victim by the actor, whether directly or through clothing, as well as the emission of ejaculate by the actor upon any part of the victim, clothed or unclothed.

4. For the purposes of this article "married" means the existence of the relationship between the actor and the victim as spouses which is recognized by law at the time the actor commits an offense proscribed by this article against the victim.

5. "Mentally disabled" means that a person suffers from a mental disease or defect which renders him or her incapable of appraising the nature of his or her conduct.

6. "Mentally incapacitated" means that a person is rendered temporarily incapable of appraising or controlling his conduct owing to the influence of a narcotic or intoxicating substance administered to him without his consent, or to any other act committed upon him without his consent.

7. "Physically helpless" means that a person is unconscious or for any other reason is physically unable to communicate unwillingness to an act.

8. "Forcible compulsion" means to compel by either:

   a. use of physical force; or

   b. a threat, express or implied, which places a person in fear of immediate death or physical injury to himself, herself or another person, or in fear that he, she or another person will immediately be kidnapped.

9. Foreign object" means any instrument or article which, when inserted in the vagina, urethra, penis, rectum or anus, is capable of causing physical injury.

10. "Sexual conduct" means sexual intercourse, oral sexual conduct, anal sexual conduct, aggravated sexual contact, or sexual contact.

11. "Aggravated sexual contact" means inserting, other than for a valid medical purpose, a foreign object in the vagina, urethra, penis, rectum or anus of a child, thereby causing physical injury to such child.

12. "Health care provider" means any person who is, or is required to be, licensed or registered or holds himself or herself out to be licensed or registered, or provides services as if he or she were licensed or registered in the profession of medicine, chiropractic, dentistry or podiatry under any of the following: article one hundred thirty-one, one hundred thirty-two, one hundred thirty-three, or one hundred forty-one of the education law.

13. "Mental health care provider" shall mean a licensed physician, licensed psychologist, registered professional nurse, licensed clinical social worker or a licensed master social worker under the supervision of a physician, psychologist or licensed clinical social worker.

HISTORY: Add, L 1965, ch 1030, § 1, eff Sept 1, 1967; amd, L 1977, ch 692, § 2, L 1978, ch 735, § 1, eff Sept 1, 1978, L 1981, ch 696, § 1, eff July 21, 1981, L 1982, ch 560, § 1, L 1983, ch 449, § 1, eff July 15, 1983, L 1984, ch 650, § 1, eff July 27, 1984, L 1996, ch 122, § 5, eff Aug 1, 1996, L 2000, ch 1, § 1-a, eff Feb 1, 2001, L 2003, ch 264, § 12, eff Nov 1, 2003, L 2004, ch 230, § 25, eff July 27, 2004, L 2009, ch 485, §§ 1, 2, eff Jan 7, 2010, L 2010, ch 193, § 1, eff Oct 13, 2010.

§ 130.05. Sex offenses; lack of consent

1. Whether or not specifically stated, it is an element of every offense defined in this article that the sexual act was committed without consent of the victim.

2. Lack of consent results from:

(a) Forcible compulsion; or

(b) Incapacity to consent; or

(c) Where the offense charged is sexual abuse or forcible touching, any circumstances, in addition to forcible compulsion or incapacity to consent, in which the victim does not expressly or impliedly acquiesce in the actor's conduct; or

(d) Where the offense charged is rape in the third degree as defined in subdivision three of section 130.25, or criminal sexual act in the third degree as defined in subdivision three of section 130.40, in addition to forcible compulsion, circumstances under which, at the time of the act of intercourse, oral sexual conduct or anal sexual conduct, the victim clearly expressed that he or she did not consent to engage in such act, and a reasonable person in the actor's situation would have understood such person's words and acts as an expression of lack of consent to such act under all the circumstances.

3. A person is deemed incapable of consent when he or she is:

(a) less than seventeen years old; or

(b) mentally disabled; or

(c) mentally incapacitated; or

(d) physically helpless; or

(e) committed to the care and custody or supervision of the state department of corrections and community supervision or a hospital, as such term is defined in subdivision two of section four hundred of the correction law, and the actor is an employee who knows or reasonably should know that such person is committed to the care and custody or supervision of such department or hospital. For purposes of this paragraph, "employee" means

(i) an employee of the state department of corrections and community supervision who, as part of his or her employment, performs duties:

(A) in a state correctional facility in which the victim is confined at the time of the offense consisting of providing custody, medical or mental health services, counseling services, educational programs, vocational training, institutional parole services or direct supervision to inmates; or

(B) of supervising persons released on community supervision and supervises the victim at the time of the offense or has supervised the victim and the victim is still under community supervision at the time of the offense; or

(ii) an employee of the office of mental health who, as part of his or her employment, performs duties in a state correctional facility or hospital, as such term is defined in subdivision two of section four hundred of the correction law in which the inmate is confined at the time of the offense, consisting of providing custody, medical or mental health services, or direct supervision to such inmates; or

(iii) a person, including a volunteer, providing direct services to inmates in a state correctional facility in which the victim is confined at the time of the offense pursuant to a contractual arrangement with the state department of corrections and community supervision or, in the case of a volunteer, a written agreement with such department, provided that the person received written notice concerning the provisions of this paragraph; or

(f) committed to the care and custody of a local correctional facility, as such term is defined in subdivision two of section forty of the correction law, and the actor is an employee, not married to such person, who knows or reasonably should know that such person is committed to the care and custody of such facility. For purposes of this paragraph, "employee" means an employee of the local correctional facility where the person is committed who performs professional duties consisting of providing custody, medical or mental health services, counseling services, educational services, or vocational training for inmates. For purposes of this paragraph, "employee" shall also mean a person, including a volunteer or a government employee of the state department of corrections and community supervision or a local health, education or probation agency, providing direct services to inmates in the local correctional facility in which the victim is confined at the time of the offense pursuant to a contractual arrangement with the local correctional department or, in the case of such a volunteer or government employee, a written agreement with such department, provided that such person received written notice concerning the provisions of this paragraph; or

(g) committed to or placed with the office of children and family services and in residential care, and the actor is an employee, not married to such person, who knows or reasonably should know that such person is committed to or placed with such office of children and family services and in residential care. For purposes of this paragraph, "employee" means an employee of the office of children and family services or of a residential facility in which such person is committed to or placed at the time of the offense who, as part of his or her employment, performs duties consisting of providing custody, medical or mental health services, counseling services, educational services, vocational training, or direct supervision to persons committed to or placed in a residential facility operated by the office of children and family services; or

(h) a client or patient and the actor is a health care provider or mental health care provider charged with rape in the third degree as defined in section 130.25, criminal sexual act in the third degree as defined in section 130.40, aggravated sexual abuse in the fourth degree as defined in section 130.65-a, or sexual abuse in the third degree as defined in section 130.55, and the act of sexual conduct occurs during a treatment session, consultation, interview, or examination; or

(i) a resident or inpatient of a residential facility operated, licensed or certified by (i) the office of mental health; (ii) the office for people with developmental disabilities; or (iii) the office of alcoholism and substance abuse services, and the actor is an employee of the facility not married to such resident or inpatient. For purposes of this paragraph, "employee" means either: an employee of the agency operating the residential facility, who knows or reasonably should know that such person is a resident or inpatient of such facility and who provides direct care services, case management services, medical or other clinical services, habilitative services or direct supervision of the residents in the facility in which the resident resides; or an officer or other employee, consultant, contractor or volunteer of the residential facility, who knows or reasonably should know that the person is a resident of such facility and who is in direct contact with residents or inpatients; provided, however, that the provisions of this paragraph shall only apply to a consultant, contractor or volunteer providing services pursuant to a contractual arrangement with the agency operating the residential facility or, in the case of a volunteer, a written agreement with such facility, provided that the person received written notice concerning the provisions of this paragraph; provided further, however, "employee" shall not include a person with a developmental disability who is or was receiving services and is also an employee of a service provider and who has sexual contact with another service recipient who is a consenting adult who has consented to such contact.

HISTORY: Add, L 1965, ch 1030, § 1, eff Sept 1, 1967; amd, L 1965, ch 1038, § 1, eff Sept 1, 1967, L 1996, ch 266, § 1, eff Aug 1, 1996, L 2000, ch 1, §§ 3, 45, eff Feb 1, 2001, L 2003, ch 264, §§ 13, 14, eff Nov 1, 2003, L 2004, ch 40, § 1, eff April 20, 2004, L 2007, ch 335, §§ 1, 2, eff Nov 1, 2007, L 2011, ch 62, § 127-q (Part C, Subpart B), eff March 31, 2011, L 2011, ch 205, §§ 1, 2, eff Nov 1, 2011, L 2012, ch 501, § 2 (Part G), eff Jan 17, 2013.

§ 130.10. Sex offenses; limitation; defenses

1. In any prosecution under this article in which the victim's lack of consent is based solely upon his or her incapacity to consent because he or she was mentally disabled, mentally incapacitated or physically helpless, it is an affirmative defense that the defendant, at the time he or she engaged in the conduct constituting the offense, did not know of the facts or conditions responsible for such incapacity to consent.

2. Conduct performed for a valid medical or mental health care purpose shall not constitute a violation of any section of this article in which incapacity to consent is based on the circumstances set forth in paragraph (h) of subdivision three of section 130.05 of this article.

3. In any prosecution for the crime of rape in the third degree as defined in section 130.25, criminal sexual act in the third degree as defined in section 130.40, aggravated sexual abuse in the fourth degree as defined in section 130.65-a, or sexual abuse in the third degree as defined in section 130.55 in which incapacity to consent is based on the circumstances set forth in paragraph (h) of subdivision three of section 130.05 of this article it shall be an affirmative defense that the client or patient consented to such conduct charged after having been expressly advised by the health care or mental health care provider that such conduct was not performed for a valid medical purpose.

4. In any prosecution under this article in which the victim's lack of consent is based solely on his or her incapacity to consent because he or she was less than seventeen years old, mentally disabled, a client or patient and the actor is a health care provider, or committed to the care and custody or supervision of the state department of corrections and community supervision or a hospital and the actor is an employee, it shall be a defense that the defendant was married to the victim as defined in subdivision four of section 130.00 of this article.

HISTORY: Add, L 1965, ch 1030, § 1, eff Sept 1, 1967; amd, L 2000, ch 1, § 4, eff Feb 1, 2001, L 2003, ch 264, § 15, eff Nov 1, 2003, L 2011, ch 205, § 3, eff Nov 1, 2011.

§ 130.15. [Repealed]

HISTORY: Add, L 1965, ch 1030, § 1, with substance derived in part from § 2013; amd, L 1972, ch 373, § 1; repealed, L 1974, ch 14, § 1, eff March 21, 1974.

§ 130.16. Sex offenses; corroboration

A person shall not be convicted of any offense defined in this article of which lack of consent is an element but results solely from incapacity to consent because of the victim's mental defect, or mental incapacity, or an attempt to commit the same, solely on the testimony of the victim, unsupported by other evidence tending to:

(a) Establish that an attempt was made to engage the victim in sexual intercourse, oral sexual conduct, anal sexual conduct, or sexual contact, as the case may be, at the time of the occurrence; and

(b) Connect the defendant with the commission of the offense or attempted offense.

HISTORY: Add, L 1974, ch 14, § 1; amd, L 1984, ch 89, § 1, eff Nov 1, 1984. Opening par, amd, L 1984, ch 89, § 1, eff Nov 1, 1984. Opening par, amd, L 2003, ch 264, § 16, eff Nov 1, 2003. Sub (a), amd, L 1984, ch 89, § 1, eff Nov 1, 1984. Sub (a), amd, L 2003, ch 264, § 16, eff Nov 1, 2003.

§ 130.20. Sexual misconduct

A person is guilty of sexual misconduct when:

1. He or she engages in sexual intercourse with another person without such person's consent; or

2. He or she engages in oral sexual conduct or anal sexual conduct with another person without such person's consent; or

3. He or she engages in sexual conduct with an animal or a dead human body.

Sexual misconduct is a class A misdemeanor.

HISTORY: Add, L 1965, ch 1030, § 1, eff Sept 1, 1967, with substance derived from §§ 690 in part, 2010. Amd, L 2000, ch 1, § 31, eff Feb 1, 2001. Sub 1, amd, L 2000, ch 1, § 31, eff Feb 1, 2001. Sub 2, amd, L 2000, ch 1, § 31, eff Feb 1, 2001, L 2003, ch 264, § 17, eff Nov 1, 2003. Sub 3, amd, L 2000, ch 1, § 31, eff Feb 1, 2001.

§ 130.25. Rape in the third degree

A person is guilty of rape in the third degree when:

1. He or she engages in sexual intercourse with another person who is incapable of consent by reason of some factor other than being less than seventeen years old;

2. Being twenty-one years old or more, he or she engages in sexual intercourse with another person less than seventeen years old; or

3. He or she engages in sexual intercourse with another person without such person's consent where such lack of consent is by reason of some factor other than incapacity to consent.

Rape in the third degree is a class E felony.

HISTORY: Add, L 1965, ch 1030, § 1, eff Sept 1, 1967, with substance derived from § 2010. Amd, L 2000, ch 1, § 32, eff Feb 1, 2001. Opening par, amd, L 1987, ch 510, § 1, eff Nov 1, 1987. Sub 1, amd, L 1987, ch 510, § 1, eff Nov 1, 1987. Sub 1, amd, L 2000, ch 1, § 32, eff Feb 1, 2001. Sub 2, amd, L 1987, ch 510, § 1, eff Nov 1, 1987. Sub 2, amd, L 2000, ch 1, § 32, eff Feb 1, 2001. Sub 3, add, L 2000, ch 1, § 32, eff Feb 1, 2001.

§ 130.30. Rape in the second degree

A person is guilty of rape in the second degree when:

1. being eighteen years old or more, he or she engages in sexual intercourse with another person less than fifteen years old; or

2. he or she engages in sexual intercourse with another person who is incapable of consent by reason of being mentally disabled or mentally incapacitated.

It shall be an affirmative defense to the crime of rape in the second degree as defined in subdivision one of this section that the defendant was less than four years older than the victim at the time of the act.

Rape in the second degree is a class D felony.

HISTORY: Add, L 1965, ch 1030, § 1, eff Sept 1, 1967. Amd, L 2000, ch 1, § 33, eff Feb 1, 2001. First undesignated par, amd, L 1987, ch 510, § 2, eff Nov 1, 1987. Opening par, formerly part of first undesignated par, so designated opening par and amd, L 2000, ch 1, § 33, eff Feb 1, 2001. Sub 1, formerly part of first undesignated par, so designated sub 1 and amd, L 2000, ch 1, § 33, eff Feb 1, 2001. Sub 2, add, L 2000, ch 1, § 33, eff Feb 1, 2001. Second undesignated par, add, L 2000, ch 1, § 33, eff Feb 1, 2001.

§ 130.35. Rape in the first degree

A person is guilty of rape in the first degree when he or she engages in sexual intercourse with another person:

1. By forcible compulsion; or

2. Who is incapable of consent by reason of being physically helpless; or

3. Who is less than eleven years old; or

4. Who is less than thirteen years old and the actor is eighteen years old or more.

Rape in the first degree is a class B felony.

HISTORY: Add, L 1965, ch 1030, § 1, eff Sept 1, 1967, with substance derived in part from § 2010. Amd, L 2000, ch 1, § 34, eff Feb 1, 2001. Opening par, amd, L 2000, ch 1, § 34, eff Feb 1, 2001. Sub 3, amd, L 2000, ch 1, § 34, eff Feb 1, 2001. Sub 4, add, L 2000, ch 1, § 34, eff Feb 1, 20001.

§ 130.38. [Repealed]

HISTORY: Add, L 1965, ch 1038, § 2, eff Sept 1, 1967. Repealed, L 2000, ch 1, § 6, eff Feb 1, 2001.

§ 130.40. Criminal sexual act in the third degree

A person is guilty of criminal sexual act in the third degree when:

1. He or she engages in oral sexual conduct or anal sexual conduct with a person who is incapable of consent by reason of some factor other than being less than seventeen years old;

2. Being twenty-one years old or more, he or she engages in oral sexual conduct or anal sexual conduct with a person less than seventeen years old; or

3. He or she engages in oral sexual conduct or anal sexual conduct with another person without such person's consent where such lack of consent is by reason of some factor other than incapacity to consent.

Criminal sexual act in the third degree is a class E felony.

HISTORY: Add, L 1965, ch 1030, § 1, eff Sept 1, 1967, with substance derived from § 690 in part. Amd, L 2000, ch 1, § 35, eff Feb 1, 2001, L 2003, ch 264, § 18, eff Nov 1, 2003. Section heading amd, L 2003, ch 264, § 18, eff Nov 1, 2003. Opening par, amd, L 2003, ch 264, § 18, eff Nov 1, 2003. Sub 1, amd, L 2000, ch 1, § 35, eff Feb 1, 2001, L 2003, ch 264, § 18, eff Nov 1, 2003. Sub 2, amd, L 2000, ch 1, § 35, eff Feb 1, 2001, L 2003, ch 264, § 18, eff Nov 1, 2003. Sub 3, add, L 2000, ch 1, § 35, eff Feb 1, 2001; amd, L 2003, ch 264, § 18, eff Nov 1, 2003. Closing par, amd, L 2003, ch 264, § 18, eff Nov 1, 2003.

§ 130.45. Criminal sexual act in the second degree

A person is guilty of criminal sexual act in the second degree when:

1. being eighteen years old or more, he or she engages in oral sexual conduct or anal sexual conduct with another person less than fifteen years old; or

2. he or she engages in oral sexual conduct or anal sexual conduct with another person who is incapable of consent by reason of being mentally disabled or mentally incapacitated.

It shall be an affirmative defense to the crime of criminal sexual act in the second degree as defined in subdivision one of this section that the defendant was less than four years older than the victim at the time of the act.

Criminal sexual act in the second degree is a class D felony.

> **HISTORY:** Add, L 1965, ch 1030, § 1, eff Sept 1, 1967. Amd, L 2000, ch 1, § 36, eff Feb 1, 2001, L 2003, ch 264, § 19, eff Nov 1, 2003. Section heading, amd, L 2003, ch 264, § 19, eff Nov 1, 2003. Opening par, formerly part of first undesignated par, so designated opening par and amd, L 2000, ch 1, § 36, eff Feb 1, 2001; amd, L 2003, ch 264, § 19, eff Nov 1, 2003. Sub 1, formerly part of first undesignated par, so designated sub 1 and amd, L 2000, ch 1, § 36, eff Feb 1, 2001; amd, L 2003, ch 264, § 19, eff Nov 1, 2003. Sub 2, add, L 2000, ch 1, § 36, eff Feb 1, 2001; amd, L 2003, ch 264, § 19, eff Nov 1, 2003. Second undesignated par, add, L 2000, ch 1, § 36, eff Feb 1, 2001; amd, L 2003, ch 264, § 19, eff Nov 1, 2003. Closing par, amd, L 2003, ch 264, § 19, eff Nov 1, 2003.

§ 130.50. Criminal sexual act in the first degree

A person is guilty of criminal sexual act in the first degree when he or she engages in oral sexual conduct or anal sexual conduct with another person:

1. By forcible compulsion; or

2. Who is incapable of consent by reason of being physically helpless; or

3. Who is less than eleven years old; or

4. Who is less than thirteen years old and the actor is eighteen years old or more.

Criminal sexual act in the first degree is a class B felony.

> **HISTORY:** Add, L 1965, ch 1030, § 1, eff Sept 1, 1967, with substance derived from § 690 in part. Amd, L 2000, ch 1, § 37, eff Feb 1, 2001, L 2003, ch 264, § 20, eff Nov 1, 2003. Section heading, amd, L 2003, ch 264, § 20, eff Nov 1, 2003. Opening par, amd, L 2000, ch 1, § 37, eff Feb 1, 2001, L 2003, ch 264, § 20, eff Nov 1, 2003. Sub 3, amd, L 2000, ch 1, § 37, eff Feb 1, 2001. Sub 4, add, L 2000, ch 1, § 37, eff Feb 1, 2001. Closing par, amd, L 2003, ch 264, § 20, eff Nov 1, 2003.

§ 130.52. Forcible touching

A person is guilty of forcible touching when such person intentionally, and for no legitimate purpose, forcibly touches the sexual or other intimate parts of another person for the purpose of degrading or abusing such person; or for the purpose of gratifying the actor's sexual desire.

For the purposes of this section, forcible touching includes squeezing, grabbing or pinching.

Forcible touching is a class A misdemeanor.

> **HISTORY:** Add, L 2000, ch 1, § 53, eff Feb 1, 2001; amd, L 2003, ch 264, § 21, eff Nov 1, 2003. Opening par, formerly part of subs 1 and 2, so designated opening par and amd, L 2003, ch 264, § 21, eff Nov 1, 2003. Sub 1, redesignated part of opening par, L 2003, ch 264, § 21, eff Nov 1, 2003. Sub 2, redesignated part of opening par, L 2003, ch 264, § 21, eff Nov 1, 2003. Second undesignated par, amd, L 2003, ch 264, § 21, eff Nov 1, 2003.

§ 130.53. Persistent sexual abuse

A person is guilty of persistent sexual abuse when he or she commits the crime of forcible touching, as defined in section 130.52 of this article, sexual abuse in the third degree, as defined in section 130.55 of this article, or sexual abuse in the second degree, as defined in section 130.60 of this article, and, within the previous ten year period, excluding any time during which such person was incarcerated for any reason, has been convicted two or more times, in separate criminal transactions for which sentence was imposed on separate occasions, of forcible touching, as defined in section 130.52 of this article, sexual abuse in the third degree as defined in section 130.55 of this article, sexual abuse in the second degree, as defined in section 130.60 of this article, or any offense defined in this article, of which the commission or attempted commission thereof is a felony.

Persistent sexual abuse is a class E felony.

HISTORY: Add, L 2000, ch 1, § 38, eff Feb 1, 2001; amd, L 2003, ch 264, § 22, eff Nov 1, 2003, L 2014, ch 192, § 1, eff Nov 1, 2014.

§ 130.55. Sexual abuse in the third degree

A person is guilty of sexual abuse in the third degree when he or she subjects another person to sexual contact without the latter's consent; except that in any prosecution under this section, it is an affirmative defense that (a) such other person's lack of consent was due solely to incapacity to consent by reason of being less than seventeen years old, and (b) such other person was more than fourteen years old, and (c) the defendant was less than five years older than such other person.

Sexual abuse in the third degree is a class B misdemeanor.

HISTORY: Add, L 1965, ch 1030, § 1, eff Sept 1, 1967, with substance derived from §§ 483-a, 483-b. Amd, L 2000, ch 1, § 39, eff Feb 1, 2001. Opening par, amd, L 2000, ch 1, § 39, eff Feb 1, 2001.

§ 130.60. Sexual abuse in the second degree

A person is guilty of sexual abuse in the second degree when he or she subjects another person to sexual contact and when such other person is:

1. Incapable of consent by reason of some factor other than being less than seventeen years old; or

2. Less than fourteen years old.

Sexual abuse in the second degree is a class A misdemeanor.

HISTORY: Add, L 1965, ch 1030, § 1, eff Sept 1, 1967, with substance derived from §§ 483-a, 483-b. Amd, L 2000, ch 1, § 40, eff Feb 1, 2001. Opening par, amd, L 2000, ch 1, § 40, eff Feb 1, 2001.

§ 130.65. Sexual abuse in the first degree

A person is guilty of sexual abuse in the first degree when he or she subjects another person to sexual contact:

1. By forcible compulsion; or

2. When the other person is incapable of consent by reason of being physically helpless; or

3. When the other person is less than eleven years old; or

4. When the other person is less than thirteen years old and the actor is twenty-one years old or older.

Sexual abuse in the first degree is a class D felony.

HISTORY: Add, L 1965, ch 1030, § 1, eff Sept 1, 1967, with substance derived from §§ 483-a,

483-b; amd, L 2000, ch 1, § 41, eff Feb 1, 2001, L 2000, ch 1, § 41, eff Feb 1, 2001, L 2011, ch 26, § 1, eff Nov 1, 2011.

§ 130.65-a. Aggravated sexual abuse in the fourth degree

1. A person is guilty of aggravated sexual abuse in the fourth degree when:

(a) He or she inserts a foreign object in the vagina, urethra, penis, rectum or anus of another person and the other person is incapable of consent by reason of some factor other than being less than seventeen years old; or

(b) He or she inserts a finger in the vagina, urethra, penis, rectum or anus of another person causing physical injury to such person and such person is incapable of consent by reason of some factor other than being less than seventeen years old.

2. Conduct performed for a valid medical purpose does not violate the provisions of this section. Aggravated sexual abuse in the fourth degree is a class E felony.

> **HISTORY:** Add, L 2000, ch 1, § 42, eff Feb 1, 2001. Sub 1, amd, L 2009, ch 485, § 3, eff Jan 7, 2010.

§ 130.66. Aggravated sexual abuse in the third degree

1. A person is guilty of aggravated sexual abuse in the third degree when he or she inserts a foreign object in the vagina, urethra, penis, rectum or anus of another person:

(a) By forcible compulsion; or

(b) When the other person is incapable of consent by reason of being physically helpless; or

(c) When the other person is less than eleven years old.

2. A person is guilty of aggravated sexual abuse in the third degree when he or she inserts a foreign object in the vagina, urethra, penis, rectum or anus of another person causing physical injury to such person and such person is incapable of consent by reason of being mentally disabled or mentally incapacitated.

3. Conduct performed for a valid medical purpose does not violate the provisions of this section. Aggravated sexual abuse in the third degree is a class D felony.

> **HISTORY:** Add, L 1996, ch 181, § 2, eff Nov 1, 1996. Sub 1, opening par, amd, L 2009, ch 485, § 4, eff Jan 7, 2010. Sub 2, add, L 2000, ch 1, § 43, eff Feb 1, 2001; amd, L 2009, ch 485, § 4, eff Jan 7, 2010. Former sub 2, redesignated sub 3, L 2000, ch 1, § 43, eff Feb 1, 2001. Sub 3, formerly sub 2, so designated sub 3, L 2000, ch 1, § 43, eff Feb 1, 2001.

§ 130.67. Aggravated sexual abuse in the second degree

1. A person is guilty of aggravated sexual abuse in the second degree when he or she inserts a finger in the vagina, urethra, penis, rectum, or anus of another person causing physical injury to such person:

(a) By forcible compulsion; or

(b) When the other person is incapable of consent by reason of being physically helpless; or

(c) When the other person is less than eleven years old.

2. Conduct performed for a valid medical purpose does not violate the provisions of this section. Aggravated sexual abuse in the second degree is a class C felony.

HISTORY: Add, L 1988, ch 450, § 1, eff Nov 1, 1988. Sub 1, opening par, amd, L 2009, ch 485, § 5, eff Jan 7, 2010.

§ 130.70. Aggravated sexual abuse in the first degree

1. A person is guilty of aggravated sexual abuse in the first degree when he or she inserts a foreign object in the vagina, urethra, penis, rectum or anus of another person causing physical injury to such person:

(a) By forcible compulsion; or

(b) When the other person is incapable of consent by reason of being physically helpless; or

(c) When the other person is less than eleven years old.

2. Conduct performed for a valid medical purpose does not violate the provisions of this section.

Aggravated sexual abuse in the first degree is a class B felony.

HISTORY: Add, L 1978, ch 723, § 1; amd, L 1981, ch 696, § 2, L 1988, ch 450, § 2, eff Nov 1, 1988. Section heading, amd, L 1988, ch 450, § 2, eff Nov 1, 1988. Sub 1, opening par, amd, L 2009, ch 485, § 6, eff Jan 7, 2010. Sub 1, amd, L 1988, ch 450, § 2, eff Nov 1, 1988. Concluding par, formerly sub 3, so designated and amd, L 1988, ch 450, § 2, eff Nov 1, 1988. Former sub 3, redesignated as concluding par, L 1988, ch 450, § 2, eff Nov 1, 1988.

§ 130.75. Course of sexual conduct against a child in the first degree

1. A person is guilty of course of sexual conduct against a child in the first degree when, over a period of time not less than three months in duration:

(a) he or she engages in two or more acts of sexual conduct, which includes at least one act of sexual intercourse, oral sexual conduct, anal sexual conduct or aggravated sexual contact, with a child less than eleven years old; or

(b) he or she, being eighteen years old or more, engages in two or more acts of sexual conduct, which include at least one act of sexual intercourse, oral sexual conduct, anal sexual conduct or aggravated sexual contact, with a child less than thirteen years old.

2. A person may not be subsequently prosecuted for any other sexual offense involving the same victim unless the other charged offense occurred outside the time period charged under this section.

Course of sexual conduct against a child in the first degree is a class B felony.

HISTORY: Add, L 1996, ch 122, § 6, eff Aug 1, 1996. Amd, L 2000, ch 1, § 44, eff Feb 1, 2001. Sub 1, formerly sub (a), so designated sub 1, L 2000, ch 1, § 44, eff Feb 1, 2001. Sub 1, opening par, amd, L 2000, ch 1, § 44, eff Feb 1, 2001. Sub 1, par (a), amd, L 2000, ch 1, § 44, eff Feb 1, 2001, L 2003, ch 264, § 23, eff Nov 1, 2003. Sub 1, par (b), add, L 2000, ch 1, § 44, eff Feb 1, 2001 L 2003, ch 264, § 23, eff Nov 1, 2003. Sub 2, formerly sub (b), so designated sub 2, L 2000, ch 1, § 44, eff Feb 1, 2001. Sub (a), redesignated sub 1, opening par and par (a), L 2000, ch 1, § 44, eff Feb 1, 2001. Sub (b), redesignated sub 2, L 2000, ch 1, § 44, eff Feb 1, 2001.

§ 130.80. Course of sexual conduct against a child in the second degree

1. A person is guilty of course of sexual conduct against a child in the second degree when, over a period of time not less than three months in duration:

(a) he or she engages in two or more acts of sexual conduct with a child less than eleven years old; or

(b) he or she, being eighteen years old or more, engages in two or more acts of sexual conduct with a child less than thirteen years old.

2. A person may not be subsequently prosecuted for any other sexual offense involving the same victim unless the other charged offense occurred outside the time period charged under this section.

Course of sexual conduct against a child in the second degree is a class D felony.

HISTORY: Add, L 1996, ch 122, § 6, eff Aug 1, 1996. Amd, L 2000, ch 1, § 44, eff Feb 1, 2001. Sub 1, formerly sub (a), so designated sub 1, L 2000, ch 1, § 44, eff Feb 1, 2001. Sub 1, opening par, amd, L 2000, ch 1, § 44, eff Feb 1, 2001. Sub 1, par (a), amd, L 2000, ch 1, § 44, eff Feb 1, 2001. Sub 1, par (b), add, L 2000, ch 1, § 44, eff Feb 1, 2001. Sub 2, formerly sub (b), so designated sub 2, L 2000, ch 1, § 44, eff Feb 1, 2001. Sub (a), redesignated sub 1, opening par and par (a), L 2000, ch 1, § 44, eff Feb 1, 2001. Sub (b), redesignated sub 2, L 2000, ch 1, § 44, eff Feb 1, 2001.

§ 130.85. Female genital mutilation

1. A person is guilty of female genital mutilation when:

(a) a person knowingly circumcises, excises, or infibulates the whole or any part of the labia majora or labia minora or clitoris of another person who has not reached eighteen years of age; or

(b) being a parent, guardian or other person legally responsible and charged with the care or custody of a child less than eighteen years old, he or she knowingly consents to the circumcision, excision or infibulation of whole or part of such child's labia majora or labia minora or clitoris.

2. Such circumcision, excision, or infibulation is not a violation of this section if such act is:

(a) necessary to the health of the person on whom it is performed, and is performed by a person licensed in the place of its performance as a medical practitioner; or

(b) performed on a person in labor or who has just given birth and is performed for medical purposes connected with that labor or birth by a person licensed in the place it is performed as a medical practitioner, midwife, or person in training to become such a practitioner or midwife.

3. For the purposes of paragraph (a) of subdivision two of this section, no account shall be taken of the effect on the person on whom such procedure is to be performed of any belief on the part of that or any other person that such procedure is required as a matter of custom or ritual.

Female genital mutilation is a class E felony.

HISTORY: Add, L 1997, ch 618, § 2, eff Nov 1, 1997.

§ 130.90. Facilitating a sex offense with a controlled substance

A person is guilty of facilitating a sex offense with a controlled substance when he or she:

1. knowingly and unlawfully possesses a controlled substance or any preparation, compound, mixture or substance that requires a prescription to obtain and administers such substance or preparation, compound, mixture or substance that requires a prescription to obtain to another person without such person's consent and with intent to commit against such person conduct constituting a felony defined in this article; and

2. commits or attempts to commit such conduct constituting a felony defined in this article.

Facilitating a sex offense with a controlled substance is a class D felony.

HISTORY: Add, L 2000, ch 1, § 49, eff Feb 1, 2001. Sub 1, amd, L 2003, ch 264, § 24, eff Nov 1, 2003. Sub 2, amd, L 2003, ch 264, § 24, eff Nov 1, 2003.

§ 130.91. Sexually motivated felony

1. A person commits a sexually motivated felony when he or she commits a specified offense for the purpose, in whole or substantial part, of his or her own direct sexual gratification.

2. A "specified offense" is a felony offense defined by any of the following provisions of this chapter: assault in the second degree as defined in section 120.05, assault in the first degree as defined in section 120.10, gang assault in the second degree as defined in section 120.06, gang assault in the first degree as defined in section 120.07, stalking in the first degree as defined in section 120.60, strangulation in the second degree as defined in section 121.12, strangulation in the first degree as defined in section 121.13, manslaughter in the second degree as defined in subdivision one of section 125.15, manslaughter in the first degree as defined in section 125.20, murder in the second degree as defined in section 125.25, aggravated murder as defined in section 125.26, murder in the first degree as defined in section 125.27, kidnapping in the second degree as defined in section 135.20, kidnapping in the first degree as defined in section 135.25, burglary in the third degree as defined in section 140.20, burglary in the second degree as defined in section 140.25, burglary in the first degree as defined in section 140.30, arson in the second degree as defined in section 150.15, arson in the first degree as defined in section 150.20, robbery in the third degree as defined in section 160.05, robbery in the second degree as defined in section 160.10, robbery in the first degree as defined in section 160.15, promoting prostitution in the second degree as defined in section 230.30, promoting prostitution in the first degree as defined in section 230.32, compelling prostitution as defined in section 230.33, disseminating indecent material to minors in the first degree as defined in section 235.22, use of a child in a sexual performance as defined in section 263.05, promoting an obscene sexual performance by a child as defined in section 263.10, promoting a sexual performance by a child as defined in section 263.15, or any felony attempt or conspiracy to commit any of the foregoing offenses.

HISTORY: Add, L 2007, ch 7, § 29, eff April 13, 2007; amd, L 2010, ch 405, § 14, eff Nov 11, 2010.

§ 130.92. Sentencing

1. When a person is convicted of a sexually motivated felony pursuant to this article, and the specified felony is a violent felony offense, as defined in section 70.02 of this chapter, the sexually motivated felony shall be deemed a violent felony offense.

2. When a person is convicted of a sexually motivated felony pursuant to this article, the sexually motivated felony shall be deemed to be the same offense level as the specified offense the defendant committed.

3. Persons convicted of a sexually motivated felony as defined in section 130.91 of this article, must be sentenced in accordance with the provisions of section 70.80 of this chapter.

HISTORY: Add, L 2007, ch 7, § 29, eff April 13, 2007.

§ 130.95. Predatory sexual assault

A person is guilty of predatory sexual assault when he or she commits the crime of rape in the first degree, criminal sexual act in the first degree, aggravated sexual abuse in the first degree, or course of sexual conduct against a child in the first degree, as defined in this article, and when:

1. In the course of the commission of the crime or the immediate flight therefrom, he or she:

    (a) Causes serious physical injury to the victim of such crime; or

    (b) Uses or threatens the immediate use of a dangerous instrument; or

2. He or she has engaged in conduct constituting the crime of rape in the first degree, criminal sexual act in the first degree, aggravated sexual abuse in the first degree, or course of sexual

conduct against a child in the first degree, as defined in this article, against one or more additional persons; or

3. He or she has previously been subjected to a conviction for a felony defined in this article, incest as defined in section 255.25 of this chapter or use of a child in a sexual performance as defined in section 263.05 of this chapter.

Predatory sexual assault is a class A-II felony.

HISTORY: Add, L 2006, ch 107, § 1, eff June 23, 2006.

§ 130.96. Predatory sexual assault against a child

A person is guilty of predatory sexual assault against a child when, being eighteen years old or more, he or she commits the crime of rape in the first degree, criminal sexual act in the first degree, aggravated sexual abuse in the first degree, or course of sexual conduct against a child in the first degree, as defined in this article, and the victim is less than thirteen years old.

Predatory sexual assault against a child is a class A-II felony.

HISTORY: Add, L 2006, ch 107, § 2, eff June 23, 2006.

ARTICLE 135   KIDNAPPING, COERCION AND RELATED OFFENSES

HISTORY: Add L 1965, ch 1030, § 1, eff Sept 1, 1967.

§ 135.00. Unlawful imprisonment, kidnapping and custodial interference; definitions of terms

The following definitions are applicable to this article:

1. "Restrain" means to restrict a person's movements intentionally and unlawfully in such manner as to interfere substantially with his liberty by moving him from one place to another, or by confining him either in the place where the restriction commences or in a place to which he has been moved, without consent and with knowledge that the restriction is unlawful. A person is so moved or confined "without consent" when such is accomplished by (a) physical force, intimidation or deception, or (b) any means whatever, including acquiescence of the victim, if he is a child less than sixteen years old or an incompetent person and the parent,

guardian or other person or institution having lawful control or custody of him has not acquiesced in the movement or confinement.

2. "Abduct" means to restrain a person with intent to prevent his liberation by either (a) secreting or holding him in a place where he is not likely to be found, or (b) using or threatening to use deadly physical force.

3. "Relative" means a parent, ancestor, brother, sister, uncle or aunt.

HISTORY: Add, L 1965, ch 1030, § 1, eff Sept 1, 1967.

§ 135.05. Unlawful imprisonment in the second degree

A person is guilty of unlawful imprisonment in the second degree when he restrains another person.

Unlawful imprisonment in the second degree is a class A misdemeanor.

HISTORY: Add, L 1965, ch 1030, § 1, eff Sept 1, 1967.

§ 135.10. Unlawful imprisonment in the first degree

A person is guilty of unlawful imprisonment in the first degree when he restrains another person under circumstances which expose the latter to a risk of serious physical injury.

Unlawful imprisonment in the first degree is a class E felony.

HISTORY: Add, L 1965, ch 1030, § 1, eff Sept 1, 1967.

§ 135.15. Unlawful imprisonment; defense

In any prosecution for unlawful imprisonment, it is an affirmative defense that (a) the person restrained was a child less than sixteen years old, and (b) the defendant was a relative of such child, and (c) his sole purpose was to assume control of such child.

HISTORY: Add, L 1965, ch 1030, § 1, eff Sept 1, 1967.

§ 135.20. Kidnapping in the second degree

A person is guilty of kidnapping in the second degree when he abducts another person.

Kidnapping in the second degree is a class B felony.

HISTORY: Add, L 1965, ch 1030, § 1, eff Sept 1, 1967.

§ 135.25. Kidnapping in the first degree

A person is guilty of kidnapping in the first degree when he abducts another person and when:

1. His intent is to compel a third person to pay or deliver money or property as ransom, or to engage in other particular conduct, or to refrain from engaging in particular conduct; or

2. He restrains the person abducted for a period of more than twelve hours with intent to:

(a) Inflict physical injury upon him or violate or abuse him sexually; or

(b) Accomplish or advance the commission of a felony; or

(c) Terrorize him or a third person; or

(d) Interfere with the performance of a governmental or political function; or

3. The person abducted dies during the abduction or before he is able to return or to be returned to safety. Such death shall be presumed, in a case where such person was less than sixteen years old or an incompetent person at the time of the abduction, from evidence that his parents, guardians or other lawful custodians did not see or hear from him following the

termination of the abduction and prior to trial and received no reliable information during such period persuasively indicating that he was alive. In all other cases, such death shall be presumed from evidence that a person whom the person abducted would have been extremely likely to visit or communicate with during the specified period were he alive and free to do so did not see or hear from him during such period and received no reliable information during such period persuasively indicating that he was alive.

Kidnapping in the first degree is a class A-I felony.

HISTORY: Add, L 1965, ch 1030, § 1; amd, L 1967, ch 791, § 12, eff Sept 1, 1967. Concluding par, amd, L 1973, ch 276, § 14, eff Sept 1, 1973.

§ 135.30. Kidnapping; defense

In any prosecution for kidnapping, it is an affirmative defense that (a) the defendant was a relative of the person abducted, and (b) his sole purpose was to assume control of such person.

HISTORY: Add, L 1965, ch 1030, § 1, eff Sept 1, 1967.

§ 135.35. Labor trafficking

A person is guilty of labor trafficking if he or she compels or induces another to engage in labor or recruits, entices, harbors, or transports such other person by means of intentionally:

1. unlawfully providing a controlled substance to such person with intent to impair said person's judgment;

2. requiring that the labor be performed to retire, repay, or service a real or purported debt that the actor has caused by a systematic ongoing course of conduct with intent to defraud such person;

3. withholding, destroying, or confiscating any actual or purported passport, immigration document, or any other actual or purported government identification document, of another person with intent to impair said person's freedom of movement; provided, however, that this subdivision shall not apply to an attempt to correct a social security administration record or immigration agency record in accordance with any local, state, or federal agency requirement, where such attempt is not made for the purpose of any express or implied threat;

4. using force or engaging in any scheme, plan or pattern to compel or induce such person to engage in or continue to engage in labor activity by means of instilling a fear in such person that, if the demand is not complied with, the actor or another will do one or more of the following:

(a) cause physical injury, serious physical injury, or death to a person; or

(b) cause damage to property, other than the property of the actor; or

(c) engage in other conduct constituting a felony or unlawful imprisonment in the second degree in violation of section 135.05 of this chapter; or

(d) accuse some person of a crime or cause criminal charges or deportation proceedings to be instituted against such person; provided, however, that it shall be an affirmative defense to this subdivision that the defendant reasonably believed the threatened charge to be true and that his or her sole purpose was to compel or induce the victim to take reasonable action to make good the wrong which was the subject of such threatened charge; or

(e) expose a secret or publicize an asserted fact, whether true or false, tending to subject some person to hatred, contempt or ridicule; or

(f) testify or provide information or withhold testimony or information with respect to another's legal claim or defense; or

(g) use or abuse his or her position as a public servant by performing some act within or related to his or her official duties, or by failing or refusing to perform an official duty, in such manner as to affect some person adversely.

Labor trafficking is a class D felony.

HISTORY: Add, L 2007, ch 74, § 3, eff Nov 1, 2007. Former § 15.35, add, L 1965, ch 1030, § 1; repealed, L 1967, ch 791, § 13, eff Sept 1, 1967.

§ 135.36. Labor trafficking; accomplice

In a prosecution for labor trafficking, a person who has been compelled or induced or recruited, enticed, harbored or transported to engage in labor shall not be deemed to be an accomplice.

HISTORY: Add, L 2007, ch 74, § 3, eff Nov 1, 2007.

§ 135.40. [Repealed]

HISTORY: Add, L 1965, ch 1030, § 1; repealed, L 1967, ch 791, § 13, eff Sept 1, 1967.

§ 135.45. Custodial interference in the second degree

A person is guilty of custodial interference in the second degree when:

1. Being a relative of a child less than sixteen years old, intending to hold such child permanently or for a protracted period, and knowing that he has no legal right to do so, he takes or entices such child from his lawful custodian; or

2. Knowing that he has no legal right to do so, he takes or entices from lawful custody any incompetent person or other person entrusted by authority of law to the custody of another person or institution.

Custodial interference in the second degree is a class A misdemeanor.

HISTORY: Add, L 1965, ch 1030, § 1, eff Sept 1, 1967, with substance derived in part from § 1250-a.

§ 135.50. Custodial interference in the first degree

A person is guilty of custodial interference in the first degree when he commits the crime of custodial interference in the second degree:

1. With intent to permanently remove the victim from this state, he removes such person from the state; or

2. Under circumstances which expose the victim to a risk that his safety will be endangered or his health materially impaired.

It shall be an affirmative defense to a prosecution under subdivision one of this section that the victim had been abandoned or that the taking was necessary in an emergency to protect the victim because he has been subjected to or threatened with mistreatment or abuse. Custodial interference in the first degree is a class E felony.

HISTORY: Add, L 1965, ch 1030, § 1, with substance derived from § 1250-a; amd, L 1981, ch 785, § 1, eff July 27, 1981. Opening par, amd, L 1981, ch 785, § 1, eff July 27, 1981. Sub 1, add, L 1981, ch 785, § 1, eff July 27, 1981. Sub 2, formerly part of entire section, so designated and amd, L 1981, ch 785, § 1, eff July 27, 1981. Sub 2, second unnumbered par, add, L 1981, ch 785, § 1, eff July 27, 1981.

§ 135.55. Substitution of children

A person is guilty of substitution of children when, having been temporarily entrusted with a child less than one year old and intending to deceive a parent, guardian or other lawful custodian of such child, he substitutes, produces or returns to such parent, guardian or custodian a child other than the one entrusted.

Substitution of children is a class E felony.

HISTORY: Add, L 1965, ch 1030, § 1, eff Sept 1, 1967, with substance derived from § 923.

§ 135.60. Coercion in the second degree

A person is guilty of coercion in the second degree when he or she compels or induces a person to engage in conduct which the latter has a legal right to abstain from engaging in, or to abstain from engaging in conduct in which he or she has a legal right to engage, or compels or induces a person to join a group, organization or criminal enterprise which such latter person has a right to abstain from joining, by means of instilling in him or her a fear that, if the demand is not complied with, the actor or another will:

1. Cause physical injury to a person; or

2. Cause damage to property; or

3. Engage in other conduct constituting a crime; or

4. Accuse some person of a crime or cause criminal charges to be instituted against him or her; or

5. Expose a secret or publicize an asserted fact, whether true or false, tending to subject some person to hatred, contempt or ridicule; or

6. Cause a strike, boycott or other collective labor group action injurious to some person's business; except that such a threat shall not be deemed coercive when the act or omission compelled is for the benefit of the group in whose interest the actor purports to act; or

7. Testify or provide information or withhold testimony or information with respect to another's legal claim or defense; or

8. Use or abuse his or her position as a public servant by performing some act within or related to his or her official duties, or by failing or refusing to perform an official duty, in such manner as to affect some person adversely; or

9. Perform any other act which would not in itself materially benefit the actor but which is calculated to harm another person materially with respect to his or her health, safety, business, calling, career, financial condition, reputation or personal relationships.

Coercion in the second degree is a class A misdemeanor.

HISTORY: Add, L 1965, ch 1030, § 1, eff Sept 1, 1967, with substance derived from §§ 530, 853, 1323, 1324, 1454, 2070, 2073. Amd, L 2008, ch 426, § 1, eff Nov 1, 2008. Opening par, amd, L 2008, ch 426, § 1, eff Nov 1, 2008. Sub 4, amd, L 2008, ch 426, § 1, eff Nov 1, 2008. Sub 8, amd, L 2008, ch 426, § 1, eff Nov 1, 2008. Sub 9, amd, L 2008, ch 426, § 1, eff Nov 1, 2008.

§ 135.65. Coercion in the first degree

A person is guilty of coercion in the first degree when he or she commits the crime of coercion in the second degree, and when:

1. He or she commits such crime by instilling in the victim a fear that he or she will cause physical injury to a person or cause damage to property; or

2. He or she thereby compels or induces the victim to:

(a) Commit or attempt to commit a felony; or

(b) Cause or attempt to cause physical injury to a person; or

(c) Violate his or her duty as a public servant.

Coercion in the first degree is a class D felony.

HISTORY: Add, L 1965, ch 1030, § 1, eff Sept 1, 1967, with substance derived from §§ 530, 853, 860, 1323, 1324, 1824, 2070, 2073. Amd, L 2008, ch 426, § 2, eff Nov 1, 2008. Opening par, amd, L 2008, ch 426, § 2, eff Nov 1, 2008. Sub 1, amd, L 2008, ch 426, § 2, eff Nov 1, 2008. Sub 2, amd, L 2008, ch 426, § 2, eff Nov 1, 2008. Sub 2, opening par, amd, L 2008, ch 426, § 2, eff Nov 1, 2008. Sub 2, par (c), amd, L 2008, ch 426, § 2, eff Nov 1, 2008.

§ 135.70. Coercion; no defense

The crimes of (a) coercion and attempt to commit coercion, and (b) bribe receiving by a labor official as defined in section 180.20, and bribe receiving as defined in section 200.05, are not mutually exclusive, and it is no defense to a prosecution for coercion or an attempt to commit coercion that, by reason of the same conduct, the defendant also committed one of such specified crimes of bribe receiving.

HISTORY: Add, L 1965, ch 1030, § 1, eff Sept 1, 1967.

§ 135.75. Coercion; defense

In any prosecution for coercion committed by instilling in the victim a fear that he or another person would be charged with a crime, it is an affirmative defense that the defendant reasonably believed the threatened charge to be true and that his sole purpose was to compel or induce the victim to take reasonable action to make good the wrong which was the subject of such threatened charge.

HISTORY: Add, L 1965, ch 1030, § 1, eff Sept 1, 1967.

TITLE I   Offenses Involving Damage to and Intrusion Upon Property

ARTICLE 140
BURGLARY AND RELATED OFFENSES

ARTICLE 145
CRIMINAL MISCHIEF AND RELATED OFFENSES

ARTICLE 150
ARSON

HISTORY: Add, L 1965, ch 1030, § 1, eff Sept 1, 1967.

ARTICLE 140   BURGLARY AND RELATED OFFENSES

HISTORY: Add, L 1965, ch 1030, § 1, eff Sept 1, 1967.

§ 140.00. Criminal trespass and burglary; definitions of terms

The following definitions are applicable to this article:

1. "Premises" includes the term "building," as defined herein, and any real property.

2. "Building," in addition to its ordinary meaning, includes any structure, vehicle or watercraft used for overnight lodging of persons, or used by persons for carrying on business therein, or used as an elementary or secondary school, or an inclosed motor truck, or an inclosed motor truck trailer. Where a building consists of two or more units separately secured or occupied, each unit shall be deemed both a separate building in itself and a part of the main building.

3. "Dwelling" means a building which is usually occupied by a person lodging therein at night.

4. "Night" means the period between thirty minutes after sunset and thirty minutes before sunrise.

5. "Enter or remain unlawfully." A person "enters or remains unlawfully" in or upon premises when he is not licensed or privileged to do so. A person who, regardless of his intent, enters or remains in or upon premises which are at the time open to the public does so with license and privilege unless he defies a lawful order not to enter or remain, personally communicated to him by the owner of such premises or other authorized person. A license or privilege to enter or remain in a building which is only partly open to the public is not a license or privilege to enter or remain in that part of the building which is not open to the public. A person who enters or remains upon unimproved and apparently unused land, which is neither fenced nor otherwise enclosed in a manner designed to exclude intruders, does so with license and privilege unless notice against trespass is personally communicated to him by the owner of such land or other

authorized person, or unless such notice is given by posting in a conspicuous manner. A person who enters or remains in or about a school building without written permission from someone authorized to issue such permission or without a legitimate reason which includes a relationship involving custody of or responsibility for a pupil or student enrolled in the school or without legitimate business or a purpose relating to the operation of the school does so without license and privilege.

HISTORY: Add, L 1965, ch 1030, § 1, eff Sept 1, 1967, with substance derived from §§ 400, 401. Sub 2, amd, L 1967, ch 791, § 14, L 1969, ch 1151, § 1, L 1979, ch 698, § 2, eff Sept 1, 1979. Sub 5, amd, L 1979, ch 698, § 3, eff Sept 1, 1979.

§ 140.05. Trespass

A person is guilty of trespass when he knowingly enters or remains unlawfully in or upon premises.

Trespass is a violation.

HISTORY: Add, L 1965, ch 1030, § 1; amd, L 1969, ch 341, § 3, L 1971, ch 307, eff Sept 1, 1971. Section heading, amd, L 1969, ch 341, § 3, L 1971, ch 307, eff Sept 1, 1971.

§ 140.10. Criminal trespass in the third degree

A person is guilty of criminal trespass in the third degree when he knowingly enters or remains unlawfully in a building or upon real property

(a) which is fenced or otherwise enclosed in a manner designed to exclude intruders; or

(b) where the building is utilized as an elementary or secondary school or a children's overnight camp as defined in section one thousand three hundred ninety-two of the public health law or a summer day camp as defined in section one thousand three hundred ninety-two of the public health law in violation of conspicuously posted rules or regulations governing entry and use thereof; or

(c) located within a city with a population in excess of one million and where the building or real property is utilized as an elementary or secondary school in violation of a personally communicated request to leave the premises from a principal, custodian or other person in charge thereof; or

(d) located outside of a city with a population in excess of one million and where the building or real property is utilized as an elementary or secondary school in violation of a personally communicated request to leave the premises from a principal, custodian, school board member or trustee, or other person in charge thereof; or

(e) where the building is used as a public housing project in violation of conspicuously posted rules or regulations governing entry and use thereof; or

(f) where a building is used as a public housing project in violation of a personally communicated request to leave the premises from a housing police officer or other person in charge thereof; or

(g) where the property consists of a right-of-way or yard of a railroad or rapid transit railroad which has been designated and conspicuously posted as a no-trespass railroad zone.

Criminal trespass in the third degree is a class B misdemeanor.

HISTORY: Add, L 1965, ch 1030, § 1; amd, L 1969, ch 341, § 4, L 1979, ch 698, § 4, L 1983, ch 813, § 1, L 1987, ch 192, § 1, eff Nov 1, 1987, L 1992, ch 434, § 1, eff Nov 1, 1992 L 1997, ch 338, §§ 2, 3, eff Nov 1, 1997, L 2000, ch 533, § 1, eff Oct 4, 2000, L 2001, ch 350, § 1, eff Sept 19, 2001, L 2011, ch 176, § 1, eff Jan 16, 2012.

§ 140.15. Criminal trespass in the second degree

A person is guilty of criminal trespass in the second degree when:

1. he or she knowingly enters or remains unlawfully in a dwelling; or

2. being a person required to maintain registration under article six-C of the correction law and designated a level two or level three offender pursuant to subdivision six of section one hundred sixty-eight-l of the correction law, he or she enters or remains in a public or private elementary, parochial, intermediate, junior high, vocational or high school knowing that the victim of the offense for which such registration is required attends or formerly attended such school. It shall not be an offense subject to prosecution under this subdivision if: the person is a lawfully registered student at such school; the person is a lawful student participant in a school sponsored event; the person is a parent or a legal guardian of a lawfully registered student at such school and enters the school for the purpose of attending their child's or dependent's event or activity; such school is the person's designated polling place and he or she enters such school building for the limited purpose of voting; or if the person enters such school building for the limited purposes authorized by the superintendent or chief administrator of such school.

Criminal trespass in the second degree is a class A misdemeanor.

HISTORY: Add, L 1965, ch 1030, § 1; amd, L 1969, ch 341, § 5, eff Sept 1, 1969. Section heading, amd, L 1969, ch 341, § 5, eff Sept 1, 1969. Amd, L 2010, ch 315, § 1, eff Nov 1, 2010.

§ 140.17. Criminal trespass in the first degree

A person is guilty of criminal trespass in the first degree when he knowingly enters or remains unlawfully in a building, and when, in the course of committing such crime, he:

1. Possesses, or knows that another participant in the crime possesses, an explosive or a deadly weapon; or

2. Possesses a firearm, rifle or shotgun, as those terms are defined in section 265.00, and also possesses or has readily accessible a quantity of ammunition which is capable of being discharged from such firearm, rifle or shotgun; or

3. Knows that another participant in the crime possesses a firearm, rifle or shotgun under circumstances described in subdivision two.

Criminal trespass in the first degree is a class D felony.

HISTORY: Add, L 1969, ch 341, § 6, eff Sept 1, 1969.

§ 140.20. Burglary in the third degree

A person is guilty of burglary in the third degree when he knowingly enters or remains unlawfully in a building with intent to commit a crime therein.

Burglary in the third degree is a class D felony.

HISTORY: Add, L 1965, ch 1030, § 1, eff Sept 1, 1967, with substance derived from §§ 404, 405.

§ 140.25. Burglary in the second degree

A person is guilty of burglary in the second degree when he knowingly enters or remains unlawfully in a building with intent to commit a crime therein, and when:

1. In effecting entry or while in the building or in immediate flight therefrom, he or another participant in the crime:

(a) Is armed with explosives or a deadly weapon; or

(b) Causes physical injury to any person who is not a participant in the crime; or

(c) Uses or threatens the immediate use of a dangerous instrument; or

(d) Displays what appears to be a pistol, revolver, rifle, shotgun, machine gun or other firearm; or

2. The building is a dwelling.

Burglary in the second degree is a class C felony.

HISTORY: Add, L 1965, ch 1030, § 1, eff Sept 1, 1967, with substance derived from §§ 403, 404. Sub 1, par (c), add, L 1967, ch 791, § 15, eff Sept 1, 1967. Sub 1, par (d), add, L 1969, ch 1012, § 1; amd, L 1973, ch 374, § 1, eff Sept 1, 1973. Sub 2, amd, L 1981, ch 361, § 1, eff Sept 1, 1981.

§ 140.30. Burglary in the first degree

A person is guilty of burglary in the first degree when he knowingly enters or remains unlawfully in a dwelling with intent to commit a crime therein, and when, in effecting entry or while in the dwelling or in immediate flight therefrom, he or another participant in the crime:

1. Is armed with explosives or a deadly weapon; or

2. Causes physical injury to any person who is not a participant in the crime; or

3. Uses or threatens the immediate use of a dangerous instrument; or

4. Displays what appears to be a pistol, revolver, rifle, shotgun, machine gun or other firearm; except that in any prosecution under this subdivision, it is an affirmative defense that such pistol, revolver, rifle, shotgun, machine gun or other firearm was not a loaded weapon from which a shot, readily capable of producing death or other serious physical injury, could be discharged. Nothing contained in this subdivision shall constitute a defense to a prosecution for, or preclude a conviction of, burglary in the second degree, burglary in the third degree or any other crime.

Burglary in the first degree is a class B felony.

HISTORY: Add, L 1965, ch 1030, § 1, with substance derived from § 402; amd, L 1967, ch 791, § 16, L 1969, ch 1012, § 2, L 1973, ch 374, § 2, eff Sept 1, 1973. Opening par, amd, L 1981, ch 361, § 2, eff Sept 1, 1981. Sub 3, add, L 1967, ch 791, § 16, eff Sept 1, 1967. Sub 4, add, L 1969, ch 1012, § 2, eff Sept 1, 1969.

§ 140.35. Possession of burglar's tools

A person is guilty of possession of burglar's tools when he possesses any tool, instrument or other article adapted, designed or commonly used for committing or facilitating offenses involving forcible entry into premises, or offenses involving larceny by a physical taking, or offenses involving theft of services as defined in subdivisions four, five and six of section 165.15, under circumstances evincing an intent to use or knowledge that some person intends to use the same in the commission of an offense of such character.

Possession of burglar's tools is a class A misdemeanor.

HISTORY: Add, L 1965, ch 1030, § 1, eff Sept 1, 1967, with substance derived from § 408.

§ 140.40. Unlawful possession of radio devices

As used in this section, the term "radio device" means any device capable of receiving a wireless voice transmission on any frequency allocated for police use, or any device capable of transmitting and receiving a wireless voice transmission. A person is guilty of unlawful possession of a radio device when he possesses a radio device with the intent to use that device in the commission of robbery, burglary, larceny, gambling or a violation of any provision of article two hundred twenty of the penal law.

Unlawful possession of a radio device is a class B misdemeanor.

HISTORY: Add, L 1970, ch 754, § 1, eff Sept 1, 1970.

ARTICLE 145   CRIMINAL MISCHIEF AND RELATED OFFENSES

HISTORY: Add, L 1965, ch 1030, § 1, eff Sept 1, 1967.

§ 145.00. Criminal mischief in the fourth degree

A person is guilty of criminal mischief in the fourth degree when, having no right to do so nor any reasonable ground to believe that he or she has such right, he or she:

1. Intentionally damages property of another person; or

2. Intentionally participates in the destruction of an abandoned building as defined in section one thousand nine hundred seventy-one-a of the real property actions and proceedings law; or

3. Recklessly damages property of another person in an amount exceeding two hundred fifty dollars; or

4. With intent to prevent a person from communicating a request for emergency assistance, intentionally disables or removes telephonic, TTY or similar communication sending equipment while that person: (a) is attempting to seek or is engaged in the process of seeking emergency assistance from police, law enforcement, fire or emergency medical services personnel; or (b) is attempting to seek or is engaged in the process of seeking emergency assistance from another person or entity in order to protect himself, herself or a third person

from imminent physical injury. The fact that the defendant has an ownership interest in such equipment shall not be a defense to a charge pursuant to this subdivision.

Criminal mischief in the fourth degree is a class A misdemeanor.

HISTORY: Add, L 1965, ch 1030, § 1, with substance derived from §§ 223, 463, 464, 466, 1420, 1420-a, 1421, 1423, 1423-a, 1423-b, 1423-c, 1424, 1425, 1426, 1427(2), 1428, 1430, 1431, 1432, 1433, 1873, 1906(1, 2), 1911, 1991; amd, L 1967, ch 791, § 17, L 1971, ch 961, § 1, L 1983, ch 496, § 3, eff Sept 1, 1983. Amd, L 2008, ch 69, § 1, eff July 6, 2008. Opening par, amd, L 2008, ch 69, § 1, eff July 6, 2008. Section heading, amd, L 1971, ch 961, § 1, eff Sept 1, 1971. Sub 1, add, L 1967, ch 791, § 17, eff Sept 1, 1967. Sub 2, add, L 1983, ch 496, § 3, eff Sept 1, 1983. Sub 2, amd, L 2008, ch 69, § 1, eff July 6, 2008. Former sub 2, add, L 1967, ch 791, § 17; renumbered sub 3, L 1983, ch 496, § 3, eff Sept 1, 1983. Sub 3, formerly sub 2, add, L 1967, ch 791, § 17; renumbered sub 3, L 1983, ch 496, § 3, eff Sept 3, 1983. Sub 3, amd, L 2008, ch 69, § 1, eff July 6, 2008. Sub 4, add, L 2008, ch 69, § 1, eff July 6, 2008.

§ 145.05. Criminal mischief in the third degree

A person is guilty of criminal mischief in the third degree when, with intent to damage property of another person, and having no right to do so nor any reasonable ground to believe that he or she has such right, he or she:

1. damages the motor vehicle of another person, by breaking into such vehicle when it is locked with the intent of stealing property, and within the previous ten year period, has been convicted three or more times, in separate criminal transactions for which sentence was imposed on separate occasions, of criminal mischief in the fourth degree as defined in section 145.00, criminal mischief in the third degree as defined in this section, criminal mischief in the second degree as defined in section 145.10, or criminal mischief in the first degree as defined in section 145.12 of this article; or

2. damages property of another person in an amount exceeding two hundred fifty dollars.

Criminal mischief in the third degree is a class E felony.

HISTORY: Add; L 1965, ch 1030, § 1, with substance derived from §§ 223, 463, 464, 466, 1420, 1420-a, 1421, 1423, 1423-a, 1423-b, 1423-c, 1424, 1425, 1426, 1427(2), 1428, 1430, 1431, 1432, 1433, 1873, 1906(1, 2), 1911, 1991; amd, L 1971, ch 961, § 2, eff Sept 1, 1971. Section heading, amd, L 1971, ch 961, § 2, eff Sept 1, 1971. Amd, L 2003, ch 276, § 1, eff Nov 1, 2003. Opening par, formerly part of first undesignated par, so designaged opening par and amd, L 2003, ch 276, § 1, eff Nov 1, 2003. Sub 1, add, L 2003, ch 276, § 1, eff Nov 1, 2003. Sub 2, formerly part of first undesignated par, so designated sub 2, L 2003, ch 276, § 1, eff Nov 1, 2003. First undesignated par, redesignated opening par and sub 2, L 2003, ch 276, § 1, eff Nov 1, 2003.

§ 145.10. Criminal mischief in the second degree

A person is guilty of criminal mischief in the second degree when with intent to damage property of another person, and having no right to do so nor any reasonable ground to believe that he has such right, he damages property of another person in an amount exceeding one thousand five hundred dollars.

Criminal mischief in the second degree is a class D felony.

HISTORY: Add, L 1965, ch 1030, § 1, with substance derived from §§ 223, 463, 464, 466, 1420, 1420-a, 1421, 1423, 1423-a, 1423-b, 1423-c, 1424, 1425, 1426, 1427(2), 1428, 1430, 1431, 1432, 1433, 1873, 1906(1, 2), 1911, 1991; amd, L 1971, ch 961, § 3, eff Sept 1, 1971.

§ 145.12. Criminal mischief in the first degree

A person is guilty of criminal mischief in the first degree when with intent to damage property of another person, and having no right to do so nor any reasonable ground to believe that he has such right, he damages property of another person by means of an explosive.

Criminal mischief in the first degree is a class B felony.

HISTORY: Add, L 1971, ch 961, § 4, eff Sept 1, 1971.

§ 145.13. Definitions

For the purposes of sections 145.00, 145.05, 145.10 and 145.12 of this article:

"Property of another" shall include all property in which another person has an ownership interest, whether or not a person who damages such property, or any other person, may also have an interest in such property.

HISTORY: Add, L 2008, ch 601, § 1, eff Nov 1, 2008. Second undesignated par, amd, L 2009, ch 45, § 1, eff May 29, 2009.

§ 145.14. Criminal tampering in the third degree

A person is guilty of criminal tampering in the third degree when, having no right to do so nor any reasonable ground to believe that he has such right, he tampers with property of another person with intent to cause substantial inconvenience to such person or to a third person.

Criminal tampering in the third degree is a class B misdemeanor.

HISTORY: Add, L 1978, ch 420, § 1, eff Jan 1, 1979.

§ 145.15. Criminal tampering in the second degree

A person is guilty of criminal tampering in the second degree when, having no right to do so nor any reasonable ground to believe that he has such right, he or she tampers or makes connection with property of a gas, electric, sewer, steam or water-works corporation, telephone or telegraph corporation, common carrier, nuclear powered electric generating facility, or public utility operated by a municipality or district; except that in any prosecution under this section, it is an affirmative defense that the defendant did not engage in such conduct for a larcenous or otherwise unlawful or wrongful purpose.

Criminal tampering in the second degree is a class A misdemeanor.

HISTORY: Add, L 1965, ch 1030, § 1, with substance derived from §§ 463, 1422, 1423-a, 1423-b, 1424, 1427, 1431, 1432, 1432-a, 1433, 1911, 1991; amd, L 1969, ch 862, § 1, L 1978, ch 420, § 2, eff Jan 1, 1979. Amd, L 2006, ch 585, § 1, eff Aug 16, 2006. Opening par, amd, L 2006, ch 585, § 1, eff Aug 16, 2006.

§ 145.20. Criminal tampering in the first degree

A person is guilty of criminal tampering in the first degree when, with intent to cause a substantial interruption or impairment of a service rendered to the public, and having no right to do so nor any reasonable ground to believe that he or she has such right, he or she damages or tampers with property of a gas, electric, sewer, steam or water-works corporation, telephone or telegraph corporation, common carrier, nuclear powered electric generating facility, or public utility operated by a municipality or district, and thereby causes such substantial interruption or impairment of service.

Criminal tampering in the first degree is a class D felony.

HISTORY: Add, L 1965, ch 1030, § 1, with substance derived from §§ 1422, 1423, 1423-a, 1431; amd, L 1969, ch 861, § 1, eff Sept 1, 1969. Amd, L 2006, ch 585, § 2, eff Aug 16, 2006. Opening par, amd, L 2006, ch 585, § 2, eff Aug 16, 2006.

§ 145.22. Cemetery desecration in the second degree

A person is guilty of cemetery desecration in the second degree when:

(a) with intent to damage property of another person, and having no right to do so nor any reasonable ground to believe that he has such right, he damages any real or personal property maintained as a cemetery plot, grave, burial place or other place of interment of human remains; or

(b) with intent to steal personal property, he steals personal property which is located at a cemetery plot, grave, burial place or other place of interment of human remains and which property is owned by the person or organization which maintains or owns such place or the estate, next-of-kin or representatives of the deceased person interred there.

Cemetery desecration in the second degree is a class A misdemeanor.

HISTORY: Add, L 1997, ch 165, § 2, eff Nov 1, 1997. Amd, L 2007, ch 353, § 1, eff July 18, 2007. Opening par, formerly part of first undesignated par, so designated opening par and amd, L 2007, ch 353, § 1, eff July 18, 2007. Sub (a), formerly part of first undesignated par, so designated sub (a) and amd, L 2007, ch 531, § 1, eff July 18, 2007. Sub (b), L 2007, ch 353, § 1, eff July 18, 2007.

§ 145.23. Cemetery desecration in the first degree

A person is guilty of cemetery desecration in the first degree when with intent to damage property of another person, and having no right to do so nor any reasonable ground to believe that he has such right, he:

(a) damages any real or personal property maintained as a cemetery plot, grave, burial place or other place of interment of human remains in an amount exceeding two hundred fifty dollars; or

(b) with intent to steal personal property, he steals personal property, the value of which exceeds two hundred fifty dollars, which is located at a cemetery plot, grave, burial place or other place of interment of human remains and which property is owned by the person or organization which maintains or owns such place or the estate, next-of-kin or representatives of the deceased person interred there; or

(c) commits the crime of cemetery desecration in the second degree as defined in section 145.22 of this article and has been previously convicted of the crime of cemetery desecration in the second degree within the preceding five years.

Cemetery desecration in the first degree is a class E felony.

HISTORY: Add, L 1997, ch 165, § 2, eff Nov 1, 1997. Amd, L 2007, ch 353, § 2, eff July 18, 2007. Sub (b), add, L 2007, ch 353, § 2, eff July 18, 2007. Former sub (b), redesignated sub (c), L 2007, ch 353, § 2, eff July 18, 2007. Sub (c), formerly sub (b), so designated sub (c), L 2007, ch 353, § 2, eff July 18, 2007.

§ 145.25. Reckless endangerment of property

A person is guilty of reckless endangerment of property when he recklessly engages in conduct which creates a substantial risk of damage to the property of another person in an amount exceeding two hundred fifty dollars.

Reckless endangerment of property is a class B misdemeanor.

HISTORY: Add, L 1965, ch 1030, § 1, eff Sept 1, 1967.

§ 145.26. Aggravated cemetery desecration in the second degree

A person is guilty of aggravated cemetery desecration in the second degree when, having no right to do so nor any reasonable ground to believe that he or she has such right, he or she opens a casket, crypt, or similar vessel containing a human body or human remains which has been buried or otherwise interred in a cemetery and unlawfully removes therefrom a body, bodily part, any human remains or any object contained in such casket, crypt or similar vessel for the purpose of obtaining unlawful possession of such body, bodily part, human remains or object for such person or a third person.

Aggravated cemetery desecration in the second degree is a class E felony.

HISTORY: Add, L 2007, ch 376, § 1, eff Nov 11, 2007.

§ 145.27. Aggravated cemetery desecration in the first degree

A person is guilty of aggravated cemetery desecration in the first degree when such person commits the crime of aggravated cemetery desecration in the second degree and has been previously convicted within the past five years of the crime of cemetery desecration in the second degree as defined in section 145.22 of this article, cemetery desecration in the first degree as defined in section 145.23 of this article or aggravated cemetery desecration in the second degree as defined in section 145.26 of this article.

Aggravated cemetery desecration in the first degree is a class D felony.

HISTORY: Add, L 2007, ch 376, § 1, eff Nov 11, 2007.

§ 145.30. Unlawfully posting advertisements

1. A person is guilty of unlawfully posting advertisements when, having no right to do so nor any reasonable ground to believe that he has such right, he posts, paints or otherwise affixes to the property of another person any advertisement, poster, notice or other matter designed to benefit a person other than the owner of the property.

2. Where such matter consists of a commercial advertisement, it shall be presumed that the vendor of the specified product, service or entertainment is a person who placed such advertisement or caused it to be placed upon the property.

Unlawfully posting advertisements is a violation.

HISTORY: Add, L 1965, ch 1030, § 1, eff Sept 1, 1967, with substance derived from § 2036-a.

§ 145.35. Tampering with a consumer product; consumer product defined

For the purposes of sections 145.40 and 145.45 of this article, "consumer product" means any drug, food, beverage or thing which is displayed or offered for sale to the public, for administration into or ingestion by a human being or for application to any external surface of a human being.

HISTORY: Add, L 1986, ch 359, § 1, eff Oct 1, 1986.

§ 145.40. Tampering with a consumer product in the second degree

A person is guilty of tampering with a consumer product in the second degree when, having no right to do so nor any reasonable ground to believe that he has such right, and with intent to cause physical injury to another or with intent to instill in another a fear that he will cause such physical injury, he alters, adulterates or otherwise contaminates a consumer product.

Tampering with a consumer product in the second degree is a class A misdemeanor.

HISTORY: Add, L 1986, ch 359, § 1, eff Oct 1, 1986.

§ 145.45. Tampering with a consumer product in the first degree

A person is guilty of tampering with a consumer product in the first degree when, having no right to do so nor any reasonable ground to believe that he has such right, and with intent to cause physical injury to another or with intent to instill in another a fear that he will cause such physical injury, he alters, adulterates or otherwise contaminates a consumer product and thereby creates a substantial risk of serious physical injury to one or more persons.

Tampering with a consumer product in the first degree is a class E felony.

HISTORY: Add, L 1986, ch 359, § 1, eff Oct 1, 1986.

§ 145.50. Penalties for littering on railroad tracks and rights-of-way

1. No person shall throw, dump, or cause to be thrown, dumped, deposited or placed upon any railroad tracks, or within the limits of the rights-of-way of any railroad, any refuse, trash, garbage, rubbish, litter or any nauseous or offensive matter.

2. Where a highway or road lies in whole or part within a railroad rights-of-way, nothing in this section shall be construed as prohibiting the use in a reasonable manner of ashes, sand, salt or other material for the purpose of reducing the hazard of, or providing traction on snow, ice or sleet situated on such highway or road.

3. A violation of the provisions of subdivision one of this section shall be punishable by a fine not to exceed two hundred fifty dollars and/or a requirement to perform services for a public or not-for-profit corporation, association, institution or agency not to exceed eight hours and for any second or subsequent violation by a fine not to exceed five hundred dollars and/or a requirement to perform services for a public or not-for-profit corporation, association, institution or agency not to exceed eight hours.

4. Nothing in this section shall be deemed to apply to a railroad or its employees when matter deposited by them on the railroad tracks or rights-of-way is done pursuant to railroad rules, regulations or procedures.

HISTORY: Add, L 1987, ch 266, § 1, eff Nov 1, 1987. Sub 3, amd, L 1991, ch 186, § 4, eff Nov 1, 1991.

§ 145.60. Making graffiti

1. For purposes of this section, the term "graffiti" shall mean the etching, painting, covering, drawing upon or otherwise placing of a mark upon public or private property with intent to damage such property.

2. No person shall make graffiti of any type on any building, public or private, or any other property real or personal owned by any person, firm or corporation or any public agency or instrumentality, without the express permission of the owner or operator of said property.

Making graffiti is a class A misdemeanor.

HISTORY: Add, L 1992, ch 458, § 2, eff Nov 1, 1992.

§ 145.65. Possession of graffiti instruments

A person is guilty of possession of graffiti instruments when he possesses any tool, instrument, article, substance, solution or other compound designed or commonly used to etch, paint, cover, draw upon or otherwise place a mark upon a piece of property which that person has no permission or authority to etch, paint, cover, draw upon or otherwise mark, under circumstances evincing an intent to use same in order to damage such property.

Possession of graffiti instruments is a class B misdemeanor.

HISTORY: Add, L 1992, ch 458, § 2, eff Nov 1, 1992.

§ 145.70. Criminal possession of a taximeter accelerating device

1. For purposes of this section, a "taximeter" means an instrument or device that automatically calculates and displays the charge to a passenger in a vehicle that is licensed to transport members of the public for hire pursuant to local law.

2. For purposes of this section, a "taximeter accelerating device" means an instrument or device

that causes a taximeter to increase the charge displayed by such taximeter to an amount greater than the maximum amount permitted by local law.

3. A person is guilty of criminal possession of a taximeter accelerating device when he knowingly possesses, with intent to use unlawfully, a taximeter accelerating device. If such a device is knowingly possessed there is a rebuttable presumption that it is intended to be used unlawfully.

Criminal possession of a taximeter accelerating device is a class A misdemeanor.

HISTORY: Add, L 1999, ch 603, § 1, eff Nov 9, 1999.

ARTICLE 150　ARSON

HISTORY: Add, L 1965, ch 1030, § 1, eff Sept 1, 1967.

§ 150.00. Arson; definitions

As used in this article,

1. "Building", in addition to its ordinary meaning, includes any structure, vehicle or watercraft used for overnight lodging of persons, or used by persons for carrying on business therein. Where a building consists of two or more units separately secured or occupied, each unit shall not be deemed a separate building.

2. "Motor vehicle", includes every vehicle operated or driven upon a public highway which is propelled by any power other than muscular power, except (a) electrically-driven invalid chairs being operated or driven by an invalid, (b) vehicles which run only upon rails or tracks, and (c) snowmobiles as defined in article forty-seven of the vehicle and traffic law.

HISTORY: Add, L 1965, ch 1030, § 1, with substance derived from § 220; amd, L 1979, ch 225, § 17, eff Sept 1, 1979. Section heading, amd, L 1979, ch 225, § 17, eff Sept 1, 1979. Sub 1, formerly part of section, so designated and amd, L 1979, ch 225, § 17, eff Sept 1, 1979. Sub 2, add, L 1979, ch 225, § 17, eff Sept 1, 1979.

§ 150.01. Arson in the fifth degree

A person is guilty of arson in the fifth degree when he or she intentionally damages property of another without consent of the owner by intentionally starting a fire or causing an explosion.

Arson in the fifth degree is a class A misdemeanor.

HISTORY: Add, L 2001, ch 224, § 1, eff Nov 1, 2001.

§ 150.05. Arson in the fourth degree

1. A person is guilty of arson in fourth degree when he recklessly damages a building or motor vehicle by intentionally starting a fire or causing an explosion.

2. In any prosecution under this section, it is an affirmative defense that no person other than the defendant had a possessory or proprietary interest in the building or motor vehicle.

Arson in the fourth degree is a class E felony.

HISTORY: Add, L 1965, ch 1030, § 1; amd, L 1971, ch 961, § 5, L 1979, ch 225, § 18, eff Sept 1, 1979. Section heading, amd, L 1971, ch 961, eff Sept 1, 1971.

§ 150.10. Arson in the third degree

1. A person is guilty of arson in the third degree when he intentionally damages a building or motor vehicle by starting a fire or causing an explosion.

2. In any prosecution under this section, it is an affirmative defense that (a) no person other than the defendant had a possessory or proprietary interest in the building or motor vehicle, or if other persons had such interests, all of them consented to the defendant's conduct, and (b) the defendant's sole intent was to destroy or damage the building or motor vehicle for a lawful and proper purpose, and (c) the defendant had no reasonable ground to believe that his conduct might endanger the life or safety of another person or damage another building or motor vehicle.

Arson in the third degree is a class C felony.

> **HISTORY:** Add, L 1965, ch 1030, § 1; amd, L 1971, ch 961, § 6, L 1979, ch 225, § 18, eff Sept 1, 1979. Section heading, amd, L 1971, ch 961, § 6, eff Sept 1, 1971.

§ 150.15. Arson in the second degree

A person is guilty of arson in the second degree when he intentionally damages a building or motor vehicle by starting a fire, and when (a) another person who is not a participant in the crime is present in such building or motor vehicle at the time, and (b) the defendant knows that fact or the circumstances are such as to render the presence of such a person therein a reasonable possibility.

Arson in the second degree is a class B felony.

> **HISTORY:** Add, L 1965, ch 1030, § 1; amd, L 1967, ch 791, § 18, L 1971, ch 961, § 7, L 1979, ch 225, § 18, eff Sept 1, 1979. Section heading, amd, L 1971, ch 961, § 7, eff Sept 1, 1971.

§ 150.20. Arson in the first degree

1. A person is guilty of arson in the first degree when he intentionally damages a building or motor vehicle by causing an explosion or a fire and when (a) such explosion or fire is caused by an incendiary device propelled, thrown or placed inside or near such building or motor vehicle; or when such explosion or fire is caused by an explosive; or when such explosion or fire either (i) causes serious physical injury to another person other than a participant, or (ii) the explosion or fire was caused with the expectation or receipt of financial advantage or pecuniary profit by the actor; and when (b) another person who is not a participant in the crime is present in such building or motor vehicle at the time; and (c) the defendant knows that fact or the circumstances are such as to render the presence of such person therein a reasonable possibility.

2. As used in this section, "incendiary device" means a breakable container designed to explode or produce uncontained combustion upon impact, containing flammable liquid and having a wick or a similar device capable of being ignited.

Arson in the first degree is a class A-I felony.

> **HISTORY:** Add, L 1980, ch 152, § 1; amd, L 1984, ch 950, § 1, eff Nov 1, 1984. Former § 150.20, add, L 1971, ch 961, § 8; amd, L 1973, ch 276, § 15, L 1979, ch 225, § 19; repealed, L 1980, ch 152, § 1, eff Sept 1, 1980. Sub 1, amd, L 1981, ch 71, § 1, eff Sept 1, 1981.

TITLE J   Offenses Involving Theft

ARTICLE 155
LARCENY

ARTICLE 156
OFFENSES INVOLVING COMPUTERS; DEFINITION OF TERMS

ARTICLE 158
WELFARE FRAUD

ARTICLE 160
ROBBERY

ARTICLE 165
OTHER OFFENSES RELATING TO THEFT

HISTORY: Add, L 1965, ch 1030, § 1, eff Sept 1, 1967.

ARTICLE 155   LARCENY

HISTORY: Add, L 1965, ch 1030, § 1, eff Sept 1, 1967.

§ 155.00. Larceny; definitions of terms

The following definitions are applicable to this title:

1. "Property" means any money, personal property, real property, computer data, computer program, thing in action, evidence of debt or contract, or any article, substance or thing of value, including any gas, steam, water or electricity, which is provided for a charge or compensation.

2. "Obtain" includes, but is not limited to, the bringing about of a transfer or purported transfer of property or of a legal interest therein, whether to the obtainer or another.

3. "Deprive." To "deprive" another of property means (a) to withhold it or cause it to be withheld from him permanently or for so extended a period or under such circumstances that the major portion of its economic value or benefit is lost to him, or (b) to dispose of the property in such manner or under such circumstances as to render it unlikely that an owner will recover such property.

4. "Appropriate." To "appropriate" property of another to oneself or a third person means (a) to exercise control over it, or to aid a third person to exercise control over it, permanently or for so extended a period or under such circumstances as to acquire the major portion of its

economic value or benefit, or (b) to dispose of the property for the benefit of oneself or a third person.

5. "Owner." When property is taken, obtained or withheld by one person from another person, an "owner" thereof means any person who has a right to possession thereof superior to that of the taker, obtainer or withholder.

A person who has obtained possession of property by theft or other illegal means shall be deemed to have a right of possession superior to that of a person who takes, obtains or withholds it from him by larcenous means.

A joint or common owner of property shall not be deemed to have a right of possession thereto superior to that of any other joint or common owner thereof.

In the absence of a specific agreement to the contrary, a person in lawful possession of property shall be deemed to have a right of possession superior to that of a person having only a security interest therein, even if legal title lies with the holder of the security interest pursuant to a conditional sale contract or other security agreement.

6. "Secret scientific material" means a sample, culture, micro-organism, specimen, record, recording, document, drawing or any other article, material, device or substance which constitutes, represents, evidences, reflects, or records a scientific or technical process, invention or formula or any part or phase thereof, and which is not, and is not intended to be, available to anyone other than the person or persons rightfully in possession thereof or selected persons having access thereto with his or their consent, and when it accords or may accord such rightful possessors an advantage over competitors or other persons who do not have knowledge or the benefit thereof.

7. "Credit card" means any instrument or article defined as a credit card in section five hundred eleven of the general business law.

7-a. "Debit card" means any instrument or article defined as a debit card in section five hundred eleven of the general business law.

7-b. "Public benefit card" means any medical assistance card, food stamp assistance card, public assistance card, or any other identification, authorization card or electronic access device issued by the state or a social services district as defined in subdivision seven of section two of the social services law, which entitles a person to obtain public assistance benefits under a local, state or federal program administered by the state, its political subdivisions or social services districts.

7-c. "Access device" means any telephone calling card number, credit card number, account number, mobile identification number, electronic serial number or personal identification number that can be used to obtain telephone service.

8. "Service" includes, but is not limited to, labor, professional service, a computer service, transportation service, the supplying of hotel accommodations, restaurant services, entertainment, the supplying of equipment for use, and the supplying of commodities of a public utility nature such as gas, electricity, steam and water. A ticket or equivalent instrument which evidences a right to receive a service is not in itself service but constitutes property within the meaning of subdivision one.

9. "Cable television service" means any and all services provided by or through the facilities of any cable television system or closed circuit coaxial cable communications system, or any microwave or similar transmission service used in connection with any cable television system

or other similar closed circuit coaxial cable communications system.

HISTORY: Add, L 1965, ch 1030, § 1, eff Sept 1, 1967. Sub 1, amd, L 1967, ch 791, § 19, L 1978, ch 420, § 3, L 1986, ch 514, § 2, eff Nov 1, 1986. Sub 6, add, L 1967, ch 791, § 20, eff Sept 1, 1967. Sub 7, add, L 1969, ch 115, § 1, eff July 23, 1969. Sub 7-a, add, L 1987, ch 556, § 7, eff Jan 1, 1988. Sub 7-b, add, L 1995, ch 81, § 169, eff Nov 1, 1995. Former sub 7-b, add, L 1992, ch 41, § 109; repealed, L 1995, ch 81, § 169, eff Nov 1, 1995. Sub 7-c, add, L 1992, ch 491, § 1; amd, L 1993, ch 171, § 1, eff Nov 1, 1993. Sub 8, add, L 1969, ch 115, § 1; amd, L 1986, ch 514, § 3, eff Nov 1, 1986. Sub 9, add, L 1975, ch 530, § 1, eff Oct 27, 1975.

§ 155.05. Larceny; defined

1. A person steals property and commits larceny when, with intent to deprive another of property or to appropriate the same to himself or to a third person, he wrongfully takes, obtains or withholds such property from an owner thereof.

2. Larceny includes a wrongful taking, obtaining or withholding of another's property, with the intent prescribed in subdivision one of this section, committed in any of the following ways:

(a) By conduct heretofore defined or known as common law larceny by trespassory taking, common law larceny by trick, embezzlement, or obtaining property by false pretenses;

(b) By acquiring lost property.

A person acquires lost property when he exercises control over property of another which he knows to have been lost or mislaid, or to have been delivered under a mistake as to the identity of the recipient or the nature or amount of the property, without taking reasonable measures to return such property to the owner;

(c) By committing the crime of issuing a bad check, as defined in section 190.05;

(d) By false promise.

A person obtains property by false promise when, pursuant to a scheme to defraud, he obtains property of another by means of a representation, express or implied, that he or a third person will in the future engage in particular conduct, and when he does not intend to engage in such conduct or, as the case may be, does not believe that the third person intends to engage in such conduct.

In any prosecution for larceny based upon a false promise, the defendant's intention or belief that the promise would not be performed may not be established by or inferred from the fact alone that such promise was not performed. Such a finding may be based only upon evidence establishing that the facts and circumstances of the case are wholly consistent with guilty intent or belief and wholly inconsistent with innocent intent or belief, and excluding to a moral certainty every hypothesis except that of the defendant's intention or belief that the promise would not be performed;

(e) By extortion.

A person obtains property by extortion when he compels or induces another person to deliver such property to himself or to a third person by means of instilling in him a fear that, if the property is not so delivered, the actor or another will:

(i) Cause physical injury to some person in the future; or

(ii) Cause damage to property; or

(iii) Engage in other conduct constituting a crime; or

(iv) Accuse some person of a crime or cause criminal charges to be instituted against him; or

(v) Expose a secret or publicize an asserted fact, whether true or false, tending to subject some person to hatred, contempt or ridicule; or

(vi) Cause a strike, boycott or other collective labor group action injurious to some person's business; except that such a threat shall not be deemed extortion when the property is demanded or received for the benefit of the group in whose interest the actor purports to act; or

(vii) Testify or provide information or withhold testimony or information with respect to another's legal claim or defense; or

(viii) Use or abuse his position as a public servant by performing some act within or related to his official duties, or by failing or refusing to perform an official duty, in such manner as to affect some person adversely; or

(ix) Perform any other act which would not in itself materially benefit the actor but which is calculated to harm another person materially with respect to his health, safety, business, calling, career, financial condition, reputation or personal relationships.

HISTORY: Add, L 1965, ch 1030, § 1, eff Sept 1, 1967, with substance derived in part from § 1290.

§ 155.10. Larceny; no defense

The crimes of (a) larceny committed by means of extortion and an attempt to commit the same, and (b) bribe receiving by a labor official as defined in section 180.20, and bribe receiving as defined in section 200.05, are not mutually exclusive, and it is no defense to a prosecution for larceny committed by means of extortion or for an attempt to commit the same that, by reason of the same conduct, the defendant also committed one of such specified crimes of bribe receiving.

HISTORY: Add, L 1965, ch 1030, § 1, eff Sept 1, 1967.

§ 155.15. Larceny; defenses

1. In any prosecution for larceny committed by trespassory taking or embezzlement, it is an affirmative defense that the property was appropriated under a claim of right made in good faith.

2. In any prosecution for larceny by extortion committed by instilling in the victim a fear that he or another person would be charged with a crime, it is an affirmative defense that the defendant reasonably believed the threatened charge to be true and that his sole purpose was to compel or induce the victim to take reasonable action to make good the wrong which was the subject of such threatened charge.

HISTORY: Add, L 1965, ch 1030, § 1, eff Sept 1, 1967, with substance derived from § 1306.

§ 155.20. Larceny; value of stolen property

For the purposes of this title, the value of property shall be ascertained as follows:

1. Except as otherwise specified in this section, value means the market value of the property at the time and place of the crime, or if such cannot be satisfactorily ascertained, the cost of replacement of the property within a reasonable time after the crime.

2. Whether or not they have been issued or delivered, certain written instruments, not including those having a readily ascertainable market value such as some public and corporate bonds and securities, shall be evaluated as follows:

(a) The value of an instrument constituting an evidence of debt, such as a check, draft or promissory note, shall be deemed the amount due or collectable thereon or thereby, such figure ordinarily being the face amount of the indebtedness less any portion thereof which has been satisfied.

(b) The value of a ticket or equivalent instrument which evidences a right to receive a transportation, entertainment or other service shall be deemed the price stated thereon, if any; and if no price is stated thereon the value shall be deemed the price of such ticket or equivalent instrument which the issuer charges the general public.

(c) The value of any other instrument which creates, releases, discharges or otherwise affects any valuable legal right, privilege or obligation shall be deemed the greatest amount of economic loss which the owner of the instrument might reasonably suffer by virtue of the loss of the instrument.

3. Where the property consists of gas, steam, water or electricity, which is provided for charge or compensation, the value shall be the value of the property stolen in any consecutive twelve-month period.

4. When the value of property cannot be satisfactorily ascertained pursuant to the standards set forth in subdivisions one and two of this section, its value shall be deemed to be an amount less than two hundred fifty dollars.

HISTORY: Add, L 1965, ch 1030, § 1, eff Sept 1, 1967, with substance derived from §§ 1303–1305. Sub 2, par (b), add, L 1969, ch 115, § 2, eff July 23, 1969. Former sub 2, par (b), relettered sub 2, par (c), L 1969, ch 115, § 2, eff July 23, 1969. Sub 2, par (c), formerly sub 2, par (b), relettered sub 2 par (c), L 1969, ch 115, § 2, eff July 23, 1969. Sub 3, add, L 1978, ch 420, § 4, eff Jan 1, 1979. Former sub 3, renumbered sub 4, L 1978, ch 420, § 4, eff Jan 1, 1979. Sub 4, formerly sub 3, renumbered sub 4, L 1978, ch 420, § 4, eff Jan 1, 1979.

§ 155.25. Petit larceny

A person is guilty of petit larceny when he steals property.

Petit larceny is a class A misdemeanor.

HISTORY: Add, L 1965, ch 1030, § 1, eff Sept 1, 1967, with substance derived from §§ 1296(1), 1298, 1299.

§ 155.30. Grand larceny in the fourth degree

A person is guilty of grand larceny in the fourth degree when he steals property and when:

1. The value of the property exceeds one thousand dollars; or

2. The property consists of a public record, writing or instrument kept, filed or deposited according to law with or in the keeping of any public office or public servant; or

3. The property consists of secret scientific material; or

4. The property consists of a credit card or debit card; or

5. The property, regardless of its nature and value, is taken from the person of another; or

6. The property, regardless of its nature and value, is obtained by extortion; or

7. The property consists of one or more firearms, rifles or shotguns, as such terms are defined in section 265.00 of this chapter; or

8. The value of the property exceeds one hundred dollars and the property consists of a motor vehicle, as defined in section one hundred twenty-five of the vehicle and traffic law, other than

a motorcycle, as defined in section one hundred twenty-three of such law; or

9. The property consists of a scroll, religious vestment, a vessel, an item comprising a display of religious symbols which forms a representative expression of faith, or other miscellaneous item of property which:

(a) has a value of at least one hundred dollars; and

(b) is kept for or used in connection with religious worship in any building, structure or upon the curtilage of such building or structure used as a place of religious worship by a religious corporation, as incorporated under the religious corporations law or the education law.

10. The property consists of an access device which the person intends to use unlawfully to obtain telephone service.

11. The property consists of anhydrous ammonia or liquified ammonia gas and the actor intends to use, or knows another person intends to use, such anhydrous ammonia or liquified ammonia gas to manufacture methamphetamine.

Grand larceny in the fourth degree is a class E felony.

HISTORY: Add, L 1965, ch 1030, § 1, with substance derived from §§ 850, 851, 852, 856, 1296, 1297; amd, L 1967, ch 791, § 21, eff Sept 1, 1967, L 1969, ch 115, § 3, L 1969, ch 352, § 1, L 1982, ch 234, § 1, eff June 15, 1982, L 1986, ch 515, § 1, eff Nov 1, 1986, L 1987, ch 556, § 8, eff Jan 1, 1988, L 1990, ch 450, § 1, eff Nov 1, 1990, L 1992, ch 491, § 2, eff Nov 1, 1992, L 2005, ch 394, § 1, eff Oct 1, 2005, L 2010, ch 479, § 1, eff Aug 30, 2010.

§ 155.35. Grand larceny in the third degree

Grand larceny in the third degree is a class D felony.

A person is guilty of grand larceny in the third degree when he or she steals property and:

1. when the value of the property exceeds three thousand dollars, or

2. the property is an automated teller machine or the contents of an automated teller machine.

Grand larceny in the third degree is a class D felony.

HISTORY: Add, L 1965, ch 1030, § 1, with substance derived from §§ 1294(3), 1295; amd, L 1986, ch 515, § 2, eff Nov 1, 1986, L 2010, ch 464, § 1, eff Nov 1, 2010.

§ 155.40. Grand larceny in the second degree

A person is guilty of grand larceny in the second degree when he steals property and when:

1. The value of the property exceeds fifty thousand dollars; or

2. The property, regardless of its nature and value, is obtained by extortion committed by instilling in the victim a fear that the actor or another person will (a) cause physical injury to some person in the future, or (b) cause damage to property, or (c) use or abuse his position as a public servant by engaging in conduct within or related to his official duties, or by failing or refusing to perform an official duty, in such manner as to affect some person adversely.

Grand larceny in the second degree is a class C felony.

HISTORY: Add, L 1965, ch 1030, § 1, with substance derived from §§ 850, 851, 852, 856; amd, L 1986, ch 515, § 2, eff Nov 1, 1986. Section heading, amd, L 1986, ch 515, § 2, eff Nov 1, 1986.

§ 155.42. Grand larceny in the first degree

A person is guilty of grand larceny in the first degree when he steals property and when the value of the property exceeds one million dollars.

Grand larceny in the first degree is a class B felony.

HISTORY: Add, L 1986, ch 515, § 3, eff Nov 1, 1986.

§ 155.43. Aggravated grand larceny of an automated teller machine

A person is guilty of aggravated grand larceny of an automated teller machine when he or she commits the crime of grand larceny in the third degree, as defined in subdivision two of section 155.35 of this article and has been previously convicted of grand larceny in the third degree within the previous five years.

Aggravated grand larceny of an automated teller machine is a class C felony.

HISTORY: Add, L 2010, ch 464, § 2, eff Nov 1, 2010.

§ 155.45. Larceny; pleading and proof

1. Where it is an element of the crime charged that property was taken from the person or obtained by extortion, an indictment for larceny must so specify. In all other cases, an indictment, information or complaint for larceny is sufficient if it alleges that the defendant stole property of the nature or value required for the commission of the crime charged without designating the particular way or manner in which such property was stolen or the particular theory of larceny involved.

2. Proof that the defendant engaged in any conduct constituting larceny as defined in section 155.05 is sufficient to support any indictment, information or complaint for larceny other than one charging larceny by extortion. An indictment charging larceny by extortion must be supported by proof establishing larceny by extortion.

HISTORY: Add, L 1965, ch 1030, § 1, eff Sept 1, 1967, with substance derived from § 261.

ARTICLE 156   OFFENSES INVOLVING COMPUTERS; DEFINITION OF TERMS

HISTORY: Add, L 1986, ch 514, § 1, eff Nov 1, 1986.

§ 156.00. Offenses involving computers; definition of terms

The following definitions are applicable to this chapter except where different meanings are expressly specified:

1. "Computer" means a device or group of devices which, by manipulation of electronic,

magnetic, optical or electrochemical impulses, pursuant to a computer program, can automatically perform arithmetic, logical, storage or retrieval operations with or on computer data, and includes any connected or directly related device, equipment or facility which enables such computer to store, retrieve or communicate to or from a person, another computer or another device the results of computer operations, computer programs or computer data.

2. "Computer program" is property and means an ordered set of data representing coded instructions or statements that, when executed by computer, cause the computer to process data or direct the computer to perform one or more computer operations or both and may be in any form, including magnetic storage media, punched cards, or stored internally in the memory of the computer.

3. "Computer data" is property and means a representation of information, knowledge, facts, concepts or instructions which are being processed, or have been processed in a computer and may be in any form, including magnetic storage media, punched cards, or stored internally in the memory of the computer.

4. "Computer service" means any and all services provided by or through the facilities of any computer communication system allowing the input, output, examination, or transfer, of computer data or computer programs from one computer to another.

5. "Computer material" is property and means any computer data or computer program which:

(a) contains records of the medical history or medical treatment of an identified or readily identifiable individual or individuals. This term shall not apply to the gaining access to or duplication solely of the medical history or medical treatment records of a person by that person or by another specifically authorized by the person whose records are gained access to or duplicated; or

(b) contains records maintained by the state or any political subdivision thereof or any governmental instrumentality within the state which contains any information concerning a person, as defined in subdivision seven of section 10.00 of this chapter, which because of name, number, symbol, mark or other identifier, can be used to identify the person and which is otherwise prohibited by law from being disclosed. This term shall not apply to the gaining access to or duplication solely of records of a person by that person or by another specifically authorized by the person whose records are gained access to or duplicated; or

(c) is not and is not intended to be available to anyone other than the person or persons rightfully in possession thereof or selected persons having access thereto with his, her or their consent and which accords or may accord such rightful possessors an advantage over competitors or other persons who do not have knowledge or the benefit thereof.

6. "Computer network" means the interconnection of hardwire or wireless communication lines with a computer through remote terminals, or a complex consisting of two or more interconnected computers.

7. "Access" means to instruct, communicate with, store data in, retrieve from, or otherwise make use of any resources of a computer, physically, directly or by electronic means.

8. "Without authorization" means to use or to access a computer, computer service or computer network without the permission of the owner or lessor or someone licensed or privileged by the owner or lessor where such person knew that his or her use or access was without permission or after actual notice to such person that such use or access was without

permission. It shall also mean the access of a computer service by a person without permission where such person knew that such access was without permission or after actual notice to such person, that such access was without permission.

Proof that such person used or accessed a computer, computer service or computer network through the knowing use of a set of instructions, code or computer program that bypasses, defrauds or otherwise circumvents a security measure installed or used with the user's authorization on the computer, computer service or computer network shall be presumptive evidence that such person used or accessed such computer, computer service or computer network without authorization.

9. "Felony" as used in this article means any felony defined in the laws of this state or any offense defined in the laws of any other jurisdiction for which a sentence to a term of imprisonment in excess of one year is authorized in this state.

HISTORY: Add, L 1986, ch 514, § 1, eff Nov 1, 1986. Amd, L 2006, ch 558, § 1, eff Nov 1, 2006. Sub 5, par (c), amd, L 2006, ch 558, § 1, eff Nov 1, 2006. Sub 6, add, L 2006, ch 558, § 1, eff Nov 1, 2006. Former sub 6, deleted, L 2006, ch 558, § 1, eff Nov 1, 2006. Sub 7, add, L 2006, ch 558, § 1, eff Nov 1, 2006. Former sub 7, redesignated sub 9, L 2006, ch 558, § 1, eff Nov 1, 2006. Sub 8, add, L 2006, ch 558, § 1, eff Nov 1, 2006. Sub 9, formerly sub 7, so designated sub 9, L 2006, ch 558, § 1, eff Nov 1, 2006.

§ 156.05. Unauthorized use of a computer

A person is guilty of unauthorized use of a computer when he or she knowingly uses, causes to be used, or accesses a computer, computer service, or computer network without authorization.

Unauthorized use of a computer is a class A misdemeanor.

HISTORY: Add, L 1986, ch 514, § 1, eff Nov 1, 1986. Amd, L 2006, ch 558, § 2, eff Nov 1, 2006. Opening par, amd, L 2006, ch 558, § 2, eff Nov 1, 2006.

§ 156.10. Computer trespass

A person is guilty of computer trespass when he or she knowingly uses, causes to be used, or accesses a computer, computer service, or computer network without authorization and:

1. he or she does so with an intent to commit or attempt to commit or further the commission of any felony; or

2. he or she thereby knowingly gains access to computer material.

Computer trespass is a class E felony.

HISTORY: Add, L 1986, ch 514, § 1, eff Nov 1, 1986. Amd, L 2006, ch 558, § 2, eff Nov 1, 2006. Opening par, amd, L 2006, ch 558, § 2, eff Nov 1, 2006. Sub 1, amd, L 2006, ch 558, § 2, eff Nov 1, 2006. Sub 2, amd, L 2006, ch 558, § 2, eff Nov 1, 2006.

§ 156.20. Computer tampering in the fourth degree

A person is guilty of computer tampering in the fourth degree when he or she uses, causes to be used, or accesses a computer, computer service, or computer network without authorization and he or she intentionally alters in any manner or destroys computer data or a computer program of another person.

Computer tampering in the fourth degree is a class A misdemeanor.

HISTORY: Add, L 1986, ch 514, § 1, eff Nov 1, 1986. Amd, L 2006, ch 558, § 3, eff Nov 1, 2006. Section heading, amd, L 1993, ch 89, § 1, eff Nov 1, 1993. First undesignated par, amd, L 1993, ch 89, § 1, eff Nov 1, 1993. First undesignated par, amd, L 2006, ch 558, § 3, eff Nov 1, 2006. Second undesignated par, amd, L 1993, ch 89, § 1, eff Nov 1, 1993.

§ 156.25. Computer tampering in the third degree

A person is guilty of computer tampering in the third degree when he commits the crime of computer tampering in the fourth degree and:

1. he does so with an intent to commit or attempt to commit or further the commission of any felony; or

2. he has been previously convicted of any crime under this article or subdivision eleven of section 165.15 of this chapter; or

3. he intentionally alters in any manner or destroys computer material; or

4. he intentionally alters in any manner or destroys computer data or a computer program so as to cause damages in an aggregate amount exceeding one thousand dollars.

Computer tampering in the third degree is a class E felony.

HISTORY: Add, L 1986, ch 514, § 1; amd, L 1993, ch 89, § 2, eff Nov 1, 1993. Section heading, amd, L 1993, ch 89, § 2, eff Nov 1, 1993. Opening par, amd, L 1993, ch 89, § 2, eff Nov 1, 1993. Sub 2, amd, L 1997, ch 376, § 1, eff Nov 1, 1997. Sub 4, amd, L 1993, ch 89, § 2, eff Nov 1, 1993. Closing par, amd, L 1993, ch 89, § 2, eff Nov 1, 1993.

§ 156.26. Computer tampering in the second degree

A person is guilty of computer tampering in the second degree when he or she commits the crime of computer tampering in the fourth degree and he or she intentionally alters in any manner or destroys:

1. computer data or a computer program so as to cause damages in an aggregate amount exceeding three thousand dollars; or

2. computer material that contains records of the medical history or medical treatment of an identified or readily identifiable individual or individuals and as a result of such alteration or destruction, such individual or individuals suffer serious physical injury, and he or she is aware of and consciously disregards a substantial and unjustifiable risk that such serious physical injury may occur.

Computer tampering in the second degree is a class D felony.

HISTORY: Add, L 1993, ch 89, § 3, eff Nov 1, 1993. Amd, L 2008, ch 590, § 1, eff Nov 1, 2008. First undesignated par, opening par, formerly entire first undesignated par, so designated first undesignated par, opening par and amd, L 2008, ch 590, § 1, eff Nov 1, 2008. First undesignated par, sub 1, formerly part of first undesignated par, so designated first undesignated par, sub 1 and amd, L 2008, ch 590, § 1, eff Nov 1, 2008. First undesignated par, sub 2, add, L 2008, ch 590, § 1, eff Nov 1, 2008.

§ 156.27. Computer tampering in the first degree

A person is guilty of computer tampering in the first degree when he commits the crime of computer tampering in the fourth degree and he intentionally alters in any manner or destroys computer data or a computer program so as to cause damages in an aggregate amount exceeding fifty thousand dollars.

Computer tampering in the first degree is a class C felony.

HISTORY: Add, L 1993, ch 89, § 3, eff Nov 1, 1993.

§ 156.29. Unlawful duplication of computer related material in the second degree

A person is guilty of unlawful duplication of computer related material in the second degree when having no right to do so, he or she copies, reproduces or duplicates in any manner computer material that contains records of the medical history or medical treatment of an identified or readily identifiable individual or individuals with an intent to commit or further the commission of any crime under this chapter.

Unlawful duplication of computer related material in the second degree is a class B misdemeanor.

HISTORY: Add, L 2008, ch 590, § 2, eff Nov 1, 2008.

§ 156.30. Unlawful duplication of computer related material in the first degree

A person is guilty of unlawful duplication of computer related [material]* in the first degree [material]** when having no right to do so, he or she copies, reproduces or duplicates in any manner:

1. any computer data or computer program and thereby intentionally and wrongfully deprives or appropriates from an owner thereof an economic value or benefit in excess of two thousand five hundred dollars; or

2. any computer data or computer program with an intent to commit or attempt to commit or further the commission of any felony.

Unlawful duplication of computer related material in the first degree is a class E felony.

HISTORY: Add, L 1986, ch 514, § 1, eff Nov 1, 1986. Amd, L 2008, ch 590, § 3, eff Nov 1, 2008. Section heading, amd, L 2008, ch 590, § 3, eff Nov 1, 2008. Opening par, amd, L 2008, ch 590, § 3, eff Nov 1, 2008. Closing par, amd, L 2008, ch 590, § 3, eff Nov 1, 2008.

§ 156.35. Criminal possession of computer related material

A person is guilty of criminal possession of computer related material when having no right to do so, he knowingly possesses, in any form, any copy, reproduction or duplicate of any computer data or computer program which was copied, reproduced or duplicated in violation of section 156.30 of this article, with intent to benefit himself or a person other than an owner thereof.

Criminal possession of computer related material is a class E felony.

HISTORY: Add, L 1986, ch 514, § 1, eff Nov 1, 1986.

§ 156.40. Operating an unlawful electronic sweepstakes

1. As used in this section the following words and terms shall have the following meanings:

(a) "Electronic machine or device" means a mechanically, electrically or electronically operated machine or device that is owned, leased or otherwise possessed by a sweepstakes sponsor or promoter, or any sponsors, promoters, partners, affiliates, subsidiaries or contractors thereof; that is intended to be used by a sweepstakes entrant; that uses energy; and that displays the results of a game entry or game outcome to a participant on a screen or other mechanism at a business location, including a private club; provided, that an electronic machine or device may, without limitation:

(1) be server-based;

(2) use a simulated game terminal as a representation of the prizes associated with the results of the sweepstakes entries;

(3) utilize software such that the simulated game influences or determines the winning or value of the prize;

---

* The bracketed word was inadvertently omitted by the Legislature.

** The bracketed word was inadvertently inserted by the Legislature.

(4) select prizes from a predetermined finite pool of entries;

(5) utilize a mechanism that reveals the content of a predetermined sweepstakes entry;

(6) predetermine the prize results and stores those results for delivery at the time the sweepstakes entry results are revealed;

(7) utilize software to create a game result;

(8) require deposit of any money, coin or token, or the use of any credit card, debit card, prepaid card or any other method of payment to activate the electronic machine or device;

(9) require direct payment into the electronic machine or device, or remote activation of the electronic machine or device;

(10) require purchase of a related product having legitimate value;

(11) reveal the prize incrementally, even though it may not influence if a prize is awarded or the value of any prize awarded;

(12) determine and associate the prize with an entry or entries at the time the sweepstakes is entered; or

(13) be a slot machine or other form of electrical, mechanical, or computer game.

(b) "Enter" or "entry" means the act or process by which a person becomes eligible to receive any prize offered in a sweepstakes.

(c) "Entertaining display" means any visual information, capable of being seen by a sweepstakes entrant, that takes the form of actual game play or simulated game play.

(d) "Prize" means any gift, award, gratuity, good, service, credit or anything else of value, which may be transferred to a person, whether possession of the prize is actually transferred, or placed on an account or other record as evidence of the intent to transfer the prize.

(e) "Sweepstakes" means any game, advertising scheme or plan, or other promotion, which, with or without payment of any consideration, a person may enter to win or become eligible to receive any prize, the determination of which is based upon chance.

2. A person is guilty of operating an unlawful electronic sweepstakes when he or she knowingly possesses with the intent to operate, or place into operation, an electronic machine or device to:

(a) conduct a sweepstakes through the use of an entertaining display, including the entry process or the reveal of a prize; or

(b) promote a sweepstakes that is conducted through the use of an entertaining display, including the entry process or the reveal of a prize.

3. Nothing in this section shall be construed to make illegal any activity which is lawfully conducted as the New York state lottery for education as authorized by article thirty-four of the tax law; pari-mutuel wagering on horse races as authorized by articles two, three, four, five-A, and ten of the racing, pari-mutuel wagering and breeding law; the game of bingo as authorized pursuant to article fourteen-H of the general municipal law; games of chance as authorized pursuant to article nine-A of the general municipal law; gaming as authorized by article thirteen of the racing, pari-mutuel wagering and breeding law; or pursuant to the federal Indian Gaming Regulatory Act.

Operating an unlawful electronic sweepstakes is a class E felony.

HISTORY: Add, L 2013, ch 174, § 11, eff July 30, 2013.

§ 156.50. Offenses involving computers; defenses

In any prosecution:

1. under section 156.05 or 156.10 of this article, it shall be a defense that the defendant had reasonable grounds to believe that he had authorization to use the computer;

2. under section 156.20, 156.25, 156.26 or 156.27 of this article it shall be a defense that the defendant had reasonable grounds to believe that he had the right to alter in any manner or destroy the computer data or the computer program;

3. under section 156.29 or 156.30 of this article it shall be a defense that the defendant had reasonable grounds to believe that he had the right to copy, reproduce or duplicate in any manner the computer data or the computer program.

HISTORY: Add, L 1986, ch 514, § 1; amd, L 1993, ch 89, § 4, eff Nov 1, 1993. Sub 2, amd, L 1993, ch 89, § 4, eff Nov 1, 1993. Sub 3, amd, L 2008, ch 590, § 4, eff Nov 1, 2008.

ARTICLE 158   WELFARE FRAUD

HISTORY: Add, L 1995, ch 81, § 168, eff Nov 1, 1995.

§ 158.00. Definitions; presumption; limitation

1. Definitions. The following definitions are applicable to this article: .

(a) "Public benefit card" means any medical assistance card, food stamp assistance card, public assistance card, or any other identification, authorization card or electronic access device issued by the state or a social services district, as defined in subdivision seven of section two of the social services law, which entitles a person to obtain public assistance benefits under a local, state, or federal program administered by the state, its political subdivisions, or social services districts.

(b) "Fraudulent welfare act" means knowingly and with intent to defraud, engaging in an act or acts pursuant to which a person:

(1) offers, presents or causes to be presented to the state, any of its political subdivisions or social services districts, or any employee or agent thereof, an oral or written application or request for public assistance benefits or for a public benefit card with knowledge that the application or request contains a false statement or false information, and such statement or information is material, or

(2) holds himself or herself out to be another person, whether real or fictitious, for the purpose of obtaining public assistance benefits, or

(3) makes a false statement or provides false information for the purpose of (i) establishing or maintaining eligibility for public assistance benefits or (ii) increasing or preventing reduction of public assistance benefits, and such statement or information is material.

(c) "Public assistance benefits" means money, property or services provided directly or indirectly through programs of the federal government, the state government or the government of any political subdivision within the state and administered by the department of social services or social services districts.

2. Rebuttable presumption.

(a) A person who possesses five or more public benefit cards in a name or names other than his or her own is presumed to possess the same with intent to defraud, deceive or injure another.

(b) The presumption established by this subdivision shall not apply to:

(1) any employee or agent of the department of social services to the extent that he or she possesses such cards in the course of his or her official duties; or

(2) any person to the extent that he [or]* she possesses a public benefit card or cards issued to a member or members of his or her immediate family or household with the consent of the cardholder; or

(3) any person providing home health services or personal care services pursuant to title eleven of article five of the social services law, or any agent or employee of a congregate care or residential treatment facility or foster care provider, to the extent that in the course of his or her duties, he or she possesses public assistance cards issued to persons under his or her care.

(c) The presumption established by this subdivision is rebuttable by evidence tending to show that the defendant did not possess such public benefit card or cards with intent to defraud, deceive or injure another. In any action tried before a jury, the jury shall be so instructed.

(d) The foregoing presumption shall apply to prosecutions for criminal possession of public benefit cards.

3. Limitation. Nothing contained in this article shall be construed to prohibit a recipient of public assistance benefits from pledging his or her public assistance benefits or using his or her public benefit card as collateral for a loan.

HISTORY: Add, L 1995, ch 81, § 168, eff Nov 1, 1995.

§ 158.05. Welfare fraud in the fifth degree

A person is guilty of welfare fraud in the fifth degree when he or she commits a fraudulent welfare act and thereby takes or obtains public assistance benefits.

Welfare fraud in the fifth degree is a class A misdemeanor.

HISTORY: Add, L 1995, ch 81, § 168, eff Nov 1, 1995.

§ 158.10. Welfare fraud in the fourth degree

A person is guilty of welfare fraud in the fourth degree when he or she commits a fraudulent welfare act and thereby takes or obtains public assistance benefits, and when the value of the public

---

* The bracketed word has been inserted by the Publisher.

assistance benefits exceeds one thousand dollars.

Welfare fraud in the fourth degree is a class E felony.

HISTORY: Add, L 1995, ch 81, § 168, eff Nov 1, 1995.

§ 158.15. Welfare fraud in the third degree

A person is guilty of welfare fraud in the third degree when he or she commits a fraudulent welfare act and thereby takes or obtains public assistance benefits, and when the value of the public assistance benefits exceeds three thousand dollars.

Welfare fraud in the third degree is a class D felony.

HISTORY: Add, L 1995, ch 81, § 168, eff Nov 1, 1995.

§ 158.20. Welfare fraud in the second degree

A person is guilty of welfare fraud in the second degree when he or she commits a fraudulent welfare act and thereby takes or obtains public assistance benefits, and when the value of the public assistance benefits exceeds fifty thousand dollars.

Welfare fraud in the second degree is a class C felony.

HISTORY: Add, L 1995, ch 81, § 168, eff Nov 1, 1995.

§ 158.25. Welfare fraud in the first degree

A person is guilty of welfare fraud in the first degree when he or she commits a fraudulent welfare act and thereby takes or obtains public assistance benefits, and when the value of the public assistance benefits exceeds one million dollars.

Welfare fraud in the first degree is a class B felony.

HISTORY: Add, L 1995, ch 81, § 168, eff Nov 1, 1995.

§ 158.30. Criminal use of a public benefit card in the second degree

A person is guilty of criminal use of a public benefit card in the second degree when he or she knowingly:

　　1. Loans money or otherwise provides property or services on credit, and accepts a public benefit card as collateral or security for the repayment of such loan or for the provision of such property or services;

　　2. Obtains a public benefit card in exchange for a benefit; or

　　3. Transfers or delivers a public benefit card to another (a) in exchange for money or a controlled substance as defined in subdivision five of section 220.00, or (b) for the purpose of committing an unlawful act.

Criminal use of a public benefit card in the second degree is a class A misdemeanor.

HISTORY: Add, L 1995, ch 81, § 168, eff Nov 1, 1995.

§ 158.35. Criminal use of a public benefit card in the first degree

A person is guilty of criminal use of a public benefit card in the first degree when he or she, pursuant to an act or a series of acts, knowingly (i) obtains three or more public benefit cards from another or others in exchange for a benefit, or (ii) transfers or delivers three or more public benefit cards to another or others in exchange for money or a controlled substance as defined in subdivision five of section 220.00 of this chapter.

Criminal use of a public benefit card in the first degree is a class E felony.

HISTORY: Add, L 1995, ch 81, § 168, eff Nov 1, 1995.

§ 158.40. Criminal possession of public benefit cards in the third degree

A person is guilty of criminal possession of public benefit cards in the third degree when he or she with intent to defraud, deceive or injure another, knowingly possesses five or more public benefit cards in a name or names other than the person's own name.

Criminal possession of public benefit cards in the third degree is a class E felony.

HISTORY: Add, L 1995, ch 81, § 168, eff Nov 1, 1995.

§ 158.45. Criminal possession of public benefit cards in the second degree

A person is guilty of criminal possession of public benefit cards in the second degree when he or she with intent to defraud, deceive or injure another, knowingly possesses ten or more public benefit cards in a name or names other than the person's own name.

Criminal possession of public benefit cards in the second degree is a class D felony.

HISTORY: Add, L 1995, ch 81, § 168, eff Nov 1, 1995.

§ 158.50. Criminal possession of public benefit cards in the first degree

A person is guilty of criminal possession of public benefit cards in the first degree when he or she with intent to defraud, deceive or injure another, knowingly possesses twenty-five or more public benefit cards in a name or names other than the person's own name.

Criminal possession of public benefit cards in the first degree is a class C felony.

HISTORY: Add, L 1995, ch 81, § 168, eff Nov 1, 1995.

ARTICLE 160   ROBBERY

§ 160.00.	Robbery; defined
§ 160.05.	Robbery in the third degree
§ 160.10.	Robbery in the second degree
§ 160.15.	Robbery in the first degree

HISTORY: Add, L 1965, ch 1030, § 1, eff Sept 1, 1967.

§ 160.00. Robbery; defined

Robbery is forcible stealing. A person forcibly steals property and commits robbery when, in the course of committing a larceny, he uses or threatens the immediate use of physical force upon another person for the purpose of:

1. Preventing or overcoming resistance to the taking of the property or to the retention thereof immediately after the taking; or

2. Compelling the owner of such property or another person to deliver up the property or to engage in other conduct which aids in the commission of the larceny.

HISTORY: Add, L 1965, ch 1030, § 1, eff Sept 1, 1967, with substance derived from §§ 2120, 2121, 2122, 2123.

§ 160.05. Robbery in the third degree

A person is guilty of robbery in the third degree when he forcibly steals property.

Robbery in the third degree is a class D felony.

HISTORY: Add, L 1965, ch 1030, § 1, eff Sept 1, 1967, with substance derived from § 2126.

§ 160.10. Robbery in the second degree

A person is guilty of robbery in the second degree when he forcibly steals property and when:

1. He is aided by another person actually present; or

2. In the course of the commission of the crime or of immediate flight therefrom, he or another participant in the crime:

(a) Causes physical injury to any person who is not a participant in the crime; or

(b) Displays what appears to be a pistol, revolver, rifle, shotgun, machine gun or other firearm; or

3. The property consists of a motor vehicle, as defined in section one hundred twenty-five of the vehicle and traffic law.

Robbery in the second degree is a class C felony.

HISTORY: Add, L 1965, ch 1030, § 1, with substance derived from § 2124(2); amd, L 1969, ch 1012, § 3, L 1973, ch 374, § 3, eff Sept 1, 1973. Sub 2, add, L 1969, ch 1012, § 3, eff Sept 1, 1969. Sub 2, par (b), amd, L 1995, ch 308, § 1, eff Nov 1, 1995. Sub 3, add, L 1995, ch 308, § 1, eff Nov 1, 1995.

§ 160.15. Robbery in the first degree

A person is guilty of robbery in the first degree when he forcibly steals property and when, in the course of the commission of the crime or of immediate flight therefrom, he or another participant in the crime:

1. Causes serious physical injury to any person who is not a participant in the crime; or

2. Is armed with a deadly weapon; or

3. Uses or threatens the immediate use of a dangerous instrument; or

4. Displays what appears to be a pistol, revolver, rifle, shotgun, machine gun or other firearm; except that in any prosecution under this subdivision, it is an affirmative defense that such pistol, revolver, rifle, shotgun, machine gun or other firearm was not a loaded weapon from which a shot, readily capable of producing death or other serious physical injury, could be discharged. Nothing contained in this subdivision shall constitute a defense to a prosecution for, or preclude a conviction of, robbery in the second degree, robbery in the third degree or any other crime.

Robbery in the first degree is a class B felony.

HISTORY: Add, L 1965, ch 1030, § 1, with substance derived from § 2124(1, 3); amd, L 1969, ch 1012, § 4, L 1973, ch 374, § 4, eff Sept 1, 1973. Sub 3, amd, L 1967, ch 791, § 22, eff Sept 1, 1967. Sub 4, add, L 1969, ch 1012, § 4, eff Sept 1, 1969.

ARTICLE 165   OTHER OFFENSES RELATING TO THEFT

PL

HISTORY: Add, L 1965, ch 1030, § 1, eff Sept 1, 1967.

§ 165.00. Misapplication of property

1. A person is guilty of misapplication of property when, knowingly possessing personal property of another pursuant to an agreement that the same will be returned to the owner at a future time,

(a) he loans, leases, pledges, pawns or otherwise encumbers such property without the consent of the owner thereof in such manner as to create a risk that the owner will not be able to recover it or will suffer pecuniary loss; or

(b) he intentionally refuses to return personal property valued in excess of one hundred dollars to the owner pursuant to the terms of the rental agreement provided that the owner shall have made a written demand for the return of such personal property in person or by certified mail at an address indicated in the rental agreement and he intentionally refuses to return such personal property for a period of thirty days after such demand has been received or should reasonably have been received by him. Such written demand shall state: (i) the date and time at which the personal property was to have been returned under the rental agreement; (ii) that the owner does not consent to the continued withholding or retaining of such personal property and demands its return; and (iii) that the continued withholding or retaining of the property may constitute a class A misdemeanor punishable by a fine of up to one thousand dollars or by a sentence to a term of imprisonment for a period of up to one year or by both such fine and imprisonment.

(c) as used in paragraph (b) of this subdivision and in subdivision three of this section, the terms owner, personal property, and rental agreement shall be defined as in subdivision one of section three hundred ninety-nine-w of the general business law.

2. In any prosecution under paragraph (a) of subdivision one of this section, it is a defense that, at the time the prosecution was commenced, (a) the defendant had recovered possession of the property, unencumbered as a result of the unlawful disposition, and (b) the owner had suffered no material economic loss as a result of the unlawful disposition.

3. In any prosecution under paragraph (b) of subdivision one of this section, it is a defense that

at the time the prosecution was commenced, (a) the owner had recovered possession of the personal property and suffered no material economic loss as a result of the unlawful retention; or (b) the defendant is unable to return such personal property because it has been accidentally destroyed or stolen; or (c) the owner failed to comply with the provisions of section three hundred ninety-nine-w of the general business law.

Misapplication of property is a class A misdemeanor.

HISTORY: Add, L 1965, ch 1030, § 1, with substance derived from §§ 941, 1310; amd, L 1995, ch 372, § 1, eff Nov 1, 1995. Sub 1, opening par, formerly part of entire sub 1, so designated, L 1995, ch 372, § 1, eff Nov 1, 1995. Sub 1, par (a), formerly part of entire sub 1, so designated and amd, L 1995, ch 372, § 1, eff Nov 1, 1995. Sub 1, par (b), add, L 1995, ch 372, § 1, eff Nov 1, 1995. Sub 1, par (c), add, L 1995, ch 372, § 1, eff Nov 1, 1995. Sub 2, amd, L 1995, ch 372, § 1, eff Nov 1, 1995. Sub 3, add, L 1995, ch 372, § 1, eff Nov 1, 1995.

§ 165.05. Unauthorized use of a vehicle in the third degree

A person is guilty of unauthorized use of a vehicle in the third degree when:

1. Knowing that he does not have the consent of the owner, he takes, operates, exercises control over, rides in or otherwise uses a vehicle. A person who engages in any such conduct without the consent of the owner is presumed to know that he does not have such consent; or

2. Having custody of a vehicle pursuant to an agreement between himself or another and the owner thereof whereby he or another is to perform for compensation a specific service for the owner involving the maintenance, repair or use of such vehicle, he intentionally uses or operates the same, without the consent of the owner, for his own purposes in a manner constituting a gross deviation from the agreed purpose; or

3. Having custody of a vehicle pursuant to an agreement with the owner thereof whereby such vehicle is to be returned to the owner at a specified time, he intentionally retains or withholds possession thereof, without the consent of the owner, for so lengthy a period beyond the specified time as to render such retention or possession a gross deviation from the agreement.

For purposes of this section "a gross deviation from the agreement" shall consist of, but not be limited to, circumstances wherein a person who having had custody of a vehicle for a period of fifteen days or less pursuant to a written agreement retains possession of such vehicle for at least seven days beyond the period specified in the agreement and continues such possession for a period of more than two days after service or refusal of attempted service of a notice in person or by certified mail at an address indicated in the agreement stating (i) the date and time at which the vehicle was to have been returned under the agreement; (ii) that the owner does not consent to the continued withholding or retaining of such vehicle and demands its return; and that continued withholding or retaining of the vehicle may constitute a class A misdemeanor punishable by a fine of up to one thousand dollars or by a sentence to a term of imprisonment for a period of up to one year or by both such fine and imprisonment.

Unauthorized use of a vehicle in the third degree is a class A misdemeanor.

HISTORY: Add, L 1965, ch 1030, § 1, with substance derived from § 1293-a; amd, L 1978, ch 626, § 1, L 1981, ch 602, § 1, L 1982, ch 413, § 1, eff Sept 1, 1982. Section heading, amd, L 1981, ch 602, § 1, L 1982, ch 413, § 1, eff Sept 1, 1982.

§ 165.06. Unauthorized use of a vehicle in the second degree

A person is guilty of unauthorized use of a vehicle in the second degree when:

He commits the crime of unauthorized use of a vehicle in the third degree as defined in subdivision one of section 165.05 of this article and has been previously convicted of the crime of unauthorized use of a vehicle in the third degree as defined in subdivision one of section 165.05 or second degree within the preceding ten years.

Unauthorized use of a vehicle in the second degree is a class E felony.

HISTORY: Add, L 1981, ch 602, § 2; amd, L 1982, ch 413, § 2, eff Sept 1, 1982. Section heading, amd, L 1982, ch 413, § 2, eff Sept 1, 1982.

§ 165.07. Unlawful use of secret scientific material

A person is guilty of unlawful use of secret scientific material when, with intent to appropriate to himself or another the use of secret scientific material, and having no right to do so and no reasonable ground to believe that he has such right, he makes a tangible reproduction or representation of such secret scientific material by means of writing, photographing, drawing, mechanically or electronically reproducing or recording such secret scientific material.

Unlawful use of secret scientific material is a class E felony.

HISTORY: Add, L 1967, ch 791, § 23, eff Sept 1, 1967.

§ 165.08. Unauthorized use of a vehicle in the first degree

A person is guilty of unauthorized use of a vehicle in the first degree when knowing that he does not have the consent of the owner, he takes, operates, exercises control over, rides in or otherwise uses a vehicle with the intent to use the same in the course of or the commission of a class A, class B, class C or class D felony or in the immediate flight therefrom. A person who engages in any such conduct without the consent of the owner is presumed to know he does not have such consent.

Unauthorized use of a vehicle in the first degree is a class D felony.

HISTORY: Add, L 1982, ch 413, § 3, eff Sept 1, 1982.

§ 165.09. Auto stripping in the third degree

A person is guilty of auto stripping in the third degree when:

1. He or she removes or intentionally destroys or defaces any part of a vehicle, other than an abandoned vehicle, as defined in subdivision one of section one thousand two hundred twenty-four of the vehicle and traffic law, without the permission of the owner; or

2. He or she removes or intentionally destroys or defaces any part of an abandoned vehicle, as defined in subdivision one of section one thousand two hundred twenty-four of the vehicle and traffic law, except that it is a defense to such charge that such person was authorized to do so pursuant to law or by permission of the owner.

Auto stripping in the third degree is a class A misdemeanor.

HISTORY: Add, L 1984, ch 390, § 1, eff Nov 1, 1984. Section heading, amd, L 1996, ch 494, § 1, eff Nov 1, 1996. Opening par, amd, L 1996, ch 494, § 1, eff Nov 1, 1996. Sub 1, amd, L 1996, ch 494, § 1, eff Nov 1, 1996. Sub 2, amd, L 1996, ch 494, § 1, eff Nov 1, 1996. Closing par, amd, L 1996, ch 494, § 1, eff Nov 1, 1996.

§ 165.10. Auto stripping in the second degree

A person is guilty of auto stripping in the second degree when:

1. He or she commits the offense of auto stripping in the third degree and when he or she has been previously convicted within the last five years of having violated the provisions of section 165.09 or this section; or

2. He or she removes or intentionally destroys, defaces, disguises, or alters any part of two or more vehicles, other than abandoned vehicles, as defined in subdivision one of section one thousand two hundred twenty-four of the vehicle and traffic law, without the permission of the

owner, and the value of the parts of vehicles removed, destroyed, defaced, disguised, or altered exceeds an aggregate value of one thousand dollars.

Auto stripping in the second degree is a class E felony.

> **HISTORY:** Add, L 1984, ch 390, § 1, eff Nov 1, 1984. Former § 165.10, add, L 1965, ch 1030, § 1; amd, L 1967, ch 791, § 24; repealed, L 1969, ch 115, § 4, eff July 23, 1969, with substance transferred to § 155.00(7, 8). Section heading, amd, L 1996, ch 494, § 2, eff Nov 1, 1996. Opening par, formerly part of first undesignated par, so designated as opening par and amd, L 1996, ch 494, § 2, eff Nov 1, 1996. Sub 1, formerly part of first undesignated par, so designated sub 1 and amd, L 1996, ch 494, § 2, eff Nov 1, 1996. Sub 2, add, L 1996, ch 494, § 2, eff Nov 1, 1996. Closing par, amd, L 1996, ch 494, § 2, eff Nov 1, 1996.

§ 165.11. Auto stripping in the first degree

A person is guilty of auto stripping in the first degree when he or she removes or intentionally destroys, defaces, disguises, or alters any part of three or more vehicles, other than abandoned vehicles, as defined in subdivision one of section one thousand two hundred twenty-four of the vehicle and traffic law, without the permission of the owner, and the value of the parts of vehicles removed, destroyed, defaced, disguised, or altered exceeds an aggregate value of three thousand dollars.

Auto stripping in the first degree is a class D felony.

> **HISTORY:** Add, L 1996, ch 494, § 3, eff Nov 1, 1996.

§ 165.15. Theft of services

A person is guilty of theft of services when:

1. He obtains or attempts to obtain a service, or induces or attempts to induce the supplier of a rendered service to agree to payment therefor on a credit basis, by the use of a credit card or debit card which he knows to be stolen.

2. With intent to avoid payment for restaurant services rendered, or for services rendered to him as a transient guest at a hotel, motel, inn, tourist cabin, rooming house or comparable establishment, he avoids or attempts to avoid such payment by unjustifiable failure or refusal to pay, by stealth, or by any misrepresentation of fact which he knows to be false. A person who fails or refuses to pay for such services is presumed to have intended to avoid payment therefor; or

3. With intent to obtain railroad, subway, bus, air, taxi or any other public transportation service without payment of the lawful charge therefor, or to avoid payment of the lawful charge for such transportation service which has been rendered to him, he obtains or attempts to obtain such service or avoids or attempts to avoid payment therefor by force, intimidation, stealth, deception or mechanical tampering, or by unjustifiable failure or refusal to pay; or

4. With intent to avoid payment by himself or another person of the lawful charge for any telecommunications service, including, without limitation, cable television service, or any gas, steam, sewer, water, electrical, telegraph or telephone service which is provided for a charge or compensation, he obtains or attempts to obtain such service for himself or another person or avoids or attempts to avoid payment therefor by himself or another person by means of (a) tampering or making connection with the equipment of the supplier, whether by mechanical, electrical, acoustical or other means, or (b) offering for sale or otherwise making available, to anyone other than the provider of a telecommunications service for such service provider's own use in the provision of its service, any telecommunications decoder or descrambler, a principal function of which defeats a mechanism of electronic signal encryption, jamming or individually addressed switching imposed by the provider of any such telecommunications service to restrict

the delivery of such service, or (c) any misrepresentation of fact which he knows to be false, or (d) any other artifice, trick, deception, code or device. For the purposes of this subdivision the telecommunications decoder or descrambler described in paragraph (b) above or the device described in paragraph (d) above shall not include any non-decoding and non-descrambling channel frequency converter or any television receiver type-accepted by the federal communications commission. In any prosecution under this subdivision, proof that telecommunications equipment, including, without limitation, any cable television converter, descrambler, or related equipment, has been tampered with or otherwise intentionally prevented from performing its functions of control of service delivery without the consent of the supplier of the service, or that telecommunications equipment, including, without limitation, any cable television converter, descrambler, receiver, or related equipment, has been connected to the equipment of the supplier of the service without the consent of the supplier of the service, shall be presumptive evidence that the resident to whom the service which is at the time being furnished by or through such equipment has, with intent to avoid payment by himself or another person for a prospective or already rendered service, created or caused to be created with reference to such equipment, the condition so existing. A person who tampers with such a device or equipment without the consent of the supplier of the service is presumed to do so with intent to avoid, or to enable another to avoid, payment for the service involved. In any prosecution under this subdivision, proof that any telecommunications decoder or descrambler, a principal function of which defeats a mechanism of electronic signal encryption, jamming or individually addressed switching imposed by the provider of any such telecommunications service to restrict the delivery of such service, has been offered for sale or otherwise made available by anyone other than the supplier of such service shall be presumptive evidence that the person offering such equipment for sale or otherwise making it available has, with intent to avoid payment by himself or another person of the lawful charge for such service, obtained or attempted to obtain such service for himself or another person or avoided or attempted to avoid payment therefor by himself or another person; or

5. With intent to avoid payment by himself or another person of the lawful charge for any telephone service which is provided for a charge or compensation he (a) sells, offers for sale or otherwise makes available, without consent, an existing, canceled or revoked access device; or (b) uses, without consent, an existing, canceled or revoked access device; or (c) knowingly obtains any telecommunications service with fraudulent intent by use of an unauthorized, false, or fictitious name, identification, telephone number, or access device. For purposes of this subdivision access device means any telephone calling card number, credit card number, account number, mobile identification number, electronic serial number or personal identification number that can be used to obtain telephone service.

6. With intent to avoid payment by himself or another person for a prospective or already rendered service the charge or compensation for which is measured by a meter or other mechanical device, he tampers with such device or with other equipment related thereto, or in any manner attempts to prevent the meter or device from performing its measuring function, without the consent of the supplier of the service. In any prosecution under this subdivision, proof that a meter or related equipment has been tampered with or otherwise intentionally prevented from performing its measuring function without the consent of the supplier of the service shall be presumptive evidence that the person to whom the service which is at the time being furnished by or through such meter or related equipment has, with intent to avoid payment by himself or another person for a prospective or already rendered service, created or caused to be created with reference to such meter or related equipment, the condition so existing. A person who tampers with such a device or equipment without the consent of the

supplier of the service is presumed to do so with intent to avoid, or to enable another to avoid, payment for the service involved; or

7. He knowingly accepts or receives the use and benefit of service, including gas, steam or electricity service, which should pass through a meter but has been diverted therefrom, or which has been prevented from being correctly registered by a meter provided therefor, or which has been diverted from the pipes, wires or conductors of the supplier thereof. In any prosecution under this subdivision proof that service has been intentionally diverted from passing through a meter, or has been intentionally prevented from being correctly registered by a meter provided therefor, or has been intentionally diverted from the pipes, wires or conductors of the supplier thereof, shall be presumptive evidence that the person who accepts or receives the use and benefit of such service has done so with knowledge of the condition so existing; or

8. With intent to obtain, without the consent of the supplier thereof, gas, electricity, water, steam or telephone service, he tampers with any equipment designed to supply or to prevent the supply of such service either to the community in general or to particular premises; or

9. With intent to avoid payment of the lawful charge for admission to any theatre or concert hall, or with intent to avoid payment of the lawful charge for admission to or use of a chair lift, gondola, rope-tow or similar mechanical device utilized in assisting skiers in transportation to a point of ski arrival or departure, he obtains or attempts to obtain such admission without payment of the lawful charge therefor.

10. Obtaining or having control over labor in the employ of another person, or of business, commercial or industrial equipment or facilities of another person, knowing that he is not entitled to the use thereof, and with intent to derive a commercial or other substantial benefit for himself or a third person, he uses or diverts to the use of himself or a third person such labor, equipment or facilities.

11. With intent to avoid payment by himself, herself, or another person of the lawful charge for use of any computer, computer service, or computer network which is provided for a charge or compensation he or she uses, causes to be used, accesses, or attempts to use or access a computer, computer service, or computer network and avoids or attempts to avoid payment therefor. In any prosecution under this subdivision proof that a person overcame or attempted to overcome any device or coding system a function of which is to prevent the unauthorized use of said computer or computer service shall be presumptive evidence of an intent to avoid payment for the computer or computer service.

Theft of services is a class A misdemeanor, provided, however, that theft of cable television service as defined by the provisions of paragraphs (a), (c) and (d) of subdivision four of this section, and having a value not in excess of one hundred dollars by a person who has not been previously convicted of theft of services under subdivision four of this section is a violation, that theft of services under subdivision nine of this section by a person who has not been previously convicted of theft of services under subdivision nine of this section is a violation and provided further, however, that theft of services of any telephone service under paragraph (a) or (b) of subdivision five of this section having a value in excess of one thousand dollars or by a person who has been previously convicted within five years of theft of services under paragraph (a) of subdivision five of this section is a class E felony.

HISTORY: Add, L 1965, ch 1030, § 1, eff Sept 1, 1967, with substance derived from §§ 925, 967, 1293-c, 1431, 1432, 1990, 1990-b. Sub 1, add, L 1969, ch 115, § 5; amd, L 1987, ch 556, § 9, L 1992, ch 41, § 110, L 1995, ch 81, § 170, eff Nov 1, 1995. Former sub 1, repealed, L 1969, ch 115, § 5, eff July 23, 1969. Sub 2, amd, L 1967, ch 791, § 25, eff Sept 1, 1967. Sub 4, amd, L 1975, ch 530, § 2, L 1978, ch 420, § 5, L 1983, ch 521, § 1, L 1983, ch 522, § 1, eff Sept 1, 1983. Sub

5, add, L 1992, ch 491, § 3; amd, L 1993, ch 171, § 2, L 1996, ch 357, § 2, eff Nov 1, 1996. Former sub 5, amd, L 1967, ch 791, § 25, L 1976, ch 768, §§ 1, 2; redesignated sub 6, L 1992, ch 491, § 3, eff Nov 1, 1992. Sub 6, formerly sub 5, amd, L 1967, ch 791, § 25, L 1976, ch 768, §§ 1, 2; so designated as sub 6, L 1992, ch 491, § 3, eff Nov 1, 1992. Former sub 6, add, L 1976, ch 768, §§ 1, 2; redesignated sub 7, L 1992, ch 491, § 3, eff Nov 1, 1992. Another sub 6, amd, L 1967, ch 791, § 25; redesignated sub 7, L 1976, ch 768, eff Sept 1, 1976. Sub 7, formerly sub 6, add, L 1976, ch 768, §§ 1, 2; so designated as sub 7, L 1992, ch 491, § 3, eff Nov 1, 1992. Former sub 7, redesignated sub 8, L 1992, ch 491, § 3, eff Nov 1, 1992. Another sub 7, formerly sub 6, redesignated sub 7, L 1976, ch 768, eff Sept 1, 1976. Sub 8, formerly sub 6, amd, L 1967, ch 791, § 25; so designated as sub 7, L 1976, ch 768; so designated as sub 8, L 1992, ch 491, § 3, eff Nov 1, 1992. Former sub 8, add, L 1986, ch 15, § 1; redesignated sub 9, L 1992, ch 491, § 3, eff Nov 1, 1992. Previous sub 8, redesignated as sub 9, L 1986, ch 15, § 1, eff Nov 1, 1986. Sub 9, formerly sub 8, add, L 1986, ch 15, § 1; so designated as sub 9, L 1992, ch 491, § 3, eff Nov 1, 1992. Former sub 9, formerly sub 8, renumbered sub 9, L 1986, ch 15, § 1; redesignated sub 10, L 1992, ch 491, § 3, eff Nov 1, 1992. Sub 10, formerly sub 7, so designated as sub 8, L 1976, ch 678; so designated as sub 9, L 1986, ch 15, § 1; so designated as sub 10, L 1992, ch 491, § 3, eff Nov 1, 1992. Former sub 10, add, L 1986, ch 514, § 4; redesignated sub 11, L 1992, ch 491, § 3, eff Nov 1, 1992. Sub 11, formerly sub 10, add, L 1986, ch 514, § 4; so designated as sub 11, L 1992, ch 491, § 3, eff Nov 1, 1992. Sub 11, amd, L 2006, ch 558, § 4, eff Nov 1, 2006. Closing par, amd, L 1983, ch 521, § 2, L 1983, ch 522, § 2, L 1986, ch 15, § 2, L 1987, ch 753, § 1, L 1992, ch 491, § 4, eff Nov 1, 1992.

§ 165.16. Unauthorized sale of certain transportation services

1. A person is guilty of unauthorized sale of certain transportation services when, with intent to avoid payment by another person to the metropolitan transportation authority, New York city transit authority or a subsidiary or affiliate of either such authority of the lawful charge for transportation services on a railroad, subway, bus or mass transit service operated by either such authority or a subsidiary or affiliate thereof, he or she, in exchange for value, sells access to such transportation services to such person, without authorization, through the use of an unlimited farecard or doctored farecard. This section shall apply only to such sales that occur in a transportation facility, as such term is defined in subdivision two of section 240.00 of this chapter, operated by such metropolitan transportation authority, New York city transit authority or subsidiary or affiliate of such authority, when public notice of the prohibitions of its section and the exemptions thereto appears on the face of the farecard or is conspicuously posted in transportation facilities operated by such metropolitan transportation authority, New York city transit authority or such subsidiary or affiliate of such authority.

2. It shall be a defense to a prosecution under this section that a person, firm, partnership, corporation, or association: (a) selling a farecard containing value, other than a doctored farecard, relinquished all rights and privileges thereto upon consummation of the sale; or (b) sold access to transportation services through the use of a farecard, other than a doctored farecard, when such sale was made at the request of the purchaser as an accommodation to the purchaser at a time when a farecard was not immediately available to the purchaser, provided, however, that the seller lawfully acquired the farecard and did not, by means of an unlawful act, contribute to the circumstances that caused the purchaser to make such request.

3. For purposes of this section:

(a) "farecard" means a value-based, magnetically encoded card containing stored monetary value from which a specified amount of value is deducted as payment of a fare;

(b) "unlimited farecard" means a farecard that is time-based, magnetically encoded and which permits entrance an unlimited number of times into facilities and conveyances for a specified period of time; and

(c) "doctored farecard" means a farecard that has been bent or manipulated or altered so as to facilitate a person's access to transportation services without paying the lawful charge.

Unauthorized sale of transportation service is a class B misdemeanor.

> **HISTORY:** Add, L 2005, ch 57, § 1 (Part T), eff July 11, 2005.

§ 165.17. Unlawful use of credit card, debit card or public benefit card

A person is guilty of unlawful use of credit card, debit card or public benefit card when in the course of obtaining or attempting to obtain property or a service, he uses or displays a credit card, debit card or public benefit card which he knows to be revoked or cancelled.

Unlawful use of a credit card, debit card or public benefit card is a class A misdemeanor.

> **HISTORY:** Add, L 1969, ch 115, § 6; amd, L 1987, ch 556, § 10, L 1995, ch 81, § 171, eff Nov 1, 1995. Section heading, amd, L 1987, ch 556, § 10, L 1992, ch 41, § 111, L 1995, ch 81, § 171, eff Nov 1, 1995. First undesignated par, amd, L 1992, ch 41, § 111, L 1995, ch 81, § 171, eff Nov 1, 1995. Second undesignated par, amd, L 1992, ch 41, § 111, L 1995, ch 81, § 171, eff Nov 1, 1995.

§ 165.20. Fraudulently obtaining a signature

A person is guilty of fraudulently obtaining a signature when, with intent to defraud or injure another or to acquire a substantial benefit for himself or a third person, he obtains the signature of a person to a written instrument by means of any misrepresentation of fact which he knows to be false.

Fraudulently obtaining a signature is a class A misdemeanor.

> **HISTORY:** Add, L 1965, ch 1030, § 1, eff Sept 1, 1967, with substance derived from §§ 932, 934, 935, 937-a.

§ 165.25. Jostling

A person is guilty of jostling when, in a public place, he intentionally and unnecessarily:

    1. Places his hand in the proximity of a person's pocket or handbag; or

    2. Jostles or crowds another person at a time when a third person's hand is in the proximity of such person's pocket or handbag.

Jostling is a class A misdemeanor.

> **HISTORY:** Add, L 1965, ch 1030, § 1, eff Sept 1, 1967, with substance derived from § 722(6).

§ 165.30. Fraudulent accosting

    1. A person is guilty of fraudulent accosting when he accosts a person in a public place with intent to defraud him of money or other property by means of a trick, swindle or confidence game.

    2. A person who, either at the time he accosts another in a public place or at some subsequent time or at some other place, makes statements to him or engages in conduct with respect to him of a kind commonly made or performed in the perpetration of a known type of confidence game, is presumed to intend to defraud such person of money or other property.

Fraudulent accosting is a class A misdemeanor.

> **HISTORY:** Add, L 1965, ch 1030, § 1, eff Sept 1, 1967, with substance derived from § 722(6). Sub 1, formerly entire section, so designated and amd, L 1971, ch 772, § 1, eff Sept 1, 1971. Sub 2, add, L 1971, ch 772, § 1, eff Sept 1, 1971.

§ 165.35. Fortune telling

A person is guilty of fortune telling when, for a fee or compensation which he directly or indirectly solicits or receives, he claims or pretends to tell fortunes, or holds himself out as being able, by claimed or pretended use of occult powers, to answer questions or give advice on personal matters or to exorcise, influence or affect evil spirits or curses; except that this section does not apply to a person who engages in the aforedescribed conduct as part of a show or exhibition solely for the purpose of entertainment or amusement.

Fortune telling is a class B misdemeanor.

HISTORY: Add, L 1965, ch 1030, § 1, eff Sept 1, 1967.

§ 165.40. Criminal possession of stolen property in the fifth degree

A person is guilty of criminal possession of stolen property in the fifth degree when he knowingly possesses stolen property, with intent to benefit himself or a person other than an owner thereof or to impede the recovery by an owner thereof.

Criminal possession of stolen property in the fifth degree is a class A misdemeanor.

HISTORY: Add, L 1965, ch 1030, § 1, with substance derived from § 1308; amd, L 1986, ch 515, § 4, eff Nov, 1986. Section heading, amd, L 1986, ch 515, § 4, eff Nov 1, 1986.

§ 165.45. Criminal possession of stolen property in the fourth degree

A person is guilty of criminal possession of stolen property in the fourth degree when he knowingly possesses stolen property, with intent to benefit himself or a person other than an owner thereof or to impede the recovery by an owner thereof, and when:

1. The value of the property exceeds one thousand dollars; or

2. The property consists of a credit card, debit card or public benefit card; or

3. He is a collateral loan broker or is in the business of buying, selling or otherwise dealing in property; or

4. The property consists of one or more firearms, rifles and shotguns, as such terms are defined in section 265.00 of this chapter; or

5. The value of the property exceeds one hundred dollars and the property consists of a motor vehicle, as defined in section one hundred twenty-five of the vehicle and traffic law, other than a motorcycle, as defined in section one hundred twenty-three of such law; or

6. The property consists of a scroll, religious vestment, vessel or other item of property having a value of at least one hundred dollars kept for or used in connection with religious worship in any building or structure used as a place of religious worship by a religious corporation, as incorporated under the religious corporations law or the education law.

7. The property consists of anhydrous ammonia or liquified ammonia gas and the actor intends to use, or knows another person intends to use, such anhydrous ammonia or liquified ammonia gas to manufacture methamphetamine.

Criminal possession of stolen property in the fourth degree is a class E felony.

HISTORY: Add, L 1965, ch 1030, § 1, with substance derived from § 1308(2); amd, L 1969, ch 354, § 1, L 1986, ch 515, § 5, eff Nov 1, 1986. Section heading, amd, L 1986, ch 515, § 5, eff Nov 1, 1986. Opening par, amd, L 1986, ch 515, § 5, eff Nov 1, 1986. Sub 1, amd, L 1986, ch 515, § 5, eff Nov 1, 1986. Sub 2, add, L 1969, ch 115, § 7; amd, L 1986, ch 515, § 5, L 1987, ch 556, § 11, L 1995, ch 81, § 172, eff Nov 1, 1995. Former sub 2, renumbered sub 3, L 1969, ch 115, § 7, eff July 23, 1969. Sub 3, formerly sub 2, renumbered sub 3, L 1969, ch 115, § 7; amd, L 1983, ch 321, § 8, eff June 21, 1983. Another sub 3, add, L 1969, ch 354, § 1; renumbered sub 4, L 1979, ch 329, § 1, eff June 28, 1979. Sub 4, formerly sub 3, add, L 1969, ch 354, § 1; renumbered sub 4, L 1979, ch 329, § 1; amd, L 1986, ch 515, § 5, eff Nov, 1986. Sub 5, add, L 1986, ch 515, § 5; amd, L 1990, ch 450, § 2, eff Nov 1, 1990. Sub 6, add, L 1990, ch 450, § 2, eff Nov 1, 1990. Sub 7, add, L 2005, ch 394, § 2, eff Oct 1, 2005. Closing par, amd, L 1986, ch 515, § 5, eff Nov 1, 1986.

§ 165.50. Criminal possession of stolen property in the third degree

A person is guilty of criminal possession of stolen property in the third degree when he knowingly possesses stolen property, with intent to benefit himself or a person other than an owner thereof or to impede the recovery by an owner thereof, and when the value of the property exceeds three thousand dollars.

Criminal possession of stolen property in the third degree is a class D felony.

> **HISTORY:** Add, L 1965, ch 1030, § 1; amd, L 1986, ch 515, § 6, eff Nov 1, 1986. Section heading, amd, L 1986, ch 515, § 6, eff Nov 1, 1986.

§ 165.52. Criminal possession of stolen property in the second degree

A person is guilty of criminal possession of stolen property in the second degree when he knowingly possesses stolen property, with intent to benefit himself or a person other than an owner thereof or to impede the recovery by an owner thereof, and when the value of the property exceeds fifty thousand dollars.

Criminal possession of stolen property in the second degree is a class C felony.

> **HISTORY:** Add, L 1986, ch 515, § 7, eff Nov 1, 1986.

§ 165.54. Criminal possession of stolen property in the first degree

A person is guilty of criminal possession of stolen property in the first degree when he knowingly possesses stolen property, with intent to benefit himself or a person other than an owner thereof or to impede the recovery by an owner, and when the value of the property exceeds one million dollars.

Criminal possession of stolen property in the first degree is a class B felony.

> **HISTORY:** Add, L 1986, ch 515, § 7, eff Nov 1, 1986.

§ 165.55. Criminal possession of stolen property; presumptions

1. A person who knowingly possesses stolen property is presumed to possess it with intent to benefit himself or a person other than an owner thereof or to impede the recovery by an owner thereof.

2. A collateral loan broker or a person in the business of buying, selling or otherwise dealing in property who possesses stolen property is presumed to know that such property was stolen if he obtained it without having ascertained by reasonable inquiry that the person from whom he obtained it had a legal right to possess it.

3. A person who possesses two or more stolen credit cards, debit cards or public benefit cards is presumed to know that such credit cards, debit cards or public benefit cards were stolen.

4. A person who possesses three or more tickets or equivalent instrument for air transportation service, which tickets or instruments were stolen by reason of having been obtained from the issuer or agent thereof by the use of one or more stolen or forged credit cards, is presumed to know that such tickets or instruments were stolen.

> **HISTORY:** Add, L 1965, ch 1030, § 1, eff Sept 1, 1967, with substance derived in part from § 1308(3). Sub 2, amd, L 1983, ch 321, § 9, eff June 21, 1983. Sub 3, add, L 1969, ch 115, § 8; amd, L 1987, ch 556, § 12, L 1995, ch 81, § 173, eff Nov 1, 1995. Sub 4, add, L 1969, ch 115, § 8, eff July 23, 1969.

§ 165.60. Criminal possession of stolen property; no defense

In any prosecution for criminal possession of stolen property, it is no defense that:

1. The person who stole the property has not been convicted, apprehended or identified; or

2. The defendant stole or participated in the larceny of the property; or

3. The larceny of the property did not occur in this state.

    HISTORY: Add, L 1965, ch 1030, § 1; amd, L 1976, ch 375, § 1, eff Sept 1, 1976 and not applicable to offenses committed before Sept 2, 1976, with substance derived in part from § 1309.

§ 165.65. Criminal possession of stolen property; corroboration

1. A person charged with criminal possession of stolen property who participated in the larceny thereof may not be convicted of criminal possession of such stolen property solely upon the testimony of an accomplice in the larceny unsupported by corroborative evidence tending to connect the defendant with such criminal possession.

2. Unless inconsistent with the provisions of subdivision one of this section, a person charged with criminal possession of stolen property may be convicted thereof solely upon the testimony of one from whom he obtained such property or solely upon the testimony of one to whom he disposed of such property.

    HISTORY: Add, L 1965, ch 1030, § 1, eff Sept 1, 1967, with substance derived in part from § 1308-a. Sub 1, amd, L 1971, ch 1097, § 77, eff Sept 1, 1971.

§ 165.70. Definitions

As used in sections 165.71, 165.72, 165.73 and 165.74, the following terms have the following definitions:

1. The term "trademark" means (a) any word, name, symbol, or device, or any combination thereof adopted and used by a person to identify goods made by a person and which distinguish them from those manufactured or sold by others which is in use and which is registered, filed or recorded under the laws of this state or of any other state or is registered in the principal register of the United States patent and trademark office; or (b) the symbol of the International Olympic Committee, consisting of five interlocking rings; the emblem of the United States Olympic Committee, consisting of an escutcheon having a blue chief and vertically extending red and white bars on the base with five interlocking rings displayed on the chief; any trademark, trade name, sign, symbol, or insignia falsely representing association with, or authorization by, the International Olympic Committee or the United States Olympic Committee; or the words "Olympic", "Olympiad", "Citius Altius Fortius", or any combination thereof tending to cause confusion, to cause mistake, to deceive, or to falsely suggest a connection with the United States Olympic Committee or any International Olympic Committee or United States Olympic Committee activity.

2. The term "counterfeit trademark" means a spurious trademark or an imitation of a trademark that is:

    (a) used in connection with trafficking in goods; and

    (b) used in connection with the sale, offering for sale or distribution of goods that are identical with or substantially indistinguishable from a trademark as defined in subdivision one of this section.

The term "counterfeit trademark" does not include any mark used in connection with goods for which the person using such mark was authorized to use the trademark for the type of goods so manufactured or produced by the holder of the right to use such mark or designation, whether or not such goods were manufactured or produced in the United States or in another country, and does not include imitations of trade dress or packaging such as color, shape and the like unless those features have been registered as trademarks as defined in subdivision one of this section.

3. The term "traffic" means to transport, transfer, or otherwise dispose of, to another, as consideration for anything of value, or to obtain control of with intent to so transport, transfer, or otherwise dispose of.

4. The term "goods" means any products, services, objects, materials, devices or substances which are identified by the use of a trademark.

HISTORY: Add, L 1992, ch 490, § 1, eff Nov 1, 1992. Sub 1, amd, L 1993, ch 155, § 1, eff June 28, 1993.

§ 165.71. Trademark counterfeiting in the third degree

A person is guilty of trademark counterfeiting in the third degree when, with the intent to deceive or defraud some other person or with the intent to evade a lawful restriction on the sale, resale, offering for sale, or distribution of goods, he or she manufactures, distributes, sells, or offers for sale goods which bear a counterfeit trademark, or possesses a trademark knowing it to be counterfeit for the purpose of affixing it to any goods.

Trademark counterfeiting in the third degree is a class A misdemeanor.

HISTORY: Add, L 1992, ch 490, § 1, eff Nov 1, 1992.

§ 165.72. Trademark counterfeiting in the second degree

A person is guilty of trademark counterfeiting in the second degree when, with the intent to deceive or defraud some other person or with the intent to evade a lawful restriction on the sale, resale, offering for sale, or distribution of goods, he or she manufactures, distributes, sells, or offers for sale goods which bear a counterfeit trademark, or possesses a trademark knowing it to be counterfeit for the purpose of affixing it to any goods, and the retail value of all such goods bearing counterfeit trademarks exceeds one thousand dollars.

Trademark counterfeiting in the second degree is a class E felony.

HISTORY: Add, L 1992, ch 490, § 1; amd, L 1995, ch 535, § 1, eff Nov 1, 1995. First undesignated par, amd, L 1995, ch 535, § 1, eff Nov 1, 1995.

§ 165.73. Trademark counterfeiting in the first degree

A person is guilty of trademark counterfeiting in the first degree when, with the intent to deceive or defraud some other person, or with the intent to evade a lawful restriction on the sale, resale, offering for sale, or distribution of goods, he or she manufactures, distributes, sells, or offers for sale goods which bear a counterfeit trademark, or possesses a trademark knowing it to be counterfeit for the purpose of affixing it to any goods, and the retail value of all such goods bearing counterfeit trademarks exceeds one hundred thousand dollars.

Trademark counterfeiting in the first degree is a class C felony.

HISTORY: Add, L 1992, ch 490, § 1; amd, L 1995, ch 535, § 2, eff Nov 1, 1995. First undesignated par, amd, L 1995, ch 535, § 2, eff Nov 1, 1995.

§ 165.74. Seizure and destruction of goods bearing counterfeit trademarks

Any goods manufactured, sold, offered for sale, distributed or produced in violation of this article may be seized by any police officer. The magistrate must, within forty-eight hours after arraignment of the defendant, determine whether probable cause exists to believe that the goods had been manufactured, sold, offered for sale, distributed or produced in violation of this article, and upon a finding that probable cause exists to believe that the goods had been manufactured, sold, offered for sale, distributed, or produced in violation of this article, the court shall authorize such articles to be retained as evidence pending the trial of the defendant. Upon conviction of the defendant, the articles in respect whereof the defendant stands convicted shall be destroyed. Destruction shall not include auction, sale or distribution of the items in their original form.

HISTORY: Add, L 1992, ch 490, § 1; amd, L 1995, ch 535, § 3, eff Nov 1, 1995.

TITLE K   Offenses Involving Fraud
ARTICLE 170
FORGERY AND RELATED OFFENSES

ARTICLE 175
OFFENSES INVOLVING FALSE WRITTEN STATEMENTS

ARTICLE 176
INSURANCE FRAUD

ARTICLE 177
HEALTH CARE FRAUD

ARTICLE 178
CRIMINAL DIVERSION OF PRESCRIPTION MEDICATIONS AND PRESCRIPTIONS

ARTICLE 179
[EXPIRES AND REPEALED JULY 5, 2021] CRIMINAL DIVERSION OF MEDICAL MARIHUANA

ARTICLE 180
BRIBERY NOT INVOLVING PUBLIC SERVANTS, AND RELATED OFFENSES

ARTICLE 185
FRAUDS ON CREDITORS

ARTICLE 187
RESIDENTIAL MORTGAGE FRAUD

ARTICLE 190
OTHER FRAUDS

HISTORY: Add, L 1965, ch 1030, § 1, eff Sept 1, 1967.

ARTICLE 170   FORGERY AND RELATED OFFENSES

---

* So in original. Does not agree with section heading.

HISTORY: Add, L 1965, ch 1030, § 1, eff Sept 1, 1967.

§ 170.00. Forgery; definitions of terms

1. "Written instrument" means any instrument or article, including computer data or a computer program, containing written or printed matter or the equivalent thereof, used for the purpose of reciting, embodying, conveying or recording information, or constituting a symbol or evidence of value, right, privilege or identification, which is capable of being used to the advantage or disadvantage of some person.

2. "Complete written instrument" means one which purports to be a genuine written instrument fully drawn with respect to every essential feature thereof. An endorsement, attestation, acknowledgment or other similar signature or statement is deemed both a complete written instrument in itself and a part of the main instrument in which it is contained or to which it attaches.

3. "Incomplete written instrument" means one which contains some matter by way of content or authentication but which requires additional matter in order to render it a complete written instrument.

4. "Falsely make." A person "falsely makes" a written instrument when he makes or draws a complete written instrument in its entirety, or an incomplete written instrument, which purports to be an authentic creation of its ostensible maker or drawer, but which is not such either because the ostensible maker or drawer is fictitious or because, if real, he did not authorize the making or drawing thereof.

5. "Falsely complete." A person "falsely completes" a written instrument when, by adding, inserting or changing matter, he transforms an incomplete written instrument into a complete one, without the authority of anyone entitled to grant it, so that such complete instrument appears or purports to be in all respects an authentic creation of or fully authorized by its ostensible maker or drawer.

6. "Falsely alter." A person "falsely alters" a written instrument when, without the authority of anyone entitled to grant it, he changes a written instrument, whether it be in complete or incomplete form, by means of erasure, obliteration, deletion, insertion of new matter, transposition of matter, or in any other manner, so that such instrument in its thus altered form appears or purports to be in all respects an authentic creation of or fully authorized by its ostensible maker or drawer.

7. "Forged instrument" means a written instrument which has been falsely made, completed or altered.

8. "Electronic access device" means a mobile identification number or electronic serial number that can be used to obtain telephone service.

HISTORY: Add, L 1965, ch 1030, § 1, eff Sept 1, 1967, with substance derived from § 880. Sub 1, amd, L 1986, ch 514, § 5, eff Nov 1, 1986. Sub 8, add, L 1996, ch 357, § 4, eff Nov 1, 1996.

§ 170.05. Forgery in the third degree

A person is guilty of forgery in the third degree when, with intent to defraud, deceive or injure another, he falsely makes, completes or alters a written instrument.

Forgery in the third degree is a class A misdemeanor.

HISTORY: Add, L 1965, ch 1030, § 1, eff Sept 1, 1967, with substance derived from §§ 660, 889(2, 3), 889-b, 926(1).

§ 170.10. Forgery in the second degree

A person is guilty of forgery in the second degree when, with intent to defraud, deceive or injure another, he falsely makes, completes or alters a written instrument which is or purports to be, or which is calculated to become or to represent if completed:

1. A deed, will, codicil, contract, assignment, commercial instrument, credit card, as that term is defined in subdivision seven of section 155.00, or other instrument which does or may evidence, create, transfer, terminate or otherwise affect a legal right, interest, obligation or status; or

2. A public record, or an instrument filed or required or authorized by law to be filed in or with a public office or public servant; or

3. A written instrument officially issued or created by a public office, public servant or governmental instrumentality; or

4. Part of an issue of tokens, public transportation transfers, certificates or other articles manufactured and designed for use as symbols of value usable in place of money for the purchase of property or services; or

5. A prescription of a duly licensed physician or other person authorized to issue the same for any drug or any instrument or device used in the taking or administering of drugs for which a prescription is required by law.

Forgery in the second degree is a class D felony.

HISTORY: Add, L 1965, ch 1030, § 1, eff Sept 1, 1967, with substance derived from §§ 884(1, 2, 4, 6), 887(1, 2, 4), 889(4), 889-a, 889-b, 890, 891, 1325, 1326. Sub 1, amd, L 1984 ch 949, § 1, eff Nov 1, 1984.

§ 170.15. Forgery in the first degree

A person is guilty of forgery in the first degree when, with intent to defraud, deceive or injure another, he falsely makes, completes or alters a written instrument which is or purports to be, or which is calculated to become or to represent if completed:

1. Part of an issue of money, stamps, securities or other valuable instruments issued by a government or governmental instrumentality; or

2. Part of an issue of stock, bonds or other instruments representing interests in or claims against a corporate or other organization or its property.

Forgery in the first degree is a class C felony.

HISTORY: Add, L 1965, ch 1030, § 1, eff Sept 1, 1967, with substance derived from §§ 884(3, 5), 892.

§ 170.20. Criminal possession of a forged instrument in the third degree

A person is guilty of criminal possession of a forged instrument in the third degree when, with knowledge that it is forged and with intent to defraud, deceive or injure another, he utters or possesses a forged instrument.

Criminal possession of a forged instrument in the third degree is a class A misdemeanor.

HISTORY: Add, L 1965, ch 1030, § 1, eff Sept 1, 1967, with substance derived from §§ 661, 881(3), 889(3), 889-b, 926(2).

§ 170.25. Criminal possession of a forged instrument in the second degree

A person is guilty of criminal possession of a forged instrument in the second degree when, with knowledge that it is forged and with intent to defraud, deceive or injure another, he utters or possesses any forged instrument of a kind specified in section 170.10.

Criminal possession of a forged instrument in the second degree is a class D felony.

HISTORY: Add, L 1965, ch 1030, § 1, eff Sept 1, 1967, with substance derived from §§ 662, 881(1, 3), 887(4), 889(4), 891.

§ 170.27. Criminal possession of a forged instrument in the second degree; presumption

A person who possesses two or more forged instruments, each of which purports to be a credit card or debit card, as those terms are defined in subdivisions seven and seven-a of section 155.00, is presumed to possess the same with knowledge that they are forged and with intent to defraud, deceive or injure another.

HISTORY: Add, L 1969, ch 115, § 9; amd, L 1987, ch 556, § 13, eff Jan 1, 1988.

§ 170.30. Criminal possession of a forged instrument in the first degree

A person is guilty of criminal possession of a forged instrument in the first degree when, with knowledge that it is forged and with intent to defraud, deceive or injure another, he utters or possesses any forged instrument of a kind specified in section 170.15.

Criminal possession of a forged instrument in the first degree is a class C felony.

HISTORY: Add, L 1965, ch 1030, § 1, eff Sept 1, 1967, with substance derived from §§ 881(2), 892, 894.

§ 170.35. ˙ Criminal possession of a forged instrument; no defense

In any prosecution for criminal possession of a forged instrument, it is no defense that the defendant forged or participated in the forgery of the instrument in issue; provided that a person may not be convicted of both criminal possession of a forged instrument and forgery with respect to the same instrument.

HISTORY: Add, L 1965, ch 1030, § 1, eff Sept 1, 1967.

§ 170.40. Criminal possession of forgery devices

A person is guilty of criminal possession of forgery devices when:

1. He makes or possesses with knowledge of its character any plate, die or other device, apparatus, equipment, or article specifically designed for use in counterfeiting or otherwise forging written instruments; or

2. With intent to use, or to aid or permit another to use, the same for purposes of forgery, he makes or possesses any device, apparatus, equipment or article capable of or adaptable to such use.

Criminal possession of forgery devices is a class D felony.

HISTORY: Add, L 1965, ch 1030, § 1, eff Sept 1, 1967, with substance derived from §§ 881, 887(3, 5).

§ 170.45. Criminal simulation

A person is guilty of criminal simulation when:

1. With intent to defraud, he makes or alters any object in such manner that it appears to have

---

˙ So in original. Does not agree with Article 170 analysis.

an antiquity, rarity, source or authorship which it does not in fact possess; or

2. With knowledge of its true character and with intent to defraud, he utters or possesses an object so simulated.

Criminal simulation is a class A misdemeanor.

HISTORY: Add, L 1965, ch 1030, § 1, eff Sept 1, 1967.

§ 170.47. Criminal possession of an anti-security item

A person is guilty of criminal possession of an anti-security item, when with intent to steal property at a retail mercantile establishment as defined in article twelve-B of the general business law, he knowingly possesses in such an establishment an item designed for the purpose of overcoming detection of security markings or attachments placed on property offered for sale at such an establishment.

Criminal possession of an anti-security item is a class B misdemeanor.

HISTORY: Add, L 1983, ch 580, § 1, eff Sept 1, 1983.

§ 170.50. Unlawfully using slugs; definitions of terms

The following definitions are applicable to sections 170.55 and 170.60:

1. "Coin machine" means a coin box, turnstile, vending machine or other mechanical or electronic device or receptacle designed (a) to receive a coin or bill or a token made for the purpose, and (b) in return for the insertion or deposit thereof, automatically to offer, to provide, to assist in providing or to permit the acquisition of some property or some service.

2. "Slug" means an object or article which, by virtue of its size, shape or any other quality, is capable of being inserted or deposited in a coin machine as an improper substitute for a genuine coin, bill or token.

3. "Value" of a slug means the value of the coin, bill or token for which it is capable of being substituted.

HISTORY: Add, L 1965, ch 1030, § 1, eff Sept 1, 1967.

§ 170.55. Unlawfully using slugs in the second degree

A person is guilty of unlawfully using slugs in the second degree when:

1. With intent to defraud the owner of a coin machine, he inserts or deposits a slug in such machine; or

2. He makes, possesses or disposes of a slug with intent to enable a person to insert or deposit it in a coin machine.

Unlawfully using slugs in the second degree is a class B misdemeanor.

HISTORY: Add, L 1965, ch 1030, § 1, eff Sept 1, 1967, with substance derived from § 1293-d.

§ 170.60. Unlawfully using slugs in the first degree

A person is guilty of unlawfully using slugs in the first degree when he makes, possesses or disposes of slugs with intent to enable a person to insert or deposit them in a coin machine, and the value of such slugs exceeds one hundred dollars.

Unlawfully using slugs in the first degree is a class E felony.

HISTORY: Add, L 1965, ch 1030, § 1, eff Sept 1, 1967, with substance derived from § 1293-d.

§ 170.65. Forgery of a vehicle identification number

A person is guilty of forgery of a vehicle identification number when:

(1) He knowingly destroys, covers, defaces, alters or otherwise changes the form or appearance of a vehicle identification number on any vehicle or component part thereof, except tires; or

(2) He removes any such number from a vehicle or component part thereof, except as required by the provisions of the vehicle and traffic law; or

(3) He affixes a vehicle identification number to a vehicle, except in accordance with the provisions of the vehicle and traffic law.

(4) He or she, with intent to defraud, knowingly manufactures, produces or reproduces a vehicle identification number label, sticker or plate which was not manufactured, produced or reproduced in accordance with the rules and regulations promulgated by the United States National Highway Safety Administration and/or in accordance with the provisions of the state vehicle and traffic law.

Forgery of a vehicle identification number is a class E felony.

HISTORY: Add, L 1970, ch 880, § 1; amd, L 1977, ch 488, § 1, eff Aug 31, 1977, L 2013, ch 186, § 1, eff Nov 1, 2013.

§ 170.70. Illegal possession of a vehicle identification number

A person is guilty of illegal possession of a vehicle identification number when:

(1) He knowingly possesses a vehicle identification number label, sticker or plate which has been removed from the vehicle or vehicle part to which such label, sticker or plate was affixed by the manufacturer in accordance with 49 U.S.C. section 32101, et seq. and regulations promulgated thereunder or in accordance with the provisions of the vehicle and traffic law; or

(2) He knowingly possesses a vehicle or vehicle part to which is attached a vehicle identification number label, sticker or plate or on which is stamped or embossed a vehicle identification number which has been destroyed, covered, defaced, altered or otherwise changed, or a vehicle or vehicle part from which a vehicle identification number label, sticker or plate has been removed, which label, sticker or plate was affixed in accordance with 49 U.S.C. section 32101, et seq. or regulations promulgated thereunder, except when he has complied with the provisions of the vehicle and traffic law and regulations promulgated thereunder; or

(3) He knowingly possesses a vehicle, or part of a vehicle to which by law or regulation must be attached a vehicle identification number, either (a) with a vehicle identification number label, sticker, or plate which was not affixed by the manufacturer in accordance with 49 U.S.C. section 32101, et seq. or regulations promulgated thereunder, or in accordance with the provisions of the vehicle and traffic law or regulations promulgated thereunder, or (b) on which is affixed, stamped or embossed a vehicle identification number which was not affixed, stamped or embossed by the manufacturer, or in accordance with 49 U.S.C. section 32101, et seq. or regulations promulgated thereunder or in accordance with the provisions of the vehicle and traffic law or regulations promulgated thereunder.

Illegal possession of a vehicle identification number is a class E felony.

HISTORY: Add, L 1970, ch 880, § 2; amd, L 1977, ch 488, § 2, L 1984, ch 81, § 1, L 1992, ch 317, § 1, eff Nov 1, 1992. Amd, L 2001, ch 540, § 1, eff Nov 1, 2002. Section heading, amd, L 1984, ch 81, § 1, eff Nov 1, 1984. Opening par, amd, L 1984, ch 81, § 1, eff Nov 1, 1984. Sub (1), amd,

L 1992, ch 317, § 1, eff Nov 1, 1992. Sub (1), amd, L 2001, ch 540, § 1, eff Nov 1, 2002. Sub (2), amd, L 1981, ch 976, § 6, L 1992, ch 317, § 1, eff Nov 1, 1992. Sub (2), amd, L 2001, ch 540, § 1, eff Nov 1, 2002. Sub (3), amd, L 1992, ch 317, § 1, eff Nov 1, 1992. Sub (3), amd, L 2001, ch 540, § 1, eff Nov 1, 2002. Closing par, amd, L 1984, ch 81, § 1, eff Nov 1, 1984.

§ 170.71. Illegal possession of a vehicle identification number; presumptions

(1) A person is presumed to knowingly possess a vehicle or vehicle part in violation of subdivision two of section 170.70, when he possesses any combination of five such whole vehicles or individual vehicle parts, none of which are attached to or contained in the same vehicle.

(2) A person is presumed to knowingly possess a vehicle or vehicle part in violation of subdivision three of section 170.70, when he possesses any combination of five such whole vehicles or individual vehicle parts, none of which are attached to or contained in the same vehicle.

HISTORY: Add, L 1984, ch 81, § 2, eff Nov 1, 1984. Sub (1), amd, L 1984, ch 576, § 1, eff Nov 1, 1984. Sub (2), amd, L 1984, ch 576, § 1, eff Nov 1, 1984.

§ 170.75. Fraudulent making of an electronic access device in the second degree

A person is guilty of fraudulent making of an electronic access device in the second degree when, with intent to defraud, deceive or injure another, he falsely makes, completes or alters two or more electronic access devices, as that term is defined in subdivision eight of section 170.00 of this article.

Fraudulent making of an electronic access device in the second degree is a class D felony.

HISTORY: Add, L 1996, ch 357, § 5, eff Nov 1, 1996.

ARTICLE 175　　OFFENSES INVOLVING FALSE WRITTEN STATEMENTS

HISTORY: Add, L 1965, ch 1030, § 1, eff Sept 1, 1967.

§ 175.00. Definitions of terms

The following definitions are applicable to this article:

1. "Enterprise" means any entity of one or more persons, corporate or otherwise, public or private, engaged in business, commercial, professional, industrial, eleemosynary, social, political or governmental activity.

2. "Business record" means any writing or article, including computer data or a computer program, kept or maintained by an enterprise for the purpose of evidencing or reflecting its condition or activity.

3. "Written instrument" means any instrument or article, including computer data or a

computer program, containing written or printed matter or the equivalent thereof, used for the purpose of reciting, embodying, conveying or recording information, or constituting a symbol or evidence of value, right, privilege or identification, which is capable of being used to the advantage or disadvantage of some person.

> **HISTORY:** Add, L 1965, ch 1030, § 1; amd, L 1978, ch 233, § 1, eff June 5, 1978. Section heading, amd, L 1978, ch 233, § 1, eff June 5, 1978. Sub 2, amd, L 1986, ch 514, § 6, eff Nov 1, 1986. Sub 3, add, L 1978, ch 233, § 1; amd, L 1986, ch 514, § 6, eff Nov 1, 1986.

§ 175.05. Falsifying business records in the second degree

A person is guilty of falsifying business records in the second degree when, with intent to defraud, he:

1. Makes or causes a false entry in the business records of an enterprise; or

2. Alters, erases, obliterates, deletes, removes or destroys a true entry in the business records of an enterprise; or

3. Omits to make a true entry in the business records of an enterprise in violation of a duty to do so which he knows to be imposed upon him by law or by the nature of his position; or

4. Prevents the making of a true entry or causes the omission thereof in the business records of an enterprise.

Falsifying business records in the second degree is a class A misdemeanor.

> **HISTORY:** Add, L 1965, ch 1030, § 1, eff Sept 1, 1967, with substance derived from §§ 665(2, 3, 4), 887(2), 889(A1, B1-4), 1865(2, 3).

§ 175.10. Falsifying business records in the first degree

A person is guilty of falsifying business records in the first degree when he commits the crime of falsifying business records in the second degree, and when his intent to defraud includes an intent to commit another crime or to aid or conceal the commission thereof.

Falsifying business records in the first degree is a class E felony.

> **HISTORY:** Add, L 1965, ch 1030, § 1, eff Sept 1, 1967, with substance derived from §§ 665(2, 3, 4), 887(2), (A1, B1–4), 1865(2, 3).

§ 175.15. Falsifying business records; defense

In any prosecution for falsifying business records, it is an affirmative defense that the defendant was a clerk, bookkeeper or other employee who, without personal benefit, merely executed the orders of his employer or of a superior officer or employee generally authorized to direct his activities.

> **HISTORY:** Add, L 1965, ch 1030, § 1, eff Sept 1, 1967, with substance derived from § 889(B4).

§ 175.20. Tampering with public records in the second degree

A person is guilty of tampering with public records in the second degree when, knowing that he does not have the authority of anyone entitled to grant it, he knowingly removes, mutilates, destroys, conceals, makes a false entry in or falsely alters any record or other written instrument filed with, deposited in, or otherwise constituting a record of a public office or public servant.

Tampering with public records in the second degree is a Class A misdemeanor.

> **HISTORY:** Add, L 1965, ch 1030, § 1, eff Sept 1, 1967, with substance derived from §§ 1836, 1838(1), 2050.

§ 175.25. Tampering with public records in the first degree

A person is guilty of tampering with public records in the first degree when, knowing that he does not have the authority of anyone entitled to grant it, and with intent to defraud, he knowingly removes, mutilates, destroys, conceals, makes a false entry in or falsely alters any record or other written instrument filed with, deposited in, or otherwise constituting a record of a public office or public servant.

Tampering with public records in the first degree is a class D felony.

> **HISTORY:** Add, L 1965, ch 1030, § 1, eff Sept 1, 1967, with substance derived from §§ 1836, 1838(1), 2050.

§ 175.30. Offering a false instrument for filing in the second degree

A person is guilty of offering a false instrument for filing in the second degree when, knowing that a written instrument contains a false statement or false information, he offers or presents it to a public office or public servant with the knowledge or belief that it will be filed with, registered or recorded in or otherwise become a part of the records of such public office or public servant.

Offering a false instrument for filing in the second degree is a class A misdemeanor.

> **HISTORY:** Add, L 1965, ch 1030, § 1, eff Sept 1, 1967, with substance derived from §§ 460, 1872, 1872-a, 2051, 2321.

§ 175.35. Offering a false instrument for filing in the first degree

A person is guilty of offering a false instrument for filing in the first degree when:

1. knowing that a written instrument contains a false statement or false information, and with intent to defraud the state or any political subdivision, public authority or public benefit corporation of the state, he or she offers or presents it to a public office, public servant, public authority or public benefit corporation with the knowledge or belief that it will be filed with, registered or recorded in or otherwise become a part of the records of such public office, public servant, public authority or public benefit corporation; or

2. (a) he or she commits the crime of offering a false instrument for filing in the second degree; and

(b) such instrument is a financing statement the contents of which are prescribed by section 9-502 of the uniform commercial code, the collateral asserted to be covered in such statement is the property of a person who is a state or local officer as defined by section two of the public officers law or who otherwise is a judge or justice of the unified court system, such financing statement does not relate to an actual transaction, and he or she filed such financing statement in retaliation for the performance of official duties by such person.

Offering a false instrument for filing in the first degree is a class E felony.

> **HISTORY:** Add, L 1965, ch 1030, § 1, with substance derived from §§ 460, 1872, 1872-a, 2051, 2321; amd, L 1998, ch 99, § 1, eff Nov 1, 1998, L 2013, ch 490, § 3, eff Nov 1, 2014.

Editor's Note:

Laws 2013, ch. 490, § 5, eff Nov 13, 2013, provides as follows:

This act shall take effect immediately; provided that section three of this act shall take effect on the first of November next succeeding the date on which it shall have become a law; provided, further, subdivision 2 of section 175.35 of the penal law, as added by section three of this act, shall apply solely to the filing or amendment of financing statements under subpart 1 of part 5 of article 9 of the uniform commercial code on or after such effective date.

§ 175.40. Issuing a false certificate

A person is guilty of issuing a false certificate when, being a public servant authorized by law to make or issue official certificates or other official written instruments, and with intent to defraud, deceive or injure another person, he issues such an instrument, or makes the same with intent that it be issued, knowing that it contains a false statement or false information.

Issuing a false certificate is a class E felony.

HISTORY: Add, L 1965, ch 1030, § 1, eff Sept 1, 1967, with substance derived from §§ 461, 1860, 1861.

§ 175.45. Issuing a false financial statement

A person is guilty of issuing a false financial statement when, with intent to defraud:

1. He knowingly makes or utters a written instrument which purports to describe the financial condition or ability to pay of some person and which is inaccurate in some material respect; or

2. He represents in writing that a written instrument purporting to describe a person's financial condition or ability to pay as of a prior date is accurate with respect to such person's current financial condition or ability to pay, whereas he knows it is materially inaccurate in that respect.

Issuing a false financial statement is a class A misdemeanor.

HISTORY: Add, L 1965, ch 1030, § 1, eff Sept 1, 1967, with substance derived from §§ 665(3), 1293-b.

§ 175.50. [Repealed]

HISTORY: Add, L 1965, ch 1030, § 1, with substance derived from § 1202; repealed, L 1981, ch 720, § 4, eff Nov 1, 1981.

§ 175.55. [Repealed]

HISTORY: Add, L 1979, ch 692, § 5; repealed, L 1981, ch 720, § 4, eff Nov 1, 1981.

ARTICLE 176   INSURANCE FRAUD

HISTORY: Add, L 1981, ch 720, § 3, eff Nov 1, 1981.

§ 176.00. Insurance fraud; definition of terms

The following definitions are applicable to this article:

1. "Insurance policy" has the meaning assigned to insurance contract by subsection (a) of section one thousand one hundred one of the insurance law except it shall include reinsurance

contracts, purported insurance policies and purported reinsurance contracts.

2. "Statement" includes, but is not limited to, any notice, proof of loss, bill of lading, invoice, account, estimate of property damages, bill for services, diagnosis, prescription, hospital or doctor records, x-ray, test result, and other evidence of loss, injury or expense.

3. "Person" includes any individual, firm, association or corporation.

4. "Personal insurance" means a policy of insurance insuring a natural person against any of the following contingencies:

(a) loss of or damage to real property used predominantly for residential purposes and which consists of not more than four dwelling units, other than hotels, motels and rooming houses;

(b) loss of or damage to personal property which is not used in the conduct of a business;

(c) losses or liabilities arising out of the ownership, operation, or use of a motor vehicle, predominantly used for non-business purposes;

(d) other liabilities for loss of, damage to, or injury to persons or property, not arising from the conduct of a business;

(e) death, including death by personal injury, or the continuation of life, or personal injury by accident, or sickness, disease or ailment, excluding insurance providing disability benefits pursuant to article nine of the workers' compensation law.

A policy of insurance which insures any of the contingencies listed in paragraphs (a) through (e) of this subdivision as well as other contingencies shall be personal insurance if that portion of the annual premium attributable to the listed contingencies exceeds that portion attributable to other contingencies.

5. "Commercial insurance" means insurance other than personal insurance, and shall also include insurance providing disability benefits pursuant to article nine of the workers' compensation law, insurance providing workers' compensation benefits pursuant to the provisions of the workers' compensation law and any program of self insurance providing similar benefits.

HISTORY: Add, L 1981, ch 720, § 3, eff Nov 1, 1981. Sub 1, amd, L 1984, ch 805, § 46, eff Sept 1, 1984. Sub 5, amd, L 1996, ch 635, § 24, eff Sept 10, 1996.

§ 176.05. Insurance fraud; defined

A fraudulent insurance act is committed by any person who, knowingly and with intent to defraud presents, causes to be presented, or prepares with knowledge or belief that it will be presented to or by an insurer, self insurer, or purported insurer, or purported self insurer, or any agent thereof:

1. any written statement as part of, or in support of, an application for the issuance of, or the rating of a commercial insurance policy, or certificate or evidence of self insurance for commercial insurance or commercial self insurance, or a claim for payment or other benefit pursuant to an insurance policy or self insurance program for commercial or personal insurance that he or she knows to:

(a) contain materially false information concerning any fact material thereto; or

(b) conceal, for the purpose of misleading, information concerning any fact material thereto; or

2. any written statement or other physical evidence as part of, or in support of, an application for the issuance of a health insurance policy, or a policy or contract or other authorization that provides or allows coverage for, membership or enrollment in, or other services of a public or private health plan, or a claim for payment, services or other benefit pursuant to such policy, contract or plan that he or she knows to:

　　(a) contain materially false information concerning any material fact thereto; or

　　(b) conceal, for the purpose of misleading, information concerning any fact material thereto.

Such policy or contract or plan or authorization shall include, but not be limited to, those issued or operating pursuant to any public or governmentally-sponsored or supported plan for health care coverage or services or those otherwise issued or operated by entities authorized pursuant to the public health law. For purposes of this subdivision an "application for the issuance of a health insurance policy" shall not include (i) any application for a health insurance policy or contract approved by the superintendent of insurance pursuant to the provisions of sections three thousand two hundred sixteen, four thousand three hundred four, four thousand three hundred twenty-one or four thousand three hundred twenty-two of the insurance law or any other application for a health insurance policy or contract approved by the superintendent of insurance in the individual or direct payment market; or (ii) any application for a certificate evidencing coverage under a self-insured plan or under a group contract approved by the superintendent of insurance.

　　HISTORY: Add, L 1981, ch 720, § 3; amd, L 1996, ch 635, § 23, eff Sept 10, 1996; amd, 1998, ch 2, § 42, eff Nov 1, 1998, L 2011, ch 211 § 2, eff July 20, 2011.

§ 176.10. Insurance fraud in the fifth degree

A person is guilty of insurance fraud in the fifth degree when he commits a fraudulent insurance act.

Insurance fraud in the fifth degree is a class A misdemeanor.

　　HISTORY: Add, L 1981, ch 720, § 3; amd, L 1986, ch 515, § 8, eff Nov 1, 1986. Section heading, amd, L 1986, ch 515, § 8, eff Nov 1, 1986.

§ 176.15. Insurance fraud in the fourth degree

A person is guilty of insurance fraud in the fourth degree when he commits a fraudulent insurance act and thereby wrongfully takes, obtains or withholds, or attempts to wrongfully take, obtain or withhold property with a value in excess of one thousand dollars.

Insurance fraud in the fourth degree is a class E felony.

　　HISTORY: Add, L 1981, ch 720, § 3; amd, L 1986, ch 515, § 8, eff Nov 1, 1986. Section heading, amd, L 1986, ch 515, § 8, eff Nov 1, 1986.

§ 176.20. Insurance fraud in the third degree

A person is guilty of insurance fraud in the third degree when he commits a fraudulent insurance act and thereby wrongfully takes, obtains or withholds, or attempts to wrongfully take, obtain or withhold property with a value in excess of three thousand dollars.

Insurance fraud in the third degree is a class D felony.

　　HISTORY: Add, L 1981, ch 720, § 3; amd, L 1986, ch 515, § 8, eff Nov 1, 1986. Section heading, amd, L 1986, ch 515, § 8, eff Nov 1, 1986.

§ 176.25. Insurance fraud in the second degree

A person is guilty of insurance fraud in the second degree when he commits a fraudulent insurance act and thereby wrongfully takes, obtains or withholds, or attempts to wrongfully take, obtain or withhold property with a value in excess of fifty thousand dollars.

Insurance fraud in the second degree is a class C felony.

HISTORY: Add, L 1986, ch 515, § 9, eff Nov 1, 1986.

§ 176.30. Insurance fraud in the first degree

A person is guilty of insurance fraud in the first degree when he commits a fraudulent insurance act and thereby wrongfully takes, obtains or withholds, or attempts to wrongfully take, obtain or withhold property with a value in excess of one million dollars.

Insurance fraud in the first degree is a class B felony.

HISTORY: Add, L 1986, ch 515, § 9, eff Nov 1, 1986.

§ 176.35. Aggravated insurance fraud

A person is guilty of aggravated insurance fraud in the fourth degree when he commits a fraudulent insurance act, and has been previously convicted within the preceding five years of any offense, an essential element of which is the commission of a fraudulent insurance act.

Aggravated insurance fraud in the fourth degree is a class D felony.

HISTORY: Add, L 1996, ch 635, § 21, eff Sept 10, 1996.

§ 176.40. Fraudulent life settlement act; defined

A fraudulent life settlement act is committed by any person who, knowingly and with intent to defraud, presents, causes to be presented, or prepares with knowledge or belief that it will be presented to, or by, a life settlement provider, life settlement broker, life settlement intermediary, or any agent thereof, or to any owner any written statement or other physical evidence as part of, or in support of, an application for a life settlement contract, a claim for payment or other benefit under a life settlement contract, which the person knows to:

(1) contain materially false information concerning any material fact thereto; or

(2) conceal, for the purpose of misleading, information concerning any fact material thereto.

HISTORY: Add, L 2009, ch 499, § 19, eff May 18, 2010.

§ 176.45. Life settlement fraud in the fifth degree

A person is guilty of life settlement fraud in the fifth degree when he or she commits a fraudulent life settlement act.

Life settlement fraud in the fifth degree is a class A misdemeanor.

HISTORY: Add, L 2009, ch 499, § 19, eff May 18, 2010.

§ 176.50. Life settlement fraud in the fourth degree

A person is guilty of life settlement fraud in the fourth degree when he or she commits a fraudulent life settlement act and thereby wrongfully takes, obtains or withholds, or attempts to wrongfully take, obtain or withhold property with a value in excess of twenty-five thousand dollars.

Life settlement fraud in the fourth degree is a class E felony.

HISTORY: Add, L 2009, ch 499, § 19, eff May 18, 2010.

§ 176.55. Life settlement fraud in the third degree

A person is guilty of life settlement fraud in the third degree when he or she commits a fraudulent life settlement act and thereby wrongfully takes, obtains or withholds, or attempts to wrongfully take, obtain or withhold property with a value in excess of fifty thousand dollars.

Life settlement fraud in the third degree is a class D felony.

HISTORY: Add, L 2009, ch 499, § 19, eff May 18, 2010.

§ 176.60. Life settlement fraud in the second degree

A person is guilty of life settlement fraud in the second degree when he or she commits a fraudulent life settlement act and thereby wrongfully takes, obtains or withholds, or attempts to wrongfully take, obtain or withhold property with a value in excess of one hundred thousand dollars.

Life settlement fraud in the second degree is a class C felony.

HISTORY: Add, L 2009, ch 499, § 19, eff May 18, 2010.

§ 176.65. Life settlement fraud in the first degree

A person is guilty of life settlement fraud in the first degree when he or she commits a fraudulent life settlement act and thereby wrongfully takes, obtains or withholds, or attempts to wrongfully take, obtain or withhold property with a value in excess of one million dollars.

Life settlement fraud in the first degree is a class B felony.

HISTORY: Add, L 2009, ch 499, § 19, eff May 18, 2010.

§ 176.70. Aggravated life settlement fraud

A person is guilty of aggravated life settlement fraud when he or she commits a fraudulent life settlement act, and has been previously convicted within the preceding five years of any offense, an essential element of which is the commission of a fraudulent life settlement act.

Aggravated life settlement fraud is a class D felony.

HISTORY: Add, L 2009, ch 499, § 19, eff May 18, 2010.

ARTICLE 177   HEALTH CARE FRAUD

HISTORY: Add, L 2006, ch 442, § 9, eff Nov 1, 2006.

§ 177.00. Definitions

The following definitions are applicable to this article:

1. "Health plan" means any publicly or privately funded health insurance or managed care plan or contract, under which any health care item or service is provided, and through which payment may be made to the person who provided the health care item or service. The state's medical assistance program (Medicaid) shall be considered a single health plan. For purposes of this article, a payment made pursuant to the state's managed care program as defined in paragraph (c) of subdivision one of section three hundred sixty-four-j of the social services law shall be deemed a payment by the state's medical assistance program (Medicaid).

2. "Person" means any individual or entity, other than a recipient of a health care item or service under a health plan unless such recipient acts as an accessory to such an individual or entity.

HISTORY: Add, L 2006, ch 442, § 9, eff Nov 1, 2006.

§ 177.05. Health care fraud in the fifth degree

A person is guilty of health care fraud in the fifth degree when, with intent to defraud a health plan, he or she knowingly and willfully provides materially false information or omits material information for the purpose of requesting payment from a health plan for a health care item or service and, as a result of such information or omission, he or she or another person receives payment in an amount that he, she or such other person is not entitled to under the circumstances.

Health care fraud in the fifth degree is a class A misdemeanor.

HISTORY: Add, L 2006, ch 442, § 9, eff Nov 1, 2006.

§ 177.10. Health care fraud in the fourth degree

A person is guilty of health care fraud in the fourth degree when such person, on one or more occasions, commits the crime of health care fraud in the fifth degree and the payment or portion of the payment wrongfully received, as the case may be, from a single health plan, in a period of not more than one year, exceeds three thousand dollars in the aggregate.

Health care fraud in the fourth degree is a class E felony.

HISTORY: Add, L 2006, ch 442, § 9, eff Nov 1, 2006.

§ 177.15. Health care fraud in the third degree

A person is guilty of health care fraud in the third degree when such person, on one or more occasions, commits the crime of health care fraud in the fifth degree and the payment or portion of the payment wrongfully received, as the case may be, from a single health plan, in a period of not more than one year, exceeds ten thousand dollars in the aggregate.

Health care fraud in the third degree is a class D felony.

HISTORY: Add, L 2006, ch 442, § 9, eff Nov 1, 2006.

§ 177.20. Health care fraud in the second degree

A person is guilty of health care fraud in the second degree when such person, on one or more occasions, commits the crime of health care fraud in the fifth degree and the payment or portion of the payment wrongfully received, as the case may be, from a single health plan, in a period of not more than one year, exceeds fifty thousand dollars in the aggregate.

Health care fraud in the second degree is a class C felony.

HISTORY: Add, L 2006, ch 442, § 9, eff Nov 1, 2006.

§ 177.25. Health care fraud in the first degree

A person is guilty of health care fraud in the first degree when such person, on one or more occasions, commits the crime of health care fraud in the fifth degree and the payment or portion of the payment wrongfully received, as the case may be, from a single health plan, in a period of not more than one year, exceeds one million dollars in the aggregate.

Health care fraud in the first degree is a class B felony.

HISTORY: Add, L 2006, ch 442, § 9, eff Nov 1, 2006.

§ 177.30. Health care fraud; affirmative defense

In any prosecution under this article, it shall be an affirmative defense that the defendant was a clerk, bookkeeper or other employee, other than an employee charged with the active management and control, in an executive capacity, of the affairs of the corporation, who, without personal benefit, merely executed the orders of his or her employer or of a superior employee generally authorized to direct his or her activities.

HISTORY: Add, L 2006, ch 442, § 9, eff Nov 1, 2006.

ARTICLE 178   CRIMINAL DIVERSION OF PRESCRIPTION MEDICATIONS AND PRESCRIPTIONS

HISTORY: Add, L 1995, ch 81, § 94, eff Nov 1, 1995.

§ 178.00. Criminal diversion of prescription medications and prescriptions; definitions

The following definitions are applicable to this article:

1. "Prescription medication or device" means any article for which a prescription is required in order to be lawfully sold, delivered or distributed by any person authorized by law to engage in the practice of the profession of pharmacy.

2. "Prescription" means a direction or authorization by means of a written prescription form or an oral prescription which permits a person to lawfully obtain a prescription medication or device from any person authorized to dispense such prescription medication or device.

3. "Criminal diversion act" means an act or acts in which a person knowingly:

(a) transfers or delivers, in exchange for anything of pecuniary value, a prescription medication or device with knowledge or reasonable grounds to know that the recipient has no medical need for it; or

(b) receives, in exchange for anything of pecuniary value, a prescription medication or device with knowledge or reasonable grounds to know that the seller or transferor is not authorized by law to sell or transfer such prescription medication or device; or

(c) transfers or delivers a prescription in exchange for anything of pecuniary value; or

(d) receives a prescription in exchange for anything of pecuniary value.

HISTORY: Add, L 1995, ch 81, § 94, eff Nov 1, 1995.

§ 178.05. Criminal diversion of prescription medications and prescriptions; limitation

1. The provisions of this article shall not apply to:

(a) a duly licensed physician or other person authorized to issue a prescription acting in good faith in the lawful course of his or her profession; or

(b) a duly licensed pharmacist acting in good faith in the lawful course of the practice of pharmacy; or

(c) a person acting in good faith seeking treatment for a medical condition or assisting another person to obtain treatment for a medical condition.

2. No provision of this article relating to the sale of a prescription medication or device shall be deemed to authorize any act prohibited by article thirty-three of the public health law or article two hundred twenty of this chapter.

HISTORY: Add, L 1995, ch 81, § 94, eff Nov 1, 1995.

§ 178.10. Criminal diversion of prescription medications and prescriptions in the fourth degree

A person is guilty of criminal diversion of prescription medications and prescriptions in the fourth degree when he or she commits a criminal diversion act.

Criminal diversion of prescription medications and prescriptions in the fourth degree is a class A misdemeanor.

HISTORY: Add, L 1995, ch 81, § 94, eff Nov 1, 1995.

§ 178.15. Criminal diversion of prescription medications and prescriptions in the third degree

A person is guilty of criminal diversion of prescription medications and prescriptions in the third degree when he or she:

1. commits a criminal diversion act, and the value of the benefit exchanged is in excess of one thousand dollars; or

2. commits the crime of criminal diversion of prescription medications and prescriptions in the fourth degree, and has previously been convicted of the crime of criminal diversion of prescription medications and prescriptions in the fourth degree.

Criminal diversion of prescription medications and prescriptions in the third degree is a class E felony.

HISTORY: Add, L 1995, ch 81, § 94, eff Nov 1, 1995.

§ 178.20. Criminal diversion of prescription medications and prescriptions in the second degree

A person is guilty of criminal diversion of prescription medications and prescriptions in the second degree when he or she commits a criminal diversion act, and the value of the benefit exchanged is in excess of three thousand dollars.

Criminal diversion of prescription medications and prescriptions in the second degree is a class D felony.

HISTORY: Add, L 1995, ch 81, § 94, eff Nov 1, 1995.

§ 178.25. Criminal diversion of prescription medications and prescriptions in the first degree

A person is guilty of criminal diversion of prescription medications and prescriptions in the first degree when he or she commits a criminal diversion act, and the value of the benefit exchanged is in excess of fifty thousand dollars.

Criminal diversion of prescription medications and prescriptions in the first degree is a class C felony.

HISTORY: Add, L 1995, ch 81, § 94, eff Nov 1, 1995.

§ 178.26. Fraud and deceit related to controlled substances

1. No person shall willfully:

(a) obtain or attempt to obtain a controlled substance, a prescription for a controlled substance or an official New York state prescription form,

(i) by fraud, deceit, misrepresentation or subterfuge; or

(ii) by the concealment of a material fact; or

(iii) by the use of a false name or the giving of a false address;

(b) make a false statement in any prescription, order, application, report or record required by article thirty-three of the public health law;

(c) falsely assume the title of, or represent himself or herself to be a licensed manufacturer, distributor, pharmacy, pharmacist, practitioner, researcher, approved institutional dispenser, owner or employee of a registered outsourcing facility or other authorized person, for the purpose of obtaining a controlled substance as these terms are defined in article thirty-three of the public health law;

(d) make or utter any false or forged prescription or false or forged written order;

(e) affix any false or forged label to a package or receptacle containing controlled substances; or

(f) imprint on or affix to any controlled substance a false or forged code number or symbol.

2. Possession of a false or forged prescription for a controlled substance by any person other than a pharmacist in the lawful pursuance of his or her profession shall be presumptive evidence of his or her intent to use the same for the purpose of illegally obtaining a controlled substance.

3. Possession of a blank official New York state prescription form by any person to whom it was not lawfully issued shall be presumptive evidence of such person's intent to use same for the purpose of illegally obtaining a controlled substance.

4. Any person who, in the course of treatment, is supplied with a controlled substance or a prescription therefor by one practitioner and who with the intent to deceive, intentionally withholds or intentionally fails to disclose the fact, is supplied during such treatment with a controlled substance or a prescription therefor by another practitioner shall be guilty of a violation of this article.

5. The provisions of subdivision one of section thirty-three hundred ninety-six of the public health law shall apply to this section.

Fraud and deceit related to controlled substances is a class A misdemeanor.

    HISTORY: Add, L 2014, ch 36, § 1, eff June 23, 2014.

ARTICLE 179   [EXPIRES AND REPEALED JULY 5, 2021] CRIMINAL DIVERSION OF MEDICAL MARIHUANA

    HISTORY: Add, L 2014, ch 90, § 9, eff July 3, 2014, expires and repealed July 5, 2021.

§ 179.00. [Expires and repealed July 5, 2021] Criminal diversion of medical marihuana; definitions

The following definitions are applicable to this article:

1. "Medical marihuana" means medical marihuana as defined in subdivision eight of section thirty-three hundred sixty of the public health law.

2. "Certification" means a certification, made under section thirty-three hundred sixty-one of the public health law.

HISTORY: Add, L 2014, ch 90, § 9, eff July 3, 2014, expires and repealed July 5, 2021.

§ 179.05. [Expires and repealed July 5, 2021] Criminal diversion of medical marihuana; limitations

The provisions of this article shall not apply to:

1. a practitioner authorized to issue a certification who acted in good faith in the lawful course of his or her profession; or

2. a registered organization as that term is defined in subdivision nine of section thirty-three hundred sixty of the public health law who acted in good faith in the lawful course of the practice of pharmacy; or

3. a person who acted in good faith seeking treatment for medical condition or assisting another person to obtain treatment for a medical condition.

HISTORY: Add, L 2014, ch 90, § 9, eff July 3, 2014, expires and repealed July 5, 2021.

§ 179.10. [Expires and repealed July 5, 2021] Criminal diversion of medical marihuana in the first degree

A person is guilty of criminal diversion of medical marihuana in the first degree when he or she is a practitioner, as that term is defined in subdivision twelve of section thirty-three hundred sixty of the public health law, who issues a certification with knowledge of reasonable grounds to know that (i) the recipient has no medical need for it, or (ii) it is for a purpose other than to treat a serious condition as defined in subdivision seven of section thirty-three hundred sixty of the public health law.

Criminal diversion of medical marihuana in the first degree is a class E felony.

HISTORY: Add, L 2014, ch 90, § 9, eff July 3, 2014, expires and repealed July 5, 2021.

§ 179.11. [Expires and repealed July 5, 2021] Criminal diversion of medical marihuana in the second degree

A person is guilty of criminal diversion of medical marihuana in the second degree when he or she sells, trades, delivers, or otherwise provides medical marihuana to another with knowledge or reasonable grounds to know that the recipient is not registered under title five-A of article thirty-three of the public health law.

Criminal diversion of medical marihuana in the second degree is a class B misdemeanor.

HISTORY: Add, L 2014, ch 90, § 9, eff July 3, 2014, expires and repealed July 5, 2021.

§ 179.15. [Expires and repealed July 5, 2021] Criminal retention of medical marihuana

A person is guilty of criminal retention of medical marihuana when, being a certified patient or designated caregiver, as those terms are defined in subdivisions three and five of section thirty-three hundred sixty of the public health law, respectively, he or she knowingly obtains, possesses, stores or maintains an amount of marihuana in excess of the amount he or she is authorized to possess under the provisions of title five-A of article thirty-three of the public health law.

Criminal retention of medical marihuana is a class A misdemeanor.

HISTORY: Add, L 2014, ch 90, § 9, eff July 3, 2014, expires and repealed July 5, 2021.

ARTICLE 180　BRIBERY NOT INVOLVING PUBLIC SERVANTS, AND RELATED OFFENSES

HISTORY: Add, L 1965, ch 1030, § 1, eff Sept 1, 1967.

§ 180.00. Commercial bribing in the second degree

A person is guilty of commercial bribing in the second degree when he confers, or offers or agrees to confer, any benefit upon any employee, agent or fiduciary without the consent of the latter's employer or principal, with intent to influence his conduct in relation to his employer's or principal's affairs.

Commercial bribing in the second degree is a class A misdemeanor.

HISTORY: Add, L 1965, ch 1030, § 1, with substance derived from § 439; amd, L 1976, ch 458, § 1, L 1983, ch 577, § 1, eff Sept 1, 1983. Section heading, amd, L 1976, ch 458, § 1, eff Sept 1, 1976.

§ 180.03. Commercial bribing in the first degree

A person is guilty of commercial bribing in the first degree when he confers, or offers or agrees to confer, any benefit upon any employee, agent or fiduciary without the consent of the latter's employer or principal, with intent to influence his conduct in relation to his employer's or principal's affairs, and when the value of the benefit conferred or offered or agreed to be conferred exceeds one thousand dollars and causes economic harm to the employer or principal in an amount exceeding two hundred fifty dollars.

Commercial bribing in the first degree is a class E felony.

HISTORY: Add, L 1976, ch 458, § 2; amd, L 1983, ch 577, § 1, eff Sept 1, 1983.

§ 180.05. Commercial bribe receiving in the second degree

An employee, agent or fiduciary is guilty of commercial bribe receiving in the second degree when, without the consent of his employer or principal, he solicits, accepts or agrees to accept any benefit from another person upon an agreement or understanding that such benefit will influence his conduct in relation to his employer's or principal's affairs.

Commercial bribe receiving in the second degree is a class A misdemeanor.

HISTORY: Add, L 1965, ch 1030, § 1, with substance derived from § 439; amd, L 1976, ch 458, § 3, L 1983, ch 577, § 1, eff Sept 1, 1983. Section heading, amd, L 1976, ch 458, § 3, eff Sept 1, 1976.

§ 180.08. Commercial bribe receiving in the first degree

An employee, agent or fiduciary is guilty of commercial bribe receiving in the first degree when, without the consent of his employer or principal, he solicits, accepts or agrees to accept any benefit from another person upon an agreement or understanding that such benefit will influence his conduct in relation to his employer's or principal's affairs, and when the value of the benefit solicited, accepted or agreed to be accepted exceeds one thousand dollars and causes economic harm to the employer or principal in an amount exceeding two hundred fifty dollars.

Commercial bribe receiving in the first degree is a class E felony.

HISTORY: Add, L 1976, ch 458, § 4; amd, L 1983, ch 577, § 1, eff Sept 1, 1983.

§ 180.10. Bribery of labor official; definition of term

As used in this article, "labor official" means any duly appointed representative of a labor organization or any duly appointed trustee or representative of an employee welfare trust fund.

HISTORY: Add, L 1965, ch 1030, § 1, eff Sept 1, 1967.

§ 180.15. Bribing a labor official

A person is guilty of bribing a labor official when, with intent to influence a labor official in respect to any of his acts, decisions or duties as such labor official, he confers, or offers or agrees to confer, any benefit upon him.

Bribing a labor official is a class D felony.

HISTORY: Add, L 1965, ch 1030, § 1, eff Sept 1, 1967, with substance derived from § 380(1).

§ 180.20. Bribing a labor official; defense

In any prosecution for bribing a labor official, it is a defense that the defendant conferred or agreed to confer the benefit involved upon the labor official as a result of conduct of the latter constituting larceny committed by means of extortion, or an attempt to commit the same, or coercion, or an attempt to commit coercion.

HISTORY: Add, L 1965, ch 1030, § 1, eff Sept 1, 1967.

§ 180.25. Bribe receiving by a labor official

A labor official is guilty of bribe receiving by a labor official when he solicits, accepts or agrees to accept any benefit from another person upon an agreement or understanding that such benefit will influence him in respect to any of his acts, decisions, or duties as such labor official.

Bribe receiving by a labor official is a class D felony.

HISTORY: Add, L 1965, ch 1030, § 1, eff Sept 1, 1967, with substance derived from § 380(2).

§ 180.30. Bribe receiving by a labor official; no defense

The crimes of (a) bribe receiving by a labor official, and (b) larceny committed by means of extortion, attempt to commit the same, coercion or attempt to commit coercion, are not mutually exclusive, and it is no defense to a prosecution for bribe receiving by a labor official that, by reason of the same conduct, the defendant also committed one of such other specified crimes.

HISTORY: Add, L 1965, ch 1030, § 1, eff Sept 1, 1967.

§ 180.35. Sports bribery and tampering; definitions of terms

As used in this article:

1. "Sports contest" means any professional or amateur sport or athletic game or contest viewed by the public.

2. "Sports participant" means any person who participates or expects to participate in a sports contest as a player, contestant or member of a team, or as a coach, manager, trainer or other person directly associated with a player, contestant or team.

3. "Sports official" means any person who acts or expects to act in a sports contest as an umpire, referee, judge or otherwise to officiate at a sports contest.

4. "Pari-mutuel betting" is such betting as is authorized under the provisions of the pari-mutuel revenue law as set forth in chapter 254* of the laws of 1940 with amendments.

5. "Pari-mutuel horse race" means any horse race upon which betting is conducted under the provision of the pari-mutuel revenue law as set forth in chapter 254** of the laws of 1940.

HISTORY: Add, L 1965, ch 1030, § 1; amd, L 1982, ch 382, § 1, eff Aug 27, 1982. Section heading, amd, L 1982, ch 382, § 1, eff Aug 27, 1982. Sub 4, add, L 1982, ch 382, § 1, eff Aug 27, 1982. Sub 5, add, L 1982, ch 382, § 1, eff Aug 27, 1982.

§ 180.40. Sports bribing

A person is guilty of sports bribing when he:

1. Confers, or offers or agrees to confer, any benefit upon a sports participant with intent to influence him not to give his best efforts in a sports contest; or

2. Confers, or offers or agrees to confer, any benefit upon a sports official with intent to influence him to perform his duties improperly.

Sports bribing is a class D felony.

HISTORY: Add, L 1965, ch 1030, § 1, eff Sept 1, 1967, with substance derived from § 382(1).

§ 180.45. Sports bribe receiving

A person is guilty of sports bribe receiving when:

1. Being a sports participant, he solicits, accepts or agrees to accept any benefit from another person upon an agreement or understanding that he will thereby be influenced not to give his best efforts in a sports contest; or

---

* Repealed, April 1, 1983, L 1982, ch 865 § 1.

** Repealed, April 1, 1983, L 1982, ch 865, § 1.

2. Being a sports official, he solicits, accepts or agrees to accept any benefit from another person upon an agreement or understanding that he will perform his duties improperly.

Sports bribe receiving is a class E felony.

HISTORY: Add, L 1965, ch 1030, § 1, eff Sept 1, 1967, with substance derived from § 382(2).

§ 180.50. Tampering with a sports contest in the second degree

A person is guilty of tampering with a sports contest when, with intent to influence the outcome of a sports contest, he tampers with any sports participant, sports official or with any animal or equipment or other thing involved in the conduct or operation of a sports contest in a manner contrary to the rules and usages purporting to govern such a contest.

Tampering with a sports contest in the second degree is a class A misdemeanor.

HISTORY: Add, L 1965, ch 1030, § 1, with substance derived from § 190-a; amd, L 1982, ch 382, § 1, eff Aug 27, 1982. Section heading, amd, L 1982, ch 382, § 1, eff Aug 27, 1982.

§ 180.51. Tampering with a sports contest in the first degree

A person is guilty of tampering with a sports contest in the first degree when, with intent to influence the outcome of a pari-mutuel horse race:

1. He affects any equine animal involved in the conduct or operation of a pari-mutuel horse race by administering to the animal in any manner whatsoever any controlled substance listed in section thirty-three hundred six of the public health law; or

2. He knowingly enters or furnishes to another person for entry or brings into this state for entry into a pari-mutuel horse race, or rides or drives in any pari-mutuel horse race any running, trotting or pacing horse, mare, gelding, colt or filly under an assumed name, or deceptively out of its proper class, or that has been painted or disguised or represented to be any other or different horse, mare, gelding, colt or filly from that which it actually is; or

3. He knowingly and falsely registers with the jockey club, United States trotting association, American quarterhorse association or national steeplechase and hunt association a horse, mare, gelding, colt or filly previously registered under a different name; or

4. He agrees with one or more persons to enter such misrepresented or drugged animal in a pari-mutuel horse race. A person shall not be convicted of a violation of this subdivision unless an overt act is alleged and proved to have been committed by one of said persons in furtherance of said agreement.

Tampering with a sports contest in the first degree is a class E felony.

HISTORY: Add, L 1982, ch 382, § 2, eff Aug 27, 1982.

§ 180.52. Impairing the integrity of a pari-mutuel betting system in the second degree

A person is guilty of impairing the integrity of a pari-mutuel betting system in the second degree when, with the intent to obtain either any payment for himself or for a third person or with the intent to defraud any person he:

1. Alters, changes or interferes with any equipment or device used in connection with pari-mutuel betting; or

2. Causes any false, inaccurate, delayed or unauthorized data, impulse or signal to be fed into, or transmitted over, or registered in or displayed upon any equipment or device used in connection with pari-mutuel betting.

Impairing the integrity of a pari-mutuel betting system in the second degree is a class E felony.

HISTORY: Add, L 1982, ch 382, § 2, eff Aug 27, 1982.

§ 180.53. Impairing the integrity of a pari-mutuel betting system in the first degree

A person is guilty of impairing the integrity of a pari-mutuel betting system in the first degree when, with the intent to obtain either any payment for himself or for a third person or with the intent to defraud any person, and when the value of the payment exceeds one thousand five hundred dollars he:

1. Alters, changes or interferes with any equipment or device used in connection with pari-mutuel betting; or

2. Causes any false, inaccurate, delayed or unauthorized data, impulse or signal to be fed into, or transmitted over, or registered in or displayed upon any equipment or device used in connection with pari-mutuel betting.

Impairing the integrity of a pari-mutuel betting system in the first degree is a class D felony.

HISTORY: Add, L 1982, ch 382, § 2, eff Aug 27, 1982.

§ 180.54. Rent gouging; definition of term

As used in this article, "lawful rental and other lawful charges" means registered, reported or contracted for rent pursuant to chapter four hundred three of the laws of nineteen hundred eighty-three, article two of the private housing finance law or section eight of the federal housing act of nineteen hundred sixty-eight, or, rent contained in a court approved stipulation of settlement, even if such rent or charges are subsequently decreased by order of the department of housing and community renewal or a court of competent jurisdiction.

HISTORY: Add, L 1991, ch 584, § 1, eff Nov 1, 1991.

§ 180.55. Rent gouging in the third degree

A person is guilty of rent gouging in the third degree when, in connection with the leasing, rental or use of real property, he solicits, accepts or agrees to accept from a person some consideration of value, less than two hundred fifty dollars, in addition to lawful rental and other lawful charges, upon an agreement or understanding that the furnishing of such consideration will increase the possibility that any person may obtain or renew the lease, rental or use of such property, or that a failure to furnish it will decrease the possibility that any person may obtain or renew the same.

Rent gouging in the third degree is a class B misdemeanor.

HISTORY: Add, L 1965, ch 1030, § 1, eff Sept 1, 1967, with substance derived from § 965. Section heading, amd, L 1991, ch 584, § 2, eff Nov 1, 1991. First undesignated par, amd, L 1991, ch 584, § 2, eff Nov 1, 1991. Second undesignated par, amd, L 1991, ch 584, § 2, eff Nov 1, 1991.

§ 180.56. Rent gouging in the second degree

A person is guilty of rent gouging in the second degree when, in connection with the leasing, rental or use of real property, he solicits, accepts or agrees to accept from a person some consideration of value, of two hundred fifty dollars or more, in addition to lawful rental and other lawful charges, upon an agreement or understanding that the furnishing of such consideration will increase the possibility that any person may obtain or renew the lease, rental or use of such property, or that a failure to furnish it will decrease the possibility that any person may obtain or renew the same.

Rent gouging in the second degree is a class A misdemeanor.

HISTORY: Add, L 1991, ch 584, § 3, eff Nov 1, 1991.

§ 180.57. Rent gouging in the first degree

A person is guilty of rent gouging in the first degree when, in the course of a scheme constituting a systematic ongoing course of conduct in connection with the leasing, rental or use of three or more apartment units, the rental price of which is regulated pursuant to the provisions of federal, state or local law, he solicits, accepts or agrees to accept from one or more persons in three separate transactions some consideration of value, knowing that such consideration is in addition to lawful rental and other lawful charges established pursuant to the provisions of such federal, state or local law, and upon an agreement or understanding that the furnishing of such consideration will increase the possibility that any person may obtain or renew the lease, rental or use of such property, or that a failure to furnish it will decrease the possibility that any person may obtain or renew same, and thereby obtains such consideration from one or more persons.

Rent gouging in the first degree is a class E felony.

> **HISTORY:** Add, L 1991, ch 584, § 4, eff Nov 1, 1991.

ARTICLE 185   FRAUDS ON CREDITORS

> **HISTORY:** Add, L 1965, ch 1030, § 1, eff Sept 1, 1967.

§ 185.00. Fraud in insolvency

1. As used in this section, "administrator" means an assignee or trustee for the benefit of creditors, a liquidator, a receiver or any other person entitled to administer property for the benefit of creditors.

2. A person is guilty of fraud in insolvency when, with intent to defraud any creditor and knowing that proceedings have been or are about to be instituted for the appointment of an administrator, or knowing that a composition agreement or other arrangement for the benefit of creditors has been or is about to be made, he

    (a) conveys, transfers, removes, conceals, destroys, encumbers or otherwise disposes of any part of or any interest in the debtor's estate; or

    (b) obtains any substantial part of or interest in the debtor's estate; or

    (c) presents to any creditor or to the administrator any writing or record relating to the debtor's estate knowing the same to contain a false material statement; or

    (d) misrepresents or fails or refuses to disclose to the administrator the existence, amount or location of any part of or any interest in the debtor's estate, or any other information which he is legally required to furnish to such administrator.

Fraud in insolvency is a class A misdemeanor.

> **HISTORY:** Add, L 1965, ch 1030, § 1, eff Sept 1, 1967, with substance derived from §§ 1170, 1171, 1172, 1173.

§ 185.05. Fraud involving a security interest

A person is guilty of fraud involving a security interest when, having executed a security agreement creating a security interest in personal property securing a monetary obligation owed to a secured party, and:

    1. Having under the security agreement both the right of sale or other disposition of the

property and the duty to account to the secured party for the proceeds of disposition, he sells or otherwise disposes of the property and wrongfully fails to account to the secured party for the proceeds of disposition; or

2. Having under the security agreement no right of sale or other disposition of the property, he knowingly secretes, withholds or disposes of such property in violation of the security agreement.

Fraud involving a security interest is a class A misdemeanor.

HISTORY: Add, L 1965, ch 1030, § 1, eff Sept 1, 1967, with substance derived from § 940-a.

§ 185.10. Fraudulent disposition of mortgaged property

A person is guilty of fraudulent disposition of mortgaged property when, having theretofore executed a mortgage of real or personal property or any instrument intended to operate as such, he sells, assigns, exchanges, secretes, injures, destroys or otherwise disposes of any part of the property, upon which the mortgage or other instrument is at the time a lien, with intent thereby to defraud the mortgagee or a purchaser thereof.

Fraudulent disposition of mortgaged property is a class A misdemeanor.

HISTORY: Add, L 1965, ch 1030, § 1, eff Sept 1, 1967, with substance derived from §§ 940(1), 1291(2).

§ 185.15. Fraudulent disposition of property subject to a conditional sale contract

A person is guilty of fraudulent disposition of property subject to a conditional sale contract when, prior to the performance of the condition of a conditional sale contract and being the buyer or any legal successor in interest of the buyer, he sells, assigns, mortgages, exchanges, secretes, injures, destroys or otherwise disposes of the goods subject to the conditional sale contract under claim of full ownership, with intent thereby to defraud another.

Fraudulent disposition of property subject to a conditional sale contract is a class A misdemeanor.

HISTORY: Add, L 1965, ch 1030, § 1, eff Sept 1, 1967, with substance derived from § 940(2).

ARTICLE 187   RESIDENTIAL MORTGAGE FRAUD

HISTORY: Add, L 2008, ch 472, § 19, eff Nov 1, 2008.

§ 187.00. Definitions

As used in this article:

1. "Person" means any individual or entity.

2. "Residential mortgage loan" means a loan or agreement to extend credit, including the renewal, refinancing or modification of any such loan, made to a person, which loan is primarily secured by either a mortgage, deed of trust, or other lien upon any interest in residential real

property or any certificate of stock or other evidence of ownership in, and a proprietary lease from, a corporation or partnership formed for the purpose of cooperative ownership of residential real property.

3. "Residential real property" means real property improved by a one-to-four family dwelling, or a residential unit in a building including units owned as condominiums or on a cooperative basis, used or occupied, or intended to be used or occupied, wholly or partly, as the home or residence of one or more persons, but shall not refer to unimproved real property upon which such dwellings are to be constructed.

4. "Residential mortgage fraud" is committed by a person who, knowingly and with intent to defraud, presents, causes to be presented, or prepares with knowledge or belief that it will be used in soliciting an applicant for, applying for, underwriting or closing a residential mortgage loan, or filing with a county clerk of any county in the state arising out of and related to the closing of a residential mortgage loan, any written statement which:

(a) contains materially false information concerning any fact material thereto; or

(b) conceals, for the purpose of misleading, information concerning any fact material thereto.

HISTORY: Add, L 2008, ch 472, § 19, eff Nov 1, 2008; amd, L 2009, ch 507, § 20, eff Dec 15, 2009. Sub 1, amd, L 2009, ch 507, § 20, eff Dec 15, 2009. Sub 2, amd, L 2009, ch 507, § 20, eff Dec 15, 2009. Sub 4, opening par, amd, L 2009, ch 507, § 20, eff Dec 15, 2009. Sub 4, par (a), amd, L 2009, ch 507, § 20, eff Dec 15, 2009. Sub 4, par (b), amd, L 2009, ch 507, § 20, eff Dec 15, 2009.

§ 187.01. Limitation on prosecution

No individual who applies for a residential mortgage loan and intends to occupy such residential property which such mortgage secures shall be held liable under this article provided, however, any such individual who acts as an accessory to an individual or entity in committing any crime defined in this article may be charged as an accessory to such crime.

HISTORY: Add, L 2009, ch 507, § 21, eff Dec 15, 2010.

§ 187.05. Residential mortgage fraud in the fifth degree

A person is guilty of residential mortgage fraud in the fifth degree when he or she commits residential mortgage fraud.

Residential mortgage fraud in the fifth degree is a class A misdemeanor.

HISTORY: Add, L 2008, ch 472, § 19, eff Nov 1, 2008.

§ 187.10. Residential mortgage fraud in the fourth degree

A person is guilty of residential mortgage fraud in the fourth degree when he or she commits residential mortgage fraud and thereby receives proceeds or any other funds in the aggregate in excess of one thousand dollars.

Residential mortgage fraud in the fourth degree is a class E felony.

HISTORY: Add, L 2008, ch 472, § 19, eff Nov 1, 2008.

§ 187.15. Residential mortgage fraud in the third degree

A person is guilty of residential mortgage fraud in the third degree when he or she commits residential mortgage fraud and thereby receives proceeds or any other funds in the aggregate in excess of three thousand dollars.

Residential mortgage fraud in the third degree is a class D felony.

HISTORY: Add, L 2008, ch 472, § 19, eff Nov 1, 2008.

§ 187.20. Residential mortgage fraud in the second degree

A person is guilty of residential mortgage fraud in the second degree when he or she commits residential mortgage fraud and thereby receives proceeds or any other funds in the aggregate in excess of fifty thousand dollars.

Residential mortgage fraud in the second degree is a class C felony.

HISTORY: Add, L 2008, ch 472, § 19, eff Nov 1, 2008.

§ 187.25. Residential mortgage fraud in the first degree

A person is guilty of residential mortgage fraud in the first degree when he or she commits residential mortgage fraud and thereby receives proceeds or any other funds in the aggregate in excess of one million dollars.

Residential mortgage fraud in the first degree is a class B felony.

HISTORY: Add, L 2008, ch 472, § 19, eff Nov 1, 2008.

ARTICLE 190   OTHER FRAUDS

HISTORY: Add, L 1965, ch 1030, § 1, eff Sept 1, 1967.

§ 190.00. Issuing a bad check; definitions of terms

The following definitions are applicable to this article:

1. "Check" means any check, draft or similar sight order for the payment of money which is not post-dated with respect to the time of utterance.

2. "Drawer" of a check means a person whose name appears thereon as the primary obligor, whether the actual signature be that of himself or of a person purportedly authorized to draw the check in his behalf.

3. "Representative drawer" means a person who signs a check as drawer in a representative capacity or as agent of the person whose name appears thereon as the principal drawer or obligor.

4. "Utter." A person "utters" a check when, as a drawer or representative drawer thereof, he delivers it or causes it to be delivered to a person who thereby acquires a right against the drawer with respect to such check. One who draws a check with intent that it be so delivered is deemed to have uttered it if the delivery occurs.

5. "Pass." A person "passes" a check when, being a payee, holder or bearer of a check which previously has been or purports to have been drawn and uttered by another, he delivers it, for a purpose other than collection, to a third person who thereby acquires a right with respect thereto.

6. "Funds" means money or credit.

7. "Insufficient funds." A drawer has "insufficient funds" with a drawee to cover a check when he has no funds or account whatever, or funds in an amount less than that of the check; and a check dishonored for "no account" shall also be deemed to have been dishonored for "insufficient funds."

HISTORY: Add, L 1965, ch 1030, § 1, eff Sept 1, 1967.

§ 190.05. Issuing a bad check

A person is guilty of issuing a bad check when:

1. (a) As a drawer or representative drawer, he utters a check knowing that he or his principal, as the case may be, does not then have sufficient funds with the drawee to cover it, and (b) he

---

* The bracketed word has been inserted by the Publisher.

intends or believes at the time of utterance that payment will be refused by the drawee upon presentation, and (c) payment is refused by the drawee upon presentation; or

2. (a) He passes a check knowing that the drawer thereof does not then have sufficient funds with the drawee to cover it, and (b) he intends or believes at the time the check is passed that payment will be refused by the drawee upon presentation, and (c) payment is refused by the drawee upon presentation.

Issuing a bad check is a class B misdemeanor.

HISTORY: Add, L 1965, ch 1030, § 1, eff Sept 1, 1967, with substance derived from § 1292-a.

§ 190.10. Issuing a bad check; presumptions

1. When the drawer of a check has insufficient funds with the drawee to cover it at the time of utterance, the subscribing drawer or representative drawer, as the case may be, is presumed to know of such insufficiency.

2. A subscribing drawer or representative drawer, as the case may be, of an ultimately dishonored check is presumed to have intended or believed that the check would be dishonored upon presentation when:

(a) The drawer had no account with the drawee at the time of utterance; or

(b) (i) The drawer had insufficient funds with the drawee at the time of utterance, and (ii) the check was presented to the drawee for payment not more than thirty days after the date of utterance, and (iii) the drawer had insufficient funds with the drawee at the time of presentation.

3. Dishonor of a check by the drawee and insufficiency of the drawer's funds at the time of presentation may properly be proved by introduction in evidence of a notice of protest of the check, or of a certificate under oath of an authorized representative of the drawee declaring the dishonor and insufficiency, and such proof shall constitute presumptive evidence of such dishonor and insufficiency.

HISTORY: Add, L 1965, ch 1030, § 1, eff Sept 1, 1967, with substance derived from § 1292-a.

§ 190.15. Issuing a bad check; defenses

In any prosecution for issuing a bad check, it is an affirmative defense that:

1. The defendant or a person acting in his behalf made full satisfaction of the amount of the check within ten days after dishonor by the drawee; or

2. The defendant, in acting as a representative drawer, did so as an employee who, without personal benefit, merely executed the orders of his employer or of a superior officer or employee generally authorized to direct his activities.

HISTORY: Add, L 1965, ch 1030, § 1, eff Sept 1, 1967.

§ 190.20. False advertising

A person is guilty of false advertising when, with intent to promote the sale or to increase the consumption of property or services, he makes or causes to be made a false or misleading statement in any advertisement or publishes any advertisement in violation of chapter three of the act of congress entitled "Truth in Lending Act" and the regulations thereunder, as such act and regulations may from time to time be amended, addressed to the public or to a substantial number of persons; except that, in any prosecution under this section, it is an affirmative defense that the allegedly false or misleading statement was not knowingly or recklessly made or caused to be made.

False advertising is a class A misdemeanor.

> **HISTORY:** Add, L 1965, ch 1030, § 1, with substance derived from § 421; amd, L 1968, ch 1072, § 34, L 1969, ch 1141, § 14, eff July 1, 1969.

§ 190.23. False personation

A person is guilty of false personation when after being informed of the consequences of such act, he or she knowingly misrepresents his or her actual name, date of birth or address to a police officer or peace officer with intent to prevent such police officer or peace officer from ascertaining such information.

False personation is a class B misdemeanor.

> **HISTORY:** Add, L 1997, ch 69, § 1, eff Jan 1, 1998.

§ 190.25. Criminal impersonation in the second degree

A person is guilty of criminal impersonation in the second degree when he:

1. Impersonates another and does an act in such assumed character with intent to obtain a benefit or to injure or defraud another; or

2. Pretends to be a representative of some person or organization and does an act in such pretended capacity with intent to obtain a benefit or to injure or defraud another; or

3. (a) Pretends to be a public servant, or wears or displays without authority any uniform, badge, insignia or facsimile thereof by which such public servant is lawfully distinguished, or falsely expresses by his words or actions that he is a public servant or is acting with approval or authority of a public agency or department; and (b) so acts with intent to induce another to submit to such pretended official authority, to solicit funds or to otherwise cause another to act in reliance upon that pretense.

4. Impersonates another by communication by internet website or electronic means with intent to obtain a benefit or injure or defraud another, or by such communication pretends to be a public servant in order to induce another to submit to such authority or act in reliance on such pretense.

Criminal impersonation in the second degree is a class A misdemeanor.

> **HISTORY:** Add, L 1965, ch 1030, § 1, eff Sept 1, 1967, with substance derived from §§ 854, 928, 930, 931, 936-b, 942, 1278, 1846. Section heading, amd, L 1980, ch 27, § 1, eff Sept 1, 1980. Opening par, amd, L 1980, ch 27, § 1, eff Sept 1, 1980. Sub 3, amd, L 1980, ch 27, § 1, eff Sept 1, 1980. Sub 4, add, L 2008, ch 304, § 1, eff Nov 1, 2008. Closing par, amd, L 1980, ch 27, § 1, eff Sept 1, 1980.

§ 190.26. Criminal impersonation in the first degree

A person is guilty of criminal impersonation in the first degree when he:

1. Pretends to be a police officer or a federal law enforcement officer as enumerated in section 2.15 of the criminal procedure law, or wears or displays without authority, any uniform, badge or other insignia or facsimile thereof, by which such police officer or federal law enforcement officer is lawfully distinguished or expresses by his or her words or actions that he or she is acting with the approval or authority of any police department or acting as a federal law enforcement officer with the approval of any agency that employs federal law enforcement officers as enumerated in section 2.15 of the criminal procedure law; and

2. So acts with intent to induce another to submit to such pretended official authority or otherwise to act in reliance upon said pretense and in the course of such pretense commits or attempts to commit a felony; or

3. Pretending to be a duly licensed physician or other person authorized to issue a prescription for any drug or any instrument or device used in the taking or administering of drugs for which a prescription is required by law, communicates to a pharmacist an oral prescription which is required to be reduced to writing pursuant to section thirty-three hundred thirty-two of the public health law.

Criminal impersonation in the first degree is a class E felony.

HISTORY: Add, L 1980, ch 27, § 2; amd, L 1998, ch 2, § 41, eff Nov 1, 1998. Sub 1, amd, L 2008, ch 434, § 1, eff Nov 1, 2008. Sub 2, amd, L 1998, ch 2, § 41, eff Nov 1, 1998. Sub 3, add, L 1998, ch 2, § 41, eff Nov 1, 1998.

§ 190.27. Criminal sale of a police uniform

A person is guilty of criminal sale of a police uniform when he or she sells or offers for sale the uniform of any police officer to any person, unless presented with a valid photo identification card showing the purchaser to be a member of the police department which has authorized the requested uniform or an authorization to purchase specified uniforms signed by the police chief or the police commissioner of such police department accompanied by a personal photo identification. For purposes of this section, "police officer" shall include federal law enforcement officers, as defined in section 2.15 of the criminal procedure law; and "uniform" shall include all or any part of the uniform which identifies the wearer as a member of a police department, such as the uniform, shield, badge, numbers or other identifying insignias or emblems.

Criminal sale of a police uniform is a class A misdemeanor.

HISTORY: Add, L 1994, ch 99, § 1, eff Nov 1, 1994.

§ 190.30. Unlawfully concealing a will

A person is guilty of unlawfully concealing a will when, with intent to defraud, he conceals, secretes, suppresses, mutilates or destroys a will, codicil or other testamentary instrument.

Unlawfully concealing a will is a class E felony.

HISTORY: Add, L 1965, ch 1030, § 1, eff Sept 1, 1967, with substance derived from § 2052.

§ 190.35. Misconduct by corporate official

A person is guilty of misconduct by corporate official when:

1. Being a director of a stock corporation, he knowingly concurs in any vote or act of the directors of such corporation, or any of them, by which it is intended:

(a) To make a dividend except in the manner provided by law; or

(b) To divide, withdraw or in any manner pay to any stockholder any part of the capital stock of the corporation except in the manner provided by law; or

(c) To discount or receive any note or other evidence of debt in payment of an installment of capital stock actually called in and required to be paid, or with intent to provide the means of making such payment; or

(d) To receive or discount any note or other evidence of debt with intent to enable any stockholder to withdraw any part of the money paid in by him on his stock; or

(e) To apply any portion of the funds of such corporation, directly or indirectly, to the purchase of shares of its own stock, except in the manner provided by law; or

2. Being a director or officer of a stock corporation:

(a) He issues, participates in issuing, or concurs in a vote to issue any increase of its capital stock beyond the amount of the capital stock thereof, duly authorized by or in pursuance of law; or

(b) He sells, or agrees to sell, or is directly or indirectly interested in the sale of any share of stock of such corporation, or in any agreement to sell the same, unless at the time of such sale or agreement he is an actual owner of such share, provided that the foregoing shall not apply to a sale by or on behalf of an underwriter or dealer in connection with a bona fide public offering of shares of stock of such corporation.

Misconduct by corporate official is a class B misdemeanor.

HISTORY: Add, L 1965, ch 1030, § 1, with substance derived from § 664(1–6); amd, L 1967, ch 791, § 26, eff Sept 1, 1967. Section heading, amd, L 1967, ch 791, § 26, eff Sept 1, 1967. Sub 1, par (a), formerly par 1, so designated sub 1, par (a), L 1967, ch 791, § 26, eff Sept 1, 1967. Sub 1, par (b), formerly par 2, so designated sub 1, par (b), L 1967, ch 791, § 26, eff Sept 1, 1967. Sub 1, par (c), formerly par 3, so designated sub 1, par (c), L 1967, ch 791, § 26, eff Sept 1, 1967. Sub 1, par (d), formerly par 4, so designated sub 1, par (d), L 1967, ch 791, § 26, eff Sept 1, 1967. Sub 1, par (e), formerly par 5, so designated sub 1, par (e), L 1967, ch 791, § 26, eff Sept 1, 1967. Par 6, deleted, L 1967, ch 791, § 26, eff Sept 1, 1967. Sub 2, add, L 1967, ch 791, § 26, eff Sept 1, 1967.

§ 190.40. Criminal usury in the second degree

A person is guilty of criminal usury in the second degree when, not being authorized or permitted by law to do so, he knowingly charges, takes or receives any money or other property as interest on the loan or forbearance of any money or other property, at a rate exceeding twenty-five per centum per annum or the equivalent rate for a longer or shorter period.

Criminal usury in the second degree is a class E felony.

HISTORY: Add, L 1967, ch 791, § 27, with substance derived from § 2401; amd, L 1976, ch 424, § 1, eff Sept 1, 1976. Section heading, amd, L 1976, ch 424, § 1, eff Sept 1, 1976.

§ 190.42. Criminal usury in the first degree

A person is guilty of criminal usury in the first degree when, not being authorized or permitted by law to do so, he knowingly charges, takes or receives any money or other property as interest on the loan or forbearance of any money or other property, at a rate exceeding twenty-five per centum per annum or the equivalent rate for a longer or shorter period and either the actor had previously been convicted of the crime of criminal usury or of the attempt to commit such crime, or the actor's conduct was part of a scheme or business of making or collecting usurious loans.

Criminal usury in the first degree is a class C felony.

HISTORY: Add, L 1976, ch 424, § 2, eff Sept 1, 1976.

§ 190.45. Possession of usurious loan records

A person is guilty of possession of usurious loan records when, with knowledge of the contents thereof, he possesses any writing, paper, instrument or article used to record criminally usurious transactions prohibited by section 190.40.

Possession of usurious loan records is a class A misdemeanor.

HISTORY: Add, L 1967, ch 791, § 28, eff Sept 1, 1967, with substance derived from § 2403.

§ 190.50. Unlawful collection practices

A person is guilty of unlawful collection practices when, with intent to enforce a claim or judgment for money or property, he knowingly sends, mails or delivers to another person a notice, document or other instrument which has no judicial or official sanction and which in its format or appearance, simulates a summons, complaint, court order or process, or an insignia, seal or printed form of a federal, state or local government or an instrumentality thereof, or is otherwise calculated to induce a belief that such notice, document or instrument has a judicial or official sanction.

Unlawful collection practices is a class B misdemeanor.

> **HISTORY:** Add, L 1968, ch 739, § 1, eff Sept 1, 1968. Another § 190.50, add, L 1968, ch 1072, § amd, L 1969, ch 1141, § 15; renumbered § 190.55, L 1982, ch 674, § 1, eff July 22, 1982.

§ 190.55. Making a false statement of credit terms

A person is guilty of making a false statement of credit terms when he knowingly and willfully violates the provisions of chapter two of the act of congress entitled "Truth in Lending Act" and the regulations thereunder, as such act and regulations may from time to time be amended, by understating or failing to state the interest rate required to be disclosed, or by failing to make or by making a false or inaccurate or incomplete statement of other credit terms in violation of such act.

Making a false statement of credit terms is a class A misdemeanor.

> **HISTORY:** Added as § 190.50, L 1968, ch 1072, § 35; amd, L 1969, ch 1141, § 15; renumbered § 190.55, L 1982, ch 674, § 1, eff July 22, 1982.

§ 190.60. Scheme to defraud in the second degree

1. A person is guilty of a scheme to defraud in the second degree when he engages in a scheme constituting a systematic ongoing course of conduct with intent to defraud more than one person or to obtain property from more than one person by false or fraudulent pretenses, representations or promises, and so obtains property from one or more of such persons.

2. In any prosecution under this section, it shall be necessary to prove the identity of at least one person from whom the defendant so obtained property, but it shall not be necessary to prove the identity of any other intended victim.

Scheme to defraud in the second degree is a class A misdemeanor.

> **HISTORY:** Add, L 1976, ch 384, § 1; amd, L 1992, ch 491, § 5, eff Nov 1, 1992. Sub 1, amd, L 1992, ch 491, § 5, L 1993, ch 171, § 3, L 1996, ch 357, § 3, eff Nov 1, 1996.

§ 190.65. Scheme to defraud in the first degree

1. A person is guilty of a scheme to defraud in the first degree when he or she: (a) engages in a scheme constituting a systematic ongoing course of conduct with intent to defraud ten or more persons or to obtain property from ten or more persons by false or fraudulent pretenses, representations or promises, and so obtains property from one or more of such persons; or (b) engages in a scheme constituting a systematic ongoing course of conduct with intent to defraud more than one person or to obtain property from more than one person by false or fraudulent pretenses, representations or promises, and so obtains property with a value in excess of one thousand dollars from one or more such persons; or (c) engages in a scheme constituting a systematic ongoing course of conduct with intent to defraud more than one person, more than one of whom is a vulnerable elderly person as defined in subdivision three of section 260.30 of this chapter or to obtain property from more than one person, more than one of whom is a vulnerable elderly person as defined in subdivision three of section 260.30 of this chapter, by false or fraudulent pretenses, representations or promises, and so obtains property from one or more such persons.

2. In any prosecution under this section, it shall be necessary to prove the identity of at least one

person from whom the defendant so obtained property, but it shall not be necessary to prove the identity of any other intended victim, provided that in any prosecution under paragraph (c) of subdivision one of this section, it shall be necessary to prove the identity of at least one such vulnerable elderly person as defined in subdivision three of section 260.30 of this chapter.

Scheme to defraud in the first degree is a class E felony.

> **HISTORY:** Add, L 1976, ch 384, § 1, eff Jan 1, 1977. Amd, L 2008, ch 291, § 1, eff Sept 19, 2008. Sub 1, amd, L 1986, ch 515, § 10, eff Nov 1, 1986. Sub 1, amd, L 2008, ch 291, § 1, eff Sept 19, 2008. Sub 2, amd, L 2008, ch 291, § 1, eff Sept 19, 2008. Sub 2, first undesignated par, amd, L 2008, ch 291, § 1, eff Sept 19, 2008.

§ 190.70. Scheme to defraud the state by unlawfully selling prescriptions

A person is guilty of a scheme to defraud the state by unlawfully selling prescriptions when he or she engages, with intent to defraud the state, in a scheme constituting a systematic, ongoing course of conduct to make, sell, deliver for sale or offer for sale one or more prescriptions and so obtains goods or services from the state with a value in excess of one thousand dollars or causes the state to reimburse another in excess of one thousand dollars for the delivery of such goods or services.

Scheme to defraud the state by unlawfully selling prescriptions is a class A misdemeanor.

> **HISTORY:** Add, L 1992, ch 41, § 112, eff April 2, 1992.

§ 190.72. Unauthorized radio transmission

A person is guilty of an unauthorized radio transmission when such person knowingly makes or causes to be made a radio transmission in this state, on a radio frequency assigned and licensed by the federal communications commission for use by amplitude modulation (AM) radio stations between the frequencies of five hundred thirty kilohertz (kHz) to seventeen hundred kilohertz (kHz), or frequency modulation (FM) radio stations between the frequencies of eighty-eight megahertz (MHz) to one hundred eight megahertz (MHz), without authorization or having first obtained a license from the federal communications commission or duly authorized federal agency, in violation of federal law.

Unauthorized radio transmission is a class A misdemeanor.

> **HISTORY:** Add, L 2011, ch 361, § 1, eff Jan 30, 2012.

§ 190.75. Criminal use of an access device in the second degree

A person is guilty of criminal use of an access device in the second degree when he knowingly uses an access device without consent of an owner thereof with intent to unlawfully obtain telecommunications services on behalf of himself or a third person. As used in this section, access device shall have the meaning set forth in subdivision seven-c of section 155.00 of this chapter.

Criminal use of an access device in the second degree is a class A misdemeanor.

> **HISTORY:** Add, L 1996, ch 357, § 6, eff Nov 1, 1996.

§ 190.76. Criminal use of an access device in the first degree

A person is guilty of criminal use of an access device in the first degree when he knowingly uses an access device without consent of an owner thereof with intent to unlawfully obtain telecommunications services on behalf of himself or a third person, and so obtains such services with a value in excess of one thousand dollars. As used in this section, access device shall have the meaning set forth in subdivision seven-c of section 155.00 of this chapter.

Criminal use of an access device in the first degree is a class E felony.

> **HISTORY:** Add, L 1996, ch 357, § 6, eff Nov 1, 1996.

§ 190.77. Offenses involving theft of identity; definitions

1. [As amended L 2008, chs 226 and 279] For the purposes of sections 190.78, 190.79 and 190.80-a and 190.85 of this article "personal identifying information" means a person's name, address, telephone number, date of birth, driver's license number, social security number, place of employment, mother's maiden name, financial services account number or code, savings account number or code, checking account number or code, brokerage account number or code, credit card account number or code, debit card number or code, automated teller machine number or code, taxpayer identification number, computer system password, signature or copy of a signature, electronic signature, unique biometric data that is a fingerprint, voice print, retinal image or iris image of another person, telephone calling card number, mobile identification number or code, electronic serial number or personal identification number, or any other name, number, code or information that may be used alone or in conjunction with other such information to assume the identity of another person.

2. For the purposes of sections 190.78, 190.79, 190.80, 190.80-a, 190.81, 190.82 and 190.83 of this article:

a. "electronic signature" shall have the same meaning as defined in subdivision three of section three hundred two of the state technology law.

b. "personal identification number" means any number or code which may be used alone or in conjunction with any other information to assume the identity of another person or access financial resources or credit of another person.

c. "member of the armed forces" shall mean a person in the military service of the United States or the military service of the state, including but not limited to, the armed forces of the United States, the army national guard, the air national guard, the New York naval militia, the New York guard, and such additional forces as may be created by the federal or state government as authorized by law.

HISTORY: Add, L 2002, ch 619, § 3, eff Nov 1, 2002; amd, L 2008, ch 226, § 1, eff Nov 4, 2008. Sub 1, amd, L 2008, ch 226, § 1, eff Nov 4, 2008, L 2008, ch 279, § 8, eff Nov 1, 2008. Sub 2, opening par, amd, L 2008, ch 226, § 1, eff Nov 4, 2008. Sub 2, par a, amd, L 2005, ch 741, § 6, eff Oct 18, 2005. Sub 2, par c, add, L 2008, ch 226, § 1, eff Nov 4, 2008.

§ 190.78. Identity theft in the third degree

A person is guilty of identity theft in the third degree when he or she knowingly and with intent to defraud assumes the identity of another person by presenting himself or herself as that other person, or by acting as that other person or by using personal identifying information of that other person, and thereby:

1. obtains goods, money, property or services or uses credit in the name of such other person or causes financial loss to such person or to another person or persons; or

2. commits a class A misdemeanor or higher level crime.

Identity theft in the third degree is a class A misdemeanor.

HISTORY: Add, L 2002, ch 619, § 3, eff Nov 1, 2002.

§ 190.79. Identity theft in the second degree

A person is guilty of identify [identity]* theft in the second degree when he or she knowingly

---

* The bracketed word has been inserted by the Publisher.

and with intent to defraud assumes the identity of another person by presenting himself or herself as that other person, or by acting as that other person or by using personal identifying information of that other person, and thereby:

    1. obtains goods, money, property or services or uses credit in the name of such other person in an aggregate amount that exceeds five hundred dollars; or

    2. causes financial loss to such person or to another person or persons in an aggregate amount that exceeds five hundred dollars; or

    3. commits or attempts to commit a felony or acts as an accessory to the commission of a felony; or

    4. commits the crime of identity theft in the third degree as defined in section 190.78 of this article and has been previously convicted within the last five years of identity theft in the third degree as defined in section 190.78, identity theft in the second degree as defined in this section, identity theft in the first degree as defined in section 190.80, unlawful possession of personal identification information in the third degree as defined in section 190.81, unlawful possession of personal identification information in the second degree as defined in section 190.82, unlawful possession of personal identification information in the first degree as defined in section 190.83, unlawful possession of a skimmer device in the second degree as defined in section 190.85, unlawful possession of a skimmer device in the first degree as defined in section 190.86, grand larceny in the fourth degree as defined in section 155.30, grand larceny in the third degree as defined in section 155.35, grand larceny in the second degree as defined in section 155.40 or grand larceny in the first degree as defined in section 155.42 of this chapter.

Identity theft in the second degree is a class E felony.

    HISTORY: Add, L 2002, ch 619, § 3, eff Nov 1, 2002. Sub 4, amd, L 2008, ch 279, § 11, eff Nov 1, 2008.

§ 190.80. Identity theft in the first degree

A person is guilty of identity theft in the first degree when he or she knowingly and with intent to defraud assumes the identity of another person by presenting himself or herself as that other person, or by acting as that other person or by using personal identifying information of that other person, and thereby:

    1. obtains goods, money, property or services or uses credit in the name of such other person in an aggregate amount that exceeds two thousand dollars; or

    2. causes financial loss to such person or to another person or persons in an aggregate amount that exceeds two thousand dollars; or

    3. commits or attempts to commit a class D felony or higher level crime or acts as an accessory in the commission of a class D or higher level felony; or

    4. commits the crime of identity theft in the second degree as defined in section 190.79 of this article and has been previously convicted within the last five years of identity theft in the third degree as defined in section 190.78, identity theft in the second degree as defined in section 190.79, identity theft in the first degree as defined in this section, unlawful possession of personal identification information in the third degree as defined in section 190.81, unlawful possession of personal identification information in the second degree as defined in section 190.82, unlawful possession of personal identification information in the first degree as defined in section 190.83, unlawful possession of a skimmer device in the second degree as defined in section 190.85, unlawful possession of a skimmer device in the first degree as defined in section

190.86, grand larceny in the fourth degree as defined in section 155.30, grand larceny in the third degree as defined in section 155.35, grand larceny in the second degree as defined in section 155.40 or grand larceny in the first degree as defined in section 155.42 of this chapter.

Identity theft in the first degree is a class D felony.

HISTORY: Add, L 2002, ch 619, § 3, eff Nov 1, 2002. Sub 4, amd, L 2008, ch 279, § 12, eff Nov 1, 2008.

§ 190.80-a. Aggravated identity theft

A person is guilty of aggravated identity theft when he or she knowingly and with intent to defraud assumes the identity of another person by presenting himself or herself as that other person, or by acting as that other person or by using personal identifying information of that other person, and knows that such person is a member of the armed forces, and knows that such member is presently deployed outside of the continental United States and:

1. thereby obtains goods, money, property or services or uses credit in the name of such member of the armed forces in an aggregate amount that exceeds five hundred dollars; or

2. thereby causes financial loss to such member of the armed forces in an aggregate amount that exceeds five hundred dollars.

Aggravated identity theft is a class D felony.

HISTORY: Add, L 2008, ch 226, § 2, eff Nov 4, 2008.

§ 190.81. Unlawful possession of personal identification information in the third degree

A person is guilty of unlawful possession of personal identification information in the third degree when he or she knowingly possesses a person's financial services account number or code, savings account number or code, checking account number or code, brokerage account number or code, credit card account number or code, debit card number or code, automated teller machine number or code, personal identification number, mother's maiden name, computer system password, electronic signature or unique biometric data that is a fingerprint, voice print, retinal image or iris image of another person knowing such information is intended to be used in furtherance of the commission of a crime defined in this chapter.

Unlawful possession of personal identification information in the third degree is a class A misdemeanor.

HISTORY: Add, L 2002, ch 619, § 3, eff Nov 1, 2002.

§ 190.82. Unlawful possession of personal identification information in the second degree

A person is guilty of unlawful possession of personal identification information in the second degree when he or she knowingly possesses two hundred fifty or more items of personal identification information of the following nature: a person's financial services account number or code, savings account number or code, checking account number or code, brokerage account number or code, credit card account number or code, debit card number or code, automated teller machine number or code, personal identification number, mother's maiden name, computer system password, electronic signature or unique biometric data that is a fingerprint, voice print, retinal image or iris image of another person knowing such information is intended to be used in furtherance of the commission of a crime defined in this chapter.

Unlawful possession of personal identification information in the second degree is a class E felony.

HISTORY: Add, L 2002, ch 619, § 3, eff Nov 1, 2002.

§ 190.83. Unlawful possession of personal identification information in the first degree

A person is guilty of unlawful possession of personal identification information in the first degree when he or she commits the crime of unlawful possession of personal identification information in the second degree and:

1. with intent to further the commission of identity theft in the second degree, he or she supervises more than three accomplices; or

2. [As amended L 2008, chs 226 and 279] he or she has been previously convicted within the last five years of identity theft in the third degree as defined in section 190.78, identity theft in the second degree as defined in section 190.79, identity theft in the first degree as defined in section 190.80, unlawful possession of personal identification information in the third degree as defined in section 190.81, unlawful possession of personal identification information in the second degree as defined in section 190.82, unlawful possession of personal identification information in the first degree as defined in this section, unlawful possession of a skimmer device in the second degree as defined in section 190.85, unlawful possession of a skimmer device in the first degree as defined in section 190.86, grand larceny in the fourth degree as defined in section 155.30, grand larceny in the third degree as defined in section 155.35, grand larceny in the second degree as defined in section 155.40 or grand larceny in the first degree as defined in section 155.42 of this chapter; or

3. with intent to further the commission of identity theft in the second degree:

(a) he or she supervises more than two accomplices, and

(b) he or she knows that the person whose personal identification information that he or she possesses is a member of the armed forces, and

(c) he or she knows that such member of the armed forces is presently deployed outside of the continental United States.

Unlawful possession of personal identification information in the first degree is a class D felony.

HISTORY: Add, L 2002, ch 619, § 3, eff Nov 1, 2002; amd, L 2008, ch 226, § 3, eff Nov 4, 2008. Sub 2, amd, L 2008, ch 226, § 3, eff Nov 4, 2008, L 2008, ch 279, § 13, eff Nov 1, 2008. Sub 3, add, L 2008, ch 226, § 3, eff Nov 4, 2008.

§ 190.84. Defenses

In any prosecution for identity theft or unlawful possession of personal identification information pursuant to this article, it shall be an affirmative defense that the person charged with the offense:

1. was under twenty-one years of age at the time of committing the offense and the person used or possessed the personal identifying or identification information of another solely for the purpose of purchasing alcohol;

2. was under eighteen years of age at the time of committing the offense and the person used or possessed the personal identifying or identification information of another solely for the purpose of purchasing tobacco products; or

3. used or possessed the personal identifying or identification information of another person solely for the purpose of misrepresenting the person's age to gain access to a place the access to which is restricted based on age.

HISTORY: Add, L 2002, ch 619, § 3, eff Nov 1, 2002.

§ 190.85. Unlawful possession of a skimmer device in the second degree

1. A person is guilty of unlawful possession of a skimmer device in the second degree when he or she possesses a skimmer device with the intent that such device be used in furtherance of the commission of the crime of identity theft or unlawful possession of personal identification information as defined in this article.

2. For purposes of this article, "skimmer device" means a device designed or adapted to obtain personal identifying information from a credit card, debit card, public benefit card, access card or device, or other card or device that contains personal identifying information.

Unlawful possession of a skimmer device in the second degree is a class A misdemeanor.

HISTORY: Add, L 2008, ch 279, § 9, eff Nov 1, 2008.

§ 190.86. Unlawful possession of a skimmer device in the first degree

A person is guilty of unlawful possession of a skimmer device in the first degree when he or she commits the crime of unlawful possession of a skimmer device in the second degree and he or she has been previously convicted within the last five years of identity theft in the third degree as defined in section 190.78, identity theft in the second degree as defined in section 190.79, identity theft in the first degree as defined in section 190.80, unlawful possession of personal identification information in the third degree as defined in section 190.81, unlawful possession of personal identification information in the second degree as defined in section 190.82, unlawful possession of personal identification information in the first degree as defined in section 190.83, unlawful possession of a skimmer device in the second degree as defined in section 190.85, unlawful possession of a skimmer device in the first degree as defined in this section, grand larceny in the fourth degree as defined in section 155.30, grand larceny in the third degree as defined in section 155.35, grand larceny in the second degree as defined in section 155.40 or grand larceny in the first degree as defined in section 155.42 of this chapter.

Unlawful possession of a skimmer device in the first degree is a class E felony.

HISTORY: Add, L 2008, ch 279, § 10, eff Nov 1, 2008.

§ 190.87. [Eff Feb 2, 2015] Immigrant assistant [assistance]* services fraud in the second degree

A person is guilty of immigrant assistance services fraud in the second degree when, with intent to defraud another person seeking immigrant assistance services, as defined in article twenty-eight-C of the general business law, from such person, he or she violates section four hundred sixty-d of the general business law with intent to obtain property from such other person by false or fraudulent pretenses, representations or promises, and thereby wrongfully obtains such property.

Immigrant assistance services fraud in the second degree is a class A misdemeanor.

HISTORY: Add, L 2014, ch 206, § 7, eff Feb 2, 2015.

§ 190.89. [Eff Feb 2, 2015] Immigrant assistance services fraud in the first degree.

A person is guilty of immigrant assistance services fraud in the first degree when, with intent to defraud another person seeking immigrant assistance services, as defined in article twenty-eight-C of the general business law, from such person, he or she violates section four hundred sixty-d of the general business law with intent to obtain property from such other person by false or fraudulent pretenses, representations or promises, and thereby wrongfully obtains such property with a value in excess of one thousand dollars.

Immigrant assistance services fraud in the first degree is a class E felony.

---

* The bracketed word has been inserted by the Publisher.

HISTORY: Add, L 2014, ch 206, § 7, eff Feb 2, 2015.

TITLE L   Offenses Against Public Administration

ARTICLE 195
OFFICIAL MISCONDUCT AND OBSTRUCTION OF PUBLIC SERVANTS GENERALLY

ARTICLE 200
BRIBERY INVOLVING PUBLIC SERVANTS AND RELATED OFFENSES

ARTICLE 205
ESCAPE AND OTHER OFFENSES RELATING TO CUSTODY

ARTICLE 210
PERJURY AND RELATED OFFENSES

ARTICLE 215
OTHER OFFENSES RELATING TO JUDICIAL AND OTHER PROCEEDINGS

HISTORY: Add, L 1965, ch 1030, § 1, eff Sept 1, 1967.

ARTICLE 195   OFFICIAL MISCONDUCT AND OBSTRUCTION OF PUBLIC SERVANTS GENERALLY

HISTORY: Add, L 1965, ch 1030, § 1, eff Sept 1, 1967.

§ 195.00. Official misconduct

A public servant is guilty of official misconduct when, with intent to obtain a benefit or deprive another person of a benefit:

1. He commits an act relating to his office but constituting an unauthorized exercise of his official functions, knowing that such act is unauthorized; or

2. He knowingly refrains from performing a duty which is imposed upon him by law or is clearly inherent in the nature of his office.

Official misconduct is a class A misdemeanor.

HISTORY: Add, L 1965, ch 1030, § 1, with substance derived from §§ 373, 461, 462, 489, 854, 997, 1231, 1792, 1830, 1839, 1840–1844, 1847, 1857, 1862–1867, 1869, 1874–1876; amd, L 1990, ch 906, § 1, eff Nov 1, 1990. Opening par, amd, L 1990, ch 906, § 1, eff Nov 1, 1990.

§ 195.05. Obstructing governmental administration in the second degree

A person is guilty of obstructing governmental administration when he intentionally obstructs, impairs or perverts the administration of law or other governmental function or prevents or attempts to prevent a public servant from performing an official function, by means of intimidation, physical force or interference, or by means of any independently unlawful act, or by means of interfering, whether or not physical force is involved, with radio, telephone, television or other telecommunications systems owned or operated by the state, or a county, city, town, village, fire district or emergency medical service or by means of releasing a dangerous animal under circumstances evincing the actor's intent that the animal obstruct governmental administration.

Obstructing governmental administration is a class A misdemeanor.

HISTORY: Add, L 1965, ch 1030, § 1, with substance derived from §§ 196, 490, 1320, 1322, 1824, 1825, 1851; amd, L 1984, ch 956, § 1, L 1998, ch 269, § 2, eff Nov 1, 1998. First undesignated par, amd, L 1998, ch 269, § 2, eff Nov 1, 1998.

§ 195.06. Killing or injuring a police animal

A person is guilty of killing or injuring a police animal when such person intentionally kills or injures any animal while such animal is in the performance of its duties and under the supervision of a police or peace officer.

Killing or injuring a police animal is a class A misdemeanor.

HISTORY: Add, L 1986, ch 42, § 1, eff Nov 1, 1986.

§ 195.06-a. Killing a police work dog or police work horse

A person is guilty of killing a police work dog or police work horse when such person intentionally kills a police work dog or police work horse while such dog or horse is in the performance of its duties and under the supervision of a police officer. For purposes of this section, "police work dog" or "police work horse," as the case may be, shall mean any dog or horse owned or harbored by any state or municipal police department or any state or federal law enforcement agency, which has been trained to aid law enforcement officers and is actually being used for police work purposes.

Killing a police work dog or police work horse is a class E felony.

HISTORY: Add, L 2013, ch 162, § 1, eff Nov 1, 2013.

§ 195.07. Obstructing governmental administration in the first degree

A person is guilty of obstructing governmental administration in the first degree when he commits the crime of obstructing governmental administration in the second degree by means of interfering with a telecommunications system thereby causing serious physical injury to another person.

Obstructing governmental administration in the first degree is a class E felony.

HISTORY: Add, L 1984, ch 956, § 2, eff Nov 1, 1984.

§ 195.08. Obstructing governmental administration by means of a self-defense spray device

A person is guilty of obstructing governmental administration by means of a self-defense spray device when, with the intent to prevent a police officer or peace officer from performing a lawful duty, he causes temporary physical impairment to a police officer or peace officer by intentionally discharging a self-defense spray device, as defined in paragraph fourteen of subdivision a of section 265.20 of this chapter, thereby causing such temporary physical impairment.

Obstructing governmental administration by means of a self-defense spray device is a class D felony.

HISTORY: Add, L 1996, ch 354, § 1, eff Nov 1, 1996.

§ 195.10. Refusing to aid a peace or a police officer

A person is guilty of refusing to aid a peace or a police officer when, upon command by a peace or a police officer identifiable or identified to him as such, he unreasonably fails or refuses to aid such peace or a police officer in effecting an arrest, or in preventing the commission by another person of any offense.

Refusing to aid a peace or a police officer is a class B misdemeanor.

HISTORY: Add, L 1965, ch 1030, § 1, with substance derived from §§ 1848, 2095; amd, L 1980, ch 843, § 40, eff Sept 1, 1980. Section heading, amd, L 1980, ch 843, § 40, eff Sept 1, 1980.

§ 195.11. Harming an animal trained to aid a person with a disability in the second degree

A person is guilty of harming an animal trained to aid a person with a disability in the second degree when such person intentionally causes physical injury to such animal while it is in the performance of aiding a person with a disability, and thereby renders such animal incapable of providing such aid to such person, or to another person with a disability.

For purposes of this section and section 195.12 of this article, the term "disability" means "disability" as defined in subdivision twenty-one of section two hundred ninety-two of the executive law.

Harming an animal trained to aid a person with a disability in the second degree is a class B misdemeanor.

HISTORY: Add, L 1989, ch 344, § 1, eff Nov 1, 1989.

§ 195.12. Harming an animal trained to aid a person with a disability in the first degree

A person is guilty of harming an animal trained to aid a person with a disability in the first degree when such person:

    1. intentionally causes physical injury to such animal while it is in the performance of aiding a person with a disability, and thereby renders such animal permanently incapable of providing such aid to such person, or to another person with a disability; or

    2. intentionally kills such animal while it is in the performance of aiding a person with a disability.

Harming an animal trained to aid a person with a disability in the first degree is a class A misdemeanor.

HISTORY: Add, L 1989, ch 344, § 1, eff Nov 1, 1989.

§ 195.15. Obstructing firefighting operations

A person is guilty of obstructing firefighting operations when he intentionally and unreasonably obstructs the efforts of any:

    1. fireman, in extinguishing a fire, or prevents or dissuades another from extinguishing or helping to extinguish a fire; or

    2. fireman, police officer or peace officer in performing his duties in circumstances involving an imminent danger created by an explosion, threat of explosion or the presence of toxic fumes or gases.

Obstructing firefighting operations is a class A misdemeanor.

HISTORY: Add, L 1965, ch 1030, § 1, with substance derived from §§ 1906(4), 1914; amd, L 1969, ch 314, § 1, L 1981, ch 731, § 1, eff Sept 1, 1981. Sub 1, formerly part of first par, so designated and amd, L 1981, ch 731, § 1, eff Sept 1, 1981. Sub 2, add, L 1981, ch 731, § 1, eff Sept 1, 1981.

§ 195.16. Obstructing emergency medical services

A person is guilty of obstructing emergency medical services when he or she intentionally and unreasonably obstructs the efforts of any service, technician, personnel, system or unit specified in section three thousand one of the public health law in the performance of their duties.

Obstructing emergency medical services is a class A misdemeanor.

HISTORY: Add, L 2003, ch 600, § 1, eff Nov 1, 2003.

§ 195.17. Obstruction of governmental duties by means of a bomb, destructive device, explosive, or hazardous substance

A person is guilty of obstruction of governmental duties by means of a bomb, destructive device, explosive, or hazardous substance when he or she, in furtherance of a felony offense, knowingly and unlawfully installs or causes to be installed a bomb, destructive device, explosive, or hazardous substance, in any object, place, or compartment that is subject to a search so as to obstruct, prevent, hinder or delay the administration of law or performance of a government function.

Obstruction of governmental duties by means of a bomb, destructive device, explosive, or hazardous substance is a class D felony.

HISTORY: Add, L 2011, ch 327, § 1, eff Nov 1, 2011.

§ 195.20. Defrauding the government

A person is guilty of defrauding the government when, being a public servant or party officer, he or she:

(a) engages in a scheme constituting a systematic ongoing course of conduct with intent to:

(i) defraud the state or a political subdivision of the state or a governmental instrumentality within the state or to obtain property, services or other resources from the state or a political subdivision of the state or a governmental instrumentality within the state by false or fraudulent pretenses, representations or promises; or

(ii) defraud the state or a political subdivision of the state or a governmental instrumentality within the state by making use of property, services or resources of the state, political subdivision of the state or a governmental instrumentality within the state for private business purposes or other compensated non-governmental purposes; and

(b) so obtains property, services or other resources with a value in excess of one thousand dollars from such state, political subdivision or governmental instrumentality.

Defrauding the government is a class E felony.

HISTORY: Add, L 1986, ch 833, § 1, eff Nov 1, 1986. Amd, L 2010, ch 1, § 2, eff Feb 12, 2010. Opening par, amd, L 2010, ch 1, § 2, eff Feb 12, 2010. Sub (a), redesignated sub (a), opening par and sub (a), par (i), L 2010, ch 1, § 2, eff Feb 12, 2010. Sub (a), opening par, formerly part of sub (a), so designated sub (a), opening par and amd, L 2010, ch 1, § 2, eff Feb 12, 2010. Sub (a), par (i), formerly part of sub (a), so designated sub (a), par (i) and amd, L 2010, ch 1, § 2, eff Feb 12, 2010. Sub (a), par (ii), add, L 2010, ch 1, § 2, eff Feb 12, 2010. Sub (b), amd, L 2010, ch 1, § 2, eff Feb 12, 2010.

ARTICLE 200   BRIBERY INVOLVING PUBLIC SERVANTS AND RELATED OFFENSES

HISTORY: Add, L 1965, ch 1030, § 1, eff Sept 1, 1967.

§ 200.00. Bribery in the third degree

A person is guilty of bribery in the third degree when he confers, or offers or agrees to confer, any benefit upon a public servant upon an agreement or understanding that such public servant's vote, opinion, judgment, action, decision or exercise of discretion as a public servant will thereby be influenced.

Bribery in the third degree is a class D felony.

HISTORY: Add, L 1965, ch 1030, § 1, with substance derived from §§ 371, 378, 465, 1233(1), 1822; amd, L 1973, ch 276, § 21, L 1986, ch 833, § 2, eff Nov 1, 1986. Section heading, amd, L 1973, ch 276, § 21, L 1986, ch 833, § 2, eff Nov 1, 1986.

§ 200.03. Bribery in the second degree

A person is guilty of bribery in the second degree when he confers, or offers or agrees to confer, any benefit valued in excess of five thousand dollars upon a public servant upon an agreement or understanding that such public servant's vote, opinion, judgment, action, decision or exercise of discretion as a public servant will thereby be influenced.

Bribery in the second degree is a class C felony.

HISTORY: Add, L 1986, ch 833, § 3, eff Nov 1, 1986; amd, L 2014, ch 55, § 18 (Part H, Subpart A), eff April 30, 2014.

§ 200.04. Bribery in the first degree

A person is guilty of bribery in the first degree when the person confers, or offers or agrees to confer: (1) any benefit upon a public servant upon an agreement or understanding that such public servant's vote, opinion, judgment, action, decision or exercise of discretion as a public servant will thereby be influenced in the investigation, arrest, detention, prosecution or incarceration of any person for the commission or alleged commission of a class A felony defined in article two hundred twenty of this part or an attempt to commit any such class A felony; or (2) any benefit valued in excess of one hundred thousand dollars upon a public servant upon an agreement or understanding that such public servant's vote, opinion, judgment, action, decision or exercise of discretion as a public servant will thereby be influenced.

Bribery in the first degree is a class B felony.

> **HISTORY:** Add, L 1973, ch 276, § 21, eff Sept 1, 1973; amd, L 2014, ch 55, § 19 (Part H, Subpart A), eff April 30, 2014.

§ 200.05. Bribery; defense

In any prosecution for bribery, it is a defense that the defendant conferred or agreed to confer the benefit involved upon the public servant involved as a result of conduct of the latter constituting larceny committed by means of extortion, or an attempt to commit the same, or coercion, or an attempt to commit coercion.

> **HISTORY:** Add, L 1965, ch 1030, § 1, eff Sept 1, 1967.

§ 200.10. Bribe receiving in the third degree

A public servant is guilty of bribe receiving in the third degree when he or she solicits, accepts or agrees to accept any benefit from another person upon an agreement or understanding that his or her vote, opinion, judgment, action, decision or exercise of discretion as a public servant will thereby be influenced.

Bribe receiving in the third degree is a class D felony.

> **HISTORY:** Add, L 1965, ch 1030, § 1, with substance derived from §§ 372, 374, 465, 1233(3), 1823, 1826, 1829, 1833, 1839(1); amd, L 1973, ch 276, § 21, L 1986, ch 833, § 2, eff Nov 1, 1986, L 2014, ch 55, § 21 (Part H, Subpart A), eff April 20, 2014.

§ 200.11. Bribe receiving in the second degree

A public servant is guilty of bribe receiving in the second degree when he or she solicits, accepts or agrees to accept any benefit valued in excess of five thousand dollars from another person upon an agreement or understanding that his or her vote, opinion, judgment, action, decision or exercise of discretion as a public servant will thereby be influenced.

Bribe receiving in the second degree is a class C felony.

> **HISTORY:** Add, L 1986, ch 833, § 3, eff Nov 1, 1986; amd, L 2014, ch 55, § 22 (Part H, Subpart A), eff April 30, 2014.

§ 200.12. Bribe receiving in the first degree

A public servant is guilty of bribe receiving in the first degree when he or she solicits, accepts or agrees to accept: (a) any benefit from another person upon an agreement or understanding that his or her vote, opinion, judgment, action, decision or exercise of discretion as a public servant will thereby be influenced in the investigation, arrest, detention, prosecution or incarceration of any person for the commission or alleged commission of a class A felony defined in article two hundred twenty of this part or an attempt to commit any such class A felony; or (b) any benefit valued in excess of one hundred thousand dollars from another person upon an agreement or understanding that such public servant's vote, opinion, judgment, action, decision or exercise of discretion as a public servant will thereby be influenced.

Bribe receiving in the first degree is a class B felony.

> **HISTORY:** Add, L 1973, ch 276, § 21, eff Sept 1, 1973; amd, L 2014, ch 55, § 23 (Part H, Subpart A), eff April 30, 2014.

§ 200.15. Bribe receiving; no defense

1. The crimes of (a) bribe receiving, and (b) larceny committed by means of extortion, attempt to commit the same, coercion and attempt to commit coercion, are not mutually exclusive, and it is no defense to a prosecution for bribe receiving that, by reason of the same conduct, the defendant also committed one of such other specified crimes.

2. It is no defense to a prosecution pursuant to the provisions of this article that the public servant did not have power or authority to perform the act or omission for which the alleged bribe, gratuity or reward was given.

> **HISTORY:** Add, L 1965, ch 1030, § 1, eff Sept 1, 1967. Sub 1, formerly entire section, so designated sub 1, L 1986, ch 834, § 1, eff Aug 2, 1986. Sub 2, add, L 1986, ch 834, § 1, eff Aug 2, 1986.

§ 200.20. Rewarding official misconduct in the second degree

A person is guilty of rewarding official misconduct in the second degree when he knowingly confers, or offers or agrees to confer, any benefit upon a public servant for having violated his duty as a public servant.

Rewarding official misconduct in the second degree is a class E felony.

> **HISTORY:** Add, L 1965, ch 1030, § 1; amd, L 1973, ch 276, § 21, eff Sept 1, 1973. Section heading, amd, L 1973, ch 276, § 21, eff Sept 1, 1973.

§ 200.22. Rewarding official misconduct in the first degree

A person is guilty of rewarding official misconduct in the first degree when he knowingly confers, or offers or agrees to confer, any benefit upon a public servant for having violated his duty as a public servant in the investigation, arrest, detention, prosecution, or incarceration of any person for the commission or alleged commission of a class A felony defined in article two hundred twenty of the penal law or the attempt to commit any such class A felony.

Rewarding official misconduct in the first degree is a class C felony.

> **HISTORY:** Add, L 1973, ch 276, § 21, eff Sept 1, 1973.

§ 200.25. Receiving reward for official misconduct in the second degree

A public servant is guilty of receiving reward for official misconduct in the second degree when he solicits, accepts or agrees to accept any benefit from another person for having violated his duty as a public servant.

Receiving reward for official misconduct in the second degree is a class E felony.

> **HISTORY:** Add, L 1965, ch 1030, § 1; amd, L 1973, ch 276, § 21, eff Sept 1, 1973. Section heading, amd, L 1973, ch 276, § 21, eff Sept 1, 1973.

§ 200.27. Receiving reward for official misconduct in the first degree

A public servant is guilty of receiving reward for official misconduct in the first degree when he solicits, accepts or agrees to accept any benefit from another person for having violated his duty as a public servant in the investigation, arrest, detention, prosecution, or incarceration of any person for the commission or alleged commission of a class A felony defined in article two hundred twenty of the penal law or the attempt to commit any such class A felony.

Receiving reward for official misconduct in the first degree is a class C felony.

> **HISTORY:** Add, L 1973, ch 276, § 21, eff Sept 1, 1973.

§ 200.30. Giving unlawful gratuities

A person is guilty of giving unlawful gratuities when he knowingly confers, or offers or agrees to confer, any benefit upon a public servant for having engaged in official conduct which he was required or authorized to perform, and for which he was not entitled to any special or additional compensation.

Giving unlawful gratuities is a class A misdemeanor.

HISTORY: Add, L 1965, ch 1030, § 1, eff Sept 1, 1967.

§ 200.35. Receiving unlawful gratuities

A public servant is guilty of receiving unlawful gratuities when he solicits, accepts or agrees to accept any benefit for having engaged in official conduct which he was required or authorized to perform, and for which he was not entitled to any special or additional compensation.

Receiving unlawful gratuities is a class A misdemeanor.

HISTORY: Add, L 1965, ch 1030, § 1, eff Sept 1, 1967, with substance derived from §§ 855, 1826, 1831.

§ 200.40. Bribe giving and bribe receiving for public office; definition of term

As used in sections 200.45 and 200.50, "party officer" means a person who holds any position or office in a political party, whether by election, appointment or otherwise.

HISTORY: Add, L 1965, ch 1030, § 1, eff Sept 1, 1967.

§ 200.45. Bribe giving for public office

A person is guilty of bribe giving for public office when he confers, or offers or agrees to confer, any money or other property upon a public servant or a party officer upon an agreement or understanding that some person will or may be appointed to a public office or designated or nominated as a candidate for public office.

Bribe giving for public office is a class D felony.

HISTORY: Add, L 1965, ch 1030, § 1, eff Sept 1, 1967, with substance derived from § 1832(1).

§ 200.50. Bribe receiving for public office

A public servant or a party officer is guilty of bribe receiving for public office when he solicits, accepts or agrees to accept any money or other property from another person upon an agreement or understanding that some person will or may be appointed to a public office or designated or nominated as a candidate for public office.

Bribe receiving for public office is a class D felony.

HISTORY: Add, L 1965, ch 1030, § 1, eff Sept 1, 1967, with substance derived from L 1909, § 1832(2).

§ 200.55. Impairing the integrity of a government licensing examination

A person is guilty of impairing the integrity of a government licensing examination when, with intent to obtain a benefit for himself or herself, or for another person, he or she:

1. Wrongfully alters or changes an applicant's grade on a government licensing examination; or

2. Causes any false or inaccurate grade to be entered into a government licensing registry; or

3. Provides answers, with an intent to wrongfully benefit another, to current questions on a pending government licensing examination; or

4. Wrongfully provides a copy of a current test used to determine competence in a licensed profession, trade, craft or other vocation.

Impairing the integrity of a government licensing examination is a class D felony.

HISTORY: Add, L 2008, ch 463, § 2, ef Nov 1, 2008. Sub 4, amd, L 2009, ch 64, § 1, eff June 9, 2009, deemed eff on and after Nov 1, 2008.

§ 200.56. Corrupt use of position or authority

A person is guilty of corrupt use of position or authority if such person:

1. While holding public office, or being nominated or seeking a nomination therefor, corruptly uses or promises to use, directly, or indirectly, any official authority or influence possessed or anticipated, in the way of conferring upon any person, or in order to secure, or aid any person in securing, any office or public employment, or any nomination, confirmation, promotion or increase of salary, upon consideration that the vote or political influence or action of the person so to be benefited or of any other person, shall be given or used in behalf of any candidate, officer or party or upon any other corrupt condition or consideration; or

2. Being a public officer or employee of the state or a political subdivision having, or claiming to have, any authority or influence affecting the nomination, public employment, confirmation, promotion, removal or increase or decrease of salary of any public officer or employee, corruptly promises or threatens to use any such authority or influence, directly or indirectly to affect the vote or political action of any such public officer or employee, or on account of the vote or political action of such officer or employee; or

3. Corruptly makes, tenders or offers to procure, or cause any nomination or appointment for any public office or place, or accepts or requests any such nomination or appointment, upon the payment or contribution of any valuable consideration, or upon an understanding or promise thereof; or

4. Corruptly makes any gift, promise or contribution to any person, upon the condition or consideration of receiving an appointment or election to a public office or a position of public employment, or for receiving or retaining any such office or position, or promotion, privilege, increase of salary or compensation therein, or exemption from removal or discharge therefrom.

Corrupt use of position or authority is a class E felony.

HISTORY: Add, L 2014, ch 55, § 26 (Part H, Subpart A), eff April 30, 2014.

ARTICLE 205   ESCAPE AND OTHER OFFENSES RELATING TO CUSTODY

HISTORY: Add, L 1965, ch 1030, § 1, eff Sept 1, 1976.

§ 205.00. Escape and other offenses relating to custody; definitions of terms

The following definitions are applicable to this article:

1. "Detention Facility" means any place used for the confinement, pursuant to an order of a court, of a person (a) charged with or convicted of an offense, or (b) charged with being or adjudicated a youthful offender, person in need of supervision or juvenile delinquent, or (c) held for extradition or as a material witness, or (d) otherwise confined pursuant to an order of a court.

2. "Custody" means restraint by a public servant pursuant to an authorized arrest or an order of a court.

3. "Contraband" means any article or thing which a person confined in a detention facility is prohibited from obtaining or possessing by statute, rule, regulation or order.

4. "Dangerous contraband" means contraband which is capable of such use as may endanger the safety or security of a detention facility or any person therein.

HISTORY: Add, L 1965, ch 1030, § 1, eff Sept 1, 1967. Sub 1, amd, L 1972, ch 207, § 1, eff May 2, 1972.

§ 205.05. Escape in the third degree

A person is guilty of escape in the third degree when he escapes from custody.

Escape in the third degree is a class A misdemeanor.

HISTORY: Add, L 1965, ch 1030, § 1, eff Sept 1, 1967, with substance derived from § 1694.

§ 205.10. Escape in the second degree

A person is guilty of escape in the second degree when:

1. He escapes from a detention facility; or

2. Having been arrested for, charged with or convicted of a class C, class D or class E felony, he escapes from custody; or

3. Having been adjudicated a youthful offender, which finding was substituted for the conviction of a felony, he escapes from custody.

Escape in the second degree is a class E felony.

HISTORY: Add, L 1965, ch 1030, § 1, eff Sept 1, 1967, with substance derived from § 1694. Sub 2, amd, L 1983, ch 277, § 3, eff Sept 8, 1983. Sub 3, add, L 1980, ch 118, § 1, eff Sept 1, 1980.

§ 205.15. Escape in the first degree

A person is guilty of escape in the first degree when:

1. Having been charged with or convicted of a felony, he escapes from a detention facility; or

2. Having been arrested for, charged with or convicted of a class A or class B felony, he escapes from custody; or

3. Having been adjudicated a youthful offender, which finding was substituted for the conviction of a felony, he escapes from a detention facility.

Escape in the first degree is a class D felony.

HISTORY: Add, L 1965, ch 1030, § 1, with substance derived from § 1694; amd, L 1980, ch 118, § 2, L 1983, ch 277, § 4, eff Sept 8, 1983. Opening par, amd, L 1980, ch 118, § 2, eff Sept 1, 1980. Sub 1, formerly part of opening par, so designated sub 1 and amd, L 1980, ch 118, § 2, eff Sept 1, 1980. Sub 2, add, L 1980, ch 118, § 2; amd, L 1983, ch 277, § 4, eff Sept 8, 1983. Sub 3, formerly par of sub 2, so designated sub 3 and amd, L 1983, ch 277, § 4, eff Sept 8, 1983.

§ 205.16. [Expires Sept 1, 2015] Absconding from temporary release in the second degree

A person is guilty of absconding from temporary release in the second degree when having been released from confinement in a correctional institution or division for youth facility to participate in a program of work release, he intentionally fails to return to the institution or facility of his confinement at or before the time prescribed for his return.

Absconding from temporary release in the second degree is a class A misdemeanor.

HISTORY: Add, L 1969, ch 678, § 4; amd, L 1972, ch 339, § 7, expires Sept 1, 2015, L 1983, ch 460, § 2, eff July 15, 1983. Section heading, amd, L 1972, ch 339, § 7, eff June 21, 1972, expires Sept 1, 2015.

§ 205.17. [Expires Sept 1, 2015] Absconding from temporary release in the first degree

A person is guilty of absconding from temporary release in the first degree when having been released from confinement in a correctional institution under the jurisdiction of the state department of corrections and community supervision or a facility under the jurisdiction of the state office of children and family services to participate in a program of temporary release, he or she intentionally fails to return to the institution or facility of his or her confinement at or before the time prescribed for his or her return.

Absconding from temporary release in the first degree is a class E felony.

HISTORY: Add, L 1969, ch 472, § 2; amd, L 1972, ch 339, § 8, expires Sept 1, 2015, L 1983, ch 460, § 2, L 1988, ch 661, § 3, expired and repealed July 1, 1994, L 2011, ch 62, § 127-n (Part C, Subpart B), eff March 31, 2011.

§ 205.18. [Expires Sept 1, 2015] Absconding from a furlough program

A person is guilty of absconding from a furlough program when, having been released from confinement in an institution under the jurisdiction of the commissioner of correction in a city having a population of one million or more or of a county which elects to have this article apply thereto to participate in a furlough program, he intentionally fails to return to the institution of his confinement at or before the time prescribed for his return.

Absconding from a furlough program is a class A misdemeanor.

HISTORY: Add, L 1972, ch 886, § 2, expires Sept 1, 2015; amd, L 1973, ch 622, § 6, eff Aug 10, 1973.

§ 205.19. [Expires Sept 1, 2015] Absconding from a community treatment facility

A person is guilty of absconding from a community treatment facility when having been released from confinement from a correctional institution under the jurisdiction of the state department of corrections and community supervision by transfer to a community treatment facility, he or she leaves such facility without authorization or he or she intentionally fails to return to the community treatment facility at or before the time prescribed for his or her return.

Absconding from a community treatment facility is a class E felony.

HISTORY: Add, L 1986, ch 554, § 4, eff July 24, 1986, expires Sept 1, 2015; amd, L 2011, ch 62, § 127-o (Part C, Subpart B), eff March 31, 2011.

§ 205.20. Promoting prison contraband in the second degree

A person is guilty of promoting prison contraband in the second degree when:

1. He knowingly and unlawfully introduces any contraband into a detention facility; or

2. Being a person confined in a detention facility, he knowingly and unlawfully makes, obtains or possesses any contraband.

Promoting prison contraband in the second degree is a class A misdemeanor.

HISTORY: Add, L 1965, ch 1030, § 1, eff Sept 1, 1967, with substance derived from §§ 489, 1691(1, 2), 1791, 1796, 1828-a(1).

§ 205.25. Promoting prison contraband in the first degree

A person is guilty of promoting prison contraband in the first degree when:

1. He knowingly and unlawfully introduces any dangerous contraband into a detention facility; or

2. Being a person confined in a detention facility, he knowingly and unlawfully makes, obtains or possesses any dangerous contraband.

Promoting prison contraband in the first degree is a class D felony.

HISTORY: Add, L 1965, ch 1030, § 1, eff Sept 1, 1967, with substance derived from §§ 1961(3), 1796, 1828-a(2).

§ 205.30. Resisting arrest

A person is guilty of resisting arrest when he intentionally prevents or attempts to prevent a police officer or peace officer from effecting an authorized arrest of himself or another person.

Resisting arrest is a class A misdemeanor.

HISTORY: Add, L 1965, ch 1030, § 1; amd, L 1980, ch 843, § 41, eff Sept 1, 1980.

§ 205.35. [Repealed]

HISTORY: Add, L 1965, ch 1030, § 1, with substance derived from §§ 1694-a, 1694-b; repealed, L 1968, ch 510, § 1, eff Sept 1, 1968.

§ 205.40. [Repealed]

HISTORY: Add, L 1965, ch 1030, § 1, with substance derived from §§ 1694-a, 1694-b; repealed, L 1968, ch 510, § 1, eff Sept 1, 1968.

§ 205.45. [Repealed]

HISTORY: Add, L 1965, ch 1030, § 1; repealed, L 1968, ch 510, § 1, eff Sept 1, 1968.

§ 205.50. Hindering prosecution; definition of term

As used in sections 205.55, 205.60 and 205.65, a person "renders criminal assistance" when, with intent to prevent, hinder or delay the discovery or apprehension of, or the lodging of a criminal charge against, a person who he knows or believes has committed a crime or is being sought by law enforcement officials for the commission of a crime, or with intent to assist a person in profiting or benefiting from the commission of a crime, he:

1. Harbors or conceals such person; or

2. Warns such person of impending discovery or apprehension; or

3. Provides such person with money, transportation, weapon, disguise or other means of avoiding discovery or apprehension; or

4. Prevents or obstructs, by means of force, intimidation or deception, anyone from performing an act which might aid in the discovery or apprehension of such person or in the lodging of a criminal charge against him; or

5. Suppresses, by any act of concealment, alteration or destruction, any physical evidence which might aid in the discovery or apprehension of such person or in the lodging of a criminal charge against him; or

6. Aids such person to protect or expeditiously profit from an advantage derived from such crime.

HISTORY: Add, L 1965, ch 1030, § 1, eff Sept 1, 1967, with substance derived from §§ 2 (in part) and 1698.

§ 205.55. Hindering prosecution in the third degree

A person is guilty of hindering prosecution in the third degree when he renders criminal assistance to a person who has committed a felony.

Hindering prosecution in the third degree is a class A misdemeanor.

HISTORY: Add, L 1965, ch 1030, § 1, eff Sept 1, 1967, with substance derived from §§ 1698, 1934.

§ 205.60. Hindering prosecution in the second degree

A person is guilty of hindering prosecution in the second degree when he renders criminal assistance to a person who has committed a class B or class C felony.

Hindering prosecution in the second degree is a class E felony.

HISTORY: Add, L 1965, ch 1030, § 1, eff Sept 1, 1967, with substance derived from §§ 1698, 1934.

§ 205.65. Hindering prosecution in the first degree

A person is guilty of hindering prosecution in the first degree when he renders criminal assistance to a person who has committed a class A felony, knowing or believing that such person has engaged in conduct constituting a class A felony.

Hindering prosecution in the first degree is a class D felony.

HISTORY: Add, L 1965, ch 1030, § 1, with substance derived from §§ 1698, 1934; amd, L 1970, ch 398, § 1, eff Sept 1, 1970.

ARTICLE 210   PERJURY AND RELATED OFFENSES

§ 210.50. **Perjury and related offenses; requirement of corroboration**

HISTORY: Add, L 1965, ch 1030, § 1, eff Sept 1, 1967.

§ 210.00. Perjury and related offenses; definitions of terms

The following definitions are applicable to this article:

1. "Oath" includes an affirmation and every other mode authorized by law of attesting to the truth of that which is stated.

2. "Swear" means to state under oath.

3. "Testimony" means an oral statement made under oath in a proceeding before any court, body, agency, public servant or other person authorized by law to conduct such proceeding and to administer the oath or cause it to be administered.

4. "Oath required by law." An affidavit, deposition or other subscribed written instrument is one for which an "oath is required by law" when, absent an oath or swearing thereto, it does not or would not, according to statute or appropriate regulatory provisions, have legal efficacy in a court of law or before any public or governmental body, agency or public servant to whom it is or might be submitted.

5. "Swear falsely." A person "swears falsely" when he intentionally makes a false statement which he does not believe to be true (a) while giving testimony, or (b) under oath in a subscribed written instrument. A false swearing in a subscribed written instrument shall not be deemed complete until the instrument is delivered by its subscriber, or by someone acting in his behalf, to another person with intent that it be uttered or published as true.

6. "Attesting officer" means any notary public or other person authorized by law to administer oaths in connection with affidavits, depositions and other subscribed written instruments, and to certify that the subscriber of such an instrument has appeared before him and has sworn to the truth of the contents thereof.

7. "Jurat" means a clause wherein an attesting officer certifies, among other matters, that the subscriber has appeared before him and sworn to the truth of the contents thereof.

HISTORY: Add, L 1965, ch 1030, § 1, eff Sept 1, 1967, with substance derived from §§ 1621(3), 1622, 1625, 1626.

§ 210.05. Perjury in the third degree

A person is guilty of perjury in the third degree when he swears falsely.

Perjury in the third degree is a class A misdemeanor.

HISTORY: Add, L 1965, ch 1030, § 1, eff Sept 1, 1967, with substance derived from §§ 1232, 1620-b.

§ 210.10. Perjury in the second degree

A person is guilty of perjury in the second degree when he swears falsely and when his false statement is (a) made in a subscribed written instrument for which an oath is required by law, and (b) made with intent to mislead a public servant in the performance of his official functions, and (c) material to the action, proceeding or matter involved.

Perjury in the second degree is a class E felony.

HISTORY: Add, L 1965, ch 1030, § 1, eff Sept 1, 1967, with substance derived from §§ 1232, 1620-a.

§ 210.15. Perjury in the first degree

A person is guilty of perjury in the first degree when he swears falsely and when his false statement (a) consists of testimony, and (b) is material to the action, proceeding or matter in which it is made.

Perjury in the first degree is a class D felony.

HISTORY: Add, L 1965, ch 1030, § 1, eff Sept 1, 1967, with substance derived from §§ 1232, 1620-a.

§ 210.20. Perjury; pleading and proof where inconsistent statements involved

Where a person has made two statements under oath which are inconsistent to the degree that one of them is necessarily false, where the circumstances are such that each statement, if false, is perjuriously so, and where each statement was made within the jurisdiction of this state and within the period of the statute of limitations for the crime charged, the inability of the people to establish specifically which of the two statements is the false one does not preclude a prosecution for perjury, and such prosecution may be conducted as follows:

1. The indictment or information may set forth the two statements and, without designating either, charge that one of them is false and perjuriously made.

2. The falsity of one or the other of the two statements may be established by proof or a showing of their irreconcilable inconsistency.

3. The highest degree of perjury of which the defendant may be convicted is determined by hypothetically assuming each statement to be false and perjurious. If under such circumstances perjury of the same degree would be established by the making of each statement, the defendant may be convicted of that degree at most. If perjury of different degrees would be established by the making of the two statements, the defendant may be convicted of the lesser degree at most.

HISTORY: Add, L 1965, ch 1030, § 1, eff Sept 1, 1967, with substance derived from §§ 1627, 1627-a.

§ 210.25. Perjury; defense

In any prosecution for perjury, it is an affirmative defense that the defendant retracted his false statement in the course of the proceeding in which it was made before such false statement substantially affected the proceeding and before it became manifest that its falsity was or would be exposed.

HISTORY: Add, L 1965, ch 1030, § 1, eff Sept 1, 1967.

§ 210.30. Perjury; no defense

It is no defense to a prosecution for perjury that:

1. The defendant was not competent to make the false statement alleged; or

2. The defendant mistakenly believed the false statement to be immaterial; or

3. The oath was administered or taken in an irregular manner or that the authority or jurisdiction of the attesting officer who administered the oath was defective, if such defect was excusable under any statute or rule of law.

HISTORY: Add, L 1965, ch 1030, § 1, eff Sept 1, 1967, with substance derived from §§ 1621–1624.

§ 210.35. Making an apparently sworn false statement in the second degree

A person is guilty of making an apparently sworn false statement in the second degree when (a) he subscribes a written instrument knowing that it contains a statement which is in fact false and which he does not believe to be true, and (b) he intends or believes that such instrument will be uttered or delivered with a jurat affixed thereto, and (c) such instrument is uttered or delivered with a jurat affixed thereto.

Making an apparently sworn false statement in the second degree is a class A misdemeanor.

HISTORY: Add, L 1965, ch 1030, § 1, eff Sept 1, 1967.

§ 210.40. Making an apparently sworn false statement in the first degree

A person is guilty of making an apparently sworn false statement in the first degree when he commits the crime of making an apparently sworn false statement in the second degree, and when (a) the written instrument involved is one for which an oath is required by law, and (b) the false statement contained therein is made with intent to mislead a public servant in the performance of his official functions, and (c) such false statement is material to the action, proceeding or matter involved.

Making an apparently sworn false statement in the first degree is a class E felony.

HISTORY: Add, L 1965, ch 1030, § 1, eff Sept 1, 1967.

§ 210.45. Making a punishable false written statement

A person is guilty of making a punishable false written statement when he knowingly makes a false statement, which he does not believe to be true, in a written instrument bearing a legally authorized form notice to the effect that false statements made therein are punishable.

Making a punishable false written statement is a class A misdemeanor.

HISTORY: Add, L 1965, ch 1030, § 1, eff Sept 1, 1967.

§ 210.47. [Repealed]

HISTORY: Add, L 1979, ch 692, § 6; repealed, L 1981, ch 720, § 4, eff Nov 1, 1981.

§ 210.50. Perjury and related offenses; requirement of corroboration

In any prosecution for perjury, except a prosecution based upon inconsistent statements pursuant to section 210.20, or in any prosecution for making an apparently sworn false statement, or making a punishable false written statement, falsity of a statement may not be established by the uncorroborated testimony of a single witness.

HISTORY: Add, L 1965, ch 1030, § 1, eff Sept 1, 1967.

ARTICLE 215   OTHER OFFENSES RELATING TO JUDICIAL AND OTHER PROCEEDINGS

HISTORY: Add, L 1965, ch 1030, § 1, eff Sept 1, 1967.

§ 215.00. Bribing a witness

A person is guilty of bribing a witness when he confers, or offers or agrees to confer, any benefit upon a witness or a person about to be called as a witness in any action or proceeding upon an agreement or understanding that (a) the testimony of such witness will thereby be influenced, or (b) such witness will absent himself from, or otherwise avoid or seek to avoid appearing or testifying at, such action or proceeding.

Bribing a witness is a class D felony.

HISTORY: Add, L 1965, ch 1030, § 1, eff Sept 1, 1967, with substance derived from § 2440.

§ 215.05. Bribe receiving by a witness

A witness or a person about to be called as a witness in any action or proceeding is guilty of bribe receiving by a witness when he solicits, accepts or agrees to accept any benefit from another person upon an agreement or understanding that (a) his testimony will thereby be influenced, or (b) he will absent himself from, or otherwise avoid or seek to avoid appearing or testifying at, such action or proceeding.

Bribe receiving by a witness is a class D felony.

HISTORY: Add, L 1965, ch 1030, § 1, eff Sept 1, 1967, with substance derived from § 379.

§ 215.10. Tampering with a witness in the fourth degree

A person is guilty of tampering with a witness [in the fourth degree]* when, knowing that a person is or is about to be called as a witness in an action or proceeding, (a) he wrongfully induces

_____
*. The bracketed words have been inserted by the Publisher.

or attempts to induce such person to absent himself from, or otherwise to avoid or seek to avoid appearing or testifying at, such action or proceeding, or (b) he knowingly makes any false statement or practices any fraud or deceit with intent to affect the testimony of such person.

Tampering with a witness in the fourth degree is a class A misdemeanor.

> **HISTORY:** Add, L 1965, ch 1030, § 1, eff Sept 1, 1967, with substance derived from §§ 2441, 2442. Section heading, amd, L 1982, ch 664, § 1, eff Sept 1, 1982. Closing par, amd, L 1982, ch 664, § 1, eff Sept 1, 1982.

§ 215.11. Tampering with a witness in the third degree

A person is guilty of tampering with a witness in the third degree when, knowing that a person is about to be called as a witness in a criminal proceeding:

1. He wrongfully compels or attempts to compel such person to absent himself from, or otherwise to avoid or seek to avoid appearing or testifying at such proceeding by means of instilling in him a fear that the actor will cause physical injury to such person or another person; or

2. He wrongfully compels or attempts to compel such person to swear falsely by means of instilling in him a fear that the actor will cause physical injury to such person or another person.

Tampering with a witness in the third degree is a class E felony.

> **HISTORY:** Add, L 1982, ch 664, § 2, eff Sept 1, 1982. Another § 215.11, add, L 1982, ch 823, § 1; renumbered § 215.14, L 1985, ch 187, § 3, eff June 11, 1985.

§ 215.12. Tampering with a witness in the second degree

A person is guilty of tampering with a witness in the second degree when he:

1. Intentionally causes physical injury to a person for the purpose of obstructing, delaying, preventing or impeding the giving of testimony in a criminal proceeding by such person or another person or for the purpose of compelling such person or another person to swear falsely; or

2. He intentionally causes physical injury to a person on account of such person or another person having testified in a criminal proceeding.

Tampering with a witness in the second degree is a class D felony.

> **HISTORY:** Add, L 1982, ch 664, § 2, eff Sept 1, 1982.

§ 215.13. Tampering with a witness in the first degree

A person is guilty of tampering with a witness in the first degree when:

1. He intentionally causes serious physical injury to a person for the purpose of obstructing, delaying, preventing or impeding the giving of testimony in a criminal proceeding by such person or another person or for the purpose of compelling such person or another person to swear falsely; or

2. He intentionally causes serious physical injury to a person on account of such person or another person having testified in a criminal proceeding.

Tampering with a witness in the first degree is a class B felony.

> **HISTORY:** Add, L 1982, ch 664, § 2, eff Sept 1, 1982.

§ 215.14. Employer unlawfully penalizing witness or victim

1. Any person who is the victim of an offense upon which an accusatory instrument is based or, is subpoenaed to attend a criminal proceeding as a witness pursuant to article six hundred ten of

the criminal procedure law or who exercises his rights as a victim as provided by section 380.50 or 390.30 of the criminal procedure law or subdivision two of section two hundred fifty-nine-i of the executive law and who notifies his employer or agent of his intent to appear as a witness, to consult with the district attorney, or to exercise his rights as provided in the criminal procedure law, the family court act and the executive law prior to the day of his attendance, shall not on account of his absence from employment by reason of such service be subject to discharge or penalty except as hereinafter provided. Upon request of the employer or agent, the party who sought the attendance or testimony shall provide verification of the employee's service. An employer may, however, withhold wages of any such employee during the period of such attendance. The subjection of an employee to discharge or penalty on account of his absence from employment by reason of his required attendance as a witness at a criminal proceeding or consultation with the district attorney or exercise of his rights as provided under law shall constitute a class B misdemeanor.

2. For purposes of this section, the term "victim" shall include the aggrieved party or the aggrieved party's next of kin, if the aggrieved party is deceased as a result of the offense, the representative of a victim as defined in subdivision six of section six hundred twenty-one of the executive law, a good samaritan as defined in subdivision seven of section six hundred twenty-one of such law or a person pursuing an application or enforcement of an order of protection under the criminal procedure law or the family court act.

> **HISTORY:** Added as § 215.11, L 1982, ch 823, § 1; amd, L 1983, ch 101, § 1; renumbered § 215.14, L 1985, ch 187, § 3, eff June 11, 1985. Section heading, amd, L 1985, ch 187, § 2, L 1996, ch 331, § 1, eff Nov 1, 1996. Sub 1, formerly entire section, so designated sub 1 and amd, L 1996, ch 331, § 1, eff Nov 1, 1996. Sub 2, add, L 1996, ch 331, § 1, eff Nov 1, 1996.

§ 215.15. Intimidating a victim or witness in the third degree

A person is guilty of intimidating a victim or witness in the third degree when, knowing that another person possesses information relating to a criminal transaction and other than in the course of that criminal transaction or immediate flight therefrom, he:

    1. Wrongfully compels or attempts to compel such other person to refrain from communicating such information to any court, grand jury, prosecutor, police officer or peace officer by means of instilling in him a fear that the actor will cause physical injury to such other person or another person; or

    2. Intentionally damages the property of such other person or another person for the purpose of compelling such other person or another person to refrain from communicating, or on account of such other person or another person having communicated, information relating to that criminal transaction to any court, grand jury, prosecutor, police officer or peace officer.

Intimidating a victim or witness in the third degree is a class E felony.

> **HISTORY:** Add, L 1985, ch 667, § 2, eff Nov 1, 1985. Former § 215.15, renumbered § 215.19, L 1985, ch 667, § 1, eff Nov 1, 1985.

§ 215.16. Intimidating a victim or witness in the second degree

A person is guilty of intimidating a victim or witness in the second degree when, other than in the course of that criminal transaction or immediate flight therefrom, he:

    1. Intentionally causes physical injury to another person for the purpose of obstructing, delaying, preventing or impeding the communication by such other person or another person of information relating to a criminal transaction to any court, grand jury, prosecutor, police officer or peace officer or for the purpose of compelling such other person or another person to swear falsely; or

2. Intentionally causes physical injury to another person on account of such other person or another person having communicated information relating to a criminal transaction to any court, grand jury, prosecutor, police officer or peace officer; or

3. Recklessly causes physical injury to another person by intentionally damaging the property of such other person or another person, for the purpose of obstructing, delaying, preventing or impeding such other person or another person from communicating, or on account of such other person or another person having communicated, information relating to a criminal transaction to any court, grand jury, prosecutor, police officer or peace officer.

Intimidating a victim or witness in the second degree is a class D felony.

HISTORY: Add, L 1985, ch 667, § 3, eff Nov 1, 1985.

§ 215.17. Intimidating a victim or witness in the first degree

A person is guilty of intimidating a victim or witness in the first degree when, other than in the course of that criminal transaction or immediate flight therefrom, he:

1. Intentionally causes serious physical injury to another person for the purpose of obstructing, delaying, preventing or impeding the communication by such other person or another person of information relating to a criminal transaction to any court, grand jury, prosecutor, police officer or peace officer or for the purpose of compelling such other person or another person to swear falsely; or

2. Intentionally causes serious physical injury to another person on account of such other person or another person having communicated information relating to a criminal transaction to any court, grand jury, prosecutor, police officer or peace officer.

Intimidating a victim or witness in the first degree is a class B felony.

HISTORY: Add, L 1985, ch 667, § 4, eff Nov 1, 1985.

§ 215.19. Bribing a juror

A person is guilty of bribing a juror when he confers, or offers or agrees to confer, any benefit upon a juror upon an agreement or understanding that such juror's vote, opinion, judgment, decision or other action as a juror will thereby be influenced.

Bribing a juror is a class D felony.

HISTORY: Added as § 215.15, L 1965, ch 1030, § 1, with substance derived from § 371; renumbered § 215.19, L 1985, ch 667, § 1, eff Nov 1, 1985.

§ 215.20. Bribe receiving by a juror

A juror is guilty of bribe receiving by a juror when he solicits, accepts or agrees to accept any benefit from another person upon an agreement or understanding that his vote, opinion, judgment, decision or other action as a juror will thereby be influenced.

Bribe receiving by a juror is a class D felony.

HISTORY: Add, L 1965, ch 1030, § 1, eff Sept 1, 1967, with substance derived from § 374.

§ 215.22. Providing a juror with a gratuity

A person is guilty of providing a juror with a gratuity when he or she, having been a party in a concluded civil or criminal action or proceeding or having been a person with regard to whom a grand jury has taken action pursuant to any subdivision of section 190.60 of the criminal procedure law (or acting on behalf of such a party or such a person), directly or indirectly confers, offers to confer or agrees to confer upon a person whom he or she knows has served as a juror in such action or proceeding or on such grand jury any benefit with intent to reward such person for such service.

Providing a juror with a gratuity is a class A misdemeanor.

HISTORY: Add, L 2001, ch 42, § 2, eff Nov 1, 2001.

§ 215.23. Tampering with a juror in the second degree

A person is guilty of tampering with a juror in the second degree when, prior to discharge of the jury, he:

1. confers, or offers or agrees to confer, any payment or benefit upon a juror or upon a third person acting on behalf of such juror, in consideration for such juror or third person supplying information in relation to an action or proceeding pending or about to be brought before such juror; or

2. acting on behalf of a juror, accepts or agrees to accept any payment or benefit for himself or for such juror, in consideration for supplying any information in relation to an action or proceeding pending or about to be brought before such juror and prior to his discharge.

Tampering with a juror in the second degree is a class B misdemeanor.

HISTORY: Add, L 1990, ch 305, § 3, eff Nov 1, 1990.

§ 215.25. Tampering with a juror in the first degree

A person is guilty of tampering with a juror in the first degree when, with intent to influence the outcome of an action or proceeding, he communicates with a juror in such action or proceeding, except as authorized by law.

Tampering with a juror in the first degree is a class A misdemeanor.

HISTORY: Add, L 1965, ch 1030, § 1, with substance derived from §§ 376, 376-a, 860; amd, L 1990, ch 305, § 4, eff Nov 1, 1990. Section heading, amd, L 1990, ch 305, § 4, eff Nov 1, 1990.

§ 215.28. Misconduct by a juror in the second degree

A person is guilty of misconduct by a juror in the second degree when, in relation to an action or proceeding pending or about to be brought before him and prior to discharge, he accepts or agrees to accept any payment or benefit for himself or for a third person in consideration for supplying any information concerning such action or proceeding.

Misconduct by a juror in the second degree is a violation.

HISTORY: Add, L 1990, ch 305, § 5, eff Nov 1, 1990.

§ 215.30. Misconduct by a juror in the first degree

A juror is guilty of misconduct by a juror in the first degree when, in relation to an action or proceeding pending or about to be brought before him, he agrees to give a vote, opinion, judgment, decision or report for or against any party to such action or proceeding.

Misconduct by a juror in the first degree is a class A misdemeanor.

HISTORY: Add, L 1965, ch 1030, § 1, with substance derived from § 373(1); amd, L 1990, ch 305, § 6, eff Nov 1, 1990. Section heading, amd, L 1990, ch 305, § 6 eff Nov 1, 1990.

§ 215.35. Tampering with physical evidence; definitions of terms

The following definitions are applicable to section 215.40:

1. "Physical evidence" means any article, object, document, record or other thing of physical substance which is or is about to be produced or used as evidence in an official proceeding.

2. "Official proceeding" means any action or proceeding conducted by or before a legally constituted judicial, legislative, administrative or other governmental agency or official, in which evidence may properly be received.

HISTORY: Add, L 1965, ch 1030, § 1, eff Sept 1, 1967.

§ 215.40. Tampering with physical evidence

A person is guilty of tampering with physical evidence when:

1. With intent that it be used or introduced in an official proceeding or a prospective official proceeding, he (a) knowingly makes, devises or prepares false physical evidence, or (b) produces or offers such evidence at such a proceeding knowing it to be false; or

2. Believing that certain physical evidence is about to be produced or used in an official proceeding or a prospective official proceeding, and intending to prevent such production or use, he suppresses it by any act of concealment, alteration or destruction, or by employing force, intimidation or deception against any person.

Tampering with physical evidence is a class E felony.

HISTORY: Add, L 1965, ch 1030, § 1, eff Sept 1, 1967, with substance derived from §§ 810–812, 814.

§ 215.45. Compounding a crime

1. A person is guilty of compounding a crime when:

(a) He solicits, accepts or agrees to accept any benefit upon an agreement or understanding that he will refrain from initiating a prosecution for a crime; or

(b) He confers, or offers or agrees to confer, any benefit upon another person upon an agreement or understanding that such other person will refrain from initiating a prosecution for a crime.

2. In any prosecution under this section, it is an affirmative defense that the benefit did not exceed an amount which the defendant reasonably believed to be due as restitution or indemnification for harm caused by the crime.

Compounding a crime is a class A misdemeanor.

HISTORY: Add, L 1965, ch 1030, § 1, eff Sept 1, 1967, with substance derived from § 570.

§ 215.50. Criminal contempt in the second degree

A person is guilty of criminal contempt in the second degree when he engages in any of the following conduct:

1. Disorderly, contemptuous, or insolent behavior, committed during the sitting of a court, in its immediate view and presence and directly tending to interrupt its proceedings or to impair the respect due to its authority; or

2. Breach of the peace, noise, or other disturbance, directly tending to interrupt a court's proceedings; or

3. Intentional disobedience or resistance to the lawful process or other mandate of a court except in cases involving or growing out of labor disputes as defined by subdivision two of section seven hundred fifty-three-a of the judiciary law; or

4. Contumacious and unlawful refusal to be sworn as a witness in any court proceeding or, after being sworn, to answer any legal and proper interrogatory; or

5. Knowingly publishing a false or grossly inaccurate report of a court's proceeding; or

6. Intentional failure to obey any mandate, process or notice, issued pursuant to articles sixteen, seventeen*, eighteen*;, or eighteen-a*; of the judiciary law, or to rules adopted pursuant to any such statute or to any special statute establishing commissioners of jurors and prescribing their duties or who refuses to be sworn as provided therein; or

7. On or along a public street or sidewalk within a radius of two hundred feet of any building established as a courthouse, he calls aloud, shouts, holds or displays placards or signs containing written or printed matter, concerning the conduct of a trial being held in such courthouse or the character of the court or jury engaged in such trial or calling for or demanding any specified action or determination by such court or jury in connection with such trial.

Criminal contempt in the second degree is a class A misdemeanor.

HISTORY: Add, L 1965, ch 1030, § 1, with substance derived from §§ 600, 1235; amd, L 1972, ch 702, § 1, eff Sept 1, 1972. Section heading, amd, L 1972, ch 702, § 1, eff Sept 1, 1972. Sub 4, amd, L 1970, ch 734, § 1, eff Sept 1, 1970. Sub 6, amd, L 1967, ch 791, § 29, eff Sept 1, 1967.

§ 215.51. Criminal contempt in the first degree

A person is guilty of criminal contempt in the first degree when:

(a) he contumaciously and unlawfully refuses to be sworn as a witness before a grand jury, or, when after having been sworn as a witness before a grand jury, he refuses to answer any legal and proper interrogatory; or

(b) in violation of a duly served order of protection, or such order of which the defendant has actual knowledge because he or she was present in court when such order was issued, or an order of protection issued by a court of competent jurisdiction in this or another state, territorial or tribal jurisdiction, he or she:

(i) intentionally places or attempts to place a person for whose protection such order was issued in reasonable fear of physical injury, serious physical injury or death by displaying a deadly weapon, dangerous instrument or what appears to be a pistol, revolver, rifle, shotgun, machine gun or other firearm or by means of a threat or threats; or

(ii) intentionally places or attempts to place a person for whose protection such order was issued in reasonable fear of physical injury, serious physical injury or death by repeatedly following such person or engaging in a course of conduct or repeatedly committing acts over a period of time; or

(iii) intentionally places or attempts to place a person for whose protection such order was issued in reasonable fear of physical injury, serious physical injury or death when he or she communicates or causes a communication to be initiated with such person by mechanical or electronic means or otherwise, anonymously or otherwise, by telephone, or by telegraph, mail or any other form of written communication; or

(iv) with intent to harass, annoy, threaten or alarm a person for whose protection such order was issued, repeatedly makes telephone calls to such person, whether or not a conversation ensues, with no purpose of legitimate communication; or

---

* Repealed, Jan 1, 1978, L 1977, ch 316.

* Repealed, Jan 1, 1978, L 1977, ch 316.

* Repealed, Jan 1, 1978, L 1977, ch 316.

(v) with intent to harass, annoy, threaten or alarm a person for whose protection such order was issued, strikes, shoves, kicks or otherwise subjects such other person to physical contact or attempts or threatens to do the same; or

(vi) by physical menace, intentionally places or attempts to place a person for whose protection such order was issued in reasonable fear of death, imminent serious physical injury or physical injury.

(c) he or she commits the crime of criminal contempt in the second degree as defined in subdivision three of section 215.50 of this article by violating that part of a duly served order of protection, or such order of which the defendant has actual knowledge because he or she was present in court when such order was issued, under sections two hundred forty and two hundred fifty-two of the domestic relations law, articles four, five, six and eight of the family court act and section 530.12 of the criminal procedure law, or an order of protection issued by a court of competent jurisdiction in another state, territorial or tribal jurisdiction, which requires the respondent or defendant to stay away from the person or persons on whose behalf the order was issued, and where the defendant has been previously convicted of the crime of aggravated criminal contempt or criminal contempt in the first or second degree for violating an order of protection as described herein within the preceding five years; or

(d) in violation of a duly served order of protection, or such order of which the defendant has actual knowledge because he or she was present in court when such order was issued, or an order issued by a court of competent jurisdiction in this or another state, territorial or tribal jurisdiction, he or she intentionally or recklessly damages the property of a person for whose protection such order was issued in an amount exceeding two hundred fifty dollars.

Criminal contempt in the first degree is a class E felony.

HISTORY: Add, L 1970, ch 734, § 2; amd, L 1972, ch 702, § 2, L 1994, ch 222, § 47, eff Jan 1, 1995. Section heading, amd, L 1972, ch 702, § 2, eff Sept 1, 1972. Opening par, formerly part of entire section, so designated opening par and amd, L 1994, ch 222, § 47, eff Jan 1, 1995. Sub (a), formerly part of entire section, so designated sub (a), L 1994, ch 222, § 47, eff Jan 1, 1995. Sub (b), add, L 1996, ch 353, § 1, eff Sept 1, 1996. Former sub (b), add, L 1994, ch 222, § 47; repealed, L 1996, ch 353, § 1, eff Sept 1, 1996. Sub (b), opening par, amd, L 1998, ch 597, § 15, eff Dec 22, 1998. Sub (c), add, L 1994, ch 222, § 47; amd, L 1998, ch 597, § 15, eff Dec 22, 1998. Sub (c), amd, L 2003, ch 331, § 1, eff Nov 1, 2003, L 2006, ch 349, § 1, eff Nov 1, 2006. Sub (d), add, L 1994, ch 222, § 47; amd, L 1998, ch 597, § 15, eff Dec 22, 1998. Closing par, formerly part of entire section, so designated closing par, L 1994, ch 222, § 47, eff Jan 1, 1995.

§ 215.52. Aggravated criminal contempt

A person is guilty of aggravated criminal contempt when:

1. in violation of a duly served order of protection, or such order of which the defendant has actual knowledge because he or she was present in court when such order was issued, or an order of protection issued by a court of competent jurisdiction in another state, territorial or tribal jurisdiction, he or she intentionally or recklessly causes physical injury or serious physical injury to a person for whose protection such order was issued; or

2. he or she commits the crime of criminal contempt in the first degree as defined in subdivision (b) or (d) of section 215.51 of this article and has been previously convicted of the crime of aggravated criminal contempt; or

3. he or she commits the crime of criminal contempt in the first degree, as defined in paragraph (i), (ii), (iii), (v) or (vi) of subdivision (b) or subdivision (c) of section 215.51 of this article, and has been previously convicted of the crime of criminal contempt in the first degree,

. as defined in such subdivision (b), (c) or (d) of section 215.51 of this article, within the preceding five years.

Aggravated criminal contempt is a class D felony.

> **HISTORY:** Add, L 1996, ch 353, § 2; amd, L 1998, ch 597, § 16, eff Dec 22, 1998. Amd, L 2006, ch 350, § 1, eff Nov 1, 2006. Opening par, formerly part of first undesignated par, so designated opening par and amd, L 2006, ch 350, § 1, eff Nov 1, 2006. Sub 1, formerly part of first undesignated par, so designated sub 1, L 2006, ch 350, § 1, eff Nov 1, 2006. Sub 2, add, L 2006, ch 350, § 1, eff Nov 1, 2006. Sub 3, add, L 2006, ch 350, § 1, eff Nov 1, 2006. Former first undesignated par, redesignated opening par and sub 1, L 2006, ch 350, § 1, eff Nov 1, 2006.

§ 215.54. Criminal contempt; prosecution and punishment

Adjudication for criminal contempt under subdivision A of section seven hundred fifty of the judiciary law shall not bar a prosecution for the crime of criminal contempt under section 215.50 based upon the same conduct but, upon conviction thereunder, the court, in sentencing the defendant shall take the previous punishment into consideration.

> **HISTORY:** Added as § 215.55, L 1965, ch 1030, § 1, with substance derived from §§ 601, 603, 1939; renumbered § 215.54, L 1983, ch 277, § 1, eff Sept 8, 1983.

§ 215.55. Bail jumping in the third degree

A person is guilty of bail jumping in the third degree when by court order he has been released from custody or allowed to remain at liberty, either upon bail or upon his own recognizance, upon condition that he will subsequently appear personally in connection with a criminal action or proceeding, and when he does not appear personally on the required date or voluntarily within thirty days thereafter.

Bail jumping in the third degree is a class A misdemeanor.

> **HISTORY:** Add, L 1983, ch 277, § 1, eff Sept 8, 1983. Former § 215.55, add, L 1965, ch 1030, § 1; renumbered § 215.54, L 1983, ch 277, § 1, eff Sept 8, 1983.

§ 215.56. Bail jumping in the second degree

A person is guilty of bail jumping in the second degree when by court order he has been released from custody or allowed to remain at liberty, either upon bail or upon his own recognizance, upon condition that he will subsequently appear personally in connection with a charge against him of committing a felony, and when he does not appear personally on the required date or voluntarily within thirty days thereafter.

Bail jumping in the second degree is a class E felony.

> **HISTORY:** Add, L 1968, ch 510, § 2, with substance derived in part from § 205.35; amd, L 1983, ch 277, § 2, eff Sept 8, 1983.

§ 215.57. Bail jumping in the first degree

A person is guilty of bail jumping in the first degree when by court order he has been released from custody or allowed to remain at liberty, either upon bail or upon his own recognizance, upon condition that he will subsequently appear personally in connection with an indictment pending against him which charges him with the commission of a class A or class B felony, and when he does not appear personally on the required date or voluntarily within thirty days thereafter.

Bail jumping in the first degree is a class D felony.

> **HISTORY:** Add, L 1968, ch 510, § 3, with substance derived in part from § 205.40; amd, L 1983, ch 277, § 2, eff Sept 8, 1983.

§ 215.58. Failing to respond to an appearance ticket

1. A person is guilty of failing to respond to an appearance ticket when, having been personally

served with an appearance ticket, as defined in subdivision two, based upon his alleged commission of a crime, he does not appear personally in the court in which such appearance ticket is returnable on the return date thereof or voluntarily within thirty days thereafter.

2. As used in this section, an appearance ticket means a written notice, whether referred to as a summons or by any other name, issued by a police officer, peace officer or other non-judicial public servant authorized by law to issue the same, directing a designated person to appear in a designated court at a designated future time in connection with a criminal action to be instituted in such court with respect to his alleged commission of a designated offense.

3. This section does not apply to any case in which an alternative to response to an appearance ticket is authorized by law and the actor complies with such alternative procedure.

Failing to respond to an appearance ticket is a violation.

> **HISTORY:** Add, L 1968, ch 510, § 4, eff Sept 1, 1968. Sub 1, amd, L 1991, ch 378, § 1, eff Nov 1, 1991. Sub 2, amd, L 1980, ch 843, § 42, eff Sept 1, 1980.

§ 215.59. Bail jumping and failing to respond to an appearance ticket; defense

In any prosecution for bail jumping or failing to respond to an appearance ticket, it is an affirmative defense that:

1. The defendant's failure to appear on the required date or within thirty days thereafter was unavoidable and due to circumstances beyond his control; and

2. During the period extending from the expiration of the thirty day period to the commencement of the action, the defendant either:

(a) appeared voluntarily as soon as he was able to do so, or

(b) although he did not so appear, such failure of appearance was unavoidable and due to circumstances beyond his control.

> **HISTORY:** Add, L 1968, ch 510, § 5, eff Sept 1, 1968, with substance derived in part from § 205.45.

§ 215.60. Criminal contempt of the legislature

A person is guilty of criminal contempt of the legislature when, having been duly subpoenaed to attend as a witness before either house of the legislature or before any committee thereof, he:

1. Fails or refuses to attend without lawful excuse; or

2. Refuses to be sworn; or

3. Refuses to answer any material and proper question; or

4. Refuses, after reasonable notice, to produce books, papers, or documents in his possession or under his control which constitute material and proper evidence.

Criminal contempt of the legislature is a class A misdemeanor.

> **HISTORY:** Add, L 1965, ch 1030, § 1, eff Sept 1, 1967, with substance derived from §§ 1329, 1330.

§ 215.65. Criminal contempt of a temporary state commission

A person is guilty of criminal contempt of a temporary state commission when, having been duly subpoenaed to attend as a witness at an investigation or hearing before a temporary state commission, he fails or refuses to attend without lawful excuse.

Criminal contempt of a temporary state commission is a class A misdemeanor.

HISTORY: Add, L 1965, ch 1030, § 1, with substance derived from § 2448; amd, L 1970, ch 245, § 1, eff Sept 1, 1970.

§ 215.66. Criminal contempt of the state commission on judicial conduct

A person is guilty of criminal contempt of the state commission on judicial conduct when, having been duly subpoenaed to attend as a witness at an investigation or hearing before the commission or a referee designated by the commission, he fails or refuses to attend without lawful excuse.

Criminal contempt of the state commission on judicial conduct is a class A misdemeanor.

HISTORY: Add, L 1978, ch 156, § 3, eff April 1, 1978.

§ 215.70. Unlawful grand jury disclosure

A person is guilty of unlawful grand jury disclosure when, being a grand juror, a public prosecutor, a grand jury stenographer, a grand jury interpreter, a police officer or a peace officer guarding a witness in a grand jury proceeding, or a clerk, attendant, warden or other public servant having official duties in or about a grand jury room or proceeding, or a public officer or public employee, he intentionally discloses to another the nature or substance of any grand jury testimony, or any decision, result or other matter attending a grand jury proceeding which is required by law to be kept secret, except in the proper discharge of his official duties or upon written order of the court. Nothing contained herein shall prohibit a witness from disclosing his own testimony.

Unlawful grand jury disclosure is a class E felony.

HISTORY: Add, L 1965, ch 1030, § 1, with substance derived from §§ 1783, 1783-a, 1784; amd, L 1977, ch 451, § 4, L 1980, ch 843, § 43, eff Sept 1, 1980.

§ 215.75. Unlawful disclosure of an indictment

A public servant is guilty of unlawful disclosure of an indictment when, except in the proper discharge of his official duties, he intentionally discloses the fact that an indictment has been found or filed before the accused person is in custody.

Unlawful disclosure of an indictment is a class B misdemeanor.

HISTORY: Add, L 1965, ch 1030, § 1, eff Sept 1, 1967, with substance derived from § 1782.

§ 215.80. Unlawful disposition of assets subject to forfeiture

Any defendant in a forfeiture action pursuant to article thirteen-A of the civil practice law and rules who knowingly and intentionally conceals, destroys, dissipates, alters, removes from the jurisdiction, or otherwise disposes of, property specified in a provisional remedy ordered by the court or in a judgment of forfeiture in knowing contempt of said order shall be guilty of a class A misdemeanor.

HISTORY: Add, L 1984, ch 669, § 3, eff Aug 1, 1984 and applicable to crimes committed on and after Aug 1, 1984.

TITLE M   Offenses Against Public Health and Morals

ARTICLE 220
CONTROLLED SUBSTANCES OFFENSES

ARTICLE 221
OFFENSES INVOLVING MARIHUANA

ARTICLE 225
GAMBLING OFFENSES

ARTICLE 230
PROSTITUTION OFFENSES

ARTICLE 235
OBSCENITY AND RELATED OFFENSES

HISTORY: Add, L 1965, ch 1030, § 1, eff Sept 1, 1967.

ARTICLE 220   CONTROLLED SUBSTANCES OFFENSES

HISTORY: Add, L 1965, ch 1030, § 1, eff Sept 1, 1967. Art heading, add, L 1973, ch 276, § 19, eff Sept 1, 1973. Former Art heading, repealed, L 1973, ch 276, § 18, eff Sept 1, 1973.

§ 220.00. Controlled substances; definitions

1. "Sell" means to sell, exchange, give or dispose of to another, or to offer or agree to do the same.

2. "Unlawfully" means in violation of article thirty-three of the public health law.

3. "Ounce" means an avoirdupois ounce as applied to solids or semisolids, and a fluid ounce as applied to liquids.

4. "Pound" means an avoirdupois pound.

5. "Controlled substance" means any substance listed in schedule I, II, III, IV or V of section thirty-three hundred six of the public health law other than marihuana, but including concentrated cannabis as defined in paragraph (a) of subdivision four of section thirty-three hundred two of such law.

6. "Marihuana" means "marihuana" or "concentrated cannabis" as those terms are defined in section thirty-three hundred two of the public health law.

7. "Narcotic drug" means any controlled substance listed in schedule I(b), I(c), II(b) or II(c) other than methadone.

8. "Narcotic preparation" means any controlled substance listed in schedule II(b-1), III(d) or III(e).

9. "Hallucinogen" means any controlled substance listed in schedule I(d)(5), (18), (19), (20), (21) and (22).

10. "Hallucinogenic substance" means any controlled substance listed in schedule I(d) other than concentrated cannabis, lysergic acid diethylamide, or an hallucinogen.

11. "Stimulant" means any controlled substance listed in schedule I(f), II(d).

12. "Dangerous depressant" means any controlled substance listed in schedule I(e)(2), (3), II(e), III(c)(3) or IV(c)(2), (31), (32), (40).

13. "Depressant" means any controlled substance listed in schedule IV(c) except (c)(2), (31), (32), (40).

14. "School grounds" means (a) in or on or within any building, structure, athletic playing field, playground or land contained within the real property boundary line of a public or private elementary, parochial, intermediate, junior high, vocational, or high school, or (b) any area accessible to the public located within one thousand feet of the real property boundary line comprising any such school or any parked automobile or other parked vehicle located within one thousand feet of the real property boundary line comprising any such school. For the purposes of this section an "area accessible to the public" shall mean sidewalks, streets, parking lots, parks, playgrounds, stores and restaurants.

15. "Prescription for a controlled substance" means a direction or authorization, by means of an official New York state prescription form, a written prescription form or an oral prescription, which will permit a person to lawfully obtain a controlled substance from any person authorized to dispense controlled substances.

16. For the purposes of sections 220.70, 220.71, 220.72, 220.73, 220.74, 220.75 and 220.76 of this article:

(a) "Precursor" means ephedrine, pseudoephedrine, or any salt, isomer or salt of an isomer of such substances.

(b) "Chemical reagent" means a chemical reagent that can be used in the manufacture, production or preparation of methamphetamine.

(c) "Solvent" means a solvent that can be used in the manufacture, production or preparation of methamphetamine.

(d) "Laboratory equipment" means any items, components or materials that can be used in the manufacture, preparation or production of methamphetamine.

(e) "Hazardous or dangerous material" means any substance, or combination of substances, that results from or is used in the manufacture, preparation or production of methamphetamine which, because of its quantity, concentration, or physical or chemical characteristics, poses a substantial risk to human health or safety, or a substantial danger to the environment.

17. "School bus" means every motor vehicle owned by a public or governmental agency or private school and operated for the transportation of pupils, teachers and other persons acting in a supervisory capacity, to or from school or school activities or privately owned and operated for compensation for the transportation of pupils, children of pupils, teachers and other persons acting in a supervisory capacity to or from school or school activities.

18. "Controlled substance organization" means four or more persons sharing a common purpose to engage in conduct that constitutes or advances the commission of a felony under this article.

19. "Director" means a person who is the principal administrator, organizer, or leader of a controlled substance organization or one of several principal administrators, organizers, or leaders of a controlled substance organization.

20. "Profiteer" means a person who: (a) is a director of a controlled substance organization; (b) is a member of a controlled substance organization and has managerial responsibility over one or more other members of that organization; or (c) arranges, devises or plans one or more transactions constituting a felony under this article so as to obtain profits or expected profits. A person is not a profiteer if he or she is acting only as an employee; or if he or she is acting as an accommodation

to a friend or relative; or if he or she is acting only under the direction and control of others and exercises no substantial, independent role in arranging or directing the transactions in question.

HISTORY: Add, L 1973, ch 276, § 19, eff Sept 1, 1973; amd, L 1973, ch 1051, §§ 6, 7, eff Sept 1, 1973, L 1975, ch 785, § 1, L 1977, ch 360, § 4, L 1978, ch 772, § 3, L 1981, ch 455, § 3, L 1981, ch 474, § 3, L 1985, ch 341, § 1, eff Nov 1, 1985, L 1985, ch 664, § 2, eff Nov 1, 1985, L 1986, ch 118, § 1, eff Nov 1, 1986, L 1986, ch 280, § 3; amd, L 1994, ch 292, § 1, eff Nov 1, 1994, L 1998, ch 537, § 13, eff Nov 1, 1998, L 2005, ch 394, § 3, eff Oct 1, 2005, L 2006, ch 436, § 2, eff Sept 1, 2006, L 2009, ch 56, § 27 (Part AAA), eff Nov 1, 2009, L 2012, ch 477, § 18 (Part C), eff Feb 23, 2013.

§ 220.02. [Repealed]

HISTORY: Add, L 1972, ch 878, § 4; amd, L 1973, ch 163, § 23, L 1973, ch 413, § 1, L 1973, ch 1051, § 20; repealed, L 1973, ch 276, § 18, eff Sept 1, 1973.

§ 220.03. Criminal possession of a controlled substance in the seventh degree

A person is guilty of criminal possession of a controlled substance in the seventh degree when he or she knowingly and unlawfully possesses a controlled substance; provided, however, that it shall not be a violation of this section when a person possesses a residual amount of a controlled substance and that residual amount is in or on a hypodermic syringe or hypodermic needle obtained and possessed pursuant to section thirty-three hundred eighty-one of the public health law; nor shall it be a violation of this section when a person's unlawful possession of a controlled substance is discovered as a result of seeking immediate health care as defined in paragraph (b) of subdivision three of section 220.78 of the penal law, for either another person or him or herself because such person is experiencing a drug or alcohol overdose or other life threatening medical emergency as defined in paragraph (a) of subdivision three of section 220.78 of the penal law.

Criminal possession of a controlled substance in the seventh degree is a class A misdemeanor.

HISTORY: Add, L 1973, ch 276, § 19; amd, L 1978, ch 772, § 4, L 1979, ch 410, § 11, eff Sept 1, 1979, L 2010, ch 284, § 1, eff Oct 28, 2010, L 2011, ch 154, § 4, eff Sept 18, 2011.

§ 220.05. [Repealed]

HISTORY: Add, L 1978, ch 772, § 5; amd, L 1979, ch 410, § 11; repealed, L 1985, ch 341, § 2, eff Nov 1, 1985. Former § 220.05, add, L 1965, ch 1030, § 1, with substance derived from §§ 1747-b, 1747-c, 1751-a(1); amd, L 1969, ch 788, § 1; repealed, L 1973, ch 276, § 18, eff Sept 1, 1973.

§ 220.06. Criminal possession of a controlled substance in the fifth degree

A person is guilty of criminal possession of a controlled substance in the fifth degree when he knowingly and unlawfully possesses:

1. a controlled substance with intent to sell it; or

2. one or more preparations, compounds, mixtures or substances containing a narcotic preparation and said preparations, compounds, mixtures or substances are of an aggregate weight of one-half ounce or more; or

3. phencyclidine and said phencyclidine weighs fifty milligrams or more; or

4. one or more preparations, compounds, mixtures or substances containing concentrated cannabis as defined in paragraph (a) of subdivision four of section thirty-three hundred two of the public health law and said preparations, compounds, mixtures or substances are of an aggregate weight of one-fourth ounce or more; or

5. cocaine and said cocaine weighs five hundred milligrams or more.

6. ketamine and said ketamine weighs more than one thousand milligrams; or

7. ketamine and has previously been convicted of possession or the attempt to commit possession of ketamine in any amount; or

8. one or more preparations, compounds, mixtures or substances containing gamma hydroxybutyric acid, as defined in paragraph four of subdivision (e) of schedule I of section thirty-three hundred six of the public health law, and said preparations, compounds, mixtures or substances are of an aggregate weight of twenty-eight grams or more.

Criminal possession of a controlled substance in the fifth degree is a class D felony.

HISTORY: Add, L 1973, ch 276, § 19, with substance derived in part from § 220.05; amd, L 1973, ch 1051, § 8, L 1977, ch 360, § 5, L 1979, ch 410, § 11, L 1995, ch 75, § 1, eff June 10, 1995. Section heading, amd, L 1979, ch 410, § 11, eff Sept 1, 1979. Sub 2, amd, L 1995, ch 75, § 1, eff June 10, 1995. Sub 3, add, L 1978, ch 772, § 6; amd, L 1985, ch 341, § 3, L 1995, ch 75, § 1, eff June 10, 1995. Former sub 3, renumbered sub 4, L 1978, ch 772, § 6, eff Sept 1, 1978. Sub 4, formerly sub 3, renumbered sub 4, L 1978, ch 772, § 6; amd, L 1995, ch 75, § 1, L 1998, ch 537, § 14, eff Nov 1, 1998. Former sub 4, deleted, L 1977, ch 360, § 5, eff July 29, 1977, and applicable to acts committed on or after such date. Sub 5, add, L 1988, ch 178, § 1; amd, L 1995, ch 75, § 1, eff June 10, 1995. Sub 6, add, L 1997, ch 635, § 3, eff Jan 22, 1998. Sub 7, add, L 1997, ch 635, § 3, eff Jan 22, 1998. Sub 7, amd, L 2003, ch 264, § 25, eff Nov 1, 2003. Sub 8, add, L 2003, ch 264, § 25, eff Nov 1, 2003.

§ 220.09. Criminal possession of a controlled substance in the fourth degree

A person is guilty of criminal possession of a controlled substance in the fourth degree when he knowingly and unlawfully possesses:

1. one or more preparations, compounds, mixtures or substances containing a narcotic drug and said preparations, compounds, mixtures or substances are of an aggregate weight of one-eighth ounce or more; or

2. one or more preparations, compounds, mixtures or substances containing methamphetamine, its salts, isomers or salts of isomers and said preparations, compounds, mixtures or substances are of an aggregate weight of one-half ounce or more; or

3. one or more preparations, compounds, mixtures or substances containing a narcotic preparation and said preparations, compounds, mixtures or substances are of an aggregate weight of two ounces or more; or

4. a stimulant and said stimulant weighs one gram or more; or

5. lysergic acid diethylamide and said lysergic acid diethylamide weighs one milligram or more; or

6. a hallucinogen and said hallucinogen weighs twenty-five milligrams or more; or

7. a hallucinogenic substance and said hallucinogenic substance weighs one gram or more; or

8. a dangerous depressant and such dangerous depressant weighs ten ounces or more; or

9. a depressant and such depressant weighs two pounds or more; or

10. one or more preparations, compounds, mixtures or substances containing concentrated cannabis as defined in paragraph (a) of subdivision four of section thirty-three hundred two of the public health law and said preparations, compounds, mixtures or substances are of an aggregate weight of one ounce or more; or

11. phencyclidine and said phencyclidine weighs two hundred fifty milligrams or more; or

12. methadone and said methadone weighs three hundred sixty milligrams or more; or

13. phencyclidine and said phencyclidine weighs fifty milligrams or more with intent to sell it and has previously been convicted of an offense defined in this article or the attempt or conspiracy to commit any such offense; or

14. ketamine and said ketamine weighs four thousand milligrams or more; or

15. one or more preparations, compounds, mixtures or substances containing gamma hydroxybutyric acid, as defined in paragraph four of subdivision (e) of schedule I of section thirty-three hundred six of the public health law, and said preparations, compounds, mixtures or substances are of an aggregate weight of two hundred grams or more.

Criminal possession of a controlled substance in the fourth degree is a class C felony.

HISTORY: Add, L 1973, ch 276, § 19, with substance derived in part from § 220.10; amd, L 1979, ch 410, § 11, L 1985, ch 341, § 4, L 1995, ch 75, § 2, eff June 10, 1995. Section heading, amd, L 1979, ch 410, § 11, eff Sept 1, 1979. Sub 1, amd, L 1995, ch 75, § 2, eff June 10, 1995. Sub 2, amd, L 1995, ch 75, § 2, eff June 10, 1995. Sub 3, amd, L 1995, ch 75, § 2, eff June 10, 1995. Sub 4, amd, L 1973, ch 1051, § 9, L 1995, ch 75, § 2, eff June 10, 1995. Sub 5, amd, L 1973, ch 1051, § 9, L 1995, ch 75, § 2, eff June 10, 1995. Sub 6, amd, L 1973, ch 1051, § 9, L 1995, ch 75, § 2, eff June 10, 1995. Sub 7, amd, L 1973, ch 1051, § 9, L 1995, ch 75, § 2, eff June 10, 1995. Sub 8, amd, L 1973, ch 1051, § 9, L 1995, ch 75, § 2, eff June 10, 1995. Sub 9, amd, L 1973, ch 1051, § 9, L 1995, ch 75, § 2, eff June 10, 1995. Sub 10, amd, L 1973, ch 1051, § 9, L 1977, ch 360, § 6, L 1995, ch 75, § 2, L 1998, ch 537, § 15, eff Nov 1, 1998. Sub 11, add, L 1978, ch 772, § 7; amd, L 1985, ch 341, § 4, L 1995, ch 75, § 2, eff June 10, 1995. Former sub 11, amd, L 1975, ch 785, § 2; renumbered sub 12, L 1978, ch 772, § 7, eff Sept 1, 1978. Prior sub 11, deleted, L 1977, ch 360, § 6, eff July 29, 1977. Sub 12, add, L 1975, ch 785, § 2; renumbered sub 11, L 1977, ch 360, § 6; renumbered sub 12, L 1978, ch 772, § 7; amd, L 1985, ch 341, § 4, L 1995, ch 75, § 2, eff June 10, 1995. Sub 13, add, L 1985, ch 341, § 4; amd, L 1995, ch 75, § 2, L 1997, ch 635, § 4, eff Jan 22, 1998. Sub 14, add, L 1997, ch 635, § 5, eff Jan 22, 1998. Sub 14, amd, L 2003, ch 264, § 26, eff Nov 1, 2003. Sub 15, add, L 2003, ch 264, § 26, eff Nov 1, 2003.

§ 220.10. [Repealed]

HISTORY: Add, L 1965, ch 1030, § 1, with substance derived from § 1751(2); amd, L 1969, ch 788, § 2; repealed, L 1973, ch 276, § 18, eff Sept 1, 1973.

§ 220.12. [Repealed]

HISTORY: Add, L 1973, ch 276, § 19, with substance derived from § 220.15; amd, L 1978, ch 772, § 8; repealed, L 1979, ch 410, § 12, eff Sept 1, 1979.

§ 220.15. [Repealed]

HISTORY: Add, L 1965, ch 1030, § 1, with substance derived from § 1751; amd, L 1969, ch 788, § 3; repealed, L 1973, ch 276, § 18, eff Sept 1, 1973.

§ 220.16. Criminal possession of a controlled substance in the third degree

A person is guilty of criminal possession of a controlled substance in the third degree when he knowingly and unlawfully possesses:

1. a narcotic drug with intent to sell it; or

2. a stimulant, hallucinogen, hallucinogenic substance, or lysergic acid diethylamide, with intent to sell it and has previously been convicted of an offense defined in article two hundred twenty or the attempt or conspiracy to commit any such offense; or

3. a stimulant with intent to sell it and said stimulant weighs one gram or more; or

4. lysergic acid diethylamide with intent to sell it and said lysergic acid diethylamide weighs one milligram or more; or

5. a hallucinogen with intent to sell it and said hallucinogen weighs twenty-five milligrams or more; or

6. a hallucinogenic substance with intent to sell it and said hallucinogenic substance weighs one gram or more; or

7. one or more preparations, compounds, mixtures or substances containing methamphetamine, its salts, isomers or salts of isomers with intent to sell it and said preparations, compounds, mixtures or substances are of an aggregate weight of one-eighth ounce or more; or

8. a stimulant and said stimulant weighs five grams or more; or

9. lysergic acid diethylamide and said lysergic acid diethylamide weighs five milligrams or more; or

10. a hallucinogen and said hallucinogen weighs one hundred twenty-five milligrams or more; or

11. a hallucinogenic substance and said hallucinogenic substance weighs five grams or more; or

12. one or more preparations, compounds, mixtures or substances containing a narcotic drug and said preparations, compounds, mixtures or substances are of an aggregate weight of one-half ounce or more; or

13. phencyclidine and said phencyclidine weighs one thousand two hundred fifty milligrams or more.

Criminal possession of a controlled substance in the third degree is a class B felony.

HISTORY: Add, L 1973, ch 276, § 19, with substance derived from § 220.20; amd, L 1995, ch 75, § 3, eff June 10, 1995. Sub 1, amd, L 1973, ch 1051, § 10, eff Sept 1, 1973. Sub 2, add, L 1973, ch 1051, § 10, eff Sept 1, 1973. Sub 3, add, L 1973, ch 1051, § 10; amd, L 1995, ch 75, § 3, eff June 10, 1995. Former sub 3, renumbered sub 9, L 1973, ch 1051, § 10, eff Sept 1, 1973. Sub 4, add, L 1973, ch 1051, § 10; amd, L 1995, ch 75, § 3, eff June 10, 1995. Former sub 4, renumbered sub 10, L 1973, ch 1051, § 10, eff Sept 1, 1973. Sub 5, add, L 1973, ch 1051, § 10; amd, L 1995, ch 75, § 3, eff June 10, 1995. Former sub 5, renumbered sub 11, L 1973, ch 1051, § 10, eff Sept 1, 1973. Sub 6, add, L 1973, ch 1051, § 10; amd, L 1995, ch 75, § 3, eff June 10, 1995. Sub 7, add, L 1973, ch 1051, § 10; amd, L 1995, ch 75, § 3, eff June 10, 1995. Sub 8, formerly sub 2, renumbered sub 8 and amd, L 1973, ch 1051, § 10; amd, L 1995, ch 75, § 3, eff June 10, 1995. Sub 9, formerly sub 3, renumbered sub 9, and amd, L 1973, ch 1051, § 10; amd, L 1995, ch 75, § 3, eff June 10, 1995. Sub 10, formerly sub 4, renumbered sub 10 and amd, L 1973, ch 1051, § 10; amd, L 1995, ch 75, § 3, eff June 10, 1995. Sub 11, formerly sub 5, renumbered sub 11 and amd, L 1973, ch 1051, § 10; amd, L 1979, ch 410, § 13, L 1995, ch 75, § 3, eff June 10, 1995. Sub 12, add, L 1979, ch 410, § 13; amd, L 1995, ch 75, § 3, eff June 10, 1995. Sub 13, add, L 1985, ch 341, § 5; amd, L 1995, ch 75, § 3, eff June 10, 1995. Concluding par, re-enacted without change, L 1973, ch 1051, § 10; amd, L 1979, ch 410, § 13, eff Sept 1, 1979.

§ 220.18. Criminal possession of a controlled substance in the second degree

A person is guilty of criminal possession of a controlled substance in the second degree when he or she knowingly and unlawfully possesses:

1. one or more preparations, compounds, mixtures or substances containing a narcotic drug and said preparations, compounds, mixtures or substances are of an aggregate weight of four ounces or more; or

2. one or more preparations, compounds, mixtures or substances containing methamphetamine, its salts, isomers or salts of isomers and said preparations, compounds, mixtures or

substances are of an aggregate weight of two ounces or more; or

3. a stimulant and said stimulant weighs ten grams or more; or

4. lysergic acid diethylamide and said lysergic acid diethylamide weighs twenty-five milligrams or more; or

5. a hallucinogen and said hallucinogen weighs six hundred twenty-five milligrams or more; or

6. a hallucinogenic substance and said hallucinogenic substance weighs twenty-five grams or more; or

7. methadone and said methadone weighs two thousand eight hundred eighty milligrams or more.

Criminal possession of a controlled substance in the second degree is a class A-II felony.

HISTORY: Add, L 1973, ch 276, § 19, with substance derived in part from § 220.22; amd, L 1995, ch 75, § 4, eff June 10, 1995. Opening par, amd, L 2004, ch 738, § 21, eff Dec 14, 2004. Sub 1, amd, L 1979, ch 410, § 14, L 1995, ch 75, § 4, eff June 10, 1995. Sub 1, amd, L 2004, ch 738, § 21, eff Dec 14, 2004. Sub 2, amd, L 1973, ch 1051, § 11, L 1995, ch 75, § 4, eff June 10, 1995. Sub 3, amd, L 1973, ch 1051, § 11, L 1995, ch 75, § 4, eff June 10, 1995. Sub 4, amd, L 1973, ch 1051, § 11, L 1995, ch 75, § 4, eff June 10, 1995. Sub 5, amd, L 1973, ch 1051, § 11, L 1995, ch 75, § 4, eff June 10, 1995. Sub 6, amd, L 1973, ch 1051, § 11, L 1975, ch 785, § 3, L 1995, ch 75, § 4, eff June 10, 1995. Sub 7, add, L 1975, ch 785, § 3; amd, L 1995, ch 75, § 4, eff June 10, 1995.

§ 220.20. [Repealed]

HISTORY: Add, L 1965, ch 1030, § 1; amd, L 1969, ch 788, § 4; repealed, L 1973, ch 276, § 18, eff Sept 1, 1973.

§ 220.21. Criminal possession of controlled substance in the first degree

A person is guilty of criminal possession of a controlled substance in the first degree when he or she knowingly and unlawfully possesses:

1. one or more preparations, compounds, mixtures or substances containing a narcotic drug and said preparations, compounds, mixtures or substances are of an aggregate weight of eight ounces or more; or

2. methadone and said methadone weighs five thousand seven hundred sixty milligrams or more.

Criminal possession of a controlled substance in the first degree is a class A-I felony.

HISTORY: Add, L 1973, ch 276, § 19, with substance derived from § 220.23; amd, L 1973, ch 1051, § 13, L 1975, ch 785, § 4, L 1995, ch 75, § 5, eff June 10, 1995. Opening par, amd, L 2004, ch 738, § 22, eff Dec 14, 2004. Sub 1, amd, L 1979, ch 410, § 15, L 1995, ch 75, § 5, eff June 10, 1995. Sub 1, amd, L 2004, ch 738, § 22, eff Dec 14, 2004. Sub 2, amd, L 1995, ch 75, § 5, eff June 10, 1995.

§ 220.22. [Repealed]

HISTORY: Add, L 1969, ch 788, § 5; repealed, L 1973, ch 276, § 18, eff Sept 1, 1973.

§ 220.23. [Repealed]

HISTORY: Added as § 220.33, L 1969, ch 788, § 6; renumbered § 220.23, L 1970, ch 213, § 1; repealed, L 1973, ch 276, § 18, eff Sept 1, 1973.

§ 220.25. Criminal possession of a controlled substance; presumption

1. The presence of a controlled substance in an automobile, other than a public omnibus, is presumptive evidence of knowing possession thereof by each and every person in the automobile at the time such controlled substance was found; except that such presumption does not apply (a) to a duly licensed operator of an automobile who is at the time operating it for hire in the lawful and proper pursuit of his trade, or (b) to any person in the automobile if one of them, having obtained the controlled substance and not being under duress, is authorized to possess it and such controlled substance is in the same container as when he received possession thereof, or (c) when the controlled substance is concealed upon the person of one of the occupants.

2. The presence of a narcotic drug, narcotic preparation, marihuana or phencyclidine in open view in a room, other than a public place, under circumstances evincing an intent to unlawfully mix, compound, package or otherwise prepare for sale such controlled substance is presumptive evidence of knowing possession thereof by each and every person in close proximity to such controlled substance at the time such controlled substance was found; except that such presumption does not apply to any such persons if (a) one of them, having obtained such controlled substance and not being under duress, is authorized to possess it and such controlled substance is in the same container as when he received possession thereof, or (b) one of them has such controlled substance upon his person.

HISTORY: Add, L 1965, ch 1030, § 1, eff Sept 1, 1967, with substance derived from § 1751(4). Section heading, amd, L 1973, ch 276, § 20, eff Sept 1, 1973. Sub 1, formerly entire section, so designated, L 1971, ch 1044, § 1; amd, L 1973, ch 276, § 20, L 1973, ch 278, § 9, eff Sept 1, 1973. Sub 2, add, L 1971, ch 1044, § 1; amd, L 1973, ch 276, § 20, L 1978, ch 772, § 9, L 1985, ch 341, § 6, eff Nov 1, 1985.

§ 220.28. Use of a child to commit a controlled substance offense

1. A person is guilty of use of a child to commit a controlled substance offense when, being eighteen years old or more, he or she commits a felony sale or felony attempted sale of a controlled substance in violation of this article and, as part of that criminal transaction, knowingly uses a child to effectuate such felony sale or felony attempted sale of such controlled substance.

2. For purposes of this section, "uses a child to effectuate the felony sale or felony attempted sale of such controlled substance" means conduct by which the actor: (a) conceals such controlled substance on or about the body or person of such child for the purpose of effectuating the criminal sale or attempted sale of such controlled substance to a third person; or (b) directs, forces or otherwise requires such child to sell or attempt to sell or offer direct assistance to the defendant in selling or attempting to sell such controlled substance to a third person.

For purposes of this section, "child" means a person less than sixteen years of age.

Use of a child to commit a controlled substance offense is a class E felony.

HISTORY: Add, L 2006, ch 564, § 1, eff Nov 1, 2006.

§ 220.30. [Repealed]

HISTORY: Add, L 1965, ch 1030, § 1, with substance derived from §§ 1747-b, 1747-c, 1751(1); amd, L 1969, ch 787, § 1; repealed, L 1973, ch 276, § 18, eff Sept 1, 1973.

§ 220.31. Criminal sale of a controlled substance in the fifth degree

A person is guilty of criminal sale of a controlled substance in the fifth degree when he knowingly and unlawfully sells a controlled substance.

Criminal sale of a controlled substance in the fifth degree is a class D felony.

HISTORY: Add, L 1973, ch 276, § 19; amd, L 1979, ch 410, § 16, eff Sept 1, 1979. Section heading, amd, L 1979, ch 410, § 16, eff Sept 1, 1979.

§ 220.33. [Renumbered]

HISTORY: Add, L 1969, ch 788, § 6; renumbered § 220.23, L 1970, ch 213, § 1, eff April 24, 1970.

§ 220.34. Criminal sale of a controlled substance in the fourth degree

A person is guilty of criminal sale of a controlled substance in the fourth degree when he knowingly and unlawfully sells:

1. a narcotic preparation; or

2. a dangerous depressant or a depressant and the dangerous depressant weighs ten ounces or more, or the depressant weighs two pounds or more; or

3. concentrated cannabis as defined in paragraph (a) of subdivision four of section thirty-three hundred two of the public health law; or

4. phencyclidine and the phencyclidine weighs fifty milligrams or more; or

5. methadone; or

6. any amount of phencyclidine and has previously been convicted of an offense defined in this article or the attempt or conspiracy to commit any such offense; or

6-a. ketamine and said ketamine weighs four thousand milligrams or more.

7. a controlled substance in violation of section 220.31 of this article, when such sale takes place upon school grounds or on a school bus; or

8. a controlled substance in violation of section 220.31 of this article, when such sale takes place upon the grounds of a child day care or educational facility under circumstances evincing knowledge by the defendant that such sale is taking place upon such grounds. As used in this subdivision, the phrase "the grounds of a child day care or educational facility" shall have the same meaning as provided for in subdivision five of section 220.44 of this article. For the purposes of this subdivision, a rebuttable presumption shall be established that a person has knowledge that they are within the grounds of a child day care or educational facility when notice is conspicuously posted of the presence or proximity of such facility; or

9. one or more preparations, compounds, mixtures or substances containing gamma hydroxybutyric acid, as defined in paragraph four of subdivision (e) of schedule I of section thirty-three hundred six of the public health law, and said preparations, compounds, mixtures or substances are of an aggregate weight of twenty-eight grams or more.

Criminal sale of a controlled substance in the fourth degree is a class C felony.

HISTORY: Add, L 1979, ch 410, § 17; amd, L 1985, ch 341, § 7, L 1986, ch 280, § 4, L 1995, ch 75, § 6, eff June 10, 1995. Former § 220.34, add, L 1973, ch 276, § 19; amd, L 1973, ch 1051, § 12, L 1975, ch 785, § 5, L 1977, ch 360, § 7, L 1978, ch 772, § 10; repealed, L 1979, ch 410, § 17, eff Sept 1, 1979. Sub 2, amd, L 1995, ch 75, § 6, eff June 10, 1995. Sub 3, amd, L 1998, ch 537, § 16, eff Nov 1, 1998. Sub 4, amd, L 1985, ch 341, § 7, L 1995, ch 75, § 6, eff June 10, 1995. Sub 5, amd, L 1985, ch 341, § 7, eff Nov 1, 1985. Sub 6, add, L 1985, ch 341, § 7; amd, L 1986, ch 280, § 4, eff Nov 1, 1986. Sub 6-a, add, L 1997, ch 635, § 6, eff Jan 22, 1998. Sub 7, add, L 1986, ch 280, § 4; amd, L 1994, ch 292, § 2, L 1998, ch 289, § 1, eff Sept 1, 1998. Sub 7, amd, L 2006, ch 436, § 3, eff Sept 1, 2006. Sub 8, add, L 1998, ch 289, § 1, eff Sept 1, 1998. Sub 8, amd, L 2003, ch 264, § 27, eff Nov 1, 2003. Sub 9, add, L 2003, ch 264, § 27, eff Nov 1, 2003.

§ 220.35. [Repealed]

HISTORY: Add, L 1965, ch 1030, § 1, with substance derived from § 1751(1); amd, L 1969, ch 787, § 2; repealed, L 1973, ch 276, § 18, eff Sept 1, 1973.

§ 220.37. [Repealed]

> **HISTORY:** Add, L 1973, ch 276, § 19; amd, L 1978, ch 772, § 11; repealed, L 1979, ch 410, § 18, eff Sept 1, 1979.

§ 220.39. Criminal sale of a controlled substance in the third degree

A person is guilty of criminal sale of a controlled substance in the third degree when he knowingly and unlawfully sells:

1. a narcotic drug; or

2. a stimulant, hallucinogen, hallucinogenic substance, or lysergic acid diethylamide and has previously been convicted of an offense defined in article two hundred twenty or the attempt or conspiracy to commit any such offense; or

3. a stimulant and the stimulant weighs one gram or more; or

4. lysergic acid diethylamide and the lysergic acid diethylamide weighs one milligram or more; or

5. a hallucinogen and the hallucinogen weighs twenty-five milligrams or more; or

6. a hallucinogenic substance and the hallucinogenic substance weighs one gram or more; or

7. one or more preparations, compounds, mixtures or substances containing methamphetamine, its salts, isomers or salts of isomers and the preparations, compounds, mixtures or substances are of an aggregate weight of one-eighth ounce or more; or

8. phencyclidine and the phencyclidine weighs two hundred fifty milligrams or more; or

9. a narcotic preparation to a person less than twenty-one years old.

Criminal sale of a controlled substance in the third degree is a class B felony.

> **HISTORY:** Add, L 1973, ch 276, § 19; amd, L 1973, ch 278, § 5, L 1973, ch 1051, § 14, eff Sept 1, 1973. Sub 2, add, L 1973, ch 1051, § 14, eff Sept 1, 1973. Former sub 2, add, L 1973, ch 278, § 5; renumbered sub 3, L 1973, ch 1051, § 14, eff Sept 1, 1973. Prior sub 2, repealed, L 1973, ch 278, § 5, eff Sept 1, 1973. Sub 3, formerly sub 2, add, L 1973, ch 278, § 5; renumbered sub 3 and amd, L 1973, ch 1051, § 14; amd, L 1995, ch 75, § 7, eff June 10, 1995. Former sub 3, add, L 1973, ch 278, § 5, with substance derived from former sub 2; repealed, L 1973, ch 1051, § 14, eff Sept 1, 1973. Prior sub 3, repealed, L 1973, ch 278, § 5, eff Sept 1, 1973. Sub 4, add, L 1973, ch 278, § 5; amd, L 1973, ch 1051, § 14, L 1995, ch 75, § 7, eff June 10, 1995. Sub 5, formerly sub 6, add, L 1973, ch 278, § 5; renumbered sub 5 and amd, L 1973, ch 1051, § 14; amd, L 1995, ch 75, § 7, eff June 10, 1995. Former sub 5, add, L 1973, ch 278, § 5, with substance derived from former sub 3; repealed, L 1973, ch 1051, § 14, eff Sept 1, 1973. Sub 6, formerly sub 8, add, L 1973, ch 278, § 5; renumbered sub 6 and amd, L 1973, ch 1051, § 14; amd, L 1995, ch 75, § 7, eff June 10, 1995. Former sub 6, add, L 1973, ch 278, § 5; renumbered sub 5, L 1973, ch 1051, § 14, eff Sept 1, 1973. Sub 7, formerly sub 10, renumbered sub 7 and amd, L 1973, ch 1051, § 14, L 1979, ch 410, § 19; amd, L 1995, ch 75, § 7, eff June 10, 1995. Former sub 7, add, L 1973, ch 278, § 5, with substance derived from former sub 3; repealed, L 1973, ch 1051, § 14, eff Sept 1, 1973. Sub 8, add, L 1979, ch 410, § 19; amd, L 1985, ch 341, § 8, L 1995, ch 75, § 7, eff June 10, 1995. Former sub 8, add, L 1973, ch 278, § 5; renumbered sub 6, L 1973, ch 1051, § 14, eff Sept 1, 1973. Sub 9, add, L 1979, ch 410, § 19, eff Sept 1, 1979. Former sub 9, add, L 1973, ch 278, § 5, with substance derived from former sub 3; repealed, L 1973, ch 1051, § 14, eff Sept 1, 1973. Sub 10, add, L 1973, ch 278, § 5; renumbered sub 7, L 1973, ch 1051, § 14, eff Sept 1, 1973. Sub 11, add, L 1973, ch 278, § 5; repealed, L 1973, ch 1051, § 14, eff Sept 1, 1973. Closing par, amd, L 1979, ch 410, § 19, eff Sept 1, 1979.

§ 220.40. [Repealed]

> **HISTORY:** Add, L 1965, ch 1030, § 1, with substance derived from § 1751(1); amd, L 1969, ch 787, § 3; repealed, L 1973, ch 276, § 18, eff Sept 1, 1973.

§ 220.41. Criminal sale of a controlled substance in the second degree

A person is guilty of criminal sale of a controlled substance in the second degree when he knowingly and unlawfully sells:

1. one or more preparations, compounds, mixtures or substances containing a narcotic drug and the preparations, compounds, mixtures or substances are of an aggregate weight of one-half ounce or more; or

2. one or more preparations, compounds, mixtures or substances containing methamphetamine, its salts, isomers or salts of isomers and the preparations, compounds, mixtures or substances are of an aggregate weight of one-half ounce or more; or

3. a stimulant and the stimulant weighs five grams or more; or

4. lysergic acid diethylamide and the lysergic acid diethylamide weighs five milligrams or more; or

5. a hallucinogen and the hallucinogen weighs one hundred twenty-five milligrams or more; or

6. a hallucinogenic substance and the hallucinogenic substance weighs five grams or more; or

7. methadone and the methadone weighs three hundred sixty milligrams or more.

Criminal sale of a controlled substance in the second degree is a class A-II felony.

> **HISTORY:** Add, L 1973, ch 276, § 19, eff Sept 1, 1973. Sub 1, amd, L 1979, ch 410, § 20, L 1995, ch 75, § 8, eff June 10, 1995. Sub 2, amd, L 1995, ch 75, § 8, eff June 10, 1995. Sub 3, amd, L 1973, ch 1051, § 15, L 1995, ch 75, § 8, eff June 10, 1995. Sub 4, amd, L 1995, ch 75, § 8, eff June 10, 1995. Sub 5, amd, L 1973, ch 1051, § 15, L 1995, ch 75, § 8, eff June 10, 1995. Sub 6, amd, L 1973, ch 1051, § 15, L 1975, ch 785, § 6, L 1995, ch 75, § 8, eff June 10, 1995. Sub 7, add, L 1975, ch 785, § 6; amd, L 1995, ch 75, § 8, eff June 10, 1995.

§ 220.43. Criminal sale of a controlled substance in the first degree

A person is guilty of criminal sale of a controlled substance in the first degree when he knowingly and unlawfully sells:

1. one or more preparations, compounds, mixtures or substances containing a narcotic drug and the preparations, compounds, mixtures or substances are of an aggregate weight of two ounces or more; or

2. methadone and the methadone weighs two thousand eight hundred eighty milligrams or more.

Criminal sale of a controlled substance in the first degree is a class A-I felony.

> **HISTORY:** Add, L 1973, ch 276, § 19; amd, L 1975, ch 785, § 7, eff Aug 8, 1975. Sub 1, amd, L 1979, ch 410, § 21, L 1995, ch 75, § 9, eff June 10, 1995. Sub 2, amd, L 1995, ch 75, § 9, eff June 10, 1995.

§ 220.44. Criminal sale of a controlled substance in or near school grounds

A person is guilty of criminal sale of a controlled substance in or near school grounds when he knowingly and unlawfully sells:

1. a controlled substance in violation of any one of subdivisions one through six-a of section 220.34 of this article, when such sale takes place upon school grounds or on a school bus; or

2. a controlled substance in violation of any one of subdivisions one through eight of section

220.39 of this article, when such sale takes place upon school grounds or on a school bus; or

3. a controlled substance in violation of any one of subdivisions one through six of section 220.34 of this article, when such sale takes place upon the grounds of a child day care or educational facility under circumstances evincing knowledge by the defendant that such sale is taking place upon such grounds; or

4. a controlled substance in violation of any one of subdivisions one through eight of section 220.39 of this article, when such sale takes place upon the grounds of a child day care or educational facility under circumstances evincing knowledge by the defendant that such sale is taking place upon such grounds.

5. For purposes of subdivisions three and four of this section, "the grounds of a child day care or educational facility" means (a) in or on or within any building, structure, athletic playing field, a playground or land contained within the real property boundary line of a public or private child day care center as such term is defined in paragraph (c) of subdivision one of section three hundred ninety of the social services law, or nursery, pre-kindergarten or kindergarten, or (b) any area accessible to the public located within one thousand feet of the real property boundary line comprising any such facility or any parked automobile or other parked vehicle located within one thousand feet of the real property boundary line comprising any such facility. For the purposes of this section an "area accessible to the public" shall mean sidewalks, streets, parking lots, parks, playgrounds, stores and restaurants.

6. For the purposes of this section, a rebuttable presumption shall be established that a person has knowledge that they are within the grounds of a child day care or educational facility when notice is conspicuously posted of the presence or proximity of such facility.

Criminal sale of a controlled substance in or near school grounds is a class B felony.

HISTORY: Add, L 1986, ch 280, § 5; amd, L 1994, ch 292, § 3, L 1998, ch 289, § 2, eff Sept 1, 1998. Former § 220.44, add, L 1969, ch 787, § 4; repealed, L 1973, ch 276, § 18, eff Sept 1, 1973. Sub 1, amd, L 1994, ch 292, § 3, L 1997, ch 635, § 7, L 1998, ch 289, § 2, eff Sept 1, 1998. Sub 1, amd, L 2006, ch 436, § 4, eff Sept 1, 2006. Sub 2, amd, L 1994, ch 292, § 3, eff Nov 1, 1994. Sub 2, amd, L 2006, ch 436, § 4, eff Sept 1, 2006. Sub 3, add, L 1998, ch 289, § 2, eff Sept 1, 1998. Sub 4, add, L 1998, ch 289, § 2, eff Sept 1, 1998. Sub 5, add, L 1998, ch 289, § 2, eff Sept 1, 1998. Sub 6, add, L 1998, ch 289, § 2, eff Sept 1, 1998.

§ 220.45. Criminally possessing a hypodermic instrument

A person is guilty of criminally possessing a hypodermic instrument when he or she knowingly and unlawfully possesses or sells a hypodermic syringe or hypodermic needle. It shall not be a violation of this section when a person obtains and possesses a hypodermic syringe or hypodermic needle pursuant to section thirty-three hundred eighty-one of the public health law.

Criminally possessing a hypodermic instrument is a class A misdemeanor.

HISTORY: Add, L 1965, ch 1030, § 1, eff Sept 1, 1967, with substance derived from § 1747-d, L 2010, ch 284, § 2, eff Oct 28, 2010.

§ 220.46. Criminal injection of a narcotic drug

A person is guilty of criminal injection of a narcotic drug when he knowingly and unlawfully possesses a narcotic drug and he intentionally injects by means of a hypodermic syringe or hypodermic needle all or any portion of that drug into the body of another person with the latter's consent.

Criminal injection of a narcotic drug is a class E felony.

HISTORY: Add, L 1971, ch 896, § 1, eff Sept 1, 1971.

§ 220.48. Criminal sale of a controlled substance to a child

A person is guilty of criminal sale of a controlled substance to a child when, being over twenty-one years old, he or she knowingly and unlawfully sells a controlled substance in violation of section 220.34 or 220.39 of this article to a person less than seventeen years old.

Criminal sale of a controlled substance to a child is a class B felony.

    HISTORY: Add, L 2009, ch 56, § 28 (Part AAA), eff Nov 1, 2009.

§ 220.50. Criminally using drug paraphernalia in the second degree

A person is guilty of criminally using drug paraphernalia in the second degree when he knowingly possesses or sells:

1. Diluents, dilutants or adulterants, including but not limited to, any of the following: quinine hydrochloride, mannitol, mannite, lactose or dextrose, adapted for the dilution of narcotic drugs or stimulants under circumstances evincing an intent to use, or under circumstances evincing knowledge that some person intends to use, the same for purposes of unlawfully mixing, compounding, or otherwise preparing any narcotic drug or stimulant; or

2. Gelatine capsules, glassine envelopes, vials, capsules or any other material suitable for the packaging of individual quantities of narcotic drugs or stimulants under circumstances evincing an intent to use, or under circumstances evincing knowledge that some person intends to use, the same for the purpose of unlawfully manufacturing, packaging or dispensing of any narcotic drug or stimulant; or ·

3. Scales and balances used or designed for the purpose of weighing or measuring controlled substances, under circumstances evincing an intent to use, or under circumstances evincing knowledge that some person intends to use, the same for purpose of unlawfully manufacturing, packaging or dispensing of any narcotic drug or stimulant.

Criminally using drug paraphernalia in the second degree is a class A misdemeanor.

    HISTORY: Add, L 1971, ch 970, § 1; amd, L 1973, ch 276, § 20, L 1990, ch 627, § 1, eff Nov 1, 1990. Sub 1, amd, L 1990, ch 627, § 1, eff Nov 1, 1990. Sub 2, amd, L 1990, ch 627, § 1, eff Nov 1, 1990. Sub 3, add, L 1990, ch 627, § 1, eff Nov 1, 1990.

§ 220.55. Criminally using drug paraphernalia in the first degree

A person is guilty of criminally using drug paraphernalia in the first degree when he commits the crime of criminally using drug paraphernalia in the second degree and he has previously been convicted of criminally using drug paraphernalia in the second degree.

Criminally using drug paraphernalia in the first degree is a class D felony.

    HISTORY: Add, L 1971, ch 970, § 1, eff Sept 1, 1971.

§ 220.60. Criminal possession of precursors of controlled substances

A person is guilty of criminal possession of precursors of controlled substances when, with intent to manufacture a controlled substance unlawfully, he possesses at the same time:

(a) carbamide (urea) and propanedioc and malonic acid or its derivatives; or

(b) ergot or an ergot derivative and diethylamine or dimethylformamide or diethylamide; or

(c) phenylacetone (1-phenyl-2 propanone) and hydroxylamine or ammonia or formamide or benzaldehyde or nitroethane or methylamine.

(d) pentazocine and methyliodide; or

(e) phenylacetonitrile and dichlorodiethyl methylamine or dichlorodiethyl benzylamine; or

(f) diphenylacetonitrile* and dimethylaminoisopropyl chloride; or

(g) piperidine and cyclohexanone and bromobenzene and lithium or magnesium; or

(h) 2, 5-dimethoxy benzaldehyde and nitroethane and a reducing agent.

Criminal prossession [possession]** of precursor of controlled substances is a class E felony.

HISTORY: Add, L 1972, ch 730, § 1; amd, L 1973, ch 276, § 20, eff Sept 1, 1973. Section heading, amd, L 1973, ch 276, § 20, eff Sept 1, 1973. Sub (d), add, L 1973, ch 276, § 20, eff Sept 1, 1973. Sub (e), add, L 1973, ch 276, § 20; amd, L 1974, ch 394, § 1, eff Sept 1, 1974. Sub (f), add, L 1973, ch 276, § 20; amd, L 1974, ch 394, § 1, eff Sept 1, 1974. Sub (g), add, L 1974, ch 394, § 2, eff Sept 1, 1974. Sub (h), add, L 1974, ch 394, § 2, eff Sept 1, 1974.

§ 220.65. Criminal sale of a prescription for a controlled substance or of a controlled substance by a practitioner or pharmacist

A person is guilty of criminal sale of a prescription for a controlled substance or of a controlled substance by a practitioner or pharmacist when:

1. being a practitioner, as that term is defined in section thirty-three hundred two of the public health law, he or she knowingly and unlawfully sells a prescription for a controlled substance. For the purposes of this section, a person sells a prescription for a controlled substance unlawfully when he or she does so other than in good faith in the course of his or her professional practice; or

2. being a practitioner or pharmacist, as those terms are defined in section thirty-three hundred two of the public health law, he or she, acting other than in good faith, while purporting to act within the scope of the power, authority and privileges of his or her license, as that term is defined in section thirty-three hundred two of the public health law, knowingly and unlawfully sells a controlled substance.

Criminal sale of a prescription for a controlled substance or of a controlled substance by a practitioner or pharmacist is a class C felony.

HISTORY: Add, L 1986, ch 118, § 2, eff Nov 1, 1986; amd, L 2014, ch 31, § 1, eff June 23, 2014.

§ 220.70. Criminal possession of methamphetamine manufacturing material in the second degree

A person is guilty of criminal possession of methamphetamine manufacturing material in the second degree when he or she possesses a precursor, a chemical reagent or a solvent with the intent to use or knowing another intends to use such precursor, chemical reagent, or solvent to unlawfully produce, prepare or manufacture methamphetamine.

Criminal possession of methamphetamine manufacturing material in the second degree is a class A misdemeanor.

HISTORY: Add, L 2005, ch 394, § 4, eff Oct 1, 2005.

§ 220.71. Criminal possession of methamphetamine manufacturing material in the first degree

A person is guilty of criminal possession of methamphetamine manufacturing material in the

---

* So in original.

** The bracketed word has been inserted by the Publisher.

first degree when he or she commits the offense of criminal possession of methamphetamine manufacturing material in the second degree, as defined in section 220.70 of this article, and has previously been convicted within the preceding five years of criminal possession of methamphetamine manufacturing material in the second degree, as defined in section 220.70 of this article, or a violation of this section.

Criminal possession of methamphetamine manufacturing material in the first degree is a class E felony.

> **HISTORY:** Add, L 2005, ch 394, § 4, eff Oct 1, 2005.

§ 220.72. Criminal possession of precursors of methamphetamine

A person is guilty of criminal possession of precursors of methamphetamine when he or she possesses at the same time a precursor and a solvent or chemical reagent, with intent to use or knowing that another intends to use each such precursor, solvent or chemical reagent to unlawfully manufacture methamphetamine.

Criminal possession of precursors of methamphetamine is a class E felony.

> **HISTORY:** Add, L 2005, ch 394, § 4, eff Oct 1, 2005.

§ 220.73. Unlawful manufacture of methamphetamine in the third degree

A person is guilty of unlawful manufacture of methamphetamine in the third degree when he or she possesses at the same time and location, with intent to use, or knowing that another intends to use each such product to unlawfully manufacture, prepare or produce methamphetamine:

1. Two or more items of laboratory equipment and two or more precursors, chemical reagents or solvents in any combination; or

2. One item of laboratory equipment and three or more precursors, chemical reagents or solvents in any combination; or

3. A precursor:

(a) mixed together with a chemical reagent or solvent; or

(b) with two or more chemical reagents and/or solvents mixed together.

Unlawful manufacture of methamphetamine in the third degree is a class D felony.

> **HISTORY:** Add, L 2005, ch 394, § 4, eff Oct 1, 2005.

§ 220.74. Unlawful manufacture of methamphetamine in the second degree

A person is guilty of unlawful manufacture of methamphetamine in the second degree when he or she:

1. Commits the offense of unlawful manufacture of methamphetamine in the third degree as defined in section 220.73 of this article in the presence of another person under the age of sixteen, provided, however, that the actor is at least five years older than such other person under the age of sixteen; or

2. Commits the crime of unlawful manufacture of methamphetamine in the third degree as defined in section 220.73 of this article and has previously been convicted within the preceding five years of the offense of criminal possession of precursors of methamphetamine as defined in section 220.72 of this article, criminal possession of methamphetamine manufacturing material in the first degree as defined in section 220.71 of this article, unlawful disposal of methamphetamine laboratory material as defined in section 220.76 of this article, unlawful manufacture of methamphetamine in the third degree as defined in section 220.73 of this article,

unlawful manufacture of methamphetamine in the second degree as defined in this section, or unlawful manufacture of methamphetamine in the first degree as defined in section 220.75 of this article.

Unlawful manufacture of methamphetamine in the second degree is a class C felony.

HISTORY: Add, L 2005, ch 394, § 4, eff Oct 1, 2005.

§ 220.75. Unlawful manufacture of methamphetamine in the first degree

A person is guilty of unlawful manufacture of methamphetamine in the first degree when such person commits the crime of unlawful manufacture of methamphetamine in the second degree, as defined in subdivision one of section 220.74 of this article, after having previously been convicted within the preceding five years of unlawful manufacture of methamphetamine in the third degree, as defined in section 220.73, unlawful manufacture of methamphetamine in the second degree, as defined in section 220.74 of this article, or unlawful manufacture of methamphetamine in the first degree, as defined in this section.

Unlawful manufacturer of methamphetamine in the first degree is a class B felony.

HISTORY: Add, L 2005, ch 394, § 4, eff Oct 1, 2005.

§ 220.76. Unlawful disposal of methamphetamine laboratory material

A person is guilty of unlawful disposal of methamphetamine laboratory material when, knowing that such actions are in furtherance of a methamphetamine operation, he or she knowingly disposes of, or possesses with intent to dispose of, hazardous or dangerous material under circumstances that create a substantial risk to human health or safety or a substantial danger to the environment.

Unlawful disposal of methamphetamine laboratory material is a class E felony.

HISTORY: Add, L 2005, ch 394, § 4, eff Oct 1, 2005.

§ 220.77. Operating as a major trafficker

A person is guilty of operating as a major trafficker when:

1. Such person acts as a director of a controlled substance organization during any period of twelve months or less, during which period such controlled substance organization sells one or more controlled substances, and the proceeds collected or due from such sale or sales have a total aggregate value of seventy-five thousand dollars or more; or

2. As a profiteer, such person knowingly and unlawfully sells, on one or more occasions within six months or less, a narcotic drug, and the proceeds collected or due from such sale or sales have a total aggregate value of seventy-five thousand dollars or more.

3. As a profiteer, such person knowingly and unlawfully possesses, on one or more occasions within six months or less, a narcotic drug with intent to sell the same, and such narcotic drugs have a total aggregate value of seventy-five thousand dollars or more.

Operating as a major trafficker is a class A-I felony.

HISTORY: Add, L 2009, ch 56, § 29 (Part AAA), eff Nov 1, 2009.

§ 220.78. Witness or victim of drug or alcohol overdose

1. A person who, in good faith, seeks health care for someone who is experiencing a drug or alcohol overdose or other life threatening medical emergency shall not be charged or prosecuted for a controlled substance offense under article two hundred twenty or a marihuana offense under article two hundred twenty-one of this title, other than an offense involving sale for consideration or other benefit or gain, or charged or prosecuted for possession of alcohol by a person under age twenty-one years under section sixty-five-c of the alcoholic beverage control law, or for possession

of drug paraphernalia under article thirty-nine of the general business law, with respect to any controlled substance, marihuana, alcohol or paraphernalia that was obtained as a result of such seeking or receiving of health care.

2. A person who is experiencing a drug or alcohol overdose or other life threatening medical emergency and, in good faith, seeks health care for himself or herself or is the subject of such a good faith request for health care, shall not be charged or prosecuted for a controlled substance offense under this article or a marihuana offense under article two hundred twenty-one of this title, other than an offense involving sale for consideration or other benefit or gain, or charged or prosecuted for possession of alcohol by a person under age twenty-one years under section sixty-five-c of the alcoholic beverage control law, or for possession of drug paraphernalia under article thirty-nine of the general business law, with respect to any substance, marihuana, alcohol or paraphernalia that was obtained as a result of such seeking or receiving of health care.

3. Definitions. As used in this section the following terms shall have the following meanings:

(a) "Drug or alcohol overdose" or "overdose" means an acute condition including, but not limited to, physical illness, coma, mania, hysteria or death, which is the result of consumption or use of a controlled substance or alcohol and relates to an adverse reaction to or the quantity of the controlled substance or alcohol or a substance with which the controlled substance or alcohol was combined; provided that a patient's condition shall be deemed to be a drug or alcohol overdose if a prudent layperson, possessing an average knowledge of medicine and health, could reasonably believe that the condition is in fact a drug or alcohol overdose and (except as to death) requires health care.

(b) "Health care" means the professional services provided to a person experiencing a drug or alcohol overdose by a health care professional licensed, registered or certified under title eight of the education law or article thirty of the public health law who, acting within his or her lawful scope of practice, may provide diagnosis, treatment or emergency services for a person experiencing a drug or alcohol overdose.

4. It shall be an affirmative defense to a criminal sale controlled substance offense under this article or a criminal sale of marihuana offense under article two hundred twenty-one of this title, not covered by subdivision one or two of this section, with respect to any controlled substance or marihuana which was obtained as a result of such seeking or receiving of health care, that:

(a) the defendant, in good faith, seeks health care for someone or for him or herself who is experiencing a drug or alcohol overdose or other life threatening medical emergency; and

(b) the defendant has no prior conviction for the commission or attempted commission of a class A-I, A-II or B felony under this article.

5. Nothing in this section shall be construed to bar the admissibility of any evidence in connection with the investigation and prosecution of a crime with regard to another defendant who does not independently qualify for the bar to prosecution or for the affirmative defense; nor with regard to other crimes committed by a person who otherwise qualifies under this section; nor shall anything in this section be construed to bar any seizure pursuant to law, including but not limited to pursuant to section thirty-three hundred eighty-seven of the public health law.

6. The bar to prosecution described in subdivisions one and two of this section shall not apply to the prosecution of a class A-I felony under this article, and the affirmative defense described in subdivision four of this section shall not apply to the prosecution of a class A-I or A-II felony under this article.

HISTORY: Add, L 2011, ch 154, § 2, eff Sept 18, 2011.

ARTICLE 221   OFFENSES INVOLVING MARIHUANA

HISTORY: Add, L 1977, ch 360, § 3, eff July 29, 1977, and applicable to acts committed on or after such date.

§ 221.00. Marihuana; definitions

[Until July 5, 2021] Unless the context in which they are used clearly otherwise requires, the terms occurring in this article shall have the same meaning ascribed to them in article two hundred twenty of this chapter. Any act that is lawful under title five-A of article thirty-three of the public health law is not a violation of this article.

[Eff July 5, 2021] Unless the context in which they are used clearly otherwise requires, the terms occurring in this article shall have the same meaning ascribed to them in article two hundred twenty of this chapter.

HISTORY: Add, L 1977, ch 360, § 3, eff July 29, 1977 and applicable to acts committed on or after such date; amd, L 2014, ch 90, § 8, eff July 3, 2014, expires and repealed July 5, 2021.

§ 221.05. Unlawful possession of marihuana

A person is guilty of unlawful possession of marihuana when he knowingly and unlawfully possesses marihuana.

Unlawful possession of marihuana is a violation punishable only by a fine of not more than one hundred dollars. However, where the defendant has previously been convicted of an offense defined in this article or article 220 of this chapter, committed within the three years immediately preceding such violation, it shall be punishable (a) only by a fine of not more than two hundred dollars, if the defendant was previously convicted of one such offense committed during such period, and (b) by a fine of not more than two hundred fifty dollars or a term of imprisonment not in excess of fifteen days or both, if the defendant was previously convicted of two such offenses committed during such period.

HISTORY: Add, L 1977, ch 360, § 3, eff July 29, 1977 and applicable to acts committed on or after such date.

§ 221.10. Criminal possession of marihuana in the fifth degree

A person is guilty of criminal possession of marihuana in the fifth degree when he knowingly and unlawfully possesses:

1. marihuana in a public place, as defined in section 240.00 of this chapter, and such marihuana is burning or open to public view; or

2. one or more preparations, compounds, mixtures or substances containing marihuana and the preparations, compounds, mixtures or substances are of an aggregate weight of more than twenty-five grams.

Criminal possession of marihuana in the fifth degree is a class B misdemeanor.

HISTORY: Add, L 1977, ch 360, § 3; amd, L 1979, ch 265, § 1, eff Sept 1, 1979. Sub 2, amd, L 1995, ch 75, § 10, eff June 10, 1995.

§ 221.15. Criminal possession of marihuana in the fourth degree

A person is guilty of criminal possession of marihuana in the fourth degree when he knowingly and unlawfully possesses one or more preparations, compounds, mixtures or substances containing marihuana and the preparations, compounds, mixtures or substances are of an aggregate weight of more than two ounces.

Criminal possession of marihuana in the fourth degree is a class A misdemeanor.

HISTORY: Add, L 1977, ch 360, § 3; amd, L 1979, ch 265, § 1, eff Sept 1, 1979. Opening par, amd, L 1995, ch 75, § 11, eff June 10, 1995.

§ 221.20. Criminal possession of marihuana in the third degree

A person is guilty of criminal possession of marihuana in the third degree when he knowingly and unlawfully possesses one or more preparations, compounds, mixtures or substances containing marihuana and the preparations, compounds, mixtures or substances are of an aggregate weight of more than eight ounces.

Criminal possession of marihuana in the third degree is a class E felony.

HISTORY: Add, L 1977, ch 360, § 3; amd, L 1979, ch 265, § 1, eff Sept 1, 1979. Opening par, amd, L 1995, ch 75, § 12, eff June 10, 1995.

§ 221.25. Criminal possession of marihuana in the second degree

A person is guilty of criminal possession of marihuana in the second degree when he knowingly and unlawfully possesses one or more preparations, compounds, mixtures or substances containing marihuana and the preparations, compounds, mixtures or substances are of an aggregate weight of more than sixteen ounces.

Criminal possession of marihuana in the second degree is a class D felony.

HISTORY: Add, L 1977, ch 360, § 3; amd, L 1979, ch 265, § 1, eff Sept 1, 1979. Opening par, amd, L 1995, ch 75, § 13, eff June 10, 1995.

§ 221.30. Criminal possession of marihuana in the first degree

A person is guilty of criminal possession of marihuana in the first degree when he knowingly and unlawfully possesses one or more preparations, compounds, mixtures or substances containing marihuana and the preparations, compounds, mixtures or substances are of an aggregate weight of more than ten pounds.

Criminal possession of marihuana in the first degree is a class C felony.

HISTORY: Add, L 1977, ch 360, § 3; amd, L 1979, ch 265, § 1, eff Sept 1, 1979. Opening par, amd, L 1995, ch 75, § 14, eff June 10, 1995.

§ 221.35. Criminal sale of marihuana in the fifth degree

A person is guilty of criminal sale of marihuana in the fifth degree when he knowingly and unlawfully sells, without consideration, one or more preparations, compounds, mixtures or substances containing marihuana and the preparations, compounds, mixtures or substances are of an aggregate weight of two grams or less; or one cigarette containing marihuana.

Criminal sale of marihuana in the fifth degree is a class B misdemeanor.

HISTORY: Add, L 1977, ch 360, § 3; amd, L 1979, ch 265, § 1, eff Sept 1, 1979. Opening par, amd, L 1995, ch 75, § 15, eff June 10, 1995.

§ 221.40. Criminal sale of marihuana in the fourth degree

A person is guilty of criminal sale of marihuana in the fourth degree when he knowingly and unlawfully sells marihuana except as provided in section 221.35 of this article.

Criminal sale of marihuana in the fourth degree is a class A misdemeanor.

HISTORY: Add, L 1977, ch 360, § 3, eff July 29, 1977 and applicable to acts committed on or after such date.

§ 221.45. Criminal sale of marihuana in the third degree

A person is guilty of criminal sale of marihuana in the third degree when he knowingly and unlawfully sells one or more preparations, compounds, mixtures or substances containing marihuana and the preparations, compounds, mixtures or substances are of an aggregate weight of more than twenty-five grams.

Criminal sale of marihuana in the third degree is a class E felony.

HISTORY: Add, L 1977, ch 360, § 3; amd, L 1979, ch 265, § 1, eff Sept 1, 1979. Opening par, amd, L 1995, ch 75, § 16, eff June 10, 1995.

§ 221.50. Criminal sale of marihuana in the second degree

A person is guilty of criminal sale of marihuana in the second degree when he knowingly and unlawfully sells one or more preparations, compounds, mixtures or substances containing marihuana and the preparations, compounds, mixtures or substances are of an aggregate weight of more than four ounces, or knowingly and unlawfully sells one or more preparations, compounds, mixtures or substances containing marihuana to a person less than eighteen years of age.

Criminal sale of marihuana in the second degree is a class D felony.

HISTORY: Add, L 1977, ch 360, § 3; amd, L 1979, ch 265, § 1, eff Sept 1, 1979. Opening par, amd, L 1995, ch 75, § 17, eff June 10, 1995.

§ 221.55. Criminal sale of marihuana in the first degree

A person is guilty of criminal sale of marihuana in the first degree when he knowingly and unlawfully sells one or more preparations, compounds, mixtures or substances containing marihuana and the preparations, compounds, mixtures or substances are of an aggregate weight of more than sixteen ounces.

Criminal sale of marihuana in the first degree is a class C felony.

HISTORY: Add, L 1977, ch 360, § 3; amd, L 1979, ch 265, § 1, eff Sept 1, 1979. Opening par, amd, L 1995, ch 75, § 18, eff June 10, 1995.

ARTICLE 225 GAMBLING OFFENSES

HISTORY: Add, L 1965, ch 1030, § 1, eff Sept 1, 1967.

§ 225.00. Gambling offenses; definitions of terms

The following definitions are applicable to this article:

1. "Contest of chance" means any contest, game, gaming scheme or gaming devise in which the outcome depends in a material degree upon an element of chance, notwithstanding that skill of the contestants may also be a factor therein.

2. "Gambling." A person engages in gambling when he stakes or risks something of value upon the outcome of a contest of chance or a future contingent event not under his control or influence, upon an agreement or understanding that he will receive something of value in the event of a certain outcome.

3. "Player" means a person who engages in any form of gambling solely as a contestant or bettor, without receiving or becoming entitled to receive any profit therefrom other than personal gambling winnings, and without otherwise rendering any material assistance to the establishment, conduct or operation of the particular gambling activity. A person who gambles at a social game of chance on equal terms with the other participants therein does not otherwise render material assistance to the establishment, conduct or operation thereof by performing, without fee or remuneration, acts directed toward the arrangement or facilitation of the game, such as inviting persons to play, permitting the use of premises therefor and supplying cards or other equipment used therein. A person who engages in "bookmaking", as defined in this section is not a "player."

4. "Advance gambling activity." A person "advances gambling activity" when, acting other than as a player, he engages in conduct which materially aids any form of gambling activity. Such conduct includes but is not limited to conduct directed toward the creation or establishment of the particular game, contest, scheme, device or activity involved, toward the acquisition or maintenance of premises, paraphernalia, equipment or apparatus therefor, toward the solicitation or inducement of persons to participate therein, toward the actual conduct of the playing phases thereof, toward the arrangement of any of its financial or recording phases, or toward any other phase of its operation. One advances gambling activity when, having substantial proprietary or other authoritative control over premises being used with his knowledge for purposes of gambling activity, he permits such to occur or continue or makes no effort to prevent its occurrence or continuation.

5. "Profit from gambling activity." A person "profits from gambling activity" when, other than as a player, he accepts or receives money or other property pursuant to an agreement or

understanding with any person whereby he participates or is to participate in the proceeds of gambling activity.

6. "Something of value" means any money or property, any token, object or article exchangeable for money or property, or any form of credit or promise directly or indirectly contemplating transfer of money or property or of any interest therein, or involving extension of a service, entertainment or a privilege of playing at a game or scheme without charge.

7. "Gambling device" means any device, machine, paraphernalia or equipment which is used or usable in the playing phases of any gambling activity, whether such activity consists of gambling between persons or gambling by a person involving the playing of a machine. Notwithstanding the foregoing, lottery tickets, policy slips and other items used in the playing phases of lottery and policy schemes are not gambling devices.

7-a. A "coin operated gambling device" means a gambling device which operates as a result of the insertion of something of value. A device designed, constructed or readily adaptable or convertible for such use is a coin operated gambling device notwithstanding the fact that it may require adjustment, manipulation or repair in order to operate as such. A machine which awards free or extended play is not a gambling device merely because such free or extended play may constitute something of value provided that the outcome depends upon the skill of the player and not in a material degree upon an element of chance.

8. "Slot machine" means a gambling device which, as a result of the insertion of a coin or other object, operates, either completely automatically or with the aid of some physical act by the player, in such manner that, depending upon elements of chance, it may eject something of value. A device so constructed, or readily adaptable or convertible to such use, is no less a slot machine because it is not in working order or because some mechanical act of manipulation or repair is required to accomplish its adaptation, conversion or workability. Nor is it any less a slot machine because, apart from its use or adaptability as such, it may also sell or deliver something of value on a basis other than chance. A machine which sells items of merchandise which are of equivalent value, is not a slot machine merely because such items differ from each other in composition, size, shape or color.

9. "Bookmaking" means advancing gambling activity by unlawfully accepting bets from members of the public as a business, rather than in a casual or personal fashion, upon the outcomes of future contingent events.

10. "Lottery" means an unlawful gambling scheme in which (a) the players pay or agree to pay something of value for chances, represented and differentiated by numbers or by combinations of numbers or by some other media, one or more of which chances are to be designated the winning ones; and (b) the winning chances are to be determined by a drawing or by some other method based upon the element of chance; and (c) the holders of the winning chances are to receive something of value provided, however, that in no event shall the provisions of this subdivision be construed to include a raffle as such term is defined in subdivision three-b of section one hundred eighty-six of the general municipal law.

11. "Policy" or "the numbers game" means a form of lottery in which the winning chances or plays are not determined upon the basis of a drawing or other act on the part of persons conducting or connected with the scheme, but upon the basis of the outcome or outcomes of a future contingent event or events otherwise unrelated to the particular scheme.

12. "Unlawful" means not specifically authorized by law.

13. "Authorized gaming establishment" means any structure, structure and adjacent or attached structure, or grounds adjacent to a structure in which casino gaming, conducted pursuant to article thirteen of the racing, pari-mutuel wagering and breeding law, or Class III gaming, as authorized pursuant to a compact reached between the state of New York and a federally recognized Indian nation or tribe under the federal Indian Gaming Regulatory Act of 1988, is conducted and shall include all public and non-public areas of any such building, except for such areas of a building where either Class I or II gaming are conducted or any building or grounds known as a video gaming entertainment facility, including facilities where food and drink are served, as well as those areas not normally open to the public, such as where records related to video lottery gaming operations are kept, except shall not include the racetracks or such areas where such video lottery gaming operations or facilities do not take place or exist, such as racetrack areas or fairgrounds which are wholly unrelated to video lottery gaming operations, pursuant to section sixteen hundred seventeen-a and paragraph five of subdivision a of section sixteen hundred twelve of the tax law, as amended and implemented.

14. "Authorized gaming operator" means an enterprise or business entity authorized by state or federal law to operate casino or video lottery gaming.

15. "Casino gaming" means games authorized to be played pursuant to a license granted under article thirteen of the racing, pari-mutuel wagering and breeding law or by federally recognized Indian nations or tribes pursuant to a gaming compact reached in accordance with the federal Indian Gaming Regulatory Act of 1988, Pub. L. 100-497, 102 Stat. 2467, codified at 25 U.S.C. §§ 2701-21 and 18 U.S.C. §§ 1166-68.

16. "Cash equivalent" means a treasury check, a travelers check, wire transfer of funds, transfer check, money order, certified check, cashiers check, payroll check, a check drawn on the account of the authorized gaming operator payable to the patron or to the authorized gaming establishment, a promotional coupon, promotional chip, promotional cheque, promotional token, or a voucher recording cash drawn against a credit card or charge card.

17. "Cheques" or "chips" or "tokens" means nonmetal, metal or partly metal representatives of value, redeemable for cash or cash equivalent, and issued and sold by an authorized casino operator for use at an authorized gaming establishment. The value of such cheques or chips or tokens shall be considered equivalent in value to the cash or cash equivalent exchanged for such cheques or chips or tokens upon purchase or redemption.

18. "Class I gaming" and "Class II gaming" means those forms of gaming that are not Class III gaming, as defined in subsection eight of section four of the federal Indian Gaming Regulatory Act, 25 U.S.C. § 2703.

19. "Class III gaming" means those forms of gaming that are not Class I or Class II gaming, as defined in subsections six and seven of section four of the federal Indian Gaming Regulatory Act, 25 U.S.C. § 2703 and those games enumerated in the Appendix of a gaming compact.

20. "Compact" or "gaming compact" means the agreement between a federally recognized Indian tribe and the state of New York regarding Class III gaming activities entered into pursuant to the federal Indian Gaming Regulatory Act, Pub. L. 100-497, 102 Stat. 2467, codified at 25 U.S.C. §§ 2701-21 and 18 U.S.C. §§ 1166-68 (1988 & Supp. II).

21. "Gaming equipment or device" means any machine or device which is specially designed or manufactured for use in the operation of any Class III or video lottery game.

22. "Gaming regulatory authority" means, with respect to any authorized gaming establish-

ment on Indian lands, territory or reservation, the Indian nation or tribal gaming commission, its authorized officers, agents and representatives acting in their official capacities or such other agency of a nation or tribe as the nation or tribe may designate as the agency responsible for the regulation of Class III gaming, jointly with the state gaming agency, conducted pursuant to a gaming compact between the nation or tribe and the state of New York, or with respect to any casino gaming authorized pursuant to article thirteen of the racing, pari-mutuel wagering and breeding law or video lottery gaming conducted pursuant to section sixteen hundred seventeen-a and paragraph five of subdivision a of section sixteen hundred twelve of the tax law, as amended and implemented.

23. "Premises" includes any structure, parking lot, building, vehicle, watercraft, and any real property.

24. "Sell" means to sell, exchange, give or dispose of to another.

25. "State gaming agency" shall mean the New York state gaming commission, its authorized officials, agents, and representatives acting in their official capacities as the regulatory agency of the state which has responsibility for regulation with respect to video lottery gaming or casino gaming.

26. "Unfair gaming equipment" means loaded dice, marked cards, substituted cards or dice, or fixed roulette wheels or other gaming equipment which has been altered in a way that tends to deceive or tends to alter the elements of chance or normal random selection which determine the result of the game or outcome, or the amount or frequency of the payment in a game.

27. "Unlawful gaming property" means:

(a) any device, not prescribed for use in casinio gaming by its rules, which is capable of assisting a player:

(i) to calculate any probabilities material to the outcome of a contest of chance; or

(ii) to receive or transmit information material to the outcome of a contest of chance; or

(b) any object or article which, by virtue of its size, shape or any other quality, is capable of being used in casino gaming as an improper substitute for a genuine chip, cheque, token, betting coupon, debit instrument, voucher or other instrument or indicia of value; or

(c) any unfair gaming equipment.

28. "Video lottery gaming" means any lottery game played on a video lottery terminal, which consists of multiple players competing for a chance to win a random drawn prize pursuant to section sixteen hundred seventeen-a and paragraph five of subdivision a of section sixteen hundred twelve of the tax law, as amended and implemented.

29. "Voucher" means an instrument of value generated by a video lottery terminal representing a monetary amount and/or play value owed to a customer at a specific video lottery terminal based on video lottery gaming winnings and/or amounts not wagered.

HISTORY: Add, L 1965, ch 1030, § 1, eff Sept 1, 1967; amd, L 1967, ch 791, § 31, L 1987, ch 632, §§ 1, 2, eff Nov 1, 1987, L 1994, ch 550, § 1, eff Jan 22, 1995, L 2011, ch 8, § 1, eff March 25, 2011, L 2013, ch 174, § 3, eff July 30, 2013, L 2013, ch 175, § 3, eff July 30, 2013.

§ 225.05. Promoting gambling in the second degree

A person is guilty of promoting gambling in the second degree when he knowingly advances or profits from unlawful gambling activity.

Promoting gambling in the second degree is a class A misdemeanor.

HISTORY: Add, L 1965, ch 1030, § 1, eff Sept 1, 1967, with substance derived from §§ 970, 973, 974, 980, 986, 1372, 1373, 1376, 1377, 1378, 1381, 1388.

§ 225.10. Promoting gambling in the first degree

A person is guilty of promoting gambling in the first degree when he knowingly advances or profits from unlawful gambling activity by:

1. Engaging in bookmaking to the extent that he receives or accepts in any one day more than five bets totaling more than five thousand dollars; or

2. Receiving, in connection with a lottery or policy scheme or enterprise, (a) money or written records from a person other than a player whose chances or plays are represented by such money or records, or (b) more than five hundred dollars in any one day of money played in such scheme or enterprise.

Promoting gambling in the first degree is a class E felony.

HISTORY: Add, L 1965, ch 1030, § 1, eff Sept 1, 1967, with substance derived from §§ 974-a, 986-c.

§ 225.15. Possession of gambling records in the second degree

A person is guilty of possession of gambling records in the second degree when, with knowledge of the contents or nature thereof, he possesses any writing, paper, instrument or article:

1. Of a kind commonly used in the operation or promotion of a bookmaking scheme or enterprise; or

2. Of a kind commonly used in the operation, promotion or playing of a lottery or policy scheme or enterprise; except that in any prosecution under this subdivision, it is a defense that the writing, paper, instrument or article possessed by the defendant constituted, reflected or represented plays, bets or chances of the defendant himself in a number not exceeding ten.

3. Of any paper or paper product in sheet form chemically converted to nitrocellulose having explosive characteristics.

4. Of any water soluble paper or paper derivative in sheet form.

Possession of gambling records in the second degree is a class A misdemeanor.

HISTORY: Add, L 1965, ch 1030, § 1; amd, L 1969, ch 974, § 1, eff Sept 1, 1969, with substance derived in part from §§ 975, 986-b. Sub 3, add, L 1969, ch 974, § 1, eff Sept 1, 1969. Sub 4, add, L 1969, ch 974, § 1, eff Sept 1, 1969.

§ 225.20. Possession of gambling records in the first degree

A person is guilty of possession of gambling records in the first degree when, with knowledge of the contents thereof, he possesses any writing, paper, instrument or article:

1. Of a kind commonly used in the operation or promotion of a bookmaking scheme or enterprise, and constituting, reflecting or representing more than five bets totaling more than five thousand dollars; or

2. Of a kind commonly used in the operation, promotion or playing of a lottery or policy scheme or enterprise, and constituting, reflecting or representing more than five hundred plays or chances therein.

Possession of gambling records in the first degree is a class E felony.

HISTORY: Add, L 1965, ch 1030, § 1, eff Sept 1, 1967, with substance derived in part from § 985-c.

§ 225.25. Possession of gambling records; defense

In any prosecution for possession of gambling records, it is a defense that the writing, paper, instrument or article possessed by the defendant was neither used nor intended to be used in the operation or promotion of a bookmaking scheme or enterprise, or in the operation, promotion or playing of a lottery or policy scheme or enterprise.

HISTORY: Add, L 1965, ch 1030, § 1, eff Sept 1, 1967.

§ 225.30. Possession of a gambling device

a. A person is guilty of possession of a gambling device when, with knowledge of the character thereof, he or she manufactures, sells, transports, places or possesses, or conducts or negotiates any transaction affecting or designed to affect ownership, custody or use of:

1. A slot machine, unless such possession is permitted pursuant to article nine-A of the general municipal law; or

2. Any other gambling device, believing that the same is to be used in the advancement of unlawful gambling activity; or

3. A coin operated gambling device with intent to use such device in the advancement of unlawful gambling activity.

b. Possession of a slot machine shall not be unlawful where such possession and use is pursuant to a gaming compact, duly executed by the governor and an Indian tribe or Nation, under the Indian Gaming Regulatory Act, as codified at 25 U.S.C. [§§]*§§ 2701–2721 and 18 U.S.C [§§]*§§ 1166–1168, where the use of such slot machine or machines is consistent with such gaming compact and where the state receives a negotiated percentage of the net drop (defined as gross money wagered after payout, but before expenses) from any such slot machine or machines.

Possession of a gambling device is a class A misdemeanor.

c. Transportation and possession of a slot machine shall not be unlawful where such transportation and possession is necessary to facilitate the training of persons in the repair and reconditioning of such machines as are used or are to be used for operations in those casinos authorized pursuant to a tribal-state compact as provided for pursuant to section eleven hundred seventy-two of title fifteen of the United States Code in the state of New York.

d. Transportation and possession of a slot machine shall not be unlawful where such slot machine was transported into this state in a sealed container and possessed for the purpose of product development, research, or additional manufacture or assembly, and such slot machine will be or has been transported in a sealed container to a jurisdiction outside of this state for purposes which are lawful in such outside jurisdiction.

e. Transportation and possession of a gambling device shall not be unlawful where (i) the manufacturer or distributor of the gambling device has filed a statement with the state gaming commission required by subdivision twenty-one of section one hundred four of the racing, pari-mutuel wagering and breeding law, (ii) such gambling device was transported into this state in a sealed container and possessed for the purpose of exhibition or marketing in accordance with

---

* Brackets have been inserted by the Publisher around this material as it is superfluous.

* Brackets have been inserted by the Publisher around this material as it is superfluous.

such statement, and (iii) such device is thereafter transported in a sealed container to a jurisdiction outside of this state for purposes that are lawful in such outside jurisdiction.

> **HISTORY:** Add, L 1965, ch 1030, § 1, eff Sept 1, 1967, with substance derived from §§ 970-a, 970-b, 982; amd, L 1987, ch 632, § 3, eff Nov 1, 1987, L 2001, ch 383, § 4 (Part B), eff Oct 29, 2001, L 2003, ch 498, § 1, eff Oct 9, 2003, L 2010, ch 321, § 1, eff Aug 13, 2010, L 2013, ch 46, § 2, eff June 4, 2013, L 2013, ch 47, § 2, eff June 4, 2013, deemed to have been in full force and effect on and after May 1, 2013.

§ 225.32. Possession of a gambling device; defenses

1. In any prosecution for possession of a gambling device specified in subdivision one of section 225.30 of this article, it is an affirmative defense that: (a) the slot machine possessed by the defendant was neither used nor intended to be used in the operation or promotion of unlawful gambling activity or enterprise and that such slot machine is an antique; for purposes of this section proof that a slot machine was manufactured prior to nineteen hundred forty-one shall be conclusive proof that such a machine is an antique; (b) the slot machine possessed by the defendant was manufactured or assembled by the defendant for the sole purpose of transporting such slot machine in a sealed container to a jurisdiction outside this state for purposes which are lawful in such outside jurisdiction; or (c) the slot machine possessed by the defendant was neither used nor intended to be used in the operation or promotion of unlawful gambling activity or enterprise, is more than thirty years old, and such possession takes place in the defendant's home.

2. Where a defendant raises an affirmative defense provided by subdivision one hereof, any slot machine seized from the defendant shall not be destroyed, or otherwise altered until a final court determination is rendered. In a final court determination rendered in favor of said defendant, such slot machine shall be returned, forthwith, to said defendant, notwithstanding any provisions of law to the contrary.

> **HISTORY:** Add, L 1979, ch 526, § 1; amd, L 1983, ch 676, § 1, L 1997, ch 619, § 1, eff Nov 1, 1997, L 1998, ch 346, § 1, eff Nov 1, 1998, L 2010, ch 321, § 2, eff Aug 13, 2010.

§ 225.35. Gambling offenses; presumptions

1. Proof of possession of any gambling device or of any gambling record specified in sections 225.15 and 225.20, is presumptive evidence of possession thereof with knowledge of its character or contents.

2. In any prosecution under this article in which it is necessary to prove the occurrence of a sporting event, a published report of its occurrence in any daily newspaper, magazine or other periodically printed publication of general circulation shall be admissible in evidence and shall constitute presumptive proof of the occurrence of such event.

3. Possession of three or more coin operated gambling devices or possession of a coin operated gambling device in a public place shall be presumptive evidence of intent to use in the advancement of unlawful gambling activity.

> **HISTORY:** Add, L 1965, ch 1030, § 1, eff Sept 1, 1967, with substance derived in part from § 986-a. Sub 3, add, L 1987, ch 632, § 4, eff Nov 1, 1987.

§ 225.40. Lottery offenses; no defense

Any offense defined in this article which consists of the commission of acts relating to a lottery is no less criminal because the lottery itself is drawn or conducted without the state and is not violative of the laws of the jurisdiction in which it was so drawn or conducted.

> **HISTORY:** Add, L 1965, ch 1030, § 1, eff Sept 1, 1967.

§ 225.55. Gaming fraud in the second degree

A person is guilty of gaming fraud in the second degree when he or she:

1. with intent to defraud and in violation of the rules of the casino gaming, misrepresents, changes the amount bet or wagered on, or the outcome or possible outcome of the contest or event which is the subject of the bet or wager, or the amount or frequency of payment in the casino gaming; or

2. with intent to defraud, obtains anything of value from casino gaming without having won such amount by a bet or wager contingent thereon.

Gaming fraud in the second degree is a class A misdemeanor.

HISTORY: Add, L 2013, ch 174, § 4, eff July 30, 2013.

§ 225.60. Gaming fraud in the first degree

A person is guilty of gaming fraud in the first degree when he or she commits a gaming fraud in the second degree, and:

1. The value of the benefit obtained exceeds one thousand dollars; or

2. He or she has been previously convicted within the preceding five years of any offense of which an essential element is the commission of a gaming fraud.

Gaming fraud in the first degree is a class E felony.

HISTORY: Add, L 2013, ch 174, § 4, eff July 30, 2013.

§ 225.65. Use of counterfeit, unapproved or unlawful wagering instruments

A person is guilty of use of counterfeit, unapproved or unlawful wagering instruments when in playing or using any casino gaming designed to be played with, received or be operated by chips, cheques, tokens, vouchers or other wagering instruments approved by the appropriate gaming regulatory authority, he or she knowingly uses chips, cheques, tokens, vouchers or other wagering instruments other than those approved by the appropriate gaming regulating authority and the state gaming agency or lawful coin or legal tender of the United States of America.

Possession of more than one counterfeit, unapproved or unlawful wagering instrument described in this section is presumptive evidence of possession thereof with knowledge of its character or contents.

Use of counterfeit, unapproved or unlawful wagering instruments is a class A misdemeanor.

HISTORY: Add, L 2013, ch 174, § 4, eff July 30, 2013.

§ 225.70. Possession of unlawful gaming property in the third degree

A person is guilty of possession of unlawful gaming property in the third degree when he or she possesses, with intent to use such property to commit gaming fraud, unlawful gaming property at a premises being used for casino gaming.

Possession of unlawful gaming property in the third degree is a class A misdemeanor.

HISTORY: Add, L 2013, ch 174, § 4, eff July 30, 2013.

§ 225.75. Possession of unlawful gaming property in the second degree

A person is guilty of possession of unlawful gaming property in the second degree when:

1. He or she makes, sells, or possesses with intent to sell, any unlawful gaming property at a casino gaming facility, the value of which exceeds three hundred dollars, with intent that it be made available to a person for unlawful use; or

2. He or she commits possession of unlawful gaming property in the third degree as defined

in section 225.70 of this article, and the face value of the improper substitute property exceeds five hundred dollars; or

3. He or she commits the offense of possession of unlawful gaming property in the third degree and has been previously convicted within the preceding five years of any offense of which an essential element is possession of unlawful gaming property.

Possession of unlawful gaming property in the second degree is a class E felony.

HISTORY: Add, L 2013, ch 174, § 4, eff July 30, 2013.

§ 225.80. Possession of unlawful gaming property in the first degree

A person is guilty of possession of unlawful gaming property in the first degree when:

1. He or she commits the crime of unlawful possession of gaming property in the third degree as defined in section 225.70 of this article and the face value of the improper substitute property exceeds one thousand dollars; or

2. He or she commits the offense of possession of unlawful gaming property in the second degree as defined in subdivision one or two of section 225.75 of this article and has been previously convicted within the preceding five years of any offense of which an essential element is possession of unlawful gaming property.

Possession of unlawful gaming property in the first degree is a class D felony.

HISTORY: Add, L 2013, ch 174, § 4, eff July 30, 2013.

§ 225.85. Use of unlawful gaming property

A person is guilty of use of unlawful gaming property when he or she knowingly with intent to defraud uses unlawful gaming property at a premises being used for casino gaming.

Use of unlawful gaming property is a class E felony.

HISTORY: Add, L 2013, ch 174, § 4, eff July 30, 2013.

§ 225.90. Manipulation of gaming outcomes at an authorized gaming establishment

A person is guilty of manipulation of gaming outcomes at an authorized gaming establishment when he or she:

1. Knowingly conducts, operates, deals or otherwise manipulates, or knowingly allows to be conducted, operated, dealt or otherwise manipulated, cards, dice or gaming equipment or device, for themselves or for another, through any trick or sleight of hand performance, with the intent of deceiving or altering the elements of chance or normal random selection which determines the result or outcome of the game, or the amount or frequency of the payment in a game; or

2. Knowingly uses, conducts, operates, deals, or exposes for play, or knowingly allows to be used, conducted, operated, dealt or exposed for play any cards, dice or gaming equipment or device, or any combination of gaming equipment or devices, which have in any manner been altered, marked or tampered with, or placed in a condition, or operated in a manner, the result of which tends to deceive or tends to alter the elements of chance or normal random selection which determine the result of the game or outcome, or the amount or frequency of the payment in a game; or

3. Knowingly uses, or possesses with the intent to use, any cards, dice or other gaming equipment or devices other than that provided by an authorized gaming operator for current use in a permitted gaming activity; or

4. Alters or misrepresents the outcome of a game or other event on which bets or wagers have been made after the outcome is made sure but before it is revealed to players.

Possession of altered, marked or tampered with dice, cards, or gaming equipment or devices at an authorized gambling establishment is presumptive evidence of possession thereof with knowledge of its character or contents and intention to use such altered, marked or tampered with dice, cards, or gaming equipment or devices in violation of this section.

Manipulation of gaming outcomes at an authorized gaming establishment is a class A misdemeanor provided, however, that if the person has previously been convicted of this crime within the past five years this crim shall be a class E felony.

HISTORY: Add, L 2013, ch 174, § 4, eff July 30, 2013.

§ 225.95. Unlawful manufacture, sale, distribution, marking, altering or modification of equipment and devices associated with gaming

A person is guilty of unlawful manufacture, sale, distribution, marking, altering or modification of equipment and devices associated with gaming when if he or she:

1. Manufactures, sells or distributes any cards, chips, cheques, tokens, dice, vouchers, game or device and he or she knew or reasonably should have known it was intended to be used to violate any provision of this article; or

2. Marks, alters or otherwise modifies any associated gaming equipment or device in a manner that either affects the result of the wager by determining win or loss or alters the normal criteria of random selection in a manner that affects the operation of a game or determines the outcome of a game, and he or she knew or reasonably should have known that it was intended to be used to violate any provision of this article.

Unlawful manufacture, sale, distribution, marking, altering or modification of equipment and devices associated with gaming is a class A misdemeanor provided, however, that if the person has previously been convicted of this crime within the past five years this crim shall be a class E felony.

HISTORY: Add, L 2013, ch 174, § 4, eff July 30, 2013.

ARTICLE 230   PROSTITUTION OFFENSES

§ 230.35.   **Promoting or compelling prostitution; accomplice**
§ 230.36.   **Sex trafficking; accomplice**
§ 230.40.   **Permitting prostitution**

HISTORY: Add, L 1965, ch 1030, § 1, eff Sept 1, 1967.

§ 230.00. Prostitution

A person is guilty of prostitution when such person engages or agrees or offers to engage in sexual conduct with another person in return for a fee.

Prostitution is a class B Misdemeanor. [misdemeanor]*

HISTORY: Add, L 1965, ch 1030, § 1; amd, L 1969, ch 169, § 1, eff Sept 1, 1969.

§ 230.02. Patronizing a prostitute; definitions

1. A person patronizes a prostitute when:

(a) Pursuant to a prior understanding, he pays a fee to another person as compensation for such person or a third person having engaged in sexual conduct with him; or

(b) He pays or agrees to pay a fee to another person pursuant to an understanding that in return therefor such person or a third person will engage in sexual conduct with him; or

(c) He solicits or requests another person to engage in sexual conduct with him in return for a fee.

2. As used in this article, "person who is patronized" means the person with whom the defendant engaged in sexual conduct or was to have engaged in sexual conduct pursuant to the understanding, or the person who was solicited or requested by the defendant to engage in sexual conduct.

HISTORY: Added as § 230.05, L 1965, ch 1030, § 1; renumbered § 230.02 and amd, L 1978, ch 627, § 1, eff Sept 1, 1978. Section heading, amd, L 1978, ch 627, § 1, eff Sept 1, 1978. Sub 1, formerly opening par, so designated, L 1978, ch 627, § 1, eff Sept 1, 1978. Sub 1, par (a), formerly sub 1, so designated, L 1978, ch 627, § 1, eff Sept 1, 1978. Sub 1, par (b), formerly sub 2, so designated, L 1978, ch 627, § 1, eff Sept 1, 1978. Sub 1, par (c), formerly sub 3, so designated, L 1978, ch 627, § 1, eff Sept 1, 1978. Sub 2, add, L 1978, ch 627, § 1, eff Sept 1, 1978.

§ 230.03. Prostitution in a school zone

1. A person is guilty of prostitution in a school zone when, being nineteen years of age or older, and acting during the hours that school is in session, he or she commits the crime of prostitution in violation of section 230.00 of this article at a place that he or she knows, or reasonably should know, is in a school zone, and he or she knows, or reasonably should know, that such act of prostitution is within the direct view of children attending such school.

2. For the purposes of this section and section 230.19 of this article, "school zone" means (a) in or on or within any building, structure, athletic playing field, playground or land contained within the real property boundary line of a public or private elementary, parochial, intermediate, junior high, vocational, or high school, or (b) any public sidewalk, street, parking lot, park, playground or private land, located immediately adjacent to the boundary line of such school.

Prostitution in a school zone is a class A misdemeanor.

HISTORY: Add, L 2011, ch 191, § 1, eff Nov 17, 2011.

---

* The bracketed word has been inserted by the Publisher.

§ 230.04. Patronizing a prostitute in the third degree

A person is guilty of patronizing a prostitute in the third degree when he or she patronizes a prostitute.

Patronizing a prostitute in the third degree is a class A misdemeanor.

HISTORY: Add, L 1978, ch 627, § 2, eff Sept 1, 1978. Amd, L 2007, ch 74, § 5, eff Nov 1, 2007. First undesignated par, amd, L 2007, ch 74, § 5, eff Nov 1, 2007.

§ 230.05. Patronizing a prostitute in the second degree

A person is guilty of patronizing a prostitute in the second degree when, being over eighteen years of age, he patronizes a prostitute and the person patronized is less than fourteen years of age.

Patronizing a prostitute in the second degree is a class E felony.

HISTORY: Add, L 1978, ch 627, § 2, eff Sept 1, 1978. Former § 230.05, add, L 1965, ch 1030, § 1; renumbered § 230.02, L 1978, ch 627, § 1, eff Sept 1, 1978.

§ 230.06. Patronizing a prostitute in the first degree

A person is guilty of patronizing a prostitute in the first degree when he patronizes a prostitute and the person patronized is less than eleven years of age.

Patronizing a prostitute in the first degree is a class D felony.

HISTORY: Add, L 1978, ch 627, § 2, eff Sept 1, 1978.

§ 230.07. Patronizing a prostitute; defense

In any prosecution for patronizing a prostitute in the first or second degrees, it is a defense that the defendant did not have reasonable grounds to believe that the person was less than the age specified.

HISTORY: Add, L 1978, ch 627, § 2, eff Sept 1, 1978. Amd, L 2007, ch 74, § 6, eff Nov 1, 2007.

§ 230.10. Prostitution and patronizing a prostitute; no defense

In any prosecution for prostitution or patronizing a prostitute, the sex of the two parties or prospective parties to the sexual conduct engaged in, contemplated or solicited is immaterial, and it is no defense that:

1. Such persons were of the same sex; or

2. The person who received, agreed to receive or solicited a fee was a male and the person who paid or agreed or offered to pay such fee was a female.

HISTORY: Add, L 1965, ch 1030, § 1, eff Sept 1, 1967.

§ 230.15. Promoting prostitution; definitions of terms

The following definitions are applicable to this article:

1. "Advance prostitution." A person "advances prostitution" when, acting other than as a prostitute or as a patron thereof, he knowingly causes or aids a person to commit or engage in prostitution, procures or solicits patrons for prostitution, provides persons or premises for prostitution purposes, operates or assists in the operation of a house of prostitution or a prostitution enterprise, or engages in any other conduct designed to institute, aid or facilitate an act or enterprise of prostitution.

2. "Profit from prostitution." A person "profits from prostitution" when, acting other than as a prostitute receiving compensation for personally rendered prostitution services, he accepts or receives money or other property pursuant to an agreement or understanding with any person

whereby he participates or is to participate in the proceeds of prostitution activity.

HISTORY: Add, L 1965, ch 1030, § 1, eff Sept 1, 1967.

§ 230.19. Promoting prostitution in a school zone

1. A person is guilty of promoting prostitution in a school zone when, being nineteen years of age or older, he or she knowingly advances or profits from prostitution that he or she knows or reasonably should know is or will be committed in violation of section 230.03 of this article in a school zone during the hours that school is in session.

2. For purposes of this section, "school zone" shall mean "school zone" as defined in subdivision two of section 230.03 of this article.

Promoting prostitution in a school zone is a class E felony.

HISTORY: Add, L 2011, ch 191, § 2, eff Nov 17, 2011.

§ 230.20. Promoting prostitution in the fourth degree

A person is guilty of promoting prostitution in the fourth degree when he or she knowingly :

1. Advances or profits from prostitution; or

2. With intent to advance or profit from prostitution, distributes or disseminates to ten or more people in a public place obscene material, as such terms are defined by subdivisions one and two of section 235.00 of this title, or material that depicts nudity, as such term is defined by subdivision one of section 245.10 of this part.

Promoting prostitution in the fourth degree is a class A misdemeanor.

HISTORY: Add, L 1965, ch 1030, § 1, with substance derived from §§ 70(2), 1090, 1148, 2460; amd, L 1978, ch 627, § 3, eff Sept 1, 1978; L 1978, ch 627, § 3, eff Sept 1, 1978, L 2011, ch 215, § 1, eff Nov 17, 2011.

§ 230.25. Promoting prostitution in the third degree

A person is guilty of promoting prostitution in the third degree when he knowingly:

1. Advances or profits from prostitution by managing, supervising, controlling or owning, either alone or in association with others, a house of prostitution or a prostitution business or enterprise involving prostitution activity by two or more prostitutes, or a business that sells travel-related services knowing that such services include or are intended to facilitate travel for the purpose of patronizing a prostitute, including to a foreign jurisdiction and regardless of the legality of prostitution in said foreign jurisdiction; or

2. Advances or profits from prostitution of a person less than nineteen years old.

Promoting prostitution in the third degree is a class D felony.

HISTORY: Add, L 1965, ch 1030, § 1, with substance derived from §§ 70 in part, 1146, 2460; amd, L 1978, ch 627, § 3, eff Sept 1, 1978. Section heading, amd, L 1978, ch 627, § 3, eff Sept 1, 1978. Sub 1, amd, L 2007, ch 74, § 1, Nov 1, 2007.

§ 230.30. Promoting prostitution in the second degree

A person is guilty of promoting prostitution in the second degree when he knowingly:

1. Advances prostitution by compelling a person by force or intimidation to engage in prostitution, or profits from such coercive conduct by another; or

2. Advances or profits from prostitution of a person less than sixteen years old.

Promoting prostitution in the second degree is a class C felony.

HISTORY: Add, L 1965, ch 1030, § 1, with substance derived from §§ 70 in part, 1090, 2460; amd, L 1978, ch 627, § 3, eff Sept 1, 1978. Section heading, amd, L 1978, ch 627, § 3, eff Sept 1, 1978.

§ 230.32. Promoting prostitution in the first degree

A person is guilty of promoting prostitution in the first degree when he knowingly advances or profits from prostitution of a person less than eleven years old.

Promoting prostitution in the first degree is a class B felony.

HISTORY: Add, L 1978, ch 627, § 4, eff Sept 1, 1978.

§ 230.33. Compelling prostitution

A person is guilty of compelling prostitution when, being twenty-one years of age or older, he or she knowingly advances prostitution by compelling a person less than sixteen years old, by force or intimidation, to engage in prostitution.

Compelling prostitution is a class B felony.

HISTORY: Add, L 2005, ch 450, § 1, eff Nov 1, 2005.

§ 230.34. Sex trafficking

A person is guilty of sex trafficking if he or she intentionally advances or profits from prostitution by:

1. unlawfully providing to a person who is patronized, with intent to impair said person's judgment: (a) a narcotic drug or a narcotic preparation; (b) concentrated cannabis as defined in paragraph (a) of subdivision four of section thirty-three hundred two of the public health law; (c) methadone; or (d) gamma-hydroxybutyrate (GHB) or flunitrazepan, also known as Rohypnol;

2. making material false statements, misstatements, or omissions to induce or maintain the person being patronized to engage in or continue to engage in prostitution activity;

3. withholding, destroying, or confiscating any actual or purported passport, immigration document, or any other actual or purported government identification document of another person with intent to impair said person's freedom of movement; provided, however, that this subdivision shall not apply to an attempt to correct a social security administration record or immigration agency record in accordance with any local, state, or federal agency requirement, where such attempt is not made for the purpose of any express or implied threat;

4. requiring that prostitution be performed to retire, repay, or service a real or purported debt;

5. using force or engaging in any scheme, plan or pattern to compel or induce the person being patronized to engage in or continue to engage in prostitution activity by means of instilling a fear in the person being patronized that, if the demand is not complied with, the actor or another will do one or more of the following:

(a) cause physical injury, serious physical injury, or death to a person; or

(b) cause damage to property, other than the property of the actor; or

(c) engage in other conduct constituting a felony or unlawful imprisonment in the second degree in violation of section 135.05 of this chapter; or

(d) accuse some person of a crime or cause criminal charges or deportation proceedings to be instituted against some person; provided, however, that it shall be an affirmative defense to this subdivision that the defendant reasonably believed the threatened charge to be true and that his or her sole purpose was to compel or induce the victim to take reasonable action to make good the wrong which was the subject of such threatened charge; or

(e) expose a secret or publicize an asserted fact, whether true or false, tending to subject some person to hatred, contempt or ridicule; or

(f) testify or provide information or withhold testimony or information with respect to another's legal claim or defense; or

(g) use or abuse his or her position as a public servant by performing some act within or related to his or her official duties, or by failing or refusing to perform an official duty, in such manner as to affect some person adversely; or

(h) perform any other act which would not in itself materially benefit the actor but which is calculated to harm the person who is patronized materially with respect to his or her health, safety, or immigration status.

Sex trafficking is a class B felony[.]*

HISTORY: Add, L 2007, ch 74, § 2, eff Nov 1, 2007.

§ 230.35. Promoting or compelling prostitution; accomplice

In a prosecution for promoting prostitution or compellingprostitution, a person less than seventeen years of age from whose prostitution activity another person is alleged to have advanced or attempted to advance or profited or attempted to profit shall not be deemed to be an accomplice.

HISTORY: Add, L 1978, ch 627, § 5, eff Sept 1, 1978. Former § 230.35, add, L 1965, ch 1030, § 1; repealed, L 1978, ch 627, § 5, eff Sept 1, 1978. Amd, L 2005, ch 450, § 2, eff Nov 1, 2005. Section heading, amd, L 2005, ch 450, § 2, eff Nov 1, 2005.

§ 230.36. Sex trafficking; accomplice

In a prosecution for sex trafficking, a person from whose prostitution activity another person is alleged to have advanced or attempted to advance or profited or attempted to profit shall not be deemed to be an accomplice.

HISTORY: Add, L 2007, ch 74, § 2, eff Nov 1, 2007.

§ 230.40. Permitting prostitution

A person is guilty of permitting prostitution when, having possession or control of premises which he knows are being used for prostitution purposes, he fails to make reasonable effort to halt or abate such use.

Permitting prostitution is a class B misdemeanor.

HISTORY: Add, L 1965, ch 1030, § 1, eff Sept 1, 1967, with substance derived from § 1146 in part.

ARTICLE 235   OBSCENITY AND RELATED OFFENSES

---

* The bracketed punctuation has been inserted by the Publisher.

HISTORY: Add, L 1965, ch 1030, § 1, eff Sept 1, 1967.

§ 235.00. Obscenity; definitions of terms

The following definitions are applicable to sections 235.05, 235.10 and 235.15:

1. "Obscene." Any material or performance is "obscene" if (a) the average person, applying contemporary community standards, would find that considered as a whole, its predominant appeal is to the prurient interest in sex, and (b) it depicts or describes in a patently offensive manner, actual or simulated: sexual intercourse, criminal sexual act, sexual bestiality, masturbation, sadism, masochism, excretion or lewd exhibition of the genitals, and (c) considered as a whole, it lacks serious literary, artistic, political, and scientific value. Predominant appeal shall be judged with reference to ordinary adults unless it appears from the character of the material or the circumstances of its dissemination to be designed for children or other specially susceptible audience.

2. "Material" means anything tangible which is capable of being used or adapted to arouse interest, whether through the medium of reading, observation, sound or in any other manner.

3. "Performance" means any play, motion picture, dance or other exhibition performed before an audience.

4. "Promote" means to manufacture, issue, sell, give, provide, lend, mail, deliver, transfer, transmute, publish, distribute, circulate, disseminate, present, exhibit or advertise, or to offer or agree to do the same.

5. "Wholesale promote" means to manufacture, issue, sell, provide, mail, deliver, transfer, transmute, publish, distribute, circulate, disseminate or to offer or agree to do the same for purposes of resale.

6. "Simulated" means the explicit depiction or description of any of the types of conduct set forth in clause (b) of subdivision one of this section, which creates the appearance of such conduct.

7. "Criminal sexual act" means any of the types of sexual conduct defined in subdivision two of section 130.00 provided, however, that in any prosecution under this article the marital status of the persons engaged in such conduct shall be irrelevant and shall not be considered.

HISTORY: Add, L 1965, ch 1030, § 1, eff Sept 1, 1967. Sub 1, amd, L 1967, ch 791, § 32, L 1974, ch 989, § 1, eff Sept 1, 1974. Sub 1, amd, L 2003, ch 264, § 28, eff Nov 1, 2003. Sub 5, add, L 1969, ch 583, § 1, eff Sept 1, 1969. Sub 6, add, L 1974, ch 989, § 2, eff Sept 1, 1974. Sub 7, add, L 1974, ch 989, § 2, eff Sept 1, 1974. Sub 7, amd, L 2003, ch 264, § 28, eff Nov 1, 2003.

§ 235.05. Obscenity in the third degree

A person is guilty of obscenity in the third degree when, knowing its content and character, he:

1. Promotes, or possesses with intent to promote, any obscene material; or

2. Produces, presents or directs an obscene performance or participates in a portion thereof which is obscene or which contributes to its obscenity.

Obscenity in the third degree is a class A misdemeanor.

> **HISTORY:** Add, L 1965, ch 1030, § 1; amd, L 1969, ch 583, § 2, with substance derived from §§ 1140–1140-b, 1141–1141-b, 1143, L 1982, ch 649, § 2, eff Sept 1, 1982. Section heading, amd, L 1969, ch 583, § 2, L 1982, ch 649, § 2, eff Sept 1, 1982.

§ 235.06. Obscenity in the second degree

A person is guilty of obscenity in the second degree when he commits the crime of obscenity in the third degree as defined in subdivisions one and two of section 235.05 of this chapter and has been previously convicted of obscenity in the third degree.

Obscenity in the second degree is a class E felony.

> **HISTORY:** Add, L 1982, ch 649, § 1, eff Sept 1, 1982. Former § 235.06, add, L 1969, ch 583, § 3; renumbered § 235.07, L 1982, ch 649, § 1, eff Sept 1, 1982.

§ 235.07. Obscenity in the first degree

A person is guilty of obscenity in the first degree when, knowing its content and character, he wholesale promotes or possesses with intent to wholesale promote, any obscene material.

Obscenity in the first degree is a class D felony.

> **HISTORY:** Added as § 235.06, L 1969, ch 583, § 3; renumbered § 235.07, L 1982, ch 649, § 1, eff Sept 1, 1982.

§ 235.10. Obscenity; presumptions

1. A person who promotes or wholesale promotes obscene material, or possesses the same with intent to promote or wholesale promote it, in the course of his business is presumed to do so with knowledge of its content and character.

2. A person who possesses six or more identical or similar obscene articles is presumed to possess them with intent to promote the same.

The provisions of this section shall not apply to public libraries or association libraries as defined in subdivision two of section two hundred fifty-three of the education law, or trustees or employees of such public libraries or association libraries when acting in the course and scope of their duties or employment.

> **HISTORY:** Add, L 1965, ch 1030, § 1, eff Sept 1, 1967. Sub 1, amd, L 1969, ch 583, § 4, eff Sept 1, 1969. Concluding par, add, L 1980, ch 267, § 1; amd, L 1982, ch 110, § 1, eff May 18, 1982.

§ 235.15. Obscenity or disseminating indecent material to minors in the second degree; defense

1. In any prosecution for obscenity, or disseminating indecent material to minors in the second degree in violation of subdivision three of section 235.21 of this article, it is an affirmative defense that the persons to whom allegedly obscene or indecent material was disseminated, or the audience to an allegedly obscene performance, consisted of persons or institutions having scientific, educational, governmental or other similar justification for possessing, disseminating or viewing the same.

2. In any prosecution for obscenity, it is an affirmative defense that the person so charged was a motion picture projectionist, stage employee or spotlight operator, cashier, doorman, usher, candy stand attendant, porter or in any other non-managerial or non-supervisory capacity in a motion picture theatre; provided he has no financial interest, other than his employment, which

employment does not encompass compensation based upon any proportion of the gross receipts, in the promotion of obscene material for sale, rental or exhibition or in the promotion, presentation or direction of any obscene performance, or is in any way responsible for acquiring obscene material for sale, rental or exhibition.

    HISTORY: Add, L 1965, ch 1030, § 1, eff Sept 1, 1967. Section heading, amd, L 1996, ch 600, § 1, eff Nov 1, 1996. Sub 1, formerly entire section, so designated, L 1971, ch 1031, § 1; amd, L 1996, ch 600, § 1, eff Nov 1, 1996. Sub 2, add, L 1971, ch 1031, § 1, eff July 2, 1971.

§ 235.20. Disseminating indecent material to minors; definitions of terms

The following definitions are applicable to sections 235.21, 235.22, 235.23 and 235.24 of this article:

    1. "Minor" means any person less than seventeen years old.

    2. "Nudity" means the showing of the human male or female genitals, pubic area or buttocks with less than a full opaque covering, or the showing of the female breast with less than a fully opaque covering of any portion thereof below the top of the nipple, or the depiction of covered male genitals in a discernably turgid state.

    3. "Sexual conduct" means acts of masturbation, homosexuality, sexual intercourse, or physical contact with a person's clothed or unclothed genitals, pubic area, buttocks or, if such person be a female, breast.

    4. "Sexual excitement" means the condition of human male or female genitals when in a state of sexual stimulation or arousal.

    5. "Sado-masochistic abuse" means flagellation or torture by or upon a person clad in undergarments, a mask or bizarre costume, or the condition of being fettered, bound or otherwise physically restrained on the part of one so clothed.

    6. "Harmful to minors" means that quality of any description or representation, in whatever form, of nudity, sexual conduct, sexual excitement, or sado-masochistic abuse, when it:

    (a) Considered as a whole, appeals to the prurient interest in sex of minors; and

    (b) Is patently offensive to prevailing standards in the adult community as a whole with respect to what is suitable material for minors; and

    (c) Considered as a whole, lacks serious literary, artistic, political and scientific value for minors.

    7. The term "access software" means software (including client or server software) or enabling tools that do not create or provide the content of the communication but that allow a user to do any one or more of the following:

    (a) filter, screen, allow or disallow content;

    (b) pick, choose, analyze or digest content; or

    (c) transmit, receive, display, forward, cache, search, subset, organize, reorganize or translate content.

    HISTORY: Add, L 1967, ch 791, § 34, eff Sept 1, 1967, with substance derived from § 484-h(1)(a–f). Former § 235.20, add, L 1965, ch 1030, § 1, with substance derived from § 484-h; repealed, L 1967, ch 791, § 33, eff Sept 1, 1967. Opening par, amd, L 1996, ch 600, § 2, eff Nov 1, 1996. Sub 6, amd, L 1974, ch 989, § 3, eff Sept 1, 1974. Sub 6, par (a), add, L 1974, ch 989, § 3, eff Sept 1, 1974. Former sub 6, par (a), deleted, L 1974, ch 989, § 3, eff Sept 1, 1974. Sub 6, par (c), add, L 1974, ch 989, § 3, eff Sept 1, 1974. Former sub 6, par (c), deleted, L 1974, ch 989, § 3, eff Sept 1, 1974. Sub 7, add, L 1996, ch 600, § 3, eff Nov 1, 1996.

§ 235.21. Disseminating indecent material to minors in the second degree

A person is guilty of disseminating indecent material to minors in the second degree when:

1. With knowledge of its character and content, he sells or loans to a minor for monetary consideration:

(a) Any picture, photograph, drawing, sculpture, motion picture film, or similar visual representation or image of a person or portion of the human body which depicts nudity, sexual conduct or sado-masochistic abuse and which is harmful to minors; or

(b) Any book, pamphlet, magazine, printed matter however reproduced, or sound recording which contains any matter enumerated in paragraph (a) hereof, or explicit and detailed verbal descriptions or narrative accounts of sexual excitement, sexual conduct or sado-masochistic abuse and which, taken as a whole, is harmful to minors; or

2. Knowing the character and content of a motion picture, show or other presentation which, in whole or in part, depicts nudity, sexual conduct or sado-masochistic abuse, and which is harmful to minors, he:

(a) Exhibits such motion picture, show or other presentation to a minor for a monetary consideration; or

(b) Sells to a minor an admission ticket or pass to premises whereon there is exhibited or to be exhibited such motion picture, show or other presentation; or

(c) Admits a minor for a monetary consideration to premises whereon there is exhibited or to be exhibited such motion picture show or other presentation; or

3. Knowing the character and content of the communication which, in whole or in part, depicts actual or simulated nudity, sexual conduct or sado-masochistic abuse, and which is harmful to minors, he intentionally uses any computer communication system allowing the input, output, examination or transfer, of computer data or computer programs from one computer to another, to initiate or engage in such communication with a person who is a minor.

Disseminating indecent material to minors in the second degree is a class E felony.

HISTORY: Add, L 1967, ch 791, § 35, with substance derived from § 484-h(2), (3); amd, L 1969, ch 582, § 1, eff Sept 1, 1969. Section heading, amd, L 1996, ch 600, § 4, eff Nov 1, 1996. Opening par, amd, L 1996, ch 600, § 4, eff Nov 1, 1996. Sub 2, par (c), amd, L 1996, ch 600, § 4, eff Nov 1, 1996. Sub 3, add, L 1996, ch 600, § 5, eff Nov 1, 1996. Closing par, amd, L 1996, ch 600, § 4, eff Nov 1, 1996.

§ 235.22. Disseminating indecent material to minors in the first degree

A person is guilty of disseminating indecent material to minors in the first degree when:

1. knowing the character and content of the communication which, in whole or in part, depicts or describes, either in words or images actual or simulated nudity, sexual conduct or sado-masochistic abuse, and which is harmful to minors, he intentionally uses any computer communication system allowing the input, output, examination or transfer of computer data or computer programs from one computer to another, to initiate or engage in such communication with a person who is a minor; and

2. by means of such communication he importunes, invites or induces a minor to engage in sexual intercourse, oral sexual conduct or anal sexual conduct, or sexual contact with him, or

to engage in a sexual performance, obscene sexual performance, or sexual conduct for his benefit.

Disseminating indecent material to minors in the first degree is a class D felony.

> **HISTORY:** Add, L 1996, ch 600, § 6, eff Nov 1, 1996. Former § 235.22, redesignated § 235.23, L 1996, ch 600, § 6, eff Nov 1, 1996. Sub 1, amd, L 2007, ch 8, § 1, eff March 19, 2007. Sub 2, amd, L 2003, ch 264, § 29, eff Nov 1, 2003.

§ 235.23. Disseminating indecent material to minors; presumption and defenses

1. A person who engages in the conduct proscribed by section 235.21 is presumed to do so with knowledge of the character and content of the material sold or loaned, or the motion picture, show or presentation exhibited or to be exhibited.

2. In any prosecution for disseminating indecent material to minors in the second degree pursuant to subdivision one or two of section 235.21 of this article, it is an affirmative defense that:

(a) The defendant had reasonable cause to believe that the minor involved was seventeen years old or more; and

(b) Such minor exhibited to the defendant a draft card, driver's license, birth certificate or other official or apparently official document purporting to establish that such minor was seventeen years old or more.

3. In any prosecution for disseminating indecent material to minors in the second degree pursuant to subdivision three of section 235.21 of this article or disseminating indecent material to minors in the first degree pursuant to section 235.22 of this article, it shall be a defense that:

(a) The defendant made a reasonable effort to ascertain the true age of the minor and was unable to do so as a result of actions taken by the minor; or

(b) The defendant has taken, in good faith, reasonable, effective and appropriate actions under the circumstances to restrict or prevent access by minors to materials specified in such subdivision, which may involve any appropriate measures to restrict minors from access to such communications, including any method which is feasible under available technology; or

(c) The defendant has restricted access to such materials by requiring use of a verified credit card, debit account, adult access code or adult personal identification number; or

(d) The defendant has in good faith established a mechanism such that the labelling, segregation or other mechanism enables such material to be automatically blocked or screened by software or other capabilities reasonably available to responsible adults wishing to effect such blocking or screening and the defendant has not otherwise solicited minors not subject to such screening or blocking capabilities to access that material or to circumvent any such screening or blocking.

> **HISTORY:** Added as § 235.22, L 1967, ch 791, § 36; renumbered § 235.23, L 1996, ch 600, § 6; amd, L 1996, ch 600, § 7, eff Nov 1, 1996. Section heading, amd, L 1996, ch 600, § 7, eff Nov 1, 1996. Sub 2, amd, L 1996, ch 600, § 7, eff Nov 1, 1996. Sub 2, opening par, amd, L 1996, ch 600, § 7, eff Nov 1, 1996. Sub 3, add, L 1996, ch 600, § 7, eff Nov 1, 1996.

§ 235.24. Disseminating indecent material to minors; limitations

In any prosecution for disseminating indecent material to minors in the second degree pursuant to subdivision three of section 235.21 of this article or disseminating indecent material to minors in the first degree pursuant to section 235.22 of this article:

1. No person shall be held to have violated such provisions solely for providing access or

connection to or from a facility, system, or network not under that person's control, including transmission, downloading, intermediate storage, access software, or other related capabilities that are incidental to providing such access or connection that do not include the creation of the content of the communication.

(a) The limitations provided by this subdivision shall not be applicable to a person who is a conspirator with an entity actively involved in the creation or knowing distribution of communications that violate such provisions, or who knowingly advertises the availability of such communications.

(b) The limitations provided by this subdivision shall not be applicable to a person who provides access or connection to a facility, system, or network engaged in the violation of such provisions that is owned or controlled by such person.

2. No employer shall be held liable under such provisions for the actions of an employee or agent unless the employee's or agent's conduct is within the scope of his employment or agency and the employer having knowledge of such conduct, authorizes or ratifies such conduct, or recklessly disregards such conduct.

HISTORY: Add, L 1996, ch 600, § 8, eff Nov 1, 1996.

§ 235.25. [Repealed]

HISTORY: Add, L 1965, ch 1030, § 1, with substance derived from § 484-f; repealed, L 1967, ch 791, § 33, eff Sept 1, 1967.

§ 235.30. [Repealed]

HISTORY: Add, L 1965, ch 1030, § 1, with substance derived from § 484-g; repealed, L 1967, ch 791, § 33, eff Sept 1, 1967.

TITLE N   Offenses Against Public Order, Public Sensibilities and the Right to Privacy

ARTICLE 240
OFFENSES AGAINST PUBLIC ORDER

ARTICLE 241
HARASSMENT OF RENT REGULATED TENANTS [EXPIRES AND REPEALED JUNE 16, 2015]

ARTICLE 242
OFFENSES AGAINST SERVICE ANIMALS AND HANDLERS

ARTICLE 245
OFFENSES AGAINST PUBLIC SENSIBILITIES

ARTICLE 250
OFFENSES AGAINST THE RIGHT TO PRIVACY

HISTORY: Add, L 1965, ch 1030, § 1, eff Sept 1, 1967.

ARTICLE 240   OFFENSES AGAINST PUBLIC ORDER

HISTORY: Add, L 1965, ch 1030, § 1, eff Sept 1, 1967.

§ 240.00. Offenses aginst public order; definitions of terms

The following definitions are applicable to this article:

1. "Public place" means a place to which the public or a substantial group of persons has access, and includes, but is not limited to, highways, transportation facilities, schools, places of amusement, parks, playgrounds, and hallways, lobbies and other portions of apartment houses and hotels not constituting rooms or apartments designed for actual residence.

2. "Transportation facility" means any conveyance, premises or place used for or in connection with public passenger transportation, whether by air, railroad, motor vehicle or any other method. It includes aircraft, watercraft, railroad cars, buses, school buses as defined in section one hundred forty-two of the vehicle and traffic law, and air, boat, railroad and bus terminals and stations and all appurtenances thereto.

3. "School grounds" means in or on or within any building, structure, school bus as defined in section one hundred forty-two of the vehicle and traffic law, athletic playing field, playground or land contained within the real property boundary line of a public or private elementary, parochial, intermediate, junior high, vocational or high school.

4. "Hazardous substance" shall mean any physical, chemical, microbiological or radiological substance or matter which, because of its quantity, concentration, or physical, chemical or infectious characteristics, may cause or significantly contribute to an increase in mortality or an increase in serious irreversible or incapacitating reversible illness, or pose a substantial present or potential hazard to human health.

5. "Age" means sixty years old or more.

6. "Disability" means a physical or mental impairment that substantially limits a major life activity.

HISTORY: Add, L 1965, ch 1030, § 1, eff Sept 1, 1967. Sub 2, amd, L 2001, ch 395, § 1, eff Nov 1, 2001. Sub 3, add, L 1999, ch 561, § 1, eff Dec 1, 1999. Sub 4, add, L 1999, ch 561, § 1, eff Dec 1, 1999. Sub 5, add, L 2000, ch 107, § 5, eff Oct 8, 2000. Sub 6, add, L 2000, ch 107, § 5, eff Oct 8, 2000.

§ 240.05. Riot in the second degree

A person is guilty of riot in the second degree when, simultaneously with four or more other persons, he engages in tumultuous and violent conduct and thereby intentionally or recklessly causes or creates a grave risk of causing public alarm.

Riot in the second degree is a class A misdemeanor.

HISTORY: Add, L 1965, ch 1030, § 1, with substance derived from §§ 2090, 2091; amd, L

1967, ch 791, § 37, eff Sept 1, 1967. Section heading, amd, L 1967, ch 791, § 37, eff Sept 1, 1967.

§ 240.06. Riot in the first degree

A person is guilty of riot in the first degree when he:

1. Simultaneously with ten or more other persons, engages in tumultuous and violent conduct and thereby intentionally or recklessly causes or creates a grave risk of causing public alarm, and in the course of and as a result of such conduct, a person other than one of the participants suffers physical injury or substantial property damage occurs; or

2. While in a correctional facility or a local correctional facility, as those terms are defined in subdivisions four and sixteen, respectively, of section two of the correction law, simultaneously with ten or more other persons, engages in tumultuous and violent conduct and thereby intentionally or recklessly causes or creates a grave risk of causing alarm within such correctional facility or local correctional facility and in the course of and as a result of such conduct, a person other than one of the participants suffers physical injury or substantial property damage occurs.

Riot in the first degree is a class E felony.

> **HISTORY:** Add, L 1967, ch 791, § 38, eff Sept 1, 1967. Amd, L 2005, ch 294, § 1, eff Nov 1, 2005. Opening par, formerly part of first undesignated par, so designated opening par and amd, L 2005, ch 294, § 1, eff Nov 1, 2005. Sub 1, formerly part of first undesignated par, so designated sub 1 and amd, L 2005, ch 294, § 1, eff Nov 1, 2005. Sub 2, add, L 2005, ch 294, § 1, eff Nov 1, 2005; amd, L 2006, ch 13, § 1, eff March 21, 2006.

§ 240.08. Inciting to riot

A person is guilty of inciting to riot when he urges ten or more persons to engage in tumultuous and violent conduct of a kind likely to create public alarm.

Inciting to riot is a class A misdemeanor.

> **HISTORY:** Add, L 1967, ch 791, § 39, eff Sept 1, 1967.

§ 240.10. Unlawful assembly

A person is guilty of unlawful assembly when he assembles with four or more other persons for the purpose of engaging or preparing to engage with them in tumultuous and violent conduct likely to cause public alarm, or when, being present at an assembly which either has or develops such purpose, he remains there with intent to advance that purpose.

Unlawful assembly is a class B misdemeanor.

> **HISTORY:** Add, L 1965, ch 1030, § 1, with substance derived from §§ 2092, 2094; amd, L 1967, ch 791, § 40, eff Sept 1, 1967.

§ 240.15. Criminal anarchy

A person is guilty of criminal anarchy when (a) he advocates the overthrow of the existing form of government of this state by violence, or (b) with knowledge of its contents, he publishes, sells or distributes any document which advocates such violent overthrow, or (c) with knowledge of its purpose, he becomes a member of any organization which advocates such violent overthrow.

Criminal anarchy is a class E felony.

> **HISTORY:** Add, L 1965, ch 1030, § 1, eff Sept 1, 1967, with substance derived from §§ 160, 161.

§ 240.20. Disorderly conduct

A person is guilty of disorderly conduct when, with intent to cause public inconvenience, annoyance or alarm, or recklessly creating a risk thereof:

1. He engages in fighting or in violent, tumultuous or threatening behavior; or

2. He makes unreasonable noise; or

3. In a public place, he uses abusive or obscene language, or makes an obscene gesture; or

4. Without lawful authority, he disturbs any lawful assembly or meeting of persons; or

5. He obstructs vehicular or pedestrian traffic; or

6. He congregates with other persons in a public place and refuses to comply with a lawful order of the police to disperse; or

7. He creates a hazardous or physically offensive condition by any act which serves no legitimate purpose.

Disorderly conduct is a violation.

HISTORY: Add, L 1965, ch 1030, § 1, eff Sept 1, 1967, with substance derived in part from §§ 722, 1321, 1470, 2071, 2093.

§ 240.21. Disruption or disturbance of a religious service, funeral, burial or memorial service

A person is guilty of disruption or disturbance of a religious service, funeral, burial or memorial service when he or she makes unreasonable noise or disturbance while at a lawfully assembled religious service, funeral, burial or memorial service, or within three hundred feet thereof, with intent to cause annoyance or alarm or recklessly creating a risk thereof.

Disruption or disturbance of a religious service, funeral, burial or memorial service is a class A misdemeanor.

HISTORY: Add, L 1967, ch 614, § 1, eff Sept 1, 1967. Amd, L 2008, ch 566, § 1, eff Sept 25, 2008. Section heading, amd, L 2008, ch 566, § 1, eff Sept 25, 2008. Opening par, amd, L 2008, ch 566, § 1, eff Sept 25, 2008, L 2011, ch 528, § 1, eff March 21, 2012. Closing par, amd, L 2008, ch 566, § 1, eff Sept 25, 2008.

§ 240.25. Harassment in the first degree

A person is guilty of harassment in the first degree when he or she intentionally and repeatedly harasses another person by following such person in or about a public place or places or by engaging in a course of conduct or by repeatedly committing acts which places such person in reasonable fear of physical injury. This section shall not apply to activities regulated by the national labor relations act, as amended, the railway labor act, as amended, or the federal employment labor management act, as amended.

Harassment in the first degree is a class B misdemeanor.

HISTORY: Add, L 1992, ch 345, § 3; amd, L 1994, ch 109, § 1, eff May 24, 1994. Former § 240.25, renumbered § 240.26, L 1992, ch 345, § 3, eff Nov 1, 1992. First undesignated par, amd, L 1994, ch 109, § 1, eff May 24, 1994.

§ 240.26. Harassment in the second degree

A person is guilty of harassment in the second degree when, with intent to harass, annoy or alarm another person:

1. He or she strikes, shoves, kicks or otherwise subjects such other person to physical contact, or attempts or threatens to do the same; or

2. He or she follows a person in or about a public place or places; or

3. He or she engages in a course of conduct or repeatedly commits acts which alarm or seriously annoy such other person and which serve no legitimate purpose.

Subdivisions two and three of this section shall not apply to activities regulated by the national labor relations act, as amended, the railway labor act, as amended, or the federal employment labor management act, as amended.

Harassment in the second degree is a violation.

HISTORY: Added as § 240.25, L 1965, ch 1030, § 1, with substance derived in part from §§ 720, 1030; so renumbered § 240.26, L 1992, ch 345, § 3; amd, L 1994, ch 109, § 1, eff May 24, 1994. Section heading, amd, L 1992, ch 345, § 4, eff Nov 1, 1992. Opening par, amd, L 1992, ch 345, § 4, eff Nov 1, 1992. Sub 1, amd, L 1967, ch 791, § 41, L 1992, ch 345, § 4, eff Nov 1, 1992. Sub 2, formerly sub 3, so designated and amd, L 1992, ch 345, § 4, eff Nov 1, 1992. Former sub 2, deleted, L 1992, ch 345, § 4, eff Nov 1, 1992. Sub 3, formerly sub 5, so designated and amd, L 1992, ch 345, § 4, eff Nov 1, 1992. Former sub 3, redesignated sub 2, L 1992, ch 345, § 4, eff Nov 1, 1992. Sub 4, repealed, L 1988, ch 86, § 2, eff Nov 1, 1988. Sub 5, redesignated sub 3, L 1992, ch 345, § 4, eff Nov 1, 1992. Second undesignated par, add, L 1994, ch 109, § 1, eff May 24, 1994.

§ 240.30. Aggravated harassment in the second degree

A person is guilty of aggravated harassment in the second degree when:

1. With intent to harass another person, the actor either:

(a) communicates, anonymously or otherwise, by telephone, by computer or any other electronic means, or by mail, or by transmitting or delivering any other form of communication, a threat to cause physical harm to, or unlawful harm to the property of, such person, or a member of such person's same family or household as defined in subdivision one of section 530.11 of the criminal procedure law, and the actor knows or reasonably should know that such communication will cause such person to reasonably fear harm to such person's physical safety or property, or to the physical safety or property of a member of such person's same family or household; or

(b) causes a communication to be initiated anonymously or otherwise, by telephone, by computer or any other electronic means, or by mail, or by transmitting or delivering any other form of communication, a threat to cause physical harm to, or unlawful harm to the property of, such person, a member of such person's same family or household as defined in subdivision one of section 530.11 of the criminal procedure law, and the actor knows or reasonably should know that such communication will cause such person to reasonably fear harm to such person's physical safety or property, or to the physical safety or property of a member of such person's same family or household; or

2. With intent to harass or threaten another person, he or she makes a telephone call, whether or not a conversation ensues, with no purpose of legitimate communication; or

3. With the intent to harass, annoy, threaten or alarm another person, he or she strikes, shoves, kicks, or otherwise subjects another person to physical contact, or attempts or threatens to do the same because of a belief or perception regarding such person's race, color, national origin, ancestry, gender, religion, religious practice, age, disability or sexual orientation, regardless of whether the belief or perception is correct; or

4. With the intent to harass, annoy, threaten or alarm another person, he or she strikes, shoves, kicks or otherwise subjects another person to physical contact thereby causing physical injury to such person or to a family or household member of such person as defined in section 530.11 of the criminal procedure law; or

5. He or she commits the crime of harassment in the first degree and has previously been convicted of the crime of harassment in the first degree as defined by section 240.25 of this article within the preceding ten years.

Aggravated harassment in the second degree is a class A misdemeanor.

HISTORY: Add, L 1965, ch 1030, § 1, with substance derived in part from §§ 551, 555, 1423 in part; amd, L 1969, ch 290, § 1, L 1982, ch 191, § 1, L 1992, ch 345, § 5, eff Nov 1, 1992, L 2000, ch 107, § 3, eff Oct 8, 2000, L 2001, ch 385, § 1, eff Nov 1, 2001, L 2008, ch 510, § 1, eff Dec 3, 2008, L 2012, ch 491, § 4 (Part D), eff Dec 24, 2012, L 2014, ch 188, § 1, eff July 23, 2014.

§ 240.31. Aggravated harassment in the first degree

A person is guilty of aggravated harassment in the first degree when with intent to harass, annoy, threaten or alarm another person, because of a belief or perception regarding such person's race, color, national origin, ancestry, gender, religion, religious practice, age, disability or sexual orientation, regardless of whether the belief or perception is correct, he or she:

1. Damages premises primarily used for religious purposes, or acquired pursuant to section six of the religious corporation law and maintained for purposes of religious instruction, and the damage to the premises exceeds fifty dollars; or

2. Commits the crime of aggravated harassment in the second degree in the manner proscribed by the provisions of subdivision three of section 240.30 of this article and has been previously convicted of the crime of aggravated harassment in the second degree for the commission of conduct proscribed by the provisions of subdivision three of section 240.30 or he or she has been previously convicted of the crime of aggravated harassment in the first degree within the preceding ten years; or

3. Etches, paints, draws upon or otherwise places a swastika, commonly exhibited as the emblem of Nazi Germany, on any building or other real property, public or private, owned by any person, firm or corporation or any public agency or instrumentality, without express permission of the owner or operator of such building or real property;

4. Sets on fire a cross in public view; or

5. Etches, paints, draws upon or otherwise places or displays a noose, commonly exhibited as a symbol of racism and intimidation, on any building or other real property, public or private, owned by any person, firm or corporation or any public agency or instrumentality, without express permission of the owner or operator of such building or real property.

Aggravated harassment in the first degree is a class E felony.

HISTORY: Add, L 1982, ch 191, § 2; amd, 1983, ch 958, § 1, eff Sept 1, 1983. Amd, L 2006, ch 49, § 1, eff June 7, 2006. Opening par, amd, L 2000, ch 107, § 4, eff Oct 8, 2000. Sub 2, amd, L 2006, ch 49, § 1, eff June 7, 2006. Sub 3, add, L 2006, ch 49, § 1, eff June 7, 2006; amd, L 2008, ch 74, § 1, eff Nov 1, 2008. Sub 4, amd, L 2006, ch 49, § 1, eff June 7, 2006, L 2008, ch 74, § 1, eff Nov 1, 2008. Sub 5, add, L 2008, ch 74, § 1, eff Nov 1, 2008.

§ 240.32. Aggravated harassment of an employee by an inmate

An inmate or respondent is guilty of aggravated harassment of an employee by an inmate when, with intent to harass, annoy, threaten or alarm a person in a facility whom he or she knows or reasonably should know to be an employee of such facility or the board of parole or the office of mental health, or a probation department, bureau or unit or a police officer, he or she causes or attempts to cause such employee to come into contact with blood, seminal fluid, urine, feces, or the contents of a toilet bowl, by throwing, tossing or expelling such fluid or material.

For purposes of this section, "inmate" means an inmate or detainee in a correctional facility, local correctional facility or a hospital, as such term is defined in subdivision two of section four hundred of the correction law. For purposes of this section, "respondent" means a juvenile in a secure facility operated and maintained by the office of children and family services who is placed with or committed to the office of children and family services. For purposes of this section, "facility" means a correctional facility or local correctional facility, hospital, as such term is defined in subdivision two of section four hundred of the correction law, or a secure facility operated and maintained by the office of children and family services.

Aggravated harassment of an employee by an inmate is a class E felony.

> **HISTORY:** Add, L 1996, ch 92, § 2; amd, L 2000, ch 422, § 1, L 2000, ch 441, § 1, eff Nov 1, 2000, L 2011, ch 62, § 127-p (Part C, Subpart B), eff March 31, 2011.

§ 240.35. Loitering

A person is guilty of loitering when he:

1. [Repealed]

2. Loiters or remains in a public place for the purpose of gambling with cards, dice or other gambling paraphernalia; or

3. [Repealed]

4. Being masked or in any manner disguised by unusual or unnatural attire or facial alteration, loiters, remains or congregates in a public place with other persons so masked or disguised, or knowingly permits or aids persons so masked or disguised to congregate in a public place; except that such conduct is not unlawful when it occurs in connection with a masquerade party or like entertainment if, when such entertainment is held in a city which has promulgated regulations in connection with such affairs, permission is first obtained from the police or other appropriate authorities; or

5. Loiters or remains in or about school grounds, a college or university building or grounds or a children's overnight camp as defined in section one thousand three hundred ninety-two of the public health law or a summer day camp as defined in section one thousand three hundred ninety-two of the public health law, or loiters, remains in or enters a school bus as defined in section one hundred forty-two of the vehicle and traffic law, not having any reason or relationship involving custody of or responsibility for a pupil or student, or any other specific, legitimate reason for being there, and not having written permission from anyone authorized to grant the same or loiters or remains in or about such children's overnight camp or summer day camp in violation of conspicuously posted rules or regulations governing entry and use thereof; or

6. Loiters or remains in any transportation facility, unless specifically authorized to do so, for the purpose of soliciting or engaging in any business, trade or commercial transactions involving the sale of merchandise or services, or for the purpose of entertaining persons by singing, dancing or playing any musical instrument; or

7. [Repealed]

Loitering is a violation.

> **HISTORY:** Add, L 1965, ch 1030, § 1, eff Sept 1, 1967, with substance derived in part from §§ 150, 710, 711, 722 in part, 722-b, 1148, 1533, 1990-a; amd, L 1967, ch 791, § 42, L 1968, ch 668, § 1, eff Sept 1, 1968, with substance transferred to § 240.36, L 1978, ch 446, §§ 1, 2, eff July 19, 1978, L 1979, ch 698, § 1, eff Sept 1, 1979, L 2000, ch 533, § 2, eff Oct 4, 2000, L 2001, ch 350, § 2, eff Sept 19, 2001, L 2001, ch 395, § 2, eff Nov 1, 2001, L 2003, ch 264, § 30, eff Nov 1, 2003, L 2010, ch 232, § 1, eff July 30, 2010.

§ 240.36. Loitering in the first degree

A person is guilty of loitering in the first degree when he loiters or remains in any place with one or more persons for the purpose of unlawfully using or possessing a controlled substance, as defined in section 220.00 of this chapter.

Loitering in the first degree is a class B misdemeanor.

HISTORY: Add, L 1968, ch 668, § 2; amd, L 1973, ch 276, § 20, eff Sept 1, 1973.

§ 240.37. Loitering for the purpose of engaging in a prostitution offense

1. For the purposes of this section, "public place" means any street, sidewalk, bridge, alley or alleyway, plaza, park, driveway, parking lot or transportation facility or the doorways and entrance ways to any building which fronts on any of the aforesaid places, or a motor vehicle in or on any such place.

2. Any person who remains or wanders about in a public place and repeatedly beckons to, or repeatedly stops, or repeatedly attempts to stop, or repeatedly attempts to engage passers-by in conversation, or repeatedly stops or attempts to stop motor vehicles, or repeatedly interferes with the free passage of other persons, for the purpose of prostitution, or of patronizing a prostitute as those terms are defined in article two hundred thirty of the penal law, shall be guilty of a violation and is guilty of a class B misdemeanor if such person has previously been convicted of a violation of this section or of sections 230.00 or 230.05 of the penal law.

3. Any person who remains or wanders about in a public place and repeatedly beckons to, or repeatedly stops, or repeatedly attempts to stop, or repeatedly attempts to engage passers-by in conversation, or repeatedly stops or attempts to stop motor vehicles, or repeatedly interferes with the free passage of other persons, for the purpose of promoting prostitution as defined in article two hundred thirty of the penal law is guilty of a class A misdemeanor.

HISTORY: Add, L 1976, ch 344, § 2, eff July 11, 1976.

§ 240.40. Appearance in public under the influence of narcotics or a drug other than alcohol

A person is guilty of appearance in public under the influence of narcotics or a drug other than alcohol when he appears in a public place under the influence of narcotics or a drug other than alcohol to the degree that he may endanger himself or other persons or property, or annoy persons in his vicinity.

Appearance in public under the influence of narcotics or a drug other than alcohol is a violation.

HISTORY: Add, L 1965, ch 1030, § 1, with substance derived from § 1221; amd, L 1974, ch 1068, § 3, eff Jan 1, 1976. Section heading, amd, L 1974, ch 1068, § 3, eff Jan 1, 1976.

§ 240.45. Criminal nuisance in the second degree

A person is guilty of criminal nuisance in the second degree when:

1. By conduct either unlawful in itself or unreasonable under all the circumstances, he knowingly or recklessly creates or maintains a condition which endangers the safety or health of a considerable number of persons; or

2. He knowingly conducts or maintains any premises, place or resort where persons gather for purposes of engaging in unlawful conduct.

Criminal nuisance in the second degree is a class B misdemeanor.

HISTORY: Add, L 1965, ch 1030, § 1, with substance derived in part from §§ 1530, 1533 in part; amd, L 1989, ch 585, § 1, eff Nov 1, 1989. Section heading, amd, L 1989, ch 585, § 1, eff Nov 1, 1989. Opening par, amd, L 1989, ch 585, § 1, eff Nov 1, 1989. Closing par, amd, L 1989, ch 585, § 1, eff Nov 1, 1989.

§ 240.46. Criminal nuisance in the first degree

A person is guilty of criminal nuisance in the first degree when he knowingly conducts or maintains any premises, place or resort where persons come or gather for purposes of engaging in the unlawful sale of controlled substances in violation of section 220.39, 220.41, or 220.43 of this chapter, and thereby derives the benefit from such unlawful conduct.

Criminal nuisance in the first degree is a class E felony.

HISTORY: Add, L 1989, ch 585, § 2, eff Nov 1, 1989.

§ 240.48. Disseminating a false registered sex offender notice

A person is guilty of disseminating a false registered sex offender notice when, knowing the information he or she disseminates or causes to be disseminated to be false or baseless, such person disseminates or causes to be disseminated any notice which purports to be an official notice from a government agency or a law enforcement agency and such notice asserts that an individual is a registered sex offender.

Disseminating a false registered sex offender notice is a class A misdemeanor.

HISTORY: Add, L 2004, ch 106, § 2, eff Aug 7, 2004.

§ 240.50. Falsely reporting an incident in the third degree

A person is guilty of falsely reporting an incident in the third degree when, knowing the information reported, conveyed or circulated to be false or baseless, he or she:

1. Initiates or circulates a false report or warning of an alleged occurrence or impending occurrence of a crime, catastrophe or emergency under circumstances in which it is not unlikely that public alarm or inconvenience will result; or

2. Reports, by word or action, to an official or quasi-official agency or organization having the function of dealing with emergencies involving danger to life or property, an alleged occurrence or impending occurrence of a catastrophe or emergency which did not in fact occur or does not in fact exist; or

3. Gratuitously reports to a law enforcement officer or agency (a) the alleged occurrence of an offense or incident which did not in fact occur; or (b) an allegedly impending occurrence of an offense or incident which in fact is not about to occur; or (c) false information relating to an actual offense or incident or to the alleged implication of some person therein; or

4. Reports, by word or action, an alleged occurrence or condition of child abuse or maltreatment or abuse or neglect of a vulnerable person which did not in fact occur or exist to:

    (a) the statewide central register of child abuse and maltreatment, as defined in title six of article six of the social services law or the vulnerable persons' central register as defined in article eleven of such law, or

    (b) any person required to report cases of suspected child abuse or maltreatment pursuant to subdivision one of section four hundred thirteen of the social services law or to report cases of suspected abuse or neglect of a vulnerable person pursuant to section four hundred ninety-one of such law, knowing that the person is required to report such cases, and with the intent that such an alleged occurrence be reported to the statewide central register or vulnerable persons' central register.

Falsely reporting an incident in the third degree is a class A misdemeanor.

HISTORY: Add, L 1965, ch 1030, § 1, with substance derived from L 1909, §§ 727, 1250-b in part, 1424, 1786; amd, L 1971, ch 357, § 1, L 1973, ch 276, § 30, eff Sept 1, 1973, L 1976, ch 185,

§ 1, L 1979, ch 146, § 1, eff Sept 26, 1979, L 2001, ch 301, § 1, eff Sept 17, 2001, L 2001, ch 302, § 1, eff Sept 17, 2001; amd, L 2008, ch 400, § 1, eff Feb 1, 2009, L 2012, ch 501, § 1 (Part G), eff Jan 17, 2013.

§ 240.55. Falsely reporting an incident in the second degree

A person is guilty of falsely reporting an incident in the second degree when, knowing the information reported, conveyed or circulated to be false or baseless, he or she:

1. Initiates or circulates a false report or warning of an alleged occurrence or impending occurrence of a fire, explosion, or the release of a hazardous substance under circumstances in which it is not unlikely that public alarm or inconvenience will result;

2. Reports, by word or action, to any official or quasi-official agency or organization having the function of dealing with emergencies involving danger to life or property, an alleged occurrence or impending occurrence of a fire, explosion, or the release of a hazardous substance which did not in fact occur or does not in fact exist; or

3. Knowing the information reported, conveyed or circulated to be false or baseless and under circumstances in which it is likely public alarm or inconvenience will result, he or she initiates or circulates a report or warning of an alleged occurrence or an impending occurrence of a fire, an explosion, or the release of a hazardous substance upon any private premises.

Falsely reporting an incident in the second degree is a class E felony.

HISTORY: Add, L 1973, ch 276, § 30; amd, L 1989, ch 477, § 3, eff Nov 1, 1989. Opening par, amd, L 1989, ch 477, § 3, eff Nov 1, 1989. Sub 1, amd, L 1979, ch 146, § 2, L 1989, ch 477, § 3, L 1999, ch 561, § 2, eff Dec 1, 1999. Sub 2, amd, L 1979, ch 146, § 2, L 1989, ch 477, § 3, L 1999, ch 561, § 2, eff Dec 1, 1999. Sub 3, add, L 1989, ch 477, § 3, eff Nov 1, 1989. Sub 3, formerly sub 4, add, L 2001, ch 301, § 2, eff Sept 17, 2001; so designated sub 3, L 2001, ch 302, § 3, eff Sept 17, 2001. Former sub 3, repealed, L 2001, ch 302, § 2, eff Sept 17, 2001. Sub 4, redesignated sub 3, L 2001, ch 302, § 3, eff Sept 17, 2001. Closing par, amd, L 2001, ch 301, § 3, eff Sept 17, 2001.

§ 240.60. Falsely reporting an incident in the first degree

A person is guilty of falsely reporting an incident in the first degree when he:

1. commits the crime of falsely reporting an incident in the second degree as defined in section 240.55 of this article, and has previously been convicted of that crime; or

2. commits the crime of falsely reporting an incident in the third degree as defined in subdivisions one and two of section 240.50 of this article or falsely reporting an incident in the second degree as defined in subdivisions one and two of section 240.55 of this article and another person who is an employee or member of any official or quasi-official agency having the function of dealing with emergencies involving danger to life or property; or who is a volunteer firefighter with a fire department, fire company, or any unit thereof as defined in the volunteer firefighters' benefit law; or who is a volunteer ambulance worker with a volunteer ambulance corporation or any unit thereof as defined in the volunteer ambulance workers' benefit law suffers serious physical injury or is killed in the performance of his or her official duties in traveling to or working at or returning to a firehouse, police station, quarters or other base facility from the location identified in such report; or

3. commits the crime of falsely reporting an incident in the third degree as defined in subdivisions one and two of section 240.50 of this article or falsely reporting an incident in the second degree as defined in subdivisions one and two of section 240.55 of this article and another person suffers serious physical injury or is killed as a result of any vehicular or other

accident involving any emergency vehicle which is responding to, operating at, or returning from the location identified in such report.

4. An emergency vehicle as referred to in subdivision three of this section shall include any vehicle operated by any employee or member of any official or quasi-official agency having the function of dealing with emergencies involving danger to life or property and shall include, but not necessarily be limited to, an emergency vehicle which is operated by a volunteer firefighter with a fire department, fire company, or any unit thereof as defined in the volunteer firefighters' benefit law; or by a volunteer ambulance worker with a volunteer ambulance corporation, or any unit thereof as defined in the volunteer ambulance workers' benefit law.

5. Knowing the information reported, conveyed or circulated to be false or baseless and under circumstances in which it is likely public alarm or inconvenience will result, he or she initiates or circulates a report or warning of an alleged occurrence or an impending occurrence of a fire, an explosion, or the release of a hazardous substance upon school grounds and it is likely that persons are present on said grounds.

6. Knowing the information reported, conveyed or circulated to be false or baseless and under circumstances in which it is likely public alarm or inconvenience will result, he or she initiates or circulates a report or warning of an alleged occurrence or impending occurrence of a fire, explosion or the release of a hazardous substance in or upon a sports stadium or arena, mass transportation facility, enclosed shopping mall, any public building or any public place, and it is likely that persons are present. For purposes of this subdivision, the terms "sports stadium or arena, mass transportation facility or enclosed shopping mall" shall have their natural meaning and the term "public building" shall have the meaning set forth in section four hundred one of the executive law.

Falsely reporting an incident in the first degree is a class D felony.

HISTORY: Add, L 1977, ch 485, § 1; amd, L 1990, ch 576, § 1, L 1995, ch 528, § 1, eff Nov 1, 1995. Former § 240.60, add, L 1973, ch 276, § 31; amd, L 1975, ch 31, § 1; repealed, L 1977, ch 485, § 1, eff Sept 1, 1977. Opening par, formerly part of entire section, so designated and amd, L 1990, ch 576, § 1, eff Nov 1, 1990. Sub 1, formerly part of entire section, so designated and amd, L 1990, ch 576, § 1, eff Nov 1, 1990. Sub 2, add, L 1990, ch 576, § 1; amd, L 1995, ch 528, § 1, eff Nov 1, 1995. Sub 3, add, L 1995, ch 528, § 1, eff Nov 1, 1995. Sub 4, add, L 1995, ch 528, § 1, eff Nov 1, 1995. Sub 5, add, L 1999, ch 561, § 3, eff Dec 1, 1999. Sub 6, add, L 2001, ch 244, § 1, eff Nov 1, 2001; amd, L 2001, ch 301, § 4, eff Nov 1, 2001. Closing par, amd, L 2001, ch 301, § 4, eff Sept 17, 2001.

§ 240.61. Placing a false bomb or hazardous substance in the second degree

A person is guilty of placing a false bomb or hazardous substance in the second degree when he or she places, or causes to be placed, any device or object that by its design, construction, content or characteristics appears to be or to contain, a bomb, destructive device, explosive or hazardous substance, but is, in fact, an inoperative facsimile or imitation of such a bomb, destructive device, explosive or hazardous substance and which he or she knows, intends or reasonably believes will appear to be a bomb, destructive device, explosive or hazardous substance under circumstances in which it is likely to cause public alarm or inconvenience.

Placing a false bomb or hazardous substance in the second degree is a class E felony.

HISTORY: Add, L 1996, ch 355, § 1; amd, L 1999, ch 561, § 4, eff Dec 1, 1999. Section heading, amd, L 1999, ch 561, § 4, eff Dec 1, 1999. Section heading, amd, L 2004, ch 1, § 14 (Part A), eff July 23, 2004. Opening par, amd, L 1999, ch 561, § 4, eff Dec 1, 1999. Opening par, amd, L 2004, ch 1, § 14 (Part A), eff July 23, 2004. Closing par, amd, L 1999, ch 561, § 4, eff Dec 1, 1999. Closing par, amd, L 2001, ch 301, § 5, eff Sept 17, 2001, L 2004, ch 1, § 14 (Part A), eff July 23, 2004.

§ 240.62. Placing a false bomb or hazardous substance in the first degree

A person is guilty of placing a false bomb or hazardous substance in the first degree when he or she places, or causes to be placed, in or upon school grounds, a public building, or a public place any device or object that by its design, construction, content or characteristics appears to be or to contain, a bomb, destructive device, explosive or hazardous substance, but is, in fact, an inoperative facsimile or imitation of such a bomb, destructive device, explosive or hazardous substance and which he or she knows, intends or reasonably believes will appear to be a bomb, destructive device, explosive or hazardous substance under circumstances in which it is likely to cause public alarm or inconvenience. For purposes of this section the term "public building" shall have the meaning set forth in section four hundred one of the executive law.

Placing a false bomb or hazardous substance in the first degree is a class D felony.

HISTORY: Add, L 1999, ch 561, § 5, eff Dec 1, 1999. Amd, L 2001, ch 301, § 6, eff Sept 17, 2001. Section heading, amd, L 2004, ch 1, § 15 (Part A), eff July 23, 2004. Opening par, amd, L 2001, ch 301, § 6, eff Sept 17, 2001, L 2004, ch 1, § 15 (Part A), eff July 23, 2004. Closing par, amd, L 2001, ch 301, § 6, eff Sept 17, 2001, L 2004, ch 1, § 15 (Part A), eff July 23, 2004.

§ 240.63. Placing a false bomb or hazardous substance in a sports stadium or arena, mass transportation facility or enclosed shopping mall

A person is guilty of placing a false bomb or hazardous substance in a sports stadium or arena, mass transportation facility or enclosed shopping mall when he or she places, or causes to be placed, in a sports stadium or arena, mass transportation facility or enclosed shopping mall, in which it is likely that persons are present, any device or object that by its design, construction, content or characteristics appears to be or to contain a bomb, destructive device, explosive or hazardous substance, but is, in fact, an inoperative facsimile or imitation of such a bomb, destructive device, explosive or hazardous substance and which he or she knows, intends or reasonably believes will appear to be a bomb, destructive device, explosive or hazardous substance under circumstances in which it is likely to cause public alarm or inconvenience. For purposes of this section, "sports stadium or arena, mass transportation facility or enclosed shopping mall" shall have its natural meaning.

Placing a false bomb or hazardous substance in a sports stadium or arena, mass transportation facility or enclosed shopping mall is a class D felony.

HISTORY: Add, L 2001, ch 244, § 2, eff Nov 1, 2001; amd, L 2001, ch 301, § 7, Nov 1, 2001. Section heading, amd, L 2004, ch 1, § 16 (Part A), eff July 23, 2004. Opening par, amd, L 2001, ch 301, § 7, eff Nov 1, 2001, L 2004, ch 1, § 16 (Part A), eff July 23, 2004. Closing par, amd, L 2001, ch 301, § 7, eff Nov 1, 2001, L 2004, ch 1, § 16 (Part A), eff July 23, 2004.

§ 240.65. Unlawful prevention of public access to records

A person is guilty of unlawful prevention of public access to records when, with intent to prevent the public inspection of a record pursuant to article six of the public officers law, he willfully conceals or destroys any such record.

Unlawful prevention of public access to records is a violation.

HISTORY: Add, L 1989, ch 705, § 1, eff Nov 1, 1989.

§ 240.70. Criminal interference with health care services or religious worship in the second degree

1. A person is guilty of criminal interference with health services or religious worship in the second degree when:

(a) by force or threat of force or by physical obstruction, he or she intentionally injures, intimidates or interferes with, or attempts to injure, intimidate or interfere with, another person because such other person was or is obtaining or providing reproductive health services; or

(b) by force or threat of force or by physical obstruction, he or she intentionally injures, intimidates or interferes with, or attempts to injure, intimidate or interfere with, another person in order to discourage such other person or any other person or persons from obtaining or providing reproductive health services; or

(c) by force or threat of force or by physical obstruction, he or she intentionally injures, intimidates or interferes with, or attempts to injure, intimidate or interfere with, another person because such person was or is seeking to exercise the right of religious freedom at a place of religious worship; or

(d) he or she intentionally damages the property of a health care facility, or attempts to do so, because such facility provides reproductive health services, or intentionally damages the property of a place of religious worship.

2. A parent or legal guardian of a minor shall not be subject to prosecution for conduct otherwise prohibited by paragraph (a) or (b) of subdivision one of this section which is directed exclusively at such minor.

3. For purposes of this section:

(a) the term "health care facility" means a hospital, clinic, physician's office or other facility that provides reproductive health services, and includes the building or structure in which the facility is located;

(b) the term "interferes with" means to restrict a person's freedom of movement;

(c) the term "intimidates" means to place a person in reasonable apprehension of physical injury to himself or herself or to another person;

(d) the term "physical obstruction" means rendering impassable ingress to or egress from a facility that provides reproductive health services or to or from a place of religious worship, or rendering passage to or from such a facility or place of religious worship unreasonably difficult or hazardous; and

(e) the term "reproductive health services" means health care services provided in a hospital, clinic, physician's office or other facility and includes medical, surgical, counseling or referral services relating to the human reproductive system, including services relating to pregnancy or the termination of a pregnancy.

Criminal interference with health care services or religious worship in the second degree is a class A misdemeanor.

HISTORY: Add, L 1999, ch 635, § 14, eff Dec 1, 1999.

§ 240.71. Criminal interference with health care services or religious worship in the first degree

A person is guilty of criminal interference with health care services or religious worship in the first degree when he or she commits the crime of criminal interference with health care services or religious worship in the second degree and has been previously convicted of the crime of criminal interference with health care services or religious worship in the first or second degree or aggravated interference with health care services in the first or second degree.

Criminal interference with health care services or religious worship in the first degree is a class E felony.

HISTORY: Add, L 1999, ch 635, § 14, eff Dec 1, 1999. Amd, L 2009, ch 493, § 1, eff Jan 26, 2010. First undesignated par, amd, L 2009, ch 493, § 1, eff Jan 26, 2010.

§ 240.72. Aggravated interference with health care services in the second degree

A person is guilty of the crime of aggravated interference with health care services in the second degree when he or she commits the crime of criminal interference with health care services or religious worship in violation of paragraph (a) of subdivision one of section 240.70 of this article and thereby causes physical injury to such other person who was obtaining or providing, or was assisting another person to obtain or provide reproductive health services.

Aggravated interference with health care services in the second degree is a class E felony.

HISTORY: Add, L 2009, ch 493, § 2, eff Jan 26, 2010.

§ 240.73. Aggravated interference with health care services in the first degree

A person is guilty of the crime of aggravated interference with health care services in the first degree when he or she commits the crime of criminal interference with health care services or religious worship in violation of paragraph (a) of subdivision one of section 240.70 of this article and thereby causes serious physical injury to such other person who was obtaining or providing, or who was assisting another person to obtain or provide reproductive health services.

Aggravated interference with health care services in the first degree is a class C felony.

HISTORY: Add, L 2009, ch 493, § 2, eff Jan 26, 2010.

§ 240.75. Aggravated family offense

1. A person is guilty of aggravated family offense when he or she commits a misdemeanor defined in subdivision two of this section as a specified offense and he or she has been convicted of one or more specified offenses within the immediately preceding five years. For the purposes of this subdivision, in calculating the five year period, any period of time during which the defendant was incarcerated for any reason between the time of the commission of any of such previous offenses and the time of commission of the present crime shall be excluded and such five year period shall be extended by a period or periods equal to the time served under such incarceration.

2. A "specified offense" is an offense defined in section 120.00 (assault in the third degree); section 120.05 (assault in the second degree); section 120.10 (assault in the first degree); section 120.13 (menacing in the first degree); section 120.14 (menacing in the second degree); section 120.15 (menacing in the third degree); section 120.20 (reckless endangerment in the second degree); section 120.25 (reckless endangerment in the first degree); section 120.45 (stalking in the fourth degree); section 120.50 (stalking in the third degree); section 120.55 (stalking in the second degree); section 120.60 (stalking in the first degree); section 121.11 (criminal obstruction of breathing or blood circulation); section 121.12 (strangulation in the second degree); section 121.13 (strangulation in the first degree); subdivision one of section 125.15 (manslaughter in the second degree); subdivision one, two or four of section 125.20 (manslaughter in the first degree); section 125.25 (murder in the second degree); section 130.20 (sexual misconduct); section 130.30 (rape in the second degree); section 130.35 (rape in the first degree); section 130.40 (criminal sexual act in the third degree); section 130.45 (criminal sexual act in the second degree); section 130.50 (criminal sexual act in the first degree); section 130.52 (forcible touching); section 130.53 (persistent sexual abuse); section 130.55 (sexual abuse in the third degree); section 130.60 (sexual abuse in the second degree); section 130.65 (sexual abuse in the first degree); section 130.66 (aggravated sexual abuse in the third degree); section 130.67 (aggravated sexual abuse in the second degree); section 130.70 (aggravated sexual abuse in the first degree); section 130.91 (sexually motivated felony); section 130.95 (predatory sexual assault); section 130.96 (predatory

sexual assault against a child); section 135.05 (unlawful imprisonment in the second degree); section 135.10 (unlawful imprisonment in the first degree); section 135.60 (coercion in the second degree); section 135.65 (coercion in the first degree); section 140.20 (burglary in the third degree); section 140.25 (burglary in the second degree); section 140.30 (burglary in the first degree); section 145.00 (criminal mischief in the fourth degree); section 145.05 (criminal mischief in the third degree); section 145.10 (criminal mischief in the second degree); section 145.12 (criminal mischief in the first degree); section 145.14 (criminal tampering in the third degree); section 215.50 (criminal contempt in the second degree); section 215.51 (criminal contempt in the first degree); section 215.52 (aggravated criminal contempt); section 240.25 (harassment in the first degree); subdivision one, two or four of section 240.30 (aggravated harassment in the second degree); aggravated family offense as defined in this section or any attempt or conspiracy to commit any of the foregoing offenses where the defendant and the person against whom the offense was committed were members of the same family or household as defined in subdivision one of section 530.11 of the criminal procedure law.

3. The person against whom the current specified offense is committed may be different from the person against whom the previous specified offense was committed and such persons do not need to be members of the same family or household.

Aggravated family offense is a class E felony.

HISTORY: Add, L 2012, ch 491, § 2 (Part D), eff Jan 23, 2013.

§ 240.76. Directing a laser at an aircraft in the second degree

A person is guilty of directing a laser at an aircraft in the second degree when, with intent to disrupt safe air travel, he or she directs the beam of a laser:

1. onto a specific aircraft intending to thereby disrupt or interfere with such aircraft in the special aircraft jurisdiction of the United States; or

2. in the immediate vicinity of an aircraft in the special aircraft jurisdiction of the United States, and:

(a) the calculated or measured beam irradiance on the aircraft, or in the immediate vicinity of the aircraft, exceeds limits set by the FAA for the FAA-specified laser flight zone (normal, sensitive, critical, or laser-free) where the aircraft was located; and

(b) a pilot in the illuminated aircraft files a laser incident report with the FAA.

3. As used in this section:

(a) the term "laser" shall mean any device designed or used to amplify electromagnetic radiation by stimulated emission that emits a beam; and

(b) the term "FAA" shall mean the Federal Aviationb Administration.

4. This section does not prohibit directing a laser beam at an aircraft, or in the immediate vicinity of an aircraft, by:

(a) an authorized individual in the conduct of research and development or flight test operations conducted by an aircraft manufacturer, the FAA, or any other person authorized by the FAA to conduct such research and development or flight test operations; or

(b) members or elements of the United States department ofb defense or the United States department of homeland security acting in an official capacity for the purpose of research, development, operations, testing or training; or

(c) an individual in an emergency situation using a laser toc attract the attention of an aircraft for bona fide rescue purposes; or

(d) an individual whose laser operations have been submitted to and reviewed by the FAA, when:

(i) the FAA has issued a letter not objecting to the laser use; and

(ii) the laser is operated in conformity with the FAA submission.

Directing a laser at an aircraft is a class A misdemeanor.

HISTORY: Add, L 2014, ch 98, § 1, eff Nov 1, 2014.

§ 240.77. Directing a laser at an aircraft in the first degree

A person is guilty of directing a laser at an aircraft in the first degree when he or she commits the crime of directing a laser at an aircraft in the second degree in violation of section 240.76 of this article and thereby causes a significant change of course or other serious disruption to the safe travel of an aircraft that threatens the physical safety of the aircraft's passengers or crew.

Directing a laser at an aircraft in the first degree is a class E felony.

HISTORY: Add, L 2014, ch 98, § 1, eff Nov 1, 2014.

ARTICLE 241   HARASSMENT OF RENT REGULATED TENANTS
[EXPIRES AND REPEALED JUNE 16, 2015]

§ 241.00.   **[Expires and repealed June 16, 2015] Harassment of a rent regulated tenant; definition of terms**

§ 241.05.   **[Expires and repealed June 16, 2015] Harassment of a rent regulated tenant**

HISTORY: Add, L 1997, ch 116, § 28, eff July 19, 1997, expires and repealed June 16, 2015.

§ 241.00. [Expires and repealed June 16, 2015] Harassment of a rent regulated tenant; definition of terms

As used in this article:

1. "Rent regulated tenant" shall mean a person occupying a housing accommodation which is subject to the regulations and control of residential rents and evictions pursuant to the emergency housing rent control law, the local emergency housing rent control act, the emergency tenant protection act of nineteen seventy-four, the New York city rent and rehabilitation law or the New York city rent stabilization law of nineteen hundred sixty-nine, and such person is either a party to a lease or rental agreement for such housing accommodation, a statutory tenant or a person who lawfully occupies such housing accommodation with such party to a lease or rental agreement or with such statutory tenant. The definition of "rent regulated tenant" as used in this subdivision shall be applicable only to the provisions of this article and shall not be applicable to any other provision of law.

2. "Housing accommodations" shall mean housing accommodations which are subject to the regulations and control of residential rents and evictions pursuant to the emergency housing rent control law, the local emergency housing rent control act, the emergency tenant protection act of nineteen seventy-four, the New York city rent and rehabilitation law or the New York city rent stabilization law of nineteen hundred sixty-nine.

3. "Owner" shall mean an owner, lessor, sublessor, assignee, net lessee, or a proprietary lessee of a housing accommodation in a structure or premises owned by a cooperative

corporation or association, or an owner of a condominium unit or the sponsor of such cooperative corporation or association or condominium development, or any other person or entity receiving or entitled to receive rent for the use or occupation of any housing accommodation, or an agent of or any person acting on behalf of any of the foregoing.

HISTORY: Add, L 1997, ch 116, § 28, eff July 19, 1997, expires and repealed June 16, 2015.

§ 241.05. [Expires and repealed June 16, 2015] Harassment of a rent regulated tenant

An owner is guilty of harassment of a rent regulated tenant when with intent to cause a rent regulated tenant to vacate a housing accommodation, such owner:

1. With intent to cause physical injury to such tenant, causes such injury to such tenant or to a third person; or

2. Recklessly causes physical injury to such tenant or to a third person.

Harassment of a rent regulated tenant is a class E felony.

HISTORY: Add, L 1997, ch 116, § 28, eff July 19, 1997, expires and repealed June 16, 2015.

ARTICLE 242   OFFENSES AGAINST SERVICE ANIMALS AND HANDLERS

HISTORY: Add, L 2007, ch 582, § 1, eff Nov 1, 2007.

§ 242.00. Definitions

For purposes of this article:

1. "Service animal" shall mean any animal that has been partnered with a person who has a disability and has been trained or is being trained, by a qualified person, to aid or guide a person with a disability.

2. "Disability" shall have the same meaning as provided in section two hundred ninety-two of the executive law.

3. "Handler" shall mean a disabled person using a service animal.

4. "Formal training program" or "certified trainer" shall mean an institution, group or individual who has documentation and community recognition as a provider of service animals.

HISTORY: Add, L 2007, ch 582, § 1, eff Nov 1, 2007.

§ 242.05. Interference, harassment or intimidation of a service animal

A person is guilty of interference, harassment or intimidation of a service animal when he or she commits an act with intent to and which does make it impractical, dangerous or impossible for a service animal to perform its assigned responsibilities of assisting a person with a disability.

Interference, harassment or intimidation of a service animal is a class B misdemeanor.

HISTORY: Add, L 2007, ch 582, § 1, eff Nov 1, 2007.

§ 242.10. Harming a service animal in the second degree

A person is guilty of harming a service animal in the second degree when, with the intent to do so, he or she causes physical injury, or causes such injury that results in the death, of a service animal.

Harming a service animal in the second degree is a class A misdemeanor.

HISTORY: Add, L 2007, ch 582, § 1, eff Nov 1, 2007.

§ 242.15. Harming a service animal in the first degree

A person is guilty of harming a service animal in the first degree when, he or she commits the crime of harming a service animal in the second degree, and has been convicted of harming a service animal in the first or second degree within the prior five years.

Harming a service animal in the first degree is a class E felony.

HISTORY: Add, L 2007, ch 582, § 1, eff Nov 1, 2007.

ARTICLE 245   OFFENSES AGAINST PUBLIC SENSIBILITIES

 HISTORY: Add, L 1965, ch 1030, § 1, eff Sept 1, 1967.

§ 245.00. Public lewdness

A person is guilty of public lewdness when he intentionally exposes the private or intimate parts of his body in a lewd manner or commits any other lewd act (a) in a public place, or (b) in private premises under circumstances in which he may readily be observed from either a public place or from other private premises, and with intent that he be so observed.

Public lewdness is a class B misdemeanor.

 HISTORY: Add, L 1965, ch 1030, § 1, with substance derived from § 1140; amd, L 1968, ch 748, § 1, eff Sept 1, 1968.

§ 245.01. Exposure of a person

A person is guilty of exposure if he appears in a public place in such a manner that the private or intimate parts of his body are unclothed or exposed. For purposes of this section, the private or intimate parts of a female person shall include that portion of the breast which is below the top of the areola. This section shall not apply to the breastfeeding of infants or to any person entertaining or performing in a play, exhibition, show or entertainment.

Exposure of a person is a violation.

Nothing in this section shall prevent the adoption by a city, town or village of a local law prohibiting exposure of a person as herein defined in a public place, at any time, whether or not such person is entertaining or performing in a play, exhibition, show or entertainment.

 HISTORY: Add, L 1983, ch 216, § 1; amd, L 1984, ch 633, § 1, eff Oct 25, 1984. Former § 245.01, add, L 1967, ch 367, § 1, with substance derived from § 1140(b); amd, L 1970, ch 40, § 1; repealed, L 1983, ch 216, § 1, eff July 2, 1983.

§ 245.02. Promoting the exposure of a person

A person is guilty of promoting the exposure of a person when he knowingly conducts, maintains, owns, manages, operates or furnishes any public premise or place where a person in a public place appears in such a manner that the private or intimate parts of his body are unclothed or exposed. For purposes of this section, the private or intimate parts of a female person shall include that portion of the breast which is below the top of the areola. This section shall not apply to the breastfeeding of infants or to any person entertaining or performing in a play, exhibition, show or entertainment.

Promoting the exposure of a person is a violation.

Nothing in this section shall prevent the adoption by a city, town or village of a local law prohibiting the exposure of a person substantially as herein defined in a public place, at any time, whether or not such person is entertaining or performing in a play, exhibition, show or entertainment.

> **HISTORY:** Add, L 1983, ch 216, § 2; amd, L 1984, ch 633, § 2, eff Oct 25, 1984. Former § 245.02, add, L 1967, ch 367, § 1, with substance derived from § 1140(c); amd, L 1970, ch 40, § 1; repealed, L 1983, ch 216, § 2, eff July 2, 1983.

§ 245.03. Public lewdness in the first degree

A person is guilty of public lewdness in the first degree when:

1. being nineteen years of age or older and intending to be observed by a person less than sixteen years of age in a place described in subdivision (a) or (b) of section 245.00 of this article, he or she intentionally exposes the private or intimate parts of his or her body in a lewd manner for the purpose of alarming or seriously annoying such person, and he or she is thereby observed by such person in such place; or

2. he or she commits the crime of public lewdness, as defined in section 245.00 of this article, and within the preceding year has been convicted of an offense defined in such section 245.00 or this section.

Public lewdness in the first degree is a class A misdemeanor.

> **HISTORY:** Add, L 2014, ch 186, § 1, eff Nov 1, 2014.

§ 245.05. Offensive exhibition

A person is guilty of offensive exhibition when he knowingly produces, operates, manages or furnishes premises for, or in any way promotes or participates in, an exhibition in the nature of public entertainment or amusement in which:

1. A person competes continuously without respite for a period of more than eight consecutive hours in a dance contest, bicycle race or other contest involving physical endurance; or

2. A person is held up to ridicule or contempt by voluntarily submitting to indignities such as the throwing of balls or other articles at his head or body; or

3. A firearm is discharged or a knife, arrow or other sharp or dangerous instrument is thrown or propelled at or toward a person.

Offensive exhibition is a violation.

> **HISTORY:** Add, L 1965, ch 1030, § 1, with substance derived from §§ 831 in part, 832-834; amd, L 1968, ch 680, § 1, eff June 16, 1968. Sub 3, amd, L 1968, ch 680, § 1, eff June 16, 1968. Sub 4, deleted, L 1968, ch 680, § 1, eff June 16, 1968.

§ 245.10. Public display of offensive sexual material; definitions of terms

The following definitions are applicable to section 245.11:

1. "Nudity" means the showing of the human male or female genitals, pubic area or buttocks with less than a full opaque covering, or the showing of the female breast with less than a fully opaque covering of any portion thereof below the top of the nipple, or the depiction of covered male genitals in a discernibly turgid state.

2. "Sexual conduct" means an act of masturbation, homosexuality, sexual intercourse, or physical contact with a person's clothed or unclothed genitals, pubic area, buttocks or, if such person be a female, breast.

3. "Sado-masochistic abuse" means flagellation or torture by or upon a person clad in undergarments, a mask or bizzare costume, or the condition of being fettered, bound or otherwise physically restrained on the part of one so clothed.

4. "Transportation facility" means any conveyance, premises or place used for or in connection with public passenger transportation, whether by air, railroad, motor vehicle or any other method. It includes aircraft, watercraft, railroad cars, buses, and air, boat, railroad and bus terminals and stations and all appurtenances thereto.

HISTORY: Add, L 1971, ch 962, § 2, eff Sept 1, 1971. Former § 245.10, add, L 1965, ch 1030, § 1, with substance derived in part from § 180(1); repealed, L 1965, ch 1047, § 1, eff Sept 1, 1967.

§ 245.11. Public display of offensive sexual material

A person is guilty of public display of offensive sexual material when, with knowledge of its character and content, he displays or permits to be displayed in or on any window, showcase, newsstand, display rack, wall, door, billboard, display board, viewing screen, moving picture screen, marquee or similar place, in such manner that the display is easily visible from or in any: public street, sidewalk or thoroughfare; transportation facility; or any place accessible to members of the public without fee or other limit or condition of admission such as a minimum age requirement and including but not limited to schools, places of amusement, parks and playgrounds but excluding rooms or apartments designed for actual residence; any pictorial, three-dimensional or other visual representation of a person or a portion of the human body that predominantly appeals to prurient interest in sex, and that:

(a) depicts nudity, or actual or simulated sexual conduct or sado-masochistic abuse; or

(b) depicts or appears to depict nudity, or actual or simulated sexual conduct or sado-masochistic abuse, with the area of the male or female subject's unclothed or apparently unclothed genitals, pubic area or buttocks, or of the female subject's unclothed or apparently unclothed breast, obscured by a covering or mark placed or printed on or in front of the material displayed, or obscured or altered in any other manner.

Public display of offensive sexual material is a Class A misdemeanor.

HISTORY: Add, L 1971, ch 962, § 2; amd, L 1985, ch 231, § 2, eff Nov 1, 1985. Opening par, amd, L 1972, ch 814, § 1, eff Sept 1, 1972.

§ 245.15. [Repealed]

HISTORY: Add, L 1965, ch 1030, § 1, with substance derived from §§ 181, 182, 185, 186, 187, 189(1), 190, 191, 194, 194-a; repealed, L 1965, ch 1047, § 1, eff Sept 1, 1967.

§ 245.20. [Repealed]

HISTORY: Add, L 1965, ch 1030, § 1, with substance derived from § 185 in part; repealed, L 1965, ch 1047, § 1, eff Sept 1, 1967.

ARTICLE 250   OFFENSES AGAINST THE RIGHT TO PRIVACY

HISTORY: Add, L 1965, ch 1030, § 1, eff Sept 1, 1967.

§ 250.00. Eavesdropping; definitions of terms

The following definitions are applicable to this article:

1. "Wiretapping" means the intentional overhearing or recording of a telephonic or telegraphic communication by a person other than a sender or receiver thereof, without the consent of either the sender or receiver, by means of any instrument, device or equipment. The normal operation of a telephone or telegraph corporation and the normal use of the services and facilities furnished by such corporation pursuant to its tariffs or necessary to protect the rights or property of said corporation shall not be deemed "wiretapping."

2. "Mechanical overhearing of a conversation" means the intentional overhearing or recording of a conversation or discussion, without the consent of at least one party thereto, by a person not present thereat, by means of any instrument, device or equipment.

3. "Telephonic communication" means any aural transfer made in whole or in part through the use of facilities for the transmission of communications by the aid of wire, cable or other like connection between the point of origin and the point of reception (including the use of such connection in a switching station) furnished or operated by any person engaged in providing or operating such facilities for the transmission of communications and such term includes any electronic storage of such communications.

4. "Aural transfer" means a transfer containing the human voice at any point between and including the point of origin and the point of reception.

5. "Electronic communication" means any transfer of signs, signals, writing, images, sounds, data, or intelligence of any nature transmitted in whole or in part by a wire, radio, electromagnetic, photoelectronic or photo-optical system, but does not include:

(a) any telephonic or telegraphic communication; or

(b) any communication made through a tone only paging device; or

(c) any communication made through a tracking device consisting of an electronic or mechanical device which permits the tracking of the movement of a person or object; or

(d) any communication that is disseminated by the sender through a method of transmission that is configured so that such communication is readily accessible to the general public.

6. "Intercepting or accessing of an electronic communication" and "intentionally intercepted or accessed" mean the intentional acquiring, receiving, collecting, overhearing, or recording of an electronic communication, without the consent of the sender or intended receiver thereof, by means of any instrument, device or equipment, except when used by a telephone company in the ordinary course of its business or when necessary to protect the rights or property of such company.

7. "Electronic communication service" means any service which provides to users thereof the ability to send or receive wire or electronic communications.

8. "Unlawfully" means not specifically authorized pursuant to article seven hundred or seven hundred five of the criminal procedure law for the purposes of this section and sections 250.05, 250.10, 250.15, 250.20, 250.25, 250.30 and 250.35 of this article.

HISTORY: Add, L 1965, ch 1030, § 1; amd, L 1988, ch 744, § 1, eff Dec 22, 1988. Sub 1, amd, L 1988, ch 744, § 1, eff Dec 22, 1988. Sub 3, add, L 1988, ch 744, § 1, eff Dec 22, 1988. Former sub 3, amd, L 1968, ch 546, § 3, L 1969, ch 1147, § 6, L 1971, ch 1097, § 78; redesignated sub 8, L 1988, ch 744, § 1, eff Dec 22, 1988. Sub 4, add, L 1988, ch 744, § 1, eff Dec 22, 1988. Sub 5, add, L 1988, ch 744, § 1, eff Dec 22, 1988. Sub 6, add, L 1988, ch 744, § 1, eff Dec 22, 1988. Sub 7, add, L 1988, ch 744, § 1, eff Dec 22, 1988. Sub 8, formerly sub 3, amd, L 1968, ch 546, § 3, L 1969, ch 1147, § 6, L 1971, ch 1097, § 78; so designated sub 8 and amd, L 1988, ch 744, § 1, eff Dec 22, 1988. Sub 8, amd, L 2003, ch 69, § 2, eff Aug 11, 2003.

§ 250.05. Eavesdropping

A person is guilty of eavesdropping when he unlawfully engages in wiretapping, mechanical overhearing of a conversation, or intercepting or accessing of an electronic communication.

Eavesdropping is a class E felony.

HISTORY: Add, L 1965, ch 1030, § 1, with substance derived from § 738; amd, L 1988, ch 744, § 2, eff Dec 22, 1988.

§ 250.10. Possession of eavesdropping devices

A person is guilty of possession of eavesdropping devices when, under circumstances evincing an intent to use or to permit the same to be used in violation of section 250.05, he possesses any instrument, device or equipment designed for, adapted to or commonly used in wiretapping or mechanical overhearing of a conversation.

Possession of eavesdropping devices is a class A misdemeanor.

HISTORY: Add, L 1965, ch 1030, § 1, eff Sept 1, 1967, with substance derived from § 742.

§ 250.15. Failure to report wiretapping

A telephone or telegraph corporation is guilty of failure to report wiretapping when, having knowledge of the occurrence of unlawful wiretapping, it does not report such matter to an appropriate law enforcement officer or agency.

Failure to report wiretapping is a class B misdemeanor.

HISTORY: Add, L 1965, ch 1030, § 1, eff Sept 1, 1967, with substance derived from § 744.

§ 250.20. Divulging an eavesdropping warrant

A person is guilty of divulging an eavesdropping warrant when, possessing information concerning the existence or content of an eavesdropping warrant issued pursuant to article seven hundred of the criminal procedure law, or concerning any circumstances attending an application for such a warrant, he discloses such information to another person; except that such disclosure is not criminal or unlawful when permitted by section 700.65 of the criminal procedure law or when made to a state or federal agency specifically authorized by law to receive reports concerning eavesdropping warrants, or when made in a legal proceeding, or to a law enforcement officer or agency connected with the application for such warrant, or to a legislative committee or temporary state commission, or to the telephone or telegraph corporation whose facilities are involved, or to any entity operating an electronic communications service whose facilities are involved.

Divulging an eavesdropping warrant is a class A misdemeanor.

HISTORY: Add, L 1965, ch 1030, § 1, with substance derived from § 745; amd, L 1968, ch 546, § 4, L 1969, ch 1147, § 7, L 1971, ch 1097, § 79, L 1988, ch 744, § 3, eff Dec 22, 1988. Section heading, amd, L 1968, ch 546, § 4, eff June 5, 1968.

§ 250.25. Tampering with private communications

A person is guilty of tampering with private communications when:

1. Knowing that he does not have the consent of the sender or receiver, he opens or reads a sealed letter or other sealed private communication; or

2. Knowing that a sealed letter or other sealed private communication has been opened or read in violation of subdivision one of this section, he divulges without the consent of the sender or receiver, the contents of such letter or communication, in whole or in part, or a resume of any portion of the contents thereof; or

3. Knowing that he does not have the consent of the sender or receiver, he obtains or attempts to obtain from an employee, officer or representative of a telephone or telegraph corporation, by connivance, deception, intimidation or in any other manner, information with respect to the contents or nature thereof of a telephonic or telegraphic communication; except that the provisions of this subdivision do not apply to a law enforcement officer who obtains information from a telephone or telegraph corporation pursuant to section 250.35; or

4. Knowing that he does not have the consent of the sender or receiver, and being an employee, officer or representative of a telephone or telegraph corporation, he knowingly divulges to another person the contents or nature thereof of a telephonic or telegraphic communication; except that the provisions of this subdivision do not apply to such person when he acts pursuant to section 250.35.

Tampering with private communications is a class B misdemeanor.

HISTORY: Add, L 1965, ch 1030, § 1, eff Sept 1, 1967, with substance derived from §§ 553, 743.

§ 250.30. Unlawfully obtaining communications information

A person is guilty of unlawfully obtaining communications information when, knowing that he does not have the authorization of a telephone or telegraph corporation, he obtains or attempts to obtain, by deception, stealth or in any other manner, from such corporation or from any employee, officer or representative thereof:

1. Information concerning identification or location of any wires, cables, lines, terminals or other apparatus used in furnishing telephone or telegraph service; or

2. Information concerning a record of any communication passing over telephone or telegraph lines of any such corporation.

Unlawfully obtaining communications information is a class B misdemeanor.

HISTORY: Add, L 1965, ch 1030, § 1, eff Sept 1, 1967, with substance derived from § 743(2).

§ 250.35. Failing to report criminal communications

1. It shall be the duty of a telephone or telegraph corporation, or an entity operating an electronic communications service, and of any employee, officer or representative thereof having knowledge that the facilities of such corporation or entity are being used to conduct any criminal business, traffic or transaction, to furnish or attempt to furnish to an appropriate law enforcement officer or agency all pertinent information within his possession relating to such matter, and to cooperate fully with any law enforcement officer or agency investigating such matter.

2. A person is guilty of failing to report criminal communications when he knowingly violates any duty prescribed in subdivision one of this section.

Failing to report criminal communications is a class B misdemeanor.

HISTORY: Add, L 1965, ch 1030, § 1, eff Sept 1, 1967, with substance derived from § 743(1). Sub 1, amd, L 1988, ch 744, § 4, eff Dec 22, 1988.

§ 250.40. Unlawful surveillance; definitions

The following definitions shall apply to sections 250.45, 250.50, 250.55 and 250.60 of this article:

1. "Place and time when a person has a reasonable expectation of privacy" means a place and time when a reasonable person would believe that he or she could fully disrobe in privacy.

2. "Imaging device" means any mechanical, digital or electronic viewing device, camera, cellular phone or any other instrument capable of recording, storing or transmitting visual images that can be utilized to observe a person.

3. "Sexual or other intimate parts" means the human male or female genitals, pubic area or buttocks, or the female breast below the top of the nipple, and shall include such part or parts which are covered only by an undergarment.

4. "Broadcast" means electronically transmitting a visual image with the intent that it be viewed by a person.

5. "Disseminate" means to give, provide, lend, deliver, mail, send, forward, transfer or transmit, electronically or otherwise to another person.

6. "Publish" means to (a) disseminate, as defined in subdivision five of this section, with the intent that such image or images be disseminated to ten or more persons; or (b) disseminate with the intent that such images be sold by another person; or (c) post, present, display, exhibit, circulate, advertise or allows access, electronically or otherwise, so as to make an image or images available to the public; or (d) disseminate with the intent that an image or images be posted, presented, displayed, exhibited, circulated, advertised or made accessible, electronically or otherwise and to make such image or images available to the public.

7. "Sell" means to disseminate to another person, as defined in subdivision five of this section, or to publish, as defined in subdivision six of this section, in exchange for something of value.

HISTORY: Add, L 2003, ch 69, § 3, eff Aug 11, 2003. Sub 2, amd, L 2007, ch 291, § 1, eff Nov 1, 2007.

§ 250.45. Unlawful surveillance in the second degree

A person is guilty of unlawful surveillance in the second degree when:

1. For his or her own, or another person's amusement, entertainment, or profit, or for the purpose of degrading or abusing a person, he or she intentionally uses or installs, or permits the utilization or installation of an imaging device to surreptitiously view, broadcast or record a person dressing or undressing or the sexual or other intimate parts of such person at a place and time when such person has a reasonable expectation of privacy, without such person's knowledge or consent; or

2. For his or her own, or another person's sexual arousal or sexual gratification, he or she intentionally uses or installs, or permits the utilization or installation of an imaging device to surreptitiously view, broadcast or record a person dressing or undressing or the sexual or other intimate parts of such person at a place and time when such person has a reasonable expectation of privacy, without such person's knowledge or consent; or

3. (a) For no legitimate purpose, he or she intentionally uses or installs, or permits the utilization or installation of an imaging device to surreptitiously view, broadcast or record a person in a bedroom, changing room, fitting room, restroom, toilet, bathroom, washroom, shower or any room assigned to guests or patrons in a motel, hotel or inn, without such person's knowledge or consent.

(b) For the purposes of this subdivision, when a person uses or installs, or permits the utilization or installation of an imaging device in a bedroom, changing room, fitting room, restroom, toilet, bathroom, washroom, shower or any room assigned to guests or patrons in a hotel, motel or inn, there is a rebuttable presumption that such person did so for no legitimate purpose; or

4. Without the knowledge or consent of a person, he or she intentionally uses or installs, or permits the utilization or installation of an imaging device to surreptitiously view, broadcast or record, under the clothing being worn by such person, the sexual or other intimate parts of such person; or

5. For his or her own, or another individual's amusement, entertainment, profit, sexual arousal or gratification, or for the purpose of degrading or abusing a person, the actor intentionally uses or installs or permits the utilization or installation of an imaging device to surreptitiously view, broadcast, or record such person in an identifiable manner:

(a) engaging in sexual conduct, as defined in subdivision ten of section 130.00 of this part;

(b) in the same image with the sexual or intimate part of any other person; and

(c) at a place and time when such person has a reasonable expectation of privacy, without such person's knowledge or consent.

Unlawful surveillance in the second degree is a class E felony.

HISTORY: Add, L 2003, ch 69, § 3, eff Aug 11, 2003; amd, L 2003, ch 157, § 1, eff Aug 11, 2003, L 2014, ch 193, § 1, eff Nov 1, 2014.

§ 250.50. Unlawful surveillance in the first degree

A person is guilty of unlawful surveillance in the first degree when he or she commits the crime of unlawful surveillance in the second degree and has been previously convicted within the past ten years of unlawful surveillance in the first or second degree.

Unlawful surveillance in the first degree is a class D felony.

HISTORY: Add, L 2003, ch 69, § 3, eff Aug 11, 2003.

§ 250.55. Dissemination of an unlawful surveillance image in the second degree

A person is guilty of dissemination of an unlawful surveillance image in the second degree when he or she, with knowledge of the unlawful conduct by which an image or images of the sexual or other intimate parts of another person or persons were obtained and such unlawful conduct would satisfy the essential elements of the crime of unlawful surveillance in the first or second degree, as defined, respectively, in section 250.50 or 250.45 of this article, intentionally disseminates such image or images.

Dissemination of an unlawful surveillance image in the second degree is a class A misdemeanor.

HISTORY: Add, L 2003, ch 69, § 3, eff Aug 11, 2003; amd, L 2014, ch 193, § 2, eff Nov 1, 2014.

§ 250.60 Dissemination of an unlawful surveillance image in the first degree

A person is guilty of dissemination of an unlawful surveillance image in the first degree when:

1. He or she, with knowledge of the unlawful conduct by which an image or images of the sexual or other intimate parts of another person or persons were obtained and such unlawful conduct would satisfy the essential elements of the crime of unlawful surveillance in the first or second degree, as defined, respectively, in section 250.50 or 250.45 of this article, sells or publishes such image or images; or

2. Having created a surveillance image in violation of section 250.45 or 250.50 of this article, or in violation of the law in any other jurisdiction which includes all of the essential elements of either such crime, or having acted as an accomplice to such crime, or acting as an agent to the person who committed such crime, he or she intentionally disseminates such unlawfully created image; or

3. He or she commits the crime of dissemination of an unlawful surveillance image in the second degree and has been previously convicted within the past ten years of dissemination of an unlawful surveillance image in the first or second degree.

Dissemination of an unlawful surveillance image in the first degree is a class E felony.

HISTORY: Add, L 2003, ch 69, § 3, eff Aug 11, 2003; amd, L 2003, ch 157, § 2, eff Aug 11, 2003, L 2014, ch 193, § 3, eff Nov 1, 2014.

§ 250.65. Additional provisions

1. The provisions of sections 250.45, 250.50, 250.55 and 250.60 of this article do not apply with respect to any: (a) law enforcement personnel engaged in the conduct of their authorized duties; (b) security system wherein a written notice is conspicuously posted on the premises stating that a video surveillance system has been installed for the purpose of security; or (c) video surveillance devices installed in such a manner that their presence is clearly and immediately obvious.

2. With respect to sections 250.55 and 250.60 of this article, the provisions of subdivision two of section 235.15 and subdivisions one and two of section 235.24 of this chapter shall apply.

HISTORY: Add, L 2003, ch 69, § 3, eff Aug 11, 2003.

TITLE O   Offenses Against Marriage, The Family, and The Welfare of Children and Incompetents

ARTICLE 255
OFFENSES AFFECTING THE MARITAL RELATIONSHIP

ARTICLE 260
OFFENSES RELATING TO CHILDREN, DISABLED PERSONS AND VULNERABLE ELDERLY PERSONS

ARTICLE 263
SEXUAL PERFORMANCE BY A CHILD

HISTORY: Add, L 1965, ch 1030, § 1, eff Sept 1, 1967.

ARTICLE 255   OFFENSES AFFECTING THE MARITAL RELATIONSHIP

HISTORY: Add, L 1965, ch 1030, § 1, eff Sept 1, 1967.

§ 255.00. Unlawfully solemnizing a marriage

A person is guilty of unlawfully solemnizing a marriage when:

1. Knowing that he is not authorized by the laws of this state to do so, he performs a marriage ceremony or presumes to solemnize a marriage; or

2. Being authorized by the laws of this state to perform marriage ceremonies and to solemnize marriages, he performs a marriage ceremony or solemnizes a marriage knowing that a legal impediment to such marriage exists.

Unlawfully solemnizing a marriage is a class A misdemeanor.

HISTORY: Add, L 1965, ch 1030, § 1, eff Sept 1, 1967, with substance derived from § 1450.

§ 255.05. Unlawfully issuing a dissolution decree

A person is guilty of unlawfully issuing a dissolution decree when, not being a judicial officer authorized to issue decrees of divorce or annulment, he issues a written instrument reciting or certifying that he or some other purportedly but not actually authorized person has issued a valid decree of civil divorce, annulment or other dissolution of a marriage.

Unlawfully issuing a dissolution decree is a class A misdemeanor.

HISTORY: Add, L 1965, ch 1030, § 1, eff Sept 1, 1967, with substance derived from § 1451.

§ 255.10. Unlawfully procuring a marriage license

A person is guilty of unlawfully procuring a marriage license when he procures a license to marry another person at a time when he has a living spouse, or the other person has a living spouse.

Unlawfully procuring a marriage license is a class A misdemeanor.

HISTORY: Add, L 1965, ch 1030, § 1, eff Sept 1, 1967, with substance derived from § 1453.

§ 255.15. Bigamy

A person is guilty of bigamy when he contracts or purports to contract a marriage with another person at a time when he has a living spouse, or the other person has a living spouse.

Bigamy is a class E felony.

HISTORY: Add, L 1965, ch 1030, § 1, eff Sept 1, 1967, with substance derived from §§ 340, 343.

§ 255.17. Adultery

A person is guilty of adultery when he engages in sexual intercourse with another person at a time when he has a living spouse, or the other person has a living spouse.

Adultery is a class B misdemeanor.

HISTORY: Add, L 1965, ch 1037, § 1, eff Sept 1, 1967.

§ 255.20. Unlawfully procuring a marriage license, bigamy, adultery: defense

In any prosecution for unlawfully procuring a marriage license, bigamy, or adultery, it is an affirmative defense that the defendant acted under a reasonable belief that both he and the other person to the marriage or prospective marriage or to the sexual intercourse, as the case may be, were unmarried.

HISTORY: Add, L 1965, ch 1030, § 1; amd, L 1965, ch 1037, § 2, eff Sept 1, 1967.

§ 255.25. Incest in the third degree

A person is guilty of incest in the third degree when he or she marries or engages in sexual intercourse, oral sexual conduct or anal sexual conduct with a person whom he or she knows to be related to him or her, whether through marriage or not, as an ancestor, descendant, brother or sister of either the whole or the half blood, uncle, aunt, nephew or niece.

Incest in the third degree is a class E felony.

HISTORY: Add, L 1965, ch 1030, § 1, with substance derived from § 1110; amd, L 1984, ch 649, § 1, eff Nov 1, 1984. Amd, L 2006, ch 320, § 1, eff Nov 1, 2006. Section heading amd, L 2006, ch 320, § 1, eff Nov 1, 2006. Opening par, amd, L 2003, ch 264, § 31, eff Nov 1, 2003, amd, L 2006, ch 320, § 1, eff Nov 1, 2006. Closing par, amd, L 2006, ch 320, § 1, eff Nov 1, 2006.

§ 255.26. Incest in the second degree

A person is guilty of incest in the second degree when he or she commits the crime of rape in the second degree, as defined in section 130.30 of this part, or criminal sexual act in the second degree, as defined in section 130.45 of this part, against a person whom he or she knows to be related to him or her, whether through marriage or not, as an ancestor, descendant, brother or sister of either the whole or the half blood, uncle, aunt, nephew or niece.

Incest in the second degree is a class D felony.

HISTORY: Add, L 2006, ch 320, § 1, eff Nov 1, 2006.

§ 255.27. Incest in the first degree

A person is guilty of incest in the first degree when he or she commits the crime of rape in the first degree, as defined in subdivision three or four of section 130.35 of this part, or criminal sexual act in the first degree, as defined in subdivision three or four of section 130.50 of this part, against a person whom he or she knows to be related to him or her, whether through marriage or not, as an ancestor, descendant, brother or sister of either the whole or half blood, uncle, aunt, nephew or niece.

Incest in the first degree is a class B felony.

HISTORY: Add, L 2006, ch 320, § 1, eff Nov 1, 2006.

§ 255.30. Adultery and incest; corroboration

1. A person shall not be convicted of adultery or of an attempt to commit adultery solely upon the testimony of the other party to the adulterous act or attempted act, unsupported by other evidence tending to establish that the defendant attempted to engage with the other party in sexual intercourse, and that the defendant or the other party had a living spouse at the time of the adulterous act or attempted act.

2. A person shall not be convicted of incest or of an attempt to commit incest solely upon the testimony of the other party unsupported by other evidence tending to establish that the defendant married the other party, or that the defendant was a relative of the other party of a kind specified in section 255.25.

HISTORY: Add, L 1965, ch 1030, § 1; amd, L 1967, ch 791, § 43, L 1972, ch 373, § 2, L 1982, ch 659, § 1, eff July 22, 1982. Section heading, amd, L 1967, ch 791, § 43, eff Sept 1, 1967. Sub 1, formerly entire section, so designated and amd, L 1972, ch 373, § 2, eff June 21, 1972. Sub 2, add, L 1972, ch 373, § 2, eff June 21, 1972.

ARTICLE 260 OFFENSES RELATING TO CHILDREN, DISABLED PERSONS AND VULNERABLE ELDERLY PERSONS

HISTORY: Add, L 1965, ch 1030, § 1, eff Sept 1, 1967. Article heading, amd, L 1998, ch 381, § 1, eff Nov 1, 1998.

§ 260.00. Abandonment of a child

1. A person is guilty of abandonment of a child when, being a parent, guardian or other person legally charged with the care or custody of a child less than fourteen years old, he or she deserts

---

* Two versions of § 260.31 have been enacted.
* Two versions of § 260.31 have been enacted.

such child in any place with intent to wholly abandon such child.

2. A person is not guilty of the provisions of this section when he or she engages in the conduct described in subdivision one of this section: (a) with the intent that the child be safe from physical injury and cared for in an appropriate manner; (b) the child is left with an appropriate person, or in a suitable location and the person who leaves the child promptly notifies an appropriate person of the child's location; and (c) the child is not more than thirty days old.

Abandonment of a child is a class E felony.

HISTORY: Add, L 1965, ch 1030, § 1, eff Sept 1, 1967, with substance derived from § 481; amd, L 2010, ch 447, § 1, eff Aug 30, 2010.

§ 260.03. [Repealed]

HISTORY: Add, L 2000, ch 156, § 3, eff July 18, 2000; repealed, L 2010, ch 447, § 4, eff Aug 30, 2010.

§ 260.05. Non-support of a child in the second degree

A person is guilty of non-support of a child when:

1. being a parent, guardian or other person legally charged with the care or custody of a child less than sixteen years old, he or she fails or refuses without lawful excuse to provide support for such child when he or she is able to do so, or becomes unable to do so, when, though employable, he or she voluntarily terminates his or her employment, voluntarily reduces his or her earning capacity, or fails to diligently seek employment; or

2. being a parent, guardian or other person obligated to make child support payments by an order of child support entered by a court of competent jurisdiction for a child less than eighteen years old, he or she knowingly fails or refuses without lawful excuse to provide support for such child when he or she is able to do so, or becomes unable to do so, when, though employable, he or she voluntarily terminates his or her employment, voluntarily reduces his or her earning capacity, or fails to diligently seek employment.

Non-support of a child in the second degree is a class A misdemeanor.

HISTORY: Add, L 1965, ch 1030, § 1, with substance derived from § 482(1); amd, L 1972, ch 687, § 3, L 1997, ch 397, § 1, eff Sept 1, 1997. Section heading, amd, L 1997, ch 397, § 1, eff Sept 1, 1997. Second undesignated par, amd, L 1997, ch 397, § 1, eff Sept 1, 1997. Opening par, formerly part of first undesignated par, so designated opening par and amd, L 2008, ch 70, § 1, eff Nov 1, 2008. Sub 1, formerly part of first undesignated par, so designated sub 1 and amd, L 2008, ch 70, § 1, eff Nov 1, 2008. Sub 2, add, L 2008, ch 70, § 1, eff Nov 1, 2008.

§ 260.06. Non-support of a child in the first degree

A person is guilty of non-support of a child in the first degree when:

1. (a) being a parent, guardian or other person legally charged with the care or custody of a child less than sixteen years old, he or she fails or refuses without lawful excuse to provide support for such child when he or she is able to do so; or

(b) being a parent, guardian or other person obligated to make child support payments by an order of child support entered by a court of competent jurisdiction for a child less than eighteen years old, he or she fails or refuses without lawful excuse to provide support for such child when he or she is able to do so; and

2. he or she has previously been convicted in the preceding five years of a crime defined in section 260.05 of this article or a crime defined by the provisions of this section.

Non-support of a child in the first degree is a class E felony.

> **HISTORY:** Add, L 1997, ch 397, § 2, eff Sept 1, 1997. Amd, L 2007, ch 310, § 1, eff Nov 1, 2007, L 2008, ch 70, § 2, eff Nov 1, 2008. Sub 1, par (a), formerly entire sub 1, so designated sub 1, par (a) and amd, L 2008, ch 70, § 2, eff Nov 1, 2008. Sub 1, par (b), add, L 2008, ch 70, § 2, eff Nov 1, 2008. Sub 2, amd, L 2007, ch 310, § 1, eff Nov 1, 2007.

§ 260.10. Endangering the welfare of a child

A person is guilty of endangering the welfare of a child when:

1. He or she knowingly acts in a manner likely to be injurious to the physical, mental or moral welfare of a child less than seventeen years old or directs or authorizes such child to engage in an occupation involving a substantial risk of danger to his or her life or health; or

2. Being a parent, guardian or other person legally charged with the care or custody of a child less than eighteen years old, he or she fails or refuses to exercise reasonable diligence in the control of such child to prevent him or her from becoming an "abused child," a "neglected child," a "juvenile delinquent", or a "person in need of supervision," as those terms are defined in articles ten, three and seven of the family court act.

3. A person is not guilty of the provisions of this section when he or she engages in the conduct described in subdivision one of section 260.00 of this article: (a) with the intent to wholly abandon the child by relinquishing responsibility for and right to the care and custody of such child; (b) with the intent that the child be safe from physical injury and cared for in an appropriate manner; (c) the child is left with an appropriate person, or in a suitable location and the person who leaves the child promptly notifies an appropriate person of the child's location; and (d) the child is not more than thirty days old.

Endangering the welfare of a child is a class A misdemeanor.

> **HISTORY:** Add, L 1965, ch 1030, § 1, eff Sept 1, 1967, with substance derived from §§ 483, 494; amd, L 1967, ch 791, § 44, L 1970, ch 389, § 1, L 1970, ch 962, § 14, L 1982, ch 920, § 81, eff July 1, 1983, L 1990, ch 476, § 1, eff Nov 1, 1990, L 2010, ch 447, § 2, eff Aug 30, 2010.

§ 260.11. Endangering the welfare of a child; corroboration

A person shall not be convicted of endangering the welfare of a child, or of an attempt to commit the same, upon the testimony of a victim who is incapable of consent because of mental defect or mental incapacity as to conduct that constitutes an offense or an attempt to commit an offense referred to in section 130.16, without additional evidence sufficient pursuant to section 130.16 to sustain a conviction of an offense referred to in section 130.16, or of an attempt to commit the same.

> **HISTORY:** Add, L 1972, ch 373, § 3; amd, L 1974, ch 14, § 3, L 1984, ch 89, § 2, eff Nov 1, 1984.

§ 260.15. Endangering the welfare of a child; defense

In any prosecution for endangering the welfare of a child, pursuant to section 260.10of this article, based upon an alleged failure or refusal to provide proper medical care or treatment to an ill child, it is an affirmative defense that the defendant (a) is a parent, guardian or other person legally charged with the care or custody of such child; and (b) is a member or adherent of an organized church or religious group the tenets of which prescribe prayer as the principal treatment for illness; and (c) treated or caused such ill child to be treated in accordance with such tenets.

> **HISTORY:** Add, L 1965, ch 1030, § 1, with substance derived from § 495; amd, L 1967, ch 791, § 45, eff Sept 1, 1967, L 2000, ch 156, § 4, eff July 18, 2000, L 2010, ch 447, § 3, eff Aug 30, 2010.

§ 260.20. Unlawfully dealing with a child in the first degree

A person is guilty of unlawfully dealing with a child in the first degree when:

1. He knowingly permits a child less than eighteen years old to enter or remain in or upon a place, premises or establishment where sexual activity as defined by article one hundred thirty, two hundred thirty or two hundred sixty-three of this chapter or activity involving controlled substances as defined by article two hundred twenty of this chapter or involving marihuana as defined by article two hundred twenty-one of this chapter is maintained or conducted, and he knows or has reason to know that such activity is being maintained or conducted; or

2. He gives or sells or causes to be given or sold any alcoholic beverage, as defined by section three of the alcoholic beverage control law, to a person less than twenty-one years old; except that this subdivision does not apply to the parent or guardian of such a person or to a person who gives or causes to be given any such alcoholic beverage to a person under the age of twenty-one years, who is a student in a curriculum licensed or registered by the state education department, where the tasting or imbibing of alcoholic beverages is required in courses that are part of the required curriculum, provided such alcoholic beverages are given only for instructional purposes during classes conducted pursuant to such curriculum.

It is no defense to a prosecution pursuant to subdivision two of this section that the child acted as the agent or representative of another person or that the defendant dealt with the child as such.

It is an affirmative defense to a prosecution pursuant to subdivision two of this section that the defendant who sold, caused to be sold or attempted to sell such alcoholic beverage to a person less than twenty-one years old, had not been, at the time of such sale or attempted sale, convicted of a violation of this section or section 260.21 of this article within the preceding five years, and such defendant, subsequent to the commencement of the present prosecution, has completed an alcohol training awareness program established pursuant to subdivision twelve of section seventeen of the alcoholic beverage control law. A defendant otherwise qualifying pursuant to this paragraph may request and shall be afforded a reasonable adjournment of the proceedings to enable him or her to complete such alcohol training awareness program.

Unlawfully dealing with a child in the first degree is a class A misdemeanor.

HISTORY: Add, L 1965, ch 1030, § 1, eff Sept 1, 1967, with substance derived from §§ 483-c, 484; amd, L 1982, ch 159, § 4, L 1985, ch 274, § 5, L 1986, ch 107, § 2, L 1986, ch 210, § 1, L 1992, ch 362, § 1, eff Nov 1, 1992, L 2010, ch 435, § 5, eff Sept 29, 2010.

§ 260.21. Unlawfully dealing with a child in the second degree

A person is guilty of unlawfully dealing with a child in the second degree when:

1. Being an owner, lessee, manager or employee of a place where alcoholic beverages are sold or given away, he permits a child less than sixteen years old to enter or remain in such place unless:

(a) The child is accompanied by his parent, guardian or an adult authorized by a parent or guardian; or

(b) The entertainment or activity is being conducted for the benefit or under the auspices of a non-profit school, church or other educational or religious institution; or

(c) Otherwise permitted by law to do so; or

(d) The establishment is closed to the public for a specified period of time to conduct an activity or entertainment, during which the child is in or remains in such establishment, and no alcoholic beverages are sold, served, given away or consumed at such establishment during such period. The state liquor authority shall be notified in writing by the licensee of such establishment, of the intended closing of such establishment, to conduct any such activity or entertainment, not less than ten days prior to any such closing; or

2. He marks the body of a child less than eighteen years old with indelible ink or pigments by means of tattooing; or

3. He sells or causes to be sold tobacco in any form to a child less than eighteen years old.

It is no defense to a prosecution pursuant to subdivision three of this section that the child acted as the agent or representative of another person or that the defendant dealt with the child as such.

Unlawfully dealing with a child in the second degree is a class B misdemeanor.

HISTORY: Add, L 1992, ch 362, § 2, eff Nov 1, 1992. Sub 1, opening par, amd, L 1996, ch 478, § 1, eff Nov 1, 1996.

§ 260.24. Endangering the welfare of an incompetent or physically disabled person in the second degree

A person is guilty of endangering the welfare of an incompetent or physically disabled person in the second degree when he or she recklessly engages in conduct which is likely to be injurious to the physical, mental or moral welfare of a person who is unable to care for himself or herself because of physical disability, mental disease or defect.

Endangering the welfare of an incompetent or physically disabled person in the second degree is a class A misdemeanor.

HISTORY: Add, L 2012, ch 501, § 3 (Part G), eff Jan 17, 2013.

§ 260.25. Endangering the welfare of an incompetent or physically disabled person in the first degree

A person is guilty of endangering the welfare of an incompetent or physically disabled person in the first degree when he knowingly acts in a manner likely to be injurious to the physical, mental or moral welfare of a person who is unable to care for himself or herself because of physical disability, mental disease or defect.

Endangering the welfare of an incompetent or physically disabled person in the first degree is a class E felony.

HISTORY: Add, L 1965, ch 1030, § 1, eff Sept 1, 1967, with substance derived from §§ 1121, 1123; amd, L 1998, ch 381, § 2, eff Nov 1, 1998, L 2012, ch 501, § 4 (Part G), eff Jan 17, 2013.

§ 260.31. Vulnerable elderly persons; definitions*

For the purpose of sections 260.32 and 260.34 of this article, the following definitions shall apply:

1. "Caregiver" means a person who (i) assumes responsibility for the care of a vulnerable elderly person, or an incompetent or physically disabled person pursuant to a court order; or (ii) receives monetary or other valuable consideration for providing care for a vulnerable elderly person, or an incompetent or physically disabled person.

2. "Sexual contact" means any touching of the sexual or other intimate parts of a person for the purpose of gratifying sexual desire of either party. It includes the touching of the actor by the victim, as well as the touching of the victim by the actor, whether directly or through

---

* There are two sections 260.31.

clothing, as well as the emission of ejaculate by the actor upon any part of the victim, clothed or unclothed.

3. "Vulnerable elderly person" means a person sixty years of age or older who is suffering from a disease or infirmity associated with advanced age and manifested by demonstrable physical, mental or emotional dysfunction to the extent that the person is incapable of adequately providing for his or her own health or personal care.

4. "Incompetent or physically disabled person" means an individual who is unable to care for himself or herself because of physical disability, mental disease or defect.

HISTORY: Added as § 260.30, L 1998, ch 381, § 3, eff Nov 1, 1998; so designated § 260.31, L 2010, ch 14, § 1, eff May 22, 2010; amd, L 2010, ch 14, § 2, eff May 22, 2010, L 2010, ch 193, § 2, eff Oct 13, 2010.

§ 260.31. Misrepresentation by a child day care provider*

A person is guilty of misrepresentation by a child day care provider when, being a child day care provider or holding himself or herself out as such, he or she makes any willful and intentional misrepresentation, by act or omission, to a parent or guardian of a child in the care of such provider (or a child whose prospective placement in such care is being considered by such parent or guardian) to any state or local official having jurisdiction over child day care providers, or to any police officer or peace officer as to the facts pertaining to such child day care provider, including, but not limited to: (i) the number of children in the facility or home where such number is in violation of the provisions of section three hundred ninety of the social services law, (ii) the area of the facility, home, or center used for child day care, or (iii) the credentials or qualifications of any child day care provider, assistant, employee, or volunteer. A misrepresentation subject to the provisions of this section must substantially place at risk the health or safety of a child in the care of a child day care provider.

Misrepresentation by a child day care provider is a class A misdemeanor.

HISTORY: Formerly § 260.30, add, L 1998, ch 600, § 2, eff Nov 1, 1998; so designated § 260.31, L 2010, ch 117, § 11, eff June 15, 2010.

§ 260.32. Endangering the welfare of a vulnerable elderly person, or an incompetent or physically disabled person in the second degree

A person is guilty of endangering the welfare of a vulnerable elderly person, or an incompetent or physically disabled person in the second degree when, being a caregiver for a vulnerable elderly person, or an incompetent or physically disabled person:

1. With intent to cause physical injury to such person, he or she causes such injury to such person; or

2. He or she recklessly causes physical injury to such person; or

3. With criminal negligence, he or she causes physical injury to such person by means of a deadly weapon or a dangerous instrument; or

4. He or she subjects such person to sexual contact without the latter's consent. Lack of consent under this subdivision results from forcible compulsion or incapacity to consent, as those terms are defined in article one hundred thirty of this chapter, or any other circumstances in which the vulnerable elderly person, or an incompetent or physically disabled person does not expressly or impliedly acquiesce in the caregiver's conduct. In any prosecution under this

---

* There are two sections 260.31.

subdivision in which the victim's alleged lack of consent results solely from incapacity to consent because of the victim's mental disability or mental incapacity, the provisions of section 130.16 of this chapter shall apply. In addition, in any prosecution under this subdivision in which the victim's lack of consent is based solely upon his or her incapacity to consent because he or she was mentally disabled, mentally incapacitated or physically helpless, it is an affirmative defense that the defendant, at the time he or she engaged in the conduct constituting the offense, did not know of the facts or conditions responsible for such incapacity to consent.

Endangering the welfare of a vulnerable elderly person, or an incompetent or physically disabled person in the second degree is a class E felony.

HISTORY: Add, L 1998, ch 381, § 4, eff Nov 1, 1998. Amd, L 2010, ch 14, § 3, eff May 22, 2010. Section heading, amd, L 2010, ch 14, § 3, eff May 22, 2010. Opening par, amd, L 2010, ch 14, § 3, eff May 22, 2010. Sub 4, amd, L 2000, ch 1, § 5, eff Feb 1, 2001, L 2010, ch 14, § 3, eff May 22, 2010. Closing par, amd, L 2010, ch 14, § 3, eff May 22, 2010.

§ 260.34. Endangering the welfare of a vulnerable elderly person, or an incompetent or physically disabled person in the first degree

A person is guilty of endangering the welfare of a vulnerable elderly person, or an incompetent or physically disabled person in the first degree when, being a caregiver for a vulnerable elderly person, or an incompetent or physically disabled person:

1. With intent to cause physical injury to such person, he or she causes serious physical injury to such person; or

2. He or she recklessly causes serious physical injury to such person.

Endangering the welfare of a vulnerable elderly person, or an incompetent or physically disabled person in the first degree is a class D felony.

HISTORY: Add, L 1998, ch 381, § 5, eff Nov 1, 1998. Amd, L 2010, ch 14, § 3, eff May 22, 2010. Section heading, amd, L 2010, ch 14, § 3, eff May 22, 2010. Opening par, amd, L 2010, ch 14, § 3, eff May 22, 2010. Sub 2, amd, L 2010, ch 14, § 3, eff May 22, 2010.

ARTICLE 263   SEXUAL PERFORMANCE BY A CHILD

HISTORY: Add, L 1977, ch 910, § 1, eff Nov 9, 1977.

§ 263.00. Definitions

As used in this article the following definitions shall apply:

1. "Sexual performance" means any performance or part thereof which, for purposes of section 263.16 of this article, includes sexual conduct by a child less than sixteen years of age or, for purposes of section 263.05 or 263.15 of this article, includes sexual conduct by a child less than seventeen years of age.

2. "Obscene sexual performance" means any performance which, for purposes of section 263.11 of this article, includes sexual conduct by a child less than sixteen years of ageor, for purposes of section 263.10 of this article, includes sexual conduct by a child less than seventeen years of age, in any material which is obscene, as such term is defined in section 235.00 of this chapter.

3. "Sexual conduct" means actual or simulated sexual intercourse,oral sexual conduct, anal sexual conduct, sexual bestiality, masturbation, sado-masochistic abuse, or lewd exhibition of the genitals.

4. "Performance" means any play, motion picture, photograph or dance. Performance also means any other visual representation exhibited before an audience.

5. "Promote" means to procure, manufacture, issue, sell, give, provide, lend, mail, deliver, transfer, transmute, publish, distribute, circulate, disseminate, present, exhibit or advertise, or to offer or agree to do the same.

6. "Simulated" means the explicit depiction of any of the conduct set forth in subdivision three of this section which creates the appearance of such conduct and which exhibits any uncovered portion of the breasts, genitals or buttocks.

7. "Oral sexual conduct" and "anal sexual conduct" mean the conduct defined by subdivision two of section 130.00 of this chapter.

8. "Sado-masochistic abuse" means the conduct defined in subdivision five of section 235.20 of this chapter.

9. For purposes of sections 263.10, 263.11, 263.15 and 263.16 of this article, the terms "possession," "control" and "promotion" shall not include conduct by an attorney when the performance was provided to such attorney in relation to the representation of a person under investigation or charged under this chapter or as a respondent pursuant to the family court act, and is limited in use for the purpose of representation for the period of such representation.

HISTORY: Add, L 1977, ch 910, § 2, eff Nov 9, 1977. Sub 1, amd, L 2000, ch 1, § 18, eff Feb 1, 2001. Sub 2, amd, L 2000, ch 1, § 18, eff Feb 1, 2001. Sub 3, amd, L 2003, ch 264, § 32, eff Nov 1, 2003. Sub 7, amd, L 2003, ch 264, § 32, eff Nov 1, 2003. Sub 9, add, L 2012, ch 456, § 3, eff Sept 7, 2012.

§ 263.05. Use of a child in a sexual performance

A person is guilty of the use of a child in a sexual performance if knowing the character and content thereof he employs, authorizes or induces a child less than seventeen years of age to engage in a sexual performance or being a parent, legal guardian or custodian of such child, he consents to the participation by such child in a sexual performance.

Use of a child in a sexual performance is a class C felony.

HISTORY: Add, L 1977, ch 910, § 2, eff Nov 9, 1977. Amd, L 2000, ch 1, § 19, eff Feb 1, 2001. Opening par, amd, L 2000, ch 1, § 19, eff Feb 1, 2001.

§ 263.10. Promoting an obscene sexual performance by a child

A person is guilty of promoting an obscene sexual performance by a child when, knowing the character and content thereof, he produces, directs or promotes any obscene performance which includes sexual conduct by a child less than seventeen years of age.

Promoting an obscene sexual performance by a child is a class D felony.

HISTORY: Add, L 1977, ch 910, § 2, eff Nov 9, 1977. Amd, L 2000, ch 1, § 20, eff Feb 1, 2001. Opening par, amd, L 2000, ch 1, § 20, eff Feb 1, 2001.

§ 263.11. Possessing an obscene sexual performance by a child

A person is guilty of possessing an obscene sexual performance by a child when, knowing the character and content thereof, he knowingly has in his possession or control, or knowingly accesses with intent to view, any obscene performance which includes sexual conduct by a child less than sixteen years of age.

Possessing an obscene sexual performance by a child is a class E felony.

HISTORY: Add, L 1996, ch 11, § 1, eff Nov 1, 1996. Amd, L 2012, ch 456, § 1, eff Sept 7, 2012.

§ 263.15. Promoting a sexual performance by a child

A person is guilty of promoting a sexual performance by a child when, knowing the character and content thereof, he produces, directs or promotes any performance which includes sexual conduct by a child less than seventeen years of age.

Promoting a sexual performance by a child is a class D felony.

HISTORY: Add, L 1977, ch 910, § 2, eff Nov 9, 1977. Amd, L 2000, ch 1, § 21, eff Feb 1, 2001. Opening par, amd, L 2000, ch 1, § 21, eff Feb 1, 2001.

§ 263.16. Possessing a sexual performance by a child

A person is guilty of possessing a sexual performance by a child when, knowing the character and content thereof, he knowingly has in his possession or control, or knowingly accesses with intent to view, any performance which includes sexual conduct by a child less than sixteen years of age.

Possessing a sexual performance by a child is a class E felony.

HISTORY: Add, L 1996, ch 11, § 1, eff Nov 1, 1996. Amd, L 2012, ch 456, § 2, eff Sept 7, 2012.

§ 263.20. Sexual performance by a child; affirmative defenses

1. Under this article, it shall be an affirmative defense that the defendant in good faith reasonably believed the person appearing in the performance was, for purposes of section 263.11 or 263.16 of this article, sixteen years of age or over or, for purposes of section 263.05, 263.10 or 263.15 of this article, seventeen years of age or over.

2. In any prosecution for any offense pursuant to this article, it is an affirmative defense that the person so charged was a librarian engaged in the normal course of his employment, a motion picture projectionist, stage employee or spotlight operator, cashier, doorman, usher, candy stand attendant, porter or in any other non-managerial or non-supervisory capacity in a motion picture theatre; provided he has no financial interest, other than his employment, which employment does not encompass compensation based upon any proportion of the gross receipts, in the promotion of a sexual performance for sale, rental or exhibition or in the promotion, presentation or direction of any sexual performance, or is in any way responsible for acquiring such material for sale, rental or exhibition.

HISTORY: Add, L 1977, ch 910, § 2, eff Nov 9, 1977. Sub 1, amd, L 2000, ch 1, § 22, eff Feb 1, 2001.

§ 263.25. Proof of age of child

Whenever it becomes necessary for the purposes of this article to determine whether a child who participated in a sexual performance was under an age specified in this article, the court or jury may make such determination by any of the following: personal inspection of the child; inspection of a photograph or motion picture which constituted the sexual performance; oral testimony by a witness to the sexual performance as to the age of the child based upon the child's appearance; expert medical testimony based upon the appearance of the child in the sexual performance; and any other method authorized by any applicable provision of law or by the rules of evidence at common law.

HISTORY: Add, L 1977, ch 910, § 2, eff Nov 9, 1977. Amd, L 2000, ch 1, § 23, eff Feb 1, 2001.

§ 263.30. Facilitating a sexual performance by a child with a controlled substance or alcohol

1. A person is guilty of facilitating a sexual performance by a child with a controlled substance or alcohol when he or she:

(a) (i) knowingly and unlawfully possesses a controlled substance as defined in section thirty-three hundred six of the public health law or any controlled substance that requires a prescription to obtain, (ii) administers that substance to a person under the age of seventeen without such person's consent, (iii) intends to commit against such person conduct constituting a felony as defined in section 263.05, 263.10, or 263.15 of this article, and (iv) does so commit or attempt to commit such conduct against such person; or

(b) (i) administers alcohol to a person under the age of seventeen without such person's consent, (ii) intends to commit against such person conduct constituting a felony defined in section 263.05, 263.10, or 263.15 of this article, and (iii) does so commit or attempt to commit such conduct against such person.

2. For the purposes of this section, "controlled substance" means any substance or preparation, compound, mixture, salt, or isomer of any substance defined in section thirty-three hundred six of the public health law.

Facilitating a sexual performance by a child with a controlled substance or alcohol is a class B felony.

HISTORY: Add, L 2008, ch 431, § 1, eff Nov 1, 2008.

TITLE P   Offenses Against Public Safety
ARTICLE 265
FIREARMS AND OTHER DANGEROUS WEAPONS
ARTICLE 270
OTHER OFFENSES RELATING TO PUBLIC SAFETY
ARTICLE 275
OFFENSES RELATING TO UNAUTHORIZED RECORDING

HISTORY: Add, L 1965, ch 1030, § 1, eff Sept 1, 1967.

ARTICLE 265   FIREARMS AND OTHER DANGEROUS WEAPONS

HISTORY: Add, L 1965, ch 1030, § 1, eff Sept 1, 1967.

§ 265.00. Definitions

As used in this article and in article four hundred, the following terms shall mean and include:

1. "Machine-gun" means a weapon of any description, irrespective of size, by whatever name known, loaded or unloaded, from which a number of shots or bullets may be rapidly or

automatically discharged from a magazine with one continuous pull of the trigger and includes a sub-machine gun.

2. "Firearm silencer" means any instrument, attachment, weapon or appliance for causing the firing of any gun, revolver, pistol or other firearms to be silent, or intended to lessen or muffle the noise of the firing of any gun, revolver, pistol or other firearms.

3. "Firearm" means (a) any pistol or revolver; or (b) a shotgun having one or more barrels less than eighteen inches in length; or (c) a rifle having one or more barrels less than sixteen inches in length; or (d) any weapon made from a shotgun or rifle whether by alteration, modification, or otherwise if such weapon as altered, modified, or otherwise has an overall length of less than twenty-six inches; or (e) an assault weapon. For the purpose of this subdivision the length of the barrel on a shotgun or rifle shall be determined by measuring the distance between the muzzle and the face of the bolt, breech, or breechlock when closed and when the shotgun or rifle is cocked; the overall length of a weapon made from a shotgun or rifle is the distance between the extreme ends of the weapon measured along a line parallel to the center line of the bore. Firearm does not include an antique firearm.

4. "Switchblade knife" means any knife which has a blade which opens automatically by hand pressure applied to a button, spring or other device in the handle of the knife.

5. "Gravity knife" means any knife which has a blade which is released from the handle or sheath thereof by the force of gravity or the application of centrifugal force which, when released, is locked in place by means of a button, spring, lever or other device.

5-a. "Pilum ballistic knife" means any knife which has a blade which can be projected from the handle by hand pressure applied to a button, lever, spring or other device in the handle of the knife.

5-b. "Metal knuckle knife" means a weapon that, when closed, cannot function as a set of plastic knuckles or metal knuckles, nor as a knife and when open, can function as both a set of plastic knuckles or metal knuckles as well as a knife.

5-c. "Automatic knife" includes a stiletto, a switchblade knife, a gravity knife, a cane sword, a pilum ballistic knife, and a metal knuckle knife.

6. "Dispose of" means to dispose of, give, give away, lease-loan, keep for sale, offer, offer for sale, sell, transfer and otherwise dispose of.

7. "Deface" means to remove, deface, cover, alter or destroy the manufacturer's serial number or any other distinguishing number or identification mark.

8. "Gunsmith" means any person, firm, partnership, corporation or company who engages in the business of repairing, altering, assembling, manufacturing, cleaning, polishing, engraving or trueing, or who performs any mechanical operation on, any firearm, large capacity ammunition feeding device or machine-gun.

9. "Dealer in firearms" means any person, firm, partnership, corporation or company who engages in the business of purchasing, selling, keeping for sale, loaning, leasing, or in any manner disposing of, any assault weapon, large capacity ammunition feeding device, pistol or revolver.

10. "Licensing officer" means in the city of New York the police commissioner of that city; in the county of Nassau the commissioner of police of that county; in the county of Suffolk the sheriff of that county except in the towns of Babylon, Brookhaven, Huntington, Islip and

Smithtown, the commissioner of police of that county; for the purposes of section 400.01 of this chapter the superintendent of state police; and elsewhere in the state a judge or justice of a court of record having his office in the county of issuance.

11. "Rifle" means a weapon designed or redesigned, made or remade, and intended to be fired from the shoulder and designed or redesigned and made or remade to use the energy of the explosive in a fixed metallic cartridge to fire only a single projectile through a rifled bore for each single pull of the trigger.

12. "Shotgun" means a weapon designed or redesigned, made or remade, and intended to be fired from the shoulder and designed or redesigned and made or remade to use the energy of the explosive in a fixed shotgun shell to fire through a smooth bore either a number of ball shot or a single projectile for each single pull of the trigger.

13. "Cane Sword" means a cane or swagger stick having concealed within it a blade that may be used as a sword or stilletto.

14.* "Chuka stick" means any device designed primarily as a weapon, consisting of two or more lengths of a rigid material joined together by a thong, rope or chain in such a manner as to allow free movement of a portion of the device while held in the hand and capable of being rotated in such a manner as to inflict serious injury upon a person by striking or choking. These devices are also known as nunchakus and centrifugal force sticks.

14.* "Antique firearm" means:

Any unloaded muzzle loading pistol or revolver with a matchlock, flintlock, percussion cap, or similar type of ignition system, or a pistol or revolver which uses fixed cartridges which are no longer available in the ordinary channels of commercial trade.

15. "Loaded firearm" means any firearm loaded with ammunition or any firearm which is possessed by one who, at the same time, possesses a quantity of ammunition which may be used to discharge such firearm.

15-a. "Electronic dart gun" means any device designed primarily as a weapon, the purpose of which is to momentarily stun, knock out or paralyze a person by passing an electrical shock to such person by means of a dart or projectile.

15-b. "Kung Fu star" means a disc-like object with sharpened points on the circumference thereof and is designed for use primarily as a weapon to be thrown.

15-c. "Electronic stun gun" means any device designed primarily as a weapon, the purpose of which is to stun, cause mental disorientation, knock out or paralyze a person by passing a high voltage electrical shock to such person.

16. "Certified not suitable to possess a self-defense spray device, a rifle or shotgun" means that the director or physician in charge of any hospital or institution for mental illness, public or private, has certified to the superintendent of state police or to any organized police department of a county, city, town or village of this state, that a person who has been judicially adjudicated incompetent, or who has been confined to such institution for mental illness pursuant to judicial authority, is not suitable to possess a self-defense spray device, as defined in section 265.20 of this article, or a rifle or shotgun.

---

* There are two subdivisions 14.

* There are two subdivisions 14.

17. "Serious offense" means

(a) any of the following offenses defined in the former penal law as in force and effect immediately prior to September first, nineteen hundred sixty-seven: illegally using, carrying or possessing a pistol or other dangerous weapon; making or possessing burglar's instruments; buying or receiving stolen property; unlawful entry of a building; aiding escape from prison; that kind of disorderly conduct defined in subdivisions six and eight of section seven hundred twenty-two of such former penal law; violations of sections four hundred eighty-three, four hundred eighty-three-b, four hundred eighty-four-h and article one hundred six of such former penal law; that kind of criminal sexual act or rape which was designated as a misdemeanor; violation of section seventeen hundred forty-seven-d and seventeen hundred forty-seven-e of such former penal law; any violation of any provision of article thirty-three of the public health law relating to narcotic drugs which was defined as a misdemeanor by section seventeen hundred fifty-one-a of such former penal law, and any violation of any provision of article thirty-three-A of the public health law relating to depressant and stimulant drugs which was defined as a misdemeanor by section seventeen hundred forty-seven-b of such former penal law.

(b) [As amended, L 2010, ch 232, § 2] any of the following offenses defined in the penal law: illegally using, carrying or possessing a pistol or other dangerous weapon; possession of burglar's tools; criminal possession of stolen property in the third degree; escape in the third degree; jostling; fraudulent accosting; endangering the welfare of a child; the offenses defined in article two hundred thirty-five; issuing abortional articles; permitting prostitution; promoting prostitution in the third degree; stalking in the fourth degree; stalking in the third degree; the offenses defined in article one hundred thirty; the offenses defined in article two hundred twenty.

(b) [As amended, L 2010, ch 232, § 3] any of the following offenses defined in the penal law: illegally using, carrying or possessing a pistol or other dangerous weapon; possession of burglar's tools; criminal possession of stolen property in the third degree; escape in the third degree; jostling; fraudulent accosting; endangering the welfare of a child; the offenses defined in article two hundred thirty-five; issuing abortional articles; permitting prostitution; promoting prostitution in the third degree; stalking in the third degree; stalking in the fourth degree; the offenses defined in article one hundred thirty; the offenses defined in article two hundred twenty.

18. "Armor piercing ammunition" means any ammunition capable of being used in pistols or revolvers containing a projectile or projectile core, or a projectile or projectile core for use in such ammunition, that is constructed entirely (excluding the presence of traces of other substances) from one or a combination of any of the following: tungsten alloys, steel, iron, brass, bronze, beryllium copper, or uranium.

19. "Duly authorized instructor" means (a) a duly commissioned officer of the United States army, navy, marine corps or coast guard, or of the national guard of the state of New York; or (b) a duly qualified adult citizen of the United States who has been granted a certificate as an instructor in small arms practice issued by the United States army, navy or marine corps, or by the adjutant general of this state, or by the national rifle association of America, a not-for-profit corporation duly organized under the laws of this state; or (c) by a person duly qualified and designated by the department of environmental conservation under paragraph d of subdivision six of section 11-0713 of the environmental conservation law as its agent in the giving of instruction and the making of certifications of qualification in responsible hunting practices.

20. "Disguised gun" means any weapon or device capable of being concealed on the person from which a shot can be discharged through the energy of an explosive and is designed and intended to appear to be something other than a gun.

21. "Semiautomatic" means any repeating rifle, shotgun or pistol, regardless of barrel or overall length, which utilizes a portion of the energy of a firing cartridge or shell to extract the fired cartridge case or spent shell and chamber the next round, and which requires a separate pull of the trigger to fire each cartridge or shell.

22. "Assault weapon" means

(a) a semiautomatic rifle that has an ability to accept a detachable magazine and has at least one of the following characteristics:

(i) a folding or telescoping stock;

(ii) a pistol grip that protrudes conspicuously beneath the action of the weapon;

(iii) a thumbhole stock;

(iv) a second handgrip or a protruding grip that can be held by the non-trigger hand;

(v) a bayonet mount;

(vi) a flash suppressor, muzzle break, muzzle compensator, or threaded barrel designed to accommodate a flash suppressor, muzzle break, or muzzle compensator;

(vii) a grenade launcher; or

(b) a semiautomatic shotgun that has at least one of the following characteristics:

(i) a folding or telescoping stock;

(ii) a thumbhole stock;

(iii) a second handgrip or a protruding grip that can be held by the non-trigger hand;

(iv) a fixed magazine capacity in excess of seven rounds;

(v) an ability to accept a detachable magazine; or

(c) a semiautomatic pistol that has an ability to accept a detachable magazine and has at least one of the following characteristics:

(i) a folding or telescoping stock;

(ii) a thumbhole stock;

(iii) a second handgrip or a protruding grip that can be held by the non-trigger hand;

(iv) capacity to accept an ammunition magazine that attaches to the pistol outside of the pistol grip;

(v) a threaded barrel capable of accepting a barrel extender, flash suppressor, forward handgrip, or silencer;

(vi) a shroud that is attached to, or partially or completely encircles, the barrel and that permits the shooter to hold the firearm with the non-trigger hand without being burned;

(vii) a manufactured weight of fifty ounces or more when the pistol is unloaded; or

(viii) a semiautomatic version of an automatic rifle, shotgun or firearm;

(d) a revolving cylinder shotgun;

(e) a semiautomatic rifle, a semiautomatic shotgun or a semiautomatic pistol or weapon defined in subparagraph (v) of paragraph (e) of subdivision twenty-two of section 265.00 of this chapter as added by chapter one hundred eighty-nine of the laws of two thousand and otherwise lawfully possessed pursuant to such chapter of the laws of two thousand prior to September fourteenth, nineteen hundred ninety-four;

(f) a semiautomatic rifle, a semiautomatic shotgun or a semiautomatic pistol or weapon defined in paragraph (a), (b) or (c) of this subdivision, possessed prior to the date of enactment of the chapter of the laws of two thousand thirteen which added this paragraph;

(g) provided, however, that such term does not include:

(i) any rifle, shotgun or pistol that (A) is manually operated by bolt, pump, lever or slide action; (B) has been rendered permanently inoperable; or (C) is an antique firearm as defined in 18 U.S.C. 921(a)(16);

(ii) a semiautomatic rifle that cannot accept a detachable magazine that holds more than five rounds of ammunition;

(iii) a semiautomatic shotgun that cannot hold more than five rounds of ammunition in a fixed or detachable magazine; or

(iv) a rifle, shotgun or pistol, or a replica or a duplicate thereof, specified in Appendix A to 18 U.S.C. 922 as such weapon was manufactured on October first, nineteen hundred ninety-three. The mere fact that a weapon is not listed in Appendix A shall not be construed to mean that such weapon is an assault weapon;

(v) any weapon validly registered pursuant to subdivision sixteen-a of section 400.00 of this chapter. Such weapons shall be subject to the provisions of paragraph (h) of this subdivision;

(vi) any firearm, rifle, or shotgun that was manufactured at least fifty years prior to the current date, but not including replicas thereof that is validly registered pursuant to subdivision sixteen-a of section 400.00 of this chapter;

(h) Any weapon defined in paragraph (e) or (f) of this subdivision and any large capacity ammunition feeding device that was legally possessed by an individual prior to the enactment of the chapter of the laws of two thousand thirteen which added this paragraph, may only be sold to, exchanged with or disposed of to a purchaser authorized to possess such weapons or to an individual or entity outside of the state provided that any such transfer to an individual or entity outside of the state must be reported to the entity wherein the weapon is registered within seventy-two hours of such transfer. An individual who transfers any such weapon or large capacity ammunition device to an individual inside New York state or without complying with the provisions of this paragraph shall be guilty of a class A misdemeanor unless such large capacity ammunition feeding device, the possession of which is made illegal by the chapter of the laws of two thousand thirteen which added this paragraph, is transferred within one year of the effective date of the chapter of the laws of two thousand thirteen which added this paragraph.

23. "Large capacity ammunition feeding device" means a magazine, belt, drum, feed strip, or similar device, that (a) has a capacity of, or that can be readily restored or converted to

accept, more than ten rounds of ammunition, or [pars (b) and (c) are suspended and not effective as stated in Laws 2013, ch 1, § 58, sub b note below] (b) contains more than seven rounds of ammunition, or (c) is obtained after the effective date of the chapter of the laws of two thousand thirteen which amended this subdivision and has a capacity of, or that can be readily restored or converted to accept, more than seven rounds of ammunition; provided, however, that such term does not include an attached tubular device designed to accept, and capable of operating only with,.22 caliber rimfire ammunition or a feeding device that is a curio or relic. A feeding device that is a curio or relic is defined as a device that (i) was manufactured at least fifty years prior to the current date, (ii) is only capable of being used exclusively in a firearm, rifle, or shotgun that was manufactured at least fifty years prior to the current date, but not including replicas thereof, (iii) is possessed by an individual who is not prohibited by state or federal law from possessing a firearm and (iv) is registered with the division of state police pursuant to subdivision sixteen-a of section 400.00 of this chapter, except such feeding devices transferred into the state may be registered at any time, provided they are registered within thirty days of their transfer into the state. Notwithstanding paragraph (h) of subdivision twenty-two of this section, such feeding devices may be transferred provided that such transfer shall be subject to the provisions of section 400.03 of this chapter including the check required to be conducted pursuant to such section.

24. "Seller of ammunition" means any person, firm, partnership, corporation or company who engages in the business of purchasing, selling or keeping ammunition.

25. "Qualified retired New York or federal law enforcement officer" means an individual who is a retired police officer as police officer is defined in subdivision thirty-four of section 1.20 of the criminal procedure law, a retired peace officer as peace officer is defined in section 2.10 of the criminal procedure law or a retired federal law enforcement officer as federal law enforcement officer is defined in section 2.15 of the criminal procedure law, who: (a) separated from service in good standing from a public agency located in New York state in which such person served as either a police officer, peace officer or federal law enforcement officer; and (b) before such separation, was authorized by law to engage in or supervise the prevention, detection, investigation, or prosecution of, or the incarceration of any person for, any violation of law, and had statutory powers of arrest, pursuant to their official duties, under the criminal procedure law; and (c) (i) before such separation, served as either a police officer, peace officer or federal law enforcement officer for five years or more and at the time of separation, is such an officer; or (ii) separated from service with such agency, after completing any applicable probationary period of such service, due to a service-connected disability, as determined by such agency at or before the time of separation; and (d)(i) has not been found by a qualified medical professional employed by such agency to be unqualified for reasons relating to mental health; or (ii) has not entered into an agreement with such agency from which the individual is separating from service in which that individual acknowledges he or she is not qualified for reasons relating to mental health; and (e) is not otherwise prohibited by New York or federal law from possessing any firearm.

HISTORY: Add, L 1965, ch 1030, § 1, eff Sept 1, 1967, with substance derived from § 1896; amd, L 1967, ch 791, § 46, L 1969, ch 123, § 1, eff Sept 1, 1969, L 1972, ch 588, § 1, L 1972, ch 605, § 1, L 1974, ch 179, § 1, eff Sept 1, 1974, L 1974, ch 986, §§ 1, 2, L 1974, ch 1041, § 1, eff Sept 1, 1974, L 1976, ch 217, § 1, eff Sept 1, 1976, L 1982, ch 492, § 1, L 1985, ch 61, § 1, eff Nov 1, 1985, L 1986, ch 328, § 2, eff Nov 1, 1986, L 1986, ch 646, § 1, eff Nov 1, 1986, L 1988, ch 264, § 1, L 1990, ch 264, § 1, eff Nov 1, 1990, L 1995, ch 219, § 2, eff Nov 1, 1995, L 1996, ch 354, § 2, eff Nov 1, 1996, L 1999, ch 210, § 1, eff Nov 1, 1999, L 1997, ch 446, § 2, eff Aug 25, 1997, L 1998, ch 378, § 1, eff Nov 1, 1998, L 1999, ch 635, §§ 11, 15, eff Dec 1, 1999, L 2000, ch 189, §§ 8-10, eff Nov 1, 2000, L 2008, ch 257, § 3, eff Nov 1, 2008, L 2010, ch 232, §§ 2, 3, eff July 30, 2010, L 2013, ch 1, § 37, eff Jan 15, 2013, L 2013, ch 1, § 38, eff April 15, 2013, except sub 23, par (a) eff Jan 15, 2013, except sub 23, pars (b) and (c), suspended and not effective as stated in 2013 note below, L 2013, ch 1, § 39, eff March 16, 2013, L 2013, ch 98, § 1, eff July 5, 2013.

Editor's Note:

Laws 2013, ch 57, § 4 (Part FF), eff March 29, 2013, and deemed to have been in full force and effect on the same date as Laws 2013, ch 1, provides as follows:

Subdivision b of section 58 of chapter 1 of the laws of 2013 amending the criminal procedure law and other laws relating to suspension and revocation of firearms licenses, is amended to read as follows:

b. The amendments to subdivision 23 of section 265.00 of the penal law made by section thirty-eight of this act shall take effect on the ninetieth day after this act shall have become a law, except that the amendments designating paragraph (a) of subdivision 23 shall take effect immediately; and provided further that the effective date of the amendments adding paragraphs (b) and (c) to such subdivision shall be suspended and not effective[.]

§ 265.01. Criminal possession of a weapon in the fourth degree

A person is guilty of criminal possession of a weapon in the fourth degree when:

(1) He or she possesses any firearm, electronic dart gun, electronic stun gun, gravity knife, switchblade knife, pilum ballistic knife, metal knuckle knife, cane sword, billy, blackjack, bludgeon, plastic knuckles, metal knuckles, chuka stick, sand bag, sandclub, wrist-brace type slingshot or slungshot, shirken or "Kung Fu star"; or

(2) He possesses any dagger, dangerous knife, dirk, razor, stiletto, imitation pistol, or any other dangerous or deadly instrument or weapon with intent to use the same unlawfully against another; or

(3) ;* or

(4) He possesses a rifle, shotgun, antique firearm, black powder rifle, black powder shotgun, or any muzzle-loading firearm, and has been convicted of a felony or serious offense; or

(5) He possesses any dangerous or deadly weapon and is not a citizen of the United States; or

(6) He is a person who has been certified not suitable to possess a rifle or shotgun, as defined in subdivision sixteen of section 265.00, and refuses to yield possession of such rifle or shotgun upon the demand of a police officer. Whenever a person is certified not suitable to possess a rifle or shotgun, a member of the police department to which such certification is made, or of the state police, shall forthwith seize any rifle or shotgun possessed by such person. A rifle or shotgun seized as herein provided shall not be destroyed, but shall be delivered to the headquarters of such police department, or state police, and there retained until the aforesaid certificate has been rescinded by the director or physician in charge, or other disposition of such rifle or shotgun has been ordered or authorized by a court of competent jurisdiction.

(7) He knowingly possesses a bullet containing an explosive substance designed to detonate upon impact.

(8) He possesses any armor piercing ammunition with intent to use the same unlawfully against another.

Criminal possession of a weapon in the fourth degree is a class A misdemeanor.

---

* So in original.

HISTORY: Add, L 1974, ch 1041, § 3, eff Sept 1, 1974, with substance derived from former § 265.05, L 1976, ch 217, § 2, L 1981, ch 807, § 1, eff Sept 1, 1981, L 1982, ch 840, § 1, L 1983, ch 621, § 1, L 1985, ch 61, § 2, L 1986, ch 328, § 3, L 1986, ch 646, § 2, eff Nov 1, 1986, L 1988, ch 220, §§ 1, 2, L 1990, ch 264, § 2, L 1995, ch 219, § 3, eff Nov 1, 1995, L 2006, ch 199, § 1, eff Nov 1, 2006, L 2008, ch 257, § 4, eff Nov 1, 2008, L 2011, ch 357, § 1, eff Jan 30, 2012, L 2013, ch 1, § 40, eff March 16, 2013.

§ 265.01-a. Criminal possession of a weapon on school grounds

A person is guilty of criminal possession of a weapon on school grounds when he or she knowingly has in his or her possession a rifle, shotgun, or firearm in or upon a building or grounds, used for educational purposes, of any school, college, or university, except the forestry lands, wherever located, owned and maintained by the State University of New York college of environmental science and forestry, or upon a school bus as defined in section one hundred forty-two of the vehicle and traffic law, without the written authorization of such educational institution.

Criminal possession of a weapon on school grounds is a class E felony.

HISTORY: Add, L 2013, ch 1, § 41, eff March 16, 2013.

§ 265.01-b. Criminal possession of a firearm

A person is guilty of criminal possession of a firearm when he or she: (1) possesses any firearm or; (2) lawfully possesses a firearm prior to the effective date of the chapter of the laws of two thousand thirteen which added this section subject to the registration requirements of subdivision sixteen-a of section 400.00 of this chapter and knowingly fails to register such firearm pursuant to such subdivision.

Criminal possession of a firearm is a class E felony.

HISTORY: Add, L 2013, ch 1, § 41-a, eff March 16, 2013.

§ 265.02. Criminal possession of a weapon in the third degree

A person is guilty of criminal possession of a weapon in the third degree when:

(1) Such person commits the crime of criminal possession of a weapon in the fourth degree as defined in subdivision one, two, three or five of section 265.01, and has been previously convicted of any crime; or

(2) Such person possesses any explosive or incendiary bomb, bombshell, firearm silencer, machine-gun or any other firearm or weapon simulating a machine-gun and which is adaptable for such use; or

(3) Such person knowingly possesses a machine-gun, firearm, rifle or shotgun which has been defaced for the purpose of concealment or prevention of the detection of a crime or misrepresenting the identity of such machine-gun, firearm, rifle or shotgun; or

(4) [Repealed]

(5) (i) Such person possesses three or more firearms; or (ii) such person possesses a firearm and has been previously convicted of a felony or a class A misdemeanor defined in this chapter within the five years immediately preceding the commission of the offense and such possession did not take place in the person's home or place of business; or

(6) Such person knowingly possesses any disguised gun; or

(7) Such person possesses an assault weapon; or

(8) Such person possesses a large capacity ammunition feeding device. For purposes of this

subdivision, a large capacity ammunition feeding device shall not include an ammunition feeding device lawfully possessed by such person before the effective date of the chapter of the laws of two thousand thirteen which amended this subdivision, that has a capacity of, or that can be readily restored or converted to accept more than seven but less than eleven rounds of ammunition, or that was manufactured before September thirteenth, nineteen hundred ninety-four, that has a capacity of, or that can be readily restored or converted to accept, more than ten rounds of ammunition; or

(9) Such person possesses an unloaded firearm and also commits a drug trafficking felony as defined in subdivision twenty-one of section 10.00 of this chapter as part of the same criminal transaction; or

(10) Such person possesses an unloaded firearm and also commits any violent felony offense as defined in subdivision one of section 70.02 of this chapter as part of the same criminal transaction.

Criminal possession of a weapon in the third degree is a class D felony.

HISTORY: Add, L 1974, ch 1041, § 3, eff Sept 1, 1974; amd, L 1980, ch 233, § 7; amd, L 1981, ch 175, § 4, applicable to offenses committed on or after such date; amd, L 1987, ch 695, § 1, eff Nov 1, 1987, L 1998, ch 378, § 3; amd, L 2000, ch 189, § 11, eff Nov 1, 2000, L 2005, ch 764, § 2, eff Dec 21, 2005, L 2006, ch 742, § 1, eff Nov 1, 2006, L 2013, ch 1, § 41-b, eff March 13, 2013.

§ 265.03. Criminal possession of a weapon in the second degree

A person is guilty of criminal possession of a weapon in the second degree when:

(1) with intent to use the same unlawfully against another, such person:

(a) possesses a machine-gun; or

(b) possesses a loaded firearm; or

(c) possesses a disguised gun; or

(2) such person possesses five or more firearms; or

(3) such person possesses any loaded firearm. Such possession shall not, except as provided in subdivision one or seven of section 265.02 of this article, constitute a violation of this subdivision if such possession takes place in such person's home or place of business.

Criminal possession of a weapon in the second degree is a class C felony.

HISTORY: Add, L 1974, ch 1041, § 3, eff Sept 1, 1974. Opening par, amd, L 1998, ch 378, § 4, eff Nov 1, 1998. Sub (1), formerly part of opening par, so designated sub (1) and amd, L 1998, ch 378, § 4, eff Nov 1, 1998. Sub (2), formerly part of opening par, so designated sub (2) and amd, L 1998, ch 378, § 4, eff Nov 1, 1998. Sub (3), add, L 1998, ch 378, § 4, eff Nov 1, 1998. Amd, L 2005, ch 764, § 3, eff Dec 21, 2005, L 2006, ch 742, § 2, eff Nov 1, 2006. Opening par, amd, L 2005, ch 764, § 3, eff Dec 21, 2005. Sub (1), opening par, formerly part of opening par, so designated sub (1), opening par and amd, L 2005, ch 764, § 3, eff Dec 21, 2005; amd, L 2006, ch 745, § 1, eff Dec 15, 2006. Sub (1), par (a), formerly sub (1), so designated sub (1), par (a) and amd, L 2005, ch 764, § 3, eff Dec 21, 2005. Sub (1), par (b), add, L 2006, ch 745, § 1, eff Dec 15, 2006. Former sub (1), par (b), redesignated sub (1), par (c), L 2006, ch 745, § 1, eff Dec 15, 2006. Earlier sub (1), par (b), formerly sub (2), so designated sub (1), par (b) and amd, L 2005, ch 764, § 3, eff Dec 21, 2005; deleted, L 2006, ch 742, § 2, eff Nov 1, 2006. Sub (1), par (c), formerly sub (1), par (b), previously sub (1), par (c), earlier sub (3), so designated sub (1), par (c) and amd, L 2005, ch 764, § 3, eff Dec 21, 2005; so designated sub (1), par (b), L 2006, ch 742, § 2, eff Nov 1, 2006; so designated sub (1), par (c), L 2006, ch 745, § 1, eff Dec 15, 2005. Sub (2), add, L 2005, ch 764, § 3, eff Dec 21, 2005; amd, L 2006, ch 742, § 2, eff Nov 1, 2006. Former sub (2), redesignated sub (1), par (b), L 2005, ch 764, § 3, eff Dec 21, 2005. Sub (3), add, L 2006, ch 742, § 2, eff Nov 1, 2006; amd, L 2006, ch 745, § 1, eff Dec 15, 2006. Former sub (3), redesignated sub (1), par (c), L 2005, ch 764, § 3, eff Dec 21, 2005.

§ 265.04. Criminal possession of a weapon in the first degree

A person is guilty of criminal possession of a weapon in the first degree when such person:

(1) possesses any explosive substance with intent to use the same unlawfully against the person or property of another; or

(2) possesses ten or more firearms.

Criminal possession of a weapon in the first degree is a class B felony.

HISTORY: Add, L 1974, ch 1041, § 3, eff Sept 1, 1974. Amd, L 2005, ch 764, § 4, eff Dec 21, 2005. Section heading, amd, L 2005, ch 764, § 4, eff Dec 21, 2005. Opening par, formerly part of first undesignated par, so designated opening par and amd, L 2005, ch 764, § 4, eff Dec 21, 2005. Sub (1), formerly part of first undesignated par, so designated sub (1) and amd, L 2005, ch 764, § 4, eff Dec 21, 2005. Sub (2), add, L 2005, ch 764, § 4, eff Dec 21, 2005.

§ 265.05. Unlawful possession of weapons by persons under sixteen

It shall be unlawful for any person under the age of sixteen to possess any air-gun, spring-gun or other instrument or weapon in which the propelling force is a spring or air, or any gun or any instrument or weapon in or upon which any loaded or blank cartridges may be used, or any loaded or blank cartridges or ammunition therefor, or any dangerous knife; provided that the possession of rifle or shotgun or ammunition therefor by the holder of a hunting license or permit issued pursuant to article eleven of the environmental conservation law and used in accordance with said law shall not be governed by this section.

A person who violates the provisions of this section shall be adjudged a juvenile delinquent.

HISTORY: Add, L 1974, ch 1041, § 3; amd, L 1985, ch 56, § 1, eff Nov 1, 1985. Former § 265.05, add, L 1965, ch 1030, § 1, with substance derived from § 1897; amd, L 1969, ch 123, § 1, L 1969, ch 141, § 1, L 1970, ch 1012, § 1, L 1970, ch 1022, § 1, L 1971, ch 359, § 1, L 1971, ch 1097, § 80, L 1972, ch 387, § 1, L 1974, ch 179, § 1; repealed, L 1974, ch 1041, § 2, eff Sept 1, 1974.

§ 265.06. Unlawful possession of a weapon upon school grounds

It shall be unlawful for any person age sixteen or older to knowingly possess any air-gun, spring-gun or other instrument or weapon in which the propelling force is a spring, air, piston or co2 cartridge in or upon a building or grounds, used for educational purposes, of any school, college or university, without the written authorization of such educational institution. Unlawful possession of a weapon upon school grounds is a violation.

HISTORY: Add, L 1994, ch 268, § 1, eff Sept 1, 1994.

§ 265.08. Criminal use of a firearm in the second degree

A person is guilty of criminal use of a firearm in the second degree when he commits any class C violent felony offense as defined in paragraph (b) of subdivision one of section 70.02 and he either:

(1) possesses a deadly weapon, if the weapon is a loaded weapon from which a shot, readily capable of producing death or other serious injury may be discharged; or

(2) displays what appears to be a pistol, revolver, rifle, shotgun, machine gun or other firearm.

Criminal use of a firearm in the second degree is a class C felony.

HISTORY: Add, L 1980, ch 233, § 8, eff Aug 12, 1980.

§ 265.09. Criminal use of a firearm in the first degree

(1) A person is guilty of criminal use of a firearm in the first degree when he commits any class B violent felony offense as defined in paragraph (a) of subdivision one of section 70.02 and he either:

(a) possesses a deadly weapon, if the weapon is a loaded weapon from which a shot, readily capable of producing death or other serious injury may be discharged; or

(b) displays what appears to be a pistol, revolver, rifle, shotgun, machine gun or other firearm.

Criminal use of a firearm in the first degree is a class B felony.

(2) Sentencing. Notwithstanding any other provision of law to the contrary, when a person is convicted of criminal use of a firearm in the first degree as defined in subdivision one of this section, the court shall impose an additional consecutive sentence of five years to the sentence imposed on the underlying class B violent felony offense where the person convicted of such crime displays a loaded weapon from which a shot, readily capable of producing death or other serious injury may be discharged, in furtherance of the commission of such crime, provided, however, that such additional sentence shall not be imposed if the court, having regard to the nature and circumstances of the crime and to the history and character of the defendant, finds on the record that such additional consecutive sentence would be unduly harsh and that not imposing such sentence would be consistent with the public safety and would not deprecate the seriousness of the crime. Notwithstanding any other provision of law to the contrary, the aggregate of the five year consecutive term imposed pursuant to this subdivision and the minimum term of the indeterminate sentence imposed on the underlying class B violent felony shall constitute the new aggregate minimum term of imprisonment, and a person subject to such term shall be required to serve the entire aggregate minimum term and shall not be eligible for release on parole or conditional release during such term. This subdivision shall not apply where the defendant's criminal liability for displaying a loaded weapon from which a shot, readily capable of producing death or other serious injury may be discharged, in furtherance of the commission of crime is based on the conduct of another pursuant to section 20.00 of this chapter.

HISTORY: Add, L 1980, ch 233, § 9; amd, L 1996, ch 650, § 1, eff Nov 1, 1996, L 2013, ch 1, § 42, eff March 16, 2013.

§ 265.10. Manufacture, transport, disposition and defacement of weapons and dangerous instruments and appliances

1. Any person who manufactures or causes to be manufactured any machine-gun, assault weapon, large capacity ammunition feeding device or disguised gun is guilty of a class D felony. Any person who manufactures or causes to be manufactured any switchblade knife, gravity knife, pilum ballistic knife, metal knuckle knife, billy, blackjack, bludgeon, plastic knuckles, metal knuckles, Kung Fu star, chuka stick, sandbag, sandclub or slungshot is guilty of a class A misdemeanor.

2. Any person who transports or ships any machine-gun, firearm silencer, assault weapon or large capacity ammunition feeding device or disguised gun, or who transports or ships as merchandise five or more firearms, is guilty of a class D felony. Any person who transports or ships as merchandise any firearm, other than an assault weapon, switchblade knife, gravity knife, pilum ballistic knife, billy, blackjack, bludgeon, plastic knuckles, metal knuckles, Kung Fu star, chuka stick, sandbag or slungshot is guilty of a class A misdemeanor.

3. Any person who disposes of any machine-gun, assault weapon, large capacity ammunition feeding device or firearm silencer is guilty of a class D felony. Any person who knowingly buys, receives, disposes of, or conceals a machine-gun, firearm, large capacity ammunition feeding

device, rifle or shotgun which has been defaced for the purpose of concealment or prevention of the detection of a crime or misrepresenting the identity of such machine-gun, firearm, large capacity ammunition feeding device, rifle or shotgun is guilty of a class D felony.

4. Any person who disposes of any of the weapons, instruments or appliances specified in subdivision one of section 265.01, except a firearm, is guilty of a class A misdemeanor, and he is guilty of a class D felony if he has previously been convicted of any crime.

5. Any person who disposes of any of the weapons, instruments, appliances or substances specified in section 265.05 to any other person under the age of sixteen years is guilty of a class A misdemeanor.

6. Any person who wilfully defaces any machine-gun, large capacity ammunition feeding device or firearm is guilty of a class D felony.

7. Any person, other than a wholesale dealer, or gunsmith or dealer in firearms duly licensed pursuant to section 400.00, lawfully in possession of a firearm, who disposes of the same without first notifying in writing the licensing officer in the city of New York and counties of Nassau and Suffolk and elsewhere in the state the executive department, division of state police, Albany, is guilty of a class A misdemeanor.

> **HISTORY:** Add, L 1965, ch 1030, § 1, eff Sept 1, 1967, with substance derived from §§ 1898, 1902(3); amd, L 2000, ch 189, § 12, eff Nov 1, 2000. Sub 1, amd, L 1974, ch 179, § 3, L 1985, ch 61, § 3, L 1986, ch 328, § 4, L 1995, ch 219, § 4, L 1998, ch 378, § 5, L 2000, ch 189, § 12, eff Nov 1, 2000. Sub 1, amd, L 2008, ch 257, § 5, eff Nov 1, 2008. Sub 2, amd, L 1974, ch 179, § 1, L 1985, ch 61, § 3, L 1986, ch 328, § 4, L 1991, ch 174, § 1, L 1998, ch 378, § 5, L 2000, ch 189, § 12, eff Nov 1, 2000. Sub 2, amd, L 2008, ch 257, § 5, eff Nov 1, 2008. Sub 3, amd, L 1987, ch 695, § 2, L 2000, ch 189, § 12, eff Nov 1, 2000. Sub 4, amd, L 1974, ch 1041, § 4, L 1980, ch 233, § 10, eff Aug 12, 1980. Sub 5, amd, L 1978, ch 3, § 1, eff Feb 7, 1978. Sub 6, amd, L 2000, ch 189, § 12, eff Nov 1, 2000. Sub 7, amd, L 1974, ch 1041, § 4, eff Sept 1, 1974.

§ 265.11. Criminal sale of a firearm in the third degree

A person is guilty of criminal sale of a firearm in the third degree when such person is not authorized pursuant to law to possess a firearm and such person unlawfully either:

(1) sells, exchanges, gives or disposes of a firearm or large capacity ammunition feeding device to another person; or

(2) possesses a firearm with the intent to sell it.

Criminal sale of a firearm in the third degree is a class D felony.

> **HISTORY:** Add, L 1980, ch 233, § 11; amd, L 1991, ch 496, § 1, L 1995, ch 310, § 1, eff Nov 1, 1995. Amd, L 2005, ch 764, § 5, eff Dec 21, 2005. Section heading, amd, L 1991, ch 496, § 1, eff Nov 1, 1991. Opening par, amd, L 1991, ch 496, § 1, eff Nov 1, 1991. Opening par, amd, L 2005, ch 764, § 5, eff Dec 21, 2005. Sub (1), amd, L 1995, ch 310, § 1, L 2000, ch 189, § 13, eff Nov 1, 2000. Closing par, amd, L 1991, ch 496, § 1, L 1998, ch 654, § 1, eff Nov 1, 1999.

§ 265.12. Criminal sale of a firearm in the second degree

A person is guilty of criminal sale of a firearm in the second degree when such person:

(1) unlawfully sells, exchanges, gives or disposes of to another five or more firearms; or

(2) unlawfully sells, exchanges, gives or disposes of to another person or persons a total of five or more firearms in a period of not more than one year.

Criminal sale of a firearm in the second degree is a class C felony.

> **HISTORY:** Add, L 1980, ch 233, § 12, eff Aug 12, 1980. Section heading, amd, L 1991, ch 496, § 2, eff Nov 1, 1991. First undesignated par, amd, L 1991, ch 496, § 2, eff Nov 1, 1991. Second

undesignated par, amd, L 1991, ch 496, § 2, L 1998, ch 654, § 2, eff Nov 1, 1999. Amd, L 2005, ch 764, § 6, eff Dec 21, 2005. Opening par, formerly part of first undesignated par, so designated opening par and amd, L 2005, ch 764, § 6, eff Dec 21, 2005. Sub (1), formerly part of first undesignated par, so designated sub (1) and amd, L 2005, ch 764, § 6, eff Dec 21, 2005. Sub (2), add, L 2005, ch 764, § 6, eff Dec 21, 2005.

§ 265.13. Criminal sale of a firearm in the first degree

A person is guilty of criminal sale of a firearm in the first degree when such person:

(1) unlawfully sells, exchanges, gives or disposes of to another ten or more firearms; or

(2) unlawfully sells, exchanges, gives or disposes of to another person or persons a total of ten or more firearms in a period of not more than one year.

Criminal sale of a firearm in the first degree is a class B felony.

HISTORY: Add, L 1991, ch 496, § 3, eff Nov 1, 1991. Second undesignated par, amd, L 1998, ch 654, § 3, eff Nov 1, 1999. Amd, L 2005, ch 764, § 7, eff Dec 21, 2005. Opening par, formerly part of first undesignated par, so designated opening par and amd, L 2005, ch 764, § 7, eff Dec 21, 2005. Sub (1), formerly part of first undesignated par, so designated sub (1) and amd, L 2005, ch 764, § 7, eff Dec 21, 2005. Sub (2), add, L 2005, ch 764, § 7, eff Dec 21, 2005.

§ 265.14. Criminal sale of a firearm with the aid of a minor

A person over the age of eighteen years of age is guilty of criminal sale of a weapon with the aid of a minor when a person under sixteen years of age knowingly and unlawfully sells, exchanges, gives or disposes of a firearm in violation of this article, and such person over the age of eighteen years of age, acting with the mental culpability required for the commission thereof, solicits, requests, commands, importunes or intentionally aids such person under sixteen years of age to engage in such conduct.

Criminal sale of a firearm with the aid of a minor is a class C felony.

HISTORY: Add, L 1991, ch 175, § 1, eff Nov 1, 1991. Second undesignated par, amd, L 1998, ch 654, § 4, eff Nov 1, 1999.

§ 265.15. Presumptions of possession, unlawful intent and defacement

1. The presence in any room, dwelling, structure or vehicle of any machine-gun is presumptive evidence of its unlawful possession by all persons occupying the place where such machine-gun is found.

2. The presence in any stolen vehicle of any weapon, instrument, appliance or substance specified in sections 265.01, 265.02, 265.03, 265.04 and 265.05 is presumptive evidence of its possession by all persons occupying such vehicle at the time such weapon, instrument, appliance or substance is found.

3. The presence in an automobile, other than a stolen one or a public omnibus, of any firearm, large capacity ammunition feeding device, defaced firearm, defaced rifle or shotgun, defaced large capacity ammunition feeding device, firearm silencer, explosive or incendiary bomb, bombshell, gravity knife, switchblade knife, pilum ballistic knife, metal knuckle knife, dagger, dirk, stiletto, billy, blackjack, plastic knuckles, metal knuckles, chuka stick, sandbag, sandclub or slungshot is presumptive evidence of its possession by all persons occupying such automobile at the time such weapon, instrument or appliance is found, except under the following circumstances: (a) if such weapon, instrument or appliance is found upon the person of one of the occupants therein; (b) if such weapon, instrument or appliance is found in an automobile which is being operated for hire by a duly licensed driver in the due, lawful and proper pursuit of his or her trade, then such presumption shall not apply to the driver; or (c) if the weapon so found is a pistol or revolver and

one of the occupants, not present under duress, has in his or her possession a valid license to have and carry concealed the same.

4. The possession by any person of the substance as specified in section 265.04 is presumptive evidence of possessing such substance with intent to use the same unlawfully against the person or property of another if such person is not licensed or otherwise authorized to possess such substance. The possession by any person of any dagger, dirk, stiletto, dangerous knife or any other weapon, instrument, appliance or substance designed, made or adapted for use primarily as a weapon, is presumptive evidence of intent to use the same unlawfully against another.

5. The possession by any person of a defaced machine-gun, firearm, rifle or shotgun is presumptive evidence that such person defaced the same.

6. The possession of five or more firearms by any person is presumptive evidence that such person possessed the firearms with the intent to sell same.

> **HISTORY:** Add, L 1965, ch 1030, § 1, eff Sept 1, 1967, with substance derived from § 1899. Sub 2, amd, L 1974, ch 1041, § 5, eff Sept 1, 1974. Sub 3, amd, L 1970, ch 1012, § 2, L 1974, ch 179, § 4, L 1986, ch 328, § 5, L 1987, ch 695, § 3, L 1995, ch 219, § 5, L 2000, ch 189, § 14, eff Nov 1, 2000. Sub 3, amd, L 2008, ch 257, § 6, eff Nov 1, 2008. Sub 4, amd, L 1970, ch 1022, § 13, L 1974, ch 1041, § 5, eff Sept 1, 1974. Sub 5, amd, L 1987, ch 695, § 4, eff Nov 1, 1987. Sub 6, add, L 1980, ch 233, § 13, eff Aug 12, 1980.

§ 265.16. Criminal sale of a firearm to a minor

A person is guilty of criminal sale of a firearm to a minor when he is not authorized pursuant to law to possess a firearm and he unlawfully sells, exchanges, gives or disposes of a firearm to another person who is or reasonably appears to be less than nineteen years of age who is not licensed pursuant to law to possess a firearm.

Criminal sale of a firearm to a minor is a class C felony.

> **HISTORY:** Add, L 1992, ch 600, § 1, eff Nov 1, 1992. Second undesignated par, amd, L 1998, ch 654, § 5, eff Nov 1, 1999.

§ 265.17. Criminal purchase or disposal of a weapon

A person is guilty of criminal purchase or disposal of a weapon when:

1. Knowing that he or she is prohibited by law from possessing a firearm, rifle or shotgun because of a prior conviction or because of some other disability which would render him or her ineligible to lawfully possess a firearm, rifle or shotgun in this state, such person purchases a firearm, rifle or shotgun from another person; or

2. Knowing that it would be unlawful for another person to possess a firearm, rifle or shotgun, he or she purchases a firearm, rifle or shot gun for, on behalf of, or for the use of such other person; or

3. Knowing that another person is prohibited by law from possessing a firearm, rifle or shotgun because of a prior conviction or because of some other disability which would render him or her ineligible to lawfully possess a firearm, rifle or shotgun in this state, a person disposes of a firearm, rifle or shotgun to such other person.

Criminal purchase or disposal of a weapon is a class D felony.

> **HISTORY:** Add, L 2000, ch 189, § 14-a, eff Nov 1, 2000; amd, L 2013, ch 1, § 43, eff March 16, 2013.

§ 265.19. Aggravated criminal possession of a weapon

A person is guilty of aggravated criminal possession of a weapon when he or she commits the crime of criminal possession of a weapon in the second degree as defined in subdivision three of section 265.03 of this article and also commits any violent felony offense as defined in subdivision one of section 70.02 of this chapter or a drug trafficking felony as defined in subdivision twenty-one of section 10.00 of this chapter arising out of the same criminal transaction.

HISTORY: Add, L 2013, ch 1, § 45, eff March 16, 2013.

§ 265.20. Exemptions

a. Paragraph (h) of subdivision twenty-two of section 265.00 and sections 265.01, 265.01-a, subdivision one of section 265.01-b, 265.02, 265.03, 265.04, 265.05, 265.10, 265.11, 265.12, 265.13, 265.15, 265.36, 265.37 and 270.05 shall not apply to:

1. Possession of any of the weapons, instruments, appliances or substances specified in sections 265.01, 265.02, 265.03, 265.04, 265.05 and 270.05 by the following:

(a) Persons in the military service of the state of New York when duly authorized by regulations issued by the adjutant general to possess the same.

(b) Police officers as defined in subdivision thirty-four of section 1.20 of the criminal procedure law.

(c) Peace officers as defined by section 2.10 of the criminal procedure law.

(d) Persons in the military or other service of the United States, in pursuit of official duty or when duly authorized by federal law, regulation or order to possess the same.

(e) Persons employed in fulfilling defense contracts with the government of the United States or agencies thereof when possession of the same is necessary for manufacture, transport, installation and testing under the requirements of such contract.

(f) A person voluntarily surrendering such weapon, instrument, appliance or substance, provided that such surrender shall be made to the superintendent of the division of state police or a member thereof designated by such superintendent, or to the sheriff of the county in which such person resides, or in the county of Nassau or in the towns of Babylon, Brookhaven, Huntington, Islip and Smithtown in the county of Suffolk to the commissioner of police or a member of the police department thereof designated by such commissioner, or if such person resides in a city, town other than one named in this subparagraph, or village to the police commissioner or head of the police force or department thereof or to a member of the force or department designated by such commissioner or head; and provided, further, that the same shall be surrendered by such person in accordance with such terms and conditions as may be established by such superintendent, sheriff, police force or department. Nothing in this paragraph shall be construed as granting immunity from prosecution for any crime or offense except that of unlawful possession of such weapons, instruments, appliances or substances surrendered as herein provided. A person who possesses any such weapon, instrument, appliance or substance as an executor or administrator or any other lawful possessor of such property of a decedent may continue to possess such property for a period not over fifteen days. If such property is not lawfully disposed of within such period the possessor shall deliver it to an appropriate official described in this paragraph or such property may be delivered to the superintendent of state police. Such officer shall hold it and shall thereafter deliver it on the written request of such executor, administrator or other lawful possessor of such property to a named person, provided such named person is licensed to or is otherwise lawfully permitted to possess the same. If no request to deliver the property is received by such official within one year of the delivery of such property, such official shall dispose of it in accordance with the provisions of section 400.05 of this chapter.

2. Possession of a machine-gun, large capacity ammunition feeding device, firearm, switchblade knife, gravity knife, pilum ballistic knife, billy or blackjack by a warden, superintendent, headkeeper or deputy of a state prison, penitentiary, workhouse, county jail or other institution for the detention of persons convicted or accused of crime or detained as witnesses in criminal cases, in pursuit of official duty or when duly authorized by regulation or order to possess the same.

3. Possession of a pistol or revolver by a person to whom a license therefor has been issued as provided under section 400.00 or 400.01 of this chapter or possession of a weapon as defined in paragraph (e) or (f) of subdivision twenty-two of section 265.00 of this article which is registered pursuant to paragraph (a) of subdivision sixteen-a of section 400.00 of this chapter or is included on an amended license issued pursuant to section 400.00 of this chapter. In the event such license is revoked, other than because such licensee is no longer permitted to possess a firearm, rifle or shotgun under federal or state law, information sufficient to satisfy the requirements of subdivision sixteen-a of section 400.00 of this chapter, shall be transmitted by the licensing officer to the state police, in a form as determined by the superintendent of state police. Such transmission shall constitute a valid registration under such section. Further provided, notwithstanding any other section of this title, a failure to register such weapon by an individual who possesses such weapon before the enactment of the chapter of the laws of two thousand thirteen which amended this paragraph and may so lawfully possess it thereafter upon registration, shall only be subject to punishment pursuant to paragraph (c) of subdivision sixteen-a of section 400.00 of this chapter; provided, that such a license or registration shall not preclude a conviction for the offense defined in subdivision three of section 265.01 of this article or section 265.01-a of this article.

4. Possession of a rifle, shotgun, crossbow or longbow for use while hunting, trapping or fishing, by a person, not a citizen of the United States, carrying a valid license issued pursuant to section 11-0713 of the environmental conservation law.

5. Possession of a rifle or shotgun by a person other than a person who has been convicted of a class A-I felony or a violent felony offense, as defined in subdivision one of section 70.02 of this chapter, who has been convicted as specified in subdivision four of section 265.01 to whom a certificate of good conduct has been issued pursuant to section seven hundred three-b of the correction law.

6. Possession of a switchblade or gravity knife for use while hunting, trapping or fishing by a person carrying a valid license issued to him pursuant to section 11-0713 of the environmental conservation law.

7. Possession, at an indoor or outdoor shooting range for the purpose of loading and firing, of a rifle or shotgun, the propelling force of which is gunpowder by a person under sixteen years of age but not under twelve, under the immediate supervision, guidance and instruction of (a) a duly commissioned officer of the United States army, navy, air force, marine corps or coast guard, or of the national guard of the state of New York; or (b) a duly qualified adult citizen of the United States who has been granted a certificate as an instructor in small arms practice issued by the United States army, navy, air force or marine corps, or by the adjutant general of this state, or by the national rifle association of America, a not-for-profit corporation duly organized under the laws of this state; or (c) a parent, guardian, or a person over the age of eighteen designated in writing by such parent or guardian who shall have a certificate of

qualification in responsible hunting, including safety, ethics, and landowner relations-hunter relations, issued or honored by the department of environmental conservation; or (d) an agent of the department of environmental conservation appointed to conduct courses in responsible hunting practices pursuant to article eleven of the environmental conservation law.

7-a. Possession and use, at an indoor or outdoor pistol range located in or on premises owned or occupied by a duly incorporated organization organized for conservation purposes or to foster proficiency in small arms or at a target pistol shooting competition under the auspices of or approved by the national rifle association for the purpose of loading and firing the same, by a person duly licensed to possess a pistol or revolver pursuant to section 400.00 or 400.01 of this chapter of a pistol or revolver duly so licensed to another person who is present at the time.

7-b. Possession and use, at an indoor or outdoor pistol range located in or on premises owned or occupied by a duly incorporated organization organized for conservation purposes or to foster proficiency in small arms or at a target pistol shooting competition under the auspices of or approved by the national rifle association for the purpose of loading and firing the same, by a person who has applied for a license to possess a pistol or revolver and pre-license possession of same pursuant to section 400.00 or 400.01 of this chapter, who has not been previously denied a license, been previously convicted of a felony or serious offense, and who does not appear to be, or pose a threat to be, a danger to himself or to others, and who has been approved for possession and use herein in accordance with section 400.00 or 400.01 of this chapter; provided however, that such possession shall be of a pistol or revolver duly licensed to and shall be used under the supervision, guidance and instruction of, a person specified in paragraph seven of this subdivision and provided further that such possession and use be within the jurisdiction of the licensing officer with whom the person has made application therefor or within the jurisdiction of the superintendent of state police in the case of a retired sworn member of the division of state police who has made an application pursuant to section 400.01 of this chapter.

7-c. Possession for the purpose of loading and firing, of a rifle, pistol or shotgun, the propelling force of which may be either air, compressed gas or springs, by a person under sixteen years of age but not under twelve, under the immediate supervision, guidance and instruction of (a) a duly commissioned officer of the United States army, navy, marine corps or coast guard, or of the national guard of the state of New York; or (b) a duly qualified adult citizen of the United States who has been granted a certificate as an instructor in small arms practice issued by the United States army, navy or marine corps, or by the adjutant general of this state, or by the national rifle association of America, a not-for-profit corporation duly organized under the laws of this state; or (c) a parent, guardian, or a person over the age of eighteen designated in writing by such parent or guardian who shall have a certificate of qualification in responsible hunting, including safety, ethics, and landowner relations-hunter relations, issued or honored by the department of environmental conservation.

7-d. Possession, at an indoor or outdoor shooting range for the purpose of loading and firing, of a rifle, pistol or shotgun, the propelling force of which may be either air, compressed gas or springs, by a person under twelve years of age, under the immediate supervision, guidance and instruction of (a) a duly commissioned officer of the United States army, navy, marine corps or coast guard, or of the national guard of the state of New York; or (b) a duly qualified adult citizen of the United States who has been granted a certificate as an instructor in small arms practice issued by the United States army, navy or marine corps, or by the adjutant general of this state, or by the national rifle association of America, a not-for-profit corporation duly organized under the laws of this state; or (c) a parent, guardian, or a person over the age of eighteen designated in writing by such parent or guardian who shall have a certificate of qualification in responsible hunting, including safety, ethics, and landowner relations-hunter relations, issued or honored by the department of environmental conservation.

7-e. Possession and use of a pistol or revolver, at an indoor or outdoor pistol range located in or on premises owned or occupied by a duly incorporated organization organized for conservation purposes or to foster proficiency in small arms or at a target pistol shooting competition under the auspices of or approved by an association or organization described in paragraph 7-a of this subdivision for the purpose of loading and firing the same by a person at least fourteen years of age but under the age of twenty-one who has not been previously convicted of a felony or serious offense, and who does not appear to be, or pose a threat to be, a danger to himself or to others; provided however, that such possession shall be of a pistol or revolver duly licensed to and shall be used under the immediate supervision, guidance and instruction of, a person specified in paragraph seven of this subdivision.

7-f. Possession and use of a magazine, belt, feed strip or similar device, that contains more than seven rounds of ammunition, but that does not have a capacity of or can readily be restored or converted to accept more than ten rounds of ammunition, at an indoor or outdoor firing range located in or on premises owned or occupied by a duly incorporated organization organized for conservation purposes or to foster proficiency in arms; at an indoor or outdoor firing range for the purpose of firing a rifle or shotgun; at a collegiate, olympic or target shooting competition under the auspices of or approved by the national rifle association; or at an organized match sanctioned by the International Handgun Metallic Silhouette Association.

8. The manufacturer of machine-guns, firearm silencers, assault weapons, large capacity ammunition feeding devices, disguised guns, pilum ballistic knives, switchblade or gravity knives, billies or blackjacks as merchandise, or as a transferee recipient of the same for repair, lawful distribution or research and development, and the disposal and shipment thereof direct to a regularly constituted or appointed state or municipal police department, sheriff, policeman or other peace officer, or to a state prison, penitentiary, workhouse, county jail or other institution for the detention of persons convicted or accused of crime or held as witnesses in criminal cases, or to the military service of this state or of the United States; or for the repair and return of the same to the lawful possessor or for research and development.

9. The regular and ordinary transport of firearms as merchandise, provided that the person transporting such firearms, where he knows or has reasonable means of ascertaining what he is transporting, notifies in writing the police commissioner, police chief or other law enforcement officer performing such functions at the place of delivery, of the name and address of the consignee and the place of delivery, and withholds delivery to the consignee for such reasonable period of time designated in writing by such police commissioner, police chief or other law enforcement officer as such official may deem necessary for investigation as to whether the consignee may lawfully receive and possess such firearms.

9-a. a. Except as provided in subdivision b hereof, the regular and ordinary transport of pistols or revolvers by a manufacturer of firearms to whom a license as a dealer in firearms has been issued pursuant to section 400.00 of this chapter, or by an agent or employee of such manufacturer of firearms who is otherwise duly licensed to carry a pistol or revolver and who is duly authorized in writing by such manufacturer of firearms to transport pistols or revolvers on the date or dates specified, directly between places where the manufacturer of firearms regularly conducts business provided such pistols or revolvers are transported unloaded, in a locked opaque container. For purposes of this subdivision, places where the manufacturer of firearms regularly conducts business includes, but is not limited to places where the manufacturer of firearms regularly or customarily conducts development or design of pistols or revolvers, or regularly or customarily conducts tests on pistols or revolvers, or regularly or customarily participates in the exposition of firearms to the public.

b. The transportation of such pistols or revolvers into, out of or within the city of New York may be done only with the consent of the police commissioner of the city of New York. To obtain such consent, the manufacturer must notify the police commissioner in writing of the name and address of the transporting manufacturer, or agent or employee of the manufacturer who is authorized in writing by such manufacturer to transport pistols or revolvers, the number, make and model number of the firearms to be transported and the place where the manufacturer regularly conducts business within the city of New York and such other information as the commissioner may deem necessary. The manufacturer must not transport such pistols and revolvers between the designated places of business for such reasonable period of time designated in writing by the police commissioner as such official may deem necessary for investigation and to give consent. The police commissioner may not unreasonably withhold his consent.

10. Engaging in the business of gunsmith or dealer in firearms by a person to whom a valid license therefor has been issued pursuant to section 400.00.

11. Possession of a firearm or large capacity ammunition feeding device by a police officer or sworn peace officer of another state while conducting official business within the state of New York.

12. Possession of a pistol or revolver by a person who is a member or coach of an accredited college or university target pistol team while transporting the pistol or revolver into or through New York state to participate in a collegiate, olympic or target pistol shooting competition under the auspices of or approved by the national rifle association, provided such pistol or revolver is unloaded and carried in a locked carrying case and the ammunition therefor is carried in a separate locked container.

12-a. Possession and use of a pistol or revolver, at an indoor or outdoor shooting range, by a registered student of a higher education institution chartered by the state of New York, who is participating in a course in gun safety and proficiency offered by such institution, under the immediate supervision, guidance, and instruction of a person specified in paragraph seven of this subdivision.

13. Possession of pistols and revolvers by a person who is a nonresident of this state while attending or traveling to or from, an organized competitive pistol match or league competition under auspices of, or approved by, the National Rifle Association and in which he is a competitor, within forty-eight hours of such event or by a person who is a non-resident of the state while attending or traveling to or from an organized match sanctioned by the International Handgun Metallic Silhouette Association and in which he is a competitor, within forty-eight hours of such event, provided that he has not been previously convicted of a felony or a crime which, if committed in New York, would constitute a felony, and further provided that the pistols or revolvers are transported unloaded in a locked opaque container together with a copy of the match program, match schedule or match registration card. Such documentation shall constitute prima facie evidence of exemption, providing that such person also has in his possession a pistol license or firearms registration card issued in accordance with the laws of his place of residence. For purposes of this subdivision, a person licensed in a jurisdiction which does not authorize such license by a person who has been previously convicted of a felony shall be presumed to have no prior conviction. The superintendent of state police shall annually

review the laws of jurisdictions within the United States and Canada with respect to the applicable requirements for licensing or registration of firearms and shall publish a list of those jurisdictions which prohibit possession of a firearm by a person previously convicted of a felony or crimes which if committed in New York state would constitute a felony.

13-a. Except in cities not wholly contained within a single county of the state, possession of pistols and revolvers by a person who is a nonresident of this state while attending or traveling to or from, an organized convention or exhibition for the display of or education about firearms, which is conducted under auspices of, or approved by, the National Rifle Association and in which he is a registered participant, within forty-eight hours of such event, provided that he has not been previously convicted of a felony or a crime which, if committed in New York, would constitute a felony, and further provided that the pistols or revolvers are transported unloaded in a locked opaque container together with a copy of the convention or exhibition program, convention or exhibition schedule or convention or exhibition registration card. Such documentation shall constitute prima facie evidence of exemption, providing that such person also has in his possession a pistol license or firearms registration card issued in accordance with the laws of his place of residence. For purposes of this paragraph, a person licensed in a jurisdiction which does not authorize such license by a person who has been previously convicted of a felony shall be presumed to have no prior conviction. The superintendent of state police shall annually review the laws of jurisdictions within the United States and Canada with respect to the applicable requirements for licensing or registration of firearms and shall publish a list of those jurisdictions which prohibit possession of a firearm by a person previously convicted of a felony or crimes which if committed in New York state would constitute a felony.

14. Possession in accordance with the provisions of this paragraph of a self-defense spray device as defined herein for the protection of a person or property and use of such self-defense spray device under circumstances which would justify the use of physical force pursuant to article thirty-five of this chapter.

(a) As used in this section "self-defense spray device" shall mean a pocket sized spray device which contains and releases a chemical or organic substance which is intended to produce temporary physical discomfort or disability through being vaporized or otherwise dispensed in the air or any like device containing tear gas, pepper or similar disabling agent.

(b) The exemption under this paragraph shall not apply to a person who:

(i) is less than eighteen years of age; or

(ii) has been previously convicted in this state of a felony or any assault; or

(iii) has been convicted of a crime outside the state of New York which if committed in New York would constitute a felony or any assault crime.

(c) The department of health, with the cooperation of the division of criminal justice services and the superintendent of state police, shall develop standards and promulgate regulations regarding the type of self-defense spray device which may lawfully be purchased, possessed and used pursuant to this paragraph. The regulations shall include a requirement that every self-defense spray device which may be lawfully purchased, possessed or used pursuant to this paragraph have a label which states: "WARNING: The use of this substance or device for any purpose other than self-defense is a criminal offense under the law. The contents are dangerous - use with care. This device shall not be sold by anyone other than a licensed or authorized dealer. Possession of this device by any person under the age of eighteen or by anyone who has been convicted of a felony or assault is illegal. Violators may be prosecuted under the law."

15. Possession and sale of a self-defense spray device as defined in paragraph fourteen of this subdivision by a dealer in firearms licensed pursuant to section 400.00 of this chapter, a pharmacist licensed pursuant to article one hundred thirty-seven of the education law or by such other vendor as may be authorized and approved by the superintendent of state police.

(a) Every self-defense spray device shall be accompanied by an insert or inserts which include directions for use, first aid information, safety and storage information and which shall also contain a toll free telephone number for the purpose of allowing any purchaser to call and receive additional information regarding the availability of local courses in self-defense training and safety in the use of a self-defense spray device.

(b) Before delivering a self-defense spray device to any person, the licensed or authorized dealer shall require proof of age and a sworn statement on a form approved by the superintendent of state police that such person has not been convicted of a felony or any crime involving an assault. Such forms shall be forwarded to the division of state police at such intervals as directed by the superintendent of state police. Absent any such direction the forms shall be maintained on the premises of the vendor and shall be open at all reasonable hours for inspection by any peace officer or police officer, acting pursuant to his or her special duties. No more than two self-defense spray devices may be sold at any one time to a single purchaser.

16. The terms "rifle," "shotgun," "pistol," "revolver," and "firearm" as used in paragraphs three, four, five, seven, seven-a, seven-b, nine, nine-a, ten, twelve, thirteen and thirteen-a of this subdivision shall not include a disguised gun or an assault weapon.

b. Section 265.01 shall not apply to possession of that type of billy commonly known as a "police baton" which is twenty-four to twenty-six inches in length and no more than one and one-quarter inches in thickness by members of an auxiliary police force of a city with a population in excess of one million persons or the county of Suffolk when duly authorized by regulation or order issued by the police commissioner of such city or such county respectively. Such regulations shall require training in the use of the police baton including but not limited to the defensive use of the baton and instruction in the legal use of deadly physical force pursuant to article thirty-five of this chapter. Notwithstanding the provisions of this section or any other provision of law, possession of such baton shall not be authorized when used intentionally to strike another person except in those situations when the use of deadly physical force is authorized by such article thirty-five.

c. Sections 265.01, 265.10 and 265.15 shall not apply to possession of billies or blackjacks by persons:

1. while employed in fulfilling contracts with New York state, its agencies or political subdivisions for the purchase of billies or blackjacks; or

2. while employed in fulfilling contracts with sister states, their agencies or political subdivisions for the purchase of billies or blackjacks; or

3. while employed in fulfilling contracts with foreign countries, their agencies or political subdivisions for the purchase of billies or blackjacks as permitted under federal law.

d. Subdivision one of section 265.01 and subdivision four of section 265.15 of this article shall not apply to possession or ownership of automatic knives by any cutlery and knife museum established pursuant to section two hundred sixteen-c of the education law or by any director, officer, employee, or agent thereof when he or she is in possession of an automatic knife and acting in furtherance of the business of such museum.

e. Subdivision eight of section 265.02 and sections 265.36 and 265.37 of this chapter shall not apply to a qualified retired New York or federal law enforcement officer as defined in subdivision twenty-five of section 265.00 of this article, with respect to large capacity ammunition feeding devices issued to such officer or purchased by such officer in the course of his or her official duties and owned by such officer at the time of his or her retirement or comparable replacements for such devices, if: (i) the agency that employed the officer qualified such officer in the use of the weapon which accepts such device in accordance with applicable state or federal standards for active duty law enforcement officers within twelve months prior to his or her retirement; and (ii) such retired officer meets, at his or her own expense, such applicable standards for such weapon at least once within three years after his or her retirement date and at least once every three years thereafter, provided, however, that any such qualified officer who has been retired for eighteen months or more on the effective date of this subdivision shall have eighteen months from such effective date to qualify in the use of the weapon which accepts such large capacity ammunition feeding device according to the provisions of this subdivision, notwithstanding that such officer did not qualify within three years after his or her retirement date, provided that such officer is otherwise qualified and maintains compliance with the provisions of this subdivision.

HISTORY: Add, L 1965, ch 1030, § 1, with substance derived from § 1900; amd, L 1967, ch 791, § 47, L 1969, ch 341, § 2, L 1969, ch 452, § 1, eff Sept 1, 1969, L 1969, ch 674, § 1, L 1970, ch 13, § 1, L 1970, ch 233, § 1, L 1971, ch 435, eff Sept 1, 1971, L 1971, ch 1097, § 81, L 1974, ch 1041, § 6, eff Sept 1, 1974, L 1976, ch 498, § 1, L 1979, ch 90, § 1, eff May 14, 1979, L 1979, ch 667, § 1, L 1980, ch 233, § 14, 1980, ch 843, §§ 44–46, eff Sept 1, 1980, L 1981, ch 469, § 1, L 1982, ch 733, § 1, L 1983, ch 75, § 1, L 1984, ch 262, § 1, L 1984, ch 608, § 2, eff Nov 1, 1984, L 1985, ch 189, § 1, eff June 11, 1985, L 1986, ch 328, §§ 6, 7, L 1986, ch 370, § 1, eff Nov 1, 1986, L 1988, ch 141, § 75, eff June 20, 1988, L 1988, ch 150, § 1, eff Nov 1, 1988, L 1998, ch 378, §§ 6, 7, L 1988, ch 442, § 1, eff Nov 1, 1988, L 1991, ch 496, § 5, eff Nov 1, 1991, L 1995, ch 376, §§ 1, 2, eff Aug 2, 1995, L 1996, ch 651, §§ 1, 2, eff Nov 1, 1996, L 1998, ch 180, § 1, eff Jan 1, 1999, L 1999, ch 210, §§ 2–4, eff Nov 1, 1999, L 2000, ch 189, §§ 15–17, eff Nov 1, 2000, L 2003, ch 172, § 1, eff July 22, 2003, L 2006, ch 281, § 1, eff July 26, 2006, L 1996, ch 354, § 3, eff Nov 1, 1996, L 2006, ch 578, § 2, eff Nov 1, 2006, L 2007, ch 210, § 4, eff Feb 11, 2008, L 2007, ch 235, § 1, eff Oct 16, 2007, L 2010, ch 61, § 1, eff April 28, 2010, L 2012, ch 330, § 1, eff Aug 1, 2012, L 2013, ch 1, § 46, eff March 16, 2013, L 2013, ch 57, § 1 (Part FF), eff March 29, 2013, deemed in full force and eff March 16, 2013, L 2013, ch 98, § 2, eff July 5, 2013, L 2014, ch 55, § 10 (Part EE), eff April 1, 2014.

§ 265.25. Certain wounds to be reported

Every case of a bullet wound, gunshot wound, powder burn or any other injury arising from or caused by the discharge of a gun or firearm, and every case of a wound which is likely to or may result in death and is actually or apparently inflicted by a knife, icepick or other sharp or pointed instrument, shall be reported at once to the police authorities of the city, town or village where the person reporting is located by: (a) the physician attending or treating the case; or (b) the manager, superintendent or other person in charge, whenever such case is treated in a hospital, sanitarium or other institution. Failure to make such report is a class A misdemeanor. This subdivision shall not apply to such wounds, burns or injuries received by a member of the armed forces of the United States or the state of New York while engaged in the actual performance of duty.

HISTORY: Add, L 1965, ch 1030, § 1, eff Sept 1, 1967, with substance derived from § 1902(4).

§ 265.26. Burn injury and wounds to be reported

Every case of a burn injury or wound, where the victim sustained second or third degree burns to five percent or more of the body and/or any burns to the upper respiratory tract or laryngeal edema due to the inhalation of super-heated air, and every case of a burn injury or wound which is likely to or may result in death, shall be reported at once to the office of fire prevention and control. The state fire administrator shall accept the report and notify the proper investigatory agency. A written report shall also be provided to the office of fire prevention and control within seventy-two hours. The report shall be made by (a) the physician attending or treating the case; or (b) the manager, superintendent or other person in charge, whenever such case is treated in a hospital, sanitarium, institution or other medical facility.

The intentional failure to make such report is a class A misdemeanor.

HISTORY: Add, L 1985, ch 201, § 1, eff Nov 1, 1985.

§ 265.30. Certain convictions to be reported

Every conviction under this article or section 400.00, of a person who is not a citizen of the United States, shall be certified to the proper officer of the United States government by the district attorney of the county in which such conviction was had.

HISTORY: Add, L 1965, ch 1030, § 1, eff Sept 1, 1967, with substance derived from § 1902(5).

§ 265.35. Prohibited use of weapons

1. Any person hunting with a dangerous weapon in any county wholly embraced within the territorial limits of a city is guilty of a class A misdemeanor.

2. Any person who wilfully discharges a loaded firearm or any other gun, the propelling force of which is gunpowder, at an aircraft while such aircraft is in motion in the air or in motion or stationary upon the ground, or at any railway or street railroad train as defined by the public service law, or at a locomotive, car, bus or vehicle standing or moving upon such railway, railroad or public highway, is guilty of a class D felony if thereby the safety of any person is endangered, and in every other case, of a class E felony.

3. Any person who, otherwise than in self defense or in the discharge of official duty, (a) wilfully discharges any species of firearms, air-gun or other weapon, or throws any other deadly missile, either in a public place, or in any place where there is any person to be endangered thereby, or, in Putnam county, within one-quarter mile of any occupied school building other than under supervised instruction by properly authorized instructors although no injury to any person ensues; (b) intentionally, without malice, points or aims any firearm or any other gun, the propelling force of which is gunpowder, at or toward any other person; (c) discharges, without injury to any other person, firearms or any other guns, the propelling force of which is gunpowder, while intentionally without malice, aimed at or toward any person; or (d) maims or injures any other person by the discharge of any firearm or any other gun, the propelling force of which is gunpowder, pointed or aimed intentionally, but without malice, at any such person, is guilty of a class A misdemeanor.

HISTORY: Add, L 1965, ch 1030, § 1, eff Sept 1, 1967, with substance derived from § 1904. Sub 1, formerly sub 2, renumbered sub 1, L 1974, ch 1041, § 8, eff Sept 1, 1974. Former sub 1, repealed, L 1974, ch 1041, § 7, eff Sept 1, 1974. Sub 2, formerly sub 3, renumbered sub 2, L 1974, ch 1041, § 8, eff Sept 1, 1974. Former sub 2, renumbered sub 1, L 1974, ch 1041, § 8, eff Sept 1, 1974. Sub 3, formerly sub 4, renumbered sub 3, L 1974, ch 1041, § 8, eff Sept 1, 1974. Former sub 3, renumbered sub 2, L 1974, ch 1041, § 8, eff Sept 1, 1974. Sub 4, renumbered sub 3, L 1974, ch 1041, § 8, eff Sept 1, 1974.

§ 265.36. Unlawful possession of a large capacity ammunition feeding device

It shall be unlawful for a person to knowingly possess a large capacity ammunition feeding device manufactured before September thirteenth, nineteen hundred ninety-four, and if such person lawfully possessed such large capacity feeding device before the effective date of the chapter of the laws of two thousand thirteen which added this section, that has a capacity of, or that can be readily restored or converted to accept, more than ten rounds of ammunition.

An individual who has a reasonable belief that such device is of such a character that it may lawfully be possessed and who surrenders or lawfully disposes of such device within thirty days of being notified by law enforcement or county licensing officials that such possession is unlawful shall not be guilty of this offense. It shall be a rebuttable presumption that such person knows that such large capacity ammunition feeding device may not be lawfully possessed if he or she has been contacted by law enforcement or county licensing officials and informed that such device may not be lawfully possessed.

Unlawful possession of a large capacity ammunition feeding device is a class A misdemeanor.

HISTORY: Add, L 2013, ch 1, § 46-a, eff March 16, 2013.

§ 265.37. Unlawful possession of certain ammunition feeding devices

It shall be unlawful for a person to knowingly possess an ammunition feeding device where such device contains more than seven rounds of ammunition.

If such device containing more than seven rounds of ammunition is possessed within the home of the possessor, the person so possessing the device shall, for a first offense, be guilty of a violation and subject to a fine of two hundred dollars, and for each subsequent offense, be guilty of a class B misdemeanor and subject to a fine of two hundred dollars and a term of up to three months imprisonment.

If such device containing more than seven rounds of ammunition is possessed in any location other than the home of the possessor, the person so possessing the device shall, for a first offense, be guilty of a class B misdemeanor and subject to a fine of two hundred dollars and a term of up to six months imprisonment, and for each subsequent offense, be guilty of a class A misdemeanor.

HISTORY: Add, L 2013, ch 1, § 46-a, eff March 16, 2013; amd, L 2013, ch 57, § 2 (Part FF), eff March 29, 2013.

§ 265.40. Purchase of rifles and/or shotguns in contiguous states

Definitions. As used in this act:

1. "Contiguous state" shall mean any state having any portion of its border in common with a portion of the border of the state of New York;

2. All other terms herein shall be given the meaning prescribed in Public Law 90-618 known as the "Gun Control Act of 1968" (18 U.S.C. 921).

It shall be lawful for a person or persons residing in this state, to purchase or otherwise obtain a rifle and/or shotgun in a contiguous state, and to receive or transport such rifle and/or shotgun into this state; provided, however, such person is otherwise eligible to possess a rifle and/or shotgun under the laws of this state.

HISTORY: Add, L 1971, ch 900, § 1, eff June 25, 1971.

§ 265.45. Safe storage of rifles, shotguns, and firearms

No person who owns or is custodian of a rifle, shotgun or firearm who resides with an individual who such person knows or has reason to know is prohibited from possessing a firearm pursuant to 18 U.S.C. § 922(g) (1), (4), (8) or (9) shall store or otherwise leave such rifle, shotgun or firearm out of his or her immediate possession or control without having first securely locked such rifle, shotgun or firearm in an appropriate safe storage depository or rendered it incapable of being fired by use of a gun locking device appropriate to that weapon. For purposes of this section "safe storage depository" shall mean a safe or other secure container which, when locked, is incapable of being opened without the key, combination or other unlocking mechanism and is capable of preventing an unauthorized person from obtaining access to and possession of the weapon contained therein. With respect to a person who is prohibited from possessing a firearm pursuant to 18 USC § 922(g)(9), for purposes of this section, this section applies only if such person has been convicted of a crime included in subdivision one of section 370.15 of the criminal procedure law and such gun is possessed within five years from the later of the date of conviction or completion of sentence. Nothing in this section shall be deemed to affect, impair or supersede any special or local act relating to the safe storage of rifles, shotguns or firearms which impose additional requirements on the owner or custodian of such weapons.

A violation of this section shall constitute a class A misdemeanor.

HISTORY: Add, L 2013, ch 1, § 47, eff March 16, 2013; amd, L 2013, ch 57, § 3 (Part FF), eff March 29, 2013.

ARTICLE 270   OTHER OFFENSES RELATING TO PUBLIC SAFETY

§ 270.00.	Unlawfully dealing with fireworks and dangerous fireworks
§ 270.05.	Unlawfully possessing or selling noxious material
§ 270.10.	Creating a hazard
§ 270.15.	Unlawfully refusing to yield a party line
§ 270.20.	Unlawful wearing of a body vest
§ 270.25.	Unlawful fleeing a police officer in a motor vehicle in the third degree
§ 270.30.	Unlawful fleeing a police officer in a motor vehicle in the second degree
§ 270.35.	Unlawful fleeing a police officer in a motor vehicle in the first degree

HISTORY: Add, L 1965, ch 1030, § 1, eff Sept 1, 1967.

§ 270.00. Unlawfully dealing with fireworks and dangerous fireworks

1. Definition of "fireworks" and "dangerous fireworks". The term "fireworks," as used in this section, is defined and declared to be and to include any blank cartridge, blank cartridge pistol, or toy cannon in which explosives are used, firecrackers, sparklers or other combustible or explosive of like construction, or any preparation containing any explosive or inflammable compound or any tablets or other device commonly used and sold as fireworks containing nitrates, chlorates, oxalates, sulphides of lead, barium, antimony, arsenic, mercury, nitroglycerine, phosphorus or any compound containing any of the same or other explosives, or any substance or combination of substances, or article prepared for the purpose of producing a visible or an audible effect by combustion, explosion, deflagration or detonation, or other device containing any explosive substance and the term "dangerous fireworks" means any fireworks capable of causing serious physical injury and which are: firecrackers containing more than fifty milligrams of any explosive substance, torpedoes, skyrockets and rockets including all devices which employ any combustible or explosive substance and which rise in the air during discharge, Roman candles, bombs, sparklers more than ten inches in length or one-fourth of one inch in diameter, or chasers including all devices which dart or travel about the surface of the ground during discharge. "Fireworks" and "dangerous fireworks" shall not be deemed to include (1) flares of the type used by railroads or any warning lights commonly known as red flares, or marine distress signals of a type approved by the United States coast guard or (2) toy pistols, toy canes, toy guns or other devices in which paper caps containing twenty-five hundredths grains or less of explosive compound are used, providing they are so constructed that the hand cannot come in contact with the cap when in place for use, and toy pistol paper caps which contain less than twenty-hundredths grains of explosive mixture,

the sale and use of which shall be permitted at all times, or (3) bank security devices which contain not more than fifty grams of any compound or substance or any combination thereof, together with an igniter not exceeding 0.2 gram, capable of producing a lachrymating and/or visible or audible effect, where such device is stored or used only by banks, national banking associations, trust companies, savings banks, savings and loan associations, industrial banks, or credit unions, or by any manufacturer, wholesaler, dealer, jobber or common carrier for such devices and where the total storage on any one premises does not exceed one hundred devices.

2. Offense.

(a) Except as herein otherwise provided, or except where a permit is obtained pursuant to section 405.00;

(i) any person who shall offer or expose for sale, sell or furnish, any fireworks or dangerous fireworks is guilty of a class B misdemeanor;

(ii) any person who shall offer or expose for sale, sell or furnish any fireworks or dangerous fireworks valued at five hundred dollars or more shall be guilty of a class A misdemeanor;

(b) (i) Except as herein otherwise stated, or except where a permit is obtained pursuant to section 405.00, any person who shall possess, use, explode or cause to explode any fireworks or dangerous fireworks is guilty of a violation.

(ii) A person who shall offer or expose for sale, sell or furnish, any dangerous fireworks to any person who is under the age of eighteen is guilty of a class A misdemeanor.

(iii) A person who has previously been convicted of a violation of subparagraph (ii) of this paragraph within the preceding five years and who shall offer or expose for sale, sell or furnish, any dangerous fireworks to any person who is under the age of eighteen, shall be guilty of a class E felony.

(c) Possession of fireworks or dangerous fireworks valued at fifty dollars or more shall be a presumption that such fireworks were intended to be offered or exposed for sale.

3. The provisions of this section shall not apply to articles of the kind and nature herein mentioned, while in possession of railroads and transportation agencies for the purpose of transportation to points without the state, the shipment of which is not prohibited by the interstate commerce commission regulations as formulated and published from time to time, unless the same be held voluntarily by such railroads or transportation companies as warehousemen for delivery to points within the state; provided, that none of the provisions of this section shall apply to signaling devices used by railroad companies or motor vehicles referred to in subdivision seventeen of section three hundred seventy-five of the vehicle and traffic law, or to high explosives for blasting or similar purposes; provided that none of the provisions of this section shall apply to fireworks or dangerous fireworks and the use thereof by the army and navy departments of the state and federal government; nor shall anything in this act contained be construed to prohibit any manufacturer, wholesaler, dealer or jobber from manufacturing, possessing or selling at wholesale such fireworks or dangerous fireworks to municipalities, religious or civic organizations, fair associations, amusement parks, or other organizations or groups of individuals authorized to possess and use fireworks or dangerous fireworks under this act, or the sale or use of blank cartridges for a show or theatre, or for signal purposes in athletic sports, or for dog trials or dog training, or the use, or the storage, transportation or sale for use of fireworks or dangerous fireworks in the preparation for or in connection with television broadcasts; nor shall anything in this act contained be construed to prohibit the manufacture of fireworks or dangerous fireworks,

nor the sale of any kind of fireworks or dangerous fireworks, provided the same are to be shipped directly out of the state.

4. Sales of ammunition not prohibited. Nothing contained in this section shall be construed to prevent, or interfere in any way with, the sale of ammunition for revolvers or pistols of any kind, or for rifles, shot guns, or other arms, belonging or which may belong to any persons whether as sporting or hunting weapons or for the purpose of protection to them in their homes, or, as they may go abroad; and manufacturers are authorized to continue to manufacture, and wholesalers and dealers to continue to deal in and freely to sell ammunition to all such persons for such purposes.

5. Notwithstanding the provisions of subdivision four of this section, it shall be unlawful for any dealer in firearms to sell any ammunition designed exclusively for use in a pistol or revolver to any person, not authorized to possess a pistol or revolver. The violation of this section shall constitute a class B misdemeanor.

> **HISTORY:** Add, L 1965, ch 1030, § 1, with substance derived from § 1894-a; amd, L 1997, ch 180, § 1, eff Nov 1, 1997. Section heading, amd, L 1997, ch 180, § 1, eff Nov 1, 1997. Sub 1, amd, L 1978, ch 286, § 1, L 1997, ch 180, § 1, eff Nov 1, 1997. Sub 2, amd, L 1975, ch 840, § 1, L 1997, ch 180, § 1, eff Nov 1, 1997. Sub 2, par (a), formerly sub 2, so lettered and amd, L 1975, ch 840, § 1, eff Sept 1, 1975. Sub 2, par (a), opening par, formerly part of entire sub 2, par (a), so designated sub 2, par (a), opening and amd, L 1997, ch 180, § 1, eff Nov 1, 1997. Sub 2, par (a), subpar (i), formerly part of entire sub 2, par (a), so designated sub 2, par (a), subpar (i) and amd, L 1997, ch 180, § 1, eff Nov 1, 1997. Sub 2, par (a), subpar (ii), add, L 1997, ch 180, § 1, eff Nov 1, 1997. Sub 2, par (b), add, L 1975, ch 840, § 1, eff Sept 1, 1975. Sub 2, par (b), subpar (i), amd, L 1997, ch 180, § 1, eff Nov 1, 1997. Sub 2, par (b), subpar (ii), add, L 1997, ch 180, § 1, eff Nov 1, 1997. Former sub 2, par (b), subpar (ii), redesignated sub 2, par (c), L 1997, ch 180, § 1, eff Nov 1, 1997. Sub 2, par (b), subpar (iii), add, L 1997, ch 180, § 1, eff Nov 1, 1997. Sub 2, par (c), formerly sub 2, par (b), subpar (ii), so designated sub 2, par (c), L 1997, ch 180, § 1, eff Nov 1, 1997. Sub 3, amd, L 1967, ch 791, § 1, L 1986, ch 166, § 1, L 1997, ch 180, § 1, eff Nov 1, 1997. Sub 5, add, L 1969, ch 709, § 1, eff Sept 1, 1969.

§ 270.05. Unlawfully possessing or selling noxious material

1. As used in this section, "noxious material" means any container which contains any drug or other substance capable of generating offensive, noxious or suffocating fumes, gases or vapors, or capable of immobilizing a person.

2. A person is guilty of unlawfully possessing noxious material when he possesses such material under circumstances evincing an intent to use it or to cause it to be used to inflict physical injury upon or to cause annoyance to a person, or to damage property of another, or to disturb the public peace.

3. Possession of noxious material is presumptive evidence of intent to use it or cause it to be used in violation of this section.

4. Bank security devices not prohibited. Notwithstanding the provisions of subdivision one of this section, it shall not be unlawful for any bank, national banking association, trust company, savings bank, savings and loan association, industrial bank, or credit union to store, possess, transport, use or cause to discharge any bank security device as described in subdivision one of section 270.00 of this chapter; nor shall it be unlawful for any manufacturer, wholesaler, dealer, jobber or common carrier to manufacture, store, possess, transport, or sell such a device to banks, national banking associations, trust companies, savings banks, savings and loan associations, industrial banks or credit unions.

5. Self-defense spray devices not prohibited. Notwithstanding the provisions of subdivisions two and three of this section, it shall not be unlawful for a person eighteen years of age or older

to possess a self-defense spray device as defined in paragraph fourteen of subdivision a of section 265.20 of this chapter in accordance with the provisions set forth therein.

6. A person is guilty of unlawfully selling a noxious material when he or she sells a self-defense spray device as defined in paragraph fourteen of subdivision a of section 265.20 of this chapter and such sale was not authorized in accordance with the provisions of paragraph fifteen of subdivision a of section 265.20 of this chapter.

Unlawfully possessing or selling noxious material is a class B misdemeanor.

HISTORY: Add, L 1965, ch 1030, § 1, eff Sept 1, 1967, with substance derived from § 726. Section heading, amd, L 1996, ch 354, § 4, eff Nov 1, 1996. Sub 1, amd, L 1969, ch 452, § 2, eff Sept 1, 1969. Sub 4, add, L 1978, ch 286, § 2, eff June 19, 1978. Sub 5, add, L 1996, ch 354, § 4, eff Nov 1, 1996. Sub 6, add, L 1996, ch 354, § 4, eff Nov 1, 1996. Closing par, amd, L 1996, ch 354, § 4, eff Nov 1, 1996.

§ 270.10. Creating a hazard

A person is guilty of creating a hazard when:

1. Having discarded in any place where it might attract children, a container which has a compartment of more than one and one-half cubic feet capacity and a door or lid which locks or fastens automatically when closed and which cannot easily be opened from the inside, he fails to remove the door, lid, locking or fastening device; or

2. Being the owner or otherwise having possession of property upon which an abandoned well or cesspool is located, he fails to cover the same with suitable protective construction.

Creating a hazard is a class B misdemeanor.

HISTORY: Add, L 1965, ch 1030, § 1, eff Sept 1, 1967, with substance derived from §§ 1920, 1923.

§ 270.15. Unlawfully refusing to yield a party line

1. As used in this section:

(a) "Party line" means a subscriber's line telephone circuit, consisting of two or more main telephone stations connected therewith, each station with a distinctive ring or telephone number.

(b) "Emergency call" means a telephone call to a police or fire department, or for medical aid or ambulance service, necessitated by a situation in which human life or property is in jeopardy and prompt summoning of aid is essential.

2. A person is guilty of unlawfully refusing to yield a party line when, being informed that a party line is needed for an emergency call, he refuses immediately to relinquish such line.

Unlawfully refusing to yield a party line is a class B misdemeanor.

HISTORY: Add, L 1965, ch 1030, § 1, eff Sept 1, 1967, with substance derived from § 1424-a.

§ 270.20. Unlawful wearing of a body vest

1. A person is guilty of the unlawful wearing of a body vest when acting either alone or with one or more other persons he commits any violent felony offense defined in section 70.02 while possessing a firearm, rifle or shotgun and in the course of and in furtherance of such crime he wears a body vest.

2. For the purposes of this section a "body vest" means a bullet-resistant soft body armor

providing, as a minimum standard, the level of protection known as threat level I which shall mean at least seven layers of bullet-resistant material providing protection from three shots of one hundred fifty-eight grain lead ammunition fired from a.38 calibre handgun at a velocity of eight hundred fifty feet per second.

The unlawful wearing of a body vest is a class E felony.

> **HISTORY:** Add, L 1984, ch 56, § 1, eff Nov 1, 1984. Sub 1, amd, L 2001, ch 317, § 1, eff Nov 1, 2001.

§ 270.25. Unlawful fleeing a police officer in a motor vehicle in the third degree

A person is guilty of unlawful fleeing a police officer in a motor vehicle in the third degree when, knowing that he or she has been directed to stop his or her motor vehicle by a uniformed police officer or a marked police vehicle by the activation of either the lights or the lights and siren of such vehicle, he or she thereafter attempts to flee such officer or such vehicle by driving at speeds which equal or exceed twenty-five miles per hour above the speed limit or engaging in reckless driving as defined by section twelve hundred twelve of the vehicle and traffic law.

Unlawful fleeing a police officer in a motor vehicle in the third degree is a class A misdemeanor.

> **HISTORY:** Add, L 2006, ch 738, § 2, eff Nov 1, 2006.

§ 270.30. Unlawful fleeing a police officer in a motor vehicle in the second degree

A person is guilty of unlawful fleeing a police officer in a motor vehicle in the second degree when he or she commits the offense of unlawful fleeing a police officer in a motor vehicle in the third degree, as defined in section 270.25 of this article, and as a result of such conduct a police officer or a third person suffers serious physical injury.

Unlawful fleeing a police officer in a motor vehicle in the second degree is a class E felony.

> **HISTORY:** Add, L 2006, ch 738, § 2, eff Nov 1, 2006.

§ 270.35. Unlawful fleeing a police officer in a motor vehicle in the first degree

A person is guilty of unlawful fleeing a police officer in a motor vehicle in the first degree when he or she commits the offense of unlawful fleeing a police officer in a motor vehicle in the third degree, as defined in section 270.25 of this article, and as a result of such conduct a police officer or a third person is killed.

Unlawful fleeing a police officer in a motor vehicle in the first degree is a class D felony.

> **HISTORY:** Add, L 2006, ch 738, § 2, eff Nov 1, 2006.

ARTICLE 275   OFFENSES RELATING TO UNAUTHORIZED RECORDING

§ 275.00.	**Definitions**
§ 275.05.	**Manufacture of unauthorized recordings in the second degree**
§ 275.10.	**Manufacture of unauthorized recordings in the first degree**
§ 275.15.	**Manufacture or sale of an unauthorized recording of a performance in the second degree**
§ 275.20.	**Manufacture or sale of an unauthorized recording of a performance in the first degree**
§ 275.25.	**Advertisement or sale of unauthorized recordings in the second degree**
§ 275.30.	**Advertisement or sale of unauthorized recordings in the first degree**
§ 275.32.	**Unlawful operation of a recording device in a motion picture or live theater in the third degree**
§ 275.33.	**Unlawful operation of a recording device in a motion picture or live theater in the second degree**

HISTORY: Add, L 1990, ch 460, § 1, eff Nov 1, 1990. Former Art 275, add, L 1978, ch 445, § 2; repealed, L 1990, ch 460, § 1, eff Nov 1, 1990.

§ 275.00. Definitions

The following definitions are applicable to this article:

1. "Person" means any individual, firm, partnership, corporation or association.

2. "Owner" means (a) the person who owns, or has the exclusive license in the United States to reproduce or the exclusive license in the United States to distribute to the public copies of the sounds fixed in a master phonograph record, master disc, master tape, master film or any other device used for reproducing sounds on phonograph records, discs, tapes, films, videocassettes, or any other articles upon which sound is recorded, and from which the transferred recorded sounds are directly derived; or (b) the person who owns the rights to record or authorize the recording of a live performance.

3. "Fixed" means embodied in a recording by or under the authority of the author, so that the matter embodied is sufficiently permanent or stable to permit it to be perceived, reproduced, or otherwise communicated for a period of more than transitory duration.

4. "Performer" means the person or persons appearing in a performance.

5. "Performance" means, whether live before an audience or transmitted by wire or through the air by radio or television, a recitation, rendering, or playing of a series of images, musical, spoken, or other sounds, or a combination of images and sounds, in an audible sequence.

6. "Recording" means an original phonograph record, disc, tape, audio or video cassette, wire, film, hard drive, flash drive, memory card or other data storage device or any other medium on which such sounds, images, or both sounds and images are or can be recorded or otherwise stored, or a copy or reproduction that duplicates in whole or in part the original.

HISTORY: Add, L 1990, ch 460, § 1, eff Nov 1, 1990; amd, L 1995, ch 419, § 1, eff Nov 1, 1995, L 2011, ch 313, § 1, eff Nov 1, 2011.

§ 275.05. Manufacture of unauthorized recordings in the second degree

A person is guilty of the manufacture of unauthorized recordings in the second degree when such person:

1. knowingly, and without the consent of the owner, transfers or causes to be transferred any sound recording, with the intent to rent or sell, or cause to be rented or sold for profit, or used to promote the sale of any product, such article to which such recording was transferred, or

2. transports within this state, for commercial advantage or private financial gain, a recording, knowing that the sounds have been reproduced or transferred without the consent of the owner; provided, however, that this section shall only apply to sound recordings initially fixed prior to February fifteenth, nineteen hundred seventy-two.

Manufacture of unauthorized recordings in the second degree is a class A misdemeanor.

HISTORY: Add, L 1990, ch 460, § 1, eff Nov 1, 1990. Former § 275.05, add, L 1978, ch 445,

§ 2; repealed, L 1990, ch 460, § 1, eff Nov 1, 1990. Sub 2, amd, L 1995, ch 419, § 2, eff Nov 1, 1995.

§ 275.10. Manufacture of unauthorized recordings in the first degree

A person is guilty of manufacture of unauthorized recordings in the first degree when he commits the crime of manufacture of unauthorized recordings in the second degree as defined in section 275.05 of this article and either:

1. has previously been convicted of that crime within the past five years; or

2. commits that crime by the manufacture of one thousand unauthorized sound recordings; provided, however, that this section shall only apply to sound recordings initially fixed prior to February fifteenth, nineteen hundred seventy-two.

Manufacture of unauthorized recordings in the first degree is a class E felony.

HISTORY: Add, L 1990, ch 460, § 1, eff Nov 1, 1990. Former § 275.10, add, L 1978, ch 445, § 2; repealed, L 1990, ch 460, § 1, eff Nov 1, 1990. Sub 2, amd, L 1995, ch 419, § 3, eff Nov 1, 1995.

§ 275.15. Manufacture or sale of an unauthorized recording of a performance in the second degree

A person commits the crime of manufacture or sale of an unauthorized recording of a performance in the second degree when he knowingly, and without the consent of the performer, records or fixes or causes to be recorded or fixed on a recording a performance, with the intent to sell or rent or cause to be sold or rented such recording, or with the intent to use such recording to promote the sale of any product; or when he knowingly possesses, transports or advertises, for purposes of sale, resale or rental or sells, resells, rents or offers for rental, sale or resale, any recording that the person knows has been produced in violation of this section.

Manufacture or sale of an unauthorized recording of a performance in the second degree is a class A misdemeanor.

HISTORY: Add, L 1990, ch 460, § 1; amd, L 1995, ch 419, § 4, eff Nov 1, 1995. Former § 275.15, add, L 1978, ch 445, § 2; repealed, L 1990, ch 460, § 1, eff Nov 1, 1990. Section heading, amd, L 1995, ch 419, § 4, eff Nov 1, 1995. First undesignated par, amd, L 1995, ch 419, § 4, eff Nov 1, 1995. Second undesignated par, amd, L 1995, ch 419, § 4, eff Nov 1, 1995.

§ 275.20. Manufacture or sale of an unauthorized recording of a performance in the first degree

A person commits the crime of unauthorized recording of a performance in the first degree when he commits the crime of manufacture or sale of an unauthorized recording of a performance in the second degree as defined in section 275.15 of this article and either:

1. such person has previously been convicted of that crime within the past five years; or

2. commission of that crime involves at least one thousand unauthorized sound recordings or at least one hundred unauthorized audio-visual recordings.

Manufacture or sale of an unauthorized recording of a performance in the first degree is a class E felony.

HISTORY: Add, L 1990, ch 460, § 1; amd, L 1995, ch 419, § 5, eff Nov 1, 1995. Former § 275.20, add, L 1978, ch 445, § 2; repealed, L 1990, ch 460, § 1, eff Nov 1, 1990. Section heading, amd, L 1995, ch 419, § 5, eff Nov 1, 1995. Opening par, amd, L 1995, ch 419, § 5, eff Nov 1, 1995. Closing par, amd, L 1995, ch 419, § 5, eff Nov 1, 1995.

§ 275.25. Advertisement or sale of unauthorized recordings in the second degree

A person is guilty of the advertisement or sale of unauthorized recordings in the second degree when such person knowingly advertises, offers for sale, resale, or rental, or sells, resells, rents, distributes or possesses for any such purposes, any recording that has been produced or transferred without the consent of the owner; provided, however, that this section shall only apply to sound recordings initially fixed prior to February fifteenth, nineteen hundred seventy-two.

Advertisement or sale of unauthorized recordings in the second degree is a class A misdemeanor.

HISTORY: Add, L 1990, ch 460, § 1, eff Nov 1, 1990. Former § 275.25, add, L 1978, ch 445, § 2; repealed, L 1990, ch 460, § 1, eff Nov 1, 1990. First undesignated par, amd, L 1995, ch 419, § 6, eff Nov 1, 1995.

§ 275.30. Advertisement or sale of unauthorized recordings in the first degree

A person is guilty of the advertisement or sale of unauthorized recordings in the first degree when such person commits the crime of advertisement or sale of unauthorized recordings in the second degree as defined in section 275.25 of this article and either:

1. such person has previously been convicted of that crime within the past five years; or

2. commission of that crime involves at least one thousand unauthorized sound recordings or at least one hundred unauthorized audiovisual recordings.

Advertisement and sale of unauthorized recordings in the first degree is a class E felony.

HISTORY: Add, L 1990, ch 460, § 1, eff Nov 1, 1990.

§ 275.32. Unlawful operation of a recording device in a motion picture or live theater in the third degree

1. A person is guilty of unlawful operation of a recording device in a motion picture or live theater in the third degree when without authority or written permission from the operator of a motion picture theater or live theater, the person operates a recording device in such theater.

2. As used in this section

(a) "recording device" means a photographic or video camera, or any audiovisual recording function of any device used for recording the sound or picture of a motion picture;

(b) "operator" means the owner or lessee of a motion picture theater or live theater or the authorized agent or employee of such owner or lessee;

(c) "motion picture theater" means a theater, screening room, auditorium or other venue that is being utilized primarily for the exhibition of a motion picture at the time of the offense; and

(d) "live theater" means a concert hall, recital hall, theater, or auditorium in which a presentation is rendered, consisting in whole or in part of a musical, dramatic, dance, or other stage rendition by one or more professional performers who appear in person in the immediate presence of their audiences, and admission to which is limited by its operator to persons holding an admission ticket or who have other authority or written permission to enter. Live theater shall not mean or include a musical, dramatic, dance, or other stage rendition that is performed by students enrolled in a school or college or as a part of a children's camp or similar program.

Unlawful operation of a recording device in a motion picture or live theater in the third degree is a violation.

HISTORY: Add, L 1994, ch 374, § 2, eff Nov 1, 1994. Amd, L 2008, ch 639, § 3, eff Dec 6, 2008. Section heading amd, L 2008, ch 639, § 3, eff Dec 6, 2008. Sub 1, amd, L 2008, ch 639, § 3, eff Dec 6, 2008. Sub 2, par (a), formerly part of sub 2, so designated sub 2, par (a) and amd, L 2008, ch 639, § 3, eff Dec 6, 2008. Sub 2, par (b), add, L 2008, ch 639, § 3, eff Dec 6, 2008. Sub 2, par (c), formerly part of sub 2, so designated sub 2, par (c) and amd, L 2008, ch 639, § 3, eff Dec 6,

2008. Sub 2, par (d), add, L 2008, ch 639, § 3, eff Dec 6, 2008. Closing par, amd, L 2008, ch 639, § 3, eff Dec 6, 2008.

§ 275.33. Unlawful operation of a recording device in a motion picture or live theater in the second degree

A person is guilty of unlawful operation of a recording device in a motion picture or live theater in the second degree when he or she violates section 275.32 of this article:

1. for financial profit or commercial purposes; or

2. in circumstances where the material recorded is fifteen or more minutes, or all or a substantial portion, of the motion picture or live theatrical performance; or

3. in circumstances where such person has previously been convicted within the past five years of violating section 275.32 or 275.34 of this article or this section.

Unlawful operation of a recording device in a motion picture or live theater in the second degree is a class A misdemeanor.

HISTORY: Add, L 2008, ch 639, § 4, eff Dec 6, 2008.

§ 275.34. Unlawful operation of a recording device in a motion picture or live theater in the first degree

A person is guilty of unlawful operation of a recording device in a motion picture or live theater in the first degree when he or she commits the crime of unlawful operation of a recording device in a motion picture or live theater in the second degree as defined in section 275.33 of this article and has previously been convicted within the past ten years of violating section 275.33 of this article or this section.

Unlawful operation of a recording device in a motion picture or live theatre in the first degree is a class E felony.

HISTORY: Add, L 2008, ch 639, § 4, eff Dec 6, 2008.

§ 275.35. Failure to disclose the origin of a recording in the second degree

A person is guilty of failure to disclose the origin of a recording in the second degree when, for commercial advantage or private financial gain, he knowingly advertises or offers for sale, resale, or rental, or sells, resells, or rents, or possesses for such purposes, a recording the cover, box, jacket or label [of which]* does not clearly and conspicuously disclose the actual name and address of the manufacturer or the name of the performer or principal artist. The omission of the actual name and address of the manufacturer, or the omission of the name of the performer or principal artist, or the omission of both, shall constitute the failure to disclose the origin of a recording.

Failure to disclose the origin of a recording in the second degree is a class A misdemeanor.

HISTORY: Add, L 1990, ch 460, § 1, eff Nov 1, 1990. First undesignated par, amd, L 1995, ch 419, § 7, eff Nov 1, 1995.

§ 275.40. Failure to disclose the origin of a recording in the first degree

A person is guilty of failure to disclose the origin of a recording in the first degree when such person commits the crime of failure to disclose the origin of a recording in the second degree as defined in section 275.35 of this article and either:

1. such person has been convicted of failure to disclose the origin of a recording in the first or second degree within the past five years; or

---

* The bracketed words have been inserted by the Publisher.

2. commission of the crime involves at least one hundred unauthorized sound recordings or at least one hundred unauthorized audiovisual recordings.

Failure to disclose the origin of a recording in the first degree is a class E felony.

HISTORY: Add, L 1990, ch 460, § 1, eff Nov 1, 1990. Amd, L 2006, ch 682, § 1, eff Nov 1, 2006. Opening par, amd, L 2006, ch 682, § 1, eff Nov 1, 2006. Sub 1, add, L 2006, ch 682, § 1, eff Nov 1, 2006. Sub 2, add, L 2006, ch 682, § 1, eff Nov 1, 2006.

§ 275.45. Limitations of application

1. This article does not apply to:

(a) any broadcaster who, in connection with or as part of a radio, television, or cable broadcast transmission, or for the purpose of archival preservation, transfers any such recorded sounds or images; or

(b) any person who transfers such sounds or images for personal use, and without profit for such transfer.

2. This article shall neither enlarge nor diminish the rights of parties in civil litigation.

HISTORY: Add, L 1990, ch 460, § 1, eff Nov 1, 1990.

PART FOUR Administrative Provisions

Title W
**Provisions Relating to Firearms, Fireworks, Pornography Equipment and Vehicles Used
in the Transportation of Gambling Records**

Title X
Organized Crime Control Act

Title Y
Hate Crimes Act of 2000

Title Y-1
[Terrorism]*

Title Y-2
Corrupting the Government

Title Z
Laws Repealed; Time of Taking Effect

HISTORY: Add, L 1965, ch 1030, § 1, eff Sept 1, 1967.

---

* The bracketed word has been inserted by the Publisher.

TITLE W   Provisions Relating to Firearms, Fireworks, Pornography Equipment and Vehicles Used in the Transportation of Gambling Records

ARTICLE 400
LICENSING AND OTHER PROVISIONS RELATING TO FIREARMS

ARTICLE 405
LICENSING AND OTHER PROVISIONS RELATING TO FIREWORKS

ARTICLE 410
SEIZURE AND FORFEITURE OF EQUIPMENT USED IN PROMOTING PORNOGRAPHY

ARTICLE 415
SEIZURE AND FORFEITURE OF VEHICLES, VESSELS AND AIRCRAFT USED TO TRANSPORT OR CONCEAL GAMBLING RECORDS

ARTICLE 420
SEIZURE AND DESTRUCTION OF UNAUTHORIZED RECORDINGS OF SOUND AND FORFEITURE OF EQUIPMENT USED IN THE PRODUCTION THEREOF

ARTICLE 450
DISPOSAL OF STOLEN PROPERTY

HISTORY: Add, L 1965, ch 1030, § 1, eff Sept 1, 1967. Title heading, amd, L 1969, ch 920, § 1, eff Sept 1, 1969.

ARTICLE 400   LICENSING AND OTHER PROVISIONS RELATING TO FIREARMS

HISTORY: Add, L 1965, ch 1030, § 1, eff Sept 1, 1967.

§ 400.00. Licenses to carry, possess, repair and dispose of firearms

1. Eligibility. No license shall be issued or renewed pursuant to this section except by the licensing officer, and then only after investigation and finding that all statements in a proper application for a license are true. No license shall be issued or renewed except for an applicant (a) twenty-one years of age or older, provided, however, that where such applicant has been honorably discharged from the United States army, navy, marine corps, air force or coast guard, or the national guard of the state of New York, no such age restriction shall apply; (b) of good moral character; (c) who has not been convicted anywhere of a felony or a serious offense; (d) who is not a fugitive from justice; (e) who is not an unlawful user of or addicted to any controlled substance as defined in section 21 U.S.C. 802; (f) who being an alien (i) is not illegally or unlawfully in the United States or (ii) has not been admitted to the United States under a nonimmigrant visa subject to the exception in 18 U.S.C. 922(y)(2); (g) who has not been discharged from the Armed Forces under dishonorable conditions; (h) who, having been a citizen of the United States, has not renounced his or her citizenship; (i) who has stated whether he or she has ever suffered any mental illness; (j) who has not been involuntarily committed to a facility under the jurisdiction of an office of the department of mental hygiene pursuant to article nine or

fifteen of the mental hygiene law, article seven hundred thirty or section 330.20 of the criminal procedure law, section four hundred two or five hundred eight of the correction law, section 322.2 or 353.4 of the family court act, or has not been civilly confined in a secure treatment facility pursuant to article ten of the mental hygiene law; (k) who has not had a license revoked or who is not under a suspension or ineligibility order issued pursuant to the provisions of section 530.14 of the criminal procedure law or section eight hundred forty-two-a of the family court act; (l) in the county of Westchester, who has successfully completed a firearms safety course and test as evidenced by a certificate of completion issued in his or her name and endorsed and affirmed under the penalties of perjury by a duly authorized instructor, except that: (i) persons who are honorably discharged from the United States army, navy, marine corps or coast guard, or of the national guard of the state of New York, and produce evidence of official qualification in firearms during the term of service are not required to have completed those hours of a firearms safety course pertaining to the safe use, carrying, possession, maintenance and storage of a firearm; and (ii) persons who were licensed to possess a pistol or revolver prior to the effective date of this paragraph are not required to have completed a firearms safety course and test; (m) who has not had a guardian appointed for him or her pursuant to any provision of state law, based on a determination that as a result of marked subnormal intelligence, mental illness, incapacity, condition or disease, he or she lacks the mental capacity to contract or manage his or her own affairs; and (n) concerning whom no good cause exists for the denial of the license. No person shall engage in the business of gunsmith or dealer in firearms unless licensed pursuant to this section. An applicant to engage in such business shall also be a citizen of the United States, more than twenty-one years of age and maintain a place of business in the city or county where the license is issued. For such business, if the applicant is a firm or partnership, each member thereof shall comply with all of the requirements set forth in this subdivision and if the applicant is a corporation, each officer thereof shall so comply.

2. Types of licenses. A license for gunsmith or dealer in firearms shall be issued to engage in such business. A license for a pistol or revolver, other than an assault weapon or a disguised gun, shall be issued to (a) have and possess in his dwelling by a householder; (b) have and possess in his place of business by a merchant or storekeeper; (c) have and carry concealed while so employed by a messenger employed by a banking institution or express company; (d) have and carry concealed by a justice of the supreme court in the first or second judicial departments, or by a judge of the New York city civil court or the New York city criminal court; (e) have and carry concealed while so employed by a regular employee of an institution of the state, or of any county, city, town or village, under control of a commissioner of correction of the city or any warden, superintendent or head keeper of any state prison, penitentiary, workhouse, county jail or other institution for the detention of persons convicted or accused of crime or held as witnesses in criminal cases, provided that application is made therefor by such commissioner, warden, superintendent or head keeper; (f) have and carry concealed, without regard to employment or place of possession, by any person when proper cause exists for the issuance thereof; and (g) have, possess, collect and carry antique pistols which are defined as follows: (i) any single shot, muzzle loading pistol with a matchlock, flintlock, percussion cap, or similar type of ignition system manufactured in or before 1898, which is not designed for using rimfire or conventional centerfire fixed ammunition; and (ii) any replica of any pistol described in clause (i) hereof if such replica—

(1) is not designed or redesigned for using rimfire or conventional centerfire fixed ammunition, or

(2) uses rimfire or conventional centerfire fixed ammunition which is no longer manufactured in the United States and which is not readily available in the ordinary channels of commercial trade.

3. Applications.

(a) Applications shall be made and renewed, in the case of a license to carry or possess a pistol or revolver, to the licensing officer in the city or county, as the case may be, where the applicant resides, is principally employed or has his or her principal place of business as merchant or storekeeper; and, in the case of a license as gunsmith or dealer in firearms, to the licensing officer where such place of business is located. Blank applications shall, except in the city of New York, be approved as to form by the superintendent of state police. An application shall state the full name, date of birth, residence, present occupation of each person or individual signing the same, whether or not he or she is a citizen of the United States, whether or not he or she complies with each requirement for eligibility specified in subdivision one of this section and such other facts as may be required to show the good character, competency and integrity of each person or individual signing the application. An application shall be signed and verified by the applicant. Each individual signing an application shall submit one photograph of himself or herself and a duplicate for each required copy of the application. Such photographs shall have been taken within thirty days prior to filing the application. In case of a license as gunsmith or dealer in firearms, the photographs submitted shall be two inches square, and the application shall also state the previous occupation of each individual signing the same and the location of the place of such business, or of the bureau, agency, subagency, office or branch office for which the license is sought, specifying the name of the city, town or village, indicating the street and number and otherwise giving such apt description as to point out reasonably the location thereof. In such case, if the applicant is a firm, partnership or corporation, its name, date and place of formation, and principal place of business shall be stated. For such firm or partnership, the application shall be signed and verified by each individual composing or intending to compose the same, and for such corporation, by each officer thereof.

(b) Application for an exemption under paragraph seven-b of subdivision a of section 265.20 of this chapter. Each applicant desiring to obtain the exemption set forth in paragraph seven-b of subdivision a of section 265.20 of this chapter shall make such request in writing of the licensing officer with whom his application for a license is filed, at the time of filing such application. Such request shall include a signed and verified statement by the person authorized to instruct and supervise the applicant, that has met with the applicant and that he has determined that, in his judgment, said applicant does not appear to be or poses a threat to be, a danger to himself or to others. He shall include a copy of his certificate as an instructor in small arms, if he is required to be certified, and state his address and telephone number. He shall specify the exact location by name, address and telephone number where such instruction will take place. Such licensing officer shall, no later than ten business days after such filing, request the duly constituted police authorities of the locality where such application is made to investigate and ascertain any previous criminal record of the applicant pursuant to subdivision four of this section. Upon completion of this investigation, the police authority shall report the results to the licensing officer without unnecessary delay. The licensing officer shall no later than ten business days after the receipt of such investigation, determine if the applicant has been previously denied a license, been convicted of a felony, or been convicted of a serious offense, and either approve or disapprove the applicant for exemption purposes based upon such determinations. If the applicant is approved for the exemption, the licensing officer shall notify the appropriate duly constituted police authorities and the applicant. Such exemption shall terminate if the application for the license is denied, or at any earlier time based upon any information obtained by the licensing officer or the appropriate police authorities which would cause the license to be denied. The applicant and appropriate police authorities shall be notified of any such terminations.

4. Investigation. Before a license is issued or renewed, there shall be an investigation of all statements required in the application by the duly constituted police authorities of the locality where such application is made, including but not limited to such records as may be accessible to the division of state police or division of criminal justice services pursuant to section 400.02 of this article. For that purpose, the records of the appropriate office of the department of mental hygiene concerning previous or present mental illness of the applicant shall be available for inspection by the investigating officer of the police authority. In order to ascertain any previous criminal record, the investigating officer shall take the fingerprints and physical descriptive data in quadruplicate of each individual by whom the application is signed and verified. Two copies of such fingerprints shall be taken on standard fingerprint cards eight inches square, and one copy may be taken on a card supplied for that purpose by the federal bureau of investigation; provided, however, that in the case of a corporate applicant that has already been issued a dealer in firearms license and seeks to operate a firearm dealership at a second or subsequent location, the original fingerprints on file may be used to ascertain any criminal record in the second or subsequent application unless any of the corporate officers have changed since the prior application, in which case the new corporate officer shall comply with procedures governing an initial application for such license. When completed, one standard card shall be forwarded to and retained by the division of criminal justice services in the executive department, at Albany. A search of the files of such division and written notification of the results of the search to the investigating officer shall be made without unnecessary delay. Thereafter, such division shall notify the licensing officer and the executive department, division of state police, Albany, of any criminal record of the applicant filed therein subsequent to the search of its files. A second standard card, or the one supplied by the federal bureau of investigation, as the case may be, shall be forwarded to that bureau at Washington with a request that the files of the bureau be searched and notification of the results of the search be made to the investigating police authority. Of the remaining two fingerprint cards, one shall be filed with the executive department, division of state police, Albany, within ten days after issuance of the license, and the other remain on file with the investigating police authority. No such fingerprints may be inspected by any person other than a peace officer, who is acting pursuant to his special duties, or a police officer, except on order of a judge or justice of a court of record either upon notice to the licensee or without notice, as the judge or justice may deem appropriate. Upon completion of the investigation, the police authority shall report the results to the licensing officer without unnecessary delay.

4-a. Processing of license applications. Applications for licenses shall be accepted for processing by the licensing officer at the time of presentment. Except upon written notice to the applicant specifically stating the reasons for any delay, in each case the licensing officer shall act upon any application for a license pursuant to this section within six months of the date of presentment of such an application to the appropriate authority. Such delay may only be for good cause and with respect to the applicant. In acting upon an application, the licensing officer shall either deny the application for reasons specifically and concisely stated in writing or grant the application and issue the license applied for.

4-b. Westchester county firearms safety course certificate. In the county of Westchester, at the time of application, the licensing officer to which the license application is made shall provide a copy of the safety course booklet to each license applicant. Before such license is issued, such licensing officer shall require that the applicant submit a certificate of successful completion of a firearms safety course and test issued in his or her name and endorsed and affirmed under the penalties of perjury by a duly authorized instructor.

5. Filing of approved applications.

(a) The application for any license, if granted, shall be filed by the licensing officer with the clerk of the county of issuance, except that in the city of New York and, in the counties of Nassau and Suffolk, the licensing officer shall designate the place of filing in the appropriate division, bureau or unit of the police department thereof, and in the county of Suffolk the county clerk is hereby authorized to transfer all records or applications relating to firearms to the licensing authority of that county. Except as provided in paragraphs (b) through (f) of this subdivision, the name and address of any person to whom an application for any license has been granted shall be a public record. Upon application by a licensee who has changed his place of residence such records or applications shall be transferred to the appropriate officer at the licensee's new place of residence. A duplicate copy of such application shall be filed by the licensing officer in the executive department, division of state police, Albany, within ten days after issuance of the license. The superintendent of state police may designate that such application shall be transmitted to the division of state police electronically. In the event the superintendent of the division of state police determines that it lacks any of the records required to be filed with the division, it may request that such records be provided to it by the appropriate clerk, department or authority and such clerk, department or authority shall provide the division with such records. In the event such clerk, department or authority lacks such records, the division may request the license holder provide information sufficient to constitute such record and such license holder shall provide the division with such information. Such information shall be limited to the license holder's name, date of birth, gender,race, residential address, social security number and firearms possessed by said license holder. Nothing in this subdivision shall be construed to change the expiration date or term of such licenses if otherwise provided for in law. Records assembled or collected for purposes of inclusion in the database established by this section shall be released pursuant to a court order. Records assembled or collected for purposes of inclusion in the database created pursuant to section 400.02 of this chapter shall not be subject to disclosure pursuant to article six of the public officers law.

(b) Each application for a license pursuant to paragraph (a) of this subdivision shall include, on a separate written form prepared by the division of state police within thirty days of the effective date of the chapter of the laws of two thousand thirteen, which amended this section, and provided to the applicant at the same time and in the same manner as the application for a license, an opportunity for the applicant to request an exception from his or her application information becoming public record pursuant to paragraph (a) of this subdivision. Such forms, which shall also be made available to individuals who had applied for or been granted a license prior to the effective date of the chapter of the laws of two thousand thirteen which amended this section, shall notify applicants that, upon discovery that an applicant knowingly provided false information, such applicant may be subject to penalties pursuant to section 175.30 of this chapter, and further, that his or her request for an exception shall be null and void, provided that written notice containing such determination is provided to the applicant. Further, such forms shall provide each applicant an opportunity to specify the grounds on which he or she believes his or her application information should not be publicly disclosed. These grounds, which shall be identified on the application with a box beside each for checking, as applicable, by the applicant, shall be as follows:

(i) the applicant's life or safety may be endangered by disclosure because:

(A) the applicant is an active or retired police officer, peace officer, probation officer, parole officer, or corrections officer;

(B) the applicant is a protected person under a currently valid order of protection;

(C) the applicant is or was a witness in a criminal proceeding involving a criminal charge;

(D) the applicant is participating or previously participated as a juror in a criminal proceeding, or is or was a member of a grand jury; or

(E) the applicant is a spouse, domestic partner or household member of a person identified in this subparagraph or subparagraph (ii) of this paragraph, specifying which subparagraph or subparagraphs and clauses apply.

(ii) the applicant has reason to believe his or her life or safety may be endangered by disclosure due to reasons stated by the applicant.

(iii) the applicant has reason to believe he or she may be subject to unwarranted harassment upon disclosure of such information.

(c) Each form provided for recertification pursuant to paragraph (b) of subdivision ten of this section shall include an opportunity for the applicant to request an exception from the information provided on such form becoming public record pursuant to paragraph (a) of this subdivision. Such forms shall notify applicants that, upon discovery that an applicant knowingly provided false information, such applicant may be subject to penalties pursuant to section 175.30 of this chapter, and further, that his or her request for an exception shall be null and void, provided that written notice containing such determination is provided to the applicant. Further, such forms shall provide each applicant an opportunity to either decline to request the grant or continuation of an exception, or specify the grounds on which he or she believes his or her information should not be publicly disclosed. These grounds, which shall be identified in the application with a box beside each for checking, as applicable, by the applicant, shall be the same as provided in paragraph (b) of this subdivision.

(d) Information submitted on the forms described in paragraph (b) of this subdivision shall be excepted from disclosure and maintained by the entity retaining such information separate and apart from all other records.

(e) (i) Upon receiving a request for exception from disclosure, the licensing officer shall grant such exception, unless the request is determined to be null and void, pursuant to paragraph (b) or (c) of this subdivision.

(ii) A request for an exception from disclosure may be submitted at any time, including after a license or recertification has been granted.

(iii) If an exception is sought and granted pursuant to paragraph (b) of this subdivision, the application information shall not be public record, unless the request is determined to be null and void. If an exception is sought and granted pursuant to paragraph (c) of this subdivision, the information concerning such recertification application shall not be public record, unless the request is determined to be null and void.

(f) The information of licensees or applicants for a license shall not be disclosed to the public during the first one hundred twenty days following the effective date of the chapter of the laws of two thousand thirteen, which amended this section. After such period, the information of those who had applied for or been granted a license prior to the preparation of the form for requesting an exception, pursuant to paragraph (b) of this subdivision, may be released only if such individuals did not file a request for such an exception during the first sixty days following such preparation; provided, however, that no information contained in an application for licensure or recertification shall be disclosed by an entity that has not completed processing any such requests received during such sixty days.

(g) If a request for an exception is determined to be null and void pursuant to paragraph (b) or (c) of this subdivision, an applicant may request review of such determination pursuant to article seventy-eight of the civil practice laws [law]* and rules. Such proceeding must commence within thirty days after service of the written notice containing the adverse determination. Notice of the right to commence such a petition, and the time period therefor, shall be included in the notice of the determination. Disclosure following such a petition shall not be made prior to the disposition of such review.

6. License: validity. Any license issued pursuant to this section shall be valid notwithstanding the provisions of any local law or ordinance. No license shall be transferable to any other person or premises. A license to carry or possess a pistol or revolver, not otherwise limited as to place or time of possession, shall be effective throughout the state, except that the same shall not be valid within the city of New York unless a special permit granting validity is issued by the police commissioner of that city. Such license to carry or possess shall be valid within the city of New York in the absence of a permit issued by the police commissioner of that city, provided that (a) the firearms covered by such license have been purchased from a licensed dealer within the city of New York and are being transported out of said city forthwith and immediately from said dealer by the licensee in a locked container during a continuous and uninterrupted trip; or provided that (b) the firearms covered by such license are being transported by the licensee in a locked container and the trip through the city of New York is continuous and uninterrupted; or provided that (c) the firearms covered by such license are carried by armored car security guards transporting money or other valuables, in, to, or from motor vehicles commonly known as armored cars, during the course of their employment; or provided that (d) the licensee is a retired police officer as police officer is defined pursuant to subdivision thirty-four of section 1.20 of the criminal procedure law or a retired federal law enforcement officer, as defined in section 2.15 of the criminal procedure law, who has been issued a license by an authorized licensing officer as defined in subdivision ten of section 265.00 of this chapter; provided, further, however, that if such license was not issued in the city of New York it must be marked "Retired Police Officer" or "Retired Federal Law Enforcement Officer", as the case may be, and, in the case of a retired officer the license shall be deemed to permit only police or federal law enforcement regulations weapons; or provided that (e) the licensee is a peace officer described in subdivision four of section 2.10 of the criminal procedure law and the license, if issued by other than the city of New York, is marked "New York State Tax Department Peace Officer" and in such case the exemption shall apply only to the firearm issued to such licensee by the department of taxation and finance. A license as gunsmith or dealer in firearms shall not be valid outside the city or county, as the case may be, where issued.

7. License: form. Any license issued pursuant to this section shall, except in the city of New York, be approved as to form by the superintendent of state police. A license to carry or possess a pistol or revolver shall have attached the licensee's photograph, and a coupon which shall be removed and retained by any person disposing of a firearm to the licensee. Such license shall specify the weapon covered by calibre, make, model, manufacturer's name and serial number, or if none, by any other distinguishing number or identification mark, and shall indicate whether issued to carry on the person or possess on the premises, and if on the premises shall also specify the place where the licensee shall possess the same. If such license is issued to an alien, or to a person not a citizen of and usually a resident in the state, the licensing officer shall state in the

---

* The bracketed word has been inserted by the Publisher.

license the particular reason for the issuance and the names of the persons certifying to the good character of the applicant. Any license as gunsmith or dealer in firearms shall mention and describe the premises for which it is issued and shall be valid only for such premises.

8. License: exhibition and display. Every licensee while carrying a pistol or revolver shall have on his or her person a license to carry the same. Every person licensed to possess a pistol or revolver on particular premises shall have the license for the same on such premises. Upon demand, the license shall be exhibited for inspection to any peace officer, who is acting pursuant to his or her special duties, or police officer. A license as gunsmith or dealer in firearms shall be prominently displayed on the licensed premises. A gunsmith or dealer of firearms may conduct business temporarily at a location other than the location specified on the license if such temporary location is the location for a gun show or event sponsored by any national, state, or local organization, or any affiliate of any such organization devoted to the collection, competitive use or other sporting use of firearms. Any sale or transfer at a gun show must also comply with the provisions of article thirty-nine-DD of the general business law. Records of receipt and disposition of firearms transactions conducted at such temporary location shall include the location of the sale or other disposition and shall be entered in the permanent records of the gunsmith or dealer of firearms and retained on the location specified on the license. Nothing in this section shall authorize any licensee to conduct business from any motorized or towed vehicle. A separate fee shall not be required of a licensee with respect to business conducted under this subdivision. Any inspection or examination of inventory or records under this section at such temporary location shall be limited to inventory consisting of, or records related to, firearms held or disposed at such temporary locations. Failure of any licensee to so exhibit or display his or her license, as the case may be, shall be presumptive evidence that he or she is not duly licensed.

9. License: amendment. Elsewhere than in the city of New York, a person licensed to carry or possess a pistol or revolver may apply at any time to his or her licensing officer for amendment of his or her license to include one or more such weapons or to cancel weapons held under license. If granted, a record of the amendment describing the weapons involved shall be filed by the licensing officer in the executive department, division of state police, Albany. The superintendent of state police may authorize that such amendment be completed and transmitted to the state police in electronic form. Notification of any change of residence shall be made in writing by any licensee within ten days after such change occurs, and a record of such change shall be inscribed by such licensee on the reverse side of his or her license. Elsewhere than in the city of New York, and in the counties of Nassau and Suffolk, such notification shall be made to the executive department, division of state police, Albany, and in the city of New York to the police commissioner of that city, and in the county of Nassau to the police commissioner of that county, and in the county of Suffolk to the licensing officer of that county, who shall, within ten days after such notification shall be received by him or her, give notice in writing of such change to the executive department, division of state police, at Albany.

10. License: expiration, certification and renewal.

(a) Any license for gunsmith or dealer in firearms and, in the city of New York, any license to carry or possess a pistol or revolver, issued at any time pursuant to this section or prior to the first day of July, nineteen hundred sixty-three and not limited to expire on an earlier date fixed in the license, shall expire not more than three years after the date of issuance. In the counties of Nassau, Suffolk and Westchester, any license to carry or possess a pistol or revolver, issued at any time pursuant to this section or prior to the first day of July, nineteen hundred sixty-three and not limited to expire on an earlier date fixed in the license, shall expire not more than five years after the date of issuance; however, in the county of Westchester, any such license shall be certified prior to the first day of April, two thousand, in accordance with a schedule to be contained in regulations promulgated by the commissioner of the division of criminal justice services, and every such license shall be recertified every five years thereafter. For purposes of this section certification shall mean that the licensee shall provide to the licensing officer the following information only: current name, date of birth, current address, and the make, model, caliber and serial number of all firearms currently possessed. Such certification information shall be filed by the licensing officer in the same manner as an amendment. Elsewhere than in the city of New York and the counties of Nassau, Suffolk and Westchester, any license to carry or possess a pistol or revolver, issued at any time pursuant to this section or prior to the first day of July, nineteen hundred sixty-three and not previously revoked or cancelled, shall be in force and effect until revoked as herein provided. Any license not previously cancelled or revoked shall remain in full force and effect for thirty days beyond the stated expiration date on such license. Any application to renew a license that has not previously expired, been revoked or cancelled shall thereby extend the term of the license until disposition of the application by the licensing officer. In the case of a license for gunsmith or dealer in firearms, in counties having a population of less than two hundred thousand inhabitants, photographs and fingerprints shall be submitted on original applications and upon renewal thereafter only at six year intervals. Upon satisfactory proof that a currently valid original license has been despoiled, lost or otherwise removed from the possession of the licensee and upon application containing an additional photograph of the licensee, the licensing officer shall issue a duplicate license.

(b) All licensees shall be recertified to the division of state police every five years thereafter. Any license issued before the effective date of the chapter of the laws of two thousand thirteen which added this paragraph shall be recertified by the licensee on or before January thirty-first, two thousand eighteen, and not less than one year prior to such date, the state police shall send a notice to all license holders who have not recertified by such time. Such recertification shall be in a form as approved by the superintendent of state police, which shall request the license holder's name, date of birth, gender, race, residential address, social security number, firearms possessed by such license holder, email address at the option of the license holder and an affirmation that such license holder is not prohibited from possessing firearms. The form may be in an electronic form if so designated by the superintendent of state police. Failure to recertify shall act as a revocation of such license. If the New York state police discover as a result of the recertification process that a licensee failed to provide a change of address, the New York state police shall not require the licensing officer to revoke such license.

11. License: revocation and suspension.

(a) The conviction of a licensee anywhere of a felony or serious offense or a licensee at any time becoming ineligible to obtain a license under this section shall operate as a revocation of the license. A license may be revoked or suspended as provided for in section 530.14 of the criminal procedure law or section eight hundred forty-two-a of the family court act. Except for a license issued pursuant to section 400.01 of this article, a license may be revoked and cancelled at any time in the city of New York, and in the counties of Nassau and Suffolk, by the licensing officer, and elsewhere than in the city of New York by any judge or justice of a court of record; a license issued pursuant to section 400.01 of this article may be revoked and cancelled at any time by the licensing officer or any judge or justice of a court of record. The official revoking a license shall give written notice thereof without unnecessary delay to the executive department, division of state police, Albany, and shall also notify immediately the duly constituted police authorities of the locality.

(b) Whenever the director of community services or his or her designee makes a report pursuant to section 9.46 of the mental hygiene law, the division of criminal justice services shall convey such information, whenever it determines that the person named in the report possesses a license issued pursuant to this section, to the appropriate licensing official, who shall issue an order suspending or revoking such license.

(c) In any instance in which a person's license is suspended or revoked under paragraph (a) or (b) of this subdivision, such person shall surrender such license to the appropriate licensing official and any and all firearms, rifles, or shotguns owned or possessed by such person shall be surrendered to an appropriate law enforcement agency as provided in subparagraph (f) of paragraph one of subdivision a of section 265.20 of this chapter. In the event such license, firearm, shotgun, or rifle is not surrendered, such items shall be removed and declared a nuisance and any police officer or peace officer acting pursuant to his or her special duties is authorized to remove any and all such weapons.

12. Records required of gunsmiths and dealers in firearms. Any person licensed as gunsmith or dealer in firearms shall keep a record book approved as to form, except in the city of New York, by the superintendent of state police. In the record book shall be entered at the time of every transaction involving a firearm the date, name, age, occupation and residence of any person from whom a firearm is received or to whom a firearm is delivered, and the calibre, make, model, manufacturer's name and serial number, or if none, any other distinguishing number or identification mark on such firearm. Before delivering a firearm to any person, the licensee shall require him to produce either a license valid under this section to carry or possess the same, or proof of lawful authority as an exempt person pursuant to section 265.20. In addition, before delivering a firearm to a peace officer, the licensee shall verify that person's status as a peace officer with the division of state police. After completing the foregoing, the licensee shall remove and retain the attached coupon and enter in the record book the date of such license, number, if any, and name of the licensing officer, in the case of the holder of a license to carry or possess, or the shield or other number, if any, assignment and department, unit or agency, in the case of an exempt person. The original transaction report shall be forwarded to the division of state police within ten days of delivering a firearm to any person, and a duplicate copy shall be kept by the licensee. The superintendent of state police may designate that such record shall be completed and transmitted in electronic form. A dealer may be granted a waiver from transmitting such records in electronic form if the superintendent determines that such dealer is incapable of such transmission due to technological limitations that are not reasonably within the control of the dealer, or other exceptional circumstances demonstrated by the dealer, pursuant to a process established in regulation, and at the discretion of the superintendent. Records assembled or collected for purposes of inclusion in the database created pursuant to section 400.02 of this article shall not be subject to disclosure pursuant to article six of the public officers law. The record book shall be maintained on the premises mentioned and described in the license and shall be open at all reasonable hours for inspection by any peace officer, acting pursuant to his special duties, or police officer. In the event of cancellation or revocation of the license for gunsmith or dealer in firearms, or discontinuance of business by a licensee, such record book shall be immediately surrendered to the licensing officer in the city of New York, and in the counties of Nassau and Suffolk, and elsewhere in the state to the executive department, division of state police.

12-a. State police regulations applicable to licensed gunsmiths engaged in the business of assembling or manufacturing firearms. The superintendent of state police is hereby authorized to issue such rules and regulations as he deems reasonably necessary to prevent the manufacture and assembly of unsafe firearms in the state. Such rules and regulations shall establish safety standards in regard to the manufacture and assembly of firearms in the state, including specifications as to materials and parts used, the proper storage and shipment of firearms, and minimum standards of quality control. Regulations issued by the state police pursuant to this subdivision shall apply to any person licensed as a gunsmith under this section engaged in the business of manufacturing or assemblying firearms, and any violation thereof shall subject the licensee to revocation of license pursuant to subdivision eleven of this section.

12-b. [None]

12-c. Firearms records.

(a) Every employee of a state or local agency, unit of local government, state or local commission, or public or private organization who possesses a firearm or machine-gun under an exemption to the licensing requirements under this chapter, shall promptly report in writing to his employer the make, model, calibre and serial number of each such firearm or machine-gun. Thereafter, within ten days of the acquisition or disposition of any such weapon, he shall furnish such information to his employer, including the name and address of the person from whom the weapon was acquired or to whom it was disposed.

(b) Every head of a state or local agency, unit of local government, state or local commission, public authority or public or private organization to whom an employee has submitted a report pursuant to paragraph (a) of this subdivision shall promptly forward such report to the superintendent of state police.

(c) Every head of a state or local agency, unit of local government, state or local commission, public authority, or any other agency, firm or corporation that employs persons who may lawfully possess firearms or machine-guns without the requirement of a license therefor, or that employs persons licensed to possess firearms or machine-guns, shall promptly report to the superintendent of state police, in the manner prescribed by him, the make, model, calibre and serial number of every firearm or machine-gun possessed by it on the effective date of this act for the use of such employees or for any other use. Thereafter, within ten days of the acquisition or disposition of any such weapon, such head shall report such information to the superintendent of the state police, including the name and address of the person from whom the weapon was acquired or to whom it was disposed.

13. Expenses. The expense of providing a licensing officer with blank applications, licenses and record books for carrying out the provisions of this section shall be a charge against the county, and in the city of New York against the city.

14. Fees. In the city of New York and the county of Nassau, the annual license fee shall be twenty-five dollars for gunsmiths and fifty dollars for dealers in firearms. In such city, the city council and in the county of Nassau the Board of Supervisors shall fix the fee to be charged for a license to carry or possess a pistol or revolver and provide for the disposition of such fees. Elsewhere in the state, the licensing officer shall collect and pay into the county treasury the following fees: for each license to carry or possess a pistol or revolver, not less than three dollars nor more than ten dollars as may be determined by the legislative body of the county; for each amendment thereto, three dollars, and five dollars in the county of Suffolk; and for each license issued to a gunsmith or dealer in firearms, ten dollars. The fee for a duplicate license shall be five dollars. The fee for processing a license transfer between counties shall be five dollars. The fee for processing a license or renewal thereof for a qualified retired police officer as defined under subdivision thirty-four of section 1.20 of the criminal procedure law, or a qualified retired sheriff, undersheriff, or deputy sheriff of the city of New York as defined under subdivision two of section 2.10 of the criminal procedure law, or a qualified retired bridge and tunnel officer, sergeant or

lieutenant of the triborough bridge and tunnel authority as defined under subdivision twenty of section 2.10 of the criminal procedure law, or a qualified retired uniformed court officer in the unified court system, or a qualified retired court clerk in the unified court system in the first and second judicial departments, as defined in paragraphs a and b of subdivision twenty-one of section 2.10 of the criminal procedure law or a retired correction officer as defined in subdivision twenty-five of section 2.10 of the criminal procedure law shall be waived in all counties throughout the state.

15. Any violation by any person of any provision of this section is a class A misdemeanor.

16. Unlawful disposal. No person shall except as otherwise authorized pursuant to law dispose of any firearm unless he is licensed as gunsmith or dealer in firearms.

16-a. Registration.

(a) An owner of a weapon defined in paragraph (e) or (f) of subdivision twenty-two of section 265.00 of this chapter, possessed before the date of the effective date of the chapter of the laws of two thousand thirteen which added this paragraph, must make an application to register such weapon with the superintendent of state police, in the manner provided by the superintendent, or by amending a license issued pursuant to this section within one year of the effective date of this subdivision except any weapon defined under subparagraph (vi) of paragraph (g) of subdivision twenty-two of section 265.00 of this chapter transferred into the state may be registered at any time, provided such weapons are registered within thirty days of their transfer into the state. Registration information shall include the registrant's name, date of birth, gender, race, residential address, social security number and a description of each weapon being registered. A registration of any weapon defined under subparagraph (vi) of paragraph (g) of subdivision twenty-two of section 265.00 or a feeding device as defined under subdivision twenty-three of section 265.00 of this chapter shall be transferable, provided that the seller notifies the state police within seventy-two hours of the transfer and the buyer provides the state police with information sufficient to constitute a registration under this section. Such registration shall not be valid if such registrant is prohibited or becomes prohibited from possessing a firearm pursuant to state or federal law. The superintendent shall determine whether such registrant is prohibited from possessing a firearm under state or federal law. Such check shall be limited to determining whether the factors in 18 USC 922 (g) apply or whether a registrant has been convicted of a serious offense as defined in subdivision sixteen-b of section 265.00 of this chapter, so as to prohibit such registrant from possessing a firearm, and whether a report has been issued pursuant to section 9.46 of the mental hygiene law. All registrants shall recertify to the division of state police every five years thereafter. Failure to recertify shall result in a revocation of such registration.

(a-1) Notwithstanding any inconsistent provisions of paragraph (a) of this subdivision, an owner of an assault weapon as defined in subdivision twenty-two of section 265.00 of this chapter, who is a qualified retired New York or federal law enforcement officer as defined in subdivision twenty-five of section 265.00 of this chapter, where such weapon was issued to or purchased by such officer prior to retirement and in the course of his or her official duties, and for which such officer was qualified by the agency that employed such officer within twelve months prior to his or her retirement, must register such weapon within sixty days of retirement.

(b) The superintendent of state police shall create and maintain an internet website to educate the public as to which semiautomatic rifle, semiautomatic shotgun or semiautomatic pistol or weapon that are illegal as a result of the enactment of the chapter of the laws of two thousand thirteen which added this paragraph, as well as such assault weapons which are illegal pursuant to article two hundred sixty-five of this chapter. Such website shall contain information to assist the public in recognizing the relevant features proscribed by such article two hundred sixty-five, as well as which make and model of weapons that require registration.

(c) A person who knowingly fails to apply to register such weapon, as required by this section, within one year of the effective date of the chapter of the laws of two thousand thirteen which added this paragraph shall be guilty of a class A misdemeanor and such person who unknowingly fails to validly register such weapon within such one year period shall be given a warning by an appropriate law enforcement authority about such failure and given thirty days in which to apply to register such weapon or to surrender it. A failure to apply or surrender such weapon within such thirty-day period shall result in such weapon being removed by an appropriate law enforcement authority and declared a nuisance.

16-b. The cost of the software, programming and interface required to transmit any record that must be electronically transmitted by the dealer or licensing officer to the division of state police pursuant to this chapter shall be borne by the state.

17. Applicability of section. The provisions of article two hundred sixty-five of this chapter relating to illegal possession of a firearm, shall not apply to an offense which also constitutes a violation of this section by a person holding an otherwise valid license under the provisions of this section and such offense shall only be punishable as a class A misdemeanor pursuant to this section. In addition, the provisions of such article two hundred sixty-five of this chapter shall not apply to the possession of a firearm in a place not authorized by law, by a person who holds an otherwise valid license or possession of a firearm by a person within a one year period after the stated expiration date of an otherwise valid license which has not been previously cancelled or revoked shall only be punishable as a class A misdemeanor pursuant to this section.

> **HISTORY:** Add, L 1965, ch 1030, § 1, eff Sept 1, 1967, with substance derived from § 1903; amd, L 1967, ch 791, § 49, L 1971, ch 796, L 1971, ch 1097, §§ 82, 83, L 1973, ch 172, L 1973, ch 546, § 1, L 1973, ch 593, § 1, L 1974, ch 1041, §§ 10, 11, L 1974, ch 1042, § 2, eff Sept 1, 1974, L 1976, ch 584, § 1, L 1977, ch 480, § 1, L 1980, ch 233, §§ 15–17, eff Aug 12, 1980, L 1980, ch 843, §§ 47–50, eff Sept 1, 1980, L 1981, ch 175, § 5 L 1982, ch 71, § 1, L 1984, ch 739, § 1, L 1985, ch 778, § 2, eff Nov 1, 1985, L 1986, ch 539, § 1, L 1988, ch 437, § 1, L 1990, ch 707, § 1, L 1991, ch 414, § 1, L 1992, ch 320, § 1, L 1993, ch 448, §§ 1, 2, eff Nov 1, 1993, L 1993, ch 449, § 1, eff Nov 1, 1993, L 1993, ch 498, § 3, L 1994, ch 332, § 1, eff Nov 1, 1994, L 1994, ch 636, § 1, L 1994, ch 637, § 1, eff Aug 2, 1994, L 1995, ch 236, § 1, L 1995, ch 370, § 1, L 1996, ch 644, § 6, L 1997, ch 446, §§ 3–6, L 1997, ch 447, § 2, eff Aug 25, 1997, L 1998, ch 378, § 8, L 1999, ch 210, §§ 5, 6, eff Nov 1, 1999, L 2000, ch 189, §§ 18–20, eff Nov 1, 2000, L 2002, ch 318, § 5, eff Aug 6, 2002, L 2005, ch 195, § 1, eff July 12, 2005, L 2005, ch 331, § 1, eff July 26, 2005, L 2013, ch 1, § 48, eff Jan 15, 2014, except sub 5, eff Jan 15, 2013, except sub 16-a, eff April 15, 2013, L 2013, ch 98, § 3, eff April 15, 2013.

§ 400.01. License to carry and possess firearms for retired sworn members of the division of state police

1. A license to carry or possess a firearm for a retired sworn member of the division of state police shall be granted in the same manner and upon the same terms and conditions as licenses issued under section 400.00 of this article provided, however, that applications for such license shall be made to, and the licensing officer shall be, the superintendent of state police.

2. For purposes of this section, a "retired sworn member of the division of state police" shall mean a former sworn member of the division of state police, who upon separation from the division of state police was immediately entitled to receive retirement benefits under the provisions of the retirement and social security law.

3. The provisions of this section shall only apply to license applications made or renewals which

must be made on or after the effective date of this section. A license to carry or possess a pistol or revolver issued pursuant to the provisions of section 400.00 of this article to a person covered by the provisions of this section shall be valid until such license would have expired pursuant to the provisions of section 400.00 of this article; provided that, on or after the effective date of this section, an application or renewal of such license shall be made pursuant to the provisions of this section.

4. Except for the designation of the superintendent of state police as the licensing officer for retired sworn members of the division of state police, all of the provisions and requirements of section 400.00 of this article and any other provision of law shall be applicable to individuals licensed pursuant to this section. In addition all provisions of section 400.00 of this article, except for the designation of the superintendent of state police as licensing officer are hereby deemed applicable to individuals licensed pursuant to this section.

HISTORY: Add, L 1999, ch 210, § 7, eff Nov 1, 1999.

§ 400.02. Statewide license and record database

There shall be a statewide license and record database which shall be created and maintained by the division of state police the cost of which shall not be borne by any municipality. Records assembled or collected for purposes of inclusion in such database shall not be subject to disclosure pursuant to article six of the public officers law. Records containing granted license applications shall be periodically checked by the division of criminal justice services against criminal conviction, mental health, and all other records as are necessary to determine their continued accuracy as well as whether an individual is no longer a valid license holder. The division of criminal justice services shall also check pending applications made pursuant to this article against such records to determine whether a license may be granted. All state agencies shall cooperate with the division of criminal justice services, as otherwise authorized by law, in making their records available for such checks. The division of criminal justice services, upon determining that an individual is ineligible to possess a license, or is no longer a valid license holder, shall notify the applicable licensing official of such determination and such licensing official shall not issue a license or revoke such license and any weapons owned or possessed by such individual shall be removed consistent with the provisions of subdivision eleven of section 400.00 of this article. Local and state law enforcement shall have access to such database, as otherwise authorized by law, in the performance of their duties. Records assembled or collected for purposes of inclusion in the database established by this section shall be released pursuant to a court order.

HISTORY: Add, L 2013, ch 1, § 49, eff Jan 15, 2014.

§ 400.03. Sellers of ammunition

1. A seller of ammunition as defined in subdivision twenty-four of section 265.00 of this chapter shall register with the superintendent of state police in a manner provided by the superintendent. Any dealer in firearms that is validly licensed pursuant to section 400.00 of this article shall not be required to complete such registration.

2. Any seller of ammunition or dealer in firearms shall keep a record book approved as to form by the superintendent of state police. In the record book shall be entered at the time of every transaction involving ammunition the date, name, age, occupation and residence of any person from whom ammunition is received or to whom ammunition is delivered, and the amount, calibre, manufacturer's name and serial number, or if none, any other distinguishing number or identification mark on such ammunition. The record book shall be maintained on the premises mentioned and described in the license and shall be open at all reasonable hours for inspection by any peace officer, acting pursuant to his or her special duties, or police officer. Any record

produced pursuant to this section and any transmission thereof to any government agency shall not be considered a public record for purposes of article six of the public officers law.

3. No later than thirty days after the superintendent of the state police certifies that the statewide license and record database established pursuant to section 400.02 of this article is operational for the purposes of this section, a dealer in firearms licensed pursuant to section 400.00 of this article, a seller of ammunition as defined in subdivision twenty-four of section 265.00 of this chapter shall not transfer any ammunition to any other person who is not a dealer in firearms as defined in subdivision nine of such section 265.00 or a seller of ammunition as defined in subdivision twenty-four of section 265.00 of this chapter, unless:

(a) before the completion of the transfer, the licensee or seller contacts the statewide license and record database and provides the database with information sufficient to identify such dealer or seller, transferee based on information on the transferee's identification document as defined in paragraph (c) of this subdivision, as well as the amount, calibre, manufacturer's name and serial number, if any, of such ammunition;

(b) the system provides the licensee or seller with a unique identification number; and

(c) the transferor has verified the identity of the transferee by examining a valid state identification document of the transferee issued by the department of motor vehicles or if the transferee is not a resident of the state of New York, a valid identification document issued by the transferee's state or country of residence containing a photograph of the transferee.

4. If the database determines that the purchaser of ammunition is eligible to possess ammunition pursuant to state and federal laws, the system shall:

(a) assign a unique identification number to the transfer; and

(b) provide the licensee or seller with the number.

5. If the statewide license and record database notifies the licensee or seller that the information available to the database does not demonstrate that the receipt of ammunition by such other person would violate 18 U.S.C. 922(g) or state law, and the licensee transfers ammunition to such other person, the licensee shall indicate to the database that such transaction has been completed at which point a record of such transaction shall be created which shall be accessible by the division of state police and maintained for no longer than one year from point of purchase, which shall not be incorporated into the database established pursuant to section 400.02 of this article or the registry established pursuant to subdivision sixteen-a of section 400.00 of this article. The division of state police may share such information with a local law enforcement agency. Evidence of the purchase of ammunition is not sufficient to establish probable cause to believe that the purchaser has committed a crime absent other information tending to prove the commission of a crime. Records assembled or accessed pursuant to this section shall not be subject to disclosure pursuant to article six of the public officers law. This requirement of this section shall not apply (i) if a background check cannot be completed because the system is not operational as determined by the superintendent of state police, or where it cannot be accessed by the practitioner due to a temporary technological or electrical failure, as set forth in regulation, or (ii) a dealer or seller has been granted a waiver from conducting such background check if the superintendent of state police determines that such dealer is incapable of such check due to technological limitations that are not reasonably within the control of the dealer, or other exceptional circumstances demonstrated by the dealer, pursuant to a process established in regulation, and at the discretion of such superintendent.

6. If the superintendent of state police certifies that background checks of ammunition

purchasers may be conducted through the national instant criminal background check system, use of that system by a dealer or seller shall be sufficient to satisfy subdivisions four and five of this section and such checks shall be conducted through such system, provided that a record of such transaction shall be forwarded to the state police in a form determined by the superintendent.

7. No commercial transfer of ammunition shall take place unless a licensed dealer in firearms or registered seller of ammunition acts as an intermediary between the transferor and the ultimate transferee of the ammunition for the purposes of contacting the statewide license and record database pursuant to this section. Such transfer between the dealer or seller, and transferee must occur in person.

8. A seller of ammunition who fails to register pursuant to this section and sells ammunition, for a first offense, shall be guilty of a violation and subject to the fine of one thousand dollars and for a second offense, shall be guilty of a class A misdemeanor.

A seller of ammunition that fails to keep any record required pursuant to this section, for a first offense shall be guilty of a violation and subject to a fine of five hundred dollars, and for a second offense shall be guilty of a class B misdemeanor, and the registration of such seller shall be revoked.

HISTORY: Add, L 2013, ch 1, § 50, eff Jan 15, 2014.

§ 400.05. Disposition of weapons and dangerous instruments, appliances and substances

1. Any weapon, instrument, appliance or substance specified in article two hundred sixty-five, when unlawfully possessed, manufactured, transported or disposed of, or when utilized in the commission of an offense, is hereby declared a nuisance. When the same shall come into the possession of any police officer or peace officer, it shall be surrendered immediately to the official mentioned in paragraph (f) of subdivision one of section 265.20, except that such weapon, instrument, appliance or substance coming into the possession of the state police shall be surrendered to the superintendent of state police.

2. The official to whom the weapon, instrument, appliance or substance which has subsequently been declared a nuisance pursuant to subdivision one of this section is so surrendered shall, at any time but at least once each year, destroy the same or cause it to be destroyed, or render the same or cause it to be rendered ineffective and useless for its intended purpose and harmless to human life.

3. Notwithstanding subdivision two of this section, the official to whom the weapon, instrument, appliance or substance is so surrendered shall not destroy the same if (a) a judge or justice of a court of record, or a district attorney, shall file with the official a certificate that the non-destruction thereof is necessary or proper to serve the ends of justice; or (b) the official directs that the same be retained in any laboratory conducted by any police or sheriff's department for the purpose of research, comparison, identification or other endeavor toward the prevention and detection of crime.

4. In the case of any machine-gun or firearm taken from the possession of any person, the official to whom such weapon is surrendered pursuant to subdivision one of this section shall immediately notify the executive department, division of state police, Albany, giving the calibre, make, model, manufacturer's name and serial number, or if none, any other distinguishing number or identification mark. A search of the files of such division and notification of the results of the search to such official shall immediately be made.

5. Before any machine-gun or firearm is destroyed pursuant to subdivision two of this section, (a) the official to whom the same has been surrendered shall forward to the executive department,

division of state police, Albany, a notice of intent to destroy and the calibre, make, model, manufacturer's name and serial number, or if none, any other distinguishing number or identification mark of the machine-gun or firearm; (b) such division shall make and keep a record of such description together with the name and address of the official reporting the same and the date such notice was received; and (c) a search of the files of such division and notification of the results of the search to such official shall be made without unnecessary delay.

6. A firearm or other weapon which is surrendered, or is otherwise voluntarily delivered pursuant to section 265.20 of this chapter and which has not been declared a nuisance pursuant to subdivision one of this section, shall be retained by the official to whom it was delivered for a period not to exceed one year. Prior to the expiration of such time period, a person who surrenders a firearm shall have the right to arrange for the sale, or transfer, of such firearm to a dealer in firearms licensed in accordance with this chapter or for the transfer of such firearm to himself or herself provided that a license therefor has been issued in accordance with this chapter. If no lawful disposition of the firearm or other weapon is made within the time provided, the firearm or weaponconcerned shall be declared a nuisance and shall be disposed of in accordance with the provisions of this section.

HISTORY: Add, L 1965, ch 1030, § 1, eff Sept 1, 1967, with substance derived from §§ 1901, 1902. Section heading, amd, L 1986, ch 350, § 1, eff Nov 1, 1986. Sub 1, amd, L 1980, ch 843, § 51, L 1982, ch 179, § 1, L 1986, ch 350, § 2, eff Nov 1, 1986. Sub 2, amd, L 1986, ch 350, § 2, L 1991, ch 166, § 377, eff June 12, 1991. Sub 3, amd, L 1991, ch 166, § 378, eff June 12, 1991. Sub 6, add, L 1986, ch 350, § 3, eff Nov 1, 1986. Sub 6, amd, L 2006, ch 578, § 1, eff Nov 1, 2006.

§ 400.10. Report of theft or loss of a firearm, rifle or shotgun

1. (a) Any owner or other person lawfully in possession of: (i) a firearm, rifle or, shotgun who suffers the loss or theft of said weapon; (ii) ammunition as well as a firearm, rifle or shotgun who suffers the loss or theft of such ammunition as well as a firearm, rifle or shotgun; or (iii) ammunition and is a dealer in firearms or seller of ammunition who suffers the loss or theft of such ammunition shall within twenty-four hours of the discovery of the loss or theft report the facts and circumstances of the loss or theft to a police department or sheriff's office.

(b) Whenever a person reports the theft or loss of a firearm, rifle, shotgun or ammunition to any police department or sheriff's office, the officer or department receiving such report shall forward notice of such theft or loss to the division of state police via the New York Statewide Police Information Network. The notice shall contain information in compliance with the New York Statewide Police Information Network Operating Manual, including the caliber, make, model, manufacturer's name and serial number, if any, and any other distinguishing number or identification mark on the weapon.

2. The division of state police shall receive, collect and file the information referred to in subdivision one of this section. The division shall cooperate, and undertake to furnish or make available to law enforcement agencies this information, for the purpose of coordinating law enforcement efforts to locate such weapons.

3. Notwithstanding any other provision of law, a violation of paragraph (a) of subdivision one of this section shall be a class A misdemeanor.

HISTORY: Add, L 1984, ch 531, § 1, eff July 27, 1984; amd, L 2000, ch 189, § 23, eff Nov 1, 2000, L 2013, ch 1, § 51, eff March 16, 2013.

ARTICLE 405   LICENSING AND OTHER PROVISIONS RELATING TO FIREWORKS

§ 405.00.   **Permits for public displays of fireworks**

HISTORY: Add, L 1965, ch 1030, § 1, eff Sept 1, 1967.

§ 405.00. Permits for public displays of fireworks

1. Definition of "permit authority." The term "permit authority," as used in this section, means and includes the agency authorized to grant and issue the permits provided in this section. The permit authority on or within state property shall be the office of fire prevention and control. The permit authority for territory within a county park shall be the county park commission, or such other agency having jurisdiction, control and/or operation of the parks or parkways within which any fireworks are to be displayed. The permit authority in a city shall be the duly constituted licensing agency thereof and, in the absence of such agency, shall be an officer designated for the purpose by the legislative body thereof. The permit authority in a village shall be an officer designated for the purpose by the board of trustees thereof and the permit authority in the territory of a town outside of villages shall be an officer designated for the purpose by the town board thereof.

2. Permits for fireworks displays. Notwithstanding the provisions of section 270.00 of this chapter, the permit authority for state property, county parks, cities, villages, or towns may grant a permit for the display of fireworks to municipalities, fair associations, amusement parks, persons, or organizations of individuals that submit an application in writing. The application for such permit shall set forth:

(a) The name of the body sponsoring the display and the names of the persons actually to be in charge of the firing of the display who shall possess a valid certificate of competence as a pyrotechnician as required under the general business law and article sixteen of the labor law. The permit application shall further contain a verified statement from the applicant identifying the individuals who are authorized to fire the display including their certificate numbers, and that such individuals possess a valid certificate of competence as a pyrotechnician.

(b) The date and time of day at which the display is to be held.

(c) The exact location planned for the display.

(d) The number and kind of fireworks to be discharged.

(e) The manner and place of storage of such fireworks prior to the display.

(f) A diagram of the grounds on which the display is to be held showing the point at which the fireworks are to be discharged, the location of all buildings, highways and other lines of communication, the lines behind which the audience will be restrained and the location of all nearby trees, telegraph or telephone lines or other overhead obstructions.

(g) Such other information as the permit authority may deem necessary to protect persons or property.

3. Applications for permits. All applications for permits for the display of fireworks shall be

made at least five days in advance of the date of the display and the permit shall contain provisions that the actual point at which the fireworks are to be fired be in accordance with the rules promulgated by the commissioner of labor pursuant to section four hundred sixty-two of the labor law and that all the persons in actual charge of firing the fireworks shall be over the age of eighteen years, competent and physically fit for the task, that there shall be at least two such operators constantly on duty during the discharge and that at least two approved type fire extinguishers shall be kept at as widely separated points as possible within the actual area of the display. For any applications made for the display of fireworks on state property, the state fire administrator shall coordinate the issuance of such permits with the head of the police or fire department or both, where there are such departments. The legislative body of a county park, city, village or town may provide for approval of such permit by the head of the police or fire department or both where there are such departments. No permit granted and issued hereunder shall be transferable. After such permit shall have been granted, sales, possession, use and distribution of fireworks for such display shall be lawful solely therefor.

3-a. Notwithstanding the provisions of subdivision three of this section, no permit may be issued to conduct a display of fireworks upon any property where the boundary line of such property is less than five hundred yards from the boundary line of any property which is owned, leased or operated by any breeder as defined in subdivision four of section two hundred fifty-one of the racing, pari-mutuel wagering and breeding law.

4. Bonds. Before granting and issuing a permit for a display of fireworks as herein provided, the permit authority shall require an adequate bond from the applicant therefor, unless it is a state entity, county park, city, village or town, in a sum to be fixed by the permit authority, which, however, shall not be less than one million dollars, conditioned for the payment of all damages, which may be caused to a person or persons or to property, by reason of the display so permitted and arising from any acts of the permittee, his or her agents, employees, contractors or subcontractors. Such bond shall run to the state if the permit is granted for a display on state property, or to the county park, city, village or town in which the permit is granted and issued and shall be for the use and benefit of any person or persons or any owner or owners of any property so injured or damaged, and such person or persons or such owner or owners are hereby authorized to maintain an action thereon, which right of action also shall accrue to the heirs, executors, administrators, successors or assigns of such person or persons or such owner or owners. The permit authority may accept, in lieu of such bond, an indemnity insurance policy with liability coverage and indemnity protection equivalent to the terms and conditions upon which such bond is predicated and for the purposes provided in this section.

5. Local ordinances superseded. All local ordinances regulating or prohibiting the display of fireworks are hereby superseded by the provisions of this section. Every city, town or village shall have the power to enact ordinances or local laws regulating or prohibiting the use, or the storage, transportation or sale for use of fireworks in the preparation for or in connection with television broadcasts.

HISTORY: Add, L 1965, ch 1030, § 1, eff Sept 1, 1967, with substance derived from § 1894-a; amd, L 1972, ch 661, § 9, eff Sept 1, 1972, L 2002, ch 151, § 1, eff Oct 21, 2002, L 2009, ch 57, § 21 (Part CC), eff Oct 4, 2009, L 2013, ch 127, § 2, eff July 12, 2011.

§ 405.05. Seizure and destruction of fireworks

Fireworks possessed unlawfully may be seized by any peace officer, acting pursuant to his special duties, or police officer, who must deliver the same to the magistrate before whom the person arrested is required to be taken. The magistrate must, upon the examination of the defendant, or if such examination is delayed or prevented, without awaiting such examination, determine whether the fireworks had been possessed by the defendant in violation of the provisions of section 270.00; and if he finds that the fireworks had been so possessed by the defendant, he must cause such fireworks to be destroyed, in a way safe for the particular type of such fireworks, or to be delivered to the district attorney of the county in which the defendant is liable to indictment or trial, as the interests of justice and public safety may, in his opinion, require. Upon the conviction of the defendant, the district attorney must cause to be destroyed, in a way safe for the particular type of such fireworks, the fireworks in respect whereof the defendant stands convicted, and which remain in the possession or under the control of the district attorney.

HISTORY: Add, L 1965, ch 1030, § 1, with substance derived from § 1894-a; amd, L 1980, ch 843, § 52, eff Sept 1, 1980.

§ 405.10. Permits for indoor pyrotechnics

1. Definitions. For the purposes of this section, the following terms have the following meanings:

a. Airburst. A pyrotechnic device that is suspended in the air to simulate outdoor aerial fireworks shells without producing hazardous debris.

b. Areas of public assembly. All buildings or portions of buildings used for gathering together fifty or more persons for amusement, athletic, civic, dining, educational, entertainment, patriotic, political, recreational, religious, social, or similar purposes, the entire fire area of which they are a part, and the means of egress therefrom.

c. Assistant. A person who works under the supervision of the pyrotechnic operator.

d. Audience. Spectators whose primary purpose is to view a performance.

e. Building. A combination of any materials, whether portable or fixed, having a roof, to form a structure affording shelter for persons, animals, or property. The word "building" shall be construed for the purposes of this section as though followed by the words "or part or parts thereof", unless the context clearly requires a different meaning.

f. Concussion mortar. A device specifically designed and constructed to produce a loud noise and a violent jarring shock for dramatic effect without producing any damage.

g. Fallout area. The area in which any hazardous debris falls after a pyrotechnic device is fired. The fallout area is defined as a circle that, in turn, is defined by the fallout radius.

h. Fallout radius. A line that defines the fallout area of a pyrotechnic device. The line is defined by two points. The first point is at the center of a pyrotechnic device. The second point is the point most distant from the center of the pyrotechnic device at which any hazardous debris from the device can fall.

i. Fire area. The floor area of a story of a building within exterior walls, party walls, fire walls, or any combination thereof.

j. Hazardous debris. Any debris, produced or expelled by the functioning of a pyrotechnic device, that is capable of causing personal injury or unpredicted property damage. This includes, but is not limited to, hot sparks, heavy casing fragments, and unignited components. Materials such as confetti, lightweight foam pieces, feathers, or novelties are not to be construed as hazardous debris.

k. Owner. Any person, agent, firm, association, limited liability company, partnership, or corporation having a legal or equitable interest in the property.

l. Performance. The enactment of a musical, dramatic, operatic, or other entertainment production. The enactment may begin and progress to its end according to a script, plan, or other preconceived list of events, or deviate therefrom. A performance includes any encores.

m. Performer. Any person active in a performance during which pyrotechnics are used and who is not part of the audience or support personnel. Among others, performers include, but are not limited to, actors, singers, musicians, and acrobats.

n. Permit authority. The agency authorized to grant and issue the permits provided for in this section on or within state property shall be the office of fire prevention and control, in the territory within a county park shall be the county park commission, or such other agency having jurisdiction, control, and/or operation of the parks or parkways within which any pyrotechnics are to be used, in a city shall be the duly constituted licensing agency thereof and, in the absence of such agency, shall be an officer designated for the purpose by the legislative body thereof, in a village shall be an officer designated for the purpose by the board of trustees thereof, and, in the territory of a town outside of villages, shall be an officer designated for the purpose by the town board thereof.

o. Permittee.

(1) The person or persons who are responsible, as provided in subparagraph two of this paragraph, for obtaining the necessary permit or permits for the use of indoor pyrotechnics in areas of public assembly or for a production, or who are responsible for obtaining such permit or permits under an applicable local law or ordinance authorized pursuant to subdivision five of this section.

(2) The owner of a place of public assembly or building in which pyrotechnics are to be used shall be responsible for obtaining such permit or permits; provided, however, that such owner, in writing, by agreement or lease, may require or otherwise authorize a lessee, licensee, pyrotechnic operator, or other party to be responsible for obtaining such permit or permits, in which case such other party or parties shall be deemed responsible for obtaining such permit or permits and shall be the permittee for purposes of this article; provided further that the structure is otherwise appropriate for such use under the New York state fire prevention and building code or other such applicable code.

p. Producer. An individual who has overall responsibility for the operation and management of the performance where the pyrotechnics are to be used. Generally, the producer is an employee of the promotion company, entertainment company, festival, theme park, or other entertainment group.

q. Production. All the performances of a musical, dramatic, operatic, or other show or series of shows.

r. Pyrotechnic device. Any device containing pyrotechnic materials and capable of producing a special effect as defined in this subdivision.

s. Pyrotechnic material (Pyrotechnic special effects material). A chemical mixture used in the entertainment industry to produce visible or audible effects by combustion, deflagration, or detonation. Such a chemical mixture consists predominantly of solids capable of producing a controlled, self-sustaining, and self-contained exothermic chemical reaction that results in heat, gas, sound, light, or a combination of these effects. The chemical reaction functions without external oxygen.

t. Pyrotechnic operator (Special effects operator). An individual who has responsibility for pyrotechnic safety and who controls, initiates, or otherwise creates special effects.

u. Pyrotechnic special effect. A special effect created through the use of pyrotechnic materials and devices.

v. Pyrotechnics. Controlled exothermic chemical reactions that are timed to create the effects of heat, gas, sound, dispersion of aerosols, emission of visible electromagnetic radiation, or a combination of these effects to provide the maximum effect from the least volume.

w. Rocket. A pyrotechnic device that moves by the ejection of matter produced by the internal combustion of propellants.

x. Special effect. A visual or audible effect used for entertainment purposes, often produced to create an illusion. For example, smoke might be produced to create the impression of fog being present, or a puff of smoke, a flash of light, and a loud sound might be produced to create the impression that a cannon has been fired.

y. Support personnel. Any individual who is not a performer or member of the audience. Among others, support personnel include the road crew of any production, stage hands, property masters, security guards, fire watch officers, janitors, or any other employee.

z. Venue manager. An individual who has overall responsibility for the operation and management of the facility where pyrotechnics are to be used in a performance.

2. Permit requirements.

a. All uses of all pyrotechnics in areas of public assembly shall be approved by the permit authority. The permit authority shall determine that appropriate measures are established to provided [provide]* acceptable crowd management, security, fire protection, (including sprinklers), and other emergency services. All planning and use of pyrotechnics shall be coordinated with the venue manager and producer.

b. Before the performance of any production, the permittee shall submit a plan for the use of pyrotechnics to the permit authority. After a permit has been granted, the permittee shall keep the plan available at the site for safety inspectors or other designated agents of the permit authority. Any addition of pyrotechnics to a performance or any significant change in the presentation of pyrotechnics shall require approval by the permit authority, except that reducing the number or size of pyrotechnics to be used in a performance shall not be considered to be a significant change in the presentation.

c. (1) The plan for the use of pyrotechnics shall be made in writing or such other form as is required or approved by the permit authority.

(2) The plan shall provide the following:

(a) Name of the person, group, organization, or other entity sponsoring the production.

(b) Date and time of day of the production.

(c) Exact location of the production.

(d) Name of the person actually in charge of firing the pyrotechnics (i.e., the pyrotechnic operator).

---

* The bracketed word has been inserted by the Publisher.

(e) Number, names, and ages of all assistants who are to be present.

(f) Qualifications of the pyrotechnic operator.

(g) Pyrotechnic experience of the operator.

(h) Confirmation of any applicable local, state, and federal licenses held by the operator or assistant.

(i) Evidence of the permittee's insurance carrier or financial responsibility.

(j) Number and types of pyrotechnic devices and materials to be used, the operator's experience with those devices and effects, and a definition of the general responsibilities of assistants.

(k) Diagram of the grounds or facilities where the production is to be held. This diagram shall show the point at which the pyrotechnic devices are to be fired, the fallout radius for each pyrotechnic device used in the performance, the lines behind which the audience shall be restrained, and the placement of sprinkler systems.

(l) Point of on-site assembly of pyrotechnic devices.

(m) Manner and place of storage of the pyrotechnic materials and devices.

(n) Material safety data sheet (MSDS) for the pyrotechnic materials to be used.

(o) Certification that the set, scenery, and rigging materials are inherently flame-retardant or have been treated to achieve flame retardancy.

(p) Certification that all materials worn by performers in the fallout area during use of pyrotechnic effects shall be inherently flame-retardant or have been treated to achieve flame retardancy.

(3) All plans shall be submitted as soon as is possible so that the permit authority has time to be present and to notify other interested parties. In no event shall such advance notice be less than five business days.

d. A walk-through and a representative demonstration of the pyrotechnics shall be approved by the permit authority before a permit is approved. The permit authority may waive this requirement based on past history, prior knowledge, and other factors; provided that the authority is confident that the discharge of pyrotechnics can be conducted safely. The demonstration shall be scheduled with sufficient time allowed to reset/reload the pyrotechnics before the arrival of the audience.

e. All pyrotechnic operators shall be at least twenty-one years old and licensed or approved by the permit authority in accordance with all applicable laws, if any. All assistants shall be at least eighteen years old.

3. Conduct of pyrotechnic performances.

a. Two or more fire extinguishers of the proper classification and size as approved by the permit authority shall be readily accessible while the pyrotechnics are being loaded, prepared for firing, or fired. In all cases, at least two pressurized water or pump extinguishers shall be available. Additional fire extinguishing equipment shall be provided as required by the permit authority. Personnel who have a working knowledge of the use of the applicable fire extinguishers shall be present while the pyrotechnics are being handled, used, or removed. No personnel shall use or handle pyrotechnic materials or devices while under the influence of intoxicating beverages, narcotics, controlled substances, and prescription or nonprescription drugs that can impair judgment. Fire detection and life safety systems shall not be interrupted during the operation of pyrotechnic effects.

b. (1) All pyrotechnic devices shall be mounted in a secure manner to maintain their proper positions and orientations so that, when they are fired, the pyrotechnic effects described in the plan submitted by the permittee are produced. Pyrotechnic devices shall be mounted so that no fallout from the device endangers human lives, results in personal injury, or damages property. Pyrotechnic materials shall be fired only from equipment specifically constructed for the purpose of firing pyrotechnic materials. The pyrotechnic operator shall be responsible for selecting equipment and materials that are compatible.

(2) Where rockets are launched before an audience, performers, or support personnel, the rockets shall be attached securely to a guide wire or cable with both ends securely attached and placed on an impact-resistant surface located at the terminal end of the guide. This guide wire or cable shall be of sufficient strength and flame resistance to withstand the exhaust from the rocket. An effective arrangement to stop the rocket shall be provided.

(3) Pyrotechnics shall be: (a) placed so that any hazardous debris falls into a safe, flame-resistant area; (b) fired so that the trajectory of their pyrotechnic material is not carried over the audience; and (c) placed for firing so that no flammable materials are within their fallout area.

(4) Pyrotechnic devices and materials used indoors shall be specifically manufactured and marked for indoor use by the manufacturer.

(5) Airbursts shall be permitted to be fired above the assembled audience, subject to the following conditions:

(a) The airburst shall be suspended by a minimum 30-gauge metal wire that is attached securely to a secure support acceptable to the authority having jurisdiction.

(b) The airburst shall occur at a minimum height of three times the diameter of the effect.

(c) Where the effect is demonstrated, there shall be no burning or glowing particles below the fifteen-foot level above the floor.

c. Each pyrotechnic device fired during a performance shall be separated from the audience by at least fifteen feet but not by less than twice the fallout radius of the device. Concussion mortars shall be separated from the audience by a minimum of twenty-five feet. There shall be no glowing or flaming particles within ten feet of the audience.

d. (1) The facility where pyrotechnic materials and devices are handled and used shall be maintained in a neat and orderly condition and shall be kept free of any conditions that can create a fire hazard.

(2) Smoking shall not be permitted within twenty-five feet of the area where pyrotechnics are being handled or fired; provided that smoking by performers as part of the performance shall be permitted as blocked in rehearsals and if expressly approved by the pyrotechnic operator and the permit authority.

e. (1) The pyrotechnic effect operator shall advise all performers and support personnel that they are exposed to a potentially hazardous situation when performing or otherwise carrying out their responsibilities in the vicinity of a pyrotechnic effect. Performers and support personnel familiar and experienced with the pyrotechnic effects being used shall be permitted to be in the area of a pyrotechnic effect, but only voluntarily and in the performance of their duties.

(2) No part, projectile, or debris from the pyrotechnic material or device shall be propelled so that it damages overhead properties, overhead equipment, or the ceiling and walls of the facility.

(3) Immediately before any performance, the pyrotechnic operator shall make a final check of wiring, positions, hook-ups, and pyrotechnic devices to ensure that they are in proper working order. The pyrotechnic operator also shall verify safety distances.

(4) The placement and wiring of all pyrotechnic devices shall be designed to minimize the possibility of performers and support personnel disturbing the devices during a performance.

(5) The pyrotechnic operator shall exercise extreme care throughout the performance to ensure that the pyrotechnic devices function correctly and that the performers, support personnel, and audience are clear of the devices.

(6) When pyrotechnics are fired, the quantity of smoke developed shall be controlled so as not to obscure the visibility of exit signs or paths of egress.

4. Bonds. Before granting and issuing a permit for a use of pyrotechnics as provided in this section, the permit authority shall require an adequate bond from the applicant therefor, unless such applicant is a state entity, county park, city, village, or town, or from the person to whom a contract for such use shall be awarded, in a sum to be fixed by the permit authority, which, however, shall not be less than five hundred thousand dollars, conditioned for the payment of all damages which may be caused to a person or persons or to property by reason of the use so permitted and arising from any acts of the permittee, his or her agents, employees, contractors, or subcontractors. Such bond shall run to the owner of the facility for which the permit is granted and issued and shall be for the use and benefit of any person or persons or any owner or owners of any property so injured or damaged, and such person or persons or such owner or owners are hereby authorized to maintain an action thereon, which right of action also shall accrue to the heirs, executors, administrators, successors, or assigns of such person or persons or such owner or owners. The permit authority may accept, in lieu of such bond, an indemnity insurance policy with liability coverage and indemnity protection equivalent to the terms and conditions upon which such bond is predicated and for the purposes herein provided.

5. Local laws or ordinances superseded. All local laws or ordinances regulating the use of pyrotechnics within the contemplation of this section are hereby superseded by the provisions of this section, with the exception of:

a. all laws or ordinances enacted by a city of one million or more; and

b. other local laws or ordinances that prohibit the use of indoor pyrotechnics.

HISTORY: Add, L 2003, ch 584, § 1, eff Nov 1, 2003; amd, L 2013, ch 127, § 3, eff July 12, 2013.

§ 405.12. Unpermitted use of indoor pyrotechnics in the second degree

A person is guilty of unpermitted use of indoor pyrotechnics in the second degree when he or she is responsible for obtaining a necessary permit to use indoor pyrotechnics, as required by paragraph o of subdivision one of section 405.10 of this article, and, without obtaining such permit or knowing that he or she is not in compliance with the terms of a permit, he or she intentionally ignites or detonates pyrotechnics for which such permit is required, or knowingly permits another to ignite or detonate such pyrotechnics, in a building, as defined in paragraph e of subdivision one of section 405.10 of this article.

Unpermitted use of indoor pyrotechnics in the second degree is a class A misdemeanor.

HISTORY: Add, L 2003, ch 584, § 2, eff Nov 1, 2003.

§ 405.14. Unpermitted use of indoor pyrotechnics in the first degree

A person is guilty of unpermitted use of indoor pyrotechnics in the first degree when he or she commits the crime of unpermitted use of indoor pyrotechnics in the second degree, as defined in section 405.12 of this article, and, within the previous five year period, he or she has been convicted one or more times of the crime of unpermitted use of indoor pyrotechnics in the second degree, as defined in section 405.12 of this article, or unpermitted use of indoor pyrotechnics in the first degree, as defined in this section.

Unpermitted use of indoor pyrotechnics in the first degree is a class E felony.

HISTORY: Add, L 2003, ch 584, § 2, eff Nov 1, 2003.

§ 405.16. Aggravated unpermitted use of indoor pyrotechnics in the second degree

A person is guilty of aggravated unpermitted use of indoor pyrotechnics in the second degree when he or she commits the crime of unpermitted use of indoor pyrotechnics in the second degree, as defined in section 405.12 of this article, and, by means of igniting or detonating such indoor pyrotechnics, he or she recklessly: (1) causes physical injury to another person; or (2) damages the property of another person in an amount that exceeds two hundred fifty dollars.

Aggravated unpermitted use of indoor pyrotechnics in the second degree is a class E felony.

HISTORY: Add, L 2003, ch 584, § 2, eff Nov 1, 2003.

§ 405.18. Aggravated unpermitted use of indoor pyrotechnics in the first degree

A person is guilty of aggravated unpermitted use of indoor pyrotechnics in the first degree when he or she commits the crime of unpermitted use of indoor pyrotechnics in the second degree, as defined in section 405.12 of this article, and, by means of igniting or detonating such indoor pyrotechnics, he or she recklessly causes serious physical injury or death to another person.

Aggravated unpermitted use of indoor pyrotechnics in the first degree is a class D felony.

HISTORY: Add, L 2003, ch 584, § 2, eff Nov 1, 2003.

ARTICLE 410   SEIZURE AND FORFEITURE OF EQUIPMENT USED IN PROMOTING PORNOGRAPHY

§ 410.00.   Seizure and forfeiture of equipment used in photographing, filming, producing, manufacturing, projecting or distributing pornographic still or motion pictures

HISTORY: Add, L 1965, ch 1030, § 1, eff Sept 1, 1967.

§ 410.00. Seizure and forfeiture of equipment used in photographing, filming, producing, manufacturing, projecting or distributing pornographic still or motion pictures

1. Any peace officer, acting pursuant to his special duties, or police officer of this state may seize any equipment used in the photographing, filming, printing, producing, manufacturing or projecting of pornographic still or motion pictures and may seize any vehicle or other means of transportation, other than a vehicle or other means of transportation used by any person as a common carrier in the transaction of business as such common carrier, used in the distribution of such obscene prints and articles and such equipment or vehicle or other means of transportation shall be subject to forfeiture as hereinafter in this section provided.

2. The seized property shall be delivered by the police officer or peace officer having made the seizure to the custody of the district attorney of the county wherein the seizure was made, except that in the cities of New York, Yonkers and Buffalo, the seized property shall be delivered to the custody of the police department of such cities, together with a report of all the facts and circumstances of the seizure.

3. It shall be the duty of the district attorney of the county wherein the seizure was made, if elsewhere than in the cities of New York or Buffalo, and where the seizure is made in either such city it shall be the duty of the corporation counsel of the city, to inquire into the facts of the seizure so reported to him and if it appears probable that a forfeiture has been incurred, for the determination of which the institution of proceedings in the supreme court is necessary, to cause the proper proceedings to be commenced and prosecuted, at any time after thirty days from the date of seizure, to declare such forfeiture, unless, upon inquiry and examination such district attorney or corporation counsel decides that such proceedings can not probably be sustained or that the ends of public justice do not require that they should be instituted or prosecuted, in which case, the district attorney or corporation counsel shall cause such seized property to be returned to the owner thereof.

4. Notice of the institution of the forfeiture proceeding shall be served either (a) personally on the owners of the seized property or (b) by registered mail to the owners' last known address and by publication of the notice once a week for two successive weeks in a newspaper published or circulated in the county wherein the seizure was made.

5. Forfeiture shall not be adjudged where the owners established by preponderance of the evidence that (a) the use of such seized property was not intentional on the part of any owner, or (b) said seized property was used by any person other than an owner thereof, while such seized property was unlawfully in the possession of a person who acquired possession thereof in violation of the criminal laws of the United States, or of any state.

6. The district attorney or the police department having custody of the seized property, after such judicial determination of forfeiture, shall, by a public notice of at least five days, sell such forfeited property at public sale. The net proceeds of any such sale, after deduction of the lawful expenses incurred, shall be paid into the general fund of the county wherein the seizure was made except that the net proceeds of the sale of property seized in the cities of New York and Buffalo shall be paid into the respective general funds of such cities.

7. Whenever any person interested in any property which is seized and declared forfeited under the provisions of this section files with a justice of the supreme court a petition for the recovery of such forfeited property, the justice of the supreme court may restore said forfeited property upon such terms and conditions as he deems reasonable and just, if the petitioner establishes either of the affirmative defenses set forth in subdivision five of this section and that the petitioner was without personal or actual knowledge of the forfeiture proceeding. If the petition be filed after the sale of the forfeited property, any judgment in favor of the petitioner shall be limited to the net proceeds of such sale, after deduction of the lawful expenses and costs incurred by the district attorney, police department or corporation counsel.

8. No suit or action under this section for wrongful seizure shall be instituted unless such suit or action is commenced within two years after the time when the property was seized.

9. For the purposes of this section only, a pornographic still or motion picture, is defined as a still or motion picture showing acts of sexual intercourse or acts of sexual perversion. This section shall not be construed as applying to bona fide medical photographs or films.

PL

HISTORY: Add, L 1965, ch 1030, § 1, eff Sept 1, 1967, with substance derived from § 1141-c. Sub 1, amd, L 1980, ch 843, § 53, eff Sept 1, 1980. Sub 2, amd, L 1980, ch 843, § 53, L 1983, ch 608, § 1, eff July 25, 1983.

ARTICLE 415   SEIZURE AND FORFEITURE OF VEHICLES, VESSELS AND AIRCRAFT USED TO TRANSPORT OR CONCEAL GAMBLING RECORDS

§ 415.00.   **Seizure and forfeiture of vehicles, vessels and aircraft used to transport or conceal gambling records**

HISTORY: Add, L 1969, ch 920, § 2, eff Sept 1, 1969.

§ 415.00. Seizure and forfeiture of vehicles, vessels and aircraft used to transport or conceal gambling records

1. It shall be unlawful to transport, carry, convey or conceal in, upon or by means of any vehicle, vessel or aircraft, with knowledge of the contents thereof, any writing, paper, instrument or article:

   (a) Of a kind commonly used in the operation or promotion of a bookmaking scheme or enterprise, and constituting, reflecting or representing more than five bets totaling more than five thousand dollars; or

   (b) Of a kind commonly used in the operation, promotion or playing of a lottery or policy scheme or enterprise, and constituting, reflecting or representing more than five hundred plays or chances therein.

2. Any vehicle, vessel or aircraft which has been or is being used in violation of subdivision one by a person other than a bettor, player or shareholder whose bets, plays or shares are represented by all such writings, papers, instruments or articles, shall be seized by any peace officer, who is acting pursuant to his special duties, or police officer, and forfeited as provided in this section. However, such forfeiture and seizure provisions shall not apply to any vehicle, vessel or aircraft used by any person as a common carrier in the transaction of business as such common carrier.

3. The seized property shall be delivered by the police officer or peace officer having made the seizure to the custody of the district attorney of the county wherein the seizure was made, except that in the cities of New York, Yonkers and Buffalo, the seized property shall be delivered to the custody of the police department of such cities, together with a report of all the facts and circumstances of the seizure.

4. It shall be the duty of the district attorney of the county wherein the seizure is made, if elsewhere than in the cities of New York, Yonkers or Buffalo, and where the seizure is made in either such city it shall be the duty of the corporation counsel of the city, to inquire into the facts of the seizure so reported to him and if it appears probable that a forfeiture has been incurred by reason of a violation of this section, for the determination of which the institution of proceedings in the supreme court is necessary, to cause the proper proceedings to be commenced and prosecuted, at any time after thirty days from the date of seizure, to declare such forfeiture, unless, upon inquiry and examination, such district attorney or corporation counsel decides that such proceedings can not probably be sustained or that the ends of public justice do not require that they should be instituted or prosecuted, in which case, the district attorney or corporation counsel shall cause such seized property to be returned to the owner thereof.

5. Notice of the institution of the forfeiture proceeding shall be served either (a) personally on the owners of the seized property, or (b) by registered mail to the owners' last known address and by publication of the notice once a week for two successive weeks in a newspaper published or circulated in the county wherein the seizure was made.

6. Forfeiture shall not be adjudged where the owners establish by preponderance of the evidence that (a) the use of such seized property, in violation of subdivision one of this section, was not intentional on the part of any owner, or (b) said seized property was used in violation of subdivision one of this section by any person other than an owner thereof, while such seized property was unlawfully in the possession of a person who acquired possession thereof in violation of the criminal laws of the United States, or of any state.

7. The district attorney or the police department having custody of the seized property, after such judicial determination of forfeiture, shall, at their discretion, either retain such seized property for the official use of their office or department, or, by a public notice of at least five days, sell such forfeited property at public sale. The net proceeds of any such sale, after deduction of the lawful expenses incurred, shall be paid into the general fund of the county wherein the seizure was made except that the net proceeds of the sale of property seized in the cities of New York, Yonkers and Buffalo shall be paid into the respective general funds of such cities.

8. Whenever any person interested in any property which is seized and declared forfeited under the provisions of this section files with a justice of the supreme court a petition for the recovery of such forfeited property, the justice of the supreme court may restore said forfeited property upon such terms and conditions as he deems reasonable and just, if the petitioner establishes either of the affirmative defenses set forth in subdivision six of this section and that the petitioner was without personal or actual knowledge of the forfeiture proceeding. If the petition be filed after the sale of the forfeited property, any judgment in favor of the petitioner shall be limited to the net proceeds of such sale after deduction of the lawful expenses and costs incurred by the district attorney, police department or corporation counsel.

9. No suit or action under this section for wrongful seizure shall be instituted unless such suit or action is commenced within two years after the time when the property was seized.

HISTORY: Add, L 1969, ch 920, § 2, eff Sept 1, 1969. Sub 2, amd, L 1980, ch 843, § 54, eff Sept 1, 1980. Sub 3, amd, L 1980, ch 843, § 54, L 1983, ch 608, § 2, eff July 25, 1983. Sub 4, amd, L 1983, ch 608, § 2, eff July 25, 1983. Sub 7, amd, L 1983, ch 608, § 2, eff July 25, 1983.

ARTICLE 420 SEIZURE AND DESTRUCTION OF UNAUTHORIZED RECORDINGS OF SOUND AND FORFEITURE OF EQUIPMENT USED IN THE PRODUCTION THEREOF

§ 420.00.   Seizure and destruction of unauthorized recordings
§ 420.05.   Seizure and forfeiture of equipment used in the production of unauthorized recordings

HISTORY: Add, L 1978, ch 445, § 3, eff Sept 1, 1978.

§ 420.00. Seizure and destruction of unauthorized recordings

Any article produced in violation of article two hundred seventy-five of this chapter may be seized by any police officer upon the arrest of any individual in possession of same. Upon final determination of the charges, the court shall, upon proper notice by the district attorney or representative of the crime victim or victims, after prior notice to the district attorney and custodian of the seized property, enter an order preserving any goods manufactured, sold, offered for sale, distributed or produced in violation of this article, as evidence for use in other cases, including a civil action. This notice must be received within thirty days of final determination of the charges. The cost of storage, security, and destruction of goods so ordered for preservation and use as evidence in a civil action, other than a civil action under article thirteen-A of the civil practice law and rules initiated by the district attorney, shall be paid by the party seeking preservation of the evidence for a civil action. If no such order is entered within the thirty day period, the district attorney or custodian of the seized property must cause such articles to be destroyed. Destruction shall not include auction, sale, or distribution of the items in their original form.

HISTORY: Add, L 1978, ch 445, § 3, eff Sept 1, 1978. Amd, L 2001, ch 542, § 1, eff March 12, 2002, L 2002, ch 149, § 1, eff March 12, 2002. Section heading, amd, L 1990, ch 460, § 2, eff Nov 1, 1990.

§ 420.05. Seizure and forfeiture of equipment used in the production of unauthorized recordings

1. Any police officer of this state may seize any equipment, or components, used in the manufacture or production of unauthorized recordings and may seize any vehicle or other means of transportation, other than a vehicle or means of transportation used by any person as a common carrier in the transaction of business as such common carrier, used in the distribution of such unauthorized recordings and such equipment or vehicle or other means of transportation shall be subject to forfeiture as provided in this section.

2. The seized property shall be delivered by the police officer having made the seizure to the custody of the district attorney of the county wherein the seizure was made, except that in the cities of New York, Yonkers and Buffalo, the seized property shall be delivered to the custody of the police department of such cities, together with a report of all the facts and circumstances of the seizure.

3. It shall be the duty of the district attorney of the county wherein the seizure was made, if elsewhere than in the city of New York, Yonkers or Buffalo, and where the seizure is made in either such city, it shall be the duty of the corporation counsel of the city, to inquire into the facts of the seizure so reported to him and if it appears probable that a forfeiture has been incurred for the determination of which the institution of proceedings in the supreme court is necessary, to cause the proper proceedings to be commenced and prosecuted, at any time after thirty days from the date of seizure, to declare such forfeiture, unless, upon inquiry and examination such district attorney or corporation counsel decides that such proceedings cannot probably be sustained or that the ends of public justice do not require that they should be instituted or prosecuted, in which case, the district attorney or corporation counsel shall cause such seized property to be returned to the owner thereof.

4. Notice of the institution of the forfeiture proceeding shall be served either:

(a) personally on the owners of the seized property; or

(b) by registered mail to the owners' last known address and by publication of the notice once a week for two successive weeks in a newspaper published or circulated in the county wherein the seizure was made.

5. Forfeiture shall not be adjudged where the owners established by preponderance of the evidence that:

(a) the use of such seized property was not intentional on the part of any owner; or

(b) said seized property was used by any person other than an owner thereof, while such seized property was unlawfully in the possession of a person who acquired possession thereof in violation of the criminal laws of the United States, or of any state.

6. The district attorney or the police department having custody of the seized property, after such judicial determination of forfeiture, shall, by a public notice of at least five days, sell such forfeited property at public sale. The net proceeds of any such sale, after deduction of the lawful expenses incurred, shall be paid into the general fund of the county wherein the seizure was made except

that the net proceeds of the sale of property seized in the cities of New York, Yonkers and Buffalo shall be paid into the respective general funds of such cities.

7. Whenever any person interested in any property which is seized and declared forfeited under the provisions of this section files with a justice of the supreme court a petition for the recovery of such forfeited property, the justice of the supreme court may restore said forfeited property upon such terms and conditions as he deems reasonable and just, if the petitioner establishes either of the affirmative defenses set forth in subdivision five of this section and that the petitioner was without personal or actual knowledge of the forfeiture proceeding. If the petition be filed after the sale of the forfeited property, any judgment in favor of the petitioner shall be limited to the net proceeds of such sale, after deduction of the lawful expenses and costs incurred by the district attorney, police department or corporation counsel.

8. No suit or action under this section for wrongful seizure shall be instituted unless such suit or action is commenced within two years after the time when the property was seized.

> **HISTORY:** Add, L 1978, ch 445, § 3, eff Sept 1, 1978. Section heading, amd, L 1990, ch 460, § 3, eff Nov 1, 1990. Sub 1, amd, L 1990, ch 460, § 3, eff Nov 1, 1990. Sub 2, amd, L 1983, ch 608, § 3, eff July 25, 1983. Sub 3, amd, L 1983, ch 608, § 3, eff July 25, 1983. Sub 6, amd, L 1983, ch 608, § 3, eff July 25, 1983.

ARTICLE 450   DISPOSAL OF STOLEN PROPERTY
§ 450.10.   **Disposal of stolen property**
> **HISTORY:** Add, L 1971, ch 545 § 30, eff Sept 1, 1971.

§ 450.10. Disposal of stolen property

1. When property, other than contraband including but not limited to those items subject to the provisions of sections 410.00, 415.00, 420.00 and 420.05 of this chapter, alleged to have been stolen is in the custody of a police officer, a peace officer or a district attorney and a request for its release is made prior to or during the criminal proceeding, it may not be released except as provided in subdivisions two, three and four of this section. When a request is made for the return of stolen property under this section, the police officer, peace officer or district attorney in possession of such property must provide written notice to the defendant or his counsel of such request as soon as practicable. Such notice shall advise the defendant or his counsel of the date on which the property will be released and the name and address of a person with whom arrangements can be made for the examination, testing, photographing, photocopying or other reproduction of said property.

2. Both the defendant's counsel and the prosecutor thereafter shall make a diligent effort to examine, test and photograph, photocopy or otherwise reproduce the property. Either party may apply to the court for an extension of any period allowed for examination, testing, photographing, photocopying or otherwise reproducing the property. For good cause shown the court may order retention of the property for use as evidence by either party. Unless extended by a court order sought by either party on notice to the other, the property shall be released no later than the time periods for retention set forth in subdivisions three and four of this section to the person making such request after satisfactory proof of such person's entitlement to the possession thereof. Unless a court, upon applicaton [application]* of either party with notice to the other, orders otherwise, the release of property in accordance with the provisions of this section shall be unconditional.

3. Except as provided in subdivision four of this section, when a request is made for the release

---

*   The bracketed word has been inserted by the Publisher.

of property described in subdivision one of this section, the property shall be retained until either the expiration of a fifteen day period from receipt by the defendant or his counsel of the notice of the request, or the examination testing and photographing, photocopying or other reproduction of such property, by the parties, whichever event occurs first. The fifteen day period may be extended by up to five additional days by agreement between the parties.

4. (a) Except as provided in paragraphs (b) and (c) of this subdivision and in subdivision eleven of this section, when a request is made for the release of property described in subdivision one of this section, and the property shall consist of perishables, fungible retail items, motor vehicles or any other property release of which is necessary for either the operation of a business or the health or welfare of any person, the property shall be retained until either the expiration of a forty-eight hour period from the receipt by the defendant's counsel of the notice of the request, or the examination, testing and photocopying, photographing or other reproduction of such property, by the parties whichever event occurs first. The forty-eight hour period may be extended by up to twenty-four additional hours by agreement between the parties. For the purposes of this section, perishables shall mean any property likely to spoil or decay or diminish significantly in value within twenty days of the initial retention of the property.

(b) If, upon oral or written application by the district attorney with notice to the defendant or his counsel, a court determines that immediate release of property described in paragraph (a) of this subdivision is required under the attendant circumstances, the court shall issue an order releasing the property and, if requested by either party, setting, as a part of such order, any condition appropriate in the furtherance of justice.

(c) A motor vehicle alleged to have been stolen but not alleged to have been used in connection with any crime or criminal transaction other than the theft or unlawful use of said motor vehicle, which is in the custody of a police officer, a peace officer or a district attorney, may be released expeditiously to its registered owner or the owner's representative without prior notice to the defendant. Before such release, evidentiary photographs shall be taken of such motor vehicle. Such photographs shall include the vehicle identification number, registration on windshield, license plates, each side of the vehicle, including vent windows, door locks and handles, the front and back of the vehicle, the interior of the vehicle, including ignition lock, seat to floor clearance, center console, radio receptacle and dashboard area, the motor, and any other interior or exterior surfaces showing any and all damage to the vehicle. Notice of such release, and the photographs taken of said vehicle, shall be furnished to the defendant within fifteen days after arraignment or after counsel initially appears on behalf of the defendant or respondent, whichever occurs later.

5. If stolen property comes into the custody of a court, it must, unless temporary retention be deemed necessary in furtherance of justice, be delivered to the owner, on satisfactory proof of his title, and on his paying the necessary expenses incurred in its preservation, to be certified by the court.

6. If stolen property has not been delivered to the owner, the court before which a trial is had for stealing it, may, on proof of his title, order it to be restored to the owner.

7. If stolen property is not claimed by the owner, before the expiration of six months from the conviction of a person for stealing it, the court or other officer having it in custody must, on payment of the necessary expenses incurred in its preservation, deliver it to the county commissioner of social services, or in the city of New York, to the commissioner of social services, to be applied for the benefit of the poor of the county or city, as the case may be.

8. Except in the city of New York, when money or other property is taken from a defendant, arrested upon a charge of an offense, the officer taking it must, at the time, give duplicate receipts therefor, specifying particularly the amount of property taken, one of which receipts he must deliver to the defendant, and the other of which he must forthwith file with the court in which the criminal action is pending.

9. The commissioners of police of the city of New York may designate some person to take charge of all property alleged to be stolen, and which may be brought into the police office, and all property taken from the person of a prisoner, and may prescribe regulations in regard to the duties of the clerk or clerks so designated, and to require and take security for the faithful performance of the duties imposed by this subdivision, and it shall be the duty of every officer into whose possession such property may come, to deliver the same forthwith to the person so designated.

10. Where there has been a failure to comply with the provisions of this section, and where the district attorney does not demonstrate to the satisfaction of the court that such failure has not caused the defendant prejudice, the court shall instruct the jury that it may consider such failure in determining the weight to be given such evidence and may also impose any other sanction set forth in subdivision one of section 240.70 of the criminal procedure law; provided, however, that unless the defendant has convinced the court that such failure has caused him undue prejudice, the court shall not preclude the district attorney from introducing into evidence the property, photographs, photocopies, or other reproductions of the property or, where appropriate, testimony concerning its value and condition, where such evidence is otherwise properly authenticated and admissible under the rules of evidence. Failure to comply with any one or more of the provisions of this section shall not for that reason alone be grounds for dismissal of the accusatory instrument.

11. When a request for the release of stolen property is made pursuant to paragraph (a) of subdivision four of this section and the defendant is not represented by counsel the notice required pursuant to subdivision one of this section shall be personally delivered to the defendant and release of said property shall not occur for a period less than five days: from (a) the delivery of such notice; or (b) in the case of delivery to such person in custody, from the first appearance before the court, whichever is later.

HISTORY: Add, L 1971, ch 545 § 30, eff Sept 1, 1971, with substance derived from Crim C §§ 685–691. Sub 1, add, L 1984, ch 795, § 2, eff Nov 1, 1984. Former sub 1, add, L 1981, ch 567, § 1; repealed, L 1984, ch 795, § 1, eff Nov 1, 1984. Prior sub 1, amd, L 1980, ch 843, § 55; deleted, L 1981, ch 567, § 1, eff Sept 1, 1981. Sub 2, add, L 1984, ch 795, § 2, eff Nov 1, 1984. Former sub 2, add, L 1981, ch 567, § 2; repealed, L 1984, ch 795, § 1, eff Nov 1, 1984. Prior sub 2, deleted, L 1981, ch 567, § 2, eff Sept 1, 1981. Sub 2-a, add, L 1982, ch 892, § 1; repealed, L 1984, ch 795, § 1, eff Nov 1, 1984. Sub 3, add, L 1984, ch 795, § 2, eff Nov 1, 1984. Former sub 3, renumbered sub 5, L 1984, ch 795, § 1, eff Nov 1, 1984. Sub 4, add, L 1984, ch 795, § 2, eff Nov 1, 1984. Former sub 4, renumbered sub 6, L 1984, ch 795, § 1, eff Nov 1, 1984. Sub 4, par (a), amd, L 1992, ch 421, § 1, eff Nov 1, 1992. Sub 4, par (c), add, L 1992, ch 421, § 2, eff Nov 1, 1992. Sub 5, formerly sub 3, renumbered sub 5, L 1984, ch 795, § 1, eff Nov 1, 1984. Former sub 5, renumbered sub 7, L 1984, ch 795, § 1, eff Nov 1, 1984. Sub 6, formerly sub 4, renumbered sub 6, L 1984, ch 795, § 1, eff Nov 1, 1984. Former sub 6, renumbered sub 8, L 1984, ch 795, § 1, eff Nov 1, 1984. Sub 7, formerly sub 5, renumbered sub 7, L 1984, ch 795, § 1, eff Nov 1, 1984. Former sub 7, renumbered sub 9, L 1984, ch 795, § 1, eff Nov 1, 1984. Sub 8, formerly sub 6, renumbered sub 8, L 1984, ch 795, § 1, eff Nov 1, 1984. Sub 9, formerly sub 7, renumbered sub 9, L 1984, ch 795, § 1, eff Nov 1, 1984. Sub 10, add, L 1984, ch 795, § 2, eff Nov 1, 1984. Sub 11, add, L 1984, ch 795, § 2, eff Nov 1, 1984.

TITLE X   Organized Crime Control Act

ARTICLE 460
ENTERPRISE CORRUPTION

ARTICLE 470
MONEY LAUNDERING

ARTICLE 480
CRIMINAL FORFEITURE—FELONY CONTROLLED SUBSTANCE OFFENSES

HISTORY: Add, L 1986, ch 516, § 2, eff Nov 1, 1986.

ARTICLE 460   ENTERPRISE CORRUPTION

HISTORY: Add, L 1986, ch 516, § 2, eff Nov 1, 1986.

§ 460.00. Legislative findings

The legislature finds and determines as follows:

Organized crime in New York state involves highly sophisticated, complex and widespread forms of criminal activity. The diversified illegal conduct engaged in by organized crime, rooted in the illegal use of force, fraud, and corruption, constitutes a major drain upon the state's economy, costs citizens and businesses of the state billions of dollars each year, and threatens the peace, security and general welfare of the people of the state.

Organized crime continues to expand its corrosive influence in the state through illegal enterprises engaged in such criminal endeavors as the theft and fencing of property, the importation and distribution of narcotics and other dangerous drugs, arson for profit, hijacking, labor racketeering, loansharking, extortion and bribery, the illegal disposal of hazardous wastes, syndicated gambling, trafficking in stolen securities, insurance and investment frauds, and other forms of economic and social exploitation.

The money and power derived by organized crime through its illegal enterprises and endeavors is increasingly being used to infiltrate and corrupt businesses, unions and other legitimate enterprises and to corrupt our democratic processes. This infiltration takes several forms with legitimate enterprises being employed as instrumentalities, injured as victims, or taken as prizes. Through such infiltration the power of an enterprise can be diverted to criminal ends, its resources looted, or it can be taken over entirely, either on paper or de facto. Thus, for purposes of making both criminal and civil remedies available to deal with the corruption of such enterprises, the concept of criminal enterprise should not be limited to traditional criminal syndicates or crime families, and may include persons who join together in a criminal enterprise, as defined by subdivision three of section 460.10 of this article, for the purpose of corrupting such legitmate enterprises or infiltrating and illicitly influencing industries.

One major cause of the continuing growth of organized criminal activities within the state is the inadequacy and limited nature of sanctions and remedies available to state and local law enforcement officials to deal with this intricate and varied criminal conduct. Existing penal law provisions are primarily concerned with the commission of specific and limited criminal acts without regard to the relationships of particular criminal acts or the illegal profits derived therefrom, to legitimate or illicit enterprises operated or controlled by organized crime. Further, traditional penal law provisions only provide for the imposition of conventional criminal penalties, including imprisonment, fines and probation, for entrenched organized crime enterprises. Such penalties are not adequate to enable the state to effectively fight organized crime. Instead, new penal prohibitions and enhanced sanctions, and new civil and criminal remedies are necessary to deal with the unlawful activities of persons and enterprises engaged in organized crime. Comprehensive statutes enacted at the federal level and in a number of other states with significant organized crime problems, have provided law enforcement agencies with an effective tool to fight organized crime. Such laws permit law enforcement authorities (i) to charge and prove patterns of criminal activity and their connection to ongoing enterprises, legitimate or illegal, that are controlled or operated by organized crime, and (ii) to apply criminal and civil penalties designed to prevent and eliminate organized crime's involvement with such enterprises. The organized crime control act is a statute of comparable purpose but tempered by reasonable limitations on its applicability, and by due regard for the rights of innocent persons. Because of its more rigorous definitions, this act will not apply to some situations encompassed within comparable statutes in other jurisdictions. This act is vital to the peace, security and general welfare of the state.

In part because of its highly diverse nature, it is impossible to precisely define what organized crime is. This article, however, does attempt to define and criminalize what organized crime does. This article focuses upon criminal enterprises because their sophistication and organization make them more effective at their criminal purposes and because their structure and insulation protect their leadership from detection and prosecution.

At the same time, this article is not intended to be employed to prosecute relatively minor or isolated acts of criminality which, while related to an enterprise and arguably part of a pattern as defined in this article, can be adequately and more fairly prosecuted as separate offenses. Similarly, particular defendants may play so minor a role in a criminal enterprise that their culpability would be unfairly distorted by prosecution and punishment for participation in the enterprise.

The balance intended to be struck by this act cannot readily be codified in the form of restrictive definitions or a categorical list of exceptions. General, yet carefully drawn definitions of the terms "pattern of criminal activity" and "criminal enterprise" have been employed. Notwithstanding the provisions of section 5.00 of this chapter these definitions should be given their plain meaning, and should not be construed either liberally or strictly, but in the context of the legislative purposes set forth in these findings. Within the confines of these and other applicable definitions, discretion ought still be exercised. Once the letter of the law is complied with, including the essential showing that there is a pattern of conduct which is criminal under existing statutes, the question whether to prosecute under those statutes or for the pattern itself is essentially one of fairness. The answer will depend on the particular situation, and is best addressed by those institutions of government which have traditionally exercised that function: the grand jury, the public prosecutor, and an independent judiciary.

HISTORY: Add, L 1986, ch 516, § 2, eff Nov 1, 1986.

§ 460.10. Definitions

The following definitions are applicable to this article.

1. "Criminal act" means conduct constituting any of the following crimes, or conspiracy or attempt to commit any of the following felonies:

(a) Any of the felonies set forth in this chapter: sections 120.05, 120.10 and 120.11 relating to assault; sections 121.12 and 121.13 relating to strangulation; sections 125.10 to 125.27 relating to homicide; sections 130.25, 130.30 and 130.35 relating to rape; sections 135.20 and 135.25 relating to kidnapping; section 135.35 relating to labor trafficking; section 135.65 relating to coercion; sections 140.20, 140.25 and 140.30 relating to burglary; sections 145.05, 145.10 and 145.12 relating to criminal mischief; article one hundred fifty relating to arson; sections 155.30, 155.35, 155.40 and 155.42 relating to grand larceny; sections 177.10, 177.15, 177.20 and 177.25 relating to health care fraud; article one hundred sixty relating to robbery; sections 165.45, 165.50, 165.52 and 165.54 relating to criminal possession of stolen property; sections 165.72 and 165.73 relating to trademark counterfeiting; sections 170.10, 170.15, 170.25, 170.30, 170.40, 170.65 and 170.70 relating to forgery; sections 175.10, 175.25, 175.35, 175.40 and 210.40 relating to false statements; sections 176.15, 176.20, 176.25 and 176.30 relating to insurance fraud; sections 178.20 and 178.25 relating to criminal diversion of prescription medications and prescriptions; sections 180.03, 180.08, 180.15, 180.25, 180.40, 180.45, 200.00, 200.03, 200.04, 200.10, 200.11, 200.12, 200.20, 200.22, 200.25, 200.27, 200.56, 215.00, 215.05 and 215.19; sections 187.10, 187.15, 187.20 and 187.25 relating to residential mortgage fraud, sections 190.40 and 190.42 relating to criminal usury; section 190.65 relating to schemes to defraud; any felony defined in article four hundred ninety-six; sections 205.60 and 205.65 relating to hindering prosecution; sections 210.10, 210.15, and 215.51 relating to perjury and contempt; section 215.40 relating to tampering with physical evidence; sections 220.06, 220.09, 220.16, 220.18, 220.21, 220.31, 220.34, 220.39, 220.41, 220.43, 220.46, 220.55, 220.60, 220.65 and 220.77 relating to controlled substances; sections 225.10 and 225.20 relating to gambling; sections 230.25, 230.30, and 230.32 relating to promoting prostitution; section 230.34 relating to sex trafficking; sections 235.06, 235.07, 235.21 and 235.22 relating to obscenity; sections 263.10 and 263.15 relating to promoting a sexual performance by a child; sections 265.02, 265.03, 265.04, 265.11, 265.12, 265.13 and the provisions of section 265.10 which constitute a felony relating to firearms and other dangerous weapons; sections 265.14 and 265.16 relating to criminal sale of a firearm; section 275.10, 275.20, 275.30, or 275.40 relating to unauthorized recordings; and sections 470.05, 470.10, 470.15 and 470.20 relating to money laundering; or

(b) Any felony set forth elsewhere in the laws of this state and defined by the tax law relating to alcoholic beverage, cigarette, gasoline and similar motor fuel taxes; article seventy-one of the environmental conservation law relating to water pollution, hazardous waste or substances hazardous or acutely hazardous to public health or safety of the environment; article twenty-three-A of the general business law relating to prohibited acts concerning stocks, bonds and other securities, article twenty-two of the general business law concerning monopolies.

2. "Enterprise" means either an enterprise as defined in subdivision one of section 175.00 of this chapter or criminal enterprise as defined in subdivision three of this section.

3. "Criminal enterprise" means a group of persons sharing a common purpose of engaging in criminal conduct, associated in an ascertainable structure distinct from a pattern of criminal activity, and with a continuity of existence, structure and criminal purpose beyond the scope of individual criminal incidents.

4. "Pattern of criminal activity" means conduct engaged in by persons charged in an

enterprise corruption count constituting three or more criminal acts that:

(a) were committed within ten years of the commencement of the criminal action;

(b) are neither isolated incidents, nor so closely related and connected in point of time or circumstance of commission as to constitute a criminal offense or criminal transaction, as those terms are defined in section 40.10 of the criminal procedure law; and

(c) are either: (i) related to one another through a common scheme or plan or (ii) were committed, solicited, requested, importuned or intentionally aided by persons acting with the mental culpability required for the commission thereof and associated with or in the criminal enterprise.

HISTORY: Add, L 1986, ch 516, § 2, eff Nov 1, 1986; amd, L 1995, ch 401, § 1, L 1995, ch 419, § 8, L 1996, ch 102, § 1, L 1996, ch 371, § 1, L 1998, ch 2, § 39, L 1998, ch 369, § 1, L 2000, ch 489, § 2-a, eff Nov 1, 2000, L 2006, ch 442, § 10, eff Nov 1, 2006, L 2007, ch 74, § 7, eff Nov 1, 2007, L 2007, ch 568, § 1, eff Nov 1, 2007, L 2008, ch 312, § 1, eff Oct 19, 2008, L 2008, ch 472, § 21, eff Nov 1, 2008, L 2009, ch 56, § 30 (Part AAA), eff Nov 1, 2009, L 2010, ch 405, § 7, eff Nov 11, 2010, L 2014, ch 37, § 2, eff June 23, 2014, L 2014, ch 55, § 16 (Part H, Subpart A), eff April 30, 2014.

§ 460.20. Enterprise corruption

1. A person is guilty of enterprise corruption when, having knowledge of the existence of a criminal enterprise and the nature of its activities, and being employed by or associated with such enterprise, he:

(a) intentionally conducts or participates in the affairs of an enterprise by participating in a pattern of criminal activity; or

(b) intentionally acquires or maintains any interest in or control of an enterprise by participating in a pattern of criminal activity; or

(c) participates in a pattern of criminal activity and knowingly invests any proceeds derived from that conduct, or any proceeds derived from the investment or use of those proceeds, in an enterprise.

2. For purposes of this section, a person participates in a pattern of criminal activity when, with intent to participate in or advance the affairs of the criminal enterprise, he engages in conduct constituting, or, is criminally liable for pursuant to section 20.00 of this chapter, at least three of the criminal acts included in the pattern, provided that:

(a) Two of his acts are felonies other than conspiracy;

(b) Two of his acts, one of which is a felony, occurred within five years of the commencement of the criminal action; and

(c) Each of his acts occurred within three years of a prior act.

3. For purposes of this section, the enterprise corrupted in violation of subdivision one of this section need not be the criminal enterprise by which the person is employed or with which he is associated, and may be a legitimate enterprise.

Enterprise corruption is a class B felony.

HISTORY: Add, L 1986, ch 516, § 2, eff Nov 1, 1986.

§ 460.22. Aggravated enterprise corruption

A person is guilty of aggravated enterprise corruption when he or she commits the crime of enterprise corruption and two or more of the acts that constitute his or her pattern of criminal activity are class B felonies or higher, and at least two acts are armed felonies as defined in paragraph (a) of subdivision forty-one of section 1.20 of the criminal procedure law or one act is such an armed felony and one act is a violation of subdivision two of section 265.17 of this chapter or one act is a class B violent felony and two are violations of subdivision two of section 265.17 of this chapter.

Aggravated enterprise corruption is a class A-I felony.

HISTORY: Add, L 2013, ch 1, § 52, eff March 16, 2013.

§ 460.25. Enterprise corruption; limitations

1. For purposes of subdivision one of section 460.20 of this article, a person does not acquire or maintain an interest in an enterprise by participating in a pattern of criminal activity when he invests proceeds derived from a pattern of criminal activity in such enterprise.

2. For purposes of subdivision one of section 460.20 of this article, it shall not be unlawful to:

(a) purchase securities on the open market with intent to make an investment, and without the intent of controlling or participating in the control of the issuer, or of assisting another to do so, if the securities of the issuer held by the purchaser, the members of his immediate family, and his or their accomplices in any pattern of criminal activity do not amount in the aggregate to five percent of the outstanding securities of any one class and do not confer, either in the law or in fact, the power to elect one or more directors of the issuer;

(b) make a deposit in an account maintained in a savings and loan association, or a deposit in any other such financial institution, that creates an ownership interest in that association or institution;

(c) purchase shares in co-operatively owned residential or commercial property;

(d) purchase non-voting shares in a limited partnership, with intent to make an investment, and without the intent of controlling or participating in the control of the partnership.

HISTORY: Add, L 1986, ch 516, § 2, eff Nov 1, 1986.

§ 460.30. Enterprise corruption; forfeiture

1. Any person convicted of enterprise corruption may be required pursuant to this section to criminally forfeit to the state:

(a) any interest in, security of, claim against or property or contractual right of any kind affording a source of influence over any enterprise whose affairs he has controlled or in which he has participated in violation of subdivision one of section 460.20 of this article and for which he was convicted and the use of which interest, security, claim or right by him contributed directly and materially to the crime for which he was convicted unless such forfeiture is disproportionate to the defendant's gain from his association or employment with the enterprise, in which event the jury may recommend forfeiture of a portion thereof;

(b) any interest, including proceeds, he has acquired or maintained in an enterprise in violation of subdivision one of section 460.20 of this article and for which he was convicted unless such forfeiture is disproportionate to the conduct he engaged in and on which the forfeiture is based, in which event the jury may recommend forfeiture of a portion thereof; or

(c) any interest, including proceeds he has derived from an investment of proceeds in an enterprise in violation of subdivision one of section 460.20 of this article and for which he was convicted unless such forfeiture is disproportionate to the conduct he engaged in and on which the forfeiture is based, in which event the jury may recommend forfeiture of a portion thereof.

2. (a) Forfeiture may be ordered when the grand jury returning an indictment charging a person with enterprise corruption has received evidence legally sufficient to establish, and providing reasonable cause to believe, that the property or other interest is subject to forfeiture under this section. In that event, the grand jury shall file a special information, not to be disclosed to the jury in the criminal action prior to verdict on the criminal charges, specifying the property or other interest for which forfeiture is sought and containing a plain and concise factual statement which sets forth the basis for the forfeiture. Alternatively, where the defendant has waived indictment and consented to be prosecuted by superior court information pursuant to article one hundred ninety-five of the criminal procedure law, the prosecutor may file, in addition to the superior court information charging enterprise corruption, a special information specifying the property or other interest for which forfeiture is sought and containing a plain and concise factual statement which sets forth the basis for the forfeiture.

(b) After returning a verdict of guilty on an enterprise corruption count or counts, the jury shall be given the special information and hear any additional evidence which is relevant and legally admissible upon the forfeiture count or counts of the special information. After hearing such evidence, the jury shall then deliberate upon the forfeiture count or counts and, based upon all the evidence received in connection with the indictment or superior court information and the special information, may, if satisfied by proof beyond a reasonable doubt that the property or other interest, or a portion thereof, is subject to forfeiture under this section return a verdict determining such property or other interest, or portion thereof, is subject to forfeiture, provided, however, where a defendant has waived a jury trial pursuant to article three hundred twenty of the criminal procedure law, the court may hear and receive all of the evidence upon the indictment or superior court information and the special information and render a verdict upon the enterprise corruption count or counts and the forfeiture count or counts.

(c) After the verdict of forfeiture, the court shall hear arguments and may receive additional evidence upon a motion of the defendant that the verdict of forfeiture (i) is against the weight of the evidence, or (ii) is, with respect to a forfeiture pursuant to paragraph (a) of subdivision one of this section, disproportionate to the defendant's gain from his association or employment with the enterprise, or, with respect to a forfeiture pursuant to paragraph (b) or (c) of subdivision one of this section, disproportionate to the conduct he engaged in on which the forfeiture is based. Upon such a finding the court may in the interests of justice set aside, modify, limit or otherwise condition an order of forfeiture.

3. (a) An order of criminal forfeiture shall authorize the prosecutor to seize all property or other interest declared forfeited under this section upon such terms and conditions as the court shall deem proper. If a property right or other interest is not exercisable or transferable for value by the prosecutor, it shall expire and shall not revert to the convicted person. The court ordering any forfeiture may remit such forfeiture or any portion thereof.

(b) No person shall forfeit any right, title or interest in any property or enterprise under this article who has not been convicted of a violation of section 460.20 of this article. Any person other than the convicted person claiming an interest in forfeited property or other interest may bring a special proceeding to determine that claim, before or after trial, pursuant to section thirteen hundred twenty-seven of the civil practice law and rules, provided, however, that if such an action is brought before trial, it may, upon motion of the prosecutor, and in the court's discretion, be postponed by the court until completion of the trial. In addition, any person claiming an interest in property subject to forfeiture may petition for remission as provided in

PL

subdivision seven of section thirteen hundred eleven of such law and rules.

4. All property and other interests which are criminally forfeited following the commencement of an action under this article, whether by plea, verdict or other agreement, shall be disposed of in accordance with the provisions of section thirteen hundred forty-nine of the civil practice law and rules. In any case where one or more of the counts upon which a person is convicted specifically includes as a criminal act a violation of any offense defined in article two hundred twenty of this chapter, the court shall determine what portion of that property or interest derives from or relates to such criminal act, and direct that distribution of that portion be conducted in the manner prescribed for actions grounded upon offenses in violation of article two hundred twenty.

5. Any person convicted of a violation of section 460.20 of this article through which he derived pecuniary value, or by which he caused personal injury or property damage or other loss, may be sentenced to pay a fine not in excess of three times the gross value he gained or three times the gross loss he caused, whichever is greater. Moneys so collected shall be paid as restitution to victims of the crime for medical expenses actually incurred, loss of earnings or property loss or damage caused thereby. Any excess after restitution shall be paid to the state treasury. In any case where one or more of the counts upon which a person is convicted specifically includes as a criminal act a violation of any offense defined in article two hundred twenty of this chapter, the court shall determine what proportion of the entire pattern such criminal acts constitute and distribute such portion in the manner prescribed by section three hundred forty-nine of the civil practice law and rules for forfeiture actions grounded upon offenses in violation of article two hundred twenty. When the court imposes a fine pursuant to this subdivision, the court shall make a finding as to the amount of the gross value gained or the gross loss caused. If the record does not contain sufficient evidence to support such a finding the court may conduct a hearing upon the issue. In imposing a fine, the court shall consider the seriousness of the conduct, whether the amount of the fine is disproportionate to the conduct in which he engaged, its impact on victims and the enterprise corrupted by that conduct, as well as the economic circumstances of the convicted person, including the effect of the imposition of such a fine upon his immediate family.

6. The imposition of an order of criminal forfeiture pursuant to subdivision one of this section, a judgment of civil forfeiture pursuant to article thirteen-A of the civil practice law and rules, or a fine pursuant to subdivision five of this section or paragraph (b) of subdivision one of section 80.00 of this chapter, shall preclude the imposition of any other such order or judgment of forfeiture or fine based upon the same criminal conduct, provided however that where an order of criminal forfeiture is imposed pursuant to subdivision one of this section, an action pursuant to article thirteen-A of the civil practice law and rules may nonetheless be brought, and an order imposed in that action, for forfeiture of the proceeds of a crime or the substituted proceeds of a crime where such proceeds are not subject to criminal forfeiture pursuant to subdivision one of this section. The imposition of a fine pursuant to subdivision five of this section or paragraph (b) of subdivision one of section 80.00 of this chapter, shall preclude the imposition of any other fine pursuant to any other provision of this chapter.

7. Other than as provided in subdivision six, the imposition of a criminal penalty, forfeiture or fine under this section shall not preclude the application of any other criminal penalty or civil remedy under this article or under any other provision of law.

8. Any payment made as restitution to victims pursuant to this section shall not limit, preclude or impair any liability for damages in any civil action or proceeding for an amount in excess of such payment.

HISTORY: Add, L 1986, ch 516, § 2, eff Nov 1, 1986.

§ 460.40. Enterprise corruption; jurisdiction

A person may be prosecuted for enterprise corruption:

1. in any county in which the principal place of business, if any, of the enterprise was located at the time of the offense, and, if the enterprise had a principal place or business located in more than one county, then in any such county in which any conduct occurred constituting or requisite to the completion of the offense of enterprise corruption; or

2. in any county in which any act included in the pattern of criminal activity could have been prosecuted pursuant to article twenty of the criminal procedure law; provided, however, that such person may not be prosecuted for enterprise corruption in such county based on this subdivision if the jurisdiction of such county is based solely on section 20.60 of the criminal procedure law; or

3. in any county in which he:

(a) conducts or participates in the affairs of the enterprise in violation of subdivision one of section 460.20 of this article,

(b) acquires or maintains an interest in or control of the enterprise in violation of subdivision one of section 460.20 of this article,

(c) invests proceeds in an enterprise in violation of subdivision one of section 460.20 of this article; or

4. in any county in which the conduct of the actor had or was likely to have a particular effect upon such county or a political subdivision or part thereof, and was performed with intent that it would, or with knowledge that it was likely to, have such particular effect therein.

HISTORY: Add, L 1986, ch 516, § 2, eff Nov 1, 1986.

§ 460.50. Enterprise corruption; prosecution

1. Subject to the provisions of section 460.60 of this article, a charge of enterprise corruption may be prosecuted by: (a) the district attorney of any county with jurisdiction over the offense pursuant to section 460.40 of this article; (b) the deputy attorney general in charge of the statewide organized crime task force when authorized by subdivision seven of section seventy-a of the executive law; or (c) the attorney general when he is otherwise authorized by law to prosecute each of the criminal acts specifically included in the pattern of criminal activity alleged in the enterprise corruption charge.

2. For purposes of paragraph (c) of subdivision one of this section, a criminal act or an offense is specifically included in a pattern of criminal activity when the count of the accusatory instrument charging a person with enterprise corruption alleges a pattern of criminal activity and the act is alleged to be a criminal act within the pattern of criminal activity.

HISTORY: Add, L 1986, ch 516, § 2, eff Nov 1, 1986.

§ 460.60. Enterprise corruption; consent to prosecute

1. For purposes of this section, when a grand jury proceeding concerns a possible charge of enterprise corruption, or when an accusatory instrument includes a count charging a person with enterprise corruption, the affected district attorneys are the district attorneys otherwise empowered to prosecute any of the underlying acts of criminal activity in a county with jurisdiction over the offense of enterprise corruption pursuant to section 460.40 of this article, in which:

(a) there has been substantial and significant activity by the particular enterprise; or

(b) conduct occurred constituting a criminal act specifically included in the pattern of criminal activity charged in the accusatory instrument and not previously prosecuted; or

(c) the particular enterprise has its principal place of business.

2. A grand jury proceeding concerning a possible charge of enterprise corruption may be instituted only with the consent of the affected district attorneys. Should the possibility of such a charge develop after a grand jury proceeding has been instituted, the consent of the affected district attorneys shall be sought as soon as is practical, and an indictment charging a person with enterprise corruption may not be voted upon by the grand jury without such consent.

3. A person may be charged in an accusatory instrument with enterprise corruption only with the consent of the affected district attorneys. When it is impractical to obtain the consent specified in subdivision two of this section prior to the filing of the accusatory instrument, then that consent must be secured within twenty days thereafter.

4. When the prosecutor is the deputy attorney general in charge of the statewide organized crime task force, the consent required by subdivisions two and three of this section shall be in addition to that required by subdivision seven of section seventy-a of the executive law.

5. Within fifteen days after the arraignment of any person on an indictment charging a person with the crime of enterprise corruption the prosecutor shall provide a copy of the indictment to those district attorneys whose consent was required pursuant to subdivision three of this section, and shall notify the court and defendant of those district attorneys whose consent the prosecutor has secured. The court shall then review the indictment and the grand jury minutes, notify any district attorney whose consent under subdivision one of this section should have been but was not obtained, direct that the prosecutor provide that district attorney with the portion of the indictment and grand jury minutes that are relevant to a determination whether that district attorney is an "affected district attorney" within the meaning of subdivision one of this section.

6. The failure to obtain from any district attorney the consent required by subdivision two or three of this section shall not be grounds for dismissal of the accusatory instrument or for any other relief upon motion of a defendant in the criminal action.

Upon motion of a district attorney whose consent, pursuant to subdivision three of this section, the court determines was required but not obtained, the court may not dismiss the accusatory instrument or any count thereof but may grant any appropriate relief. Such relief may include, but is not limited to:

(a) ordering that any money forfeited by a defendant in the criminal action, or the proceeds from the sale of any other property forfeited in the criminal action by a defendant, which would have been paid to the county of that district attorney pursuant to section thirteen hundred forty-nine of the civil practice law and rules had the forfeiture action been prosecuted in the county of that district attorney, be paid in whole or in part to the county of that district attorney; or

(b) upon consent of the defendant, ordering the transfer of the prosecution, or any part thereof, to that district attorney or to any other prosecutor with jurisdiction over the prosecution, of the part thereof to be transferred. However, prior to ordering any transfer of the prosecution, the court shall provide to those district attorneys who have previously consented to the prosecution an opportunity to intervene and be heard concerning such transfer.

7. A district attorney whose consent, pursuant to subdivision three of this section, the court determines was required but not obtained may seek the relief described in subdivision six of this

section exclusively by a pre-trial motion in the criminal action based on the indictment charging the crime of enterprise corruption. Such relief must be sought within forty-five days of the receipt of notice from the court pursuant to subdivision five of this section.

HISTORY: Add, L 1986, ch 516, § 2, eff Nov 1, 1986.

§ 460.70. Provisional remedies

1. The provisional remedies authorized by article thirteen-A of the civil practice law and rules shall be available in all criminal actions in which criminal forfeiture or a fine pursuant to section 460.60 is sought to the extent and under the same terms and conditions as provided in article thirteen-A of such law and rules.

2. Upon the filing of an indictment and special information seeking criminal forfeiture under this article all further proceedings with respect to provisional remedies shall be heard by the judge or justice in the criminal part to which the indictment and special information are assigned.

3. For purposes of this section, the indictment and special information seeking criminal forfeiture shall constitute the summons and complaint referred to in article thirteen-A of the civil practice law and rules.

HISTORY: Add, L 1986, ch 516, § 2, eff Nov 1, 1986.

§ 460.80. Court ordered disclosure

Notwithstanding the provisions of article two hundred forty of the criminal procedure law, when forfeiture is sought pursuant to section 460.30 of this chapter, the court may order discovery of any property not otherwise disclosed which is material and reasonably necessary for preparation by the defendant with respect to the forfeiture proceeding pursuant to such section. The court may issue a protective order denying, limiting, conditioning, delaying or regulating such discovery where a danger to the integrity of physical evidence or a substantial risk of physical harm, intimidation, economic reprisal, bribery or unjustified annoyance or embarrassment to any person or an adverse effect upon the legitimate needs of law enforcement, including the protection of the confidentiality of informants, or any other factor or set of factors outweighs the usefulness of the discovery.

HISTORY: Add, L 1986, ch 516, § 2, eff Nov 1, 1986.

ARTICLE 470   MONEY LAUNDERING

HISTORY: Add, L 1988, ch 280, § 1, eff Nov 1, 1988.

§ 470.00. Definitions

The following definitions are applicable to this article.

1. "Monetary instrument" means coin and currency of the United States or of any other

country; personal checks; bank checks; traveler's checks; money orders; and investment securities and negotiable instruments, in bearer form or otherwise, in such form that title thereto passes on delivery, except that "monetary instrument" shall not include payments to attorneys for legal services.

2. "Conducts" includes initiating, concluding or participating in initiating or concluding a transaction.

3. "Transaction" includes a payment, purchase, sale, loan, pledge, transfer, or delivery, and with respect to a financial institution includes a deposit, withdrawal, transfer between accounts, exchange of currency, loan, extension of credit, purchase or sale of any stock, bond, certificate of deposit, or other monetary instrument, use of a safe deposit box, or any other payment, transfer, or delivery by, through, or to a financial institution, by whatever means effected, except that "transaction" shall not include payments to attorneys for legal services.

4. "Criminal conduct" means conduct which is a crime under the laws of this state or conduct committed in any other jurisdiction which is or would be a crime under the laws of this state.

5. "Specified criminal conduct" means criminal conduct committed in this state constituting a criminal act, as the term criminal act is defined in section 460.10 of this chapter, or constituting the crime of enterprise corruption, as defined in section 460.20 of this chapter, or conduct committed in any other jurisdiction which is or would be specified criminal conduct if committed in this state.

6. "Financial institution" means:

(a) an insured bank, as defined in section 3(b) of the Federal Deposit Insurance Act, 12 U.S.C. 1813(h);

(b) a commercial bank or trust company;

(c) a private banker;

(d) an agency or branch of a foreign bank in the United States;

(e) a credit union;

(f) a thrift institution;

(g) a broker or dealer registered with the Securities and Exchange Commission under the Securities and Exchange Act of 19 34, U.S.C. 78a et seq.;

(h) a broker or dealer in securities or commodities;

(i) an investment banker or investment company;

(j) a currency exchange;

(k) an issuer, redeemer, or cashier of travelers' checks, checks, money orders, or similar instruments;

(l) an operator of a credit card system;

(m) an insurance company;

(n) a dealer in precious metals, stones, or jewels;

(o) a pawnbroker;

(p) a loan or finance company;

(q) a travel agency;

(r) a person licensed to engage in the business of receiving money for transmission or transmitting the same by whatever means, or any other person engaged in such business as an agent of a licensee or engaged in such business without a license;

(s) a telegraph company;

(t) a business engaged in vehicle sales, including automobile, airplane and boat sales;

(u) persons involved in real estate closings and settlements;

(v) the United States Postal Service;

(w) an agency of the United States government or of a state or local government carrying out a duty or power of a business described in this subdivision;

(x) a casino, gambling casino, or gaming establishment with an annual gaming revenue of more than a million dollars which:

(i) is licensed as a casino, gambling casino or gaming establishment under the laws of any state or any political subdivision of any state; or

(ii) is an Indian gaming operation conducted under or pursuant to the Indian Gaming Regulatory Act other than an operation which is limited to class 1 gaming as defined in subdivision six of section four of such act; or

(y) any business or agency engaged in any activity which the superintendent of banks or the United States Secretary of the Treasury determines, by regulation, to be an activity which is similar to, related to, or a substitute for activity which any business as described in this subdivision is authorized to engage.

7. "Financial transaction" means a transaction involving:

(a) the movement of funds by wire or other means; or

(b) one or more monetary instruments; or

(c) the transfer of title to any real property, vehicle, vessel or aircraft; or

(d) the use of a financial institution.

8. "Represented" means any representation made by a law enforcement officer, or by another person at the direction of, or with the approval of, such law enforcement officer.

9. "Law enforcement officer" means any public servant, federal or state, who is authorized to conduct an investigation, prosecute or make an arrest for a criminal offense.

10. For the purpose of this article, each of the five counties in the city of New York shall be considered as a separate county.

HISTORY: Add, L 1988, ch 280, § 1; amd, L 2000, ch 489, § 3, eff Nov 1, 2000. Sub 1, amd, L 2000, ch 489, § 3, eff Nov 1, 2000. Sub 2, add, L 2000, ch 489, § 3, eff Nov 1, 2000. Former sub 2, deleted, L 2000, ch 489, § 3, eff Nov 1, 2000. Sub 3, amd, L 2000, ch 489, § 3, eff Nov 1, 2000. Sub 5, amd, L 2000, ch 489, § 3, eff Nov 1, 2000. Sub 6, amd, L 1990, ch 543, § 2, L 2000, ch 489, § 3, eff Nov 1, 2000. Sub 6, opening par, amd, L 2000, ch 489, § 3, eff Nov 1, 2000. Sub 6, par (e), add, L 2000, ch 489, § 3, eff Nov 1, 2000. Former sub 6, par (e), deleted, L 2000, ch 489, § 3, eff Nov 1, 2000. Sub 6, par (g), amd, L 2000, ch 489, § 3, eff Nov 1, 2000. Sub 6, par (k), amd, L 1990, ch 543, § 2, L 2000, ch 489, § 3, eff Nov 1, 2000. Sub 6, par (r), add, L 2000, ch 489, § 3, eff Nov 1, 2000. Former sub 6, par (r), amd, L 1990, ch 543, § 2; deleted, L 2000, ch 489, § 3, eff Nov 1, 2000. Sub 6, par (s), amd, L 1990, ch 543, § 2, eff Nov 1, 1990. Sub 6, par (t), add, L 1990, ch 543, § 2, eff Nov 1, 1990. Sub 6, par (u), add, L 1990, ch 543, § 2, eff Nov 1, 1990. Sub 6, par (v), add, L 1990, ch 543, § 2; amd, L 2000, ch 489, § 3, eff Nov 1, 2000. Sub 6, par (w), add, L 1990, ch 543, § 2; amd, L 2000, ch 489, § 3, eff Nov 1, 2000. Sub 6, par (x), add, L 2000, ch 489, § 3, eff Nov 1, 2000. Sub 6, par (y), add, L 2000, ch 489, § 3, eff Nov 1, 2000. Sub 7, add, L 2000, ch 489, § 3, eff Nov 1, 2000. Sub 8, add, L 2000, ch 489, § 3, eff Nov 1, 2000. Sub 9, add, L 2000, ch 489, § 3, eff Nov 1, 2000. Sub 10, add, L 2000, ch 489, § 3, eff Nov 1, 2000.

§ 470.03. Money laundering: aggregation of value; other matters

1. For purposes of subdivisions one and three of sections 470.05, 470.10, 470.15, 470.21, 470.22 and 470.23, and for purposes of subdivisions one and two of sections 470.20 and 470.24 of this article, financial transactions may be considered together and the value of the property involved may be aggregated, provided that the transactions are all part of a single "criminal transaction" as defined in subdivision two of section 40.10 of the criminal procedure law.

2. For purposes of subdivision two of sections 470.05, 470.10, 470.15, 470.21, 470.22 and 470.23 of this article, separate occasions involving the transport, transmittal or transfer of monetary instruments may be considered together and the value of the monetary instruments involved may be aggregated, provided that the occasions are all part of a single "criminal transaction" as defined in subdivision two of section 40.10 of the criminal procedure law.

3. Nothing in sections 470.05, 470.21, 470.22, 470.23 and 470.24; paragraph (b) of subdivision one, paragraph (b) of subdivision two and paragraph (b) of subdivision three of section 470.10; paragraph (b) of subdivision one, paragraph (b) of subdivision two and paragraph (b) of subdivision three of section 470.15; or paragraph (b) of subdivision one and paragraph (b) of subdivision two of section 470.20 of this article shall make it unlawful to return funds held in escrow:

    (a) as a portion of a purchase price for real property pursuant to a contract of sale; or

    (b) to satisfy the tax or other lawful obligations arising out of an administrative or judicial proceeding concerning the person who provided the escrow funds.

    HISTORY: Add, L 2000, ch 489, § 4, eff Nov 1, 2000. Amd, L 2004, ch 1, § 17 (Part A), eff July 23, 2004. Sub 1, amd, L 2004, ch 1, § 17 (Part A), eff July 23, 2004. Sub 2, amd, L 2004, ch 1, § 17 (Part A), eff July 23, 2004. Sub 3, amd, L 2004, ch 1, § 17 (Part A), eff July 23, 2004. Sub 3, opening par, amd, L 2004, ch 1, § 17 (Part A), eff July 23, 2004.

§ 470.05. Money laundering in the fourth degree

A person is guilty of money laundering in the fourth degree when:

1. Knowing that the property involved in one or more financial transactions represents the proceeds of criminal conduct:

    (a) he or she conducts one or more such financial transactions which in fact involve the proceeds of specified criminal conduct:

    (i) With intent to:

    (A) promote the carrying on of criminal conduct; or

    (B) engage in conduct constituting a felony as set forth in section eighteen hundred three, eighteen hundred four, eighteen hundred five, or eighteen hundred six of the tax law; or

(ii) Knowing that the transaction or transactions in whole or in part are designed to:

(A) conceal or disguise the nature, the location, the source, the ownership or the control of the proceeds of criminal conduct; or

(B) avoid any transaction reporting requirement imposed by law; and

(b) The total value of the property involved in such financial transaction or transactions exceeds five thousand dollars; or

2. Knowing that one or more monetary instruments represents the proceeds of criminal conduct:

(a) he or she transports, transmits, or transfers on one or more occasions, monetary instruments which in fact represent the proceeds of specified criminal conduct:

(i) With intent to promote the carrying on of criminal conduct; or

(ii) Knowing that such transportation, transmittal, or transfer is designed in whole or in part to:

(A) conceal or disguise the nature, the location, the source, the ownership, or the control of the proceeds of criminal conduct; or

(B) avoid any transaction reporting requirement imposed by law; and

(b) The total value of such monetary instrument or instruments exceeds ten thousand dollars; or

3. He or she conducts one or more financial transactions:

(a) involving property represented to be the proceeds of specified criminal conduct, or represented to be property used to conduct or facilitate specified criminal conduct, with intent to:

(i) promote the carrying on of specified criminal conduct; or

(ii) conceal or disguise the nature, the location, the source, the ownership or the control of property believed to be the proceeds of specified criminal conduct; or

(iii) avoid any transaction reporting requirement imposed by law; and

(b) the total value of the property involved in such financial transaction or transactions exceeds ten thousand dollars.

Money laundering in the fourth degree is a class E felony.

HISTORY: Add, L 2000, ch 489, § 5, eff Nov 1, 2000. Former § 470.05, add, L 1988, ch 280, § 1; repealed, L 2000, ch 489, § 5, eff Nov 1, 2000. Sub 1, amd, L 2009, ch 57, § 2 (Part V-1, Subpart I), eff April 7, 2009. Sub 1, par (a), subpar (i), cl (B), amd, L 2009, ch 57, § 2 (Part V-1, Subpart I), eff April 7, 2009.

§ 470.10. Money laundering in the third degree

A person is guilty of money laundering in the third degree when:

1. Knowing that the property involved in one or more financial transactions represents:

(a) the proceeds of the criminal sale of a controlled substance, he or she conducts one or more such financial transactions which in fact involve the proceeds of the criminal sale of a controlled substance:

(i) With intent to:

(A) promote the carrying on of specified criminal conduct; or

(B) engage in conduct constituting a felony as set forth in section eighteen hundred three, eighteen hundred four, eighteen hundred five, or eighteen hundred six of the tax law; or

(ii) Knowing that the transaction or transactions in whole or in part are designed to:

(A) conceal or disguise the nature, the location, the source, the ownership or the control of the proceeds of specified criminal conduct; or

(B) avoid any transaction reporting requirement imposed by law; and

(iii) The total value of the property involved in such financial transaction or transactions exceeds ten thousand dollars; or

(b) the proceeds of criminal conduct, he or she conducts one or more such financial transactions which in fact involve the proceeds of specified criminal conduct:

(i) With intent to:

(A) promote the carrying on of criminal conduct; or

(B) engage in conduct constituting a felony as set forth in section eighteen hundred three, eighteen hundred four, eighteen hundred five, or eighteen hundred six of the tax law; or

(ii) knowing that the transaction or transactions in whole or in part are designed to:

(A) conceal or disguise the nature, the location, the source, the ownership or the control of the proceeds of criminal conduct; or

(B) avoid any transaction reporting requirement imposed by law; and

(iii) The total value of the property involved in such financial transaction or transactions exceeds fifty thousand dollars; or

2. Knowing that one or more monetary instruments represent:

(a) the proceeds of the criminal sale of a controlled substance, he or she transports, transmits, or transfers or attempts to transport, transmit or transfer, on one or more occasions, monetary instruments which in fact represent the proceeds of the criminal sale of a controlled substance from a place in any county in this state to or through a place outside that county or to a place in any county in this state from or through a place outside that county:

(i) With intent to promote the carrying on of specified criminal conduct; or

(ii) Knowing that such transportation, transmittal or transfer is designed in whole or in part to:

(A) conceal or disguise the nature, the location, the source, the ownership or the control of the proceeds of specified criminal conduct; or

(B) avoid any transaction reporting requirement imposed by law; and

(iii) The total value of such monetary instrument or instruments exceeds ten thousand dollars; or

(b) the proceeds of criminal conduct, he or she transports, transmits, or transfers or attempts to transport, transmit or transfer, on one or more occasions monetary instruments which in fact represent the proceeds of specified criminal conduct from a place in any county in this state to or through a place outside that county or to a place in any county in this state from or through a place outside that county:

(i) With intent to promote the carrying on of criminal conduct; or

(ii) Knowing that such transportation, transmittal or transfer is designed in whole or in part to:

(A) conceal or disguise the nature, the location, the source, the ownership, or the control of the proceeds of criminal conduct; or

(B) avoid any transaction reporting requirement imposed by law; and

(iii) The total value of such monetary instrument or instruments exceeds fifty thousand dollars; or

3. He or she conducts one or more financial transactions involving property represented to be:

(a) the proceeds of the criminal sale of a controlled substance, or represented to be property used to conduct or facilitate the criminal sale of a controlled substance:

(i) With intent to:

(A) promote the carrying on of specified criminal conduct; or

(B) conceal or disguise the nature, the location, the source, the ownership or the control of property believed to be the proceeds of specified criminal conduct; or

(C) avoid any transaction reporting requirement imposed by law; and

(ii) The total value of the property involved in such financial transaction or transactions exceeds ten thousand dollars; or

(b) the proceeds of specified criminal conduct, or represented to be property used to conduct or facilitate specified criminal conduct:

(i) With intent to:

(A) promote the carrying on of specified criminal conduct; or

(B) conceal or disguise the nature, the location, the source, the ownership or the control of property believed to be the proceeds of specified criminal conduct; or

(C) avoid any transaction reporting requirement imposed by law; and

(ii) The total value of the property involved in such financial transaction or transactions exceeds fifty thousand dollars.

Money laundering in the third degree is a class D felony.

HISTORY: Add, L 2000, ch 489, § 5, eff Nov 1, 2000. Former § 470.10, add, L 1988, ch 280, § 1; amd, L 1990, ch 543, § 3; repealed, L 2000, ch 489, § 5, eff Nov 1, 2000. Sub 1, amd, L 2009, ch 57, § 3 (Part V-1, Subpart I), eff April 7, 2009. Sub 1, par (a), subpar (i), cl (B), amd, L 2009, ch 57, § 3 (Part V-1, Subpart I), eff April 7, 2009. Sub 1, par (b), subpar (i), cl (B), amd, L 2009, ch 57, § 3 (Part V-1, Subpart I), eff April 7, 2009.

§ 470.15. Money laundering in the second degree

A person is guilty of money laundering in the second degree when:

1. Knowing that the property involved in one or more financial transactions represents:

(a) the proceeds of the criminal sale of a controlled substance, he or she conducts one or more such financial transactions which in fact involve the proceeds of the criminal sale of a controlled substance:

(i) With intent to:

(A) promote the carrying on of specified criminal conduct; or

(B) engage in conduct constituting a felony as set forth in section eighteen hundred three, eighteen hundred four, eighteen hundred five, or eighteen hundred six of the tax law; or

(ii) Knowing that the transaction or transactions in whole or in part are designed to:

(A) conceal or disguise the nature, the location, the source, the ownership or the control of the proceeds of specified criminal conduct; or

(B) avoid any transaction reporting requirement imposed by law; and

(iii) The total value of the property involved in such financial transaction or transactions exceeds fifty thousand dollars; or

(b) the proceeds of specified criminal conduct, he or she conducts one or more such financial transactions which in fact involve the proceeds of specified criminal conduct:

(i) With intent to:

(A) promote the carrying on of specified criminal conduct; or

(B) engage in conduct constituting a felony as set forth in section eighteen hundred three, eighteen hundred four, eighteen hundred five, or eighteen hundred six of the tax law; or

(ii) Knowing that the transaction or transactions in whole or in part are designed to:

(A) conceal or disguise the nature, the location, the source, the ownership or the control of the proceeds of specified criminal conduct; or

(B) avoid any transaction reporting requirement imposed by law; and

(iii) The total value of the property involved in such financial transaction or transactions exceeds one hundred thousand dollars; or

2. Knowing that one or more monetary instruments represent:

(a) the proceeds of the criminal sale of a controlled substance, he or she transports, transmits, or transfers or attempts to transport, transmit or transfer, on one or more occasions, monetary instruments which in fact represent the proceeds of the criminal sale of a controlled substance from a place in any county in this state to or through a place outside that county or to a place in any county in this state from or through a place outside that county:

    (i) With intent to promote the carrying on of specified criminal conduct; or

    (ii) Knowing that such transportation, transmittal or transfer is designed in whole or in part to:

        (A) conceal or disguise the nature, the location, the source, the ownership or the control of the proceeds of specified criminal conduct; or

        (B) avoid any transaction reporting requirement imposed by law; and

    (iii) The total value of such monetary instrument or instruments exceeds fifty thousand dollars; or

  (b) the proceeds of specified criminal conduct, he or she transports, transmits, or transfers or attempts to transport, transmit or transfer, on one or more occasions, monetary instruments which in fact represent the proceeds of specified criminal conduct from a place in any county in this state to or through a place outside that county or to a place in any county in this state from or through a place outside that county:

    (i) With intent to promote the carrying on of specified criminal conduct; or

    (ii) Knowing that such transportation, transmittal or transfer is designed in whole or in part to:

        (A) conceal or disguise the nature, the location, the source, the ownership or the control of the proceeds of specified criminal conduct; or

        (B) avoid any transaction reporting requirement imposed by law; and

    (iii) The total value of such monetary instrument or instruments exceeds one hundred thousand dollars; or

3. He or she conducts one or more financial transactions involving property represented to be:

  (a) the proceeds of the criminal sale of a controlled substance, or represented to be property used to conduct or facilitate the criminal sale of a controlled substance:

    (i) With intent to:

        (A) promote the carrying on of specified criminal conduct; or

        (B) conceal or disguise the nature, the location, the source, the ownership or the control of property believed to be the proceeds of specified criminal conduct; or

        (C) avoid any transaction reporting requirement imposed by law; and

    (ii) The total represented value of the property involved in such financial transaction or transactions exceeds fifty thousand dollars; or

  (b) the proceeds of specified criminal conduct, or represented to be property used to conduct or facilitate specified criminal conduct:

    (i) With intent to:

        (A) promote the carrying on of specified criminal conduct;

(B) conceal or disguise the nature, the location, the source, the ownership or the control of property believed to be the proceeds of specified criminal conduct; or

(C) avoid any transaction reporting requirement imposed by law; and

(ii) The total represented value of the property involved in such financial transaction or transactions exceeds one hundred thousand dollars.

Money laundering in the second degree is a class C felony.

HISTORY: Add, L 2000, ch 489, § 5, eff Nov 1, 2000. Former § 470.15, add, L 1988, ch 280, § 1; repealed, L 2000, ch 489, § 5, eff Nov 1, 2000. Sub 1, amd, L 2009, ch 57, § 4 (Part V-1, Subpart I), eff April 7, 2009. Sub 1, par (a), subpar (i), cl (B), amd, L 2009, ch 57, § 4 (Part V-1, Subpart I), eff April 7, 2009. Sub 1, par (b), subpar (i), cl (B), amd, L 2009, ch 57, § 4 (Part V-1, Subpart I), eff April 7, 2009.

§ 470.20. Money laundering in the first degree

A person is guilty of money laundering in the first degree when:

1. Knowing that the property involved in one or more financial transactions represents:

(a) the proceeds of the criminal sale of a controlled substance, he or she conducts one or more such financial transactions which in fact involve the proceeds of the criminal sale of a controlled substance:

(i) With intent to:

(A) promote the carrying on of specified criminal conduct; or

(B) engage in conduct constituting a felony as set forth in section eighteen hundred three, eighteen hundred four, eighteen hundred five, or eighteen hundred six of the tax law; or

(ii) Knowing that the transaction or transactions in whole or in part are designed to:

(A) conceal or disguise the nature, the location, the source, the ownership or the control of the proceeds of specified criminal conduct; or

(B) avoid any transaction reporting requirement imposed by law; and

(iii) The total value of the property involved in such financial transaction or transactions exceeds five hundred thousand dollars; or

(b) the proceeds of a class A, B or C felony, or of a crime in any other jurisdiction that is or would be a class A, B or C felony under the laws of this state, he or she conducts one or more such financial transactions which in fact involve the proceeds of any such felony:

(i) With intent to:

(A) promote the carrying on of specified criminal conduct; or

(B) engage in conduct constituting a felony as set forth in section eighteen hundred three, eighteen hundred four, eighteen hundred five, [or]* eighteen hundred six of the tax law; or

(ii) Knowing that the transaction or transactions in whole or in part are designed to:

---

* The bracketed word has been inserted by the Publisher.

(A) conceal or disguise the nature, the location, the source, the ownership or the control of the proceeds of specified criminal conduct; or

(B) avoid any transaction reporting requirement imposed by law; and

(iii) The total value of the property involved in such financial transaction or transactions exceeds one million dollars.

2. He or she conducts one or more financial transactions involving property represented to be:

(a) the proceeds of the criminal sale of a controlled substance, or represented to be property used to conduct or facilitate the criminal sale of a controlled substance:

(i) With intent to:

(A) promote the carrying on of specified criminal conduct; or

(B) conceal or disguise the nature, the location, the source, the ownership or the control of property believed to be the proceeds of specified criminal conduct; or

(C) avoid any transaction reporting requirement imposed by law; and

(ii) The total represented value of the property involved in such financial transaction or transactions exceeds five hundred thousand dollars; or

(b) the proceeds of a class A, B or C felony or of a crime in any other jurisdiction that is or would be a class A, B or C felony under the laws of this state, or represented to be property used to conduct or facilitate such crimes:

(i) With intent to:

(A) promote the carrying on of specified criminal conduct; or

(B) conceal or disguise the nature, the location, the source, the ownership or the control of property believed to be the proceeds of specified criminal conduct; or

(C) avoid any transaction reporting requirement imposed by law; and

(ii) The total represented value of the property involved in such financial transaction or transactions exceeds one million dollars.

Money laundering in the first degree is a class B felony.

HISTORY: Add, L 2000, ch 489, § 5, eff Nov 1, 2000. Former § 470.20, redesignated § 470.25, L 2000, ch 489, § 6, eff Nov 1, 2000. Sub 1, amd, L 2009, ch 57, § 5 (Part V-1, Subpart I), eff April 7, 2009. Sub 1, par (a), subpar (i), cl (B), amd, L 2009, ch 57, § 5 (Part V-1, Subpart I), eff April 7, 2009. Sub 1, par (b), subpar (i), cl (B), amd, L 2009, ch 57, § 5 (Part V-1, Subpart I), eff April 7, 2009.

§ 470.21. Money laundering in support of terrorism in the fourth degree

A person is guilty of money laundering in support of terrorism in the fourth degree when:

1. Knowing that the property involved in one or more financial transactions represents either the proceeds of an act of terrorism as defined in subdivision one of section 490.05 of this part, or a monetary instrument given, received or intended to be used to support a violation of article four hundred ninety of this part:

(a) he or she conducts one or more such financial transactions which in fact involve either the proceeds of an act of terrorism as defined in subdivision one of section 490.05 of this part, or a monetary instrument given, received or intended to be used to support a violation of article four hundred ninety of this part:

    (i) With intent to:

        (A) promote the carrying on of criminal conduct; or

        (B) engage in conduct constituting a felony as set forth in section eighteen hundred three, eighteen hundred four, eighteen hundred five, or eighteen hundred six of the tax law; or

    (ii) Knowing that the transaction or transactions in whole or in part are designed to:

        (A) conceal or disguise the nature, the location, the source, the ownership or the control of either the proceeds of an act of terrorism as defined in subdivision one of section 490.05 of this part, or a monetary instrument given, received or intended to be used to support a violation of article four hundred ninety of this part; or

        (B) avoid any transaction reporting requirement imposed by law; and

    (b) the total value of the property involved in such financial transaction or transactions exceeds one thousand dollars; or

2. Knowing that one or more monetary instruments represents either the proceeds of an act of terrorism as defined in subdivision one of section 490.05 of this part, or a monetary instrument given, received or intended to be used to support a violation of article four hundred ninety of this part:

    (a) he or she transports, transmits, or transfers on one or more occasions, monetary instruments which in fact represent either the proceeds of an act of terrorism as defined in subdivision one of section 490.05 of this part, or a monetary instrument given, received or intended to be used to support a violation of article four hundred ninety of this part:

    (i) With intent to promote the carrying on of criminal conduct; or

    (ii) Knowing that such transportation, transmittal, or transfer is designed in whole or in part to:

        (A) conceal or disguise the nature, the location, the source, the ownership, or the control of either the proceeds of an act of terrorism as defined in subdivision one of section 490.05 of this part, or a monetary instrument given, received or intended to be used to support a violation of article four hundred ninety of this part; or

        (B) avoid any transaction reporting requirement imposed by law; and

    (b) the total value of such monetary instrument or instruments exceeds two thousand dollars; or

3. He or she conducts one or more financial transactions:

    (a) involving property represented to be either the proceeds of an act of terrorism as defined in subdivision one of section 490.05 of this part, or a monetary instrument given, received or intended to be used to support a violation of article four hundred ninety of this part, with intent to:

    (i) promote the carrying on of specified criminal conduct; or

(ii) conceal or disguise the nature, the location, the source, the ownership or the control of property believed to be either the proceeds of an act of terrorism as defined in subdivision one of section 490.05 of this part, or a monetary instrument given, received or intended to be used to support a violation of article four hundred ninety of this part; or

(iii) avoid any transaction reporting requirement imposed by law; and

(b) the total value of the property involved in such financial transaction or transactions exceeds two thousand dollars.

Money laundering in support of terrorism in the fourth degree is a class E felony.

HISTORY: Add, L 2004, ch 1, § 18 (Part A), eff July 23, 2004. Sub 1, amd, L 2009, ch 57, § 6 (Part V-1, Subpart I), eff April 7, 2009. Sub 1, par (a), subpar (i), cl (B), amd, L 2009, ch 57, § 6 (Part V-1, Subpart I), eff April 7, 2009.

§ 470.22. Money laundering in support of terrorism in the third degree

A person is guilty of money laundering in support of terrorism in the third degree when:

1. Knowing that the property involved in one or more financial transactions represents either the proceeds of an act of terrorism as defined in subdivision one of section 490.05 of this part, or a monetary instrument given, received or intended to be used to support a violation of article four hundred ninety of this part:

(a) he or she conducts one or more such financial transactions which in fact involve either the proceeds of an act of terrorism as defined in subdivision one of section 490.05 of this part, or a monetary instrument given, received or intended to be used to support a violation of article four hundred ninety of this part:

(i) With intent to:

(A) promote the carrying on of specified criminal conduct; or

(B) engage in conduct constituting a felony as set forth in section eighteen hundred three, eighteen hundred four, eighteen hundred five, or eighteen hundred six of the tax law; or

(ii) Knowing that the transaction or transactions in whole or in part are designed to:

(A) conceal or disguise the nature, the location, the source, the ownership or the control of either the proceeds of an act of terrorism as defined in subdivision one of section 490.05 of this part, or a monetary instrument given, received or intended to be used to support a violation of article four hundred ninety of this part; or

(B) avoid any transaction reporting requirement imposed by law; and

(b) the total value of the property involved in such financial transaction or transactions exceeds five thousand dollars; or

2. Knowing that one or more monetary instruments represent either the proceeds of an act of terrorism as defined in subdivision one of section 490.05 of this part, or a monetary instrument given, received or intended to be used to support a violation of article four hundred ninety of this part:

(a) he or she transports, transmits, or transfers or attempts to transport, transmit or transfer, on one or more occasions, monetary instruments which in fact represent either the proceeds of an act of terrorism as defined in subdivision one of section 490.05 of this part, or a monetary instrument given, received or intended to be used to support a violation of article four hundred ninety of this part from a place in any county in this state to or through a place outside that county or to a place in any county in this state from or through a place outside that county:

(i) With intent to promote the carrying on of specified criminal conduct; or

(ii) Knowing that such transportation, transmittal or transfer is designed in whole or in part to:

(A) conceal or disguise the nature, the location, the source, the ownership or the control of either the proceeds of an act of terrorism as defined in subdivision one of section 490.05 of this part, or a monetary instrument given, received or intended to be used to support a violation of article four hundred ninety of this part; or

(B) avoid any transaction reporting requirement imposed by law; and

(b) The total value of such monetary instrument or instruments exceeds five thousand dollars; or

3. He or she conducts one or more financial transactions involving property represented to be either the proceeds of an act of terrorism as defined in subdivision one of section 490.05 of this part, or a monetary instrument given, received or intended to be used to support a violation of article four hundred ninety of this part:

(a) With intent to:

(i) promote the carrying on of specified criminal conduct; or

(ii) conceal or disguise the nature, the location, the source, the ownership or the control of property believed to be either the proceeds of an act of terrorism as defined in subdivision one of section 490.05 of this part, or a monetary instrument given, received or intended to be used to support a violation of article four hundred ninety of this part; or

(iii) avoid any transaction reporting requirement imposed by law; and

(b) The total value of the property involved in such financial transaction or transactions exceeds five thousand dollars.

Money laundering in support of terrorism in the third degree is a class D felony.

HISTORY: Add, L 2004, ch 1, § 18 (Part A), eff July 23, 2004. Sub 1, amd, L 2009, ch 57, § 7 (Part V-1, Subpart I), eff April 7, 2009. Sub 1, par (a), subpar (i), cl (B), amd, L 2009, ch 57, § 7 (Part V-1, Subpart I), eff April 7, 2009.

§ 470.23. Money laundering in support of terrorism in the second degree

A person is guilty of money laundering in support of terrorism in the second degree when:

1. Knowing that the property involved in one or more financial transactions represents either the proceeds of an act of terrorism as defined in subdivision one of section 490.05 of this part, or a monetary instrument given, received or intended to be used to support a violation of article four hundred ninety of this part:

(a) he or she conducts one or more such financial transactions which in fact involve either the proceeds of an act of terrorism as defined in subdivision one of section 490.05 of this part, or a monetary instrument given, received or intended to be used to support a violation of article four hundred ninety of this part:

    (i) With intent to:

      (A) promote the carrying on of specified criminal conduct; or

      (B) engage in conduct constituting a felony as set forth in section eighteen hundred three, eighteen hundred four, eighteen hundred five, or eighteen hundred six of the tax law; or

    (ii) Knowing that the transaction or transactions in whole or in part are designed to:

      (A) conceal or disguise the nature, the location, the source, the ownership or the control of either the proceeds of an act of terrorism as defined in subdivision one of section 490.05 of this part, or a monetary instrument given, received or intended to be used to support a violation of article four hundred ninety of this part; or

      (B) avoid any transaction reporting requirement imposed by law; and

  (b) the total value of the property involved in such financial transaction or transactions exceeds twenty-five thousand dollars; or

2. Knowing that one or more monetary instruments represent either the proceeds of an act of terrorism as defined in subdivision one of section 490.05 of this part, or a monetary instrument given, received or intended to be used to support a violation of article four hundred ninety of this part:

  (a) he or she transports, transmits, or transfers or attempts to transport, transmit or transfer, on one or more occasions, monetary instruments which in fact represent either the proceeds of an act of terrorism as defined in subdivision one of section 490.05 of this part, or a monetary instrument given, received or intended to be used to support a violation of article four hundred ninety of this part from a place in any county in this state to or through a place outside that county or to a place in any county in this state from or through a place outside that county:

    (i) With intent to promote the carrying on of specified criminal conduct; or

    (ii) Knowing that such transportation, transmittal or transfer is designed in whole or in part to:

      (A) conceal or disguise the nature, the location, the source, the ownership or the control of either the proceeds of an act of terrorism as defined in subdivision one of section 490.05 of this part, or a monetary instrument given, received or intended to be used to support a violation of article four hundred ninety of this part; or

      (B) avoid any transaction reporting requirement imposed by law; and

  (b) the total value of such monetary instrument or instruments exceeds twenty-five thousand dollars; or

3. He or she conducts one or more financial transactions involving property represented to be either the proceeds of an act of terrorism as defined in subdivision one of section 490.05 of this part, or a monetary instrument given, received or intended to be used to support a violation of article four hundred ninety of this part:

  (a) With intent to:

(i) promote the carrying on of specified criminal conduct; or

(ii) conceal or disguise the nature, the location, the source, the ownership or the control of property believed to be either the proceeds of an act of terrorism as defined in subdivision one of section 490.05 of this part, or a monetary instrument given, received or intended to be used to support a violation of article four hundred ninety of this part; or

(iii) avoid any transaction reporting requirement imposed by law; and

(b) The total value of the property involved in such financial transaction or transactions exceeds twenty-five thousand dollars.

Money laundering in support of terrorism in the second degree is a class C felony.

HISTORY: Add, L 2004, ch 1, § 18 (Part A), eff July 23, 2004. Sub 1, amd, L 2009, ch 57, § 8 (Part V-1, Subpart I), eff April 7, 2009. Sub 1, par (a), subpar (i), cl (B), amd, L 2009, ch 57, § 8 (Part V-1, Subpart I), eff April 7, 2009.

§ 470.24. Money laundering in support of terrorism in the first degree

A person is guilty of money laundering in support of terrorism in the first degree when:

1. Knowing that the property involved in one or more financial transactions represents either the proceeds of an act of terrorism as defined in subdivision one of section 490.05 of this part, or a monetary instrument given, received or intended to be used to support a violation of article four hundred ninety of this part:

(a) he or she conducts one or more financial transactions which in fact involve either the proceeds of an act of terrorism as defined in subdivision one of section 490.05 of this part, or a monetary instrument given, received or intended to be used to support a violation of article four hundred ninety of this part:

(i) With intent to:

(A) promote the carrying on of specified criminal conduct; or

(B) engage in conduct constituting a felony as set forth in section eighteen hundred three, eighteen hundred four, eighteen hundred five, or eighteen hundred six of the tax law; or

(ii) Knowing that the transaction or transactions in whole or in part are designed to:

(A) conceal or disguise the nature, the location, the source, the ownership or the control of the proceeds of either the proceeds of an act of terrorism as defined in subdivision one of section 490.05 of this part, or a monetary instrument given, received or intended to be used to support a violation of article four hundred ninety of this part; or

(B) avoid any transaction reporting requirement imposed by law; and

(iii) The total value of the property involved in such financial transaction or transactions exceeds seventy-five thousand dollars.

2. He or she conducts one or more financial transactions involving property represented to be either the proceeds of an act of terrorism as defined in subdivision one of section 490.05 of this part, or a monetary instrument given, received or intended to be used to support a violation of article four hundred ninety of this part:

(a) With intent to:

(i) promote the carrying on of specified criminal conduct; or

(ii) conceal or disguise the nature, the location, the source, the ownership or the control of property believed to be either the proceeds of an act of terrorism as defined in subdivision one of section 490.05 of this part, or a monetary instrument given, received or intended to be used to support a violation of article four hundred ninety of this part; or

(iii) avoid any transaction reporting requirement imposed by law; and

(b) The total represented value of the property involved in such financial transaction or transactions exceeds one hundred twenty-five thousand dollars.

Money laundering in support of terrorism in the first degree is a class B felony.

HISTORY: Add, L 2004, ch 1, § 18 (Part A), eff July 23, 2004. Sub 1, amd, L 2009, ch 57, § 9 (Part V-1, Subpart I), eff April 7, 2009. Sub 1, par (a), subpar (i), cl (B), amd, L 2009, ch 57, § 9 (Part V-1, Subpart I), eff April 7, 2009.

§ 470.25. Money laundering; fines

1. Any person convicted of a violation of section 470.05, 470.10, 470.15, or 470.20 of this article may be sentenced to pay a fine not in excess of two times the value of the monetary instruments which are the proceeds of specified criminal activity. When a fine is imposed pursuant to this subdivision, the court shall make a finding as to the value of such monetary instrument or instruments. If the record does not contain sufficient evidence to support such a finding the court may conduct a hearing upon the issue. In imposing a fine, the court shall consider the seriousness of the conduct, whether the amount of the fine is disproportionate to the conduct in which he engaged, its impact on victims, as well as the economic circumstances of the convicted person, including the effect of the imposition of such a fine upon his immediate family.

2. The imposition of a fine pursuant to subdivision one of this section or paragraph b of subdivision one of section 80.00 of this chapter, shall preclude the imposition of any other order or judgment of forfeiture or fine based upon the same criminal conduct.

HISTORY: Formerly § 470.20, add, L 1988, ch 280, § 1; so designated § 470.25 and amd, L 2000, ch 489, § 6, eff Nov 1, 2000. Sub 1, amd, L 1990, ch 543, § 4, L 2000, ch 489, § 6, eff Nov 1, 2000.

ARTICLE 480   CRIMINAL FORFEITURE—FELONY CONTROLLED SUBSTANCE OFFENSES

HISTORY: Add, L 1990, ch 655, § 14, eff Nov 1, 1990.

§ 480.00. Definitions

The following definitions are applicable to this article.

1. "Felony offense" means only a felony defined in article two hundred twenty of this chapter,

or an attempt or conspiracy to commit any such felony, provided such attempt or conspiracy is punishable as a felony, or solicitation of any such felony provided such solicitation is punishable as a felony.

2. "Property" means real property, personal property, money, negotiable instruments, securities, or anything of value or an interest in a thing of value.

3. "Proceeds" means any property obtained by a defendant through the commission of a felony controlled substance offense, and includes any appreciation in value of such property.

4. "Substituted proceeds" means any property obtained by a defendant by the sale or exchange of proceeds of a felony controlled substance offense, and any gain realized by such sale or exchange.

5. "Instrumentality of a felony controlled substance offense" means any property, other than real property and any buildings, fixtures, appurtenances, and improvements thereon, whose use contributes directly and materially to the commission of a felony controlled substance offense.

6. "Real property instrumentality of a crime" means an interest in real property the use of which contributes directly and materially to the commission of a specified felony offense.

7. "Specified felony offense" means:

(a) a conviction of a person for a violation of section 220.18, 220.21, 220.41, 220.43, or 220.77 of this chapter, or where the accusatory instrument charges one or more of such offenses, conviction upon a plea of guilty to any of the felonies for which such plea is otherwise authorized by law or a conviction of a person for conspiracy to commit a violation of section 220.18, 220.21, 220.41, 220.43, or 220.77 of this chapter, where the controlled substances which are the object of the conspiracy are located in the real property which is the subject of the forfeiture action; or

(b) three or more violations of any of the felonies defined in section 220.09, 220.16, 220.18, 220.21, 220.31, 220.34, 220.39, 220.41, 220.43, 220.77, or 221.55 of this chapter, which violations do not constitute a single criminal offense as defined in subdivision one of section 40.10 of the criminal procedure law, or a single criminal transaction, as defined in paragraph (a) of subdivision two of section 40.10 of the criminal procedure law, and at least one of which resulted in a conviction of such offense, or where the accusatory instrument charges one or more of such felonies, conviction upon a plea of guilty to a felony for which such plea is otherwise authorized by law; or

(c) a conviction of a person for a violation of section 220.09, 220.16, 220.34, 220.39, or 221.30 of this chapter, or where the accusatory instrument charges any such felony, conviction upon a plea of guilty to a felony for which the plea is otherwise authorized by law, together with evidence which: (i) provides substantial indicia that the defendant used the real property to engage in a continual, ongoing course of conduct involving the unlawful mixing, compounding, manufacturing, warehousing, or packaging of controlled substances or where the conviction is for a violation of section 221.30 of this chapter, marijuana as part of an illegal trade or business for gain; and (ii) establishes, where the conviction is for possession of a controlled substance or where the conviction is for a violation of section 221.30 of this chapter, marijuana, that such possession was with the intent to sell it.

HISTORY: Add, L 1990, ch 655, § 14, eff Nov 1, 1990. Sub 7, par (a), amd, L 2009, ch 56, § 31 (Part AAA), eff Nov 1, 2009. Sub 7, par (b), amd, L 2009, ch 56, § 31 (Part AAA), eff Nov 1, 2009.

§ 480.05. Felony controlled substance offenses; forfeiture

1. When any person is convicted of a felony offense, the following property is subject to forfeiture pursuant to this article:

(a) any property constituting the proceeds or substituted proceeds of such offense, unless the forfeiture is disproportionate to the defendant's gain from or participation in the offense, in which event the trier of fact may direct forfeiture of a portion thereof; and

(b) any property constituting an instrumentality of such offense, other than a real property instrumentality of a crime, unless such forfeiture is disproportionate to the defendant's gain from or participation in the offense, in which event the trier of fact may direct forfeiture of a portion thereof.

2. When any person is convicted of a specified offense, the real property instrumentality of such specified offense is subject to forfeiture pursuant to this article, unless such forfeiture is disproportionate to the defendant's gain from or participation in the offense, in which event the trier of fact may direct forfeiture of a portion thereof.

3. Property acquired in good faith by an attorney as payment for the reasonable and bona fide fees of legal services or reimbursement of reasonable and bona fide expenses related to the representation of a defendant in connection with a civil or criminal forfeiture proceeding or a related criminal matter, shall be exempt from a judgment of forfeiture. For purposes of this subdivision, "bona fide" means that the attorney who acquired such property had no reasonable basis to believe that the fee transaction was a fraudulent or sham transaction designed to shield property from forfeiture, hide its existence from governmental investigative agencies, or was conducted for any purpose other than legitimate.

HISTORY: Add, L 1990, ch 655, § 14, eff Nov 1, 1990.

§ 480.10. Procedure

1. After the grand jury votes to file an indictment charging a person with a felony offense as that term is defined in section 480.00 of this article, it may subsequently receive evidence that property is subject to forfeiture under this article. If such evidence is legally sufficient and provides reasonable cause to believe that such property is subject to forfeiture under this article, the grand jury shall file together with the indictment a special forfeiture information specifying the property for which forfeiture is sought and containing a plain and concise factual statement which sets forth the basis for the forfeiture. Alternatively, where the defendant has waived indictment and has consented to be prosecuted for a felony offense by superior court information pursuant to article one hundred ninety-five of the criminal procedure law, the prosecutor may, in addition to the superior court information, file a special forfeiture information specifying the property for which the forfeiture is sought and containing a plain and concise factual statement which sets forth the basis for the forfeiture.

2. At any time before entry of a plea of guilty to an indictment or commencement of a trial thereof, the prosecutor may file a superseding special forfeiture information in the same court in accordance with the provisions of subdivision one of this section. Upon the filing of such a superseding forfeiture information the court must, upon application of the defendant, order any adjournment of the proceedings which may, by reason of such superseding special forfeiture information, be necessary to accord the defendant adequate opportunity to prepare his defense of the forfeiture action.

3. A motion to inspect and reduce made pursuant to section 210.20 of the criminal procedure law

may seek modification of a special forfeiture information dismissing a claim with respect to any property interest therein where the court finds the evidence before the grand jury was legally insufficient to support a claim against such interest.

4. The prosecutor shall promptly file a copy of the special forfeiture information, including the terms thereof, with the state division of criminal justice services and with the local agency responsible for criminal justice planning. Failure to file such information shall not be grounds for any relief under this chapter.

5. In addition to information required to be disclosed pursuant to article two hundred forty of the criminal procedure law, when forfeiture is sought pursuant to this article, and following the defendant's arraignment on the special forfeiture information, the court shall order discovery of any information not otherwise disclosed which is material and reasonably necessary for preparation by the defendant with respect to a forfeiture proceeding brought pursuant to this article. Such material shall include those portions of the grand jury minutes and such other information which pertain solely to the special forfeiture information and shall not include information which pertains to the criminal charges. Upon application of the prosecutor, the court may issue a protective order pursuant to section 240.40 of the criminal procedure law with respect to any information required to be disclosed pursuant to this subdivision.

6. (a) Trial of forfeiture counts by jury or by the court. Evidence which relates solely to the issue of forfeiture shall not be presented during the trial on the underlying felony offense or specified felony offense, and the defendant shall not be required to present such evidence prior to the verdict on such offense. A defendant who does not present evidence in his defense with respect to the trial of the underlying offense is not precluded on account thereof from presenting evidence during the trial of the forfeiture count or counts.

(b) Trial of forfeiture counts by the jury. After returning a verdict of guilty of a felony offense or specified felony offense, or where the defendant has pled guilty to a felony offense or a specified felony offense and has not waived a jury trial of the forfeiture count or counts pursuant to article three hundred twenty of the criminal procedure law, the jury shall be given the forfeiture information and shall hear any additional evidence which is relevant and legally admissible upon the forfeiture count or counts. After hearing such evidence, the jury shall then deliberate upon the forfeiture count or counts, and based upon all the evidence admitted in connection with the indictment or superior court information and the forfeiture information, may, if satisfied by proof beyond a reasonable doubt that the property, or a portion thereof, is subject to forfeiture pursuant to this article, return a verdict directing that such property, or portion thereof, is subject to forfeiture.

(c) Trial of forfeiture counts by the court. Where a defendant has waived a jury trial of the forfeiture count or counts pursuant to article three hundred twenty of the criminal procedure law, the court shall hear all evidence upon the forfeiture information and may, if satisfied by proof beyond a reasonable doubt that the property, or a portion thereof, is subject to forfeiture under this article, render a verdict determining that such property, or a portion thereof, is subject to forfeiture under this article.

(d) After the verdict of forfeiture, the court shall hear arguments and may receive additional evidence upon a motion of the defendant that the verdict of forfeiture (i) is against the weight of the evidence, or (ii) is, with respect to a forfeiture pursuant to this article, disproportionate to the defendant's gain from the offense, or the defendant's interest in the property, or the defendant's participation in the conduct upon which the forfeiture is based. Upon such a finding, the court may in the interest of justice set aside, modify, limit or otherwise condition the verdict of forfeiture.

7. A final judgment or order of forfeiture issued pursuant to this article shall authorize the prosecutor to seize all property directed to be forfeited under this article upon such terms and conditions as the court deems proper. If a property right is not exercisable or transferable for value by the prosecutor, it shall expire and shall not revert to the convicted person.

8. Where the forfeited property consists of real property, the court may at any time prior to a verdict of forfeiture, enter an order pursuant to subdivision four-a of section thirteen hundred eleven of the civil practice law and rules.

9. No person shall forfeit any right, title, or interest in any property under this article who has not been convicted of a felony offense or specified felony offense, as the case may be. Any person claiming an interest in property subject to forfeiture may institute a special proceeding to determine that claim, before or after the trial, pursuant to section thirteen hundred twenty-seven of the civil practice law and rules; provided, however, that if such special proceeding is initiated before trial on the forfeiture count or counts, it may, upon written motion of the prosecutor, and in the court's discretion, be postponed by the court until completion of the trial. In addition, any person claiming an interest in property subject to forfeiture may petition for remission as provided for in subdivision seven of section thirteen hundred eleven of the civil practice law and rules.

10. Testimony of the defendant or evidence derived therefrom introduced in the trial of the forfeiture count may not be used by the prosecution in any post-trial motion proceedings, appeals, or retrials relating to the defendant's criminal liability for the underlying criminal offense unless the defendant has previously referred to such evidence in such post-trial proceeding, appeal, or retrial relating to the underlying offense and the evidence is presented by the prosecutor in response thereto. Upon vacatur or reversal on appeal of a judgment of conviction upon which a verdict of forfeiture is based, any verdict of forfeiture which is based upon such conviction shall also be vacated or reversed.

HISTORY: Add, L 1990, ch 655, § 14, eff Nov 1, 1990.

§ 480.20. Disposal of property

All property which is forfeited pursuant to this article shall be disposed of in accordance with the provisions of section thirteen hundred forty-nine of the civil practice law and rules. All reports required to be filed pursuant to article thirteen-A of such law and rules by a claiming authority shall be filed by the prosecutor in a forfeiture action brought pursuant to this article.

HISTORY: Add, L 1990, ch 655, § 14, eff Nov 1, 1990.

§ 480.25. Election of remedies

The imposition of a judgment or order of forfeiture pursuant to this article with respect to a defendant's interest in property shall preclude the imposition of a judgment or order of forfeiture with respect to such interest in property pursuant to the provisions of any other state or local law based upon the same criminal conduct.

HISTORY: Add, L 1990, ch 655, § 14, eff Nov 1, 1990.

§ 480.30. Provisional remedies

1. The provisional remedies authorized by article thirteen-A of the civil practice law and rules shall be available in an action for criminal forfeiture pursuant to this article to the extent and under the same terms, conditions and limitations as provided in article thirteen-A of such law and rules, except as specifically provided herein.

2. Upon the filing of an indictment and special forfeiture information, or a superior court information and special forfeiture information, seeking forfeiture pursuant to this article, all further proceedings with respect to provisional remedies shall be heard by the judge or justice in the criminal part to which the criminal action is assigned.

3. For purposes of this section, the indictment and special forfeiture information or superior court information and special forfeiture information seeking criminal forfeiture shall constitute the summons with notice or summons and verified complaint referred to in article thirteen-A of the civil practice law and rules.

HISTORY: Add, L 1990, ch 655, § 14, eff Nov 1, 1990.

§ 480.35. Rebuttable presumption

1. In a criminal forfeiture proceeding commenced pursuant to this article, the following rebuttable presumption shall apply: all currency or negotiable instruments payable to the bearer shall be presumed to be the proceeds of a felony offense when such currency or negotiable instruments are (i) found in close proximity to a controlled substance unlawfully possessed by the defendant in an amount sufficient to constitute a violation of section 220.18 or 220.21 of the penal law, or (ii) found in close proximity to any quantity of a controlled substance or marihuana unlawfully possessed by such defendant in a room, other than a public place, under circumstances evincing an intent to unlawfully mix, compound, package, distribute or otherwise prepare for sale such controlled substance or marihuana.

2. The presumption established by this section shall be rebutted by credible and reliable evidence which tends to show that such currency or negotiable instruments payable to the bearer is not the proceeds of a felony offense. In an action tried before a jury, the jury shall be so instructed. Any sworn testimony of a defendant offered to rebut the presumption and any other evidence which is obtained as a result of such testimony, shall be inadmissible in any subsequent proceeding relating to the forfeiture action, or in any other civil or criminal action, except in a prosecution for a violation of article two hundred ten of this chapter. In an action tried before a jury, at the commencement of the trial, or at such other time as the court reasonably directs, the prosecutor shall provide notice to the court and to the defendant of its intent to request that the court charge such presumption.

HISTORY: Add, L 1990, ch 655, § 14, eff Nov 1, 1990.

TITLE Y   Hate Crimes Act of 2000

ARTICLE 485
HATE CRIMES

HISTORY: Add, L 2000, ch 107, § 2, eff Oct 8, 2000.

ARTICLE 485   HATE CRIMES

§ 485.00.   **Legislative findings**

§ 485.05.   **Hate crimes**

§ 485.10.   **Sentencing**

HISTORY: Add, L 2000, ch 107, § 2, eff Oct 8, 2000.

§ 485.00. Legislative findings

The legislature finds and determines as follows: criminal acts involving violence, intimidation and destruction of property based upon bias and prejudice have become more prevalent in New York state in recent years. The intolerable truth is that in these crimes, commonly and justly referred to as "hate crimes", victims are intentionally selected, in whole or in part, because of their race, color, national origin, ancestry, gender, religion, religious practice, age, disability or sexual orientation. Hate crimes do more than threaten the safety and welfare of all citizens. They inflict on victims incalculable physical and emotional damage and tear at the very fabric of free society. Crimes motivated by invidious hatred toward particular groups not only harm individual victims but send a powerful message of intolerance and discrimination to all members of the group to which the victim belongs. Hate crimes can and do intimidate and disrupt entire communities and vitiate the civility that is essential to healthy democratic processes. In a democratic society, citizens cannot be required to approve of the beliefs and practices of others, but must never commit criminal acts on account of them. Current law does not adequately recognize the harm to public order and individual safety that hate crimes cause. Therefore, our laws must be strengthened to provide clear recognition of the gravity of hate crimes and the compelling importance of preventing their recurrence.

Accordingly, the legislature finds and declares that hate crimes should be prosecuted and punished with appropriate severity.

HISTORY: Add, L 2000, ch 107, § 2, eff Oct 8, 2000.

§ 485.05. Hate crimes

1. A person commits a hate crime when he or she commits a specified offense and either:

(a) intentionally selects the person against whom the offense is committed or intended to be committed in whole or in substantial part because of a belief or perception regarding the race, color, national origin, ancestry, gender, religion, religious practice, age, disability or sexual orientation of a person, regardless of whether the belief or perception is correct, or

(b) intentionally commits the act or acts constituting the offense in whole or in substantial part because of a belief or perception regarding the race, color, national origin, ancestry, gender, religion, religious practice, age, disability or sexual orientation of a person, regardless of whether the belief or perception is correct.

2. Proof of race, color, national origin, ancestry, gender, religion, religious practice, age, disability or sexual orientation of the defendant, the victim or of both the defendant and the victim does not, by itself, constitute legally sufficient evidence satisfying the people's burden under paragraph (a) or (b) of subdivision one of this section

3. A "specified offense" is an offense defined by any of the following provisions of this chapter:

section 120.00 (assault in the third degree); section 120.05 (assault in the second degree); section 120.10 (assault in the first degree); section 120.12 (aggravated assault upon a person less than eleven years old); section 120.13 (menacing in the first degree); section 120.14 (menacing in the second degree); section 120.15 (menacing in the third degree); section 120.20 (reckless endangerment in the second degree); section 120.25 (reckless endangerment in the first degree); section 121.12 (strangulation in the second degree); section 121.13 (strangulation in the first degree); subdivision one of section 125.15 (manslaughter in the second degree); subdivision one, two or four of section 125.20 (manslaughter in the first degree); section 125.25 (murder in the second degree); section 120.45 (stalking in the fourth degree); section 120.50 (stalking in the third degree); section 120.55 (stalking in the second degree); section 120.60 (stalking in the first degree); subdivision one of section 130.35 (rape in the first degree); subdivision one of section 130.50 (criminal sexual act in the first degree); subdivision one of section 130.65 (sexual abuse in the first degree); paragraph (a) of subdivision one of section 130.67 (aggravated sexual abuse in the second degree); paragraph (a) of subdivision one of section 130.70 (aggravated sexual abuse in the first degree); section 135.05 (unlawful imprisonment in the second degree); section 135.10 (unlawful imprisonment in the first degree); section 135.20 (kidnapping in the second degree); section 135.25 (kidnapping in the first degree); section 135.60 (coercion in the second degree); section 135.65 (coercion in the first degree); section 140.10 (criminal trespass in the third degree); section 140.15 (criminal trespass in the second degree); section 140.17 (criminal trespass in the first degree); section 140.20 (burglary in the third degree); section 140.25 (burglary in the second degree); section 140.30 (burglary in the first degree); section 145.00 (criminal mischief in the fourth degree); section 145.05 (criminal mischief in the third degree); section 145.10 (criminal mischief in the second degree); section 145.12 (criminal mischief in the first degree); section 150.05 (arson in the fourth degree); section 150.10 (arson in the third degree); section 150.15 (arson in the second degree); section 150.20 (arson in the first degree); section 155.25 (petit larceny); section 155.30 (grand larceny in the fourth degree); section 155.35 (grand larceny in the third degree); section 155.40 (grand larceny in the second degree); section 155.42 (grand larceny in the first degree); section 160.05 (robbery in the third degree); section 160.10 (robbery in the second degree); section 160.15 (robbery in the first degree); section 240.25 (harassment in the first degree); subdivision one, two or four of section 240.30 (aggravated harassment in the second degree); or any attempt or conspiracy to commit any of the foregoing offenses.

4. For purposes of this section:

(a) the term "age" means sixty years old or more;

(b) the term "disability" means a physical or mental impairment that substantially limits a major life activity.

HISTORY: Add, L 2000, ch 107, § 2, eff Oct 8, 2000; amd, L 2003, ch 264, § 34, eff Nov 1, 2003, L 2010, ch 405, § 13, eff Nov 11, 2010.

§ 485.10. Sentencing

1. When a person is convicted of a hate crime pursuant to this article, and the specified offense is a violent felony offense, as defined in section 70.02 of this chapter, the hate crime shall be deemed a violent felony offense.

2. When a person is convicted of a hate crime pursuant to this article and the specified offense is a misdemeanor or a class C, D or E felony, the hate crime shall be deemed to be one category higher than the specified offense the defendant committed, or one category higher than the offense level applicable to the defendant's conviction for an attempt or conspiracy to commit a specified offense, whichever is applicable.

3. Notwithstanding any other provision of law, when a person is convicted of a hate crime pursuant to this article and the specified offense is a class B felony:

(a) the maximum term of the indeterminate sentence must be at least six years if the defendant is sentenced pursuant to section 70.00 of this chapter;

(b) the term of the determinate sentence must be at least eight years if the defendant is sentenced pursuant to section 70.02 of this chapter;

(c) the term of the determinate sentence must be at least twelve years if the defendant is sentenced pursuant to section 70.04 of this chapter;

(d) the maximum term of the indeterminate sentence must be at least four years if the defendant is sentenced pursuant to section 70.05 of this chapter; and

(e) the maximum term of the indeterminate sentence or the term of the determinate sentence must be at least ten years if the defendant is sentenced pursuant to section 70.06 of this chapter.

4. Notwithstanding any other provision of law, when a person is convicted of a hate crime pursuant to this article and the specified offense is a class A-1 felony, the minimum period of the indeterminate sentence shall be not less than twenty years.

5. In addition to any of the dispositions authorized by this chapter, the court may require as part of the sentence imposed upon a person convicted of a hate crime pursuant to this article, that the defendant complete a program, training session or counseling session directed at hate crime prevention and education, where the court determines such program, training session or counseling session is appropriate, available and was developed or authorized by the court or local agencies in cooperation with organizations serving the affected community.

HISTORY: Add, L 2000, ch 107, § 2, eff Oct 8, 2000, L 2010, ch 158, § 1, eff Nov 1, 2010.

TITLE Y-1   [Terrorism]*

ARTICLE 490
TERRORISM

HISTORY: Add, L 2001, ch 300, § 4, eff Sept 17, 2001.

ARTICLE 490   TERRORISM

HISTORY: Add, L 2001, ch 300, § 4, eff Sept 17, 2001.

§ 490.00. Legislative findings

The devastating consequences of the recent barbaric attack on the World Trade Center and the Pentagon underscore the compelling need for legislation that is specifically designed to combat the evils of terrorism. Indeed, the bombings of American embassies in Kenya and Tanzania in 1998, the federal building in Oklahoma City in 1995, Pan Am Flight number 103 in Lockerbie in 1988, the 1997 shooting atop the Empire State Building, the 1994 murder of Ari Halberstam on the Brooklyn Bridge and the 1993 bombing of the World Trade Center, will forever serve to remind us that terrorism is a serious and deadly problem that disrupts public order and threatens individual safety both at home and around the world. Terrorism is inconsistent with civilized society and cannot be tolerated.

Although certain federal laws seek to curb the incidence of terrorism, there are no corresponding state laws that facilitate the prosecution and punishment of terrorists in state courts. Inexplicably, there is also no criminal penalty in this state for a person who solicits or raises funds for, or provides other material support or resources to, those who commit or encourage the commission

---

* The bracketed word has been inserted by the Publisher.

of horrific and cowardly acts of terrorism. Nor do our criminal laws proscribe the making of terrorist threats or punish with appropriate severity those who hinder the prosecution of terrorists. Finally, our death penalty statute must be strengthened so that the cold-blooded execution of an individual for terrorist purposes is a capital offense.

A comprehensive state law is urgently needed to complement federal laws in the fight against terrorism and to better protect all citizens against terrorist acts. Accordingly, the legislature finds that our laws must be strengthened to ensure that terrorists, as well as those who solicit or provide financial and other support to terrorists, are prosecuted and punished in state courts with appropriate severity.

HISTORY: Add, L 2001, ch 300, § 4, eff Sept 17, 2001.

§ 490.01. Liability protection

1. Any person who makes a qualified disclosure of suspicious behavior shall be immune from civil and criminal liability for reporting such behavior.

2. For purposes of this article, "qualified disclosure of suspicious behavior" means any disclosure of allegedly suspicious behavior of another individual or individuals to any person that is made in good faith and with the reasonable belief that such suspicious behavior constitutes, is indicative of, or is in furtherance of a crime or an act of terrorism.

3. An action alleging that a statement or disclosure by a person of any suspicious transaction, activity or occurrence indicating that an individual may be engaging in or preparing to engage in suspicious behavior which constitutes, is indicative of, or is in furtherance of, a crime or an act of terrorism was not made in good faith and with the reasonable belief that such suspicious behavior constitutes, is indicative of, or is in furtherance of, a crime or an act of terrorism must be pled with particularity pursuant to subdivision (b) of rule three thousand sixteen of the civil practice law and rules.

HISTORY: Add, L 2007, ch 651, § 2, eff Aug 28, 2007.

§ 490.05. Definitions

As used in this article, the following terms shall mean and include:

1. "Act of terrorism":

(a) for purposes of this article means an act or acts constituting a specified offense as defined in subdivision three of this section for which a person may be convicted in the criminal courts of this state pursuant to article twenty of the criminal procedure law, or an act or acts constituting an offense in any other jurisdiction within or outside the territorial boundaries of the United States which contains all of the essential elements of a specified offense, that is intended to:

(i) intimidate or coerce a civilian population;

(ii) influence the policy of a unit of government by intimidation or coercion; or

(iii) affect the conduct of a unit of government by murder, assassination or kidnapping; or

(b) for purposes of subparagraph (xiii) of paragraph (a) of subdivision one of section 125.27 of this chapter means activities that involve a violent act or acts dangerous to human life that are in violation of the criminal laws of this state and are intended to:

(i) intimidate or coerce a civilian population;

(ii) influence the policy of a unit of government by intimidation or coercion; or

(iii) affect the conduct of a unit of government by murder, assassination or kidnapping.

2. "Material support or resources" means currency or other financial securities, financial services, lodging, training, safehouses, false documentation or identification, communications equipment, facilities, weapons, lethal substances, explosives, personnel, transportation, and other physical assets, except medicine or religious materials.

3. (a) "Specified offense" for purposes of this article means a class A felony offense other than an offense as defined in article two hundred twenty, a violent felony offense as defined in section 70.02, manslaughter in the second degree as defined in section 125.15, criminal tampering in the first degree as defined in section 145.20, identity theft in the second degree as defined in section 190.79, identity theft in the first degree as defined in section 190.80, unlawful possession of personal identification information in the second degree as defined in section 190.82, unlawful possession of personal identification information in the first degree as defined in section 190.83, money laundering in support of terrorism in the fourth degree as defined in section 470.21, money laundering in support of terrorism in the third degree as defined in section 470.22, money laundering in support of terrorism in the second degree as defined in section 470.23, money laundering in support of terrorism in the first degree as defined in section 470.24 of this chapter, and includes an attempt or conspiracy to commit any such offense.

(b) Notwithstanding the provisions of paragraph (a) of this subdivision, a specified offense shall not mean an offense defined in sections 490.37, 490.40, 490.45, 490.47, 490.50, and 490.55 of this article, nor shall a specified offense mean an attempt to commit any such offense.

4. "Renders criminal assistance" for purposes of sections 490.30 and 490.35 of this article shall have the same meaning as in section 205.50 of this chapter.

5. "Biological agent" means any micro-organism, virus, infectious substance, or biological product that may be engineered as a result of biotechnology, or any naturally occurring or bioengineered component of any such micro-organism, virus, infectious substance, or biological product, capable of causing:

(a) death, disease, or other biological malfunction in a human, an animal, a plant, or another living organism;

(b) deterioration of food, water, equipment, supplies, or material of any kind; or

(c) deleterious alteration of the environment.

6. "Toxin" means the toxic material of plants, animals, micro-organisms, viruses, fungi, or infectious substances, or a recombinant molecule, whatever its origin or method of production, including:

(a) any poisonous substance or biological product that may be engineered as a result of biotechnology produced by a living organism; or

(b) any poisonous isomer or biological product, homolog, or derivative of such a substance.

7. "Delivery system" means:

(a) any apparatus, equipment, device, or means of delivery specifically designed to deliver or disseminate a biological agent, toxin, or vector; or

(b) any vector.

8. "Vector" means a living organism, or molecule, including a recombinant molecule, or biological product that may be engineered as a result of biotechnology, capable of carrying a biological agent or toxin to a host.

9. "Biological weapon" means any biological agent, toxin, vector, or delivery system or combination thereof.

10. "Chemical weapon" means the following, together or separately:

(a) a toxic chemical or its precursors;

(b) a munition or device specifically designed to cause death or other harm through the toxic properties of a toxic chemical or its precursors, which would be released as a result of the employment of such munition or device;

(c) any equipment specifically designed for use directly in connection with the employment of munitions or devices; or

(d) any device that is designed to release radiation or radioactivity at a level dangerous to human life.

11. "Precursor" means any chemical reactant that takes part at any stage in the production by whatever method of a toxic chemical, including any key component of a binary or multicomponent chemical system, and includes precursors which have been identified for application of verification measures under article VI of the convention in schedules contained in the annex on chemicals of the chemical weapons convention.

12. "Key component of a binary or multicomponent chemical system" means the precursor which plays the most important role in determining the toxic properties of the final product and reacts rapidly with other chemicals in the binary or multicomponent system.

13. "Toxic chemical" means any chemical which through its chemical action on life processes can cause death, serious physical injury or permanent harm to humans or animals, including all such chemicals, regardless of their origin or of their method of production, and regardless of whether they are produced in facilities, in munitions or elsewhere, and includes toxic chemicals which have been identified by the commissioner of health and included on the list of toxic chemicals pursuant to subdivision twenty of section two hundred six of the public health law.

14. The terms "biological agent", "toxin", and "toxic chemical" do not include any biological agent, toxin or toxic chemical that is in its naturally occurring environment, if the biological agent, toxin or toxic chemical has not been cultivated, collected, or otherwise extracted from its natural source.

15. "Select chemical agent" shall mean a chemical weapon which has been identified in regulations promulgated pursuant to subdivision twenty of section two hundred six of the public health law.

16. "Select biological agent" shall mean a biological weapon which has been identified in regulations promulgated pursuant to subdivision twenty-one of section two hundred six of the public health law.

17. "Chemical weapons convention" and "convention" mean the convention on the prohibition of the development, production, stockpiling and use of chemical weapons and on their destruction, opened for signature on January thirteenth, nineteen hundred ninety-three.

HISTORY: Add, L 2001, ch 300, § 4, eff Sept 17, 2001. Sub 3, par (a), formerly entire sub 3, amd, L 2002, ch 619, § 4, eff Nov 1, 2002; so designated sub 3, par (a) and amd, L 2004, ch 1, § 7 (Part A), eff July 23, 2004. Sub 3, par (b), add, L 2004, ch 1, § 7 (Part A), eff July 23, 2004. Sub 5, add, L 2004, ch 1, § 8 (Part A), eff July 23, 2004. Sub 6, add, L 2004, ch 1, § 8 (Part A), eff July 23, 2004. Sub 7, add, L 2004, ch 1, § 8 (Part A), eff July 23, 2004. Sub 8, add, L 2004, ch 1, § 8 (Part A), eff July 23, 2004. Sub 9, add, L 2004, ch 1, § 8 (Part A), eff July 23, 2004. Sub 10, add, L 2004, ch 1, § 8 (Part A), eff July 23, 2004. Sub 11, add, L 2004, ch 1, § 8 (Part A), eff July 23, 2004. Sub 12, add, L 2004, ch 1, § 8 (Part A), eff July 23, 2004. Sub 13, add, L 2004, ch 1, § 8 (Part A), eff July 23, 2004. Sub 14, add, L 2004, ch 1, § 8 (Part A), eff July 23, 2004. Sub 15, add, L 2004, ch 1, § 8 (Part A), eff July 23, 2004. Sub 16, add, L 2004, ch 1, § 8 (Part A), eff July 23, 2004. Sub 17, add, L 2004, ch 1, § 8 (Part A), eff July 23, 2004.

§ 490.10. Soliciting or providing support for an act of terrorism in the second degree

A person commits soliciting or providing support for an act of terrorism in the second degree when, with intent that material support or resources will be used, in whole or in part, to plan, prepare, carry out or aid in either an act of terrorism or the concealment of, or an escape from, an act of terrorism, he or she raises, solicits, collects or provides material support or resources.

Soliciting or providing support for an act of terrorism in the second degree is a class D felony.

HISTORY: Add, L 2001, ch 300, § 4, eff Sept 17, 2001.

§ 490.15. Soliciting or providing support for an act of terrorism in the first degree

A person commits soliciting or providing support for an act of terrorism in the first degree when he or she commits the crime of soliciting or providing support for an act of terrorism in the second degree and the total value of material support or resources exceeds one thousand dollars.

Soliciting or providing support for an act of terrorism in the first degree is a class C felony.

HISTORY: Add, L 2001, ch 300, § 4, eff Sept 17, 2001.

§ 490.20. Making a terroristic threat

1. A person is guilty of making a terroristic threat when with intent to intimidate or coerce a civilian population, influence the policy of a unit of government by intimidation or coercion, or affect the conduct of a unit of government by murder, assassination or kidnapping, he or she threatens to commit or cause to be committed a specified offense and thereby causes a reasonable expectation or fear of the imminent commission of such offense.

2. It shall be no defense to a prosecution pursuant to this section that the defendant did not have the intent or capability of committing the specified offense or that the threat was not made to a person who was a subject thereof.

Making a terroristic threat is a class D felony.

HISTORY: Add, L 2001, ch 300, § 4, eff Sept 17, 2001.

§ 490.25. Crime of terrorism

1. A person is guilty of a crime of terrorism when, with intent to intimidate or coerce a civilian population, influence the policy of a unit of government by intimidation or coercion, or affect the conduct of a unit of government by murder, assassination or kidnapping, he or she commits a specified offense.

2. Sentencing.

(a) When a person is convicted of a crime of terrorism pursuant to this section, and the specified offense is a class B, C, D or E felony offense, the crime of terrorism shall be deemed a violent felony offense.

(b) When a person is convicted of a crime of terrorism pursuant to this section, and the specified offense is a class C, D or E felony offense, the crime of terrorism shall be deemed to be one category higher than the specified offense the defendant committed, or one category higher than the offense level applicable to the defendant's conviction for an attempt or conspiracy to commit the offense, whichever is applicable.

(c) When a person is convicted of a crime of terrorism pursuant to this section, and the specified offense is a class B felony offense, the crime of terrorism shall be deemed a class A-I felony offense and the sentence imposed upon conviction of such offense shall be in accordance with section 70.00 of this chapter.

(d) Notwithstanding any other provision of law, when a person is convicted of a crime of terrorism pursuant to this section, and the specified offense is a class A-I felony offense, the sentence upon conviction of such offense shall be life imprisonment without parole; provided, however, that nothing herein shall preclude or prevent a sentence of death when the specified offense is murder in the first degree as defined in section 125.27 of this chapter.

HISTORY: Add, L 2001, ch 300, § 4, eff Sept 17, 2001.

§ 490.30. Hindering prosecution of terrorism in the second degree

A person is guilty of hindering prosecution of terrorism in the second degree when he or she renders criminal assistance to a person who has committed an act of terrorism, knowing or believing that such person engaged in conduct constituting an act of terrorism.

Hindering prosecution of terrorism in the second degree is a class C felony.

HISTORY: Add, L 2001, ch 300, § 4, eff Sept 17, 2001.

§ 490.35. Hindering prosecution of terrorism in the first degree

A person is guilty of hindering prosecution of terrorism in the first degree when he or she renders criminal assistance to a person who has committed an act of terrorism that resulted in the death of a person other than one of the participants, knowing or believing that such person engaged in conduct constituting an act of terrorism.

Hindering prosecution of terrorism in the first degree is a class B felony.

HISTORY: Add, L 2001, ch 300, § 4, eff Sept 17, 2001.

§ 490.37. Criminal possession of a chemical weapon or biological weapon in the third degree

A person is guilty of criminal possession of a chemical weapon or biological weapon in the third degree when he or she possesses any select chemical agent or select biological agent under circumstances evincing an intent by the defendant to use such weapon to cause serious physical injury or death to another person.

Criminal possession of a chemical weapon or biological weapon in the third degree is a class C felony.

HISTORY: Add, L 2004, ch 1, § 9 (Part A), eff July 23, 2004.

§ 490.40. Criminal possession of a chemical weapon or biological weapon in the second degree

A person is guilty of criminal possession of a chemical weapon or biological weapon in the second degree when he or she possesses any chemical weapon or biological weapon with intent to use such weapon to:

1. (a) cause serious physical injury to, or the death of, another person; and

(b) (i) intimidate or coerce a civilian population;

(ii) influence the policy of a unit of government by intimidation or coercion; or

(iii) affect the conduct of a unit of government by murder, assassination, or kidnapping.

2. cause serious physical injury to, or the death of, more than two persons.

Criminal possession of a chemical weapon or biological weapon in the second degree is a class B felony.

HISTORY: Add, L 2004, ch 1, § 9 (Part A), eff July 23, 2004.

§ 490.45. Criminal possession of a chemical weapon or biological weapon in the first degree

A person is guilty of criminal possession of a chemical weapon or biological weapon in the first degree when he or she possesses:

1. any select chemical agent, with intent to use such agent to:

(a) cause serious physical injury to, or the death of, another person; and

(b) (i) intimidate or coerce a civilian population;

(ii) influence the policy of a unit of government by intimidation or coercion; or

(iii) affect the conduct of a unit of government by murder, assassination, or kidnapping.

2. any select chemical agent, with intent to use such agent to cause serious physical injury to, or the death of, more than two other persons; or

3. any select biological agent, with intent to use such agent to cause serious physical injury to, or the death of, another person.

Criminal possession of a chemical weapon or biological weapon in the first degree is a class A-I felony.

HISTORY: Add, L 2004, ch 1, § 9 (Part A), eff July 23, 2004.

§ 490.47. Criminal use of a chemical weapon or biological weapon in the third degree

A person is guilty of criminal use of a chemical weapon or biological weapon in the third degree when, under circumstances evincing a depraved indifference to human life, he or she uses, deploys, releases, or causes to be used, deployed, or released any select chemical agent or select biological agent, and thereby creates a grave risk of death or serious physical injury to another person not a participant in the crime.

Criminal use of a chemical weapon or biological weapon in the third degree is a class B felony.

HISTORY: Add, L 2004, ch 1, § 9 (Part A), eff July 23, 2004.

§ 490.50. Criminal use of a chemical weapon or biological weapon in the second degree

A person is guilty of criminal use of a chemical weapon or biological weapon in the second degree when he or she uses, deploys, releases, or causes to be used, deployed, or released, any chemical weapon or biological weapon, with intent to:

1. cause serious physical injury to, or the death of, another person; and

2. (a) intimidate or coerce a civilian population;

(b) influence the policy of a unit of government by intimidation or coercion; or

(c) to affect the conduct of a unit of government by murder, assassination, or kidnapping.

Criminal use of a chemical weapon or biological weapon in the second degree is a class A-II felony.

> **HISTORY:** Add, L 2004, ch 1, § 9 (Part A), eff July 23, 2004.

§ 490.55. Criminal use of a chemical weapon or biological weapon in the first degree

A person is guilty of criminal use of a chemical weapon or biological weapon in the first degree when:

1. with intent to:

(a) cause serious physical injury to, or the death of, another person; and

(b) (i) intimidate or coerce a civilian population;

(ii) influence the policy of a unit of government by intimidation or coercion; or

(iii) affect the conduct of a unit of government by murder, assassination, or kidnapping;

he or she uses, deploys, releases, or causes to be used, deployed, or released any select chemical agent and thereby causes serious physical injury to, or the death of, another person who is not a participant in the crime.

2. with intent to cause serious physical injury to, or the death of, more than two persons, he or she uses, deploys, releases, or causes to be used, deployed, or released any select chemical agent and thereby causes serious physical injury to, or the death of, more than two persons who are not participants in the crime; or

3. with intent to cause serious physical injury to, or the death of, another person, he or she uses, deploys, releases, or causes to be used, deployed, or released any select biological agent and thereby causes serious physical injury to, or the death of, another person who is not a participant in the crime.

Criminal use of a chemical weapon or biological weapon in the first degree is a class A-I felony.

> **HISTORY:** Add, L 2004, ch 1, § 9 (Part A), eff July 23, 2004.

§ 490.70. Limitations

1. The provisions of sections 490.37, 490.40, 490.45, 490.47, 490.50, and 490.55 of this article shall not apply where the defendant possessed or used:

(a) any household product generally available for sale to consumers in this state in the quantity and concentration available for such sale;

(b) a self-defense spray device in accordance with the provisions of paragraph fourteen of subdivision a of section 265.20 of this chapter;

(c) a chemical weapon solely for a purpose not prohibited under this chapter, as long as the type and quantity is consistent with such a purpose; or

(d) a biological agent, toxin, or delivery system solely for prophylactic, protective, bona fide research, or other peaceful purposes.

2. For the purposes of this section, the phrase "purposes not prohibited by this chapter" means

the following:

(a) any peaceful purpose related to an industrial, agricultural, research, medical, or pharmaceutical activity or other peaceful activity;

(b) any purpose directly related to protection against toxic chemicals and to protection against chemical weapons;

(c) any military purpose of the United States that is not connected with the use of a chemical weapon or that is not dependent on the use of the toxic or poisonous properties of the chemical weapon to cause death or other harm; and

(d) any law enforcement purpose, including any domestic riot control purpose and including imposition of capital punishment.

HISTORY: Add, L 2004, ch 1, § 9 (Part A), eff July 23, 2004.

TITLE Y-2 Corrupting the Government
ARTICLE 496
CORRUPTING THE GOVERNMENT

HISTORY: Add, L 2014, ch 55, § 14 (Part H, Subpart A), eff April 30, 2014.

ARTICLE 496 CORRUPTING THE GOVERNMENT

§ 496.01. Definitions

For the purposes of this article, "scheme" means any plan, pattern, device, contrivance, or course of action.

HISTORY: Add, L 2014, ch 55, § 14 (Part H, Subpart A), eff April 30, 2014.

§ 496.02. Corrupting the government in the fourth degree

A person is guilty of corrupting the government in the fourth degree when, being a public servant, or acting in concert with a public servant, he or she engages in a scheme constituting a systematic ongoing course of conduct with intent to defraud the state or one or more political subdivisions of the state or one or more governmental instrumentalities within the state to obtain property, actual services or other resources, or obtain property, actual services or other resources from the state, or any political subdivision or governmental instrumentality of the state by false or fraudulent pretenses, representations or promises, and thereby wrongfully obtains such property, actual services or other resources.

Corrupting the government in the fourth degree is a class E felony.

HISTORY: Add, L 2014, ch 55, § 14 (Part H, Subpart A), eff April 30, 2014.

§ 496.03. Corrupting the government in the third degree

A person is guilty of corrupting the government in the third degree when, being a public servant, or acting in concert with a public servant, he or she engages in a scheme constituting a systematic ongoing course of conduct with intent to defraud the state or one or more political subdivisions of the state or one or more governmental instrumentalities within the state to obtain property, actual services or other resources, or obtain property, actual services or other resources from the state, or any political subdivision or governmental instrumentality of the state by false or fraudulent pretenses, representations or promises, and thereby wrongfully obtains such property, actual services or other resources with a value in excess of one thousand dollars.

Corrupting the government in the third degree is a class D felony.

HISTORY: Add, L 2014, ch 55, § 14 (Part H, Subpart A), eff April 30, 2014.

§ 496.04. Corrupting the government in the second degree

A person is guilty of corrupting the government in the second degree when, being a public servant, or acting in concert with a public servant, he or she engages in a scheme constituting a systematic ongoing course of conduct with intent to defraud the state or one or more political subdivisions of the state or one or more governmental instrumentalities within the state to obtain property, actual services or other resources, or obtain property, actual services or other resources from the state, or any political subdivision or governmental instrumentality of the state by false or fraudulent pretenses, representations or promises, and thereby wrongfully obtains such property, actual services or other resources with a value in excess of twenty thousand dollars.

Corrupting the government in the second degree is a class C felony.

HISTORY: Add, L 2014, ch 55, § 14 (Part H, Subpart A), eff April 30, 2014.

§ 496.05. Corrupting the government in the first degree

A person is guilty of corrupting the government in the first degree when, being a public servant, or acting in concert with a public servant, he or she engages in a scheme constituting a systematic ongoing course of conduct with intent to defraud the state or one or more political subdivisions of the state or one or more governmental instrumentalities within the state to obtain property, actual services or other resources, or to obtain property, actual services or other resources from the state, or any political subdivision or governmental instrumentality of the state by false or fraudulent pretenses, representations or promises, and thereby wrongfully obtains such property, actual services or other resources with a value in excess of one hundred thousand dollars.

Corrupting the government in the first degree is a class B felony.

HISTORY: Add, L 2014, ch 55, § 14 (Part H, Subpart A), eff April 30, 2014.

§ 496.06. Public corruption

1. A person commits the crime of public corruption when: (a) (i) being a public servant he or she commits a specified offense through the use of his or her public office, or (ii) being a person acting in concert with such public servant he or she commits a specified offense, and (b) the state or any political subdivision thereof or any governmental instrumentality within the state is the owner of the property.

2. A "specified offense" is an offense defined by any of the following provisions of this chapter: section 155.25 (petit larceny); section 155.30 (grand larceny in the fourth degree); section 155.35 (grand larceny in the third degree); section 155.40 (grand larceny in the second degree); section 155.42 (grand larceny in the first degree); section 190.60 (scheme to defraud in the second degree); or section 190.65 (scheme to defraud in the first degree).

HISTORY: Add, L 2014, ch 55, § 14 (Part H, Subpart A), eff April 30, 2014.

§ 496.07. Sentencing

When a person is convicted of the crime of public corruption pursuant to section 496.06 of this article and the specified offense is a class C, D or E felony, the crime shall be deemed to be one category higher than the specified offense the defendant committed, or one category higher than the offense level applicable to the defendant's conviction for an attempt or conspiracy to commit a specified offense, whichever is applicable.

HISTORY: Add, L 2014, ch 55, § 14 (Part H, Subpart A), eff April 30, 2014.

TITLE Z   Laws Repealed; Time of Taking Effect

ARTICLE 500
LAWS REPEALED; TIME OF TAKING EFFECT

HISTORY: Add, L 1965, ch 1030, § 1, eff Sept 1, 1967.

ARTICLE 500   LAWS REPEALED; TIME OF TAKING EFFECT

§ 500.00.　　　　　　　　**[Repealed]**

§ 500.05.　　　　　　　　**Laws repealed**

§ 500.10.　　　　　　　　**Time of taking effect**

> **HISTORY:** Add, L 1965, ch 1030, § 1, eff Sept 1, 1967. Article heading, amd, L 1965, ch 1046, § 2, L 1967, ch 791, § 50, eff Sept 1, 1967.

§ 500.00. [Repealed]

> **HISTORY:** Add, L 1965, ch 1046, § 2; repealed, L 1967, ch 791, § 51, eff Sept 1, 1967. Former § 500.00, add, L 1965, ch 1030, § 1; renumbered § 500.05, L 1965, ch 1046, § 2, eff Sept 1, 1967.

§ 500.05. Laws repealed

Chapter eighty-eight of the laws of nineteen hundred nine, entitled "An act providing for the punishment of crime, constituting chapter forty of the consolidated laws," and all acts amendatory thereof and supplemental thereto, constituting the penal law as heretofore in force, are hereby repealed.

> **HISTORY:** Added as § 500.00, L 1965, ch 1030, § 1; renumbered § 500.05, L 1965, ch 1046, § 2, eff Sept 1, 1967. Former § 500.05, add, L 1965, ch 1030, § 1; renumbered § 500.10, L 1965, ch 1046, § 2, eff Sept 1, 1965.

§ 500.10. Time of taking effect

This act shall take effect September first, nineteen hundred sixty-seven.

> **HISTORY:** Added as § 500.05, L 1965, ch 1030, § 1; renumbered § 500.10, L 1965, ch 1046, § 2, eff Sept 1, 1965.

PL

PART II
SELECTED STATUTES AND COURT RULES

SELECTED SECTIONS
OF THE
CORRECTION LAW

HISTORY: Add, L 1909, ch 47.

ARTICLE 1 SHORT TITLE; DEFINITIONS

§ 1. Short title

This chapter shall be known as the "Correction Law."

> **HISTORY:** Add, L 1909, ch 47; amd, L 1929, ch 243, § 3, eff April 2, 1929.

§ 2. Definitions

When used in this chapter, unless otherwise expressly stated or the context or subject matter otherwise requires, the following terms have the following meanings:

1. "Department" means the state department of corrections and community supervision;

2. "Commissioner" means the state commissioner of corrections and community supervision;

3. "Commission" means the state commission of correction;

4. (a) "Correctional facility". Any place operated by the department and designated by the commissioner as a place for the confinement of persons under sentence of imprisonment or persons committed for failure to pay a fine. Except as provided in paragraph (b) of this subdivision, whenever reference has been or hereafter will be made in any statute, judgment, sentence, commitment, court order or otherwise to a state prison, state reformatory, reception center, diagnostic center or other institution or facility in the department, such reference shall be deemed to mean "correctional facility".

(b) The term "correctional facility" shall not, however, be deemed to mean or to include any place operated by the department for the care and confinement of persons who have been found to be mentally defective or mentally ill by a court and who are confined in such place pursuant to an order of a court based upon such finding.

(c) Whenever the term "institution" is used in this chapter or elsewhere in such context as to mean an institution in the department, such term shall be deemed to include correctional facilities and any other place operated by the department as a place for the confinement of persons.

5. "Reception center". A correctional facility for reception, classification and program-planning for purposes of confinement, treatment and transfer.

6. "Residential treatment facility". A correctional facility consisting of a community based residence in or near a community where employment, educational and training opportunities are readily available for persons who are on parole or conditional release and for persons who are or who will soon be eligible for release on parole who intend to reside in or near that community when released.

7. "Detention center". A correctional facility for the temporary detention of persons taken into custody upon violation of parole or upon violation of a condition of release, or of persons being transferred from other correctional facilities, or of persons who are assigned to other correctional facilities for confinement but whose presence is required in court or for some other purpose at a location that is distant from the institution of confinement.

8. "Correctional Camp". A correctional facility consisting of a camp maintained for the purpose of including conservation work in the program of inmates.

9. "Diagnostic and treatment center". A correctional facility operated for the purpose of providing intensive physical, mental and sociological diagnostic and treatment services including pre-parole diagnostic evaluation, where requested by the board of parole, and scientific study of the social and mental aspects of the causes of crime.

10. "General confinement facility". A correctional facility for confinement and treatment of persons under institutional programs oriented to education, vocational training and industry.

11. "Work release facility". A facility designated by the commissioner as an institution that may conduct a work release program.

12. "Superintendent". The chief administrative officer of a correctional facility. Whenever the

term "warden" appears in this chapter in such context as to mean an officer of a state correctional facility, such reference shall be deemed to mean "superintendent".

13. "Infant" or "minor" means a person who has not attained the age of eighteen years.

14. [Expires Sept 1, 2015] "Community treatment facility." A residential chemical dependence facility approved as provided in section 32.01 of the mental hygiene law or pursuant to section 32.31 of such law used exclusively to provide substance abuse treatment services to persons eligible pursuant to section seventy-two-a of this chapter and who are otherwise eligible for temporary release pursuant to subdivision two of section eight hundred fifty-one of this chapter. These facilities shall be separate and distinct so as not to replace existing substance abuse treatment services.

15. "Shock incarceration correctional facility". A correctional facility designated by the commissioner as an institution that may conduct a shock incarceration program.

16. (a) "Local correctional facility." Any place operated by a county or the city of New York as a place for the confinement of persons duly committed to secure their attendance as witnesses in any criminal case, charged with crime and committed for trial or examination, awaiting the availability of a court, duly committed for any contempt or upon civil process, convicted of any offense and sentenced to imprisonment therein or awaiting transportation under sentence to imprisonment in a correctional facility, or pursuant to any other applicable provisions of law.

(b) Whenever the term "jail", "penitentiary" or "workhouse" is used in this chapter, such term shall be deemed to mean local correctional facility.

(c) Whenever the term "sheriff" is used in this chapter, such term shall be deemed to include the warden, superintendent, or other person in charge of a local correctional facility.

17. "Alcohol and substance abuse treatment facility." A correctional facility designed to house medium security inmates as defined by department rules and regulations and operated for the purpose of providing intensive alcohol and substance abuse treatment services. Such services shall ensure comprehensive treatment for alcoholism and substance abuse to inmates who have been identified by the commissioner or his or her designee as having had or presently having a history of alcoholism or substance abuse. Such services shall be provided in the facility in accordance with minimum standards promulgated by the department after consultation with the division of alcoholism and alcohol abuse and the division of substance abuse services.

18. [Until Sept 1, 2015, as amended L 1994, ch 60, § 46(c), L 2004, ch 738, § 1, L 2009, ch 56, § 1 (Part AAA), L 2011, ch 62, § 1-a (Part C, Subpart A)] "Alcohol and substance abuse treatment correctional annex." A medium security correctional facility consisting of one or more residential dormitories, which provide intensive alcohol and substance abuse treatment services to inmates who: (i) are otherwise eligible for temporary release, or (ii) stand convicted of a felony defined in article two hundred twenty or two hundred twenty-one of the penal law, and are within six months of being an eligible inmate as that term is defined in subdivision two of section eight hundred fifty-one of this chapter including such inmates who are participating in such program pursuant to subdivision six of section 60.04 of the penal law. Notwithstanding the foregoing provisions of this subdivision, any inmate to be enrolled in this program pursuant to subdivision six of section 60.04 of the penal law shall be governed by the same rules and regulations promulgated by the department, including without limitation those rules and regulations establishing requirements for completion and those rules and regulations governing

discipline and removal from the program. No such period of court ordered corrections based drug abuse treatment pursuant to this subdivision shall be required to extend beyond the defendant's conditional release date. Such treatment services may be provided by one or more outside service providers pursuant to contractual agreements with the department, provided, however, that any such provider shall be required to continue to provide, either directly or through formal or informal agreement with other providers, alcohol and substance abuse treatment services to inmates who have successfully participated in such provider's incarcerative treatment services and who have been presumptively released, paroled, conditionally released or released to post release supervision under the supervision of the department and who are, as a condition of such release, required to participate in alcohol or substance abuse treatment. Such incarcerative services shall be provided in the facility in accordance with minimum standards promulgated by the department after consultation with the office of alcoholism and substance abuse services. Such services to parolees shall be provided in accordance with standards promulgated by the department after consultation with the office of alcoholism and substance abuse services. Notwithstanding any other provision of law, any person who has successfully completed no less than six months of intensive alcohol and substance abuse treatment services in one of the department's eight designated alcohol and substance abuse treatment correctional annexes having a combined total capacity of two thousand five hundred fifty beds may be transferred to a program operated by or at a residential treatment facility, provided however, that a person under a determinate sentence as a second felony drug offender for a class B felony offense defined in article two hundred twenty of the penal law, who was sentenced pursuant to section 70.70 of such law, shall not be eligible to be transferred to a program operated at a residential treatment facility until the time served under imprisonment for his or her determinate sentence, including any jail time credited pursuant to subdivision three of section 70.30 of the penal law, shall be at least nine months. The commissioner shall report annually to the temporary president of the senate and the speaker of the assembly commencing January first, two thousand twelve the number of inmates received by the department during the reporting period who are subject to a sentence which includes enrollment in substance abuse treatment in accordance with subdivision six of section 60.04 of the penal law, the number of such inmates who are not placed in such treatment program and the reasons for such occurrences.

18. [Eff Sept 1, 2015, as amended L 2004, ch 738, § 2, L 2011, ch 62, § 2 (Part C, Subpart A)] "Alcohol and substance abuse treatment correctional annex." A medium security correctional facility consisting of one or more residential dormitories which provide intensive alcohol and substance abuse treatment services to inmates who: (i) are otherwise eligible for temporary release, or (ii) stand convicted of a felony defined in article two hundred twenty or two hundred twenty-one of the penal law, and are within six months of being an eligible inmate as that term is defined in subdivision two of section eight hundred fifty-one of this chapter including such inmates who are participating in such program pursuant to subdivision six of section 60.04 of the penal law. Notwithstanding the foregoing provisions of this subdivision, any inmate to be enrolled in this program pursuant to subdivision six of section 60.04 of the penal law shall be governed by the same rules and regulations promulgated by the department, including without limitation those rules and regulations establishing requirements for completion and those rules and regulations governing discipline and removal from the program. No such period of court ordered corrections based drug abuse treatment pursuant to this subdivision shall be required to extend beyond the defendant's conditional release date. Such treatment services may be provided by one or more outside service providers pursuant to contractual agreements with the department, provided, however, that any such provider shall be required to continue to provide, either directly or through formal or informal agreement with other providers, alcohol and

substance abuse treatment services to inmates who have successfully participated in such provider's incarcerative treatment services and who have been presumptively released, paroled, conditionally released or released to post release supervision under the supervision of the department and who are, as a condition of such release, required to participate in alcohol or substance abuse treatment. Such incarcerative services shall be provided in the facility in accordance with minimum standards promulgated by the department after consultation with the office of alcoholism and substance abuse services. Such services to parolees shall be provided in accordance with standards promulgated by the department after consultation with the office of alcoholism and substance abuse services. The commissioner shall report annually to the majority leader of the senate and the speaker of the assembly commencing January first, two thousand twelve the number of inmates received by the department during the reporting period who are subject to a sentence which includes enrollment in substance abuse treatment in accordance with subdivision six of section 60.04 of the penal law, the number of such inmates who are not placed in such treatment program and the reasons for such occurrences.

19. "Vocational and skills training facility" means a correctional facility designated by the commissioner to provide a vocational and skills training program ("VAST") to inmates who need such service before they participate in a work release program. The VAST facility shall provide intensive assessment, counseling, job search assistance and where appropriate academic and vocational instruction to program participants. Such assistance may include an assessment of any inmate's education attainment level and skills aptitudes; career counseling and exploration; the development of a comprehensive instructional plan including identification of educational and training needs that may extend beyond the date of entry into work release; instructional programs including GED preparation or post-secondary instruction as appropriate; occupational skills training; life skills training; employment readiness including workplace behavior; and job search assistance. The department and the department of labor shall jointly develop activities providing career counseling, job search assistance, and job placement services for participants. Nothing contained in this section shall be deemed to modify the eligibility requirements provided by law applicable to inmates participating in a work release program.

20. "Drug treatment campus" means a facility operated by the department to provide a program of intensive drug treatment services for individuals sentenced to parole supervision sentences pursuant to section 410.91 of the criminal procedure law or for certain parole violators. All such treatment services shall be provided by, or with the approval of and pursuant to a plan developed in conjunction with, the office of alcoholism and substance abuse services, and which plan shall include but not be limited to provision for an appropriate continuum of care that includes a needs assessment and treatment services for individuals while at this facility and upon discharge from such facility, including an enhanced aftercare program.

Notwithstanding the foregoing, in the event that a person sentenced to parole supervision pursuant to section 410.91 of the criminal procedure law requires a degree of medical care or mental health care that cannot be provided at a drug treatment campus, the department, in writing, shall notify the person, provide a proposal describing a proposed alternative-to-the-drug-treatment-campus program, and notify him or her that he or she may object in writing to placement in such alternative-to-the-drug-treatment-campus program. If the person objects in writing to placement in such alternative-to-the-drug-treatment-campus program, the department shall notify the sentencing court, provide such proposal to the court, and arrange for the person's prompt appearance before the court. The court shall provide the proposal and notice of a court appearance to the prosecutor, the person and the appropriate defense attorney. After considering the proposal and any submissions by the parties, and after a reasonable opportunity for the prosecutor, the person and counsel to be heard, the court may modify its sentencing order accordingly, notwithstanding the provisions of section 430.10 of the criminal procedure law. A person who successfully completes an alternative-to-the-drug-treatment-campus program within the department shall be treated in the same manner as a person who has successfully completed the drug treatment campus program, as set forth herein and in section 410.91 of the criminal procedure law.

21. [Effective as stated in 2008 note below] "Residential mental health treatment unit" means housing for inmates with serious mental illness that is operated jointly by the department and the office of mental health and is therapeutic in nature. Such units shall not be operated as disciplinary housing units, and decisions about treatment and conditions of confinement shall be made based upon a clinical assessment of the therapeutic needs of the inmate and maintenance of adequate safety and security on the unit. Such units shall include, but not be limited to, the residential mental health unit model, the behavioral health unit model, the intermediate care program and the intensive intermediate care program. The models shall be defined in regulations promulgated by the department in consultation with the commissioner of mental health consistent with this subdivision and section four hundred one of this chapter. Inmates placed in a residential mental health treatment unit shall be offered at least four hours a day of structured out-of-cell therapeutic programming and/or mental health treatment, except on weekends or holidays, in addition to exercise, and may be provided with additional out-of-cell activities as are consistent with their mental health needs; provided, however, that the department may maintain no more than thirty-eight behavioral health unit beds in which the number of hours of out-of-cell structured therapeutic programming and/or mental health treatment offered to inmates on a daily basis, except on weekends or holidays, may be limited to only two hours. Out-of-cell therapeutic programming and/or mental health treatment need not be provided to an inmate for a brief orientation period following his or her arrival at a residential mental health treatment unit. The length of such orientation period shall be determined by a mental health clinician but in no event shall be longer than five business days.

22. [Effective as stated in 2008 note below] "Mental health clinician" means a psychiatrist, psychologist, social worker or nurse practitioner who is licensed by the department of education and employed by the office of mental health.

23. [Effective as stated in 2008 note below] "Segregated confinement" means the disciplinary confinement of an inmate in a special housing unit or in a separate keeplock housing unit. Special housing units and separate keeplock units are housing units that consist of cells grouped so as to provide separation from the general population, and may be used to house inmates confined pursuant to the disciplinary procedures described in regulations.

24. [Effective as stated in 2008 note below] "Joint case management committee" means a committee composed of staff from the department and the office of mental health. Such a committee shall be established at each level one and level two facility. Each committee shall consist of at least two clinical staff of the office of mental health and two officials of the department. The purpose of such committee shall be to review, monitor and coordinate the behavior and treatment plan of any inmate who is placed in segregated confinement or a residential mental health treatment unit and who is receiving services from the office of mental health.

25. [Effective as stated in 2008 note below] "Joint central office review committee" means a committee comprised of central office personnel from the department and the office of mental health as designated by the respective commissioners.

Corr. L.

26. [Effective as stated in 2008 note below] "Treatment team" means a team consisting of an equal number of individuals from the department and the office of mental health who are assigned to a residential mental health treatment unit and who will review and determine each inmate's appropriateness for movement through the various program phases, when applicable. The treatment team shall also review, monitor and coordinate the treatment plans for all inmate participants.

27. [Effective as stated in 2008 note below] "Level one facility" means a correctional facility at which staff from the office of mental health are assigned on a full-time basis and able to provide treatment to inmates with a major mental disorder. The array of available specialized services include: residential crisis treatment, residential day treatment, medication monitoring by psychiatric nursing staff, and potential commitment to the central New York Psychiatric Center.

28. [Effective as stated in 2008 note below] "Level two facility" means a correctional facility at which staff from the office of mental health are assigned on a full-time basis and able to provide treatment to inmates with a major mental disorder, but such disorder is not as acute as that of inmates who require placement at a level one facility.

29. [Effective as stated in 2008 note below] "Level three facility" means a correctional facility at which staff from the office of mental health are assigned on a part-time basis and able to provide treatment and medication to inmates who either have a moderate mental disorder, or who are in remission from a disorder, and who are determined by staff of the office of mental health to be able to function adequately in the facility with such level of staffing.

30. [Effective as stated in 2008 note below] "Level four facility" means a correctional facility at which staff from the office of mental health are assigned on a part-time basis and able to provide treatment to inmates who may require limited intervention, excluding psychiatric medications.

31. "Community supervision" means the supervision of individuals released into the community on temporary release, presumptive release, parole, conditional release, post release supervision or medical parole.

HISTORY: Add, L 1929, ch 243, § 3; amd, L 1970, ch 475, § 1, 1970, ch 476, § 1, eff July 7, 1970, L 1972, ch 567, § 1, eff May 24, 1972, L 1983, ch 418, §§ 1 and 2, eff July 8, 1983, expired July 31, 1984, L 1986, ch 554, § 1, expires Sept 1, 2015, L 1987, ch 261, § 8, eff July 13, 1987, L 1987, ch 604, § 2, L 1989, ch 338, § 7, eff July 10, 1989, L 1990, ch 681, § 4, eff Nov 1, 1990, L 1992, ch 55, § 284, expires Sept 1, 2015, L 1994, ch 60, § 41, expires Sept 1, 2015, L 1994, ch 60, § 44, L 1994, ch 63, § 130, eff April 11, 1994, deemed eff April 1, 1994, L 1995, ch 3, § 21, eff June 10, 1995, L 2004, ch 738, §§ 1 and 2, eff Dec 14, 2004, L 1999, ch 558, § 26, eff Oct 5, 1999, L 2008, ch 1, § 2, effective as stated in 2008 note below, L 2009, ch 56, § 1 (Part AAA), eff April 7, 2009, L 2010, ch 82, § 1, eff May 18, 2010, L 2011, ch 62, § 1-a (Part C, Subpart A), eff March 31, 2011, L 2011, ch 62, § 2 (Part C, Subpart B), eff Sept 1, 2013.

Editor's Note: Laws 2008, ch 1, §§ 1 and 8, pars (a) and (c), eff Jan 28, 2008, provide as follows:

[Eff as stated in § 8(a) below:] Section 1. Legislative findings. 1. The legislature finds that the needs of inmates with serious mental illness should be served by improved access to mental health treatment during incarceration. In particular, inmates with serious mental illness should be offered therapeutic care and treatment in residential mental health settings when doing so will not compromise the safety of inmates or other persons or the security of the facility. While in exceptional circumstances segregated confinement may sometimes be necessary to maintain such safety and security, even for inmates with serious mental illness, the state should strive to maintain such inmates with serious mental illness in less restrictive settings whenever it can safely do so.

2. When inmates with serious mental illness are placed in segregated confinement, they should receive a

heightened level of care, including out-of-cell therapeutic programming and/or mental health treatment, when consistent with the safety of the inmate and other persons or the security of the facility. Such inmates with serious mental illness should also undergo periodic reassessments of their mental condition to determine whether diversion from segregated confinement to a less restrictive setting is appropriate.

3. This act creates a balanced approach to care and treatment of inmates with serious mental illness and the state's ability to ensure the safety of all inmates and employees and the security of prison facilities.

§ 8. This act shall take effect immediately; provided however, that:

(a) sections one, two, three, four and five of this act and subdivisions 2 and 3 of section 401-a of the correction law as added by section six of this act shall take effect two years after the date that the commissioner of correctional services certifies to the legislative bill drafting commission that the first residential mental health unit constructed by the department of correctional services is completed and ready to receive inmates, provided, however that such sections shall take effect no later than July 1, 2011;

(c) the commissioner of mental health and the commissioner of correctional services are immediately authorized to promulgate rules and regulations necessary to implement the provisions of this act on their respective effective dates.

ARTICLE 2   DEPARTMENT OF CORRECTIONS AND COMMUNITY SUPERVISION

HISTORY: Add, L 1929, ch 243, § 4, eff April 2, 1929. Former Article 2, add, L 1909, ch 47;

---

* Section heading supplied by the editor.

renumbered Article 22, and amd, L 1929, ch 243, § 23, eff April 2, 1929. Article heading, amd, L 1970, ch 475, § 2, eff Jan 1, 1971.

§ 5. Department of corrections and community supervision; commissioner

1. There shall be in the state government a department of corrections and community supervision. The head of the department shall be the commissioner of corrections and community supervision, who shall be appointed by the governor, by and with the advice and consent of the senate, and hold office at the pleasure of the governor by whom he was appointed and until his successor is appointed and has qualified.

2. The commissioner of corrections and community supervision shall be the chief executive officer of the department.

3. The principal office of the department of corrections and community supervision shall be in the county of Albany.

4. The commissioner is hereby authorized and empowered to convert the sentence of a person serving an indeterminate sentence of imprisonment, except a person serving a sentence with a maximum term of life imprisonment, to a determinate sentence of imprisonment equal to two-thirds of the maximum or aggregate maximum term imposed where such conversion is necessary to make such person eligible for transfer either to federal custody or to foreign countries under treaties that provide for the voluntary transfer of such persons on the execution of penal sentences entered into by the government of the United States with foreign countries.

5. The commissioner upon request, may in his or her discretion, authorize the purchase and presentation of a flag of the state of New York to the person designated to dispose of the remains of a deceased correction officer or parole officer.

6. The commissioner shall have the discretion to enter into agreements with the commissioner of mental health for the provision of security services relating to article ten of the mental hygiene law.

HISTORY: Add, L 1970, ch 475, § 3, eff Jan 1, 1971; amd, L 1995, ch 547, § 1, eff Aug 2, 1995, L 2000, ch 448, § 1, eff Sept 20, 2000, L 2007, ch 7, § 21, eff April 13, 2007, L 2011, ch 62, § 4 (Part C, Subpart A), eff March 31, 2011.

§ 7. Organization of department of corrections and community supervision; officers and employees; delegation by commissioner

1. The commissioner of corrections and community supervision may, from time to time, create, abolish, transfer and consolidate divisions, bureaus and other units within the department not expressly established by law as he or she may determine necessary for the efficient operation of the department, subject to the approval of the director of the budget.

2. The commissioner of corrections and community supervision may appoint such deputies, directors, assistants and other officers and employees as may be needed for the performance of his or her duties and may prescribe their powers and duties and fix their compensation within the amounts appropriated therefor.

3. The commissioner may by order filed in the department of corrections and community supervision delegate any of his or her powers to or direct any of his or her duties to be performed by a deputy commissioner or a head of a division or bureau of such department.

4. The commissioner shall not appoint any person as a correction officer or parole officer, unless such person has attained his twenty-first birthday.

HISTORY: Add, L 1970, ch 475, § 8; amd, L 1980, ch 519, § 1, eff June 24, 1980, L 1984, ch 35, § 1, eff March 27, 1984, L 2011, ch 62, § 5 (Part C, Subpart A), eff March 31, 2011.

§ 8. [Expires Sept 1, 2015] Testing of certain applicants for employment

1. Any applicant for employment with the department as a correction officer at a facility of the department, shall be tested in accordance with the requirements of this section.

2. The department is hereby authorized to conduct, or to enter into agreements necessary for conducting tests for psychological screening of applicants covered by this section. Any such tests shall consist of at least three independent psychological instruments and shall meet the level of the art for psychological instruments to be used in a validation study developed for selection of such applicants. Such psychological instruments shall be used in testing and selection of applicants for positions referred to in subdivision one of this section. Persons who have been determined by a psychologist licensed under the laws of this state as suffering from psychotic disorders, serious character disorders, or other disorders which could hinder performance on the job may be deemed ineligible for appointment; provided, however, that other components of the employee selection process may be taken into consideration in reaching the determination as to whether a candidate is deemed eligible or ineligible for certification to a list of eligible candidates. The department's testing program shall include a component consisting of criteria related validity studies or other validity studies acceptable under relevant federal law governing equal employment.

3. The commissioner or his or her designee shall advise those candidates who have been deemed ineligible for appointment through psychological screening and shall notify such persons of their right to appeal their disqualification. A person so deemed may apply to the commissioner for a review of the findings within thirty days of the date of notification. The commissioner shall refer the matter to an independent advisory board to review any recommendation. A copy of the advisory board's recommendations shall be promptly forwarded to the parties and to the commissioner. If the advisory board's recommendation is rejected by the commissioner, wholly or in part, the commissioner shall state his or her reasons for such rejection in writing.

4. The advisory board shall consist of three members who shall be selected by the president of the civil service commission. The membership of the board shall consist of: A psychologist and a psychiatrist, both of whom shall be licensed under the laws of this state, and a third member who shall be a representative of the department of civil service. The department of civil service shall maintain a list of alternate board members comprised of psychologists and psychiatrists, licensed under the laws of this state, and representatives nominated by the president of the civil service commission, who shall sit on the advisory board in the event a designated member is unable to serve, provided, however, that at all times the advisory board must be comprised of a psychiatrist, a psychologist and a representative of the department of civil service. Each of the members of the advisory board and their alternates so selected shall serve at the pleasure of the president of the civil service commission. Each of the members and alternates so selected shall be reimbursed for services and actual costs at a per diem rate not to exceed nine hundred dollars for the psychiatrist, seven hundred dollars for the psychologist and six hundred dollars for the representative of the civil service department; provided, however, that if any member of or alternate to the advisory board is an employee of the state of New York, then such representative shall only receive reimbursement for actual costs incurred.

5. The commissioner or his or her designee shall advise the department of civil service of those persons who have been determined under this section as being eligible for appointment from any list of eligible candidates.

6. Notwithstanding any other provision of law, the results of the tests administered pursuant to

this section shall be used solely for the qualification of a candidate for correction officer and the validation of the psychological instruments utilized. For all other purposes, the results of the examination shall be confidential and the records sealed by the department of corrections and community supervision, and not be available to any other agency or person except by authorization of the applicant or, upon written notice by order of a court of this state or the United States.

7. Prior to March first of each year, the commissioner of the department of corrections and community supervision will report to the governor, president of the senate and speaker of the assembly on the conduct of the psychological testing program and the results of such program in improving the quality of correction officer candidates.

HISTORY: Add, L 1983, ch 887, § 1, eff Feb 4, 1984 and expiring Sept 1, 2015; amd, L 1984, ch 338, § 1, eff July 3, 1984, L 1986, ch 354, § 1, eff July 17, 1986, L 2002, ch 205, § 1, eff July 30, 2002, L 2011, ch 62, § 6 (Part C, Subpart A), eff March 31, 2011.

§ 9. Access to inmate information via the internet

Notwithstanding any provision of law to the contrary, any information relating to the conviction of a person, except for a person convicted of an offense that would make such person ineligible for merit time under section eight hundred three of this chapter or an offense for which registration as a sex offender is required as set forth in subdivision two or three of section one hundred sixty-eight-a of this chapter, that is posted on a website maintained by or for the department, under article six of the public officers law, may be posted on such website for a period not to exceed five years after the expiration of such person's sentence of imprisonment and any period of parole or post-release supervision; provided, however, that in the case of a person who has been committed to the department on more than one occasion, the department may post conviction information relating to any prior commitment on such website for a period not to exceed five years after the expiration of such person's sentence of imprisonment and any period of parole or post-release supervision arising from the most recent commitment to the department.

HISTORY: Add, L 2010, ch 56, § 3 (Part OO), eff July 22, 2010.

§ 10. Parole officers

1. Employees in the department who perform the duties of supervising inmates released on community supervision shall be parole officers.

2. No person shall be eligible for the position of parole officer who is under twenty-one years of age or who does not possess a baccalaureate degree conferred by a post-secondary institution accredited by an accrediting agency recognized by the United States office of education, or who is not fit physically, mentally and morally. Parole officer selection shall be based on definite qualifications as to character, ability and training with an emphasis on capacity and ability to provide a balanced approach to influencing human behavior and to use judgment in the enforcement of the rules and regulations of community supervision. Parole officers shall be persons likely to exercise a strong and helpful influence upon persons placed under their supervision while retaining the goal of protecting society.

3. The commissioner, acting in cooperation with the civil service commission, shall establish standards, preliminary requisites and requisites to govern the selection and appointment of parole officers.

3-a. [Expires Dec 31, 2015] In order to best effectuate the provisions of subdivision two of this section the commissioner shall, pursuant to subdivision one of section seventy of the civil service law, transfer any employee who held the position of facility parole officer I or facility parole officer II on January first, two thousand twelve and who wishes to accept such transfer, to fill any open position in the parole officer or senior parole officer title. The provisions of this subdivision shall apply to facility parole officer I or facility parole officer II employees for the period that the certificate attesting to satisfactory completion of the training requirements for peace officer eligibility awarded to such employee remains valid pursuant to the provisions of subdivision six of section 2.30 of the criminal procedure law. In no instance shall the department appoint a newly hired employee to a parole officer or senior parole officer position where an employee, eligible under this subdivision, is willing and able to transfer to such position. An employee transferred under this subdivision shall in no instance displace an incumbent employee in the parole officer or senior parole officer title or a person who is on a preferred list or reemployment roster for the position of parole officer or senior parole officer pursuant to section eighty-one or eighty-one-a of the civil service law.

4. A parole or warrant officer, in performing or in attempting to perform an arrest pursuant to and in conformance with the provisions of article one hundred forty of the criminal procedure law, shall be deemed to have performed such actions, relating to such arrest, in the course of employment in the department for purposes of disability or death from any injuries arising therefrom. The provisions of this subdivision shall apply whether or not such parole or warrant officer was on duty for the department at the time of performing such actions or performed such actions outside of his or her regular or usual duties within the department.

> **HISTORY:** Add, L 2011, ch 62, § 8 (Part C, Subpart A), eff March 31, 2011; amd, L 2012, ch 55, § 1 (Part T), eff March 30, 2012, expires and repealed Dec 31, 2015.

§ 15-b. Education

The present director of vocational education shall be the director of education with the powers and duties of the director of education and hereafter shall be appointed by the commissioner. The director of education, at any time appointed, shall be a person whose education, training and experience shall cover fields of penology and of professional education. The educational qualifications shall include the satisfactory completion of three years of graduate work in education, penology, and allied fields. The head of the division of education shall have the direct supervision of all educational work in the department of corrections and community supervision and shall have full authority to visit and inspect all institutions of the department to observe, study, organize, and develop the educational activities of such institutions in harmony with the general educational program of the department. He or she shall be responsible to the commissioner and deputy commissioner designated by the commissioner.

> **HISTORY:** Add, L 1935, ch 670, § 1, eff July 1, 1935; amd, L 2011, ch 62, § 1 (Part C, Subpart B), eff March 31, 2011.

§ 15-c. [Grants and gifts; acceptance and use]*

The commissioner, with the approval of the governor, may accept as agent of the state any grant, including federal grants, or any gift for any of the purposes of this article. Any moneys so received may be expended by the department to develop and promote programs for the study and treatment of crime and delinquency, education and training of inmates, staff improvement, research and evaluation, improvement of facilities, or any other lawful purpose, subject to the same limitations as to approval of expenditures and audit as are prescribed for state moneys appropriated for the purpose of this article.

> **HISTORY:** Add, L 1966, ch 647, eff June 21, 1966.

§ 16. Expense of autopsy; state charge

---

* Section heading supplied by the editor.

The reasonable expense of any inquiry, autopsy, examination or report prepared thereon conducted by a coroner, coroner's physician or medical examiner as required by law with respect to any death occurring to an inmate of an institution operated by the department shall, to the extent not otherwise reimbursed by the state, be a state charge. Reimbursement of such expense shall be made on vouchers submitted annually and certified by the chief fiscal officer of the county or city as the case may be on the audit and warrant of the comptroller.

HISTORY: Add, L 1980, ch 109, § 1, eff May 6, 1980. Former § 16 add, L 1929, ch 243, § 4, with substance transferred from St Dept Law, § 410; repealed, L 1973, ch 398, § 1, eff Sept 1, 1973. Prior § 16, add, L 1909, ch 47; renumbered § 606 and amd, L 1929, ch 243, § 23, eff April 2, 1929.

§ 18. Superintendents of correctional facilities

1. Each correctional facility shall have a superintendent who shall be appointed by the commissioner. Each such superintendent shall be in the non-competitive-confidential class but shall be appointed from employees of the department who have at least three years of experience in correctional work in the department and (i) who have a permanent civil service appointment of salary grade twenty-seven or higher or who have a salary equivalent to a salary grade of twenty-seven or higher for correctional facilities with an inmate population capacity of four hundred or more inmates, or (ii) who have a permanent civil service appointment of salary grade twenty-three or higher or who have a salary equivalent to a salary grade of twenty-three or higher for correctional facilities with an inmate population capacity of fewer than four hundred inmates; provided that for correctional facilities of either capacity, the employee shall be appointed superintendent at the hiring rate set forth in section nineteen of this article or such other rate as may be appropriate, subject to the approval of the director of the budget; provided that in no event shall the salary upon appointment exceed the job rate. Such superintendents shall serve at the pleasure of the commissioner and shall have such other qualifications as may be prescribed by the commissioner, based on differences in duties, levels of responsibility, size and character of the correctional facility, knowledge, skills and abilities required, and other factors affecting the position.

2. Subject to the rules and statutory powers of the commissioner, or rules approved by him or her, the superintendent of a correctional facility shall have the supervision and management thereof.

3. Subject to the direction of the commissioner, and of the deputy and assistant commissioners in their respective fields of supervision, the superintendent of a correctional facility shall direct the work and define the duties of all officers and subordinates of the facility.

HISTORY: Add, L 1929, ch 243, § 4, with substance transferred from St Dept Law § 411; amd, L 1941, ch 156, § 1, L 1960, ch 54, § 1, L 1970, ch 476, § 4, eff July 7, 1970, L 1975, ch 829, §§ 1, 2, L 1984, ch 708, § 1, L 1985, ch 306, § 6, eff April 1, 1985, deemed eff on and after April 1, 1985, L 2011, ch 62, § 10 (Part C, Subpart A), eff March 31, 2011.

§ 19. Salary and emoluments of superintendents

1. This section shall apply to each superintendent of a correctional facility appointed on or after August ninth, nineteen hundred seventy-five and any superintendent heretofore appointed who elects to be covered by the provisions thereof by filing such election with the commissioner.

a. The salary schedule for superintendents of a correctional facility with an inmate population capacity of four hundred or more inmates shall be as follows:

Effective April first, two thousand eleven:

Hiring Rate	Job Rate
$105,913	$144,535

Effective April first, two thousand fourteen:

Hiring Rate	Job Rate
$108,031	$147,426

Effective April first, two thousand fifteen:

Hiring Rate	Job Rate
$110,192	$150,375

b. The salary schedule for superintendents of correctional facilities with an inmate population capacity of fewer than four hundred inmates shall be as follows:

Effective April first, two thousand eleven:

Hiring Rate	Job Rate
$82,363	$104,081

Effective April first, two thousand fourteen:

Hiring Rate	Job Rate
$84,010	$106,163

Effective April first, two thousand fifteen:

Hiring Rate	Job Rate
$85,690	$108,286

2. Employees to whom the provisions of this section apply whose basic annual salary is less than the job rate herein specified may receive periodic performance advancement payments based on periodic evaluations of work performance in accordance with rules and regulations promulgated by the director of the budget; provided, however, that in no event may such a payment result in a basic annual salary in excess of the job rate of such grade. Such payments shall be part of the employee's basic annual salary. Payments pursuant to this subdivision shall commence no earlier than July first, nineteen hundred seventy-nine.

3. Employees to whom the provisions of this section apply whose basic annual salary at the time of the performance award evaluation equals or exceeds the job rate of the salary schedule of their positions may receive performance award payments in accordance with rules and regulations promulgated by the director of the budget. Such payments shall be lump sum payments and shall be in addition to and shall not be part of the employee's basic annual salary; provided, however, that any amounts payable pursuant to this subdivision shall be included as compensation for retirement purposes.

4. The salary herein provided shall be in lieu of all other compensation or emolument, benefit of entitlement of office of the office of superintendent except as may be necessarily incidental to the discharge of the duties of such office or provided by law.

HISTORY: Add, L 1979, ch 307, § 3, eff June 28, 1979, deemed eff April 1, 1979; amd, L 1981, ch 1028, § 5, L 1982, ch 460, § 3, L 1984, ch 708, § 2, L 1985, ch 306, § 7, L 1988, ch 732, § 10, eff April 1, 1988, L 1992, ch 497, § 4, eff April 1, 1993, L 1995, ch 314, § 2, L 1988, ch 732, § 10, L 2000, ch 68, § 2 (Part B), L 2004, ch 103, § 2 (Part B), eff June 4, 2004, deemed eff on and after April 1, 2003, L 2008, ch 10, § 2 (Part B), eff Jan 28, 2008, deemed eff on and after April 1, 2007, L 2011, ch 491, § 2 (Part B), eff Aug 17, 2011, deemed eff on and after April 1, 2011.

Repeal Notes:

[1981, ch 1028] Former subdivision one of section nineteen of the correction law, repealed by section five of this act, provided a salary schedule for certain superintendents of correctional facilities and is replaced by a new schedule.

[1982, ch 460] Former subdivision one of section nineteen of the correction law repealed by section three of this act, provided salary schedules for superintendents of correctional facilities and is replaced by a revised salary schedule in a new subdivision one.

[1985, ch 306] Former subdivision one of section nineteen of the correction law, repealed by section seven of this act, provided salary schedules for superintendents of correctional facilities and is replaced by revised salary schedules in a new subdivision one.

§ 20. Library

A library shall be provided in the department containing the leading books on parole, probation and other correctional activities, together with reports and other documents on correlated topics of criminology and social work.

> **HISTORY:** Add, L 1929, ch 243, § 4, eff April 2, 1929. Former § 20, add, L 1909, ch 47; renumbered § 610 and amd, L 1929, ch 243, § 23, eff April 2, 1929. Amd, L 2011, ch 62, § 4 (Part C, Subpart B), eff March 31, 2011.

§ 21. Acquisition of real property by purchase and acquisition

1. The commissioner, when an appropriation therefor has been made by the legislature, may acquire any real property which he may deem necessary for the purposes of the department by purchase or pursuant to the eminent domain procedure law. Title to any such real property shall be taken in the name of and be vested in the people of the state of New York; provided, however, that no real property shall be so acquired by purchase unless the title thereto shall be approved by the attorney general.

2. Whenever title to real property is to be acquired pursuant to the eminent domain procedure law the commissioner shall cause to be made by the state department of transportation an accurate acquisition map as so provided in said law.

3. On the approval of such map by the commissioner, the original tracing of such map shall, pursuant to the eminent domain procedure law, be filed in the main office of the department.

4. If the commissioner shall determine, prior to the filing of such map in the office of the clerk or register of the county, that changes, alterations or modifications of such map as filed in the main office of the department should be made, he or she shall, subject to the provisions of article two of the eminent domain procedure law, if applicable, direct the preparation by the department of transportation of an amended map. On the approval of such amended map by the commissioner, it shall be filed in the main office of the department and the amended map shall thereupon in all respects and for all purposes supersede the map previously filed.

5. If the commissioner shall determine, prior to the filing of a copy of such acquisition map in the office of the county clerk or register as provided in section four hundred two of the eminent domain procedure law, that such map should be withdrawn, he or she may file a certificate of withdrawal in the offices of the department and of the department of law. Upon the filing of such

certificate of withdrawal, the map to which it refers shall be cancelled and all rights thereunder shall cease and determine.

6. The commissioner shall deliver to the attorney general a copy of such acquisition map, whereupon it shall be the duty of the attorney general to advise and certify to the commissioner the names of the owners of the property, easements, interests or rights described in the said acquisition map, including the owners of any right, title or interest therein, pursuant to the requirements of section four hundred three of the eminent domain procedure law.

7. If, at or after the vesting of title to such property in the people of the state of New York, as provided for in the eminent domain procedure law, the commissioner shall deem it necessary to cause the removal of an owner or occupant from any real property so acquired, he may cause such owner or occupant to be removed therefrom by proceeding in accordance with section four hundred five of the eminent domain procedure law. The proceeding shall be brought in the name of the commissioner as agent of the state and the attorney general shall represent the petitioner in the proceedings. No execution shall issue for costs, if any, awarded against the state or the commissioner, but they shall be part of the costs of the acquisition of the real property and be paid in like manner. Proceedings may be brought separately against one or more of the owners or occupants of any such property, or one proceeding may be brought against all or several of the owners or occupants of any or all such property within the territorial jurisdiction of the same court, justice or judge; judgment shall be given for immediate removal of persons defaulting in appearance or in answering, or withdrawing their answers, if any, without awaiting the trial or decision of issues raised by contestants, if any.

8. Upon making any agreement provided for in section three hundred four of the eminent domain procedure law, the commissioner shall deliver to the comptroller such agreement and a certificate stating the amount due such owner or owners thereunder on account of such appropriation of his or their property and the amounts so fixed shall be paid out of the state treasury after audit by the comptroller from moneys appropriated for the acquisition of such real property, but not until there shall have been filed with the comptroller a certificate of the attorney general showing the person or persons claiming the amount so agreed upon to be legally entitled thereto.

9. Application for reimbursement of incidental expenses as provided in section seven hundred two of the eminent domain procedure law shall be made to the commissioner upon forms prescribed by him and shall be accompanied by such information and evidence as the commissioner may require. Upon approval of such application, the commissioner shall deliver a copy thereof to the comptroller together with a certificate stating the amount due thereof, and the amount so fixed shall be paid out of the state treasury after audit by the comptroller from moneys appropriated for the obtaining of title to property under this section.

10. The commissioner, with the approval of the director of the budget, shall establish and may from time to time amend rules and regulations authorizing the payment of actual reasonable and necessary moving expenses of occupants of property acquired pursuant to this section; of actual direct losses of tangible personal property as a result of moving or discontinuing a business or farm operation, but not exceeding an amount equal to the reasonable expenses that would have been required to relocate such property, as determined by the commissioner; and actual reasonable expenses in searching for a replacement business or farm; or in hardship cases for the advance payment of such expenses and losses. For the purposes of making payment of such expenses and losses only the term "business" means any lawful activity conducted primarily for assisting in the purchase, sale, resale, manufacture, processing or marketing of products, commodities, personal property or services by the erection and maintenance of an outdoor advertising display or displays, whether or not such display or displays are located on the premises on which any of the above

activities are conducted. Such rules and regulations may further define the terms used in this subdivision. In lieu of such actual reasonable and necessary moving expenses, any such displaced owner or tenant of residential property may elect to accept a moving expense allowance, plus a dislocation allowance, determined in accordance with a schedule prepared by the commissioner and made a part of such rules and regulations. In lieu of such actual, reasonable and necessary moving expenses, any such displaced owner or tenant of commercial property who relocates or discontinues his business or farm operation may elect to accept a fixed relocation payment in an amount equal to the average annual net earnings of the business or farm operation, except that such payment shall be not less than two thousand five hundred dollars nor more than ten thousand dollars. In the case of a business, no such fixed relocation payment shall be made unless the commissioner finds and determines that the business cannot be relocated without a substantial loss of its existing patronage, and that the business is not part of a commercial enterprise having at least one other establishment, which is not being acquired by the state or the United States, which is engaged in the same or similar business. In the case of a business which is to be discontinued but for which the findings and determinations set forth above cannot be made, the commissioner may prepare an estimate of what the actual reasonable and necessary moving expenses, exclusive of any storage charges, would be if the business were to be relocated and enter into an agreed settlement with the owner of such business for an amount not to exceed such estimate in lieu of such actual reasonable and necessary moving expenses. Application for payment under this subdivision shall be made to the commissioner upon forms prescribed by him and shall be accompanied by such information and evidence as the commissioner may require. Upon approval of such application, the commissioner shall deliver a copy thereof to the comptroller together with a certificate stating the amount due thereunder, and the comptroller from moneys appropriated for the acquisition of property under this section. As used in this subdivision the term "commercial property" shall include property owned by an individual, family, partnership, corporation, association or a nonprofit organization and includes a farm operation. As used in this subdivision the term "business" means any lawful activity, except a farm operation, conducted primarily for the purchase, sale, lease and rental of personal and real property, and for the manufacture, processing, or marketing of products, commodities, or any other personal property; for the sale of services to the public; or by a non-profit organization.

11. Authorization is hereby given to the commissioner to make supplemental relocation payments, separately computed and stated, to displaced owners and tenants of residential property acquired pursuant to this section who are entitled thereto, as determined by him. The commissioner, with the approval of the director of the budget, may establish and from time to time amend rules and regulations providing for such supplemental relocation payments. Such rules and regulations may further define the terms used in this subdivision. In the case of property acquired pursuant to this section which is improved by a dwelling actually owned and occupied by the displaced owner for not less than one hundred eighty days immediately prior to initiation of negotiations for the acquisition of such property, such payment to such owner shall not exceed fifteen thousand dollars. Such payment shall be the amount, if any, which, when added to the acquisition payment equals the average price, established by the commissioner on a class, group or individual basis, required to obtain a comparable replacement dwelling that is decent, safe and sanitary to accommodate the displaced owner, reasonably accessible to public services and places of employment and available on the private market, but in no event shall such payment exceed the difference between acquisition payment and the actual purchase price of the replacement dwelling. Such payment shall include an amount which will compensate such displaced owner for any increased interest costs which such person is required to pay for financing the acquisition of any such comparable replacement dwelling. Such amount shall be paid only if the dwelling acquired pursuant to this section was encumbered by a bona fide mortgage which was a valid lien on such

dwelling for not less than one hundred eighty days prior to the initiation of negotiations for the acquisition of such dwelling. Such amount shall be equal to the excess in the aggregate interest and other debt service costs of that amount of the principal of the mortgage on the replacement dwelling which is equal to the unpaid balance of the mortgage on the acquired dwelling, over the remainder term of the mortgage on the acquired dwelling, reduced to discounted present value. The discount rate shall be the prevailing interest rate paid on savings deposits by commercial banks in the general area in which the replacement dwelling is located. Any such mortgage interest differential payment shall, notwithstanding the provisions of section twenty-six-b of the general construction law, be in lieu of and in full satisfaction of the requirements of such section. Such payment shall include reasonable expenses incurred by such displaced owner for evidence of title, recording fees and other closing costs incident to the purchase of the replacement dwelling, but not including prepaid expenses. Such payment shall be made only to a displaced owner who purchases and occupies a replacement dwelling which is decent, safe and sanitary within one year subsequent to the date on which he is required to move from the dwelling acquired pursuant to this section or the date on which he receives from the state final payment of all costs of the acquired dwelling, whichever occurs later, except advance payment of such amount may be made in hardship cases. In the case of property acquired pursuant to this section from which an individual or family, not otherwise eligible to receive a payment pursuant to the above provisions of this subdivision, is displaced from any dwelling thereon which has been actually and lawfully occupied by such individual or family for not less than ninety days immediately prior to the initiation of negotiations for the acquisition of such property, such payment to such individual or family shall not exceed four thousand dollars. Such payment shall be the amount which is necessary to enable such individual or family to lease or rent for a period not to exceed four years, a decent, safe, and sanitary dwelling of standards adequate to accommodate such individual or family in areas not generally less desirable in regard to public utilities and public and commercial facilities and reasonably accessible to his place of employment, but shall not exceed four thousand dollars, or to make the down payment, including reasonable expenses incurred by such individual or family for evidence of title, recording fees, and other closing costs incident to the purchase of the replacement dwelling, but not including prepaid expenses, on the purchase of, a decent, safe and sanitary dwelling of standards adequate to accommodate such individual or family in areas not generally less desirable in regard to public utilities and public and commercial facilities, but shall not exceed four thousand dollars, except if such amount exceeds two thousand dollars, such person must equally match any such amount in excess of two thousand dollars, in making the down payment. Such payments may be made in installments as determined by the commissioner. Application for payment under this subdivision shall be made to the commissioner upon forms prescribed by him and shall be accompanied by such information and evidence as the commissioner may require. Upon approval of such application, the commissioner shall deliver a copy thereof to the comptroller, together with a certificate stating the amount due thereunder, and the amount so fixed shall be paid out of the state treasury after audit by the comptroller from moneys appropriated for the acquisition of property under this section.

12. The owner of any real property so acquired may present to the court of claims pursuant to section five hundred three of the eminent domain procedure law a claim for the value of such property acquired and for legal damages caused by such appropriation, as provided by law for the filing of claims with the court of claims. Awards and judgments of the court of claims shall be paid in the same manner as awards and judgments of that court for the acquisition of lands generally and shall be paid out of the state treasury after audit by the comptroller from moneys appropriated for the acquisition of such real property.

13. If the commissioner shall determine subsequent to the acquisition of a temporary easement

in any real property that the purposes for which such easement right was acquired have been accomplished and that the exercise of such easement is no longer necessary, he shall make his certificate that the exercise of such easement is no longer necessary and that such easement right is therefore terminated, released and extinguished. The commissioner shall cause such certificate to be filed in the office of the department of state and upon such filing all rights acquired by the state in such property shall cease and determine. The commissioner shall cause a certified copy of such certificate as so filed in the office of the department of state to be mailed to the owner of the property affected, as certified by the attorney general, if the place of residence of such owner is known or can be ascertained by a reasonable effort and such commissioner shall cause a further certified copy of such certificate to be filed in the office of the recording officer of each county in which the property affected or any part thereof is situated. On the filing of such certified copy of such certificate with such recording officer, it shall be his duty to record the same in his office in the books used for recording deeds and to index the same against the name of the people of the state of New York as grantor.

> **HISTORY:** Add, L 1977, ch 840, § 8, eff July 1, 1978. Former § 21, add, L 1953, ch 178, § 2; amd, L 1962, ch 310, § 88, L 1962, ch 445, § 5, L 1963, ch 336, L 1963, ch 337, § 5, L 1966, ch 860, § 5, L 1967, ch 729, § 5, L 1968, ch 420, § 81, L 1968, ch 956, § 5, L 1970, ch 249, §§ 9, 10, L 1970, ch 251, § 5, L 1970, ch 476, § 6, L 1971, ch 661, §§ 13–15, L 1971, ch 1155, § 5; repealed, L 1977, ch 840, § 8, eff July 1, 1978. Prior § 21, add, L 1939, ch 640, § 1; amd, L 1940, ch 311; repealed, L 1953, ch 178, § 1, eff March 24, 1953. Earlier § 21, add, L 1930, ch 250; repealed, L 1939, ch 640, eff May 31, 1939. An even earlier § 21, formerly § 22, add, L 1920, ch 933; renumbered § 21, L 1926, ch 702; renumbered § 611 and amd, L 1929, ch 243, § 23, eff April 2, 1929. An even earlier § 21, add, L 1909, ch 47; repealed, L 1926, ch 702. Sub 3, amd, L 1996, ch 394, § 7, eff July 30, 1996. Sub 4, amd, L 1996, ch 394, § 7, eff July 30, 1996. Sub 5, amd, L 1996, ch 394, § 7, eff July 30, 1996.

§ 21-a. [Repealed]

> **HISTORY:** Add, L 1972, ch 337, § 1; repealed, L 1974, ch 240, § 6, eff April 1, 1974.

§ 22. Institution officers not to be interested in institution contracts

A commissioner of correction, superintendent or other officer or employee, employed at any of the institutions in the department who:

    1. Shall be directly or indirectly interested in any contract, purchase or sale, for, by, or on account of such institution; or,

    2. Accepts a present from a contractor or contractor's agent, directly or indirectly, or employs the labor of an inmate or another person employed in such institution on any work for the private benefit of such commissioner, superintendent, officer or employee, is guilty of a misdemeanor.

> **HISTORY:** Add, L 1965, ch 1031, § 33, with substance derived from Penal Law § 1828; amd, L 1970, ch 476, § 7, eff July 7, 1970. Former § 22, add, L 1920, ch 933; renumbered § 21, L 1926, ch 702. Earlier § 22, add, L 1919, ch 12; renumbered § 612 and amd, L 1929, ch 243, § 23, eff April 2, 1929. Section heading, amd, L 1970, ch 476, § 7, eff July 7, 1970. Sub 2, amd, L 1975, ch 829, eff Aug 9, 1975.

§ 22-a. Qualification for employment as a correction officer

No person, on or after the effective date of this section, may be appointed to the position of a correction officer in any institution in the department who has been convicted of a felony or of any offense in any other jurisdiction which if committed in this state would constitute a felony. The commissioner may in his discretion, bar the appointment of a person, on or after the effective date of this section, to the position of correction officer in any institution in the department, who has been convicted of a misdemeanor or of any offense in any other jurisdiction which if committed in this state would constitute a misdemeanor where he has determined that the employment of such person is not in the best interest of the department. Notwithstanding the foregoing provisions of this section, no person shall be disqualified pursuant to this section unless he shall have first been furnished a written statement of the reasons for such disqualification and afforded an opportunity by the commissioner, or his designee, to make an explanation and to submit facts in opposition thereto.

HISTORY: Add, L 1984, ch 134, § 1, eff June 21, 1984.

§ 23. Transfer of inmates from one correctional facility to another; treatment in outside hospitals

1. The commissioner shall have the power to transfer inmates from one correctional facility to another. Whenever the transfer of inmates from one correctional facility to another shall be ordered by the commissioner, the superintendent of the facility from which the inmates are transferred shall take immediate steps to make the transfer. The transfer shall be in accordance with rules and regulations promulgated by the department for the safe delivery of such inmates to the designated facility.

2. The commissioner, in his or her discretion, may by written order permit inmates to receive medical diagnosis and treatment in outside hospitals, upon the recommendation of the superintendent or director that such outside treatment or diagnosis is necessary by reason of inadequate facilities within the institution. Such inmates shall remain under the jurisdiction and in the custody of the department while in said outside hospital and said superintendent or director shall enforce proper measures in each case to safely maintain such jurisdiction and custody.

3. The cost of transporting inmates between facilities and to outside hospitals shall be paid from funds appropriated to the department for such purpose.

HISTORY: Formerly § 6-a, add, L 1946, ch 216, § 1, with substance transferred from § 131; amd, L 1951, ch 711; renumbered § 23, L 1970, ch 475, § 5; amd, L 1970, ch 476, § 2, eff July 7, 1970, L 2011, ch 62, § 5 (Part C, Subpart B), eff March 31, 2011.

§ 24. Civil actions against department personnel

1. No civil action shall be brought in any court of the state, except by the attorney general on behalf of the state, against any officer or employee of the department, which for purposes of this section shall include members of the state board of parole, in his or her personal capacity, for damages arising out of any act done or the failure to perform any act within the scope of the employment and in the discharge of the duties by such officer or employee.

2. Any claim for damages arising out of any act done or the failure to perform any act within the scope of the employment and in the discharge of the duties of any officer or employee of the department shall be brought and maintained in the court of claims as a claim against the state.

3. This section shall apply with respect to claims arising on or after the effective date of this section.

HISTORY: Add, L 1972, ch 283, § 15, eff May 15, 1972; amd, L 1974, ch 537, L 1978, ch 466, §§ 2, 3, eff Sept 4, 1978, L 1994, ch 60, § 44, L 1994, ch 63, § 130, eff April 11, 1994, deemed eff April 1, 1994, L 2011, ch 62, § 11 (Part C, Subpart A), eff March 31, 2011.

§ 24-a. Actions against persons rendering health care services at the request of the department; defense and indemnification

The provisions of section seventeen of the public officers law shall apply to any person holding a license to practice a profession pursuant to article one hundred thirty-one, one hundred thirty-one-B, one hundred thirty-two, one hundred thirty-three, one hundred thirty-six, one hundred thirty-seven, one hundred thirty-nine, one hundred forty-one, one hundred forty-three, one hundred fifty-six or one hundred fifty-nine of the education law, who is rendering or has rendered professional services authorized under such license while acting at the request of the department or a facility of the department in providing health care and treatment or professional consultation to inmates of state correctional facilities, or to the infant children of inmates while such infants are cared for in facility nurseries pursuant to section six hundred eleven of this chapter, without regard to whether such health care and treatment or professional consultation is provided within or without a correctional facility.

> **HISTORY:** Add, L 1978, ch 466, § 4; amd, L 1991, ch 351, § 1, L 1992, ch 481, § 1, eff July 17, 1992. Former § 24-a, add, L 1974, ch 489; repealed, L 1978, ch 466, § 4, eff Sept 4, 1978.

§ 25. Mutual assistance by institutional and local fire fighting facilities

In cooperation with the development and operation of plans for mutual aid in cases of fire and other public emergencies, the warden or superintendent of any state institution in the department, with the approval of the commissioner, may authorize the fire department of the institution to furnish aid to such territory surrounding the institution as may be practical in cases of fire and such emergencies, having due regard to the safety of the inmates and property of the institution and to engage in practice and training programs in connection with the development and operation of such mutual aid plans. Any lawfully organized fire-fighting forces or firemen from such surrounding territory may enter upon the grounds of the institution to furnish aid in cases of fire and such emergencies.

> **HISTORY:** Formerly § 6-c, add, L 1947, ch 589, § 1; amd, L 1952, ch 396, § 1; renumbered § 25, L 1970, ch 475, § 5, eff Jan 1, 1971. Former § 25, add, L 1926, ch 702; renumbered § 615 and amd, L 1929, ch 243, § 23, eff April 2, 1929.

§ 26. Establishment of commissaries or canteens in correctional institutions

The commissioner may authorize the head of any institution in the department to establish a commissary or a canteen in such institution for the use and benefit of inmates. The moneys received by the head of the institution as profits from the sales of the commissary or canteen shall be deposited in a special fund to be known as the commissary or canteen fund and such funds shall be used for the general purposes of the institution subject to the provisions of section fifty-three of the state finance law.

> **HISTORY:** Formerly § 6-d, add, L 1948, ch 535, § 1; renumbered § 26, L 1970, ch 475, § 5; amd, L 1994, ch 487, § 1, eff July 26, 1994. Former § 26, add, L 1926, ch 702, renumbered § 616 and amd, L 1929, ch 243, § 23, eff April 2, 1929.

§ 29. Department statistics

1. The department shall continue to collect, maintain, and analyze statistical and other information and data with respect to persons subject to the jurisdiction of the department, including but not limited to: (a) the number of such persons: placed in the custody of the department, assigned to a specific department program, accorded community supervision and declared delinquent, recommitted to a state correctional institution upon revocation of community supervision, or discharged upon maximum expiration of sentence; (b) the criminal history of such persons; (c) the social, educational, and vocational circumstances of any such persons; and, (d) the institutional and community supervision programs and the behavior of such persons. Provided, however, in the event any statistical information on the ethnic background of the inmate population of a correctional facility or facilities is collected by the department, such statistical information shall contain, but not be limited to, the following ethnic categories: (i) Caucasian; (ii) Asian; (iii) American Indian; (iv) Afro-American/Black; and (v) Spanish speaking/Hispanic which category shall include, but not be limited to, the following subcategories consisting of: (1) Puerto Ricans;

(2) Cubans; (3) Dominicans; and (4) other Hispanic nationalities.

2. The commissioner shall make rules as to the privacy of records, statistics and other information collected, obtained and maintained by the department, its institutions or the board of parole and information obtained in an official capacity by officers, employees or members thereof.

3. The commissioner shall have access to records and criminal statistics collected by the division of criminal justice services and the commissioner of criminal justice services shall have access to records and criminal statistics collected by the department of corrections and community supervision, as the commissioner of corrections and community supervision and the commissioner of criminal justice services shall mutually determine.

4. (a) The commissioner shall provide an annual report to the legislature on the staffing of correction officers and correction sergeants in state correctional facilities. Such report shall include, but not be limited to the following factors: the number of security posts on the current plot plan for each facility that have been closed on a daily basis, by correctional facility security classification (minimum, medium and maximum); the number of security positions eliminated by correctional facility since two thousand compared to the number of inmates incarcerated in each such facility; a breakdown by correctional facility security classification (minimum, medium, and maximum) of the staff hours of overtime worked, by year since two thousand and the annual aggregate costs related to this overtime. In addition, such report shall be delineated by correctional facility security classification, the annual number of security positions eliminated, the number of closed posts and amount of staff hours of overtime accrued as well as the overall overtime expenditures that resulted. Such report shall be provided to the chairs of the senate finance, assembly ways and means, senate crime and corrections and assembly correction committees, and posted on the department's website, annually by February first.

(b) Such report shall also include but not be limited to: the total number of correctional facilities in operation which are maintained by the department, the security level of each facility, the number of beds at each facility as of December thirty-first of the prior year, as classified by the department, and the number of empty beds, if any, by such classification as of such date.

HISTORY: Add, L 1974, ch 654, § 1, eff May 30, 1974, with substance derived from §§ 15-a, 615; amd, L 1989, ch 411, § 1, L 1990, ch 598, § 1, eff July 18, 1990 and deemed eff Aug 15, 1989, L 2003, ch 62, § 4 (Part H); amd, L 2004, ch 56, § 1 (Part N), L 2005, ch 56, § 1 (Part R), eff April 12, 2005, deemed eff on and after April 1, 2005, L 2011, ch 62, § 12 (Part C, Subpart A), eff March 31, 2011, L 2012, ch 55, § 1 (Part U), eff March 30, 2012.

ARTICLE 3   STATE COMMISSION OF CORRECTION

HISTORY: Add, L 1975, ch 865, § 2, eff Sept 8, 1975. Former Article 3, add, L 1973, ch 398; repealed, L 1975, ch 865, § 1, eff Sept 8, 1975. Prior Article 3, add, L 1909, ch 47; amd, L 1929, ch 243, § 3; repealed, L 1973, ch 398, eff Sept 1, 1973..

§ 40. Definitions

As used in this article the following terms have the following meanings:

1. "Commission" means the state commission of correction.

2. "Local correctional facility" means any county jail, county penitentiary, county lockup, city jail, police station jail, town or village jail or lockup, court detention pen or hospital prison ward.

3. "Correctional facility" means any institution operated by the state department of corrections and community supervision, any local correctional facility, or any place used, pursuant to a contract with the state or a municipality, for the detention of persons charged with or convicted of a crime, or, for the purpose of this article only, a secure facility operated by the office of children and family services.

4. "Municipal official" means (a) the sheriff or, where a local correctional facility is under the jurisdiction of a county department, the head of such department, and clerk of the board of supervisors, in the case of a county jail; (b) the sheriff or other officer having custody or administrative jurisdiction and the clerk of the board of supervisors, in the case of a county penitentiary; (c) the clerk of the board of supervisors in the case of a county lockup; (d) the mayor and the city clerk, in the case of a city jail or police station jail; (e) the supervisor and town clerk, in the case of a town jail or lockup; (f) the mayor and village clerk, in the case of a village jail or lockup; (g) the clerk of the board of supervisors of the county wherein located and the officer having custody or control, in the case of a court detention pen or a hospital prison ward.

5. "Board" means the correction medical review board.

6. "Council" means the citizen's policy and complaint review council.

   HISTORY: Add, L 1975, ch 865, § 2, eff Sept 8, 1975; amd, L 1996, ch 309, § 55, eff July 13, 1996, L 2011, ch 62, § 13 (Part C, Subpart A), eff March 31, 2011.

§ 41. State commission of correction; organization

1. There shall be within the executive department a state commission of correction. It shall consist of three persons to be appointed by the governor, by and with the advice and consent of the senate. The governor shall designate one of the appointed members as chairman to serve as such at the pleasure of the governor. The members shall devote full time to their duties and shall hold no other salaried public position.

2. The members shall hold office for terms of five years; provided that of the three members first appointed, one shall serve for a term of two years, one shall serve for a term of three years and one shall serve for a term of five years from January first next succeeding their appointment. No member shall serve for more than ten years. Any member of the commission may be removed by the governor for cause after an opportunity to be heard in his defense.

3. Any member chosen to fill a vacancy created other than by expiration of term shall be appointed for the unexpired term of the member whom he is to succeed. Vacancies caused by expiration of term or otherwise shall be filled in the same manner as original appointments.

   HISTORY: Add, L 1975, ch 865, § 2, eff Sept 8, 1975, with substance derived in part from former § 42. Former § 41, add, L 1909, ch 47; amd, L 1929, ch 243; repealed, L 1973, ch 398, § 1, eff Sept 1, 1973.

§ 42. Citizen's policy and complaint review council; organization; functions, powers and duties

(a) 1. There shall be within the commission a citizen's policy and complaint review council. It shall consist of nine persons to be appointed by the governor, by and with the advice and consent of the senate. One person so appointed shall have served in the armed forces of the United States in any foreign war, conflict or military occupation, who was discharged therefrom under other than dishonorable conditions, or shall be a duly licensed mental health professional who has professional experience or training with regard to post-traumatic stress syndrome. One person so appointed shall be an attorney admitted to practice in this state. One person so appointed shall be a former inmate of a correctional facility. One person so appointed shall be a former correction officer. One person so appointed shall be a former resident of a division for youth secure center or a health care professional duly licensed to practice in this state. One person so appointed shall be a former employee of the office of children and family services who has directly supervised youth in a secure residential center operated by such office. In addition, the governor shall designate one of the full-time members other than the chairman of the commission as chairman of the council to serve as such at the pleasure of the governor.

2. The nine appointed members of the council shall hold office for five years; provided that of the seven members first appointed, two shall be appointed for a term of one year, two shall be appointed for a term of two years, one shall be appointed for a term of three years, one shall be appointed for a term of four years and one shall be appointed for a term of five years from January first next succeeding their appointment. Any appointed member of the council may be removed by the governor for cause after an opportunity to be heard in his defense.

3. Any member chosen to fill in a vacancy created other than by expiration of term shall be appointed for the unexpired term of the member whom he is to succeed. Vacancies caused by the expiration of term or otherwise shall be filled in the same manner as original appointments.

4. The members of the council other than the chairman shall receive no compensation for their services but each member other than the chairman shall be entitled to receive his or her actual and necessary expenses incurred in the performance of his or her duties.

5. No appointed member of the council shall qualify or enter upon the duties of his office, or remain therein, while he is an officer or employee of the department of corrections and community supervision or any correctional facility or is in a position where he exercises administrative supervision over any correctional facility. The council shall have such staff as shall be necessary to assist it in the performance of its duties within the amount of the appropriation therefor as determined by the chairman of the commission.

(b) The council and each member thereof shall have the following functions, powers and duties:

1. To investigate, review or take such other action as shall be deemed necessary or proper with respect to complaints or grievances regarding any local correctional facility or part thereof as shall be called to its attention in writing.

2. To have access, at any and all times, to any local correctional facility or part thereof and to all books, records, and data pertaining to any local correctional facility which are deemed necessary for carrying out the council's functions, powers and duties.

3. To obtain from administrators, officers or employees of any local correctional facility any information deemed necessary for the purpose of carrying out its functions, powers and duties.

4. To request and receive temporary office space in any local correctional facility for the

purpose of carrying out its functions, powers and duties.

5. To report periodically to the commission and, where appropriate, to make such recommendations as are necessary to fulfill the purposes of this article to the commission and to the administrator of any local correctional facility.

(c) In addition to the functions, powers and duties prescribed by subdivision (b) of this section, the council shall

1. Advise and assist the commission in developing policies, plans and programs for improving the commission's performance of its duties and for coordinating the efforts of the commission and of correctional officials to improve conditions of care, treatment, safety, supervision, rehabilitation, recreation, training and education in correctional facilities;

2. Foster and promote research and study in areas of correctional policy and program development deemed necessary or desirable by the commission or the council;

3. Meet at least once per calendar month at a time and place designated by the chairman of the council.

HISTORY: Add, L 1975, ch 865, § 2, eff Sept 8, 1975; amd, L 1987, ch 131, § 1, L 1992, ch 55, § 285, eff April 10, 1992, L 1994, ch 86, § 1, L 1996, ch 309, § 56, eff July 13, 1996, L 2011, ch 62, § 14 (Part C, Subpart A), eff March 31, 2011, L 2014, ch 139, § 1, eff July 22, 2014.

§ 43. Correction medical review board; organization

1. There shall be within the commission a correction medical review board. It shall consist of six persons to be appointed by the governor by and with the advice and consent of the senate. In addition, the governor shall designate one of the full-time members other than the chairman of the commission and the chairman of the council as chairman of the board to serve as such at the pleasure of the governor. Of the appointed members of the board one shall be a physician duly licensed to practice in this state; one shall be a physician duly licensed to practice in this state and a board certified forensic pathologist; one shall be a physician duly licensed to practice in this state and shall be a board certified forensic psychiatrist; one shall be an attorney admitted to practice in this state; two shall be members appointed at large.

2. The six appointed members of the board shall hold office for five years; provided that of the two members first appointed, after December thirty-first, nineteen hundred eighty-seven who are not appointed to succeed any other member of the board, one shall be appointed for a term of four years and one shall be appointed for a term of five years from January first next succeeding their appointment. Any appointed member of the board may be removed by the governor for cause after an opportunity to be heard in his defense.

3. Any member chosen to fill a vacancy created other than by expiration of term shall be appointed for the unexpired term of the member whom he is to succeed. Vacancies caused by expiration of term or otherwise shall be filled in the same manner as original appointments.

4. The members of the board shall receive no compensation for their services but each member shall be entitled to receive his actual and necessary expenses incurred in the performance of his duties.

HISTORY: Add, L 1975, ch 865, § 2, eff Sept 8, 1975. Former § 43, add, L 1909, ch 47; amd, L 1929, ch 243; repealed, L 1973, ch 398, § 1, eff Sept 1, 1973. Sub 1, amd, L 1988, ch 379, § 1, eff July 29, 1988. Sub 2, amd, L 1988, ch 379, § 1, eff July 29, 1988.

§ 44. Chairman of commission

1. The chairman shall be the executive officer of the commission, the board and the council.

2. The chairman may appoint such assistants, officers and employees, committees and consultants for the board and the council as he may determine necessary, prescribe their powers and duties, fix their compensation and provide for reimbursement of their expenses within amounts appropriated therefor.

3. The chairman may, from time to time, create, abolish, transfer and consolidate bureaus and other units within the commission, the board and the council not expressly established by law as he may determine necessary for the efficient operation of the commission, the board and the council, subject to the approval of the director of the budget.

4. The chairman may request and receive from any department, division, board, bureau, commission or other agency of the state or any political subdivision thereof or any public authority such assistance, information and data as will enable the commission, the board and the council properly to carry out its functions, powers and duties.

HISTORY: Add, L 1975, ch 865, § 2, eff Sept 8, 1975, with substance transferred from former § 46. Former § 44, add, L 1973, ch 398, § 2, deriving in part from former § 52; repealed, L 1975, ch 865, § 2, eff Sept 8, 1975. Prior § 44, add, L 1909, ch 47; amd, L 1929, ch 243; repealed, L 1973, ch 398, eff Sept 1, 1973.

§ 45. Functions, powers and duties of the commission

The commission shall have the following functions, powers and duties:

1. Advise and assist the governor in developing policies, plans and programs for improving the administration of correctional facilities and the delivery of services therein.

2. Make recommendations to administrators of correctional facilities for improving the administration of such correctional facilities and the delivery of services therein.

3. Except in circumstances involving health, safety or alleged violations of established standards of the commission, visit, and inspect correctional facilities consistent with a schedule determined by the chairman of the commission, taking into consideration available resources, workload and staffing, and appraise the management of such correctional facilities with specific attention to matters such as safety, security, health of inmates, sanitary conditions, rehabilitative programs, disturbance and fire prevention and control preparedness, and adherence to laws and regulations governing the rights of inmates.

4. Establish procedures to assure effective investigation of grievances of, and conditions affecting, inmates of local correctional facilities. Such procedures shall include but not be limited to receipt of written complaints, interviews of persons, and on-site monitoring of conditions. In addition, the commission shall establish procedures for the speedy and impartial review of grievances referred to it by the commissioner of the department of corrections and community supervision.

5. Ascertain and recommend such system of employing inmates of correctional facilities as may, in the opinion of said commission, be for the best interest of the public and of said inmates and not in conflict with the provisions of the constitution or laws of the state relating to the employment of inmates.

6. Promulgate rules and regulations establishing minimum standards for the review of the construction or improvement of correctional facilities and the care, custody, correction, treatment, supervision, discipline, and other correctional programs for all persons confined in correctional facilities. Such rules and regulations shall be forwarded to the governor, the

Corr. L.

temporary president of the senate and the speaker of the assembly no later than January first, nineteen hundred seventy-six and annually thereafter.

6-a. Promulgate rules and regulations to assure that persons in custody in local correctional facilities, including persons awaiting arraignment, are furnished or have access to the type of food required by their religious dietary rules or medically prescribed diets, if any.

6-b. Promulgate rules and regulations, in consultation with the division for youth, establishing minimum standards for the care, custody, rehabilitation, treatment, supervision, discipline and other programs for correctional facilities operated by the division for youth.

7. Place such members of its staff as it deems appropriate as monitors in any local correctional facility which, in the judgment of the commission, presents an imminent danger to the health, safety or security of the inmates or employees of such correctional facility or of the public.

8. (a) Close any correctional facility which is unsafe, unsanitary or inadequate to provide for the separation and classification of prisoners required by law or which has not adhered to or complied with the rules or regulations promulgated with respect to any such facility by the commission pursuant to the provisions of subdivision six of this section; provided, however, that before such facility may be closed due to conditions which are unsafe, unsanitary or inadequate to provide for the separation and classification of prisoners, the commission shall cause a citation to be mailed to the appropriate municipal or other official at least ten days before the return day thereof directing the responsible authorities designated to appear before such commission at the time and place set forth in the citation, and show cause why such correctional facility should not be closed. After a hearing thereon or upon the failure to appear, such commission is empowered to order such facility designated in the citation closed within twenty days, during which time the respondent authority may review such order in the manner provided in article seventy-eight of the civil practice law and rules, in the supreme court. Fifteen days after the order to close has been served by a registered letter upon the appropriate official if no court review has been taken, and fifteen days after the order of such commission has been confirmed by the court, in case of court review, such facility designated in the order shall be closed, and it shall be unlawful to confine or detain any person therein and any officer confining or detaining any person therein shall be guilty of a class A misdemeanor.

(b) Before a correctional facility as defined in subdivision four of section two of this chapter, may be closed for a reason other than those set forth in paragraph (a) of this subdivision, the provisions of section seventy-nine-a of this chapter shall be adhered to.

9, 9-a. [Repealed]

10. Approve or reject plans and specifications for the construction or improvement of correctional facilities that directly affect the health of inmates and staff, safety, or security.

11. [Repealed]

12. Make an annual report to the governor and legislature concerning its work and the work of the board and the council during the preceding year, and such further interim reports to the governor, or to the governor and legislature, as it shall deem advisable, or as shall be required by the governor.

13. Accept, with the approval of the governor, as agent of the state any grant, including federal grants, or any gift for any of the purposes of this article. Any moneys so received may

be expended by the commission to effectuate any purpose of this article, subject to the same limitations as to approval of expenditures and audit as are prescribed for state moneys appropriated for the purposes of this article.

14. Enter into contracts with any person, firm, corporation, municipality, or governmental agency.

15. Adopt, amend or rescind such rules and regulations as may be necessary or convenient to the performance of the functions, powers and duties of the commission.

16. Do all other things necessary or convenient to carry out its functions, powers and duties expressly set forth in this article.

17. [Expires and repealed Sept 1, 2017] Make an annual report to the governor, the chairman of the assembly committee on correction and the chairman of the senate committee on crime victims, crime and correction concerning inmates confined in local correctional facilities pursuant to an agreement authorized by section five hundred-o of this chapter. Such report shall include but not be limited to the number of counties maintaining such agreements and the number of inmates confined pursuant to such agreements.

> **HISTORY:** Add, L 1975, ch 865, § 2, eff Sept 8, 975, with substance transferred from former § 48; amd, L 1979, ch 577, § 1, eff Sept 8, 1979, L 1981, ch 752, § 1, eff July 27, 1981, L 1982, ch 85, § 1, eff Sept 1, 1982, L 1996, ch 309, § 57, eff July 13, 1996, L 2005, ch 57, § 1 (Part S) (amd, L 2005, ch 63, § 2 ((Part D)), eff April 12, 2005), eff April 12, 2005, L 2009, ch 56, § 4 (Part H), eff April 7, 2009, L 2009, ch 56, § 2 (Part Q), eff Oct 4, 2009, L 2009, ch 56, §§ 1, 7 (Part Q), eff April 7, 2009, L 2011, ch 62, § 15 (Part C, Subpart A), eff March 31, 2011, L 2011, ch 573, § 1, eff Sept 23, 2011, and to expire and be deemed repealed Sept 1, 2017.

§ 46. Additional functions, powers and duties of the commission

1. The commission, any member or any employee designated by the commission must be granted access at any and all times to any correctional facility or part thereof and to all books, records, inmate medical records and data pertaining to any correctional facility deemed necessary for carrying out the commission's functions, powers and duties. The commission, any member or any employee designated by the chairman may require from the officers or employees of a correctional facility any information deemed necessary for the purpose of carrying out the commission's functions, powers and duties.

2. In the exercise of its functions, powers and duties, the commission, any member, and any attorney employed by the commission is authorized to issue and enforce a subpoena and a subpoena duces tecum, administer oaths and examine persons under oath, in accordance with and pursuant to civil practice law and rules. A person examined under oath pursuant to this subdivision shall have the right to be accompanied by counsel who shall advise the person of their rights subject to reasonable limitations to prevent obstruction of, or interference with, the orderly conduct of the examination. Notwithstanding any other provision of law, a subpoena may be issued and enforced pursuant to this subdivision for the medical records of an inmate of a correctional facility, regardless of whether such medical records were made during the course of the inmate's incarceration.

3. In any case where a person in charge or control of a correctional facility or an officer or employee thereof shall fail to comply with the provisions of subdivision one, the commission may apply to the supreme court for an order directed to such person requiring compliance therewith. Upon such application the court may issue such order as may be just and a failure to comply with the order of the court shall be a contempt of court and punishable as such.

Corr. L.

4. In any case where any rule or regulation promulgated by the commission pursuant to subdivision six of section forty-five or the laws relating to the construction, management and affairs of any correctional facility or the care, treatment and discipline of its inmates, are being or are about to be violated, the commission shall notify the person in charge or control of the facility of such violation, recommend remedial action, and direct such person to comply with the rule, regulation or law, as the case may be. Upon the failure of such person to comply with the rule, regulation or law the commission may apply to the supreme court for an order directed to such person requiring compliance with such rule, regulation or law. Upon such application the court may issue such order as may be just and a failure to comply with the order of the court shall be a contempt of court and punishable as such.

> **HISTORY:** Add, L 1975, ch 865, § 2, eff Sept 8, 1975, with substance transferred from former § 50; amd, L 1981, ch 850, § 5, eff July 31, 1981, L 1994, ch 536, § 1, eff July 26, 1994, L 2012, ch 232, §§ 1, 2, eff July 18, 2012.

§ 47. Functions, powers and duties of the board

1. The board shall have the following functions, powers and duties:

(a) Investigate and review the cause and circumstances surrounding the death of any inmate of a correctional facility.

(b) Visit and inspect any correctional facility wherein an inmate has died.

(c) Cause the body of the deceased to undergo such examinations, including an autopsy, as in the opinion of the board, are necessary to determine the cause of death, irrespective of whether any such examination or autopsy shall have previously been performed.

(d) Upon review of the cause of death and circumstances surrounding the death of any inmate, the board shall submit its report thereon to the commission and, where appropriate, make recommendations to prevent the recurrence of such deaths to the commission and the administrator of the appropriate correctional facility.

(e) Investigate and report to the commission on the condition of systems for the delivery of medical care to inmates of correctional facilities and where appropriate recommend such changes as it shall deem necessary and proper to improve the quality and availability of such medical care.

2. Every administrator of a correctional facility shall immediately report to the board the death of an inmate of any such facility in such manner and form as the board shall prescribe, together with an autopsy report.

> **HISTORY:** Add, L 1975, ch 865, § 2, eff Sept 8, 1975, with substance transferred from former § 52. Former § 47, add, L 1909, ch 47; amd, L 1929, ch 243, § 1; repealed, L 1973, ch 398, eff Sept 1, 1973. Sub 2, amd, L 1987, ch 491, § 4, eff July 30, 1987.

§ 48. Preference

Any action or proceeding commenced by the commission pursuant to this article shall have a preference over all other cases, except habeas corpus proceedings, pending before the court.

> **HISTORY:** Add, L 1975, ch 865, § 2, eff Sept 8, 1975. Former § 48, add, L 1973, ch 398, deriving in part from former §§ 46, 47 and 49; repealed, L 1975, ch 865, § 2, eff Sept 8, 1975, with substance transferred to § 45. Prior § 48, add, L 1909, ch 47; amd, L 1929, ch 243, § 1; repealed, L 1973, ch 398, eff Sept 1, 1973.

* * *

ARTICLE 4   ESTABLISHMENT OF CORRECTIONAL FACILITIES, COMMITMENT TO DEPARTMENT AND CUSTODY OF INMATES

HISTORY: Add, 1970, ch 476, § 9, eff July 7, 1970.

§ 70. Establishment, use and designation of correctional facilities

1. (a) Except as provided in paragraphs (b) and (c) of this subdivision, every institution operated by the department for the confinement of persons under sentence of imprisonment, or for the confinement of persons committed for failure to pay a fine, shall be a correctional facility.

(b) An institution operated by the department for the care and confinement of persons who have been found to be mentally defective or mentally ill by a court and who are confined in such place pursuant to an order of a court based upon such finding shall not be deemed to be a correctional facility.

(c) An institution operated by the department as a drug treatment campus, as defined in subdivision twenty of section two of this chapter and used to provide intensive drug treatment services for parolees and certain parole violators, shall not be deemed to be a correctional facility.

2. Correctional facilities shall be used for the purpose of providing places of confinement and programs of treatment for persons in the custody of the department. Such use shall be suited, to the greatest extent practicable, to the objective of assisting sentenced persons to live as law abiding citizens. In furtherance of this objective the department may establish and maintain any type of institution or program of treatment, not inconsistent with other provisions of law, but with due regard to:

(a) The safety and security of the community;

(b) The right of every person in the custody of the department to receive humane treatment; and

(c) The health and safety of every person in the custody of the department.

3. (a) The commissioner may continue to maintain, as a correctional facility, any institution operated by the department prior to May eighth, nineteen hundred seventy, and may add to or close any such place, and may establish and maintain new correctional facilities, in accordance

with the needs of the department and provided expenditures for such purposes are within amounts made available therefor by appropriation; provided, however, that before the closure of any correctional facility, for reasons other than those set forth in paragraph (a) of subdivision eight of section forty-five of this chapter, the provisions of section seventy-nine-a of this article shall be adhered to.

(b) A correctional camp or a shock incarceration correctional facility may be established by the department (i) upon land controlled and designated by the commissioner, or (ii) on land controlled and designated by the commissioner of parks, recreation and historic preservation or, in the sixth park region, by the commissioner of environmental conservation.

4. Two or more correctional facilities may be maintained or established in the same building or on the same premises so long as the inmates of each are at all times kept separate and apart from each other except that the inmates of one may be permitted to have contact with inmates of the other in order to perform duties, receive therapeutic treatment, attend religious services and engage in like activities as specifically provided in the rules and regulations of the department.

5. Each correctional facility must be designated in the rules and regulations of the department and no correctional facility can be used by the department for confinement of persons unless the rules and regulations of the department specify at least the following:

(a) The name and location of the facility;

(b) Whether the facility is to be used for the confinement of males or for the confinement of females;

(c) The age range of the persons who may be confined in the facility; and

(d) The classification of the facility.

6. Correctional facilities shall be classified by the commissioner in accordance with the following types of classifications:

(a) Each facility shall be classified with respect to the type of security maintained as either a maximum, medium or minimum security facility.

(b) Each facility shall be classified with respect to the function served in accordance with one or more of the following categories: (i) reception center; (ii) residential treatment facility; (iii) detention center; (iv) correctional camp; (v) diagnostic and treatment center; (vi) general confinement facility; (vii) work release facility; (viii) shock incarceration correctional facility; (ix) alcohol and substance abuse treatment facility; (x) alcohol and substance abuse treatment correctional annex.

7. The commissioner shall have the authority to enter into leases within the amount appropriated therefor, for the purpose of maintaining or establishing any correctional facility or any adjunct thereto.

8. The commissioner is authorized to enter into contracts, within the amount appropriated therefor, with any university, social agency or qualified person to render professional services to any correctional facility.

HISTORY: Add, L 1970, ch 476, § 9, eff July 7, 1970; amd, L 1972, ch 567, L 1972, ch 661, § 2, L 1974, ch 141, § 1, eff April 1, 1974, L 1974, ch 239 § 5, L 1974, ch 660, § 2, L 1975, ch 667, § 12, L 1980, ch 471, § 26, eff July 23, 1980, L 1987, ch 261, §§ 9, 10, L 1989, ch 338, § 8, eff July 10, 1989, L 1995, ch 3, §§ 22, 23, eff June 10, 1995, L 2005, ch 57, § 2 (Part S) (amd, L 2005, ch 63, § 2 ((Part D)), eff April 12, 2005), eff April 12, 2005, L 2009, ch 56, § 2 (Part H), eff April 7,

2009, L 2011, ch 62, § 6 (Part C, Subpart B), eff March 31, 2011.

§ 71. Persons received into the custody of the department

1. [Until Sept 1, 2015] Persons committed to the custody of the department under an indeterminate or determinate sentence of imprisonment shall be delivered to correctional facilities designated as reception centers in the rules and regulations of the department. The commissioner may designate any correctional facility as a reception center subject, however, to the following criteria:

1. [Eff Sept 1, 2015] Persons committed to the custody of the department under an indeterminate or a reformatory sentence of imprisonment shall be delivered to correctional facilities designated as reception centers in the rules and regulations of the department. The commissioner may designate any correctional facility as a reception center subject, however, to the following criteria:

(a) Males and females shall not be received at the same correctional facility;

(b) Males under the age of twenty-one at the time sentence is imposed shall not be received at the same correctional facility as males who are twenty-one or over at the time sentence is imposed.

1-a. The commissioner shall ensure that each general confinement facility law library has information on international offender transfers sufficient to inform those persons who are citizens of a treaty nation of the existence of such treaties and of the means by which such persons may initiate a request for return to the person's country of citizenship for service of the sentence imposed. Such law libraries shall also contain the most recent annual Amnesty International Report published by Amnesty International describing the conditions of prisons in each treaty nation and, to the extent practicable, other materials describing such prison conditions published by the United Nations, United States Department of State or human rights organizations. In addition, to the extent practicable, such law libraries shall contain information either listing each foreign country's provisions for the reduction of the terms of confinement for penal sentences as well as the availability of inmate programs or, shall contain a list of officials in the United States Department of Justice or the embassy of the foreign country to whom an inmate may write for information. To the extent practicable, newly received inmates who are identified as foreign nationals of treaty nations shall, as part of the reception process, be advised of the existence of such treaties and the possibility of the initiation of a transfer request.

1-b. The commissioner shall promulgate rules and regulations setting forth the procedures by which an inmate may apply to be considered for transfer to a foreign nation. The commissioner, or his designee, shall retain sole and absolute authority to approve or disapprove an inmate's application for transfer. Nothing herein shall be construed to confer upon an inmate a right to be [a]* transferred to a foreign nation. Notwithstanding any other law, rule or regulation to the contrary, no inmate application for transfer shall be processed unless the inmate has first indicated his willingness and desire in writing, on a form prescribed by the commissioner, to be considered for transfer to the foreign nation. Such form shall also contain a copy of the inmate's most recent legal date computation printout indicating the term or aggregate term of the sentence originally imposed and the release dates resulting therefrom. If a request for transfer is approved by the commissioner or his designee, facility staff shall assist in the preparation and submission of all materials and forms necessary to effectuate the person's request for transfer to the United States Department of Justice for purposes of finalization of the transfer process, including verification

---

* Brackets have been inserted by the Publisher around this word as it is superfluous.

proceedings before a United States District Court Judge, United States magistrate or other appointed United States official to assure and document the inmate's voluntary request for transfer.

1-c. For purposes of this section, the term "treaty nation" means a foreign country under treaty that provides for the voluntary transfer of persons on the execution of penal sentences entered into by the government of the United States with foreign countries.

2. Persons returned to the custody of the department as parole or conditional release violators shall be delivered to institutions designated in the rules and regulations of the department.

3. Persons who are committed, transferred, certified to or placed in the care or custody of the department as mental defectives shall be delivered to a special institution maintained for the care, treatment, training and custody of mental defectives in accordance with article seventeen of this chapter.

4. Persons who are committed, transferred, certified to or placed in the care or custody of the department while mentally ill shall be delivered to a special institution maintained for the care, treatment and custody of the mentally ill in accordance with article sixteen of this chapter.

5. The commissioner of correction shall file copies of written orders with the clerk of each court having jurisdiction to commit persons to the custody of the department designating the institutions to which persons committed by such court shall be delivered. Such orders may be amended or superseded by the commissioner from time to time and any change shall become effective immediately upon receipt by the clerk of the court.

6. A commitment to a specified institution in the department, rather than to the custody of the department, which is valid in all other respects shall not be void for such reason but shall be deemed a commitment to the custody of the department and the person so committed shall be conveyed to the proper institution as prescribed by this section.

7. Whenever the department receives information that a person committed to the department is a social services recipient and a certificate of conviction and the term of the sentence imposed has not previously been delivered by the sentencing court to the local commissioner of social services pursuant to section 380.80 of the criminal procedure law, the department shall deliver the certificate of conviction and provide notification of the sentence imposed to the commissioner of social services. Such commissioner shall deliver the certificate of conviction and the term of sentence imposed to the appropriate local commissioner of social services.

8. (a) In each year in which the federal decennial census is taken but in which the United States bureau of the census does not implement a policy of reporting incarcerated persons at each such person's residential address prior to incarceration, the department of corrections and community supervision shall by September first of that same year deliver to the legislative task force on demographic research and reapportionment the following information for each incarcerated person subject to the jurisdiction of the department and located in this state on the date for which the decennial census reports population:

    (i) A unique identifier, not including the name, for each such person;

    (ii) The street address of the correctional facility in which such person was incarcerated at the time of such report;

    (iii) The residential address of such person prior to incarceration (if any); and

    (iv) Any additional information as the task force may specify pursuant to law.

(b) The department shall provide the information specified in paragraph (a) of this subdivision in such form as the legislative task force on demographic research and reapportionment shall specify.

> **HISTORY:** Add, L 1970, ch 476, § 9, eff July 7, 1970; amd, L 1974, ch 652, § 1, eff July 31, 1974, L 1995, ch 3, § 24, eff Oct 1, 1995, repealed eff Sept 1, 2015, L 1995, ch 547, § 2, eff Aug 2, 1995, L 1996, ch 700, § 1, eff Jan 7, 1997, L 2010, ch 57, § 1 (Part XX) eff Aug 11, 2010, L 2010, ch 508, § 1, eff Aug 11, 2010, L 2011, ch 62, § 16 (Part C, Subpart A), eff March 31, 2011.

§ 71-a. Transitional accountability plan

Upon admission of an inmate committed to the custody of the department under an indeterminate or determinate sentence of imprisonment, the department shall develop a transitional accountability plan. Such plan shall be a comprehensive, dynamic and individualized case management plan based on the programming and treatment needs of the inmate. The purpose of such plan shall be to promote the rehabilitation of the inmate and their successful and productive reentry and reintegration into society upon release. To that end, such plan shall be used to prioritize programming and treatment services for the inmate during incarceration and any period of community supervision. The commissioner may consult with the office of mental health, the office of alcoholism and substance abuse services, the board of parole, the department of health, and other appropriate agencies in the development of transitional case management plans.

> **HISTORY:** Add, L 2011, ch 62, § 16-a (Part C, Subpart A), eff Sept 30, 2011.

§ 72. Confinement of persons by the department

1. Except as otherwise provided in this section, all persons committed, transferred, certified to or placed in the care or custody of the department shall be confined in institutions maintained by the department until paroled, conditionally released, transferred to the care of another agency or released or discharged in accordance with the law.

2. The commissioner, or the superintendent or director of an institution in which an inmate is confined, may permit an inmate to be taken, under guard, to any place or for any purpose authorized by law, and the commissioner must provide for delivery of an inmate, under guard, to any place where his presence is required pursuant to an order of a court that has authority to require his presence.

2-a. The commissioner, superintendent, or director of an institution in which an inmate is confined, may permit an inmate, wishing to do so, to leave the institution under guard for the purpose of performing volunteer labor or services when in the public interest upon the threat or occurrence of a natural disaster, including but not limited to flood, earthquake, hurricane, landslide or fire. An inmate may also be permitted to leave the institution under guard to voluntarily perform work for a nonprofit organization pursuant to this subdivision. As used in this subdivision, the term "nonprofit organization" means an organization operated exclusively for religious, charitable, or educational purposes, no part of the net earnings of which inures to the benefit of any private shareholder or individual.

2-b. The commissioner, or his designee as authorized by the commissioner, may permit an inmate to be taken under guard to any place to participate in an industrial training program.

3. The superintendent or director of an institution may permit inmates to leave the institution for the purpose of performing maintenance work or farm work, or any other work necessary or appropriate for the upkeep, operations or business of the institution or the department.

4. Any inmate who is confined in a correctional facility and who is eligible for parole or who will become eligible for parole within two years or who has one year or less remaining to be served

under his sentence may be transferred by the commissioner to a correctional camp and may be permitted, by the superintendent, to leave the camp to engage in conservation or forestry work or for any purpose permitted under subdivisions two and three of this section.

5. [Expires Sept 1, 2015] An inmate may be permitted to leave the institution to participate in a temporary release program in accordance with the provisions of article twenty-six of this chapter.

5. [Effective Sept 1, 2015] An inmate of a work release facility may be permitted to leave the facility to participate in a work release program in accordance with the provisions of article twenty-six of this chapter.

6. An inmate of a residential treatment facility may be permitted to leave such facility in accordance with the provisions of section seventy-three of this article.

7. An inmate of a shock incarceration correctional facility may be permitted to leave the facility to participate in programs in accordance with the provisions of article twenty-six-A of this chapter.

8. In any case where the decision to permit an inmate to leave an institution is made by a person other than the commissioner or a deputy commissioner of correction such action and the manner in which it is carried out shall be in strict accordance with the rules and regulations of the department. Such rules and regulations may restrict or limit the authority of the superintendent or director in any manner deemed advisable by the commissioner.

9. The provisions of this section shall not be construed in such manner as to be in conflict with any provision of law that specifically provides for circumstances under which inmates may be permitted to leave institutions.

> **HISTORY:** Add, L 1970, ch 476, § 9, eff July 7, 1970; amd, L 1972, ch 339, § 1, eff June 21, 1972, expires Sept 1, 2015, L 1972, ch 567, § 4, eff May 24, 1972, L 1973, ch 268, § 1, eff May 1, 1973, L 1974, ch 536, § 2; amd, L 1974, ch 966, § 6, eff June 13, 1974, L 1987, ch 261, § 11, eff July 13, 1987, L 2010, ch 256, § 1, eff July 30, 2010.

§ 72-a. [Expires Sept 1, 2015] Community treatment facilities

1. Transfer of eligible inmate. Notwithstanding the provisions of section seventy-two of this chapter, any inmate confined in a correctional facility who is an "eligible inmate" as defined by subdivision two of section eight hundred fifty-one of this chapter and has been certified by the division of substance abuse services as being in need of substance abuse treatment and rehabilitation may be transferred by the commissioner to a community treatment facility.

2. Designation of facilities. A community treatment facility shall be designated by the director of the division of substance abuse services and the commissioner. Such facility shall be operated by a provider or sponsoring agency that has provided approved residential substance abuse treatment services for at least two years duration.

3. Operating standards. The commissioner, after consultation with the director of the division of substance abuse services, shall promulgate rules and regulations which provide for minimum standards of operation, including but not limited to the following:

    (a) provision for adequate security and protection of the surrounding community;

    (b) adequate physical plant standards;

    (c) provisions for adequate program services, staffing, and record keeping; and

    (d) provision for the general welfare of the inmates.

4. Community supervision. The department shall provide for the provision of community

supervision services. All inmates residing in a community treatment facility shall be assigned to parole officers for supervision. Such parole officers shall be responsible for providing such supervision.

5. Reports. The department and the division of substance abuse services shall jointly issue quarterly reports including a description of those facilities that have been designated as community treatment facilities, the number of inmates confined in each facility, a description of the programs within each facility, and the number of absconders, if any, as well as the nature and number of re-arrests, if any, during the individual's period of community supervision. Copies of such reports, as well as copies of any inspection report issued by the department or the commission of correction shall be sent to the director of the budget, the chairman of the senate finance committee, the chairman of the senate crime and correction committee, the chairman of the assembly ways and means committee and the chairman of the assembly committee on codes.

6. Reimbursement.

(a) The commissioner, in consultation with the director of the division of substance abuse services, shall enter into an agreement with the division of substance abuse services whereby the division of substance abuse services will contract with community treatment facilities for provision of services pursuant to this section within amounts made available by the department. Each contract shall provide for frequent visitation, inspection of the facility, and enforcement of the minimum standards and shall authorize the supervision of inmates residing in a community treatment facility by parole officers.

(b) The commissioner shall promulgate rules and regulations specifying those costs related to the general operation of community treatment facilities that shall be eligible for reimbursement. Such eligible costs shall not include debt service, whether principal or interest, or costs for which state or federal aid or reimbursement is otherwise available. Such rules and regulations shall be subject to the approval of the director of the budget.

(c) The department shall not contract for provision of services to more than fifty inmates at any one facility.

(d) At least thirty days prior to final approval of any such contract, a copy of the proposed contract shall be sent to the director of the budget, the chairman of the senate finance committee, the chairman of the senate crime and correction committee, the chairman of the assembly ways and means committee, and the chairman of the assembly committee on codes.

HISTORY: Add, L 1986, ch 554, § 2, eff July 24, 1986, expires Sept 1, 2015; amd, L 2011, ch 62, § 7 (Part C, Subpart B), eff March 31, 2011.

§ 72-b. Discharge of inmates to adult care facilities

1. An inmate about to be discharged to an adult home, enriched housing program or residence for adults, as defined in section two of the social services law, shall be referred only to such home, program or residence that is consistent with that person's needs and that operates pursuant to section four hundred sixty of the social services law. No inmate shall be directly referred to any facility that is required to be certified as an adult care facility under the provisions of article seven of the social services law, unless it has been determined that such facility has a valid operating certificate.

2. No inmate about to be paroled, conditionally released, transferred, released or discharged shall be referred to any adult home, enriched housing program or residence for adults, as defined in section two of the social services law, where the department of corrections and community

Corr. L.

supervision has received written notice that the facility has been placed on the "do not refer list" pursuant to subdivision fifteen of section four hundred sixty-d of the social services law.

HISTORY: Add, L 2004, ch 58, § 48 (Part B), eff Aug 20, 2004; amd, L 2011, ch 62, § 17 (Part C, Subpart A), eff March 31, 2011.

§ 72-c. [Repealed]

HISTORY: Add, L 2005, ch 410, § 1, eff Oct 1, 2005; repealed, L 2006, ch 96, § 2, eff June 7, 2006, deemed eff on and after Oct 1, 2005.

§ 73. Residential treatment facilities

1. The commissioner may transfer any inmate of a correctional facility who is eligible for community supervision or who will become eligible for community supervision within six months after the date of transfer or who has one year or less remaining to be served under his or her sentence to a residential treatment facility and such person may be allowed to go outside the facility during reasonable and necessary hours to engage in any activity reasonably related to his or her rehabilitation and in accordance with the program established for him or her. While outside the facility he or she shall be at all times in the custody of the department and under its supervision.

2. The department shall be responsible for securing appropriate education, on-the-job training and employment for inmates transferred to residential treatment facilities. The department also shall supervise such inmates during their participation in activities outside any such facility and at all times while they are outside any such facility.

3. Programs directed toward the rehabilitation and total reintegration into the community of persons transferred to a residential treatment facility shall be established. Each inmate shall be assigned a specific program by the superintendent of the facility and a written memorandum of such program shall be delivered to him or her.

4. If at any time the superintendent of a residential treatment facility is of the opinion that any aspect of the program assigned to an individual is inconsistent with the welfare or safety of the community or of the facility or its inmates, the superintendent may suspend such program or any part thereof and restrict the inmate's activities in any manner that is necessary and appropriate. Upon taking such action the superintendent shall promptly notify the commissioner and pending decision by the commissioner, the superintendent may keep such inmate under such security as may be necessary.

5. The commissioner may at any time and for any reason transfer an inmate from a residential treatment facility to another correctional facility.

6. Where a person who is an inmate of a residential treatment facility absconds, or fails to return thereto as specified in the program approved for himor her, he or she may be arrested and returned by an officer or employee of the department or by any peace officer, acting pursuant to his or her special duties, or police officer without a warrant; or a member of the board of parole or an officer designated by such board may issue a warrant for the retaking of such person. A warrant issued pursuant to this subdivision shall have the same force and effect, and shall be executed in the same manner, as a warrant issued for violation of community supervision.

7. The provisions of this chapter relating to good behavior allowances and conditional release shall apply to behavior of inmates while assigned to a residential treatment facility for behavior on the premises and outside the premises of such facility and good behavior allowances may be granted, withheld, forfeited or cancelled in whole or in part for behavior outside the premises of the facility to the same extent and in the same manner as is provided for inmates within the premises of any facility.

8. The state board of parole may grant parole to any inmate of a residential treatment facility at any time after he or she becomes eligible therefor. Such parole shall be in accordance with provisions of law that would apply if the person were still confined in the facility from which he or she was transferred, except that any personal appearance before the board may be at any place designated by the board.

9. The earnings of any inmate of a residential treatment facility shall be dealt with in accordance with the procedure set forth in section eight hundred sixty of this chapter.

10. The commissioner is authorized to use any residential treatment facility as a residence for persons who are on community supervision. Persons who reside in such a facility shall be subject to conditions of community supervision imposed by the board.

> **HISTORY:** Add, L 1970, ch 476, § 9, eff July 7, 1970, L 1980, ch 843, § 197, eff Sept 1, 1980, L 2011, ch 62, § 8 (Part C, Subpart B), eff March 31, 2011.

§ 74. Discharge on holidays, Saturdays and Sundays

Where the date of release on parole or conditional release, or where the date of discharge from the care or custody of the department, falls on Saturday or Sunday, it shall be deemed to fall on the preceding Friday. Where the date of such release or discharge falls on a legal holiday it shall be deemed to fall on the preceding day, except that when such legal holiday falls on a Monday the date of release shall be deemed to fall on the preceding Friday.

> **HISTORY:** Add, L 1970, ch 476, § 9, eff July 7, 1970. Former § 74, add, L 1909, ch 47; omitted, L 1929, ch 243, eff April 2, 1929.

§ 75. Notice of voting rights

Upon the discharge from a correctional facility of any person whose maximum sentence of imprisonment has expired or upon a person's discharge from community supervision, the department shall notify such person of his or her right to vote and provide such person with a form of application for voter registration together with written information distributed by the board of elections on the importance and the mechanics of voting.

> **HISTORY:** Add, L 2010, ch 56, § 8 (Part OO), eff July 22, 2010; amd, L 2011, ch 62, § 18 (Part C, Subpart A), eff March 31, 2011.

§ 79. Leasing of state institutions to cities or counties for the confinement of prisoners

1. The commissioner is hereby authorized and empowered to lease to any city or county, upon such terms and conditions as he may deem appropriate, all or any part of any state correctional institution or facility under his jurisdiction, to be used as an adjunct to a jail, penitentiary or correctional institution of such city or county, for the confinement of persons sentenced to such jail, penitentiary, or correctional institution. Such lease may provide for the commissioner to have the superintendence, management and control of the state correctional institution or facility, or part thereof, which is the subject of such lease. Such lease shall provide for such city or county to pay to the state the actual per capita daily cost, as certified to the appropriate local official by the commissioner, for the care of such persons for each day of confinement, but, in any case, the reimbursement rate shall not exceed five dollars per day per capita.

2. [Expired]

> **HISTORY:** Formerly § 6-g, add, L 1966, ch 651; amd, L 1968, ch 1080; redesignated § 28, L 1970, ch 475. § 5; redesignated § 79 and amd, L 1973, ch 1054, eff Aug 1, 1973. Sub 1, formerly entire section, so designated sub 1, L 1973, ch 1054, eff Aug 1, 1973. Sub 2, add, L 1973, ch 1054, eff Aug 1, 1973, expired Aug 1, 1977.

§ 79-a. Closure of correctional facilities; notice

Before the closure of any correctional facility,[,]* for reasons other than those set forth in paragraph (a) of subdivision eight of section forty-five of this chapter, the commissioner shall take the following actions:

1. confer with the department of civil service, the governor's office of employee relations and any other appropriate state agencies to develop strategies which attempt to minimize the impact of the closure on the state work force;

2. consult with the department of economic development and any other appropriate state agencies to develop strategies which attempt to minimize the impact of such closures on the local and regional economies; and

3. provide notice by certified mail to (i) all local governments of any political subdivision in which the correctional facility is located, (ii) all employee labor organizations operating within, or representing employees of, the correctional facility, and (iii) managerial and confidential employees employed within the correctional facility at least twelve months prior to any such closure.

> **HISTORY:** Add and amd, L 2005, ch 57, § 3 (Part S) (amd, L 2005, ch 63, § 2 ((Part D)), eff April 12, 2005), eff April 12, 2005. Amd, L 2009, ch 56, § 1 (Part H), eff April 7, 2009. Opening par, amd, L 2005, ch 57, § 3 (Part S) (amd, L 2005, ch 63, § 2 ((Part D)), eff April 12, 2005), eff April 12, 2005, L 2009, ch 56, § 1 (Part H), eff April 7, 2009. Sub 3, amd, L 2005, ch 57, § 3 (Part S) (amd, L 2005, ch 63, § 2 ((Part D)), eff April 12, 2005), eff April 12, 2005.

§ 79-b. Adaptive reuse plan for consideration prior to prison closure

Not later than six months prior to the effective date of closure of a correctional facility, the commissioner of economic development shall, in consultation with the commissioner, the commissioners of civil service, general services and the division of criminal justice services, the director of the governor's office of employee relations, officials of all local governments of any political subdivision in which the correctional facility is located and any other appropriate state agencies or authorities, provide a report for an adaptive reuse plan for any facility slated for closure which will evaluate the community impact of the proposed closure including but not limited to the following factors: the potential to utilize the property for another state government purpose, including for a new purpose as part of the state criminal justice system; potential for the sale or transfer of the property to a local government or other governmental entity; potential for the sale of the property to a private entity for development into a business, residential or other purpose; community input for local development; and the condition of the facility and the investments required to keep the structure in good repair, or to make it viable for reuse.

> **HISTORY:** Formerly § 79-c, add, L 2005, ch 57, § 3 (Part S) (amd, L 2005, ch 63, § 2 ((Part D)), eff April 12, 2005), eff April 12, 2005; so designated § 79-b and amd, L 2005, ch 57, § 3 (Part S) (amd, L 2005, ch 63, § 2 ((Part D)), eff April 12, 2005), eff April 12, 2005, L 2010, ch 56, § 1 (Part MM), eff June 22, 2010.

*   *   *

ARTICLE 4-B   ALTERNATE CORRECTIONAL FACILITIES FOR THE CITY OF NEW YORK

---

* Brackets have been inserted around this punctuation by the Publisher as it is superfluous.

HISTORY: Add, L 1987, ch 549, § 1, eff July 30, 1987.

§ 86. Purpose of alternate correctional facilities

The purpose of this article is to provide an extraordinary method for relieving existing emergency space pressures in New York city local correctional facilities.

HISTORY: Add, L 1987, ch 549, § 1, eff July 30, 1987.

§ 87. Definitions

As used in this article, the following terms shall have the following meanings:

1. "Alternate correctional facility" shall mean a correctional facility designed to house medium security inmates as defined by department rules and regulations, which is owned by the city of New York, operated by the department pursuant to the rules and regulations promulgated by the commissioner and in accordance with the operation agreement as defined in subdivision five of this section, and used for the confinement of eligible inmates, as defined by subdivision four of this section.

2. "Panel" shall mean the alternate-correctional facility review panel established pursuant to section eighty-nine-e of this article.

3. "Construction agreement" shall mean an agreement entered into pursuant to section eighty-eight of this article by the commissioner and the city of New York which governs the construction of two alternate correctional facilities of approximately seven hundred beds each, one at Ogdensburg and one at Cape Vincent, New York.

4. "Eligible inmates" shall mean male inmates of a New York city correctional facility who are at least nineteen years of age, who are serving a definite, but not an intermittent, sentence of imprisonment, and who do not have criminal charges pending against them.

5. "Operation agreement" shall mean an agreement entered into pursuant to section eighty-eight of this article by the commissioner and the city of New York which governs the

_____

* So in original.

operation of one or both alternate correctional facilities and addresses all related issues, including, but not limited to, general staffing levels and nature of staffing positions; composition of medical staff; availability of outside medical services; procedures and criteria for selecting eligible inmates; availability and frequency of transportation of inmates and visitors of inmates to such facility; availability, content and frequency of programming for inmates; mechanisms to establish, monitor and review operating and capital expenditures; and legal representation of both inmates and employees of such facilities.

HISTORY: Add, L 1987, ch 549, § 1, eff July 30, 1987.

§ 88. Authorization for alternate correctional facilities

1. As hereinafter provided in this article, the department is authorized and empowered to establish, operate and maintain under its jurisdiction no more than two alternate correctional facilities.

2. In carrying out the purposes of this article, the department may acquire land for and construct the alternate correctional facilities authorized pursuant to this section.

3. Any acquisition of land for or construction of an alternate correctional facility shall be governed by section twenty-one of this chapter, section one hundred twenty-seven of the state finance law and any other provisions of law applicable to the acquisition of land for and construction of state correctional facilities. The department, if it elects, shall be the lead agency for all purposes under article eight of the environmental conservation law with respect to alternate correctional facilities.

4. For each alternate correctional facility, the commissioner is hereby authorized and empowered to enter into a construction agreement, an operation agreement, and any other agreements or leases with the city of New York which are deemed by the commissioner to be necessary or convenient for the establishment, operation and maintenance of an alternate correctional facility. An operation agreement shall govern the operation of an alternate correctional facility for up to ten years after the commencement of housing of eligible inmates at such facility. The commissioner shall not operate an alternate correctional facility except pursuant to an executed operation agreement.

5. All agreements entered into by the commissioner and the city of New York pursuant to this section shall be approved by the director of the budget and filed with the chairman of the senate finance committee, the chairman of the assembly ways and means committee, the chairman of the senate crime and corrections committee and the chairman of the assembly committee on correction.

HISTORY: Add, L 1987, ch 549, § 1, eff July 30, 1987.

§ 88-a. Authorization for the city of New York to acquire and utilize alternate correctional facilities

As set forth in this article, the city of New York, acting by and through its mayor, is authorized and empowered:

1. To enter into a construction agreement as defined in this article and pursuant to such agreement to advance payment for the construction of and to acquire from the state two alternate correctional facilities, one in Ogdensburg and one in Cape Vincent, and to finance such construction and acquisition in the manner provided by law under which the city of New York is authorized to finance property acquired or constructed for public purposes regardless of the period of any operation agreement relating to such facilities.

2. To enter into an operation agreement or agreements as defined in this article and pursuant to any such agreements to utilize alternate correctional facilities for the housing of certain inmates of New York city correctional facilities.

3. To pay to the state the costs, both capital and operating, which may be required of the city of New York by the state in accordance with a construction agreement or an operation agreement in the manner set forth in any such agreement, including payment in advance of receipt of services.

4. To sell, subject to the provisions of section eighty-nine-k of this article, facilities which were originally acquired from the state as alternate correctional facilities. Upon sale for cash by the city of New York of any facility originally acquired pursuant to a construction agreement as defined in this article, an amount equal to the principal amount of any bonds then outstanding used to finance such acquisition shall be utilized by the city of New York for its general capital purposes.

5. To make provision for indemnification in any construction or operation agreement to conform with the requirements set forth in section eighty-nine-1 of this article.

6. From time to time, to authorize, issue and sell obligations, pursuant to the local finance law, to pay the costs of acquiring property, of constructing alternate correctional facilities, of constructing, reconstructing or otherwise providing other public improvements and appurtenances, including in each case architectural and engineering fees, and of purchasing original furnishings, equipment, machinery and apparatus therefor pursuant to this section. The acquisition of such property, the construction of such correctional facilities, the construction, reconstruction or other provision of other public improvements and appurtenances and the purchase of such original furnishings, equipment, machinery and apparatus are hereby declared city purposes.

HISTORY: Add, L 1987, ch 549, § 1, eff July 30, 1987.

§ 89. Establishment of alternate correctional facilities

An alternate correctional facility shall be deemed to have been established when the commissioner has filed with the secretary of state a designation of such facility which sets forth, at a minimum, the name and location of the facility, a copy of the department's rules and regulations for the operation of that facility, and a copy of all applicable agreements, including a construction agreement and an operation agreement.

HISTORY: Add, L 1987, ch 549, § 1, eff July 30, 1987.

§ 89-a. 1.* Management of alternate correctional facilities

[1.]** Superintendence, management and control of alternate correctional facilities and the eligible inmates housed therein shall be as directed by the commissioner consistent with the following: an alternate correctional facility shall be operated pursuant to rules and regulations promulgated for such facilities by the commissioner in consultation with the state commission of correction and the provisions of the operation agreement. The commissioner shall operate such facility insofar as practicable in the same manner as a general confinement facility which houses medium security state inmates. Nothing herein, however, shall preclude the commissioner from enhancing staffing or programming to accommodate the particular needs of eligible inmates

---

*   So in original.

**   The bracketed subsection designator added by the Publisher.

pursuant to the operation agreement. No inmate shall be housed in any alternate correctional facility until such facility has been established in accordance with the provisions of section eighty-nine of this article. The population in an alternate correctional facility shall not exceed its design capacity of approximately seven hundred eligible inmates except pursuant to variances permitted by law, rule or regulation or court order.

2. Notwithstanding any other provisions of law, no variance authorizing an alternate correctional facility to exceed its design capacity shall be granted after March fifteenth, nineteen hundred ninety-two unless the mayor of the city of New York submits, together with the variance request, a certificate of emergency demonstrating the need for such variance and that reasonable alternatives to the granting of the variance do not exist, and containing a detailed summary of measures that will be taken to restore compliance with such design capacity. The chairman of the state commission of correction shall transmit, in a timely manner, notice of such request to the chairmen of the senate crime and correction committee and the assembly correction committee.

HISTORY: Add, L 1987, ch 549, § 1; amd, L 1991, ch 409, § 2, eff July 19, 1991, deemed eff April 1, 1991. Section heading, amd, L 1991, ch 409, § 2, eff July 19, 1991, deemed eff April 1, 1991. Sub 2, add, L 1991, ch 409, § 2, eff July 19, 1991, deemed eff April 1, 1991.

§ 89-b. Good behavior time allowances against definite sentences served in alternate correctional facilities

Notwithstanding any other provision of law, the commissioner shall be authorized to grant, withhold, cause to be forfeited, or cancel time allowances as provided in and in compliance with section eight hundred four of the correction law.

HISTORY: Add, L 1987, ch 549, § 1, eff July 30, 1987.

§ 89-c. Use of alternate correctional facilities

1. Alternate correctional facilities shall serve only to supplement local correctional facilities within the city of New York. In considering whether to assign an eligible inmate to an alternate correctional facility or to transfer such inmate from such facility, preference shall be given to available space suitable for housing sentenced inmates at local correctional facilities within the city of New York.

2. Consistent with the provisions of this article and subject to the applicable rules and regulations for operation of alternate correctional facilities and the provisions of the operation agreement, assignment of inmates to alternate correctional facilities shall be made jointly by the commissioner and the commissioner of the New York city department of correction. In making such assignments, consideration shall be given to inmates who have a greater period of time remaining to be served on their sentences, taking into account any applicable jail time and good behavior time. No inmate who is eligible for educational services pursuant to subdivision seven of section three thousand two hundred two of the education law and who chooses to avail himself of such services shall be assigned to an alternate correctional facility.

3. Inmates assigned to alternate correctional facilities shall be returned to a local correctional facility within the city of New York at any such time as the commissioner determines:

(a) that the assignment was not in accordance with this article, or

(b) that the confinement of an inmate in an alternate correctional facility is no longer suitable because it potentially endangers the safety, security or order of the facility.

4. Any inmate who is eligible for educational services pursuant to subdivision seven of section three thousand two hundred two of the education law shall also be returned to a New York city

local correctional facility if he chooses to avail himself of such services.

5. Inmates assigned to alternate correctional facilities shall be returned to a New York city correctional facility within the city of New York no later than seven days prior to their scheduled release or discharge from incarceration.

6. Notwithstanding any other provisions of law, no inmates from jurisdictions other than the city of New York shall be housed at any time in an alternate correctional facility.

HISTORY: Add, L 1987, ch 549, § 1, eff July 30, 1987.

§ 89-d. Transportation

The state of New York shall have no responsibility, financial or otherwise, for transporting inmates between a New York city local correctional facility and an alternate correctional facility, regardless of the reason for such transfer. The city of New York shall be responsible for all such costs, as well as the actual transportation and supervision of inmates during transport.

HISTORY: Add, L 1987, ch 549, § 1, eff July 30, 1987.

§ 89-e. Alternate correctional facility review panel

1. The alternate correctional facility review panel is hereby established and shall consist of the commissioner, the chairman of the state commission of correction, the chairman of the board of parole, the director of the office of probation and correctional alternatives, the commissioner of correction of the city of New York, the president of the New York State Sheriffs' Association Institute, Inc., and the president of the Correctional Association of New York or their designees. The governor shall appoint a chairman and vice-chairman from among the members.

2. The panel shall be authorized to enter and inspect at any and all times each alternate correctional facility or any part thereof and shall have access to all books, records and data pertaining to any such facility within the possession of the department relating to subdivision three of this section.

3. The panel shall examine whether alternate correctional facilities should continue to be utilized, whether all steps practicable have been taken by the city of New York toward finding alternatives to housing eligible inmates in alternate correctional facilities, including the construction of correctional facilities within the city of New York and the development of alternatives to incarceration, and whether there has been compliance with all applicable laws, rules and regulations and the operation agreement.

4. The panel shall prepare an annual report which shall be filed with the governor, the mayor of the city of New York, the chairman of the senate crime and correction committee, and the chairman of the assembly committee on correction no later than the first day of March of each year.

HISTORY: Add, L 1987, ch 549, § 1, eff April 1, 1988; amd, L 1987, ch 550, § 2, eff April 1, 1988, L 2010, ch 56, § 47 (Part A), eff June 22, 2010.

§ 89-f. Oversight

The state commission of correction shall exercise the same powers and duties concerning each alternate correctional facility as the commission is required to exercise concerning a New York state correctional facility. The commission shall prepare an annual report on each alternate correctional facility which shall evaluate and assess the department's compliance with all rules and regulations applicable to that facility and the operation agreement and which shall include an analysis of the frequency and severity of all unusual incidents and assaults occurring in that facility. The annual reports shall be filed with the governor, the mayor of the city of New York, the chairman of the senate crime and correction committee, and the chairman of the assembly committee on correction no later than the first day of June of each year.

HISTORY: Add, L 1987, ch 549, § 1, eff July 30, 1987.

§ 89-g. Costs for establishing, operating and maintaining alternate correctional facilities

1. When the city of New York has entered into the agreements as set forth in section eighty-eight of this article, it shall be obligated, to pay, in accordance with such agreements and at such times and in such amounts as may be determined by the commissioner and approved by the director of the budget, all direct and indirect costs associated with the acquisition, construction, establishment, capital repairs and improvements, operation and maintenance of the alternate correctional facility.

2. Upon completion of the acquisition, construction and establishment of an alternate correctional facility, the commissioner shall make a final determination of the cost of such project and shall certify such cost to the comptroller and to the city of New York. Notwithstanding any other provision of law to the contrary, upon receipt of such certification of the commissioner, the comptroller shall forthwith refund any amounts received from the city of New York in excess of the costs so certified to the city of New York, including interest accrued thereon.

3. On or before October fifteenth of each year, the comptroller shall certify to the commissioner the actual operation and maintenance costs of each alternate correctional facility for the preceding state fiscal year and the amounts paid by the city of New York for such operation and maintenance costs. To the extent that the amounts so paid by the city of New York are less than the operation and maintenance costs for such state fiscal year, the commissioner shall include the amount of such underpayment in the next payment required to be received from the city of New York, or if operation by the state has terminated, the commissioner shall bill the city of New York for the amounts due and such amounts shall be paid by the city within thirty days of receipt of such a bill. To the extent that the amounts so paid by the city of New York are more than the operation and maintenance costs for such state fiscal year, the commissioner shall reduce the next scheduled payment to be received from the city of New York by the amount of the overpayment or if operation by the state has terminated, the commissioner shall refund the overpayment within sixty days of the determination of overpayment.

HISTORY: Add, L 1987, ch 549, § 1, eff July 30, 1987.

§ 89-h. Alternate correctional facilities operating fund

1. There is hereby established in the joint custody of the state comptroller and the commissioner of taxation and finance a special revenue fund to be known as the alternate correctional facilities operating fund.

2. Such fund shall consist of all moneys received by the commissioner pursuant to the operation agreement and all monies received pursuant to section eighty-nine-l of this article. Any interest accruing on amounts deposited in this fund shall be credited to this fund by the state comptroller and shall reduce the amounts the city of New York would otherwise be obligated to pay pursuant to this article. Upon termination of the operation agreement, any balance in the fund less any amount due from the city of New York hereunder shall be paid to the city of New York within sixty days.

3. In the event that any amounts owed by the city of New York pursuant to section eighty-nine-g of this article are not paid to the commissioner within thirty days of the time such payment is due, the commissioner shall certify the unpaid amount to the state comptroller and the comptroller shall, to the extent not otherwise prohibited by law and subject to any other provision of law providing for withholding of payments to the city of New York which shall take precedence over this subdivision, withhold any such unpaid amount from the next succeeding payments of state aid or

local assistance otherwise payable to the city of New York. The amounts so withheld by the comptroller shall be deposited by the comptroller to the fund established by this section.

4. All payments from this account shall be made on the audit of the comptroller on vouchers certified or approved by the commissioner or an employee of the department designated by the commissioner.

> **HISTORY:** Add, L 1987, ch 549, § 1, eff July 30, 1987.

§ 89-i. Local taxes

Alternate correctional facilities shall be exempt from all local property taxes while fee title to such facilities is vested in the city of New York.

> **HISTORY:** Add, L 1987, ch 549, § 1, eff July 30, 1987.

§ 89-j. Title to facilities

Upon payment by the city of New York of the costs of acquisition and construction, the state of New York shall transfer title in fee simple absolute to the city of New York without additional consideration. Notwithstanding the foregoing, as long as an operation agreement entered into pursuant to this article is in effect, the department shall have sole and exclusive authority to operate, manage and maintain such facility including but not limited to the authority to authorize or make without obtaining approval from the city of New York any capital repairs or improvements deemed necessary.

> **HISTORY:** Add, L 1987, ch 549, § 1; amd, L 1987, ch 550, § 3, eff July 30, 1987.

§ 89-k. Termination of operation agreement

At the termination of the operation agreement as to either or both alternate correctional facilities, the department shall have an exclusive option to purchase, from the city of New York, the facility or facilities for which the operation agreement has terminated, at a fair market value price or prices which shall be negotiated by the state office of general services and the city of New York. The duration of the state's option to purchase shall commence on the date notice is received from the city of New York of its intent to terminate such agreement and shall continue for a period of six months or until the next succeeding April first, whichever is longer. Such option to purchase shall be deemed exercised upon execution of an agreement to purchase. Notwithstanding any other provision of law, these facilities shall not be operated as correctional facilities except by the department.

> **HISTORY:** Add, L 1987, ch 549, § 1, eff July 30, 1987.

§ 89-l. Indemnification

The city of New York shall indemnify and hold harmless the state of New York in any action or proceeding arising out of the construction, maintenance or operation of an alternate correctional facility which is constructed, maintained or operated in accordance with the provisions of this article. The obligation to indemnify and hold harmless imposed herein shall include reasonable attorneys' fees, court costs, and costs of litigation including witness fees, incurred by the state of New York in connection with the defense of any such action or proceeding. Such obligation shall extend to any expenses incurred by the state of New York pursuant to section seventeen of the public officers law for the defense and indemnification of state officers and employees in any action or proceeding arising out of the construction, maintenance or operation of any such facility constructed, maintained and operated in accordance with the provisions of this article and the operating agreement or agreements. The city of New York's obligation to indemnify and hold harmless the state of New York shall in no way be construed as relieving the state of its obligation to comply with any and all orders or injunctions issued by any court of competent jurisdiction.

HISTORY: Add, L 1987, ch 549, § 1, eff July 30, 1987.

*   *   *

ARTICLE 5-A   INTERSTATE CORRECTIONS COMPACT

     HISTORY: Add, L 1984, ch 400, § 1, eff July 19, 1984.

§ 100. Compact

The interstate corrections compact as set forth in this article is hereby adopted and entered into with all jurisdictions joining therein.

     HISTORY: Add, L 1984, ch 400, § 1, eff July 19, 1984. Former § 100, add, L 1909, ch 47; renumbered § 95, L 1929, ch 243, eff April 2, 1929.

§ 101. Short title; purpose

This article shall be known and may be cited as the "interstate corrections compact". The party states, desiring common action to fully utilize and improve their institutional facilities and provide adequate programs for the confinement, treatment and rehabilitation of various types of offenders, declare that it is the policy of each of the party states to provide such facilities and programs on a basis of cooperation with one another, thereby serving the best interests of such offenders and of society and effecting economies in capital expenditures and operational costs. The purpose of this compact is to provide for the mutual development and execution of such programs of cooperation for the confinement, treatment and rehabilitation of offenders with the most economical use of human and material resources.

     HISTORY: Add, L 1984, ch 400, § 1, eff July 19, 1984.

§ 102. Definitions

As used in this compact, unless the context clearly requires otherwise:

     (a) "State" means a state of the United States; the United States of America; a territory or possession of the United States; the District of Columbia; the Commonwealth of Puerto Rico.

     (b) "Sending state" means a state party to this compact in which conviction or court commitment was had.

     (c) "Receiving state" means a state party to this compact to which an inmate is sent for confinement other than a state in which conviction or court commitment was had.

     (d) "Inmate" means a male or female offender who is committed, under sentence to or confined in a penal or correctional institution.

     (e) "Institution" means any penal or correctional facility, including but not limited to a facility for the mentally ill or mentally defective, in which inmates as defined in subdivision (d) hereof may lawfully be confined.

HISTORY: Add, L 1984, ch 400, § 1, eff July 19, 1984.

§ 103. Contracts

(a) Each party state may make one or more contracts with any one or more of the other party states for the confinement of inmates on behalf of a sending state in institutions situated within receiving states. Any such contract shall provide for:

1. Its duration.

2. Payments to be made to the receiving state by the sending state for inmate maintenance, extraordinary medical and dental expenses, and any participation in or receipt by inmates of rehabilitative or correctional services, facilities, programs or treatment not reasonably included as part of normal maintenance.

3. Participation in programs of inmate employment, if any; the disposition or crediting of any payments received by inmates on account thereof; and the crediting of proceeds from or disposal of any products resulting therefrom.

4. Delivery and retaking of inmates.

5. Such other matters as may be necessary and appropriate to fix the obligations, responsibilities and rights of the sending and receiving states.

(b) The terms and provisions of this compact shall be a part of any contract entered into by the authority of or pursuant thereto, and nothing in any such contract shall be inconsistent therewith.

HISTORY: Add, L 1984, ch 400, § 1, eff July 19, 1984.

§ 104. Procedures and rights

(a) Whenever the duly constituted authorities in a state party to this compact, and which has entered into a contract pursuant to section one hundred three of this article, shall decide that confinement in, or transfer of an inmate to, an institution within the territory of another party state is necessary or desirable in order to provide adequate quarters and care or an appropriate program of rehabilitation or treatment, said officials may direct that the confinement be within an institution within the territory of said other party state, the receiving state to act in that regard solely as agent for the sending state.

(b) The appropriate officials of any state party to this compact shall have access, at all reasonable times, to any institution in which it has a contractual right to confine inmates for the purpose of inspecting the facilities thereof and visiting such of its inmates as may be confined in the institution.

(c) Inmates confined in an institution pursuant to the terms of this compact shall at all times be subject to the jurisdiction of the sending state and may at any time be removed therefrom for transfer to a prison or other institution within the sending state, for transfer to another institution in which the sending state may have a contractual or other right to confine inmates, for release on probation or parole, for discharge, or for any other purpose permitted by the laws of the sending state; provide that the sending state shall continue to be obligated to such payments as may be required pursuant to the terms of any contract entered into under the terms contained in section one hundred three of this article.

(d) Each receiving state shall provide regular reports to each sending state on the inmates of that sending state in institutions pursuant to this compact including a conduct record of each inmate and certify said record to the official designated by the sending state, in order that each inmate may have official review of his or her record in determining and altering the disposition of said inmate in accordance with the law which may obtain in the sending state and in order that the same may be a source of information for the sending state.

(e) All inmates who may be confined in an institution pursuant to the provisions of this compact shall be treated in a reasonable and humane manner and shall be treated equally with such similar inmates of the receiving state as may be confined in the same institution. The fact of confinement in a receiving state shall not deprive any inmate so confined of any legal rights which said inmate would have had if confined in an appropriate institution of the sending state.

(f) Any hearing or hearings to which an inmate confined pursuant to this compact may be entitled by the laws of the sending state may be had before the appropriate authorities of the sending state, or of the receiving state if authorized by the sending state. The receiving state shall provide adequate facilities for such hearings as may be conducted by the appropriate officials of a sending state. In the event such hearing or hearings are had before officials of the receiving state, the governing law shall be that of the sending state and a record of the hearing or hearings as prescribed by the sending state shall be made. Said record together with any recommendations of the hearing officials shall be transmitted forthwith to the official or officials before whom the hearing would have been had if it had taken place in the sending state. In any and all proceedings had pursuant to the provisions of this subdivision, the officials of the receiving state shall act solely as agents of the sending state and no final determination shall be made in any matter except by the appropriate officials of the sending state.

(g) Any inmate confined pursuant to this compact shall be released within the territory of the sending state unless the inmate, and the sending and receiving states, shall agree upon release in some other place. The sending state shall bear the cost of such return to its territory.

(h) Any inmate confined pursuant to the terms of this compact shall have any and all rights to participate in and derive any benefits or incur or be relieved of any obligations or have such obligations modified or his status changed on account of any action or proceeding in which he could have participated if confined in any appropriate institution of the sending state located within such state.

(i) The parent, guardian, trustee, or other person or persons entitled under the laws of the sending state to act for, advise, or otherwise function with respect to any inmate shall not be deprived of or restricted in his exercise of any power in respect to any inmate confined pursuant to the terms of this compact.

HISTORY: Add, L 1984, ch 400, § 1, eff July 19, 1984.

§ 105. Acts not reviewable in receiving state; extradition

(a) Any decision of the sending state in respect to any matter over which it retains jurisdiction pursuant to this compact shall be conclusive upon and not reviewable within the receiving state, but if at the time the sending state seeks to remove an inmate from an institution in the receiving state there is pending against the inmate within such state any criminal charge or if the inmate is formally accused of having committed within such state a criminal offense, the inmate shall not be returned without the consent of the receiving state until discharged from prosecution or other form of proceeding, imprisonment or detention for such offense. The duly accredited officers of the sending state shall be permitted to transport inmates pursuant to this compact through any and all states party to this compact without interference.

(b) Any inmate who escapes from an institution in which he is confined pursuant to this compact shall be deemed a fugitive from the sending state and from the state in which the institution is situated. In the case of any escape to a jurisdiction other than the sending or receiving state, the responsibility for institution of extradition or rendition proceedings shall be that of the sending state, but nothing contained herein shall be construed to prevent or affect the activities of officers and agencies of any jurisdiction directed toward the apprehension and return of the escapee.

HISTORY: Add, L 1984, ch 400, § 1, eff July 19, 1984.

§ 106. Federal aid

Any state party to this compact may accept federal aid for use in connection with any institution or program, the use of which is or may be affected by this compact or any contract pursuant hereto and any inmate in a receiving state pursuant to this compact may participate in any such federally aided program or activity for which the sending and receiving states have made contractual provision, provided that if such program or activity is not part of the customary correctional regimen, the express consent of the appropriate official of the sending state shall be required therefor.

HISTORY: Add, L 1984, ch 400, § 1, eff July 19, 1984.

§ 107. Entry into force

This compact shall enter into force and become effective and binding upon the states so acting when it has been enacted into law by any two states. Thereafter, this compact shall enter into force and become effective and binding as to any other of said states upon similar action by such state.

HISTORY: Add, L 1984, ch 400, § 1, eff July 19, 1984.

§ 108. Withdrawal and termination

This compact shall continue in force and remain binding upon a party state until it shall have enacted a statute repealing the same and providing for the sending of formal written notice of withdrawal from the compact to the appropriate officials of all other party states. An actual withdrawal shall not take effect until one year after the notices provided in said statute have been sent. Such withdrawal shall not relieve the withdrawing state from its obligations assumed hereunder prior to the effective date of withdrawal. Before the effective date of withdrawal, a withdrawing state shall remove to its territory, at its own expense, such inmates as it may have confined pursuant to the provisions of this compact.

HISTORY: Add, L 1984, ch 400, § 1, eff July 19, 1984.

§ 109. Construction and severability

(a) Nothing contained in this compact shall be construed to abrogate or impair any agreement or other arrangement which a party state may have with a nonparty state for the confinement, rehabilitation or treatment of inmates nor to repeal any other laws of a party state authorizing the making of cooperative institutional arrangements.

(b) The provisions of this compact shall be liberally construed and shall be severable. If any phrase, clause, sentence or provision of this compact is declared to be contrary to the constitution of any participating state or of the United States or the applicability thereof to any government, agency, person or circumstance is held invalid, the validity of the remainder of this compact and the applicability thereof to any government, agency, person or circumstance shall not be affected thereby. If this compact shall be held contrary to the constitution of any state participating therein, the compact shall remain in full force and effect as to the remaining states and in full force and effect as to the state affected as to all severable matters.

HISTORY: Add, L 1984, ch 400, § 1, eff July 19, 1984.

* * *

ARTICLE 6-A   WORK RELEASE PROGRAM IN NEW YORK CITY CORRECTIONAL INSTITUTIONS

HISTORY: Add, L 1968, ch 788, § 1, eff June 16, 1968.

§ 150. Definitions

As used in this article:

1. "City" means the City of New York.

2. "Commissioner" means the commissioner of correction of the city provided, however, that if there shall be established by law a correctional administration in the city, "commissioner" shall mean the correctional administrator of the City.

3. "Department" means the department of correction of the city provided, however, that if there shall be established by law a correctional administration in the city, "department" shall mean such administration.

4. "Work release program" means a program in which the limits of place of confinement are extended for the purpose of seeking or engaging in employment or self-employment, attending an educational institution, participating in a training program, or obtaining medical treatment not otherwise available, caring for the prisoner's household and family or for some other compelling reason consistent with the public interest.

HISTORY: Add, L 1968, ch 788, § 1, eff June 16, 1968. Former § 150, add, L 1909, ch 47; renumbered § 136 and amd, L 1929, ch 243, eff April 2, 1929. Sub 4, amd, L 1971, ch 625, § 1, L 1976, ch 71, § 1, eff Sept 1, 1976.

§ 151. Work Release Program

The department shall establish work release programs for prisoners sentenced to New York City correctional institutions. The commissioner may extend the limits of the place of confinement of a prisoner as to whom there is reasonable cause to believe he will honor his trust by authorizing him to participate in a work release program in the community on a voluntary basis while continuing as a prisoner of the institution or facility in which he is confined. An extension of limits shall be under such prescribed conditions and for such reasonable hours or reasonable periods of time as the commissioner deems necessary. Such extension of limits may be withdrawn at any time.

HISTORY: Add, L 1968, ch 788, § 1, eff June 16, 1968. Former § 151, add, L 1909, ch 47; renumbered § 137 and amd, L 1929, ch 243, eff April 2, 1929.

§ 152. Employment

The department shall endeavor to secure employment for a prisoner deemed eligible to participate in a work release program and assist him in contacting prospective employers. In carrying out this function, the department shall coordinate its efforts with other departments or agencies furnishing employment placement services.

> **HISTORY:** Add, L 1968, ch 788, § 1, eff June 16, 1968. Former § 152, add, L 1909, ch 47; renumbered § 138 and amd, L 1929, ch 243, eff April 2, 1929.

§ 153. Conditions of Employment

1. A prisoner shall be permitted to be employed only if:

(a) The rates of pay and other conditions of employment will not be less than those paid or provided for work of similar nature in the locality in which the work is to be performed.

(b) The commissioner finds, after consultation with representatives of local union central bodies or similar labor union organizations, that such employment will not result in the displacement of employed workers, impair existing contracts for services, or be applied, except where a prisoner is to be hired by an employer for whom he worked prior to his conviction, in skills, crafts, or trades in which there is a surplus of available gainful labor in the locality.

2. The State Department of Labor shall exercise the same supervision over conditions of employment for prisoners participating in work release programs as such department does over conditions of employment for free persons.

3. In no event shall a prisoner be employed in an establishment which has a labor dispute.

> **HISTORY:** Add, L 1968, ch 788, § 1, eff June 16, 1968. Former § 153, add, L 1909, ch 47; renumbered § 139 and amd, L 1929, ch 243, eff April 2, 1929.

§ 154. Disposition of Earnings

The earnings of a prisoner participating in a work release program, less any payroll deductions required or authorized by law, shall be deposited with the department in a trust fund account. Such earnings shall not be subject to attachment or garnishment in the hands of the department. The commissioner is authorized to provide for disbursements from the trust fund account for any or all of the following purposes:

1. Such costs incident to the prisoner's confinement as the commissioner deems appropriate and reasonable.

2. Such costs related to the prisoner's work release program as the commissioner deems appropriate and reasonable.

3. Support of the prisoner's dependents.

4. Payment of court fines, mandatory surcharge, sex offender registration fee, DNA databank fee, restitution or reparation, or forfeitures.

The balance of such earnings, if any, after disbursements for any of the foregoing purposes shall be paid to the prisoner upon termination of his imprisonment.

> **HISTORY:** Add, L 1968, ch 788, § 1, eff June 16, 1968. Former § 154, add, L 1909, ch 47; renumbered § 140 and amd, L 1929, ch 243, eff April 2, 1929. Sub 4, amd, L 1988, ch 661, § 2, L 2003, ch 62, § 3 (Part F), eff May 15, 2003.

§ 156. Liability for a Prisoner on Work Release

No prisoner participating in a work release program or whose place of confinement is extended pursuant to this article shall be deemed an agent, employee or involuntary servant of the department or the city while employed or going to and from such employment or released from confinement pursuant to this article; provided, however, that where a prisoner is employed and paid by the city, his relationship to the city arising out of such employment shall be determined in the same manner as if he were a free person so employed.

> **HISTORY:** Add, L 1968, ch 788, § 1, eff June 16, 1968. Former § 156, add, L 1909, ch 47; renumbered § 142 and amd, L 1929, ch 243, eff April 2, 1929.

§ 157. Rules and Regulations

The commissioner may make such rules and regulations as he shall deem necessary and appropriate to carry out the purposes of this article.

> **HISTORY:** Add, L 1968, ch 788, § 1, eff June 16, 1968. Former § 157, add, L 1909, ch 47, renumbered § 143 and amd, L 1929, ch 243, eff April 2, 1929.

§ 158. Designation of Place of Confinement

The commissioner may designate as a place of confinement of a prisoner any available, suitable and appropriate correctional institution or facility whether maintained by the city, state or federal government and may at any time transfer a prisoner from one place of confinement to another. Where such designation or transfer is to either a state or federal correctional institution or facility, it shall be subject to the prior approval of the appropriate person or agency having jurisdiction and control over such facility and upon such terms and conditions as such person or agency deems appropriate.

> **HISTORY:** Add L 1968, ch 788, § 1, eff June 16, 1968. Former § 158, add, L 1909, ch 47; renumbered § 144 and amd, L 1929, ch 243, eff April 2, 1929.

§ 159. Eligibility for Other Programs

The participation of any prisoner in a work release program established pursuant to this article shall in no way prejudice his eligibility for conditional release, parole or discretionary reduction of sentence.

> **HISTORY:** Add L 1968, ch 788, § 1, eff June 16, 1968. Former § 159, add, L 1909, ch 47; renumbered § 145 and amd, L 1929, ch 243, eff April 2, 1929.

§ 160. Annual Report of Commissioner

The commissioner shall annually prepare a report of the work release program which shall be transmitted to the legislature on or before the first day of March in each year. Such annual report shall include a summary of the operations and activities of the program for the preceding year and such recommendations for the improvement of the program as the commissioner shall deem necessary and proper.

> **HISTORY:** Add, L 1968, ch 788, § 1, eff June 16, 1968. Former § 160, add, L 1909, ch 47; renumbered § 146 and amd, L 1929, ch 243, eff April 2, 1929.

*   *   *

ARTICLE 6-C   SEX OFFENDER REGISTRATION ACT

HISTORY: Add, L 1995, ch 192, § 2, eff Jan 21, 1996.

§ 168. Short title

This article shall be known and may be cited as the "Sex Offender Registration Act".

HISTORY: Add, L 1995, ch 192, § 2, eff Jan 21, 1996.

§ 168-a. Definitions

As used in this article, the following definitions apply:

1. "Sex offender" includes any person who is convicted of any of the offenses set forth in subdivision two or three of this section. Convictions that result from or are connected with the same act, or result from offenses committed at the same time, shall be counted for the purpose of this article as one conviction. Any conviction set aside pursuant to law is not a conviction for purposes of this article.

2. "Sex offense" means:

(a) (i) a conviction of or a conviction for an attempt to commit any of the provisions of sections 120.70, 130.20, 130.25, 130.30, 130.40, 130.45, 130.60, 230.34, 250.50, 255.25, 255.26 and 255.27 or article two hundred sixty-three of the penal law, or section 135.05, 135.10, 135.20 or 135.25 of such law relating to kidnapping offenses, provided the victim of such kidnapping or related offense is less than seventeen years old and the offender is not the parent of the victim, or section 230.04, where the person patronized is in fact less than seventeen years of age, 230.05 or 230.06, or subdivision two of section 230.30, or section 230.32 or 230.33 of the penal law, or (ii) a conviction of or a conviction for an attempt to commit any of the provisions of section 235.22 of the penal law, or (iii) a conviction of or a conviction for an attempt to commit any provisions of the foregoing sections committed or attempted as a hate crime defined in section 485.05 of the penal law or as a crime of terrorism defined in section 490.25 of such law or as a sexually motivated felony defined in section 130.91 of such law; or

(b) a conviction of or a conviction for an attempt to commit any of the provisions of section 130.52 or 130.55 of the penal law, provided the victim of such offense is less than eighteen years of age; or

(c) a conviction of or a conviction for an attempt to commit any of the provisions of section 130.52 or 130.55 of the penal law regardless of the age of the victim and the offender has previously been convicted of: (i) a sex offense defined in this article, (ii) a sexually violent offense defined in this article, or (iii) any of the provisions of section 130.52 or 130.55 of the penal law, or an attempt thereof; or

(d) a conviction of (i) an offense in any other jurisdiction which includes all of the essential elements of any such crime provided for in paragraph (a), (b) or (c) of this subdivision or (ii) a felony in any other jurisdiction for which the offender is required to register as a sex offender in the jurisdiction in which the conviction occurred or, (iii) any of the provisions of 18 U.S.C. 2251, 18 U.S.C. 2251A, 18 U.S.C. 2252, 18 U.S.C. 2252A, 18 U.S.C. 2260, 18 U.S.C. 2422(b), 18 U.S.C. 2423, or 18 U.S.C. 2425, provided that the elements of such crime of conviction are substantially the same as those which are a part of such offense as of the date on which this subparagraph takes effect.

(e) a conviction of or a conviction for an attempt to commit any of the provisions of subdivision two, three or four of section 250.45 of the penal law, unless upon motion by the defendant, the trial court, having regard to the nature and circumstances of the crime and to the history and character of the defendant, is of the opinion that registration would be unduly harsh and inappropriate.

3. "Sexually violent offense" means:

(a) (i) a conviction of or a conviction for an attempt to commit any of the provisions of sections 130.35, 130.50, 130.65, 130.66, 130.67, 130.70, 130.75, 130.80, 130.95 and 130.96 of the penal law, or (ii) a conviction of or a conviction for an attempt to commit any of the provisions of sections 130.53, 130.65-a and 130.90 of the penal law, or (iii) a conviction of or a conviction for an attempt to commit any provisions of the foregoing sections committed or attempted as a hate crime defined in section 485.05 of the penal law or as a crime of terrorism defined in section 490.25 of such law; or

(b) a conviction of an offense in any other jurisdiction which includes all of the essential elements of any such felony provided for in paragraph (a) of this subdivision or conviction of a felony in any other jurisdiction for which the offender is required to register as a sex offender in the jurisdiction in which the conviction occurred.

4. "Law enforcement agency having jurisdiction" means: (a) (i) the chief law enforcement officer in the village, town or city in which the offender expects to reside upon his or her discharge, probation, parole, release to post-release supervision or upon any form of state or local conditional release; or (ii) if there be no chief law enforcement officer in such village, town or city, the chief law enforcement officer of the county in which the offender expects to reside; or (iii) if there be no chief enforcement officer in such village, town, city or county, the division of state police and (b) in the case of a sex offender who is or expects to be employed by, enrolled in, attending or employed, whether for compensation or not, at an institution of higher education, (i) the chief law enforcement officer in the village, town or city in which such institution is located; or (ii) if there be no chief law enforcement officer in such village, town or city, the chief law enforcement officer of the county in which such institution is located; or (iii) if there be no chief law enforcement officer in such village, town, city or county, the division of state police; and (iv) if such institution operates or employs a campus law

enforcement or security agency, the chief of such agency and (c) in the case of a sex offender who expects to reside within a state park or on other land under the jurisdiction of the office of parks, recreation and historic preservation, the state regional park police.

5. "Division" means the division of criminal justice services as defined by section eight hundred thirty-seven of the executive law.

6. "Hospital" means: (a) a hospital as defined in subdivision two of section four hundred of this chapter and applies to persons committed to such hospital by order of commitment made pursuant to article sixteen of this chapter; or (b) a secure treatment facility as defined in section 10.03 of the mental hygiene law and applies to persons committed to such facility by an order made pursuant to article ten of the mental hygiene law.

7. (a) "Sexual predator" means a sex offender who has been convicted of a sexually violent offense defined in subdivision three of this section and who suffers from a mental abnormality or personality disorder that makes him or her likely to engage in predatory sexually violent offenses.

(b) "Sexually violent offender" means a sex offender who has been convicted of a sexually violent offense defined in subdivision three of this section.

(c) "Predicate sex offender" means a sex offender who has been convicted of an offense set forth in subdivision two or three of this section when the offender has been previously convicted of an offense set forth in subdivision two or three of this section.

8. "Mental abnormality" means a congenital or acquired condition of a person that affects the emotional or volitional capacity of the person in a manner that predisposes that person to the commission of criminal sexual acts to a degree that makes the person a menace to the health and safety of other persons.

9. "Predatory" means an act directed at a stranger, or a person with whom a relationship has been established or promoted for the primary purpose of victimization.

10. "Board" means the "board of examiners of sex offenders" established pursuant to section one hundred sixty-eight-l of this article.

11. "Local correctional facility" means a local correctional facility as that term is defined in subdivision sixteen of section two of this chapter.

12. Probation means a sentence of probation imposed pursuant to article sixty-five of the penal law and shall include a sentence of imprisonment imposed in conjunction with a sentence of probation.

13. "Institution of higher education" means an institution in the state providing higher education as such term is defined in subdivision eight of section two of the education law.

14. "Nonresident worker" means any person required to register as a sex offender in another jurisdiction who is employed or carries on a vocation in this state, on either a full-time or a part-time basis, with or without compensation, for more than fourteen consecutive days, or for an aggregate period exceeding thirty days in a calendar year.

15. "Nonresident student" means a person required to register as a sex offender in another jurisdiction who is enrolled on a full-time or part- time basis in any public or private educational institution in this state including any secondary school, trade or professional institution or institution of higher education.

16. "Authorized internet entity" means any business, organization or other entity providing or offering a service over the internet which permits persons under eighteen years of age to access, meet, congregate or communicate with other users for the purpose of social networking. This definition shall not include general e-mail services.

17. "Internet access provider" means any business, organization or other entity engaged in the business of providing a computer and communications facility through which a customer may obtain access to the internet, but does not include a business, organization or other entity to the extent that it provides only telecommunications services.

18. "Internet identifiers" means electronic mail addresses and designations used for the purposes of chat, instant messaging, social networking or other similar internet communication.

HISTORY: Add, L 1995, ch 192, § 2, eff Jan 21, 1996. Sub 2, par (a), amd, L 1999, ch 453, § 1, L 2002, ch 11, § 1, L 2003, ch 69, § 4, eff Aug 11, 2003. Sub 2, par (a), subpar (i), amd, L 2006, ch 91, § 1, eff June 7, 2006, L 2006, ch 320, § 8, eff Nov 1, 2006, L 2007, ch 7, § 22, eff April 13, 2007, L 2007, ch 74, § 9, eff Nov 1, 2007, L 2008, ch 405, § 2, eff Oct 4, 2008. Sub 2, par (b), add, L 2002, ch 11, § 1, eff March 11, 2002. Former sub 2, par (b), redesignated sub 2, par (d), L 2002, ch 11, § 1, eff March 11, 2002. Sub 2, par (c), add, L 2002, ch 11, § 1, eff March 11, 2002. Sub 2, par (d), formerly sub 2, par (b), amd, L 1999, ch 453, § 1; so designated sub 2, par (d) and amd, L 2002, ch 11, § 1; amd, L 2004, ch 146, § 1, eff July 13, 2004. Sub 2, par (d), supbar (iii), amd, L 2008, ch 232, § 1, eff July 7, 2008. Sub 2, par (e), add, L 2003, ch 69, § 4, eff Aug 11, 2003, amd, L 2011, ch 513, § 1, eff Sept 23, 2011. Sub 3, par (a), amd, L 1999, ch 453, § 2, L 2002, ch 11, § 2, eff March 11, 2002. Sub 3, par (a), amd, L 2006, ch 107, § 9, eff June 23, 2006. Sub 3, par (b), amd, L 1999, ch 453, § 2, L 2002, ch 11, § 2, eff March 11, 2002. Sub 4, amd, L 1999, ch 453, § 3, L 2002, ch 11, § 3, eff March 11, 2002. Sub 4, amd, L 2008, ch 303, § 1, eff July 21, 2008. Sub 6, amd, L 2007, ch 7, § 10, eff April 13, 2007. Sub 7, add, L 2002, ch 11, § 4, eff March 11, 2002. Former sub 7, amd, L 1999, ch 453, § 5; deleted, L 2002, ch 11, § 4, eff March 11, 2002. Sub 12, add, L 1999, ch 453, § 4, eff Jan 1, 2000. Sub 13, add, L 2002, ch 11, § 5, eff March 11, 2002. Sub 14, add, L 2002, ch 11, § 5, eff March 11, 2002. Sub 15, add, L 2002, ch 11, § 5, eff March 11, 2002. Sub 16, add, L 2008, ch 67, § 3, eff April 28, 2008. Sub 17, add, L 2008, ch 67, § 3, eff April 28, 2008. Sub 18, add, L 2008, ch 67, § 3, eff April 28, 2008.

§ 168-b. Duties of the division; registration information

1. The division shall establish and maintain a file of individuals required to register pursuant to the provisions of this article which shall include the following information of each registrant:

(a) The sex offender's name, all aliases used, date of birth, sex, race, height, weight, eye color, driver's license number, home address and/or expected place of domicile, any internet accounts with internet access providers belonging to such offender and internet identifiers that such offender uses.

(b) A photograph and set of fingerprints. For a sex offender given a level three designation, the division shall, during the period of registration, update such photograph once each year. For a sex offender given a level one or level two designation, the division shall, during the period of registration, update such photograph once every three years. The division shall notify the sex offender by mail of the duty to appear and be photographed at the specified law enforcement agency having jurisdiction. Such notification shall be mailed at least thirty days and not more than sixty days before the photograph is required to be taken pursuant to subdivision two of section one hundred sixty-eight-f of this article.

(c) A description of the offense for which the sex offender was convicted, the date of conviction and the sentence imposed including the type of assigned supervision and the length of time of such supervision.

(d) The name and address of any institution of higher education at which the sex offender is or expects to be enrolled, attending or employed, whether for compensation or not, and whether such offender resides in or will reside in a facility owned or operated by such institution.

(e) If the sex offender has been given a level two or three designation, such offender's employment address and/or expected place of employment.

(f) Any other information deemed pertinent by the division.

2. a. The division is authorized to make the registry available to any regional or national registry of sex offenders for the purpose of sharing information. The division shall accept files from any regional or national registry of sex offenders and shall make such files available when requested pursuant to the provisions of this article.

b. The division shall also make registry information available to: (i) the department of health, to enable such department to identify persons ineligible to receive reimbursement or coverage for drugs, procedures or supplies pursuant to subdivision seven of section twenty-five hundred ten of the public health law, paragraph (e) of subdivision four of section three hundred sixty-five-a of the social services law, paragraph (e-1) of subdivision one of section three hundred sixty-nine-ee of the social services law, and subdivision one of section two hundred forty-one of the elder law; (ii) the department of financial services to enable such department to identify persons ineligible to receive reimbursement or coverage for drugs, procedures or supplies pursuant to subsection (b-1) of section four thousand three hundred twenty-two and subsection (d-1) of section four thousand three hundred twenty-six of the insurance law; and (iii) a court, to enable the court to promptly comply with the provisions of paragraph (a-1) of subdivision one of section two hundred forty of the domestic relations law, subdivision (e) of section six hundred fifty-one of the family court act, and subdivision (g) of section 81.19 of the mental hygiene law.

c. The department of health and the department of insurance may disclose to plans providing coverage for drugs, procedures or supplies for the treatment of erectile dysfunction pursuant to section three hundred sixty-nine-ee of the social services law or sections four thousand three hundred twenty-one, four thousand three hundred twenty-two or four thousand three hundred twenty-six of the insurance law registry information that is limited to the names, dates of birth, and social security numbers of persons who are ineligible by law to receive payment or reimbursement for specified drugs, procedures and supplies pursuant to such provisions of law. Every such plan shall identify to the department of health or the department of insurance, in advance of disclosure, each person in its employ who is authorized to receive such information provided, however, that such information may be disclosed by such authorized employee or employees to other personnel who are directly involved in approving or disapproving reimbursement or coverage for such drugs, procedures and supplies for such plan members, and provided further that no person receiving registry information shall redisclose such information except to other personnel who are directly involved in approving or disapproving reimbursement or coverage for such drugs, procedures and supplies.

d. No official, agency, authorized person or entity, whether public or private, shall be subject to any civil or criminal liability for damages for any decision or action made in the ordinary course of business of that official, agency, authorized person or entity pursuant to paragraphs b and c of this subdivision, provided that such official, agency, authorized person or entity acted reasonably and in good faith with respect to such registry information.

e. The division shall require that no information included in the registry shall be made available except in the furtherance of the provisions of this article.

3. The division shall develop a standardized registration form to be made available to the appropriate authorities and promulgate rules and regulations to implement the provisions of this section. Such form shall be written in clear and concise language and shall advise the sex offender of his or her duties and obligations under this article.

4. The division shall mail a nonforwardable verification form to the last reported address of the person for annual verification requirements.

5. The division shall also establish and operate a telephone number as provided for in section one hundred sixty-eight-p of this article.

6. The division shall also establish a subdirectory pursuant to section one hundred sixty-eight-q of this article.

7. The division shall also establish a public awareness campaign to advise the public of the provisions of this article.

8. The division shall charge a fee of ten dollars each time a sex offender registers any change of address or any change of his or her status of enrollment, attendance, employment or residence at any institution of higher education as required by subdivision four of section one hundred sixty-eight-f of this article. The fee shall be paid to the division by the sex offender. The state comptroller is hereby authorized to deposit such fees into the general fund.

9. The division shall, upon the request of any children's camp operator, release to such person any information in the registry relating to a prospective employee of any such person or entity in accordance with the provisions of this article. The division shall promulgate rules and regulations relating to procedures for the release of information in the registry to such persons.

10. The division shall, upon the request of any authorized internet entity, release to such entity internet identifiers that would enable such entity to prescreen or remove sex offenders from its services or, in conformity with state and federal law, advise law enforcement and/or other governmental entities of potential violations of law and/or threats to public safety. Before releasing any information the division shall require an authorized internet entity that requests information from the registry to submit to the division the name, address and telephone number of such entity and the specific legal nature and corporate status of such entity. Except for the purposes specified in this subdivision, an authorized internet entity shall not publish or in any way disclose or redisclose any information provided to it by the division pursuant to this subdivision. The division may charge an authorized internet entity a fee for access to registered internet identifiers requested by such entity pursuant to this subdivision. The division shall promulgate rules and regulations relating to procedures for the release of information in the registry, including but not limited to, the disclosure and redisclosure of such information, and the imposition of any fees.

11. The division shall promptly notify each sex offender whose term of registration and verification would otherwise have expired prior to March thirty-first, two thousand seven of the continuing duty to register and verify under this article.

12. The division shall make registry information regarding level two and three sex offenders available to municipal housing authorities, as established pursuant to article three of the public housing law, to enable such authorities to identify persons ineligible to reside in public housing. The division shall, at least monthly, release to each municipal housing authority information about level two and three sex offenders with a home address and/or expected place of domicile within the corresponding municipality. The division may promulgate rules and regulations relating to procedures for the release of information in the registry to such authorities.

HISTORY: Add, L 1995, ch 192, § 2, eff Jan 21, 1996; amd, L 2000, ch 1, § 15, eff Feb 1, 2001, L 2002, ch 11, § 6, eff March 11, 2002, L 2002, ch 694, § 1, L 2003, ch 10, §§ 1, 2, eff May 30, 2003, L 2003, ch 62, § 4 (Part F), eff May 15, 2003, L 2004, ch 361, § 2, eff Sept 9, 2004, L 2005, ch 56, § 1 (Part O), eff April 12, 2006, L 2005, ch 260, § 5, eff Aug 18, 2005, L 2005, ch 645, § 6, eff Aug 30, 2005, L 2006, ch 1, § 2, eff Jan 18, 2006, L 2006, ch 106, § 4, eff June 23, 2006, L 2008, ch 67, §§ 4, 5, eff April 28, 2008, L 2008, ch 595, § 4, eff Jan 23, 2009, L 2010, ch 278, § 1, eff Sept 28, 2010, L 2011, ch 507, § 1, eff Sept 23, 2011, L 2011, ch 532, § 1, eff Sept 23, 2011, L 2012, ch 475, § 1, eff April 1, 2013.

§ 168-c. Sex offender; relocation; notification

1. In the case of any sex offender, it shall be the duty of the department, hospital or local correctional facility at least ten calendar days prior to the release or discharge of any sex offender from a correctional facility, hospital or local correctional facility to notify the division of the contemplated release or discharge of such sex offender, informing the division in writing on a form provided by the division indicating the address at which he or she proposes to reside and the name and address of any institution of higher education at which he or she expects to be enrolled, attending or employed, whether for compensation or not, and whether he or she resides in or will reside in a facility owned or operated by such institution. If such sex offender changes his or her place of residence while on parole, such notification of the change of residence shall be sent by the sex offender's parole officer within forty-eight hours to the division on a form provided by the division. If such sex offender changes the status of his or her enrollment, attendance, employment or residence at any institution of higher education while on parole, such notification of the change of status shall be sent by the sex offender's parole officer within forty-eight hours to the division on a form provided by the division.

2. In the case of any sex offender on probation, it shall be the duty of the sex offender's probation officer to notify the division within forty-eight hours of the new place of residence on a form provided by the division. If such sex offender changes the status of his or her enrollment, attendance, employment or residence at any institution of higher education while on probation, such notification of the change of status shall be sent by the sex offender's probation officer within forty-eight hours to the division on a form provided by the division.

3. In the case in which any sex offender escapes from a state or local correctional facility or hospital, the designated official of the facility or hospital where the person was confined shall notify within twenty-four hours the law enforcement agency having had jurisdiction at the time of his or her conviction, informing such law enforcement agency of the name and aliases of the person, and the address at which he or she resided at the time of his or her conviction, the amount of time remaining to be served, if any, on the full term for which he or she was sentenced, and the nature of the crime for which he or she was sentenced, transmitting at the same time a copy of such sex offender's fingerprints and photograph and a summary of his or her criminal record.

4. The division shall provide general information, in registration materials and annual correspondence, to registrants concerning notification and registration procedures that may apply if the registrant is authorized to relocate and relocates to another state or United States possession, or commences employment or attendance at an education institution in another state or United States possession. Such information shall include addresses and telephone numbers for relevant agencies from which additional information may be obtained.

HISTORY: Add, L 1995, ch 192, § 2; amd, L 2002, ch 11, § 7, eff July 1, 2002. Sub 1, amd, L 2002, ch 11, § 7, eff July 1, 2002. Sub 2, amd, L 2002, ch 11, § 7, eff July 1, 2002. Sub 3, formerly sub 4, so designated sub 3 and amd, L 2002, ch 11, § 7, eff July 1, 2002. Former sub 3, deleted, L 2002, ch 11, § 7, eff July 1, 2002. Sub 4, add, L 2004, ch 410, § 1, eff Nov 15, 2004. Former sub 4, redesignated sub 3, L 2002, ch 11, § 7, eff July 1, 2002.

Corr. L.

§ 168-d. Duties of the court

1. (a) Except as provided in paragraphs (b) and (c) of this subdivision, upon conviction of any of the offenses set forth in subdivision two or three of section one hundred sixty-eight-a of this article the court shall certify that the person is a sex offender and shall include the certification in the order of commitment, if any, and judgment of conviction, except as provided in paragraph (e) of subdivision two of section one hundred sixty-eight-a of this article. The court shall also advise the sex offender of his or her duties under this article. Failure to include the certification in the order of commitment or the judgment of conviction shall not relieve a sex offender of the obligations imposed by this article.

(b) Where a defendant stands convicted of an offense defined in paragraph (b) of subdivision two of section one hundred sixty-eight-a of this article or where the defendant was convicted of patronizing a prostitute in the third degree under section 230.04 of the penal law and the defendant controverts an allegation that the victim of such offense was less than eighteen years of age or, in the case of a conviction under section 230.04 of the penal law, less than seventeen years of age, the court, without a jury, shall, prior to sentencing, conduct a hearing, and the people may prove by clear and convincing evidence that the victim was less than eighteen years of age or less than seventeen years of age, as applicable, by any evidence admissible under the rules applicable to a trial of the issue of guilt. The court in addition to such admissible evidence may also consider reliable hearsay evidence submitted by either party provided that it is relevant to the determination of the age of the victim. Facts concerning the age of the victim proven at trial or ascertained at the time of entry of a plea of guilty shall be deemed established by clear and convincing evidence and shall not be relitigated. At the conclusion of the hearing, or if the defendant does not controvert an allegation that the victim of the offense was less than eighteen years of age or less than seventeen years of age, as applicable, the court must make a finding and enter an order setting forth the age of the victim. If the court finds that the victim of such offense was under eighteen years of age or under seventeen years of age, as applicable, the court shall certify the defendant as a sex offender, the provisions of paragraph (a) of this subdivision shall apply and the defendant shall register with the division in accordance with the provisions of this article.

(c) Where a defendant stands convicted of an offense defined in paragraph (c) of subdivision two of section one hundred sixty-eight-a of this article and the defendant controverts an allegation that the defendant was previously convicted of a sex offense or a sexually violent offense defined in this article or has previously been convicted of or convicted for an attempt to commit any of the provisions of section 130.52 or 130.55 of the penal law, the court, without a jury, shall, prior to sentencing, conduct a hearing, and the people may prove by clear and convincing evidence that the defendant was previously convicted of a sex offense or a sexually violent offense defined in this article or has previously been convicted of or convicted for an attempt to commit any of the provisions of section 130.52 or 130.55 of the penal law, by any evidence admissible under the rules applicable to a trial of the issue of guilt. The court in addition to such admissible evidence may also consider reliable hearsay evidence submitted by either party provided that it is relevant to the determination of whether the defendant was previously convicted of a sex offense or a sexually violent offense defined in this article or has previously been convicted of or convicted for an attempt to commit any of the provisions of section 130.52 or 130.55 of the penal law. At the conclusion of the hearing, or if the defendant does not controvert an allegation that the defendant was previously convicted of a sex offense or a sexually violent offense defined in this article or has previously been convicted of or convicted for an attempt to commit any of the provisions of section 130.52 or 130.55 of the penal law, the court must make a finding and enter an order determining whether the defendant was previously convicted of a sex offense or a sexually violent offense defined in this article or has previously been convicted of or convicted for an attempt to commit any of the provisions of section 130.52 or 130.55 of the penal law. If the court finds that the defendant has such a previous conviction, the court shall certify the defendant as a sex offender, the provisions of paragraph (a) of this subdivision shall apply and the defendant shall register with the division in accordance with the provisions of this article.

2. Any sex offender, who is released on probation or discharged upon payment of a fine, conditional discharge or unconditional discharge shall, prior to such release or discharge, be informed of his or her duty to register under this article by the court in which he or she was convicted. At the time sentence is imposed, such sex offender shall register with the division on a form prepared by the division. The court shall require the sex offender to read and sign such form and to complete the registration portion of such form. The court shall on such form obtain the address where the sex offender expects to reside upon his or her release, and the name and address of any institution of higher education he or she expects to be employed by, enrolled in, attending or employed, whether for compensation or not, and whether he or she expects to reside in a facility owned or operated by such an institution, and shall report such information to the division. The court shall give one copy of the form to the sex offender and shall send two copies to the division which shall forward the information to the law enforcement agencies having jurisdiction. The court shall also notify the district attorney and the sex offender of the date of the determination proceeding to be held pursuant to subdivision three of this section, which shall be held at least forty-five days after such notice is given. This notice shall include the following statement or a substantially similar statement: "This proceeding is being held to determine whether you will be classified as a level 3 offender (risk of repeat offense is high), a level 2 offender (risk of repeat offense is moderate), or a level 1 offender (risk of repeat offense is low), or whether you will be designated as a sexual predator, a sexually violent offender or a predicate sex offender, which will determine how long you must register as a sex offender and how much information can be provided to the public concerning your registration. If you fail to appear at this proceeding, without sufficient excuse, it shall be held in your absence. Failure to appear may result in a longer period of registration or a higher level of community notification because you are not present to offer evidence or contest evidence offered by the district attorney." The court shall also advise the sex offender that he or she has a right to a hearing prior to the court's determination, that he or she has the right to be represented by counsel at the hearing and that counsel will be appointed if he or she is financially unable to retain counsel. If the sex offender applies for assignment of counsel to represent him or her at the hearing and counsel was not previously assigned to represent the sex offender in the underlying criminal action, the court shall determine whether the offender is financially unable to retain counsel. If such a finding is made, the court shall assign counsel to represent the sex offender pursuant to article eighteen-B of the county law. Where the court orders a sex offender released on probation, such order must include a provision requiring that he or she comply with the requirements of this article. Where such sex offender violates such provision, probation may be immediately revoked in the manner provided by article four hundred ten of the criminal procedure law.

3. For sex offenders released on probation or discharged upon payment of a fine, conditional discharge or unconditional discharge, it shall be the duty of the court applying the guidelines established in subdivision five of section one hundred sixty-eight-l of this article to determine the level of notification pursuant to subdivision six of section one hundred sixty-eight-l of this article and whether such sex offender shall be designated a sexual predator, sexually violent offender, or predicate sex offender as defined in subdivision seven of section one hundred sixty-eight-a of this article. At least fifteen days prior to the determination proceeding, the district attorney shall

provide to the court and the sex offender a written statement setting forth the determinations sought by the district attorney together with the reasons for seeking such determinations. The court shall allow the sex offender to appear and be heard. The state shall appear by the district attorney, or his or her designee, who shall bear the burden of proving the facts supporting the determinations sought by clear and convincing evidence. Where there is a dispute between the parties concerning the determinations, the court shall adjourn the hearing as necessary to permit the sex offender or the district attorney to obtain materials relevant to the determinations from any state or local facility, hospital, institution, office, agency, department or division. Such materials may be obtained by subpoena if not voluntarily provided to the requesting party. In making the determinations, the court shall review any victim's statement and any relevant materials and evidence submitted by the sex offender and the district attorney and the court may consider reliable hearsay evidence submitted by either party provided that it is relevant to the determinations. Facts previously proven at trial or elicited at the time of entry of a plea of guilty shall be deemed established by clear and convincing evidence and shall not be relitigated. The court shall render an order setting forth its determinations and the findings of fact and conclusions of law on which the determinations are based. A copy of the order shall be submitted by the court to the division. Upon application of either party, the court shall seal any portion of the court file or record which contains material that is confidential under any state or federal statute. Either party may appeal as of right from the order pursuant to the provisions of articles fifty-five, fifty-six and fifty-seven of the civil practice law and rules. Where counsel has been assigned to represent the sex offender upon the ground that the sex offender is financially unable to retain counsel, that assignment shall be continued throughout the pendency of the appeal, and the person may appeal as a poor person pursuant to article eighteen-B of the county law.

4. If a sex offender, having been given notice, including the time and place of the determination proceeding in accordance with this section, fails to appear at this proceeding, without sufficient excuse, the court shall conduct the hearing and make the determinations in the manner set forth in subdivision three of this section.

HISTORY: Add, L 1995, ch 192, § 2; amd, L 1999, ch 453, § 6, L 2002, ch 11, § 8, eff March 11, 2002. Sub 1, par (a), formerly entire sub 1, amd, L 1999, ch 453, § 6; so designated sub 1, par (a) and amd, L 2002, ch 11, § 8; amd, L 2003, ch 69, § 5, eff Aug 11, 2003. Sub 1, par (b), add, L 2002, ch 11, § 8, eff March 11, 2002. Sub 1, par (b), amd, L 2007, ch 74, § 10, eff Nov 1, 2007. Sub 1, par (c), add, L 2002, ch 11, § 8, eff March 11, 2002. Sub 2, amd, L 1999, ch 453, § 6, L 2002, ch 11, § 8, eff July 1, 2002. Sub 2, amd, L 2005, ch 684, § 1, eff Oct 4, 2005. Sub 3, amd, L 1999, ch 453, § 6, L 2002, ch 11, § 8, eff March 11, 2002. Sub 4, add, L 2005, ch 684, § 2, eff Oct 4, 2005.

§ 168-e. Discharge of sex offender from correctional facility; duties of official in charge

1. Any sex offender, to be discharged, paroled, released to post-release supervision or released from any state or local correctional facility, hospital or institution where he or she was confined or committed, shall at least fifteen calendar days prior to discharge, parole or release, be informed of his or her duty to register under this article, by the facility in which he or she was confined or committed. The facility shall require the sex offender to read and sign such form as may be required by the division stating the duty to register and the procedure for registration has been explained to him or her and to complete the registration portion of such form. The facility shall obtain on such form the address where the sex offender expects to reside upon his or her discharge, parole or release and the name and address of any institution of higher education he or she expects to be employed by, enrolled in, attending or employed, whether for compensation or not, and whether he or she expects to reside in a facility owned or operated by such an institution, and shall report such information to the division. The facility shall give one copy of the form to the sex offender, retain one copy and shall send one copy to the division which shall provide the

information to the law enforcement agencies having jurisdiction. The facility shall give the sex offender a form prepared by the division, to register with the division at least fifteen calendar days prior to release and such form shall be completed, signed by the sex offender and sent to the division by the facility at least ten days prior to the sex offender's release or discharge.

2. The division shall also immediately transmit the conviction data and fingerprints to the Federal Bureau of Investigation if not already obtained.

HISTORY: Add, L 1995, ch 192, § 2, eff Jan 21, 1996. Sub 1, amd, L 1999, ch 453, § 7, L 2002, ch 11, § 9, eff July 1, 2002.

§ 168-f. Duty to register and to verify

1. Any sex offender shall, (a) at least ten calendar days prior to discharge, parole, release to post-release supervision or release from any state or local correctional facility, hospital or institution where he or she was confined or committed, or, (b) at the time sentence is imposed for any sex offender released on probation or discharged upon payment of a fine, conditional discharge or unconditional discharge, register with the division on a form prepared by the division.

2. For a sex offender required to register under this article on each anniversary of the sex offender's initial registration date during the period in which he is required to register under this section the following applies:

(a) The sex offender shall mail the verification form to the division within ten calendar days after receipt of the form.

(b) The verification form shall be signed by the sex offender, and state that he still resides at the address last reported to the division.

(b-1) If the sex offender has been given a level two or three designation, such offender shall sign the verification form, and state that he or she still is employed at the address last reported to the division.

(b-2) If the sex offender has been given a level three designation, he or she shall personally appear at the law enforcement agency having jurisdiction within twenty days of the first anniversary of the sex offender's initial registration and every year thereafter during the period of registration for the purpose of providing a current photograph of such offender. The law enforcement agency having jurisdiction shall photograph the sex offender and shall promptly forward a copy of such photograph to the division. For purposes of this paragraph, if such sex offender is confined in a state or local correctional facility, the local law enforcement agency having jurisdiction shall be the warden, superintendent, sheriff or other person in charge of the state or local correctional facility.

(b-3) If the sex offender has been given a level one or level two designation, he or she shall personally appear at the law enforcement agency having jurisdiction within twenty days of the third anniversary of the sex offender's initial registration and every three years thereafter during the period of registration for the purpose of providing a current photograph of such offender. The law enforcement agency having jurisdiction shall photograph the sex offender and shall promptly forward a copy of such photograph to the division. For purposes of this paragraph, if such sex offender is confined in a state or local correctional facility, the local law enforcement agency having jurisdiction shall be the warden, superintendent, sheriff or other person in charge of the state or local correctional facility.

(c) If the sex offender fails to mail the signed verification form to the division within ten calendar days after receipt of the form, he or she shall be in violation of this section unless he proves that he or she has not changed his or her residence address.

(c-1) If the sex offender, to whom a notice has been mailed at the last reported address pursuant to paragraph b of subdivision one of section one hundred sixty-eight-b of this article, fails to personally appear at the law enforcement agency having jurisdiction, as provided in paragraph (b-2) or (b-3) of this subdivision, within twenty days of the anniversary of the sex offender's initial registration, or an alternate later date scheduled by the law enforcement agency having jurisdiction, he or she shall be in violation of this section. The duty to personally appear for such updated photograph shall be temporarily suspended during any period in which the sex offender is confined in any hospital or institution, and such sex offender shall personally appear for such updated photograph no later than ninety days after release from such hospital or institution, or an alternate later date scheduled by the law enforcement agency having jurisdiction.

3. The provisions of subdivision two of this section shall be applied to a sex offender required to register under this article except that such sex offender designated as a sexual predator or having been given a level three designation must personally verify his or her address with the local law enforcement agency every ninety calendar days after the date of release or commencement of parole or post-release supervision, or probation, or release on payment of a fine, conditional discharge or unconditional discharge. At such time the law enforcement agency having jurisdiction may take a new photograph of such sex offender if it appears that the offender has had a change in appearance since the most recent photograph taken pursuant to paragraph (b-2) of subdivision two of this section. If such photograph is taken, the law enforcement agency shall promptly forward a copy of such photograph to the division. The duty to personally verify shall be temporarily suspended during any period in which the sex offender is confined to any state or local correctional facility, hospital or institution and shall immediately recommence on the date of the sex offender's release.

4. Any sex offender shall register with the division no later than ten calendar days after any change of address, internet accounts with internet access providers belonging to such offender, internet identifiers that such offender uses, or his or her status of enrollment, attendance, employment or residence at any institution of higher education. A fee of ten dollars, as authorized by subdivision eight of section one hundred sixty-eight-b of this article, shall be submitted by the sex offender each time such offender registers any change of address or any change of his or her status of enrollment, attendance, employment or residence at any institution of higher education. Any failure or omission to submit the required fee shall not affect the acceptance by the division of the change of address or change of status.

5. The duty to register under the provisions of this article shall not be applicable to any sex offender whose conviction was reversed upon appeal or who was pardoned by the governor.

6. Any nonresident worker or nonresident student, as defined in subdivisions fourteen and fifteen of section one hundred sixty-eight-a of this article, shall register his or her current address and the address of his or her place of employment or educational institution attended with the division within ten calendar days after such nonresident worker or nonresident student commences employment or attendance at an educational institution in the state. Any nonresident worker or nonresident student shall notify the division of any change of residence, employment or educational institution address no later than ten days after such change. The division shall notify the law enforcement agency where the nonresident worker is employed or the educational institution is located that a nonresident worker or nonresident student is present in that agency's jurisdiction.

HISTORY: Add, L 1995, ch 192, § 2, eff Jan 21, 1996; amd, L 1999, ch 453, §§ 8–10, eff Jan 1, 2000, L 2001, ch 11, § 11, L 2002, ch 11, § 12, eff July 1, 2002, L 2002, ch 694, § 2; amd, L 2003, ch 10, § 3, eff May 30, 2003, L 2003, ch 62, § 5 (Part F), eff May 15, 2003, L 2005, ch 56, § 2 (Part O), eff April 12, 2006, L 2008, ch 67, § 6, eff April 28, 2008, L 2011, ch 532, § 2, eff Sept 23, 2011, L 2012, ch 364, § 1, eff Aug 31, 2012.

§ 168-g. Prior convictions; duty to inform and register

1. The department or office of probation and correctional alternatives in accordance with risk factors pursuant to section one hundred sixty-eight-l of this article shall determine the duration of registration and notification for every sex offender who on the effective date of this article is then on community supervision or probation for an offense provided for in subdivision two or three of section one hundred sixty-eight-a of this article.

2. Every sex offender who on the effective date of this article is then on community supervision or probation for an offense provided for in subdivision two or three of section one hundred sixty-eight-a of this article shall within ten calendar days of such determination register with his parole or probation officer. On each anniversary of the sex offender's initial registration date thereafter, the provisions of section one hundred sixty-eight-f of this article shall apply. Any sex offender who fails or refuses to so comply shall be subject to the same penalties as otherwise provided for in this article which would be imposed upon a sex offender who fails or refuses to so comply with the provisions of this article on or after such effective date.

3. It shall be the duty of the parole or probation officer to inform and register such sex offender according to the requirements imposed by this article. A parole or probation officer shall give one copy of the form to the sex offender and shall, within three calendar days, send two copies electronically or otherwise to the department which shall forward one copy electronically or otherwise to the law enforcement agency having jurisdiction where the sex offender resides upon his or her community supervision, probation, or local conditional release.

4. A petition for relief from this section is permitted to any sex offender required to register while released to community supervision or probation pursuant to section one hundred sixty-eight-o of this article.

> **HISTORY:** Add, L 1995, ch 192, § 2, eff Jan 21, 1996; amd, L 2011, ch 62, § 18 (Part C, Subpart B), eff March 31, 2011.

§ 168-h. Duration of registration and verification

1. The duration of registration and verification for a sex offender who has not been designated a sexual predator, or a sexually violent offender, or a predicate sex offender, and who is classified as a level one risk, or who has not yet received a risk level classification, shall be annually for a period of twenty years from the initial date of registration.

2. The duration of registration and verification for a sex offender who, on or after March eleventh, two thousand two, is designated a sexual predator, or a sexually violent offender, or a predicate sex offender, or who isclassified as a level two or level three risk, shall be annually for life. Notwithstanding the foregoing, a sex offender who is classified as a level two risk and who is not designated a sexual predator, a sexually violent offender or a predicate sex offender, may be relieved of the duty to register and verify as provided by subdivision one of section one hundred sixty-eight-o of this article.

3. Any sex offender having been designated a level three risk or a sexual predator shall also personally verify his or her address every ninety calendar days with the local law enforcement agency having jurisdiction where the offender resides.

HISTORY: Add, L 1995, ch 192, § 2; amd, L 1999, ch 453, § 11, eff Jan 1, 2000. Section heading, amd, L 1999, ch 453, § 11, eff Jan 1, 2000. Sub 1, formerly entire section, so designated sub 1 and amd, L 2002, ch 11, § 13, eff March 11, 2002. Sub 1, amd, L 2006, ch 1, § 3, eff Jan 18, 2006. Sub 2, add, L 2002, ch 11, § 13, eff March 11, 2002. Sub 2, amd, L 2006, ch 1, § 3, eff Jan 18, 2006. Sub 3, add, L 2002, ch 11, § 13, eff March 11, 2002.

§ 168-i. Registration and verification requirements

Registration and verification as required by this article shall consist of a statement in writing signed by the sex offender giving the information that is required by the division and the division shall enter the information into an appropriate electronic data base or file.

HISTORY: Add, L 1995, ch 192, § 2; amd, L 1999, ch 453, § 11, eff Jan 1, 2000. Section heading, amd, L 1999, ch 453, § 11, eff Jan 1, 2000.

§ 168-j. Notification of local law enforcement agencies of change of address

1. Upon receipt of a change of address by a sex offender required to register under this article, the division shall notify the local law enforcement agency having jurisdiction of the new place of residence and the local law enforcement agency where the sex offender last resided of the new place of residence.

2. Upon receipt of change of address information, the local law enforcement agency having jurisdiction of the new place of residence shall adhere to the notification provisions set forth in subdivision six of section one hundred sixty-eight-l of this article.

3. The division shall, if the sex offender changes residence to another state, notify the appropriate agency within that state of the new place of residence.

4. Upon receipt of a change in the status of the enrollment, attendance, employment or residence at an institution of higher education by a sex offender required to register under this article, the division shall notify each law enforcement agency having jurisdiction which is affected by such change.

5. Upon receipt of change in the status of the enrollment, attendance, employment or residence at an institution of higher education by a sex offender required to register under this article, each law enforcement agency having jurisdiction shall adhere to the notification provisions set forth in subdivision six of section one hundred sixty-eight-l of this article.

HISTORY: Add, L 1995, ch 192, § 2; amd, L 1999, ch 453, § 11, L 2002, ch 11, § 14, eff March 11, 2002. Sub 1, formerly sub (a), amd, L 1999, ch 453, § 11; so designated sub 1, L 2002, ch 11, § 14, eff March 11, 2002. Sub 2, formerly sub (c), so designated sub (b), L 1999, ch 453, § 11; so designated sub 2, L 2002, ch 11, § 14, eff March 11, 2002. Sub 3, add, L 2002, ch 11, § 14, eff March 11, 2002. Sub 4, add, L 2002, ch 11, § 14, eff July 1, 2002. Sub 5, add, L 2002, ch 11, § 14, eff July 1, 2002. Sub (a), redesignated sub 1, L 2002, ch 11, § 14, eff March 11, 2002. Sub (b), formerly sub (c), redesignated sub (b), L 1999, ch 453, § 11; redesignated sub 2, L 2002, ch 11, § 14, eff March 11, 2002. Former sub (b), deleted, L 1999, ch 453, § 11, eff Jan 1, 2000. Sub (c), redesignated sub (b), L 1999, ch 453, § 11, eff Jan 1, 2000.

§ 168-k. Registration for change of address from another state

1. A sex offender who has been convicted of an offense which requires registration under paragraph (d) of subdivision two or paragraph (b) of subdivision three of section one hundred sixty-eight-a of this article shall notify the division of the new address no later than ten calendar days after such sex offender establishes residence in this state.

2. The division shall advise the board that the sex offender has established residence in this state. The board shall determine whether the sex offender is required to register with the division. If it is determined that the sex offender is required to register, the division shall notify the sex offender

of his or her duty to register under this article and shall require the sex offender to sign a form as may be required by the division acknowledging that the duty to register and the procedure for registration has been explained to the sex offender. The division shall obtain on such form the address where the sex offender expects to reside within the state and the sex offender shall retain one copy of the form and send two copies to the division which shall provide the information to the law enforcement agency having jurisdiction where the sex offender expects to reside within this state. No later than thirty days prior to the board making a recommendation, the sex offender shall be notified that his or her case is under review and that he or she is permitted to submit to the board any information relevant to the review. After reviewing any information obtained, and applying the guidelines established in subdivision five of section one hundred sixty-eight-l of this article, the board shall within sixty calendar days make a recommendation regarding the level of notification pursuant to subdivision six of section one hundred sixty-eight-l of this article and whether such sex offender shall be designated a sexual predator, sexually violent offender, or predicate sex offender as defined in subdivision seven of section one hundred sixty-eight-a of this article. This recommendation shall be confidential and shall not be available for public inspection. It shall be submitted by the board to the county court or supreme court and to the district attorney in the county of residence of the sex offender and to the sex offender. It shall be the duty of the county court or supreme court in the county of residence of the sex offender, applying the guidelines established in subdivision five of section one hundred sixty-eight-l of this article, to determine the level of notification pursuant to subdivision six of section one hundred sixty-eight-l of this article and whether such sex offender shall be designated a sexual predator, sexually violent offender, or predicate sex offender as defined in subdivision seven of section one hundred sixty-eight-a of this article. At least thirty days prior to the determination proceeding, such court shall notify the district attorney and the sex offender, in writing, of the date of the determination proceeding and the court shall also provide the district attorney and sex offender with a copy of the recommendation received from the board and any statement of the reasons for the recommendation received from the board. This notice shall include the following statement or a substantially similar statement: "This proceeding is being held to determine whether you will be classified as a level 3 offender (risk of repeat offense is high), a level 2 offender (risk of repeat offense is moderate), or a level 1 offender (risk of repeat offense is low), or whether you will be designated as a sexual predator, a sexually violent offender or a predicate sex offender, which will determine how long you must register as a sex offender and how much information can be provided to the public concerning your registration. If you fail to appear at this proceeding, without sufficient excuse, it shall be held in your absence. Failure to appear may result in a longer period of registration or a higher level of community notification because you are not present to offer evidence or contest evidence offered by the district attorney." The court shall also advise the sex offender that he or she has a right to a hearing prior to the court's determination, that he or she has the right to be represented by counsel at the hearing and that counsel will be appointed if he or she is financially unable to retain counsel. A returnable form shall be enclosed in the court's notice to the sex offender on which the sex offender may apply for assignment of counsel. If the sex offender applies for assignment of counsel and the court finds that the offender is financially unable to retain counsel, the court shall assign counsel to represent the sex offender pursuant to article eighteen-B of the county law. If the district attorney seeks a determination that differs from the recommendation submitted by the board, at least ten days prior to the determination proceeding the district attorney shall provide to the court and the sex offender a statement setting forth the determinations sought by the district attorney together with the reasons for seeking such determinations. The court shall allow the sex offender to appear and be heard. The state shall appear by the district attorney, or his or her designee, who shall bear the burden of proving the facts supporting the determinations sought by clear and convincing evidence. It shall be the duty of the court applying the guidelines

Corr. L.

established in subdivision five of section one hundred sixty-eight-l of this article to determine the level of notification pursuant to subdivision six of section one hundred sixty-eight-l of this article and whether such sex offender shall be designated a sexual predator, sexually violent offender, or predicate sex offender as defined in subdivision seven of section one hundred sixty-eight-a of this article. Where there is a dispute between the parties concerning the determinations, the court shall adjourn the hearing as necessary to permit the sex offender or the district attorney to obtain materials relevant to the determinations from the state board of examiners of sex offenders or any state or local facility, hospital, institution, office, agency, department or division. Such materials may be obtained by subpoena if not voluntarily provided to the requesting party. In making the determinations the court shall review any victim's statement and any relevant materials and evidence submitted by the sex offender and the district attorney and the recommendation and any material submitted by the board, and may consider reliable hearsay evidence submitted by either party, provided that it is relevant to the determinations. If available, facts proven at trial or elicited at the time of a plea of guilty shall be deemed established by clear and convincing evidence and shall not be relitigated. The court shall render an order setting forth its determinations and the findings of fact and conclusions of law on which the determinations are based. A copy of the order shall be submitted by the court to the division. Upon application of either party, the court shall seal any portion of the court file or record which contains material that is confidential under any state or federal statute. Either party may appeal as of right from the order pursuant to the provisions of articles fifty-five, fifty-six and fifty-seven of the civil practice law and rules. Where counsel has been assigned to represent the sex offender upon the ground that the sex offender is financially unable to retain counsel, that assignment shall be continued throughout the pendency of the appeal, and the person may appeal as a poor person pursuant to article eighteen-B of the county law.

3. The division shall undertake an information campaign designed to provide information to officials and appropriate individuals in other states and United States possessions concerning the notification procedures required by this article. Such information campaign shall be ongoing, and shall include, but not be limited to, letters, notice forms and similar materials providing relevant information about this article and the specific procedures required to effect notification. Such materials shall include an address and telephone number which such officials and individuals in other states and United States possessions may use to obtain additional information.

4. If a sex offender, having been given notice, including the time and place of the determination proceeding in accordance with this section, fails to appear at this proceeding, without sufficient excuse, the court shall conduct the hearing and make the determinations in the manner set forth in subdivision two of this section.

   HISTORY: Add, L 1995, ch 192, § 2; amd, L 1999, ch 453, § 11, eff Jan 1, 2000. Sub 1, formerly entire section, so designated sub 1 and amd, L 1999, ch 453, § 11; amd, L 2004, ch 146, § 2, eff July 13, 2004. Sub 2, add, L 1999, ch 453, § 11; amd, L 2002, ch 11, § 15, eff March 11, 2002. Sub 2, amd, L 2005, ch 684, § 3, eff Oct 4, 2005. Sub 3, add, L 2004, ch 410, § 2, eff Nov 15, 2004. Sub 4, add, L 2005, ch 684, § 4, eff Oct 4, 2005.

§ 168-l. Board of examiners of sex offenders

1. There shall be a board of examiners of sex offenders which shall possess the powers and duties hereinafter specified. Such board shall consist of five members appointed by the governor. All members shall be employees of the department and shall be experts in the field of the behavior and treatment of sex offenders. The term of office of each member of such board shall be for six years; provided, however, that any member chosen to fill a vacancy occurring otherwise than by expiration of term shall be appointed for the remainder of the unexpired term of the member whom he or she is to succeed. In the event of the inability to act of any member, the governor may appoint

some competent informed person to act in his or her stead during the continuance of such disability.

2. The governor shall designate one of the members of the board as chairman to serve in such capacity at the pleasure of the governor or until the member's term of office expires and a successor is designated in accordance with law, whichever first occurs.

3. Any member of the board may be removed by the governor for cause after an opportunity to be heard.

4. Except as otherwise provided by law, a majority of the board shall constitute a quorum for the transaction of all business of the board.

5. The board shall develop guidelines and procedures to assess the risk of a repeat offense by such sex offender and the threat posed to the public safety. Such guidelines shall be based upon, but not limited to, the following:

    (a) criminal history factors indicative of high risk of repeat offense, including:

        (i) whether the sex offender has a mental abnormality or personality disorder that makes him or her likely to engage in predatory sexually violent offenses;

        (ii) whether the sex offender's conduct was found to be characterized by repetitive and compulsive behavior, associated with drugs or alcohol;

        (iii) whether the sex offender served the maximum term;

        (iv) whether the sex offender committed the felony sex offense against a child;

        (v) the age of the sex offender at the time of the commission of the first sex offense;

    (b) other criminal history factors to be considered in determining risk, including:

        (i) the relationship between such sex offender and the victim;

        (ii) whether the offense involved the use of a weapon, violence or infliction of serious bodily injury;

        (iii) the number, date and nature of prior offenses;

    (c) conditions of release that minimize risk or [of]* re-offense, including but not limited to whether the sex offender is under supervision; receiving counseling, therapy or treatment; or residing in a home situation that provides guidance and supervision;

    (d) physical conditions that minimize risk of re-offense, including but not limited to advanced age or debilitating illness;

    (e) whether psychological or psychiatric profiles indicate a risk of recidivism;

    (f) the sex offender's response to treatment;

    (g) recent behavior, including behavior while confined;

    (h) recent threats or gestures against persons or expressions of intent to commit additional offenses; and

---

* The bracketed word has been inserted by the Publisher.

Corr. L.

(i) review of any victim impact statement.

6. Applying these guidelines, the board shall within sixty calendar days prior to the discharge, parole, release to post-release supervision or release of a sex offender make a recommendation which shall be confidential and shall not be available for public inspection, to the sentencing court as to whether such sex offender warrants the designation of sexual predator, sexually violent offender, or predicate sex offender as defined in subdivision seven of section one hundred sixty-eight-a of this article. In addition, the guidelines shall be applied by the board to make a recommendation to the sentencing court which shall be confidential and shall not be available for public inspection, providing for one of the following three levels of notification depending upon the degree of the risk of re-offense by the sex offender.

(a) If the risk of repeat offense is low, a level one designation shall be given to such sex offender. In such case the law enforcement agency or agencies having jurisdiction and the law enforcement agency or agencies having had jurisdiction at the time of his or her conviction shall be notified and may disseminate relevant information which may include a photograph and description of the offender and which may include the name of the sex offender, approximate address based on sex offender's zip code, background information including the offender's crime of conviction, modus of operation, type of victim targeted, the name and address of any institution of higher education at which the sex offender is enrolled, attends, is employed or resides and the description of special conditions imposed on the offender to any entity with vulnerable populations related to the nature of the offense committed by such sex offender. Any entity receiving information on a sex offender may disclose or further disseminate such information at its discretion.

(b) If the risk of repeat offense is moderate, a level two designation shall be given to such sex offender. In such case the law enforcement agency or agencies having jurisdiction and the law enforcement agency or agencies having had jurisdiction at the time of his or her conviction shall be notified and may disseminate relevant information which shall include a photograph and description of the offender and which may include the exact name and any aliases used by the sex offender, exact address, background information including the offender's crime of conviction, mode of operation, type of victim targeted, the name and address of any institution of higher education at which the sex offender is enrolled, attends, is employed or resides and the description of special conditions imposed on the offender to any entity with vulnerable populations related to the nature of the offense committed by such sex offender. Any entity receiving information on a sex offender may disclose or further disseminate such information at its discretion. In addition, in such case, the information described herein shall also be provided in the subdirectory established in this article and notwithstanding any other provision of law, such information shall, upon request, be made available to the public.

Such law enforcement agencies shall compile, maintain and update a listing of vulnerable organizational entities within its jurisdiction. Such listing shall be utilized for notification of such organizations in disseminating such information on level two sex offenders pursuant to this paragraph. Such listing shall include and not be limited to: superintendents of schools or chief school administrators, superintendents of parks, public and private libraries, public and private school bus transportation companies, day care centers, nursery schools, preschools, neighborhood watch groups, community centers, civic associations, nursing homes, victim's advocacy groups and places of worship.

(c) If the risk of repeat offense is high and there exists a threat to the public safety a level three designation shall be given to such sex offender. In such case, the law enforcement agency or agencies having jurisdiction and the law enforcement agency or agencies having had jurisdiction at the time of his or her conviction shall be notified and may disseminate relevant information which shall include a photograph and description of the offender and which may include the sex offender's exact name and any aliases used by the offender, exact address, address of the offender's place of employment, background information including the offender's crime of conviction,mode of operation, type of victim targeted, the name and address of any institution of higher education at which the sex offender is enrolled, attends, is employed or resides and the description of special conditions imposed on the offender to any entity with vulnerable populations related to the nature of the offense committed by such sex offender. Any entity receiving information on a sex offender may disclose or further disseminate such information at its discretion. In addition, in such case, the information described herein shall also be provided in the subdirectory established in this article and notwithstanding any other provision of law, such information shall, upon request, be made available to the public.

Such law enforcement agencies shall compile, maintain and update a listing of vulnerable organizational entities within its jurisdiction. Such listing shall be utilized for notification of such organizations in disseminating such information on level three sex offenders pursuant to this paragraph. Such listing shall include and not be limited to: superintendents of schools or chief school administrators, superintendents of parks, public and private libraries, public and private school bus transportation companies, day care centers, nursery schools, preschools, neighborhood watch groups, community centers, civic associations, nursing homes, victim's advocacy groups and places of worship.

7. Upon request by the court, pursuant to section one hundred sixty-eight-o of this article, the board shall provide an updated report pertaining to the sex offender petitioning for relief of the duty to register or for a modification of his or her level of notification.

8. A failure by a state or local agency or the board to act or by a court to render a determination within the time period specified in this article shall not affect the obligation of the sex offender to register or verify under this article nor shall such failure prevent a court from making a determination regarding the sex offender's level of notification and whether such offender is required by law to be registered for a period of twenty years or for life. Where a court is unable to make a determination prior to the date scheduled for a sex offender's discharge, parole, release to post-release supervision or release, it shall adjourn the hearing until after the offender is discharged, paroled, released to post-release supervision or released, and shall then expeditiously complete the hearing and issue its determination.

HISTORY: Add, L 1995, ch 192, § 2, eff Jan 21, 1996; amd, L 1999, ch 453, §§ 12–14, L 2002, ch 11, § 17, L 2002, ch 11, §§ 16–19, eff March 11, 2002, L 2003, ch 10, § 4, L 2003, ch 316, § 1, eff Nov 1, 2003, L 2005, ch 318, § 1, eff Oct 24, 2005, L 2005, ch 680, § 1, eff Nov 1, 2005, L 2006, ch 1, § 4, eff Jan 18, 2006, L 2006, ch 106, § 1, eff June 23, 2006, L 2011, ch 62, § 19 (Part C, Subpart B), eff March 31, 2011, L 2011, ch 513, § 2, eff Sept 23, 2011.

§ 168-m. Review

Notwithstanding any other provision of law to the contrary, any state or local correctional facility, hospital or institution, district attorney, law enforcement agency, probation department, state board of parole, court or child protective agency shall forward relevant information pertaining to a sex offender to be discharged, paroled, released to post-release supervision or released to the board for review no later than one hundred twenty days prior to the release or discharge and the board shall make recommendations as provided in subdivision six of section one hundred sixty-eight-l of this article within sixty days of receipt of the information. Information may include, but may not be limited to all or a portion of the arrest file, prosecutor's file, probation or parole file, child protective file, court file, commitment file, medical file and treatment file pertaining to such person. Such person shall be permitted to submit to the board any information relevant to the review. Upon application of the sex offender or the district attorney, the court shall seal any portion of the board's file pertaining to the sex offender that contains material that is confidential under any state or federal law; provided, however, that in any subsequent proceedings in which the sex offender who is the subject of the sealed record is a party and which requires the board to provide a recommendation to the court pursuant to this article, such sealed record shall be available to the sex offender, the district attorney, the court and the attorney general where the attorney general is a party, or represents a party, in the proceeding.

    HISTORY: Add, L 1995, ch 192, § 2; amd, L 1999, ch 453, § 15, eff Jan 1, 2000, L 2011, ch 62, § 20 (Part C, Subpart B), eff March 31, 2011.

§ 168-n. Judicial determination

1. A determination that an offender is a sexual predator, sexually violent offender, or predicate sex offender as defined in subdivision seven of section one hundred sixty-eight-a of this article shall be made prior to the discharge, parole, release to post-release supervision or release of such offender by the sentencing court applying the guidelines established in subdivision five of section one hundred sixty-eight-l of this article after receiving a recommendation from the board pursuant to section one hundred sixty-eight-l of this article.

2. In addition, applying the guidelines established in subdivision five of section one hundred sixty-eight-l of this article, the sentencing court shall also make a determination with respect to the level of notification, after receiving a recommendation from the board pursuant to section one hundred sixty-eight-l of this article. Both determinations of the sentencing court shall be made thirty calendar days prior to discharge, parole or release.

3. No later than thirty days prior to the board's recommendation, the sex offender shall be notified that his or her case is under review and that he or she is permitted to submit to the board any information relevant to the review. Upon receipt of the board's recommendation, the sentencing court shall determine whether the sex offender was previously found to be eligible for assigned counsel in the underlying case. Where such a finding was previously made, the court shall assign counsel to represent the offender, pursuant to article eighteen-B of the county law. At least twenty days prior to the determination proceeding, the sentencing court shall notify the district attorney, the sex offender and the sex offender's counsel, in writing, of the date of the determination proceeding and shall also provide the district attorney, the sex offender and the sex offender's counsel with a copy of the recommendation received from the board and any statement of the reasons for the recommendation received from the board. This notice shall include the following statement or a substantially similar statement: "This proceeding is being held to determine whether you will be classified as a level 3 offender (risk of repeat offense is high), a level 2 offender (risk of repeat offense is moderate), or a level 1 offender (risk of repeat offense is low), or whether you will be designated as a sexual predator, a sexually violent offender or a predicate sex offender, which will determine how long you must register as a sex offender and how much information can be provided to the public concerning your registration. If you fail to appear at this proceeding, without sufficient excuse, it shall be held in your absence. Failure to appear may result in a longer period of registration or a higher level of community notification because you are not present to offer evidence or contest evidence offered by the district attorney." The written notice to the sex offender shall also advise the offender that he or she has a right to a hearing prior to the court's determination, and that he or she has the right to be represented by counsel at the hearing. If counsel has been assigned to represent the offender at the determination proceeding, the notice shall also provide the name, address and telephone number of the assigned counsel. Where counsel has not been assigned, the notice shall advise the sex offender that counsel will be appointed if he or she is financially unable to retain counsel, and a returnable form shall be

enclosed in the court's notice to the sex offender on which the sex offender may apply for assignment of counsel. If the sex offender applies for assignment of counsel and the court finds that the offender is financially unable to retain counsel, the court shall assign counsel to represent the sex offender pursuant to article eighteen-B of the county law. If the district attorney seeks a determination that differs from the recommendation submitted by the board, at least ten days prior to the determination proceeding the district attorney shall provide to the court and the sex offender a statement setting forth the determinations sought by the district attorney together with the reasons for seeking such determinations. The court shall allow the sex offender to appear and be heard. The state shall appear by the district attorney, or his or her designee, who shall bear the burden of proving the facts supporting the determinations sought by clear and convincing evidence. Where there is a dispute between the parties concerning the determinations, the court shall adjourn the hearing as necessary to permit the sex offender or the district attorney to obtain materials relevant to the determinations from the state board of examiners of sex offenders or any state or local facility, hospital, institution, office, agency, department or division. Such materials may be obtained by subpoena if not voluntarily provided to the requesting party. In making the determinations the court shall review any victim's statement and any relevant materials and evidence submitted by the sex offender and the district attorney and the recommendation and any materials submitted by the board, and may consider reliable hearsay evidence submitted by either party, provided that it is relevant to the determinations. Facts previously proven at trial or elicited at the time of entry of a plea of guilty shall be deemed established by clear and convincing evidence and shall not be relitigated. The court shall render an order setting forth its determinations and the findings of fact and conclusions of law on which the determinations are based. A copy of the order shall be submitted by the court to the division. Upon application of either party, the court shall seal any portion of the court file or record which contains material that is confidential under any state or federal statute. Either party may appeal as of right from the order pursuant to the provisions of articles fifty-five, fifty-six and fifty-seven of the civil practice law and rules. Where counsel has been assigned to represent the sex offender upon the ground that the sex offender is financially unable to retain counsel, that assignment shall be continued throughout the pendency of the appeal, and the person may appeal as a poor person pursuant to article eighteen-B of the county law.

4. Upon determination that the risk of repeat offense and threat to public safety is high, the sentencing court shall also notify the division of such fact for the purposes of section one hundred sixty-eight-q of this article.

5. Upon the reversal of a conviction of a sexual offense defined in paragraphs (a) and (b) of subdivision two or three of section one hundred sixty-eight-a of this article, the appellate court shall remand the case to the lower court for entry of an order directing the expungement of any records required to be kept herein.

6. If a sex offender, having been given notice, including the time and place of the determination proceeding in accordance with this section, fails to appear at this proceeding, without sufficient excuse, the court shall conduct the hearing and make the determinations in the manner set forth in subdivision three of this section.

HISTORY: Add, L 1995, ch 192, § 2, eff Jan 21, 1996. Sub 1, amd, L 1999, ch 453, § 16, L 2002, ch 11, § 20, eff March 11, 2002. Sub 2, amd, L 1999, ch 453, § 16, eff Jan 1, 2000. Sub 3, add, L 1999, ch 453, § 16; amd, L 2002, ch 11, § 21, eff March 11, 2002. Former sub 3, deleted, L 1999, ch 453, § 16, eff Jan 1, 2000. Sub 3, amd, L 2005, ch 684, § 5, eff Oct 4, 2005. Sub 5, amd, L 1999, ch 453, § 17, eff Jan 1, 2000. Sub 6, add, L 2005, ch 684, § 6, eff Oct 4, 2005.

§ 168-o. Petition for relief or modification

1. Any sex offender who is classified as a level two risk, and who has not been designated a sexual predator, or a sexually violent offender, or a predicate sex offender, who is required to register or verify pursuant to this article and who has been registered for a minimum period of thirty years may be relieved of any further duty to register upon the granting of a petition for relief by the sentencing court or by the court which made the determination regarding duration of registration and level of notification. The sex offender shall bear the burden of proving by clear and convincing evidence that his or her risk of repeat offense and threat to public safety is such that registration or verification is no longer necessary. Such petition, if granted, shall not relieve the petitioner of the duty to register pursuant to this article upon conviction of any offense requiring registration in the future. Such a petition shall not be considered more than once every two years. In the event that the sex offender's petition for relief is granted, the district attorney may appeal as of right from the order pursuant to the provisions of articles fifty-five, fifty-six and fifty-seven of the civil practice law and rules. Where counsel has been assigned to represent the sex offender upon the ground that the sex offender is financially unable to retain counsel, that assignment shall be continued throughout the pendency of the appeal, and the person may appeal as a poor person pursuant to article eighteen-B of the county law.

2. Any sex offender required to register or verify pursuant to this article may petition the sentencing court or the court which made the determination regarding the level of notification for an order modifying the level of notification. The petition shall set forth the level of notification sought, together with the reasons for seeking such determination. The sex offender shall bear the burden of proving the facts supporting the requested modification by clear and convincing evidence. Such a petition shall not be considered more than annually. In the event that the sex offender's petition to modify the level of notification is granted, the district attorney may appeal as of right from the order pursuant to the provisions of articles fifty-five, fifty-six and fifty-seven of the civil practice law and rules. Where counsel has been assigned to represent the sex offender upon the ground that the sex offender is financially unable to retain counsel, that assignment shall be continued throughout the pendency of the appeal, and the person may appeal as a poor person pursuant to article eighteen-B of the county law.

3. The district attorney may file a petition to modify the level of notification for a sex offender with the sentencing court or with the court which made the determination regarding the level of notification, where the sex offender (a) has been convicted of a new crime, or there has been a determination after a proceeding pursuant to section 410.70 of the criminal procedure law or section two hundred fifty-nine-i of the executive law that the sex offender has violated one or more conditions imposed as part of a sentence of a conditional discharge, probation, parole or post-release supervision for a designated crime, and (b) the conduct underlying the new crime or the violation is of a nature that indicates an increased risk of a repeat sex offense. The petition shall set forth the level of notification sought, together with the reasons for seeking such determination. The district attorney shall bear the burden of proving the facts supporting the requested modification, by clear and convincing evidence. In the event that the district attorney's petition is granted, the sex offender may appeal as of right from the order, pursuant to the provisions of articles fifty-five, fifty-six and fifty-seven of the civil practice law and rules. Where counsel has been assigned to represent the offender upon the ground that he or she is financially unable to retain counsel, that assignment shall be continued throughout the pendency of the appeal, and the person may proceed as a poor person, pursuant to article eighteen-B of the county law.

4. Upon receipt of a petition submitted pursuant to subdivision one, two or three of this section, the court shall forward a copy of the petition to the board and request an updated recommendation pertaining to the sex offender and shall provide a copy of the petition to the other party. The court shall also advise the sex offender that he or she has the right to be represented by counsel at the

hearing and counsel will be appointed if he or she is financially unable to retain counsel. A returnable form shall be enclosed in the court's notice to the sex offender on which the sex offender may apply for assignment of counsel. If the sex offender applies for assignment of counsel and the court finds that the offender is financially unable to retain counsel, the court shall assign counsel to represent the offender, pursuant to article eighteen-B of the county law. Where the petition was filed by a district attorney, at least thirty days prior to making an updated recommendation the board shall notify the sex offender and his or her counsel that the offender's case is under review and he or she is permitted to submit to the board any information relevant to the review. The board's updated recommendation on the sex offender shall be confidential and shall not be available for public inspection. After receiving an updated recommendation from the board concerning a sex offender, the court shall, at least thirty days prior to ruling upon the petition, provide a copy of the updated recommendation to the sex offender, the sex offender's counsel and the district attorney and notify them, in writing, of the date set by the court for a hearing on the petition. After reviewing the recommendation received from the board and any relevant materials and evidence submitted by the sex offender and the district attorney, the court may grant or deny the petition. The court may also consult with the victim prior to making a determination on the petition. The court shall render an order setting forth its determination, and the findings of fact and conclusions of law on which the determination is based. If the petition is granted, it shall be the obligation of the court to submit a copy of its order to the division. Upon application of either party, the court shall seal any portion of the court file or record which contains material that is confidential under any state or federal statute.

> **HISTORY:** Add, L 1995, ch 192, § 2; amd, L 1999, ch 453, § 18, eff Jan 1, 2000. Section heading, amd, L 1999, ch 453, § 18, eff Jan 1, 2000. Sub 1, formerly entire section, so designated sub 1 and amd, L 1999, ch 453, § 18; amd, L 2002, ch 11, § 22, eff March 11, 2002. Sub 1, amd, L 2006, ch 1 § 5, eff Jan 18, 2006. Sub 2, add, L 1999, ch 453, § 18; amd, L 2002, ch 11, § 22, eff March 11, 2002. Sub 3, add, L 1999, ch 453, § 18; amd, L 2002, ch 11, § 22, eff March 11, 2002. Sub 4, add, L 1999, ch 453, § 18, eff Jan 1, 2000.

§ 168-p. Special telephone number

1. Pursuant to section one hundred sixty-eight-b of this article, the division shall also operate a telephone number that members of the public may call free of charge and inquire whether a named individual required to register pursuant to this article is listed. The division shall ascertain whether a named person reasonably appears to be a person so listed and provide the caller with the relevant information according to risk as described in subdivision six of section one hundred sixty-eight-l of this article. The division shall decide whether the named person reasonably appears to be a person listed, based upon information from the caller providing information that shall include (a) an exact street address, including apartment number, driver's license number or birth date, along with additional information that may include social security number, hair color, eye color, height, weight, distinctive markings, ethnicity; or (b) any combination of the above listed characteristics if an exact birth date or address is not available. If three of the characteristics provided include ethnicity, hair color, and eye color, other identifying characteristics shall be provided. Any information identifying the victim by name, birth date, address or relation to the person listed by the division shall be excluded by the division.

2. When the telephone number is called, a preamble shall be played which shall provide the following information:

(a) notice that the caller's telephone number will be recorded;

(b) that there is no charge for use of the telephone number;

(c) notice that the caller is required to identify himself or herself to the operator and provide current address and shall be maintained in a written record;

(d) notice that the caller is required to be eighteen years of age or older;

(e) a warning that it is illegal to use information obtained through the telephone number to commit a crime against any person listed or to engage in illegal discrimination or harassment against such person;

(f) notice that the caller is required to have the birth date, driver's license or identification number, or address or other identifying information regarding the person about whom information is sought in order to achieve a positive identification of that person;

(g) a statement that the number is not a crime hotline and that any suspected criminal activity should be reported to local authorities;

(h) a statement that an information package which will include a description of the law and sex abuse and abduction prevention materials is available upon request from the division. Such information package shall include questions and answers regarding the most commonly asked questions about the sex offender registration act, and current sex abuse and abduction prevention material.

2-a. (a) The division shall establish a program allowing non-profit and not-for-profit youth services organizations to pre-register with the division for use of the telephone number. Pre-registration shall include the identification of up to two officials of the organization who may call the telephone number and obtain information on behalf of the organization. A pre-registered certificate issued under this subdivision shall be valid for two years, unless earlier revoked by the division for good cause shown. No fee shall be charged to an applicant for the issuance of a pre-registered certificate pursuant to this subdivision.

(b) An organization granted a pre-registered certificate pursuant to this subdivision may, upon calling the telephone number, inquire whether multiple named individuals are listed on the sex offender registry. Notwithstanding any per call limitation the division may place on calls by private individuals, the division shall allow such pre-registered organizations to inquire about up to twenty prospective coaches, leaders or volunteers in each call to the telephone number.

(c) For purposes of this subdivision, "youth services organization" shall mean a formalized program operated by a corporation pursuant to subparagraph five of paragraph (a) of section one hundred two of the not-for-profit corporation law that functions primarily to: (a) provide children the opportunity to participate in adult-supervised sporting activities; or (b) match children or groups of children with adult volunteers for the purpose of providing children with positive role models to enhance their development.

3. Whenever there is reasonable cause to believe that any person or group of persons is engaged in a pattern or practice of misuse of the telephone number, the attorney general, any district attorney or any person aggrieved by the misuse of the number is authorized to bring a civil action in the appropriate court requesting preventive relief, including an application for a permanent or temporary injunction, restraining order or other order against the person or group of persons responsible for the pattern or practice of misuse. The foregoing remedies shall be independent of any other remedies or procedures that may be available to an aggrieved party under other provisions of law. Such person or group of persons shall be subject to a fine of not less than five hundred dollars and not more than one thousand dollars.

4. The division shall submit to the legislature an annual report on the operation of the telephone number. The annual report shall include, but not be limited to, all of the following:

(a) number of calls received;

(b) a detailed outline of the amount of money expended and the manner in which it was expended for purposes of this section;

(c) number of calls that resulted in an affirmative response and the number of calls that resulted in a negative response with regard to whether a named individual was listed;

(d) number of persons listed; and

(e) a summary of the success of the telephone number program based upon selected factors.

HISTORY: Add, L 1995, ch 192, § 2; amd, L 2004, ch 361, § 1, eff Sept 9, 2004. Section heading, amd, L 2004, ch 361, § 1, eff Sept 9, 2004. Sub 1, amd, L 2004, ch 361, § 1, eff Sept 9, 2004. Sub 2, amd, L 2000, ch 1, § 16, L 2000, ch 608, § 1, L 2004, ch 361, § 1, eff Sept 9, 2004. Sub 2, opening par, amd, L 2004, ch 361, § 1, eff Sept 9, 2004. Sub 2, par (b), amd, L 2000, ch 1, § 16, L 2000, ch 608, § 1 (repealed L 2001, ch 95, § 19), L 2004, ch 361, § 1, eff Sept 9, 2004. Sub 2, par (e), amd, L 2004, ch 361, § 1, eff Sept 9, 2004. Sub 2, par (g), amd, L 2000, ch 1, § 16, L 2000, ch 608, § 1, eff April 28, 2001. Sub 2, par (h), add, L 2000, ch 1, § 16, eff Feb 1, 2001. Another sub 2, par (h), add, L 2000, ch 608, § 1; repealed, L 2001, ch 95, § 19, eff July 13, 2001. Sub 2-a, add, L 2004, ch 361, § 1, eff Sept 9, 2004. Former sub 2-a, add, L 2000, ch 1, § 17, eff Feb 1, 2001, expired and deemed repealed Sept 1, 2001. Sub 3, amd, L 2004, ch 361, § 1, eff Sept 9, 2004. Sub 4, opening par, amd, L 2004, ch 361, § 1, eff Sept 9, 2004. Sub 4, par (b), formerly sub 4, par (c), so designated sub 4, par (b), L 2004, ch 361, § 1, eff Sept 9, 2004. Former sub 4, par (b), deleted, L 2004, ch 361, § 1, eff Sept 9, 2004. Sub 4, par (c), formerly sub 4, par (d), so designated sub 4, par (c), L 2004, ch 361, § 1, eff Sept 9, 2004. Former sub 4, par (c), redesignated sub 4, par (b), L 2004, ch 361, § 1, eff Sept 9, 2004. Sub 4, par (d), formerly sub 4, par (e), so designated sub 4, par (d), L 2004, ch 361, § 1, eff Sept 9, 2004. Former sub 4, par (d), redesignated sub 4, par (c), L 2004, ch 361, § 1, eff Sept 9, 2004. Sub 4, par (e), formerly sub 4, par (f), so designated sub 4, par (e) and amd, L 2004, ch 361, § 1, eff Sept 9, 2004. Former sub 4, par (e), redesignated sub 4, par (d), L 2004, ch 361, § 1, eff Sept 9, 2004. Sub 4, par (f), redesignated sub 4, par (e), L 2004, ch 361, § 1, eff Sept 9, 2004.

§ 168-q. Subdirectory; internet posting

1. The division shall maintain a subdirectory of level two and three sex offenders. The subdirectory shall include the exact address, address of the offender's place of employment and photograph of the sex offender along with the following information, if available: name, physical description, age and distinctive markings. Background information including the sex offender's crime of conviction, modus of operation, type of victim targeted, the name and address of any institution of higher education at which the sex offender is enrolled, attends, is employed or resides and a description of special conditions imposed on the sex offender shall also be included. The subdirectory shall have sex offender listings categorized by county and zip code. Such subdirectory shall be made available at all times on the internet via the division homepage. Any person may apply to the division to receive automated e-mail notifications whenever a new or updated subdirectory registration occurs in a geographic area specified by such person. The division shall furnish such service at no charge to such person, who shall request e-mail notification by county and/or zip code on forms developed and provided by the division. E-mail notification is limited to three geographic areas per e-mail account.

2. Any person who uses information disclosed pursuant to this section in violation of the law shall in addition to any other penalty or fine imposed, be subject to a fine of not less than five hundred dollars and not more than one thousand dollars. Unauthorized removal or duplication of the subdirectory from the offices of local, village or city police department shall be punishable by a fine not to exceed one thousand dollars. In addition, the attorney general, any district attorney, or any person aggrieved is authorized to bring a civil action in the appropriate court requesting preventive relief, including an application for a permanent or temporary injunction, restraining

order, or other order against the person or group of persons responsible for such action. The foregoing remedies shall be independent of any other remedies or procedures that may be available to an aggrieved party under other provisions of law.

HISTORY: Add, L 1995, ch 192, § 2, eff Jan 21, 1996. Section heading, amd, L 1999, ch 453, § 19, L 2002, ch 11, § 23, eff July 1, 2002. Section heading, amd, L 2006, ch 106, § 2, eff June 23, 2006. Sub 1, amd, L 1999, ch 113, § 1, L 1999, ch 453, § 19, L 2000, ch 490, § 1, L 2002, ch 11, § 23, L 2002, ch 694, § 4 (repealed L 2003, ch 10, § 5, eff May 30, 2003). Sub 1, amd, L 2006, ch 106, § 2, eff June 23, 2006, L 2009, ch 478, § 1, eff March 15, 2010, L 2011, ch 532, § 3, eff Sept 23, 2011.

§ 168-r. Immunity from liability

1. No official, employee or agency, whether public or private, shall be subject to any civil or criminal liability for damages for any discretionary decision to release relevant and necessary information pursuant to this section, unless it is shown that such official, employee or agency acted with gross negligence or in bad faith. The immunity provided under this section applies to the release of relevant information to other employees or officials or to the general public.

2. Nothing in this section shall be deemed to impose any civil or criminal liability upon or to give rise to a cause of action against any official, employee or agency, whether public or private, for failing to release information as authorized in this section unless it is shown that such official, employee or agency acted with gross negligence or in bad faith.

HISTORY: Add, L 1995, ch 192, § 2, eff Jan 21, 1996.

§ 168-s. Annual report

The division shall on or before February first in each year file a report with the governor, and the legislature detailing the program, compliance with provisions of this article and effectiveness of the provisions of this article, together with any recommendations to further enhance the intent of this article.

HISTORY: Add, L 1995, ch 192, § 2, eff Jan 21, 1996.

§ 168-t. Penalty

Any sex offender required to register or to verify pursuant to the provisions of this article who fails to register or verify in the manner and within the time periods provided for in this article shall be guilty of a class E felony upon conviction for the first offense, and upon conviction for a second or subsequent offense shall be guilty of a class D felony. Any sex offender who violates the provisions of section one hundred sixty-eight-v of this article shall be guilty of a class A misdemeanor upon conviction for the first offense, and upon conviction for a second or subsequent offense shall be guilty of a class D felony. Any such failure to register or verify may also be the basis for revocation of parole pursuant to section two hundred fifty-nine-i of the executive law or the basis for revocation of probation pursuant to article four hundred ten of the criminal procedure law.

HISTORY: Add, L 1995, ch 192, § 2; amd, L 1999, ch 453, § 20, eff Jan 1, 2000. Amd, L 2005, ch 604, § 2, eff Aug 30, 2005, L 2007, ch 373, § 1, eff Aug 17, 2007. Section heading, amd, L 1999, ch 453, § 20, eff Jan 1, 2000. Section heading, add, L 2005, ch 604, § 2, eff Aug 30, 2005. Former section heading deleted, L 2005, ch 604, § 2, eff Aug 30, 2005.

§ 168-u. Unauthorized release of information

The unauthorized release of any information required by this article shall be a class B misdemeanor.

HISTORY: Add, L 1995, ch 192, § 2, eff Jan 21, 1996.

§ 168-v. Prohibition of employment on motor vehicles engaged in retail sales of frozen desserts

No person required to maintain registration under this article (sex offender registration act) shall operate, be employed on or dispense goods for sale at retail on a motor vehicle engaged in retail sales of frozen desserts as defined in subdivision thirty-seven of section three hundred seventy-five of the vehicle and traffic law.

> **HISTORY:** Add, L 2005, ch 604, § 1, eff Aug 30, 2005. Former § 168-v, added as 168-v, L 1995, ch 192, § 2; redesignated § 168-w, L 2003, ch 200, § 1; redesignated § 168-v, L 2004, ch 106, § 1, eff Aug 7, 2004; redesignated § 168-w, L 2005, ch 604, § 1, eff Aug 30, 2005.

§ 168-w. Separability

If any section of this article, or part thereof shall be adjudged by a court of competent jurisdiction to be invalid, such judgment shall not affect, impair or invalidate the remainder or any other section or part thereof.

> **HISTORY:** Added as 168-v, L 1995, ch 192, § 2; redesignated § 168-w, L 2003, ch 200, § 1; redesignated § 168-v, L 2004, ch 106, § 1, eff Aug 7, 2004; so designated § 168-w, L 2005, ch 604, § 1, eff Aug 30, 2005.

*   *   *

ARTICLE 11   EXECUTIVE CLEMENCY

§ 261.	**Subpoena on application for executive clemency**
§ 262.	**Appointment of person to hear application**
§ 263.	**Oath of [to]* witnesses**
§ 264.	**Form and service of subpoena; witness fees**
§ 265.	**Penalty for failure of witness to appear**
§ 266.	**Disbursements**

> **HISTORY:** Formerly Article 10, add, L 1909, ch 47; renumbered Article 11 and amd, L 1929, ch 243, § 14, eff April 2, 1929. Former Article 11, add, L 1909, ch 47; renumbered Article 12 and amd, L 1929, ch 243, § 15, eff April 2, 1929.

§ 261. Subpoena on application for executive clemency

The governor shall have the power in any matter pertaining to an application for clemency, to issue a subpoena to compel the attendance of a person before him at a time and place designated in said subpoena; and he shall also have the power to compel the production of any book, paper or writing by a subpoena duces tecum, directed to a person in whose custody either may be, at a time and place designated in said subpoena. But the provisions of this article shall not apply to any book, paper or writing filed in any office of record in any civil division of this state.

> **HISTORY:** Add, L 1909, ch 47; amd, L 1929, ch 243, eff April 2, 1929.

§ 262. Appointment of person to hear application

The governor may appoint a person to conduct a hearing in a matter pertaining to an application for clemency, and his compensation shall not exceed ten dollars for each day's actual service. Such person, upon the conclusion of such hearing, shall forward to the governor without delay, the testimony taken before him. The governor may direct that a person subpoenaed by him, in conformity to the provisions of the preceding section, appear before a person designated by him to conduct a hearing as provided by this section; and a person so subpoenaed shall produce any book, paper or writing before said person so designated by the governor, in conformity with the

---

* The bracketed word has been inserted by the Publisher.

Corr. L.

provisions of the preceding section of this article.

HISTORY: Add, L 1909, ch 47; amd, L 1929, ch 243, eff April 2, 1929.

§ 263. Oath of [to]* witnesses

The governor or a person designated by him to conduct a hearing in a matter pertaining to an application for clemency, shall have power to administer an oath to a person brought before him.

HISTORY: Add, L 1909, ch 47; amd, L 1929, ch 243, eff April 2, 1929.

§ 264. Form and service of subpoena; witness fees

A subpoena, or subpoena duces tecum, issued in conformity with the provisions of this article, shall be signed by the governor's secretary, and be attested by the privy seal of the state. A subpoena issued under this section shall be regulated by the civil practice law and rules.

HISTORY: Add, L 1909, ch 47; amd, L 1929, ch 243, L 1962, ch 310, § 91, eff Sept 1, 1963.

§ 265. Penalty for failure of witness to appear

A person subpoenaed who fails to appear, refuses to answer, or produce a book, paper or writing as provided in this article, shall upon conviction be adjudged guilty of a criminal contempt. And in addition thereto a person so subpoenaed shall be subject to all the provisions of law which now or may hereafter exist, relating to witnesses in civil or criminal actions at law; and the governor shall possess all the powers in relation to said provisions which are possessed by any court or judge, but he shall be limited to the matters arising under the provisions of this article.

HISTORY: Add, L 1909, ch 47; amd, L 1929, ch 243, eff April 2, 1929.

§ 266. Disbursements

Any disbursements necessary to be made for any of the purposes mentioned in this article shall be paid from the treasury upon the approval of the governor's secretary, on the audit and warrant of the comptroller, out of any moneys in the treasury not otherwise appropriated.

HISTORY: Add, L 1909, ch 47; amd, L 1929, ch 243, eff April 2, 1929.

ARTICLE 12   LOCAL CONDITIONAL RELEASE COMMISSION

HISTORY: Add, L 2009, ch 56, § 1 (Part SS), eff April 7, 2009. Former Article 12, add, L 1989, ch 79, § 1, eff May 1, 1989, expired and repealed Sept 1, 2005. Prior Article 12, add, L 1931, ch 455, § 1; repealed, L 1970, ch 476, § 48, eff July 7, 1970. Earlier Article 12, formerly Article 11, add, L 1909, ch 47; renumbered Article 12 and amd, L 1929, ch 243, § 15; repealed, L 1931, ch 455, § 1, eff April 16, 1931. Earliest Article 12, add, L 1909, ch 47; renumbered Article 19 and amd, L 1929, ch 243, § 20, eff April 2, 1929. Former another Article 12, add, L 1931, ch 455, § 1; amd, L 1933, ch 151, L 1939, ch 661, § 2, L 1957, ch 802, §§ 1, 12; repealed, L 1970, ch 476, § 48, eff July 7, 1970. Prior another Article 12, formerly Art 11, renumbered and amd, L 1929, ch 243, § 15; repealed, L 1931, ch 455, § 1, eff Apr 16, 1931. Earlier another Article 12, add, L 1909, ch 47,

---

* The bracketed word has been inserted by the Publisher.

renumbered Art 19 and amd, L 1929, ch 243, § 20, eff April 2, 1929.

§ 270. Definitions

As used in this article, the following terms have the following meanings:

1. "Commission" means the local conditional release commission.

2. "County" means each county in the state, except a county within the city of New York.

3. "County executive" means the county commissioner, county manager, county director or county president.

4. "Division" means the division of criminal justice services.

HISTORY: Add, L 2009, ch 56, § 1 (Part SS), eff April 7, 2009; amd, L 2010, ch 56, § 48 (Part A), eff June 22, 2010.

§ 271. Local conditional release commission; organization

1. Every county, and the city of New York, may adopt a local law establishing a local conditional release commission. Such commission shall be appointed by the county executive, upon the advice and consent of the county legislature, or in the case of the city of New York, such commission shall be appointed by the mayor, upon the advice and consent of the city council. Each such commission shall consist of at least five members. Each member of the commission shall have graduated from an accredited four year college or university and shall have had at least five years of experience in the field of criminology, administration of criminal justice, law enforcement, probation, parole, law, social work, social science, psychology, psychiatry or corrections.

2. The term of office of each member of such commission shall be for four years; provided, however, that any member chosen to fill a vacancy occurring otherwise than by expiration of term shall be appointed for the remainder of the unexpired term of the member whom the person is to succeed. Vacancies caused by expiration of term or otherwise shall be filled in the same manner as original appointments.

3. No member of the commission shall serve as a representative of any political party on an executive committee or other governing body thereof, as an executive officer or employee of any political committee, organization or association, nor be a judge or justice, a sheriff or district attorney.

4. Any member may be removed by the county executive, or the mayor in the case of the city of New York, for cause, after notice and an opportunity to be heard.

5. The director of the local probation department, or such director's designee, shall serve as an ex-officio, non-voting member of the commission.

6. The local probation department shall assign staff support to the commission.

HISTORY: Add, L 2009, ch 56, § 1 (Part SS), eff April 7, 2009. Former § 271, add, L 1989, ch 79, § 1, eff May 1, 1989, expired and repealed Sept 1, 2005. Prior § 271, add, L 1931, ch 455, § 1, with substance transferred from § 281; amd, L 1933, ch 151, § 4, L 1954, ch 803, § 6; repealed, L 1970, ch 476, § 48, eff July 7, 1970.

§ 272. Local conditional release commission; function, powers and duties

The commission shall:

1. have the power and duty of determining which persons sentenced within the county, or the city of New York, and serving a definite sentence of imprisonment and eligible for conditional release pursuant to subdivision two of section 70.40 of the penal law may be released on

Corr. L.

conditional release and when and under what conditions in accordance with section two hundred seventy-three of this article;

2. have the power to determine, as each inmate applies for conditional release, the need for supplemental investigation of the background of such inmate and cause such investigation as may be necessary to be made as soon as practicable. The commission may require that the probation department located in the jurisdiction of the commission conduct such supplemental investigation. The results of such investigation together with all other information compiled by the local correctional facility and the complete criminal record and family court record of such inmate shall be readily available when the conditional release of such inmate is being considered. Such information shall include a complete statement of the crime for which the inmate has been sentenced, the circumstances of such crime, all presentence memoranda, the nature of the sentence, the court in which such inmate was sentenced, the name of the judge and district attorney and copies of such probation reports as may have been made as well as reports as to the inmate's social, physical, mental and psychiatric condition and history;

3. have the legal custody of persons conditionally released and placed under the supervision of the local probation department for a period of one year, or until returned to the custody of the local correctional facility located in the jurisdiction of the commission, as the case may be;

4. have the power to revoke the conditional release of any person in the legal custody of the commission and to issue declarations of delinquency and authorize the issuance of a warrant for the retaking of such person, as provided for in section two hundred seventy-four of this article;

5. for the purpose of any investigation necessary in the performance of its duties, have the power to issue subpoenas, to compel the attendance of witnesses and the production of books, papers, and other documents pertinent to the subject of its inquiry. The minutes of all commission meetings must be recorded and such records shall be retained according to applicable standards;

6. have the power to authorize any members thereof to administer oaths and take the testimony of persons under oath;

7. notify, in writing, the initial sentencing court, the district attorney and defense counsel within five business days of receipt of an application for a local conditional release filed under this article and provide a fifteen day period for comment on such application. Comments submitted under this subdivision shall be provided to the commission and all parties;

8. notify in writing the appropriate local probation department prior to release of a conditionally released person of such department's responsibilities to supervise such person;

Such notice shall include the name and residence of the person, the date of release, the conditions of release, and all necessary records maintained on such person to aid the local probation department in the performance of its responsibilities pursuant to subdivision six of section two hundred fifty-six of the executive law;

9. have the power to transfer the legal custody of persons conditionally released in accordance with the provisions of section two hundred seventy-five of this article;

10. present an annual report to the county legislature, or in the case of the city of New York, to the city council, of its findings and actions on submitted applications.

HISTORY: Add, L 2009, ch 56, § 1 (Part SS), eff April 7, 2009. Former § 272, add, L 1989, ch 79, § 1, eff May 1, 1989, expired and repealed Sept 1, 2005; amd, L 2000, ch 1, § 9, eff Feb 1, 2001; amd, L 2005, ch 544, § 3, eff Sept 1, 2006. Prior § 272, add, L 1931, ch 455, § 1, with substance transferred from § 284; repealed, L 1970, ch 476, § 48, eff July 7, 1970.

§ 273. Conditional release; procedures for application and determinations

1. Any inmate who is eligible for conditional release by a commission pursuant to subdivision two of section 70.40 of the penal law and who has served a minimum period of sixty days in a local correctional facility may apply for conditional release. Eligibility criteria shall be limited to inmates:

(a) who have not been previously convicted and who do not stand convicted of any crime which would make such inmate ineligible for the receipt of merit time pursuant to section eight hundred three of this chapter, any crime pursuant to article two hundred thirty-five of the penal law when the victim of such offense was under the age of eighteen at the time of the offense, or any crime which the commission determines constituted a crime of domestic violence;

(b) having jail records which make them eligible for a reduction of sentence under section eight hundred four of this chapter;

(c) having verified community ties in one of the following areas: employment, permanent residence and family.

Application shall be made in writing, on forms prescribed by the division, to the commission in the county where the sentence was imposed.

2. The commission shall review and make a determination on each application within thirty days of receipt of such application. No determination granting or denying such application shall be valid unless made by a majority vote of at least three commission members present. No release shall be granted unless there is a reasonable probability that, if such inmate is released, he or she shall live and remain at liberty without violating the law, and that his or her release is not incompatible with the welfare of society and shall not so deprecate the seriousness of his or her crime as to undermine respect for law.

3. If conditional release is granted, the commission shall set the conditions for release of the person in accordance with rules and regulations promulgated by the division. Such person shall be given a copy of the conditions of release. Such conditions shall, where appropriate, include a requirement that the person comply with any restitution order previously imposed by a court of competent jurisdiction that applies to the person.

4. No person who has been granted conditional release shall be released until such person has served a minimum period of incarceration of ninety days, in accordance with subdivision two of section 70.40 of the penal law, and unless such person has agreed in writing to the conditions set by the commission. Such agreement shall state in plain, easily understandable language the consequences of a violation of one or more of the conditions of release.

5. Persons who have been granted conditional release by the commission established pursuant to this article shall, while on conditional release, be in the legal custody of the commission for a period of one year, or until returned to the custody of the local correctional facility located in the jurisdiction of the commission, as the case may be. The probation department located in the jurisdiction of the commission has the duty of supervising the person during the period of such conditional release. The commission shall impose a minimum of four supervision contacts per month while the person is on conditional release, unless the commission determines that fewer contacts are appropriate in any individual case.

6. If conditional release is not granted, the commission shall inform the person in writing of the factors and reasons for such denial of conditional release within fifteen days of the decision. Such reasons shall be given in detail and not in conclusory terms. Inmates denied conditional release are

eligible to reapply sixty days after the date of the denial.

HISTORY: Add, L 2009, ch 56, § 1 (Part SS), eff April 7, 2009. Former § 273, add, L 1989, ch 79, § 1, eff May 1, 1989, expired and repealed Sept 1, 2005. Prior § 273, add, L 1931, ch 455, § 1, with substance transferred from § 286; amd, L 1934, ch 423, L 1954, ch 803, § 7, L 1957, ch 381, § 2, L 1957, ch 802, § 4; repealed, L 1970, ch 476, § 48, eff July 7, 1970.

§ 274. Conditional release; procedures for violation, delinquency, warrants and revocation

1. If at any time during the period of conditional release, the commission, or any member thereof, has reasonable cause to believe that a person who has been conditionally released has lapsed into criminal ways or company, or has violated one or more conditions of conditional release, the commission or such member may declare such person delinquent and issue a written declaration of delinquency. Upon such declaration, such commission or such member may issue a warrant for the retaking and temporary detention of such person.

2. A warrant issued pursuant to this section shall constitute sufficient authority to the chief administrative officer of any local correctional facility to whom it is delivered to hold in temporary detention the person named therein.

3. A warrant issued pursuant to this section may be executed by any probation officer or any officer authorized to serve criminal process or any peace officer, who is acting pursuant to his or her special duties, or any police officer. Any such officer to whom such warrant shall be delivered is authorized and required to execute such warrant by taking such person and having him or her detained as provided for in this section.

4. The alleged violator shall, within five days of the execution of the warrant, be given written notice of the time, place and purpose of the hearing. The notice shall state what conditions of conditional release are alleged to have been violated and in what manner and shall inform the alleged violator of his or her right to counsel as provided for in subdivision seven of this section.

5. The alleged conditional release violator shall appear before the commission within twenty days of the execution of the warrant. At the time of such appearance the commission shall ask the alleged violator whether he or she wishes to make any statement with respect to the violation. If the alleged violator makes a statement, the commission may accept it and base a decision thereon. If the commission does not accept it, or if the alleged violator does not make a statement, the commission shall proceed with the hearing.

6. The commission may receive any relevant evidence. The alleged violator may cross examine witnesses and may present evidence on his or her own behalf.

7. The alleged violator is entitled to counsel at all stages of any proceeding under this section and the commission shall advise him or her of such right upon delivering to the alleged violator written notice, required pursuant to subdivision four of this section.

8. At the conclusion of the hearing, the commission shall issue a finding. If the commission is not satisfied that there is a preponderance of evidence in support of the violation, the commission shall dismiss the violation, cancel delinquency and restore the person to supervision. If the commission is satisfied that there is a preponderance of evidence that the alleged violator violated one or more conditions of conditional release in an important respect, the commission shall so find.

9. Upon a finding in support of the violation, the commission may revoke the conditional release, or continue or modify the conditions of such conditional release. Where the commission revokes a person's conditional release, such person shall be committed to the custody of the chief administrative officer of the local correctional facility to serve the time remaining on his or her

sentence, in accordance with subdivision three of section 70.40 of the penal law. Where the commission modifies the conditions of the conditional release, the commission shall inform the person, in writing, of such modified conditions.

10. Any actions by the commission pursuant to this article shall be deemed a judicial function and shall not be reviewable if done in accordance with law.

> **HISTORY:** Add, L 2009, ch 56, § 1 (Part SS), eff April 7, 2009. Former § 274, add, L 1989, ch 79, § 1, eff May 1, 1989, expired and repealed Sept 1, 2005. Prior § 274, add, L 1931, ch 455, § 1, with substance transferred from § 287; amd, L 1954, ch 803, § 8, L 1957, ch 802, § 1; repealed, L 1970, ch 476, § 48, eff July 7, 1970.

§ 275. Transfer of custody and supervision of conditional releasee

1. If a person who has been granted conditional release pursuant to this article resides or desires to reside in a place other than the one located within the jurisdiction of the commission which has legal custody of such person, such commission, or any member thereof, may designate any other commission established pursuant to this article, or the department, to assume custody of such person and may so transfer custody upon the consent of such other commission or the department.

2. Where custody of a person who has been granted conditional release pursuant to this article is transferred pursuant to subdivision one of this section, upon designation and prior to transfer, the commission making the designation shall notify the commission which has been designated to receive custody of such transfer or the department. The commission making the designation shall immediately forward its entire case record regarding such person to the receiving commission or the department. The commission to which legal custody has been transferred, or the department, shall assume the same powers and duties exercised by the designating commission and shall have the sole custody of such person.

3. The commission making the designation shall, upon designation and prior to transfer, notify the local probation department located in the jurisdiction of the receiving commission of the duties of supervision and conditions of release of such person. Upon such notification, such probation department shall assume responsibilities of supervision. The commission making the designation shall immediately forward its entire case record regarding such person to such probation department.

> **HISTORY:** Add, L 2009, ch 56, § 1 (Part SS), eff April 7, 2009. Former § 275, add, L 1989, ch 79, § 1, eff May 1, 1989, expired and repealed Sept 1, 2005. Prior § 275, add, L 1931, ch 455, § 1, with substance transferred from § 294; amd, L 1942, ch 738, § 14, L 1954, ch 803, § 9; repealed, L 1970, ch 476, § 48, eff July 7, 1970, L 2011, ch 62, § 24 (Part C, Subpart B), eff March 31, 2011.

§ 276. Regulations and report

The division shall promulgate regulations in conformance with the provisions of this article which ensure that local conditional release commissions operate in accordance with the requirements provided in this article. The division shall report annually to the speaker of the assembly and to the temporary president of the senate concerning the operations of local conditional release commissions.

> **HISTORY:** Add, L 2009, ch 56, § 1 (Part SS), eff April 7, 2009. Former § 276, add, L 1931, ch 455, § 1, with substance transferred from § 291; amd, L 1954, ch 803, § 10, L 1957, ch 802, § 6; repealed, L 1970, ch 476, § 48, eff July 7, 1970.

* * *

ARTICLE 20   LOCAL CORRECTIONAL FACILITIES

HISTORY: Formerly Article 13, add, L 1909, ch 47; renumbered Article 20 and amd, L 1929, ch 243, § 21, eff April 2, 1929. Former Article 20, formerly Article 16, add, L 1909, ch 47; renumbered Article 17, L 1917, ch 712, § 1; renumbered Article 20, L 1927, ch 426, § 14; renumbered Article 25 and amd, L 1929, ch 243, § 24, eff April 2, 1929. Article heading, amd, L 1987, ch 604, § 3, eff Sept 2, 1987.

§ 500. Application of article

The provisions of this article shall apply to all local correctional facilities as defined by subdivision sixteen of section two of this chapter.

HISTORY: Add, L 1987, ch 604, § 4, eff Sept 2, 1987; amd, L 2014, ch 131, § 1, eff July 22, 2014.

§ 500-a. Use of jails

1. Each county jail shall be used:

(a) For the detention of persons duly committed to secure their attendance as witnesses in any criminal case;

(b) For the detention of persons charged with crime, and committed for trial or examination;

(c) For the detention of persons awaiting the availability of a court, pursuant to the provisions of section 210.10, subdivision two of section 530.70 or subdivision two of section 410.40 of the criminal procedure law;

(d) For the confinement of persons duly committed for any contempt, or upon civil process;

(e) For the confinement of persons convicted of any offense and sentenced to imprisonment therein, or awaiting transportation under sentence to imprisonment in another county;

(f) For the confinement of persons during any proceedings pursuant to article ten of the mental hygiene law.

(g) [Expires and repealed Sept 1, 2017] For the confinement of persons committed pursuant to an agreement authorized by section five hundred-o of this article.

2. The Onondaga county jail may also be used for the detention of persons under arrest being held for arraignment.

2-a. Notwithstanding any other provision of law, the city council of the city of Elmira may enter into an agreement with the county of Chemung by which the county, through its facilities at the Chemung county jail, shall undertake to provide services pertaining to the confinement of individuals arrested or detained by police officers or other law enforcement officers within the city of Elmira who have been detained and are awaiting arraignment or initial court appearances.

2-b. The Erie county holding center and the Erie county correctional facility may also be used for the detention of persons under arrest being held for arraignment.

2-c. The Yates county jail may also be used for the detention of persons under arrest being held for arraignment in any court located in the county of Yates.

2-d.* Notwithstanding any other law, rule or regulation to the contrary, the Cortland county jail may also be used for the detention of persons under arrest and being held for arraignment in any court located in the county of Cortland.

2-d.* The Putnam county jail may also be used for the detention of persons under arrest being held for arraignment in any court located in the county of Putnam.

2-e. Notwithstanding any other provision of law, the city of Rochester may enter into an agreement with the county of Monroe by which the county, through its facilities at the Monroe county jail, shall undertake to provide services pertaining to the confinement of individuals arrested or detained by police officers or other law enforcement officers within the city of Rochester who have been detained and are awaiting arraignment or initial court appearances.

2-f. The Warren county jail may also be used for the detention of persons under arrest being held for arraignment in any court located in the county of Warren.

2-g.** The Niagara county jail may also be used for the detention of persons under arrest being

---

* There are two subdivisions 2-d.

* There are two subdivisions 2-d.

** There are two subdivisions 2-g.

held for arraignment in any court located in the county of Niagara.

2-g.** The Genesee county jail may also be used for the detention of persons under arrest being held for arraignment in any court located in the county of Genesee.

2-h. The Allegany county correctional facility may also be used for the detention of persons under arrest being held for arraignment in any court located in the county of Allegany.

2-i. The Seneca county correctional facility may also be used for the detention of persons under arrest being held for arraignment in any court located in the county of Seneca.

2-j.** The Montgomery county correctional facility may also be used for the detention of persons under arrest being held for arraignment in any court located in the county of Montgomery.

2-j.** The Chautauqua county correctional facility may also be used for the detention of persons under arrest being held for arraignment in any court located in the county of Chautauqua.

2-k. The Ontario county correctional facility may also be used for the detention of persons under arrest being held for arraignment in any court located in the county of Ontario.

2-l. The Albany county correctional facility may also be used for the detention of persons under arrest being held for arraignment in any court located in the county of Albany.

2-m. The Jefferson county correctional facility may also be used for the detention of persons under arrest being held for arraignment in any court located in the county of Jefferson.

3. The buildings, now used as jails of the counties of the state, shall continue to be the jails of those counties respectively, until other buildings have been designated or erected for that purpose, according to law.

4. Notwithstanding any other provision of law, a county jail may be used for the electronic acquisition and transmission of fingerprint and other identification records pursuant to article one hundred sixty of the criminal procedure law.

> **HISTORY:** Add, L 1950, ch 695, with substance transferred from County Law § 90; amd, L 1968, ch 226, L 1990, ch 681, § 5, eff Nov 1, 1990, L 1993, ch 161, § 2, L 1994, ch 541, § 1, eff July 26, 1994, L 1997, ch 633, § 1, eff Sept 24, 1997, L 2002, ch 413, § 1, eff Aug 13, 2002, L 2003, ch 135, § 1, eff July 22, 2003, L 2003, ch 171, § 1, L 2003, ch 189, § 1, L 2004, ch 555, §§ 1–3, eff Oct 5, 2004, L 2004, ch 559, § 1, eff Oct 5, 2004, L 2005, ch 84, § 1, eff June 7, 2005, L 2005, ch 258, § 1, eff July 19, 2005, L 2005, ch 311, § 1, eff July 26, 2005, L 2007, ch 7, § 24-a, eff April 13, 2007, L 2007, ch 336, § 1, eff July 18, 2007, L 2007, 377, § 1, eff July 18, 2007, expires and repealed March 31, 2010, L 2009, ch 271, § 1, eff July 28, 2009, L 2010, ch 249, § 1, eff July 30, 2010, L 2010, ch 260, § 1, eff July 30, 2010, L 2011, ch 299, § 1, eff Aug 3, 2011, L 2011, ch 573, § 2, eff Sept 23, 2011, expires and repealed Sept 1, 2017, L 2012, ch 343, § 1, eff Aug 1, 2012; L 2014, ch 346, § 1, eff Sept 4, 2014.

§ 500-b. [Repealed Sept 1, 2015] Housing of prisoners and other persons in custody

1. As used in this section, the term "chief administrative officer" shall mean the person responsible pursuant to section five hundred-c of this article for receiving and safely keeping persons committed to a county jail.

2. In any case in which the chief administrative officer has more than one jail under his

---

** There are two subdivisions 2-g.

** There are two subdivisions 2-j.

** There are two subdivisions 2-j.

jurisdiction, he may confine a civil or criminal prisoner in any such jail and may remove the prisoner from one jail to another, within the county, whenever he deems it necessary for his safekeeping, or for the prisoner's appearance at court.

3. No female confined in a county jail shall be assigned to or housed in a facility housing unit with a male; and if detained on civil process, or for contempt, or as a witness, she shall not be put or kept in the same room with a man, except her husband.

4. No person under eighteen years of age shall be placed or kept or allowed to be at any time with any prisoner or prisoners eighteen years of age or older, in any room, dormitory, cell or tier of the buildings of such institution unless separately grouped to prevent access to persons under eighteen years of age by prisoners eighteen years of age or older.

5. [Repealed]

6. The commission shall promulgate rules and regulations in accordance with subdivisions seven and eight of this section to assure that persons in custody in local correctional facilities will be afforded appropriate precautions for their personal safety and welfare in assignment to housing.

7. (a) Consistent with the commission's rules and regulations regarding the assignment of inmates to housing units, the chief administrative officer shall exercise good judgment and discretion and shall take all reasonable steps to ensure that the assignment of persons to facility housing units:

(1) fosters the safety, security and good order of the jail; and

(2) affords appropriate precautions for the personal safety and welfare of persons in custody with particular attention to those who are known to be vulnerable to assault or any physical or mental abuse.

(b) The chief administrative officer shall consider the following in complying with this subdivision:

(1) prior victimization in jail or prison;

(2) prior history of mental illness;

(3) prior history of sex offenses;

(4) prior history of a hostile relationship with another inmate;

(5) prior attempts at self-injury or suicide;

(6) prior attempted escapes;

(7) any mental or physical handicapping condition; and

(8) any other information concerning the safety or welfare of the inmate.

(c) In considering the above information, the chief administrative officer shall examine the following:

(1) records made available to such officer at the time of the commitment by the court or law enforcement agency;

(2) determinations made upon an interview with an inmate at the time of classification;

(3) records, to the extent relevant and known to the chief administrative officer,

Corr. L.

maintained by the department of corrections and community supervision and/or any local correctional facility in this state and which are accessible and available to the chief administrative officer; and

(4) any other relevant information brought to the attention of the chief administrative officer by any person with knowledge of the conditions of the defendant.

8. Where the commission finds substantial noncompliance with commission rules and regulations with regard to (a) minimum staffing requirements; or (b) maximum jail capacity and security requirements; or (c) where it is determined that the county does not have an approved service plan in effect pursuant to article thirteen-A of the executive law or is found to be in non-compliance therewith, as provided in section two hundred sixty-three of such law, it shall prohibit the commingling of any of the following categories of inmates:

(1) persons in custody on civil process, or committed for contempt, or detained as witnesses with persons detained for trial or examination upon a criminal charge with convicts under sentence;

(2) persons detained for trial or examination upon a criminal charge with convicts under sentence;

(3) persons under eighteen years of age with persons eighteen years of age or older; or

(4) a woman detained in any county jail or penitentiary upon a criminal charge or as a convict under sentence with a man; and if detained on civil process, or for contempt, or as a witness in a room in which there are no other prisoners with a man, except with her husband.

Such prohibition shall continue until such time as the commission finds that the county is no longer in substantial noncompliance with paragraphs (a), (b) and (c) of this subdivision.

Notwithstanding the provisions of this subdivision to the contrary, classification as authorized pursuant to this section may occur without compliance with paragraphs (b) and (c) of this subdivision for a period not to exceed six months immediately following the submission of a plan to the division pursuant to section two hundred sixty-two of the executive law. During such six month period the commission shall undertake to review, observe and assess the classification of inmates in local correctional facilities as authorized under this section to thereby ascertain safeguards which should be incorporated in its rules and regulations. Further, during such six month period in which such classification shall be permitted pursuant to this subdivision, the commission shall evaluate whether a local correctional facility is in substantial noncompliance with rules and regulations regarding the requirements specified in paragraphs (a), (b) and (c) of this subdivision and shall determine at the end of such six month period whether substantial noncompliance exists. At the expiration of the six month period if the commission finds a local facility in substantial noncompliance, the commission shall order that the prohibition set forth in this subdivision immediately take effect. The commissioner shall advise the chief administrative officer of such facility of the specific nature of the noncompliance and the specific measures which should be undertaken to remedy the noncompliance. When such measures have been implemented, the chief administrative officer shall certify same to the commissioner and upon the verification thereof by the commissioner, shall permit the chief administrative officer to classify inmates as provided under this section. In the event substantial noncompliance is not found at the expiration of the six month period, then the local correctional facility may continue to classify inmates as authorized in this section.

9. The chief administrative officer shall forward to the commission a quarterly report relative to the housing of inmates. The report shall include, but not be limited to:

(a) all unusual incidents or assaults occurring in a housing unit;

(b) staffing;

(c) daily prisoner population counts;

(d) verification that the locality is maintaining security and supervision records as mandated pursuant to the commission's rules and regulations;

(e) court orders which have been issued and which relate to staffing, jail capacity or security requirements; and

(f) any other information requested by the commission and available to the chief administrative officer with respect to this section.

10. The commission shall conduct on-site inspections and review reports required by this section to monitor the assignment of persons to facility housing units as governed by this section.

11. The commission shall submit to the governor, the temporary president of the senate, the speaker of the assembly, the chairman of the senate crime and correction committee and the chairman of the assembly committee on codes, by March first of each year, its evaluation and assessment of housing in county jails, together with any recommendations with respect to the proper operation or improvement of housing in county jails.

12. The provisions of this section shall govern only the assignment of persons to facility housing units and shall not be construed to prohibit the commingling of persons during their participation in any facility program or activity, including meals and visitations.

13. Where in the opinion of the chief administrative officer an emergency overcrowding condition exists in a local correctional facility caused in part by the prohibition against the commingling of persons under eighteen years of age with persons eighteen years of age or older or the commingling of persons eighteen years of age or older with persons under eighteen years of age, the chief administrative officer may apply to the commission for permission to commingle the aforementioned categories of inmates for a period not to exceed thirty days as provided herein. The commission shall acknowledge to the chief administrative officer the receipt of such application upon its receipt. The chief administrative officer shall be permitted to commingle such inmates upon acknowledgment of receipt of the application by the commission. The commission shall assess the application within seven days of receipt. The commission shall deny any such application and shall prohibit the continued commingling of such inmates where it has found that the local correctional facility does not meet the criteria set forth in this subdivision and further is in substantial noncompliance with minimum staffing requirements as provided in commission rules and regulations. In addition, the commission shall determine whether the commingling of such inmates presents a danger to the health, safety or welfare of any such inmate. If no such danger exists the chief administrative officer may continue the commingling until the expiration of the aforementioned thirty day period or until such time as he determines that the overcrowding which necessitated the commingling no longer exists, whichever occurs first. In the event the commission determines that such danger exists, it shall immediately notify the chief administrative officer, and the commingling of such inmates shall cease. Such notification shall include specific measures which should be undertaken by the chief administrative officer, to correct such dangers. The chief administrative officer may correct such dangers and reapply to the commission for permission to commingle; however, no commingling may take place until such time as the commission certifies that the facility is now in compliance with the measures set forth in the notification under this subdivision. When such certification has been received by the chief

administrative officer, the commingling may continue for thirty days, less any time during which the chief administrative officer commingled such inmates following his application to the commission, or until such time as he determines that the overcrowding which necessitated the commingling no longer exists, whichever occurs first. The chief administrative officer may apply for permission to commingle such inmates for up to two additional thirty day periods, in conformity with the provisions and the requirements of this subdivision, in a given calendar year. For the period ending December thirtieth, nineteen hundred eighty-four, a locality may not apply for more than one thirty day commingling period.

> **HISTORY:** Add, L 1984, ch 907, § 4, eff Aug 6, 1984 and repealed Sept 1, 2015; amd, L 1984, ch 908, § 3, L 1985, ch 574, §§ 1–9, eff July 26, 1985, L 1987, ch 754, § 3, eff Aug 5, 1987, L 2011, ch 62, § 36 (Part C, Subpart A), eff March 31, 2011, L 2014, ch 55, §§ 1–3 (Part M), eff March 31, 2014, and shall be deemed repealed with this section.

§ 500-c. [Repealed Sept 1, 2015] Custody and control of prisoners

1. Except as provided in subdivision two of this section, the sheriff of each county shall have custody of the county jail of such county.

2. In the counties within the city of New York, the city commissioner of correction shall have custody of the correctional facilities within the jurisdiction of the New York city department of correction. In the county of Westchester, the county commissioner of correction shall have custody of all county correctional facilities.

3. Whenever a person is committed to the custody of the sheriff, such commitment shall be deemed to be to the custody of the person designated in subdivisions one and two of this section hereinafter referred to as the chief administrative officer.

4. The chief administrative officer shall receive and safely keep in the county jail of his county each person lawfully committed to his custody pursuant to the provisions of sections five hundred-a and five hundred four of this article and any other applicable provisions of law. Such officer shall not be held personally liable for receiving or detaining any person under and in accordance with a commitment issued by a judicial officer; nor shall he, without lawful authority, let any such person out of jail.

5. All persons confined in a county jail or penitentiary shall, as far as practicable, be allowed to converse with their counsel, or religious advisor, under such reasonable regulations and restrictions as the chief administrative officer may fix. The chief administrative officer may prevent all other conversation by any prisoner in the jail when he shall deem it necessary and proper.

6. Notwithstanding any other provision of law, in the county of Onondaga all of the provisions of this section shall equally apply in any case where the sheriff is holding a person under arrest, for arraignment, prior to commitment, as if such person had been judicially committed to the custody of the sheriff and such person may be held in the Onondaga county jail.

7. A sheriff, the New York city commissioner of correction, or the Westchester county commissioner of correction, as the case may be, shall maintain an institutional fund account on behalf of every lawfully sentenced inmate or prisoner in his custody and shall for the benefit of the person make deposits into said accounts of any prisoner funds. As used in this section, the term "prisoner funds" means (i) funds in the possession of the prisoner at the time of admission into the institution; (ii) funds earned by a prisoner as provided in section one hundred eighty-seven of this chapter; and (iii) any other funds received by or on behalf of the prisoner and deposited with such sheriff or municipal official in accordance with the written procedures established by the commission. Whenever the total value of unencumbered funds in a prisoner's account exceeds ten

thousand dollars, such sheriff or official shall give written notice to the office of victim services.

8. A sheriff, the New York city commissioner of correction, or the Westchester county commissioner of correction, as the case may be, shall provide written notice to all inmates serving a definite sentence for a specified crime defined in paragraph (e) of subdivision one of section six hundred thirty-two-a of the executive law who may be subject to any requirement to report to the office of victim services any funds of a convicted person as defined in section six hundred thirty-two-a of the executive law, the procedures for such reporting and any potential penalty for a failure to comply.

9. Notwithstanding any other provision of law, in the county of Erie all of the provisions of this section shall equally apply in any case where the sheriff is holding a person under arrest for arraignment, prior to commitment, as if such person had been judicially committed to the custody of the sheriff and such person may be held in the Erie county holding center or the Erie county correctional facility.

10. Notwithstanding any other provision of law, in the county of Yates all of the provisions of this section shall equally apply in any case where the sheriff is holding a person under arrest for arraignment, prior to commitment, as if such person had been judicially committed to the custody of the sheriff and such person may be held in the Yates county jail.

11.* Notwithstanding any other provision of law, in the county of Cortland, all of the provisions of this section shall equally apply in any case where the sheriff is holding a person under arrest for arraignment, prior to commitment, as if such person had been judicially committed to the custody of the sheriff.

11.* Notwithstanding any other provision of law, in the county of Putnam, all of the provisions of this section shall equally apply in any case where the sheriff is holding a person under arrest for arraignment, prior to commitment, as if such person had been judicially committed to the custody of the sheriff and such person may be held in the Putnam county jail.

12. Notwithstanding any other provision of law, in the county of Warren all the provisions of this section shall equally apply in any case where the sheriff is holding a person under arrest for arraignment prior to commitment, as if such person had been judicially committed to the custody of the sheriff and such person may be held in the Warren county jail.

13.** Notwithstanding any other provision of law, in the county of Niagara, all of the provisions of this section shall equally apply in any case where the sheriff is holding a person under arrest for arraignment, prior to commitment, as if such person had been judicially committed to the custody of the sheriff and such person may be held in the Niagara county jail.

13.** Notwithstanding any other provision of law, in the county of Genesee all the provisions of this section shall equally apply in any case where the sheriff is holding a person under arrest for arraignment prior to commitment, as if such person had been judicially committed to the custody of the sheriff and such person may be held in the Genesee county jail.

14. Notwithstanding any other provision of law, in the county of Allegany all the provisions of

---

*   There are two subdivisions 11.

*   There are two subdivisions 11.

**   There are two subdivisions 13.

**   There are two subdivisions 13.

this section shall equally apply in any case where the sheriff is holding a person under arrest for arraignment prior to commitment, as if such person had been judicially committed to the custody of the sheriff and such person may be held in the Allegany county correctional facility.

15. Notwithstanding any other provision of law, in the county of Seneca all the provisions of this section shall equally apply in any case where the sheriff is holding a person under arrest for arraignment prior to commitment, as if such person had been judicially committed to the custody of the sheriff and such person may be held in the Seneca county correctional facility.

16.* Notwithstanding any other provision of law, in the county of Montgomery all the provisions of this section shall equally apply in any case where the sheriff is holding a person under arrest for arraignment prior to commitment, as if such person had been judicially committed to the custody of the sheriff and such person may be held in the Montgomery county correctional facility.

16.* Notwithstanding any other provision of law, in the county of Chautauqua all the provisions of this section shall equally apply in any case where the sheriff is holding a person under arrest for arraignment prior to commitment, as if such person has been judicially committed to the custody of the sheriff and such person may be held in the Chautauqua county correctional facility.

17. Notwithstanding any other provision of law, in the county of Ontario all the provisions of this section shall equally apply in any case where the sheriff is holding a person under arrest for arraignment prior to commitment, as if such person has been judicially committed to the custody of the sheriff and such person may be held in the Ontario county correctional facility.

18. Notwithstanding any other provision of law, in the county of Albany, all the provisions of this section shall equally apply in any case where the sheriff is holding a person under arrest for arraignment prior to commitment, as if such person has been judicially committed to the custody of the sheriff and such person may be held in the Albany county correctional facility.

19. Notwithstanding any other provision of law, in the county of Jefferson, all the provisions of this section shall equally apply in any case where the sheriff is holding a person under arrest for arraignment prior to commitment, as if such person has been judicially committed to the custody of the sheriff and such person may be held in the Jefferson county correctional facility.

HISTORY: § 500-c, add, L 1984, ch 907, § 5, eff Aug 6, 1984, repealed Sept 1, 2015, amd, L 1985, ch 574, § 10, eff July 26, 1985, L 1991, ch 508, § 5, eff July 19, 1991, L 1994, ch 541, § 2, eff July 26, 1994, L 2001, ch 62, § 7, eff June 25, 2001, L 2002, ch 413, § 2, eff Aug 13, 2002, L 2003, ch 135, § 2, eff July 22, 2003, L 2003, ch 171, § 2, L 2004, ch 555, § 4, eff Oct 5, 2004, L 2004, ch 555, § 5, eff Oct 5, 2004, L 2004, ch 559, § 2, eff Oct 5, 2004, L 2005, ch 84, § 2, eff June 7, 2005, L 2005, ch 258, § 2, eff July 19, 2005, L 2005, ch 311, § 2, eff July 26, 2005, repealed Sept 1, 2015, L 2007, ch 336, § 2, eff July 18, 2007, repealed Sept 1, 2015, L 2010, ch 56, § 43 (Part A-1), eff June 22, 2010, L 2010, ch 249, § 2, eff July 30, 2010, L 2010, ch 260, § 2, eff July 30, 2010, L 2011, ch 299, § 2, eff Aug 3, 2011, L 2012, ch 343, § 2, eff Aug 1, 2012; L 2014, ch 346, § 2, eff Sept 4, 2014, and shall be deemed repealed with this section.

§ 500-d. Food and labor

(1) Prisoners detained for trial, and those under sentence, shall be provided with a sufficient quantity of plain but wholesome food, at the expense of the county; such foods shall be purchased in the manner and subject to the regulations provided in section four hundred eight of the county law; but prisoners detained for trial may, at their own expense, and under the direction of the keeper, be supplied with any other proper articles of food.

---

* There are two subdivisions 16.

* There are two subdivisions 16.

(2) Such keeper shall cause each prisoner committed to his jail for imprisonment under sentence, to be constantly employed at hard labor when practicable, during every day, except Sunday but the Sunday exception shall not apply where a prisoner under sentence of intermittent imprisonment serves less than the five preceding days in the jail and the keeper has adopted an employment program designed especially for intermittent imprisonment, and the board of supervisors of the county, or judge of the county, may prescribe the kind of labor at which such prisoner shall be employed; and the keeper shall account, at least annually, with the board of supervisors of the county, for the proceeds of such labor.

(3) Such keeper may, with the consent of the board of supervisors of the county, or the county judge, from time to time, cause such of the convicts under his charge as are capable of hard labor, to be employed outside of the jail in the same, or in an adjoining county, upon such terms as may be agreed upon between the keepers and the officers, or persons, under whose direction such convicts shall be placed, subject to such regulations as the board or judge may prescribe; and the board of supervisors of the several counties are authorized to employ convicts under sentence to confinement in the county jails, in building and repairing penal institutions of the county and in building and repairing the highways in their respective counties or in preparing the materials for such highways for sale to and for the use of the state, counties, towns, villages or cities, and in cutting wood and performing other work which is commonly carried on at a prison camp, and to make rules and regulations for their employment; and the said board of supervisors are hereby authorized to cause money to be raised by taxation for the purpose of furnishing materials and carrying this provision into effect; and the courts of this state are hereby authorized to sentence convicts committed to detention in the county jails to such hard labor as may be provided for them by the boards of supervisors. This section as amended shall not affect a county wholly included within a city. Notwithstanding any other provision of law, an inmate may be permitted to leave the institution under guard to voluntarily perform work for a nonprofit organization pursuant to this subdivision. As used in this section, the term "nonprofit organization" means an organization operated exclusively for religious, charitable, or educational purposes, no part of the net earnings of which inures to the benefit of any private shareholder or individual.

HISTORY: Add, L 1950, ch 695, with substance transferred from County Law § 93; amd, L 1951, ch 487, § 1, L 1986, ch 403, § 1, eff July 21, 1986, L 2010, ch 246, § 4, eff July 30, 2010.

§ 500-e. Reading matter; divine service

Each keeper shall provide a bible to be kept in each room of the jail in his charge, and he shall permit the persons therein confined to be supplied with other suitable and proper books and papers, and if practicable, he shall cause divine service to be conducted for the benefit of the prisoners, at least once each Sunday, if there shall be room in the prison that may be safely used for that purpose.

HISTORY: Add, L 1950, ch 695, eff Jan 1, 1951, with substance transferred from County Law, § 94.

§ 500-f. Record of commitments and discharges

Each keeper shall keep a daily record, to be provided at the expense of the county, of the commitments and discharges of all prisoners delivered to his charge, which shall contain the date of entrance, name, offense, term of sentence, fine, age, sex, place of birth, color, social relations, education, secular and religious, for what and by whom committed, how and when discharged, trade or occupation, whether so employed when arrested, number of previous convictions. The daily record shall be a public record, and shall be kept permanently in the office of the keeper.

HISTORY: Add, L 1950, ch 695, with substance transferred from County Law § 95; amd, L

Corr. L.

1968, ch 251, § 7, L 1985, ch 413, § 1, eff July 19, 1985.

§ 500-g. Commitment by United States courts

[Until Sept 1, 2015, § 500-g reads as set out below:]

The chief administrative officer shall receive and keep in his jail every person duly committed thereto, for any offense against the United States, by any court or officer of the United States, until he shall be duly discharged, the United States supporting such person during his confinement; provided such official shall not violate any of the provisions of section five hundred-b of this article in receiving or detaining such persons; and the provisions of this article relative to the mode of confining prisoners shall apply to all persons so committed by any court or officer of the United States.

[Eff Sept 1, 2015, § 500-g reads as set out below:]

Such keeper shall receive and keep in his jail every person duly committed thereto, for any offense against the United States, by any court or officer of the United States, until he shall be duly discharged; the United States supporting such person during his confinement; provided such keeper shall not violate any of the provisions of section five hundred-c of this article in receiving or detaining such persons; and the provisions of this article relative to the mode of confining prisoners and convicts, shall apply to all persons so committed by any court or officer of the United states.

> **HISTORY:** Add, L 1950, ch 695, with substance transferred from County Law § 96; amd, L 1951, ch 487, § 1, L 1984, ch 907, § 6, repealed Sept 1, 2015, L 1985, ch 574, § 11, eff July 26, 1985.

§ 500-h. Payment of costs for medical and dental services

1. Diagnoses, tests, studies or analyses for the diagnosis of a disease or disability, and care and treatment by a hospital, as defined in article twenty-eight of the public health law, or by a physician, or by a dentist to inmates of a local correctional facility which are provided by a county or the city of New York shall be available without cost or charge to the inmates receiving such examinations, care or treatment.

2. Notwithstanding the provisions of subdivision one of this section, any county or the city of New York may, by local law, provide that such entity may be reimbursed for costs paid pursuant to subdivision one of this section from any third party coverage or indemnification carried by an inmate. Such third party coverage or indemnification shall first be applied against the total cost to the hospital or other provider as established in accordance with the provisions of section twenty-eight hundred seven of the public health law relating to rates of payment of an individual's care and treatment, as provided herein.

> **HISTORY:** Add, L 1991, ch 481, § 1, eff July 19, 1991. Former § 500-h, add, L 1950, ch 695, with substance transferred from County Law § 99, amd, L 1968, ch 251, § 7; repealed L 1976, ch 244, eff Sept 1, 1976.

§ 500-i. County workhouses

The board of supervisors of any county may establish and maintain a workhouse for the confinement of persons convicted within the county of crimes and criminal offenses, the punishment for which is imprisonment in the county jail, and may provide for the imprisonment and employment therein of all persons sentenced thereto, and any court or judicial officer may sentence such person to such workhouse instead of to the county jail.

> **HISTORY:** Add, L 1950, ch 695, eff Jan 1, 1951, with substance transferred from County Law, § 100.

§ 500-j. Who may visit local correctional facilities

The following persons may visit at pleasure all local correctional facilities: The governor and lieutenant-governor, secretary of state, comptroller and attorney-general, members of the legislature, judges of the court of appeals, justices of the supreme court and county judges, district attorneys and every clergyman or minister, as such terms are defined in section two of the religious corporations law, having charge of a congregation in the county in which such facility is located. No other person not otherwise authorized by law shall be permitted to enter the rooms of a local correctional facility in which convicts are confined, unless under such regulations as the sheriff of the county, or in counties within the city of New York, the commissioner of correction of such city, or in the county of Westchester, the commissioner of correction of such county shall prescribe.

> **HISTORY:** Add, L 1950, ch 695, with substance transferred from County Law § 101; amd, L 1968, ch 251, § 7, L 1980, ch 400, § 2, L 1991, ch 508, § 2, eff July 19, 1991, L 2009, ch 291, § 2, eff Aug 11, 2009.

§ 500-k. Treatment of inmates

[Until as stated in 2008 note below, § 500-k reads as set out below]

Subdivisions five and six of section one hundred thirty-seven of this chapter relating to the treatment of inmates in state correctional facilities are applicable to inmates confined in county jails; except that the report required by paragraph (d) of subdivision six of such section shall be made to a person designated to receive such report in the rules and regulations of the state commission of correction, or in any county or city where there is a department of correction, to the head of such department.

[Effective as stated in 2008 note below, § 500-k reads as set out below]

Subdivisions five and six of section one hundred thirty-seven of this chapter, except paragraphs (d) and (e)of subdivision six of such section, relating to the treatment of inmates in state correctional facilities are applicable to inmates confined in county jails; except that the report required by paragraph (f) of subdivision six of such section shall be made to a person designated to receive such report in the rules and regulations of the state commission of correction, or in any county or city where there is a department of correction, to the head of such department.

> **HISTORY:** Add, 1968, ch 226, § 2; amd, L 1970, ch 476, § 70, eff July 7, 1970. Amd, L 2008, ch 2, § 1, effective as stated in 2008 note below. Section heading, amd, L 1970, ch 476, § 70, eff July 7, 1970.

> **Editor's Note:** Laws 2008, ch 1, §§ 1 and 8, pars (a) and (c), eff Jan 28, 2008, provide as follows:

[Eff as stated in § 8(a) below:] Section 1. Legislative findings. 1. The legislature finds that the needs of inmates with serious mental illness should be served by improved access to mental health treatment during incarceration. In particular, inmates with serious mental illness should be offered therapeutic care and treatment in residential mental health settings when doing so will not compromise the safety of inmates or other persons or the security of the facility. While in exceptional circumstances segregated confinement may sometimes be necessary to maintain such safety and security, even for inmates with serious mental illness, the state should strive to maintain such inmates with serious mental illness in less restrictive settings whenever it can safely do so.

2. When inmates with serious mental illness are placed in segregated confinement, they should receive a heightened level of care, including out-of-cell therapeutic programming and/or mental health treatment, when consistent with the safety of the inmate and other persons or the security of the facility. Such inmates with serious mental illness should also undergo periodic reassessments of their mental condition to determine whether diversion from segregated confinement to a less restrictive setting is appropriate.

3. This act creates a balanced approach to care and treatment of inmates with serious mental illness and the state's ability to ensure the safety of all inmates and employees and the security of prison facilities.

Corr. L.

§ 8. This act shall take effect immediately; provided however, that:

(a) sections one, two, three, four and five of this act and subdivisions 2 and 3 of section 401-a of the correction law as added by section six of this act shall take effect two years after the date that the commissioner of correctional services certifies to the legislative bill drafting commission that the first residential mental health unit constructed by the department of correctional services is completed and ready to receive inmates, provided, however that such sections shall take effect no later than July 1, 2011;

(c) the commissioner of mental health and the commissioner of correctional services are immediately authorized to promulgate rules and regulations necessary to implement the provisions of this act on their respective effective dates.

§ 500-l. Release on holidays, Saturdays and Sundays

When the date of release from imprisonment in any county jail or jail farm, any city prison or workhouse, falls on Saturday or Sunday, it shall be deemed to fall on the preceding Friday. When the date of such release falls on a legal holiday it shall be deemed to fall on the preceding day, except that when such legal holiday falls on a Monday the date of release shall be deemed to fall on the preceding Friday. This section shall also apply to civil prisoners confined in any jail or prison. This section shall not apply to a sentence of intermittent imprisonment imposed pursuant to article eighty-five or paragraph (d) of subdivision two of section 60.01 of the penal law.

> **HISTORY:** Formerly § 255, add, L 1941, ch 793; amd, L 1943, ch 144, L 1959, ch 286; renumbered § 500-l, L 1970, ch 476, § 46; amd, L 1987, ch 304, § 1, eff Sept 18, 1987.

§ 500-m. Special provision relating to city of New York

Unless specifically provided by law to the contrary, within the city of New York or the counties constituting such city the term sheriff as set forth in this chapter shall be deemed to mean the commissioner of correction of such city.

> **HISTORY:** Add, L 1977, ch 189, eff June 1, 1977.

§ 500-n. Prisoners; unlawful fees prohibited

[Until Sept 1, 2015, § 500-n reads as follows:]

1. Except as otherwise provided by law, a sheriff or other person in charge of a correctional facility or any person employed at such facility shall not charge a prisoner or other person in custody with any sum of money, or demand or receive from him money or any valuable thing for any drink, food or other thing furnished or provided for such prisoner or person at any correctional facility.

2. A sheriff or other public officer or employee shall not demand or receive from a prisoner or other person, while in his custody, a gratuity or reward, upon any pretense or for any purpose.

3. A sheriff, or other public officer or employee, shall not demand or receive from a prisoner or other person in custody, money or any valuable thing for rent in a jail or any fee, compensation, or reward for the commitment, detaining in custody, release, or discharge of a prisoner, other than the fees expressly allowed therefor by law.

[Effective Sept 1, 2015, § 500-n reads as follows and its catchline reads "Civil prisoners":]

1. A sheriff or other officer shall not charge a civil prisoner with any sum of money, or demand or receive from him money, or any valuable thing, for any drink, victuals or other thing, furnished or provided for the officer or the prisoner, at any public house.

2. A sheriff or other officer shall not demand or receive from a civil prisoner, while in his custody, a gratuity or reward, upon any pretense or for any purpose.

3. If a person arrested in a civil cause is kept in a house, other than the jail of the county, the officer arresting him, or the person in whose custody he is, shall not demand or receive from him any greater sum, for lodging, drink, victuals, or any other thing, than has been theretofore prescribed by the court of sessions or county court of the county; or, if no rate has been prescribed by the court of sessions or county court, than is allowed by a justice of the peace of the same town or city, upon proof that the lodging or other thing was actually furnished, at the request of the prisoner.

4. A civil prisoner arrested and kept in a house, other than the jail of the county, may send for and have drink and necessary food, and such bedding, linen and other necessary things, as he thinks fit, from whom he pleases, without detention of the same or any part thereof by, or paying for the same, or any part thereof to, the officer arresting him, or the person in whose custody he is.

5. A sheriff, jailer, or other officer, shall not demand or receive money, or any valuable thing, for chamber rent in a jail; or any fee, compensation, or reward, for the commitment, detaining in custody, release, or discharge of a civil prisoner, other than the fees expressly allowed therefor by law.

6. A prisoner, arrested in a civil cause, must not be kept in a room, in which any prisoner, detained on a criminal charge or conviction, is confined.

7. Male and female civil prisoners must not be put in the same room; except that a husband and his wife may be put or kept together, in a room wherein there are no other prisoners.

8. The sheriff of a county, in which there is more than one jail, or in the county of Westchester the commissioner of correction of such county in the case of a criminal prisoner and the sheriff in the case of a civil prisoner, may confine a civil or criminal prisoner in either or any of such county jails; and may remove him from one jail to another, within the county, whenever he deems it necessary for his safe-keeping, or for his appearance at court.

HISTORY: § 500-n [first setout], formerly § 500, add, L 1984, ch 907, § 3, repealed Sept 1, 2015; amd, L 1984, ch 908, § 2; renumbered § 500-n, L 1987, ch 604, § 4, eff Sept 2, 1987. § 500-n [second setout], formerly §§ 340–347, add, L 1909, ch 47; renumbered § 500, L 1929, ch 243; amd, L 1968, ch 251, § 5; renumbered as § 500-n, L 1987, ch 604, § 4, eff Sept 2, 1987.

§ 500-o. [Expires and repealed Sept 1, 2017] Agreements for custody of inmates from other states

1. The sheriff, warden, superintendent, local commissioner of correction or other person in charge of a local correctional facility may enter into an agreement with a correctional institution located in another state to provide for the custody in such local correctional facility in this state of persons sentenced to a period of imprisonment for an offense in such other state to a term in excess of ninety days but no more than one year. Any such agreement, except one that is made by the city of New York, shall be subject to the approval of the county legislature, the chief executive officer of the county and the commission. An agreement made by the city of New York shall be subject to the approval of the city council, the mayor and the commission.

2. Inmates who are confined in a local correctional facility pursuant to an agreement under this section shall be dealt with in all respects in the same manner as inmates committed to the custody of a local correctional facility pursuant to paragraph (e) of section five hundred-a of this article. All rules and regulations promulgated by the commission regarding the treatment of inmates confined in a local correctional facility shall be applicable to inmates confined pursuant to this section. An inmate confined in a local correctional facility pursuant to an agreement under this

section shall not be deprived of any legal rights which such inmate would have had if confined in a correctional institution in the jurisdiction in which he or she was convicted.

3. Nothing in this section shall be construed to allow persons duly committed and confined to a local correctional facility in this state to serve such confinement in another state.

4. Notwithstanding subdivision one of this section, the sheriff of Albany county may enter into an agreement with a correctional institution located in another state to provide for the custody in the Albany county correctional facility of persons sentenced to a period of imprisonment in such other state to a term in excess of ninety days but no more than two years, subject to the approval of the county legislature, the chief executive officer and the commission.

> **HISTORY:** Add, L 2011, ch 573, § 3, eff Sept 23, 2011, expires and repealed Sept 1, 2017; amd, L 2012, ch 433, § 1, eff Aug 17, 2012.

§ 501. Jail physician

The board of supervisors of each county, except New York, must appoint some reputable physician, duly authorized to practice medicine, as the physician to the jail of the county. If there is more than one jail they must appoint a physician to each. The physician to a jail holds his office at the pleasure of the board which appointed him, except in the county of Kings. In that county, the term of his office is three years.

> **HISTORY:** Formerly § 348, add, L 1909, ch 47; renumbered § 501 and amd, L 1929, ch 243, § 21, eff April 2, 1929. Former § 501, formerly § 421, renumbered § 451, L 1917, ch 712; renumbered § 501, L 1927, ch 426, § 14; renumbered § 801 and amd, L 1929, ch 243, § 24, eff April 2, 1929.

§ 502. Use of liquor in jails

Spirituous, fermented or other liquor shall not be brought into a jail for the use of a person confined therein, except as authorized by federal statute and then only upon a written permit by the physician to the jail, which must be delivered to and kept by the keeper thereof, specifying the quantity and kind of liquor which may be furnished, the name of the civil prisoner for whom, and the time during which the same may be furnished.

> **HISTORY:** Formerly § 349, add, L 1909, ch 47; renumbered § 502 and amd, L 1929, ch 243, § 21, eff April 2, 1929.

§ 503. Permit to bring liquor into jail

A permit by a jail physician as specified in the last section shall not be granted, unless the physician is satisfied, that the liquor allowed to be furnished is necessary for the health of the civil prisoner, for whose use it is permitted and that fact must be stated in the permit.

> **HISTORY:** Formerly § 350, add, L 1909, ch 47; renumbered § 503 and amd, L 1929, ch 243, § 21, eff April 2, 1929.

§ 504. Designation of substitute jail

1. If there is no jail in a county, or the jail becomes unfit or unsafe for the confinement of some or all of the inmates, civil or criminal, or is destroyed by fire or otherwise, or if a pestilential disease breaks out in the jail or in the vicinity of the jail and the physician to the jail certifies that it is likely to endanger the health of any or all of the inmates in the jail, the state commission of correction, upon application, must, by an instrument in writing, filed with the clerk of the county, designate another suitable place within the county, or the jail of any other county, for the confinement of some or all of the inmates, as the case requires. The place so designated thereupon becomes, to all intents and purposes, except as otherwise prescribed in this article, the jail of the county for which it has been so designated, and the purposes expressed in the instrument

designating the same. The designation may be amended, modified or revoked by the state commission of correction by a subsequent instrument in writing filed with the clerk of the county.

2. Where the jail in a county becomes unfit or unsafe for the confinement of some or all of the inmates due to an inmate disturbance or other extraordinary circumstances, including but not limited to a natural disaster, unanticipated deficiencies in the structural integrity of a facility or the inability to provide one or more inmates with essential services such as medical care, upon the request of the municipal official as defined in subdivision four of section forty of this chapter and no other suitable place within the county nor the jail of any other county is immediately available to house some or all of the inmates, the commissioner of corrections and community supervision may, in his or her sole discretion, make available, upon such terms and conditions as he or she may deem appropriate, all or any part of a state correctional institution for the confinement of some or all of such inmates as an adjunct to the county jail for a period not to exceed thirty days. However, if the county jail remains unfit or unsafe for the confinement of some or all of such inmates beyond thirty days, the state commission of correction, with the consent of the commissioner of corrections and community supervision, may extend the availability of a state correctional institution for one or more additional thirty day periods. The state commission of correction shall promulgate rules and regulations governing the temporary transfer of inmates to state correctional institutions from county jails, including but not limited to provisions for confinement of such inmates in the nearest correctional facility, to the maximum extent practicable, taking into account necessary security. The commissioner of corrections and community supervision may, in his or her sole discretion, based on standards promulgated by the department, determine whether a county shall reimburse the state for any or all of the actual costs of confinement as approved by the director of the division of the budget. On or before the expiration of each thirty day period, the state commission of correction must make an appropriate designation pursuant to subdivision one if the county jail remains unfit or unsafe for the confinement of some or all of the inmates and consent to the continued availability of a state correctional institution as required for herein. The superintendence, management and control of a state correctional institution or part thereof made available pursuant hereto and the inmates housed therein shall be as directed by the commissioner of corrections and community supervision.

3. The county clerk must serve a copy of the designation, duly certified by him or her, under his or her official seal, on the sheriff and keeper of the jail of the county designated. The sheriff of that county must, upon the delivery of the sheriff of the county for which the designation is made, receive into his or her jail, and there safely keep, all persons who may be lawfully confined therein, pursuant to this article; and he or she is responsible for their safekeeping, as if he or she was sheriff of the county for which the designation is made.

4. In any county where a jail is under the jurisdiction of a commissioner of correction the term sheriff as set forth in this section shall be deemed to mean the commissioner of correction of such county.

5. As provided in this section, any designation of the state commission of correction, or any amendment, modification or revocation thereto, may be issued by the commission, any member, or any attorney employed by the commission.

HISTORY: Formerly § 351, add, L 1909, ch 47; renumbered § 504 and amd, L 1929, ch 243, § 21; amd, L 1966, ch 245, eff April 26, 1966, L 1974, ch 799; amd, L 1982, ch 506, § 1, eff July 13, 1982, L 2009, ch 56, § 8 (Part Q), eff April 7, 2009, L 2011, ch 62, § 28 (Part C, Subpart B), eff March 31, 2011, L 2013, ch 133, § 1, eff July 12, 2013.

§ 505. Provision of routine medical, dental and mental health services and treatment

1. Where an inmate who is not yet eighteen years of age has been committed to the custody of the sheriff or other person in charge of a local correctional facility and no medical consent has been obtained prior to commitment, the commitment order shall be deemed to grant to the minor the capacity to consent to routine medical, dental and mental health services and treatment to himself or herself.

2. Subject to the regulations of the department of health, routine medical, dental and mental health services and treatment is defined for the purposes of this section to mean any routine diagnosis or treatment, including without limitation the administration of medications or nutrition, the extraction of bodily fluids for analysis, and dental care performed with a local anesthetic. Routine mental health treatment shall not include psychiatric administration of medication unless it is part of an ongoing mental health plan or unless it is otherwise authorized by law.

3. (a) At any time prior to the date the inmate becomes eighteen years of age, the inmate's parent or legal guardian may institute legal proceedings pursuant to section 70.20 of the penal law objecting to the provision of routine medical, dental or mental health services and treatment being provided to the inmate.

(b) A notice of motion shall be served on the inmate and the sheriff or other person in charge of the local correctional facility not less than seven days prior to the return date of the motion. The person on whom the notice of motion is served shall answer the motion not less than two days before the return date. On examining the motion and answer and, in its discretion, after hearing argument, the court shall enter an order, granting or denying the motion.

4. Nothing in this section shall preclude an inmate from consenting on his or her own behalf to any medical, dental or mental health services and treatment where otherwise authorized by law to do so.

HISTORY: Add, L 2013, ch 437, § 2, eff Oct 23, 2013.

§ 507. Removal of prisoners in case of fire

If, by reason of a jail, or a building near a jail, being on fire, there is reason to apprehend that some or all of the prisoners confined in the jail, may be injured, or may escape, the sheriff or keeper of the jail may, in his discretion, remove them to some safe and convenient place, and there confine them, until they can be safely returned to the jail or, if the jail is destroyed, or so injured, that it is unfit or unsafe for the confinement of the prisoners, until a designation is made, as prescribed in section five hundred and four of this article.

HISTORY: Formerly § 354, add, L 1909, ch 47; renumbered § 507 and amd, L 1929, ch 243, § 21, eff April 2, 1929.

§ 508. Removal of sick prisoners from jail

1. A sheriff, in his discretion, may by written order permit inmates confined in a local correctional facility to receive medical diagnosis and treatment in outside hospitals, upon the determination that such outside treatment and diagnosis is necessary by reason of inadequate facilities within the local correctional facility. Such inmates shall remain under the jurisdiction and in the custody of said sheriff while in a hospital and said sheriff shall enforce proper measures in each case to safely maintain such jurisdiction and custody.

2. a. If a physician to a jail or in case of a vacancy a physician acting as such and the warden or jailer certify in writing that a prisoner confined in a jail either in a civil cause or upon a criminal charge is in such a state of mental health that he is in need of involuntary care and treatment and in their opinion should be removed to a psychiatric hospital for treatment, the warden or jailer shall immediately notify the director who shall have the responsibility for

providing treatment for such prisoner. If such director after examination of the prisoner by an examining physician designated by him shall determine that such prisoner is in need of involuntary care and treatment, the director shall file an application for the involuntary hospitalization of such prisoner pursuant to article nine of the mental hygiene law in a hospital operated by the department of mental hygiene or in the case of a prisoner confined in a jail in a city or county which maintains or operates a general hospital containing a psychiatric prison ward approved by the department of mental hygiene to such prison ward for care and treatment or to any other psychiatric hospital if such prison ward is filled to capacity. Such application shall be supported by the certificate of two physicians in accordance with the requirements of section 9.27 of the mental hygiene law and thereupon such prisoner shall be admitted forthwith to the hospital in which such application is filed, and the procedures of the mental hygiene law governing the hospitalization of such prisoner. The jailer or warden having custody of the prisoner shall deliver the prisoner to the hospital with which the director has filed the application. If such jailer or warden shall certify that such prisoner has a mental illness which is likely to result in serious harm to himself or others and for which care in a psychiatric hospital is appropriate such jailer or warden shall effect the admission of such prisoner to a hospital forthwith in accordance with the provisions of section 9.37 or 9.39 of the mental hygiene law and the hospital shall admit such prisoner. Upon admission of the prisoner, pursuant to section 9.37 or 9.39 of the mental hygiene law, the jailer or warden shall notify the director, the prisoner's attorney, and his family, where information about the family is available. While the prisoner is in the hospital he shall remain in the custody under sufficient guard of the jailer or warden in charge of the jail from which he came. A prisoner admitted to a psychiatric hospital pursuant to section 9.27, 9.37 or 9.39 of the mental hygiene law may be retained at the hospital pursuant to the provisions of the mental hygiene law until he has improved sufficiently in his mental illness so that hospitalization is no longer necessary or until ordered by the court to be returned to the jail whichever comes first and in either event, the prisoner shall thereupon be returned to jail. The cost of the care and treatment of such prisoners in the hospital shall be defrayed in accordance with the provisions of the mental hygiene law in such cases provided.

From the time of admission of a prisoner to a hospital under this section the retention of such prisoner for care and treatment shall be subject to the provisions for notice, hearing, review and judicial approval of continued retention or transfer and continued retention provided by article nine of the mental hygiene law for the admission and retention of involuntary patients.

b. As used in this section, the following terms shall have the following meanings:

(i) "Director" means (a) the director of a state hospital operated by the department of mental hygiene, or (b) the director of a hospital operated by any local government of the state that has been certified by the commissioner of mental hygiene as having adequate facilities to treat a mentally ill person or (c) the director of community mental health services or the designees of any of the foregoing. The appropriate director to whom a jailer or warden shall certify the need for involuntary care and treatment and who shall have the responsibility for such care and treatment shall be determined in accordance with rules jointly adopted by the judicial conference and the commissioner of mental hygiene.

(ii) "Mental illness" shall mean an affliction with a mental disease or mental condition which is manifested by a disorder or a disturbance in behavior, feeling, thinking, or judgement to such an extent that the person afflicted requires care and treatment.

(iii) "In need of involuntary care and treatment" shall mean that a person has a mental illness for which care and treatment as a patient in a hospital is essential to such person's welfare and whose judgement is so impaired that he is unable to understand the need for such care and treatment.

(iv) "Likelihood to result in serious harm" shall mean (1) substantial risk of physical harm to himself as manifested by threats of or attempts at suicide or serious bodily harm or other conduct demonstrating that he is dangerous to himself or (2) a substantial risk of physical harm to other persons as manifested by homicidal or other violent behavior by which others are placed in reasonable fear or serious physical harm.

c. If at any time the hospital in which a prisoner is hospitalized pursuant to this subdivision determines that the prisoner is not in such state of mental health to be in need of involuntary care and treatment the prisoner shall be returned to the jail forthwith.

d. If at any time the director of a hospital in which a prisoner is hospitalized pursuant to this subdivision has reason to believe that the prisoner may be an incapacitated defendant as defined in article seven hundred thirty of the criminal procedure law he shall so notify the court in which the criminal charges are pending and such court shall thereupon issue an examination order pursuant to the provisions of article seven hundred thirty of the criminal procedure law.

e. Nothing in this subdivision shall prevent the release of the prisoner from custody where appropriate by recognizance, bail, or otherwise as the court may direct.

HISTORY: Formerly § 355, add, L 1909, ch 47; renumbered § 508 and amd, L 1929, ch 243, § 21; amd, L 1946, ch 700, L 1961, ch 151, L 1962, ch 536, L 1968, ch 251, § 9, eff Jan 1, 1969. Sub 1, formerly entire section, so designated sub 1, L 1968, ch 251, § 9, eff Jan 1, 1969. Sub 2, add, L 1988, ch 240, § 1, eff July 8, 1988. Former sub 2, add, L 1968, ch 251, § 9; repealed, L 1988, ch 240, § 1, eff July 8, 1988. Sub 3, add, L 1974, ch 656, eff May 30, 1974. Sub 3, par a, first undesignated par, amd, L 2002, ch 283, § 1, eff Aug 6, 2002. Sub 3, par a, second undesignated par, amd, L 2002, ch 283, § 1, eff Aug 6, 2002. Sub 1, formerly sub 2, so designated sub 1, L 2009, ch 33, § 1, eff May 19, 2009; amd, L 2009, ch 33, § 2, eff May 19, 2009. Former sub 1, repealed, L 2009, ch 33, § 1, eff May 19, 2009. Sub 2, formerly sub 3, so designated sub 2, L 2009, ch 33, § 1, eff May 19, 2009. Former sub 2, redesignated sub 1, L 2009, ch 33, § 1, eff May 19, 2009. Sub 3, redesignated sub 2, L 2009, ch 33, § 1, eff May 19, 2009.

§ 509. Absence of inmate for funeral and deathbed visits

The sheriff of a local correctional facility or his designee may permit any inmate confined in his local correctional facility to attend the funeral of his or her father, mother, guardian or former guardian, child, brother, sister, husband, wife, grandparent, grandchild, ancestral uncle or ancestral aunt within the state, or to visit such individual during his or her illness if death be imminent; but the exercise of such power shall be subject to such rules and regulations as the commission shall prescribe, respecting the granting of such permission, duration of absence from the institution, custody, transportation and care of the inmate, and guarding against escape.

HISTORY: Add, L 1987, ch 229, § 1; amd, L 1989, ch 419, § 1, eff Aug 15, 1989. Former § 509, formerly § 356, add, L 1909, ch 47; renumbered § 509 and amd, L 1929, ch 243, § 21; repealed, L 1974, ch 799, eff June 7, 1974.

§ 514. Confinement of civil prisoner

A civil prisoner, committed to jail upon process for contempt, or committed for misconduct in a case prescribed by law, must be actually confined and detained within the jail, until he is discharged by due course of law, or is removed to another jail or place of confinement, in a case prescribed by law. A sheriff or keeper of a jail, who suffers such a prisoner to go or be at large out of his jail; except by virtue of a writ of habeas corpus, or by the special direction of the court committing him, or in a case specially prescribed by law; is liable to the party aggrieved, for his damages sustained thereby, and is guilty of a misdemeanor. If the commitment was for the nonpayment of a sum of money, the amount thereof, with interest, is the measure of damages.

HISTORY: Formerly § 361, add, L 1920, ch 933; renumbered § 514 and amd, L 1929, ch 243, § 21, eff April 2, 1929.

§ 523. Revocation of designation of jail

When a jail is erected for the county, for whose use the designation pursuant to section five hundred and four of this chapter was made, or its jail is rendered fit and safe for the confinement of prisoners, or the reason for the designation of another jail or place has otherwise ceased to be operative, the designation must be revoked, as prescribed in this article and section five hundred and five of this chapter.

HISTORY: Formerly § 369, add, L 1920, ch 933; renumbered § 523 and amd, L 1929, ch 243, § 21, eff April 2, 1929.

§ 524. Manner and effect of revocation

The county clerk must immediately serve a copy of the revocation, duly certified by him under his official seal, upon the sheriff of the same county; who must remove the civil and criminal prisoners belonging to his custody, and confined without his county, to his proper jail. If a prisoner has been admitted to the jail liberties in the other county, he must also be removed; and he is entitled to the liberties of the jail of the county, to which he is removed, without a new bond, as if he had been originally admitted to the jail liberties in that county; and the bond given by him applies accordingly to those liberties.

HISTORY: Formerly § 369-a, add, L 1920, ch 933; renumbered § 524 and amd, L 1929, ch 243, § 21, eff April 2, 1929.

§ 529. Term of imprisonment of a recaptured prisoner

A prisoner arrested or committed in a civil action or proceeding, who escapes from custody, upon his voluntary return or recapture, shall be imprisoned for a term equal to that portion of his original term of imprisonment which remains unexpired at the time of his escape.

HISTORY: Add, L 1943, ch 143, eff March 20, 1943.

* * *

ARTICLE 22-A [EXPIRES SEPT 1, 2015] PRISONER FURLOUGHS

HISTORY: Add, L 1972, ch 886, § 1, eff Aug 7, 1972, expires Sept 1, 2015.

Editor's Note: Laws 1972, ch 886, § 3, eff June 8, 1972, provides as follows: § 3. This act shall take effect 60 days after it shall have become law and shall remain in effect until September 1, 2015. (Amd, L 1974, ch 299, § 1, L 1977, ch 691, § 9, L 1978, ch 691, L 1979, ch 485, § 2, L 1980, ch 296, § 2, L 1981, ch 495, § 3, L 1982, ch 137, § 2, L 1983, ch 519, § 2, L 1984, ch 983, § 2, L 1985, ch 573, § 2, L 1986, ch 395, § 2, L 1987, ch 261, § 19, L 1991, ch 511, § 6, L 1994, ch 61, § 9, L 1995, ch 3, § 47, L 1997, ch 435, § 47, L 1999, ch 452, § 1, L 2001, ch 95, § 3, L 2003, ch 16, § 3, L 2005, ch 56, § 3 (Part D), eff April 12, 2005, deemed eff on and after April 1, 2005, L 2007, ch 56, § 3 (Part C), eff April 9, 2007, deemed eff on and after March 31, 2007, L 2009, ch 56, § 3 (Part U), eff April 7, 2009, L 2011, ch 57, § 3 (Part A), eff March 31, 2011.).

§ 630. [Expires Sept 1, 2015] Applicability

This article shall be applicable only to prisoners sentenced to institutions operated by a department of correction in cities having a population of one million or more or by a county which elects to have this article apply thereto.

HISTORY: Add, L 1972, ch 886, § 1, eff Aug 7, 1972, expires Sept 1, 2015.

§ 631. [Expires Sept 1, 2015] Definitions

As used in this article the following terms shall have the following meanings:

1. "Institution" means any institution under the jurisdiction of the commissioner of correction in any city having a population of one million or more or of a county which elects to have this article apply thereto.

2. "Eligible inmate" means a person confined in a city prison or reformatory in a city having a population of one million or more or in a county jail and penitentiaries of a county which elects to have this article apply thereto where a furlough program has been established who is sentenced to a definite period of six months or more or to a reformatory sentence of imprisonment and has served a minimum of six months of any such sentence.

3. "Furlough program" means a program under which eligible inmates may be granted the privilege of leaving the premises of a prison for a period not exceeding seventy-two hours for the purpose of seeking employment, maintaining family ties, solving family problems, to undergo surgery or to receive medical treatment or dental treatment not available in the correctional institution, or for any matter necessary to the furtherance of any such purposes.

4. "Extended bounds of confinement" means the area in which an inmate participating in a furlough program may travel, the routes he is permitted to use, the places he is authorized to visit, and the hours, days, or specially defined period during which he is permitted to be absent from the premises of the institution. An extension of limits shall be under such prescribed conditions as the commissioner deems necessary. Such extension of limits may be withdrawn at any time.

5. "Furlough committee" means the body of persons which may include members of the public, appointed pursuant to regulations promulgated by the commissioner for the purposes of formulating, modifying and revoking furlough programs at an institution.

6. "Warden" means the person in charge of an institution by whatever title he may be known.

7. "Commissioner" means the commissioner of correction in a city having a population of one million or more or that official having similar duties in any county which elects to have this article apply thereto, by whatever title he may be known.

8. "Department" means the applicable department of correction or, where no such department exists, the office of the commissioner.

HISTORY: Add, L 1972, ch 886, § 1, eff Aug 7, 1972, expires Sept 1, 2015. Sub 2, amd, L 1973, ch 411, § 1, L 1973, ch 622, § 3, eff Aug 10, 1973. Sub 7, add, L 1973, ch 622, eff Aug 10, 1973. Sub 8, add, L 1973, ch 622, § 3, eff Aug 10, 1973.

§ 632. [Expires Sept 1, 2015] Establishment of a furlough program

1. The commissioner shall designate, in the rules and regulations of the department, appropriate employees or an appropriate unit of the department, to be responsible for (a) securing education, on-the-job training and employment opportunities for inmates who are eligible to participate in a furlough program and (b) supervising inmates during their participation in a furlough program outside the premises of the institution.

2. [None]

HISTORY: Add, L 1972, ch 886, § 1, eff Aug 7, 1972, expires Sept 1, 2015.

§ 633. [Expires Sept 1, 2015] Procedure for furlough release of eligible inmates

1. A person confined in a city prison or a county jail and penitentiaries of a county which elects to have this article apply thereto who is, or who within thirty days will become, an eligible inmate, may make application to the furlough release committee of the institution for permission to participate in a furlough program.

2. Any eligible inmate may make application to the furlough committee for leave of absence provided, however, that in exigent circumstances such application may be made directly to the warden of the institution and the warden may exercise all of the powers of the furlough committee subject, however, to any limitations or requirements set forth in the rules and regulations of the department and subject further to the discretion of the commissioner.

3. If the furlough committee determines that a furlough program for the applicant is consistent with the safety of the community, is in the best interests of rehabilitation of the applicant, and is consistent with the rules and regulations of the department, the committee, with the assistance of the employees designated by the commissioner pursuant to section six hundred thirty-two of this chapter, shall develop a suitable furlough program for the applicant.

4. The committee shall then prepare a memorandum setting forth the details of the furlough program including the extended bounds of confinement and any other matter required by the rules and regulations of the department. Such memorandum shall be transmitted to the warden who may approve or reject the program. If the warden approves the program, he shall indicate such approval in writing by signing the memorandum. If the warden rejects the program, such decision shall be reviewed by the commissioner.

5. In order for the applicant to accept the furlough program, he shall agree to be bound by all the terms and conditions thereof and shall indicate such agreement by signing the memorandum of the program immediately below a statement reading as follows:

"I accept the foregoing program and agree to be bound by the terms and conditions thereof. I understand I will be under the supervision of the department while I am away from the premises of the institution and I agree to comply with the instructions of any employee of the department assigned to supervise me. I will carry a copy of this memorandum on my person at all times while I am away from the premises of the institution and I will exhibit it to any peace officer or police officer upon his request. I understand that my participation in the program is a privilege which may be revoked at any time, and that if I violate any provision of the program I may be taken into custody by any peace officer or police officer and I will be subject to disciplinary procedures. I further understand that if I intentionally fail to return to the institution at or before the time specified in the memorandum I may be found guilty of a misdemeanor."

6. After approving the program of furlough, the warden may then permit an eligible inmate who has accepted such program to go outside the premises of the institution within the limits of the extended bounds of confinement described in the memorandum; provided, however, that no such permission shall become effective in the case of a furlough program prior to the time at which the person to be released becomes an eligible inmate.

7. Participation in a furlough release program shall be a privilege. Nothing contained in this article may be construed to confer upon any inmate the right to participate, or to continue to participate in a furlough program. The warden of the institution may at any time, and upon

Corr. L.

recommendation of the furlough committee or of the commissioner, revoke any inmate's privilege to participate in a program of furlough.

> **HISTORY:** Add, L 1972, ch 886, § 1, eff Aug 7, 1972, expires Sept 1, 2015. Sub 1, amd, L 1973, ch 622, § 4, eff Aug 10, 1973. Sub 3, amd, L 1973, ch 411, § 2, L 1973, ch 622, § 4, eff Aug 10, 1973. Sub 5, amd, L 1973, ch 622, § 4, L 1980, ch 843, § 199, eff Sept 1, 1980.

§ 634. [Expires Sept 1, 2015] Conduct of inmates participating in furlough program

1. An inmate who is permitted to leave the premises of an institution to participate in a furlough program shall have on his person a copy of the memorandum of that program as signed by the warden of the institution and shall exhibit such copy to any peace officer or police officer upon request of such officer.

2. If the inmate violates any provision of the program, or any rule, or regulation promulgated by the commissioner for conduct of inmates participating in furlough programs, he shall be subject to disciplinary measures to the same extent as if he violated a rule or regulation of the commissioner for conduct of inmates within the premises of the institution.

3. The provisions of this section relating to good behavior of inmates while participating in furlough programs outside the premises of institutions, and such allowances may be granted, withheld, forfeited or cancelled in whole or part for behavior outside the premises of an institution to the same extent and in the same manner as is provided for behavior of inmates within the premises of the institutions.

4. An inmate who is in violation of the provisions of his furlough program may be taken into custody by any peace officer or police officer and, in such event the inmate shall be returned forthwith to the institution that released him. In any case where the institution is in a county other than the one in which the inmate is apprehended, the officer may deliver the inmate to the nearest institution, jail or lockup and it shall be the duty of the person in charge of said facility to hold such inmate securely until such time as he is delivered into the custody of an officer of the institution from which he was released. Upon delivering the inmate to an institution, jail or lockup, other than the one from which he was released, the officer who apprehended the inmate shall forthwith notify the warden of the institution from which the inmate was released and it shall be the duty of the warden to effect the expeditious return of the inmate to the institution.

> **HISTORY:** Add, L 1972, ch 886, eff Aug 7, 1972, expires Sept 1, 2015. Sub 1, amd, L 1980, ch 843, § 200, eff Sept 1, 1980. Sub 2, amd, L 1973, ch 622, § 5, eff Aug 10, 1973. Sub 4, amd, L 1980, ch 843, § 201, eff Sept 1, 1980.

ARTICLE 22-B   THE DEATH PENALTY

§ 662.   **Disposition of body**

> **HISTORY:** Add, L 1995, ch 1, § 32, eff Sept 1, 1995. Former Article 22-B, add, L 1971, ch 545, § 11; repealed, L 1995, ch 1, § 32, eff Sept 1, 1995.

§ 650. Warrant for execution of death sentence

1. When a person is sentenced to the punishment of death, the justice or judge who presided at the sentencing proceeding, or if that justice or judge is unavailable for any reason, then any justice of the supreme court of the department in which the defendant was sentenced, must, within seven days, make out, sign and deliver to the sheriff of the county, a warrant directed to the commissioner or to the superintendent of an institution in the department designated by the commissioner. Such warrant shall state the conviction and sentence, appoint a week on which the sentence shall be executed, and command the commissioner to execute the sentence within that week. In counties within the city of New York, or in the county of Westchester, such warrant shall be made out as aforesaid, signed and delivered to the commissioner of correction of such city or county.

2. If the execution of the sentence shall be delayed while the conviction or sentence is being appealed, a justice or judge authorized to act pursuant to subdivision one of this section, at the conclusion of the state appellate process, if the conviction or sentence is not set aside, must, within seven days, make out, sign and deliver another warrant as provided in subdivision one of this section. If the execution of the sentence on the date appointed is delayed by any other cause, the justice or judge shall, as soon as such cause ceases to exist, make out, sign and deliver another warrant.

> **HISTORY:** Add, L 1995, ch 1, § 32, eff Sept 1, 1995. Former § 650, add, L 1971, ch 545, § 11, with substance derived from Crim C § 491; amd, L 1974, ch 367, § 17, L 1980, ch 400, § 4, L 1991, ch 508, § 4; repealed, L 1995, ch 1, § 32, eff Sept 1, 1995.

§ 651. Time of execution

The week of execution appointed in the warrant shall be not less than thirty days and not more than sixty days after the issuance of the warrant. The date of execution within said week shall be left to the discretion of the commissioner, but the date and hour of the execution shall be announced publicly no later than seven days prior to said execution.

> **HISTORY:** Add, L 1995, ch 1, § 32, eff Sept 1, 1995. Former § 651, add, L 1971, ch 545, § 11, with substance derived from Crim C § 492; repealed, L 1995, ch 1, § 32, eff Sept 1, 1995.

§ 652. Delivery of warrant and confinement

1. Within ten days after the issuance of a warrant as provided in section six hundred fifty of this article, the sheriff or the commissioner of correction, if within the city of New York or county of Westchester, must deliver the warrant and the person sentenced, if that person is not already in the custody of the department, to the department or to the superintendent of the state institution designated by the commissioner. Upon the issuance of the warrant the court shall cause a copy to be personally delivered to the convicted person and shall send a copy of the warrant to the convicted person's last attorney of record.

2. From the time of the delivery of the warrant and until the imposition of the punishment of death upon the convicted person, unless discharged from the sentence, such person may, in the commissioner's discretion, either be kept isolated from the general prison population in a designated institution or confined as otherwise provided by law. The commissioner, in his discretion, may determine that the safety and security of the facility, or of the inmate population, or of the staff, or of the inmate, would not be jeopardized by the inmate's confinement within the general prison population.

3. The commissioner may promulgate rules and regulations concerning visitation of inmates sentenced to death. Such rules and regulations may provide that inmates sentenced to death are subject to different visitation policies and procedures than inmates who are not sentenced to death.

> **HISTORY:** Add, L 1995, ch 1, § 32, eff Sept 1, 1995. Former § 652, add, L 1971, ch 545, § 11, with substance derived from Crim C § 493; repealed, L 1995, ch 1, § 32, eff Sept 1, 1995.

§ 653. Transmittal of record to the governor

Within a reasonable time following the issuance of the warrant as provided in section six hundred fifty of this article, the clerk of the court in the county in which the person was sentenced to death shall transmit to the governor a statement of conviction and sentence, and the transcripts of both the trial and the sentencing proceedings, including, to the extent practicable, any exhibits introduced therein.

> **HISTORY:** Add, L 1995, ch 1, § 32, eff Sept 1, 1995. Former § 653, add, L 1971, ch 545, § 11, with substance derived from Crim C § 494; repealed, L 1995, ch 1, § 32, eff Sept 1, 1995.

§ 654. Governor may consult

The governor is authorized to request the opinion of the attorney general, the district attorney, and the convicted person's counsel, or any of them, as to whether the execution of the person should be reprieved or suspended.

> **HISTORY:** Add, L 1995, ch 1, § 32, eff Sept 1, 1995. Former § 654, add, L 1971, ch 545, § 11, with substance derived from Crim C § 495; repealed, L 1995, ch 1, § 32, eff Sept 1, 1995.

§ 655. Governor only to reprieve

No judge, court, or officer, other than the governor, can reprieve the execution of a person sentenced to death. This section does not apply to a stay authorized by law.

> **HISTORY:** Add, L 1995, ch 1, § 32, eff Sept 1, 1995. Former § 655, add, L 1971, ch 545, § 11, with substance derived from Crim C § 495-a; repealed, L 1995, ch 1, § 32, eff Sept 1, 1995.

§ 656. Proceeding when person under sentence of death may be incompetent

1. The state may not execute an inmate who is incompetent. An inmate is "incompetent" when, as a result of mental disease or defect, he lacks the mental capacity to understand the nature and effect of the death penalty and why it is to be carried out.

2. Upon the filing of a petition in the supreme court in either the county in which an inmate sentenced to death is confined or in the county in which the inmate was prosecuted alleging that the inmate is incompetent, the court shall issue an order staying the execution if and to the extent a stay is necessary to permit determination of the petition. Upon application of either the inmate's counsel or the district attorney the petition may be transferred to the court in which the inmate was convicted unless such transfer would be unduly burdensome or impracticable. Promptly upon filing the petition, the court shall appoint a commission of three psychiatric examiners, hereinafter referred to as "the psychiatric commissioners," to inquire into the inmate's competence and report to the court as to the inmate's competence. The psychiatric commissioners shall be impartial and must be qualified psychiatrists or certified psychologists. Before commencing an inquiry, the psychiatric commissioners must take the oath prescribed in rule forty-three hundred fifteen of the civil practice law and rules to be taken by referees. The petition may be filed by the inmate, the inmate's counsel, an employee of the department, the inmate's legal guardian, a member of such inmate's immediate family or, in the event that the inmate does not have regular contact with a member of his or her immediate family, a bona fide friend who has maintained regular contact with the inmate. The petition must be accompanied by an affidavit of at least one qualified psychiatrist or certified psychologist who, based at least in part on personal examination, attests that in the psychiatrist's or psychologist's professional opinion the inmate is incompetent and lists the

pertinent facts therefor. For purposes of this section the terms "qualified psychiatrist" and "certified psychologist" have the meaning set forth in section 730.10 of the criminal procedure law.

3. The petition shall be served upon either the district attorney who prosecuted the inmate or upon the district attorney for the county in which the inmate is confined. If the petition is served upon the district attorney for the county in which the inmate is confined, the court shall promptly notify the district attorney who prosecuted the inmate. Immediately upon appointing the psychiatric commissioners, the court shall direct that an examination of the convicted person promptly take place with all three of the psychiatric commissioners present at the same time. The court shall also direct, upon application of the inmate or the district attorney, that the inmate be examined by a qualified psychiatrist or certified psychologist designated by the inmate or the district attorney. Counsel for the inmate and the district attorney shall have the right to be present at each such examination. Upon the filing of a petition pursuant to subdivision two of this section, if the inmate does not have counsel and is financially unable to obtain counsel the court shall appoint competent counsel experienced in the trial of criminal matters to represent the inmate.

4. The psychiatric commissioners must receive and consider evidence offered by the inmate's counsel and the district attorney, including written submissions, testimony and expert psychiatric evidence. The proceeding before the psychiatric commissioners shall be conducted on the record but need not be conducted in accordance with the rules governing the admission of evidence at trial, but counsel for the people and the inmate shall have the right to cross-examine witnesses.

5. When the proceeding before the psychiatric commissioners has been concluded, they must forthwith provide a transcript of the proceeding, together with their findings of fact, to the court with their opinion thereon. Unless impracticable, the psychiatric commissioners shall so act within sixty days from the filing of the petition. When an inmate shall be found incompetent by a majority of the psychiatric commissioners, the court shall accept such finding unless clearly erroneous, and promptly enter an order finding the inmate to be incompetent, staying the execution of the inmate and directing that the inmate be committed to a secure facility under the jurisdiction of the office of mental health if the inmate's incompetency is the result of mental illness. In all other cases, the inmate shall remain in the custody of the department. When an inmate is found competent by a majority of the psychiatric commissioners, the court shall accept such finding unless clearly erroneous, promptly enter an order finding the inmate to be competent and vacating any stay previously issued, and the court shall promptly inform the judge or justice who issued the warrant for the execution of the inmate of the court's finding. Upon being so informed, the judge or justice shall promptly issue a new warrant in accordance with subdivision two of section six hundred fifty of this article. Any other provision of law notwithstanding, no other review, judicial or otherwise, shall be available with respect to an order finding the inmate to be incompetent or competent. If the court rejects the finding of a majority of the psychiatric commissioners on the ground that it is clearly erroneous, the court shall appoint another commission to proceed as provided in this section.

6. When an inmate has been committed to a secure facility pursuant to this section, the inmate shall remain there until the facility administrator determines that the inmate may be competent. Upon so determining, the facility administrator shall promptly notify the court that entered the order finding the inmate to be incompetent, and the court shall promptly notify counsel and the district attorneys and appoint another commission to proceed as provided in this section.

7. The court shall allow reasonable fees to the psychiatric commissioners. The court shall allow reasonable fees for time spent in court and for time reasonably expended out of court to counsel appointed pursuant to this section. The court shall allow all reasonably necessary costs, including without limitation the costs attendant to fees for the examination of the inmate by a qualified

Corr. L.

psychiatrist or certified psychologist, incurred by the inmate and the district attorney in connection with a petition pursuant to this section. Each claim for compensation and reimbursement shall be supported by a sworn statement specifying the time expended, services rendered, expenses incurred and reimbursement or compensation applied for or received in the same case from any other source. All such fees and costs shall be a state charge payable on vouchers approved by the court after audit by and on the warrant of the comptroller.

8. When a petition has previously been filed and determined pursuant to this section, the court in which a subsequent petition is filed or to which a subsequent petition is transferred, shall not issue an order staying the execution of the inmate unless the court finds, after notice to the district attorney who prosecuted the inmate and after affording the district attorney a reasonable opportunity to be heard in writing, that there is reasonable cause to believe that the inmate is incompetent; provided, however, that the court may issue an order staying the execution of the inmate, to the extent a stay is necessary to afford the district attorney an opportunity to be heard and such reasonable cause determination to be made.

> **HISTORY:** Add, L 1995, ch 1, § 32, eff Sept 1, 1995. Former § 656, add, L 1971, ch 545, § 11, with substance derived from Crim C § 498; repealed, L 1995, ch 1, § 32, eff Sept 1, 1995.

§ 657. Proceeding when person under sentence of death is pregnant

1. A sentence of death may not be carried out upon a woman while she is pregnant.

2. When the superintendent of the correctional facility where the inmate is confined is informed that reasonable grounds exist that a convicted person under sentence of death may be pregnant, the superintendent shall appoint a qualified physician to examine the convicted person and determine if she is pregnant.

3. Upon being informed by the superintendent that such convicted person is pregnant, the governor shall stay execution of the warrant to the extent necessary.

> **HISTORY:** Add, L 1995, ch 1, § 32, eff Sept 1, 1995. Former § 657, add, L 1971, ch 545, § 11, with substance derived from Crim C § 499; repealed, L 1995, ch 1, § 32, eff Sept 1, 1995.

§ 658. Death penalty inflicted by lethal injection

The punishment of death shall be inflicted by lethal injection; that is, by the intravenous injection of a substance or substances in a lethal quantity into the body of a person convicted until such person is dead.

> **HISTORY:** Add, L 1995, ch 1, § 32, eff Sept 1, 1995. Former § 658, add, L 1971, ch 545, § 11, with substance derived from Crim C § 500; repealed, L 1995, ch 1, § 32, eff Sept 1, 1995.

§ 659. Facility

The commissioner shall provide and maintain a suitable and efficient facility, enclosed from public view, within the confines of a designated correctional institution for the imposition of the punishment of death. That facility shall contain the apparatus and equipment necessary for the carrying out of executions by lethal injection.

> **HISTORY:** Add, L 1995, ch 1, § 32, eff Sept 1, 1995. Former § 659, add, L 1971, ch 545, § 11, with substance derived from Crim C § 501; repealed, L 1995, ch 1, § 32, eff Sept 1, 1995.

§ 660. Persons authorized to be present at execution

1. The commissioner, any persons designated by the commissioner to act as execution technicians or otherwise to assist in the execution, including correction officers, and a licensed physician or physicians may be present at the execution. The commissioner shall also select and invite the presence, by at least three days' prior notice, of a justice of the supreme court, the

counsel for the convicted person, the district attorney and the sheriff of the county where the conviction was had, together with six adult citizens. The names of the execution technician or technicians shall never be disclosed, notwithstanding any other provision of law to the contrary, including article six of the public officers law. The names of the six adult citizens who witnessed the execution shall not be disclosed until after the execution.

2. The commissioner shall, at the request of the person sentenced to death, authorize and permit two clergymen to be present at the execution.

3. The inmate sentenced to death may name four relatives or bona fide friends to witness the execution, and the commissioner shall authorize said named relatives or friends of the inmate to witness the execution unless the commissioner determines that the presence of any named relative or friend at the execution would pose a threat to the safety or security of the designated correctional institution. No person under eighteen years of age shall be permitted to witness any execution.

HISTORY: Add, L 1995, ch 1, § 32, eff Sept 1, 1995. Former § 660, add, L 1971, ch 545, § 11, with substance derived from Crim C § 502; repealed, L 1995, ch 1, § 32, eff Sept 1, 1995.

§ 661. Examination of convicted person's body and certificate

1. Immediately after the execution an examination of the body of the convicted person shall be made by the licensed physicians present at the execution and their report in writing stating the nature of the examination and occurrence of death, so made by them, shall be annexed to the certificate provided for in subdivision two of this section and filed therewith.

2. The commissioner shall prepare and sign a certificate setting forth the time and place of the execution and stating that the execution was conducted in conformity to the sentence of the court and the provisions of this article. The commissioner shall cause the certificate to be filed, within ten days after the execution, with the office of clerk of the court in which the conviction was had.

3. The commissioner may appoint a deputy with the department to execute the warrant of execution and to perform all other duties imposed upon the commissioner under this article.

HISTORY: Add, L 1995, ch 1, § 32, eff Sept 1, 1995. Former § 661, add, L 1971, ch 545, § 11, with substance derived from Crim C § 503; repealed, L 1995, ch 1, § 32, eff Sept 1, 1995.

§ 662. Disposition of body

1. Prior to the execution, the convicted person shall be given the opportunity to decide in writing to whom his or her body shall be delivered after the execution. The commissioner or his or her designee shall sign and authorize the convicted person's request if the request is not contrary to law. If the convicted person does not indicate to whom such person's body shall be delivered, or if the person's request is contrary to law, the commissioner may deliver the convicted person's body to a relative by blood or marriage or a bona fide friend. If the body is not claimed by a relative or bona fide friend within seven days after execution, the body shall be delivered to a duly authorized and incorporated pathological and anatomical association in the state, if requested by an authorized association.

2. If the body of the convicted person is not claimed by a relative, bona fide friend, or a duly authorized and incorporated pathological and anatomical association, the commissioner shall cause the body to be disposed of in the same manner as are bodies of prisoners dying in the institution. Notwithstanding any other provision of law, no autopsy shall be required for the body of an inmate upon whom a sentence of death has been carried out.

HISTORY: Add, L 1995, ch 1, § 32, eff Sept 1, 1995. Former § 662, add, L 1971, ch 545, § 11, with substance derived from Crim C § 505; repealed, L 1995, ch 1, § 32, eff Sept 1, 1995.

ARTICLE 23 DISCRETIONARY RELIEF FROM FORFEITURES AND DISABILITIES AUTOMATICALLY IMPOSED BY LAW

HISTORY: Add, L 1966, ch 654, eff Oct 1, 1966. Article heading, amd, L 1972, ch 342, eff May 22, 1972.

§ 700. Definitions and rules of construction

1. As used in this article the following terms have the following meanings:

(a) "Eligible offender" shall mean a person who has been convicted of a crime or of an offense, but who has not been convicted more than once of a felony.

(b) "Felony" means a conviction of a felony in this state, or of an offense in any other jurisdiction for which a sentence to a term of imprisonment in excess of one year, or a sentence of death, was authorized.

(c) "Revocable sentence" means a suspended sentence or a sentence upon which execution was suspended pursuant to the penal law in effect prior to September first, nineteen hundred sixty-seven; or a sentence of probation or of conditional discharge imposed pursuant to the penal law in effect after September first, nineteen hundred sixty-seven.

2. For the purposes of this article the following rules of construction shall apply:

(a) Two or more convictions of felonies charged in separate counts of one indictment or information shall be deemed to be one conviction;

(b) Two or more convictions of felonies charged in two or more indictments or informations, filed in the same court prior to entry of judgment under any of them, shall be deemed to be one conviction; and

(c) A plea or a verdict of gulity [guilty]* upon which sentence or the execution of sentence has been suspended or upon which a sentence of probation, conditional discharge, or unconditional discharge has been imposed shall be deemed to be a conviction.

HISTORY: Add, L 1966, ch 654; amd, L 1972, ch 342, eff May 22, 1972. Section heading, amd, L 1972, ch 342, eff May 22, 1972.

§ 701. Certificates of relief from disabilities

1. A certificate of relief from disabilities may be granted as provided in this article to relieve an eligible offender of any forfeiture or disability, or to remove any bar to his employment, automatically imposed by law by reason of his conviction of the crime or of the offense specified

---

* The bracketed word has been inserted by the Publisher.

therein. Such certificate may be limited to one or more enumerated forfeitures, disabilities or bars, or may relieve the eligible offender of all forfeitures, disabilities and bars. Provided, however, that no such certificate shall apply, or be construed so as to apply, to the right of such person to retain or to be eligible for public office.

2. Notwithstanding any other provision of law, except subdivision five of section twenty-eight hundred six of the public health law or paragraph (b) of subdivision two of section eleven hundred ninety-three of the vehicle and traffic law, a conviction of a crime or of an offense specified in a certificate of relief from disabilities shall not cause automatic forfeiture of any license, other than a license issued pursuant to section 400.00 of the penal law to a person convicted of a class A-I felony or a violent felony offense, as defined in subdivision one of section 70.02 of the penal law, permit, employment, or franchise, including the right to register for or vote at an election, or automatic forfeiture of any other right or privilege, held by the eligible offender and covered by the certificate. Nor shall such conviction be deemed to be a conviction within the meaning of any provision of law that imposes, by reason of a conviction, a bar to any employment, a disability to exercise any right, or a disability to apply for or to receive any license, permit, or other authority or privilege covered by the certificate; provided, however, that a conviction for a second or subsequent violation of any subdivision of section eleven hundred ninety-two of the vehicle and traffic law committed within the preceding ten years shall impose a disability to apply for or receive an operator's license during the period provided in such law; and provided further, however, that a conviction for a class A-I felony or a violent felony offense, as defined in subdivision one of section 70.02 of the penal law, shall impose a disability to apply for or receive a license or permit issued pursuant to section 400.00 of the penal law. A certificate of relief from a disability imposed pursuant to subparagraph (v) of paragraph b of subdivision two and paragraphs i and j of subdivision six of section five hundred ten of the vehicle and traffic law may only be issued upon a determination that compelling circumstances warrant such relief.

3. A certificate of relief from disabilities shall not, however, in any way prevent any judicial, administrative, licensing or other body, board or authority from relying upon the conviction specified therein as the basis for the exercise of its discretionary power to suspend, revoke, refuse to issue or refuse to renew any license, permit or other authority or privilege.

> **HISTORY:** Add, L 1966, ch 654; amd, L 1972, ch 342, § 3, eff May 22, 1972; amd, L 1983, ch 584, § 2, L 1985, ch 718, § 2, L 1988, ch 47, § 2, L 1993, ch 533, § 7, eff Sept 30, 1993, L 2007, ch 235, § 2, eff Oct 18, 2007.

§ 702. Certificates of relief from disabilities issued by courts

1. Any court of this state may, in its discretion, issue a certificate of relief from disabilities to an eligible offender for a conviction that occurred in such court, if the court either (a) imposed a revocable sentence or (b) imposed a sentence other than one executed by commitment to an institution under the jurisdiction of the state department of corrections and community supervision. Such certificate may be issued (i) at the time sentence is pronounced, in which case it may grant relief from forfeitures, as well as from disabilities, or (ii) at any time thereafter, in which case it shall apply only to disabilities. Where such court either imposes a revocable sentence or imposes a sentence other than one executed by commitment to an institution under the jurisdiction of the state department of corrections and community supervision, the court, upon application and in accordance with subdivision two of this section, shall initially determine the fitness of an eligible offender for such certificate prior to or at the time sentence is pronounced.

2. Such certificate shall not be issued by the court unless the court is satisfied that:

(a) The person to whom it is to be granted is an eligible offender, as defined in section seven hundred;

(b) The relief to be granted by the certificate is consistent with the rehabilitation of the eligible offender; and

(c) The relief to be granted by the certificate is consistent with the public interest.

3. Where a certificate of relief from disabilities is not issued at the time sentence is pronounced it shall only be issued thereafter upon verified application to the court. The court may, for the purpose of determining whether such certificate shall be issued, request its probation service to conduct an investigation of the applicant, or if the court has no probation service it may request the probation service of the county court for the county in which the court is located to conduct such investigation. Any probation officer requested to make an investigation pursuant to this section shall prepare and submit to the court a written report in accordance with such request.

4. Where the court has imposed a revocable sentence and the certificate of relief from disabilities is issued prior to the expiration or termination of the time which the court may revoke such sentence, the certificate shall be deemed to be a temporary certificate until such time as the court's authority to revoke the sentence has expired or is terminated. While temporary, such certificate (a) may be revoked by the court for violation of the conditions of the sentence, and (b) shall be revoked by the court if it revokes the sentence and commits the person to an institution under the jurisdiction of the state department of corrections and community supervision. Any such revocation shall be upon notice and after an opportunity to be heard. If the certificate is not so revoked, it shall become a permanent certificate upon expiration or termination of the court's authority to revoke the sentence.

5. Any court that has issued a certificate of relief from disabilities may at any time issue a new certificate to enlarge the relief previously granted, provided, however, that the provisions of subdivisions one through four of this section shall apply to the issuance of any such new certificate.

6. Any written report submitted to the court pursuant to this section is confidential and may not be made available to any person or public or private agency except where specifically required or permitted by statute or upon specific authorization of the court. However, upon the court's receipt of such report, the court shall provide a copy of such report, or direct that such report be provided to the applicant's attorney, or the applicant himself, if he or she has no attorney. In its discretion, the court may except from disclosure a part or parts of the report which are not relevant to the granting of a certificate, or sources of information which have been obtained on a promise of confidentiality, or any other portion thereof, disclosure of which would not be in the interest of justice. The action of the court excepting information from disclosure shall be subject to appellate review. The court, in its discretion, may hold a conference in open court or in chambers to afford an applicant an opportunity to controvert or to comment upon any portions of the report. The court may also conduct a summary hearing at the conference on any matter relevant to the granting of the application and may take testimony under oath.

   HISTORY: Add, L 1966, ch 654, amd, L 1971, ch 748, eff June 25, 1971, L 1972, ch 342, § 4; eff May 22, 1972, L 1976, ch 931, § 2, eff Jan 1, 1977, L 1982, ch 121, § 1, eff May 24, 1982, L 1985, ch 134, § 24, eff April 1, 1985, L 2006, ch 98, § 2, eff June 7, 2006, L 2006, ch 720, § 1, eff June 7, 2006, L 2010, ch 56, § 64 (Part A), eff June 22, 2010, L 2011, ch 62, § 32 (Part C, Subpart B), eff March 31, 2011, L 2011, ch 488, § 1, eff Aug 17, 2011.

§ 703. Certificates of relief from disabilities issued by the department of corrections and community supervision

1. The department of corrections and community supervision shall have the power to issue a certificate of relief from disabilities to:

(a) any eligible offender who has been committed to an institution under the jurisdiction of the state department of corrections and community supervision. Such certificate may be issued by the department at the time the offender is released from such institution under the department's supervision or otherwise or at any time thereafter;

(b) any eligible offender who resides within this state and whose judgment of conviction was rendered by a court in any other jurisdiction.

2. Where the department has issued a certificate of relief from disabilities, the department may at any time issue a new certificate enlarging the relief previously granted.

3. The department shall not issue any certificate of relief from disabilities pursuant to subdivisions one or two, unless the department is satisfied that:

(a) The person to whom it is to be granted is an eligible offender, as defined in section seven hundred;

(b) The relief to be granted by the certificate is consistent with the rehabilitation of the eligible offender; and

(c) The relief to be granted by the certificate is consistent with the public interest.

4. Any certificate of relief from disabilities issued by the department to an eligible offender who at time of the issuance of the certificate is under the department's supervision, shall be deemed to be a temporary certificate until such time as the eligible offender is discharged from the department's supervision, and, while temporary, such certificate may be revoked by the department for violation of the conditions of community supervision. Revocation shall be upon notice to the releasee, who shall be accorded an opportunity to explain the violation prior to decision thereon. If the certificate is not so revoked, it shall become a permanent certificate upon expiration or termination of the department's jurisdiction over the individual.

5. In granting or revoking a certificate of relief from disabilities the action of the department shall be deemed a judicial function and shall not be reviewable if done according to law.

6. For the purpose of determining whether such certificate shall be issued, the department may conduct an investigation of the applicant.

7. Presumption based on federal recommendation. Where a certificate of relief from disabilities is sought pursuant to paragraph (b) of subdivision one of this section on a judgment of conviction rendered by a federal district court in this state and the department is in receipt of a written recommendation in favor of the issuance of such certificate from the chief probation officer of the district, the department shall issue the requested certificate, unless it finds that the requirements of paragraphs (a), (b) and (c) of subdivision three of this section have not been satisfied; or that the interests of justice would not be advanced by the issuance of the certificate.

HISTORY: Add, L 1966, ch 654; amd, L 1971, ch 748, § 2, L 1972, ch 342, § 5, eff May 22, 1972, L 1974, ch 475, § 1, eff May 23, 1974, L 1976, ch 931, § 3, eff Jan 1, 1977, L 1988, ch 378, § 1, eff July 29, 1988, L 2010, ch 56, § 3 (Part OO), eff July 22, 2010, L 2011, ch 62, § 34 (Part C, Subpart B), eff March 31, 2011.

§ 703-a. Certificate of good conduct

1. A certificate of good conduct may be granted as provided in this section to relieve an individual of any disability, or to remove any bar to his employment, automatically imposed by law by reason of his conviction of the crime or of the offense specified therein. Such certificate may

be limited to one or more enumerated disabilities or bars, or may relieve the individual of all disabilities and bars.

2. Notwithstanding any other provision of law, a conviction of a crime or of an offense specified in a certificate of good conduct shall not be deemed to be a conviction within the meaning of any provision of law that imposes, by reason of a conviction, a bar to any employment, a disability to exercise any right, or a disability to apply for or to receive any license, permit, or other authority or privilege covered by the certificate; and provided, however, that a conviction for a class A-I felony or a violent felony offense, as defined in subdivision one of section 70.02 of the penal law, shall impose a disability to apply for or receive a license or permit issued pursuant to section 400.00 of the penal law.

3. A certificate of good conduct shall not, however, in any way prevent any judicial administrative, licensing or other body, board or authority from considering the conviction specified therein in accordance with the provisions of article twenty-three-a of this chapter.

HISTORY: Add, L 1976, ch 931, § 4, eff Jan 1, 1977. Sub 2, amd, L 2007, ch 235, § 3, eff Oct 16, 2007.

§ 703-b. Issuance of certificate of good conduct

1. The department of corrections and community supervision shall have the power to issue a certificate of good conduct to any person previously convicted of a crime in this state, when the department is satisfied that:

(a) The applicant has conducted himself or herself in a manner warranting such issuance for a minimum period in accordance with the provisions of subdivision three of this section;

(b) The relief to be granted by the certificate is consistent with the rehabilitation of the applicant; and

(c) The relief to be granted is consistent with the public interest.

2. The department shall have the power to issue a certificate of good conduct to any person previously convicted of a crime in any other jurisdiction, when the department is satisfied that:

(a) The applicant has demonstrated that there exist specific facts and circumstances, and specific sections of New York state law that have an adverse impact on the applicant and warrant the application for relief to be made in New York; and

(b) The provisions of paragraphs (a), (b) and (c) of subdivision one of this section have been met.

3. The minimum period of good conduct by the individual referred to in paragraph (a) of subdivision one of this section, shall be as follows: where the most serious crime of which the individual was convicted is a misdemeanor, the minimum period of good conduct shall be one year; where the most serious crime of which the individual was convicted is a class C, D or E felony, the minimum period of good conduct shall be three years; and, where the most serious crime of which the individual was convicted is a class B or A felony, the minimum period of good conduct shall be five years. Criminal acts committed outside the state shall be classified as acts committed within the state based on the maximum sentence that could have been imposed based upon such conviction pursuant to the laws of such foreign jurisdiction. Such minimum period of good conduct by the individual shall be measured either from the date of the payment of any fine imposed upon him or her or the suspension of sentence, or from the date of his or her unrevoked release from custody by parole, commutation or termination of his or her sentence. The department

shall have power and it shall be its duty to investigate all persons when such application is made and to grant or deny the same within a reasonable time after the making of the application.

4. Where the department has issued a certificate of good conduct, the department may at any time issue a new certificate enlarging the relief previously granted.

5. Any certificate of good conduct by the department to an individual who at time of the issuance of the certificate is under the department's supervision, shall be deemed to be a temporary certificate until such time as the individual is discharged from the department's supervision, and, while temporary, such certificate may be revoked by the department for violation of the conditions of community supervision. Revocation shall be upon notice to the releasee, who shall be accorded an opportunity to explain the violation prior to decision thereon. If the certificate is not so revoked, it shall become a permanent certificate upon expiration or termination of the department's jurisdiction over the individual.

> **HISTORY:** Add, L 1976, ch 931, § 4, eff Jan 1, 1977; amd, L 1985, ch 386, §§ 1, 2, eff July 19, 1985, L 2011, ch 62, § 35 (Part C, Subpart B), eff March 31, 2011.

§ 704. Effect of revocation; use of revoked certificate

1. Where a certificate of relief from disabilities is deemed to be temporary and such certificate is revoked, disabilities and forfeitures thereby relieved shall be reinstated as of the date upon which the person to whom the certificate was issued receives written notice of such revocation. Any such person shall upon receipt of such notice surrender the certificate to the issuing court or board.

2. A person who knowingly uses or attempts to use, a revoked certificate of relief from disabilities in order to obtain or to exercise any right or privilege that he would not be entitled to obtain or to exercise without a valid certificate shall be guilty of a misdemeanor.

> **HISTORY:** Add, L 1966, ch 654, eff Oct 1, 1966.

§ 705. Forms and filing

1. All applications, certificates and orders of revocation necessary for the purposes of this article shall be upon forms prescribed pursuant to agreement among the state commissioner of corrections and community supervision, the chairman of the state board of parole and the administrator of the state judicial conference. Such forms relating to certificates of relief from disabilities shall be distributed by the office of probation and correctional alternatives and forms relating to certificates of good conduct shall be distributed by the commissioner of the department of corrections and community supervision.

2. Any court or department issuing or revoking any certificate pursuant to this article shall immediately file a copy of the certificate, or of the order of revocation, with the New York state identification and intelligence system.

> **HISTORY:** Add, L 1966, ch 654, eff Oct 1, 1966; amd, L 1971, ch 748, § 3, L 1985, ch 134, § 25, L 1991, ch 193, § 1, eff July 21, 1991, L 2010, ch 56, § 49 (Part A), eff June 22, 2010, L 2011, ch 62, § 36 (Part C, Subpart B), eff March 31, 2011.

§ 706. Certificate not to be deemed to be a pardon

Nothing contained in this article shall be deemed to alter or limit or affect the manner of applying for pardons to the governor, and no certificate issued hereunder shall be deemed or construed to be a pardon.

> **HISTORY:** Add, L 1966, ch 654, eff Oct 1, 1966.

ARTICLE 23-A   LICENSURE AND EMPLOYMENT OF PERSONS PREVIOUSLY CONVICTED OF ONE OR MORE CRIMINAL OFFENSES

HISTORY: Add, L 1976, ch 931, § 5, eff Jan 1, 1977.

§ 750. Definitions

For the purposes of this article, the following terms shall have the following meanings:

(1) "Public agency" means the state or any local subdivision thereof, or any state or local department, agency, board or commission.

(2) "Private employer" means any person, company, corporation, labor organization or association which employs ten or more persons.

(3) "Direct relationship" means that the nature of criminal conduct for which the person was convicted has a direct bearing on his fitness or ability to perform one or more of the duties or responsibilities necessarily related to the license, opportunity, or job in question.

(4) "License" means any certificate, license, permit or grant of permission required by the laws of this state, its political subdivisions or instrumentalities as a condition for the lawful practice of any occupation, employment, trade, vocation, business, or profession. Provided, however, that "license" shall not, for the purposes of this article, include any license or permit to own, possess, carry, or fire any explosive, pistol, handgun, rifle, shotgun, or other firearm.

(5) "Employment" means any occupation, vocation or employment, or any form of vocational or educational training. Provided, however, that "employment" shall not, for the purposes of this article, include membership in any law enforcement agency.

HISTORY: Add, L 1976, ch 931, § 5, eff Jan 1, 1977. Sub (3), amd, L 2007, ch 284, § 1, eff July 18, 2007.

§ 751. Applicability

The provisions of this article shall apply to any application by any person for a license or employment at any public or private employer, who has previously been convicted of one or more criminal offenses in this state or in any other jurisdiction, and to any license or employment held by any person whose conviction of one or more criminal offenses in this state or in any other jurisdiction preceded such employment or granting of a license, except where a mandatory forfeiture, disability or bar to employment is imposed by law, and has not been removed by an executive pardon, certificate of relief from disabilities or certificate of good conduct. Nothing in this article shall be construed to affect any right an employer may have with respect to an intentional misrepresentation in connection with an application for employment made by a prospective employee or previously made by a current employee.

HISTORY: Add, L 1976, ch 931, § 5, eff Jan 1, 1977. Amd, L 2007, ch 284, § 2, eff July 18, 2007.

§ 752. Unfair discrimination against persons previously convicted of one or more criminal offenses prohibited

No application for any license or employment, and no employment or license held by an individual, to which the provisions of this article are applicable, shall be denied or acted upon adversely by reason of the individual's having been previously convicted of one or more criminal offenses, or by reason of a finding of lack of "good moral character" when such finding is based upon the fact that the individual has previously been convicted of one or more criminal offenses, unless:

(1) there is a direct relationship between one or more of the previous criminal offenses and the specific license or employment sought or held by the individual; or

(2) the issuance or continuation of the license or the granting or continuation of the employment would involve an unreasonable risk to property or to the safety or welfare of specific individuals or the general public.

> **HISTORY:** Add, L 1976, ch 931, § 5, eff Jan 1, 1977. Opening par, amd, L 2007, ch 284, § 3, eff July 18, 2007. Sub (1), amd, L 2007, ch 284, § 3, eff July 18, 2007. Sub (2), amd, L 2007, ch 284, § 3, eff July 18, 2007.

§ 753. Factors to be considered concerning a previous criminal conviction; presumption

1. In making a determination pursuant to section seven hundred fifty-two of this chapter, the public agency or private employer shall consider the following factors:

(a) The public policy of this state, as expressed in this act, to encourage the licensure and employment of persons previously convicted of one or more criminal offenses.

(b) The specific duties and responsibilities necessarily related to the license or employment sought or held by the person.

(c) The bearing, if any, the criminal offense or offenses for which the person was previously convicted will have on his fitness or ability to perform one or more such duties or responsibilities.

(d) The time which has elapsed since the occurrence of the criminal offense or offenses.

(e) The age of the person at the time of occurrence of the criminal offense or offenses.

(f) The seriousness of the offense or offenses.

(g) Any information produced by the person, or produced on his behalf, in regard to his rehabilitation and good conduct.

(h) The legitimate interest of the public agency or private employer in protecting property, and the safety and welfare of specific individuals or the general public.

2. In making a determination pursuant to section seven hundred fifty-two of this chapter, the public agency or private employer shall also give consideration to a certificate of relief from disabilities or a certificate of good conduct issued to the applicant, which certificate shall create a presumption of rehabilitation in regard to the offense or offenses specified therein.

> **HISTORY:** Add, L 1976, ch 931, § 5, eff Jan 1, 1977. Sub 1, par (b), amd, L 2007, ch 284, § 4, eff July 18, 2007.

§ 754. Written statement upon denial of license or employment

At the request of any person previously convicted of one or more criminal offenses who has been denied a license or employment, a public agency or private employer shall provide, within thirty days of a request, a written statement setting forth the reasons for such denial.

HISTORY: Add, L 1976, ch 931, § 5, eff Jan 1, 1977.

§ 755. Enforcement

1. In relation to actions by public agencies, the provisions of this article shall be enforceable by a proceeding brought pursuant to article seventy-eight of the civil practice law and rules.

2. In relation to actions by private employers, the provisions of this article shall be enforceable by the division of human rights pursuant to the powers and procedures set forth in article fifteen of the executive law, and, concurrently, by the New York city commission on human rights.

HISTORY: Add, L 1976, ch 931, § 5, eff Jan 1, 1977.

ARTICLE 24   PROVISIONS APPLICABLE TO SENTENCES IMPOSED UNDER THE [THE]* REVISED PENAL PLAN

§ 800.	Applicability
§ 803.	Good behavior allowances against indeterminate and determinate sentences
§ 803-a.	Certain calculations
§ 803-b.	Limited credit time allowances for inmates serving indeterminate or determinate sentences imposed for specified offenses
§ 804.	Good behavior allowances against definite sentences
§ 804-a.	Good behavior allowances for certain civil commitments
§ 805.	[Repealed Sept 1, 2015] Earned eligibility program
§ 806.	[Repealed Sept 1, 2015] Presumptive release program for nonviolent inmates

HISTORY: Add, L 1967, ch 680, § 147, eff Sept 1, 1967.

§ 800. Applicability

The provisions of this article shall apply, to the exclusion of all other provisions of this chapter relating to good behavior allowances, where sentence has been imposed pursuant to the provisions of the penal law as enacted by chapter ten hundred thirty of the laws of nineteen hundred sixty-five, as amended, or where the sentence is a reformatory sentence of imprisonment. Matters not expressly covered herein or covered in such penal law shall be governed by such other provisions of law as may be applicable.

HISTORY: Add, L 1967, ch 680, § 147; amd, L 1970, ch 476, § 72, L 1974, ch 653, § 4, eff May 30, 1974. Another § 800, formerly § 420, renumbered § 450, L 1917, ch 712; renumbered § 500, Laws 1927, ch 426, § 14; renumbered § 800 and amd, L 1929, ch 243, § 24; renumbered § 1000, L 1969, ch 317, eff April 27, 1969.

§ 803. Good behavior allowances against indeterminate and determinate sentences

[Until Sept 1, 2015, § 803 reads as set out below:]

1. (a) Every person confined in an institution of the department or a facility in the department of mental hygiene serving an indeterminate or determinate sentence of imprisonment, except a person serving a sentence with a maximum term of life imprisonment, may receive time allowance against the term or maximum term of his or her sentence imposed by the court. Such allowances may be granted for good behavior and efficient and willing performance of duties

---

* Brackets have been inserted by the Publisher around this word as it is superfluous.

assigned or progress and achievement in an assigned treatment program, and may be withheld, forfeited or canceled in whole or in part for bad behavior, violation of institutional rules or failure to perform properly in the duties or program assigned.

(b) A person serving an indeterminate sentence of imprisonment may receive time allowance against the maximum term of his or her sentence not to exceed one-third of the maximum term imposed by the court.

(c) A person serving a determinate sentence of imprisonment may receive time allowance against the term of his or her sentence not to exceed one-seventh of the term imposed by the court.

(d) [Expires and repealed Sept 1, 2015]

(i) Except as provided in subparagraph (ii) of this paragraph, every person under the custody of the department or confined in a facility in the department of mental hygiene serving an indeterminate sentence of imprisonment with a minimum period of one year or more or a determinate sentence of imprisonment of one year or more imposed pursuant to section 70.70 or 70.71 of the penal law, may earn a merit time allowance.

(ii) Such merit time allowance shall not be available to any person serving an indeterminate sentence authorized for an A-I felony offense, other than an A-I felony offense defined in article two hundred twenty of the penal law, or any sentence imposed for a violent felony offense as defined in section 70.02 of the penal law, manslaughter in the second degree, vehicular manslaughter in the second degree, vehicular manslaughter in the first degree, criminally negligent homicide, an offense defined in article one hundred thirty of the penal law, incest, or an offense defined in article two hundred sixty-three of the penal law, or aggravated harassment of an employee by an inmate.

(iii) The merit time allowance credit against the minimum period of the indeterminate sentence shall be one-sixth of the minimum period imposed by the court except that such credit shall be one-third of the minimum period imposed by the court for an A-I felony offense defined in article two hundred twenty of the penal law. In the case of such a determinate sentence, in addition to the time allowance credit authorized by paragraph (c) of this subdivision, the merit time allowance credited against the term of the determinate sentence pursuant to this paragraph shall be one-seventh of the term imposed by the court.

(iv) Such merit time allowance may be granted when an inmate successfully participates in the work and treatment program assigned pursuant to section eight hundred five of this article and when such inmate obtains a general equivalency diploma, an alcohol and substance abuse treatment certificate, a vocational trade certificate following at least six months of vocational programming or performs at least four hundred hours of service as part of a community work crew.

Such allowance shall be withheld for any serious disciplinary infraction or upon a judicial determination that the person, while an inmate, commenced or continued a civil action, proceeding or claim that was found to be frivolous as defined in subdivision (c) of section eight thousand three hundred three-a of the civil practice law and rules, or an order of a federal court pursuant to rule 11 of the federal rules of civil procedure imposing sanctions in an action commenced by a person, while an inmate, against a state agency, officer or employee.

(v) The provisions of this paragraph shall apply to persons in custody serving an indeterminate sentence on the effective date of this paragraph as well as to persons sentenced

Corr. L.

to an indeterminate sentence on and after the effective date of this paragraph and prior to September first, two thousand five and to persons sentenced to a determinate sentence prior to September first, two thousand eleven for a felony as defined in article two hundred twenty or two hundred twenty-one of the penal law.

2. If a person is serving more than one sentence, the authorized allowances may be granted separately against the term or maximum term of each sentence or, where consecutive sentences are involved, against the aggregate maximum term. Such allowances shall be calculated as follows:

(a) A person serving two or more indeterminate sentences which run concurrently may receive time allowance not to exceed one-third of the indeterminate sentence which has the longest unexpired time to run.

(b) A person serving two or more indeterminate sentences which run consecutively may receive time allowance not to exceed one-third of the aggregate maximum term.

(c) A person serving two or more determinate sentences which run concurrently may receive time allowance not to exceed one-seventh of the determinate sentence which has the longest unexpired time to run.

(d) A person serving two or more determinate sentences which run consecutively may receive time allowance not to exceed one-seventh of the aggregate maximum term.

(e) A person serving one or more indeterminate sentence and one or more determinate sentence which run concurrently may receive time allowance not to exceed one-third of the indeterminate sentence which has the longest unexpired term to run or one-seventh of the determinate sentence which has the longest unexpired time to run, whichever allowance is greater.

(f) A person serving one or more indeterminate sentence and one or more determinate sentence which run consecutively may receive time allowance not to exceed the sum of one-third of the maximum or aggregate maximum of the indeterminate sentence or sentences and one-seventh of the term or aggregate maximum of the determinate sentence or sentences.

2-a. [Expires and repealed Sept 1, 2015] If a person is serving more than one sentence, the authorized merit time allowances may be granted against the period or aggregate minimum period of the indeterminate sentence or sentences, or against the term or aggregate term of the determinate sentence or sentences, or where consecutive determinate and indeterminate sentences are involved, against the aggregate minimum period as calculated pursuant to subparagraph (iv) of paragraph (a) of subdivision one of section 70.40 of the penal law. Such allowances shall be calculated as follows:

(a) A person serving two or more indeterminate sentences which run concurrently may receive a merit time allowance not to exceed one-sixth of the minimum period of the indeterminate sentence imposed for an offense other than an A-I felony offense defined in article two hundred twenty of the penal law, or one-third of the minimum period of the indeterminate sentence imposed for an A-I felony offense defined in article two hundred twenty of the penal law, whichever allowance results in the longest unexpired time to run.

(b) A person serving two or more indeterminate sentences which run consecutively may receive a merit time allowance not to exceed the amount of one-third of the minimum or aggregate minimum period of the sentences imposed for an A-I felony offense defined in article two hundred twenty of the penal law, plus one-sixth of the minimum or aggregate minimum period of the sentences imposed for an offense other than such A-I felony offense.

(c) A person serving two or more determinate sentences for an offense defined in article two hundred twenty or two hundred twenty-one of the penal law which run concurrently may receive a merit time allowance not to exceed one-seventh of the term of the determinate sentence which has the longest unexpired time to run.

(d) A person serving two or more determinate sentences for an offense defined in article two hundred twenty or two hundred twenty-one of the penal law which run consecutively may receive a merit time allowance not to exceed one-seventh of the aggregate term of such determinate sentences.

(e) A person serving one or more indeterminate sentences and one or more determinate sentences for an offense defined in article two hundred twenty or two hundred twenty-one of the penal law which run concurrently may receive a merit time allowance not to exceed one-sixth of the minimum period of the indeterminate sentence imposed for an offense other than an A-I felony offense defined in article two hundred twenty of the penal law, one-third of the minimum period of the indeterminate sentence imposed for an A-I felony offense defined in article two hundred twenty of the penal law, or one-seventh of the term of the determinate sentence, whichever allowance results in the largest unexpired time to run.

(f) A person serving one or more indeterminate sentences and one or more determinate sentences which run consecutively may receive a merit time allowance not to exceed the sum of one-sixth of the minimum or aggregate minimum period of the indeterminate sentence or sentences imposed for an offense other than an A-I felony offense defined in article two hundred twenty of the penal law, one-third of the minimum or aggregate minimum period of the indeterminate sentence or sentences imposed for an A-I felony offense defined in article two hundred twenty of the penal law and one-seventh of the term or aggregate term of the determinate sentence or sentences.

(g) The provisions of this subdivision shall apply to persons in custody serving an indeterminate sentence on the effective date of this subdivision as well as to persons sentenced to an indeterminate sentence on and after the effective date of this subdivision and prior to September first, two thousand five and to persons sentenced to a determinate sentence prior to September first, two thousand eleven for a felony as defined in article two hundred twenty or two hundred twenty-one of the penal law.

2-b. [Repealed Sept 1, 2015] Notwithstanding the foregoing, if a person is serving more than one indeterminate sentence, at least one of which is imposed for a class A-I felony offense defined in article two hundred twenty of the penal law, the authorized merit time allowance granted pursuant to paragraph (d) of subdivision one of this section shall be calculated as follows:

(a) In the event a person is serving two or more indeterminate sentences with different minimum periods which run concurrently, the merit time allowance shall be based upon the sentence with the longest unexpired minimum period. If the sentence with the longest unexpired minimum period was imposed for a class A-I felony, the merit time credit shall be one-third of such sentence's minimum period; if such sentence was imposed for an offense other than a class A-I felony, such merit time credit shall be one-sixth of such sentence's minimum period. Provided, however, that where the minimum period of any other concurrent indeterminate sentence is greater than such reduced minimum period, the minimum period of such other concurrent indeterminate sentence shall also be reduced but only to the extent that the minimum period of such other concurrent sentence, as so reduced, is equal to the reduced minimum period of such sentence with the longest unexpired minimum period to run.

(b) A person serving two or more indeterminate sentences with the same minimum periods which run concurrently, and no concurrent indeterminate sentence with any greater minimum period, shall have the minimum period of each such sentence reduced in the amount of one-third of such minimum period if all such sentences were imposed for a class A-I felony.

(c) A person serving two or more indeterminate sentences that run consecutively shall have the aggregate minimum period of such sentences reduced in the amount of one-third of such aggregate minimum period of the sentences imposed for a class A-I felony, plus one-sixth of such aggregate minimum period of the sentences imposed for an offense other than a class A-I felony.

3. The commissioner of corrections and community supervision shall promulgate rules and regulations for the granting, withholding, forfeiture, cancellation and restoration of allowances authorized by this section in accordance with the criteria herein specified. Such rules and regulations shall include provisions designating the person or committee in each correctional institution delegated to make discretionary determinations with respect to the allowances, the books and records to be kept, and a procedure for review of the institutional determinations by the commissioner.

4. No person shall have the right to demand or require the allowances authorized by this section. The decision of the commissioner of corrections and community supervision as to the granting, withholding, forfeiture, cancellation or restoration of such allowances shall be final and shall not be reviewable if made in accordance with law.

5. Time allowances granted prior to any release to community supervision shall be forfeited and shall not be restored if the released person is returned to an institution under the jurisdiction of the state department of corrections and community supervision for violation of community supervision or by reason of a conviction for a crime committed while on community supervision. A person who is so returned may, however, subsequently receive time allowances against the remaining portion of his or her term, maximum term or aggregate maximum term pursuant to this section and provided such remaining portion of his or her term, maximum term, or aggregate maximum term is more than one year.

6. Upon commencement of an indeterminate or a determinate sentence the provisions of this section shall be furnished to the person serving the sentence and the meaning of same shall be fully explained to him by a person designated by the commissioner to perform such duty.

[Eff Sept 1, 2015, § 803 reads as set out below and its section heading reads as follows: "Good behavior allowances against indeterminate sentences"]

1. (a) Every person confined in an institution of the department or a facility in the department of mental hygiene serving an indeterminate sentence of imprisonment, except a person serving a sentence with a maximum term of life imprisonment, may receive time allowance against the maximum term or period of his sentence not to exceed in the aggregate one-third of the term or period imposed by the court. Such allowances may be granted for good behavior and efficient and willing performance of duties assigned or progress and achievement in an assigned treatment program, and may be withheld, forfeited or canceled in whole or in part for bad behavior, violation of institutional rules or failure to perform properly in the duties or program assigned.

(b), (c) [None]

(d) [Eff Sept 1, 2015]

(i) Except as provided in subparagraph (ii) of this paragraph, every person under the custody of the department or confined in a facility in the department of mental hygiene serving an indeterminate sentence of imprisonment with a minimum period of one year or more or a determinate sentence of imprisonment of one year or more imposed pursuant to section 70.70 or 70.71 of the penal law, may earn a merit time allowance.

(ii) Such merit time allowance shall not be available to any person serving an indeterminate sentence authorized for an A-I felony offense, other than an A-I felony offense defined in article two hundred twenty of the penal law, or any sentence imposed for a violent felony offense as defined in section 70.02 of the penal law, manslaughter in the second degree, vehicular manslaughter in the second degree, vehicular manslaughter in the first degree, criminally negligent homicide, an offense defined in article one hundred thirty of the penal law, incest, or an offense defined in article two hundred sixty-three of the penal law, or aggravated harassment of an employee by an inmate.

(iii) The merit time allowance credit against the minimum period of the indeterminate sentence shall be one-sixth of the minimum period imposed by the court except that such credit shall be one-third of the minimum period imposed by the court for an A-I felony offense defined in article two hundred twenty of the penal law. In the case of such a determinate sentence, in addition to the time allowance credit authorized by paragraph (c) of this subdivision, the merit time allowance credited against the term of the determinate sentence pursuant to this paragraph shall be one-seventh of the term imposed by the court.

(iv) Such merit time allowance may be granted when an inmate successfully participates in the work and treatment program assigned pursuant to section eight hundred five of this article and when such inmate obtains a general equivalency diploma, an alcohol and substance abuse treatment certificate, a vocational trade certificate following at least six months of vocational programming or performs at least four hundred hours of service as part of a community work crew.

Such allowance shall be withheld for any serious disciplinary infraction or upon a judicial determination that the person, while an inmate, commenced or continued a civil action, proceeding or claim that was found to be frivolous as defined in subdivision (c) of section eight thousand three hundred three-a of the civil practice law and rules, or an order of a federal court pursuant to rule 11 of the federal rules of civil procedure imposing sanctions in an action commenced by a person, while an inmate, against a state agency, officer or employee.

(v) The provisions of this paragraph shall apply to persons in custody serving an indeterminate sentence on the effective date of this paragraph as well as to persons sentenced to an indeterminate sentence on and after the effective date of this paragraph and prior to September first, two thousand five and to persons sentenced to a determinate sentence prior to September first, two thousand eleven for a felony as defined in article two hundred twenty or two hundred twenty-one of the penal law.

1-a. [Eff Sept 1, 2015] A person serving a determinate sentence imposed pursuant to section 70.70 or 70.71 of the penal law may receive a time allowance against the term of his or her sentence not to exceed one-seventh of the term imposed by the court.

2. If a person is serving more than one sentence, the authorized allowances may be granted separately against the maximum term of each sentence or, where consecutive sentences are involved, against the aggregate maximum term. In no case, however, shall the total of all allowances granted to any such person under this section exceed one-third of the time he would

be required to serve, computed without regard to this section.

2-a. [Eff Sept 1, 2015] If a person is serving more than one sentence, the authorized merit time allowances may be granted against the period or aggregate minimum period of the indeterminate sentence or sentences, or against the term or aggregate term of the determinate sentence or sentences, or where consecutive determinate and indeterminate sentences are involved, against the aggregate minimum period as calculated pursuant to subparagraph (iv) of paragraph (a) of subdivision one of section 70.40 of the penal law. Such allowances shall be calculated as follows:

(a) A person serving two or more indeterminate sentences which run concurrently may receive a merit time allowance not to exceed one-sixth of the minimum period of the indeterminate sentence imposed for an offense other than an A-I felony offense defined in article two hundred twenty of the penal law, or one-third of the minimum period of the indeterminate sentence imposed for an A-I felony offense defined in article two hundred twenty of the penal law, whichever allowance results in the longest unexpired time to run.

(b) A person serving two or more indeterminate sentences which run consecutively may receive a merit time allowance not to exceed the amount of one-third of the minimum or aggregate minimum period of the sentences imposed for an A-I felony offense defined in article two hundred twenty of the penal law, plus one-sixth of the minimum or aggregate minimum period of the sentences imposed for an offense other than such A-I felony offense.

(c) A person serving two or more determinate sentences for an offense defined in article two hundred twenty or two hundred twenty-one of the penal law which run concurrently may receive a merit time allowance not to exceed one-seventh of the term of the determinate sentence which has the longest unexpired time to run.

(d) A person serving two or more determinate sentences for an offense defined in article two hundred twenty or two hundred twenty-one of the penal law which run consecutively may receive a merit time allowance not to exceed one-seventh of the aggregate term of such determinate sentences.

(e) A person serving one or more indeterminate sentences and one or more determinate sentences for an offense defined in article two hundred twenty or two hundred twenty-one of the penal law which run concurrently may receive a merit time allowance not to exceed one-sixth of the minimum period of the indeterminate sentence imposed for an offense other than an A-I felony offense defined in article two hundred twenty of the penal law, one-third of the minimum period of the indeterminate sentence imposed for an A-I felony offense defined in article two hundred twenty of the penal law, or one-seventh of the term of the determinate sentence, whichever allowance results in the largest unexpired time to run.

(f) A person serving one or more indeterminate sentences and one or more determinate sentences which run consecutively may receive a merit time allowance not to exceed the sum of one-sixth of the minimum or aggregate minimum period of the indeterminate sentence or sentences imposed for an offense other than an A-I felony offense defined in article two hundred twenty of the penal law, one-third of the minimum or aggregate minimum period of the indeterminate sentence or sentences imposed for an A-I felony offense defined in article two hundred twenty of the penal law and one-seventh of the term or aggregate term of the determinate sentence or sentences.

(g) The provisions of this subdivision shall apply to persons in custody serving an indeterminate sentence on the effective date of this subdivision as well as to persons sentenced to an indeterminate sentence on and after the effective date of this subdivision and prior to

September first, two thousand five and to persons sentenced to a determinate sentence prior to September first, two thousand eleven for a felony as defined in article two hundred twenty or two hundred twenty-one of the penal law.

3. The commissioner of corrections and community supervision shall promulgate rules and regulations for the granting, withholding, forfeiture, cancellation and restoration of allowances authorized by this section in accordance with the criteria herein specified. Such rules and regulations shall include provisions designating the person or committee in each correctional institution delegated to make discretionary determinations with respect to the allowances, the books and records to be kept, and a procedure for review of the institutional determinations by the commissioner.

4. No person shall have the right to demand or require the allowances authorized by this section. The decision of the commissioner of corrections and community supervision as to the granting, withholding, forfeiture, cancellation or restoration of such allowances shall be final and shall not be reviewable if made in accordance with law.

5. Time allowances granted prior to any release to community supervision shall be forfeited and shall not be restored if the released person is returned to an institution under the jurisdiction of the state department of corrections and community supervision for violation of community supervision or by reason of a conviction for a crime committed while on community supervision. A person who is so returned may, however, subsequently receive time allowances against the remaining portion of his maximum or aggregate maximum term or period not to exceed in the aggregate one-third of such portion provided such remaining portion of his or her maximum or aggregate maximum term or period is more than one year.

6. Upon commencement of an indeterminate sentence the provisions of this section shall be furnished to the person serving the sentence and the meaning of same shall be fully explained to him by a person designated by the commissioner to perform such duty.

HISTORY: [First setout of section] add, L 1967, ch 680, § 147; amd, L 1969, ch 270, § 2, L 1974, ch 653, § 5, L 1975, ch 148, § 3, L 1976, ch 766; L 1987, ch 126, § 1, L 1995, ch 3, § 27, eff Oct 1, 1995, repealed Sept 1, 2015, L 1997, ch 435, §§ 43, 44; amd, L 2003, ch 62, §§ 1, 2 (Part E), L 2003, ch 62, § 3 (Part E), eff May 15, 2003, deemed eff on and after April 1, 2003 and repealed Sept 1, 2015, L 2004, ch 553, § 1, L 2004, ch 738, §§ 7, 9, eff Dec 14, 2004, expires and repealed Sept 1, 2015, L 2011, ch 62, § 37 (Part C, Subpart B), eff March 31, 2011. [Second setout of section] add, L 1967, ch 680, § 147; amd, L 1969, ch 270, § 2, L 1974, ch 653, § 5, eff May 30, 1974, L 1975, ch 148, § 3, L 1976, ch 766, L 1987, ch 126, § 1, eff June 15, 1987, L 2004, ch 738, §§ 10-a, 11, eff Sept 1, 2015, L 2011, ch 62, § 38 (Part C, Subpart B), eff Sept 1, 2015.

§ 803-a. Certain calculations

Notwithstanding the provisions of any other law, no merit time allowance accrued, earned or credited to any person, pursuant to any existing or former section eight hundred three of this article, while in the custody of the commissioner, shall be withdrawn, cancelled, forfeited or otherwise lost by virtue of the sunset or expiration of any provision of law.

HISTORY: Add, L 2004, ch 738, § 11-a, eff Dec 14, 2004.

§ 803-b. Limited credit time allowances for inmates serving indeterminate or determinate sentences imposed for specified offenses

1. Definitions. As used in this section the following terms shall have the following meanings:

(a) "eligible offender" means a person under the custody of the department or confined in a facility in the department of mental hygiene, other than a person who is subject to a sentence imposed for murder in the first degree as defined in section 125.27 of the penal law, an offense

Corr. L.

defined in article one hundred thirty of such law, or an attempt or a conspiracy to commit any such offense, who is otherwise subject to:

(i) an indeterminate sentence imposed for any class A-I felony offense other than criminal possession of a controlled substance in the first degree as defined in section 220.21 of the penal law or criminal sale of a controlled substance in the first degree as defined in section 220.43 of such law or an attempt or a conspiracy to commit such controlled substance offense; or

(ii) an indeterminate or determinate sentence imposed for an offense listed in subdivision one of section 70.02 of the penal law; or

(iii) an indeterminate or determinate sentence imposed for an offense defined in article one hundred twenty-five of the penal law.

(b) "limited credit time benefit" means:

(i) in the case of an eligible offender who is subject to an indeterminate sentence with a maximum term of life imprisonment, such offender shall be eligible for release six months before the completion of the controlling minimum period of imprisonment as defined by subdivision one of section 70.40 of the penal law; or

(ii) (A) in the case of an eligible offender who is not subject to an indeterminate sentence with a maximum term of life imprisonment, such offender shall be eligible for conditional release six months earlier than as provided by paragraph (b) of subdivision one of section 70.40 of the penal law, provided that the department determines such offender has earned the full amount of good time authorized by section eight hundred three of this article; the withholding of any good behavior time credit by the department shall render an inmate ineligible for the credit defined herein;

(B) in the event the limited credit time benefit defined herein causes such conditional release date to precede the parole eligibility date as calculated pursuant to subdivision one of section 70.40 of the penal law, a limited credit time benefit shall also be applied to the parole eligibility date, but only to the extent necessary to cause such parole eligibility date to be the same date as the conditional release date;

(C) an inmate shall not be eligible for the credit defined herein if he or she is returned to the department pursuant to a revocation of presumptive release, parole, conditional release, or post-release supervision and has not been sentenced to an additional indeterminate or determinate term of imprisonment.

(iii) Regardless of the number of sentences to which an eligible offender is subject, the limited credit time benefit authorized pursuant to this section shall be limited to a single six-month credit applied to such person's parole eligibility date pursuant to subparagraph (i) of this paragraph or to such person's conditional release date pursuant to subparagraph (ii) of this paragraph. Except as provided in clause (B) of subparagraph (ii) of this paragraph, the limited credit time benefit authorized pursuant to this section shall not be applied to an eligible offender's parole eligibility date and conditional release date.

(c) "significant programmatic accomplishment" means that the inmate:

(i) participates in no less than two years of college programming; or

(ii) obtains a masters of professional studies degree; or

(iii) successfully participates as an inmate program associate for no less than two years; or

(iv) receives a certification from the state department of labor for his or her successful participation in an apprenticeship program; or

(v) successfully works as an inmate hospice aid for a period of no less than two years; or

(vi) successfully works in the division of correctional industries' optical program for no less than two years and receives a certification as an optician from the American board of opticianry; or

(vii) receives an asbestos handling certificate from the department of labor upon successful completion of the training program and then works in the division of correctional industries' asbestos abatement program as a hazardous materials removal worker or group leader for no less than eighteen months; or

(viii) successfully completes the course curriculum and passes the minimum competency screening process performance examination for sign language interpreter, and then works as a sign language interpreter for deaf inmates for no less than one year; or

(ix) successfully works in the puppies behind bars program for a period of no less than two years.

(d) "serious disciplinary infraction" or "overall poor institutional record" shall be defined in regulations promulgated by the commissioner and need not be the same as the regulations promulgated for the meaning of serious disciplinary infraction pursuant to paragraph (d) of subdivision one of section eight hundred three of this article.

(e) "disqualifying judicial determination" means a judicial determination that the person, while an inmate, commenced or continued a civil action or proceeding or claim that was found to be frivolous as defined in subdivision (c) of section eight thousand three hundred three-a of the civil practice law and rules, or an order of a federal court pursuant to rule 11 of the federal rules of civil procedure imposing sanctions in an action commenced by a person while an inmate against a state agency, officer or employee.

2. Every eligible offender under the custody of the department or confined in a facility in the department of mental hygiene may earn a limited credit time allowance if such offender successfully participates in the work and treatment program assigned pursuant to section eight hundred five of this article and:

(a) successfully completes one or more significant programmatic accomplishments; and

(b) has not committed a serious disciplinary infraction or maintained an overall negative institutional record as defined in rules and regulations promulgated by the commissioner; and

(c) has not received a disqualifying judicial determination.

3. No person shall have the right to demand or require the credit authorized by this section. The commissioner may revoke at any time such credit for any disciplinary infraction committed by the inmate or for any failure to continue to participate successfully in any assigned work and treatment program after the certificate of earned eligibility has been awarded. Any action by the commissioner pursuant to this section shall be deemed a judicial function and shall not be reviewable if done in accordance with law.

Corr. L.

HISTORY: Add, L 2009, ch 56, § 4 (Part L), eff April 7, 2009; amd, L 2010, ch 412, § 1, eff Aug 13, 2010.

§ 804. Good behavior allowances against definite sentences

1. Every person confined in an institution serving a definite sentence of imprisonment may receive time allowances as discretionary reductions of the term of his sentence not to exceed in the aggregate one-third of the term imposed by the court. Such allowances may be granted for good behavior and efficient and willing performance of duties assigned or progress and achievement in an assigned treatment program, and may be withheld, forfeited or cancelled in whole or in part for bad behavior, violation of institutional rules or failure to perform properly in the duties or program assigned.

2. If a person is serving more than one sentence, the authorized allowances may be granted separately against the term of each sentence or, where consecutive sentences are involved, against the aggregate term. Allowances based upon sentences of less than one month may be granted, and in such case the maximum allowance shall be one day for every three days of the sentence. In no case, however, shall the total of all allowances granted to any such person exceed one-third of the time he would be required to serve, computed without regard to this section.

3. No person shall have the right to demand or require the allowances authorized by this section. The decision of the sheriff, superintendent, warden or other person in charge of the institution, or where such institution is under the jurisdiction of a county or city department the decision of the head of such department, as to the granting, withholding, forfeiture, cancellation or restoration of such allowances shall be final and shall not be reviewable if made in accordance with law.

4. A person who has earned a reduction of sentence pursuant to this section and who has been conditionally released under subdivision two of section 70.40 of the penal law shall not forfeit such reduction by reason of conduct causing his return to the institution. Provided, nevertheless, that such reduction may be forfeited by reason of subsequent conduct while serving the remainder of his term.

5. The state commission of correction shall promulgate record keeping rules and regulations for the granting, withholding, forfeiture, cancellation and restoration of allowances authorized by this section.

6. Notwithstanding anything to the contrary in this section, in any case where a person is serving a definite sentence in an institution under the jurisdiction of the state department of corrections and community supervision, subdivisions three and four of section eight hundred three of this chapter shall apply.

7. Upon commencement of any definite sentence the provisions of this section shall be furnished to the person serving the sentence and the meaning of same shall be fully explained to him by an officer designated in the regulation to perform such duty.

HISTORY: Add, L 1967, ch 680, § 147, eff Sept 1, 1967; amd, L 1976, ch 145, eff July 1, 1976, L 2011, ch 62, § 39 (Part C, Subpart B), eff March 31, 2011.

§ 804-a. Good behavior allowances for certain civil commitments

1. Every person confined in an institution serving a civil commitment for a fixed period of time, whose release is not conditional upon any act within his power to perform, may receive time allowances as discretionary reductions of the term of his commitment not to exceed, in the aggregate, one-third of the term imposed by the court. Such allowances may be granted for good behavior and efficient and willing performance of duties assigned or progress and achievement in

an assigned treatment program, and may be withheld, forfeited or cancelled in whole or in part for bad behavior, violation of institutional rules or failure to perform properly in the duties or program assigned.

2. Allowances based upon commitments of less than one month may be granted, and in such case the maximum allowances shall be one day for every three days of the commitment. In no case, however, shall the total of all allowances granted to any such person exceed one-third of the time he would be required to serve, computed without regard to this section.

3. No person shall have the right to demand or require the allowances authorized by this section. The decision of the sheriff, superintendent, warden or other person in charge of the institution, or where such institution is under the jurisdiction of a county or city department the decision of the head of such department, as to the granting, withholding, forfeiture, cancellation, or restoration of such allowances shall be final and shall not be reviewable if made in accordance with law.

4. The state commission of correction shall promulgate record keeping rules and regulations for the granting, withholding, forfeiture, cancellation and restoration of allowances authorized by this section.

5. Upon commencement of any civil commitment as described in subdivision one of this section, the provisions of this section shall be furnished to the person serving the commitment and the meaning of same shall be fully explained to him by an officer designated in the regulation to perform such duty.

HISTORY: Add, L 1987, ch 220, § 1, eff Sept 5, 1987.

§ 805. [Repealed Sept 1, 2015] Earned eligibility program

Persons committed to the custody of the department under an indeterminate or determinate sentence of imprisonment shall be assigned a work and treatment program as soon as practicable. No earlier than two months prior to the inmate's eligibility to be paroled pursuant to subdivision one of section 70.40 of the penal law, the commissioner shall review the inmate's institutional record to determine whether he has complied with the assigned program. If the commissioner determines that the inmate has successfully participated in the program he may issue the inmate a certificate of earned eligibility. Notwithstanding any other provision of law, an inmate who is serving a sentence with a minimum term of not more than eight years and who has been issued a certificate of earned eligibility, shall be granted parole release at the expiration of his minimum term or as authorized by subdivision four of section eight hundred sixty-seven of this chapter unless the board of parole determines that there is a reasonable probability that, if such inmate is released, he will not live and remain at liberty without violating the law and that his release is not compatible with the welfare of society. Any action by the commissioner pursuant to this section shall be deemed a judicial function and shall not be reviewable if done in accordance with law.

HISTORY: Add, L 1987, ch 261, § 13, expires Sept 1, 2015; amd, L 1987, ch 262, § 2, expires Sept 1, 2015, L 1995, ch 3, § 28, repealed Sept 1, 2015, L 2003, ch 62, § 4 (Part E), eff May 15, 2003, deemed eff on and after April 1, 2003. Former § 805, add, L 1967, ch 680, § 147; amd, L 1969, ch 270; renumbered § 212, L 1970, ch 476, § 43, eff July 7, 1970.

§ 806. [Repealed Sept 1, 2015] Presumptive release program for nonviolent inmates

1. Notwithstanding any other provision of law to the contrary and except as provided in subdivision two of this section, an inmate who has been awarded a certificate of earned eligibility by the commissioner as set forth in section eight hundred five of this article may be entitled to presumptive release at the expiration of the minimum or aggregate minimum period of his or her indeterminate term of imprisonment, provided that:

(i) the inmate has not been convicted previously of, nor is presently serving a sentence imposed for a class A-I felony, a violent felony offense as defined in section 70.02 of the penal law, manslaughter in the second degree, vehicular manslaughter in the second degree, vehicular manslaughter in the first degree, criminally negligent homicide, an offense defined in article one hundred thirty of the penal law, incest, or an offense defined in article two hundred sixty-three of the penal law,

(ii) the inmate has not committed any serious disciplinary infraction, and

(iii) there has been no judicial determination that the person while an inmate commenced or continued a civil action, proceeding or claim that was found to be frivolous as defined in subdivision (c) of section eight thousand three hundred three-a of the civil practice law and rules, or an order has not been issued by a federal court pursuant to rule 11 of the federal rules of civil procedure imposing sanctions in an action commenced by the inmate against a state agency, officer or employee.

2. In the case of an inmate who meets the criteria set forth in subdivision one of this section and who also meets the criteria for merit time as provided for in paragraph (d) of subdivision one of section eight hundred three of this article, such inmate may be entitled to presumptive release, as provided in this section, at the expiration of five-sixths of the minimum or aggregate minimum period of his or her indeterminate term of imprisonment.

3. Any inmate eligible for presumptive release pursuant to this section shall be required to apply for such release pursuant to section two hundred six of this chapter.

4. The commissioner shall promulgate rules and regulations for the granting, withholding, cancellation and recission of presumptive release authorized by this section in accordance with law.

5. No person shall have the right to demand or require presumptive release authorized by this section. The commissioner may revoke at any time an inmate's scheduled presumptive release pursuant to this section for any disciplinary infraction committed by the inmate or for any failure to continue to participate successfully in any assigned work and treatment program after the certificate of earned eligibility has been awarded. The commissioner may deny presumptive release to any inmate whenever the commissioner determines that such release may not be consistent with the safety of the community or the welfare of the inmate. Any action by the commissioner pursuant to this section shall be deemed a judicial function and shall not be reviewable if done in accordance with law.

6. Any eligible inmate who is not released pursuant to subdivision one or two of this section shall be considered for discretionary release on parole pursuant to the provisions of section eight hundred five of this article or section two hundred fifty-nine-i of the executive law, whichever is applicable.

7. Any reference to parole and conditional release in this chapter shall also be deemed to include presumptive release.

HISTORY: Add, L 2003, ch 62, § 5 (Part E), eff May 15, 2003, deemed eff on and after April 1, 2003, repealed Sept 1, 2015; amd, L 2011, ch 62, § 40 (Part C, Subpart B), eff March 31, 2011, L 2012, ch 45, § 2, eff May 31, 2012.

*   *   *

**ARTICLE 26   [UNTIL SEPT 1, 2015] TEMPORARY RELEASE PROGRAMS
FOR STATE CORRECTIONAL INSTITUTIONS
[EFF SEPT 1, 2015] WORK RELEASE PROGRAMS FOR STATE
CORRECTIONAL INSTITUTIONS**

HISTORY: Add, L 1969, ch 472, eff Jan 1, 1970. Article heading, amd, L 1972, ch 339, § 2, eff June 21, 1972, expires Sept 1, 2015.

§ 851. [Expires Sept 1, 2015] Definitions

[Until Sept 1, 2015, § 851 reads as set out below]

As used in this article the following terms have the following meanings:

1. "Institution" means any institution under the jurisdiction of the state department of corrections and community supervision or an institution designated by the commissioner pursuant to section seventy-two-a of this chapter.

2. [As amended L 2005, ch 252, § 1 and L 2006, ch 320, § 9] "Eligible inmate" means: a person confined in an institution who is eligible for release on parole or who will become eligible for release on parole or conditional release within two years. Provided, however, that a person under sentence for an offense defined in paragraphs (a) and (b) of subdivision one of section 70.02 of the penal law, where such offense involved the use or threatened use of a deadly weapon or dangerous instrument shall not be eligible to participate in a work release program until he or she is eligible for release on parole or who will be eligible for release on parole or conditional release within eighteen months. Provided, further, however, that a person under a determinate sentence as a second felony drug offender for a class B felony offense defined in article two hundred twenty of the penal law, who was sentenced pursuant to section 70.70 of such law, shall not be eligible to participate in a temporary release program until the time served under imprisonment for his or her determinate sentence, including any jail time credited pursuant to the provisions of article seventy of the penal law, shall be at least eighteen months. In the case of a person serving an indeterminate sentence of imprisonment imposed pursuant to the penal law in effect after September one, nineteen hundred sixty-seven, for the purposes of this article parole eligibility shall be upon the expiration of the minimum period of imprisonment fixed by the court or where the court has not fixed any period, after service of the minimum period fixed by the state board of parole. If an inmate is denied release on parole, such inmate shall not be deemed an eligible inmate until he or she is within two years of his or her next scheduled appearance before the state parole board. In any case where an inmate is denied release on parole while participating in a temporary release program, the department shall review the status of the inmate to determine if continued placement in the program is appropriate. No person convicted of any escape or absconding offense defined in article two hundred five of the penal law shall be eligible for temporary release. Further, no person under

sentence for aggravated harassment of an employee by an inmate as defined in section 240.32 of the penal law for, any homicide offense defined in article one hundred twenty-five of the penal law, for any sex offense defined in article one hundred thirty of the penal law, or for an offense defined in section 255.25, 255.26 or 255.27 of the penal law shall be eligible to participate in a work release program as defined in subdivision three of this section. Nor shall any person under sentence for any sex offense defined in article one hundred thirty of the penal law be eligible to participate in a community services program as defined in subdivision five of this section. Notwithstanding the foregoing, no person who is an otherwise eligible inmate who is under sentence for a crime involving: (a) infliction of serious physical injury upon another as defined in the penal law or (b) any other offense involving the use or threatened use of a deadly weapon may participate in a temporary release program without the written approval of the commissioner. The commissioner shall promulgate regulations giving direction to the temporary release committee at each institution in order to aid such committees in carrying out this mandate.

The governor, by executive order, may exclude or limit the participation of any class of otherwise eligible inmates from participation in a temporary release program. Nothing in this paragraph shall be construed to affect either the validity of any executive order previously issued limiting the participation of otherwise eligible inmates in such program or the authority of the commissioner to impose appropriate regulations limiting such participation.

2-a. Notwithstanding subdivision two of this section, the term "eligible inmate" shall also include a person confined in an institution who is eligible for release on parole or who will become eligible for release on parole or conditional release within two years, and who was convicted of a homicide offense as defined in article one hundred twenty-five of the penal law or an assault offense defined in article one hundred twenty of the penal law, and who can demonstrate to the commissioner that: (a) the victim of such homicide or assault was a member of the inmate's immediate family as that term is defined in section 120.40 of the penal law or had a child in common with the inmate; (b) the inmate was subjected to substantial physical, sexual or psychological abuse committed by the victim of such homicide or assault; and (c) such abuse was a substantial factor in causing the inmate to commit such homicide or assault. With respect to an inmate's claim that he or she was subjected to substantial physical, sexual or psychological abuse committed by the victim, such demonstration shall include corroborative material that may include, but is not limited to, witness statements, social services records, hospital records, law enforcement records and a showing based in part on documentation prepared at or near the time of the commission of the offense or the prosecution thereof tending to support the inmate's claim. Prior to making a determination under this subdivision, the commissioner is required to request and take into consideration the opinion of the district attorney who prosecuted the underlying homicide or assault offense and the opinion of the sentencing court. If such opinions are received within forty-five days of the request, the commissioner shall take them into consideration. If such opinions are not so received, the commissioner may proceed with the determination. Any action by the commissioner pursuant to this subdivision shall be deemed a judicial function and shall not be reviewable in any court.

2-b. When calculating in advance the date on which a person is or will be eligible for release on parole or conditional release, for purposes of determining eligibility for temporary release or for placement at an alcohol and substance abuse treatment correctional annex, the commissioner shall consider and include credit for all potential credits and reductions including but not limited to merit time and good behavior allowances. Nothing in this subdivision shall be interpreted as precluding the consideration and inclusion of credit for all potential credits and reductions including, but not limited to, merit time and good behavior allowances when calculating in advance for any other purpose the date on which a person is or will be eligible for release on parole or conditional release.

3. "Work release program" means a program under which eligible inmates may be granted the privilege of leaving the premises of an institution for a period not exceeding fourteen hours in any day for the purpose of on-the-job training or employment, or for any matter necessary to the furtherance of any such purposes. No person shall be released into a work release program unless prior to release such person has a reasonable assurance of a job training program or employment. If after release, such person ceases to be employed or ceases to participate in the training program, the inmate's privilege to participate in such work release program may be revoked in accordance with rules and regulations promulgated by the commissioner.

4. "Furlough program" means a program under which eligible inmates may be granted the privilege of leaving the premises of an institution for a period not exceeding seven days for the purpose of seeking employment, maintaining family ties, solving family problems, seeking post-release housing, attending a short-term educational or vocational training course, or for any matter necessary to the furtherance of any such purposes.

5. "Community services program" means a program under which eligible inmates may be granted the privilege of leaving the premises of an institution for a period not exceeding fourteen hours in any day for the purpose of participation in religious services, volunteer work, or athletic events, or for any matter necessary to the furtherance of any such purposes.

6. "Leave of absence" means a privilege granted to an inmate, who need not be an "eligible inmate," to leave the premises of an institution for the period of time necessary:

(a) to visit his or her spouse, child, brother, sister, grandchild, parent, grandparent or ancestral aunt or uncle during his or her last illness if death appears to be imminent;

(b) to attend the funeral of such individual;

(c) to undergo surgery or to receive medical or dental treatment not available in the correctional institution only if deemed absolutely necessary to the health and well-being of the inmate and whose approval is granted by the commissioner or his designated representative.

7. "Educational leave" means a privilege granted to an eligible inmate to leave the premises of an institution for a period not exceeding fourteen hours in any day for the purpose of education or vocational training, or for any matter necessary to the furtherance of any such purposes.

8. "Industrial training leave" means a privilege granted to an eligible inmate to leave the premises of an institution for a period not exceeding fourteen hours in any day for the purpose of participating in an industrial training program, or for any matter necessary to the furtherance of any such purpose.

9. "Temporary release program" means a "work release program," a "furlough program," a "community services program," an "industrial training leave," an "educational leave," or a "leave of absence."

10. "Extended bounds of confinement" means the area in which an inmate participating in a temporary release program may travel, the routes he or she is permitted to use, the places he or she is authorized to visit, and the hours, days, or specially defined period during which he

or she is permitted to be absent from the premises of the institution.

11. "Temporary release committee" means the body of persons, which may include members of the public, appointed pursuant to regulations promulgated by the commissioner to serve at the pleasure of the commissioner for the purpose of formulating, modifying and revoking temporary release programs at an institution.

12. "Superintendent" means the person in charge of an institution, by whatever title he or she may be known.

[Eff Sept 1, 2015 and until the expiration of L 1972, Ch 339 § 10, L 1986, ch 554, § 3 and L 1994, ch 60, § 42, § 851 reads as set out below]

As used in this article the following terms have the following meanings:

1. "Institution" means any institution under the jurisdiction of the state department of corrections and community supervision.

2. [As amended L 2005, ch 252, § 2] "Eligible inmate" means: a person confined in an institution who is eligible for release on parole or who will become eligible for release on parole or conditional release within two years. Provided, that a person under a determinate sentence as a second felony drug offender for a class B felony offense defined in article two hundred twenty of the penal law, who was sentenced pursuant to section 70.70 of such law, shall not be eligible to participate in a temporary release program until the time served under imprisonment for his or her determinate sentence, including any jail time credited pursuant to the provisions of article seventy of the penal law, shall be at least eighteen months. In the case of a person serving an indeterminate sentence of imprisonment imposed pursuant to the penal law in effect after September one, nineteen hundred sixty-seven, for the purposes of this article parole eligibility shall be upon the expiration of the minimum period of imprisonment fixed by the court or where the court has not fixed any period, after service of the minimum period fixed by the state board of parole. If an inmate is denied release on parole, such inmate shall not be deemed an eligible inmate until he or she is within two years of his or her next scheduled appearance before the state parole board. In any case where an inmate is denied release on parole while participating in a temporary release program, the department shall review the status of the inmate to determine if continued placement in the program is appropriate. No person convicted of any escape or absconding offense defined in article two hundred five of the penal law shall be eligible for temporary release. Nor shall any person under sentence for any sex offense defined in article one hundred thirty of the penal law be eligible to participate in a community services program as defined in subdivision five of this section. Notwithstanding the foregoing, no person who is an otherwise eligible inmate who is under sentence for a crime involving: (a) infliction of serious physical injury upon another as defined in the penal law, (b) a sex offense involving forcible compulsion, or (c) any other offense involving the use or threatened use of a deadly weapon may participate in a temporary release program without the written approval of the commissioner. The commissioner shall promulgate regulations giving direction to the temporary release committee at each institution in order to aid such committees in carrying out this mandate.

The governor, by executive order, may exclude or limit the participation of any class of otherwise eligible inmates from participation in a temporary release program. Nothing in this paragraph shall be construed to affect either the validity of any executive order previously issued limiting the participation of otherwise eligible inmates in such program or the authority of the commissioner to impose appropriate regulations limiting such participation.

2-a. Notwithstanding subdivision two of this section, the term "eligible inmate" shall also include a person confined in an institution who is eligible for release on parole or who will become eligible for release on parole or conditional release within two years, and who was convicted of a homicide offense as defined in article one hundred twenty-five of the penal law or an assault offense defined in article one hundred twenty of the penal law, and who can demonstrate to the commissioner that: (a) the victim of such homicide or assault was a member of the inmate's immediate family as that term is defined in section 120.40 of the penal law or had a child in common with the inmate; (b) the inmate was subjected to substantial physical, sexual or psychological abuse committed by the victim of such homicide or assault; and (c) such abuse was a substantial factor in causing the inmate to commit such homicide or assault. With respect to an inmate's claim that he or she was subjected to substantial physical, sexual or psychological abuse committed by the victim, such demonstration shall include corroborative material that may include, but is not limited to, witness statements, social services records, hospital records, law enforcement records and a showing based in part on documentation prepared at or near the time of the commission of the offense or the prosecution thereof tending to support the inmate's claim. Prior to making a determination under this subdivision, the commissioner is required to request and take into consideration the opinion of the district attorney who prosecuted the underlying homicide or assault offense and the opinion of the sentencing court. If such opinions are received within forty-five days of the request, the commissioner shall take them into consideration. If such opinions are not so received, the commissioner may proceed with the determination. Any action by the commissioner pursuant to this subdivision shall be deemed a judicial function and shall not be reviewable in any court.

2-b. When calculating in advance the date on which a person is or will be eligible for release on parole or conditional release, for purposes of determining eligibility for temporary release or for placement at an alcohol and substance abuse treatment correctional annex, the commissioner shall consider and include credit for all potential credits and reductions including but not limited to merit time and good behavior allowances. Nothing in this subdivision shall be interpreted as precluding the consideration and inclusion of credit for all potential credits and reductions including, but not limited to, merit time and good behavior allowances when calculating in advance for any other purpose the date on which a person is or will be eligible for release on parole or conditional release.

3. "Work release program" means a program under which eligible inmates may be granted the privilege of leaving the premises of an institution for a period not exceeding fourteen hours in any day for the purpose of on-the-job training or employment, or for any matter necessary to the furtherance of any such purposes. No person shall be released into a work release program unless prior to release such person has a reasonable assurance of a job training program or employment. If after release, such person ceases to be employed or ceases to participate in the training program, the inmate's privilege to participate in such work release program may be revoked in accordance with rules and regulations promulgated by the commissioner.

4. "Furlough program" means a program under which eligible inmates may be granted the privilege of leaving the premises of an institution for a period not exceeding seven days for the purpose of seeking employment, maintaining family ties, solving family problems, seeking post-release housing, attending a short-term educational or vocational training course, or for any matter necessary to the furtherance of any such purposes.

5. "Community services program" means a program under which eligible inmates may be granted the privilege of leaving the premises of an institution for a period not exceeding fourteen hours in any day for the purpose of participation in religious services, volunteer work,

or athletic events, or for any matter necessary to the furtherance of any such purposes.

6. "Leave of absence" means a privilege granted to an inmate, who need not be an "eligible inmate," to leave the premises of an institution for the period of time necessary:

(a) to visit his or her spouse, child, brother, sister, grandchild, parent, grandparent or ancestral aunt or uncle during his or her last illness if death appears to be imminent;

(b) to attend the funeral of such individual;

(c) to undergo surgery or to receive medical or dental treatment not available in the correctional institution only if deemed absolutely necessary to the health and well-being of the inmate and whose approval is granted by the commissioner or his designated representative.

7. "Educational leave" means a privilege granted to an eligible inmate to leave the premises of an institution for a period not exceeding fourteen hours in any day for the purpose of education or vocational training, or for any matter necessary to the furtherance of any such purposes.

8. "Industrial training leave" means a privilege granted to an eligible inmate to leave the premises of an institution for a period not exceeding fourteen hours in any day for the purpose of participating in an industrial training program, or for any matter necessary to the furtherance of any such purpose.

9. "Temporary release program" means a "work release program," a "furlough program," a "community services program," an "industrial training leave," an "educational leave," or a "leave of absence."

10. "Extended bounds of confinement" means the area in which an inmate participating in a temporary release program may travel, the routes he or she is permitted to use, the places he or she is authorized to visit, and the hours, days, or specially defined period during which he or she is permitted to be absent from the premises of the institution.

11. "Temporary release committee" means the body of persons, which may include members of the public, appointed pursuant to regulations promulgated by the commissioner to serve at the pleasure of the commissioner for the purpose of formulating, modifying and revoking temporary release programs at an institution.

12. "Superintendent" means the person in charge of an institution, by whatever title he or she may be known.

[Effective only upon expiration of L 1972, ch 339, § 10, L 1986, ch 554, § 3, L 1994, ch 60, § 42; § 851 reads as set out below]

As used in this article the following terms have the following meanings:

1. "Institution" means any institution under the jurisdiction of the state department of corrections and community supervision.

2. "Eligible inmate" means a person confined in an institution where a work release program has been established who is eligible for release on parole or who will become eligible for release on parole within one year.

3. "Work release program" means a program under which eligible inmates may be granted the privilege of leaving the premises of an institution for the purpose of education, on-the-job training or employment.

4. "Extended bounds of confinement" means the area in which an inmate participating in a work release program may travel, the routes he is permitted to use, the places he is authorized to visit, and the hours, not exceeding fourteen hours in any day, he is permitted to be absent from the premises of the institution.

5. "Work release committee" means the body of persons, which may include members of the public, appointed pursuant to regulations promulgated by the commissioner for the purpose of formulating, modifying and revoking work release programs at an institution.

6. "Warden" means the person in charge of an institution, by whatever title he may be known.

HISTORY: Add, L 1969, ch 472, § 1; amd, L 1972, ch 339, § 3, expires Sept 1, 2015, L 1973, ch 269, § 2, L 1974, ch 966, § 1, L 1977, ch 691, § 1, eff Sept 1, 1977, L 1983, ch 107, § 1, eff May 17, 1983, L 1983, ch 418, § 5, expired July 31, 1984, L 1986, ch 554, § 3, eff July 24, 1986, expires Sept 1, 2015, L 1987, ch 261, § 14, L 1991, ch 447, § 1, L 1994, ch 60, § 42, expires Sept 1, 2015, L 1994, ch 60, § 43, eff Oct 1, 1995, L 1995, ch 3, § 29, eff June 10, 1995, L 1996, ch 92, § 4, expires Sept 1, 2015, L 2002, ch 251, § 1, eff July 30, 2002, L 2004, ch 738, § 12, eff Jan 13, 2005, L 2004, ch 738, § 13, eff Dec 14, 2004, L 2005, ch 252, § 1, eff July 19, 2005, expires and repealed Sept 1, 2015, L 2005, ch 252, § 2, eff July 19, 2005, L 2006, ch 320, § 9, eff Nov 1, 2006, L 2011, ch 62, §§ 41, 42 (Part C, Subpart B), eff March 31, 2011, L 2011, ch 62, §§ 41-a, 43 (Part C, Subpart B), eff Sept 1, 2015, L 2011, ch 62, §§ 41-b, 43-a (Part C, Subpart B), eff upon expiration of L. 1972, Ch. 339, § 10, L. 1986, Ch. 554, § 3, and L. 1994, Ch. 60, § 42.

§ 852. Establishment of temporary release
[Until Sept 1, 2015, § 852 reads as set out below:]

1. The commissioner, guided by consideration for the safety of the community and the welfare of the inmate, shall review and evaluate all existing rules, regulations and directives relating to current temporary release programs and consistent with the provisions of this article for the administration of temporary release programs shall by January first, nineteen hundred seventy-eight promulgate new rules and regulations for the various forms of temporary release. Such rules and regulations shall reflect the purposes of the different programs and shall include but not be limited to selection criteria, supervision and procedures for the disposition of each application.

2. The commissioner shall appoint or cause to be appointed a temporary release committee for each institution which shall meet on a regularly scheduled basis to review all applications for temporary release.

3. Work release programs may be established only at institutions classified by the commissioner as work release facilities. Educational release programs may be established only at those educational institutions which shall maintain attendance records for participating inmates.

4. The commissioner shall designate in the rules and regulations of the department appropriate employees or an appropriate unit of the department to be responsible for (a) securing education, on-the-job training and employment opportunities for inmates who are eligible to participate in a work release program, and (b) assisting such inmates in such other manner as necessary or desirable to assure the success of the program.

5. All inmates participating in temporary release programs shall be assigned to parole officers for supervision. As part of the parole officer's supervisory functions he or she shall be required to provide reports every two months on each inmate under his or her supervision. Such reports shall include but not be limited to:

(a) an evaluation of the individual's participation in such program;

(b) a statement of any problems and the manner in which such problems were resolved relative to an individual's participation in such programs; and

(c) a recommendation with respect to the individual's continued participation in the program.

6. [Repealed]

[Eff Sept 1, 2015, § 852 reads as set out below:]

§ 852. Establishment of work release

1. The commissioner of correction shall designate one or more institutions for the conduct of work release programs. Upon such designation the commissioner, with the approval of the chairman of the board of parole, shall promulgate rules and regulations consistent with the provisions of this article for the administration of work release programs at any institution designated, and shall appoint or cause to be appointed a work release committee for such institution.

2. The department shall be responsible for securing appropriate education, on-the-job training and employment opportunities for eligible inmates and shall supervise inmates during their participation in work release programs outside the premises of institutions.

> **HISTORY:** Add, L 1969, ch 472; amd, L 1972, ch 339, § 4, expires Sept 1, 2015, L 1977, ch 691, § 2,L 1981, ch 495, § 1, eff Sept 1, 1981, L 2011, ch 62, §§ 44, 44-a (Part C, Subpart B), eff March 31, 2011, L 2011, ch 62, § 45 (Part C, Subpart B), eff Sept 1, 2013.

§ 853. Reporting and information

To ensure the accurate maintenance and availability of statistics and records with respect to participation in temporary release programs, the department shall maintain the following information relative to the operation of temporary release programs:

(a) number of inmate participants in each temporary release program;

(b) number of imates participating in temporary release for whom written approval of the commissioner was required pursuant to subdivision two of section eight hundred fifty-one of this chapter;

(c) number and type of individual programs approved for each participant;

(d) approved participating employers and educational institutions;

(e) number of inmates arrested;

(f) inmates involuntarily returned for violations by institution;

(g) absconders still at large;

(h) number of disciplinary proceedings initiated and the results thereof;

(i) number of temporary release committee decisions appealed and the results thereof by institution;

(j) reports or information made available to the department with respect to the participation of individuals in such programs, including any incidents of absconding or re-arrest.

The department shall also forward to the state commission of correction quarterly reports including, but not limited to, the information identified in subdivisions (a), (b), (d), (e), (f) and (g) of this section and such other information requested by the commission or available to the department with respect to such programs.

> **HISTORY:** Add, L 1977, ch 691, § 3; amd, L 1981, ch 757, § 1, eff July 27, 1981. Former § 853, renumbered § 855, L 1977, ch 691, § 4, eff Sept 1, 1977.

§ 854. Evaluation and recommendation

In recognition of the need for an independent evaluation of, and recommendations with respect to, temporary release, the commission of correction shall evaluate and assess the administration and operation of all temporary release programs conducted pursuant to this article and shall submit to the governor and the legislature by March first, nineteen hundred seventy-eight, its findings together with any recommendations with respect to the proper operation or the improvement of such temporary release programs.

> **HISTORY:** Add, L 1977, ch 691, § 3, eff Sept 1, 1977. Former § 854, renumbered § 856, L 1977, ch 691, § 5, eff Sept 1, 1977.

§ 855. Procedure for temporary release of inmates

[Until Sept 1, 2015, § 855 reads as set out below:]

1. A person confined in an institution designated for the conduct of work release programs who is an eligible inmate, may make application to the work release committee of the institution for permission to participate in a work release program.

2. Any eligible inmate may make application to the temporary release committee for participation in a furlough program or community services program, or for an industrial training leave or educational leave.

3. Any inmate may make application to the temporary release committee for a leave of absence provided, however, that in exigent circumstances such application may be made directly to the superintendent of the institution and the superintendent may exercise all of the powers of the temporary release committee subject, however, to any limitation or requirement set forth in the rules and regulations of the department and subject further to the discretion of the commissioner. All leave of absences provided in exigent circumstances shall state the reasons for approval or disapproval of the application and shall be included in the inmate's institutional parole file.

4. If the temporary release committee determines that a temporary release program for the applicant is consistent with the safety of the community and the welfare of the applicant, and is consistent with rules and regulations of the department, the committee, with the assistance of the employees or unit designated by the commissioner pursuant to subdivision four of section eight hundred fifty-two of this article, shall develop a suitable program of temporary release for the applicant. Consistent with these provisions, any educational leave program shall consider the scheduling of classes to insure a reduction of release time not spent in educational pursuits.

5. The committee shall then prepare a memorandum setting forth the details of the temporary release program including the extended bounds of confinement and any other matter required by rules or regulations of the department. Such memorandum shall be transmitted to the superintendent who may approve or reject the program, subject to rules and regulations promulgated by the commissioner. If the superintendent approves the program, he shall indicate such approval in writing by signing the memorandum. If the superintendent rejects the program, he shall state his reasons in writing and a copy of his statement shall be given to the inmate and to the commissioner and such decision shall be reviewed by the commissioner. If the commissioner rejects the program, he shall state his reasons in writing. A copy of such statement shall be filed in the inmate's institutional file.

6. In order for an applicant to accept a program of temporary release, such inmate shall agree to be bound by all the terms and conditions thereof and shall indicate such agreement by signing the memorandum of the program immediately below a statement reading as follows: "I accept the foregoing program and agree to be bound by the terms and conditions thereof. I understand that I will be under the supervision of the state department of corrections and community supervision while I am away from the premises of the institution and I agree to comply with the instructions

of any parole officer or other employee of the department assigned to supervise me. I understand that my participation in the program is a privilege which may be revoked at any time, and that if I violate any provision of the program I may be taken into custody by any peace officer or police officer and I will be subject to disciplinary procedures. I further understand that if I intentionally fail to return to the institution at or before the time specified in the memorandum I may be found guilty of a felony." Such agreement shall be placed on file at the institution from which such temporary release is granted.

7. After approving the program of temporary release, the superintendent may then permit an inmate who has accepted such program to go outside the premises of the institution within the limits of the extended bounds of confinement described in the memorandum; provided, however, that no such permission shall become effective in the case of a work release or furlough program prior to the time at which the person to be released becomes an eligible inmate.

8. At least three days before releasing an inmate on a temporary release program, the superintendent shall notify in writing the sheriff or chief of police of the community into which the inmate is to be released.

9. Participation in a temporary release program shall be a privilege. Nothing contained in this article may be construed to confer upon any inmate the right to participate, or to continue to participate, in a temporary release program. The superintendent of the institution may at any time, and upon recommendation of the temporary release committee or of the commissioner or of the chairman of the state board of parole or his designee shall, revoke any inmate's privilege to participate in a program of temporary release in accordance with regulations promulgated by the commissioner.

[Eff Sept 1, 2015, § 855 reverts to § 853 and reads as set out below:]

§ 853. Procedure for release of eligible inmates

1. A person confined in an institution designated for the conduct of work release programs who is, or who within ninety days will become, an eligible inmate, may make application to the work release committee of the institution for permission to participate in a work release program.

2. If the work release committee determines that a work release program for the applicant is consistent with the safety of the community, is in the best interests of rehabilitation of the applicant, and is consistent with rules and regulations of the commissioner, the committee shall develop a suitable program of work release for the applicant.

3. The committee shall then prepare a memorandum setting forth the details of the work release program, including the extended bounds of confinement and any other matter required by rules or regulations of the commissioner. Such memorandum shall be transmitted to the warden who may approve or reject the program. If the warden approves the program, he or she shall indicate such approval in writing by signing the memorandum. If the warden rejects the program, such decision shall be reviewed by the commissioner.

4. In order for an applicant to accept a program of work release, he or she shall agree to be bound by all the terms and conditions thereof and shall indicate such agreement by signing the memorandum of the program immediately below a statement reading as follows: "I accept the foregoing program and agree to be bound by the terms and conditions thereof. I understand that I will be under the supervision of the department of corrections and community supervision while I am away from the premises of the institution and I agree to comply with the instructions of any parole officer assigned to supervise me. I will carry a copy of this memorandum on my person at all times while I am away from the premises of the institution and I will exhibit it to any peace

officer upon his or her request. I understand that my participation in the program is a privilege which may be revoked at any time, and that if I violate any provision of the program I may be taken into custody by any peace officer and I will be subject to disciplinary procedures. I further understand that if I intentionally fail to return to the institution at or before the time specified in the memorandum I may be found guilty of a felony."

5. After approving the program of work release, the warden may then permit an eligible inmate who has accepted such program to go outside the premises of the institution within the limits of the extended bounds of confinement described in the memorandum.

6. Participation in a work release program shall be a privilege. Nothing contained in this article may be construed to confer upon any inmate the right to participate, or to continue to participate, in a work release program. The warden of the institution may at any time, and upon recommendation of the work release committee or of the chairman of the state board of parole or his designee shall, revoke any inmate's privilege to participate in a program of work release.

HISTORY: Formerly § 853, add, L 1969, ch 472; amd, L 1972, ch 339, § 5, expires Sept 1, 2015, L 1974, ch 966, § 2, eff June 13, 1974; renumbered § 855 and amd, L 1977, ch 691, § 4, eff Sept 1, 1977; amd, L 1980, ch 843, § 202, eff Sept 1, 1980, L 2011, ch 62, § 47 (Part C, Subpart B), eff March 31, 2011, L 2011, ch 62, § 48 (Part C, Subpart B), eff Sept 1, 2013.

§ 856. Conduct of inmates participating in a temporary release program
[Until Sept 1, 2015, § 856 reads as set out below:]

1. An inmate who is permitted to leave the premises of an institution to participate in a temporary release program shall have on his or her person a card identifying him or her as a participant in a temporary release program as signed by the superintendent of the institution at all times while outside the premises of the institution and shall exhibit such card to any peace officer or police officer upon request of such officer. The commissioner may, by regulation, require such information, including effective dates, to be included in such card as he shall deem necessary and proper.

2. If the inmate violates any provision of the program, or any rule or regulation promulgated by the commissioner for conduct of inmates participating in temporary release programs, such inmate shall be subject to disciplinary measures to the same extent as if he or she violated a rule or regulation of the commissioner for conduct of inmates within the premises of the institution. The failure of an inmate to voluntarily return to the institution of his confinement more than ten hours after his prescribed time of return shall create a rebuttable presumption that the failure to return was intentional. Any inmate who is found to have intentionally failed to return pursuant to this subdivision shall be an absconder in violation of his temporary release program and will not be an eligible inmate as defined in subdivision two of section eight hundred fifty-one of this chapter. The creation of such rebuttable presumption shall not be admissible in any court of law as evidence of the commission of any crime defined in the penal law. A full report of any such violation, a summary of the facts and findings of the disciplinary hearing and disciplinary measures taken, shall be made available to the board for the inmate's next scheduled appearance before the state board of parole including any defense or explanation offered by the inmate in response at such hearing.

3. The provisions of this chapter relating to good behavior allowances shall apply to behavior of inmates while participating in temporary release programs outside the premises of institutions, and such allowances may be granted, withheld, forfeited or cancelled in whole or in part for behavior outside the premises of an institution to the same extent and in the same manner as is provided for behavior of inmates within the premises of institutions.

Corr. L.

4. An inmate who is in violation of the provisions of his or her temporary release program may be taken into custody by any peace officer or police officer and, in such event, the inmate shall be returned forthwith to either the institution that released him or her, or to the nearest secure facility where greater security is indicated. In any case where the institution is in a county other than the one in which the inmate is apprehended, the officer may deliver the inmate to the nearest institution, jail or lockup and it shall be the duty of the person in charge of said facility to hold such inmate securely until such time as he or she is delivered into the custody of an officer of the institution from which he or she was released. Upon delivering the inmate to an institution, jail or lockup, other than the one from which the inmate was released, the officer who apprehended the inmate shall forthwith notify the superintendent of the institution from which the inmate was released and it shall be the duty of the superintendent to effect the expeditious return of the inmate to the institution.

5. Upon the conclusion or termination of a temporary release program, a full report of the inmate's performance in such program shall be prepared in accordance with regulations of the commissioner. Such report shall include but not be limited to: adjustment to release, supervision contacts, statement of any violations of the terms and conditions of release and of any disciplinary actions taken, and an assessment of the inmate's suitability for parole. Such report shall be made available to the state board of parole for the inmate's next scheduled appearance before such board. [Eff Sept 1, 2015, § 856 reverts to § 854 and reads as set out below:]

§ 854. Conduct of inmates participating in work release program

1. An inmate who is permitted to leave the premises of an institution to participate in a program of work release shall have on his person a copy of the memorandum of that program as signed by the warden of the institution at all times while outside the premises of the institution and shall exhibit such copy to any peace officer upon request of the officer.

2. If the inmate violates any provision of the program, or any rule or regulation promulgated by the commissioner of corrections and community supervision for conduct of inmates participating in work release programs, he or she shall be subject to disciplinary measures to the same extent as if he or she violated a rule or regulation of the commissioner for conduct of inmates within the premises of the institution.

3. The provisions of this chapter relating to good behavior allowances shall apply to behavior of inmates while participating in work release programs outside the premises of institutions, and such allowances may be granted, withheld, forfeited or cancelled in whole or in part for behavior outside the premises of an institution to the same extent and in the same manner as is provided for behavior of inmates within the premises of institutions.

4. An inmate who is in violation of the provisions of his work release program may be taken into custody by any peace officer and, in such event, the inmate shall be returned forthwith to the institution that released him. In any case where the institution is in a county other than the one in which the inmate is apprehended, the officer may deliver the inmate to the nearest institution, jail or lockup and it shall be the duty of the person in charge of said facility to hold such inmate securely until such time as he is delivered into custody of an officer of the institution from which he was released. Upon delivering the inmate to an institution, jail or lockup, other than the one from which he was released, the peace officer who apprehended the inmate shall forthwith notify the warden of the institution from which the inmate was released and it shall be the duty of the warden to effect the expeditious return of the inmate to the institution.

HISTORY: Formerly § 854, add, L 1969, ch 472, § 1; amd, L 1972, ch 339, § 6, expires Sept 1, 2015; renumbered § 856 and amd, L 1977, ch 691, § 5, eff Sept 1, 1977; amd, L 1980, ch 843,

§ 203, eff Sept 1, 1980, L 1980, ch 843, § 204, eff Sept 1, 1980, L 2011, ch 62, § 46 (Part C, Subpart B), eff Sept 1, 2013.

§ 857. Complaint and abuse review

Any person may submit to the commission of correction any complaint he or she may have concerning programmatic abuses. The commission of correction shall evaluate such complaints and, where indicated, conduct any needed investigation. If the commission concludes that a complaint is valid, the commission shall make recommendations to the department for corrective action. Where the commission believes sufficient evidence exists to support a criminal charge, the commission shall report such evidence to the appropriate law enforcement agencies.

> **HISTORY:** Add, L 1977, ch 691, § 6, eff Sept 1, 1977. Former § 857, renumbered § 860, L 1977, ch 691, § 7, eff Sept 1, 1977.

§ 858. Application of labor laws

The laws of the state and its political subdivisions with respect to employment conditions shall apply to inmates participating in work release programs.

> **HISTORY:** Formerly § 855, add, L 1969, ch 472; renumbered § 858, L 1977, ch 691, § 7, eff Sept 1, 1977.

§ 859. When employment prohibited

No employment under a work release program may be approved or continued if (a) such employment results in the displacement of employed workers, or is applied in skills, crafts or trades in which there is a surplus of available labor in the locality, or (b) the rates of pay and other conditions of employment are not at least equal to those paid or provided for work of similar nature in the locality in which the work is to be performed, or (c) there is any labor strike or lockout in the establishment in which the inmate is employed.

> **HISTORY:** Formerly § 856, add, L 1969, ch 472; renumbered § 859, L 1977, ch 691, § 7, eff Sept 1, 1977.

§ 860. Disposition of earnings

The earnings of an inmate participating in a work release program, less any payroll deductions required or authorized by law, shall be turned over to the warden who shall deposit such receipts as inmates' funds pursuant to section one hundred sixteen of this chapter. Such receipts shall not be subject to attachment or garnishment in the hands of the warden. The commissioner of correction may authorize the warden to make disbursements of such receipts, and such receipts may be disbursed, for any or all of the following purposes:

    1. Appropriate and reasonable costs related to the inmate's participation in the work release program;

    2. Support of the inmate's dependents;

    3. Payment of fines imposed by any court;

    4. Payment of any court ordered restitution or reparation to the victim of the inmate's crime.

    5. Purchases by the inmate from the commissary of the institution.

The balance of such receipts, if any, after disbursements for the foregoing purposes shall be paid to the inmate upon termination of his imprisonment.

> **HISTORY:** Formerly § 857, add, L 1969, ch 472; renumbered § 860, L 1977, ch 691, § 7, eff Sept 1, 1977. Opening par, amd, L 1974, ch 966, § 3, eff June 13, 1974, and expired Sept 1, 1977. Sub 1, amd, L 1974, ch 966, § 3, eff June 13, 1974, and expired Sept 1, 1977. Sub 4, add, L 1985, ch 233, § 6, eff Nov 1, 1985. Former sub 4, redesignated sub 5, L 1985, ch 233, § 6, eff Nov 1, 1985.

Sub 5, formerly sub 4, redesignated sub 5, L 1985, ch 233, § 6, eff Nov 1, 1985.

§ 861. Inmate not agent of state

An inmate participating in a work release program shall not, merely by reason of such participation, be deemed an agent, employee or servant of the state while outside the premises of an institution pursuant to the terms of a work release program.

> **HISTORY:** Formerly § 858, add, L 1969, ch 472; amd, L 1974, ch 966, § 4, expired Sept 1, 1977; renumbered § 861, L 1977, ch 691, § 7, eff Sept 1, 1977.

ARTICLE 26-A SHOCK INCARCERATION PROGRAM FOR STATE CORRECTIONAL INMATES

§ 865.   **Definitions**
§ 866.   **Establishment of shock incarceration program**
§ 867.   **Procedure for selection of participants in shock incarceration program**

> **HISTORY:** Add, L 1987, ch 261, § 15, eff July 13, 1987.

§ 865. Definitions

As used in this article, the following terms mean:

1. "Eligible inmate" means a person sentenced to an indeterminate term of imprisonment who will become eligible for release on parole within three years or sentenced to a determinate term of imprisonment who will become eligible for conditional release within three years, who has not reached the age of fifty years, who has not previously been convicted of a violent felony as defined in article seventy of the penal law, or a felony in any other jurisdiction which includes all of the essential elements of any such violent felony, upon which an indeterminate or determinate term of imprisonment was imposed and who was between the ages of sixteen and fifty years at the time of commission of the crime upon which his or her present sentence was based. Notwithstanding the foregoing, no person who is convicted of any of the following crimes shall be deemed eligible to participate in this program: (a) a violent felony offense as defined in article seventy of the penal law, (b) an A-I felony offense, (c) any homicide offense as defined in article one hundred twenty-five of the penal law, (d) any felony sex offense as defined in article one hundred thirty of the penal law and (e) any escape or absconding offense as defined in article two hundred five of the penal law.

2. "Shock incarceration program" means a program pursuant to which eligible inmates are selected to participate in the program and serve a period of six months in a shock incarceration facility, which shall provide rigorous physical activity, intensive regimentation and discipline and rehabilitation therapy and programming. Such inmates may be selected either: (i) at a reception center; or (ii) at a general confinement facility when the otherwise eligible inmate then becomes eligible for release on parole within three years in the case of an indeterminate term of imprisonment, or then becomes eligible for conditional release within three years in the case of a determinate term of imprisonment.

> **HISTORY:** Add, L 1987, ch 261, § 15, eff July 13, 1987, L 1987, ch 262, § 3, L 1988, ch 59, § 5, L 1988, ch 636, § 1, L 1989, ch 338, § 9, L 1992, ch 55, § 292, L 1999, ch 412, § 1 (Part B), L 2003, ch 264, § 52, L 2004, ch 738, § 14, eff Jan 13, 2005, L 2009, ch 56, §§ 1 2, (Part L), eff April 7, 2009, L 2010, ch 377, § 1, eff Aug 13, 2010.

§ 866. Establishment of shock incarceration program

1. The commissioner, guided by consideration for the safety of the community and the welfare of the inmate, shall promulgate rules and regulations for the shock incarceration program. Such rules and regulations shall reflect the purpose of the program and shall include, but not be limited

to, selection criteria, inmate discipline, programming and supervision, and program structure and administration.

2. The commissioner shall appoint or cause to be appointed a shock incarceration selection committee at one or more designated correctional facilities, which shall meet on a regularly scheduled basis to review all eligible inmates transferred to such facility for screening and all applications for the shock incarceration program.

3. Shock incarceration programs may be established only at institutions classified by the commissioner as shock incarceration facilities.

4. The department may contract with the division of substance abuse services for the provision of such services as may be required to assure the success of the program.

5. The department shall conduct an ongoing evaluation of the program to ensure that the programmatic objectives are met. The department shall undertake studies and prepare reports periodically on the impact of the program.

HISTORY: Add, L 1987, ch 261, § 15, eff July 13, 1987. Sub 2, amd, L 2009, ch 56, § 3 (Part L), eff April 7, 2009.

§ 867. Procedure for selection of participants in shock incarceration program

1. An eligible inmate may make an application to the shock incarceration screening committee for permission to participate in the shock incarceration program.

2. If the shock incarceration screening committee determines that an inmate's participation in the shock incarceration program is consistent with the safety of the community, the welfare of the applicant and the rules and regulations of the department, the committee shall forward the application to the commissioner or his designee for approval or disapproval.

2-a. Subdivisions one and two of this section shall apply to a judicially sentenced shock incarceration inmate only to the extent that the screening committee may determine whether the inmate has a medical or mental health condition that will render the inmate unable to successfully complete the shock incarceration program, and the facility in which the inmate will participate in such program. Notwithstanding subdivision five of this section, an inmate sentenced to shock incarceration shall promptly commence participation in the program when such inmate is an eligible inmate pursuant to subdivision one of section eight hundred sixty-five of this article.

3. Applicants cannot participate in the shock incarceration program unless they agree to be bound by all the terms and conditions thereof and indicate such agreement by signing the memorandum of the program immediately below a statement reading as follows:

"I accept the foregoing program and agree to be bound by the terms and conditions thereof. I understand that my participation in the program is a privilege that may be revoked at any time at the sole discretion of the commissioner. I understand that I must successfully complete the entire program to obtain a certificate of earned eligibility upon the completion of said program, and in the event that I do not successfully complete said program, for any reason, I will be transferred to a nonshock incarceration correctional facility to continue service of my sentence."

4. An inmate who has successfully completed a shock incarceration program shall be eligible to receive such a certificate of earned eligibility pursuant to section eight hundred five of this chapter. Notwithstanding any other provision of law, an inmate sentenced to a determinate sentence of imprisonment who has successfully completed a shock incarceration program shall be

Corr. L.

eligible to receive such a certificate of earned eligibility and shall be immediately eligible to be conditionally released.

5. Participation in the shock incarceration program shall be a privilege. Nothing contained in this article may be construed to confer upon any inmate the right to participate or continue to participate therein.

> **HISTORY:** Add, L 1987, ch 261, § 15, eff July 13, 1987. Sub 1, amd, L 1989, ch 338, § 10, L 1992, ch 55, § 293, eff April 10, 1992. Sub 2-a, add, L 2009, ch 56, § 2 (Part AAA), eff April 7, 2009. Sub 4, amd, L 1989, ch 338, § 10, L 1992, ch 55, § 293, L 2004, ch 738, § 15, eff Jan 13, 2005.

ARTICLE 27   WORK RELEASE PROGRAM FOR COUNTY JAILS

> **HISTORY:** Add, L 1968, ch 786, § 1, eff Jan 1, 1969.

§ 870. Establishment of program

The sheriff, upon approval of the legislative body of the county, may establish a work release program pursuant to which prisoners, sentenced to and confined in any county jail under his jurisdiction, may be granted the privilege of leaving confinement for the purpose of working at gainful employment, participating in a privately or publicly sponsored program of vocational training, with or without compensation, or attending an educational institution. The work release program may also include the release from confinement during necessary and reasonable hours for the purpose of caring for the prisoner's family.

> **HISTORY:** Add, L 1968, ch 786, § 1; amd, L 1976, ch 71, § 2, eff Sept 1, 1976.

§ 871. Procedures

(a) Any prisoner sentenced to and confined in any jail for which the sheriff has established a work release program may apply to the sheriff for permission to participate in such program. Pursuant to rules and regulations promulgated by the sheriff and approved by the state commission of correction, the sheriff may approve or disapprove the application. In the event of approval, the sheriff shall prepare a specific, written work release plan for the prisoner which shall contain such terms and conditions as shall be deemed reasonably proper and necessary. The prisoner shall signify in writing his agreement to the terms of the work release plan in such form as the sheriff shall specify and a copy of the work release plan shall be delivered to the prisoner prior to his participation therein. The work release plan may be revoked, suspended or modified by the sheriff at any time for good cause, with or without notice to the prisoner. Any disapproval, revocation, suspension or modification of a work release application or plan shall be reviewable by the state commission of correction upon written request of the prisoner which shall be forwarded immediately to the commission by the sheriff. The decision of the commission shall be final and not be subject to judicial review.

(b) The sheriff shall appoint a committee, to be known as the work release committee, composed of at least one member of the county department of probation and of such members of the staff of the jail of confinement as he shall deem proper. The work release committee may also include such other persons whom the sheriff may deem proper, and such persons shall be selected upon the basis of their knowledge and experience in the field of penology, law, medicine, labor, commerce, theology or social services. The committee shall advise and assist the sheriff in administering the work release program, provided, however, that any determination to approve, disapprove, revoke, suspend or modify any work release application or plan shall rest solely in the discretion of the sheriff subject to review by the commission of correction as set forth in subdivision (a) of this section.

(c) The sheriff and work release committee may assist prisoners seeking admission to the work release program in securing gainful employment or participation in a publicly or privately sponsored program of vocational training.

(d) A work release plan may include employment within a county other than that in which the jail of confinement is located. The sheriff may arrange with the sheriff or the superintendent or other person in charge of a jail or penitentiary of any other county which has adopted a work release program to maintain custody of any prisoner employed in such other county during the period of employment or until his discharge from confinement, whichever shall occur first. In such event, the sheriff or superintendent of the jail or penitentiary having such custody of the prisoner shall dispose of the earnings of the prisoner pursuant to section eight hundred seventy-two of this article.

HISTORY: Add, L 1968, ch 786, § 2, eff Jan 1, 1969.

§ 872. Disposition of earnings

(a) The wages or salary of a prisoner participating in the work release program, less payroll deductions required by law, shall be deposited with the sheriff in a trust fund account, which fund shall not be subject to garnishment or attachment. The sheriff shall keep a ledger of the account of each prisoner and he may disburse from the said trust fund account:

(1) such sum as the prisoner may be legally obligated to pay for the support of his dependents as recommended by the department of social services of the county in which such dependents reside, provided, however, that the prisoner may authorize that a sum greater than that so recommended be disbursed for this purpose;

(2) a sum determined by the sheriff to be the cost to the county of providing food, lodging and clothing for such prisoner subject, however, to approval by the state commission of correction;

(3) a sum determined by the sheriff to be the cost to the county of the actual and necessary food, travel and other expenses of such prisoner when released from confinement for the purpose of participating in the work release program;

(4) such sums as may be necessary to satisfy any fines outstanding against the prisoner;

(5) such sums as may be necessary to satisfy any outstanding legal obligations of the prisoner, acknowledged by him in writing and filed with the sheriff in such form as the sheriff shall specify.

(b) Any balance remaining in the trust fund account after such disbursements shall be paid to the prisoner upon his discharge from confinement.

(c) On or before the thirty-first day of January of each year, the sheriff shall prepare a summary of receipts and disbursements of all accounts kept during the previous year and shall forward the summary to the chief executive officer of the county. The summary shall be a public record.

HISTORY: Add, L 1968, ch 786, § 1, eff Jan 1, 1969. Sub (c), add, L 1984, ch 236, § 1, eff June 19, 1984.

§ 873. Separate housing

The sheriff may designate separate facilities within the jail for the quartering of prisoners, participating in the work release program.

HISTORY: Add, L 1968, ch 786, § 1, eff Jan 1, 1969.

§ 874. When employment prohibited

(a) No employment under the work release program for any prisoner shall be approved if:

(1) it is ascertained by the sheriff that such employment will result in the displacement of employed workers, or be applied in skills, crafts or trades in which there is a surplus of available labor in the locality, except in the case of a prisoner who is to be employed by an employer for whom he was employed as a free person prior to the commencement of his sentence, and;

(2) the rates of pay and other conditions of employment are not at least equal to those paid or provided for work of a similar nature in the locality in which the work is to be performed.

(b) The state department of labor shall exercise the same supervision over conditions of employment for prisoners participating in the work release program as such department does over conditions of employment for free persons.

(c) In no event shall any work release program be permitted when there is any labor strike or lock-out in the establishment in which the prisoner is, or is to be, employed.

HISTORY: Add, L 1968, ch 786, § 1, eff Jan 1, 1969.

§ 876. Eligibility for reduction of sentence, parole or conditional release

Nothing in this article shall be construed to prejudice the eligibility of any prisoner participating in a work release program for the purposes of discretionary reduction of sentence, parole or conditional release except absconding from work release as defined by section 205.16 of the penal law; provided, however, that the participation of any prisoner in such program may be considered favorably for such purposes if such participation has assisted in the rehabilitation of such prisoner.

HISTORY: Add, L 1968, ch 786, § 1; amd, L 1969, ch 678, eff Jan 1, 1970.

§ 877. Prisoner not an agent of county

No prisoner participating in a work release program shall be deemed an agent, employee or involuntary servant of the county while released from the jail of confinement pursuant to the terms of any work release plan; provided, however, that when a prisoner is employed by the state or a local municipality, his relationship to the state or local municipality arising out of such employment shall be determined in the same manner as if he were a free person so employed.

HISTORY: Add, L 1968, ch 786, § 1, eff Jan 1, 1969.

§ 878. Annual report

The sheriff shall annually prepare a report of the work release program which shall be transmitted to the legislature on or before the first day of March in each year. Such annual report shall include a summary of the operations and activities of the program for the preceding year and such recommendations for the improvement of the program as the sheriff shall deem necessary and proper.

HISTORY: Add, L 1968, ch 786, § 1, eff Jan 1, 1969.

§ 879. Application of article

This article shall not apply to any sheriff in the city of New York or to the commissioner of correction in the city of New York.

HISTORY: Add, L 1968, ch 786, § 1, eff Jan 1, 1969.

Corr. L.

SELECTED SECTIONS
OF THE
EXECUTIVE LAW

ARTICLE 12-B STATE BOARD OF PAROLE

HISTORY: Add, L 1977, ch 904, § 3, eff Aug 11, 1977.

§ 259. Definitions

When used in this article, the following terms shall have the following meanings:

  1. "Board" means the state board of parole.

2. "Commissioner" means the commissioner of the department of corrections and community supervision.

3. "Community supervision" means the supervision of individuals released into the community on temporary release, presumptive release, parole, conditional release, post release supervision or medical parole.

4. "Department" means the department of corrections and community supervision.

HISTORY: Add, L 2011, ch 62, § 37 (Part C, Subpart A), eff March 31, 2011.

§ 259-a. State board of parole; funding

The annual budget submitted by the governor shall separately state the recommended appropriations for the state board of parole. Upon enactment, these separately stated appropriations for the state board of parole shall not be decreased by interchange with any other appropriation, notwithstanding section fifty-one of the state finance law.

HISTORY: Add, L 2011, ch 62, § 38 (Part C, Subpart A), eff March 31, 2011.

§ 259-b. State board of parole; organization

1. There shall be in the department a state board of parole which shall possess the powers and duties hereinafter specified. The board shall function independently of the department regarding all of its decision-making functions, as well as any other powers and duties specified in this article, provided, however, that administrative matters of general applicability within the department shall be applicable to the board. Such board shall consist of not more than nineteen members appointed by the governor with the advice and consent of the senate. The term of office of each member of such board shall be for six years; provided, however, that any member chosen to fill a vacancy occurring otherwise than by expiration of term shall be appointed for the remainder of the unexpired term of the member whom he is to succeed. In the event of the inability to act of any member, the governor may appoint some competent informed person to act in his stead during the continuance of such disability.

2. Each member of the board shall have been awarded a degree from an accredited four-year college or university or a graduate degree from such college or university or accredited graduate school and shall have had at least five years of experience in one or more of the fields of criminology, administration of criminal justice, law enforcement, sociology, law, social work, corrections, psychology, psychiatry or medicine.

3. The governor shall designate one of the members of the board as chairman to serve in such capacity at the pleasure of the governor or until the member's term of office expires and a successor is designated in accordance with law, whichever first occurs. The chairman shall be responsible for the administrative functions and daily operations of the parole board and its staff, except as otherwise provided by law.

4. The members of the board shall not hold any other public office; nor shall they, at any time of their appointment nor during their incumbency, serve as a representative of any political party on an executive committee or other governing body thereof, nor as an executive officer or employee of any political committee, organization or association.

5. Each member of the board shall receive for his services an annual salary to be fixed by the governor within the amount appropriated therefor. Each member of such board shall also receive his necessary expenses actually incurred in the discharge of his duties.

6. Any member of the board may be removed by the governor for cause after an opportunity to

be heard.

7. Except as otherwise provided by law, a majority of the board shall constitute a quorum for the transaction of all business of the board.

> **HISTORY:** Add, L 1977, ch 904, § 3, eff Aug 11, 1977; amd, L 1983, ch 714, § 1, L 1987, ch 123, § 1, eff June 15, 1987, L 2011, ch 62, § 38-a (Part C, Subpart A), eff March 31, 2011, L 2013, ch 135, § 1, eff July 12, 2013.

§ 259-c. State board of parole; functions, powers and duties

The state board of parole shall:

1. [Until Sept 1, 2015] have the power and duty of determining which inmates serving an indeterminate or determinate sentence of imprisonment may be released on parole, or on medical parole pursuant to section two hundred fifty-nine-r or section two hundred fifty-nine-s of this article, and when and under what conditions;

1. [Eff Sept 1, 2015] have the power and duty of determining which inmates serving an indeterminate or reformatory sentence of imprisonment may be released on parole and when and under what conditions;

2. [Until Sept 1, 2015] have the power and duty of determining the conditions of release of the person who may be presumptively released, conditionally released or subject to a period of post-release supervision under an indeterminate or determinate sentence of imprisonment;

2. [Eff Sept 1, 2015] have the power and duty of determining the conditions of release of the person who may be conditionally released or subject to a period of post-release supervision under an indeterminate or determinate sentence of imprisonment and of determining which inmates serving a definite sentence of imprisonment may be conditionally released and when and under what conditions;

3. determine, as each inmate is received by the department, the need for further investigation of the background of such inmate. Upon such determination, the department shall cause such investigation as may be necessary to be made as soon as practicable, the results of such investigation together with all other information compiled by the department and the complete criminal record and family court record of such inmate to be filed so as to be readily available when the parole of such inmate is being considered;

4. establish written procedures for its use in making parole decisions as required by law. Such written procedures shall incorporate risk and needs principles to measure the rehabilitation of persons appearing before the board, the likelihood of success of such persons upon release, and assist members of the state board of parole in determining which inmates may be released to parole supervision;

5. through its members, officers and employees, study or cause to be studied the inmates confined in institutions over which the board has jurisdiction, so as to determine their ultimate fitness to be paroled;

6. have the power to revoke thecommunity supervision status of any person and to authorize the issuance of a warrant for the re-taking of such persons;

7. [Deleted]

8. have the power and perform the duty, when requested by the governor, of reporting to the governor the facts, circumstances, criminal records and social, physical, mental and psychiatric conditions and histories of inmates under consideration by the governor for pardon or

commutation of sentence and of applicants for restoration of the rights of citizenship;

9. for the purpose of any investigation in the performance of duties made by it or any member thereof, have the power to issue subpoenas, to compel the attendance of witnesses and the production of books, papers, and other documents pertinent to the subject of its inquiry;

10. have the power to authorize any members thereof and hearing officers to administer oaths and take the testimony of persons under oath;

11. make rules for the conduct of its work, a copy of such rules and of any amendments thereto to be filed by the chairman with the secretary of state;

12. to facilitate the supervision of all inmates released on community supervision the chairman of the state board of parole shall consider the implementation of a program of graduated sanctions, including but not limited to the utilization of a risk and needs assessment instrument that would be administered to all inmates eligible for parole supervision. Such a program would include various components including the use of alternatives to incarceration for technical parole violations;

13. transmit a report of the work of the state board of parole for the preceding calendar year to the governor and the legislature annually;

14. notwithstanding any other provision of law to the contrary, where a person serving a sentence for an offense defined in article one hundred thirty, one hundred thirty-five or two hundred sixty-three of the penal law or section 255.25, 255.26 or 255.27 of the penal law and the victim of such offense was under the age of eighteen at the time of such offense or such person has been designated a level three sex offender pursuant to subdivision six of section one hundred sixty-eight-l of the correction law, is released on parole or conditionally released pursuant to subdivision one or two of this section, the board shall require, as a mandatory condition of such release, that such sentenced offender shall refrain from knowingly entering into or upon any school grounds, as that term is defined in subdivision fourteen of section 220.00 of the penal law, or any other facility or institution primarily used for the care or treatment of persons under the age of eighteen while one or more of such persons under the age of eighteen are present, provided however, that when such sentenced offender is a registered student or participant or an employee of such facility or institution or entity contracting therewith or has a family member enrolled in such facility or institution, such sentenced offender may, with the written authorization of his or her parole officer and the superintendent or chief administrator of such facility, institution or grounds, enter such facility, institution or upon such grounds for the limited purposes authorized by the parole officer and superintendent or chief officer. Nothing in this subdivision shall be construed as restricting any lawful condition of supervision that may be imposed on such sentenced offender.

15. Notwithstanding any other provision of law to the contrary, where a person is serving a sentence for an offense for which registration as a sex offender is required pursuant to subdivision two or three of section one hundred sixty-eight-a of the correction law, and the victim of such offense was under the age of eighteen at the time of such offense or such person has been designated a level three sex offender pursuant to subdivision six of section one hundred sixty-eight-l of the correction law or the internet was used to facilitate the commission of the crime, is released on parole or conditionally released pursuant to subdivision one or two of this section, the board shall require, as mandatory conditions of such release, that such sentenced offender shall be prohibited from using the internet to access pornographic material, access a commercial social networking website, communicate with other individuals or groups

for the purpose of promoting sexual relations with persons under the age of eighteen, and communicate with a person under the age of eighteen when such offender is over the age of eighteen, provided that the board may permit an offender to use the internet to communicate with a person under the age of eighteen when such offender is the parent of a minor child and is not otherwise prohibited from communicating with such child. Nothing in this subdivision shall be construed as restricting any other lawful condition of supervision that may be imposed on such sentenced offender. As used in this subdivision, a "commercial social networking website" shall mean any business, organization or other entity operating a website that permits persons under eighteen years of age to be registered users for the purpose of establishing personal relationships with other users, where such persons under eighteen years of age may: (i) create web pages or profiles that provide information about themselves where such web pages or profiles are available to the public or to other users; (ii) engage in direct or real time communication with other users, such as a chat room or instant messenger; and (iii) communicate with persons over eighteen years of age; provided, however, that, for purposes of this subdivision, a commercial social networking website shall not include a website that permits users to engage in such other activities as are not enumerated herein.

15-a. Notwithstanding any other provision of law, where a person is serving a sentence for a violation of section 120.03, 120.04, 120.04-a, 125.12, 125.13 or 125.14 of the penal law, or a felony as defined in paragraph (c) of subdivision one of section eleven hundred ninety-three of the vehicle and traffic law, if such person is released on parole or conditional release the board shall require as a mandatory condition of such release, that such person install and maintain, in accordance with the provisions of section eleven hundred ninety-eight of the vehicle and traffic law, an ignition interlock device in any motor vehicle owned or operated by such person during the term of such parole or conditional release for such crime. Provided further, however, the board may not otherwise authorize the operation of a motor vehicle by any person whose license or privilege to operate a motor vehicle has been revoked pursuant to the provisions of the vehicle and traffic law.

16. determine which inmates serving a definite sentence of imprisonment may be conditionally released from an institution in which he or she is confined in accordance with subdivision two of section 70.40 of the penal law.

17. within amounts appropriated, appoint attorneys to serve as its legal advisors. Such attorneys shall report directly to the board, provided, however, that administrative matters of general applicability within the department shall be applicable to such attorneys.

HISTORY: Add, L 1977, ch 904, § 3, eff Aug 11, 1977; amd, L 1989, ch 79, § 4, eff May 1, 1989, expired and repealed Sept 1, 2005, L 1992, ch 55, § 287, eff April 10, 1992, L 1995, ch 3, § 38, eff Oct 1, 1995, repealed Sept 1, 2015, L 1998, ch 1, §§ 22, 23, eff Aug 6, 1998, L 2000, ch 1, § 8, eff Feb 1, 2001, L 2001, ch 62, § 14, eff June 25, 2001, L 2003, ch 62, § 7 (Part E), eff May 15, 2003, deemed eff April 1, 2003, L 2005, ch 544, § 2, eff Sept 1, 2006, L 2006, ch 320, § 23, eff Nov 1, 2006, L 2006, ch 96, § 1, eff June 7, 2006, deemed eff on and after Oct 1, 2005, L 2008, ch 67, § 9, eff April 28, 2008, L 2009, ch 56, § 8 (Part J), eff April 7, 2009, L 2009, ch 56, § 2 (Part N), eff April 7, 2009, deemed eff on and after March 1, 2009, L 2009, ch 496, § 11, eff Dec 18, 2009, L 2010, ch 56, § 14 (Part A-1), eff June 22, 2010, L 2011, ch 62, § 38-b (Part C, Subpart A), eff March 31, 2011, except subd 4, amd, eff Sept 30, 2011.

§ 259-d. Hearing officers

1. The state board of parole shall appoint and shall have the power to remove, in accordance with the provisions of the civil service law, hearing officers who shall be authorized to conduct parole revocation proceedings. Hearing officers shall function independently of the department regarding all of their decision-making functions, and shall report directly to the board, provided,

Exec. L.

however, that administrative matters of general applicability within the department shall be applicable to all hearing officers. A hearing officer conducting such proceedings shall, when delegated such authority by the board in rules adopted by the board, be required to make a written decision in accordance with standards and rules adopted by the board. Nothing in this article shall be deemed to preclude a member of the state board of parole from exercising all of the functions, powers and duties of a hearing officer upon request of the chairman.

2. The board, acting in cooperation with the civil service commission, shall establish standards, preliminary requisites and requisites to govern the selection, appointment and removal of hearing officers. Such standards and requisites shall be designed to assure that persons selected as hearing officers have the ability to conduct parole revocation proceedings fairly and impartially. Such standards shall not require prior experience as a parole officer. The board shall have the authority to establish procedures necessary to implement this section.

HISTORY: Add, L 1977, ch 904, § 3, eff Aug 11, 1977; amd, L 1991, ch 166, § 360, eff June 12, 1991, L 2011, ch 62, § 38-b-2 (Part C, Subpart A), eff March 31, 2011.

§ 259-e. Institutional parole services

The department shall provide institutional parole services. Such services shall include preparation of reports and other data required by the state board of parole in the exercise of its functions with respect to release on presumptive release, parole, conditional release or post-release supervision of inmates. Employees of the department who collect data, interview inmates and prepare reports for the state board of parole in institutions under the jurisdiction of the department shall work under the direct supervision of the deputy commissioner of the department in charge of program services. Data and reports submitted to the board shall address the statutory factors to be considered by the board pursuant to the relevant provisions of section two hundred fifty-nine-i of this article.

HISTORY: Add, L 1977, ch 904, § 3; amd, L 1985, ch 34, § 1, eff April 1, 1985; amd, L 1998, ch 1, § 24, eff Aug 6, 1998, L 2003, ch 62, § 8 (Part E), eff April 1, 2003, L 2011, ch 62, § 38-c (Part C, Subpart A), eff March 31, 2011.

§ 259-f. [Repealed]

HISTORY: Add, L 1977, ch 904, § 3, eff Aug 11, 1977. **Repealed,** L 2011, ch 62, § 38-d (Part C, Subpart A), eff March 31, 2011. Sub 1, amd, L 1985, ch 34, § 2, eff April 1, 1985. Sub 1, amd, L 1998, ch 1, § 25, eff Aug 6, 1998, L 2003, ch 62, § 9 (Part E), eff April 1, 2003. Sub 2, amd, L 2003, ch 62, § 9 (Part E), eff April 1, 2003. Sub 4, add, L 1981, ch 501, § 1, eff July 15, 1981.

§ 259-g. [Repealed]

HISTORY: Add, L 1977, ch 904, § 3, eff Aug 11, 1977. **Repealed,** L 2011, ch 62, § 38-e (Part C, Subpart A), eff March 31, 2011. Section heading, amd, L 2003, ch 62, § 10 (Part E), eff April 1, 2003. Sub 1, amd, L 2003, ch 62, § 10 (Part E), eff April 1, 2003. Sub 2, amd, L 2003, ch 62, § 10 (Part E), eff April 1, 2003.

§ 259-h. Parole eligibility for certain inmates sentenced for crimes committed prior to September first, nineteen hundred sixty-seven

1. The provisions of this subdivision shall apply in any case where a person is under one or more of the following sentences imposed pursuant to the penal law in effect prior to September first, nineteen hundred sixty-seven:

(a) Life imprisonment for the crime of murder in the first degree pursuant to section ten hundred forty-five or ten hundred forty-five-a of such law;

(b) Life imprisonment for the crime of kidnapping pursuant to section twelve hundred fifty of such law; or

(c) Death commuted to life imprisonment for the crime of murder in the first degree or for the crime of kidnapping pursuant to one of the above sections.

Any such person who is not otherwise or who will not sooner become eligible for release on parole under such sentence shall be or become eligible for release on parole after service of a minimum period of imprisonment of twenty years.

2. The provisions of this subdivision shall apply in any case where a person is under one or more of the following sentences imposed pursuant to the penal law in effect prior to September first, nineteen hundred sixty-seven:

(a) A minimum term of twenty years or more and a maximum of natural life for the crime of murder in the second degree pursuant to section ten hundred forty-eight of such law;

(b) A minimum term of twenty years or more and a maximum of natural life for the crime of kidnapping imposed pursuant to section twelve hundred fifty of such law;

(c) A minimum term of fifteen years or more and a maximum of natural life for a third conviction of a felony under laws relating to narcotic drugs pursuant to section nineteen hundred forty-one of such law; or

(d) A minimum term of fifteen years or more and a maximum of natural life for a fourth conviction of a felony pursuant to section nineteen hundred forty-two of such law.

Any person who is not otherwise or who will not sooner become eligible for release on parole under such sentence shall be or become eligible for release on parole after service of a minimum period of imprisonment of fifteen years.

3. The provisions of this subdivision shall apply in any case where a person is under a sentence imposed pursuant to the penal law in effect prior to September first, nineteen hundred sixty-seven, other than a sentence specified in subdivisions one and two of this section. Any person who is not otherwise or who will not sooner become eligible for release on parole shall be or become eligible for release on parole under such sentence after service of a minimum period of imprisonment of eight years and four months.

Notwithstanding the provisions of subdivisions one and two hereof, inmates convicted of murder, second degree, and sentenced pursuant to the provisions of the penal law in effect prior to September first, nineteen hundred sixty-seven, who are not otherwise or who will not sooner become eligible for release on parole, shall be eligible for release on parole under such sentence after service of a minimum period of imprisonment of eight years and four months.

4. In calculating time required to be served prior to eligibility for parole under the minimum periods of imprisonment established by this section the following rules shall apply:

(a) Service of such time shall be deemed to have commenced on the day the inmate was received in an institution under the jurisdiction of the department pursuant to the sentence;

(b) Where an inmate is under more than one sentence, (i) if the sentences run concurrently, the time served under imprisonment on any of the sentences shall be credited against the minimum periods of all the concurrent sentences, and (ii) if the sentences run consecutively, the minimum periods of imprisonment shall merge in and be satisfied by service of the period that has the longest unexpired time to run;

(c) No credit shall be allowed for "good conduct and efficient and willing performance of duties," under former section two hundred thirty of the correction law, repealed by chapter four hundred seventy-six of the laws of nineteen hundred seventy and continued in effect as to certain inmates, or under any other provision of law;

(d) Calculations with respect to "jail time"[,]* "time served under vacated sentence" and interruption for "escape" shall be in accordance with the provisions of subdivisions three, five and six of section 70.30 of the penal law as enacted by chapter ten hundred thirty of the laws of nineteen hundred sixty-five, as amended.

5. The provisions of this section shall not be construed as diminishing the discretionary authority of the board of parole to determine whether or not an inmate is to be paroled.

HISTORY: Add, L 1977, ch 904, § 3, eff Aug 11, 1977.

§ 259-i. Procedures for the conduct of the work of the state board of parole

1. [Repealed]

2. Parole.

(a) [Until Sept 1, 2015]

(i) [As amended L 2003, ch 62, § 11 (Part E), ch 62, § 9 (Part F) and L 2011, ch 62, § 38-f-1 (Part C, Subpart A)] Except as provided in subparagraph (ii) of this paragraph, at least one month prior to the date on which an inmate may be paroled pursuant to subdivision one of section 70.40 of the penal law, a member or members as determined by the rules of the board shall personally interview such inmate and determine whether he should be paroled in accordance with the guidelines adopted pursuant to subdivision four of section two hundred fifty-nine-c of this article. If parole is not granted upon such review, the inmate shall be informed in writing within two weeks of such appearance of the factors and reasons for such denial of parole. Such reasons shall be given in detail and not in conclusory terms. The board shall specify a date not more than twenty-four months from such determination for reconsideration, and the procedures to be followed upon reconsideration shall be the same. If the inmate is released, he shall be given a copy of the conditions of parole. Such conditions shall where appropriate, include a requirement that the parolee comply with any restitution order, mandatory surcharge, sex offender registration fee and DNA databank fee previously imposed by a court of competent jurisdiction that applies to the parolee. The conditions shall indicate which restitution collection agency established under subdivision eight of section 420.10 of the criminal procedure law, shall be responsible for collection of restitution, mandatory surcharge, sex offender registration fees and DNA databank fees as provided for in section 60.35 of the penal law and section eighteen hundred nine of the vehicle and traffic law.

(ii) Any inmate who is scheduled for presumptive release pursuant to section eight hundred six of the correction law shall not appear before the board as provided in subparagraph (i) of this paragraph unless such inmate's scheduled presumptive release is forfeited, canceled, or rescinded subsequently as provided in such law. In such event, the inmate shall appear before the board for release consideration as provided in subparagraph (i) of this paragraph as soon thereafter as is practicable.

(a) [Eff Sept 1, 2015] At least one month prior to the expiration of the minimum period or periods of imprisonment fixed by the court or board, a member or members as determined by the rules of the board shall personally interview an inmate serving an indeterminate sentence and determine whether he should be paroled at the expiration of the minimum period or periods

---

* The bracketed punctuation has been inserted by the Publisher.

in accordance with the procedures adopted pursuant to subdivision four of section two hundred fifty-nine-c. If parole is not granted upon such review, the inmate shall be informed in writing within two weeks of such appearance of the factors and reasons for such denial of parole. Such reasons shall be given in detail and not in conclusory terms. The board shall specify a date not more than twenty-four months from such determination for reconsideration, and the procedures to be followed upon reconsideration shall be the same. If the inmate is released, he shall be given a copy of the conditions of parole. Such conditions shall where appropriate, include a requirement that the parolee comply with any restitution order and mandatory surcharge previously imposed by a court of competent jurisdiction that applies to the parolee. The conditions shall indicate which restitution collection agency established under subdivision eight of section 420.10 of the criminal procedure law, shall be responsible for collection of restitution and mandatory surcharge as provided for in section 60.35 of the penal law and section eighteen hundred nine of the vehicle and traffic law.

(b) Persons presumptively released, paroled, conditionally released or released to post-release supervision from an institution under the jurisdiction of the department, the department of mental hygiene or the office of children and family services shall, while on presumptive release, parole, conditional release or post-release supervision, be in the legal custody of the department until expiration of the maximum term or period of sentence, or expiration of the period of supervision, including any period of post-release supervision, or return to imprisonment in the custody of the department, as the case may be.

(c) (A) Discretionary release on parole shall not be granted merely as a reward for good conduct or efficient performance of duties while confined but after considering if there is a reasonable probability that, if such inmate is released, he will live and remain at liberty without violating the law, and that his release is not incompatible with the welfare of society and will not so deprecate the seriousness of his crime as to undermine respect for law. In making the parole release decision, the procedures adopted pursuant to subdivision four of section two hundred fifty-nine-c of this article shall require that the following be considered: (i) the institutional record including program goals and accomplishments, academic achievements, vocational education, training or work assignments, therapy and interactions with staff and inmates; (ii) performance, if any, as a participant in a temporary release program; (iii) release plans including community resources, employment, education and training and support services available to the inmate; (iv) any deportation order issued by the federal government against the inmate while in the custody of the department and any recommendation regarding deportation made by the commissioner of the department pursuant to section one hundred forty-seven of the correction law; (v) any statement made to the board by the crime victim or the victim's representative, where the crime victim is deceased or is mentally or physically incapacitated; (vi) the length of the determinate sentence to which the inmate would be subject had he or she received a sentence pursuant to section 70.70 or section 70.71 of the penal law for a felony defined in article two hundred twenty or article two hundred twenty-one of the penal law; (vii) the seriousness of the offense with due consideration to the type of sentence, length of sentence and recommendations of the sentencing court, the district attorney, the attorney for the inmate, the pre-sentence probation report as well as consideration of any mitigating and aggravating factors, and activities following arrest prior to confinement; and (viii) prior criminal record, including the nature and pattern of offenses, adjustment to any previous probation or parole supervision and institutional confinement. The board shall provide toll free telephone access for crime victims. In the case of an oral statement made in accordance with subdivision one of section 440.50 of the criminal procedure law, the parole board member shall present a written report of the statement to the parole board. A crime victim's representative shall mean the crime victim's closest surviving relative, the committee or guardian of such person, or the legal representative of any such person. Such statement submitted by the victim or victim's representative may include information concerning threatening or intimidating conduct toward the victim, the victim's representative, or the victim's family, made by the person sentenced and occurring after the sentencing. Such information may include, but need not be limited to, the threatening or intimidating conduct of any other person who or which is directed by the person sentenced.

(B) Where a crime victim or victim's representative as defined in subparagraph (A) of this paragraph, or other person submits to the parole board a written statement concerning the release of an inmate, the parole board shall keep that individual's name and address confidential.

(d) (i) Notwithstanding the provisions of paragraphs (a), (b) and (c) of this subdivision, after the inmate has served his minimum period of imprisonment imposed by the court, or at any time after the inmate's period of imprisonment has commenced for an inmate serving a determinate or indeterminate term of imprisonment, provided that the inmate has had a final order of deportation issued against him and provided further that the inmate is not convicted of either an A-I felony offense other than an A-I felony offense as defined in article two hundred twenty of the penal law or a violent felony offense as defined in section 70.02 of the penal law, if the inmate is subject to deportation by the United States Bureau of Immigration and Customs Enforcement, in addition to the criteria set forth in paragraph (c) of this subdivision, the board may consider, as a factor warranting earlier release, the fact that such inmate will be deported, and may grant parole from an indeterminate sentence or release for deportation from a determinate sentence to such inmate conditioned specifically on his prompt deportation. The board may make such conditional grant of early parole from an indeterminate sentence or release for deportation from a determinate sentence only where it has received from the United States Bureau of Immigration and Customs Enforcement assurance (A) that an order of deportation will be executed or that proceedings will promptly be commenced for the purpose of deportation upon release of the inmate from the custody of the department of correctional services, and (B) that the inmate, if granted parole or release for deportation pursuant to this paragraph, will not be released from the custody of the United States Bureau of Immigration and Customs Enforcement, unless such release be as a result of deportation without providing the board a reasonable opportunity to arrange for execution of its warrant for the retaking of such person.

(ii) An inmate who has been granted parole from an indeterminate sentence or release for deportation from a determinate sentence pursuant to this paragraph shall be delivered to the custody of the United States Bureau of Immigration and Customs Enforcement along with the board's warrant for his retaking to be executed in the event of his release from such custody other than by deportation. In the event that such person is not deported, the board shall execute the warrant, effect his return to imprisonment in the custody of the department and within sixty days after such return, provided that the person is serving an indeterminate sentence and the minimum period of imprisonment has been served, personally interview him to determine whether he should be paroled in accordance with the provisions of paragraphs (a), (b) and (c) of this subdivision. The return of a person granted parole from an indeterminate sentence or release for deportation from a determinate sentence pursuant to this paragraph for the reason set forth herein shall not be deemed to be a parole delinquency and the interruptions specified in subdivision three of section 70.40 of the penal law shall not apply, but the time spent in the custody of the United States Bureau of Immigration and

Customs Enforcement shall be credited against the term of the sentence in accordance with the rules specified in paragraph (c) of that subdivision. Notwithstanding any other provision of law, any inmate granted parole from an indeterminate sentence or release for deportation from a determinate sentence pursuant to this paragraph who is subsequently committed to imprisonment in the custody of the department for a felony offense committed after release pursuant to this paragraph shall have his parole eligibility date on the indeterminate sentence for the new felony offense, or his conditional release date on the determinate sentence for the new felony offense, as the case may be, extended by the amount of time between the date on which such inmate was released from imprisonment in the custody of the department pursuant to this paragraph and the date on which such inmate would otherwise have completed service of the minimum period of imprisonment on the prior felony offense.

(e) Notwithstanding the requirements of paragraph (a) of this subdivision, the determination to parole an inmate who has successfully completed the shock incarceration program pursuant to section two hundred sixty-seven of the correction law may be made without a personal interview of the inmate and shall be made in accordance with procedures set forth in the rules of the board. If parole is not granted, the time period for reconsideration shall not exceed the court imposed minimum.

3. Revocation of presumptive release, parole, conditional release and post-release supervision.

(a) (i) If the parole officer having charge of a presumptively released, paroled or conditionally released person or a person released to post-release supervision or a person received under the uniform act for out-of-state parolee supervision shall have reasonable cause to believe that such person has lapsed into criminal ways or company, or has violated one or more conditions of his presumptive release, parole, conditional release or post-release supervision, such parole officer shall report such fact to a member of the board, or to any officer of the department designated by the board, and thereupon a warrant may be issued for the retaking of such person and for his temporary detention in accordance with the rules of the board. The retaking and detention of any such person may be further regulated by rules and regulations of the department not inconsistent with this article. A warrant issued pursuant to this section shall constitute sufficient authority to the superintendent or other person in charge of any jail, penitentiary, lockup or detention pen to whom it is delivered to hold in temporary detention the person named therein; except that a warrant issued with respect to a person who has been released on medical parole pursuant to section two hundred fifty-nine-r of this article and whose parole is being revoked pursuant to paragraph (h) of subdivision four of such section shall constitute authority for the immediate placement of the parolee only into imprisonment in the custody of the department to hold in temporary detention. A warrant issued pursuant to this section shall also constitute sufficient authority to the person in charge of a drug treatment campus, as defined in subdivision twenty of section two of the correction law, to hold the person named therein, in accordance with the procedural requirements of this section, for a period of at least ninety days to complete an intensive drug treatment program mandated by the board as an alternative to presumptive release or parole or conditional release revocation, or the revocation of post-release supervision, and shall also constitute sufficient authority for return of the person named therein to local custody to hold in temporary detention for further revocation proceedings in the event said person does not successfully complete the intensive drug treatment program. The board's rules shall provide for cancellation of delinquency and restoration to supervision upon the successful completion of the program.

(ii) A warrant issued for a presumptive release, a parole, a conditional release or a

Exec. L.

post-release supervision violator may be executed by any parole officer or any officer authorized to serve criminal process or any peace officer, who is acting pursuant to his special duties, or police officer. Any such officer to whom such warrant shall be delivered is authorized and required to execute such warrant by taking such person and having him detained as provided in this paragraph.

(iii) Where the alleged violator is detained in another state pursuant to such warrant and is not under parole supervision pursuant to the uniform act for out-of-state parolee supervision or where an alleged violator under parole supervision pursuant to the uniform act for out-of-state parolee supervision is detained in a state other than the receiving state, the warrant will not be deemed to be executed until the alleged violator is detained exclusively on the basis of such warrant and the department has received notification that the alleged violator (A) has formally waived extradition to this state or (B) has been ordered extradited to this state pursuant to a judicial determination. The alleged violator will not be considered to be within the convenience and practical control of the department until the warrant is deemed to be executed.

(iv) [Redesignated]

(b) A person who shall have been taken into custody pursuant to this subdivision for violation of one or more conditions of presumptive release, parole, conditional release or post-release supervision shall, insofar as practicable, be incarcerated in the county or city in which the arrest occurred.

(c) (i) Within fifteen days after the warrant for retaking and temporary detention has been executed, unless the releasee has been convicted of a new crime committed while under presumptive release, parole, conditional release or post-release supervision, the board of parole shall afford the alleged presumptive release, parole, conditional release or post-release supervision violator a preliminary revocation hearing before a hearing officer designated by the board of parole. Such hearing officer shall not have had any prior supervisory involvement over the alleged violator.

(ii) The preliminary presumptive release, parole, conditional release or post-release supervision revocation hearing shall be conducted at an appropriate correctional facility, or such other place reasonably close to the area in which the alleged violation occurred as the board may designate.

(iii) The alleged violator shall, within three days of the execution of the warrant, be given written notice of the time, place and purpose of the hearing unless he or she is detained pursuant to the provisions of subparagraph (iv) of paragraph (a) of this subdivision. In those instances, the alleged violator will be given written notice of the time, place and purpose of the hearing within five days of the execution of the warrant. The notice shall state what conditions of presumptive release, parole, conditional release or post-release supervision are alleged to have been violated, and in what manner; that such person shall have the right to appear and speak in his or her own behalf; that he or she shall have the right to introduce letters and documents; that he or she may present witnesses who can give relevant information to the hearing officer; that he or she has the right to confront the witnesses against him or her. Adverse witnesses may be compelled to attend the preliminary hearing unless the prisoner has been convicted of a new crime while on supervision or unless the hearing officer finds good cause for their non-attendance. As far as practicable or feasible, any additional documents having been collected or prepared that support the charge shall be delivered to the alleged violator.

(iv) The preliminary hearing shall be scheduled to take place no later than fifteen days from the date of execution of the warrant. The standard of proof at the preliminary hearing shall be probable cause to believe that the presumptive releasee, parolee, conditional releasee or person under post-release supervision has violated one or more conditions of his or her presumptive release, parole, conditional release or post-release supervision in an important respect. Proof of conviction of a crime committed while under supervision shall constitute probable cause for the purposes of this section.

(v) At the preliminary hearing, the hearing officer shall review the violation charges with the alleged violator, direct the presentation of evidence concerning the alleged violation, receive the statements of witnesses and documentary evidence on behalf of the prisoner, and allow cross examination of those witnesses in attendance.

(vi) At the conclusion of the preliminary hearing, the hearing officer shall inform the alleged violator of his or her decision as to whether there is probable cause to believe that the presumptive releasee, parolee, conditional releasee or person on post-release supervision has violated one or more conditions of his or her release in an important respect. Based solely on the evidence adduced at the hearing, the hearing officer shall determine whether there is probable cause to believe that such person has violated his or her presumptive release, parole, conditional release or post-release supervision in an important respect. The hearing officer shall in writing state the reasons for his or her determination and the evidence relied on. A copy of the written findings shall be sent to both the alleged violator and his or her counsel.

(vii) If the hearing officer is satisfied that there is no probable cause to believe that such person has violated one or more conditions of release in an important respect, he or she shall dismiss the notice of violation and direct such person be restored to supervision.

(viii) If the hearing officer is satisfied that there is probable cause to believe that such person has violated one or more conditions of release in an important respect, he or she shall so find.

(d) [Until Sept 1, 2015] If a finding of probable cause is made pursuant to this subdivision either by a determination at a preliminary hearing or by the waiver thereof, or if the releasee has been convicted of a new crime while under presumptive release, parole, conditional release or post-release supervision, the board's rules shall provide for (i) declaring such person to be delinquent as soon as practicable and shall require reasonable and appropriate action to make a final determination with respect to the alleged violation or (ii) ordering such person to be restored to presumptive release, parole, conditional release or post-release supervision under such circumstances as it may deem appropriate or (iii) when a presumptive releasee, parolee, conditional releasee or person on post-release supervision has been convicted of a new felony committed while under such supervision and a new indeterminate or determinate sentence has been imposed, the board's rules shall provide for a final declaration of delinquency. The inmate shall then be notified in writing that his release has been revoked on the basis of the new conviction and a copy of the commitment shall accompany said notification. The inmate's next appearance before the board shall be governed by the legal requirements of said new indeterminate or determinate sentence, or shall occur as soon after a final reversal of the conviction as is practicable.

(d) [Eff Sept 1, 2015] If a finding of probable cause is made pursuant to this subdivision either by determination at a preliminary hearing or by the waiver thereof, or if the releasee has been convicted of a new crime while under his present parole or conditional release supervision, the board's rules shall provide for (i) declaring such person to be delinquent as soon as practicable and shall require reasonable and appropriate action to make a final determination with respect to the alleged violation or (ii) ordering such person to be restored to parole supervision under such circumstances as it may deem appropriate or (iii) when a parolee or conditional releasee has been convicted of a new felony committed while under his present parole or conditional release supervision and a new indeterminate sentence has been imposed, the board's rules shall provide for a final declaration of delinquency. The inmate shall then be notified in writing that his release has been revoked on the basis of the new conviction and a copy of the commitment shall accompany said notification. The inmate's next appearance before the board shall be governed by the legal requirements of said new indeterminate sentence, or shall occur as soon after a final reversal of the conviction as is practicable.

(e) (i) If the alleged violator requests a local revocation hearing, he or she shall be given a revocation hearing reasonably near the place of the alleged violation or arrest if he or she has not been convicted of a crime committed while under supervision. However, the board may, on its own motion, designate a case for a local revocation hearing.

(ii) If there are two or more alleged violations, the hearing may be conducted near the place of the violation chiefly relied upon as a basis for the issuance of the warrant as determined by the board.

(iii) If a local revocation hearing is not ordered pursuant to subparagraph (i) of this paragraph the alleged violator shall be given a revocation hearing upon his or her return to a state correctional facility.

(f) (i) Revocation hearings shall be scheduled to be held within ninety days of the probable cause determination. However, if an alleged violator requests and receives any postponement of his revocation hearing, or consents to a postponed revocation proceeding initiated by the board, or if an alleged violator, by his actions otherwise precludes the prompt conduct of such proceedings, the time limit may be extended.

(ii) The revocation hearing shall be conducted by a presiding officer who may be a member or a hearing officer designated by the board in accordance with rules of the board.

(iii) Both the alleged violator and an attorney who has filed a notice of appearance on his behalf in accordance with the rules of the board of parole shall be given written notice of the date, place and time of the hearing as soon as possible but at least fourteen days prior to the scheduled date.

(iv) The alleged violator shall be given written notice of the rights enumerated in subparagraph (iii) of paragraph (c) of this subdivision as well as of his right to present mitigating evidence relevant to restoration to presumptive release, parole, conditional release or post-release supervision and his right to counsel.

(v) The alleged violator shall be permitted representation by counsel at the revocation hearing. In any case where such person is financially unable to retain counsel, the criminal court of the city of New York, the county court or district court in the county where the violation is alleged to have occurred or where the hearing is held, shall assign counsel in accordance with the county or city plan for representation placed in operation pursuant to article eighteen-B of the county law. He shall have the right to confront and cross-examine adverse witnesses, unless there is good cause for their non-attendance as determined by the presiding officer; present witnesses and documentary evidence in defense of the charges; and present witnesses and documentary evidence relevant to the question whether reincarceration of the alleged violator is appropriate.

(vi) At the revocation hearing, the charges shall be read and the alleged violator shall be permitted to plead not guilty, guilty, guilty with explanation or to stand mute. As to each charge, evidence shall be introduced through witnesses and documents, if any, in support of that charge. At the conclusion of each witness's direct testimony, he shall be made available for cross-examination. If the alleged violator intends to present a defense to the charges or to present evidence of mitigating circumstances, the alleged violator shall do so after presentation of all the evidence in support of a violation of presumptive release, parole, conditional release or post-release supervision.

(vii) All persons giving evidence at the revocation hearing shall be sworn before giving any testimony as provided by law.

(viii) At the conclusion of the hearing the presiding officer may sustain any or all of the violation charges or may dismiss any or all violation charges. He may sustain a violation charge only if the charge is supported by a preponderance of the evidence adduced.

(ix) If the presiding officer is not satisfied that there is a preponderance of evidence in support of the violation, he shall dismiss the violation, cancel the delinquency and restore the person to presumptive release, parole, conditional release or post-release supervision.

(x) If the presiding officer is satisfied that there is a preponderance of evidence that the alleged violator violated one or more conditions of release in an important respect, he or she shall so find. For each violation so found, the presiding officer may (A) direct that the presumptive releasee, parolee, conditional releasee or person serving a period of post-release supervision be restored to supervision; (B) as an alternative to reincarceration, direct the presumptive releasee, parolee, conditional releasee or person serving a period of post-release supervision be placed in a parole transition facility for a period not to exceed one hundred eighty days and subsequent restoration to supervision; (C) in the case of presumptive releasees, parolees or conditional releasees, direct the violator's reincarceration and fix a date for consideration by the board for re-release on presumptive release, or parole or conditional release, as the case may be; or (D) in the case of persons released to a period of post-release supervision, direct the violator's reincarceration up to the balance of the remaining period of post-release supervision, not to exceed five years; provided, however, that a defendant serving a term of post-release supervision for a conviction of a felony sex offense defined in section 70.80 of the penal law may be subject to a further period of imprisonment up to the balance of the remaining period of post-release supervision. For the violator serving an indeterminate sentence who while re-incarcerated has not been found by the department to have committed a serious disciplinary infraction, such violator shall be re-released on the date fixed at the revocation hearing. For the violator serving an indeterminate sentence who has been found by the department to have committed a serious disciplinary infraction while re-incarcerated, the department shall refer the violator to the board for consideration for re-release to community supervision. Upon such referral the board may waive the personal interview between a member or members of the board and the violator to determine the suitability for re-release when the board directs that the violator be re-released upon expiration of the time assessment. The board shall retain the authority to suspend the date fixed for re-release based on the violator's commission of a serious disciplinary infraction and shall in such case require a personal interview be conducted within a reasonable time between a panel of members of the board and the violator to determine suitability for re-release. If an interview is required, the board shall notify the violator in advance of the date and time of such interview in accordance with the rules and regulations of the board.

(xi) If the presiding officer sustains any violations, he must prepare a written statement, to be made available to the alleged violator and his counsel, indicating the evidence relied upon and the reasons for revoking presumptive release, parole, conditional release or post-release supervision, and for the disposition made.

(g) Revocation of presumptive release, parole, conditional release or post-release supervision shall not prevent re-parole or re-release provided such re-parole or re-release is not inconsistent with any other provisions of law. When there has been a revocation of the period of post-release supervision imposed on a felony sex offender who owes three years or more on such period imposed pursuant to subdivision two-a of section 70.45 of the penal law, and a time assessment of three years or more has been imposed, the violator shall be reviewed by the board of parole and may be restored to post-release supervision only after serving three years of the time assessment, and only upon a determination by the board of parole made in accordance with the procedures set forth in this section. Even if the hearing officer has imposed a time assessment of a certain number of years of three years or more, the violator shall not be released at or before the expiration of that time assessment unless the board authorizes such release, the period of post-release supervision expires, or release is otherwise authorized by law. If a time assessment of less than three years was imposed upon such a defendant, the defendant shall be released upon the expiration of such time assessment, unless he or she is subject to further imprisonment or confinement under any other law.

(h) If the alleged violation is not sustained and the alleged violator is restored to supervision, the interruptions specified in subdivision three of section 70.40 of the penal law shall not apply, but the time spent in custody in any state or local correctional institution shall be credited against the term of the sentence in accordance with the rules specified in paragraph (c) of such subdivision.

(i) Where there is reasonable cause to believe that a presumptive releasee, parolee, conditional releasee or person under post-release supervision has absconded from supervision the board may declare such person to be delinquent. This paragraph shall not be construed to deny such person a preliminary revocation hearing upon his retaking, nor to relieve the department of any obligation it may have to exercise due diligence to retake the alleged absconder, nor to relieve the parolee or releasee of any obligation he may have to comply with the conditions of his release.

4. Appeals.

(a) Except for determinations made upon preliminary hearings upon allegations of violation of presumptive release, parole, conditional release or post-release supervision, all determinations made pursuant to this section may be appealed in accordance with rules promulgated by the board. Any board member who participated in the decision from which the appeal is taken may not participate in the resolution of that appeal. The rules of the board may specify a time within which any appeal shall be taken and resolved.

(b) Upon an appeal to the board, the inmate may be represented by an attorney. Where the inmate is financially unable to provide for his own attorney, upon request an attorney shall be assigned pursuant to the provisions of subparagraph (v) of paragraph (f) of subdivision three of this section.

5. Actions of the board. Any action by the board or by a hearing officer pursuant to this article

shall be deemed a judicial function and shall not be reviewable if done in accordance with law.

6. Record of proceedings.

(a) (i) The board shall provide for the making of a verbatim record of each parole release interview, except where a decision is made to release the inmate to parole supervision, and each preliminary and final revocation hearing, except when the decision of the presiding officer after such hearings result in a dismissal of all charged violations of parole, conditional release or post release supervision.

(ii) Notwithstanding the provisions of subparagraph (i) of this paragraph, the board shall provide for the making of a verbatim record of each parole release interview in all proceedings where the inmate is a detained sex offender as such term is defined in subdivision (g) of section 10.03 of the mental hygiene law. Such record shall be provided to the office of mental health for use by the multidisciplinary staff and the case review panel pursuant to section 10.05 of the mental hygiene law.

(b) The chairman of the board of parole shall maintain records of all parole interviews and hearings for a period of twenty-five years from the date of the parole release interview or until expiration of the maximum term of sentence.

7. Deaf person before the board. Whenever any deaf person participates in an interview, parole release hearing, preliminary hearing or revocation hearing, there shall be appointed a qualified interpreter who is certified by a recognized national or New York state credentialing authority to interpret the proceedings to and the statements or testimony of such deaf person. The board shall determine a reasonable fee for all such interpreting services, the cost of which shall be a charge upon the division of parole.

HISTORY: Add, L 1977, ch 904, § 3, eff Aug 11, 1977; amd, 1978, ch 499, § 3, L 1980, ch 76, § 1, L 1980, ch 412, § 1, eff June 23, 1980, L 1980, ch 843, § 62, eff Sept 1, 1980, L 1981, ch 430, § 2, L 1983, ch 417, § 2, L 1984, ch 238, § 1, L 1984, ch 413, §§ 1, 2, eff Nov 1, 1984, L 1984, ch 435, § 1, eff Nov 1, 1984, L 1985, ch 78, § 1, L 1985, ch 372, § 1, eff July 19, L 1985, L 1985, ch 494, § 3, L 1986, ch 230, § 1, eff July 1, 1986, L 1986, ch 466, § 1, L 1987, ch 261, § 17, L 1987, ch 262, § 4, eff July 13, 1987, L 1987, ch 396, § 1, eff July 23, 1987, L 1989, ch 73, § 1, L 1989, ch 432, § 1, eff Sept 14, 1989, L 1991, ch 166, §§ 361–363, eff June 12, 1991, L 1991, ch 703, § 2, eff Aug 2, 1991, L 1992, ch 55, § 288, eff April 10, 1992, L 1992, ch 55, § 294, eff April 10, 1992, L 1994, ch 559, § 2, eff Nov 1, 1994, L 1995, ch 3, §§ 39, 42, eff Oct 1, 1995, repealed Sept 1, 2015, L 1995, ch 3, §§ 40, 41, eff June 10, 1995, L 1997, ch 581, § 1, eff Jan 1, 1998, L 1998, ch 1, §§ 26–39, eff Aug 6, 1998, L 1999, ch 40, § 1, eff May 10, 1999, L 1999, ch 126, § 1, eff June 29, 1999, L 2003, ch 62, § 11 (Part E), eff May 15, 2003, deemed eff April 1, 2003, L 2003, ch 62, § 9 (Part F), eff May 15, 2003, L 2003, ch 62, § 1 (Part T), eff May 15, 2003, deemed eff April 1, 2003, L 2004, ch 56, § 1 (Part J), eff Aug 20, 2004, L 2007, ch 7, §§ 42, 43, 43-a, eff April 13, 2007, L 2007, ch 56, §§ 1–3 (Part E), eff April 9, 2007, deemed eff on and after April 1, 2007, L 2007, ch 239, § 1, eff July 18, 2007, L 2009, ch 56, § 1 (Part M), eff April 7, 2009, deemed eff on and after April 1, 2009, L 2009, ch 56, § 12 (Part AAA), eff April 7, 2009, L 2011, ch 62, §§ 38-f, 38-f-1 (Part C, Subpart A), eff March 31, 2011, L 2011, ch 62, § 38-f-2 (Part C, Subpart A), eff Sept 1, 2015, L 2012, ch 363, § 1, eff Aug 31, 2012.

§ 259-j. Discharge of sentence

1. Except where a determinate sentence was imposed for a felony other than a felony defined in article two hundred twenty or article two hundred twenty-one of the penal law, if the board of parole is satisfied that an absolute discharge from presumptive release, parole, conditional release or release to a period of post-release supervision is in the best interests of society, the board may grant such a discharge prior to the expiration of the full term or maximum term to any person who has been on unrevoked community supervision for at least three consecutive years. A discharge granted under this section shall constitute a termination of the sentence with respect to which it was

granted. No such discharge shall be granted unless the board is satisfied that the parolee or releasee, otherwise financially able to comply with an order of restitution and the payment of any mandatory surcharge, sex offender registration fee or DNA databank fee previously imposed by a court of competent jurisdiction, has made a good faith effort to comply therewith.

2. The chairman of the board of parole shall promulgate rules and regulations governing the issuance of discharges from community supervision pursuant to this section to assure that such discharges are consistent with public safety.

3. Notwithstanding any other provision of this section to the contrary, where a term of post-release supervision in excess of five years has been imposed on a person convicted of a crime defined in article one hundred thirty of the penal law, including a sexually motivated felony, the board of parole may grant a discharge from post-release supervision prior to the expiration of the maximum term of post-release supervision. Such a discharge may be granted only after the person has served at least five years of post-release supervision, and only to a person who has been on unrevoked post-release supervision for at least three consecutive years. No such discharge shall be granted unless the board of parole or the department acting pursuant to its responsibility under subdivision one of section two hundred one of the correction law consults with any licensed psychologist, qualified psychiatrist, or other mental health professional who is providing care or treatment to the supervisee; and the board: (a) determines that a discharge from post-release supervision is in the best interests of society; and (b) is satisfied that the supervisee, otherwise financially able to comply with an order of restitution and the payment of any mandatory surcharge, sex offender registration fee, or DNA data bank fee previously imposed by a court of competent jurisdiction, has made a good faith effort to comply therewith. Before making a determination to discharge a person from a period of post-release supervision, the board of parole may request that the commissioner of the office of mental health arrange a psychiatric evaluation of the supervisee. A discharge granted under this section shall constitute a termination of the sentence with respect to which it was granted.

3-a. [Deleted]

4–6. [Redesignated]

HISTORY: [First setout of section] Add, L 1977, ch 904, § 3; amd, L 1986, ch 466, § 2, L 1987, ch 396, § 2, eff July 23, 1987, L 1995, ch 3, § 43, eff Oct 1, 1995, L 1998, ch 1, § 40, eff Aug 6, 1998, L 2003, ch 62, § 10 (Part F), eff May 15, 2003, L 2003, ch 62, § 11 (Part F), L 2003, ch 62, § 1 (Part N), eff May 15, 2003, deemed eff April 1, 2003, L 2004, ch 738, § 37, eff Feb 12, 2005, L 2004, ch 738, § 38, L 2007, ch 7, § 44, eff April 13, 2007, L 2008, ch 310, § 1, eff July 21, 2008, L 2008, ch 486, § 1, eff Aug 5, 2008, L 2009, ch 56, § 13 (Part AAA), eff April 7, 2009, L 2011, ch 62, § 38-g (Part C, Subpart A), eff March 31, 2011.

Editor's Notes:

Laws 2004, ch 738, § 41 (j), eff Dec 14, 2004, provides as follows:

§ 41. This act shall take effect immediately, provided that:

(j) the amendments to section 259-j of the executive law, made by section thirty-seven of this act shall not affect the expiration of such section pursuant to chapter 3 of the laws of 1995, as amended, and shall expire therewith, when upon such date the provisions of section thirty-eight shall take effect.

Laws 2007, ch 7, §§ 1 and 52 (a), (e), eff April 13, 2007, provide as follows:

Section 1. Short title. This act shall be known and may be cited as the "sex offender management and treatment act."

§ 52. This act shall take effect on the thirtieth day after it shall have become a law; provided, however, that:

(a) the provisions of sections thirteen, twenty-nine, thirty, thirty-one, thirty-two, thirty-three, thirty-four, thirty-five, thirty-six, thirty-seven, thirty-eight, thirty-nine, thirty-nine-a, forty, forty-one, forty-two, forty-three, forty-four, forty-five, forty-six, forty-seven, forty-eight, forty-nine and fifty of this act shall only apply to crimes committed after the effective date of this act;

(e) the amendments to section 259-j of the executive law made by section forty-four of this act shall not affect the expiration of such section, and shall expire and be deemed repealed therewith, when upon such date the provisions of section forty-five of this act shall take effect.

§ 259-jj. [Repealed]

    HISTORY: Add, L 2010, ch 56, § 9 (Part OO), eff July 22, 2010. **Repealed,** L 2011, ch 62, § 38-h (Part C, Subpart A), eff March 31, 2011.

§ 259-k. Access to records and institutions

1. All case files shall be maintained by the department for use by the department and board. The department and board and authorized officers and employees thereof shall have complete access to such files and the board of parole shall have the right to make such entries as the board of parole shall deem appropriate in accordance with law.

2. The board shall make rules for the purpose of maintaining the confidentiality of records, information contained therein and information obtained in an official capacity by officers, employees or members of the board of parole.

3. Members of the board and officers and employees of the department providing community supervision services and designated by the commissioner shall have free access to all inmates confined in institutions under the jurisdiction of the department, the office of children and family services and the department of mental hygiene in order to enable them to perform their functions, provided, however, that the department of mental hygiene may temporarily restrict such access where it determines, for significant clinical reasons, that such access would interfere with its care and treatment of the mentally ill inmate. If under the provisions of this subdivision an inmate is not accessible for release consideration by the board, that inmate shall be scheduled to see the board in the month immediately subsequent to the month within which he was not available.

4. Upon a determination by the department and board of parole that records regarding an individual presently under the supervision of the department are relevant to an investigation of child abuse or maltreatment conducted by a child protective service pursuant to title six of article six of the social services law, the department and board shall provide the records determined to be relevant to the child protective service conducting the investigation. The department and board shall promulgate rules for the transmission of records required to be provided under this section.

    HISTORY: Add, L 1977, ch 904, § 3, eff Aug 11, 1977; amd, L 1986, ch 230, § 2, eff July 1, 1986, L 1992, ch 707, § 3, eff Oct 1, 1992, L 2011, ch 62, § 38-i (Part C, Subpart A), eff March 31, 2011.

§ 259-l. Cooperation

1. It shall be the duty of the commissioner of corrections and community supervision to insure that all officers and employees of the department shall at all times cooperate with the board of parole and shall furnish to such members of the board and employees of the board such information as may be appropriate to enable them to perform their independent decision making functions. It is also his or her duty to ensure that the functions of the board of parole are not hampered in any way, including but not limited to: a restriction of resources including staff assistance; limited access to vital information; and presentation of inmate information in a manner that may inappropriately influence the board in its decision making.

2. The official in charge of each institution wherein any person is confined under a definite

sentence of imprisonment, all officers and employees thereof and all other public officials shall at all times cooperate with the board of parole, and shall furnish to such board, its officers and employees such information as may be required by the board to perform its functions hereunder. The members of the board, its officers and employees shall at all times be given free access to all persons confined in any such institution under such sentence and shall be furnished with appropriate working space in such institution for such purpose without charge therefor.

3. It shall be the duty of the clerk of the court, the commissioner of mental hygiene and all probation officers and other appropriate officials to send such information as may be in their possession or under their control to the chairman of the board upon request in order to facilitate the work of the board.

HISTORY: Add, L 1977, ch 904, § 3, eff Aug 11, 1977; amd, L 2011, ch 62, § 38-j (Part C, Subpart A), eff March 31, 2011.

§ 259-m. [Repealed as stated in 2003 note below] Compacts with other states for out-of-state parolee supervision

1. The governor is hereby authorized and directed to enter into a compact on behalf of the state of New York with any state of the United States legally joining therein in the form substantially as follows:

A COMPACT

Entered into by and among the contracting states, signatories hereto, with the consent of the Congress of the United States of America, granted by an act entitled "An act granting the consent of Congress to any two or more states to enter into agreements or compacts for cooperative effort and mutual assistance in the prevention of crime and for other purposes."

The contracting states solemnly agree:

(1) That it shall be competent for the duly constituted judicial and administrative authorities of a state party to this compact (herein called "sending state") to permit any person convicted of an offense within such state and placed on probation or released on parole to reside in any other state party to this compact (herein called "receiving state") while on probation or parole, if

(a) Such person is in fact a resident of or has his family residing within the receiving state and can obtain employment there;

(b) Though not a resident of the receiving state and not having his family residing there, the receiving state consents to such person being sent there.

Before granting such permission, opportunity shall be granted to the receiving state to investigate the home and prospective employment of such person.

A resident of the receiving state, within the meaning of this section, is one who has been an actual inhabitant of such state continuously for more than one year prior to his coming to the sending state and has not resided within the sending state more than six continuous months immediately preceding the commission of the offense for which he has been convicted.

(2) That each receiving state will assume the duties of visitation of and supervision over probationers or parolees of any sending state and in the exercise of those duties will be governed by the same standards that prevail for its own probationers and parolees.

(3) That duly accredited officers of a sending state may at all times enter a receiving state and there apprehend and retake any person on probation or parole. For that purpose no

formalities will be required other than establishing the authority of the officer and the identity of the person to be retaken. All legal requirements to obtain extradition of fugitives from justice are hereby expressly waived on the part of states party hereto, as to such persons. The decision of the sending state to retake a person on probation or parole shall be conclusive upon and not reviewable within the receiving state; provided, however, that if at the time when a state seeks to retake a probationer or parolee there should be pending against him within the receiving state any criminal charge, or he should be suspected of having committed within such state a criminal offense, he shall not be retaken without the consent of the receiving state until discharged from prosecution or from imprisonment for such offense.

(4) That the duly accredited officers of the sending state will be permitted to transport prisoners being retaken through any and all states parties to this compact, without interference.

(5) That the governor of each state may designate an officer who, acting jointly with like officers of other contracting states, if and when appointed, shall promulgate such rules and regulations as may be deemed necessary to more effectively carry out the terms of this compact.

(6) That this compact shall become operative immediately upon its ratification by any state as between it and any other state or states so ratifying. When ratified it shall have the full force and effect of law within such state, the form of ratification to be in accordance with the laws of the ratifying state.

(7) That this compact shall continue in force and remain binding upon each ratifying state until renounced by it. The duties and obligations hereunder of a renouncing state shall continue as to parolees or probationers residing therein at the time of withdrawal until retaken or finally discharged by the sending state. Renunciation of this compact shall be by the same authority which ratified it, by sending six months' notice in writing of its intention to withdraw from the compact to the other states party hereto.

2. The chairman of the board of parole shall have power and shall be charged with the duty of promulgating such rules and regulations as may be deemed necessary to carry out the terms of a compact entered into by the state pursuant to this section.

3. If any section, sentence, subdivision or clause of this section is for any reason held invalid or to be unconstitutional, such decision shall not affect the validity of the remaining portions of this section.

4. This section may be cited as the uniform act for out-of-state parolee supervision.

HISTORY: Add, L 1977, ch 904, § 3, eff Aug 11, 1977; repealed as stated in 2003 note below.

Editor's Note: Laws 2003, ch 688, § 3, eff Oct 21, 2003, as amended, provides as follows:

§ 3. This act shall take effect immediately, except that section one of this act shall take effect on the first of January next succeeding the date on which it shall have become a law, and shall remain in effect until the first of September, 2015, upon which date this act shall be deemed repealed and have no further force and effect; provided that section one of this act shall only take effect with respect to any compacting state which has enacted an interstate compact entitled "Interstate compact for adult offender supervision" and having an identical effect to that added by section one of this act and provided further that with respect to any such compacting state, upon the effective date of section one of this act, section 259-m of the executive law is hereby deemed REPEALED and section 259-mm of the executive law, as added by section one of this act, shall take effect; and provided further that with respect to any state which has not enacted an interstate compact entitled

"Interstate compact for adult offender supervision" and having an identical effect to that added by section one of this act, section 259-m of the executive law shall take effect and the provisions of section one of this act, with respect to any such state, shall have no force or effect until such time as such state shall adopt an interstate compact entitled "Interstate compact for adult offender supervision" and having an identical effect to that added by section one of this act in which case, with respect to such state, effective immediately, section 259-m of the executive law is deemed repealed and section 259-mm of the executive law, as added by section one of this act, shall take effect. (Amd, L 2004, ch 368, § 2, eff Aug 17, 2004, L 2007, ch 56, § 27 (Part C), eff April 9, 2007, deemed eff on and after March 31, 2007, L 2009, ch 56, § 20 (Part U), eff April 7, 2009.).

§ 259-mm. [Effective as stated in 2003 note below] Interstate compact for adult offender supervision

The interstate compact for adult offender supervision as set forth in this section is hereby adopted, enacted into law and entered into with all other jurisdictions joining therein. The compact shall be as follows:

INTERSTATE COMPACT FOR ADULT OFFENDER SUPERVISION

ARTICLE I. Purpose.

ARTICLE II. Definitions.

ARTICLE III. The compact commission.

ARTICLE IV. The state council.

ARTICLE V. Powers and duties of the interstate commission.

ARTICLE VI. Organization and operation of the interstate commission.

ARTICLE VII. Activities of the interstate commission.

ARTICLE VIII. Rulemaking functions of the interstate commission.

ARTICLE IX. Oversight, enforcement and dispute resolution by the interstate commission.

ARTICLE X. Finance.

ARTICLE XI. Compacting states, effective date and amendment.

ARTICLE XII. Withdrawal, default, termination and judicial enforcement.

ARTICLE XIII. Severability and construction.

ARTICLE XIV. Binding effect of compact and other laws.

ARTICLE I
PURPOSE

The compacting states to this interstate compact recognize that each state is responsible for the supervision of adult offenders in the community who are authorized pursuant to the bylaws and rules of this compact to travel across state lines both to and from each compacting state in such a manner as to track the location of offenders, transfer supervision authority in an orderly and efficient manner, and when necessary return offenders to the originating jurisdictions. The compacting states also recognize that Congress, by enacting the Crime Control Act, 4 U.S.C. Section 112 (1965), has authorized and encouraged compacts for cooperative efforts and mutual assistance in the prevention of crime. It is the purpose of this compact and the interstate commission created pursuant to this compact, through means of joint and cooperative action among the compacting states: to provide the framework for the promotion of public safety and protect the rights of victims through the control and regulation of the interstate movement of offenders in the community; to provide for the effective tracking, supervision and rehabilitation of these offenders by the sending and receiving states; and to equitably distribute the costs, benefits and obligations of the compact among the compacting states. In addition, this compact will: create an interstate commission which will establish uniform procedures to manage the movement between states of adults placed under community supervision and released to the community under the jurisdiction of courts, paroling authorities, corrections or other criminal justice agencies which will promulgate rules to achieve the purpose of this compact; ensure an opportunity for input and timely notice to victims and to jurisdictions where defined offenders are authorized to travel or to relocate across state lines; establish a system of uniform data collection, access to information on active cases by authorized criminal justice officials, and regular reporting of compact activities to heads of state councils, state executive, judicial and legislative branches, and criminal justice administrators; monitor compliance with rules governing interstate movement of offenders and initiate interventions to address and correct non-compliance; and coordinate training and education regarding regulations of interstate movement of offenders for officials involved in such activity. The compacting states recognize that there is no "right" of any offender to live in another state and that duly accredited officers of a sending state may at all times enter a receiving state and there apprehend and retake any offender under supervision subject to the provisions of this compact and bylaws and rules promulgated thereto. It is the policy of the compacting states that the activities conducted by the interstate commission created by this compact are the formation of public policies and are therefore public business.

ARTICLE II

DEFINITIONS

As used in this compact, unless the context clearly requires a different construction:

(a) "Adult" means both individuals legally classified as adults and juveniles treated as adults by court order, statute or operation of law.

(b) "By-laws" means those by-laws established by the interstate commission for its governance, or for directing or controlling the interstate commission's actions or conduct.

(c) "Compact administrator" means the individual in each compacting state appointed pursuant to the terms of this compact responsible for the administration and management of the state's supervision and transfer of offenders subject to the terms of this compact, the rules adopted by the interstate commission and policies adopted by the state council under this compact.

(d) "Compacting state" means any state which has enacted the enabling legislation for this compact.

(e) "Commissioner" means the voting representative of each compacting state appointed pursuant to article III of this compact.

(f) "Interstate commission" means the interstate commission for adult offender supervision established by this compact.

(g) "Member" means the commissioner of a compacting state or designee, who shall be a person officially connected with the commissioner.

(h) "Non-compacting state" means any state which has not enacted the enabling legislation for this compact.

(i) "Offender" means an adult placed under, or subject to, supervision as the result of the commission of a criminal offense and released to the community under the jurisdiction of courts, paroling authorities, corrections or other criminal justice agencies.

(j) "Person" means any individual, corporation, business enterprise or other legal entity, either public or private.

(k) "Rules" means acts of the interstate commission, duly promulgated pursuant to article VIII of this compact, substantially affecting interested parties in addition to the interstate commission, which shall have the force and effect of law in the compacting states.

(l) "State" means a state of the United States, the District of Columbia and any other territorial possessions of the United States.

(m) "State council" means the resident members of the state council for interstate adult offender supervision created by each state under article IV of this compact.

ARTICLE III
THE COMPACT COMMISSION

The compacting states hereby create the "interstate commission for adult offender supervision". The interstate commission shall be a body corporate and joint agency of the compacting states. The interstate commission shall have all the responsibilities, powers and duties set forth in this compact, including the power to sue and be sued, and such additional powers as may be conferred upon it by subsequent action of the respective legislatures of the compacting states in accordance with the terms of this compact.

The interstate commission shall consist of commissioners selected and appointed by resident members of a state council for interstate adult offender supervision for each state. In addition to the commissioners who are the voting representatives of each state, the interstate commission shall include individuals who are not commissioners but who are members of interested organizations; such non-commissioner members must include a member of the national organizations of governors, legislators, state chief justices, attorneys general and crime victims. All non-commissioner members of the interstate commission shall be ex-officio (nonvoting) members. The interstate commission may provide in its by-laws for such additional, ex-officio, non-voting members as it deems necessary.

Each compacting state represented at any meeting of the interstate commission is entitled to one vote. A majority of the compacting states shall constitute a quorum for the transaction of business, unless a larger quorum is required by the by-laws of the interstate commission. The interstate commission shall meet at least once each calendar year. The chairperson may call additional meetings and, upon the request of twenty-seven or more compacting states, shall call additional meetings. Public notice shall be given of all meetings and meetings shall be open to the public.

The interstate commission shall establish an executive committee which shall include commission officers, members and others as shall be determined by the by-laws. The executive committee shall have the power to act on behalf of the interstate commission during periods when the interstate commission is not in session, with the exception of rulemaking and/or amendment to the compact. The executive committee oversees the day-to-day activities managed by the executive director and interstate commission staff; administers enforcement and compliance with the provisions of the compact, its by-laws and as directed by the interstate commission and performs other duties as directed by the commission or set forth in the by-laws.

ARTICLE IV
THE STATE COUNCIL

Each member state shall create a state council for interstate adult offender supervision which shall be responsible for the appointment of the commissioner who shall serve on the interstate commission from that state. Each state council shall appoint as its commissioner the compact administrator from that state to serve on the interstate commission in such capacity under or pursuant to applicable law of the member state. While each member state may determine the membership of its own state council, its membership must include at least one representative from the legislative, judicial and executive branches of government, victims groups and compact administrators. Each compacting state retains the right to determine the qualifications of the compact administrator who shall be appointed by the state council or by the governor in consultation with the legislature and the judiciary. In addition to appointment of its commissioner to the national interstate commission, each state council shall exercise oversight and advocacy concerning its participation in interstate commission activities and other duties as may be determined by each member state including but not limited to, development of policy concerning operations and procedures of the compact within that state. The compact administrator shall be appointed by the governor in consultation with the temporary president of the senate, the speaker of the assembly and the chief judge of the court of appeals. The state council shall appoint the compact administrator to serve on the interstate commission pursuant to this section.

ARTICLE V
POWERS AND DUTIES OF THE INTERSTATE COMMISSION

The interstate commission shall have the following powers:

(a) to adopt a seal and suitable by-laws governing the management and operation of the interstate commission;

(b) to promulgate rules which shall have the force and effect of statutory law and shall be binding in the compacting states to the extent and in the manner provided in this compact;

(c) to oversee, supervise and coordinate the interstate movement of offenders subject to the terms of this compact and any by-laws adopted and rules promulgated by the compact commission;

(d) to enforce compliance with compact provisions, interstate commission rules, and by-laws using all necessary and proper means, including but not limited to, the use of judicial order;

(e) to establish and maintain offices;

(f) to purchase and maintain insurance and bonds;

(g) to borrow, accept or contract for services of personnel, including, but not limited to, members and their staffs;

(h) to establish and appoint committees and hire staff which it deems necessary for the carrying out of its functions including, but not limited to, an executive committee as required by article III of this compact which shall have the power to act on behalf of the interstate commission in carrying out its powers and duties pursuant to this compact;

(i) to elect or appoint such officers, attorneys, employees, agents or consultants, and to fix their compensation, define their duties and determine their qualifications; and to establish the interstate commission's personnel policies and programs relating to, among other things, conflicts of interest, rates of compensation and qualifications of personnel;

(j) to accept any and all donations and grants of money, equipment, supplies, materials and services, and to receive, utilize and dispose of same;

(k) to lease, purchase, accept contributions or donations of, or otherwise to own, hold, improve or use any property, real, personal or mixed;

(l) to sell, convey, mortgage, pledge, lease, exchange, abandon or otherwise dispose of any property, real, personal or mixed;

(m) to establish a budget and make expenditures and levy dues as provided in article X of this compact;

(n) to sue and be sued;

(o) to provide for dispute resolution among compacting states;

(p) to perform such functions as may be necessary or appropriate to achieve the purposes of this compact;

(q) to report annually to the legislatures, governors, judiciary and state councils of the compacting states concerning the activities of the interstate commission during the preceding year. Such reports shall also include any recommendations that may have been adopted by the interstate commission;

(r) to coordinate education, training and public awareness regarding the interstate movement of offenders for officials involved in such activity; and

(s) to establish uniform standards for the reporting, collecting and exchanging of data.

ARTICLE VI
ORGANIZATION AND OPERATION OF THE INTERSTATE COMMISSION

(a) By-laws. The interstate commission shall, by a majority of the members, within twelve months of the first interstate commission meeting, adopt by-laws to govern its conduct as may be necessary or appropriate to carry out the purposes of the compact, including, but not limited to:

1. establishing the fiscal year of the interstate commission;

2. establishing an executive committee and such other committees as may be necessary;

3. providing reasonable standards and procedures:

   a. for the establishment of committees, and

   b. governing any general or specific delegation of any authority or function of the interstate commission;

4. providing reasonable procedures for calling and conducting meetings of the interstate commission, and ensuring reasonable notice of each such meeting;

5. establishing the titles and responsibilities of the officers of the interstate commission;

6. providing reasonable standards and procedures for the establishment of the personnel policies and programs of the interstate commission. Notwithstanding any civil service or other similar laws of any compacting state, the by-laws shall exclusively govern the personnel policies and programs of the interstate commission;

7. providing a mechanism for winding up the operations of the interstate commission and the equitable return of any surplus funds that may exist upon the termination of the compact after the payment and/or reserving of all of its debts and obligations;

8. providing transition rules for "start up" administration of the compact; and

9. establishing standards and procedures for compliance and technical assistance in carrying out the compact.

(b) Officers and staff. The interstate commission shall, by a majority of the members, elect from among its members a chairperson and a vice chairperson, each of whom shall have such authorities and duties as may be specified in the by-laws. The chairperson or, in his or her absence or disability, the vice chairperson, shall preside at all meetings of the interstate commission. The officers so elected shall serve without compensation or remuneration from the interstate commission; provided that, subject to the availability of budgeted funds, the officers shall be reimbursed for any actual and necessary costs and expenses incurred by them in the performance of their duties and responsibilities as officers of the interstate commission.

The interstate commission shall, through its executive committee, appoint or retain an executive director for such period, upon such terms and conditions and for such compensation as the interstate commission may deem appropriate. The executive director shall serve as secretary to the interstate commission, and hire and supervise such other staff as may be authorized by the interstate commission, but shall not be a member.

(c) Corporate records of the interstate commission. The interstate commission shall maintain its corporate books and records in accordance with the by-laws.

(d) Qualified immunity, defense and indemnification. The members, officers, executive director and employees of the interstate commission shall be immune from suit and liability, either personally or in their official capacity, for any claim for damage to or loss of property or personal injury or other civil liability cause or arising out of any actual or alleged act, error or omission that occurred within the scope of interstate commission employment, duties or responsibilities; provided, that nothing in this subdivision shall be construed to protect any such person from suit and/or liability for any damage, loss, injury or liability caused by the intentional or willful and wanton misconduct of any such person. The interstate commission shall defend the commissioner of a compacting state, or his or her representatives or employees, or the interstate commission's representatives or employees, in any civil action seeking to impose liability, arising out of any actual or alleged act, error or omission that occurred within the scope of interstate commission employment, duties or responsibilities, or that the defendant had a reasonable basis for believing occurred within the scope of interstate commission employment, duties or responsibilities; provided, that the actual or alleged act, error or omission did not result from intentional wrongdoing on the part of such person.

The interstate commission shall indemnify and hold the commissioner of a compacting state, the appointed designee or employees, or the interstate commission's representatives or employees, harmless in the amount of any settlement or judgment obtained against such persons arising out of any actual or alleged act, error or omission that occurred within the scope of interstate commission employment, duties or responsibilities, or that such persons had a reasonable basis for believing occurred within the scope of interstate commission employment, duties or responsibilities, provided, that the actual or alleged act, error or omission did not result from gross negligence or intentional wrongdoing on the part of such person.

ARTICLE VII
ACTIVITIES OF THE INTERSTATE COMMISSION

The interstate commission shall meet and take such actions as are consistent with the provisions of this compact.

Except as otherwise provided in this compact and unless a greater percentage is required by the by-laws, in order to constitute an act of the interstate commission, such act shall have been taken at a meeting of the interstate commission and shall have received an affirmative vote of a majority of the members present.

Each member of the interstate commission shall have the right and power to cast a vote to which that compacting state is entitled and to participate in the business and affairs of the interstate commission. A member shall vote in person on behalf of the state and shall not delegate a vote to another member state. However, a state council shall appoint another authorized representative, in the absence of the commissioner from that state, to cast a vote on behalf of the member state at a specified meeting. The by-laws may provide for members' participation in meetings by telephone or other means of telecommunication or electronic communication. Any voting conducted by telephone, or other means of telecommunication or electronic communication shall be subject to the same quorum requirements of meetings where members are present in person.

The interstate commission shall meet at least once during each calendar year. The chairperson of the interstate commission may call additional meetings at any time and, upon the request of a majority of the members, shall call additional meetings.

The interstate commission's by-laws shall establish conditions and procedures under which the interstate commission shall make its information and official records available to the public for inspection or copying. The interstate commission may exempt from disclosure any information or official records to the extent they would adversely affect personal privacy rights or proprietary interests. In promulgating such rules, the interstate commission may make available to law enforcement agencies records and information otherwise exempt from disclosure, and may enter into agreements with law enforcement agencies to receive or exchange information or records subject to nondisclosure and confidentiality provisions.

Public notice shall be given of all meetings and all meetings shall be open to the public, except as set forth in the rules or as otherwise provided in the compact. The interstate commission shall promulgate rules consistent with the principles contained in the "Government in Sunshine Act," 5 U.S.C. Section 552(b), as may be amended. The interstate commission and any of its committees may close a meeting to the public where it determines by a two-thirds vote that an open meeting would be likely to:

(a) relate solely to the interstate commission's internal personnel practices and procedures;

(b) disclose matters specifically exempted from disclosure by statute;

(c) disclose trade secrets or commercial or financial information which is privileged or confidential;

(d) involve accusing any person of a crime, or formally censuring any person;

(e) disclose information of a personal nature where disclosure would constitute a clearly unwarranted invasion of personal privacy;

(f) disclose investigatory records compiled for law enforcement purposes;

(g) disclose information contained in or related to examination, operating or condition reports prepared by, or on behalf of or for the use of, the interstate commission with respect to a regulated entity for the purpose of regulation or supervision of such entity;

(h) disclose information, the premature disclosure of which would significantly endanger the life of a person or the stability of a regulated entity; or

(i) specifically relate to the interstate commission's issuance of a subpoena, or its participation in a civil action or proceeding.

For every meeting closed pursuant to this article, the interstate commission's chief legal officer shall publicly certify that, in his or her opinion, the meeting may be closed to the public, and shall reference each relevant exemptive provision. The interstate commission shall keep minutes which shall fully and clearly describe all matters discussed in any meeting and shall provide a full and accurate summary of any actions taken, and the reasons therefor, including a description of each of the views expressed on any item and the record of any rollcall vote (reflected in the vote of each member on the question). All documents considered in connection with any action shall be identified in such minutes.

The interstate commission shall collect standardized data concerning the interstate movement of offenders as directed through its by-laws and rules which shall specify the data to be collected, the means of collection and data exchange and reporting requirements.

ARTICLE VIII

RULEMAKING FUNCTIONS OF THE INTERSTATE COMMISSION

The interstate commission shall promulgate rules in order to effectively and efficiently achieve the purposes of the compact including transition rules governing administration of the compact during the period in which it is being considered and enacted by the states.

Rulemaking shall occur pursuant to the criteria set forth in this article and the by-laws and rules adopted pursuant thereto. Such rulemaking shall substantially conform to the principles of the federal Administrative Procedure Act, 5 U.S.C.S. section 551 et seq., and the Federal Advisory Committee Act, 5 U.S.C.S. app. 2, section 1 et seq., as may be amended (hereinafter referred to as "APA"). All rules and amendments shall become binding as of the date specified in each rule or amendment.

If a majority of the legislatures of the compacting states rejects a rule, by enactment of a statute or resolution in the same manner used to adopt the compact, then such rule shall have no further force and effect in any compacting state.

When promulgating a rule, the interstate commission shall:

(a) publish the proposed rule stating with particularity the text of the rule which is proposed and the reason for the proposed rule;

(b) allow persons to submit written data, facts, opinions and arguments, which information shall be publicly available;

(c) provide an opportunity for an informal hearing; and

(d) promulgate a final rule and its effective date, if appropriate, based on the rulemaking record.

Not later than sixty days after a rule is promulgated, any interested person may file a petition in the United States District Court for the District of Columbia or in the Federal District Court where the interstate commission principal office is located for judicial review of such rule. If the court finds that the interstate commission's action is not supported by substantial evidence, (as defined in the APA), in the rulemaking record, the court shall hold the rule unlawful and set it aside. Subjects to be addressed within twelve months after the first meeting must at a minimum include:

1. notice to victims and opportunity to be heard;

2. offender registration and compliance;

3. violations/returns;

4. transfer procedures and forms;

5. eligibility for transfer;

6. collection of restitution and fees from offenders;

7. data collection and reporting;

8. the level of supervision to be provided by the receiving state;

9. transition rules governing the operation of the compact and the interstate commission during all or part of the period between the effective date of the compact and the date on which the last eligible state adopts the compact; and

10. mediation, arbitration and dispute resolution.

The existing rules governing the operation of the previous compact superceded by this compact shall be null and void twelve months after the first meeting of the interstate commission created pursuant to this compact.

Upon determination by the interstate commission that an emergency exists, it may promulgate an emergency rule which shall become effective immediately upon adoption, provided that the usual rulemaking procedures provided hereunder shall be retroactively applied to said rule as soon as reasonably possible, in no event later than ninety days after the effective date of the rule.

ARTICLE IX

OVERSIGHT, ENFORCEMENT AND DISPUTE RESOLUTION BY THE INTERSTATE COMMISSION

(a) Oversight. The interstate commission shall oversee the interstate movement of adult offenders in the compacting states and shall monitor such activities being administered in non-compacting states which may significantly affect compacting states.

The courts and executive agencies in each compacting state shall enforce this compact and shall take all actions necessary and appropriate to effectuate the compact's purposes and intent. In any judicial or administrative proceeding in a compacting state pertaining to the subject matter of this compact which may affect the powers, responsibilities or actions of the interstate commission, the interstate commission shall be entitled to receive all service of process in any such proceeding, and shall have standing to intervene in the proceeding for all purposes.

(b) Dispute resolution. The compacting states shall report to the interstate commission on issues or activities of concern to them, and cooperate with and support the interstate commission in the discharge of its duties and responsibilities.

The interstate commission shall attempt to resolve any disputes or other issues which are subject to the compact and which may arise among compacting states and non-compacting states.

The interstate commission shall enact a by-law or promulgate a rule providing for both mediation and binding dispute resolution for disputes among the compacting states.

(c) Enforcement. The interstate commission, in the reasonable exercise of its discretion, shall enforce the provisions of this compact using any or all means set forth in article XII, subdivision (b), of this compact.

ARTICLE X

FINANCE

The interstate commission shall pay or provide for the payment of the reasonable expenses of its establishment, organization and ongoing activities.

The interstate commission shall levy on and collect an annual assessment from each compacting state to cover the cost of the internal operations and activities of the interstate commission and its staff which must be in a total amount sufficient to cover the interstate commission's annual budget as approved each year. The aggregate annual assessment amount shall be allocated based upon a formula to be determined by the interstate commission, taking into consideration the population of the state and the volume of interstate movement of offenders in each compacting state and shall promulgate a rule binding upon compacting states which governs said assessment.

The interstate commission shall not incur any obligations of any kind prior to securing the funds adequate to meet the same; nor shall the interstate commission pledge the credit of any of the compacting states, except by and with the authority of the compacting state.

The interstate commission shall keep accurate accounts of all receipts and disbursements. The receipts and disbursements of the interstate commission shall be subject to the audit and accounting procedures established under its by-laws. However, all receipts and disbursements of funds handled by the interstate commission shall be audited yearly by a certified or licensed public accountant and the report of the audit shall be included in and become part of the annual report of the interstate commission.

ARTICLE XI
COMPACTING STATES, EFFECTIVE DATE AND AMENDMENT

Any state, as defined in article II of this compact, is eligible to become a compacting state. The compact shall become effective and binding upon legislative enactment of the compact into law by no less than thirty-five of the states. The initial effective date shall be the later of July first, two thousand three, or upon enactment into law by the thirty-fifth jurisdiction. Thereafter it shall become effective and binding, as to any other compacting state and in the state of New York, upon enactment of the compact into law by that state. The governors of non-member states or their designees will be invited to participate in interstate commission activities on a non-voting basis prior to adoption of the compact by all states and territories of the United States.

Amendments to the compact may be proposed by the interstate commission for enactment by the compacting states. No amendment shall become effective and binding upon the interstate commission and the compacting states unless and until it is enacted into law by unanimous consent of the compacting states.

ARTICLE XII
WITHDRAWAL, DEFAULT, TERMINATION AND JUDICIAL ENFORCEMENT

(a) Withdrawal. Once effective, the compact shall continue in force and remain binding upon each and every compacting state; provided, that a compacting state may withdraw from the compact ("withdrawing state") by enacting a statute specifically repealing the statute which enacted the compact into law.

The effective date of withdrawal is the effective date of the repeal.

The withdrawing state shall immediately notify the chairperson of the interstate commission in writing upon the introduction of legislation repealing this compact in the withdrawing state. The interstate commission shall notify the other compacting states of the withdrawing state's intent to withdraw within sixty days of its receipt thereof.

The withdrawing state is responsible for all assessments, obligations and liabilities incurred through the effective date of withdrawal, including any obligations, the performance of which extend beyond the effective date of withdrawal. Reinstatement following withdrawal of any compacting state shall occur upon the withdrawing state reenacting the compact or upon such later date as determined by the interstate commission.

(b) Default. If the interstate commission determines that any compacting state has at any time defaulted ("defaulting state") in the performance of any of its obligations or responsibilities under this compact, the by-laws or any duly promulgated rules the interstate commission may impose any or all of the following penalties:

Exec. L.

1. Fines, fees and costs in such amounts as are deemed to be reasonable as fixed by the interstate commission;

2. Remedial training and technical assistance as directed by the interstate commission;

3. Suspension and termination of membership in the compact. Suspension shall be imposed only after all other reasonable means of securing compliance under the by-laws and rules have been exhausted. Immediate notice of suspension shall be given by the interstate commission to the governor, the chief justice or chief judicial officer of the state, the majority and minority leaders of the defaulting state's legislature, and the state council.

The grounds for default include, but are not limited to, failure of a compacting state to perform such obligations or responsibilities imposed upon it by this compact, interstate commission by-laws, or duly promulgated rules. The interstate commission shall immediately notify the defaulting state in writing of the penalty imposed by the interstate commission on the defaulting state pending a cure of the default. The interstate commission shall stipulate the conditions and the time period within which the defaulting state must cure its default. If the defaulting state fails to cure the default within the time period specified by the interstate commission, in addition to any other penalties imposed herein, the defaulting state may be terminated from the compact upon an affirmative vote of a majority of the compacting states and all rights, privileges and benefits conferred by this compact shall be terminated from the effective date of suspension. Within sixty days of the effective date of termination of a defaulting state, the interstate commission shall notify the governor, the chief justice or chief judicial officer, the majority and minority leaders of the defaulting state's legislature, and the state council of such termination.

The defaulting state is responsible for all assessments, obligations and liabilities incurred through the effective date of termination including any obligations, the performance of which extends beyond the effective date of termination.

The interstate commission shall not bear any costs relating to the defaulting state unless otherwise mutually agreed upon between the interstate commission and the defaulting state.

Reinstatement following termination of any compacting state requires both a reenactment of the compact by the defaulting state and the approval of the interstate commission pursuant to the rules.

(c) Judicial enforcement. The interstate commission may, by majority vote of the members, initiate legal action in the United States District Court for the District of Columbia or, at the discretion of the interstate commission, in the federal district where the interstate commission has its offices to enforce compliance with the provisions of the compact, its duly promulgated rules and by-laws, against any compacting state in default. In the event judicial enforcement is necessary the prevailing party shall be awarded all costs of such litigation including reasonable attorneys' fees.

(d) Dissolution of compact. The compact dissolves effective upon the date of the withdrawal or default of the compacting state which reduces membership in the compact to one compacting state.

Upon the dissolution of this compact, the compact becomes null and void and shall be of no further force or effect, and the business and affairs of the interstate commission shall be wound up and any surplus funds shall be distributed in accordance with the by-laws.

ARTICLE XIII

SEVERABILITY AND CONSTRUCTION

The provisions of this compact shall be severable, and if any phrase, clause, sentence or provision is deemed unenforceable, the remaining provisions of the compact shall be enforceable.

The provisions of this compact shall be liberally constructed to effectuate its purposes.

ARTICLE XIV

BINDING EFFECT OF COMPACT AND OTHER LAWS

(a) Other laws. Nothing in this compact prevents the enforcement of any other law of a compacting state that is not inconsistent with this compact.

All compacting states' laws conflicting with this compact are superseded to the extent of the conflict.

(b) Binding effect of the compact. All lawful actions of the interstate commission, including all rules and by-laws promulgated by the interstate commission, are binding upon the compacting states.

All agreements between the interstate commission and the compacting states are binding in accordance with their terms.

Upon the request of a party to a conflict over meaning or interpretation of interstate commission actions, and upon a majority vote of the compacting states, the interstate commission may issue advisory opinions regarding such meaning or interpretation.

In the event any provision of this compact exceeds the constitutional limits imposed on the legislature of any compacting state, the obligations, duties, powers or jurisdiction sought to be conferred by such provision upon the interstate commission shall be ineffective and such obligations, duties, powers or jurisdiction shall remain in the compacting state and shall be exercised by the agency thereof to which such obligations, duties, powers or jurisdiction are delegated by law in effect at the time this compact becomes effective.

HISTORY: Add, L 2003, ch 688, § 1, effective as stated in 2003 note below. ARTICLE IV, amd, L 2004, ch 368, § 1, eff Aug 17, 2004.

Editor's Note: Laws 2003, ch 688, § 3, eff Oct 21, 2003, as amended, provides as follows:

§ 3. This act shall take effect immediately, except that section one of this act shall take effect on the first of January next succeeding the date on which it shall have become a law, and shall remain in effect until the first of September, 2015, upon which date this act shall be deemed repealed and have no further force and effect; provided that section one of this act shall only take effect with respect to any compacting state which has enacted an interstate compact entitled "Interstate compact for adult offender supervision" and having an identical effect to that added by section one of this act and provided further that with respect to any such compacting state, upon the effective date of section one of this act, section 259-m of the executive law is hereby deemed REPEALED and section 259-mm of the executive law, as added by section one of this act, shall take effect; and provided further that with respect to any state which has not enacted an interstate compact entitled "Interstate compact for adult offender supervision" and having an identical effect to that added by section one of this act, section 259-m of the executive law shall take effect and the provisions of section one of this act, with respect to any such state, shall have no force or effect until such time as such state shall adopt an interstate compact entitled "Interstate compact for adult offender supervision" and having an identical effect to that added by section one of this act in which case, with respect to such state, effective immediately, section 259-m of the executive law is deemed repealed and section 259-mm of the executive law, as added by section one of this act, shall take effect. (Amd, L 2004, ch 368, § 2, eff Aug 17, 2004, L 2007, ch 56, § 27 (Part C), eff April 9, 2007, deemed eff on and after March 31, 2007, L 2009, ch 56, § 20 (Part U), eff April 7, 2009.).

§ 259-o. Interstate hearings for parole violations

1. For the purposes of this section, "preliminary violation hearing" means a hearing to determine whether there are reasonable grounds to believe that a person released on parole has violated the conditions of his parole.

2. Whenever there is reasonable cause to believe that a person released on parole in another state but under the parole supervision of this state pursuant to section two hundred fifty-nine-m of this

article has violated the conditions thereof, a member or designee of the board of parole, upon request of the sending state, may conduct a preliminary violation hearing unless such hearing is waived by the parolee.

3. Whenever there is reasonable cause to believe that a person released on parole in this state but under the parole supervision of another state pursuant to section two hundred fifty-nine-m of this article has violated the conditions thereof, any person duly authorized in such other state to conduct preliminary violation hearings, upon request of the chairman of the board of parole, may conduct such hearing, unless such hearing is waived by the parolee. The preliminary violation hearing and the determinations made thereat shall have the same force and effect as preliminary violation hearing conducted in this state by the board of parole or a member, hearing officer or panel thereof.

4. Whenever a preliminary violation hearing is conducted in another state pursuant to this section, the alleged violator must be afforded a final hearing within ninety days from the date of his return to this state.

HISTORY: Add, L 1977, ch 904, § 3; amd, L 1985, ch 211, § 1, eff June 18, 1985. Sub 2, amd, L 1985, ch 211, § 1, eff June 18, 1985. Sub 3, amd, L 1985, ch 211, § 1, eff June 18, 1985. Sub 4, add, L 1984, ch 435, § 2; amd, L 1985, ch 211, § 1, eff June 18, 1985.

§ 259-p. [Repealed]

HISTORY: Add, L 1977, ch 904, § 3, eff Aug 11, 1977. **Repealed,** L 2011, ch 62, § 38-k (Part C, Subpart A), eff March 31, 2011.

§ 259-q. Civil actions against division personnel

1. No civil action shall be brought in any court of the state, except by the attorney general on behalf of the state, against any officer or employee of the board of parole or former division of parole, in his personal capacity, for damages arising out of any act done or the failure to perform any act within the scope of the employment and in the discharge of the duties by such officer or employee.

2. Any claim for damages arising out of any act done or the failure to perform any act within the scope of the employment and in the discharge of the duties of any officer or employee of the board of parole or former division of parole shall be brought and maintained in the court of claims as a claim against the state.

3. The state shall save harmless and indemnify any officer or employee of the board of parole or former division of parole from financial loss resulting from a claim filed in a court of the United States for damages arising out of an act done or the failure to perform any act that was (a) within the scope of the employment and in the discharge of the duties of such officer or employee, and (b) not done or omitted with the intent to violate any rule or regulation of the division or of any statute or governing case law of the state or of the United States at the time the damages were sustained; provided that the officer or employee shall comply with the provisions of subdivision four of section seventeen of the public officers law.

4. (a) The provisions of this section shall supplement, and be available in addition to, the provisions of section seventeen of the public officers law and, insofar as this section is inconsistent with section seventeen of the public officers law, the provisions of this section shall be controlling.

(b) The provisions of this section shall not be construed in any way to impair, modify or abrogate any immunity available to any officer or employee of the board of parole or former division of parole under the statutory or decisional law of the state or the United States.

5. This section shall not in any way impair, limit or modify the rights and obligations of any insurer under any policy of insurance.

6. The benefits of subdivision three hereof shall inure only to officers and employees of the board of parole or former division of parole and shall not enlarge or diminish the rights of any other party.

7. This section shall apply with respect to claims arising on or after the effective date of this section. Claims arising prior thereto shall be governed by section seventeen of the public officers law or section twenty-four of the correction law as the case may be.

> **HISTORY:** Add, L 1977, ch 904, § 3, eff Aug 11, 1977; amd, L 1978, ch 466, §§ 7, 8, eff Sept 4, 1978, L 2011, ch 62, § 38-k-1 (Part C, Subpart A), eff March 31, 2011.

§ 259-r. Release on medical parole for terminally ill inmates

1. (a) [Until Sept 1, 2015] The board shall have the power to release on medical parole any inmate serving an indeterminate or determinate sentence of imprisonment who, pursuant to subdivision two of this section, has been certified to be suffering from a terminal condition, disease or syndrome and to be so debilitated or incapacitated as to create a reasonable probability that he or she is physically or cognitively incapable of presenting any danger to society, provided, however, that no inmate serving a sentence imposed upon a conviction for murder in the first degree or an attempt or conspiracy to commit murder in the first degree shall be eligible for such release, and provided further that no inmate serving a sentence imposed upon a conviction for any of the following offenses shall be eligible for such release unless in the case of an indeterminate sentence he or she has served at least one-half of the minimum period of the sentence and in the case of a determinate sentence he or she has served at least one-half of the term of his or her determinate sentence: murder in the second degree, manslaughter in the first degree, any offense defined in article one hundred thirty of the penal law or an attempt to commit any of these offenses. Solely for the purpose of determining medical parole eligibility pursuant to this section, such one-half of the minimum period of the indeterminate sentence and one-half of the term of the determinate sentence shall not be credited with any time served under the jurisdiction of the department prior to the commence-ment of such sentence pursuant to the opening paragraph of subdivision one of section 70.30 of the penal law or subdivision two-a of section 70.30 of the penal law, except to the extent authorized by subdivision three of section 70.30 of the penal law.

(a) [Eff Sept 1, 2015] The board shall have the power to release on medical parole any inmate serving an indeterminate or determinate sentence of imprisonment who, pursuant to subdivision two of this section, has been certified to be suffering from a terminal condition, disease or syndrome and to be so debilitated or incapacitated as to create a reasonable probability that he or she is physically or cognitively incapable of presenting any danger to society, provided, however, that no inmate serving a sentence imposed upon a conviction for murder in the first degree or an attempt or conspiracy to commit murder in the first degree shall be eligible for such release, and provided further that no inmate serving a sentence imposed upon a conviction for any of the following offenses shall be eligible for such release unless in the case of an indeterminate sentence he or she has served at least one-half of the minimum period of the sentence and in the case of a determinate sentence he or she has served at least one-half of the term of his or her determinate sentence: murder in the second degree, manslaughter in the first degree, any offense defined in article one hundred thirty of the penal law or an attempt to commit any of these offenses. Solely for the purpose of determining medical parole eligibility pursuant to this section, such one-half of the minimum period of the indeterminate sentence and one-half of the term of the determinate sentence shall not be credited with any time served

Exec. L.

under the jurisdiction of the department prior to the commencement of such sentence pursuant to the opening paragraph of subdivision one of section 70.30 of the penal law or subdivision two-a of section 70.30 of the penal law, except to the extent authorized by subdivision three of section 70.30 of the penal law.

(b) Such release shall be granted only after the board considers whether, in light of the inmate's medical condition, there is a reasonable probability that the inmate, if released, will live and remain at liberty without violating the law, and that such release is not incompatible with the welfare of society and will not so deprecate the seriousness of the crime as to undermine respect for the law, and shall be subject to the limits and conditions specified in subdivision four of this section. Except as set forth in paragraph (a) of this subdivision, such release may be granted at any time during the term of an inmate's sentence, notwithstanding any other provision of law.

(c) The board shall afford notice to the sentencing court, the district attorney and the attorney for the inmate that the inmate is being considered for release pursuant to this section and the parties receiving notice shall have fifteen days to comment on the release of the inmate. Release on medical parole shall not be granted until the expiration of the comment period provided for in this paragraph.

2. (a) The commissioner, on the commissioner's own initiative or at the request of an inmate, or an inmate's spouse, relative or attorney, may, in the exercise of the commissioner's discretion, direct that an investigation be undertaken to determine whether a diagnosis should be made of an inmate who appears to be suffering from a terminal condition, disease or syndrome. Any such medical diagnosis shall be made by a physician licensed to practice medicine in this state pursuant to section sixty-five hundred twenty-four of the education law. Such physician shall either be employed by the department, shall render professional services at the request of the department, or shall be employed by a hospital or medical facility used by the department for the medical treatment of inmates. The diagnosis shall be reported to the commissioner and shall include but shall not be limited to a description of the terminal condition, disease or syndrome suffered by the inmate, a prognosis concerning the likelihood that the inmate will not recover from such terminal condition, disease or syndrome, a description of the inmate's physical or cognitive incapacity which shall include a prediction respecting the likely duration of the incapacity, and a statement by the physician of whether the inmate is so debilitated or incapacitated as to be severely restricted in his or her ability to self-ambulate or to perform significant normal activities of daily living. This report also shall include a recommendation of the type and level of services and treatment the inmate would require if granted medical parole and a recommendation for the types of settings in which the services and treatment should be given.

(b) The commissioner, or the commissioner's designee, shall review the diagnosis and may certify that the inmate is suffering from such terminal condition, disease or syndrome and that the inmate is so debilitated or incapacitated as to create a reasonable probability that he or she is physically or cognitively incapable of presenting any danger to society. If the commissioner does not so certify then the inmate shall not be referred to the board for consideration for release on medical parole. If the commissioner does so certify, then the commissioner shall, within seven working days of receipt of such diagnosis, refer the inmate to the board for consideration for release on medical parole. However, no such referral of an inmate to the board shall be made unless the inmate has been examined by a physician and diagnosed as having a terminal condition, disease or syndrome as previously described herein at some time subsequent to such inmate's admission to a facility operated by the department of correctional services.

(c) When the commissioner refers an inmate to the board, the commissioner shall provide an appropriate medical discharge plan established by the department. The department is authorized to request assistance from the department of health and from the county in which the inmate resided and committed his or her crime, which shall provide assistance with respect to the development and implementation of a discharge plan, including potential placements of a releasee. The department and the department of health shall jointly develop standards for the medical discharge plan that are appropriately adapted to the criminal justice setting, based on standards established by the department of health for hospital medical discharge planning. The board may postpone its decision pending completion of an adequate discharge plan, or may deny release based on inadequacy of the discharge plan.

3. Any certification by the commissioner or the commissioner's designee pursuant to this section shall be deemed a judicial function and shall not be reviewable if done in accordance with law.

4. (a) Medical parole granted pursuant to this section shall be for a period of six months.

(b) The board shall require as a condition of release on medical parole that the releasee agree to remain under the care of a physician while on medical parole and in a hospital established pursuant to article twenty-eight of the public health law, a hospice established pursuant to article forty of the public health law or any other placement that can provide appropriate medical care as specified in the medical discharge plan required by subdivision two of this section. The medical discharge plan shall state that the availability of the placement has been confirmed, and by whom. Notwithstanding any other provision of law, when an inmate who qualifies for release under this section is cognitively incapable of signing the requisite documentation to effectuate the medical discharge plan and, after a diligent search no person has been identified who could otherwise be appointed as the inmate's guardian by a court of competent jurisdiction, then, solely for the purpose of implementing the medical discharge plan, the facility health services director at the facility where the inmate is currently incarcerated shall be lawfully empowered to act as the inmate's guardian for the purpose of effectuating the medical discharge.

(c) Where appropriate, the board shall require as a condition of release that medical parolees be supervised on intensive caseloads at reduced supervision ratios.

(d) The board shall require as a condition of release on medical parole that the releasee undergo periodic medical examinations and a medical examination at least one month prior to the expiration of the period of medical parole and, for the purposes of making a decision pursuant to paragraph (e) of this subdivision, that the releasee provide the board with a report, prepared by the treating physician, of the results of such examination. Such report shall specifically state whether or not the parolee continues to suffer from a terminal condition, disease, or syndrome, and to be so debilitated or incapacitated as to be severely restricted in his or her ability to self-ambulate or to perform significant normal activities of daily living.

(e) Prior to the expiration of the period of medical parole the board shall review the medical examination report required by paragraph (d) of this subdivision and may again grant medical parole pursuant to this section; provided, however, that the provisions of paragraph (c) of subdivision one and subdivision two of this section shall not apply.

(f) If the updated medical report presented to the board states that a parolee released pursuant to this section is no longer so debilitated or incapacitated as to create a reasonable probability that he or she is physically or cognitively incapable of presenting any danger to society or if the releasee fails to submit the updated medical report then the board may not make a new grant

Exec. L.

of medical parole pursuant to paragraph (e) of this subdivision. Where the board has not granted medical parole pursuant to such paragraph (e) the board shall promptly conduct through one of its members, or cause to be conducted by a hearing officer designated by the board, a hearing to determine whether the releasee is suffering from a terminal condition, disease or syndrome and is so debilitated or incapacitated as to create a reasonable probability that he or she is physically or cognitively incapable of presenting any danger to society and does not present a danger to society. If the board makes such a determination then it may make a new grant of medical parole pursuant to the standards of paragraph (b) of subdivision one of this section. At the hearing, the releasee shall have the right to representation by counsel, including the right, if the releasee is financially unable to retain counsel, to have the appropriate court assign counsel in accordance with the county or city plan for representation placed in operation pursuant to article eighteen-B of the county law.

(g) The hearing and determination provided for by paragraph (f) of this subdivision shall be concluded within the six month period of medical parole. If the board does not renew the grant of medical parole, it shall order that the releasee be returned immediately to the custody of the department.

(h) In addition to the procedures set forth in paragraph (f) of this subdivision, medical parole may be revoked at any time upon any of the grounds specified in paragraph (a) of subdivision three of section two hundred fifty-nine-i of this article, and in accordance with the procedures specified in subdivision three of section two hundred fifty-nine-i of this article.

(i) A releasee who is on medical parole and who becomes eligible for parole pursuant to the provisions of subdivision two of section two hundred fifty-nine-i of this article shall be eligible for parole consideration pursuant to such subdivision.

5. A denial of release on medical parole or expiration of medical parole in accordance with the provisions of paragraph (f) of subdivision four of this section shall not preclude the inmate from reapplying for medical parole or otherwise affect an inmate's eligibility for any other form of release provided for by law.

6. To the extent that any provision of this section requires disclosure of medical information for the purpose of processing an application or making a decision, regarding release on medical parole or renewal of medical parole, or for the purpose of appropriately supervising a person released on medical parole, and that such disclosure would otherwise be prohibited by article twenty-seven-F of the public health law, the provisions of this section shall be controlling.

7. The commissioner and the chairman of the board shall be authorized to promulgate rules and regulations for their respective agencies to implement the provisions of this section.

8. Any decision made by the board pursuant to this section may be appealed pursuant to subdivision four of section two hundred fifty-nine-i of this article.

9. The chairman shall report annually to the governor, the temporary president of the senate and the speaker of the assembly, the chairpersons of the assembly and senate codes committees, the chairperson of the senate crime and corrections committee, and the chairperson of the assembly corrections committee the number of inmates who have applied for medical parole; the number who have been granted medical parole; the nature of the illness of the applicants, the counties to which they have been released and the nature of the placement pursuant to the medical discharge plan; the categories of reasons for denial for those who have been denied; the number of releasees who have been granted an additional period or periods of medical parole and the number of such grants; the number of releasees on medical parole who have been returned to imprisonment in the

custody of the department and the reasons for return.

HISTORY: Add, L 1992, ch 55, § 289, eff April 10, 1992; amd, L 1994, ch 503, §§ 1, 2, eff July 26, 1994, L 1995, ch 3, § 44, eff Oct 1, 1995, repealed Sept 1, 2015, L 2009, ch 56, §§ 1, 3–5 (Part J), eff April 7, 2009, L 2009, ch 56, § 2 (Part J), eff Sept 1, 2015, L 2009, ch 495, § 3, eff Nov 16, 2009, L 2009, ch 495, § 4, eff Sept 1, 2015, L 2011, ch 62, § 38-1 (Part C, Subpart A), eff March 31, 2011, L 2011, ch 62, § 38-1-1 (Part C, Subpart A), eff Sept 1, 2015.

§ 259-s. Release on medical parole for inmates suffering significant debilitating illnesses

1. (a) The board shall have the power to release on medical parole any inmate serving an indeterminate or determinate sentence of imprisonment who, pursuant to subdivision two of this section, has been certified to be suffering from a significant and permanent non-terminal condition, disease or syndrome that has rendered the inmate so physically or cognitively debilitated or incapacitated as to create a reasonable probability that he or she does not present any danger to society, provided, however, that no inmate serving a sentence imposed upon a conviction for murder in the first degree or an attempt or conspiracy to commit murder in the first degree shall be eligible for such release, and provided further that no inmate serving a sentence imposed upon a conviction for any of the following offenses shall be eligible for such release unless in the case of an indeterminate sentence he or she has served at least one-half of the minimum period of the sentence and in the case of a determinate sentence he or she has served at least one-half of the term of his or her determinate sentence: murder in the second degree, manslaughter in the first degree, any offense defined in article one hundred thirty of the penal law or an attempt to commit any of these offenses. Solely for the purpose of determining medical parole eligibility pursuant to this section, such one-half of the minimum period of the indeterminate sentence and one-half of the term of the determinate sentence shall not be credited with any time served under the jurisdiction of the department prior to the commence-ment of such sentence pursuant to the opening paragraph of subdivision one of section 70.30 of the penal law or subdivision two-a of section 70.30 of the penal law, except to the extent authorized by subdivision three of section 70.30 of the penal law.

(b) Such release shall be granted only after the board considers whether, in light of the inmate's medical condition, there is a reasonable probability that the inmate, if released, will live and remain at liberty without violating the law, and that such release is not incompatible with the welfare of society and will not so deprecate the seriousness of the crime as to undermine respect for the law, and shall be subject to the limits and conditions specified in subdivision four of this section. In making this determination, the board shall consider: (i) the nature and seriousness of the inmate's crime; (ii) the inmate's prior criminal record; (iii) the inmate's disciplinary, behavioral and rehabilitative record during the term of his or her incarceration; (iv) the amount of time the inmate must serve before becoming eligible for release pursuant to section two hundred fifty-nine-i of this article; (v) the current age of the inmate and his or her age at the time of the crime; (vi) the recommendations of the sentencing court, the district attorney and the victim or the victim's representative; (vii) the nature of the inmate's medical condition, disease or syndrome and the extent of medical treatment or care that the inmate will require as a result of that condition, disease or syndrome; and (viii) any other relevant factor. Except as set forth in paragraph (a) of this subdivision, such release may be granted at any time during the term of an inmate's sentence, notwithstanding any other provision of law.

(c) The board shall afford notice to the sentencing court, the district attorney, the attorney for the inmate and, where necessary pursuant to subdivision two of section two hundred fifty-nine-i of this article, the crime victim, that the inmate is being considered for release pursuant to this section and the parties receiving notice shall have thirty days to comment on the release of the inmate. Release on medical parole shall not be granted until the expiration of the comment period provided for in this paragraph.

2. (a) The commissioner, on the commissioner's own initiative or at the request of an inmate, or an inmate's spouse, relative or attorney, may, in the exercise of the commissioner's discretion, direct that an investigation be undertaken to determine whether a diagnosis should be made of an inmate who appears to be suffering from a significant and permanent non-terminal and incapacitating condition, disease or syndrome. Any such medical diagnosis shall be made by a physician licensed to practice medicine in this state pursuant to section sixty-five hundred twenty-four of the education law. Such physician shall either be employed by the department, shall render professional services at the request of the department, or shall be employed by a hospital or medical facility used by the department for the medical treatment of inmates. The diagnosis shall be reported to the commissioner and shall include but shall not be limited to a description of the condition, disease or syndrome suffered by the inmate, a prognosis concerning the likelihood that the inmate will not recover from such condition, disease or syndrome, a description of the inmate's physical or cognitive incapacity which shall include a prediction respecting the likely duration of the incapacity, and a statement by the physician of whether the inmate is so debilitated or incapacitated as to be severely restricted in his or her ability to self-ambulate or to perform significant normal activities of daily living. This report also shall include a recommendation of the type and level of services and treatment the inmate would require if granted medical parole and a recommendation for the types of settings in which the services and treatment should be given.

(b) The commissioner, or the commissioner's designee, shall review the diagnosis and may certify that the inmate is suffering from such condition, disease or syndrome and that the inmate is so debilitated or incapacitated as to create a reasonable probability that he or she is physically or cognitively incapable of presenting any danger to society. If the commissioner does not so certify then the inmate shall not be referred to the board for consideration for release on medical parole. If the commissioner does so certify, then the commissioner shall, within seven working days of receipt of such diagnosis, refer the inmate to the board for consideration for release on medical parole. However, no such referral of an inmate to the board of parole shall be made unless the inmate has been examined by a physician and diagnosed as having a condition, disease or syndrome as previously described herein at some time subsequent to such inmate's admission to a facility operated by the department.

(c) When the commissioner refers an inmate to the board, the commissioner shall provide an appropriate medical discharge plan established by the department. The department is authorized to request assistance from the department of health and from the county in which the inmate resided and committed his or her crime, which shall provide assistance with respect to the development and implementation of a discharge plan, including potential placements of a releasee. The department and the department of health shall jointly develop standards for the medical discharge plan that are appropriately adapted to the criminal justice setting, based on standards established by the department of health for hospital medical discharge planning. The board may postpone its decision pending completion of an adequate discharge plan, or may deny release based on inadequacy of the discharge plan.

3. Any certification by the commissioner or the commissioner's designee pursuant to this section shall be deemed a judicial function and shall not be reviewable if done in accordance with law.

4. (a) Medical parole granted pursuant to this section shall be for a period of six months.

(b) The board shall require as a condition of release on medical parole that the releasee agree to remain under the care of a physician while on medical parole and in a hospital established pursuant to article twenty-eight of the public health law, a hospice established pursuant to article forty of the public health law or any other placement, including a residence with family or others, that can provide appropriate medical care as specified in the medical discharge plan required by subdivision two of this section. The medical discharge plan shall state that the availability of the placement has been confirmed, and by whom. Notwithstanding any other provision of law, when an inmate who qualifies for release under this section is cognitively incapable of signing the requisite documentation to effectuate the medical discharge plan and, after a diligent search no person has been identified who could otherwise be appointed as the inmate's guardian by a court of competent jurisdiction, then, solely for the purpose of implementing the medical discharge plan, the facility health services director at the facility where the inmate is currently incarcerated shall be lawfully empowered to act as the inmate's guardian for the purpose of effectuating the medical discharge.

(c) Where appropriate, the board shall require as a condition of release that medical parolees be supervised on intensive caseloads at reduced supervision ratios.

(d) The board shall require as a condition of release on medical parole that the releasee undergo periodic medical examinations and a medical examination at least one month prior to the expiration of the period of medical parole and, for the purposes of making a decision pursuant to paragraph (e) of this subdivision, that the releasee provide the board with a report, prepared by the treating physician, of the results of such examination. Such report shall specifically state whether or not the parolee continues to suffer from a significant and permanent non-terminal and debilitating condition, disease, or syndrome, and to be so debilitated or incapacitated as to be severely restricted in his or her ability to self-ambulate or to perform significant normal activities of daily living.

(e) Prior to the expiration of the period of medical parole the board shall review the medical examination report required by paragraph (d) of this subdivision and may again grant medical parole pursuant to this section; provided, however, that the provisions of paragraph (c) of subdivision one and subdivision two of this section shall not apply.

(f) If the updated medical report presented to the board states that a parolee released pursuant to this section is no longer so debilitated or incapacitated as to create a reasonable probability that he or she is physically or cognitively incapable of presenting any danger to society or if the releasee fails to submit the updated medical report then the board may not make a new grant of medical parole pursuant to paragraph (e) of this subdivision. Where the board has not granted medical parole pursuant to such paragraph (e) the board shall promptly conduct through one of its members, or cause to be conducted by a hearing officer designated by the board, a hearing to determine whether the releasee is suffering from a significant and permanent non-terminal and incapacitating condition, disease or syndrome and is so debilitated or incapacitated as to create a reasonable probability that he or she is physically or cognitively incapable of presenting any danger to society and does not present a danger to society. If the board makes such a determination then it may make a new grant of medical parole pursuant to the standards of paragraph (b) of subdivision one of this section. At the hearing, the releasee shall have the right to representation by counsel, including the right, if the releasee is financially unable to retain counsel, to have the appropriate court assign counsel in accordance with the county or city plan for representation placed in operation pursuant to article eighteen-B of the county law.

(g) The hearing and determination provided for by paragraph (f) of this subdivision shall be concluded within the six month period of medical parole. If the board does not renew the grant

Exec. L.

of medical parole, it shall order that the releasee be returned immediately to the custody of the department of correctional services.

(h) In addition to the procedures set forth in paragraph (f) of this subdivision, medical parole may be revoked at any time upon any of the grounds specified in paragraph (a) of subdivision three of section two hundred fifty-nine-i of this article, and in accordance with the procedures specified in subdivision three of section two hundred fifty-nine-i of this article.

(i) A releasee who is on medical parole and who becomes eligible for parole pursuant to the provisions of subdivision two of section two hundred fifty-nine-i of this article shall be eligible for parole consideration pursuant to such subdivision.

5. A denial of release on medical parole or expiration of medical parole in accordance with the provisions of paragraph (f) of subdivision four of this section shall not preclude the inmate from reapplying for medical parole or otherwise affect an inmate's eligibility for any other form of release provided for by law.

6. To the extent that any provision of this section requires disclosure of medical information for the purpose of processing an application or making a decision, regarding release on medical parole or renewal of medical parole, or for the purpose of appropriately supervising a person released on medical parole, and that such disclosure would otherwise be prohibited by article twenty-seven-F of the public health law, the provisions of this section shall be controlling.

7. The commissioner and the chair of the board shall be authorized to promulgate rules and regulations for their respective agencies to implement the provisions of this section.

8. Any decision made by the board pursuant to this section may be appealed pursuant to subdivision four of section two hundred fifty-nine-i of this article.

9. The chair of the board shall report annually to the governor, the temporary president of the senate and the speaker of the assembly, the chairpersons of the assembly and senate codes committees, the chairperson of the senate crime and corrections committee, and the chairperson of the assembly corrections committee the number of inmates who have applied for medical parole under this section; the number who have been granted medical parole; the nature of the illness of the applicants, the counties to which they have been released and the nature of the placement pursuant to the medical discharge plan; the categories of reasons for denial for those who have been denied; the number of releasees who have been granted an additional period or periods of medical parole and the number of such grants; the number of releasees on medical parole who have been returned to imprisonment in the custody of the department and the reasons for return.

  HISTORY: Add, L 2009, ch 56, § 6 (Part J), eff April 7, 2009; amd, L 2009, ch 495, § 5, eff Nov 16, 2009, L 2011, ch 62, § 38-m (Part C, Subpart A), eff March 31, 2011.

* * *

ARTICLE 22 OFFICE OF VICTIM SERVICES

HISTORY: Add, L 1966, ch 894, § 1, eff Aug 1, 1966. Another Art 22, add, L 1966, ch 828, § 1; repealed, L 1972, ch 664, § 15, eff Sept 1, 1972. A third Art 22, add, L 1966, ch 986, § 1; renumbered Art 26, L 1970, ch 385, § 1; repealed, L 1975, ch 34, § 1, eff April 1, 1975. Article heading, amd, L 1982, ch 17, § 3, eff March 15, 1982.

§ 620. Declaration of policy and legislative intent

The legislature recognizes that many innocent persons suffer personal physical injury or death as a result of criminal acts. Such persons or their dependents may thereby suffer disability, incur financial hardships, or become dependent upon public assistance. The legislature finds and determines that there is a need for government financial assistance for such victims of crime. Accordingly, it is the legislature's intent that aid, care and support be provided by the state, as a matter of grace, for such victims of crime.

HISTORY: Add, L 1966, ch 894, § 1, eff Aug 1, 1966. Another § 620, add, L 1966, ch 828, § 1; repealed, L 1972, ch 664, § 15, eff Sept 1, 1972.

§ 621. Definitions

For the purposes of this article:

1. "Office" shall mean the office of victim services.

2. "Claimant" shall mean the person filing a claim pursuant to this article.

3. "Crime" shall mean

(a) an act committed in New York state which would, if committed by a mentally competent criminally responsible adult, who has no legal exemption or defense, constitute a crime as defined in and proscribed by law; or

(b) an act committed outside the state of New York against a resident of the state of New York which would be compensable had it occurred within the state of New York and which occurred in a state which does not have an eligible crime victim compensation program as such term is defined in the federal victims of crime act of 1984; or

(c) an act of terrorism, as defined in section 2331 of title 18, United States Code, committed outside of the United States against a resident of New York state.

4. "Family", when used with reference to a person, shall mean (a) any person related to such person within the third degree of consanguinity or affinity, (b) any person maintaining a sexual

relationship with such person, or (c) any person residing in the same household with such person.

5. "Victim" shall mean (a) a person who suffers personal physical injury as a direct result of a crime; (b) a person who is the victim of either the crime of (1) unlawful imprisonment in the first degree as defined in section 135.10 of the penal law, (2) kidnapping in the second degree as defined in section 135.20 of the penal law, (3) kidnapping in the first degree as defined in section 135.25 of the penal law, (4) labor trafficking as defined in section 135.35 of the penal law, or (5) sex trafficking as defined in section 230.34 of the penal law; or a person who has had a frivolous lawsuit filed against them.

6. "Representative" shall mean one who represents or stands in the place of another person, including but not limited to an agent, an assignee, an attorney, a guardian, a committee, a conservator, a partner, a receiver, an administrator, an executor or an heir of another person, or a parent of a minor.

7. "Good samaritan" shall mean a person who, other than a law enforcement officer, acts in good faith (a) to apprehend a person who has committed a crime in his presence or who has in fact committed a felony, (b) to prevent a crime or an attempted crime from occurring, or (c) to aid a law enforcement officer in effecting an arrest.

8. "Essential personal property" shall mean articles of personal property necessary and essential to the health, welfare or safety of the victim.

9. "Elderly victim" shall mean a person sixty years of age or older who suffers loss, or damage as a direct result of a crime.

10. "Disabled victim" shall mean a person who has (a) physical, mental or medical impairment from anatomical, physiological or neurological conditions which prevents the exercise of a normal bodily function or is demonstrable by medically accepted clinical or laboratory diagnostic techniques or (b) a record of such an impairment or (c) a condition regarded by others as such an impairment.

11. For purposes of this article "child victim" shall mean a person less than eighteen years of age who suffers physical, mental or emotional injury, or loss or damage, as a direct result of a crime or as a result of witnessing a crime.

12. "Frivolous lawsuit" shall mean a lawsuit brought by the individual who committed a crime against the victim of the crime, found to be frivolous, meritless and commenced to harass, intimidate or menace the victim by a court and costs were imposed upon the plaintiff pursuant to section eighty-three hundred three-a of the civil practice law and rules.

13. "Crime scene cleanup" shall mean removing, or attempting to remove from the crime scene, blood, dirt, stains, debris, odors, or other impurities caused by the crime or the processing of the crime scene and the repair or replacement of permanent fixtures and floor coverings, soiled, damaged, or rendered unusable or uncleanable by the crime, the processing of the crime scene, or by being taken into evidence.

14. "Securing a crime scene" shall mean taking immediate, emergency steps to return the residence where the crime occurred to the level of safety present prior to the crime. It shall include, but not be limited to, the repair or replacement of doors, windows, screens and locks or other points of entry damaged or rendered unusable by the crime.

15. "Livery" shall mean a for-hire vehicle duly licensed by the appropriate local licensing

authority, designed to carry no more than five passengers for direct cash payment by such passenger and which is affiliated with a livery car base. The term "livery" shall not include a vehicle driven by a "black car operator", as defined in section one hundred sixty-cc of this chapter.

16. "Livery car base" shall mean a central facility, wherever located, that dispatches the livery operator to both pick-up and discharge passengers in the state.

17. "Livery operator" shall mean the registered owner of a livery, or a driver designated by such registered owner to operate the registered owner's livery as the registered owner's authorized designee, whose status as a livery operator victim arose out of and in the course of providing services while affiliated with a livery car base. The term "livery operator" shall not include a "black car operator", as defined in section one hundred sixty-cc of this chapter.

18. "Livery operator victim" shall mean a livery operator homicide victim or a livery operator assault victim.

19. "Livery operator assault victim" shall mean a livery operator who is the victim of a violent felony offense, as defined in subdivision one of section 70.02 of the penal law, which offense directly results in a serious physical injury, as defined in subdivision ten of section 10.00 of the penal law.

20. "Livery operator homicide victim" shall mean a livery operator who is the victim of a homicide, as defined in article one hundred twenty-five of the penal law.

21. "Local licensing authority" shall mean the governmental agency in the state, if any, that is authorized to license a livery and/or a livery car base.

22. "Financial counselling" shall mean financial services provided by an experienced financial counsellor or adviser which may include, but are not limited to: analysis of a victim's financial situation such as income producing capacity and crime related financial obligations, assistance with restructuring budget and debt, assistance in accessing insurance, public assistance and other benefits, assistance in completing the financial aspects of victim impact statements, and assistance in settling estates and handling guardianship matters.

23. "Relocation expenses" shall mean the cost of relocating a crime victim, when relocation is necessary for the health or safety of the victim. An award for relocation expenses of a victim shall include the reasonable cost of moving and transportation expenses for (a) the victim, which may include the relocation expenses of their spouse and any other person dependent for his or her principal support upon the victim or spouse who lives in the same residence as the victim, or (b) if the victim is a child victim eligible for such an award pursuant to this article, the child victim, which may include the relocation expenses of their parent, stepparent, guardian and any other person dependent for his or her principal support upon such parent, stepparent, and guardian who lives in the same residence as the child victim.

HISTORY: Add, L 1966, ch 894, § 1, eff Aug 1, 1966; amd, L 1981, ch 445, § 1, eff July 7, 1981, L 1982, ch 17, § 1, eff March 15, 1982, L 1982, ch 351, § 1, eff June 21, 1982, and applicable to all claims filed on or after the date on which it shall have become a law; amd, L 1983, ch 197, § 1, eff May 31, 1983, and applicable to claims submitted and based upon crimes committed on or after such date; amd, L 1985, ch 688, §§ 8, 9, L 1986, ch 263, § 2, L 1988, ch 56, § 1, eff Nov 1, 1988, L 1989, ch 163, § 1, eff June 17, 1989, L 1995, ch 543, § 1, eff Aug 2, 1995, L 1996, ch 710, § 1, eff Oct 9, 1996, L 1997, ch 620, §§ 1, 2, eff Nov 1, 1997, L 1998, ch 81, § 1, eff June 2, 1998, L 2000, ch 148, § 1, eff July 12, 2000, deemed eff on and after Jan 1, 2000, L 2003, ch 391, § 1, eff Aug 19, 2003, L 2005, ch 377, § 1, eff Aug 2, 2005, L 2007, ch 74, § 12, eff Nov 1, 2007, L 2010, ch 56, § 6 (Part A-1), eff June 22, 2010, L 2013, ch 261, § 1, eff Aug 30, 2013.

Exec. L.

§ 622. Office of victim services

There is hereby created in the executive department the office of victim services, hereinafter in this article referred to as the "office". The office shall be headed by a director, who shall be appointed by the governor for a term of three years. The director shall coordinate and recommend policy relating to the provision of services to crime victims. The director shall appoint staff and perform such other functions to ensure the efficient operation of the office within the amounts made available therefor by appropriation.

HISTORY: Add, L 2010, ch 56, § 7 (Part A-1), eff June 22, 2010.

§ 623. Powers and duties of the office

The office shall have the following powers and duties:

1. To establish and maintain a principal office and such other offices within the state as it may deem necessary.

2. To appoint a secretary, counsel, clerks and such other employees and agents as it may deem necessary, fix their compensation within the limitations provided by law, and prescribe their duties.

3. To adopt, promulgate, amend and rescind suitable rules and regulations to carry out the provisions and purposes of this article, including rules for the determination of claims, rules for the approval of attorneys' fees for representation before the office and/or before the appellate division upon judicial review as provided for in section six hundred twenty-nine of this article, and rules for the authorization of qualified persons to assist claimants in the preparation of claims for presentation to the office.

4. To request from the division of state police, from county or municipal police departments and agencies and from any other state or municipal department or agency, or public authority, and the same are hereby authorized to provide, such assistance and data as will enable the office to carry out its functions and duties.

5. To hear and determine all claims for awards filed with the office pursuant to this article, and to reinvestigate or reopen cases as necessary.

6. To direct medical examination of victims.

7. To hold hearings, administer oaths or affirmations, examine any person under oath or affirmation and to issue subpoenas requiring the attendance and giving of testimony of witnesses and require the production of any books, papers, documentary or other evidence. The powers provided in this subdivision may be delegated by the director to any member or employee of the office. A subpoena issued under this subdivision shall be regulated by the civil practice law and rules.

8. To take or cause to be taken affidavits or depositions within or without the state.

9. To establish and maintain a special investigative unit to expedite processing of claims by senior citizens and special emergency situations, and to promote the establishment of a volunteer program of home visitation to elderly and invalid victims of violent crime.

10. To advise and assist the governor in developing policies designed to recognize the legitimate rights, needs and interests of crime victims.

11. To coordinate state programs and activities relating to crime victims.

12. To cooperate with and assist political subdivisions of the state and not-for-profit

organizations in the development of local programs for crime victims.

13. To study the operation of laws and procedures affecting crime victims and recommend to the governor and legislature proposals to improve the administration and effectiveness of such laws.

14. To establish an advisory council to assist in formulation of policies on the problems of crime victims and to provide recommendations to the director to improve the delivery of services to victims by the office.

15. To work with national associations, statewide coalitions, regional coalitions, victim service providers, and other advocates to address and advance the rights and interests of crime victims of the state.

16. To promote and conduct studies, research, analyses and investigations of matters affecting the interests of crime victims.

17. To coordinate training opportunities for crime victim advocates and service providers.

18. To serve as a clearinghouse for information relating to crime victims' problems and programs.

19. To accept, with the approval of the governor, as agent of the state, any grant including federal grants, or any gift for the purposes of this article. Any monies so received may be expended by the office to effectuate any purpose of this article, subject to the applicable provisions of the state finance law.

20. To render each year to the governor and to the legislature, on or before December first of each year, a written report on the office's activities including, but not limited to, specific information on each of the subdivisions of this section, and the manner in which the rights, needs and interests of crime victims are being addressed by the state's criminal justice system. Such report shall also include, but not be limited to:

(a) [As amended L 2010, ch 56, §§ 37, 71 (Part A) and ch 56, § 8 (Part A-1)] Information transmitted by the office of probation and correctional alternatives under subdivision five of section 390.30 of the criminal procedure law and subdivision seven of section 351.1 of the family court act which the office shall compile, review and make recommendations on how to promote the use of restitution and encourage its enforcement.

(b) Information relating to the implementation of and compliance with article twenty-three of this chapter by the criminal justice agencies and the "crime victim-related agencies" of the state. Such report shall also include but not be limited to information regarding crime victim service programs, including:

(1) the programs funded by the office;

(2) other sources of funding for crime victims service programs;

(3) an assessment of the adequacy of the current level of appropriation to the office to meet the reasonable needs of crime victims service programs for funding under section six hundred thirty-one-a of this article; and

(4) an estimate of the reasonable needs of programs in the next fiscal year.

21. To make grants to local crime victim service programs and carry out related duties under section six hundred thirty-one-a of this article.

22. To delegate to specified employees of the office the power to disallow claims under circumstances where regulations of the office provide for disallowance without prejudice to the reopening of claims.

HISTORY: Add, L 1966, ch 894, § 1, eff Aug 1, 1966; amd, L 1976, ch 952, § 2, L 1979, ch 415, §§ 2, 3, L 1985, ch 14, § 7, L 1985, ch 688, § 14, eff Aug 1, 1985, L 1986, ch 74, §§ 1, 2, eff May 12, 1986, L 1986, ch 346, § 1, eff Sept 15, 1986, L 1986, ch 418, § 4, eff Nov 1, 1986, L 2010, ch 56, §§ 37, 71, eff June 22, 2010, L 2010, ch 56, § 8 (Part A-1), eff June 22, 2010.

§ 624. Eligibility

1. Except as provided in subdivision two of this section, the following persons shall be eligible for awards pursuant to this article:

(a) a victim of a crime;

(b) a surviving spouse, grandparent, parent, stepparent, guardian, brother, sister, stepbrother, stepsister, child or stepchild of a victim of a crime who died as a direct result of such crime;

(c) any other person dependent for his principal support upon a victim of a crime who died as a direct result of such crime;

(d) any person who has paid for or incurred the burial expenses of a victim who died as a direct result of such crime, except such person shall not be eligible to receive an award for other than burial expenses unless otherwise eligible under paragraph (a), (b) or (c) of this subdivision;

(e) an elderly victim of a crime;

(f) a disabled victim of a crime;

(g) a child victim of a crime;

(h) a parent, stepparent, grandparent, guardian, brother, sister, stepbrother or stepsister of a child victim of a crime;

(i) a surviving spouse of a crime victim who died from causes not directly related to the crime when such victim died prior to filing a claim with the office or subsequent to filing a claim but prior to the rendering of a decision by the office. Such award shall be limited to out-of-pocket loss incurred as a direct result of the crime; and

(j) a spouse, child or stepchild of a victim of a crime who has sustained personal physical injury as a direct result of a crime.

(k) a surviving spouse, child or stepchild of a victim of a crime who died as a direct result of such crime and where such crime occurred in the residence shared by such family member or members and the victim.

2. A person who is criminally responsible for the crime upon which a claim is based or an accomplice of such person shall not be eligible to receive an award with respect to such claim. A member of the family of a person criminally responsible for the crime upon which a claim is based or a member of the family of an accomplice of such person, shall be eligible to receive an award, unless the office determines pursuant to regulations promulgated to carry out the provisions and purposes of this article, that the person criminally responsible will receive substantial economic benefit or unjust enrichment from the compensation. In such circumstances the award may be reduced or structured in such way as to remove the substantial economic benefit or unjust enrichment to such person or the claim may be denied.

HISTORY: Add, L 1966, ch 894, § 1, eff Aug 1, 1966; amd, L 1968, ch 661, § 1; amd, L, 1982, ch 205, § 1, L 1983, ch 197, § 2, L 1983, ch 811, § 1, L 1983, ch 805, § 2, L 1984, ch 729, § 1, L 1986, ch 74, § 3, L 1986, ch 263, § 3, L 1989, ch 307, § 1, eff July 10, 1989, L 1990, ch 859, § 1, eff Oct 1, 1990, L 1998, ch 276, § 1, eff July 10, 1998, L 1999, ch 427, § 1, eff Aug 31, 1999, L 2010, ch 56, § 9 (Part A-1), eff June 22, 2010, L 2012, ch 233, § 1, eff July 18, 2012, L 2013, ch 119, § 1, eff Aug 11, 2013.

§ 625. Filing of claims

1. A claim may be filed by a person eligible to receive an award, as provided in section six hundred twenty-four of this article, or, if such person is under the age of eighteen years, an incompetent, or a conservatee, by his relative, guardian, committee, conservator, or attorney.

2. A claim must be filed by the claimant not later than one year after the occurrence or discovery of the crime upon which such claim is based, one year after a court finds a lawsuit to be frivolous, or not later than one year after the death of the victim, provided, however, that upon good cause shown, the office may extend the time for filing. The office shall extend the time for filing where the claimant received no notice pursuant to section six hundred twenty-five-a of this article and had no knowledge of eligibility pursuant to section six hundred twenty-four of this article.

3. Claims shall be filed in person, by mail or electronically, in such manner as the office may prescribe. The office shall accept for filing all claims submitted by persons eligible under subdivision one of this section and alleging the jurisdictional requirements set forth in this article and meeting the requirements as to form in the rules and regulations promulgated to carry out the provisions and purposes of this article.

4. Upon filing of a claim pursuant to this article, the office shall promptly notify the district attorney of the county wherein the crime is alleged to have occurred. If, within ten days after such notification, such district attorney advises the office that a criminal prosecution is pending upon the same alleged crime and requests that action by the office be deferred, the office shall defer all proceedings under this article until such time as such criminal prosecution has been concluded and shall so notify such district attorney and the claimant. When such criminal prosecution has been concluded, such district attorney shall promptly so notify the office. Nothing in this section shall limit the authority of the office to grant emergency awards pursuant to section six hundred thirty of this article.

HISTORY: Add, L 1966, ch 894, § 1, eff Aug 1, 1966; amd, L 1969, ch 726, § 1, eff May 22, 1969, L 1972, ch 287, § 1, L 1974, ch 906, § 3, L 1976, ch 952, § 1, L 1981, ch 115, § 50, eff May 18, 1981, L 1984, ch 330, § 1, L 1985, ch 688, § 2, eff Aug 1, 1985, L 1997, ch 620, § 3, eff Nov 1, 1997, L 2001, ch 359, § 1, eff Oct 3, 2001, L 2010, ch 56, § 10 (Part A-1), eff June 22, 2010.

§ 625-a. Information relative to claims; application forms

1. Every police station, precinct house, any appropriate location where a crime may be reported and any location required by the rules and regulations of the office shall have available informative booklets, pamphlets and other pertinent written information, including information cards, to be supplied by the office, relating to the availability of crime victims compensation including all necessary application blanks required to be filed with the office and shall display prominently posters giving notification of the existence and general provisions of this article, those provisions of the penal law that prohibit the intimidation of crime victims and the location of the nearest crime victim service program. The office may issue guidelines for the location of such display and shall provide posters, application forms, information cards and general information. Every victim who reports a crime in any manner whatsoever shall be given notice about the rights of crime victims and the existence of all relevant local victim's assistance programs and services pursuant to section six hundred twenty-five-b of this article, and supplied by the person receiving the report with information, application blanks, and information cards which shall clearly state: (a) that crime

victims may be eligible for state compensation benefits; (b) the address and phone number of the office; (c) that police and district attorneys can help protect victims against harassment and intimidation; (d) the addresses and phone numbers of local victim service programs, where appropriate, or space for inserting that information; or (e) any other information the office deems appropriate. Such cards shall be designed by the office in consultation with local police, and shall be printed and distributed by the office. The office shall develop a system for distributing a sufficient supply of the information cards referred to in this subdivision, to all the appropriate designated locations, which shall include a schedule for meeting that requirement.

1-a. Every general hospital established under the laws of this state, which maintains facilities for providing out-patient emergency medical care, shall display prominently in its emergency room posters giving notification of the existence and general provisions of this chapter. The board may issue guidelines for the location of such display and shall provide posters, application forms and general information regarding the provision of this chapter to each such hospital.

2. No cause of action of whatever nature or kind arising out of a failure to give or receive the notice required by this section shall accrue to any person against the state or any of its agencies or local subdivisions, or, any police officer or other agent, servant or employee thereof, or any hospital or agents or employees thereof, nor shall any such failure be deemed or construed to affect or alter any time limitation or other requirement contained in this article for the filing or payment of a claim hereunder.

HISTORY: Add, L 1976, ch 952, § 7, eff Jan 1, 1977; amd, L 1979, ch 416, §§ 1, 2, eff July 5, 1979, L 1983, ch 77, § 1, L 1985, ch 688, § 3, eff Aug 1, 1985, L 2006, ch 173, § 1, eff Jan 1, 2007, L 2010, ch 56, § 15 (Part A-1), eff June 22, 2010.

§ 625-b. Standardized victim notification and verification procedures for police officers

1. The commissioner of the division of criminal justice services in cooperation with the office shall develop and implement a standardized procedure to be used by police officers, county sheriffs' departments and state police officers whereby victims of crime are notified about the rights of crime victims and the existence of programs designed to assist crime victims.

2. In establishing a victims assistance notification procedure, consideration shall be given to (a) developing a uniform method of informing victims of crime of their rights and services available, (b) including notification as part of a routine task performed in the course of law enforcement duties, and (c) documenting a victim's receipt of such notice.

3. All state or municipal printed forms for a police primary investigation report shall include a space to indicate that the victim did or did not receive information on victim's rights, office of victim services assistance and relevant local assistance pursuant to subdivision one of section six hundred twenty-five-a of this article.

HISTORY: Add, L 2006, ch 173, § 2, eff Jan 1, 2007; amd, L 2006, ch 173, § 3, eff Jan 1, 2007, L 2010, ch 56, § 16 (Part A-1), eff June 22, 2010.

§ 626. Out-of-pocket loss; definition

1. Out-of-pocket loss shall mean unreimbursed and unreimbursable expenses or indebtedness reasonably incurred for medical care or other services necessary as a result of the injury upon which such claim is based, including such expenses incurred as a result of the exacerbation of a pre-existing disability or condition directly resulting from the crime or causally related to the crime. Such expenses or indebtedness shall include the cost of counseling for the eligible spouse, grandparents, parents, stepparents, guardians, brothers, sisters, stepbrothers, stepsisters, children or stepchildren of a homicide victim, and crime victims who have sustained a personal physical injury

as the direct result of a crime and the spouse, children or stepchildren of such physically injured victim. For the purposes of this subdivision, the victim of a sex offense as defined in article one hundred thirty of the penal law is presumed to have suffered physical injury. Such counseling may be provided by local victim service programs, where available. It shall also include the cost of residing at or utilizing services provided by shelters for battered spouses and children who are eligible pursuant to subdivision two of section six hundred twenty-four of this article, and the cost of reasonable attorneys' fees for representation before the office and/or before the appellate division upon judicial review not to exceed one thousand dollars.

2. Out-of-pocket loss shall also include the cost of counseling for a child victim and the parent, stepparent, grandparent, guardian, brother, sister, stepbrother or stepsister of such victim, pursuant to regulations promulgated to carry out the provisions and purposes of this article.

3. Notwithstanding any inconsistent provision of this article, and without regard to the financial difficulty of the claimant, out-of-pocket loss also shall include the cost of unreimbursed and unreimbursable counseling expense or indebtedness reasonably incurred by relief workers who worked at the World Trade Center site in the immediate aftermath of the September eleventh, two thousand one terrorist attacks, or incurred by individuals who personally witnessed such attacks, where such counseling expense or indebtedness is incurred as a direct result of such work or of the witnessing of such attacks, and is incurred on or before December thirty-first, two thousand seven.

HISTORY: Add, L 1966, ch 894, § 1; amd, L 1976, ch 952, § 3, L 1983, ch 198, § 1, L 1985, ch 688, § 1, L 1986, ch 263, § 4, L 1986, ch 312, § 1, eff Nov 14, 1986, L 1986, ch 263, § 4, eff Jan 1, 1987, L 1989, ch 324, § 1, eff Nov 7, 1989, L 1998, ch 276, § 2, eff July 10, 1998, L 1998, ch 276, § 2, eff July 10, 1998, L 1999, ch 427, § 2, eff Aug 31, 1999, L 2005, ch 408, § 1, eff Aug 2, 2005, L 2007, ch 21, § 1, eff April 17, 2007, L 2010, ch 56, § 17 (Part A-1), eff June 22, 2010.

§ 627. Determination of claims

1. The office shall determine claims in accordance with rules and regulations promulgated by the director. Such rules and regulations must provide for:

(a) written notification to an applying victim of their right to representation by counsel, as well as their potential eligibility for an award of attorney's fees pursuant to subdivision one of section six hundred twenty-six of this article;

(b) administrative procedures regarding the intake and initial processing of claims, including mandatory timelines for the initiation of investigation of a properly filed claim;

(c) the investigation and determination of claims regardless of whether the alleged criminal has been apprehended or prosecuted for or convicted of any crime based upon the same incident, or has been acquitted, or found not guilty of the crime in question owing to criminal irresponsibility or other legal exemption;

(d) the rebuttable presumption that a child reported missing for a time period exceeding seven days is a victim of a crime;

(e) the generation of a written decision for each properly filed claim, and written notice to the claimant of the written decision and their right to a copy of such a decision, as well as any rights to appeal that the claimant may have of the decision and a projected date of payment in the case of an award to the claimant;

(f) expedited determination of claims with respect to a livery operator within thirty days of the date upon which the claim was accepted for filing, as well as standards for awards of loss of earnings or support granted pursuant to rules and regulations promulgated in accordance with

Exec. L.

the provisions of this subdivision and subdivision three of section six hundred thirty-one of this article. Each award for loss of earnings pursuant to rules and regulations promulgated in accordance with this subdivision made with respect to a claim involving a livery operator assault victim shall be for such period of time as the office determines that the livery operator assault victim is unable to work and has lost earnings as a result of such assault, in an amount not to exceed twenty thousand dollars. Such award shall be distributed in increments of five hundred dollars per week. Each award for loss of support pursuant to rules and regulations promulgated in accordance with this subdivision made with respect to a claim involving a livery operator homicide victim shall be in the amount of twenty thousand dollars, distributed in increments of five hundred dollars per week; and

(g) provisions for any claimant to submit an additional claim for any loss of earnings or support in excess of the amount awarded pursuant to rules and regulations in accordance with paragraph (f) of this subdivision, or an additional claim for any other award pursuant to rules and regulations promulgated in accordance with this article, in each case pursuant to and in accordance with the other provisions of this article or any rules and regulations promulgated in accordance thereof and subject to any applicable maximum award limitations contained in this article.

2. The claimant may, within thirty days after receipt of the decision of the office regarding a claim, make an application in writing to the director of the office for reconsideration of such decision. The director, or his or her designee, shall consider such applications in accordance with rules and regulations promulgated by the director and may affirm or modify the decision. The decision of the director, or his or her designee, shall become the final determination of the office regarding the claim.

HISTORY: Add, L 2010, ch 56, § 18 (Part A-1), eff June 22, 2010.

§ 628. [Repealed]

HISTORY: Add, L 1966, ch 894, § 1; amd, L 1973, ch 491, § 1, eff June 5, 1973, L 1976, ch 952, § 4, eff Jan 1, 1977, L 1986, ch 74, § 4, eff May 12, 1986, L 1986, ch 346, § 3, eff Sept 15, 1986, L 2005, ch 408, § 3, eff Aug 2, 2005; repealed, L 2010, ch 56, § 19 (Part A-1), eff June 22, 2010. Section heading, amd, L 1973, ch 491, § 1, eff June 5, 1973. Sub 2, amd, L 1986, ch 346, § 3, eff Sept 15, 1986. Sub 3, amd, L 1976, ch 952, § 4, eff Jan 1, 1977. Sub 4, amd, L 1986, ch 74, § 4, eff May 12, 1986. Sub 4, amd, L 2005, ch 408, § 3, eff Aug 2, 2005.

§ 629. Judicial review

1. Within fifteen days after receipt of the copy of the report containing the final decision of the office, the comptroller shall, if in his judgment the award is illegal or excessive, notify the office of his conclusion, state the reasons for that conclusion, and provide specific recommendations for modification. Upon receiving such notification, the office shall have fifteen days within which to review and either modify or re-affirm its award. If after such modification or reaffirmation the comptroller continues to adjudge the award to be illegal or excessive, he may within fifteen days after receipt of such modification or reaffirmation, commence a proceeding in the appellate division of the supreme court, third department, to review the decision of the office. Such proceeding shall be heard in a summary manner and shall have precedence over all other civil cases in such court. Any claimant aggrieved by a final decision of the office may commence a proceeding to review that decision pursuant to article seventy-eight of the civil practice law and rules.

2. Any such proceeding shall be commenced in accordance with the civil practice law and rules.

HISTORY: Add, L 1966, ch 894, § 1, eff Aug 1, 1966; amd, L 1976, ch 952, § 5, L 1985, ch 688, § 11, eff Aug 1, 1985, L 2010, ch 56, § 20 (Part A-1), eff June 22, 2010.

§ 630. Emergency awards

1. Notwithstanding the provisions of section six hundred twenty-seven of this article, if it appears to the office, that such claim is one with respect to which an award probably will be made, and undue hardship will result to the claimant if immediate payment is not made, the office may make one or more emergency awards to the claimant pending a final decision of the office or payment of an award in the case, provided, however, that the total amount of such emergency awards shall not exceed twenty-five hundred dollars. The amount of such emergency awards shall be deducted from any final award made to the claimant, and the excess of the amount of any such emergency award over the amount of the final award, or the full amount of any emergency awards if no final award is made, shall be repaid by the claimant to the office.

2. Notwithstanding the provisions of section six hundred twenty-seven of this article, local crime victim service programs shall be authorized to provide emergency awards to crime victims for essential personal property, medical treatment, shelter costs, security services, counseling and transportation the total amount of such emergency awards not to exceed five hundred dollars. These programs shall be reimbursed by the office, pursuant to the provisions of this article, if it is subsequently determined that the victim is an eligible claimant. Local crime victim service programs shall be authorized to establish special accounts for this purpose. The office shall initiate a program to assist local crime victim service programs in establishing special accounts to provide emergency awards, within amounts designated for that purpose.

> **HISTORY:** Add, L 1966, ch 894, § 1; amd, L 1979, ch 417, § 1, eff July 5, 1979, L 1986, ch 346, § 5, eff Sept 15, 1986, L 2007, ch 318, § 1, eff July 18, 2007, L 2010, ch 56, § 21 (Part A-1), eff June 22, 2010.

§ 631. Awards

1. No award shall be made unless the office finds that (a) a crime was committed, (b) such crime directly resulted in personal physical injury to or the exacerbation of a preexisting disability, or condition, or death of, the victim, and (c) criminal justice agency records show that such crime was promptly reported to the proper authorities; and in no case may an award be made where the criminal justice agency records show that such report was made more than one week after the occurrence of such crime unless the office, for good cause shown, finds the delay to have been justified; provided, however, in cases involving an alleged sex offense as contained in article one hundred thirty of the penal law or incest as defined in section 255.25, 255.26 or 255.27 of the penal law or labor trafficking as defined in section 135.35 of the penal law or sex trafficking as defined in section 230.34 of the penal law or an offense chargeable as a family offense as described in section eight hundred twelve of the family court act or section 530.11 of the criminal procedure law, the criminal justice agency report need only be made within a reasonable time considering all the circumstances, including the victim's physical, emotional and mental condition and family situation. For the purposes of this subdivision, "criminal justice agency" shall include, but not be limited to, a police department, a district attorney's office, and any other governmental agency having responsibility for the enforcement of the criminal laws of the state provided, however, that in cases involving such sex offense a criminal justice agency shall also mean a family court, a governmental agency responsible for child and/or adult protective services pursuant to title six of article six of the social services law and/or title one of article nine-B of the social services law, and any medical facility established under the laws of the state that provides a forensic physical examination for victims of rape and sexual assault.

1-a. No award shall be made for a frivolous lawsuit unless the office finds that the victim has been awarded costs pursuant to section eighty-three hundred three-a of the civil practice law and rules and the individual responsible for the payment of costs is unable to pay such costs provided, however, that in no event shall the amount of such costs exceed two thousand five hundred dollars.

2. Any award made pursuant to this article shall be in an amount not exceeding out-of-pocket expenses, including indebtedness reasonably incurred for medical or other services necessary as a result of the injury upon which the claim is based; loss of earnings or support resulting from such injury not to exceed thirty thousand dollars; burial expenses not exceeding six thousand dollars of a victim who died as a direct result of a crime; the costs of crime scene cleanup and securing of a crime scene not exceeding twenty-five hundred dollars; reasonable relocation expenses not exceeding twenty-five hundred dollars; and the unreimbursed cost of repair or replacement of articles of essential personal property lost, damaged or destroyed as a direct result of the crime. An award for loss of earnings shall include earnings lost by a parent or guardian as a result of the hospitalization of a child victim under age eighteen for injuries sustained as a direct result of a crime. In addition to the medical or other services necessary as a result of the injury upon which the claim is based, an award may be made for rehabilitative occupational training for the purpose of job retraining or similar employment-oriented rehabilitative services based upon the claimant's medical and employment history. For the purpose of this subdivision, rehabilitative occupational training shall include but not be limited to educational training and expenses. An award for rehabilitative occupational training may be made to a victim, or to a family member of a victim where necessary as a direct result of a crime.

3. Any award made for loss of earnings or support shall, unless reduced pursuant to other provisions of this article, be in an amount equal to the actual loss sustained, provided, however, that no such award shall exceed six hundred dollars for each week of lost earnings or support. Awards with respect to livery operator victims pursuant to paragraphs (f) and (g) of subdivision one of section six hundred twenty-seven of this article shall be granted in the amount and in the manner provided therein. The aggregate award for all such losses pursuant to this subdivision, including any awards made pursuant to paragraphs (f) and (g) of subdivision one of section six hundred twenty-seven of this article, shall not exceed thirty thousand dollars. If there are two or more persons entitled to an award as a result of the death of a person which is the direct result of a crime, the award shall be apportioned by the office among the claimants.

4. Any award made pursuant to this article shall be reduced by the amount of any payments received or to be received by the claimant as a result of the injury (a) from or on behalf of the person who committed the crime, (b) under insurance programs mandated by law, (c) from public funds, (d) under any contract of insurance wherein the claimant is the insured or beneficiary, (e) as an emergency award pursuant to section six hundred thirty of this article. Notwithstanding the foregoing, where the person injured is a livery operator victim, because undue hardship may result to the claimant if immediate payment is not made, any award pursuant to paragraphs (f) and (g) of subdivision one of section six hundred twenty-seven of this article shall be granted without reduction for workers' compensation benefits to be received, if any.

5. (a) In determining the amount of an award, the office shall determine whether, because of his conduct, the victim of such crime contributed to the infliction of his injury, and the office shall reduce the amount of the award or reject the claim altogether, in accordance with such determination.

(b) Notwithstanding the provisions of paragraph (a) of this subdivision, the office shall disregard for this purpose the responsibility of the victim for his own injury where the record shows that the person injured was acting as a good samaritan, as defined in this article.

(c) Notwithstanding any inconsistent provision of this article, where the person injured acted as a good samaritan, the office may, without regard to the financial difficulty of the claimant, make an award for out-of-pocket losses. Such award may also include compensation for any loss of property up to five thousand dollars suffered by the victim during the course of his actions as a good samaritan.

(d) Notwithstanding any inconsistent provision of this article, where a person acted as a good samaritan, and was killed as a direct result of the crime, the office may, without regard to the financial difficulty of the claimant, make a lump sum award to such claimant for actual loss of support not to exceed thirty thousand dollars.

(e) Notwithstanding any inconsistent provision of this article, where a police officer or firefighter, both paid and volunteer, dies from injuries received in the line of duty as a direct result of a crime, the office may, without regard to the financial difficulty of the claimant, make an award for the unreimbursed counseling expenses of the eligible spouse, parents, brothers, sisters or children of such victim, and/or the reasonable burial expenses incurred by the claimant.

6. (a) Claims may be approved only if the office finds that unless the claimant's award is approved he will suffer financial difficulty. However, no finding of financial difficulty is required for a claim for an emergency award or an award less than five thousand dollars. In determining financial difficulty, the office shall consider all relevant factors, including but not limited to:

(1) the number of claimant's dependents;

(2) reasonable living expenses of the claimant and his family;

(3) any special health, rehabilitative or educational needs of the claimant and his dependents;

(4) the claimant's employment situation including income and potential earning capacity;

(5) the claimant's net financial resources after authorized deduction as provided in paragraphs (b) and (c) of this subdivision;

(6) whether claimant's financial resources will become exhausted during his lifetime; and

(7) the nature and the amount of claimant's total debt and liabilities, including the amount of debt incurred or to be incurred to pay for losses and expenses of the crime, and the extent to which claimant's essential assets will have to be liquidated.

(b) Claimant's net financial resources do not include the present value of future earnings, and shall be determined by the office by deducting from his total financial resources the value, within reasonable limits, of the following items:

(1) a homestead, not exceeding five hundred thousand dollars, or a total of ten years' rent for a renter;

(2) personal property consisting of clothing and strictly personal effects;

(3) household furniture, appliances and equipment;

(4) tools and equipment necessary for the claimant's trade, occupation or business;

(5) a family automobile;

(6) life insurance, except in death claims; and

(7) retirement, education and health plans or contributions to a retirement or pension program including but not limited to contributions to: (i) employee profit sharing plans, (ii) employee money purchase plans, (iii) 401 (k) plans, (iv) simplified employee pensions (SEP), (v) individual retirement accounts (IRA), (vi) 403 (b) plans, (vii) 457 plans, (viii) Keogh plans, (self employed), and (ix) any other plan or account for which contributions are made primarily for retirement purposes.

(c) The office, after taking into consideration the claimant's financial resources, may exempt that portion of the victim's or claimant's annual income required to meet reasonable living expenses and the value of inventory or other property necessary for the claimant's business or occupation or the production of income required to meet reasonable living expenses. In no event shall the aggregate value of exemptions under this paragraph exceed one hundred thousand dollars.

(d) Nothing contained in this subdivision shall be construed to mean that the office must maintain the same standard of living enjoyed by the claimant prior to the death or injury.

(e) The director shall promulgate such rules and regulations as are necessary for the implementation of this section.

7. Notwithstanding the provisions of subdivision six of this section, an award shall include out-of-pocket expenses, including indebtedness reasonably incurred by the victim of a sex offense or the person responsible for the victim of such sex offense, as such sex offense is defined in article one hundred thirty of the penal law, for a hospital or medical examination in connection with the investigation or prosecution of any such offense.

8. Notwithstanding the provisions of subdivisions one, two and three of this section, an elderly or disabled victim who has not been physically injured as a direct result of a crime, shall only be eligible for an award that includes the unreimbursed cost of repair or replacement of essential personal property that has been lost, damaged or destroyed as a direct result of a crime, transportation expenses incurred for necessary court appearances in connection with the prosecution of such crimes and the unreimbursed cost of counselling provided to the elderly or disabled victim on account of mental or emotional stress or financial counselling provided to the elderly or disabled victim on account of financial difficulty resulting from the incident in which the crime occurred if such counselling or financial counselling is commenced within one year from the date of the incident.

9. Any award made for the cost of repair or replacement of essential personal property, including cash losses of essential personal property, shall be limited to an amount of five hundred dollars, except that all cash losses of essential personal property shall be limited to the amount of one hundred dollars.

10. Notwithstanding any contrary provision of law, an award shall include reasonable transportation expenses incurred for necessary court appearances in connection with the prosecution of such crimes upon which the claim is based.

11. Notwithstanding the provisions of subdivisions one, two and three of this section, an individual who was a victim of either the crime of unlawful imprisonment in the first degree as defined in section 135.10 of the penal law, kidnapping in the second degree as defined in section 135.20 of the penal law or kidnapping in the first degree as defined in section 135.25 of the penal law who has not been physically injured as a direct result of such crime shall only be eligible for an award that includes loss of earnings or support and the unreimbursed costs of counseling

provided to such victim on account of mental or emotional stress resulting from the incident in which the crime occurred.

12. Notwithstanding the provisions of subdivisions one, two and three of this section, an individual who was a victim of either the crime of menacing in the second degree as defined in subdivision two or three of section 120.14 of the penal law, menacing in the first degree as defined in section 120.13 of the penal law, criminal obstruction of breathing or blood circulation as defined in section 121.11 of the penal law, harassment in the second degree as defined in subdivision two or three of section 240.26 of the penal law, harassment in the first degree as defined in section 240.25 of the penal law, aggravated harassment in the second degree as defined in subdivision five of section 240.30 of the penal law, aggravated harassment in the first degree as defined in subdivision two of section 240.31 of the penal law, criminal contempt in the first degree as defined in paragraph (ii) or (iv) of subdivision (b) or subdivision (c) of section 215.51 of the penal law, or stalking in the fourth, third, second or first degree as defined in sections 120.45, 120.50, 120.55 and 120.60 of the penal law, respectively, who has not been physically injured as a direct result of such crime shall only be eligible for an award that includes loss of earning or support, the unreimbursed cost of repair or replacement of essential personal property that has been lost, damaged or destroyed as a direct result of such crime, the unreimbursed cost for security devices to enhance the personal protection of such victim, transportation expenses incurred for necessary court expenses in connection with the prosecution of such crime, the unreimbursed costs of counseling provided to such victim on account of mental or emotional stress resulting from the incident in which the crime occurred, reasonable relocation expenses, and for occupational or job training.

13. Notwithstanding any other provision of law, rule, or regulation to the contrary, when any New York state accredited hospital, accredited sexual assault examiner program, or licensed health care provider furnishes services to any sexual assault survivor, including but not limited to a health care forensic examination in accordance with the sex offense evidence collection protocol and standards established by the department of health, such hospital, sexual assault examiner program, or licensed healthcare provider shall provide such services to the person without charge and shall bill the office directly. The office, in consultation with the department of health, shall define the specific services to be covered by the sexual assault forensic exam reimbursement fee, which must include at a minimum forensic examiner services, hospital or healthcare facility services related to the exam, and related laboratory tests and necessary pharmaceuticals; including but not limited to HIV post-exposure prophylaxis provided by a hospital emergency room at the time of the forensic rape examination pursuant to paragraph (c) of subdivision one of section twenty-eight hundred five-i of the public health law. Follow-up HIV post-exposure prophylaxis costs shall continue to be reimbursed according to established office procedure. The office, in consultation with the department of health, shall also generate the necessary regulations and forms for the direct reimbursement procedure. The rate for reimbursement shall be the amount of itemized charges not exceeding eight hundred dollars, to be reviewed and adjusted annually by the office in consultation with the department of health. The hospital, sexual assault examiner program, or licensed health care provider must accept this fee as payment in full for these specified services. No additional billing of the survivor for said services is permissible. A sexual assault survivor may voluntarily assign any private insurance benefits to which she or he is entitled for the healthcare forensic examination, in which case the hospital or healthcare provider may not charge the office. A hospital, sexual assault examiner program or licensed health care provider shall, at the time of the initial visit, request assignment of any private health insurance benefits to which the sexual assault survivor is entitled on a form prescribed by the office; provided, however, such sexual assault survivor shall be advised orally and in writing that he or she may decline to provide such

information regarding private health insurance benefits if he or she believes that the provision of such information would substantially interfere with his or her personal privacy or safety and in such event, the sexual assault forensic exam fee shall be paid by the office. Such sexual assault survivor shall also be advised that providing such information may provide additional resources to pay for services to other sexual assault victims. If he or she declines to provide such health insurance information, he or she shall indicate such decision on the form provided by the hospital, sexual assault examiner program or licensed health care provider, which form shall be prescribed by the office.

14. Notwithstanding any inconsistent provision of this article, where a victim dies from injuries received as a direct result of the World Trade Center terrorist attacks on September eleventh, two thousand one, the office may make an award for the unreimbursed and unreimbursable expense or indebtedness reasonably incurred for the cost of counseling for the eligible spouse, grandparents, parents, stepparents, guardians, brothers, sisters, stepbrothers, stepsisters, children, or stepchildren of such victim. Any award for such expense incurred on or before December thirty-first, two thousand seven, shall be made without regard to the financial difficulty of the claimant.

15. Notwithstanding any inconsistent provision of this article, where a victim is injured as a direct result of the World Trade Center terrorist attacks on September eleventh, two thousand one, the office may make an award for the unreimbursed and unreimbursable expense or indebtedness reasonably incurred by the claimant for medical care or counseling services necessary as a result of such injury. Any award for such expense or indebtedness incurred on or before December thirty-first, two thousand seven, shall be made without regard to the financial difficulty of the claimant.

16. Notwithstanding any inconsistent provision of this article, and without regard to the financial difficulty of the claimant, where a victim dies from injuries received as a direct result of the World Trade Center terrorist attacks on September eleventh, two thousand one, the office may make an award of reasonable burial expenses for such victim.

17. Notwithstanding the provisions of subdivision one of this section, where a child victim has not been physically injured as a direct result of a crime, or has witnessed a crime in which no physical injury occurred, the claimant shall only be eligible for an award that includes the unreimbursed cost of repair or replacement of essential personal property of the child victim that has been lost, damaged or destroyed as a direct result of a crime, transportation expenses incurred by the claimant for necessary court appearances of the child victim in connection with the prosecution of such crimes, and, if counseling is commenced within one year from the date of the incident or its discovery, (1) the unreimbursed cost of counseling provided to the child victim on account of mental or emotional stress resulting from the incident in which the crime occurred, and/or (2) the unreimbursed cost of counseling provided to the claimant eligible under paragraph (h) of subdivision one of section six hundred twenty-four of this article and resulting from the incident in which the crime occurred.

18. Notwithstanding any inconsistent provision of this article and subject to any applicable maximum award limitations contained in this section, where a victim has died as a direct result of the crime upon which the claim is based and the crime occurred in the residence of a person eligible pursuant to paragraph (k) of subdivision one of section six hundred twenty-four of this article, the office may make no more than one award for crime scene clean-up related to such residence.

HISTORY: Add, L 1966, ch 894, § 1, eff Aug 1, 1966; amd, L 1970, ch 376, § 1, L 1974, ch 392, § 1, L 1976, ch 952, § 6, L 1977, ch 693, § 1, L 1979, ch 418, § 1, eff July 5, 1979, L 1982, ch 351, § 2, eff June 21, 1982, L 1982, ch 885, § 1, L 1983, ch 85, § 1, L 1983, ch 197, § 4, eff May 31,

1983, L 1983, ch 810, § 1, eff Sept 28, 1983, L 1983, ch 197, § 3, L 1985, ch 688, §§ 6, 7, 10,, L 1986, ch 74, § 5, eff May 12, 1986, L 1986, ch 309, § 1, L 1986, ch 327, § 1, L 1990, ch 720, § 1, eff July 22, 1990L 1986, ch 465, § 1, L 1991, ch 400, § 1, eff July 15, 1991, L 1988, ch 368, § 1, L 1989, ch 345, § 1, L 1991, ch 166, §§ 364–367, L 1990, ch 763, § 1, eff July 22, 1990, L 1992, ch 55, §§ 295–298, eff April 10, 1992, L 1994, ch 244, § 1, eff July 6, 1994, L 1995, ch 543, § 2, eff Aug 2, 1995, L 1996, ch 141, § 1, eff Nov 1, 1996, L 1996, ch 309, §§ 55–60, eff July 13, 1996, L 1997, ch 620, § 4, eff Nov 1, 1997, L 1998, ch 58, § 30 (Part E), eff May 28, 1998, L 1998, ch 81, § 2, eff June 2, 1998, L 1998, ch 443, § 1, eff July 22, 1998, L 1999, ch 635, § 6, eff Dec 1, 1999, L 2000, ch 1, § 28, eff Feb 1, 2001, L 2000, ch 148, §§ 3, 4, eff July 12, 2000, L 2003, ch 264, § 68, eff April 1, 2005, L 2003, ch 391, § 2, eff Aug 19, 2003, L 2005, ch 322, § 1, eff July 26, 2005, L 2005, ch 377, § 2, eff Aug 2, 2005, L 2005, ch 408, § 4, eff Aug 2, 2005, L 2006, ch 320, § 24, eff Nov 1, 2006, L 2007, ch 21, § 2, eff April 17, 2007, L 2007, ch 74, § 13, eff Nov 1, 2007, L 2008, ch 162, § 1, eff Sept 1, 2008, L 2009, ch 56, § 1 (Part E), eff April 7, 2009, L 2009, ch 272, § 1, eff July 28, 2009, L 2010, ch 56, § 22 (Part A-1), eff June 22, 2010, L 2011, ch 534, § 1, eff Dec 22, 2011, L 2012, ch 39, § 2, eff Nov 27, 2012, L 2013, ch 119, § 2, eff Aug 11, 2013, L 2014, ch 188, § 2, eff July 23, 2014.

§ 631-a. Crime victim service programs

1. The office shall make grants, within amounts appropriated for that purpose, for crime victim service programs to provide services to crime victims and witnesses. These programs shall be operated at the community level by not-for-profit organizations, by agencies of local government or by any combination thereof. Crime victim service programs may be designed to serve crime victims and witnesses in general in a particular community, or may be designed to serve a category of persons with special needs relating to a particular kind of crime.

2. The director shall promulgate regulations, relating to these grants, including guidelines for its determinations.

(a) These regulations shall be designed to promote:

(i) alternative funding sources other than the state, including local government and private sources;

(ii) coordination of public and private efforts to aid crime victims; and

(iii) long range development of services to all victims of crime in the community and to all victims and witnesses involved in criminal prosecutions.

(b) These regulations shall also provide for services including, but not limited to:

(i) assistance to claimants seeking crime victims compensation benefits;

(ii) referrals, crisis intervention and other counseling services;

(iii) services to elderly victims and to child victims and their families;

(iv) transportation and household assistance; and

(v) outreach to the community and education and training of law enforcement and other criminal justice officials to the needs of crime victims.

3. [Repealed]

HISTORY: Add, L 1985, ch 688, § 12, eff Aug 1, 1985; amd, L 1986, ch 263, § 6, eff Jan 1, 1987, provided that all rules and regulations necessary for the implementation of this act are to be made on or before Jan 1, 1987; amd, L 2010, ch 56, §§ 27, 28 (Part A-1), eff June 22, 2010.

§ 632. Manner of payment

1. The award shall be paid in a lump sum, except that in the case of death or protracted disability

the award shall provide for periodic payments to compensate for loss of earnings or support. No award made pursuant to this article shall be subject to execution or attachment other than for expenses resulting from the injury which is the basis for the claim.

2. Where a person entitled to receive an award is a person under the age of eighteen years, an incompetent, or a conservatee, the award may be paid to a relative, guardian, committee, conservator, or attorney of such person on behalf of and for the benefit of such person. In such case the payee shall be required to file a periodic accounting of the award with the office and to take such other action as the office shall determine is necessary and appropriate for the benefit of the person under the age of eighteen years, incompetent or conservatee.

HISTORY: Add, L 1966, ch 894, § 1, eff Aug 1, 1966; amd, L 1972, ch 287, § 2, eff May 15, 1972, L 1974, ch 906, § 4, L 1981, ch 115, § 51, eff May 18, 1981, L 2010, ch 56, § 23 (Part A-1), eff June 22, 2010.

§ 632-a. Crime victims

1. For the purposes of this section:

(a) "Crime" means (i) any felony defined in the laws of the state; or (ii) an offense in any jurisdiction which includes all of the essential elements of any felony defined in the laws of this state and: (A) the crime victim, as defined in subparagraph (i) of paragraph (d) of this subdivision, was a resident of this state at the time of the commission of the offense; or (B) the act or acts constituting the offense occurred in whole or in part in this state.

(b) "Profits from a crime" means (i) any property obtained through or income generated from the commission of a crime of which the defendant was convicted; (ii) any property obtained by or income generated from the sale, conversion or exchange of proceeds of a crime, including any gain realized by such sale, conversion or exchange; and (iii) any property which the defendant obtained or income generated as a result of having committed the crime, including any assets obtained through the use of unique knowledge obtained during the commission of, or in preparation for the commission of, a crime, as well as any property obtained by or income generated from the sale, conversion or exchange of such property and any gain realized by such sale, conversion or exchange.

(c) "Funds of a convicted person" means all funds and property received from any source by a person convicted of a specified crime, or by the representative of such person as defined in subdivision six of section six hundred twenty-one of this article excluding child support and earned income, where such person:

(i) is an inmate serving a sentence with the department of corrections and community supervision or a prisoner confined at a local correctional facility or federal correctional institute, and includes funds that a superintendent, sheriff or municipal official receives on behalf of an inmate or prisoner and deposits in an inmate account to the credit of the inmate pursuant to section one hundred sixteen of the correction law or deposits in a prisoner account to the credit of the prisoner pursuant to section five hundred-c of the correction law; or

(ii) is not an inmate or prisoner but who is serving a sentence of probation or conditional discharge or is presently subject to an undischarged indeterminate, determinate or definite term of imprisonment or period of post-release supervision or term of supervised release, but shall include earned income earned during a period in which such person was not in compliance with the conditions of his or her probation, parole, conditional release, period of post-release supervision by the department of corrections and community supervision or term of supervised release with the United States probation office or United States parole commission. For purposes of this subparagraph, such period of non-compliance shall be measured, as applicable, from the earliest date of delinquency determined by the department of corrections and community supervision, or from the earliest date on which a declaration of delinquency is filed pursuant to section 410.30 of the criminal procedure law and thereafter sustained, or from the earliest date of delinquency determined in accordance with applicable federal law, rules or regulations, and shall continue until a final determination sustaining the violation has been made by the trial court, the department of corrections and community supervision, or appropriate federal authority; or

(iii) is no longer subject to a sentence of probation or conditional discharge or indeterminate, determinate or definite term of imprisonment or period of post-release supervision or term of supervised release, and where within the previous three years: the full or maximum term or period terminated or expired or such person was granted a discharge by the state board of parole or the department of corrections and community supervision pursuant to applicable law, or granted a discharge or termination from probation pursuant to applicable law or granted a discharge or termination under applicable federal or state law, rules or regulations prior to the expiration of such full or maximum term or period; and includes only: (A) those funds paid to such person as a result of any interest, right, right of action, asset, share, claim, recovery or benefit of any kind that the person obtained, or that accrued in favor of such person, prior to the expiration of such sentence, term or period; (B) any recovery or award collected in a lawsuit after expiration of such sentence where the right or cause of action accrued prior to the expiration or service of such sentence; and (C) earned income earned during a period in which such person was not in compliance with the conditions of his or her probation, parole, conditional release, period of post-release supervision by the department of corrections and community supervision or term of supervised release with the United States probation office or United States parole commission. For purposes of this subparagraph, such period of non-compliance shall be measured, as applicable, from the earliest date of delinquency determined by the department of corrections and community supervision, or from the earliest date on which a declaration of delinquency is filed pursuant to section 410.30 of the criminal procedure law and thereafter sustained, or from the earliest date of delinquency determined in accordance with applicable federal law, rules or regulations, and shall continue until a final determination sustaining the violation has been made by the trial court, the department of corrections and community supervision, or appropriate federal authority.

(d) "Crime victim" means (i) the victim of a crime; (ii) the representative of a crime victim as defined in subdivision six of section six hundred twenty-one of this article; (iii) a good samaritan as defined in subdivision seven of section six hundred twenty-one of this article; (iv) the office of victim services or other governmental agency that has received an application for or provided financial assistance or compensation to the victim.

(e) (i) "Specified crime" means:

(A) a violent felony offense as defined in subdivision one of section 70.02 of the penal law;

(B) a class B felony offense defined in the penal law;

(C) an offense for which a merit time allowance may not be received against the sentence pursuant to paragraph (d) of subdivision one of section eight hundred three of the correction law;

(D) an offense defined in the penal law that is titled in such law as a felony in the first degree;

(E) grand larceny in the fourth degree as defined in subdivision six of section 155.30 or grand larceny in the second degree as defined in section 155.40 of the penal law;

(F) criminal possession of stolen property in the second degree as defined in section 165.52 of the penal law; or

(G) an offense in any jurisdiction which includes all of the essential elements of any of the crimes specified in clauses (A) through (F) of this subparagraph and either the crime victim as defined in subparagraph (i) of paragraph (d) of this subdivision was a resident of this state at the time of the commission of the offense or the act or acts constituting the crime occurred in whole or in part in this state.

(ii) Notwithstanding the provisions of subparagraph (i) of this paragraph a "specified crime" shall not mean or include an offense defined in any of the following articles of the penal law: articles one hundred fifty-eight, one hundred seventy-eight, two hundred twenty, two hundred twenty-one, two hundred twenty-five, and two hundred thirty.

(f) "Earned income" means income derived from one's own labor or through active participation in a business as distinguished from income from, for example, dividends or investments.

2. (a) Every person, firm, corporation, partnership, association or other legal entity, or representative of such person, firm, corporation, partnership, association or entity, which knowingly contracts for, pays, or agrees to pay: (i) any profits from a crime as defined in paragraph (b) of subdivision one of this section, to a person charged with or convicted of that crime, or to the representative of such person as defined in subdivision six of section six hundred twenty-one of this article; or (ii) any funds of a convicted person, as defined in paragraph (c) of subdivision one of this section, where such conviction is for a specified crime and the value, combined value or aggregate value of the payment or payments of such funds exceeds or will exceed ten thousand dollars, shall give written notice to the office of the payment or obligation to pay as soon as practicable after discovering that the payment or intended payment constitutes profits from a crime or funds of a convicted person.

(b) Notwithstanding subparagraph (ii) of paragraph (a) of this subdivision, whenever the payment or obligation to pay involves funds of a convicted person that a superintendent, sheriff or municipal official receives or will receive on behalf of an inmate serving a sentence with the department of corrections and community supervision or prisoner confined at a local correctional facility and deposits or will deposit in an inmate account to the credit of the inmate or in a prisoner account to the credit of the prisoner, and the value, combined value or aggregate value of such funds exceeds or will exceed ten thousand dollars, the superintendent, sheriff or municipal official shall also give written notice to the office.

Further, whenever the state or subdivision of the state makes payment or has an obligation to pay funds of a convicted person, as defined in subparagraph (ii) or (iii) of paragraph (c) of subdivision one of this section, and the value, combined value or aggregate value of such funds exceeds or will exceed ten thousand dollars, the state or subdivision of the state shall also give written notice to the office.

In all other instances where the payment or obligation to pay involves funds of a convicted person, as defined in subparagraph (ii) or (iii) of paragraph (c) of subdivision one of this section, and the value, combined value or aggregate value of such funds exceeds or will exceed ten thousand dollars, the convicted person who receives or will receive such funds, or the representative of such person as defined in subdivision six of section six hundred twenty-one of this article, shall give written notice to the office.

(c) The office, upon receipt of notice of a contract, an agreement to pay or payment of profits from a crime or funds of a convicted person pursuant to paragraph (a) or (b) of this subdivision, or upon receipt of notice of funds of a convicted person from the superintendent, sheriff or municipal official of the facility where the inmate or prisoner is confined pursuant to section one hundred sixteen or five hundred-c of the correction law, shall notify all known crime victims of the existence of such profits or funds at their last known address.

3. Notwithstanding any inconsistent provision of the estates, powers and trusts law or the civil practice law and rules with respect to the timely bringing of an action, any crime victim shall have the right to bring a civil action in a court of competent jurisdiction to recover money damages from a person convicted of a crime of which the crime victim is a victim, or the representative of that convicted person, within three years of the discovery of any profits from a crime or funds of a convicted person, as those terms are defined in this section. Notwithstanding any other provision of law to the contrary, a judgment obtained pursuant to this section shall not be subject to execution or enforcement against the first one thousand dollars deposited in an inmate account to the credit of the inmate pursuant to section one hundred sixteen of the correction law or in a prisoner account to the credit of the prisoner pursuant to section five hundred-c of the correction law. In addition, where the civil action involves funds of a convicted person and such funds were recovered by the convicted person pursuant to a judgment obtained in a civil action, a judgment obtained pursuant to this section may not be subject to execution or enforcement against a portion thereof in accordance with subdivision (k) of section fifty-two hundred five of the civil practice law and rules. If an action is filed pursuant to this subdivision after the expiration of all other applicable statutes of limitation, any other crime victims must file any action for damages as a result of the crime within three years of the actual discovery of such profits or funds, or within three years of actual notice received from or notice published by the office of such discovery, whichever is later.

4. Upon filing an action pursuant to subdivision three of this section, the crime victim shall give notice to the office of the filing by delivering a copy of the summons and complaint to the office. The crime victim may also give such notice to the office prior to filing the action so as to allow the office to apply for any appropriate provisional remedies which are otherwise authorized to be invoked prior to the commencement of an action.

5. Upon receipt of a copy of a summons and complaint, or upon receipt of notice from the crime victim prior to filing the action as provided in subdivision four of this section, the office shall immediately take such actions as are necessary to:

(a) notify all other known crime victims of the alleged existence of profits from a crime or funds of a convicted person by certified mail, return receipt requested, where the victims' names and addresses are known by the office;

(b) publish, at least once every six months for three years from the date it is initially notified by a victim, pursuant to subdivision four of this section, a legal notice in newspapers of general circulation in the county wherein the crime was committed and in counties contiguous to such county advising any crime victims of the existence of profits from a crime or funds of a convicted person. For crimes committed in a county located within a city having a population of one million or more, the notice shall be published in newspapers having general circulation in such city. The office may, in its discretion, provide for such additional notice as it deems necessary;

(c) avoid the wasting of the assets identified in the complaint as the newly discovered profits from a crime or as funds of a convicted person, in any manner consistent with subdivision six of this section.

6. The office, acting on behalf of the plaintiff and all other victims, shall have the right to apply for any and all provisional remedies that are also otherwise available to the plaintiff.

(a) The provisional remedies of attachment, injunction, receivership and notice of pendency available to the plaintiff under the civil practice law and rules, shall also be available to the office in all actions under this section.

(b) On a motion for a provisional remedy, the moving party shall state whether any other provisional remedy has previously been sought in the same action against the same defendant. The court may require the moving party to elect between those remedies to which it would otherwise be entitled.

7. (a) (i) Whenever it appears that a person or entity has knowingly and willfully failed to give notice in violation of paragraph (a) or (b) of subdivision two of this section, other than the state, a subdivision of the state, or a person who is a superintendent, sheriff or municipal official required to give notice pursuant to this section or section one hundred sixteen or section five hundred-c of the correction law, the office shall be authorized to serve a notice of hearing upon the person or entity by personal service or by registered or certified mail. The notice shall contain the time, place and purpose of the hearing. In addition, the notice shall be accompanied by a petition alleging facts of an evidentiary character that support or tend to support that the person or entity, who shall be named therein as a respondent, knowingly and willfully failed to give notice in violation of paragraph (a) or (b) of subdivision two of this section. Service of the notice and petition shall take place at least fifteen days prior to the date of the hearing.

(ii) The director or any individual designated by the director, shall preside over the hearing, shall administer oaths, may issue subpoenas and shall not be bound by the rules of evidence or civil procedure, but his or her determination shall be based on a preponderance of the evidence. At the hearing, the burden of proof shall be on the office. The office shall produce witnesses and present evidence in support of the alleged violation, which may include relevant hearsay evidence. The respondent, who may appear personally at the hearing, shall have the right of counsel and may cross-examine witnesses and produce evidence and witnesses in his or her behalf, which may include relevant hearsay evidence. The issue of whether the person who received an alleged payment or obligation to pay committed the underlying crime shall not be re-litigated at the hearing. Where the alleged violation is the failure to give notice of a payment amount involving two or more payments the combined value or aggregate value of which exceeds ten thousand dollars, no violation shall be found unless it is shown that such payments were intentionally structured to conceal their character as funds of a convicted person, as defined in this section.

(iii) At the conclusion of the hearing, if the director or designated individual is not satisfied that there is a preponderance of evidence in support of a violation, the director or designated individual shall dismiss the petition. If the director or designated individual is satisfied that there is a preponderance of the evidence that the respondent committed one or more violations, the director or designated individual shall so find. Upon such a finding, the director or designated individual shall prepare a written statement, to be made available to the respondent and respondent's counsel, indicating the evidence relied on and the reasons for finding the violation.

(iv) The director shall adopt, promulgate, amend and repeal administrative rules and regulations governing the procedures to be followed with respect to hearings, including rules and regulations for the administrative appeal of a decision made pursuant to this paragraph, provided such rules and regulations are consistent with the provisions of this subdivision.

(b) (i) Whenever it is found pursuant to paragraph (a) of this subdivision that a respondent knowingly and willfully failed to give notice in violation of paragraph (a) or (b) of subdivision two of this section, the office shall impose an assessment of up to the amount of the payment or obligation to pay and a civil penalty of up to one thousand dollars or ten percent of the payment or obligation to pay, whichever is greater. If a respondent fails to pay the assessment and civil penalty imposed pursuant to this paragraph, the assessment and civil penalty may be recovered from the respondent by an action brought by the attorney general, upon the request of the office, in any court of competent jurisdiction. The office shall deposit the assessment in an escrow account pending the expiration of the three year statute of limitations authorized by subdivision three of this section to preserve such funds to satisfy a civil judgment in favor of a person who is a victim of a crime committed by the convicted person to whom such failure to give notice relates. The office shall pay the civil penalty to the state comptroller who shall deposit the money in the state treasury pursuant to section one hundred twenty-one of the state finance law to the credit of the criminal justice improvement account established by section ninety-seven-bb of the state finance law.

(ii) The office shall then notify any crime victim or crime victims, who may have a claim against the convicted person, of the existence of such moneys. Such notice shall instruct such person or persons that they may have a right to commence a civil action against the convicted person, as well as any other information deemed necessary by the office.

(iii) Upon a crime victim's presentation to the office of a civil judgment for damages incurred as a result of the crime, the office shall satisfy up to one hundred percent of that judgment, including costs and disbursements as taxed by the clerk of the court, with the escrowed fund obtained pursuant to this paragraph, but in no event shall the amount of all judgments, costs and disbursements satisfied from such escrowed funds exceed the amount in escrow. If more than one such crime victim indicates to the office that they intend to commence or have commenced a civil action against the convicted person, the office shall delay satisfying any judgment, costs and disbursements until the claims of all such crime victims are reduced to judgment. If the aggregate of all judgments, costs and disbursement obtained exceeds the amount of escrowed funds, the amount used to partially satisfy each judgment shall be reduced to a pro rata share.

(iv) After expiration of the three year statute of limitations period established in subdivision three of this section, the office shall review all judgments that have been satisfied from such escrowed funds. In the event no claim was filed or judgment obtained prior to the expiration of the three year statute of limitations, the office shall return the escrowed amount to the respondent. In the event a claim or claims are pending at the expiration of the statute of limitations, such funds shall remain escrowed until the final determination of all such claims to allow the office to satisfy any judgment which may be obtained by the crime victim. Upon the final determination of all such claims and the satisfaction of up to one hundred percent of such claims by the office, the office shall be authorized to impose an additional civil penalty of up to one thousand dollars or ten percent of the payment or obligation to pay, whichever is greater. Prior to imposing any such penalty, the office shall serve a notice upon the respondent by personal service or by registered or certified mail of the intent of the office to impose such penalty thirty days after the date of the notice and of

Exec. L.

the opportunity to submit documentation concerning the office's determination. After imposing and deducting any such additional civil penalty, the office shall distribute such remaining escrowed funds, if any, as follows: fifty percent to the state comptroller, who shall deposit the money in the state treasury pursuant to section one hundred twenty-one of the state finance law to the credit of the criminal justice improvement account established by section ninety-seven-bb of the state finance law; and fifty percent to the respondent.

(v) Notwithstanding any provision of law, an alleged failure by a convicted person to give notice under this section may not result in proceedings for an alleged violation of the conditions of probation, parole, conditional release, post release supervision or supervised release unless: one or more claims were made by a crime victim against the convicted person pursuant to this section, and the office imposes an assessment and/or penalty upon the convicted person pursuant to this section, and the convicted person fails to pay the total amount of the assessment and/or penalty within sixty days of the imposition of such assessment and/or penalty.

(vi) Records maintained by the office and proceedings by the office based thereon regarding a claim submitted by a victim or a claimant shall be deemed confidential, subject to the exceptions that appear in subdivision one of section six hundred thirty-three of this article.

HISTORY: Add, L 1992, ch 618, § 10, eff July 24, 1992; amd, L 2001, ch 62, § 1, eff June 25, 2001, L 2010, ch 56, § 24 (Part A-1), eff June 22, 2010, L 2011, ch 62, §§ 100, 101 (Part C, Subpart B), eff March 31, 2011.

§ 633. Confidentiality of records

1. Records maintained by the office and proceedings by the office based thereon regarding a claim submitted by a victim or a claimant shall be deemed confidential with the following exceptions:

(a) requests for information based upon legitimate criminal justice purposes;

(b) judicial subpoenas;

(c) requests for information by the victim or claimant or his or her authorized representative;

(d) for purposes necessary and proper for the administration of this article.

2. All other records, including but not limited to, records maintained pursuant to sections six hundred thirty-one-a and six hundred thirty-two-a of this article and proceedings by the office based thereon shall be public record.

3. Any report or record obtained by the office, the confidentiality of which is protected by any other law or regulation, shall remain confidential subject to such law or regulation.

HISTORY: Add, L 1998, ch 64, § 1, eff May 21, 1998; amd, L 2010, ch 56, § 25 (Part A-1), eff June 22, 2010.

§ 634. Subrogation

1. (a) Acceptance of an award made pursuant to this article shall subrogate the state, to the extent of such award, to any right or right of action accruing to the claimant or the victim to recover payments on account of losses resulting from the crime with respect to which the award is made. Upon the payment of an award, the office may, by writing, notify the claimant that such claimant has ninety days, or thirty days prior to the date of expiration of the applicable statute of limitations, whichever period is shorter, within which to commence an action against his

assailant or any third party who, as a result of the crime, may be liable in damages to the claimant. If the claimant fails to commence an action within the time provided herein, such failure shall, after written notification by the office to the claimant, operate as an assignment of the claimant's cause of action against the assailant or such other third party to the state; provided, however, that should the claimant's cause of action be in an amount in excess of the office's award, such assignment shall be for only that portion of the cause of action which equals the amount of the award.

(b) The office of victim services shall review those claims that have been approved by the office and that have resulted in an award in excess of one thousand dollars for the purpose of identifying those causes of action that are likely to result in recovery of the state's payment to the victim. The office shall submit a list of these claims on a monthly basis to the attorney general with all necessary information relating to the case including whether the claimant's cause of action has been assigned to the office.

(c) The attorney general may commence an action against the defendant convicted of the crime or third party for money damages to the extent of the award paid, and the claimant shall retain a right of action, subject to defenses, to recover damages for the full amount of loss incurred by him as a result of the crime less the amount assigned to the state by operation of this subdivision. Notwithstanding any other provision of law, an action brought by the attorney general pursuant to this paragraph against the defendant convicted of the crime must be commenced within seven years of the crime or pursuant to the time frames authorized in subdivision three of section six hundred thirty-two-a of this article. A claimant who retains such right of action shall be permitted to intervene in any action brought pursuant to this subdivision by the attorney general. Any action brought by the attorney general may be compromised or settled provided the attorney general and the office find that such action is in the best interests of the state.

2. Acceptance of an award made pursuant to this article shall create a lien in favor of the state on the proceeds of any recovery from the person or persons liable for the injury or death giving rise to the award by the office, whether by judgment, settlement or otherwise, after the deduction of the reasonable and necessary expenditures, including attorney's fees, incurred in effecting such recovery, to the total amount of the award made by the office. Such lien shall attach to any moneys received or to be received by the claimant or victim on account of losses resulting from the crime. Should the claimant or victim secure a recovery from the person or persons liable for the injury or death giving rise to the award by the office, whether by judgment, settlement or otherwise, such claimant may, upon notice to the office, apply to the court in which the action was instituted, or to any court of competent jurisdiction if no action was instituted, for an order apportioning the reasonable and necessary expenditures, including attorney's fees, incurred in effecting such recovery. Such expenditures shall be equitably apportioned by the court between the claimant and the office. A copy of such lien shall be mailed to the clerk of the county within which the crime occurred and such clerk will file the copy in accordance with the duties of such clerk as set forth in section five hundred twenty-five of the county law. The amount of such lien may be compromised or settled by the office provided the office finds that such action is in the best interests of the state, or payment of the full amount of the lien to the state would cause undue hardship for the victim.

3. Any claimant who has received an award under this article, or his guardian, judicially appointed personal representative, or his estate, who brings an action for damages against the person or persons liable for the injury or death giving rise to an award by the office under this article shall give written notice to the office of the commencement of such action at the time such

action is commenced. Such notice shall be served personally or by certified mail, return receipt requested.

4. The attorney general may intervene, as of right, in any such action on behalf of the state of New York for the purpose of recovering the subrogated interest due the state of New York under the provisions of this article.

5. The director shall adopt rules and regulations to carry out the provisions and purposes of this section.

6. The office shall compile information on the number of cases submitted to the attorney general, the number of actions instituted by the attorney general to recover payments made to crime victims, the dollar amount of recoveries made in such actions both on behalf of the state and any awards made to victims who intervene in such actions. The office shall include this information, and any recommendations to the governor and legislature to improve the collection of awards, in its annual report.

> **HISTORY:** Add, L 1966, ch 894, § 1, eff Aug 1, 1966; amd, L 1982, ch 513, § 1, Oct 11, 1982, L 1985, ch 688, § 13, L 1986, ch 74, § 7, eff May 12, 1986, L 1986, ch 477, §§ 1, 2, eff July 21, 1986, L 1991, ch 401, § 1, L 1993, ch 397, § 1, eff July 21, 1993, L 2010, ch 56, § 26 (Part A-1), eff June 22, 2010.

§ 635. Severability of provisions

If any provision of this article or the application thereof to any person or circumstances is held invalid, the remainder of this article and the application of such provision to other persons or circumstances shall not be affected thereby.

> **HISTORY:** Add, L 1966, ch 894, § 1, eff Aug 1, 1966.

ARTICLE 23   FAIR TREATMENT STANDARDS FOR CRIME VICTIMS

> **HISTORY:** Add, L 1984, ch 94, § 1, eff April 24, 1984. Former Art 23, add, L 1967, ch 167, § 1; repealed, L 1971, ch 134, § 1, eff April 14, 1971.

§ 640. Fair treatment standards for crime victims

1. The commissioner of the division of criminal justice services, in consultation with the director of the office of victim services and other appropriate officials, shall promulgate standards for the

---

* There are two sections 646.

* There are two sections 646.

treatment of the innocent victims of crime by the agencies which comprise the criminal justice system of the state.

2. For the purposes of this article the term "criminal justice" shall include juvenile justice and the objectives and criteria set forth in sections six hundred forty-one and six hundred forty-two of this article shall apply to presentment agencies as defined in subdivision twelve of section 301.2 of the family court act.

> **HISTORY:** Add, L 1984, ch 94, § 1, eff April 24, 1984; amd, L 1985, ch 414, § 1, eff Sept 17, 1985, L 2010, ch 56, § 31 (Part A-1), eff June 22, 2010.

§ 641. Objectives of fair treatment standards

The object of such fair treatment standards shall be to:

1. Ensure that crime victims routinely receive emergency social and medical services as soon as possible and are given information pursuant to section six hundred twenty-five-a of this chapter on the following:

(a) availability of crime victim compensation;

(b) availability of appropriate public or private programs that provide counseling, treatment or support for crime victims, including but not limited to the following: rape crisis centers, victim/witness assistance programs, elderly victim services, victim assistance hotlines and domestic violence shelters;

(c) the role of the victims in the criminal justice process, including what they can expect from the system as well as what the system expects from them; and

(d) stages in the criminal justice process of significance to a crime victim, and the manner in which information about such stages can be obtained.

2. Ensure routine notification of a victim or witness as to steps that law enforcement officers or district attorneys can take to protect victims and witnesses from intimidation.

3. Ensure notification of victims, witnesses, relatives of those victims and witnesses who are minors, and relatives of homicide victims, if such persons provide the appropriate official with a current address and telephone number, either by phone or by mail, if possible, of judicial proceedings relating to their case, including:

(a) the arrest of an accused;

(b) the initial appearance of an accused before a judicial officer;

(c) the release of an accused pending judicial proceedings; and

(d) proceedings in the prosecution of the accused including entry of a plea of guilty, trial, sentencing, but prior to sentencing specific information shall be provided regarding the right to seek restitution and reparation, and where a term of imprisonment is imposed, specific information shall be provided regarding maximum and minimum terms of such imprisonment.

> **HISTORY:** Add, L 1984, ch 94, § 1, eff April 24, 1984. Former § 641, add, L 1967, ch 167, § 1; repealed, L 1971, ch 134, § 1, eff April 14, 1971. Sub 1, opening par, amd, L 1985, ch 688, § 4, eff Aug 1, 1985. Sub 3, par (d), amd, L 1992, ch 618, § 11, eff Nov 1, 1992.

§ 642. Criteria for fair treatment standards

Such fair treatment standards shall provide that:

1. The victim of a violent felony offense, a felony involving physical injury to the victim, a felony involving property loss or damage in excess of two hundred fifty dollars, a felony involving attempted or threatened physical injury or property loss or damage in excess of two hundred fifty dollars or a felony involving larceny against the person shall, unless he or she refuses or is unable to cooperate or his or her whereabouts are unknown, be consulted by the district attorney in order to obtain the views of the victim regarding disposition of the criminal case by dismissal, plea of guilty or trial. In such a case in which the victim is a minor child, or in the case of a homicide, the district attorney shall, unless the family refuses or is unable to cooperate or his, her or their whereabouts are unknown, consult for such purpose with the family of the victim. In addition, the district attorney shall, unless he or she (or, in the case in which the victim is a minor child or a victim of homicide, his or her family) refuses or is unable to cooperate or his, her or their whereabouts are unknown, consult and obtain the views of the victim or family of the victim, as appropriate, concerning the release of the defendant in the victim's case pending judicial proceedings upon an indictment, and concerning the availability of sentencing alternatives such as community supervision and restitution from the defendant. The failure of the district attorney to so obtain the views of the victim or family of the victim shall not be cause for delaying the proceedings against the defendant nor shall it affect the validity of a conviction, judgment or order.

2. The victims and other prosecution witnesses shall, where possible, be provided, when awaiting court appearances, a secure waiting area that is separate from all other witnesses.

2-a. (a) All police departments, as that term is defined in subdivision a of section eight hundred thirty-seven-c of this chapter, district attorneys' offices and presentment agencies, as that term is defined in subdivision twelve of section 301.2 of the family court act, shall provide a private setting for interviewing victims of a crime defined in article one hundred thirty or section 255.25, 255.26 or 255.27 of the penal law. For purposes of this subdivision, "private setting" shall mean an enclosed room from which the occupants are not visible or otherwise identifiable, and whose conversations cannot be heard, from outside such room. Only (i) those persons directly and immediately related to the interviewing of a particular victim, (ii) the victim, (iii) a social worker, rape crisis counselor, psychologist or other professional providing emotional support to the victim, unless the victim objects to the presence of such person and requests the exclusion of such person from the interview, and (iv) where appropriate, the parent or parents of the victim, if requested by the victim, shall be present during the interview of the victim.

(b) All police departments, as that term is defined in subdivision a of section eight hundred thirty-seven-c of this chapter, shall provide victims of a crime defined in article one hundred thirty of the penal law with the name, address, and telephone of the nearest rape crisis center in writing.

3. Law enforcement agencies and district attorneys shall promptly return property held for evidentiary purposes unless there is a compelling reason for retaining it relating to proof at trial.

4. The victim or witness who so requests shall be assisted by law enforcement agencies and district attorneys in informing employers that the need for victim and witness cooperation in the prosecution of the case may necessitate absence of that victim or witness from work. In addition, a victim or witness who, as a direct result of a crime or of cooperation with law enforcement agencies or the district attorney in the investigation or prosecution of a crime is unable to meet obligations to a creditor, creditors or others should be assisted by such agencies or the district attorney in providing to such creditor, creditors or others accurate information about the circumstances of the crime, including the nature of any loss or injury suffered by the

victim, or about the victim's or witness' cooperation, where appropriate.

5. Victim assistance education and training, with special consideration to be given to victims of domestic violence, sex offense victims, elderly victims, child victims, and the families of homicide victims, shall be given to persons taking courses at state law enforcement training facilities and by district attorneys so that victims may be promptly, properly and completely assisted.

HISTORY: Add, L 1984, ch 94, § 1, eff April 24, 1984. Former § 642, add, L 1967, ch 167, § 1; amd, L 1968, ch 431, § 1, L 1969, ch 490, § 1; repealed, L 1971, ch 134, § 1, eff April 14, 1971. Sub 1, amd, L 2005, ch 186, § 2, eff Sept 1, 2005, L 2006, ch 193, § 1, eff Sept 1, 2005. Sub 2-a, add, L 1989, ch 45, § 1, eff April 1, 1990. Sub 2-a, par (a), formerly entire sub 2-a, so designated sub 2-a, par (a), L 1991, ch 301, § 1, eff April 1, 1992. Sub 2-a, par (a), amd, L 2006, ch 320, § 25, eff Nov 1, 2006. Sub 2-a, par (b), add, L 1991, ch 301, § 1, eff April 1, 1992. Sub 3, amd, L 1986, ch 893, § 1, eff Aug 5, 1986. Sub 5, amd, L 1986, ch 263, § 7, eff Jan 1, 1987, provided that all rules and regulations necessary for the implementation of this act are to be made on or before Jan 1, 1987.

§ 642-a. Fair treatment of child victims as witnesses

To the extent permitted by law, criminal justice agencies, crime victim-related agencies, social services agencies and the courts shall comply with the following guidelines in their treatment of child victims:

1. To minimize the number of times a child victim is called upon to recite the events of the case and to foster a feeling of trust and confidence in the child victim, whenever practicable and where one exists, a multi-disciplinary team as established pursuant to subdivision six of section four hundred twenty-three of the social services law and/or a child advocacy center shall be used for the investigation and prosecution of child abuse cases involving abuse of a child, as described in paragraph (i), (ii) or (iii) of subdivision (e) of section one thousand twelve of the family court act, sexual abuse of a child or the death of a child.

2. Whenever practicable, the same prosecutor should handle all aspects of a case involving an alleged child victim.

3. To minimize the time during which a child victim must endure the stress of his involvement in the proceedings, the court should take appropriate action to ensure a speedy trial in all proceedings involving an alleged child victim. In ruling on any motion or request for a delay or continuance of a proceeding involving an alleged child victim, the court should consider and give weight to any potential adverse impact the delay or continuance may have on the well-being of the child.

4. The judge presiding should be sensitive to the psychological and emotional stress a child witness may undergo when testifying.

5. In accordance with the provisions of article sixty-five of the criminal procedure law, when appropriate, a child witness as defined in subdivision one of section 65.00 of such law should be permitted to testify via live, two-way closed-circuit television.

6. In accordance with the provisions of section 190.32 of the criminal procedure law, a person supportive of the "child witness" or "special witness" as defined in such section should be permitted to be present and accessible to a child witness at all times during his testimony, although the person supportive of the child witness should not be permitted to influence the child's testimony.

7. A child witness should be permitted in the discretion of the court to use anatomically

Exec. L.

correct dolls and drawings during his testimony.

HISTORY: Add, L 1986, ch 263, § 8, eff Jan 1, 1987, provided that all rules and regulations necessary for the implementation of this act are to be made on or before Jan 1, 1987. Section heading, amd, L 2008, ch 574, § 3, eff March 24, 2009. Sub 1, amd, L 2006, ch 517, § 3, eff Feb 12, 2007, L 2008, ch 574, § 3, eff March 24, 2009.

§ 643. Fair treatment standards for crime victims; agencies generally

1. As used in this section, "crime victim-related agency" means any agency of state government which provides services to or deals directly with crime victims, including (a) the office of children and family services, the office for the aging, the division of veterans affairs, the office of probation and correctional alternatives, the department of corrections and community supervision, the office of victim services, the department of motor vehicles, the office of vocational rehabilitation, the workers' compensation board, the department of health, the division of criminal justice services, the office of mental health, every transportation authority and the division of state police, and (b) any other agency so designated by the governor within ninety days of the effective date of this section.

2. Each crime victim-related agency shall review its practices, procedures, services, regulations and laws to determine the adequacy and appropriateness of its services with respect to crime victims, including victims with special needs, particularly the elderly, disabled or victims of child abuse, domestic violence or sex-related offenses. Such review shall include reasonable opportunity for public comment and consultation with crime victims or their representatives, and may include public hearings.

3. After the review, and not later than one hundred eighty days after the effective date of this section, each crime victim-related agency shall submit a report to the governor and the legislature, setting forth the findings of the review including a description of the services provided by the agency and recommendations for changes in its practices, procedures, services, regulations and laws to improve its services to crime victims and to establish and implement fair treatment standards for crime victims.

4. Subject to the direction of the governor, and to the extent practicable, each crime victim-related agency shall expeditiously implement the recommendations of its report.

HISTORY: Add, L 1984, ch 94, § 1, eff April 24, 1984; amd, L 2010, ch 56, § 38 (Part A), eff June 22, 2010, L 2010, ch 56, § 1 (Part A-1), eff June 22, 2010, L 2011, ch 62, § 107 (Part C, Subpart B), eff March 31, 2011.

§ 644. Implementation

The commissioner of the division of criminal justice services and the director of the office of victim services shall assist criminal justice agencies in implementing the guidelines promulgated by the commissioner.

HISTORY: Add, L 1984, ch 94, § 1, eff April 24, 1984; amd, L 2010, ch 56, § 33 (Part A-1), eff June 22, 2010.

§ 645. Fair treatment standards for crime victims in the courts

The chief administrator of the courts, in consultation with the commissioner of the division of criminal justice services, the director of the office of victim services and other appropriate officials, shall promulgate standards for the treatment of the innocent victims of crime by the unified court system. These standards shall conform to and be consistent with the regulations promulgated pursuant to section six hundred forty of this article.

HISTORY: Add, L 1986, ch 893, § 2, eff Aug 5, 1986; amd, L 2010, ch 56, § 34 (Part A-1), eff June 22, 2010.

§ 646. Police reports*

1. A victim of crime shall be entitled, regardless of physical injury, without charge to a copy of a police report of the crime.

2. An individual whose identity was assumed or whose personal identifying information, as defined in section 190.77 of the penal law, was used in violation of section 190.78, 190.79 or 190.80 of the penal law, or any person who has suffered a financial loss as a direct result of the acts of a defendant in violation of section 190.78, 190.79, 190.80, 190.82 or 190.83 of the penal law, who has learned or reasonably suspects that his or her personal identifying information has been unlawfully used by another, may make a complaint to the local law enforcement agency of the county in which any part of the offense took place regardless of whether the defendant was actually present in such county, or in the county in which the person who suffered financial loss resided at the time of the commission of the offense, or in the county where the person whose personal identification information was used in the commission of the offense resided at the time of the commission of the offense as provided in paragraph (l) of subdivision four of section 20.40 of the criminal procedure law. Said local law enforcement agency shall take a police report of the matter and provide the complainant with a copy of such report free of charge.

> **HISTORY:** Add, L 1986, ch 548, § 1, eff Sept 1, 1986. Former § 646, add, L 1967, ch 167, § 1; repealed, L 1971, ch 134, § 1, eff April 14, 1971. Sub 1, formerly entire section, so designated sub 1, L 2007, ch 346, § 1, eff July 18, 2007. Sub 2, add, L 2007, ch 346, § 1, eff July 18, 2007.

§ 646. Objectives*

The object of these fair treatment standards shall be to:

1. Ensure that crime victims are given information on the following:

(a) the role of the victims in the criminal justice process, including what they can expect from the system as well as what the system expects from them;

(b) stages in the criminal justice process of significance to a crime victim, and the manner in which information about such stages can be obtained; and

(c) how the court can address the needs of the victims at sentencing.

2. Ensure routine notification of a victim or witness as to steps that the court can take to protect victims and witnesses from intimidation, including the issuance of orders of protection and temporary orders of protection.

3. Ensure notification of victims, witnesses, relatives of those victims and witnesses who are minors, and relatives of homicide victims, if such persons provide the appropriate court official with a current address and telephone number, either by phone or by mail, if possible, of judicial proceedings relating to their case, including:

(a) the initial appearance of an accused before a judicial officer;

(b) the release of an accused pending judicial proceedings;

(c) proceedings in the prosecution of the accused, including entry of a plea of guilty, trial, sentencing, and where a term of imprisonment is imposed, specific information shall be provided regarding maximum and minimum terms of such imprisonment; and

---

* There are two sections 646.

* There are two sections 646.

(d) the reversal or modification of the judgment by an appellate court.

HISTORY: Add, L 1986, ch 893, § 2, eff Aug 5, 1986. Former § 646, add, L 1967, ch 167, § 1; repealed, L 1971, ch 134, § 1, eff April 14, 1971.

§ 646-a. Information relative to the fair treatment standards; pamphlet

1. The district attorney shall provide the victim, at the earliest time possible, with an informational pamphlet detailing the rights of crime victims which shall be prepared by the division of criminal justice services in consultation with the director of the office of victim services and distributed to each district attorney's office.

2. The pamphlet shall summarize provisions of this article. It shall also include specific information with appropriate statutory references on the following:

(a) the rights of crime victims to compensation and services;

(b) the rights of crime victims to routine notification of judicial proceedings relating to their case as provided in section six hundred forty-one of this article, in section 330.20, and section 440.50 of the criminal procedure law and section one hundred forty-nine-a of the correction law;

(c) the rights of crime victims to be protected from intimidation and to have the court, where appropriate, issue protective orders as provided in sections 530.12 and 530.13 of the criminal procedure law and sections 215.15, 215.16 and 215.17 of the penal law;

(d) the rights of crime victims to submit, where appropriate, a victim impact statement for the pre-sentencing report and the parole hearing as provided in section 390.30 of the criminal procedure law and section two hundred fifty-nine-i of this chapter;

(e) the rights of crime victims, where a defendant is being sentenced for a felony, to request the right to make a statement at the time of sentencing as provided in section 380.50 of the criminal procedure law; and

(f) the rights of crime victims to request restitution and have the district attorney present such request to the court and assist the crime victim in the filing and collection of a restitution order in cooperation with the designated agency of the court as provided in section 420.10 of the criminal procedure law and section 60.27 of the penal law.

(g) the rights of crime victims to be aware of the defendant's incarceration status by providing the division of parole's contact information, including the division's toll-free telephone number, as provided for in subdivision two of section two hundred fifty-nine-i of this chapter. Such notice shall advise the crime victim to use the division's toll-free telephone number to update contact information.

3. This pamphlet shall provide space for the insertion of the following information:

(a) the address and phone number of the office of victim services;

(b) the address and phone numbers of local victim service programs, where appropriate;

(c) the name, phone number and office location of the person in the district attorney's office to whom inquiries concerning the victims case may be directed; and

(d) any other information the division deems appropriate.

4. (a) The commissioner of the division of criminal justice services in consultation with the director of the office of victim services shall develop and prepare a standardized form for the

use of district attorney offices for the purpose of reporting compliance with this section. The form is to be distributed to each district attorney. Every district attorney's office in the state shall complete the reporting form annually and send it to the director of the office of victim services by the first day of January each year subsequent to the effective date of this subdivision.

(b) A copy of the report shall be retained by the district attorney and upon request, a victim of a crime or relative of a victim shall be entitled to receive from the district attorney a copy of their district attorney's annual report without charge. Any other person requesting a copy of the report shall pay a fee not to exceed the actual cost of reproduction.

HISTORY: Add, L 1994, ch 67, § 1, eff Jan 1, 1995; amd, L 2005, ch 186, § 1, eff Sept 1, 2005, L 2006, ch 173, §§ 4, 5, eff Jan 1, 2007, L 2010, ch 56, § 35 (Part A-1), eff June 22, 2010.

§ 647. Criteria

Fair treatment standards for crime victims in the courts shall provide that:

1. The court shall consider the views of the victim of a violent felony offense, a felony involving physical injury to the victim, a felony involving property loss or damage in excess of two hundred fifty dollars, a felony involving attempted or threatened physical injury or property loss or damage in excess of two hundred fifty dollars or a felony involving larceny against the person, or of the family of a homicide victim or minor child, regarding discretionary decisions relating to the criminal case, including, but not limited to, plea agreements and sentence. In addition, the court shall consider the views of the victim or family of the victim, as appropriate, concerning the release of the defendant in the victim's case pending judicial proceedings upon an indictment, and concerning the availability of sentencing alternatives such as community supervision and restitution from the defendant. The failure of the court to consider the views of the victim or family of the victim shall not be cause for delaying the proceedings against the defendant nor shall it affect the validity of a conviction, judgment or order.

2. The victims and other prosecution witnesses shall, where possible, be provided, when awaiting court appearances, a secure waiting area that is separate from all other witnesses.

3. The court shall assist in and expedite the return of property held for evidentiary purposes unless there is a compelling reason for retaining it relating to proof at trial.

4. Victim assistance education shall be given to judicial and nonjudicial personnel of the unified court system so that victims may be promptly, properly and completely assisted.

HISTORY: Add, L 1986, ch 893, § 2, eff Aug 5, 1986. Former § 647, add, L 1967, ch 167, § 1; repealed, L 1971, ch 134, § 1, eff April 14, 1971.

§ 648. Review; report and implementation

1. The chief administrator of the unified court system shall review court practices, procedures, services, regulations and laws to determine the adequacy and appropriateness of its services with respect to crime victims, including victims with special needs, particularly the elderly, disabled or victims of child abuse, domestic violence or sex-related offenses. Such review shall include reasonable opportunity for public comment and consultation with crime victims or their representatives, and may include public hearings.

2. After the review, and not later than two hundred seventy days after the effective date of this section, the chief administrator of the unified court system shall submit a report to the governor and the legislature, setting forth the findings of the review, including a description of the services provided by the components of the unified court system and recommendations for changes in its

procedures, services, regulations and laws to improve its services to crime victims and to establish and implement fair treatment standards for crime victims.

3. Subject to the direction of the chief administrator, the components of the unified court system shall expeditiously implement the recommendations of its report.

HISTORY: Add, L 1986, ch 893, § 2, eff Aug 5, 1986.

§ 649. Miscellaneous

Nothing in this article shall be construed as creating a cause of action for damages or injunctive relief against the state or any of its political subdivisions or officers or any agency thereof.

HISTORY: Formerly § 645, add, L 1984, ch 94, § 1; renumbered § 649, L 1986, ch 893, § 2, eff Aug 5, 1986.

* * *

ARTICLE 38 NATIONAL CRIME PREVENTION AND PRIVACY COMPACT

§ 850. Enactment of compact

HISTORY: Add, L 2013, ch 55, § 1 (Part D), eff March 28, 2013.

§ 850. Enactment of compact

The national crime prevention and privacy compact is hereby enacted into law and entered into with all other jurisdictions legally joining therein in the form substantially as follows:

The Contracting Parties agree to the following:

NATIONAL CRIME PREVENTION AND PRIVACY COMPACT

ARTICLE I. Definitions.

ARTICLE II. Purposes.

ARTICLE III. Responsibilities of compact parties.

ARTICLE IV. Authorized record disclosures.

ARTICLE V. Record request procedures.

ARTICLE VI. Establishment of compact council.

ARTICLE VII. Ratification of compact.

ARTICLE VIII. Miscellaneous provisions.

ARTICLE IX. Renunciation.

ARTICLE X. Severability.

ARTICLE XI. Adjudication of disputes.

OVERVIEW

(a) In general, this compact organizes an electronic information sharing system among the federal government and the states to exchange criminal history records for noncriminal justice purposes authorized by federal or state law, such as background checks for governmental licensing and employment.

(b) Under this compact, the FBI and the party states agree to maintain detailed databases of their respective criminal history records, including arrests and dispositions, and to make them available to the federal government and to party states for authorized purposes. The FBI shall also manage the federal data facilities that provide a significant part of the infrastructure for the system.

ARTICLE I—DEFINITIONS

As used in this compact:

(a) "Attorney general" means the attorney general of the United States.

(b) "Compact officer" means:

1. with respect to the federal government, an official so designated by the director of the FBI; and

2. with respect to a party state, the chief administrator of the state's criminal history record repository or a designee of the chief administrator who is a regular full-time employee of the repository.

(c) "Council" means the compact council established under article VI.

(d) "Criminal history records":

1. means information collected by criminal justice agencies on individuals consisting of identifiable descriptions and notations of arrests, detentions, indictments, or other formal criminal charges, and any disposition arising therefrom, including acquittal, sentencing, correctional supervision, or release; and

2. does not include identification information such as fingerprint records if such information does not indicate involvement of the individual with the criminal justice system.

(e) "Criminal history record repository" means the state agency designated by the governor or other appropriate executive official or the legislature of a state to perform centralized recordkeeping functions for criminal history records and services in the state.

(f) "Criminal justice" includes activities relating to the detection, apprehension, detention, pretrial release, post-trial release, prosecution, adjudication, correctional supervision, or rehabilitation of accused persons or criminal offenders. The administration of criminal justice includes criminal identification activities and the collection, storage, and dissemination of criminal history records.

(g) "Criminal justice agency":

1. means:

a. courts; and

b. a governmental agency or any subunit thereof that:

(i) performs the administration of criminal justice pursuant to a statute or executive order; and

(ii) allocates a substantial part of its annual budget to the administration of criminal justice; and

2. includes federal and state inspectors general offices.

(h) "Criminal justice services" means services provided by the FBI to criminal justice agencies in response to a request for information about a particular individual or as an update to information previously provided for criminal justice purposes.

(i) "Criterion offense" means any felony or misdemeanor offense not included on the list of nonserious offenses published periodically by the FBI.

(j) "Direct access" means access to the national identification index by computer terminal or other automated means not requiring the assistance of or intervention by any other party or agency.

(k) "Executive order" means an order of the president of the United States or the chief executive officer of a state that has the force of law and that is promulgated in accordance with applicable law.

(l) "FBI" means the Federal Bureau of Investigation.

(m) "Interstate identification index system" or "III system":

1. means the cooperative federal-state system for the exchange of criminal history records; and

2. includes the national identification index, the national fingerprint file and, to the extent of their participation in such system, the criminal history record repositories of the states and the FBI.

(n) "National fingerprint file" means a database of fingerprints, or other uniquely personal identifying information, relating to an arrested or charged individual maintained by the FBI to provide positive identification of record subjects indexed in the III system.

(o) "National identification index" means an index maintained by the FBI consisting of names, identifying numbers, and other descriptive information relating to record subjects about whom there are criminal history records in the III system.

(p) "National indices" means the national identification index and the national fingerprint file.

(q) "Nonparty state" means a state that has not ratified this compact.

(r) "Noncriminal justice purposes" means uses of criminal history records for purposes authorized by federal or state law other than purposes relating to criminal justice activities, including employment suitability, licensing determinations, immigration and naturalization matters, and national security clearances.

(s) "Party state" means a state that has ratified this compact.

(t) "Positive identification" means a determination, based upon a comparison of fingerprints or other equally reliable biometric identification techniques, that the subject of a record search is the same person as the subject of a criminal history record or records indexed in the III system. Identifications based solely upon a comparison of subjects' names or other nonunique identification characteristics or numbers, or combinations thereof, shall not constitute positive identification.

(u) "Sealed record information" means:

1. with respect to adults, that portion of a record that is:

a. not available for criminal justice uses;

b. not supported by fingerprints or other accepted means of positive identification; or

c. subject to restrictions on dissemination for noncriminal justice purposes pursuant to a court order related to a particular subject or pursuant to a federal or state statute that requires action on a sealing petition filed by a particular record subject; and

2. with respect to juveniles, whatever each state determines is a sealed record under its own law and procedure.

(v) "State" means any state, territory, or possession of the United States, the district of Columbia, and the commonwealth of Puerto Rico.

ARTICLE II—PURPOSES

The purposes of this compact are to:

(a) provide a legal framework for the establishment of a cooperative federal-state system for the interstate and federal-state exchange of criminal history records for noncriminal justice uses;

(b) require the FBI to permit use of the national identification index and the national fingerprint file by each party state, and to provide, in a timely fashion, federal and state criminal history records to requesting states, in accordance with the terms of this compact and with rules, procedures, and standards established by the council under article VI;

(c) require party states to provide information and records for the national identification index and the national fingerprint file and to provide criminal history records, in a timely fashion, to criminal history record repositories of other states and the federal government for noncriminal justice purposes, in accordance with the terms of this compact and with rules, procedures, and standards established by the council under article VI;

(d) provide for the establishment of a council to monitor III system operations and to prescribe system rules and procedures for the effective and proper operation of the III system for noncriminal justice purposes; and

(e) require the FBI and each party state to adhere to III system standards concerning record dissemination and use, response times, system security, data quality, and other duly established standards, including those that enhance the accuracy and privacy of such records.

ARTICLE III—RESPONSIBILITIES OF COMPACT PARTIES

(a) The director of the FBI shall:

1. appoint an FBI compact officer who shall:

a. administer this compact within the department of justice and among federal agencies and other agencies and organizations that submit search requests to the FBI pursuant to subdivision (c) of article V;

b. ensure that compact provisions and rules, procedures, and standards prescribed by the council under article VI are complied with by the department of justice and the federal agencies and other agencies and organizations referred to in subparagraph a of paragraph one of this subdivision; and

c. regulate the use of records received by means of the III system from party states when such records are supplied by the FBI directly to other federal agencies;

2. provide to federal agencies and to state criminal history record repositories, criminal history records maintained in its database for the noncriminal justice purposes described in article IV, including:

a. information from nonparty states; and

b. information from party states that is available from the FBI through the III system,

Exec. L.

but is not available from the party state through the III system;

c. provide a telecommunications network and maintain centralized facilities for the exchange of criminal history records for both criminal justice purposes and the noncriminal justice purposes described in article IV, and ensure that the exchange of such records for criminal justice purposes has priority over exchange for noncriminal justice purposes; and

d. modify or enter into user agreements with nonparty state criminal history record repositories to require them to establish record request procedures conforming to those prescribed in article V.

(b) Each party state shall:

1. appoint a compact officer who shall:

a. administer this compact within that state;

b. ensure that compact provisions and rules, procedures, and standards established by the council under article VI are complied with in the state; and

c. regulate the in-state use of records received by means of the III system from the FBI or from other party states;

2. establish and maintain a criminal history record repository, which shall provide:

a. information and records for the national identification index and the national fingerprint file; and

b. the state's III system-indexed criminal history records for noncriminal justice purposes described in article IV; and

c. participate in the national fingerprint file; and

d. provide and maintain telecommunications links and related equipment necessary to support the services set forth in this compact.

(c) Compliance with III system standards. In carrying out their responsibilities under this compact, the FBI and each party state shall comply with III system rules, procedures, and standards duly established by the council concerning record dissemination and use, response times, data quality, system security, accuracy, privacy protection, and other aspects of III system operation.

(d) 1. Use of the III system for noncriminal justice purposes authorized in this compact shall be managed so as not to diminish the level of services provided in support of criminal justice purposes.

2. Administration of compact provisions shall not reduce the level of service available to authorized noncriminal justice users on the effective date of this compact.

ARTICLE IV—AUTHORIZED RECORD DISCLOSURES

(a) State criminal history record repositories. To the extent authorized by section five hundred fifty-two-a of title five of the United States code, (commonly known as the "Privacy Act of 1974"), the FBI shall provide on request criminal history records (excluding sealed records) to state criminal history record repositories for noncriminal justice purposes allowed by federal statute, federal executive order, or a state statute that has been approved by the attorney general and that authorizes national indices checks.

(b) The FBI, to the extent authorized by section five hundred fifty-two-a of title five of the United States code, (commonly known as the "Privacy Act of 1974"), and state criminal history record repositories shall provide criminal history records (excluding sealed records) to criminal justice agencies and other governmental or nongovernmental agencies for noncriminal justice purposes allowed by federal statute, federal executive order, or a state statute that has been approved by the attorney general, that authorizes national indices checks.

(c) Any record obtained under this compact may be used only for the official purposes for which the record was requested. Each compact officer shall establish procedures, consistent with this compact, and with rules, procedures, and standards established by the council under article VI, which procedures shall protect the accuracy and privacy of the records, and shall:

1. ensure that records obtained under this compact are used only by authorized officials for authorized purposes;

2. require that subsequent record checks are requested to obtain current information whenever a new need arises; and

3. ensure that record entries that may not legally be used for a particular noncriminal justice purpose are deleted from the response and, if no information authorized for release remains, an appropriate "no record" response is communicated to the requesting official.

ARTICLE V—RECORD REQUEST PROCEDURES

(a) Subject fingerprints or other approved forms of positive identification shall be submitted with all requests for criminal history record checks for noncriminal justice purposes.

(b) Each request for a criminal history record check utilizing the national indices made under any approved state statute shall be submitted through that state's criminal history record repository. A state criminal history record repository shall process an interstate request for noncriminal justice purposes through the national indices only if such request is transmitted through another state criminal history record repository or the FBI.

(c) Each request for criminal history record checks utilizing the national indices made under federal authority shall be submitted through the FBI or, if the state criminal history record repository consents to process fingerprint submissions, through the criminal history record repository in the state in which such request originated. Direct access to the national identification index by entities other than the FBI and state criminal history records repositories shall not be permitted for noncriminal justice purposes.

(d) A state criminal history record repository or the FBI:

1. may charge a fee, in accordance with applicable law, for handling a request involving fingerprint processing for noncriminal justice purposes; and

2. may not charge a fee for providing criminal history records in response to an electronic request for a record that does not involve a request to process fingerprints.

(e) 1. If a state criminal history record repository cannot positively identify the subject of a record request made for noncriminal justice purposes, the request, together with fingerprints or other approved identifying information, shall be forwarded to the FBI for a search of the national indices.

2. If, with respect to a request forwarded by a state criminal history record repository under paragraph one of this subdivision, the FBI positively identifies the subject as having a III system-indexed record or records:

a. the FBI shall so advise the state criminal history record repository; and

b. the state criminal history record repository shall be entitled to obtain the additional criminal history record information from the FBI or other state criminal history record repositories.

ARTICLE VI—ESTABLISHMENT OF COMPACT COUNCIL

(a) 1. In general, there is established a council to be known as the "compact council", which shall have the authority to promulgate rules and procedures governing the use of the III system for noncriminal justice purposes, not to conflict with FBI administration of the III system for criminal justice purposes.

2. The council shall:

a. continue in existence as long as this compact remains in effect;

b. be located, for administrative purposes, within the FBI; and

c. be organized and hold its first meeting as soon as practicable after the effective date of this compact.

(b) The council shall be composed of fifteen members, each of whom shall be appointed by the attorney general, as follows:

1. Nine members, each of whom shall serve a two-year term, who shall be selected from among the compact officers of party states based on the recommendation of the compact officers of all party states, except that, in the absence of the requisite number of compact officers available to serve, the chief administrators of the criminal history record repositories of nonparty states shall be eligible to serve on an interim basis.

2. Two at-large members, nominated by the director of the FBI, each of whom shall serve a three-year term, of whom:

a. one shall be a representative of the criminal justice agencies of the federal government and may not be an employee of the FBI; and

b. one shall be a representative of the noncriminal justice agencies of the federal government.

3. Two at-large members, nominated by the chairman of the council, once the chairman is elected pursuant to subdivision (c) of this article, each of whom shall serve a three-year term, of whom:

a. one shall be a representative of state or local criminal justice agencies; and

b. one shall be a representative of state or local noncriminal justice agencies.

4. One member, who shall serve a three-year term, and who shall simultaneously be a member of the FBI's advisory policy board on criminal justice information services, nominated by the membership of that policy board.

5. One member, nominated by the director of the FBI, who shall serve a three-year term, and who shall be an employee of the FBI.

(c) 1. In general, from its membership, the council shall elect a chairman and a vice chairman of the council, respectively. Both the chairman and vice chairman of the council:

a. shall be a compact officer, unless there is no compact officer on the council who is willing to serve, in which case the chairman may be an at-large member; and

b. shall serve a two-year term and may be reelected to only one additional two-year term.

2. The vice chairman of the council shall serve as the chairman of the council in the absence of the chairman.

(d) 1. In general, the council shall meet at least once each year at the call of the chairman. Each meeting of the council shall be open to the public. The council shall provide prior public notice in the federal register of each meeting of the council, including the matters to be addressed at such meeting.

2. A majority of the council or any committee of the council shall constitute a quorum of the council or of such committee, respectively, for the conduct of business. A lesser number may meet to hold hearings, take testimony, or conduct any business not requiring a vote.

(e) The council shall make available for public inspection and copying at the council office within the FBI, and shall publish in the federal register, any rules, procedures, or standards established by the council.

(f) The council may request from the FBI such reports, studies, statistics, or other information or materials as the council determines to be necessary to enable the council to perform its duties under this compact. The FBI, to the extent authorized by law, may provide such assistance or information upon such a request.

(g) The chairman may establish committees as necessary to carry out this compact and may prescribe their membership, responsibilities, and duration.

ARTICLE VII—RATIFICATION OF COMPACT

This compact shall take effect upon being entered into by two or more states as between those states and the federal government. Upon subsequent entering into this compact by additional states, it shall become effective among those states and the federal government and each party state that has previously ratified it. When ratified, this compact shall have the full force and effect of law within the ratifying jurisdictions.The form of ratification shall be in accordance with the laws of the executing state.

ARTICLE VIII—MISCELLANEOUS PROVISIONS

(a) Administration of this compact shall not interfere with the management and control of the director of the FBI over the FBI's collection and dissemination of criminal history records and the advisory function of the FBI's advisory policy board chartered under the federal advisory committee act (5 U.S.C. App.) for all purposes other than noncriminal justice.

(b) Nothing in this compact shall require the FBI to obligate or expend funds beyond those appropriated to the FBI.

(c) Nothing in this compact shall diminish or lessen the obligations, responsibilities, and authorities of any state, whether a party state or a nonparty state, or of any criminal history record repository or other subdivision or component thereof, under the departments of state, justice, and commerce, the judiciary, and related agencies appropriation act, 1973 (Public Law 92-544), or regulations and guidelines promulgated thereunder, including the rules and

Exec. L.

procedures promulgated by the council under subdivision (a) of article VI, regarding the use and dissemination of criminal history records and information.

ARTICLE IX—RENUNCIATION

(a) In general, this compact shall bind each party state until renounced by the party state.

(b) Any renunciation of this compact by a party state shall:

1. be effected in the same manner by which the party state ratified this compact; and

2. become effective one hundred eighty days after written notice of renunciation is provided by the party state to each other party state and to the federal government.

ARTICLE X—SEVERABILITY

The provisions of this compact shall be severable, and if any phrase, clause, sentence, or provision of this compact is declared to be contrary to the constitution of any participating state, or to the constitution of the United States, or the applicability thereof to any government, agency, person, or circumstance is held invalid, the validity of the remainder of this compact and the applicability thereof to any government, agency, person, or circumstance shall not be affected thereby. If a portion of this compact is held contrary to the constitution of any party state, all other portions of this compact shall remain in full force and effect as to the remaining party states and in full force and effect as to the party state affected, as to all other provisions.

ARTICLE XI—ADJUDICATION OF DISPUTES

(a) The council shall:

1. have initial authority to make determinations with respect to any dispute regarding:

    a. interpretation of this compact;

    b. any rule or standard established by the council pursuant to article VI; and

    c. any dispute or controversy between any parties to this compact; and

2. hold a hearing concerning any dispute described in paragraph one of this subdivision at a regularly scheduled meeting of the council and only render a decision based upon a majority vote of the members of the council. Such decision shall be published pursuant to the requirements of subdivision (e) of article VI.

(b) The FBI shall exercise immediate and necessary action to preserve the integrity of the III system, maintain system policy and standards, protect the accuracy and privacy of records, and to prevent abuses, until the council holds a hearing on such matters.

(c) The FBI or a party state may appeal any decision of the council to the attorney general, and thereafter may file suit in the appropriate district court of the United States, which shall have original jurisdiction of all cases or controversies arising under this compact. Any suit arising under this compact and initiated in a state court shall be removed to the appropriate district court of the United States in the manner provided by section fourteen hundred forty-six of title twenty-eight of the United States code, or other statutory authority.

HISTORY: Add, L 2013, ch 55, § 1 (Part D), eff March 28, 2013.

ARTICLE 49-B   COMMISSION ON FORENSIC SCIENCE AND ESTABLISHMENT OF DNA IDENTIFICATION INDEX

§ 995-b.	**Powers and duties of the commission**
§ 995-c.	**State DNA identification index**
§ 995-d.	**Confidentiality**
§ 995-e.	**Applicability**
§ 995-f.	**Penalties**

HISTORY: Add, L 1994, ch 737, § 1, eff Aug 2, 1994.

§ 995. Definitions

When used in this article, the following words and terms shall have the meanings ascribed to them in this section:

1. For purposes of general forensic analysis the term "forensic laboratory" shall mean any laboratory operated by the state or unit of local government that performs forensic testing on evidence in a criminal investigation or proceeding or for purposes of identification provided, however, that the examination of latent fingerprints by a police agency shall not be subject to the provisions of this article.

2. For purposes of forensic DNA analysis, the term "forensic DNA laboratory" shall mean any forensic laboratory operated by the state or unit of local government, that performs forensic DNA testing on crime scenes or materials derived from the human body for use as evidence in a criminal proceeding or for purposes of identification and the term "forensic DNA testing" shall mean any test that employs techniques to examine deoxyribonucleic acid (DNA) derived from the human body for the purpose of providing information to resolve issues of identification. Regulation pursuant to this article shall not include DNA testing on materials derived from the human body pursuant to title five of article five of the public health law for the purpose of determining a person's genetic disease or medical condition and shall not include a laboratory operated by the federal government.

3. "DNA testing methodology" means methods and procedures used to extract and analyze DNA material, as well as the methods, procedures, assumptions, and studies used to draw statistical inferences from the test results.

4. "Blind external proficiency testing" means a test sample that is presented to a forensic laboratory for forensic DNA testing through a second agency, and which appears to the analysts to involve routine evidence submitted for forensic DNA testing.

5. "DNA" means deoxyribonucleic acid.

6. "State DNA identification index" means the DNA identification record system for New York state established pursuant to this article.

7. "Designated offender" means a person convicted of any felony defined in any chapter of the laws of the state or any misdemeanor defined in the penal law except that where the person is convicted under section 221.10 of the penal law, only a person convicted under subdivision two of such section, or a person convicted under subdivision one of such section who stands previously convicted of any crime as defined in subdivision six of section 10.00 of the penal law.

8. "DNA record" means DNA identification information prepared by a forensic DNA laboratory and stored in the state DNA identification index for purposes of establishing identification in connection with law enforcement investigations or supporting statistical interpretation of the results of DNA analysis. A DNA record is the objective form of the results of a DNA analysis sample.

9. "DNA subcommittee" shall mean the subcommittee on forensic DNA laboratories and forensic DNA testing established pursuant to subdivision thirteen of section nine hundred ninety-five-b of this article.

10. "Commission" shall mean the commission on forensic science established pursuant to section nine hundred ninety-five-a of this article.

HISTORY: Add, L 1994, ch 737, § 1, eff Aug 2, 1994; amd, L 1999, ch 560, § 1, eff Dec 1, 1999, L 2000, ch 8, § 1, eff March 6, 2000, deemed eff Dec 1, 1999, L 2004, ch 138, § 1, eff July 6, 2004, L 2004, ch 1, § 13 (Part A), eff July 23, 2004, L 2004, ch 576, § 1, eff July 6, 2004, L 2006, ch 2, § 1, eff June 23, 2006, L 2006, ch 91, § 2, eff June 7, 2006, L 2006, ch 320, § 26, eff Nov 1, 2006, L 2010, ch 405, § 6, eff Nov 11, 2010, L 2012, ch 19, § 5, eff Aug 1, 2012.

§ 995-a. Commission on forensic science

1. There is hereby created in the executive department, the commission on forensic science, which shall consist of the following fourteen members:

(a) the commissioner of the division of criminal justice services who shall be chair of the commission and the commissioner of the department of health or his or her designee, who shall serve as an ex-officio member of the commission;

(b) twelve members appointed by the governor.

2. Of the members appointed by the governor,

(a) one member shall be the chair of the New York state crime laboratory advisory committee;

(b) one member shall be the director of a forensic laboratory located in New York state;

(c) one member shall be the director of the office of forensic services within the division of criminal justice services;

(d) two members shall be a scientist having experience in the areas of laboratory standards or quality assurance regulation and monitoring and shall be appointed upon the recommendation of the commissioner of health;

(e) one member shall be a representative of a law enforcement agency and shall be appointed upon the recommendation of the commissioner of criminal justice services;

(f) one member shall be a representative of prosecution services who shall be appointed upon the recommendation of the commissioner of criminal justice services;

(g) one member shall be a representative of the public criminal defense bar who shall be appointed upon the recommendation of an organization representing public defense services;

(h) one member shall be a representative of the private criminal defense bar who shall be appointed upon the recommendation of an organization of such bar;

(i) two members shall be members-at-large, one of whom shall be appointed upon the recommendation of the temporary president of the senate, and one of whom shall be appointed upon the recommendation of the speaker of the assembly; and

(j) one member, who shall be an attorney or judge with a background in privacy issues and biomedical ethics, shall be appointed upon the recommendation of the chief judge of the court of appeals.

3. Of the members appointed by the governor, each member shall be appointed to serve a three

year term. Any member appointed by the governor may be reappointed for additional three year terms.

4. Any member chosen to fill a vacancy created otherwise than by expiration of term shall be appointed by the governor for the unexpired term of the member he or she is to succeed. Any such vacancy shall be filled in the same manner as the original appointment.

5. The commission shall meet at least four times each year and may establish its own rules and procedures concerning the conduct of its meetings and other affairs not inconsistent with law.

6. No member of the commission on forensic science shall be disqualified from holding any public office or employment, nor shall he or she forfeit any such office or employment, by reason of his or her appointment hereunder, and members of the commission shall not be required to take and file oaths of office before serving on the commission.

7. Members of the commission shall receive no compensation for their services but shall be allowed their actual and necessary expenses incurred in the performance of their functions hereunder.

HISTORY: Add, L 1994, ch 737, § 1, eff Aug 2, 1994.

§ 995-b. Powers and duties of the commission

1. The commission shall develop minimum standards and a program of accreditation for all forensic laboratories in New York state, including establishing minimum qualifications for forensic laboratory directors and such other personnel as the commission may determine to be necessary and appropriate, and approval of forensic laboratories for the performance of specific forensic methodologies. Nothing in this article shall be deemed to preclude forensic laboratories from performing research and validation studies on new methodologies and technologies which may not yet be approved by the commission at that time.

In designing a system of accreditation pursuant to this article, the commission shall evaluate other systems of accreditation.

2. The minimum standards and program of accreditation shall be designed to accomplish the following objectives:

(a) increase and maintain the effectiveness, efficiency, reliability, and accuracy of forensic laboratories, including forensic DNA laboratories;

(b) ensure that forensic analyses, including forensic DNA testing, are performed in accordance with the highest scientific standards practicable;

(c) promote increased cooperation and coordination among forensic laboratories and other agencies in the criminal justice system;

(d) ensure compatibility, to the extent consistent with the provisions of this article and any other applicable provision of law pertaining to privacy or restricting disclosure or redisclosure of information, with other state and federal forensic laboratories to the extent necessary to share and exchange information, data and results of forensic analyses and tests; and

(e) set forth minimum requirements for the quality and maintenance of equipment.

2-a. Any program of forensic laboratory accreditation with respect to a DNA laboratory pursuant to this section shall be under the direction of the DNA subcommittee established pursuant to subdivision thirteen of this section. Such subcommittee shall have the sole authority to grant, deny, review or modify a DNA forensic laboratory accreditation pursuant to this article, provided that

Exec. L.

such authority shall be effectuated through binding recommendations made by the DNA subcommittee to the commission. In the event the commission disagrees with any of the binding recommendations of the DNA subcommittee made pursuant to this article, the commission may so notify such subcommittee and request such subcommittee to reasonably review such binding recommendations. The DNA subcommittee shall conduct such review and either forward revised binding recommendations to the commission or indicate, with the reasons therefor, that following such review such subcommittee has determined that such binding recommendations shall not be revised.

3. The program of forensic laboratory accreditation shall include, at a minimum, the following requirements:

(a) an initial laboratory inspection, and routine inspections, as necessary, to ensure compliance with accreditation requirements;

(b) routine internal and external proficiency testing of all laboratory personnel involved in forensic analysis, including blind external proficiency testing if the commission, or the DNA subcommittee as the case may be, determines such a blind proficiency testing program to be practicable and appropriate. In determining whether a blind proficiency testing program is practicable and appropriate, the commission, or the DNA subcommittee as the case may be, shall consider such factors as accuracy and reliability of laboratory results, cost-effectiveness, time, allocation of resources, and availability;

(c) quality control and quality assurance protocols, a method validation procedure and a corrective action and remedial program;

(d) annual certification to the commission by the forensic laboratories of their continued compliance with the requirements of the accreditation program which certification, in the case of a forensic DNA laboratory, shall be forwarded to the DNA subcommittee;

(e) the accreditation of a forensic laboratory may be revoked, suspended or otherwise limited, upon a determination by the commission or, in the case of a forensic DNA laboratory, upon the binding recommendation of the DNA subcommittee, that the laboratory or one or more persons in its employ:

(i) is guilty of misrepresentation in obtaining a forensic laboratory accreditation;

(ii) rendered a report on laboratory work actually performed in another forensic laboratory without disclosing the fact that the examination or procedure was performed by such other forensic laboratory;

(iii) showed a pattern of excessive errors in the performance of forensic laboratory examination procedures;

(iv) failed to file any report required to be submitted pursuant to this article or the rules and regulations promulgated pursuant thereto; or

(v) violated in a material respect any provision of this article or the rules and regulations promulgated pursuant thereto; and

(f) no forensic laboratory accreditation shall be revoked, suspended, or otherwise limited without a hearing. The commission shall serve written notice of the alleged violation, together with written notice of the time and place of the hearing, which notice shall be mailed by certified mail to the holder of the forensic laboratory accreditation at the address of such holder at least twenty-one days prior to the date fixed for such hearing. An accredited laboratory may file a written answer to the charges with the commission, not less than five days prior to the hearing.

4. A laboratory director who knowingly operates a laboratory without obtaining the accreditation required by this article, or who, with the intent to mislead or deceive, misrepresents a material fact to the commission or DNA subcommittee, shall be subject to a civil penalty not to exceed seventy-five hundred dollars and such other penalties as are prescribed by the law.

5. The commission and the DNA subcommittee established pursuant to subdivision thirteen of this section may require and receive from any agency of the state or any political subdivision thereof such assistance and data as may be necessary to enable the commission or DNA subcommittee to administer the provisions of this article. The commission or DNA subcommittee may enter into such cooperative arrangements with the division of criminal justice services, the department of health, and any other state agency, each of which is authorized to enter into such cooperative arrangements as shall be necessary or appropriate. Upon request of the commission or DNA subcommittee, any state agency may transfer to the commission such officers and employees as the commission or DNA subcommittee may deem necessary from time to time to assist the commission or DNA subcommittee in carrying out its functions and duties. Officers and employees so transferred shall not lose their civil service status or rights, and shall remain in the negotiating unit, if any, established prior to such transfer.

6. All of the commission's records, reports, assessments, and evaluation with respect to accreditation, implementation of quality assurance standards (including proficiency testing) and monitoring thereof, shall be archived by the commission.

7. The commission and DNA subcommittee may establish, appoint, and set terms of members to as many advisory councils as it deems necessary to provide specialized expertise to the commission with respect to new forensic technologies including DNA testing methodologies.

8. The commission or DNA subcommittee shall designate one or more entities for the performance of proficiency tests required pursuant to the provisions of this article.

9. After reviewing recommendations from the division of criminal justice services, the commission, in consultation with the DNA subcommittee, shall promulgate a policy for the establishment and operation of a DNA identification index consistent with the operational requirements and capabilities of the division of criminal justice services. Such policy shall address the following issues:

(a) the forensic DNA methodology or methodologies to be utilized in compiling the index;

(b) procedures for assuring that the state DNA identification index contains the following safeguards:

(i) that any records maintained as part of such an index are accurate and complete;

(ii) that effective software and hardware designs are instituted with security features to prevent unauthorized access to such records;

(iii) that periodic audits will be conducted to ensure that no illegal disclosures of such records have taken place;

(iv) that access to record information system facilities, systems operating environments, data file contents whether while in use or when stored in a media library is restricted to authorized personnel only;

Exec. L.

(v) that operation programs are used that will prohibit inquiry, record updates, or destruction of records from any source other than an authorized source of inquiry, update, or destruction of records;

(vi) that operational programs are used to detect and store for the output of authorized employees only all unauthorized attempts to penetrate the state DNA identification index;

(vii) that adequate and timely procedures exist to insure that any subject of the state DNA identification index has the right of access to and review of records relating to such individual contained in such index for the purpose of ascertaining their accuracy and completeness, including procedures for review of information maintained about such individuals and administrative review (including procedures for administrative appeal) and the necessary documentation to demonstrate that the information is inaccurate or incomplete;

(viii) that access to the index will be granted to an agency authorized by this article to have such access only pursuant to a written use and dissemination agreement, a copy of which is filed with the commission, which agreement sets forth the specific procedures by which such agency shall implement the provisions of subparagraphs (i) through (vii) of this paragraph, as applicable, and which agreement specifically prohibits the redisclosure by such agency of any information obtained from the DNA identification index; and

(ix) such policy shall provide for the mutual exchange, use and storage of DNA records with the system of DNA identification utilized by the federal bureau of investigation provided that the commission determines that such exchange, use and storage are consistent with the provisions of this article and applicable provisions of law.

10. Review, and if necessary, recommend modifications to, a plan for implementation of the DNA identification index submitted by the commissioner of criminal justice services pursuant to section nine hundred ninety-five-c of this article.

11. Upon the recommendation of the DNA subcommittee established pursuant to subdivision thirteen of this section, the commission shall designate one or more approved methodologies for the performance of forensic DNA testing, and shall review and act upon applications by forensic DNA laboratories for approval to perform forensic DNA testing.

12. Promulgate standards for a determination of a match between the DNA records contained in the state DNA identification index and a DNA record of a person submitted for comparison therewith.

13. (a) The commission shall establish a subcommittee on forensic DNA laboratories and forensic DNA testing. The chair of the subcommittee shall be appointed by the chair of the commission. The chair of the subcommittee shall appoint six other members to the subcommittee, one of whom shall represent the discipline of molecular biology and be appointed upon the recommendation of the commissioner of the department of health, one of whom shall represent the discipline of population genetics and be appointed upon the recommendation of the commissioner of the department of health, one of whom shall be representative of the discipline of laboratory standards and quality assurance regulation and monitoring and be appointed upon the recommendation of the commissioner of the department of health, one of whom shall be a forensic scientist and be appointed upon the recommendation of the commissioner of the department of health, one of whom shall be representative of the discipline of population genetics and be appointed upon the recommendation of the commissioner of criminal justice services and one of whom shall be representative of the discipline of forensic

science and be appointed upon the recommendation of the commissioner of criminal justice services. Members of the DNA subcommittee shall serve for three year terms and be subject to the conditions of service specified in section nine hundred ninety-five-a of this article.

(b) The DNA subcommittee shall assess and evaluate all DNA methodologies proposed to be used for forensic analysis, and make reports and recommendations to the commission as it deems necessary. The DNA subcommittee shall make binding recommendations for adoption by the commission addressing minimum scientific standards to be utilized in conducting forensic DNA analysis including, but not limited to, examination of specimens, population studies and methods employed to determine probabilities and interpret test results. The DNA subcommittee may require a demonstration by an independent laboratory of any proposed forensic DNA testing methodology proposed to be used by a forensic laboratory.

(c) The DNA subcommittee shall make binding recommendations for adoption by the commission with regard to an accreditation program for laboratories performing forensic DNA testing in accordance with the provisions of the state administrative procedure act. Such recommendations shall include the adoption and implementation of internal and external proficiency testing programs, including, if possible, a blind external proficiency testing program for forensic laboratories performing forensic DNA testing. The DNA subcommittee shall also provide the commission with a list of accepted proficiency testers.

(d) The DNA subcommittee shall be authorized to advise the commission on any other matters regarding the implementation of scientific controls and quality assurance procedures for the performance of forensic DNA testing, or on any other matters referred to it by the commission.

HISTORY: Add, L 1994, ch 737, § 1, eff Aug 2, 1994. Sub 13, par (a), amd, L 1999, ch 560, § 2, eff Dec 1, 1999.

§ 995-c. State DNA identification index

1. Following the promulgation of a policy by the commission pursuant to subdivision nine of section nine hundred ninety-five-b of this article, the commissioner of criminal justice services is authorized to promulgate a plan for the establishment of a computerized state DNA identification index within the division of criminal justice services.

2. Following the review and approval of the plan by the DNA subcommittee and the commission and the filing of such plan with the speaker of the assembly and the temporary president of the senate, the commissioner of criminal justice services is hereby authorized to establish a computerized state DNA identification index pursuant to the provisions of this article.

3. (a) Any designated offender subsequent to conviction and sentencing for a crime specified in subdivision seven of section nine hundred ninety-five of this article, shall be required to provide a sample appropriate for DNA testing to determine identification characteristics specific to such person and to be included in a state DNA identification index pursuant to this article.

(b) (i) In the case of a designated offender who is sentenced to a term of imprisonment, such sample shall be collected by the public servant to whose custody the designated offender has been committed.

(ii) In the case of a designated offender who is sentenced to a term of probation, including a sentence of probation imposed in conjunction with a sentence of imprisonment when a sample has not already been taken, such sample shall be collected by the probation department supervising the designated offender.

(iii) In the case of a designated offender whose sentence does not include either a term of imprisonment or a term of probation, outside of the city of New York, the court shall order that a court officer take a sample or that the designated offender report to an office of the sheriff of that county, and when the designated offender does so, such sample shall be collected by the sheriff's office. Within the city of New York, the court shall order that the sample be collected by a court officer.

(iv) Nothing in this paragraph shall prohibit the collection of a DNA sample from a designated offender by any court official, state or local correction official or employee, probation officer, parole officer, police officer, peace officer, other law enforcement official, or designated personnel of the division of criminal justice services who has been notified by the division of criminal justice services that such designated offender has not provided a DNA sample. Upon notification by the division of criminal justice services that a designated offender has not provided a DNA sample, such court official, state or local correction official or employee, probation officer, parole officer, police officer, peace officer or other law enforcement official, or designated personnel of the division of criminal justice services shall collect the DNA sample.

4. The commissioner of the division of criminal justice services, in consultation with the commission, the commissioner of health, the director of the office of probation and correctional alternatives and the department of corrections and community supervision, shall promulgate rules and regulations governing the procedures for notifying designated offenders of the requirements of this section.

5. The sample shall be collected, stored and forwarded to any forensic DNA laboratory which has been authorized by the commission to perform forensic DNA testing and analysis for inclusion in the state DNA identification index. Such laboratory shall promptly perform the requisite testing and analysis, and forward the resulting DNA record only to the state DNA identification index in accordance with the regulations of the division of criminal justice services. Such laboratory shall perform DNA analysis only for those markers having value for law enforcement identification purposes. For the purposes of this article, the term "marker" shall have the meaning generally ascribed to it by members of the scientific community experienced in the use of DNA technology.

6. DNA records contained in the state DNA identification index shall be released only for the following purposes:

(a) to a federal law enforcement agency, or to a state or local law enforcement agency or district attorney's office for law enforcement identification purposes upon submission of a DNA record in connection with the investigation of the commission of one or more crimes or to assist in the recovery or identification of specified human remains, including identification of missing persons, provided that there exists between the division and such agency a written agreement governing the use and dissemination of such DNA records in accordance with the provisions of this article;

(b) for criminal defense purposes, to a defendant or his or her representative, who shall also have access to samples and analyses performed in connection with the case in which such defendant is charged;

(c) after personally identifiable information has been removed by the division, to an entity authorized by the division for the purpose of creating or maintaining a population statistics database or for identification research and protocol development for forensic DNA analysis or quality control purposes.

7. Requests for DNA records must be in writing, or in a form prescribed by the division authorized by the requesting party, and, other than a request pursuant to paragraph (b) of subdivision six of this section, maintained on file at the state DNA identification index in accordance with rules and regulations promulgated by the commissioner of the division of criminal justice services.

8. The defendant, including the representative of a defendant, in a criminal action or proceeding shall have access to information in the state DNA identification index relating to the number of requests previously made for a comparison search and the name and identity of any requesting party.

9. (a) Upon receipt of notification of a reversal or a vacatur of a conviction, or of the granting of a pardon pursuant to article two-A of this chapter, of an individual whose DNA record has been stored in the state DNA identification index in accordance with this article by the division of criminal justice services, the DNA record shall be expunged from the state DNA identification index, and such individual may apply to the court in which the judgment of conviction was originally entered for an order directing the expungement of any DNA record and any samples, analyses, or other documents relating to the DNA testing of such individual in connection with the investigation or prosecution of the crime which resulted in the conviction that was reversed or vacated or for which the pardon was granted. A copy of such application shall be served on the district attorney and an order directing expungement may be granted if the court finds that all appeals relating to the conviction have been concluded; that such individual will not be retried, or, if a retrial has occurred, the trier of fact has rendered a verdict of complete acquittal, and that expungement will not adversely affect the investigation or prosecution of some other person or persons for the crime. The division shall, by rule or regulation, prescribe procedures to ensure that the DNA record in the state DNA identification index, and any samples, analyses, or other documents relating to such record, whether in the possession of the division, or any law enforcement or police agency, or any forensic DNA laboratory, including any duplicates or copies thereof, at the discretion of the possessor thereof, are either destroyed or returned to such individual, or to the attorney who represented him or her at the time such reversal, vacatur or pardon, was granted. The commissioner shall also adopt by rule and regulation a procedure for the expungement in other appropriate circumstances of DNA records contained in the index.

(b) As prescribed in this paragraph, if an individual, either voluntarily or pursuant to a warrant or order of a court, has provided a sample for DNA testing in connection with the investigation or prosecution of a crime and (i) no criminal action against the individual relating to such crime was commenced within the period specified by section 30.10 of the criminal procedure law, or (ii) a criminal action was commenced against the individual relating to such crime which resulted in a complete acquittal, or (iii) a criminal action against the individual relating to such crime resulted in a conviction that was subsequently reversed or vacated, or for which the individual was granted a pardon pursuant to article two-A of this chapter, such individual may apply to the supreme court or the court in which the judgment of conviction was originally entered for an order directing the expungement of any DNA record and any samples, analyses, or other documents relating to the DNA testing of such individual in connection with the investigation or prosecution of such crime. A copy of such application shall be served on the district attorney and an order directing expungement may be granted if the court finds that the individual has satisfied the conditions of one of the subparagraphs of this paragraph; that if a judgment of conviction was reversed or vacated, all appeals relating thereto have been concluded and the individual will not be retried, or, if a retrial has occurred, the trier of fact has rendered a verdict of complete acquittal, and that expungement will not adversely affect the investigation or prosecution of some other person or persons for the crime. If an order directing the expungement of any DNA record and any samples, analyses or other documents relating to the DNA testing of such individual is issued, such record and any samples, analyses, or other documents shall, at the discretion of the possessor thereof, be destroyed or returned to such individual or to the attorney who represented him or her in connection with the application for the order of expungement.

HISTORY: Add, L 1994, ch 737, § 1, eff Jan 1, 1996; amd, L 1999, ch 560, §§ 3, 4, eff Dec 1, 1999, L 2002, ch 524, § 1, eff Sept 17, 2002, L 2004, ch 576, § 2, eff July 6, 2004, L 2010, ch 56, § 65 (Part A), eff June 22, 2010, L 2011, ch 62, § 104 (Part C, Subpart B), eff March 31, 2011, L 2012, ch 19, § 6, eff Aug 1, 2012, L 2012, ch 55, § 1 (Part A), eff Aug 1, 2012.

§ 995-d. Confidentiality

1. All records, findings, reports, and results of DNA testing performed on any person shall be confidential and may not be disclosed or redisclosed without the consent of the subject of such DNA testing. Such records, findings, reports and results shall not be released to insurance companies, employers or potential employers, health providers, employment screening or personnel companies, agencies, or services, private investigation services, and may not be disclosed in response to a subpoena or other compulsory legal process or warrant, or upon request or order of any agency, authority, division, office, corporation, partnership, or any other private or public entity or person, except that nothing contained herein shall prohibit disclosure in response to a subpoena issued on behalf of the subject of such DNA record or on behalf of a party in a civil proceeding where the subject of such DNA record has put such record in issue.

2. Notwithstanding the provisions of subdivision one of this section, records, findings, reports, and results of DNA testing, other than a DNA record maintained in the state DNA identification index, may be disclosed in a criminal proceeding to the court, the prosecution, and the defense pursuant to a written request on a form prescribed by the commissioner of the division of criminal justice services. Notwithstanding the provisions of subdivision one of this section, a DNA record maintained in the state DNA identification index may be disclosed pursuant to section nine hundred ninety-five-c of this article.

HISTORY: Add, L 1994, ch 737, § 1, eff Aug 2, 1994. Sub 2, amd, L 1999, ch 560, § 5, eff Dec 1, 1999.

§ 995-e. Applicability

This article shall not apply to a forensic DNA laboratory operated by any agency of the federal government, or to any forensic DNA test performed by any such federal laboratory.

HISTORY: Add, L 1994, ch 737, § 1, eff Aug 2, 1994.

§ 995-f. Penalties

Any person who (a) intentionally discloses a DNA record, or the results of a forensic DNA test or analysis, to an individual or agency other than one authorized to have access to such records pursuant to this article or (b) intentionally uses or receives DNA records, or the results of a forensic DNA test or analysis, for purposes other than those authorized pursuant to this article or (c) any person who knowingly tampers or attempts to tamper with any DNA sample or the collection container without lawful authority shall be guilty of a class E felony.

HISTORY: Add, L 1994, ch 737, § 1, eff Aug 2, 1994. Amd, L 1999, ch 560, § 6, eff Dec 1, 1999.

SELECTED SECTIONS
OF THE
JUDICIARY LAW

Article

5-B.   **Special Narcotics Parts of the Supreme Court in Cities with a Population of One Million or More**

21-A.   **Community Dispute Resolution Centers Program**

ARTICLE 5-B   SPECIAL NARCOTICS PARTS OF THE SUPREME COURT IN CITIES WITH A POPULATION OF ONE MILLION OR MORE

§ 177-a.   **Declaration of legislative findings and intent**

§ 177-b.   **Special narcotics parts; establishment**

§ 177-c.   **Special narcotics parts; prosecutorial organization**

§ 177-d.   **Special narcotics parts; procedure**

§ 177-e.   **[Repealed]**

    HISTORY: Add, L 1971, ch 462, eff June 17, 1971. Article heading, amd, L 1972, ch 633, § 1, eff May 24, 1972.

§ 177-a.   Declaration of legislative findings and intent

The legislature hereby finds and declares that an emergency of grave dimensions exists in narcotics law enforcement in cities having a population of one million or more. The overall law enforcement effort has not been successful in stemming the distribution of narcotic drugs. The legislature finds that the ineffectiveness of official efforts to contain the narcotics traffic is due in significant part to the inability of the overburdened criminal justice system to cope with the enormous volume of narcotics cases.

The legislature further finds that this crisis, which transcends the traditional jurisdictional boundaries of the counties wholly contained within such cities having a population of one million or more, demands coordinated prosecution, centralized direction and the infusion of massive new resources.

The legislature declares that without these new directions and resources, this crisis will intensify and very shortly overwhelm the already strained criminal justice system.

Based upon the above findings the legislature hereby declares that an emergency narcotics court program is required.

It is the intent of the legislature that the emergency narcotics program should be coordinated by the division of criminal justice of the office of planning services in cooperation with the criminal justice coordinating councils of such cities. The program would be implemented by the joint efforts of the district attorneys of the counties within cities having a population of one million or more, the judiciary, and other criminal justice services acting in accordance with a mutually agreed upon plan. The legislature contemplates that the program authorized herein shall consist of the establishment of special narcotics parts in the supreme court in cities having a population of one million or more to hear and determine narcotic cases from within counties wholly contained in a city having a population of one million or more, commencing not later than the September nineteen hundred seventy-two term and continuing thereafter during the duration of the emergency.

The legislature declares that the resources necessary for these special narcotics parts of the supreme court can be made available only through a combination of federal funds from the law enforcement assistance administration of the United States department of justice, and state and local funds, services and facilities. To this end the legislature declares that in order to utilize presently appropriated federal funds, all necessary agreements shall be entered into forthwith.

HISTORY: Add, L 1971, ch 462; amd, L 1972, ch 633, § 2, eff May 24, 1972.

§ 177-b. Special narcotics parts; establishment

1. There shall be established in cities having a population of one million or more in the supreme court special narcotics parts in such numbers and at such locations as shall be designated by the administrative board of the judicial conference of the state of New York to effectuate the purposes of this article. Such parts shall hear and determine narcotics indictments assigned thereto from any part of the supreme court in any county within such cities.

As used in this article, "narcotics indictment" means an indictment charging a crime that is prosecutable in any county wholly contained in a city within cities having a population of one million or more involving the sale or possession of a narcotic drug and any other offense properly joined therewith.

2. Notwithstanding any other provision of law, upon or after arraignment on a narcotics indictment filed in the supreme court in any county within such cities and before entry of a plea of guilty or commencement of trial, such supreme court may order that the indictment and action be assigned to a special narcotics part of the supreme court.

3. The trial of an indictment in a special narcotics part shall for all purposes be deemed to be a trial in the county in which the indictment was filed, but the administrative board of the judicial conference may promulgate rules, orders or regulations to be applicable to such parts in place and instead of the rules, orders or regulations applicable to courts in the county where the indictment was filed. The administrative board shall provide by rule, order or regulation for at least the following matters: the procedure of the part; its auxiliary services; the assignment of judicial personnel; the appointment of terms; and transmittal of all papers in the action, including all undertakings for appearances of the defendant and of the witnesses, to the part of the supreme court to which the action has been assigned.

HISTORY: Add, L 1971, ch 462; amd, L 1972, ch 633, § 2, eff May 24, 1972.

§ 177-c. Special narcotics parts; prosecutorial organization

The district attorneys of the counties wholly contained in a city having a population of one million or more shall formulate and adopt a plan designed to effect the purposes of this article. The plan shall provide for the following matters:

(i) the appointment of an assistant district attorney to the staff of one of the district attorneys to administer the program established pursuant to the plan;

(ii) the appointment of a staff to operate under the direction and supervision of the assistant district attorney appointed pursuant to paragraph (i);

(iii) the establishment of standards, administrative policies, and procedures to govern the performance of the prosecutorial functions in connection with narcotics cases, including but not limited to guidelines governing applications by the assistant district attorney appointed pursuant to paragraph (i) for the impaneling of a grand jury; and

(iv) any other matters, pertaining to the effective administration of the program and fulfillment of the purposes of this article.

HISTORY: Add, L 1971, ch 462; amd, L 1972, ch 633, § 2, eff May 24, 1972.

§ 177-d. Special narcotics parts; procedure

Notwithstanding any other provision of law,

(i) a narcotics indictment returned in any county within such cities may be prosecuted in the special narcotics part to which it is assigned pursuant to section one hundred seventy-seven-b irrespective of the county in which the part is held and in which the crime charged was committed;

(ii) any assistant district attorney appointed pursuant to the plan authorized by section one hundred seventy-seven-c may prosecute all offenses cognizable by any special narcotics part irrespective of the county in which the part is held and in which the crime charged was committed; and

(iii) upon the application of the assistant district attorney in charge of the special narcotics parts appointed pursuant to the plan authorized by section one hundred seventy-seven-c, one or more grand juries may be drawn and impaneled for a special narcotics part upon the order of the justice assigned to such part, which grand jury may exercise all the powers of a grand jury in the county in which it is impaneled and may in addition exercise its powers with respect to the alleged commission of an offense in any county wholly contained in a city having a population of one million or more involving the sale or possession of a narcotic drug and any other offense that could be properly joined therewith in an indictment.

HISTORY: Add, L 1971, ch 462; amd, L 1972, ch 633, § 2, eff May 24, 1972.

§ 177-e. [Repealed]

HISTORY: Add, L 1971, ch 462; amd, L 1972, ch 633, § 2, L 1985, ch 134, § 19, eff April 1, 1985. **Repealed** by L. 2010, Ch. 56 (Part A), § 56, eff. June 22, 2010.

*   *   *

ARTICLE 21-A   COMMUNITY DISPUTE RESOLUTION CENTERS PROGRAM

HISTORY: Add, L 1981, ch 847, § 3, eff July 27, 1981.

§ 849-a. Definitions

For the purposes of this article:

1. "Center" means a community dispute center which provides conciliation, mediation, arbitration or other forms and techniques of dispute resolution.

2. "Mediator" means an impartial person who assists in the resolution of a dispute.

3. "Grant recipient" means any nonprofit organization that administers a community dispute resolution center pursuant to this article, and is organized for the resolution of disputes or for religious, charitable or educational purposes.

HISTORY: Add, L 1981, ch 847, § 3, eff July 27, 1981.

§ 849-b. Establishment and administration of centers

1. There is hereby established the community dispute resolution center program, to be administered and supervised under the direction of the chief administrator of the courts, to provide funds pursuant to this article for the establishment and continuance of dispute resolution centers on the basis of need in neighborhoods.

2. Every center shall be operated by a grant recipient.

3. All centers shall be operated pursuant to contract with the chief administrator and shall comply with all provisions of this article. The chief administrator shall promulgate rules and regulations to effectuate the purposes of this article, including provisions for periodic monitoring and evaluation of the program.

4. A center shall not be eligible for funds under this article unless:

(a) it complies with the provisions of this article and the applicable rules and regulations of the chief administrator;

(b) it provides neutral mediators who have received at least twenty-five hours of training in conflict resolution techniques;

(c) it provides dispute resolution without cost to indigents and at nominal or no cost to other participants;

(d) it provides that during or at the conclusion of the dispute resolution process there shall be a written agreement or decision setting forth the settlement of the issues and future responsibilities of each party and that such agreement or decision shall be available to a court which has adjourned a pending action pursuant to section 170.55 of the criminal procedure law;

(e) it does not make monetary awards except upon consent of the parties and such awards do not exceed the monetary jurisdiction of the small claims part of the justice court, except that where an action has been adjourned in contemplation of dismissal pursuant to section 215.10 of the criminal procedure law, a monetary award not in excess of five thousand dollars may be made; and

(f) it does not accept for dispute resolution any defendant who is named in a filed felony complaint, superior court information, or indictment, charging: (i) a class A felony, or (ii) a violent felony offense as defined in section 70.02 of the penal law, or (iii) any drug offense as defined in article two hundred twenty of the penal law, or (iv) a felony upon the conviction of which defendant must be sentenced as a second felony offender, a second violent felony offender, or a persistent violent felony offender pursuant to sections 70.06, 70.04 and 70.08 of the penal law, or a felony upon the conviction of which defendant may be sentenced as a persistent felony offender pursuant to section 70.10 of such law.

5. Parties must be provided in advance of the dispute resolution process with a written statement relating:

(a) their rights and obligations;

(b) the nature of the dispute;

(c) their right to call and examine witnesses;

(d) that a written decision with the reasons therefor will be rendered; and

(e) that the dispute resolution process will be final and binding upon the parties.

6. Except as otherwise expressly provided in this article, all memoranda, work products, or case files of a mediator are confidential and not subject to disclosure in any judicial or administrative proceeding. Any communication relating to the subject matter of the resolution made during the resolution process by any participant, mediator, or any other person present at the dispute resolution shall be a confidential communication.

HISTORY: Add, L 1981, ch 847, § 3, eff July 27, 1981. Sub 4, par (e), amd, L 1985, ch 91, § 1, L 1986, ch 837, § 4, eff Nov 1, 1986. Sub 4, par (f), amd, L 1986, ch 837, § 4, eff Nov 1, 1986.

§ 849-c. Application procedures

1. Funds appropriated or available for the purposes of this article may be allocated for programs proposed by eligible centers. Nothing in this article shall preclude existing resolution centers from applying for funds made available under this article provided that they are otherwise in compliance with this article.

2. Centers shall be selected by the chief administrator from applications submitted.

3. The chief administrator shall require that applications submitted for funding include, but need not be limited to the following:

(a) The cost of each of the proposed centers components including the proposed compensation of employees.

(b) A description of the proposed area of service and number of participants who may be served.

(c) A description of available dispute resolution services and facilities within the proposed geographical area.

(d) A description of the applicant's proposed program, including support of civic groups, social services agencies and criminal justice agencies to accept and make referrals; the present availability of resources; and the applicant's administrative capacity.

(e) Such additional information as is determined to be needed pursuant to rules of the chief administrator.

HISTORY: Add, L 1981, ch 847, § 3, eff July 27, 1981.

§ 849-d. Payment procedures

1. Upon the approval of the chief administrator, funds appropriated or available for the purposes of this article shall be used for the costs of operation of approved programs. The methods of payment or reimbursement for dispute resolution costs shall be specified by the chief administrator and may vary among centers. All such arrangements shall conform to the eligibility criteria of this article and the rules and regulations of the chief administrator.

2. The state share of the cost of any center approved under this section shall include a basic grant of up to forty thousand dollars for each county served by the center and may include an additional amount not exceeding fifty per centum of the difference between the approved estimated cost of the program and the basic grant.

HISTORY: Add, L 1981, ch 847, § 3, eff July 27, 1981. Sub 2, amd, L 1987, ch 281, § 1, eff April 1, 1987. Sub 2, amd, L 2006, ch 451, § 1, eff April 1, 2007.

§ 849-e. Funding

1. The chief administrator may accept and disburse from any public or private agency or person, any money for the purposes of this article.

2. The chief administrator may also receive and disburse federal funds for purposes of this article, and perform services and acts as may be necessary for the receipt and disbursement of such federal funds.

    (a) A grant recipient may accept funds from any public or private agency or person for the purposes of this article.

    (b) The state comptroller, the chief administrator and their authorized representatives, shall have the power to inspect, examine and audit the fiscal affairs of the program.

    (c) Centers shall, whenever reasonably possible, make use of public facilities at free or nominal cost.

    HISTORY: Add, L 1981, ch 847, § 3, eff July 27, 1981.

§ 849-f. Rules and regulations

The chief administrator shall promulgate rules and regulations to effectuate the purposes of this article.

    HISTORY: Add, L 1981, ch 847, § 3, eff July 27, 1981.

§ 849-g. Reports

Each resolution center funded pursuant to this article shall annually provide the chief administrator with statistical data regarding the operating budget, the number of referrals, categories or types of cases referred, number of parties serviced, number of disputes resolved, nature of resolution, amount and type of awards, rate of compliance, returnees to the resolution process, duration and estimated costs of hearings and such other information the chief administrator may require and the cost of hearings as the chief administrator requires. The chief administrator shall thereafter report annually to the governor and the temporary president of the senate, speaker of the assembly, and chairpersons of the judiciary and children and families committees regarding the operation and success of the centers funded pursuant to this article. The chief administrator shall include in such report all the information for each center that is required to be in the report from each center to the chief administrator. Such annual report shall also evaluate and make recommendations regarding the operation and success of such center.

    HISTORY: Add, L 1981, ch 847, § 3, eff July 27, 1981. Amd, L 2005, ch 524, § 31, eff Nov 14, 2005.

SELECTED SECTIONS
OF THE
PUBLIC HEALTH LAW

ARTICLE 33   CONTROLLED SUBSTANCES

HISTORY: Add, L 1972, ch 878, § 2, eff April 1, 1973. Former Art 33 (consisting of §§ 3300-3366), add, L 1953, ch 879, § 1; repealed, L 1972, ch 878, § 1, eff April 1, 1973.

HISTORY: Add, L 1972, ch 878, § 2, eff April 1, 1973. Former Title I, add, L 1953, ch 879, § 1; repealed, L 1972, ch 878, § 1, eff April 1, 1973.

§ 3300. Short title

This article shall be known as the New York State Controlled Substances Act.

HISTORY: Add, L 1972, ch 878, § 2, eff April 1, 1973, with substance derived from former §§ 3300, 3370. Former § 3300, add, L 1953, ch 879, § 1, with substance derived from former § 420; repealed, L 1972, ch 878, § 1, eff April 1, 1973.

§ 3300-a. Legislative purposes

The purposes of this article are:

1. to combat illegal use of and trade in controlled substances; and

2. to allow legitimate use of controlled substances in health care, including palliative care; veterinary care; research and other uses authorized by this article or other law; under appropriate regulation and subject to this article, title eight of the education law, and other applicable law.

HISTORY: Add, L 1998, ch 537, § 2, eff Nov 1, 1998.

§ 3301. Applicability of this article to actions and matters occurring or arising before and after the effective date

Unless otherwise expressly provided, or unless the context otherwise requires:

(a) the provisions of this article shall govern and control the possession, manufacture, dispensing, administering, and distribution of controlled substances with respect to any matter, act or omission, arising or occurring on or after the effective date hereof;

(b) the provisions of this article do not apply to or govern any matter, act, or omission arising or occurring prior to the effective date hereof. Such matters, acts, or omissions must be governed and construed according to provisions of law existing at the time such matter, act or omission arose or occurred in the same manner as if this article had not been enacted.

HISTORY: Add, L 1972, ch 878, § 2, eff April 1, 1973. Former § 3301, add, L 1961, ch 206, § 1; amd, L 1962, ch 597, L 1970, ch 700, L 1971, ch 997, §§ 1, 2; repealed, L 1972, ch 878, § 1, eff April 1, 1973. See now § 3302. Original § 3301, add, L 1953, ch 879, with substance derived from § 421; amd, L 1956, ch 230, L 1957, ch 564; repealed, L 1961, ch 206.

§ 3302. Definitions of terms of general use in this article

Except where different meanings are expressly specified in subsequent provisions of this article, the following terms have the following meanings:

1. "Addict" means a person who habitually uses a controlled substance for a non-legitimate or unlawful use, and who by reason of such use is dependent thereon.

2. "Administer" means the direct application of a controlled substance, whether by injection, inhalation, ingestion, or any other means, to the body of a patient or research subject.

3. "Agent" means an authorized person who acts on behalf of or at the direction of a manufacturer, distributor, or dispenser. No person may be authorized to so act if under title VIII of the education law such person would not be permitted to engage in such conduct. It does not include a common or contract carrier, public warehouseman, or employee of the carrier or warehouseman when acting in the usual and lawful course of the carrier's or warehouseman's business.

4. "Concentrated Cannabis" means

(a) the separated resin, whether crude or purified, obtained from a plant of the genus Cannabis; or

(b) a material, preparation, mixture, compound or other substance which contains more than two and one-half percent by weight of delta-9 tetrahydrocannabinol, or its isomer, delta-8 dibenzopyran numbering system, or delta-1 tetrahydrocannabinol or its isomer, delta 1 (6) monoterpene numbering system.

5. "Controlled substance" means a substance or substances listed in section thirty-three hundred six of this chapter.

6. "Commissioner" means commissioner of health of the state of New York.

7. "Deliver" or "delivery" means the actual, constructive or attempted transfer from one person to another of a controlled substance, whether or not there is an agency relationship.

8. "Department" means the department of health of the state of New York.

9. "Dispense" means to deliver a controlled substance to an ultimate user or research subject by lawful means, including by means of the internet, and includes the packaging, labeling, or compounding necessary to prepare the substance for such delivery.

10. "Distribute" means to deliver a controlled substance, including by means of the internet, other than by administering or dispensing.

11. "Distributor" means a person who distributes a controlled substance.

12. "Diversion" means manufacture, possession, delivery or use of a controlled substance by a person or in a manner not specifically authorized by law.

13. "Drug" means

(a) substances recognized as drugs in the official United States Pharmacopoeia, official Homeopathic Pharmacopoeia of the United States, or official National Formulary, or any supplement to any of them;

(b) substances intended for use in the diagnosis, cure, mitigation, treatment, or prevention of disease in man or animals; and

(c) substances (other than food) intended to affect the structure or a function of the body of man or animal. It does not include devices or their components, parts, or accessories.

14. "Federal agency" means the Drug Enforcement Administration, United States Department of Justice, or its successor agency.

15. "Federal controlled substances act" means the Comprehensive Drug Abuse Prevention and Control Act of 1970, Public Law 91-513, and any act or acts amendatory or supplemental thereto or regulations promulgated thereunder.

16. "Federal registration number" means such number assigned by the Federal agency to any person authorized to manufacture, distribute, sell, dispense or administer controlled substances.

17. "Habitual user" means any person who is, or by reason of repeated use of any controlled substance for non-legitimate or unlawful use is in danger of becoming, dependent upon such substance.

18. "Institutional dispenser" means a hospital, veterinary hospital, clinic, dispensary, maternity home, nursing home, mental hospital or similar facility approved and certified by the department as authorized to obtain controlled substances by distribution and to dispense and administer such substances pursuant to the order of a practitioner.

19. "License" means a written authorization issued by the department or the New York state department of education permitting persons to engage in a specified activity with respect to controlled substances.

20. "Manufacture" means the production, preparation, propagation, compounding, cultivation, conversion or processing of a controlled substance, either directly or indirectly or by extraction from substances of natural origin, or independently by means of chemical synthesis, or by a combination of extraction and chemical synthesis, and includes any packaging or repackaging of the substance or labeling or relabeling of its container, except that this term does not include the preparation, compounding, packaging or labeling of a controlled substance:

(a) by a practitioner as an incident to his administering or dispensing of a controlled substance in the course of his professional practice; or

(b) by a practitioner, or by his authorized agent under his supervision, for the purpose of, or as an incident to, research, teaching, or chemical analysis and not for sale; or

(c) by a pharmacist as an incident to his dispensing of a controlled substance in the course of his professional practice.

21. "Marihuana" means all parts of the plant of the genus Cannabis, whether growing or not; the seeds thereof; the resin extracted from any part of the plant; and every compound, manufacture, salt, derivative, mixture, or preparation of the plant, its seeds or resin. It does not include the mature stalks of the plant, fiber produced from the stalks, oil or cake made from the seeds of the plant, any other compound, manufacture, salt, derivative, mixture, or preparation of the mature stalks (except the resin extracted therefrom), fiber, oil, or cake, or the sterilized seed of the plant which is incapable of germination.

22. "Narcotic drug" means any of the following, whether produced directly or indirectly by extraction from substances of vegetable origin, or independently by means of chemical synthesis, or by a combination of extraction and chemical synthesis:

(a) opium and opiate, and any salt, compound, derivative, or preparation of opium or opiate;

(b) any salt, compound, isomer, derivative, or preparation thereof which is chemically equivalent or identical with any of the substances referred to in subdivision (a), but not including the isoquinoline alkaloids of opium;

(c) opium poppy and poppy straw.

23. "Opiate" means any substance having an addiction-forming or addiction-sustaining liability similar to morphine or being capable of conversion into a drug having addiction-forming or addiction-sustaining liability. It does not include, unless specifically designated as controlled under section 3306 of this article, the dextrorotatory isomer of 3-methoxy-n-methylmorphinan and its salts (dextromethorphan). It does include its racemic and levorotatory forms.

24. "Opium poppy" means the plant of the species Papaver somniferum L., except its seeds.

25. "Person" means individual, institution, corporation, government or governmental subdivision or agency, business trust, estate, trust, partnership or association, or any other legal entity.

26. "Pharmacist" means any person licensed by the state department of education to practice pharmacy.

27. "Pharmacy" means any place registered as such by the New York state board of pharmacy and registered with the Federal agency pursuant to the federal controlled substances act.

28. "Poppy straw" means all parts, except the seeds, of the opium poppy, after mowing.

29. "Practitioner" means:

A physician, dentist, podiatrist, veterinarian, scientific investigator, or other person licensed, or otherwise permitted to dispense, administer or conduct research with respect to a controlled substance in the course of a licensed professional practice or research licensed pursuant to this article. Such person shall be deemed a "practitioner" only as to such substances, or conduct relating to such substances, as is permitted by his license, permit or otherwise permitted by law.

30. "Prescribe" means a direction or authorization, by prescription, permitting an ultimate user lawfully to obtain controlled substances from any person authorized by law to dispense such substances.

31. "Prescription" shall mean an official New York state prescription, an electronic prescription, an oral prescription, an out-of-state prescription, or any one.

32. "Sell" means to sell, exchange, give or dispose of to another, or offer or agree to do the same.

33. "Ultimate user" means a person who lawfully obtains and possesses a controlled substance for his own use or the use by a member of his household or for an animal owned by him or in his custody. It shall also mean and include a person designated, by a practitioner on a prescription, to obtain such substance on behalf of the patient for whom such substance is intended.

34. "Internet" means collectively computer and telecommunications facilities which comprise the worldwide network of networks that employ a set of industry standards and protocols, or any predecessor or successor protocol to such protocol, to exchange information of all kinds.

"Internet," as used in this article, also includes other networks, whether private or public, used to transmit information by electronic means.

35. "By means of the internet" means any sale, delivery, distribution, or dispensing of a controlled substance that uses the internet, is initiated by use of the internet or causes the internet to be used.

36. "Online dispenser" means a practitioner, pharmacy, or person in the United States that sells, delivers or dispenses, or offers to sell, deliver, or dispense, a controlled substance by means of the internet.

37. "Electronic prescription" means a prescription issued with an electronic signature and transmitted by electronic means in accordance with regulations of the commissioner and the commissioner of education and consistent with federal requirements. A prescription generated on an electronic system that is printed out or transmitted via facsimile is not considered an electronic prescription and must be manually signed.

38. "Electronic" means of or relating to technology having electrical, digital, magnetic, wireless, optical, electromagnetic or similar capabilities. "Electronic" shall not include facsimile.

39. "Electronic record" means a paperless record that is created, generated, transmitted, communicated, received or stored by means of electronic equipment and includes the preservation, retrieval, use and disposition in accordance with regulations of the commissioner and the commissioner of education and in compliance with federal law and regulations.

40. "Electronic signature" means an electronic sound, symbol, or process, attached to or logically associated with an electronic record and executed or adopted by a person with the intent to sign the record, in accordance with regulations of the commissioner and the commissioner of education.

41. "Registry" or "prescription monitoring program registry" means the prescription monitoring program registry established pursuant to section thirty-three hundred forty-three-a of this article.

42. "Compounding" means the combining, admixing, mixing, diluting, pooling, reconstituting, or otherwise altering of a drug or bulk drug substance to create a drug with respect to an outsourcing facility under section 503B of the federal Food, Drug and Cosmetic Act and further defined in this section.

43. "Outsourcing facility" means a facility that:

(a) is engaged in the compounding of sterile drugs as defined in section sixty-eight hundred two of the education law;

(b) is currently registered as an outsourcing facility pursuant to article one hundred thirty-seven of the education law; and

(c) complies with all applicable requirements of federal and state law, including the Federal Food, Drug and Cosmetic Act.

Notwithstanding any other provision of law to the contrary, when an outsourcing facility distributes or dispenses any drug to any person pursuant to a prescription, such outsourcing facility shall be deemed to be providing pharmacy services and shall be subject to all laws, rules and regulations governing pharmacies and pharmacy services.

HISTORY: Add, L 1972, ch 878, § 2, eff April 1, 1973, with substance derived from former §§ 3301, 3371; amd, L 1973, ch 163, §§ 1–3, eff April 1, 1973, L 1998, ch 537, § 3, eff Nov 1, 1998, L 2004, ch 58, § 4 (Part A), eff Oct 20, 2004, L 2010, ch 178, §§ 1, 2, eff July 15, 2010, L 2012, ch 447, § 6 (Part A), eff Aug 27, 2013, L 2014, ch 60, § 13 (Part D), eff June 29, 2014.

§ 3304. Prohibited acts

[As amended by L 1981, ch. 547, § 1, § 3304 reads as set out below:]

1. It shall be unlawful for any person to manufacture, sell, prescribe, distribute, dispense, administer, possess, have under his control, abandon, or transport a controlled substance except as expressly allowed by this article.

2. It shall be unlawful for any person to possess or have under his control an official New York state prescription form except as expressly allowed by this article.

[As amended by L 1981, ch. 795, § 1, § 3304 reads as set out below:]

a. It shall be unlawful for any person to manufacture, sell, prescribe, distribute, dispense, administer, possess, have under his control, abandon, or transport a controlled substance except as expressly allowed by this article.

b. It shall be unlawful for any physician practicing medicine as defined in section sixty-five hundred twenty-one of the education law to prescribe, dispense or administer any amphetamines or sympathomimetic amine drug or compound thereof, designated as a schedule II controlled substance pursuant to section thirty-three hundred six of this article for the exclusive treatment of obesity, weight control or weight loss. A violation of the provisions of this subdivision shall not be grounds for prosecution under article two hundred twenty of the penal law.

HISTORY: [First setout] Add, L 1972, ch 878, § 2; amd L 1981, ch 547, § 1, eff Sept 1, 1981. [Second setout] Add, L 1972, ch 878, § 2; amd, L 1981, ch 795, § 1, eff Sept 1, 1981. Former § 3304, add, L 1953, ch 879, § 1, with substance derived from former § 421-a; repealed, L 1972, ch 878, § 1, eff April 1, 1973. See now § 3373.

§ 3305. Exemptions

1. The provisions of this article restricting the possession and control of controlled substances and official New York state prescription forms shall not apply:

(a) to common carriers or to warehousemen, while engaged in lawfully transporting or storing such substances, or to any employee of the same acting within the scope of his employment; or

(b) to public officers or their employees in the lawful performance of their official duties requiring possession or control of controlled substances; or

(c) to temporary incidental possession by employees or agents of persons lawfully entitled to possession, or by persons whose possession is for the purpose of aiding public officers in performing their official duties.

(d) to a duly authorized agent of an incorporated society for the prevention of cruelty to animals or a municipal animal control facility for the limited purpose of buying, possessing, and dispensing to registered and certified personnel, ketamine hydrochloride to anesthetize animals and/or sodium pentobarbital to euthanize animals, including but not limited to dogs and cats. The department shall, consistent with the public interest, register such duly authorized agent and such agent shall file, on a quarterly basis, a report of purchase, possession, and use of ketamine hydrochloride and/or sodium pentobarbital, which report shall be certified by the society for the prevention of cruelty to animals or municipal animal control facility as to its accuracy and validity. This report shall be in addition to any other record keeping and reporting requirements of state and federal law and regulation. The department shall adopt rules and regulations providing for the registration and certification of any individual who, under the direction of the duly authorized and registered agent of an incorporated society for the prevention of cruelty to animals, or municipal animal control facility, uses ketamine hydrochloride to anesthetize animals and/or sodium pentobarbital to euthanize animals, including but not limited to dogs and cats. The department may also adopt such other rules and regulations as shall provide for the safe and efficient use of ketamine hydrochloride and/or sodium pentobarbital by incorporated societies for the prevention of cruelty to animals and animal control facilities. Nothing in this paragraph shall be deemed to waive any other requirement imposed on incorporated societies for the prevention of cruelty to animals and animal control facilities by state and federal law and regulation.

2. The commissioner may, by regulation, provide for the exemption from all or part of the requirements of this article the possession of substances in schedule III or IV and use thereof as part of an industrial process or manufacture of substances other than drugs. The commissioner may impose such conditions upon the granting of such exemption as may be necessary to protect against diversion or misuse of the controlled substance.

3. The commissioner is hereby authorized and empowered to make any rules, regulations and determinations permitting the following categories of persons to obtain, dispense and administer controlled substances under such conditions and in such manner as he shall prescribe:

(a) a person in the employ of the United States government or of any state, territory, district, county, municipal, or insular government, obtaining, possessing, dispensing and administering controlled substances by reason of his official duties;

(b) a master of a ship or a person in charge of any aircraft upon which no physician is regularly employed, or to a physician or surgeon duly licensed in any state, territory, or the District of Columbia to practice his profession, or to a retired commissioned medical officer of the United States army, navy, or public health service, employed upon such ship or aircraft, for the actual medical needs of persons on board such ship or aircraft when not in port.

(c) a person in a foreign country in compliance with the provisions of this article.

4. The provisions of this article with respect to the payment of fees and costs shall not apply to the state of New York or any political subdivision thereof or any agency or instrumentality of either.

HISTORY: Add, L 1972, ch 878, § 2, eff April 1, 1973. Former § 3305, add, L 1953, ch 879, § 1, with substance derived from former § 422; repealed, L 1972, ch 878, § 1, eff April 1, 1973. See now § 3304. Sub 1, amd, L 1981, ch 547, § 2, eff Sept 1, 1981. Sub 1, par (c), amd, L 1973, ch 163, § 4, eff April 1, 1973. Sub 1, par (d), add, L 1987, ch 619, § 6; amd, L 1992, ch 18, § 1, eff March 20, 1992. Sub 1, par (d), amd, L 1997, ch 635, § 1, eff Jan 22, 1998. Sub 3, opening par, amd, L 1991, ch 166, § 359, eff June 12, 1991 and expired June 30, 1995. Sub 3, par (a), amd, L 1991, ch 166, § 359, eff June 12, 1991 and expired June 30, 1995.

§ 3306. Schedules of controlled substances

There are hereby established five schedules of controlled substances, to be known as schedules I, II, III, IV and V respectively. Such schedules shall consist of the following substances by whatever name or chemical designation known:

Schedule I.

(a) Schedule I shall consist of the drugs and other substances, by whatever official name, common or usual name, chemical name, or brand name designated, listed in this section.

(b) Opiates. Unless specifically excepted or unless listed in another schedule, any of the following opiates, including their isomers, esters, ethers, salts, and salts of isomers, esters, and ethers, whenever the existence of such isomers, esters, ethers and salts is possible within the specific chemical designation (for purposes of 3-methylfentanyl only, the term isomer includes the optical and geometric isomers):

(1) Acetyl-alpha-methylfentanyl (N-{1-(-methyl-2-phenethyl) -4-piperidinyl} -N-phenylacetamide.

(2) Acetylmethadol.

(3) Allylprodine.

(4) Alphacetylmethadol (except levo-alphacetylmethadol also known as levo-alpha-acetylmethadol, levomethadyl acetate or LAAM).

(5) Alphameprodine.

(6) Alphamethadol.

(7) Alpha-methylfentanyl (N-{1-(alpha-methyl-beta-phenyl) ethyl-4-piperidyl} propionanilide; 1-(1-methyl-2-phenylethyl) -4-(N-propanilido) piperidine).

(8) Alpha-methylthiofentanyl (N-{1-methyl-2)2-thienyl) ethyl-4-piperidinyl} -N-phenylpropanamide).

(9) Beta-hydroxyfentanyl (N-{1-2 (2-hydroxy-2-phenethyl)- 4-piperidinyl} -N-phenylpropanamide).

(10) Beta-hydroxy-3-methylfentanyl (other name: N-{1- (2-hydroxy-2-phenethyl) -3-methyl-4-piperidinyl} -N-phenylpropanamide.

(11) Benzethidine.

(12) Betacetylmethadol.

(13) Betameprodine.

(14) Betamethadol.

(15) Betaprodine.

(16) Clonitazene.

(17) Dextromoramide.

(18) Diampromide.

(19) Diethylthiambutene.

(20) Difenoxin.

(21) Dimenoxadol.

(22) Dimepheptanol.

(23) Dimethylthiambutene.

(24) Dioxaphetyl butyrate.

(25) Dipipanone.

(26) Ethylmethylthiambutene.

(27) Etonitazene.

(28) Etoxeridine.

(29) Furethidine.

(30) Hydroxypethidine.

(31) Ketobemidone.

(32) Levomoramide.

(33) Levophenacylmorphan.

(34) 3-Methylfentanyl (N-{3-methyl-1- (2- phenylethyl -4-piperidyl} -N-phenylpropanamide).

(35) 3-Methylthiofentanyl (N-{3-methyl-1- (2-thienyl)ethyl -4-piperidinyl} -N-phenylpropanamide).

(36) Morpheridine.

(37) MPPP (1-methyl -4-phenyl -4-propionoxypiperidine).

(38) Noracymethadol.

(39) Norlevorphanol.

(40) Normethadone.

(41) Norpipanone.

(42) Para-fluorofentanyl (N- (4-fluorophenyl) -N-{1- (2-phenethyl) -4-piperidinyl} -propanamide.

(43) PEPAP (1- (-2-phenethyl) -4-phenyl -4-acetoxypiperidine.

(44) Phenadoxone.

(45) Phenampromide.

(46) Phenomorphan.

(47) Phenoperidine.

(48) Piritramide.

(49) Proheptazine.

(50) Properidine.

(51) Propiram.

(52) Racemoramide.

(53) Thiofentanyl (N-phenyl-N-{1- (2-thienyl) ethyl -4- piperidinyl} -propanamide.

(54) Tilidine.

(55) Trimeperidine.

(c) Opium derivatives. Unless specifically excepted or unless listed in another schedule, any of the following opium derivatives, its salts, isomers, and salts of isomers whenever the existence of such salts, isomers, and salts of isomers is possible within the specific chemical designation:

(1) Acetorphine.

(2) Acetyldihydrocodeine.

(3) Benzylmorphine.

(4) Codeine methylbromide.

(5) Codeine-N-oxide.

(6) Cyprenorphine.

(7) Desomorphine.

(8) Dihydromorphine.

(9) Drotebanol.

(10) Etorphine (except hydrochloride salt).

(11) Heroin.

(12) Hydromorphinol.

(13) Methyldesorphine.

(14) Methyldihydromorphine.

(15) Morphine methylbromide.

(16) Morphine methylsulfonate.

(17) Morphine-N-oxide.

(18) Myrophine.

(19) Nicocodeine.

(20) Nicomorphine.

(21) Normorphine.

(22) Pholcodine.

(23) Thebacon.

(d) Hallucinogenic substances. Unless specifically excepted or unless listed in another schedule, any material, compound, mixture, or preparation, which contains any quantity of the following hallucinogenic substances, or which contains any of its salts, isomers, and salts of isomers whenever the existence of such salts, isomers, and salts of isomers is possible within the specific chemical designation (for purposes of this paragraph only, the term "isomer" includes the optical, position and geometric isomers):

(1) 4-bromo-2, 5-dimethoxy-amphetamine Some trade or other names: 4-bromo-2, 5-dimethoxy-a-methylphenethylamine; 4-bromo-2, 5-DMA.

(2) 2, 5-dimethoxyamphetamine Some trade or other names: 2, 5-dimethoxy-a-methylphenethylamine; 2, 5-DMA.

(3) 4-methoxyamphetamine Some trade or other names: 4-methoxy-a-methylphenethylamine; paramethoxyamphetamine, PMA.

(4) 5-methoxy-3, 4-methylenedioxy-amphetamine.

(5) 4-methyl-2, 5-dimethoxy-amphetamine Some trade and other names: 4-methyl-2, 5-dimethoxy-a-methylphenethylamine; "DOM"; and "STP".

(6) 3, 4-methylenedioxy amphetamine.

(7) 3, 4, 5-trimethoxy amphetamine.

(8) Bufotenine Some trade and other names: 3-(B-dimethylaminoethyl)-5 Hydroxin-dole; 3-(2-dimethylaminoethyl)-5-indolol; N, N-dimethylserotonin; -5-hydroxy-N, N-dimethyltryptamine; mappine.

(9) Diethyltryptamine Some trade and other names: N, N-diethyltryptamine; DET.

(10) Dimethyltryptamine Some trade or other names: DMT.

(11) Ibogane Some trade and other names: 7-ethyl-6, 6B, 7, 8, 9, 10, 12, 13-octahydro-2-methoxy-6, 9-methano-5h-pyrido {1 ', 2 ': 1,2} azepino {5,4-b} indole: tabernanthe iboga.

(12) Lysergic acid diethylamide.

(13) Marihuana.

(14) Mescaline.

(15) Parahexyl. Some trade or other names: 3-Hexyl-1-hydroxy-7, 8, 9, 10-tetra hydro-6, 6, 9-trimethyl-6H-dibenfo{b,d} pyran.

(16) Peyote. Meaning all parts of the plant presently classified botanically as Lophophora williamsii Lemaire, whether growing or not, the seeds thereof, any extract from any part of such plant, and every compound, manufacture, salts, derivative, mixture, or preparation of such plant, its seeds or extracts.

(17) N-ethyl-3-piperidyl benzilate.

(18) N-methyl-3-piperidyl benzilate.

(19) Psilocybin.

(20) Psilocyn.

(21) Tetrahydrocannabinols. Synthetic equivalents of the substances contained in the plant, or in the resinous extractives of cannabis, sp. and/or synthetic substances, derivatives, and their isomers with similar chemical structure and pharmacological activity such as the following:

Δ1 cis or trans tetrahydrocannabinol, and their optical isomers

Δ6 cis or trans tetrahydrocannabinol, and their optical isomers

Δ3, 4 cis or trans tetrahydrocannabinol, and its optical isomers (since nomenclature of these substances is not internationally standardized, compounds of these structures, regardless of numerical designation of atomic positions covered).

(22) Ethylamine analog of phencyclidine. Some trade or other names: N-ethyl-1-phenylcyclohexylamine, (1-phenylcyclohexyl) ethylamine, N-(1-phenylcyclohexyl) ethylamine cyclohexamine, PCE.

(23) Pyrrolidine analog of phencyclidine. Some trade or other names 1-(1-phenylcyclohexyl)-pyrrolidine; PCPy, PHP.

(24) Thiophene analog of phencyclidine. Some trade or other names: 1-{1-(2-thienyl)-cyclohexyl}-piperidine, 2-thienylanalog of phencyclidine, TPCP, TCP.

(25) 3,4-methylenedioxymethamphetamine (MDMA).

(26) 3,4-methylendioxy-N-ethylamphetamine (also known as N-ethyl-alpha-methyl-3,4 (methylenedioxy) phenethylamine, N-ethyl MDA, MDE, MDEA.

(27) N-hydroxy-3,4-methylenedioxyamphetamine (also known as N-hydroxy-alpha-methyl-3,4 (methylenedioxy) phenethylamine, and N-hydroxy MDA.

(28) 1-{1- (2-thienyl) cyclohexyl} pyrrolidine. Some other names: TCPY.

(29) Alpha-ethyltryptamine. Some trade or other names: etryptamine; Monase; Alpha-ethyl-1H-indole-3-ethanamine; 3- (2-aminobutyl) indole; Alpha-ET or AET.

(30) 2,5-dimethoxy-4-ethylamphetamine. Some trade or other names: DOET.

(31) 4-Bromo-2,5-dimethoxyphenethylamine. Some trade or other names: 2-(4-bromo-2,5-dimethoxyphenyl)-1-aminoethane; alpha-desmethyl DOB; 2C-B, Nexus.

(32) 2,5-dimethoxy-4-(n)-propylthiophenethylamine (2C-T-7), its optical isomers, salts and salts of isomers.

(e) Depressants. Unless specifically excepted or unless listed in another schedule, any material, compound, mixture, or preparation which contains any quantity of the following substances having a depressant effect on the central nervous system, including its salts, isomers, and salts of isomers whenever the existence of such salts, isomers, and salts of isomers is possible within the specific chemical designation:

(1) Mecloqualone.

(2) Methaqualone.

(3) Phencyclidine.

(4) Gamma hydroxybutyric acid, and salt, hydroxybutyric compound, derivative or preparation of gamma hydroxybutyric acid, including any isomers, esters and ethers and salts of isomers, esters and ethers of gamma hydroxybutyric acid, except gamma-butyrolactone, whenever the existence of such isomers, esters and ethers and salts is possible within the specific chemical.

(5) Gamma-butyrolactone, including butyrolactone; butyrolactone gamma; 4-butyrolactone; 2(3H)-furanone dihydro; dihydro-2(3H)-furanone; tetrahydro-2-furanone; 1,2-butanolide; 1,4-butanolide; 4-butanolide; gamma-hydroxybutyric acid lactone; 3-hydroxybutyric acid lactone and 4-hydroxybutanoic acid lactone with Chemical Abstract Service number (96-48-0) when any such substance is intended for human consumption.

(6) 1,4 butanediol, including butanediol; butane-1,4-diol; 1,4-butylene glyco; butylene glycol; 1,4-dihydroxybutane; 1,4-tetramethyleneglycol; tetramethylene glycol; tetramethylene Abstract Service number (110-63-4) when any such substance is intended for human consumption.

(f) Stimulants. Unless specifically excepted or unless listed in another schedule, any material, compound, mixture, or preparation which contains any quantity of the following substances having a stimulant effect on the central nervous system, including its salts, isomers, and salts of isomers:

(1) Fenethylline.

(2) N-ethylamphetamine.

(3) (+ -)cis-4-methylaminorex ((+ -)cis-4,5-dihydro-4-methyl -5-phenyl -2-oxazolamine).

(4) N,N-dimethylamphetamine (also known as N,N-alpha- trimethyl-benzeneethanamine; N,N-alpha- trimethylphenethylamine).

(5) Methcathinone (some other names: 2-(methylamino) - propiophenone; alpha-(methylamino) propiophenone; 2-(methylamino) -1-phenylpropan- 1 -one; alpha-N-methylaminopropiophenone; monomethylpropion; ephedrone, N-methylcathinone, methylcathinone; AL-464; AL-422; AL-463 and UR1432), its salts, optical isomers and salts of optical isomers.

(6) Aminorex. Some other names: aminoxaphen; 2-amino-5-phenyl -2-oxazoline; or 4,5-dihydro-5-phenyl-2-oxazolamine.

(7) Cathinone. Some trade or other names: 2-amino-1-phenyl-1-propanone, alpha-aminopropiophenone, 2-aminopropiophenone, and norephedrone.

(8) N-benzylpiperazine (some other names: BZP; 1-benzylpiperazine), its optical isomers, salts and salts of isomers.

(9) 4-methyl-N-methylcathinone or 4-Methylmethcathinone, also known as Mephedrone.

(10) 3,4-methylenedioxypyrovalerone or Methylenedioxypyrovalerone, also known as MDPV.

(11) 3,4-methylenedioxy-N-methylcathinone (some other names: methylone).

(12) 4-Methoxymethcathinone.

(13) 3-Fluoromethcathinone.

(14) 4-Fluoromethcathinone.

(15) Ethylpropion (Ethcathinone).

(16) 2-(2,5-Dimethoxy-4-ethylphenyl)ethanamine (2C-E).

(17) 2-(2,5-Dimethoxy-4-methylphenyl)ethanamine (2C-D).

(18) 2-(4-Chloro-2,5-dimethoxyphenyl)ethanamine (2C-C).

(19) 2-(4-Iodo-2,5-dimethoxyphenyl)ethanamine (2C-I).

(20) 2-{4-(Ethylthio)-2,5-dimethoxyphenyl}ethanamine (2C-T-2).

(21) 2-{4-(Isopropylthio)-2,5-dimethoxyphenyl}ethanamine (2C-T-4).

(22) 2-(2,5-Dimethoxyphenyl)ethanamine (2C-H).

(23) 2-(2,5-Dimethoxy-4-nitro-phenyl)ethanamine (2C-N).

(24) 2-(2,5-Dimethoxy-4-(n)-propylphenyl)ethanamine (2C-P).

Schedule II.

(a) Schedule II shall consist of the drugs and other substances, by whatever official name, common or usual name, chemical name, or brand name designated, listed in this section.

(b) Substances, vegetable origin or chemical synthesis. Unless specifically excepted or unless listed in another schedule, any of the following substances whether produced directly or indirectly by extraction from substances of vegetable origin, or independently by means of chemical synthesis, or by a combination of extraction and chemical synthesis:

(1) Opium and opiate, and any salt, compound, derivative, or preparation of opium or opiate, excluding apomorphine, dextrorphan, nalbuphine, nalmefene, naloxone, and naltrexone, and their respective salts, but including the following:

1. Raw opium.

2. Opium extracts.

3. Opium fluid.

4. Powdered opium.

5. Granulated opium.

6. Tincture of opium.

7. Codeine.

8. Ethylmorphine.

9. Etorphine hydrochloride.

10. Hydrocodone (also known as dihydrocodeinone).

11. Hydromorphone.

12. Metopon.

13. Morphine.

14. Oxycodone.

15. Oxymorphone.

16. Thebaine.

17. Dihydroetorphine.

18. Oripavine.

(2) Any salt, compound, derivative, or preparation thereof which is chemically equivalent or identical with any of the substances referred to in this section, except that

these substances shall not include the isoquinoline alkaloids of opium.

(3) Opium poppy and poppy straw.

(4) Coca leaves and any salt, compound, derivative, or preparation of coca leaves, and any salt, compound, derivative, or preparation thereof which is chemically equivalent or identical with any of these substances including cocaine and ecgonine, their salts, isomers, and salts of isomers, except that the substances shall not include decocainized coca leaves or extraction of coca leaves, which extractions do not contain cocaine or ecgonine.

(5) Concentrate of poppy straw (the crude extract of poppy straw in either liquid, solid or powder form which contains the phenanthrene alkaloids of the opium poppy).

(6) [*Repealed*]

(b-1) Unless specifically excepted or unless listed in another schedule, any material, compound, mixture, or preparation containing any of the following, or their salts calculated as the free anhydrous base or alkaloid, in limited quantities as set forth below:

(1) Not more than three hundred milligrams of dihydrocodeinone (hydro-codone) per one hundred milliliters or not more than fifteen milligrams per dosage unit, with a fourfold or greater quantity of an isoquinoline alkaloid of opium.

(2) Not more than three hundred milligrams of dihydrocodeinone (hydro-codone) per one hundred milliliters or not more than fifteen milligrams per dosage unit, with one or more active nonnarcotic ingredients in recognized therapeutic amounts.

(c) Opiates. Unless specifically excepted or unless in another schedule any of the following opiates, including its isomers, esters, ethers, salts and salts of isomers, esters and ethers whenever the existence of such isomers, esters, ethers, and salts is possible within the specific chemical designation, dextrorphan and levopropoxyphene excepted:

(1) Alfentanil.

(2) Alphaprodine.

(3) Anileridine.

(4) Bezitramide.

(5) Bulk dextropropoxyphene (non-dosage forms).

(6) Carfentanil.

(7) Dihydrocodeine.

(8) Diphenoxylate.

(9) Fentanyl.

(10) Isomethadone.

(11) Levo-alphacetylmethadol (also known as levo-alpha-acetylmethadol, levometh-adyl acetate or LAAM).

(12) Levomethorphan.

(13) Levorphanol.

(14) Metazocine.

(15) Methadone.

(16) Methadone-intermediate, 4-cyano-2-dimethylamino-4, 4-di-phenyl butane.

(17) Moramide-intermediate, 2-methyl-3-morpholino-1, 1-di- phenylpropane-carboxylic acid.

(18) Pethidine (meperidine).

(19) Pethidine-intermediate-A, 4-cyano-1-methyl-4-phenyl- piperidine.

(20) Pethidine-intermediate-B, ethyl-4-phenylpiperidine-4-carboxylate.

(21) Pethidine-intermediate-C, 1-methyl-4- phenylpiperidine-4-carboxylic acid.

(22) Phenazocine.

(23) Piminodine.

(24) Racemethorphan.

(25) Racemorphan.

(26) Sufentanil.

(27) Remifentanil.

(28) Tapentadol.

(d) Stimulants. Unless specifically excepted or unless listed in another schedule, any material, compound, mixture, or preparation which contains any quantity of the following substances having a stimulant effect on the central nervous system, including its salts, isomers, and salts of isomers:

(1) Amphetamine.

(2) Methamphetamine.

(3) Phenmetrazine.

(4) Methylphenidate.

(5) Lisdexamfetamine.

(e) Depressants. Unless specifically excepted or unless listed in another schedule, any material, compound, mixture, or preparation which contains any quantity of the following substances having a depressant effect on the central nervous system, including its salts, isomers, and salts of isomers whenever the existence of such salts, isomers, and salts of isomers is possible within the specific chemical designation:

(1) Amobarbital.

(2) Glutethimide.

(3) Pentobarbital.

(4) Secobarbital.

(f) Hallucinogenic substances.

Nabilone: Another name for nabilone: (+,-)-trans- 3-(1,1-dimethylheptyl)-6, 6a, 7, 8, 10, 10a-hexahydro-1-hydroxy-6, 6-dimethyl-9H-dibenzo {b,d} pyran-9-one.

(g) Immediate precursors. Unless specifically excepted or unless listed in another schedule, any material, compound, mixture or preparation which contains any quantity of the following substances:

(1) Immediate precursor to amphetamine and methamphetamine:

(i) Phenylacetone Some trade or other names: phenyl-2-propanone; P2P; benzyl methyl ketone; methyl benzyl ketone;

(2) Immediate precursors to phencyclidine (PCP):

(i) 1-phenylcyclohexylamine;

(ii) 1-piperidinocyclohexanecarbonitrile (PCC).

(3) Immediate precursor to fentanyl:

(i) 4-anilino-N-phenethyl-4-piperidine (ANPP).

(h) Anabolic steroids. Unless specifically excepted or unless listed in another schedule, "anabolic steroid" shall mean any drug or hormonal substance, chemically and pharmacologically related to testosterone (other than estrogens, progestins, corticosteroids and dehydroepiandros- terone) and includes:

(1) 3{beta}, 17-dihydroxy-5a-androstane.

(2) 3{alpha}, 17{beta}-dihydroxy-5a-androstane.

(3) 5{alpha}-androstan-3,17-dione.

(4) 1-androstenediol (3{beta},17{beta}-dihydroxy-5{alpha}-androst-1-ene).

(5) 1-androstenediol (3{alpha},17{beta}-dihydroxy-5{alpha}-androst-1-ene).

(6) 4-androstenediol (3{beta}, 17{beta}-dihydroxy-androst-4-ene).

(7) 5-androstenediol (3{beta}, 17{beta}-dihydroxy-androst-5-ene).

(8) 1-androstenedione ({5{alpha]}-androst-1-en-3,17-dione).

(9) 4-androstenedione (androst-4-en-3,17-dione).

(10) 5-androstenedione (androst-5-en-3,17-dione).

(11) Bolasterone (7{alpha},17{alpha}-dimethyl-17{beta}-hydroxyandrost-4-en-3-one).

(12) Boldenone (17{beta}-hydroxyandrost-1, 4,-diene-3-one).

(13) Boldione (androsta-1,4-diene-3,17-dione).

(14) Calusterone (7{beta}, 17{alpha}-dimethyl-17{beta}-hydroxyandrost-4-en-3-one).

(15) Clostebol (4-chloro-17{beta}-hydroxyandrost-4-en-3-one).

(16) Dehydrochloromethyltestosterone (4-chloro-17{beta}-hydroxy-17 {alpha}-methyl-androst-1, 4-dien-3-one).

(17) {Delta} 1-dihydrotestosterone (a.k.a. '1-testosterone') (17 {beta}-hydroxy-5{alpha}-androst-1-en-3-one).

(18) 4-dihydrotestosterone (17{beta}-hydroxy-androstan-3-one).

(19) Drostanolone (17{beta}-hydroxy-2{alpha}-methyl-5{alpha}-androstan-3-one).

(20) Ethylestrenol (17{alpha}-ethyl-17{beta}-hydroxyestr-4-ene).

(21)   Fluoxymesterone   (9-fluoro-17{alpha}-methyl-11{beta},   17{beta}-dihydroxyandrost-4-en-3-one).

(22)   Formebolone   (2-formyl-17{alpha}-methyl-11{alpha},   17{beta}-dihydroxyandrost-1, 4-dien-3-one).

(23) Furazabol (17{alpha}-methyl-17{beta}-hydroxyandrostano {2, 3-c}-furazan).

(24) 13{beta}-ethyl-17{beta}-hyroxygon-4-en-3-one.

(25) 4-hydroxytestosterone (4, 17{beta}-dihydroxy-androst-4-en-3-one).

(26) 4-hydroxy-19-nortestosterone (4,17{beta}-dihydroxy-estr-4-en-3-one).

(27) desoxymethyltestosterone (17{alpha}-methyl-5{alpha}-androst-2-en-17{beta}-ol) (a.k.a., madol).

(28) Mestanolone (17{alpha}-methyl-17{beta}-hydroxy-5-androstan-3-one).

(29) Mesterolone (1{alpha} methyl-17{beta}-hydroxy- {5}alpha}}-androstan-3-one).

(30) Methandienone (17{alpha}-methyl-17{beta}-hydroxyandrost-1, 4-dien-3-one).

(31) Methandriol (17{alpha}-methyl-3{beta}, 17{beta}-dihydroxyandrost-5-ene).

(32) Methenolone (1-methyl-17{beta}-hydroxy-5{alpha}-androst-1-en-3-one).

(33) 17{alpha}-methyl-3{beta},17{beta}-dihydroxy-5a-androstane.

(34) 17{alpha}-methyl-3{alpha}, 17{beta}-dihydroxy-5a-androstane.

(35) 17{alpha}-methyl-3{beta}, 17{beta}-dihydroxyandrost-4-ene.

(36)   17{alpha}-methyl-4-hydroxynandrolone   (17{alpha}-methyl-4-hydroxy-17{beta}-hydroxyestr-4-en-3-one).

(37) Methyldienolone (17{alpha}-methyl-17{beta}-hydroxyestra-4,9(10)-dien-3-one).

(38) Methyltrienolone (17{alpha}-methyl-17{beta}-hydroxyestra-4, 9-11-trien-3-one).

(39) Methyltestosterone (17{alpha{-methyl-17{beta}-hydroxyandrost- 4-en-3-one).

(40) Mibolerone (7{alpha},17{alpha}-dimethyl-17{beta}-hydroxyestr- 4-en-3-one).

(41) 17{alpha}-methyl-{Delta} 1-dihydrotestosterone (17b{beta}-hydroxy-17{alpha}-methyl-5{alpha}-androst-1-en-3-one) (a.k.a. '17-{alpha}-methyl-1-testosterone').

(42) Nandrolone(17{beta}-hydroxyestr-4-en-3-one).

(43) 19-nor-4-androstenediol (3{beta},17{beta}-dihydroxyestr-4-ene).

(44) 19-nor-4-androstenediol (3{alpha},17{beta:-dihydroxyestr-4-ene).

(45) 19-nor-5-androstenediol (3{beta},17{beta}-dihydroxyestr-5-ene).

(46) 19-nor-5-androstenediol (3{alpha},17{beta}-dihydroxyestr-5-ene).

(47) 19-nor-4,9(10)-androstadienedione (estra-4,9(10)-diene-3,17-dione).

(48) 19-nor-4-androstenedione (estr-4-en-3,17-dione).

(49) 19-nor-5-androstenedione (estr-5-en-3,17-dione).

(50) Norbolethone (13{beta}, 17{alpha}-diethyl-17{beta}-hydroxygon-4-en-3-one).

(51) Norclostebol (4-chloro-17{beta}-hydroxyestr-4-en-3-one).

(52) Norethandrolone (17{alpha}-ethyl-17{beta}-hydroxyestr-4-en-3-one).

(53) Normethandrolone (17{alpha}-methyl-17{beta}-hydroxyestr-4-en-3-one).

(54) Oxandrolone (17{alpha}-methyl-17{beta}-hydroxy-2-oxa- {5}alpha}}-androstan-3-one).

(55) Oxymesterone (17{alpha}-methyl-4, 17{beta}-dihydroxy androst-4-en-3-one).

(56) Oxymetholone (17{alpha{{-methyl-2-hydroxymethylene-17{beta}-hydroxy-{5}alpha}}- androstan-3-one).

(57) Stanozolol (17{alpha}-methyl-17{beta}-hydroxy-{5{alpha}}-androst-2-eno{3, 2-c}-pyrazole).

(58) Stenbolone (17{beta}-hydroxy-2-methyl-{5{alpha}}-androst-1-en-3-one).

(59) Testolactone (13-hydroxy-3-oxo-13, 17-secoandrosta-1, 4-dien-17-oic acid lactone).

(60) Testosterone (17{beta}-hydroxyandrost-4-en-3-one).

(61) Tetrahydrogestrinone (13{beta}, 17{alpha}-diethyl-17{beta}-hydroxygon-4, 9, 11-trien-3-one).

(62) Trenbolone (17{beta}-hydroxyestr-4, 9, 11-trien-3-one).

(63) Any salt, ester or ether of a drug or substance described or listed in this subdivision.

(i) Subdivision (h) of this section shall not include any substance containing anabolic steroids expressly intended for administration through implants to cattle or other nonhuman species and that are approved by the federal food and drug administration solely for such use. Any individual who knowingly and willfully administers to himself or another person, prescribes, dispenses or distributes such substances for other than implantation to cattle or nonhuman species shall be subject to the same penalties as a practitioner who violates the provisions of this section or any other penalties prescribed by law.

(j) [*Repealed*]

Schedule III.

(a) Schedule III shall consist of the drugs and other substances, by whatever official name, common or usual name, chemical name, or brand name designated, listed in this section.

(b) Stimulants. Unless specifically excepted or unless listed in another schedule, any material, compound, mixture, or preparation which contains any quantity of the following substances having a stimulant effect on the central nervous system, including its salts, isomers (whether optical, position, or geometric), and salts of such isomers whenever the existence of such salts, isomers, and salts of isomers is possible within the specific chemical designation:

(1) Those compounds, mixtures, or preparations in dosage unit form containing any stimulant substances listed in schedule II which compounds, mixtures, or preparations were listed on August twenty-five, nineteen hundred seventy-one, as excepted compounds under title twenty-one, section 308.32 of the code of federal regulations and any other drug of the quantitive composition shown in that list for those drugs or which is the same except that it contains a lesser quantity of controlled substances.

(2) Benzphetamine.

(3) Chlorphentermine.

(4) Clortermine.

(5) [*Repealed*]

(6) Phendimetrazine.

(c) Unless specifically excepted or unless listed in another schedule, any material, compound, mixture, or preparation which contains any quantity of the following substances having a depressant effect on the central nervous system, including its salts, isomers, and salts of isomers:

(1) Any compound, mixture or preparation containing:

    (i) Amobarbital;

    (ii) Secobarbital;

    (iii) Pentobarbital;

or any salt thereof and one or more other active medicinal ingredients which are not listed in any schedule.

(2) Any suppository dosage form containing:

    (i) Amobarbital;

    (ii) Secobarbital;

    (iii) Pentobarbital;

or any salt of any of these drugs and approved by the federal food and drug administration for marketing only as a suppository.

(3) Any substance which contains any quantity of a derivative of barbituric acid or any salt thereof.

(4) Chlorhexadol.

(5) Lysergic acid.

(6) Lysergic acid amide.

(7) Methyprylon.

(8) Sulfondiethylmethane.

(9) Sulfonethylmethane.

(10) Sulfonmethane.

(11) Tiletamine and zolazepam or any salt thereof. Some trade or other names for a tiletamine-zolazepam combination product: Telazol. Some trade or other names for tiletamine: 2-(ethylamino) -2-(2-thienyl) -cyclohexanone. Some trade or other names for zolazepam: 4-(2-fluorophenyl) -6,8-dihydro -1, 3, 8i-trimethylpyrazolo-[3,4-e] [1,4]-diazepin-7(1H)-one, flupyrazapon.

(12) Gamma hydroxybutyric acid, and salt, hydroxybutyric compound, derivative or4 preparation of gamma hydroxybutyric acid, including any isomers, esters and ethers and salts of isomers, esters and ethers of gamma hydroxybutyric acid, contained in a drug product for which an application has been approved under section 505 of the federal food, drug and cosmetic act.

(13) Ketamine, its salts, isomers and salts of isomers (some other names for ketamine: (±)-2-(2-chlorophenyl)-2-(methylamino)- cyclohexanone).

(14) Embutramide.

(d) Nalorphine.

(e) Narcotic drugs. Unless specifically excepted or unless listed in another schedule, any material, compound, mixture, or preparation containing any of the following narcotic drugs, or their salts calculated as the free anhydrous base or alkaloid, in limited quantities as set forth below:

(1) Not more than 1.8 grams of codeine per one hundred milliliters or not more than ninety milligrams per dosage unit, with an equal or greater quantity of an isoquinoline alkaloid of opium.

(2) Not more than 1.8 grams of codeine per one hundred milliliters or not more than ninety milligrams per dosage unit, with one or more active, nonnarcotic ingredients in recognized therapeutic amounts.

(3) Not more than 1.8 grams of dihydrocodeine per one hundred milli liters or not more than ninety milligrams per dosage unit, with one or more active nonnarcotic ingredients in recognized therapeutic amounts.

(4) Not more than three hundred milligrams of ethylmorphine per one hundred milliliters or not more than fifteen milligrams per dosage unit, with one or more active, nonnarcotic ingredients in recognized therapeutic amounts.

(5) Not more than five hundred milligrams of opium per one hundred milliliters or per one hundred grams or not more than twenty-five milligrams per dosage unit, with one or more active, nonnarcotic ingredients in recognized therapeutic amounts.

(6) Not more than fifty milligrams of morphine per one hundred milliliters or per one hundred grams, with one or more active, nonnarcotic ingredients in recognized therapeutic amounts.

(7) Buprenorphine in any quantities.

(8), (9) [Redesignated]

(f) Dronabinol (synthetic) in sesame oil and encapsulated in a soft gelatin capsule in a U.S. Food and Drug Administration approved product. Some other names for dronabinol include: (6aR-trans)-6a, 7, 8, 10a-tetrahydro-6, 6, 9-trimethyl-3-pentyl-6H-dibenzo{b,d} pyran-1-o1, or (-)-delta-9-(trans) - tetrahydrocannabinol.

(g) Chorionic gonadotropin. Unless specifically excepted or unless listed in another schedule any material, compound, mixture, or preparation which contains any amount of chorionic gonadotropin.

Schedule IV.

(a) Schedule IV shall consist of the drugs and other substances, by whatever official name, common or usual name, chemical name, or brand name designated, listed in this section.

(b) Narcotic drugs. Unless specifically excepted or unless listed in another schedule, any material, compound, mixture, or preparation containing any of the following narcotic drugs, or their salts calculated as the free anhydrous base or alkaloid, in limited quantities as set forth below:

(1) Not more than one milligram of difenoxin and not less than twenty-five micrograms of atropine sulfate per dosage unit.

(2) Dextropropoxyphene (alpha-(+)-4-dimethylamino-1, 2-diphenyl-3-methyl-2-propionoxybutane).

(c) Depressants. Unless specifically excepted or unless listed in another schedule, any material, compound, mixture, or preparation which contains any quantity of the following substances, including its salts, isomers, and salts of isomers whenever the existence of such salts, isomers, and salts of isomers is possible within the specific chemical designation:

(1) Alprazolam.

(2) Barbital.

(3) Bromazepam.

(4) Camazepam.

(5) Chloral betaine.

(6) Chloral hydrate.

(7) Chlordiazepoxide.

(8) Clobazam.

(9) Clonazepam.

(10) Clorazepate.

(11) Clotiazepam.

(12) Cloxazolam.

(13) Delorazepam.

(14) Diazepam.

(15) Estazolam.

(16) Ethchlorvynol.

(17) Ethinamate.

(18) Ethyl Loflazepate.

(19) Fludiazepam.

(20) Flunitrazepam.

(21) Flurazepam.

(22) Halazepam.

(23) Haloxazolam.

(24) Ketazolam.

(25) Loprazolam.

(26) Lorazepam.

(27) Lormetazepam.

(28) Mebutamate.

(29) Medazepam.

(30) Meprobamate.

(31) Methohexital.

(32) Methylphenobarbital (mephobarbital).

(33) Nimetazepam.

(34) Nitrazepam.

(35) Nordiazepam.

(36) Oxazepam.

(37) Oxazolam.

(38) Paraldehyde.

(39) Petrichoral.

(40) Phenobarbital.

(41) Pinazepam.

(42) Prazepam.

(43) Temazepam.

(44) Tetrazepam.

(45) Triazolam.

(46) Midazolam.

(47) Quazepam.

(48) Zolpidem.

(49) Dichloralphenazone.

(50) Zaleplon.

(51) Zopiclone (eszopiclone).

(52) Fospropofol.

(53) Carisoprodol.

(d) [*Repealed upon the removal of fenfluramine and its salts and isomers from Schedule IV of the federal Controlled Substances Act.*] Fenfluramine. Any material, compound, mixture, or preparation which contains any quantity of the following substances, including its salts, isomers (whether optical, position, or geometric), and salts of such isomers, whenever the existence of such salts, isomers and salts of isomers is possible:

(1) Fenfluramine.

(e) Stimulants. Unless specifically excepted or unless listed in another schedule, any material, compound, mixture, or preparation which contains any quantity of the following substances having a stimulant effect on the central nervous system, including its salts, isomers, and salts of such isomers:

(1) Cathine ((+) - norpseudoephedrine).

(2) Diethylpropion.

(3) Fencamfamin.

(4) Fenproporex.

(5) Mazindol.

(6) Mefenorex.

(7) Pemoline (including organometallic complexes and chelates thereof).

(8) Phentermine.

(9) Pipradrol.

(10) SPA ((-))-1-dimethylamino-1, 2-diphenylethane).

(11) Modafinil.

(12) Sibutramine.

(f) Other substances. Unless specifically excepted or unless listed in another schedule, any material, compound, mixture or preparation which contains any quantity of the following substances, including its salts:

(1) Pentazocine.

(2) Butorphanol (including its optical isomers).

(3) Tramadol in any quantities.

Schedule V.

(a) Schedule V shall consist of the drugs and other substances, by whatever official name, common or usual name, chemical name, or brand name designated, listed in this section.

(b) Narcotic drugs containing nonnarcotic active medicinal ingredients. Any compound, mixture, or preparation containing any of the following narcotic drugs, or their salts calculated as the free anhydrous base or alkaloid, in limited quantities as set forth below, whichshall include one or more nonnarcotic active medicinal ingredients insufficient proportion to confer upon the compound, mixture, or preparation valuable medicinal qualities other than those possessed by narcotic drugs alone:

(1) Not more than two hundred milligrams of codeine per one hundred milliliters or per one hundred grams.

(2) Not more than one hundred milligrams of dihydrocodeine per one hundred milliliters or per one hundred grams.

(3) Not more than one hundred milligrams of ethylmorphine per one hundred milliliters or per one hundred grams.

(4) Not more than 2.5 milligrams of diphenoxylate and not less than twenty-five micrograms of atropine sulfate per dosage unit.

(5) Not more than one hundred milligrams of opium per one hundred milliliters or per one hundred grams.

(6) Not more than 0.5 milligram of difenoxin and not less than twenty-five micrograms of atropine sulfate per dosage unit.

(c) Stimulants. Unless specifically exempted or excluded or unless listed in another schedule, any material, compound, mixture, or preparation which contains any quantity of the following substances having a stimulant effect on the central nervous system, including its salts, isomers and salts of isomers:

(1) Pyrovalerone.

(d) Depressants. Unless specifically exempted or excluded or unless listed in another schedule, any material, compound, mixture, or preparation which contains any quantity of the following substances having a depressant effect on the central nervous system, including its salts, isomers, and salts of isomers:

(1) Ezogabine {N-{2-amino-4-(4-fluorobenzylamino)-phenyl}-carbamic acid ethyl ester}.

(2) Lacosamide {(R)-2-acetoamido-N-benzyl-3-methoxy-propionamide}.

(3) Pregabalin{(S)-3-(aminomethyl)-5-methylhexanoic acid}.

HISTORY: Add, L 1985, ch 664, § 1, eff Nov 1, 1985; amd, L 1986, ch 826, § 1, eff Sept 1, 1986, L 1987, ch 44, §§ 1, 2, eff April 21, 1987, L 1989, ch 418, § 1, L 1990, ch 640, §§ 1, 2, L 1992, ch 115, § 1, eff June 1, 1992, L 1993, ch 473, § 1, eff July 26, 1993, L 1995, ch 452, §§ 1, 2, L 1996, ch 443, § 1, eff Aug 2, 1996, L 1996, ch 589, §§ 1–10, eff Feb 4, 1997, L 1997, ch 635, § 2, eff Jan 22, 1998, L 2000, ch 1, §§ 29, 30, eff Feb 1, 2001, L 2001, ch 565, § 1, eff Jan 1, 2002, L 2001, ch 575, §§ 1–3, eff Dec 19, 2001, L 2003, ch 264, §§ 56, 57, eff Nov 1, 2003, L 2003, ch 591, §§ 1, 2, eff Sept 22, 2003, L 2006, ch 457, §§ 1–15, eff Aug 16, 2006, L 2010, ch 178, §§ 13–18, eff Oct 13, 2010, L 2011, ch 130, § 1, eff Aug 14, 2011, L 2012, ch 447, §§ 2, 10, 14 (Part C), eff Feb 23, 2013, L 2012, ch 447, §§ 1, 4–9, 11–13, 16 (Part C), eff Nov 25, 2012, L 2012, ch 447, § 15 (Part C), eff Aug 27, 2012; L 2013, ch 341, § 1, eff Dec 11, 2013.

§ 3307. Exception from schedules

1. The commissioner may, by regulation, except any compound, mixture, or preparation containing any depressant substance in paragraph (a) of schedule III or in schedule IV from the application of all or any part of this article if (1) the compound, mixture, or preparation contains one or more active medicinal ingredients not having a depressant effect on the central nervous system, and (2) such ingredients are included therein in such combinations, quantity, proportion, or concentration as to vitiate the potential for abuse of the substances which do have a depressant effect on the central nervous system.

2. The commissioner may, by regulation, reclassify as a schedule III substance, any compound, mixture or preparation containing any stimulant substance listed in paragraph (c) of schedule II, if

(a) the compound, mixture or preparation contains one or more active medicinal ingredients not having a stimulant effect on the central nervous system; and

(b) such ingredients are included therein in such combinations, quantity, proportion or concentration as to vitiate the potential for abuse of the substances which do have a stimulant effect on the central nervous system.

3. The commissioner may, by regulation, except any compound, mixture or preparation containing a narcotic antagonist substance from the application of all or any part of this article if (1) such compound, mixture or preparation has no potential for abuse, and (2) such compound, mixture or preparation has been excepted or exempted from control under the Federal Controlled Substances Act.

4. The commissioner may by regulation exempt or reclassify any compound, mixture or preparation containing any substance listed in subdivision (h) or (j) of Schedule II of section three thousand three hundred six of this article as a Schedule III, IV or V substance if (a) the compound, mixture or preparation contains one or more active medicinal ingredients not found in subdivision (h) or (j) of Schedule II of section three thousand three hundred six of this article; and (b) such ingredients are included therein in such combinations, quantity, proportion or concentration as to substantially reduce the potential for abuse.

5. The commissioner shall establish minimum standards for the storage, reporting, ordering and record keeping of controlled substances specified in subdivision (b-1) of schedule II of section thirty-three hundred six of this article by manufacturers and distributors as if such substances were set forth in schedule III of section thirty-three hundred six of this article.

HISTORY: Add, L 1972, ch 878, § 2, eff April 1, 1973, with substance derived from former § 3374; amd, L 1972, ch 879, § 1, eff April 1, 1973, L 1973, ch 163, §§ 6, 7, eff April 1, 1973, L 1990, ch 640, § 3, eff July 18, 1990, deemed eff Jan 12, 1990, L 2012, ch 447, § 3 (Part C), eff Feb 23, 2013.

§ 3308. Powers and duties of the commissioner

1. The commissioner, and any representative authorized by him, shall have the power to administer oaths, compel the attendance of witnesses and the production of books, papers and records and to take proof and testimony concerning all matters within the jurisdiction of the department.

2. The commissioner is hereby authorized and empowered to make any rules, regulations and determinations which in his judgment may be necessary or proper to supplement the provisions of this article to effectuate the purposes and intent thereof or to clarify its provisions so as to provide

the procedure or details to secure effective and proper enforcement of its provisions.

3. No rule or regulation hereunder shall become effective unless, at least twenty-one days prior to the proposed effective date, persons who have conveyed to the department in writing a request to be notified of proposed changes and additions to the department's rules and regulations under this article have been provided with the text of such proposed rules and regulations and have been given an opportunity to comment in writing thereon.

4. The rules, regulations and determinations, when made and promulgated by the commissioner, shall be the rules, regulations and determinations of the department and, until modified or rescinded, shall have the force and effect of law. It shall be the duty of the department, to enforce all of the provisions of this article and all of the rules, regulations and determinations made thereunder.

5. Notwithstanding any inconsistent provision of this article, the commissioner in consultation with the commissioner of education is hereby authorized to promulgate regulations regarding the prescribing, dispensing, use and transmission of electronic prescriptions, which may be prescribed and dispensed in lieu of an official New York state prescription.

6. The commissioner in consultation with the commissioner of education is hereby authorized to promulgate regulations regarding the dispensing of out-of-state prescriptions.

> **HISTORY:** Add, L 1972, ch 878, § 2, eff April 1, 1973. Sub 5, add, L 2004, ch 58, § 5 (Part A), eff Oct 20, 2004. Sub 6, add, L 2004, ch 58, § 5 (Part A), eff Oct 20, 2004.

§ 3309. Opioid overdose prevention

1. The commissioner is authorized to establish standards for approval of any opioid overdose prevention program, and opioid antagonist prescribing, dispensing, distribution, possession and administration pursuant to this section which may include, but not be limited to, standards for program directors, appropriate clinical oversight, training, record keeping and reporting.

2. Notwithstanding any inconsistent provisions of section sixty-five hundred twelve of the education law or any other law, the purchase, acquisition, possession or use of an opioid antagonist pursuant to this section shall not constitute the unlawful practice of a profession or other violation under title eight of the education law or this article.

3.* Any distribution of opioid antagonists through this program shall include an informational card or sheet. The informational card or sheet shall include, at a minimum, information on:

    (a) how to recognize symptoms of an opioid overdose;

    (b) steps to take prior to and after an opioid antagonist is administered, including calling first responders;

    (c) the number for the toll free office of alcoholism and substance abuse services HOPE line;

    (d) how to access the office of alcoholism and substance abuse services' website; and

    (e) any other information deemed relevant by the commissioner.

The educational card shall be provided in languages other than English as deemed appropriate by the commissioner. The department shall make such informational cards available to the opioid overdose prevention programs.

---

* There are two subdivisions three.

3.* (a) As used in this section:

(i) "Opioid antagonist" means a drug approved by the Food and Drug Administration that, when administered, negates or neutralizes in whole or in part the pharmacological effects of an opioid in the body. "Opioid antagonist" shall be limited to naloxone and other medications approved by the department for such purpose.

(ii) "Health care professional" means a person licensed, registered or authorized pursuant to title eight of the education law to prescribe prescription drugs.

(iii) "Pharmacist" means a person licensed or authorized to practice pharmacy pursuant to article one hundred thirty-seven of the education law.

(iv) "Opioid antagonist recipient" or "recipient" means a person at risk of experiencing an opioid-related overdose, or a family member, friend or other person in a position to assist a person experiencing or at risk of experiencing an opioid-related overdose, or an organization registered as an opioid overdose prevention program pursuant to this section.

(b) (i) A health care professional may prescribe by a patient-specific or non-patient-specific prescription, dispense or distribute, directly or indirectly, an opioid antagonist to an opioid antagonist recipient.

(ii) A pharmacist may dispense an opioid antagonist, through a patient-specific or non-patient-specific prescription pursuant to this paragraph, to an opioid antagonist recipient.

(iii) An opioid antagonist recipient may possess an opioid antagonist obtained pursuant to this paragraph, may distribute such opioid antagonist to a recipient, and may administer such opioid antagonist to a person the recipient reasonably believes is experiencing an opioid overdose.

(iv) The provisions of this paragraph shall not be deemed to require a prescription for any opioid antagonist that does not otherwise require a prescription; nor shall it be deemed to limit the authority of a health care professional to prescribe, dispense or distribute, or of a pharmacist to dispense, an opioid antagonist under any other provision of law.

4. Use of an opioid antagonist pursuant to this section shall be considered first aid or emergency treatment for the purpose of any statute relating to liability.

A recipient or opioid overdose prevention program under this section, acting reasonably and in good faith in compliance with this section, shall not be subject to criminal, civil or administrative liability solely by reason of such action.

5. The commissioner shall publish findings on statewide opioid overdose data that reviews overdose death rates and other information to ascertain changes in the cause and rates of fatal opioid overdoses. The report may be part of existing state mortality reports issued by the department, and shall be submitted annually to the governor, the temporary president of the senate, the speaker of the assembly, and the chairs of the senate and assembly health committees. The report shall include, at a minimum, the following information:

(a) information on opioid overdose deaths, including age, gender, ethnicity, and geographic location;

---

* There are two subdivisions three.

(b) data on emergency room utilization for the treatment of opioid overdose;

(c) data on utilization of pre-hospital services;

(d) data on utilization of opioid antagonists; and

(e) any other information necessary to ascertain the success of the program and ways to further reduce overdoses.

HISTORY: Add, L 2005, ch 413, § 1, eff April 1, 2006; amd, L 2014, ch 34, § 1, eff June 23, 2014, L 2014, ch 42, § 1, eff June 24, 2014.

§ 3309-a. Prescription pain medication awareness program

1. There is hereby established within the department a prescription pain medication awareness program to educate the public and health care practitioners about the risks associated with prescribing and taking controlled substance pain medications.

2. Within the amounts appropriated, the commissioner, in consultation with the commissioner of the office of alcoholism and substance abuse services, shall:

(a) Develop and conduct a public health education media campaign designed to alert youth, parents and the general population about the risks associated with prescription pain medications and the need to properly dispose of any unused medication. In developing this campaign, the commissioner shall consult with and use information provided by the work group established pursuant to subdivision (b) of this section and other relevant professional organizations. The campaign shall include an internet website providing information for parents, children and health care professionals on the risks associated with taking opioids and resources available to those needing assistance with prescription pain medication addiction. Such website shall also provide information regarding where individuals may properly dispose of controlled substances in their community and include active links to further information and resources. The campaign shall begin no later than September first, two thousand twelve.

(b) Establish a work group, no later than June first, two thousand twelve, which shall be composed of experts in the fields of palliative and chronic care pain management and addiction medicine. Members of the work group shall receive no compensation for their services, but shall be allowed actual and necessary expenses in the performance of their duties pursuant to this section. The work group shall:

(i) Report to the commissioner regarding the development of recommendations and model courses for continuing medical education, refresher courses and other training materials for licensed health care professionals on appropriate use of prescription pain medication. Such recommendations, model courses and other training materials shall be submitted to the commissioner, who shall make such information available for the use in medical education, residency programs, fellowship programs, and for use in continuing medication education programs no later than January first, two thousand thirteen. Such recommendations also shall include recommendations on: (A) educational and continuing medical education requirements for practitioners appropriate to address prescription pain medication awareness among health care professionals; (B) continuing education requirements for pharmacists related to prescription pain medication awareness; and (C) continuing education in palliative care as it relates to pain management, for which purpose the work group shall consult the New York state palliative care education and training council;

(ii) No later than January first, two thousand thirteen, provide outreach and assistance to health care professional organizations to encourage and facilitate continuing medical education training programs for their members regarding appropriate prescribing practices for the best patient care and the risks associated with overprescribing and underprescribing pain medication;

(iii) Provide information to the commissioner for use in the development and continued update of the public awareness campaign, including information, resources, and active web links that should be included on the website; and

(iv) Consider other issues deemed relevant by the commissioner, including how to protect and promote the access of patients with a legitimate need for controlled substances, particularly medications needed for pain management by oncology patients, and whether and how to encourage or require the use or substitution of opioid drugs that employ tamper-resistance technology as a mechanism for reducing abuse and diversion of opioid drugs.

3. On or before September first, two thousand twelve, the commissioner, in consultation with the commissioner of the office of alcoholism and substance abuse services, the commissioner of education, and the executive secretary of the state board of pharmacy, shall add to the workgroup such additional members as appropriate so that the workgroup may provide guidance in furtherance of the implementation of the I-STOP act. For such purposes, the workgroup shall include but not be limited to consumer advisory organizations, health care practitioners and providers, oncologists, addiction treatment providers, practitioners with experience in pain management, pharmacists and pharmacies, and representatives of law enforcement agencies.

4. The commissioner shall report to the governor, the temporary president of the senate and the speaker of the assembly no later than March first, two thousand thirteen, and annually thereafter, on the work group's findings. The report shall include information on opioid overdose deaths, emergency room utilization for the treatment of opioid overdose, the utilization of pre-hospital addiction services and recommendations to reduce opioid addiction and the consequences thereof. The report shall also include a recommendation as to whether subdivision two of section thirty-three hundred forty-three-a of this article should be amended to require practitioners prescribing or dispensing certain identified schedule V controlled substances to comply with the consultation requirements of such subdivision.

HISTORY: Add, L 2012, ch 56, § 52 (Part D), eff March 30, 2012, deemed eff on and after April 1, 2012, L 2012, ch 447, §§ 1, 2 (Part D), eff Aug 27, 2012.

HISTORY: Add, L 1972, ch 878, § 2, eff April 1, 1973. Former Title II, add, L 1953, ch 879, § 1; repealed, L 1972, ch 878, § 1, eff April 1, 1973.

§ 3310. Licenses for manufacture or distribution of controlled substances

1. No person shall manufacture or distribute a controlled substance in this state without first having obtained a license to do so from the department.

2. A license issued under this section shall be valid for two years from the date of issue, except that in order to facilitate the renewals of such licenses, the commissioner may upon the initial application for a license, issue some licenses which may remain valid for a period of time greater than two years but not exceeding an additional eleven months.

3. The fee for a license under this section shall be one thousand two hundred dollars; provided however, if the license is issued for a period greater than two years the fee shall be increased, pro rata, for each additional month of validity.

4. Licenses issued under this section shall be effective only for and shall specify:

    (a) the name and address of the licensee;

    (b) the nature of the controlled substances, either by name or schedule, or both, which may be manufactured or distributed;

    (c) whether manufacture or distribution or both such activities are permitted by the license.

5. Upon application of a licensee, a license may be amended to allow the licensee to relocate within the state or to add a manufacturing or distributing activity or to add further substances or schedules to the manufacturing or distribution activity permitted thereunder. The fee for such amendment shall be two hundred fifty dollars.

HISTORY: Add, L 1972, ch 878, § 2, eff April 1, 1973, with substance derived from former §§ 3310, 3375. Former § 3310, add, L 1953, ch 879, § 1, with substance derived from former § 425-a; amd, L 1958, ch 925, § 1; repealed, L 1972, ch 878, § 1, eff April 1, 1973. Sub 3, amd, L 1981, ch 103, § 148, L 1989, ch 61, § 257, eff April 19, 1989. Sub 5, amd, L 1981, ch 103, § 148, L 1983, ch 269, § 1, L 1989, ch 61, § 257, eff April 19, 1989.

§ 3311. Authority to issue initial licenses, amended licenses, and to renew licenses

1. Subject to the provisions of this article the commissioner is authorized to issue licenses authorizing the manufacture or distribution of controlled substances.

2. An application for a license, amendment of a license, or renewal of a license which, if granted, would authorize the manufacture or distribution of a controlled substance which the applicant is not then authorized to manufacture or distribute shall, with respect to any such additional authorization, be treated as an application for an initial license.

3. An application for a license which, if granted, would authorize a licensee to continue to manufacture or distribute a controlled substance shall, with respect to such continued manufacture or distribution only, be treated as an application for renewal of a license.

4. A late-filed application for the renewal of a license may, in the discretion of the commissioner, be treated as an application for an initial license.

HISTORY: Add, L 1972, ch 878, § 2, eff April 1, 1973. Former § 3311, add, L 1953, ch 879, § 1, with substance derived from former § 423; amd, L 1958, ch 925, § 1, L 1961, ch 884, § 1, L 1962, ch 597, § 2; repealed, L 1972, ch 878, § 1, eff April 1, 1973. See now §§ 3305(4), 3325, 3341. Sub 2, amd, L 1973, ch 163, § 8, eff April 1, 1973.

§ 3312. Application for initial license

1. An applicant for an initial license to manufacture or distribute controlled substances shall furnish to the department such information as it shall require and evidence that the applicant:

(a) and its managing officers are of good moral character;

(b) possesses sufficient land, buildings and equipment to properly carry on the activity described in the application;

(c) is able to maintain effective control against diversion of the controlled substances for which the license is sought;

(d) is able to comply with all applicable state and federal laws and regulations relating to the manufacture or distribution of the controlled substances for which the license is sought.

2. The application shall include the name, residence address and title of each of the officers and directors and the name and residence address of any person having a ten percentum or greater proprietary, beneficial, equitable or credit interest in the applicant. Each such person, if an individual, or lawful representative if a legal entity, shall submit an affidavit with the application setting forth:

(a) any position of management or ownership during the preceding ten years of a ten percentum or greater interest in any other business, located in or outside this state, manufacturing or distributing drugs; and

(b) whether such person or any such business has been convicted, fined, censured or had a license suspended or revoked in any administrative or judicial proceeding relating to or arising out of the manufacture or distribution of drugs; and

(c) such other information as the commisisoner [commissioner]* may require.

3. The applicant shall be under a continuing duty to report to the department any change in facts or circumstances reflected in the application on any newly discovered or occurring fact or circumstance which is required to be included in the application.

HISTORY: Add, L 1972, ch 878, § 2, eff April 1, 1973, with substance derived from former §§ 3312, 3377. Former § 3312, add, L 1953, ch 879, § 1, with substance derived from former

---

* The bracketed word has been inserted by the Publisher.

§ 421-a; amd, L 1958, ch 925, § 1; repealed, L 1972, ch 878, § 1, eff April 1, 1973. Sub 2, par (b), amd, L 1973, ch 163, § 9, eff April 1, 1973.

§ 3313. Granting of initial license

1. The commisisoner [commissioner]* shall grant an initial license or amendment to a license as to one or more of the substances or activities enumerated in the application if he is satisfied that:

(a) the applicant will be able to maintain effective control against diversion of controlled substances;

(b) the applicant will be able to comply with all applicable state and federal laws;

(c) the applicant and its officers are ready, willing and able to properly carry on the manufacturing or distributing activity for which a license is sought;

(d) the applicant possesses sufficient land, buildings and equipment to properly carry on the activity described in the application;

(e) it is in the public interest that such license be granted; and

(f) the applicant and its managing officers are of good moral character.

2. If the commissioner is not satisfied that the applicant should be issued an initial license, he shall notify the applicant in writing of those factors upon which further evidence is required. Within thirty days of the receipt of such notification, the applicant may submit additional material to the commissioner or demand a hearing or both.

HISTORY: Add, L 1972, ch 878, § 2, eff April 1, 1973, with substance derived from former § 3314. Former § 3313, add, L 1953, ch 879, § 1, with substance derived from former § 423; amd, L 1958, ch 925, § 1; repealed, L 1972, ch 878, § 1 eff April 1, 1973.

§ 3315. Applications for renewal of licenses to manufacture or distribute controlled substances

1. An application for the renewal of any license issued pursuant to this title shall be filed with the department not more than six months nor less than four months prior to the expiration thereof.

2. The application for renewal shall include such information prepared in such manner and detail as the commissioner may require, including but not limited to:

(a) any material change in the circumstances or factors listed in section thirty-three hundred twelve of this article;

(b) every known charge or investigation, pending or concluded during the period of the license, by any governmental agency with respect to:

(i) each incident or alleged incident involving the theft, loss, or possible diversion of controlled substances manufactured or distributed by the applicant; and

(ii) compliance by the applicant with the requirements of the federal controlled substances act, or the laws of any state with respect to any substance listed in section thirty-three hundred six of this article.

3. An applicant for renewal shall be under a continuing duty to report to the department any change in facts or circumstances reflected in the application or any newly discovered or occurring

---

* The bracketed word has been inserted by the Publisher.

fact or circumstance which is required to be included in the application.

4. If the commissioner is not satisfied that the applicant is entitled to a renewal of such license, he shall within forty-five days after the filing of the application serve upon the applicant or his attorney of record in person or by registered or certified mail an order directing the applicant to show cause why his application for renewal should not be denied. Such order shall specify in detail the respects in which the applicant has not satisfied the commissioner that the license should be renewed.

5. Within thirty days of service of such order, the applicant may either submit additional material to the commissioner or demand a hearing or both. If a hearing is demanded the commissioner shall fix a date for hearing not sooner than fifteen days nor later than thirty days after receipt of the demand, unless such time limitation is waived by the applicant.

    HISTORY: Add, L 1972, ch 878, § 2, eff April 1, 1973, with substance derived from former §§ 3310(1) (b), 3375(1)(b). Former § 3315, add, L 1965, ch 1031, § 173, with substance derived from former Penal Law § 1753; repealed, L 1972, ch 878, § 1, eff April 1, 1973. See now § 3382. Sub 2, par (b), subpar (ii), amd, L 1973, ch 163, § 10, eff April 1, 1973.

§ 3316. Granting of renewal of licenses

1. The commissioner shall renew a license unless he determines and finds that the applicant:

    (a) is unlikely to maintain or be able to maintain effective control against diversion; or

    (b) is unlikely to comply with all federal and state laws applicable to the manufacture or distribution of the controlled substance or substances for which the license is sought.

2. For purposes of this section, proof that a licensee, during the period of his license, has failed to maintain effective control against diversion or has knowingly or negligently failed to comply with applicable federal or state laws relating to the manufacture or distribution of controlled substances, shall constitute substantial evidence that the applicant will be unlikely to maintain effective control against diversion or be unlikely to comply with the applicable federal or state statutes during the period of proposed renewal.

    HISTORY: Add, L 1972, ch 878, § 2, eff April 1, 1973.

§ 3318. Identification of controlled substances

1. No controlled substance may be manufactured or delivered within this state in solid or capsule form unless it has clearly marked or imprinted upon each such capsule or solid:

    (a) an individual symbol or number assigned to the person who manufactured the controlled substance in such form, and

    (b) a code number or symbol assigned by the commissioner identifying such substance or combination of substances.

2. No controlled substance contained within a bottle, vial, carton or other container, or in any way affixed or appended to or enclosed within a package of any kind, and designed or intended for delivery in such container or package to an ultimate consumer, shall be manufactured, delivered or distributed within this state unless such container or package has clearly and permanently marked or imprinted upon it:

    (a) an individual symbol or number assigned to the person who packaged the controlled substance in such form; and

    (b) a code number or symbol assigned by the commissioner identifying such substance or combination of substances.

3. The commissioner shall assign a code number or symbol to each controlled substance, and in his discretion for combinations of substances, so as to provide ready identification of such substance. Upon application by a manufacturer of controlled substances, the commissioner shall assign to such manufacturer an identifying number or symbol. Wherever possible and practical, the commissioner shall assign code numbers which conform to the national drug code system.

> HISTORY: Add, L 1972, ch 878, § 2, eff April 1, 1973; amd, L 1973, ch 163, § 11, eff April 1, 1973, L 2014, ch 60, § 14 (Part D), eff June 29, 2014.

§ 3319. Distribution of free samples

It shall be unlawful to distribute free samples of controlled substances, except to persons licensed pursuant to title III of this article.

> HISTORY: Add, L 1972, ch 878, § 2, eff April 1, 1973.

§ 3320. Authorized distribution

1. Controlled substances may be lawfully distributed within this state only to licensed distributors or manufacturers, practitioners, pharmacists, pharmacies, institutional dispensers, registered outsourcing facilities, and laboratory, research or instructional facilities authorized by law to possess the particular substance distributed.

2. A person authorized to obtain a controlled substance by distribution may lawfully receive such substance only from a distributor licensed pursuant to this article.

> HISTORY: Add, L 1972, ch 878, § 2, eff April 1, 1973, with substance derived from former §§ 3310(2), 3375(2); amd, L 2014, ch 60, § 15 (Part D), eff June 29, 2014.

§ 3321. Exempt distribution

1. The commissioner by regulation or ruling may exempt from the licensing requirements of this title:

(a) the return of controlled substances to a manufacturer, registered outsourcing facility or distributor by a practitioner or pharmacy;

(b) the sale of controlled substances by a pharmacy or practitioner to a pharmacy or practitioner for the immediate needs of the pharmacy or practitioner receiving such substances; and

(c) the disposition of controlled substances by a person in lawful possession thereof who, not in the ordinary course of business, wishes to discontinue such possession.

2. Records of such transactions shall be prepared and maintained and reports filed in such manner as the commissioner shall require.

> HISTORY: Add, L 1972, ch 878, § 2, eff April 1, 1973, with substance derived from former §§ 3322(3), 3381(2); amd, L 1973, ch 163, § 12, L 1974, ch 965, § 8, eff July 13, 1974, L 2014, ch 60, § 16 (Part D), eff June 29, 2014.

§ 3322. Reports and records

1. Persons licensed under this title or operating a registered outsourcing facility shall maintain records of all controlled substances manufactured, compounded, received, disposed of, delivered or distributed by them. The record shall show the date of receipt or delivery, the name and address, and registration number of the person from whom received or to whom delivered or distributed, the kind and quantity of substance received and delivered or distributed, the kind and quantity of

substance produced or removed from the process of manufacture and the date thereof.

2. Any person licensed under this title or operating a registered outsourcing facility shall prepare and maintain a biennial report setting forth the current inventory of controlled substances, the quantities of controlled substances manufactured, compounded, delivered or distributed within the state during the period covered by the report and such other information as the commissioner shall by regulation prescribe. Maintaining for inspection a biennial inventory of controlled substances prepared and maintained in compliance with federal statutes and regulations shall be deemed in compliance with this section.

3. Any person licensed under this title or operating a registered outsourcing facility shall forthwith notify the department of any incident involving the theft, loss or possible diversion of controlled substances manufactured, compounded, delivered or distributed by the licensee or operator.

4. The records and reports required by this section shall be prepared, preserved, or filed in such manner and detail as the commissioner shall by regulation prescribe.

HISTORY: Add, L 1972, ch 878, § 2, eff April 1, 1973, with substance derived from former §§ 3333(2), 3388(2); amd, L 1975, ch 108, § 1, eff May 20, 1975, L 2014, ch 60, § 17 (Part D), eff June 29, 2014.

TITLE III   Research, Instructional Activities, and Chemical Analysis Relating to Controlled Substances

HISTORY: Add, L 1972, ch 878, § 2, eff April 1, 1973. Former Title III, add, L 1953, ch 879, § 1; repealed, L 1972, ch 878, § 1, eff April 1, 1973.

§ 3324. Licenses to engage in research, instructional activities, and chemical analysis relating to controlled substances

1. No person within this state shall manufacture, obtain, possess, administer or dispense a controlled substance for purposes of scientific research, instruction or chemical analysis without having first obtained a license to do so from the department.

2. A license issued under this title shall be valid for two years from the date of issue.

3. The fee for a license under this title shall be forty dollars.

4. Licenses issued under this title shall be effective only for and shall specify:

(a) the name and address of the licensee;

(b) the nature of the project or projects permitted by the license;

(c) the nature of the controlled substance or substances to be used in the project, by name if in schedule I, and by name or schedule or both if in any other schedule;

(d) whether dispensing to human subjects is permitted by the license.

5. Upon application of a person licensed pursuant to this title, a license may be amended to add a further activity or to add further substances or schedules to the project permitted thereunder. The fee for such amendment shall be twenty dollars.

HISTORY: Add, L 1972, ch 878, § 2, eff April 1, 1973. Former § 3324, add, L 1953, ch 879, § 1, with substance derived from former § 428; amd, L 1957, ch 38, § 1, L 1961, ch 884, § 1, L 1965, ch 323, § 2, L 1968, ch 137, § 1, L 1968, ch 171, § 1; repealed, L 1972, ch 878, § 1, eff April 1, 1973. Sub 1, amd, L 1974, ch 965, § 9, eff July 13, 1974. Sub 3, amd, L 1981, ch 103, § 149, L 1989, ch 61, § 258, eff April 19, 1989. Sub 5, amd, L 1981, ch 103, § 149, L 1989, ch 61, § 258, eff April 19, 1989.

§ 3325. Authority to issue licenses; applications

1. Subject to the provisions of this title, the commissioner is authorized to license a person to manufacture, obtain and possess, dispense, and administer controlled substances for purposes of scientific research, chemical analysis or instruction.

2. A license or amendment of a license shall be issued by the department unless the applicant therefor has failed to furnish a satisfactory protocol pursuant to subdivision three of this section, or a satisfactory statement pursuant to section 3326, and proof that the applicant:

(a) and its managing officers are of good moral character;

(b) possesses or is capable of acquiring facilities, staff and equipment sufficient to carry on properly the proposed project detailed in the protocol or statement accompanying the application;

(c) is able to maintain effective control against diversion of the controlled substances for which the license is sought;

(d) is able to comply with all applicable state and federal laws and regulations relating to the controlled substances for which the license is sought.

3. An application for a license or for an amendment to a license shall be accompanied by a detailed protocol setting forth:

(a) the nature of the proposed project;

(b) the proposed quantity or quantities of each controlled substance involved;

(c) the qualifications and competence of the applicant to engage in such project;

(d) specific provisions for the safe administration or dispensing of controlled substances to humans, if such is contemplated, and the proposed method of selecting humans;

(e) such other additional information as the commissioner may require.

4. The application for a license pursuant to this title shall include copies of all papers filed with the Bureau, the Federal Food and Drug Administration and any other governmental agency, whether state or federal, in connection with the applicant's proposed project.

HISTORY: Add, L 1972, ch 878, § 2, eff April 1, 1973, with substance derived from former §§ 3311, 3376. Former § 3325, add, L 1953, ch 879, § 1, with substance derived from former § 431; amd, L 1960, ch 527, § 1, L 1961, ch 884, § 5, L 1971, ch 997, § 5; repealed, L 1972, ch 878, § 1, eff April 1, 1973. See now §§ 3331(4), 3333(2).

§ 3326. Institutional research licenses

1. Subject to the provisions of this title, the commissioner is authorized to license an institution, which regularly engages in research, to approve specific projects conducted under its immediate auspices.

2. An institution seeking a license pursuant to this section shall make application in the same manner as an applicant for a license pursuant to section 3325. However, such institution shall submit, in lieu of a detailed protocol of a specific project, a statement including:

(a) the qualifications and such other data as the commissioner may require regarding each member of the committee within the institution which will approve specific projects;

(b) a description of the system within the institution for approving, supervising and evaluating such projects.

3. Upon approval of each specific project, such institution shall forward to the commissioner a description of the project, the names and qualifications of the individuals working thereon and of those individuals designated to supervise the project. If administration or dispensing to human subjects is contemplated, there shall also be included a description of the provisions for safe administration or dispensing.

4. Such institution shall forward to the commissioner periodic progress reports and evaluations of, as well as amendments to each project, in such manner and in such detail as the commissioner may prescribe.

HISTORY: Add, L 1972, ch 878, § 2, eff April 1, 1973, with substance derived from former §§ 3312, 3314, 3377.

§ 3327. Procedure

1. A license or amendment to a license shall be issued or refused by the department within ninety days from the date of filing of a completed application.

2. Within thirty days of notification of such refusal, the applicant may either submit additional material to the commissioner or demand a hearing or both. If a hearing is demanded the commissioner shall fix a date for hearing not sooner than fifteen days nor later than thirty days after receipt of the demand, unless such time limitation is waived by the applicant.

HISTORY: Add, L 1972, ch 878, § 2, eff April 1, 1973.

§ 3328. Exemptions from title

The following persons engaging in the following activities shall be exempt from the provisions of this title:

1. A practitioner lawfully administering, dispensing, or prescribing a controlled substance in the course of his professional practice to an ultimate user for a recognized medical purpose;

2. A licensed manufacturer engaged in research upon non-human subjects or chemical analysis conducted on the premises specified in the manufacturer's license;

3. A licensed distributor engaged in quality control analysis at the premises specified in his license.

4. A practitioner or patient participating in a clinical research program on the therapeutic use of marijuana or tetrahydrocannabinols.

(a) Each such clinical research program shall have received protocol approval from the United States Food and Drug Administration, shall possess an effective investigational new drug application and shall have been registered by the Drug Enforcement Administration, United States Department of Justice.

(b) Each such clinical research program authorized under the provisions of article thirty-three-A of this chapter.

HISTORY: Add, L 1972, ch 878, § 2, eff April 1, 1973. Sub 4, add, L 1980, ch 810, § 3, eff Sept 1, 1980.

§ 3329. Reports and records

1. Persons licensed under this title shall keep records showing the receipt, administration, dispensing, or destruction of all controlled substances and maintain the records in such manner and detail as the commissioner, by regulation, shall require.

2. Persons licensed under this title shall submit reports to the department summarizing the activity conducted under the license. Included in such report shall be a detailed inventory of controlled substances, and an accounting for all such substances received or disposed of during the period covered by the report and such other information as the commissioner shall, by regulation, require. Such reports shall be filed with the department at such times as the commissioner may require.

HISTORY: Add, L 1972, ch 878, § 2, eff April 1, 1973, with substance of sub 1 derived from former §§ 3333(5), 3388(5).

TITLE IV   Dispensing to Ultimate Users

> **HISTORY:** Add, L 1972, ch 878, § 2, eff April 1, 1973. Former Title IV, add, L 1953, ch 879, § 1; repealed, L 1972, ch 878, § 1, eff April 1, 1973.

§ 3330. Schedule I substances

No prescription may be made or filled for any controlled substance in schedule I nor may such substance be possessed, distributed, dispensed or administered except pursuant to title III of this article.

> **HISTORY:** Add, L 1972, ch 878, § 2, eff April 1, 1973. Former § 3330, add, L 1953, ch 879, § 1, with substance derived from former §§ 425, 427; amd, L 1971, ch 997, § 6; repealed, L 1972, ch 878, § 1, eff April 1, 1973. See now §§ 3305(3), 3331(2), (3).

§ 3331. Scheduled substances administering and dispensing by practitioners

1. Except as provided in titles III or V of this article, no substance in schedules II, III, IV, or V may be prescribed for or dispensed or administered to an addict or habitual user.

2. A practitioner, in good faith, and in the course of his or her professional practice only, may prescribe, administer and dispense substances listed in schedules II, III, IV, and V, or he or she may cause the same to be administered by a designated agent under his or her direction and supervision.

3. A veterinarian, in good faith, and in the course of the practice of veterinary medicine only, may prescribe, administer and dispense substances listed in schedules II, III, IV, and V or he may cause them to be administered by a designated agent under his direction and supervision.

4. No such substance may be dispensed unless it is enclosed within a suitable and durable container, and:

    (a) Affixed to such container is a label upon which is indelibly typed, printed or otherwise legibly written the following:

        (i) the name and address of the ultimate user for whom the substance is intended, or, if intended for use upon an animal, the species of such animal and the name and address of the owner or person in custody of such animal;

(ii) the name, address, and telephone number of the dispensing practitioner;

(iii) specific directions for use, including but not limited to the dosage and frequency of dosage, and the maximum daily dosage;

(iv) the legend, prominently marked or printed in either boldface or upper case lettering: "CONTROLLED SUBSTANCE, DANGEROUS UNLESS USED AS DIRECTED";

(v) the date of dispensing;

(vi) either the name of the substance or such code number assigned by the department for the particular substance pursuant to section thirty-three hundred eighteen of this article;

(b) Such container shall be identified as a controlled substance by either:

(i) an orange label;

(ii) a label of another color over which is superimposed an orange transparent adhesive tape; or

(iii) an auxiliary orange label affixed to the front of such container and bearing the legend, prominently marked or printed "Controlled Substance, Dangerous Unless Used As Directed";

(c) Any label, transparency, or auxiliary label shall be applied in a manner which would inhibit its removal.

5. No more than a thirty day supply or, pursuant to regulations of the commissioner enumerating conditions warranting specified greater supplies, no more than a three month supply of a schedule II, III or IV substance, as determined by the directed dosage and frequency of dosage, may be dispensed by an authorized practitioner at one time.

6. A practitioner dispensing a controlled substance shall file information pursuant to such dispensing with the department by electronic means in such manner and detail as the commissioner shall, by regulation, require. This requirement shall not apply to the dispensing by a practitioner pursuant to subdivision five of section thirty-three hundred fifty-one of this article.

7. A practitioner may not administer, prescribe or dispense any substance referred to in subdivision (h) of Schedule II, and subdivision (g) of Schedule III, of section three thousand three hundred six of this article for other than therapeutic purposes. A practitioner may not administer, prescribe or dispense any such substance to any individual without first obtaining the informed consent of such individual, or where the individual lacks capacity to give such consent, a person legally authorized to consent on his or her behalf.

HISTORY: Add, L 1972, ch 878, § 2, eff April 1, 1973, L 1974, ch 965, § 10, eff July 13, 1974, L 1981, ch 415, § 1, with substance derived from former § 3383(3), L 1973, ch 728, § 1, L 1986, ch 433, § 1, eff July 21, 1986, L 1989, ch 418, § 2; amd, L 1990, ch 640, § 4, eff July 18, 1990, deemed eff Jan 12, 1990, L 1998, ch 537, § 4, eff Nov 1, 1998, L 2004, ch 58, § 6 (Part A), eff Oct 20, 2004, L 2010, ch 178, § 6, eff July 15, 2010, L 2012, ch 447, § 17 (Part C), eff Aug 27, 2012.

§ 3332. Making of official New York state prescriptions or electronic prescriptions for scheduled substances

1. No controlled substance may be prescribed by a practitioner except on an official New York

state prescription or on an electronic prescription, and in good faith and in the course of his or her professional practice only.

2. Such prescription shall be prepared on an official New York state prescription form, written with ink, indelible pencil or, apart from the practitioner's signature, typewriter or electronic printer, or to the extent authorized by federal requirements, on an electronic prescription. The original official New York state prescription or the electronic prescription must contain the following:

(a) the name, address, and age of the ultimate user for whom the substance is intended, or, if the ultimate user is an animal, the species of such animal and the name and address of the owner or person having custody of such animal;

(b) the name, address, Federal registration number, telephone number, and handwritten signature of the prescribing practitioner, except that an electronic prescription must contain the electronic signature of the prescribing practitioner;

(c) specific directions for use, including but not limited to the dosage and frequency of dosage and the maximum daily dosage;

(d) the date upon which such prescription was actually signed by the prescribing practitioner.

3. No such prescription shall be made for a quantity of controlled substances which would exceed a thirty day supply if the controlled substance were used in accordance with the directions for use specified on the prescription. A practitioner may, however, issue a prescription for up to a three month supply of a controlled substance provided that the controlled substance has been prescribed to treat one of the conditions that have been enumerated by the commissioner pursuant to regulations as warranting the prescribing of greater than a thirty day supply of a controlled substance and that the practitioner specifies the condition on the face of the prescription. No additional prescriptions for a controlled substance may be issued by a practitioner to an ultimate user within thirty days of the date of any prescription previously issued unless and until the ultimate user has exhausted all but a seven day supply of the controlled substance provided by any previously issued prescription. A practitioner may, however, issue a prescription for up to a six month supply of any substance listed in subdivision (h) of Schedule II of section thirty-three hundred six of this article provided that such substance has been prescribed to treat one of the conditions that have been enumerated by the commissioner pursuant to regulations as warranting the prescribing of a six month supply and that the practitioner specifies the condition on the prescription or on the electronic prescription.

4. The practitioner shall deliver the original official New York state prescription to the ultimate user or shall transmit the electronic prescription to the pharmacy.

HISTORY: Add, L 1972, ch 878, § 2, eff April 1, 1973; amd, L 1974, ch 965, § 11, L 1986, ch 118, § 3, L 1990, ch 640, § 5, eff July 18, 1990 and deemed eff Jan 12, 1990, L 1998, ch 537, § 5, eff Nov 1, 1998, L 2004, ch 58, § 7 (Part A), eff Oct 20, 2004, L 2010, ch 178, § 7, eff July 15, 2010.

§ 3333. Dispensing upon official New York state prescription or electronic prescription

1. A licensed pharmacist may, in good faith and in the course of his or her professional practice, sell and dispense to an ultimate user controlled substances only upon the delivery of an official New York state prescription or the receipt of an electronic prescription to such pharmacist, within thirty days of the date such prescription was signed by an authorized practitioner; provided, however, a pharmacist may dispense a part or portion of such prescription in accordance with regulations of the commissioner in consultation with the commissioner of education. No pharmacy or pharmacist may sell or dispense greater than a thirty day supply of a controlled substance to an

ultimate user unless and until the ultimate user has exhausted all but a seven day supply of the controlled substance provided pursuant to any previously issued prescription, except that a pharmacy or pharmacist may sell or dispense up to a three month supply of a controlled substance if there appears, on the official New York state prescription or electronic prescription, a statement that the controlled substance has been prescribed to treat one of the conditions that have been enumerated by the regulations of the commissioner as warranting the prescribing of greater than a thirty day supply of a controlled substance. A pharmacy or pharmacist may sell or dispense up to a six month supply of any substance listed in subdivision (h) of Schedule II of section thirty-three hundred six of this article if there appears, on the official New York state prescription or on an electronic prescription, a statement that the substance has been prescribed to treat one of the conditions that have been enumerated by the regulations of the commissioner as warranting the prescribing of a specified greater supply.

2. No controlled substance may be so dispensed or sold unless it is enclosed within a suitable container, and:

(a) Affixed to such container is a label upon which is indelibly typed, printed, or otherwise legibly written the following:

(i) the name and address of the ultimate user for whom the substance is intended, or if intended for use upon an animal, the species of such animal and the name and address of the owner or person in custody of such animal;

(ii) the name, address, and telephone number of the pharmacy from which such substance is dispensed;

(iii) specific directions for use as stated on the prescription;

(iv) the name of the prescribing practitioner;

(v) the legend, prominently marked or printed in either boldface or upper case lettering: "CONTROLLED SUBSTANCE, DANGEROUS UNLESS USED AS DIRECTED";

(vi) the number of the prescription under which it is recorded in the pharmacist's prescription file;

(vii) such code number assigned by the department for the particular substance pursuant to section thirty-three hundred eighteen of this article, or when requested by the practitioner, the name of such substance;

(b) Such container shall be identified as a controlled substance by either:

(i) an orange label;

(ii) a label of another color over which is superimposed an orange transparent adhesive tape; or

(iii) an auxiliary orange label affixed to the front of such container and bearing the legend, prominently marked or printed "Controlled Substance, Dangerous Unless Used As Directed";

(c) Any label, transparency, or auxiliary label shall be applied in a manner which would inhibit its removal.

3. The pharmacist filling the controlled substance prescription shall endorse upon the original

official New York state prescription the date of delivery and his or her signature or, if an electronic prescription, his or her electronic signature.

4. The endorsed original prescription shall be retained by the proprietor of the pharmacy for a period of five years. The proprietor of the pharmacy shall file or cause to be filed such prescription information with the department by electronic means on a real time basis as the commissioner in consultation with the commissioner of education shall, by regulation, require; provided, however, that the commissioner may, pursuant to a process established in regulation, grant a waiver allowing a pharmacy to make such filings within a longer period of time if and to the extent that the commissioner finds it warranted, in his or her discretion, due to economic hardship, technological limitations that are not reasonably within the control of the pharmacy, or other exceptional circumstance demonstrated by the pharmacy; and provided, further, however, that such regulations shall specify the manner in which such requirements shall apply to the delivery of controlled substances to individuals in this state by means of mail or licensed express delivery services.

5. When filing prescription information electronically pursuant to subdivision four of this section, the proprietor of the pharmacy shall dispose of any electronically recorded prescription information in such manner as the commissioner shall by regulation require.

HISTORY: Add, L 1972, ch 878, § 2, eff April 1, 1973; amd, L 1986, ch 118, § 4, L 1990, ch 640, § 6, eff July 18, 1990 and deemed eff Jan 12, 1990, L 1981, ch 415, § 2, with substance derived from former §§ 3325(2), 3383(2), L 1998, ch 537, § 6, eff Nov 1, 1998, L 2004, ch 58, § 8 (Part A), eff Oct 20, 2004, L 2010, ch 178, § 8, eff July 15, 2010, L 2012, ch 447, § 3 (Part A), eff Aug 27, 2013.

§ 3334. Emergency oral prescriptions for schedule II drugs and certain other controlled substances

1. In an emergency situation, as defined by rule or regulation of the department, a practitioner may orally prescribe and a pharmacist may dispense to an ultimate user controlled substances in schedule II and those schedule III or schedule IV controlled substances as the commissioner may, by regulation, require; provided however the pharmacist shall:

(a) contemporaneously reduce such prescription to writing or to the extent authorized by federal requirements, to an electronic record;

(b) dispense the substance in conformity with the labeling requirements applicable to the type of prescription which would be required but for the emergency; and

(c) make a good faith effort to verify the practitioner's identity, if the practitioner is unknown to the pharmacist.

2. No oral prescription shall be filled for a quantity of controlled substances which would exceed a five day supply if the substance were used in accordance with the directions for use.

3. Within seventy-two hours after authorizing an emergency oral prescription, the prescribing practitioner shall cause to be delivered to the pharmacist the original of an official New York state prescription or an electronic prescription. Such prescription shall, in addition to the information otherwise required, also have upon the official New York state prescription or upon the electronic prescription the words: "Authorization for emergency dispensing." If the pharmacist fails to receive such prescription he or she shall notify the department in writing or electronically within seven days from the date of dispensing the substance.

4. Such official New York state prescription or electronic prescription shall be endorsed, and retained and filed in the same manner as is otherwise required for such prescriptions.

HISTORY: Add, L 1972, ch 878, § 2, eff April 1, 1973, with substance derived from former §§ 3371(19), 3381; amd, L 1998, ch 537, § 7, eff Nov 1, 1998, L 2004, ch 58, § 9 (Part A), eff Oct 20, 2004, L 2010, ch 178, § 10, eff July 15, 2010.

§ 3335. Dispensing by online dispensers of controlled substances

A controlled substance may be sold, delivered, or dispensed by means of the internet but only in accordance with this article. An online dispenser shall file with the department by electronic means information concerning the dispensing by means of the internet, of any controlled substances in such manner as the commissioner by regulation shall require.

HISTORY: Add, L 2010, ch 178, § 3, eff Jan 11, 2011.

§ 3336. [Repealed]

HISTORY: Add, L 1972, ch 878, § 2, eff April 1, 1973, with substance derived from former §§ 3322, 3381. Sub 1, amd, L 1986, ch 118, § 6, eff Nov 1, 1986. Amd, L 1998, ch 537, § 9, eff Nov 1, 1998, L 2003, ch 591, § 3, eff Sept 22, 2003; repealed, L 2004, ch 58, § 10 (Part A), eff Oct 20, 2004.

§ 3337. Oral prescriptions schedule III, IV and V substances

1. Except as provided in section thirty-three hundred thirty-four of this title, a practitioner may orally prescribe and a pharmacist may dispense to an ultimate user controlled substances in schedules III, IV or V provided however the pharmacist shall:

(a) contemporaneously reduce such prescription to writing or, to the extent authorized by federal requirements, an electronic record;

(b) dispense the substance in conformity with the labeling requirements applicable to a prescription; and

(c) make a good faith effort to verify the practitioner's identity, if the practitioner is unknown to the pharmacist.

2. No oral prescription shall be filled for a quantity of controlled substances which would exceed a five day supply if the controlled substance were used in accordance with the directions for use, except that with respect to a schedule IV substance such prescription shall not exceed a thirty-day supply or one hundred dosage units, whichever is less; provided, however, that this provision shall not apply to any schedule IV controlled substance limited to a five day supply by section thirty-three hundred thirty-four of this title.

3. Within seventy-two hours after authorizing such an oral prescription, the prescribing practitioner shall cause to be delivered to the pharmacist an official New York state prescription or an electronic prescription. If the pharmacist fails to receive such prescription he or she shall make a record of such fact in such manner and detail as the commissioner in consultation with the commissioner of education, by regulation, shall require.

4. Such official New York state prescription or electronic prescription shall be endorsed, retained and filed in the same manner as is otherwise required for such prescriptions.

HISTORY: Add, L 1972, ch 878, § 2, eff April 1, 1973, with substance derived from former §§ 3371(19), 3381; amd, L 1974, ch 960, § 1, L 1974, ch 961, § 1, eff June 13, 1974, L 1974, ch 965, § 13, eff July 13, 1974, L 2004, ch 58, § 11 (Part A), eff Oct 20, 2004, L 2010, ch 178, § 11, eff July 15, 2010.

§ 3338. Official New York state prescription forms

1. Official New York state prescription forms shall be prepared and issued by the department in the manner and detail as the commissioner in consultation with the commissioner of education

may, by regulation, require, and, each form shall be serialized. Such forms shall be furnished to practitioners authorized to write such prescriptions and to institutional dispensers. Such prescription blanks shall not be transferable.

2. Except as expressly authorized by section thirty-three hundred thirty-four or thirty-three hundred thirty-seven of this article, controlled substances may be prescribed or dispensed only upon an official New York state prescription or, pursuant to regulations, an electronic prescription or out-of-state prescription.

3. The commissioner in consultation with the commissioner of education is hereby authorized and empowered to make rules and regulations, not inconsistent with this article, with respect to the retention or filing of such official New York state prescription forms,electronic prescriptions and out-of-state prescriptions, including information required to be filed with the department, the maximum number of official prescription forms which may be issued at any one time, the manner in which such forms shall be issued, the period of time after issuance by the department that such form shall remain valid for use, and the manner in which practitioners associated with institutional dispensers may use such forms, or any other matter of procedure or detail necessary to effectuate or clarify the provisions of this section and to secure proper and effective enforcement of the provisions of this article.

4. Upon a finding by the commissioner that a person has willfully failed to comply with the provisions of this article, the commissioner may revoke, cancel or withhold official New York state prescription forms which have been issued or for which application has been made.

5. [Redesignated]

HISTORY: Add, L 1972, ch 878, § 2, eff April 1, 1973. Sub 1, amd, L 1981, ch 103, § 150, L 1982, ch 129, § 1, eff Jan 1, 1983. Sub 1, amd, L 1997, ch 433, § 43, eff Aug 20, 1997, L 1998, ch 537, § 10, eff Nov 1, 1998, L 2004, ch 58, § 12 (Part A), eff Oct 20, 2004. Sub 2, amd, L 2004, ch 58, § 12 (Part A), eff Oct 20, 2004. Sub 3, formerly sub 4, amd, L 1998, ch 537, § 10, eff Nov 1, 1998; so designated sub 4 and amd, L 2004, ch 58, § 12 (Part A), eff Oct 20, 2004. Former sub 3, deleted, L 2004, ch 58, § 12 (Part A), eff Oct 20, 2004. Sub 4, formerly sub 5, so designated sub 4 and amd, L 2004, ch 58, § 12 (Part A), eff Oct 20, 2004. Former sub 4, redesignated sub 3, L 2004, ch 58, § 12 (Part A), eff Oct 20, 2004. Sub 5, redesignated sub 4, L 2004, ch 58, § 12 (Part A), eff Oct 20, 2004.

§ 3339. Refilling of prescriptions for controlled substances

1. Prescriptions for a schedule II controlled substance and those schedule III or schedule IV controlled substances which the commissioner may require by regulation may not be refilled.

2. A prescription, except for a schedule II controlled substance or those schedule III or schedule IV controlled substances which the commissioner may require by regulation may be refilled not more than the number of times specifically authorized by the prescriber upon the prescription, provided however no such authorization shall be effective for a period greater than six months from the date the prescription is signed. In the event that the prescription authorizes the dispensing of more than a thirty day supply of schedule III, schedule IV or schedule V substances pursuant to regulations of the commissioner enumerating conditions warranting specified greater supplies, the prescription may be refilled only once.

3. Unless an earlier refilling is authorized by the prescriber, no prescription for a controlled substance may be refilled earlier than seven days prior to the date the previously dispensed supply would be exhausted if used in conformity with the directions for use.

HISTORY: Add, L 1972, ch 878, § 2, eff April 1, 1973, with substance derived from former § 3322(1)(d). Sub 1, amd, L 2004, ch 58, § 13 (Part A), eff Oct 20, 2004. Sub 2, amd, L 1974, ch

965, § 14, eff July 13, 1974. Sub 2, amd, L 2004, ch 58, § 13 (Part A), eff Oct 20, 2004. Sub 3, amd, L 2004, ch 58, § 13 (Part A), eff Oct 20, 2004.

§ 3341. Institutional dispensers certificates of approval

1. No institutional dispenser as hereinbefore defined, shall receive, possess or cause controlled substances to be administered or dispensed without first having been issued a certificate of approval authorizing such activity by the commissioner.

2. Upon application of an institutional dispenser for a certificate of approval, the commissioner shall issue such certificate if he is satisfied that:

    (a) the applicant and its managing officers are of good moral character;

    (b) the applicant possesses the necessary land, building, paraphernalia and staff to properly carry on the activities described in the application;

    (c) the applicant will be able to maintain effective control against diversion of controlled substances; and

    (d) the applicant will be able to comply with all applicable state and federal laws.

3. Institutional dispensers to whom such certificates have been issued shall thereafter register biennially with the department. The fee for such certificate and for each biennial registration shall be one hundred dollars.

4. Certificates and registrations issued under this section shall be effective only for and shall specify:

    (a) the name and address of the institutional dispenser;

    (b) the nature of the controlled substance, or substances, either by name or schedule, or both, for which the certificate or registration is issued.

    HISTORY: Add, L 1972, ch 878, § 2, eff April 1, 1973, with substance derived from former §§ 3311, 3314, 3376. Sub 3, amd, L 1981, ch 103, § 151, L 1989, ch 61, § 259, eff April 19, 1989.

§ 3342. Dispensing and administering by institutional dispensers

1. An institutional dispenser may cause controlled substances to be administered or dispensed for use on its premises or for the immediate care or treatment of a patient lawfully being transferred in an emergency situation, as defined by rule or regulation of the commissioner, to an alternative medical facility only pursuant to a written order by a practitioner for medication. Such orders shall be made and preserved in the manner and form as the commissioner shall, by regulation, prescribe.

2. An institutional dispenser may dispense controlled substances for use off its premises only pursuant to a prescription, prepared and filed in conformity with this title, provided, however, that, in an emergency situation as defined by rule or regulation of the department, a practitioner in a hospital without a full-time pharmacy may dispense controlled substances to a patient in a hospital emergency room for use off the premises of the institutional dispenser for a period not to exceed twenty-four hours.

3. An institutional dispenser shall maintain records of all controlled substances dispensed and administered in such manner as the commissioner shall, by regulation, require.

    HISTORY: Add, L 1972, ch 878, § 2, eff April 1, 1973. Former § 3342, add, L 1953, ch 879, § 1; repealed, L 1972, ch 878, § 1, eff April 1, 1973. Sub 1, with substance derived from former §§ 3333(4), (6), (7), 3388(4), (6), amd, L 1974, ch 965, § 15, eff July 13, 1974. Sub 2, amd, L 1976, ch 692, § 1, eff July 24, 1976. Sub 3, add, L 1973, ch 163, § 13, eff April 1, 1973.

§ 3343. Reports and records

1. Prescriptions and copies of prescriptions shall be preserved in the following manner:

(a) dispensing practitioners filing information electronically pursuant to subdivision six of section thirty-three hundred thirty-one of this article, shall dispose of any electronically recorded information in such manner as the commissioner in consultation with the commissioner of education shall by regulation require;

(b) pharmacists dispensing controlled substances upon prescription shall preserve such prescriptions in such manner as the commissioner in consultation with the commissioner of education shall, by regulation, require.

2. Practitioners and pharmacies shall maintain records in all controlled substances received and dispensed in such manner as the commissioner shall, by regulation, require.

> **HISTORY:** Add, L 1972, ch 878, § 2, eff April 1, 1973, with substance derived from former §§ 3333(1), 3388(1). Former § 3343, add, L 1953, ch 879, § 1; repealed, L 1972, ch 878, § 1, eff April 1, 1973. Sub 1, amd, L 2004, ch 58, § 14 (Part A), eff Oct 20, 2004. Sub 1, par (a), amd, L 1998, ch 537, § 11, eff Nov 1, 1998, L 2004, ch 58, § 14 (Part A), eff Oct 20, 2004. Sub 1, par (b), amd, L 2004, ch 58, § 14 (Part A), eff Oct 20, 2004.

§ 3343-a. Prescription monitoring program registry

1. Establishment of system.

(a) The commissioner shall, in accordance with the provisions of this section, establish and maintain an electronic system for collecting, monitoring and reporting information concerning the prescribing and dispensing of controlled substances, to be known as the prescription monitoring program registry. The registry shall include information reported by pharmacies on a real time basis, as set forth in subdivision four of section thirty-three hundred thirty-three of this article.

(b) The registry shall include, for each person to whom a prescription for controlled substances has been dispensed, all patient-specific information covering such period of time as is deemed appropriate and feasible by the commissioner, but no less than six months and no more than five years. Such patient-specific information shall be obtained from the prescription information reported by pharmacies pursuant to subdivision four of section thirty-three hundred thirty-three of this article and by practitioners who dispense pursuant to subdivision six of section thirty-three hundred thirty-one of this article, and shall be processed and included in the registry by the department without undue delay. For purposes of this article, "patient-specific information" means information pertaining to individual patients included in the registry, which shall include the following information and such other information as is required by the department in regulation:

(i) the patient's name;

(ii) the patient's residential address;

(iii) the patient's date of birth;

(iv) the patient's gender;

(v) the date on which the prescription was issued;

(vi) the date on which the controlled substance was dispensed;

(vii) the metric quantity of the controlled substance dispensed;

(viii) the number of days supply of the controlled substance dispensed;

(ix) the name of the prescriber;

(x) the prescriber's identification number, as assigned by the drug enforcement administration;

(xi) the name or identifier of the drug that was dispensed; and

(xii) the payment method.

(c) The registry shall be secure, easily accessible by practitioners and pharmacists, and compatible with the electronic transmission of prescriptions for controlled substances, as required by section two hundred eighty-one of this chapter, and section sixty-eight hundred ten of the education law, and any regulations promulgated pursuant thereto. To the extent practicable, implementation of the electronic transmission of prescriptions for controlled substances shall serve to streamline consultation of the registry by practitioners and reporting of prescription information by pharmacists. The registry shall be interoperable with other similar registries operated by federal or state governments, to the extent deemed appropriate by the commissioner, and subject to the provisions of section thirty-three hundred seventy-one-a of this article.

(d) The department shall establish and implement such protocols as are reasonably necessary to ensure that information contained in the registry is maintained in a secure and confidential manner and is accessible only by practitioners, pharmacists or their designees for the purposes established in subdivisions two and three of this section, or as otherwise set forth in sections thirty-three hundred seventy-one and thirty-three hundred seventy-one-a of this article. Such protocols shall include a mechanism for the department to monitor and record access to the registry, which shall identify the authorized individual accessing and each controlled substance history accessed.

2. Duty to consult prescription monitoring program registry; practitioners.

(a) Every practitioner shall consult the prescription monitoring program registry prior to prescribing or dispensing any controlled substance listed on schedule II, III or IV of section thirty-three hundred six of this article, for the purpose of reviewing a patient's controlled substance history as set forth in such registry; provided, however, that nothing in this section shall preclude an authorized practitioner, other than a veterinarian, from consulting the registry at his or her option prior to prescribing or dispensing any controlled substance. The duty to consult the registry shall not apply to:

(i) veterinarians;

(ii) a practitioner dispensing pursuant to subdivision three of section thirty-three hundred fifty-one of this article;

(iii) a practitioner administering a controlled substance;

(iv) a practitioner prescribing or ordering a controlled substance for use on the premises of an institutional dispenser pursuant to section thirty-three hundred forty-two of this title;

(v) a practitioner prescribing a controlled substance in the emergency department of a general hospital, provided that the quantity of controlled substance prescribed does not exceed a five day supply if the controlled substance were used in accordance with the directions for use;

(vi) a practitioner prescribing a controlled substance to a patient under the care of a hospice, as defined by section four thousand two of this chapter;

(vii) a practitioner when:

(A) it is not reasonably possible for the practitioner to access the registry in a timely manner;

(B) no other practitioner or designee authorized to access the registry, pursuant to paragraph (b) of this subdivision, is reasonably available; and

(C) the quantity of controlled substance prescribed does not exceed a five day supply if the controlled substance were used in accordance with the directions for use;

(viii) a practitioner acting in compliance with regulations that may be promulgated by the commissioner as to circumstances under which consultation of the registry would result in a patient's inability to obtain a prescription in a timely manner, thereby adversely impacting the medical condition of such patient;

(ix) a situation where the registry is not operational as determined by the department or where it cannot be accessed by the practitioner due to a temporary technological or electrical failure, as set forth in regulation; or

(x) a practitioner who has been granted a waiver due to technological limitations that are not reasonably within the control of the practitioner, or other exceptional circumstance demonstrated by the practitioner, pursuant to a process established in regulation, and in the discretion of the commissioner.

(b) For purposes of this section, a practitioner may authorize a designee to consult the prescription monitoring program registry on his or her behalf, provided that: (i) the designee so authorized is employed by the same professional practice or is under contract with such practice; (ii) the practitioner takes reasonable steps to ensure that such designee is sufficiently competent in the use of the registry; (iii) the practitioner remains responsible for ensuring that access to the registry by the designee is limited to authorized purposes and occurs in a manner that protects the confidentiality of the information obtained from the registry, and remains responsible for any breach of confidentiality; and (iv) the ultimate decision as to whether or not to prescribe or dispense a controlled substance remains with the practitioner and is reasonably informed by the relevant controlled substance history information obtained from the registry. The commissioner shall establish in regulation reasonable parameters with regard to a practitioner's ability to authorize designees pursuant to this section, which shall include processes necessary to allow the department to: (A) grant access to the registry in a reasonably prompt manner to as many designees as are authorized by practitioners, up to the number deemed appropriate by the commissioner for particular professional practices or types of practices, taking into account the need to maintain security of the registry and the patient-specific information maintained therein, and the objective of minimizing burdens to practitioners to the extent practicable; (B) require that practitioners notify the department upon terminating the authorization of any designee; and (C) establish a mechanism to prevent such terminated designees from accessing the registry in a reasonably prompt manner following such notification.

3. Authority to consult prescription monitoring program registry; pharmacists.

(a) A pharmacist may consult the prescription monitoring program registry in order to review the controlled substance history of an individual for whom one or more prescriptions for controlled substances is presented to such pharmacist.

(b) For purposes of this section, a pharmacist may designate another pharmacist, a pharmacy intern, as defined by section sixty-eight hundred six of the education law, or other individual as may be permitted by the commissioner in regulation, to consult the prescription monitoring program registry on the pharmacist's behalf, provided that such designee is employed by the same pharmacy or is under contract with such pharmacy. The commissioner shall establish in regulation reasonable parameters with regard to a pharmacist's ability to authorize designees pursuant to this section, which shall include processes necessary to allow the department to: (A) grant access to the registry in a reasonably prompt manner to as many designees as are authorized by pharmacists, up to the number deemed appropriate by the commissioner for particular pharmacies, taking into account the need to maintain security of the registry and the patient-specific information maintained therein, and the objective of minimizing burdens to pharmacists to the extent practicable; (B) require that pharmacists notify the department upon terminating the authorization of any designee; and (C) establish a mechanism to prevent such terminated designees from accessing the registry in a reasonably prompt manner following such notification.

4. Immunity. No practitioner or pharmacist, and no person acting on behalf of such practitioner or pharmacist as permitted under this section, acting with reasonable care and in good faith shall be subject to civil liability arising from any false, incomplete or inaccurate information submitted to or reported by the registry or for any resulting failure of the system to accurately or timely report such information; provided, however, that nothing in this subdivision shall be deemed to alter the obligation to submit or report prescription information to the department as otherwise set forth in this article or in regulations promulgated pursuant thereto.

5. Guidance to practitioners and pharmacists. The commissioner shall, in consultation with the commissioner of education, provide guidance to practitioners, pharmacists, and pharmacies regarding the purposes and uses of the registry established by this section and the means by which practitioners and pharmacists can access the registry. Such guidance shall reference educational information available pursuant to the prescription pain medication awareness program established pursuant to section thirty-three hundred nine-a of this article.

6. Individual access to controlled substance histories. The commissioner shall establish procedures by which an individual may: (a) request and obtain his or her own controlled substances history consisting of patient-specific information or, in appropriate circumstances, that of a patient who lacks capacity to make health care decisions and for whom the individual has legal authority to make such decisions and would have legal access to the patient's health care records; or (b) seek review of any part of his or her controlled substances history or, in appropriate circumstances, that of a patient who lacks capacity to make health care decisions and for whom the individual has legal authority to make such decisions and would have legal access to the patient's health care records, that such individual disputes. Such procedures shall require the department to promptly revise any information accessible through the registry that the department determines to be inaccurate. Such procedures shall be described on the department's website and included with the controlled substances history provided to an individual pursuant to a request made under this subdivision or under subparagraph (iv) of paragraph (a) of subdivision two of section thirty-three hundred seventy-one of this article.

7. Department analysis of data. The department shall periodically analyze data contained in the prescription monitoring program registry to identify information that indicates that a violation of

law or breach of professional standards may have occurred and, as warranted, provide any relevant information to appropriate entities as permitted under section thirty-three hundred seventy-one of this article. The department shall keep a record of the information provided, including, but not limited to, the specific information provided and the agency to which such information was provided, including the name and title of the person to whom such information was provided and an attestation from such person that he or she has authority to receive such information.

8. Funding the prescription monitoring program registry.

(a) The commissioner shall make reasonable efforts to apply for monies available from the federal government and other institutions, to the extent deemed appropriate by the commissioner, and use any monies so obtained to supplement any other monies made available for the purposes of this title.

(b) Operation of the registry established by this section shall not be funded, in whole or in part, by fees imposed specifically for such purposes upon practitioners, pharmacists, designees or patients subject to this section.

9. Rules and regulations. The commissioner shall promulgate such rules and regulations as are necessary to effectuate the provisions of this section, in consultation with the work group established pursuant to subdivision three of section thirty-three hundred nine-a of this article.

HISTORY: Add, L 2012, ch 447, § 2 (Part A), eff Aug 27, 2013.

§ 3343-b. Safe disposal of unused controlled substances

1. The department shall establish a program for the safe disposal of unused controlled substances by consumers in accordance with federal law. The program shall permit individual members of the public to voluntarily surrender controlled substances listed on schedule II, III, IV or V of section thirty-three hundred six of this article in a secure manner, without identifying themselves, and shall be publicized consistent with the prescription pain medication awareness program established pursuant to section thirty-three hundred nine-a of this article.

2. The surrender of a controlled substance pursuant to the program established pursuant to this section shall not constitute the possession, transfer or sale of such controlled substance for purposes of this article or the penal law.

3. In developing such program, the department shall consider the following: appropriate sites for disposal throughout the state; the role of law enforcement and federal authorities, as appropriate; and the manner in which potential costs to localities or to the state will be addressed. Disposal sites shall be operated by law enforcement agencies and pharmacies on a voluntary basis in collaboration with the department. Nothing in this section shall require any political subdivision of the state to participate in the program established in this section.

4. A licensed pharmacy designated by the commissioner may be a disposal site under this section for the functions of accepting surrender of controlled substances from consumers, temporarily storing the controlled substances, and transferring the controlled substances to an authorized disposal site.

5. The commissioner shall make regulations under this section, including (in consultation with the commissioner of education) regulations relating to pharmacies in the program.

HISTORY: Add, L 2012, ch 447, § 1 (Part E), eff Aug 27, 2012; amd, L 2013, ch 343, § 1, eff Sept 27, 2014.

§ 3345. Possession of controlled substances by ultimate users original container

Except for the purpose of current use by the person or animal for whom such substance was prescribed or dispensed, it shall be unlawful for an ultimate user of controlled substances to possess such substance outside of the original container in which it was dispensed.

Violation of this provision shall be an offense punishable by a fine of not more than fifty dollars.

HISTORY: Add, L 1972, ch 878, § 2, eff April 1, 1973, with substance derived from former §§ 3331(1), 3386(1).

TITLE V   Dispensing to Addicts and Habitual Users

§ 3350.   **Dispensing prohibition**
§ 3351.   **Dispensing for medical use**
§ 3352.   **Reports and records**

HISTORY: Add, L 1972, ch 878, § 2, eff April 1, 1973. Former Title V, add, L 1953, ch 879, § 1; repealed, L 1972, ch 878, § 1, eff April 1, 1973.

§ 3350. Dispensing prohibition

Controlled substances may not be prescribed for, or administered or dispensed to addicts or habitual users of controlled substances, except as provided by this title or title III.

HISTORY: Add, L 1972, ch 878, § 2, eff April 1, 1973. Former § 3350, add, L 1953, ch 879, § 1, with substance derived from former §§ 421-a, 443; repealed, L 1972, ch 878, § 1, eff April 1, 1973.

§ 3351. Dispensing for medical use

1. Controlled substances may be prescribed for, or administered or dispensed to an addict or habitual user:

(a) during emergency medical treatment unrelated to abuse of controlled substances;

(b) who is a bona fide patient suffering from an incurable and fatal disease such as cancer or advanced tuberculosis;

(c) who is aged, infirm, or suffering from serious injury or illness and the withdrawal from controlled substances would endanger the life or impede or inhibit the recovery of such person.

2. Controlled substances may be ordered for use by an addict or habitual user by a practitioner and administered by a practitioner or registered nurse to relieve acute withdrawal symptoms.

3. Methadone, or such other controlled substance designated by the commissioner as appropriate for such use, may be ordered for use of an addict by a practitioner and dispensed or administered by a practitioner or his designated agent as interim treatment for an addict on a waiting list for admission to an authorized maintenance program.

4. Methadone, or such other controlled substance designated by the commissioner as appropriate for such use, may be administered to an addict by a practitioner or by his designated agent acting under the direction and supervision of a practitioner, as part of a regime designed and intended to withdraw a patient from addiction to controlled substances.

5. Methadone, or such other controlled substance designated by the commissioner as appropriate for such use, may be administered to an addict by a practitioner or by his designated agent acting under the direction and supervision of a practitioner, as part of a substance abuse or chemical dependence program approved pursuant to article twenty-three or thirty-two of the mental hygiene law.

HISTORY: Add, L 1972, ch 878, § 2, eff April 1, 1973. Former § 3351, add, L 1953, ch 879, § 1, with substance derived from former §§ 438, 442; amd, 1961, ch 884, § 9; repealed, L 1972, ch 878, § 1, eff April 1, 1973. Sub 5, add, L 1986, ch 433, § 2, eff July 21, 1986. Sub 5, amd, L 1999, ch 558, § 40, eff Oct 5, 1999.

§ 3352. Reports and records

Persons certified pursuant to article thirty-two of the mental hygiene law to operate methadone maintenance treatment programs shall keep records showing the receipt, administration, dispensing, or destruction of all controlled substances and documenting each incident or alleged incident involving the theft, loss or possible diversion of controlled substances and shall maintain the records in such manner and detail as the commissioner, by regulation, shall require.

A person certified to conduct a maintenance program shall immediately file a report with the department of each incident or alleged incident involving the theft, loss or possible diversion of controlled substances.

HISTORY: Add, L 1986, ch 433, § 4, eff July 21, 1986; amd, L 1999, ch 558, § 41, eff Oct 5, 1999, L 2010, ch 178, § 19, eff Jan 11, 2011.

HISTORY: Add, L 2014, ch 90, § 1, eff July 3, 2014, expires and repealed July 5, 2021.

§ 3360. [Expires and repealed July 5, 2021] Definitions

As used in this title, the following terms shall have the following meanings, unless the context clearly requires otherwise:

1. "Certified medical use" means the acquisition, possession, use, or, transportation of medical marihuana by a certified patient, or the acquisition, possession, delivery, transportation or administration of medical marihuana by a designated caregiver, for use as part of the treatment of the patient's serious condition, as authorized in a certification under this title including enabling the patient to tolerate treatment for the serious condition. A certified medical use does not include smoking.

2. "Caring for" means treating a patient, in the course of which the practitioner has completed a full assessment of the patient's medical history and current medical condition.

3. "Certified patient" means a patient who is a resident of New York state or receiving care and treatment in New York state as determined by the commissioner in regulation, and is certified under section thirty-three hundred sixty-one of this title.

4. "Certification" means a certification, made under section thirty-three hundred sixty-one of this title.

5. "Designated caregiver" means the individual designated by a certified patient in a registry application. A certified patient may designate up to two designated caregivers.

6. "Public place" means a public place as defined in regulation by the commissioner.

7. (a) "Serious condition" means:

(i) having one of the following severe debilitating or life-threatening conditions: cancer, positive status for human immunodeficiency virus or acquired immune deficiency syndrome, amyotrophic lateral sclerosis, Parkinson's disease, multiple sclerosis, damage to the nervous tissue of the spinal cord with objective neurological indication of intractable spasticity, epilepsy, inflammatory bowel disease, neuropathies, Huntington's disease, or as added by the commissioner; and

(ii) any of the following conditions where it is clinically associated with, or a complication of, a condition under this paragraph or its treatment: cachexia or wasting syndrome; severe or chronic pain; severe nausea; seizures; severe or persistent muscle spasms; or such conditions as are added by the commissioner.

(b) No later than eighteen months from the effective date of this section, the commissioner shall determine whether to add the following serious conditions: Alzheimer's, muscular dystrophy, dystonia, posttraumatic stress disorder and rheumatoid arthritis.

8. "Medical marihuana" means marihuana as defined in subdivision twenty-one of section thirty-three hundred two of this article, intended for a certified medical use, as determined by the commissioner in his or her sole discretion. Any form of medical marihuana not approved by the commissioner is expressly prohibited.

9. "Registered organization" means a registered organization under sections thirty-three hundred sixty-four and thirty-three hundred sixty-five of this title.

10. "Registry application" means an application properly completed and filed with the department by a certified patient under section thirty-three hundred sixty-three of this title.

11. "Registry identification card" means a document that identifies a certified patient or designated caregiver, as provided under section thirty-three hundred sixty-three of this title.

12. "Practitioner" means a practitioner who (i) is a physician licensed by New York state and practicing within the state, (ii) who by training or experience is qualified to treat a serious condition as defined in subdivision seven of this section; and (iii) has completed a two to four hour course as determined by the commissioner in regulation and registered with the department; provided however, a registration shall not be denied without cause. Such course may count toward board certification requirements. The commissioner shall consider the inclusion of nurse practitioners under this title based upon considerations including access and availability. After such consideration the commissioner is authorized to deem nurse practitioners as practitioners under this title.

13. "Terminally ill" means an individual has a medical prognosis that the individual's life expectancy is approximately one year or less if the illness runs its normal course.

14. "Labor peace agreement" means an agreement between an entity and a labor organization that, at a minimum, protects the state's proprietary interests by prohibiting labor organizations and members from engaging in picketing, work stoppages, boycotts, and any other economic interference with the registered organization's business.

15. "Individual dose" means a single measure of raw medical marihuana or non-infused concentrates to be determined and clearly identified by a patient's practitioner for the patient's specific certified condition. For ingestible or sub-lingual medical marihuana products, no individual dose may contain more than ten milligrams of tetrahydrocannabinol.

16. "Form of medical marihuana" means characteristics of the medical marihuana recommended or limited for a particular certified patient, including the method of consumption and

any particular strain, variety, and quantity or percentage of marihuana or particular active ingredient.

17. "Applicant" means a for-profit entity or not-for-profit corporation and includes: board members, officers, managers, owners, partners, principal stakeholders and members who submit an application to become a registered organization.

HISTORY: Add, L 2014, ch 90, § 1, eff July 3, 2014, expires and repealed July 5, 2021.

§ 3361. [Expires and repealed July 5, 2021] Certification of patients

1. A patient certification may only be issued if: (a) a practitioner has been registered with the department to issue a certification as determined by the commissioner; (b) the patient has a serious condition, which shall be specified in the patient's health care record; (c) the practitioner by training or experience is qualified to treat the serious condition; (d) the patient is under the practitioner's continuing care for the serious condition; and (e) in the practitioner's professional opinion and review of past treatments, the patient is likely to receive therapeutic or palliative benefit from the primary or adjunctive treatment with medical use of marihuana for the serious condition.

2. The certification shall include (a) the name, date of birth and address of the patient; (b) a statement that the patient has a serious condition and the patient is under the practitioner's care for the serious condition; (c) a statement attesting that all requirements of subdivision one of this section have been satisfied; (d) the date; and (e) the name, address, federal registration number, telephone number, and the handwritten signature of the certifying practitioner. The commissioner may require by regulation that the certification shall be on a form provided by the department. The practitioner may state in the certification that, in the practitioner's professional opinion, the patient would benefit from medical marihuana only until a specified date. The practitioner may state in the certification that, in the practitioner's professional opinion, the patient is terminally ill and that the certification shall not expire until the patient dies.

3. In making a certification, the practitioner shall consider the form of medical marihuana the patient should consume, including the method of consumption and any particular strain, variety, and quantity or percentage of marihuana or particular active ingredient, and appropriate dosage. The practitioner shall state in the certification any recommendation or limitation the practitioner makes, in his or her professional opinion, concerning the appropriate form or forms of medical marihuana and dosage.

4. Every practitioner shall consult the prescription monitoring drug program registry prior to making or issuing a certification, for the purpose of reviewing a patient's controlled substance history. For purposes of this section, a practitioner may authorize a designee to consult the prescription monitoring program registry on his or her behalf, provided that such designation is in accordance with section thirty-three hundred forty-three-a of this article.

5. The practitioner shall give the certification to the certified patient, and place a copy in the patient's health care record.

6. No practitioner shall issue a certification under this section for himself or herself.

7. A registry identification card based on a certification shall expire one year after the date the certification is signed by the practitioner.

8. (a) If the practitioner states in the certification that, in the practitioner's professional opinion, the patient would benefit from medical marihuana only until a specified earlier date, then the registry identification card shall expire on that date;

(b) If the practitioner states in the certification that in the practitioner's professional opinion the patient is terminally ill and that the certification shall not expire until the patient dies, then the registry identification card shall state that the patient is terminally ill and that the registration card shall not expire until the patient dies;

(c) If the practitioner re-issues the certification to terminate the certification on an earlier date, then the registry identification card shall expire on that date and shall be promptly returned by the certified patient to the department;

(d) If the certification so provides, the registry identification card shall state any recommendation or limitation by the practitioner as to the form or forms of medical marihuana or dosage for the certified patient; and

(e) The commissioner shall make regulations to implement this subdivision.

HISTORY: Add, L 2014, ch 90, § 1, eff July 3, 2014, expires and repealed July 5, 2021.

§ 3362. [Expires and repealed July 5, 2021] Lawful medical use

1. The possession, acquisition, use, delivery, transfer, transportation, or administration of medical marihuana by a certified patient or designated caregiver possessing a valid registry identification card, for certified medical use, shall be lawful under this title; provided that:

(a) the marihuana that may be possessed by a certified patient shall not exceed a thirty day supply of the dosage as determined by the practitioner, consistent with any guidance and regulations issued by the commissioner, provided that during the last seven days of any thirty day period, the certified patient may also possess up to such amount for the next thirty day period;

(b) the marihuana that may be possessed by designated caregivers does not exceed the quantities referred to in paragraph (a) of this subdivision for each certified patient for whom the caregiver possesses a valid registry identification card, up to five certified patients;

(c) the form or forms of medical marihuana that may be possessed by the certified patient or designated caregiver pursuant to a certification shall be in compliance with any recommendation or limitation by the practitioner as to the form or forms of medical marihuana or dosage for the certified patient in the certification; and

(d) the medical marihuana shall be kept in the original package in which it was dispensed under subdivision twelve of section thirty-three hundred sixty-four of this title, except for the portion removed for immediate consumption for certified medical use by the certified patient.

2. Notwithstanding subdivision one of this section:

(a) possession of medical marihuana shall not be lawful under this title if it is smoked, consumed, vaporized, or grown in a public place, regardless of the form of medical marihuana stated in the patient's certification.

(b) a person possessing medical marihuana under this title shall possess his or her registry identification card at all times when in immediate possession of medical marihuana.

HISTORY: Add, L 2014, ch 90, § 1, eff July 3, 2014, expires and repealed July 5, 2021.

§ 3363. [Expires and repealed July 5, 2021] Registry identification cards

1. Upon approval of the certification, the department shall issue registry identification cards for certified patients and designated caregivers. A registry identification card shall expire as provided

in section thirty-three hundred sixty-one of this title or as otherwise provided in this section. The department shall begin issuing registry identification cards as soon as practicable after the certifications required by section thirty-three hundred sixty-nine-b are granted. The department may specify a form for a registry application, in which case the department shall provide the form on request, reproductions of the form may be used, and the form shall be available for downloading from the department's website.

2. To obtain, amend or renew a registry identification card, a certified patient or designated caregiver shall file a registry application with the department. The registry application or renewal application shall include:

(a) in the case of a certified patient:

(i) the patient's certification (a new written certification shall be provided with a renewal application);

(ii) the name, address, and date of birth of the patient;

(iii) the date of the certification;

(iv) if the patient has a registry identification card based on a current valid certification, the registry identification number and expiration date of that registry identification card;

(v) the specified date until which the patient would benefit from medical marihuana, if the certification states such a date;

(vi) the name, address, federal registration number, and telephone number of the certifying practitioner;

(vii) any recommendation or limitation by the practitioner as to the form or forms of medical marihuana or dosage for the certified patient; and

(viii) other individual identifying information required by the department;

(b) in the case of a certified patient, if the patient designates a designated caregiver, the name, address, and date of birth of the designated caregiver, and other individual identifying information required by the department;

(c) in the case of a designated caregiver:

(i) the name, address, and date of birth of the designated caregiver;

(ii) if the designated caregiver has a registry identification card, the registry identification number and expiration date of that registry identification card; and

(iii) other individual identifying information required by the department;

(d) a statement that a false statement made in the application is punishable under section 210.45 of the penal law;

(e) the date of the application and the signature of the certified patient or designated caregiver, as the case may be;

(f) a fifty dollar application fee, provided, that the department may waive or reduce the fee in cases of financial hardship; and

(g) any other requirements determined by the commissioner.

3. Where a certified patient is under the age of eighteen:

(a) The application for a registry identification card shall be made by an appropriate person over twenty-one years of age. The application shall state facts demonstrating that the person is appropriate.

(b) The designated caregiver shall be (i) a parent or legal guardian of the certified patient, (ii) a person designated by a parent or legal guardian, or (iii) an appropriate person approved by the department upon a sufficient showing that no parent or legal guardian is appropriate or available.

4. No person may be a designated caregiver if the person is under twenty-one years of age unless a sufficient showing is made to the department that the person should be permitted to serve as a designated caregiver. The requirements for such a showing shall be determined by the commissioner.

5. No person may be a designated caregiver for more than five certified patients at one time.

6. If a certified patient wishes to change or terminate his or her designated caregiver, for whatever reason, the certified patient shall notify the department as soon as practicable. The department shall issue a notification to the designated caregiver that their registration card is invalid and must be promptly returned to the department. The newly designated caregiver must comply with all requirements set forth in this section.

7. If the certification so provides, the registry identification card shall contain any recommendation or limitation by the practitioner as to the form or forms of medical marihuana or dosage for the certified patient.

8. The department shall issue separate registry identification cards for certified patients and designated caregivers as soon as reasonably practicable after receiving a complete application under this section, unless it determines that the application is incomplete or factually inaccurate, in which case it shall promptly notify the applicant.

9. If the application of a certified patient designates an individual as a designated caregiver who is not authorized to be a designated caregiver, that portion of the application shall be denied by the department but that shall not affect the approval of the balance of the application.

10. A registry identification card shall:

(a) contain the name of the certified patient or the designated caregiver as the case may be;

(b) contain the date of issuance and expiration date of the registry identification card;

(c) contain a registry identification number for the certified patient or designated caregiver, as the case may be and a registry identification number;

(d) contain a photograph of the individual to whom the registry identification card is being issued, which shall be obtained by the department in a manner specified by the commissioner in regulations; provided, however, that if the department requires certified patients to submit photographs for this purpose, there shall be a reasonable accommodation of certified patients who are confined to their homes due to their medical conditions and may therefore have difficulty procuring photographs;

(e) be a secure document as determined by the department;

(f) plainly state any recommendation or limitation by the practitioner as to the form or forms of medical marihuana or dosage for the certified patient; and

(g) any other requirements determined by the commissioner.

11. A certified patient or designated caregiver who has been issued a registry identification card shall notify the department of any change in his or her name or address or, with respect to the patient, if he or she ceases to have the serious condition noted on the certification within ten days of such change. The certified patient's or designated caregiver's registry identification card shall be deemed invalid and shall be returned promptly to the department.

12. If a certified patient or designated caregiver loses his or her registry identification card, he or she shall notify the department and submit a twenty-five dollar fee within ten days of losing the card to maintain the registration. The department may establish higher fees for issuing a new registry identification card for second and subsequent replacements for a lost card, provided, that the department may waive or reduce the fee in cases of financial hardship. The department shall issue a new registry identification card as soon as practicable, which may contain a new registry identification number, to the certified patient or designated caregiver, as the case may be. The certified patient or designated caregiver shall not be able to obtain medical marihuana until the certified patient receives a new card.

13. The department shall maintain a confidential list of the persons to whom it has issued registry identification cards. Individual identifying information obtained by the department under this title shall be confidential and exempt from disclosure under article six of the public officers law. Notwithstanding this subdivision, the department may notify any appropriate law enforcement agency of information relating to any violation or suspected violation of this title.

14. The department shall verify to law enforcement personnel in an appropriate case whether a registry identification card is valid.

15. If a certified patient or designated caregiver willfully violates any provision of this title as determined by the department, his or her registry identification card may be suspended or revoked. This is in addition to any other penalty that may apply.

    HISTORY: Add, L 2014, ch 90, § 1, eff July 3, 2014, expires and repealed July 5, 2021.

§ 3364. [Expires and repealed July 5, 2021] Registered organizations

1. A registered organization shall be a for-profit business entity or not-for-profit corporation organized for the purpose of acquiring, possessing, manufacturing, selling, delivering, transporting, distributing or dispensing marihuana for certified medical use.

2. The acquiring, possession, manufacture, sale, delivery, transporting, distributing or dispensing of marihuana by a registered organization under this title in accordance with its registration under section thirty-three hundred sixty-five of this title or a renewal thereof shall be lawful under this title.

3. Each registered organization shall contract with an independent laboratory to test the medical marihuana produced by the registered organization. The commissioner shall approve the laboratory and require that the laboratory report testing results in a manner determined by the commissioner. The commissioner is authorized to issue regulation requiring the laboratory to perform certain tests and services.

4. (a) A registered organization may lawfully, in good faith, sell, deliver, distribute or dispense medical marihuana to a certified patient or designated caregiver upon presentation to the registered organization of a valid registry identification card for that certified patient or

designated caregiver. When presented with the registry identification card, the registered organization shall provide to the certified patient or designated caregiver a receipt, which shall state: the name, address, and registry identification number of the registered organization; the name and registry identification number of the certified patient and the designated caregiver (if any); the date the marihuana was sold; any recommendation or limitation by the practitioner as to the form or forms of medical marihuana or dosage for the certified patient; and the form and the quantity of medical marihuana sold. The registered organization shall retain a copy of the registry identification card and the receipt for six years.

(b) The proprietor of a registered organization shall file or cause to be filed any receipt and certification information with the department by electronic means on a real time basis as the commissioner shall require by regulation. When filing receipt and certification information electronically pursuant to this paragraph, the proprietor of the registered organization shall dispose of any electronically recorded prescription information in such manner as the commissioner shall by regulation require.

5. (a) No registered organization may sell, deliver, distribute or dispense to any certified patient or designated caregiver a quantity of medical marihuana larger than that individual would be allowed to possess under this title.

(b) When dispensing medical marihuana to a certified patient or designated caregiver, the registered organization (i) shall not dispense an amount greater than a thirty day supply to a certified patient until the certified patient has exhausted all but a seven day supply provided pursuant to a previously issued certification, and (ii) shall verify the information in subparagraph (i) of this paragraph by consulting the prescription monitoring program registry under section thirty-three hundred forty-three-a of this article.

(c) Medical marihuana dispensed to a certified patient or designated caregiver by a registered organization shall conform to any recommendation or limitation by the practitioner as to the form or forms of medical marihuana or dosage for the certified patient.

6. When a registered organization sells, delivers, distributes or dispenses medical marihuana to a certified patient or designated caregiver, it shall provide to that individual a safety insert, which will be developed and approved by the commissioner and include, but not be limited to, information on:

(a) methods for administering medical marihuana in individual doses,

(b) any potential dangers stemming from the use of medical marihuana,

(c) how to recognize what may be problematic usage of medical marihuana and obtain appropriate services or treatment for problematic usage, and

(d) other information as determined by the commissioner.

7. Registered organizations shall not be managed by or employ anyone who has been convicted of any felony of sale or possession of drugs, narcotics, or controlled substances provided that this subdivision only applies to (a) managers or employees who come into contact with or handle medical marihuana, and (b) a conviction less than ten years (not counting time spent in incarceration) prior to being employed, for which the person has not received a certificate of relief from disabilities or a certificate of good conduct under article twenty-three of the correction law.

8. Manufacturing of medical marihuana by a registered organization shall only be done in an indoor, enclosed, secure facility located in New York state, which may include a greenhouse. The

commissioner shall promulgate regulations establishing requirements for such facilities.

9. Dispensing of medical marihuana by a registered organization shall only be done in an indoor, enclosed, secure facility located in New York state, which may include a greenhouse. The commissioner shall promulgate regulations establishing requirements for such facilities.

10. A registered organization shall determine the quality, safety, and clinical strength of medical marihuana manufactured or dispensed by the registered organization, and shall provide documentation of that quality, safety and clinical strength to the department and to any person or entity to which the medical marihuana is sold or dispensed.

11. A registered organization shall be deemed to be a "health care provider" for the purposes of title two-D of article two of this chapter.

12. Medical marihuana shall be dispensed to a certified patient or designated caregiver in a sealed and properly labeled package. The labeling shall contain: (a) the information required to be included in the receipt provided to the certified patient or designated caregiver by the registered organization; (b) the packaging date; (c) any applicable date by which the medical marihuana should be used; (d) a warning stating, "This product is for medicinal use only. Women should not consume during pregnancy or while breastfeeding except on the advice of the certifying health care practitioner, and in the case of breastfeeding mothers, including the infant's pediatrician. This product might impair the ability to drive. Keep out of reach of children."; (e) the amount of individual doses contained within; and (f) a warning that the medical marihuana must be kept in the original container in which it was dispensed.

13. The commissioner is authorized to make rules and regulations restricting the advertising and marketing of medical marihuana, which shall be consistent with the federal regulations governing prescription drug advertising and marketing.

　　HISTORY: Add, L 2014, ch 90, § 1, eff July 3, 2014, expires and repealed July 5, 2021.

§ 3365. [Expires and repealed July 5, 2021] Registering of registered organizations

1. Application for initial registration.

　(a) An applicant for registration as a registered organization under section thirty-three hundred sixty-four of this title shall include such information prepared in such manner and detail as the commissioner may require, including but not limited to:

　　(i) a description of the activities in which it intends to engage as a registered organization;

　　(ii) that the applicant:

　　　(A) is of good moral character;

　　　(B) possesses or has the right to use sufficient land, buildings, and other premises (which shall be specified in the application) and equipment to properly carry on the activity described in the application, or in the alternative posts a bond of not less than two million dollars;

　　　(C) is able to maintain effective security and control to prevent diversion, abuse, and other illegal conduct relating to the marihuana;

　　　(D) is able to comply with all applicable state laws and regulations relating to the activities in which it intends to engage under the registration;

　　(iii) that the applicant has entered into a labor peace agreement with a bona-fide labor organization that is actively engaged in representing or attempting to represent the applicant's employees. The maintenance of such a labor peace agreement shall be an ongoing material condition of certification.

(iv) the applicant's status under subdivision one of section thirty-three hundred sixty-four of this title; and

(v) the application shall include the name, residence address and title of each of the officers and directors and the name and residence address of any person or entity that is a member of the applicant. Each such person, if an individual, or lawful representative if a legal entity, shall submit an affidavit with the application setting forth:

(A) any position of management or ownership during the preceding ten years of a ten per centum or greater interest in any other business, located in or outside this state, manufacturing or distributing drugs;

(B) whether such person or any such business has been convicted of a felony or had a registration or license suspended or revoked in any administrative or judicial proceeding; and

(C) such other information as the commissioner may reasonably require.

2. Duty to report. The applicant shall be under a continuing duty to report to the department any change in facts or circumstances reflected in the application or any newly discovered or occurring fact or circumstance which is required to be included in the application.

3. Granting of registration.

(a) The commissioner shall grant a registration or amendment to a registration under this section if he or she is satisfied that:

(i) the applicant will be able to maintain effective control against diversion of marihuana;

(ii) the applicant will be able to comply with all applicable state laws;

(iii) the applicant and its officers are ready, willing and able to properly carry on the manufacturing or distributing activity for which a registration is sought;

(iv) the applicant possesses or has the right to use sufficient land, buildings and equipment to properly carry on the activity described in the application;

(v) it is in the public interest that such registration be granted; the commissioner may consider whether the number of registered organizations in an area will be adequate or excessive to reasonably serve the area;

(vi) the applicant and its managing officers are of good moral character;

(vii) the applicant has entered into a labor peace agreement with a bona-fide labor organization that is actively engaged in representing or attempting to represent the applicant's employees; and

(viii) the applicant satisfies any other conditions as determined by the commissioner.

(b) If the commissioner is not satisfied that the applicant should be issued a registration, he or she shall notify the applicant in writing of those factors upon which further evidence is required. Within thirty days of the receipt of such notification, the applicant may submit additional material to the commissioner or demand a hearing, or both.

(c) The fee for a registration under this section shall be a reasonable amount determined by the department in regulations; provided, however, if the registration is issued for a period greater than two years the fee shall be increased, pro rata, for each additional month of validity.

(d) Registrations issued under this section shall be effective only for the registered organization and shall specify:

(i) the name and address of the registered organization;

(ii) which activities of a registered organization are permitted by the registration;

(iii) the land, buildings and facilities that may be used for the permitted activities of the registered organization; and

(iv) such other information as the commissioner shall reasonably provide to assure compliance with this title.

(e) Upon application of a registered organization, a registration may be amended to allow the registered organization to relocate within the state or to add or delete permitted registered organization activities or facilities. The fee for such amendment shall be two hundred fifty dollars.

4. A registration issued under this section shall be valid for two years from the date of issue, except that in order to facilitate the renewals of such registrations, the commissioner may upon the initial application for a registration, issue some registrations which may remain valid for a period of time greater than two years but not exceeding an additional eleven months.

5. Applications for renewal of registrations.

(a) An application for the renewal of any registration issued under this section shall be filed with the department not more than six months nor less than four months prior to the expiration thereof. A late-filed application for the renewal of a registration may, in the discretion of the commissioner, be treated as an application for an initial license.

(b) The application for renewal shall include such information prepared in the manner and detail as the commissioner may require, including but not limited to:

(i) any material change in the circumstances or factors listed in subdivision one of this section; and

(ii) every known charge or investigation, pending or concluded during the period of the registration, by any governmental or administrative agency with respect to:

(A) each incident or alleged incident involving the theft, loss, or possible diversion of marihuana manufactured or distributed by the applicant; and

(B) compliance by the applicant with the laws of the state with respect to any substance listed in section thirty-three hundred six of this article.

(c) An applicant for renewal shall be under a continuing duty to report to the department any change in facts or circumstances reflected in the application or any newly discovered or occurring fact or circumstance which is required to be included in the application.

(d) If the commissioner is not satisfied that the applicant is entitled to a renewal of the registration, he or she shall within a reasonably practicable time as determined by the commissioner, serve upon the applicant or his or her attorney of record in person or by registered or certified mail an order directing the applicant to show cause why his or her application for renewal should not be denied. The order shall specify in detail the respects in which the applicant has not satisfied the commissioner that the registration should be renewed.

(e) Within a reasonably practicable time as determined by the commissioner of such order, the applicant may submit additional material to the commissioner or demand a hearing or both. If a hearing is demanded the commissioner shall fix a date as soon as reasonably practicable.

6. Granting of renewal of registrations.

(a) The commissioner shall renew a registration unless he or she determines and finds that:

(i) the applicant is unlikely to maintain or be able to maintain effective control against diversion; or

(ii) the applicant is unlikely to comply with all state laws applicable to the activities in which it may engage under the registration; or

(iii) it is not in the public interest to renew the registration because the number of registered organizations in an area is excessive to reasonably serve the area; or

(iv) the applicant has either violated or terminated its labor peace agreement.

(b) For purposes of this section, proof that a registered organization, during the period of its registration, has failed to maintain effective control against diversion, violates any provision of this article, or has knowingly or negligently failed to comply with applicable state laws relating to the activities in which it engages under the registration, shall constitute grounds for suspension or termination of the registered organization's registration as determined by the commissioner. The registered organization shall also be under a continuing duty to report to the department any material change or fact or circumstance to the information provided in the registered organization's application.

7. The department may suspend or terminate the registration of a registered organization, on grounds and using procedures under this article relating to a license, to the extent consistent with this title. The department shall suspend or terminate the registration in the event that a registered organization violates or terminates the applicable labor peace agreement. Conduct in compliance with this title which may violate conflicting federal law, shall not be grounds to suspend or terminate a registration.

8. The department shall begin issuing registrations for registered organizations as soon as practicable after the certifications required by section thirty-three hundred sixty-nine-b of this title are given.

9. The commissioner shall register no more than five registered organizations that manufacture medical marihuana with no more than four dispensing sites wholly owned and operated by such registered organization. The commissioner shall ensure that such registered organizations and dispensing sites are geographically distributed across the state. The commission may register additional registered organizations.

HISTORY: Add, L 2014, ch 90, § 1, eff July 3, 2014, expires and repealed July 5, 2021.

§ 3366. [Expires and repealed July 5, 2021] Reports by registered organizations

1. The commissioner shall, by regulation, require each registered organization to file reports by the registered organization during a particular period. The commissioner shall determine the information to be reported and the forms, time, and manner of the reporting.

2. The commissioner shall, by regulation, require each registered organization to adopt and

maintain security, tracking, record keeping, record retention and surveillance systems, relating to all medical marihuana at every stage of acquiring, possession, manufacture, sale, delivery, transporting, distributing, or dispensing by the registered organization, subject to regulations of the commissioner.

HISTORY: Add, L 2014, ch 90, § 1, eff July 3, 2014, expires and repealed July 5, 2021.

§ 3367. [Expires and repealed July 5, 2021] Evaluation; research programs; report by department

1. The commissioner may provide for the analysis and evaluation of the operation of this title. The commissioner may enter into agreements with one or more persons, not-for-profit corporations or other organizations, for the performance of an evaluation of the implementation and effectiveness of this title.

2. The department may develop, seek any necessary federal approval for, and carry out research programs relating to medical use of marihuana. Participation in any such research program shall be voluntary on the part of practitioners, patients, and designated caregivers.

3. The department shall report every two years, beginning two years after the effective date of this title, to the governor and the legislature on the medical use of marihuana under this title and make appropriate recommendations.

HISTORY: Add, L 2014, ch 90, § 1, eff July 3, 2014, expires and repealed July 5, 2021.

§ 3368. [Expires and repealed July 5, 2021] Relation to other laws

1. (a) The provisions of this article shall apply to this title, except that where a provision of this title conflicts with another provision of this article, this title shall apply.

(b) Medical marihuana shall not be deemed to be a "drug" for purposes of article one hundred thirty-seven of the education law.

2. Nothing in this title shall be construed to require an insurer or health plan under this chapter or the insurance law to provide coverage for medical marihuana. Nothing in this title shall be construed to require coverage for medical marihuana under article twenty-five of this chapter or article five of the social services law.

HISTORY: Add, L 2014, ch 90, § 1, eff July 3, 2014, expires and repealed July 5, 2021.

§ 3369. [Expires and repealed July 5, 2021] Protections for the medical use of marihuana

1. Certified patients, designated caregivers, practitioners, registered organizations and the employees of registered organizations shall not be subject to arrest, prosecution, or penalty in any manner, or denied any right or privilege, including but not limited to civil penalty or disciplinary action by a business or occupational or professional licensing board or bureau, solely for the certified medical use or manufacture of marihuana, or for any other action or conduct in accordance with this title.

2. Non-discrimination. Being a certified patient shall be deemed to be having a "disability" under article fifteen of the executive law (human rights law), section forty-c of the civil rights law, sections 240.00, 485.00, and 485.05 of the penal law, and section 200.50 of the criminal procedure law. This subdivision shall not bar the enforcement of a policy prohibiting an employee from performing his or her employment duties while impaired by a controlled substance. This subdivision shall not require any person or entity to do any act that would put the person or entity in violation of federal law or cause it to lose a federal contract or funding.

3. The fact that a person is a certified patient and/or acting in accordance with this title, shall not be a consideration in a proceeding pursuant to applicable sections of the domestic relations law, the social services law and the family court act.

4. Certification applications, certification forms, any certified patient information contained within a database, and copies of registry identification cards shall be deemed exempt from public disclosure under sections eighty-seven and eighty-nine of the public officers law.

HISTORY: Add, L 2014, ch 90, § 1, eff July 3, 2014, expires and repealed July 5, 2021.

§ 3369-a. [Expires and repealed July 5, 2021] Regulations

The commissioner shall make regulations to implement this title.

HISTORY: Add, L 2014, ch 90, § 1, eff July 3, 2014, expires and repealed July 5, 2021.

§ 3369-b. [Expires and repealed July 5, 2021] Effective date

Registry identification cards or registered organization registrations shall be issued or become effective no later than eighteen months from signing or until such time as the commissioner and the superintendent of state police certify that this title can be implemented in accordance with public health and safety interests, whichever event comes later.

HISTORY: Add, L 2014, ch 90, § 1, eff July 3, 2014, expires and repealed July 5, 2021.

§ 3369-c. [Expires and repealed July 5, 2021] Suspend; terminate

Based upon the recommendation of the commissioner and/or the superintendent of state police that there is a risk to the public health or safety, the governor may immediately terminate all licenses issued to registered organizations.

HISTORY: Add, L 2014, ch 90, § 1, eff July 3, 2014, expires and repealed July 5, 2021.

§ 3369-d. [Expires and repealed July 5, 2021] Pricing

1. Every sale of medical marihuana shall be at the price determined by the commissioner. Every charge made or demanded for medical marihuana not in accordance with the price determined by the commissioner, is prohibited.

2. The commissioner is hereby authorized to set the per dose price of each form of medical marihuana sold by any registered organization. In setting the per dose price of each form of medical marihuana, the commissioner shall consider the fixed and variable costs of producing the form of marihuana and any other factor the commissioner, in his or her discretion, deems relevant to determining the per dose price of each form of medical marihuana.

HISTORY: Add, L 2014, ch 90, § 1, eff July 3, 2014, expires and repealed July 5, 2021.

§ 3369-e. [Expires and repealed July 5, 2021] Severability

If any clause, sentence, paragraph, section or part of this act shall be adjudged by any court of competent jurisdiction to be invalid, the judgment shall not affect, impair, or invalidate the remainder thereof, but shall be confined in its operation to the clause, sentence, paragraph, section or part thereof directly involved in the controversy in which the judgment shall have been rendered.

HISTORY: Add, L 2014, ch 90, § 1, eff July 3, 2014, expires and repealed July 5, 2021.

TITLE VI　Records and Reports

HISTORY: Add, L 1972, ch 878, § 2, eff April 1, 1973. Former Title VI, add, L 1953, ch 879, § 1; repealed, L 1972, ch 878, § 1, eff April 1, 1973.

§ 3370. Preserving and inspection of records

1. Any record, including prescriptions, required to be kept or maintained by this article shall be preserved for a period of at least five years following the date of the event or transaction recorded, unless a shorter period of time is specifically provided.

2. Such records shall be made available during business hours for inspection and copying by any officer or employee of the department who is charged with the enforcement of this article and to any officer or employee of this state charged with the duty of regulating or licensing of any person who by virtue of such license is authorized to obtain, distribute, dispense or administer controlled substances.

3. Every record, including prescriptions, required to be kept under this article shall be maintained at the premises where the licensed activity is conducted.

4. The department shall cause to be expunged or otherwise destroyed, within five years from the date of receipt thereof, any record of the name of any patient received by it pursuant to the filing requirements of subdivision six of section thirty-three hundred thirty-one, subdivision four of section thirty-three hundred thirty-three, and subdivision four of section thirty-three hundred thirty-four of this article.

5. Electronic prescription records shall be maintained and preserved in accordance with regulations of the commissioner.

HISTORY: Add, L 1972, ch 878, § 2, eff April 1, 1973, with substance derived from former §§ 3333(8), (9), 3388(7); amd, L 1974, ch 58, § 1, eff March 12, 1974, L 1974, ch 965, § 16, eff July 13, 1974, L 2010, ch 178, § 9, eff July 15, 2010.

§ 3371. Confidentiality of certain records, reports, and information

1. No person, who has knowledge by virtue of his or her office of the identity of a particular patient or research subject, a manufacturing process, a trade secret or a formula shall disclose such knowledge, or any report or record thereof, except:

(a) to another person employed by the department, for purposes of executing provisions of this article;

(b) pursuant to judicial subpoena or court order in a criminal investigation or proceeding;

(c) to an agency, department of government, or official board authorized to regulate, license or otherwise supervise a person who is authorized by this article to deal in controlled substances, or in the course of any investigation or proceeding by or before such agency, department or board;

(d) to the prescription monitoring program registry and to authorized users of such registry as set forth in subdivision two of this section;

(e) to a practitioner to inform him or her that a patient may be under treatment with a controlled substance by another practitioner for the purposes of subdivision two of this section, and to facilitate the department's review of individual challenges to the accuracy of controlled substances histories pursuant to subdivision six of section thirty-three hundred forty-three-a of this article;

(f) to a pharmacist to provide information regarding prescriptions for controlled substances presented to the pharmacist for the purposes of subdivision two of this section and to facilitate the department's review of individual challenges to the accuracy of controlled substances histories pursuant to subdivision six of section thirty-three hundred forty-three-a of this article;

(g) to the deputy attorney general for medicaid fraud control, or his or her designee, in furtherance of an investigation of fraud, waste or abuse of the Medicaid program, pursuant to an agreement with the department;

(h) to a local health department for the purpose of conducting public health research or education: (i) pursuant to an agreement with the commissioner; (ii) when the release of such information is deemed appropriate by the commissioner; (iii) for use in accordance with measures required by the commissioner to ensure that the security and confidentiality of the data is protected; and (iv) provided that disclosure is restricted to individuals within the local health department who are engaged in the research or education;

(i) to a medical examiner or coroner who is an officer of or employed by a state or local government, pursuant to his or her official duties; and

(j) to an individual for the purpose of providing such individual with his or her own controlled substance history or, in appropriate circumstances, in the case of a patient who lacks capacity to make health care decisions, a person who has legal authority to make such decisions for the patient and who would have legal access to the patient's health care records, if requested from the department pursuant to subdivision six of section thirty-three hundred forty-three-a of this article or from a treating practitioner pursuant to subparagraph (iv) of paragraph (a) of subdivision two of this section.

2. *[Until July 5, 2021, sub 2, reads as set out below]*

The prescription monitoring program registry may be accessed, under such terms and conditions as are established by the department for purposes of maintaining the security and confidentiality of the information contained in the registry, by:

(a) a practitioner, or a designee authorized by such practitioner pursuant to paragraph (b) of subdivision two of section thirty-three hundred forty-three-a or section thirty-three hundred sixty-one of this article, for the purposes of: (i) informing the practitioner that a patient may be under treatment with a controlled substance by another practitioner; (ii) providing the practitioner with notifications of controlled substance activity as deemed relevant by the department, including but not limited to a notification made available on a monthly or other periodic basis through the registry of controlled substances activity pertaining to his or her patient; (iii) allowing the practitioner, through consultation of the prescription monitoring program registry, to review his or her patient's controlled substances history as required by section thirty-three hundred forty-three-a or section thirty-three hundred sixty-one of this article; and (iv) providing to his or her patient, or person authorized pursuant to paragraph (j) of subdivision one of this section, upon request, a copy of such patient's controlled substance history as is available to the practitioner through the prescription monitoring program registry; or

(b) a pharmacist, pharmacy intern or other designee authorized by the pharmacist pursuant to paragraph (b) of subdivision three of section thirty-three hundred forty-three-a of this article, for the purposes of: (i) consulting the prescription monitoring program registry to review the controlled substances history of an individual for whom one or more prescriptions for controlled substances or certifications for marihuana is presented to the pharmacist, pursuant to section thirty-three hundred forty-three-a of this article; and (ii) receiving from the department such notifications of controlled substance activity as are made available by the department; or

(c) an individual employed by a registered organization for the purpose of consulting the prescription monitoring program registry to review the controlled substances history of an individual for whom one or more certifications for marihuana is presented to that registered organization, pursuant to section thirty-three hundred sixty-four of this article. Unless otherwise authorized by this article, an individual employed by a registered organization will be provided access to the prescription monitoring program in the sole discretion of the commissioner.

2. *[Eff July 5, 2021, sub 2, reads as set out below]*

The prescription monitoring program registry may be accessed, under such terms and conditions as are established by the department for purposes of maintaining the security and confidentiality of the information contained in the registry, by:

(a) a practitioner, or a designee authorized by such practitioner pursuant to paragraph (b) of subdivision two of section thirty-three hundred forty-three-a of this article, for the purposes of: (i) informing the practitioner that a patient may be under treatment with a controlled substance by another practitioner; (ii) providing the practitioner with notifications of controlled substance activity as deemed relevant by the department, including but not limited to a notification made available on a monthly or other periodic basis through the registry of controlled substances activity pertaining to his or her patient; (iii) allowing the practitioner, through consultation of the prescription monitoring program registry, to review his or her patient's controlled substances history as required by section thirty-three hundred forty-three-a of this article; and (iv) providing to his or her patient, or person authorized pursuant to paragraph (j) of subdivision one of this section, upon request, a copy of such patient's controlled substance history as is available to the practitioner through the prescription monitoring program registry; or

(b) a pharmacist, pharmacy intern or other designee authorized by the pharmacist pursuant to paragraph (b) of subdivision three of section thirty-three hundred forty-three-a of this article, for the purposes of: (i) consulting the prescription monitoring program registry to review the controlled substances history of an individual for whom one or more prescriptions for controlled substances is presented to the pharmacist, pursuant to section thirty-three hundred forty-three-a of this article; and (ii) receiving from the department such notifications of controlled substance activity as are made available by the department.

3. Where it has reason to believe that a crime related to the diversion of controlled substances has been committed, the department may notify appropriate law enforcement agencies and provide relevant information about the suspected criminal activity, including controlled substances prescribed or dispensed, as reasonably appears to be necessary. The department shall keep a record of the information provided, including, but not limited to: the specific information provided and the agency to which such information was provided, including the name and title of the person to whom such information was provided and an attestation from such person that he or she has authority to receive such information.

4. In the course of any proceeding where such information is disclosed, except when necessary to effectuate the rights of a party to the proceeding, the court or presiding officer shall take such action as is necessary to insure that such information, or record or report of such information is not made public.

> **HISTORY:** Add, L 1972, ch 878, § 2, eff April 1, 1973, with substance derived from former §§ 3334, 3389(2); amd, L 1973, ch 163, § 19, eff April 1, 1973, L 1974, ch 965, § 17, eff July 13, 1974, L 2004, ch 58, § 15 (Part A), eff Oct 20, 2004, L 2010, ch 178, § 4, eff July 15, 2010, L 2012, ch 447, §§ 4, 5 (Part A), eff Aug 27, 2013, L 2014, ch 90, § 3, eff July 3, 2014, expires and repealed July 5, 2021.

§ 3371-a. Disclosure of certain records, reports, and information to another state

1. The commissioner is authorized to disclose records, reports and information filed pursuant to sections thirty-three hundred thirty-one and thirty-three hundred thirty-three of this article:

    (a) to another state's controlled substance monitoring program or other authorized agency with which the department has established an interoperability agreement, pursuant to judicial subpoena or court order in a criminal investigation or proceeding in that state;

    (b) to another state's agency, department, or board with which the department has established an interoperability agreement and which is authorized to regulate, license, register or otherwise supervise a person who is authorized by law to deal in controlled substances, in the course of any investigation or proceeding by or before such agency, department or board;

    (c) to another state's controlled substance monitoring program or other authorized agency with which the department has established an interoperability agreement to inform a practitioner in another state that a patient may be under treatment with a controlled substance by another practitioner; or

    (d) to another state's controlled substance monitoring program or other authorized agency with which the department has established an interoperability agreement to inform a pharmacy in another state that a person who presents or has presented a prescription for one or more controlled substances at the pharmacy may have also obtained controlled substances at another pharmacy where the circumstances indicate a possibility of drug abuse or diversion, potential harm to the person, or similar grounds under regulations of the commissioner.

2. Records, reports, and information disclosed under the provisions of this section shall be in accordance with regulations promulgated by the commissioner and shall include, but not be limited to:

    (a) the authentication of the person requesting such information;

    (b) an attestation from the person requesting the information that he or she has authority to request and receive such information, and that such information will only be used consistent with the purpose of the request for such information;

    (c) a statement of the purpose of the request for such information; and

    (d) ensuring that such information is, or will be, transmitted in a secure manner.

3. Every agreement under subdivision one of this section shall:

    (a) require reciprocity with the department on the part of every other party to the agreement;

    (b) guarantee protection for the confidentiality of information disclosed at least as strong as the protections that would apply to the information when in the possession of the department, including remedies for breaches of confidentiality; and

(c) be subject to renewal not less frequently than every two years.

HISTORY: Add, L 2010, ch 178, § 5, eff July 15, 2010.

§ 3372. Practitioner patient reporting

It shall be the duty of every attending practitioner and every consulting practitioner to report promptly to the commissioner, or his duly designated agent, the name and, if possible, the address of, and such other data as may be required by the commissioner with respect to, any person under treatment if he finds that such person is an addict or a habitual user of any narcotic drug. Such report shall be kept confidential and may be utilized only for statistical, epidemiological or research purposes, except that those reports which originate in the course of a criminal proceeding other than under section 81.25 of the mental hygiene law* .shall be subject only to the confidentiality requirements of section thirty-three hundred seventy-one of this article.

HISTORY: Add, L 1972, ch 878, § 2, with substance derived from former § 3344; amd, L 1973, ch 195, § 39, eff April 25, 1973. Former § 3372, add, L 1965, ch 323, § 1; repealed, L 1972, ch 878, § 1, eff April 1, 1973. See now § 3308(2). Another § 3372, add, L 1965, ch 1031, § 174, with substance derived from former Penal § 1747-e; repealed, L 1967, ch 680, § 111, eff Sept 1, 1967.

§ 3373. Confidential communications

For the purposes of duties arising out of this article, no communication made to a practitioner shall be deemed confidential within the meaning of the civil practice law and rules relating to confidential communications between such practitioner and patient.

HISTORY: Add, L 1972, ch 878, § 2, eff April 1, 1973, with substance derived from former §§ 3304(2), 3334(3), 3389(3). Former § 3373, add, L 1965, ch 323, § 1; repealed, L 1972, ch 878, § 1, eff April 1, 1973. See now § 3304.

§ 3374. Notification by licensee

Persons licensed or certified pursuant to this article shall be under a continuing duty to promptly notify the department of:

1. Each incident or alleged incident of theft, loss or possible diversion of controlled substances manufactured, ordered, distributed or possessed by such person;

2. Any charge or proceeding brought in any court or before any governmental agency, state or federal, in which it is alleged that the licensee, its employees, subsidiaries, managing officers, or directors has failed to comply with the provisions of the federal controlled substances act or the laws of any state relating to controlled substances.

HISTORY: Add, L 1972, ch 878, § 2, eff April 1, 1973. Former § 3374, add, L 1966, ch 868, § 1; repealed, L 1972, ch 878, § 1, eff April 1, 1973. See now § 3307.

---

* Renumbered § 23.11, L 1977, ch 978, § 15; repealed, L 1980, ch 471, § 10, eff July 23, 1980.

TITLE VII   Offenses, Violations and Enforcement

HISTORY: Add, L 1972, ch 878, § 2, eff April 1, 1973. Former Title VII, add, L 1953, ch 879, § 1; repealed, L 1968, ch 373, § 1, eff May 31, 1968.

§ 3380. Inhalation of certain toxic vapors or fumes, and certain hazardous inhalants; sale of glue and hazardous inhalants in certain cases

1. (a) As used in this section the phrase "glue containing a solvent having the property of releasing toxic vapors or fumes" shall mean and include any glue, cement, or other adhesive containing one or more of the following chemical compounds: acetone, cellulose acetate, benzene, butyl alcohol, ethyl alcohol, ethylene dichloride, ethylene trichloride, isopropyl alcohol, methyl alcohol, methyl ethyl ketone, pentachlorophenol, petroleum ether, toluene or such other similar material as the commissioner shall by regulation prescribe.

(b) As used in this section hazardous inhalants shall mean and include any of the preparations of compounds containing one or more of the chemical compounds; amyl nitrite, isoamyl nitrite, butyl nitrite, isobutyl nitrite, pentyl nitrite or any other akyl nitrite compound that is either designed to be used, or commonly used, as an inhalant.

2. No person shall, for the purpose of causing a condition of intoxication, inebriation, excitement, stupefaction, or the dulling of his brain or nervous system, intentionally smell or inhale the fumes from any hazardous inhalants or from any glue containing a solvent having the property of releasing toxic vapors or fumes; provided, that nothing in this section shall be interpreted as applying to the inhalation of any anesthesia or inhalant for medical or dental purposes.

3. No person shall, for the purpose of violating subdivision two, use, or possess for the purpose of so using, any hazardous inhalants or any glue containing a solvent having the property of releasing toxic vapors or fumes.

4. No person shall sell, or offer to sell, to any other person any tube or other container of any

hazardous inhalants or glue containing a solvent having the property of releasing toxic vapors or fumes:

(a) if he has knowledge that the product sold, or offered for sale, will be used for the purpose set forth in subdivision two of this section; or

(b) unless there has been added to such glue a sufficient quantity of an additive, approved by the commission, which shall act as a deterrent to inhalation, and not be harmful or toxic to the human body. This provision shall not apply to hazardous inhalants or glue manufactured and sold for industrial use.

5. (a) No person shall use nitrous oxide for purposes of causing intoxication, inebriation, excitement, stupefaction or the dulling of the brain or nervous system of himself or another.

(b) No person shall sell any canister or other container of nitrous oxide unless granted an exemption pursuant to this subdivision. In no event shall any canister or other container of nitrous oxide be sold to a person under the age of twenty-one years.

(c) This subdivision shall not apply to the use of nitrous oxide in industrial, medical or dental applications, or to specific products which must use nitrous oxide as a propellant provided such products shall in no event be sold at retail to the public, as shall be determined by the commissioner pursuant to paragraph (d) of this subdivision.

(d) The commissioner is directed to promulgate regulations to exempt specific products which must use nitrous oxide, or a mixture of nitrous oxide with other gases, as a propellant from the provisions of this chapter provided such regulations shall prohibit the sale of such products at retail to the public.

(e) The provisions of this section shall not be deemed to prohibit the sale of food products containing nitrous oxide provided such products comply with the provisions of section sixteen-a of the agriculture and markets law.

(f) The commissioner may, upon the application of a manufacturer or seller of a product containing nitrous oxide and intended for sale at retail, authorize the sale of such a product if there is no evidence of substantial misuse of the product as defined by this subdivision and if the manufacturer or seller takes the following steps to:

(i) clearly indicate the legitimate purpose or use of the product on the package;

(ii) display prominently on the package in heavy type print language which warns of health dangers resulting from the misuse of nitrous oxide;

(iii) demonstrate that the product bears a distinctive feature or features enabling it to be clearly distinguished from the nitrous oxide products of other manufacturers;

(iv) educate wholesale and retail businesses which sell the product of the dangers of nitrous oxide and the need to monitor its sale; and

(v) prevent their sale of the product to any person, firm or corporation who or which sells drug-related paraphernalia as such term is defined by subdivision two of section eight hundred fifty of the general business law.

6. (a) Any person who violates any provision of subdivision two or three of this section shall be guilty of an offense and upon conviction thereof shall be punished by a fine of not more than fifty dollars or by imprisonment for not more than five days, or by both such fine and imprisonment.

(b) Any person who violates any provision of subdivision four or five of this section shall be guilty of a class A misdemeanor.

HISTORY: Add, L 1972, ch 878, § 2, with substance derived from former § 3396; amd, L 1985, ch 234, § 1, eff Aug 17, 1985. Former § 3380, add, L 1965, ch 323, § 1; amd, L 1966, ch 868, § 3; repealed, L 1972, ch 878, § 1, eff April 1, 1973. Section heading, amd, L 1985, ch 234, § 1, eff Aug 17, 1985. Sub 1, par (b), add, L 1985, ch 234, § 1, eff Aug 17, 1985. Sub 4, amd, L 1972, ch 880, § 1, eff April 1, 1973. Sub 5, add, L 1982, ch 771, § 2; amd, L 1989, ch 667, § 1, eff Nov 1, 1989. Former sub 5, renumbered sub 6, L 1982, ch 771, § 1, eff Jan 1, 1983. Sub 5, par (b), amd, L 1989, ch 667, § 1, L 1990, ch 551, § 2, eff July 18, 1990. Sub 5, par (c), amd, L 1989, ch 667, § 1, eff Nov 1, 1989. Sub 5, par (d), amd, L 1989, ch 667, § 1, eff Nov 1, 1989. Sub 5, par (e), add, L 1989, ch 667, § 1, eff Nov 1, 1989. Sub 5, par (f), add, L 1989, ch 667, § 1; amd, L 1990, ch 551, § 1, eff July 18, 1990. Sub 5, par (f), subpars (i)–(v), add, L 1990, ch 551, § 1, eff July 18, 1990. Sub 6, formerly sub 5, so renumbered and amd, L 1982, ch 771, § 1, eff Jan 1, 1983.

§ 3381. Sale and possession of hypodermic syringes and hypodermic needles

1. It shall be unlawful for any person to sell or furnish to another person or persons, a hypodermic syringe or hypodermic needle except:

(a) pursuant to a prescription of a practitioner, which for the purposes of this section shall include a patient specific prescription form as provided for in the education law; or

(b) to persons who have been authorized by the commissioner to obtain and possess such instruments; or

(c) by a pharmacy licensed under article one hundred thirty-seven of the education law, health care facility licensed under article twenty-eight of this chapter or a health care practitioner who is otherwise authorized to prescribe the use of hypodermic needles or syringes within his or her scope of practice; provided, however, that such sale or furnishing: (i) shall only be to a person eighteen years of age or older; (ii) shall be limited to a quantity of ten or less hypodermic needles or syringes; and (iii) shall be in accordance with subdivision five of this section.

2. It shall be unlawful for any person to obtain or possess a hypodermic syringe or hypodermic needle unless such possession has been authorized by the commissioner or is pursuant to a prescription, or is pursuant to subdivision five of this section.

3. Any person selling or furnishing a hypodermic syringe or hypodermic needle pursuant to a prescription shall record upon the prescription, his or her signature or electronic signature, and the date of the sale or furnishing of the hypodermic syringe or hypodermic needle. Such prescription shall be retained on file for a period of five years and be readily accessible for inspection by any public officer or employee engaged in the enforcement of this section. Such prescription may be refilled not more than the number of times specifically authorized by the prescriber upon the prescription, provided however no such authorization shall be effective for a period greater than two years from the date the prescription is signed.

4. The commissioner shall, subject to subdivision five of this section, designate persons, or by regulation, classes of persons who may obtain hypodermic syringes and hypodermic needles without prescription and the manner in which such transactions may take place and the records thereof which shall be maintained.

5. (a) A person eighteen years of age or older may obtain and possess a hypodermic syringe or hypodermic needle pursuant to paragraph (c) of subdivision one of this section.

(b) Subject to regulations of the commissioner, a pharmacy licensed under article one hundred thirty-seven of the education law, a health care facility licensed under article twenty-eight of this chapter or a health care practitioner who is otherwise authorized to prescribe the use of hypodermic needles or syringes within his or her scope of practice, may obtain and possess hypodermic needles or syringes for the purpose of selling or furnishing them pursuant to paragraph (c) of subdivision one of this section or for the purpose of disposing of them, provided that such pharmacy, health care facility or health care practitioner has registered with the department.

(c) Sale or furnishing of hypodermic syringes or hypodermic needles to direct consumers pursuant to this subdivision by a pharmacy, health care facility, or health care practitioner shall be accompanied by a safety insert. Such safety insert shall be developed or approved by the commissioner and shall include, but not be limited to, (i) information on the proper use of hypodermic syringes and hypodermic needles; (ii) the risk of blood borne diseases that may result from the use of hypodermic syringes and hypodermic needles; (iii) methods for preventing the transmission or contraction of blood borne diseases; (iv) proper hypodermic syringe and hypodermic needle disposal practices; (v) information on the dangers of injection drug use, and how to access drug treatment; (vi) a toll-free phone number for information on the human immunodeficiency virus; and (vii) information on the safe disposal of hypodermic syringes and hypodermic needles including the relevant provisions of the environmental conservation law relating to the unlawful release of regulated medical waste. The safety insert shall be attached to or included in the hypodermic syringe and hypodermic needle packaging, or shall be given to the purchaser at the point of sale or furnishing in brochure form.

(d) In addition to the requirements of paragraph (c) of subdivision one of this section, a pharmacy licensed under article one hundred thirty-seven of the education law may sell or furnish hypodermic needles or syringes only if such pharmacy: (i) does not advertise to the public the availability for retail sale or furnishing of hypodermic needles or syringes without a prescription; and (ii) at any location where hypodermic needles or syringes are kept for retail sale or furnishing, stores such needles and syringes in a manner that makes them available only to authorized personnel and not openly available to customers.

(e) The commissioner shall promulgate rules and regulations necessary to implement the provisions of this subdivision which shall include a requirement that such pharmacies, health care facilities and health care practitioners cooperate in a safe disposal of used hypodermic needles or syringes.

(f) The commissioner may, upon the finding of a violation of this section, suspend for a determinate period of time the sale or furnishing of syringes by a specific entity.

6. The provisions of this section shall not apply to farmers engaged in livestock production or to those persons supplying farmers engaged in livestock production, provided that:

(a) Hypodermic syringes and needles shall be stored in a secure, locked storage container.

(b) At any time the department may request a document outlining:

(i) the number of hypodermic needles and syringes purchased over the past calendar year;

(ii) a record of all hypodermic needles used over the past calendar year; and

(iii) a record of all hypodermic needles and syringes destroyed over the past calendar year.

(c) Hypodermic needles and syringes shall be destroyed in a manner consistent with the provisions set forth in section thirty-three hundred eighty-one-a of this article.

7. [Redesignated]

HISTORY: Add, L 1972, ch 878, § 2, eff April 1, 1973, with substance derived from former § 3395; amd, L 1973, ch 163, § 20, eff April 1, 1973, L 1996, ch 639, § 121, eff Sept 12, 1996, deemed eff on and after July 1, 1996, L 2000, ch 56, § 1 (Part G), eff Jan 1, 2001, L 2002, ch 668, § 1, eff Dec 9, 2002, L 2007, ch 58, § 9-a (Part B), eff April 9, 2007, deemed eff on and after April 1, 2007, L 2010, ch 178, § 12, eff July 15, 2010.

§ 3381-a. Destruction of hypodermic syringes and needles

All hypodermic syringes, needles and disposable hypodermic units which are no longer usable or required shall be crushed, broken or otherwise rendered inoperable in the process of disposal.

The department may specify procedures for disposal of such hypodermic syringes, needles and disposable units as may be necessary to protect public health including, but not limited to, placement of such syringes, needles and units in a leak-proof, puncture resistant container prior to disposal.

HISTORY: Add, L 1980, ch 429, § 1; amd, L 1985, ch 220, § 1, L 1990, ch 861, § 2, eff July 25, 1990, expired and repealed eff Aug 1, 1994. First unnumbered par, formerly sub 1, so designated, L 1990, ch 861, § 2, eff July 25, 1990, expired and repealed eff Aug 1, 1994. Second unnumbered par, formerly sub 2, so designated, L 1990, ch 861, § 2, eff July 25, 1990, expired and repealed eff Aug 1, 1994. Sub 3, add, L 1990, ch 861, § 2, eff July 25, 1990, expired and repealed eff Aug 1, 1994; amd, L 1992, ch 184, § 1, eff June 16, 1992.

§ 3382. Growing of the plant known as Cannabis by unlicensed person

A person who, without being licensed so to do under this article, grows the plant of the genus Cannabis or knowingly allows it to grow on his land without destroying the same, shall be guilty of a class A misdemeanor.

HISTORY: Add, L 1972, ch 878, § 2, eff April 1, 1973, with substance derived from former § 3315. Former § 3382, add, L 1965, ch 323, § 1; repealed, L 1972, ch 878, § 1, eff April 1, 1973.

§ 3383. Imitation controlled substances

1. For purposes of this section, the following terms shall have the following meanings:

a. "Manufacture" means the production, preparation, compounding, tableting, processing, encapsulating, packaging, repackaging, labeling or relabeling of an imitation controlled substance.

b. "Markings" means a simulated trademark, trade name, imprinting or other mark, or likeness thereof, of the manufacturer, distributor or dispenser of a controlled substance or a simulated code number or symbol or likeness thereof identifying a controlled substance or combination of such substances.

c. "Imitation controlled substance" means a substance, other than a drug for which a prescription is required pursuant to article one hundred thirty-seven of the education law, that is not a controlled substance, which by dosage unit appearance, including color, shape and size and by a representation is represented to be a controlled substance, as defined in the penal law. Evidence of representations that the substance is a controlled substance may include but is not limited to oral or written representations by the manufacturer or seller, as the case may be, about the substance with regard to:

(i) its price, nature, use or effect as a controlled substance; or

(ii) its packaging in a manner normally used for illicit controlled substances; or

(iii) markings on the substance.

2. It shall be unlawful for any person to manufacture, sell or possess with the intent to sell, an imitation controlled substance.

3. It shall be unlawful for any person to possess or use any punch, die, plate, stone or any other equipment in order to print, imprint, or reproduce the trademark, trade name or other identifying mark, imprint or device of another or any likeness of any of the foregoing upon any substance or container or labeling thereof with intent to manufacture an imitation controlled substance.

4. No liability shall be imposed by virtue of this section on any person licensed pursuant to article one hundred thirty-one of the education law or licensed under this article who manufactures, distributed [distributes],* sells, prescribes, dispenses or possesses an imitation controlled substance for use as a placebo or for use in clinical research conducted pursuant to the federal food, drug and cosmetic act.

5. Nothing in this section shall apply to a noncontrolled substance that was initially introduced into commerce prior to the initial introduction into commerce of the controlled substance which it is alleged to imitate.

6. In any prosecution under this section it shall be necessary to prove that the imitation controlled substance was represented to be a controlled substance; however, it shall not be a defense to a prosecution under this section that the accused believed the imitation controlled substance to be a controlled substance.

7. A violation of subdivision two or three of this section shall be a class A misdemeanor. A violation of subdivision two or three of this section by a person previously convicted of a violation of this section within the preceding five years shall be a class E felony.

8. If any provision or part of this section or application thereof is held invalid, the invalidity shall not affect other provisions, parts or applications of this section which can be given effect without the invalid provisions or application, and to this end the provisions of this section are severable.

> **HISTORY:** Add, L 1982, ch 494, § 1, eff Sept 1, 1982. Former § 3383 add, L 1965, ch 323, § 1; amd, L 1966, ch 868, §§ 5, 6; repealed, L 1972, ch 878, § 1, eff April 1, 1973. See now §§ 3331(4), 3333(2).

§ 3384. Information program for retailers

The department shall develop and maintain a program to inform retailers about the methamphetamine problem in New York state.

> **HISTORY:** Add, L 2005, ch 394, § 11, eff Nov 1, 2005.

§ 3385. Enforcement

1. (a) The department and its representatives shall have access during business hours to all orders, prescriptions or records required to be kept under this article.

(b) Orders, prescriptions and records required to be kept under this article shall be maintained at the premises where the licensed activity is conducted.

2. For the purposes of enforcing the provisions of this article, each employee of the department designated by the commissioner shall possess all of the powers of a peace officer as set forth in section 2.20 of the criminal procedure law.

> **HISTORY:** Add, L 1972, ch 878, § 2, eff April 1, 1973, with substance derived from former

---

*   The bracketed word has been inserted by Publisher.

§§ 3350(1), (2), 3390(1), (2). Former § 3385, add, L 1965, ch 323, § 1; repealed, L 1972, ch 878, § 1, eff April 1, 1973. See now §§ 3305(3), 3331(2), (3). Sub 1, par (a), formerly entire sub 1, so designated and amd, L 1974, ch 58, § 2, eff March 12, 1974. Sub 1, par (b), add, L 1974, ch 58, § 2, eff March 12, 1974. Sub 2, amd, L 1980, ch 843, § 140, eff Sept 1, 1980.

§ 3385-a. Access to criminal history information

Upon such terms and conditions as the commissioner of the division of criminal justice services agrees, authorized employees of the department's bureau of narcotic enforcement, designated by the commissioner pursuant to subdivision two of section three thousand three hundred eighty-five of this title, may access criminal history information in the central data facility established pursuant to subdivision six of section eight hundred thirty-seven of the executive law upon request to the director of the bureau of narcotic enforcement demonstrating the necessity for such access as part of an identified, ongoing criminal investigation. Any information obtained as a result of such access shall not be disseminated to persons not authorized to access such criminal history information.

HISTORY: Add, L 2014, ch 35, § 1, eff June 23, 2014.

§ 3387. Seizure and forfeiture of controlled substances, imitation controlled substances and official New York state prescription forms; disposition

1. Any controlled substance or imitation controlled substance which has been manufactured, distributed, dispensed or acquired in violation of this article, or the lawful possession of which cannot be immediately ascertained, and any official New York state prescription form which has been printed, distributed or acquired in violation of this article or the lawful possession of which cannot be immediately ascertained are hereby declared to be public nuisances and may be seized by a peace officer, acting pursuant to his special duties, or a police officer and shall be forfeited, and disposed of as follows:

(a) except as in this section otherwise provided, the commissioner, the court or magistrate having jurisdiction shall order such controlled substance or imitation controlled substance forfeited or destroyed. A record of the quantity and nature of the substance, of the place where said substance was seized, and of the time, place and manner of destruction, shall be kept, and a return under oath, reporting said destruction, shall be made to the person ordering such destruction by the officer who destroys them;

(b) upon written application by the commissioner, the court or magistrate by whom the forfeiture of controlled substances or imitation controlled substances has been decreed may order the delivery of any of them, except substances listed in schedule I of section thirty-three hundred six, to such commissioner for distribution or destruction, as hereinafter provided;

(c) upon application by any hospital within this state, not operated for private gain, the commissioner may in his discretion deliver any controlled substance or imitation controlled substance that has come into his custody by authority of this section to the applicants for medicinal use;

(d) the commissioner may from time to time deliver excess stocks of controlled substances or imitation controlled substances to the Bureau or shall destroy the same;

(e) controlled substances or imitation controlled substances which are excess or undesired by persons lawfully possessing the same may be disposed of in such manner as the commissioner shall by regulation require;

(f) official New York state prescription forms which have been seized as provided by this section shall be disposed of by express prepaid shipment to the "State Department of Health,

Bureau of Prescription Analysis, Albany, New York," or by delivery to an authorized narcotic control representative of the department.

2. The commissioner shall keep a full and complete record of all controlled substances or imitation controlled substances received and of all controlled substances or imitation controlled substances disposed of, showing the exact kinds, quantities and forms of such substances; the persons from whom received and to whom delivered; by whose authority received, delivered and destroyed; and the dates of the receipt, disposal or destruction. This record shall be open to inspection by all federal or state officers charged with the enforcement of federal and state laws relating to controlled substances or imitation controlled substances.

3. Any raw material product, container or equipment of any kind which is used, or intended for use, in manufacturing, distributing, dispensing or administering a controlled substance or imitation controlled substance in violation of this article shall be seized by any peace officer, acting pursuant to his special duties, or police officer and forfeited in the same manner as property subject to seizure and forfeiture pursuant to section thirty-three hundred eighty-eight of this article, except that such property shall not be retained for use by any official.

HISTORY: Add, L 1972, ch 878, § 2, with substance derived from former §§ 3352, 3392; amd, L 1982, ch 494, § 2, eff Sept 1, 1982. Former § 3387, add, L 1965, ch 323, § 1; amd, L 1966, ch 868, § 7; repealed, L 1972, ch 878, § 1, eff April 1, 1973. See now § 3305(1). Section heading, amd, L 1981, ch 547, § 3, L 1982, ch 494, § 2, eff Sept 1, 1982. Sub 1, amd, L 1981, ch 547, § 3, eff Sept 1, 1981. Sub 1, opening par, amd, L 1980, ch 843, § 141, eff Sept 1, 1980. Sub 1, par (f), add, L 1981, ch 547, § 3, eff Aug 14, 1981. Sub 3, amd, L 1980, ch 843, § 142, eff Sept 1, 1980. Sub 1, par (e), amd, L 1998, ch 537, § 12, eff Nov 1, 1998.

§ 3388. Seizure and forfeiture of vehicles, vessels or aircraft unlawfully used to conceal, convey or transport controlled substances

1. Except as authorized in this article, it shall be unlawful to:

(a) transport, carry, or convey any controlled substance in, upon, or by means of any vehicle, vessel or aircraft; or

(b) conceal or possess any controlled substance in or upon any vehicle, vessel or aircraft, or upon the person of anyone in or upon any vehicle, vessel or aircraft; or

(c) use any vehicle, vessel or aircraft to facilitate the transportation, carriage, conveyance, concealment, receipt, possession, purchase, or sale of any controlled substance.

2. Any vehicle, vessel or aircraft which has been or is being used in violation of subdivision one, except a vehicle, vessel or aircraft used by any person as a common carrier in the transaction of business as such common carrier shall be seized by any peace officer, acting pursuant to his special duties, or police officer, and forfeited as hereinafter in this section provided. A vehicle, vessel or aircraft is not subject to forfeiture unless used in connection with acts or conduct which would constitute a felony under article 220 of the penal law.

3. The seized property shall be delivered by the officer having made the seizure to the custody of the district attorney of the county wherein the seizure was made, except that in the cities of New York, Yonkers, Rochester and Buffalo the seized property shall be delivered to the custody of the police department of such cities and such property seized by a member or members of the state police shall be delivered to the custody of the superintendent of state police, together with a report of all the facts and circumstances of the seizure.

4. It shall be the duty of the attorney general in seizures by members of the state police, otherwise it shall be the duty of the district attorney of the county wherein the seizure is made, if

elsewhere than in the cities of New York, Yonkers, Rochester or Buffalo, and where the seizure is made in such cities it shall be the duty of the corporation counsel of the city, to inquire into the facts of the seizure so reported to him and if it appears probable that a forfeiture has been incurred by reason of a violation of this section, for the determination of which the institution of proceedings in the supreme court is necessary, to cause the proper proceedings to be commenced and prosecuted, not later than twenty days after written demand by a person claiming ownership thereof, to declare such forfeiture, unless, upon inquiry and examination, such district attorney, attorney general or corporation counsel decides that such proceedings cannot probably be sustained or that the ends of public justice do not require that they should be instituted or prosecuted, in which case, the district attorney, the attorney general or corporation counsel shall cause such seized property to be returned to the owner thereof. The procedure for proceedings instituted under this section shall conform as much as possible to the procedure for attachment.

5. Notice of the institution of the forfeiture proceeding shall be served either:

(a) personally on the owners of the seized property; or

(b) by registered mail to the owners' last known address and by publication of the notice once a week for two successive weeks in a newspaper published or circulated in the county wherein the seizure was made.

6. Forfeiture shall not be adjudged where the owners establish by preponderance of the evidence that:

(a) the use of such seized property, in violation of subdivision one of this section, was not intentional on the part of any owner; or

(b) said seized property was used in violation of subdivision one of this section by any person other than an owner thereof, while such seized property was unlawfully in the possession of a person who acquired possession thereof in violation of the criminal laws of the United States, or of any state.

7. The district attorney, the superintendent of state police or the police department having custody of the seized property, after such judicial determination of forfeiture, shall, at their discretion, either retain such seized property for the official use of their office, division or department, or, by a public notice of at least five days, sell such forfeited property at public sale; provided, however, that where such property is subject to a perfected lien such property may not be retained for their official use unless all such liens on the property to be retained have been or will be satisfied. The net proceeds of any such sale, after deduction of the lawful expenses incurred, shall be paid into the general fund of the county wherein the seizure was made except that the net proceeds of the sale of property seized in the cities of New York, Yonkers, Rochester and Buffalo shall be paid into the respective general funds of such cities, and of the sale of property seized by the state police into the general fund of the state.

8. Whenever any person interested in any property which is seized and declared forfeited under the provisions of this section files with a justice of the supreme court a petition for the recovery of such forfeited property, the justice of the supreme court may restore said forfeited property upon such terms and conditions as he deems reasonable and just, if the petitioner establishes either of the affirmative defenses set forth in subdivision six of this section and that the petitioner was without personal or actual knowledge of the forfeiture proceeding. If the petition be filed after the sale of the forfeited property, any judgment in favor of the petitioner shall be limited to the net proceeds of such sale, after deduction of the lawful expenses and costs incurred by the district attorney, police department or corporation counsel.

9. No suit or action under this section for wrongful seizure shall be instituted unless such suit or action is commenced within two years after the time when the property was seized.

HISTORY: Add, L 1972, ch 878, § 2, eff April 1, 1973, with substance derived from former § 3353. Former § 3388, add, L 1965, ch 323, § 1; amd, L 1966, ch 868, §§ 8, 9; repealed, L 1972, ch 878, § 1, eff April 1, 1973. See now §§ 3322, 3333(4), 3342(1), 3343, 3370. Sub 2, amd, L 1980, ch 843, § 143, eff Sept 1, 1980. Sub 3, amd, L 1980, ch 843, § 143, L 1984, ch 717, § 1, L 1985, ch 621, § 1, L 1986, ch 419, § 1, eff July 21, 1986. Sub 4, amd, L 1984, ch 717, § 2, L 1985, ch 621, § 1, L 1986, ch 419, § 1, L 1987, ch 527, § 1, eff July 30, 1987. Sub 7, amd, L 1984, ch 717, § 3, L 1985, ch 621, § 1, L 1990, ch 655, § 18, eff Nov 1, 1990.

§ 3390. Revocation of licenses and certificates of approval

Any license or certificate of approval granted pursuant to this article may be revoked by the commissioner in whole or in part upon a finding that the licensee or certificate holder has:

1. falsified any application, report, or record required by this article;

2. wilfully failed to furnish the department with timely reports or information required to be filed with the department;

3. been convicted of an offense in any jurisdiction relating to any substance listed in this article as a controlled substance;

4. wilfully or negligently failed to comply with any of the provisions of the federal controlled substances act, this article, or the regulations promulgated thereunder;

5. failed to maintain effective control against diversion of controlled substances; or

6. wilfully and unreasonably refused to permit an inspection authorized by this article.

HISTORY: Add, L 1972, ch 878, § 2, eff April 1, 1973, with substance derived from former §§ 3313, 3378. Former § 3390, add, L 1965, ch 323, § 1; repealed, L 1972, ch 878, § 1, eff April 1, 1973. See now § 3385(1), (2).

§ 3391. Revocation and suspension of license or certificate of approval procedure

1. A proceeding to revoke a license or certificate of approval shall be commenced by a notice served personally or by registered or certified mail upon the licensee or holder of a certificate of approval directing him to show cause why his license or certificate should not be revoked. Such notice shall set forth in detail the grounds for the proposed revocation and shall fix a date for hearing not less than fifteen nor more than thirty days from the date of such notice.

2. Simultaneous with the commencement of a proceeding to revoke a license or certificate or during the course of such proceeding, the commissioner may in the case of a clear and imminent danger to the public health or safety forthwith suspend without prior notice any license or certificate theretofore issued.

3. If the commissioner suspends or revokes a license or certificate, all controlled substances owned or possessed by the licensee or holder of a certificate of approval and in the state of New York at the time of the suspension or the effective date of the revocation and which such licensee or holder of a certificate of approval is no longer authorized to possess, shall be seized or placed under seal in the manner provided in this article.

4. In lieu of revocation of a license or certificate, the commissioner may impose a civil penalty not in excess of ten thousand dollars. Such penalty may be imposed in lieu of revocation only if the commissioner is satisfied that the imposition and payment of such penalty will serve as a sufficient deterrent to future violations.

HISTORY: Add, L 1972, ch 878, § 2, eff April 1, 1973. Former § 3391, add, L 1965, ch 323, § 1; repealed, L 1972, ch 878, § 1, eff April 1, 1973.

§ 3393. Formal hearings procedure

1. The commissioner or any person designated by him for this purpose, shall have the power to administer oaths, compel the attendance of witnesses and the production of books, records and documents and to take proof and testimony concerning all matters within the jurisdiction of the department.

2. Notice of hearing shall be served at least fifteen days prior to the date of the hearing, provided, however, whenever the commissioner has made a preliminary order suspending a license or directing the cessation of any activity pending the hearing, the commissioner shall provide the person affected thereby with an opportunity to be heard within five days.

3. At a hearing any person who is a party thereto may appear personally, shall have the right of counsel, and may cross-examine witnesses and produce evidence and witnesses in his own behalf.

4. Following a hearing, the commissioner shall make appropriate findings of fact and determinations and shall issue an order in accordance therewith.

5. The person conducting the hearing shall not be bound by the rules of evidence but any determination must be founded upon sufficient legal evidence to sustain it.

6. The commissioner may adopt such rules and regulations governing the procedures to be followed with respect to the hearings as may be consistent with the fair and effective administration of this article.

7. Any notice, application, order or other paper required to be served upon any party to a proceeding hereunder may be served in person, by registered mail or by certified mail upon either the party or an attorney who has appeared on his behalf.

HISTORY: Add, L 1972, ch 878, § 2, eff April 1, 1973. Former § 3393, add, L 1965, ch 323, § 1; amd, L 1971, ch 386, § 2; repealed, L 1972, ch 878, § 1, eff April 1, 1973. See now § 3396.

§ 3394. Judicial review

1. All orders or determinations hereunder shall be subject to judicial review as provided in article seventy-eight of the civil practice law and rules. In any such proceeding findings of fact made by the commissioner, if supported by substantial evidence, shall be conclusive.

2. Application for such review must be made within sixty days after service of the order or determination upon the person whose license, certificate, right or privilege is affected thereby or upon the attorney of record for such person.

3. An order, or the enforcement of an order revoking or suspending a license or revoking or cancelling official forms issued by the department, if accompanied by a finding of a clear and imminent danger to the public health or safety, may not be temporarily stayed or restrained prior to a determination on the merits of the application for judicial review.

HISTORY: Add, L 1972, ch 878, § 2, eff April 1, 1973.

§ 3396. Violations; penalties

1. In any civil, criminal or administrative action or proceeding brought for the enforcement of any provision of this article, it shall not be necessary to negate or disprove any exception, excuse, proviso or exemption contained in this article, and the burden of proof of any such exception, excuse, proviso, or exemption shall be upon the person claiming its benefit.

2. Violation of any provision of this article for which a penalty is specifically provided herein shall be punishable as provided herein. Violation of any provision of this article for which no penalty is provided herein shall be punishable as provided in section twelve-b of article one of this chapter or in the penal law.

3. No person shall be prosecuted for a violation of any provision of this article if such person has been acquitted or convicted under the federal controlled substances act, of the same act or omission which, it is alleged, constitutes a violation of this article.

4. Upon the conviction of any person for violating any provision of this article, a copy of the judgment and sentence, and of the opinion of the court or judge, if any opinion be filed, shall be sent by the clerk of the court, or by the judge, to the board or officer, if any, by whom the convicted defendant has been licensed or registered to practice his profession, or to carry on his business.

5. Upon the imposition of any penalty, warning, reprimand or other sanction against any person for violating any provision of this article, a copy of the order, finding or opinion, if any is made or rendered, shall be sent by the person authorized by law to make such determination, to the board or officer by whom the respondent is licensed or registered to practice a profession or to carry on a business.

HISTORY: Add, L 1972, ch 878, § 2, eff April 1, 1973, with substance derived from former §§ 3354, 3393. Former § 3396, add, L 1967, ch 680, § 112, with substance derived from former Penal Law § 1747-f; amd, L 1968, ch 357, § 1, L 1971, ch 341, § 1, L 1972, ch 127, § 1, L 1972, ch 969, § 1; repealed, L 1972, ch 878, § 1, eff April 1, 1973. See now § 3380. Sub 1, amd, L 1973, ch 163, § 21, L 1974, ch 965, § 18, eff July 13, 1974.

§ 3397. Fraud and deceit

1. No person shall:

(a) obtain or attempt to obtain a controlled substance, a prescription for a controlled substance or an official New York State prescription form,

(i) by fraud, deceit, misrepresentation or subterfuge; or

(ii) by the concealment of a material fact; or

(iii) by the use of a false name or the giving of a false address;

(b) wilfully make a false statement in any prescription, order, application, report or record required by this article;

(c) falsely assume the title of, or represent himself to be a licensed manufacturer, distributor, pharmacy, pharmacist, practitioner, researcher, approved institutional dispenser, owner or employee of a registered outsourcing facility or other authorized person, for the purpose of obtaining a controlled substance;

(d) make or utter any false or forged prescription or false or forged written order;

(e) affix any false or forged label to a package or receptacle containing controlled substances; or

(f) imprint on or affix to any controlled substance a false or forged code number or symbol.

2. Possession of a false or forged prescription for a controlled substance by any person other than a pharmacist in the lawful pursuance of his profession shall be presumptive evidence of his intent to use the same for the purpose of illegally obtaining a controlled substance.

3. Possession of a blank official New York state prescription form by any person to whom it was not lawfully issued shall be presumptive evidence of such person's intent to use same for the purpose of illegally obtaining a controlled substance.

4. Any person who, in the course of treatment, is supplied with a controlled substance or a prescription therefor by one practitioner and who, without disclosing the fact, is supplied during such treatment with a controlled substance or a prescription therefor by another practitioner shall be guilty of a violation of this article.

HISTORY: Add, L 1973, ch 163, § 22; amd, L 1981, ch 547, § 4, eff Sept 1, 1981, L 2014, ch 60, § 18 (Part D), eff June 29, 2014.

SELECTED SECTIONS
OF THE
VEHICLE AND TRAFFIC LAW

TITLE I   Words and Phrases Defined
ARTICLE 1
WORDS AND PHRASES DEFINED

HISTORY: Add, L 1959, ch 775, eff Oct 1, 1960, with substance transferred from former Title II.

ARTICLE 1   WORDS AND PHRASES DEFINED
(Selected Section)

§ 155.   **Traffic infraction**

HISTORY: Add, L 1959, ch 775, eff Oct 1, 1960, with substance transferred from former Arts 1 and 10.

§ 155. Traffic infraction

The violation of any provision of this chapter, except articles forty-seven and forty-eight, or of any law, ordinance, order, rule or regulation regulating traffic which is not declared by this chapter or other law of this state to be a misdemeanor or a felony. A traffic infraction is not a crime and the punishment imposed therefor shall not be deemed for any purpose a penal or criminal punishment and shall not affect or impair the credibility as a witness or otherwise of any person convicted thereof. This definition shall be retroactive and shall apply to all acts and violations heretofore committed where such acts and violations would, if committed subsequent to the taking effect of this section, be included within the meaning of the term "traffic infraction" as herein defined. Except in those portions of Suffolk county for which a district court has been established, outside of cities having a population in excess of two hundred thousand in which administrative tribunals have heretofore been established, courts and judicial officers heretofore having jurisdiction over such violations shall continue to do so and for such purpose such violations shall be deemed misdemeanors and all provisions of law relating to misdemeanors except as provided in section eighteen hundred five of this chapter and except as herein otherwise expressly provided shall apply except that no jury trial shall be allowed for traffic infractions. In those portions of Suffolk county for which a district court has been established, and in cities having a population in excess of two hundred thousand in which administrative tribunals have heretofore been established, the criminal courts of such cities or portions of Suffolk county in which a district court has been established shall have jurisdiction to hear and determine any complaint alleging a violation constituting a traffic infraction, except that administrative tribunals heretofore established in such cities or portions of Suffolk county in which a district court has been established shall have jurisdiction to hear and determine any charge of an offense which is a traffic infraction, except parking, standing or stopping. In cities having a population in excess of two hundred thousand in which administrative tribunals have heretofore been established, and any such administrative tribunal established by the city of Yonkers, the city of Peekskill, or the city of Syracuse, such tribunals shall have jurisdiction to hear and determine any charge of an offense which is a parking, standing or stopping violation. Any fine imposed by an administrative tribunal shall be a civil penalty. For purposes of arrest without a warrant, pursuant to article one hundred forty of the criminal procedure law, a traffic infraction shall be deemed an offense.

HISTORY: Add, L 1959, ch 775, with substance transferred from former § 155; amd, L 1962, ch 698, § 37, L 1969, ch 1075, § 1, L 1970, ch 337, § 1, L 1971, ch 1097, § 128, L 1972, ch 359, § 1, L 1972, ch 715, § 1, L 1973, ch 379, § 1, L 1973, ch 839, § 2, L 1976, ch 675, § 1, L 1978, ch 536, § 1, L 1981, ch 44, § 1, L 1990, ch 519, § 1, eff July 18, 1990. Amd, L 1993, ch 287, § 1, eff July 21, 1993, L 2002, ch 628, § 1, eff Oct 9, 2002.

TITLE III   Safety Responsibility; Financial Security; Equipment; Inspection; Size and Weight; and Other Provisions

ARTICLE 12
OTHER PROVISIONS

HISTORY: Add, L 1959, ch 775, eff Oct 1, 1960, with substance transferred from former Arts 6-A and 6-B.

ARTICLE 12   OTHER PROVISIONS
(Selected Sections)

HISTORY: Add, L 1959, ch 775, eff Oct 1, 1960.

§ 392. False statements, alteration of records or substitution in connection with any examination

Any person knowingly making a false statement in an application for any document issued by the commissioner or in any proof or statement in writing in connection with such an application, or who shall deceive or substitute or cause another to deceive or substitute in connection with any examination hereunder, or who shall wilfully alter a number plate (except for restoration purposes pursuant to schedule G of subdivision seven of section four hundred one of this chapter), or make a material alteration on any document issued pursuant to this chapter, or unlawfully use a validating device on a certificate of registration, license or any other form, shall be guilty of a misdemeanor. A person who operates a motor vehicle upon the public highway displaying or using any document that he or she knows has been obtained in violation of this section, shall be guilty of a misdemeanor. Nothing contained in this section shall prohibit the imposition of a charge of any other offense set forth in this chapter or any other provision of law for any acts arising out of the same incident.

HISTORY: Add, L 1959, ch 775, with substance transferred from former § 70(8); amd, L 1960, ch 300, § 1, L 1978, ch 40, § 1, eff Sept 1, 1978. Amd, L 1994, ch 307, § 1, eff Sept 18, 1994, L 2004, ch 710, § 1, eff Nov 16, 2004.

§ 392-a. Sale or purchase of stolen, false or fraudulent license, identification card, certificate of registration, or number plate

A person who knowingly sells or offers to sell or buys or offers to buy a false, fraudulent or stolen license, identification card, certificate of registration or number plate, shall be guilty of a misdemeanor as a first offense and a class E felony as a second or subsequent offense committed within ten years of the prior offense.

HISTORY: Add, L 1966, ch 532, § 1; amd, L 1975, ch 154, § 10, L 1981, ch 569, § 8, eff Sept 1, 1982. Amd, L 1994, ch 307, § 2, eff Sept 18, 1994.

§ 397. Equipping motor vehicles with radio receiving sets capable of receiving signals on the frequencies allocated for police use

A person, not a police officer or peace officer, acting pursuant to his special duties, who equips a motor vehicle with a radio receiving set capable of receiving signals on the frequencies allocated for police use or knowingly uses a motor vehicle so equipped or who in any way knowingly interferes with the transmission of radio messages by the police without having first secured a permit so to do from the person authorized to issue such a permit by the local governing body or board of the city, town or village in which such person resides, or where such person resides outside of a city or village in a county having a county police department by the board of supervisors of such county, is guilty of a misdemeanor, punishable by a fine not exceeding one thousand dollars, or imprisonment not exceeding six months, or both. Nothing in this section contained shall be construed to apply to any person who holds a valid amateur radio operator's license issued by the federal communications commission and who operates a duly licensed portable mobile transmitter and in connection therewith a receiver or receiving set on frequencies exclusively allocated by the federal communications commission to duly licensed radio amateurs.

> **HISTORY:** Add, L 1965, ch 1031, § 193, deriving from Penal Law § 1916; amd, L 1966, ch 620, § 2, L 1980, ch 843, § 90, eff Sept 1, 1980. Section heading, amd, L 1966, ch 620, § 2, eff Sept 1, 1967.

§ 397-a. Radar detectors and laser detectors prohibited

1. No radar detector or laser detector shall be used in any motor vehicle with a gross vehicle weight rating of more than eighteen thousand pounds or in any commercial vehicle with a gross vehicle weight rating of more than ten thousand pounds. The presence in such vehicle of a radar detector or laser detector connected to a power source and in an operable condition is presumptive evidence of its use by any person operating such vehicle. Such presumption shall be rebutted by any credible and reliable evidence which tends to show that such radar detector or laser detector was not in use.

2. The provisions of this section shall not be construed as authorizing the seizure or forfeiture of a radar detector or laser detector, unless otherwise provided by law.

3. A violation of the provisions of this section shall constitute a traffic infraction punishable by a fine of not less than twenty-five nor more than one hundred dollars.

> **HISTORY:** Add, L 1990, ch 173, § 20, eff Aug 19, 1990. Amd, L 1996, ch 524, § 1, eff Nov 1, 1996. Section heading, amd, L 1996, ch 524, § 1, eff Nov 1, 1996. Sub 1, amd, L 1996, ch 524, § 1, eff Nov 1, 1996. Sub 2, amd, L 1996, ch 524, § 1, eff Nov 1, 1996.

TITLE V   Drivers' Licenses

ARTICLE 20
SUSPENSION AND REVOCATION

ARTICLE 21
ALCOHOL AND DRUG REHABILITATION PROGRAM

HISTORY: Add, L 1959, ch 775; amd, L 1972, ch 780, § 7, eff April 1, 1973.

ARTICLE 20   SUSPENSION AND REVOCATION

HISTORY: Add, L 1959, ch 775, eff Oct 1, 1960.

§ 510. Suspension, revocation and reissuance of licenses and registrations

1. Who may suspend or revoke. Any magistrate, justice or judge, in a city, in a town, or in a village, any supreme court justice, any county judge, any judge of a district court, the superintendent of state police and the commissioner of motor vehicles or any person deputized by him, shall have power to revoke or suspend the license to drive a motor vehicle or motorcycle of any person, or in the case of an owner, the registration, as provided herein.

A learner's permit, or a license which has expired but is renewable, shall be deemed a license within the meaning of this section.

2. Mandatory revocations and suspensions.

a. Mandatory revocations. Such licenses shall be revoked and such registrations may also be revoked where the holder is convicted:

(i) of homicide or assault arising out of the operation of a motor vehicle or motorcycle or criminal negligence in the operation of a motor vehicle or motorcycle resulting in death, whether the conviction was had in this state or elsewhere;

(ii) pursuant to section twenty-three hundred eighty-five of title eighteen of the United States code, of the crime of advocating the overthrow of government, whether the conviction was had in this state or elsewhere;

(iii) of any violation of subdivision two of section six hundred or section three hundred ninety-two or of a local law or ordinance making it unlawful to leave the scene of an accident without reporting;

(iv) of a third or subsequent violation, committed within a period of eighteen months, of any provision of section eleven hundred eighty of this chapter, any ordinance or regulation limiting the speed of motor vehicles and motorcycles or any provision constituted a misdemeanor by this chapter, not included in subparagraphs (i) or (iii) of this paragraph, except violations of subdivision one of section three hundred seventy-five of this chapter or of subdivision one of section four hundred one of this chapter and similar violations under any local law, ordinance or regulation committed by an employed driver if the offense occurred while operating, in the course of his employment, a vehicle not owned by said driver, whether such three or more violations were repetitions of the same offense or were different offenses;

(v) of a violation for the conviction of which any such license is subject to revocation under subdivision two of section five hundred ten-b;

(vi) of a violation of any provision of section eleven hundred eighty-two of this chapter;

(vii) of a second violation of any provision of section eleven hundred eighty-two committed within a period of three years of a previous violation of the aforesaid section shall result in a license revocation of one year;

(viii) of a third violation, committed within a period of three years, of any provision of subdivision a of section eleven hundred seventy-four of this chapter;

(ix) of a violation of section twelve hundred twenty-four of this chapter, other than a violation adjudicated by the environmental control board of a city having a population of one million or more pursuant to subdivision seven of such section, and fails to pay the fine imposed thereon pursuant to subdivision seven of such section;

(x) of a traffic infraction for a subsequent violation of article twenty-six of this chapter and the commission of such violation caused serious physical injury to another person and such subsequent violation occurred within eighteen months of a prior violation of any provision of article twenty-six of this chapter where the commission of such prior violation caused the serious physical injury or death of another person;

(xi) of a traffic infraction for a subsequent violation of article twenty-six of this chapter and the commission of such violation caused the death of another person and such subsequent violation occurred within eighteen months of a prior violation of any provision of article twenty-six of this chapter where the commission of such prior violation caused the serious physical injury or death of another person;

(xii) of a second or subsequent conviction of a violation of section twelve hundred twenty-five-c or section twelve hundred twenty-five-d of this chapter committed where such person is the holder of a probationary license, as defined in subdivision four of section five hundred one of this title, at the time of the commission of such violation and such second or subsequent violation was committed within six months following the restoration or issuance of such probationary license; or

(xiii) of a second or subsequent conviction of a violation of section twelve hundred twenty-five-c or section twelve hundred twenty-five-d of this chapter committed where such person is the holder of a class DJ or MJ learner's permit or a class DJ or MJ license at the time of the commission of such violation and such second or subsequent violation was committed within six months following the restoration of such permit or license.

b. Mandatory suspensions. Such licenses shall be suspended, and such registrations may also be suspended:

(i) for a period of sixty days where the holder is convicted of a violation for the conviction of which such license is subject to suspension pursuant to subdivision one of section five hundred ten-b;

(ii) when the holder forfeits bail given upon being charged with any of the offenses mentioned in this subdivision, until the holder submits to the jurisdiction of the court in which he forfeited bail; and

(iii) such registrations shall be suspended when necessary to comply with subdivision nine of section one hundred forty or subdivision four of section one hundred forty-five of the transportation law. The commissioner shall have the authority to deny a registration or renewal application to any other person for the same vehicle and may deny a registration or renewal application for any other motor vehicle registered in the name of the applicant where it has been determined that such registrant's intent has been to evade the purposes of this subdivision and where the commissioner has reasonable grounds to believe that such registration or renewal will have the effect of defeating the purposes of this subdivision.

(iv) For a period of not less than thirty nor greater than one hundred eighty days where the holder is convicted of the crime of assault in the first, second or third degree as defined in article one hundred twenty of the penal law, where such offense was committed against a traffic enforcement agent employed by the city of New York or the city of Buffalo while such agent was enforcing or attempting to enforce the traffic regulations of such city.

(v) For a period of six months where the holder is convicted of, or receives a youthful offender or other juvenile adjudication in connection with, any misdemeanor or felony defined in article two hundred twenty or two hundred twenty-one of the penal law, any violation of the federal controlled substances act, any crime in violation of subdivision four of section eleven hundred ninety-two of this chapter or any out-of-state or federal misdemeanor or felony drug-related offense; provided, however, that any time actually served in custody pursuant to a sentence or disposition imposed as a result of such conviction or youthful offender or other juvenile adjudication shall be credited against the period of such suspension and, provided further, that the court shall determine that such suspension need not be imposed where there are compelling circumstances warranting an exception.

(vi) Pursuant to subparagraph (v) of this paragraph, the magistrate, justice or judge shall order such suspension or render its findings that are compelling circumstances warranting an exception at the time of sentencing. At that time, the judge, justice or magistrate may also issue an order making said license suspension take effect twenty days after the date of sentencing and, if this is done, the license holder shall be given a copy of the order permitting the continuation of driving privileges.

(vii) In no event shall the commissioner suspend a driver's license pursuant to subparagraph (v) of this paragraph absent a copy of an order by the magistrate, justice or judge as provided in subparagraph (vi) of this paragraph.

(viii) for a period of sixty days where the holder is convicted of a violation of section twelve hundred twenty-b of this chapter within a period of eighteen months of a previous violation of such section.

(ix) For a period of three months where the holder is sentenced to a license suspension pursuant to paragraph (a) of subdivision five of section sixty-five-b of the alcoholic beverage control law, provided however, that, in accordance with such subdivision five, such suspension shall be only a license suspension.

(x) For a period of six months where the holder is sentenced to a license suspension pursuant to paragraph (b) of subdivision five of section sixty-five-b of the alcoholic beverage control law, provided however, that, in accordance with such subdivision five, such suspension shall be only a license suspension.

(xi) For a period of one year or until the holder reaches the age of twenty-one, whichever is the greater period of time, where the holder is sentenced to a license suspension pursuant to paragraph (c) of subdivision five of section sixty-five-b of the alcoholic beverage control law, provided however, that, in accordance with such subdivision five, such suspension shall be only a license suspension.

(xii) for [For]* a period of one year where the holder is convicted of, or receives a youthful offender or juvenile delinquency adjudication in connection with a violation of section 240.62 or subdivision five of section 240.60 of the penal law.

(xiii) for a period of sixty days where the holder is convicted of two or more violations of paragraph two of subdivision (d) or subdivision (f) of section eleven hundred eighty of this chapter.

(xiv) for a period of forty-five days where the holder is convicted of a traffic infraction for a first violation of article twenty-six of this chapter and the commission of such violation caused serious physical injury to another person, except: (A) where the holder is convicted of a traffic infraction for a first violation of section eleven hundred forty-six of this chapter and the commission of such violation caused serious physical injury to another person, the suspension shall be for a period of six months; and (B) where the holder is convicted of a traffic infraction for a second violation of section eleven hundred forty-six of this chapter and the commission of such violation caused serious physical injury to another person, and such person has previously been convicted of a traffic infraction for a violation of section

---

* The bracketed word has been inserted by the Publisher.

eleven hundred forty-six of this chapter and the commission of such violation caused serious physical injury to another person within five years, the suspension shall be for a period of one year.

(xv) for a period of seventy-five days where the holder is convicted of a traffic infraction for a first violation of article twenty-six of this chapter and the commission of such violation caused the death of another person.

(xvi) for a period of one hundred twenty days where the holder is convicted of a violation of section twelve hundred twenty-five-c or section twelve hundred twenty-five-d of this chapter when such violation was committed while such holder had a probationary license, as defined in subdivision four of section five hundred one of this title.

(xvii) for a period of one hundred twenty days where the holder is convicted of a violation of section twelve hundred twenty-five-c or section twelve hundred twenty-five-d of this chapter when such violation was committed while such holder had a class DJ or MJ learner's permit or a class DJ or MJ license.

c. Application of mandatory revocations and suspensions to non-residents and to unlicensed persons. Whenever a non-resident or a person who is unlicensed is convicted of any violation or receives a youthful offender or juvenile delinquency adjudication in conjunction with a violation of section 240.62 or subdivision five of section 240.60 of the penal law, which would require the revocation or suspension of a license, pursuant to the provisions of this chapter, if the person so convicted or adjudicated was the holder of a license issued by the commissioner, such non-resident's privilege of operating a motor vehicle in this state or such unlicensed person's privilege of obtaining a license issued by the commissioner shall be revoked or suspended, and such non-resident's privilege of operation within this state of any motor vehicle owned by such person or such unlicensed person's privilege of obtaining a registration issued by the commissioner may be suspended as if such non-resident or unlicensed person was the holder of a license issued by the commissioner. The provisions of subdivisions six and seven of this section shall be applicable to any such suspension or revocation.

d. Mandatory suspensions; vehicles over eighteen thousand pounds. A license or privilege shall be suspended by the commissioner for a period of sixty days, where the holder is convicted of a violation of subdivision (g) of section eleven hundred eighty of this chapter, and (i) the recorded or entered speed upon which the conviction was based exceeded the applicable speed limit by more than twenty miles per hour or (ii) the recorded or entered speed upon which the conviction was based exceeded the applicable speed limit by more than ten miles per hour and the vehicle was either (A) in violation of any rules or regulations involving an out-of-service defect relating to brake systems, steering components and/or coupling devices, or (B) transporting flammable gas, radioactive materials or explosives. Whenever a license is suspended pursuant to this paragraph, the commissioner shall immediately issue a restricted license provided the holder of such license is otherwise eligible to receive such restricted license, except that no such restricted license shall be valid for the operation of a vehicle with a GVWR of more than eighteen thousand pounds and further provided that issuing a license to such person does not create a substantial traffic safety hazard.

2-a. Mandatory suspension and revocation of a license and registration in certain cases.

(a) Within seven days after conviction for a violation of any local law which prohibits the knowing operation or offering to operate or permitting the operation for hire of any vehicle as a taxicab, livery, as defined in section one hundred twenty-one-e of this chapter, coach, limousine, van or wheelchair accessible van or tow truck within the state without first having obtained an appropriate license therefor from the appropriate licensing authority and appropriate for-hire insurance from the appropriate insurance agency, the taxi and limousine commission or other local body having jurisdiction over such offenses with respect to such vehicles shall provide notice of such conviction to the commissioner in a manner agreed upon between any such local body and the commissioner. Upon receipt of such notice, the commissioner shall suspend the license of such operator and the registration of such vehicle for a period of sixty days.

(b) Within seven days after conviction for a violation of any local law which prohibits the knowing operation or offering to operate or permitting the operation for hire of any vehicle as a taxicab, livery, as defined in section one hundred twenty-one-e of this chapter, coach, limousine, van or wheelchair accessible van or tow truck within the state without first having obtained an appropriate license therefor from the appropriate licensing authority and appropriate for-hire insurance from the appropriate insurance agency where the operator has, within the previous five years, been convicted of any such violation, the taxi and limousine commission or other local body having jurisdiction over such offenses with respect to such vehicles shall provide notice to the commissioner in a manner agreed upon between any such local body and the commissioner. Upon receipt of such notice, the commissioner shall revoke the license of such operator.

(c) Within seven days after conviction for a violation of any local law which prohibits the knowing operation or offering to operate or permitting the operation for hire of any vehicle as a taxicab, delivery, as defined in section one hundred twenty-one-e of this chapter, coach, limousine, van or wheelchair accessible van or tow truck within the state without first having obtained an appropriate license therefor from the appropriate licensing authority and appropriate for-hire insurance from the appropriate insurance agency where the registrant has, within the previous five years, been convicted of any such violation, the taxi and limousine commission or other local body having jurisdiction over such offenses with respect to such vehicles shall provide notice to the commissioner in a manner agreed upon between any such local body and the commissioner. Upon receipt of such notice, the commissioner shall revoke the registration of such vehicle, and no new registration shall be issued for at least six months, nor thereafter, except in the discretion of the commissioner.

(d) The provisions of this subdivision shall not apply to any taxicab or livery as defined in section one hundred twenty-one-e of this chapter, coach, limousine, van or wheelchair accessible vanor tow truck licensed or permitted for such operation by the appropriate local body of any other municipality, the department of transportation, the metropolitan transportation authority or the interstate commerce commission.

3. Permissive suspensions and revocations. Such licenses and registrations and the privilege of a non-resident of operating a motor vehicle in this state and of operation within this state of any motor vehicle owned by him and the privilege of an unlicensed person of obtaining a license issued by the commissioner and of obtaining a registration issued by the commissioner may be suspended or revoked:

a. for any violation of the provisions of this chapter, except section eleven hundred ninety-two, or for any violation of a local ordinance or regulation prohibiting dangerous driving as shall, in the discretion of the officer acting hereunder, justify such revocation or suspension;

b. because of some physical or mental disability of the holder, the court commitment of the holder to an institution under the jurisdiction of the department of mental hygiene or the disability of the holder by reason of intoxication or the use of drugs;

c. because of the conviction of the holder at any time of a felony;

d. for habitual or persistent violation of any of the provisions of this chapter, or of any lawful ordinance, rule or regulation made by local authorities in relation to traffic;

e. for gross negligence in the operation of a motor vehicle or motorcycle or operating a motor vehicle or motorcycle in a manner showing a reckless disregard for life or property of others;

f. for knowingly permitting or suffering any motor vehicle or motorcycle under the direction or control of the holder to be used in aid or furtherance of the commission of any crime;

g. for preventing lawful identification of any motor vehicle or motorcycle under the holder's direction or control, or evading lawful arrest or prosecution while operating such motor vehicle or motorcycle;

h. for wilfully evading lawful prosecution in this state or in another state or jurisdiction for an offense committed therein against the motor vehicle or traffic laws thereof;

i. for habitual or persistent violation of any provisions of this chapter, and/or any lawful ordinance, rule or regulation made by local authorities in relation to traffic, and/or violations committed in a commercial motor vehicle of any law, statute, ordinance, rule or regulation in relation to traffic made by any other state, District of Columbia, Canadian province or local authority of such state, district or province;

j. except as provided in subdivision one herein or section eleven hundred ninety-three of this chapter upon the conviction of a person under eighteen years of age of any crime or in the case of an adjudication of youthful offender under nineteen years of age, such license or registration may be suspended or revoked for a maximum period of one year by the judge or justice sentencing him;

k. for a period of up to ninety days because of the conviction of the holder of the offenses of menacing as defined in section 120.15 of the penal law, where such offense was committed against a traffic enforcement agent employed by the city of New York or the city of Buffalo while such agent was enforcing or attempting to enforce the traffic regulations of such city.

3-a. Opportunity to be heard and temporary suspensions. Where revocation or suspension is permissive, the holder, unless he shall waive such right, shall have an opportunity to be heard except where such revocation or suspension is based solely on a court conviction or convictions or on a court commitment to an institution under the jurisdiction of the department of mental hygiene. A license or registration, or the privilege of a non-resident of operating a motor vehicle in this state or of the operation within this state of any motor vehicle owned by him, may, however, be temporarily suspended without notice, pending any prosecution, investigation or hearing.

4. Administrative action pursuant to interstate compact.

a. Such licenses may be suspended where pursuant to any compact or agreement authorized by section five hundred seventeen of this chapter the holder thereof is issued a summons for a moving traffic violation, is not detained or required to furnish bail or collateral and fails to appear in response to such summons. Such suspension shall remain in effect only until such holder submits to the jurisdiction of the court in which such summons is returnable.

b. If notification is received by the commissioner pursuant to any compact or agreement authorized by section five hundred sixteen-b of this article that the holder of a New York license or an unlicensed New York resident has been convicted of an offense set forth in such compact or agreement, such conviction, for the purpose of administrative action which must or may be taken by the commissioner pursuant to the provisions of this section, shall be deemed to be a conviction of an offense committed within this state in accordance with the provisions of such compact or agreement.

4-a. Suspension for failure to answer an appearance ticket or to pay a fine.

(a) Upon receipt of a court notification of the failure of a person to appear within sixty days of the return date or new subsequent adjourned date, pursuant to an appearance ticket charging said person with a violation of any of the provisions of this chapter (except one for parking, stopping, or standing), of any violation of the tax law or of the transportation law regulating traffic or of any lawful ordinance or regulation made by a local or public authority, relating to traffic (except one for parking, stopping, or standing) or the failure to pay a fine imposed by a court the commissioner or his or her agent may suspend the driver's license or privileges of such person pending receipt of notice from the court that such person has appeared in response to such appearance ticket or has paid such fine. Such suspension shall take effect no less than thirty days from the day upon which notice thereof is sent by the commissioner to the person whose driver's license or privileges are to be suspended. Any suspension issued pursuant to this paragraph shall be subject to the provisions of paragraph (j-l) of subdivision two of section five hundred three of this chapter.

(b) The provisions of paragraph (a) of this subdivision shall not apply to a registrant who was not operating a vehicle, but who was issued a summons or an appearance ticket for a violation of section three hundred eighty-five, section four hundred one or section five hundred eleven-a of this chapter. Upon the receipt of a court notification of the failure of such person to appear within sixty days of the return date or a new subsequent adjourned date, pursuant to an appearance ticket charging said person with such violation, or the failure of such person to pay a fine imposed by a court, the commissioner or his or her agent may suspend the registration of the vehicle or vehicles involved in such violation or privilege of operation of any motor vehicle owned by the registrant pending receipt of notice from the court that such person has appeared in response to such appearance ticket or has paid such fine. Such suspension shall take effect no less than thirty days from the day upon which notice thereof is sent by the commissioner to the person whose registration or privilege is to be suspended. Any suspension issued pursuant to this paragraph shall be subject to the provisions of paragraph (j-1) of subdivision two of section five hundred three of this chapter.

(c) Upon receipt of notification from a traffic and parking violations agency of the failure of a person to appear within sixty days of the return date or new subsequent adjourned date, pursuant to an appearance ticket charging said person with a violation of:

(i) any of the provisions of this chapter except one for parking, stopping or standing and except those violations described in paragraphs (a), (b), (d), (e) and (f) of subdivision two of section three hundred seventy-one of the general municipal law;

(ii) section five hundred two or subdivision (a) of section eighteen hundred fifteen of the tax law;

(iii) section fourteen-f (except paragraph (b) of subdivision four of section fourteen-f), two hundred eleven or two hundred twelve of the transportation law; or

(iv) any lawful ordinance or regulation made by a local or public authority relating to traffic (except one for parking, stopping or standing) or the failure to pay a fine imposed for such a violation by a traffic and parking violations agency, the commissioner or his or her agent may suspend the driver's license or privileges of such person pending receipt of notice from the agency that such person has appeared in response to such appearance ticket or has paid such fine. Such suspension shall take effect no less than thirty days from the day upon which notice thereof is sent by the commissioner to the person whose driver's license or privileges are to be suspended. Any suspension issued pursuant to this paragraph shall be subject to the provisions of paragraph (j-1) of subdivision two of section five hundred three of this chapter.

4-b. Suspension of registration for failure to answer or to pay fines with respect to certain violations. Upon receipt of certification from a court or administrative tribunal of appropriate jurisdiction that the owner of a motor vehicle or his representative failed to appear on the return date or dates or any subsequent adjourned date or dates or failed to comply with the rules and regulations of an administrative tribunal following entry of a final decision or decisions in response to twenty-five or more summonses or other process, issued within an eighteen month period charging that such motor vehicle is parked, stopped or standing in violation of any of the provisions of this chapter or of any law, ordinance, rule or regulation made by a local authority, the commissioner shall suspend the registration of such motor vehicle. Such suspension shall take effect no less than thirty days from the date on which notice thereof is sent by the commissioner to the person whose registration is to be suspended and shall remain in effect as long as the summmons [summons]* or summonses remain unanswered, or in the case of an administrative tribunal, the registrant fails to comply with the rules and regulations following the entry of a final decision or decisions.

4-c. [Repealed Sept 1, 2015] Suspension of registration for failure to answer or to pay fines with respect to parking, stopping and standing violations. Upon receipt of certification from a court or administrative tribunal of appropriate jurisdiction in a city with a population in excess of one hundred thousand persons according to the nineteen hundred eighty United States census that the owner of a motor vehicle or his representative following compliance by such city with the notice provisions of subdivision two of section two hundred thirty-five of this chapter, failed to appear on the return date or dates or any subsequent adjourned date or dates or failed to comply with the rules and regulations of an administrative tribunal following entry of a final decision or decisions, in response to five or more summonses or other process, issued within a twelve month period charging that such motor vehicle is parked, stopped or standing in violation of any of the provisions of this chapter or of any law, ordinance, rule or regulation made by a local authority, the commissioner shall suspend the registration of such motor vehicle. Such suspension shall take effect no less than thirty days from the date on which notice thereof is sent by the commissioner to the person whose registration is to be suspended and shall remain in effect as long as the summons or summonses remain unanswered, or in the case of an administrative tribunal, the registrant fails to comply with the rules and regulations following the entry of a final decision or decisions.

4-d. Suspension of registration for failure to answer or pay penalties with respect to certain violations. Upon the receipt of a notification from a court or an administrative tribunal that an owner of a motor vehicle failed to appear on the return date or dates or a new subsequent adjourned date or dates or failed to pay any penalty imposed by a court or failed to comply with the rules and regulations of an administrative tribunal following entry of a final decision or decisions, in response to five or more notices of liability or other process, issued within an eighteen month

* The bracketed word has been inserted by the Publisher.

period charging such owner with a violation of toll collection regulations in accordance with the provisions of section two thousand nine hundred eighty-five of the public authorities law or sections sixteen-a, sixteen-b and sixteen-c of chapter seven hundred seventy-four of the laws of nineteen hundred fifty, the commissioner or his agent shall suspend the registration of the vehicle or vehicles involved in the violation or the privilege of operation of any motor vehicle owned by the registrant. Such suspension shall take effect no less than thirty days from the date on which notice thereof is sent by the commissioner to the person whose registration or privilege is suspended and shall remain in effect until such registrant has appeared in response to such notices of liability or has paid such penalty or in the case of an administrative tribunal, the registrant has complied with the rules and regulations following the entry of a final decision or decisions.

4-e. [Repealed June 30, 2015] Suspension and disqualification for failure to make child support payments or failure to comply with a summons, subpoena or warrant relating to a paternity or child support proceeding.

(1) The commissioner, on behalf of the department, shall enter into a written agreement with the commissioner of the office of temporary and disability assistance, on behalf of the office of temporary and disability assistance, which shall set forth the procedures for suspending the driving privileges of individuals who have failed to make payments of child support or combined child and spousal support.

(2) Such agreement shall include:

(i) the procedure under which the office of temporary and disability assistance shall notify the department of an individual's liability for support arrears;

(ii) the procedure under which the department shall be notified by the office of temporary and disability assistance that an individual has satisfied or commenced payment of his or her support arrears; or has made satisfactory payment arrangements thereon and shall have the suspension of his or her driving privileges terminated;

(iii) the procedure for reimbursement of the department and its agents by the office of temporary and disability assistance for the full additional costs of carrying out the procedures authorized by this section, and may include, subject to the approval of the director of the budget, a procedure for reimbursement of necessary additional costs of collecting social security numbers pursuant to section five hundred two of this title;

(iv) provision for the publicizing of sanctions for nonpayment of child support including the potential for the suspension of delinquent support obligors' driving privileges if they fail to pay child support or combined child and spousal support; and

(v) such other matters as the parties to such agreement shall deem necessary to carry out provisions of this section.

(3) Upon receipt of notification from the office of temporary and disability assistance of a person's failure to satisfy support arrears or to make satisfactory payment arrangements thereon pursuant to paragraph (e) of subdivision twelve of section one hundred eleven-b of the social services law or notification from a court issuing an order pursuant to section four hundred fifty-eight-a of the family court act or section two hundred forty-four-b of the domestic relations law, the commissioner or his or her agent shall suspend the license of such person to operate a motor vehicle. In the event such person is unlicensed, such person's privilege of obtaining a license shall be suspended. Such suspension shall take effect no later than fifteen days from the date of the notice thereof to the person whose license or privilege of obtaining a license is to

be suspended, and shall remain in effect until such time as the commissioner is advised that the person has satisfied the support arrears or has made satisfactory payment arrangements thereon pursuant to paragraph (e) of subdivision twelve of section one hundred eleven-b of the social services law or until such time as the court issues an order to terminate such suspension;

(4) From the time the commissioner is notified by the office of temporary and disability assistance of a person's liability for support arrears under this section, the commissioner shall be relieved from all liability to such person which may otherwise arise under this section, and such person shall have no right to commence a court action or proceeding or to any other legal recourse against the commissioner to recover such driving privileges as authorized by this section. In addition, notwithstanding any other provision of law, such person shall have no right to a hearing or appeal pursuant to this chapter with respect to a suspension of driving privileges as authorized by this section. However, nothing herein shall be construed to prohibit such person from proceeding against the support collection unit pursuant to article seventy-eight of the civil practice law and rules.

(5) Any person whose license has been suspended pursuant to subdivision three of this section may apply for the issuance of a restricted use license as provided in section five hundred thirty of this title.

4-f. Suspension for failure to pay past-due tax liabilities.

(1) The commissioner shall enter into a written agreement with the commissioner of taxation and finance, as provided in section one hundred seventy-one-v of the tax law, which shall set forth the procedures for suspending the drivers' licenses of individuals who have failed to satisfy past-due tax liabilities as such terms are defined in such section.

(2) Upon receipt of notification from the department of taxation and finance that an individual has failed to satisfy past-due tax liabilities, or to otherwise make payment arrangements satisfactory to the commissioner of taxation and finance, or has failed to comply with the terms of such payment arrangements more than once within a twelve month period, the commissioner or his or her agent shall suspend the license of such person to operate a motor vehicle. In the event such person is unlicensed, such person's privilege of obtaining a license shall be suspended. Such suspension shall take effect no later than fifteen days from the date of the notice thereof provided to the person whose license or privilege of obtaining a license is to be suspended, and shall remain in effect until such time as the commissioner is advised that the person has satisfied his or her past-due tax liabilities, or has otherwise made payment arrangements satisfactory to the commissioner of taxation and finance.

(3) From the time the commissioner is notified by the department of taxation and finance under this section, the commissioner shall be relieved from all liability to such person which may otherwise arise under this section, and such person shall have no right to commence a court action or proceeding or to any other legal recourse against the commissioner to recover such driving privileges as authorized by this section. In addition, notwithstanding any other provision of law, such person shall have no right to a hearing or appeal pursuant to this chapter with respect to a suspension of driving privileges as authorized by this section.

(4) Notwithstanding any provision of law to the contrary, the department shall furnish the department of taxation and finance with the information necessary for the proper identification of an individual referred to the department for the purpose of driver's license suspension pursuant to this section and section one hundred seventy-one-v of the tax law. This shall include

the individual's name, social security number and any other information the commissioner of motor vehicles deems necessary.

(5) Any person whose driver's license is suspended pursuant to paragraph two of this subdivision may apply for the issuance of a restricted use license as provided in section five hundred thirty of this title.

5. Restoration. A license or registration may be restored by direction of the commissioner but not otherwise. Reversal on appeal, of any conviction because of which any license or registration has been revoked or suspended, shall entitle the holder to restoration thereof forthwith. The privileges of a non-resident may be restored by direction of the commissioner in his discretion but not otherwise.

6. Restrictions.

a. Where revocation is mandatory hereunder, no new license shall be issued for at least six months or, in certain cases a longer period as specified in this chapter, nor thereafter, except in the discretion of the commissioner of motor vehicles.

b. Except as otherwise provided in paragraph c of this subdivision, where revocation is mandatory pursuant to subparagraph (iii) of paragraph a of subdivision two of this section, no new commercial driver's license shall be issued for at least one year nor thereafter except in the discretion of the commissioner, except that if such person has previously been found to have refused a chemical test pursuant to section eleven hundred ninety-four of this chapter or has a prior conviction of any of the following offenses any violation of section eleven hundred ninety-two of this chapter; any violation of subdivision one or two of section six hundred of this chapter; or has a prior conviction of any felony involving the use of a motor vehicle pursuant to paragraph (a) of subdivision one of section five hundred ten-a of this article, then such commercial driver's license revocation shall be permanent.

c. Where revocation is mandatory pursuant to subdivision one of section five hundred ten-a of this chapter or subparagraph (iii) of paragraph a of subdivision two of this section and the violation of subdivision two of section six hundred of this chapter was committed while operating a commercial motor vehicle transporting hazardous materials, no new commercial driver's license shall be issued for at least three years nor thereafter except in the discretion of the commissioner, except that if such person has previously been found to have refused a chemical test pursuant to section eleven hundred ninety-four of this chapter or has a prior conviction of any of the following offenses: any violation of section eleven hundred ninety-two of this chapter; any violation of subdivisionone or two of section six hundred of this chapter; or has a prior conviction of any felony involving the use of a motor vehicle pursuant to paragraph (a) of subdivision one of section five hundred ten-a of this article, then such commercial driver's license revocation shall be permanent.

d. The permanent commercial driver's license revocation required by paragraphs b and c of this subdivision may be waived by the commissioner after a period of ten years has expired from such sentence provided:

(i) that during such ten year period such person has not been found to have refused a chemical test pursuant to section eleven hundred ninety-four of this chapter and has not been convicted of any one of the following offenses: any violation of section eleven hundred ninety-two of this chapter; any violation of subdivision one or two of section six hundred of this chapter; or has a prior conviction of any felony involving the use of a motor vehicle pursuant to paragraph (a) of subdivision one of section five hundred ten-a of this article;

(ii) if any of the grounds upon which the permanent commercial driver's license revocation is based involved a finding of refusal to submit to a chemical test pursuant to section eleven hundred ninety-four of this chapter or a conviction of a violation of any subdivision of section eleven hundred ninety-two of this chapter, that such person provides acceptable documentation to the commissioner that such person has voluntarily enrolled in and successfully completed an appropriate rehabilitation program; and

(iii) after such documentation, if required, is accepted, that such person is granted a certificate of relief from disabilities or a certificate of good conduct pursuant to article twenty-three of the correction law by the court in which such person was last penalized.

e. Upon a third finding of refusal and/or conviction of any of the offenses which require a permanent commercial driver's license revocation, such permanent revocation may not be waived by the commissioner under any circumstances.

f. Where revocation is mandatory hereunder, based upon a conviction had outside this state, no new license shall be issued until after sixty days from the date of such revocation, nor thereafter, except in the discretion of the commissioner.

g. Except as provided in paragraph k of this subdivision, where revocation is permissive, no new license or certificate shall be issued by such commissioner to any person until after thirty days from the date of such revocation, nor thereafter, except in the discretion of the commissioner after an investigation or upon a hearing, provided, however, that where the revocation is based upon a failure in a reexamination pursuant to section five hundred six of this chapter, a learner's permit may be issued immediately and provided further, that where revocation is based upon a conviction of a felony, other than a felony relating to the operation of a motor vehicle or motorcycle, a license shall be issued immediately, if the applicant is otherwise qualified and if the application for such license is accompanied by consent in writing issued by the parole or probation authority having jurisdiction over such applicant.

h. The provisions of this subdivision shall not apply to revocations issued pursuant to sections eleven hundred ninety-three and eleven hundred ninety-four of this chapter.

i. Where suspension of a driver's license is mandatory hereunder based upon a conviction of, or youthful offender or other juvenile adjudication in connection with, any misdemeanor or felony as defined in article two hundred twenty or two hundred twenty-one of the penal law, any violation of the federal controlled substances act, any crime in violation of subdivision four of section eleven hundred ninety-two of this chapter or any out-of-state or federal misdemeanor or felony drug-related offense, the commissioner may issue a restricted use license pursuant to section five hundred thirty of this chapter.

j. Where suspension of a driver's license is mandatory hereunder based upon a conviction of, or youthful offender or other juvenile adjudication in connection with, any misdemeanor or felony as defined in article two hundred twenty or two hundred twenty-one of the penal law, any violation of the federal controlled substances act, any crime in violation of subdivision four of section eleven hundred ninety-two of this chapter or any out-of-state or federal misdemeanor or felony drug-related offense and the individual does not have a driver's license or the individual's driver's license was suspended at the time of conviction or youthful offender or other juvenile adjudication, the commissioner shall not issue a new license nor restore the former license for a period of six months after such individual would otherwise have become eligible to obtain a new license or to have the former license restored; provided, however, that during such delay period the commissioner may issue a restricted use license pursuant to section five hundred thirty of this chapter to such previously suspended licensee.

k. Where revocation is permissive hereunder, based upon a finding of a violation of section three hundred ninety-two or section three hundred ninety-two-a of this chapter, no new license or certificate shall be issued until after one year from the date of such revocation, nor thereafter, except in the discretion of the commissioner.

l. Where revocation is mandatory pursuant to subparagraph (x) of paragraph a of subdivision two of this section, no new license shall be issued for at least seventy-five days, nor thereafter except in the discretion of the commissioner.

m. Where revocation is mandatory pursuant to subparagraph (xi) of paragraph a of subdivision two of this section, no new license shall be issued for at least one hundred twenty days, nor thereafter except in the discretion of the commissioner.

n. Notwithstanding the provisions of paragraph a of this subdivision, subdivision two of section five hundred ten-b of this article or paragraph (b) of subdivision one of section five hundred ten-c of this article, where revocation is mandatory pursuant to subparagraph (xii) or subparagraph (xiii) of paragraph a of subdivision two of this section, no new license shall be issued for at least one year, nor thereafter except in the discretion of the commissioner.

7. Miscellaneous provisions. Except as expressly provided, a court conviction shall not be necessary to sustain a revocation or suspension. Revocation or suspension hereunder shall be deemed an administrative act reviewable by the supreme court as such. Notice of revocation or suspension, as well as any required notice of hearing, where the holder is not present, may be given by mailing the same in writing to him or her at the address contained in his or her license, certificate of registration or at the current address provided by the United States postal service, as the case may be. Proof of such mailing by certified mail to the holder shall be presumptive evidence of the holder's receipt and actual knowledge of such notice. Attendance of witnesses may be compelled by subpoena. Failure of the holder or any other person possessing the license card or number plates, to deliver the same to the suspending or revoking officer is a misdemeanor. Suspending or revoking officers shall place such license cards and number plates in the custody of the commissioner except where the commissioner shall otherwise direct. If any person shall fail to deliver a license card or number plates as provided herein, any police officer, bridge and tunnel officer of the Triborough bridge and tunnel authority, or agent of the commissioner having knowledge of such facts shall have the power to secure possession thereof and return the same to the commissioner, and the commissioner may forthwith direct any police officer, bridge and tunnel officer of the Triborough bridge and tunnel authority, acting pursuant to his or her special duties, or agent of the commissioner to secure possession thereof and to return the same to the commissioner. Failure of the holder or of any person possessing the license card or number plates to deliver to any police officer, bridge and tunnel officer of the Triborough bridge and tunnel authority, or agent of the commissioner who requests the same pursuant to this subdivision shall be a misdemeanor. Notice of revocation or suspension of any license or registration shall be transmitted forthwith by the commissioner to the chief of police of the city or prosecuting officer of the locality in which the person whose license or registration so revoked or suspended resides. In case any license or registration shall expire before the end of any period for which it has been revoked or suspended, and before it shall have been restored as provided in this chapter, then and in that event any renewal thereof may be withheld until the end of such period of suspension or until restoration, as the case may be.

The revocation of a learner's permit shall automatically cancel the application for a license of the holder of such permit.

No suspension or revocation of a license or registration shall be made because of a judgment of conviction if the suspending or revoking officer is satisfied that the magistrate who pronounced the judgment failed to comply with subdivision one of section eighteen hundred seven of this chapter. In case a suspension or revocation has been made and the commissioner is satisfied that there was such failure, the commissioner shall restore the license or registration or both as the case may be.

8. Cancellation. Upon receipt of a license which has been surrendered to the licensing authority of any other jurisdiction as a prerequisite to the issuance of a license by such other jurisdiction in accordance with the provisions of the Driver License Compact or any other laws of such jurisdiction, the commissioner shall cancel such license. Provided, however, that such license shall not be cancelled if the licensee is a resident of this state.

9. Railroad vehicle violations. Upon certification by the commissioner of transportation that there has been a violation of section seventy-six-b of the railroad law, the commissioner of motor vehicles may rescind, cancel or suspend the registration of any motor vehicle described in subdivision one of section seventy-six-b of the railroad law and may rescind, cancel, suspend or take possession of the current registration certificate and number plates of any such motor vehicle.

10. Where a youth is determined to be a youthful offender, following a conviction of a violation for which a license suspension or revocation is mandatory or where a youth receives a juvenile delinquency adjudication in conjunction with a violation of section 240.62 or subdivision five of section 240.60 of the penal law, the court shall impose such suspension or revocation as is otherwise required upon conviction and, further, shall notify the commissioner of said suspension or revocation and its finding that said violator is granted youthful offender status as is required pursuant to section five hundred thirteen of this chapter or received a juvenile delinquency adjudication.

11. Notwithstanding any contrary provision of law, the division of criminal justice services is authorized to share with the commissioner such criminal history information in its possession as may be necessary to effect the provisions of this chapter.

HISTORY: Add, L 1959, ch 775, with substance transferred from former § 71; amd, L 1960, ch 184, §§ 3–5, L 1961 ch 962, § 1, L 1962, ch 779, § 1, L 1963, ch 869, § 3, L 1964, ch 447, § 1, L 1964, ch 905, § 1, L 1965, ch 651, § 2, L 1966, ch 86 § 1, L 1966, ch 759, § 1, L 1966, ch 963, § 2, L 1967, ch 79, § 1, eff Oct 1, 1967, L 1968, ch 36, § 1, L 1969, ch 445, § 3, eff Jan 1, 1970, applicable only to licenses issued on and after that date; amd, L 1970, ch 275, § 1, L 1971, ch 1106, § 1, L 1972, ch 99, § 3, L 1972, ch 243, § 2, L 1973, ch 156, § 1, L 1973, ch 168, § 5, L 1973, ch 541, § 2, L 1974, ch 129, § 1, L 1974, ch 772, § 1, L 1975, ch 143, § 3, L 1976, ch 282, § 1, L 1976, ch 404, §§ 1, 2, L 1976, ch 670, § 2, L 1977, ch 163, § 1, L 1979, ch 195, § 1, eff June 4, 1979, L 1979, ch 594, § 2, L 1980, ch 381, § 2, L 1980, ch 722, § 2, eff June 30, 1980, L 1980, ch 806, §§ 2, 3, L 1980, ch 807, § 1, L 1980, ch 843, § 98, L 1981, ch 428, § 1, L 1981, ch 477, § 1, L 1981, ch 912, § 1, L 1982, ch 861, § 1, L 1982, ch 888, §§ 1, 2, L 1983, ch 802, § 1, L 1983, ch 890, § 2, L 1983, ch 892, §§ 1–3, L 1984, ch 192, § 1, L 1984, ch 977, §§ 1, 2, L 1984, ch 978, § 2, eff Nov 1, 1984, L 1985, ch 707, § 1, L 1985, ch 718, § 1, L 1986, ch 132, §§ 5–11, eff June 2, 1986, L 1986, ch 411, § 20, L 1986, ch 492, §§ 1, 2, L 1986, ch 649, § 4, L 1986, ch 731, § 1, eff July 30, 1986, L 1987, ch 188, § 1, L 1987, ch 338, § 3, eff Jan 1, 1988, L 1987, ch 594, §§ 2, 3, L 1987, ch 687, §§ 1, 2, L 1988, ch 47, §§ 5–9, eff Nov 1, 1988, L 1988, ch 183, §§ 1–5, eff Nov 1, 1988, L 1988, ch 197, § 3, eff Nov 1, 1988, L 1988, ch 254, § 2, L 1989, ch 625, § 1, eff Nov 1, 1989, L 1989, ch 703, § 1, eff Sept 22, 1989, L 1989, ch 779, §§ 3, 4, eff July 1, 1990, L 1990, ch 173, §§ 23, 51-a, eff Aug 19, 1990, L 1990, ch 173, §§ 52, 53, eff Feb 19, 1991, L 1990, ch 173, § 54, eff April 1, 1991, L 1990, ch 496, § 6, eff July 18, 1990, L 1991, ch 166, § 373, expires and repealed Sept 1, 2015, L 1992, ch 124, §§ 1, 2, eff Nov 1, 1992, L 1992, ch 379, § 15, eff July 17, 1992, L 1992, ch 605, § 2, eff Nov 21, 1992, L 1993, ch 349, § 3, eff July 21, 1993, L 1993, ch 533, §§ 1–3, eff Sept 30, 1993, L 1993, ch 606, § 1, eff Nov 1, 1993, L 1994, ch 307, §§ 5, 6, eff Sept 18, 1994, L 1994, ch 313, § 2, eff Nov 1, 1994, L, 1994, ch 429, § 2, eff July 20, 1994, L 1995, ch 3, § 72, eff June 10, 1995 and deemed eff on and after April 1, 1995, L 1995, ch 81, § 211, eff July 1, 1995,

L 1997, ch 398, § 133, eff Jan 1, 1998, L 1997, ch 505, § 1, eff Oct 3, 1997, L 1998, ch 383, § 9, eff April 1, 1999, L 1998, ch 652, § 1, eff April 1, 1999, expired and repealed Jan 1, 2002, 1999, ch 166, § 373, L 1999, ch 412, § 5 (Part J), eff Aug 9, 1999, deemed eff on and after April 1, 1999, expired and repealed Sept 1, 2002, L 1999, ch 561, §§ 6–8, eff Dec 1, 1999, L 2003, ch 62, § 10 (Part J), eff Sept 12, 2003, L 2005, ch 60, § 12 (Part E), eff Sept 30, 2005, L 2005, ch 223, § 2, eff Nov 1, 2005, L 2006, ch 571, §§ 1–4, eff Nov 1, 2006, L 2007, ch 601, § 23, eff Aug 15, 2007, L 2010, ch 56, § 29 (Part LL), eff June 22, 2010, L 2010, ch 59, § 5 (Part K), eff June 22, 2010, L 2010, ch 409, § 2, eff Aug 13, 2010, L 2013, ch 59, § 2 (Part P), eff March 28, 2013, L 2014, ch 55, §§ 1–3 (Part B), eff Nov 1, 2014.

§ 510-a. Suspension and revocation of commercial driver's licenses

1. Revocation. A commercial driver's license shall be revoked by the commissioner whenever the holder is convicted within or outside of this state (a) of a felony involving the use of a motor vehicle except a felony as described in paragraph (b) of this subdivision; (b) of a felony involving manufacturing, distributing or dispensing a drug as defined in section one hundred fourteen-a of this chapter or possession of any such drug with intent to manufacture, distribute or dispense such drug in which a motor vehicle was used; (c) of a violation of subdivision one or two of section six hundred of this chapter; (d) of operating a commercial motor vehicle when, as a result of prior violations committed while operating a commercial motor vehicle, the driver's commercial driver's license is revoked, suspended, or canceled, or the driver is disqualified from operating a commercial motor vehicle; (e) has been convicted of causing a fatality through the negligent operation of a commercial motor vehicle, including but not limited to the crimes of vehicular manslaughter or criminally negligent homicide; or (f) the commissioner determines that the holder has made a false statement regarding information: (i) required by the federal motor carrier safety improvement act of 1999 and Subpart J of Part 383 of title 49 of the code of federal regulations relating to a commercial driver's license document in an application for a commercial driver's license; (ii) required by the federal motor carrier safety improvement act of 1999 and Part 383.71 (a) and (g) of title 49 of the code of federal regulations relating to an initial commercial driver's license or existing commercial driver's license holder's self-certification in any of the self-certifications regarding the type of driving engaged or to be engaged in by the holder or regarding the non-applicability to the holder of the physical qualification requirements of the federal motor carrier safety improvement act of 1999 and Part 391 of title 49 of the code of federal regulations relating to qualifications of drivers; or (iii) required by the federal motor carrier safety improvement act of 1999 and Part 383.71(h) of title 49 of the code of federal regulations relating to commercial driver's license requirements in any medical certificate.

2. Duration of revocation.

(a) Except as otherwise provided in paragraph (b) of this subdivision, where revocation of a commercial driver's license is mandatory pursuant to paragraph (a), (c), (d), (e) or (f) of subdivision one of this section no new commercial driver's license shall be issued for at least one year nor thereafter except in the discretion of the commissioner, except that for revocations pursuant to paragraph (a), (c), (d) or (e) of subdivision one of this section, if such person has previously been found to have refused a chemical test pursuant to section eleven hundred ninety-four of this chapter or has a prior conviction of any of the following offenses: any violation of section eleven hundred ninety-two of this chapter, any violation of subdivision one or two of section six hundred of this chapter, or any felony involving the use of a motor vehicle pursuant to paragraph (a) of subdivision one of this section, or has been convicted of operating a commercial motor vehicle when, as a result of prior violations committed while operating a commercial motor vehicle, the driver's commercial driver's license is revoked, suspended, or canceled, or the driver is disqualified from operating a commercial motor vehicle, or has been convicted of causing a fatality through the negligent operation of a commercial motor vehicle, including but not limited to the crimes of vehicular manslaughter or criminally negligent homicide, then such commercial driver's license revocation shall be permanent.

(b) Where revocation is mandatory pursuant to paragraph (a), (c), (d) or (e) of subdivision one of this section and the commercial motor vehicle was transporting hazardous materials, no new commercial driver's license shall be issued for at least three years nor thereafter except in the discretion of the commissioner, except that if such person has previously been found to have refused a chemical test pursuant to section eleven hundred ninety-four of this chapter or has a prior conviction of any of the following offenses: any violation of section eleven hundred ninety-two of this chapter, any violation of subdivision one or two of section six hundred of this chapter, or any felony involving the use of a motor vehicle pursuant to paragraph (a) of subdivision one of this section, or been convicted of operating a commercial motor vehicle when, as a result of prior violations committed while operating a commercial motor vehicle the driver's commercial driver's license is revoked, suspended, or canceled, or the driver is disqualified from operating a commercial motor vehicle, or has been convicted of causing a fatality through the negligent operation of a commercial motor vehicle, including but not limited to the crimes of vehicular manslaughter or criminally negligent homicide, then such commercial driver's license revocation shall be permanent.

(c) The permanent commercial driver's license revocation required by paragraphs (a) and (b) of this subdivision may be waived by the commissioner after a period of ten years has expired from such sentence provided:

(i) that during such ten year period such person has not been found to have refused a chemical test pursuant to section eleven hundred ninety-four of this chapter and has not been convicted of any one of the following offenses: any violation of section eleven hundred ninety-two of this chapter, any violation of subdivision one or two of section six hundred of this chapter, or any felony involving the use of a motor vehicle pursuant to paragraph (a) of subdivision one of this section, or has been convicted of operating a commercial motor vehicle when, as a result of prior violations committed while operating a commercial motor vehicle, the driver's commercial driver's license is revoked, suspended, or canceled, or the driver is disqualified from operating a commercial motor vehicle; or has been convicted of causing a fatality through the negligent operation of a commercial motor vehicle, including but not limited to the crimes of vehicular manslaughter or criminally negligent homicide;

(ii) if any of the grounds upon which the permanent commercial driver's license revocation is based involved a finding of refusal to submit to a chemical test pursuant to section eleven hundred ninety-four of this chapter or a conviction of a violation of any subdivision of section eleven hundred ninety-two of this chapter, that such person provides acceptable documentation to the commissioner that such person has enrolled in and successfully completed an appropriate rehabilitation program; and

(iii) after such documentation, if required, is accepted, that such person is granted a certificate of relief from disabilities or a certificate of good conduct pursuant to article twenty-three of the correction law by the court in which such person was last penalized.

(d) Upon a third finding of refusal and/or conviction of any of the offenses which require a permanent commercial driver's license revocation, such permanent revocation may not be waived by the commissioner under any circumstances.

(e) Where revocation is mandatory pursuant to paragraph (b) of subdivision one of this section such revocation shall be permanent and may not be waived by the commissioner under any circumstances.

3. Suspension.

(a) A commercial driver's license shall be suspended by the commissioner for a period of sixty days where the holder is convicted of two serious traffic violations as defined in subdivision four of this section committed within a three year period, in separate incidents whether such convictions occurred within or outside of this state.

(b) A commercial driver's license shall be suspended by the commissioner for a period of one hundred twenty days where the holder is convicted of three serious traffic violations as defined in subdivision four of this section committed within a three year period, in separate incidents whether such convictions occurred within or outside of this state. Such suspension shall take effect upon the termination of any other suspension already in effect pursuant to paragraph (a) of this subdivision or this paragraph.

(c) A commercial drivers license shall be suspended by the commissioner for a period of sixty days where the holder is convicted of a violation of subdivision (g) of section eleven hundred eighty of this chapter, and (i) the recorded or entered speed upon which the conviction was based exceeded the applicable speed limit by more than twenty miles per hour or (ii) the recorded or entered speed upon which the conviction was based exceeded the applicable speed limit by more than ten miles per hour and the vehicle was either (A) in violation of any rules or regulations involving an out-of-service defect relating to brake systems, steering components and/or coupling devices, or (B) transporting flammable gas, radioactive materials or explosives.

(d) A commercial driver's license shall be suspended by the commissioner:

(i) for a period of one hundred eighty days where the holder was found to have operated a commercial motor vehicle designed or used to transport property as defined in subparagraphs (i) and (ii) of paragraph (a) of subdivision four of section five hundred one-a of this title, in violation of an out-of-service order as provided for in the rules and regulations of the department of transportation whether such violation was committed within this state or was the same or a similar violation involving an out-of-service order committed outside of this state;

(ii) for a period of two years if, during any ten-year period, the holder is found to have committed two such violations not arising from the same incident whether such violations were committed within or outside of the state;

(iii) for a period of three years if, during any ten-year period, the holder is convicted of three or more such violations not arising from the same incident whether such violations were committed within or outside of the state;

(iv) for a period of one hundred eighty days if the holder is found to have operated a commercial motor vehicle designed or used to transport passengers or property as defined in subparagraphs (iii) and (v) of paragraph (a) of subdivision four of section five hundred one-a of this title, in violation of an out-of-service order, as provided for in the rules and regulations of the department of transportation, while transporting hazardous materials or passengers whether such violation was committed within this state or was the same or a similar violation committed outside of this state;

(v) for a period of three years if, during any ten-year period, the holder is found to have committed two or more violations, not arising from the same incident, of operating a commercial motor vehicle designed or used to transport passengers or property as defined in subparagraphs (iii) and (v) of paragraph (a) of subdivision four of section five hundred one-a of this title, in violation of an out-of-service order, as provided for in the rules and regulations of the department of transportation, while transporting hazardous materials or passengers whether such violation was committed within this state or was the same or asimilar violation involving an out-of-service order committed outside of this state.

(e) A commercial driver's license shall be suspended by the commissioner:

(i) for a period of sixty days where the holder is convicted of a violation of section eleven hundred seventy-one or section eleven hundred seventy-six of this chapter whether such violation was committed within this state or was the same or a similar violation involving railroad grade crossings committed outside of this state.

(ii) for a period of one hundred twenty days where the holder is convicted of a second violation of section eleven hundred seventy-one or section eleven hundred seventy-six of this chapter whether such violations were committed within or outside of this state, both of which were committed within a three year period.

(iii) for a period of one year where the holder is convicted of a third violation of section eleven hundred seventy-one or section eleven hundred seventy-six of this chapter whether such violations were committed within or outside of this state, all of which were committed within a three year period.

(f) [Repealed]

4. Serious traffic violations.

(a) A serious traffic violation shall mean operating a commercial motor vehicle in violation of any provision of this chapter or the laws or ordinances of any other state or locality outside of this state that restricts or prohibits the use of a hand-held mobile telephone or a portable electronic device while operating a commercial motor vehicle or in violation of any provision of this chapter or the laws of any other state, the District of Columbia or any Canadian province which (i) limits the speed of motor vehicles, provided the violation involved fifteen or more miles per hour over the established speed limit; (ii) is defined as reckless driving by state or local law or regulation; (iii) prohibits improper or erratic lane change; (iv) prohibits following too closely; (v) relates to motor vehicle traffic (other than parking, standing or stopping) and which arises in connection with a fatal accident; (vi) operating a commercial motor vehicle without first obtaining a commercial driver's license as required by section five hundred one of this title; (vii) operating a commercial motor vehicle without a commercial driver's license in the driver's possession; or (viii) operating a commercial motor vehicle without the proper class of commercial driver's license and/or endorsement for the specific vehicle being operated or for the passengers or type of cargo being transported.

(b) Whether any specific violation which occurs without this state is a serious violation shall be dependent upon whether the state or province in which the violation occurs, reports such violation to the commissioner as, or deems it to be, a serious traffic violation under the provisions of the federal commercial motor vehicle safety act of nineteen hundred eighty-six, public law 99-570, title XII or the motor carrier safety improvement act of 1999, public law 106-159 and regulations promulgated thereunder.

4-a. Dismissal. The court shall dismiss any charge of operating a commercial motor vehicle without a commercial driver's license in the driver's possession if, between the date the driver is charged with such violation and the appearance date for such violation, the driver supplies the court with proof that he or she held a valid commercial driver's license on the date of such violation. Such driver must also supply such proof to the law enforcement authority that issued the citation, prior to such driver's appearance in court.

5. Limitation of effect of revocation or suspension. Any revocation or suspension of a commercial driver's license issued pursuant to this section shall be applicable only to that portion of the holder's driver's license or privilege which permits the operation of commercial motor vehicles, and the commissioner shall immediately issue a license, other than a commercial driver's license, to such person, provided that such person is otherwise eligible to receive such license and further provided that issuing a license to such person does not create a substantial traffic safety hazard.

6. Application of section to persons not holding a commercial driver's license. Whenever a person who is not the holder of a commercial driver's license issued by the commissioner is convicted of a violation arising out of the operation of a commercial motor vehicle which would require the mandatory revocation or suspension of a commercial driver's license pursuant to this section or clause (i) or (ii) of subparagraph five of paragraph (b) or clause b of subparagraph three of paragraph (e) of subdivision two of section eleven hundred ninety-three, or clause c of subparagraph one of paragraph (d) of subdivision two of section eleven hundred ninety-four of this chapter, the privilege of such person to operate a commercial motor vehicle and/or to obtain a commercial driver's license issued by the commissioner will be suspended or revoked for the same periods of time and subject to the same conditions provided in this section, or clause (i) or (ii) of subparagraph five of paragraph (b) or clause b of subparagraph three of paragraph (e) of subdivision two of section eleven hundred ninety-three, or clause c of subparagraph one of paragraph (d) of subdivision two of section eleven hundred ninety-four of this chapter, which would be applicable to the holder of a commercial driver's license.

7. Other revocation or suspension action not prohibited. The provisions of this section shall not be construed to prevent any person who has the authority to suspend or revoke a license to drive or privilege of operating pursuant to section five hundred ten of this chapter from exercising any such authority based upon a conviction for which suspension or revocation of a commercial driver's license by the commissioner is mandated.

8. Disqualifications based upon record review.

(a) Where the commissioner conducts a state record review pursuant to section 384.206 of title 49 of the code of federal regulations and he or she determines that: (i) a person applying for a commercial driver's license was convicted outside of this state of an offense set forth in section 383.51 of title 49 of the code of federal regulations while holding a commercial driver's license issued by another state; and (ii) such other state failed to impose the commercial driver's license disqualification, suspension or revocation set forth in section 383.51 of title 49 of the code of federal regulations for such offense, then the commissioner shall immediately suspend such person's commercial driver's license or privilege of operating a commercial motor vehicle. Provided, however, that where such licenses would have been subject to revocation upon a conviction for such conduct had it occurred in this state, the commissioner shall revoke such license. Such suspension or revocation shall be for the applicable period of time set forth for a conviction for such offense in such section 383.51 as it existed on the date of the violation.

(b) Any suspension or revocation of a commercial driver's license issued pursuant to paragraph (a) of this subdivision shall be applicable only to that portion of the holder's driver's license or privilege which permits the operation of commercial motor vehicles, and the commissioner shall immediately issue a license, other than a commercial driver's license, to such person provided that such person is otherwise eligible to receive such license and further provided that issuing a license to such person does not create a substantial traffic safety hazard.

> **HISTORY:** Add, L 1990, ch 173, § 55, eff April 1, 1992; amd, L 1993, ch 550, § 2, eff Jan 24, 1994, L 1999, ch 412, § 1 (Part K), eff Nov 1, 1999, L 2001, ch 422, § 1, eff April 29, 2002, L 2002, ch 569, §§ 1, 2, eff Dec 23, 2002, L 2005, ch 60, §§ 13, 14 (Part E), eff Sept 30, 2005, L 2006, ch 59, § 2 (Part J), eff April 11, 2006, L 2007, ch 251, §§ 3, 4, eff July 18, 2007, L 2009, ch 59, §§ 6–9 (Part K), eff April 7, 2009, L 2010, ch 56, § 30 (Part LL), eff June 22, 2010, L 2011, ch 58, §§ 4–6 (Part CC), eff Jan 30, 2012, L 2012, ch 58, § 3 (Part D), eff March 30, 2012, L 2013, ch 58, § 1 (Part C), eff Oct 28, 2013.

§ 510-aa. Downgrade of commercial driver's licenses

A commercial driver's license shall be downgraded to a non-commercial driver's license by the commissioner within sixty days of the holder's medical certification status becoming "not-certified" based upon the expiration of the holder's medical certification or medical variance documentation required by the federal motor carrier safety improvement act of 1999 and Part 383.71(h) of title 49 of the code of federal regulations, or upon the holder's failure to submit such medical certification or medical variance documentation at such intervals as required by the federal motor carrier safety improvement act of 1999 and Part 383.71(h) of title 49 of the code of federal regulations and in a manner prescribed by the commissioner. A commercial driver's license shall also be downgraded to a non-commercial driver's license by the commissioner within sixty days of the holder's medical certification status becoming "not-certified" based upon receipt of information from the issuing medical examiner or the federal motor carrier safety administration that a medical certification or medical variance was issued in error or rescinded. Such downgrade shall be terminated, and the commercial driver's license restored, upon: (1) the holder's submission of the required valid medical examiner's certificate or medical variance documentation; or (2) the holder's self-certification specifying the type of commercial motor vehicle operation he or she engages, or expects to engage in, and that the holder is therefore not subject to the physical qualification requirements of the federal motor carrier safety improvement act of 1999 and Part 383.71(h) of title 49 of the code of federal regulations. The commissioner shall, upon a holder's status becoming "not-certified", notify the holder of such commercial driver's license by first class mail to the address of such person on file with the department or at the current address provided by the United States postal service of his or her "not-certified" medical certification status and that his or her commercial driver's license will be downgraded to a non-commercial driver's license unless he or she submits a current medical certificate and/or medical variance in accordance with Part 383.71(h) of title 49 of the code of federal regulations or changes his or her self-certification to driving only in excepted or intrastate commerce in accordance with Part 383.71(b)(ii)(B), (C) or (D) of title 49 of the code of federal regulations.

> **HISTORY:** Add, L 2012, ch 58, § 4 (Part D), eff March 30, 2012.

§ 510-b. Suspension and revocation for violations committed during probationary periods

1. A license, other than a class DJ or class MJ license, shall be suspended, for a period of sixty days, (i) upon the first conviction of the licensee of a violation, committed during the probationary period provided for in subdivision four of section five hundred one of this title, of any provision of section eleven hundred twenty-nine of this chapter, section eleven hundred eighty of this chapter or any ordinance or regulation limiting the speed of motor vehicles and motorcycles, section eleven hundred eighty-two of this chapter, subdivision one of section eleven hundred ninety-two of this chapter or section twelve hundred twelve of this chapter; or (ii) upon the second conviction of the licensee of a violation, committed during the aforesaid probationary period, of any other provision of this chapter or of any other law, ordinance, order, rule or regulation relating to traffic.

2. A license, other than a class DJ or class MJ license, considered probationary pursuant to subdivision three of this section shall be revoked upon the conviction of the licensee of a violation or violations committed within six months following the restoration or issuance of such license, which conviction or convictions would result in the suspension of a probationary license pursuant to subdivision one of this section or subparagraph (xvi) of paragraph b of subdivision two of section five hundred ten of this article.

3. Any license, other than a class DJ or class MJ license, which is restored or issued to a person who has had his last valid license suspended or revoked pursuant to the provisions of this section or the provisions of subparagraph (xii) of paragraph a or subparagraph (xvi) of paragraph b of subdivision two of section five hundred ten of this article shall be considered probationary until the expiration of six months following the date of restoration or issuance thereof.

4. The provisions of subdivisions one, five, six and seven of section five hundred ten of this chapter shall apply to any suspension or revocation under this section. However, the provisions of this section shall not operate to prevent a mandatory revocation or suspension for a greater period of time under subdivision two of section five hundred ten of this chapter or section eleven hundred ninety-three of this chapter; nor shall the provisions of this section prevent revocation or suspension under subdivisions two and three of section five hundred ten based upon two or more violations, including the same violation which was the basis for suspension or revocation under this section.

HISTORY: Add, L 1969, ch 445, § 4, eff Jan 1, 1970, applicable only to licenses issued on and after that date; amd, L 1973, ch 229, § 6, L 1988, ch 47, §§ 10, 11, eff Nov 1, 1988, L 2002, ch 644, § 10, eff Sept 1, 2003, L 2009, ch 403, § 8, eff Feb 22, 2010, L 2013, ch 91, § 1, eff July 1, 2013, L 2014, ch 55, § 4 (Part B), eff Nov 1, 2014.

§ 510-c. Suspension and revocation of learner's permits and driver's licenses for violations committed by holders of class DJ or class MJ learner's permits or licenses

1. (a) A learner's permit or a driver's license shall be suspended for a period of sixty days:

(i) upon a conviction or finding of a serious traffic violation as defined in subdivision two of this section, when such violation was committed while the holder had a class DJ or class MJ learner's permit or a class DJ or MJ license; or

(ii) upon the second conviction or finding of such permit or license holder of a violation of any other provision of this chapter or any other law, ordinance, order, rule or regulation relating to traffic, and when such violation was committed while such holder had a class DJ or class MJ learner's permit or a class DJ or MJ license.

(b) A learner's permit or a driver's license shall be revoked for a period of sixty days upon the conviction or finding of the permit or license holder of a violation or violations, committed within six months after the restoration of such permit or license suspended pursuant to paragraph (a) of this subdivision, which convictions or findings would result in the suspension of such permit or license pursuant to paragraph (a) of this subdivision.

2. For purposes of this section, the term "serious traffic violation" shall mean operating a motor vehicle in violation of any of the following provisions of this chapter: articles twenty-five and twenty-six; subdivision one of section six hundred; section six hundred one; sections eleven hundred eleven, eleven hundred seventy, eleven hundred seventy-two and eleven hundred seventy-four; subdivisions (a), (b), (c), (d) and (f) of section eleven hundred eighty, provided that the violation involved ten or more miles per hour over the established limit; section eleven hundred eighty-two; subdivision three-a of section twelve hundred twenty-nine-c for violations involving

use of safety belts or seats by a child under the age of sixteen; and section twelve hundred twelve of this chapter.

3. Any suspension or revocation required for a violation of section twelve hundred twenty-five-c or section twelve hundred twenty-five-d of this chapter shall be subject to the provisions of subdivisions two and six of section five hundred ten of this article.

4. [Redesignated]

HISTORY: Add, L 2002, ch 644, § 11, eff Sept 1, 2003; amd, L 2009, ch 403, § 9, eff Feb 22, 2010, L 2013, ch 91, § 2, eff July 1, 2013, L 2014, ch 55, § 5 (Part B), eff Nov 1, 2014.

§ 511. Operation while license or privilege is suspended or revoked; aggravated unlicensed operation

1. Aggravated unlicensed operation of a motor vehicle in the third degree.

(a) A person is guilty of the offense of aggravated unlicensed operation of a motor vehicle in the third degree when such person operates a motor vehicle upon a public highway while knowing or having reason to know that such person's license or privilege of operating such motor vehicle in this state or privilege of obtaining a license to operate such motor vehicle issued by the commissioner is suspended, revoked or otherwise withdrawn by the commissioner.

(b) Aggravated unlicensed operation of a motor vehicle in the third degree is a misdemeanor. When a person is convicted of this offense, the sentence of the court must be: (i) a fine of not less than two hundred dollars nor more than five hundred dollars; or (ii) a term of imprisonment of not more than thirty days; or (iii) both such fine and imprisonment.

(c) When a person is convicted of this offense with respect to the operation of a motor vehicle with a gross vehicle weight rating of more than eighteen thousand pounds, the sentence of the court must be: (i) a fine of not less than five hundred dollars nor more than fifteen hundred dollars; or (ii) a term of imprisonment of not more than thirty days; or (iii) both such fine and imprisonment.

2. Aggravated unlicensed operation of a motor vehicle in the second degree.

(a) A person is guilty of the offense of aggravated unlicensed operation of a motor vehicle in the second degree when such person commits the offense of aggravated unlicensed operation of a motor vehicle in the third degree as defined in subdivision one of this section; and

(i) has previously been convicted of an offense that consists of or includes the elements comprising the offense committed within the immediately preceding eighteen months; or

(ii) the suspension or revocation is based upon a refusal to submit to a chemical test pursuant to section eleven hundred ninety-four of this chapter, a finding of driving after having consumed alcohol in violation of section eleven hundred ninety-two-a of this chapter or upon a conviction for a violation of any of the provisions of section eleven hundred ninety-two of this chapter; or

(iii) the suspension was a mandatory suspension pending prosecution of a charge of a violation of section eleven hundred ninety-two of this chapter ordered pursuant to paragraph (e) of subdivision two of section eleven hundred ninety-three of this chapter or other similar statute; or

(iv) such person has in effect three or more suspensions, imposed on at least three separate dates, for failure to answer, appear or pay a fine, pursuant to subdivision three of section two hundred twenty-six or subdivision four-a of section five hundred ten of this chapter.

(b) Aggravated unlicensed operation of a motor vehicle in the second degree is a misdemeanor. When a person is convicted of this crime under subparagraph (i) of paragraph (a) of this subdivision, the sentence of the court must be: (i) a fine of not less than five hundred dollars; and (ii) a term of imprisonment not to exceed one hundred eighty days; or (iii) where appropriate a sentence of probation as provided in subdivision six of this section; or (iv) a term of imprisonment as a condition of a sentence of probation as provided in the penal law and consistent with this section. When a person is convicted of this crime under subparagraph (ii), (iii) or (iv) of paragraph (a) of this subdivision, the sentence of the court must be: (i) a fine of not less than five hundred dollars nor more than one thousand dollars; and (ii) a term of imprisonment of not less than seven days nor more than one hundred eighty days, or (iii) where appropriate a sentence of probation as provided in subdivision six of this section; or (iv) a term of imprisonment as a condition of a sentence of probation as provided in the penal law and consistent with this section.

3. Aggravated unlicensed operation of a motor vehicle in the first degree.

(a) A person is guilty of the offense of aggravated unlicensed operation of a motor vehicle in the first degree when such person:

(i) commits the offense of aggravated unlicensed operation of a motor vehicle in the second degree as provided in subparagraph (ii), (iii) or (iv) of paragraph (a) of subdivision two of this section and is operating a motor vehicle while under the influence of alcohol or a drug in violation of subdivision one, two, two-a, three, four, four-a or five of section eleven hundred ninety-two of this chapter; or

(ii) commits the offense of aggravated unlicensed operation of a motor vehicle in the third degree as defined in subdivision one of this section; and is operating a motor vehicle while such person has in effect ten or more suspensions, imposed on at least ten separate dates for failure to answer, appear or pay a fine, pursuant to subdivision three of section two hundred twenty-six of this chapter or subdivision four-a of section five hundred ten of this article; or

(iii) commits the offense of aggravated unlicensed operation of a motor vehicle in the third degree as defined in subdivision one of this section; and is operating a motor vehicle while under permanent revocation as set forth in subparagraph twelve of paragraph (b) of subdivision two of section eleven hundred ninety-three of this chapter; or

(iv) operates a motor vehicle upon a public highway while holding a conditional license issued pursuant to paragraph (a) of subdivision seven of section eleven hundred ninety-six of this chapter while under the influence of alcohol or a drug in violation of subdivision one, two, two-a, three, four, four-a or five of section eleven hundred ninety-two of this chapter.

(b) Aggravated unlicensed operation of a motor vehicle in the first degree is a class E felony. When a person is convicted of this crime, the sentence of the court must be: (i) a fine in an amount not less than five hundred dollars nor more than five thousand dollars; and (ii) a term of imprisonment as provided in the penal law, or (iii) where appropriate and a term of imprisonment is not required by the penal law, a sentence of probation as provided in subdivision six of this section, or (iv) a term of imprisonment as a condition of a sentence of probation as provided in the penal law.

4. Defense. In any prosecution under this section or section five hundred eleven-a of this chapter,

it is a defense that the person operating the motor vehicle has at the time of the offense a license issued by a foreign country, state, territory or federal district, which license is valid for operation in this state in accordance with the provisions of section two hundred fifty of this chapter.

5. Limitation on pleas. Where an accusatory instrument charges a violation of this section, any plea of guilty entered in satisfaction of such charge must include at least a plea of guilty of one of the offenses defined by this section and no other disposition by plea of guilty to any other charge in satisfaction of such charge shall be authorized; provided, however, that if the district attorney upon reviewing the available evidence determines that the charge of a violation of this section is not warranted, he may set forth upon the record the basis for such determination and consent to a disposition by plea of guilty to another charge in satisfaction of such charge, and the court may accept such plea.

6. Sentence of probation. In any case where a sentence of probation is authorized by this section, the court may in its discretion impose such sentence, provided however, if the court is of the opinion that a program of alcohol or drug treatment may be effective in assisting in prevention of future offenses of a similar nature upon imposing such sentence, the court shall require as a condition of the sentence that the defendant participate in such a program.

7. Exceptions. When a person is convicted of a violation of subdivision one or two of this section, and the suspension was issued pursuant to (a) subdivision four-e of section five hundred ten of this article due to a support arrears, or (b) subdivision four-f of section five hundred ten of the [this]* article due to past-due tax liabilities, the mandatory penalties set forth in subdivision one or two of this section shall not be applicable if, on or before the return date or subsequent adjourned date, such person presents proof that such support arrears or past-due tax liabilities have been satisfied as shown by certified check, notice issued by the court ordering the suspension, or notice from a support collection unit or department of taxation and finance as applicable. The sentencing court shall take the satisfaction of arrears or the payment of the past-due tax liabilities into account when imposing a sentence for any such conviction. For licenses suspended for nonpayment of past-due tax liabilities, the court shall also take into consideration proof, in the form of a notice from the department of taxation and finance, that such person has made payment arrangements that are satisfactory to the commissioner of taxation and finance.

HISTORY: Add, L 1985, ch 756, § 1, eff Nov 1, 1985; amd, L 1986, ch 227, § 1, eff Nov 1, 1986, L 1988, ch 47, § 12, L 1989, ch 420, § 1, eff Oct 14, 1989, L 1990, ch 173, § 24, eff Aug 19, 1990, L 1990, ch 173, § 55-a, eff April 1, 1992, L 1990, ch 786, §§ 1, 2, eff Nov 1, 1990, L 1990, 892, § 1, eff July 30, 1990, L 1993, ch 607, §§ 4–7, eff Nov 1, 1993, L 1995, ch 81, § 212, eff Oct 1, 1995, L 1996, ch 196, § 6, eff Nov 1, 1996, L 2004, ch 673, § 1, eff Nov 1, 2005, L 2006, ch 732, § 25, eff Nov 1, 2006, L 2006, ch 746, § 6, eff Dec 15, 2006, L 2013, ch 59, § 3 (Part P), eff March 28, 2013, L 2013, ch 169, § 1, eff Nov 1, 2013.

§ 511-a. Facilitating aggravated unlicensed operation of a motor vehicle

1. A person is guilty of the offense of facilitating aggravated unlicensed operation of a motor vehicle in the third degree when such person consents to the operation upon a public highway of a motor vehicle registered in such person's name knowing or having reason to know that the operator of such vehicle is a person whose license or privilege of operating such motor vehicle in this state or privilege of obtaining a license issued to operate such motor vehicle by the commissioner is suspended, revoked or otherwise withdrawn by the commissioner and the vehicle is operated upon a public highway by such person.

---

* The word has been inserted by the Publisher.

2. Facilitating aggravated unlicensed operation of a motor vehicle in the third degree is a traffic infraction. When a person is convicted thereof the sentence of the court must be: (i) a fine of not less than two hundred dollars nor more than five hundred dollars or (ii) a term of imprisonment of not more than fifteen days, or (iii) both.

3. A person is guilty of facilitating aggravated unlicensed operation of a motor vehicle in the second degree when such person:

(a) commits the offense of facilitating aggravated unlicensed operation of a motor vehicle in the third degree as defined in subdivision one of this section after having been convicted of such offense within the preceding eighteen months; or

(b) consents to the operation upon a public highway of a motor vehicle registered in such person's name knowing or having reason to know that the operator of such vehicle is a person who has in effect three or more suspensions, imposed on at least three separate dates, for failure to answer, appear or pay a fine, pursuant to subdivision three of section two hundred twenty-six or subdivision four-a of section five hundred ten of this chapter; or

(c) commits the crime of facilitating aggravated unlicensed operation of a motor vehicle in the third degree after having been convicted of such an offense two or more times within the preceding five years.

For purposes of this subdivision, "motor vehicle" shall mean any vehicle for hire, including a taxicab, livery, as defined in section one hundred twenty-one-e of this chapter, coach, limousine, van or wheelchair accessible van, tow truck, bus or commercial motor vehicle as defined* section five hundred nine-a of this chapter.

Facilitating aggravated unlicensed operation of a motor vehicle in the second degree is a misdemeanor. When a person is convicted of this crime pursuant to paragraphs (a) or (b) of this subdivision, the sentence of the court must be: (i) a fine of not less than five hundred dollars, nor more than seven hundred fifty dollars; or (ii) a term of imprisonment not to exceed sixty days; or (iii) both a fine and imprisonment; or (iv) where appropriate, a sentence of probation; or (v) a term of imprisonment as a condition of a sentence of probation as provided in the penal law. When a person is convicted of this crime pursuant to paragraph (c) of this subdivision, the sentence of the court must be: (i) a fine of not less than five hundred, nor more than one thousand dollars; or (ii) a term of imprisonment not to exceed one hundred eighty days; or (iii) both a fine and imprisonment; or (iv) where appropriate, a sentence of probation; or (v) a term of imprisonment as a condition of probation as provided in the penal law.

4. A person is guilty of facilitating aggravated unlicensed operation of a motor vehicle in the first degree when such person consents to the operation upon a public highway of a motor vehicle registered in such person's name knowing or having reason to know that the operator of such vehicle is a person who has in effect ten or more suspensions, imposed on at least ten separate dates, for failure to answer, appear or pay a fine, pursuant to subdivision three of section two hundred twenty-six or subdivision four-a of section five hundred ten of this chapter.

For purposes of this subdivision, "motor vehicle" shall mean any vehicle for hire, including a taxicab, livery, as defined in section one hundred twenty-one-e of this chapter, coach, limousine, van or wheelchair accessible van, tow truck, bus or commercial motor vehicle as defined in section five hundred nine-a of this chapter.

Facilitating aggravated unlicensed operation of a motor vehicle in the first degree is a class E

---

* So in original.

felony. When a person is convicted of this crime, the sentence of the court must be: (i) a fine in an amount not less than one thousand dollars nor more than five thousand dollars; and (ii) a term of imprisonment as provided in the penal law; or (iii) where appropriate, a sentence of probation; or (iv) a term of imprisonment as a condition of a sentence of probation as provided in the penal law.

5. Upon a conviction of a violation of subdivision three or four of this section the commissioner shall revoke the registration of the motor vehicle for which the defendant's consent is given and shall only be restored pursuant to the provisions of subdivision five of section five hundred ten of this article. If such defendant is a corporation, partnership, association or other group, none of its officers, principals, directors or stockholders owning more than ten percent of the outstanding stock of the corporation shall be eligible to register the motor vehicle.

> **HISTORY:** Add, L 1985, ch 756, § 1, eff Nov 1, 1985. Sub 1, amd, L 1990, ch 173, § 55-b, eff April 1, 1992. Amd, L 1993, ch 606, § 2, eff Nov 1, 1993. Sub 1, amd, L 1993, ch 606, § 2, eff Nov 1, 1993. Sub 2, formerly sub 2, opening par and pars (a) and (b), so designated and amd, L 1993, ch 606, § 2, eff Nov 1, 1993. Subs 3–5, add, L 1993, ch 606, § 2, eff Nov 1, 1993.

§ 511-b. Seizure and redemption of unlawfully operated vehicles

1. Upon making an arrest or upon issuing a summons or an appearance ticket for the crime of aggravated unlicensed operation of a motor vehicle in the first or second degree committed in his presence, an officer shall remove or arrange for the removal of the vehicle to a garage, automobile pound, or other place of safety where it shall remain impounded, subject to the provisions of this section if: (a) the operator is the registered owner of the vehicle or the vehicle is not properly registered; or (b) proof of financial security is not produced; or (c) where a person other than the operator is the registered owner and, such person or another properly licensed and authorized to possess and operate the vehicle is not present. The vehicle shall be entered into the New York statewide police information network as an impounded vehicle and the impounding police department shall promptly notify the owner and the local authority that the vehicle has been impounded.

2. A motor vehicle so impounded shall be in the custody of the local authority and shall not be released unless:

(a) The person who redeems it has furnished satisfactory evidence of registration and financial security;

(b) Payment has been made for the reasonable costs of removal and storage of the motor vehicle. The registered owner of the vehicle shall be responsible for such payment provided, however, that if he was not the operator at the time of the offense he shall have a cause of action against such operator to recover such costs. Payment prior to release of the vehicle shall not be required in cases where the impounded vehicle was stolen or was rented or leased pursuant to a written agreement for a period of thirty days or less, however the operator of such a vehicle shall be liable for the costs of removal and storage of the vehicle to any entity rendering such service.

(c) Where the motor vehicle was operated by a person who at the time of the offense was the owner thereof, (i) satisfactory evidence that the registered owner or other person seeking to redeem the vehicle has a license or privilege to operate a motor vehicle in this state, and (ii) (A) satisfactory evidence that the criminal action founded upon the charge of aggravated unlicensed operation of a motor vehicle has been terminated and that any fine imposed as a result of a conviction thereon has been paid, or (B) a certificate issued by the court in which the criminal action was commenced ordering release of the vehicle prior to the judgment or compliance therewith in the interest of justice, or (C) a certificate issued by the district attorney or other officer authorized to prosecute such charge waiving the requirement that the vehicle be held as security for appearance before and compliance with the judgment of the court.

3. When a vehicle seized and impounded pursuant to this section has been in the custody of the local authority for thirty days, such authority shall make inquiry in the manner prescribed by the commissioner as to the name and address of the owner and any lienholder and upon receipt of such information shall notify the owner and the lienholder, if any, at his last known address by certified mail, return receipt requested, that if the vehicle is not retrieved pursuant to subdivision two of this section within thirty days from the date the notice is given, it will be forfeited. If the vehicle was registered in New York the last known address shall be that address on file with the commissioner. If the vehicle was registered out-of-state or never registered, notification shall be made in the manner prescribed by the commissioner.

4. A motor vehicle that has been seized and not retrieved pursuant to the foregoing provisions of this section shall be forfeited to the local authority upon expiration of the period of the notice set forth in subdivision three of this section provided, however, in computing such period, the period of time during which a criminal prosecution is or was pending against the owner for a violation of this section shall be excluded. A proceeding to decree such forfeiture and to recover towing and storage costs, if any, to the extent such costs exceed the fair market value of the vehicle may be brought by the local authority in the court in which the criminal action for aggravated unlicensed operation of a motor vehicle was commenced by petition for an order decreeing forfeiture of the motor vehicle accompanied by an affidavit attesting to facts showing that forfeiture is warranted. If the identity and address of the owner and/or lienholder is known to the local authority, ten days notice shall be given to such party, who shall have an opportunity to appear and be heard prior to entry of an order decreeing forfeiture. Where the court is satisfied that forfeiture of a motor vehicle is warranted in accordance with this section, it shall enter an order decreeing forfeiture of such vehicle. Provided, however, that the court at any time prior to entry of such an order may authorize release of the vehicle in accordance with subdivision two of this section upon a showing of good cause for failure to retrieve same prior to commencement of the proceeding to decree forfeiture, but if the court orders release of the motor vehicle as herein provided and the vehicle is not redeemed within ten days from the date of such order, the vehicle shall be deemed to have been abandoned and the court upon application of the local authority must enter an order decreeing its forfeiture.

5. A motor vehicle forfeited in accordance with the provisions of this section shall be and become the property of the local authority, subject however to any lien that was recorded prior to the seizure.

6. For the purposes of this section, the term "local authority" means the municipality in which the motor vehicle was seized; except that if the motor vehicle was seized on property of the New York state thruway authority or property under the jurisdiction of the office of parks, recreation and historic preservation, the department of transportation, or a public authority or commission, the term "local authority" means such authority, office, department, or commission. A county may provide by local law that the county may act as the agent for a local authority under this section.

7. When a vehicle has been seized and impounded pursuant to this section, the local authority or any person having custody of the vehicle shall make the vehicle available or grant access to it to any owner or any person designated or authorized by such owner for the purpose of (i) taking possession of any personal property found within the vehicle and (ii) obtaining proof of registration, financial security, title or documentation in support thereof.

HISTORY: Add, L 1985, ch 756, § 1, eff Nov 1, 1985. Sub 1, amd, L 1989, ch 425, § 1, eff Oct 14, 1989. Sub 2, par (b), add, L 1989, ch 425, § 2, eff Oct 14, 1989. Former sub 2, par (b), repealed, L 1989, ch 425, § 2, eff Oct 14, 1989. Sub 3, amd, L 1989, ch 425, § 3, eff Oct 14, 1989. Sub 4, amd, L 1989, ch 425, § 3, eff Oct 14, 1989. Sub 6, amd, L 1989, ch 425, § 3, eff Oct 14, 1989. Sub 1, amd, L 1993, ch 607, § 8, eff Nov 1, 1993.

§ 511-c. Seizure and forfeiture of vehicles used in the unlicensed operation of a motor vehicle under certain circumstances

1. For purposes of this section:

(a) The term "owner" shall mean an owner as defined in section one hundred twenty-eight and in subdivision three of section three hundred eighty-eight of this chapter.

(b) The term "security interest" shall mean a security interest as defined in subdivision (k) of section two thousand one hundred one of this chapter.

(c) The term "termination of the criminal proceeding" shall mean the earliest of (i) thirty-one days following the imposition of sentence; or (ii) the date of acquittal of a person arrested for an offense; or (iii) where leave to file new charges or to resubmit the case to a new grand jury is required and has not been granted, thirty-one days following the dismissal of the last accusatory instrument filed in the case, or, if applicable, upon expiration of the time granted by the court or permitted by statute for filing new charges or resubmitting the case to a new grand jury; or (iv) where leave to file new charges or to resubmit the case to a new grand jury is not required, thirty-one days following the dismissal of the last accusatory instrument filed in the case, or, if applicable, upon expiration of the time granted by the court or permitted by statute for filing new charges or resubmitting the case to a new grand jury; or (v) six months from the issuance of an "adjournment in contemplation of dismissal" order pursuant to section 170.55 of the criminal procedure law, where the case is not restored to the court's calendar within the applicable six-month period; or (vi) the date when, prior to the filing of an accusatory instrument against a person arrested for an offense, the prosecuting authority elects not to prosecute such person.

2. Any motor vehicle which has been or is being used in violation of paragraph (a) of subdivision three of section five hundred eleven of this article may be seized by any peace officer, acting pursuant to his or her special duties, or police officer, and forfeited as hereinafter provided in this section.

3. A vehicle may be seized upon service of a notice of violation upon the owner or operator of a vehicle. The seized motor vehicle shall be delivered by the officer having made the seizure to the custody of the district attorney of the county wherein the seizure was made, except that in the cities of New York, Yonkers, Rochester and Buffalo the seized motor vehicle shall be delivered to the custody of the police department of such cities and such motor vehicle seized by a member or members of the state police shall be delivered to the custody of the superintendent of state police, together with a report of all the facts and circumstances of the seizure. Within one business day after the seizure, notice of such violation and a copy of the notice of violation shall be mailed to the owner of such vehicle at the address for such owner set forth in the records maintained by the department of motor vehicles or, for vehicles not registered in New York state, such equivalent record in such state of registration.

4. (a) The attorney general in seizures by members of the state police, or the district attorney of the county wherein the seizure is made, if elsewhere than in the cities of New York, Yonkers, Rochester or Buffalo, or where the seizure is made in such cities, the corporation counsel of the city shall inquire into the facts of the seizure so reported to him or her. If it appears that there

is a basis for the commencement and prosecution of a forfeiture proceeding pursuant to this section, any such forfeiture proceeding shall be commenced in supreme court not later than twenty days after the date of receipt of a written demand by a person claiming ownership of the motor vehicle accompanied by the documentation required to be presented upon release of the vehicle pursuant to subparagraphs (i), (ii), and (iv) of paragraph (a) of subdivision five of this section.

(b) Where forfeiture proceedings are commenced and prosecuted pursuant to this section, the motor vehicle which is the subject of such proceedings shall remain in the custody of such district attorney, police department or superintendent of state police, as applicable, pending the final determination of such proceedings.

(c) To the extent applicable, the procedures of article thirteen-A of the civil practice law and rules shall govern proceedings and actions under this section.

5. A motor vehicle seized pursuant to this section shall be released when:

(a) (i) Such attorney general, district attorney or corporation counsel has made a determination not to institute forfeiture proceedings pursuant to this section or the time period within which a forfeiture proceeding could have been commenced pursuant to this section has elapsed and no such forfeiture proceeding was commenced or the criminal proceeding has been terminated in favor of the accused, as defined in subdivision three of section 160.50 of the criminal procedure law; and

(ii) The person seeking to claim the motor vehicle has furnished satisfactory evidence of registration and financial security and, if the person was the operator of the vehicle at the time of the violation of paragraph (a) of subdivision three of section five hundred eleven of this article, satisfactory evidence of payment of any fines or penalties imposed in connection therewith; and

(iii) Payment has been made for the reasonable costs of removal and storage of the motor vehicle. The owner of the motor vehicle shall be responsible for such payment provided, however, that if he or she was not the operator at the time of the offense, such person shall have a cause of action against such operator to recover such costs. Payment prior to release of the motor vehicle shall not be required in cases where the seized motor vehicle was stolen or rented or leased pursuant to a written agreement for a period of thirty days or less, however the operator of such a motor vehicle shall be liable for the costs of removal and storage of the motor vehicle to any entity rendering such service; and

(iv) If the motor vehicle is held as evidence, the person seeking to claim the motor vehicle has presented a release from the prosecuting authority providing that the motor vehicle is not needed as evidence.

(b) (i) Pending completion of forfeiture proceedings which have been commenced, the person seeking to claim the motor vehicle has posted a bond in a form satisfactory to such attorney general, district attorney or corporation counsel in an amount that shall not exceed an amount sufficient to cover the maximum fines or civil penalties which may be imposed for the violation underlying the seizure and all reasonable costs for removal and storage of such vehicle; and

(ii) The persons seeking to claim the motor vehicle has* furnished satisfactory evidence

---

* So in original.

of registration and financial security.

6. Where a demand for the return of a motor vehicle is not made within ninety days after the termination of the criminal proceeding founded upon the charge of aggravated unlicensed operation of a motor vehicle in the first degree, such motor vehicle shall be deemed to be abandoned. Such vehicle shall be disposed of by the county, cities of New York, Yonkers, Rochester or Buffalo or the state, as applicable, in accordance with section twelve hundred twenty-four of this chapter or as otherwise provided by law.

7. Notice of the institution of the forfeiture proceeding shall be served:

(a) By personal service pursuant to the civil practice law and rules upon all owners of the seized motor vehicle listed in the records maintained by the department, or for vehicles not registered in New York state, in the records maintained by the state of registration; and

(b) By first class mail upon all individuals who have notified such attorney general, district attorney or corporation counsel that they are an owner of the vehicle and upon all persons holding a security interest in such motor vehicle which security interest has been filed with the department pursuant to the provisions of title ten of this chapter, at the address set forth in the records of such department, or for motor vehicles not registered in New York state, all persons holding a security interest in such motor vehicle which security interest has been filed with such state of registration, at the address provided by such state of registration.

8. Any owner who receives notice of the institution of a forfeiture action who claims an interest in the motor vehicle subject to forfeiture shall assert a claim for the recovery of the motor vehicle or satisfaction of the owner's interest in such motor vehicle by intervening in the forfeiture action in accordance with subdivision (a) of section one thousand twelve of the civil practice law and rules. Any person with a security interest in such vehicle who receives notice of the institution of the forfeiture action shall assert a claim for the satisfaction of such person's security interest in such vehicle by intervening in the forfeiture action in accordance with subdivision (a) of section one thousand twelve of the civil practice law and rules. If the action relates to a vehicle in which a person holding a security interest has intervened pursuant to this subdivision, the burden shall be upon the designated official to prove by clear and convincing evidence that such intervenor knew that such vehicle was or would be used for the commission of a violation of subparagraph (ii) of paragraph (a) of subdivision three of section five hundred eleven of the vehicle and traffic law and either (a) knowingly and unlawfully benefitted from such conduct or (b) voluntarily agreed to the use of the vehicle for the commission of such violation by consent freely given. For purposes of this subdivision, such intervenor knowingly and unlawfully benefited from the commission of such violation when he or she derived in exchange for permitting the use of such vehicle by a person or persons committing such specified violation a substantial benefit that would otherwise not have accrued as a result of the lawful use of such vehicle. "Benefit" means benefit as defined in subdivision seventeen of section 10.00 of the penal law.

9. No motor vehicle shall be forfeited under this section to the extent of the interest of a person who claims an interest in the motor vehicle, where such person pleads and proves that:

(a) The use of such motor vehicle for the conduct that was the basis for a seizure occurred without the knowledge of such person, or if such person had knowledge of such use, without the consent of such person, and that such person did not knowingly obtain such interest in the motor vehicle in order to avoid the forfeiture of such vehicle; or

(b) The conduct that was the basis for such seizure was committed by any person other than such person claiming an interest in the motor vehicle, while such motor vehicle was unlawfully in the possession of a person who acquired possession thereof in violation of the criminal laws of the United States or any state.

10. The court in which a forfeiture action is pending may dismiss said action in the interests of justice upon its own motion or upon an application as provided for herein.

(a) At any time during the pendency of a forfeiture action, the designated official who instituted the action, or a defendant may apply for an order dismissing the complaint and terminating the forfeiture action in the interest of justice.

(b) Such application for the relief provided in paragraph (a) of this subdivision must be made in writing and upon notice to all parties. The court may, in its discretion, direct that notice be given to any other person having an interest in the property.

(c) An application for the relief provided for in paragraph (a) of this subdivision must be brought exclusively in the superior court in which the forfeiture action is pending.

(d) The court may grant the relief provided in paragraph (a) of this subdivision if it finds that such relief is warranted by the existence of some compelling factor, consideration or circumstance demonstrating that forfeiture of the property or any part thereof, would not serve the ends of justice. Among the factors, considerations and circumstances the court may consider, among others, are:

(i) the seriousness and circumstances of the crime to which the property is connected relative to the impact of forfeiture of property upon the person who committed the crime; or

(ii) the adverse impact of a forfeiture of property upon innocent persons.

(e) The court must issue a written decision stating the basis for an order issued pursuant to this subdivision.

11. The district attorney, police department or superintendent of state police having custody of the seized motor vehicle, after such judicial determination of forfeiture, shall, by a public notice of at least twenty days, sell such forfeited motor vehicle at public sale. The net proceeds of any such sale, after deduction of the lawful expenses incurred, shall be paid into the general fund of the county wherein the seizure was made, provided, however, that the net proceeds of the sale of a motor vehicle seized in the cities of New York, Yonkers, Rochester and Buffalo shall be paid into the respective general funds of such cities, and provided further that the net proceeds of the sale of a motor vehicle seized by the state police shall be paid into the state police seized assets account.

12. In any action commenced pursuant to this section, where the court awards a sum of money to one or more persons in satisfaction of such person's or persons' interest or interests in the forfeited motor vehicle, the total amount awarded to satisfy such interest or interests shall not exceed the amount of the net proceeds of the sale of the forfeited motor vehicle, after deduction of the lawful expenses incurred by the county, cities of New York, Yonkers, Rochester or Buffalo or the state, as applicable, and storage of the motor vehicle between the time of seizure and the date of sale.

13. At any time within two years after the seizure, any person claiming an interest in a motor vehicle which has been forfeited pursuant to this section who was not sent notice of the commencement of the forfeiture action pursuant to subdivision seven of this section, or who did not otherwise receive actual notice of the forfeiture action, may assert in an action commenced before the justice of the supreme court before whom the forfeiture action was held such claim as could have been asserted in the forfeiture action pursuant to this section. The court may grant the

relief sought upon such terms and conditions as it deems reasonable and just if the person claiming an interest in the motor vehicle establishes that he or she was not sent notice of the commencement of the forfeiture action and was without actual knowledge of the forfeiture action, and establishes either of the affirmative defenses set forth in subdivision nine of this section.

14. No action under this section for wrongful seizure shall be instituted unless such action is commenced within two years after the time when the motor vehicle was seized.

HISTORY: Add, L 1993, ch 607, § 9, eff Nov 1, 1993.

§ 511-d. Aggravated failure to answer appearance tickets or pay fines imposed

1. A person is guilty of the offense of aggravated failure to answer appearance tickets or pay fines imposed when such person has in effect twenty or more suspensions, imposed on at least twenty separate dates, for failure to answer, appear or pay a fine pursuant to subdivision three of section two hundred twenty-six or subdivision four-a of section five hundred ten of this chapter.

2. A person may be prosecuted for a violation of this section in any court of competent jurisdiction in any county: (a) in which more than ten tickets which resulted in suspension for failures to answer, appear or pay fines were issued, or (b) in which the twentieth or any subsequent ticket which resulted in a suspension for failure to answer, appear or pay a fine was issued. The provisions of this subdivision shall not apply to any suspension which has been terminated prior to the defendant's being charged with a violation of this section.

3. Aggravated failure to answer appearance tickets or pay fines imposed is a misdemeanor. When a person is convicted of this crime, the sentence of the court must be: (i) a fine of not less than five hundred dollars; or (ii) a term of imprisonment of not more than one hundred eighty days; or (iii) both such fine and imprisonment.

HISTORY: Add, L 1993, ch 607, § 9, eff Nov 1, 1993.

§ 512. Operation while registration or privilege is suspended or revoked

Any person who operates any motor vehicle upon a public highway while the certificate of registration of such motor vehicle or privilege of operation of such motor vehicle in this state or privilege of obtaining a certificate of registration issued by the commissioner is suspended or revoked shall be guilty of a misdemeanor, and upon conviction shall be subject to a fine of not less than fifty dollars nor more than one hundred dollars or by imprisonment for not exceeding thirty days or by both such fine and imprisonment for conviction of a first offense; by a fine of not less than one hundred dollars nor more than two hundred dollars or by imprisonment for not exceeding ninety days or by both such fine and imprisonment for a conviction of a second offense committed within a period of eighteen months; by a fine of not less than two hundred dollars nor more than five hundred dollars or by imprisonment for not exceeding one hundred eighty days or by both such fine and imprisonment for a conviction of a third or subsequent offense committed within a period of eighteen months.

HISTORY: Add, L 1959, ch 775, with substance transferred from former § 70(7); amd, L 1976, ch 404, § 4, L 1985, ch 756, § 2, eff Nov 1, 1985. Section heading, amd, L 1976, ch 404, § 4, eff Oct 1, 1976.

§ 513. Certificate of magistrate

(a) Upon the suspension or revocation of any license or certificate of registration for any reason specified in sections five hundred ten and eleven hundred ninety-three of this chapter as a ground for such suspension or revocation, the magistrate or other officer suspending or revoking the same shall, within ninety-six hours, transmit to the commissioner a certificate stating: (a) whether such license or certificate has been suspended or revoked and, if suspended, the period of such suspension; (b) the name and address of the person whose license or certificate has been suspended or revoked; (c) the nature of the offense committed, or other reason for the suspension or revocation; (d) the number and character of the violations of the provisions of this chapter, or of any lawful local ordinance, rule or regulation in relation to motor vehicle or motorcycle speed or traffic, of which such licensee has been convicted, so far as practicable. Such certificate shall be presumptive evidence of the facts recited therein. At such time, said magistrate or officer shall transmit such license, if surrendered at sentencing, to the commissioner.

(b) Where a person has been granted youthful offender status, the certificate required by subdivision (a) of this section shall specify (i) whether such license or certificate has been suspended or revoked, and if suspended, the period of such suspension; if revoked, the time period within which no new license may be issued; (ii) the name and address of the person whose license or certificate has been revoked; and (iii) such other information as the commissioner may require by regulation.

> **HISTORY:** Add, L 1959, ch 775, with substance transferred from former § 72, amd, L 1964, ch 138, § 1, L 1983, ch 892, § 4, eff Jan 1, 1984. Sub (a), formerly entire section, so lettered, L 1984, ch 978, § 3; amd, L 1988, ch 47, § 13, eff Nov 1, 1988. Sub (b), add, L 1984, ch 978, § 3, eff Nov 1, 1984.

§ 514. Certifying convictions, forfeitures and nonappearances to the commissioner and recording convictions

1. (a) Upon a judgment of conviction of any person of (a) homicide or assault arising out of the operation of a motor vehicle, (b) criminally negligent homicide arising out of the operation of a motor vehicle, (c) a felony involving the use of a commercial motor vehicle, (d) a violation of any of the provisions of this chapter (except one relating to parking, stopping or standing) or (e) a violation of any law, ordinance, rule or regulation made by local authorities in relation to traffic (except one relating to parking, stopping or standing) or upon the forfeiture of bail given upon a charge of violating any such provision, law, ordinance, rule or regulation, the court or the clerk thereof shall within fifteen days certify the facts of the case to the commissioner in such form and in such manner as may be prescribed by the commissioner, whoshall record the same in his office. Such certificate shall be presumptive evidence of the facts recited therein. If any such conviction shall be reversed upon appeal therefrom, or shall be vacated or set aside, the person whose conviction has been so reversed, vacated or set aside may serve on the commissioner a certified copy of the appropriate order and the commissioner shall thereupon record the same in connection with the record of such conviction.

(b) Notwithstanding the provisions of paragraph (a), upon a judgment of conviction for any offense for which a mandatory suspension or revocation is required to be imposed, or a permissive suspension or revocation is imposed by the court, the court or the clerk thereof shall within ninety-six hours of the imposition of sentence file the certificate required by paragraph (a) along with the license, when surrendered at sentencing.

(c) Notwithstanding the provisions of paragraphs (a) and (b), the commissioner may prescribe time limitations for the reporting of judgments of conviction and transmission of such license that are longer than those prescribed by this section for any courts to which this section is applicable.

(d) Notwithstanding the provisions of paragraphs (a), (b) and (c) of this subdivision, upon a judgment of conviction for a violation of any provisions of this chapter or of any local law, rule, ordinance or regulation relating to traffic (except one related to parking, stopping or standing), the court or the clerk thereof shall, within ninety-six hours of the imposition of the sentence, file the certificate required by paragraph (a) of this subdivision, if the person convicted: (i) is the holder of a commercial driver's license issued by another state; or (ii) does not hold a commercial driver's license, but has been issued a license by another state and is convicted of a violation that was committed in a commercial motor vehicle, as defined in subdivision four of section five hundred one-a of this title.

2. [Repealed]

3. (a) Upon the failure of a person to appear or answer, within sixty days of the return date or any subsequent adjourned date, or the failure to pay a fine imposed by a court, pursuant to a summons charging him or her with a violation of any of the provisions of this chapter (except one for parking, stopping or standing), section five hundred two or five hundred twelve of the tax law, section fourteen-f, two hundred eleven or two hundred twelve of the transportation law or of any law, ordinance, rule or regulation made by a local authority, relating to traffic (except for parking, stopping or standing), the trial court or the clerk thereof shall within ten days certify that fact to the commissioner, in the manner and form prescribed by the commissioner, who shall record the same in his or her office. Thereafter and upon the appearance of any such person in response to such summons or the receipt of the fine by the court, the trial court or the clerk thereof shall forthwith certify that fact to the commissioner, in the manner and form prescribed by the commissioner; provided, however, no such certification shall be madeunless the court has collected the termination of suspension feerequired to be paid pursuant to paragraph (j-1) of subdivision two of section five hundred three of this chapter.

(b) Upon the failure of a person to appear or answer, within sixty days of the return date or any subsequent adjourned date, or the failure to pay a fine imposed by a traffic and parking violations agency pursuant to a summons charging him or her with a violation of:

(1) any of the provisions of this chapter except one for parking, stopping or standing and except those violations described in paragraphs (a), (b), (d), (e) and (f) of subdivision two of section three hundred seventy-one of the general municipal law;

(2) section five hundred two or subdivision (a) of section eighteen hundred fifteen of the tax law;

(3) section fourteen-f (except paragraph (b) of subdivision four of section fourteen-f), two hundred eleven or two hundred twelve of the transportation law; or

(4) any lawful ordinance or regulation made by a local or public authority relating to traffic (except one for parking, stopping or standing);

the clerk thereof shall within ten days certify that fact to the commissioner, in the manner and form prescribed by the commissioner, who shall record the same in his or her office. Thereafter and upon the appearance of any such person in response to such summons or the receipt of the fine by the agency, the traffic and parking violations agency or the clerk thereof shall forthwith certify that fact to the commissioner, in the manner and form prescribed by the commissioner; provided, however, no such certification shall be made unless the traffic and parking violations agency has collected the termination of suspension feerequired to be paid pursuant to paragraph (j-1) of subdivision two of section five hundred three of this chapter.

4. (a) Upon the failure of the owner of a motor vehicle registered in this state or his representative to appear or answer, on the return date or any subsequent adjourned date, or in the case of an administrative tribunal fails to comply with the rules and regulations of said tribunal following entry of a final decision in response to three or more summonses or other process issued within an eighteen month period, charging that said motor vehicle was parked,

stopped or standing in violation of the provisions of this chapter or any law, ordinance, rule or regulation made by a local authority, the trial court or administrative tribunal of appropriate jurisdiction may certify that fact to the commissioner in the manner and form prescribed by the commissioner, who may record the same in his office.

(b) Upon such certification, the trial court, the clerk thereof, or the administrative tribunal shall notify the registrant by certified or registered mail, return receipt requested, that the commissioner shall deny the registration or renewal application until proof from the court wherein the charges were pending is provided to the commissioner by such court, administrative tribunal, or registrant that such registrant has answered or appeared, or in the case of an administrative tribunal provides proof that such registrant has complied with the rules and regulations of said tribunal following entry of a final decision. Thereafter and upon the appearance or answer of any such person in response to such summonses the trial court or clerk thereof shall forthwith certify that fact to the registrant, and to the commissioner in a manner and form prescribed by the commissioner. In the case of an administrative tribunal such certification shall be made to the registrant and to the commissioner upon compliance with the rules and regulations of such tribunal. Provided, however, that proof provided to the commissioner by a registrant in the form of a certification provided to such registrant pursuant to this paragraph shall have the same effect as proof provided to the commissioner by such court or administrative tribunal.

(c) At least sixty days prior to renewal date the commissioner shall notify the registrant that unless he complies with the provisions of this section as set forth above, his registration or renewal thereof, will be denied.

4-a. (a) Upon the failure of the owner of a motor vehicle registered in this state or his representative to appear or answer, on the return date or dates or any subsequent adjourned date or dates, or in the case of an administrative tribunal, fails to comply with the rules and regulations of said tribunal following entry of a final decision or decisions, in response to twenty or more summonses or other process issued within an eighteen month period, charging that said motor vehicle was parked, stopped or standing in violation of the provisions of this chapter or any law, ordinance, rule or regulation made by a local authority, the trial court or administrative tribunal of appropriate jurisdiction may certify that fact to the commissioner in the manner and form prescribed by the commissioner.

(b) Thereafter and upon the appearance or answer of any such person in response to such summonses the trial court or clerk thereof shall forthwith certify that fact to the registrant, and to the commissioner in a manner and form prescribed by the commissioner. In the case of an administrative tribunal, such certification shall be made to the registrant and to the commissioner upon compliance with the rules and regulations of such tribunal. Provided, however, that proof provided to the commissioner by a registrant in the form of a certification provided to such registrant pursuant to this paragraph shall have the same effect as proof provided to the commissioner by such court or administrative tribunal.

5. Upon the conviction of any person under eighteen years of age who resides within the household of his parent or guardian, the trial court or clerk shall forthwith transmit written notice of such conviction to the parent or guardian of such minor person; provided, however, that transmittal of such notice of conviction shall not be required in any case in which notice of arraignment of such person upon the charge or charges of which convicted is required by, and shall have been previously transmitted as provided in, subdivision two of section eighteen hundred seven of this chapter.

6. Notwithstanding any inconsistent provision of this section, the commissioner may exempt by regulation additional provisions of this chapter or of other laws, ordinances, rules or regulations from the requirements of subdivisions one and two.

7. Any person chargeable with the duty of reporting to the commissioner a conviction, bail forfeiture, the fact that a person failed to appear or answer pursuant to a summons, or the fact that a person has answered or appeared, or in the case of an administrative tribunal that a person has complied with the rules and regulations of said tribunal following entry of a final decision, who wilfully fails or neglects to do so, shall be punishable by a fine of not more than twenty-five dollars for each separate offense.

> **HISTORY:** Add, L 1970, ch 164, § 2,eff June 1, 1970; amd, L 1971, ch 451, § 1, eff June 17, 1971, L 1971, ch 1097, § 129, eff Sept 1, 1971, L 1973, ch 168, § 6, L 1976, ch 142, § 1, L 1980, ch 381, § 1, L 1983, ch 890, § 3, L 1983, ch 892, § 5, eff Jan 1, 1984, L 1987, ch 338, § 4, eff Jan 1, 1988, L 1987, ch 339, § 5, eff Jan 1, 1988, L 1990, ch 173, §§ 56, 57, eff Feb 19, 1991, L 1990, ch 496, § 7, eff July 18, 1990, L 2001, ch 406, §§ 5, 6, eff Jan 29, 2002, L 2003, ch 62, § 11 (Part J), eff Sept 12, 2003, L 2008, ch 163, §§ 1–3, eff Nov 1, 2008, L 2011, ch 58, § 7 (Part CC), eff May 30, 2011.

§ 514-a. Notification of convictions, suspensions, revocations, cancellations and disqualifications by commercial motor vehicle operators

1. Each person who operates a commercial motor vehicle for a New York state employer who is convicted of violating within or outside of this state, in any type of motor vehicle, a state or local law relating to motor vehicle traffic control (other than a parking violation), shall notify his/her current employer of such conviction. Any person who holds a commercial driver's license issued by the commissioner who does not operate a commercial motor vehicle for a New York state employer or who operates a commercial motor vehicle while self-employed who is convicted in any other state, the District of Columbia or a Canadian province of violating any law relating to motor vehicle traffic control (other than a parking violation) while operating a commercial motor vehicle shall notify the commissioner of such conviction. Such notification must be made within thirty days after the date that the person has been convicted except that if a person is a bus driver as defined in section five hundred nine-a of this chapter, such notification must be made within five days after the date the person has been convicted as required by section five hundred nine-i of this chapter. The above notification must be made in writing and contain the following information: (a) driver's full name; (b) driver's license number; (c) date of conviction; (d) the specific criminal or other offense(s), serious traffic violation(s) of state or local law relating to motor vehicle traffic control, for which the person was convicted and any suspension, revocation, cancellation of any driving privileges or disqualification from operating a commercial motor vehicle which resulted from such conviction(s); (e) indication whether the violation was in a commercial motor vehicle; (f) location of offense; (g) court or tribunal in which the conviction occurred; and (h) driver's signature.

2. Each person who operates a commercial motor vehicle for a New York state employer who has a driver's license suspended, revoked, or canceled by the commissioner or by the appropriate authorities of any other state, District of Columbia or Canadian province, or who loses the right to operate a commercial motor vehicle in any state or jurisdiction for any period, or who is disqualified from operating a commercial motor vehicle for any period, shall notify his/her current employer of such suspension, revocation, cancellation, lost privilege, or disqualification.

> **HISTORY:** Add, L 1990, ch 173, § 58, eff Feb 19, 1991.

§ 514-b. Certification of convictions, suspensions, revocations and disqualifications

Whenever the commissioner receives information relating to a conviction or notice of a suspension, revocation, cancellations and disqualifications of a license or disqualification from operating a commercial motor vehicle through direct notification by the appropriate officials of another state, District of Columbia or Canadian province or through an information system established pursuant to the commercial motor vehicle safety act of nineteen hundred eighty-six, public law 99-570, title XII and regulations promulgated thereunder or through an admission made by an applicant for a driver's license, such information shall be presumptive evidence of the facts contained therein, and the commissioner shall take action as may be required and may take action as may be permitted by this chapter based upon such conviction or notice.

HISTORY: Add, L 1990, ch 173, § 59, eff Feb 19, 1991.

§ 514-c. Notification of non-resident commercial operator convictions

Within ten days of the conviction of:

(a) any holder of a commercial driver's license issued by another state for any violation of state or local law regulating traffic, other than a parking, stopping or standing violation, committed while operating a motor vehicle in this state; or

(b) any holder of a driver's license issued by another state for any violation of state or local law regulating traffic, other than a parking, stopping or standing violation, committed while operating a commercial motor vehicle in this state, the commissioner shall provide notice of such conviction to the state which issued such holder's commercial driver's license or driver's license.

HISTORY: Add, L 2007, ch 251, § 5, eff July 18, 2007.

§ 515. Alteration of convictions endorsed on licenses

No person shall wilfully erase or otherwise make illegible, the record of a conviction which has been endorsed on a license pursuant to the provisions of section five hundred fourteen.

HISTORY: Add, L 1959, ch 775, with substance transferred from former § 70(13).

§ 516. Driver license compact

1. The driver license compact is hereby enacted into law and entered into with all other jurisdictions joining therein in the form substantially as follows:

DRIVER LICENSE COMPACT

ARTICLE I

Findings and Declaration of Policy

(a) The party states find that:

(1) The safety of their streets and highways is materially affected by the degree of compliance with state and local laws and ordinances relating to the operation of motor vehicles.

(2) Violation of such a law or ordinance is evidence that the violator engages in conduct which is likely to endanger the safety of persons and property.

(3) The continuance in force of a license to drive is predicated upon compliance with laws and ordinances relating to the operation of motor vehicles, in whichever jurisdiction the vehicle is operated.

(b) It is the policy of each of the party states to:

(1) Promote compliance with the laws, ordinances, and administrative rules and

regulations relating to the operation of motor vehicles by their operators in each of the jurisdictions where such operators drive motor vehicles.

(2) Make the reciprocal recognition of licenses to drive and eligibility therefor more just and equitable by considering the overall compliance with motor vehicle laws, ordinances and administrative rules and regulations as a condition precedent to the continuance or issuance of any license by reason of which the licensee is authorized or permitted to operate a motor vehicle in any of the party states.

ARTICLE II
Definitions

As used in this compact:

(a) "State" means a state, territory or possession of the United States, the District of Columbia, the Commonwealth of Puerto Rico, or a province of Canada.

(b) "Home state" means the state which has issued and has the power to suspend or revoke the use of the license or permit to operate a motor vehicle.

(c) "Conviction" means a conviction of any offense related to the use or operation of a motor vehicle which is prohibited by state law, municipal ordinance or administrative rule or regulation, or a forfeiture of bail, bond or other security deposited to secure appearance by a person charged with having committed any such offense, and which conviction or forfeiture is required to be reported to the licensing authority.

ARTICLE III
Reports of Conviction

The licensing authority of a party state shall report each conviction of a person from another party state occurring within its jurisdiction to the licensing authority of the home state of the licensee. Such report shall clearly identify the person convicted; describe the violation specifying the section of the statute, code or ordinance violated; identify the court in which action was taken; indicate whether a plea of guilty or not guilty was entered, or the conviction was a result of the forfeiture of bail, bond or other security; and shall include any special findings made in connection therewith.

ARTICLE IV
Effect of Conviction

(a) The licensing authority in the home state, for the purposes of suspension, revocation or limitation of the license to operate a motor vehicle, shall give the same effect to the conduct reported, pursuant to article III of this compact, as it would if such conduct had occurred in the home state, in the case of convictions for:

(1) Manslaughter or negligent homicide resulting from the operation of a motor vehicle;

(2) Driving a motor vehicle while under the influence of intoxicating liquor or a narcotic drug, or under the influence of any other drug to a degree which renders the driver incapable of safely driving a motor vehicle;

(3) Any felony in the commission of which a motor vehicle is used;

(4) Failure to stop and render aid in the event of a motor vehicle accident resulting in the death or personal injury of another.

(b) If the laws of a party state do not provide for offenses or violations denominated or described in precisely the words employed in subdivision (a) of this article, such party state shall construe the denominations and descriptions appearing in subdivision (a) hereof as being applicable to and identifying those offenses or violations of a substantially similar nature and the laws of such party state shall contain such provisions as may be necessary to ensure that full force and effect is given to this article.

ARTICLE V

Applications for New Licenses

Upon application for a license to drive, the licensing authority in a party state shall ascertain whether the applicant has ever held, or is the holder of a license to drive issued by any other party state. The licensing authority in the state where application is made shall not issue a license to drive to the applicant if:

(1) The applicant has held such a license, but the same has been suspended by reason, in whole or in part, of a violation and if such suspension period has not terminated.

(2) The applicant has held such a license, but the same has been revoked by reason, in whole or in part, of a violation and if such revocation has not terminated, except that after the expiration of one year from the date the license was revoked, such person may make application for a new license if permitted by law. The licensing authority may refuse to issue a license to any such applicant if, after investigation, the licensing authority determines that it will not be safe to grant to such person the privilege of driving a motor vehicle on the public highways.

(3) The applicant is the holder of a license to drive issued by another party state and currently in force unless the applicant surrenders such license.

ARTICLE VI

Applicability of Other Laws

Except as expressly required by provisions of this compact, nothing contained herein shall be construed to affect the right of any party state to apply any of its other laws relating to licenses to drive to any person or circumstance, nor to invalidate or prevent any driver license agreement or other cooperative arrangement between a party state and a non-party state.

ARTICLE VII

Compact Administrator and Interchange of Information

(a) The head of the licensing authority of each party state shall be the administrator of this compact for his state. The administrators, acting jointly, shall have the power to formulate all necessary and proper procedures for the exchange of information under this compact.

(b) The administrator of each party state shall furnish to the administrator of each other party state any information or documents reasonably necessary to facilitate the administration of this compact.

ARTICLE VIII

Entry Into Force and Withdrawal

(a) This compact shall enter into force and become effective as to any state when it has enacted the same into law.

(b) Any party state may withdraw from this compact by enacting a statute repealing the same, but no such withdrawal shall take effect until six months after the executive head of the withdrawing state has given notice of the withdrawal to the executive heads of all other party states. No withdrawal shall affect the validity or applicability by the licensing authorities of states remaining party to the compact of any report of conviction occurring prior to the withdrawal.

ARTICLE IX

Construction and Severability

This compact shall be liberally construed so as to effectuate the purposes thereof. The provisions of this compact shall be severable and if any phrase, clause, sentence or provision of this compact is declared to be contrary to the constitution of any party state or of the United States or the applicability thereof of any government, agency, person or circumstance is held invalid, the validity of the remainder of this compact and the applicability thereof to any government, agency, person or circumstance shall not be affected thereby. If this compact shall be held contrary to the constitution of any state party thereto, the compact shall remain in full force and effect as to the remaining states and in full force and effect as to the state affected as to all severable matters.

(1) As used in the compact, the term "licensing authority" with reference to this state shall mean the department of motor vehicles. Said department shall furnish to the appropriate authorities of any other party state any information or documents reasonably necessary to facilitate the administration of the compact.

(2) The compact administrator provided for in article seven of the compact shall not be entitled to any additional compensation on account of his service as such administrator, but shall be entitled to expenses incurred in connection with his duties and responsibilities as such administrator, in the same manner as for expenses incurred in connection with any other duties or responsibilities of his office or employment.

(3) As used in the compact, with reference to this state, the term "executive head" shall mean the governor.

(4) The conduct to which effect shall be given pursuant to article four-a of the compact shall be conduct which, if it had occurred in this state, would have constituted an offense or violation within the meaning of subparagraphs (i) and (iii) of paragraph (a) of subdivision two, paragraph (f) of subdivision three of section five hundred ten and subparagraph seven of paragraph (b) of subdivision two of section eleven hundred ninety-three of the vehicle and traffic law.

(5) In any case where the application of subdivision five of section five hundred ten of the vehicle and traffic law would require or authorize a result different from that required by article five of the compact, said article five shall govern.

HISTORY: Add, L 1965, ch 650, § 1, eff Sept 1, 1965. Compact, Art II, sub (a), amd, L 1986, ch 731, § 2, eff July 30, 1986. Compact, Art IX, sub (4), amd, L 1966, ch 184, § 2, L 1986, ch 731, § 3, L 1988, ch 47, § 14, eff Nov 1, 1988.

§ 516-a. Reciprocal driver license agreements with provinces of Canada

The commissioner may execute a reciprocal compact or agreement not inconsistent with the provisions of this chapter with the motor vehicle administrator or other authorized official of any province of Canada to effectuate the purposes set forth in subdivision (b) of article one of section five hundred sixteen of this article.

HISTORY: Add, L 1986, ch 731, § 4, eff July 30, 1986.

§ 516-b. Reciprocal agreements concerning reporting of traffic offenses and administrative action thereon

(a) The commissioner may execute a reciprocal compact or agreement not inconsistent with the provisions of this chapter with the motor vehicle administrator or other authorized official of another state concerning the reporting of convictions for traffic offenses occurring in each state by a person licensed in, or a resident of, the other state to such licensing or residence state and the treating of any such reported conviction in the same manner as if the conviction occurred in the licensing or residence state for the purpose of administrative action. Any such compact or agreement shall specify the offenses subject to the compact or agreement, and shall include a determination of comparable offenses in each state if any such offenses are of a substantially similar nature but are not denominated or described in precisely the same words in each party state.

(b) The word "state" when used in this section shall mean any state, territory, a possession of the United States, District of Columbia or any province of Canada.

(c) Traffic offenses which may be subject to a reciprocal compact or agreement entered into pursuant to this section shall be limited to the follwing [following]* types of offenses in this state and equivalent offenses in each party state:

(1) Manslaughter, criminally negligent homicide and assault arising from the operation of a motor vehicle;

(2) Operating a motor vehicle while under the influence of alcohol or a drug;

(3) Any felony in the commission of which a motor vehicle is used;

(4) Leaving the scene of a personal injury or fatal incident without reporting;

(5) Any speeding offense;

(6) Any offense consisting of disobeying any traffic control device;

(7) Any offense involving failure to yield the right-of-way;

(8) Any offense involving direction of traffic, overtaking or passing;

9[(9)]. Any offense involving failure to use a safety belt or child restraint device;

(10) Reckless driving; and

(11) Passing a stopped school bus.

(d) Nothing in this section shall be construed to prohibit the reporting or recording of convictions or youthful offender or other juvenile adjudications other than those included in a reciprocal compact or agreement executed pursuant to this section when the laws of either state require or permit action to be taken or sanctions to be imposed on the basis of such convictions or youthful offender or other juvenile adjudications.

HISTORY: Add, L 1986, ch 731, § 4, eff July 30, 1986. Sub (c), par 9, add, L 1991, ch 298, § 1, eff July 15, 1991. Former sub (c), par (9), redesignated sub (c), par (10), L 1991, ch 298, § 1, eff July 15, 1991. Sub (c), par (10), formerly sub (c), par (9), so designated, L 1991, ch 298, § 1, eff July 15, 1991. Former sub (c), par (10), redesignated sub (c), par (11), L 1991, ch 298, § 1, eff July 15, 1991. Sub (c), par (11), formerly sub (c), par (10), so designated, L 1991, ch 298, § 1, eff July

---

* The bracketed word has been inserted by the Publisher.

15, 1991. Sub (d), add, L 1991, ch 298, § 2, eff July 15, 1991. Sub (d), amd, L 1993, ch 533, § 4, eff Sept 30, 1993.

§ 517. Interstate compact guaranteeing appearance

a. The commissioner may execute a reciprocal compact or agreement not inconsistent with the provisions of this chapter with the motor vehicle administrator or other authorized official of another state concerning the appearance of a person licensed in one state to answer a summons or an appearance ticket for a moving traffic violation issued by the other state. Such compact shall provide that if a person licensed by either state is issued a summons or an appearance ticket by the other state for a moving traffic violation covered by the compact or agreement, he shall not be detained or required to furnish bail or collateral, and that if he fails to appear in response to such summons or appearance ticket, his license may be suspended by the state that issued the license until he submits to the jurisdiction of the court or administrative tribunal in which such summons or appearance ticket is returnable. Such compact shall also provide such terms and procedures as are necessary and proper to facilitate its administration.

b. Such interstate compacts may also provide that if a registration or renewal of a motor vehicle would be denied pursuant to either subdivision five-a of section four hundred one of this chapter, for failing to answer summonses or other processes issued for parking infractions, or subdivision four of section one hundred forty-five of the transportation law, with respect to the transportation of household goods, returnable in any court or an administrative tribunal of the department of transportation or for failing to comply with the rules and regulations of any administrative tribunal of appropriate jurisdiction following entry of a final determination with respect to such summons or process, the state issuing the registration or renewal shall likewise deny the registration or renewal, until such applicant submits to the jurisdiction of the court or administrative tribunal in which such summonses or other processes are returnable.

c. The word "state" when used in this section shall mean any state, territory or possession of the United States, the District of Columbia or any province of the Dominion of Canada.

HISTORY: Add, L 1965, ch 651, § 1; amd, L 1975, ch 155, eff July 1, 1975. Sub a, formerly entire section, so lettered, L 1975, ch 277, § 1,eff July 24, 1975. Sub b, add, L 1975, ch 277, § 1, eff July 24, 1975, applicable only to summonses or tickets issued on or after that date. Sub b, amd, L 2000, ch 117, § 1, eff July 11, 2000. Sub c, add, L 1982, ch 138, § 1, eff June 1, 1982.

ARTICLE 21   ALCOHOL AND DRUG REHABILITATION PROGRAM

HISTORY: Add, L 1975, ch 291, § 1, eff June 24, 1975. Former Article 21, add, L 1968, ch 464, § 1; repealed, L 1975, ch 291, § 1, eff June 24, 1975. Prior Article 21, add, L 1959, ch 775, consisting of §§ 520 and 521, which sections were renumbered §§ 394 and 395 by L 1960, ch 300, §§ 44 and 45, eff Oct 1, 1960. Section 520 was also renumbered § 394 by L 1960, ch 464, § 26, eff Jan 1, 1961.

§ 520. Statement of findings and declaration of purpose

The ever-increasing number of accidents, personal injuries and deaths resulting from alcohol or drug-related traffic offenses is a matter of great concern to the legislature. The diminished perception of intoxicated and impaired operators of motor vehicles presents a constant and intolerable threat to the lives and well-being of the citizens of the state. Efforts aimed at alleviating this threat have proven inadequate. The public interest in the cause of highway safety will be well served by the implementation of a permanent program of rehabilitation for those operators convicted of alcohol or drug-related traffic offenses and certain operators who have been adjudicated youthful offenders for alcohol or drug-related traffic offenses. The commissioner of motor vehicles should have the authority to offer to such operators an opportunity for rehabilitation, thereby reducing the threat aimed at themselves and the people of the state.

> **HISTORY:** Add, L 1975, ch 291, § 1; amd, L 1979, ch 607, § 1, eff July 10, 1979. Former § 520, add, L 1968, ch 464, § 1; repealed, L 1975, ch 291, § 1, eff June 24, 1975. Prior § 520, add, L 1959, ch 775, with substance transferred from former § 7; renumbered § 394, L 1960, ch 300, § 44, and by L 1960, ch 464, eff Jan 1, 1961.

§ 521. [Repealed]

> **HISTORY:** Add, L 1975, ch 291, § 1; amd, L 1979, ch 607, § 2, L 1981, ch 344, § 1, L 1981, ch 347, § 1, L 1981, ch 910, § 3, L 1982, ch 192, §§ 1-3, L 1983, ch 892, § 6, L 1984, ch 190, § 1, L 1984, ch 977, § 3, L 1985, ch 145, § 1, L 1985, ch 755 § 1, L 1986, ch 588, § 1, L 1986, ch 649, § 5; repealed, L 1988, ch 47, § 15, eff Nov 1, 1988. Former § 521, add, L 1968, ch 464, § 1; amd, L 1970, ch 679, § 5, L 1970, ch 755, § 1, L 1973, ch 220, § 1; repealed, L 1975, ch 291, § 1, eff June 24, 1975. Prior § 521, add, L 1959, ch 775, with substance transferred from former § 7-a, renumbered § 395, L 1960, ch 300, § 45, eff Oct 1, 1960.

§ 522. [Repealed]

> **HISTORY:** Add, L 1975, ch 291, § 1, eff June 24, 1975. Repealed, L 1992, ch 55, § 228, eff April 10, 1992. Former § 522, add, L 1968, ch 464, § 1; repealed, L 1975, ch 291, eff June 24, 1975.

§ 523. Reports

The commissioner shall report to the governor and to the legislature annually with respect to the status of the alcohol and drug rehabilitation program, including therein, among other things, the scope and results of procedures for screening and referral of program participants exhibiting an early stage, of alcoholism or chronic life problem with alcohol, providing that such report shall not contain the name of or otherwise identify participants in such program.

> **HISTORY:** Add, L 1975, ch 291, § 1; amd, L 1977, ch 594, § 1, eff Aug 1, 1977. Former § 523, add, L 1968, ch 464, § 1; amd, L 1973, ch 612, § 1; repealed, L 1975 ch 291, § 1, eff June 24, 1975.

§ 523-a. Driver improvement clinic programs

In addition to the driver rehabilitation program authorized by section eleven hundred ninety-six of this chapter, the commissioner may establish, by regulation, guidelines for alcohol and highway safety programs. The purpose of such programs should be to inform participants of the effects of alcohol on driving, to discuss problem drinking and its effects, to provide assistance to individuals with referral to alcoholism treatment agencies and to provide instruction with respect to proper driving techniques and driver attitude. The commissioner shall establish criteria for requiring attendance at such clinics, and may, pending attendance at such clinic, suspend the driver's license or privilege of any person who fails to attend such clinic as required by such regulations. Such criteria may provide for the required attendance at such clinic of any person who, as a result of the conviction for a moving traffic violation, is referred by the trial court for such attendance. The commissioner shall establish a fee to be paid by any person who attends any such program. Such fee shall be used to defray the ongoing expenses of the program. Where the commissioner has approved any driver improvement program conducted by local authorities, any such fee shall be paid to the agency conducting such program.

> **HISTORY:** Add, L 1975, ch 296, § 1; amd, L 1977, ch 793, § 6, L 1988, ch 47, § 16, eff Nov 1, 1988.

§ 523-b. Experimental driver safety programs

The commissioner may study the feasibility of programs to improve driver behavior, attitude, performance or skills in order to reduce motor vehicle accidents and traffic violations, and to promote highway safety. He shall have the authority to establish such programs on a limited, experimental basis in order to assist in such feasibility study provided any such program is funded by any source other than state funds, or if any such program is to be funded with state funds, then he may establish such program only with the approval of the director of the division of the budget.

HISTORY: Add, L 1975, ch 596, § 1, eff Aug 1, 1975.

VTL

TITLE VI   Accidents and Accident Reports

ARTICLE 22
ACCIDENTS AND ACCIDENT REPORTS

HISTORY: Add, L 1959, ch 775, eff Oct 1, 1960.

ARTICLE 22   ACCIDENTS AND ACCIDENT REPORTS
(Selected Sections)

HISTORY: Add, L 1959, ch 775, eff Oct 1, 1960.

§ 600. Leaving scene of an incident without reporting

1. Property damage. a. Any person operating a motor vehicle who, knowing or having cause to know that damage has been caused to the real property or to the personal property, not including animals, of another, due to an incident involving the motor vehicle operated by such person shall, before leaving the place where the damage occurred, stop, exhibit his or her license and insurance identification card for such vehicle, when such card is required pursuant to articles six and eight of this chapter, and give his or her name, residence, including street and number, insurance carrier and insurance identification information including but not limited to the number and effective dates of said individual's insurance policy, and license number to the party sustaining the damage, or in case the person sustaining the damage is not present at the place where the damage occurred then he or she shall report the same as soon as physically able to the nearest police station, or judicial officer.

b. It shall be the duty of any member of a law enforcement agency who is at the scene of the accident to request the said operator or operators of the motor vehicles, when physically capable of doing so, to exchange the information required hereinabove and such member of a law enforcement agency shall assist such operator or operators in making such exchange of information in a reasonable and harmonious manner.

A violation of the provisions of paragraph a of this subdivision shall constitute a traffic infraction punishable by a fine of up to two hundred fifty dollars or a sentence of imprisonment for up to fifteen days or both such fine and imprisonment.

2. Personal injury[.]* a. Any person operating a motor vehicle who, knowing or having cause to know that personal injury has been caused to another person, due to an incident involving the motor vehicle operated by such person shall, before leaving the place where the said personal injury occurred, stop, exhibit his or her license and insurance identification card for such vehicle, when such card is required pursuant to articles six and eight of this chapter, and give his or her name, residence, including street and street number, insurance carrier and insurance identification information including but not limited to the number and effective dates of said individual's insurance policy and license number, to the injured party, if practical, and also to a police officer, or in the event that no police officer is in the vicinity of the place of said injury, then, he or she shall report said incident as soon as physically able to the nearest police station or judicial officer.

b. It shall be the duty of any member of a law enforcement agency who is at the scene of the accident to request the said operator or operators of the motor vehicles, when physically capable

---

* The bracketed punctuation has been inserted by the Publisher.

of doing so, to exchange the information required hereinabove and such member of a law enforcement agency shall assist such operator or operators in making such exchange of information in a reasonable and harmonious manner.

c. A violation of the provisions of paragraph a of this subdivision resulting solely from the failure of an operator to exhibit his or her license and insurance identification card for the vehicle or exchange the information required in such paragraph shall constitute a class B misdemeanor punishable by a fine of not less than two hundred fifty nor more than five hundred dollars in addition to any other penalties provided by law. Any subsequent such violation shall constitute a class A misdemeanor punishable by a fine of not less than five hundred nor more than one thousand dollars in addition to any other penalties provided by law. Any violation of the provisions of paragraph a of this subdivision, other than for the mere failure of an operator to exhibit his or her license and insurance identification card for such vehicle or exchange the information required in such paragraph, shall constitute a class A misdemeanor, punishable by a fine of not less than five hundred dollars nor more than one thousand dollars in addition to any other penalties provided by law. Any such violation committed by a person after such person has previously been convicted of such a violation shall constitute a class E felony, punishable by a fine of not less than one thousand nor more than two thousand five hundred dollars in addition to any other penalties provided by law. Any violation of the provisions of paragraph a of this subdivision, other than for the mere failure of an operator to exhibit his or her license and insurance identification card for such vehicle or exchange the information required in such paragraph, where the personal injury involved (i) results in serious physical injury, as defined in section 10.00 of the penal law, shall constitute a class E felony, punishable by a fine of not less than one thousand nor more than five thousand dollars in addition to any other penalties provided by law, or (ii) results in death shall constitute a class D felony punishable by a fine of not less than two thousand nor more than five thousand dollars in addition to any other penalties provided by law.

HISTORY: Add, L 1959, ch 775, with substance transferred from former § 70(5-a); amd, L 1967, ch 247, § 5, L 1971, ch 1025, § 6, L 1973, ch 18, § 2, L 1976, ch 405, § 1, L 1976, ch 670, § 1, L 1985, ch 736, § 1, eff Nov 1, 1985. Section heading, amd, L 1976, ch 670, § 1, eff Sept 1, 1976. Sub 1, amd, L 1980, ch 228, § 1, eff Sept 1, 1980. Sub 1, par a, formerly first par of sub 1, so lettered and amd, L 1980, ch 228, § 1; amd, L 1985, ch 215, § 1, L 1986, ch 599, § 1, eff July 24, 1986. Sub 1, par b, add, L 1980, ch 228, § 1, eff Sept 1, 1980. Sub 2, amd, L 1980, ch 228, § 1, L 1980, ch 229, § 1, eff Sept 1, 1980. Sub 2, par a, formerly first par of sub 2, so lettered and amd, L 1980, ch 228, § 1; amd, L 1985, ch 215, § 2, L 1986, ch 599, § 2, eff July 24, 1986. Sub 2, par b, add, L 1980, ch 228, § 1, eff Sept 1, 1980. Amd, L 2005, ch 49, § 1, eff June 17, 2005. Sub 1, subsect heading, add, L 2005, ch 49, § 1, eff June 17, 2005. Sub 1, par a, amd, L 2005, ch 49, § 1, eff June 17, 2005. Sub 2, subsect heading, add, L 2005, ch 49, § 1, eff June 17, 2005. Sub 2, par a, amd, L 2005, ch 49, § 1, eff June 17, 2005. Sub 2, par c, formerly closing par, so designated sub 2, par c and amd, L 2005, ch 49, § 1, eff June 17, 2005. Closing par, redesignated sub 2, par c, L 2005, ch 49, § 1, eff June 17, 2005.

§ 601. Leaving scene of injury to certain animals without reporting

Any person operating a motor vehicle which shall strike and injure any horse, dog, cat or animal classified as cattle shall stop and endeavor to locate the owner or custodian of such animal or a police, peace or judicial officer of the vicinity, and take any other reasonable and appropriate action so that the animal may have necessary attention, and shall also promptly report the matter to such owner, custodian or officer (or if no one of such has been located, then to a police officer of some other nearby community), exhibiting his or her license and insurance identification card for such vehicle, when such card is required pursuant to articles six and eight of this chapter, giving his or her name and residence, including street and street number, insurance carrier and insurance identification information and license number. Violation of this section shall be punishable by a fine of not more than one hundred dollars for a first offense and by a fine of not less than fifty nor more than one hundred fifty dollars for a second offense and each subsequent offense; provided, however where the animal that has been struck and injured is a guide dog, hearing dog or service dog, as such terms are defined in section forty-seven-b of the civil rights law which is actually engaged in aiding or guiding a person with a disability, a violation of this section shall be publishable [punishable]* by a fine of not less than fifty nor more than one hundred fifty dollars for a first offense and by a fine of not less than one hundred fifty dollars nor more than three hundred dollars for a second offense and each subsequent offense.

HISTORY: Add, L 1959, ch 775, with substance transferred from former § 70(5-b); amd, L 1960, ch 300, § 46, L 1971, ch 1025, § 7, L 1973, ch 18, § 3, L 1976, ch 405, § 2, L 1989, ch 61, § 46, effective and applicable to violations committed on and after May 19, 1989. Amd, L 1997, ch 508, § 1, eff Jan 1, 1998, L 2004, ch 672, § 1, eff Nov 1, 2005.

§ 602. Arrest for violations of sections six hundred and six hundred one

A peace officer, acting pursuant to his special duties, or a police officer may, without a warrant, arrest a person, in case of violation of section six hundred and section six hundred one, which in fact have been committed, though not in his presence, when he has reasonable cause to believe that the violation was committed by such person.

HISTORY: Add, L 1959, ch 775, with substance derived from former § 70(5-c); amd, L 1980, ch 843, § 99, eff Sept 1, 1980.

---

* The bracketed word has been inserted by the Publisher.

TITLE VII   Rules of the Road
ARTICLE 30
SPEED RESTRICTIONS
ARTICLE 31
ALCOHOL AND DRUG-RELATED OFFENSES AND PROCEDURES APPLICABLE THERETO

HISTORY: Add, L 1959, ch 775, eff Oct 1, 1960, with substance transferred from former Title III.

ARTICLE 30   SPEED RESTRICTIONS
(Selected Sections)

§ 1180.   **Basic rule and maximum limits**
§ 1182.   **Speed contests and races**

HISTORY: Add, L 1959, ch 775, eff Oct 1, 1960, with substance transferred from former Art 5.

§ 1180. Basic rule and maximum limits

(a) No person shall drive a vehicle at a speed greater than is reasonable and prudent under the conditions and having regard to the actual and potential hazards then existing.

(b) Except as provided in subdivision (g) of this section and except when a special hazard exists that requires lower speed for compliance with subdivision (a) of this section or when maximum speed limits have been established as hereinafter authorized, no person shall drive a vehicle at a speed in excess of fifty-five miles per hour.

(c) Except as provided in subdivision (g) of this section, whenever maximum school speed limits have been established on a highway adjacent to a school as authorized in section sixteen hundred twenty, sixteen hundred twenty-two, sixteen hundred thirty, sixteen hundred forty-three or sixteen hundred sixty-two-a, no person shall drive in excess of such maximum school speed limits during:

(1) school days at times indicated on the school zone speed limit sign, provided, however, that such times shall be between the hours of seven o'clock A.M. and six o'clock P.M. or alternative times within such hours; or

(2) a period when the beacons attached to the school zone speed limit sign are flashing and such sign is equipped with a notice that indicates that the school zone speed limit is in effect when such beacons are flashing, provided, however, that such beacons shall only flash during student activities at the school and up to thirty minutes immediately before and up to thirty minutes immediately after such student activities.

(d) 1. Except as provided in subdivision (g) of this section, whenever maximum speed limits, other than school speed limits, have been established as authorized in sections sixteen hundred twenty, sixteen hundred twenty-two, sixteen hundred twenty-three, sixteen hundred twenty-seven, sixteen hundred thirty, sixteen hundred forty-three, sixteen hundred forty-four, sixteen hundred fifty-two, sixteen hundred sixty-two-a, sixteen hundred sixty-three, and sixteen hundred seventy, no person shall drive in excess of such maximum speed limits at any time.

2. Except as provided in subdivision (g) of this section, whenever maximum speed limits, other than school speed limits, have been established with respect to any restricted highway as authorized in section sixteen hundred twenty-five, no person shall drive in excess of such maximum speed limits at any time.

(e) The driver of every vehicle shall, consistent with the requirements of subdivision (a) of this section, drive at an appropriate reduced speed when approaching and crossing an intersection or railway grade crossing, when approaching and going around a curve, when approaching a hill crest, when approaching and passing by an emergency situation involving any authorized emergency vehicle which is parked, stopped or standing on a highway and which is displaying one or more red or combination red, white, and/or blue lights pursuant to the provisions of paragraph two and subparagraph b of paragraph four of subdivision forty-one of section three hundred seventy-five of this chapter, when traveling upon any narrow or winding roadway, and when any special hazard exists with respect to pedestrians, or other traffic by reason of weather or highway conditions, including, but not limited to a highway construction or maintenance work area.

(f) Except as provided in subdivision (g) of this section and except when a special hazard exists that requires lower speed for compliance with subdivision (a) or (e) of this section or when a lower maximum speed limit has been established, no person shall drive a vehicle through a highway construction or maintenance work area at a speed in excess of the posted work area speed limit. The agency having jurisdiction over the affected street or highway may establish work area speed limits which are less than the normally posted speed limits; provided, however, that such normally posted speed limit may exceed the work area speed limit by no more than twenty miles per hour; and provided further that no such work area speed limit may be established at less than twenty-five miles per hour.

(g) (i) No person who uses a radar or laser detector in a vehicle with a gross vehicle weight rating of more than eighteen thousand pounds, or a commercial motor vehicle with a gross vehicle weight rating of more than ten thousand pounds, shall drive at a speed in excess of fifty-five miles per hour or, if a maximum speed limit other than fifty-five miles per hour as hereinbefore authorized has been established, at a speed in excess of such speed limit. The presence in any such vehicle of either: (1) a radar or laser detector connected to a power source and in an operable condition; or (2) a concealed radar or laser detector where a part of such detector is securely affixed to some part of the vehicle outside of the cab, in a manner which renders the detector not readily observable, is presumptive evidence of its use by any person operating such vehicle. Either such presumption shall be rebutted by any credible and reliable evidence which tends to show that such radar or laser detector was not in use.

(ii) The provisions of this section shall not be construed as authorizing the seizure or forfeiture of a radar or laser detector, unless otherwise provided by law.

(h) Upon a conviction for a violation of subdivision (b), (c), (d), (f) or (g) of this section, the court shall record the speed upon which the conviction was based on the certificate required to be filed with the commissioner pursuant to section five hundred fourteen of this chapter, or if the conviction occurs in an administrative tribunal established pursuant to article two-A of this chapter, the speed upon which the conviction was based shall be entered in the department's records.

1. Every person convicted of a violation of subdivision (b) or paragraph one of subdivision (d) of this section shall be punished as follows:

(i) Where the court or tribunal records or enters that the speed upon which the conviction was based exceeded the applicable speed limit by not more than ten miles per hour, by a fine of not less than forty-five nor more than one hundred fifty dollars;

(ii) Where the court or tribunal records or enters that the speed upon which the conviction was based exceeded the applicable speed limit by more than ten miles per hour but not more than thirty miles per hour, by a fine of not less than ninety nor more than three hundred dollars or by imprisonment for not more than fifteen days or by both such fine and imprisonment;

(iii) Where the court or tribunal records or enters that the speed upon which the conviction was based exceeded the applicable speed limit by more than thirty miles per hour, by a fine of not less than one hundred eighty nor more than six hundred dollars, or by imprisonment for not more than thirty days, or by both such fine and imprisonment.

2. Every person convicted of a violation of subdivision (a) or (e) of this section shall be punished by a fine of not less than forty-five nor more than one hundred fifty dollars, or by imprisonment for not more than fifteen days, or by both such fine and imprisonment.

3. Every person convicted of a violation of paragraph two of subdivision (d), subdivision (f) or (g) of this section shall be punished as follows:

(i) Where the court or tribunal records or enters that the speed upon which the conviction was based exceeded the applicable speed limit by not more than ten miles per hour, by a fine of not less than ninety nor more than one hundred fifty dollars;

(ii) Where the court or tribunal records or enters that the speed upon which the conviction was based exceeded the applicable speed limit by more than ten miles per hour, but not more than thirty miles per hour, by a fine of not less than one hundred eighty nor more than three hundred dollars or by imprisonment for not more than thirty days, or by both such fine and imprisonment, provided, however, that where the vehicle is either (A) in violation of any rules or regulations involving an out-of-service defect relating to brake systems, steering components and/or coupling devices, or (B) transporting flammable gas, radioactive materials or explosives, the fine shall be three hundred dollars or imprisonment for not more than thirty days, or both such fine and imprisonment;

(iii) Where the court or tribunal records or enters that the speed upon which the conviction was based exceeded the applicable speed limit by more than thirty miles per hour, by a fine of not less than three hundred sixty nor more than six hundred dollars or by imprisonment for not more than thirty days or by both such fine and imprisonment, provided, however, that where the vehicle is either (A) in violation of any rules or regulations involving an out-of-service defect relating to brake systems, steering components and/or coupling devices, or (B) transporting flammable gas, radioactive materials or explosives, the fine shall be six hundred dollars or imprisonment for not more than thirty days, or both such fine and imprisonment.

4. Every person convicted of a violation of subdivision (c) of this section when such violation occurs in a school speed zone during a school day between the hours of seven o'clock A.M. and six o'clock P.M., shall be punished as follows:

(i) Where the court or tribunal records or enters that the speed upon which the conviction was based exceeded the applicable speed limit by not more than ten miles per hour, by a fine of not less than ninety nor more than three hundred dollars;

(ii) Where the court or tribunal records or enters that the speed upon which the conviction was based exceeded the applicable speed limit by more than ten miles per hour but not more than thirty miles per hour, by a fine of not less than one hundred eighty nor more than six hundred dollars or by imprisonment for not more than fifteen days or by both such fine and imprisonment;

(iii) Where the court or tribunal records or enters that the speed upon which the conviction was based exceeded the applicable speed limit by more than thirty miles per hour, by a fine of not less than three hundred sixty nor more than one thousand two hundred dollars, or by imprisonment for not more than thirty days, or by both such fine and imprisonment.

5. Notwithstanding the foregoing provisions of this subdivision, the maximum fine provided herein for the violation for which the person is sentenced may be increased by an additional one hundred fifty dollars if the conviction is for a second violation of any subdivision of this section where both violations were committed within an eighteen month period, and the maximum fine provided herein for the violation for which the person is sentenced may be increased by an additional three hundred seventy-five dollars if the conviction is for a third or subsequent violation of any subdivision of this section where all such violations were committed within an eighteen month period. Where an additional fine is provided by this paragraph, a sentence of imprisonment for not more than thirty days may be imposed in place of or in addition to any fine imposed.

HISTORY: Add, L 1959, ch 775, with substance transferred from former § 56; amd, L 1960, ch 300, § 51, L 1960, ch 601, § 1, L 1960, ch 602, § 1, L 1961 ch 308, § 1, L 1960, ch 934, § 1, L 1966, ch 950, § 1, L 1990, ch 173, § 61, eff Aug 19, 1990. Sub (b), amd, L 1969, ch 83, § 1, L 1990, ch 173, § 61, eff Aug 19, 1990. Sub (b), par 1, amd, L 1964, ch 773, § 1; deleted, L 1966, ch 950, § 1, eff Oct 1, 1966. Sub (b), par 2, deleted, L 1966, ch 950, § 1, eff Oct 1, 1966. Sub (b), par 3, amd, L 1961, ch 519, § 3, L 1963, ch 938, § 12; relettered sub (d), L 1966, ch 950, § 1. Sub (c), add, L 1966, ch 950, § 1; amd, L 1981, ch 297, § 1, L 1990, ch 173, § 61, eff Aug 19, 1990. Former sub (c), amd, L 1962, ch 880, § 1; relettered sub (e), L 1966, ch 950, § 1, eff Oct 1, 1966. Sub (d), formerly sub (b), par 3, so lettered and amd, L 1966, ch 950, § 1, L 1968, ch 420, § 400, L 1990, ch 173, § 61, eff Aug 19, 1990. Sub (e), formerly sub (c), so lettered, L 1966, ch 950, § 1; amd, L 1983, ch 249, § 1, L 1984, ch 92, § 2, eff April 24, 1984. Sub (f), add, L 1989, ch 173, § 1; amd, L 1990, ch 173, § 61, eff Aug 19, 1990. Former sub (f), add, L 1989, ch 61, § 47; redesignated sub (g), L 1989, ch 173, § 1, eff June 19, 1989. Prior sub (f), add, L 1970, ch 679, § 8; amd, L 1981, ch 162, § 1; repealed, L 1989, ch 61, § 47, effective and applicable to violations committed on and after May 19, 1989. Sub (g), add, L 1990, ch 173, § 61, eff Aug 19, 1990. Former sub (g), relettered sub (h), L 1990, ch 173, § 612, eff Aug 19, 1990. Sub (h), formerly sub (g), formerly sub (f), add, L 1989, ch 61, § 47, so designated, L 1989, ch 173, § 1; relettered sub (h) and amd, L 1990, ch 173, § 61, eff Aug 19, 1990. Sub (h), opening par, amd, L 1990, ch 173, § 61, eff Aug 19, 1990. Sub (h), par 1, opening par, amd, L 1990, ch 173, § 61, eff Aug 19, 1990. Sub (h), par 1, subpar (ii), amd, L 1990, ch 173, § 61, eff Aug 19, 1990. Sub (h), par 3, add, L 1990, ch 173, § 61, eff Aug 19, 1990. Former sub (h), par 3, renumbered sub (h), par 4, L 1990, ch 173, § 61, eff Aug 19, 1990. Sub (h), par 4, formerly sub (h), par (3), so renumbered, L 1990, ch 173, § 61, eff Aug 19, 1990. Sub (c), opening par, formerly entire sub (c), so designated sub (c) opening par and amd, L 2002, ch 563, § 1, eff Sept 24, 2003. Sub (c), par (1), add, L 2002, ch 563, § 1, eff Sept 24, 2003. Sub (c), par (2), add, L 2002, ch 563, § 1, eff Sept 24, 2003. Sub (d), par 1, formerly entire sub (d), so designated par 1 and amd, L 1997, ch 432, § 72, eff Nov 18, 1997. Sub (d), par 2, add, L 1997, ch 432, § 72, eff Nov 18, 1997. Sub (e), amd, L 2004, ch 211, § 1, eff Nov 1, 2004. Sub (f), amd, L 1993, ch 81, § 1, eff Aug 30, 1993, L 1997 ch 432, § 75, eff Nov 18, 1997. Sub (g), par (i), amd, L 1999, ch 101, § 1, eff Nov 1, 1999. Sub (g), par (ii), amd, L 1999, ch 101, § 1, eff Nov 1, 1999. Sub (h), par 1, amd, L 2003, ch 62, § 4 (Part C), eff May 15, 2003. Sub (h), par 1, opening par, amd, L 1995, ch 446, § 2, eff Sept 1, 1995, L 1997 ch 432, § 73, eff Nov 18, 1997; L 1999, ch 484, § 1. eff Nov 1, 1999. Sub (h), par 1, subpar (i), amd, L 2003, ch 62, § 4 (Part C), eff May 15, 2003. Sub (h), par 1, subpar (ii), amd, L 2003, ch 62, § 4 (Part C), eff May 15, 2003. Sub (h), par 1, subpar (iii), amd, L 2003, ch 62, § 4 (Part C), eff May 15, 2003. Sub (h), par 2, amd, L 2003, ch 62, § 5 (Part C), eff May 15, 2003. Sub (h), par 3, amd, L 2003, ch 62, § 6 (Part C), eff May 15, 2003. Sub (h), par 3, opening par, amd, L 1995, ch 446, § 3, eff Sept 1, 1995, L 1997 ch 432, § 74, eff Nov 18, 1997. Sub (h), par 3, par (i), amd, L 2003, ch 62, § 6 (Part C), eff May 15, 2003. Sub (h), par 3, par (ii), amd, L 2003, ch 62, § 6 (Part C), eff May 15, 2003. Sub (h), par 3, par (iii), amd, L 2003, ch 62, § 6 (Part C), eff May 15, 2003. Sub (h), par 4, add, L 1999, ch 484, § 2, eff Nov 1, 1999; amd, L 2003, ch 62, § 7 (Part C), eff May 15, 2003. Former sub (h), par 4, redesignated sub (h), par 5, L 1999, ch 484, § 2, eff Nov 1, 1999. Sub (h), par 4, subpar (i), amd, L 2003, ch 62, § 7 (Part C), eff May 15, 2003. Sub (h), par 4, subpar (ii), amd, L 2003, ch 62, § 7 (Part C), eff May 15, 2003. Sub (h), par 4, subpar (iii), amd, L 2003, ch 62, § 7 (Part C), eff May 15, 2003. Sub (h), par 5, formerly sub (h), par 4, so designated sub (h), par 5, L 1999, ch 484, § 2, eff Nov 1, 1999; amd, L 2003, ch 62, § 8 (Part C), eff May 15, 2003. Sub. (e), amd, L. 2010, ch. 465, § 1, eff. Aug. 30, 2010.

§ 1182. Speed contests and races

1. Except as provided in section eleven hundred eighty-two-a of this article or section sixteen hundred thirty, sixteen hundred forty, sixteen hundred forty-two or sixteen hundred sixty of this chapter, no races, exhibitions or contests of speed shall be held and no person shall engage in or aid or abet in any motor vehicle or other speed contest or exhibition of speed on a highway. Such event, if held, shall be fully and efficiently patrolled for the entire distance over which such race, exhibition or contest for speed is to be held. Participants in a race, exhibition or contest of speed are exempted from compliance with any traffic laws otherwise applicable thereto, but shall exercise reasonable care. A violation of any of the provisions of this section shall constitute a misdemeanor and be punishable by imprisonment of not more than thirty days or a fine of not less than three hundred dollars nor more than five hundred twenty-five dollars, or both such fine and imprisonment.

2. A second conviction within twelve months of a violation of this section shall be punishable by imprisonment of not more than six months or a fine of not less than five hundred twenty-five dollars nor more than seven hundred fifty dollars, or both such fine and imprisonment.

> **HISTORY:** Formerly § 1183, add, L 1959, ch 775; renumbered § 1182 and amd, L 1960, ch 934, § 3; amd, L 1967, ch 19, § 1, L 1987, ch 594, § 1, eff Nov 1, 1987. Former § 1182, add, L 1959, ch 775, with substance transferred from former § 56-a; renumbered § 1181, L 1960, ch 934, § 2, eff Oct 1, 1961. Sub 1, formerly entire section, so numbered and amd, L 1973, ch 541, § 1; amd, L 1987, ch 593, § 1, L 1987, ch 594, § 1, L 1991, ch 247, § 1, eff Jan 1, 1992. Sub 1, amd, L 2003, ch 62, § 9 (Part C), eff May 15, 2003. Sub 2, add, L 1973, ch 541, § 1; amd, L 1987, ch 594, § 1, eff Nov 1, 1987. Sub 2, amd, L 2003, ch 62, § 9 (Part C), eff May 15, 2003.

ARTICLE 31   ALCOHOL AND DRUG-RELATED OFFENSES AND PROCEDURES APPLICABLE THERETO

> **HISTORY:** Add, L 1988, ch 47, § 18, eff Nov 1, 1988. Former Art 31 (§§ 1190-1196), add, L 1959, ch 775, with substance transferred from former Art 5; repealed, L 1988, ch 47, § 18, eff Nov 1, 1988.

§ 1190. [Repealed]

HISTORY: Add, L 1959, ch 775, with substance transferred from former § 58; repealed, L 1988, ch 47, § 18, eff Nov 1, 1988.

§ 1191. [Repealed]

HISTORY: Add, L 1959, ch 775, with substance transferred from former § 55-a; amd, L 1960, ch 300, § 52; repealed, L 1988, ch 47, § 18, eff Nov 1, 1988.

§ 1192. Operating a motor vehicle while under the influence of alcohol or drugs

1. Driving while ability impaired. No person shall operate a motor vehicle while the person's ability to operate such motor vehicle is impaired by the consumption of alcohol.

2. Driving while intoxicated; per se. No person shall operate a motor vehicle while such person has .08 of one per centum or more by weight of alcohol in the person's blood as shown by chemical analysis of such person's blood, breath, urine or saliva, made pursuant to the provisions of section eleven hundred ninety-four of this article.

2-a. Aggravated driving while intoxicated.

(a) Per se. No person shall operate a motor vehicle while such person has .18 of one per centum or more by weight of alcohol in such person's blood as shown by chemical analysis of such person's blood, breath, urine or saliva made pursuant to the provisions of section eleven hundred ninety-four of this article.

(b) With a child. No person shall operate a motor vehicle in violation of subdivision two, three, four or four-a of this section while a child who is fifteen years of age or less is a passenger in such motor vehicle.

3. Driving while intoxicated. No person shall operate a motor vehicle while in an intoxicated condition.

4. Driving while ability impaired by drugs. No person shall operate a motor vehicle while the person's ability to operate such a motor vehicle is impaired by the use of a drug as defined in this chapter.

4-a. Driving while ability impaired by the combined influence of drugs or of alcohol and any drug or drugs. No person shall operate a motor vehicle while the person's ability to operate such motor vehicle is impaired by the combined influence of drugs or of alcohol and any drug or drugs.

5. Commercial motor vehicles: per se - level I. Notwithstanding the provisions of section eleven hundred ninety-five of this article, no person shall operate a commercial motor vehicle while such person has .04 of one per centum or more but not more than .06 of one per centum by weight of alcohol in the person's blood as shown by chemical analysis of such person's blood, breath, urine or saliva, made pursuant to the provisions of section eleven hundred ninety-four of this article; provided, however, nothing contained in this subdivision shall prohibit the imposition of a charge of a violation of subdivision one of this section, or of section eleven hundred ninety-two-a of this article where a person under the age of twenty-one operates a commercial motor vehicle where a chemical analysis of such person's blood, breath, urine, or saliva, made pursuant to the provisions of section eleven hundred ninety-four of this article, indicates that such operator has .02 of one per centum or more but less than .04 of one per centum by weight of alcohol in such operator's blood.

6. Commercial motor vehicles; per se - level II. Notwithstanding the provisions of section eleven hundred ninety-five of this article, no person shall operate a commercial motor vehicle while such person has more than .06 of one per centum but less than .08 of one per centum by weight of

alcohol in the person's blood as shown by chemical analysis of such person's blood, breath, urine or saliva, made pursuant to the provisions of section eleven hundred ninety-four of this article; provided, however, nothing contained in this subdivision shall prohibit the imposition of a charge of a violation of subdivision one of this section.

7. Where applicable. The provisions of this section shall apply upon public highways, private roads open to motor vehicle traffic and any other parking lot. For the purposes of this section "parking lot" shall mean any area or areas of private property, including a driveway, near or contiguous to and provided in connection with premises and used as a means of access to and egress from a public highway to such premises and having a capacity for the parking of four or more motor vehicles. The provisions of this section shall not apply to any area or areas of private property comprising all or part of property on which is situated a one or two family residence.

8. Effect of prior out-of-state conviction. A prior out-of-state conviction for operating a motor vehicle while under the influence of alcohol or drugs shall be deemed to be a prior conviction of a violation of this section for purposes of determining penalties imposed under this section or for purposes of any administrative action required to be taken pursuant to subdivision two of section eleven hundred ninety-three of this article; provided, however, that such conduct, had it occurred in this state, would have constituted a misdemeanor or felony violation of any of the provisions of this section.Provided, however, that if such conduct, had it occurred in this state, would have constituted a violation of any provisions of this section which are not misdemeanor or felony offenses, then such conduct shall be deemed to be a prior conviction of a violation of subdivision one of this section for purposes of determining penalties imposed under this section or for purposes of any administrative action required to be taken pursuant to subdivision two of section eleven hundred ninety-three of this article.

8-a. Effect of prior finding of having consumed alcohol. A prior finding that a person under the age of twenty-one has operated a motor vehicle after having consumed alcohol pursuant to section eleven hundred ninety-four-a of this article shall have the same effect as a prior conviction of a violation of subdivision one of this section solely for the purpose of determining the length of any license suspension or revocation required to be imposed under any provision of this article, provided that the subsequent offense is committed prior to the expiration of the retention period for such prior offense or offenses set forth in paragraph (k) of subdivision one of section two hundred one of this chapter.

9. Conviction of a different charge. A driver may be convicted of a violation of subdivision one, two or three of this section, notwithstanding that the charge laid before the court alleged a violation of subdivision two or three of this section, and regardless of whether or not such conviction is based on a plea of guilty.

10. Plea bargain limitations.

    (a) (i) In any case wherein the charge laid before the court alleges a violation of subdivision two, three, four or four-a of this section, any plea of guilty thereafter entered in satisfaction of such charge must include at least a plea of guilty to the violation of the provisions of one of the subdivisions of this section, other than subdivision five or six, and no other disposition by plea of guilty to any other charge in satisfaction of such charge shall be authorized; provided, however, if the district attorney, upon reviewing the available evidence, determines that the charge of a violation of this section is not warranted, such district attorney may consent, and the court may allow a disposition by plea of guilty to another charge in satisfaction of such charge; provided, however, in all such cases, the court shall set forth upon the record the basis for such disposition.

(ii) In any case wherein the charge laid before the court alleges a violation of subdivision two, three, four or four-a of this section, no plea of guilty to subdivision one of this section shall be accepted by the court unless such plea includes as a condition thereof the requirement that the defendant attend and complete the alcohol and drug rehabilitation program established pursuant to section eleven hundred ninety-six of this article, including any assessment and treatment required thereby; provided, however, that such requirement may be waived by the court upon application of the district attorney or the defendant demonstrating that the defendant, as a condition of the plea, has been required to enter into and complete an alcohol or drug treatment program prescribed pursuant to an alcohol or substance abuse screening or assessment conducted pursuant to section eleven hundred ninety-eight-a of this article or for other good cause shown. The provisions of this subparagraph shall apply, notwithstanding any bars to participation in the alcohol and drug rehabilitation program set forth in section eleven hundred ninety-six of this article; provided, however, that nothing in this paragraph shall authorize the issuance of a conditional license unless otherwise authorized by law.

(iii) In any case wherein the charge laid before the court alleges a violation of subdivision one of this section and the operator was under the age of twenty-one at the time of such violation, any plea of guilty thereafter entered in satisfaction of such charge must include at least a plea of guilty to the violation of such subdivision; provided, however, such charge may instead be satisfied as provided in paragraph (c) of this subdivision, and, provided further that, if the district attorney, upon reviewing the available evidence, determines that the charge of a violation of subdivision one of this section is not warranted, such district attorney may consent, and the court may allow a disposition by plea of guilty to another charge in satisfaction of such charge; provided, however, in all such cases, the court shall set forth upon the record the basis for such disposition.

(b) In any case wherein the charge laid before the court alleges a violation of subdivision one or six of this section while operating a commercial motor vehicle, any plea of guilty thereafter entered in satisfaction of such charge must include at least a plea of guilty to the violation of the provisions of one of the subdivisions of this section and no other disposition by plea of guilty to any other charge in satisfaction of such charge shall be authorized; provided, however, if the district attorney upon reviewing the available evidence determines that the charge of a violation of this section is not warranted, he may consent, and the court may allow, a disposition by plea of guilty to another charge is satisfaction of such charge.

(c) Except as provided in paragraph (b) of this subdivision, in any case wherein the charge laid before the court alleges a violation of subdivision one of this section by a person who was under the age of twenty-one at the time of commission of the offense, the court, with the consent of both parties, may allow the satisfaction of such charge by the defendant's agreement to be subject to action by the commissioner pursuant to section eleven hundred ninety-four-a of this article. In any such case, the defendant shall waive the right to a hearing under section eleven hundred ninety-four-a of this article and such waiver shall have the same force and effect as a finding of a violation of section eleven hundred ninety-two-a of this article entered after a hearing conducted pursuant to such section eleven hundred ninety-four-a. The defendant shall execute such waiver in open court, and, if represented by counsel, in the presence of his attorney, on a form to be provided by the commissioner, which shall be forwarded by the court to the commissioner within ninety-six hours. To be valid, such form shall, at a minimum, contain clear and conspicuous language advising the defendant that a duly executed waiver: (i) has the same force and effect as a guilty finding following a hearing pursuant to section eleven hundred ninety-four-a of this article; (ii) shall subject the defendant to the imposition of sanctions pursuant to such section eleven hundred ninety-four-a; and (iii) may subject the defendant to increased sanctions upon a subsequent violation of this section or section eleven hundred ninety-two-a of this article. Upon receipt of a duly executed waiver pursuant to this paragraph, the commissioner shall take such administrative action and impose such sanctions as may be required by section eleven hundred ninety-four-a of this article.

(d) In any case wherein the charge laid before the court alleges a violation of subdivision two-a of this section, any plea of guilty thereafter entered in satisfaction of such charge must include at least a plea of guilty to the violation of the provisions of subdivision two, two-a or three of this section, and no other disposition by plea of guilty to any other charge in satisfaction of such charge shall be authorized; provided, however, if the district attorney, upon reviewing the available evidence, determines that the charge of a violation of this section is not warranted, such district attorney may consent and the court may allow a disposition by plea of guilty to another charge in satisfaction of such charge, provided, however, in all such cases, the court shall set forth upon the record the basis for such disposition. Provided, further, however, that no such plea shall be accepted by the court unless such plea includes as a condition thereof the requirement that the defendant attend and complete the alcohol and drug rehabilitation program established pursuant to section eleven hundred ninety-six of this article, including any assessment and treatment required thereby; provided, however, that such requirement may be waived by the court upon application of the district attorney or the defendant demonstrating that the defendant, as a condition of the plea, has been required to enter into and complete an alcohol or drug treatment program prescribed pursuant to an alcohol or substance abuse screening or assessment conducted pursuant to section eleven hundred ninety-eight-a of this article or for other good cause shown. The provisions of this paragraph shall apply, notwithstanding any bars to participation in the alcohol and drug rehabilitation program set forth in section eleven hundred ninety-six of this article; provided, however, that nothing in this paragraph shall authorize the issuance of a conditional license unless otherwise authorized by law.

11. No person other than an operator of a commercial motor vehicle may be charged with or convicted of a violation of subdivision five or six of this section.

12. Driving while intoxicated or while ability impaired by drugs—serious physical injury or death or child in the vehicle.

(a) In every case where a person is charged with a violation of subdivision two, two-a, three, four or four-a of this section, the law enforcement officer alleging such charge shall make a clear notation in the "Description of Violation" section of a simplified traffic information (i) if, arising out of the same incident, someone other than the person charged was killed or suffered serious physical injury as defined in section 10.00 of the penal law; such notation shall be in the form of a "D" if someone other than the person charged was killed and such notation shall be in the form of a "S.P.I." if someone other than the person charged suffered serious physical injury; and (ii) if a child aged fifteen years or less was present in the vehicle of the person charged with a violation of subdivision two, two-a, three, four or four-a of this section; such notation shall be in the form of "C.I.V.". Provided, however, that the failure to make such notations shall in no way affect a charge for a violation of subdivision two, two-a, three, four or four-a of this section.

(b) Where a law enforcement officer alleges a violation of paragraph (b) of subdivision two-a of this section and the operator of the vehicle is a parent, guardian, or custodian of, or other person legally responsible for, a child aged fifteen years or less who is a passenger in such vehicle, then the officer shall report or cause a report to be made, if applicable, in accordance with title six of article six of the social services law.

HISTORY: Add, L 1988, ch 47, § 18, eff Nov 1, 1988. Former § 1192, add, L 1970, ch 275, § 3; amd, L 1971, ch 495, § 1, L 1972, ch 450, § 1, L 1975, ch 154, § 12, L 1981, ch 910, § 4, L 1981, ch 913, § 3, L 1982, ch 391, § 1, L 1982, ch 487, § 1, L 1984, ch 166, § 3, L 1985, ch 694, § 1, L 1985, ch 729, § 1, L 1986, ch 226, § 1, L 1986, ch 287, § 1, L 1986, ch 649 §§ 1-3, L 1987, ch 687, § 4; repealed, L 1988, ch 47, § 18, eff Nov 1, 1988. Sub 5, add, L 1990, ch 173, § 62, eff April 1, 1992. Former sub 5, renumbered sub 7, L 1990, ch 173, § 62, eff April 1, 1992. Sub 6, add, L 1990, ch 173, § 62, eff April 1, 1992. Former sub 6, renumbered sub 8, L 1990, ch 173, § 62, eff April 1, 1992. Sub 7, formerly sub 5, so renumbered, L 1990, ch 173, § 62, eff April 1, 1992. Former sub 7, renumbered sub 9, L 1990, ch 173, § 62, eff April 1, 1992. Sub 8, formerly sub 6, so renumbered, L 1990, ch 173, § 62, eff April 1, 1992. Former sub 8, renumbered sub 10, L 1990, ch 173, § 62, eff April 1, 1992. Sub 9, formerly sub 7, so renumbered, L 1990, ch 173, § 62, eff April 1, 1992. Sub 10, formerly sub 8, amd, L 1988, ch 406, § 1; renumbered sub 10, L 1990, ch 173, § 62, eff April 1, 1992. Sub 10, par (a), formerly entire subdivision, so designated and amd, L 1990, ch 173, § 63, eff April 1, 1992. Sub 10, par (b), add, L 1990, ch 173, § 63, eff April 1, 1992. Sub 11, add, L 1990, ch 173, § 62, eff April 1, 1992. Sub 2, amd, L 2002, ch 3, § 1, eff July 1, 2003. Sub 2-a, add, L 2006, ch 732, § 1, eff Nov 1, 2006; amd, L 2006, ch 746, § 1, eff Dec 15, 2006. Sub 2-a, opening par, formerly part of sub 2-a, so designated sub 2-a, opening par and amd, L 2009, ch 496, § 1, eff Dec 18, 2009. Sub 2-a, par (a), formerly part of sub 2-a, so designated sub 2-a, par (a) and amd, L 2009, ch 496, § 1, eff Dec 18, 2009. Sub 2-a, par (b), add, L 2009, ch 496, § 1, eff Dec 18, 2009. Sub 4-a, add, L 2006, ch 732, § 2, eff Nov 1, 2006. Sub 5, amd, L 1996, ch 196, § 7, eff Nov 1, 1996, L 2003, ch 236, § 1, eff Nov 1, 2003. Sub 6, amd, L 1996, ch 196, § 7, eff Nov 1, 1996, L 2002, ch 3, § 2, eff July 1, 2003, L 2003, ch 236, § 1, eff July 1, 2003. Sub 8, amd, L 2006, ch 231, § 1, eff Nov 1, 2006. Sub 8-a, add, L 1996, ch 196, § 8, eff Nov 1, 1996. Sub 10, par (a), subpar (i), formerly part of sub 10, par (a), amd, L 1996, ch 196, § 9, eff Nov 1, 1996; so designated sub 10, par (a), subpar (i) and amd, L 2006, ch 732, § 16, eff Nov 1, 2006. Sub 10, par (a), subpar (ii), add, L 2006, ch 732, § 16, eff Nov 1, 2006. Sub 10, par (a), subpar (iii), formerly part of sub 10, par (a), so designated sub 10, par (a), subpar (iii), L 2006, ch 732, § 16, eff Nov 1, 2006. Sub 10, par (c), add, L 1996, ch 196, § 10, eff Nov 1, 1996. Sub 10, par (d), add, L 2006, ch 732, § 3, eff Nov 1, 2006. Sub 12, add, L 1992, ch 449, § 1, eff Nov 14, 1992; amd, L2006, ch 732, § 4, eff Nov 1, 2006. Sub 12, opening par, formerly part of sub 12, so designated sub 12, opening par and amd, L 2009, ch 496, § 2, eff Dec 18, 2009. Sub 12, par (a), formerly part of sub 12, so designated sub 12, par (a) and amd, L 2009, ch 496, § 2, eff Dec 18, 2009. Sub 12, par (b), add, L 2009, ch 496, § 2, eff Dec 18, 2009.

§ 1192-a. Operating a motor vehicle after having consumed alcohol; under the age of twenty-one; per se

No person under the age of twenty-one shall operate a motor vehicle after having consumed alcohol as defined in this section. For purposes of this section, a person under the age of twenty-one is deemed to have consumed alcohol only if such person has .02 of one per centum or more but not more than .07 of one per centum by weight of alcohol in the person's blood, as shown by chemical analysis of such person's blood, breath, urine or saliva, made pursuant to the provisions of section eleven hundred ninety-four of this article. Any person who operates a motor vehicle in violation of this section, and who is not charged with a violation of any subdivision of section eleven hundred ninety-two of this article arising out of the same incident shall be referred to the department for action in accordance with the provisions of section eleven hundred ninety-four-a of this article. Except as otherwise provided in subdivision five of section eleven hundred ninety-two of this article, this section shall not apply to a person who operates a commercial motor vehicle. Notwithstanding any provision of law to the contrary, a finding that a person under the age of twenty-one operated a motor vehicle after having consumed alcohol in violation of this section is not a judgment of conviction for a crime or any other offense.

HISTORY: Add, L 1996, ch 196, § 11, eff Nov 1, 1996.

§ 1193. Sanctions

1. Criminal penalties.

(a) Driving while ability impaired. A violation of subdivision one of section eleven hundred ninety-two of this article shall be a traffic infraction and shall be punishable by a fine of not less than three hundred dollars nor more than five hundred dollars or by imprisonment in a penitentiary or county jail for not more than fifteen days, or by both such fine and imprisonment. A person who operates a vehicle in violation of such subdivision after having been convicted of a violation of any subdivision of section eleven hundred ninety-two of this article within the preceding five years shall be punished by a fine of not less than five hundred dollars nor more than seven hundred fifty dollars, or by imprisonment of not more than thirty days in a penitentiary or county jail or by both such fine and imprisonment. A person who operates a vehicle in violation of such subdivision after having been convicted two or more times of a violation of any subdivision of section eleven hundred ninety-two of this article within the preceding ten years shall be guilty of a misdemeanor, and shall be punished by a fine of not less than seven hundred fifty dollars nor more than fifteen hundred dollars, or by imprisonment of not more than one hundred eighty days in a penitentiary or county jail or by both such fine and imprisonment.

(b) Driving while intoxicated or while ability impaired by drugs or while ability impaired by the combined influence of drugs or of alcohol and any drug or drugs; aggravated driving while intoxicated; misdemeanor offenses.

(i) A violation of subdivision two, three, four or four-a of section eleven hundred ninety-two of this article shall be a misdemeanor and shall be punishable by a fine of not less than five hundred dollars nor more than one thousand dollars, or by imprisonment in a penitentiary or county jail for not more than one year, or by both such fine and imprisonment. A violation of paragraph (a) of subdivision two-a of section eleven hundred ninety-two of this article shall be a misdemeanor and shall be punishable by a fine of not less than one thousand dollars nor more than two thousand five hundred dollars or by imprisonment in a penitentiary or county jail for not more than one year, or by both such fine and imprisonment.

(ii) In addition to the imposition of any fine or period of imprisonment set forth in this paragraph, the court shall also sentence such person convicted of, or adjudicated a youthful offender for, a violation of subdivision two, two-a or three of section eleven hundred ninety-two of this article to a term of probation or conditional discharge, as a condition of which it shall order such person to install and maintain, in accordance with the provisions of section eleven hundred ninety-eight of this article, an ignition interlock device in any motor vehicle owned or operated by such person during the term of such probation or conditional discharge imposed for such violation of section eleven hundred ninety-two of this article and in no event for a period of less than twelve months; provided, however, that such period of interlock restriction shall terminate upon submission of proof that such person installed and maintained an ignition interlock device for at least six months, unless the court ordered such person to install and maintain an ignition interlock device for a longer period as authorized by this subparagraph and specified in such order. The period of interlock restriction shall commence from the earlier of the date of sentencing, or the date that an ignition interlock device was installed in advance of sentencing. Provided, however, the court may not authorize the operation of a motor vehicle by any person whose license or privilege to operate a motor vehicle has been revoked pursuant to the provisions of this section.

(c) Felony offenses.

(i) A person who operates a vehicle (A) in violation of subdivision two, two-a, three, four or four-a of section eleven hundred ninety-two of this article after having been convicted of a violation of subdivision two, two-a, three, four or four-a of such section or of vehicular assault in the second or first degree, as defined, respectively, in sections 120.03 and 120.04 and aggravated vehicular assault as defined in section 120.04-a of the penal law or of vehicular manslaughter in the second or first degree, as defined, respectively, in sections 125.12 and 125.13 and aggravated vehicular homicide as defined in section 125.14 of such law, within the preceding ten years, or (B) in violation of paragraph (b) of subdivision two-a of section eleven hundred ninety-two of this article shall be guilty of a class E felony, and shall be punished by a fine of not less than one thousand dollars nor more than five thousand dollars or by a period of imprisonment as provided in the penal law, or by both such fine and imprisonment.

(ii) A person who operates a vehicle in violation of subdivision two, two-a, three, four or four-a of section eleven hundred ninety-two of this article after having been convicted of a violation of subdivision two, two-a, three, four or four-a of such section or of vehicular assault in the second or first degree, as defined, respectively, in sections 120.03 and 120.04 and aggravated vehicular assault as defined in section 120.04-a of the penal law or of vehicular manslaughter in the second or first degree, as defined, respectively, in sections 125.12 and 125.13 and aggravated vehicular homicide as defined in section 125.14 of such law, twice within the preceding ten years, shall be guilty of a class D felony, and shall be punished by a fine of not less than two thousand dollars nor more than ten thousand dollars or by a period of imprisonment as provided in the penal law, or by both such fine and imprisonment.

(ii-a) A person who operates a vehicle in violation of subdivision two, two-a, three, four or four-a of section eleven hundred ninety-two of this article after having been convicted of a violation of subdivision two, two-a, three, four or four-a of such section or of vehicular assault in the second or first degree, as defined, respectively, in sections 120.03 and 120.04 and aggravated vehicular assault as defined in section 120.04-a of the penal law or of vehicular manslaughter in the second or first degree, as defined, respectively, in sections 125.12 and 125.13 and aggravated vehicular homicide as defined in section 125.14 of such law, three or more times within the preceding fifteen years, shall be guilty of a class D felony, and shall be punished by a fine of not less than two thousand dollars nor more than ten thousand dollars or by a period of imprisonment as provided in the penal law, or by both such fine and imprisonment.

(iii) In addition to the imposition of any fine or period of imprisonment set forth in this paragraph, the court shall also sentence such person convicted of, or adjudicated a youthful offender for, a violation of subdivision two, two-a or three of section eleven hundred ninety-two of this article to a period of probation or conditional discharge, as a condition of which it shall order such person to install and maintain, in accordance with the provisions of section eleven hundred ninety-eight of this article, an ignition interlock device in any motor vehicle owned or operated by such person during the term of such probation or conditional discharge imposed for such violation of section eleven hundred ninety-two of this article and in no event for a period of less than twelve months; provided, however, that such period of interlock restriction shall terminate upon submission of proof that such person installed and maintained an ignition interlock device for at least six months, unless the court ordered such person to install and maintain a ignition interlock device for a longer period as authorized by this subparagraph and specified in such order. The period of interlock restriction shall commence from the earlier of the date of sentencing, or the date that an ignition interlock device was installed in advance of sentencing. Provided, however, the court may not authorize the operation of a motor vehicle by any person whose license or privilege to operate a motor vehicle has been revoked pursuant to the provisions of this section.

(d) Alcohol or drug related offenses; special vehicles.

(1) Except as provided in subparagraph four of this paragraph, a violation of subdivision one, two, three, four or four-a of section eleven hundred ninety-two of this article wherein the violator is operating a taxicab as defined in section one hundred forty-eight-a of this chapter, or livery as defined in section one hundred twenty-one-e of this chapter, and such taxicab or livery is carrying a passenger for compensation, or a truck with a GVWR of more than eighteen thousand pounds but not more than twenty-six thousand pounds and which is not a commercial motor vehicle shall be a misdemeanor punishable by a fine of not less than five hundred dollars nor more than fifteen hundred dollars or by a period of imprisonment as provided in the penal law, or by both such fine and imprisonment. A violation of subdivision two-a of section eleven hundred ninety-two of this article wherein the violator is operating a taxicab as defined in section one hundred forty-eight-a of this chapter, or livery as defined in section one hundred twenty-one-e of this chapter, and such taxicab or livery is carrying a passenger for compensation, or a truck with a GVWR of more than eighteen thousand pounds but not more than twenty-six thousand pounds and which is not a commercial motor vehicle shall be a class E felony punishable by a fine of not less than one thousand dollars nor more than five thousand dollars or by a period of imprisonment as provided in the penal law, or by both such fine and imprisonment.

(1-a) A violation of subdivision one of section eleven hundred ninety-two of this article wherein the violator is operating a school bus as defined in section one hundred forty-two of this chapter and such school bus is carrying at least one student passenger shall be a misdemeanor punishable by a fine of not less than five hundred dollars nor more than fifteen hundred dollars or by a period of imprisonment as provided in the penal law, or by both such fine and imprisonment.

(2) A violation of subdivision five of section eleven hundred ninety-two of this article shall be a traffic infraction punishable as provided in paragraph (a) of this subdivision. Except as provided in subparagraph three or five of this paragraph, a violation of subdivision one, two, three, four, four-a or six of section eleven hundred ninety-two of this article wherein the violator is operating a commercial motor vehicle, or any motor vehicle registered or registerable under schedule F of subdivision seven of section four hundred one of this chapter shall be a misdemeanor. A violation of subdivision one, two, three, four or four-a of section eleven hundred ninety-two of this article shall be punishable by a fine of not less than five hundred dollars nor more than fifteen hundred dollars or by a period of imprisonment as provided in the penal law, or by both such fine and imprisonment. A violation of subdivision six of section eleven hundred ninety-two of this article shall be punishable by a fine of not less than five hundred dollars nor more than fifteen hundred dollars or by a period of imprisonment not to exceed one hundred eighty days, or by both such fine and imprisonment. A person who operates any such vehicle in violation of such subdivision six after having been convicted of a violation of subdivision one, two, two-a, three, four, four-a or six of section eleven hundred ninety-two of this article within the preceding five years shall be punishable by a fine of not less than five hundred dollars nor more than fifteen hundred dollars or by a period of imprisonment as provided in the penal law, or by both such fine and imprisonment. A violation of subdivision two-a of section eleven hundred ninety-two of this article wherein the violator is operating a commercial motor vehicle, or any motor vehicle registered or registerable under schedule F of

subdivision seven of section four hundred one of this chapter shall be a class E felony punishable by a fine of not less than one thousand dollars nor more than five thousand dollars or by a period of imprisonment as provided in the penal law, or by both such fine and imprisonment.

(3) A violation of subdivision one of section eleven hundred ninety-two of this article wherein the violator is operating a motor vehicle with a gross vehicle weight rating of more than eighteen thousand pounds which contains flammable gas, radioactive materials or explosives shall be a misdemeanor punishable by a fine of not less than five hundred dollars nor more than fifteen hundred dollars or by a period of imprisonment as provided in the penal law, or by both such fine and imprisonment.

(4) (i) A person who operates a vehicle in violation of subdivision one, two, two-a, three, four or four-a of section eleven hundred ninety-two of this article and which is punishable as provided in subparagraph one, one-a, two or three of this paragraph after having been convicted of a violation of any such subdivision of section eleven hundred ninety-two of this article and penalized under subparagraph one, one-a, two or three of this paragraph within the preceding ten years, shall be guilty of a class E felony, which shall be punishable by a fine of not less than one thousand dollars nor more than five thousand dollars, or by a period of imprisonment as provided in the penal law, or by both such fine and imprisonment. A person who operates a vehicle in violation of subdivision six of section eleven hundred ninety-two of this article after having been convicted of two or more violations of subdivisions one, two, two-a, three, four, four-a or six of section eleven hundred ninety-two of this article within the preceding five years, any one of which was a misdemeanor, shall be guilty of a class E felony, which shall be punishable by a fine of not less than one thousand dollars nor more than five thousand dollars, or by a period of imprisonment as provided in the penal law, or by both such fine and imprisonment. In addition, any person sentenced pursuant to this subparagraph shall be subject to the disqualification provided in subparagraph three of paragraph (e) of subdivision two of this section.

(ii) A person who operates a vehicle in violation of subdivision one, two, two-a, three, four or four-a of section eleven hundred ninety-two of this article and which is punishable as provided in subparagraph one, one-a, two or three of this paragraph after having been convicted of a violation of any such subdivision of section eleven hundred ninety-two of this article and penalized under subparagraph one, one-a, two or three of this paragraph twice within the preceding ten years, shall be guilty of a class D felony, which shall be punishable by a fine of not less than two thousand dollars nor more than ten thousand dollars, or by a period of imprisonment as provided in the penal law, or by both such fine and imprisonment. A person who operates a vehicle in violation of subdivision six of section eleven hundred ninety-two of this article after having been convicted of three or more violations of subdivisions one, two, two-a, three, four, four-a or six of section eleven hundred ninety-two of this article within the preceding five years, any one of which was a misdemeanor, shall be guilty of a class D felony, which shall be punishable by a fine of not less than two thousand dollars nor more than ten thousand dollars, or by a period of imprisonment as provided in the penal law, or by both such fine and imprisonment. In addition, any person sentenced pursuant to this subparagraph shall be subject to the disqualification provided in subparagraph three of paragraph (e) of subdivision two of this section.

(4-a) A violation of subdivision two, three, four or four-a of section eleven hundred ninety-two of this article wherein the violator is operating a school bus as defined in section one hundred forty-two of this chapter and such school bus is carrying at least one student passenger shall be a class E felony punishable by a fine of not less than one thousand dollars nor more than five thousand dollars, or by a period of imprisonment as provided in the penal law, or by both such fine and imprisonment. A violation of subdivision two-a of section eleven hundred ninety-two of this article wherein the violator is operating a school bus as defined in section one hundred forty-two of this chapter and such school bus is carrying at least one student passenger shall be a class D felony punishable by a fine of not less than two thousand dollars nor more than ten thousand dollars, or by a period of imprisonment as provided in the penal law, or by both such fine and imprisonment.

(5) A violation of subdivision two, three, four or four-a of section eleven hundred ninety-two of this article wherein the violator is operating a motor vehicle with a gross vehicle weight rating of more than eighteen thousand pounds which contains flammable gas, radioactive materials or explosives, shall be a class E felony punishable by a fine of not less than one thousand dollars and such other penalties as provided for in the penal law; provided, however, that a conviction for such violation shall not be considered a predicate felony pursuant to section 70.06 of such law, or a previous felony conviction pursuant to section 70.10 of such law. A violation of subdivision two-a of section eleven hundred ninety-two of this article wherein the violator is operating a motor vehicle with a gross vehicle weight rating of more than eighteen thousand pounds which contains flammable gas, radioactive materials or explosives, shall be a class D felony punishable by a fine of not less than two thousand nor more than ten thousand dollars and such other penalties as provided for in the penal law; provided, however, that a conviction for such violation shall not be considered a predicate felony pursuant to section 70.06 of such law, or a previous felony conviction pursuant to section 70.10 of such law.

(6) The sentences required to be imposed by subparagraph one, one-a, two, three, four, four-a or five of this paragraph shall be imposed notwithstanding any contrary provision of this chapter or the penal law.

(7) Nothing contained in this paragraph shall prohibit the imposition of a charge of any other felony set forth in this or any other provision of law for any acts arising out of the same incident.

(e) Certain sentences prohibited. Notwithstanding any provisions of the penal law, no judge or magistrate shall impose a sentence of unconditional discharge for a violation of any subdivision of section eleven hundred ninety-two of this article nor shall a judge or magistrate impose a sentence of conditional discharge or probation unless such conditional discharge or probation is accompanied by a sentence of a fine as provided in this subdivision.

(f) Where the court imposes a sentence for a violation of section eleven hundred ninety-two of this article, the court may require the defendant, as a part of or as a condition of such sentence, to attend a single session conducted by a victims impact program. For purposes of this section, "victims impact program" means a program operated by a county, a city with a population of one million or more, by a not-for-profit organization authorized by any such county or city, or a combination thereof, in which presentations are made concerning the impact of operating a motor vehicle while under the influence of alcohol or drugs to one or more persons who have been convicted of such offenses. A description of any such program shall be filed with the commissioner and with the coordinator of the special traffic options program for driving while intoxicated established pursuant to section eleven hundred ninety-seven of this article, and shall be made available to the court upon request. Nothing contained herein shall be construed to require any governmental entity to create such a victim impact program.

(g) The office of probation and correctional alternatives shall recommend to the commissioner of the division of criminal justice services regulations governing the monitoring of compliance by persons ordered to install and maintain ignition interlock devices to provide standards for monitoring by departments of probation, and options for monitoring of compliance by such persons, that counties may adopt as an alternative to monitoring by a department of probation.

1-a. Additional penalties.

(a) Except as provided for in paragraph (b) of this subdivision, a person who operates a vehicle in violation of subdivision two or three of section eleven hundred ninety-two of this article after having been convicted of a violation of subdivision two or three of such section within the preceding five years shall, in addition to any other penalties which may be imposed pursuant to subdivision one of this section, be sentenced to a term of imprisonment of five days or, as an alternative to such imprisonment, be required to perform thirty days of service for a public or not-for-profit corporation, association, institution or agency as set forth in paragraph (h) of subdivision two of section 65.10 of the penal law as a condition of sentencing for such violation. Notwithstanding the provisions of this paragraph, a sentence of a term of imprisonment of five days or more pursuant to the provisions of subdivision one of this section shall be deemed to be in compliance with this subdivision.

(b) A person who operates a vehicle in violation of subdivision two or three of section eleven hundred ninety-two of this article after having been convicted on two or more occasions of a violation of any of such subdivisions within the preceding five years shall, in addition to any other penalties which may be imposed pursuant to subdivision one of this section, be sentenced to a term of imprisonment of ten days or, as an alternative to such imprisonment, be required to perform sixty days of service for a public or not-for-profit corporation, association, institution or agency as set forth in paragraph (h) of subdivision two of section 65.10 of the penal law as a condition of sentencing for such violation. Notwithstanding the provisions of this paragraph, a sentence of a term of imprisonment of ten days or more pursuant to the provisions of subdivision one of this section shall be deemed to be in compliance with this subdivision.

(c) A court sentencing a person pursuant to paragraph (a) or (b) of this subdivision shall: (i) order the installation of an ignition interlock device approved pursuant to section eleven hundred ninety-eight of this article in any motor vehicle owned or operated by the person so sentenced. Such devices shall remain installed during any period of license revocation required to be imposed pursuant to paragraph (b) of subdivision two of this section, and, upon the termination of such revocation period, for an additional period as determined by the court; and (ii) order that such person receive an assessment of the degree of their alcohol or substance abuse and dependency pursuant to the provisions of section eleven hundred ninety-eight-a of this article. Where such assessment indicates the need for treatment, such court is authorized to impose treatment as a condition of such sentence except that such court shall impose treatment as a condition of a sentence of probation or conditional discharge pursuant to the provisions of subdivision three of section eleven hundred ninety-eight-a of this article. Any person ordered to install an ignition interlock device pursuant to this paragraph shall be subject to the provisions of subdivisions four, five, seven, eight and nine of section eleven hundred ninety-eight of this article.

(d) Confidentiality of records. The provisions of subdivision six of section eleven hundred ninety-eight-a of this article shall apply to the records and content of all assessments and treatment conducted pursuant to this subdivision.

2. License sanctions.

(a) Suspensions. Except as otherwise provided in this subdivision, a license shall be suspended and a registration may be suspended for the following periods:

(1) Driving while ability impaired. Ninety days, where the holder is convicted of a violation of subdivision one of section eleven hundred ninety-two of this article;

(2) Persons under the age of twenty-one; driving after having consumed alcohol. Six months, where the holder has been found to have operated a motor vehicle after having consumed alcohol in violation of section eleven hundred ninety-two-a of this article where such person was under the age of twenty-one at the time of commission of such violation.

(b) Revocations. A license shall be revoked and a registration may be revoked for the following minimum periods:

(1) Driving while ability impaired; prior offense. Six months, where the holder is convicted of a violation of subdivision one of section eleven hundred ninety-two of this article committed within five years of a conviction for a violation of any subdivision of section eleven hundred ninety-two of this article.

(1-a) Driving while ability impaired; misdemeanor offense. Six months, where the holder is convicted of a violation of subdivision one of section eleven hundred ninety-two of this article committed within ten years of two previous convictions for a violation of any subdivision of section eleven hundred ninety-two of this article.

(2) Driving while intoxicated or while ability impaired by drugs or while ability impaired by the combined influence of drugs or of alcohol and any drug or drugs; aggravated driving while intoxicated. Six months, where the holder is convicted of a violation of subdivision two, three, four or four-a of section eleven hundred ninety-two of this article. One year where the holder is convicted of a violation of subdivision two-a of section eleven hundred ninety-two of this article.

(3) Driving while intoxicated or while ability impaired by drugs or while ability impaired by the combined influence of drugs or of alcohol and any drug or drugs; aggravated driving while intoxicated; prior offense. One year, where the holder is convicted of a violation of subdivision two, three, four or four-a of section eleven hundred ninety-two of this article committed within ten years of a conviction for a violation of subdivision two, three, four or four-a of section eleven hundred ninety-two of this article. Eighteen months, where the holder is convicted of a violation of subdivision two-a of section eleven hundred ninety-two of this article committed within ten years of a conviction for a violation of subdivision two, two-a, three, four or four-a of section eleven hundred ninety-two of this article; or where the holder is convicted of a violation of subdivision two, three, four or four-a of section eleven hundred ninety-two of this article committed within ten years of a conviction for a violation of subdivision two-a of section eleven hundred ninety-two of this article.

(4) Special vehicles other than school buses. One year, where the holder is convicted of a violation of any subdivision of section eleven hundred ninety-two of this article and is sentenced pursuant to subparagraph one of paragraph (d) of subdivision one of this section.

(4-a) School buses.

(A) One year, where the holder is convicted of a violation of any subdivision of section eleven hundred ninety-two of this article, such violation was committed while the holder was driving a school bus, and the holder is sentenced pursuant to subparagraph one, one-a or four-a of paragraph (d) of subdivision one of this section.

(B) Three years where the holder is convicted of a violation of any subdivision of section eleven hundred ninety-two of this article, such violation was committed while the holder was driving a school bus, and the holder is sentenced pursuant to subparagraph four of paragraph (d) of subdivision one of this section.

(C) Notwithstanding the provisions of the opening paragraph of this paragraph (b), the commissioner shall not revoke the registration of a school bus driven in violation of section eleven hundred ninety-two of this article.

(5) Holder of a commercial driver's license.

(i) Except as otherwise provided in this subparagraph, one year where the holder of a commercial driver's license is convicted of a violation of any subdivision of section eleven hundred ninety-two of this article or if such holder is convicted of an offense consisting of operating a motor vehicle under the influence of alcohol or drugs where such conviction was had outside of this state.

(ii) Three years, where the holder is convicted of a violation of any subdivision of section eleven hundred ninety-two of this article, such violation was committed while the holder was operating a commercial motor vehicle transporting hazardous materials or if such holder is convicted of an offense consisting of operating a motor vehicle under the influence of alcohol or drugs where such conviction was had outside of this state.

(6) Persons under the age of twenty-one. One year, where the holder is convicted of or adjudicated a youthful offender for a violation of any subdivision of section eleven hundred ninety-two of this article, or is convicted of or receives a youthful offender or other juvenile adjudication for an offense consisting of operating a motor vehicle under the influence of intoxicating liquor where the conviction, or youthful offender or other juvenile adjudication was had outside this state, where such person was under the age of twenty-one at the time of commission of such violation.

(7) Persons under the age of twenty-one; prior offense or finding. One year or until the holder reaches the age of twenty-one, whichever is the greater period of time, where the holder has been found to have operated a motor vehicle after having consumed alcohol in violation of section eleven hundred ninety-two-a of this article, or is convicted of, or adjudicated a youthful offender for, a violation of any subdivision of section eleven hundred ninety-two of this article, or is convicted of or receives a youthful offender or juvenile adjudication for an offense consisting of operating a motor vehicle under the influence of intoxicating liquor where the conviction, or youthful offender or other juvenile adjudication was had outside this state, where such person was under the age of twenty-one at the time of commission of such violation and has previously been found to have operated a motor vehicle after having consumed alcohol in violation of section eleven hundred ninety-two-a of this article, or has previously been convicted of, or adjudicated a youthful offender for, any violation of section eleven hundred ninety-two of this article not arising out of the same incident, or has previously been convicted of or received a youthful offender or juvenile adjudication for an offense consisting of operating a motor vehicle under the influence of intoxicating liquor when the conviction, or youthful offender or other juvenile adjudication was had outside this state and not arising out of the same.

(8) Out-of-state offenses. Except as provided in subparagraph six or seven of this paragraph: (i) ninety days, where the holder is convicted of an offense consisting of operating a motor vehicle under the influence of intoxicating liquor where the conviction was had outside this state and (ii) six months, where the holder is convicted of, or receives a youthful offender or other juvenile adjudication, which would have been a misdemeanor or felony if committed by an adult, in connection with, an offense consisting of operating a motor vehicle under the influence of or while impaired by the use of drugs where the conviction or youthful offender or other juvenile adjudication was had outside this state.

(9) Effect of rehabilitation program. No period of revocation arising out of subparagraph four, five, six or seven of this paragraph may be set aside by the commissioner for the reason that such person was a participant in the alcohol and drug rehabilitation program set forth in section eleven hundred ninety-six of this chapter.

(10) Action required by commissioner. Where a court fails to impose, or incorrectly imposes, a suspension or revocation required by this subdivision, the commissioner shall, upon receipt of a certificate of conviction filed pursuant to section five hundred fourteen of this chapter, impose such mandated suspension or revocation, which shall supersede any such order which the court may have imposed.

(11) Limitation of certain mandatory revocations. Where revocation is mandatory pursuant to subparagraph five of this paragraph for a conviction of a violation of subdivision five of section eleven hundred ninety-two of this article, such revocation shall be issued only by the commissioner and shall be applicable only to that portion of the holder's driver's license or privilege which permits the operation of commercial motor vehicles, and the commissioner shall immediately issue a license, other than a commercial driver's license, to such person provided that such person is otherwise eligible to receive such license and further provided that issuing a license to such person does not create a substantial traffic safety hazard.

(12) Permanent revocation.

(a) Notwithstanding any other provision of this chapter to the contrary, whenever a revocation is imposed upon a person for the refusal to submit to a chemical test pursuant to the provisions of section eleven hundred ninety-four of this article or conviction for any violation of section eleven hundred ninety-two of this article for which a sentence of imprisonment may be imposed, and such person has: (i) within the previous four years been twice convicted of any provisions of section eleven hundred ninety-two of this article or a violation of the penal law for which a violation of such section eleven hundred ninety-two is an essential element and at least one such conviction was for a crime, or has twice been found to have refused to submit to a chemical test pursuant to section eleven hundred ninety-four of this article, or has any combination of two such convictions and findings of refusal not arising out of the same incident; or (ii) within the previous eight years been convicted three times of any provision of section eleven hundred ninety-two of this article for which a sentence of imprisonment may be imposed or a violation of the penal law for which a violation of such section eleven hundred ninety-two is an essential element and at least two such convictions were for crimes, or has been found, on three separate occasions, to have refused to submit to a chemical test pursuant to section eleven hundred ninety-four of this article, or has any combination of such convictions and findings of refusal not arising out of the same incident, such revocation shall be permanent.

(b) The permanent driver's license revocation required by clause (a) of this subparagraph shall be waived by the commissioner after a period of five years has expired since the imposition of such permanent revocation, provided that during such five-year period such person has not been found to have refused a chemical test pursuant to section eleven hundred ninety-four of this article while operating a motor vehicle and has not been convicted of a violation of any subdivision of section eleven hundred ninety-two of this article or section five hundred eleven of this chapter or a violation of the penal law for which a violation of any subdivision of such section eleven hundred ninety-two is an essential element and either:

(i) that such person provides acceptable documentation to the commissioner that such person has voluntarily enrolled in and successfully completed an appropriate rehabilitation program; or

(ii) that such person is granted a certificate of relief from disabilities or a certificate of good conduct pursuant to article twenty-three of the correction law.

Provided, however, that the commissioner may, on a case by case basis, refuse to restore a license which otherwise would be restored pursuant to this item, in the interest of the public safety and welfare.

(c) For revocations imposed pursuant to clause (a) of this subparagraph, the commissioner may adopt rules to permit conditional or restricted operation of a motor vehicle by any such person after a mandatory revocation period of not less than three years subject to such criteria, terms and conditions as established by the commissioner.

(d) Upon (i) a finding of refusal after having been convicted three times within four years of a violation of any subdivision of section eleven hundred ninety-two of this article or of the penal law for which a violation of any subdivision of such section eleven hundred ninety-two is an essential element or any combination of three such convictions not arising out of the same incident within four years or (ii) a fourth conviction of any subdivision of section eleven hundred ninety-two of this article after having been convicted of any such subdivision of such section eleven hundred ninety-two or of the penal law for which a violation of any of such subdivisions of such section eleven hundred ninety-two is an essential element or any combination of three such convictions not arising out of the same incident within four years or (iii) a finding of refusal after having been convicted four times within eight years of a violation of any subdivision of section eleven hundred ninety-two of this article or of the penal law for which a violation of any of such subdivisions of such section eleven hundred ninety-two is an essential element or any combination of four such convictions not arising out of the same incident within eight years or (iv) a fifth conviction of any subdivision of section eleven hundred ninety-two of this article after having been convicted of such subdivision or of the penal law for which a violation of any of such subdivisions of such section eleven hundred ninety-two is an essential element or any combination of four such convictions not arising out of the same incident within eight years, such revocation shall be permanent.

(e) The permanent driver's license revocation required by clause (d) of this subparagraph may be waived by the commissioner after a period of eight years has expired since the imposition of such permanent revocation provided:

(i) that during such eight-year period such person has not been found to have refused a chemical test pursuant to section eleven hundred ninety-four of this article while operating a motor vehicle and has not been convicted of a violation of any subdivision of section eleven hundred ninety-two of this article or section five hundred eleven of this chapter or a violation of the penal law for which a violation of any such subdivisions of such section eleven hundred ninety-two is an essential element; and

(ii) that such person provides acceptable documentation to the commissioner that such person has voluntarily enrolled in and successfully completed an appropriate rehabilitation program; and

(iii) after such documentation is accepted, that such person is granted a certificate of relief from disabilities or a certificate of good conduct pursuant to article twenty-three of the correction law.

Notwithstanding the provisions of this clause, nothing contained in this clause shall be deemed to require the commissioner to restore a license to an applicant who otherwise has complied with the requirements of this item, in the interest of the public safety and welfare.

(f) Nothing contained in this subparagraph shall be deemed to reduce a license revocation period imposed pursuant to any other provision of law.

(c) Reissuance of licenses; restrictions.

(1) Except as otherwise provided in this paragraph, where a license is revoked pursuant to paragraph (b) of this subdivision, no new license shall be issued after the expiration of the minimum period specified in such paragraph, except in the discretion of the commissioner.

(2) Where a license is revoked pursuant to subparagraph two, three or eight of paragraph (b) of this subdivision for a violation of subdivision four of section eleven hundred ninety-two of this article, and where the individual does not have a driver's license or the individual's license was suspended at the time of conviction or youthful offender or other juvenile adjudication, the commissioner shall not issue a new license nor restore the former license for a period of six months after such individual would otherwise have become eligible to obtain a new license or to have the former license restored; provided, however, that during such delay period the commissioner may issue a restricted use license pursuant to section five hundred thirty of this chapter.

(3) In no event shall a new license be issued where a person has been twice convicted of a violation of subdivision three, four or four-a of section eleven hundred ninety-two of this article or of driving while intoxicated or of driving while ability is impaired by the use of a drug or of driving while ability is impaired by the combined influence of drugs or of alcohol and any drug or drugs where physical injury, as defined in section 10.00 of the penal law, has resulted from such offense in each instance.

(d) Suspension or revocation; sentencing.

(1) Notwithstanding anything to the contrary contained in a certificate of relief from disabilities or a certificate of good conduct issued pursuant to article twenty-three of the correction law, where a suspension or revocation, other than a revocation required to be issued by the commissioner, is mandatory pursuant to paragraph (a) or (b) of this subdivision, the magistrate, justice or judge shall issue an order suspending or revoking such license upon sentencing, and the license holder shall surrender such license to the court. Except as hereinafter provided, such suspension or revocation shall take effect immediately.

(2) Except where the license holder has been charged with a violation of article one hundred twenty or one hundred twenty-five of the penal law arising out of the same incident

or convicted of such violation or a violation of any subdivision of section eleven hundred ninety-two of this article within the preceding five years, the judge, justice or magistrate may issue an order making said license suspension or revocation take effect twenty days after the date of sentencing. The license holder shall be given a copy of said order permitting the continuation of driving privileges for twenty days after sentencing, if granted by the court. The court shall forward to the commissioner the certificates required in sections five hundred thirteen and five hundred fourteen of this chapter, along with a copy of any order issued pursuant to this paragraph and the license, within ninety-six hours of sentencing.

(e) Special provisions.

(1) Suspension pending prosecution; procedure.

a. Without notice, pending any prosecution, the court shall suspend such license, where the holder has been charged with a violation of subdivision two, two-a, three, four or four-a of section eleven hundred ninety-two of this article and either (i) a violation of a felony under article one hundred twenty or one hundred twenty-five of the penal law arising out of the same incident, or (ii) has been convicted of any violation under section eleven hundred ninety-two of this article within the preceding five years.

b. The suspension under the preceding clause shall occur no later than twenty days after the holder's first appearance before the court on the charges or at the conclusion of all proceedings required for the arraignment. In order for the court to impose such suspension it must find that the accusatory instrument conforms to the requirements of section 100.40 of the criminal procedure law and there exists reasonable cause to believe that the holder operated a motor vehicle in violation of subdivision two, two-a, three, four or four-a of section eleven hundred ninety-two of this article and either (i) the person had been convicted of any violation under such section eleven hundred ninety-two of this article within the preceding five years; or (ii) that the holder committed a violation of a felony under article one hundred twenty or one hundred twenty-five of the penal law. At such time the holder shall be entitled to an opportunity to make a statement regarding the enumerated issues and to present evidence tending to rebut the court's findings. Where such suspension is imposed upon a pending charge of a violation of a felony under article one hundred twenty or one hundred twenty-five of the penal law and the holder has requested a hearing pursuant to article one hundred eighty of the criminal procedure law, the court shall conduct such hearing. If upon completion of the hearing, the court fails to find that there is reasonable cause to believe that the holder committed a felony under article one hundred twenty or one hundred twenty-five of the penal law and the holder has not been previously convicted of any violation of section eleven hundred ninety-two of this article within the preceding five years the court shall promptly notify the commissioner and direct restoration of such license to the license holder unless such license is suspended or revoked pursuant to any other provision of this chapter.

(2) Bail forfeiture. A license shall be suspended where the holder forfeits bail upon a charge of a violation of any subdivision of section eleven hundred ninety-two of this article. Such suspension shall not be terminated until the holder submits to the jurisdiction of the court in which the bail was forfeited.

(3) Permanent disqualification from operating certain motor vehicles.

a. Except as otherwise provided herein, in addition to any revocation set forth in subparagraph four or five of paragraph (b) of this subdivision, any person sentenced pursuant to subparagraph three of paragraph (d) of subdivision one of this section shall be permanently disqualified from operating any vehicle set forth in such paragraph. In addition, the commissioner shall not issue such person a license valid for the operation of any vehicle set forth therein by such person. The commissioner may waive such disqualification and prohibition hereinbefore provided after a period of five years has expired from such sentencing provided:

    (i) that during such five year period such person has not violated any of the provisions of section eleven hundred ninety-two of this article or any alcohol or drug related traffic offense in this state or in any jurisdiction outside this state;

    (ii) that such person provides acceptable documentation to the commissioner that such person is not in need of alcohol or drug treatment or has satisfactorily completed a prescribed course of such treatment; and

    (iii) after such documentation is accepted, that such person is granted a certificate of relief from disabilities or a certificate of good conduct pursuant to article twenty-three of the correction law.

    b. Any person who holds a commercial driver's license and is convicted of a violation of any subdivision of section eleven hundred ninety-two of this article who has had a prior finding of refusal to submit to a chemical test pursuant to section eleven hundred ninety-four of this article or has had a prior conviction of any of the following offenses: any violation of section eleven hundred ninety-two of this article; any violation of subdivision one or two of section six hundred of this chapter; or has a prior conviction of any felony involving the use of a motor vehicle pursuant to paragraph (a) of subdivision one of section five hundred ten-a of this chapter, shall be permanently disqualified from operating a commercial motor vehicle. The commissioner may waive such disqualification and prohibition hereinbefore provided after a period of ten years has expired from such sentence provided:

    (i) that during such ten year period such person has not been found to have refused a chemical test pursuant to section eleven hundred ninety-four of this article while operating a motor vehicle and has not been convicted of any one of the following offenses while operating a motor vehicle: any violation of section eleven hundred ninety-two of this article; any violation of subdivision one or two of section six hundred of this chapter; or has a prior conviction of any felony involving the use of a motor vehicle pursuant to paragraph (a) of subdivision one of section five hundred ten-a of this chapter;

    (ii) that such person provides acceptable documentation to the commissioner that such person is not in need of alcohol or drug treatment or has satisfactorily completed a prescribed course of such treatment; and

    (iii) after such documentation is accepted, that such person is granted a certificate of relief from disabilities or a certificate of good conduct pursuant to article twenty-three of the correction law.

    c. Upon a third finding of refusal and/or conviction of any of the offenses which require a permanent commercial driver's license revocation, such permanent revocation may not be waived by the commissioner under any circumstances.

(4) Youthful offenders. Where a youth is determined to be a youthful offender, following

a conviction of a violation of section eleven hundred ninety-two of this article for which a license suspension or revocation is mandatory, the court shall impose such suspension or revocation as is otherwise required upon conviction and, further, shall notify the commissioner of said suspension or revocation and its finding that said violator is granted youthful offender status as is required pursuant to section five hundred thirteen of this chapter.

(5) Probation. When a license to operate a motor vehicle has been revoked pursuant to this chapter, and the holder has been sentenced to a period of probation pursuant to section 65.00 of the penal law for a violation of any provision of this chapter, or any other provision of the laws of this state, and a condition of such probation is that the holder thereof not operate a motor vehicle or not apply for a license to operate a motor vehicle during the period of such condition of probation, the commissioner may not restore such license until the period of the condition of probation has expired.

(6) Application for new license. Where a license has been revoked pursuant to paragraph (b) of this subdivision, or where the holder is subject to a condition of probation as provided in subparagraph five of this paragraph, application for a new license may be made within forty-five days prior to the expiration of such minimum period of revocation or condition of probation, whichever expires last.

(7) Suspension pending prosecution; excessive blood alcohol content.

a. Except as provided in clause a-1 of this subparagraph, a court shall suspend a driver's license, pending prosecution, of any person charged with a violation of subdivision two, two-a, three or four-a of section eleven hundred ninety-two of this article who, at the time of arrest, is alleged to have had .08 of one percent or more by weight of alcohol in such driver's blood as shown by chemical analysis of blood, breath, urine or saliva, made pursuant to subdivision two or three of section eleven hundred ninety-four of this article.

a-1. A court shall suspend a class DJ or MJ learner's permit or a class DJ or MJ driver's license, pending prosecution, of any person who has been charged with a violation of subdivision one, two, two-a and/or three of section eleven hundred ninety-two of this article.

b. [As amended by Laws 2002, chs 3 and 571] The suspension occurring under clause a of this subparagraph shall occur no later than at the conclusion of all proceedings required for the arraignment and the suspension occurring under clause a-1 of this subparagraph shall occur immediately after the holder's first appearance before the court on the charge which shall, whenever possible, be the next regularly scheduled session of the court after the arrest or at the conclusion of all proceedings required for the arraignment; provided, however, that if the results of any test administered pursuant to section eleven hundred ninety-four of this article are not available within such time period, the complainant police officer or other public servant shall transmit such results to the court at the time they become available, and the court shall, as soon as practicable following the receipt of such results and in compliance with the requirements of this subparagraph, suspend such license. In order for the court to impose such suspension it must find that the accusatory instrument conforms to the requirements of section 100.40 of the criminal procedure law and there exists reasonable cause to believe either that (a) the holder operated a motor vehicle while such holder had .08 of one percent or more by weight of alcohol in his or her blood as was shown by chemical analysis of such person's blood, breath, urine or saliva, made pursuant to the provisions of section eleven hundred ninety-four of this article or (b) the person was the holder of a class DJ or MJ learner's permit or a class DJ or MJ driver's license and operated a motor vehicle while such holder was in violation of subdivision one, two and/or three of section eleven hundred ninety-two of this article. At the time of such license suspension the holder shall be entitled to an opportunity to make a statement regarding these two issues and to present evidence tending to rebut the court's findings.

c. Nothing contained in this subparagraph shall be construed to prohibit or limit a court from imposing any other suspension pending prosecution required or permitted by law.

d. Notwithstanding any contrary provision of this chapter, if any suspension occurring under this subparagraph has been in effect for a period of thirty days, the holder may be issued a conditional license, in accordance with section eleven hundred ninety-six of this article, provided the holder of such license is otherwise eligible to receive such conditional license. A conditional license issued pursuant to this subparagraph shall not be valid for the operation of a commercial motor vehicle. The commissioner shall prescribe by regulation the procedures for the issuance of such conditional license.

e. If the court finds that the suspension imposed pursuant to this subparagraph will result in extreme hardship, the court must issue such suspension, but may grant a hardship privilege, which shall be issued on a form prescribed by the commissioner. For the purposes of this clause, "extreme hardship" shall mean the inability to obtain alternative means of travel to or from the licensee's employment, or to or from necessary medical treatment for the licensee or a member of the licensee's household, or if the licensee is a matriculating student enrolled in an accredited school, college or university travel to or from such licensee's school, college or university if such travel is necessary for the completion of the educational degree or certificate. The burden of proving extreme hardship shall be on the licensee who may present material and relevant evidence. A finding of extreme hardship may not be based solely upon the testimony of the licensee. In no event shall arraignment be adjourned or otherwise delayed more than three business days solely for the purpose of allowing the licensee to present evidence of extreme hardship. The court shall set forth upon the record, or otherwise set forth in writing, the factual basis for such finding. The hardship privilege shall permit the operation of a vehicle only for travel to or from the licensee's employment, or to or from necessary medical treatment for the licensee or a member of the licensee's household, or if the licensee is a matriculating student enrolled in an accredited school, college or university travel to or from such licensee's school, college or university if such travel is necessary for the completion of the educational degree or certificate. A hardship privilege shall not be valid for the operation of a commercial motor vehicle.

(f) Notice of charges to parent or guardian. Notwithstanding the provisions of subdivision two of section eighteen hundred seven of this chapter, upon the first scheduled appearance of any person under eighteen years of age who resides within the household of his or her parent or guardian upon a charge of a violation of subdivision one, two and/or three of section eleven hundred ninety-two of this article, the local criminal court before which such first appearance is scheduled shall forthwith transmit written notice of such appearance or failure to make such appearance to the parent or guardian of such minor person; provided, however, that if an arraignment and conviction of such person follows such appearance upon the same day, or in case such person waives arraignment and enters a plea of guilty to the offense as charged in accordance with the provisions of section eighteen hundred five of this chapter, transmittal of notice of his or her conviction as provided in section five hundred fourteen of this chapter shall be sufficient and the notice required by this paragraph need not be given; provided further that the failure of a local criminal court to transmit the notice required by this paragraph shall in no manner affect the validity of a conviction subsequently obtained.

HISTORY: Add, L 1988, ch 47, § 18, eff Nov 1, 1988; amd, 1988, ch 294, § 1, eff Nov 1, 1988, L 1988, ch 406, §§ 2–6, eff Nov 1, 1988, L 1988, ch 664, § 1, eff Nov 1, 1988, L 1990, ch 173, § 27, eff Aug 19, 1990, L 1990, ch 173, § 64, eff Feb 19, 1991, L 1990, ch 173, §§ 65, 67–70 eff April 1, 1992, L 1990, ch 173, § 66, eff May 21, 1990, L 1990, ch 696, §§ 7, 8, eff Feb 19, 1991, L 1990, ch 714, § 1, eff Oct 20, 1990, L 1992, ch 420, § 1, eff Nov 1, 1992, L 1993, ch 533, §§ 5, 6, eff Sept 30, 1993, L 1994, ch 75, §§ 1, 2, eff Nov 1, 1994, L 1994, ch 312, § 1, eff July 24, 1994, L 1994, ch 312, § 2, eff Sept 3, 1993, L 1994, ch 314, § 3, eff Nov 1, 1994, L 1994, ch 312, § 4, eff Nov 1, 1994, L 1996, ch 26, §§ 1, 2, eff Nov 1, 1996, L 1996, ch 196, §§ 12, 13, eff Nov 1, 1996, L 1996, ch 652, §§ 1, 2, eff Nov 1, 1996, L 2000, ch 287, § 1, eff Nov 1, 2000, L 2002, ch 3, § 3, eff July 1, 2003, L 2002, ch 571, §§ 1–4, eff Dec 23, 2002, L 2002, ch 691, § 1, eff Sept 30, 2003, L 2005, ch 60, §§ 16, 17 (Part E), eff Sept 30, 2005, L 2006, ch 59, § 3 (Part J), eff April 11, 2006, L 2006, ch 732, §§ 5–10, 17, 18, 26, eff Nov 1, 2006, L 2007, ch 251, §§ 6, 7, eff July 18, 2007, L 2007, ch 345, § 7, eff Nov 1, 2007, L 2007, ch 668, § 2, eff Oct 27, 2007, L 2007, ch 669, § 2, eff Oct 27, 2007, L 2009, ch 496, § 3, eff Dec 18, 2009, L 2010, ch 56, § 57 (Part A), eff June 22, 2010, L 2010, ch 56, §§ 32–36 (Part LL), eff June 22, 2010, L 2013, ch 169, § 2, eff Nov 1, 2013, L 2014, ch 191, § 2, eff Nov 1, 2014.

§ 1194. Arrest and testing

1. Arrest and field testing.

(a) Arrest. Notwithstanding the provisions of section 140.10 of the criminal procedure law, a police officer may, without a warrant, arrest a person, in case of a violation of subdivision one of section eleven hundred ninety-two of this article, if such violation is coupled with an accident or collision in which such person is involved, which in fact has been committed, though not in the police officer's presence, when the officer has reasonable cause to believe that the violation was committed by such person.

(b) Field testing. Every person operating a motor vehicle which has been involved in an accident or which is operated in violation of any of the provisions of this chapter shall, at the request of a police officer, submit to a breath test to be administered by the police officer. If such test indicates that such operator has consumed alcohol, the police officer may request such operator to submit to a chemical test in the manner set forth in subdivision two of this section.

2. Chemical tests.

(a) When authorized. Any person who operates a motor vehicle in this state shall be deemed to have given consent to a chemical test of one or more of the following: breath, blood, urine, or saliva, for the purpose of determining the alcoholic and/or drug content of the blood provided that such test is administered by or at the direction of a police officer with respect to a chemical test of breath, urine or saliva or, with respect to a chemical test of blood, at the direction of a police officer:

(1) having reasonable grounds to believe such person to have been operating in violation of any subdivision of section eleven hundred ninety-two of this article and within two hours after such person has been placed under arrest for any such violation; or having reasonable grounds to believe such person to have been operating in violation of section eleven hundred ninety-two-a of this article and within two hours after the stop of such person for any such violation,

(2) within two hours after a breath test, as provided in paragraph (b) of subdivision one of this section, indicates that alcohol has been consumed by such person and in accordance

with the rules and regulations established by the police force of which the officer is a member;

(3) for the purposes of this paragraph, "reasonable grounds" to believe that a person has been operating a motor vehicle after having consumed alcohol in violation of section eleven hundred ninety-two-a of this article shall be determined by viewing the totality of circumstances surrounding the incident which, when taken together, indicate that the operator was driving in violation of such subdivision. Such circumstances may include any visible or behavioral indication of alcohol consumption by the operator, the existence of an open container containing or having contained an alcoholic beverage in or around the vehicle driven by the operator, or any other evidence surrounding the circumstances of the incident which indicates that the operator has been operating a motor vehicle after having consumed alcohol at the time of the incident; or

(4) notwithstanding any other provision of law to the contrary, no person under the age of twenty-one shall be arrested for an alleged violation of section eleven hundred ninety-two-a of this article. However, a person under the age of twenty-one for whom a chemical test is authorized pursuant to this paragraph may be temporarily detained by the police solely for the purpose of requesting or administering such chemical test whenever arrest without a warrant for a petty offense would be authorized in accordance with the provisions of section 140.10 of the criminal procedure law or paragraph (a) of subdivision one of this section.

(b) Report of refusal.

(1) If: (A) such person having been placed under arrest; or (B) after a breath test indicates the presence of alcohol in the person's system; or (C) with regard to a person under the age of twenty-one, there are reasonable grounds to believe that such person has been operating a motor vehicle after having consumed alcohol in violation of section eleven hundred ninety-two-a of this article; and having thereafter been requested to submit to such chemical test and having been informed that the person's license or permit to drive and any non-resident operating privilege shall be immediately suspended and subsequently revoked, or, for operators under the age of twenty-one for whom there are reasonable grounds to believe that such operator has been operating a motor vehicle after having consumed alcohol in violation of section eleven hundred ninety-two-a of this article, shall be revoked for refusal to submit to such chemical test or any portion thereof, whether or not the person is found guilty of the charge for which such person is arrested or detained, refuses to submit to such chemical test or any portion thereof, unless a court order has been granted pursuant to subdivision three of this section, the test shall not be given and a written report of such refusal shall be immediately made by the police officer before whom such refusal was made. Such report may be verified by having the report sworn to, or by affixing to such report a form notice that false statements made therein are punishable as a class A misdemeanor pursuant to section 210.45 of the penal law and such form notice together with the subscription of the deponent shall constitute a verification of the report.

(2) The report of the police officer shall set forth reasonable grounds to believe such arrested person or such detained person under the age of twenty-one had been driving in violation of any subdivision of section eleven hundred ninety-two or eleven hundred ninety-two-a of this article, that said person had refused to submit to such chemical test, and that no chemical test was administered pursuant to the requirements of subdivision three of this section. The report shall be presented to the court upon arraignment of an arrested person, provided, however, in the case of a person under the age of twenty-one, for whom a test was authorized pursuant to the provisions of subparagraph two or three of paragraph

(a) of this subdivision, and who has not been placed under arrest for a violation of any of the provisions of section eleven hundred ninety-two of this article, such report shall be forwarded to the commissioner within forty-eight hours in a manner to be prescribed by the commissioner, and all subsequent proceedings with regard to refusal to submit to such chemical test by such person shall be as set forth in subdivision three of section eleven hundred ninety-four-a of this article.

(3) For persons placed under arrest for a violation of any subdivision of section eleven hundred ninety-two of this article, the license or permit to drive and any non-resident operating privilege shall, upon the basis of such written report, be temporarily suspended by the court without notice pending the determination of a hearing as provided in paragraph (c) of this subdivision. Copies of such report must be transmitted by the court to the commissioner and such transmittal may not be waived even with the consent of all the parties. Such report shall be forwarded to the commissioner within forty-eight hours of such arraignment.

(4) The court or the police officer, in the case of a person under the age of twenty-one alleged to be driving after having consumed alcohol, shall provide such person with a scheduled hearing date, a waiver form, and such other information as may be required by the commissioner. If a hearing, as provided for in paragraph (c) of this subdivision, or subdivision three of section eleven hundred ninety-four-a of this article, is waived by such person, the commissioner shall immediately revoke the license, permit, or non-resident operating privilege, as of the date of receipt of such waiver in accordance with the provisions of paragraph (d) of this subdivision.

(c) Hearings. Any person whose license or permit to drive or any non-resident driving privilege has been suspended pursuant to paragraph (b) of this subdivision is entitled to a hearing in accordance with a hearing schedule to be promulgated by the commissioner. If the department fails to provide for such hearing fifteen days after the date of the arraignment of the arrested person, the license, permit to drive or non-resident operating privilege of such person shall be reinstated pending a hearing pursuant to this section. The hearing shall be limited to the following issues: (1) did the police officer have reasonable grounds to believe that such person had been driving in violation of any subdivision of section eleven hundred ninety-two of this article; (2) did the police officer make a lawful arrest of such person; (3) was such person given sufficient warning, in clear or unequivocal language, prior to such refusal that such refusal to submit to such chemical test or any portion thereof, would result in the immediate suspension and subsequent revocation of such person's license or operating privilege whether or not such person is found guilty of the charge for which the arrest was made; and (4) did such person refuse to submit to such chemical test or any portion thereof. If, after such hearing, the hearing officer, acting on behalf of the commissioner, finds on any one of said issues in the negative, the hearing officer shall immediately terminate any suspension arising from such refusal. If, after such hearing, the hearing officer, acting on behalf of the commissioner finds all of the issues in the affirmative, such officer shall immediately revoke the license or permit to drive or any non-resident operating privilege in accordance with the provisions of paragraph (d) of this subdivision. A person who has had a license or permit to drive or non-resident operating privilege suspended or revoked pursuant to this subdivision may appeal the findings of the hearing officer in accordance with the provisions of article three-A of this chapter. Any person may waive the right to a hearing under this section. Failure by such person to appear for the scheduled hearing shall constitute a waiver of such hearing, provided, however, that such person may petition the commissioner for a new hearing which shall be held as soon as practicable.

(d) Sanctions.

(1) Revocations.

a. Any license which has been revoked pursuant to paragraph (c) of this subdivision shall not be restored for at least one year after such revocation, nor thereafter, except in the discretion of the commissioner. However, no such license shall be restored for at least eighteen months after such revocation, nor thereafter except in the discretion of the commissioner, in any case where the person has had a prior revocation resulting from refusal to submit to a chemical test, or has been convicted of or found to be in violation of any subdivision of section eleven hundred ninety-two or section eleven hundred ninety-two-a of this article not arising out of the same incident, within the five years immediately preceding the date of such revocation; provided, however, a prior finding that a person under the age of twenty-one has refused to submit to a chemical test pursuant to subdivision three of section eleven hundred ninety-four-a of this article shall have the same effect as a prior finding of a refusal pursuant to this subdivision solely for the purpose of determining the length of any license suspension or revocation required to be imposed under any provision of this article, provided that the subsequent offense or refusal is committed or occurred prior to the expiration of the retention period for such prior refusal as set forth in paragraph (k) of subdivision one of section two hundred one of this chapter.

b. Any license which has been revoked pursuant to paragraph (c) of this subdivision or pursuant to subdivision three of section eleven hundred ninety-four-a of this article, where the holder was under the age of twenty-one years at the time of such refusal, shall not be restored for at least one year, nor thereafter, except in the discretion of the commissioner. Where such person under the age of twenty-one years has a prior finding, conviction or youthful offender adjudication resulting from a violation of section eleven hundred ninety-two or section eleven hundred ninety-two-a of this article, not arising from the same incident, such license shall not be restored for at least one year or until such person reaches the age of twenty-one years, whichever is the greater period of time, nor thereafter, except in the discretion of the commissioner.

c. Any commercial driver's license which has been revoked pursuant to paragraph (c) of this subdivision based upon a finding of refusal to submit to a chemical test, where such finding occurs within or outside of this state, shall not be restored for at least eighteen months after such revocation, nor thereafter, except in the discretion of the commissioner, but shall not be restored for at least three years after such revocation, nor thereafter, except in the discretion of the commissioner, if the holder of such license was operating a commercial motor vehicle transporting hazardous materials at the time of such refusal. However, such person shall be permanently disqualified from operating a commercial motor vehicle in any case where the holder has a prior finding of refusal to submit to a chemical test pursuant to this section or has a prior conviction of any of the following offenses: any violation of section eleven hundred ninety-two of this article; any violation of subdivision one or two of section six hundred of this chapter; or has a prior conviction of any felony involving the use of a motor vehicle pursuant to paragraph (a) of subdivision one of section five hundred ten-a of this chapter. Provided that the commissioner may waive such permanent revocation after a period of ten years has expired from such revocation provided:

(i) that during such ten year period such person has not been found to have refused a chemical test pursuant to this section and has not been convicted of any one of the following offenses: any violation of section eleven hundred ninety-two of this article; refusal to submit to a chemical test pursuant to this section; any violation of subdivision one or two of section six hundred of this chapter; or has a prior conviction of any felony involving the use of a motor vehicle pursuant to paragraph (a) of subdivision one of section five hundred ten-a of this chapter;

(ii) that such person provides acceptable documentation to the commissioner that such person is not in need of alcohol or drug treatment or has satisfactorily completed a prescribed course of such treatment; and

(iii) after such documentation is accepted, that such person is granted a certificate of relief from disabilities or a certificate of good conduct pursuant to article twenty-three of the correction law by the court in which such person was last penalized.

d. Upon a third finding of refusal and/or conviction of any of the offenses which require a permanent commercial driver's license revocation, such permanent revocation may not be waived by the commissioner under any circumstances.

(2) Civil penalties. Except as otherwise provided, any person whose license, permit to drive, or any non-resident operating privilege is revoked pursuant to the provisions of this section shall also be liable for a civil penalty in the amount of five hundred dollars except that if such revocation is a second or subsequent revocation pursuant to this section issued within a five year period, or such person has been convicted of a violation of any subdivision of section eleven hundred ninety-two of this article within the past five years not arising out of the same incident, the civil penalty shall be in the amount of seven hundred fifty dollars. Any person whose license is revoked pursuant to the provisions of this section based upon a finding of refusal to submit to a chemical test while operating a commercial motor vehicle shall also be liable for a civil penalty of five hundred fifty dollars except that if such person has previously been found to have refused a chemical test pursuant to this section while operating a commercial motor vehicle or has a prior conviction of any of the following offenses while operating a commercial motor vehicle: any violation of section eleven hundred ninety-two of this article; any violation of subdivision two of section six hundred of this chapter; or has a prior conviction of any felony involving the use of a commercial motor vehicle pursuant to paragraph (a) of subdivision one of section five hundred ten-a of this chapter, then the civil penalty shall be seven hundred fifty dollars. No new driver's license or permit shall be issued, or non-resident operating privilege restored to such person unless such penalty has been paid. All penalties collected by the department pursuant to the provisions of this section shall be the property of the state and shall be paid into the general fund of the state treasury.

(3) Effect of rehabilitation program. No period of revocation arising out of this section may be set aside by the commissioner for the reason that such person was a participant in the alcohol and drug rehabilitation program set forth in section eleven hundred ninety-six of this article.

(e) Regulations. The commissioner shall promulgate such rules and regulations as may be necessary to effectuate the provisions of subdivisions one and two of this section.

(f) Evidence. Evidence of a refusal to submit to such chemical test or any portion thereof shall be admissible in any trial, proceeding or hearing based upon a violation of the provisions of section eleven hundred ninety-two of this article but only upon a showing that the person was given sufficient warning, in clear and unequivocal language, of the effect of such refusal and that the person persisted in the refusal.

(g) Results. Upon the request of the person who was tested, the results of such test shall be made available to such person.

3. Compulsory chemical tests.

(a) Court ordered chemical tests. Notwithstanding the provisions of subdivision two of this section, no person who operates a motor vehicle in this state may refuse to submit to a chemical test of one or more of the following: breath, blood, urine or saliva, for the purpose of determining the alcoholic and/or drug content of the blood when a court order for such chemical test has been issued in accordance with the provisions of this subdivision.

(b) When authorized. Upon refusal by any person to submit to a chemical test or any portion thereof as described above, the test shall not be given unless a police officer or a district attorney, as defined in subdivision thirty-two of section 1.20 of the criminal procedure law, requests and obtains a court order to compel a person to submit to a chemical test to determine the alcoholic or drug content of the person's blood upon a finding of reasonable cause to believe that:

(1) such person was the operator of a motor vehicle and in the course of such operation a person other than the operator was killed or suffered serious physical injury as defined in section 10.00 of the penal law; and

(2) a. either such person operated the vehicle in violation of any subdivision of section eleven hundred ninety-two of this article, or

b. a breath test administered by a police officer in accordance with paragraph (b) of subdivision one of this section indicates that alcohol has been consumed by such person; and

(3) such person has been placed under lawful arrest; and

(4) such person has refused to submit to a chemical test or any portion thereof, requested in accordance with the provisions of paragraph (a) of subdivision two of this section or is unable to give consent to such a test.

(c) Reasonable cause; definition. For the purpose of this subdivision "reasonable cause" shall be determined by viewing the totality of circumstances surrounding the incident which, when taken together, indicate that the operator was driving in violation of section eleven hundred ninety-two of this article. Such circumstances may include, but are not limited to: evidence that the operator was operating a motor vehicle in violation of any provision of this article or any other moving violation at the time of the incident; any visible indication of alcohol or drug consumption or impairment by the operator; the existence of an open container containing an alcoholic beverage in or around the vehicle driven by the operator; any other evidence surrounding the circumstances of the incident which indicates that the operator has been operating a motor vehicle while impaired by the consumption of alcohol or drugs or intoxicated at the time of the incident.

(d) Court order; procedure.

(1) An application for a court order to compel submission to a chemical test or any portion thereof, may be made to any supreme court justice, county court judge or district court judge in the judicial district in which the incident occurred, or if the incident occurred in the city

of New York before any supreme court justice or judge of the criminal court of the city of New York. Such application may be communicated by telephone, radio or other means of electronic communication, or in person.

(2) The applicant must provide identification by name and title and must state the purpose of the communication. Upon being advised that an application for a court order to compel submission to a chemical test is being made, the court shall place under oath the applicant and any other person providing information in support of the application as provided in subparagraph three of this paragraph. After being sworn the applicant must state that the person from whom the chemical test was requested was the operator of a motor vehicle and in the course of such operation a person, other than the operator, has been killed or seriously injured and, based upon the totality of circumstances, there is reasonable cause to believe that such person was operating a motor vehicle in violation of any subdivision of section eleven hundred ninety-two of this article and, after being placed under lawful arrest such person refused to submit to a chemical test or any portion thereof, in accordance with the provisions of this section or is unable to give consent to such a test or any portion thereof. The applicant must make specific allegations of fact to support such statement. Any other person properly identified, may present sworn allegations of fact in support of the applicant's statement.

(3) Upon being advised that an oral application for a court order to compel a person to submit to a chemical test is being made, a judge or justice shall place under oath the applicant and any other person providing information in support of the application. Such oath or oaths and all of the remaining communication must be recorded, either by means of a voice recording device or verbatim stenographic or verbatim longhand notes. If a voice recording device is used or a stenographic record made, the judge must have the record transcribed, certify to the accuracy of the transcription and file the original record and transcription with the court within seventy-two hours of the issuance of the court order. If the longhand notes are taken, the judge shall subscribe a copy and file it with the court within twenty-four hours of the issuance of the order.

(4) If the court is satisfied that the requirements for the issuance of a court order pursuant to the provisions of paragraph (b) of this subdivision have been met, it may grant the application and issue an order requiring the accused to submit to a chemical test to determine the alcoholic and/or drug content of his blood and ordering the withdrawal of a blood sample in accordance with the provisions of paragraph (a) of subdivision four of this section. When a judge or justice determines to issue an order to compel submission to a chemical test based on an oral application, the applicant therefor shall prepare the order in accordance with the instructions of the judge or justice. In all cases the order shall include the name of the issuing judge or justice, the name of the applicant, and the date and time it was issued. It must be signed by the judge or justice if issued in person, or by the applicant if issued orally.

(5) Any false statement by an applicant or any other person in support of an application for a court order shall subject such person to the offenses for perjury set forth in article two hundred ten of the penal law.

(6) The chief administrator of the courts shall establish a schedule to provide that a sufficient number of judges or justices will be available in each judicial district to hear oral applications for court orders as permitted by this section.

(e) Administration of compulsory chemical test. An order issued pursuant to the provisions of this subdivision shall require that a chemical test to determine the alcoholic and/or drug content of the operator's blood must be administered. The provisions of paragraphs (a), (b) and (c) of subdivision four of this section shall be applicable to any chemical test administered pursuant to this section.

4. Testing procedures.

(a) Persons authorized to withdraw blood; immunity; testimony.

(1) At the request of a police officer, the following persons may withdraw blood for the purpose of determining the alcoholic or drug content therein: (i) a physician, a registered professional nurse, a registered physician assistant, a certified nurse practitioner, or an advanced emergency medical technician as certified by the department of health; or (ii) under the supervision and at the direction of a physician, registered physician assistant or certified nurse practitioner acting within his or her lawful scope of practice, or upon the express consent of the person eighteen years of age or older from whom such blood is to be withdrawn: a clinical laboratory technician or clinical laboratory technologist licensed pursuant to article one hundred sixty-five of the education law; a phlebotomist; or a medical laboratory technician or medical technologist employed by a clinical laboratory approved under title five of article five of the public health law. This limitation shall not apply to the taking of a urine, saliva or breath specimen.

(2) No person entitled to withdraw blood pursuant to subparagraph one of this paragraph or hospital employing such person, and no other employer of such person shall be sued or held liable for any act done or omitted in the course of withdrawing blood at the request of a police officer pursuant to this section.

(3) Any person who may have a cause of action arising from the withdrawal of blood as aforesaid, for which no personal liability exists under subparagraph two of this paragraph, may maintain such action against the state if any person entitled to withdraw blood pursuant to paragraph (a) hereof acted at the request of a police officer employed by the state, or against the appropriate political subdivision of the state if such person acted at the request of a police officer employed by a political subdivision of the state. No action shall be maintained pursuant to this subparagraph unless notice of claim is duly filed or served in compliance with law.

(4) Notwithstanding the foregoing provisions of this paragraph an action may be maintained by the state or a political subdivision thereof against a person entitled to withdraw blood pursuant to subparagraph one of this paragraph or hospital employing such person for whose act or omission the state or the political subdivision has been held liable under this paragraph to recover damages, not exceeding the amount awarded to the claimant, that may have been sustained by the state or the political subdivision by reason of gross negligence or bad faith on the part of such person.

(5) The testimony of any person other than a physician, entitled to withdraw blood pursuant to subparagraph one of this paragraph, in respect to any such withdrawal of blood made by such person may be received in evidence with the same weight, force and effect as if such withdrawal of blood were made by a physician.

(6) The provisions of subparagraphs two, three and four of this paragraph shall also apply with regard to any person employed by a hospital as security personnel for any act done or omitted in the course of withdrawing blood at the request of a police officer pursuant to a court order in accordance with subdivision three of this section.

(b) Right to additional test. The person tested shall be permitted to choose a physician to administer a chemical test in addition to the one administered at the direction of the police officer.

(c) Rules and regulations. The department of health shall issue and file rules and regulations approving satisfactory techniques or methods of conducting chemical analyses of a person's blood, urine, breath or saliva and to ascertain the qualifications and competence of individuals to conduct and supervise chemical analyses of a person's blood, urine, breath or saliva. If the analyses were made by an individual possessing a permit issued by the department of health, this shall be presumptive evidence that the examination was properly given. The provisions of this paragraph do not prohibit the introduction as evidence of an analysis made by an individual other than a person possessing a permit issued by the department of health.

HISTORY: Add, L 1988, ch 47, § 18, eff Nov 1, 1988. Former § 1194, add, L 1959, ch 775, with substance transferred from former § 71-a; amd, L 1960, ch 184, § 2, L 1960, ch 896, § 1, L 1966, ch 615, § 1, L 1966, ch 963, § 3, L 1968, ch 36, § 2, L 1968, ch 85, § 1, L 1969, ch 669, § 1, L 1969, ch 1027, § 2, L 1970, ch 275, § 4, L 1971, ch 445, §§ 1, 2, L 1971, ch 928 § 1, L 1972, ch 449, § 1, L 1973, ch 351, § 1, L 1974, ch 248, § 1, L 1976, ch 298, §§ 1, 2, L 1978, ch 252, § 1, L 1980, ch 807, § 2, L 1980, ch 808, § 1, L 1981, ch 347, §§ 2, 3, L 1983, ch 481, § 1, L 1983, ch 802, § 2, L 1985, ch 592, §§ 1-4, L 1985, ch 755, §§ 2-4, L 1986, ch 623, § 1, L 1986, ch 876, §§ 1, 2; repealed, L 1988, ch 47, § 18, eff Nov 1, 1988. Sub 1, par (d), subpar (1), cl c, add, L 1990, ch 173, § 71, eff April 1, 1992. Sub 1, par (d), subpar (1), cl d, add, L 1990, ch 173, § 71, eff April 1, 1992. Sub 2, par (a), amd, L 1988, ch 406, § 7, eff Nov 1, 1988. Sub 2, par (b), amd, L 1988, ch 406, § 8, eff Nov 1, 1988. Sub 2, par (d), subpar (1), cl c, add, L 1990, ch 173, § 71, eff April 1, 1992. Sub 2, par (d), subpar (1), cl d, add, L 1990, ch 173, § 71, eff April 1, 1992. Sub 2, par (d), subpar (2), amd, L 1990, ch 173, § 72, eff April 1, 1992, L 1990, ch 299, eff July 1, 1990. Sub 4, par (a), subpar (1), amd, L 1988, ch 406, § 9, eff Nov 1, 1988. Sub 2, par (a), amd, L 1996, ch 196, § 14, eff Nov 1, 1996. Sub 2, par (a), subpar (1), amd, L 1996, ch 196, § 14, eff Nov 1, 1996. Sub 2, par (a), subpar (2), amd, L 1996, ch 196, § 14, eff Nov 1, 1996. Sub 2, par (a), subpar (3), add, L 1996, ch 196, § 14, eff Nov 1, 1996. Sub 2, par (a), subpar (4), add, L 1996, ch 196, § 14, eff Nov 1, 1996. Sub 2, par (b), amd, L 1996, ch 196, § 14, eff Nov 1, 1996. Sub 2, par (b), subpar (1), formerly part of sub 2, par (b), so designated and amd, L 1996, ch 196, § 14, eff Nov 1, 1996. Sub 2, par (b), subpar (2), formerly part of sub 2, par (b), so designated and amd, L 1996, ch 196, § 14, eff Nov 1, 1996. Sub 2, par (b), subpar (3), formerly part of sub 2, (b), so designated and amd, L 1996, ch 196, § 14, eff Nov 1, 1996. Sub 2, par (b), subpar (4), formerly part of sub 2, (b), so designated and amd, L 1996, ch 196, § 14, eff Nov 1, 1996. Sub 2, par (d), subpar (1), amd, L 2006, ch 732, § 23, eff Nov 1, 2006. Sub 2, par (d), subpar (1), cl a, amd, L 1996, ch 196, § 16, eff Nov 1, 1996, L 2006, ch 732, § 23, eff Nov 1, 2006. Sub 2, par (d), subpar (1), cl b, amd, L 1996, ch 196, § 15, eff Nov 1, 1996. Sub 2, par (d), subpar (1), cl c, amd, L 2005, ch 60, § 18 (Part E), eff Sept 30, 2005, L 2006, ch 59, § 4 (Part J), eff April 11, 2006. Sub 2, par (d), subpar (1), cl c, opening par, amd, L 2005, ch 60, § 18 (Part E), eff Sept 30, 2005, L 2006, ch 59, § 4 (Part J), eff April 11, 2006, L 2006, ch 732, § 23, eff Nov 1, 2006. Sub 2, par (d), subpar (1), cl c, subcl (i), amd, L 2005, ch 60, § 18 (Part E), eff Sept 30, 2005. Sub 2, par (d), subpar (2), amd, L 1994, ch 169, § 122, eff June 9, 1994, deemed eff April 1, 1994, L 1996, ch 449, § 1, eff Nov 1, 1996, L 2006, ch 732, § 24, eff Nov 1, 2006. Sub. 2(d)(1)(c)(iii), amd, L. 2010, ch 56 (Part LL), § 37, eff. June 22, 2010. Sub. 4(a)(1), amd, L. 2010, Ch. 169, § 1, eff. July 13, 2010.

§ 1194-a. Driving after having consumed alcohol; under twenty-one; procedure

1. Chemical test report and hearing.

(a) Whenever a chemical test of the breath, blood, urine or saliva of an operator who is under the age of twenty-one indicates that such person has operated a motor vehicle in violation of section eleven hundred ninety-two-a of this article, and such person is not charged with violating any subdivision of section eleven hundred ninety-two arising out of the same incident, the police officer who administered the test shall forward a report of the results of such test to the department within twenty-four hours of the time when such results are available in a manner prescribed by the commissioner, and the operator shall be given a hearing notice as provided in subdivision one-a of this section, to appear before a hearing officer in the county where the chemical test was administered, or in an adjoining county under such circumstances as prescribed by the commissioner, on a date to be established in accordance with a schedule promulgated by the commissioner. Such hearing shall occur within thirty days of, but not less than forty-eight hours from, the date that the chemical test was administered, provided, however, where the commissioner determines, based upon the availability of hearing officers and the anticipated volume of hearings at a particular location, that the scheduling of such hearing within thirty days would impair the timely scheduling or conducting of other hearings pursuant to this chapter, such hearing shall be scheduled at the next hearing date for such particular location. When providing the operator with such hearing notice, the police officer shall also give to the operator, and shall, prior to the commencement of the hearing, provide to the department, copies of the following reports, documents and materials: any written report or document, or portion thereof, concerning a physical examination, a scientific test or experiment, including the most recent record of inspection, or calibration or repair of machines or instruments utilized to perform such scientific tests or experiments and the certification certificate, if any, held by the operator of the machine or instrument, which tests or examinations were made by or at the request or direction of a public servant engaged in law enforcement activity. The report of the police officer shall be verified by having the report sworn to, or by affixing to such report a form notice that false statements made therein are punishable as a class A misdemeanor pursuant to section 210.45 of the penal law and such form notice together with the subscription of the deponent shall constitute verification of the report.

(b) Every person under the age of twenty-one who is alleged to have operated a motor vehicle after having consumed alcohol as set forth in section eleven hundred ninety-two-a of this article, and who is not charged with violating any subdivision of section eleven hundred ninety-two of this article arising out of the same incident, is entitled to a hearing before a hearing officer in accordance with the provisions of this section. Unless otherwise provided by law, the license or permit to drive or any non-resident operating privilege of such person shall not be suspended or revoked prior to the scheduled date for such hearing.

(i) The hearing shall be limited to the following issues: (1) did such person operate the motor vehicle; (2) was a valid request to submit to a chemical test made by the police officer in accordance with the provisions of section eleven hundred ninety-four of this article; (3) was such person less than twenty-one years of age at the time of operation of the motor vehicle; (4) was the chemical test properly administered in accordance with the provisions of section eleven hundred ninety-four of this article; (5) did the test find that such person had driven after having consumed alcohol as defined in section eleven hundred ninety-two-a of this article; and (6) did the police officer make a lawful stop of such person. The burden of proof shall be on the police officer to prove each of these issues by clear and convincing evidence.

(ii) Every person who is entitled to a hearing pursuant to this subdivision has the right to be present at the hearing; the right to be represented by attorney, or in the hearing officer's discretion, by any other person the operator chooses; the right to receive and review discovery materials as provided in this subdivision; the right not to testify; the right to present evidence and witnesses in his own behalf, the right to cross examine adverse witnesses, and the right to appeal from an adverse determination in accordance with article three-A of this chapter. Any person representing the operator must conform to the standards of conduct required of attorneys appearing before state courts, and failure to conform to these standards will be grounds for declining to permit his continued appearance in the hearing.

(iii) Hearings conducted pursuant to this subdivision shall be in accordance with this subdivision and with the provisions applicable to the adjudication of traffic infractions pursuant to the following provisions of part 124 of title fifteen of the codes, rules and regulations of the state of New York: paragraph (b) of section 124.1 regarding the opening statement; paragraph (b) of section 124.2 regarding the right to representation and to remain silent and paragraphs (a) through (e) of section 124.4 regarding the conduct of the hearing, procedure and recusal; provided, however, that nothing contained in this subparagraph shall be deemed to preclude a hearing officer from changing the order of a hearing conducted pursuant to this subdivision as justice may require and for good cause shown.

(iv) The rules governing receipt of evidence in a court of law shall not apply in a hearing conducted pursuant to this subdivision except as follows:

(1) on the merits of the charge, and whether or not a party objects, the hearing officer shall exclude from consideration the following: a privileged communication; evidence which, for constitutional reasons, would not be admissible in a court of law; evidence of prior misconduct, incompetency or illness, except where such evidence would be admissible in a court of law; evidence which is irrelevant or immaterial;

(2) no negative inference shall be drawn from the operator's exercising the right not to testify.

(v) If, after such hearing, the hearing officer, acting on behalf of the commissioner, finds all of the issues set forth in this subdivision in the affirmative, the hearing officer shall suspend or revoke the license or permit to drive or non-resident operating privilege of such person in accordance with the time periods set forth in subdivision two of section eleven hundred ninety-three of this article. If, after such hearing, the hearing officer, acting on behalf of the commissioner, finds any of said issues in the negative, the hearing officer must find that the operator did not drive after having consumed alcohol.

(vi) A person who has had a license or permit to drive or non-resident operating privilege suspended or revoked pursuant to the provisions of this section may appeal the finding of the hearing officer in accordance with the provisions of article three-A of this chapter.

(c) Unless an adjournment of the hearing date has been granted, upon the operator's failure to appear for a scheduled hearing, the commissioner shall suspend the license or permit to drive or non-resident operating privilege until the operator petitions the commissioner and a rescheduled hearing is conducted, provided, however, the commissioner shall restore such person's license or permit to drive or non-resident operating privilege if such rescheduled hearing is adjourned at the request of a person other than the operator. Requests for adjournments shall be made and determined in accordance with regulations promulgated by the commissioner. If such a request by the operator for an adjournment is granted, the commissioner shall notify the operator of the rescheduled hearing, which shall be scheduled for the next hearing date. If a second or subsequent request by the operator for an adjournment is granted, the operator's license or permit to drive or non-resident operating privilege may be suspended pending the hearing at the time such adjournment is granted; provided, however, that the records of the department or the evidence already admitted furnishes reasonable grounds to believe such suspension is necessary to prevent continuing violations or a substantial traffic safety hazard; and provided further, that such hearing shall be scheduled for the next hearing date.

If a police officer does not appear for a hearing, the hearing officer shall have the authority to dismiss the charge. Any person may waive the right to a hearing under this subdivision, in a form and manner prescribed by the commissioner, and may enter an admission of guilt, in person or by mail, to the charge of operating a motor vehicle in violation of section eleven hundred ninety-two-a of this article. Such admission of guilt shall have the same force and effect as a finding of guilt entered following a hearing conducted pursuant to this subdivision.

1-a. Hearing notice. The hearing notice issued to an operator pursuant to subdivision one of this section shall be in a form as prescribed by the commissioner. In addition to containing information concerning the time, date and location of the hearing, and such other information as the commissioner deems appropriate, such hearing notice shall also contain the following information: the date, time and place of the offense charged; the procedures for requesting an adjournment of a scheduled hearing as provided in this section, the operator's right to a hearing conducted pursuant to this section and the right to waive such hearing and plead guilty, either in person or by mail, to the offense charged.

2. Civil penalty. Unless otherwise provided, any person whose license, permit to drive, or any non-resident operating privilege is suspended or revoked pursuant to the provisions of this section shall also be liable for a civil penalty in the amount of one hundred twenty-five dollars, which shall be distributed in accordance with the provisions of subdivision nine of section eighteen hundred three of this chapter.

3. Refusal report and hearing.

(a) Any person under the age of twenty-one who is suspected of operating a motor vehicle after having consumed alcohol in violation of section eleven hundred ninety-two-a of this chapter, and who is not charged with violating any subdivision of section eleven hundred ninety-two of this article arising out of the same incident, and who has been requested to submit to a chemical test pursuant to paragraph (a) of subdivision two of section eleven hundred ninety-four of this article and after having been informed that his license or permit to drive and any non-resident operating privilege shall be revoked for refusal to submit to such chemical test or any portion thereof, whether or not there is a finding of driving after having consumed alcohol, and such person refuses to submit to such chemical test or any portion thereof, shall be entitled to a hearing in accordance with a schedule promulgated by the commissioner, and such hearing shall occur within thirty days of, but not less than forty-eight hours from, the date of such refusal, provided, however, where the commissioner determines, based upon the availability of hearing officers and the anticipated volume of hearings at a particular location, that the scheduling of such hearing within thirty days would impair the timely scheduling or conducting of other hearings pursuant to this chapter, such hearing shall be scheduled at the next hearing date for such particular location.

(b) Unless an adjournment of the hearing date has been granted, upon the operator's failure to appear for a scheduled hearing, the commissioner shall suspend the license or permit to drive or non-resident operating privilege until the operator petitions the commissioner and a rescheduled hearing is conducted, provided, however, the commissioner shall restore such person's license or permit to drive or non-resident operating privilege if such rescheduled hearing is adjourned at the request of a person other than the operator. Requests for adjournments shall be made and determined in accordance with regulations promulgated by the commissioner. If such a request by the operator for an adjournment is granted, the commissioner shall notify the operator of the rescheduled hearing, which shall be scheduled for the next hearing date. If a second or subsequent request by the operator for an adjournment is granted, the operator's license or permit to drive or non-resident operating privilege may be suspended pending the hearing at the time such adjournment is granted; provided, however, that the records of the department or the evidence already admitted furnishes reasonable grounds to believe such suspension is necessary to prevent continuing violations or a substantial traffic safety hazard; and provided further, that such hearing shall be scheduled for the next hearing date.

If a police officer does not appear for a hearing, the hearing officer shall have the authority to dismiss the charge. Any person may waive the right to a hearing under this subdivision.

(c) The hearing on the refusal to submit to a chemical test pursuant to this subdivision shall be limited to the following issues: (1) was a valid request to submit to a chemical test made by the police officer in accordance with the provisions of section eleven hundred ninety-four of this article; (2) was such person given sufficient warning, in clear or unequivocal language, prior to such refusal that such refusal to submit to such chemical test or any portion thereof, would result in the revocation of such person's license or permit to drive or nonresident operating privilege, whether or not such person is found to have operated a motor vehicle after having consumed alcohol; (3) did such person refuse to submit to such chemical test or any portion thereof; (4) did such person operate the motor vehicle; (5) was such person less than twenty-one years of age at the time of operation of the motor vehicle; (6) did the police officer make a lawful stop of such person. If, after such hearing, the hearing officer, acting on behalf of the commissioner, finds on any one said issue in the negative, the hearing officer shall not revoke the operator's license or permit to drive or non-resident operating privilege and shall immediately terminate any outstanding suspension of the operator's license, permit to drive or non-resident operating privilege arising from such refusal. If, after such hearing, the hearing officer, acting on behalf of the commissioner, finds all of the issues in the affirmative, such hearing officer shall immediately revoke the license or permit to drive or any non-resident operating privilege in accordance with the provisions of paragraph (d) of subdivision two of section eleven hundred ninety-four of this article. A person who has had a license or permit to drive or non-resident operating privilege suspended or revoked pursuant to the provisions of this section may appeal the findings of the hearing officer in accordance with the provisions of article three-A of this chapter.

HISTORY: Add, L 1996, ch 196, § 17, eff Nov 1, 1996. Former § 1194-a, add, L 1983, ch 481, § 2; amd, L 1985, ch 592, § 5, L 1985, ch 755, § 5, L 1986, ch 623, §§ 2–4, L 1986, ch 876, § 3; repealed, L 1988, ch 47, § 18, eff Nov 1, 1988.

§ 1195. Chemical test evidence

1. Admissibility. Upon the trial of any action or proceeding arising out of actions alleged to have been committed by any person arrested for a violation of any subdivision of section eleven hundred ninety-two of this article, the court shall admit evidence of the amount of alcohol or drugs in the defendant's blood as shown by a test administered pursuant to the provisions of section eleven hundred ninety-four of this article.

2. Probative value. The following effect shall be given to evidence of blood-alcohol content, as determined by such tests, of a person arrested for violation of section eleven hundred ninety-two of this article:

(a) Evidence that there was .05 of one per centum or less by weight of alcohol in such person's blood shall be prima facie evidence that the ability of such person to operate a motor vehicle was not impaired by the consumption of alcohol, and that such person was not in an intoxicated condition;

(b) Evidence that there was more than .05 of one per centum but less than .07 of one per centum by weight of alcohol in such person's blood shall be prima facie evidence that such person was not in an intoxicated condition, but such evidence shall be relevant evidence, but shall not be given prima facie effect, in determining whether the ability of such person to operate a motor vehicle was impaired by the consumption of alcohol; and

(c) Evidence that there was .07 of one per centum or more but less than .08 of one per centum by weight of alcohol in such person's blood shall be prima facie evidence that such person was not in an intoxicated condition, but such evidence shall be given prima facie effect in determining whether the ability of such person to operate a motor vehicle was impaired by the consumption of alcohol.

3. Suppression. A defendant who has been compelled to submit to a chemical test pursuant to the provisions of subdivision three of section eleven hundred ninety-four of this article may move for the suppression of such evidence in accordance with article seven hundred ten of the criminal procedure law on the grounds that the order was obtained and the test administered in violation of the provisions of such subdivision or any other applicable law.

> **HISTORY:** Add, L 1988, ch 47, § 18, eff Nov 1, 1988. Former § 1195, add, L 1970, ch 275, § 5; amd, L 1971, ch 495, §§ 2–4, L 1972, ch 450, § 2, L 1974, ch 248, §§ 2, 3, L 1983, ch 481, § 3, L 1985, ch 755, § 6; repealed, L 1988, ch 47, § 18, eff Nov 1, 1988. Sub 2, par (b), amd, L 2003, ch 153, § 1, eff July 1, 2003. Sub 2, par (c), amd, L 2002, ch 3, § 4, eff July 1, 2003, L 2003, ch 153, § 1, eff July 1, 2003.

§ 1196. Alcohol and drug rehabilitation program

1. Program establishment. There is hereby established an alcohol and drug rehabilitation program within the department of motor vehicles. The commissioner shall establish, by regulation, the instructional and rehabilitative aspects of the program. Such program shall consist of at least fifteen hours and include, but need not be limited to, classroom instruction in areas deemed suitable by the commissioner. No person shall be required to attend or participate in such program or any aspect thereof for a period exceeding eight months except upon the recommendation of the department of mental hygiene or appropriate health officials administering the program on behalf of a municipality.

2. Curriculum. The form, content and method of presentation of the various aspects of such program shall be established by the commissioner. In the development of the form, curriculum and content of such program, the commissioner may consult with the commissioner of mental health, the director of the division of alcoholism and alcohol abuse, the director of the division of substance abuse services and any other state department or agency and request and receive assistance from them. The commissioner is also authorized to develop more than one curriculum and course content for such program in order to meet the varying rehabilitative needs of the participants.

3. Where available. A course in such program shall be available in at least every county in the state, except where the commissioner determines that there is not a sufficient number of alcohol or drug-related traffic offenses in a county to mandate the establishment of said course, and that provisions be made for the residents of said county to attend a course in another county where a course exists.

4. Eligibility. Participation in the program shall be limited to those persons convicted of alcohol or drug-related traffic offenses or persons who have been adjudicated youthful offenders for alcohol or drug-related traffic offenses, or persons found to have been operating a motor vehicle after having consumed alcohol in violation of section eleven hundred ninety-two-a of this article, who choose to participate and who satisfy the criteria and meet the requirements for participation as established by this section and the regulations promulgated thereunder; provided, however, in the exercise of discretion, the judge imposing sentence may prohibit the defendant from enrolling

in such program. The commissioner or deputy may exercise discretion, to reject any person from participation referred to such program and nothing herein contained shall be construed as creating a right to be included in any course or program established under this section. In addition, no person shall be permitted to take part in such program if, during the five years immediately preceding commission of an alcohol or drug-related traffic offense or a finding of a violation of section eleven hundred ninety-two-a of this article, such person has participated in a program established pursuant to this article or been convicted of a violation of any subdivision of section eleven hundred ninety-two of this article other than a violation committed prior to November first, nineteen hundred eighty-eight, for which such person did not participate in such program. In the exercise of discretion, the commissioner or a deputy shall have the right to expel any participant from the program who fails to satisfy the requirements for participation in such program or who fails to satisfactorily participate in or attend any aspect of such program. Notwithstanding any contrary provisions of this chapter, satisfactory participation in and completion of a course in such program shall result in the termination of any sentence of imprisonment that may have been imposed by reason of a conviction therefor; provided, however, that nothing contained in this section shall delay the commencement of such sentence.

5. Effect of completion. Except as provided in subparagraph nine of paragraph (b) of subdivision two of section eleven hundred ninety-three or in subparagraph three of paragraph (d) of subdivision two of section eleven hundred ninety-four of this article, upon successful completion of a course in such program as certified by its administrator, a participant may apply to the commissioner on a form provided for that purpose, for the termination of the suspension or revocation order issued as a result of the participant's conviction which caused the participation in such course. In the exercise of discretion, upon receipt of such application, and upon payment of any civil penalties for which the applicant may be liable, the commissioner is authorized to terminate such order or orders and return the participant's license or reinstate the privilege of operating a motor vehicle in this state. However, the commissioner shall not issue any new license nor restore any license where said issuance of restoral is prohibited by subdivision two of section eleven hundred ninety-three of this article.

6. Fees. The commissioner shall establish a schedule of fees to be paid by or on behalf of each participant in the program, and may, from time to time, modify same. Such fees shall defray the ongoing expenses of the program. Provided, however, that pursuant to an agreement with the department a municipality, department thereof, or other agency may conduct a course in such program with all or part of the expense of such course and program being borne by such municipality, department or agency. In no event shall such fee be refundable, either for reasons of the participant's withdrawal or expulsion from such program or otherwise.

7. Conditional license.

(a) Notwithstanding any inconsistent provision of this chapter, participants in the program, except those penalized under paragraph (d) of subdivision one of section eleven hundred ninety-three of this article for any violation of subdivision two, three, or four of section eleven hundred ninety-two of this article, may, in the commissioner's discretion, be issued a conditional driver's license, or if the holder of a license issued by another jurisdiction valid for operation in this state, a conditional privilege of operating a motor vehicle in this state. Such a conditional license or privilege shall be valid only for use, by the holder thereof, (1) enroute to and from the holder's place of employment, (2) if the holder's employment requires the operation of a motor vehicle then during the hours thereof, (3) enroute to and from a class or an activity which is an authorized part of the alcohol and drug rehabilitation program and at which his attendance is required, (4) enroute to and from a class or course at an accredited school, college or university or at a state approved institution of vocational or technical training, (5) to or from court ordered probation activities, (6) to and from a motor vehicle office for the transaction of business relating to such license or program, (7) for a three hour consecutive daytime period, chosen by the administrators of the program, on a day during which the participant is not engaged in usual employment or vocation, (8) enroute to and from a medical examination or treatment as part of a necessary medical treatment for such participant or member of the participant's household, as evidenced by a written statement to that effect from a licensed medical practitioner, and (9) enroute to and from a place, including a school, at which a child or children of the holder are cared for on a regular basis and which is necessary for the holder to maintain such holder's employment or enrollment at an accredited school, college or university or at a state approved institution of vocational or technical training. Such license or privilege shall remain in effect during the term of the suspension or revocation of the participant's license or privilege unless earlier revoked by the commissioner.

(b) The conditional license or privilege described in paragraph (a) of this subdivision shall be in a form prescribed by the commissioner, and shall have indicated thereon the conditions imposed by such paragraph.

(c) Upon receipt of a conditional license issued pursuant to this section, any order issued by a judge, justice or magistrate pursuant to paragraph (c) of subdivision two of section eleven hundred ninety-three of this article shall be surrendered to the department.

(d) The commissioner shall require applicants for a conditional license to pay a fee of seventy-five dollars for processing costs. Such fees assessed under this subdivision shall be paid to the commissioner for deposit to the general fund and shall be in addition to any fees established by the commissioner pursuant to subdivision six of this section to defray the costs of the alcohol and drug rehabilitation program.

(e) The conditional license or privileges described in this subdivision may be revoked by the commissioner, for sufficient cause including, but not limited to, failure to register in the program, failure to attend or satisfactorily participate in the sessions, conviction of any traffic infraction other than one involving parking, stopping or standing or conviction of any alcohol or drug-related traffic offense, misdemeanor or felony. In addition, the commissioner shall have the right, after a hearing, to revoke the conditional license or privilege upon receiving notification or evidence that the offender is not attempting in good faith to accept rehabilitation. In the event of such revocation, the fee described in subdivision six of this section shall not be refunded.

(f) It shall be a traffic infraction for the holder of a conditional license or privilege to operate a motor vehicle upon a public highway for any use other than those authorized pursuant to paragraph (a) of this subdivision. When a person is convicted of this offense, the sentence of the court must be a fine of not less than two hundred dollars nor more than five hundred dollars or a term of imprisonment of not more than fifteen days or both such fine and imprisonment. Additionally, the conditional license or privileges described in this subdivision shall be revoked by the commissioner upon receiving notification from the court that the holder thereof has been convicted of this offense.

(g) Notwithstanding anything to the contrary contained in a certificate of relief from disabilities or a certificate of good conduct issued pursuant to article twenty-three of the correction law, any conditional license or privilege issued to a person convicted of a violation of any subdivision of section eleven hundred ninety-two of this article shall not be valid for the operation of any commercial motor vehicle. In addition, no such conditional license or privilege shall be valid for the operation of a taxicab as defined in this chapter.

(h) Notwithstanding any inconsistent provision of this chapter, the conditional license described in this subdivision may, pursuant to regulations established by the commissioner, be issued to a person whose license has been suspended pending prosecution pursuant to subparagraph seven of paragraph (e) of subdivision two of section eleven hundred ninety-three of this article.

> **HISTORY:** Add, L 1988, ch 47, § 18, eff Nov 1, 1988. Former § 1196, add, L 1970, ch 275, § 6; amd, L 1980, ch 806, § 1; repealed, L 1988, ch 47, § 18, eff Nov 1, 1988. Sub 4, amd, L 1988, ch 406, § 10, eff Nov 1, 1988. Sub 7, par (a), amd, L 1988, ch 406, § 11, L 1990, ch 539, § 3, eff Aug 17, 1990. Sub 7, par (d), amd, L 1989, ch 61, § 25, L 1990, ch 190, § 300, eff July 1, 1990. Sub 7, par (f), add, L 1989, ch 420, § 2, eff Oct 14, 1989. Sub 7, par (g), add, L 1990, ch 173, § 73, eff Feb 19, 1991. Sub 4, amd, L 1996, ch 196, § 18, eff Nov 1, 1996. Sub 5, amd, L 1996, ch 196, § 19, eff Nov 1, 1996. Sub 7, par (d), amd, L 1996, ch 309, § 97, eff Aug 31, 1996. Sub 7, par (g), amd, L 1993, ch 571, § 2, eff Jan 24, 1994, L 2005, ch 60, § 19 (Part E), eff Sept 30, 2005. Sub 7, par (h), add, L 1994, ch 312, § 5, eff Nov 1, 1994. Sub. 7(g), amd, L. 2010, ch 56 (Part LL), § 38, eff. June 22, 2010.

§ 1197. Special traffic options program for driving while intoxicated

"The program", as used in this section, shall mean the special traffic options program for driving while intoxicated, a program established pursuant to this section, and approved by the commissioner of motor vehicles.

1. Program establishment.

(a) Where a county establishes a special traffic options program for driving while intoxicated, pursuant to this section, it shall receive fines and forfeitures collected by any court, judge, magistrate or other officer within that county, including, where appropriate, a hearing officer acting on behalf of the commissioner[,]*: (1) imposed for violations of subparagraphs (ii) and (iii) of paragraph (a) of subdivision two or subparagraph (i) of paragraph (a) of subdivision three of section five hundred eleven of this chapter; (2) imposed in accordance with the provisions of section eleven hundred ninety-three and civil penalties imposed pursuant to subdivision two of section eleven hundred ninety-four-a of this article, including, where appropriate, a hearing officer acting on behalf of the commissioner, from violations of sections eleven hundred ninety-two, eleven hundred ninety-two-a and findings made under section eleven hundred ninety-four-a of this article; and (3) imposed upon a conviction for: aggravated vehicular assault, pursuant to section 120.04-a of the penal law; vehicular assault in the first degree, pursuant to section 120.04 of the penal law; vehicular assault in the second degree, pursuant to section 120.03 of the penal law; aggravated vehicular homicide, pursuant to section 125.14 of the penal law; vehicular manslaughter in the first degree, pursuant to section 125.13 of the penal law; and vehicular manslaughter in the second degree, pursuant to section 125.12 of the penal law, as provided in section eighteen hundred three of this chapter. Upon receipt of these moneys, the county shall deposit them in a separate account entitled "special traffic options program for driving while intoxicated" and they shall be under the exclusive care, custody and control of the chief fiscal officer of each county participating in the program.

(b) Expenditures from such account shall only be made pursuant to the approval of a county program by the commissioner of motor vehicles. The chief fiscal officer of each participating county shall, on a quarterly basis, forward to the commissioner a written

---

* Brackets have been inserted around this punctuation by the Publisher as it is superfluous.

certificate of moneys expended from such account.

2. Program organization.

(a) Where a program is established by a county, it shall be organized by a coordinator for the special traffic options program for driving while intoxicated, who shall be designated by the chief executive officer of the county, if there be one, otherwise the chairman of the governing board of the county, or in the city of New York, a person designated by the mayor thereof. Where a coordinator is designated, the coordinator shall receive such salary and expenses as the board of legislators or other governing body of such county may fix and properly account for such expenses and shall serve at the pleasure of such appointing body or officer.

(b) In counties having a county traffic safety board, the chief executive officer, if there be one, otherwise the chairman of the governing board of the county or the mayor of the city of New York, may designate the chairman of the board or a member thereof as coordinator of the program.

3. Purposes.

(a) The program shall provide a plan for coordination of county, town, city and village efforts to reduce alcohol-related traffic injuries and fatalities.

(b) The program shall, where approved by the county board or other governing body, provide funding for such activities as the board or other body may approve, for the above-described purposes.

4. Duties of the coordinator; reports.

(a) It shall be the duty of the coordinator to:

(1) Render annually or at the request of the county legislature or other governing body of the county, a verified account of all moneys received and expended by the coordinator or under the coordinator's direction and an account of other pertinent matters.

(2) Submit annually or upon request of the chief fiscal officer of each county participating in the program, in such manner as may be required by law, an estimate of the funds required to carry out the purposes of this section.

(3) Make an annual report to the commissioner, which shall be due on or before the first day of April of each year following the implementation of said program, and shall include the following:

a. the progress, problems and other matters related to the administration of said program; and

b. an assessment of the effectiveness of the program within the geographic area of the county participating therein and any and all recommendations for expanding and improving said program.

(b) Any annual report shall also contain the following, in a form prescribed by the commissioner:

(1) Number of arrests for violations of section eleven hundred ninety-two of this article and subdivision two of section five hundred eleven of this chapter;

(2) Number and description of dispositions resulting therefrom;

(3) Number of suspensions issued in the county for alleged refusals to submit to chemical tests;

(4) Total fine moneys returned to the participating county in connection with the program;

(5) Contemplated programs;

(6) Distribution of moneys in connection with program adminstration [administration]*;

(7) Any other information required by the commissioner.

5. Functions of the coordinator. In addition to the duties of the coordinator as provided in subdivision four of this section, the coordinator shall perform the following functions:

(a) Formulate a special traffic options program for driving while intoxicated and coordinate efforts of interested parties and agencies engaged in alcohol traffic safety, law enforcement, adjudication, rehabilitation and preventive education.

(b) Receive proposals from county, town, city or village agencies or non-governmental groups for activities related to alcohol traffic safety and to submit them to the county board of legislators or other such governing body, together with a recommendation for funding of the activity if deemed appropriate.

(c) Cooperate with and assist local officials within the county in the formulation and execution of alcohol traffic safety programs including enforcement, adjudication, rehabilitation and education.

(d) Study alcohol traffic safety problems with the county and recommend to the appropriate legislative bodies, departments or commissions, such changes in rules, orders, regulations and existing law as the coordinator may deem advisable.

(e) Promote alcohol and drug-related traffic safety education for drivers.

(f) Obtain and assemble data on alcohol-related accident arrests, convictions and accidents and to analyze, study, and consolidate such data for educational, research and informational purposes.

6. County purpose and charge. The provisions of this section and expenditures made hereunder shall be deemed a county purpose and charge.

7. Program approval. The program, including a proposed operational budget, shall be submitted by each county coordinator to the commissioner for approval. The commissioner shall consider the following before approving said program:

(a) The interrelationship of such program with existing drunk driving related programs in areas including, but not limited to, law enforcement, prosecution, adjudication and education.

(b) Avoidance of duplication of existing programs funded or operated by either the state or any municipality including, but not limited to, the alcohol and drug rehabilitation program, established under section eleven hundred ninety-six of this article.

---

* The bracketed word has been inserted by the Publisher.

(c) All other factors which the commissioner shall deem necessary.

8. Duties of the commissioner.

(a) The commissioner shall compile the reports submitted by the county coordinators and shall issue a comprehensive report on such programs to the governor and to the legislature.

(b) The commissioner shall monitor all programs to ensure satisfactory implementation in conjunction with the established program application goals.

9. Program cessation. When a participating county wishes to cease its program, the coordinator shall notify the commissioner in writing of the date of termination and all money remaining in the fund established by that county pursuant to subdivision one of this section on such date shall be transferred to the general fund of the state treasury. All fines and forfeitures collected pursuant to the provisions of this section on and after the termination date shall be disposed of in accordance with subdivision one of section eighteen hundred three of this chapter.

10. Program audit. The comptroller is authorized to conduct audits of any program established pursuant to this section for the purposes of determining compliance with the provisions of this section and with generally accepted accounting principles.

HISTORY: Add, L 1988, ch 47, § 18, eff Nov 1, 1988. Sub 1, par (a), amd, L 1988, ch 406, § 12, eff Nov 1, 1988. Sub 5, par (e), amd, L 1988, ch 748, § 2, eff Nov 1, 1989. Sub 7, opening par, amd, L 1991, ch 707, § 1, eff Aug 2, 1991. Sub 10, add, L 1991, ch 707, § 2, eff Aug 2, 1991. Sub 1, amd, L 1993, ch 607, § 10, eff Nov 1, 1993. Sub 1, par (a), amd, L 1993, ch 607, § 10, eff Nov 1, 1993, L 1996, ch 196, § 20, eff Nov 1, 1996, L 1996, ch 688, § 1, eff Nov 1, 1996, L 2007, ch 345, § 8, eff Nov 1, 2007. Sub 7, opening par, amd, L 1998, ch 469, § 4, eff July 22, 1998.

§ 1198. [Expires and repealed Sept 1, 2015] Installation and operation of ignition interlock devices

1. Applicability. The provisions of this section shall apply throughout the state to each person required or otherwise ordered by a court as a condition of probation or conditional discharge to install and operate an ignition interlock device in any vehicle which he or she owns or operates.

2. Requirements.

(a) In addition to any other penalties prescribed by law, the court shall require that any person who has been convicted of a violation of subdivision two, two-a or three of section eleven hundred ninety-two of this article, or any crime defined by this chapter or the penal law of which an alcohol-related violation of any provision of section eleven hundred ninety-two of this article is an essential element, to install and maintain, as a condition of probation or conditional discharge, a functioning ignition interlock device in accordance with the provisions of this section and, as applicable, in accordance with the provisions of subdivisions one and one-a of section eleven hundred ninety-three of this article; provided, however, the court may not authorize the operation of a motor vehicle by any person whose license or privilege to operate a motor vehicle has been revoked except as provided herein. For any such individual subject to a sentence of probation, installation and maintenance of such ignition interlock device shall be a condition of probation.

(b) Nothing contained in this section shall prohibit a court, upon application by a probation department, from modifying the conditions of probation of any person convicted of any violation set forth in paragraph (a) of this subdivision prior to the effective date of this section, to require the installation and maintenance of a functioning ignition interlock device, and such person shall thereafter be subject to the provisions of this section.

(c) Nothing contained in this section shall authorize a court to sentence any person to a period of probation or conditional discharge for the purpose of subjecting such person to the provisions of this section, unless such person would have otherwise been so eligible for a sentence of probation or conditional discharge.

3. Conditions.

(a) Notwithstanding any other provision of law, the commissioner may grant a post-revocation conditional license, as set forth in paragraph (b) of this subdivision, to a person who has been convicted of a violation of subdivision two, two-a or three of section eleven hundred ninety-two of this article and who has been sentenced to a period of probation or conditional discharge, provided the person has satisfied the minimum period of license revocation established by law and the commissioner has been notified that such person may operate only a motor vehicle equipped with a functioning ignition interlock device. No such request shall be made nor shall such a license be granted, however, if such person has been found by a court to have committed a violation of section five hundred eleven of this chapter during the license revocation period or deemed by a court to have violated any condition of probation or conditional discharge set forth by the court relating to the operation of a motor vehicle or the consumption of alcohol. In exercising discretion relating to the issuance of a post-revocation conditional license pursuant to this subdivision, the commissioner shall not deny such issuance based solely upon the number of convictions for violations of any subdivision of section eleven hundred ninety-two of this article committed by such person within the ten years prior to application for such license. Upon the termination of the period of probation or conditional discharge set by the court, the person may apply to the commissioner for restoration of a license or privilege to operate a motor vehicle in accordance with this chapter.

(b) Notwithstanding any inconsistent provision of this chapter, a post-revocation conditional license granted pursuant to paragraph (a) of this subdivision shall be valid only for use by the holder thereof, (1) enroute to and from the holder's place of employment, (2) if the holder's employment requires the operation of a motor vehicle then during the hours thereof, (3) enroute to and from a class or course at an accredited school, college or university or at a state approved institution of vocational or technical training, (4) to and from court ordered probation activities, (5) to and from a motor vehicle office for the transaction of business relating to such license, (6) for a three hour consecutive daytime period, chosen by the department, on a day during which the participant is not engaged in usual employment or vocation, (7) enroute to and from a medical examination or treatment as part of a necessary medical treatment for such participant or member of the participant's household, as evidenced by a written statement to that effect from a licensed medical practitioner, (8) enroute to and from a class or an activity which is an authorized part of the alcohol and drug rehabilitation program and at which participant's attendance is required, and (9) enroute to and from a place, including a school, at which a child or children of the participant are cared for on a regular basis and which is necessary for the participant to maintain such participant's employment or enrollment at an accredited school, college or university or at a state approved institution of vocational or technical training.

(c) The post-revocation conditional license described in this subdivision may be revoked by the commissioner for sufficient cause including but not limited to, failure to comply with the terms of the condition of probation or conditional discharge set forth by the court, conviction of any traffic offense other than one involving parking, stopping or standing or conviction of any alcohol or drug related offense, misdemeanor or felony or failure to install or maintain a court ordered ignition interlock device.

(d) Nothing contained herein shall prohibit the court from requiring, as a condition of probation or conditional discharge, the installation of a functioning ignition interlock device in any vehicle owned or operated by a person sentenced for a violation of subdivision two, two-a, or three of section eleven hundred ninety-two of this chapter, or any crime defined by this chapter or the penal law of which an alcohol-related violation of any provision of section eleven hundred ninety-two of this chapter is an essential element, if the court in its discretion, determines that such a condition is necessary to ensure the public safety. Imposition of an ignition interlock condition shall in no way limit the effect of any period of license suspension or revocation set forth by the commissioner or the court.

(e) Nothing contained herein shall prevent the court from applying any other conditions of probation or conditional discharge allowed by law, including treatment for alcohol or drug abuse, restitution and community service.

(f) The commissioner shall note on the operator's record of any person restricted pursuant to this section that, in addition to any other restrictions, conditions or limitations, such person may operate only a motor vehicle equipped with an ignition interlock device.

4. Proof of compliance and recording of condition.

(a) Following imposition by the court of the use of an ignition interlock device as a condition of probation or conditional discharge it shall require the person to provide proof of compliance with this section to the court and the probation department or other monitor where such person is under probation or conditional discharge supervision. If the person fails to provide for such proof of installation, absent a finding by the court of good cause for that failure which is entered in the record, the court may revoke, modify, or terminate the person's sentence of probation or conditional discharge as provided under law. Good cause may include a finding that the person is not the owner of a motor vehicle if such person asserts under oath that such person is not the owner of any motor vehicle and that he or she will not operate any motor vehicle during the period of interlock restriction except as may be otherwise authorized pursuant to law. "Owner" shall have the same meaning as provided in section one hundred twenty-eight of this chapter.

(b) When a court imposes the condition specified in subdivision one of this section, the court shall notify the commissioner in such manner as the commissioner may prescribe, and the commissioner shall note such condition on the operating record of the person subject to such conditions.

5. Cost, installation and maintenance.

(a) The cost of installing and maintaining the ignition interlock device shall be borne by the person subject to such condition unless the court determines such person is financially unable to afford such cost whereupon such cost may be imposed pursuant to a payment plan or waived. In the event of such waiver, the cost of the device shall be borne in accordance with regulations issued under paragraph (g) of subdivision one of section eleven hundred ninety-three of this article or pursuant to such other agreement as may be entered into for provision of the device. Such cost shall be considered a fine for the purposes of subdivision five of section 420.10 of the criminal procedure law. Such cost shall not replace, but shall instead be in addition to, any fines, surcharges, or other costs imposed pursuant to this chapter or other applicable laws.

(b) The installation and service provider of the device shall be responsible for the installation, calibration, and maintenance of such device.

6. Certification.

(a) The commissioner of the department of health shall approve ignition interlock devices for installation pursuant to subdivision one of this section and shall publish a list of approved devices.

(b) After consultation with manufacturers of ignition interlock devices and the national highway traffic safety administration, the commissioner of the department of health, in consultation with the commissioner and the office of probation and correctional alternatives, shall promulgate regulations regarding standards for, and use of, ignition interlock devices. Such standards shall include provisions for setting a minimum and maximum calibration range and shall include, but not be limited to, requirements that the devices:

(1) have features that make circumventing difficult and that do not interfere with the normal or safe operation of the vehicle;

(2) work accurately and reliably in an unsupervised environment;

(3) resist tampering and give evidence if tampering is attempted;

(4) minimize inconvenience to a sober user;

(5) require a proper, deep, lung breath sample or other accurate measure of blood alcohol content equivalence;

(6) operate reliably over the range of automobile environments;

(7) correlate well with permissible levels of alcohol consumption as may be established by the sentencing court or by any provision of law; and

(8) are manufactured by a party covered by product liability insurance.

(c) The commissioner of the department of health may, in his discretion, adopt in whole or relevant part, the guidelines, rules, regulations, studies, or independent laboratory tests performed on and relied upon for the certification or approval of ignition interlock devices by other states, their agencies or commissions.

7. Use of other vehicles.

(a) Any requirement of this article or the penal law that a person operate a vehicle only if it is equipped with an ignition interlock device shall apply to every motor vehicle operated by that person including, but not limited to, vehicles that are leased, rented or loaned.

(b) No person shall knowingly rent, lease, or lend a motor vehicle to a person known to have had his or her driving privilege restricted to vehicles equipped with an ignition interlock device unless the vehicle is so equipped. Any person whose driving privilege is so restricted shall notify any other person who rents, leases, or loans a motor vehicle to him or her of such driving restriction.

(c) A violation of paragraph (a) or (b) of this subdivision shall be a misdemeanor.

8. Employer vehicle. Notwithstanding the provisions of subdivision one and paragraph (d) of subdivision nine of this section, if a person is required to operate a motor vehicle owned by said person's employer in the course and scope of his or her employment, the person may operate that vehicle without installation of an approved ignition interlock device only in the course and scope of such employment and only if the employer has been notified that the person's driving privilege has been restricted under the provisions of this article or the penal law and the person whose privilege has been so restricted has provided the court and probation department with written documentation indicating the employer has knowledge of the restriction imposed and has granted

permission for the person to operate the employer's vehicle without the device only for business purposes. The person shall notify the court and the probation department of his or her intention to so operate the employer's vehicle. A motor vehicle owned by a business entity which business entity is all or partly owned or controlled by a person otherwise subject to the provisions of this article or the penal law is not a motor vehicle owned by the employer for purposes of the exemption provided in this subdivision. The provisions of this subdivision shall apply only to the operation of such vehicle in the scope of such employment.

9. Circumvention of interlock device.

(a) No person whose driving privilege is restricted pursuant to this article or the penal law shall request, solicit or allow any other person to blow into an ignition interlock device, or to start a motor vehicle equipped with the device, for the purpose of providing the person so restricted with an operable motor vehicle.

(b) No person shall blow into an ignition interlock device or start a motor vehicle equipped with the device for the purpose of providing an operable motor vehicle to a person whose driving privilege is so restricted.

(c) No person shall tamper with or circumvent an otherwise operable ignition interlock device.

(d) No person subject to a court ordered ignition interlock device shall operate a motor vehicle without such device.

(e) In addition to any other provisions of law, any person convicted of a violation of paragraph (a), (b), (c), or (d) of this subdivision shall be guilty of a Class A misdemeanor.

10. Warning label. The department of health shall design a warning label which the manufacturer shall affix to each ignition interlock device upon installation in the state. The label shall contain a warning that any person tampering, circumventing, or otherwise misusing the device is guilty of a misdemeanor and may be subject to civil liability.

HISTORY: Add, L 1988, ch 713, § 3, eff April 1, 1989, expires and repealed Sept 1, 2015; amd, L 1992, ch 276, § 1, eff June 30, 1992, L 1994, ch 413, §§ 1, 2, eff July 20, 1994, L 1995, ch 168, §§ 1–3, eff July 19, 1995, L 1997, ch 150, § 1, eff June 30, 1997, L 1998, ch 359, § 1, eff Aug 13, 1998, L 1999, ch 135, § 1, eff June 29, 1999, L 2001, ch 86, § 1, eff June 29, 2001, L 2006, ch 732, §§ 12, 13, eff Nov 1, 2006, L 2007, ch 669, § 3, eff Oct 27, 2007, L 2009, ch 496, § 5, eff Aug 15, 2010, L 2009, ch 496, § 5-a, eff Dec 18, 2009, L 2010, ch 56, § 41 (Part A), eff June 22, 2010, L 2013, ch 169, § 3, eff Nov 1, 2013.

§ 1198-a. Special procedures and disposition involving alcohol and substance abuse assessment and treatment

1. Definitions. For purposes of this section, the following terms shall have the following meanings:

(a) "Alcohol and substance abuse professional" shall mean persons credentialed by the office of alcoholism and substance abuse services to provide alcohol and substance abuse services pursuant to the mental hygiene law and persons licensed by the state education department in an appropriate health field, including licensed clinical social worker, licensed master social worker, licensed mental health counselor, nurse practitioner, physician, physician's assistant, psychiatrist, psychologist, and registered nurse.

(b) "Licensed agency" shall mean an agency licensed by the office of alcoholism and substance abuse services to provide alcohol and substance abuse services pursuant to the mental hygiene law.

2. Procedure.

(a) Mandatory screening; when authorized. Upon the arraignment of, or at the discretion of the court, prior to the sentencing of any person who (i) at arraignment is charged with or prior to sentencing convicted of a first violation of operating a motor vehicle in violation of subdivision one, two or three or paragraph (b) of subdivision two-a of section eleven hundred ninety-two of this article while such person has less than.15 of one per centum by weight of alcohol in the person's blood as shown by chemical analysis of such person's blood, breath, urine or saliva made pursuant to the provisions of section eleven hundred ninety-four of this article, or in violation of subdivision four of such section eleven hundred ninety-two, or (ii) has refused to submit to a chemical test pursuant to section eleven hundred ninety-four of this article, the court shall order such person to submit to screening for alcohol or substance abuse and dependency using a standardized written screening instrument developed by the office of alcoholism and substance abuse services, to be administered by an alcohol or substance abuse professional.

(b) Mandatory assessment; when authorized. The court shall order a defendant to undergo a formal alcohol or substance abuse and dependency assessment by an alcohol or substance abuse professional or a licensed agency: (i) when the screening required by paragraph (a) of this subdivision indicates that a defendant is abusing or dependent upon alcohol or drugs; (ii) following the arraignment of any person charged with or, at the discretion of the court, prior to the sentencing of any person convicted of a violation of subdivision one, two, three, four or four-a of section eleven hundred ninety-two of this article after having been convicted of a violation of any subdivision of section eleven hundred ninety-two of this article or of vehicular assault in the second or first degree, as defined, respectively, in sections 120.03 and 120.04 of the penal law or of aggravated vehicular assault, as defined in section 120.04-a of the penal law or of vehicular manslaughter in the second or first degree, as defined, respectively, in sections 125.12 and 125.13 of the penal law or of aggravated vehicular homicide, as defined in section 125.14 of such law within the preceding five years or after having been convicted of a violation of any subdivision of such section or of vehicular assault in the second or first degree, as defined, respectively, in sections 120.03 and 120.04 of the penal law or of aggravated vehicular assault, as defined in section 120.04-a of the penal law or of vehicular manslaughter in the second or first degree, as defined, respectively, in sections 125.12 and 125.13 of the penal law or of aggravated vehicular homicide, as defined in section 125.14 of such law, two or more times within the preceding ten years; or (iii) following the arraignment of any person charged with or, at the discretion of the court, prior to the sentencing of any person convicted of operating a motor vehicle in violation of subdivision two or three or paragraph (b) of subdivision two-a of section eleven hundred ninety-two of this article while such person has.15 of one per centum or more by weight of alcohol in the person's blood as shown by a chemical analysis of such person's blood, breath, urine or saliva made pursuant to the provisions of section eleven hundred ninety-four of this article or in violation of paragraph (a)of subdivision two-a of section eleven hundred ninety-two of this article.

(c) Mandatory assessment; procedure. The assessment ordered by a court pursuant to this section shall be performed by an alcohol or substance abuse professional or a licensed agency which shall forward the results, in writing, to the court and to the defendant or his or her counsel within thirty days of the date of such order.

3. Authorized disposition. When a sentence of probation or a conditional discharge is imposed

upon a person who has been required to undergo an alcohol or substance abuse and dependency assessment pursuant to subdivision two of this section and where such assessment indicates that such person is in need of treatment for alcohol or substance abuse or dependency, the court shall require, as a condition of such sentence, that such person participate in and successfully complete such treatment. Such treatment shall be provided by an alcohol or substance abuse professional or a licensed agency.

4. Any case wherein a court has accepted a plea pursuant to the provisions of subparagraph (ii) of paragraph (a) of subdivision ten of section eleven hundred ninety-two of this article and such plea includes as a condition thereof that the defendant attend and complete the alcohol and drug rehabilitation program established pursuant to section eleven hundred ninety-six of this article, including any assessment and treatment required thereby, shall be deemed to be in compliance with the provisions of this section.

5. The chief administrator of the office of court administration shall make available to all courts in this state with jurisdiction in criminal cases a list of alcohol and substance abuse professionals and licensed agencies as provided by the office of alcoholism and substance abuse services pursuant to subdivision (g) of section 19.07 of the mental hygiene law.

6. Confidentiality of records.

(a) The records and content of all screenings, assessments and treatment conducted pursuant to this section, including the identity, diagnosis and prognosis of each individual who is the subject of such records, and including any statements or admissions of such individual made during the course of such screenings, assessments and treatment, shall be confidential, shall not be disclosed except as authorized by this subdivision, and shall not be entered or received as evidence at any civil, criminal or administrative trial, hearing or proceeding. No person, other than a defendant to whom such records are disclosed, may redisclose such records.

(b) Consistent with Section 290 dd-2 of Title 42 of the United States Code, as such law may, from time to time, be amended, such records and content may only be disclosed as follows:

(i) to a court for the sole purpose of requiring a defendant charged with or convicted of a violation of subdivision one, two, two-a, three, four or four-a of section eleven hundred ninety-two of this article to undergo alcohol or substance abuse or dependency assessment or treatment;

(ii) to the defendant or his or her authorized representative; and

(iii) to medical personnel to the extent necessary to mee a bona fide medical emergency.

7. Effect of completion of treatment. Except as provided in subparagraph nine of paragraph (b) of subdivision two of section eleven hundred ninety-three or in subparagraph three of paragraph (d) of subdivision two of section eleven hundred ninety-four of this article, upon successful completion of treatment ordered pursuant to this section as certified by the alcohol or substance abuse professional or licensed agency which provided such treatment, the defendant may apply to the commissioner on a form provided for that purpose, for the termination of the suspension or revocation order issued as a result of the defendant's conviction. In the exercise of discretion, upon receipt of such application, and upon payment of any civil penalties for which the defendant may be liable, the commissioner is authorized to terminate such order or orders and return the defendant's license or reinstate the privilege of operating a motor vehicle in this state. However, the commissioner shall not issue any new license nor restore any license where said issuance or restoration is prohibited by subdivision two of section eleven hundred ninety-three of this article.

HISTORY: Add, L 2006, ch 732, § 19, eff Nov 1, 2006. Sub 1, par (a), amd, L 2007, ch 669, § 4, eff Oct 27, 2007. Sub 2, amd, L 2009, ch 496, § 6, eff Dec 18, 2009. Sub 2, par (a), amd, L 2009, ch 496, § 6, eff Dec 18, 2009. Sub 2, par (b), amd, L 2007, ch 345, § 9, eff Nov 1, 2007. Sub 3, amd, L 2006, ch 746, § 2, eff Dec 15, 2006. Sub 5, amd, L 2007, ch 669, § 4, eff Oct 27, 2007.

§ 1199. Driver responsibility assessment

1. In addition to any fines, fees, penalties and surcharges authorized by law, any person convicted of a violation of any subdivision of section eleven hundred ninety-two of this article, or any person found to have refused a chemical test in accordance with section eleven hundred ninety-four of this article not arising out of the same incident as a conviction for a violation of any of the provisions of section eleven hundred ninety-two of this article, shall become liable to the department for payment of a driver responsibility assessment as provided in this section.

2. The amount of the driver responsibility assessment under this section shall be two hundred fifty dollars per year for a three-year period.

3. Upon receipt of evidence that a person is liable for the driver responsibility assessment required by this section, the commissioner shall notify such person by first class mail to the address of such person on file with the department or at the current address provided by the United States postal service of the amount of such assessment, the time and manner of making required payments, and that failure to make payment shall result in the suspension of his or her driver's license or privilege of obtaining a driver's license.

4. If a person shall fail to pay any driver responsibility assessment as provided in this section, the commissioner shall suspend such person's driver's license or privilege of obtaining a license. Such suspension shall remain in effect until any and all outstanding driver responsibility assessments have been paid in full.

5. The provisions of this section shall also be applicable to any person convicted of any violation of section forty-nine-a of the navigation law, any person convicted of a violation of section 25.24 of the parks, recreation and historic preservation law, or any person found to have refused a chemical test in accordance with the applicable provisions of either the navigation law or the parks, recreation and historic preservation law not arising out of the same incident as such conviction.

HISTORY: Add, L 2004, ch 59, § 1 (Part E), eff Nov 18, 2004.

TITLE IX   Penalties and Disposition of Fines and Forfeitures

ARTICLE 45

PENALTIES AND DISPOSITION OF FINES AND FORFEITURES

HISTORY: Add, L 1959, ch 775, eff Oct 1, 1960, with substance transferred from former Title V.

HISTORY: Add, L 1959, ch 775, eff Oct 1, 1960, with substance transferred from former Art 32.

§ 1800. Penalties for traffic infractions

(a) It is a traffic infraction for any person to violate any of the provisions of this chapter or of any local law, ordinance, order, rule or regulation adopted pursuant to this chapter, unless such violation is by this chapter or other law of this state declared to be a misdemeanor or a felony.

(b) 1. Every person convicted of a traffic infraction for a violation of any of the provisions of this chapter or of any ordinance, order, rule or regulation adopted pursuant to section sixteen hundred thirty or sixteen hundred thirty-one of this chapter for which another penalty is not provided shall for a first conviction thereof be punished by a fine of not more than one hundred fifty dollars or by imprisonment for not more than fifteen days or by both such fine and imprisonment; for a conviction of a second violation, both of which were committed within a period of eighteen months, such person shall be punished by a fine of not more than three hundred dollars or by imprisonment for not more than forty-five days or by both such fine and imprisonment; upon a conviction of a third or subsequent violation, all of which were committed within a period of eighteen months, such person shall be punished by a fine of not more than four hundred fifty dollars or by imprisonment for not more than ninety days or by both such fine and imprisonment, except that a person convicted of a traffic infraction for a violation of paragraph one of subdivision (d) of section one thousand one hundred eleven of this chapter outside of a city having a population of one million or more shall, for a first conviction thereof, be punished by a fine of not less than seventy-five dollars nor more than two hundred twenty-five dollars or by imprisonment for not more than fifteen days or by both such fine and imprisonment; for a conviction of a second violation, both of which were committed within a period of eighteen months, such person shall be punished by a fine of not less than one hundred fifty dollars nor more than three hundred seventy-five dollars or by imprisonment for not more than forty-five days or by both such fine and imprisonment; upon a conviction of a third or subsequent violation, all of which were committed within a period of eighteen months, such person shall be punished by a fine of not less than three hundred seventy-five dollars nor more than six hundred seventy-five dollars or by imprisonment for not more than ninety days or by both such fine and imprisonment except that a person convicted for a violation of paragraph one of subdivision (d) of section one thousand one hundred eleven of this chapter shall, for a first conviction thereof, be punished by a fine of not less than one hundred fifty dollars nor more than four hundred fifty dollars or by imprisonment for not more than fifteen days or by both such fine and imprisonment; for a conviction of a second violation, both of which were committed within a period of eighteen months, such person shall be punished by a fine of not less than three hundred dollars nor more than seven hundred fifty dollars or by imprisonment for not more than forty-five days or by both such fine and imprisonment; upon a conviction of a third or subsequent violation, all of which were committed within a period of eighteen months, such person shall be punished by a fine of not less than seven hundred fifty dollars nor more than one thousand five hundred dollars or by imprisonment for not more than ninety days or by both such fine and imprisonment.

2. Notwithstanding the provisions of paragraph one of this subdivision, a person convicted of a traffic infraction for a violation of paragraph two of subdivision (b) of section twelve hundred two of this chapter shall for a first conviction thereof be punished by a fine of not more than four hundred dollars or by imprisonment for not more than fifteen days or by both such fine and imprisonment. Upon a conviction for a second violation, both of which were committed within a period of eighteen months, such person shall be punished by a fine of not more than six hundred dollars or by imprisonment for not more than forty-five days or by both such fine and imprisonment; upon a conviction of a third or subsequent violation, all of which were committed within a period of eighteen months, such person shall be punished by a fine of not more than seven hundred fifty dollars or by imprisonment for not more than ninety days or by both such fine and imprisonment.

(c) Every person convicted of a traffic infraction for a violation of any local law, ordinance, order, rule, regulation or administrative code provision adopted pursuant to this chapter by any local authority or continued in effect by this chapter, except those adopted pursuant to sections sixteen hundred thirty and sixteen hundred thirty-one, shall be punished in the same manner as has heretofore been prescribed by law unless or until otherwise prescribed by local law, ordinance or state statute.

(d) A conviction of violation of any provision of this chapter shall not be a bar to a prosecution for an assault or for a homicide committed by any person in operating a motor vehicle or motorcycle.

(e) Every person convicted of a violation of the provisions of section eleven hundred forty-four of this chapter shall for a first conviction thereof be punished by a fine of not more than two hundred seventy-five dollars or by imprisonment for not more than fifteen days or by both such fine and imprisonment. For a conviction of a second violation, both of which were committed within a period of eighteen months, such person shall be punished by a fine of not more than four hundred fifty dollars or by imprisonment for not more than forty-five days or by both such fine and imprisonment. For a conviction of a third violation and all subsequent violations, all of which were committed within a period of eighteen months, such person shall be punished by a fine of not more thanseven hundred fifty dollars or by imprisonment for not more than ninety days or by both such fine and imprisonment.

(f) Every person convicted of operating a truck, tractor or tractor-trailer combination having a total gross weight in excess of ten thousand pounds in violation of a local law, ordinance, rule or regulation enacted by the legislative body of any city with a population in excess of one million pursuant to the provisions of paragraph ten of subdivision (a) of section sixteen hundred forty of this chapter shall, for a first offense thereof, be punished by a fine of not less than two hundred dollars nor more than five hundred dollars or by imprisonment for not more than fifteen days or by both such fine and imprisonment. For a conviction of a second violation, both of which were committed within a period of eighteen months, such person shall be punished by a fine of not less than five hundred dollars nor more than one thousand dollars or by imprisonment for not more than forty-five days or by both such fine and imprisonment. For a conviction of a third violation and all subsequent violations, all of which were committed within a period of eighteen months, such person shall be punished by a fine of not less than one thousand dollars nor more than two thousand dollars, or by imprisonment for not more than ninety days or by both such fine and imprisonment.

(g) Notwithstanding the provisions of subdivisions (b) and (c) of this section, a person convicted of a traffic infraction for a violation of any ordinance, order, rule, regulation or local law adopted pursuant to one or more of the following provisions of this chapter: paragraphs two and nine of subdivision (a) of section sixteen hundred twenty-one; subdivision three of section sixteen hundred thirty; or subdivision five of section seventy-one of the transportation law, prohibiting the operation on a highway or parkway of a motor vehicle registered as a commercial vehicle and having a gross vehicle weight rating of less than twenty-six thousand pounds shall, for a first conviction thereof, be punished by a fine of not more than two hundred fifty dollars or by imprisonment of not more than fifteen days or by both such fine and imprisonment; for a conviction of a second violation, both of which were committed within a period of eighteen months, such person shall be punished by a fine of not more than five hundred dollars or by imprisonment for not more than forty-five days or by both such fine and imprisonment; upon a conviction of a third or subsequent violation, all of which were committed within a period of eighteen months, such person shall be punished by a fine of not more than seven hundred fifty dollars or by imprisonment of not more than ninety days or by both such fine and imprisonment. Provided, however, the provisions of this subdivision shall not apply to a commercial motor vehicle as such term is defined in paragraph (a) of subdivision four of section five hundred one-a of this chapter.

(h) Notwithstanding the provisions of subdivisions (b) and (c) of this section, a person convicted of a traffic infraction for a violation of any ordinance, order, rule, regulation or local law adopted pursuant to one or more of the following provisions of this chapter: paragraphs two and nine of subdivision (a) of section sixteen hundred twenty-one; subdivision three of section sixteen hundred thirty; or subdivision five of section seventy-one of the transportation law, prohibiting the operation on a highway or parkway of a commercial motor vehicle as defined in paragraph (a) of subdivision four of section five hundred one-a of this chapter, for a first conviction thereof, be punished by a fine of not more than three hundred fifty dollars or by imprisonment of not more than fifteen days or by both such fine and imprisonment; for a conviction of a second violation, both of which were committed within a period of eighteen months, such person shall be punished by a fine of not more than seven hundred dollars or by imprisonment for not more than forty-five days or by both such fine and imprisonment; upon a conviction of a third or subsequent violation, all of which were committed within a period of eighteen months, such person shall be punished by a fine of not more than one thousand dollars or by imprisonment of not more than ninety days or by both such fine and imprisonment.

HISTORY: Add, L 1959, ch 775, eff Oct 1, 1960, with substance transferred from former §§ 70(12), 1800. Sub (b), amd, L 1981, ch 162, § 2, L 1983, ch 926, § 1, L 1983, ch 927, § 1, L 1989, ch 61, § 48, effective and applicable to violations committed on and after May 19, 1989. Sub (e), add, L 1967, ch 783, § 3; amd, L 1968, ch 186, § 1, L 1969, ch 1075, § 2; repealed, L 1970, ch 337, § 8, eff July 1, 1970. Sub (b), par 1, formerly entire sub (b), amd, L 1995, ch 202, § 1, eff Aug 25, 1995, L 2003, ch 62, § 1 (Part C), eff May 15, 2003; so designated sub (b), par 1 and amd, L 2006, ch 574, § 2, eff Nov 1, 2006. Sub (b), par 2, add, L 2006, ch 574, § 2, eff Nov 1, 2006. Sub (e), add, L 1993, ch 540, § 1, eff Nov 1, 1993; amd, L 2003, ch 62, § 1 (Part C), eff May 15, 2003. Sub (f), add, L 2003, ch 203, § 1, eff Nov 1, 2003. Sub (g), add, L 2008, ch 221, § 1, eff Nov 1, 2008. Sub (h), add, L 2008, ch 221, § 1, eff Nov 1, 2008.

§ 1801. Penalties for misdemeanors

1. Every person convicted of a misdemeanor for a violation of any of the provisions of this chapter for which another penalty is not provided shall for a first conviction thereof be punished by a fine of not more than three hundred dollars or by imprisonment for not more than thirty days or by both such fine and imprisonment; for a conviction of a second violation, both of which were committed within a period of eighteen months, such person shall be punished by a fine of not more than five hundred twenty-five dollars or by imprisonment for not more than ninety days or by both such fine and imprisonment; upon a conviction of a third or subsequent violation, all of which were committed within a period of eighteen months, such person shall be punished by a fine of not more than one thousand one hundred twenty-five dollars or by imprisonment for not more than one hundred eighty days or by both such fine and imprisonment, except that any fine imposed upon conviction of a violation of section twelve hundred twelve of this chapter shall be not less than one hundred dollars.

2. Notwithstanding the provisions of subdivision one of this section, every operator or registered owner of a motor vehicle having a registered maximum gross weight of eighteen thousand pounds or more convicted of a misdemeanor for a violation of the provisions of the closing paragraph of subdivision one of section three hundred seventy-five of this chapter with respect to the knowing disconnection of any set of service brakes on such motor vehicle, shall be punished by a fine of not more than two thousand two hundred fifty dollars.

HISTORY: Add, L 1959, ch 775, with substance transferred from former § 1801; amd, L 1981, ch 162, § 3, L 1986, ch 816, § 2, eff Oct 31, 1986. Sub 1, formerly entire section, so designated sub 1, L 1986, ch 816, § 2; amd, L 1989, ch 61, § 49, effective and applicable to violations committed on and after May 19, 1989. Sub 1, amd, L 2003, ch 62, § 2 (Part C), eff May 15, 2003. Sub 2, add, L 1986, ch 816, § 2, eff Oct 31, 1986. Sub 2, amd, L 2003, ch 62, § 2 (Part C), eff May 15, 2003.

§ 1801-a. [Repealed]

HISTORY: Add, L 1960, ch 934, § 20, with substance transferred from § 1181; repealed, L 1970, ch 679, § 10, eff Jan 1, 1971.

§ 1802. Receipts for fines or bail

Upon receipt of the payment of any fine or penalty collected under a sentence or judgment of conviction of a violation of any of the provisions of this chapter or any local law, ordinance, order, rule or regulation made by local authorities in relation to traffic or the deposit of bail of a person charged with a violation of any such provision, local law, ordinance, order, rule or regulation, the officer or employee receiving such payment or deposit shall issue a receipt therefor when the payment or deposit is made in cash. Whenever any such payment or deposit is made by check, money order or in other property, the officer or employee shall issue a receipt therefor upon request; provided, however, no such receipt shall be issued where a fine or penalty is paid by mail unless the name and address of the payee is known to such officer or employee or enclosed with the payment.

HISTORY: Add, L 1959, ch 775, eff Oct 1, 1960, with substance transferred from former § 1802.

§ 1803. Disposition of fines and forfeitures

1. Except as otherwise provided in subdivision five of section two hundred twenty-seven of this chapter and as provided in section eleven hundred ninety-seven of this chapter, section ninety of the state finance law and sections fourteen-f and one hundred forty of the transportation law, all fines and penalties collected under a sentence or judgment of conviction of a violation of this chapter or of any act relating to the use of highways by motor vehicles or trailers, now in force or hereafter enacted, shall be distributed in the following manner:

a. for a violation which occurs in a city, town or suburban town, any fine or penalty shall be paid to the city, town or suburban town in which the violation occurs, when such violation is of (1) any of the provisions of title seven of this chapter, but including violations of section eleven hundred eighty only when occurring in state parks for which the office of parks, recreation and historic preservation has established maximum speed limits pursuant to section sixteen hundred thirty and the violations could have been charged under either such established maximum speed limits or another section of this chapter, and when involving maximum speed limits established pursuant to section sixteen hundred forty-three, sixteen hundred forty-four, sixteen hundred sixty-two-a, sixteen hundred sixty-three or sixteen hundred seventy, and excluding violations of sections eleven hundred eighty-two, eleven hundred ninety-two and twelve hundred twelve of this chapter, or (2) any ordinance, order, rule or regulation adopted pursuant to article two-E of the transportation law or section sixteen hundred thirty of this chapter by the East Hudson Parkway Authority or by its successor, or the County of Westchester Department of Parks, Recreation and Conservation, or the state office of parks, recreation and historic preservation. For purposes of this paragraph, violations shall be deemed to be violations of any such ordinance, order, rule or regulation when they occur on highways under the jurisdiction of the enumerated entities and the violations could have been charged under either such ordinance, order, rule or regulation or another section of this chapter.

b. for a violation which occurs in a village in which the office of village justice is established, any fine or penalty shall be paid to the village in which the violation occurs, when such violation is of (1) any of the provisions of title seven of this chapter, but including violations of section eleven hundred eighty only when occurring in state parks for which the office of parks, recreation and historic preservation has established maximum speed limits pursuant to section sixteen hundred thirty and the violations could have been charged under either such established maximum speed limits or another section of this chapter, and when involving maximum speed limits established pursuant to section sixteen hundred forty-three, sixteen hundred forty-four or sixteen hundred seventy, and excluding violations of sections eleven hundred eighty-two, eleven hundred ninety-two and twelve hundred twelve of this chapter, or (2) any ordinance, order, rule or regulation adopted pursuant to article two-E of the transportation law or section sixteen hundred thirty of this chapter by the East Hudson Parkway

Authority or by its successor, or the County of Westchester Department of Parks, Recreation and Conservation, or the state office of parks, recreation and historic preservation. For purposes of this paragraph, violations shall be deemed to be violations of any such ordinance, order, rule or regulation when they occur on highways under the jurisdiction of the enumerated entities and the violations could have been charged under either such ordinance, order, rule or regulation, or another section of this chapter. Notwithstanding the foregoing provisions of this paragraph, all fines, penalties and forfeitures for violation of a village ordinance, local law or regulation adopted pursuant to the authorization of paragraph six of subdivision (a) of section sixteen hundred forty of this chapter prohibiting, restricting or limiting the stopping, standing or parking of vehicles shall be paid to such village whether or not the village has established the office of village justice.

c. for compliance with or violations of subdivision nineteen of section three hundred eighty-five of this chapter, notwithstanding any inconsistent provision of law, except as provided in section ninety of the state finance law, the fees and fines collected by the state pursuant to sections two hundred twenty-seven, three hundred eighty-five and eighteen hundred three of this chapter and section ninety-nine-a of the state finance law, shall be made available to the state comptroller for deposit in the general fund except that fines collected within a city not wholly included within one county shall be paid to such city in accordance with the procedures set forth in subdivision four of section two hundred twenty-seven of this chapter for deposit into the general fund of such city.

d. for violations of section eleven hundred eighty which are not included in paragraph a or paragraph b of this subdivision, violations of sections eleven hundred eighty-two, eleven hundred ninety-two, except in those counties adopting a special traffic option program for driving while intoxicated pursuant to section eleven hundred ninety-seven of this chapter, and section twelve hundred twelve of this chapter, and violations of this chapter or of any act relating to the use of highways by motor vehicles or trailers, now in force or hereafter enacted, for which no other distribution is prescribed, all fines, penalties and forfeitures shall be paid to the state.

e. for a violation which occurs within a county which has established a traffic and parking violations agency pursuant to section three hundred seventy of the general municipal law, other than parking, standing or stopping violations except for those set forth in section four hundred two of this chapter, and which violation is disposed of by such agency, any fine or penalty shall be paid to the county in which the violation occurs, when such violation is of any of the provisions of title seven of this chapter, but including violations of section eleven hundred eighty of this chapter only when involving maximum speed limits in state parks established by the office of parks, recreation and historic preservation pursuant to section sixteen hundred thirty of this chapter and when involving maximum speed limits established pursuant to section sixteen hundred forty-three, sixteen hundred forty-four, sixteen hundred sixty-two-a, sixteen hundred sixty-three or sixteen hundred seventy of this chapter, and excluding violations of sections eleven hundred eighty-two, eleven hundred ninety-two and twelve hundred twelve of this chapter.

2. Whenever a defendant is arrested and arraigned before a judicial officer authorized to conduct any proceedings in or in connection with any prosecution triable in any local court of inferior jurisdiction of a city or before a town court, or a village court on a charge in which the state is entitled to all fines and penalties under a sentence or judgment of conviction such city, town or village shall be entitled to receive the fees set forth in section ninety-nine-l of the general

municipal law and such fees shall be a state charge and paid as provided in section ninety-nine-a of the state finance law.

3. All fines, penalties and forfeitures paid to a city, town or village pursuant to the provisions of paragraph a of subdivision one of this section shall be credited to the general fund of such city, town or village, unless a different disposition is prescribed by charter, special law, local law or ordinance.

4. All fines, penalties and forfeitures collected in a city, upon conviction or upon forfeiture of bail by any person charged with a violation of any local law, ordinance, order, rule, regulation, administrative code provision or sanitary or health code provision adopted or continued pursuant to this chapter, shall be paid to the city and credited to its general fund, unless a different disposition is prescribed by charter, special law, local law or ordinance.

5. All fines, penalties and forfeitures for violations of section eleven hundred eighty of this chapter, which relate to maximum speed limits established by a village pursuant to sections sixteen hundred forty-three and sixteen hundred forty-four or by a suburban town pursuant to section sixteen hundred sixty-two-a of this chapter, and all bail forfeited by the non-appearance of defendants charged with such violations shall be paid over to the state comptroller by the court, justice or other officer collecting the same within the first ten days of the month following the collection, except as otherwise provided by subdivision three of section ninety-nine-a of the state finance law. Whenever such fines, penalties and forfeitures, including bail forfeited, in any year commencing July first shall aggregate in excess of five dollars for each inhabitant of the village or suburban town, as the case may be, according to the last preceding federal census, such excess shall be the property of the state and shall be paid into the general fund of the state treasury.

6. The comptroller from the moneys received pursuant to this section shall, within six years from the receipt thereof, refund any fine received pursuant to this section which was imposed by a judgment of conviction that has been reversed and any fine, penalty or forfeiture received by the comptroller, payment of which was not required by this section. In any action by the state to recover fines, penalties, or forfeitures collected more than six years before the commencement of the action, the defendant shall be entitled to set off a claim for refund of any such item paid to the state during the ten years preceding the commencement of the action.

7. [Repealed]

8. All fines, penalties and forfeitures referred to in subdivision one of this section, except fines, penalties and forfeitures paid to the commissioner of taxation and finance as required by section thirty-nine of the judiciary law, and except as otherwise provided in subdivision three of section ninety-nine-a of the state finance law, shall be paid to the state comptroller by the court, judge, magistrate or other officer within the first ten days of the month following collection. Every such payment to the comptroller shall be accompanied by a statement in such form and detail as the comptroller shall prescribe.

9. Where a county establishes a special traffic options program for driving while intoxicated, approved by the commissioner of motor vehicles, pursuant to section eleven hundred ninety-seven of this chapter, all fines, penalties and forfeitures collected from violations of subparagraphs (ii) and (iii) of paragraph (a) of subdivision two or subparagraph (i) of paragraph (a) of subdivision three of section five hundred eleven, all fines, penalties and forfeitures imposed in accordance with section eleven hundred ninety-three of this chapter collected from violations of section eleven hundred ninety-two of this chapter; and any fines or forfeitures collected by any court, judge, magistrate or other officer imposed upon a conviction for: aggravated vehicular assault, pursuant

to section 120.04-a of the penal law; vehicular assault in the first degree, pursuant to section 120.04 of the penal law; vehicular assault in the second degree, pursuant to section 120.03 of the penal law; aggravated vehicular homicide, pursuant to section 125.14 of the penal law; vehicular manslaughter in the first degree, pursuant to section 125.13 of the penal law; and vehicular manslaughter in the second degree, pursuant to section 125.12 of the penal law and civil penalties imposed pursuant to subdivision two of section eleven hundred ninety-four-a of this chapter, shall be paid to such county.

(a) Any such fine, penalty, or forfeiture collected by any court, judge, magistrate or other officer referred to in subdivision one of section thirty-nine of the judiciary law, establishing a unified court budget, shall be paid to that county within the first ten days of the month following collection.

(b) Any such fine, penalty, or forfeiture collected by any other court, judge, magistrate or other officer, including, where appropriate, a hearing officer acting on behalf of the commissioner, shall be paid to the state comptroller within the first ten days of the month following collection. Every such payment to the comptroller shall be accompanied by a statement in such form and detail as the comptroller shall provide. The comptroller shall pay these funds to the county in which the violation occurs.

(c) Upon receipt of any monies referred to in this section, the county shall deposit them in a separate account entitled "special traffic options program for driving while intoxicated".

HISTORY: Add, L 1965, ch 1064, § 2; amd, L 1970, ch 679, § 13, eff Jan 1, 1971. Former § 1803, add, L 1959, ch 775, with substance transferred from former § 1803; amd, L 1960, ch 300, § 63, L 1960, ch 578, § 1, L 1961, ch 421, § 3, L 1961, ch 586, § 1, L 1962, ch 727, §§ 1-3, L 1962, ch 1009, § 7, L 1963, ch 938, § 14; repealed, L 1965, ch 1064, § 1, eff July 1, 1965. Sub 1, amd, L 1969, ch 1074, § 3, eff July 1, 1970, applicable to all violations occurring on and after such date. Sub 1, opening par, amd, L 1981, ch 910, § 5, L 1988, ch 47, § 21, L 1990, ch 173, § 29, L 1991, ch 520, § 2, eff July 19, 1991. Sub 1, par a, amd, L 1988, ch 47, § 22, L 1991, ch 460, § 5, eff Nov 1, 1991. Sub 1, par b, amd, L 1988, ch 47, § 22, L 1991, ch0 460, § 5, eff Nov 1, 1991. Sub 1, par c, add, L 1985, ch 549, § 9, eff Jan 1, 1986. Former sub 1, par c, relettered sub 1, par d, L 1985, ch 549, § 9, eff Jan 1, 1986. Sub 1, par d, formerly sub 1, par c, amd, L 1981, ch 910, § 5; relettered sub 1, par d, L 1985, ch 549, § 9; amd, L 1988, ch 47, § 23, L 1988, ch 406, § 13, eff Nov 1, 1988. Sub 2, amd, L 1971, ch 1097, § 130, eff Sept 1, 1971. Sub 5, amd, L 1987, ch 426, § 1, eff July 27, 1987. Sub 7, amd, L 1968, ch 420, § 350, L 1971, ch 274, § 3, L 1985, ch 549, § 10, eff Jan 1, 1986. Sub 8, add, L 1968, ch 118, § 1; amd, L 1980, ch 292, § 3, eff Jan 1, 1981. Sub 9, add, L 1981, ch 910, § 6; amd, L 1986, ch 537, § 2, eff Nov 1, 1986. Sub 9, opening par, amd, L 1986, ch 537, § 2, L 1988, ch 47, § 24, L 1988, ch 406, § 14, eff Nov 1, 1988. Sub 1, amd, L 1999, ch 385, § 1, eff July 27, 1999. Sub 1, par a, amd, L 1999, ch 385, § 1, eff July 27, 1999. Sub 1, par b, amd, L 1999, ch 385, § 1, eff July 27, 1999. Sub 1, par c, amd, L 1997, ch 432, § 70, eff Aug 20, 1997, deemed eff on and after April 1, 1997. Sub 1, par e, add, L 1993, ch 261, § 15, eff July 13, 1993; amd, L 1999, ch 385, § 1, eff July 27, 1999. Sub 5, amd, L 1998, ch 465, § 6, eff July 22, 1998. Sub 7, repealed, L 1997 ch 432, § 71, eff Aug 20, 1997, deemed eff on and after April 1, 1997. Sub 8, amd, L 1998, ch 465, § 7, eff July 22, 1998. Sub 9, amd, L 1996, ch 196, § 21, eff Nov 1, 1996. Sub 9, opening par, amd, L 1993, ch 607, § 11, eff Nov 1, 1993, L 1996, ch 196, § 21, eff Nov 1, 1996, L 1996, ch 688, § 2, eff Nov 1, 1996, L 2007, ch 345, § 10, eff Nov 1, 2007. Sub 9, par (b), amd, L 1996, ch 196, § 21, eff Nov 1, 1996.

§ 1805. Plea of guilty, how put in

The provisions of section 170.10 of the criminal procedure law and the provisions of section eighteen hundred seven of this article may be waived, to the extent hereinafter indicated, by a defendant charged with a violation of any provision of the tax law or the transportation law regulating traffic, or a traffic infraction, as defined in this chapter, other than a third or subsequent speeding violation committed within a period of eighteen months, provided that he shall submit to the local criminal court having jurisdiction, in person, by duly authorized agent, by first class mail or by registered or certified mail, return receipt requested, an application setting forth (a) the nature of the charge, (b) the information or instructions required by section eighteen hundred seven of this article to be given defendant upon arraignment, (c) that defendant waives arraignment in open court and the aid of counsel, (d) that he pleads guilty to the offense as charged, (e) that defendant elects and requests that the charge be disposed of and the fine or penalty fixed by the court, pursuant to this section, (f) any statement or explanation that the defendant may desire to make concerning the offense charged and (g) that defendant makes all statements with respect to such application under penalty of perjury. This application shall be in such form as the commissioner shall prescribe and a copy thereof shall be handed to the defendant by the officer charging him with such offense. Thereupon the local criminal court may proceed as though the defendant had been convicted upon a plea of guilty in open court, provided, however, that any imposition of fine or penalty hereunder shall be deemed tentative until such fine or penalty shall have been paid and discharged in full, prior to which time such court, in its discretion, may annul any proceedings hereunder, including such tentative imposition of fine or penalty, and deny the application, in which event the charge shall be disposed of pursuant to the applicable provisions of law, as though no proceedings had been had under this section. If upon receipt of the aforesaid application such court shall deny the same, it shall thereupon inform the defendant of this fact, and that he is required to appear before the said court at a stated time and place to answer the charge which shall thereafter be disposed of pursuant to the applicable provisions of law.

> **HISTORY:** Add, L 1971, ch 545, § 34, deriving from Crim C § 335(2); amd, L 1973, ch 477, § 1, L 1981, ch 139, § 1, L 1983, ch 890, § 4, L 1986, ch 411, § 21, L 1990, ch 173, § 30, eff Aug 19, 1990. Amd, L 2001, ch 406, § 7, eff Jan 29, 2002, L 2004, ch 182, § 1, eff July 20, 2004.

§ 1806. Plea of not guilty by a defendant charged with a traffic infraction

In addition to appearing personally to enter a plea of not guilty to a violation of any provision of the tax law or the transportation law regulating traffic, or to a traffic infraction for the violation of any of the provisions of the vehicle and traffic law or of any local law, ordinance, order, rule or regulation relating to the operation of motor vehicles or motorcycles, a defendant may enter a plea of not guilty by mailing to the court of appropriate jurisdiction the ticket making the charge and a signed statement indicating such plea. Such plea must be sent: (a) by registered or certified mail, return receipt requested or by first class mail; and (b) within forty-eight hours after receiving such ticket. Upon receipt of such ticket and statement, the court shall advise the violator, by first class mail, of an appearance at which no testimony shall be taken. If the motorist requests a trial, the court shall set a trial date on a date subsequent to the date of the initial appearance and shall notify the defendant of the date by first class mail but no warrant of arrest for failure to appear can be issued until the violator is notified of a new court appearance date by registered or certified mail, return receipt requested, and fails to appear.

> **HISTORY:** Add, L 1971, ch 545, § 35, deriving from Crim C § 335-b; amd, L 1976, ch 676, § 1, L 1981, ch 139, § 2, L 1983, ch 890, § 5, L 1986, ch 411, § 22, L 1990, ch 173, § 30, eff Aug 19, 1990, L 2009, ch 56, § 1 (Part TT), eff April 7, 2009, L 2012, ch 55, § 1 (Part C), eff March 30, 2012.

§ 1806-a. Default judgment in cases of failure to answer

1. In the event a person charged with a traffic infraction does not answer within the time specified, the court having jurisdiction, other than a court in a city over one million population may, in addition to any other action authorized by law, enter a plea of guilty on behalf of the defendant and render a default judgment of a fine determined by the court within the amount authorized by law. Any judgment entered pursuant to default shall be civil in nature, but shall be treated as a conviction for the purposes of this section. However, at least thirty days after the expiration of the original date prescribed for entering a plea and before a plea of guilty and a

default judgment may be rendered, the traffic violations bureau or, if there be none, the clerk of the court, shall notify the defendant by certified mail: (a) of the violation charged; (b) of the impending plea of guilty and default judgment; (c) that such judgement will be filed with the county clerk of the county in which the operator or registrant is located, and (d) that a default or plea of guilty may be avoided by entering a plea or making an appearance within thirty days of the sending of such notice. Pleas entered within that period shall be in a manner prescribed in the notice. In no case shall a default judgment and plea of guilty be rendered more than two years after the expiration of the time prescribed for originally entering a plea. When a person has entered a plea of not guilty and has demanded a hearing, no fine or penalty shall be imposed for any reason, prior to the holding of the hearing which shall be scheduled by the court of such city, village or town within thirty days of such demand.

2. The filing of the default judgment with the county clerk shall have the full force and effect of a judgment duly docketed in the office of such clerk and may be enforced in the same manner and with the same effect as that provided by law in respect to executions issued against property upon judgments of a court of record and such judgment shall remain in full force and effect for eight years notwithstanding any other provision of law.

3. Notwithstanding the provisions of subdivision one of this section, a traffic violations bureau or, if there be none, the clerk of the court, shall have two years from the effective date of this act to serve notice upon an operator or owner of a motor vehicle charged with a traffic violation who has not answered within the time specified and prior to the effective date of this act.

4. In the event a person charged with a parking violation does not answer within the time specified, a traffic and parking violations agency may, in addition to any other action authorized by law, enter a plea of guilty on behalf of the defendant and render a default judgment of a fine determined by the judicial hearing officer within the amount authorized by law. Any judgment entered pursuant to default shall be civil in nature, but shall be treated as a conviction for the purposes of this section. However, at least thirty days after the expiration of the original date prescribed for entering a plea and before a plea of guilty and a default judgment may be rendered, the traffic and parking violations agency shall notify the defendant by certified mail: (a) of the violation charged; (b) of the impending plea of guilty and default judgment; (c) that such judgment will be filed with the county clerk of the county in which the operator or registrant is located, and (d) that a default or plea of guilty may be avoided by entering a plea or making an appearance within thirty days of the sending of such notice. Pleas entered within that period shall be in a manner prescribed in the notice. In no case shall a default judgment and plea of guilty be rendered more than two years after the expiration of the time prescribed for originally entering a plea. When a person has entered a plea of not guilty and has demanded a hearing, no fine or penalty shall be imposed for any reason, prior to the holding of the hearing which shall be scheduled by the traffic and parking violations agency within thirty days of such demand.

5. If a motor vehicle which is owned by a rental or leasing company is ticketed for a traffic infraction, the municipality shall not enter a default judgement under this section against the rental or leasing company if, when the municipality sends the notice to the company, the company sends to the municipality within fifteen days a copy of the rental or leasing agreement covering that vehicle on that date with the name and address of the lessee clearly legible. If this information is not sent to the municipality within such fifteen day time period, the municipality shall proceed under this section to enter a default judgement and the rental or leasing company shall be liable for the traffic infraction.

HISTORY: Add, L 1984, ch 841, § 1, eff July 1, 1985. Sub 4, add, L 1990, ch 496, § 9, eff July 18, 1990. Former sub 4, redesignated sub 5, L 1990, ch 496, § 9, eff July 18, 1990. Sub 5, formerly sub 4, redesignated sub 5, L 1990, ch 496, § 9, eff July 18, 1990. Sub 1, amd, L 1993, ch 261, § 16, eff July 13, 1993, expires and deemed repealed April 1, 1997, L 1995, ch 83, § 199, eff June 20, 1995, deemed eff on and after April 1, 1995, expires and deemed repealed April 1, 1997.

§ 1807. Provisions applicable to arraignments for traffic violations

1. The local criminal court, upon the arraignment in this state of a resident of this state charged with a violation of the vehicle and traffic law, or other law or ordinance relating to the operation of motor vehicles or motor cycles, and before accepting a plea, or in the case of such a defendant who has previously pleaded not guilty, as provided in section eighteen hundred six of this chapter, and who wishes to change or withdraw such plea, must inform the defendant at the time of his arraignment or appearance for trial in the substance as follows:

A plea of guilty to this charge is equivalent to a conviction after trial. If you are convicted, not only will you be liable to a penalty, but in addition your license to drive a motor vehicle or motor cycle, and your certificate of registration, if any, are subject to suspension and revocation as prescribed by law.

The giving of the foregoing instructions by means of a statement printed in a noticeably distinct manner and in bold type in a size equal to at least twelve point type, upon a summons or ticket issued to a person charged with any such offense shall constitute compliance with the requirements of this section.

The foregoing provisions of this section may be waived as provided in section eighteen hundred five of this chapter.

2. Upon the arraignment of any person under eighteen years of age who resides within the household of his parent or guardian upon a charge of a violation of the vehicle and traffic law or other law or ordinance relating to the operation of motor vehicles or motor cycles, except a violation relating to parking, stopping or standing, the local criminal court which arraigns him shall forthwith transmit written notice of such arraignment to the parent or guardian of such minor person; provided, however, that if a conviction of such person follows such arraignment upon the same day, or in case such person waives arraignment and enters a plea of guilty to the offense as charged in accordance with the provisions of section eighteen hundred five of this chapter, transmittal of notice of his conviction as provided in section five hundred fourteen of this chapter shall be sufficient and the notice of arraignment hereunder need not be given; provided further that the failure of a local criminal court to transmit such notice of arraignment shall in no manner affect the validity of a conviction subsequently obtained.

HISTORY: Add, L 1971, ch 545, § 36, eff Sept 1, 1971, deriving from Crim C § 335-a. Sub 1, third undesignated par, amd, L 1999, ch 493, § 1, eff Nov 1, 1999.

§ 1808. Effect of stay order on appeal from judgment of conviction of an offense under this chapter

(a) When an appeal is taken to an intermediate appellate court from a conviction of an offense under this chapter resulting in the suspension or revocation of the defendant's motor vehicle operator's license, and a stay of execution is granted ordering reinstatement of such license during the pendency and until the determination of such appeal, service of a certified copy of such stay order by mail upon the commissioner of motor vehicles shall be binding upon the commissioner; and during a period of ninety days from the date such stay order was granted, or until such appeal is determined, if sooner than ninety days, such commissioner shall be stayed from taking any proceedings under the vehicle and traffic law to suspend or revoke such license on account of such conviction; and such order shall contain appropriate provisions to that effect.

(b) For good cause shown, such stay may be extended by the court, in its discretion, for additional periods not to exceed ninety days each; such extension order or orders, when served upon the commissioner of motor vehicles in the same manner as the original stay order, shall be binding upon him to the same extent as the original stay order for such additional period or periods.

(c) A stay order or orders issued pursuant to section 460.50 of the criminal procedure law which purport to reinstate a license during the pendency of an appeal from a conviction resulting in the suspension or revocation of a license shall, for the purposes of such reinstatement, be deemed to be issued in accordance with the provisions of this section and the ninety day stay period authorized by this section shall apply.

> **HISTORY:** Add, L 1971, ch 545, § 37, deriving from Crim C § 753(2); amd, L 1974, ch 204, § 1, eff June 15, 1974. Sub (a), formerly first par, so lettered and amd, L 1974, ch 204, § 1, eff June 15, 1974. Sub (b), formerly second par, so lettered and amd, L 1974, ch 204, § 1, eff June 15, 1974. Sub (c), add, L 1974, ch 204, § 1, eff June 15, 1974.

§ 1809. Mandatory surcharge and crime victim assistance fee required in certain cases

1. [Until Sept 1, 2015, sub 1, opening par as amended L 2014, chs 43, 99, 101, 123] Whenever proceedings in an administrative tribunal or a court of this state result in a conviction for an offense under this chapter or a traffic infraction under this chapter, or a local law, ordinance, rule or regulation adopted pursuant to this chapter, other than a traffic infraction involving standing, stopping, or parking or violations by pedestrians or bicyclists, or other than an adjudication of liability of an owner for a violation of subdivision (d) of section eleven hundred eleven of this chapter in accordance with section eleven hundred eleven-a of this chapter, or other than an adjudication of liability of an owner for a violation of subdivision (d) of section eleven hundred eleven of this chapter in accordance with section eleven hundred eleven-b of this chapter, or other than an adjudication in accordance with section eleven hundred eleven-c of this chapter for a violation of a bus lane restriction as defined in such section, or other than an adjudication of liability of an owner for a violation of subdivision (d) of section eleven hundred eleven of this chapter in accordance with section eleven hundred eleven-d of this chapter, or other than an adjudication of liability of an owner for a violation of subdivision (b), (c), (d), (f) or (g) of section eleven hundred eighty of this chapter in accordance with section eleven hundred eighty-b of this chapter, or other than an adjudication of liability of an owner for a violation of subdivision (b), (c), (d), (f) or (g) of section eleven hundred eighty of this chapter in accordance with section eleven hundred eighty-c of this chapter, there shall be levied a crime victim assistance fee and a mandatory surcharge, in addition to any sentence required or permitted by law, in accordance with the following schedule:

(a) Whenever proceedings in an administrative tribunal or a court of this state result in a conviction for a traffic infraction pursuant to article nine of this chapter, there shall be levied a crime victim assistance fee in the amount of five dollars and a mandatory surcharge, in addition to any sentence required or permitted by law, in the amount of twenty-five dollars.

(b) Whenever proceedings in an administrative tribunal or a court of this state result in a conviction for a misdemeanor or felony pursuant to section eleven hundred ninety-two of this chapter, there shall be levied, in addition to any sentence required or permitted by law, a crime victim assistance fee in the amount of twenty-five dollars and a mandatory surcharge in accordance with the following schedule:

    (i) a person convicted of a felony shall pay a mandatory surcharge of three hundred dollars;

    (ii) a person convicted of a misdemeanor shall pay a mandatory surcharge of one hundred seventy-five dollars.

(c) [As amended L 2014, chs 43, 99, 101, 123] Whenever proceedings in an administrative tribunal or a court of this state result in a conviction for an offense under this chapter other than a crime pursuant to section eleven hundred ninety-two of this chapter, or a traffic infraction under this chapter, or a local law, ordinance, rule or regulation adopted pursuant to this chapter, other than a traffic infraction involving standing, stopping, or parking or violations by pedestrians or bicyclists, or other than an adjudication of liability of an owner for a violation of subdivision (d) of section eleven hundred eleven of this chapter in accordance with section eleven hundred eleven-a of this chapter, or other than an adjudication of liability of an owner for a violation of subdivision (d) of section eleven hundred eleven of this chapter in accordance with section eleven hundred eleven-b of this chapter, or other than an adjudication of liability of an owner for a violation of subdivision (d) of section eleven hundred eleven of this chapter in accordance with section eleven hundred eleven-d of this chapter, or other than an infraction pursuant to article nine of this chapter or other than an adjudication of liability of an owner for a violation of toll collection regulations pursuant to section two thousand nine hundred eighty-five of the public authorities law or sections sixteen-a, sixteen-b and sixteen-c of chapter seven hundred seventy-four of the laws of nineteen hundred fifty or other than an adjudication in accordance with section eleven hundred eleven-c of this chapter for a violation of a bus lane restriction as defined in such section, or other than an adjudication of liability of an owner for a violation of subdivision (b), (c), (d), (f) or (g) of section eleven hundred eighty of this chapter in accordance with section eleven hundred eighty-b of this chapter, or other than an adjudication of liability of an owner for a violation of subdivision (b), (c), (d), (f) or (g) of section eleven hundred eighty of this chapter in accordance with section eleven hundred eighty-c of this chapter, there shall be levied a crime victim assistance fee in the amount of five dollars and a mandatory surcharge, in addition to any sentence required or permitted by law, in the amount of fifty-five dollars.

1. [Eff Sept 1, 2015 and until Dec 1, 2019 as amended L 2014, chs 43, 99, 101, 123] Whenever proceedings in an administrative tribunal or a court of this state result in a conviction for a crime under this chapter or a traffic infraction under this chapter, or a local law, ordinance, rule or regulation adopted pursuant to this chapter, other than a traffic infraction involving standing, stopping, parking or motor vehicle equipment or violations by pedestrians or bicyclists, or other than an adjudication of liability of an owner for a violation of subdivision (d) of section eleven hundred eleven of this chapter in accordance with section eleven hundred eleven-a of this chapter, or other than an adjudication of liability of an owner for a violation of subdivision (d) of section eleven hundred eleven of this chapter in accordance with section eleven hundred eleven-b of this chapter, or other than an adjudication in accordance with section eleven hundred eleven-c of this chapter for a violation of a bus lane restriction as defined in such section, or other than an adjudication of liability of an owner for a violation of subdivision (d) of section eleven hundred eleven of this chapter in accordance with section eleven hundred eleven-d of this chapter, or other than an adjudication of liability of an owner for a violation of subdivision (b), (c), (d), (f) or (g) of section eleven hundred eighty of this chapter in accordance with section eleven hundred eighty-b of this chapter, or other than an adjudication of liability of an owner for a violation of subdivision (b), (c), (d), (f) or (g) of section eleven hundred eighty of this chapter in accordance with section eleven hundred eighty-c of this chapter, there shall be levied a mandatory surcharge, in addition to any sentence required or permitted by law, in the amount of twenty-five dollars.

1. [Eff Dec 1, 2019 and until Sept 20, 2015 as amended L 2014, chs 43, 99, 101, 123] Whenever proceedings in an administrative tribunal or a court of this state result in a conviction for a crime under this chapter or a traffic infraction under this chapter other than a traffic infraction involving standing, stopping, parking or motor vehicle equipment or violations by pedestrians or bicyclists,

or other than an adjudication in accordance with section eleven hundred eleven-c of this chapter for a violation of a bus lane restriction as defined in such section, or other than an adjudication of liability of an owner for a violation of subdivision (d) of section eleven hundred eleven of this chapter in accordance with section eleven hundred eleven-d of this chapter, or other than an adjudication of liability of an owner for a violation of subdivision (b), (c), (d), (f) or (g) of section eleven hundred eighty of this chapter in accordance with section eleven hundred eighty-b of this chapter, or other than an adjudication of liability of an owner for a violation of subdivision (b), (c), (d), (f) or (g) of section eleven hundred eighty of this chapter in accordance with section eleven hundred eighty-c of this chapter, there shall be levied a mandatory surcharge, in addition to any sentence required or permitted by law, in the amount of seventeen dollars.

1. [Eff Sept 20, 2015 and until Aug 30, 2018 as amended L 2014, ch 43, 99, 101, 123] Whenever proceedings in an administrative tribunal or a court of this state result in a conviction for a crime under this chapter or a traffic infraction under this chapter other than a traffic infraction involving standing, stopping, parking or motor vehicle equipment or violations by pedestrians or bicyclists, or other than an adjudication of liability of an owner for a violation of subdivision (b), (c), (d), (f) or (g) of section eleven hundred eighty of this chapter in accordance with section eleven hundred eighty-b of this chapter, or other than an adjudication of liability of an owner for a violation of subdivision (b), (c), (d), (f) or (g) of section eleven hundred eighty of this chapter in accordance with section eleven hundred eighty-c of this chapter, or other than an adjudication of liability of an owner for a violation of subdivision (d) of section eleven hundred eleven of this chapter in accordance with section eleven hundred eleven-d of this chapter, there shall be levied a mandatory surcharge, in addition to any sentence required or permitted by law, in the amount of seventeen dollars.

1. [Eff Aug 30, 2018 and until July 25, 2018 as amended L 2014, ch 43] Whenever proceedings in an administrative tribunal or a court of this state result in a conviction for a crime under this chapter or a traffic infraction under this chapter other than a traffic infraction involving standing, stopping, parking or motor vehicle equipment or violations by pedestrians or bicyclists, or other than an adjudication of liability of an owner for a violation of subdivision (b), (c), (d), (f) or (g) of section eleven hundred eighty of this chapter in accordance with section eleven hundred eighty-c of this chapter, or other than an adjudication of liability of an owner for a violation of subdivision (d) of section eleven hundred eleven of this chapter in accordance with section eleven hundred eleven-d of this chapter, there shall be levied a mandatory surcharge, in addition to any sentence required or permitted by law, in the amount of seventeen dollars.

1. [Eff July 25, 2018 and until Aug 21, 2019 as amended L 2014, chs 99, 101, 123] Whenever proceedings in an administrative tribunal or a court of this state result in a conviction for a crime under this chapter or a traffic infraction under this chapter other than a traffic infraction involving standing, stopping, parking or motor vehicle equipment or violations by pedestrians or bicyclists, or other than an adjudication of liability of an owner for a violation of subdivision (d) of section eleven hundred eleven of this chapter in accordance with section eleven hundred eleven-d of this chapter, there shall be levied a mandatory surcharge, in addition to any sentence required or permitted by law, in the amount of seventeen dollars.

1. [Eff Aug 21, 2019] Whenever proceedings in an administrative tribunal or a court of this state result in a conviction for a crime under this chapter or a traffic infraction under this chapter other than a traffic infraction involving standing, stopping, parking or motor vehicle equipment or violations by pedestrians or bicyclists, there shall be levied a mandatory surcharge, in addition to any sentence required or permitted by law, in the amount of seventeen dollars.

2. [Until Sept 1, 2015] Where a person is convicted of two or more such crimes or traffic

infractions committed through a single act or omission, or through an act or omission which in itself constituted one of the crimes or traffic infractions and also was a material element of the other, the court or administrative tribunal shall impose a crime victim assistance fee and a mandatory surcharge mandated by subdivision one of this section for each such conviction; provided however, that in no event shall the total amount of such crime victim assistance fees and mandatory surcharges imposed pursuant to paragraph (a) or (c) of subdivision one of this section exceed one hundred ninety-six dollars.

2. [Eff Sept 1, 2015] Where a person is convicted of two or more such crimes or traffic infractions committed through a single act or omission, or through an act or omission which in itself constituted one of the crimes or traffic infractions and also was a material element of the other, the court or administrative tribunal shall impose only one mandatory surcharge mandated by subdivision one of this section.

3. The mandatory surcharge provided for in subdivision one of this section shall be paid to the clerk of the court or administrative tribunal that rendered the conviction. Within the first ten days of the month following collection of the mandatory surcharge the collecting authority shall determine the amount of mandatory surcharge collected and, if it is an administrative tribunal or a town or village justice court, it shall pay such money to the state comptroller who shall deposit such money in the state treasury pursuant to section one hundred twenty-one of the state finance law to the credit of the general fund. If such collecting authority is any other court of the unified court system, it shall, within such period, pay such money to the state commissioner of taxation and finance to the credit of the criminal justice improvement account established by section ninety-seven-bb of the state finance law. The crime victim assistance fee provided for in subdivision one of this section shall be paid to the clerk of the court or administrative tribunal that rendered the conviction. Within the first ten days of the month following collection of the crime victim assistance fee, the collecting authority shall determine the amount of crime victim assistance fee collected and, if it is an administrative tribunal or a town or village justice court, it shall pay such money to the state comptroller who shall deposit such money in the state treasury pursuant to section one hundred twenty-one of the state finance law to the credit of the criminal justice improvement account established by section ninety-seven-bb of the state finance law.

4. Any person who has paid a mandatory surcharge or crime victim assistance fee under the authority of this section which is ultimately determined not to be required by this section shall be entitled to a refund of such mandatory surcharge or crime victim assistance fee upon application to the state comptroller. The state comptroller shall require such proof as it is necessary in order to determine whether a refund is required by law.

5. When a person who is convicted of a crime or traffic infraction and sentenced to a term of imprisonment has failed to pay the mandatory surcharge or crime victim assistance fee required by this section, the clerk of the court or the administrative tribunal that rendered the conviction shall notify the superintendent or the municipal official of the facility where the person is confined. The superintendent or the municipal official shall cause any amount owing to be collected from such person during his term of imprisonment from moneys to the credit of an inmates' fund or such moneys as may be earned by a person in a work release program pursuant to section eight hundred sixty of the correction law. Such moneys shall be paid over to the state comptroller to the credit of the criminal justice improvement account established by section ninety-seven-bb of the state finance law, except that any such moneys collected which are surcharges or crime victim assistance fees levied in relation to convictions obtained in a town or village justice court shall be paid within thirty days after the receipt thereof by the superintendent or municipal official of the facility to the justice of the court in which the conviction was obtained. For the purposes of collecting such

mandatory surcharge or crime victim assistance fee, the state shall be legally entitled to the money to the credit of an inmates' fund or money which is earned by an inmate in a work release program. For purposes of this subdivision, the term "inmates' fund" shall mean moneys in the possession of an inmate at the time of his admission into such facility, funds earned by him as provided for in section one hundred eighty-seven of the correction law and any other funds received by him or on his behalf and deposited with such superintendent or municipal official.

5-a. The provisions of subdivision four-a of section five hundred ten, subdivision three of section five hundred fourteen and subdivision three of section two hundred twenty-seven of this chapter governing actions which may be taken for failure to pay a fine or penalty shall be applicable to a mandatory surcharge or crime victim assistance fee imposed pursuant to this section.

6. Notwithstanding any other provision of this section, where a person has made restitution or reparation pursuant to section 60.27 of the penal law, such person shall not be required to pay a mandatory surcharge or crime victim assistance fee.

7. Notwithstanding any other provision of this section, where a mandatory surcharge or crime victim assistance fee is imposed pursuant to the provisions of section 60.35 of the penal law, no mandatory surcharge or crime victim assistance fee shall be imposed pursuant to the provisions of this section.

8. The provisions of this section shall only apply to offenses committed on or before September first, two thousand fifteen.

9. Notwithstanding the provisions of subdivision one of this section, in the event a proceeding is in a town or village court, the court shall add an additional five dollars to the surcharges imposed by such subdivision one of this section.

10. For the purposes of this section, the term conviction means and includes the conviction of a felony or a misdemeanor for which a youthful offender finding was substituted and upon such a finding there shall be levied a mandatory surcharge and a crime victim assistance fee to the same extent and in the same manner and amount provided by this section for conviction of the felony or misdemeanor, as the case may be, for which such youthful offender finding was substituted.

HISTORY: Add, L 1983, ch 15, § 52, eff April 1, 1983, and applicable to convictions for acts or omissions occurring on and after such date; amd, L 1983, ch 16, § 2, L 1983, ch 945, §§ 2, 3,L 1988, ch 746, § 13, expires and is repealed Dec 1, 2019, L 1989, ch 62, § 85, eff April 19, 1989, L 1990, ch 190, § 318, L 1991, ch 166, §§ 337, 338, eff June 12, 1991 and expires Sept 1, 2015, L 1991, ch 166, § 339, eff June 12, 1991, L 1992, ch 55, § 385, eff April 10, 1992, L 1992, ch 379, § 16, eff July 17, 1992, L 1994, ch 61, § 10, eff April 18, 1994, deemed eff April 1, 1994, L 1996, ch 309, § 70, eff Aug 31, 1996, L 1997, ch 435, § 65, eff Aug 20, 1997, L 1997, ch 452, § 3, eff Jan 1, 1998, L 1999, ch 385, § 5, eff July 27, 1999, L 1999, ch 452, §§ 13, 14, Sept 1, 1999, deemed eff on and after April 1, 1999, L 2000, ch 57, § 2 (Part L), eff May 15, 2000, deemed eff on and after April 1, 2000, L 2001, ch 95, § 17, eff July 13, 2001, L 2003, ch 16, § 16, eff March 31, 2003, deemed eff on and after March 31, 2003, L 2003, ch 62, §§ 2, 3 (Part M), eff Nov 11, 2003, L 2003, ch 261, § 4, eff July 29, 2003, L 2004, ch 56, § 3 (Part F), eff Feb 16, 2004, L 2005, ch 56, § 14 (Part D), eff April 12, 2005, deemed eff on and after April 1, 2005, L 2007, ch 56, § 14 (Part C), eff April 9, 2007, deemed eff on and after March 31, 2007, L 2008, ch 56, § 2 (Part DD), eff July 1, 2008, L 2009, ch 19, § 4, eff May 28, 2009, expires and repealed Sept 1, 2015, L 2009, ch 19, § 5, eff Sept 1, 2011 and expires and repealed Dec 1, 2019, L 2009, ch 20, § 17, eff May 28, 2009, expires and repealed Sept 1, 2015, L 2009, ch 20, § 18, eff Sept 1, 2011, expires and repealed Dec 1, 2019,L 2009, ch 21, § 17, eff May 28, 2009, expires and repealed Sept 1, 2015, L 2009, ch 21, § 18, eff Sept 1, 2013, expires and repealed Dec 1, 2014, L 2009, ch 22, § 17, eff May 28, 2009, expires and repealed Sept 1, 2015, L 2009, ch 22, § 18, eff Sept 1, 2015, expires and repealed Dec 1, 2019, L 2009, ch 23, § 4, eff May 28, 2009, expires and repealed Sept 1, 2015, L 2009, ch 23, § 5, eff Sept 1, 2015, expires and repealed Dec 1, 2019, L 2009, ch 56, § 14 (Part U), eff April 7,

2009, L 2009, ch 59, § 1 (Part I), eff July 6, 2009, L 2009, ch 383, § 17, eff Sept 25, 2009, expires and repealed Sept 1, 2015, L 2009, ch 383, § 18, eff Sept 1, 2013, expires and repealed Dec 1, 2014, L 2010, ch 59, § 10 (Part II), eff Sept 20, 2010, expires and repealed Sept 1, 2015, L 2010, ch 59, § 10-a (Part II), eff Dec 1, 2014, expires and repealed Dec 1, 2019, L 2010, ch 59, § 10-b (Part II), eff Dec 1, 2014, expires and repealed Sept 20, 2015, L 2011, ch 57, § 14 (Part A), eff March 31, 2011, L 2013, ch 55, § 6 (Part C), eff July 26, 2013, L 2013, ch 55, § 13 (Part E), eff March 28, 2013, L 2013, ch 189, § 11, eff Aug 30, 2013, expires and repealed Sept 1, 2015, L 2013, ch 189, § 11-a, eff Sept 1, 2015, expires and repealed Dec 1, 2019, L 2013, ch 189, § 11-b, eff Dec 1, 2014, expires and repealed Sept 20, 2015, L 2013, ch 189, § 11-c, eff Sept 20, 2015, expires and repealed Aug 30, 2018, L 2014, ch 43, § 3, eff July 25, 2014, expires Sept 1, 2015, L 2014, ch 43, § 3-a, eff Sept 1, 2015, expires Dec 1, 2014, L 2014, ch 43, § 3-b, eff Dec 1, 2014, expires Sept 20, 2015, L 2014, ch 43, § 3-c, eff Sept 20, 2015, expires and repealed Aug 30, 2018, L 2014, ch 43, § 3-d, eff Aug 30, 2018, expires July 25, 2018, L 2014, ch 99, § 10, eff Aug 21, 2014, expires and repealed Sept 1, 2015, L 2014, ch 99, § 10-a, eff Sept 1, 2015, expires and repealed Dec 1, 2019, L 2014, ch 99, § 10-b, eff Dec 1, 2019, expires and repealed Sept 20, 2015, L 2014, ch 99, § 10-c, eff Sept 20, 2015, expires and repealed Aug 30, 2018, L 2014, ch 99, § 10-d, eff July 25, 2018, expires Aug 21, 2019, L 2014, ch 101, § 10, eff Aug 21, 2014, expires and repealed Sept 1, 2015, L 2014, ch 101, § 10-a, eff Sept 1, 2015, expires and repealed Dec 1, 2019, L 2014, ch 101, § 10-b, eff Dec 1, 2019, expires and repealed Sept 20, 2015, L 2014, ch 101, § 10-c, eff Sept 20, 2015, expires and repealed Aug 30, 2018, L 2014, ch 101, § 10-d, eff July 25, 2018, expires Aug 21, 2019, L 2014, ch 123, § 10, eff Aug 21, 2014, expires and repealed Sept 1, 2015, L 2014, ch 123, § 10-a, eff Sept 1, 2015, expires and repealed Dec 1, 2019, L 2014, ch 123, § 10-b, eff Dec 1, 2019, expires and repealed Sept 20, 2015, L 2014, ch 123, § 10-c, eff Sept 20, 2015, expires and repealed Aug 30, 2018, L 2014, ch 123, § 10-d, eff July 25, 2018, expires Aug 21, 2019.

§ 1809-a. [Repealed Sept 1, 2015] Mandatory surcharge required in certain cities for parking, stopping and standing violations

1. The provisions of any other general or special law notwithstanding, whenever, in a city having a population of one hundred thousand or more according to the nineteen hundred eighty United States census, proceedings in an administrative tribunal or a court result in a finding of liability, or conviction for the violation of any statute, local law, ordinance or rule involving the parking, stopping or standing of a motor vehicle, there shall be levied a mandatory surcharge in addition to any other sentence, fine or penalty otherwise permitted or required, in the amount of fifteen dollars. Such surcharge shall not be deemed a monetary penalty for the purposes of section two hundred thirty-seven of this chapter or section 19-203 of the administrative code of the city of New York.

2. The mandatory surcharge provided for in subdivision one of this section shall be paid to the clerk of the court or administrative tribunal that made the determination of liability.

(a) Except as provided in paragraph (b) of this subdivision within the first ten days of the month next succeeding the collection of such surcharge, the collecting authority shall pay seven dollars and fifty cents of each surcharge to the justice court fund held by the state comptroller pursuant to section ninety-nine-a of the state finance law which monies shall then be deposited to the credit of the general fund. Each such payment shall be accompanied by a true and complete report in such form and detail as the comptroller shall prescribe. The remaining amount of the surcharge shall be paid to the chief fiscal officer of the municipality and used by the municipality from which it originated for its local criminal justice programs and purposes.

(b) Within the first ten days of the month next succeeding the collection of such surcharge, the collecting authority in cities having a population of one hundred thousand or more but less than one million shall pay such surcharge to the chief fiscal officer of the municipality and such surcharge shall be used by the municipality from which it originated for its local criminal justice programs and purposes.

3. Any person who has paid a mandatory surcharge under the authority of this section which is ultimately determined not to be required by this section shall be entitled to a refund of such mandatory surcharge upon written application to the collecting authority. The collecting authority shall require such proof as is necessary in order to determine whether a refund is required by law. If the collecting authority shall refund any portion of the surcharge previously paid to the justice court fund pursuant to subdivision two of this section, the collecting authority may offset an equal amount from a subsequent remittance to the justice court fund, provided, however, that the collecting authority shall prepare such reports and provide such information with respect to such refunds as the comptroller shall direct, and provided, further, that the comptroller, upon review of such reports and information, may direct that any appropriate adjustments be made in future payments to the justice court fund pursuant to subdivision two of this section.

4. Notwithstanding any other provision of this section, where a mandatory surcharge is imposed pursuant to the provisions of section 60.35 of the penal law or section eighteen hundred nine or eighteen hundred nine-b of this article, no mandatory surcharge shall be imposed pursuant to the provisions of this section.

> **HISTORY:** Add, L 1991, ch 166, § 374, eff June 12, 1991, repealed eff Sept 1, 2015. Sub 1, amd, L 2003, ch 62, § 21 (Part J), eff Nov 11, 2003. Sub 2, amd, L 1996, ch 309, § 71, eff Aug 31, 1996, L 1996, ch 690, § 2, eff Dec 31, 1996, L 2003, ch 62, § 21, eff Nov 11, 2003, L 2007, ch 57, § 1 (Part M), eff Jan 1, 2008. Sub 2, opening par, formerly part of sub 2, so designated sub 2, opening par and amd, L 2007, ch 57, § 1 (Part M), eff Jan 1, 2008. Sub 2, par (a), formerly part of sub 2, so designated sub 2, par (a) and amd, L 2007, ch 57, § 1 (Part M), eff Jan 1, 2008. Sub 2, par (b), add, L 2007, ch 57, § 1 (Part M), eff Jan 1, 2008. Sub 3, amd, L 1991, ch 526, § 2, eff July 19, 1991, L 1996, ch 690, § 4, eff Dec 31, 1996. Sub 4, amd, L 1999, ch 497, § 2, eff April 1, 2000.

§ 1809-aa. Mandatory surcharge required for certain parking violations

1. Notwithstanding any other provision of law, whenever proceedings in an administrative tribunal or court result in a conviction for a violation of section twelve hundred, twelve hundred one or twelve hundred two of this chapter, there shall be levied a mandatory surcharge in addition to any other sentence, fine or penalty otherwise permitted or required, in the amount of twenty-five dollars.

2. The mandatory surcharge provided for in subdivision one of this section shall be paid to the clerk of the court or administrative tribunal that rendered the conviction. Within the first ten days of the month following collection of the surcharge the collecting authority shall pay such money to the state comptroller who shall deposit such money in the state treasury pursuant to section one hundred twenty-one of the state finance law to the credit of the general fund.

> **HISTORY:** Add, L 2013, ch 55, § 7 (Part C), eff July 26, 2013.

§ 1809-b. Mandatory surcharge required for certain violations relating to handicapped parking spaces

1. Notwithstanding any other provision of law, whenever proceedings in an administrative tribunal or a court result in a finding of liability, or conviction for a violation of section twelve hundred three-a, twelve hundred three-b or twelve hundred three-c of this chapter or any other statute, local law, ordinance or rule involving the parking, stopping or standing of motor vehicles registered pursuant to section four hundred four-a of this chapter or those possessing a special vehicle identification parking permit issued in accordance with section one thousand two hundred three-a of this chapter, there shall be levied a mandatory surcharge in addition to any other sentence, fine or penalty otherwise permitted or required, in the amount of thirty dollars. Such surcharge shall not be deemed a monetary penalty for the purposes of section two hundred thirty-seven of this chapter or section 19-203 of the administrative code of the city of New York.

2. The mandatory surcharge provided for in subdivision one of this section shall be paid to the clerk of the court or administrative tribunal that made the determination of liability. Within the first ten days of the month next succeeding the collection of such surcharge, the collecting authority shall pay fifteen dollars of such surcharge to the chief fiscal officer of the county in which such violation occurred or of the city of New York, for deposit to the credit of the handicapped parking education fund of such county or city established pursuant to section twelve hundred three-g of this chapter which shall be used by such county or city solely for a handicapped parking education program pursuant to such section. The remaining amount of the surcharge shall be paid to the chief fiscal officer of the municipality from which it originated and used by such municipality for its local criminal justice programs and purposes; provided, however, that such municipality shall use ten percent of such funds for developing and implementing a disability awareness program for local law enforcement agencies for the purpose of training local law enforcement personnel to recognize and appropriately respond to persons with disabilities with whom such personnel come into contact in the course of their duties.

HISTORY: Add, L 1999, ch 497, § 3, eff April 1, 2000.

§ 1809-c. Additional surcharge required for certain violations relating to driving while intoxicated and driving while impaired

1. Notwithstanding any other provision of law, whenever proceedings in a court of this state result in a conviction pursuant to section eleven hundred ninety-two of this chapter, there shall be levied, in addition to any sentence or other surcharge required or permitted by law, an additional surcharge of twenty-five dollars.

2. The additional surcharge provided for in subdivision one of this section shall be paid to the clerk of the court that rendered the conviction. Within the first ten days of the month following collection of the surcharge the collecting authority shall determine the amount of surcharge collected and it shall pay such money to the state comptroller who shall deposit such money in the state treasury pursuant to section one hundred twenty-one of the state finance law to the credit of the general fund.

3. The provisions of subdivision three of section two hundred twenty-seven, subdivision four-a of section five hundred ten, and subdivision three of section five hundred fourteen of this chapter governing actions which may be taken for failure to pay a fine or penalty shall be applicable to the additional surcharge imposed pursuant to this section.

4. For the purposes of this section, the term conviction means and includes the conviction of a felony or a misdemeanor for a violation of section eleven hundred ninety-two of this chapter for which a youthful offender finding was substituted and upon such a finding there shall be levied an additional surcharge, in addition to any sentence or other surcharge required or permitted by law, to the same extent and in the same manner and amount provided by this section for conviction of the felony or misdemeanor, as the case may be, for which such youthful offender finding was substituted.

HISTORY: Add, L 2003, ch 62, § 37 (Part J), eff Nov 11, 2003. Sub 4, add, L 2004, ch 56, § 4 (Part F), eff Feb 16, 2005.

§ 1809-d. Mandatory surcharge for violation of maximum speed limits in highway construction or maintenance work areas

1. Notwithstanding any other provision of law, whenever proceedings in an administrative tribunal or court result in a finding of liability or conviction for a violation of paragraph two of subdivision (d) or subdivision (f) of section eleven hundred eighty of this chapter or any other

statute, local law, ordinance or rule involving the maximum speed limits in highway construction or maintenance work areas, there shall be levied a mandatory surcharge in addition to any other sentence, fine or penalty otherwise permitted or required, in the amount of fifty dollars. Such surcharge shall not be deemed a monetary penalty for the purposes of section two hundred thirty-seven of this chapter or section 19-203 of the administrative code of the city of New York.

2. The mandatory surcharge provided for in subdivision one of this section shall be paid to the clerk of the court or administrative tribunal that made the determination of liability. Within the first ten days of the month next succeeding the collection of such surcharge, the collecting authority shall pay such money to the state comptroller to be deposited in the highway construction and maintenance safety education fund established by section ninety-nine-n of the state finance law.

HISTORY: Add, L 2005, ch 223, § 3, eff Nov 1, 2005. Former § 1809, add, L 2004, ch 56, § 2 (Part G), eff Sept 1, 2004, expires and repealed Sept 1, 2005; repealed, L 2004, ch 740, § 2, ef Dec 15, 2004, deemed eff Sept 1, 2004.

§ 1809-e. Additional surcharge required for certain violations

1. a. [Until Dec 1, 2019 as amended, chs 43, 99, 101, 123] Notwithstanding any other provision of law, whenever proceedings in a court or an administrative tribunal of this state result in a conviction for an offense under this chapter, except a conviction pursuant to section eleven hundred ninety-two of this chapter, or for a traffic infraction under this chapter, or a local law, ordinance, rule or regulation adopted pursuant to this chapter, except a traffic infraction involving standing, stopping, or parking or violations by pedestrians or bicyclists, and except an adjudication of liability of an owner for a violation of subdivision (d) of section eleven hundred eleven of this chapter in accordance with section eleven hundred eleven-a of this chapter or in accordance with section eleven hundred eleven-d of this chapter, and except an adjudication of liability of an owner for a violation of subdivision (d) of section eleven hundred eleven of this chapter in accordance with section eleven hundred eleven-b of this chapter, and except an adjudication in accordance with section eleven hundred eleven-c of this chapter of a violation of a bus lane restriction as defined in such section, and except an adjudication of liability of an owner for a violation of subdivision (b), (c), (d), (f) or (g) of section eleven hundred eighty of this chapter in accordance with section eleven hundred eighty-b of this chapter, and except an adjudication of liability of an owner for a violation of subdivision (b), (c), (d), (f) or (g) of section eleven hundred eighty of this chapter in accordance with section eleven hundred eighty-c of this chapter, and except an adjudication of liability of an owner for a violation of toll collection regulations pursuant to section two thousand nine hundred eighty-five of the public authorities law or sections sixteen-a, sixteen-b and sixteen-c of chapter seven hundred seventy-four of the laws of nineteen hundred fifty, there shall be levied in addition to any sentence, penalty or other surcharge required or permitted by law, an additional surcharge of twenty-eight dollars.

1. a. [Eff Dec 1, 2019 and until Sept 20, 2015 as amended, chs 43, 99, 101, 123] Notwithstanding any other provision of law, whenever proceedings in a court or an administrative tribunal of this state result in a conviction for an offense under this chapter, except a conviction pursuant to section eleven hundred ninety-two of this chapter, or for a traffic infraction under this chapter, or a local law, ordinance, rule or regulation adopted pursuant to this chapter, except a traffic infraction involving standing, stopping, or parking or violations by pedestrians or bicyclists, and except an adjudication of liability of an owner for a violation of subdivision (d) of section eleven hundred eleven of this chapter in accordance with section eleven hundred eleven-a of this chapter or in accordance with section eleven hundred eleven-d of this chapter, and except an adjudication in accordance with section eleven hundred eleven-c

of this chapter of a violation of a bus lane restriction as defined in such section, and except an adjudication of liability of an owner for a violation of subdivision (b), (c), (d), (f) or (g) of section eleven hundred eighty of this chapter in accordance with section eleven hundred eighty-b of this chapter, and except an adjudication of liability of an owner for a violation of subdivision (b), (c), (d), (f) or (g) of section eleven hundred eighty of this chapter in accordance with section eleven hundred eighty-c of this chapter, and except an adjudication of liability of an owner for a violation of toll collection regulations pursuant to section two thousand nine hundred eighty-five of the public authorities law or sections sixteen-a, sixteen-b and sixteen-c of chapter seven hundred seventy-four of the laws of nineteen hundred fifty, there shall be levied in addition to any sentence, penalty or other surcharge required or permitted by law, an additional surcharge of twenty-eight dollars.

1. a. [Eff Sept 20, 2015 and until Aug 30, 2018 as amended, chs 43, 99, 101, 123] Notwithstanding any other provision of law, whenever proceedings in a court or an administrative tribunal of this state result in a conviction for an offense under this chapter, except a conviction pursuant to section eleven hundred ninety-two of this chapter, or for a traffic infraction under this chapter, or a local law, ordinance, rule or regulation adopted pursuant to this chapter, except a traffic infraction involving standing, stopping, or parking or violations by pedestrians or bicyclists, and except an adjudication of liability of an owner for a violation of subdivision (d) of section eleven hundred eleven of this chapter in accordance with section eleven hundred eleven-a of this chapter or in accordance with section eleven hundred eleven-d of this chapter, and except an adjudication of liability of an owner for a violation of subdivision (b), (c), (d), (f) or (g) of section eleven hundred eighty of this chapter in accordance with section eleven hundred eighty-b of this chapter, and except an adjudication of liability of an owner for a violation of subdivision (b), (c), (d), (f) or (g) of section eleven hundred eighty of this chapter in accordance with section eleven hundred eighty-c of this chapter, and except an adjudication of liability of an owner for a violation of toll collection regulations pursuant to section two thousand nine hundred eighty-five of the public authorities law or sections sixteen-a, sixteen-b and sixteen-c of chapter seven hundred seventy-four of the laws of nineteen hundred fifty, there shall be levied in addition to any sentence, penalty or other surcharge required or permitted by law, an additional surcharge of twenty-eight dollars.

1. a. [Eff Aug 30, 2018 and until July 25, 2018 as amended L 2014, ch 43] Notwithstanding any other provision of law, whenever proceedings in a court or an administrative tribunal of this state result in a conviction for an offense under this chapter, except a conviction pursuant to section eleven hundred ninety-two of this chapter, or for a traffic infraction under this chapter, or a local law, ordinance, rule or regulation adopted pursuant to this chapter, except a traffic infraction involving standing, stopping, or parking or violations by pedestrians or bicyclists, and except an adjudication of liability of an owner for a violation of subdivision (d) of section eleven hundred eleven of this chapter in accordance with section eleven hundred eleven-a of this chapter or in accordance with section eleven hundred eleven-d of this chapter, and except an adjudication of liability of an owner for a violation of subdivision (b), (c), (d), (f) or (g) of section eleven hundred eighty of this chapter in accordance with section eleven hundred eighty-c of this chapter, and except an adjudication of liability of an owner for a violation of toll collection regulations pursuant to section two thousand nine hundred eighty-five of the public authorities law or sections sixteen-a, sixteen-b and sixteen-c of chapter seven hundred seventy-four of the laws of nineteen hundred fifty, there shall be levied in addition to any sentence, penalty or other surcharge required or permitted by law, an additional surcharge of twenty-eight dollars.

1. a. [Eff July 25, 2018 and until Aug 21, 2019 as amended L 2014, chs 99, 101, 123]

Notwithstanding any other provision of law, whenever proceedings in a court or an administrative tribunal of this state result in a conviction for an offense under this chapter, except a conviction pursuant to section eleven hundred ninety-two of this chapter, or for a traffic infraction under this chapter, or a local law, ordinance, rule or regulation adopted pursuant to this chapter, except a traffic infraction involving standing, stopping, or parking or violations by pedestrians or bicyclists, and except an adjudication of liability of an owner for a violation of subdivision (d) of section eleven hundred eleven of this chapter in accordance with section eleven hundred eleven-a of this chapter or in accordance with section eleven hundred eleven-d of this chapter, and except an adjudication of liability of an owner for a violation of toll collection regulations pursuant to section two thousand nine hundred eighty-five of the public authorities law or sections sixteen-a, sixteen-b and sixteen-c of chapter seven hundred seventy-four of the laws of nineteen hundred fifty, there shall be levied in addition to any sentence, penalty or other surcharge required or permitted by law, an additional surcharge of twenty-eight dollars.

1. a. [Eff Aug 21, 2019] Notwithstanding any other provision of law, whenever proceedings in a court or an administrative tribunal of this state result in a conviction for an offense under this chapter, except a conviction pursuant to section eleven hundred ninety-two of this chapter, or for a traffic infraction under this chapter, or a local law, ordinance, rule or regulation adopted pursuant to this chapter, except a traffic infraction involving standing, stopping, or parking or violations by pedestrians or bicyclists, and except an adjudication of liability of an owner for a violation of subdivision (d) of section eleven hundred eleven of this chapter in accordance with section eleven hundred eleven-a of this chapter, and except an adjudication of liability of an owner for a violation of toll collection regulations pursuant to section two thousand nine hundred eighty-five of the public authorities law or sections sixteen-a, sixteen-b and sixteen-c of chapter seven hundred seventy-four of the laws of nineteen hundred fifty, there shall be levied in addition to any sentence, penalty or other surcharge required or permitted by law, an additional surcharge of twenty-eight dollars.

b. Notwithstanding any other provision of law, whenever proceedings in a court of this state result in a conviction pursuant to section eleven hundred ninety-two of this chapter, there shall be levied, in addition to any sentence or other surcharge required or permitted by law, an additional surcharge of one hundred seventy dollars.

2. The additional surcharges provided for in subdivision one of this section shall be paid to the clerk of the court or administrative tribunal that rendered the conviction. Within the first ten days of the month following collection of such surcharges, the collecting authority shall pay such money to the state comptroller to be deposited to the general fund.

3. The provisions of subdivision four-a of section five hundred ten, subdivision three of section five hundred fourteen and subdivision three of section two hundred twenty-seven of this chapter governing actions which may be taken for failure to pay a fine or penalty shall be applicable to the additional surcharge imposed pursuant to this section.

HISTORY: Add, L 2008, ch 56, § 1 (Part EE), eff August 1, 2008; amd, L 2009, ch 19, § 6, eff May 28, 2009, expires and repealed Dec 1, 2014, L 2009, ch 20, § 19, eff May 28, 2009, expires and repealed Dec 1, 2019, L 2009, ch 22, § 19, eff May 28, 2009, expires and repealed Dec 1, 2019, L 2009, ch 23, § 6, eff May 28, 2009, expires and repealed Dec 1, 2019, L 2009, ch 383, § 19, eff Sept 25, 2009, expires and repealed Dec 1, 2019, L 2010, ch 59, § 11 (Part II), eff Sept 20, 2010, expires and repealed Dec 1, 2019, L 2010, ch 59, § 11-a (Part II), eff Dec 1, 2014, expires and repealed Sept 20, 2015, L 2013, ch 55, § 3 (Part C), eff July 26, 2013, expires and repealed Dec 1, 2019, L 2013, ch 55, § 4 (Part C), eff Dec 1, 2019, expires and repealed Sept 20, 2015, L 2013, ch 55, § 5 (Part C), eff Sept 20, 2015, L 2013, ch 189, § 12, eff Aug 30, 2013, expires and repealed Dec 1, 2019, L 2013, ch 189, § 12-a, eff Dec 1, 2019 and expires and repealed Sept 20, 2015, L

2013, ch 189, § 12-b, eff Sept 20, 2015, expires and repealed Aug 30, 2018, L 2013, ch 189, § 12-c, eff Aug 30, 2018, L 2014, ch 43, § 4, eff July 25, 2014, expires Dec 1, 2014, L 2014, ch 43, § 4-a, eff Dec 1, 2014, expires Sept 20, 2015, L 2014, ch 43, § 4-b, eff Sept 20, 2015, expires Aug 30, 2018, L 2014, ch 43, § 4-c, eff Aug 30, 2018 and expires and repealed July 25, 2018, L 2014, ch 99, § 11, eff Aug 21, 2014, expires and repealed Dec 1, 2019, L 2014, ch 99, § 11-a, eff Dec 1, 2019 and expires and repealed Sept 20, 2015, L 2014, ch 99, § 11-b, eff Sept 20, 2015, expires and repealed Aug 30, 2018, L 2014, ch 99, § 11-c, eff July 25, 2018, expires and repealed Aug 21, 2019, L 2014, ch 101, § 11, eff Aug 21, 2014, expires and repealed Dec 1, 2019, L 2014, ch 101, § 11-a, eff Dec 1, 2019 and expires and repealed Sept 20, 2015, L 2014, ch 101, § 11-b, eff Sept 20, 2015, expires and repealed Aug 30, 2018, L 2014, ch 101, § 11-c, eff July 25, 2018, expires and repealed Aug 21, 2019, L 2014, ch 123, § 11, eff Aug 21, 2014, expires and repealed Dec 1, 2019, L 2014, ch 123, § 11-a, eff Dec 1, 2019 and expires and repealed Sept 20, 2015, L 2014, ch 123, § 11-b, eff Sept 20, 2015, expires and repealed Aug 30, 2018, L 2014, ch 123, § 11-c, eff July 25, 2018, expires and repealed Aug 21, 2019.

§ 1810. Compensation of officers shall not depend upon apprehension or arrests

(a) No city or village shall employ any officer, agent or person whose compensation shall in any way depend upon the apprehension or arrest of any person or persons for violating any ordinance adopted pursuant to section sixteen hundred four of this chapter or for reckless driving as defined in section twelve hundred twelve of this chapter. If any person be apprehended or arrested or haled before a magistrate for a violation of a local ordinance adopted pursuant to section sixteen hundred four or for reckless driving as defined by section twelve hundred twelve of this chapter by any officer, agent or employee of any city or village who is so employed, the fact of such employment at the time shall be a defense to any charge made for violation of such ordinance or for reckless driving.

(b) No county or town shall employ any officer, agent or person, whether such employee be elected or appointed, whose compensation shall in any way depend upon the apprehension or arrest of any person for reckless driving as defined in section twelve hundred twelve of this chapter. If any person be apprehended or arrested or haled before a magistrate for reckless driving as so defined, by any officer, agent or employee of any county or town who is so employed, the fact of such employment at the time shall be a defense to any charge made for reckless driving as defined in section twelve hundred twelve of this chapter.

HISTORY: Add, L 1988, ch 47, § 25, eff Nov 1, 1988.

UNIFORM RULES FOR THE NEW YORK STATE TRIAL COURTS

PART 200—UNIFORM RULES FOR COURTS EXERCISING CRIMINAL JURISDICTION

RULES APPLICABLE TO ALL COURTS

§ 200.1   Application; definitions.

(a) The rules of this Part shall govern procedures in each criminal court of the State.

(b) For purposes of this Part:

(1) *Chief Administrator of the Courts* shall include the designee of the Chief Administrator.

(2) *Clerk* as used in this Part, shall mean the chief clerk or the appropriate clerk of the trial court, unless the context otherwise requires.

(3) Other words or expressions used in this Part shall have the same meanings as they have under provisions of the Criminal Procedure Law.

§ 200.2   Terms and parts of court.

(a) *Terms of court.* A term of court is a four-week session of court, and there shall be 13 terms of court in a year, unless otherwise provided in the annual schedule of terms established by the Chief Administrator of the Courts, which also shall specify the dates of such terms.

(b) *Parts of court.* A part of court is a designated unit of the court in which specified business of the court is to be conducted by a judge or quasi-judicial officer. There shall be such parts of court as may be authorized to be established from time to time by the Chief Administrator of the Courts.

§ 200.3   Papers filed in a criminal court; form.

In addition to complying with the applicable provisions of CPLR 2101, every paper filed in court, other than an exhibit or printed form, shall contain writing on one side only, and if typewritten, shall have at least double space between each line, except for quotations and the names and addresses of attorneys appearing in the action, and shall have at least one-inch margins.

§ 200.4   Submission of papers to judge of a criminal court.

All papers for signature or consideration of the court shall be presented to the clerk of the trial court in the appropriate courtroom or clerk's office, except that where the clerk is unavailable or the judge so directs, papers may be submitted to the judge and a copy filed with the clerk at the first available opportunity. All papers for any judge that are filed in the clerk's office shall be promptly delivered to the judge by the clerk. The papers shall be clearly addressed to the judge for whom they are intended and prominently show the nature of the papers, the title and the identification number of the accusatory instrument or instruments by which defendant is charged, the name of the assigned judge, if any, the name of the attorney or party submitting them and the return date of any motion to which the papers refer.

§ 200.5   Appearance of counsel in criminal actions.

Each attorney appearing in a criminal action is required to file a written notice of appearance on or before the time of the attorney's first appearance in court or not later than 10 days after appointment or retainer, whichever is sooner. The notice shall contain the attorney's name, office address and telephone number, the name of the person on whose behalf he or she is appearing, and the identification number of the accusatory instrument or instruments by which such person is charged.

§ 200.6   Engagement of counsel.

No adjournment shall be granted on the ground of engagement of counsel except in accordance with Part 125 of the Rules of the Chief Administrator of the Courts (22 NYCRR Part 125).

Unif. Rules

§ 200.7   Authorization to administer oaths.

(a) All court clerks employed in court parts devoted in whole or in part to the disposition of criminal actions, and such other employees as the judge presiding therein may designate in accordance with section 105 of the Uniform District Court Act, section 105 of the Uniform City Court Act, section 109 of the Uniform Justice Court Act and section 23(1) of the New York City Criminal Court Act, are authorized to administer oaths, take acknowledgments and sign the process of the court under the seal thereof.

(b) Copies of written authorizations to administer oaths required by section 58 of the New York City Criminal Court Act to be filed with the New York City Criminal Court are to be filed with the chief clerk thereof.

§ 200.8   Official forms.

The forms set forth in Chapter VI of Subtitle D of this Title, designated "Forms for use in courts exercising criminal jurisdiction," shall be the official forms of those courts and shall, in substantially the same form as set forth, be uniformly used throughout the State.

§ 200.9   Certificate of relief from disabilities; notification of eligibility.

(a) In all criminal causes, whenever a pre-sentence probation report is submitted to the court, such report shall contain information bearing upon the eligibility of the defendant to obtain a certificate of relief from forfeitures and disabilities under article 23 of the Correction Law and shall further contain a recommendation as to the appropriateness of granting such discretionary relief at the time sentence is pronounced. Whenever a defendant has been sentenced to a period of probation, and has not received such discretionary relief, and if such defendant is apparently eligible for consideration of such discretionary relief, the probation officer supervising such defendant, prior to the termination of the probation period, shall inform the defendant, of his right to make application to the court for a certificate of relief from disabilities, and shall provide such defendant with the required forms in order to enable him or her to make application to the court if he or she should wish to do so.

(b) In all criminal causes, whenever a defendant who is eligible to receive a certificate of relief from disabilities under article 23 of the Correction Law is sentenced, the court, in pronouncing sentence, unless it grants a certificate at that time, shall advise the defendant of his or her eligibility to make application at a later time for such relief.

(c) Failure to comply with the requirements of subdivision (a) or (b) of this section shall not affect the validity of any sentence.

RULES APPLICABLE TO SUPERIOR COURTS

§ 200.10   Applicability of sections 200.10–200.14.

The rules of these sections shall be applicable to each superior court.

§ 200.11   Assignment of criminal actions.

Criminal actions shall be assigned as follows:

(a) *General.* Except as the Chief Administrator of the Courts may otherwise provide, all criminal actions in Supreme Court and in County Court shall be heard and disposed of in accordance with an individual assignment system.

(b) *Arraignment-conference part.* The Chief Administrator of the Courts may authorize the establishment of an arraignment-conference part for any superior court. Where an arraignment-conference part has been established, upon commencement of a criminal action in the superior court, the action shall be assigned to such part. The judge presiding therein shall arraign the defendant and hear and determine any bail application. If no plea of guilty is entered within 14 calendar days of the defendant's arraignment, or if the judge presiding determines that it is unlikely that a plea of guilty will be entered, the action shall be assigned to a judge as provided in subdivision (c) of this section. If a plea of guilty is entered within such time period, the action shall remain in the arraignment-conference part for sentencing and any further proceedings therein.

(c) *Assignment of actions to individual assignment judges.* Except as provided in subdivision (b) of this section, upon commencement of a criminal action in the superior court, the action shall be assigned to a judge by the clerk of the court in which it is pending pursuant to a method of random selection authorized by the Chief Administrator. The judge thereby assigned shall be known as the "assigned judge" with respect to such action and, except as otherwise provided in subdivision (d) of this section, shall conduct all further proceedings therein.

(d) *Exceptions.*

(1) Where the requirements of matters already assigned to a judge are such as to limit the ability of that judge to handle additional cases, the Chief Administrator may authorize that new assignments to that judge be suspended until the judge is able to handle additional cases.

(2) The Chief Administrator may authorize the assignment of one or more special reserve trial judges. Such judges may be assigned matters for trial in exceptional circumstances where the needs of the courts require such assignment.

(3) Matters requiring immediate disposition may be assigned to a judge designated to hear such matters when the assigned judge is not available.

(4) The Chief Administrator may authorize the transfer of any action and any matter relating to an action from one judge to another in accordance with the needs of the court.

§ 200.12   Preliminary conference.

As soon as practicable after the assignment of an action to an individual assignment judge, the assigned judge shall conduct a preliminary conference. The matters to be considered at such conference shall include establishment of a timetable for completion of discovery and filing and hearing of motions, fixing a date for commencement of trial, and consideration of any other matters that the court may deem relevant. At the conclusion of the conference, the directions by the court to the parties and any stipulations by counsel shall be placed on the record or incorporated in a written court order. In the discretion of the court, failure of a party to comply with these directions shall result in the imposition of such sanctions as are authorized by law. The court may direct the holding of additional preliminary conferences as may be needed.

§ 200.13   Impaneling of grand juries.

There shall be a grand jury drawn and impaneled for such terms of a superior court as may be provided on the annual schedule of terms established by the Chief Administrator of the Courts. Whenever the public interest requires, additional grand juries may be drawn and impaneled as authorized by the Chief Administrator.

§ 200.14   Transfer of indictments between superior courts.

Upon authorization by the Chief Administrator:

(a) An indictment pending in the Supreme Court at a term held in a county outside the City of New York may, prior to entry of a plea of guilty thereto or commencement of a trial thereof, be removed to the County Court of such county.

(b) An indictment pending in a County Court may similarly be removed to the Supreme Court at a term held or to be held in the same county.

§ 200.15   Appointment of a special district attorney.

Any party filing with a superior court an application for appointment of a special district attorney, pursuant to section 701 of the County Law, shall make the application to the Chief Administrator of the Courts or to an appropriate Deputy Chief Administrative Judge. The Chief Administrator, Deputy Chief Administrative Judge, or appropriate Administrative Judge shall assign a superior court judge to consider the application as provided by law, selected from a list of judges established for that purpose that has been approved by the Chief Administrator and the Presiding Justice of the appropriate Appellate Division.

Amended eff. July 2, 2014.

§§ 200.16–200.19   [Reserved]

RULES APPLICABLE TO LOCAL CRIMINAL COURTS

§ 200.20   Applicability of sections 200.20–200.22.

The rules of these sections shall be applicable to each local criminal court.

§ 200.21   Procedure in local criminal courts; local court rules.

Procedure in each local criminal court shall be as provided by the Criminal Procedure Law and such local court rules as may be adopted in compliance with Part 9 of the Rules of the Chief Judge (22 NYCRR Part 9).

§ 200.22   Assignment of criminal actions.

Criminal actions in a criminal term shall be assigned to judges in a manner authorized by the Chief Administrator of the Courts.

§ 200.23   Recordkeeping requirements for town and village courts.

(a) Each town and village court shall maintain:

(1) case files containing all appears filed, orders issued, any minutes or notes made by the court of proceedings or testimony, and a copy of any original documents or papers forwarded to another court or agency;

(2) an index of cases with a unique number assigned to each case when filed; and

(3) a cashbook which shall chronologically itemize all receipts and disbursements.

(b) In each case, except for parking violations, the court shall assign a unique case number for each defendant. In addition to the papers filed and orders issued, the court shall maintain records which shall include the following information:

(1) the defendant's name, address, and date of birth if under the age of 19;

(2) the State law or local ordinance, including section number, of each offense charged;

(3) a brief description of each offense charged and the date of its alleged commission;

(4) the date of arrest;

(5) the name of the arresting agency or officer;

(6) the date of arraignment;

(7) the name and address of the prosecutor and the defendant's attorney;

(8) a record of the arraignment proceedings, including the following entries: whether the charges were read to the defendant; the constitutional and statutory rights of which defendant was advised; whether counsel was assigned; the plea entered by defendant; a summary of other actions taken by the court at arraignment, including the form of release and amount of bail set; and the date of the next scheduled appearance;

(9) the defendant's NYSID number and court control number, where available, for fingerprintable offenses;

(10) a summary of all other actions taken and proceedings conducted before trial;

(11) the names and addresses of all witnesses sworn;

(12) whether the defendant waived a jury;

(13) each disposition after trial, and each disposition other than by trial and the reasons therefor;

(14) whether a pre-sentence report was ordered and made available to the defendant or the defendant's attorney;

(15) any sentence imposed by the court; and

(16) a summary of all post-judgment proceedings.

(c) A model recordkeeping system which complies with the requirements of this Part will be prepared and distributed by the Office of Court Administration.

§ 200.24   Recordkeeping in city courts.

Each city court may, consistent with the provisions of section 2019 of the Uniform City Court Act, maintain records of all criminal actions and proceedings in accordance with section 200.23 of this Part.

§ 200.25   Procedure for accepting guilty pleas by mail in the New York City Criminal Court.

(a) *Establishment.* The Administrative Judge of the New York City Criminal Court may establish a procedure for accepting guilty pleas by mail whereby a defendant charged in an information with a designated petty offense defined outside of the Penal Law may enter a plea of guilty to such petty offense, and be sentenced by the Court to pay a fine and any applicable surcharge on the resulting conviction, without making a personal appearance in the action. For purposes of this section, the term "petty offense" shall have the same meaning as in subdivision (39) of section 1.20 of the Criminal Procedure Law.

(b) *Applicability.* The procedure established pursuant to subdivision (a) shall apply only where a defendant has been served with an appearance ticket in lieu of an arrest, returnable in the Summons Part of the New York City Criminal Court, for a petty offense defined outside of the Penal Law that has been specifically designated by the Administrative Judge of the New York City Criminal Court as appropriate for disposition under this section.

(c) *Appearance ticket; form and content.*

(1) The appearance ticket shall be in a form prescribed by the Administrative Judge of the

New York City Criminal Court, in consultation with appropriate criminal justice agencies, and shall be served upon the defendant by the issuing officer. The appearance ticket shall contain the nature of the charge, the range of applicable penalties if convicted of the charge, a procedure for pleading guilty by mail, and such other information as may be prescribed by the Administrative Judge.

(2) With respect to the procedure for the entry of a plea of guilty by mail, the appearance ticket shall contain the exact amount of the fine and surcharge to be imposed by the Court, and the manner in which and date by which such fine and surcharge must be paid. The appearance ticket also shall include a provision advising the defendant that, by entering a plea of guilty by mail to the charge, he or she:

(i) waives arraignment in open court, the right to receive a copy of the accusatory instrument and the right to the aid of counsel;

(ii) pleads guilty to the offense as charged;

(iii) understands that a plea of guilty to the charge is equivalent to a conviction after trial;

(iv) agrees that the charge be disposed of by payment of the fine and any applicable surcharge in accordance with the amounts designated in the appearance ticket; and

(v) understands that the Court may refuse to accept the plea of guilty, because of the defendant's prior criminal record or other special circumstance, in which case, if ultimately convicted, he or she may be sentenced to the full range of penalties set forth in the appearance ticket.

(d) *Procedure.* A defendant served with an appearance ticket pursuant to this section charging the defendant with a designated petty offense defined outside of the Penal Law may enter a plea of guilty by mail by indicating, in accordance with the instructions in the appearance ticket, that he or she pleads guilty to the charge, and by signing and mailing the completed ticket, by first class, registered or certified mail, to the Court at the address provided on the ticket, together with payment of the amount of the fine and surcharge set forth on the ticket for the offense charged. Provided an information has been filed charging such offense, the Court then may dispose of the case as though the defendant had been convicted upon a plea of guilty in open court, or, because of the defendant's prior criminal record or other special circumstance, may refuse to accept the plea of guilty. If the plea is so refused, the Court shall inform the defendant in writing that he or she is required to appear before the Court at a stated time and place to answer the charge, which shall thereafter be disposed of pursuant to the applicable provisions of law, and shall return to the defendant any fine or surcharge payment that may have accompanied the defendant's proffered plea of guilty. Where an information charging a designated petty offense is dismissed by the court, any plea of guilty to such offense entered pursuant to this section shall be refused, and the court shall inform the defendant of the fact of the dismissal and shall return to the defendant any fine or surcharge payment that may have accompanied the defendant's proffered plea of guilty. A plea of guilty to a designated petty offense that is refused pursuant to this section shall be deemed a nullity.

§ 200.26   Issuance of certain securing orders in town and village courts; duties of the court, assignment of and notification to counsel; notification to pretrial services agency.

(a) Where, following an arrest, a defendant is brought, pursuant to CPL § 120.90, 140.20 or 140.27, before a town or village court for arraignment on an accusatory instrument filed with such court, counsel for the defendant shall be given an opportunity to be heard before the court issues a securing order fixing bail or committing the defendant to the custody of the sheriff.

(b) If the defendant appears at such time without counsel, the court shall:

(i) permit the defendant to communicate free of charge by telephone for the purposes of obtaining counsel and informing a relative or friend that he or she has been charged with an offense.

(ii) prior to issuing a securing order fixing bail or committing the defendant to the custody of the sheriff, make an initial determination as to the defendant's eligibility for assigned counsel, provided, however, that this paragraph, as well as subdivisions (c) and (d) of this section, shall not apply where the court determines that the defendant has sufficient funds available to him or her to immediately post bail with the court in the amount and form to be fixed by the court, and such bail is so posted with the court.

(c) Where it appears, pursuant to paragraph (ii) of subdivision (b) of this section, that the defendant is financially unable to obtain counsel, the court shall, prior to issuing a securing order fixing bail or committing the defendant to the custody of the sheriff, assign counsel. Such assignment shall be in accordance with the plan for representation adopted by the county pursuant to County Law § 722, and shall, in accordance with such plan:

(i) direct the administrator of the assigned counsel program to, without delay, select and assign to the defendant, subject to the court's approval, an appropriate attorney from the administrator's list of eligible attorneys:

(ii) direct the local public defender office or legal aid society to represent the defendant; or

(iii) designate a named attorney to represent the defendant. Where assigned counsel is not present in court at the time of the assignment, the court may issue such securing order in the absence of counsel, and in such case shall provide the defendant, in writing, with the name, business address and telephone number of such assigned counsel, or of the administrator of the assigned counsel program or director of the local public defender office or legal aid society, as appropriate. Upon issuing such securing order in the absence of counsel, or, if not practicable, within 24 hours thereafter, but no later than 48 hours thereafter if extraordinary circumstances so require, the court shall notify such counsel, administrator or director, as well as the director of the local pretrial services agency or head of the pretrial services unit of the county probation department, if any, by telephone, and in writing or by written fax, of the court's assignment, and shall include in such notification the defendant's name, the names of any codefendants, the charge or charges contained in the accusatory instrument, the docket or case number, if available, the adjourn date and time, the terms of the securing order and such other information as the court deems appropriate. The court shall include with such written or faxed notification to such counsel, administrator of the assigned counsel program or director of the local public defender office or legal aid society a copy of the accusatory instrument.

(d) Where it appears, pursuant to paragraph (ii) of subdivision (b) of this section, that the defendant is financially able to retain counsel, the court shall inquire whether the defendant intends to retain counsel, and whether there is a particular attorney the defendant intends to retain. If the defendant identifies a particular attorney he or she intends to retain, the court shall, where such information is readily available, provide the defendant, in writing, with the telephone number of such attorney. Where the defendant does not identify a particular attorney, or where the attorney so identified is not present in court at the time the court intends to issue the securing order fixing bail or committing the defendant to the custody of the sheriff, the court may issue such securing order in the absence of counsel. Upon issuing such securing order in the absence of counsel, or, if not practicable, within 24 hours thereafter, but no later than 48 hours thereafter if extraordinary circumstances so require, the court shall notify the director of the local pretrial services agency or head of the pretrial services unit of the county probation department, if any, and the administrator of the assigned counsel program or director of the local public defender office or legal aid society, as appropriate, by telephone, and in writing or by written fax, of the defendant's appearance before the court and of the court's preliminary determination that the defendant appears to be financially able to retain counsel.

Such notification shall also include the defendant's name, the names of any codefendants, the charge or charges contained in the accusatory instrument, the docket or case number, if available, the adjourn date and time, the terms of the securing order and such other information as the court deems appropriate. The court shall include with such written or faxed notification to the administrator of the assigned counsel program or director of the local public defender office or legal aid society a copy of the accusatory instrument.

(e) Each town and village court shall obtain from the administrator of the assigned counsel program, public defender, legal aid society or other provider of indigent criminal defense legal services in that jurisdiction, and from the director of the local pretrial services agency or head of the pretrial services unit of the county probation department, if any, the names, addresses, telephone numbers and fax numbers required to effectuate the notification provisions of subdivisions (c) and (d) of this section.

(f) Nothing contained in this section shall be deemed to preclude the court from:

(i) terminating an assignment of counsel made pursuant to subdivision (c) of this section in accordance with the provisions of County Law § 722-d; or

(ii) issuing a securing order releasing the defendant on his or her own recognizance in accordance with CPL § 170.70, 180.80 or any other relevant provision of the Criminal Procedure Law; or

(iii) issuing a securing order releasing the defendant on bail or on his or her own recognizance in accordance with CPL § 30.30(2); or

(iv) entertaining an application for recognizance or bail made pursuant to CPL § 510.20.

(g) Nothing contained in this section shall be deemed to relieve the court of any obligation imposed pursuant to CPL §§ 170.10 and 180.10.

(h) Each town and village court shall maintain a record in the case file of any communications and correspondence initiated or received by the court pursuant to this section, and shall make such records available to the defendant's counsel and the prosecutor upon request.

(i) The Office of Court Administration shall prepare and distribute to each town and village court such forms as may be necessary to implement the notification provisions of this section.

§§ 200.27–200.29   [Reserved]

CRIMINAL APPEALS TO COUNTY COURTS

§ 200.30   Applicability of sections 200.30–200.33.

The rules of these sections shall govern procedures in appeals to county courts in criminal actions.

§ 200.31   Judges who may stay judgment pending appeal to county court.

Upon an appeal to county court from a judgment of sentence of a local criminal court, an order pursuant to CPL 460.50, staying or suspending execution of the judgment pending termination of the appeal and either releasing defendant on his own recognizance or fixing bail, may be issued by a judge of the county court to which the appeal has been taken or a justice of the supreme court in the judicial district in which the local court is located. In the case of any appeal as of right from a judgment or sentence of a city court, such order also may be issued by a judge of such city court.

§ 200.32   Duration of order staying or suspending execution of judgment.

(a) An order issued pursuant to CPL 460.50 shall contain a statement that, if an appeal has not been perfected within 120 days after the issuance of the order, the operation of such order terminates and the defendant must surrender himself to the criminal court in which the judgment was entered in order that execution of the judgment be commenced or resumed.

(b) No extension of the 120-day period specified in CPL 460.50 shall be granted except by the county court.

§ 200.33   Perfection of criminal appeals.

(a) When a notice of appeal is filed with a local court, a copy shall be filed with the county clerk by the person filing with the local court. After an appeal has been taken pursuant to CPL 460.10(2), and within 10 days after two transcripts of the stenographic minutes of the proceedings shall have been filed with the local criminal court pursuant to CPL 460.70(1), the local criminal court shall file with the clerk of the county court the notice of appeal, a transcript of the proceedings, a copy of the accusatory instrument and any decision on pretrial motions, and shall notify the appellant and the respondent. If the local criminal court does not file the notice of appeal and transcript within the prescribed period, or if the transcript is defective, the county court, upon application of appellant or respondent, shall order the local criminal court to file them or shall order the parties to settle the transcript before the local court in the manner prescribed by CPLR 5525(c) within a designated time which the county court deems reasonable.

(b) Within 20 days after the affidavit of errors and the return of the lower court have been filed with the county court, where an appeal has been taken pursuant to CPL 460.10(3), or within 20 days after the notice of appeal and transcript have been filed with the county court, where an appeal has been taken pursuant to CPL 460.10(2), appellant shall notice the appeal for the next term or special term of county court by filing with the judge of the county court, not less than 14 days prior to the date for which the appeal has been notice, a brief and notice of argument with proof of service of a copy of each upon respondent. If the defendant is the appellant and the district attorney did not appear in the local criminal court, defendant shall also file proof of service of a copy of the brief and notice of argument upon the district attorney. Respondent's brief, or the district attorney's brief, if any, shall be filed with the judge of the county court within 12 days after service of appellant's brief, with proof of service of a copy upon appellant.

(c) If appellant does not comply herewith, the county court may, upon respondent's motion, or upon its own motion, dismiss the appeal.

(d) Upon motion, the county court judge hearing the appeal may, for good cause shown, extend the time to a subsequent term or special term, in which case the appellant must notice the appeal for such subsequent term. Unless otherwise ordered by the court, appeals may be submitted without oral argument. Motions for reargument may be made after decision is rendered, and must be made within 30 days after service upon the moving party of a copy of the order entered on the decision, with written notice of its entry.

§§ 200.34–200.39   [Reserved]

§ 200.40   Obligation of the court to advise of right to counsel on People's appeal.

(a) When a criminal court issues an order suppressing evidence, dismissing an accusatory instrument, setting aside a verdict or sentence, vacating a judgment or denying a motion made pursuant to CPL section 440.40, where such order may be appealed as of right by the People pursuant to CPL § 450.20, the court promptly shall advise the defendant, on the record or in writing, (1) that the People have the right to take an appeal; (2) that the defendant has the right to retain counsel to represent him or her on the appeal or to respond to the appeal pro se; (3) if the defendant can show no financial ability to pay for the cost of counsel on appeal, the defendant may make application to the appellate court for assignment of counsel to respond to the appeal; and (4) that the defendant must provide the court and the defendant's trial counsel with an address where he or she can be contacted should the People appeal the order of the criminal court.

(b) In addition to the circumstances set forth in subdivision (a) of this section, where a court imposes a sentence, and where the People have indicated to the sentencing court their belief that the sentence is invalid as a matter of law and may be appealed by them on that ground, the court, upon imposing the sentence, shall advise the defendant of the rights enumerated in subdivision (a).

PART III
SENTENCING GUIDES

SENTENCING GUIDES

by Hon. Barry Kamins*

SYNOPSIS

---

* Hon. Barry Kamins, a retired Supreme Court Justice, is the author of *New York Search and Seizure* (LexisNexis Matthew Bender).

Sent. Gds.

I. INTRODUCTION TO USE OF THE SENTENCING GUIDES

The following guides are designed to assist the practitioner in understanding the sentencing statutes contained in the Penal Law and Criminal Procedure Law. These guides include classifications of felonies, misdemeanors, and violations as designated under the New York Penal Law. The terms of imprisonment for these crimes are enumerated, as are specified crimes for youthful and juvenile offenders.*

To use the Sentencing Guides, certain terminology should be defined:

(1) Indeterminate Sentence of Imprisonment (PL § 70.00(1)). An indeterminate sentence is imposed by the court for a felony. A minimum and a maximum period are fixed in the sentence, the maximum being the completion of the term. The minimum period may not be less than one year and the maximum period may not be less than three years.

(2) Definite Sentence of Imprisonment (PL § 70.15). A definite sentence is a term of imprisonment for a specific time not to exceed one year. Typically, such a sentence is imposed for misdemeanors and lesser crimes.

(3) Sentence of Intermittent Imprisonment (PL § 85.00). A sentence of intermittent imprisonment is a revocable sentence of imprisonment to be served on days or during certain periods of days, or both, specified by the court as part of the sentence. The duration of the sentence of intermittent imprisonment may be for any term that could be imposed as a definite sentence of imprisonment. The sentence of intermittent imprisonment may be used when: (1) the court is imposing sentence on a person other than a second or persistent felony offender, for a Class D or E felony or for any offense that is not a felony; (2) the court is not imposing any other sentence of imprisonment on the defendant at the same time; and (3) the defendant is not under any other sentence of imprisonment with a term in excess of 15 days imposed by any other court.

(4) Determinate Sentence (PL § 70.06(6)). A determinate sentence is a fixed period of years and fractions thereof, which must be imposed on: (1) first time violent felony offenders; (2) second violent felony offenders and (3) those individuals who are convicted of a violent felony and who also have a previous nonviolent felony conviction.

---

* For a chart outlining the New York court structure, see Part IV *infra*.

II. SENTENCING GUIDE FOR FELONIES

NOTE: *Class A felonies carry mandatory determinate sentences (for drug offenses) and mandatory indeterminate sentences (for non-drug offenses). Class B and Class C (violent) felonies carry mandatory determinate sentences. Certain Class C nonviolent felonies (PL § 60.05(4)) carry mandatory imprisonment which must be indeterminate sentences (no definite or intermittent) but Class C drug felonies also permit definite sentences (PL § 70.00(4)). All Class D felonies have permissible definite or intermittent terms of up to 1 year (see PL § 70.02(2)(b)). All Class E felonies have permissible definite or intermittent terms of up to 1 year (PL §§ 70.00(4), 85.00(2)(a), (3)). Where a definite sentence is permitted, a sentence from one day to six months incarceration plus probation (a "split" sentence) is permitted. (PL §§ 60.01(2)(d), 60.05(4), 70.00.) Where an intermittent sentence is permitted, a period of up to four months incarceration plus probation (a "split" sentence) is permitted. (PL § 60.01(2)(d).) Where imprisonment is not mandatory, a period of probation not to exceed five years may be imposed as well as the following sentences: probation plus a fine; an unconditional discharge; a conditional discharge of three years; a conditional discharge plus a fine. (PL §§ 60.01(2)(c); 65.00(1)(a), (3)(a); 65.20(1).)*

NOTE: *Effective February 1, 2001, probation periods for a felony sexual assault (PL art. 130 or 263 offense or incest) will be 10 years. The period for a misdemeanor sexual assault will be 6 years. (PL § 65.00(3); see Sexual Assault Reform Act, Chap. 1, Laws 2000.)*

NOTE: *Effective November 1, 2000, a court may enhance a sentence by 3 to 5 years when a defendant is convicted of a "specified offense" against a driver of a "for-hire" vehicle (PL § 60.07).*

NOTE: *Effective January 13, 2005, sentences for drug offenses have changed pursuant to PL §§ 70.70 and 70.71 (see chart).*

NOTE: *A determinate sentence includes a period of post-release supervision (PRS). For a person convicted of a Class B or Class C violent felony, PRS is from 2½ to 5 years; for a Class D or E violent felony, PRS is 1½ to 3 years. (See chart for PRS on felony drug offenses.) See Chap. 141, Laws 2008, for resentencing procedures involving post-release supervision.*

Sent. Gds.

Classification of Crime	Section	Term of Imprisonment	
CLASS A		**Minimum**	**Maximum**
I (Murder-1)	§ 125.27	A defendant can receive life imprisonment without parole or a minimum of 20 to 25 years and a maximum of life imprisonment. § 70.00(3)(a)(i)	

Classification of Crime	Section	Term of Imprisonment	
CLASS A		**Minimum**	**Maximum**
I (Excluding Murder-1)	§ 70.00(1)	Not Less than 15 yrs. Not More than 25 yrs. § 70.00(3)(a)(i)	Life § 70.00(2)(a)
Arson-1	§ 150.20	Not Less than 15 yrs. Not More than 25 yrs. § 70.00(3)(a)(i)	Life § 70.00(2)(a)
Kidnapping-1	§ 135.25	Not Less than 15 yrs. Not More than 25 yrs. § 70.00(3)(a)(i)	Life § 70.00(2)(a)
Conspiracy-1	§ 105.17	Not Less than 15 yrs. Not More than 25 yrs. § 70.00(3)(a)(i)	Life § 70.00(2)(a)
Aggravated Enterprise Corruption	§ 460.22	Not Less than 15 yrs. Not More than 25 yrs. § 70.00(3)(a)(i)	Life § 70.00(2)(a)
Sale Drugs-1 (A-I)	§ 220.43	Determinate Sentence between 8–20 yrs.	
Possession Drugs-1 (A-I)	§ 220.21	Determinate Sentence between 8–20 yrs.	
Sale Drugs-2 (A-II)	§ 220.41	Determinate Sentence between 3–10 yrs.	
Possession Drugs-2 (A-II)	§ 220.18	Determinate Sentence between 3–10 yrs.	
Predatory Sexual Assault (A-II)	§ 130.95	10 to 25 yrs. (first offense)	Life

Classification of Crime	Section	Term of Imprisonment	
CLASS A		**Minimum**	**Maximum**
		10 to 25 yrs. (second felony offender)	Life
		25 yrs. (persistent felony offender)	Life
Predatory Sexual Assault Against a Child (A-II)	§ 130.96	10 to 25 yrs. (first offense)	Life
		10 to 25 yrs. (second felony offender)	Life
		25 yrs. (persistent felony offender)	Life

NOTE: *When a defendant is convicted of Murder in the Second Degree and the victim is killed during the course of certain enumerated sex crimes, the victim is less than fourteen years of age and the defendant is over eighteen, the defendant must be sentenced to life imprisonment without the possibility of parole. PL §§ 60.06, 70.00(5)(3), 70.00(3)(a)(i), 125.25(5).*

NOTE: *For A-II drug felonies lifetime probation is permitted where defendant gives material assistance. PL §§ 60.05(3), 65.00.*

NOTE: *When a defendant is convicted of Aggravated Murder Involving a Child, the victim is under the age of fourteen, and the defendant is more than eighteen years old at the time of the crime, the sentence shall be life imprisonment without possibility of parole. PL § 125.26(2).*

NOTE: *A sentence of imprisonment imposed upon a person convicted of an A-1 felony shall run consecutively to a previously imposed, undischarged sentence of imprisonment. PL § 70.25(2–a).*

Classification of Crime	Section	Term of Imprisonment
CLASS B	§ 70.00	
Violent Felony	§ 70.02(1)(a)	Determinate Sentence between 5–25 years (for crimes committed after 9/1/98; prior crimes require an indeterminate sentence) § 70.02(3)

Sent. Gds.

Classification of Crime	Section	Term of Imprisonment
(1) Attempt to Commit A-I Felony, Murder-2	§ 125.25	

NOTE: *In domestic violence cases, can be an indeterminate sentence. Maximum sentence must be 6–25 years and minimum must be ½ maximum. § 60.12.*

(2) Kidnapping-2	§ 135.20	Determinate Sentence	
(3) Manslaughter-1	§ 125.20	between 5–25 years	§ 70.02(3)
(4) Burglary-1	§ 140.30		
(5) Arson-2	§ 150.15		
(6) Possession of Weapon-1	§ 265.04		
(7) Robbery-1	§ 160.15		
(8) Firearm Use-1	§ 265.09 (*but see* § 265.09(2))		
(9) Aggravated Assault on Peace Officer	§ 120.11		
(10) Intimidating a Victim or Witness-1	§ 215.17		
(11) Course of sexual conduct against a child in the first degree	§ 130.75		
(12) Gang assault in the first degree	§ 120.07		
(13) Assault in the first degree	§ 120.10		
(14) Crim. Firearm Sale-1	§ 265.13		

Nonviolent Felony	§ 55.05(1)	**Minimum**	**Maximum**

Classification of Crime	Section	Term of Imprisonment	
All other Class B felonies not enumerated above.		Not Less than 1 year (Minimum time cannot exceed ⅓ of the maximum term.) See § 70.00(2), (3)(b)	Not Less than 3 yrs. Not More than 25 yrs. § 70.00(2), (2)(b)

NOTE: *When a Class B second felony drug offender gives material assistance, lifetime probation is permitted. When a Class B felony drug offender gives material assistance, probation for 25 years is permitted.*

An individual who is convicted of Criminal Use of a Firearm in the First Degree, for using a weapon during the commission of a Class B violent felony for which the defendant is also convicted, must be sentenced to an additional consecutive sentence of 5 years which is added to the minimum term of the indeterminate sentence imposed on the underlying Class B violent felony, unless the court finds it would be "unduly harsh" to do so.

NOTE: *An enhanced sentence is required for a "hate crime." PL § 485.05.*

Sent. Gds.

Classification of Crime	Section	Term of Imprisonment
CLASS C		
Violent Felony	§ 70.02(1)(b)	Determinate Sentence between 3½ –15 years (for crimes committed after 9/1/98; prior crimes require an indeterminate sentence) § 70.02(3)
(1) Any attempt to commit Class B Violent Felony	§ 70.02(1)(b)	
(2) Burglary-2	§ 140.25	
(3) Robbery-2	§ 160.10	
(4) Weapon Possession-2	§ 265.03(3)	
(5) Firearm Use-2	§ 265.08	
(6) Crim. Firearm Sale—aid by minor	§ 265.14	

Classification of Crime	Section	Term of Imprisonment	
(7) Crim. Firearm Sale—to minor	§ 265.16		
(8) Gang assault in the second degree	§ 120.06		
(9) Assault on a peace officer, police officer, fireman or emergency medical service professional	§ 120.08		

Classification of Crime	Section	Term of Imprisonment	
Nonviolent Felony *(NOTE: See PL § 60.05 for various classifications)*	§ 55.05(1)	**Minimum** Not Less than 1 yr. Not More than ⅓ of maximum (See PL § 70.00) (Exception: Manslaughter-2, where victim is operator of "for hire" vehicle— PL § 60.07)	**Maximum** Not Less than 3 yrs. Not More than 15 yrs.

NOTE: *In domestic violence cases, can be an indeterminate sentence. Maximum must be 4½ –15 years and minimum must be ½ maximum. PL § 60.12.*

NOTE: *Definite sentence is permitted in Class C drug conviction; thus split sentence is also permitted. PL §§ 60.01(2)(d), 60.05(4), 70.00.*

NOTE: *Enhanced sentence if victim is operator of a "for hire" vehicle. PL § 60.07.*

Classification of Crime	Section	Term of Imprisonment
CLASS D		
Violent Felony	§ 70.02(1)(c)	Determinate Sentence between 2–7 years (for crimes committed after 9/1/98; prior crimes require an indeterminate sentence) § 70.02(3)
(1) Assault-2	§ 120.05	

Classification of Crime	Section	Term of Imprisonment
(2)	Crim. Firearm Sale-2	§ 265.12
(3)	Attempt to Commit Any Class C Violent Felony	§ 70.02(1)(c)
(4)	Intimidating Witness/Victim-2	§ 215.16
(5)	Aggravated Sexual Abuse in the Third Degree	§ 130.66
(6)	Reckless Assault of a Child	§ 120.02

NOTE: *In domestic violence cases, can be an indeterminate sentence. Maximum must be 3–7 years and minimum must be ½ maximum. PL § 60.12.*

NOTE: *The following D violent felonies carry mandatory jail sentences, but can be satisfied in several ways:*

Assault-2: definite sentence available as well as an intermittent sentence of up to four months plus probation or a definite jail sentence of up to 6 months plus probation. PL §§ 70.00(4), 70.02(2)(b), (c), 85.00(2)(a), (3).

Nonviolent Felony	§ 55.05(1)	Minimum	Maximum
		Not Less than 1 year	Not less than 3 yrs.
		Not More than 2⅓ yrs.	Not More than 7 yrs.
		(Minimum time cannot exceed ⅓ maximum term) § 70.00(3)	§ 70.00(2)

NOTE: *(See PL § 60.05(5)). Class D nonviolent felonies carry the same range of sentences as Class D violent felonies, i.e., definite and intermittent sentences are permitted.*

Classification of Crime	Section	Term of Imprisonment	

CLASS E

| Violent Felony | § 70.02(1)(d) | Determinate Sentence between 1½ to 4 years (for crimes committed after 9/1/98; prior crimes require an indeterminate sentence)   § 70.02(3) | |

NOTE: *A lesser term may be imposed for a definite period. (See PL §§ 70.00(4), 85.00(2)(a), (3)).*

NOTE: *In domestic violence cases, can be an indeterminate sentence. Maximum must be 3–4 years and minimum must be ½ maximum, PL § 60.12.*

Nonviolent Felony	§ 55.05(1)	**Minimum**	**Maximum**
		Not Less than 1 year (Minimum time may not exceed ⅓ maximum term) See § 70.00(3)(b), (4)	Not Less than 3 yrs. Not More than 4 yrs. § 70.00(2)(e)

NOTE: *Class E violent and nonviolent offenses carry definite and intermittent sentences.*

A. JAIL SENTENCES FOR FELONY DRUG OFFENSES (PL §§ 70.70, 70.71)

Effective April 7, 2009, for crimes committed on or after that date.

The following are determinate sentences:

Class A-I Felony

First Offender:	8–20 years
Prior Nonviolent Felony:	12–24 years
Prior Violent Felony:	15–30 years

Class A-II Felony

First Offender:	3–10 years
Prior Nonviolent Felony:	6–14 years
Prior Violent Felony:	8–17 years

Class B Felony

First Offender:	1–9 years (2–9 years if near a school)
Prior Nonviolent Felony:	2–12 years
Prior Violent Felony:	6–15 years

Class C Felony

First Offender:	1–5½ years
Prior Nonviolent Felony:	1½–8 years
Prior Violent Felony:	3½ –9 years

Class D Felony

First Offender:	1–2½ years
Prior Nonviolent Felony:	1½ –4 years
Prior Violent Felony:	2½ –4½ years

Class E Felony

First Offender:	1–1½ years
Prior Nonviolent Felony:	1½ –2 years
Prior Violent Felony:	2–2½ years

Sent. Gds.

A. JAIL SENTENCES FOR FELONY DRUG OFFENSES (PL §§ 70.70, 70.71)

Post-Release Supervision Periods

Class A-I and Class A-II Offender:	5 years
Class B or C First Offender:	1–2 years
Class D or E First Offender:	1 year
Class B or C Second Offender (prior nonviolent felony):	1½ –3 years
Class D or E Second Offender (prior nonviolent felony):	1–2 years
Class B or C Violent Felony Offender (prior violent felony):	1½–3 years
Class D or E Violent Felony Offender (prior violent felony):	1–2 years

NOTE: *1) The weight thresholds for Class A-I and A-II possession crimes have been doubled from 4 ounces to 8 ounces for class A-I felonies and from 2 ounces to 4 ounces for class A-II felonies.*

2) Class A-I felony offenders serving sentences of 15–25 years to life can apply for a resentencing consistent with the new sentencing structure for A-I felonies. An inmate can appeal either a denial of a resentencing application or a grant of resentencing with which the inmate does not agree.

*3) Class A-II felony offenders can also apply for a resentencing consistent with the new sentencing structure of A-II felonies. The resentencing provision applies to those inmates who are more than three years from a parole eligibility date (and 12 months from work release eligibility) and who are **eligible** for merit time.*

4) When a defendant is sentenced on a conviction for a drug felony and receives a state prison sentence, the court must, on motion of the defendant, order the Department of Correctional Services to enroll the defendant in a comprehensive alcohol and substance abuse treatment program provided that the defendant satisfies the eligibility criteria (see Corr. Law § 2(18) and PL § 60.04(6)).

5) Effective April 7, 2009, probation is available, over the objection of the prosecutor, to first-time Class B felony drug offenders and Class C second felony drug offenders with a prior nonviolent felony conviction.

6) Effective April 7, 2009, Class B felony drug offenders are eligible for a definite sentence of one year or less.

B.   **SECOND FELONY OFFENDER** (Where second felony is not a violent felony offense and first felony is either a nonviolent or violent felony)

Classification of Crime	Section	Term of Imprisonment	
		Minimum	**Maximum**
Class B			
(Nonviolent)	§ 70.06	Minimum time may not exceed ½ maximum § 70.06(4)(b)	Not Less than 9 yrs. Not More than 25 yrs. § 70.06(3)(b)
Class C			
(Nonviolent)	§ 70.06	Minimum time may not exceed ½ the maximum § 70.06(4)(b)	Not Less than 6 yrs. Not More than 15 yrs. § 70.06(3)(c)
Class D			
(Nonviolent)	§ 70.06	Minimum time may not exceed ½ the maximum § 70.06(4)(b)	Not Less than 4 yrs. Not More than 7 yrs. § 70.06(3)(d)
Class E			
(Nonviolent)	§ 70.06	Minimum time may not exceed ½ the maximum § 70.06(4)(b)	Not Less than 3 yrs. Not More than 4 yrs. § 70.06(3)(e)

NOTE: *Certain Second Felony Offenders are eligible for a sentence of "parole supervision." See PL § 410.91 (eff. Oct. 1, 1995).*

NOTE: *For a Class B "hate" crime, the maximum term of the indeterminate sentence must be at least 10 years. In addition, for the Class C felony of Manslaughter in the Second Degree where the victim was operating a "for hire" vehicle, the sentence is enhanced. § 60.07(1), (2).*

NOTE: *See chart for drug offense sentences.*

SECOND FELONY OFFENDER (Where second felony is a violent offense but first felony is not a violent offense)

Classification of Crime	Section	Term of Imprisonment
		Determinate Sentence Between
Class B VFO	§ 70.06(6)	8–25 yrs.
Class C VFO	§ 70.06(6)	5–15 yrs.
Class D VFO	§ 70.06(6)	3–7 yrs.

SECOND FELONY OFFENDER (Where second felony is a violent offense but first felony is not a violent offense)

Classification of Crime	Section	Term of Imprisonment
		Determinate Sentence Between
Class E VFO	§ 70.06(6)	2–4 yrs.

NOTE: *Sentence can be in fractions of years.*

NOTE: *See chart for drug offense sentences.*

C. SECOND VIOLENT FELONY OFFENDER

Classification of Crime	Section	Term of Imprisonment
		Determinate Sentence Between
Class B		
(Violent) *(Listed § 70.02(1)(a))*	§ 70.04(3)	10–25 yrs.
Class C		
(Violent) *(Listed § 70.02(1)(b))*	§ 70.04(3)	7–15 yrs.
Class D		
(Violent) *(Listed § 70.02(1)(c))*	§ 70.04(3)	5–7 yrs.
Class E		
(Violent)	§ 70.04(3)	3–4 yrs.

NOTE: *Sentence must be in whole or half years. PL § 70.04(2).*

NOTE: *There are enhanced sentences for Class B violent "hate crimes" and Class B or C violent felonies where the victim was operating a "for hire" vehicle. PL § 60.07(1).*

NOTE: *See chart for drug offense sentences.*

D. PERSISTENT FELONY OFFENDER (3 or more felony convictions).

NOTE: *Where defendant's conviction is a third felony conviction, the court may impose an indeterminate sentence authorized for a Class A-I felony (15–25 years to life). If the court does not impose an A-I sentence, then the court must sentence the defendant as a second felony offender.*

NOTE: *For a Class C felony of manslaughter in the second degree, there are enhanced sentences when the victim of the crime was operating a "for hire" vehicle. PL § 60.07(1).*

E. PERSISTENT VIOLENT FELONY OFFENDER

Classification of Crime	Section	Term of Imprisonment	

NOTE: *Where defendant's conviction is a third <u>violent</u> felony offense (as defined in PL § 70.02), the court <u>must</u> sentence the defendant as follows*

		Minimum	Maximum
Class B			
(Violent) *(Listed § 70.02(1)(a))*	§ 70.08	Not Less than 20 yrs. Not More than 25 yrs. § 70.08(3)(a)	Life § 70.08(2)
Class C			
(Violent) *(Listed § 70.02(1)(b))*	§ 70.08	Not Less than 16 yrs. Not More than 25 yrs. § 70.08(3)(b)	Life § 70.08(2)
Class D			
(Violent) *(Listed § 70.02(1)(c))*	§ 70.08	Not Less than 12 yrs. Not More than 25 yrs. § 70.08(3)(c)	Life § 70.08(2)
Class E			
(Violent)	§ 70.08	Not Less than 3 yrs.; Not More than 4 yrs. *See* People v. Tolbert, 93 N.Y.2d 86 (1999)	Life § 70.08(2)

NOTE: *For a Class B or C violent felony there are enhanced sentences when the victim of the crime was operating a "for hire" vehicle. PL § 60.07(1).*

Sent. Gds.

F. SECOND CHILD SEXUAL ASSAULT FELONY OFFENDER (eff. Feb. 1, 2000)

(Where a person stands convicted of a felony sex offense (PL art. 130 or 263 or § 255.25) involving a victim under the age of 15 and within the preceding 15 years (exclusive of time in jail) was previously convicted of a felony sex offense involving a victim under the age of 15 (PL § 70.07).)

Present Conviction	Predicate Conviction	New Sentence Range
Class A-II or B	Class A-II, B, or C felony	15–25 years to Life (indeterminate)
Class B	Class D or E felony	12–30 years (determinate)
Class C	Class A-II, B, or C felony	12–30 years (determinate) or 15–25 years to Life (indeterminate)
Class C	Class D or E felony	10–25 years (determinate)
Class D	Any degree felony	5–15 years (determinate)
Class E	Any degree felony	4–12 years (determinate)

NOTE: *A determinate sentence includes a period of post-release supervision. PL §§ 70.45(2-a)(j), 70.80(3).*

G. INCREASED SENTENCES FOR HATE CRIMES (eff. Oct. 8, 2000)

(When an individual is convicted of a specified offense that is found to be a hate crime (PL §§ 485.05, 485.10).)

Specified Offense	Minimum Sentence
A-1 Felony	20 years to Life
Class B Violent (first felony)	8 years (determinate)
Class B Violent (second felony)	12 years (determinate)
Class B Nonviolent (first felony)	6 years (indeterminate) i.e., 2 to 6 years
Class B Nonviolent (second felony)	10 years (determinate)
Class B (juvenile offender)	4 years (indeterminate) i.e., 1⅓ to 4 years

NOTE: *Courts are now authorized to require, as part of a sentence imposed for a hate crime, that a defendant complete a program, training session, or counseling session directed at hate crime prevention and education. PL § 485.10(5).*

H. PROBATION AND CONDITIONAL DISCHARGE

1. <u>Periods of Probation</u> (PL § 65.00(3))

H.   PROBATION AND CONDITIONAL DISCHARGE

(a) <u>Felonies</u>

Class A-II Drug Felony (PL art. 220) **when defendant cooperates**	Lifetime
Class B Drug Felony (PL art. 220) **when defendant cooperates**	25 years (PL § 220.48)
Felony Defined in PL art. 130 or 263 or PL § 255.25	10 years
Any Other Felony (see Note below for exceptions)	3, 4, or 5 years

(b) <u>Misdemeanors</u>

Class A Misdemeanor in PL art. 130 or 263	6 years
Any Other Class A Misdemeanor	2 or 3 years
Class B Misdemeanor in PL § 245.00 (Public Lewdness)	1–3 years
Any Other Class B Misdemeanor	1 year
Unclassified Misdemeanor	1 year (except 3 years if authorized definite sentence exceeds 3 months)

2. Periods of Conditional Discharge
(PL § 65.05(3))

Felony	3 years
Misdemeanor (A, B, and Unclassified)	1 year

NOTE: *A pre-sentence report is not required in cities with a population of one million or more, where a defendant is convicted of a misdemeanor when there is a negotiated sentence of 365 days or less.*

NOTE: *No probation permitted for:*
- *A - I drug felony.*
- *Non-Drug, Class A felony.*
- *Class B and C felony sex offenses under PL art. 130.*
- *Class B non-drug, non-sex, non-violent felony.*
- *Class A, B, and C violent felonies (certain Class D violent felonies require* *mandatory imprisonment).*

I.   CRIMES AGAINST POLICE OFFICERS AND PEACE OFFICERS (as defined in CPL §§ 2.10 and 2.15) (eff. Dec. 21, 2005)

New Crime	Maximum Sentence
Menacing a Police Officer or Peace Officer (Class D Violent Felony, PL § 120.18)	2 to 8 Years (determinate)
Aggravated Criminally Negligent Homicide (Class C Violent Felony, PL § 125.11)	3½ to 20 Years (determinate)
Aggravated Manslaughter in the Second Degree (Class C Violent Felony, PL § 125.21)	7 to 20 Years (determinate)

Sent. Gds.

I. CRIMES AGAINST POLICE OFFICERS AND PEACE OFFICERS (as defined in CPL §§ 2.10 and 2.15) (eff. Dec. 21, 2005)

New Crime	Maximum Sentence
Aggravated Manslaughter in the First Degree (Class B Violent Felony, PL § 125.22)	10 to 30 Years (determinate)
Aggravated Murder (Class A-1 Felony, PL § 125.26)	Life Without Parole
Attempted Aggravated Murder (Class B Violent Felony, PL art. 110, § 125.26)	20 to 40 Years to Life

J. INCREASED PENALTIES FOR CURRENT CRIMES AGAINST POLICE OFFICERS AND PEACE OFFICERS

Current Crime	New Sentence
Aggravated Assault of a Police Officer or Peace Officer (Class B Violent Felony, PL § 120.11)	10 to 30 Years (determinate)
Attempted Aggravated Assault of a Police Officer or Peace Officer (Class C Violent Felony, PL art. 110, § 120.11)	7 to 20 Years (determinate)

K. DEFINITIONS OF POSSESSION OR SALE OF FIREARMS (eff. Dec. 21, 2005)

Crime	New Definition
Criminal Sale of a Firearm in the First Degree (Class B Violent Felony, PL § 265.13)	10 guns sold on one occasion or a total of 10 guns sold in one year
Criminal Sale of a Firearm in the Second Degree (Class C Violent Felony, PL § 265.12)	5 guns sold on one occasion or a total of 5 guns sold in one year
Criminal Sale of a Firearm in the Third Degree (Class D Felony, PL § 265.11)	Becomes a D Violent Felony
Criminal Possession of a Weapon in the First Degree (Class B Violent Felony, PL § 265.04)	10 or more firearms
Criminal Possession of a Weapon in the Second Degree (Class C Violent Felony, PL § 265.03(2))	5 to 9 firearms
Criminal Possession of a Weapon in the Third Degree (Class D Violent Felony, PL § 265.02(5))	3 to 4 firearms

L. SENTENCES FOR FELONY SEX OFFENSES (eff. Apr. 13, 2007)

As of 4/13/07, sentences for all current felony sex offenses in PL art. 130 have been changed to permit an increase in post-release supervision. In addition, certain specified offenses not listed in PL art. 130 are deemed to be "sexually motivated felonies" if a person commits the offense for the purpose, in whole or substantial part, of his or her sexual gratification. These specified offenses are listed in PL § 130.91(2). As of 4/13/07, current sex felonies listed in PL art. 130 and "sexually motivated" felonies are known as "felony sex offenses." The sentences for felony sex offenses are listed below.

NON-VIOLENT CLASS B, C, D, E FELONY SEX OFFENSE
NO PRIOR FELONY (PL § 70.80(4))

Felony	Determinate Jail Sentence	Post-Release Supervision	Other Sentence
Class B	5–25 years	5–20 years	No
Class C	3½ –15 years	5–15 years	No
Class D	2–7 years	3–10 years	Probation or 1 year definite
Class E	1½ –4 years	3–10 years	Probation or 1 year definite

PRIOR NON-VIOLENT FELONY (PL § 70.80(5))

Felony	Determinate Jail Sentence	Post-Release Supervision	Other Sentence
Class B	8–25 years	10–25 years	No
Class C	5–15 years	7–20 years	No
Class D	3–7 years	5–15 years	No
Class E	2–4 years	5–15 years	No

PRIOR VIOLENT FELONY (PL § 70.80(5))

Felony	Determinate Jail Sentence	Post-Release Supervision	Other Sentence
Class B	9–25 years	10–25 years	No
Class C	6–15 years	7–20 years	No
Class D	4–7 years	5–15 years	No
Class E	2½ –4 years	5–15 years	No

VIOLENT CLASS B, C, D, E FELONY SEX OFFENSE
NO PRIOR FELONY (PL § 70.02)

Felony	Determinate Jail Sentence	Post-Release Supervision	Other Sentence
Class B	5–25 years	5–20 years	No
Class C	3½ –15 years	5–15 years	No
Class D	2–7 years	3–10 years	No
Class E	1½ –4 years	3–10 years	No

PRIOR VIOLENT FELONY (PL §§ 70.04, 70.06)

Sent. Gds.

L.   SENTENCES FOR FELONY SEX OFFENSES (eff. Apr. 13, 2007)

Felony	Determinate Jail Sentence	Post-Release Supervision	Other Sentence
Class B	10–25 years	10–25 years	No
Class C	7–15 years	7–20 years	No
Class D	5–7 years	5–15 years	No
Class E	3–4 years	5–15 years	No

III. SENTENCING GUIDE FOR MISDEMEANORS AND VIOLATIONS

Classification of Offense	Section	Jail Sentence	Non-Jail Sentence
CLASS A MISDE-MEANOR	§ 55.10 (2)(a)	Up to 1 year §§ 70.15(1), 85.00(2)(a), (3)	Probation (up to 3 years) (but see chart on previous page for exceptions); probation plus fine; probation plus up to 60 days in jail; probation plus up to 4 months intermittent sentence; conditional discharge (one year) with or without a fine up to $1000. PL §§ 60.01(2)(c), (d), (3)(d), 65.00(1), (3)(b), 65.03(3)(b), 65.05(1), 65.20(1)
CLASS B MISDE-MEANOR	§ 55.10 (2)(a)	Up to 3 months §§ 70.15(2), 85.00(2)(a)	Probation (up to one year) (but see chart on previous page for exceptions); all sentences for A misdemeanor except an intermittent sentence cannot exceed 3 months
UNCLASSIFIED MISDEMEANOR (Outside Penal Law where a sentence is provided)	§ 55.10 (2)(c)	Shall be in accordance with sentence specified in law that defines crime	Shall be in accordance with sentence specified in law that defines crime
UNCLASSIFIED MISDEMEANOR (Outside Penal Law where no sentence is provided)	§ 55.10 (2)(b)	Up to 1 year	Same as sentences for Class A misdemeanor
VIOLATION	§ 55.10(3) § 70.15(4) § 85.00(2) (a), (3)	Up to 15 days	Conditional discharge (up to 1 year); unconditional discharge; fine up to $250
MARIHUANA VIOLATIONS			

Classification of Offense	Section	Jail Sentence	Non-Jail Sentence
First Offense (no previous drug or marihuana conviction in 3 yrs.)	§ 221.05	None	Up to $100 fine
Second Offense (within 3 years)	§ 221.05	None	Up to $200 fine
Third Offense (within 3 years)	§ 221.05	Up to 15 days	Up to $250 fine

IV. SENTENCING GUIDE FOR JUVENILE OFFENDERS

PART I—CLASSIFICATIONS

Age	Class of Felony	Felony
13	Class A-I Felony	**Murder-2** (Excluding Felony Murder)
14, 15	Class A Felony	**Murder-2** (Felony Murder if Underlying Felony Is a Juvenile Offender Felony)
		Arson-1
		Kidnapping-1
14, 15	Class B Felony	**Aggravated Sexual Abuse** (§ 130.70)
		Arson-2
		Attempted Kidnapping-1
		Attempted Murder-2
		Burglary-1
		Manslaughter-1
		Rape-1 (§ 130.35)
		Robbery-1
		Criminal Sexual Act-1 (formerly Sodomy-1) (§ 130.50(1), (2))
14, 15	Class C Felony	**Assault-1** (Intentional § 120.10(1), (2))
		Burglary-2 (§ 140.25(1))
		Robbery-2 (§ 160.10(2)(a), (b))
		Crim. Poss. Weapon-2 (§ 265.03) (On School Grounds)
14, 15	Class D Felony	**Crim. Poss. Weapon-3** (§ 265.02(4)) (On School Grounds)

Sent. Gds.

TERMS OF IMPRISONMENT—JUVENILE OFFENDERS

Classification of Crime By Juvenile Offender	Mandatory Term of Imprisonment	
	Minimum	**Maximum**

NOTE: *Under PL § 70.05, there shall be an indeterminate sentence for the following felonies committed by a juvenile offender. Imprisonment is mandatory unless Youthful Offender Treatment is granted.*

(a)   Class A Felony

     (i)   Murder-2

	Minimum	**Maximum**
Intentional Murder	Not less than 7½ yrs. Not more than 15 yrs.	Life
Depraved Indifference Murder	Not less than 7½ yrs. Not more than 15 yrs.	Life
Felony Murder	Not less than 5 yrs. Not more than 9 yrs. § 70.05(3)(a)	Life
(ii) Arson-1 Kidnapping-1	Not less than 4 yrs Not more than 6 yrs. § 70.05(3)(b)	Not less than 12 yrs. Not more than 15 yrs. § 70.05(2)(c)
(b) Class B Felony	No more than ⅓ the Maximum Sentence § 70.05(3)(c)	Not less than 3 yrs. Not more than 10 yrs. § 70.05(2)(c)
(c) Class C Felony	No more than ⅓ the Maximum Sentence § 70.05(3)(c)	Not less than 3 yrs. Not more than 7 yrs. § 70.05(2)(d)
(d) Class D Felony	No more than ⅓ the Maximum Sentence § 70.05(3)(c)	Not less than 3 yrs. Not more than 4 yrs. § 70.05(2)(e)

V. SENTENCING GUIDE FOR YOUTHFUL OFFENDERS

WHO QUALIFIES AS A YOUTHFUL OFFENDER

Eligibility   (CPL art. 720)

A person is eligible for youthful offender treatment if he or she is between the ages of 14 and 19 at the time a crime is committed and stands convicted of any crime *except* an A-I or A-II felony. If a person stands convicted of an armed felony, Rape in the First Degree, Criminal Sexual Act in the First Degree (Sodomy) or Aggravated Sexual Abuse, a person is eligible if he or she can establish mitigating factors. A person is not eligible for youthful offender treatment if he or she has been sentenced on a prior felony conviction, was adjudicated as a youthful offender for a felony, or has a previous juvenile delinquent adjudication based on a Family Court Act Designated Felony.

TERMS OF IMPRISONMENT FOR YOUTHFUL OFFENDERS

Crimes by Youthful Offenders

Classification of Crime	Definite or Intermittent Term
(a) Misdemeanors	

(Note: There are no indeterminate terms allowed in the statute for misdemeanors by youthful offenders (see PL § 60.02(1)). Alternative, non-jail sentences, which are available to adult offenders, are available to youthful offenders.

(i) Class A	Up to 1 year for Discretionary Youthful Offenders (PL §§ 60.01(3)(a), 70.15(1)) Up to 6 months for Mandatory Youthful Offenders (CPL § 720.20(1)(b); PL § 60.02(2))
(ii) Class B	Up to 3 months for all Youthful Offenders (PL §§ 60.01(3)(a), 70.15(2))
(iii) Unclassified	A sentence of imprisonment for an unclassified misdemeanor shall be a definite sentence. When such a sentence is imposed, the term shall be fixed by the court and shall be in accordance with the sentence specified in the law or ordinance that defines the crime (PL §§ 60.01(3)(a), 70.15(3))

TERMS OF IMPRISONMENT FOR YOUTHFUL OFFENDERS
(Continued)

(b) Felonies	Section	Definite or Intermittent Term	Indeterminate Term	
			Minimum	**Maximum**
(i) Class B	§ 60.02 § 70.00	Up to 1 year § 85.00	Not less than 1 year Not more than 1⅓ yrs.	Not less than 3 yrs. Not more than 4 yrs.
(ii) Class C	§ 60.02 § 70.00	Up to 1 year § 85.00	Not less than 1 year Not more than 1⅓ yrs	Not less than 3 yrs. Not more than 4 yrs.
(iii) Class D	§ 60.02 § 70.00	Up to 1 year § 85.00	Not less than 1 year Not more than 1⅓ yrs.	Not less than 3 yrs. Not more than 4 yrs.
(iv) Class E	§ 60.02 § 70.00	Up to 1 year § 85.00	Not less than 1 year Not more than 1⅓ yrs.	Not less than 3 yrs. Not more than 4 yrs.

NOTE: *Alternative non-jail sentences, which are available to adult offenders for felony convictions, are available to youthful offenders.*

NOTE: *Consecutive terms of imprisonment cannot exceed the authorized maximum term of imprisonment (four years) for a Class E felony.*

VI. PLEA BARGAINING RESTRICTIONS
(Reduction of Charge)

A. Limitations on reducing a Felony complaint to a Misdemeanor.

When a local criminal court determines that there is reasonable cause to believe a defendant has committed either a Class A felony other than those defined in PL art. 220[*] of the Penal Law **or** any armed felony as defined in CPL § 1.20(41), the court **may not reduce** such felony to a misdemeanor. **See CPL §§ 180.50, 180.70.**

B. Post-indictment limitations on pleas of Guilty to a Felony charge under CPL art. 220.

Crime Charged	Lowest Possible Plea
Class A-I Felony (controlled substances as defined in PL art. 220)	Class B Felony (See CPL § 220.10(5)(a)(i))
Other Class A-I Felonies (except Murder-I)	Class C Violent Felony (See CPL § 220.10(5)(d)(i))
Class A-I Felony (Murder-I)	Class A-I (with consent of court and People; sentence of life without parole or 20–25 years to life)
Class A-II Felony (controlled substances as defined in PL art. 220)	Class B Felony (See CPL § 220.10(5)(a)(ii))
Class B Violent and Armed Felony	Class C violent felony offense (See CPL § 220.10(5)(d)(i))
Class B Violent Felony	Class D violent felony offense (See CPL § 220.10(5)(d)(ii))
Class B Felony (controlled substances as defined in PL art. 220)	Class D Felony (See CPL § 220.10(5)(a)(iii))
Any Other Class B Felony	Class E Felony (See CPL § 220.10(5)(b))

---

[*] For definitions and schedules of controlled substances, see Pub. Health Law §§ 3302 and 3306, reproduced in Part II *supra*.

Crime Charged	Lowest Possible Plea *(continued)*
Class C Violent Felony	Class D Violent Felony (See CPL § 220.10(5)(d)(ii))
Any Other Class C Felony	No limitations (**exception:** if defendant has predicate felony conviction, then Class E) (See CPL § 220.10(5)(c) and PL § 70.06)
Class C Violent Felony (Criminal Possession of Weapon-2d degree as defined in PL § 265.03(3))	Class D Violent Felony (PL § 70.02(2)(c), (4))
Class D Violent Felony (Criminal Possession of Weapon-3rd degree as defined in PL § 265.02(5), (7), or (8))	Class E Violent Felony (See CPL § 220.10(5)(d)(iv))
Any Other Class D Felony	No limitations (**exception:** if defendant has predicate felony conviction, then Class E Felony (See CPL § 220.10(5)(c) and PL § 70.06)
Class E Felony of Aggravated Harassment of an Employee by an Inmate	Class E Felony (See CPL § 220.10(5)(h))
Any Other Class E felony	No limitations (**exception:** if defendant has predicate felony conviction, then Class E Felony (See CPL § 220.10(5)(c) and PL § 70.06)

NOTE: *(1) A defendant may always plead guilty (as a matter of right) to the crime charged except for Murder-1. (See CPL §§ 220.10(2), (5)(e), 220.30(3)(b)(vii).)*

(2) A defendant may plead to a "lesser included offense" or any one of multiple counts in satisfaction of an entire indictment or in satisfaction of one or more other indictments. (See CPL §§ 220.10(3), (4), 220.30(3)(a)(i).)

(3) Consent of the District Attorney and the Court is required for all pleas except a plea of guilty to an entire indictment. (See CPL §§ 180.50, 180.70, 220.10(2), 220.30.)

VII. ADJOURNMENT IN CONTEMPLATION OF DISMISSAL IN FELONY CASES

(CPL art. 215)

NOTE: *Effective 11/1/02, a superior court can grant an adjournment in contemplation of dismissal, when the sole remaining count or counts of an indictment charge only a Misdemeanor offense and both parties consent. (CPL § 210.47.)*

(A) The court, with the consent of both sides, and with reasonable notice to the victim of the crime and an opportunity for the victim to be heard, and after arraignment of an action in a local criminal court or superior court, and before final disposition, may adjourn in contemplation of dismissal for the purpose of referring certain selected felonies (see below for exceptions) to a community dispute center, as established pursuant to Jud. Law art. 21-A. However, when the court makes a determination that an Adjournment in Contemplation of Dismissal is not proper for the reason outlined, *infra,* the court may restore the action in the time limits specified.

(B) <u>Who is not eligible</u>—defendant who is charged with:

    (a) a class A felony;

    (b) a violent felony offense as defined under PL § 70.02;

    (c) any drug offense as defined under PL art. 220;

    (d) a felony upon the conviction of which a defendant must be sentenced as a second felony offender or persistent felony offender as defined by PL §§ 70.04, 70.06, 70.08, or 70.10.

(C) <u>Restoration of Action to Calendar</u>

Situation	Time Limit
(a) Resolution Center must inform district attorney as to whether changes against defendant have been resolved.	Not more than 45 days
(b) Application to restore action to calendar upon determination that dismissal of accusatory instrument would not be in furtherance of justice.	Not more than 6 months
(c) Application to restore action where defendant has agreed to pay a fine, restitution or reparation and has failed to.	Not more than 1 year

Sent. Gds.

(D) <u>Action Not Restored To Calendar</u>

Situation

(a) No application made within 6 months to restore action to calendar; **or**—

(b) Defendant agreed to pay fine, restitution or reparation but has not paid such within one year of the issuance of an order adjourning an action in contemplation of dismissal.

Effect

Accusatory instrument deemed to have been dismissed by court in furtherance of justice at expiration of 6 months or one year period. The arrest and prosecution is deemed a nullity, and defendant is restored to status he or she was at before arrest and prosecution.

VIII.   MANDATORY SURCHARGE AND FEES

NOTE: *These are in addition to fines imposed after conviction for specific offenses.*

	Mandatory Surcharge	
Felony	Misdemeanor	Violation
$300	$175	$95
	Crime Victim Assistance Fee	
Felony	Misdemeanor	Violation
$25	$25	$25

Sex Offender Registration Fee: $50

DNA Databank Fee: $50

Supplemental Sex Offender Victim Fee: $1000 (imposed upon each person convicted of a felony or misdemeanor under PL art. 130)

NOTE: *A youthful offender sentence must include the crime victim assistance fee and the mandatory surcharge, but it must not include a DNA fee, sex offender registration fee, or supplemental sex offender victim fee (see PL §§ 60.02(3), 60.35, 60.35(10)).*

NOTE: *A court shall waive any mandatory surcharge and crime victim assistance fee when the court finds that a defendant is a victim of sex trafficking under PL § 230.34 or 22 U.S.C. ch. 78 (CPL § 420.35(2)).*

Sent. Gds.

IX. DRIVER'S LICENSE REVOCATION AND SUSPENSION

Based on certain convictions, a defendant's driver's license may be revoked or suspended. The following convictions will result in revocation or suspension for the period indicated:

Conviction	Action Taken
1) Homicide or Assault Arising out of Operating a Motor Vehicle	Revocation (VTL § 510(2)(a)(i))
2) Drug Conviction or Youthful Offender Adjudication for any Felony or Misdemeanor Under PL art. 220 or 221	6 mo. Suspension (VTL § 510(2)(b)(v)) (absent compelling circumstances)
3) Conviction or Youthful Offender Adjudication for Placing a False Bomb in the First Degree (PL § 240.62) or Falsely Reporting an Incident in the First Degree (PL §§ 240.60, 240.62)	6 mo. Suspension (VTL § 510(2)(b)(xii))
4) Conviction for Assault in the First, Second, or Third Degree When Committed Against a Traffic Enforcement Agent Employed by the City of New York or the City of Buffalo in the Course of the Agent's Duties	30–180 days Suspension (VTL § 510(2)(b)(iv))

PART IV
NEW YORK COURT SYSTEM CHART AND DIRECTORY

New York Court Structure

New York

Court of Appeals — COLR *S*

CSP Case Types:
- Appeal by right civil, administrative agency. Interlocutory appeals in civil, administrative agency.
- Appeal by permission criminal, civil, administrative agency. Interlocutory appeals in criminal, civil, administrative agency.
- Exclusive original proceeding judicial qualification, certified question.

link

Appellate Divisions of Supreme Court — IAC A *S*

CSP Case Types:
- Appeal by right criminal, civil, administrative agency. Interlocutory appeals in criminal, civil, administrative agency.
- Appeal by permission criminal, civil, administrative agency. Interlocutory appeals in criminal, civil, administrative agency.
- Exclusive original proceeding application for writ, bar/judiciary.

link

Appellate Terms of Supreme Court — IAC *S*

CSP Case Types:
- Appeal by right criminal, civil. Interlocutory appeal in criminal, civil.
- Appeal by permission criminal, juvenile. Interlocutory appeals in criminal, juvenile.

link

Supreme Court — GJC A *S*
Jury trials

CSP Case Types:
- Tort, contract, real property, miscellaneous civil.
- Exclusive marriage dissolution.
- Felony, misdemeanor.

link

County Court — GJC *S*
Jury trials

CSP Case Types:
- Tort, contract, real property ($0 - $25,000), civil appeals, miscellaneous civil.
- Criminal.

link

Court of Claims — LJC *S*
No jury trials

CSP Case Types:
- Tort, contract, real property.

link

District Court — LJC *S*
Jury trials except in traffic

CSP Case Types:
- Tort, contract, real property ($0 - $15,000), small claims (up to $5,000)
- Felony, preliminary hearings, misdemeanor.
- Traffic infractions, ordinance violations.

City Court — LJC *S*
Jury trials for highest level misdemeanor

CSP Case Types:
- Tort, contract, real property ($0 - $15,000), small claims (up to $5,000)
- Felony, preliminary hearings, misdemeanor.
- Traffic infractions, ordinance violations.

Family Court — LJC *S*
No jury trials

CSP Case Types:
- Guardianship.
- Support, paternity, adoption.
- Exclusive domestic violence.
- Exclusive juvenile.

Civil Court of the City of New York — LJC *S*
Jury trials

CSP Case Types:
- Tort, contract, real property ($0 - $25,000), small claims, (up to $5,000), miscellaneous civil.

link

Criminal Court of the City of New York — LJC *S*
Jury trials for highest level misdemeanor

CSP Case Types:
- Preliminary hearings, misdemeanor.
- Traffic infractions, ordinance violations.

link

Town and Village Justice Court — LJC *M*
Jury trials in most cases

CSP Case Types:
- Tort, contract, real property ($0 - $3,000), small claims (up to $3,000)
- Preliminary hearings, misdemeanor.
- Traffic/other violations.

link

Surrogates' Court — LJC *S*
Jury trials in probate/estate

CSP Case Types:
- Probate/estate.
- Adoption.

Legend

☐ = Appellate level
☐ = Trial level
↑ = Route of appeal

COLR = Court of Last Resort
IAC = Intermediate Appellate Court
GJC = General Jurisdiction Court
LJC = Limited Jurisdiction Court

A = Appeal from Admin. Agency
S = State funded
£ = Locally funded
M = Mixed: state and locally funded

AOC Web site:
www.courts.state.ny.us

Reprinted with the permission of the Court Statistics Project, National Center for State Courts (Williamsburg, VA).

COURT DIRECTORY

STATE-WIDE COURT ADMINISTRATIVE OFFICES

Office of Court Administration

25 Beaver Street–Room 852
New York, New York 10004
Honorable A. Gail Prudenti, Chief Administrative Judge
(212) 428-2700 (New York City Office)
Internet: http://www.courts.state.ny.us

Commission on Judicial Conduct

61 Broadway, New York, New York 10006
(646) 386–4800
Fax: (646) 458–0037
www.cjc@cjc.ny.gov (for all offices)

New York State Unified Court System Office of Court Administration
Empire State Plaza
Albany, New York
4ESP Suite 2001
Albany, New York 12223–1450
(518) 453-8560
www.questions@nycourts.gov

Lawyers' Fund for Client Protection

119 Washington Avenue
Albany, New York 12210
(518) 434-1935
(800) 442-3863
Fax: (518) 434-5641
E-mail: info@nylawfund.org
Internet: http://www.nylawfund.org

Department of State

One Commerce Plaza
99 Washington Avenue
Albany, New York 12231-1001
(518) 474-4752; (518) 474-6740
Fax: (518) 474-4597
E-mail: info@dos.state.ny.us; counsel@dos.ny.gov
Internet: http://www.dos.ny.gov

New York City Regional Office

123 William Street

Ct. Dir.

New York, New York 10038
(212) 417-5800
Fax: (212) 417-2383
www.dos.ny.gov

Division of Corporations and State Records

One Commerce Plaza
99 Washington Avenue
Albany, New York 12231-1001
(518) 473-2492
Fax: (518) 474-1418
State Records: (518) 473–0730
Uniform Commercial Code: (518) 474-4763
Fax: (518) 474-4478
Email: corporations@dos.ny.gov
Internet: http://www.dos.ny.gov

NEW YORK STATE COURTS
www.nycourts.gov (Information for all NYS courts)

Court of Appeals

Court of Appeals Hall
20 Eagle Street
Albany, New York 12207-1095
(518) 455-7700
Internet: http://www.courts.state.ny.us/ctapps

Appellate Division

First Department

27 Madison Avenue
New York, New York 10010
(212) 340-0400
Fax: (212) 889-4412
Hon. Luis. A Gonzalez

Second Department

45 Monroe Place
Brooklyn, New York 11201
(718) 875-1300
www.nycourts.gov/courts/ad2
Hon.Randall T. Eng

Third Department

Robert Abrams Building for Law and Justice
Empire State Plaza, Fifth Floor, Room 511
Albany, New York 12223

(518) 471-4777
Fax: (518) 471-4750
www.nycourts.gov/ad3/

mailing address:
Capitol Station
P.O. Box 7288
Albany, New York 12224–0288
Hon. Karen K. Peters

Fourth Department

50 East Avenue
Rochester, New York 14604
(585) 530-3100
www.nycourts.gov/courts/ad4
Hon. Henry J. Scudder

Court of Claims

Robert Abrams Building for Law and Justice
P.O. Box 7344
Capitol Station
Albany, New York 12224-0902
(518) 432-3411
Acting Chief Clerk: Scott M. Murphy
Fax for filing: (866) 413-1069
www.nyscourtofclaims.state.ny.us

26 Broadway, 10th Floor
New York, New York 10004
(212) 361-8100
Receptionist: (212) 361-8150
Fax: (212) 361-8163

COUNTY DIRECTORY

Albany County

(Third Department, Third Judicial District)
www.nycourts.gov

Supreme Court

Albany County Courthouse
16 Eagle Street Albany, New York 12207
(518) 285–8989
Fax: (518) 487-5020
County Clerk: (518) 487–5100

Criminal Court

Public Safety Building

One Morton Avenue
Albany, New York 12202
(518) 453–5520
Fax: (518) 453–8989

Surrogate's Court

16 Eagle Street
Albany, New York 12207
(518) 285–8585
Fax: (518) 462–0194

County Court

Albany County Judicial Center
6 Lodge Street
Albany, New York 12207
(518) 285-8777
Fax: (518) 487–3986

Family Court

30 Clinton Avenue
Albany, New York 12207
(518) 285-8600
Fax: (518) 462-4248

City Court

Civil Court

24 Eagle Street
City Hall
Albany, New York 12207
Civil Court: Room 209
Traffic Court: Basement
Civil (518) 453-4640
Traffic (518) 453-4630
www.nycourts.gov

97 Mohawk Street
Cohoes, New York 12047
(518) 453–5501
Fax: (518) 233-8202

No. 2 15th Street
Watervliet, New York 12189
Chief Clerk: Robin Robillard
(518) 453–5550
Fax: (518) 453-8995

Sheriff

16 Eagle Street
Albany, New York 12207
(518) 487-5400
Fax: (518) 487-5037

Allegany County

(Fourth Department, Eighth Judicial District)

Supreme Court

Courthouse
7 Court Street
Belmont, New York 14813–1084
Phone (585) 268-5800
Fax: (585) 268-7090

Surrogate's Court

Courthouse
7 Court Street
Belmont, New York 14813
(585) 268-5815
Fax: (585) 268-7090

County Court

Courthouse
7 Court Street
Belmont, New York 14813–1084
Phone (585) 268-5800
Fax: (585) 268-7090

Family Court

Courthouse
7 Court Street
Belmont, New York 14813
(585) 268-5876
Fax: (585) 268-7090

Sheriff

4884 State Route 19
Belmont, New York 14813-9506
(585) 268-9200
Fax: (585) 268-9484

Bronx County

(First Department, Twelfth Judicial District)

Supreme Court

Civil Term
851 Grand Concourse, Rm 217
Bronx, New York 10451
Civil Division: (718) 618-1400
Civil General Information: (646) 386-5700
Civil (718) 618-2561
Small Claims (718) 618-2517
Criminal Term
265 East 161st Street
Bronx, New York 10451
(718) 618–3100
Fax: (718) 618–3585
Internet: www.nycourts.gov

Surrogate's Court

851 Grand Concourse
Bronx, New York 10451
(718) 618–2300
Fax: (718) 537-5158

Family Court

900 Sheridan Avenue
Bronx, New York 10451
(718) 618-2098
Fax: (718) 590-7875

Civil Court

851 Grand Concourse
Bronx, New York 10451
General Information
(718) 618–2500
Fax: (718) 590-7294

Broome County

(Third Department, Sixth Judicial District)

Supreme Court

92 Court Street
Courthouse
Binghamton, New York 13901
(607) 240-5800

Fax: (607) 240–5940

Surrogate's Court

92 Court Street
Binghamton, New York 13901
Malmquist
(607) 240-5789

County Court

65 Hawley Street
Binghamton, New York 13901
(607) 240–5800
Fax: (607) 240–5940

Family Court

65 Hawley Street
Binghamton, New York 13901
(607) 240–5799
Fax: (607) 240–5904

City Court

City Hall Governmental Plaza
38 Hawley Street 5th Floor
Binghamton, New York 13901
(607) 772-7006
Fax: (607) 772-7041

Sheriff

155 Lt. Van Winkle Drive
Binghamton, New York 13905
(607) 778-1911
Fax: (607) 778-2100

Cattaraugus County

(Fourth Department, Eighth Judicial District)

Supreme Court

County Courthouse
One Leo Moss Drive
Olean, New York 14760
(716) 373-8035
Fax: (716) 373-0449

Surrogate's Court

303 Court Street

Little Valley, New York 14755
(716) 938-9111
Fax: (716) 938-6413
Chief Clerk: Christine Wrona
E-mail: cwrona@nycourts.gov

County Court

County Center
303 Court Street
Little Valley, New York 14755
(716) 938-9111, Ext. 388
Fax: (716) 938-6413
County Clerk: (716) 938-9111, Ext. 2297

Family Court

One Leo Moss Drive
Olean, New York 14760
(716) 373-8035
Fax: (716) 373-0449
Chief Clerk: Denise Filjones
E-mail: dfiljone@nycourts.gov

City Court

101 East State Street
P.O. Box 631
Olean, New York 14760
(716) 376-5620
Fax: (716) 376-5623
Acting Chief Clerk: Rhonda Eaton
Email: reaton@nycourts.gov.

225 Wildwood Avenue
Salamanca, New York 14779
(716) 945-4153, (716) 945-0573
Fax: (716) 945-2362
Chief Clerk: Stella S. Johnston
Email:ssjohnst@courts.state.ny.us

Sheriff

County Center
301 Court Street
Little Valley, New York 14755
(716) 938-2599

Cayuga County

(Fourth Department, Seventh Judicial District)

Supreme Court

152 Genesee Street
Auburn, New York 13021
(315) 237-6450
Fax: (315) 237–6451
Internet: www.nycourts.gov
County Clerk: (315) 253-1271

Surrogate's Court

152 Genesee Street
Auburn, New York 13021
(315) 237–6210
Fax: (315) 237–6211

County Court

152 Genesee Street
Auburn, New York 13021
(315) 237–6450
Fax: (315) 237–6451

Family Court

Old Historic Post Office Building
157 Genesee Street, 2nd Floor
Auburn, New York 13021
(315) 237–6400
Fax: (315) 237–6401

City Court

157 Genesee Street
Auburn, New York 13021
(315) 237-6420
Fax: (315) 237–6421

Sheriff

Public Safety Building
7445 County House Road
Auburn, New York 13021
(315) 253-1222
Fax: (315) 253-1192

Chautauqua County

(Fourth Department, Eighth Judicial District)

Supreme Court

Hon. Deborah A. Chimes
P.O. Box 292
3 North Erie Street
Mayville, New York 14757-0292
(716) 753-4266
Fax: (716) 753-4993
County Clerk: (716) 753-4835

Surrogate's Court

3 North Erie Street
Mayville, New York 14757
(716) 753-4339
Fax: (716) 753-4600

County Court

Courthouse
3 North Erie Street
P.O. Box 292
Mayville, New York 14757-0292
(716) 753-4266
Fax: (716) 753-4993

Family Court

2 Academy Street Suite 5
Mayville, New York 14757
(716) 753-4351
Fax: (716) 753-4350

City Court

Dunkirk City Court—City Hall
342 Central Avenue
Dunkirk, New York 14048-2122
(716) 366-2055
Fax: (716) 366-3622
Email: jdill@nycourts.gov

City Hall
Municipal Building
200 East 3rd Street
Jamestown, New York 14701
(716) 483-7561
Fax: (716) 483-7519

Sheriff

Sheriff's Office
15 East Chautauqua Street
Mayville, New York 14757
(716) 753-4232

Chemung County

(Third Department, Sixth Judicial District)

Supreme Court

Hazlett Building
224 Lake Street
P.O. Box 588
Elmira, New York 14902–0588
(607) 873–9450
Fax: (646) 963–6605

Surrogate's Court

224 Lake Street
P.O. Box 588
Elmira, New York 14902–0588
(607) 873-9440
Fax: (646) 963-6606
E-mail: 6juchmsurr@courts.state.ny.us

County Court

Hazlett Building
224 Lake Street
P.O. Box 588
Elmira, New York 14902–0588
(607) 873–9450
Fax: (646) 963–6605

Family Court

Justice Building
203–209 William Street
P.O. Box 588
Elmira, New York 14902–0588
(607) 873–9500
Fax: (212) 884-8950

City Court
City Hall
317 East Church Street
Elmira, New York 14901
(607) 873–9520

Ct. Dir.

Fax: (212) 401-9240
E-mail: ElmiraCityCourt@courts.state.ny.us

Sheriff

Justice Building
203-209 William Street
Elmira, New York 14901
(607) 737-2987
Fax: (607) 737-2930

Chenango County
(Third Department, Sixth Judicial District)

Supreme Court

Chenango County Court House
West Park Place
Norwich, New York 13815
(607) 337-1457
Fax: (917) 522–3477

Chenango County Office Building
5 Court Street
Norwich, New York 13815

Surrogate's Court

County Office Building
5 Court Street
Norwich, New York 13815
(607) 337-1827
Fax: (646) 983-6603

County Court

County Office Building
5 Court Street
Norwich, New York 13815
(607) 337-1825
Fax: (917) 522–3477
E-mail: cshell@courts.state.ny.us

Family Court

County Office Building
5 Court Street
Norwich, New York 13815
(607) 337-1824
Fax: (607) 337-1835

City Court

1 Court Plaza

Norwich, New York 13815
(607) 334-1224
Fax: (607) 334-8494

Sheriff

279 County Road 46
Norwich, New York 13815
(607) 334-2000

Clinton County

(Third Department, Fourth Judicial District)

Supreme Court

Clerk's Office

County Government Center
137 Margaret Street
Plattsburgh, New York 12901
(518) 562–1446
Fax: (518) 562–1792

Surrogate's Court

County Government Center
137 Margaret Street,
Plattsburgh, New York 12901
(518) 565-4630
Fax: (518) 565-4769

County Court

County Government Center
137 Margaret Street
Plattsburgh, New York 12901
(518) 565-4657
Fax: (518) 565–4887

Family Court

County Government Center
137 Margaret Street
Plattsburgh, New York 12901
(518) 565-4404
Fax: (518) 565-4688

City Court

24 U.S. Oval
Plattsburgh, New York 12903
(518) 563-7870

Fax: (518) 453-8624

Sheriff

25 McCarthy Drive
Plattsburgh, New York 12901
(518) 561-4300
Fax: (518) 565-4333

Columbia County

(Third Department, Third Judicial District)

Supreme Court

621 State Route 23 B
Claverack, New York 12513 (Temporary Courthouse)
(518) 267-3150
Fax: (518) 851–7615

Surrogate's Court

621 State Route 23 B
Claverack, New York 12513 (Temporary Courthouse)
(518) 267-3150
Fax: (518) 851–7615

County Court

621 State Route 23 B
Claverack, New York 12513 (Temporary Courthouse)
(518) 267-3150
Fax: (518) 851–7615

Family Court

621 State Route 23 B
Claverack, New York 12513 (Temporary Courthouse)
(518) 267-3150
Fax: (518) 851–7615

City Court

429 Warren Street
Hudson, New York 12534
(518) 828-3100
Fax: (518) 828–3628
E-mail: HudsonCityCourt@nycourts.gov

Sheriff

85 Industrial Tract
Hudson, New York 12534

Emergency: (518) 828-3344
Business: (518) 828-0601

Cortland County
(Third Department, Sixth Judicial District)

Supreme Court

46 Greenbush Street, Suite 301
Cortland, New York 13045–2772
(607) 753-5013
Fax: (646) 963-6452 (Chief Clerk)
E-mail: kjordan@nycourts.gov

Surrogate's Court

46 Greenbush Street, Suite 301
Cortland, New York 13045–2725
(607) 753-5355
Fax: (212) 457-2661 (Chief Clerk)
E-mail: lday@courts.state.ny.us

County Court

46 Greenbush Street, Suite 301
Cortland, New York 13045–2772
(607) 753-5013
Fax: (646) 963-6452
E-mail: kjordan@courts.state.ny.us

Family Court

46 Greenbush Street, Suite 301
Cortland, New York 13045–2772
(607) 753-5353
Fax: (646) 963-6452
E-mail: lcase@courts.state.ny.us

City Court

City Hall
25 Court Street
Cortland, New York 13045
(607) 428-5420
Fax: (607) 428-5435

Sheriff

Courthouse
54 Greenbush Street
Cortland, New York 13045-5590

Ct. Dir.

Fax: (607) 758–6150

Delaware County

(Third Department, Sixth Judicial District)

Supreme Court

Delaware County Courthouse
3 Court Street
Delhi, New York 13753
(607) 746-2131
Fax: (646) 963–6402

Surrogate's Court

Delaware County Courthouse
3 Court Street
Delhi, New York 13753
(607) 746-2126
Fax: (646) 963–6403

County Court

Delaware County Courthouse
3 Court Street
Delhi, New York 13753
(607) 746-2131
Fax: (646) 963–6402

Family Court

Delaware County Courthouse
3 Court Street
Delhi, New York 13753
(607) 746-2298
Fax: (646) 963–6400

Sheriff

280 Phoebe Lane
Suite 1
Delhi, New York 13753
(607) 746-2336
(607) 746-2632

Dutchess County

(Second Department, Ninth Judicial District)

Supreme Court

10 Market Street

Poughkeepsie, New York 12601
(845) 431–1710
Fax: (845) 431–1743

Surrogate's Court

10 Market Street
Poughkeepsie, New York 12601
(845) 431–1770
Fax: (845) 476-3659

County Court

10 Market Street
Poughkeepsie, New York 12601
(845) 431–1710
Fax: (845) 431–1743

Family Court

50 Market Street
Poughkeepsie, New York 12601
(845) 431–1850
Fax: (845) 486-2510

City Court

1 Municipal Plaza
Suite 2
Beacon, New York 12508
Phone:(845) 431–1900
Fax: (845) 838–5041

62 Civic Center Plaza
Poughkeepsie, New York 12601
(845) 483–8200
Fax: (845) 451-4094

Sheriff

150 North Hamilton Street
Poughkeepsie, New York 12601
(845) 486-3800
Fax: (845) 452-2987

Erie County

(Fourth Department, Eighth Judicial District)

Supreme Court

25 Delaware Avenue
Buffalo, New York 14202

(716) 845-9300
Fax: (716) 851-3293

Surrogate's Court

92 Franklin Street
Buffalo, New York 14202
(716) 845-2560
Fax: (716) 845–7565

County Court

25 Delaware Avenue
Buffalo, New York 14202
(716) 845-9300
Fax: (716) 851-3293

Family Court

1 Niagara Plaza
Buffalo, New York 14202
(716) 845-7400
Fax: (716) 858-8432

City Court

50 Delaware Avenue
Buffalo, New York 14202
(716) 845-2600
Fax: (716) 847-8257
E-mail: sthomas@nycourts.gov

City Hall

714 Ridge Road
Lackawanna, New York 14218
(716) 827–6486
Fax: (716) 825–1874

City Hall

200 Niagara Street
Tonawanda, New York 14150
(716) 845-2160
Fax: (716) 845-7590

Sheriff

10 Delaware Avenue
Buffalo, New York 14202
(716) 858-7608

Essex County

(Third Department, Fourth Judicial District)

Supreme Court

7559 Court Street
P.O. Box 217
Elizabethtown, New York 12932
(518) 873-3370
Fax: (518) 451–8738

Surrogate's Court

7559 Court Street
Elizabethtown, New York 12932
(518) 873-3384
Fax: (518) 451–8740

County Court

7559 Court Street
P.O. Box 217
Elizabethtown, New York 12932
(518) 873-3370
Fax: (518) 451–8738

Family Court

7559 Court Street
P.O. Box 217
Elizabethtown, New York 12932
(518) 873-3320
Fax: (518) 451-8739

Sheriff

702 Stowersville Road
Lewis, New York 12950
(518) 873-6321

Franklin County

(Third Department, Fourth Judicial District)

Supreme Court

355 West Main Street
Malone, New York 12953
(518) 285-8788
Fax: (518) 285-4513

Surrogate's Court

355 West Main Street

Malone, New York 12953
(518) 481-1736
Fax: (518) 481-1443

County Court

355 West Main Street
Malone, New York 12953
(518) 481-1732
Fax: (518) 481-6704

Family Court

355 West Main Street
Malone, New York 12953
(518) 481-1742
Fax: (518) 481–5453

Commissioner of Jurors

Courthouse
355 West Main Street
Malone, New York 12953
(518) 481-1756
Fax: (518) 481-6204

Sheriff

Courthouse
45 Bare Hill Road
Malone, New York 12953
(518) 483-3304

Fulton County

(Third Department, Fourth Judicial District)

Supreme Court

223 West Main Street
Johnstown, New York 12095
(518) 736-5662
Fax: (518) 762-5078

Surrogate's Court

223 West Main Street
Johnstown, New York 12095
(518) 736-5685
Fax: (518) 451–8746

County Court

223 West Main Street

Johnstown, New York 12095
(518) 736-5662
Fax: (518) 762-5078

Family Court

11 North William Street
Johnstown, New York 12095
(518) 762-3840
Fax: (518) 451–8745

City Court

City Hall
3 Frontage Road
Gloversville, New York 12078
(518) 773-4527
Fax: (518) 773-4599

City Hall
33-41 East Main Street
Johnstown, New York 12095
(518) 762-0007
(518) 453-8651

Sheriff

2712 State Highway 29
P.O. Box 20
Johnstown, New York 12095
(518) 736-2100
Fax: (518) 736-2126

Genesee County

(Fourth Department, Eighth Judicial District)

Supreme Court

Courts Facility Building
1 West Main Street
Batavia, New York 14020
(585) 344-2550
Fax: (585) 344-8517

Surrogate's Court

Courts Facility Building
1 West Main Street
Batavia, New York 14020
(585) 344-2550
Fax: (585) 344-8517

County Court

Courts Facility Building
1 West Main Street
Batavia, New York 14020
(585) 344-2550
Fax: (585) 344-8517

Family Court

Courts Facility Building
1 West Main Street
Batavia, New York 14020
(585) 344-2550, ext. 2233
Fax: (585) 344-8520

City Court

Courts Facility Building
1 West Main Street
Batavia, New York 14020
(585) 344-2550, ext. 2417
Fax: (585) 344-8556

Sheriff

165 Park Road
Batavia, New York 14020-1283
(585) 345–3000
Fax: (585) 343-9129

Greene County

(Third Department, Third Judicial District)

Supreme Court

320 Main Street
Catskill, New York 12414
Michelle Carroll, Chief Clerk
(518) 625–3160

Surrogate's Court

320 Main Street
Catskill, New York 12414
(518) 625–3150

County Court

320 Main Street
Catskill, New York 12414
(518) 625–3160

Family Court

320 Main Street
Catskill, New York 12414
(518) 625–3180

Sheriff

80 Bridge Street
Catskill, New York 12414
(518) 943-3300
Fax: (518) 943-6832

Hamilton County

(Third Department, Fourth Judicial District)

Supreme Court

No sessions held *(See Fulton County for information)*
Hamilton County Court Law Library
Hamilton County Court House
102 County View Drive
Lake Pleasant, New York 12108
(518) 736-5539
Fax: (518) 451-8744

Surrogate's Court
mailing address:
139 White Birch Lane P.O. Box 780
Indian Lake, New York 12842-0780
(518) 648–5411
Fax: (518) 453-8687

Court sessions held at:
223 W. Main Street
Johnstown, New York 12095
(518) 736–5539
Fax: (518) 451–8744

County Court
mailing address:
139 White Birch Lane P.O. Box 780
Indian Lake, New York 12842-0780
(518) 648–5411
Fax: (518) 453–8687

Court sessions held at: 223 W. Main Street
Johnstown, New York 12095
(518) 736–5539
Fax:(518) 451-8744

Family Court
mailing address:
139 White Birch Lane
P.O. Box 780
Indian Lake, New York 12842-0780
(518) 648–5411
Fax: (518) 453-8687

Court sessions held at:
233 W. Main Street
Johnstown, New York 12095
(518) 736-5539
Fax: (518) 451–8744

Sheriff

P.O. Box 210
102 County View Drive
Lake Pleasant, New York 12108
(518) 548-3113
Fax: (518) 548-5704

Herkimer County

(Fourth Department, Fifth Judicial District)

Supreme Court

Herkimer County Office and Courts Facility
301 North Washington Street
Herkimer, New York 13350
Civil Phone: (315) 867-1209
Criminal Phone: (315) 867-1282
Fax: (315) 866-1802

Surrogate's Court

Herkimer County Office and Courts Facility
301 North Washington Street
Herkimer, New York 13350
(315) 867-1170
Fax: (315) 866-1722

County Court

Herkimer County Office and Courts Facility
301 North Washington Street
Herkimer, New York 13350
Civil Phone: (315) 867-1175
Criminal Phone: (315) 867-1282
Fax: (315) 866-1722

Family Court

Herkimer County Office and Court Facility
301 North Washington Street, Suite 2501
Herkimer, New York 13350–2935
(315) 867-1139
Fax: (315) 867-1369

City Court

City Hall
659 East Main Street
Little Falls, New York 13365
(315) 823-1690
Fax: (315) 266–4711

Sheriff

320 North Main Street
Herkimer, New York 13350
(315) 867-1167
Fax: (315) 867-1354

Jefferson County

Fourth Department, Fifth Judicial District)

Supreme Court

Dulles State Office Building
317 Washington Street
Watertown, New York 13601
(315) 785-7906
Fax: (315) 266–4779

Surrogate's Court

Jefferson County Court Complex
163 Arsenal Street
Watertown, New York 13601
(315) 785-3019
Fax: (315) 785-5194

County Court

Jefferson County Court Complex
163 Arsenal Street
Watertown, New York 13601
(315) 785-3044
Fax: (315) 786-7409

Family Court

Jefferson County Court Complex

163 Arsenal Street
Watertown, New York 13601
(315) 785-3001
Fax: (315) 266–4776

City Court

Municipal Building, 245 Washington Street
Watertown, New York 13601
(315) 785-7785
Fax: (315) 785-7856

Sheriff

753 Waterman Drive
Watertown, New York 13601
(315) 788–1441
Fax: (315) 786-2709

Kings County

(Second Department, Second Judicial District)

Supreme Court

Civil Term
360 Adams Street
Brooklyn, New York 11201
(718) 675–7699

Criminal Term

320 Jay Street
Brooklyn, New York 11201
(347) 296-1076

Surrogate's Court

2 Johnson Street
Brooklyn, New York 11201
Public access may be had through Supreme Court, Kings County main
entrance at 360 Adams Street
(347) 404-9700
Fax: (718) 643-6237

Family Court

330 Jay Street
Brooklyn, New York 11201
(347) 401-9600
Fax: (347) 401-9609

Civil Court

141 Livingston Street

Brooklyn, New York 11201
General Information: (212) 791–6000
Civil: (347) 404–9123
Housing General Information: (347) 404-9201
Red Hook—Housing: (718) 923–8270
Small Claims: (347) 404-9021

Criminal Court

120 Schermerhorn Street
Brooklyn New York 11201
(646) 386-4500
Fax: (718) 643-7733

Under Sheriff

Municipal Building
210 Joralemon Street
Brooklyn, New York 11201
(718) 802-3545
Fax: (718) 802-3715

Lewis County

(Fourth Department, Fifth Judicial District)

Supreme Court

7660 North State Street
Lowville, New York 13367
(315) 376-5366
Fax: (315) 376-4145

Surrogate's Court

7660 North State Street, Second Floor
Lowville, New York 13367
(315) 376-5344
Fax: (315) 376-1647

County Court

7660 North State Street, Third Floor
Lowville, New York 13367
(315) 376-5380
Fax: (315) 376-1656

Family Court

7660 State Street, First Floor
Lowville, New York 13367
(315) 376-5345

Fax: (315) 376-5189

Sheriff

Public Safety Building
5252 Outer Stowe Street
P.O. Box 233
Lowville, New York 13367
(315) 376-3511
Fax: (315) 376-5232

Livingston County

(Fourth Department, Seventh Judicial District)

Supreme Court

2 Court Street
Geneseo, New York 14454–1030
(585) 371–3920
Fax: (585) 371–3935

Surrogate's Court

2 Court Street
Geneseo, New York 14454
(585) 371–3921
Fax: (585) 371–3936

County Court

2 Court Street
Geneseo, New York 14454
(585) 371–3920
Fax: (585) 371–3935

Family Court

2 Court Street
Geneseo, New York 14454
(585) 371–3919
Fax: (585) 371–3933

Sheriff

4 Court Street
Geneseo, New York 14454
(585) 243-7100
Fax: (585) 243-7104

Madison County

(Third Department, Sixth Judicial District)

Supreme Court

North Court Street

P.O. Box 545
Wampsville, New York 13163
(315) 366-2267
Fax: (646) 963-6588

Surrogate's Court

138 North Court Street
P.O. Box 607
Wampsville, New York 13163
(315) 366-2392
Fax: (646) 963-6594

County Court

North Court Street
P.O. Box 545
Wampsville, New York 13163
(315) 366-2266
Fax: (646) 963-6588

Family Court

North Court Street
P.O. Box 607
Wampsville, New York 13163
(315) 366-2291
Fax: (646) 963-6589

City Court

Oneida Justice Building
108 Main Street
Oneida, New York 13421
(315) 266-4740
Fax: (646) 963-6435

Sheriff

P.O. Box 16
Wampsville, New York 13163
(315) 366-2318
Fax: (315) 366-2286

Monroe County

(Fourth Department, Seventh Judicial District)

Supreme Court

Hall of Justice
Room 545

99 Exchange Boulevard
Rochester, New York 14614
(585) 371–3758
Fax: (585) 371–3780

Surrogate's Court

Hall of Justice
Room 541
99 Exchange Boulevard
Rochester, New York 14614
(585) 371-3310
Fax: (212) 371-3313

County Court

Hall of Justice
99 Exchange Boulevard
Rochester, New York 14614
(585) 371–3758
Fax: (585) 371–3780

Family Court

Hall of Justice
Room 360
99 Exchange Boulevard
Rochester, New York 14614
(585) 371–3544
Fax: (585) 371-3585

City Court

Room 6 – Hall of Justice
99 Exchange Boulevard
Rochester, New York 14614
Criminal: (585) 371-3412
Fax: (585) 371–3427

Sheriff

130 South Plymouth Avenue
Rochester, New York 14614
(585) 753–4178
Fax: (585) 753-4524

Montgomery County

(Third Department, Fourth Judicial District)

Supreme Court

58 Broadway

P.O. Box 1500
Fonda, New York 12068
(518) 853-4432
Fax: (518) 853-8378

Surrogate's Court

58 Broadway
P.O. Box 1500
Fonda, New York 12068
(518) 853-8108
Fax: (518) 853-8230

County Court

58 Broadway
P.O. Box 1500
Fonda, New York 12068
(518) 853-3834
Fax: (518) 853-3596

Family Court

58 Broadway
P.O. Box 1500
Fonda, New York 12068
(518) 853-8133
Fax: (518) 853-4390

City Court

1 Guy Park Avenue Extension
Amsterdam, New York 12010
(518) 842-9510
Fax: (518) 843-8646

Sheriff

Sheriff's Office
200 Clark Drive
Fultonville, New York 12072
Civil: (518) 853-5525
Sheriff Fax: (518) 853-4096

Nassau County

(Second Department, Tenth Judicial District)

Supreme Court

100 Supreme Court Drive
Mineola, New York 11501

(516) 493-3400

Surrogate's Court

262 Old Country Road
Mineola, New York 11501
(516) 493-3800

County Court

262 Old Country Road
Mineola, New York 11501
(516) 493–3710

Family Court

1200 Old Country Road
Westbury, New York 11590
(516) 493-4000

District Court

99 Main Street
Hempstead, New York 11550
Civil: (516) 493-4113
Criminal:
North: (516) 493–4049
South: s(516) 493-4201

City Court

13 Glen Street
Glen Cove, New York 11542
(516) 403-2441
Fax: (516) 676-1570

1 West Chester Street
Long Beach, New York 11561
(516) 442-8545
Fax: (516) 889–3511

Sheriff

100 Carmen Avenue
East Meadow, New York 11554
Civil Enforcement: (516) 571-2120
Corrections Division: (516) 572-4100

New York County

(First Department, First Judicial District)

Supreme Court

Civil Term:

60 Centre Street
New York, New York 10007
80 Centre Street
New York, New York 10013
111 Centre Street
New York, New York 10013
71 Thomas Street
New York, New York 10013
(646) 386–3600
Fax: (212) 374–3326
Criminal Term:
100 Centre Street
New York, New York 10013
Courtroom also located at 111 Centre Street
(646) 386-3685
Fax: (212) 374-0667
111 Centre Street
(646) 386-4301
Fax: (212) 374-2637

Children's Center

111 Centre Street Room 103
(212) 577-8769

Surrogate's Court

31 Chambers Street
New York, New York 10007
(646) 386-5000
Fax: (212) 374-3250

Family Court

60 Lafayette Street
New York, New York 10013
(646) 386-5206
Fax: (212) 374-4567

Civil Court

111 Centre Street
New York, New York 10013
Civil General Information: (646) 386-5700
Civil (646) 386-5600
Housing General Information: (646) 386-5480
Small Claims: (646) 386-5484

Criminal Court

100 Centre Street

New York, New York 10013
(646) 386-4500
Fax: (212) 374-5293

Sheriff

66 John Street 13th Floor
New York, New York 10038
(212) 487-9734
Fax: (212) 487-5567

Niagara County

(Fourth Department, Eighth Judicial District)

Supreme Court

Angelo DelSignore Civil Building
775 Third Street
Niagara Falls, New York 14301
(716) 278-1800
Fax: (716) 278-1809

Surrogate's Court

175 Hawley Street
Lockport, New York 14094
(716) 439-7130
Fax: (716) 439-7319

County Court

175 Hawley Street
Lockport, New York 14094
(716) 439-7148
Fax: (716) 439-7157

Family Court

Two Locations:
175 Hawley Street, Lockport, New York 14094
(716) 439-7172
Fax: (716) 439-7170
775 Third Street, Niagara Falls, New York 14301
(716) 278-1880
Fax: (716) 248-1877

City Court

One Locks Plaza
Lockport, New York 14094
Criminal: (716) 439-6660 ext. 501

Civil: (716) 439-6660 ext. 502
Traffic: (716) 439-6660 ext. 503
Fax: (716) 439-6684

Niagara Falls Municipal Complex
1925 Main Street
Niagara Falls, New York 14305
(716) 278-9800
Fax: (716) 278-9809

City Hall
216 Payne Avenue
North Tonawanda, New York 14120
(716) 845-7240
Fax: (716) 743-1754

Sheriff

P.O. Box 496
5526 Niagara Street Ext.
Lockport, New York 14095-0496
(716) 438-3393
Fax: (716) 438-3302

Oneida County

(Fourth Department, Fifth Judicial District)

Supreme Court

Oneida County Courthouse
200 Elizabeth Street
Utica, New York 13501
(315) 266–4200
Fax: (315) 798-6436

Oneida County Courthouse
302 North James Street
Rome, New York 13440

Surrogate's Court

Oneida County Office Building
800 Park Avenue, 8th Floor
Utica, New York 13501
(315) 266-4550
Fax: (315) 797-9237

County Court

Oneida County Courthouse
200 Elizabeth Street

Utica, New York 13501
Fax: (315) 793-6047

Family Court

Oneida County Courthouse
200 Elizabeth Street 1st Floor
Utica, New York 13501
Phone: (315) 266-4444
Fax: (315) 798-6404
Oneida County Courthouse
301 West Dominick Street
Rome, New York 13440
(315) 266-4500
Fax: (315) 336-3828

City Court

100 West Court Street
Rome, New York 13440
(315) 337-6440
Fax: (315) 338-0343

373 Sherrill Road
Sherrill, New York 13461
(315) 363-0996
Fax: (315) 363-1176

411 Oriskany Street West
Utica, New York 13502
Civil: (315) 266-4603
Criminal: (315) 266-4602
Traffic (315) 266-4601
Fax:
Civil: (315) 792-8038
Criminal: (315) 724-0762
Traffic: (315) 724-0762

Sheriff

Law Enforcement Building
6065 Judd Road
Oriskany, New York 13424
(315) 768-7804
Fax: (315) 765-2205

Onondaga County
(Fourth Department, Fifth Judicial District)

Supreme Court

Onondaga County Courthouse

401 Montgomery Street
Syracuse, New York 13202
(315) 671-1030
Fax: (315) 671-1176

Surrogate's Court

Onondaga County Courthouse
401 Montgomery Street
Syracuse, New York 13202
(315) 671-2100
Fax: (315) 671-1162

County Court

Onondaga County/City of Syracuse Criminal Courthouse
505 South State Street
Syracuse, New York 13202–2104
(315) 671-1020
Fax: (315) 671-1191

Family Court

Onondaga County Courthouse
401 Montgomery Street
Syracuse, New York 13202
(315) 671-2000
Fax: (315) 671-1163

City Court

Onondaga County/City of Syracuse Criminal Courthouse
505 South State Street
Syracuse, New York 13202–2104
Criminal: (315) 671-2760
Civil: (315) 671-2782
Traffic: (315) 671-2770
Fax:
Criminal: (315) 671-2744
Civil: (315) 671-2741
Traffic: (315) 671-2743

Sheriff

407 South State Street
Syracuse, New York 13202
(315) 435-3044
Fax: (315) 435-2942

Ontario County

(Fourth Department, Seventh Judicial District)

Supreme Court

27 North Main Street
Canandaigua, New York 14424
(585) 396-4239
Fax: (585) 396-4576

Surrogate's Court

27 North Main Street
Canandaigua, New York 14424
(585) 396-4055
Fax: (585) 396-4576

County Court

27 North Main Street
Canandaigua, New York 14424
(585) 396-4239
Fax: (585) 396-4576

Family Court

27 North Main Street
Canandaigua, New York 14424
(585) 412-5299
Fax: (585) 412-5327
E-mail: ontariofamilycourt@ courts.state.ny.us

City Court

2 North Main Street
Canandaigua, New York 14424
(585) 396-5011
Fax: (585) 396-5012

Geneva City Court Building
255 Exchange Street
Geneva, New York 14456
(315) 789-237-6575
Fax: (315) 237-6415
E-mail: jguard@courts.state.ny.us

Sheriff

Sheriff's Office
74 Ontario Street
Canandaigua, New York 14424

(585) 394-4560
Fax: (585) 394-3245

Orange County

(Second Department, Ninth Judicial District)

Supreme Court

285 Main Street
Goshen, New York 10924
(845) 476-3500
Fax: (845) 291-2595

Surrogate's Court

30 Park Place
Goshen, New York 10924
Jeanne Smith, Chief Clerk
Amy Miller, Deputy Chief Clerk
(845) 476-3655
Fax: (845) 291-2196

County Court

285 Main Street
Goshen, New York 10924
(845) 476–3500
Fax: (845) 291-2595

Family Court

285 Main Street
Goshen, New York 10924
(845) 476-3520
Fax: (845) 291-3054

City Court

2 James Street
Middletown, New York 10940
Linda Padden, Chief Clerk
Robin Siegel, Deputy Chief Clerk
(845) 476-3630
Fax: (845) 343-5737

300 Broadway
Newburgh, New York 12550
Jasmin Reyes-Finch, Chief Clerk
Irene Grant, Deputy Chief Clerk
(845) 483-8100
Fax: Civil/Traffic/Housing—(845) 565-0230

Criminal: (845) 565-0241

20 Hammond Street
Port Jervis, New York 12771
Catherine Quinn, Chief Clerk
(845) 476-3700
Fax: (845) 476-3691

Sheriff

110 Wells Farm Road
Goshen, New York 10924
(845) 294-4033
Fax: (845) 294-1590

Orleans County

(Fourth Department, Eighth Judicial District)

Supreme Court

1 South Main Street, Suite 3
Albion, New York 14411–1497
(585) 589-5458
Fax: (585) 589-0632

Surrogate's Court

1 South Main Street, Suite 3
Albion, New York 14411–1497
(585) 589-4457
Fax: (585) 589-0632
Deborah Berry, Chief Clerk
E-mail: dberry@courts.state.ny.us

County Court

1 South Main Street, Suite 3
Albion, New York 14411–1497
(585) 589-5458

Family Court

1 South Main Street, Suite 3
Albion, New York 14411–1497
(585) 589-4457
Fax: (585) 589-0632
Laurie Bower, Chief Clerk
E-mail: lbower@courts.state.ny.us

Sheriff

400 Public Safety Building

13925 Route 31
Albion, New York 14411
(585) 589-5527
Fax: (585) 590-4178

Oswego County

(Fourth Department, Fifth Judicial District)

Supreme Court

Oswego County Courthouse
25 East Oneida Street
Oswego, New York 13126
(315) 349-3277
Fax: (315) 266-4519

Surrogate's Court

Oswego County Courthouse
25 East Oneida Street
Oswego, New York 13126
(315) 349-3295
Fax: (315) 349-8514

County Court

Oswego County Courthouse
25 East Oneida Street
Oswego, New York 13126
(315) 349-3280
Fax: (315) 266-4519

Family Court

Public Safety Center
39 Churchill Road
Oswego, New York 13126
(315) 349-3350
Fax: (315) 349-3457

City Court

Conway Municipal Building
20 West Oneida Street
Oswego, New York 13126
(315) 343-0415
Fax: (315) 266-4752
E-mail: osw_city_ct@courts.state.ny.us

Municipal Building
141 South First Street

Fulton, New York 13069
(315) 593-8400
Fax: (315) 266-4753
E-mail: fulton_city@courts.state.ny.us

Sheriff

39 Churchill Road
Oswego, New York 13126
(315) 349-3302
Fax: (315) 349-3303

Otsego County

(Third Department, Sixth Judicial District)

Supreme Court

Ostego County Annex Building
32 Chestnut Street
Cooperstown, New York 13326
(607) 547-4364
Fax: (607) 963-6663

Surrogate's Court

197 Main Street
Cooperstown, New York 13326
(607) 547-4213
Fax: (607) 547-7566

County Court

197 Main Street
Cooperstown, New York 13326
(607) 547-4364
Fax: (607) 547-6663

Family Court

Otsego County Annex Building
32 Chestnut Street
Cooperstown, New York 13326
(607) 547-4264
Fax: (212) 457-2956

City Court

Public Safety Building
81 Main Street
Oneonta, New York 13820
(607) 432-4480

Fax: (646) 963-6433

Sheriff

Sheriff's Office
172 County Highway 33 West
Cooperstown, New York 13326
(607) 547-4271
Fax: (607) 547-6413

Putnam County

(Second Department, Ninth Judicial District)

Supreme Court

County Office Building
20 County Center
Carmel, New York 10512
Phone: (845) 208-7800
Fax: (845) 208-7869

Surrogate's Court

Historic Courthouse
44 Gleneida Avenue
Carmel, New York 10512
Phone: (845) 208-7860
Fax: (845) 228-5761

County Court

County Office Building
20 County Center
Carmel, New York 10512
(845) 208-7800
Fax: (845) 208-7869

Family Court

County Office Building
20 County Center
Carmel, New York 10512
(845) 208-7800
Fax: (845) 228-9614

Sheriff

3 County Center
Carmel, New York 10512
(845) 225-4300
Fax: (845) 225-4399

Queens County

(/Second Department, Eleventh Judicial District)

Supreme Court

Civil Term:

88-11 Sutphin Boulevard
Queens County Courthouse
Jamaica, New York 11435
(718) 298-1000

25–10 Court Square
Long Island City, New York 11101
718-298-1000

Criminal Term:

125-01 Queens Boulevard
Kew Gardens, New York 11415
(718) 298-1000

Surrogate's Court

88-11 Sutphin Boulevard 7th Floor
Queens County Courthouse
Jamaica, New York 11435
(718) 298-0500

Family Court

151-20 Jamaica Avenue
Jamaica, New York 11432
(718) 298-0197
Fax: (718) 297-2826

Civil Court

89-17 Sutphin Boulevard
Jamaica, New York 11435
Civil General Information: (212) 791–6000
Civil: (718) 262-7100
Fax: (718) 262-7107

Criminal Court

125-01 Queens Boulevard
Kew Gardens, New York 11415
(212) 374-5880
Fax: (718) 520-4712

Sheriff

144-06 94th Avenue

Jamaica, New York 11435
(718) 298-7500
Fax: (718) 298-7470

Rensselaer County

(Third Department, Third Judicial District)

Supreme Court

80 Second Street
Troy, New York 12180
(518) 285-5025
Fax: (518) 270-3714

Surrogate's Court

80 Second Street
Troy, New York 12180
(518) 285-6100
Fax: (518)272–5452

County Court

80 Second Street
Troy, New York 12180
(518) 285-5025
Fax: (518) 270-3714

Family Court

1504 Fifth Avenue
Troy, New York 12180-4107
(518) 453-5515
Fax: (518) 272-6573

City Court

62 Washington Street
Rensselaer, New York 12144
(518) 453-4680
Fax: (518) 453-8996

Civil
51 State Street, Third Floor
Troy, New York 12180
(518) 453–5900
Fax: (518) 274-2816

Criminal and Traffic
51 State Street, Second Floor
Troy, New York 12180

(518) 453–5900
Fax: (518) 274-2816

Sheriff

4000 Main Street
Troy, New York 12181-0389
(518) 2266-1900
Fax: (518) 270-5447

Richmond County

(Second Department, Second Judicial District)

Supreme Court

Civil Term
18 Richmond Terrace
Richmond County Courthouse
Staten Island, New York 10301
(718) 675–8700
Fax: (718) 390-5435

130 Stuyvesant Place
Staten Island, NY 10301

23 Hyatt Street

Staten Island, NY 10301
(718) 657-8700

Criminal Court

18 Richmond Terrace
Richmond County Courthouse
Staten Island, New York 10304
(718) 675–8760

Surrogate's Court

18 Richmond Terrace
Staten Island, New York 10301
(718) 675-8500
Fax: (718) 390-8741

Family Court

100 Richmond Terrace
Staten Island, New York 10301
(718) 675-8800
Fax: (718) 390-5247

NYC Civil Court

927 Castleton Avenue

Staten Island, New York 10310
Civil: (646) 386-5700
Fax: (718) 390-8108

Sheriff

350 Saint Marks Avenue
Staten Island, New York 10301
(718) 815-8407
Fax: (718) 815-8412

Rockland County

(Second Department, Ninth Judicial District)

Supreme Court

1 South Main Street
New City, New York 10956
(845) 483-8310
Fax: (845) 638-5312

Surrogate's Court

1 South Main Street 2nd Floor
New City, New York 10956
(845) 483–8260
Fax: (845) 638-5632

County Court

1 South Main Street
New City, New York 10956
(845) 483-8310
Fax: (845) 638-5312

Family Court

1 South Main Street Suite 300
New City, New York 10956
(845) 483–8210
Fax: (845) 638-5319

Sheriff

55 New Hempstead Road
New City, New York 10956
(845) 638-5400

St. Lawrence County

(Third Department, Fourth Judicial District)

Supreme Court

48 Court Street

Ct. Dir.

Canton, New York 13617-1194
(315) 379-0326
Fax: (315) 379-2311

Surrogate's Court

48 Court Street
Canton, New York 13617
(315) 379-2217
Fax: (315) 379-2372

County Court

48 Court Street
Canton, New York 13617-1194
(315) 379-2214
Fax: (315) 379-9934

Family Court

48 Court Street
Canton, New York 13617-1194
(315) 379-2410
Fax: (315) 386-3197

City Court

330 Ford Street
Ogdensburg, New York 13669
(315) 393-3941
Fax: (315) 393-6839

Sheriff

48 Court Street
Canton, New York 13617
(315) 379-2222
Fax: (315) 379-0335

Saratoga County

(Third Department, Fourth Judicial District)

Supreme Court

Municipal Center
30 McMaster Street, Building Three
Ballston Spa, New York 12020
(518) 451-8840
Fax: (518) 453-5937

Surrogate's Court

Municipal Center

30 McMaster Street, Building Three
Ballston Spa, New York 12020
(518) 451-8830
Fax: (518) 453-8693

County Court

Municipal Center
30 McMaster Street, Building Three
Ballston Spa, New York 12020
(518) 451-8840
Fax: (518) 453-5937

Family Court

35 West High Street
Ballston Spa, New York 12020
(518) 451-8888
Fax: (518) 453-5942

City Court

City Hall
36 North Main Street
Mechanicville, New York 12118
(518) 453-5959
Fax: (518) 453-8678

City Hall
474 Broadway
Saratoga Springs, New York 12866
(518) 451–8780
Fax: (518) 453-8686

Sheriff

6010 County Farm Road
Ballston Spa, New York 12020-0600
(518) 885-2450
Fax: (518) 885-2453

Schenectady County
(Third Department, Fourth Judicial District)

Supreme Court

612 State Street
Schenectady, New York 12305
(518) 285-8401
Fax: (518) 451–8731

Surrogate's Court

612 State Street

Schenectady, New York 12305
(518) 285-8455
Fax: (518) 451-8732

County Court

Schenectady County Judicial Building
612 State Street
Schenectady, New York 12305
(518) 285-8401
Fax: (518) 451-8731

Family Court

620 State Street
Schenectady, New York 12305
(518) 285-8435
Fax: (518) 393-1565

City Court

Civil Division:
City Hall
Jay Street
Schenectady, New York 12305
(518) 453-6989
Fax: (518) 453-8984

Criminal Division:
531 Liberty Street
Schenectady, New York 12305
(518) 453-6989
Fax: (518) 285-8983

Sheriff

Schenectady County Correctional Facility
320 Veeder Avenue
Schenectady, New York 12307
(518) 388-4596
Civil: (518) 388-4300
Fax: (518) 388-4593

Schoharie County

(Third Department, Third Judicial District)

Supreme Court

290 Main Street
Schoharie County Courthouse
PO Box 669

Schoharie, New York 12157
(518) 453-6998

Surrogate's Court

290 Main Street
Schoharie County Courthouse
PO Box 669
Schoharie, New York 12157
(518) 453-6986

County Court

290 Main Street
Schoharie County Courthouse
PO Box 669
Schoharie, New York 12157
(518) 454-6998
Fax: (518) 295-7226

Family Court

290 Main Street
Schoharie County Courthouse
PO Box 669
Schoharie, New York 12157
(518) 453-6982

Sheriff

157 Depot Lane
P.O. Box 689
Schoharie, New York 12157-0089
(518) 295-2266
Fax: (518) 295-2278

Schuyler County

(Third Department, Sixth Judicial District)

Supreme Court

105 Ninth Street Unit 35
Watkins Glen, New York 14891
(607) 535-7760
Fax: (607) 535–8160

Surrogate's Court

105 Ninth Street Unit 35
Watkins Glen, New York 14891
(607) 535-7144

Fax: (607) 535-8160

County Court

105 Ninth Street Unit 35
Watkins Glen, New York 14891
(607) 535-7760
Fax: (607) 535-8160

Family Court

105 Ninth Street Unit 35
Watkins Glen, New York 14891
(607) 535-7143
(607) 535-8160

Sheriff

106 10th Street
Watkins Glen, New York 14891
(607) 535-8222
Fax: (607) 535-8216

Seneca County

(Fourth Department, Seventh Judicial District)

Supreme Court

48 West Williams Street
Waterloo, New York 13165
(315) 539-7021
Fax: (315) 539-3267

Surrogate's Court

48 West Williams Street
Waterloo, New York 13165
(315) 539-7531
Fax: (315) 539-7929

County Court

48 West Williams Street
Waterloo, New York 13165
(315) 539-7021
Fax: (315) 539-3267

Family Court

48 West Williams Street
Waterloo, New York 13165
(315) 539-4917

Fax: (315) 539-3267

Sheriff

6150 State Route 96
Romulus NY, 14551
(315) 220-3200
Fax: (315) 220-3478

Steuben County

(Fourth Department, Seventh Judicial District)

Supreme Court

3 East Pulteney Square
Bath, New York 14810
(607) 622-8219
Fax: (607) 622-8244

Surrogate's Court

3 East Pulteney Square
Bath, New York 14810
(607) 622-8221
Fax: (607) 622-8243

County Court

3 East Pulteney Square
Bath, New York 14810
(607) 622–8219
Fax: (607) 622–8244

Family Court

3 East Pulteney Square
Bath, New York 14810
(607) 622-8218
Fax: (607) 622-8239

City Court

12 Civic Center Plaza
Corning, New York 14830
(607) 654-6033
Fax: (607) 654-6030

82 Main Street P.O. Box 627
Hornell, New York 14843-0627
(607) 324-7531
Fax: (607) 324-6325

Sheriff

7007 Rumsey Street Extension

Bath, New York 14810
(607) 622-3901

Suffolk County

(Second Department, Tenth Judicial District)

Supreme Court

1 Court Street
Riverhead, New York 11901
(631) 852-2333
Fax: (631) 852-2340

Surrogate's Court

County Center Building
320 Center Drive
Riverhead, New York 11901
(631) 852-1746
Fax: (631) 852-1777

County Court

Cromarty Court Complex
210 Center Drive
Riverhead, New York 11901
(631) 852-2120
Fax: (631) 852-2568

District Court

First District Court

Civil:
3105 Veterans Memorial Highway
Ronkonkoma, New York 11779
(631) 854-9676
Fax: (631) 854-9681
Criminal: 400 Carleton Avenue P.O. Box 9075
Central Islip, New York 11722
(631) 853-7500

Second District Court

30 East Hoffman Avenue
Lindenhurst, New York 11757
(631) 854-1121
Fax: (631) 854-1127

Third District Court

1850 New York Avenue

Huntington Station, New York 11746
(631) 854-4545
Fax: (631) 854-4549

Fourth District Court

Building 158, North County Complex
Veterans Memorial Highway
Hauppauge, New York 11787
(631) 853-5408
Fax: (631) 853-5951

Fifth District Court

Civil: 3105 Veterans Memorial Highway
Ronkonkoma, New York 11779
(631) 854-9676
Fax: (631) 854-9681

Criminal: 400 Carleton Avenue
Central Islip, New York 11722
(631) 853-7500

Sixth District Court

150 West Main Street
Patchogue, New York 11772
(631) 854-1440
Fax: (631) 854-1444

Family Court

400 Carleton Avenue
Central Islip, New York 11722
899 East Main Street, Suite 308
Riverhead, New York 11901
Islip: (631) 853-4289
Fax: (631) 853-4283
Riverhead: (631) 852-3905
Fax: (631) 852-2851

Sheriff

100 Center Drive
Riverhead, New York 11901
(631) 852-2200

Sullivan County
(Third Department, Third Judicial District)

Supreme Court

414 Broadway

Monticello, New York 12701
Supreme: (845) 794-4066
County: (845) 794-4066
Fax: (845) 791-6170

Surrogate's Court

Sullivan County Government Center
100 North Street
Monticello, New York 12701
(845) 807-0690
Fax: (845) 794-0310

County Court

414 Broadway
Monticello, New York 12701
(845) 794-4066
Fax: (845) 791-6170

Family Court

Sullivan County Government Center
100 North Street
Monticello, New York 12701
(845) 807-0650
Fax: (845) 794-0199

Sheriff

County Jail
4 Bushnell Avenue
Monticello, New York 12701
(845) 794-7100
Fax: (845) 794-0810

Tioga County

(Third Department, Sixth Judicial District)

Supreme Court

16 Court Street
P.O. Box 307
Owego, New York 13827
(607) 689-6102
Fax: (212) 401-5970

Surrogate's Court

Court Annex
20 Court Street

Owego, New York 13827
(607) 689-6099
Fax: (607) 963–6398

County Court

20 Court Street
P.O. Box 307
Owego, New York 13827
(607) 689-6102
Fax: (212) 401-5970

Family Court

Court Annex
20 Court Street
Owego, New York 13827
(607) 689-6077
Fax: (646) 963-6399

Sheriff

Tioga County Public Safety Building
103 Corporate Drive
Owego, New York 13827
(607) 689-1010

Tompkins County

(Third Department, Sixth Judicial District)

Supreme Court

320 North Tioga Street
Ithaca, New York 14851-0070
(607) 272-0466
Fax: (212) 216-6610

Surrogate's Court

320 North Tioga Street
P.O. Box 70
Ithaca, New York 14851-0070
(607) 216-6655
Fax: (212) 457-2952

County Court

320 North Tioga Street
P.O. Box 70
Ithaca, New York 14851-0070
(607) 216-6610

Fax: (212) 401-9071

Family Court

320 North Tioga Street
P.O. Box 70
Ithaca, New York 14851-0070
(607) 216-6640
Fax: (607) 457-2951

City Court

118 East Clinton Street
Ithaca, New York 14850
(607) 216-6660
Fax: (607) 277-3702

Sheriff

779 Warren Road
Ithaca, New York 14850
(607) 257-1345

Ulster County

(Third Department, Third Judicial District)

Supreme Court

285 Wall Street
Kingston, New York 12401
(845) 340-3377
Fax: (845) 340-3387

Surrogate's Court

240 Fair Street 3rd Floor
Kingston, New York 12401
(845) 340-3348
Fax: (845) 340-3352

County Court

285 Wall Street
Kingston, New York 12401
(845) 340-3377
Fax: (845) 340-3387

Family Court

16 Lucas Avenue
Kingston, New York 12401
(845) 340-3600

Fax: (845) 340-3626

City Court

1 Garraghan Drive
Kingston, New York 12401
(845) 338-2974
Fax: (845) 338-1443

Sheriff

Ulster County Law Enforcement Facility
380 Boulevard
Kingston, New York 12401
(845) 338-3640
Fax: (845) 331-2810

Warren County

(Third Department, Fourth Judicial District)

Supreme Court

Warren County Municipal Center
1340 State Route 9
Lake George, New York 12845
(518) 761-6431
Fax: (518) 761-6253

Surrogate's Court

Warren County Municipal Center
1340 State Route 9
Lake George, New York 12845
(518) 761-6514
Fax: (518) 761-6511

County Court

Warren County Municipal Center
1340 State Route 9
Lake George, New York 12845
(518) 761-6431
Fax: (518) 761-6253

Family Court

Warren County Municipal Center
1340 State Route 9
Lake George, New York 12845
(518) 761-6500
Fax: (518) 761-6230

City Court

City Hall
42 Ridge Street, Third Floor
Glens Falls, New York 12801
(518) 798-4714
Fax: (518) 453-8623

Sheriff

Warren County Municipal Center
1400 State Route 9
Lake George, New York 12845
(518) 743-2500

Washington County

(Third Department, Fourth Judicial District)

Supreme Court

383 Broadway
Fort Edward, New York 12828
(518) 746-2521
Fax: (518) 746-2519

Surrogate's Court

383 Broadway
Fort Edward, New York 12828
(518) 746-2545
Fax: (518) 746-2547

County Court

383 Broadway
Fort Edward, New York 12828
(518) 746-2521
Fax: (518) 746-2519

Family Court

383 Broadway
Fort Edward, New York 12828
(518) 746-2501
Fax: (518) 746-2503

Sheriff

399 Broadway
Fort Edward, New York 12828
(518) 746-2475

Wayne County

(Fourth Department, Seventh Judicial District)

Supreme Court

Hall of Justice
54 Broad Street
Lyons, New York 14489
(315) 946-5459
Fax: (315) 946-5456

Surrogate's Court

Hall of Justice
54 Broad Street
Lyons, New York 14489
(315) 946-5430
Fax: (315) 946-5433

County Court

Hall of Justice
54 Broad Street
Lyons, New York 14489
(315) 946-5459
Fax: (315) 946-5456

Family Court

Hall of Justice
54 Broad Street
Lyons, New York 14489
(315) 946-5420
Fax: (315) 946-5456

Sheriff

7368 Route 31
Lyons, New York 14489
(315) 946-9711
Fax: (315) 946-5811

Westchester County

(Second Department, Ninth Judicial District)

Supreme Court

111 Dr. Martin Luther King, Jr. Boulevard
White Plains, New York 10601
General: (914) 824–5840
Civil: (914) 824-5300

Ct. Dir.

Fax: (914) 824-5873
Criminal: (914) 824–5400
Fax: (914) 824-5065

Surrogate's Court

111 Dr. Martin Luther King Jr. Boulevard
19th Floor
White Plains, New York 10601
(914) 824-5656
Fax: (914) 995-3728

County Court

111 Dr. Martin Luther King, Jr. Boulevard
White Plains, New York 10601
General: (914) 824–5840
Civil: (914) 824-5300
Fax: (914) 824-5873
Criminal: (914) 824–5400
Fax: (914) 824-5065

Family Court

111 Dr. Martin Luther King, Jr. Boulevard
White Plains, New York 10601
(914) 824-5500
Fax: (914) 995-8650

420 North Avenue
New Rochelle, New York 10801
(914) 831-6590
Fax: (914) 813-5580

53 South Broadway
3rd Floor
Yonkers, New York 10701
(914) 831-6555
Fax: (914) 831-6409

City Court

Ronald A. Blackwood Building
2 Roosevelt Square North, 2nd Floor
Mount Vernon, New York 10550
Phone: (914) 831–6440
Fax: (914) 824-5511

475 North Avenue
New Rochelle, New York 10801
(914) 358-8000

Fax: (914) 654-0344

2 Nelson Avenue
Peekskill, New York 10566
(914) 831-6480
Fax: (914) 736-1889

21 McCullough Place
Rye, New York 10580
(914) 831-6400
Fax: (914) 831-6546

77 South Lexington Avenue
White Plains, New York 10601
(914) 824-5675
Fax: (914) 824-5858

100 South Broadway
Yonkers, New York 10701
(914) 831-6450
Fax: (914) 377-6395

Sheriff

Westchester County Police
1 Saw Mill River Parkway
Hawthorne, New York 10532
(914) 864-7700
Fax: (914) 995-4095

Wyoming County

(Fourth Department, Eighth Judicial District)

Supreme Court

147 North Main Street
Warsaw, New York 14569
(585) 786-3148
Fax: (585) 786-2818

Surrogate's Court

147 North Main Street
Warsaw, New York 14569
(585) 786-3148
Fax: (585) 786-3800

County Court

147 North Main Street
Warsaw, New York 14569
(585) 786-3148

Ct. Dir.

Fax: (585) 786-2818
Commissioner of Jurors: (585) 786-8756
Fax: (585) 786-2818

Family Court

147 North Main Street
Warsaw, New York 14569
(585) 786-3148
Fax: (585) 786-3800

Sheriff

151 North Main Street
Warsaw, New York 14569
(716) 786-8989
Fax: (716) 786-8961

Yates County

(Fourth Department, Seventh Judicial District)

Supreme Court

415 Liberty Street
Penn Yan, New York 14527
(315) 536-5126
Fax: (315) 536-5190

Surrogate's Court

415 Liberty Street
Penn Yan, New York 14527
(315) 536-5130
Fax: (315) 536-5190

County Court

415 Liberty Street
Penn Yan, New York 14527
(315) 536-5126
Fax: (315) 536-5190

Family Court

415 Liberty Street
Penn Yan, New York 14527
(315) 536-5127
Fax: (315) 536-5190

Sheriff

227 Main Street

Penn Yan, New York 14527-1720
(315) 536-4438
Fax: (315) 536-5191

INDEX

References in the Index to the Consolidated Laws are abbreviated as follows:

COR   Correction Law

CPL   Criminal Procedure Law

EXEC   Executive Law

JUD   Judiciary Law

PHL   Public Health Law

PL   Penal Law

VTL   Vehicle and Traffic Law

INDEX

[References are to sections of Consolidated Laws as abbreviated on Page i.]

A

ABANDONMENT OF CHILD
Generally . . . PL 260.00

ABORTION
Articles, issuing abortional . . . PL 125.60
Definition . . . PL 125.05
First degree . . . PL 125.45
Issuing abortional articles . . . PL 125.60
Second degree . . . PL 125.40
Self-abortion
First degree . . . PL 125.55
Second degree . . . PL 125.50

ABSCONDING FROM CUSTODY (See CUSTODY)

ABSENCE OF INMATES
Deathbed visits . . . COR 509
Funeral service . . . COR 509
Local correctional facilities . . . COR 509

ACCESSORIAL CONDUCT
Generally . . . PL 20.00
Convictions . . . PL 20.15
Corporations, liability of
Generally . . . PL 20.20
Individual's liability for corporate conduct
. . . PL 20.25
Defense, lack of . . . PL 20.05
Exemptions . . . PL 20.10

ACCIDENTS AND ACCIDENT REPORTS
Animals, leaving scene of accident without reporting injury to . . . VTL 601
Arrest for leaving scene of accident without reporting . . . VTL 602
Leaving scene of accident without reporting
Generally . . . VTL 600
Animals, injury to certain . . . VTL 601
Arrest for violations . . . VTL 602

ACCOMPLICES
Corroboration of accomplice testimony, evidentiary rules on . . . CPL 60.22
Prostitution, promotion of . . . PL 230.35
Trafficking
Labor . . . PL 135.36
Sex . . . PL 230.36

ACCUSATORY INSTRUMENTS
Appearance ticket, local criminal court accusatory instrument requirements after issuance of
. . . CPL 150.50

ACCUSATORY INSTRUMENTS—Cont.
Arrest without warrant, dismissal of insufficient accusatory instrument in case involving
. . . CPL 140.45
District attorney on local criminal court accusatory instrument, notice to . . . CPL 110.20
Local criminal court accusatory instrument
Appearance ticket, requirements after issuance of . . . CPL 150.50
Arrest without warrant, dismissal of insufficient accusatory instrument in case involving
. . . CPL 140.45
Definition . . . CPL 100.10
District attorney, notice to . . . CPL 110.20
Filing procedures . . . CPL 100.55
Sufficiency on face . . . CPL 100.40
Youthful offender, sealing of accusatory instrument filed against . . . CPL 720.15
New trial, accusatory instrument status upon order of . . . CPL 470.55
Pre-pleading status, accusatory instrument status upon restoration of action to . . . CPL 470.55
Warrant of arrest, attachment of accusatory instrument to . . . CPL 120.40

ACQUITTAL
Discharge of defendant after verdict of . . . CPL 330.10

ADJUDICATION
Youthful offenders (See YOUTHFUL OFFENDERS)

ADMISSIBILITY OF EVIDENCE
Defendant's statements . . . CPL 60.45
Sex offense cases
Dress, victim's manner of . . . CPL 60.48
Sexual conduct of victim . . . CPL 60.42
Sexual conduct of victim
Non-sex offense cases . . . CPL 60.43
Sex offense cases . . . CPL 60.42

ADULTERY
Generally . . . PL 255.17
Corroboration . . . PL 255.30
Defense . . . PL 255.20

ADVERTISEMENTS
False advertising . . . PL 190.20
Posting, unlawful . . . PL 145.30
Recordings of sound, unauthorized
First degree . . . PL 275.30
Second degree . . . PL 275.25

AGENCIES
Crime victim-related, fair treatment standards for
. . . EXEC 643

I-1

[References are to sections of Consolidated Laws as abbreviated on Page i.]

AGGRAVATED ASSAULT (See ASSAULT)

AGGRAVATED FAMILY OFFENSE
Generally . . . PL 240.75
Indictment or information for . . . CPL 200.63

AGGRAVATED GRAND LARCENY
Automated teller machines, of . . . PL 155.43

AGGRAVATED HARASSMENT (See HARASS-
MENT)

**AGGRAVATED INTERFERENCE WITH
HEALTH CARE SERVICE**
First degree . . . PL 240.73
Second degree . . . PL 240.72

AGGRAVATED LIFE SETTLEMENT FRAUD
Generally . . . PL 176.70

AGGRAVATED MURDER
Generally . . . PL 125.26

AIRCRAFT
Forfeiture of aircraft used to transport gambling
records . . . PL 415.00
Laser beam, directing at
First degree . . . PL 240.77
Second degree . . . PL 240.76
Seizure and forfeiture of aircraft used to transport
gambling records . . . PL 415.00

ALCOHOL
Chemical tests for alcohol and drugs . . . VTL
1195
Judicial diversion program
Definitions . . . CPL 216
Procedures . . . CPL 216.05
Local correctional facilities, use of alcoholic bever-
ages in . . . COR 502; COR 503
Overdose or other medical emergency, witness or
victim seeking health care for . . . PL 220.78
Rehabilitation program (See ALCOHOL AND
DRUG REHABILITATION PROGRAM)
Vehicle and Traffic Law (See VEHICLE AND
TRAFFIC LAW)

**ALCOHOL AND DRUG REHABILITATION
PROGRAM**
Generally . . . VTL 1196
Age of 21, persons under . . . VTL 1196
Clinic programs, driver improvement . . . VTL
523–a
Declaration of purpose . . . VTL 520
Parole
Revocation of, drug treatment program as alter-
native to . . . EXEC 259–i
Sentence of parole supervision, drug treatment
program as part of . . . CPL 410.91
Reports . . . VTL 523
Safety programs, experimental driver . . . VTL
523–b

**ALCOHOL AND DRUG REHABILITATION
PROGRAM**—Cont.
Sealing of records after completion . . . CPL
160.58
Statement of findings . . . VTL 520

ALIBI
Notice of . . . CPL 250.20

**ALTERNATE CORRECTIONAL FACILITIES:
NEW YORK CITY**
Acquisition of, authorization for . . . COR 88–a
Authorization for . . . COR 88; COR 88–a
Commissioner of Correction, management by
. . . COR 89–a
Commission of Correction, powers and duties of
. . . COR 89–f
Costs for establishment, operation and maintenance
of . . . COR 89–g
Definitions . . . COR 87
Establishment of
Generally . . . COR 89
Costs for . . . COR 89–g
Good behavior time allowances against definite
sentences served in . . . COR 89–b
Indemnification . . . COR 89–l
Local taxes . . . COR 89–i
Maintenance of, costs for . . . COR 89–g
Management of . . . COR 89–a
Operation of
Costs for . . . COR 89–g
Fund for . . . COR 89–h
Termination of operation agreement . . . COR
89–k
Purpose of . . . COR 86
Review panel . . . COR 89–e
Title to facilities . . . COR 89–j
Transportation of inmates to . . . COR 89–d
Use of . . . COR 89–c
Utilization of, authorization for . . . COR 88–a

AMMUNITION SELLERS
Generally . . . PL 400.03

ANARCHY
Criminal . . . PL 240.15

ANIMALS
Accident without reporting injury to animal, leav-
ing scene of . . . VTL 601
Police animal, killing or injuring . . . PL 195.06–a
Service, offenses against
Definitions . . . PL 242.00
First degree . . . PL 242.15
Harassment . . . PL 242.05
Interference . . . PL 242.05
Second degree . . . PL 242.10
Trained animal to aid persons with disability, harm-
ing
First degree . . . PL 195.12

[References are to sections of Consolidated Laws as abbreviated on Page i.]

[References are to sections of Consolidated Laws as abbreviated on Page i.]

APPEARANCE—Cont.
Inmates (See INMATES)
Prisoners (See INMATES)
Probation and conditional discharge
    Court, appearance before . . . CPL 410.60
    Notice to appear . . . CPL 410.40
Securing appearance of defendant
    Generally . . . CPL 550.10
    Corporate defendants . . . CPL 600.10
    Extradition (See EXTRADITION)
    Inmates (See INMATES)
    Prisoners (See INMATES)
    Uniform Criminal Extradition Act (See EXTRA-
    DITION)
Service of summons, defendant's failure to appear
    after . . . CPL 130.50
Subpoenas (See SUBPOENAS)
Ticket (See APPEARANCE TICKET)
Uniform Criminal Extradition Act (See EXTRADI-
    TION)
Witnesses, securing appearance of (See WIT-
    NESSES)

APPEARANCE TICKET
Generally . . . CPL 150.75
Bail requirements, pre-arraignment . . . CPL
    150.30
Content . . . CPL 150.10
Definition . . . CPL 150.10
Failure to appear, defendant's . . . CPL 150.60
Failure to respond to
    Generally . . . PL 215.58
    Defense . . . PL 215.59
    Suspension due to . . . VTL 510
Fingerprinting of defendant . . . CPL 150.70
Form and content . . . CPL 150.10
Local criminal court accusatory instrument require-
    ments . . . CPL 150.50
Persons authorized to issue . . . CPL 150.20
Pre-arraignment bail requirements . . . CPL 150.30
Return of . . . CPL 150.40
Service of . . . CPL 150.40
Simplified information, ticket issued in conjunction
    with offense charged in . . . CPL 100.25
When issuable . . . CPL 150.20

ARRAIGNMENT
Appearance of defendant
    Indictment . . . CPL 210.10
    Local criminal courts . . . CPL 110.10
    Pre-arraignment bail, issuance and service of
        appearance ticket upon posting of . . . CPL
        150.30
Felony complaint, proceedings upon . . . CPL
    180.10
Indictment
    Appearance of defendant, securing . . . CPL
        210.10
    Procedure . . . CPL 210.15

ARRAIGNMENT—Cont.
Information . . . CPL 170.10
Local criminal courts for arraignment, methods of
    requiring defendant's appearance in . . . CPL
    110.10
Material witness order . . . CPL 620.40
Misdemeanor complaint . . . CPL 170.10
Pre-arraignment bail, issuance and service of ap-
    pearance ticket upon posting of . . . CPL 150.30
Prosecutor's information on misdemeanor com-
    plaint . . . CPL 170.10
Simplified traffic information . . . CPL 170.10
Traffic violations . . . VTL 1807

ARREST
Extradition, arrest for (See EXTRADITION)
Physical force, use of
    Escape, prevention of . . . PL 35.30
    Making of arrest, prohibitions against use of
        physical force in . . . PL 35.30
    Resisting arrest, prohibitions against use of
        physical force in . . . PL 35.27
Resisting arrest
    Generally . . . PL 205.30
    Physical force in, prohibitions against use of
        . . . PL 35.27
Vehicle and Traffic Law (See VEHICLE AND
    TRAFFIC LAW)
Warrant of (See WARRANT OF ARREST)
Without warrant (See ARREST WITHOUT WAR-
    RANT)

ARREST WITHOUT WARRANT
Generally . . . CPL 140.05
Extradition, arrest for . . . CPL 570.34
Local criminal court accusatory instrument, dis-
    missal of insufficient . . . CPL 140.45
Parole officer's arrest without warrant as action in
    course of employment . . . COR 10
Peace officers, arrest by
    Generally . . . CPL 140.25
    Close pursuit, by officers of other states in
        . . . CPL 140.55
    Post-arrest procedure . . . CPL 140.27
    Procedure for . . . CPL 140.27
    When authorized . . . CPL 140.30
    Where authorized . . . CPL 140.30
Police officers, arrest by
    Post-arrest procedure . . . CPL 140.20
    Procedure for . . . CPL 140.15
    When authorized . . . CPL 140.10
    Where authorized . . . CPL 140.10
Private persons, arrest by
    Post-arrest procedure . . . CPL 140.40
    Procedure for . . . CPL 140.35
    When authorized . . . CPL 140.30
    Where authorized . . . CPL 140.30
Public places, temporary questioning of persons in
    . . . CPL 140.50

[References are to sections of Consolidated Laws as abbreviated on Page i.]

ARREST WITHOUT WARRANT—Cont.
Search for weapons . . . CPL 140.50
Temporary questioning of persons in public places . . . CPL 140.50
Uniform Close Pursuit Act . . . CPL 140.55

ARSON
Definitions . . . PL 150.00
Fifth degree . . . PL 150.01
First degree . . . PL 150.20
Fourth degree . . . PL 150.05
Reparation . . . PL 60.27
Restitution . . . PL 60.27
Second degree . . . PL 150.15
Third degree . . . PL 150.10

ASSAULT
Aggravated assault
    Eleven years of age, upon person less than . . . PL 120.12
    Peace officers, upon . . . PL 120.11
    Police officers, upon . . . PL 120.11
Emergency medical services professional, on . . . PL 120.08
Firefighter, on . . . PL 120.08
First degree . . . PL 120.10
Gang assault
    First degree . . . PL 120.07
    Second degree . . . PL 120.06
Judge, assault on . . . PL 120.09
Minors (See MINORS)
Paramedic, on . . . PL 120.08
Peace officer, on . . . PL 120.08
Police officer, on . . . PL 120.08
Second degree . . . PL 120.05
Sexual assault on a child (See MINORS)
Third degree . . . PL 120.00
Vehicular assault (See VEHICULAR ASSAULT)

ATTEMPT TO COMMIT CRIME
Generally . . . PL 110.00
Defense, lack of . . . PL 110.10
Punishment . . . PL 110.05

ATTENDANCE (See APPEARANCE)

ATTORNEY GENERAL
Death penalty cases, consultation of Governor with Attorney General in . . . COR 654

ATTORNEYS
District attorney (See DISTRICT ATTORNEY)
Grand jury proceedings, witness' right to attorney in . . . CPL 190.52

**AUTHORIZED DISPOSITIONS OF OFFEND-
ERS**
Generally . . . PL 60.01
Applicability of provisions . . . PL 60.00
Cemetery desecration . . . PL 60.29
Civil penalties . . . PL 60.30

**AUTHORIZED DISPOSITIONS OF
OFFENDERS**—Cont.
Class A, B, certain C and D felonies . . . PL 60.04; PL 60.05
Controlled substance offenders
    Felony offenses . . . PL 60.04
    Resentencing of . . . CPL 440.46; PL 60.08; PL 60.09
    Treatment for substance abuse . . . PL 60.04
Corporations . . . PL 60.25
Domestic violence cases . . . PL 60.12
Driving while intoxicated . . . PL 60.21; PL 60.36
Eligible persons charged with certain cyber crimes may be placed in education reform program under Social Services Law § 488-l . . . PL 60.37
Fines (See FINES AND PENALTIES)
Graffiti, making of; possession of graffiti instruments . . . PL 60.28
Juvenile offenders . . . PL 60.10
Marijuana
    Felony offenses . . . PL 60.04; PL 60.05
    Multiple felony offender . . . PL 60.04; PL 60.05
Multiple felony offender . . . PL 60.04; PL 60.05
Murder in first degree . . . PL 60.06
Operators of for-hire vehicles, criminal attack on . . . PL 60.07
Penalties (See FINES AND PENALTIES)
Possession of weapon (See subhead: Weapon, possession of)
Reparation . . . PL 60.27
Resentencing of . . . CPL 440.46; PL 60.08; PL 60.09
Restitution . . . PL 60.27
Sex offenses . . . PL 60.13
Traffic infractions . . . PL 60.20
Treatment for substance abuse . . . PL 60.04
Weapon, possession of
    Fourth degree . . . PL 60.11
    Third degree . . . PL 60.11–a
Youthful offenders . . . PL 60.02

AUTOMOBILES
Assault, vehicular
    First degree . . . PL 120.04
    Second degree . . . PL 120.03
Auto stripping
    First degree . . . PL 165.11
    Second degree . . . PL 165.10
    Third degree . . . PL 165.09
Fleeing from police officer in (See POLICE OFFICERS)
Identification numbers
    Forgery . . . PL 170.65
    Illegal possession of
       Generally . . . PL 170.70
       Presumptions . . . PL 170.71
    Presumptions as to illegal possession of . . . PL 170.71

[References are to sections of Consolidated Laws as abbreviated on Page i.]

AUTOMOBILES—Cont.

Manslaughter, vehicular
   First degree . . . PL 125.13
   Second degree . . . PL 125.12
Operators of for-hire vehicles
   Authorized disposition of offenders for attack on
   . . . PL 60.07
   Special information . . . CPL 200.61
Presumptions as to illegal possession of identification numbers . . . PL 170.71
Seizure and forfeiture of vehicles used to transport gambling records . . . PL 415.00
Stripping, auto (See subhead: Auto stripping)
Taximeter accelerating device, criminal possession of . . . PL 145.70
Unauthorized use of
   First degree . . . PL 165.08
   Second degree . . . PL 165.06
   Third degree . . . PL 165.05
Vehicle and Traffic Law (See VEHICLE AND TRAFFIC LAW)

AUTOPSY

Inmates, state liability for expense of autopsy on
   . . . COR 16

B

BAIL

Application for recognizance or bail
   Criteria controlling determination . . . CPL 510.30
   Procedure . . . CPL 510.20
   Rules of law and criteria controlling determination . . . CPL 510.30
   Securing order, determination by . . . CPL 510.40
Authorized form of . . . CPL 520.10
Bond (See BAIL BOND)
Cash bail
   Posting of . . . CPL 520.15
   Transfer from local criminal court to superior court . . . CPL 520.40
Conviction and before sentence, order of recognizance or bail after . . . CPL 530.45
Definitions . . . CPL 500.10
Extradition proceedings (See EXTRADITION)
Felony complaint, proceedings upon . . . CPL 180.10
Fixing bail, methods of . . . CPL 520.10
Forfeiture of
   Generally . . . CPL 540.10
   Local criminal courts . . . CPL 540.20
   Remission of . . . CPL 540.30
Jumping (See BAIL JUMPING)
Local criminal courts
   Forfeiture of bail . . . CPL 540.20
   Order of recognizance or bail pending action . . . CPL 530.20

BAIL—Cont.

Order of recognizance or bail
   Generally . . . CPL 530.10
   After conviction and before sentence . . . CPL 530.45
   Appeal, during pendency of . . . CPL 530.50
   Before sentence, after conviction and . . . CPL 530.45
   Bench warrant . . . CPL 530.70
   Family offense matters, procedures for . . . CPL 530.11
   Local criminal court, pending action by . . . CPL 530.20
   Pending action
      Local criminal court, order by . . . CPL 530.20
      Superior court, order by . . . CPL 530.30; CPL 530.40
   Revocation . . . CPL 530.60
   Surrender of defendant . . . CPL 530.80
   Victims of crimes, protection of . . . CPL 530.13
   Victims of family offenses, protection of . . . CPL 530.12
Pre-arraignment bail, issuance and service of appearance ticket upon posting of . . . CPL 150.30
Receipts for . . . VTL 1802
Recognizance, release on own
   Application for (See subhead: Application for recognizance or bail)
   Definition . . . CPL 500.10
   Order of recognizance or bail (See subhead: Order of recognizance or bail)
Securing order
   Application for recognizance or bail, determination of . . . CPL 510.40
   Enforcement of . . . CPL 510.50
   Requirement . . . CPL 510.10
Sufficiency, examination as to . . . CPL 520.30

BAIL BOND

Affidavits, justifying . . . CPL 520.20
Content . . . CPL 520.20
Form and content . . . CPL 520.20
Posting of . . . CPL 520.20
Sufficiency, examination as to . . . CPL 520.30

BAIL JUMPING

Defense . . . PL 215.59
First degree . . . PL 215.57
Second degree . . . PL 215.56
Third degree . . . PL 215.55

BIGAMY

Generally . . . PL 255.15
Defense . . . PL 255.20

BILL OF PARTICULARS

Indictment . . . CPL 200.95
Information . . . CPL 100.45

[References are to sections of Consolidated Laws as abbreviated on Page i.]

BILL OF PARTICULARS—Cont.
Misdemeanor complaint . . . CPL 100.45
Prosecutor's information . . . CPL 100.45

BIOLOGICAL WEAPONS (See TERRORISM, CRIMES OF)

BLOOD TESTS
DNA testing (See DNA TESTING)
HIV-related testing requirement . . . CPL 390.15

BOARD OF PAROLE (See PAROLE BOARD)

BOMBS
False bomb, placement of
    Generally . . . PL 240.63
    Eavesdropping or video surveillance warrants, false reporting of incident as designated offense for purposes of . . . CPL 700.05
    First degree . . . PL 240.62
    Second degree . . . PL 240.61
Obstruction of governmental duties by use of . . . PL 195.17

BRIBERY
Commercial bribery
    First degree
        Generally . . . PL 180.03
        Receiving in . . . PL 180.08
    Second degree
        Generally . . . PL 180.00
        Receiving in . . . PL 180.05
Jurors
    Generally . . . PL 215.19
    Gratuities to . . . PL 215.22
    Receiving bribe . . . PL 215.20
Labor officials, bribery of
    Generally . . . PL 180.15
    Defenses . . . PL 180.20; PL 180.30
    Definition . . . PL 180.10
    Lack of defense . . . PL 180.30
    Receiving bribe . . . PL 180.25
Public servants, bribery involving (See PUBLIC SERVANTS)
Rent gouging (See RENT GOUGING)
Sports bribery (See SPORTS)
Witnesses (See WITNESSES)

BURDEN OF PROOF
Defenses . . . PL 25.00

BURGLARY
Definition . . . PL 140.00
First degree . . . PL 140.30
Physical force; justification for use in defense of person in course of burglary . . . PL 35.20
Possession of burglar's tools . . . PL 140.35
Second degree . . . PL 140.25
Third degree . . . PL 140.20
Tools, possession of burglar's . . . PL 140.35

BURN INJURIES
Failure to report . . . PL 265.26

BUSINESS RECORDS
Falsifying (See WRITTEN FALSE STATEMENTS)

C

CANADA
Driver's license, suspension and revocation of; reciprocal agreements . . . VTL 516–a

CAPITAL PUNISHMENT (See DEATH PENALTY)

CAREGIVER
Endangering welfare of vulnerable elderly, incompetent or physically disabled person
    First degree . . . PL 260.34
    Second degree . . . PL 260.32

CEMETERY DESECRATION
Aggravated
    First degree . . . PL 145.27
    Second degree . . . PL 145.26
Authorized disposition of offenders . . . PL 60.29
Conditional discharge . . . PL 65.10
First degree
    Generally . . . PL 145.23
    Aggravated . . . PL 145.27
Second degree
    Generally . . . PL 145.22
    Aggravated . . . PL 145.26

CERTIFICATES AND CERTIFICATION
Appeal, certificate granting leave to
    Court of appeals, to . . . CPL 460.20
    Intermediate appellate court, to . . . CPL 460.15
Controlled substances, revocation and suspension of certificate of approval for . . . PHL 3390–3396
Conviction, certificate concerning judgment of . . . CPL 60.60
Correctional facility or children and family services facility, delivery of certificate of conviction to . . . CPL 380.65
Disabilities, certificate of relief from (See DISABILITIES)
Execution, certificate as to . . . COR 661
False certificates, issuing . . . PL 175.40
Fingerprints . . . CPL 60.60
Good conduct . . . COR 703–a; COR 703–b
Social services, delivery of certificate of conviction to commissioner of . . . COR 71; CPL 380.80
Vehicle and Traffic Law (See VEHICLE AND TRAFFIC LAW)

CHALLENGES (See JURY AND JURORS)

CHARGE TO JURY (See JURY AND JURORS)

[References are to sections of Consolidated Laws as abbreviated on Page i.]

[References are to sections of Consolidated Laws as abbreviated on Page i.]

COMMUNICATIONS—Cont.
Eavesdropping (See EAVESDROPPING)
Privacy, right to (See PRIVACY, RIGHT TO)

COMMUNITY DISPUTE RESOLUTION CENTER PROGRAM
Administration of centers . . . JUD 849–b
Application procedures . . . JUD 849–c
Definitions . . . JUD 849–a
Establishment . . . JUD 849–b
Findings . . . JUD 849–e
Payment procedures . . . JUD 849–d
Regulations . . . JUD 849–f
Reports . . . JUD 849–g
Rules and regulations . . . JUD 849–f

COMMUNITY TREATMENT FACILITIES
Absconding from . . . PL 205.19
Transfer of eligible inmates to . . . COR 72–a

COMMUTATION OF SENTENCE (See EXECUTIVE CLEMENCY)

COMPLAINT REVIEW COUNCIL
Role of . . . COR 42

COMPOUNDING A CRIME
Generally . . . PL 215.45

COMPUTER CRIMES
Defenses . . . PL 156.50
Definitions . . . PL 156.00
Duplication of computer related material, unlawful . . . PL 156.30
Electronic sweepstakes, operation of unlawful . . . PL 156.40
Notice of defenses involving . . . CPL 250.30
Related material, computer
    Duplication, unlawful . . . PL 156.30
    Possession, criminal . . . PL 156.35
Tampering
    First degree . . . PL 156.27
    Second degree . . . PL 156.26
    Third degree . . . PL 156.25
    Fourth degree . . . PL 156.20
Trespass . . . PL 156.10
Unauthorized use of computer . . . PL 156.05

CONDITIONAL DISCHARGE (See PROBATION AND CONDITIONAL DISCHARGE)

CONDITIONAL SALE CONTRACTS
Fraudulent dispositions of property subject to . . . PL 185.05

CONFIDENTIALITY
Controlled substances, records or reports relating to . . . PHL 3371; PHL 3373
DNA testing . . . EXEC 995–d
HIV-related testing requirement
    Indictment . . . CPL 210.16
    Pre-sentence reports . . . CPL 390.15

CONFIDENTIALITY—Cont.
Pre-sentence reports
    Generally . . . CPL 390.50
    HIV-related testing requirement . . . CPL 390.15
Victim services office records . . . EXEC 633

CONSPIRACY
Defense, lack of . . . PL 105.30
Enterprise corruption . . . PL 105.35
Evidence . . . PL 105.20
Fifth degree . . . PL 105.05
First degree . . . PL 105.17
Fourth degree . . . PL 105.10
Jurisdiction and venue . . . PL 105.25
Overt act, necessity of . . . PL 105.20
Pleading and proof . . . PL 105.20
Second degree . . . PL 105.15
Sixth degree . . . PL 105.00
Third degree . . . PL 105.13
Venue . . . PL 105.25

CONSTITUTIONALITY
Extradition . . . CPL 570.66

CONSUMER PRODUCTS
Definition . . . PL 145.35
Tampering with
    Consumer product defined . . . PL 145.35
    First degree . . . PL 145.45
    Second degree . . . PL 145.40

CONTEMPT
Aggravated criminal contempt . . . PL 215.52
First degree . . . PL 215.51
Judicial conduct, criminal contempt of state commission on . . . PL 215.66
Legislature, of . . . PL 215.60
Prosecution and punishment . . . PL 215.54
Punishment . . . PL 215.54
Second degree . . . PL 215.50
State commission on judicial conduct, of . . . PL 215.66
Temporary state commission, of . . . PL 215.65

CONTRACTS
Conditional sale contract, fraudulent disposition of property subject to . . . PL 185.05
Employees' interest in contracts for institution, penalty for . . . COR 22
Interstate Corrections Compact . . . COR 103
Labor time of inmates in correctional facilities, prohibitions against contracts for . . . COR 103
Officers and employees' interest in contracts for institution, penalty for . . . COR 22

CONTROLLED SUBSTANCES
Addicts and habitual users, dispensing to
    Medical use, dispensing for . . . PHL 3351
    Prohibitions . . . PHL 3350
    Records . . . PHL 3352

[References are to sections of Consolidated Laws as abbreviated on Page i.]

[References are to sections of Consolidated Laws as abbreviated on Page i.]

[References are to sections of Consolidated Laws as abbreviated on Page i.]

[References are to sections of Consolidated Laws as abbreviated on Page i.]

CORRECTION LAW (GENERALLY)—Cont.

Local correctional facilities (See LOCAL COR-
RECTIONAL FACILITIES)

Pardons (See EXECUTIVE CLEMENCY)

Shock incarceration program (See SHOCK IN-
CARCERATION PROGRAM)

Short title . . . COR 1

Temporary release program (See TEMPORARY
RELEASE PROGRAM)

Work release program (See WORK RELEASE
PROGRAM)

CORRECTION OFFICERS AND EMPLOYEES

Appointment by commissioner . . . COR 7

Civil action against . . . COR 24

Commissioner, appointment by . . . COR 7

Contracts for institution, penalty for interest in
. . . COR 22

Qualification for employment as correction officer
. . . COR 22–a

Superintendents of correctional facilities (See SU-
PERINTENDENTS OF CORRECTIONAL FA-
CILITIES)

Testing of certain applicants for employment
. . . COR 8

CORRECTIONS AND COMMUNITY SUPER-
VISION DEPARTMENT

"Community supervision" defined . . . EXEC 259

Confinement of persons by . . . COR 72

Custody of, persons received into . . . COR 71

Employees (See CORRECTION OFFICERS AND
EMPLOYEES)

Library of . . . COR 20

Officers and employees (See CORRECTION OFFI-
CERS AND EMPLOYEES)

Organization of . . . COR 7

Parole officers . . . COR 10

Real property, acquisition of . . . COR 21

Social services, notification of conviction to commissioner of . . . COR 71; CPL 380.80

Statistical analysis . . . COR 29

Testing of certain applicants for employment
. . . COR 8

CORROBORATION

Accomplice testimony . . . CPL 60.22

Adultery . . . PL 255.30

Child, endangering welfare of . . . PL 260.11

Defendant's statements . . . CPL 60.50

Facilitation, criminal . . . PL 115.15

Incest . . . PL 255.30

Perjury . . . PL 210.50

Sex offenses . . . PL 130.16

Stolen property, criminal possession of . . . PL
165.65

CORRUPTION

Enterprise corruption (See ENTERPRISE COR-
RUPTION)

CORRUPTION—Cont.

Position or authority, corrupt use of . . . PL
200.56

COSTS AND FEES

Alternate correctional facilities for New York City;
costs for establishment, operation and maintenance . . . COR 89–g

Crime victim assistance fee . . . CPL 420.35

Discovery . . . CPL 240.70

Extradition, expense of . . . CPL 570.56

Health care in local correctional facilities, costs for
. . . COR 500–h

Inmates, costs for
Autopsy, state liability for expense of . . . COR
16
Health care costs for inmates in local correctional facilities . . . COR 500–h

Local correctional facilities, health care costs for
. . . COR 500–h

Mandatory surcharge
Generally . . . CPL 420.35; PL 60.35
Deferral of . . . CPL 420.40

Sex offender registration, fee charged upon change
of address for . . . COR 168–b

Witnesses
Material witness . . . CPL 620.80
Subpoenaed witness . . . CPL 610.50

COUNTERFEITING (See TRADEMARK
COUNTERFEITING)

COUNTIES

Correctional facilities (See LOCAL CORREC-
TIONAL FACILITIES)

Geographical jurisdiction of offenses . . . CPL
20.40

Jails
Generally (See LOCAL CORRECTIONAL FA-
CILITIES)
Work release program for (See WORK RE-
LEASE PROGRAM, subhead: County jails)

Leasing of state institutions to cities or counties for
confinement of prisoners . . . COR 79

Work release program for (See WORK RELEASE
PROGRAM, subhead: County jails)

COUNTY COURTS

Removal of action to and from supreme court
. . . CPL 230.10; CPL 230.20

COURT OF APPEALS

Criminal courts, appeals taken directly upon judgments and orders of . . . CPL 470.30

Death sentence, motion for setting aside
Generally . . . CPL 450.70; CPL 450.80
Judicial review, basis of . . . CPL 470.30
Racial bias . . . CPL 470.30
Stay of judgment . . . CPL 460.40

Defendant, appeal by . . . CPL 450.70

[References are to sections of Consolidated Laws as abbreviated on Page i.]

[References are to sections of Consolidated Laws as abbreviated on Page i.]

[References are to sections of Consolidated Laws as abbreviated on Page i.]

DEATH PENALTY—Cont.

Confinement of persons under death sentence—Cont.

  Incompetent persons . . . COR 656

Court of Appeals (See COURT OF APPEALS)

Execution of

  Certificate of . . . COR 661

  Disposition of body . . . COR 662

  Lethal injection as method . . . COR 658

  Place of . . . COR 659

  Post-mortem examination of body . . . COR 661

  Time for . . . COR 651

  Warrant for

    Generally . . . COR 650

    Delivery of . . . COR 652

  Witnesses to execution . . . COR 660

Governor, role of

  Consultation with attorney general, district attorney, and counsel . . . COR 654

  Record to, transmittal of . . . COR 653

  Reprieve, granting of . . . COR 655

Incompetent persons, procedures for . . . COR 656

Intent to seek, notice of . . . CPL 250.40

Jurors in capital cases (See JURY AND JURORS, subhead: Capital cases)

Lethal injection as method of execution . . . COR 658

Notice of intent to seek . . . CPL 250.40

Place of execution . . . COR 659

Post-mortem certificate . . . COR 661

Pregnant convicts, procedures for . . . COR 657

Pre-sentence proceedings . . . CPL 400.27

Racial bias

  Court of Appeals, review by . . . CPL 470.30

  Prospective jurors, of . . . CPL 270.16

Reprieve, granting . . . COR 655

Setting aside of sentence, motion for

  Generally . . . CPL 440.20

  Court of appeals, to (See COURT OF APPEALS)

Time for execution of . . . COR 651

Warrant for execution of

  Generally . . . COR 650

  Delivery of . . . COR 652

Witnesses to execution . . . COR 660

DEBIT CARDS

Unlawful use of . . . PL 165.17

DEFENSES

Adultery . . . PL 255.20

Appearance ticket, failure to respond to . . . PL 215.59

Attempt to commit crime . . . PL 110.10

Bad checks, issuance of . . . PL 190.15

Bail jumping . . . PL 215.59

Bigamy . . . PL 255.20

DEFENSES—Cont.

Bribery involving public servants . . . PL 200.05; PL 200.15

Burden of proof . . . PL 25.00

Business records, falsifying . . . PL 175.15

Child, endangering welfare of . . . PL 260.15

Coercion . . . PL 135.70; PL 135.75

Computer crimes . . . PL 156.50

Conspiracy . . . PL 105.30

Culpability, defenses involving lack of (See CULPABILITY)

Entrapment, defense of . . . PL 40.05

Facilitation, lack of . . . PL 115.10

Forged instrument, criminal possession of . . . PL 170.35

Gambling offenses (See GAMBLING OFFENSES)

Imprisonment, unlawful . . . PL 135.15

Infancy, defense of . . . PL 30.00

Justification (See JUSTIFICATION)

Kidnapping . . . PL 135.30

Labor officials, bribery of . . . PL 180.20; PL 180.30

Lack of

  Attempt to commit crime . . . PL 110.10

  Coercion . . . PL 135.70

  Conspiracy . . . PL 105.30

  Facilitation, lack of . . . PL 115.10

  Forged instrument, criminal possession of . . . PL 170.35

  Labor officials, bribery of . . . PL 180.30

  Larceny . . . PL 155.10

  Lottery offenses . . . PL 225.40

  Perjury . . . PL 210.30

  Prostitute, patronizing . . . PL 230.10

  Public servants, receipt of bribery by . . . PL 200.15

  Solicitation, criminal . . . PL 100.15

  Stolen property, criminal possession of . . . PL 165.60

Larceny . . . PL 155.10; PL 155.15

Lottery offenses . . . PL 225.40

Marriage license, unlawfully procuring . . . PL 255.20

Minors, dissemination of indecent material to . . . PL 235.23

Obscenity . . . PL 235.15

Perjury . . . PL 210.25; PL 210.30

Prostitute, patronizing . . . PL 230.07; PL 230.10

Public servants, bribery involving . . . PL 200.05

Renunciation, defense of . . . PL 40.10

Sex offenses . . . PL 130.10

Sexual performance by child; affirmative defenses . . . PL 263.20

Solicitation, criminal . . . PL 100.15

Stolen property, criminal possession of . . . PL 165.60

Unlawful imprisonment . . . PL 135.15

[References are to sections of Consolidated Laws as abbreviated on Page i.]

DEFINITE SENTENCE
Alternate correctional facilities, good behavior time allowances against definite sentences served in; New York City . . . COR 89–b
Good behavior allowances against; revised Penal Law provisions . . . COR 804

DELIBERATIONS (See JURY AND JURORS)

DEPARTMENT OF CORRECTIONS AND COMMUNITY SUPERVISION (See COR-RECTIONS AND COMMUNITY SUPERVI-SION DEPARTMENT)

DEPOSITION
Supporting (See SUPPORTING DEPOSITION)

DESTRUCTION
Counterfeit goods . . . PL 165.74
Dangerous drugs (See CONTROLLED SUB-STANCES)
Fireworks . . . PL 405.05
Recording of sound, unauthorized . . . PL 420.00

DETAINERS
Agreement on . . . CPL 580.20

DETENTION FACILITY
Escape from (See CUSTODY, subhead: Escape from)

DISABILITIES
Certificate of relief from
   Generally . . . COR 701
   Courts, issued by . . . COR 702
   Definitions . . . COR 700
   Filing . . . COR 705
   Forms . . . COR 705
   Pardon, no status as . . . COR 706
   Parole board, issued by . . . COR 703
   Revocation of . . . COR 704
Definitions . . . COR 700
Relief from, certificate of (See subhead: Certificate of relief from)

DISABLED PERSONS
Animal trained to aid, harming
   First degree . . . PL 195.12
   Restitution to person with disability . . . PL 60.27
   Second degree . . . PL 195.11
Endangering welfare of physically disabled persons
   First degree . . . PL 260.25; PL 260.34
   Second degree . . . PL 260.24; PL 260.32

DISCLOSURE
Discovery (See DISCOVERY)
DNA testing
   Generally . . . EXEC 995–d
   Penalties for disclosure . . . EXEC 995–f
Eavesdropping, information obtained through . . . CPL 700.65

DISCLOSURE—Cont.
Enterprise corruption; court ordered disclosure . . . PL 460.80
Grand jury disclosure, unlawful . . . PL 215.70
HIV-related testing requirement . . . CPL 390.15
Indictment, unlawful disclosure of . . . PL 215.75
Video surveillance, information obtained through . . . CPL 700.65

DISCOVERY
Continuing duty to disclose . . . CPL 240.60
Court order . . . CPL 240.40
Criminal acts, disclosure of prior uncharged . . . CPL 240.43
Criminal history of witnesses, discovery upon trial of . . . CPL 240.45
Defendant's demand . . . CPL 240.20
Definitions . . . CPL 240.10
Demand for
   Defendant's demand . . . CPL 240.20
   Procedure . . . CPL 240.80
   Prosecutor's demand . . . CPL 240.30
   Refusal of . . . CPL 240.35; CPL 240.80
Duty to disclose, continuing . . . CPL 240.60
Fees . . . CPL 240.70
Immoral acts, disclosure of prior uncharged . . . CPL 240.43
Interrogatories of witnesses on commission . . . CPL 680.50
Motion procedure . . . CPL 240.90
Pre-trial discovery, prosecution of information and . . . CPL 340.30
Pre-trial hearing, upon . . . CPL 240.44
Prior statements of witnesses, discovery upon trial of . . . CPL 240.45
Prior uncharged acts, disclosure of . . . CPL 240.43
Prosecutor's demand . . . CPL 240.30
Protective orders . . . CPL 240.50
Refusal of demand . . . CPL 240.35
Sanctions . . . CPL 240.70
Supporting deposition (See SUPPORTING DEPO-SITION)
Vicious or immoral acts, disclosure of prior uncharged . . . CPL 240.43
Violations . . . CPL 240.75
Witnesses, discovery upon trial of prior statements and criminal history of . . . CPL 240.45

DISCRETIONARY REDUCTIONS OF SEN-TENCE
Work release program for county jails, eligibility of person participating in . . . COR 876

DISCRIMINATION
Death penalty cases, racial bias issues in
   Court of Appeals, review by . . . CPL 470.30
   Prospective jurors, of . . . CPL 270.16

[References are to sections of Consolidated Laws as abbreviated on Page i.]

DISCRIMINATION—Cont.

Prior convictions, application for license or employment by persons with; prohibitions against unfair discrimination . . . COR 752

DISMISSAL OF CHARGES

Adjournment in contemplation of dismissal
  Dispute resolution, for purposes of referral to . . . CPL 215.30
  Marijuana cases . . . CPL 170.56; CPL 210.46
Dispute resolution, adjournment in contemplation of dismissal for purposes of referral to . . . CPL 215.30
Effect of . . . CPL 215.40
Grand jury . . . CPL 190.75
Marijuana cases, adjournment in contemplation of dismissal of charges in . . . CPL 170.56; CPL 210.46

DISORDERLY CONDUCT

Generally . . . PL 240.20

DISPOSITION OF CASE

Notice to crime victims of . . . CPL 440.50

DISPOSITIONS OF OFFENDERS, AUTHORIZED (See AUTHORIZED DISPOSITIONS OF OFFENDERS)

DISPUTE RESOLUTION

Adjournment in contemplation of dismissal . . . CPL 215.30
Referral of selected felonies to
  Adjournment in contemplation of dismissal for purposes of . . . CPL 215.30
  Procedure . . . CPL 215.10
Restoration of action to calendar . . . CPL 215.30
Victim defined . . . CPL 215.20

DISTRICT ATTORNEY

Death penalty, governor's consultation with district attorney pending decision of reprieval or suspension of . . . COR 654
Grand jury proceedings, duties and authority in . . . CPL 190.55
Local criminal court accusatory instrument, notice to district attorney on . . . CPL 110.20
Removal from local criminal court to superior court, request for . . . CPL 170.20

DIVISION OF CRIMINAL JUSTICE SERVICES (See CRIMINAL JUSTICE SERVICES DIVISION)

DNA IDENTIFICATION INDEX

State identification index . . . EXEC 995–c

DNA TESTING

Application of article . . . EXEC 995–e
Confidentiality . . . EXEC 995–d
Databank fee
  Generally . . . PL 60.35

DNA TESTING—Cont.

Databank fee—Cont.
  Deferral based on financial hardship . . . CPL 420.40
Definitions . . . EXEC 995
Disclosure
  Generally . . . EXEC 995–d
  Penalties for . . . EXEC 995–f
Identification index . . . EXEC 995–c
Penalties for disclosure or tampering . . . EXEC 995–f
Tampering, penalties for . . . EXEC 995–f

DOMESTIC VIOLENCE

Authorized dispositions of offenders . . . PL 60.12
Determining whether certain misdemeanors are crimes of domestic violence under federal law . . . CPL 370.15; CPL 380.97
Indeterminate sentence of imprisonment . . . PL 60.12
Notice to division of criminal justice services that misdemeanor is crime of domestic violence under federal law . . . CPL 380.97

DOUBLE JEOPARDY (See PREVIOUS PROSECUTION)

DRIVER'S LICENSE

Downgrade of commercial driver's license for medical certification status becoming "noncertified" . . . VTL 510–aa
Suspension or revocation of driver's license (See DRIVER'S LICENSE: SUSPENSION AND REVOCATION)

DRIVER'S LICENSE: SUSPENSION AND REVOCATION

Generally . . . VTL 510
Aggravated unlicensed operation of vehicle, facilitating . . . VTL 511; VTL 511–a
Alcohol, operation of vehicle by persons under age 21 after consumption of . . . VTL 1194
Appearance (See APPEARANCE)
Certification of . . . VTL 514–b
Child support payments, failure to make . . . VTL 510
Commercial driver's licenses . . . VTL 510–a
Compact, driver license . . . VTL 516
Fines, failure to pay . . . VTL 511–d
Forfeiture
  Certification to commissioner . . . VTL 514
  Unlicensed operation of vehicle under certain circumstances, seizure and forfeitures for . . . VTL 511–c
Fraudulent license, sale or purchase of . . . VTL 392–a
Nonappearance, certification of . . . VTL 514
Notification of . . . VTL 514–a; VTL 514–c
Probationary periods, for violations committed during . . . VTL 510–b

DRIVER'S LICENSE: SUSPENSION AND REVOCATION—Cont.

Reciprocal agreements

Canada, agreements with provinces of . . . VTL 516–a

Traffic offenses, reporting of . . . VTL 516–b

Redemption of unlawfully operated vehicles, seizure and . . . VTL 511–b

Reissuance . . . VTL 510

Seizures

Unlawfully operated vehicles, seizure and redemption of . . . VTL 511–b

Unlicensed operation of vehicle under certain circumstances . . . VTL 511–c

Stolen or fraudulent license, sale or purchase of . . . VTL 392–a

DRIVING WHILE INTOXICATED

Vehicle and Traffic Law (See VEHICLE AND TRAFFIC LAW, subhead: Alcohol and drug-related offenses)

DRUGS (See CONTROLLED SUBSTANCES)

DURESS

Defense of . . . PL 40.00

E

EAVESDROPPING

Generally . . . PL 250.05

Definitions . . . PL 250.00

Devices, possession of . . . PL 250.10

Electronic access device; defined . . . PL 170.00

Failure to report . . . PL 250.15

Warrants (See EAVESDROPPING OR VIDEO SURVEILLANCE WARRANTS)

Wiretapping, failure to report . . . PL 250.15

EAVESDROPPING OR VIDEO SURVEILLANCE WARRANTS

Generally . . . CPL 700.10

Administrative office of United States courts, reports to . . . CPL 700.60

Amendment, order of . . . CPL 700.65

Application

Generally . . . CPL 700.20

Content . . . CPL 700.20

Custody of . . . CPL 700.55

Determination of . . . CPL 700.25

Content . . . CPL 700.30

Custody of warrants, applications and recordings . . . CPL 700.55

Definitions . . . CPL 700.05

Determination of application . . . CPL 700.25

Disclosure and use of information . . . CPL 700.65

Divulging warrant . . . PL 250.20

Emergency situations, temporary authorization for . . . CPL 700.21

EAVESDROPPING OR VIDEO SURVEILLANCE WARRANTS—Cont.

Execution, manner and time of . . . CPL 700.35

Extension, order of . . . CPL 700.40

Form and content . . . CPL 700.30

Intention to use, notice of . . . CPL 700.70

Issuance of . . . CPL 700.15

Manner of execution . . . CPL 700.35

Notice . . . CPL 700.50; CPL 700.70

Order of extension . . . CPL 700.40

Progress reports . . . CPL 700.50

Recordings, custody of . . . CPL 700.55

Reports

Administrative office of United States courts, reports to . . . CPL 700.60

Progress reports . . . CPL 700.50

Temporary authorization for emergency situations . . . CPL 700.21

Time of execution . . . CPL 700.35

Use of information, disclosure and . . . CPL 700.65

EDUCATION

Director of, appointment of . . . COR 15–b

Education department where licensed professional convicted of felony, notice to . . . CPL 440.55

ELDERLY PERSONS

Endangering welfare of vulnerable elderly person

First degree . . . PL 260.34

Second degree . . . PL 260.32

Vulnerable elderly person

Definition . . . PL 260.30

Endangering welfare of

First degree . . . PL 260.34

Second degree . . . PL 260.32

ELECTRONIC APPEARANCE (See APPEARANCE)

ELECTRONIC PRESCRIPTIONS (See PRESCRIPTIONS, subhead: Electronic prescriptions)

ELECTRONIC SURVEILLANCE (See EAVESDROPPING)

EMERGENCY MEDICAL SERVICES PROFESSIONAL

Assault on . . . PL 120.08

EMINENT DOMAIN

Correctional Services Department, acquisition of real property by . . . COR 21

EMPLOYERS AND EMPLOYEES

Bribery (See BRIBERY)

Correction officers and employees (See CORRECTION OFFICERS AND EMPLOYEES)

Government employees (See PUBLIC SERVANTS)

[References are to sections of Consolidated Laws as abbreviated on Page i.]

[References are to sections of Consolidated Laws as abbreviated on Page i.]

EXECUTIVE CLEMENCY—Cont.

Oath of witnesses, administration of . . . COR 263

Subpoenas

    Application for clemency . . . COR 261

    Requirements . . . COR 261

Witnesses

    Fees . . . COR 264

    Oath of witnesses, administration of . . . COR 263

    Penalty for failure to appear . . . COR 265

Subpoenas

    Application for clemency . . . COR 261

    Requirements . . . COR 264

EXECUTIVE LAW (GENERALLY)

Board of parole (See PAROLE BOARD)

Crime victims board (See VICTIM SERVICES OF-FICE)

DNA testing (See DNA TESTING)

Fair treatment standards for crime victims (See FAIR TREATMENT STANDARDS FOR CRIME VICTIMS)

Forensic science commission (See FORENSIC SCIENCE COMMISSION)

Office of victim services (See VICTIM SERVICES OFFICE)

Parole board (See PAROLE BOARD)

Victim services (See VICTIM SERVICES OFFICE)

EXEMPTIONS

Previous prosecution, exemption of prosecution by reason of (See PREVIOUS PROSECUTION)

EXPLOSIVES (See BOMBS)

EXTRADITION

Arrest for

    Authority of arresting officer . . . CPL 570.22

    Requisition, before making . . . CPL 570.32

    Warrant of (See subhead: Warrant of arrest)

    Without warrant . . . CPL 570.34

Awaiting trial, persons . . . CPL 570.12

Bail

    Conditions . . . CPL 570.38

    Forfeiture . . . CPL 570.42

    Posting . . . CPL 570.36

Civil actions in connection with, immunity from service of process in . . . CPL 570.58

Compulsion, persons who left demanding state under . . . CPL 570.14

Confinement

    Jail, confinement of accused in . . . CPL 570.28

    Passing through state, persons . . . CPL 570.30

Constitutionality . . . CPL 570.66

Definitions . . . CPL 570.04

Demand, requirements for . . . CPL 570.08

Duty of governor as to delivery of fugitive . . . CPL 570.06; CPL 570.52

Expense of . . . CPL 570.56

EXTRADITION—Cont.

Extension of time for commitment . . . CPL 570.40

Foreign countries, defendants in . . . CPL 590.10

Guilt or innocence of accused, inquiry into . . . CPL 570.46

Habeas corpus proceeding . . . CPL 570.24

Immunity

    Other criminal prosecutions while in this state . . . CPL 570.60

    Service of process in civil actions in connection with extradition proceedings . . . CPL 570.58

Imprisoned or awaiting trial, persons . . . CPL 570.12; CPL 580.10

Innocence or guilt of accused, inquiry into . . . CPL 570.46

Interpretation of statute . . . CPL 570.64

Interstate Corrections Compact provisions . . . COR 105

Investigation by governor . . . CPL 570.10

Requisition

    Application for issuance of . . . CPL 570.54

    Arrest of accused before making . . . CPL 570.32

    Commitment to await . . . CPL 570.36

    Content . . . CPL 570.54

    Criminal prosecution pending in this state at time of . . . CPL 570.44

    Issuance of . . . CPL 570.54

Rights of accused

    Habeas corpus proceeding . . . CPL 570.24

    Violation of, penalties for . . . CPL 570.26

Service of process, immunity from . . . CPL 570.58

Short title . . . CPL 570.02

Time of commission of crime, extraditions of persons not present in demanding state at . . . CPL 570.16

Waiver

    Non-waiver . . . CPL 570.62

    Written waiver . . . CPL 570.50

Warrant of arrest

    Alias warrant . . . CPL 570.48

    Execution of . . . CPL 570.20

    Issuance of . . . CPL 570.18

F

FACILITATION, CRIMINAL (See CRIMINAL FACILITATION)

FAIR TREATMENT STANDARDS FOR CRIME VICTIMS

Generally . . . EXEC 640; EXEC 649

Agencies providing services to victims . . . EXEC 643

Applicability . . . EXEC 640; EXEC 649

Child victims as witnesses, guidelines for . . . EXEC 642–a

[References are to sections of Consolidated Laws as abbreviated on Page i.]

FAIR TREATMENT STANDARDS FOR CRIME VICTIMS—Cont.
Courts, treatment of victims by . . . EXEC 645
Criteria for . . . EXEC 642; EXEC 647
Establishment of . . . EXEC 642
Felony offense . . . EXEC 642
Implementation . . . EXEC 644; EXEC 648
Informational pamphlet, providing victim with . . . EXEC 646–a
Limitations on application . . . EXEC 649
Objectives of . . . EXEC 641; EXEC 646; EXEC 647
Pamphlet, providing informational . . . EXEC 646–a
Police reports . . . EXEC 646
Purpose of . . . EXEC 641
Requirements for . . . EXEC 642
Review . . . EXEC 648
Witnesses, child victims as . . . EXEC 642–a

FALSE STATEMENTS
Eavesdropping or video surveillance warrants, false reporting of incident as designated offense for purposes of . . . CPL 700.05
Perjury (See PERJURY)
Written false statements (See WRITTEN FALSE STATEMENTS)

FAMILY COURT
Family offenses; evidentiary rules for proceedings in family court . . . CPL 60.46
Juvenile offenders (See JUVENILE OFFENDERS, subhead: Removal of proceeding to family court)
Local criminal courts, effect of family court proceeding on commencing action in . . . CPL 100.07

FAMILY OFFENSES
Aggravated family offense
    Generally . . . PL 240.75
    Indictment or information for . . . CPL 200.63
Procedures . . . CPL 530.11
Rules of evidence for proceedings in family court . . . CPL 60.46
Victims of family offenses, protection for . . . CPL 530.12

FEDERAL LAW ENFORCEMENT OFFICERS
Peace officers, status as . . . CPL 2.15
Powers of . . . CPL 2.15

FEES (See COSTS AND FEES)

FELONY (See also specific crimes)
Authorized dispositions of offenders (See AUTHORIZED DISPOSITIONS OF OFFENDERS)
Classification of . . . PL 55.05
Complaint (See FELONY COMPLAINT)
Definitions . . . COR 700
Fines . . . PL 80.00

FELONY (See also specific crimes)—Cont.
Imprisonment (See IMPRISONMENT SENTENCE)
Judicial diversion program
    Definitions . . . CPL 216
    Procedures . . . CPL 216.05
Persistent offender . . . CPL 400.16; CPL 400.21
Predicate felony conviction, hearing on . . . CPL 220.35
Second felony offender (See SECOND FELONY OFFENDERS)
Sentence . . . PL 55.05
Violent felony offense (See IMPRISONMENT SENTENCE, subhead: Violent felony offense)

FELONY COMPLAINT
Arraignment . . . CPL 180.10
Bail matters . . . CPL 180.10
Content . . . CPL 100.15
Court's instructions . . . CPL 180.10
Defendant's rights . . . CPL 180.10
Disposition of
    Hearing, disposition after . . . CPL 180.70
    Release of defendant from custody upon failure of timely . . . CPL 180.80
Form and content . . . CPL 100.15
Hearing
    Conduct of . . . CPL 180.60
    Disposition of felony after . . . CPL 180.70
    Superior court, application in . . . CPL 180.40
    Waiver of hearing
        Procedure upon . . . CPL 180.30
        Superior court, application in . . . CPL 180.40
Juvenile offenders . . . CPL 180.75
Reduction of charges . . . CPL 180.50
Release of defendant from custody upon failure of timely disposition . . . CPL 180.80
Removal of action from one local criminal court to another . . . CPL 180.20
Termination of prosecution . . . CPL 180.85
Verification . . . CPL 100.30

FEMALE INMATES (See WOMEN)

FIFTH DEGREE OFFENSES (See specific headings)

FINANCIAL STATEMENTS
False statements, issuing . . . PL 175.45

FINANCING STATEMENTS
False statements, notice to secretary of state of filing of . . . CPL 440.70

FINES AND PENALTIES
Attempt to commit crime . . . PL 110.05
Civil penalties . . . PL 60.30
Collection of
    Generally . . . CPL 420.10
    Corporation, fines imposed on . . . . CPL 420.20

FINES AND PENALTIES—Cont.

Corporation, fines imposed on . . . CPL 420.20; PL 80.10

Credit card, payment by . . . CPL 420.05

Crime victim assistance fee . . . CPL 420.35; PL 60.35

Crime victims board (See VICTIM SERVICES OFFICE)

Defendant's gain from offense, based on . . . CPL 400.30

DNA databank fee . . . PL 60.35

DNA tests or analysis, penalties for disclosure or tampering of . . . EXEC 995-f

Extradition proceedings, penalties for violation of rights of accused in . . . CPL 570.26

Felony . . . PL 80.00

Leaving scene of accident without reporting injury to certain animals . . . VTL 601

Littering on railroad tracks and rights-of-ways . . . PL 145.50

Mandatory surcharge
  Generally . . . CPL 420.35; PL 60.35
  Deferral of . . . CPL 420.40

Misdemeanors . . . PL 80.05

Money laundering . . . PL 470.20

Multiple offenses . . . PL 80.15

Office of Victim Services (See VICTIM SERVICES OFFICE)

Railroad tracks, littering on . . . PL 145.50

Remission of . . . CPL 420.30

Rights-of-ways, littering on . . . PL 145.50

Sex offender registration fee (See SEX OFFENDER REGISTRATION ACT)

Supplemental sex offender victim fee . . . PL 60.35

Vehicle and Traffic Law (See VEHICLE AND TRAFFIC LAW)

Victim services (See VICTIM SERVICES OFFICE)

Violations . . . PL 80.05

FINGERPRINTING

Appearance ticket, fingerprinting in conjunction with . . . CPL 150.70

Certificates concerning, evidentiary rules on . . . CPL 60.60

Criminal justice services division
  Duties of . . . CPL 160.30
  Transmission of report received by police . . . CPL 160.40

Forwarding of . . . CPL 160.20

Pre-sentence report . . . CPL 390.10

Procedure . . . CPL 160.20

Requirements . . . CPL 160.10

Summons procedure, fingerprinting . . . CPL 130.60

Termination of criminal action, return of fingerprints upon . . . CPL 160.50; CPL 160.55

FIRE

Arson (See ARSON)

Burn injuries, failure to report . . . PL 265.26

Correctional facility, fire in . . . COR 25; COR 507

Mutual assistance by institutional and local fire fighting facilities . . . COR 25

Removal of inmates in case of . . . COR 507

FIREARMS (See also WEAPONS)

Ammunition sellers, requirements for . . . PL 400.03

Criminal possession . . . PL 265.01–b

Criminal sale of (See subhead: Sale of, criminal)

Criminal use of (See subhead: Use of, criminal)

Definitions . . . PL 265.00

Licenses to carry, possess, repair and dispose of
  Applications . . . PL 400.00
  Certification . . . PL 400.00
  Eligibility . . . PL 400.00
  Expiration . . . PL 400.00
  Gunsmiths and dealers, records required of . . . PL 400.00
  Investigations . . . PL 400.00
  Registration . . . PL 400.00
  Renewal . . . PL 400.00
  Requirements . . . PL 400.00
  Retired sworn members of state police, granting to . . . PL 400.01
  Revocation and suspension . . . PL 400.00
  Statewide license and record database . . . PL 400.02
  Suspension and revocation . . . CPL 530.14

Loss of, report of . . . PL 400.10

Minors
  Aid of minor, sale with . . . PL 265.14
  Possession by . . . PL 265.20
  Sale to . . . PL 265.16

Purchase of
  Contiguous states, rifles and/or shotguns in . . . PL 265.40
  Criminal purchase . . . PL 265.17

Report of theft or loss of . . . PL 400.10

Safe storage of . . . PL 265.45

Sale of, criminal
  First degree . . . PL 265.13
  Minors
    Aid of minor, sale with . . . PL 265.14
    Sale to . . . PL 265.16
  Second degree . . . PL 265.12
  Third degree . . . PL 265.11

Sentencing court's obligation to demand surrender of . . . CPL 380.96

Statewide license and record database . . . PL 400.02

Suspension and revocation of licenses to carry, possess, repair and dispose of . . . CPL 530.14

Theft, report of . . . PL 400.10

[References are to sections of Consolidated Laws as abbreviated on Page i.]

FIREARMS (See also WEAPONS)—Cont.
Use of, criminal
    First degree . . . PL 265.09
    Second degree . . . PL 265.08

FIREFIGHTERS AND FIREFIGHTING
Assault on firefighter . . . PL 120.08
Obstruction of firefighting operations . . . PL
    195.15

FIREWORKS
Dangerous fireworks, unlawfully dealing with
    . . . PL 270.00
Destruction of, seizure and . . . PL 405.05
Seizure and destruction of . . . PL 405.05
Unlawfully dealing with . . . PL 270.00

**FIRST DEGREE OFFENSES (See specific head-
ings)**

**FITNESS TO PROCEED (See MENTAL DIS-
EASE OR DEFECT)**

FOREIGN COUNTRIES
Extradition of defendants in . . . CPL 590.10
Transfer of inmates to, availability of information
    in correctional facility library on . . . COR 71

FORENSIC SCIENCE COMMISSION
Generally . . . EXEC 995–a
Definitions . . . EXEC 995
DNA testing (See DNA TESTING)
Duties . . . EXEC 995–b
Powers . . . EXEC 995–b

FORFEITURE
Aircraft used to transport or conceal gambling re-
    cords . . . PL 415.00
Bail (See BAIL)
Controlled substances (See CONTROLLED SUB-
    STANCES)
Dispositions of assets subject to, unlawful . . . PL
    215.80
Driver's license, suspension and revocation of
    Certification of forfeitures to commissioner
        . . . VTL 514
    Unlicensed operation of vehicle under certain
        circumstances . . . VTL 511–c
Enterprise corruption . . . PL 460.30
Gambling records; seizure of any vehicles, vessels
    or aircraft used to transport or conceal . . . PL
    415.00
Pornography, equipment used to promote . . . PL
    410.00
Recording of sound, equipment used in unauthor-
    ized . . . PL 420.05
Unlicensed operation of vehicle under certain cir-
    cumstances . . . VTL 511–c
Vehicle and Traffic Law
    Dispositions . . . VTL 1803

FORFEITURE—Cont.
Vehicle and Traffic Law—Cont.
    Driver's license, suspension and revocation of
        Certification of forfeitures to commissioner
        . . . VTL 514
        Unlicensed operation of vehicle under certain
        circumstances . . . VTL 511–c
Vehicles, vessels or aircraft used to transport gam-
    bling records . . . PL 415.00
Vessels
    Controlled substances, any vehicles or vessels
        used for transportation or conveyance of
        . . . PHL 3388
    Gambling records, vessels used to transport
        . . . PL 415.00

FORGERY
Definitions . . . PL 170.00
Devices, possession of forgery . . . PL 170.40
First degree . . . PL 170.15
Possession of forged instrument, criminal
    Defense, lack of . . . PL 170.35
    Devices, possession of forgery . . . PL 170.40
    First degree . . . PL 170.30
    Presumptions, second degree . . . PL 170.27
    Second degree
        Generally . . . PL 170.25
        Presumptions . . . PL 170.27
    Third degree . . . PL 170.20
Second degree . . . PL 170.10
Third degree . . . PL 170.05
Vehicle identification numbers . . . PL 170.65

FORTUNE TELLING
Definition . . . PL 165.35

**FOURTH DEGREE OFFENSES (See specific
headings)**

FRAUD
Accosting, fraudulent . . . PL 165.30
Anti-security items, criminal possession of . . . PL
    170.47
Bad checks, issuance of
    Generally . . . PL 190.05
    Defenses . . . PL 190.15
    Definitions . . . PL 190.00
    Presumptions . . . PL 190.10
Bribery (See BRIBERY)
Collection practices, unlawful . . . PL 190.50
Conditional sale contract, fraudulent disposition of
    property subject to . . . PL 185.15
Controlled substances, obtaining . . . PHL 3397;
    PL 178.26
Corporate official, misconduct by . . . PL 190.35
Creditors
    Conditional sale contract, fraudulent disposition
        of property subject to . . . PL 185.15
    Insolvency, fraud in . . . PL 185.00

[References are to sections of Consolidated Laws as abbreviated on Page i.]

FRAUD—Cont.
Creditors—Cont.
  Mortgaged property, fraudulent disposition of
    . . . PL 185.10
    Security interests . . . PL 185.05
False advertising . . . PL 190.20
False personation . . . PL 190.23
False written statements (See WRITTEN FALSE
  STATEMENTS)
Forgery (See FORGERY)
Gaming fraud
  First degree . . . PL 225.60
  Second degree . . . PL 225.55
Government, defrauding . . . PL 195.20
Health care (See HEALTH CARE)
Immigrant assistant services fraud
  First degree . . . PL 190.89
  Second degree . . . PL 190.87
Impersonation, criminal
  First degree . . . PL 190.26
  Second degree . . . PL 190.25
Insolvency, fraud in . . . PL 185.00
Insurance fraud (See INSURANCE FRAUD)
Misconduct by corporate official . . . PL 190.35
Mortgaged property, fraudulent disposition of
  . . . PL 185.10
Police uniforms, criminal sale of . . . PL 190.27
Prescriptions, unlawful sale of . . . PL 190.70
Scheme to defraud
  First degree . . . PL 190.65
  Prescriptions, unlawful sale of . . . PL 190.70
  Second degree . . . PL 190.60
Security interests . . . PL 185.05
Signatures, fraudulently obtaining . . . PL 165.20
Simulation, criminal . . . PL 170.45
Slugs, unlawfully using (See SLUGS, subhead:
  Unlawfully using)
Usury, criminal
  First degree . . . PL 190.42
  Second degree . . . PL 190.40
Welfare (See WELFARE FRAUD)
Wills, unlawful concealment of . . . PL 190.30
Written false statements (See WRITTEN FALSE
  STATEMENTS)

FUNERAL SERVICE
Absence of inmate for . . . COR 509

FURLOUGHS
Generally . . . COR 630
Absconding from furlough program . . . PL
  205.18
Conduct of inmates participating in program
  . . . COR 634
Definitions . . . COR 631
Eligible inmates, procedure for furlough release of
  . . . COR 633
Establishment of furlough program . . . COR 632

G

GAMBLING OFFENSES
Counterfeit, unapproved or unlawful wagering in-
  struments, use of . . . PL 225.65
Defenses
  Devices, possession of gambling . . . PL
    225.32
  Lottery offenses . . . PL 225.40
  Records, possession of gambling . . . PL
    225.25
Definitions . . . PL 225.00
Devices, possession of gambling
  Generally . . . PL 225.30
  Defenses . . . PL 225.32
Fraud
  First degree . . . PL 225.60
  Second degree . . . PL 225.55
Gaming property
  Possession of unlawful gaming property
    First degree . . . PL 225.80
    Second degree . . . PL 225.75
    Third degree . . . PL 225.70
  Use of unlawful gaming property . . . PL
    225.85
Lottery offenses . . . PL 225.40
Manipulation of gaming outcomes at unauthorized
  gaming establishment . . . PL 225.90
Manufacture, sale, distribution, marking, altering or
  modification of equipment and devices associated
  with gambling . . . PL 225.95
Presumptions . . . PL 225.35
Promotion of gambling
  First degree . . . PL 225.10
  Second degree . . . PL 225.05
Records, possession of gambling
  Defenses . . . PL 225.25
  First degree . . . PL 225.20
  Second degree . . . PL 225.15

GANG ASSAULT
First degree . . . PL 120.07
Second degree . . . PL 120.06

GEOGRAPHICAL JURISDICTION OF OF-
  FENSES
Cities . . . CPL 20.50
Communications between jurisdictions . . . CPL
  20.60
Counties . . . CPL 20.40
Definitions . . . CPL 20.10
Partly committed within state, offense . . . CPL
  20.30
State jurisdiction . . . CPL 20.20
Towns . . . CPL 20.50
Transportation of property between jurisdictions
  . . . CPL 20.60
Villages . . . CPL 20.50

[References are to sections of Consolidated Laws as abbreviated on Page i.]

GIFTS
Commissioner of correction, acceptance by
. . . COR 15–c

GOOD BEHAVIOR
Alternate correctional facilities, good behavior time
allowances against definite sentences served in;
New York City . . . COR 89–b
Certificate of good conduct . . . COR 703–a; COR
703–b
Civil commitments, provisions for certain
. . . COR 804–a
Definite sentences, good behavior allowances
against . . . COR 804
Determinate sentences, good behavior allowances
against . . . COR 803–a
Indeterminate sentence, good behavior allowances
against . . . COR 803–a

GOVERNMENT
Corruption of
Definitions . . . PL 496.01
First degree . . . PL 496.05
Fourth degree . . . PL 496.02
Public corruption . . . PL 496.06
Second degree . . . PL 496.04
Sentencing . . . PL 496.03
Third degree . . . PL 496.03
Defrauding . . . PL 195.20
Public corruption . . . PL 496.06

GOVERNMENT EMPLOYEES (See PUBLIC
SERVANTS)

GOVERNOR
Death penalty cases, role in (See DEATH PEN-
ALTY)
Extradition of fugitive (See EXTRADITION)

GRAFFITI
Authorized disposition of offenders . . . PL 60.28
Conditional discharge . . . PL 60.28; PL 65.10
Making graffiti . . . PL 145.60
Possession of graffiti instruments . . . PL 145.65

GRAND JURY
Generally . . . CPL 190.05
Actions to be taken by . . . CPL 190.60
Appeal from order concerning grand jury reports
. . . CPL 190.90
Courts drawn from . . . CPL 190.10
Definition . . . CPL 190.05; CPL 190.35
Direction to file
Family court, request for removal to . . . CPL
190.71
Prosecutor's information and related matters
. . . CPL 190.70
Discharge . . . CPL 190.15
Disclosure, unlawful . . . PL 215.70
Dismissal of charges . . . CPL 190.75

GRAND JURY—Cont.
District attorney, duties and authority of . . . CPL
190.55
Duration of term . . . CPL 190.15
Duties of . . . CPL 190.20
Evidence
Compulsion of . . . CPL 190.40
Definitions . . . CPL 50.10
District attorney, duties and authority of
. . . CPL 190.55
Examination of . . . CPL 190.55
Insufficiency of, motion to dismiss or reduce
indictment on ground of . . . CPL 210.30
Rules of . . . CPL 190.30
Witnesses (See subhead: Witnesses)
Family court, direction to file request for removal
to . . . CPL 190.71
Formation . . . CPL 190.20
Function of . . . CPL 190.05
Hearing of evidence in . . . CPL 190.55
Immunity
Generally . . . CPL 190.40
Waiver of immunity . . . CPL 190.45
Indictment (See INDICTMENT)
Minutes, motion to inspect . . . CPL 210.30
Operation and proceedings . . . CPL 190.25
Organization . . . CPL 190.20
Proceedings and operation . . . CPL 190.25
Prosecutor's information, direction to file . . . CPL
190.70
Release of defendant upon failure of timely grand
jury action . . . CPL 190.80
Reports
Generally . . . CPL 190.85
Appeal from order concerning . . . CPL 190.90
Timely grand jury action, release of defendant upon
failure of . . . CPL 190.80
Videotaped examination . . . CPL 190.32
Waiver
Immunity, waiver by witness . . . CPL 190.45
Indictment (See INDICTMENT)
Witnesses
Generally . . . CPL 190.40
Attorney, right to . . . CPL 190.52
Defendant as witness . . . CPL 190.50
Immunity
Generally . . . CPL 190.40
Waiver of . . . CPL 190.45
Videotaped examination . . . CPL 190.32
Who may call . . . CPL 190.50

GRAND LARCENY
Aggravated grand larceny of automated teller ma-
chine . . . PL 155.43
Evidence . . . PL 155.45
First degree . . . PL 155.42
Fourth degree . . . PL 155.30
Pleading and proof . . . PL 155.45
Second degree . . . PL 155.40

[References are to sections of Consolidated Laws as abbreviated on Page i.]

GRAND LARCENY—Cont.
Third degree . . . PL 155.35

GRANTS
Commissioner of correction, acceptance by
. . . COR 15–c

GRATUITIES
Public servants, unlawful gratuities to
Giving . . . PL 200.30
Receiving . . . PL 200.35

GUNS (See FIREARMS)

H

HABEAS CORPUS
Extradition proceedings . . . CPL 570.24

HARASSMENT
Aggravated harassment
First degree . . . PL 240.31
Inmate, harassment of employee by . . . PL
240.32
Second degree . . . PL 240.30
Employee by inmate, aggravated harassment of
. . . PL 240.32
First degree . . . PL 240.25
Inmate, aggravated harassment of employee by
. . . PL 240.32
Rent regulated tenants
Generally . . . PL 241.05
Definition . . . PL 241.00
Second degree . . . PL 240.26

HATE CRIMES
Definitions . . . PL 485.05
Legislative findings . . . PL 485.00
Sentencing . . . PL 485.10

HAZARDOUS SUBSTANCES
False, placement of
Generally . . . PL 240.63
First degree . . . PL 240.62
Second degree . . . PL 240.61
Obstruction of governmental duties by use of
. . . PL 195.17

HAZING
First degree . . . PL 120.16
Second degree . . . PL 120.17

HEALTH CARE
Aggravated interference with health care service
First degree . . . PL 240.73
Second degree . . . PL 240.72
Criminal interference with health care service
First degree . . . PL 240.71
Second degree . . . PL 240.70
Fraud
Affirmative defense . . . PL 177.30

HEALTH CARE—Cont.
Fraud—Cont.
Definitions . . . PL 177.00
Fifth degree . . . PL 177.05
First degree . . . PL 177.25
Fourth degree . . . PL 177.10
Second degree . . . PL 177.20
Third degree . . . PL 177.15
Interference with, aggravated (See subhead: Aggra-
vated interference with health care service)
Local correctional facilities, costs for medical and
dental services for inmates in . . . COR 500–h
Medical review board (See MEDICAL REVIEW
BOARD)
Minors' right of consent to medical care, incarcer-
ated . . . PL 70.20
Outside hospitals, requirements for permitting in-
mates treatment in . . . COR 23
Persons rendering services at request of Depart-
ment, action against . . . COR 24–a
Strangulation, occurrence for medical or dental pur-
pose . . . PL 121.14

HEARING
Chemical test report and hearing for persons oper-
ating vehicle after consumption of alcohol
. . . VTL 1194–a
Clemency, appointment of persons to hear applica-
tion for . . . COR 262
Conditional discharge sentence, violation of
. . . CPL 410.70
Controlled substances, procedures regarding
. . . PHL 3393
Discovery upon pre-trial . . . CPL 240.44
Felony complaint (See FELONY COMPLAINT)
Financial hardship, deferral of mandatory surcharge
based on . . . CPL 420.40
Grand jury proceeding, hearing of evidence in
. . . CPL 190.55
Mandatory surcharge based on financial hardship,
deferral of . . . CPL 420.40
Material witness, adjudgment of . . . CPL 620.50
Parole violations, interstate hearings for
. . . EXEC 259–o
Predicate felony conviction . . . CPL 220.35
Probation sentence, violation of . . . CPL 410.70

HEARING OFFICERS
Parole board . . . EXEC 259–d

HINDERING PROSECUTION
Definition . . . PL 205.50
First degree . . . PL 205.65
Second degree . . . PL 205.60
Third degree . . . PL 205.55

HIV-RELATED TESTING
Indictments . . . CPL 210.16
Pre-sentence reports . . . CPL 390.15

HOMICIDE
Criminally negligent . . . PL 125.10
Definition . . . PL 125.00; PL 125.05
Manslaughter (See MANSLAUGHTER)
Murder (See MURDER)
Victim of; defined . . . PL 125.05

HORSE RACING
Pari-mutuel betting system, impairing integrity of
    First degree . . . PL 180.53
    Second degree . . . PL 180.52

HOSPITALS
Mental disease or defect, commitment of inmates
    with (See MENTAL DISEASE OR DEFECT)
Outside hospitals, requirements for permitting in-
    mates treatment in . . . COR 23
Pre-sentence report to accompany defendant to
    mental health facility . . . CPL 390.60

HYPODERMIC INSTRUMENTS
Criminal possession of (See subhead: Possession
    of, criminal)
Destruction of . . . PHL 3381–a
Distribution of single-use syringes . . . PHL 3381
Narcotic drugs, criminal injection of . . . PL
    220.46
Possession of, criminal
    Exceptions to charge . . . PL 220.03; PL
    220.45
    Sale and . . . PHL 3381
Sale and possession of . . . PHL 3381

I

IDENTITY THEFT
Aggravated . . . PL 190.80–a
Defenses . . . PL 190.84
Definitions . . . PL 190.77
First degree offense . . . PL 190.80
Geographical jurisdiction of . . . CPL 20.40
Personal identification information, unlawful pos-
    session of
    Defenses . . . PL 190.84
    First degree offense . . . PL 190.83
    Second degree offense . . . PL 190.82
    Third degree offense . . . PL 190.81
Restitution and reparations for . . . PL 60.27
Second degree offense . . . PL 190.79
Skimmer device, unlawful possession of
    First degree . . . PL 190.86
    Second degree . . . PL 190.85
Terrorism, defined as specified offense for . . . PL
    490.05
Third degree offense . . . PL 190.78
Warrants for eavesdropping and video surveillance,
    designated offense for . . . CPL 700.05

IGNITION INTERLOCK DEVICE PROGRAM
Generally . . . PL 60.21; PL 60.36; VTL 1198

**IMMIGRANT ASSISTANCE SERVICES
    FRAUD**
First degree, in . . . PL 190.89
Second degree, in . . . PL 190.87

IMMUNITY
Compulsion of evidence by offer of
    Generally . . . CPL 50.20
    Court as competent authority to confer immunity
    . . . CPL 50.30
    Definitions . . . CPL 50.10
Extradition
    Other criminal prosecutions while in this state
    . . . CPL 570.60
    Service of process in civil actions in connection
    with . . . CPL 570.58
Grand jury proceedings
    Generally . . . CPL 190.40
    Waiver of immunity . . . CPL 190.45

IMPEACHMENT
Contradictory statement, impeachment of own wit-
    ness by proof of prior . . . CPL 60.35

IMPERSONATION
Criminal impersonation
    First degree . . . PL 190.26
    Physician, as; first degree . . . PL 190.26
    Police officer, as; first degree . . . PL 190.26
    Second degree . . . PL 190.25

IMPRISONMENT
Inmates (See INMATES)
Sentence (See IMPRISONMENT SENTENCE)
Unlawful imprisonment (See UNLAWFUL IM-
    PRISONMENT)

IMPRISONMENT SENTENCE
Calculation of terms of . . . PL 70.30
Certificate of conviction or a sentence and commit-
    ment delivered to facility where defendant is
    committed after sentencing . . . CPL 380.65
Change after commencement . . . CPL 430.10
Child sexual assault felony, for second . . . PL
    70.07
Class A felony drug offender . . . PL 70.71
Class B, C, D, and E felony drug offender . . . PL
    70.70
Commitment of defendant . . . CPL 430.20
Concurrent terms . . . PL 70.25
Conditional release . . . PL 70.40
Consecutive terms . . . PL 70.25
Definite and indeterminate sentences, merger of
    . . . PL 70.35
Determinate sentence law, transitional exception to
    . . . PL 70.85
Duty to deliver defendant . . . CPL 430.30
Felonies
    Generally . . . PL 70.00
    Class A felony drug offender . . . PL 70.71

[References are to sections of Consolidated Laws as abbreviated on Page i.]

[References are to sections of Consolidated Laws as abbreviated on Page i.]

[References are to sections of Consolidated Laws as abbreviated on Page i.]

INSOLVENCY
Creditors, fraud by . . . PL 185.00

INSURANCE FRAUD
Aggravated . . . PL 176.35
Definitions . . . PL 176.00; PL 176.05
Fifth degree . . . PL 176.10
First degree . . . PL 176.30
Fourth degree . . . PL 176.15
Life settlement fraud
    Aggravated . . . PL 176.70
    Definitions . . . PL 176.40
    Fifth degree . . . PL 176.45
    First degree . . . PL 176.65
    Fourth degree . . . PL 176.50
    Second degree . . . PL 176.60
    Third degree . . . PL 176.55
Second degree . . . PL 176.25
Third degree . . . PL 176.20

INTENT
Definition . . . PL 15.05

INTERMEDIATE APPELLATE COURT
Certificate granting leave to appeal to . . . CPL 460.15
Court of appeals, appeal to (See COURT OF APPEALS)
Defendant, appeal by . . . CPL 450.10; CPL 450.15
Determination of appeals
    Generally . . . CPL 470.15
    Content of order . . . CPL 470.25
    Corrective action upon reversal or modification
      . . . CPL 470.20; CPL 470.40
    Court of appeals, determination by . . . CPL 470.35; CPL 470.40
    Form and content of order . . . CPL 470.25
    Modification or reversal, corrective action upon . . . CPL 470.20; CPL 470.40
    Reversal or modification, corrective action upon . . . CPL 470.20; CPL 470.40
People, appeal by . . . CPL 450.20
Stay of judgment pending appeal to or from . . . CPL 460.50; CPL 460.60
Taking appeal to . . . CPL 450.60

INTERMITTENT IMPRISONMENT (See IMPRISONMENT SENTENCE)

INTERNET
Inmate lookup information access via the . . . COR 9
Prescriptions, dispensing of . . . PHL 3302

INTERROGATORIES
Commission, examination of witnesses on . . . CPL 680.50

INTERSTATE CORRECTIONS COMPACT
Acts not reviewable in receiving state . . . COR 105
Adoption of . . . COR 100
Construction of . . . COR 109
Contracts . . . COR 103
Definitions . . . COR 102
Entry into force . . . COR 107
Extradition provisions . . . COR 105
Federal aid . . . COR 106
Force, entry into . . . COR 107
Procedures . . . COR 104
Purpose of . . . COR 101
Rights of inmates . . . COR 104
Severability of provisions . . . COR 109
Short title . . . COR 101
Termination of . . . COR 108
Withdrawal of . . . COR 108

INTOXICATION
Criminal liability, effect on . . . PL 15.25

J

JAILS (See CORRECTIONAL FACILITIES)

JOSTLING
Definition . . . PL 165.25

JUDGE
Assault on . . . PL 120.09

JUDGMENT
Appeals (See APPEALS)
Certificates concerning judgments of conviction and fingerprints . . . CPL 60.60
Vacation of, motion for
    Generally . . . CPL 440.10
    Procedure . . . CPL 440.30
Vehicle and Traffic Law provisions for fines and penalties
    Default judgment . . . VTL 1806–a
    Stay order on appeal from judgment of conviction of offense, effect of . . . VTL 1808

JUDICIARY LAW
Community dispute resolution center program (See COMMUNITY DISPUTE RESOLUTION CENTER PROGRAM)
Special narcotics parts of supreme court in cities with population of one million or more
    Declaration . . . JUD 177–a
    Establishment . . . JUD 177–b
    Intent . . . JUD 177–a
    Legislative findings . . . JUD 177–a
    Probation services . . . JUD 177–e
    Procedure . . . JUD 177–d
    Prosecutional organization . . . JUD 177–c

JURISDICTION
Conspiracy . . . PL 105.25

[References are to sections of Consolidated Laws as abbreviated on Page i.]

[References are to sections of Consolidated Laws as abbreviated on Page i.]

JUVENILE OFFENDERS—Cont.
Commitment of principal under sixteen years of age . . . CPL 510.15
Declaration of delinquency . . . CPL 410.30
Felony complaint, proceedings upon . . . CPL 180.75
Imprisonment sentence . . . PL 70.05
Records
Removal of records to family court, procedure for . . . CPL 725.20
Sealing of records . . . CPL 725.15
Removal of proceeding to family court
Generally . . . CPL 725.10
Applicability of statute . . . CPL 725.00
Grand jury's direction to file request for . . . CPL 190.71
Indictment, motion for removal after . . . CPL 210.43
Order of removal . . . CPL 725.05
Records
Procedure for removal of . . . CPL 725.20
Sealing of records . . . CPL 725.15
Sealing of records . . . CPL 725.15

K

KIDNAPPING
Defense . . . PL 135.30
Definition . . . PL 135.00
First degree . . . PL 135.25
Second degree . . . PL 135.20

KNOWLEDGE
Definition . . . PL 15.05

L

LABOR
Bribery of officials (See BRIBERY)
Trafficking
Generally . . . PL 135.35
Accomplice . . . PL 135.36

LARCENY
Defenses . . . PL 155.10; PL 155.15
Definitions . . . PL 155.00; PL 155.05
Grand larceny (See GRAND LARCENY)
Petit larceny . . . PL 155.25
Physical force; justification for use to prevent or terminate larceny . . . PL 35.25
Value of stolen property . . . PL 155.20

LASER BEAMS
Aircraft, directing at
First degree . . . PL 240.77
Second degree . . . PL 240.76

LASER DETECTORS
Prohibitions . . . VTL 397–a

LESSER INCLUDED OFFENSES
Indictment, submission of . . . CPL 300.50
Plea . . . CPL 220.20

LIBRARIES
Correctional facility library, availability of information on international offender transfers . . . COR 71
Correctional Services Department, of . . . COR 20

LICENSES
Controlled substances
Cannabis grown by unlicensed persons . . . PHL 3382
Chemical analysis (See subhead: Research, instructional activities and chemical analysis relating to controlled substances)
Distribution of (See subhead: Controlled substances, manufacture and distribution of)
Instructional activities (See subhead: Research, instructional activities and chemical analysis relating to controlled substances)
Manufacture and distribution of (See subhead: Controlled substances, manufacture and distribution of)
Research activities (See subhead: Research, instructional activities and chemical analysis relating to controlled substances)
Revocation of licenses . . . PHL 3390; PHL 3391
Suspension of licenses . . . PHL 3391
Controlled substances, manufacture and distribution of
Generally . . . PHL 3310
Amended licenses . . . PHL 3311
Initial licenses
Application for . . . PHL 3312
Authority to issue . . . PHL 3311
Granting of . . . PHL 3313
Renewal of licenses
Applications for . . . PHL 3315
Authority to issue . . . PHL 3311
Granting of . . . PHL 3316
Driver's license, suspension and revocation (See DRIVER'S LICENSE: SUSPENSION AND REVOCATION)
Firearms, license to carry, possess, repair and dispose of (See FIREARMS)
Fireworks, permits for public display of . . . PL 405.00
Marriage license, unlawfully procuring
Generally . . . PL 255.10
Defense . . . PL 255.20
Permits for public display of fireworks . . . PL 405.00
Prior convictions, application for license by persons with (See PRIOR CONVICTIONS, subhead: License or employment application by persons with)

[References are to sections of Consolidated Laws as abbreviated on Page i.]

LICENSES—Cont.

Public display of fireworks, permits for . . . PL 405.00

Research, instructional activities and chemical analysis relating to controlled substances

Generally . . . PHL 3324

Applications . . . PHL 3325

Authority to issue licenses . . . PHL 3325

Exemptions from title . . . PHL 3328

Institutional research licenses . . . PHL 3326

Procedure . . . PHL 3327

Records . . . PHL 3329

Reports and records . . . PHL 3329

Suspension and revocation

Driver's license (See DRIVER'S LICENSE: SUSPENSION AND REVOCATION)

Firearms; licenses to carry, possess, repair or dispose . . . CPL 530.14

LIQUOR (See ALCOHOL)

LITTERING

Railroad tracks, penalties for littering on . . . PL 145.50

Rights-of-way, penalties for littering on . . . PL 145.50

LOCAL CORRECTIONAL FACILITIES

Absence of inmate for funeral or deathbed visits . . . COR 509

Aggravated harassment of employee by inmate . . . PL 240.32

Alcoholic beverages, use of . . . COR 502; COR 503

Application of article . . . COR 500

Civil prisoners . . . COR 500–n; COR 514

Custody and control of inmates . . . COR 500–c

Deathbed visits, absence of inmate for . . . COR 509

Dental services

Payment of costs for . . . COR 500–h

Routine dental services and treatment, provision of . . . COR 505

Designation of jail

Revocation of . . . COR 523; COR 524

Substitute jail . . . COR 504

Fire, removal of inmates in case of . . . COR 507

Food provisions . . . COR 500–d

Funeral service, absence of inmate for . . . COR 509

Health care costs . . . COR 500–h

Holidays, release on . . . COR 500–l

Housing of inmates and other persons . . . COR 500–b

Labor . . . COR 500–d

Liquor in jails, use of . . . COR 502; COR 503

Medical services

Payment of costs for . . . COR 500–h

Routine medical services and treatment, provision of . . . COR 505

LOCAL CORRECTIONAL FACILITIES—Cont.

Mental health services and treatment, provision of . . . COR 505

Minors, provision of routine medical, dental, and mental health services to . . . COR 505

New York City, special provision relating to . . . COR 500–m

Physicians, appointment of . . . COR 501

Reading matter . . . COR 500–e

Recaptured prisoner, term of imprisonment of . . . COR 529

Record of commitments and discharges . . . COR 500–f

Release on holidays, Saturdays and Sundays . . . COR 500–l

Religious services . . . COR 500–e

Revocation of designation of jail . . . COR 523; COR 524

Saturdays, release on . . . COR 500–l

Segregation of inmates, rooms for . . . COR 500–b

Sick persons, removal of . . . COR 508

Substitute jail, designation of . . . COR 504

Sundays, release on . . . COR 500–l

Treatment of inmates . . . COR 500–k

United States courts, commitment by . . . COR 500–g

Unlawful fees, prohibitions against charging to inmates . . . COR 500–n

Use of jails . . . COR 500–a

Visitations . . . COR 500–j

Workhouses

Generally . . . COR 500–i

Visitations . . . COR 500–j

Work release program (See WORK RELEASE PROGRAM, subhead: County jails)

LOCAL CRIMINAL COURTS

Accusatory instruments (See ACCUSATORY INSTRUMENTS)

Arraignment, methods of requiring defendant's appearance in local court for . . . CPL 110.10

Bail

Forfeiture of . . . CPL 540.20

Recognizance or, order when action pending . . . CPL 530.20

Cash bail transfer to superior court from . . . CPL 520.40

Commencement of action

Generally . . . CPL 100.05

Family court proceeding, effect of . . . CPL 100.07

Deposition, supporting (See SUPPORTING DEPOSITION)

Felony complaint (See FELONY COMPLAINT)

Information (See INFORMATION)

Jurisdiction of

Generally . . . CPL 10.30

LOCAL CRIMINAL COURTS—Cont.
Jurisdiction of—Cont.
Divestiture of jurisdiction by indictment
. . . CPL 170.20; CPL 170.25
Misdemeanor complaint (See MISDEMEANOR
COMPLAINT)
Prosecutor's information (See PROSECUTOR'S
INFORMATION)
Recognizance or bail, order when action pending
. . . CPL 530.20
Removal of action to or from (See REMOVAL OF
ACTION)
Simplified information (See SIMPLIFIED INFOR-
MATION)
Supporting deposition (See SUPPORTING DEPO-
SITION)
Warrant of arrest, issuance of . . . CPL 120.30

LOITERING
Generally . . . PL 240.35
First degree . . . PL 240.36
Prostitution offense, for purposes of engaging in
. . . PL 240.37

LOTTERY OFFENSES
Defense, lack of . . . PL 225.40

M

**MANAGEMENT OF CORRECTIONAL FA-
CILITIES**
Alternate facilities . . . COR 89–a

MANSLAUGHTER
First degree . . . PL 125.20
Second degree . . . PL 125.15
Vehicular manslaughter (See VEHICULAR MAN-
SLAUGHTER)

MARIJUANA
Adjournment in contemplation of dismissal of
charges . . . CPL 170.56; CPL 210.46
Definitions . . . PL 221.00
Felony
Multiple felony offender . . . PL 60.04; PL
60.05
Offenses . . . PL 60.04; PL 60.05
Medical marijuana
Certification of patients . . . PHL 3361
Criminal diversion of
First degree diversion . . . PL 179.10
Limitations . . . PL 179.05
Retention of, criminal . . . PL 179.05
Second degree diversion . . . PL 179.11
Criminal retention of . . . PL 179.15
Definitions . . . PHL 3360
Effective date . . . PHL 3369–b
Evaluation of implementation and effectiveness
of title . . . PHL 3367
Lawful medical use . . . PHL 3362

MARIJUANA—Cont.
Medical marijuana—Cont.
Patients, certification of . . . PHL 3361
Pricing . . . PHL 3369–d
Protections for use of . . . PHL 3369
Registered organizations
Generally . . . PHL 3364
Registering of . . . PHL 3365
Reports by . . . PHL 3366
Registry identification cards . . . PHL 3363
Regulations . . . PHL 3369–a
Relation to other laws . . . PHL 3368
Severability . . . PHL 3369–e
Suspension or termination of licenses . . . PHL
3369–c
Multiple felony offender . . . PL 60.04; PL 60.05
Possession of
First degree . . . PL 221.30
Second degree . . . PL 221.25
Third degree . . . PL 221.20
Fourth degree . . . PL 221.15
Fifth degree . . . PL 221.10
Unlawful possession of . . . PL 221.05
Sale of
First degree . . . PL 221.55
Second degree . . . PL 221.50
Third degree . . . PL 221.45
Fourth degree . . . PL 221.40
Fifth degree . . . PL 221.35
Sealing of record after completion of diversion pro-
gram . . . CPL 160.58
Treatment for substance abuse . . . PL 60.04
Unlawful possession of . . . PL 221.05

MARRIAGE
Adultery (See ADULTERY)
Bigamy
Generally . . . PL 255.15
Defense . . . PL 255.20
Dissolution decree, unlawfully issuing . . . PL
255.05
Incest (See INCEST)
License, unlawfully procuring
Generally . . . PL 255.10
Defense . . . PL 255.20
Solemnizing marriage unlawfully . . . PL 255.00

MATERIAL WITNESS ORDER
Amendment . . . CPL 620.60
Appearance of prospective witness . . . CPL
620.30
Arraignment . . . CPL 620.40
Authorization . . . CPL 620.20
Commencement of proceedings . . . CPL 620.30
Courts authorized to issue . . . CPL 620.20
Definition . . . CPL 620.10
Determination and execution of . . . CPL 620.50
Duration of . . . CPL 620.20
Execution of . . . CPL 620.50

[References are to sections of Consolidated Laws as abbreviated on Page i.]

MATERIAL WITNESS ORDER—Cont.
Failure to appear on, compelling appearance of witness for . . . CPL 620.70
Fees of material witness . . . CPL 620.80
Hearing . . . CPL 620.50
Modification . . . CPL 620.60
Procurement of appearance of prospective witness . . . CPL 620.30
Vacation . . . CPL 620.60

MEDICAL REVIEW BOARD
Duties . . . COR 47
Functions . . . COR 47
Organization . . . COR 43
Powers . . . COR 47

MEDICAL TREATMENT (See HEALTH CARE)

MEGAN'S LAW (See SEX OFFENDER REGISTRATION ACT)

MENACING
First degree . . . PL 120.13
Second degree . . . PL 120.14
Third degree . . . PL 120.15

MENTAL DISEASE OR DEFECT
Custody of defendant by commissioner, procedure following
  Generally . . . CPL 730.60
  Termination of . . . CPL 730.70
Death sentence, incompetent persons under . . . COR 656
Defense . . . PL 40.15
Endangering welfare of incompetent persons
  First degree . . . PL 260.25; PL 260.34
  Second degree . . . PL 260.24; PL 260.32
Evidentiary rules for giving testimony . . . CPL 60.20
Examination (See subhead: Fitness to proceed)
Fitness to proceed
  Generally . . . CPL 730.20
  Custody of defendant by commissioner, procedure following
    Generally . . . CPL 730.60
    Termination of . . . CPL 730.70
  Definitions . . . CPL 730.10
  Indictment . . . CPL 730.50
  Local criminal court accusatory instrument . . . CPL 730.40
  Order of examination . . . CPL 730.30
Indictment; fitness to proceed following mental examination . . . CPL 730.50
Murder in first degree, pre-sentence proceeding for defendant convicted of . . . CPL 400.27
Notice of intent to proffer psychiatric evidence . . . CPL 250.10
Plea of not responsible by reason of
  Generally . . . CPL 220.15
  Procedure following . . . CPL 330.20

MENTAL DISEASE OR DEFECT—Cont.
Pre-sentence proceeding for defendant convicted of murder in first degree . . . CPL 400.27
Pre-sentence report to accompany defendant to mental health facility . . . CPL 390.60
Verdict of not responsible by reason of, procedure following . . . CPL 330.20
Victim services office, awards to incompetents by . . . EXEC 632

METHAMPHETAMINE
Information program for retailers . . . PHL 3384
Laboratory material, disposal of . . . PL 220.76
Manufacture, unlawful
  First degree . . . PL 220.75
  Second degree . . . PL 220.74
  Third degree . . . PL 220.73
Manufacturing material, criminal possession of
  First degree . . . PL 220.71
  Second degree . . . PL 220.70
Precursors of methamphetamine, criminal possession of . . . PL 220.72

METROCARD
Sale of transportation service, unauthorized . . . PL 165.16
Tampering of farecard . . . PL 165.16

MINORS
Abandonment . . . PL 260.00
Aggravated assault upon person less than eleven years old . . . PL 120.12
Alcohol by persons under age of 21, consumption of (See VEHICLE AND TRAFFIC LAW, subhead: Alcohol and drug-related offenses)
Assault
  Aggravated assault upon person less than eleven years old . . . PL 120.12
  Child day care provider upon person less than eleven years old, assault by . . . PL 120.01
  Reckless assault on minor causing serious physical injury to brain . . . PL 120.02
  Sexual assault (See subhead: Sexual assault)
Child day care provider
  Assault by provider upon person less than eleven years old, by . . . PL 120.01
  Misrepresentation by . . . PL 120.01
Child protective agencies of conviction for certain crimes against child, notice to . . . CPL 440.65
Closed-circuit television for child witnesses
  Application, procedure for . . . CPL 65.20
  Definitions . . . CPL 65.00
  Determination for allowing, grounds for . . . CPL 65.20
  Special testimonial procedure . . . CPL 65.30
  Vulnerability, declaration of . . . CPL 65.10
Controlled substance offenses
  Sale to child . . . PL 220.48
  Use of child to commit . . . PL 220.28

[References are to sections of Consolidated Laws as abbreviated on Page i.]

[References are to sections of Consolidated Laws as abbreviated on Page i.]

MISDEMEANOR COMPLAINT—Cont.
Dismissal of, motion for—Cont.
   Justice, in interest of . . . CPL 170.40
   Procedure . . . CPL 170.45
Form and content . . . CPL 100.15
Information, replacement by
   Generally . . . CPL 170.65
   Release of defendant upon failure to replace
     . . . CPL 170.70
   Waiver of . . . CPL 170.65
Prosecutor's information on, arraignment upon
   . . . CPL 170.10
Removal of action (See REMOVAL OF ACTION)
Severance . . . CPL 100.45
Verification . . . CPL 100.30

MISTRIAL
Generally . . . CPL 280.10
Indictment status upon new trial . . . CPL 280.20

MONEY LAUNDERING
Definitions . . . PL 470.00
Fines . . . PL 470.20
First degree . . . PL 470.15
Second degree . . . PL 470.10
Terrorism, in support of (See TERRORISM,
   CRIMES OF)
Third degree . . . PL 470.05

MORTGAGED PROPERTY
Fraudulent disposition of . . . PL 185.10

MOTION PICTURE THEATERS
Recording device in, unauthorized operation of
   . . . PL 275.32

MOTIONS (See specific subject headings, e.g.,
   PRE-TRIAL MOTIONS)

MOTOR VEHICLES (See AUTOMOBILES)

MULTIPLE OFFENSES
Fines . . . PL 80.15

MURDER
Aggravated murder . . . PL 125.26
Authorized dispositions of offenders for first degree
   murder . . . PL 60.06
First degree
   Generally . . . PL 125.27
   Authorized dispositions of offenders . . . PL
     60.06
   Life imprisonment without parole, sentence of
     . . . PL 70.00
   Pre-sentence proceedings . . . CPL 400.27
Life imprisonment without parole for first degree
   murder, sentence of . . . PL 70.00
Second degree . . . PL 125.25
Suicide attempt, promoting; when punishable as
   attempt to commit murder . . . PL 120.35

N

NARCOTICS (See CONTROLLED SUB-
   STANCES)

**NATIONAL CRIME PREVENTION AND PRI-
VACY COMPACT**
Enactment of . . . EXEC 850

NEW YORK CITY
Alternate correctional facilities (See ALTERNATE
   CORRECTIONAL FACILITIES: NEW YORK
   CITY)
Local correctional facilities, special provision relat-
   ing to . . . COR 500–m
Work release program (See WORK RELEASE
   PROGRAM)

NON-JURY TRIAL
Authorization of . . . CPL 320.10
Conduct of . . . CPL 320.20
Judicial hearing officer, trial by . . . CPL 350.20
Procedure . . . CPL 320.20
Single judge trial, conduct of . . . CPL 350.10
Waiver of jury trial and consent to . . . CPL
   320.10

NOTICE
Absconding from custody, victim notification of
   violent offender . . . CPL 380.50
Alibi, notice of . . . CPL 250.20
Child protective agencies of conviction for certain
   crimes against child, notice to . . . CPL 440.65
Computer crimes, defenses involving . . . CPL
   250.30
Conditional discharge, notice to appear for
   . . . CPL 410.40
Conditional examination of witnesses, service of
   notice for . . . CPL 660.40
Conditional release of violent felony offender, vic-
   tim notification upon . . . CPL 380.50
Correctional facilities, notice of closure of
   . . . COR.79–a
Death penalty, intent to seek . . . CPL 250.40
Destruction of dangerous drugs . . . CPL 715.20
Disposition of case . . . CPL 440.50
Domestic violence under federal law, notice to divi-
   sion of criminal justice services that misde-
   meanor is crime of . . . CPL 380.97
Eavesdropping or video surveillance warrants
   . . . CPL 700.50; CPL 700.70
Education Department notified where licensed pro-
   fessional convicted of felony . . . CPL 440.55
Escaped violent felony offender, victim notification
   of . . . CPL 380.50
False financing statement, notice to secretary of
   state of . . . CPL 440.70
Information, notice of defenses on prosecution of
   . . . CPL 340.30
Intermittent imprisonment . . . PL 85.10

[References are to sections of Consolidated Laws as abbreviated on Page i.]

O

P

[References are to sections of Consolidated Laws as abbreviated on Page i.]

PARDONS (See EXECUTIVE CLEMENCY)

PAROLE
Board of (See PAROLE BOARD)
Disabilities, certificates of relief from; issuance by parole board . . . COR 703
Drug treatment program
　Sentence of parole supervision, part of . . . CPL 410.91
Requirements . . . PL 70.40
Sentence of parole supervision, drug treatment program as part of . . . CPL 410.91
Victim notification of parole of violent felony offender . . . CPL 380.50
Work release program for county jails, eligibility of person participating in . . . COR 876

PAROLE BOARD
Access to records and institutions . . . EXEC 259–k
Civil actions against board personnel . . . EXEC 259–q
"Community supervision" defined . . . EXEC 259
Conduct of work of state board of parole, procedures for . . . EXEC 259–i
Cooperation . . . EXEC 259–l
Definitions . . . EXEC 259
Discharge from parole . . . EXEC 259–j
Drug treatment program
　Revocation of parole, program as alternative to . . . EXEC 259–i
　Sentence of parole supervision . . . CPL 410.91
Duties . . . EXEC 259–c
Eligibility for inmates sentenced for crimes committed prior to September 1, 1967 . . . EXEC 259–h
Functions . . . EXEC 259–c
Funding . . . EXEC 259–a
Hearing for parole violations, interstate . . . EXEC 259–o
Hearing officers . . . EXEC 259–d
Institutional parole service . . . EXEC 259–e
Institutions, access to . . . EXEC 259–k
Interstate
　Compact for adult offender supervision . . . EXEC 259–mm
　Hearings for parole violations . . . EXEC 259–o
Medical parole, release on
　Non-terminal condition . . . EXEC 259–s
　Terminal condition . . . EXEC 259–r
Merit termination of parole . . . EXEC 259–j
Organization . . . EXEC 259–b
Out-of-state parolee supervision, compacts with other states for . . . EXEC 259–m
Post-release supervision . . . PL 70.45
Powers . . . EXEC 259–c
Records, access to . . . EXEC 259–k

PAROLE BOARD—Cont.
Revocation, drug treatment program as alternative to parole . . . EXEC 259–i
Sentence of parole supervision . . . CPL 410.91
State board of parole
　Conduct of work of, procedures for . . . EXEC 259–i
　Duties . . . EXEC 259–c
　Functions . . . EXEC 259–c
　Organization . . . EXEC 259–b
　Powers . . . EXEC 259–c

PAROLE OFFICERS
Arrest without warrant as in course of employment . . . COR 10
Definition . . . COR 10
Warrant of arrest, execution by . . . CPL 120.55

PEACE OFFICERS
Aggravated assault upon . . . PL 120.11
Arrest
　Warrant of arrest (See WARRANT OF ARREST, subhead: State university appointed police and peace officers)
　Without warrant (See ARREST WITHOUT WARRANT)
Assault on . . . PL 120.08
Designated persons . . . CPL 2.10
Federal law enforcement officers as . . . CPL 2.15
Fire department members as . . . CPL 2.10
Kaleida Health security officers, peace officer status of . . . CPL 2.10
Persons designated as . . . CPL 2.10
Powers of . . . CPL 2.20
Refusal to aid . . . PL 195.10
Rockland County, officers or agents of society for the prevention of cruelty to children in . . . CPL 2.10
Southampton, peace officer status of uniformed court officers of . . . CPL 2.10
Syracuse University, peace officer status of certain employees of . . . CPL 2.10
Training requirements . . . CPL 2.30
University of Rochester security services officers, peace officer status of . . . CPL 2.10
Warrant of arrest (See WARRANT OF ARREST, subhead: State university appointed police and peace officers)
Watershed protection and enforcement officers . . . CPL 2.16

PENAL LAW (GENERALLY)
Abortion (See ABORTION)
Accessorial conduct (See ACCESSORIAL CONDUCT)
Application of
　Limitations . . . PL 5.05; PL 5.10
　Offenses committed before and after enactment . . . PL 5.05
Arson (See ARSON)

[References are to sections of Consolidated Laws as abbreviated on Page i.]

PHOTOGRAPHS
Termination of criminal action
    Fingerprints upon, return of . . . CPL 160.55
    Return upon . . . CPL 160.50

PHYSICAL FORCE
Arrest (See ARREST)
Justification for use of (See JUSTIFICATION)

PHYSICAL INJURY (See ASSAULT)

PHYSICIANS
Impersonation as; first degree . . . PL 190.26
Local correctional facilities, appointment at
    . . . COR 501

PLEA
Change of . . . CPL 220.60
Deportation of non-citizen defendant; guilty plea
    . . . CPL 220.50
Entry of . . . CPL 220.50
Guilty plea
    Deportation of non-citizen defendant . . . CPL
      220.50
    Part of indictment, guilty plea to . . . CPL
      220.30
    Public official's pension, notice of possible loss
      of . . . CPL 220.51
Information
    Prosecution of . . . CPL 340.20
    Requirements for . . . CPL 170.60
Lesser included offense for purposes of . . . CPL
    220.20
Mental disease or defect, plea of not responsible by
    reason of
    Generally . . . CPL 220.15
    Procedure following . . . CPL 330.20
Non-citizen defendant, deportation of; guilty plea
    . . . CPL 220.50
Not guilty plea . . . CPL 220.40
Part of indictment, guilty plea to . . . CPL 220.30
Predicate felony conviction, hearing on . . . CPL
    220.35
Prosecutor's information, requirements for
    . . . CPL 170.60
Public official's pension, notice of effect of guilty
    plea on . . . CPL 220.51
Requirement . . . CPL 210.50
Simplified information, requirements for . . . CPL
    170.60
Types of . . . CPL 220.10

PLEADING
Conspiracy . . . PL 105.20
Grand larceny . . . PL 155.45
Inconsistent statements, pleading as to . . . PL
    210.20

POLICE ANIMALS
Killing or injuring . . . PL 195.06–a

POLICE OFFICERS
Aggravate assault upon . . . . PL 120.11
Arrest
    Warrant of (See WARRANT OF ARREST, sub-
      head: State university appointed police and
      peace officers)
    Without warrant (See ARREST WITHOUT
      WARRANT)
Assault on . . . PL 120.08
Fleeing from an officer in motor vehicle, unlawful
    First degree . . . PL 270.35
    Second degree . . . PL 270.30
    Third degree . . . PL 270.25
Impersonation as; first degree . . . PL 190.26
License to carry and possess firearms for retired
    sworn members of state police . . . PL 400.01
Records and reports . . . EXEC 646
Refusal to aid . . . PL 195.10
Reports . . . EXEC 646
Retired sworn members of state police license to
    carry and possess firearms, granting . . . PL
    400.01
Victim assistance notification procedure
    . . . EXEC 625–b
Warrant of arrest (See WARRANT OF ARREST,
    subhead: State university appointed police and
    peace officers)

POLICE RECORDS AND REPORTS
Fair treatment standards . . . EXEC 646

POLICE UNIFORMS
Criminal sale of . . . PL 190.27

POLYGRAPH TESTS
Prohibitions against use . . . CPL 160.45

PORNOGRAPHY
Equipment used to promote, seizure and forfeiture
    of . . . PL 410.00

POST-RELEASE SUPERVISION
Generally . . . PL 70.45
Sex offenders, felony . . . PL 70.45
Victim notification upon release of violent felony
    offender to . . . CPL 380.50

PREMISES
Physical force; justification for use in defense of
    premises . . . PL 35.20

PRESCRIPTIONS
Criminal sale prescription for controlled substances
    . . . PL 220.65
Diversion, criminal
    Definitions . . . PL 178.00
    First degree . . . PL 178.25
    Fourth degree . . . PL 178.10
    Fraud and deceit related to controlled substances
      . . . PL 178.26
    Limitations . . . PL 178.05

[References are to sections of Consolidated Laws as abbreviated on Page i.]

PRIOR CONVICTIONS—Cont.

License or employment application by persons with—Cont.

Discrimination, prohibitions against . . . COR 752

Enforcement of Article 23-A provisions . . . COR 755

Factors to consider . . . COR 753

Presumptions . . . COR 753

Written statement upon denial of . . . COR 754

Sentencing, determination of prior convictions for purposes of

Generally . . . CPL 400.40

Murder in first degree, defendant convicted of; pre-sentence proceeding . . . CPL 400.27

Sex Offender Registration Act, duty to inform of prior convictions under . . . COR 168–g

Vehicular alcohol and drug-related offenses by persons under 21 . . . VTL 1192

PRISON CONTRABAND

First degree . . . PL 205.25

Second degree . . . PL 205.20

PRISONERS (See INMATES)

PRIVACY, RIGHT TO

Criminal communications, failure to report . . . PL 250.35

Eavesdropping (See EAVESDROPPING)

Tampering with private communications . . . PL 250.25

Unlawfully obtaining communications information . . . PL 250.30

Unlawful surveillance (See UNLAWFUL SURVEILLANCE)

PRIVILEGED COMMUNICATIONS

Controlled substances, records and reports on . . . PHL 3373

PROBATION AND CONDITIONAL DISCHARGE

Generally . . . PL 65.00; PL 65.05

Absence of inmates (See ABSENCE OF INMATES)

Appearance

Court, before . . . CPL 410.60

Notice to appear . . . CPL 410.40

Calculation of periods of . . . PL 65.15

Cemetery desecration . . . PL 65.10

Conditions of . . . PL 65.10

Custody and supervision of probationers . . . CPL 410.50

Delinquency, declaration of . . . CPL 410.30

Detainer warrants pilot project, sex offenders . . . CPL 410.92

Electronic monitoring as condition of probation . . . PL 65.10

Enlargement of conditions . . . CPL 410.20

PROBATION AND CONDITIONAL DISCHARGE—Cont.

Graffiti-related offense . . . PL 60.28; PL 65.10

Hearing on violation . . . CPL 410.70

Interim probation supervision . . . CPL 390.30

Invalid sentence of probation, notification of . . . CPL 440.60

Modification or enlargement of conditions . . . CPL 410.20

Notice to appear . . . CPL 410.40

Parole (See PAROLE)

Parole board (See PAROLE BOARD)

Requirements . . . PL 70.40

Sex offenders

Detainer warrants pilot project, sex offenders . . . CPL 410.92

Mandatory conditions for . . . PL 65.10

Notification requirement upon conditional release of . . . COR 168–c

Specification of conditions of sentence . . . CPL 410.10

Supervision of probationers

Custody and . . . CPL 410.50

Transfer of . . . CPL 410.80

Temporary release program (See TEMPORARY RELEASE PROGRAM)

Termination of sentence . . . CPL 410.90

Warrants

Detainer warrants for sex offenders . . . CPL 410.92

Issuing . . . CPL 410.40

Work release program (See WORK RELEASE PROGRAM)

PROBATION OFFICERS

Warrant of arrest, execution by . . . CPL 120.55

PROSECUTOR'S INFORMATION

Amendment . . . CPL 100.45

Appeal by people from order directing filing . . . CPL 450.55

Arraignment upon prosecutor's information on misdemeanor complaint . . . CPL 170.10

Bill of particulars . . . CPL 100.45

Consolidation . . . CPL 100.45

Content . . . CPL 100.35

Dismissal of, motion for

Generally . . . CPL 170.30

Adjournment in contemplation of dismissal

Generally . . . CPL 170.55

Marijuana cases . . . CPL 170.56

Defective information . . . CPL 170.35

Justice, in interest of . . . CPL 170.40

Procedure . . . CPL 170.45

Superior court, motion in . . . CPL 170.50

Form and content . . . CPL 100.35

Grand jury proceedings, direction to file information in . . . CPL 190.70

[References are to sections of Consolidated Laws as abbreviated on Page i.]

PROSECUTOR'S INFORMATION—Cont.

Misdemeanor complaint, arraignment upon prosecutor's information on . . . CPL 170.10

Plea requirements . . . CPL 170.60

Removal of action (See REMOVAL OF ACTION)

Severance . . . CPL 100.45

Superseding information . . . CPL 100.50

PROSTITUTION

Generally . . . PL 230.00

Compelling . . . PL 230.33

Defense to patronizing prostitutes . . . PL 230.07; PL 230.10

Loitering for purposes of engaging in prostitution offense . . . PL 240.37

Patronizing prostitutes

    Defense . . . PL 230.07; PL 230.10

    Definitions . . . PL 230.02

    First degree . . . PL 230.06

    Fourth degree . . . PL 230.03

    Second degree . . . PL 230.05

    Third degree . . . PL 230.04

Permitting . . . PL 230.40

Person in need of supervision proceeding, conversion to . . . CPL 170.80

Promotion of

    Accomplice . . . PL 230.35

    Definitions . . . PL 230.15

    First degree . . . PL 230.32

    Fourth degree . . . PL 230.20

    School zone, prostitution in . . . PL 230.19

    Second degree . . . PL 230.30

    Third degree . . . PL 230.25

School zone, prostitution in . . . PL 230.03; PL 230.19

Sexually exploited child . . . CPL 170.80

Sixteen and seventeen year olds, provisions for . . . CPL 170.80

Specialized services for underage prostitutes . . . CPL 170.80

Trafficking, sex

    Generally . . . PL 230.34

    Accomplice . . . PL 230.36

PROTECTION ORDERS

Delivery of copy of order to facility where defendant is committed after sentencing . . . CPL 380.65

Discovery . . . CPL 240.50

Victims of crimes, protection of . . . CPL 530.13

Victims of family offenses, protection of . . . CPL 530.12

PSYCHIATRISTS

Evidentiary rules on testimony by . . . CPL 60.55

Mental disease or defect, psychiatric examination for (See MENTAL DISEASE OR DEFECT, subhead: Fitness to proceed)

PUBLIC BENEFIT CARDS

Unlawful use of . . . PL 165.17

Welfare fraud (See WELFARE FRAUD)

PUBLIC HEALTH LAW

Controlled substances (See CONTROLLED SUBSTANCES)

PUBLIC ORDER, OFFENSES AGAINST

Anarchy, criminal . . . PL 240.15

Appearance in public under the influence of narcotics or drugs other than alcohol . . . PL 240.40

Assembly, unlawful . . . PL 240.10

Bomb, placement of false

    First degree . . . PL 240.62

    Second degree . . . PL 240.61

Definitions . . . PL 240.00

Disorderly conduct . . . PL 240.20

Drugs, appearance in public under the influence of . . . PL 240.40

Falsely reporting

    First degree . . . PL 240.60

    Second degree . . . PL 240.55

    Third degree . . . PL 240.50

Harassment (See HARASSMENT)

Hazardous substances, placement of false

    First degree . . . PL 240.62

    Second degree . . . PL 240.61

Loitering (See LOITERING)

Narcotics, appearance in public under the influence of . . . PL 240.40

Nuisance

    First degree . . . PL 240.46

    Second degree . . . PL 240.45

Records, unlawful prevention of public access to . . . PL 240.65

Religious services, disruption or disturbance of . . . PL 240.21

PUBLIC SAFETY, OFFENSES AGAINST

Body vest, unlawful wearing of . . . PL 270.20

Dangerous fireworks, unlawfully dealing with . . . PL 270.00

Fireworks, unlawfully dealing with . . . PL 270.00

Fleeing police officer in motor vehicle (See POLICE OFFICERS)

Hazard, creation of . . . PL 270.10

Noxious material, possession of . . . PL 270.05

Party line, refusal to yield to . . . PL 270.15

Weapons

    Generally (See WEAPONS)

    Firearms (See FIREARMS)

PUBLIC SENSIBILITIES, OFFENSES AGAINST

Exposure of person . . . PL 245.01; PL 245.02; PL 245.03

Lewdness

    Generally . . . PL 245.00

    First degree . . . PL 245.03

[References are to sections of Consolidated Laws as abbreviated on Page i.]

PUBLIC SENSIBILITIES, OFFENSES AGAINST—Cont.
Obscenity (See OBSCENITY)
Offensive exhibition . . . PL 245.05
Sexual material, public display of offensive
   . . . PL 245.10; PL 245.11

PUBLIC SERVANTS
Bribery
   Defenses . . . PL 200.05; PL 200.15
   First degree . . . PL 200.04; PL 200.12
   Gratuities, unlawful
      Giving . . . PL 200.30
      Receiving . . . PL 200.35
   Official misconduct, reward for (See subhead:
      Official misconduct)
   Public office
      Giving for . . . PL 200.40; PL 200.45
      Receiving for . . . PL 200.40; PL 200.50
   Receiving bribe
      Defense, lack of . . . PL 200.15
      First degree . . . PL 200.12
      Public office, for . . . PL 200.40; PL 200.50
      Second degree . . . PL 200.11
      Third degree . . . PL 200.10
   Second degree . . . PL 200.03; PL 200.11
   Third degree . . . PL 200.00; PL 200.10
Defrauding government . . . PL 195.20
Gratuities, unlawful
   Giving . . . PL 200.30
   Receiving . . . PL 200.35
Misconduct, official (See subhead: Official miscon-
   duct)
Obstruction of (See OBSTRUCTION OF PUBLIC
   SERVANTS)
Official misconduct
   Generally . . . PL 195.00
   Receiving reward for
      First degree . . . PL 200.27
      Second degree . . . PL 200.25
   Rewarding
      First degree . . . PL 200.22
      Second degree . . . PL 200.20
Peace officers (See PEACE OFFICERS)
Pension of public official, notice of effect of con-
   viction or guilty plea on . . . CPL 220.51
Police officers (See POLICE OFFICERS)

R

RADAR DETECTORS
Prohibitions . . . VTL 397–a

RADIO DEVICES
Equipping motor vehicles with sets capable of receiving signals on frequencies allocated for police use . . . VTL 397
Unlawful possession of . . . PL 140.40

RADIO TRANSMISSIONS
Unauthorized radio transmissions . . . PL 190.72

RAILROAD TRACKS
Littering on, penalties for . . . PL 145.50

RAPE
First degree . . . PL 130.35
Rape crisis counselor evidence . . . CPL 60.76
Second degree . . . PL 130.30
Third degree . . . PL 130.25

REAL PROPERTY
Commissioner of correction, acquisition by
   . . . COR 21
Rent gouging (See RENT GOUGING)

RECKLESS ENDANGERMENT
First degree . . . PL 120.25
Property, of . . . PL 145.25
Second degree . . . PL 120.20

RECKLESSNESS
Definition . . . PL 15.05

RECOGNIZANCE, RELEASE ON OWN (See
   BAIL)

RECORDINGS
Advertisement or sale of unauthorized recording of
   sound
      First degree . . . PL 275.30
      Second degree . . . PL 275.25
Definitions . . . PL 275.00
Destruction of equipment used in unauthorized re-
   cording of sound . . . PL 420.00
Forfeiture of equipment used in production of re-
   cordings, seizure and . . . PL 420.05
Manufacturer of unauthorized recordings of sound
      First degree . . . PL 275.10
      Second degree . . . PL 275.05
Motion picture theater, unauthorized operation of
   recording device in . . . PL 275.32
Performances, unauthorized recording of
      First degree . . . PL 275.20
      Second degree . . . PL 275.15
Sale of unauthorized recording of sound
      First degree . . . PL 275.30
      Second degree . . . PL 275.25
Unauthorized recording of sound
   Advertisement or sale of
      First degree . . . PL 275.30
      Second degree . . . PL 275.25
   Definitions . . . PL 275.00
   Destruction of equipment used in . . . PL
      420.00
   Equipment used in, seizure and forfeiture of
      . . . PL 420.05
   Forfeiture of equipment used in production of
      recordings, seizure and . . . PL 420.05

RECORDINGS—Cont.
Unauthorized recording of sound—Cont.
Limitations of application of statute . . . PL 275.45
Manufacturer of
First degree . . . PL 275.10
Second degree . . . PL 275.05
Origin of recording, failure to disclose
First degree . . . PL 275.40
Second degree . . . PL 275.35
Performances
First degree . . . PL 275.20
Second degree . . . PL 275.15
Sale of
First degree . . . PL 275.30
Second degree . . . PL 275.25
Seizures
Destruction and . . . PL 420.00
Equipment used in production of recordings . . . PL 420.05

RECORDS AND REPORTS
Accident reports (See ACCIDENTS AND ACCIDENT REPORTS)
Alcohol and drug rehabilitation program . . . VTL 523
Business records, falsifying (See WRITTEN FALSE STATEMENTS)
Chemical test report of persons operating vehicle after consumption of alcohol . . . VTL 1194–a
Confidentiality of office of victim services records . . . EXEC 633
Controlled substances (See CONTROLLED SUBSTANCES)
Eavesdropping or video surveillance warrants
Administrative office of United States courts, reports to . . . CPL 700.60
Progress reports . . . CPL 700.50
False statements (See WRITTEN FALSE STATEMENTS)
Firearms, theft or loss of . . . PL 400.10
Gambling records, possession of (See GAMBLING OFFENSES)
Grand jury
Generally . . . CPL 190.85
Appeal from order concerning grand jury reports . . . CPL 190.90
Juvenile offenders
Removal of records to family court, procedure for . . . CPL 725.20
Sealing of records . . . CPL 725.15
Loan records, possession of usurious . . . PL 190.45
Local correctional facilities . . . COR 500–f
Parole board, access by . . . EXEC 259–k
Police reports . . . EXEC 646
Pre-sentence reports (See PRE-SENTENCE REPORTS)

RECORDS AND REPORTS—Cont.
Public access to, unlawful prevention of . . . PL 240.65
Public records, tampering with (See subhead: Tampering with public records)
Rehabilitation program . . . VTL 523
Sealing of records
Controlled substance offenses, post-diversion program sealing of record of . . . CPL 160.58
Juvenile offenders . . . . CPL 725.15
Sentences of students, notification to school officials of convictions and . . . CPL 380.90
Tampering with public records
First degree . . . PL 175.25
Second degree . . . PL 175.20
Temporary release programs . . . COR 853
Victims
Police reports . . . EXEC 646
Victims services office records, confidentiality of . . . EXEC 633
Video surveillance warrants (See subhead: Eavesdropping or video surveillance warrants)
Waiver, termination of criminal action by entry of; sealed records . . . CPL 160.55
Youthful offender adjudication . . . CPL 720.35

REDUCTION OF SENTENCE, DISCRETIONARY (See DISCRETIONARY REDUCTIONS OF SENTENCE)

RELIGION AND RELIGIOUS SERVICES
Criminal interference with service
First degree . . . PL 240.71
Second degree . . . PL 240.70
Disruption or disturbance of . . . PL 240.21
Local correctional facilities . . . COR 500–e

REMOVAL OF ACTION
County court to supreme court . . . CPL 230.10; CPL 230.20
Determinations and rulings before and after . . . CPL 230.40
Grand jury's direction to file request for removal to family court . . . CPL 190.71
Juvenile offenders, removal to family court (See JUVENILE OFFENDERS)
Local criminal court to another, removal from
Generally . . . CPL 170.15
Felony complaint, proceedings upon . . . CPL 180.20
Rulings and determinations before and after . . . CPL 230.40
Stay of trial pending motion . . . CPL 230.30
Superior court, removal from local criminal court to
Defendant's request . . . CPL 170.25
District attorney's request . . . CPL 170.20
Supreme court to county court . . . CPL 230.10
Venue, change of . . . CPL 230.20

[References are to sections of Consolidated Laws as abbreviated on Page i.]

REMOVAL OF ACTION—Cont.
Verdict, after . . . CPL 330.25

RENT GOUGING
Definition . . . PL 180.54
First degree . . . PL 180.57
Second degree . . . PL 180.56
Third degree . . . PL 180.55

RENT REGULATED TENANTS
Harassment of
Generally . . . PL 241.05
Rent regulated tenant defined . . . PL 241.00

RENUNCIATION
Defense of . . . PL 40.10

REPARATION
Generally . . . PL 60.27
Arson . . . PL 60.27
Collection of
Generally . . . CPL 420.10
Corporation, reparation imposed on . . . CPL 420.20
Corporation, collection of reparation imposed on . . . CPL 420.20
Remission of . . . CPL 420.30

REPORTS (See RECORDS AND REPORTS)

RESIDENTIAL TREATMENT FACILITIES
Coordinated use of state and local institutions . . . COR 94
Transfer of eligible inmates to . . . COR 73

RESTITUTION
Generally . . . PL 60.27
Animal trained to aid person with disability, restitution for harming . . . PL 60.27
Arson . . . PL 60.27
Collection of
Generally . . . CPL 420.10
Corporation, collection of restitution imposed on . . . CPL 420.20
Corporation, collection of restitution imposed on . . . CPL 420.20
Remission of . . . CPL 420.30

REVOCATION OF DRIVER'S LICENSE (See DRIVER'S LICENSE: SUSPENSION AND REVOCATION)

RIGHTS-OF-WAY
Littering on, penalties for . . . PL 145.50

RIGHT TO PRIVACY (See PRIVACY, RIGHT TO)

RIOTS
First degree . . . PL 240.06
Inciting to . . . PL 240.08
Second degree . . . PL 240.05

ROBBERY
Definition . . . PL 160.00
First degree . . . PL 160.15
Second degree . . . PL 160.10
Third degree . . . PL 160.05

S

SANCTIONS
Alcohol and drug-related offenses . . . VTL 1193
Discovery . . . CPL 240.70
Drug-related offenses . . . VTL 1193

SCHOOLS
Adjudication of youthful offenders to, notification of . . . CPL 720.35
Controlled substances, criminal sale in or near school grounds of . . . PL 220.44
Prostitution in school zone . . . PL 230.03; PL 230.19
Sentences of students convicted of crimes to, reporting . . . CPL 380.90
Teacher's conviction for sex offense, notification to commissioner of education of . . . CPL 380.95
Weapons upon school grounds
Criminal possession . . . PL 265.01–a
Unlawful possession of . . . PL 265.06

SCIENTIFIC MATERIAL
Unauthorized use of secret scientific material . . . PL 165.07

SEARCH WARRANTS
Generally . . . CPL 690.05
Addressing . . . CPL 690.25
Application for
Determination of . . . CPL 690.40
Oral application, special provisions governing . . . CPL 690.36
Requirements . . . CPL 690.35
Content . . . CPL 690.45
Definition . . . CPL 690.05
Execution of
Persons authorized to execute . . . CPL 690.25
Place of execution . . . CPL 690.20
Procedure . . . CPL 690.50
Time of . . . CPL 690.30
Form and content . . . CPL 690.45
Persons subject to . . . CPL 690.15
Place or premises subject to . . . CPL 690.15
Property subject to seizure . . . CPL 690.10
Seizure of property
Generally . . . CPL 690.10
Disposition of seized property . . . CPL 690.55

[References are to sections of Consolidated Laws as abbreviated on Page i.]

[References are to sections of Consolidated Laws as abbreviated on Page i.]

[References are to sections of Consolidated Laws as abbreviated on Page i.]

SEXUAL ABUSE—Cont.
Aggravated sexual abuse—Cont.
    Third degree . . . PL 130.66
First degree . . . PL 130.65
Persistent sexual abuse . . . PL 130.53
Second degree . . . PL 130.60
Statute of limitations for prosecution of course
    sexual conduct against child . . . CPL 30.10
Third degree . . . PL 130.55

SEXUAL PERFORMANCE BY CHILD
Generally . . . PL 263.05
Affirmative defenses . . . PL 263.20
Age of child, proof of . . . PL 263.25
Control of performance . . . PL 263.16
Definitions . . . PL 263.00
Obscene sexual performance by child
    Control of performance . . . PL 263.11
    Defined . . . PL 263.00
    Possession of performance . . . PL 263.11
    Promotion of . . . PL 263.10
Possession of performance . . . PL 263.16
Promotion of . . . PL 263.10; PL 263.15

SHOCK INCARCERATION PROGRAM
Definitions . . . COR 865
Establishment of . . . COR 866
Selection of participants, procedure for . . . COR
    867

SIGNATURES
Fraudulently obtaining . . . PL 165.20

SIMPLIFIED INFORMATION
Appearance ticket, issuance of . . . CPL 100.25
Dismissal of, motion for
    Generally . . . CPL 170.30
    Adjournment in contemplation of dismissal
        Generally . . . CPL 170.55
        Marijuana cases involving . . . CPL 170.56
    Defective information . . . CPL 170.35
    Traffic information
        Justice, dismissal in interest of . . . CPL
        170.40
        Procedure . . . CPL 170.45
Form and content . . . CPL 100.25
Notice requirement . . . CPL 100.25
Plea requirements . . . CPL 170.60
Removal of action (See REMOVAL OF ACTION)
Supporting deposition of defendant arraigned upon
    . . . CPL 100.25
Traffic information
    Arraignment upon . . . CPL 170.10
    Dismissal of, motion for
        Justice, dismissal in interest of . . . CPL
        170.40
        Procedure . . . CPL 170.45

SIMULATION
Criminal . . . PL 170.45

SLUGS
Definitions . . . PL 170.50
Unlawfully using
    Definitions . . . PL 170.50
    First degree . . . PL 170.60
    Second degree . . . PL 170.55

SOLICITATION, CRIMINAL (See CRIMINAL
SOLICITATION)

SOUND RECORDINGS (See RECORDINGS)

SPEED RESTRICTIONS (See VEHICLE AND
TRAFFIC LAW)

SPEEDY TRIAL
Generally . . . CPL 30.20
Time limitations . . . CPL 30.30

SPORTS
Bribery
    Generally . . . PL 180.40
    Definitions . . . PL 180.35
    Receiving bribe . . . PL 180.45
    Tampering (See subhead: Tampering)
Pari-mutuel betting system, impairing integrity of
    First degree . . . PL 180.53
    Second degree . . . PL 180.52
Tampering
    Definitions . . . PL 180.35
    First degree . . . PL 180.51
    Pari-mutuel betting system, impairing integrity
    of
        First degree . . . PL 180.53
        Second degree . . . PL 180.52
    Second degree . . . PL 180.50

SPRAY DEVICE (See SELF-DEFENSE SPRAY
DEVICE)

STALKING
Definitions . . . PL 120.40
First degree . . . PL 120.60
Second degree . . . PL 120.55
Third degree . . . PL 120.50
Fourth degree . . . PL 120.45

STATE BOARD OF PAROLE (See PAROLE
BOARD)

STATE COMMISSION OF CORRECTION (See
COMMISSION OF CORRECTION)

STATISTICS
Corrections and Community Supervision Depart-
    ment statistical analysis . . . COR 29

STATUTE OF LIMITATIONS
Prosecutions . . . CPL 30.10
Sex offenses committed against child, prosecution
    of . . . CPL 30.10
Speedy trial . . . CPL 30.30

[References are to sections of Consolidated Laws as abbreviated on Page i.]

SUPPORTING DEPOSITION—Cont.
Verification . . . CPL 100.30

SUPPRESSION OF EVIDENCE
Generally . . . CPL 710.20; CPL 710.40
Appeal by people from order for . . . CPL 450.50
Courts determining motion . . . CPL 710.50
Definitions . . . CPL 710.10
Determination of motion . . . CPL 710.40
Failure to make motion . . . CPL 710.70
Grounds for . . . CPL 710.20
Intention to offer evidence, notice to defendant of
. . . CPL 710.30
Making of motion for . . . CPL 710.40; CPL
710.50
Notice to defendant of intention to offer evidence
. . . CPL 710.30
Orders for . . . CPL 710.70
Procedure . . . CPL 710.60
Time for motion . . . CPL 710.40

SUPREME COURT
Removal action to and from county courts
. . . CPL 230.10; CPL 230.20

SUSPENSION OF DRIVER'S LICENSE (See
DRIVER'S LICENSE: SUSPENSION AND RE-
VOCATION)

SWEEPSTAKES
Operation of unlawful electronic sweepstakes
. . . PL 156.40

SWORN FALSE STATEMENT (See PERJURY)

T

TAMPERING
Communications, private . . . PL 250.25
Computer tampering (See COMPUTER CRIMES)
Consumer products, tampering with (See CON-
SUMER PRODUCTS)
DNA testing, penalties for tampering with
. . . EXEC 995–f
Evidence, physical
Generally . . . PL 215.40
Definitions . . . PL 215.35
Farecard of mass transit service . . . PL 165.16
First degree . . . PL 145.20
Jurors, with
First degree . . . PL 215.25
Second degree . . . PL 215.23
Private communications . . . PL 250.25
Public records
First degree . . . PL 175.25
Second degree . . . PL 175.20
Second degree . . . PL 145.15
Sports (See SPORTS)
Third degree . . . PL 145.14
Witnesses, with (See WITNESSES)

TELECOMMUNICATIONS
Access device, criminal use of
First degree . . . PL 190.76
Second degree . . . PL 190.75
Electronic access device
Defined . . . PL 170.00
Fraudulent making of; second degree . . . PL
170.75

TEMPORARY RELEASE PROGRAM
Absconding from
First degree . . . PL 205.17
Second degree . . . PL 205.16
Absence of inmates (See ABSENCE OF IN-
MATES)
Abuses, review of complaint of . . . COR 857
Agent of state, status of inmate as . . . COR 861
Complaint and abuse review . . . COR 857
Conduct of inmates participating in . . . COR 856
Definitions . . . COR 851
Employment, prohibitions against . . . COR 859
Establishment of . . . COR 852
Evaluation and recommendation . . . COR 854
Furloughs (See FURLOUGHS)
Information on, maintenance of . . . COR 853
Procedure . . . COR 855
Recommendation for . . . COR 854
Records . . . COR 853
Reports, maintenance of . . . COR 853
Work release programs (See WORK RELEASE
PROGRAM)

TERMINATION OF CRIMINAL ACTION
Administrative findings . . . CPL 160.55
Favor of accused
Effect of termination in . . . CPL 160.60
Order upon termination in . . . CPL 160.50
Orders
Favor of accused, order upon termination in
. . . CPL 160.55
Noncriminal offenses, order upon termination by
conviction for . . . CPL 160.55
Waiver, termination upon entry of . . . CPL 160.55

TERRORISM, CRIMES OF
Generally . . . PL 490.25
Biological and chemical weapons
Defined . . . PL 490.05
Disposition of offender, authorized . . . CPL
700.05
Eavesdropping and video surveillance warrants,
defined as designated offense for . . . CPL
700.05
Possession of
Exclusions . . . PL 490.70
First degree . . . PL 490.45
Second degree . . . PL 490.40
Third degree . . . PL 490.37
Use of
Exclusions . . . PL 490.70

[References are to sections of Consolidated Laws as abbreviated on Page i.]

[References are to sections of Consolidated Laws as abbreviated on Page i.]

TRAP AND TRACE DEVICES—Cont.
Order authorizing use of—Cont.
    Application for—Cont.
        Determination of . . . CPL 705.20
        Extensions . . . CPL 705.25
        Issuance of . . . CPL 705.10
        Time period . . . CPL 705.25

TRESPASS
Generally . . . PL 140.05
Computer trespass . . . PL 156.10
Criminal (See CRIMINAL TRESPASS)

TRIAL
Discovery upon trial of prior statements and criminal history of witnesses . . . CPL 240.45
Information, prosecution of (See INFORMATION, subhead: Prosecution of information)
Jury trial (See JURY TRIAL)
Non-jury trial (See NON-JURY TRIAL)
Removal of action, stay of trial pending motion for . . . CPL 230.30
Speedy trial
    Generally . . . CPL 30.20
    Time limitations . . . CPL 30.30
Transcript of examination of witness on commission, use of . . . CPL 680.80

U

UNCONDITIONAL DISCHARGE
Sentence of . . . PL 65.20

UNIFORM CLOSE PURSUIT ACT
Provisions . . . CPL 140.55

UNIFORM CRIMINAL EXTRADITION ACT
(See EXTRADITION)

UNIFORMS
Police uniforms, criminal sale of . . . PL 190.27

UNLAWFUL IMPRISONMENT
Defense . . . PL 135.15
Definition . . . PL 135.00
First degree . . . PL 135.10
Second degree . . . PL 135.05

UNLAWFUL SURVEILLANCE
Generally . . . PL 250.40
Additional provisions . . . PL 250.65
Dissemination of image
    First degree . . . PL 250.60
    Second degree . . . PL 250.55
First degree . . . PL 250.50
Second degree . . . PL 250.45

USURY
Criminal usury
    First degree . . . PL 190.42
    Second degree . . . PL 190.40

USURY—Cont.
Loan records, possession of usurious . . . PL 190.45

V

VEHICLE AND TRAFFIC LAW
Accidents and accident reports (See ACCIDENTS AND ACCIDENT REPORTS)
Age of 21, consumption of alcohol by persons under (See subhead: Alcohol and drug-related offenses)
Alcohol and drug-related offenses
    Age of 21, persons under
        Chemical tests . . . VTL 1192–a; VTL 1194–a
        Prior convictions . . . VTL 1192
        Procedure . . . VTL 1194–a
        Rehabilitation program . . . VTL 1196
        Restrictions . . . VTL 1192–a
        Sanctions . . . VTL 1194
    Arrests . . . VTL 1194
    Assessment . . . VTL 1198–a
    Chemical tests (See CHEMICAL TESTS)
    Driver responsibility assessment . . . VTL 1199
    Ignition interlock device program (See IGNITION INTERLOCK DEVICE PROGRAM)
    Operation of vehicle under influence of . . . VTL 1192
    Rehabilitation program (See ALCOHOL AND DRUG REHABILITATION PROGRAM)
    Sanctions . . . VTL 1193
    School bus driver . . . VTL 1193
    Special traffic options for driving while intoxicated . . . VTL 1197
    Surcharges for, additional . . . VTL 1809–c
    Treatment . . . VTL 1198–a
Alteration of records in connection with examination . . . VTL 392
Arrests
    Alcohol and drug-related offenses . . . VTL 1194
    Compensation of officers not dependent upon apprehension or arrests . . . VTL 1810
    Drug-related offenses . . . VTL 1194
    Scene of accident, leaving without reporting . . . VTL 602
Certificate of magistrate . . . VTL 513
Certificate of registration
    Fraudulent, sale or purchase of . . . VTL 392–a
    Reissuance of . . . VTL 510
    Revoked, operation while registration or privilege . . . VTL 512
    Stolen or fraudulent, sale or purchase of . . . VTL 392–a
    Suspended or revoked, operation while registration or privilege . . . VTL 512
Chemical tests (See CHEMICAL TESTS)

[References are to sections of Consolidated Laws as abbreviated on Page i.]

[References are to sections of Consolidated Laws as abbreviated on Page i.]

VERDICT

Acquittal, discharge of defendant after verdict of . . . CPL 330.10

Checking of . . . CPL 310.80

Defective verdict, reconsideration of . . . CPL 310.50

Discharge of defendant after verdict of acquittal . . . CPL 330.10

Discharge of jury before rendition of verdict, effect of . . . CPL 310.60

Form . . . CPL 310.50

Guilty verdict where defendant not criminally responsible . . . CPL 310.85

Information, prosecution of

Generally . . . CPL 360.55

Sentence, proceedings from verdict to . . . CPL 370.10

Mental disease or defect, procedure following verdict or plea of not responsible by reason of . . . CPL 330.20

Partial verdict, effect of . . . CPL 310.70

Polling of jury . . . CPL 310.80

Procedure for rendition of . . . CPL 310.40

Recording and checking of . . . CPL 310.80

Removal of action after . . . CPL 330.25

Setting aside

Grounds for . . . CPL 330.30

Motion for

Order granting motion . . . CPL 330.50

Procedure . . . CPL 330.40

VESSELS

Seizures and forfeitures

Controlled substances, any vehicles or vessels used for transportation or conveyance of . . . PHL 3388

Gambling records, vessels used to transport . . . PL 415.00

VICTIMS

Audiotaped, videotaped or written victim impact statement, notice to crime victim of right to submit . . . CPL 440.50

Bail or recognizance for protection of, order of . . . CPL 530.13

Crime victim assistance fee . . . CPL 420.35; PL 60.35; VTL 1809

Crime victims board (See VICTIM SERVICES OFFICE)

Disposition of case, notice to crime victims of . . . CPL 440.50

Dispute resolution, defined for purposes of . . . CPL 215.20

Fair treatment standards for crime victims (See FAIR TREATMENT STANDARDS FOR CRIME VICTIMS)

Financial assistance for (See VICTIM SERVICES OFFICE)

Homicide victim defined . . . PL 125.05

VICTIMS—Cont.

Intimidation of

First degree . . . PL 215.17

Second degree . . . PL 215.16

Third degree . . . PL 215.15

Notification upon release of violent felony offender . . . CPL 380.50

Office of victim services (See VICTIM SERVICES OFFICE)

Protection orders

Family offenses . . . CPL 530.12

Other crimes . . . CPL 530.13

Sex offenses, of

Dress, admissibility of victim's manner of . . . CPL 60.48

Sexual conduct, admissibility of victim's . . . CPL 60.42

Videotaped, audiotaped or written victim impact statement, notice to crime victim of right to submit . . . CPL 440.50

VICTIM SERVICES OFFICE

Application forms for filing claims . . . EXEC 625–a

Assistance notification procedure for police officers, victim . . . EXEC 625–b

Awards

Children, to . . . EXEC 632

Conservatee, to . . . EXEC 632

Eligibility to receive . . . EXEC 624; EXEC 631

Emergency awards . . . EXEC 630

Filing of claims . . . EXEC 625–a

Incompetents, to . . . EXEC 632

Limitations . . . EXEC 631

Lump sum payments . . . EXEC 632

Manner of payment . . . EXEC 632

Out-of-pocket loss . . . EXEC 626

Profits from crime . . . EXEC 632–a

Reduction of . . . EXEC 631

Subrogation . . . EXEC 634

Children, awards to . . . EXEC 632

Compensation board . . . EXEC 622

Composition of . . . EXEC 622

Confidentiality of records . . . EXEC 633

Conservatee, awards to . . . EXEC 632

Crime defined . . . EXEC 621

Declaration of policy . . . EXEC 620

Definitions . . . EXEC 621

Determination of claims . . . EXEC 627

Duties of . . . EXEC 623

Eligibility for financial assistance . . . EXEC 624

Emergency awards . . . EXEC 630

Filing of claims . . . EXEC 625–a

Incompetents, awards to . . . EXEC 632

Information relative to claim . . . EXEC 625–a

Investigation of claims . . . EXEC 627

Judicial review of decisions by . . . EXEC 629

Legislative intent . . . EXEC 620

[References are to sections of Consolidated Laws as abbreviated on Page i.]

WARRANTS—Cont.

Arrest—Cont.

Without warrant (See ARREST WITHOUT WARRANT)

Bench warrant . . . CPL 530.70

Conditional discharge . . . CPL 410.40

Death penalty, warrant for execution of

Generally . . . COR 650

Delivery of . . . COR 652

Detainer warrants pilot project for sex offenders . . . CPL 410.92

Eavesdropping or video surveillance (See EAVESDROPPING OR VIDEO SURVEILLANCE WARRANTS)

Intermittent imprisonment . . . PL 85.10

Probation or conditional discharge

Detainer warrants pilot project for sex offenders . . . CPL 410.92

Issuance of warrant on defendant under sentence of . . . CPL 410.40

Search warrants (See SEARCH WARRANTS)

Video surveillance (See EAVESDROPPING OR VIDEO SURVEILLANCE WARRANTS)

WATERSHED PROTECTION AND ENFORCEMENT OFFICERS

Peace officers, status as . . . CPL 2.16

WEAPONS

Ammunition feeding devices, unlawful possession of

Large capacity ammunition feeding device . . . PL 265.36

Seven rounds of ammunition, devices containing more than . . . PL 265.37

Contiguous states, purchase in . . . PL 265.40

Convictions related to use of, reporting . . . PL 265.30

Criminal possession of (See subhead: Possession of)

Criminal use of . . . PL 265.09

Defacement . . . PL 265.10

Definitions . . . PL 265.00

Disposition of . . . PL 265.10; PL 400.05

Firearms (See FIREARMS)

Intent, presumptions of unlawful . . . PL 265.15

Large capacity ammunition feeding device, unlawful possession of . . . PL 265.36

Loss of, report of . . . PL 400.10

Manufacturing . . . PL 265.10

Minors

Firearms, sale of

Aid of minor . . . PL 265.14

Criminal sale to minor . . . PL 265.16

Sixteen years of age, possession by persons under . . . PL 265.05; PL 265.06

Possession of

Aggravated criminal possession . . . PL 265.19

WEAPONS—Cont.

Possession of—Cont.

Ammunition feeding devices, unlawful possession of

Large capacity ammunition feeding device . . . PL 265.36

Seven rounds of ammunition, devices containing more than . . . PL 265.37

Exemptions . . . PL 265.20

First degree . . . PL 265.04

Fourth degree . . . PL 60.11; PL 265.01

Presumptions . . . PL 265.15

School grounds

Criminal possession . . . PL 265.01–a

Unlawful possession upon . . . PL 265.06

Second degree . . . PL 265.03

Self-defense spray device . . . PL 265.20; PL 270.05

Sixteen years of age, possession by persons under . . . PL 265.05

Third degree . . . PL 60.11–a; PL 265.02

Presumptions of possession, unlawful intent and defacement . . . PL 265.15

Prohibited use of . . . PL 265.35

Purchase of

Contiguous states, in . . . PL 265.40

Criminal purchase . . . PL 265.17

Safe storage of . . . PL 265.45

School grounds

Criminal possession . . . PL 265.01–a

Unlawful possession upon . . . PL 265.06

Search for weapons without warrant . . . CPL 140.50

Self-defense spray device, use of (See SELF-DEFENSE SPRAY DEVICE)

Sixteen years of age, possession by persons under . . . PL 265.05; PL 265.06

Theft or loss of, report of . . . PL 400.10

Transportation . . . PL 265.10

Wounds from, reporting of . . . PL 265.25

WELFARE FRAUD

Definitions . . . PL 158.00

Fifth degree . . . PL 158.05

First degree . . . PL 158.25

Fourth degree . . . PL 158.10

Public benefit cards

Possession of, criminal

First degree . . . PL 158.50

Second degree . . . PL 158.45

Third degree . . . PL 158.40

Use of, criminal

First degree . . . PL 158.35

Second degree . . . PL 158.30

Second degree . . . PL 158.20

Third degree . . . PL 158.15

WILLS

Concealment of, unlawful . . . PL 190.30

[References are to sections of Consolidated Laws as abbreviated on Page i.]

[References are to sections of Consolidated Laws as abbreviated on Page i.]

WORK RELEASE PROGRAM—Cont.
Confinement, designation of place of . . . COR 158
County jails
Generally . . . COR 879
Agent of county, prisoner as . . . COR 877
Annual report . . . COR 878
Conditional release, eligibility for . . . COR 876
Earnings, disposition of . . . COR 872
Establishment of program . . . COR 870
Parole, eligibility for . . . COR 876
Procedures . . . COR 871
Prohibitions . . . COR 874
Sentence reduction, eligibility for . . . COR 876
Separate housing . . . COR 873
Earnings, disposition of
Generally . . . COR 860
County jail program . . . COR 872
New York City program . . . COR 154
Labor laws, application of . . . COR 858
Liability for prisoner . . . COR 156
New York City
Generally . . . COR 151; COR 152
Annual report of commissioner . . . COR 160
Conditions of employment . . . COR 153
Confinement, designation of place of . . . COR 158
Definitions . . . COR 150
Designation of place of confinement . . . COR 158
Earnings, disposition of . . . COR 154
Eligibility for other programs . . . COR 159
Liability for prisoner . . . COR 156
Rules and regulations . . . COR 157
Securing employment for prisoner . . . COR 152
Rules and regulations . . . COR 157

WRITTEN FALSE STATEMENTS
Business records, falsifying
Defense . . . PL 175.15
First degree . . . PL 175.10
Second degree . . . PL 175.05
Certificates, issuing false . . . PL 175.40

WRITTEN FALSE STATEMENTS—Cont.
Credit terms, making false statement of . . . PL 190.55
Defense to falsifying business records . . . PL 175.15
Definitions . . . PL 175.00
Filing, offering false instrument for
First degree . . . PL 175.35
Second degree . . . PL 175.30
Financial statements . . . PL 175.45
Public records, tampering with
First degree . . . PL 175.25
Second degree . . . PL 175.20
Punishable statement . . . PL 210.45
Records
Business records (See subhead: Business records, falsifying)
Public records, tampering with
First degree . . . PL 175.25
Second degree . . . PL 175.20
Tampering with public records (See subhead: Public records, tampering with)

Y

YOUTHFUL OFFENDERS
Accusatory instrument, sealing of . . . CPL 720.15
Adjudication
Appeals . . . CPL 720.30
Effect of . . . CPL 720.35
Exemptions . . . CPL 720.25
Post-judgment motions . . . CPL 720.30
Records . . . CPL 720.35
School officials, notification to . . . CPL 720.35
Alcohol, operation of motor vehicle by persons under age 21 after consumption of (See VEHICLE AND TRAFFIC LAW, subhead: Alcohol and drug-related offenses)
Appeal of adjudication . . . CPL 720.30
Authorized dispositions of . . . PL 60.02
Definitions . . . CPL 720.10
Determination eligibility as . . . CPL 720.20
Eligibility as, determination of . . . CPL 720.20
Privacy of proceedings . . . CPL 720.15
Records . . . CPL 720.35
Sealing of accusatory instrument . . . CPL 720.15